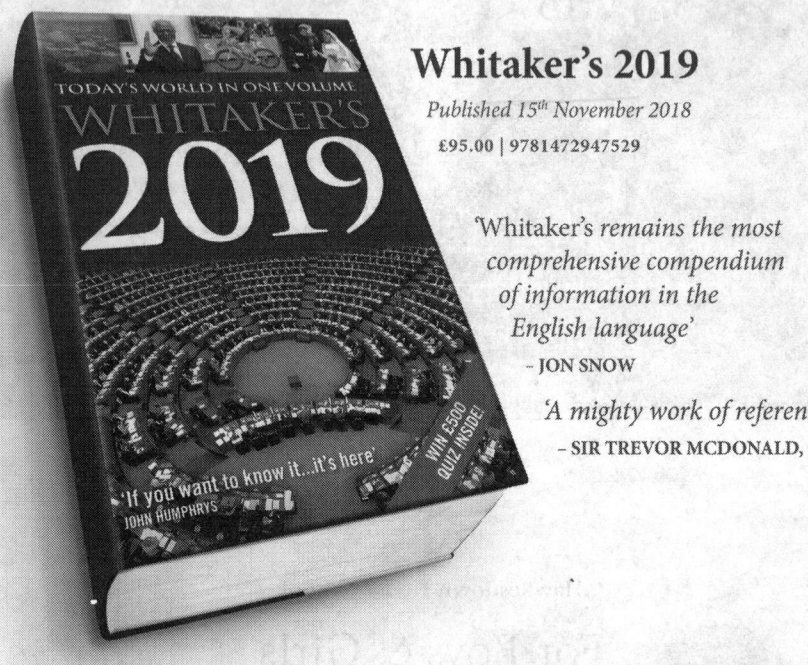

INDEPENDENT SCHOOLS YEARBOOK

2018–2019

Boys Schools, Girls Schools,
Co-educational Schools and
Preparatory Schools

Details of Schools whose Heads are in membership of
one or more of the following
Constituent Associations of the
Independent Schools Council (ISC):

Headmasters' and Headmistresses' Conference (HMC)
Girls' Schools Association (GSA)
The Society of Heads
Independent Association of Prep Schools (IAPS)
Independent Schools Association (ISA)

Edited by
JUDY MOTT

Tel: 020 7631 5600; email: isyb@acblack.com
website: www.isyb.co.uk

BLOOMSBURY YEARBOOKS
LONDON · OXFORD · NEW YORK · NEW DELHI · SYDNEY

BLOOMSBURY YEARBOOKS
Bloomsbury Publishing Plc
50 Bedford Square, London, WC1B 3DP, UK

BLOOMSBURY, BLOOMSBURY YEARBOOKS and the Diana
logo are trademarks of Bloomsbury Publishing Plc

First published in Great Britain 1889
This edition published 2019

A catalogue record for this book is available from the British Library.

ISBN: PB 978-1-4729-6212-6

2 4 6 8 10 9 7 5 3 1

Printed and bound in Great Britain by CPI Group (UK) Ltd,
Croydon CR0 4YY

FSC
www.fsc.org
MIX
Paper from
responsible sources
FSC® C019777

To find out more about our authors and books visit www.bloomsbury.com
and sign up for our newsletters.

INDEPENDENT SCHOOLS YEARBOOK 2018–2019

CONTENTS

PART I: HEADMASTERS' AND HEADMISTRESSES' CONFERENCE

314 schools for pupils from age 11 to 18, whose Heads are members of HMC; 56 of these are international members. They are all-boys schools (some admitting girls to the Sixth Form), co-educational schools, "Diamond" schools (girls and boys taught separately in the 11–16 age range), and some are all-girls schools. Many of the schools also have a Preparatory/Junior school or department.

PART II: GIRLS' SCHOOLS ASSOCIATION

113 schools for pupils from age 11 to 16/18, whose Heads are members of GSA. They are all-girls schools in the 11–16 age range, some admit boys to the Sixth Form and some are "Diamond" schools (girls and boys taught separately in the 11–16 age range). Some of the schools also have a Preparatory/Junior school or department.

. . ./continued

PART III: THE SOCIETY OF HEADS

83 schools for pupils from age 11 to 18 whose Heads are members of The Society of Heads. The majority are co-educational schools, but Membership is open to boys and girls schools. Many of the schools also have a Preparatory/Junior school or department.

PART IV: INDEPENDENT ASSOCIATION OF PREP SCHOOLS

558 schools whose Heads are members of IAPS; 19 of these are overseas members. Most of the schools are co-educational; some cater for boys only or girls only. The preparatory school age range is 7 to 11/13, but many of the schools have a pre-preparatory department for children up to age 7.

PART V: INDEPENDENT SCHOOLS ASSOCIATION

229 schools in membership of ISA. Schools in this Association are not confined to one age range and can cater for any age range of pupils up to 18/19 years.

ISC
INDEPENDENT SCHOOLS COUNCIL
www.isc.co.uk

"Working with its members to promote and preserve the quality, diversity and excellence of UK independent education"

ISC is established:
- to support the aims and objectives of its seven member associations;
- to provide authoritative research and intelligence about the sector;
- to be a leading source of legal and regulatory information/guidance;
- to promote public affairs and parliamentary engagement on behalf of the sector;
- to provide online access and support informing parental decisions;
- to promote the sector through agreed national messaging and communications;
- to provide a meeting place in central London for members.

The Constituent Associations of ISC are:

Association of Governing Bodies of Independent Schools (AGBIS)
Girls' Schools Association (GSA)
Headmasters' and Headmistresses' Conference (HMC)
Independent Association of Prep Schools (IAPS)
Independent Schools Association (ISA)
Independent Schools' Bursars Association (ISBA)
The Society of Heads

Secretariat

Chairman
Barnaby Lenon

General Secretary
Julie Robinson

Independent Schools Council
First Floor, 27 Queen Anne's Gate, London SW1H 9BU

Tel: 020 7766 7070
Website: www.isc.co.uk

HMC
HEADMASTERS' AND HEADMISTRESSES' CONFERENCE
www.hmc.org.uk

The HMC dates from 1869, when the celebrated Edward Thring of Uppingham asked thirty-seven of his fellow headmasters to meet at his house to consider the formation of a 'School Society and Annual Conference'. Twelve headmasters accepted the invitation. From that date there have been annual meetings. Thring's intention was to provide an opportunity for discussion at regular intervals, both on practical issues in the life of a school and on general principles in education. He believed that his guests would discharge their practical business more effectively at a residential meeting where they could also enjoy being in the company of like-minded men. Annual Meetings of the HMC still combine formal debate on current educational questions with the second element of conversational exchanges in an agreeable environment. These gatherings, which up to 1939 were usually at individual schools, then took place at a University. Nowadays they are held in major hotels and conference centres in the Autumn term. In addition to these annual conferences attended by all members, there are local meetings each term arranged by the ten branches or Divisions into which the country is divided.

Present full membership of the HMC is a total of two hundred and ninety-two, which now includes headmasters and headmistresses of boys', girls' and co-educational schools. In considering applications for election to membership, the Committee has regard to the degree of independence enjoyed by the Head and his/her school. Eligibility also depends on the academic standards obtaining in the school, as reflected by the proportion of pupils in the Sixth Form pursuing a course of study beyond GCSE and by the school's public examination results, including A Levels, the International Baccalaureate and the Cambridge Pre-U.

The Constitution provides that the full membership shall consist only of heads of independent schools in the UK and Ireland. At the same time, it is held to be a strength that the Conference includes heads of schools from the maintained sector as well as other influential figures from the world of education. There is provision therefore for the election of a small number of HMC Associates.

In addition the HMC has a number of International members, who are heads of high-quality schools from around the world. The International division meets on two occasions during the academic year and the Chair is a member of the HMC Committee. There is also a small number of Honorary Associates who have been elected to life membership on retirement.

The HMC is closely associated with the other independent sector associations that also belong to the Independent Schools Council (ISC), and with the Association of School and College Leaders (ASCL), which represents the Heads and senior staff of secondary schools and colleges in both the maintained and independent sectors.

The HMC Committee 2018–2019

Elected Members

Chair	Shaun Fenton	Reigate Grammar School
Vice-Chair	Sally-Anne Huang	James Allen's Girls' School
Chair-Elect	Fiona Boulton	Guildford High School
Treasurer	Stephen Holliday	Queen Elizabeth's Hospital

Divisional Members

Chairman – East	Chris Staley	Wisbech Grammar School
Secretary – East	Bill Penty	Trent College
Chairman – Irish	Robert Robinson	Campbell College
Secretary – Irish	Elizabeth Huddleson	Bangor Grammar School
Chair – London	Heather Hanbury	The Lady Eleanor Holles School
Secretary – London	Suzie Longstaff	Putney High School
Chairman – North East	David Craig	Queen Elizabeth Grammar School
Secretary – North East	Anton Maree	Ackworth School
Chairman – North West	Michael Kennedy	St Mary's College
Secretary – North West	Simon Hyde	The King's School Macclesfield
Chairman – Scottish	Simon Mills	Robert Gordon's College
Secretary – Scottish	Johanna Urquhart	Urquhart School
Chair – South Central	Jesse Elzinga	Reading Blue Coat School
Secretary – South Central	Adam Williams	Lord Wandsworth College
Chairman – South East	Angela Drew	Bromley High School
Secretary – South East	Julie Lodrick	Kent College, Pembury
Chairman – South West	Jonathan Standen	Plymouth College
Secretary – South West	Andrew Gordon-Brown	Truro School
Chairman – West	Nick Gregory	Wycliffe College
Secretary – West	Alastair Land	Repton School
Chairman – International		
Secretary – International	Mark Steed	JESS, Dubai

Co-opted Members

Chairman of Academic Policy	Martin Collier	Haileybury
Chairman of Professional Development	John Watson	Bablake School
Chairman of Universities	Chris Ramsey	Whitgift School
Chair of Inspection	Emma Hattersley	Godolphin School
Chairman of Communications	Philip Britton	Bolton School
Chairman of Membership	Brendan Wignall	Ellesmere College
Chairman of Sports	David Elstone	Hymers College
	Mary Breen	St Mary's School Ascot

Executive Director: Michael Buchanan (Tel: 01858 469059)
Membership Secretary: Ian Power, MA (Tel: 01858 465260)

Headmasters' and Headmistresses' Conference
12 The Point, Rockingham Road, Market Harborough, Leicestershire LE16 7QU
Tel: 01858 465260 · Fax: 01858 465759 · email: gensec@hmc.org.uk

GSA

GIRLS' SCHOOLS ASSOCIATION

www.gsa.uk.com

The Girls' Schools Association represents the heads of many of the top-performing day and boarding schools in the UK, and is a member of the Independent Schools Council.

The GSA encourages high standards of education for girls and promotes the benefits of being taught in a largely girls-only environment. GSA schools are internationally respected and have an impressive global reputation for excellence in and out of the classroom; with academic rigour, innovative practice and wide-ranging extra-curricular activities attracting pupils from around the world. They are also widely recognised for their exceptional record of examination achievements, with high results in STEM subjects and 96% of pupils progressing to university.

Twenty-first century girls' schools come in many different shapes and sizes. Whether they are day, boarding, junior, senior, large, small, urban or rural, the educational provision they provide ensures girls don't just have equal opportunities, but that they have every opportunity to realise their potential as active, equal, confident and competent leaders, participants and contributors. Former GSA school pupils are among the most noteworthy high achievers of the UK and indeed the world. They include world leading scientists, international charity campaigners, famous actresses, foreign correspondents, Olympic medallists and business women at the highest levels.

Members of the GSA share a commitment to the values and benefits of single-sex schools for girls, and a belief that the needs and aspirations of girls is always the main focus. Staff in GSA schools are specialists in the teaching of girls, and provide positive role models to encourage girls in all that they do.

The GSA provides its members and their staff with a full programme of professional development and support, to assist them in remaining fully up-to-date with all aspects of their profession. The Association also aims to inform and influence national educational debate and is a powerful and well-respected voice within the educational establishment, advising and lobbying educational policy makers on core education issues as well as those relating to girls' schools and the education of girls.

Officers 2018

President:	Gwen Byrom	Loughborough High School
Vice-President:	Charlotte Avery	St Mary's School, Cambridge
President Elect 2019:	Sue Hincks	Bolton School (Girls' Division)
Treasurer:	Antonia Beary	Mayfield Girls

Officers 2019

President:	Sue Hincks	Bolton School (Girls' Division)
Vice-President:	Charlotte Avery	St Mary's School, Cambridge
President Elect 2020:	Jane Prescott	Portsmouth High School GDST
Treasurer:	Antonia Beary	Mayfield Girls

Committee Chairs

Boarding:	Samantha Price	Benenden School
Education:	Ruth Weeks	Edgbaston High School for Girls
Membership & Accreditation:	Claire Hewitt	Manchester High School for Girls
Professional Development:	Nicola Botterill	Bruton School for Girls
Sport and Wellness:	Ashley Clancy	The Ladies' College
Universities:	Rachel Dent	The Abbey School

Regional Representatives

East:	Elizabeth Thomas	Abbot's Hill School
London:	Millan Sachania	Streatham & Clapham High School GDST
Midlands:	Ann Clark	King Edward VI High School for Girls
North East:	Sylvia Brett	Harrogate Ladies' College
North West:	Sarah Haslam	Withington Girls' School
Scotland:	Dorothy MacGinty	Kilgraston School
South Central:	Jane Gandee	St Swithun's School
South East:	Anna King	Notre Dame School
South West & Wales:	Felicia Kirk	St Mary's Calne

Secretariat

Chief Executive:	Vivienne Durham
Membership Director:	Jane Carroll
Executive Assistant to the Chief Executive:	Jeven Sharma
Membership Manager:	Jannette Davison
Conference & Events Manager:	Emily Hall (maternity leave)
Conference & Events Manager:	Davina Chester (maternity cover)
Digital Manager:	Imogen Vanderpump
Communications Manager:	Rachel Kerr
Finance Manager:	Janice Lightley

Girls' Schools Association
Suite 105, 108 New Walk, Leicester, LE1 7PG
Tel: 0116 254 1619 · email: office@gsa.uk.com

THE SOCIETY OF HEADS
www.thesocietyofheads.org.uk

The Society is an Association of Heads of over 110 well-established independent schools. It was founded in 1961 at a time when the need arose from the vitality and growth of the independent sector in the 1950s and the wish of a group of Heads to share ideas and experience.

The Society continues to provide a forum for the exchange of ideas and consideration of the particular needs of its schools. All members value their independence, breadth in education and the pursuit of excellence, particularly in relation to academic standards.

The Society's policy is to maintain high standards in member schools, to ensure their genuine independence, to foster an association of schools which contributes to the whole independent sector by its distinctive character and flexibility, to provide an opportunity for the sharing of ideas and common concerns, to promote links with the wider sphere of higher education, to strengthen relations with the maintained sector and with local communities.

Within the membership there is a wide variety of educational experience. Some schools are young, some have evolved from older foundations, some have behind them a long tradition of pioneer and specialist education, the great majority are now co-educational but we also have all-boys and all-girls schools. A good number of the member schools have a strong boarding element and others are day schools. Some have specific religious foundations and some are non-denominational. All offer a stimulating Sixth Form experience and at the same time give a sound and balanced education to pupils of widely varying abilities and interests.

The Society is one of the constituent Associations of the Independent Schools Council. Every Full Member school has been accredited through inspection by the Independent Schools Inspectorate (or Estyn in Wales and HMIE in Scotland) and is subject to regular visits to monitor standards and ensure that good practice and sound academic results are maintained. The Society is also represented on many other educational bodies.

All members are in membership of the Association of School and College Leaders (ASCL) or other union for school leaders and Full Member schools belong to AGBIS or an equivalent professional body supporting governance.

There are also categories of Alliance and Alliance Overseas Membership to which Heads are elected whose schools do not fulfil all the criteria for Full Membership but whose personal contribution to the Society is judged to be invaluable. They are recorded separately at the end of the entries.

The Society has a one-day meeting for members in the autumn and summer terms and organises a two-day residential conference in the Easter term.

Officers 2018–2019
Chair: Lynne Horner, Westholme School
Vice-Chair: Gregg Davies, Shiplake College
Chair Designate: Roland Martin, City of London Freemen's School
Hon. Treasurer: Adrian Meadows, The Peterborough School

Committee 2018–2019
Lynne Horner, Westholme School
Gregg Davies, Shiplake College
Roland Martin, City of London Freemen's School
Adrian Meadows, The Peterborough School
Guy Ayling, Llandovery College
Frank Butt, Langley School
Andy Colpus, St Joseph's College, Reading
Christine Cunniffe, LVS Ascot
Damian Ettinger, Cokethorpe School
Sue Hannam, Lichfield Cathedral School
Emma-Kate Henry, d'Overbroecks
David Holland, Hill House School
Sarah Raffray, St Augustine's Priory
Annette Roberts, Kirkham Grammar School

Secretariat
General Secretary: Clive Rickart

The Society of Heads
12 The Point, Rockingham Road, Market Harborough, Leicestershire LE16 7QU
Tel: 01858 433760 · email: gensec@thesocietyofheads.org.uk

Members who are also members of the Headmasters' and Headmistresses' Conference:

Anton Maree, Ackworth School
Magnus Bashaarat, Bedales Schools
Jaideep Barot, Bristol Grammar School
Roland Martin, City of London Freemen's School
Joanne Thomson, Clayesmore School
Damian Ettinger, Cokethorpe School
James Davies, Halliford School
Alex Wilson, Hull Collegiate School
Daniel Berry, Kirkham Grammar School
Dominic Findlay, Langley School
Matthew Judd, Leighton Park School

Mark Wallace, Lincoln Minster School
Jonathan Forster, Moreton Hall
Jesse Elzinga, Reading Blue Coat School
Mark Hoskins, Reed's School
Rob Jones, Rendcomb College
David Buxton, St Columba's College
John Green, Seaford College
Gregg Davies, Shiplake College
Philip Rowe, Silcoates School
Mark Mortimer, Warminster School
Chris Staley, Wisbech Grammar School

Members who are also members of the Girls' Schools Association:
Jonathan Forster, Moreton Hall
Sarah Raffray, St Augustine's Priory School

Honorary Members
(former post in brackets)

John Aguilar (Principal, Padworth College)
Stephen Aiano (Headmaster, Bearwood College)
Geoffrey Allen (Headmaster, The Roman Ridge School)
Steph Bailey (Headmaster, The Royal Wolverhampton School)
Ron Balaam (Headmaster, Royal Russell School)
Mark Bedford (Headmaster, Thetford Grammar School)
David Beeby (Headmaster, Clayesmore School)
Nicholas Beesley (Headmaster, Beechwood Sacred Heart School)
Kathryn Bell (Head, Burgess Hill Girls)
Lee Bergin (Headmaster, North Cestrian Grammar School)
Graham Best (Headmaster, St John's College, Southsea)
David Boddy (Headmaster, St James Senior Boys' School)
Peter Bodkin (General Secretary, The Society of Heads)
Sue Bradley (Head, Stover School)
David Bryson (Headmaster, St Andrew's School)
Keith Budge (Headmaster, Bedales School)
Philip Cantwell (Headmaster, The King's School, Tynemouth)
David Chapman (Headmaster, Hampshire Collegiate School)
Anna Chaudhri (Head, Walden School)
Nicholas Chisholm (Headmaster, Yehudi Menuhin School)
Roger Clark (Headmaster, Battle Abbey School)
Sami Cohen (Headmaster, d'Overbroecks)
Timothy Cook (Headmaster, Portland Place School)
Martin Cooke (Headmaster, Clayesmore School)
Philip Cottam (Headmaster, Halliford School)
David Crawford (Headmaster, Colston's School)
Nicholas Dorey (Headmaster, Bethany School)
John Dunston (Headmaster, Leighton Park School)
Mark Eagers (Headmaster, Box Hill School)
Nick England (Headmaster, Ryde School)
Sarah Evans (Principal, King Edward VI High School for Girls)
Steve Fairclough (Headmaster, Abbotsholme School)
Darrell Farrant (Headmaster, Abbotsholme School)
Sue Freestone (Principal, King's Ely)
Michael Goodwin (Headmaster, Sibford School)
Allan Graham (Headmaster, Windermere St Anne's School)
Richard Hadfield (Headmaster, The Read School)
Tony Halliwell (Principal, Welbeck Defence Sixth Form College)
Nick Hammond (Headmaster, Wisbech Grammar School)
Paul Harvey (Headmaster, St Edward's School)
Carole Hawkins (Head, Royal School, Hampstead)
Rob Haworth (Headmaster, Hull Collegiate School)
Stuart Hay (Headmaster, St David's College)
John Hewitt (Headmaster, Bredon School)
Stuart Higgins (Principal, King's College Saint Michael's)
Richard Hillier (Headmaster, The Yehudi Menuhin School)
Gerry Holden (Headmaster, Dover College)
Jonathan Insall-Reid (Headmaster, Claremont Fan Court School)
Catherine James (Headmistress, Farringtons School)
David Jarrett (Headmaster, Reed's School)

Charles Johnson (Headmaster, The Duke of York's Royal Military School)
Stephen Jones (Headmaster, Dover College)
Trevor Kernohan (Headmaster, Fulneck School)
Iain Kilpatrick (Headmaster, Sidcot School)
Michael Kirk (Headmaster, Royal Hospital School)
Tim Kirkup (Headmaster, Scarborough College)
Aaron Lennon (Headmaster, Beechwood Sacred Heart School)
Geoff Link (Headmaster, Stanbridge Earls School)
Martyn Long (Headmaster, Tettenhall College)
Chris Lumb (Headmaster, St Joseph's College, Ipswich)
Tim Manning (Headmaster, Longridge Towers School)
James McArthur (Headmaster, Reading Blue Coat School)
Alex McGrath (Headmaster, Leighton Park School)
Linde Melhuish (Principal, Padworth College)
Edward Mitchell (Headmaster, Abbey Gate College)
Stephen Morris (Headmaster of The Cathedral School, Llandaff)
Howard Moxon (Headmaster, Stanbridge Earls School)
Ian Mullins (Licenced Victuallers' School)
Deborah Newman (Principal, Fulneck School)
Isobel Nixon (Head, Scarborough College)
Thomas Packer (Headmaster, Teesside High School)
John Payne (Headmaster, Pierrepoint School)
Joe Peake (Headmaster, St George's College, Weybridge)
The Hon Martin Penney (Headmaster, Bearwood College)
Ian Power (Headmaster, Lord Wandsworth College)
Gareth Price (Headmaster, Thetford Grammar School)
Martin Priestley (Headmaster, Warminster School)
Colin Reid (Headmaster, St Christopher School)
Lynne Renwick (Head, Our Lady's Abingdon School)
Bob Repper (Headmaster, Wisbech Grammar School)
David Richardson (General Secretary, The Society of Heads)
Douglas Robb (Headmaster, Oswestry School)
Christopher Robinson (Headmaster, Hipperholme Grammar School)
Michael Scullion (Headmaster, Our Lady of Sion School)
John Shinkwin (Headmaster, Princethorpe College)
Philip Skelker (Headmaster, Immanuel College)
Paul Spillane (Headmaster, Silcoates School)
John Sweetman (Headmaster, The Read School)
Michael Symonds (Headmaster, Bedstone College)
Elizabeth Thomas (Head, Stonar School)
Nigel Thorne (Headmaster, St John's College, Southsea)
Andrew Tibble (Headmaster, Ewell Castle School)
John Tolputt (Headmaster, The Purcell School)
David Vanstone (Headmaster, North Cestrian Grammar School)
Richard Walker (Headmaster, Portland Place School)
David Ward (Principal, Bredon School)
Nick Ward (Headmaster, The Royal Hospital School)
Andy Waters (Headmaster, Kingsley School)
Nigel Williams (Head, Leighton Park School)
Simon Wilson (Headmaster, Halliford School)
Michael Windsor (Headmaster, Reading Blue Coat School)
Simon Wormleighton (Headmaster, Grenville College)

IAPS
INDEPENDENT ASSOCIATION OF PREP SCHOOLS
www.iaps.uk

IAPS is the voice of independent prep school education. We work with and lobby governments on an international stage to ensure the needs of our members, and the independent sector as a whole, are met.

Schools can only join IAPS if they have been accredited through a satisfactory inspection and the head is suitably qualified. In addition, they must demonstrate the highest standards of education and care. Our member schools offer an all-round, values-led, broad education which produces confident, adaptable, motivated children with a lifelong passion for learning.

While the values may be the same, each of our schools is independent and distinct: we have single-sex and co-educational, boarding, day and mixed, urban and rural. Sizes vary from more than 800 pupils to around 100.

We have one of the independent sector's top training programmes which includes a broad range of professional development courses. New members are offered an experienced head as a mentor and members are divided into district groups by geographical location, giving them the chance to meet with fellow heads on a regular basis.

With around 630 members in the UK and around 50 abroad, IAPS offers excellent opportunities to members for fellowship and networking.

The Council and Officers for 2018–2019

Chairman of IAPS: Chris Davies
Vice-Chairman: Helen Todd

Members of Council:

Jeremy Banks	Luke Harrison
Edward Balfour	Sebastian Hepher
Mark Brearey	Rebecca Lyons-Smith
Clare Bruce	Andrew Nott
Christopher Cann	James Reid
Mike Crossley	Christopher Schanschieff
Maureen Cussans	Howard Tuckett
John Gilmour	Tim Wheeler
Mark Hammond	Jane Whittingham

Officers:

Chief Executive: Christopher King
Director of Education: Mark Brotherton
Finance and Operations Director: Richard Flower
Membership Secretary: Petra Hancock
Association Administrator: Christine McCrudden

Independent Association of Prep Schools
11 Waterloo Place, Leamington Spa CV32 5LA
Tel: 01926 887833 · email: iaps@iaps.uk

ISA

INDEPENDENT SCHOOLS ASSOCIATION

www.isaschools.org.uk

The Independent Schools Association is a registered charity with a service-led approach to supporting its Members and the wider educational community. The Association's dedication to its Members, including the delivery of instant 24/7 expert advice, has resulted in growth of over 76% in the last seven years and ISA is now regarded as the most representative of any organisation within the sector. Its growth is simply unprecedented within the sector.

Membership is open to independent school Heads and Proprietors provided they meet the necessary criteria, which include accreditation by any government-approved inspectorate. ISA makes no requirements upon Members for other memberships or affiliations, or for schools to operate in any specific way, beyond the requirements of the appropriate regulations. A strong regional network of fellow Heads supports each Member, and all Members receive a free high-level compliance check in the run-up to their next scheduled inspection, as well as an annual pastoral visit from a dedicated regional representative. An extensive programme of training events and conferences helps Members and their staff to keep up-to-date with the latest thinking on teaching and learning.

ISA celebrates a wide-ranging membership, not confined to any one type of school, but including all: nursery, pre-preparatory, junior, preparatory and senior, all-through schools, specialist sixth-forms, co-educational, single-sex, boarding, day, and performing arts and special schools.

Promoting best practice and fellowship for Members remains at the core of the Association, just as it did when it began 140 years ago. The 470 Members and their schools enjoy high quality national conferences and courses that foster excellence in independent education. The Association's Annual ISA Awards ceremony celebrates the best of good practice across Members' schools. ISA's central office also supports Members and provides expert advice in areas such as HR, curriculum, finance, leadership and governance, and represents the views of its membership at national and governmental levels. Pupils in ISA schools enjoy a wide variety of competitions, including a wealth of sporting, artistic and academic activities at Area and National level, often at world-class venues.

Council and Officers for 2018–2019

President: Lord Lexden OBE

Vice-Presidents:
Mrs Angela Culley
Mr Barry Huggett
Mr Paul Moss
Mr John Wood

Honorary Officers:
Mr Matthew Adshead (*Chair*)
Mr Alex Gear (*Vice-Chair*)
Mrs Claire Osborn (*Vice-Chair*)

Elective Councillors:

Mr Adrian Blake	Mr Stephen McKernan
Miss Elizabeth Brown	Mr John Southworth
Mrs Helen Chalmers	Mrs Helen Stanton-Tonner
Mrs Penny Ford	Mr Richard Walden
Mr Andrew Hampton	Mr Craig Wardle
Mrs Pam Hutley	Mr James Wilding
Dr Sarah Lockyer	Ms Tracey Wilson

Area Coordinators:

East Anglia: Mrs Pauline Wilson	Midlands: Mr David Preston
London North: Mrs Kaye Lovejoy	North: Mr Jeff Shaw
London South: Mr Phil Soutar	South West: Mrs Dionne Seagrove
London West: (tbc)	

Officials
Chief Executive Officer: Neil Roskilly
Deputy Chief Executive Officer: Peter Woodroffe
Professional Development Officer: Alice Thompson
Office Manager and PA to the CEO: Karen Goddard

Independent Schools Association
ISA House, 5–7 Great Chesterford Court, Great Chesterford, Essex CB10 1PF
Tel: 01799 523619 · email: isa@isaschools.org.uk

AGBIS
ASSOCIATION OF GOVERNING BODIES OF INDEPENDENT SCHOOLS
REGISTERED CHARITY NO. 1108756

www.agbis.org.uk

The Object of the Association is to advance education in independent schools and, in furtherance of that object, but not otherwise, the Association shall have power:

(a) to discuss matters concerning the policy and administration of such schools and to encourage cooperation between their Governing Bodies;
(b) to consider the relationship of such schools to the general educational interests of the community;
(c) to consider and give guidance on matters of general or individual concern to the Governing Bodies of such schools;
(d) to promote good governance in such schools;
and
(e) to express the views of the Governing Bodies of such schools on any of the foregoing matters and to take such action as may be appropriate in their interests.

Membership

There are two categories of membership: full membership and associate membership. Schools in England and Wales applying for either category will have heads in full membership of one of the five Independent Schools Council (ISC) Heads' Associations or expecting to be so within one year. If the school is not a charitable trust, it must have either a governing body or an advisory or management committee which fulfils a similar function and is constituted in such a fashion as to provide a significant degree of oversight.

FULL MEMBERSHIP

To be accepted as full members, schools will need to demonstrate that the composition of the Governing Body and governance procedures meet the principles of good governance practice set out in the AGBIS publication 'Guidelines for Governors'. All schools must be able to demonstrate that they are financially viable and must also be able to provide a satisfactory current inspection report issued by a recognised inspectorate

ASSOCIATE MEMBERSHIP

Schools which do not meet all of the criteria above for full membership may be offered associate membership at the discretion of the AGBIS Board. The offer of associate membership can be temporary and may require a school to rectify a perceived shortcoming or weakness. Once this condition has been met, the school may apply to be considered for full membership.

Association of Governing Bodies of Independent Schools
The Grange, 3 Codicote Road, Welwyn, Hertfordshire AL6 9LY
Tel: 01438 840730 · email: admin@agbis.org.uk

ISBA

INDEPENDENT SCHOOLS' BURSARS ASSOCIATION

www.theisba.org.uk

The Independent Schools' Bursars Association (ISBA) is the only national association to represent school bursars and business managers of independent schools, providing them with the professional support they need to manage their schools successfully and provide a world class education to their pupils.

The association can trace its history back seventy years to the founding of the Public Schools Bursars' Association which held its first general meeting on 26 April 1932 at the offices of Epsom College. Its name then changed to the Independent Schools' Bursars Association in 1983.

The ISBA now has more than 1000 independent school members, covering more than 1000 schools, including some 40 overseas associate members, from smaller preparatory schools to larger and well-renowned senior schools, including both boarding and day schools. Although it is the school and not the bursar who becomes a member of the association, it is usually the bursar or equivalent who is the school's nominated representative.

The association is one of the constituent members of the Independent Schools Council (ISC) and also works closely with the other seven constituent associations of the ISC. It is represented on the ISC Governing Council and a number of ISC committees and is also often called on to represent the ISC at meetings with the Department for Education, Health & Safety Executive and Teachers' Pensions providing advice on bursarial matters.

Full membership of the ISBA is open to schools who are members of one of the constituent associations in membership of the ISC. Associate membership is open to certain other schools/organisations which are recognised as educational charities.

Day-to-day the ISBA advises many different staff within a school's senior management team including the bursar, finance director, chief operations officer, business manager, deputy or assistant with areas of responsibility encompassing accounting, financial management and reporting, risk management, regulatory compliance, facilities management, HR, technology, environmental sustainability, auxiliary services and more. As part of its range of support services the association offers schools:

- guidance and legislative briefings, and model policies to download from its online reference library;
- a comprehensive professional development programme covering finance, legal, HR, inspections and other key operational issues and tailored to suit staff at all levels;
- information, advice and networking opportunities at the ISBA Annual Conference (the 2019 conference will be held at the Manchester Central Convention Complex on Tuesday 21st and Wednesday 22nd May 2019);
- a 'Bursar's Guide' – providing the latest information on legislation affecting schools;
- termly copies of the ISBA's magazine – The Bursar's Review – and monthly e-newsletters covering the latest legal, financial and HR news and more;
- an online job vacancies page where schools can advertise any of their vacant bursary management roles for free.

The ISBA Board consists of the Chairman of the Association, John Pratten, Bursar at Box Hill School, and the bursars of 12 other leading independent schools.

The Independent Schools' Bursars Association is a Registered Charity, number 1121757, and a Company Limited by Guarantee, registered in England and Wales, number 6410037.

Chief Executive: Mr David Woodgate

Independent Schools' Bursars Association
Bluett House, Unit 11–12, Manor Farm, Cliddesden, Basingstoke, Hampshire RG25 2JB
Tel: 01256 330369 · email: office@theisba.org.uk

BSA

BOARDING SCHOOLS' ASSOCIATION

www.boarding.org.uk

The Boarding Schools' Association (BSA) champions boarding and promotes boarding excellence.

The BSA represents over 560 independent and state boarding schools in the UK and overseas. BSA services include professional development, government relations, communications, media, publications, conferences, training and events.

Aims

The BSA exists to:

- Champion boarding and promote boarding excellence
- Help member schools provide the best quality of boarding education and meet the highest standards of welfare for boarders by providing a comprehensive programme of professional development for all staff and governors of boarding schools
- Conduct appropriate research and produce regular publications on boarding issues and good practice in boarding
- Liaise with other bodies concerned with boarding – the Independent Schools Inspectorate, the Independent Schools Council, the Scottish Council for Independent Schools, Ofsted etc
- Engage in a regular dialogue with government on boarding issues
- Provide a platform informing parents and prospective boarders of the benefits of twenty-first century boarding and offer a conduit to individual member schools for further enquiry
- Forge links with associations of boarding schools worldwide
- Speak for boarding in today's world.

Membership

Membership is open to all schools with boarders which are members of Associations within the Independent Schools Council (ISC), to schools in membership of the Scottish Council of Independent Schools (SCIS), and also to state boarding schools. Membership may also be offered to boarding schools overseas at Associate or Affiliate level. Please contact Chris Ryan, Membership and Marketing Manager (chris@boarding.org.uk) for further details. Current membership comprises over 550 schools (full boarding, weekly/flexi boarding, or day schools with boarding provision; co-educational or single-sex; preparatory or secondary).

Support for Schools

THE PROFESSIONAL DEVELOPMENT PROGRAMME

The BSA has established a Professional Development Programme for all staff working in boarding schools. These BSA courses lead to validated Certificates of Professional Practice in Boarding Education. There is a programme of Day Courses on a range of topics including Child Protection, Anti-Bullying strategies, the role of GAP Assistants, Boarding Legislation and Good Practice and Boarding Governance.

Individual courses and INSET tailored to the particular needs of a school or group of schools is also offered. BSA training is available to all staff who work in boarding schools and to the Governors of boarding schools.

BSA Training Programmes are also used by schools and boarding associations throughout the world.

RESIDENTIAL CONFERENCES

Conferences are held annually for:
Boarding House Staff
Deputy Heads & Heads of Boarding
MAGIC – Marketing, Admissions, Guardianship and International Conference
Heads
State Boarding Schools
Nurses & Matrons

PUBLICATIONS

These include:

- *Running a School Boarding House – A Legal Guide for Housemasters and Housemistresses*
- *Duty of Care*
- *Parenting the Boarder*
- *Being a Boarder*
- *Mirror Mirror – Reflections on Boarding Practice 2014*
- *Truly World Class*
- *Boarding Briefing Papers* – are published at regular intervals on matters concerning boarding legislation and good practice

NATIONAL BOARDING STANDARDS

The Association liaises with the Department for Education, Ofsted, and the Independent Schools Inspectorate on the inspection of boarding schools under the National Minimum Standards for Boarding schools in England and Wales, and the Care Commission in Scotland.

LIAISON WITH NATIONAL BODIES

The Association meets regularly with the Department for Education to discuss issues concerned with boarding. It also liaises with Local Government, ISI (Independent Schools Inspectorate), Ofsted (Office for Standards in Education), CEAS (Children's Education Advisory Service) and all the national educational organisations.

Organisation

At the Annual General Meeting, held at the Heads' Annual Conference, Officers of the Association are elected together with the Executive Committee The Honorary Treasurer is usually a Bursar from a member school.

Chief Executive
Robin Fletcher, email: robin@boarding.org.uk

The Boarding Schools' Association
4th Floor, 134–136 Buckingham Palace Road, London SW1W 9SA
Tel: +44 (0)20 7798 1580 · email: bsa@boarding.org.uk

ISEB
INDEPENDENT SCHOOLS EXAMINATIONS BOARD

www.iseb.co.uk

COMMON ENTRANCE

COMMON PRE-TESTS

COMMON ACADEMIC SCHOLARSHIP

Executive Chairman:
Mr D Barnes, BA Hons, PGCE

Chief Administrator:
Mrs K Allen, BSc Hons, PGCE

COMMON ENTRANCE

The Common Entrance Examinations are used for transfer to senior schools at the ages of 11+ and 13+. The syllabuses are devised and regularly monitored by the Independent Schools Examinations Board which comprises members of the Headmasters' and Headmistresses' Conference, the Girls' Schools Association and the Independent Association of Prep Schools.

The papers are set by examiners appointed by the Board, but the answers are marked by the senior school for which a candidate is entered. Common Entrance is not a public examination as, for example, GCSE, and candidates may normally be entered only if they have been offered a place at a senior school, subject to their passing the examination.

Candidates normally take the examination in their own junior or preparatory schools, either in the UK or overseas.

Common Entrance at 11+ consists of papers in English, Mathematics and Science. At 13+, in addition to these core subjects, a wide range of additional papers is available in modern and classical languages, and the humanities subjects. Tiered papers are available for many subjects.

Mandarin Chinese is offered as an online examination which can be taken at any age.

Dates

The 11+ examination is held in early November or mid-January.

The 13+ examination commences either on the first Monday in November, the last Monday in January or on the first Tuesday in June.

Entries

In cases where candidates are at schools in membership of the Independent Association of Prep Schools, it is usual for heads of these schools to make arrangements for entering candidates for the appropriate examination after consultation with parents and senior school heads. In the case of candidates at schools which do not normally enter candidates, it is the responsibility of parents to arrange for candidates to be entered for the appropriate examination in accordance with the requirements of senior schools.

Conduct of the Examination

Regulations for the conduct of the examination are laid down by the Independent Schools Examinations Board.

Past Papers and Other Resources

Copies of past Common Entrance papers can be purchased from Galore Park:

website: www.galorepark.co.uk

email: customer.services@galorepark.co.uk

Tel: 01235 400555

ISEB-endorsed Common Entrance textbooks, revision guides and practice exercises are available from a number of publishers, listed on the ISEB website.

COMMON PRE-TESTS

The Common Pre-Tests are age-standardised tests used to assess pupils' attainment and potential when they are in Year 6 or Year 7, prior to entry to their senior schools. Pupils who sit the tests will normally still be required to sit the Common Entrance examinations.

ISEB commissions the tests from GL Assessment which has long been associated with providing high-quality and reliable assessments in education. The tests are taken online, usually in the pupil's current school, and include multiple-choice tests in Mathematics, English, verbal and non-verbal reasoning. Senior schools will inform parents if their son or daughter needs to be entered for the tests.

No special preparation is needed for the tests and no past papers are available, although a short familiarisation test is provided for candidates. Examples and practice questions are provided during the test itself so that candidates understand what they have to do.

Further details are available for schools in the Schools section of the ISEB website and for parents in the Parents section of the ISEB website.

COMMON ACADEMIC SCHOLARSHIP

ISEB sets Scholarship examination papers at 13+ which a number of independent senior schools use to assess potential scholars. Papers are set in English, Mathematics, Science, History, Geography, Religious Studies, French and Latin. Questions are based on the Common Entrance syllabuses and past papers are available from Galore Park.

Candidates are entered by the senior schools for which they are registered and the papers are marked by the senior schools themselves.

Fees

The Independent Schools Examinations Board decides the fees to be charged for each candidate. Schools are notified annually in the spring term of fees payable for the following three terms. Parents seeking information about current fees should look on the ISEB website or contact the ISEB office.

Correspondence

Correspondence about academic matters relating to the Common Entrance examinations and requests for further information about the administration of the examinations should be addressed to the Chief Administrator.

Independent Schools Examinations Board
Suite 3, Endeavour House, Crow Arch Lane, Ringwood, Hampshire BH24 1HP
Tel: 01425 470555 · email: enquiries@iseb.co.uk

COBIS
COUNCIL OF BRITISH INTERNATIONAL SCHOOLS
www.cobis.org.uk
twitter: @COBISorg · @COBIS_CEO

Representing over 450 member organisations, COBIS is the global association for international British schools overseas. The organisation has developed markedly since its foundation, changing to meet the needs and aspirations of its growing global school membership base.

COBIS exists to serve, support and represent its member schools – their leaders, governors, staff and students by:

- Providing Quality Assurance in member schools via The Patron's Accreditation and Compliance scheme
- Representing member schools with the British Government, educational bodies and the corporate sector
- Providing effective professional development for senior leaders, governors, teachers and support staff
- Facilitating, coordinating and supporting professional networking opportunities for British International schools
- Promoting child protection and safer recruitment and employment practices
- Engaging, challenging and inspiring students of all ages and abilities by delivering excellent interschool student competitions and events
- Providing access to information about trends and developments in UK education
- Facilitating high impact 'Member to Member' professional networking
- Promoting career opportunities within the global COBIS network
- Connecting suppliers and companies operating in the education sector with international British schools overseas in its role as Trade Challenge Partner of the Department for International Trade (DIT)
- Brokering a cost-effective consultancy service between schools and approved educational support service providers

Patron
HRH The Duke of York, KG

COBIS Executive 2018–2019

Honorary President
Sir Roger Fry CBE

Honorary Vice Presidents
The Rt Hon Lord Andrew Adonis
Sir Mervyn Brown KCMG OBE
Michael Cooper OBE
Lord Lexden OBE
The Rt Hon the Lord Macgregor OBE
Dame Judith Mayhew Jonas DBE
Jean Scott
Lord Sharman OBE
The Rt Hon the Lord Knight of Weymouth

COBIS Head Office
CEO: Colin Bell

COBIS Board
Elected:

Chairman: Trevor Rowell, Governor, British International School Cairo
Vice Chairman: Dr Steffen Sommer, Principal, Doha College, Qatar
Kai Vacher, Principal, British School Muscat, Oman
Dawn Akyurek, Chief Academic Officer, King's Group, Spain
Eamonn Mullally, Executive Head/CEO, The Edron Academy, Mexico City
Janet Brock, Headteacher, The British International School of Kuala Lumpur
Craig Heaton, Headteacher, St Saviour's School Ikoyi
Paul Morgan, Principal, The British School of Amsterdam

Co-opted:

Professor Deborah Eyre, Author, World Class Educator
Dr Martin Coles, Former CEO, The British School in The Netherlands and Former Vice-Dean, The National College for School Leadership (*Treasurer*)
Jennifer Bray MBE, Former Principal in Hong Kong and Brussels (*Inspections and Quality Officer*)
Simon O'Grady, Principal, GEMS International School, Metropark Kuala Lumpur
Clive Pierrepont, Director of Communications, Taaleem

Council of British International Schools
55-56 Russell Square, Bloomsbury, London WC1B 4HP
Tel: +44 (0)20 3826 7190 · email: pa@cobis.org.uk

INDEPENDENT SCHOOLS INSPECTORATE
AND ISI CONSULTANCY LTD
www.isi.net

School inspections undertaken by the Independent Schools Inspectorate (ISI) have two principal objectives: to nurture and encourage school improvement and to report on whether independent schools comply with the regulatory requirements of government. Its overriding aim is to help ensure that every child receives education and care of the highest quality in the schools it inspects.

ISI is the body approved by the Secretary of State to inspect schools in England in membership of Associations within the Independent Schools Council (ISC). Inspections are conducted in accordance with the Education and Skills Act 2008, the Childcare Act 2006 and the Children Act 1989. The Office for Standards in Education, Children's Services and Skills (Ofsted) monitors ISI's work on behalf of the Department for Education (DfE).

Schools are inspected regularly on a schedule agreed with the DfE. Inspection reports are published to parents and made available, with other related material, on the ISI website: www.isi.net.

What gives ISI inspections their unique quality is the element of 'peer review'. Inspections are led by professional Reporting Inspectors, mainly either former HMI or Ofsted Inspectors or former head teachers who have trained and qualified for the role. The inspection team is composed of serving head teachers or other senior staff from ISC schools, who are also trained by ISI. This peer review combines professional rigour, an understanding of the reality of modern independent schools and an up-to-date grasp of current educational developments.

ISI also inspects private Further Education and English Language providers. Inspection under this voluntary scheme for colleges satisfies the inspection requirements necessary to apply for or renew a Tier 4 licence to sponsor international students under the UKVI Points Based System. ISI also inspects schools in more than 30 countries worldwide, using a framework appropriate to the schools' international setting, and is approved to inspect schools under the UK government scheme for British Schools Overseas (BSO).

Through its subsidiary company ISI Consultancy Ltd, ISI offers a range of seminars, INSET and consultancy services to schools, other organisations and governments in the UK and overseas on matters related to inspection and school improvement.

Independent Schools Inspectorate
CAP House, 9-12 Long Lane, London EC1A 9HA
Tel: 020 7600 0100 · Fax: 020 7776 8849 · email: info@isi.net

METHODIST INDEPENDENT SCHOOLS TRUST
www.methodistschools.org.uk
Chairman: Revd Dr John Barrett
General Secretary: Mr David Humphreys
Director of Finance and Company Secretary: Mr John Weaving

Trust Schools

Culford School, Bury St Edmunds, Suffolk	Queen's College, Taunton, Somerset
Farringtons School, Chislehurst, Kent	Shebbear College, Beaworthy, Devon
Kent College, Canterbury, Kent	Truro School, Truro, Cornwall
Kent College Pembury, Tunbridge Wells, Kent	Woodhouse Grove School, Apperley Bridge, West Yorks
Kingsley School, Bideford, North Devon	

Acquired Schools

Lorenden Preparatory School, Faversham, Kent	St Petroc's School, Bude, Cornwall
Moorlands School, Leeds, West Yorkshire	Truro High School, Truro, Cornwall
Roselyon School, Par, Cornwall	

Associated Schools

Ashville College, Harrogate, North Yorks	Rydal Penrhos School, Colwyn Bay, North Wales
Kingswood School, Bath, Somerset	

Affiliated Schools

The Leys School, Cambridge	St Faith's School, Cambridge
Queenswood School, Hatfield, Herts	Kent College Dubai

In cases of need applications may be made to a Methodist Bursary Fund for financial help to enable Methodist children to attend these schools. This fund is available to day pupils as well as boarding pupils. Details are available from the Schools.

Information regarding other sources of assistance with fees may be obtained from The Independent Schools Council, First Floor, 27 Queen Anne's Gate, London SW1H 9BU. Tel: 020 7766 7070; email: office@isc.co.uk

Methodist Independent Schools Trust
Methodist Church House, 25 Marylebone Road, London NW1 5JR
Tel: 020 7935 3723 · email: admin@methodistschools.org.uk

GDST

THE GIRLS' DAY SCHOOL TRUST

www.gdst.net

Chair:	Juliet Humphries
Deputy Chair:	Helen Williams, CB, MA
Chief Executive:	Cheryl Giovannoni

The GDST is a family of 23 independent schools and two academies located across England and Wales. Our schools represent the very best in teaching and pastoral care. We foster academic excellence but also build character, helping girls to be confident, resilient and fearless. Whatever her disposition and direction in life, we strive to create environments where each girl can learn without limits and thrive in her own way.

The Trust was founded in 1872 and throughout our history we have been at the forefront of education for girls and a strong voice in promoting opportunities for young women.

Today, the GDST is a vibrant, successful organisation and our schools are some of the very best in the country. Each one has its own distinct identity, but they all share a common purpose: to help every girl fulfil her potential and make her dreams a reality, for the benefit of everyone. Each school is characterised by a broad curriculum, academic excellence and rich programme of co-curricular activities.

GDST schools

Blackheath High School	Oxford High School
Brighton & Hove High School	Portsmouth High School
Bromley High School	Putney High School
Croydon High School	The Royal High School, Bath
Howell's School Llandaff, Cardiff	Sheffield High School for Girls
Kensington Prep School	Shrewsbury High School
Newcastle High School for Girls	South Hampstead High School
Northampton High School	Streatham & Clapham High School
Northwood College for Girls	Sutton High School
Norwich High School for Girls	Sydenham High School
Notting Hill & Ealing High School	Wimbledon High School
Nottingham Girls' High School	

GDST academies

The Belvedere Academy, Liverpool
Birkenhead High School Academy

Information on the schools can be found in the Yearbook or on the GDST website: www.gdst.net

The Girls' Day School Trust is a Registered Charity, number 306983.

The Girls' Day School Trust
100 Rochester Row, London SW1P 1JP
Tel: 020 7393 6666 · email: info@wes.gdst.net

CISC
CATHOLIC INDEPENDENT SCHOOLS' CONFERENCE
www.catholicindependentschools.com

The Catholic Independent Schools' Conference is a dynamic and forward-thinking family of schools with members in England, Scotland, Ireland, France, Spain, Gibraltar, Italy and Singapore. There are 135 schools in CISC and the number is growing. In total, CISC schools educate more than 40,000 pupils from nursery age through to eighteen.

There is a wide variety of types of school in CISC, with co-educational, single-sex, day, boarding, junior, prep, senior and all-through. We also have in our family of schools ten special schools (two independent and eight non-maintained special schools) serving a wide range of complex needs from profound physical disability to visual impairment and autism. For more information on our special schools please follow the link from Schools on the homepage.

Most of our schools have their foundation in a Religious Order or Congregation. These orders, many from the Continent, set up Catholic schools in Britain when there was little educational provision for the Catholic population. Despite the great variety of these religious foundations there is a strong common goal to serve the mission of the Church by educating young men and women to take their place in society as young disciples, or for those who are not of the Catholic faith, principled citizens with values based on the Gospel who will work for the common good.

CISC is very much part of this living tradition and is committed to playing its part in the mission of the Church in education. A priority for us is to support the formation of our members, i.e. the heads of our Catholic independent schools. We are also committed to developing the next generation of Catholic leaders and our programme for their formation, Introduction to the Leadership of a Catholic School, is very popular with our schools.

CISC is a charitable organisation and the main beneficiaries are our members and their colleagues. While we support opportunities for the pupils in our schools (e.g. through competitions) we do not provide services or supervise any activities for our pupils. CISC is governed by a committee currently consisting of nine members, all serving heads, who are trustees of the charity. CISC employs a Secretariat who is responsible for delivering on the strategic aims of the organisation. Every year at the annual conference CISC members have an opportunity to attend the Annual General Meeting, to view the annual accounts and statement from the trustees, and share their views on the direction and priorities of the charity.

For more information on joining as a Member, please visit our website or contact Dr Maureen Glackin, by email: info@catholicindependentschools.com.

Catholic Independent Schools' Conference
19 South Road, Hampton, Middlesex TW12 3PE
Tel: 07595 089928 · email: info@catholicindependentschools.com

CHOIR SCHOOLS' ASSOCIATION

www.choirschools.org.uk

Patron: The Duchess of Kent

Committee:

Chairman: Neil Chippington, St John's College School, Cambridge

Vice-Chairman: Paul Smith, Hereford Cathedral School

Yvette Day, King's College School, Cambridge
Clive Marriott, Salisbury Cathedral School
Stephen Morris, St Edward's College, Liverpool

Clare Turnbull, Lanesborough School, Guildford
Richard White, Director of Development

CSA Full and Associate Members

Ampleforth College, York
Blackburn Cathedral
Bristol Cathedral Choir School
The Cathedral School, Llandaff
Chapel Royal, Hampton Court
Chetham's School of Music, Manchester
The Chorister School, Durham
Christ Church Cathedral School, Oxford
City of London School
Dean Close Preparatory School, Cheltenham
Exeter Cathedral School
Hereford Cathedral School
King's College School, Cambridge
King's Ely Junior, Ely
King's Rochester Preparatory School
The King's School, Gloucester
The King's School, Peterborough
The King's School, Worcester

Lanesborough School, Guildford
Leicester Cathedral
Lichfield Cathedral School
Lincoln Cathedral
Lincoln Minster School
The London Oratory School
Magdalen College School, Oxford
The Minster School, Southwell
The Minster School, York
New College School, Oxford
Norwich School
The Old Palace School, Croydon
The Pilgrims' School, Winchester
Polwhele House School, Truro
The Portsmouth Grammar School
The Prebendal School, Chichester
Queen Elizabeth Grammar School, Wakefield
Reigate St Mary's Choir School
Ripon Cathedral

Runnymede St Edward's School, Liverpool
Salisbury Cathedral School
Sheffield Cathedral
St Cedd's School, Chelmsford
St Edmund's Junior School, Canterbury
St Edward's College, Liverpool
St George's School, Windsor
St John's College School, Cambridge
St John's College, Cardiff
St Mary's Music School, Edinburgh
St Nicholas Cathedral, Newcastle-upon-Tyne
St Paul's Cathedral School, London
St Peter's Church, Wolverhampton
Wells Cathedral School
Westminster Abbey Choir School, London
Westminster Cathedral Choir School, London
Whitgift School, Croydon

Overseas Members:
St Patrick's Cathedral Choir School, Dublin
The Cathedral Grammar School, Christchurch, New Zealand
National Cathedral School, Washington DC, USA
St Paul's Choir School, Cambridge, MA, USA
St Thomas Choir School, New York, USA

The Choir Schools' Association celebrated its Centenary in 2018.

46 schools in the UK educate some or all of the choristers at cathedrals, churches or college chapels all over the country. Between them they educate well over 20,000 pupils, including some 1,300 choristers. Westminster Abbey Choir School is the only school to educate choristers and probationers only. The Association's associate membership includes cathedrals and churches without choir schools.

Choir schools offer a very special opportunity for children who enjoy singing. They receive a first-class academic and all-round education combined with excellent music training. The experience and self-discipline choristers acquire remain with them for life. There is a wide range of schools: some cater for children aged 7–13, others are junior schools with senior schools to 18; most are Church of England but the Roman Catholic, Scottish and Welsh churches are all represented.

Most CSA members are fee-paying schools and Deans and Chapters provide fee assistance while Government support comes in the shape of the Choir Schools' Scholarship Scheme. Under the umbrella of the Music and Dance Scheme, funds are available to help those who cannot afford even the reduced school fees. Government funding through the Music and Dance Scheme (MDS), along with other monies in its Bursary Trust Fund, is administered by the CSA. Applications are means-tested and an award made once a child has secured a place at a choir school.

Each CSA member school has its own admissions procedure for choristers. However, every child will be assessed both musically and academically. A growing number of children are given informal voice tests which enable the organist or director of music to judge whether they have the potential to become choristers. Some are offered places immediately or will be urged to enter the more formal voice trial organised by the school. In some cases a family may be advised not to proceed. Alternatively, the child's voice may be more suitable for one of the other choir schools.

A number of special ingredients help make a good chorister: potential, a keen musical ear and an eagerness to sing. A clutch of music examination certificates is not vital – alertness and enthusiasm are! At the same time, school staff must be satisfied that a new recruit can cope with school work and the many other activities on offer as well as the demanding choir workload.

To find out more about choir schools please visit the CSA website: **www.choirschools.org.uk**

CSA members can be contacted direct or you can write, email or telephone
for further information about choir schools to:

Jane Capon, Information Officer, Village Farm, The Street, Market Weston, Diss, Norfolk IP22 2NZ
Telephone: 01359 221333; email: info@choirschools.org.uk

Mrs Susan Rees, Administrator, 39 Grange Close, Winchester, Hampshire SO23 9RS
Tel: 01962 890530; email: csamds@tiscali.co.uk

CIFE
COUNCIL FOR INDEPENDENT EDUCATION
www.cife.org.uk

President:
Lord Lexden OBE

Vice President:
Hugh Monro, MA

Chairman:
Tim Naylor, BA Hons, MSc, PGCE

Vice-Chairman:
Mark Shingleton, BA, MA, PGCE

Independent sixth-form colleges are extremely well placed to offer what is needed for students preparing for university and beyond. The best such colleges are generally members of CIFE, the Council for Independent Education, an organisation which was founded more than 40 years ago. There are 24 CIFE colleges, geographically spread across the country, each one offering individual features but all subject to high standards of accreditation. For example, there are some colleges that specialise in students wishing to retake in order to improve exam grades, some offering GCSE and pre-GCSE programmes as well as full A Level courses, which may be residential, homestay, day, or a mix of all three. Several colleges offer foundation programmes and are twinned with universities. In short, CIFE colleges offer a wide range of educational environments in which students can succeed.

Teaching in CIFE colleges really helps and supports students since teaching groups are small and teachers highly experienced and specialists in their subject. The 'tutorial' system derives directly from Oxbridge where it continues to be world famous. A student in a small group receives a greater degree of individual attention. Regular testing ensures that she/he maintains good progress, and the emphasis on study skills provides essential support for the AS/A Level subjects.

It is not surprising that a student gains confidence and self-belief within such an environment. Colleges engender a strong work ethic in their student communities. Many of the minor rules and regulations essential for schools are not necessary at CIFE colleges. Good manners and an enthusiastic attitude are every bit as important, but uniform, strict times for eating or homework, assemblies or games participation are not part of the picture. It can be seen from the large numbers of students going on to higher education from CIFE colleges that universities regard our students highly.

Increasing numbers of young people are deciding to move school at the age of 16, not because they are unhappy with their school, but because they see the need for a change at this stage. It may be that they wish to study a subject which their school does not offer, such as Accounting, Law, Psychology or Photography. Perhaps they are looking for a more adult environment or one where they can focus on their academic subjects to the exclusion of other things. However, it would be misleading to suggest that CIFE colleges are lacking in extracurricular activities, as every CIFE college recognises the need for enrichment of all sorts, sporting, social and creative. The difference is that activities are at the choice of the student.

As with schools, choosing a college calls for careful research. CIFE colleges undergo regular inspection either by the Independent Schools Inspectorate, Ofsted and/or the British Accreditation Council, recognised bodies which regulate the provision and standards of teaching, safety and pastoral care. While each college has its own individual character, all share the desire to provide each individual student with a superb preparation for higher education.

Members of CIFE

Acorn House College, London
Ashbourne Independent Sixth-form College, London
Bales College, London
Bath Academy, Bath
Bosworth Independent College, Northampton
Brooke House College, Market Harborough
Cambridge Centre for Sixth-form Studies, Cambridge
Cambridge Tutors College, London
Carfax College, Oxford
CATS College, Cambridge
CATS College, London
Chelsea Independent College, London
Cherwell College, Oxford
Collingham, London
David Game College, London
DLD College, London
LSI Independent Sixth Form College, London
Mander Portman Woodward, Birmingham
Mander Portan Woodward, Cambridge
Mander Portman Woodward, London
Oxford International College, Oxford
Oxford Tutorial College, Oxford
Regent College, London
Westminster Tutors, London

Further information can be obtained from:

CIFE
Tel: 020 8767 8666 · email: enquiries@cife.org.uk

UNITED LEARNING
www.unitedlearning.org.uk

United Learning Independent Schools

Our Ethos

United Learning is a group of schools committed to providing excellent education through which all pupils are able to progress, achieve and go on to succeed in life. Our approach is underpinned by a sense of moral purpose and commitment to doing what is right for children and young people, supporting colleagues to achieve excellence and acting with integrity in all our dealings within and beyond the organisation, in the interests of young people everywhere. We summarise this ethos as 'The Best in Everyone'.

This ethos underpins our core values:

- Ambition – to achieve the best for ourselves and others;
- Confidence – to have the courage of our convictions and to take risks in the right cause;
- Creativity – to imagine possibilities and make them real;
- Respect – of ourselves and others in all that we do;
- Enthusiasm – to seek opportunity, find what is good and pursue talents and interests;
- Determination – to overcome obstacles and reach success.

As a single organisation, we seek to bring together the best of independent and state sectors, respecting both traditions and learning from each. We believe that each of our schools is and should be distinctive – each is committed to developing its own strengths and identity while sharing our core values as institutions which promote service, compassion and generosity.

Academic scholarships, exhibitions and bursaries are awarded at all schools. The tuition fees vary according to age and school; for example, tuition fees per annum in the senior schools range from £10,899 to £16,800 (day), and £25,305 to £33,750 (full boarding).

United Learning comprises: UCST (Registered in England No: 2780748. Charity No. 1016538) and ULT (Registered in England No. 4439859. An Exempt Charity). Companies limited by guarantee. VAT number 834 8515 12.

United Learning
Worldwide House, Thorpe Wood, Peterborough, PE3 6SB
Tel: 01832 864444 · Fax: 01832 864455 · email: enquiries@unitedlearning.org.uk

INSPIRING FUTURES

**Working in partnership with independent UK and
international schools to provide the full range of careers
education and development support for their students**

www.inspiringfutures.org.uk

Contacts

Who to ask for information and help
Contact the Area or Regional Director for your area (see below) or the Information Helpline on 01491 820382

For further information on *The Inspiring Futures Foundation* or on *Inspiring Futures Careers* please contact:
Executive Director: Sarah Frend (email: sarah.frend@inspiringfutures.org.uk, tel: 01491 820381)

Purpose and Aims

Inspiring Futures (IF) is a leading provider of careers information, advice and guidance for young people both in the UK and internationally. It exists to help young people make decisions and develop skills which maximize their potential, enhance their employment opportunities and allow them to make a fulfilling contribution to the world in which they live. Their charity group, Inspiring Futures Foundation, oversees a School Careers Award Scheme that provides free careers support for aspiring pupils from low-income schools.

In order to do this, Inspiring Futures works with like-minded people and organisations to provide expert careers guidance, innovative learning resources and personal skills training to young people from all backgrounds, particularly those entering higher education. Inspiring Futures offers a range of professional services to support students and schools' careers staff.

Inspiring Futures Membership for independent and international schools provides a range of careers and higher education related services to complement and reinforce school programmes with impartial and professional expertise.

Services also include Futurewise, a personalised careers guidance programme for students aged 15 to 23. The web-based psychometric profile and one-to-one interview is followed by a wealth of resources and support for the student helping them with subject choices, routes to HE and alternative pathways to a career. The programme is flexible making it suitable for easy lesson planning.

Inspiring Futures Careers : Area and Regional Directors

Scotland & International

Area Director: Margaret Graham (Tel: 07717 530459; email: margaret.graham@inspiringfutures.org.uk)

E Scotland: Jane Ambrose (Tel: 07887 758166; email: jane.ambrose@inspiringfutures.org.uk)

N, W & Central Scotland: David Chapman (Tel: 07387 091078; email: david.chapman@inspiringfutures.org.uk)

International: James Davidson (Tel: 07545 734105; email: james.davidson@inspiringfutures.org.uk)

England & Wales

North, North East & Midlands

Area Director: Kate Coles (Tel: 07717 468074; email: kate.coles@inspiringfutures.org.uk)

Shropshire & Midlands: Sally Hayward (Tel: 07887 758649; email: sally.hayward@inspiringfutures.org.uk)

Wales: Jane Johns (Tel: 07387 091080; email: jane.johns@inspiringfutures.org.uk)

East: Rowena James (Tel: 07387 091074; email: rowena.james@inspiringfutures.org.uk)

London & South East

Area Director: Emma-Marie Fry (Tel: 07702 226271; email: emma-marie.fry@inspiringfutures.org.uk)

Sussex, Kent, Hampshire & Surrey: Elizabeth Armstrong (Tel: 07909 972769; email: elizabeth.armstrong@inspiringfutures.org.uk)

North London & Herts: Helen Barham (Tel: 07917 712603; email: hel.barham@inspiringfutures.org.uk)

South West

South West: Vicki MacDonald (Tel: 07717 496523; email: vicki.macdonald@inspiringfutures.org.uk)

High quality education in an actively Christian environment for all

w⊗odard schools

Information on all of the schools can be found at www.woodard.co.uk

Woodard schools form the largest group of Anglican schools in England and Wales. In addition to the above list of incorporated schools, a number of schools in the independent and maintained sectors choose to be associated or affiliated, respectively. Woodard also sponsors academies. The schools are not exclusive and take pupils of all faiths and of none. In total over 30,000 pupils are taught in schools throughout the group.

This unique partnership of schools, independent and state, boarding and day, junior and senior, co-educational and single-sex, is united by a determination to provide a first-class holistic education within a distinctive Christian ethos. The schools were founded by Nathaniel Woodard in the nineteenth century and aim to prepare children from a wide variety of backgrounds for responsibility, leadership and service in today's world.

The schools seek to provide flexible, stimulating, demanding and appropriate schemes of academic study together with a rich variety of sporting, artistic and recreational opportunities. We encourage personal success, self-confidence and self-respect whilst also stressing the importance of responsible citizenship, high moral values and a commitment to use one's gifts in the service of others.

With the geographical spread and diversity of schools included in the group it is able to offer parents a wide range of educational options for their children. Woodard incorporated schools operate bursary and scholarship schemes including all classes of concession. Fees vary from school to school and are set locally.

The Woodard Corporation is a Registered Charity (No. 1096270) and Company (No. 4659710). The objects of the charity are to promote and extend education (including spiritual, moral, social, cultural and physical education) in accordance with the doctrines and principles of the Church of England/Church in Wales by directly or indirectly carrying on schools

ASSOCIATION FOR ADMISSIONS, MARKETING AND COMMUNICATIONS IN INDEPENDENT SCHOOLS (AMCIS)

FOUNDED 1993

www.amcis.co.uk

Objectives:
- To promote and develop good marketing practice in admissions, marketing and communications in independent education
- To help increase the effectiveness of the admissions, marketing and communications representatives of member schools
- To encourage personal development within the schools' admissions, marketing and communications departments

Achieved through:
- Seminars and workshops on a variety of admissions, marketing and communications-led subjects held throughout the year
- Annual residential conference
- Regional networking lunches
- Training – Diploma in Schools' Marketing & Certificate in Admissions Management
- Helpline
- Website with member-only resource section
- LinkedIn Group Forum
- On-line News bulletins throughout the year
- Speakers provided for conferences, inset days and similar

Membership:
- School Membership, renewable annually by subscription
- Corporate Membership, renewable annually by subscription

The Association is directed by a Chairman, Vice Chairman and Treasurer together with a Board of Directors.

Managing Director: Tory Gillingham

AMCIS
57A Market Place, Malton, North Yorkshire YO17 7LX
Tel: 01653 699800 · email: enquiries@amcis.co.uk

ASSOCIATION OF REPRESENTATIVES OF OLD PUPILS' SOCIETIES (AROPS)

Founded in 1971

www.arops.org.uk

President:
Bill Gillen (Old Arnoldians and Belfast Old Instonians' Association)
Vice-Presidents:
Margaret Carter-Pegg (Old Crohamian), Guy Cliff (Old Silcoatian), Michael Freegard (Old Haileyburian),
Tim Neale (Radleian Society), Trish Woodhouse (GSA)

Committee
Chairman: Peter Jakobek (Old Bristolians)
Treasurer: Keith Balkham (KGS Friends)
Secretary: Vijay Khullar (Old Roffensian)
and 10 committee members

Aim: To provide a friendly forum for the exchange of views and experiences between representatives of school alumni societies.

Membership: Open to representatives of any school alumni society. New members are always welcome. Details are available on the website – www.arops.org.uk – where you can also find information on events and member societies' news, regularly updated. Please contact us by email to: arops@arops.org.uk.

Meetings: The Conference in May is our main event and an ideal opportunity to meet up with other representatives and to share thoughts on current topics. Our very successful Conference in 2018 took place at St Dunstan's College, Catford, London where sessions included: *Are you ready for GDPR, Mastering Communications, Engaging Younger Alumni, The Alumni Society – Where next, Alumni Engagement with ToucanTech, Digital Archiving with SDS Group, Data Protection – detailed Q&A.*

The Conferences always end with a lively forum and a dinner. The 2019 Conference will be held at Magdalen College School, Oxford on Saturday 11th May 2019.

Apart from the Conference and the AGM (held in London in October), AROPS now organises a series of *regional networking meetings* around the country which allow representatives to meet neighbouring members in a less formal environment. These have proved very popular for members to discuss items concerning alumni engagement on an informal basis.

Subscription: £50 per year (with discounts for smaller societies). Please email the Treasurer, Keith Balkham, on kbalkham@hotmail.com or write to him at: 14 Cromwell Road, Alperton, Middlesex HA0 1JS.

MOSA
MEDICAL OFFICERS OF SCHOOLS ASSOCIATION

FOUNDED 1884

www.mosa.org.uk

Objects

It is the objective of the Association to offer guidance and support and to encourage the application of the highest of medical standards in the educational environment. MOSA offers its members mutual assistance in promoting school health and the holding of meetings for consideration of all subjects connected with the special work of medical officers of schools.

Membership

Medical officers of schools and medical and dental practitioners and nurses especially concerned with the health of the schoolchild are eligible for membership, and members of the teaching profession, and those related to independent school management, for associate membership. The membership currently stands at 174.

The work of the Association

The Council meets three times a year and is chaired by the current President, Dr Stephen Haynes, MO to Bloxham School. MOSA council members are available for advice to members and non-members. Members have access to a secure online discussion forum where questions and topics are discussed giving access to up-to-date resources and peer support.

Clinical meetings are arranged each year together with an annual summer visit to a school. Research projects are carried out individually and collectively. The Association strongly recommends that all independent schools appoint medical officers to carry out preventative medicine duties which are undertaken in maintained schools by the School Health Service.

MOSA Consultancy Service

MOSA offers a consultancy service for any school which will offer a review of the medical care provided within the school environment.

This can be tailored to the school's needs but tends to be one of two types:

• A general review of the overall medical/nursing provision in the school

• A review of a specific area of concern.

Initially there will be discussion between the MOSA team leader and the school representative so that the Terms of Reference can be drawn up. MOSA will then provide the necessary team to perform the investigation with the most suitably qualified professionals, being able to draw from a pool of highly experienced school doctors and nurses. The team will then visit the appropriate areas of the school and carry out any necessary interviews.

If you are interested in this service, please contact the Executive Secretary, email: mosa.execsec@gmail.com.

Publications

The Association publishes administrative and clinical guidelines for its Medical Officers; these are found on the Association's website and updated regularly.

For further information about the Association and other related business enquiries should in the first instance be directed to:

The Hon Secretary: Dr Rebecca Pryse, MB BS, MRCGP, DCH, DRCOG, DFSRH
email: mosa.honsec@gmail.com

For administrative information and background please contact:
The Executive Secretary
Tel: 01375 483102 • email: mosa.execsec@gmail.com

ESU

THE ENGLISH-SPEAKING UNION

UK REGISTERED CHARITY NO. 273136

www.esu.org/sse

Secondary School Exchange Scholarships to the USA

A gap year with a difference – since 1928 the English-Speaking Union has offered young people the opportunity to spend a life-changing year or six months at a private American high school. The ESU offers the following Secondary School Exchange Scholarships:

Three-term scholarships

- The closing date for applications is in February (in your final year of A Levels or equivalent)
- Interviews are in March
- Leave for the US in September (after completion of your A Levels or equivalent)

Two-term scholarships

- The closing date for applications is in September (after completion of your A Levels or equivalent)
- Interviews are in September/October
- Leave for the US in early January

About the Scholarship

Each scholarship covers the cost of tuition, board and lodging, worth $40,000-$65,000. Scholars are fully fledged students at their host school, with access to world class facilities and a range of extra-curricular activities. Alumni of the programme include singer KT Tunstall, Sir Ian Blair, former Metropolitan Police Commissioner, Sir Richard Dearlove KCMG OBE, former head of MI6, 'City Superwoman' Nicole Horlick, the actress and comedienne Dawn French, and former HSBC chairman, Sir John Bond.

SSE is both an academic and cultural gap year programme. Scholars study a range of subjects at their host schools including some they dropped at GCSE, subjects they will study at university, and even subjects that don't feature in UK schools. The skills that can be gained from the exchange have proven to be beneficial at University: American teaching emphasises independence of thought, and discussions play a large part in the classroom. Scholars also enjoy American rites of passage such as spring break, prom, and graduation.

Scholars are responsible for additional costs including travel, insurance, and expenses. The ESU offers means-tested assistance to help towards these additional costs to successful applicants who would otherwise be unable to take up a scholarship. It also offers one full award, designed to cover all the additional costs related to the scholarship. Grants are given in the range of £250-£4,000. Many scholars use the summer holidays or the six-month gap between finishing school and leaving the US to save money for their time abroad.

Eligibility

- You must have completed your A Levels (or equivalent) and be intending to study at a UK university on your return Your place does not need to be confirmed or deferred, and some scholars reapply during their scholarship year
- Applications from students intending to study at a US university at undergraduate level will not be accepted
- You must have a minimum of 3 Grade Cs at A Level or equivalent
- You should be under 19 years and 6 months old when you take up the scholarship
- Scholars are expected to commit to the full term of their scholarship (two-term: 6 months; three-term: 9 months)
- You must be a British or Irish Citizen and have studied/be studying A Levels (or equivalent) at a school in the UK

About the English-Speaking Union

Founded in 1918, the ESU is an international educational charity and membership organisation that promotes mutual understanding, and fosters friendship and exchange throughout the world.

The English-Speaking Union
37 Charles Street, London W1J 5ED
Tel: 020 7529 1550 · email: education@esu.org

 Crowe

Listening to you

Crowe UK is a leading advisor to independent schools.

How we can help you:

- Technical advice in a clear and pragmatic way.
- We focus on your needs, investing time in understanding your school and being proactive in our approach.
- Always working with clear and transparent lines of communication.

Start the conversation

Tina Allison
London
Head of Education
tina.allison@crowe.co.uk
+44 (0)20 7842 7276

Vicky Szulist
Manchester
Partner
vicky.szulist@crowe.co.uk
+44 (0)161 214 7500

Alastair Lyon
Thames Valley
Partner
alastair.lyon@crowe.co.uk
+44 (0)118 959 7222

Guy Biggin
Cheltenham
Partner
guy.biggin@crowe.co.uk
+44 (0)124 223 4421

Helen Drew
Midlands
Partner
helen.drew@crowe.co.uk
+44 (0)121 543 1900

Audit / Tax / Advisory / Risk

Smart decisions. Lasting value.

www.crowe.co.uk

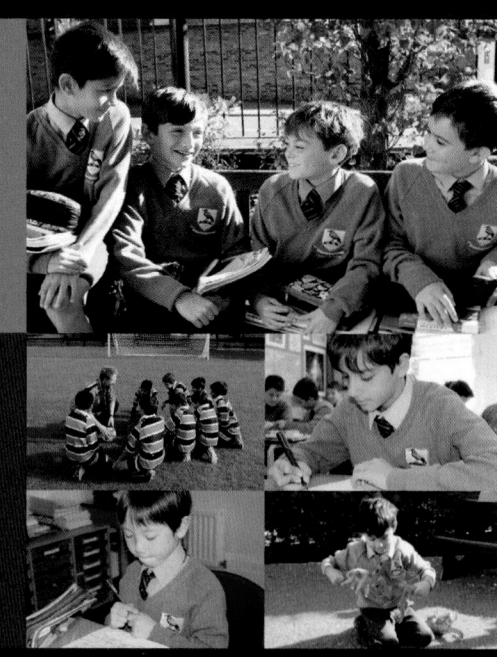

BOOKS FOR MENTAL HEALTH AND WELLBEING FROM

BLOOMSBURY EDUCATION

TEACHERS' MENTAL HEALTH AND WELLBEING

9781472941688 • £18.99

9781472949790 • £16.99

9781472961655 • £19.99

9781472951502 • £19.99

CHILDREN'S MENTAL HEALTH AND WELLBEING

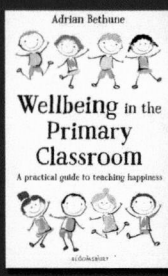

9781472951540 • £19.99

9781472921406 • £18.99

9781472944955 • £14.99

9781472917317 • £24.99

9781472949806 • £9.99

9781472906090 • £10.99

9781472959232 • £10.99

9781472955340 • £10.99

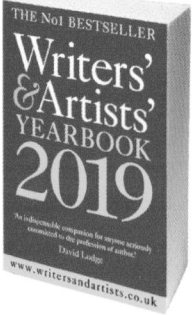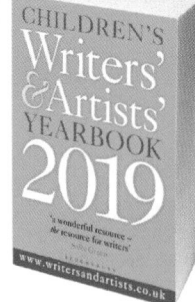

PART I
Schools whose Heads are members of the Headmasters' and Headmistresses' Conference

ALPHABETICAL LIST OF SCHOOLS

The following schools, whose Heads are members of both HMC and GSA, can be found in the GSA section:

Edgbaston High School
Howell's School Llandaff
Lady Eleanor Holles
Putney High School
St Paul's Girls' School
St Swithun's School
South Hampstead High School
Wimbledon High School

HMC
GEOGRAPHICAL LIST OF SCHOOLS

Symbols used in Staff Listings

* Head of Department   § Part Time or Visiting
† Housemaster/Housemistress   ¶ Old Pupil
‡ See below list of staff for meaning

Individual School Entries

Abingdon School

Park Road, Abingdon, Oxfordshire OX14 1DE

Tel:	01235 521563 School
	01235 849041 Registry
	01235 849022 Bursar
Fax:	01235 849079 School
email:	heads.pa@abingdon.org.uk
	admissions@abingdon.org.uk
	bursars.sec@abingdon.org.uk
website:	www.abingdon.org.uk
Twitter:	@abingdonschool
Facebook:	@abingdonschool

The foundation of the School appears to date from the twelfth century; the first clear documentary reference occurs in 1256. After the dissolution of Abingdon Abbey, the School was re-endowed in 1563 by John Roysse, of the Mercers' Company in London. It was rebuilt in 1870 on its present site, and many further buildings have been added including extensive facilities for the arts and sport and a new science centre in 2015. A new sixth form centre, library and art department are the latest additions to the campus in a new 3-storey development that opened in September 2018. Abingdon Preparatory School is situated close by at Frilford (*see entry in IAPS section*).

The total establishment numbers about 1,260 boys. In the Senior School there are about 1,018 boys aged 11–18, of whom approximately 138 are boarders. Boarding starts from age 13.

Boarding is organised in three houses: School House (Mr Mike Litchfield), Austin House (Mr James Golding) and Crescent House (Mr Matthew Kendry). The School values its boarding element very highly and weekly boarding features strongly as part of a policy aimed at asserting a distinctive regional identity for the School.

Pastoral Care. The Lower School has a self-contained system of pastoral care, led by the Lower School Housemaster. All boys join a senior house on entering the Middle School. Within the house system there are distinct tutoring arrangements for Middle School and Upper School boys, which are coordinated by the Middle Master and Upper Master respectively. Special emphasis is placed on the value of parental involvement and also on the provision of careers guidance at appropriate points in a boy's development. Great importance is attached to pastoral care and the School's teaching philosophy is based on a tutorial approach.

Land and Buildings. The School is surrounded by 35 acres of its own grounds, yet is within a few hundred yards of the historic centre of Abingdon, which lies 6 miles down the Thames from Oxford. A further 30 acres of playing fields are located at the Preparatory School, three miles from Abingdon. The School has additional extensive sports facilities at the Tilsley Park Sports Centre in Abingdon.

The last quarter-century has seen a considerable expansion in the School's stock of buildings. A major development in the 1990s was Mercers' Court, which celebrated the School's historical link with the Mercers' Company of London. In 2003 a £3m Arts Centre was opened which houses music and drama. 2008 saw the addition of a new Sports Centre and in autumn 2015 the School opened an impressive Science Centre which transformed the science facilities and enabled redevelopment of the existing science block for other subjects. In 2018 the sixth form facilities were given a tremendous boost with the opening of a new sixth form centre in Beech Court which also houses a new library and art department.

Sports facilities have been greatly enhanced by the £8m sports centre with a superb 8-lane swimming pool, fitness suites, classroom space, squash courts, climbing wall and a martial arts and fencing studio. This follows the opening in 2003 of a beautiful timber-framed boathouse situated on the River Thames a short distance from the School. In 2014 the School took over the lease for Tilsley Park Sports Centre which enhances the School's facilities still further with all-weather surfaces for rugby, hockey, football and athletics.

Courses of Study. The School is essentially academic in character and intention and levels of both expectation and achievement are high. Subjects taught include English, DT, History, French, German, Spanish, Mandarin Chinese, Latin, Greek, Ancient History, Economics, Business Studies, Geography, Mathematics, Physics, Chemistry, Biology, Art, Religious Studies, Psychology, Music and Theatre Studies. Over the last few years there has been increasing collaboration with the School of St Helen and St Katharine with joint tuition particularly in Theatre Studies and Government and Politics. The School is well equipped with computing facilities and audio-visual teaching aids.

All boys spend three years in the Middle School (13 to 16 year olds), in which many different subject combinations are possible, and there is no specialisation before the Sixth Form. In the Sixth Form many boys combine courses in arts and sciences; four subjects are normally taken in the Lower Sixth, followed by three or four in the Upper Sixth. Classroom teaching at all levels is supplemented by a programme of specialist lectures and outside visits. In general terms, the curriculum aims to combine academic discipline and excellence with the fullest encouragement of a wide range of interests and pursuits.

Games and Activities. The School enjoys some 80 acres of playing fields and has its own sports centre, swimming pool, fitness suites, climbing wall, squash and tennis courts and a boathouse on the River Thames. The major sports are rowing, rugby, cricket, hockey, football, tennis, athletics and cross-country. Particular success has been achieved recently in rowing, fencing, badminton, swimming and shooting. Other sports include sailing, golf and Real Tennis.

Importance is attached to the development of a sense of social responsibility, through voluntary membership of Community Service and the Duke of Edinburgh's Award schemes. There is a contingent of the Combined Cadet Force based on voluntary recruitment.

There are numerous societies catering for all kinds of interests and enthusiasms. Music is particularly strong, with over half the boys taking instrumental or vocal lessons in school. In addition to the Chapel Choir, Choral Society and three orchestras, there are excellent opportunities for ensemble playing, including jazz.

Religion. The School is Anglican by tradition, but boys of other denominations are welcome, and normally attend, by year group, a short non-denominational service approximately once a week.

Health. The School has its own doctor and counselling service and there is a well-equipped health centre in the school grounds. In cases of emergency boys are admitted to one of the local hospitals.

Admission. The normal ages of entry to the Senior School are 11, 13 and 16; there are occasionally vacancies at other ages. About half of each year's intake enter the School at age 11 and most of the rest at age 13. Registration by the October of the year prior to joining is recommended. Abingdon Preparatory School has its own entrance arrangements (*see entry in IAPS section*).

Details of the entrance examination procedures for all age groups are available on the School's website. Entry to the Sixth Form, at 16, generally depends on promising GCSE grades and written tests where it is appropriate, as well as on interviews and a report from the previous school.

Term of Entry. September is the usual date of entry and is preferred by the School. Boys may be accepted in any of the three terms, if vacancies occur in their age group.

Fees per term (2018–2019). The tuition fee, for dayboys, is £6,650. This includes the cost of lunches and textbooks.

For boarders, the total fee (including tuition and all extras except for instrumental music lessons and some disbursements directly incurred by individual boys) is £11,070 (weekly) and £13,250 (full).

Scholarships and Bursaries. The School offers a number of scholarships and means-tested bursaries at ages 11, 13 and 16; Scholarships and awards categories include: Academic, All-Rounder, Music, Art and Design, Sport and Drama.

Full details are available, on application, from the Registry or from our website www.abingdon.org.uk/scholarships or /bursaries.

The majority of awards are made at 13+ entry and are open to external and internal candidates. Some additional awards are available on entry to Sixth Form and to the Lower School. Scholarships carry an entitlement to a nominal fee remission of £300 per year plus remission of up to 100% of the tuition fee on a means-tested bursary basis. Music Scholarships also carry an entitlement to remission on instrument tuition fees.

Honours. Numerous places are won each year at Oxford and Cambridge and on other highly selective university courses.

Old Abingdonian Club. Administrator: c/o Abingdon School.

Charitable status. Abingdon School Limited is a Registered Charity, number 1071298. It exists to provide educational opportunities which are open to talented boys without regard to their families' economic standing. Its curriculum is designed to promote intellectual rigour, personal versatility and social responsibility.

Governing Body:
Professor Michael Stevens (*Chairman*)
Mr Andrew Saunders-Davies, MRICS, MBA (*Vice Chairman*)
Mr Damian Tracey (*Vice Chairman*)

Mr Robbie Barr
Mrs Glynne Butt
Mr Jonathan Carroll
Miss Penny Chapman
Mr Mark Lascelles
Mrs Olga Senior, MSc
Mr Matthew Tate
Mr Ken Welby

Clerk to the Governors: Mr Tom Ayling, MA

Head: Mr Michael Windsor, BA Hons, MA, PGCE

Second Master: Mr David Dawswell, BSc
Deputy Head, Academic: Mr Graeme May, MA
Deputy Head, Pastoral: Mr Mark Hindley, LLB, UCL, MA
Director of Teaching & Learning: Mrs Ronnie Reading, BA
Chaplain: Revd Dr Simon Steer, BA, MDiv, PhD
Upper Master: Mr Nick O'Doherty, BSc
Middle Master: Mr Andrew Crisp, BA
Lower School Housemaster: Mr Adam Jenkins, BA
Director of eLearning: Mr Ben Whitworth, MA
Curriculum Director: Mr Oliver Lomax, MA
Master of Scholars: Dr Chris Burnand, MA, DPhil
Master i/c the Other Half: Mr Stuart Evans, BA

Housemasters:

Boarders:
Head of Boarding and Crescent House: Mr Matthew Kendry, MA, MEng
School House: Mr Mike Litchfield, BSc
Austin House: Mr James Golding, BSc

Dayboys:
Mr David Border, BSc
Mr David Franklin, MA
Mr Simon James, MA
Mr Adam Jenkins, MA (*Lower School*)
Mr Henry Morgan, MA
Mrs Emily O'Doherty, MA
Mr Richard Pygott, MA, MSc, PGCE

Teaching Staff:
* *Head of Department*

Art and Design:
*Mr Paul Williamson, BA, PGCE
Mrs Emily O'Doherty, MA
Ms Kate Byrne, BA
Ms Elizabeth Hancock, BA

Classics:
*Dr Chris Burnand, MA, DPhil
Mrs Jenny Fishpool, MA
Mr David Franklin, MA
Mr Adam Jenkins, MA
Miss Amanda Moore, BA, MA
Mr Hugh Price, BA

Computing (ICT):
Ben Whitworth, BA

Design and Technology:
*Mr Dan Hughes, BA
Mr David James, BEng, PGCE
Mr Mark Johnson, MEng
Mr Mike Webb, BSc

Drama:
*Mr Ben Phillips, BA
Mr Graeme May, MA
Mr Joe McDonnell, MA
Mr Jeremy Taylor, MA

Economics and Business Studies:
*Mr Adam Hepworth, BSc, PGCE
Mr Dean Evans, BA
Mr Simon Grills, BSc, MSc, MPhil
Dr Laura Haar, BSc, MSc, PhD
Mrs Jackie Simpson, MSc

English:
*Mr Matthew Cooline, BA, MA, PGCE
Mrs Jo Bridgeworth, BA
Mrs Katherine Burrows, BA, MA
Mr Stuart Evans, BA
Mr Mark Hindley, LLB, MA

Mr Andrew Jamison, BA, MLitt, PGCE
Mr Duncan Miller, BA, MA, PGCE
Miss Rena Papadopoulos, BA, MA
Miss Katyana Rocker-Cook, BA, MA
Miss Emma Williamson, BA, MA

Geography:
*Mr Ian Fishpool, BSc, FRGS
Miss Amy Atkinson, BA
The Reverend Paul Gooding, MA, Dip Theo, Dip Min
Mr Peter Moore, BSc
Mr Nick O'Doherty, BSc
Mr Richard Pygott, MA, MSc, PGCE
Mr Robin Southwell-Sander, BA
Mrs Kathy Yarker, BSc, PGCE

History:
*Mr Nicholas Knowland, BA, MA, PGCE
Mr Tom Allen, BA, PGCE
Mr David McGill, BA
Mr Timonthy Chase, BA
Mr Mark Earnshaw, BA, MA
Mr Richard Jackson, MA
Mrs Lucy Moonen, MA, MSc, PGCE
Mrs Helen Wenham, MA

Mathematics:
*Mrs Samantha Coull, BA, MA
Mr Nick Ball, BSc, PGCE
Mr Graham Cook, MMath
Mr David Dawswell, BSc, ACGI
Mr Julian Easterbrook, BA
Mr Andrew English, BA, MLitt
Mrs Eleanor Kaye, BSc
Mr Matthew Kendry, MA, MEng
Mr Henry Morgan, MMath
Mrs Catherine Muller, BSc
Mr David Panter, MEng, PGCE
Mr Martin Poon, MMath
Mr Jason Taylor, DPhil
Mr Harry Williams, MMath, PGCE

Modern Languages:
Mr James Ambrose, BA, MSt, DPhil
Mrs Maud Cottrell, PGCE (*French*)
Mr Andrew Crisp, BA
Mrs Regina Engel-Hart, MA (*Spanish*)
Mrs Victoria Middleton, MA
Mrs Sophie Payne, MA (*Spanish*)
Mrs Esther Peternek, MA, PGCE
Miss Sarah-Jane Poole, BSc (*German*)
Mrs Victoria Pradas Muñoz, BA
Mrs Ronnie Reading, BA, PGCE
Mr Nick Revill, BA
Ms Alexandra von Widdern, BA
Ms Gao Zhang, MSc

Music:
*Mr Michael Stinton, MA, LRAM, ARCM
Mr Christopher Fletcher-Campbell, MA
Mr Jason Preece, BMus, MSt
Mrs Mariette Pringle, MMus, FTCL, LRAM, LRSM
Mrs Lynette Stulting
Mr Andrew Treadaway, BA, MA
Mr Andrew Yeats

Physical Education:
*Mr Pete Bignell, BEd
Mr Andrew Broadbent, BEd
Mr Elliot Birkbeck, BSc
Mr Matthew Gold, BA
Mr Mike Davies, BSc, MSc
Mr Oliver Deasy, BSc, MSc

Mr Tom Donnelly, BSc
Mr James Golding, BSc
Mr James Latham, BA

Religious Studies:
*Mr Tom Eames-Jones, BA, PGCE
Mr Henry Barnes, BA
Miss Natalie Spurling-Holt, BA
The Reverend Dr Simon Steer, BA, MDiv, PhD

Science:

Biology:
*Mr Simon Bliss, BSc
Mr Mathew Dempsey, BSc
Mrs Sarah Gibbard, BSc
Dr Robert Jeffreys, BSc, PhD
Mrs Su McRae, BSc
Mr Richard Taylor, BA
Mr Ben Whitworth, BA

Chemistry:
*Mr Michael Frampton, MA, DPhil
Mr Ian Middleton, MA
Mr David Border, BSc
Mr Richard Fisher, BSc
Mr Timothy Goodman, MBiochem, PGCE
Dr Rebecca Howe, MSc, DPhil
Mrs Kate Ley, BSc
Mr Mike Litchfield, BSc
Dr Mark Simpson, BA, MA, DPhil

Physics:
*Mr Ben Simmons, BSc
Mr Lawrence Barber, BSc
Mr John Brooks, BSc
Mrs Victoria Griffiths, BSc
Mr Simon James, MPhys
Mr Oliver Lomax, MA
Miss Alice Perry, BSc
Miss Nelly Petrov, BSc
Miss Melanie Snedden, BSc
Mr Jeremy Thomas, BSc, MSc
Dr AP Willis, BSc, PhD

Psychology:
Mrs Deborah Bennison, BSc

Librarians:
Dr Graham Gardner, BA, PhD
Mrs Wendy Hole, BSc
Mrs Lynn Mills

EFL:
Miss Katy Lee, BSocSc, MEd
Ms Vanessa Clark, BSc
Mrs Amanda Streatfield, BEd

Learning Support:
*Mrs Celia Collins, MA
Mrs Sarah Beynon, MA, MSc
Mrs Hettie Preiss-Chapman, BA

Director of Finance and Operations: Mr Justin Hodges, MSc
Director of Admissions and Marketing: Mrs Jane Jørgensen, MA

AKS Lytham
United Learning

Clifton Drive South, Lytham St Annes, Lancashire
FY8 1DT

Tel: 01253 784100
Fax: 01253 784150
email: headmaster@akslytham.com
            info@akslytham.com
website: www.akslytham.com
Twitter: @aksschool
Facebook: @AKSSchoolLytham

In September 2012, Arnold (Blackpool) and KEQMS (Lytham) merged as ArnoldKEQMS (AKS), part of the United Learning group of independent schools and academies. With over 300 years of history and tradition, the school has a reputation for high standards and excellence in achievement, both academic and non-academic, as well as encouraging participation within an inclusive and caring community environment. Hockey has triumphed at national level, while rugby and drama also hold prestigious awards, and music has an international reputation. Sports teams tour in the UK, Europe and the Southern Hemisphere, and a large number of pupils participate in the Duke of Edinburgh's Award scheme at bronze, silver and gold level. The school also has a popular CCF and a thriving House structure, and charity features prominently in school actions, both in support of local needs as well as international needs. AKS recently became a full global member of Round Square International.

Our Location. AKS dominates an impressive position in Lytham, overlooking the sand dunes and the Fylde coast. Preston, the Ribble Valley, the Lake District and Manchester are all within easy reach by direct motorway.

Our Opportunities. Through our membership of United Learning all teaching staff benefit from a high standard of professional training. All schools within the United Learning group communicate frequently and mutual support is always available, at all levels. International exchange opportunities are available through Round Square.

Our Co-curricular. Whilst the pursuit of high academic standards is undoubtedly important, all our pupils take advantage of the broad range of experience which our school offers, to nurture creativity and to encourage a spirit of voluntary contribution to the school and the wider community. Our main games are rugby, football, hockey, cricket and athletics, with strong fixture lists and several national and regional titles. This extensive programme provides competition and challenge for all pupils and touring sides have travelled as far afield as Argentina, Chile, the Caribbean, Canada, Australia and South Africa. As well as sport we also offer a Combined Cadet Force, Duke of Edinburgh's Award, Tycoon in Schools, World Challenge, debating, dance, chess and much more. Drama and music also feature prominently and inspire countless pupils each year to take part in top-quality productions, concerts and recitals.

Admission. Prospectus and Admissions forms can be obtained from the Admissions Secretary.

All entries to the Senior School are made through the Headmaster. Pupils are admitted to the Senior School on the basis of the School's own examinations in English, Mathematics and Non-Verbal Reasoning. The main intake to the Senior School is at 11, though entry at other times is possible depending on availability of places.

For entry at Sixth Form level, respectable GCSE grades in at least five subjects are normally expected in addition to a satisfactory report from the pupil's current Head.

Entry into the Junior School (2–11 years) is normally at the ages of 2, 4 and 7. Enquiries should be made to the Admissions Secretary.

Fees per term (2018–2019). Tuition (including books and stationery): Seniors £3,929; Juniors £2,965. Extras are minimal.

Entrance Scholarships. Several scholarships (including those for Music, Drama and Sport) are available for entry at 11+ and in the Sixth Form. Bursaries and Assisted Places are also available. Further particulars from the Admissions Secretary (01253 784104).

Registration. Pupils may be registered at any time although this should be as early as possible if entry is requested at ages other than 2, 4, 7 or 11 years. Candidates will be called for examination in the year of entry, although those who live at a distance may have the papers sent to their schools.

Charitable status. AKS is part of United Learning which comprises: UCST (a Company Limited by Guarantee, Registered in England, number 2780748, and a Registered Charity, number 1016538) and ULT (a Company Limited by Guarantee, Registered in England, number 4439859, and an Exempt Charity).

Local Governing Body:
Chairman: Mr C R Dickson
Vice Chairman: Mrs M Towers
Mr A E P Baines, BA, BArch, RIBA
Ms L Grant, LLB
Mrs L Hoiles, BA
Mr A Hoskisson, Dip PFS, Cert PFS [MP&ER]
Mr A Iredale, BA, MCIM
Mrs H Lucking, LLB
Revd D Lyon
Mr P M Owen, ACIB
Mr L Smith
Mr D Stanhope, FCCA

Bursar and Clerk to the Governors: Mrs A Sanderson

Senior School Management:

Headmaster: Mr M H P Walton, BA, MA Ed, PGCE, NPQH

Deputy Head: Mr A McKeown, BSc
Head of Junior School: Mrs A Ilhan, BEd
Director of External Relations: Mr P Crouch, BSc
Admissions Secretary: Mrs E Wyatt
Head of Sixth Form: Mr K Maund, BA
Head of Middle School: Mr P Rudd, BSc
Head of Lower School: Mrs H House, BA
Assistant Head (Pastoral): Mr P Hayden, BA
Assistant Head (Teaching & Learning): Dr C Jessop, BSc, PhD
Assistant Head (Curriculum & Organisation): Mr D Culpan, BSc
Assistant Head (Staff & Student Development): Mrs F Marland, BA
Examinations Officer: Mr P Klenk, BA

Head of Art: Mrs J Wild, BA
Head of Biology: Mrs J Arnold, BSc
Head of Business Education: Mr G McIntyre, BA
Head of Careers: Mr K Maund, BA
Head of Chemistry: Dr C Jessop, BSc, PhD
Head of Computing & DT: Mr D Culpan, BSc
Head of Drama: Mr N Lewis, BA
Head of English: Mr J Bridges, BA
Head of Geography: Mr N O'Loughlin, MA
Head of History: Mr I Cowlishaw, BA
Head of Learning Support: Mrs E Luke, BEd
Head of Mathematics: Mr L Sobey, BSc

Head of MFL: Mrs F Burnett, BA
Director of Music: Mr M Waterhouse, BMus
Head of Physics: Mr J Riding, BEng
Head of PSHE: Mrs H House, BA
Head of Psychology: Mr S Collings, BA
Head of Religious Studies: Mr M Harding, BEd
Head of Science: Mr S Downey, BSc
Director of Sport: Mr R Jones, BEd

Aldenham School

Elstree, Herts WD6 3AJ

Tel: 01923 858122
email: enquiries@aldenham.com
website: www.aldenham.com

Motto: *In God is all our Trust*

The School was founded in 1597 by Richard Platt, 'Cytyzen and Brewer of London'.

Number in School. 700, of which 170 are boarders and 438 day pupils. Around one-third are girls.

Aldenham is situated in its own beautiful grounds of more than 110 acres in the Hertfordshire green belt, with excellent access to London (Thameslink/Jubilee Line) and within the M25, close to the M1. Aldenham's particular reputation as a close-knit, small and supportive community with a strong boarding ethos makes it the very best environment for a high-quality all-round education. The achievement of every child's academic potential remains central but the building of confidence comes too from sports, music and drama, and by living and working together within the disciplined and vigorous community that is Aldenham today.

Admission. Prospective parents are encouraged to visit the School with their sons and daughters, either individually or at one of the school's 2 open days in June and October.

At 11, entry is by tests and interview, at 13 by interview and reference and at 16 by interview and GCSE results. Every effort is made to meet parents' wishes as regards which House is chosen for their son or daughter.

Registration fee £100; Deposit £1,000.

Fees per term (2018–2019). Boarders £7,597–£11,078; Day Pupils £5,497–£7,538.

Scholarships and Exhibitions are awarded to boys and girls who have demonstrated outstanding achievement and who have the potential to make a special contribution to the School. In addition to Academic there are also opportunities for Music, Art, Sport and Design Technology scholarships and exhibitions.

Music scholarships and exhibitions offer free tuition for one instrument. Any combination of choral and instrumental ability may be offered for the audition.

Art: A small number of awards at 13+ and 16+ are available each year. These are based on the candidate's portfolio and a short exercise at the school on a mutually convenient date.

Bursaries are also available to help boys and girls who will benefit from education at Aldenham but whose parents would not otherwise be able to afford the full fees.

Curriculum. From 11 to 16 the timetable closely reflects the National Curriculum. Boys and girls are prepared for GCSEs across a range of subjects including Maths, English, French, Science and a number of other Arts and language options. Care is taken that all pupils include Art, Music, Technology and Computer Science in their programme and there is a progressive course of Theology throughout the School with GCSE taken in Year 11. The Inspiring Futures

programme of tests and interviews are used as a basis for career planning and A Level choice in Year 11.

Students will take 3–4 A Levels. The majority of students go on to degree courses at universities. There are regular successes at Oxford and Cambridge.

Games and Other Activities. Great value is placed on the participation of every pupil in an extensive Games and Activities programme. Football, Hockey, Cricket and Athletics are the major sports for boys, whilst girls benefit from a breadth of in- and out-of-school activities including Hockey, Tennis, Badminton, Dance, Squash, Netball, Rounders, Trampolining, Aerobics and Sailing. In addition there is a full programme of House and School competitions in Squash, Eton Fives, Basketball, Tennis, Sailing, Table Tennis, and Cross Country. Volleyball, Climbing, Judo and Golf are also available. The Sports Centre provides excellent facilities for expert and novice alike and incorporates a full-size indoor hockey pitch, dance studio, martial arts room, and keep-fit suite. Time is set apart for activities and societies; these include CCF, The Duke of Edinburgh's Award scheme, Community Service, Electronics, Chess, Computing, Motor Club, Photography and Model Railway. The Debating and Philosophy societies meet regularly throughout the year

Music and Drama. Music flourishes in the School. There is a Chapel Choir, School Orchestra and wind and brass groups. A spring concert is performed annually in the School Chapel. A number of boys and girls learn to play on the fine, modern, 3-manual pipe organ in the Chapel. The music school has a recital room, practice and performance facilities and music technology classrooms.

The school theatre encourages a high calibre of Drama students. In addition to an annual School Play there are Senior and Junior House Play competitions and boys and girls have the opportunity to produce and design as well as to perform in the various productions. The School's proximity to London makes possible frequent visits to theatres and concerts. Drama is offered as a full A Level subject.

Organisation. Whilst the framework of the School is contemporary, it takes as its basis the long-established 'House' system. Each House creates an extended family and provides the formal and social focus of the School. There are four boarding and two day Houses together with a distinct yet fully integrated Junior House for 11–13 year olds. Each has a Housemaster or Housemistress and a team of tutors so every pupil has a personal tutor. In the Boarding Houses the Housemaster/mistress, his/her family and tutors live at the centre of the community ensuring the well-being of each child.

Boarding. Aldenham's unique array of day and boarding options enables it to provide the educational benefits of a boarding school to Day and Day Boarding pupils and to offer real flexibility with its arrangements for boarders, the vast majority of whom live within 20 miles of the School. Boys and girls may board from entry at 11+.

Religion. Aldenham is a Church of England foundation and seeks to maintain a strong Christian ethos to which those of other faiths are warmly welcomed.

Old Aldenhamian Society. There is a thriving Old Aldenhamian Society, details from the OA Office at the School.

Charitable status. The Aldenham Foundation is a Registered Charity, number 298140. It exists to provide high quality education and pastoral care to enable children to achieve their full potential in later life.

Governing Body:
Chairman: J T Barton [OA]
Deputy Chairman: Mrs V Shah

A J Bingham [OA]	S Nokes
A J S Cox [OA]	Col M O'Dwyer
A Day [OA]	Ms H Simmons
I A Dewar	TC ff B Sligo-Young
A Hellman	The Ven J Smith
Cllr D Lambert	D T Tidmarsh
R Mashru	T F Wells
Mrs D Nicholes	

[OA] *Old Aldenhamian*

Headmaster: **J C Fowler**, MA

Head of Senior School: A M Williams, BSc
Deputy Head (Academic): Dr P J Reid
Deputy Head (Pastoral): Mrs S H Wilson, BSc
Deputy Head (Co-curricular, Sixth Form & External Affairs): Mrs E Murray, MA

Heads of Department:
Art: Miss E J Lang, MA
Biology: Dr A D Camenzuli, MA
Business: L M Flindall, BA
Chemistry: A Shead, BSc
Classics: T M Hoskins, BA
Computing: C J Chandler, BSc
Design Technology: Miss C E C Macdonald, BA
Drama: E Avdijian, BA
English: C R Jenkins, MA
Geography: R Wildsmith, BSc
History: J R Kerslake, BA
Learning Support: Ms H J Southgate, BSc, MA
Mathematics: Mrs C J O Fulford, BSc
Languages: Srta M B Bustamante
Director of Music: J Rayfield, BMus
Philosophy, Religion & Ethics: Mrs A L Perry, BA
Physical Education: D L Breeze, BA
Physics: I R Webber, BSc
Psychology: Mrs V Evagora, MTh, ThM
Sciences: A T Shead, BSc

Head of Prep School: Mrs V Gocher, BA

Houses and Housemasters:

Boarding Houses:
McGill's: M I Yeabsley, BSc
Beevor's: S Pennycook, BSc
Kennedy's: R W Pineo, BSc
Paull's: Ms E C Gratton, BA

Day Houses:
Leeman's: G L Cornock, BA
Riding's: Miss L O W Jones, BA
Martineau's: Mrs L Gall, BEd

Chaplain: Revd J C Perris, BSc
Librarian: A Nelson, MA, DLIS, ALA
Bursar: K Mahon, MA

Alleyn's School

Townley Road, Dulwich, London SE22 8SU

Tel: 020 8557 1500
email: enquiries@alleyns.org.uk
website: www.alleyns.org.uk
Twitter: @Alleyns_School
Facebook: @Alleynsschool

Motto: *God's Gift*

Alleyn's is one of London's leading co-educational day schools for boys and girls aged 11–18, where academic excellence goes hand-in-hand with an extensive co-curriculum and the strongest possible pastoral care. Celebrating the School's 400th anniversary in 2019, we are a progressive school, built upon a long and proud heritage in the heart of London.

Our holistic approach to education aims to nurture every pupil to fulfil his or her potential while making lasting friendships and enjoying life to the full.

Entrance. A registration fee of £100 is charged for 11+ and 13+ applications, £50 for 16+ applications, and £200 for all overseas applications. These fees are waived for applicants who qualify for the Pupil Premium. Candidates should be entered for the School before the middle of November (and in October for 16+), for admission the following September.

Admission to Year 7 is by competitive examination at age 11. Entrance is decided on the basis of the entrance/scholarship examination held in January for entry the following September. Reports are requested from the Heads of the applicants' schools and, if they reach a satisfactory standard in the examination, boys and girls are invited for interview. The examination consists of Reasoning, English and Mathematics papers.

There is a smaller entry by examination for boys and girls at age 13, and the procedure is similar to that for entry at 11.

For entry at 16+, the examination is in early November and all candidates sit three general papers that test their skills in Critical Writing, and Qualitative and Quantitative Reasoning, regardless of their A Level choices. All candidates are considered for an academic scholarship.

Fees per term (2018–2019). £6,617 (£19,851 per annum).

Scholarships, Exhibitions and Bursaries.

Academic Scholarships, worth up to £4,000 p.a., are available at 11+, 13+ and 16+ and awarded based on the results of the entrance examination and interview.

Music Scholarships, worth up to £4,000 p.a. plus free tuition on principal instrument, are available at all entry points, and Music Exhibitions (free tuition on principal instrument) are available at 11+ and 13+.

Art Scholarships, worth up to £4,000 p.a., are available at 11+.

Sports Scholarships, worth up to £4,000 p.a., and Sports Exhibitions (£250 p.a.) are available at 11+ and 13+.

Bursaries: Academic Bursary Places (up to 100% fee remission, means-tested) are available for academically able candidates at 11+, 13+ and 16+. Means-tested bursaries (up to 100% fee remission) are also available to supplement a scholarship award.

Curriculum. All pupils follow a broad and balanced curriculum in the first three years, including English, Mathematics, Spanish, Latin and/or additional foreign languages (German or French), Biology, Chemistry, Physics, Geography, History, Religious Studies, Art, Computer Studies, Music, Design Technology, Drama, Dance, and the Alleyn's Learners' Programme. In Years 10–11, pupils take nine or ten GCSE subjects including English, English Literature, Mathematics, Biology, Chemistry and Physics and a modern language. In addition, they choose three option subjects. In Year 12, four subjects are followed. In Year 13, three or four A Levels are taken. In addition to those subjects listed above, Classical Civilisation, Economics, Classical Greek, History of Art, Media Studies, Philosophy, Politics, Psychology, Physical Education and Drama and Theatre Studies are also available.

Pupils go on to universities, medical and dental schools, music and art colleges. Almost all enter higher education. Selected pupils are prepared and entered for colleges at

Oxford and Cambridge, where a very good record of places is maintained each year.

Organisation. The Lower School (Years 7 and Year 8) has its own building and its own Head. The Middle School (Years 9–11) and Upper School (Years 12–13) each has its own Head, and pupils from Year 9 up belong to one of eight Houses. Each Head of House is responsible, under the leadership of the Head of School section, for the welfare of each of their pupils during their time in the School. This care is supplemented by a system of form tutors for supervision of academic progress and pastoral support. Parents are invited to Consultation Evenings during the year, at which pupils' work and progress are discussed with the teaching staff. From Year 10 upwards, the children themselves attend these evenings.

Games. The School stands in its own grounds of 30 acres and offers a wide variety of sports and games, including Football, Hockey, Cricket, Swimming, Athletics, Netball, Cross-Country Running, Rugby Fives, Water Polo, Gymnastics, Badminton, Fencing, Golf, Basketball, Tennis, Rounders, Trampolining, Aerobics, Fitness and Personal Training, Table Tennis, Squash, Cycling and Climbing.

Religious Education. Alleyn's is a Church of England Foundation and warmly welcomes boys and girls from all backgrounds, whatever their faith position. Religious Education of a non-denominational nature is given throughout the School, and pupils attend worship in Assembly and once each term in the Foundation Chapel or in St Barnabas Church. The Chaplain holds voluntary Holy Communion Services during term time. Pupils, if they wish, are prepared for Confirmation in an annual service. The Chaplain is assisted by an Assistant Chaplain and the Chaplaincy area is used as a place of relaxation and reflection.

Buildings. The original building dates from 1887. In addition, there is a brand new Lower School, accommodating a six-form entry in Year 7, a fully-equipped sports hall, with cardiovascular room, a refurbished indoor swimming pool (with a tiered viewing gallery and Olympic timing system), an art department with kiln and multimedia art provision, a technology centre, a music school, two digital language laboratories, a large library, a refurbished science block with rooftop observatory, a new all-weather playing surface, a sports hall and pavilion, a gym, computer rooms and a RIBA Award-winning performing arts centre (the Edward Alleyn Building), containing a 350-seat theatre, a Sixth Form study centre, lecture theatre, film classroom, and a studio for the National Youth Theatre.

Music, Drama, Art and Dance feature very strongly in the life of the School. There are various major concerts each year, including an annual concert at St John's Smith Square and Jazz Night at Hideaway. There are multiple orchestras, bands, and choirs, including over 30 Chamber groups. A number of dramatic productions are staged each year, from the Lower, Middle and Upper School plays to our student-led Bearpit productions, including a show that Upper School students take to Edinburgh each year. Dance goes from strength to strength and the standard of choreography is very high. The annual Dance Show regularly features over 100 boys and girls from across the year groups. Creative arts are cherished and well-supported at Alleyn's. From traditional fine art and ceramics to the powerful use of film, photography and installation, pupils' work is ambitious, and our annual Art, Design and Media Show spotlights our boys' and girls' talents across an increasing breadth of media.

Pupils are offered an extensive and diverse range of **co-curricular activities** each term with over 200 opportunities outside the classroom each week. There are over 60 weekly sports clubs and over 50 weekly matches and fixtures, including mixed Cricket and Football, Water Polo, Fencing and Fives, in addition to Hockey, Basketball, Netball and Swimming. There are more than ten weekly Art, Film and Photography clubs and plenty of Drama, including the Technical and Creative Team and LAMDA. Pupils have many other co-curricular options to choose from, including Design and Make-It, Classics, Debating, Chess, Science Club and Boys' Dance, to name just a few.

Pupils can choose an optional year of **Combined Cadet Force** in Year 9 and then choose between **CCF, The Duke of Edinburgh's Award** and **Volunteering** in the community in Year 10.

A full programme of **Careers Education** and guidance is offered to pupils throughout their School journey. This includes dedicated careers lessons and activities, inspirational talks, aptitude testing and careers interviews with independent advisors from COA and a very popular annual Year 11 work experience scheme. In Year 12 students make a mock application for various professions and are interviewed by alumni and parents.

A School Council and Learning Council, with members from each section of the School, represents pupils' views to the Headmaster.

Relations with Parents. The Alleyn's Parents' Association is a dynamic and enthusiastic parent organisation which nurtures close links between parents and the School and raises considerable funds for the benefit of the School's Pupil Support Fund.

The Edward Alleyn Club. The official foundation meeting of the Edward Alleyn Club was held on 18 April 1884. All past pupils are given membership to the Edward Alleyn Club. This enables them to take part in sporting and social activities, and receive regular updates from the School, including a biannual newsletter and invitations to year group reunions, bespoke networking events and important fundraising activities. Please get in touch on alumni@alleyns.org.uk.

Charitable status. Alleyn's School is a Registered Charity, number 1161864, and a Charitable Company Limited by Guarantee, registered in England and Wales, number 09401357. Registered office: Townley Road, SE22 8SU.

Chairman of Governors: Mr I Barbour, BSc Econ Hons, ACIB

Headmaster: **Dr G J Savage**, MA Cantab, PhD, FRSA

Senior Deputy Head: Mr A W A Skinnard, MA Oxon (*Designated Lead for Safeguarding*)

Deputy Head (Personnel & Administration): Ms S P Chandler, BSc, PG Dip

Deputy Head (Academic): Mrs A McAuliffe, BA

Assistant Heads:

Head of Upper School: Dr R C J Atkinson, PhD, MSci, MA Cantab

Assistant Head Co-Curricular & Partnerships: Mr N J G Green, BEd

Teaching & Learning: Mrs C L Heindl, BA

Head of Middle School: Mrs M A Joel, BA

Head of Lower School: Mr S W Turner, BSc, MEd

Bursar: Mr S R Born, BA

Director of Finance and Deputy Bursar: Claire Morgan, BSc, FCA

Registrar: Ms L Mawer, LLB

Ampleforth College

York, North Yorkshire YO62 4ER

Tel: 01439 766000
Fax: 01439 788330
email: admin@ampleforth.org.uk
website: www.ampleforth.org.uk/college

Motto: *Dieu le Ward*

Ampleforth Abbey was founded in 1607 at Dieulouard in Lorraine by English Benedictine monks who had strong links with the mediaeval Benedictines of Westminster Abbey. After the French Revolution the monastic community was resettled at Ampleforth in 1802 and the present School was started there soon after.

The Community is dedicated, first to prayer, and then to religious and charitable works. Ampleforth College and St Martin's Ampleforth are the works of St Laurence Educational Trust. The other works of the Community include parishes in Yorkshire, Lancashire and Cumbria, St Benet's Hall in Oxford and pastoral involvement both at Ampleforth and elsewhere.

Governance. The Abbot of Ampleforth is elected by the Community for eight years at a time and presides over the Community and its works.

The Abbot is Chairman of the Ampleforth Abbey Trustees, which is the legal institute that owns and governs its foundation. St Laurence Education Trust is a separate limited company formed by the Abbey Trust. This also has charitable status and is responsible for both Ampleforth College and St Martin's Ampleforth.

The governance of these works is the responsibility of the Abbot who, with structured advice, appoints the officials, monastic and lay, who are in charge of their administration.

Number in School. There are around 544 students, of whom 83% are Boarders, 37% are girls and 17% are Day Boys and Girls.

Our aims are:

• to share with parents in the spiritual, moral and intellectual formation of their children, in a Christian community focussed on Benedictine values with which their families may be joined in friendship and prayer for the rest of their lives.

• to educate the young in the tradition and sacramental life of the Church and to encourage each towards a joyful, free and self-disciplined life of faith and virtue.

• to work for excellence in all our endeavours, academic, sporting and cultural. We ask students to give of their best. We ask much of the gifted and we encourage the weak. Each is taught to appreciate the value of learning and the pursuit of the truth.

• to help Ampleforth boys and girls grow up mature and honourable, inspired by high ideals and capable of leadership, so that they may serve others generously, be strong in friendship, and loving and loyal towards their families.

Organisation. The upper school has 6 houses for boys aged 13 to 18 and three houses for girls aged 13 to 18. Houses are kept small and are home to approximately 60 boarders and there are some day students in each.

Each house has its own separate accommodation. All students eat their lunch in separate house refectories. They eat breakfast and supper in a central cafeteria with the House staff, chaplains and tutors.

The work and games of the whole school are centrally organised. At least five tutors are allocated to each house to supervise students' work and provide the appropriate guidance at each stage in their school career. The Head of

Careers provides information and assistance and can arrange expert advice for pupils, parents and tutors. Some of the non-teaching life of the school is organised around the houses. House competitions help to create a strong house loyalty. We have a central school chaplaincy that acts as a social meeting place for the middle school and a sixth form social centre, the Windmill, just off the campus.

Curriculum. The first year (year 9) provides a broad basis from which to make informed GCSE choices. In the second and third years, a core of English, Mathematics, Science and Christian Theology is studied to GCSE, together with a balanced selection from a wide range of subjects. In the first year of the sixth form (year 12), up to four subjects may be studied at A Level. One of those subjects may be A Level Christian Theology, but, if not, students follow a Christian Theology short course. Normally three subjects will be taken on to completion in the second year (year 13). A comprehensive health education programme is provided in all years.

Games and Activities. There are opportunities to play a wide variety of representative sports at all levels with excellent indoor and outdoor facilities. Many activities and games take place during the week and weekends, including drama, debating, outdoor pursuits, creative arts and a wide variety of sports. These sports range from lacrosse to rugby. The school has its own outstanding 9-hole golf course and has recently completed a new all-weather hockey surface and new tennis courts. In addition, the college has its own all-weather athletics track.

Music, which is a strong academic subject, plays a major part in the extracurricular life of the school. The Schola Cantorum, our liturgical choir, sing for Mass in the Abbey and perform sacred music in Britain and abroad. They have been responsible for the production of several commercial CDs in recent years. The Schola Puellarum, our girls choir, sings with the Schola Cantorum on alternate Sundays and has its own repertoire. It has undertaken tours both at home and abroad and has also released its own CD.

Further enquiries may be made directly to the Director of Sport on 01439 766885 or the Music Department on 01439 766701.

Admission. Applications may be made through the Admissions Office. Registration Fee: £100.

Fees per term (2018–2019). Boarders £11,808; Day Boys/Girls £8,212.

The fees are inclusive, the only normal extras being for individual tuition in Music: £31 per lesson, £29 for a second instrument; EAL £915 per term (Y12 and Y13).

Entrance Scholarships. Scholarships are awarded annually on the results of examinations held at Ampleforth. Exceptional scholars can be awarded a 10% remission on fees, twenty such awards being available each year. Other scholarships are honorary. The award of a scholarship can support a means-tested bursary application. Discounts for HM Armed Forces and HM Diplomatic Services are also available.

Academic Scholarships at 11+: Examinations are held in February

Academic Scholarships at 13+: ISEB Common Academic Scholarship examinations are sat in February.

Sixth Form Entry: Academic Scholarship examinations are held in November.

Music Scholarships are available for entry to the College at ages 11, 13 and 16. All scholarships carry free music tuition.

Extracurricular Scholarships at 13+: The Basil Hume Scholarships for candidates who have a strong commitment to extracurricular activities.

Further details can be obtained from The Admissions Office, Tel: 01439 766863, email: admissions@ampleforth.org.uk.

Charitable status. St Laurence Educational Trust is a Registered Charity, number 1063808. Its aim is to advance Roman Catholic religion.

Governing Body:
The Abbot of Ampleforth is the Chairman of Governors acting with the Council and Chapter of Ampleforth Abbey. He is assisted by a lay Advisory Body.

***Acting Head Teacher*: Miss D Rowe**, MA, NPQH, CCRS

Acting Deputy Head Pastoral: Mr A P Smerdon, BSc
Director of Studies: Dr H R Pomroy, BSc, PhD
Director of Professional Development: Mr A S Thorpe, BSc, CChem, MRSC
Senior Admissions Registrar: Mrs H C McKell, BA
Head of Sixth Form: Mr W F Lofthouse, MA
Head of Middle School: Dr R Warren, BSc, PhD
Head of Careers: Mrs A Toone
School Chaplain: Rev C Boulton, OSB, BA
Guestmaster: Rev H Lewis-Vivas, OSB, MA

Academic Departments:

Christian Theology:
*Mrs H E Pepper, BA
Mr J Grenham, BA
Mrs G M O McGovern, MA
†Mr J D Rainer, BA
Mr R M Hudson, MA

Christian Living:
†Mrs A Le Gall, MA
Mrs M B Carter, BSc
Mrs A Rogerson, BTh

Classics:
*Dr C Goddard, BA, PhD
†Mr J B Mutton, MA
Mr W F Lofthouse, MA
Miss J Sutcliffe, BA

History:
*Mr P T Connor, MA
†Mr G D Thurman, BEd
Mrs M F Rainer, BA
Miss K F Germany, BA
†Miss G S Foster, BA

English:
*Dr C G Vowles, BA, PhD
Mr A C Carter, MA
Mr D J Davison, MA
†Mrs C R Day, BA
Miss E B H Richmond, BA
Mrs V Browning, BA (*EAL*)
Mrs J S Adams, BA (*EAL*)
Mrs A Mihkelson (*Learning Support*)
Ms D Brown, BA, MPhil (*Learning Support*)

Modern Languages:
*Mrs J Knowles, BA
Mr S R Owen, MA
Mr J P Ridge, MA
Mr M Torrens-Burton, BA (*EAL*)
Rev A McCabe, OSB, MA
Mrs F Garcia-Ortega, BA

Mrs S M G Baseley, MA
Miss S Normand
†Dr J M Depnering, DPhil

Geography:
*Mrs C R M Dent, BSc
Mr A P Smerdon, BSc
Mrs H E Graham, BSc
Mr B McNiff, BA

Modern Studies:
*Miss H Thompson, BA, MSc
Miss J M C Simmonds, BSc
Mrs J Stannard, BA

Mathematics:
*Dr J W Large, BSc, PhD
Dr H R Pomroy, BSc, PhD
Mrs P J Melling, BSc, BA
Dr R Warren, BSc, PhD (*Head of Middle School*)
Mr D Willis, BEd, MEd
Dr J M Weston, BSc, DPhil
Mr E Reid, BSc
Mr P S P Butler, BEng

Physics:
*Mrs R L Dale, BSc
Dr L M Kessell, BSc, PhD
Mr B Townend, MPh
†Mr J Cochrane, BSc
Miss M Hindle, MA

Chemistry:
*Mr S J Howard, BSc
Mr A S Thorpe, BSc, CChem, MRSC
Mrs E A Coop, BA
Dr D G Free, PhD
Dr T Keslake, PhD

Biology:
*Mr P W Anderson, BSc
Dr O S Beveridge, BSc, PhD
Mr D J Cocks, BSc
Miss K Giles, BSc

Music:
Mr W J Dore, MA, FRCO
Mr A Hardie, MA (*Assistant Head of Music*)
Miss K Medway, BMus
Ms F Kelleher, BMus, Dip CSM (*Head of Keyboard*)
Ms N Hicks (*Head of Strings*)
†Miss A M A I Brown, BA

Design and Technology:
*Mr B J Anglim, BEng
Mrs V Anglim, BEng
Mr J Hart, BEng

ICT:
†Mr P Curran, BSc
Mr C M Higgs, BSc
Mr DJ Bradbury, BSc

Art:
*Mrs L Frith-Powell, BA
Mr T J W Walsh, MA
Miss A R Lister, BA

Drama and Theatre:
*Miss E Naylor, BA
Mrs R Clough, BA
Miss L Walsh (*Dance*)

PE and Games:
*Miss G L Atkins, BSc
Mr J J Owen, BEd (*Head of Hockey*)
Mr C Booth, BSc
Mr W James (*Head of Rugby*)
Miss J Rose, BA (*Head of Netball*)
Mr M Slingsby, BA

Houses and Housemasters/Housemistresses:
St Aidan's (*girls*): Mrs A Le Gall, MA
St Bede's (*girls*): Mrs Caroline Day, BA
St Margaret's (*girls*): Miss G S Foster, BA
St Cuthbert's: Mr J D Rainer, BA
St Dunstan's: Mr G D Thurman, BEd
St Hugh's: Dr J M Depnering, DPhil
St John's: Mr P Curran, BSc
St Oswald's: Mr J Cochrane, BSc
St Thomas': Mr J B Mutton, MA

Counsellor: Mr J G J Allistone, BA

Medical Officer: Dr G Black, MBChB, MRCGP, DRCOG

Headmaster's PA: Mrs H L Richardson

Ardingly College
A Woodard School

Haywards Heath, West Sussex RH17 6SQ

Tel: 01444 893000
Fax: 01444 893001
email: head@ardingly.com
website: www.ardingly.com

Motto: *Beati Mundo Corde*

Ardingly is a co-educational school in the Woodard Family founded to teach the Christian Faith. We work with our children to discover their qualities and prepare them for their future beyond school.

History and development of the College. Ardingly College, the third of Nathaniel Woodard's schools, was founded in Shoreham in 1858 and moved to its present beautiful site in Mid Sussex, about halfway between Gatwick and Brighton, in 1870. The College now consists of a Nursery, Pre-Prep day School, a weekly boarding and day Prep School, for boys and girls between the ages of 2 and 13, and a boarding and day Senior School for boys and girls aged between 13 and 18.

In the Prep School, there are 305 pupils. In the Senior School, there are 325 pupils and a further 261 in the Sixth Form. There is a relatively even balance between boys and girls and boarders and day pupils.

For further details about Ardingly Prep and Pre-Prep Schools, see entry in the IAPS section.

Academic. Ardingly has an extremely good academic record in both arts and science subjects achieved by boys and girls who come from a wide spectrum of ability. Both the International Baccalaureate and A Levels are offered.

Results for 2018. GCSE: A*–A 75%, A*–B 90%, A*–C 99%. A Level: A* 18%, A*–A 46%, A*–B 80%, A*–C 94%. IB: Average points score 38.6, Graded 7–6 88%, Graded 7–5 98%, Graded 7–4 100%.

Curriculum. *First year*: A broad course in which all pupils do virtually everything; second Modern Language (German or Spanish); Expressive Arts; and all undertake iMind research and inquiry lessons whilst completing their own chosen personal project.

GCSE (2nd and 3rd years): All take IGCSEs in English and English Literature, Maths, Sciences and the usual wide range of options.

Sixth Form Curriculum: Standard choices in a highly flexible block system at AS/A2 or in the International Baccalaureate Diploma Programme. ICT skills are developed through AS/A2 and IB courses. All Lower Sixth students follow a development course which covers life skills, careers and HE study skills. All Sixth Form students, whether following the A Level route or the IB route, complete the IB Core (Extended Essay, Theory of Knowledge, and Creativity, Action and Service) which is highly valued by universities both in the UK and around the globe. BTEC courses are also offered.

Pastoral. There are 8 Houses, four for boys and three for girls, which contain everyone from the first year to the Lower Sixth. In the Upper Sixth all boys and girls transfer to a separate, newly-built, integrated co-educational House, "Woodard", in which they are able to concentrate more fully on their studies and can be given greater responsibility for themselves and be better prepared for life at University or in the outside world. Each House has its own Housemaster or Housemistress, Assistant and House Tutors. In addition every boy and girl will have a Tutor who has responsibility for the work, progress, choices and many other aspects of the pupil's life. Tutorials are regular, weekly group tutorials and fortnightly individual tutorials. Tutors work closely with careers staff to incorporate careers guidance into their tutorials.

In Year 9 and Year 10 pupils study and discuss personal, social and health education, careers topics in small mixed groups as part of a specially designed course called Eudaimonia meaning 'human flourishing' and through Eudaimonia days in the Fifth Form.

There is an efficient Medical Centre in the centre of the school with a residential Sister in charge. The School Doctor takes three surgeries a week in the School and is always on call.

Since September 2005 School on Saturdays has been discontinued.

Expressive Arts. *Music*: Choir, Chamber Choir, Schola Cantorum, Jazz Singers, Orchestras, Concert Band, Jazz Band, Chamber Music. Instrumental lessons taken by about half the boys and girls.

Art: Painting, drawing, printing, ceramics, sculpture, fashion & textiles, photography, etching.

Design Technology: Real design problems solved in a variety of materials and forms.

Photography: Offered at A Level.

Drama: Many productions in the course of the year for all ages. Large flexible theatre space and a small workshop theatre.

The expressive arts are studied throughout Year 9, are options for GCSE and A Level and offer scholarships for talented candidates, at both 13+ and for the Sixth Form.

Sport. Boys play Football, Hockey, Rugby 7s, Cricket, Tennis, Athletics; Girls play Hockey, Netball, Tennis, Rounders, Athletics. (Football and cricket are also available for girls.) Hockey and football are particularly strong at Ardingly with many country and regional competitions won and the 1XI ISFA National Boodles Cup, the most prestigious title in independent schools football. Ardingly prides itself on developing these teams in extra coaching sessions without compromising studies.

Also (for both boys and girls) there is Cross Country, Swimming, Shooting, Golf, Volleyball, Horse Riding, Clay Pigeon Shooting, Basketball, Badminton, Karate, Croquet, Sailing, etc.

The indoor pool is open to both Prep and Senior Schools and pupils who cannot swim are taught to do so.

Activities. Extensive Enrichment Programme, The Duke of Edinburgh's Award, Beekeeping, Modern Dance, Photography, Computers, Fencing, Astronomy, Debating, Charity Focus, Amnesty International etc.

Admission to the Senior School normally takes place at 13+ or directly into the Sixth Form at 16+. Admission is also possible at 14+ but is not advisable at the beginning of the years in which GCSE or A Levels are taken unless there are very special reasons. A Pre-IB course is offered in the Sixth Form.

ISEB Common Pre-Test taken in Lent Term of Year 6 for 2021 entry and beyond. Offers made in May of Year 6 for Year 9 entry. Common Entrance used for setting purposes, but not for admission. Pupils coming from non-prep schools will be required to sit our own assessments. We also require a report and reference from the pupil's previous school. The headmaster likes to interview prospective pupils if practicable.

The selection of candidates for direct entry to the Sixth Form takes place in November of the year prior to entry. All candidates are interviewed and take an English paper and a Maths paper. A report from their Head is also required. Places will then be offered subject to the candidate gaining a minimum of 6 grade Bs or above at GCSE. Modifications of these procedures and of the timing for individuals at any stage are almost always possible.

The Prep School has entry at 7+ and 11+ or at any other time between the ages of 7 and 11.

Scholarships. A number of Scholarships are offered for annual competition at 13+ and 16+. They include Academic, Art, Drama, Music and Sports Awards. Ashdown Awards for all-rounders are offered for those entering at 13+. The Prep School offers Academic, Art, Music and Sports Awards at 11+. Along with other HMC schools, the maximum value of a scholarship is 40% of the basic fees pa but all may be supplemented by a means-tested bursary if need can be shown.

A limited number of bursaries are available for the children of the Clergy.

Please address all enquiries about admissions, scholarships and bursaries to the Registrar (Tel: 01444 893320; fax: 01444 893001; email: registrar@ardingly.com).

Term of Entry. Main 13+ and Sixth Form intake in September. Intake at other ages and other times on an individual basis.

Registration. The School Prospectus may be obtained from the Registrar. Registration (where a non-returnable fee of £150 is charged) can be made at any age subject to the availability of places. No separate registration is required for children transferring from the Prep to the Senior School.

Fees per term (2018–2019). Senior School: Boarding £11,135–£11,470, Flexi Boarding £9,345, Day Pupils £7,665–£7,870. Occasional Boarding: £48 per night. Prep School: Boarding £300 (1 night) to £1,100 (weekly) in addition to Day Fees; Prep Day Pupils £4,370–£5,250; Occasional Boarding £36 per night. Pre-Prep: £3,065.

Fees are inclusive.

Further Particulars. For further information, application should be made to the Registrar.

Charitable status. Ardingly College Limited is a Registered Charity, number 1076456. It exists to provide high quality education for boys and girls aged 2½ to 18.

School Council:

Mr Jim F Sloane, BSc (*Chairman, Chair of Nominations Committee*)

Mr Graham N Turner, BSc, FCIOB (*Deputy Chairman, Chair of Finance and General Purposes Committee, Governor with Responsibility for Health & Safety*)

Mrs Jane Armstrong, BA Hons

Mr Robert H Brown, BSc, MSc Econ (*Chair of Development Committee*)

Mr Peter N Bryan, BA, ACA

Mrs Siân L Champkin

Mr Guy W Dixon, BA Hons, Dip TP, MRTPI

Mrs Liz Hewer, MA, PGCE

Mrs Mary E Ireland, BSc Hons, Dip Ed, FRSA, CBiol, MRSB (*Chair of the Education Committee*)

Mr Douglas H T Johnson-Poensgen, BEng Hons (*Chair of the Estates Committee*)

Dr Simon Kay, PhD (*Governor with Responsibility for Compliance*)

Mrs Louise E Lindsay, FCIPD, LLM, BA Hons (*Governor with Responsibility for Safeguarding*)

Professor Helen E Smith, BMedSci, BMBS, MSc, DM, FFPHM, MRCGP

Ms Kate E C Sweeney, MA Cantab

Headmaster: Ben Figgis, MA, MEd

Deputy Headmaster: James Johnson, BA, MPhil

Deputy Head Academic and Head of Sixth Form: Georgina Dore, MA

Assistant Head and Head of Middle School: Nicola Burns, BSc

Head of Student & Staff Support: Leonie Gurd, BSc

Director of Finance and Resources: Tracey Trotter

Director of Admissions, Marketing & Communications: Pamela Bower-Nye, BA, DipM, MCIM, FIDM

HR Manager: Nicola Smart, BA, MCIPD

Head of the Prep School: Harry Hastings, BA Hons, MEd Oxon

Chaplain: The Revd A J Stark-Ordish, MA, BA

Medical Officer: Dr B Lambert

Ashford School
United Learning

East Hill, Ashford, Kent TN24 8PB

Tel:	01233 625171
Fax:	01233 647185
email:	registrar@ashfordschool.co.uk
website:	www.ashfordschool.co.uk
Twitter:	@AshfordSchool
Facebook:	@AshfordSchool
LinkedIn:	/ashford-school

Ashford School was founded in 1898 as an independent, day and boarding school and provides education for boys and girls from 3 months to 18 years. There are over 450 students in the Senior School and over 350 in the Prep School (age 3–11). There are around 155 boarders in the school

cared for by resident teachers and support staff in extensive accommodation that includes en-suite rooms for many. Twenty-five nationalities are represented and specialist English tuition is provided for those who require it. There are no lessons on Saturdays.

The school recently opened an International Centre which houses another 20 or so boarders who enjoy intensive English language tuition with iGCSEs before entering mainstream British education.

Ashford School is a member of a group of independent schools run by United Learning which provides a first-class education for more than 25,000 pupils. United Learning aims to be at the forefront of educational development, bringing the very best resources, both human and physical, to the children in its schools.

The Senior School occupies a 25-acre site in a prominent position close to the centre of Ashford and near to the International Station. A green and secure haven in a busy and growing town, Ashford is 37 minutes from London by rail and also benefits from rapid access to Paris, Lyon, Brussels, Amsterdam, Cologne and Frankfurt on the Eurostar. With easy access to the M20 motorway and local train services, the central location and easy accessibility provides an ideally located school whether you live in the UK or anywhere across the globe.

With playing fields on site, a brand new Sports Centre, two gyms, indoor swimming pool, floodlit Astroturf, tennis and netball courts, boarding houses and dining hall, the School enjoys all the specialist teaching facilities you would expect of an independent school and has embarked on a programme to refurbish and extend the facilities. The Pre-Nursery, Bridge House, is located on the Senior School site and the Prep School is located in the nearby picturesque village of Great Chart and has recently undergone major redevelopment to double its size and further improve facilities and opportunities for pupils at the school.

Almost half of the students entering the Senior School at 11+ join direct from the Prep School and the remainder from other primary and prep schools. There are normally three classes per year through to GCSE with additional students joining other years and the Sixth Form. All Sixth Form students go on to take degree courses at leading universities in the UK and abroad.

Over the last three years an average of two thirds of A Level students have gone to Russell Group universities and one fifth to World Top Ten such as Imperial College, LSE, Durham, Warwick, Birmingham, Bristol, UCL, Nottingham, Leeds, York and Newcastle.

An inspection by the Independent Schools Inspectorate in March 2014 found the school to be 'outstanding' or 'excellent' in every category.

The Senior School curriculum is broad and provides many opportunities in the classroom and in activities. The school has interactive whiteboards in every teaching room and modern facilities throughout. Pupils follow a broad curriculum to keep their options open and in addition to the core subjects of English, maths, the sciences and a language they may study additional languages, history, geography, religious studies, information technology, art and textiles, music, drama and physical education. Throughout the Senior School, subjects are set by ability where possible and there is a strong pastoral system based around six Houses.

The school prides itself on its adventurous approach to learning.

External Examinations. Most pupils take 9/10 subjects at GCSE. Many A Level combinations are available to the Sixth Form, all of whom go on to Higher Education before entering a varied range of careers including music, design, advertising, banking, engineering, journalism, law, management, the media, medicine and veterinary science. There is a consistently high external examination success rate and pupils are prepared for Oxbridge in all subjects.

Entry requirements. School report, subject entrance tests and interview for the Sixth Form, supporting six or more 9–5 (A*–B) grades at GCSE with at least a 9–7 (A) grade in the subjects chosen to study at A Level. School report and written tests in English, Mathematics, Science and Non Verbal Reasoning at Years 7 and 9. Places are generally available throughout the year in all other year groups.

Scholarships. Academic, art & design technology, sport, drama and music scholarships are available in Years 7, 9 and 12 with theatre arts additionally in Year 12. Further details may be obtained from the Head.

Fees per term (2018–2019). Senior: £5,600 (day), £8,000 (weekly boarding), £12,000 (full boarding); Prep: £5,000; Pre-Prep: £3,500; Nursery: £753 (one full day per week), £3,500 (full-time).

Charitable status. Ashford School is part of United Learning which comprises: UCST (a Company Limited by Guarantee, Registered in England, number 2780748, and a Registered Charity, number 1016538) and ULT (a Company Limited by Guarantee, Registered in England, number 4439859, and an Exempt Charity).

School Council:
Chairman: Mr W Peppitt
Professor P Freemont
Mrs D Geering
Mrs E Langlands-Pearse
Mr A J Rawlins
Mr J B Rimmer
Mrs E Rose
The Ven S Taylor
Mrs L van der Bijl

Head: **Mr Michael Hall**, BA Liverpool, MA

Head of the Senior School: Mr T Wilding, BA Exeter
Deputy Head, Pastoral: Mrs N Timms, BEng Loughborough
Deputy Head, Teaching and Learning: Mrs J Russell, BA Leeds
Deputy Head, Co-Curricular and Community Partnerships: Mr T Wilde, MA Warwick, BSc Brighton
Head of the Prep School: Mrs P Willetts, BPrimEd
Deputy Head of the Prep School, Teaching and Learning: Mrs R Clifford
Deputy Head of the Prep School, Pastoral: Mr C Neesham

Bablake School

Coundon Road, Coventry CV1 4AU

Tel: 024 7627 1200
Fax: 024 7627 1290
email: info@bablake.coventry.sch.uk
website: www.bablake.com
Twitter: @bablakeschool
Facebook: @BablakeSchool

Bablake School was originally part of the College of the same name founded by Queen Isabella in 1344. After the dissolution of the monasteries, it was refounded in 1560 by the city; it is chiefly associated with the name of Thomas Wheatley, whose indentures of 1563 put its finances on a firm foundation.

Number in School. There are approximately 754 Day Pupils (including 196 in the Sixth Form) and 360 in the Junior School and Pre Prep.

Buildings. In the Home Field of 11 acres stand the main buildings which have been considerably extended to include a Sports Centre, heated indoor swimming pool and a purpose-built Modern Languages block. A purpose-built English, Music and Drama block was completed in July 2000. In 1993 Bablake Junior School was opened on the Home Field site for pupils aged 7–11 and Cheshunt Prep became Bablake Pre Prep, for pupils ages 3–7, in 2009 (*for further details, see Bablake Junior School and Pre Prep entry in IAPS section*). The school has its own nationally recognised weather station. At Hollyfast Road there are 27 acres of playing fields, a large pavilion, and two all-weather hockey pitches.

Curriculum. Pupils take and must pass the Governors' Examination for entry to the Senior School. The Senior School provides courses leading to the GCSE examinations and GCE A Levels. Subjects available include: English, Mathematics, History, Geography, French, German, Spanish, Religious Studies, Latin, Classical Civilisation, Physics, Chemistry, Biology, Music, Art, Food, Design Technology, Information Technology and Drama. Design Technology and Food and Textiles courses are followed by both boys and girls. The separate sciences or Science and Additional Science are taught up to IGCSE. Most pupils study 10 subjects at GCSE, the majority progressing into the Sixth Form where the new A Level curriculum is followed with three subjects being examined at the end of the two years. All pupils study an academic enrichment programme, leading to an additional qualification, for example AS Law or an Extended Project Qualification (EPQ). There is a wide range of Enrichment Studies options including Art, Astronomy, Chinese, Computing, Cookery, Design, Drama, Music, Photography and many others. All pupils follow a structured programme of PE and Games.

Games and Activities. Rugby, Hockey, Netball, Basketball, Cross-Country Running, Athletics, Rounders, Tennis, Cricket, Football, Squash and Swimming. The school has an extensive artificial turf games area, used mainly for hockey, but providing in the summer an additional 24 tennis courts. A wide range of co curricular activities is offered, and there are approximately 50 societies and clubs. Drama and Music are strong features. All pupils are involved in the charity work of the school and there is a large Community Service programme for the Senior pupils in the Fifth and Sixth Forms.

Scholarships. The Governors award annually a number of Entrance bursaries each year for those entering at 11+. These are dependent on academic ability and on parental means. Academic, Art and Music scholarships are also available.

Academic, Sports and Music scholarships are also available in the Sixth Form.

Fees per term (2018–2019). Senior School £3,898; Junior School £2,981; Pre Prep £2,376.

Admission. Entry is via the School's own Entrance Examination held annually in October (11+) and January (all other age groups) for entrance the following September. The normal age of entry is 11 but there are smaller intakes at 12, 13 and 14. Entry to the Sixth Form is based on gaining at least five GCSE passes at grade 6 or above (with a grade 7 preferred in the subjects chosen to study at A Level, and required in some cases) and an interview with the Headmaster and Head of Sixth Form. Enquiries about admissions should be addressed to the Admissions Office.

Charitable status. Coventry School Foundation is a Registered Charity, number 528961. It exists to provide quality education for boys and girls.

The Governing Body is Coventry School Foundation, on which are represented Sir Thomas White's Charity, the

Coventry Church Charities, Coventry General Charities, Oxford and Warwick Universities and the University of Coventry. There are also several co-opted governors.

Chairman of Governors: Mrs J McNaney

Headmaster: Mr J W Watson, MA

Deputy Heads:
Mr C R Seeley, BA, MPhil
Mr A Wright, BSc (*Academic*)
Mrs G Press, BEd (*Pastoral*)

Assistant Head: Mr J G Burns, MA

Director of Admissions & Marketing: Mrs S V Harris, BSc

Head of Sixth Form: Mrs A J Tumber, BA
Head of Fifth Year: Mrs S M Smith, BEd
Head of Fourth Year: Mrs L A French, BSc
Head of Third Year: Mrs H E Sawyer, BSc
Head of Second Year: Mr J C Hobday, BSc
Head of Shells: Mr M W Spencer, BSc
Chaplain: Revd S Slavic, DEUG

Director of Finance & Operations: Mrs J Hammond, CGMA

Assistant staff:
* Head of Department

Art:
*Mr P Cleaver, MA
Miss R Brandrick, BA
Mrs A S Cassell, BA

Biology:
*Mr A M Hall, BSc
Mrs L B Alexander, BSc
Mrs L R T Lawrence, MA
Mr C W Mohamed, BSc
Miss C Billingham, MSc

Careers:
*Mr M G A Woodward, BA

Chemistry:
*Dr P J Knight, PhD
Dr T C Casey, PhD
Mr I S Kalsi, MChem
Mrs A H Learmont Henry, MA
Mr S S Sahota, BSc

Classics:
*Mr D C Menashe, BA
Mr N Fontana, MA
Mr C R Seeley, MPhil
Mr J W Watson, MA

Design Technology –
Resistant Materials,
Food & Textiles:
*Mr C R West, BEd
Mrs H L Bamforth, BA
Mrs J L Solomon, BA
Mr P Nicholson, BEd
Mr S J Roberts, BA

Economics & Business
Studies:
*Mrs L J Alderson, LLB
Mr J G Burns, MA
Mr P Scanlon, BA

English and Drama:
*Mrs K G Duke, MA
Miss K E Blackie, MA

Mrs C E Lynch, BA
Mrs C A Martlew, BA
Mr G L Park, BA
Mrs L J Reddish, BA
Mr B D Wall, BA

Geography:
*Mr S P Enstone, BSc
Mrs A L P Bradshaw, MEd
Mrs J MacGibbon, MSc
Mrs G Press, BEd

History:
*Mrs H Skilton, MA
Mr J M Grantham, BA
Mrs K L Lenihan, BA
Mrs C A Rees, BA
Mr C R Seeley, MPhil

ICT:
*Mr M G Bull, MEng
Mr L Atwal, BSc
Miss R M Blattner, BSc

Learning Support:
*Dr L S Greenway, PhD
Mrs E L Hollick, BSc
Mrs H E Sawyer, BSc

Mathematics:
*Mr K J Tyas, BEd
Dr P B M Archer, PhD
Mr J M Drury, BSc
Miss K V French, MMath
Mrs L A French, BSc
Mrs N D Green, BSc
Mrs G S Heath, MEng
Mr S Memon, BSc
Mrs H E Sawyer, BSc
Mrs S M Smith, BEd
Mr A M Wright, BSc

Modern Languages:
*Mrs J May, MA
Mrs H M Billings, MA
Mrs M O'Neill, MA
Mrs R I Bilsland, BA

Mrs S V Harris, BSc
Mr P R Neale, MA
Ms C Pfennig, MEd

Director of Performing
Arts:
Ms V Bradley, BA

Music:
Ms N Brass, MMus
Mr S J Cooper, GLCM
Mrs C Scott-Burt, Dip TCL

Physical Education – Boys:
*Mr R L Burdett, BSc
Mr T Freemantle, BSc
Mr A C Phillips, MSc
Mr B G Wilson, BEd

Junior School & Pre Prep

Headmaster: Mr N Price, BA

Deputy Head: Mr L Holder, BEd

Head of Pre Prep: Mrs T Horton, BEd

Headmaster's Personal Assistant: Mrs R Mohomed
Administrator: Mrs H Rypma, BA

Physical Education – Girls:
*Mrs J Russell, BSc
Miss L J Mullan, BSc
Mrs S M Smith, BEd
Miss L C Watts, BA

Physics:
*Mr T Hyde, BSc
Mr J C Hobday, BSc
Mr M W Spencer, BSc

Psychology:
*Mrs J Barratt, BSc

Religious Studies:
*Dr T M P Smith, PhD
Miss K E Blackie, MA
Revd S Slavic, DEUG
Mrs A J Tumber, BA

Bancroft's School

High Road, Woodford Green, Essex IG8 0RF

Tel: 020 8505 4821
email: office@bancrofts.org
website: www.bancrofts.org

Motto: *Unto God only be honour and glory*

By the Will of Francis Bancroft (1727) all his personal estate was bequeathed on trust to the Worshipful Company of Drapers of the City of London to build and endow almshouses for 24 old men, with a chapel and schoolroom for 100 poor boys and 2 dwelling-houses for masters. The Foundation was originally situated at Mile End, but by a scheme established by the Charity Commissioners in 1884 the almshouses were abolished and the School transferred to Woodford Green, Essex. In 1976 the School reverted to independence, and became a fully co-educational day school, with a Preparatory School being added in 1990.

Bancroft's School is a co-educational day school of about 1,100 pupils. It stands in its own grounds with about five acres of playing fields and it has a further 16 acres of playing fields near Woodford Station. Its buildings have successfully combined the spacious style of the original architecture with the constant additions demanded by developing needs. These include a swimming pool, enhanced science facilities, music resources and art rooms. In 2006 a new building, housing kitchens, additional teaching space and a new Sixth Form Centre, was opened; a new sports centre and performing arts studio were opened in 2007. A digital language lab and a new ICT suite were added in 2009. 2011 saw the addition of an enhanced Sixth Form study area, new Arts and Ceramics Workshops and additional science laboratories. In 2015 and 2017 the workshop and classroom facilities for Design Technology were increased and enhanced.

Meals are taken in a well-equipped central dining room, and there is a good variety of menu with self-service on the cafeteria principle.

Pupils are grouped in four Houses – North, East, West and School. Each of the Houses has its own Housemaster or Housemistress and a tutorial system.

The School offers a wide range of subjects at GCSE and A Level and has a strong record of academic success. Virtually all Bancroftians progress to university, with about 12 each year to Oxford or Cambridge. On average 75% of pupils will go on to study at Russell Group institutions. Bancroft's has a very strong record of pupils studying medicine and dentistry.

The major sports for girls are hockey, netball, tennis and athletics; the main curricular games for boys are rugby, hockey, cricket and athletics. Swimming, soccer, badminton and basketball are also provided. The Physical Education programme includes gymnastics, trampolining, basketball and badminton.

The School has a Contingent of the CCF (both Army and RAF sections), a Sea Scout Unit, a branch of the Duke of Edinburgh's Award scheme, and a Social Service Group, each of which caters both for girls and boys. The wide programme of concerts and plays throughout the school year offers opportunities for pupils of all age groups.

Preparatory School. The Prep School opened in September 1990 occupying purpose-built accommodation on a separate site within the school grounds. There are 12 classrooms, a hall, a library, a performing arts studio and specialist rooms for art and science. Although self-contained, the Prep School makes extensive use of the Senior School's sports, music and drama facilities.

(*For further details, see Preparatory School entry in IAPS section.*)

Admission. 65 places are available each year for boys and girls wishing to enter the Preparatory Department at 7+; entry tests take place in the January. Transfer to the Senior School is guaranteed. At 11+ there are another 60 places available for children entering Bancroft's who sit an examination in Mathematics and English in mid-January. For candidates of other ages individual arrangements are made. Applications for 7+ and 11+ entry must be made before 1 December in the year prior to entry. There is a direct entry for boys and girls into the Sixth Form dependent upon GCSE results and performance in the School's 16+ entrance examination which is sat in the November of Year 11.

Scholarships. Each year up to 15 Scholarships, worth typically one half, one third or one quarter of the full fees, are awarded to candidates at 11+ on the basis of performance in the School's own 11+ Entrance Examination. Two will generally be awarded as Music Scholarships to children of outstanding musical talent; these are worth up to 50% of fees plus extra music tuition. Five Academic Scholarships, each worth up to 50% of the full fees, are available to external candidates entering the Sixth Form. A Music Scholarship is also awarded for entrants into the Sixth Form. A further three academic awards are available to internal candidates.

Means-tested awards (including Francis Bancroft Scholarships and Foundation Awards) are available at age 11, which can cover the full fees. These are awarded based on disclosure of family finances and performance in the Entrance Examination. Two means-tested Francis Bancroft Scholarships are available for entrants to the Prep School at age 7; these only cover Prep School fees. Means-tested awards may also be available for entrants into the Sixth Form.

Fees per term (2018–2019). Senior School £6,041, Prep School £4,917. Fees include lunch and books.

Old Bancroftians' Association. Hon Secretary: Mrs C Lavender, obasecretary@bancroftsnet. School contact: susan.day@bancrofts.org.

There is a strong Old Bancroftians' Association, organising a variety of social, sporting and networking event throughout the year including an annual dinner at the School and OBs Day in the summer term.

Charitable status. Bancroft's School is a Registered Charity, number 1068532. It exists to provide an academic education to able children.

The Worshipful Company of Drapers

President: The Master of the Drapers' Company

Trustees and Governors:

Appointed by the Drapers' Company:
Prof P Kopelman, MD, FRCP, FFPH (*Chairman*)
J Rose, BA
R Williamson, BA, FRGS
Ms L Wingham, MA

Appointed by the London Borough of Redbridge:
M J Stark

Appointed by Essex CC:
R Gooding, IEng, ACIBSE

Co-opted:
Mrs B Conroy, MA [OB]
R Bhumbra, BSc, PhD, MBBS, MRCS, FRCS
Dr A V Philp, MA, MB BChir (*Deputy Chair*)
E Sautter, MA [OB]
Mrs S Siddiqui, BA, TEP

[OB] Old Bancroftian

Head: **S R J Marshall**, MA, MA, MPhil

Deputy Head: Mrs D Picton, MA
Deputy Head (*Academic*): J T Silvester, MA

Senior Tutor: R B de Renzy Channer, MA

Assistant Heads:
Mrs E F de Renzy Channer, MA
C A F Butler, BSc
Mrs A M Scurfield, BSc

Head of Sixth Form: N E Lee, BSc
Head of Section, Middle School: Mrs P R Tindall, BA
Head of Section, Lower School: J P Dickinson, MEng
Director of Teaching & Learning Mrs V Talbot, BA

Assistant Director of Studies: C J Atkinson, MA

Head, Preparatory School: J P Layburn, MA, QTS

Assistant Staff:
* *Head of Department/Subject*
† *Housemaster/mistress*

Art:
*A D Ford, MA
Mrs S O'Sullivan, MA
Mrs N Vetta, BA
Ms I Ward, MA

Biology:
Miss R Adams, BA
Mrs A C Carter, BSc
Miss A Grimwood, BSc
Mrs S C Hampson, BSc
*J H Raw, MA

Chemistry:
Dr A Ahmed, MScI
J Choy, MSci (*Head of Medics*)
*N Goalby, MEng
Dr G M Ismail, BSc (**Junior Science*)
Miss H Korcz, BSc, MEd
†Miss H J Prescott-Morrin, BSc

Classics:
*Mrs M J Baker, BA
†Mrs L J Coyne, BA

A J Smethurst, MA
Miss H E Stewart, BA

Computer Science & ICT:
*Mr A D Shaw, BSc

Drama:
Ms G Entwhistle, BA
Miss H C Gartland, MA
*Miss E M Middleton, BA

Economics & Business Studies:
*Mrs L R Anthony, BSc
Miss S L Brand, BA
Mr J S Chapman, BA
Mrs K J Dean, BA, ACA
Mr A Gocoldas, BSc
Mrs A Haysman, BA
Mrs S Strand, MA
Mr H C Tiler, MA

English:
†Miss C G Edwards, BA
Miss N Evans, MEd (*Junior English*)
K P Gallagher, BA
*Miss H C Gartland, MA
T R C Jones, MA (*Second in Department*)
Dr A J Mill, MA
R E Young, BA

Geography:
Miss S L Brand, BA
*Miss R S Burridge, BSc
C A F Butler, BSc (*Assistant Head Co-Curricular*)
J S Foley, BSc
†R M Hitching, BA
N E Lee, BSc (*Head of Sixth Form*)
*Mrs V Talbot, BA (*Director of Teaching & Learning*)
†R M Hitching, BA

Politics:
Mrs K J Dean, BA, ACA
†R M Hitching, BA
*Dr S A Hunn, BA, MSt

History:
*L J Brennand, BA
Miss G M Carnell, BA
R B de Renzy Channer, MA
†Miss K A Hughes, MA
Dr S A Hunn, BA, MSt
Mrs M Sparkes, MA
†Miss A M H Wainwright, BA

Learning Support:
*†Mrs A Fryer-Green, BSc
Mrs J Collins
Mrs A Hubbard

Mathematics:
C J Atkinson, MA
P A Caira, BSc
Miss G K Chana, BSc
A M Conington, BSc
J P Dickinson, MEng (*Head of Section, Lower School*)
*M J Flaherty, MA
Dr J D Larwood, BSc
P A McGuiggan, BSc (*Junior Mathematics*)
Mr J E Osborne, BSc
Mrs A M Scurfield, BSc (*Assistant Head Academic*)
S P Taylor, BEng (*Sixth Form Mathematics*)
R Tse, MSc
Mrs E J Tynan, MEng (*KS4 Mathematics*)

Modern Languages:
Mrs A Abbott-Imboden, BA (*German*)

Mrs E F de Renzy Channer, MA (*Assistant Head Pastoral*)
Miss J Grossman, Staatsexamen (*French*)
Miss M Harringon, PGD
*Ms S Hancock, MA
R M A Hay, BA
Miss J K Robbins, BA
Mrs S Savjani, BA
Mrs P R Tindall, BA (*Head of Section, Middle School*)
Mr I Urreaga Gorostidi, BA (*Spanish*)
Mrs L Whalley, BA
Miss L G Williams, BA

Music:
*Mrs C J Foinette, BA
J D Kelsall, BA, MMus
Mrs J Whitbread, MA (*Director of Music*)

Physical Education:
Mrs C Ablitt (*Swimming Coach*)
D J Argyle, BEd
Mrs S Cheshire (*Swimming Coach*)
*N P Doherty, MSc (*Director of Sport*)
A Eghoyan, BSc (*Strength & Conditioning Coach*)
R Faiers, BA (*Academic PE and Rugby*)
Mrs J Fryer-Green, BA (*Examinations Officer, *Girls' Hockey*)
C Greenidge (*Cricket*)
R M A Hay, BA (*Boys' Hockey*)
Miss S Johnston, BSc (*Graduate Sports Assistant, Sports Therapist*)
J K Lever, MBE, Essex CCC and England
Mrs H E Marchant (*Netball*)
Mr H Markatis, BSc (*Graduate Sports Assistant*)
J C Pollard, BEd (*PE*)
†Miss A M H Wainwright, MA (*Tennis*)
Mr D Webster (*Hockey Coach*)

Physics:
A N Busch, MSci
J Ceeraz, BSc
N A Jaques, MA (*Science*)
L Pollock, BSc
*J Prole, BSc

Religious Studies:
Mr T Bigglestone, BA
*Miss L Jones, BA
†Miss H C Mead, BA
Revd I Moore, MA, BTh (*School Chaplain, *PSHE*)
J T Silvester, MA (*Deputy Head Academic*)

Technology:
S Burton, BA
T Peddle, BEng
*M J Rogers, BA
A Whitbread, DipEd
S P Woolley, BSc

Preparatory School:

Mrs A Adams, BA	Mrs T Jones (*Learning*
D Archer, BA	*Support Assistant*)
A D Baum, BA	Mrs A Kanolik, BA
Mrs S K Bhangal, BEd	J P Layburn, MA (*Head*)
Mrs C Biston, BA	Mrs L Life, BA (*Assistant*
Mrs H A Chilvers, MA, BEd	*Head*)
Mrs L Dalton, BA	Mrs K McNelis, BSc
Mrs N Doctors, BA	Miss E Mitchell, BA
Miss L Ellery, MSc	(*Graduate Sports*
C P Hall, BSc	*Assistant*)
Miss E Hewitt, BSc	Ms A Moor, BA
Mrs J M Hitching, BA	Mrs S O'Sullivan, BA
Miss K Johnston, BSc	T Paramour, BA
Mrs S M Jones, BA	C Pearson, BA
	Miss L C Phelps, BA

M Piper, BA (*Assistant Head*)
Mrs B Rathod, BA
Mrs S Strong, MA

Miss H Sylvester, BA
N Thomas, BCom, MA (*Assistant Head*)
Mrs K Yelverton, BA

Bursar: L Green

Matron: Mrs A Hancock

Barnard Castle School

Newgate, Barnard Castle, County Durham DL12 8UN

Tel: 01833 690222
Fax: 01833 638985
email: genoffice@barneyschool.org.uk
website: www.barnardcastleschool.org.uk

Motto: *Parvis imbutus tentabis grandia tutus*

The St John's Hospital in Barnard Castle was founded in the 13th century by John Baliol, whose widow founded the Oxford College. By a Scheme of the Charity Commissioners, bequests under the will of Benjamin Flounders of Yarm were combined with the funds of the St John's Hospital and public subscriptions to build and endow the present foundation in 1883. Originally known as the North Eastern County School, the name was changed to Barnard Castle School in 1924.

Barnard Castle is a day and boarding school for boys and girls between the ages of 4 and 18.

Organisation and Numbers. There are 505 pupils aged 11–18 in the Senior School, of whom 136 are boarders. The Preparatory School comprises a Pre-Prep Department of 48 pupils between the ages of 4 and 7, and 134 pupils between the ages of 7 and 11, of whom 8 are boarders. (*See also Preparatory School entry in IAPS section.*) The Senior and Preparatory Schools are located on adjacent sites and operate separately on a day-to-day basis whilst enjoying the mutual benefits of being able to share a number of resources and facilities. Girls were first admitted in 1981 and the School has been fully co-educational since 1993.

Location. The School is situated in its own extensive grounds on the outskirts of an historic market town in an area of outstanding natural beauty. The area is well served by Durham Tees Valley and Newcastle airports and by Darlington railway station. The School also operates its own bus service for pupils from a wide area.

Curriculum. This is designed to provide a broad, balanced and flexible programme, avoiding undue specialisation at too early a stage. In the Prep School emphasis is given to literacy and numeracy skills, as well as Science, History, Geography, French (from age 8), Religious Education, Technology, Art, Music, Information Technology, Physical Education (including swimming) and Games. These subjects are developed further in the Senior School, with the addition of Latin or Classical Civilisation, Personal, Social and Health Education, and three separate sciences. German or Spanish is added at age 12, whilst Business Studies and Engineering increase the list of GCSE options at age 14. There are some twenty A, AS or Pre-U Level subjects which give a wide choice in the Sixth Form. Almost all Sixth Form leavers go on to University or College courses. A Learning Support Department provides specialist help for those who need it in both the Preparatory and Senior Schools, and tuition is offered in English as a Second Language.

Religious Education. The School is a Christian foundation and the Chapel stands at the heart of the School in more than just a geographical sense. The School Chaplain, who plays an important role in the pastoral structure of the School as well as being responsible for Religious Studies and Chapel worship, is an ordained member of the Church of England, but the School is a multi-denominational one which welcomes and supports pupils of all faiths and none. Pupils attend weekday morning assemblies in Chapel, and there is a Sunday service for boarders.

Boarding and Day Houses. There are eight single-sex Houses within the Senior School – three boarding and five day – each small enough for pupils to know each other well, but large enough to allow a mixture of interests, backgrounds and abilities, as well as opportunities for leadership. Housemasters and Housemistresses, each supported by a team of Tutors and Assistants, are responsible for the welfare and progress of each pupil in their charge.

Junior Boarders (boys and girls aged 7–11) and Senior Girl Boarders live in their own modern Houses in the School grounds, alongside their Houseparents, Boarding Tutors and Matrons. The two Senior Boys' Boarding Houses have recently undergone a major programme of restructuring and refurbishment, and offer comfortable accommodation within the main building of the School. The resident Housemasters are supported by resident boarding tutors and matrons, and by the School Sister in the School's Medical Centre. The School Doctor visits daily.

Cultural and other activities. The School has a flourishing music department in which the Chapel Choir, Orchestras, Wind and Jazz Bands and smaller ensembles perform regularly.

Drama is also prominent, with a regular programme of productions taking place throughout the year. There is a strong tradition of after-school activities; both day and boarding pupils take part in a wide range of clubs and societies, selecting from over 100 weekly activities.

Games. Rugby, Hockey, Netball, Cricket, Athletics, Squash, Cross-Country Running, Tennis and Swimming are the main sports, and other options such as soccer, badminton, basketball and golf are available. The School has extensive playing fields, a modern Sports Hall, and Fitness Centre, squash and tennis courts, and a heated indoor swimming pool. A full-size, floodlit AstroTurf-style pitch is available for all to use. Regular inter-school matches are arranged at all levels.

Outdoor Activities. There is a strong emphasis on providing instruction, opportunity and challenge in a wide range of outdoor activities. Much of this takes place under the auspices of a flourishing Cadet Force (Army and RAF sections) or The Duke of Edinburgh's Gold and Silver Award schemes.

Careers. There is a well-equipped Careers Room, and a team of careers staff work together with the Higher Education Coordinator to provide pupils at all stages of the School with expert advice and help in decision-making and application procedures.

Admission. Pupils are admitted at all stages either via the School's own Entrance Assessments. There is also direct entry into the Sixth Form subject to satisfactory performance at GCSE level. Details of the application procedure are obtainable from the Admissions Secretary (admissions@barneyschool.org.uk).

Scholarships and Assisted Places. Academic Scholarships and Exhibitions are awarded to entrants to the Senior School at Year 7, Year 9 and the Sixth Form, on the basis of the School's own entrance examinations held in February.

Music Scholarships and Exhibitions: There are two Music Exhibitions available in Year 7, a further two Scholarships in Year 9 and in the Sixth Form.

Sport Exhibitions based on potential are available at Year 7 and Scholarships are available at Year 9 and in the Sixth Form. Four Exhibitions may be awarded in Year 7, followed by up to four Scholarships in Year 9 and a further two Scholarships in the Sixth Form.

Art Scholarships and Exhibitions are available from Year 9 and in the Sixth Form.

Drama Scholarships and Exhibitions are available to candidates entering the Sixth Form.

Awards may be supplemented by means-tested Bursaries.

The School is also able to offer a small number of means-tested assisted places. Details are available from the Admissions Secretary.

Fees per term (2018–2019). Senior School (Years 7–13): Day £4,650; Junior Boarder (Years 7–8) £7,850; Junior International Boarder (Years 7–8) £8,900; Senior Boarder (Years 9–13) £8,400; International Boarder £9,500. Fees are inclusive and subject to annual review.

Charitable status. Barnard Castle School is a Registered Charity, number 1125375, whose aim is the education of boys and girls.

The Governing Body:
Chairman: Mr P Mothersill
Vice-Chairs: Dr J Elphick & Mrs C J Sunley JP
Chair of House & Finance Sub-Committee: Mrs S Sunley
Chair of Education & Welfare Sub-Committee: Mrs R Dent
Chair of Estates & Development Sub-Committee: Mr D Osborne

Mr C Dennis	Mrs K Pratt
Mr A Fielder	Councillor Richardson
Mr P Hodges	Mr D F Starr
Mr J Hunter	Dr N Thorpe
Mr I Moffatt	Mrs D Vinsome
Ms C Newnam	

Clerk to the Governors: Mrs S Metcalf, BA, FCCA

Headmaster: Tony C Jackson, BA (*History*)

Second Master: Martin Pepper, BA (*PE*)
Deputy Head (i/c of Sixth Form): David Cresswell, MA Oxon (*Modern Languages*)
Deputy Head (Pastoral): Peter Lavery, BA Hons (*Modern Foreign Languages*)
Deputy Head (Academic): Michael R Truss, MPhys Oxon, PhD, FRAS (*Physics*)
Chaplain: Revd Darren Moore, MA (*History*)

Assistant Staff:
* *Head of Department*
† *Housemaster/mistress*

†Gary Bishop, BA (**Economics & Business Studies*)
Stuart Everall, BEd (**PE*)
John D N Gedye, BA (**Classics*)
Mike H Nicholson, BSc, BA (**Mathematics*)
Fiona Norrie, BEd (*PE, Head of Games*)
Caroline L Shovlin, BA, ALA (*Librarian, Head of Careers*)
†David W Dalton, MA (**Geography*)
Mick Donnelly, FLCM, Cert Ed (*Music*)
†Ben C Usher, BSc (*Mathematics*)
Mandy Gorman, BA (**English, History*)
Charles H Alderson, BSc (*Geography*)
Martin P Ince, BA (**History*)
Neil Toyne, BSc (*Mathematics*)
Alan M Beaty, BSc (**Design & Technology*)
Tanya C Broadbent, BA (*PE*)
Andrea J Campbell, BA (*History & Politics*)
Ian M Butterfield, PhD, BSc (**Chemistry*)
Alan R Jacobs, MA (*Modern Languages*)
Kate Baptist, BA (**Art*)
Erin E Beaty, BA (*English, History and Classics*)
Judith Brown, MSc (**ICT*)
†Luke D Monument, BSc (*PE*)

†Lesley J Burgess, BEd (*PE*)
Alan J Maude, BSc (*Mathematics*)
Michelle Abela, BA, LLCM, ALCM (*Music*)
Nick J Connor, BA (*Bus Studies and ICT*)
Caroline Connor, BSc (*Biology*)
Lucy Nicholson, Mgr, Dip Trans, MCIL, DPSI (*EAL*)
Caroline J Snaith, MA, LLB (*RS, Classics, Psychology, *PSHE*)
Steven J F Tomlinson, BA (*Modern Languages*)
Sheila Butler, BA (*Religious Studies*)
Andy M Dunn, MSc, MPhil (*Physics*)
Scott Edwards, BA (*English, *Theatre Studies*)
Henry W Fairwood, BSc (*ICT*)
Elaine E McDermott, PhD, BSc (*Chemistry*)
David S Walton, PhD (**Physics*)
Sarah Rothwell, MA (*Art*)
†Carrie Riley, MA (*Modern Languages*)
Alexander Still, BA (*Modern Languages*)
Kevin B Cosstick, JP, PhD, BSc (*Chemistry*)
Janine Wilson, MA (*Chemistry*)
Simon P Dearsley, MA, MMus, BA (**Music*)
Sam S Forsyth, BSc (*Biology*)
Sebastian T Nichols, PhD (*Classics*)
Rebecca K B Gibson, MSc, BSc (**Biology*)
Helen D Kent, MPhil, BA (**Modern Languages*)
Holly Creevy (*Geography*)
Diana L M Everall (*English*)
Judith Gibbons (*Learning Support*)
Edward Hodgson (*Physics*)
Olivia Hovington (*PE/Games*)

Combined Cadet Force:
Commanding Officer: Major Caroline E Hall, BSc
SSI: Martyn G Lewis, WO1

Preparatory School

Headmistress: Laura E R Turner, MA

Deputy Head: Mark Langley, BSc
Director of Studies: Simon Ayres, BA
Head of Pastoral: Rebecca A Robertson, BEd

Simon T Ayres, BA
Claire L Bale, BA
Lizzie J F Hairsine, BA
Fiona M Killeen, BA
Michael Killeen
Lauren Laverick
Tabitha J Michelin, BA
Claire N Priestley, BEd
Kate Roberts-Lilley
Louise E Rowlandson, BA
Sue M Seddon, BEd
Emma J Small, BA
Jennifer D Strachan
Donna J Thirling, BA, SAC Dip
Ruth Thompson, BEd
Ben E Wicling, BA
Alexandra A White, BSc Hons

Admissions Secretary: Jo Barkes

Medical Officer: Dr Robert Carter
Medical Centre:
Catherine Bainbridge, RGN

Bedales School

Church Road, Steep, Petersfield, Hampshire GU32 2DG

Tel: 01730 300100
            Registrar: 01730 711733
            Assistant Registrar: 01730 711569
Fax: 01730 300500
email: admissions@bedales.org.uk
website: www.bedales.org.uk
Twitter: @BedalesSchool
Facebook: @BedalesSchool
LinkedIn: /bedales-school

Number in school. 463 pupils: 210 boys; 253 girls; 309 boarders.

Bedales stands in an estate of 120 acres in the heart of the Hampshire countryside in the South Downs National Park. Although only one hour from London by train, this is one of the most beautiful corners of rural England. Founded in 1893, Bedales is one of the oldest co-educational boarding schools. The community is a stimulating and happy one, in which tolerance and supportive relationships thrive at all levels.

The school has strong traditions in both the Humanities and the Sciences, in Art, Design, Drama and Music. The school estate supports a thriving 'Outdoor Work' programme, including the management of livestock and a variety of traditional crafts; a stunning new Art & Design facility was opened in 2016.

The school is known for its liberal values, the individualism and creativity of its students, and a sense that the students are generally at ease with who they are. The atmosphere is relaxed (first-name terms for staff and students; no uniform), but it is underpinned by a firm structure of values, rules, guidance and support.

Admission. Entry to the school is from 3+, 7+ (Bedales Pre-prep, Dunannie), 8+, 11+ (Bedales Prep, Dunhurst), 13+ and 16+ (Bedales). Once in the school, pupils are assessed before proceeding to the next stage.

Entry tests. Entry for newcomers at 10+, 11+ and 13+ takes the form of residential tests in the January approximately 20 months before entry. Entry at 16+ is by a series of interviews on a single day. Contact the Registrar in the first instance.

Senior School (13 to 18). Our Block 3 (Year 9) curriculum revolves around our 'head, hand and heart' ethos, and is a rich, experiential year based in small groups of 8–12. These are led by their 'Badley tutor' – named after our founder, and two of our senior (6.2) students per group. In addition to work in the classroom, students are given prep to complete in their own time. Prep can be done at various times in the week, some of them designated and supervised. During the course of Block 3 it is expected that each student will establish effective working habits and an appropriate balance between academic work and other pursuits.

Bedales has a long tradition of leading the way in educational change. Its determination to do what is right for its students led to the creation of a unique curriculum, Bedales Assessed Courses (BACs), for Blocks 4 and 5 with a range of innovative courses designed to complement a core of IGCSEs. The curriculum is built around a compulsory group of five core IGCSE subjects and two non-examined courses, plus a choice of Bedales Assessed Courses and other GCSEs. Well regarded by universities, the content of BACs is broad and stimulating, offering significant cross-curricular and independent-learning opportunities. Since its aim to develop a broad range of skills through the delivery of BACs, internal assessment includes a mixture of written assignments, presentations, projects and performances, together with terminal examinations as appropriate. Each course is externally moderated.

In class, and particularly in the Bedales Assessed Courses, students are encouraged to question, to challenge, to think for themselves – visitors comment on a 'no fear' classroom atmosphere.

The Sixth Form at Bedales offers an unusually broad and stimulating environment in which to spend the final years at school and to prepare for life beyond. Serious academic responsibility and opportunities for leadership combine to create a challenging and rewarding experience.

In particular, inspired by the success of the BAC courses, Bedales has developed an additional strand of the curriculum to stand as an alternative to a fourth A Level. The Bedales Enrichment Programme consists of a series of one-term courses chosen from a broad range of offerings developed by enthusiastic staff and shaped by student requests. Courses are grouped under the Bedalian banner of 'head, hand and heart', and students are expected to pursue at least one course in each area.

Each student's programme will also include a combination of academic study, sport, Outdoor Work, cultural and current affairs, service to the community, and global awareness. Sixth Form students are also expected to take on positions of responsibility in the school, such as contributing to one of the many student committees or acting as role model and mentor to younger students.

Bedales Prep School, Dunhurst (8 to 13). (*See Dunhurst entry in IAPS section*).

Bedales Pre-prep School, Dunannie (3 to 8). Currently 80 pupils. Entrance at 3+ is by date of registration; after this acceptances are made following informal assessments, should vacancies arise. Dunannie has six classes including a nursery. Its aim is for children to develop a lifetime's love of learning in a stimulating environment.

Dunannie aims to inspire children by learning through doing in a community based on mutual respect. Children help to form the rules of caring behaviour towards one another and are on first name terms with teachers. The children are encouraged to have confidence to make their own decisions and to formulate their own ideas in class, supported by their teachers.

The children at Dunannie benefit from the indoor swimming pool, tennis courts, sports hall, pitches, farm and theatre which are all close by on the Bedales estate. The outdoor play areas include a stunning orchard with a climbing frame, Sound Garden of outdoor instruments and a hill fort.

The children have many opportunities to thrive and flourish. Dunannie offers a rich and varied curriculum that allows for rigour in basic skills, but also embraces creativity. Children are encouraged to think and be independent in their response to cross-curricular activities. First-hand experiences are an integral part of learning. All children from Nursery to Year 3 go on inspiring visits that enrich their classroom experiences. There are close links between Dunannie, Dunhurst and Bedales. Children in Year 3 can automatically transfer from Dunannie to Dunhurst unless there are exceptional circumstances. Sport is a strength with a comprehensive programme of activities including swimming, gymnastics, tennis, netball, football and orienteering. Year 3 children have sport with Dunhurst Group 1 children and have the opportunity to play inter-school matches. Dunannie is a very friendly school with happy, confident children who relish being at school.

Scholarships. Personal development is central to the Bedales concept of scholarship. It aims to align scholarship beneficiaries closely with the school's aim "to develop inquisitive thinkers with a love of learning who cherish independent thought".

The school has introduced a scheme for pupils with particular talents in Art, Design, Music, Drama, Sport and other academic subjects to encourage their appetite for research, enquiry and development. Depending on their specialist subject, most scholarship holders have access to a research fund to support their individual scholarly projects. There is no reduction in school fees – research grants are non-means tested and hence have a relatively small financial value (up to £500 per year for 2018/19). The award of a scholarship is reviewed annually based on student performance.

Bursaries. Ranging from part-fee contributions up to full 100% bursaries (with further support for additional costs), these awards enable pupils (generally from 11+ upwards) with an appetite for learning to attend Bedales Prep School, Dunhurst and Bedales who otherwise would have been unable to pay the fees. Awards are based on an assessment of the family's financial means.

Pupils can benefit from the award of either a scholarship or a bursary, or both. Although bursary financial assistance is not dependent on a scholarship award, the school aims to enable pupils with particularly strong talents to attend the school, therefore a number of bursary beneficiaries also benefit from scholarship awards. Please contact the Registrar Janie Jarman (email: jjarman@bedales.org.uk; tel: 01730 711733) if you would like to discuss suitability for a scholarship or bursary to Bedales Prep School, Dunhurst or Bedales School.

Fees per term (2018–2019). Bedales: Boarders £12,095, Day £9,505. Bedales Prep, Dunhurst: Boarders £8,310, Half-boarding (3 nights) £7,405, Day £5,640–£6,255. Bedales Pre-prep, Dunannie: £3,175–£4,105.

Charitable status. Bedales School is a Registered Charity, number 307332. Its aims and objectives are to educate children as broadly as possible in a creative and caring environment.

Governors:

Clare Bradbury, BSc, PGCE

Felix Grey, MChem, MPhil

Avril Hardie, BEd, JP

Owen Jonathan, LLB Hons

Michele Johnson, BA

Dr Anna Keay, PhD

Rear Admiral John Lippiett, CB, CBE

Matthew Rice, BA (*Chairman*)

Steve Nokes

Professor Geoffrey Ward

Charles Watson, BA

Timothy Wise

Head: **Magnus Bashaarat**, MA Edinburgh, PGCE King's College London

Senior Deputy, Operational and Pastoral: Louise Wilson, BA King's College London, MA Bath

Head, Bedales Prep, Dunhurst: Colin Baty, NPQH, BEd, Dip Teach Waikato University NZ, BPP Roehampton

Head, Bedales Pre-prep, Dunannie: Victoria Homewood, BA Goldsmiths London

Bursar and Clerk to the Governors: Richard Lushington, BA, MCIPD Thames Polytechnic London

Director of External Relations: Rob Reynolds, BSc Royal Holloway London, MBA Strathclyde, MCIM

Bede's Senior School

Upper Dicker, East Sussex BN27 3QH

Tel: 01323 843252
email: school.office@bedes.org
website: www.bedes.org
Twitter: @bedesnews
Facebook: @bedesseniorschool

Founded in 1978 Bede's discovers the talents of each student through breadth of academic curriculum and co-curricular. It is academically ambitious for all and the pastoral care, delivered through the House and Tutor systems, is inspiring and nurturing and ensures Bede's sends its young people into the outside world self-aware, happy and confident in what they can achieve and looking forward to the challenges they will meet.

The Senior School owes its existence in part to the success and vitality of Bede's Preparatory School in Eastbourne, one of the first boys' Preparatory Schools to become fully co-educational and now one of the largest co-educational Preparatory Schools in the country. The Senior School has 760 students. Of these 310 are boarders (full and weekly), 450 are day students, 340 are Sixth Formers, 60 per cent are boys and 40 per cent are girls. Bede's enjoys an enviable reputation internationally. Currently 20% of our students are from over 40 countries.

The School takes great pride in the variety of its students and the outstanding range of opportunities available to them. The breadth of choice means every student can find what they naturally excel at. Students at Bede's pick from a wide array of over 100 clubs and activities, guided by personal tutors.

Aims. Bede's aims include the provision of an outstanding education, in an inclusive co-educational environment. That education is predicated on flexibility for the student; a broad and varied curriculum; personalisation of study programmes and respect for students' choices and aptitudes. Coupled with this is the provision of an extensive and exceptional variety of co-curricular activities that allows students to find, nurture and develop their interests and talents. The programme caters for everyone, from elite performers to hobbyists, and no activity is considered more important than another.

Bede's provides pastoral care that aims to support and safeguard each student, and in so doing, develops values of respect and humanity within a framework of friendly, non-confrontational relationships between all people, adults and students alike.

Facilities. Bede's buildings are friendly, in enviable settings and a far cry from the overbearing, institutional character of much school architecture. In 2007 the School opened two innovative and award-winning boarding houses and two more were opened in February 2012. The multi-purpose Hall, also opened in 2007, is used for School Assemblies, examinations and many sports, including basketball, badminton, cricket, football, netball and tennis. The Performing Arts Centre, in a beautiful setting next to the lake, provides studio space for both drama and dance and 2008 saw the opening of a new Music Centre. A new multi-purpose games area, water-based astro and cricket pavilion were all opened in 2015. The zoo – which originally opened in 2011 – currently hosts over 70 species of mammals, birds, amphibians, reptiles, fish and invertebrates. In 2018 it was extended with six brand-new enclosures, housing African birds, Madagascan lemurs, and South American squirrel monkeys.

Curriculum. A new first year curriculum launched in September 2015 offering a range of new, fresh courses. The programme has an emphasis on the core skills of literacy, numeracy and scientific discovery and also includes "21st Century Studies", encompassing "soft skills" such as team work and time management as well as "hard skills" including cooking and first aid. All children also study a carousel of subjects as part of a course entitled "The World", which will cover global politics, history and geography. There is also an emphasis on creative subjects with children given the opportunity to experience art in many forms.

In the Fifth Form (Year 10) most students begin two-year courses leading to the GCSE (Key Stage 4) examinations. Students usually follow nine subjects of a possible 40 at GCSE; Mathematics, Science and English are compulsory subjects. Potential optional courses include: Art and Design, Business Studies, Dance, Design & Technology, Drama, Geography, History, Home Economics, Information Technology, Latin and Greek, Media Studies, Modern Languages (French, Spanish, German), Music, Performing Arts (Dance), Physical Education, Religious Studies, Science (Triple Award), Science (Double Award), Science (Single Award). Some IGCSEs are also offered along with some short-course GCSEs. A Pre-Sixth course is offered for those who need a year of intensive English before embarking on an A Level course.

During the first three years those with particular needs, such as those with any form of Dyslexia and those who are non-native speakers of English, can follow organised programmes within the timetable taught by suitably qualified teachers.

In the Sixth Form students can follow the traditional three or four A Level courses and some Pre-U courses, which can provide a broader education. Most GCSE subjects are offered at A Level plus Economics, Media Studies, Government & Politics, Philosophy and Ethics and Theatre Studies. Bede's also offers Cambridge Pre-U in a number of subjects. Sixth Form students can also take the Extended Project Qualification, Level 2 Award in Sports Leadership, Level 2 Certificate in Financial Education or Arts Award Gold.

Vocational provision: BTEC National Certificate in Sport, Music Performance, Animal Management and Business Management.

Bede's also runs the Legat Professional Dance Course which is fully integrated with the academic programme.

Current class sizes average 16 up to GCSE level and 12 at A Level.

Co-Curricular Programme including Games. The extensive programme includes the many sporting and games playing opportunities open to students, The Duke of Edinburgh's Award scheme, numerous outdoor pursuits and a daily programme of activities within the fields of Art, Drama, Music, Journalism, Science, Technology, Engineering and Social Service. There are currently over 14 Club Activities running each week and an average daily choice from 40 options. Games and Sports include Aerobics, Archery, Athletics, Badminton, Basketball, Canoeing, Climbing, Cricket, Cross-Country, Fishing, Football, Golf (the School has its own practice course), Hockey, Dance, Netball, Orienteering, Photography, Riding, Rounders, Rugby, Squash, Swimming, Target Rifle Shooting, Tennis and Volleyball. Bede's has a fine sporting reputation with students past and present representing their country at cricket, football, rugby, hockey, athletics and showjumping. The Emerging Talent Programme brings together pupils across different sports who have potential to become professional sports people and provides training in areas such as nutrition, sports psychology and media handling.

Pastoral Care. There are three boys' boarding houses and two girls' houses, the numbers in each house averaging 60, with three resident staff in each. An appropriately selected tutor provides a mentor for each student during their time at the School. These tutors are responsible for ensuring that each student's academic and social well-being is carefully looked after. Tutors act in liaison with Housemasters and Housemistresses and are readily available for discussions with parents. All parents have several formal opportunities each year to meet those who teach or otherwise look after their sons or daughters. In 2015 a Day Boarding concept was launched allowing day pupils to be part of a boarding house, complete prep in house and return home on the late bus service.

Religion. The School maintains the Village Church for the local community. Confirmation classes are available, if requested. All students attend weekly meetings in the church which are appropriate to boys and girls of all religions and are of outstanding variety. Bede's does not impose any singular religious observance on its students but would rather either that their existing faith is further strengthened by their being full members of the congregation of local churches or that they grow to appreciate and value the importance of a strong spiritual life through the thoughtful and varied programme of 'School Meetings'. There is a choice of four types of observance on Sundays: the Multi-Religious School Meeting, Church of England, Roman Catholic and Free Church.

Admission. The usual points of entry are at Year 9 and Year 12, although a small number of places are usually available for entry into Year 10. Pupils entering Year 9 will be invited to attend a Bede's Experience Day in Year 7 when pupils will take part in group activities, take a cognitive test, be interviewed and participate in an activity of choice. School reports and references are also taken into account. Entry into the Sixth Form will be conditional on GCSE results, reports and references.

Scholarships and Bursaries. Bede's invests in excess of ten per cent of its annual income in means-tested fee remission and academic, art, dance, drama, music and sports scholarships. Prospective students who wish to join outside of the scholarship process are able to apply for means-tested fee remission.

Further details regarding scholarships and bursaries are available from the Admissions Office, email: admissions@bedes.org.

Fees per term (2018–2019). Full Boarders £11,720, Weekly Boarders £11,020, Day Pupils £7,370, Day Boarding £7,470.

Charitable status. St Bede's School Trust Sussex is a Registered Charity, number 278950. It exists to provide quality education.

Governors:
Mrs Geraldine Watkins, JP (*Chair*)
Mr John Burbidge, BA Hons, ACA
Mr Andrew Corbett, MA Hons, PGCE
Dr Matthew Crummack, BSc Hons
Mr Christopher Doidge, MA Oxon
Mrs Sarah Jelly
Mr Dermot Keegan
Mrs Katharine Lees-Jones, JP, MCSP
Professor Andrew Lloyd, MA Cantab, PhD
Mr Mark MacFadden, MRICS, ACIArb
Mr Nicholas Mercer, BA Hons
Mrs Kate Nash, BEd
Mr Xavier Van Hove, BA Hons Oxon
Mrs Jenifer Woodhouse, Cert Ed London
Mr Christopher Yates, BA Hons, MBA

Senior Management:
Headmaster: **Mr P Goodyer**, BSc

Senior Management:
Principal Deputy Headmaster: Mr J Lewis, BA Hons, MA, PGCE
Deputy Head, Academic: Mr J Tuson, MA, GTP
Deputy Head, Staff: Mr R Frame, BA Hons, HDE
Deputy Head, Co-Curricular: Ms R Woollett, BA Hons, PGCE
School Chaplain: Revd T Buckler, BA, MA Hons, PGCE
Assistant Head of Compliance & Welfare: Mrs L M Belrhiti, BEd Hons, Dip TEFL
Senior Registrar: Mr R Mills, BA Hons, PGCE
Principal of Summer School: Mr S Wood
Director of Curriculum Management: Mr A Hayes, BSc Hons, PGCE
Director of Marketing and Admissions: Mrs R Nairne, BA Hons
Bursar: Dr Jonathan Northway, MB, FRCS

Housemasters and Housemistresses:
Bloomsbury House: Mrs M Leggett, BA Hons, MA, PGCE
Camberlot House: Mr F McKeefry, BA Hons, PGCE
Crossways House: Mrs J Lambeth, BSc Hons, PGCE
Charleston House: Mrs M Martin, BA Hons, PGCE, MA Ed, Dip TEFL
Deis House: Mr N Driver, BCom, PGCE
Dicker House: Mr C Abraham, BSc Hons, Dip Law, PGCE
Dorms House: Mr P Juniper, BSc Hons, PGCE, CBiol, MSB
Dorter House: Mrs A Murphy, MTeach, BA Hons, PGCE DT
Knights House: Mr A Waterhouse, HDE Secondary
Stud House: Mr P Jones, BSc Hons, MSc, PGCE

Heads of Departments/Subjects:

Mr J Turner, BA Hons, PGCE (*Head of Art; Photography*)
Mr A Hammond, BA Hons, MA, GTP (*Head of Ceramics*)
Miss E Excell, BA Hons, GTP (*Head of Photography*)
Mr G Parfitt, MBA (*Head of Business Studies & Economics*)
Mr N Potter, BSc Hons, PGCE (*Head of Design & Technology*)
Mrs K Lewis, BA Hons, PGCE (*Director of Performing Arts; Theatre Studies*)
Mr J Cook, RSA, TEFLA (*Head of EAL*)
Mr M Oliver, BA Hons, PGCE (*Head of English*)
Mr Jonathan Slinger, BA, MA, PGCE (*Head of Geography*)
Mr P Gibbs, BA Hons, PGCE (*Director of Higher Education*)
Mr J Whittaker, BA Hons, PGCE (*Head of History*)
Mr G Parker, BA Hons (*Head of Government and Politics*)
Mr C Betts, BSc Hons (*Head of Computing and Information Technology*)
Mrs C MacGregor, BSc, QTS, PGCE (*Director of Learning Enhancement*)
Mr N Abrams, BSc Hons, PGCE (*Head of STEM; Further Mathematics*)
Mr R Williams, BA Hons, GTP, Dip Media Ed (*Head of Media Studies*)
Mrs Elizabeth Wyles (*Head of MFL*)
Mr Robert Scamardella, MMus, MMP, FRSM, FRCO (*Director of Music*)
Mrs Mary-Jane Newbery BA Hons (*Head of Physical Education*)
Mr David Byrne, BA Hons (*Head of Sport*)
Mr Savvas Costi, BA Hons, PGCE (*Head of Religion & Philosophy*)
Mr M Costley, BSc Hons, MSc, PGCE (*Head of Chemistry*)
Mrs N Morton-Freeman, BSc Hons, PGCE (*Head of Biology*)

Mr C Hiscox, BSc Hons, PGCE (*Head of Physics*)
Mr P Juniper, BSc Hons, PGCE CBiol, MSB (*Head of Animal Management*)
Legat School of Dance:
Mr L Smikle (*Principal and Artistic Director*)
Mrs A Murphy, BA Hons, PGCE (*Head of Academic Dance*)

Year Heads:
Head of First Year: Mr L Backler, BA Hons, PGCE
Director of Studies (GCSE): Ms J French, BSc, PGCE
Head of Sixth Form: Mr J Henham, BSc Hons, PGCE
Deputy Head of Sixth Form & Pre-Sixth: Mr B Jackson, BSc, PGCE

Bedford Modern School

Manton Lane, Bedford, Bedfordshire MK41 7NT

Tel: 01234 332500
Fax: 01234 332550
email: info@bedmod.co.uk
website: www.bedmod.co.uk
Twitter: @BedfordModern
Facebook: @BedfordModernSchool
LinkedIn: /bedford-modern-school

Bedford Modern School is one of the Harpur Trust Schools in Bedford, sharing equally in the educational endowment bequeathed for the establishment of a school in Bedford by Sir William Harpur in 1566. Bedford Modern School was a Direct Grant Grammar School which became independent in 1976. It became co-educational in September 2003.

Number of Pupils. There are 253 pupils in the Junior School (aged 7–11) and 956 pupils in the Senior School (aged 11–18).

(*See also Bedford Modern Junior School entry in IAPS section.*)

Facilities. The School occupies an attractive forty-acre wooded site to the north of Bedford. The main buildings date from 1974 and there have been substantial additions since that time, most notably a new assembly hall, performance arena and classrooms to the Junior School (2002); a Sixth Form Study Centre and Refectory (The Rutherford Building – 2006) and new Library Resource Centre (2007). There are extensive facilities for Science, Technology and Information Technology. There have been recent extensions to the Music School and Performing Arts Centre. Each year group has its own common room.

A new, state-of-the-art Science Centre opened in September 2017. The exciting design provides current and future generations of BMS students with an inspirational learning environment.

The playing fields are all on the School site with extensive facilities for Rugby, Football, Cricket and Athletics. There is also a large swimming pool, a fitness suite, gym and sports hall. Recent additions include two large all-weather training areas and netball courts. The School shares a large and well-stocked Boathouse with the other Harpur Trust Schools on the River Ouse.

Admissions. Pupils are admitted between the ages of 7 and 16. The School conducts its own entrance assessments which are held in January of the year prior to September entry.

Registration fee is £100.

Fees per term (2018–2019). Tuition: Junior School £3,257, Senior School and Sixth Form £4,468.

Assistance with Fees. The School offers Modern Scholarships which are available to pupils joining the School from Year 7 (11+) upwards and have been designed to provide opportunities for children with potential academically, in sport, performance arts, music and art/design and information technology. All scholarships are means-tested and are also dependent on a pupil's academic success in the entrance assessments. Further details may be obtained from the School.

Curriculum. The Junior School (ages 7–11) curriculum covers Mathematics, English, Humanities (History, Geography and RE), Science, Information and Communication Technology (ICT), Modern Foreign Languages, PE, Art, Drama, PSHE and Games. Pupils benefit both from a purpose-built practical skills centre containing art and science rooms as well as specialist computer and technology rooms, and from the Senior School, music, PE and games facilities including the swimming pool.

In the Senior School, the curriculum includes all the core subjects, as well as Technology, IT, RE, PE, Music, Art and Drama. All pupils experience French, German, and Spanish in Year 7 and Latin in Year 8 before making choices. Pupils opt for ten GCSE subjects. For the Sixth Form, pupils select four from a wide range of 29 subjects. In addition to all the traditional options, the choice of subjects also includes Computer Science, Government and Politics, Economics, Business, Religious Studies, Philosophy, DT Systems and Control, DT Product Design, Classical Civilisation, Theatre Studies, PE, Psychology, Film Studies and Music Technology. All students will sit AS exams at the end of Year 12 in all their subjects and the majority will continue three to A Level.

ICT Facilities. The School boasts a range of ICT facilities offering both staff and pupils an individual network account and email address so that they are able to access over 400 networked PCs across the School in addition to high-speed broadband Internet access, wireless classroom laptop sets, networked printing, and an extensive subject software library including a range of training courseware material.

All standard classrooms are equipped with a computer linked to ceiling mounted data projector and speakers. There are a number of interactive whiteboards and additional presentation equipment is also available for use. The School's website can be viewed at www.bedmod.co.uk.

Religious and Moral Education. The School is multifaith and multicultural, and religious and moral education is given throughout. Personal, social and health education is a fundamental and well-established part of the timetable.

Individual Care. Every pupil has a personal tutor, who supervises and takes an interest in his or her academic progress, co-curricular activities and sporting interests. Tutors meet with their tutees on a daily basis and there is at least one longer pastoral session each week. Each Year Group has its own common room for use at break and lunchtimes and other non-taught times with a study area and recreational facilities.

We believe that common sense and courtesy lie at the heart of pastoral care. We stress self-discipline and high standards of personal conduct. The tutorial system and the academic organisation are discrete, working in parallel to complement each other. Teaching class sizes are a maximum of twenty-four and often many fewer. We aim to provide a relaxed but purposeful environment; a culture in which all feel at ease and are ambitious to achieve their best.

Drama. There are several large-scale productions each year, a Drama Festival hosted for local schools, and several smaller events. There are separate drama and dance studios and a 300-seat theatre. Speech and Drama is offered throughout the School, leading to LAMDA examinations.

Ballet, tap and modern dance lessons follow the ISTD syllabus.

Music. Pupils can learn all the orchestral and band instruments as well as piano, keyboard, guitar/electric guitar and singing. The School has a large variety of choirs, orchestra, bands and ensembles. Pupils can follow courses for GCSE and A Level Music as well as A Level Music Technology. Music accommodation includes a music technology suite with ten Apple computers and state-of-the-art recording facilities.

Activities. There are many school societies and clubs catering for a variety of tastes and interests. The voluntary Combined Cadet Force is strong with Army, Navy, RAF and Marine sections. There is a structured programme of outdoor education which includes residential trips from Years 6, 7 and 8 with international expeditions available for older students. Outreach including community service and the Duke of Edinburgh's Award scheme are very popular.

Sport. Rugby, football, cricket and rowing are major sports for boys; hockey, netball and rowing for girls. Additional activities include: table tennis, water polo, badminton, hockey (boys), equestrian, snowsports, cycling, cross-country, weights and fitness, fencing, fives, sevens, swimming, dance, athletics, rounders, tennis, climbing, shooting, and gymnastics. There is regular representation at national, divisional and regional levels.

Higher Education. The great majority of sixth form leavers go on to a degree course at their chosen university. More than 30% take courses in STEM (Science, Technology, Engineering and Mathematics) subjects.

Old Bedford Modernians' Club. For further details see the OBM section of the School website or please contact externalrelations@bedmod.co.uk.

Charitable status. Bedford Modern School is part of the Harpur Trust which is a Registered Charity, number 1066861. It includes in its aims the provision of high quality education for boys and girls.

Governors and Staff:
Chairman of School Governors: Shirley Jackson

Headmaster: **Mr A N J Tate**, MA

Senior Deputy Head: Mrs S E Davis, MA, PGCE
Deputy Head Academic: Mr M R Price, MA, PGCE
Deputy Head Pastoral: Mrs J Goodacre, BA Hons, PGCE, MBA
Head of Junior School: Mrs J C Rex, BA, PGCE
Director of Sixth Form: Mr J P White, BEd
Director of External Relations: Ms J Ridge, BA
Director of Operations: Mr R Pooley, BA Hons

Heads of Year:
Head of Year 7: Mrs S J Sanctuary, BSc, PGCE
Head of Year 8: Mr J P Searle, BTh, PGCE
Head of Year 9: Mr T E Rex, BEd Hons
Head of Year 10: Mrs L L Neville, BA Hons
Head of Year 11: Mr J P Fitton, BSc, PGCE

Heads of Houses:
Senior Head of House: Mrs P Edwards, BA, MA, PGCE
Head of Bell House: Mr A G Higgens, BSc, QTS
Head of Farrar House: Mr J M Sadler, BSc, PGCE
Head of Mobbs House: Mr E Kerr
Head of Oatley House: Mrs V Jenkins
Head of Rose House: Mr A Slater, BEng, PGCE
Head of Tilden House: Ms S Sobrado

Teaching Staff:

Faculty of Art, Design & Information Technology: Miss S E Milton, BA, PGCE

Art:
Mr J McGregor, BA, PG Dip, PGCE
Mrs P Edwards, BA, MA, PGCE

Design Technology:
Mr A H Jones
Mrs L Neville
Mr A Rock, BSc Hons, PGCE
Mr J P White, BEd
Mr E Kerr

ICT:
Mr A Leach, BA
Miss J Hollingsworth, PGCE
Mr W Reed

Faculty of English: Mr S D Bywater, BA, MLitt, PGCE

Dr J P Barnes, PhD, PGCE
Ms J Chumbley, BA, PGCE
Dr T Foster, BA, MA, PhD, PGCE
Mrs J L Kilbey, BA, MA, PGCE
Mr O L Roberts
Mr J J Sanders, BA, PGCE
Mrs H Denison, BA Hons, PGCE

Film Studies:
Mr J J Sanders, BA, PGCE
Dr T Foster, BA, MA, PhD, PGCE

Faculty of Humanities: Miss R Gleeson

Geography:
Mr T Barwood
Mrs D R Mistrano, BA, PGCE
Mr M R Price, MA Cantab, PGCE
Mrs A Kelly, BSc Hons, MA, PGCE
Miss A Smith, BSc, PGCE, MEd

History:
Mrs S E Wright, MA, PGCE
Dr S Boa BA, MPhil, PhD, PGCE
Dr S Reid, BA Hons, MA, PhD, PGCE
Mr A D Tapper, BSc, MSt Oxon
Ms C Webb, BA, PGCE

Religious Studies and Theology:
Mr J L Hooper, BA, PGCE
Mr J P Searle, BTh, PGCE
Mrs J Shaw

Faculty of Languages and Classics: Miss R Crawley, BA,
 PGCE, LGSM, MEd

Classics:
Miss J Newton, MA, PGCE
Mrs S E Davis, MA, PGCE
Miss E Swallow
Miss A Hutchinson

French:
Miss R Crawley, BA, PGCE, LGSM, MEd

German:
Mr R J Killen, MA, PGCE, TEFL, DipSp & DipFr

Spanish:
Miss S Celani
Mrs R Reed, BA, PGCE, TEFL
Miss S Sobrado, Licenciatura, PGCE

Languages Teachers:
Mlle G Amoros, Licence Civilisation * Lit, PGCE
Mr G Watkins, BA
Mrs J Williams, BA, PGCE

Faculty of Mathematics: Mr N D Shackleton, BSc, PGCE
Mr S A Brocklehurst, BA, PGCE
Mrs N Fisher, BSc Hons, PGCE

Miss E J Ginns
Mr N Hussain, BSc, PGCE
Mr R Kay, BSc, PGCE
Mr D M King, BSc, PGCE
Mr A Leach, BA
Mr R Millar
Mr A Slater, BEng, PGCE
Miss K Ward, BSc Hons, QTS

Faculty of Music: Mr J Mower, GRSM, ARCO, ARCM,
 Dip RAM

Assistant Director of Music: Mrs M Perry, BMus, PGCE,
 DipABRSM

Music Technology:

Faculty of Performance Arts: Miss L Coltman, BA Hons

Drama:
Mrs V Jenkins
Mrs L Wright
Mrs J Goodacre, BA, PGCE, MBA

Speech and Drama:
Mrs S Leather, BA
Miss S Brooks
Mr W Moss

Dance:
Miss R Bradley, AISTD, FDI

Faculty of Politics, Philosophy and Economics (PPE): Mr
 D Bareham

Economics:
Mr P J Davis
Mr R Smith, BA, PGCE

Business:
Mr R Smith, BA, PGCE

Government & Politics:
Mr S Baker, BSc, PGCE

Philosophy:
Mrs J Morris

Faculty of Science: Mr N R Else, BEd, MA

Biology:
Mr R J Brand, BSc, PGCE
Mr D Donoghue, BA, PGCE, MA
Mrs H Lakhani, BSc, PGCE
Miss E McEwan
Miss D Randhawa
Mrs S Sanctuary, BSc, PGCE
Mrs S Sumal, BSc MSc, PGCE

Chemistry:
Dr C M Oswald, BSc, PhD, PGCE
Mrs N K Cordell, BEd Hons
Mr J P Fitton, BSc, PGCE
Mr J Sadler, BSc, PGCE
Mrs V Shehu, BSc, GTP

Physics:
Mrs V Ecart, MD, BSc Hons, PGCE
Mr D C Honnor, BA Oxon, GTP
Mrs W D Hallett, BA, MA, PGCE
Mr J Krishna, BSc Hons, MSc, PGCE, MInstP
Mr T P Mullan, BSc, PGCE
Mr T E Rex, BEd Hons

Psychology:
Miss H J Kelly, BSc, PGCE

Faculty of Sport:
Head of Junior School Sport Development: Mr T W
 Bucktin, BSc

Director of Cricket: Mr P J Woodroffe, BA
Director of Rowing: Mr M Bavington
Director of Rugby: Mr B Richmond
Coordinator of Girls Games: Miss H L Gilbert, BA, MA, PGCE

PE Teachers:
Mr A G Higgens, BSc, QTS
Mr A D Tapper, BSc, MSt Oxon
Mr M Park

Waterpolo and Swimming:
Mr A Bygraves

Other Areas:
Careers: Miss S Burns, DipCG
Examinations: Mrs J Lemon
Librarian: Mrs M S Brown, BSc, Dip Lib, CNNA Dist, MCILIP
PSHE: Mrs D Tapper, BA, PGCE
Welfare Liaison Manager: Mrs L Arif
Head of Enrichment: Dr T Foster, BA Hons, MA, PhD, PGCE
Health and Fitness Manager: Mrs L Williams, LLB, MSc
Technical Theatre Manager: Mr N Parker, BA
Theatre Technician: Mr J Hundy, BA Hons

Director of Academic Support: Dr Sean Reid
SENCO: Miss L J Hendry

SpLD Academic Support:
Mrs D Costello, BA, MA, CertSpLD
Mrs C Setchfield, BA, PGCE, CertSpLD
Mrs M Tew, BA, PGCE

Junior School:
Head of Junior School: Mrs J Rex, BA, PGCE
Deputy Head of Junior School: Mrs P Pacyna, BA, QTS
Junior School Heads Secretary: Mrs K Smith
Head of Junior School Sports Development: Mr T Bucktin, BSc, PGCE
Director of Studies: Mrs K Harpin, BA Hons

Junior School Teachers:

Miss J Barlow, BEd
Mr C Barrow, BEd
Mr R Bishop
Mrs A Crawford-Smith, BEd Hons
Mrs M Fox, BA, PGCE
Mrs F Gale, BEd
Mrs M Garton
Mrs K Hale, BA, QTS
Miss E Hayman, BSc Hons, PGCE
Miss C Hendrie, BA Hons, PGCE
Mrs J Leydon, BEd
Mrs L Mills, BS, QTS
Mrs S J Nicholls, BA, Cert Ed
Mrs M Phillips, BEd
Mr M Redmond, BA Hons QTS, MA
Mrs C Toumazou
Mr E Warren, BA, QTS

Administration Assistant: Mrs C Mayfield
Cover Supervisor: Mrs S Westbrook
Learning Support Assistant: Mrs H Draycott
Learning Support Assistant: Mrs B Sehmbi

Bedford School

De Parys Avenue, Bedford MK40 2TU
Tel: 01234 362216
email: admissions@bedfordschool.org.uk
website: www.bedfordschool.org.uk
Twitter: @bedfordschool
Facebook: @Bedford-School

Bedford School is a leading boarding and day school for boys aged 13–18. The school is situated in an extensive 50-acre estate in the heart of Bedford and is just 45 minutes from London by train.

Established in 1552, Bedford School has a reputation for academic excellence and all boys are encouraged to aspire to the highest possible standards and to exceed their expectations.

The school's success is demonstrated by a long history of impressive exam results at GCSE, A Level, and in the International Baccalaureate Diploma (IB). Bedford is also renowned for its strengths in music, the arts and sport.

From the classroom to the sports field, in laboratories and theatres, on excursions and exchanges, boys are challenged academically, socially and culturally. They learn exciting new skills and knowledge, and how to prepare themselves for a successful future as well-rounded young men with confidence, compassion and critical minds.

Number in School. 717 boys aged between 13–18 years: 238 weekly and full boarders, 479 day boys.

Boarders and Day Boys. There is a balanced mix of day boys, weekly boarders and full boarders, who combine in lessons, games and all other school activities. There are six Senior Boarding Houses, each containing up to 51 boys.

Academic. Academic excellence is central to life at Bedford School. Consistent high exam results at GCSE, A Level and the IB set the standard for academic achievement throughout the school. The curriculum extends learning well beyond the national requirements and is structured to provide a balanced and varied choice of subjects, which will challenge each boy's strengths.

Boys are encouraged to achieve through a balance of different teaching techniques, small class sizes and (where appropriate) setting, well-resourced and subject-specific classrooms, specialist teachers, prep setting, regular lecture series and visiting speakers, lunchtime and after school academic clinics. ICT and mobile device technology is used extensively to support and enhance learning, but literacy and numeracy skills remain fundamental to all that we do.

University and Careers. A strong Careers and UCAS provision enables all boys, throughout their school years, to access tailored, professional experience and advice. In addition to an annual careers fair, regular information evenings, lectures and seminars are also held. The school is a member of the Independent Schools Careers Organisation and was awarded E2E Gold status in 2016 and a Career Mark in 2017.

Almost all leavers go on to higher education. In 2018, two-thirds of boys went on to Russell Group Universities including Oxbridge.

Extracurricular. The school offers a diverse programme of extracurricular activities every evening between 4.15 pm and 6.00 pm for boarders and day boys alike, many of which involve girls from Harpur Trust sister school, Bedford Girls' School. Activities include the Combined Cadet Force (CCF), Duke of Edinburgh's Award scheme, community service, fundraising groups, and more than 60 other clubs and societies from Astronomy to Young Enterprise. Concerts, plays, lectures and film performances are given in the Great Hall, the Recital Hall, the Erskine May Hall and the Quarry Theatre.

Sport. The school aims to inspire a lifelong interest in sport, promoting teamwork, well-being, fitness and fun. A team of dedicated, passionate specialist teachers and coaches are on hand to provide high-quality guidance and help each boy to develop his skills. Many boys go on to excel at sport, and the majority of major sport first teams are of county standard or beyond.

The school's major sports are rugby, hockey, rowing and cricket but the range of sports on offer extends to athletics, badminton, basketball, cross country, fencing, fives, golf, sailing, soccer, squash, swimming, tennis, water polo and weight training/conditioning.

First-class facilities include a twin Astroturf complex with floodlights, an indoor 25m swimming pool, 28 tennis courts, four squash courts, a climbing wall and immaculate grass pitches.

Music. All boys have the opportunity to explore and perform, with a wide range of musical instruments and groups to choose from. As well as the two Senior Symphony Orchestras, a Chamber Orchestra, a Concert Band and a large Choral Society, there is a Chapel Choir trained in the English Cathedral tradition, two Junior Orchestras, a Dance Band, Jazz Band, Rock Band, a large number of chamber music groups, and a Music Club. There is a full music programme throughout each year, with at least one concert a week.

The Music department is situated in a £3 million, state-of-the-art, purpose-built development, which includes a superb recital hall, music technology suite, multi-track recording studio and the school's radio station.

Drama. All boys can get involved in Bedford School's vibrant drama scene, whether on stage or behind the scenes. Each year a range of formal and informal dramatic productions are performed by all age groups.

The drama department is housed in the school's new £6m Quarry Theatre, which officially opened in June 2015 in the former St Luke's Church. The 286-seat theatre and 60-seat studio-theatre provide a superb venue for school productions and the extensive programme performed by visiting touring companies.

Art and Design. The art department works to develop each boy's individual artistic talents and encourages pupils to engage with and appreciate the world around them. Boys are encouraged to develop a lifelong appreciation of the creative arts with visits to museums and galleries, annual study tours abroad, weekly life drawing classes and a series of art lectures.

The Art School, located in a characterful mid-1750s Georgian building, has three specialist studios for painting, printmaking and sculpture. All three Art Staff are practising artists.

Admissions. The majority of boys enter the Preparatory School from seven and the Upper School at 13 or 16 years of age. The Preparatory School has its own Headmaster and specialist staff. (*See Bedford Preparatory School entry in IAPS section.*)

Parents wishing to send their sons to Bedford School should apply to the Director of Admissions. All applicants are expected to provide evidence of good character and suitability from their previous school. Year 9 applicants from Preparatory Schools wishing to enter the Upper School are assessed in Year 6 or Year 7 by an initial Pre-test and interview. In Year 8 all applicants undertake a computer-based test (designed to measure raw academic potential) at the school, along with English and Mathematics papers.

Boys looking to join the Sixth Form are invited for an assessment day in the January before entry. Applicants sit a Verbal Reasoning paper and have an interview with a senior member of staff. In addition, the school takes up a reference with the boy's current school and considers his application along with his predicted grades at GCSE.

Additional information is also available on the website: www.bedfordschool.org.uk/admissions.

Scholarships and Bursaries. The school offers a range of Scholarships and Bursaries to boys who excel academically or show outstanding talent in art, drama, music or sport (including golf). Up to 20 Scholars receive up to a maximum of 10% of annual school fees from The Harpur Trust.

18 of these Scholars receive up to a further 25% of annual school fees if they demonstrate exceptional talent. This additional funding, from the Brian Saville and Professor John Roach Scholarship Funds, gives a total award of up to 35% of annual school fees. Any amount required beyond this is awarded on a means-tested basis through the school's Bursary scheme.

Awards are available for boys joining the school at our 13+ and 16+ entry points. For more information, please visit www.bedfordschool.org.uk/scholarships.

Fees per term (2018–2019). Day Boys £6,344; Full Boarders £10,730; Weekly Boarders £10,375.

Old Bedfordians Club. Tel: 01234 362262; email: obclub@bedfordschool.org.uk. For further details, visit www.bedfordschool.org.uk/the-club.

Charitable status. Bedford School is part of the Harpur Trust which is a Registered Charity, number 1066861.

School Governors:
Chairman: Sir Clive Loader

Mrs Kirsty Bourne	Mrs Jenny Pelling
Mr Simon Briggs	Mr Rajkumar Roy
Mr Rob Campbell	Mrs Jennifer Sauborah Till
Mrs Rhian Castell	Mr Mark Slater
Dr Anne Egan	Revd Paula Vennells
Mrs Lucy Hubber	Mr Phil Wallace
Mr Ali Malek	

Chairman of the Harpur Trust: Mr Murray Stewart
Deputy Chairman of the Harpur Trust: Mr Stephen Mayson

Head Master: Mr J S Hodgson, BA

Vice Master: Mr D Koch, BA, DPhil
Deputy Head (Academic): Mr S Baldock, MA, FRSB
Bursar and Clerk to the Governors: Mr S Holliday
Director of Teaching & Learning: Mr W Montgomery, BSc
Director of Bedford School Association: Mr R Garrett, BA

Director of Admissions: Mrs A Steiger
Director of International Baccalaureate: Mr A Finch, MA
Senior Boarding Housemaster: Mr C J Bury, BA
Undermaster: Mr I B Armstrong, BSc, MSc
Director of Digital Learning: Dr A Wallace, FBCS, FSRA

Assistant staff:
* *Head of Department*

Academic Support (ESOL & SPLD):
*Ms J Spir, BA, RSA Preparatory Cert TEFL
Mrs K Chevallier, MA, Cert TEFL, OCNW Level 4 Cert ESOL
Mrs J Greening, BPhil, Cert TEFL
Ms J Hutt, BEd, RSA Dip SpLD, SENCo National Award
Mr T Kehoe, BA, MSt, PGCE, QTS
Mr B O'Connor, Cert Ed, Cert TEFL
Mrs M Nayar, BSc, Cert Ed
Mrs S Manning, LLB, CELTA
Mrs L Patel, BA, Cert ESOL
Mr N Pieris, MA, CELTA, MCollT
Mrs L Saunders MA, Dip TEFL
Miss T Thompson, BA

Art:
*Mr M Croker, BA
Mr J Nicholl, BA
Mrs K Nicholson, BA, MA
Mrs F Whiteman, BA, MA

Biology:
*Mr M Beale, BSc, MEd (*Head of Science*)
Mr S Baldock, BA
Mrs F Bell, BSc
Ms J Mainstone, BS
Mr C Palmer, BSc, MA
Ms A Swallow, BA
Mr P Whatling, BSc, BEng

Chemistry:
*Mr S Knight, BA
Miss K Begum
Mr B Johnson, MA, MSc, PhD
Mr P Lumley-Wood, BSc, CChem, MRSC
Mr K Peters, MChem
Dr W Suthers, BSc, MSc, PhD

Classics:
*Mr A Melvill, BA
Mr N Allen, BA
Dr G McCormick, BA, MPhil, DPhil

Computing:
*Dr D Wild, BSc, PhD

Design Technology:
*Mr I Armstrong, BSc, MSc
Mr L Holt, BA
Mr M Huddlestone, BA
Mr G Waite, MEng

Economics & Business Studies:
*Mr P Waterhouse, BSc
Mr C Bury, BA
Mr M Cassell, BSc
Mr R Heale, BSc
Mr H Taylor, BSc

English:
*Mr N Hopton, MA, MEd
Miss H Bassa, BA
Miss K Betterton, BA, MA
Mr A Grimshaw, BA
Mrs K Philpott, BA
Mrs A Smith, BA
Mrs R Wainwright, BA, MA

Geography:
*Mr T Rees, BSc
Mr R Campbell, BA
Miss E Goodman, BSc
Mr M Gracie, BSc
Mr J Marriott, BA
Mr W Montgomery, BSc
Mr M Ruta, BSc
Ms S Spyropoulos, BA

History:
*Ms E Parcell, BA
Mr N Allen, BA
Mr C Fisher, MA
Mr M Graham, BA, MA Ed
Miss G Tooth, BSc
Mr H Vann, BA, MA Cantab

Mathematics:
*Mrs J C Beale, BSc, MA
Mr S Adams, MPhys
Mr S Boul, BSc, MSc
Mr B Burgess, BA Ed
Mrs T Harbinson, BSc
Miss R Jackson, BSc
Mr A Midwinter, BSc
Miss L Owens, BA, BSc
Mr C Prior, BSc
Mrs N Tekell-Mellor, BSc
Mr J Watson, MA
Dr D Wild, BSc, PhD

Modern Languages:
*Mr F Graeff, Dipl Kfm (*Head of German*)
Mr A Huxford, MA (*Head of Spanish*)
Miss V Fletcher, MA (*Acting Head of French*)
Mr A Braithwaite, BA

Mrs M Buergo, MA
Dr A Chen, MBA, PhD
Mr M Dawson, BA
Ms C Geneve, MA
Miss J Law, BA
Mr V Sánchez Jimenez, BA

Music:
*Mr J Sanders, BA
Mr B Bantock, BMus, PPRNCM
Mr D Childs, BMus
Mr T Rooke, MMus, BA
Mr J Rouse, MA, FRCO
Mr R Thompson, BMus, PG Dip MM

Physical Education:
*Mr B Burgess, BA Ed
Mr R Midgley, BA Ed
Mr J Hinkins (*Director of Rugby*)
Mr S Mee (*Director of Hockey*)
Mr P Mulkerrins (*Director of Rowing*)
Mr G Steer (*Director of Cricket*)

Physics:
*Mr G Monaghan
Mr M Crisp, MEng
Mr S Everitt, MEng
Mr G Green, BSc
Mr L Guise, BA
Dr E Palmer, MSci, PhD
Mr A Watson, MSci

Religious Education:
*Mr M Bolton, MA
Mr A Finch, MA
Mr N McCleery, BA (*Chaplain*)
Mr B Rowland

Theatre Studies:
Mrs A Keylock, BA (*Head of Academic Drama*)
Mrs C Millington, BA
Mr J Pharoah, BA (*Theatre Manager*)

Houses and Housemasters:

Boarding Housemasters:
Burnaby: Mr R E Heale, BSc
Pemberley: Mr H Taylor, BSc
Phillpotts: Mr C Fisher, MA
Redburn: Mr J Marriott, BA
Sanderson's: Mr R Midgley, BA Ed
Talbot's: Mr M Gracie, BSc

Day Housemasters:
Ashburnham: S Everitt, MEng
Bromham: Mr P Whatling, BSc, BEng
Crescent: Ms A Swallow, BA
Paulo Pontine: Mrs F Whiteman, BA, MA
St Cuthbert's: Mr L M Holt, BA
St Peter's: Mr M Cassell, BSc

Chaplain: Mr N McCleery, BA

Benenden School

Cranbrook, Kent TN17 4AA

Tel:	01580 240592
Fax:	01580 240280
email:	registry@benenden.kent.sch.uk
	schooloffice@benenden.kent.sch.uk
website:	www.benenden.kent.sch.uk
Twitter:	@benendenschool

Benenden aims to give each girl a complete education in which she achieves her academic potential and grows as an individual. We want her to relish all that school life has to offer so that she leaves us as a confident, positive young woman truly prepared for her future.

We expect each girl to be a responsible and considerate citizen who is outward looking, courageous and compassionate. We support her in being aspirational and in developing her interests and talents whilst learning to achieve balance in her life.

By emphasising the importance of spiritual growth, we hope that each girl will enjoy making a contribution to our supportive school and to be inspired to make a difference throughout her life in her future communities.

In all that we do at Benenden, we aim to foster:

Belief in oneself, belief in others, commitment to learning, commitment to the community.

We aim to do this by providing:

- An inspiring, challenging and relevant academic curriculum which balances the best of tradition and innovation.
- Excellent and motivating teaching designed to encourage girls to become independent, enquiring and critical thinkers.
- A framework of individual support devised to help each girl experience and benefit from a full programme of study balanced with a wide variety of cultural, creative, physical and fun activities.
- A culture of encouragement, opportunity and challenge designed to develop self-reliance, resilience, confidence and physical and emotional wellbeing.
- The experience of learning to understand other people, working and living together with understanding and compromise and appreciating diversity.
- A wide range of opportunities for leadership.
- Careers and higher education guidance designed to help every girl achieve her own personal goals, equipped with the requisite skills for university and beyond in their professional lives.
- A close partnership with parents so that school and home can work together to help every girl make the most of her time at Benenden.

General Information. The School is an independent boarding school for 555 girls between the ages of 11 and 18 years, standing in its own parkland of 250 acres.

As a non-stop, thriving boarding school, girls at Benenden benefit from a bespoke curriculum which achieves excellent academic results and which provides huge added value in an environment where girls are stretched without being stressed by School life.

All girls are full-time boarders and boarding is a partnership between school and home. Girls can be at home, on average, every second weekend if they choose and parents are always welcome on site. Benenden believes in close cooperation between School and parents and there is regular contact with them, including a weekly email newsletter. Formal reports are sent four times a year. Parents are encouraged to visit the School for concerts, plays and other events, as well as to take their daughters out for meals or weekend exeats. There is a flourishing programme of social events for parents.

On any given weekend, around two-thirds of girls are in School – which is perhaps no surprise considering Benenden offers the country's finest programme of Weekend activities. There is also a breathtaking array of co-curricular opportunities and numerous curriculum trips, with more than 150 activities on offer every week.

Benenden is a happy and safe home from home with excellent pastoral care and 24/7 medical care. Its food is much admired and would not be out of place in a top hotel.

Benenden has the perfect location: nestled in the middle of the Garden of England, the School's beautiful campus is also within easy reach of London, with the capital less than an hour by train from nearby Staplehurst Station. Girls at Benenden get the best of both worlds: life in a safe and picturesque rural location with regular trips into large towns, to the seaside and into London.

Every weekend the School organises train travel to London for girls returning home and at Exeats and other school holidays it also arranges coaches to transport girls to Sussex, London, Essex and Suffolk. It also provides transfers to Heathrow, Gatwick and City Airport at Half Term and End of Term.

Benenden has an Anglican tradition and the key Christian principle of loving our neighbour is at the heart of our shared life. Members of other communions and beliefs are welcomed to the School and every effort is made to help them in the practice of their own faith, in an atmosphere of respect and tolerance for the views of others. The School is committed to every girl being a global citizen, which is achieved through the bespoke global awareness programme and a strong focus in Prayers and Form gatherings on current national and global issues.

Girls are taught by highly qualified staff of over 100 men and women, many of whom are leaders in their particular fields.

Each student belongs to a House in which she sleeps and spends much of her private study and leisure time: it is, in effect, her home from home. There are six Houses for 11 to 16-year-olds, while Sixth Form students live in the Founders' Sixth Form Centre in one of four Sixth Form Houses.

Each House has a resident Housemistress or Housemaster, who is also a member of the teaching staff and responsible for the academic and pastoral well-being of each student in the House. Much of the day-to-day work is shared with Deputies and Day and Resident Matrons, while other non-resident members of the teaching staff are Personal Academic Tutors.

Headmistress. Mrs Samantha Price began as Headmistress in January 2014. Previously Headmistress at Godolphin School, Mrs Price was educated at Malvern Girls' College and Edinburgh University, where she read History of Art (with modules of European History). Having graduated, she joined the Tate Britain and was responsible for marketing for Members and Patrons and became heavily involved with the Patrons of what is now the Tate Modern.

She started her teaching career in 1999 as a History of Art and History teacher at Reading Blue Coat School, where she stayed for a number of years. She then joined King's Canterbury as a Housemistress, History and History of Art teacher. Her next post was to be Deputy Head at Hereford Cathedral School and from there she became Head of Godolphin in 2010.

Samantha is married with a daughter and a son. Her husband is an Army Chaplain.

Curriculum. In 2018 Benenden gained impressive A Level results, with 63% A*/A grades and 86% A*–B grades. At GCSE, 81% of all grades were A* or A.

The most popular university destinations for Benenden students are Oxford, Cambridge, London, Edinburgh, Durham, Bristol and Exeter, and more than a dozen girls from the past three years are studying in Canada and the States.

80% of girls gain their first-choice university, with the vast majority being Russell Group or equivalent, and 36% of girls going to a university in the UK Top 10, and 9% World Top 10. Some girls go on to prestigious art or drama courses. About 25% of Sixth Formers will make a post-A Level application, with a superb careers support service for students who have left the School, including a university mentoring programme.

There are three full-time members of the Higher Education and Professional Guidance team, with a robust and inspirational careers programme which begins in Year 7.

The curriculum is innovative and imaginative, and highly bespoke for each student.

In 2016 Benenden introduced the Professional Skills Programme, teaching Sixth Formers practical skills that are vital for the workplace. These include teamworking, giving a business pitch, developing business plans and reading complex financial information and much of the content is delivered by recruitment consultants, business professionals and blue chip companies such as PwC and Deloitte.

The School has also developed the Benenden Diploma – our bespoke curriculum for the Fourths and Upper Fourths (the two youngest year groups). Unique to Benenden, this is a two-year curriculum designed to capture the sense of awe and wonder that students of this age still have about discovering new knowledge and skills.

Year 9 (LV) also has an enquiry focus at its heart with each term being connected to the theme of Service (to the school and community, to your country, to the world) and departments regularly collaborating on investigative real-life problem-solving which allows girls to apply, connect and synthesise the work covered in the subject-based lessons.

Benenden uses five themes to frame the hundreds of enrichment, co-curricular, weekend and boarding opportunities: Physical Health and Wellbeing, Mind and Spirit, Life Skills, Global Citizenship and Creativity and Culture. Students are encouraged to undertake activities from all five areas and move beyond their comfort zone, and their participation is accredited in a record of achievement.

Facilities. In Spring 2019 we are due to begin construction of our new School Hall and Music School – the most ambitious development project in Benenden's history, creating a state-of-the-art facility offering girls and audiences a truly professional performance experience. The Music School will include a music recital hall, more than 20 music practice rooms and classrooms, as well as a smaller performance room, IT suite and recording and performance booths. The Music School will be linked to the School Hall by a bridge through a stunning atrium which will flow into the new courtyard outside, creating a tranquil and beautiful space in which girls will relax and gather with friends.

Other notable facilities include the All-Weather Pitch (opened in 2016; Benenden won the National School Lacrosse Championships after one season training on the new pitch!), the state-of-the-art Science Centre, a beautiful eco-classroom and impressive Theatre and Drama teaching complex.

As well as the All-Weather Pitch, which is primarily used for Lacrosse and Hockey, for physical recreation there are nine Lacrosse pitches, 11 all-weather Tennis courts, a sports hall containing a further full-sized tennis court, an indoor heated swimming pool, a second sports hall (also used for Badminton, Volleyball, Netball and Fencing), a fitness centre and gym, two Squash courts and a grass running track.

Curriculum. All the usual subjects are taught and all students' programmes also include academic extension programmes: careers education, information technology, physical education, religious education, personal, social and health education, global awareness and, for the Sixth Form, Professional Skills.

Sport. Lacrosse, netball, tennis, hockey, swimming, rounders, badminton, athletics and cross country, squash, gym, dance, fencing, rugby, judo, karate, trampolining, exercise and fitness, equestrian, scuba diving and cricket.

Opportunities in Music. Tuition is available in all orchestral and keyboard instruments as well as singing. Numerous opportunities exist for instrumental and choral performance. The School is home to a full youth symphony orchestra, in which students from other schools also play. Benenden also enjoys a strong choral tradition and hosts recitals by musicians of international calibre.

The planned new School Hall and Music School will offer enhanced Music facilities to further improve the standard and experience of the talented musicians at Benenden.

Opportunities in Speech and Drama. Students are able to pursue drama as an extracurricular activity throughout their School career by participating in drama workshops, House and Lower and Upper School plays. Speech and drama lessons are available and students are prepared for both Trinity and LAMDA examinations. Many pupils are involved in MUN clubs and represent the school at MUN conferences in the UK and abroad.

Optional Extras. The Duke of Edinburgh's Award, Combined Cadet Force, Science, Technology, Engineering and Maths projects, Arabic, karate, journalism and marketing, philosophy, creative writing, satellite project, ballet, modern dance, yoga, clay pigeon shooting and many others.

Fees per term (2018–2019). £12,650 payable before the start of term. The fees include the country's finest programme of Weekend Activities at no extra charge, as well as a breathtaking array of co-curricular opportunities and numerous curriculum trips.

Admission. Prospective parents are encouraged to visit the School, either individually or with others at a Prospective Parents' Morning. Prospectuses and full details of entry and scholarship requirements may be obtained from the Registry.

Entrance to the School is after internal assessment at Preview Weekend, (11+ a year ahead, 13+ two years ahead), but dependent upon candidates meeting the School's standard at 11+ Common Entrance or in entrance papers. 13+ firm offers may be made following Preview Weekend. There is also a small intake at Sixth Form level, with competitive entry by the School's own examination. All of the School's students are expected to qualify for degree courses, leaving School with at least three A Levels and eight to twelve subjects at GCSE. (A full careers programme is a key component of the Personal Development Programme, aimed to foster the widest range of skills.)

Scholarships. *Academic Scholarships – Lower School Entry (11–13)*: The examinations are held in January preceding the date of entry.

Academic Scholarships – Sixth Form Entry: Examinations are held in November preceding entry in September. Candidates take two papers in subjects which they intend to study at A Level.

Music Scholarships – Lower School Entry (11–13): The examinations are held in January preceding the date of entry. Candidates should have reached the standard of Grade V (or equivalent) or show great potential. Those offering piano or singing as a principal study should be fluent in an orchestral instrument. Candidates will be required to undertake practical tests and will be interviewed; they are also required to show that they have reached the general academic standards of any entrant either by sitting entrance papers, or by taking the academic scholarship examination.

Music Scholarships – Sixth Form Entry: Examinations are held in November preceding entry in September. The requirements for a Sixth Form Music Scholarship are very much the same as for Lower School candidates (see above entry), but candidates should have reached the standard of Grade VII (or equivalent). Candidates are also required to show that they have reached the general academic standard required of any entrant by taking two qualifying papers in subjects which they intend to study at A Level.

Art and Design – 13+: Examinations are held in January preceding entry in September. The examination for the Art Scholarship will consist of one hour on a set-piece drawing followed by an interview based on the candidate's portfolio on which particular emphasis will be placed for evidence of commitment and enthusiasm.

Design and Technology – 13+: Scholarships are offered to girls who show exceptional promise and commitment in this area, supported by good academic results in the normal entry papers. Applicants will be asked to produce evidence of three kinds: a record or portfolio of previous work or achievements; a response to a challenge set at Benenden; and an interview.

Sports Scholarships – 13+: Scholarships are offered to girls who show exceptional promise and commitment in this area, supported by good academic results in the normal entry papers. Candidates will undertake a test to measure levels of fitness, participate in a range of games to show physical ability and tactical awareness, and be given an opportunity to demonstrate their chosen specialism.

Trust Award Programme: Bursary support of up to 100% of fees (subject to means-testing) to one or more local primary school pupils at 11+ or to a Sixth Form candidate at 16+.

For further information, please contact the Director of Admissions.

Charitable status. Benenden School (Kent) Limited is a Registered Charity, number 307854. It is a charitable foundation for the education of girls.

Governing Council:

The Hon Mrs A Birkett MA, MBA (*Chairman of the Governing Council and Chairman of Nominations Committee*)

Mr S S Smart, BSc, FCA (*Vice Chairman of the Governing Council and Chairman of Remuneration and Investment Committees*)

Mrs W M Carey, BA Hons (*Chairman of Safeguarding and Education Committees*)

Dr F Cornish, MA, FRCGP

Dr R Evenett, MA, MSc, PhD, FCA (*Chairman of Risk Committee*)

Ms L Gallagher, MSc (*Chairman of Estates Committee*)

Mrs A McNab, BA Hons, FCA (*Chairman of Finance Committee*)

Mr J McParland, BD, PGCE, MA, NPQH

Mrs A J Mogridge, BA Hons, FCIPR, FPRCA

Mr C G Nicolle, MA Oxon

Mr J Pearce, BA Oxon

Mr G Pugh, MA, ACMA, MBA

Mr P Simpkin, MA Hons

Mr J V Strong MRICS

Prof L Ta

Mr M Lander, BSc, MA (*Clerk*)

Senior Management Team:

Headmistress: Mrs S A Price, MA Edinburgh, PGCE

Deputy Head Boarding and Pastoral Care: Miss A Steven, BA Bristol

Deputy Head Academic: Mrs L Tyler, MA Oxon, PGCE London

Deputy Head Staff and Co-Curricular: Mr M Commander, BEng Cardiff, MEd Buckingham

Director of Finance and Operations: Mr M C Lander, MA London

Director of Development: Mr K A Johnson, BA Leicester

Berkhamsted

133 High Street, Berkhamsted, Hertfordshire HP4 2DJ

Tel: 01442 358000 (General enquiries)
      01442 358001 (Admissions)
Fax: 01442 358040
email: enquiries@berkhamsted.com
      admissions@berkhamsted.com
website: www.berkhamsted.com
Twitter: @berkhamstedsch
Facebook: @berkhamstedschool
LinkedIn: /Berkhamsted-School

Our family of six schools offers a 'Diamond model' with co-educational and single-sex tuition for boys and girls, providing the best of both worlds in one family of Schools. At the Pre-Prep and Prep, boys and girls are taught together until the age of 11, separately from 11–16 (Berkhamsted Boys and Berkhamsted Girls), before coming back together again in a joint Sixth. Heatherton provides a co-educational nursery class (3–4) and single-sex education for girls from age 4 to 11. *Please also refer to separate entries for Berkhamsted Prep, Berkhamsted Pre-Prep and Heatherton.*

We are a family of Schools with a long history and proud traditions, yet we have a firm eye on current best educational practice and use of leading-edge teaching technologies. We are proud of our excellent academic standards without being academic hothouses. The Berkhamsted family of Schools have all the advantages of access to large-school resources with a small school sense of community and individual care. Our House system places academic progress and pastoral care at the centre of your child's education. There is a range of options to make life easier for time-pressured families: a day nursery that operates 50 weeks a year from 07.30 to 18.30, wrap-around care and extended hours, the choice of flexible, weekly or full boarding, coach routes and a multi-activity holiday camp and other courses on offer during the main school holidays through Berkhamsted BASECAMP.

There are 397 pupils in the flourishing co-educational Sixth; between the ages of 11 and 16, 470 boys at the Boys School (Castle) and 384 girls at the Girls School (Kings) are taught in single-sex groups.

The Principal is a member of both HMC and GSA.

Aims. At Berkhamsted we believe that excellent academic results do not have to be won at the expense of the wider attributes of a good education. All pupils are supported and encouraged to reach their full potential, with appropriate teaching environments for each age group and a structure that offers the best of both co-educational and single-sex tuition. In addition to the development of the intellect, social, sporting and cultural activities play an important part within the framework of a disciplined and creative community based on Christian values. It is important that pupils come to value both the individual and the Community through school life. The School seeks to encourage spiritual and moral values and a sense of responsibility as an essential part of the pursuit of excellence.

Location. The School stands in the heart of Berkhamsted, an historic and thriving town only 30 miles from London. It enjoys excellent communications to London, the airports, to the Midlands and the communities of Buckinghamshire, Bedfordshire and Hertfordshire.

Facilities. The original site has at its heart a magnificent Tudor Hall used as a schoolroom for over 300 years. Other buildings are from late Victorian to modern periods and of architectural interest (especially the Chapel modelled on the Church of St Maria dei Miracoli in Venice). With separate Pre-Prep and Prep sites, and two Senior School campuses, the School is well equipped with a range of facilities. There are new Science laboratories, Library and Learning Resources Centres, Information Technology suites, Sixth Form centres located on the two Senior School campuses, Careers libraries, Dining halls, Medical centre, House rooms, Deans' Hall (an Assembly Hall) and Centenary Theatre (a modern 500-seat theatre also used for concerts and theatre productions). Recreational and sports facilities include extensive playing fields, Eton Fives courts, Squash courts, Tennis courts, Gymnasium, Drama studio, Music school and Art studios. Additional facilities include a Sports Hall and 25m indoor swimming pool and a state-of-the-art Design Centre as well as the Nash-Harris Building at Kings comprising a new dining facility, classrooms and Chapel. More recent additions include a new sports pavilion and changing rooms at the School's Chesham Road Playing Fields and upgrades to the Football and Rugby pitches, as well as a high ropes course at the Haresfoot site and a brand new, floodlit astroturf Lacrosse pitch at Kings.

Curriculum. The Senior School curriculum includes: English, English Literature, Mathematics, Biology, Chemistry, Physics, History, Geography, Religious Studies, French/Spanish, Latin/Classics, Mandarin (available for Years 7, 8 and 9 in September 2018), Music, Art, Physical Education and Design and Technology. Up to eleven subjects may be taken for GCSE. In the Sixth Form, courses are offered in 27 subjects and all students benefit from an Enrichment Programme with the option to complete an Extended Project Qualification or a Mini-MBA, delivered in partnership with Ashridge Executive Education at Hult International Business School. Pupils are prepared for university entrance, including Oxbridge. Careers guidance and personal tutoring are offered throughout.

Day and Boarding. Pupils may be full boarders, weekly boarders, flexible boarders or day pupils. The two Boarding houses, accommodating boys and girls separately, are well-equipped and within a few minutes' walk of the main campus. There are up to 60 boarding places. Day pupils come from both Berkhamsted and the surrounding area of Hertfordshire, Buckinghamshire and Bedfordshire.

Pastoral Care and Discipline. The main social and pastoral unit is the House; the Head of House and House Tutors provide continuity of support and advice and monitor each individual pupil's progress. The aim is to encourage self-discipline so that pupils work with a sense of responsibility and trust. Pupils are expected to be considerate, courteous, honest and industrious.

Pupil wellbeing is of vital importance at Berkhamsted. A Deputy Head, Pupil Wellbeing supports teaching staff across the whole school in implementing a proactive strategy that focuses primarily on keeping pupils well and looking for early signs of potential issues. There is a Medical Centre with qualified staff. The School Medical Officer has special responsibility for boarders. Qualified Counsellors are available to all pupils for confidential counselling. The School also has a full-time Chaplain.

Sport and Leisure Activities. Major sports for Girls are Lacrosse, Netball and Tennis and for Boys, Rugby, Football and Cricket. A number of other sports are also pursued including Athletics, Badminton, Cross-Country, Equestrian, Eton Fives, Golf, Hockey, Judo, Rowing, Shooting, Squash and Swimming. Team games are encouraged and pupils are selected for regional and national squads.

There is a flourishing Duke of Edinburgh's Award at all levels. The CCF, community service, work experience and Young Enterprise are offered. The format of the school day allows pupils in the Senior School to choose from a wide range of clubs, societies or courses, which are attended during school hours. Regular school theatre productions, orchestral and choral concerts achieve high standards of performance.

Enrichment. At Berkhamsted, we recognise that intelligence takes many forms and we encourage all our pupils to pursue their talents and interests through the many enrichment opportunities on offer for each age group. These opportunities are available for academic subjects and co-curricular topics. For the more academically adventurous, there are a number of avenues through which to fulfil their potential at each school.

Careers. A team of advisors, internal and external, is directed by the Head of Careers who also arranges Careers Lunches, Applying to Higher Education training sessions, Medicine and Law Careers Taster Days and an annual Higher Education, Careers, Apprenticeships and GAP Year Fair. Heads of House oversee pupils' applications for higher education, together with parents and Careers advisors. The great majority of leavers proceeds to university and higher education.

Entry. Entry to the Pre-Prep School is from the age of 3, entry to the Prep School from 7, and entry to the Senior Boys & Girls from 11. Children are assessed for entry to the Nursery year group during a meeting with the Headteacher and attend an informal assessment day for Year 2 entry. The School's Entrance Assessments and an interview are required for entry to the Prep and Senior Boys and Girls.

The minimum entrance requirement for the Sixth Form is 45 points based on the student's best 8 subject scores, with a B or Grade 6 in the subjects he/she wishes to study (conversion to numbers using the scale A*=8, A=7, B=6, C=5, D=4, E=3 where necessary). There are also specific admission requirements relating to certain courses, although competition amongst external candidates means that it is the norm that top grades are required.

Scholarships and Bursaries. It is the Governors' policy to award Scholarships and Exhibitions on merit to pupils whom the Governors wish to attract to Berkhamsted because of the contribution that they are able to make to School life, be that academic, musical, sporting, creative or as potential leaders.

Academic Scholarships are awarded on the basis of academic merit alone on entrance to the School.

Who can apply? Applications are welcome from pupils who qualify from their performance in the Entrance Examination and sit Scholarship Examinations in English, Mathematics and other appropriate subjects. These are usually only at 11+, 13+ and 16+.

Incent Awards are made to talented pupils from financially or socially disadvantaged backgrounds.

They are awarded to enable pupils who would not otherwise be able to attend Berkhamsted, to afford to do so.

Candidates must demonstrate academic potential or have a particular talent(s) or skill(s) so that they will make a significant contribution to some other area of School life.

The Award shall be up to 100% of the school fees, and, where appropriate, will also include financial assistance for School uniform and sports kit, travel to and from school, school trips and expeditions, extra lessons e.g. Music, Drama etc if applicable.

Whilst most applications for Incent Awards will be received from candidates who are presently in maintained sector schools, Berkhamsted does work with a number of feeder schools in the independent sector who offer awards on a similar basis and thus will entertain applications from pupils who are presently in receipt of means-tested awards of this nature.

Music, Drama, Art and Sports Scholarships are also offered.

Where there is a demonstrated need, additional means-tested funding may be available to those awarded Scholarships.

More information about Scholarships and Bursaries may be obtained from the Admissions Manager or on the School website.

Fees per term (2018–2019). Day Pupils: £5,755–£6,880. Boarding Pupils: £11,530 (full), £9,540 (weekly 4 nights).

Further information about the School's aims, its academic curriculum, facilities, activities, admissions, scholarships and awards is published in the School's prospectus and is available on the School website. Admissions enquiries should be made in the first instance to the Admissions Manager, who will be pleased to arrange for parents to visit the School.

Old Berkhamstedians. There is a vibrant and growing community of Old Berkhamstedians: www.theoldberkhamstedians.org. President: Mrs Emma Jeffrey.

Charitable status. Berkhamsted Schools Group is a Registered Charity, number 310630.

Principal: **Mr R P Backhouse**, MA Cantab

Vice Principal: Mr M Bond, BA
Chief Operating Officer: Mr J Anthony, BSc, FCA
Chief People Officer: Mrs T L Evans, CIPD, FInstLM
Assistant Vice-Principal (*External Relations*): Mr R Thompson, BA
Headteacher, Berkhamsted Sixth: Mr M Walker, BA
Headteacher, Berkhamsted Boys (*Boys 11–16*): Mrs M-C Startin, BA, MA
Headteacher, Berkhamsted Girls (*Girls 11–16*): Mrs E A Richardson, BA
Deputy Head, Berkhamsted Sixth: Mr D G Richardson, BSc
Deputy Head, Berkhamsted Boys (*Boys 11–16*): Mr G Anker, BA, MA
Deputy Head, Berkhamsted Girls (*Girls 11–16*): Mrs L Simson, BA Cantab
Deputy Head, Curriculum: Mr W R C Gunary, BSc
Deputy Head, Teaching & Innovation: Mrs H Butland, MA
Deputy Head, Academic Performance: Mr A Ford, BA
Deputy Head, Pupil Wellbeing, Ms E Watson, BEng
Director of IT: Mr P Samtani
Finance Director: Mr S Elliff

Birkdale School

Oakholme Road, Sheffield S10 3DH

Tel:	0114 266 8408
	Admissions: 0114 266 8409
Fax:	0114 267 1947
email:	headmaster@birkdaleschool.org.uk
	admissions@birkdaleschool.org.uk
	enquiries@birkdaleschool.org.uk
website:	www.birkdaleschool.org.uk
Twitter:	@BirkdaleSchool
Facebook:	@BirkdaleSchool

Motto: *Res non verba*

Birkdale School is an HMC day school for 850 pupils, boys from age 4 to 18 with a co-educational Sixth Form of over 200 pupils. The age 4–11 Prep School is on a separate campus nearby. (*For further details see IAPS section.*) The

Governing Body is in membership of the Association of Governing Bodies of Independent Schools.

Set in a pleasant residential area near the University 1.5 miles from the city centre, and 5 miles from the Peak District National Park, the school has expanded in recent years to provide for Sheffield and South Yorkshire the only independent secondary school for boys, with a co-educational Sixth Form. Birkdale Prep School for 300 boys is on a separate campus half a mile from the Senior School. School coaches bring pupils from Worksop, Chesterfield, North Derbyshire, Rotherham and Barnsley.

Birkdale is a Christian school, reflecting its foundation in the evangelical tradition. There is nothing exclusive about this: entrance is open to all, and there is no denominational emphasis. We seek to develop the full potential of each individual: body, mind and spirit. Within a framework of high academic standards, pastoral care is given a high priority, balanced by an emphasis on sport and outdoor pursuits, music and drama with a wide range of extracurricular activities available.

At 18, over 95% of pupils go on to university, with a good proportion each year gaining places at prestigious universities including Oxford and Cambridge.

Admission. The main ages of admission are at 4, 7, 11 and 16, although it is possible to admit pupils at other ages if a place is available. Entrance examinations for candidates at 11 are held annually towards the end of January. Entrance to the co-educational Sixth Form is subject to interview and a satisfactory performance in GCSE examinations. In the first instance, enquiries should be addressed to the Registrar.

Academic Curriculum. Over 20 subjects are offered at A Level. A full range of academic subjects are offered to GCSE. All pupils study English Language and Literature, Mathematics, Double Award Science, at least one Modern Foreign Language (French, German, Spanish) and at least one of the Humanities subjects (Classical Studies, Geography, History, RE). Optional subjects include Art, DT: Electronic Products, DT: Resistant Materials, Latin, Drama and Music. The wider curriculum includes ICT, Religious Education, Health Education, Careers and Economic Awareness. Latin, German and Spanish are compulsory subjects in the Lower School (11–13) in addition to the usual range of National Curriculum subjects.

Games and Outdoor Pursuits. The major games are Rugby, Soccer, Cricket and Athletics, with Cross Country, Hockey, Netball, Tennis, Squash, Basketball, Volleyball, Swimming and Golf also available. The playing fields are a short bus ride away from the school. A 10-lane cricket net facility, constructed to full English Cricket Board standards was opened in 2012. The netting system is retractable and so the area can also be fully utilised for football and hockey outside of the cricket season. All members of the school play games weekly. Additional team practices take place on Saturdays or at other times, and there is a full fixture list in the major sports. The school enjoys regular use of the university swimming pool nearby. Additionally, we use two local international venues, Ponds Forge and the English Institute of Sport for basketball, netball, dance and athletics. Birkdale's Sports Hall is at the centre of the Senior School campus.

Outdoor Pursuits play an important part in the overall leadership training programme. All members of the school participate in regular training sessions leading in each age group to a major expedition. This programme culminates in the 4th Form camp held annually in Snowdonia. Virtually all members of the Third Form undertake the Bronze Award of the Duke of Edinburgh's Award scheme, and an increasing number progress to Silver and Gold awards.

Music and the Arts. Music, Art and Drama flourish both within and outside the formal curriculum. A full annual programme of dramatic and musical productions is arranged. Over 120 pupils receive weekly instrumental music lessons at school, and a wide range of orchestras and choirs provide opportunities for pupils to experience group musical activities at an appropriate level.

Extracurricular Activities. In addition to the activities above there is a broad range of clubs and societies which meet at lunchtime and outside the formal school day, providing opportunities for members of the school to explore and excel in activities such as Chess, Debating, Design and Enterprise, as well as in the usual activities such as Sport, Drama, Outdoor Pursuits, Art and Music. Awards are often won in local and national competitions.

Careers. The school is a member of the Inspiring Futures careers guidance service and there is a well equipped Careers Centre on site. A biennial Careers Convention is held in the school and regular visits are made by services liaison officers and others to give advice and help to pupils under the guidance of the school's careers staff.

Fees per term (2018–2019). Sixth Form £4,380; Senior School: £4,330 (Years 9–11), £4,255 (Years 7 and 8); Prep School £3,555; Pre-Prep Department £2,900 including lunches, textbooks and stationery (with the exception of Sixth Form textbooks).

Scholarships and Bursaries. Academic and Music Scholarships are normally available at 11 and 16. Bursaries are available to increase awards up to 100% of fees in cases of proven financial need. In addition we offer the Arkwright Scholarship at 16+.

Charitable status. Birkdale School is a Registered Charity, number 1018973, and a Company Limited by Guarantee, registered in England, number 2792166. It exists to develop the full potential of its members within a Christian community.

Chairman of Governors: P Houghton, FCA

Bursar and Clerk to the Governors: D H Taylor, BSc

Head Master: P Harris, MSc

Deputy Head: W P N Pietrek, BA

Director of Studies: P R King, BA

Heads of Departments:
Art: A Armitage, BA, Dip Ed Management
Biology: Mrs B Holder, MA, BSc
Careers: C J Cook, BSc
Classics: Mrs M A Daly, BA
Design & Technology: P S Offer, BA
Drama: A G Low, BA
Economics & Business Studies: S B Stoddard, BA
English: Mrs S J Burt, BA
Geography: H Parker, BSc
History: M S Clarke, MA
ICT: G Morton, BSc
Mathematics: M E Roach, BSc
Modern Languages: Mrs K M Higham, BA, MEd
Music: A M Jordan, BMus
Outdoor Pursuits, Chaplain: J D Allen, BSc
Physical Education: R D Heaton, BEd
Science & Physics: Dr P C Jukes, PhD, MA
Religious Education: T J Pearson, BA
Chemistry: Dr P D Myatt, BSc, DPhil
SENCO: Mrs L E Marsh, BA
Counsellor: Miss S E Brown, PG Dip Counselling

Prep School:
Head of Prep School: C J Burch, BA, PGCE
Deputy Head: J R Leighton, BEd

Director of Studies: A J Oakey, MScEd, BA
Senior Mistress: Mrs E J Arcari, BA/Mrs J Kitchen, MEd, BEd

Birkenhead School

58 Beresford Road, Oxton, Birkenhead, Merseyside CH43 2JD

Tel: 0151 652 4014
Fax: 0151 651 3091
email: enquire@birkenheadschool.co.uk
website: www.birkenheadschool.co.uk
Twitter: @BirkenheadSchl
Facebook: @birkenheadschool

Motto: *Beati mundo corde*

Birkenhead School is one of the country's leading co-educational independent schools situated in Oxton, Wirral. The School offers outstanding educational opportunities for girls and boys from three months to eighteen years and attracts students from Wirral, Cheshire, Merseyside and North Wales.

The School was established in 1860 and at the heart of the School is a strong and welcoming student and parent community.

The Good Schools Guide visited in 2017 and commented 'A happy school consistently producing confident and considerate individuals as well as top results. Birkenhead may appear traditional from the outside but there is a strong streak of innovation running through all areas that shows it does not rest on past successes.'

School buildings are grouped around a spacious campus with a beautiful 'village green' at the centre of it. The different parts of the School have their own distinct areas and the School offers an educational journey from Nursery to Sixth Form and children move seamlessly from one year to the next.

Exam results position the School as one of the leading independent schools within the North West. The aim is academic excellence for all through inspirational teaching that looks to embed a lifelong love of learning. By knowing each individual, the School looks to recognise and celebrate each student's unique skills and passions, adding value at every stage of the educational journey. Details of the curriculum at each key stage are available on the school website.

The education goes beyond the confines of the National Curriculum and students enjoy an extensive co-curricular programme of clubs and activities alongside programmes such as 'Enrich and Explore', 'Future Skills' and 'Beyond the Curriculum'. The Nicholls Lecture Series regularly welcomes high profile speakers to talk to Sixth Form students and recent guests include Members of Parliament and the Archbishop of York, alongside business leaders and professionals from a wide range of industries. A Prep Lecture programme is starting in 2018 offering the younger pupils interesting and informative talks across a range of subjects.

The School works closely within its community and has links with, amongst others, the local MP, business organisations, the Chamber of Commerce and charities. The School offers a range of author talks and visits throughout the year to both local schools and members of the public, as well as hosting activities for the local brownies and cub groups.

The School has a strong parent community and the Parents' Association organises a range of events throughout the year. A Parent Seminar Programme was introduced in 2017 to offer a range of useful and informative talks aimed at parents. Topics have included digital awareness, e-safety, emotional wellbeing and study skills.

There is a strong tradition of drama, with regular Prep and Senior productions, alongside annual House Drama and House Music competitions.

Music plays an important role at the School, with pupils encouraged to learn a musical instrument from a young age. There is a wide range of musical bands to join including both Prep and Seniors Orchestras, Concert Band, Big Band and Brass Ensemble.

The School has its own Chapel and School Chaplain. The School has a reputation for Choral music and offers a Chapel Choir that sings at weekday services and the weekly Sunday Evensong service.

Sports offered at the School include rugby, hockey, netball and lacrosse during the winter terms and cricket, athletics, tennis, rounders and golf during the summer. There are representative teams at all levels and the playing fields cover about 40 acres on three different sites. Facilities include a floodlit AstroTurf surface, squash court, fitness suites and a climbing wall.

The School has its own Duke of Edinburgh's Award scheme. Outdoor pursuits form part of the curriculum and from Year Six upwards, pupils attend annual residential outdoor pursuits camps.

The legacy of an education at the School is about confidence, social awareness, and a breadth of knowledge that will stay with students for a lifetime and set them apart from their peers. The School has a strong reputation for producing medical students, with the majority of students continuing their learning at Russell Group universities including Oxbridge. Upon leaving the School, The Old Birkonian Society offers young people membership of an established and extensive community and a range of alumni events provide valuable networking opportunities.

Fees per term (2018–2019). Seniors £3,710–£3,998; Prep £2,670–£3,015.

Admissions. Both the Headmaster and Head of Prep meet personally with prospective parents to discuss individual children's needs and admissions are managed by their respective PAs. Prospective families are welcomed and encouraged to visit the School for a personalised visit at any time during the year and early application is encouraged. The School hosts Open Days during the Michaelmas and Lent terms. Entrance into the Prep is through individual assessments and interviews. Entry into Seniors at age 11 is by progression from the Prep and Assessment and Taster Days hosted by the School. Entry into the Sixth Form is based on GCSE grades and interview.

Scholarships and Bursaries. The Birkenhead School Foundation Trust was established in 1998 to provide Bursaries and Funded Places. Scholarships are also available. Particulars may be obtained from the Headmaster's PA.

Charitable status. Birkenhead School is a Registered Charity, number 1093419. The charitable status means the School not only accepts fee-paying pupils but can offer places to able children from less advantaged backgrounds.

Visitor: The Rt Revd Dr Peter Forster, The Lord Bishop of Chester
President: Sir Andreas Whittam Smith, CBE

Chair of Governors: Mr A Cross, LLB Hons

Company Secretary and Clerk to the Governors: Mr M J Turner, MA Oxon, MInstLM (*Bursar*)

Headmaster: Mr P R Vicars, MA

Deputy Head: Mrs K Pankhurst, BA
Deputy Head (*Academic*): Mr T Whitworth, BA

Head of Prep: Mr H R FitzHerbert, BA
Deputy Head of Prep: Mr R A Halpin, BSc

Bishop's Stortford College

10 Maze Green Road, Bishop's Stortford, Hertfordshire CM23 2PJ

Tel: 01279 838575
email: admissions@bishopsstortfordcollege.org
website: www.bishopsstortfordcollege.org
Twitter: @BSCollege
Facebook: @bishopsstortfordcollege

Motto: *Soli Deo Gloria*

Bishop's Stortford College is a friendly, co-educational, day and boarding community providing high academic standards, good discipline and an excellent all-round education. We aim to equip our pupils with the vital qualifications, skills, adaptability and, above all, confidence to thrive as adults in a rapidly changing world. A flourishing Prep School and Pre-Prep, sharing many facilities with the Senior School, give all the advantages of educational continuity whilst retaining their own distinctive characters.

The College welcomes boys and girls of all denominations and faiths, and, while the majority of current pupils' homes are in the Home Counties and East Anglia, a substantial number of parents work and live overseas.

There are typically 600 pupils in the Senior School (boarders and day), 460 pupils in the Prep School and 120 in the Pre-Prep.

Location. Bishop's Stortford is midway between London and Cambridge and can be reached quickly via Liverpool Street Station, M25 and M11. Stansted Airport is a ten-minute drive. The College is situated on the edge of the town adjacent to open countryside. The gardens and grounds cover about 130 acres.

Facilities. Purpose-built Pre-Prep accommodation, Prep and Senior School libraries, extensive ICT facilities and campus-wide Wi-Fi, outstanding sports facilities, well-resourced centres for Design and Technology, the Sciences, Languages, Music and Drama and a superb Art Centre. The main school Library and state-of-the-art indoor Swimming Pool are notable features. All school Houses offer a welcoming, family-like environment.

At the centre of the campus stands the Memorial Hall, used daily for Assembly. Originally built in 1921, it stands in memory of Old Stortfordians who served and fell during the Wars.

Academic Organisation. The Curriculum is designed to give as broad a course of study as possible up to the specialisation at A Level and Oxbridge entry.

In addition to the three Sciences, French, Spanish, English, Maths, Geography and History, all new pupils joining the Fourth Form (Year 9) take Design and Technology, ICT, Art and Music as well as one period each of Ethics Philosophy and Theology, and PE/Swimming. Most also begin German and a significant number continue with Latin.

All Lower and Upper Fifth Forms (Years 10 and 11), take 'core' subjects; English, English Literature, Maths and the three Sciences. Four other subjects, one of which must be a modern foreign language, are chosen from History, Geography, Design and Technology, Latin, French, Spanish, German, Art and Design, Music, Drama and Ethics Philosophy and Theology. Pupils also have one period each of non-GCSE courses in PE, Swimming and Personal, Social and Health Education.

At all stages, progress is carefully monitored by House-masters, Housemistresses and Tutors, Heads of Department, and in Staff Meetings. Throughout the Senior School, grades for Effort and Attainment are given twice termly, and full written reports are sent home twice a year for each year group.

Careers. A purpose-built Higher Education and Careers Centre is open daily with three specialist staff. The College has close ties with Inspiring Futures, local commerce and industry and the Hertfordshire Careers Service. Links with local businesses are strong and there is an extensive programme of Work Experience organised for pupils in the Upper Fifth and Lower Sixth Forms.

The Sixth Form. Pupils choose between three and four subjects in the Lower Sixth, before specialising in the Upper Sixth. Sixth Formers select from the following subjects: Art, Biology, Business, Chemistry, Classical Civilisation, Design and Technology: Product Design, Drama and Theatre Studies, Economics, English Literature, Ethics Philosophy and Theology, French, Geography, German, History, Maths, Further Maths, Media Studies, Music, Physical Education, Physics, Politics, Psychology, Religious Education and Spanish. Latin will be reintroduced to the A Level syllabus from 2019.

Pupils can take an Extended Project Qualification (EPQ) which requires independent study into an area of individual interest, perhaps an extension of a particular aspect of the syllabus or something outside the curriculum. The structure of EPQ works to prepare pupils for Higher Education and employment while inspiring and motivating them.

An extensive PSHEE programme operates throughout the school and there is a weekly Upper Sixth Form lecture.

Each department organises visits and invites guest speakers to meetings of Societies, which are held in lunch hours or evenings. These, together with small group teaching, seminars and excellent resources, encourages pupils to develop their self-reliance, analytical skills and their spirit of academic enquiry to equip them for Higher Education and beyond.

Progress is closely monitored, as in Senior School, with the addition of overall supervision from the Head of Sixth Form. Parents are closely involved and regular Parents' Meetings are held.

Worship. The Religious Instruction, Sunday Worship and occasional weekday services are interdenominational. The opportunity of exploring faith and being prepared for adult membership of particular churches (including Confirmation) is offered each year through the Chaplain.

Activities. Our young people are involved in an environment of wholehearted participation. A diverse range of extracurricular activities alongside high academic standards provides the opportunity for every child to discover areas of interest.

In addition to the meetings of Clubs and Societies, Wednesday and Friday afternoons are set aside within the timetable for Activities, including The Duke of Edinburgh's Award scheme. We encourage pupils to pursue their own interests as well as introducing them to others; many carry these on into their spare time, beyond School. Projects which promote a willingness to serve others are an important aspect of the breadth of activity offered.

Music and Drama. An interest in and appreciation for all kinds of music is encouraged throughout the school. In Form One and Form Two (Years 3 and 4), all Prep School pupils are taught an instrument in class and those who show promise are encouraged to continue individually in the Senior School.

There are numerous ensembles including Orchestra, Wind Band, guitar and string quartets, brass group, a Choral Society, and Choirs. Pupils are also encouraged to make music in small groups from the earliest stages. The College has a fully equipped Recording Studio. The Music Staff includes 27 visiting teachers of singing and all the main instruments, together with the Acting Director of Music, an Assistant Director and a Musician in Residence. The House Music Competition is a major event in the school year and involves all pupils. There are regular opportunities to perform in public at Pupils' Concerts and in School Assemblies. Overseas tours also offer excellent experience.

Drama is an area of strength with significant developments in recent years to the theatre facilities, curriculum and performing opportunities in which all pupils can participate. A Level Theatre Studies is offered, as is GCSE Drama.

Sport. The College has an excellent reputation in all areas of sporting achievement. Physical Education is taught in the Fourth and Fifth Forms and facilities include a Sports Hall, an impressive indoor swimming pool, all-weather surface courts for netball and tennis, two floodlit astro pitches for hockey and tennis, and 100 acres of playing fields.

Health. The Medical Centre is staffed by a resident full-time Nurse, part-time Nurse and full-time Health Care Assistant. Regular surgeries are held by the School's Medical Officer.

Varied and wholesome meals, included in the fees, are provided for all pupils in the College Dining Hall; the catering team has been awarded a Gold CAP Award for six consecutive years.

Prep School. The organisation of the Prep School (for pupils up to age 13+) is largely separate from that of the Senior School, but the curricula of the two Schools are carefully integrated. Pupils are able to share resources in Sport, Design and Technology, Music and Drama.

(*For further details see entry in IAPS section.*)

Admission. The main ages of admission are 4, 7, 11, 13 and 16, but entry at intermediate stages is possible. Entry to the Senior School at 13+ is based on school reference, interview and entry test results. Sixth Form Entry Interviews and Examinations are held in the November before year of entry.

Scholarships. The following annual awards are available:

Under 11 (Year 6): Academic, Music

Under 12 (Year 7): Academic, Music, Art, Sport

Under 14 (Year 9): Academic, Music, Art, Sport

Sixth Form: Academic, Music, Art, Sport

Financial Assistance. Means-tested bursaries are awarded based on individual need. Awards range from partial assistance of 5% up to (in exceptional circumstances) 100% of the full fees.

Fees per term (2018–2019). Senior School: Full Boarders £10,176–£10,237; Overseas Boarders £10,580–£10,641; Weekly Boarders £10,076–£10,137; Day £6,554–£6,613.

Prep School: Full Boarders £7,109–£7,714; Overseas Boarders £7,428–£8,034; Weekly Boarders £7,034–£7,637; Day £4,678–£5,243.

Pre-Prep £3,030–£3,089.

Fees are inclusive except for individual music tuition.

Charitable status. The Incorporated Bishop's Stortford College Association is a Registered Charity, number 311057. Its aims and objectives are to provide high quality Independent Day and Boarding education for boys and girls from age 4 to 18.

Governing Council:

Mr G E Baker, BSc, MRICS (*Chairman*)

Mrs I M Pearman, MA, MRICS (*Vice Chairman*)

Sir Stephen Lander, KCB, MA, PhD, LLD, DSc

Mrs M Goitiandia, BSc, MBA, FCIPD

Mrs P Mullender, MA

Mr R Wells, BEd, BA, Dip PE

Mr D F Thomson, BAcc, CA
Mr C P Solway, BSc, MRICS
Mr R C V Harrison, BCom, ACA
Mr A J W Conti, BEng, FCA
Mr D Alexander
Dr S Nurbhai, MB ChB, MRCP (*UK*)
Mr P Dodd, BSc

***Headmaster*: Mr Jeremy Gladwin**, BSc, MEd

Deputy Head (*Academic*): Mr Graham Brooks, BA
Deputy Head (*Boarding*): Mr Chris Woodhouse, BSc
Deputy Head (*Pastoral*): Ms Jane Daly, BA
Head of Sixth Form: Mrs Linda Dickinson, BA
Examinations Officer: Mr Tim Herbert, MA
Senior Teacher: Mr Keith Irvine, BA
Policy Coordinator: Mrs Beth Wheeler, BSc
Educational Data: Mr Mark McGrath

Housemasters/Housemistresses:
Alliott House: Mrs Sarah Wilson, BA
Benson House: Miss Kate Gregory, BA
Collett House: Mr Alex Swart-Wilson, MA
Hayward House: Mr Simon Lipscombe, BA
Robert Pearce House: Mr Richard Honey, MA
Rowe House: Mr Peter Griffin, BSc
Sutton House: Mr Tom Atkinson, BA
Tee House: Mrs Janet Oldfield, BSc
Trotman House: Mrs Sarah Wyatt
Young House: Mrs Tina Hood, BSc, BEd

Heads of Department:
Art: Mr Richard Honey, MA
Biology: Mrs Beth Wheeler, BSc
Chemistry: Mr Charlie Bannister, MA
Classics: Dr Lucy Cresswell, PhD
Design & Technology: Mr John Trant, BA
Director of Drama: Mr Richard Norman, BA
Economics & Business Studies: Mr John Birchall, MA
English as a Second Language: Mrs Heather McNaughton
English: Mrs Claire Bond, MA
Ethics, Philosophy and Theology: Mr Patrick Winter, MEd
French: Mrs Marie-Lorraine Cunin
Geography: Mr Nicholas Tether
German: Miss Kate Gregory, BA
Higher Education and Careers: Mrs Deborah Hearne
History: Mr Tom Stuart, MA
Director of IT: Mr Stephen Bacon, BSc
Mathematics: Mr Mark McGrath
Media Studies: Mr Mike Tomkys, BA
Music (*Senior School*): Mrs Helen Pervez, BA
Physics: Mr Adrian Baker, BSc
Politics: Mrs Alison Self, BA
PSHE: Mr Chris Woodhouse, BSc
Psychology: Mrs Jenny Marshall, BSc
Science: Dr Stuart McPeake, PhD
Spanish: Mrs Ruth Bravo
Swimming: Mrs Deborah Huggett
Director of College Sport: Mrs Lyndsay Shepherd, BEd

Senior School Librarian: Mrs Maggie Garrett, MCLIP

Prep School:
Head of Prep School: W J Toleman, BA
Deputy Head: Mr Graham Millard, BA
Head of Shell: Mrs Kirsty Brooks, BA
Senior Teacher (*Pastoral*): Mr Richard Clough, BA
Head of Mathematics, Communications Coordinator: Mr
  Neil Eddom, BEd
Housemaster, Grimwade House & Senior Teacher
  (*Operations*): Mr Adrian Hathaway, BEd
Director of Studies: Mrs Wendy Sharman, MSc

Heads of Department:
Art: Mr Aaran Donlevy, BA
English: Miss Jane Mitchell
French: Miss Emmanuelle Carme, MA
Geography: Mr Richard Clough, BA
German: Mrs Imogen Cowan, BA
History: Mrs Laura Davies
ICT: Mrs Frances Sharpsmith, BSc
Latin: Mrs Jennie North
Mathematics: Mr Neil Eddom, BEd
Acting Director of Music: Mrs Helen Pervez
PSHEE: Mr Rupert Snow
RE: Mrs Livia Fraser
KS3 Science: Mrs Zoe Barford
KS2 Science: Mrs Julia Krosny-Reed
Spanish: Mrs Fiona Jones, BA
Swimming: Mrs Deborah Huggett

Prep School Librarian: Mrs Rosie Pike, BA

Learning Support:
Head of Learning Support: Mrs Elizabeth Bridle, MA
Mrs Rita Gearing, CertEd, Dip SpLD
Mrs Gerda Miller, CertEd, Dip SpLD

Pre-Prep:
Head of Pre-Prep: Miss Belinda Callow, BEd
Miss C Cuthbert
Mrs C Martin, MA
Miss A Strouts, BA
Miss R Smith, BA
Mrs K Cordell
Miss G Fricker

Learning Support:
Mrs Anita Foy

College Chaplain: Mr Ian Morris
Bursar: Mr Paul Stanley
Senior School Admissions Officer: Mrs Marie-Louise
  Gough
Prep School Admissions Officer: Mrs Fiona Brett
Pre-Prep Admissions Officer: Mrs Sally McGuiness
Marketing Manager: Mrs Sarah Gowans

Blundell's School

Tiverton, Devon EX16 4DN

Tel: 01884 252543
Fax: 01884 243232
email: info@blundells.org
website: www.blundells.org
Twitter: @BlundellsSchool
Facebook: @blundellsschool

The School, with its attendant connection to Balliol and
Sidney Sussex Colleges, was built and endowed in 1604 at
the sole charge of the estate of Mr Peter Blundell, Clothier,
of Tiverton, by his executor the Lord Chief Justice, Sir John
Popham. In 1882 the School was moved to its present site on
the outskirts of Tiverton. It is now a thriving co-educational
day and boarding school combining strong academic
achievement and excellent facilities in a secure and happy
environment. The deep and enduring friendships formed at
Blundell's, fostered by the school's fantastic community
spirit, together with the intellectual, physical and cultural
interests they develop here, provide pupils with skills for
life.
Admission. Entry is at 11, 13 and 16 for most pupils.
This is via the Blundell's Entrance Test or the Common

Entrance Examination. Most join the School in September, though a January entry is welcome.

Numbers. There are 604 pupils of whom 257 are girls; 400 board (full, weekly, flexi). There are three boys' Houses and two girls' Houses for Years 9–12 and a separate Upper Sixth House. Years 7 and 8 have a separate House with separate pastoral and academic leadership. They have no lessons on Saturdays.

Fees per term (2018–2019). Full Boarding £8,020–£11,735; Weekly Boarding £7,190–£10,220; Day £4,710–£7,470. Flexi boarding is also available. A basic tuition fee is charged for those living within ten miles of Blundell's (over the age of 13).

Scholarships and Bursaries. Open Scholarships and Exhibitions: Up to half of the chosen designation fee (i.e. boarding, weekly, flexi, day) are offered on the basis of our own examinations held in January (13+) and November (Sixth Form). Awards for Art, Music, Drama, Sport and All-round ability are also made. At 11+ Junior Exhibitions only are awarded for academic and musical ability (January examination) and are deducted from the basic tuition fees.

Services Package available to the sons and daughters of serving members of the Armed Forces and Diplomatic Corps.

Awards may occasionally be supplemented by means-tested bursaries at the discretion of the Head.

Full details of all scholarships and bursaries are available from the Registrars.

School Work. There are four forms at age 11 and five at age 13. During the first three years most pupils will study Art, Biology, Chemistry, Design and Technology, Divinity, Drama, English, French, Geography, History, Information Technology, Mathematics, Music (Class), Personal and Social Development, Physical Education and Physics. Latin, Greek, German and Spanish are also available.

During the GCSE years the range of subjects remains broad. Extensive advice is provided by the School to assist both GCSE and A Level choices. Parents are advised to enter their children for Inspiring Futures' Futurewise programme and there is a comprehensive work experience scheme on offer.

Sixth Form options enable a wide combination of subjects to be taken. Four of the following are taken to AS Level and three to A Level: Art, Biology, Business Studies, Chemistry, Classical Civilisations, Design Technology, Drama, Economics, English, Film Studies, French, Geography, German, History (Modern & Early Modern options), ICT (AS only), Latin, Mathematics and Further Mathematics, Music, Photography, Physical Education, Physics, Psychology, Religious Studies (Ethics) and Spanish.

Mark Orders, Tutorial System and Reports. Good communication is a central concept. Frequent Mark Orders and Staff Meetings are held to monitor each pupil's work. All pupils have academic tutors. Parents receive termly formal written feedback in addition to receiving Mark Order summaries every few weeks. There are regular parents' meetings and information forums.

Music and Drama. Blundell's music is excellent. Based in our own music school there are several choirs, an orchestra and varying musical ensembles. These range from a jazz band through a chamber choir to brass, woodwind and string groups. The Department has state-of-the-art recording equipment. In addition to School concerts there are visits from professional musicians. The Choir undertakes a European tour at Christmas; recent destinations have included Prague, Paris, Oslo, and Venice.

Similarly, Drama plays a key role in the School. There are three major School Plays each year, as well as House plays. The magnificent, purpose-built Ondaatje Hall offers the combined facilities of a theatre, a concert hall and an art stu-

dio. Frequent visits are made by theatre companies and Blundell's is a cultural venue for Mid-Devon.

Games and Physical Training. Boys play rugby football in the Autumn Term whilst girls play hockey. Spring Term sports include cross-country, squash, rugby, fives, hockey, soccer, fencing, basketball, netball and rugby sevens. In the Summer Term cricket, tennis, swimming, athletics and golf take place. The Sports Hall gives further scope to the range of sport, as does the all-weather floodlit pitch; there is also a Fitness Suite. Elite sportsmen and women are supported with specialised fitness programmes. A variety of other sports, such as clay pigeon shooting, fly fishing, canoeing and miniature range shooting, are available through the extensive activity programme.

Computing and Technology. All Blundellians have access to the school IT network and will develop a range of skills during their time at school to support their studies.

Recent New Facilities. There have been extensive developments at Blundell's over the past two decades which include upgrading the Science Departments, provision of advanced technological and careers arrangements as part of the resources included in the redesigned Library, a new Modern Languages block, ongoing refurbishment of all boarding houses, a Fitness Suite, a Music School, IT suites and extension to the U6 Boarding House to incorporate new study areas and a library. With the relocation of St Aubyn's School (now called Blundell's Preparatory School) onto the Blundell's site, the whole campus provides education from the age of 2½ to 18 years.

Community Service. The School is involved in a wide variety of activities, both local and national, and pupils regularly raise around £20,000 per annum for a variety of charities, as well as taking part in practical tasks locally and 'befriending' etc.

Adventure Training. Blundell's is well placed to make full use of Dartmoor and Exmoor, the coast and rivers of the area, for academic fieldwork or adventure training. For many years the School has entered teams for the Ten Tors Expedition on Dartmoor, canoes the Devizes–Westminster race and takes part in The Duke of Edinburgh's Award scheme up to Gold level.

CCF. Everyone in Year 10 serves for a year in the CCF. Thereafter it is voluntary and comprises senior pupils who provide the NCO Instructors. There are links with the 18 Cadet Training Team, Derriford, and the Rifle Volunteers.

Boarding. Blundell's is built around the ethos of boarding and all pupils (full boarding, weekly, flexi boarding and day) are accommodated in one of seven houses on the campus. A full range of weekend activities is offered including a Leadership Programme, Ten Tors, sport and a range of local trips and activities.

Religion. The School maintains a Christian tradition, while welcoming members of other faiths. All pupils are expected to attend weekday morning Chapel and boarders go to the School Service on Sundays. The Chaplain prepares boys and girls who wish to be confirmed; the Confirmation Service takes place annually in the Spring Term.

Accessibility. Blundell's is close to the M5, and is served by Tiverton Parkway Station, two hours from Paddington, London. Airports at Bristol and Exeter are close at hand.

Prospectus. Fuller details of School life are given in the prospectus, available from the Registrars. Prospective parents are invited to visit the School, when they will meet the Head and a Housemaster or Housemistress and have a full tour of the School with a current pupil. The Blundell's website (www.blundells.org) is regularly updated throughout the academic year and as well as giving details of the school and academic departments, lists the main sporting, musical and dramatic events of each term and some match results.

Preparatory School. Blundell's Preparatory School for children aged 2½ to 11 years is on its own extensive site at Blundell's. For further information apply to the Headmaster, Mr A D Southgate. (*See also entry in IAPS section*).

Charitable status. Blundell's School is a Registered Charity, number 1081249. It exists to provide education for children.

Board of Governors:
Mr C M Clapp, FCA (*Chairman*)
Mr N P Hall, MA, FCA (*Vice Chairman*)
Mr B J Hurst-Bannister, MA
Mr N Arnold, BA, App Dip Crim
Dr S B Ansell, MB Bch, MA Hons
Mr N J Cryer, BEng, MCIBSE
Mr P M Johnson, MA, FRSA
Mrs M MacNiece, BCL
Mr J K Macpherson, BEd
Mrs J M A Mannix, MA
Fr R Maudsley
Rt Revd N McKinnel, BA, MA
Mr I R G Thomas, AFPS
Dr M E Wood, BA, MA, DPhil

Mr R W Thane, BA (*Representative Governor*)
Sir Christopher Ondaatje, OC, CBE (*Honorary Governor Emeritus*)

Bursar and Clerk to the Governors: Mrs Annika Hedrich-Wiggans, MA, MSt, ACA

Head: **Mr B Wielenga**, BCom Natal & Johannesburg, BEd (*Economics*)

* *Head of Department*
† *Housemaster/Housemistress*

Second Master: Mr M R J Radley, MA Oxon, MEd Cambridge, PGCE (*History*)
Deputy Head (Academic): Mr C H List, BSc Durham, PGCE (*Chemistry*)
Deputy Head (Co-curricular): Mr E K S Saunders, BA Leeds, PGCE (*Physical Education*)
Designated Safeguarding Lead: Mrs N J Klinkenberg, BSc Swansea, PGCE (*Mathematics*)
Senior Master: Mr A J R Berrow, MA St Peter's College Oxford, PGCE (**Religious Studies*)
Head of IT: Mr M P Dyer, MSc Dundee, PGCE (*ICT*)
Academic Head of Sixth Form: Mr G J Baily, BSc Aston, PGCE (*Biology, Chemistry*)
Head of School House: Mrs K L Corbin, MSc C & G College, PGCE (*LS*)

Mrs G Armstrong Williams, BA Stourbridge, GDST (**Art and Design*)
Dr J T Balsdon, BSc PhD London, PGCE (*Biology*)
Mr L P N B Barnes, BSc Gloucestershire, PGCE (*Biology*)
Mr R O Barrowcliffe, BA Newcastle, MA (*Physics*)
Mrs G M L Batting, BEng Exeter, PGCE (**Chemistry*)
Mr H J Bloomfield, BSc Cardiff (*Graduate Assistant*)
Mr G A Bucknell, BSc Durham (**Geography*)
Mrs T E Bright, BA Staffordshire, MSc, PGCE (*Economics & B Studies*)
M G Cachia, LLB Leeds, MA, PCGE (*Maths*)
Mrs A T Candler, BSc Loughborough, PGCE (*PE*)
Mr T E Candler, BA Plymouth (**Business Studies, ICT*)
Mrs S J Clark, BA UNISA (*LS*)
Mrs J K Cole, BSc Birmingham, QTS, MA (*Psychology*)
Mrs A M Cox, MA Bristol, PGCE (*Classics*)
Mrs R J Crease, BEd Plymouth (*PSHE, RS*)
Miss L Douglas, BA Exeter, PG Dip (*Classics*)
Ms C E L Flavelle, MA New Hall Cambridge, PGCE (*History, Politics*)
Mrs C E Francis, BA De Montfort, PGCE (*D & T, Art*)

Mr T S Frappart, BA Plymouth, PGCE (*D & T*)
Mr C L L Gabbitass, BEd St Paul's (*PE*)
Ms V J Gill, MEd Birmingham, PGCE (**PE*)
Miss J Gillman, BA Kingston, PGCE (*English*)
Mr P H Gordon, BA Rhodes, BEd (*Mathematics*)
Miss E J Gore-Lloyd, BA Bristol, MA (**EAL*)
Mr T E Grant, BA UWI, PGCE (*Art & Design*)
Mrs T R Griffiths, BA London, GTP (*Classics, English*)
Miss C R Hall, BA Newcastle, PGCE (*English*)
Mr C M Hamilton, BA Anglia, PGCE (*Geography*)
Mr J C Hatton, BA Salford (*Spanish*)
Miss M Ho, BSc MEd Exeter (*Mathematics*)
Mrs S Holman, BA Exeter, PGCE (*Geography*)
The Reverend T C Hunt, BD Wales-Cardiff, MTh, MRICS (*RS, Chaplain*)
Mr K D W Insull, BA UWCN, PGCE (*Art & Photography*)
Miss R S Isdell-Carpenter, BA Wales, PGCE (**English*)
Mr S P Johnson, BSc Bath, MA, PGCE (*History, Politics*)
Mr H D Jones, BSc, MSc UWE Bristol (*PE*)
Mr P M Jones, CELTA Kent (*EAL*)
Mr P G Klinkenberg, BEd Exeter (*Registrar*)
Miss E M Lacki, BA, MA Exeter, CELTA, DELTA (*EAL*)
Mr A Lambert, MPhys Durham (**Physics*)
Dr O J Leaman, BMus, PhD Edinburgh (**Music*)
Mr N M Y Lecharpentier, BA Caen, MA, PGCE (**French*)
Mr L J Lewis, BSc Loughborough, PGCE (*Business Studies*)
Mr M G Lodge, BSc Exeter, PGCE (*Physics*)
Mr D P Marshman, BSc Loughborough, PGCE (*Mathematics*)
Mr S J Mault, BSc Liverpool, PGCE (*Mathematics*)
Mr A J Mead, BSc Bath, PGCE (**Chemistry*)
Mr L Menheneott, BEd St Paul's, MBA (*PE, Proctor*)
Miss C E Mercer, BA Cardiff, PGCE (*English*)
Mrs R C Milne, BA Wales, PGCE (*Speech & Drama*)
Mrs R E Milne, MA Exeter, PGCE (**Classics*)
Mr R E T Moore, BA Manchester, PGCE (**History and Politics*)
Mr D E Morrison, MEng Bristol (*Physics*)
Mr T M Mycock, BSc Plymouth (*Chemistry*)
Mrs B A Nuttall-Owen, BSc Durham, PGCE (*Geography*)
C E Olive, BSc Aberystwyth, PGCE (*Biology*)
Miss E C Partington, BSc Bristol, MSc, PGCE (*Geography*)
Dr D Quinlivan-Brewer (*Film Studies*)
Dr J A Ratcliffe, BSc Nottingham, PhD, PGCE (**Biology*)
Mr P F Rivett, MA Exhibitioner of The Queen's College Oxford, PGCE (*Mathematics*)
Mr J A Rochfort (*Drama*)
Miss E P Sage, BA Durham, PGCE (*Classics*)
Miss I G Scott, BA Reading, MA, PGCE (*German, French*)
Mr J S Shrimpton, BA Bristol (*English*)
Mr D J Smart, BSc Birmingham, PGCE (*Biology, Chemistry*)
Mrs S J Soutar, BA Lancaster, PGCE (**Learning Support*)
Miss J Spencer BA, MEd Newcastle, PGCE (*Drama*)
Mrs L R M Stanton, BA Sheffield, PGCE (*French*)
Mrs A M Taylor-Ross, BA, MA Nottingham, PGCE (**PSHE*)
Miss G A Trivett BSc Gloucester, PGCE (*PE*)
Mr O J Tysoe, BA, Dip ABRSM, Durham (*Music*)
Mr S A Uddin, BSc Greenwich (*Chemistry*)
Mrs E V Weaver, BSc Cardiff, PGCE (**Psychology*)
Mrs L E Webster, BSc Exeter, PGCE (*Physics*)
Mr B Wheatley, MA Loughborough, PGCE (**D & T, Academic Head of Yrs 7–11*)
Mrs K J Wheatley, BA Swansea, PGCE (*French*)
Mrs L J Wielenga, BEd Natal (*LS, English*)
Mrs T L Winsley, BA Exeter (**Drama*)
Miss G H G Withers, BA Rose Bruford, PGCE (*Drama*)

Mrs L Yang, MBS Sunderland (*Mandarin*)
Miss H L Youngs, BTec Somerset College (*LS*)

Director of Development: Mr B Boswell
Director of Marketing and Communications: Mrs S Mann

Head's PA: Mrs H L Tucker

Registrars:
Mr P J Klinkenberg, BEd
Mrs T L Frankpitt, BEng, MBA

Medical Officer: Dr S-J Seymour, MA, MD, BChir

Bolton School Boys' Division

Chorley New Road, Bolton BL1 4PA

Tel:	01204 840201
Fax:	01204 849477
email:	seniorboys@boltonschool.org
website:	www.boltonschool.org/seniorboys
Twitter:	@BoltonSchool
	@Philip_Britton
Facebook:	@boltonschool.org
LinkedIn:	/bolton-school

Motto: *Mutare vel timere sperno*

Bolton School Boys' Division, founded ante 1516 as Bolton Grammar School for Boys, was rebuilt and endowed by Robert Lever in 1644. In 1913 the first Viscount Leverhulme gave a generous endowment to the Bolton Grammar School for Boys and the High School for Girls on condition that the two schools should be equal partners known as Bolton School (Boys' and Girls' Divisions).

Bolton School is a family of schools, where children can enjoy an all-through education, joining our co-educational Nursery for 3 and 4 year olds or Infant School before moving up to our single-sex Junior and Senior Schools with Sixth Forms. We are strong believers that girls and boys from 7+ perform best in a single-sex environment, but one where there are co-educational activities – the best of both worlds.

Situated in imposing sandstone buildings on a thirty-two acre site, Bolton School Boys' Division educates over 1,100 boys, all day pupils. Of these, over 200 are members of the Junior School which is housed in an adjacent separate building close to the main site providing education for boys aged 7–11. In the Senior School of 900, 220 are in the Sixth Form.

Bolton School Boys' Division seeks to realise the potential of each pupil. We provide challenge, encourage initiative, promote teamwork and develop leadership capabilities. It is our aim that students leave the School as self-confident young people equipped with the knowledge, skills and attributes that will allow them to lead happy and fulfilled lives and to make a difference for good in the wider community.

We do this through offering a rich and stimulating educational experience which encompasses academic, extra-curricular and social activities. We provide a supportive and industrious learning environment for pupils selected on academic potential, irrespective of means and background.

Curriculum. The GCSE programme comprises a core curriculum of English Language, English Literature, Mathematics, Biology, Chemistry, Physics and Sport. In addition, pupils select a further 4 options chosen from Art, Drama, French, Geography, German, Greek, History, Latin, Music, Philosophy and Ethics, RE, Russian, Science Enrichment, Spanish and Technology. One of these choices must be a foreign language. At A Level approximately 30 different subjects are currently on offer. Boys study four subjects to AS Level, with the majority reducing to three A2 Levels in Year 13. In addition all boys have the option of taking General Studies to A2 Level. While many boys elect to take standard combinations of either Arts or Science subjects in the Sixth Form, a high degree of flexibility ensures that any desired combination of subjects can be offered. Throughout both years of the Sixth Form, there is an additional and extensive programme of academic work which supports the GCE Advanced curriculum. Some boys will take the AQA Bacc qualification and all boys do an enrichment course and take part in community service. In 2017 the School won the Queen's Award for Voluntary Service, the MBE for organisations.

Facilities and Organisation. The Boys' and Girls' Divisions of Bolton School are housed in separate buildings on the same site and, though the organisation of the two Divisions provides single-sex schools, there are many opportunities for boys and girls to meet and to cooperate in the life of the school community. This is particularly so in the new Riley Sixth Form Centre, where boys and girls share a Common Room, cafe and learning areas equipped with the very latest technology. Single-sex teaching remains the norm in the Sixth Form, although in a very few subjects co-educational arrangements are in operation. The buildings of the Boys' Division include the Great Hall, two libraries, gymnasium, sports hall, swimming pool, laboratories, art rooms, sixth form common room and ICT learning centre, design technology centre, performing arts centre, MFL laboratory, classrooms and dining hall. The Junior School building has recently been extended and refurbished and contains eight form rooms and specialist rooms for ICT, art & design and science & technology together with a gymnasium, library and its own dining accommodation. Use of the sports hall, the adjacent 25-metre swimming pool and the arts centre is shared by all sections of the school.

Games and PE. The extensive playing fields which adjoin the School contain thirteen pitches. Principal games are football, rugby and cricket. Tennis, hockey, swimming, water polo, badminton, athletics, golf and orienteering are also all played at representative school level. All boys also undertake a gymnastics programme and play volleyball and basketball. The School is divided into four Houses for the purpose of internal competitions.

Art, Drama, Design, Music. In addition to timetabled sessions in each discipline there are many opportunities for extra-curricular activities in all these pursuits. Facilities in the art department include a pottery room with kiln; within the very active musical life of the School there are choral groups, orchestras and ensembles catering for all ages and abilities. In addition arrangements can be made for individual lessons on all orchestral instruments, piano, organ and in singing. Drama is an important part of the work of the English department and boys are encouraged to develop their talents in the drama studio and arts centre. The annual major school play, musical or opera is produced in cooperation with the Girls' Division. Design and technology features strongly in the curriculum in both Junior and Senior Schools with considerable success each year in the A Level technology courses, many boys gaining industrial sponsorships as a result. In addition, a wide variety of extracurricular opportunities exists in both the design technology base and the computer rooms. All boys are encouraged to take part in the extensive lunchtime programme when over 120 clubs, societies and practices are offered to different groups.

Outdoor Pursuits. All junior school pupils and all students up to and including Year 12 in the senior school undertake an annual period of outdoor education within curriculum time. In addition, camps, trips, exchanges and expeditions go to 63 destinations over two years, 17 of them abroad. The School has its own 60-bed Outdoor Pursuits

Centre, Patterdale Hall in Cumbria, used by parties of boys regularly for curriculum, weekend, holiday and fieldwork expeditions. In Year 8 boys have the opportunity to undertake sail training lessons on Tenacity of Bolton, the boat built by boys at the School. There is a large and active Scout Group with its own modern headquarters on school premises.

Religion. The School is non-denominational; all boys have periods devoted to religious education. In assemblies the basic approach is Christian although a great variety of readings and methods of presentation are adopted.

Careers and Higher Education. Careers education and guidance, and life-long learning are key elements of the curriculum. In Year 8 pupils take part in a Work Sampling Day. As an aid to Sixth Form choices, the Morrisby Test with follow-up interviews and extensive feedback is undertaken in Years 10 and 11. All pupils take part in Work Experience placements at the end of Year 11 and throughout the Sixth Form.

In Year 12, all pupils attend a 3 day residential business training course at Patterdale Hall and take part in an e-business competition. Mock interviews are conducted on Interview Skills Evenings. Year 13 pupils are guided through UCAS procedures and careers advice is always available from two full-time Careers Assistants in the Careers Library. The Head of Careers oversees all these events and can be consulted by all parents and pupils.

Transport. The School provides an extensive coach service which offers secure and easy access for pupils from a wide surrounding catchment area. Over twenty routes are operated by either the School's own fleet of coaches or by contract hire arrangements.

Admission. An entrance examination is held in January annually for boys over 7 and under 8 on August 31st of the year of admission. Fifty places are available at 7+ and a few additional places thereafter. Admission to the first year of the Senior School (140 places) is by entrance examination held annually in mid-January. Boys who are over 10 and under 12 on August 31st of the year of entry are eligible. Entry to the Sixth Form is available to boys who have taken GCSE examinations elsewhere on the basis of interview and agreed levels of performance in these public examinations. Boys are also admitted at other ages when vacancies occur; in these cases admission is gained through satisfactory interview and test performances. There is a co-educational pre-preparatory section – Beech House Infants' School – which has recently moved to new purpose-built, state-of-the-art premises. Admission is from the age of 4 and enquiries should be made to infants@boltonschool.org. There is also a nursery providing facilities for children from 3 months to 4 years old.

Fees per term (2018–2019). Senior School and Sixth Form £3,992; Infant and Junior Schools £3,193. Fees include lunches.

Fee Assistance. Means-tested Foundation Grants are available and one in five Senior School pupils receives assistance with fees. Scholarships are also available and are offered regardless of parental income, to those pupils whose achievement in the Entrance Examination and the Interviews places them at the top of the cohort.

Prospectus and Open Day. The School holds an annual Open Morning for the benefit of prospective candidates and their parents. This is normally in mid-October. Individual tours can be arranged on working days throughout the year. Further information concerning all aspects of the School is contained in the School Prospectus, copies of which may be obtained from the Admissions Registrar. More detail can be found on the School website. Enquiries concerning admission are welcome at any time of the School year.

Charitable status. The Bolton School is a Registered Charity, number 1110703. Under the terms of the Charity it is administered as two separate Divisions providing for boys and girls under a separate Headmaster and Headmistress.

Chairman of Governors: M T Griffiths, BA, FCA

Headmaster: P J Britton, MBE, MEd

Deputy Head (*Pastoral*): Mrs H M Brandon, MA
Deputy Head (*Academic*): N L Ford, BSc
Deputy Head (*Admissions & Achievement*): Dr F H Mullins, BSc, PhD
Assistant Head: K M Hiepko, MA
Senior Teacher: Miss H Tunstall, BSc, MSc

Heads of Department:
Art and Design: Mrs M A Ryder, BA & Mrs L Turner, BA
Biology: Dr N Morgan, BSc, PhD
Business Studies: Mrs C M Edge, BSc
Chemistry: Dr M Yates, BSc, PhD
Classics: Mr D V B Lamb, MA
Economics: D W Kettle, BA
English: Ms H Thomson, BA, MA
French: A C Robson, BA
Geography: P Newbold, BA
German: R A Catterall, MA
History: Miss S V Burgess, MA
ICT: P J Humphrey, BSc
Mathematics: D N Palmer, BSc
Music: J Bleasdale, BA
Physical Education:
P Fernside, BA (*Head of Games*)
M Johnson, BSc (*Head of PE*)
Physics: M R Ormerod, BSc
Religious Studies: Mrs C E Fox, BA
Russian: P G Davidson, BA
Spanish: Mrs J L Cotton, BA, MA
Technology: C J Walker, BA

Instrumental Music Staff:
Brass, Cello, Clarinet, Guitar, Oboe, Organ, Percussion, Piano, Saxophone, Singing, Viola, Violin

Junior School (*Age 7–11*):
Head: Mrs S A Faulkner, BA, MA
Deputy Head: F Morris, BA

Headmaster's Personal Assistant: Mrs J Higham
Headmaster's Secretary & Admissions Registrar: Mrs S Yates

Bootham School

Bootham, York YO30 7BU

Tel:	01904 623261 (School)
	01904 623261 (Headmaster)
Fax:	01904 652106
email:	office@boothamschool.com
website:	www.boothamschool.com

Bootham offers Full and Weekly Boarding and Day Education to both boys and girls from 11–18, together with day education from the age of 3 at Bootham Junior School. There are now over 470 pupils in the Senior School and 130 day pupils in the Junior School (*see entry in IAPS section*).

The School was founded in 1823 by Quakers, but pupils of all denominations or none are welcomed. All pupils attend Meetings for Worship and arrangements are made for pupils to be prepared for confirmation or membership of their own churches.

Curriculum. In Years 7–9 all pupils pursue a course of study which includes English, History, Religious Studies, Geography, Classics, Latin, French, German, Spanish, Mathematics, the three separate Sciences, Music, Drama, Art and Craft, Physical Education, Design & Technology, Computer Science, Careers, Health and the Environment and Thinking Skills.

In Years 10 and 11 pupils follow a curriculum leading to 10 subjects at GCSE.

The College Classes (Sixth Form) are preparatory to university entrance. The majority of pupils remain at school until the age of 18 and each year there is a strong Oxbridge entry. A wide choice of subjects is offered. It is usual to study 3 or 4 examination subjects and to study subjects of wider interest.

Students are able to choose from a wide variety of subjects. These are: Mathematics, Further Mathematics, Physics, Chemistry, Psychology, Biology, English, French, German, Spanish, History, Classics, Latin, Geography, Economics, Business Studies, Music, Art, Design Technology, Religious Studies, Drama and Theatre Studies, and Sports Studies and Physical Education.

Site and Buildings. The School is situated close to York Minster. From the road it appears as an impressive line of Georgian houses but behind this is the spacious main school campus. There is a steady programme of development, and the buildings now include 8 well-equipped Laboratories, an impressive Arts Centre (open 2014) with Auditorium and Darkroom (photography), 2 ICT Suites, 2 DT workshops, an Astronomical Observatory, an up-to-date Physical Education Department with Sports Hall, Indoor Swimming Pool, Fitness Suite and Squash Courts, and a modern Assembly Hall, which received a national RIBA award. There are many facilities for leisure time pursuits which are an important feature of the lives of pupils at the School. The buildings are complemented by formal gardens and a beautiful Cricket Field, overlooked by the Minster. Another large Playing Field is situated nearby, in Clifton, which also houses Bootham Junior School in a new purpose-built complex.

Pastoral Care. As a Quaker School, Bootham places great emphasis on caring relationships within a friendly community. There are three boarding houses, under the special care of House staff. Each House has its own recreational facilities. Throughout the School, both boarding and day pupils are supervised and guided by form tutors. In College, pupils have Personal Tutors who are responsible for both academic and pastoral matters, and guidance towards Higher Education.

Admission. Pupils usually enter Bootham at the age of 11. Entry is also usually possible at 12, 13 and 14. The main entrance assessment is held annually in January and this forms the basis of Scholarship and Bursary selection. Sixth form entry is welcomed and selection is on the bases of school report and GCSE performance. In special circumstances late entrants can be considered.

Leisure Time Activities. The School has long been recognised as a pioneer in the right use of leisure. The Natural History Society, founded in 1832, claims to be the oldest society of its kind with an unbroken history in this country. Other clubs and societies include Debates, Drama, Bridge, Chess, Cookery and Jazz. There are around 100 activities offered each week. Pupils follow the Duke of Edinburgh's Award scheme and are involved in Community Services.

Music. The Director of Music and his assistant are supported by 25 visiting teachers. Tuition is arranged in a wide variety of instruments and a strong tradition of music in the School is maintained. A recent leaver was named 'Young Composer of the Year' and there is a strong record of success in gaining Music College and University scholarships.

Games. Association Football, Hockey, Tennis, Fencing, Cricket, Swimming, Athletics, Netball, Basketball, Badminton, Squash, Rounders. There is no cadet force.

Fees per term (2018–2019). Boarding: £6,295–£10,155. Day: £2,310–£5,995.

Fees for instrumental music lessons are extra. Enquiries for up-to-date information are welcome.

Scholarships and Bursaries. *Academic* Scholarships (honorary and without fee reduction) are awarded on an annual basis at the end of each academic year and are based on performance throughout the year. Academic Scholarships are subject to annual reviews.

Sixth Form: We offer a means-tested scholarship/bursary to candidates from state-maintained schools who gain a minimum of 8 A/A* grades at GCSE.

Music Scholarships of up to 50% fee remission are available for candidates of good all-round musical and academic ability or potential. These are available for entry at 11+ and 13+ (Years 7 and 9) and are awarded on the basis of performance in the entrance assessment, and in tests and an audition with the Director of Music.

Means-tested Bursaries (supported by the Bootham Trust) are available:

- to assist Friend (Quaker) children, or the children of Friend (Quaker) parents, to attend the School;
- to assist children, whose families would not be able to afford an independent school education, to attend the School.

Applicants will be assessed by academic performance in the entrance assessment at 11+ and 13+ and in addition, for Music Scholars, their performance at the Music Scholarship tests and audition. Applications for bursaries need to be made in the Autumn term prior to entry to the school.

Bootham Old Scholars' Association. There is an annual Reunion in York during the second weekend in May. The Bootham Old Scholars' Association has branches in all parts of the country and Eire. The Secretary may be contacted through the School.

Charitable status. Bootham School is a Registered Charity, number 513645.

Head: **Christopher Jeffery**, BA, FRSA

Deputy Head: Martyn Beer, BA, PGCE, NPQH

Academic Deputy: Ruth Crabtree, BA, MA

Head of Junior School: Helen Todd, BA, MA Ed, QTS

Assistant Heads:
William Lewis, MA
James Ratcliffe, BSc

Boarding Coordinator: Beth Steer

Bursar: Gavin Blackstone, CPFA, BA

Assistant Staff:
* Head of Department
† Housemaster/mistress

Sarah Allen, BEd, BD (*Religious Studies*)
Mathew D Aston, BEd (**Mathematics*)
Joan Attwell, BA (*Drama*)
Richard M Barnes, BA, MA (*Art*)
Andrew Bell, BA Ed (*Physical Education, English*)
Simon Benson, BA, MA (**Drama*)
Dina Bonner (*German Language Assistant*)
Elizabeth Brown, BSc, PhD (**Geography*)
Richard N Burton, BA (*Music*)
Carol L Campbell, BA (*French, Spanish*)
Angelica Coates (*Spanish Language Assistant*)
Kirsten S Cooper, MPhys (**Physics*)
Tracey Copestake, BA (**Religious Studies*)

Ben Coxon, BA (*Physical Education*)
Steve J Elsworth, BA (*Mathematics*)
Harriet Ennis, BSc (**Psychology*, *Biology*)
Paul Feehan, BA (**Director of Music*)
Elizabeth Gallagher-Coates, BA (*English*, *Psychology*)
Robert Gardiner, BSc (**Biology*)
Emma Glover, BA (*English*)
Robert E Graham, BEd (*Physical Education*, *Geography*)
Sally Gray, BA (*Classics*)
Kerri Haynes-McDonnell, BA, MA, PG Cert/NASCO
  (*Learning Support*)
Elisabeth Hooley, BA (*Physical Education*, *Mathematics*)
Freya Horsley, BA, MA (*Art*)
Helen Landau, BA (*Learning Support*)
Claire Little, BMus (*Music*)
Jack MacKenzie, BA (*Music*)
Kelly McCarthy, BA, MA (*EAL*)
Elizabeth McCulloch, MA (**History*)
Eamonn Molloy, BEd (**Design & Technology*)
Catherine Morin (*French Language Assistant*)
Amanda Naylor, BSc (*Mathematics*)
Russell Newlands, MSc, BEng (*Physics*, †*Evelyn House*)
Sarah O'Keeffe, BSc (**Economics & Business Studies*)
Christina Oliver, BA, MA (**French*, *German*)
Anne Partridge, BSc (*Geography*)
Peter Rankin, BEng (*Information Technology*, *Physics*)
Lindsey Robertson, BSc (*Chemistry*)
Mark Robinson, BA, MA (**Chemistry*)
Sarah Robinson, BA (**Classics*)
Catherine Rowell, BSc, PhD (*Biology*, *Chemistry*, *Physics*)
Helen Sharpe, BA, MA (*English*)
Michael Shaw, BSc (*Biology*)
Mark Shuttleworth, BA (*French*)
Gill Simpson, BA, MA (**English*)
David Swales, BA (**Art*, †*Fox House*)
Emma Thomas , BA, MA (*French and Spanish*)
Jay Thorpe (*Outdoor Education Instructor*)
Sue Tomlinson, BSc (*Chemistry*, *Biology*)
George Trifan (*Sports Assistant*)
Shazma White, BA (*Economics*)
Anne Whittle, BSc (*Mathematics*)
Catherine Wilson, BA (*History*)
Angela Woods, BEd (*Geography*, *Physical Education*)

Admissions Registrar: Jenny Daly

Librarian: Laura Herring, BA, MSc

Bradfield College

Bradfield, Berkshire RG7 6AU

Tel: General Enquiries: 0118 964 4500
           Admissions: 0118 964 4516
           Bursar: 0118 964 4530
email: admissions@bradfieldcollege.org.uk
website: www.bradfieldcollege.org.uk
Twitter: @BradfieldCol
Facebook: @BradfieldCollege
LinkedIn: /bradfield-college-enterprises-ltd

Motto: *Benedictus es, O Domine; Doce me Statuta Tua ~ Blessed are you, our Lord; teach me your laws* (from Psalm 119).

Bradfield College was founded in 1850 by Thomas Stevens, Rector and Lord of the Manor of Bradfield.

We define our ethos by the outcome of our pupils as they leave Bradfield. We actively promote personal integrity, tolerance, understanding and independence of thought. We encourage young people to work with and learn from each

other, as well as to show moral courage to stand up for what they believe in. The breadth of a Bradfield education supports our pupils in challenging themselves and develops their abilities to communicate with others. The College is a co-educational boarding school dedicated to the provision of the highest possible care for all its pupils.

Location. Bradfield College occupies the village of Bradfield, 8 miles west of Reading and 9 miles east of Newbury. It is 2 miles from Junction 12 of the M4 (the Theale access point). There are good road and rail communications with Reading, Oxford, London and Heathrow.

Organisation. The College is a fully co-educational boarding school with approximately 810 pupils, of whom about 76 are day pupils. At 13+ entry girls and boys spend their first year in Faulkner's, a purpose-built co-educational house with its own facilities and dining hall. Thereafter, the College is divided into 11 houses (7 for Boys and 4 for Girls). Day pupils are full members of the boarding houses. The Housemaster/mistress is assisted by House Tutors and a Matron. Meals are served in the central Dining Hall. About fifty girls and boys join the large and vibrant Sixth Form through 16+ entry.

Admission. 13+ candidates qualify by taking either the Common Entrance Examination, the Common Academic or Bradfield College Scholarship Examination, or the Bradfield Entrance Examination (if not taking Common Entrance); candidates are interviewed by the a Housemaster/mistress and an Admissions tutor, and school reports and references are required. All candidates are required to take the ISEB Common Pre-Test in October of Year 7. Admission to the Sixth Form is by Assessment; this comprises English and Maths tests and pastoral and academic interviews. In addition, school reports and references are required. Scholarships and Exhibitions are available.

A school prospectus and details of the entry procedure may be obtained from the Admissions Office or College website.

Fees per term (2018–2019). Boarders £12,468; Day pupils £9,975.

A fee is payable on registration. 20 months before the date of entry a Guaranteed Place fee of £1,000, which is later credited against the final account, is payable.

Entrance Scholarships. *Academic*: At 13+ scholarships are awarded on the results of a competitive examination held at the College in the Lent Term. Candidates must be under the age of 14 on 1 September. Further Honorary scholarships conferring the status and privileges of a scholar are awarded at the end of the Year 11 (post GCSE).

At 16+ Scholarships are awarded annually after competitive examinations in the Michaelmas Term.

Music Scholarships are awarded at 13+ and 16+.

Dr Gray All Rounder Scholarships are awarded at 13+ and 16+ for achievement and potential in their all-round ability, which would take into account their academic achievement as well as their aptitude in any combination of other disciplines (including Music). Individual Scholarships are also available for distinction in Art, Drama or Sport.

All awards are augmentable according to financial need. Further information and entrance forms can be obtained on application to the Admissions Office.

Academic Organisation. Pupils enter the College in September and follow a three-year course to GCSE examinations, and then a two-year course to A Level or IB.

In the first three years all the normal subjects are taught in a core curriculum, but there is also opportunity to emphasise the linguistic or the aesthetic or the practical elements through a system of options.

In the Sixth Form GCE A Level courses are offered in all subjects studied for GCSE with the addition of Economics,

Film Studies, Politics, History of Art, Business and Computer Science. Sixth Formers can also choose to study the IB Diploma Programme.

A brand new state-of-the-art and environmentally-friendly Science Centre opened its doors to pupils and the local community in September 2010. It includes ten sophisticated laboratories, a living grass roof, a conservatory and a biomass boiler providing an educationally and environmentally exciting space for the teaching of science.

Academic Staff. There are 128 members of the Academic Staff who cover all the main subjects. These are almost entirely graduates recruited from British universities, although there are also native speakers of German, French and Spanish in the Modern Languages department.

Careers. The Careers Department – Bradfield Horizons – provides a wide range of careers education, information, advice and guidance to all year groups, particularly at key decision points. The College is a full member of Inspiring Futures and through them, all pupils in the Fifth Form (and new pupils in the Lower Sixth) undertake Futurewise (Morrisby) psychometric profiling, follow-up interviews and receive a detailed personal report to help them plan for the future. In the Sixth Form, pupils have opportunities to find out about various professions, industries and the Armed Services through talks, visits and courses. Specialist advice is available on University entrance in the UK and overseas, Gap Years and work-related learning.

Sports. The main Sports for girls are hockey in the Michaelmas term, netball in the Lent term and tennis and rounders in the Summer term. Girls also have the chance to play competitive lacrosse, football and cricket.

The main Sports for boys are football in the Michaelmas term, hockey in the Lent term and cricket and tennis in the Summer term.

In addition, teams represent the College at squash, fives, cross-country, fencing, athletics, golf, sailing, swimming, shooting, badminton, basketball, water polo, clay pigeon shooting, showjumping, eventing and polo. There are also opportunities to take part in dance classes, Zumba and aerobics.

There are 2 all-weather artificial grass pitches used for hockey, football and tennis, a 3-court indoor Tennis Centre, 6 other hard tennis courts, 5 netball courts, 2 fives courts, 4 squash courts and a very large and modern Sports Complex, including an indoor swimming pool. The College grounds extend to nearly 250 acres and include fine playing fields, a nine-hole golf course and fly fishing on the river Pang.

Recreation, Drama and Music. Every encouragement is given to pupils to develop their interests and talents in a wide variety of creative activities. There are modern and well-equipped studios for Art, Sculpture and Textiles, an Information Technology Centre, a purpose-built and very extensive Design and Technology Centre and a Music School with a Concert Hall and practice rooms. The Drama department stages a diverse number of productions each term and a classical Greek Play is produced every three years. In addition, there are about 30 Societies covering a wide range of other interests from Young Enterprise to Knitting.

Religion. Chapel services are those of the Church of England, and Religious Education is part of the core curriculum in Year 9. Confirmation Services are held each year for Anglicans in the College Chapel and for Catholics in the local parish.

Combined Cadet Force. The College maintains a contingent of the Combined Cadet Force which all pupils have the opportunity of joining. There is a full range of alternative activities, including Community Service and The Duke of Edinburgh's Award. All pupils take part in a programme of Adventure Training.

The Bradfield Society. The College values its links with its former pupils and parents, and a series of social and sporting occasions is held each year to enable friendships to be maintained and renewed. Address: The Bradfield Society, Bradfield College, Reading, Berkshire RG7 6AU.

Charitable status. Bradfield College is a Registered Charity, number 309089.

Visitor: The Right Revd The Lord Bishop of Oxford

Council:

Ms S Bergqvist (*Warden*)	S Clarkson Webb
M A Jones	B N Tomlinson
P B Saunders	Mrs C J Hartz
I M Wood-Smith	Mrs E R Barker
H P Gangsted	Dr N Hodson
Mrs J Scarrow	D Mundy
Mrs S Scrope	A Aird
Professor R Van De Noort	

Clerk of the Council: Mrs H J F Perkins

Headmaster: Dr C C Stevens, MA, DPhil

Second Master: A A G Logan, BA, MEd

Senior Deputy Head (*Admissions and Marketing*): Mrs A M C Acton, BA

Deputy Head (*Academic*): N M Burch, MSci

Bursar: D Barnett (*Acting*)

Houses and Housemasters:
A – *Loyd*: J R Preston, BSc
C – *Army*: A S Golding, BA
D – *House on the Hill*: R P Sanford, BSc
E – *Stone House*: J C Saunders, BA
F – *Hillside*: C A Carlier, MA
G – *House on the Hill*: T E Goad, BA
H – *The Close*: J C Hanbury, BA
I – *Palmer House* (*Girls*): Miss L E Rowlands, BSc
J – *Armstrong House* (*Girls*): Mrs A L Cocksworth, MA
K – *Stevens House* (*Girls*): Mrs C van der Westhuizen, MSc
M – *Stanley House* (*Girls*): Mrs H B Peters, LLB
L – *Faulkner's* (*Year 9*): M J Blackburn BA and Mrs F J Wall BA

Assistant Staff:
* *Head of Department*

Creative Arts Faculty:
*M K Holmes, MA
Art:
Miss A M Cowan, BA
J A Green, MA
Ms D S Rodgers, BA
A L Whittaker, MFA
Design & Technology:
*J F Fuller, BA
M K Goodwin, MA

Business Studies:
*M R Rippon, BA
L A Webb, BSc

Careers and Higher Education:
*Mrs S Leijten, BA

Classics:
*Mrs P M H Caffrey, MA
P C Armstrong, BA

Economics:
*C G Irvine, BA
L W Beith, BComm

J C Fox, BA
C W Sykes, MA

English and Film Faculty:
*J M Longmore, LLB
English:
A M Cocksworth, MA
A R C Copeman, MSc
Ms S R Davies, BA
Mrs E V Earnshaw, BA
Mrs A L Gregory, BA
A S Golding, BA
Mrs H A Morris, BA
Mrs H B Peters, LLB
Miss Z A Preston, BA
Miss A J Routledge, BA
J M C Saunders, BA
English Language and EAL:
*Mrs H E Bebbington, BA, MA
Film Studies:
Ms J Stables, BA

Geography:
*T J Kidson, BSc
M S Hill, BA
R Keeley, MA
A A G Logan, BA, MEd
J R Preston, BSc
G M Turner, MSc
R J Wall, BA

History:
*C M Best, BA
Mrs M Y Best, BSc
C J Booth, LLB
S H Rees, BA, PhD
L S Scott, BA
J P Shafe, BA

History of Art:
*Mrs B H Bond, BA
T E Goad, BA

Mathematics and Computing Faculty:
*N A Thorpe, BSc
Computing:
*A H Roush, MSc
Mathematics:
Mrs N C Armstrong, BA
D M Brooks, BSc
J A Carle, BSc
Mrs C du Boulay, BA
M J Green, BEng
S S Gumbs, BSc
A P Jaffe, BSc
Mrs P A Peck, BSc
Mrs C Shaikh, CertEd
C J Sharp, BSc
C R Stoneman, MA
N J Taylor, BSc
Mrs C van der Westhuizen, MSc
S N Whalley, BSc

Modern Languages Faculty:
*Mrs B E D'Cruz, MA (*Head of German*)
Mrs A M C Acton, BA
Mrs B Benito Lozano, BA
C A Carlier, MA
M E Denhart (*Head of Spanish*)
M M Etherington, BA
Mrs I Golding
J R Haighton, BA
J C Hanbury, BA
Mrs E R Hayes, MA (*Head of French*) [maternity leave]

Mrs C Jones [maternity cover]
Mrs L E Page, BA
Mrs K L Parker, BA
R Somma, BA (*Head of Italian*)
Miss C M Southall BSc
Miss A H Spillane MSc
Mrs F J C Wall, BA
Mrs J M Walsh, BA

Performing Arts Faculty:
Dance:
Mrs M Hunkin
Drama:
M J Blackburn, BA
D E Quinn, BA
*N J Saunders, BA
Miss L R Rees, BA
Music:
M Lowe MMus (*Director*)
Miss E A Harre, BA
*Mrs V S Hughes, BA [maternity leave]

PE:
M M Ruxton, BSc (*Director*)
*D J Clark, BA
D J Mitchell, BSc
Miss K Papps, BSc
Miss L E Rowlands, BSc
R P P Sanford, BSc
Miss C M Southall, BSc

Politics:
*S H Rees, BA, PhD
Mrs M Y Best, BSc
C J Booth, LLB
A R MacEwen, MA

Religion, Philosophy and Ethics:
*J P A Ball, MA (*acting*)
Mrs M Baynton-Perret, BD Dip
Mrs P M Donnelly, BA
Reverend Dr P M Hansell, PhD (*Chaplain*)
S P Williams, MA, MLitt

Science Faculty:
Dr D J Brooks, BSc, PhD
Biology:
*Mrs C C Doherty, BSc
Ms E J Appleby, BSc
Dr S J Bevan, DPhil
P J J Clegg, BSc
Mrs J O Etherington, MSc
Mrs J P Foad, BSc
Dr R J Johnston, PhD
Dr K J Ogbe, BSc, PhD
Dr L S Vat, BSc, PhD
S D Whitehead, BSc
Chemistry:
*Dr J A F Burnside, MChem, PhD
N M Burch, MSci
A J Hardwicke, BSc, MA
Dr L C Hutchins, PhD
A J Singh, BSc
Physics:
*G C Stead BA
Miss L Allen-Mirehouse, BEng
C P Coghlan, BEng
Mrs I J Rickard, BSc
T C O'Toole, BSc

Support and Study Skills:
*Dr K A Spaulding, PhD, MSc
Mrs S S Bunyan, BA
Mrs P Donnelly, BA

Mrs K E Howells, Cert SpLD
Dr L C Hutchins, BSc, PhD
Miss L M Morey, BA
Mrs I Smith, BEd, Dip SpLD
Mrs G K Thompson, BEd, Dip SpLD
Mrs C Wright, BA, Dip SpLD

Wellbeing:
*Mrs V Rae, RGN
Mrs M S Hunkin

Bradford Grammar School

Keighley Road, Bradford, West Yorkshire BD9 4JP

Tel: 01274 542492; Headmaster: 01274 553701
Fax: 01274 548129
email: admissions@bradfordgrammar.com
website: www.bradfordgrammar.com
Twitter: @BradfordGrammar
Facebook: @bradfordgrammarschool
LinkedIn: /bradfordgrammar

Motto: *Hoc Age*

Northern independent school of the year 2018 – The Sunday Times.

With a heritage dating back to 1548, Bradford Grammar School (BGS) is one of the oldest and most respected institutions in Yorkshire. Our illustrious past spans hundreds of years. In 1662 Charles II granted BGS's Charter, a document that the school proudly displays. Having occupied three locations since our establishment, the iconic building that BGS inhabits today was opened in 1949. A long history of excellence inspires BGS pupils to fulfil their potential and make their own mark upon the future of BGS.

With a 'first-class, academic and outward-looking approach' (Good Schools Guide), BGS is one of the UK's leading independent schools, providing an outstanding education for more than 1,051 girls and boys aged six to 18. The school is fully co-educational: girls have been admitted to the Sixth Form since 1984 and in all intakes from 1999.

BGS provides every opportunity for its Junior, Senior and Sixth Form pupils to embrace academic, sporting and creative excellence within an aspirational, caring environment in which happiness is the key to an individual's success. With its impressive 'value added' provision, academic excellence is available to all.

Pupil Numbers. 1,044 day pupils (576 boys, 468 girls). Junior School (6–11): 181 pupils (96 boys, 85 girls). Senior School (11–18): 863 pupils (480 boys, 383 girls).

Location and Facilities. The school, comprising six main buildings and a separate junior school building, stands in extensive grounds situated just a mile from Bradford city centre. The School thrives upon the opportunities created by this dynamic hub of enterprise and innovation.

The majority of our pupils travel by bus or train from areas such as Ilkley, Skipton, Leeds, Halifax and Huddersfield. We provide dedicated buses from a number of locations, including Huddersfield, Halifax and the Calder Valley, Bramhope, Headingley, Horsforth, Oakworth, Rawdon and Oxenhope.

Frizinghall train station is within a five-minute walk of the school and we provide a daily patrol team who ensure that pupils walk between the station and the school safely and sensibly. There are direct rail connections from Frizinghall train station to Leeds, Airedale and Wharfedale, Skipton, Ilkley and Apperley Bridge.

Nestling on the edge of the Yorkshire Dales, and within striking distance of the Lake District, opportunities abound for outdoor visits and residential trips.

Facilities include a 25m competition swimming pool, sports pavilion, all-weather sports pitch, squash and tennis courts, a dedicated Sixth Form centre with full Wi-Fi, the Hockney Theatre, Design Technology workshops, Computer Aided Design (CAD) suites, fitness suite with rowing machines, cycling machines, treadmills and weights, a music auditorium, recording studio, debating chamber, dedicated Science building and a new state-of-the-art Library, completed in 2015. The Price Hall is the centrepiece of the main school building and provides a magnificent setting for assemblies, concerts and other major events.

Bradford Grammar Junior School occupies Clock House, a seventeenth century Manor House within the school grounds, where it enjoys its own assembly hall, Computing and Design Technology facilities and teaching accommodation. *For further details, please see separate entry in IAPS section.*

Senior School Curriculum. In Years Seven and Eight all pupils study English, Mathematics, French, German, Latin, Biology, Physics, Chemistry, Geography, History, Art, Music, Design and Technology (DT), Religious Studies (RS), Personal Development and Games.

In Year Nine pupils follow a common core of English, Mathematics, Geography, History, Physics, Chemistry, Biology, RS, Personal Development and Games, choose one core Modern Foreign Language from a choice of French, German or Spanish and choose three optional subjects from a choice of German, Russian, Latin, Greek, Art, Music, Spanish and Computer Science.

In Years Ten and Eleven pupils follow ten GCSE courses. All pupils follow a common core of English Language, English Literature, Mathematics, Biology, Chemistry, Physics, and Games, choose a core Modern Foreign Language from French, German or Spanish, and choose three optional subjects from Geography, History, German, Computer Science, Russian, Latin, Spanish, Greek, Art, Music, DT and RS.

Year 12 (Lower Sixth Form). Pupils choose four AS Level subjects from Art, Biology, Business Studies, Chemistry, Classical Civilisation, DT, Economics, Electronics, English Literature, English Language, English Language and Literature, French, Further Mathematics, Geography, Geology, German, Greek, History, Computer Science, Latin, Mathematics, Music, Music Technology, Physics, Politics, Psychology, RS, Russian, Spanish and Theatre Studies. In addition, they also take two eleven-week General Studies courses from a wide range of non-examined options, or Japanese, AS Further Mathematics or the Extended Project Qualification (EPQ).

Year 13 (Upper Sixth Form). Pupils take three or four of their AS Level courses through to A Level. It is possible to replace the fourth subject with another AS course. Pupils may follow a non-examinable General Studies course if they wish.

For further details please see the booklets A Guide to GCSE Courses and A Guide to Sixth Form Courses both of which can be downloaded from our website at www.bradfordgrammar.com.

Results.

A Level: Terrifically successful at A and AS Levels, BGS was recognised as having the highest average University admission points per student of any school in West Yorkshire. In 2018 123 A Level students celebrated outstanding success with 17% of all exams awarded A* and 54% A*/A grades.

GCSEs: At GCSE, our results far exceed the national average. A record-breaking 76% of all exams taken in 2018 were awarded A/A* or 9–7 grades, well over three times higher than the national average of recent years. (Pupils at BGS take a mixture of IGCSEs and GCSEs, graded either 9–1 or A*–G.)

Co-curricular Activities. We actively encourage pupils to engage in co-curricular activities. Pupils in the Senior School currently have a choice of over 50 clubs and societies covering a wide range of sports, drama, music, academic subjects and other areas of interest – from rowing, orienteering, war games, debating, Biomedical and Classics Societies to Micro:bit, Games and Handmade Clubs, there is something for everyone. Pupils can take part in The Duke of Edinburgh's Award scheme, the Combined Cadet Force (both RAF and Army) and World Challenge expeditions.

Pastoral Care. Outstanding pastoral support contributes to the happiness of Bradford Grammar School pupils, creating a positive, friendly atmosphere for all. The school works closely with parents to ensure each child receives the best possible pastoral care during their time at BGS. The team of form tutors, Heads of Year, school nurses, counsellors and Learning Support Department work together to promote pupils' happiness and progress. They ensure that every child receives the attention they deserve. Pupils who need extra help are quickly identified by our pastoral team, who work with a team of trained mentors from Year 13 to support each child as they make their way up the school.

Beyond the classroom BGS encourages pupils to participate in physical exercise and pursue a wide range of co-curricular interests with an extensive in-house counselling programme helping pupils to avoid and overcome problems.

Admission. Boys and girls can join the school at the ages of 6, 7, 8, 9, 10 in the Junior School or 11, 12, 13 or 16 in the Senior School. Pupils are admitted into the Sixth Form on the basis of their GCSE results (at least 20 points, grade B, preferably A, in sixth form subjects), an interview and a satisfactory reference from the candidate's current school. Candidates for entry into Year 2 (6+), Year 3 (7+) and Year 4 (8+) will be invited to spend an informal day in the Junior School. Admission for all other ages is by examination in Mathematics and English in January each year.

Bursaries. Bursaries are awarded on a means-tested basis, each case being reviewed annually. The award depends on parental circumstances, the amount of capital available at the time of the examination and the academic ability of the candidate.

Fees per term (2018–2019). Junior School £3,305, Senior School £4,223, Sixth Form £4,223.

Former Pupils include Olympic heroes Alistair and Jonathan Brownlee, Team GB cyclist Abby-Mae Parkinson, actress Georgie Henley, England rugby legend Charlie Hodgson and artist David Hockney.

Old Bradfordians Association. President: Mr I Holland, c/o Bradford Grammar School.

The Parents' Association (previously BGS Society). Chairman: Mrs C Hanafin and Mr T Tullie, c/o Bradford Grammar School.

Charitable status. Bradford Grammar School (The Free Grammar School of King Charles II at Bradford) is a Registered Charity, number 529113. It exists to provide education for children.

Governors:
Chairman: Lady Morrison, LLB
Vice-Chairman: Professor C Mellors, OBE, BA, MA, PhD, FAcSS, FHEA, FRSA
President: A H Jerome, MBE, MA [OB]

Ex-officio:
The Dean of Bradford, the Very Revd J J Lepine, BA

Co-optative:
P Cogan, BA, FCA
A C Craig, DL, DCR
V L Davey, LLB
D J Davies, MBE, BEng, MA
S R Davies, BA, FRSA
Professor A Francis, BSc, ACGI, FBAM, CCMI, AcSS
C Hamilton Stewart, MBE
His Honour J A Lewis
I McAleese, FCIPD
C M Wontner-Smith, BA, FCA [OB]
Sir David Wootton MA [OB]

Representing Leeds University:
Professor Sir Alexander F Markham, BSc, PhD, MBBS, DSc, FRCP, FRCPath

Representing Chamber of Commerce:
S R Watson, MCIPR

Governors Emeriti:
J E Barker, MA [OB]
P J M Bell ,JP, FCIS, CText, FTI, FRSA [OB]
R G Bowers, DL, BSc, CEng, FRSA [OB]
I Crawford, FCA
J D Fenton, MCSP, SRP
J G Ridings, FCA

[OB] *Old Bradfordian*

Bursar and Clerk to the Governors: G Monnickendam, BA, ACA

Headmaster: Dr S Hinchliffe, BA, MEd, PhD, FRSA

Deputy Headmaster: L G d'Arcy, MChem
Assistant Head, Pastoral: M J Chapman, MA
Assistant Head, Curriculum: G P Woods, MA
Assistant Head, Development: P Merckx, BSc
HR Manager: C Macdonald
Headmistress, Junior School: Miss K L Howes, BSc, MSc

Brentwood School

Middleton Hall Lane, Brentwood, Essex CM15 8EE

Tel:	01277 243243
Fax:	01277 243299
email:	headmaster@brentwood.essex.sch.uk
website:	www.brentwoodschool.co.uk

Motto: *Virtue, Learning and Manners*

Brentwood School was founded in 1557 and received its charter as the Grammar School of Antony Browne, Serjeant at Law, on 5th July, 1558. The Founder became Chief Justice of Common Pleas shortly before the death of Queen Mary, and was knighted a few months before his death in 1567. The Foundation Stone over the door of Old Big School was laid on 10th April, 1568, by Edmund Huddleston and his wife Dorothy, who was the step-daughter of the Founder. The Elizabethan silver seal of the School Corporation is still in the possession of the Governors. In 1622 Statutes were drawn up for the School by Sir Antony Browne, kinsman of the Founder, George Monteigne, Bishop of London, and John Donne, Dean of St Paul's.

Brentwood School is a co-educational school with a total of 1,600 pupils including 409 in the Preparatory School. The Preparatory School is fully co-educational as is the Sixth Form (of 314 pupils), but boys and girls are taught separately between the ages of 11 and 16. Boarding is available for boys and girls from 11.

Buildings and Grounds. The School occupies a 75-acre site on high ground at the northern end of the town some 20 miles north-east of London. Old Big School, the original School room, is still in regular use thus maintaining a direct link with the School's founder. Over recent years a major building programme has seen extensions to the Science and Modern Languages buildings and Dining Halls; Boarding Houses and Sixth Form accommodation; the building of the magnificent Brentwood School Sports Centre; a Performing Arts Centre, an all-weather pitch, an Art and Design Centre and an indoor heated swimming pool. In November 2011, HRH Prince Edward The Earl of Wessex formally opened the School's new Sixth Form Centre and Wessex Auditorium. The Sixth Form Centre, which has become the intellectual powerhouse of the School, provides an exemplary educational environment for the International Baccalaureate Diploma programme. Facilities include common rooms and private study areas, 16 additional classrooms, a dedicated computer suite and multi-purpose 400-seat auditorium. The award-winning Bean Academic Centre, the intellectual heart of the School, was opened to pupils at the end of March 2016. With large classroom spaces, a lecture theatre & café, it provides a state-of-the-art environment within which pupils can develop independent learning. A multimillion pound development is under way at the Preparatory School.

Organisation. The School is one community within which, for good educational reasons, girls and boys are taught separately from age 11 to 16. They are encouraged to participate together in all co-curricular activities. The Senior School is divided into Year Groups. Each Year Group has a Head of Year and Deputy who oversee it. The vast majority of pupils join the School at 11 after successfully completing our Entrance Examination. A broad curriculum is followed through the first three years and this continues through careful choice of GCSE and IGCSE subjects to the end of the Fifth Year. Entry to the Sixth Form is conditional upon success in the GCSE examinations. In the Sixth Form students take either four of the 27 AS Level subjects or follow the International Baccalaureate Diploma programme. Most go on to University. Pass rates at A Level reach 100% and many pupils gain places at Oxford and Cambridge each year.

Religion. Although Brentwood is a Christian School, pupils and staff from all faiths, or none, are welcome. There is a resident Chaplain and pupils attend Chapel weekly. Regular Communion Services are held.

Boarding. There are two Boarding Houses, both of which have been thoroughly modernised. The boys reside in Hough House which can accommodate up to 42 students; the girls reside in Mill Hill House where 27 can be accommodated. The public rooms are spacious and both Houses generously staffed. Full and weekly boarding are available. A qualified Matron runs an efficient Sanatorium.

Pastoral Care. Brentwood School has an outstanding level of pastoral care which is provided by Heads of Year, Tutors and our Pastoral Team, ably supported by the delegated senior manager, Mrs Jenkin, and by all colleagues, who together create the enabling, supportive ethos. Tutors combine pastoral care with detailed academic monitoring, thus treating the whole person. Their encouragement to their pupils to participate in a wide range of activities successfully engenders greater self-confidence and self-awareness. In addition to Mrs Jenkin, Deputy Head (Pastoral), Heads of Year and Tutors, there are two pastoral managers.

Music, Drama and Art. Music plays an important part in the life of the School, as do Drama and Art. There are four orchestras and several ensembles and jazz groups. The Big Band is internationally acclaimed. There are at least three dramatic productions each year, together with regular Art Exhibitions.

Careers. There is an excellent University Entrance and Careers Department where students receive advice and can obtain information about courses and/or careers. Aptitude Tests; Work Experience; visits to colleges, universities and places of work; visiting speakers are all part of the provision. A careers convention is held in March each year.

CCF and CSU. All pupils either join the Combined Cadet Force or, through the Community Service Unit, engage in a wide-ranging series of activities which bring them into contact with the Community. The Duke of Edinburgh's Award scheme runs alongside these activities.

School Societies. There are many flourishing societies covering a wide range of interests, catering for all ages. The Sir Antony Browne Society (SABS) at Brentwood School is a society for Sixth Form students, which provides them with an opportunity for intellectual discussion and cultural interest.

Sports Facilities. Brentwood School was one of the official training venues for the London 2012 Games. The playing fields are part of the School complex and provide ample space for soccer, cricket, hockey, rugby and tennis. There is a world-class all-weather athletics track. The Brentwood School Sports Centre includes an indoor soccer/hockey pitch, six badminton courts, indoor cricket nets, basketball courts and a fencing salle, as well as squash courts and a fitness suite. There is a heated indoor swimming pool and an all-weather pitch. Provision is made for golf, sailing and table tennis. The two Astroturfs and netball courts are floodlit for use in winter

Preparatory School. *See entry in IAPS section for details.*

Entry. Entrance Examinations for both boys and girls aged 11 are held at the School in January each year. Entries are also accepted at 13 plus, following the Common Entrance Examination, vacancies permitting. Transfers at other ages are also possible. Sixth Form entry is through GCSE success, and interview.

Scholarships and Bursaries. In addition to Academic scholarships the School offers Music, Drama, Dance, Art, Chess, Sport and Choral scholarships at 11+. These may be supplemented by means-tested Bursaries.

The School offers a considerable number of Bursaries in addition to the awards described above. Over a fifth of pupils receive such assistance.

Fees per term (2018–2019). Day £6,315, Boarding £12,376.

Old Brentwoods Society. There is a flourishing Society for pupils to stay in touch once they have left the School; email: oldbrentwoods@brentwood.essex.sch.uk.

Charitable status. Brentwood School (part of Sir Antony Browne's School Trust, Brentwood) is a Registered Charity, number 1153605. It is a Charitable Trust for the purpose of educating children.

Governors:
Sir Michael Snyder, DSc, FCA, FRSA [OB] (*Chairman*)
R I McLintock, MSc, DMS, DipEd (*Vice-Chairman*)
P C Beresford, FNAEA, MARLA
Lord Black of Brentwood, MA, MCIPR, FRSA [OB]
M Bolton, MBE, BA Hons
Mrs J Bryan, CTA, LLB
Miss A Chapman, ACMA
Mrs S Dalgarno, MA, PGCE, JP
D J Elms, MA, FCA, FCSI
Professor B J W Evans, BSc Hons, PhD [OB]
Lord Flight of Worcester, MA, MBA [OB]
J Griffith-Jones, MA, ACA, TD
Mrs A Hardy, QC, LLB Hons, LLM Tax, AKC
Mrs J M Jones, BA Hons, ARCM
The Venerable D Lowman, BD, AKC

Ms R Martin, MEd, NPQH
J M May, MA, LLB [OB]
Dr C Tout, MA, PhD [OB]
J Tumbridge, CC, MCIArb, LLB Hons

[OB] *Old Brentwood*

Bursar and Clerk to the Governors: c/o Mrs S Lenferna De La Motte

Headmaster: D I Davies, MA Oxon, FRSA

Deputy Head (Staff Development & Co-Curricular): J Cohen, BSc, MEd
Deputy Head (Pastoral): Mrs N Jenkin, BA, MA
Deputy Head (Academic): J Barfield Moore, MA

Heads of Year:
Sixth Form, Director of Sixth Form, Head of Upper Sixth: R Higgins, BA, MA
Sixth Form, Head of Lower Sixth: T Sellers, BA
Fifth Year: I Wignall, BA
Fourth Year: Mrs J Khush, MSc
Third Year: Mrs M E Belsham, BSc
Second Year: Miss Siobhan Coady, BSc
First Year: Miss K Crane, BA [OB]

Houses & Housemasters/mistresses:
East: J McCann, BEng
Hough: S Taylor, LLB
Mill Hill: M Monro, BA & Mrs J Monro
North: S Salisbury, BA
South: C M Long, BA
Weald: D Wright, BSc, QTS
West: Mrs A Wall, BA

* *Head of Department*

Art:
*Miss N J Bixby, MA
Miss V Cooper, BA
Miss K Gellard, BA
Miss E Stimpson, BA

Biology:
*Dr E Parades, PhD
Miss E Aherne, BSc
Mrs R Bentley, BSc
Miss J P Byrne, BSc
Dr K Dingwell, BSc
Mrs P Ebden, BSc, MSc
Miss E Faulkner
K Gray, BSc
Miss V Kerslake, BSc
Mrs G Robertson, BSc [OB]
Ms S St Clair Jones, BA

Business Studies:
*Miss M Sorohan, BA, MA
N Carr, MA, MA Econ Ed, ACEM
Mrs M Farrugia,
A Giles, BA
Ms K Miller, BA
Miss R Ryan, BA
C Wakeling, BSc

Chemistry:
*D Endlar, MChem
Miss E Faulkner
S L Gonsalves, BSc
Mrs J Khush, MSc
Revd Dr A McConnaughie, BA, MA, PhD, BA
Dr I Ross, MA, PhD

J Seaman, BSc, MSc, CChem, MRSC
A Siam, MSc
Miss C Thomas, MSci
D Wightman, BSc, MSc

Classics:
*Mr B Clark, BA
Miss K L Crane, BA [OB]
Miss Z D'Souza, BA
Miss Z Fleming, MA
Mrs J Gray, BA
Miss C Martin, BA [OB]
B Roberts, MA
Miss M Swettenham,
Miss C Tsaknaki, BA, MSt
M Whetnall, BA

Computing & ICT:
*G Kiff, BSc
Miss I Lovelock, BA
J McCann, BEng
Miss J Scotland, BSc Hons

Design & Technology:
*Miss L Hall, BA, MA
M Lewis, BEd
D Murphy, BEd
T Walland, BA

Drama:
*M Bulmer, BA, MA (*Director of Performing Arts*)
Miss D Foster, BA
Mrs S Martin, BA
Ms R Worth, MA, BA

Economics:
*A Dean, BSc, MA
N J Carr, MA, MA EconEd, ACEM, FRSA
J Cohen, BSc, MEd
A Giles, BA
P Rees, BA
C Wakeling, BSc

English:
*Dr S Evans, BA, PhD
Mrs C Bowley, BA, MA
M Bulmer, BA
Mrs M Callender, MA
Mrs V Denman, BA
R Higgins, BA, MA
R Irvine, BA
Miss A Kwolek, BA, MA, UG Dip
S Levien
Mrs P Morris-Jeffery, BA
S Salisbury, BA
Mrs S Schwar, BSc
Miss F Spriggs, MA
S Taylor, LLB
Miss C Tiernan, BA, BS, MA

EAL:
*C Berkley, BA
B Clements, BA, MPhil, Dip RSA
Ms K North

Food & Nutrition:
*Mrs C Picton, BEd
Mrs B Daly, BEd
Mrs J Franklin, BSc

Geography:
*Miss H O'Neill, BSc
L Berale, MSc, SCITT
Mrs S Davis, BSc
Miss S Kilkenny-Brown, BSc
C M Long, BA
D Wight, BSc, QTS

History:
*Ms B Fuller, BA
Mrs M E Belsham, BSc
C Berkley, BA
M Clark, BA
Mrs R Coppell, MA
Dr C Harvey, BA, PhD
M Howard, BA, MA
T Sellers, BA
Mrs S Sharpe, BA
M V Willis, BA

Learning Development:
Ms D Porovic, MSc (*Director of Teaching & Learning*)
*Ms A Hope
Miss R Coates, BA
Mrs S Schwar, BSc
D M Taylor, GRSM Hons, LRAM Hons, FASC, FRSA

Mathematics:
*Ms Louise Ward, BSc, MSc

*Miss E Warnes, BSc, MEd (*Acting Head of Mathematics*)
T Beedell, BSc, MA
P Bolton, BSc
Dr T Bourne, MA, PhD
Mrs K Bowes, BSc
M Childs, BA
Mrs R Dryden, BSc
E Essuman, BSc
R Ewin, BSc
P Forster, BSc
Miss G Furnell, BSc
Miss S Hunter, BSc
T Lai, BSc
B Paredes, BA, MA
Ms D Porovic, MSc
Miss E Preston, BSc
C Wakeling, BSc
Miss L Williams, BSc
D Wood, BSc, MSc

Modern Languages:
*I Walton, MA (*Senior Head of Languages*, *German)
Mrs N Piejko, BTS, BEd (*French)
Mrs J Rodgers, MSc (*Mandarin)
Mr G Smith, BA, MA (*Spanish)
Mrs M D Taylor, BA (*Italian)
M Bauer, MA
Mrs C Bowley, BA, MA
J Bowley, MA, Maîtrise, MIL, FCIEA, FRSA
Miss R Campbell, BA
Mrs L G M Dearmer-Decup, BA
Mrs A Hall, BA
Mrs N Jenkin, BA, MA
Miss C Lacotte, DEUG, BA
Mrs M Morris, BA, MA
Ms K North
Ms Q Oztoprak
Mrs I Penalver-Edwards, BA
Dr B Priest, BA Hons, MPhil
R Pritchard, BA
Mrs S J Roast, BEd
Miss B Selfridge, BA
Mrs A Wall, BA
Mrs M Watts-Jimenez, BA

Music:
Director of Music: F Cooper, BA [OB]
Assistant Director of Music: D Revels, MA Oxon, MMus, LRSM
T Heard, MA, BMus

Physics:
*R Jukes, MA
Mrs C Astolfi, MA
C Beadling, BSc
Miss S Coady, BSc
R Ewin, BSc

L C Jenkins, MSc, FRAS
B Letts, BSc
Miss C Panteli, BSc
Dr I Ross, PhD, MA
Ms L Ward, BSc, MSc

Physical Education & Games:
Director of Sport, I Wignall, BA
Mrs J McLeod, BSc (*Head of Academic PE*)
W Castleman (*Master i/c Rugby*)
C Galesloot, FIE (*Master i/c Fencing*)
Miss K Herterich, ISTD (*Head of Dance Academy*)
B Juhasz (*Fencing Coach*)
Mrs W L Juniper, BEd
Miss J Lazenby, BSc (*Head of Hockey*)
C M Long, BA (*Head of Golf & Squash*)
J Mikelburgh (*Cricket Coach*)
M Miller, BSc (*Head of Boys' Games & Football*)
Miss L Morrell (*Head of Girls' Games*)

Director of IB: J Barfield Moore, MA
Admissions Registrar: Mrs S Hilton
Headmaster's PA: Mrs S Gilder
School Medical Officer: Dr Nasif

S Salisbury, BA (*Master i/c Cricket*)
Miss A Simpson, BSc (*Head of Tennis & Netball*) [OB]
C Smith, BSc
C Warburton (*Head of Cross Country*)
Mrs N Watson, HND (*Head of Swimming & Water Polo*)

Politics:
*M V Willis, BA
Dr C Bryan,
Mrs R Coppell, MA
Dr C Harvey, BA, PhD
M Howard, BA, MA

Psychology:
*Mrs A Morris, BSc, MA
Miss J Atkinson, BSc
Dr C Bryan
Mrs J O'Connell, BSc

Religion & Philosophy:
*M Willingham, BA, MA
J Barfield Moore, MA
B Clements, BA, MPhil, Dip RSA
Miss R Bishop, BA
R Jenkins, BA
M Monro, BA, AKA
Mrs H Barfield Moore, BA, AKC

Brighton College

Eastern Road, Brighton BN2 0AL

Tel:	01273 704200
	01273 704339 Head Master
	01273 704260 Bursar
	01273 704210 Prep School
	01273 704259 Pre-Prep School
Fax:	01273 704204
email:	admissions@brightoncollege.net
website:	www.brightoncollege.org.uk
Twitter:	@BrightonCollege
Facebook:	@BrightonCollegeUK

Motto: ΤΟ Δ'ΕΥ ΝΙΚΑΤΩ ~ *Let the right prevail*

Thoroughly progressive, academic, inclusive and, above all, focused on the importance of kindness, Brighton College has become a powerhouse in independent education. Founded in 1845 in the heart of Brighton's Kemp Town area, its historic quad and listed buildings speak of a rich educational heritage. Its dynamic head teacher Richard Cairns, however, is far more interested in the future and has become known nationally for his ground-breaking approach both educationally and pastorally.

Mr Cairns has overseen an ambitious capital project during his tenure which includes a new 20-classroom Yeoh Building, including a Creative Learning Centre. Construction is now under way on a £55 million Sports and Science Centre, which will open in September 2019.

The College regularly achieves the best GCSE and A Level results in Sussex and some of the highest in the country. In 2018, 90% pupils achieved grades 9–7 in the new GCSE exams. At A Level, 99% of pupils achieved A*/B, the highest result in the country. Overall there were 559 A*/A grades and 29 pupils took up places at Oxford or Cambridge.

The school has been the recipient of many awards: named 'United Kingdom Independent School of the Year 2013–14' at the Independent School Awards, and Mr Cairns was named 'Public School Headmaster of the Year 2012–13' by Tatler magazine. The Week have called Brighton College the 'most forward thinking school in Britain' for two years running in 2017/18 and 2018/19.

There is a wealth of extracurricular activities on offer, in particular sport, music and the performing arts. There are now some 1090 pupils, of whom a third are boarders. In its most recent inspection in 2015, the Independent Schools Inspectorate gave Brighton College and its Prep & Pre-Prep School the highest possible grade across every single inspection category, with a rare 'Exceptional' for Achievement and Learning.

Buildings. An extensive programme of development is currently taking place which has seen many of the new builds win architectural awards. In 2015 the new Music School opened, home to state-of-the-art recording facilities and a 150-seat recital hall. In September 2017, the tenth new building in ten years opened, the Hopkins-designed Yeoh Building, with its innovative top-floor double-height Creative Learning Centre.

Admission. Pupils are admitted to the Lower Third at the age of 11 via assessments held at the College in January; to the Fourth Form between the ages of 13 and 14 via the Common Entrance examination, the Academic Scholarship examination or by special assessment and interview; and into the Sixth Form for A Levels between the ages of 16 and 17. In all cases pupils must also produce evidence of good character and conduct from their previous school. The College prospectus and registration form can be obtained from the Director of Admissions.

Houses. An extensive refurbishment programme is nearing completion across the day and boarding houses. A third of the pupils are boarders in the school and weekly boarding is increasingly popular, giving pupils the opportunity to go home on Friday afternoon and return either on Sunday evening or Monday morning.

Health. There is a Central Health Centre with a team of qualified nurses, and the Medical Officer visits regularly.

Catering. There is self-service dining room, managed by a qualified Catering Manager.

Holidays. School holidays are around three weeks each at Christmas and Easter, and eight weeks in the Summer. There is a half-term holiday of one week in all three terms.

Religion. A short morning service is held in Chapel on two days a week, with one service aimed to embrace all faiths.

Curriculum. The School is divided into seven forms: Lower Third, Upper Third, Fourth, Lower Fifth, Upper Fifth, Lower Sixth and Upper Sixth. In the Sixth Form almost 30 subjects are available at A Level. For GCSE, pupils select their subjects – usually 10 – at the end of the Fourth Form. 99% of pupils proceed to university. Preparation for the UCAS process begins in the second term of the Lower Sixth, and pupils are guided towards appropriate choices by the Head of Sixth Form in conjunction with the individual pupil's tutor.

Sport. The College enjoys a strong record of excellence at sports. The main playing field (the Home Ground) is part of the College campus and the Jubilee Ground is a mile away at East Brighton Park. All pupils take part in the College's extensive games programme. The main sports for boys are rugby and cricket and for girls, netball, hockey and cricket. In addition, a host of other options are available including football, squash, tennis, golf, beach volleyball, aerobics, rounders, yoga, athletics and cross country.

Service. All pupils from the Lower Fifth onwards are expected to participate in a service activity on one afternoon a week. Pupils may participate in charity work or, in the Sixth Form, Community Service; alternatively they may join The Duke of Edinburgh's Award scheme or enter one of the three sections of the CCF.

Music. There is a strong musical tradition and pupils reach a very high level of performance. The Choir, Chamber Orchestra, Symphony Orchestra, Concert Band and Swing Band perform regularly both inside and outside the College. There are several Chamber groups, and the Choral Society and Orchestra usually perform major works at the annual Brighton Festival.

Drama. The College has a strong tradition of excellence in drama, and there are opportunities for anyone to be involved. In addition to the regular calendar of a musical, Sixth Form studio production, Sixth Form play, Fourth Form play, Lower School play and House Drama festival, there are also many productions mounted entirely by pupils.

Activities. Creative activities are encouraged both in and out of school time, and the College has its own Art School and Gallery. Dance is a very popular activity with many pupils performing in regional and national productions.

Careers. The Head of Careers with a team of tutors advise pupils on careers. The College is a member of the Independent Schools Careers Organisation.

Scholarships. The following Scholarships are available:

11+ Entry: Academic, All-Rounder (Art, Dance, Drama, Music and Sport), Chess, and Choral.

13+ Entry: Academic, All-Rounder, Art & Photography, Chess, Choral, Dance, Drama, DT, Music, and Sport.

Sixth Form Entry: Academic, Sport and Expressive Arts (Art, Dance, Drama, Music).

For further details about scholarships, please contact the Admissions Office.

Fees per term (2018–2019). Weekly Boarding: £11,130 (Fourth Form) to £11,470 (Upper 6th). Full Boarding: £12,490 (Fourth Form EU) to £13,190 (Upper 6th Non-EU). Day: £5,600 (Lower Third) to £8,180 (Upper Sixth).

The Old Brightonians, the College's alumni network, has annual dinners and a number of flourishing sports clubs.

Preparatory School. The College has its own co-educational Nursery, Pre-Prep & Prep School. (*For details see entry in IAPS section.*)

Charitable status. Brighton College is a Registered Charity, number 307061.

Chair of Governors: The Lord Mogg, KCMG

Senior Management Team:

Head Master: Mr R J Cairns, MA, FRSA

Director of Finance & Deputy Headmaster: Mr P Westbrook, BA, FCA
Deputy Headmaster: Mr N J Fraser, MA
Deputy Headmistress: Miss L Hamblett, MA
Deputy Headmaster: Mr S Marshall-Taylor, BA
Deputy Headmaster, Head of Lower School and Executive Head of Prep Schools: Mr G R Owton, BA
Deputy Headmistress: Mrs J A Riley, MA
Deputy Headmaster: Mr M C Sloan, BA

Assistant Head (Sixth Form): Mr A T Patton, MA
Assistant Head (Middle School): Mr C Fowler, BA
Assistant Head (Co-Curriculum): Miss N J Collins, MA

Assistant Head (Director of Social Responsibility): Mr K A Grocott, MA
Director of Boarding: Mrs J Hamblett-Jahn, LLB
Director of Admissions/Registrar: Mr J Carr-Hill, MSc
Deputy Director of Admissions: Mrs A Withers
Chaplain: Revd R Easton, BA, MTheol

Bristol Grammar School

University Road, Bristol BS8 1SR

Tel:	0117 973 6006
Fax:	0117 946 7485
email:	headmaster@bgs.bristol.sch.uk
website:	www.bristolgrammarschool.co.uk
Twitter:	@bgsbristol
Facebook:	@bgsbristol

Motto: Ex Spinis Uvas

'The Grammar School in Bristowe' existed under a lay master in 1532 in which year, under a charter of Henry VIII, it was endowed with the estates of St Bartholomew's Hospital by the merchant and geographer Robert Thorne and others. The trust was placed in the care of the Corporation of Bristol and then the Trustees of the Bristol Municipal Charities. In September 2004 the School incorporated as a company limited by guarantee with registered charitable status and is now governed under Memorandum and Articles of Association approved by the Charity Commission in 2004.

Co-educational since 1980, Bristol Grammar School is a day school providing a wide-ranging and challenging education for c. 1,000 boys and girls aged between 11 and 18, while BGS Infants and Juniors, based on the same site, caters for those in the 4–11 age range.

Pupils learn in an atmosphere that motivates them to enjoy their education and as a result BGS has a deserved reputation as one of the leading academic schools in the South West. The School has a friendly and lively environment and pupils are encouraged to make the most of the wide-ranging opportunities available to them. When pupils join the School at 11+, they are based in the same building in their House form groups, which helps ease their transition to senior school, as well as providing an important opportunity for the year group to bond socially. In Years 8–11, each House group has its own base, although teaching is spread throughout the School's specialist facilities.

Close to the city centre and adjacent to the University, Bristol Grammar School is well placed to take advantage of the city's many amenities. It is also committed to a continuing programme of investment to ensure its own facilities continue to offer the best possible opportunities to its pupils.

The Houses. The School is divided into six Houses, each organised by a Head of House, with the assistance of a Deputy Head of House and House Form Tutors. Form Tutors will typically remain with pupils throughout their time in the Senior School from Years 7–11. Older pupils become leaders within their House, while social, theatrical, musical, sporting and other opportunities allow those from all year groups to work together in a friendly and cooperative atmosphere. As well as providing continuity of pastoral care and enhancing school/home links, the Houses operate as families within the School community, encouraging a real sense of belonging among pupils.

Curriculum. The School takes note of the National Curriculum but, in keeping with its academic ethos and focus on every learner being enabled to make the most of their individual ability, a far wider range of subjects and opportunities is offered. Setting is used in Maths, Science and some Modern and Classical languages to ensure optimal individual progress, but there is no streaming. In Year 7 all pupils follow a curriculum which includes English, Mathematics, Science, French, Spanish, History, Geography, Technology, Food & Nutrition, ICT, Latin, Philosophy, Religion and Ethics, Art, Textiles, Music, Drama, Dance, and Physical Education. In Year 8 the core curriculum is continued but pupils are offered a further choice of languages to include German and Russian. In Year 9 pupils personalise their curriculum making choices from all subjects studied thus far and other areas such as Classical Civilisation, Greek, Business Studies and Computer Science, and pupils then choose their GCSE options from this broad base. Most pupils take eleven GCSEs at the end of Year 11 in the core subjects of English, Mathematics, Biology, Chemistry, Physics, a humanities subject and a modern language, together with a selection of other subjects, chosen from a carefully balanced range of options.

BGS currently offers the IGCSE in Mathematics; the Sciences; Geography; History; French; German; Spanish; Business Studies; Food & Nutrition; and Philosophy, Religion & Ethics. The Sixth Form provides a the opportunity to study the International Baccalaureate (IB) Diploma Programme or A Levels. They have a wide range of options chosen from English (Language and Literature), Mathematics and Further Mathematics, the Sciences, Design & Technology, French, German, Russian, Spanish, Latin, Greek, Classical Civilisation, History, Global Politics (IB only) Geography, Economics, Business Studies, Computer Science, Psychology, Philosophy and Theology, Drama & Theatre Studies, Dance, Physical Education, Art, Music, and Music Technology. In addition, many pupils prepare for the Extended Project Qualification and Gold Duke of Edinburgh's Award. All pupils follow enrichment courses and attend a richly diverse programme of weekly lectures by visiting speakers; and many attend enrichment lessons to support university preparation for Russell Group and Oxbridge Universities, including for Medicine, Veterinary Science and Law. Two experienced Higher Education and Careers Advisors guide pupils to proceed on a pathway that is best suited to their ambitions, whether that be an apprenticeship, the world of work or to a wide range of universities in the UK and abroad, with the majority securing places at their first-choice universities.

There are frequent opportunities for parents to consult Form Tutors and Heads of Houses and regular meetings are held for parents to meet the teaching staff. The School also has three teachers to support pupils with SEN (including dyslexia and EAL).

Games. The games options – which vary for different age groups – include rugby, hockey, football, cross-country, cricket, athletics, swimming, tennis, netball and weight training. Facilities for orienteering, aerobics, climbing, dance, judo, fencing, badminton and squash are also available. There is a Pavilion and extensive playing fields at Failand, which includes an all-weather 3G pitch, two Astroturf hockey pitches and netball and tennis areas. Below the Sixth Form, all pupils participate in School games sessions; the full range of sports is available to Sixth-form pupils. Major sports tours are run on a three-year cycle: recent destinations have been New Zealand, South America and, Sri Lanka and Malaysia.

Activities and Societies. Pupils take part in a wide-ranging programme of activities (this forms part of the compulsory curriculum for some year groups) and there are many clubs and societies at lunchtimes and after school, including Astronomy Club, Model United Nations (MUN), Beekeeping, and Architecture Club. There are flourishing choirs and orchestras; tuition can also be arranged on a large number of instruments. Drama productions are regularly staged by different age levels and by the Houses. Regular excursions are made abroad, as well as cultural visits. Pupils may join The Duke of Edinburgh's Award scheme in Year 10 and there is an active Community Service Unit.

Admission. Entry to the School is normally in September at age 11+ following a satisfactory performance in the entrance examination held in the previous spring and a creditable school report or reference. All Year 7 applicants are also invited in to meet with a member of staff to discuss their school work, interests and hobbies. An additional 10–15 places become available each year at age 13+, with a further 30–40 places at 16+. Pupils may also be accepted into the School during the year, subject to the availability of places.

Applications should be made to the Admissions Office at the School. Prospective entrants and their families are always welcome to visit; please see the website for information about open days, tours and taster days.

Bursaries. The School's Assisted Places Scheme is able to offer substantial financial assistance towards the fees of able pupils whose parents have limited means. The scheme is kept under regular review by the Governors who constantly seek to extend it.

Scholarships. Scholarships are available for entry at 11+, 13+ and 16+ and are awarded for academic ability; all applicants who take the entrance assessments in January are automatically considered for these, there is no separate assessment. Scholarships are also available at 11+ and 13+ for Sports and Creative & Performing Arts.

The School runs a Scholars' Programme designed to meet the educational needs of its most gifted pupils. This programme offers extended individual learning opportunities, group activities and mentoring in and out of School by the Director of Scholars. At 16+ pupils may apply to become Subject Scholars and work more closely with Heads of Subject.

Fees per term (2018–2019). Senior School £4,870. Juniors: Years 3–6 £3,320. Infants: Years 1 & 2 £3,085, Reception £2,825. Fees include the cost of most textbooks and stationery and lunch for Reception to Year 11 pupils.

BGS Infants and Juniors. The Junior School extended its provision to include infants, with its first Reception class in September 2010. The School admits children from 4–11 and is housed in its own buildings on the same site as the Senior School. (*For further details see entry in IAPS section.*)

Old Bristolians Society. Close contact is maintained with former pupils through the Old Bristolians Society whose Honorary Secretary can be contacted at the School.

Charitable status. Bristol Grammar School is a Registered Charity, number 1104425. It has existed since 1532 to provide an education for Bristol children.

Governors:
Mrs A J Arlidge, BA
A Barr, LLB
Professor N Canagarajah, BA Hons Cantab, PhD Cantab
Ms M Crayton, BA, MCIM
Mrs C Gil, BSc, ACA
Dr J D Knox, BSc, PhD
P Meehan, BEd Hons, FPFS
Dr J O'Gallagher, MBChB, MRCP, FRCPCH, FHEA
D Pester, BA Hons
N Pickersgill, BSc, FCA
Ms K Redshaw, BA Hons Oxon
Prof J Selwyn, BA Hons, MSc Econ, PhD
D Shelton, FCIM
J Sisman, BSc Hons, MRICS
Dr D Thompson, MBChB, MRCGP Dist
J Vafadari

R Vaitilingam, BA Hons Oxon, MBE (*Chairman*)
M Wilson, BSc Hons, MRICS

Senior Leadership Team:

Headmaster: J M Barot, MA, MSc

Headmaster, BGS Infants and Juniors: P R Huckle, BA, MEd
Deputy Head: P R Roberts, BSc, MSc
Deputy Head: M J Bennett, BSc
Deputy Head: Miss F A Ripley, BSc
Deputy Head: D J Stone, BSc
Bursar: G Mitchell, BA

Assistant Head: G S Clark, BSc
Assistant Head: P Z Jakobek, BEd
Assistant Head: L Goodman, BA
Assistant Head: B Schober, BSc, MA
Assistant Head: Dr M G Ransome, BA, PhD
Assistant Head: J S Harford, BSc
Assistant Head: Mrs K H Jones, BSc
Assistant Head: O L Chambers, BSc
Assistant Head: A N Gunawardana, BA

* *Head of Department*

Art:
Mrs B D Barnacle, BA
Mrs S M Cooper, BA
Miss D M Davies, BA
P Z Jakobek, BEd
*E Hume-Smith, BA
Mrs J H Troup, BA

Biology:
Miss E Barr, BSc
M J Bennett, BSc
A P Bolton, BA
Mrs R Cullen, BSc
Ms N A Diamond, BSc
N S Fuller, BSc, MSc, CBiol, MIBiol
*A J Goodland, BSc
J S Harford, BSc (*Director of Sixth Form*)
B Schober, MA, BSc
Ms K Surry, MA

Careers:
Mrs A L Smith, BA
D C Ruck

Chemistry:
T P Carpenter, BSc
Mrs A J Hutchings, BSc (*Head of SPD*)
Dr J B Macro BA, MA
A J Nalty, MSc
Miss S L Ricketts, MSci
Dr H F Rowlands, BSc, PhD
D J Stone, BSc
*Dr J C Stone, BSc, PhD
C Watson, BSc

Classics:
Miss E M Cox, BA
*A J Keen, BA
G C King, MA, BA
A Moraca, MA
Mrs L M Ray, BA
D J Watkins, BA

Computer Science:
Mrs A L Finney, BA
R S Jones, BSc
*I Jones, BSc
Mrs N Ramanadi, MA

Dance:
Miss L E Sampson, BA
*Mrs K M White, BA

Design & Technology:
M W Hilliard, BSc (*Head of House*)
Ms L-J Knights, BA
Mrs S Muirhead, BSc
P Thomas, BA
*P M Whitehouse, BSc

Drama:
K Bradshaw-Smith, BA
L G McKenzie, BA
*Mrs J A Walker, BA

Economics/Business Studies:
*Mrs S Biggin, BA
N Morris, MA
D P Wiltshire, BA

English:
T A Biddle, BA, MA
D L Briggs, BA
*Miss R Lunt, BA
D S Mair, BA
Ms S E Robinson, BA
Miss S E Thomas, MA
Mrs J Whitehead, BAMs
Mrs E M Yemenakis, BA

EPQ:
*Mrs R Atkins, BSc

Food & Nutrition:
*Mrs L D Bolton, Cert Ed

Geography:
Mrs R L Atkins, BSc
*Miss K J Brimming, BSc
Dr A J Dimberline, BSc, PhD
L Goodman, BA
A J Short, BSc (*Head of House*)

Miss A E Strutt, BSc
Miss T Yates, BA

History:
Ms S J Bassett, BA
Mrs E D Clare, BA
O R T Edwards, BA (*Head of House*)
*R M Hambly, BA, MA
Mrs P Lobo, BA
Dr R A Massey, BA, PhD (*Director of Scholars and Academic Challenge*)

Learning Support:
Mrs J Benn, BA
Mrs A S Denny, MA
*Dr M G Ransome, BA, PhD

Mathematics:
J F Carr, BSc
Mrs J L Carter, BCom Grad Dip TCHG
O L Chambers, BSc
G S Clark, BSc
B S Fellows, MEng
Mrs L M Hancock, BSc
G R Iwi, MSc
Mrs K H Jones, BSc
Miss H Klimach, MSc
S M Mitchell, BSc
Miss A Niamir, BSc (*Head of House*)
Miss C O'Gallagher
M Pearson, MEng
*Miss S M Poole, BSc
P R Roberts, BSc, MSc
A D Thackray, BSc

Modern Languages:
*Ms E Corrigan, BA (*Head of French*)
*R J Hawkins, BA (*Head of Russian*)
Miss C M Höelzer, MA
Miss L Hughes, BA
Mrs C Kent, BA
*Mrs A C Macro, BA (*Head of Spanish*)
Miss N Parratt, BA
Mrs A A Pestell, BA
Dr M G Ransome, BA, PhD

PA to Headmaster: Miss C Davies
Admissions and Marketing Manager: Mrs H Matthews

Miss E J Vance, BA, MA
*J Wall, BA (*Head of German*)
Miss M C Whatmough, Hons

Music:
C Morris, BA
*D A Franks, BA, MMus (*Director of Music*)
*Mrs E Rees, BA, MA (*Head of Academic Music*)
J W Rees, BA, MA

Outdoor Education:
*Mrs K Murphy, BSc

PE/Games:
K R Blackburn, BSc
J M Corsi, BSc
Mrs V L Dixon, BEd
P Z Jakobek, BEd
Mrs R E John, BA
*T M Lacey, BSc (*Head of PE and Games*)
Miss F A Ripley, BSc
Miss L E Sampson, MSc, LABAN
B Scott, BEd (*Head of House*)
*R Williams, BSc (*Director of Sport*)
Miss R J Wintle, Hons

Physics:
C R Bramley, MChem
S E Carruthers, BSc
Miss L Glenn, BEng (*Head of House*)
*S T Harper, BSc
R F Jervis, MEng
T Murray, BSc

Psychology:
*Mrs L Dilley, BSc
Miss L Mcleod, BSc
Miss L Self, BSc

Philosophy, Religion and Ethics:
A N Gunawardana, BA
*R M Smith, BA
C P Wadey, MA
J H Williams, BA

Bromley High School
GDST

Blackbrook Lane, Bickley, Bromley, Kent BR1 2TW
Tel: 020 8781 7000
email: bhs@bro.gdst.net
website: www.bromleyhigh.gdst.net
Twitter: @bromleyhs
Facebook: @bromleyhighschoolGDST

Bromley High School is a selective school offering an exceptional education to girls aged 4–18 years. The school is part of the GDST (Girls' Day School Trust), the leading network of independent girls' schools in the UK. For further information about the Trust visit www.gdst.net.

Founded in 1883, Bromley High School was originally situated in the centre of Bromley. In 1981 it moved to Bickley to occupy modern purpose-built buildings set in 24 acres of leafy parkland. Sharing the same site, both Senior and Junior departments benefit from first-rate facilities.

Bromley High School provides a beautiful and buzzy environment where bright girls will flourish. In the classroom, each girl's intellectual potential is challenged and developed by inspirational teachers whose concern for your daughter ranges infinitely beyond her performance in examinations; teachers who have a capacity to develop a love of learning, a spirit of enquiry and an independence of mind. Girls learn to collaborate and to compete; to be creative and intellectually curious and their learning is underpinned by the school's ethos of achievement for all and by the subject passion, enthusiasm and expertise of their teachers.

Results are consistently superb. In 2018, 25% of new GCSE Grades were 9s with 45% of all GCSEs A* (9/8). The school is most proud of its consistently impressive Value Added results at GCSE and A Level which demonstrate the care taken to bring out the best in every girl. In the 2016 ISI Inspection Report, Learning and Achievement were graded as Exceptional.

However, outstanding success at Bromley High School is not purely academic. Bromley High girls are resilient and well-rounded young women participating with enthusiasm and commitment in Music, Drama, Sport, Duke of Edinburgh's Award and an overabundant range of activities – and where they have interest or talent or enthusiasm, it is nurtured so that they learn to excel. Sport is exceptional with recent leavers gaining sports scholarships to Princeton and Yale.

Pastoral care is thoughtful and developmental, actively encouraging girls to develop key attributes: Confidence, Courage, Composure, and Commitment. Every house takes on the responsibility of supporting its own charity and the school has a highly valued tradition of volunteering and charitable activity.

Bromley High School girls are confident, cheerful, considerate and enthusiastic about the myriad of opportunities their school has to offer.

Pupil Numbers. Senior School (ages 11–18): 580 (including the Sixth Form). Junior School (ages 4–11): 312.

The Junior School. Our two-form entry Junior School provides a stimulating and happy environment in which our pupils are encouraged to strive for excellence in all they do and to derive satisfaction from their achievements both great and small. From the earliest years we offer a broad curriculum which encourages, challenges and excites the young mind. Our aim is to foster a love of learning, develop independent thinking and promote a spirit of enquiry that leads to a depth of understanding. In our approach to teaching and learning we blend the traditional with progressive insights into learning styles and the particular needs of young girls as learners in a modern world. We teach the full range of the National Curriculum, including French, Spanish, German and also Latin and accord sports and the creative arts a significant place in the timetable, whilst ensuring that the foundations of the core subjects are well established. Class lessons are differentiated and we offer extension and support where appropriate and specialist teaching, sometimes from Senior School staff, in a number of subjects.

Bromley High believes in preparing girls for the challenges beyond school and values the importance of a holistic approach. The school provides many varied opportunities within a vibrant co-curricular programme including sporting, musical, dramatic and other creative activities. We make the most of our beautiful school grounds to provide opportunities for outdoor learning, in which our Forest School is a vital part.

Forest School is a planned programme that takes place in a woodland environment with the aim of developing opportunities for the learner to encounter the beauty, joy, awe and wonder of the natural environment. The approach is 'hands on' and seeks to promote the holistic development of the unique child, including physical, spatial, linguistic, emotional and spiritual aspects. Self-confidence and independence are increased through freedom, time and space to learn. A safe and secure environment allows the girls to extend their learning beyond their comfort zone; to challenge their existing boundaries and ideas and to tackle investigations and tasks which in the classroom may not be possible. Collaboration and cooperation between the learners, their peers and the forest school leader is at the core of the Forest School programme. Social skills develop through risk-taking and an understanding of the consequences of your own actions, whilst self-awareness, self-regulation and empathy for others are also developed. Forest School enables children to be active participants in their own education and development.

In the delivery of our curriculum we are well served by outstanding facilities which, in addition to comprehensively equipped classrooms, include a music wing, a library, ICT suite, a science room, and an art and technology room, a sensory garden and outdoor 'classrooms'. We share many other facilities with the Senior School including a swimming pool, gymnasium, sports hall, tennis courts and an all-weather pitch. Our pupils have their lunch in the main school dining room where a wide variety of hot dishes or sandwiches are served.

The Senior School. Bromley High combines a tradition of scholarship with an innovative curriculum and expansive co-curricular provision. In the classroom, an emphasis on independent learning and growth mindset is designed to inculcate a spirit of enquiry, an independence of mind and a love of learning. Girls participate with enthusiasm and commitment in Music, Drama, Sport and an overabundant range of activities – and where they have interest or talent or enthusiasm, it is nurtured so that they learn to excel. In 2018 the school was awarded the EBA (Education Business Awards) for Outstanding Progress in an Independent School and the award for Best STEM (Science, Technology, Engineering and Mathematics) Provision in the UK.

Consistent investment has developed new science facilities, library, sixth form centre, drama studio, and specialist teaching rooms for the creative arts enabling departments to have their own dedicated spaces for teaching and extracurricular activities. Visual and creative arts are highly valued with Photography, Drama and Dance offered to A level and students regularly progressing to study at Central St Martin's and other prestigious Arts Foundation courses and to Ballet Schools.

Academic. Languages, both ancient and modern, are a particular strength with French, German and Spanish offered from Year 7. Latin and Classics are both popular A Level choices, with Ancient Greek offered as an optional extra GCSE. As a girls' school, Bromley High lays great emphasis on STEM subjects – Science, Technology, Engineering and Mathematics. Teaching rooms are equipped with Smart Boards and all have Wi-Fi and digital projector facilities which allow pupils to use iPads, Chrome Books, or their own mobile computer devices. Teachers are encouraged to enrich the curriculum and teach lively, challenging lessons. Myriad trips and activities, including music tours abroad from Year 7, and Lower School trips to Florence, Venice and Iceland. The modern foreign languages department has links with France, Germany and Spain and arranges exchanges, visits and work experience placements.

Girls study 10 GCSE subjects including Mathematics, Biology, Chemistry, Physics, English and English Literature and a Modern Language. Three further options are chosen from French, Spanish and German, Latin and Classical Civilisation; Computer Science, Music, Art, Photography, Drama, Dance, Design Technology, Economics, Geography, History, Physical Education.

Sport. Sports facilities on the school's 25-acre site are superb including a large, well-equipped Sports Hall, a new fitness suite, a gymnasium, a 400-metre athletics track, two grass hockey pitches, a fine indoor heated swimming pool, and floodlit Astroturf pitches and courts. Sport is both integral to the curriculum and an important part of the extracurricular life of the school. The school is proud of its tradition of producing national level athletes and swimmers and the number of girls who play county level hockey, netball, swimming, tennis and athletics. In 2018, the U16 Hockey Team reached the U16 National Indoor Hockey Finals as East of England Champions.

Sixth Form. The Sixth Form Centre provides a bright, modern setting for traditional scholarship. Students select from a broad range of A levels supplemented by Extended Project, AS Thinking Skills and electives such as Young Enterprise, Magazine Editing, Fashion, etc. Careers education, supported by the extensive GDST network of more than 70,000 alumnae. Sixth Formers benefit from GDST-wide initiatives, such as leadership and Oxbridge conferences and residential course on topics such as Engineering and Environmental Sustainability.

Extracurricular Activities. A great emphasis is put on an enthusiastic involvement in music, art, sport and drama. The annual Dance production is a significant event in the school calendar and in recent years the school has staged concerts in major London venues such as the Royal Albert Hall, Southwark Cathedral and The Swiss Church.

Girls contribute to local, national and international charities and to community service. Almost all girls participate in The Duke of Edinburgh's Award scheme in Y10 with some continuing to completion of Gold Award in Sixth Form. The Eco Society promotes a keen interest in environmental issues. There are regular exchanges to France, Germany and Spain as well as Geography and Biology field trips as far as Iceland. Annual World Challenge expeditions have recently visited Madagascar, Mongolia and Costa Rica. The Year 6 and 7 Music Tours have recently visited Paris, Brussels, Normandy and Bruges with the Senior Music Tour performing in Berlin, Prague, New York and Los Angeles. It is the only all-girls senior school in the world to have all Steinway status and musicians benefit from a Musician-in-Residence.

Fees per term (2018–2019). Senior School £5,697, Junior School £4,594.

Fees cover tuition, stationery, textbooks and scientific and games materials as well as entry fees for GCSE and GCE Advanced Level examinations. Extra tuition in Music and Speech and Drama is available at recognised rates.

Bursaries. Bursaries are means-tested and provide, for successful applicants, assistance with fees to enable bright girls to benefit from a GDST education. For those receiving full remission of fees, the award may include uniform and trips allowances.

Scholarships. There are Academic, Art, Music and Sport scholarships for the most successful candidates in the assessments at 11+ and for entry into the Sixth Form.

Admission and Entrance Examination. Admission into the school is at 4+ (Reception) and 7+ (Year 3) by assessment and testing. Pupils from the Junior School progress automatically to the Senior School but external applicants, or those wishing to be considered for scholarship or bursary

are assessed at 11+. The examination tests verbal and non-verbal skills, as well as creative writing. Entry to the Sixth Form is dependent on interview and school reference, including predicted grades and is contingent on results at GCSE.

Charitable status. Bromley High School is part of The Girls' Day School Trust, which is a Registered Charity, number 306983.

Chairman of the Local Governors: Mrs P Emburey, BA, ACA

Headmistress: **Angela Drew**, BA Hons, MBA Dunelm

Deputy Head (Pastoral): Mrs H Elkins, BA King's College London

Deputy Head (Academic): Dr S Lindfield, BSc Oxon, PhD Liverpool

Assistant Head (Head of Sixth Form): Mrs C Bird, BA Manchester

Assistant Head (Organisation): Mr P Isted, BA Bristol

Director of Finance & Operations: Mr J Crisp, FCIMA

Head of Junior School: Mrs C Dickerson, BA Anglia

Deputy Head of Junior School: Mrs K Powell, BEd Primary Ed Greenwich

Admissions Registrar: Mrs L Clarke

Director of Marketing and Communications: Maria Dark, BA Oxon

Bromsgrove School

Worcester Road, Bromsgrove, Worcestershire B61 7DU

Tel: 01527 579679
email: admissions@bromsgrove-school.co.uk
website: www.bromsgrove-school.co.uk
Twitter: @bromsschool
Facebook: @bromsgroveschool

Motto: *Deo Regi Vicino*

The date of the School's Foundation is unknown but it was reorganised by Edward VI in 1553 and was granted a Royal Charter 6 years later. It was refounded in 1693 by Sir Thomas Cookes, Bt, at the same time as Worcester College, Oxford (formerly Gloucester Hall). The link between School and College has been maintained ever since.

Location. This co-educational boarding and day school is situated some 13 miles north of the Cathedral City of Worcester and an equal distance south of Birmingham. Birmingham International Airport and Station are a 20-minute drive by motorway. The M5, M6, M42 and M40 motorways provide easy access to the School.

The School stands in 100 acres of grounds on the south side and within walking distance of the market town of Bromsgrove.

Facilities. The School's impressive ongoing building and development programme includes a new Performing Arts complex which was formally opened in November 2017. Two 300-seat theatres have been created, linked by an avenue which connects the Preparatory and Senior Schools.

Historic Routh Hall on the Senior campus has been transformed into a concert hall, tuned exclusively for musical performances and making use of its exceptional acoustic qualities. Adjacent, a new Music School houses a suite of specialist classrooms, recording studios and 12 instrumental practice rooms, as well as a reception foyer and box office.

The Performing Arts Avenue leads to an equivalent home for Drama, built where Cobham Hall once stood in the Preparatory School. Flexible seating and a hydraulic thrust stage allow for a wide range of dramatic and dance performances. From intimate plays to large-scale productions, the new facility will provide fully-equipped technical galleries and safe access to all lighting and flying facilities, encouraging students into technical aspects of theatre as well as performance. The facility boasts a 90-seat performance studio, with large scenic workshops, props stores and modern dressing rooms available for both lessons and productions.

A major sports complex with an arena which holds eight badminton courts, dance studios, gym, teaching rooms and hospitality suite/sports viewing room enhances the existing all-weather, floodlit sports facilities. The School has outstanding academic facilities including an award-winning Art, Design and Technology building, a twenty-classroom Humanities building and eighteen recently built or refurbished Science laboratories.

Boarding. Bromsgrove Senior School's boarding community is made up of boarders from over 50 nationalities accommodated between six Houses, one of which is in the town. The boarding environment is happy, stable, disciplined and nurturing. Pupils are very loyal to their House and competitions between day and boarding Houses including sport, music and debating are keenly contested.

The stability and continuity that enable boarders to thrive are provided by resident houseparents (all academic members of staff) and their families, assistant houseparents, housemothers and a team of house-based tutors. A new dining hall complete with state-of-the-art kitchens was opened in summer 2015 and all meals are taken centrally in the School, with the exception of the evening meal at the off-campus Sixth Form boarding house, Housman Hall. Boarding facilities have been enhanced by one completely new girls' boarding house and total refurbishment of the existing boys' and girls' houses to a very high standard. New wings have been built at Housman Hall and the existing building, formerly home of OB and poet A E Housman, has been sympathetically refurbished.

Numbers. There are over 950 pupils in the Senior School, of whom 545 are boys. The Preparatory, Pre-Preparatory and Pre-School has a further 703 pupils aged 3 to 13. (*See also Preparatory & Pre-Preparatory School entry in IAPS section.*)

Curriculum. In the Preparatory School a broadly based curriculum is followed. In addition to the usual academic subjects, time is given to Art, Music, ICT, Drama, Design Technology and to a full programme of Physical Education. Languages on offer include French, German, Spanish and Latin.

As pupils move up the School, GCSE choices are made for the start of Year 9. Eleven subjects is the norm at GCSE, with a broad core including the three separate sciences, a modern language and three further three optional subjects. The minimum qualification for automatic entry into the Sixth Form is a six point (B grade) average at GCSE with areas of strength also evident. Pupils may study the IB Diploma or take the A Level route whilst BTECs are also available in Sports Science and Business Studies. Flexibility in timetabling aims to ensure that all pupils' subject choices are catered for whatever the combination. Many A Level subjects are available including, Art, Biology, Business, Chemistry, Classics, Design and Technology, Drama and Theatre Studies, Design, Economics, Engineering, English, French, Geography, German, Latin, Mathematics and Further Mathematics, Music, Physical Education, Physics, Politics, Religious Studies, Spanish and Textiles. Under the IB umbrella, Italian, Environmental Systems, Mandarin, Global Politics and Psychology are also on offer. With two-

thirds of students achieving A*/A at both GCSE and A Level and an IB average of 39 points, virtually all our pupils proceed to degree courses usually at Russell Group universities. The most popular university destinations in recent years have been University and King's Colleges in London followed by Exeter, Bath and Bristol.

Performing Arts. The performing arts are well supported at Bromsgrove School and rightly thrive. The School boasts a new Performing Arts Centre which includes a state-of-the-art concert hall, full sized theatre, a large drama studio and a suite of new music classrooms and practice areas.

Music and Drama flourish both within and outside the formal curriculum. House Music Competitions, Jazz Gigs and a variety of informal concerts happen throughout the year. There is plenty of scope for involvement in the School Orchestra and String, Wind and Brass Ensembles, Chamber Groups, Jazz Bands, a 50-strong Chapel Choir and large Choral Society. The timetable is sufficiently flexible to allow special arrangements to be made for outstanding musicians. The Year 3 String Scheme and Year 5 Wind and Brass Scheme are opportunities for these pupils to experience learning and playing an instrument for a year. Each year, the Chamber Choir takes the opportunity to sing in some spectacular cathedrals and chapels, including singing Evensong at Worcester College Oxford, Hereford Cathedral and St Paul's Cathedral. Our recent musical productions of Hair Spray and Sweeney Todd are also highlights. School musicians take part in festivals, which last year included the Upton Jazz Festival and Cheltenham Festival of Arts and there is a strong Choral Society which performs in venues including Birmingham Town Hall.

Discrete Drama forms part of the curriculum for every student from Year 5 until Year 9 when the option is available for students to take the subject to GCSE level. Within the Sixth Form, the school offers A Level Theatre Studies. Senior, Fourth Form and Prep School productions, alongside a number of House Drama Competitions at all levels, form the main spine of co-curricular Drama at Bromsgrove which has a reputation for very high production standards. This has been greatly enhanced by the recent opening of a state-of-the-art theatre in the School. A high level of training for aspiring theatre technicians and designers, ensures a vibrant dramatic life within the School for both performers and those wishing to work backstage.

Drama Scholarships are awarded to students joining at 13+ and 16+ whilst Music Scholarships are available at 11+, 13+ and 16+.

Careers. The School employs a fully qualified, full-time Careers Advisor and a comprehensive careers counselling programme is available to pupils of all ages.

Co-currricular activities. A wide range of sports and activities is offered, giving opportunities to participate at a competitive level in Rugby, Hockey, Netball, Athletics, Badminton, Basketball, Clay Pigeon Shooting, Cricket, Cross Country, Debating, Fencing, Golf, Horse Riding, Rounders, Soccer, Squash, Swimming, Table Tennis, Tennis and Young Enterprise.

The Saturday timetable, in conjunction with the weekday programme, allows the activities programme more flexibility to offer both recreational and academic choices. Pupils may select from a diverse range of recreational activities including Academic extension and support, Revision for GCSE, A Levels, IB, SATs and Oxbridge, Biology, Chemistry and Physics Olympiad, Aerobics, Art, Badminton, Board Game Design, Body Balance, Chess, Coding, Cookery, Corps of Drums, Design Technology, Drama, EPP (Economics, Politics and Philosophy), Engineering, Forest Schools, Golf driving range, Handicrafts, History Society, Horse Riding, ICT, Literary Society, MedVet Society, Military skills, Music, Outdoor pursuits (including climbing, high ropes, kayaking, orienteering, raft building, sailing), Mahjong, Park Run, Photography, Plaster Modelling, School Magazine, Table tennis, Website design, Weight training and Ultimate Frisbee. There are opportunities to gain qualifications in Life saving, First Aid, LAMDA, Sports/Dance Leader Awards and Martial Arts. In addition to the activities programme, Year 9 pupils participate in Bromsgrove Badge, comprising a selection of activities that help to prepare them for the Bronze Duke of Edinburgh's Award and culminating in a four-day camp at the end of the year. There is a thriving Combined Cadet Force (Army and RAF), and many pupils are involved in The Duke of Edinburgh's Award scheme. The School's Bromsgrove Service programme caters for large numbers of pupils and provides a wide range of activities; examples include working in local schools and charity shops, visiting residential homes, acting as Learning Mentors and Student Listeners, helping in animal sanctuaries, supporting conservation projects and fundraising for charities.

Admission. Entrance at 13 is by Bromsgrove School Entrance Examinations. Boys and Girls may be admitted to the Preparatory School at any age from 7 to 12 inclusive. 11+ Entrance Tests take place in November and mid-January for entry into other years. Places are available in the Sixth Form for boys and girls who have had their GCSE education elsewhere.

Scholarships and Bursaries. Awards are made on the results of open examinations held at the School in January. A significant number of scholarships, means-tested bursaries and Foundation bursaries for pupils of academic, artistic, sporting and all-round ability are awarded at 11+, 13+ and 16+. A number of Music scholarships and exhibitions are awarded each year at ages 11, 13 and 16, offering free tuition on up to two instruments. Means-tested bursaries may be used to supplement any scholarship. Full details are available from the Admissions Department.

Fees per term (2018–2019). Senior School (age 13+): £12,430 full boarding, £8,250 weekly boarding, £5,555 day inc lunch. Preparatory School (age 7–13): £8,080–£9,965 full boarding, £5,895–£7,130 weekly boarding, £3,880–£5,035 day inc lunch. Pre-Preparatory (age 4–7): £2,660–£2,930 day. Pre-School (age 3–4): £2,950 full-time.

Charitable status. Bromsgrove School is a Registered Charity, number 1098740. It exists to provide education for boys and girls.

Patron: A Denham-Cookes

President: T M Horton, BA

A Vice-President: J A Hall, FCA
A Vice-President: N J Birch, MIMechE
A Vice-President: Prof K B Haley, BSc, PhD, FIMA, CMath, FIEE, CEng
A Vice-President: V S Anthony, BSc, Hon DEd, Hon FCP, FRSA

Governing Body:
P West (*Chairman*)

C Barnett	M Luckman
R Brookes	J W Roden
A Cleary	I Stringer
C Cameron	G Strong
R D Brookes, FRICS	Dr N Venning, BSc, PhD,
R Lane, MA	MBA
J Loynton	D Walters, MA, FCA
Dr C Lidbury	D Waltier

Company Secretary: J Sommerville, MA

Headmaster: P Clague, BA, MBA

Bursar: Mrs L Brookes, ACMA
Assistant Head: Miss R M Scannell, BA, PGCE

Deputy Head (*Academic*): P S Ruben, BSc, MPhil, MBA
Deputy Head (*Co-Curricular*): P S T Mullan, BA, PGCE
Deputy Head (*Pastoral*): A McClure, BA, PGCE
Director of Staffing (*Whole School*): S Challoner, BSc, PGCE
Senior Mistress: Dr M R Werrett, GRSC, PhD, PGCE
School Medical Officer: Dr D Law, MA, MBChB Oxon, MRCGP, DRCOG, DFFP

Staff:
* *Head of Department*
† *Houseparent*

S J Kingston, BEd (*Examinations Officer*)
Mrs C E Turner, BA, PGCE
C A Dowling MA Cantab, PGCE (*Academic Database Coordinator*)
Mrs J A Holden, MA Oxon, PGCE
Mrs S Shinn, BSc, PGCE (*Timetabler*)
Dr A R Johns, BSc, PhD, PGCE (*Head of Sixth Form – Pupil Progress*)
Ms S J Cronin, BA, DMS, PGCE (*Business Studies)
Mrs F K Bateman, BSc, PGCE (*Head of Lower Sixth Form*; *Head of Sixth Form Enrichment Curriculum*)
Mrs S E Ascough, BSc, PGCE (*President of the Common Room*; *i/c Activities*; *Head of Fifth Form*)
Miss K E Tansley, BA, MA, PGCE
†D G Wilkins, BA, SCITT
M A C Beet, MA Cantab, PGCE (*Modern Languages; *i/c Oxbridge*)
Miss F E Diver, BA, PGCE (*Head of Lower Fourth Form*)
Miss Z L Leech, BA (*Senior Mistress*; *PSHE; *UCAS)
N C J Riley, BSc, PGCE (*Mathematics)
Mrs E L E Buckingham, BA (**Girls' PE & Games*)
Miss S A Franks, BSc, PGCE
Miss M M Smith, BA, PGCE (*Spanish)
Mrs T L Helmore, BA, PGCE
O A Matthews, BEng, PGCE (**Design and Technology*)
Dr M Thompson, BSc, PhD, MInstP, PGCE (*IB Coordinator*)
Revd P Hedworth, BEd, BA (*Chaplain*)
Dr M K Ruben, BA, PhD, PGCE (**Gifted and Talented*)
Miss S J McWilliams, BA, PGCE
Miss S Morgans, BA, PGCE, Dip ND (*Art)
G N Delahunty, BA, PGCE (*Politics)
Ms E L Densem, BA, PGCE
†H Bell, MA, PGCE
Mrs S James, BSc, PGCE
Miss J Zafar, BA, PGCE (*History)
S Broadbent, BA, QTS
D Tamplin, BSc, PGCE
Mrs M Parkinson, BA, PGCE
†Mrs T Tweddle, BSc, CertEd FE (*Senior Boarding Houseparent*)
Mrs K Hands, BA, PGCE (**Religious Studies*)
†D Fallows (*Director of Cricket*)
Ms G Tyrrell, BA, PGCE
D Williams, BA, PGCE
A Carrington-Windo (*Director of Rugby*)
Miss L Davenport, BSc, PGCE
†S Noble, BSc, PGCE
Miss A Baker, BSc, PGCE NQT
J Baldrey, BA, PGCE
Mrs L Newton, BEng, PGCE (*i/c DofE Silver*)
Miss E Harper, BA, PGCE
A Helmore, BA, MA, PGCE
J Holdsworth, BSC, PGCE
Miss E Johnston, BSc, PGCE (*Upper Fourth)
Miss J Lesniak, BA, PGCE
S Matthews, BA, PGCE (*Senior Master*)
Mrs D Sutherland, BA, HDipMaths, QTS
Mrs J Holdsworth, BA, PGCE

J McKelvey, BA, PGCE (*Director of Music*)
†Mrs K Hannah, BA, PGCE
†T Clinton, BSc
Mrs J Boonnak, BA, MA, PGCE (**International Education*)
L Mullan, BSc, PGCE (**Boys' PE*)
Mrs A Buckley, MA, PGCE
Miss L Hunter, BA, PGCE
†M Giles, BSc, PGCE
Miss S Brain, BSc, PGCE
Mrs G Bruce, BA, PGCE
Miss R Green, BSc, PGCE (*Director of GCSE*)
Ms G Hanson, BA, PGCE
S Higgins, BEd
Miss N Langford, BA, GTTP
A Laskowski, BSc, MSc, PGCE
Miss F McCanlis, BMus, PGCE
H Pothecary, BSc, PGCE
†Dr R Whitbread, MA, PhD (*i/c Extended Project Qualification*)
Mrs G Wright, BSc, PGCE (**Biology*)
†Mrs V Adams, BA,MA, PGCE
D Atkinson, BSc, MSc, PGCE
Miss C Berment, BA, PGCE (**French*)
Mrs A Eaton, MA, GTP
†G Evans, BSc, PGCE
T Hinde, BA, MA
Ms F Jung, MA, PGCE
A Kelly, BSc, MDip Ed
Ms A Linehan, BSC, MEd, PG Dip Ed
Mrs N Reid, BA, PGCE
Dr D Rimmer, PhD, MA
Dr R Short, MChem, PhD, PGCE
Miss C Wadley, BA
Miss P Woolley, MChem, PGCE
Mrs J Bradford, BA (**Drama*)
O Burton, BA, PGCE
P Dinnen, MA (**English*)
R Doak, BA, PGCE (**Geography*)
M Egan, BA, PGCE (**Economics*)
MIss L Honey, BSc
S Kettle, BSc, PGCE (**Science, *Physics*)
Miss J Partridge, MA, PGCE
T Norton, BA (**Performing Arts*)
R Vernon, BA, GTP
A Gooderham (*Director of Hockey*)
S Coleman, BSc, PGCE
D Corns, MPhil (**Classics*)
Dr A Davies, PhD, PGCE
Miss E Hill, BSc, PGCE
T Holdsworth, BSc, PGCE
Ms H Popescu, MA
A Summerfield, MSc
G Tasker, BSc, PGCE
R Unterhalter, BA, PGCE
B Vice, MChem (**Chemistry*)
Mrs A Webb, BA, PGCE
Ms S Williams, BA, PGCE
Miss G Aldridge, BA, MA, PGCE
O Astley, BA, MA, PGCE
Miss G Aust, BA, PGCE
MIss S Burt, BSc, PGCE
T Couliou, BA, MA, PGCE
J Huckle, BA, PGCE
Dr M Jewkes, BA, MA, PhD
I Jones, BSc, MSc, PGCE
Dr D West, BSc, PhD, MA, PGCE (**Business*)
MIss E Williams
J Wingfield, BA, PGCE (*Director of A Level*)

Houses and Houseparents:
Boarding:
Elmshurst (*Boys*): D Fallows
Housman Hall (*Sixth Form*): S Noble
Mary Windsor (*Girls*): Mrs T Tweddle
Oakley (*Girls*): Mrs V Adams
Webber (*Sixth Form*): Mrs J Courtney
Wendron-Gordon (*Boys*): D Wilkins

Day:
Hazeldene (*Girls*): Dr R Whitbread
Lupton (*Boys*): G Evans
Lyttelton (*Boys*): M Giles
School (*Boys*): T Clinton
Thomas Cookes (*Girls*): Mrs K Hannah
Walters (*Boys*): H Bell

Music Staff:
J McKelvey, BA, PGCE (*Director of Music*)
Mrs M Corrie (**Music, Preparatory School*)
Ms F McCanlis, BMus, PGCE
T Martin, BA, Dip ABRSM (*Head of Contemporary Music*)
Mrs J Russell, BA, PGCE
L Stockton, BA, MA (*Organ, Piano*)
Ms F Swadling, BA, ABSM, GBSM (*Head of Strings*)
MIss S Vango, BMus, PG Cert, Cons (*Head of Vocal Studies*)

Visiting Music Staff:
N Barry, GGSM, LTCL (*Piano*)
B Barlow (*Singing*)
Miss H Bool, GBSM, ABSM, BTech Nat (*Percussion*)
Ms N Brass, MMus, PGCE (*Double Reed, Piano*)
Miss V Brawn (*Oboe*)
M Broadhead LTCL, DipTCL (*Cello*)
Mrs R Brown (*Singing*)
R Bull (*Guitar*)
P Cambell-Kelly, GMus, RNCM, PG Dip RNCM, PPRNCM (*Violin*)
Mrs S Chatt, GBSM (*Percussion*)
Miss S Clark, (*Violin*)
J Dunlop, BA, GBSM, ABSM (*Flute*)
Mrs K Fawcett, BA, MA, PG Dip (*Viola, Violin*)
A Gittens, BTec, HND (*Electric Guitar*)
Mrs J A Hattersley, CT ABRSM, LRSM (*Brass*)
Mrs J Hiles, GBSM, ABSM (*Flute, Piano*)
Ms J Pearson (*Double Bass*)
M Roberts, BA Music (*Trumpet*)
M Rooney, Ba, Dip ABRSM (*Piano*)
Miss K Stevens, MMus, BMus (*Clarinet*)
A D C Thayer, MA, BMus, PG Dip (*Piano*)
Mrs K Thompson, PG Dip RNCM, PPRNCM, ARCM, LRSM, RNCM (*Piano*)
J Topp (*French Horn*)

Preparatory & Pre-Preparatory School

Headmistress: Mrs J Deval-Reed, BEd

Deputy Head (*Pastoral*): M Marie, BA, PGCE
Deputy Head (*Academic*): Mrs J Holden, MA Oxon, PGCE
Deputy Head (*Operations*): Mrs K Ison, BEd

Mrs C S Abraham, BA, MA, QTS
Mrs R Al-Nakeeb, BEd, MA
Miss V Barron, BA, MA, PGCE, BIAD (**Art, Head of Year 8*)
Mrs G BIllig, BSc, PGCE
Mrs R Boardman, BA, PGCE (**Spanish/German*)
Miss S Cadwallader, BA, PGCE (*Head of Year 6*)
Mr G Clark, BEd (*Head of Year 7*)
Mrs M Corrie, GTCL, LTCL (**Music*)
Mrs S Dakin, BA (**Forest School*)

Mrs J Danks, BMus, PGCE (*Girls' PE*)
Mrs A Davis, BA, PGCE, CCET (*Curriculum Support*)
Mr G Evans, BSc, PGCE (*Mathematics*)
Mrs T Faulkner-Petrova, BA, BSc, MSc, PGCE
Mrs K Finnegan, BA, PCGE (*French*)
Miss M Gonzalez, BA, PGCE
Mrs C Goodall, BA, PGCE
Mrs S Grove, BEd
Mr J P Grumball, BSc, PGCE (*IT*)
Mrs D Hepburn, BSc, MA, PGCE
Mrs R Ivison, BA, PGCE (*Head of Year 3, *Junior Dept.*)
Miss S Jeffrey, BSc, PGCE (*Science*)
Mr G Jones, BA, PGCE (*Boys' PE*)
Mrs G Judson, BSc, PGCE
Mrs S Keynes, BA, OTS (*Head of Year 5*)
Mr C D Kippax, BA, PGCE (*MFL*)
Mrs E Lally, BA, PGCE
Mr A Lane, BSc, PGCE
Mrs R Laurenson, BA, PGCE (*Head of Year 4*)
Mrs C Leather, BSc, PGCE
Mrs S Lewis, BA, PGCE
Miss M Mimberg, BA, PGCE
Mrs E Mullan, BEd (*PSHEE*)
Mr D Pover, BA, PGCE
Miss A Read, BTec, BA, PGCE
Miss C Roskell, BEng, PGCE
Mrs J C Russell, BA, PGCE
Mrs A Scheppel, BA, PGCE (*History*)
Mr R Shone, BA, PGCE
Mrs L Singh, BDes, PGCE (*RE*)
Mr P Sutherland, HD Ed (*Design & Technology*)
Mr M Turner, BSc, PGCE (*Activities Coordinator*)
Mrs S Webley, BSc, PGCE, MEd (*Head of Year 8*)
Mr R Widdop, BA, Dip SpPsy (*Geography*)
Mr C Woollhead, BA, PGCE (*Drama*)
Mrs H Worton, BA, PGCE

Boarding House and Houseparents:
Page (*boys and girls*): Mr & Mrs T Windo

Pre-Preparatory Staff:
Deputy Head Pastoral, Head of Pre-Preparatory Department: B Etty-Leal, BSc, PGCE
Deputy Head Academic: Mrs K Western, BEd

Head of Pre-School: Mrs J Townsend, BA, PGCE
Mrs C Cattell, BA, PGCE (*Head of Year 1*)
Mrs C Dunlop, BEd (*Head of Reception*)
Mrs L Finlay, HDip Ed (*Head of Year 2*)
Mrs J Kingston, BMus, PGCE
Miss E Lewis, BA Ed
Mrs J Lockhart, BEd
Mrs N. Marie, BA, PGCE
Mrs M Martin, BA, GTP
Mrs N St John, BA, PGCE
Mrs S Symonds, BA

Bryanston School

Blandford, Dorset DT11 0PX

Tel:	01258 452411
Fax:	01258 484661
email:	head@bryanston.co.uk
website:	www.bryanston.co.uk
Twitter:	@BryanstonSchool
Facebook:	@bryanstonschool

Motto: *Et nova et vetera*

Founded in 1928, Bryanston School's aim is that Bryanstonians will leave as well-balanced 18-year-olds, ready to go out into the wider world, to lead happy and fulfilling lives and to contribute, positively and generously. We believe a school can have no more joyful, dynamic ambition. A broad, flexible academic and extracurricular programme together with an extensive network of support encourages pupils to discover interests and talents, and explore these to the best of their abilities, as well as to adapt positively to the demands of the society of which they are part. Creativity, individuality and opportunity are the school's key notes, but a loving community is the school's most important quality.

Situation. The school is located in beautiful Dorset countryside near the market town of Blandford. There are 400 acres of grounds, which include a stretch of river used for rowing and canoeing, playing fields, woodland and parkland.

Numbers. There are approximately 380 boys and 300 girls in the school.

Admission. Boys and girls are normally admitted between 13 and 14 years of age. Prospective pupils will be required to sit the ISEB pre-test during the autumn term of year 7. The results of the test will allow the school to make an offer of a place on either the Main Entry List or on the Development List. The ISEB pre-test is not considered a pass or fail assessment, as the school recognises that children develop at different stages.

Sixth form entrants are admitted after testing and interview, conditional upon securing at least 40 points at GCSE.

Scholarships. Academic, Art, D&T, Music, Performing Arts, Sport and the Richard Hunter All-Rounder Scholarships are available annually for entry at 13+.

Academic and Music Scholarships, and Udall Awards for Sport are available annually for entry to the sixth form.

Scholarships range in value and may be supplemented by means-tested bursaries. Music Scholarships carry free musical tuition, optional Alexander Technique lessons and a weekly accompaniment lesson.

Further details may be obtained from the Admissions Registrar.

Organisation. The school is organised on a house basis with five senior boys' houses, five girls' houses, and two junior boys' houses, although the house system is less rigid and formal at Bryanston than in many senior schools. All pupils have a personal tutor throughout their time in the school, with whom they meet on a one-to-one basis at least once a week. All sixth-form pupils in their final year have individual study-bedrooms, while lower-sixth formers usually share study-bedrooms. All meals are served centrally in the Dining Hall, providing additional opportunities for friendships to be formed across house and year groups.

Religion. Christian inspiration and Christian ideals are fundamental to the Bryanston philosophy, but the school recognises that pupils may come from homes which follow other faiths or have no strong religious affiliation. There is, therefore, no attempt to impose worship on pupils, rather the intention is to provide an atmosphere in which spiritual values can be discovered and developed.

School Work. The school aims to lead pupils, over a period of five years, from the comparative dependence on class teaching when they join the school, to a position where they are capable of working on their own, for a university degree or professional qualification, or in business. In addition to traditional class teaching, there is, therefore, increasing time given to private work as a pupil moves up the school in the form of assignments to be completed within a week or a fortnight. Teachers are available to give individual help when required, and tutors supervise pupils' work and activities in general on a one-to-one basis.

Every pupil is encouraged to explore a range of opportunities. All pupils follow the same broad and challenging curriculum in D (Year 9), if at all possible. This curriculum includes Latin, Modern Languages, three separate Sciences, Creative Arts, Technology and Music as well as English and Mathematics. GCSEs are taken after three years when a pupil is in B (Year 11). There is a highly flexible choice of subjects at this level and subjects are setted independently. In the sixth form pupils can choose between A Levels and the International Baccalaureate Diploma. All lower-sixth formers follow a compulsory Personal and Social Education course and the academic enrichment programme provides supplementary sessions to develop key skills and approaches to learning.

Music. Bryanston has an exceptional musical tradition, and music is at the heart of school life. Inclusion and participation, as well as excellence, are core values and to achieve these every pupil in D (year 9) learns an instrument for the entire year. An extraordinary range of concerts, recitals and musical groups take place, with over 600 individual music lessons taught each week.

Drama. A well-equipped, modern theatre provides the venue for the many school productions which take place during the year as well as for touring professional companies. In addition to acting, pupils are involved in stage management, stage lighting and sound, and front-of-house work. There is also a large Greek Theatre in the grounds.

Sport and Leisure. A wide variety of sports is on offer at the school, including athletics, archery, badminton, canoeing, climbing, cricket, cross country, fencing, fives, hockey, indoor hockey, kayaking, lacrosse, netball, riding, rowing, rugby, rugby 7s, sailing, squash, swimming and tennis. Extensive playing fields between the school and the River Stour provide 42 tennis courts, two AstroTurf pitches, nine netball courts, a grass athletics track and grass pitches for all major sports, an all-weather riding manège and cross-country course. A sports complex provides an indoor heated 25m, six-lane swimming pool, Performance Sports gym with dual axis force platforms and 360-degree motion cameras, 40m indoor sprint track, two large indoor sports halls, four squash courts, three indoor fives courts, spinning studio, 200 sqm fitness suite, bouldering wall, multi-purpose studios, analysis room, physio room, and an outdoor and adventure hall and storage. Sailing takes place at Poole Harbour which is in addition to a huge number of clubs and societies, catering for a wide range of interests, meeting in the evenings and at weekends.

Additional Activities. To encourage pupils to contribute to their community, use their time proactively and develop a growing self-reliance, all pupils take part in all or some of the following:

- Community and Social Service
- Extracurricular activities chosen from a wide range of options
- The Duke of Edinburgh's Award
- Adventure Training

Dress. There is no school uniform but there is a dress code.

Careers. The Sixth Form and Careers Department include four members of staff who work closely with tutors, houses and departmental heads to provide guidance for pupils at every academic age and stage of development, at a pace that is right for each individual. Our goal is to empower pupils to develop confidence and self-awareness, to reflect on their abilities and aspirations, and to gain insights into their future career options and higher education pathways. Work-related learning is actively included as part of curriculum development, with psychometric profiling offered in year 11. Higher Education and 'next steps' events are organised annually, providing the chance to meet with employers, academic subject specialists and overseas universities. Ongoing support is provided one-to-one, in small groups, via PSRE and guidance events. Bespoke support is available for those who are applying to university overseas.

Further Education. The vast majority of pupils in the sixth form gain admission to universities or other academies of further education.

Fees per term (2018–2019). Boarders £12,728, Day Pupils £10,438.

Charitable status. Bryanston School Incorporated is a Registered Charity, number 306210. It is a charitable trust for the purpose of educating children.

Governors:
J R Greenhill, MA, QC (*Chair*)
N Bickford, BA
S F Bowes
B P Broad, BA
S O Conran
Dr K M Fleming, MA, MPhil, PhD
J A F Fortescue, BA
S Foulser, BA
Revd L J Holt, MA
B M Irvani, MA, FCA
M A S Laurence
C G Martin, ACA, MA
V M McDonaugh, MA, DL
M E McKeown, BA, MSc
Dr H Pharaoh, MBBS, DRCOG, MRCGP, DFSRH
A R Poulton, BA
L M V Soden, BA, MA
D M Trick

Chief Operating Officer and Clerk to the Governors: M McGovern

Head: S J Thomas, BA

Second Master: P J Hardy, JP, MA, PGCE (*Economics and Business*)
Deputy Head, Academic: Dr D A James, BA, MA, PhD, PGCE (*English*)
Director of Academic Administration: P A L Rioch, BMus (*Music*)

Staff:
* *Head of Department*
† *Housemaster/Housemistress*

Art:
*D G Knight, BA, PGCE
G J Cedeira, BA
A Connolly, BA, PGCE
†H E Dean, BA, PGCE
†J A K Dickson, BA, PCGE
J E Jehu, BA, PGCE
M Hilde, BA
S M Macpherson, MA
M L Sinclair-Smith, BA, PGCE

Classics:
*C T Holland, MA
†Dr H L Fearnley, BA, PhD
D Fowler-Watt, MA (*Director of Performing Arts*)
L M Jones, BA, MA
A J Sanghrajka, BA (*IB ToK Coordinator*)
S J Thomas, BA, PGCE

Drama, Theatre Studies and Film:
*J F Quan, BA, MA (*Director of Drama*)
†K J Scott, BA, PGCE
S N Wheeler, BA, PGCE (*Head of Film*)
G A Martin, BA Videographer

Economics and Business Studies:
*B E Leigh, LLB, MSc
Dr P S Bachra, MA, EdD (*Head of Pastoral*)
†J J A Beales, BA, PGCE
A N R Bray, BA (*Head of Work-Related Learning*)
†M S Christie, MA, PGCE
G E S Drake, BSc, PGCE
P J Hardy, JP, MA, PGCE
R H Ings, BSc, PGCE
N L Payne, BA, PGCE

English:
*H E J Weatherby, MA
C R Bentinck, BA, PGCE (*Admissions Tutor*)
L R Boothman, BA, PGCE (*D Coordinator*)
A R Croot, BA, PGCE
†S H Davies, MA
Dr D A James, BA, MA, PhD, PGCE
N M Kelly, BA, PGCE
I W McClary, MA, PGCE (*Director of Academic Administration Elect*)
O Nicholson, BA, MA, PGCE

Geography:
*K E Andrews, BA, PGCE
R J Boulton, BA, PGCE
V L Chappell, BA, MEd
M S Deketelaere, BA, MSc & DIC, PGCE (*Head of Curriculum Planning*)
L C Kearney, BEd (*International Coordinator*)
J E G Ralphs, BA, PGCE (*Head of Sixth Form*)

History and Politics:
*A L Smith, BA, MSc, PGCE
W J Bridges, BSc, PGCE
P C A Dunne, BA, MSc
P Quarrell, BA, PGCE (*Senior Tutor*)
A B L de Steiger Khandwala, MA, MA, MPhil, PGCE
J G Strange, MA, PGCE
T Strongman, BA, PGCE
S M Vincent, BA, PGCE (*Admissions Tutor*)

History of Art:
*J M C Lyne, BA, MA
S A E Stacpoole, BA
S A Wilson, BA, MA

Mathematics:
*A C Hartley, MMath, PGCE
C B Craig, BSc (*B/C Coordinator*)
†S B Green, BSc, PGCE
P A Griffin, BSc, PGCE
C L Lorek, BSc, PGCE
K M Lewin, BSc, MSc, PGCE
D J Melbourne, BSc, PGCE
C E Murray, BSc, PGCE
V R M Peck, BSc
A K Tarafder, BSc, PGCE

Modern Foreign Languages:
*L C Johnson, MA (*Head of German, Senior Tutor*)
C Dechirot, BA, MA (*Head of French*)
A E Gutierrez Aldana, BA, PGCE (*Head of Spanish*)
D Acosta Vizcaíno, BA, MA, MA
L C Blanco, BA
S D Duncker, 1 & 2 State Examination (*IB Diploma Coordinator*)
A J Gilbert, BA, PGCE
L R Haynes, BA, PGCE
F Mateo-Sanz, BA, PGCE
R A Pakenham-Walsh, BA, PGCE
L K Tate Johnson, BA, PGCE, CAES
†J M I Velasco, BA, PGCE

Music:
*S J Williams, BA (*Director of Music*)
G M Scott, BA, PGCE, Premier Prix, ARCO, LTCL (*Deputy Director of Music*)
X C Iles, MA, PGCE (*Assistant Director of Music – Academic*)
W P Ings, MA, PGCE, ARCO (*Head of Teaching and Learning*)
C S Scott, BMus, PGCE, FTCL, ARCM, LTCL (*Head of Strings*)
P A Carpenter, BA, MMus
P A L Rioch, BMus
D A Clark (*Head of Woodwind and Brass*)
R B K Rowntree, BMus (*Singing Coordinator*)

Philosophy and Religious Studies:
*L J D Pollard, BA
Revd Canon A M J Haviland, BEd, Dip CMM (*Chaplain*)
R S Irving, BA, PGCE (*Head of PSRE*)

PE and Sport Studies:
*A Fermor-Dunman, BSc, MA (*Director of Sport*)
M Boote, BSc, PGCE
†C L Bray, BSc, PGCE
A J Chapman, BSc MSc
M Lancaster, BSc, PGCE
C L Miller, BA Ed (*Head of Boarding*)
J E Morris
S E Morris, BSc, PGCE
B C Rodford, BSc, PGCE

Psychology:
Dr H A Hogarth, BSc, MSc, PhD (*IB Extended Essay Coordinator*)

Science:
*N G Welford, BSc, PGCE
C A Çava, MPhys (*Head of Physics*)
A J Elliot, BSc, PGCE (*Head of Chemistry*)
E L Silcock, BSc, PGCE (*Head of Biology*)
C G Bloomfield, BSc, PGCE
R J Collcott, MEng, MSc, PGCE
G S Elliot, BA, PGCE
S J Fazakerley, BA, PGCE
R M Hallam, MPhys, PGCE
A M Harwood, BSc, PGCE
P L Haywood, BSc, PGCE
J P Heritage, BSc, PGCE
S Y James, BA, PGCE
†R J Johnson, BSc, PGCE
S H Jones, BSc, PGCE
Dr M T Kearney, MA, PhD, CEng, MRAeS, CPhys, MInstP
A J Pattison, BSc, MSc, PGCE
R J Perkins, HND
J D Pritchard, MSc, PGCE
S J Turrill, BSc, PGCE

Technology:
*A J Barnes, BA, CertEd (*Director of Technology*)
M J Davi,s BSc, PGCE (*Head of Computer Science*)
*C J Mills, BA, PGCE (*Head of Design and Technology*)
†M T Bolton, BA
N J Davies, BEd
R H Ings, BSc, PGCE
J Ladd-Gibbon, BA, MA
S P Nicholls, BA, PGCE
P A Sillett-Scoggins, BEd
H L Southby, BSc

Careers:
S B Sutton, BA (*Careers Officer*)
A N R Bray, BA (*Head of Work-Related Learning*)
L C Kearney, BEd (*International Coordinator*)

Academic Support:
*L A Marriott, BSc, PGCE, Cert SpLD
M F Barlow, BA, PGCE, MA
J S Bell, MA
A J Casely, BA, PGCE, Dip SpLD
K E Heminsley
C Steven-Fountain, BA, PGCE, Cert SpLD

Library:
E C Minter, BA, PG Dip ISM, MCLIP

Outdoor Education:
D P T Curry, BSc

Admissions Registrar: A Megdiche
Head's PA: A Haney

Bury Grammar School Boys

Tenterden Street, Bury, Lancs BL9 0HN

Tel: 0161 696 9600
Fax: 0161 763 4655
email: communications@burygrammar.com
website: www.burygrammar.com
Twitter: @bgsboys
Facebook: @BuryGrammarSchoolBoys
LinkedIn: /burygrammarschools

Motto: *Sanctas clavis fores aperit*

The School, formerly housed in the precincts of the Parish Church of St Mary the Virgin, was first endowed by Henry Bury in 1634, but there is evidence that it existed before that date. It was re-endowed in 1726 by the Revd Roger Kay and moved to its current site in 1966. The school is a selective grammar school which aims to provide a first-class academic and extracurricular education; to nurture the whole person in a safe, stimulating, challenging and friendly community in which each individual is encouraged to fulfil his potential; and to prepare each boy for an adulthood of fulfilling work, creative leisure and responsible citizenship.

Numbers of Boys. 461 aged 7 to 18.

Admission, Scholarships and Bursaries. Admission is by examination and interview. Most boys join the school at either 7 or 11, although, subject to places being available, admission is possible at other ages. A number of means-tested bursaries, based on academic performance and financial need, are awarded each year.

Fees per term (2018–2019). Senior School £3,585; Junior School £2,664.

Facilities and Development. Bury Grammar School has a distinguished history of excellence dating back to the 1570s. Proud of its historic links with the town of Bury and the surrounding area, Bury Grammar School possesses a full range of modern facilities. These facilities enable the School to offer a broad and rich academic curriculum and extra-curricular programme. Since 1993 the Junior School has occupied its own site opposite the Senior School. Junior School pupils are able to take advantage of the additional specialist facilities and resources in the Senior School. A new Learning Resource Centre, consisting of a Library, extensive ICT provision and private study facilities, was opened in 2002, and a new Art Centre in 2004. State-of-the-art Science laboratories were completed in 2010 and a new university-style Sixth Form Centre for both boys and girls opened in 2014. In 2016 brand new sports facilities were opened to include a 3G artificial pitch and a multi-use games area so that sports can continue in inclement weather. Bury Grammar School is constantly striving to improve its facilities and to provide the best possible educational experience for all its pupils.

Pastoral Care. Bury Grammar School prides itself on excellent pastoral care and its ability to work as a family to nurture and care for every individual. It cares for and respects its students and, in turn, expects them to care for and respect others. The BGS philosophy for pastoral care is simple: BGS students should be happy, secure and ready for all that life has to offer. BGS offers individualised pastoral support for every student and is always keenly aware that it is a privilege to work alongside young people. BGS is fortunate to have on site a highly dedicated and skilled School Health Team who work closely with pupils, parents and staff to ensure that the medical, health and wellbeing needs are met. BGS also offers the services of a qualified counsellor who is on site on a weekly basis to provide confidential support and advice to those students who need it. Each boy has a Form Tutor who has primary responsibility for his pastoral care and for oversight of his academic progress and his extra-curricular programme. Form Tutors are led by Heads of Year who also oversee a boy's academic progress. There is also a strong House system for a wide range of sporting, musical and cultural inter-house competitions.

Curriculum. Bury Grammar School is immensely proud of its traditions and happy to be a modern school, continually embracing new technologies and innovative teaching methods. BGS is a leading school in the area where pupils continually reach outstanding academic standards, achieving exceptional examination results at GCSE and A Level and gaining places on competitive courses at elite universities. In response to the increasing demands of newly-reformed GCSE and A Level qualifications, BGS has introduced a new enhanced curriculum model throughout the School to strengthen further the quality of education it offers – ensuring breadth alongside academic challenge – to enable pupils to obtain the very best examination results of which they are capable and to open doors to even greater opportunities in the future. It also delivers an enhanced extra-curricular and co-curricular offering, to maintain the School's strong tradition of nurturing fully-rounded individuals.

Art. Well-equipped facilities in BGS' Schools allow all pupils to develop skills in print making, ceramics, sculpture, painting, drawing, textiles, new media and animation. There are frequent visits to galleries, both locally and further afield. Pupils' artwork is proudly displayed throughout the school and BGS hosts regular exhibitions which are opened to the School community.

Music and Drama. Music is an important part of school life. As an academic subject it is offered at GCSE and A Level. At least three major musical events take place each year. Visiting peripatetic teachers teach over 170 pupils. Boys have the opportunity to involve themselves in musical groups such as orchestra, concert band, dance orchestra and BGS Beatz and Lads' Vocal. As well as this, boys can take part in show-stopping musical productions which showcase the incredible musical talents of girls and boys across both Senior Schools and Sixth Form.

Physical Education and Games. Bury Grammar School has long had a tradition of sporting excellence and engagement. Superb sports facilities on the 45-acre campus means that all students have the opportunity to engage in purposeful and competitive sporting activity on site throughout the week. All sporting activities aim to allow pupils to participate recreationally or to compete locally, regionally, and even nationally! The excellent sporting facilities include:

- 18-metre indoor swimming pool
- 50-metre high jump, long jump and triple jump track
- A new suite of artificial playing surfaces, including exceptional 3G all-weather pitches for football, rugby, cricket, futsal and hockey
- Two multi-use games areas
- Tennis and netball courts

- Full-sized volleyball and basketball courts

Outdoor Education. In the Senior School, the Outdoor Activities programme includes a residential course for all First Form boys at the National Watersports Centre at Plas Menai in Wales. Boys in the Fifth, Lower Sixth and Upper Sixth Forms can choose Outdoor Activities as part of their Games programme. This includes a variety of activities and trips, including climbing, kayaking, dry-slope skiing and cycling. Bury Grammar School Boys is also delighted to be able to offer participation in the Duke of Edinburgh's Award scheme and World Challenge Expeditions.

CCF. The Bury Grammar School CCF was established in 1892 and is one of the oldest CCFs in the country. Originally affiliated to the local regiment, the Lancashire Fusiliers, the Contingent is now affiliated to the Royal Regiment of Fusiliers and the cadets wear its badge and hackle with pride. The current strength of the Contingent is 214 cadets. The CCF helps the boys develop qualities such as self-discipline, resourcefulness and perseverance, a sense of responsibility and skills of management and leadership.

Careers. The Careers Department aims to provide all boys with access to the information and advice they need to make informed and sensible decisions about their futures. In addition to an excellent careers library, guidance is provided by individual interviews. There are regular careers conventions and mock interview mornings. All boys are also required to complete a period of work experience during Year 10.

Bury Grammar School Old Boys' Association. The BGS journey carries through to the Old Boys' Association; friendships formed at Bury Grammar School really do last a lifetime. Secretary: Martin Entwistle, email: martinentwistle@me.com.

Charitable status. Bury Grammar Schools Charity is a Registered Charity, number 526622. The aim of the charity is to promote educational opportunities for boys and girls living in or near Bury.

Governing Body:
Chair of Governors: Mrs G Winter
Vice Chair of Governors: Mr M Edge

Mr M J Entwistle	Mr A H Spencer
Mrs S Gauge	Mr S Wild
Mrs C Hulme-McGibbon	Mr D Baker
Mr A Marshall	Mr D Long
Dr J G S Rajasansir	

Bursar and Clerk to the Governors: Mrs J Stevens, BFocFC, ACA

Principal of The Bury Grammar Schools, Headmistress of Bury Grammar School Girls: Mrs J Anderson, BA, MEd, PGCE

Vice Principal, Headmaster of Bury Grammar School Boys: Mr D P Cassidy, BSc

Assistant Principal, Director of Academic Provision: Mrs V Leaver, BSc (*Geography*)
Head of Sixth Form: Mr S Prest, MA (*History & Politics*)
Deputy Head, Pastoral, DSL: Mr R Lees, BA (*MFL*)
Deputy Head, Staff Development & Digital Strategy: Mrs H Campion, BA (*Head of Business Studies and Economics*)
Deputy Head, Administration and Enrichment: Mr A Dennis, BSc (*Mathematics, Head of Outdoor Activities*)
Deputy Head, Curriculum: Mr T J Nicholson, BA (*Mathematics*)
Deputy Head, Sixth Form: Mrs H Hammond, BA (*Drama*)

Teaching Staff:
Mr M Ahmad, BSc (*Physics*)
Mr B Alldred, MSc (*Mathematics*)
Mr M Andrews, BA (*Director of Sport – BGSB*)

Mr D Ashworth, BA (*ICT*)
Dr A Austin, PhD (*Mathematics*)
Miss E L Bailey, BSc (*Biology*)
Mrs C Banks, Licence (*Modern Foreign Languages*)
Miss G Barber, BSc (*Mathematics*)
Mrs L Barron (*Swimming*)
Dr E Bennett, PhD (*Chemistry*)
Mrs C Bevis, BA (*History*)
Mrs M Boulton, BA (*CDT*)
Mr M R Boyd, BA (*Head of French*)
Miss R Britton, BMus (*Music*)
Mrs M Bonilla-Marti, Licence (*Modern Foreign Languages*)
Mrs S G Cawtherley, BA (*Religious Studies, Head of Fifth Year*)
Miss R Charlesworth, BA (*Drama and English*)
Miss C Clarke, BA (*English*)
Mr M Cooper-Latham, BSc (*Biology*)
Mr P F Curry, BSc (*Head of Physics*)
Miss A Davenport, BA (*English*)
Mrs V Davitt, BA (*Food and Nutrition*)
Mrs F Dickson, BMus (*Music*)
Mrs K Dowling, BSc (*Mathematics*)
Miss J H Downing, BMus (*Director of Music*)
Mrs M Eady, BA (*Physical Education*)
Mr J Eastham, BA (*History, Head of Third Year*)
Miss J Elliot, BA (*English*)
Mr R Entwistle, BSc (*Biology*)
Mrs D Evans, BA (*Religious Studies*)
Mrs G L Fern, BSc (*Chemistry*)
Miss V L Frisby, BA (*French*)
Miss K A Gore, BA (*Head of Art*)
Miss E Gumbley, BSc (*Mathematics*)
Mr G Hall, BSc (*PE & Sport, Head of Second Year*)
Mr O Griffiths, BSc (*Physical Education*)
Miss O Halstead, BA (*History and Politics*)
Mrs R Hartley, BA (*Economics and Business Studies*)
Mr M J Hone, MA (*Head of History & Politics*)
Mr P Howard, BA (*Mathematics*)
Mrs S J Howard, BA (*French & German, Head of First Year, E-Safety Officer*)
Ms U Imtiaz, BA (*Modern Foreign Languages*)
Mrs L Irwen, BA (*Chemistry*)
Miss L Jackson, BSc (*Chemistry*)
Miss R Jones, BA (*Classics*)
Mrs J Kay, BA (*History*)
Mrs K Kershaw, BA (*Art*)
Mrs K Lewis, MSc (*Physics*)
Mrs K Lynch, BA (*English*)
Mr P Meakin, BSc (*Head of Computing*)
Ms C McDermott, BA (*Psychology*)
Mrs G Mehta, BA (*Geography*)
Mrs R Newbold, BSc (*Physical Education and Geography*)
Mr D T Newbury, BSc (*Geography, Head of Fourth Year*)
Mrs E Nicholls, BEng (*Physics*)
Mrs S Norman, BMU (*Music*)
Mr P O'Sullivan, BA (*Head of Mathematics*)
Mrs H Poulson, BA (*English*)
Mrs J Rumboldt, BA (*Religious Studies*)
Mr T Seed, BA (*English*)
Mrs J Slade, BSc (*Physical Education*)
Mrs J G Smith, BA (*English*)
Miss E A Stansfield, BA (*English, Head of Third Year*)
Mrs A Tait Hanlon, MSc (*Psychology*)
Miss V Tandon, BSc (*Mathematics*)
Mrs G Taylor, BA (*Modern Foreign Languages*)
Mrs S Taylor, BSc (*Chemistry and Careers*)
Mrs T J Taylor, MA (*Head of Geography*)
Ms J Tomkinson, BSc (*Geography*)
Mr A D Watts, BSc (*Head of Biology*)
Mrs M Whitlow, BA (*Economics and Business Studies*)

Mr B Wong, PhD (*Chemistry*)
Dr J Yates, PhD (*Chemistry*)

Junior School:
Headmaster of Boys' Junior School: Mr M Turner, BSc
Deputy Head of Boys' Junior School: Mr S Sheikh, BA
Mrs C M Murphy, BA
Ms R Pepper. BSc
Mrs V Melia, BA
Mr J Minta, BSc
Miss G Allen, BA

Headmaster's PA: Mrs Z Royle
Head of Admissions: Mrs S Lewis

Campbell College

Belmont Road, Belfast, Co Antrim BT4 2ND, Northern Ireland

Tel: +44 (0)28 9076 3076
Fax: +44 (0)28 9076 1894
email: hmoffice@campbellcollege.co.uk
website: www.campbellcollege.co.uk
Twitter: @CampbellCollege
Facebook: @Campbell-College

Motto: *Ne Obliviscaris*

Campbell College, which was opened in 1894, was founded and endowed in accordance with the will of Henry James Campbell, Esq (Linen Merchant) of Craigavad, Co Down. It has a reputation as one of the leading educational environments in the country. Our commitment is to welcome, challenge and inspire each and every pupil to be the very best they can be, to push themselves and to stand tall as contributors to a global society.

Ethos. Our commitment is to welcome, challenge and inspire each and every pupil to be the very best they can be, to push themselves and to stand tall as contributors to a global society.

Confidence, commitment and achievement are at the heart of everything we do. From the classroom to the extra-curricular activities, we are dedicated to ensuring that boys make the most of their talents within Campbell and beyond.

We nurture the individual and prepare them for the world. Academic achievements are important and we expect our pupils to strive for high grades; it is also our duty to harness the potential in every pupil whether it is academic, creative, physical or otherwise.

We want boys to leave the school with an assured set of values; we want them to believe they can truly make a difference in society. We want our boys to leave the school with things that are going to matter to them for the rest of their lives.

Pastoral Care. We believe that pupils learn best when they are happy, safe and secure and the purpose of our pastoral care is to provide such an environment. The strong, caring ethos of the College is demonstrated by its commitment to the welfare of the pupils and staff.

In Senior School all boys are allocated a Personal Tutor as the first point of contact for parents and our comprehensive Child Protection Policy is issued to all parents before their child commences school. Above and beyond this level of care we have a dedicated medical centre on campus led by the College Matron and a School Doctor who visits our boarders three times a week.

Boarding. We have a successful boarding department which brings an international dimension and unique character to the College; this will enable our pupils to thrive in the increasingly global world in which we all must live and work. We have approximately 150 boarders.

The Curriculum. This is focused upon giving our boys the maximum opportunity to produce the best possible examination results from a varied choice of subjects which meet the needs of the 21st century.

Class sizes are capped at 26 throughout Key Stage 3 to allow boys to grow in confidence and security in their learning as they make the transition from Primary School to Senior School. The teacher to pupil ratio is a generous 1:14, and the curriculum followed at Year 8 comprises English, Maths, Science, Geography, History, Religious Education, French, Art, Drama, Music, Technology, ICT, PE and Learning for Life and Work.

The Campus. Campbell College stands in a secure and impressive 100-acre wooded estate where the academic, boarding, artistic and sporting pursuits are all catered for on site. The College has its own indoor swimming pool, Astro-Turf pitches, squash courts, shooting range, running track and numerous rugby and cricket pitches. It has a variety of sports and assembly halls, drama studio, computer suites and technology areas.

Other Activities. Campbell College is able to provide boys with a host of activities which naturally complement the culture of learning promoted within the school. Whilst the College is widely acknowledged for its sporting excellence, especially in rugby, hockey and cricket, there are many other opportunities available. Alongside a diverse range of sports there are opportunities to participate in The Combined Cadet Force, Duke of Edinburgh's Award scheme, Drama and Music productions and the Charity Action Group.

A competitive House system allows all boys to compete, with camaraderie and collegiality, in numerous inter-House competitions so all have an opportunity to represent their House as well as their school.

Holidays. There are three annual holidays: two weeks at Christmas and Easter, and eight in the summer. In the Christmas and Easter terms there is a half-term break of one week, during which parents of boarders are required to make provision for their sons to be away from school.

Admissions. Campbell College welcomes students at a variety of entry levels. Day boys can begin in Kindergarten and stay through to Sixth Form; boarders may start at Year 8. The school structure is designed to offer our students easy transitions as they grow and mature; they begin in Junior School, then move aged 11 to Middle School, before progressing to Senior School to prepare for their public examinations (GCSE, AS and A2 Level).

There are approximately 912 students in the Senior School of whom 150 are boarders, and 267 students in the Junior School.

Fees per annum (2018–2019) Boarding Fees (Years 8–14): £14,745 (EU citizens), £20,570 (non-EU citizens).

As a Voluntary B Grammar School, Campbell College charges an annual fee to all pupils for development and maintenance. The Board of Governors seeks to support applications to the College by offering scholarships and bursaries, the details of which may be found in the Prospectus.

Prospectus. Further information is included in our prospectus which can be obtained from the College Office or you may download a copy from the College website.

Old Campbellian Society. There is a link from the College website.

Charitable status. Campbell College is registered with the Inland Revenue as a charity, number XN45154/1. It exists to provide education for boys.

Governors:
Mr I D Jordan, FCA, MA Cantab (*Chair*)

His Honour Judge A F W Devlin (*Vice-Chair*)
Mrs F C G Chamberlain, MA
Mr J Andrews, BSc Hons, FCA
Mr G C Browne, BEng Hons, CEng, FIStructE, MICE, MaPS, MConsE
Mr M G B Campbell, BA Hons (*Parent Governor*)
Mr M E J Graham, BSc, MSc, FCIOB, FICE
Mr G F Hamilton, BA, FIFP
Mr J R Hassard, MA, BEd, DASE, AdvCertEd, PQH
Mr J Andrews, BSc Hons Chem, FCA
Mr A Colmer, LLB Barrister at Law
Mr G Elliott, BSc Hons, MRIC
Mrs J Kelly, BA Hons, FCA
Mrs CM Van der Feltz, BA Hons MCIPD
Mr A Wilson, BA Hons, MSc, ACMA
Mr H J McKinney, BSc, CertEd (*Teachers' Governor*)

Headmaster: **Mr R M Robinson**, MBE, BSc, PGCE, MEd, PQH NI

Vice-Principals:
Mr W E Keown, MA, PGCE
Mr C G Oswald, BSc, PGCE, AdvCertEd, MEd

Senior Teachers:
Mr H J McKinney, BSc, CertEd
Mr H H Robinson, BSc, PGCE
Mrs K E Sheppard, MSc, BSc, PGCE (*Learning Support*)
Mrs S L Coetzee, BMus, PCGE, PGCE Careers
Mr C McIvor, MA, PGCE

Assistant Teachers:
Mr A Doherty, BMus Hons, PGCE
Mr C G A Farr, BA, DASE, AdvCertEd, MEd, CertPD
Mr D M McKee, BA, PGCE, DipModLit
Ms B M Coughlin, BEd, PGCertComp
Mrs G E Wilson, BMus, MTD
Mr D Styles, BA, PGCE, Dip IndStudies
Mr B F Robinson, BA, PGCE, MSc
Mr A W Templeton, BSc, PGCE
Mr N R Ashfield, BSc, PGCE
Mr S P Collier, BA, PGCE
Mrs R McNaught, MA, PGCE
Mr G Fry, BA, PGCE
Mr D Walker, BEd
Mr J McCurdy, BD, MA, PGCE
Mr M Cousins, BSc, PGCE
Mrs L Haughian, BA, PGCE
Mr M G Chalkley, BA, PGCE, MEd, PQH
Mr N McGarry, BA, PGCE
Mrs M Debbadi, BA, PGCE, MSc
Dr J A Breen, BSc, PGCE, PhD
Mr R D Hall, BSc, PGCE
Mrs E McIlvenny, BA, PGCE
Mrs K Magreehan, BA, PGCE
Ms L Anderson, BA, QTS
Mrs J Bailie, BA, PGCE
Mrs C A M Irwin, BSc, PGCE
Mr P D A Campbell, BEd
Mr T R Thompson, BSc, PGCE
Mr A McCrea, BEng, PGCE
Mrs W Pearson, BEd
Mr J H Rea, BSc, PGCE
Mrs K Murphy, BSc, PGCE
Mrs V Spottiswoode, BA, PGCE
Mr F N Mukula, BSc, AssDipTh, PGCE
Miss G Lamont, BEd, MSSc
Mr G P Young, BEd
Mr J P Cupitt, BSc, PGCE
Mrs W Shannon, BA, PGCE
Ms K M Marshall, MA, QTS
Mrs K McGarvey, MSci, PGCE
Mr J McNerlin, BSc, PGCE

Mr J Smyth, BSc, PGCE
Mrs J L Hempstead, MA, PGCE
Ms S Kirsch, BA, PGCE
Dr A Dunne, MA, PhD, PGCE
Mrs E McInerney, BSC, MEd
Mr M Brown, MA, PGCE
Ms L Donly, MA, PGCE
Ms D Chada, MA, PGCE
Ms P McCaul, MA, PGCE
Mrs E Reynolds, BSc, PGCE
Mr R McMaster, BSc. PGCE
Miss A Beckett, BSc, PGCE
Mr D Ledwich, BSc, PGCE
Ms E Anderson, BA, PGCE
Mr M Snodden, BA, PGCE
Miss V Wightman, BSc, PGCE

Visiting Music Teachers:
Mrs M Fenn (*Woodwind*)
Mrs J Leslie (*Brass and Piano*)
Mrs K Lowry (*Lower Strings*)
Mrs H Neale (*Upper Strings and Piano*)
Mr M Wilson (*Brass*)
Mrs L Lynch (*Percussion*)
Mr R Nellis (*Guitar*)

Bursar: K J Wilson, FCA
Headmaster's Secretary: Mrs L Crawford
Medical Officers:
Dr G Millar, BMSc, MBChB, MRCGP
Matron: Mrs E M Hoey, SRN

Junior School:
Head: Miss A Brown, BA, PGCE, MEd, PQH
Mrs E M Gwynne, BEd
Mrs H M Jennings, BEd (*Hons*), Dip PD
Mrs S Lismore, MEd, BEd (*Hons*)
Mr A Russell, BA (*Hons*), PGCE
Mr M Boyd, BEd (*Hons*)
Mr A P Jemphrey, BEd, DASE
Mr S Bolingbroke, BA (*Hons*), PGCE
Mr C Irvine, LLB, QTS
Mrs S Nickels, BSc, PGCE
Miss K Courtney, MA, PGCE
Mrs P McGarry, BEd
Mrs L M Leyland, MEd, BEd
Miss K Courtney, MA, PGCE
Miss L Reid, LLB, PGCE
Ms C Martin, BA, PGCE
Mrs S Smith, BSc, PGCE
Mr P Martin, MEd, BA (*Hons*), PGCE

Caterham School

Harestone Valley Road, Caterham, Surrey CR3 6YA

Tel:	01883 343028
Fax:	01883 347795
email:	enquiries@caterhamschool.co.uk
	admissions@caterhamschool.co.uk
website:	www.caterhamschool.co.uk

Motto: *Veritas Sine Timore*

Caterham School is one of the leading co-educational schools in the country. We are committed to providing an environment in which all pupils are challenged to be the best they can be and one in which pastoral care and well-being underpin academic, co-curricular and sporting excellence. The majority of our pupils are day pupils but we are also a thriving boarding community, which enriches the educational opportunity and experience for all. We believe in providing an education for life for all Caterhamians and we seek to ensure that the learning experience at our school blends the best of tradition with the exciting opportunities provided by new technology. Learning how to learn is a key facet of a Caterham education and is in our view an essential skill for life in the twenty-first century. We believe that a truly excellent school is about more than academic achievement alone: it is also about developing a passion for learning, a capacity for independent and critical thinking, self-awareness and resilience, self-confidence without arrogance and genuine interests that extend beyond the confines of the classroom.

Number in School. In the Senior School there are around 900 pupils, of whom 170 are boarders. In the Preparatory School there are 300 pupils.

Aims. At Caterham School we focus on developing the whole person, aiming to ensure that each pupil leaves here ready for the challenges of life at university and beyond and understanding their responsibilities towards others. We want our pupils to leave Caterham well equipped to engage positively with a rapidly changing world as accomplished problem-solvers and innovators, confident in their ability to lead and with a clear appreciation of and respect for the views and potential of others. In so doing we remain true to our founding Christian principles and values.

Situation. Caterham School is in a rural location in north Surrey just 22 miles from the centre of London. The 200-acre campus is in the beautiful, wooded Harestone Valley, less than a mile from the centre of Caterham, and only five minutes' drive from Junction 6 of the M25. The journey by taxi to London Gatwick airport is 20 minutes and about 50 minutes to London Heathrow.

Caterham Railway Station is a 15-minute walk – a morning shuttle bus to school is available. The frequent trains to London (Victoria or London Bridge) make connections to the capital easy and convenient.

There are separate boarding houses for boys (Townsend and Viney) and girls (Beech Hanger). Common rooms, dormitories (for younger pupils) and study-bedrooms are comfortably furnished, many with en-suite facilities.

In recent years there has been a substantial building and development programme. The boarding accommodation has been extended and refurbished. A new sports pavilion opened in 2017 and the sports centre with indoor pool, fully-equipped fitness suite and sports hall, language laboratory and IT facilities have all benefited from extensive investment. A new all-weather pitch and an expanded performing arts centre with two theatres opened in 2016.

The Preparatory School. *Please see entry in IAPS section.* Continuity of education is provided as boys and girls move from the Preparatory School to the Senior School at the age of eleven.

Admission. Intake is by selection on academic merit and on assessment of a pupil's likely positive contribution through good behaviour to the aims, ethos and co-curricular life of the School. All candidates must sit our examinations.

For day pupils the main intake ages are 11+ years, 13+ years and for the Sixth Form. All day pupil candidates are required to attend an interview and a report from the pupil's current school will be required prior to an offer of a place being made in addition to sitting the School's entrance examinations.

Places in the Sixth Form are offered subject to 44 points (or equivalent) from their best GCSE/IGCSE subjects. Additionally, pupils will be expected to meet the specific subject entry requirements for their AS and A Level choices.

All international applicants for boarding places must pass our examinations which are usually taken at the offices of the British Council or one of our overseas agents. For all international applicants we require a school report at registration.

For further details please contact the Registrar, Mrs A Jones, Tel: 01883 335058, email: admissions@caterham school.co.uk.

Details concerning the admission of pupils to the Pre-Preparatory and Preparatory School are published separately (*see entry in IAPS section*).

Term of Entry. Pupils are normally accepted for entry in September each year, but vacancies may sometimes occur at other times.

Scholarships. Scholarships are assessed with a view to encouraging pupils. The breadth and depth of the awards can vary each year depending on the quantity and quality of applicants.

Academic Scholarships: These are awarded at 11+, 13+ and 16+ and can represent up to 50% of the fees

At 11+ and 13+: All external candidates who have registered, and those pupils progressing from Caterham Preparatory School, are automatically considered for an Academic Scholarship. The scholarships are awarded solely on the basis of our entrance examinations, interviews and Head Teacher reports.

At 16+: Candidates applying for Academic Scholarships are required to sit a general paper and two other papers in subjects of their choice that they will be studying at A Level. Examinations and interviews take place in the November preceding entry the following academic year. These scholarships are available to all external candidates, and to internal candidates not already holding an award. Candidates must still satisfy the entry requirement for Sixth Form. In addition to Academic Scholarships, awards may be made for specific subjects, e.g. languages.

All Rounder Scholarships: These are awarded at 11+ and 13+ and can represent up to 25% of the fees. These scholarships are awarded to candidates who are academically sound and achieve scholarship standard in two of the following subjects: Art, Drama, Music or Sport. They should be a genuine 'all-rounder' with real evidence of potential leadership.

Art & Design Scholarships: These are awarded at 11+, 13+ and 16+ and can represent up to 25% of the fees. Candidates wishing to be considered for a scholarship will initially be asked to submit a portfolio of their work for assessment by the Head of Department. The portfolio should reflect the breadth and depth of personal interest and may include paintings, prints, drawings and photographs of three-dimensional work. Portfolios will be returned. Successful candidates will be invited to attend a scholarship interview and to undertake a practical examination. Sketchbooks and a selection of the work from the portfolio should be made available at the interview. All Art & Design Scholars are expected to be fully committed to the school's Art & Design programme.

Music Scholarships & Awards: Music Scholarships are awarded at 11+, 13+ and 16+ and can represent up to 25% of the fees. In addition, up to four exhibitions may be offered, each to the value of free instrumental music tuition on one or more instruments in school. These awards are made on the basis of musical potential as well as actual achievement. As a guide we would expect students to have achieved grade 4 or above aged 11+; grade 5 or above at 13+ and grade 7/8 at 16+ on their principal instrument. Auditions take place early in the Spring Term during which candidates are required to perform one substantial piece (or two shorter pieces) on their principal instrument, and one piece on a second instrument (if studied). There are also sight-reading, aural tests and an informal viva voce with members of the Music department.

All Music award holders are expected to be ambassadors for the music department taking part in the annual music award holders concert and playing active roles in the co-curricular music programme.

Performing Arts Scholarships: These are awarded at 11+ and 13+ and can represent up to 25% of the fees. They are awarded on the basis of performance in the entrance examination and interview, together with performance in the following disciplines: dance, drama or music. Candidates will be expected to excel in two of these disciplines, with potential to develop the third.

Sports Scholarships: These are awarded at 11+, 13+ and 16+ and can represent up to 25% of the fees. Candidates are expected to show exceptional promise in at least one sport and have an established record of achievement in one of Caterham School's major sports at their current school, and at club/county level. Candidates will be required to take part in drills and game situations to show evidence of their positional and tactical awareness as well as skill, agility and fitness level. Records of achievement and school recommendations will be taken into consideration. All Sports Scholars are expected to be fully committed to the School's annual sports programme.

Boarding/International Scholarships: We are prepared to consider awarding a scholarship of up to 25% of the fees to a pupil who is judged to have the potential to make a significant contribution to the boarding community. If applicable at 16+, arrangements can be made for Academic Scholarship assessments to take place overseas. Please contact the Registrar for details.

Science Scholarships: These are awarded at 16+ and can represent up to 25% of the fees. Candidates are expected to show exceptional promise in at least two subjects (chosen from Biology, Physics, Chemistry or Maths) and have an established record of achievement in the subjects at their current school. The Head of Science will interview candidates. All Science Scholars are expected to be fully committed to the School's curricular and co-curricular science activities.

Drama Scholarships: These are awarded at 16+ and can represent up to 25% of the fees. Candidates will be required to perform and discuss two contrasting monologues, one of which must be from the classical repertoire. They will be required to attend an interview to which they should bring a portfolio of their experiences and achievements.

Bursaries. We wish to ensure that Caterham School is accessible to talented students, irrespective of parental income. Therefore, any prospective pupil from a low-income family is eligible to apply for a Caterham Bursary to obtain means-tested financial support in respect of day fees. Bursaries do not preclude pupils from holding a scholarship award.

Bursaries can be offered to new pupils and those who are already in the school and whose families have suffered sudden and unexpected financial hardship. All Bursaries are reassessed annually.

A fully-funded day place for a Sixth Form student is provided by a Wilberforce Bursary. Bursaries are also available for the sons and daughters of URC Clergy, Regular Forces and FCO personnel.

Fees per term (2018–2019). Full Boarding £11,570–£12,190; Weekly Boarding £10,312–£10,871; Day £6,015–£6,300. Lunch for Day Pupils: £240.

Curriculum. Preparatory School: A wide range of subjects is provided following National Curriculum guidelines. (*For further details see entry in IAPS section.*)

Senior School: For GCSE the core curriculum is English Language and Literature, Mathematics, Physics, Chemistry, Biology and a Modern Language as well as PE and Games and RPSE. To this core is added three further subjects from Latin, Greek, Modern Languages (French, German, Spanish, Italian), Art, 3D Design, Music, Drama, GCSE PE, Economics and Business Studies, History, Geography and Religious Studies. All of the subjects offered at GCSE are available at A Level, as well as Further Mathematics, Economics, Business Studies, Photography, Psychology, Politics and Textiles. The curriculum is supplemented by an innovative, non-examined 'Forum' programme that includes expert led lectures and seminars designed to prepare students for the opportunities and responsibilities of adult life. Sixth Form students can also participate in the Caterham Award which recognises public speaking, community service and leadership development.

Music, Drama and Creative Arts. Music is an important feature of the life of the School. Individual lessons are given on the piano, in string, brass and wind instruments, and the organ. The Choral Society performs at least one major choral work each year. Each term there are several School concerts and a programme of recitals is arranged. Drama is also well-supported and popular. Each year there are three major productions which involve a large number of pupils both on and off stage. The expertise within the Art Department is broad, including painting, printmaking, textiles, fashion, ceramics, photography, digital media and sculpture and pupils are encouraged to pursue their interests in creative work, as diverse as ceramics, textiles, digital manipulation, drypoint etching and mixed media.

Societies and Hobbies. All pupils are encouraged to pursue a hobby or constructive outside interest, and there are a large number of active School Societies, including: Art, CCF, Chess, Amnesty International, Astronomy, Dance, Debating, Duke of Edinburgh's Award, Film, Greek, ICT Club, Kit Car Club (Caterham 7), Moncrieff-Jones (Sixth Form Science), Music, Circus, Textiles, Young Enterprise. The School has an active charity committee and significant funds are raised annually to support partner schools in Tanzania and Ukraine.

Games. Most of the playing fields adjoin the School including an all-weather synthetic grass pitch for Lacrosse, Hockey and Tennis. Overall there are many sporting activities, but in each term at least one major game is played. For boys it is Rugby in the Autumn Term, Hockey in the Spring Term and Cricket in the Summer. Girls play Lacrosse, Netball, Rounders and Tennis. Pupils can also participate in Athletics, Fencing, Equestrian, Swimming, Badminton, Basketball, Cross Country, Squash, Soccer, Taekwondo and, in the Summer Term, Sailing, Windsurfing and Canoeing.

Health. There is a well-equipped Health Centre with a SRN Sister. The School Doctor attends regularly.

Careers. The Careers staff are available to give advice. The School has membership of the Independent Schools Careers Organisation and parents are encouraged to enter their sons or daughters for the Inspiring Futures Aptitude Test in the Sixth Form year. The School arranges Careers and Higher Education Forums and the Headmaster and Careers staff are available to discuss careers with parents.

Old Caterhamians' and Parents' Associations. The School has flourishing Old Caterhamians' and Parents' Associations. Information about these may be obtained from the School.

Charitable status. Caterham School is a Registered Charity, number 1109508. Its aim is to develop the academic and personal potential of each pupil in a Christian context.

The Reverend N J Furley-Smith
Mr J Joiner [OC]
Mr M H P Smith
Mrs S M Whittle
Mrs P H Wilkes
Mr A P Wilson

Clerk to the Trustees: Mr J C L King, MBE

[OC] *Old Caterhamian*

The School Staff:

Headmaster: **Mr Ceri Jones**, MA Cantab

Principal Deputy Head: Mr Daniel Gabriele, MA Oxon
Deputy Head (Academic): Mr Tom Murphy, MA Oxon
Deputy Head (Pastoral and Well Being): Mrs Sarah Griffiths, MA Oxon
Deputy Head (Co-Curricular): Mrs Catherine Drummond, BA Hons
Deputy Head (External Relations): Mr Matthew Godfrey, MA
Director of Learning and Teaching: Mr Kim Wells, MA Cantab

Senior Teacher (Social Responsibility and Engagement): Mr Anthony Fahey, BA
Senior Teacher (Safeguarding): Mrs Gaelle Sullivan
Senior Teacher (Operations): Mr Andrew Taylor, BSc
Senior Teacher (Academic): Mr Rob Saleem, MA Oxon
Senior Teacher (Director of Innovation): Mr Adam Webster, BA Oxon

Mr Magnus Anderson, MA Cantab, MEng (*Physics, Head of Third Year*)
Mr Adam Assen, BMus (*Director of Music*)
Dr Rachel Avery, PhD (*Psychology*)
Mr Jonathan Batty, BSc (*Master in charge of Cricket and Assistant Director of Sport*)
Mrs Charlotte Bell, MA (*Head of Art and History of Art*)
Mr Christopher Bovet-White, BSc (*Biology*)
Mrs Clare Brown (*Head of Careers, PSHEE, Assistant Head of Sixth Form*)
Mr Peter Buchan, MA Oxon (*Mathematics*)
Mr Javier Cores-Estevez, MBiochem Oxon (*Chemistry*)
Mr Rob Clarke, BSc (*Director of Sport*)
Mrs Catherine Clifton, BA (*Head of German*)
Mr Demos Christou (*Graduate Assistant Boys' Games*)
Mr Philip Comerford, MSc (*Physics*)
Mr Toby Cooper, MA, AKC (*Head of Politics, History*)
Miss Angela Cox, BA (*English*)
Mr Nick Crombie, BA (*English, Second in Department*)
Miss Nancy Dawrant, MA Oxon (*Mathematics, House Coordinator*)
Mrs Victoria de Silva, BA (*Business and Economics*)
Mr Michael Dimakos, PhD (*Mathematics*)
Mr Richard Evans, MA (*Chemistry*)
Mrs Louise Fahey, BA Hons (*Head of Drama & Theatre Studies*)
Mr Anthony Fahey, MA (*Senior Teacher – Social & Collective Responsibility, Business Studies & Economics*)
Mr Peter Friend, BSc (*Hockey Academy Manager*)
Mr Carlos Garcia, BA Hons (*Spanish, Modern Languages Coordinator*)
Miss Elisabeth Gibbs, MA (*Head of EAL*)
Miss Rebecca Goddard, BSc Hons (*Biology, Head of Harestone*)
Mr Tim Graham, BA Cantab (*Teacher of Classics, Graduate Assistant Boys Games*)
Dr Emily Gray, PhD, ESOL, PhD Philos, MA (*English*)
Mr Tristan Hall, BMus Hons, PG Dip, Dip ABRSM (*Music, Assistant Head of Newington*)

Dr Kate Hanford, PhD (*Chemistry, Assistant Head of Underwood*)
Miss Rachel Hart, BA Hons (*PE, Head of Third Year*)
Mrs Holly Howden, BA Hons (*English, Assistant Head of Fifth Year*)
Mrs Harriet Howgego, MChem Hons (*Chemistry*)
Mrs Becky Hunter, BA Oxon (*Classics, Religious Studies*)
Mr Colin James, BSc Hons, MBA (*Business Studies and Economics, Director of Sixth Form – Upper Sixth*)
Mrs Katy James, BA (*History and Politics*)
Mr Warren Jones, BA (*Modern Foreign Languages*)
Mr David Keyworth, MSc (*Head of Chemistry*)
Mrs Katie Koi, BA (*Head of Lacrosse, PE, Head of Underwood*)
Mr Stephen Lander, MA Oxon, MSc (*Mathematics 2nd in Dept, Assistant Head of Fifth Year*)
Dr Anthony Langdon, PhD (*Head of Mathematics*)
Miss Jaclyn Leach, BSc Hons (*Head of Examination, PE, Assistant Head of Second Year*)
Mr Adrian Lewis (*Business and Economics*)
Mrs Natalie Lomas, BA Hons (*Head of First Year, PE*)
Mr John Mansell, BA Oxon (*Head of Physics*)
Mr Steven Marlow, MBioChem Oxon (*Biology*)
Miss Kirsty McLaren, BA (*History*)
Mrs Nicole McVitty, DEUG, Licence d'Anglais (*Head of French, Spanish, Deputy Director of Sixth Form – Lower Sixth*)
Mrs Vanessa Mesher, MA (*Geography*)
Mr Nick Mills, BA Hons (*Head of Viney, History*)
Mr Alexander Moore, BSc (*Acting Head of Business Studies, Dance, Assistant Head of First Year*)
Mr Robert Mugridge, BA Hons (*Geography, Head of Aldercombe*)
Miss Alice O'Donnell, MA (*Head of English*)
Mr James Ogilvie, BSc (*Mathematics, Internal School Examinations Officer*)
Mr Mathew Owen, MA Oxon (*Classics, CCF*)
Mr Neil Parker, MSc Econ (*Head of Spanish, Italian, Head of Newington*)
Mrs Penny Parker, BA Hons, MEd (*Mathematics, Assistant Head of Fourth Year*)
Mrs Sarah Parsloe, BA Hons (*Teacher of Art*) [Maternity Cover]
Miss Collette Pateman, BA Hons (*Head of 3D Design*)
Mr Andrew Patterson, MA (*Coordinator of Sports and Events*)
Mrs Rachel Pearce, MA Hons (*Mathematics, Head of Fourth Year*)
Mrs Clare Quinton, Licentiate Hons (*Head of Beech Hanger*)
Mr Dan Quinton, MA Oxon, FSB (*Head of Science, Head of Biology*)
Mr John Ranford (*Chemistry*)
Mr Daniel Richards, BA (*Head of Rugby, History, Politics*)
Mrs Helena Richards, BMus Hons (*Assistant Director of Music, Composer in Residence, Dance*)
Mrs Zoe Roberts, BA Hons (*Spanish, Assistant Head of First Year*)
Dr Jamie Robinson, PhD (*Biology, Duke of Edinburgh's Award Bronze Leader*)
Rob Salem, MA Oxon (*Senior Teacher Academic, Head of History*)
Nicholas Sharman, BA Hons (*3D Design Teacher*)
Mrs Louise Sheridan, BA (*Textiles*)
Mrs Fiona Scott, BSc (*Mathematics, Resident Boarding Tutor Beech Hanger*)
Dr Marc Scott, MPhys Hons, PhD (*Physics*)
Mrs Aimee Seal, BSc (*Biology, Head of First Year*)
Miss Jennifer Simpson (*Lacrosse Coach, Assistant Head of Ridgefield*)
Dr Christopher Sinclair, MSc, PhD (*Physics*)

Miss Rebecca Smith, BA Hons (*Religious Studies, Head of Ridgefield*)

Mr Ross Smith, BSc Hons (*Swimming Academy Manager*)

Dr Robert Soltysiak, MChem (*Chemistry, Assistant Head of Harestone*)

Mr Richard Stamper, BA Hons, MA, TESOL (*Teacher of EAL*)

Ms Catherine Stedman, MA Cantab, BA, PGCE (*English*)

Mr Neil Stokes, BSc, MA (*Head of Computing and Digital Creativity*)

Mrs Gaelle Sullivan, MA (*SENDCo, Assistant Director of Learning and Teaching*)

Mr Alistair Taylor, BSc Hons (*Games & PE, Sports Coach and Head of Strength & Conditioning, Deputy Head of Viney House*)

Mr Stuart Terrell, MPhil (*Head of Geography, Deputy Director of Sixth Form – Upper Sixth*)

Mr Daryl Todd, MA Oxon (*Mathematics, Head of Lewisham*)

Miss Hayley Troughton, BA (*Art*)

Miss Emily Unwin, BA Cantab (*French and Spanish*)

Mr Andion van Niekerk, BA (*Head of Townsend, English, Geography*)

Mrs Rachel Veldtman (*Faculty Leader for the Visual Arts*)

Mr Kristian Waite, MA Oxon (*Head of Classics*)

Mrs Cathriona Wallace, BA Hons, ACIB (*Business Studies and Economics*)

Miss Hannah Walters, BSc (*Physics*)

Mr Conrad Ware, BSc Hons (*Mathematics*)

Mr Adam Webster, BA Oxon (*Director of Digital Learning, English*)

Mrs Samantha Webster, BA Oxon (*Head of Philosophy and Theology*)

Mr John Weiner, ACA, LLB (*Head of Economic and Business Studies*)

Mrs Isis Whitwell, BSc Hons (*Biology, Head of Harestone*)

Mr Jan Whyatt, MA (*Religious Studies*)

Ms Hannah Wildsmith, BA Hons (*English*)

Mr Ben Wilkinson, BA Hons (*Head of Outdoor Learning, 3D Design, Duke of Edinburgh's Award Silver and Coordinator*)

Mrs Alexandra Yankova, BA Hons (*English, Drama*)

Registrar: Mrs Alison Jones

Preparatory School:
Head: Mr Howard Tuckett, MA
Deputy Head: Mrs Annie Ingrassia, BA Hons, Grad Dip Ed

Charterhouse

Godalming, Surrey GU7 2DX

Tel:	Admissions: 01483 291501
	General Enquiries: 01483 291500
email:	admissions@charterhouse.org.uk
	reception@charterhouse.org.uk
website:	www.charterhouse.org.uk
Twitter:	@CharterhouseSch
Facebook:	@charterhousesch
LinkedIn:	/charterhouse

Motto: *Deo Dante Dedi*

Founded in 1611, Charterhouse is one of the UK's leading independent boarding schools. With four centuries of history behind it, the School is committed to being at the forefront of educational progress in the twenty-first century.

Building on the success of its mixed Sixth Form, the School is moving to full co-education from the age of 13, and will welcome the first girls into Year 9 in September

2021. There will be girls in every year group from September 2023.

The pupil roll will grow over the next decade from 800 today to around 1,000, with the increase representing additional places for girls.

Campus. The School moved from London to Godalming, Surrey in 1872, and is set within an inspirational 250-acre campus, conveniently located close to London and within 50 minutes of Heathrow and Gatwick airports. With 17 grass sports pitches, 3 full-sized Astroturf pitches, an athletics stadium, a sports centre, 24 tennis courts and a 9-hole golf course, not to mention beautiful lawns and gardens, the campus is one of the best, if not the best, in the country. Combined with a 235-seat theatre and separate music performance and art display spaces, the School's setting encourages pupils to contribute, and provides a safe community in which to explore and grow.

Academic. Charterhouse's curriculum promotes academic rigour, develops intellectual curiosity and fosters the ability to learn independently. The curriculum follows the normal path to (I)GCSEs in Year 11, followed by a choice of A Level courses or the IB Diploma Programme in the Sixth Form. The School also offers a taught series of timetabled extended projects and academic enrichment electives. The university destinations of leavers reflect both their abilities and the quality of the education provided at the School.

Co-curricular activities. With more than 80 different sports and activities, including music, drama and other creative opportunities, everyone is encouraged to develop existing interests to exciting levels or take up new ones. A great many clubs and societies are pupil-led, offering real leadership opportunities and few limits to what can be pursued. Outdoor education, including a thriving DofE programme and a growing community and partnerships agenda, foster teamwork, service and leadership.

Boarding. Charterhouse is one of the very few schools now that is almost 100% boarding, with daily life for all pupils revolving around the Houses. The Housemasters and their families live in the Houses and are supported by resident Matrons, Assistant Housemasters and a team of tutors. Each tutor has a small number of pupils with whom he or she meets at least once a week to provide the help and encouragement that enables every pupil to make the most of life at the School. They take an active interest in their tutees, attending concerts, plays and sporting events in which they participate.

Admissions.

13+ entry. Most children arrive at Charterhouse from prep schools at the age of thirteen. Children should be registered by 1 October, when they are in Year 6.

Some children are admitted from other schools in the United Kingdom and overseas after taking our own tests, usually in the January of the year of entry.

Sixth Form. Parents wishing their children to enter Charterhouse in the Sixth Form should contact the Admissions Office at the beginning of the summer term in the year before the September entry, to register their interest.

Visits. Prospective parents and their children are warmly invited to visit Charterhouse to meet the Headmaster and his staff.

Full details on the Admissions processes are available on the School website: www.charterhouse.org.uk/admissions.

Fees per term (2018–2019). Boarders £13,055, Day Boarders £10,788. The Governing Body reserves the right to alter the School fee at its discretion. At least one term's notice is required before the removal of a pupil from the School.

Scholarships and Bursaries. Scholarships, Exhibitions and Awards are available for entry at Year 9 and Year 12 entry. They are offered in Academic, All-Rounder (Year 9

entry), Art, Design and Innovation (Year 12 entry), Music and Sport.

Year 9 Entrance Bursaries are awarded annually through academic competition for pupils in Year 6.

There are also a number of bursaries each year for pupils entering either Year 9 or Year 12, with preference given to those who gain a Scholarship or an Award (not including Exhibitions), who would benefit from a boarding education, but whose parents are unable to afford the fees.

Charitable status. Charterhouse School is a Registered Charity, number 312054. Its aims and objectives are the provision of education through the medium of a secondary boarding school for boys and girls.

Chair of Governors: Mr P M R Norris, MA
Mrs C Baldwin, MA
Mr E D Barnes, BA
Mr J N B Bovill, BA
Professor M J Collins, MA, DPhil
Cllr Clare M Curran, BSc
Professor V C Emery, PhD, FSB
The Very Revd D Gwilliams, BA, MA
Mr J D F Ide, LLM
Mr D F Jennings, MA, Dip Arch, RIBA
Mr D Macey, FCA
Mr C Oulton, MA
Mr A Reid, MA, MBA
Mr D Royds, BSc
Dr R Townsend, MA, DPhil

Clerk to the Governing Body: Ms L Gowland, BSc, MA Ed, ACIS

Headmaster: **Dr A L R Peterken**, BA, MA, EdD

Second Master: Mr A J Turner, BA, LLM
Deputy Head (Academic): Mr S J Brian, MA
Deputy Head (Pastoral): Ms K L Davies, MA, MBA
Assistant Head (Academic): Mr S P M Allen, MA, MEd
Assistant Head (Pastoral): Miss A J A Hawkins, BA
Assistant Head (Pupil Welfare): Mr J M Richardson, BA

Assistant Staff:
Mr T J Aberneithie, BA (*Head of Design & Technology*)
Miss P Aguado, BA (*Head of Modern Languages and Spanish*)
Dr A Aidonis, MA, PhD (*Head of Scholars*)
Mrs S C Allen, MA
Mrs A Alonso, BA
Mr P A Bagley, MA (*Head of Biology*)
Dr G Balasubramanian, MSc, PhD
Miss L F Batty, BSc
Dr W R Baugniet, LLB, LLM, LLD
Mr N E Beasant, BA
Mr M J Begbie, MA (*Master of Creative Arts*)
Mr M P Bicknell
Mr J A H Bingham, MA
Miss M Boggian (*Head of Italian*)
Mr S F C Brennan, BA (*Lay Chaplain*)
Miss A C Brooking, MA
Mr K D Brown, BSc
Mr N Budden, BA, Dip in Law GDL, MA (*Head of French*)
Mr B Cahill-Nicholls, MA, AMusTCL, FRSA (*Director of Community & Partnerships*)
The Revd C A Case, BA MTh (*The Senior Chaplain*)
Mr R Castro, BSc, MDiv
Miss J L Christian, BE, BEd
Mr N L Coopper, BSc, MA
Mr M J Crosby
Mr N J A Dagnall, BA, MSc
Mrs H K Dennis, BSc
Mr M J Dobson, BA

Mr M K Elston, BSc (*Head of Mathematics*)
Mr I Findlay-Palmer, BSc
Miss E A Fletcher, BA
Mr D R Fox, BA
Miss E J Fox, BA (*Master of the Under School*)
Mr J D Freeman, BA
Mr J P Freeman, MA (*Director of Drama*)
Mr P Funcasta, MA, MSc (*Head of Economics*)
Mr J Furness-Gibbon, MA
Mr W J C Gaisford, MA (*Head of English*)
Mr N S Georgiakakis, MSc
Mr G H M Gergaud, L-ès-L
Mr M R Gillespie, BA
Dr R Goorts, BA, MA, PhD
Mr E Hadley, BA (*Head of Theology, Philosophy & Ethics*)
Mr C R G Hall, MA
Mr R W T Haynes, MA
Mr S Hayward, BSc (*Director of Football*)
Mr J S Hazeldine, BA (*Head of Higher Education & Careers; Master of the Specialists*)
Mr S T Hearn, MSc, MInstP
Mr D Hewitt, Dip Ed
Mr T Hingston, MChem (*Head of Science*)
Mr A R Hunt, MA
Dr F Hutton-Williams, MA, MPhil, DPhil
Mr S D James, MA
Mr A G Johnson, MSc (*Master of Examinations*)
Dr A Johnston, MA, PhD (*Master of the Specialists and Head of Academic Monitoring*)
Dr G M Kemp, MSc, MMath, PhD
Miss M Klingberg Insoll, BSc
Dr D Lancefield, CPhys, MInstP, MIEE, MIEEE, PhD (*Head of Academic IT and Head of Physics*)
Dr P J Langman, MEd, PhD,
Mrs A C Lawrence, MA, CPE, LPC
Dr T Marlow, PhD
Mr C W Marsh, MA
Dr S P Marshall, MMath, DPhil
Mr A Marshall-Taylor, MA
Mr R N C Massey, MPhys (*Head of the Remove and Fifth Form*)
Mr D J McCombes, MA
Mrs C L McDonald, MA (*Head of History*)
Ms E McGowan, BSc
Mrs E D McIntyre, MA
Mr L R Merrony, BJuris/LLB, DipEd
Mr R C D Millard, MA, MPhil (*Head of Academic Music*)
Mr P Monkman, MA (*Director of Art*)
Mr T Monroe, MA
Mr R W Morgan, BSc (*Head of Chemistry*)
Mr M W Nash, BA
Mr J Nelmes, MA (*Head of Classics*)
Mrs E P Nelson, MSc
Dr S J Northwood, BA, PhD
Mrs M H Orson, BA
Mrs J Oxley, BA (*Head of Business & Management*)
Mr R J Paler, MA (*Director of IB and Head of Government & Politics*)
Mrs M Peacock, BA (*Head of German*)
Mr R F Peacock, BSc
Mr N S Pelling, MA
Miss H E Pinkney, BA
Mr S R Plater, BSc
Miss C L R Pounder, BSc
Mr E F Poynter, BA
Mr J L Price, BA
Mr P Price, MA (*Head of Geography*)
Mrs S J Pritchard, BA, MA, MCLIP (*Senior & Research Librarian*)
Dr P J Rand, BA, PhD
Mr E J Reid, MMath

Mr A N Reston, BA, MSt
Mr T E Reynolds, MA, MSc
Mr I S Richards, MA
Mr J M Richardson, BA (*Designated Safeguarding Lead*)
Mrs A J Rusholme, BSc
Mr B A Shah, BA, MMath (*Head of Academic IT*)
Mr M N Shepherd, MA, FRCO, ARCM (*Director of Music*)
Mr J M Silvester, BSc
Mr R W Smeeton, ARCM, LRPS, MLC (*Head of Woodwind*)
Dr R H Snell, BSc, MChem, DPhil
Mr C A M Sparrow, MA (*Head of the Yearlings*)
Mr P S Stimpson, MEng
Mrs A M Sutcliffe, MA
Mr J J Sutton, BA, BMus, ARCO
Mr W T Taylor, MSci, MA
Mr W R Tink, MPhil
Miss J Tod, MSc
Mr J C Troy, BSc, MBA
Mr J F A Tully, BEng, FICS, FRGS
Mrs L J Wakeling, MA (*Head of Higher Education*)
Miss A Waters, BSc
The Revd A J M Watkinson, BA, MA (*Chaplain*)
Mr S K Woolley, MA
Dr F P H Wragg, MA, MSci, PhD
Mr D G Wright, LTCL (*Head of Brass*)
Miss L Zhang, MA
Ms M Zhu, BA, MA

Archivist: Mrs C R I Smith, BA, MAA

Medical Officers:
Dr H Carr
Dr A Cerullo
Dr S Clarke
Dr G Dalton
Dr K Green

Senior Chaplain: The Revd C A Case, BA, MTh

Counsellors:
Ms J Symes, BA, MBACP, UKCP, SRN, CQSW
Mr R Watters, BA, FdSc Counselling, MBACP

Director of Finance & Strategy: Mr D S Armitage, MBE, MSc
Director of Business Development and External Relations: Mr J D Davey, MEng
Director of Admissions: Mrs I Hutchinson, BA
Estate Bursar: Mrs E Humphreys, RIBA
Finance Bursar: Mrs V Western, BA, FCA

Director of Sport: Mr N E Beasant, BA
Deputy Director of Sport: Mr K D Brown, BSc
Director of Cricket: Mr M P Bicknell
Director of Football: Mr S Hayward, BSc
Director of Hockey: Mr D R Fox, BA
Head of Racquets: Mr M J Crosby
Head of Swimming & Water Polo: Ms E McGowan, BSc
Sports Development Coach: Mr S R Plater, BSc
Sports Development Coach: Miss C Pounder, BSc

Houses and Housemasters:
Saunderites: Mrs S C Allen
Verites: Mr E J Reid
Gownboys: Mr A N Reston
Girdlestoneites: Dr P J Langman
Lockites: Mr A R Hunt
Weekites: Mr E F Poynter
Hodgsonites: Mr I S Richards
Daviesites: Mr J F A Tully
Bodeites: Dr A Aidonis
Pageites: Mr N S Pelling

Robinites: Mr S T Hearn
Fletcherites: Miss A C Brooking

Cheltenham College

Bath Road, Cheltenham, Gloucestershire GL53 7LD

Tel: 01242 265600
Fax: 01242 265630
email: admissions@cheltenhamcollege.org
website: www.cheltenhamcollege.org
Twitter: @cheltcollege
Facebook: @cheltcollege

Motto: *Labor Omnia Vincit* "Work Conquers All"

Situated in 72 acres of beautiful grounds in the heart of Regency Cheltenham Spa, Cheltenham College is one of the country's leading co-educational independent schools for boarding and day pupils aged 13–18. Combining a strong academic record with a considerable reputation for sport, drama, music and outward-bound activities, Cheltenham College offers an outstanding all-round education. Founded in 1841, it was the first of the great Victorian public schools.

Location. Stunning buildings and first-class playing fields provide a magnificent setting near the heart of the beautiful Cotswolds. There are excellent road and rail connections with London and the major airports, and Cheltenham College offers all the advantages of life in a thriving town community, whilst maintaining a separate campus life.

Numbers. Boys: 330 Boarders; 67 Day Boys. Girls: 249 Boarders; 62 Day Girls.

Admission. Entry to College is into Third Form at 13+ or Lower Sixth at 16+. A small number of pupils may also be admitted into the Fourth Form at 14+. Entry at 13+ can be secured in three ways: Common Entrance, College Entrance papers or College Academic Scholarship papers. Entry at 16+ can be secured by scholarship and entry tests in November or March, good GCSE predictions and a testimonial from the previous school. Full details, prospectuses and application forms can be obtained from the Admissions Office who will always be glad to welcome parents who wish to see College. There is a registration fee of £150 and a final acceptance fee of £1,000 (for pupils aged 13–16) or £1,350 (for Sixth Form entrants) which is deducted from the final term's account.

Scholarships and Bursaries. Scholarships and exhibitions are available for entry at both 13+ and 16+. They are offered in Academic, Art, Drama, Music (including 16+ Organ and Choral awards) and Sport. Generous discounts for Armed Forces families and bursaries are also available.

Fees per term (2018–2019). Boarders £12,260, Day Pupils £9,195. Sixth Form: Boarders £12,590, Day Pupils £9,525.

Chapel. There is a ten-minute service in the Chapel most weekday mornings and the main service each Sunday. There is a Confirmation service every year.

Houses. The 11 Houses, eight Boarding, two Boarding and Day, and two Day, are at the heart of College life and are all located around the Cheltenham College campus. Girls are in five Houses and boys are in six Houses. Accommodation and pastoral care are outstanding for both boys and girls. Cheltenham College opened a new girls' day and boarding house in September 2017 to meet growing demand for quality co-education in Gloucestershire.

Planned Developments. There has been a significant £25 million investment in Cheltenham College since 2010, with refurbishment of the library 'Big Modern', the theatre 'Big Classical', the Science Centre, a new girls' House, and new catering facilities already completed. Looking forward, a rolling programme of Boarding House refurbishment will continue whilst at the same time completing many exciting new development projects including the creation of a new Business and Economics learning centre.

Curriculum. On entry at 13+, pupils follow a broad course for one year, before embarking upon GCSEs in the Fourth Form. The core of the curriculum comprises English Language and English Literature, Mathematics, and at least two Sciences. All then choose at least one Modern Language (French, German, Spanish); and four options from Art, Classical Civilisation, Design Technology (Resistant Materials, Textiles), Drama, Geography, Greek, History, Latin, Music, PE and Theology, Philosophy and Ethics. In the Sixth Form, over 25 A Level subjects are offered and all students complete an EPQ to enhance their UCAS application. Boys and girls are given extensive preparation for entrance to Oxford, Cambridge and other top Russell Group universities. Over 98% of leavers go on to university.

Cultural Activities. The arts are central to the life of College, with at least six plays being staged each year. Pupils are encouraged to attend concerts, plays, films and lectures not only in Cheltenham but in nearby Oxford, Stratford, Bristol and London. Cheltenham College is fortunate to have the renowned Cheltenham Jazz, Science, Literature and Music Festivals on its doorstep, which pupils can take advantage of. Art is housed in an elegant early 19th-century mansion, with a dedicated gallery that exhibits current art and also serves as an excellent chamber music concert hall, housing the superb Steinway concert grand piano. The beautiful Chapel holds a magnificent 3-manual Harrison & Harrison organ. Music plays a vital part in College life, with pupils able to learn just about every orchestral instrument imaginable, even bagpipes. The Chapel Choir, Chamber Choir and numerous other groups enable singers to reach very high standards and many achieve university Choral Scholarships. The numerous instrumental groups and ensembles, from the Orchestra, Chamber Orchestra and Wind Band to the Jazz Bands and String Quartets, perform in Cheltenham's Town Hall and Pump Rooms, as well as in the College Chapel and other venues.

Sports. Cheltenham College is one of the strongest schools nationally in a wide cross-section of sports and benefits from top-level sports professionals and coaches. Last year, the 1st XV and U14 rugby teams enjoyed unbeaten seasons, and four girls currently play international level hockey. The main boys' games are rugby, hockey, tennis, cricket and rowing. The main girls' games are hockey, netball, tennis and rowing. In addition to the two astroturf pitches, the Sports Hall and swimming pool, there are excellent facilities for other sports available, which include rackets, squash, equestrian, golf, athletics, cross country, badminton, polo, and shooting.

Activities. On entry to College, a structured programme of outdoor pursuits, team building exercises and leadership initiatives are provided for one year. Options such as CCF, the Duke of Edinburgh's Award at Bronze and Gold level, and a wide range of expeditions are available. Up to 30 clubs operate weekly, including shooting, dance, pottery, film-making and drama.

Service. There is a strong Community Service scheme which serves the town, including schools, hospitals and care homes. The College's Humanitarian Aid Project raises funds for building and refurbishment work in a number of orphanages and schools and the members of the group regularly visit Romania and Kenya to provide practical assistance. Wherever possible, all College facilities are made available to the town, particularly to the festivals and other schools.

University entry and careers. There is a dedicated Higher Education and Careers department and students are introduced to the guidance offered from their first year at Cheltenham College. There is a well-stocked, welcoming and informative Careers Library, which is committed to offering information and guidance on: gap years; degree courses; universities and institutes, both in the UK and abroad; work experience; other alternatives to higher education, including apprenticeships and specialist colleges; and career ideas and planning. Each Sixth Former has a tutor who is charged with ensuring that he or she is fully aware of the opportunities and challenges available.

Cheltonian Society. Tel: 01242 265694.

Cheltenham College Preparatory School. *For details see entry in IAPS section.*

Charitable status. Cheltenham College is a Registered Charity, number 311720. As a charity, it is established for the purpose of providing an efficient course of education for boys and girls.

The Council:
President: Mr W J Straker-Nesbit
Deputy President: Mr H Monro

Mr R Badham-Thornhill	Mrs R Lewis
Mr M Chicken	Mr T Smith
Mr C Cooper	Reverend Canon K
Mrs G Elwood	Wilkinson
Mrs E Goldsmith	Dr P Wingfield
Mrs K Hickey	Mr M Wynne
Mr L Humphreys-Davies	

Head: Mrs Nicola Huggett, MA Oxford

Senior Deputy Head: Mr Crispin Dawson, BA Bristol
Deputy Head (Academic): Mr Tim Brewis, BA Exeter, MEd Buckingham, MSc Oxford
Deputy Head (Pastoral): Mrs Anna Cutts, BEd Middlesex
Deputy Head (Learning and Wellbeing): Dr Mary Plint, BEd Johannesburg, MEd, PhD Gloucestershire
Assistant Head (Co-curricular): Mr Stephen McQuitty, BSc Nottingham
Bursar: Mr Phil Attwell, BA Sussex, MSc Sheffield

Registrar: Mr Simon Conner, BSc Durham

Cheltenham Ladies' College

Bayshill Road, Cheltenham, Glos GL50 3EP

Tel:	01242 520691
email:	enquiries@cheltladiescollege.org
website:	www.cheltladiescollege.org
Twitter:	@cheltladiescoll
Facebook:	@CheltLadiesColl

A College education gives girls the best possible opportunities to achieve their potential in both the academic and personal spheres.

Academic excellence forms the basis of College life, but just as important is the formation of character. We recognise also that a 21st century education needs to inspire, prepare and equip young women to sustain a lifetime of independently sought learning, and to give them the flexibility and resourcefulness to flourish in our rapidly changing world.

We believe the wellbeing of our girls is as important as their academic outcomes. The wellbeing of pupils has a direct bearing on the quality of the engagement and interactions, including their receptiveness as learners. Pupils are encouraged to be self-determining and caring towards others, building the foundations of character and self-sufficiency for success and fulfilment in the years beyond school.

Girls are encouraged to embrace a broad range of co-curricular activities to suit their interests, from the sporting to the intellectual and cultural. A global outlook encourages girls to play a part in the wider world, creating young women who value and contribute to their communities. Life at College promotes mutual respect, integrity and courage, while nurturing intellectual curiosity, creativity, confidence and an enduring love of learning.

Girls are at the heart of all College does; we are ambitious for their futures, collectively and individually.

Numbers. Approximately 170 day and 680 boarding.

Fees per term (2018–2019). Day £8,270, Boarding £12,315. New Entrants to Sixth Form: Day £9,410, Boarding £13,870. Some extras are charged, e.g. music, riding.

Admission. Entry at 11+, 12+, 13+ and 16+ via College's own examinations. An interview is also required for some entry points.

Academic. Our curriculum aims to instil in each girl a curiosity about the world in which she lives and equip her with tools to question, reason and communicate articulately. Our Lower College curriculum provides exceptional breadth, building foundations for the GSCE years. The girls study separate sciences, computing, humanities and a language acquisition course, as well as music, drama, art and design, and engineering, enterprise and technology. As a large school, College is able to offer extraordinary advantages in resources and choices. Girls have a free choice of options for GCSE but are encouraged to maintain a broad curriculum, while tailored to their individual strengths and interests. In Sixth Form, girls have the option of taking A Levels or the International Baccalaureate (IB) Diploma Programme. Our GCSE and A Level exam results are consistently outstanding and College has been named top girls boarding school in the UK for IB results for three consecutive years.

Pastoral Care and Wellbeing. As a large school, College is able to offer extraordinary advantages in resources and choices, but we are also divided into small groups too, through the three academic Divisions (LC, UC & SFC), Tutor groups and Houses. These create interlocking layers of pastoral care, which work alongside our whole-school Wellbeing Programme, to enable every girl, the reserved as well as the extrovert, to find opportunities to lead a confident, fulfilled and enjoyable life at College. This network is backed up by an experienced and well-resourced Medical Centre based in College, an informed and skilled Catering department and the support of the College Chaplain. Pastoral care isn't something that happens when things go wrong; it's a constant support network for every girl throughout her time in College.

Buildings and Grounds. College is set in a 36-acre dispersed estate in the centre of Cheltenham. The single teaching site is built in a Gothic revival style, complete with the stunning Princess Hall, and complemented by the more recent Art and Technology block, housing College's Engineering, Enterprise and Technology Department, the Parabola Arts Centre, with a 325-seat theatre, and College's new Health and Fitness Centre, which opened in 2018. This sports complex and the Day and Boarding Houses are located in nearby residential areas within a short walking distance of the main site.

Houses. There are six Junior Boarding Houses and three Junior Day Houses. All girls then move into one of six Houses in Sixth Form, which is an excellent stepping stone to university life. Each House is run by a Housemistress, Deputy Housemistress and a team of staff, as well as a dedicated Chef. All Houses have dining rooms, common rooms, prep rooms, computer rooms, space for music practice and laundry facilities. Day girls are fully integrated into all College activities, regularly joining boarders on weekend trips and expeditions.

Music, Drama and Dance. More than 1,000 individual music lessons take place each week, which are scheduled around the curriculum to ensure girls do not miss academic lessons. There are also many choirs, orchestras and concerts throughout the year and at least five drama productions, with Sixth Form girls performing an open air Shakespeare play in the Summer Term. Dance and gymnastics are also available and very popular.

Sport and Co-curricular. At College, we are deeply committed to promoting the health, fitness and wellbeing of all pupils and to developing talent and a lifelong enthusiasm for sport and exercise, regardless of ability or expertise. The main sports are hockey, lacrosse, netball, swimming, athletics and tennis, but College aims to provide what girls enjoy and more than 30 different sports are offered. Alongside the existing 25m swimming pool, tennis and netball facilities, and AstroTurf pitches, the new Health and Fitness Centre includes a second sports hall, multi-purpose studios, a dance studio, and a gym and fitness suite. More than 160 co-curricular opportunities are on offer, including art and design, fencing, debating, journalism, yoga, ethical hacking, martial arts, Model UN, philosophy, engineering, Young Enterprise, medical and ethical club, Kit Car club and international society.

Scholarships and Bursaries. A number of Academic, Art, Day Girl, Music and Sport Scholarships and other awards are made annually for girls of all ages.

Applications for bursaries are welcome from girls whose parents require financial assistance in order to help their daughter join College.

Beyond College. Our dedicated Professional Guidance Centre provides specialist careers and higher education advice to girls throughout their time at College. Sixth Form tutors also provide significant support in this area. The majority of our girls gain places at Russell Group universities, including Oxbridge, or at top US universities to study a diverse range of subjects.

Former Pupils (Guild). There are over 8,000 Guild members in more than 70 different countries across the world, and many are actively involved in helping current girls prepare for the future, including supporting networking dinners, interview preparation, hosting careers and networking events, and arranging speakers from universities and the professions.

Charitable status. Cheltenham Ladies' College is a Registered Charity, number 311722. It exists to provide a high standard of education for girls.

Chairman of the Council: Ms Libby Bassett, MA, ACA

Principal: **Ms Eve Jardine-Young**, MA

Vice-Principal: Mr Richard Dodds, BSc
Vice-Principal (Academic): Miss Jackie Adams, BSc

Chief Operating Officer: Mr Nigel Richards, BSc
Director of Admissions: Dr Hilary Laver, BSc
Director of External Relations: Mrs Dragana Hartley, BSc
Curriculum Director: Mr James Pothecary, MSci
Head of Pastoral Care: Miss Caroline Ralph, BEd
Head of Sixth Form College: Mr Jonathan Marchant, BA, MA
Head of Upper College: Dr David Gamblin, MChem, MRSC
Head of Lower College: Mrs Charlotte Oosthuizen, BEd Hons

Chetham's School of Music

Long Millgate, Manchester M3 1SB
Tel: 0161 834 9644
Fax: 0161 839 3609
email: chets@chethams.com
website: www.chethams.com

Chetham's is a co-educational school for boarding and day students aged eight to eighteen. The School teaches a broad curriculum set within a framework of music. At the centre of every child's course is a 'musical core' of experiences rooted in a determination to educate the whole person. Originally founded in 1653, through the Will of Humphrey Chetham, as a Bluecoat orphanage, the School was reconstituted in 1969 as a specialist music school.

The School numbers 306 students, of whom 170 are girls. There are 210 boarders. Admission is solely by musical audition, and any orchestral instrument, plus keyboard, guitar, voice or composition, may be studied. Each student studies two instrumental studies, or voice and one instrument, as well as following academic courses which lead to GCSE and A Levels and to university entrance and music college. The School stands on the site of Manchester's original 12th century Manor House adjacent to the Cathedral, and is housed partly in the fine 15th century College Buildings, and partly in the New School (2012) which houses all the instrumental, musical and academic teaching, an Outreach Centre and two performance spaces.

Music. Instrumental tuition is guided and monitored by the advisers in each specialism, who visit regularly to survey students' work, conduct internal examinations and give masterclasses. Internationally renowned musicians hold residences at the School for string, wind, brass, percussion and keyboard players. The Director of Music has responsibility for the full-time Music Staff and also for about 100 visiting tutors. All students receive three sessions of individual instrumental tuition each week. Practice is rigorously set and supervised. Academic Music is normally studied at A Level.

Boarding. There are two boarding houses for girls and boys aged 13 to 18 and one for Juniors aged 8 to 13. Each House is run by House Parents in residence, with resident assistants. All full-time teachers act as Tutors and are involved with pastoral care. In addition, when necessary, students have open access to the School Counsellors.

Recreation. Chetham's School of Music offers students a pioneering 'Fit to Perform' programme – a bespoke programme, for each individual student, which is closely aligned with their motivations and requirements, not only in terms of conditioning and general fitness, but also in respect of injury prevention as young musicians.

Chetham's is a specialist music school with student wellbeing at its heart. Our holistic approach to student wellbeing is delivered by a number of personal trainers and specialist activity leaders throughout the day and evenings following individual, initial information-gathering and needs analysis. The School's medical staff, physiotherapist and caterers also contribute to the programme.

Applications, Visits. Entry is by audition only. Preliminary assessment auditions are held throughout the year, with final auditions in the Christmas and Spring terms.

The Prospectus and application forms are sent on request and are available on the School's website. Parents and prospective students are welcome to visit the School by arrangement with the Head's PA.

Fees, Grants. All entrants from the United Kingdom are eligible for grants under the Department for Education's Music and Dance Scheme. Parental contributions are calculated according to means and parents on low incomes qualify automatically for full fee remission. The Bursar will be glad to advise about the scales.

Choristers. The School is a member of the Choir Schools' Association and Choristerships at Manchester Cathedral for day boys and girls are available under a separate scheme. Choristers' Fee: £9,480 pa (subject to Cathedral Bursaries).

Charitable status. Chetham's School of Music is a Registered Charity, number 526702. It exists to educate exceptionally gifted young musicians.

Governors:
M Edge (*Chairman*)

Mrs S Barnes	K Jaquiss
Ms C Baxendale	Prof L Merrick
Dr B Brennan	Ms Newman
Ms A Corcoran	N Shepherd
Councillor J Davies	Canon M Wall
Mrs T Dixon	S Webb

Staff:

Principal: Mr Alun Jones, LTCL, LWCMD

Vice Principal: Miss N Smith, BA, NPQH

Director of Music: S Threlfall, GRNCM Hons, FRSA
Bursar: Mrs S C Newman, BSc Hons, FCA
Head of Sixth Form: Mrs J Harrison, MA
Head of Middle School: C Newman, MA, MSc
Head of Lower School: Mrs S Hales, BA

Music:

PA to the Director of Music: Mrs J Scott
Music Department Coordinator: I Mayer
Concert Coordinator: Miss N Prestt
Concerts Administrator: Miss A Mallon
Music Department Timetabler: Ms J Hunter
Auditions and Administration Secretary: Mrs A Herbert
Music Department Secretary: Ms B Taylor

Key:
Chamber Music Tutor
[Hallé] *Member of Hallé Orchestra*
[BBC] *Member of BBC Philharmonic*
* *Tutor at Royal Northern College of Music*
[O.North] *Member of Opera North Company*
[RLPO] *Member of Royal Liverpool Philharmonic Orchestra*
X *Manchester Camerata*
[CBSO] *Member of City of Birmingham Symphony Orchestra*

Brass:
Head of Department: David Chatterton
Euphonium Tutors: Bill Millar #, David Thornton #*
Horn Tutors: Julian Plummer [Hallé], Richard Bourn, Tom Redmond, Lindsey Stoker, Tim Jackson, Helen Varley
Percussion Tutors: Sophie Hastings (*Latin percussion and Kit*), David Hext [Hallé], Paul Patrick [BBC]#*, Andrea Vogler, Le Yu
Trombone Tutors: Robert Burtenshaw #[O.North], Katy Jones, Les Storey #
Trumpet Staff: David Chatterton #
Tutors: John Dickinson *#, Neil Fulton, Murray Greig *#[O.North], Tom Osborne, Tracey Redfern #X, Gareth Small [Hallé]#
Tuba Tutors: Brian Kingsley *#[O.North]

Keyboard:
Head of Department: Dr Murray McLachlan *

Tutors: Gemma Beeson, Simon Bottomley #, Sam Brook, Graham Caskie, Hazel Fanning, Jill Fogden, Benjamin Frith #, Duncan Glenday, John Gough, Alison Havard, Marta Karbownicka, Helen Krizos *, BingBing Li, Jonathan Middleton, Kathryn Page, Dina Parakhina *, Ben Powell, Marie-Louise Taylor, Charlotte Turner, Lulu Yang, Jeremy Young #
Harpsichord Tutor: Charlotte Turner
Jazz Piano Tutor: Les Chisnall
Organ Tutors: Simon Passmore, Christopher Stokes
Chamber Tutors: Benjamin Frith, Jeremy Young

Strings:
Head of Department: Nicholas Jones
Assistant: Owen Cox
Senior Chamber Music Tutor: Graham Oppenheimer
Chamber Music Tutor: Pavel Fischer
Violin Staff: Owen Cox
Tutors: Jiafeng Chen, Connie del Vecchio [RLPO], Krystoffer Dolatko, Ruth Hahn, Benedict Holland *, Linda Janowska, Jan Repko *, Yumi Sasaki, Katie Stillman, Deirdre Ward, Qian Wu #
Viola Tutors: Sebastian Mueller, Graham Oppenheimer #
Viola da Gamba: Roberto Carrillo-Garcia
Cello Staff: Nicholas Jones # *, Stephen Threlfall #
Tutors: Barbara Grunthal X, Jennifer Langridge, Li Lu, Anna Menzies, David Smith #, Gillian Thoday
Double Bass Tutor: Yi Xin Salvage [Hallé], Steve Berry (*jazz*)
Harp Tutor: Eleanor Hudson, Marie Leenhardt [Hallé]
Guitar Tutors: Jim Faulkner (*jazz*), Wendy Jackson #

Woodwind:
Head of Department: Belinda Gough, Martyn Shaw [job share]
Recorder/Baroque Ensembles Tutor: Chris Orton
Baroque Flute and Historical Performance: Martyn Shaw
Oboe Tutors: Rachael Clegg X, Matthew Jones, Stephane Rancourt [Hallé]
Flute Tutors: Katherine Bryan, Rachel Forgreive *, Fiona Fulton, Belinda Gough #
Clarinet Tutors: Rosa Campos-Fernandez, Sergio Castello-Lopez, Jim Muirhead [Hallé]#, Marianne Rawles, Tom Verity,
Saxophone Tutors: Iain Dixon (*Jazz/improvisation*), Jim Muirhead [Hallé], Carl Raven * (*Jazz/improvisation*), Andrew Wilson #
Bassoon Tutors: Ben Hudson [Hallé], Graham Salvage *, Elena Comelli, Adam Mackenzie
Contra-Bassoon Tutor: Simon Davies

Vocal Department:
Tutors: Helen Francis #, Margaret McDonald, Stuart Overington, Diana Palmerston #

Staff Accompanists:
Heads of Department: Brenda Blewett, Nicholas Oliver
Staff: Elena Namilova, Martyn Parkes, Simon Passmore

Composition:
Head of Department: Dr Jeremy Pike, MA, MPhil, PhD, LRAM, Hon ARAM
D Mason, BA
Music Technology:
Adrian Horn, BMus
Dr Jeremy Pike, MA, MPhil, PhD, LRAM, Hon ARAM

Practice Team Leaders:
Kristine Healy
Dannii Meagher

Big Band:
Directors: Richard Iles, Jim Muirhead [Hallé]

Improvisation:
Steve Berry *, Les Chisnall (*Keyboard*), Iain Dixon

Alexander Technique:
Patrick Grundy-White, Anne Whitehead

Academic Music:
S King, BA, MA, MPhil, PhD
Ms R Aldred, BMus
Miss C Campbell Smith, MA
J LeGrove, BA
D Mason, BA
Dr S Murphy, PhD, BA
Mrs S Oliver, BA

Art:
Miss A Boothroyd, BA
Mrs M Taube, BTEC

Compensatory Education/Special Needs:
Mrs B L Owen, BEd, RSA Dip SpLD
Miss L Fogg, MA
Miss C Lynch, BA
Learning Support Assistants

Drama & Theatre Studies:
Mrs J Sherlock, MA

English:
Mrs J Harrison, MA
Miss L Jones, BA
J Runswick-Cole, MEd
Mrs J Sherlock, MA

Humanities & PSHE:
A Kyle, BA
M Clarke, BSc
Mrs S Cox, BA
C Newman, MA

Information Technology:
Mrs F Holker, BSc
Miss C Whittaker, BA

Junior Department:
D Harris, BA
Miss C Tomlinson, PGCE

Languages:
Ms N Greschwendt, PGCE
P Chillingworth, BA
Mrs S Hales, BA
Mrs R Jordan, BA
Dr C Law, PhD, MA

Mathematics:
Mrs A Marsden, BSc
C Bramall, BA
Mrs F Holker, BSc
Mrs S Wegg

Recreation:
Miss E Burwell, BA
A Watson
Miss C Whittaker, BA

Sciences:
A Henderson, BA
J Blundell, BSc
Mrs L Gartside, BSc
Mrs C Shiells, BSc
Ms E Storey, BSc

Librarian: Mrs G Wood, BMus

Careers:
Dr S Murphy, PhD, MMus, BA (*Music Colleges*)
Mrs J Harrison, MA (*Universities*)

Houses:
Mr & Mrs J Runswick-Cole (*Boys' House*)
Mrs A Martinez Navarrate (*Girls' House*)
Mr G Taylor (*Victoria House*)

School Doctor: Dr J Tankel
Nurse: Mrs K Scott, RGN
Principal's PA: Mrs L Haslam

Chigwell School

Chigwell, Essex IG7 6QF

Tel: 020 8501 5700
Fax: 020 8500 6232
email: hm@chigwell-school.org
website: www.chigwell-school.org
Twitter: @chigwellschool

Motto: *Aut viam inveniam aut faciam ~ Find a Way or Make a Way*

The School was founded in 1629 by Samuel Harsnett, Archbishop of York, "to supply a liberal and practical education, and to afford instruction in the Christian religion, according to the doctrine and principles of the Church of England". William Penn, founder of Pennsylvania, is the most famous Old Chigwellian.

Today the School welcomes boys and girls from all backgrounds and is a lively, happy community in which pupils are encouraged to develop all their talents to the full.

The School became co-educational in September 1997 and currently there are over 940 pupils aged 4 to 18 pupils, including 25 international boarders.

Location. Chigwell School stands in a superb green belt location in 100 acres of playing fields and woodlands, midway between Epping and Hainault Forests and enjoys excellent communications. It is easily accessible from London (by Central Line Underground network). Both the M25 and M11 motorways are close by, while Heathrow, Gatwick, City of London, Stansted and Luton Airports are all reachable from the School within the hour.

Buildings. The original building is still in use and houses the Senior School Swallow Library. There has been a considerable amount of building in the past years and all the older buildings have been modernised while retaining their character. New facilities include a Junior School classroom block, a new Junior School library, a state-of-the-art Drama Centre, new catering facilities, upgraded boys' boarding houses, a superb floodlit all-weather pitch, refurbished science block and a purpose-built Pre-Prep School. The latest additions are the stunning Risham Sarao Sixth Form Centre and the extended Dining Hall which opened in January 2018.

Organisation. The School is divided into the Senior, Junior and Pre-Prep Schools and is administered as a single unit with a common teaching staff.

The Head of the Junior School is responsible for all pupils between the ages of 7 and 13, although teaching from Year 7 upwards is coordinated by the Senior School. The Junior School is on the same site as the Senior School and all facilities and grounds are used by Junior pupils. Assembly, Games and Lunch are all arranged separately from the Senior School. (For further details, see Junior School entry in IAPS section.)

The Head of Pre-Prep is responsible for children aged 4 to 7 and they are largely self-contained in the new Pre-Prep School.

In the Senior School, all the day pupils and boarders are divided into four Day Houses. Each House has a large House room and a Housemaster's or Housemistress's study.

Sixth Formers have use of the new sixth form centre which has classroom, study and social spaces and is open into the evening.

Curriculum. Pupils follow a broad based course leading to GCSE. Maths, English, Science and one modern language form the common core of subjects. Science is taken either as three separate subjects (Physics, Biology, Chemistry) or as Coordinated Science. In addition, a wide range of options is taken at GCSE including Art and Design, Graphic Design, Design Technology, French, German, Spanish, Latin, Greek, Geography, History, Religious Studies, Drama and Music.

Sixth Form. Subjects taken include, Latin, Greek, Classical Civilisation, French, German, Spanish, English, Economics, History, Geography, Maths, Further Maths, Physics, Chemistry, Biology, Music, Art, Design and Technology, Psychology, Religious Studies and Theatre Studies.

Games and Activities. Cricket, Football (Boys and Girls), Netball, Hockey (Boys and Girls), Athletics, Cross-Country Running, Swimming, Tennis, Golf, Basketball and Badminton. There are numerous School Societies and a Scout Troop. Many pupils join The Duke of Edinburgh's Award scheme as early as Year 9. There is a swimming pool, two Sports Halls and extensive playing fields on site.

Art & Design, Ceramics, and D & T. Art is taught throughout the School and there is excellent provision for Ceramics and D & T which form part of the curriculum for all pupils between the ages of 10 and 14.

Music. There are three Orchestras, two Wind Bands, one Swing Band and six Choirs. Many other ensembles flourish and perform at major concerts during the year, some of which take place in the local community. Pupils may learn any instrument (including the Organ).

Boarding. Sixth Form Boy Boarders are accommodated in Church House, run by Mr and Mrs Rabbitte, and Harsnett's House, run by Mr and Mrs Saunders. Sandon Lodge, set in the middle of the beautiful School Grounds, accommodates Sixth Form Girl Boarders under the care of Dr and Mr Lord. Hainault House, under the supervision of Mr and Mrs Goddard, lies adjacent to the Junior School and offers accommodation for the other Sixth Form Girl Boarders.

Fees per term (2018–2019). Full boarding £10,295; Day pupils £3,995–£5,995. Fees vary depending on age. Fees are inclusive of all tuition, meals (lunch and afternoon tea), textbooks, societies and most clubs.

Admission. Pupils usually join Chigwell School at 4+, 7+, 11+, 13+ or 16+.

Scholarships and Bursaries. Academic scholarships are awarded each year, primarily at 11+ and 16+ but occasionally at 13+ too. They are awarded in recognition of academic merit, irrespective of financial means. A competitive examination for Academic scholarships is held each year during the Lent Term for pupils aged 11+ and during the Michaelmas Term for pupils aged 16+.

Music scholarships are offered each year at 11+ and sometimes at 13+ and 16+ and these make a substantial contribution to school fees. In return, scholars are expected to play a full role in the performing life of the department.

Art and Drama scholarships are available at 16+.

Chigwell has always tried to ensure that children who would benefit from an education at the School are not excluded for financial reasons. A number of means-tested Bursaries are offered.

Further details can be obtained from the Admissions Registrar (email: admissions@chigwell-school.org).

The Old Chigwellians' Association. c/o Development Office, Chigwell School, Essex.

Charitable status. Chigwell School is an Incorporated Charity, registration number 1115098. It exists to provide a rounded education of the highest quality for its pupils.

Governing Body:
Chair: Mrs S L Aliker, BA, MBA, ACMA
Vice Chairman: D Morriss Esq, BSc, CEng, FIET, FBCS, CITP
Mrs E Brett, ACA
J Cullis Esq, MBE, BA, MSc
Revd C M Davies, BA, Dip SW
Dr G Dixon, MA, BMus, PhD, MBA, ARAM, FRCO, FRSA
N Garnish Esq, BSc, MBA, CMgr, FCMI, MCSI
Mrs J Gwinn, BSc
M Higgins Esq
R Howard Esq, MA
A N Howat Esq
M Jones, BA
Revd B W King, BA, MA
Mrs I Peck, BA
Miss M Ragha, MA, LLB
Mrs P Sen, BA, MA, MBA

Clerk to the Governors: C Jones, LLB, JP

Bursar: J Rea, MA, FCA, CTA

Headmaster: M E Punt, MA, MSc, PGCE

Deputy Head: D J Gower, BSc, PGCE

Deputy Head, Staff and Systems: Mrs A Savage, FTLC, GTCL, PGCE

Head of the Junior School: A Stubbs, BA, PGCE

Deputy Head of the Junior School: Mrs J Botham, BSc

Head of the Pre Prep School: E Gibbs, BA, PGCE, NPQH

Assistant Staff:
* *Head of Department*
† *Housemaster/mistress*

Mrs N A Aanonson-Rawlings, BA
Mrs A M Aitken, MA
E Aitken, MA (*Art and Design)
C G Anderson, BSc, PGCE
Mrs E D Anderson, BSc, PGCE
Mrs H I Arrowsmith, BA, PGCE
Miss H Baber, BSc, PGCE
Mrs M Baldwin, BSc (**Girls' Games*)
Ms S Bell, BA, PGCE (†*Caswalls*)
Mrs K S Bint, BSc, PGCE
Miss J E Bonner, BA, PGCE
Miss G Brien, MA, BSc, PGCE
A J Bruce, BA, PGCE
Miss C A Cassell, BSc, MSc, PGCE
Mrs M F Chan, BA, PGCE
S M Chaudhary, MA, PGCE (*Mathematics)
Mrs L Chery, MA
Dr P G Clayton, PhD, DIC, ARCS
S Coppell, MA, PGCE (*Head of Sixth Form*)
Miss G Crawford, BSc
Ms E Creber, BSc, PGCE
W P Eardley, BSc (*Biology)
H J G Ebden, BA, PGCE (*Music)
K Ennis, BA, PGCE, BSc
K Farrant, BEd (*Boys Games, *PE)
Mrs E M P Feeney, L-ès-L, PGCE (*French)
Ms N E Feeney, BA, PGCE
Dr E M Ferreira, PhD, MSc, PGCE
Mrs L C FitzGerald, BA, PGCE

Miss J R Foster, BA, PGCE (†*Penn's*)
E Gamwells, BA, PGCE
A Goddard BSc, PGCE (*Boarding)
I C Goddard, BA (†*Lambourne*, *History)
Dr G M Groszewski, BA, PG Dip, MPhil, PhD
J W Harley, BA, PGCE (*Economics)
D J L Harston, MA, DCEG, PGCE
D W Hartland, MA, PGCE, FRGS
Dr C Hirst, BSc, MRes, PhD
S A J Hirst, BA, BSc, MA, QTS (*Psychology)
R J Hume, MEd, BSc, PGCE
Mrs S Inch, BEd
Miss J L Ireland, MA, PGCE
Mrs J James, BA, PGCE
Mrs V C James, BEd
Mrs N A Jermyn, MEd, BA, PGCE (**Design & Technology*)
Mrs T Kwiecinska, MA, BA, PGCE
Mrs S L Lawrence, BSc, GTP
Miss F M Leach, BMus
Mrs A D Lewis, BEd
A Long, MSc
R A F Lonsdale, MA, DipEd
C J Lord, MA (*Classics)
H J Lukesch, 1st & 2nd STEX (*German)
J L Maingot, BA, PGCE (*Drama)
R D Maynes, BSc
J P Morris, BSc, PGCE, FRGS
Miss K V Morris, BA, PGCE
Miss S L Munro, BA, PGCE
Ms C M Nairac, BA
Dr I R Nitescu, PhD, MSc, BSc, PGCE
Miss A M J Ochana, MSc, BEng, PGCE
D I Patel, BSc, PGCE
Ms G Pearson, BSc, PGCE
C G Peebles, BSc
Mrs E Peebles, BEd, MA
S B Pepper, MA, PGCE (**Government & Politics*)
Miss R A Pettingill, BSc, PGCE (*Chemistry)
Mrs P Pewsey, BSEd, Dip EFL, PGCE
Mrs R J Philip, BEd
B W Porter, BSc, PGCE (*Physics)
Miss F Porter, BA, PGCE
Ms S C Proctor, BA, PGCE
D P Rabbitte, BA, LLB, PGCE (*Geography)
Mrs E R Rea, MA, PGCE (*English)
Ms P S Rex, BA, PGCE (**Religious Studies*)
R C Richardson, BA, MA, PGCE (†*Swallow's*)
Miss A L Ross, BA, PGCE
Mrs M A Saunders, BA, PGCE
N M Saunders, BSc, PGCE (*Director of Studies*)
The Revd G Scott, BD, PGCE (*Chaplain*)
G J Sexton, BSc
R S Spicer, BA, MSc, PGCE
Mrs L Standen, BSc, PGCE
Mrs E C Stoker, BA, PGCE
Mrs J Summers, BEd
Miss E D Taylor, MSc, BSc, GTTP (*Psychology)
Mrs L M Thurtle, BA, PGCE
Mrs C E Tilbrook, BEd, Dip SEA
W Tomsett, BSc
J J Twinn, BA, PGCE (*Spanish, *Modern Languages)
Mrs T Tyson, BA, PGCE
Miss S E Wales, MA
Mrs S E Welsford, BEd, Dip IT
Mrs R E Williams, MA, BA, PGCE (**Teaching & Learning*)
Mrs R L Williams, HND, PGCE
S C Wilson, MEd, BSc (*Science)
M D Wright, BA, BMus, PGCE
Dr M Zrinzo, LLD, BA

Christ College

Brecon

Brecon, Powys LD3 8AF

Tel: 01874 615440 (Head)
          01874 615440 (Bursar)
Fax: 01874 625174
email: enquiries@christcollegebrecon.com
website: www.christcollegebrecon.com

Motto: *Possunt quia posse videntur*

Founded by Henry VIII, 1541. Reconstituted by Act of Parliament, 1853.

Christ College, Brecon lies in a setting of outstanding natural beauty at the foot of the Brecon Beacons on the edge of the small market town of Brecon, two minutes' walk away on the opposite side of the river. The River Usk flows alongside the playing fields providing good canoeing and fishing while the nearby Llangorse Lake is available for sailing and windsurfing.

The school was founded by King Henry VIII in 1541 when he dissolved the Dominican Friary of St Nicholas. The 13th Century Chapel and Dining Hall are at the centre of school life and the school's mix of important, historic buildings and modern architecture represents the continuity of education at the school.

Estyn, Her Majesty's Inspectorate for Education & Training in Wales, inspected the school in 2017 and rated the school's current performance as 'Excellent'.

Organisation. Christ College was a boys only school until 1987 when girls were admitted to the Sixth Form. In 1995 the school became fully co-educational. There are 383 pupils in the school of whom 221 are boys and 162 girls. Approximately 60% of pupils board and there are two senior boys' houses, School House and Orchard House, two senior girls' houses, Donaldsons House and de Winton House, one co-educational house St Davids, and a lower school house, Alway House, for 11–13 year old boys and girls. Alway House also offers weekly boarding for our younger boarders in St Nicholas House. St Nicholas House is a junior day and boarding section for boys and girls aged 7–11 years.

Chapel. Chapel services are conducted in accordance with the liturgy of the Anglican church, but entrance to Christ College is open to boys and girls of all faiths. The ownership of Chapel by the boys and girls, demonstrated through their participation in services and their singing, is a feature of the school. Pupils are prepared for Confirmation by the School's Chaplain who lives on site.

Curriculum. Year 11 pupils follow a balanced curriculum leading to GCSE at which most pupils take 10 subjects. Options are chosen at the end of Year 9.

The Sixth Form follow the linear A Level syllabus. The Extended Project Qualification (EPQ) is also available for pupils.

Alongside their A Levels, pupils follow our second curriculum – Curriculum for Life. The curriculum offers a varied programme to enable them to thrive in their chosen career and personal life. The core timetable provides a series of sessions and guest lectures covering a range of life skill topics including financial literacy, preparing for university/work and health and wellbeing, politics and society. Pupils are exposed to a wide variety of influential external speakers who have been handpicked to complement the course to demonstrate how pupils may achieve their goals and work towards the next stage of their lives. The second section of the programme provides pupils with time to further develop life skills, such as participating in outdoor pursuits, Duke of Edinburgh's Award, community involvement, independent academic study, creative and music practice and physical strength and conditioning.

Class sizes rarely exceed 20 up to GCSE and average fewer than 10 at A Level.

Games. The main school games are Rugby Football, Cricket, Hockey, Soccer, Netball, Cross-Country and Athletics. Tennis, Badminton, Squash, Volleyball, Basketball, Golf, Fishing, Swimming, Shooting, Mountain Biking, Canoeing, Fencing, Indoor Cricket, Climbing, Triathlon and Aerobics are also available. The playing fields are extensive and lie adjacent to the school. Christ College has entered into a corporate partnership with Cradoc Golf Club, two miles outside of Brecon, to encourage pupils of all ages and experience in the fundamentals of the game of golf. The opportunity to play at Cradoc Golf Club and receive professional instruction is also extended to all parents of pupils attending Christ College.

Thursday Afternoons. On Thursday afternoons the CCF Contingent meets. There is a choice between Army and Royal Air Force sections and the CCF has its own Headquarters, Armoury and covered 30m Range in the school grounds. Pupils take their proficiency certificate after two years and may then choose to continue as Instructors, undergo training for the Duke of Edinburgh's Award scheme or leave the CCF and may become involved in community service.

Music. The Chapel Choir is large and enjoys an excellent reputation with radio and television broadcasts as well as overseas tours to its credit. As befits a school in Wales singing on all school occasions is committed, energetic and frequently with natural harmony. The school has a Chamber Choir, plus multiple wind, brass and string ensembles and its pupils play a prominent role in the South Powys Youth Orchestra and works in partnership with the Welsh Sinfonia to provide opportunities for pupils to play alongside professional musicians. There are many other opportunities to play in ensemble groups throughout the school. Individual instrumental and singing lessons are delivered by visiting musicians.

Activities. In addition to sporting pastimes a wide range of activities are available to pupils including Sixth Form Film Society, Advanced Chemistry, Art, Badminton, Basketball, Brass Group, Canoeing, Chamber Choir, Chess, Choir, Climbing, Community Service, Disability Sport, Drama, Fencing, Fitness, Golf, Indoor Cricket, IT Projects, Mandarin Chinese, Modern Dance/Jazz, Modern Language Film Society, Music Practice, Music Theory, Percussion Group, Project Science, Railway Modelling, Shooting, Stage Management, String Group, String Quartet, Technology, Wado Kai Karate, Wind Sinfonia, and Young Enterprise. The Duke of Edinburgh's Award scheme has been popular for many years and the majority of pupils gain at least a Bronze award, and a significant number go on to achieve the Gold award.

Overseas Travel is frequent and extensive. In recent years tours, expeditions and exchanges have taken place to Beijing, Canada, Japan, China, New York and South Africa as well as a number of European destinations.

Careers. Two members of staff also serve in the Careers department which also enlists the help of the Independent Schools Careers Organisation as well as the local Careers organisations. Former pupils return annually for Careers evenings and in this the Old Breconian Association is very helpful.

Entrance. Pupils are admitted at the age of 7+, 11+, 13+ and 16+ following the school's own entrance papers in English and Mathematics plus an IQ test, school report and interview. These tests are usually held in Jan/Feb, but individual arrangements can be made. The majority of 11 year old entrants come from local State Primary Schools, those at 13 from Preparatory schools when, instead of the Common Entrance examination, pupils face the same entrance procedures as at 11. Boys and girls also enter the Sixth Form on the basis of GCSE grade estimates, an IQ test and an interview. Although these are standard entry points, pupils will be considered for entry in Years 4, 5, 6, 8 and Year 10.

Term of Entry. Pupils are accepted in the Michaelmas, Lent and Summer terms.

Scholarships. Scholarships are available for entry at age 11, 13 and 16.

Competitive Scholarships – 11+, 13+, 6th Form Award
All Rounder – Up to 20%
Academic – Up to 20%
Art – Up to 20%
Drama – Up to 20%
Music – Up to 20%
Science – Up to 20%
Sport
Process: Interview and Assessment.

Bursaries are available at all ages and are subject to a means test.

There is a 25% fee remission for sons and daughters of the Clergy, and 10% bursaries are available each year for the children of serving members of the Armed Forces in receipt of CEA.

Fees per term (2018–2019). Years 3–6: Day £3,055–£4,012, Boarding £5,848–£6,035; Years 7 and 8: Day £5,174, Boarding £7,214; Years 9–11: Day £5,892, Boarding £9,217; Years 12–13: Day £6,182, Boarding £9,681.

Charitable status. Christ College, Brecon is a Registered Charity, number 525744. Its aims and objectives are to provide a fully rounded education for boys and girls between the ages of 7 and 18.

Visitor: Her Majesty The Queen

Chair of Governors: Sir E P Silk

Head: **Mr Gareth Pearson**, BEng

Deputy Head (*Academic*): Mr J D Bush, MA Cantab
Deputy Head (*Welfare*): Mr S Hill, BA Hons
Bursar: Mr M Allen
Marketing and Admissions: Mrs L Griffin
Admissions Registrar: Mrs M L Stephens
Development Director: Mr M Thomas

Christ's Hospital

Horsham, West Sussex RH13 0LJ

Tel: 01403 211293
Fax: 01403 255283
email: hmsec@christs-hospital.org.uk
website: www.christs-hospital.org.uk

Christ's Hospital was founded in the City of London by King Edward VI in 1552. In 1902 the boys moved to Horsham, where they were joined by the girls from their Hertford school in 1985.

Christ's Hospital is now a fully co-educational 11–18 boarding and day school for up to 900 pupils set in over 1000 acres of magnificent Sussex countryside.

Christ's Hospital is in many ways unique, offering an independent education of the highest calibre to children with academic potential, from all walks of life in a caring, boarding and day environment.

Pupils' fees are assessed according to family income, so that it is a child's ability and potential to benefit from a

Christ's Hospital education that determines their selection. This results in a social and cultural diversity that enriches our school community and offers our pupils unique opportunities as we prepare them to take their place in the modern world.

We believe in the benefits of a rounded and balanced education for our pupils. In practice, this means that as well as a challenging academic programme, pupils are also involved in music, art, drama, public speaking, community action and sport.

The School has an impressive history of high academic achievement with an average of 10 pupils each year taking up places at Oxford or Cambridge, and 98% of leavers going on to top Universities in this country and abroad.

Facilities. The Christ's Hospital campus is nothing short of majestic. From the moment you arrive you'll see that it is a very special place. Sweeping sports fields, beautiful buildings and our spectacular Quad are immediately visible.

We also have 16 boarding houses, two Upper Sixth Form residences, our own purpose-built theatre, modern sports centre, music school and art school. The School has in place an ongoing programme of renovation and rebuilding, which has included a complete refurbishment of the boarding houses.

The majority of pupils and teachers live on site, creating a community where pupils are happy and secure, with a wide range of activities on their doorstep. The seven-day week boarding school environment provides the time and space for pupils to develop their interests and talents, and to live and work successfully with others from a diverse range of backgrounds.

Christ's Hospital welcomes day pupils who are within a commutable distance from the School. Day pupils enjoy all the advantages of a top boarding school with access to an exceptional co-curricular programme.

Admission. Normally entry to Christ's Hospital is at Year 7, Year 9 or Sixth Form. Occasionally, we can admit children at Year 8 or 10. The Admissions Office will be able to advise you if places are available.

We encourage you to visit CH on one of our termly Open Mornings to enable you to see the school in action.

Our selection process is designed to determine whether a child will flourish in a busy boarding school environment with a strong academic ethos, enjoying the wide range of opportunities on offer, and feel at home at Christ's Hospital.

Parents are advised to start the Admissions process as early as possible and ideally at least eighteen months before their child would be due to enter the school.

Places at the school are academically selective and are offered on the basis of Christ's Hospital's own assessments.

Year 7 Entry. We are looking for candidates working at the higher end of the ability range: those currently working above the expected level in English, Maths and Science.

Year 9 Entry. Candidates should be targeted to achieve an average of 60% at Common Entrance or a current working grade of 6 or above in English, Maths and Science.

Sixth Form Entry. Applicants should be predicted to achieve an A or A* grade at GCSE in the subjects that they wish to continue on to A Level or Higher Level for International Baccalaureate (a 7 for those subjects now awarded 1 to 9). In addition students will also need to achieve a minimum of four B grades in other subjects at GCSE (a 6 for those subjects now awarded 1 to 9).

Additional Entry Information. In all cases reports will be requested from a candidate's current school and it is recommended that parents contact their child's current school early in the admissions process to ask about their child's predicted SATs/Common Entrance/GCSE results.

Fees per term (2018–2019). Boarding £11,480; Day £5,930 (Years 7–8), £7,470 (Years 9–13).

Charitable status. Christ's Hospital School is a Registered Charity, number 1120090, supported by the Christ's Hospital Foundation, Registered Charity number 306975.

Head Master: Simon Reid, BA

Deputy Heads:
J E Perriss, BA (*Geography*)
Mrs M A Fleming, BA (*Classics*)

Assistant Heads:
Assistant Head (Academic): Dr M I Medley, MSc, PhD
Assistant Head (Admissions): Dr A R Wines, MA, PhD
Assistant Head (Broader Curriculum): S J O'Boyle, BSc, ARCS
Assistant Head (Pastoral): D M L Kirby, BA

Chaplain:
Revd S Golding, BA, MA (*Theology & Philosophy*)

Assistant Staff:
* Head of Department

Mrs R A Ahmed-Geere, BA (*English*)
Miss N A Albrecht, MPhil (*History*)
Ms M Alcaras (*French Language Assistant*)
R Allcorn, MSc (*Biology*)
N Anthony (*Artist in Residence*)
R A K Ashley, BA (*Mathematics*)
Miss J Azancot, BA (*Design & Technology*)
Dr R Brading, BA, MA, PhD (*English*)
Ms E Browne, BSc (*Designer in Residence*)
P J Bryant, BA (**Economics*)
Miss H C Burt, BTh (*Theology & Philosophy*)
B J Callaghan, BA (*Classics*)
J B Callas, BSc (**Biology*)
Miss A Cassidy, MA (**French*)
Mrs J E Cave, MA (*French*)
G N Chandler, BA (*German, French*)
Mrs C M Chanin-Cowley, BA (*EFL*)
Ms J D Charles, BSc (*Undergraduate Sports Assistant*)
S A Cowley, BA (**Art*)
I E Davies, MSc (*Chemistry, Sport*)
P Deller, BA (**Art*)
Mrs N D Dotor Cespedes, BSc (*Biology*)
P R Drummond, MA (*English*)
J D Duffield, BSc (*Mathematics*)
P L Dutton, MA, ARCO (*Music*)
Mrs V C Dutton, BEng, MSc (*Physics*)
D J Farnfield, BA (*Geography*)
Ms W Feng (*Mandarin*)
Mrs D A Field, BA (*English ESL*)
Mrs M A Fleming, BA (*Classics*)
S Fritsch, (*German*)
Miss J E Gall, BEd (*Biology, Sports Science & PE*)
Miss S Gamba, BMus (*Music*)
Revd S Golding, BA, MA (*Theology & Philosophy*)
J-M Gonzalez, BA (*Spanish*)
Mrs J I Green, BSc (*Chemistry*)
D Griffiths, BSc (*Mathematics*)
J A Grindrod, BA (**Sports Science & PE*)
Ms Y Guo (*Mandarin Language Assistant*)
P H Hall-Palmer, BA (**Design & Technology*)
Dr K H Hannavy, BSc, DPhil (*Chemistry*)
E W G Hatton, BA (**Classics*)
C G Hawkins, MA (*English*)
Mrs C M Hennock, MA (*Mathematics*)
A E Henocq, BSc (*Chemistry*)
Miss H I Hestermann (*German Language Assistant*)
Mrs H V Hillier, BSc (*Teaching & Learning Skills Support*)
Mrs C Y Hitchcock, BA (*Economics*)

Miss R D Hodges, MA (*Theology & Philosophy*)
P A Hodgkinson, MA (**Music*)
Mrs O B Hodgkinson, BA (*Mathematics*)
Miss E F Holmes, BA (*Mathematics*)
M R Jennings, BA, PhD (*History*)
J S Johnson, MA (**Drama & Theatre Studies*)
E Jones, MA (**Music*)
M C Jones, MA (*English*)
J P Keet, MA (*History*)
Mrs C E Kelley, BA (*Drama*)
W T Kerr-Dineen, BA (*PE & Sports Science, Director of Hockey*)
D M L Kirby, BA (*English, Theology & Philosophy*)
Mrs R J Krebs, BA (**Geography*)
M K Lacewing, BA, BPhil, PhD (*Theology & Philosophy*)
Mrs P J Laughton, BA (**Food & Nutrition*)
Miss F MacKenzie, MA (**Librarian*)
Miss R L Manby, BA (*Geography*)
Miss A Manresa Amo (*Spanish Language Assistant*)
E A Marquez, BSc (**Spanish*)
Mrs E J Marsden, BMus MA (*Head of Strings*)
Miss J M Marshall, BSc (*Food & Nutrition*)
N W Martin, MSt (**History*)
S Mason, BSc (**Physics*)
K McArtney, BA (**Computer Studies*)
N McGovern, BA (*Sports Assistant*)
F McKenna, BTech (*Computer Studies, Design & Technology*)
G C McPheat, BSc (**Teaching & Learning Skills Support, Mathematics*)
Dr M I Medley, MSc, PhD (*Chemistry*)
D H Messenger, BA (**Director of Sport*)
D J Mulae, BSc (*Biology, General Science*)
Miss Z M Munday, BA (*Drama & Theatre Studies*)
A J Naylor, BA (*Art*)
Miss H N Nwandu, BSc (*Sports Science & Physical Education*)
S J O'Boyle, BSc, ARCS (*Mathematics*)
Ms J O'Connor, MA (*Biology*)
P I O'Regan, BSc (*Physics*)
Mrs C E P Page, BSc (*PE & Sport*)
H Parker, BSc (*Mathematics*)
Miss S R Patel, BA (*Classics*)
J E Perriss, BA, MEd (*Geography*)
Ms D L Petford-Naish, BSc (**Geography*)
A J Presland, BSc (*Mathematics*)
Miss E M Purvis, BA (*English*)
P Radley, BSc (*Mathematics*)
Mrs L V Ransley, BA (*French*)
Mrs M Reid, BA (*French*)
S H C Reid, BA (*English*)
W A Richards, BSc (*Physics*)
Mrs L B Russell, MA (*Biology*)
A Saha, MA, BA (*English*)
J P Salisbury, BSc (*Chemistry*)
T D Scrivener, MSc (*Economics*)
G R Seddon, BSc (*Sports Assistant*)
R D Sharkey, BA (*Economics*)
Mrs D J Stamp, BEd (*Mathematics*)
I N Stannard, BA (**Theology & Philosophy*)
M K Stephens, BSc (*Chemistry*)
M S Stephens, BSc (*Mathematics*)
R W Stuart, MA, PhD (*English*)
Ms S E Stuart, MA (*History*)
A G Taylor, BA (*Theology & Philosophy*)
Mrs C E Thomson, MA (**Chemistry*)
Dr S R Thomson, BA, DPhil (*Classics*)
Miss L E A Thornton, MA (*History*)
S M Titchener, BA, MMus (*Music*)
Mrs C Villalba Garrido, MA (*Spanish*)
S W Walsh, MA (**English*)

Mrs C Ward, MA (*Teaching & Learning Skills Support*)
Miss A Wardle (*Graduate Music Assistant*)
Ms R L Watson, BSc (*Design & Technology*)
Dr P J Webb, BA, PhD (*Physics*)
L Wegg, BSc (**Mathematics*)
G P Whitely, BA (*Art*)
T W Whittingham, BA, LTCL (*Music, Bandmaster*)
Mrs J A Williams (*Chemistry*)
A R Wines, MA, PhD (*History*)
Mrs D Yan, MSc (**Mandarin*)
Mrs M E Young, BSc (*Geography*)
S C Young, MSc (*Chemistry*)

Clerk and Chief Operating Officer: N J Tesseyman
Bursar: K J Willder, MBE
Headmaster's PA: Mrs K J Bernaldo de Quirós

Churcher's College

Ramshill, Petersfield, Hampshire GU31 4AS

Tel: 01730 263033
email: admissions@churcherscollege.com
website: www.churcherscollege.com
Twitter: @churchers1722
Facebook: @ChurchersCollege

Motto: *Credita Cælo ~ Entrusted to Heaven*

Churcher's College is an independent day school for girls and boys offering Nursery, Junior, Senior and Sixth Form education. With around 880 pupils at the Senior School and 225 pupils at the Junior School (excluding the Nursery) of approximately equal numbers of boys and girls aged 3 to 18 years old, Churcher's College enjoys recognition as one of the most accomplished independent, co-educational day schools in the country.

The school is hosted on two campus sites in Hampshire enabling the Junior School and Nursery pupils to flourish in their own beautiful grounds in Liphook, whilst maintaining close links with the Senior School and Sixth Form located in nearby Petersfield. Both sites offer on-site playing fields and unrivalled facilities, providing the comfort and opportunities of an open, healthy environment.

Admissions. We welcome girls and boys from the age of 3 into our Nursery. Other key entry points are 7+ (Year 3) at the Junior School or 11+ (Year 7) and 16+ (Sixth Form) at the Senior School.

Our Admissions Team are always happy to help, so for any enquiries please contact admissions@churchers college.com

The Sixth Form. The Sixth Form offers a wide variety of strong, widely-recognised A Level courses. The Churcher's Sixth Form curriculum allows you to build a portfolio of excellence, demonstrating to university admissions tutors and employers a depth and breadth of understanding in a wide range of fields.

Although precise programmes of study vary, based on the individual, most students will study three A Level qualifications, with Further Maths being taken as an additional fourth. In addition to this, a number of the most academically-inquisitive pupils will complete the Extended Project Qualification.

A Level course subjects include: Ancient History, Art, Biology, Business, Chemistry, Computing, Design & Technology, Drama, Economics, English Literature, French, Geography, German, History, Latin, Mathematics, Further Mathematics, Music, including the Advanced Musicians Course, Physics, Politics, Psychology, Religion & Philosophy, Spanish, Sports Science.

There is a fully-equipped Sixth Form Centre, for both study and recreation, a floor of the Library dedicated to Sixth Form private study, an excellent Careers Library and full-time Careers Officer and specialist Sixth Form teaching rooms and ICT facilities.

Years 1–5. From the 11+ entry all pupils follow a common academic programme comprising Mathematics, English, Physics, Chemistry, Biology, Latin, Classical Civilisation, Geography, Religion and Philosophy, Music, Art, Design & Technology, ICT, Drama and PE. In the First Year, all pupils study Spanish alongside their personal choice between French and German. In Year 2 an additional Modern European language (German or Spanish) is added to the programme. All pupils follow a broad curriculum and are not asked to specialise until they reach GCSE. All pupils follow GCSE courses in Mathematics, English, Language and Literature, a Modern Language, a Humanity and at least 2 additional optional subjects. All pupils begin the AQA GCSE "Trilogy" course in the third year, which leads to two GCSE grades, but at the end of the Third year, some pupils are offered the opportunity to transfer onto the Separate Sciences course, based upon aptitude and ability.

Pupils are tested and examined regularly with formal assessment procedures each half term and each end of term.

Facilities. Churcher's academic facilities include impressive purpose-built teaching accommodation, ICT suites, drama studios, art and design studios, design technology workshops, music centre and science block. Sports facilities include a swimming pool, sports halls and on-site tennis courts, netball courts, rugby pitches, all-weather hockey pitches and cricket squares. Churcher's has the facilities and resources to support an extensive range of extracurricular activities. The Sixth Form enjoys extensive recreational and teaching facilities. The Junior School is situated on its own spacious 10-acre site in Liphook, close to Petersfield.

Games and other Activities. The major sports played are Rugby, Hockey, Netball, Cricket and Rounders. There are also facilities for Swimming, Badminton, Basketball, Volleyball, Tennis, Athletics, Aerobics and Cross-country, to name but a few. The School has a strong CCF unit with Army, Air Force and Naval Sections, and a flourishing Duke of Edinburgh's Award programme. Other activities include Mountain Biking, Canoeing, Gliding, Climbing, Adventurous Training, Young Enterprise Companies, Dance, Karate, Fencing, Football, Sailing, Horse Riding, Bridge, Chess, Debating, Drama and Photography.

Music, drama and dance are very strong in the school with School and House plays produced regularly and a wide range of out-of-school activities. The school also has a significant range of orchestras, wind bands and choirs and many more ensembles.

Careers. Planning for a successful future is an essential part of education and Churcher's College strives to provide a first-class Careers and Higher Education service for its students. Churcher's has a full-time Careers Adviser who is available to all students for advice and information at any stage of their school career. CEIAG is provided through the Head of Careers and HE, PSHE programme, annual Careers Convention, specialised careers testing and careers visits. HE information is delivered through interviews, talks, tutorials and opportunities to attend various external conventions and exhibitions. In addition, the Head of Careers attends parents' evenings at appropriate times in the academic year but is available throughout the year to pupils and parents.

Parents' Association. The Parents' Association's main purpose is to promote a positive school community, build an effective partnership between home and school and raise funds for various initiatives, events or needed school items. They meet once a term at school.

Fees per term (2018–2019). Senior School £5,140, Junior School £3,305–£3,530. Fees include charges for examination fees and textbooks, but exclude lunches and individual music lessons.

Charitable status. Churcher's College is a Registered Charity, number 1173833, and a Charitable Company Limited by Guarantee, registered in England and Wales, company number 10813349.

Governing Body:
M J Gallagher, DipArch Hons, RIBA, MIOD, FIMgt (*Chairman*)
Mrs J Bloomer, LLB (*Vice-Chairman*)
S Barrett
S Beecham
Mrs D Cornish, BA, MLitt
A Cox, BA Hons, FCA (*Nominated Governor for Parents' Association, Senior School*)
S Flint, BSc, MBA
J Franklin, BA, MA
Mrs C Herraman-Stowers
W A Jones, MA
R May, MIOD
Mrs D Moses, FCA
A Robinson, BSc, PGCE, MCGI
Ms A J Spirit, BA Hons, AMCM
Mrs L Wetzel (*Nominated Governor for Parents' Association, Junior School*)

Headmaster: S H L Williams, BSc, MA

Deputy Heads:
Mrs S M J Dixon, BSc (*Staff and Co-curricular*)
C D P Jones, MA (*Pastoral*)
I G Knowles, BSc (*Academic*)

Head of Sixth Form: W Baker, BA, MSc, FRSA
Senior Teacher (*Pastoral*): Mrs J E Jamouneau, BEd, MSc
Senior Teacher (*Staff*): Mrs J B Millard, BSc, MSc, ARCS
Director of Studies: Mrs S Cockerill, BSc
Academic Registrar: I M Crossman, BA

Creative Arts Faculty:
Head of Faculty/Art: A Saralis, BA
Mrs G Heath, BA
Mrs G Roff, BA
D Heath, BA

English Faculty:
Head of Faculty: Dr D P Cave, BA, PhD (*i/c The Academy*)
Miss P Harper, BA, PG Dip
Mrs S Herrington, BA (*Head of Drake House*)
Ms J Jarrett, BA
Mrs A Jones, BA
Mrs C Lilley, BA
S Reeves, MA
Mrs L Wade, BA
Mrs S-J Naym, BA

Humanities Faculty:
Head of Faculty/Classics: J Hegan, BA
Head of Economics: M Hill, BA (*Deputy Head of Sixth Form, i/c Young Enterprise*)
Head of Business: R A West, BSc, PG Dip (*Assistant Head of Sixth Form*)
Head of Geography: D J Nighy, BSc, FRGS (*PSHE Coordinator*)
Head of Religion & Philosophy: T Ostersen, BA
Head of Psychology, Head of Teaching & Learning: G Glasspool, BSc, MA
Head of Politics: P Cheshire, MA, BA
W Baker, BA, MSc, FRSA (*Head of Sixth Form*)
Mrs S M J Dixon, BSc (*Deputy Head Staff and Co-curricular*)

J Harris, BSc
M Hoebee, MA
Mrs L A Buttar, MA
S Gibbins, BA
C D P Jones, MA (*Deputy Head Pastoral*)
Miss L Jenkinson, BA
Head of History: Mrs H Jolliffe, MA
J Lofthouse, BA, MMus, PG Dip
J McLearie, MA
Mrs N Plewes, BSc (*Deputy Head of Sixth Form*)
B Seal, BA, MBA (*Head of Collingwood House*)
P Shipley, BA
Ms L K Yardley, BSc, MA

Mathematics Faculty:
Head of Faculty: Mrs T L Greenaway, BSc
Miss L A Holmes, BSc, ACA
Dr N Jackson, DPhil, MSc
J Seaton, BA (*Head of Grenville House*)
Mrs L J Selby, BSc
Miss R Blewett, BSc (*Assistant Head of House*)
Mrs A Thomas, BSc
Mrs J Trench, BSc
G Wilson, BSc

Modern Languages Faculty:
Head of Faculty/French: Mrs K A Shaw, BA
Head of German: Dr A Broomfield, BA, MA, PhD
Head of Spanish: Mrs A-M Giffin, BA
Head of French: Mrs N Sparks, BA (*OSCA*)
I M Crossman, BA (*Academic Registrar*)
V J Leysen, BA, MA
Mrs C H Mann, BA
Mrs M Robertson, BSc
H Sutherland, BA

Performing Arts Faculty:
Head of Faculty: Mrs H J Purchase, BA (*Director of Music*)
Head of Drama (*Curriculum*): Ms P Hadzis, BA
Head of Drama (*Performance*): Miss S Carty, BA, MA
P Cree, BA (*Assistant Director of Music Academic*)
J James, BA (*Assistant Director of Music, Contemporary*)
Mrs R Northey, BA
I Webb-Taylor, MA (*Assistant Director of Music, Performance*)

Science Faculty:
Head of Faculty: Ms M J Westwood, BSc (*Head of Biology*)
Head of Chemistry: D J Dunster, MA
Head of Physics: M C Kelly, BSc
Mrs S L Cockerill, BSc (*Director of Studies*)
G Glasspool, BSc, MA
R M Hoe, BSc (*Head of Nelson House, Director of Pupil Well-Being*)
Mrs J E Jamouneau, BEd, MSc (*Senior Teacher Pastoral*)
I Knowles, BSc (*Deputy Head Academic*)
J Lucraft, MBA, MEng, CEng
Mrs J B Millard, BSc, MSc, ARCS (*Senior Teacher Staff*)
Dr V Raeside, BSc, PhD
Dr F H Perry, PSc, PhD
Mrs N Rivett, BSc
W Statham, BSc
R West, BEng
Dr R Whittle, MEng (*i/c STEAM*)
J G Yugin-Power, BSc (*Head of Rodney House*)

Sports Faculty:
Director of Sport: Mrs L J A Taylor, BSc
P Beard, BA
R Cardwell, BA (*Assistant Head of Collingwood*)
J Daniel, BSc (*Assistant Head of Drake, First Challenge*)

Miss S Gardner, BSc, MSc
Miss L K Howe, BSc (*Head of Sports Science, Fifth Year Pastoral Coordinator*)
Mrs T Jenkins (*i/c tennis*)
K Magurie, BA (*Assistant Head of House*)
R Maier (*Assistant Head of Grenville, i/c Cricket*)

Technology Faculty:
Head of Faculty: Mrs K McCathie, BSc (*Head of Computing & ICT*)
Head of Design & Technology: S Edington, BEd
S N Bond, BA
Miss C Evans, BA
Miss S J Murrall, BA
A Sangster, BSc

Adventure Faculty:
Head of Faculty: P Pearson, ML, SPA (*Head of Adventurous Activities, OSCA, DofE Manager, i/c Expeditions*)
M J B Adams, BEd (*i/c CCF Navy Section, Devizes to Westminster Canoe Marathon*)
R Cardwell, BA
J Daniel, BSc (*First Challenge*)
A P N Rowley, BSc (*Assistant Head of Adventurous Activities*)
Mrs N Sparks, BA (*OSCA*)
R Snowball, CCF
W J Statham, BSc

Curriculum Support:
Mrs L Blackman, BEd, Dip SpLD, Dip Counselling Children and Adolescents (*Head of Curriculum Support, School Counsellor*)
Mrs N Cooper, BA

Junior School

Head of Junior School: Mrs F Robinson, BA, MA

Deputy Head: Mrs P Yugin-Power, BSc, MA Ed, QTS
Head of Nursery: Mrs A Knowles, BSc
Head of Infant Department: Miss K M Humphreys, BEd
Senior Teacher Middle School: Mrs S J Moore, ARCM, GRSM
Senior Teacher Upper School: N Rushin, BSc, MSc
Director of Studies: Mrs R Drummond, BSocSc

Mrs K Stuzer, BA
Miss H Parry, BA
C Taylor, BSc
Miss K M Humphreys, BEd
Mrs J Gillard
Miss K Shipton, BA
Miss S Thompson, BA, BSc
Ms K Pendry, BA
Mrs S J Moore, ARCM, GRCM
Mrs K Tkaczynska, BEd
Mrs S Roberts, BEd
N Rushin, BSc, MSc
Mrs S Evans (*Head of Learning Enrichment*)
Miss C Stone (*Head of Music*)
M Forbes, BSc (*Head of Sport and Outdoor Learning*)
Mrs A C Chilton, BEd (*PE*)
Mrs C Murphy, MA, BSc
Mrs G Becker (*MFL*)
Mrs L M Eddy, BA (*English, PE*)
Mrs C Foley, BA

Librarians:
Mrs L M Robbins, BSc, MIEH (*Junior School*)
Mrs D T Greenall, BA
Mrs V Johnson, BSc

Bursar: D T Robbins, BSc Econ, FCCA

City of London Freemen's School

Ashtead Park, Surrey KT21 1ET

Tel: 01372 277933
Fax: 01372 276165
email: admissions@freemens.org
website: www.freemens.org
Twitter: @HelloFreemens
Facebook: @HelloFreemens

Motto: *Domine dirige nos*

The City of London Freemen's School is an independent co-educational day and boarding school which provides continuity of education for children aged 7 to 18. The School was founded in Brixton in 1854 by the Corporation of the City of London to provide 'a religious and virtuous education' for the orphaned children of Freemen of the City of London; Christian principles remain at the heart of its ethos, although the School is non-denominational. It is one of 3 schools governed and maintained by the City of London Corporation.

In 1926 the School moved to Ashtead Park, its present site and now educates approximately 915 girls and boys. Most of these pupils are day pupils, but the School remains firmly committed to the provision of boarding for a number of its pupils.

Alongside excellent academic results, our innovative enrichment programme is at the heart of our commitment to developing the whole person. We have the facilities, staff and grounds to ensure our students are happy, secure and fulfilled. We place particular emphasis on the individual and their needs and in providing the opportunities to identify and develop their skills to flourish throughout their time at Freemen's, and beyond.

There are 913 pupils in the School, approximately equal numbers of boys and girls, including up to 30 female and 30 male boarders. There are 515 pupils over the age of 13, including a Sixth Form of approximately 225.

The School stands in 57 acres of playing fields and parkland between Epsom and Leatherhead with easy access to Heathrow and Gatwick – both of which are only 22 miles away – via the M25. Buildings include a central Georgian Mansion, an Assembly Hall, a floodlit all-weather pitch and a Sports Hall complex completed in 1995. A multimillion pound building programme in the 1990s saw the addition of a Sixth Form Centre, an Art and Design Centre and a Science and Technology Centre. New teaching facilities for all subject Departments including Library and IT facilities were completed with the opening of the Haywood Centre in September 2000. A Studio Theatre was opened in October 2001, providing an auditorium for all productions, recitals, concerts and lecture facilities. The all-weather pitch has been replaced, bringing both up to modern national representative standards. A state-of-the-art music school, including a Steinway-D concert grand piano, and a co-educational boarding house for 60 pupils were completed and opened in 2014. Work has begun on the rebuilding of the swimming pool, which will be followed by the refurbishment of Main House.

Junior School. Since September 1988 the Junior School, ages 7–13, has been accommodated in a new complex in Ashtead Park. This provides 20 classrooms for up to 400 pupils. The Junior School is fully integrated within the framework and policies of the whole school and other facilities include specialist rooms for Art and Design, Science, Music and an integrated Technology Centre as well as an Assembly Hall and extended Library.

See Junior School entry in IAPS section.

Organisation and Entry. The School is divided into two sections but is administered as a single unit. The Junior Department has its own specially trained staff and its own self-contained building, but otherwise all staff teach throughout the School.

Junior entry is by the School's own examination at 7+ or 11+ (normally in January).

Senior School entry is by passing the Common Entrance examination, normally at the age of 13+, or by the School's own 13+ examination. Screening tests for Senior School entry have been introduced for Year 6 and Year 7 pupils; these take place in January. Freemen's Junior School pupils may expect to transfer satisfactorily to the Senior School at 13+ without sitting a special examination.

Sixth Form entry: If you are sitting eight or more GCSEs, you will not need to sit entrance exams. Your offer will be conditional on your GCSE results. For current Year 10 (Lower 5) pupils: 55 points across 10 GCSE subjects. Grades will be converted as they have in the past and grade numbers will be added to these grade conversions. For example, five A grades and five 7 grades would add up to 70 points. Pupils must achieve at least grade 5 in English and Mathematics and meet the subject specific requirements for their subject choices at A Level. Current Year 9 (Upper 4) pupils: 55 points across 10 GCSE subjects. We will only accept grade 5 and above in all subjects and pupils must meet the subject specific requirements for their subject choices at A Level. A Drama grade will be converted.

Foundation entry is open to orphan children of Freemen at any age from 7+ to 16+, subject to satisfactory academic potential.

(Except for Foundationers, it is not necessary for applicants to be children of Freemen of the City.)

Curriculum. The first four years (7+ to 10+ in Years 3 to 6) are largely taught by class teachers up to Key Stage 2 following the broad outlines of the National Curriculum. Up to the age of about 14 all pupils have substantially the same curriculum which comprises English, French/German/Spanish, Mathematics, Physics, Chemistry, Biology, History, Geography, Religious Education, Latin, Design Technology, Computing, Food Technology, Art and Music. Thereafter, apart from a common core of English, French or German or Spanish, Mathematics and the 3 separate Sciences, selection is made for the course to GCSE from 15 other subjects including Spanish, German, French, Computing, Drama, Geography, History, Latin, Sociology and Design Technology so that the average pupil will offer 10 subjects. The principles of the National Curriculum are followed at all levels. Physical Education and Personal, Social and Health Education are included in the curriculum at all levels and all age groups have an Enrichment afternoon.

Sixth Form courses include the following: English Literature, Mathematics, Further Mathematics, Physics, Chemistry, Biology, History, Geography, Government & Politics, Classical Civilisation, French, German, Spanish, Art & Design, Business Studies, Drama, Music, Physical Education, Design Technology, Economics, Psychology and Philosophy and Theology. Pre-U courses are also offered in Art & Design. The Sixth Form also study the Free Minds Programme: a course to run alongside A Levels that allows students to study a range of subjects to provide an even broader base to students' knowledge.

All pupils follow an Enrichment Curriculum which consists of an Extended Project, Physical Education, Leadership Skills and Community Service. Computing is well equipped and established, with specialist rooms in both the Junior and Senior Schools.

The School has an excellent academic record. Recent GCSE results have been excellent, with more than 88% of examinations awarded A* or A grades. A Level results have been equally impressive with over 90% of examinations awarded A or B grades, and nearly all leavers go on to degree courses at universities or other higher education institutes.

Each pupil is allocated to a House comprising a cross-section of boys and girls, both day and boarding, throughout the School. House teams compete in all forms of sport as well as music, drama and debating.

Games. *For Boys*: Principally Rugby, Cricket, Football, Athletics, Fencing, squash, Swimming, and Tennis.

For Girls: Principally Hockey, Netball, Tennis, Athletics, Rounders, Fencing, Squash, Swimming and Horse Riding.

There is a very wide choice of extracurricular activities throughout the School. The Duke of Edinburgh's Award scheme is a very popular option in the Senior School.

Fees per term (2018–2019). Senior School: £6,081 (day), £10,260 (boarding); Junior School: £4,466–£4,914 (day). Instrumental Music lessons: £229.

Scholarships and Bursaries. Scholarship awards are intended to attract and reward pupils of high academic ability and talent. Parents of scholars will be offered up to a maximum 5% discount of the fees. Bursary funds are available for those families requiring support to meet school fees and can be as much as 100% of the school fees. City of London Scholarships, open to both internal and external applicants, are awarded as follows:

At 11+ Scholarships of not more than 5% of the tuition fee, tenable for seven years. These Scholarships are awarded on the basis of performance in the School's Entrance Examination, school reports and an interview.

At 13+ Scholarships of not more than 5% of the tuition fee, tenable for five years. These Scholarships are awarded on the basis of performance in the 13+ Scholarship examinations, school reports and an interview.

At 16+ (Sixth Form entry) Scholarships are awarded of not more than 5% of the tuition fee tenable for two years. These Scholarships are awarded on the basis of performance in the Sixth Form Scholarship papers, school reports and an interview.

Music Scholarships are awarded as follows:

At 11+ awards of not more than 5% of the tuition fee. Applicants must have reached Grade 3 in one instrument and be able to offer a second study. Auditions and interviews are held with the Director of Music.

At 13+ awards of not more than 5% of the tuition fee. Applicants must have reached Grade 5 in one instrument and be able to offer a second study. Auditions and interviews are held with the Director of Music.

At 16+ (Sixth Form) awards of not more than 5% of the tuition fee. Applicants must have reached Grade 7 in one instrument and be able to offer a second study. Auditions and interviews are held with the Director of Music.

In all cases, music scholarships include free tuition in one instrument provided by teachers at the School.

A significant number of Bursaries, from our Bursary funds and Livery Companies, are also available.

The Bhargava Award is also available. As a 'Women in STEM' initiative, made possible by a generous legacy, girls applying for entry into the Sixth Form to study Mathematics at A Level are invited to consider applying for the Bhargava Award. Applicants need to love Maths and be looking to study STEM subjects at university. They should live within fifteen miles of the school (KT21 1ET) in keeping with Mrs Bhargava's own links with Ashtead and Leatherhead. They should be currently attending a maintained sector school or academy. The Bhargava Award can cover the school day fee and extras in order that a deserving candidate from a financially limited background would not need to worry about covering fees, transport, uniform and trips costs.

Board of Governors:
Roger Arthur Holden Chadwick, OBE, Deputy (*Chairman*)
Philip Woodhouse, Deputy (*Deputy Chairman*)
Stuart John Fraser, CBE
John Bennett, Deputy
Nicholas Goddard (*co-opted*)
Brian Harris (*co-opted*)
Michael Hudson
Shravan Joshi
Alastair John Naisbitt King, MSc (*Alderman*)
Susan Langley, OBE (*Alderman*)
Vivienne Littlechild MBE JP
Andrew McMillan (*co-opted*)
Hugh Fenton Morris
Graham David Packham
Elizabeth Rogula, Deputy
Councillor Chris Townsend (*co-opted*)
Gillian Yarrow (*co-opted*)
Clare James MA, Deputy (*Ex-Officio Member*)
Deputy James Michael Douglas Thomson (*Ex-Officio Member*)

Clerk to the Governors: Alistair MacLellan

Headmaster: Mr Roland Martin

Deputy Head: Mr Stuart Bachelor
Academic Deputy Head: Mr Paul Bridges
Head of Sixth Form: Mr Richard Dolan
Head of Upper School: Miss Sophie Blair
Head of Junior School: Mr Matthew Robinson
Bursar: Mrs Susan Williams
Director of External Relations: Mr Jason Harrison-Miles
Head of Boarding & Co-Curricular: Mrs Jemima Edney
Director of Teaching, Learning and Innovation: Mr James Felgate
Deputy Houseparent: Mr Alan Auld
Assistant Head (Junior School): Mrs Louise Jowitt
Assistant Head (Sixth Form): Mr Adrian Parkin
Head of Year 9: Mrs Georgia Middlehurst
Head of Year 10: Mr Alan Auld
Head of Year 11: Mr Robbie Davies
Head of Year 12: Mrs Sarah Stewart
Head of Year 13: Mr James Hallam

Subject departments:
* *Head of Department*
§ *Part-time*

English:
*Mrs Sarah Parkin
Mr Christopher Bloomer (*2nd in Dept*)
Mr Paul Carabine
Mrs Kathryn de Villiers
Mr M Hughes
Mrs Sarah Stewart
Mrs Charlotte Unsworth-Hughes
Ms Fiona Moncur (*KS2 Coordinator*)
Mr Patrick New
Miss Ashleigh Callow (*EAL Teacher*)

Mathematics:
*Mr Ewan Bramhall
Mrs Marie Cast (*2nd in Dept*)
Mrs Zara Field
Mrs Stella Hippolyte
§Mrs Louise Sharpe
§Mrs Cecilia Inns

Mrs Louise Jowitt (*KS2 Coordinator*)
Mr Tom Marsden
Mrs Elizabeth Newhouse
Mr Adrian Parkin
Mr Kenneth Rose
§Mrs Elizabeth Rowlands
§Mr David Murray

Modern Languages:
*Mrs Sarah Hankin

French and German:
*Mrs Sarah Hankin
Mrs Linda Headon
§Mrs Catherine Leighton
§Mrs Julia Rosin (*KS2 Coordinator*)
Miss Lorna Vickers
Miss Rebecca Willis
§Ms Karolin Gericke

Spanish:
*Mrs Christina Salisbury
Miss Rebecca Willis

Mrs Maria Willis-Jones
§Ms Carol Creevey

Classics:
*Mr Alan Chadwick
§Mrs Ida Ashworth
§Mr William Ash

Science:
*Mr James Hallam
Mrs Michelle Restall (*KS2 Coordinator*)

Biology:
*Mrs Judith Vatcher
Mrs Raylene Fox
Mr John Graham
Mrs Susan Meek

Chemistry:
*Dr Sarah Pinniger
§Mrs Torna Burton
Mrs Joanna Dickson
Mr Simon Dodd

Physics:
*Mr James Hallam
Mrs Helen Irwin
Mr Mark Newcome
Mr Brandon O'Donnell
Mrs Penni Thornton
Dr Sarah Wheeler

Technology:
*Mr Steve Sarsfield

Design Technology:
Mr Rami Al-juboori
Mrs Joy Heafford (*KS2 Coordinator*)
Mr Max Hicks

Electronics:
Mr Steve Sarsfield

Food Technology:
§Mrs Tina Judge

Art & Design:
*Mrs Bridget Downing
Mrs Rebecca Houseman
§Ms Ginny Humphreys
Mrs Vanessa Symonds (*KS2 Coordinator*)

Economics and Business:
*Mrs Justine Marvin
Mr Paul Bridges
Mr Stuart Davis
Mr Richard Dolan
Mrs Kate Jepson-Taylor

Computing & Information Technology:
*Mr Ian Bartram
Mr Oliver James (*KS2 Coordinator*)
(*vacant*)

Drama:
*Miss Joanne Warburton
Miss Jessica Barrowman
Ms Andrea Gillie
Mr Alex Powell

Enrichment:
*Mrs Elizabeth Newhouse
Netball Coach: Mrs Natalie

Revd Jon Prior (*2nd in Charge*)
Miss Harriet Pennington (*EPQ Coordinator*)
Mrs Janet Wilby-King (*KS2 Coordinator*)

Geography:
*Mrs Ofelia Bueno-Lopez
Mrs Georgia Middlehurst
Mrs Harriet Pennington
§Mrs Emma Smith (*KS2 Coordinator*)
§Mrs Philippa Whiteley

History & Politics:
*Mr Andrew Weston
Mrs Katherine Edwards
Miss Rosemary Kempster (*KS2 Coordinator*)
Mr Robbie Davies
Mrs Elizabeth Joss

Music & Music Technology:
Director: Mr Paul Dodds
Assistant Director: Mrs Natalka Eaglestone
§Mrs Ida Ashworth
Mrs Sarah Gillespie (*KS2 Coordinator*)

Philosophy and Religion:
*Mr Tim Wright
Miss Nicola Bax
Mr Andrew Illingworth
Mrs Louise Jowitt
Mrs Catherine Williams (*KS2 Coordinator*)

Psychology:
*Miss Joanna Vinall
Mrs Joanna Wright

PE and Games:
*Mr Tim Deakin
Mr Jamie Shore-Nye
§Mrs Alison Bennett
Mrs Rachel Keightley
Mr Peter McKee
Miss Sophie Hughes
Head of Cricket: (*vacant*)
Head of Rugby/Temp Head of Boys' PE: Mr Jon Moore
Head of Hockey: Miss Frankie Paul
Head of Tennis and Athletics/Temp Head of Girls' PE: Mrs Louise Shaill
§Mrs Philippa Whiteley

Physical Education A Level (Sport Studies):
*Mr Jon Moore
Mrs Louise Shaill

Cricket Coach: Mr Neil Stewart
Hockey Coach: Mr James Earl
Netball Coach: Mrs Alison Bennett Marchant

Tennis Coach: Mr John Thistlethwaite
Rugby Coach: Mr Mike Cudmore
Rugby Coach: Mr Marc Crump
Squash Coach: Mr Jeremy Colton

PSHE:
Sixth Form Coordinator: Mr Adrian Parkin
Upper School Coordinator: Mrs Sue Meek
Junior School Coordinator: Mrs Louise Jowitt

Careers:
Head of Sixth Form Careers: Miss Rebecca Willis
Assistant Careers Advisor: Miss Lorna Vickers

Learning Support:
Learning Support Manager: Mr Andrew Illingworth
Learning Support Coordinator (Junior School): Ms Fiona Moncur

Junior School:

Year 3 (Form 1):
Head of Year: Mrs Janet Wilby-King
§Mrs Emma Smith
§Mrs Jenny Cooper

Year 4 (L2):
Head of Year: Mrs Sarah Gillespie
Mr Simon Davies
Mrs Catherine Williams

Year 5 (U2):
Head of Year: Mrs Vanessa Symonds
Miss Rosemary Kempster
Mr Martin Valkenburg

Year 6 (L3):
Head of Year: Mr Ali Raja
§Mrs Michelle Restall
§Mrs Vanessa Ielpi
Mr Richard Metcalfe

Year 7 (U3):
Head of Year: Mrs Fiona Moncur
Mrs Emma Leigh
Mrs Rachel Keightley
Mr Tom Marsden
§Mrs Philippa Whiteley
Mr Jamie Shore-Nye
Mr Max Hicks
§Mrs Louise Sharpe

Year 8 (L4):
Head of Year: Mrs Sophie Hughes
Mr Peter McKee
Ms Zara Field
Miss Jessica Barrowman
Mrs Charlotte Unsworth-Hughes
Mr Joshua McCune
Mr Patrick New
Mrs Louise Shaill

Heads of Houses:

Gresham:
Miss Nicola Bax
Mrs Catherine Williams

Hale:
Mrs Helen Irwin
Mrs Rachel Keightley

Whittington:
Mr Peter McKee

Staff Induction:
New Staff Induction Coordinator: Mrs Natalka Eaglestone
NQT Coordinator: Miss Joanna Vinall
NQT Coordinator (temporary): Mrs Charlotte Unsworth-Hughes

Duke of Edinburgh's Award:
D of E Senior Coordinator: Mr Patrick New

Boarding House:
Head of Boarding: Mrs Jemima Edney
Deputy Houseparent: Mr Alan Auld
Day Matron: Mrs Lin Retzlaff
Day Matron: Miss Angele Kauffmann
Boarding House Tutor: Miss Francesca Paul
Boarding House Tutor: Mrs Georgia Middlehurst
Boarding House Tutor: Mr Patrick New

Combined Cadet Force:
CCF Staff in charge of CCF: Miss Rosemary Kempster
CCF School Staff Instructor: Mr Colin Davies

Medical Centre:
School Nurse Manager: §Mrs Kate Barron
School Nurse Manager: §Mrs Elizabeth Holmden
School Nurse: §Mrs Bernadette O'Connor
School Nurse: §Mrs Priscilla Mills

Non-Teaching Staff:
Mrs Susan Williams (*Bursar*)
Mrs Kelly Montague (*Headmaster's PA*)
Mrs Anna Atkins (*HR Manager*)
Miss Helen Lambert (*HR Officer*)
Mrs Gillian Daniel (*Finance Manager*)
Mrs Debbie Widmer (*Finance Officer – Fees*)
§Mrs Jane Arnett (*Finance Officer – Creditors*)
§Mrs Suzanne Wilding (*Lettings Administrator/Bursary Assistant*)
Mr Jason Harrison-Miles (*Director of External Relations*)
Mrs Nicola Navamani (*International Admissions Officer*)
Mrs Kerri Martin (*Outreach Officer*)
Mrs Jo Patel (*Development Officer*)
Mrs Amanda Moss (*Senior Management Secretariat Team Leader*)
Miss Sarah Corlett (*Deputy Head's Secretary*)
Mrs Lucy Ryckaert (*Senior School Secretary*)
Mrs Tracey Clarke (*Senior School Receptionist*)
Mrs Gillian Anklesaria (*Secretary to Head of Junior School*)
Miss Natalie Holdway (*Junior School Administrator*)
§Mrs Samantha Grover (*Music Administrator*)
Mrs Antonietta Caprano-Wint (*Sports Administrator*)
Mrs Nicketa Williams (*Examinations Officer*)
Mrs Sue Dawes (*Senior Librarian*)
§Mrs Nicola Mason (*Assistant Librarian*)
Ms Charlotte Bellsham-Revell (*Assistant Librarian*)
§Mrs Julie Mayhew (*Senior Science Technician*)
Mrs Joanna Wojcik (*Technician – Chemistry*)
§Mrs Jane Dallyn (*Technician – Science, Junior School*)
Mr David Dunn (*Technician – General Science*)
§Ms Emma Hughes-Phillips (*Technician – Art & Design*)
§Mr Geoff Coates (*Technician – Art & Design*)
§Mr Rami Al-juboori (*Technician – Design Technology*)
§Mrs Sarah Baxter (*Technician – Food Technology*)
Mrs Mary Marrett (*Technician – Physics*)
Mr Chris Ruby (*Facilities Technician – Theatre Facilities*)
§Mr Karim Shabankareh (*Music Technician*)
Mr Adam Cohen (*Director of Technical Services*)
Mr Anthony Richmond (*Data Manager*)
Mr Stephen Miller (*ICT Technician*)
Mr Giles Tilley (*ICT Technician*)
Mr Gary Marshall (*Head of Grounds & Gardens*)
Mr Clive Fisher (*Senior Groundsperson*)
Mr Stuart Dare (*Groundsperson*)
Mr Craig Morgan (*Gardener/Groundsperson*)
Mr Lawrence Aggett (*Gardener*)
Mr Edward Kennedy (*Facilities Manager*)
Mr Karl Webb (*Deputy Facilities Manager*)
Mr Michael Bartlett (*Maintenance Assistant*)
Mr Richard Parke (*Maintenance Assistant*)
Mr Andrew Mills (*Maintenance Assistant*)
Mr Ian Foster (*Maintenance Assistant*)
Revd Jonathan Prior (*Chaplain*)

Visiting Music Teachers:
Ms Nicola Berg (*Singing*)
Mrs Alice Bishop (*Singing*)
Mrs Victoria Brockless (*Violin, Viola*)
Miss Ruth Chappell (*Flute*)
Mrs Hilary Dilnot (*Piano*)
Mr David Eaglestone (*Trombone, Tuba, French Horn*)
Ms Jennifer Janse (*Cello, Double Bass*)
Miss Jan Lewis (*Piano*)
Miss Sally MacTaggart (*Clarinet, Saxophone*)

Mr James O'Carroll (*Percussion, Drums*)
Ms Elenlucia Pappalardo (*Piano*)
Mr Tim Peake (*Piano*)
Miss Leah Perona-Wright (*Singing*)
Mr Nigel Perona-Wright (*Flute, Singing*)
Mr Paul Smith (*Saxophone, Clarinet, Oboe, Piano*)
Mr Simon Sturgeon-Clegg (*Trumpet, Trombone, Euphonium*)
Mrs Hilary Taylor (*Piano*)
Miss Gillian Wallace (*Violin*)
Mr John Wallace (*Guitar*)

City of London School

Queen Victoria Street, London EC4V 3AL

Tel: 020 3680 6300
email: admissions@cityoflondonschool.org.uk
            reception@cityoflondonschool.org.uk
website: www.cityoflondonschool.org.uk
Twitter: @CityofLdnSchool
Facebook: @CityofLondonSchool

The City of London School occupies a unique Thameside location in the heart of the capital and has up to 940 day boys between the ages of 10 and 18 from all parts of the capital. It traces its origin to bequests left for the education of poor boys in 1442 by John Carpenter, Town Clerk of the City. The Corporation of London was authorised by Act of Parliament in 1834 to use this and other endowments to establish and maintain a School for boys. This opened in 1837 in Milk Street, Cheapside, and moved to the Victoria Embankment in 1883. In 1986 the School moved again, to excellent purpose-built premises provided by the Corporation on a fine riverside site in the City, to which a new Technology building was added in 1990. The School lies on the riverside next to the Millennium Bridge with St Paul's Cathedral to the north and the Globe Theatre and Tate Modern across the Thames to the south. The School's Board of Governors is a committee of the Court of Common Council, the City of London's governing body and four independent co-opted members.

Admissions. Pupils are admitted aged 10, 11 and 13 (as on 1st September of year of entry), on the results of the School's own entrance examinations held each year in January. Note that boys applying for entry at age 13 are examined when they are in Year 6. Those admitted at 16 into the Sixth Form are selected by test and interview in the previous November. Applicants must register for examinations using our online system.

Fees per term (2018–2019). £5,967.

Entrance Scholarships. Academic, Music and Sports Scholarships are awarded annually.

Candidates for entry to the School may also apply for Choristerships at the Temple Church or the Chapel Royal, St James's Palace (the choristers of both choirs are pupils at the School). Choristers receive Choral Bursaries. Potential choristers may also take voice auditions and academic tests in Year 4; successful applicants will be offered a conditional place in the School for the year after their 10th birthday.

Bursaries. The School offers bursaries, up to the value of full fees, to assist those parents of academically very bright boys, who otherwise could not access private education. These awards are only available at 11+ and 16+.

Curriculum. All boys follow the same broad curriculum up to and including the Third Form. In the Third Form boys spend eight afternoons throughout the year on educational visits to institutions and places of interest in and around the City. Latin, French and Mandarin are started by all in the First Form and two choices from Greek, Classical Civilisation, Drama, German and Spanish may be added as options in the Third Form. Fourth and Fifth Form boys take a core of English, Mathematics, three Sciences (the core subjects are all IGCSEs), and at least one Modern Foreign Language (which can include Russian), and choose three other subjects from a wide range of subjects available for study to GCSE/IGCSE. In the Sixth Form boys study either four A Level subjects, or three and an EPQ (Extended Project Qualification). Virtually all boys leaving the Sixth Form proceed to their first or second choice of Russell Group University or Medical School.

Games. The School's 20 acres of playing fields, at Grove Park in south-east London, offer excellent facilities for football, cricket, athletics, and tennis. Sporting facilities on the School site include an astroturf pitch, sports hall, a gymnasium with conditioning room, three squash courts, a fencing salle, and a 25-metre swimming pool.

School Societies. There is a large number of School Societies, catering for a very wide range of interests, and a Freshers' Fair is held early each year to allow societies to promote themselves. Every opportunity is taken to benefit from the School's central position by participation in the cultural and educational life of London, and of the City in particular. The School has a strong musical tradition; tuition is available in a large range of instruments, and membership of the School choirs and orchestras is encouraged. Choristers of the Temple Church and of the Chapel Royal are educated at the School as bursaried scholars provided that they satisfy the entrance requirements. There is much interest in Drama, and the School has a fully-equipped Theatre and a Drama Studio. There is a large CCF Contingent which boys may join from the age of 13, with Army, Navy and RAF Sections. There is also a successful Community Service programme. Many boys also take part in the Duke of Edinburgh's Award scheme.

Alumni Association. The Old Boys' Society known as the John Carpenter Club, website: www.jcc.org.uk.

Chairman of Governors: Mr J Thomson

Head: A R Bird, MSc

Senior Deputy Head: R M Brookes, MChem, DPhil
Deputy Head Pastoral: Mrs C B Stephenson, MA
Assistant Head Academic: Miss N H Murphy, BA
Assistant Head Admissions & Communications: P S Marshall, MA
Assistant Head Co-Curricular & Professional Development: A J V McBroom, BA
Assistant Head Head of Sixth Form & Outreach: I Emerson, BSSc
Assistant Head Teaching and Learning: A Zivanic, BA, MA
Bursar: C B Griffiths, LLB
Director of Development: Ms K Ostermann, BA

Head of Sixth Form: I Emerson, BSSc, MA
Deputy Head of Sixth Form: Miss Z L Connolly, MA
Deputy Head of Sixth Form: M N Everard-Pennell, MChem, PhD
Deputy Head of Sixth Form: C R Webb, BSc
Head of Fifth Form: S S Fernandes, BSc, MA
Deputy Head of Fifth Form: Mrs K L Pattison, BSc, PhD
Head of Fourth Form: J Norman, MA
Deputy Head of Fourth Form: J E McArdle, MA
Head of Third Form: M P Kerr, BA
Deputy Head of Third Form: S A Swann, BA MSc
Head of Second Form: N C Hudson, BA
Deputy Head of Second Form: M J Edgar-Andrews, BA
Head of First Form and Old Grammar: C E Apaloo, BSc
Deputy Head of First Form: Miss M L Franklin, BA

Deputy Head of Old Grammar: Miss C A Hudson, BSc

* Head of Department

Art & Design:
**P P Sanders, MA, MEd
Miss A E Gill, BA
Miss B Easton, BA
Miss N Cleary, BA
S R Lewington, Master
Craftsman LCGI

Classics:
**W Ellis-Rees, MA
Miss C L Rose, BA
Miss Z L Connolly, MA
J E Pile, BA
S A Swann, BA, MPhil
J E McArdle, MA
Mrs C B Stephenson, MA

Drama:
**Miss S H Dobson, BA
Miss M L Franklin, BA

Economics:
**D P Rey, BSc, MA
M Wacey, BSc
C R Webb, BSc

English:
**R A Riggs, BA, MA
J Norman, MA
Miss H M Sénéchal, MA
N C Hudson, BA
Miss E J Green, BA
Miss L O Longhurst, BA
Mrs H C Sebban, BA
Miss K K Murkett, BA

Geography:
**M S Hadley, MA
O J Davies, BSc, MSc
P S Marshall, MA
Miss A F McFarlane, BA

History and Politics:
**A J Bracken, BA
Miss N H Murphy, BA
A J V McBroom, BA
Miss K A Saunt, BA
S J Brown, BA, MA
J T Crowther, MA
J N Millard, BA
P J Mander, BA
M J Edgar-Andrews, BA
P J Wright, BA

Information Technology:
**Mrs S L Ralph, BA
Mrs A MacDonagh, BSc,
BSc

Mathematics:
**D R Eade, BA
Miss C A Hudson, BSc
S S Fernandes, BSc, MA
Mrs C S Musgrove, MA
Miss J C L Mesure, MA
Miss E L McCallan, MA
S J Dugdale, BSc, PhD
Ms N Bigden, BSc, MSc
Mr B P Broadhurst, MSc
T G Betchley, BSc, MA

Miss S Golleck, PhD,
MPhil
Miss Y Feng, BSc, MPhil

Modern Languages:
**R Edmundson, MA
P A Allwright, MA
G J Dowler, JP, MA
Miss V Vincent, MA
Mrs A L Robinson, BA
P R Eteson, BA (**French*)
Ms M J Ciechanowicz, MA
I Emerson, BSSc, MA
B Pollard, MA (**German*)
Miss F G Easton, BA
T H White, BA, MA
Mrs E Bunnage, BA, MA
(**Mandarin*)
A M Thomson, BA

Music:
**P Harrison, GLCM, MA
Miss J E Jones, BA
A J Crockatt, BA, BMus
J McHardy, BMus
(**Director of Music,*
Chapel Royal)

Physical Education:
**N F Cornwell, BEd
M P Kerr, BSc, MSc
B J Silcock, BPE
J P Santry, BEng
C E Apaloo, BSc
J J Ortiz, MA

Religious Education:
**J M Fenton, MA
Mrs K E Weare, MA, MA
Mrs A Giannorou, BSc,
BA, MPhil
Miss S K Wallace, MA

Science:
Mrs P C McCarthy, BSc
(**Chemistry, * Science*)
A A Wood, MSci
(**Physics*)
A Zivanic, BA, MA
(**Biology*)
R Mackrell, BSc
G W Dawson, BSc
K P Rogers, MChem
Mrs K L Pattison, BSc,
PhD
G H Browne, BA, BSc
M N Everard-Pennell,
MChem, PhD
R J Dharamshi, BA
R M Brookes, MChem,
DPhil
A Jackson, BSc, MA,
MPhil
T L Robinson, BSc
Miss H Stanley, BSc
Miss E L Pollock, BSc,
MEd
S L Clifford, BSc
S A Hall, BSc

There are Visiting Music Teachers for Bassoon, Cello, Double Bass, French Horn, Flute, Guitar, Jazz, Oboe, Organ, Percussion, Piano, Saxophone, Singing, Trombone, Trumpet, Tuba, Viola, Violin.

Learning Support:
**Ms A C DiStefano Power, BAH, BEd
Mrs A J Fountaine, MSci, MA, Dip RSA
Mrs J de Stacpoole, Hornsby Dip SpLD
M C Biltcliffe, BA
Mrs K J Ireland, BA

Library:
**D A Rose, BA, Dip Lib, ALA
Ms J Grantham, MA
Miss R Stocks, BA
M Evans
Mrs R Howley
Ms K Symonds (*Archivist*)
Mr T J Osborne (*Bookshop Manager*)

Registrar: Mrs V J Haley, LLB
Assistant Registrar: Ms C Cassin, BA

City of London School for Girls

St Giles' Terrace, Barbican, London EC2Y 8BB
Tel: 020 7847 5500
email: info@clsg.org.uk
website: www.clsg.org.uk
Twitter: @clsggirls
Facebook: @clsggirls
LinkedIn: /city-of-london-school-for-girls

Motto: *Domine Dirige Nos*

City of London School for Girls is an academically selective, non-denominational, independent day school for girls aged 7–18. There is an infectious vibrancy and energy at "City". Its distinctive location in the Barbican Centre provides immediate access to the wealth of London's educational and cultural opportunities, while the teaching staff and girls imbue the place with a sense of happiness, purpose, enthusiasm and fulfilment.

The School Course includes English Language and Literature, History, Geography, Religion, Philosophy and Ethics, Latin, Greek, French, German, Spanish, Mathematics, Biology, Chemistry, Physics, Economics and Politics, Art, Music, Physical Education, Classical Civilisation, Design and Technology, Theatre Studies, and Chinese.

Pupils are prepared for GCSE and A Level Examinations offered by Edexcel, OCR and AQA. They are also prepared for entrance to Oxford, Cambridge and other Universities. The Sixth Form courses are designed to meet the needs of girls wishing to proceed to other forms of specialised training.

Facilities are provided for outdoor and indoor games and the school has its own indoor swimming pool and an all-weather sports pitch. Extracurricular activities before school, in the lunch hour or at the end of afternoon school include Debating, Football, Drama, Science, Technology, Fencing, Netball, Gymnastics, Swimming, Tennis, Climbing and classes in Chinese, as well as many more. Guest speakers are frequently invited to the school, especially in the Sixth Form. There are also Junior and Senior Choirs, a Madrigal group, a Barbershop group, Junior and Senior Orchestras, a Wind Ensemble, a Chamber Orchestra and a Swing Band. Lunch hour music recitals, with visiting professional players, are encouraged. Many girls take the Duke of Edinburgh's Award scheme at bronze, silver and gold level.

Admission. Main entry points to the school are at 7 and 11 and 16 years of age. For girls over 11 years old, vacancies are only occasional. The entrance examinations for age 11 admission in September will usually be held in the previous January. For age 7 the entrance exam is held in the Autumn Term. Admission to the Sixth Form is also by written examination and interview during the Autumn Term.

Applications for 11+ and 16+ should reach the Admissions Officer by the start of the previous October. Specific deadlines can be found on the website.

Scholarships and Bursaries. The School has a variety of art, music and drama scholarships and means-tested bursaries for entry at 11+ and 16+.

Further details may be obtained from the Admissions Officer.

Fees per term (2018–2019). Preparatory Department: £6,128 (including lunch); Main School: £6,128 (excluding lunch).

Senior School lunches are paid for with a cashless system based on credited payment cards. Pupils in the Preparatory Department are expected to take school lunch for which there is no extra charge. After-school supervision is also available at £190 per term.

Extra Subjects: Pianoforte, Violin, Cello, Flute, Clarinet, Organ, Guitar and a wide variety of other instruments, including Singing: £268 per term (fees are all payable in advance).

School Governors:
Chairman: Mrs Clare James, MA, CC
Deputy Chairman: Mr Nicholas Michael Bensted-Smith, JP

Headmistress: Mrs E Harrop, BA Salamanca, MA Munich, MPhil Cantab, MA London

Senior Deputy Head (Staff and Special Projects): Mrs J Venditti, BEng Swansea

Deputy Head (Pastoral): Mrs K N Brice, MA Cantab

Deputy Head (Academic): Mr N Codd, BA Hons Oxon

Assistant Head Teaching, Learning and Research & Development: Mr B Chappell, BA Loughborough, MA London

Head of Sixth Form: Miss R Lockyear, BA Hons Cantab

Assistant Head of Sixth Form: Mrs C Williamson, BA Cantab

Head of Senior School: Mrs S Gilham, BA Oxon

Assistant Heads of Senior School:
Ms M Garnham, MA Sheffield
Mrs G Hankinson, BSc Staffordshire

Head of Lower School: Ms J Singleton, BEng Hons Southampton

Assistant Head of Lower School: Ms S Colbourne, BA Hons King's College

Head of Preparatory School: Mrs R Hadfield, BA Dunelm

Deputy Head of Preparatory Department: Mrs L Hall, BA Hons Bristol, MA Herts

Heads of Department:

Art:
Miss J Curtis, BA Hons St Martin's School of Art London, ATC London

Classical Languages:
Mr D Themistocleous, BA Oxon

Drama:
Mr S Morley, Dip Acting CCSD

Economics:
Mr A Kanwar, BA Oxon

Politics:
Miss R Lockyear, BA Hons Cantab

English:
Mr B Ward, BA Ulster

Geography:
Miss E A Moore, BA Liverpool, FRGS

History:
Mr J Murray, MA Oxon

Mathematics:
Mr T Bateup, BSc Warwick

Modern Languages:
French: Mr G Tyrrell, BA Oxford Brookes, MA
German: Mrs C Humphreys, BA London
Spanish: Ms A Golzarri de Diego, BA Pais Vasco
Italian: Miss E Perkins, BA Leeds
Chinese: Ms E Garner, BA Hons York, MA SOAS, MSc Manchester

Music:
Dr S Berryman, BMus Wales, MMus London, PhD Wales, FRSA

Physical Education:
Mrs O Helm, BA Leeds

Religion, Philosophy and Ethics:
Mrs K Bullard, MA Cantab

Sciences:
Biology: Miss N Brown, BSc Hons Edinburgh, MRes Edinburgh
Chemistry: Ms K Hotchkiss, MChem Oxon
Physics: Mr M Wilkinson, BSc Hons Nottingham

Technology:
Mr A Wright, BSc Bournemouth

ICT:
Mr D Libby, BSc West of England

Careers and PSHCEE:
Miss E Perkins, BA Leeds

Library:
Mrs R Trevor, BA Hons, MCLIP

Bursar: Mr A Bubbear, MBA Open
Facilities Manager: Mr J Valentine
Finance Manager: Ms S Mitha, FCCA
Registrar: Ms J Bonthron, BSc Sheffield, MSc Newcastle, MBA London Business School
Senior Administrative Officer: Mrs V Pyke

Health & Support Network:
School Doctor: Dr D Soldi, MB, ChB, DCH

School Counsellors:
Ms D Marcus, BA Counselling Tavistock Institute, Dip Psychodynamic Counselling Westminster Pastoral Foundation
Ms C Nancarrow, Dip Rational Emotive Behavioural Therapy Centre for Stress Management UK, MSc Rational Emotive Behavioural Therapy Goldsmiths College London

Learning Support Coordinators:
Ms K O'Connor, BS Ulster, Dip SpLD London
Mrs C Cole, BA East Anglia, RSA Dip London
Ms E Heseltine, BA Cantab, MA Leicester, BSc Open

Clayesmore School

Iwerne Minster, Blandford Forum, Dorset DT11 8LL

Tel:	01747 812122
email:	admissions@clayesmore.com
website:	www.clayesmore.com
Twitter:	@clayesmore

Supporting and challenging every pupil to fulfil their potential and contribute to the world with confidence, ambition and compassion.

Infused with an atmosphere of warmth and friendliness, Clayesmore is a flourishing co-educational school with Senior and Preparatory sharing the same stunning 62-acre site. The Senior School was founded in 1896 and in 1975 was joined by the Prep at Iwerne Minster. Despite Clayesmore being one big happy family, the two schools each have their own Head, staff and separate teaching areas.

Buildings and Grounds. The excellent facilities have been radically improved in recent years providing even greater opportunities for pupils. The attractive main building functions as the school's HQ with the upper floors used as a girls' boarding house. The ground floor features a charming library complete with computer facilities for private study and research, as well as delightful reception rooms for a variety of uses.

Recent development has included a £2.8m state-of-the-art Business School, a greatly expanded Design & Technology facility, and a girls' boarding house to accommodate growing pupil numbers. This stylish Business School houses teaching facilities for Business Studies, Economics, Psychology and a Careers Centre. Future development plans include the building of a new theatre, sports pavilion, English & Drama faculty and boys' boarding house.

The Sports Centre has a 25m indoor pool, squash courts, fitness suite, four badminton courts and indoor cricket nets. Outside, as well as the many pitches and netball courts, there is a floodlit, all-weather hockey pitch that provides 12 tennis courts for summer use.

There is a dedicated Music School and self-contained Art School, as well as a Chapel. The parkland grounds are quite outstanding, with extensive playing fields, a lake, and wonderful views towards Hambledon Hill.

Houses and Pastoral Care. The Senior School has five houses (three for boys and two for girls) each with resident, married house staff, and resident tutor, who provide nurturing pastoral care. Boarding pupils and day pupils live and learn together – there are no day houses and all pupils have a tutor to oversee academic progress and support them through school. Clayesmore has a real family feel and its comparatively small size enables the Headmaster and the staff to really get to know the pupils.

Academic work. Year 9 serves as a useful foundation year prior to GCSE courses starting in Years 10 and 11. Sixth Form students study four AS Levels in the Lower Sixth, taking three of these on to A2 in the Upper Sixth. The school has also introduced new A Level subjects and a number of BTEC options to broaden choice. The Sixth Form really helps to prepare students for life after Clayesmore, with supportive tutors, work experience opportunities and expert careers advice.

Clayesmore pays close attention to the needs of individual pupils, both in academic as well as other spheres, and the school has earned a strong reputation for successfully helping pupils with dyslexia.

Scholarships. A wide range of scholarships and bursaries can open doors, including those for HM Forces families.

The wider life at Clayesmore. Sport is well supported at Clayesmore with rugby, hockey, cricket, athletics, netball, swimming and cross-country complemented by popular subsidiary sports such as badminton, squash, sailing and orienteering.

Year 10 and 11 pupils can experience the challenges and excitement of the Combined Cadet Force with many enthusiasts continuing as NCOs into the Sixth Form. Clayesmore also offers the chance to achieve the well-respected Duke of Edinburgh's Award, as well as a marvellous mix of other activities.

Music and drama play a vibrant role in the life of the school and provide pupils with numerous opportunities to perform. Encouragement is given to pupils of all ages to learn instruments and sing in choirs. There are all sorts of ensembles and new ones are formed to match different pupil interests. The purpose-built theatre is a practical, intimate space, used with great imagination, not only for various termly productions, but also for GCSE Drama and the BTEC in Performing or Production Arts.

Entry arrangements. Entrance to Clayesmore Senior School is at 13 with those from preparatory schools taking the Common Entrance examination. For entrants from maintained schools, there are tests in English, Mathematics, Science and French. Girls and boys may join Clayesmore earlier if they attend Clayesmore Preparatory School and it is quite normal for new pupils to arrive at age 11 and undertake Years 7 and 8 at the Prep School. Each year, between 10 and 20 young people join as Sixth Formers, and the total number in the Sixth Form is roughly 170.

Clayesmore Preparatory School. Clayesmore is an 'all-through' school with both Prep and Senior sharing the same idyllic setting and it offers a seamless transition at 13 that is perfect for parents, particularly of boarders, who are keen to keep siblings together. Entrance to the Preparatory School may take place into any year group assuming a place is available, and is dependent upon an interview with the Head and a report from the pupil's present school.

Fees per term (2018–2019). Senior School: £11,910 (boarding), £8,740 (day). Preparatory School: £5,890–£8,370 (boarding), £2,570–£6,250 (day).

Charitable status. Clayesmore School is a Registered Charity, number 306214.

Chairman of Governors: Mr J Andrews, LLB (*Chairman of F&GP*)

Head: Mrs Joanne Thomson, BA

Senior School Leadership Team:
Senior Deputy Head: Mr J R Carpenter, BA, FRSA
Deputy Head Pastoral: Mrs E M Bailey, BA, PGCE
Assistant Head, Teaching & Learning: Mrs A Cowley, BSc, PGCE, MEd SEN, Dip SpLD, AMBDA
Assistant Head, Sixth Form: Mrs S J Newland, BSc, PGCE
Assistant Head, Personal Development: Mrs H Christmas, BA, PGCE
Assistant Head, Planning and Organisation: Mr M I Newland, MA, PGCE
Assistant Head, Middle Years: Mr M M McKeown, BA, PGCE
Director of Academic Progress: Mr J A Reach, BEng, PGCE
Director of Finance and Operations: Mrs A Hughes, BSc, ACA
Chaplain: Mr A R West, BA

Prep School Leadership Team:

Deputy Head: Mr S Reeves, BA, QTS

Deputy Head, Academic: Mrs E L Reach, BA, Cert SpLD

Assistant Head, Teaching & Learning: Mrs A Cowley, BSc, PGCE, MEd SEN, PG Dip SpLD, AMBDA

Head of Pre-Prep & Nursery: Mrs C Townsend, MA, PGCE

Head of Boarding: Mr D J Browse, BA, QTS

Registrar: Mrs R Rutherford

Clifton College

Guthrie Road, Clifton, Bristol BS8 3EZ

Tel: +44 (0)117 3157 000
       +44 (0)117 911 8940 (Admissions)
Fax: +44 (0)117 3157 101
email: admissions@cliftoncollege.com
       prepadmissions@cliftoncollege.com
website: www.cliftoncollege.com
Twitter: @Clifton_College
Facebook: @CliftonCollegeUK
LinkedIn: /Clifton-College

Motto: *Spiritus intus alit*

Clifton College was founded in 1862, and incorporated by Royal Charter in 1877. It is situated in the city of Bristol, on the edge of Clifton Down and not far from open country. The School is well placed to take advantage of the many cultural and educational activities of the city, and to gain much else of value from its civic and industrial life. There are friendly links with the Universities and with other schools of various types.

Admission. Boy and girl boarders and day pupils are normally admitted in September between the ages of 13 and 14, and most are required to pass the Common Entrance examination, which can be taken at their Preparatory Schools. Credentials of good character and conduct are required. Registration Forms can be obtained from the Director of Upper School Admissions, Guthrie Road, Clifton, Bristol, BS8 3EZ.

Houses. It is usual for a pupil to be entered for a particular House, but where parents have no preference or where no vacancy exists in the House chosen, the Head Master will make the necessary arrangements.

Day Pupils and Day Boarders. Day boys are divided into Houses: North Town, South Town and East Town. Day girls enter West Town, Hallward's or Holland's House. The town Houses have the same status as Boarding Houses and day pupils are encouraged to take a full part in the various activities of the School. A number of day boarder places are available for boys and girls.

Catering is managed by our own experienced caterers and boarders take all meals in the School Dining Hall. Day pupils and day boarders are required to have their midday meal at School, and arrangements are made for their tea and supper at the School when necessary.

Fees per term (2018–2019). Years 9–13: Boarders £12,020–£12,390; Day Boarders (4 nights) £10,835–£11,140; Day Pupils £8,100–£8,230. Sixth Form Joiners (from other schools): Boarders £13,135; Day Boarders (4 nights) £11,400; Day Pupils £8,530.

Scholarships, Bursaries and Awards. All awards on merit are limited to 25% of the fees, but they may be augmented by means-tested bursaries. The following awards are offered each year:

13+ entry: Academic, Music, Drama, Art and Sport scholarships. Boys and girls who are already in the School may compete for all 13+ scholarships and awards.

Sixth Form entry: Up to 10 Academic scholarships per year are available for entrants from other schools to the Sixth Form. A limited number of Sport, Art, Drama and Music scholarships and an Organ scholarship are also available.

All Music awards include free tuition in two instruments (one of which may be singing).

Bursaries: These are means-tested awards and may be awarded in addition to scholarships (or in their own right). In exceptional circumstances, bursaries may be awarded up to 100% of the fees.

Academic structure. Boys and girls enter the School in the Third Form, following a general course for their first year. Most GCSEs are taken at the end of the Fifth Form.

Thereafter boys and girls enter Block I (Sixth Form) and typically take an advanced course consisting of 3 or 4 subjects at A Level. A great many combinations of subjects are possible.

Service. All pupils are given a course in outdoor pursuits and other skills in the Third Form. In the Fourth Form they are given more advanced training, which may include involvement in The Duke of Edinburgh's Award scheme, and at the end of the year they decide whether to join the Army, Navy or Air Force sections of the CCF or to take part in Community Service. There is regular use of a property owned by the School in the Brecon Beacons for all these activities.

Societies. Voluntary membership of Scientific, Historical, Literary, Dramatic, Geographical, Debating and many other societies is encouraged.

Music and Art. The musical activities of the School are wide and varied, and are designed for musicians of all standards. They include the Chapel Choir, Choral Society and Chamber Choir, a full orchestra, 2 string orchestras, 2 wind bands, a jazz band, as well as numerous chamber music activities. Visiting concert artists regularly run masterclasses, and there are wide opportunities for performance. Teaching is available on virtually all instruments and in all styles. Instrumental and vocal competitions are held at House level and individually annually. The well-equipped and recently refurbished Music School includes practice facilities, computers, recording studio, an extensive sheet music library and a large record/compact disc library.

Drawing, Painting, Sculpture, Pottery, Textiles and various Crafts are taught under the supervision of the Director of Art in the Art School. There is an annual House Art Competition and various exhibitions throughout the year.

Theatre. Drama and Dance play an important part in the life of the School with an increasing number of pupils achieving success in LAMDA, PCERT LAM and RAD examinations. The Redgrave Theatre is used for School plays, the House Drama Festival, and for other plays that may be put on (e.g. by individual Houses, the staff or the Modern Language Society). Each House produces a play each year. It is also used for teaching purposes, and in addition for concerts, lectures and meetings.

Information and Communication Technology. The ICT Centre at the heart of the School houses the most advanced internet facility of any school in the South West.

Physical Education. Sport is part of the regular School curriculum and games are played at least twice per week by all age groups.

In the Michaelmas Term, boys play Rugby and girls play Hockey. There is a multi-sport option for seniors who are not in team squads. In the Lent Term, Hockey and Football are the main options for the boys whilst the girls mostly play Netball. Rowing, Running, Squash, Swimming, Shooting,

Climbing and Rackets are among the alternative options for senior boys and girls. In the Summer Term, Cricket is the main sport for the boys and Tennis for the girls, with Tennis, Athletics, Rowing, Swimming and Shooting as alternatives for seniors. The Clifton College playing fields in Abbots Leigh include three floodlit all-weather Hockey and Football pitches, six floodlit Tennis courts, a 3G artificial pitch for Football and Rugby, a water-based Hockey pitch with training D, and a Real Tennis court. An indoor facility for Tennis and Netball is one of the best in the region.

Careers. Careers advice is the shared responsibility of the Head Master, Housemasters, Housemistresses, Heads of Departments and the Head of Sixth Form. The School is a subscribing member of the Independent Schools Careers Organisation and of the Careers Research and Advisory Centre at Cambridge. The proximity of the city of Bristol enables the Careers Department and other members of staff to keep in close touch with Universities, business firms and professional bodies about all matters affecting boys' and girls' careers.

Clifton College Preparatory School. *Headmaster*: J Milne, BA, MBA

The Preparatory School has separate buildings (including its own Science laboratories, Arts Centre, ICT Centres and Music School) and is kept distinct from the Upper School. The two Schools nevertheless work closely together and share some facilities, including the Chapel, Theatre, sports complex, all-weather playing surfaces and swimming pool. Most boys and girls proceed from the Preparatory School to the Upper School. Pupils are also prepared for schools other than Clifton. There is a Pre-Prep School for day pupils aged between 2 and 8. Boys and girls are accepted at all ages and scholarships are available at age 11.

For further details see entries for Clifton College Preparatory School in IAPS section.

The Cliftonian Society. *Administrator*: L Nash, 32 College Road, Clifton, Bristol BS8 3JH (Tel: 0117 3157 665).

Charitable status. Clifton College is a Registered Charity, number 311735. It is a charitable trust providing boarding and day education for boys and girls aged 2–18.

Council:
President: Dr J Cottrell, PhD, MA, FCA
Chairman: Mrs A Streatfeild-James, MA
Vice-Chairman: Mr Nick Tolchard, BSc
Treasurer: Mr S Smith, BSc, DPhil, FCA

Mr R Cartwright, CTA
Ms T Fisk, MA, FCA
Mr H Harper, MA
Mrs L Harradine, BA
Mr P McCarthy, BSc, MBA, CEng, FI ET
Brig R J Morris, BA
Sir H Sants, MA
Mr C Trembath, BSc
Mr J Hemming, MA, LLM
Mr J Glassberg
Mrs F Francombe
Mrs J Hemming

Secretary and Bursar: Mrs Sheenagh Dose, CMgr, FCMI

Head Master: **Dr T M Greene**, MA, DPhil

Deputy Head (*Pastoral*): Mr E Swanwick, MEd
Deputy Head (*Co-curricular & Planning*): Mrs A Tebay, BSc
Deputy Head (*Academic*): Mr G E Simmons, BSc
Chaplain: Mr Simon Chapman, BA
Director of Admissions: Mr J S Tait, BA, MA
Head of Sixth Form: Mr J H Greenbury, MA

Heads of Department:
Art: Mr A J Wilkie, BA
Biology: Mrs R Poland, MA, PhD
Boys' Games: Mr J C Bobby, BA
Chemistry: Mr J Older, BA, PhD
Classics: Mr T Patrick, MA, DPhil
Design & Technology: Mrs V Jackson, BA Ed
Director of Drama: Mrs R Orzell, BA
Economics & Business Studies: Mr J Adams, BSc
English: Miss S A Clarke, MA
French: Miss C Bloor, BA
Geography: Mr S, Rath, BSc
German: Mr O G Lewis, MA
Girls' Games: Mrs L A Catchpole, BA
History: Mrs A John, BA, MA
Information Technology: Mr D Dean, MA, PhD
Mandarin: Ms E L Cordwell, BA
Mathematics: Mr G E Simmons, BSc
Modern Languages: Mr L Siddons, MA
Director of Music: Mr D Robson, BA
Physical Education: Mr A Wagstaff, MA
Physics and Science: Mr A Hasthorpe, MSc
Politics: Mr P G Lidington, BA
PSHE and Psychology: Ms S Griffin, BSc
Religious Studies and Philosophy: Mrs J M Greenbury, BA
Spanish: Miss M Harris, BA
Director of Sport: Mr A Wagstaff, BEd

Houses and Housemasters/mistresses:

Boys Boarding:
Moberly's: Mr G J Catchpole, MEng
Watson's: Mr N Doran, BA
School House: Mr J H Hughes, MA
Wiseman's: Mr W J Huntington, MA

Girls Boarding:
Worcester: Mrs A J Ballance, BSc
Oakeley's: Mrs K A Jeffery, BSc
Hallward's: Mrs K J Pickles, BA

Boys Day:
North Town: Mr A Copp, BSc
South Town: Mr J, Williams, BA
East Town: Mr N Mills, BA

Girls Day:
West Town: Mrs M Beever, BA
Holland's House: Mrs K Parnell, BA

Clongowes Wood College

Clane, Co Kildare, Ireland

Tel: 00 353 45 868202
Fax: 00 353 45 861042
email: reception@clongowes.net
website: www.clongowes.net

Motto: *Aeterna non Caduca*

Clongowes Wood College was founded in 1814 in a rebuilt Pale castle – Castle Brown in North Kildare, about 25 miles from Dublin. A boarding school for boys from 12–18, the school has developed steadily ever since and now has circa 500 pupils on the rolls, all of whom are seven-day boarders.

The College is situated on 150 acres of land, mostly comprising sports fields and a 9-hole golf course. It is surrounded by about 300 acres of farmland. Clongowes is listed as an historic building.

Admission. Application for admission should be made to the Headmaster. There is a registration fee of €50. An assessment day is held in May prior to the year of entry and entry is determined by a variety of factors including: suitability of the student to boarding life, family association, geographical spread including Northern Ireland and abroad, date of registration, and an understanding of the values that animate the College. Normal entry is at the age of 12; entry in later years is possible if a place becomes available.

Curriculum. A wide choice of subjects is available throughout the school and pupils are prepared for the Irish Junior Certificate and the Irish Leaving Certificate. This latter is the qualifying examination for entry to Irish Universities and other third-level institutions. It is acceptable for entry to almost all Universities in the United Kingdom, provided the requisite grades are obtained. All pupils take a Transition Year programme following the Junior Certificate. This programme is recommended by the Department of Education in Ireland. Work experience modules, social outreach programmes, exchanges with other countries and opportunities to explore different areas of study are all included in this programme.

Religious Teaching. Clongowes is a Jesuit school in the Roman Catholic tradition and there are regular formal and informal liturgies. Boys are given a good grounding in Catholic theology and are encouraged to participate in retreats, prayer groups and pilgrimages (Taize, Lourdes). Social Outreach is part of the curriculum in Transition Year and is encouraged throughout the school. A small number of boys of other faiths are pupils in the school.

Sport. All boys play rugby in their first year in school. They then have the choice to continue in that game or to play other games. There are several rugby pitches, a golf course, tennis courts, soccer pitches, squash courts, a cross-country track, an athletics and cricket oval, a gymnasium and a new swimming pool; these facilities provide plenty of opportunity for a variety of activities. Athletics, Gaelic football and cricket are popular activities in the third term. Clongowes has a strong rugby tradition and has won the Leinster Championship twice in the last decade.

Other activities. Following the Jesuit tradition, the school has a fine reputation for debating and has won competitions in three different languages (English, Irish, French) in the last decade. A large school orchestra and school choir gives a formal concert at Christmas and another before the summer holidays. Drama productions take place at every level within the school. A large-scale summer project for charity has been undertaken each year. A residential holiday project for children with disabilities takes place in the school each summer and is animated by teachers and pupils. The College has recently created link programmes with schools in Hungary and Romania.

Pastoral Care. The school is organised horizontally into Lines. Two 'prefects', or housemasters look after each year within a Line, composed of two years, with a Line Prefect in charge of the Line itself. In addition, an Academic Year Head oversees the academic work of each of the 70 pupils within each year. A Spiritual Father or Chaplain is attached to each line. There is a strong and positive relationship with parents and a good community spirit throughout the school. The school seeks to foster competence, conscience and compassionate commitment in each of the boys in its care.

Fees per annum (2018–2019). €19,890. Parents are also asked to support the continuing development of the College through various fundraising activities.

Clongowes Union. This association of past pupils of the school can be contacted through: The Secretary, The Clongowes Union, Clongowes Wood College, Clane, Co Kildare; email: development@clongowes.net.

Cokethorpe School

Witney, Oxfordshire OX29 7PU

Tel:	01993 703921
email:	hmsec@cokethorpe.org
	admissions@cokethorpe.org
website:	www.cokethorpe.org.uk
Twitter:	@CokethorpeSch
Facebook:	@CokethorpeSch

Motto: *Inopiam Ingenio Pensant*

Cokethorpe School, founded in 1957, is a vibrant and dynamic day school for around 660 girls and boys aged 4 to 18. It is set in 150 acres of parkland, two miles from Witney and ten from Oxford. There are 124 children in the Junior School and 539 pupils in the Senior School (including 151 Sixth Formers).

Aims. Our ethos is to deliver a liberal education in a vibrant, kind and academically challenging environment that will extend the potential of every pupil. We aim to promote the individual and challenge every pupil to achieve their best academically. We give our pupils the opportunity, skills and guidance to make good choices and aim for every pupil to leave Cokethorpe with strong self-esteem, high personal expectation, and with tolerance and respect for others based on our Christian values.

The School succeeds in creating a community of rounded, considerate and confident young men and women with high personal expectations by: building strong relationships with families and the local community; providing a high quality of pastoral care; achieving positive, affirmative relationships between staff and pupils, ensuring that all pupils make above-average progress, resulting in above-average levels of achievement.

Curriculum. A curriculum is offered that gives pupils the chance to pursue individual passions, with both traditional and modern subjects, those that are highly academic and others that are more practical. The National Curriculum is broadly followed up to GCSE. All pupils study core subjects of English, Maths and Science at GCSE and have a wide choice of subject options. There is also a full programme of personal, social and health education.

Sixth Formers typically choose four subjects to study at A Level and complete the EPQ. The small size of teaching groups is particularly conducive to individual attention and encouragement. The usual courses are supplemented by Economics, Government and Politics, Philosophy and Classical Civilisation.

The Junior School offers a fully balanced curriculum with the focus on developing high standards and providing intellectual challenges. Whilst the National Curriculum is followed, the freedom to offer breadth is embraced. (*See Cokethorpe Junior School entry in IAPS section.*)

Parents are kept closely informed of their child's progress and achievement, both academically and socially.

Facilities. Teaching takes place in a range of modern buildings set around the elegant Queen Anne Mansion House. The most recent addition is the Dining Hall and dedicated Sixth Form Centre that sit alongside the contemporary glass and stone library. A 200-seat auditorium is the centre for Performing Arts and a perfect setting for visiting speakers. As well as extensive sport pitches, astroturf pitches, tennis and netball courts, a nine-hole golf course, climbing tower and clay pigeon shoot, Cokethorpe also has a full-size Sports Hall with a fitness suite. The Sports facilities are rounded off with the Boat House situated close to the School on the River Thames.

Pastoral. The House system, personal tutoring (including day-to-day care, pastoral welfare and academic progress), year group specific social and health programmes and a joint Anglican and Roman Catholic foundation creates an excellent support structure. Small classes and dedicated teachers help pupils champion their strengths and challenge their weaknesses.

Sport. The School has a strong and successful sporting tradition. Principal sports include rugby, hockey, netball, football, cricket and tennis. A wide variety of subsidiary sports are also available including kayaking, clay pigeon shooting, badminton, athletics, cross-country, golf, judo, squash, swimming and sailing, designed to suit all tastes and abilities. All pupils do PE as part of the curriculum. There are regular county, national and international successes. The most talented pupils will be considered for the School Sports Academy.

Other Activities. The extracurricular programme (known as 'AOB') plays a prominent part in a pupil's timetable and includes over 150 activities such as Dance, Engineering, Dissection Club, Fencing, Web Design, Chess, Debating, Climbing and The Duke of Edinburgh's Award scheme. There is also a strong tradition of fundraising. Other activities include language exchanges, ski trips, sports tours abroad and cultural trips to Africa and Greece.

Music, Drama and Creative Arts. The Arts are extremely important at Cokethorpe. All pupils are encouraged to learn a musical instrument and join the choir or one of the range of orchestras and ensembles. Peripatetic teachers cover a very wide range of instruments, and there are regular concerts and recitals during the year. Drama flourishes with two to three whole-School productions and the Inter-House competition annually, numerous GCSE and A Level performances, a programme of lunchtime recitals from all years and frequent trips to the theatre. Art, Textiles and Design Technology (Resistant Materials and Graphic Design) are all offered at GCSE and A Level. There is also a vibrant and varied range of art, design and craft activities as part of the extended curriculum.

Higher Education and Careers. The majority of Sixth Form leavers go on to Higher Education, enrolling in a wide variety of foundation courses, degrees or apprenticeships. A careers programme is followed throughout the Senior School, including work experience, careers conventions and psychometric profiling. Help and advice is given by experienced Careers teachers and the latest literature is available in the Careers Library.

Admission. Pupils usually enter the Junior School at age 4 or 7 (the latter based on an assessment day in January) and the Senior School either at age 11, 13 or 16. There are occasionally vacancies at other ages. Candidates at age 11 are required to sit assessments in Maths and English, at age 13 either assessments or Common Entrance and at age 16 GCSEs or equivalent. Places are offered on the basis of these results, plus interviews and school reports. There is a registration fee of £100. Registration forms and details of entrance examination procedures are available from the Registrar.

Scholarships. Scholarships are assessed separately and awarded annually. Academic, Art, Design and Technology, Music, Sport and Drama scholarships and awards are available.

Bursaries. Financial assistance is available, through the award of means-tested bursaries, to those families entering the School from ages 11 through to 18 (and occasionally into the Junior School). The value of the bursary can be up to 100% of fees.

Fees per term (2018–2019). Junior School: £4,200 Reception–Year 2, £4,500 Years 3–4, £4,700 Years 5–6; Senior School £6,400. Fees include lunch. Extras are kept to a minimum.

The Cokethorpe Society. c/o Development and Events Officer: Melanie Hudson, Cokethorpe School, email: society@cokethorpe.org.

Charitable Status. Cokethorpe Educational Trust Limited is a Registered Charity, number 309650. It aims to provide a first-class education for each individual pupil.

Governing Body:
Chairman: Mr R F Jonckheer, LLB Hons
Vice-Chairman: Mrs R Gunn, MA Cantab
Mr A Bark, ACIB
Mr M Booty
Mrs W E Hart, CFQ, MA, ICAEW
Dr W W Lau, PhD, MSc, BSc
Mrs G McAndrew, CQSW, BA
Mr P G Riman, BA, LL Dip
Mr P Tolley, BSc, FRICS
Mr J Bennett, BSc
The Right Revd C Fletcher
Governor Emeritus: Mr M St John Parker, MA

Headmaster: **D J Ettinger**, BA, MA, PGCE, FRSA

Deputy Headmaster: J C Stevens, BEng, FRSA
Bursar: Mrs H J Stapleton, FCCA
Head of Junior School: Mrs N A Black, BA
Director of Studies: A E Uglow, BA, PGCE
Director of Co-Curricular: G J Sheer, BA, PGCE
Head of Sixth Form: S D White, BA, PGCE
Deputy Head of Sixth Form: Mrs J C Gregory-Newman, BA, BSc
Deputy Head of Sixth Form: A P Gale, BSc, PGCE

Housemasters and Housemistresses:
Feilden: S G Carter, MA, PGCE
Gascoigne: Mrs E Semenzato, DLit, PGCE
Harcourt: W G Lawson, BA, PGCE
Queen Anne: Mrs S A Orton, BA, PGCE
Swift: Mrs M H D Cooper, BA, PGCE
Vanbrugh: Ms L A Mountain, MA, PGCE
Lower House: M J P O'Connor, BEd

Heads of Departments:
Art: Ms E F Williams, BA, PGCE
Business Studies and Economics: Mrs N Silversides, BEd, CELTA
Classics: Miss K E Murray, BA, MA
Design Technology: Mrs H V Brown, BA, PGCE
Drama: Mrs C L Hooper, Dip Act, DCL
English: Miss D C H Jackson, BEd, Dip EFL, FRSA
Geography: J A W Capel, MA, PGCE
History: P J B Rudge, BA, PGCE
Learning Support: Mrs S J Arbuckle, BA, PGCE
Mathematics: A G M Ladell-Stuart, MMath, PGCE
Modern Foreign Languages: Miss M Bertholle, BA, PGCE
Music: J E Hughes, BA, BMus
Physical Education: Miss A M Woodcock, BSc
Psychology: Miss K J Rogers, BSc, PGCE
Religious Studies: Revd R R J Lapwood, BA, PGCE
Science: Dr C Flaherty, PhD, MSc, PGCE, MRSC

70 full-time academic teaching staff, plus 19 part-time.

20 visiting teachers for Piano, String, Wind and Brass instruments, Percussion and Singing.
24 part-time sports coaches.

Colfe's School

Horn Park Lane, London SE12 8AW

Tel: 020 8852 2283
Fax: 020 8852 2283
email: head@colfes.com
website: www.colfes.com
Twitter: @ColfesSchool
Facebook: @ColfesSchool

Colfe's is an independent day school for girls and boys from age 3–18. It is one of London's oldest schools and was nearly 100 years old when Abraham Colfe, Vicar of Lewisham, re-established it in 1652. In his will, he entrusted the care of Colfe's to the Leathersellers' livery company, which governs the school to this day.

Entrance is selective and academic standards are high, with more than 80% of A Levels graded A* to B in the last three years. Our pupils regularly gain places on the most competitive courses at university. 61% of GCSE grades are awarded A* or A and over 20% the new top grade 9. We have an exceptional and popular programme of activities outside the classroom.

Colfe's has a strong reputation for all-round quality and innovation – in December 2016 the school was rated as 'Excellent' by the Independent Schools Council following an ISI inspection. We have also been awarded two TES Awards for Education Initiative of the Year (2014 and 2016) for our outstanding pastoral programmes.

The Leathersellers' Scholarship programme enables us to select up to 14 scholars each year on fully-funded bursaries for direct entry to the Sixth Form. In so doing we draw on strong working relationships with a number of local comprehensive schools in two of London's most deprived boroughs.

We are proud of our 360-year history but we are not burdened or defined by it. Colfe's doesn't promote a single mould. It is very much a school of the present day.

Admissions. There are 700 pupils in the Senior School, including 160 in the Sixth Form. The Junior School caters for a further 450 pupils. All sectors of the school are fully co-educational. The main points of entry to the Junior School are 3+ and 4+ (EYFS, KS1). The majority of the Junior School pupils transfer to the Senior School at 11. Approximately 65 pupils from a range of local state primary and prep schools enter the Senior School directly at 11 and there are a limited number of places available to pupils wishing to join in the Sixth Form at Year 12.

Buildings. All the teaching accommodation is modern and purpose built. Specialist on-site facilities include the Sports and Leisure Centre, comprising sports hall, swimming pool, and fitness suite. The Leathersellers' Sports Ground, located less than a mile from the main school campus, provides extensive playing fields and related facilities. The school also holds the freehold of the Old Colfeians ground at Horn Park. The opening of the Stewart Building in 2015, comprising a purpose-built Sixth Form suite and eight hi-tech classrooms, marked the end of a £10 million phase of site improvement.

Curriculum. The curriculum follows the spirit of the National Curriculum in both Junior and Senior Schools. Pupils are entered for the separate Sciences at GCSE and follow the IGCSE Mathematics course. A wide range of subjects is available at A Level, 25 in total, including

Drama, Politics, Media Studies, Psychology and Philosophy.

Physical Education and Games. Physical Education and Games are compulsory for all pupils up to and including Year 11. Full use is made of the wide range of facilities available on site, including a fully-equipped Sports Centre, swimming pool and all-weather surface.

Both boys and girls play rugby, cricket, football and athletics. Other sports available include swimming, gymnastics, basketball, health-related fitness and tennis.

Music and Drama. Music and Drama thrive alongside each other in the purpose-built Performing Arts Centre. The music department is home to a wide range of performance groups ranging from beginners to advanced ensembles in both classical and contemporary genres. There are regular performance opportunities given throughout the year, some held in the purpose-built recital hall and others in external venues. A team of 20 visiting instrumental teachers provide further opportunities for pupils to enjoy making music. Drama is a popular subject at both GCSE and A Level, with large numbers of pupils also involved outside the classroom.

Careers. The Careers and Higher Education Department is staffed on a full-time basis. Regular events include University Information Evenings and Careers Fairs.

Fees per term (2018–2019). Senior School £5,643 (excluding lunch); Junior School (KS2) £4,665 (excluding lunch); KS1 £4,410 (including lunch); EYFS £4,221 (including lunch).

Scholarships. Scholarships are awarded mainly on the basis of outstanding performance in the Entrance Examination. The exam is designed to identify and reward academic potential, as well as achievement.

Means-tested scholarships are also available at 11+ and 16+. These may, in exceptional circumstances, cover the total cost of tuition fees. Application forms are available from the Admissions department.

A limited number of Art, Drama, Music and Sports awards are also available at 11+ and 16+. In the case of Music scholars, free instrumental tuition may accompany the award. Details of Music and Sports awards can be obtained from the Admissions department.

Junior School. The purpose-built Junior School was opened by HRH Prince Michael of Kent in 1988. Specialist rooms of the Senior School are also used. While the curricular emphasis is on high standards in basic Mathematics and English, a wide range of other subjects is taught, including Science and French. There is also a range of activities similar to those enjoyed by the Senior School and all pupils are expected to participate. All pupils proceed to the Senior School if they achieve the qualifying standard.

(*For further details see entry in IAPS section.*)

The Colfeian Society. Enquiries to the Alumni Relations Officer, Colfe's School, London SE12 8AW; email: development@colfes.com.

Charitable status. Colfe's School is a Registered Charity, number 1109650. It exists to provide education for boys and girls.

Visitor: HRH Prince Michael of Kent

The current Governors provide between them a broad range of relevant experience and qualifications. A majority are Members or appointees of the Leathersellers' Company to which Abraham Colfe entrusted the School in his will when he died in 1657.

The activities of the Leathersellers are many and varied but the School and its fortunes continue to feature prominently on the Company's agenda. The Master of the Company is, *ex officio*, a member of the Board of Governors.

Board of Governors:
Mr Mike Bradly-Russell (*Master of the Leathersellers' Company*)
Mr Matthew Pellereau, BSc, FRICS (*Chairman*)
Mr Andrew B Strong, BSc
Mr Sean Williams, MA Oxon, MPA Harvard
Mr Mark Williams
Mr James Russell
Mr Timothy Lister, FCA
Mr Daniel Coulson, BSc Hons, MA, MRICS
Prof Angela Brueggemann, DPhil
Dr Robert Abayasekara, BSc, PhD
Mr John Guyatt, MA Oxon
Mrs Belinda Canham, BA
Mr David Sheppard, BA
Mrs J Bradley, LLB
Mr Christopher Ramsey, MA

Headmaster: Mr R Russell, MA Cantab

Deputy Head: Mrs D Graham, GRSM, LRAM
Bursar and Clerk to the Governors: Mrs J Lerbech, MA Cantab, MSci, CA
Director of Studies: Mr L Rogers, MA Cantab
Director of Pastoral Care: Mrs J German, BA Hons
Director of Sixth Form: Mr S Drury, BA Hons, MA
Director of Teaching and Learning: Mrs J Sansome, BSc Hons, MSc
Head, Junior School: Miss C Macleod, MSc
Director of Admissions and Communications: Mrs K Bridgman, BA Hons

Heads of Departments:
Art: Mrs N Gudge, BA Hons
Classics: Mr H Cullen, MA Hons
Design & Technology: Mrs C Cox, BA Hons
Drama: Ms N Maher, BA Hons
Economics & Business Studies: Mr R Otley, BA Hons
English: Miss M Schramm, BA, MA
Geography: Mrs H Nissinen, BSc Hons, MA
Government & Politics: Mr M Poolton, BA Hons , MSc
History: Mrs O Crummay, MSc
Learning Support: Miss A Coode, BA Hons, DTLLS Literacy
Maths: Mr A Guy, MEng Hons
Media Studies, General Studies: Mr C Foxall, BA Hons
Modern Foreign Languages: Mr M Koutsakis, MA
French: Miss E Harris, BMus with French
German: Mr M Koutsakis, MA
Spanish: Mr A Seddon, BA Hons, MIL
Music: Mr B Holmes, BA Hons, MA
Outdoor Education: Major C Cherry, BSc Hons
Physical Education: Mrs N Rayes, BEd Hons, EMBA
Religion & Philosophy: Miss E Henderson, BA Hons
Biology: Dr G Zimmermann, BSc, PhD
Chemistry: Mr D Fisher, MA
Physics: Mr J Fishwick, BSc Hons
Psychology: Dr J Lea, PhD, BSc Hons

Colston's

Bell Hill, Stapleton, Bristol BS16 1BJ

Tel: 0117 965 5207
Fax: 0117 958 5652
email: admissions@colstons.org
website: www.colstons.org
Twitter: @colstonsschool
Facebook: @Colstons-School

Motto: *Go, and do thou likewise*

Colston's is a thriving co-educational day school for pupils aged 3 to 18 located on a spacious 30-acre site in Stapleton village in north Bristol. Our traditional pastoral structures and house system promote a sense of community and belonging amongst pupils.

A Colston's education extends far beyond the classroom with opportunities for sport, music, service and co-curricular activities all playing their part in creating the unique experience on offer at the school.

Organisation. There are approximately 750 pupils at Colston's. The Lower School, which caters for the 3–11 age range, includes a nursery and is adjacent to the main site which accommodates the Upper School, which pupils attend from 11–18.

For details of the Lower School, see entry in IAPS section.

Admission. Pupils are admitted at 11+ and 13+ through the school's own examinations. Pupils also join the school for the Sixth Form. Academic scholarships are available as well as scholarships for pupils excelling in art, drama, music and sport. Bursaries are also available which are means tested.

Work. Colston's offers a wide ranging and engaging curriculum which avoids premature specialisation and is in line with the provisions of the National Curriculum. Art, Business Studies, Computing, Drama, Design Technology, French, Geography, History, Music, Physical Education, Religious Studies, Spanish are optional subjects. There is a wide choice of A Level subjects and some BTECs available in the Sixth Form.

Chapel. Colston's is a Church of England Foundation, and use is made of neighbouring Stapleton Parish Church for morning assemblies and other services. Pupils of other denominations are also warmly welcomed.

Sport and Games. Colston's has a shining sporting legacy, perhaps unsurprisingly given the impressive on-site facilities that are unique in Bristol. Sport plays a huge part in the life of pupils and while excellence is pursued for those with talent, everyone is encouraged, regardless of ability, to get involved. Opportunities to represent the school are abundant and an impressive number of teams are fielded each week. The main sports for boys are rugby, hockey and cricket and hockey, netball and rounders for girls.

Music and Drama. The drama department is one of the most successful in the country. It is based in the Harry Crook Theatre which offers an exceptionally well-equipped 200-seat auditorium. Music is vibrant and inclusive, with one-third of pupils taking individual instrumental lessons. Performances are given regularly in the dedicated concert hall.

Careers. Colston's is proud of its careers provision which is available to all pupils. The school is a member of the Independent Schools Careers Organisation. Through a highly successful programme of careers guidance, pupils are helped to make the right decisions to ensure success. The careers library and interactive resources help pupils think about career options and the Head of Careers and Employability meets with each pupil regularly throughout their time at Colston's.

Service and Community. Pupils are given many opportunities to contribute to the wider community. Colston's Combined Cadet Force, one of the most successful in the South West, allows cadets to regularly take part in expeditions and activities. Pupils also undertake The Duke of Edinburgh's Award which seeks to develop lifelong skills. Pupils relish the opportunity to get involved in a diverse range of volunteering projects across the city.

Fees per term (2018–2019). £4,650 (Lunch £215).

Modernisation. An extensive building programme has been carried out to provide new teaching classrooms, a 210-seat concert hall and purpose-built CCF headquarters. Additionally the library, laboratories and Sixth Form facilities have been completely refurbished to create a 21st century learning environment.

Situation. Colston's is located in Stapleton village which is within the city of Bristol, and enjoys the advantage of having all its playing fields and facilities on site. The 30-acre campus provides a wonderful environment for pupils to explore, learn and excel.

The school is large enough to sustain a wide range of activities at a high level and yet small enough for each boy or girl to contribute actively and be known as an individual. Every effort is made to provide for and develop pupils' abilities in academic, cultural and other co-curricular activities. The school aims to encourage a strong sense of community and service, and to fully develop and extend the talents of every boy and girl.

Charitable status. Colston's School is a Registered Charity, number 1079552. Its aims and objectives are the provision of education.

Governors:
Chair of Governors: Mr T Ross

Mr N Baker	Mr D Mace
Mrs A Burrell	Prof J McGeehan
Mrs G Cross	Dr A Seddon
Mrs C Duckworth	Mrs J Worthington
Mr M Hughes	Mr J Wright
Mr C Lucas	

Headmaster: **Mr J McCullough**, MA Oxon

Deputy Headmaster: Dr P Hill, BSc, PhD
Assistant Head, Co-Curricular: Mr E Beavington, MA
Assistant Head, Curriculum: Dr K Dawson, BA, PhD
Head of Sixth Form: Miss S Matthews, MA Oxon
Assistant Head, Academic: Dr J Tovey, BA, PhD
Assistant Head, Pastoral: Miss A Willis, BA
Director of Finance: Mrs E Jennings, FCA, BSc
Director of External Communications: Mrs K Hassan, BA Dunelm, MSc, MInstF[Cert]

Cranleigh School

Horseshoe Lane, Cranleigh, Surrey GU6 8QQ

Tel:	01483 273666
Fax:	01483 267398
email:	admissions@cranleigh.org
website:	www.cranleigh.org
Twitter:	@cranleighschool
Facebook:	@cranleigh-school

Motto: *Ex cultu robur*

Cranleigh is a leading co-educational weekly boarding and day school set in a stunning rural location in more than 280 acres on the edge of the Surrey Hills. Cranleigh's beautiful campus is exceptionally well equipped, with outstanding classrooms, studio, performance and sports facilities, including three theatres, twelve rehearsal and performance spaces, competition pitches, stables, sports centres, golf course, outdoor education centre and swimming pool.

There are strong links between the School and nearby Cranleigh Preparatory School and pupils also join from a wide variety of other prep schools across London and the home counties, creating a lively, House-based community of young people who are drawn together by their inherent love of life and getting involved in everything Cranleigh has to offer.

Cranleigh School's principal aim is to provide an environment in which pupils can flourish, enabling them to cap-

italise on the diverse range of opportunities offered by the School and to achieve to the best of their ability within a framework of shared values and standards. The School's 280-acre site, situated eight miles from Guildford on the Surrey-West Sussex border, lies on the outskirts of Cranleigh Village and within 45 minutes of London. The School is fully co-educational, with some 230 girls and 400 boys between the ages of 13 and 18, including a Sixth Form of about 250. It is a predominantly boarding community, attracting boarders from both the local area and further afield; it also, however, welcomes day pupils, who are fully integrated into the Cranleigh community, playing their part in the activities of their respective Houses and benefiting from the advantages thereby offered.

Each House (separate for boys and girls) has a resident Housemaster or Housemistress, a resident Deputy, a Warden, two Matrons and a team of tutors for both the Lower School and Sixth Form. There is also a strong and active partnership between parents and the School.

Cranleighans are encouraged to relish a challenge, to feel they are known as individuals, and to become talented and wise adults with an inherent ability to adapt to a fast-changing world. Aligned with this, the School boasts an impressive record in academic achievement. Almost all pupils achieve three A2 Levels (with a record number of A*s in 2015), and in recent years more than 99% have gone on to university, with 80% to their first-choice university (including Oxbridge and Russell Group universities).

Academic Patterns. Our aim is to act within the spirit of the National Curriculum, but to offer more, taking full advantage of our independence and the extra time available to a boarding school. We, therefore, retain a very broad curriculum in the Fourth Form and have an options system in the Lower and Upper Fifth Forms which enables a pupil to take between nine and eleven GCSE subjects before moving on to A Levels in the Sixth Form. We offer the opportunity to do Double or Triple Award Science, as well as giving good linguists the chance to take two foreign languages (with Latin if they wish). In the Sixth Form, pupils can select from a wide choice of subjects.

Work on languages, with an emphasis on commercial and colloquial fluency, is encouraged for non-specialist linguists, and much use is made of the Language Laboratory. Exchanges take place with pupils in schools in France, Spain and Germany. We have comprehensive facilities for Science, with an emphasis on experimental work. All members of the Lower Sixth Form study a course in Critical Thinking, or attend a series of lectures on a variety of topics, to help broaden their education.

Information Technology is incorporated into the teaching of all other subjects, with each academic department having its own IT policy, coordinated by the Director of IT. Most teaching rooms have networked PCs, and every House and academic department has PCs available for use, all linked to the School's network and the Internet.

Creative and Performing Arts. Cranleigh has maintained an enviable reputation for Music over many years, and the Merriman Music School offers pupils some of the finest facilities available. We send Choral Scholars to Oxford, Cambridge and major Music Departments and Colleges elsewhere; boys and girls of all ages successfully take part in national competitions and well over a third of the School learns a musical instrument. Keyboard players have access to our Mander two-manual tracker organ, purposefully designed for versatility and teaching, and to two Steinway concert grand pianos. Our exciting Cranleigh Music initiative is now well established, bringing together the Music Departments of Cranleigh School and Cranleigh Preparatory School under a single performing, management and administrative structure. Whilst facilities remain on separate sites (both sides of Horseshoe Lane), the ethos is that of a single Music Faculty encompassing the full 7–18 age range, whose cohesive structure will help to nurture and progress talent from a very young age, so ensuring that all pupils are able to perform in an environment commensurate with their individual ability.

Cranleigh also boasts a strong Drama tradition. Regular large-scale productions take place in the Speech Hall, to which is linked a studio theatre, the Vivian Cox Theatre, while a flourishing Technical Theatre department encourages the development of 'backstage' skills. The School's proximity to London allows for regular attendance at professional theatre, music and opera productions.

Art and Design Engineering. Both subject areas house a talented mix of practising artists, teachers and designers. The Woodyer Art Studios provide some of the best school art facilities in the country and is spread over several buildings, with a mix of dedicated airy studios. Six large art studios provide specialist provision for painting, printmaking, photography, sculpture and ceramics. A Sixth Form studio enables each student to have their own working space; two suites of computers provide digital facilities while photography is also equipped with a traditional darkroom. The printmaking studio is equipped for relief printing, acid-based etching, and screen-printing. A large project studio provides for a weekly Sixth Form life class and for exhibitions of student work.

The Design Engineering department boasts three fully equipped design studios and workshops. Each design studio features a suite of both PCs and Macs running the latest 2D and 3D CAD software, alongside ample space for the delivery of theoretical content and sketching. Each studio is equipped with a 3D Printer allowing for the rapid prototyping of 3D models created on Autodesk Fusion 360. The department also features a CAM mezzanine which is an excellent space for building 3D printers, housing the large format printer and vinyl plotter. The main Design Engineering workshop is housed within the school's original sports hall which allows for a considerably sized, open-plan workshop kitted out with the required tools and machinery. Branching from the main workshop space is an electronics lab for soldering and electronic circuit development, a CAM area consisting of a large format CNC Router and a Laser Cutter, and a heat treatment bay for welding and brazing.

The studios are open every day and appropriate use is made of the Faculty library, ICT and digital video and photo facilities. External visits are encouraged (both nationally and internationally) and all students exhibit throughout the year.

Sport. Cranleigh has an extensive range of extremely high-standard sporting facilities. During their time at Cranleigh, pupils will have the chance to try a variety of sports. Due to our Sport for All philosophy, all pupils will have the opportunity to train and compete regularly as part of a team throughout the year.

The School possesses an impressive array of sports facilities, including 3 full-size Astroturf pitches (one of which is floodlit), a 9-hole golf course, Cricket Pavilion and 5 outdoor Cricket Squares, with one all-weather match pitch, an Equestrian Centre with two sand schools, one 30m x 60m, one 20m x 40m, both with floodlights, cross-country jumping field and on-site hacking, 6 fives courts, 12 hard tennis courts, 9 astro tennis courts, 8 netball courts, an indoor swimming pool and eco-friendly, purpose-built fitness gym with a range of cardiovascular and weighted equipment as well as a physiotherapy room. For Rugby, Football and Cricket, Cranleigh also has 10 grass pitches on site, including an International standard 1st XV pitch. The large Sports Hall complex, the Trevor Abbott Sports Centre, provides a popular venue for netball, tennis, badminton and basketball,

and also includes a separate dance studio. There is also a separate Indoor Cricket Bubble for year-round development.

High standards are set for the numerous competitive teams, with an extensive programme of fixtures at all levels and for all ages. 'Sport for All' is a key philosophy at the School, supported by an experienced and talented team of coaches, many of whom have competed themselves at county, national and Olympic level. The School has witnessed some outstanding team and individual successes in recent years, including National representation in hockey, rugby, riding and cricket; taking National titles in horse riding (show jumping and dressage), kayaking, cricket, rugby 7s, swimming and hockey and also seeing several recent Old Cranleighans continue to compete in the international arena and as Olympic hopefuls.

In the Michaelmas term the majority sports are hockey for girls and rugby for boys; in the Lent term, the majority sports are netball for girls and hockey for boys. During the winter terms, pupils can also compete in lacrosse, cross-country, golf, water polo, soccer, fives, rugby-sevens, basketball, riding and squash, plus badminton and canoeing for the Sixth Form. All pupils in the Fourth and Lower Fifth Forms take part in the majority sport, while an element of choice is gradually introduced for the older pupils. All pupils in the School take part in sport, even in the Sixth Form.

In the Summer term, the main team sport for boys is cricket, whilst some boys compete in tennis, swimming, athletics and golf. For girls, the main sport is tennis, with competitive swimming, athletics, rounders and cricket popular additional offerings.

Service Activities. There are opportunities for pupils to take part in a range of 'service' activities. Boys and girls may join the CCF or get involved with community service, ecology or first-aid training. Cranleighans help local elderly people in community settings and also have links with local schools for children with learning difficulties and with a home for adults with similar difficulties. All Houses and the Fundraising Group raise money for various charities.

Wider initiatives also include the School's 'Beyond Cranleigh' partnership – a key partnership between Cranleigh School and Beyond Ourselves, a London-based charity that works to improve the lives of disadvantaged young people in both London and in Zambia. This partnership has led to Cranleigh's sponsorship of a primary school in Kawama, to which Sixth Form pupils regularly make visits to help with building and teaching initiatives. Cranleigh has also pledged to support social enterprise projects in Kawama to provide jobs and skills training for locals post-education. Such initiatives are designed to focus pupils' thoughts on life beyond the School.

Outdoor Education. Cranleigh operates a large Duke of Edinburgh's Award scheme, with many pupils completing the Gold Award before leaving school. By way of introduction, all Fifth Form pupils undergo an Outdoor Education programme in order to improve their self-awareness and confidence. There are many other opportunities for Outdoor Education through the CCF, there is a well-attended climbing club (which has its own bouldering wall), and the School enters the annual International Devizes-to-Westminster Canoe Race (which the School won in 2015).

Religion. The striking, neo-Gothic Chapel was built as a central point of the School, and Cranleigh maintains its concern to present the Christian way of life. It welcomes pupils of all faiths and none.

Developments. The School produced a new master plan during 2016 which has informed the Governing Body and Senior Managers of the options for developing the School estate and facilities in order to continue to improve provision for pupils. The plan envisages three phases each of five years from 2016.

Van Hasselt Centre (vHC): The new academic centre to house the English, Humanities, Business Studies and Economics Departments, as well as Careers, will be named after former headmaster, Marc van Hasselt, hence vHC. The innovative design by leading architects Allies and Morrison on the site of the squash courts sees the new classroom building surround the squash court building which will, in turn, be converted into a café for pupils with a Sixth Form leisure area in a first-floor mezzanine. The design of this building was finalised in January and February 2017 and will be completed at the end of 2018.

Fourth Girls' Boarding Hous (4G): The move of academic departments into the new vHC will free space in the Connaught block at the front of the School. This will then enable the conversion of this area back to its original purpose as a boarding house and specifically the fourth girls' house. A design is being drawn up at the moment and it is hoped to finalise plans by the end of 2017 so that work can commence in the second half of 2018, for completion by September 2019.

Planning for our Pupils' Future. Cranleigh takes the future of its pupils very seriously. It maintains good contacts with various professions, industry and commerce, through links developed as part of the careers advice structure. All pupils are regularly assessed during their time at the School, and this process includes a period of Work Experience at the end of the Upper Fifth year. Closely linked with the Old Cranleighan Society and the School, the Cranleigh Network oversees skills training, CV advice, postgraduate work experience and mentoring.

Admission and Registration. If you do not already know Cranleigh, we strongly recommend an initial visit during one of our small group visits or open mornings, dependent on the age of entry. These will enable you and your child to have a tour of the school, ground and facilities and meet a few key members of staff to answer any initial questions. Our visits and open mornings are very popular and so advance booking via the Admissions office is essential to avoid disappointment.

To arrange a personal appointment or to request to join a Saturday morning Small Group Appointment, please call the Admissions Office on 01483 276377.

Awards. The Master of Scholars has a specific responsibility for all Scholars. They are members of their Houses and attend normal lessons, but also have an additional programme throughout their time at the School that covers a wide variety of academic, cultural, social and commercial areas beyond the syllabus and which encourages independent thinking and research.

At age 13, Cranleigh School offers a variety of awards and scholarships. In certain circumstances, additional consideration may be given to sons or daughters of public servants, members of the armed forces and the clergy of the Church of England.

Fees per term (2018–2019). Boarders £12,635, Day Pupils £10,390.

It is the policy of the School to keep extras down to an absolute minimum, and limited to such charges as individual music tuition. Textbooks are supplied until the Sixth Form, at which point pupils are encouraged to buy their own so that they may take them on to university. A scheme is available for the payment of fees in advance.

Preparatory School. Cranleigh is closely linked with Cranleigh Preparatory School, where boys and girls are normally admitted at seven or eight, but also at other ages. For further information, apply to the Headmaster of the Preparatory School (*see entry in IAPS section*).

Charitable status. Cranleigh School is a Registered Charity, number 1070856. It exists to provide education for children aged 13–18 and the Preparatory School for those aged 7–13.

Governing Body:
Chairman: A J Lajtha, MA, FCIB
Deputy Chairman: Mrs M M S Fisher, MA
S E Bayliss, MA
J A Brown, MA Oxon
M P Cathcart, BVMS, BSC, MVM, CERTeM, DIPECEIM, MRCVS
Dr R M Chesser, MA, MB BChir, MRCP
M Foster, MA
P S P Going, BSC, MRICS
S Gunapala, BEng, MEng, FCA
R L Johnson, BSc, MRAeS
J A M Knight, BA Hons
A J Lye, BA
E Stanton, BSc, ACA
N D L Sweet, Dip LA, MA, MLI
S J Watkinson, BSc, ACA
O A R Weiss, MA
D G Westcott, BA, BCL, QC
S J Whitehouse, BA Cantab
D A E Williams, BA, FCA
P M Wells, BEd
M J Williamson
The Rt Revd Andrew Watson, Bishop of Guildford

Bursar and Clerk to the Governors: Mr P T Roberts, MBE, DChA

Headmaster: Mr Martin Reader, MA Oxon, MPhil, MBA

Deputy Head: Mr S D Bird, BA, MEd, QTS
Deputy Head (Pastoral): Dr A Saxel, BSc, PhD
Deputy Head (Academic): Mr D R Boggitt, BEng, PGCE
Assistant Head (Co-Curricular): Mr C H D Boddington, BA, PGCSE, MEd
Assistant Head (Director of IT): Mr D J Futcher, BSc, MBCS, QTS
Assistant Head (Learning, Teaching and Innovation): Dr J L Taylor, BA, BPhil, PhD, PGCSE
Head of Admissions: Mr S J Batchelor
Head of External Relations: Mrs J R Cooksley, BA Hons, MA

Members of Common Room:
† *Housemaster/mistress*
Mrs M C Allison, BEd
Miss E M Andrew
Miss M Baffou, BA
Mr A K Barker, BSc, PGCE
Mrs R L Barker, BSc, PGCE
Mr J Bartlett, BA
Mrs S E Baumann, BA, PGCE
Mr R R R B Bellak, BA, PGCE
Mrs P M Bigg
Mr S D Bird, BA, MA
Mr C H D Boddington, BA, PGCE
Mr D R Boggitt, BEng, PGCE, MEd
Mr E J P Bradnock, BA, PGCE
Mr S L Brearley
Mr B W Browne, BSc, PGCE
Mrs G L Bukowska, MSc, PGCE
Mrs O Burt, BA, MA
Mr E J Carson, BSc
Mr S T Cooke, BA (†*Cubitt*)
Mr W E Chadwick, BA, PGCE
Mr O A Chisholm, MA
Mrs C L Constable, MA, PGCE
Mr T M D Constable, BSc, PGCE

Mr S T Cooke, MA Oxon, MEd, PGCE
Mrs N J R Davison, BA, IPGCE
Mrs E G M Dellière, BA
Mr N Drake, BA, PG Dip, PGCE
Mr M P D Emley, BA, QTS, MA
Mr A T I Evans, BA, MSc, PGCE
Mr T R Fearn, BSc, PGCE
Mrs K J Flack, BA, HND
Mr A P Forsdike, MA, PGCE (†*North*)
Miss C E Frude, BA
Mr D J Futcher, BSc, QTS
Mrs C Gangemi, BSc, PGCE
Miss R S Gibson, BTh, MA
Mrs R Godber
Ms C S Gray, BA, PGCE
Miss S L Greenwood, BA
Mr A J Guppy, BA
Miss C R Hall, BA, PGCE
Mrs A J Hassett
Mr G Helliwell, BEd
Mr A G C Hillen, BA, MA, MA, PGCE
Dr D A W Hogg, MA, MSt, DPhil, PGCE
Miss E M Holland, BA, PGCE
Mr B P Hopcroft, BA
Mr A R Houston, BSc, GTP
Mr R C E K Kefford, BSc, PGCE
Dr S L Kemp, BSc, PhD, PGCE
Mr C W Kinnersly, BA, MA, GTP
Mr R G Lane, MEng, PGCE (†*Loveday*)
Mr F P A Laughton, BSc, PGCE
Miss S J Leach, BA, PGCE
Mr P M Leamon, BA, PGAS, PGCE
Mr T G Leeke, BSc
Revd T M P Lewis, MA, MTh, QTS
Mrs B L Lewis, MA, MSc, GTP (†*Rhodes*)
Mrs C J Lock, BSc, PGCE, PGDIPP (†*South*)
Mrs E R McGhee, BA, PGCE
Mrs G L McMillan, BSc, PGCE
Mrs L Mercer, BA, PGCE
Miss H K Merry, BSc, PGCE
Mr N G A Miller, BA, GTP, QTS
Mr J B Nairne, BFA, PGCE
Mr G J N Neill, BA, MA, PGCE
Miss S Ni'man, BA
Miss C E Nicholls, MA, PGCE
Mr M C Pashley, BMus
Mr E J E Peerless, BSc, PGCE
Mr G V Pritchard, BSc, PGCE
Mr S G Quinn, BSc, PD, PGCE
Mrs O D Ravilious, BA, PGCE
Mrs A E Reader, BA, PGCE
Mr D C Reed, BA, MSc
Mr A D Robinson, MA, PGCE
Mr I P Rossiter, BSc, PGCE
Mr A S J Rothwell, MPhil, PGCE, MA
Mr G C Royall, BSc
Dr A P Saxel, BSc, PhD
Mr R J Saxel, BA, DipRam, LRAM, ARAM
Mr J H Schofield-Newton, BA, MA
Mr P N Scriven, BA, MA, LRAM, MM (*Organist in Residence*)
Mr J Scott, BA, PGCE, MBA
Mrs R J Scott, BA
Miss R E Simmons, BA, PGCE
Miss R J Singleton, BEng
Mrs A C Smuts, BSc, GTP
Mr C P G Stearn, BA, MPhil, QTS
Dr J L Taylor, BA, BPhil, PGCE, DPhil
Mr J J Taylor, BA, QTS
Dr A L J Thomas, BMus, MPhil, PhD
Dr B R Tyrrell, MChem, DPhil

Mr D N Vaiani, BA
Mr R J O Venables, MA, PGCE
Mr R Verdon, BA, MBA, PGCE
Miss E L Wallis, BA, PGCE
Dr M Ward, BA, PhD, LGSM, MMus, Dip RCM, ARCM
Mr K W Weaver, BA Music, PG Dip
Miss S L Webb, BA
Mr M J Weighton, BA, PGCE
Mr S D Welch
Miss J D Wiles, BSc, PGCE
Mrs R A C Williams, BSc, PGCE
Mr I D Winterbottom, BSc, MSc, PGCE
Mr J M Witcombe, BSc, PGCE (†*East*)
Mr M A Worsley, LL.B
Mrs A W Worsley, BSc, PGCE (†*West*)
Mrs U C Yardley, BA, PGCE
Dr S A H Young, BSc, MSc, PhD, PGCE

Culford School

Bury St Edmunds, Suffolk IP28 6TX

Tel: 01284 728615
Fax: 01284 728631
email: admissions@culford.co.uk
website: www.culford.co.uk
Twitter: @CulfordSchool
Facebook: @officialculfordscool

Motto: *Viriliter Agite Estote Fortes*

Culford School was founded in 1881 in Bury St Edmunds and moved to its present site on the Culford estate in 1935. The School is one of twelve owned by the Methodist Independent Schools Trust and is administered by a Board of Governors, to whom local control is devolved.

About Culford School. Culford is a co-educational boarding and day school for 730 pupils aged between 1 and 18 across three schools: the Pre Prep & Nursery, Prep and Senior Schools, all of which are situated within 480 acres of beautiful Suffolk parkland.

Where is Culford School? Culford is conveniently located four miles north of Bury St Edmunds and is within easy reach of Cambridge and Norwich (to which the school runs a daily bus shuttle service), Ipswich and Stansted Airport, and Heathrow and Gatwick airports are within two hours of Culford.

Teaching & Learning. We believe education should be challenging, enriching and fun and are committed to helping our pupils achieve excellence in all areas of school life. Hard work in the classroom is complemented by full sporting and extracurricular programmes.

Curriculum. We aim to give a broad and balanced education that enables every pupil to fulfil their academic potential. Core subjects at GCSE are English Language and Literature, Mathematics, the three sciences and a foreign language. Pupils can choose additional subjects from a wide range of options and receive guidance from the Deputy Head, their teachers and personal tutor who, along with the Housemaster or Housemistress, has responsibility for their academic and social progress. To support this Culford pupils also experience Personal, Social, Health and Citizenship Education (PSHCE) courses.

Culford Sixth Formers usually study three or four subjects at A Level. The majority of students go on to university, including Oxbridge and the prestigious Russell Group universities. Sixth Formers may also study for an Extended Project Qualification (EPQ) which enables students to study beyond the confines of A Level specifications; it can be an essay, a film, a composition or even something created in Design and Technology.

Facilities. Culford is centred on the magnificent Culford Hall, an 18th century mansion formerly the seat of Marquis Cornwallis and Earl Cadogan. The Hall houses Culford's Music School and purpose-built Studio Theatre. In September 2015 the facilities were further enhanced with a brand new £2.2m landmark library at the academic heart of the school.

Teaching Facilities. Teachers are specialists in their fields and are united by a passion to help the children in their care achieve their goals, whatever they may be. Classrooms are modern and well equipped, and in the case of specialist subjects, such as languages and sciences, have the latest technologies installed. The School also has excellent Art, Design and Technology facilities in the Pringle Centre which boasts its own exhibition gallery. In 2019, the School will open a brand new art studio.

Sports Facilities. Culford's fantastic £2m Sports and Tennis Centre is a state-of-the-art facility which comprises a four-court, championship-standard Indoor Tennis Centre, a 25m indoor pool, gym, strength and conditioning suite, golf swing studio and a large sports hall with a climbing wall and indoor cricket nets. Outside there are further tennis courts, two of which are seasonally covered, two artificial turf pitches (one in partnership with Bury Hockey Club) and numerous rugby and hockey pitches.

Pupils can also pursue athletics, horse riding, canoeing, sailing, scuba diving and even fishing in our own lake. Culford launched a new Football Academy programme in 2018 to sit alongside its already well-established high-profile Tennis, Golf and Swimming programmes.

Boarding. Culford accepts boarders aged 7 to 18 and for a whole host of reasons, including an 'Excellent' ISI rating, boarding is extremely popular with over half of Senior pupils boarding. Boarders enjoy an amazing range of weekend activities and have full access to Culford's impressive Sports and Tennis Centre.

Culford's boarding Houses offer children a comfortable, secure and fun place to live during term time. Boarders in their first year share study-bedrooms and move into single rooms in the Upper Sixth. Culford offers flexible arrangements for other boarders where possible: part and occasional boarding is available providing space is free. We do not have an enforced exeat at the weekends; children may stay at school throughout the term, going home at the weekend or to stay with friends only when they or their parents wish them to.

All pupils have access to our fully-equipped Medical Centre, supervised by a resident nurse, and this includes provision for residential care when necessary.

Culford Pre-Prep & Nursery School. Our purpose-designed Nursery accepts children from age 1 to 3 and perfectly prepares them for School life. Culford's Nursery opened in 2017 and is available for 50 weeks per year.

Culford Pre-Prep occupies a combination of new and entirely refurbished buildings and provides teaching for 80 children from Nursery at age three through to age seven in a delightful setting within the grounds.

Both Pre-Prep and Nursery schools take part in Forest School activities, a way of learning outdoors that helps children to develop personal, social and technical skills in a woodland setting.

Music & Drama. Music plays an important part in the life of the School. There are numerous choirs, orchestras and bands and regular concerts are held to give pupils the chance to perform in public. Individual music tuition is offered in voice, piano, organ and all orchestral instruments. Drama is also very popular and there are regular House plays and concerts as well as major productions: these include musicals and plays for different sections of the School.

Activities. There is a huge array of clubs and societies on offer – from academic and creative to sporting and community. Pupils are encouraged to take part in Community Service Activities and many participate in the Duke of Edinburgh's Award Scheme or choose to join the Combined Cadet Force (CCF).

Staff regularly take pupils out on visits and expeditions too, and every summer a group of Sixth Formers and teachers spend 3 weeks in Malawi helping with various development projects; a trip that is universally viewed as a life-changing experience. Other recent trips have included tours to New York, skiing in France and scuba diving in Tobago as well as sports tours worldwide.

Entry. The majority of pupils join in September at ages 1–7 (Pre-Prep), 7+, 8+ and 11+ (Preparatory School); and at 13+ and 16+ (Senior School). Entrance examinations are held in January and February of the year of entry or pupils may enter having passed Common Entrance in June. Entry to the Sixth Form is on the basis of GCSE performance or its equivalent for overseas candidates.

Entry to Culford Pre-Preparatory School is by informal assessment just prior to enrolment.

Applications are welcome from individuals throughout the year, subject to places being available.

Visiting Culford School. If you would like to visit Culford, the Headmaster will be delighted to welcome you. Please contact the Admissions Office to arrange an appointment and a tour on 01284 385308 or to request a copy of the School prospectus. We also hold regular Open Mornings each term, please visit www.culford.co.uk to find out more. Please follow this link to view the School Videos: www.culford.co.uk/video.

Scholarships and Exhibitions. Culford holds its Scholarship examinations between November (Sixth Form) and January/February for entry in the following September. Scholarships and Exhibitions are awarded according to merit in the following categories:

11+: Academic, Music, Swimming, Tennis, Cricket and Golf

13+: Headmaster's Foundation Scholarship, Academic, Art, Design & Technology, Drama, Music, Hockey, Rugby, Swimming, Tennis and Sport

16+: Headmaster's Foundation Scholarship, Professor Watson Scholarship, Academic, Art, Drama, Music, Design & Technology, Hockey, Rugby, Swimming, Tennis, Golf and Sport

11+, 13+ and 16+: Jubilee Scholarships for all-rounders who board are worth up to 25% of boarding fees.

16+: The William Miller Scholarship for a pupil studying sciences is worth up to 25% of tuition fees. The Arkwright Scholarship for a pupil studying Design & Technology allows an amount over two years to be shared between the pupil and the School.

Swimming and Tennis Scholarships and Exhibitions may be available at any age from 10+.

The Headmaster's Foundation Scholarship is worth up to 50% of tuition fees; the Professor Watson Scholarship (restricted to pupils coming from state schools) is worth 25% of day or boarding fees; all other scholarships are worth up to 25% of tuition fees, and Exhibitions are worth up to 10%.

Bursaries are available to those in genuine financial need.

A generous Forces Allowance is available to parents who are serving members of the Armed Forces and are in receipt of the MOD CEA.

For further details please apply to The Registrar, Tel: 01284 385308, Fax: 01284 385513 or email: admissions@culford.co.uk.

Fees per term (2018–2019). Day £6,500, Boarding £9,995–£10,580.

Charitable status. Culford School is part of the Methodist Independent Schools Trust, which is a Registered Charity, number 1142794.

Chairman of Governors: Air Vice Marshall S Abbott, CBE, MPhil, BA

Headmaster: J F Johnson-Munday, MA, MBA

Prep School Headmaster: M Schofield, BEd

Pre-Prep Headmistress: S Preston, BA

Deputy Head: Dr J Guntrip, BSc, PhD

Assistant Head: D V Watkin, BEd

Dauntsey's School

West Lavington, Devizes, Wiltshire SN10 4HE

Tel:	01380 814500
Fax:	01380 814501
email:	info@dauntseys.org
website:	www.dauntseys.org
Twitter:	@DauntseysSchool
Facebook:	@DauntseysSchool
LinkedIn:	/dauntsey's-school

Dauntsey's was founded back in 1542, here in Wiltshire, under the will of Alderman William Dauntesey, Master of the Worshipful Company of Mercers. Today it has grown into a thriving, friendly, co-educational boarding and day school of some 800 11–18 year olds with continued close links to the Mercers' Company. They are actively involved in the School and several members of the Company sit as Governors. Warmth, laughter and lasting friendships built on trust and mutual respect are the hallmarks of daily life at Dauntsey's. Perhaps this is due in some part to the spirit of our Mercer founder.

Number. 800 Pupils aged between 11–18 years: 407 boys, 393 girls, 37.5% boarding.

Situation. The School is set in an estate of over 100 acres in the Vale of Pewsey in Wiltshire. The Manor House, a mansion with its own woodland and playing fields, is the co-educational Junior boarding house for pupils in the First to Third Forms.

The Community. Our house system is the cornerstone of our community, giving pupils a secure source of support and guidance on every aspect of life, as well as the chance to get together and have fun. Every pupil joins either a boarding or day house, which are co-educational in the Lower School (ages 11 to 13) and single sex in the Upper School (ages 14 to 18). Each house is run by a housemaster or housemistress and a team of tutors who take a close and active interest in pupils' academic and social development, as well as encouraging them to make the most of the activities on offer. Above all, they really do make sure that the house is a home from home.

Curriculum. Throughout the School, the curriculum is broad and balanced, offering the opportunity to study an extensive range of subjects. The academic curriculum is well balanced, very wide ranging and offers a good amount of choice. The timetable offers a great deal of flexibility, with well-structured weekly lessons and extensive options that cater for the different interests and aptitudes of all our pupils. Dauntsey's especially promotes independent learn-ing, enabling pupils to fulfil their potential and develop the key skills they will need in later life. Gifted and talented pupils have access to work and experiences at the higher cognitive levels, to stimulate interest and develop advanced thinking skills, while pupils with mild learning difficulties get expert help and support from a dedicated team of specialist teachers.

Games. The major sports are Rugby, Football, Hockey, Cricket and Netball. Other games options include Tennis, Squash, Athletics, Swimming, Soccer, Water Polo, Fencing, Badminton and Basketball. In the Sixth Form further options include Triathlon training, Canoeing, Basketball, Rifle-shooting, Yoga, Cross-Country, Ballet, Dance, Conditioning and Riding. Sixth Formers can also choose to do volunteer work within the community. Special attention is given to Physical Education.

Extra-Curricular Activities. Our adventure education and extra-curricular programmes set us apart, encouraging pupils to try new experiences. From drama, dance, music, sport and a huge range of clubs and societies, to our lecture series, adventure programmes and volunteering initiatives – there are opportunities to suit everyone. We aim to push our pupils out of their comfort zone, inside and outside the classroom, and we bring that spirit of adventure to everything we do.

Fees per term (2018–2019). Boarders £10,480; Day Pupils £6,330. There are no compulsory extras.

Admission. Boys and girls are admitted at 11 and 13 (boarding only) by examination, school report and interview; to the Sixth Form by I/GCSE grade predictions or equivalent and interview.

Scholarships and Bursaries. Scholarships and awards are available for boarding and day places at 11+, 13+ and 16+ and carry a maximum fee remission of 10%. Scholarship supplements are available to those who have been awarded a scholarship and provide financial help with the school fees.

Bursaries: The school funds three new, 100% bursary places each year to pupils whose parents would otherwise be unable to fund any portion of the school fees. In addition, there is a fund to provide short-term bursarial support for current pupils whose parents or guardians who meet financial difficulties.

For further details please contact the Registrar.

Charitable status. Dauntsey's School is a Registered Charity, number 1115638. It is dedicated to the education of boys and girls.

Governors:
Mrs L F Walsh Waring, BA (*Chairman*)
Mr N B Elliott, QC (*Vice Chairman*)
Mr R M Bernard, CBE
Mrs S R Broadhead, BSc
Mrs K G Bruges
Mr A H Collins, AIWSc
Mr N J S Fisk, BA, ACA
Mr D Goodhew, BA
Mrs J L Green, BA
Air Chief Marshal Sir Richard Johns, GCB, KCVO
Mrs E A Light
Mr P J Lough, MA
Mr C H de N Lucas, FRICS, FAAV
Mr A S Macpherson, MBE, BA, ACA
Mrs V P Nield, BSc, MBA
Mr I Parker, BSc, MBA
Dr R E L Quarrel, BA, MA, DPhil
Brigadier P P Rawlins, MBE
Mr F W Scarborough
Mr I T Thomas, BSc, DMS

Head Master: Mark Lascelles, BA

Deputy Head (Pastoral): Mrs A L Jackson, BA

Second Master: Mr M C B McFarland, BA

Deputy Head (Academic): Mr J M Tyler, BA

Head of Lower School: Miss E S Conidaris, BSc

Heads of Department:
Adventure Education: Mr S Moore
Art: Mrs V A Rose, BA Bath Spa
Careers: Mr J F O'Hanlon, BSc Wales
Classics: Mr D Hodgkinson
Computing: Mr D A T Fraser, BSc Bangor, MSc Cardiff
Design Technology: Mr A Pickford, BA Wales
Drama and Dance: Mr R M Jackson, BA Warwick
Economics and Business Studies: Mr A Poole, BA West of England
English: Mr A Brown, BA Warwick
EFL: Mrs D A Whitchurch, BA Swansea, TESOL
Geography: Mr A J Palmer, BSc London, FCIEA
History: Mr B H Sandell, BA Exeter
Language Development: Ms J Leeming, BA Southampton
Mathematics: Mr P A Mobbs, BSc Bath, MSc LSE
French: Ms P J Harrison, BA Birmingham
German: Mrs V A H Wilks, BA Exeter
Spanish: Mrs D C Hills, BA Bristol
Music: Mr G G Harris, BMus Manchester
Physical Education: Mr J Devney, BSc Cardiff and Met
Religious Studies: Ms K Pratt, BA Surrey
Science: Mr A J Crossley, BSc Newcastle
Biology: Mr V R Muir, BSc Canterbury NZ, BSc Open, MIBiol
Chemistry: Mr M Kinder, MChem Oxford
Physics: Mr J L Johns, BSc Cardiff
Sailing: Mr T R Marris, DTP, YME
A Level PE: Mr J Devney, BSc Cardiff and Met

Houses and Housemasters/Housemistresses:

Upper School:
Evans: Mrs E M Crozier
Farmer: Mr W P J Whyte
Fitzmaurice: Mr D R D Darwall
Hemens: Mrs V A H Wilks
Jeanne: Mrs A L Evans
King-Reynolds: Mrs G S Ward
Lambert: Mrs K S Clark
Mercers: Mr M Kinder

Lower School:
Manor: Mrs A E Sampson
Forbes: Mrs E C Gardiner
Rendell: Mr M Olsen
Scott: Mrs S k Walton-Knight

Chaplain: Revd D R Johnson, MA, BSc
Bursar: Air Cdr S Lilley, RAF Retd
Registrar: Mrs J H Sagers, BA
Head Master's Secretary: Mrs D Caiger

Dean Close School

Shelburne Road, Cheltenham, Gloucestershire GL51 6HE

Tel: 01242 258000
email: registrar@deanclose.org.uk
website: www.deanclose.org.uk
Twitter: @DeanCloseSchool
Facebook: @DeanCloseSchool

Motto: *Verbum Dei Lucerna*

Sitting on a beautifully landscaped 50-acre site in the Regency town of Cheltenham, Dean Close School is an attractive mixture of old, traditional buildings and modern, hi-tech structures. The School was opened in 1886 in memory of Francis Close, Rector of Cheltenham 1826–55 and later Dean of Carlisle, and has been co-educational since 1967. Dean Close is a Christian school which believes that education is as much about building character and relationships as it is about gaining knowledge. An independent Preparatory School was established in 1949.

Admission and Withdrawal. Admission to the Senior School at 13 is through Common Entrance or direct entrance tests in English, Maths and Verbal Reasoning. Sixth Form: examination and interview, 6 Bs minimum at GCSE. We advise pupils to have at least an A in the subjects they wish to study at A Level. Prospectus and application forms are available from the Registrar who is also happy to arrange a visit at a time to suit. There is a non-returnable registration fee of £100 and a returnable deposit of £750 (day pupils) £1,500 (boarding/dayboarding pupils) payable one year before entry. One term's notice is required before a pupil is withdrawn from the School.

Fees per term (2018–2019). Boarding £11,485–£11,939, International Boarding £12,005–£12,458, Sixth Form Boarding (new entrants) £12,471, Flexi Boarding £8,822–£9,900, Day £7,772–£8,200.

Term of Entry. We prefer to accept pupils in September but will make exceptions at any time of year, even in the middle of a term, if a good reason exists.

Scholarships and Bursaries. The School offers scholarships, exhibitions and bursaries at age 13 and for entry into the Sixth Form. The six areas of talent which are recognised are academic, music, sport, drama, art and product design technology. The size of award is set according to performance. Dean Close Preparatory School also offers scholarships at ages 7 and 11.

Academic: The 13+ ISEB Common Scholarship Examination, for which specimen papers are available from the ISEB, is held annually at the school in February. Candidates for academic scholarships from state schools should contact the Admissions team. The Sixth Form Scholarship examination takes place in November.

Music (including Choral and Organ) and Drama Scholarships are based on audition, interviews and exam (Drama). Individual specialist tuition is free to all scholars and exhibitioners.

Art and Product Design Technology Scholarships may be awarded, based on portfolio, drawing / technical test and interview.

Sports Scholarships are awarded to reflect all-round sporting ability and commitment. Assessment by conditioning tests, skills tests in two or more sports and interviews.

Means-tested bursaries for sons and daughters of clergy and missionaries. Automatic discounts, known as Thierry Awards, are offered to parents serving in HM Armed Forces on a scale according to rank. Foundation Bursaries for families in the locality unable otherwise to benefit from a Dean Close education.

Number and Organisation. There are 475 in the Senior School (13–18). The Sixth Form comprises approximately 40% of the School. There are ten Houses: three for boarding boys (one Sixth Form only), two for day boys, three for boarding girls (one Sixth Form only) and two for day girls. Housemasters take immediate responsibility for pupils' work, careers, applications for universities and further education. A tutorial system ensures that all pupils have a member of the teaching staff who takes a particular interest in them, both academically and pastorally. There is a Careers department. The Preparatory School (2–13) has approximately 453 pupils of whom 222 are girls.

Work. In the lower part of the School pupils are set rather than streamed. Included in the Lower School timetable is a Creative Studies course introducing pupils to a wide range of artistic and creative subjects, embracing DT, Art, Drama, Music and Physical Education. The language centre, music school, art school, sports hall, modern laboratories, IT Suite, electronics and creative workshops combine excellent teaching and leisure facilities which are available both in timetabled and extra-curricular time. Much of the accommodation has been built in the last twenty years and is modern and purpose-built. A professional 550-seat theatre houses an ambitious programme of productions. There is also an open-air theatre. As well as several orchestras, wind band, many ensembles and the Chapel Choir, the School has a Choral Society which performs a major work at least once a year. The Strings Department is headed up by the internationally renowned Carducci Quartet. Tuition in any number of musical instruments is available as an extra. Free tuition is provided for music award holders and high-grade musicians. The theatre also affords first-class concert facilities.

Religious Education. The teaching and Chapel services are in accordance with the Church of England and the School's strong Evangelical tradition is maintained. The Chaplain prepares members of the School for confirmation each year. Most services are in the School Chapel.

Games. The School has a 25m indoor swimming pool and a £3m sports hall, both used all the year round. There are two international standard astroturf pitches and a large number of tennis courts. Hockey, rugby, cricket, netball, athletics, tennis, and cross-country are the main sports.

Health. The School has three qualified Sisters with Assistants and visiting Doctors. There is a surgery and a medical centre.

Outside Activities. There is a huge range of clubs, activities and societies, from climbing to creative writing, salsa dancing to Warhammer, theatre tech to horse riding. A very active Combined Cadet Force with RN and Army sections trains every Wednesday afternoon and some pursue Bronze and Gold Duke of Edinburgh's Award. There is an active outward bound club and a large Community Action group gets involved with projects on a local, national and international level, particularly with a link school in Uganda.

President of Council of Members: The Lord Ribeiro, CBE

Board of Trustees:
S Bullingham, MSc, BSc
Mrs K Carden, MPhil, BA (*Chairman*)
M J Cartwright, BA, FCA (*Treasurer*)
The Revd R M Coombs, BSc, MA
Mrs H Daltry, BA
C S S Drew, MA
I Duffin, FCA, BCom
R S Harman, MA
Mrs S L Hirst, BEd
Mrs A Marsden, MSc, BSc
Mrs K Riding, LLB
M P Smith, MA
Maj E Taylor, RA, BA

The Trustees are elected by the Members of Council and oversee the overall governance of the School. They carry a substantial burden of financial and legal responsibility on an entirely voluntary basis and the School is greatly indebted to them.

Warden: Mrs Emma Taylor, MA

Headmaster: B J Salisbury, MEd, PGCE

Deputy Headmaster: A S Hall, BA (*HMS*)
Director of External Relations: D R Evans, MA
Deputy Head Pastoral: Mrs J A Davis, MA, PGCE

Deputy Head Academic: J A Hole, MA
Bursar: A P Bowcher, MBA, FCIB, DipFS

Director of Studies, Sixth Form: M W Wilkes, BA, PGCE
Director of Studies, Years 10 & 11: Miss R J Donaldson, BSc, PGCE
Director of Studies, Year 9: A J George, MA, PGCE
Assistant Director of Studies: Dr M Bradley, MBiochem, DPhil, PGCE
Chaplain: Revd J Ash, BA
Head of Admissions: Miss C Heffernan

Housemasters & Housemistresses:
Brook Court: J M Pitt, BA
Dale: B P Price, BSc, PGCE
Fawley: Mrs J Briggs, BA
Field: P S Montgomery, MA, PGCE
Gate: M W Wilkes, BA, PGCE
Hatherley: Mrs K E Milne, BA
Mead: Mrs C M Feltham, MA, PGCE
Shelburne: Mrs J D Kent, GDLM
Tower: B S Poxon, MA, PGCE
Turner: Mrs C Allen, ALCM, LGSM, PGCE, BMus

Heads of Department:
Art & Design: Mrs C J Evans, BA, PGCE
Biology: Dr A D E Martin, BSc, PhD, PGCE
Chemistry: D K Chapman, BSc, PGCE
Classics: J M Allen, MA, PGCE
Drama: L S Allington, BA
Economics & Business: J Hardaker, BA, PGCE
ELT: Miss R J Vest, BA, PGCE, CELTA
e-Learning & Computer Science: D F Fitzgerald, BSc, PGCE
English: Mrs K Ledlie, MA, PGCE
Equestrianism: Mrs F Cradock, BA
Geography: Mrs C L Bourne, BA, PGCE
History & Politics: J Sheldon, MA, BA, PGCE
Learning Support: Mrs M Watts, BA, PGCE, PG Cert Literacy Difficulties
Mathematics: P J J Garner, MA, PGCE
Modern Languages: J M A Sumner, BA, PGCE
Music: Mrs H L Porter, BA, LRAM, PGCE (*Director of Music*)
Choral Music: S A H Bell, MMus, BMus, FRCO
Sport: G N Baber-Williams, BA, PGCE (*Director of Sport*)
Academic PE: Miss R J Donaldson, BSc, PGCE
Physics: M J McKechnie, MEng
Product Design Technology: D D Evans, BSc
PSHE: Miss D-M Richards, BSc, PGCE
Psychology: Miss T L Williams, BSc, PGCE, GTP
Religion, Philosophy & Ethics: D Mochan, MA, BA, PGCE, FRSA
Science: A R Needs, BSc, PGCE, MRSC
Speech & Drama: Ms R M O Vines, MA, FVCM, FRSA, LALAM, ALAM, STSD
Careers & Head Librarian: Z Suckle, MA, PGCE
UCAS Coordinator: D Mochan, MA, BA, PGCE, FRSA
Examinations Officer: Mrs M Franklin, BSc

Medical Officers (*both Schools*):
Dr J Wilson & Partners, MBBS, DRCOG, Dip Pall Med, FRCGP
Overton Park Surgery

SSI, CCF: WO1 B G Lloyd

Preparatory School:
(*see entry in IAPS section*)
Headmaster: P Moss, BA
Deputy Head Operations: J Harris, BA, PGCE
Deputy Head Academic: M Walters, BA QTS
Senior Master: E Harris, BEd
Senior Mistress: Mrs E Bailey, BSc, PGCE

Pre-Preparatory School:
(*see entry in IAPS section*)
Headmistress: Dr C A Shelley, PhD
Deputy Head: J E Cowling, BA, PGCE
Early Years Foundation Stage Coordinator: Miss A
   Moorhouse, BEd (*Hons*)

Interim Financial Controller: J Swift
Operations Bursar (Estates): S Ewence
Registrar (Senior): Mrs K Serjeant, BA
Director of Marketing: Mrs T C Colbert-Smith, BA, MCIM
Admissions (Prep): Mrs R Chaplin, BSc
Headmaster's PA (Senior): Mrs J Bond
Headmaster's PA (Prep): Ms S Clark

Denstone College
A Woodard School

Uttoxeter, Staffs ST14 5HN

Tel: 01889 590484
Fax: 01889 591295
email: admissions@denstonecollege.net
website: www.denstonecollege.org
Twitter: @DenstoneCollege
Facebook: @DenstoneCollege

Motto: *Lignum Crucis Arbor Scientiae*

Achievement, Confidence and Happiness are central to the College philosophy, through which girls and boys are always encouraged to aim high and so reach their full potential. Founded in 1868, the College is rich in tradition and history, but combines this with a forward thinking approach to education.

Denstone College offers a rounded education, where proper emphasis is placed on academic achievement and high standards are the top priority. A wide range of other opportunities, however, ensures that every individual finds and develops his or her own special talents. Denstonians emerge with a degree of self-esteem and confidence, possible only as a result of so much opportunity and challenge. They have the qualifications, skills and personality to make their mark in today's competitive world.

Location. Denstone College is situated on the Staffordshire/Derbyshire border, 6 miles north of Uttoxeter in 100 acres of grounds. The site is located in magnificent countryside, but is well served by road, rail and air.

Organisation. The College is divided into the following units: Junior School (ages 11–14, Years 7, 8 and 9), Middle School (ages 14–16, Years 10 and 11), and Senior School (ages 17–18, Sixth Form which typically numbers around 200 pupils).

All girls and boys are in one of the six houses, each numbering about 100 members, with a total roll of 617. Weekly boarding is a popular option. Just over a quarter of our pupils board, and one third are girls, who have separate boarding accommodation. The College does not believe in vertical boarding.

Denstone College Preparatory School at Smallwood Manor, also a Woodard School, is 9 miles away. Age range 3–11.

Buildings. The main building contains classrooms, day and boarding areas, studies, Dining Hall, Chapel, Theatre and resident staff accommodation. A great deal of school life is thus centred in this main block, which also includes IT facilities and a library.

The Sports Hall, laboratories, other classrooms, indoor heated swimming pool, Art Centre, Design and Technology Centre, and other buildings, such as the Medical Centre and School Shop, are elsewhere in the grounds.

Recent and Future Developments. In recent years the College has benefited from a £10m development programme, with a new Music School and additional classrooms opened in September 2010. Further extensive classroom facilities and the Adamson's sports complex were completed and opened in June 2012. Then in September 2013 the doors opened to a beautiful library which is at the heart of teaching and learning at Denstone. More recently a brand new classroom block, housing Maths and Modern Foreign Languages, was completed in the summer term 2017 and is now in use. The day and boarding accommodation undergoes regular improvement and redecoration, and impressive IT teaching facilities have been developed, along with general classroom refurbishments to a high standard. A large sports hall allows for a wide range of minority and unusual sports. Other recent improvements include a second Astroturf, and all-weather cricket facilities.

Future plans include enhancing teaching space for Art and DT including gallery areas, and creating still further sports provision by increasing the number of astroturf pitches.

Curriculum. In the Junior School (ages 11 to 14, Years 7, 8 and 9) all follow roughly the same spread of subjects: English, Drama, French, Spanish, Mathematics, Physics, Chemistry, Biology, History, Geography, Art, Music, DT, Religious Studies, Information Technology, and PE.

Girls and boys enter the Middle School at the beginning of Year 10. Subjects are studied in option blocks. Mathematics, English Language and Literature, a Modern Language, RS and Science are core subjects, and three others are chosen from those listed above, along with Business and Economics GCSE.

Girls and boys then specialise in A Levels, chosen in an option system appropriate to the current discussions regarding Sixth Form Curriculum nationally. Four A Levels will normally be taken in the Sixth Form. Subjects offered are Mathematics, Further Maths, Physics, Chemistry, Biology, English Language, English Literature, French, Spanish, History, Geography, Economics, Business, Psychology, Politics, Art, Theatre Studies, and DT. There will also be a minority who will study, in varying numbers from year to year, Music and Religious Studies. We also offer EPQ, Sport (BTEC) and ICT (Cambridge Technical). An extremely flexible timetable is possible and we aim to offer as many combinations of subjects as possible.

The vast majority of pupils take A Levels, with the aim of going on to University. Each year, some girls and boys are prepared for Oxford or Cambridge entrance. A majority of the Upper Sixth are typically accepted into one of the Russell Group Universities and almost all to their first-choice or second-choice university.

The School is well-equipped with computer rooms, laboratories, and a 200-seat Theatre. Each department remains up-to-date with subject development and members of staff regularly attend courses and conferences.

Class sizes are relatively small. Up to Year 11, 20 is an average class size, and in the Sixth Form sets vary from 6 to 14.

In addition to having a Head of School and Head of House each pupil has a Tutor with whom he or she meets regularly to discuss work and progress, and both half termly and end of term grades and reports are issued.

Pupils in both Junior and Middle School have a number of staff supervised Homework sessions incorporated into the school day. Boarding members of Fifth Form, Lower Sixth and Upper Sixth have shared or single studies.

Out of Class Activities. The aim is to provide as wide a variety of opportunities for pupils of differing aptitudes and inclinations as possible.

Games: The College has 2 full-size all-weather hockey pitches, one of which is floodlit and provides 9 tennis courts in the Summer Term. Our new netball court facility has 10 courts that also provides tennis courts in the Summer. A nine-hole handicap-standard golf course has been laid out to the west of the College. There is an indoor heated swimming pool, and the main Sports Hall accommodates indoor sports as well as our Strength and Conditioning Centre. The Drill Hall provides further games space and a CV gymnasium, with cycle machines, running machines and rowing machines.

The main sports in the Michaelmas Term are rugby for the boys and hockey for the girls, with opportunities for other games. In the Lent Term these change to hockey and football for the boys and netball for the girls, along with swimming, cross country, aerobics, and others. In the summer there is a degree of choice between cricket, athletics, swimming, golf, and tennis and rounders for girls.

In the course of the year there is opportunity for boys and girls to take part in a wide variety of sports, in which they can represent both their House and the School.

CCF and Pioneers: There is also a Combined Cadet Force with Army and Royal Air Force sections and The Duke of Edinburgh's Award scheme.

The Arts: There are set times each week when priority is given to non-sporting clubs and activities, giving pupils opportunities in a wide range of experiences. Music plays a central role in College life. There is a School Orchestra, Swing Band, and Jazz Ensemble. There is a Girls chamber choir, and the Chapel choir sings at the main service each Friday. In addition, there are also other specialist ensembles and small instrumental groups. Music is included in the curriculum of Years 7–9 and in addition tuition in most instruments from both resident and visiting staff is available. A number of musical events takes place annually, including the Junior School Music concert, and the Summer Serenade, the showcase concert, held in May.

Traditionally there is a major play or musical at the end of the Michaelmas term. The College has a proud record of 104 Shakespearean productions. The 2017 School Play was *Jesus Christ Superstar*. Each year there is also a Junior School Play (*Robin Hood and The Truth Behind the Green Tights* 2018), the Junior Drama Festival and performances from GCSE Drama and A Level Theatre Studies students.

The DT Department is fully equipped with Art and Pottery centres. These facilities are housed in the Centenary Building and allow pupils to fulfil abilities in design, woodwork, metalwork, painting, drawing, ceramics, and printing.

Entrance. Pupils wishing to join Year 7 (age 11+) or Year 9 (age 13+) sit examinations at the College in January. Pupils wishing to join Year 9 (age 13+) from Independent Preparatory Schools offering Common Entrance, sit the Common Entrance examination in June. There is also entry in the Sixth Form, an increasingly popular option for girls and boys after their GCSEs.

Occasionally pupils enter at other ages and times. They need to show that they have attained the necessary academic standard either by public examination results or by sitting papers set by the College.

The Registration Fee is £50 and the deposit is £400.

Scholarships, Exhibitions and Bursaries. Scholarships and Exhibitions are available in the following categories – Academic, Art, Design and Technology, Drama, Music (instrumental and choral), Sport and All-Rounder – and are at the discretion of the Headmaster. They are awarded at the ages of 11, 13 and for Sixth Form entry. Scholarships carry a remission of up to 20% of the fees which may be supple-mented by means-tested Bursaries. Recently launched awards, which are usually made annually, are the Alastair Hignell Scholarship and the Governors' Award.

In all Scholarships, in addition to academic excellence, all-round ability and out-of-school activities and interests are taken into account.

A number of bursaries may be awarded to those in genuine financial need. Special consideration is given to the children of Clergy, Old Denstonians and members of the Armed Forces.

Fees per term (2018–2019). Boarding: £6,344 (Year 7), £8,123 (Years 8 & 9), £8,407 (Years 10–13) including items of board and education other than music lessons and extra tuition. Day: £4,379 (Years 7–9), £5,293 (Years 10–13).

The Old Denstonian Club. *Secretary*: Mr Richard Lewis, Denstone College, Uttoxeter, Staffs. Regional Clubs based in London, Manchester and at the College.

Charitable status. Denstone College is a Registered Charity, number 1102588. It exists to provide Christian education for children.

Visitor: The Bishop of Lichfield

School Council:
K P Threlfall (*Custos*)
The Revd Canon B D Clover MA, LTCL (*Senior Provost*)
A D Coley
J S F Cash, BSc, MRICS
C J Lewis
Mrs J Dickson, BSc, OT
Mrs B McNally-Young
Mrs E Bell
Mrs E Evans
M F Coffin MA, FCA
B W Hinton, MBA, FCIPD, MCIM
D T Brown, ACA
N T Ratcliffe

Headmaster: M R M Norris, MA

Second Master: J Hartley, BA (*Registrar*)

Deputy Heads:
T J Bell, BA (*Academic*)
Mrs K Hood, BSc (*Pastoral*)
D P Baker, MA, MPhil, PhD (*Co-curricular, Operations and Partnerships*)

Senior Master: G A Jones

Assistant Heads:
B J R Duerden, BSc (*Staff Development, Teaching & Learning*)
T A H Williams, BSc (*Co-curricular*)

Chaplain: The Revd Dr R Angelici, PhD, MA

Masters and Mistresses:

M P Raisbeck, BA, CNAA	Mrs C L Burrows, BA
Miss J H Plewes, BA	(†*Woodard House*)
(*Senior Pastoral Lead*)	Mrs C G Bailey, MA
A J Wray, BA	(†*Meynell House*)
J M Tomlinson, BSc	A D Pearson, BSc (†*Selwyn*
A C Bonell, BEd (*Head of*	*House*)
Junior School)	J I Young, BA (*Head of*
C J Sassi, MA (†*Philips*)	*Middle School*)
Mrs K Rylance, BSc	Mrs A M Jones, BA
S R Francis, BSc	(†*Heywood House*)
Miss A K Greenwood, BA	Mrs S Chadfield, BA
Mrs M Silvey, BA	N Horan, BA (*Head of*
Mrs J A Teather (†*Moss*	*Senior School*)
Moor)	R Lightfoot, MSc
Mrs C A Tuxford, BA	Mrs L A Gater, BA, MA
I A K Sherwani	R C Neal, BSc, MEd
	Mrs G Butler, BSc

Mrs R E Maddocks, BA
Mrs R C Abson, BA
Miss O J Barraclough, BA
R H W Hinton, MA
    (*Curriculum & Academic
    Data Manager*)
Mrs V Sykes, MSc, BSc
P Nye, BSc (†*Shrewsbury
    House*)
M E H Rankin, BA
Mrs L E Stanley, BSc
Mrs J Westacott, MSc
T Quinlan, BSc
Mrs D Williams-Jenks, BA
S Guy
T W Forster, BSc
Miss K E Lea, MA
N C M Lyle, MA

J J Moran, BA
Mrs L Vakis, BSc
Mrs C Dawson, MA
M Gregoire, BA
Mrs J Davis, BA
Ms P Plant, BA
C Green, BA
Mrs J C Breen, BSc
Miss S F McDowell, MA
Mrs K A Philips, BA
Miss H R Gill, BSc
Miss E A Jones, BA
C P McDade, BA
Dr E Stansfield, PhD
Mrs B Hibbert, BEd
R K Stockton, BA
Mrs J A Seward, BA

Visiting Music Staff:
Mrs A O'Brien, DRSAMD, PG Dip RSAMD, ARCM
    (*piano, voice*)
R Shaw, BA, GBSM, PG Dip, ARCM, ABSM (*saxophone,
    clarinet*)
S J Ryde, ARCM, ARCO (*piano*)
G Walker, MA Oxon, ARCO, FRSA (*organ, piano*)
W Raffle, BA Keele, LVCM, AVCM (*guitar*)
Ms L Kaniewski, BA Keele, Dip Mus (*cello, guitar*)
Ms R Theobald, LRAM, ALCM (*voice, piano, oboe*)
Mrs R Melland, GRSM RCM, PG Dip RNCM (*brass*)
D Priest, MA, BMus Hons, PGCE (*drums, percussion*)
Mrs S Theart, BMus (*organ, piano*)
Ms K Riddle, BMus Hons, PG Dip RNCM
R Murray, BA Hons Music (*brass*)
Mrs S England, BMus Hons, PG Dip
Mrs H Paterson, BMus Hons
Mrs I Hurley, BA Hons, ALCM
E Pezcek, BMus Hons

Chapel Organist: G Walker, MA, ARCO, FRSA
Finance Bursar and Clerk to the School Council: D M
    Martin, ACIB
HR Manager: Miss C McNamara
Headmaster's PA: Mrs D Mills
Admissions Secretary: Miss Ruth Millington and Miss Jade
    Campbell

*Denstone College Preparatory School at Smallwood
    Manor*:
Headmaster: J Gear, BEd
(*For further details about the Preparatory School, see
    entry in IAPS section.*)

Downe House

Cold Ash, Thatcham, Berks RG18 9JJ

Tel: 01635 200286
Fax: 01635 202026
email: correspondence@downehouse.net
website: www.downehouse.net
Twitter: @DowneHouse1
Facebook: @downehouse

Founded 1907.
Numbers on roll. 550 Boarding girls, 19 Day girls.
Age Range. 11–18.
Downe House is situated in a 110-acre woodland estate,
five miles from Newbury and within easy reach of the M4;
Heathrow Airport is 50 minutes by car. The school's prox-

imity to Oxford, Reading and London allows the girls to
take part in a rich variety of cultural activities.

Buildings. The school has three Lower School Houses
for girls aged 11+ and 12+ with a fourth in Veyrines, France
where girls board for one term in Lower IV (Year 8). Upper
School houses consist of three mixed-age Houses for those
between 13 and 16. When girls enter the Sixth Form they
move into one of two Sixth Form Houses, where they have
twin-shared or single study-bedrooms and facilities appropriate to their needs. All the Housemistresses are members
of the teaching staff and are responsible for the coordination
of the academic, pastoral, social and moral development of
the girls in their care.

The jewel in the school's crown is the new Centre for
Learning building which consists of a performance area
with tiered seating and sprung floor to accommodate dance
and gymnastics as well as a gallery, digital library, learning
pods, cafe and shop.

The main school buildings include Laboratories, an Art
School, a Design and Technology suite, a Music School, an
indoor Swimming Pool and Squash Courts and a Library.
The games facilities are excellent and include a Sports Centre and all-weather pitches. The school also has a Performing Arts Centre and a Concert Room which are used for
lectures, concerts and plays, as well as a recording studio.

Religion. Downe House is a Church of England school
with its own chapel, which girls attend for prayers and for a
service of either Matins or Evensong on Sunday. Holy Communion is celebrated once a week and girls are prepared for
confirmation if they wish. Other denominations are warmly
welcomed and many faiths are celebrated. Girls can attend
mass on Sundays and are prepared for Roman Catholic confirmation.

Curriculum and Activities. The curriculum includes the
study of English, History, Geography, Religious Studies,
French, German, Spanish, Italian, Mandarin Chinese, Latin,
Greek, Mathematics, Physics, Chemistry, Biology, Design
and Technology, Information & Communication Technology, Music, Art, Drama and Theatre Studies, Food and
Nutrition and Textiles. In addition, Classical Civilisation,
Business Studies, Sports Science, Politics, Economics, Photography and History of Art are offered at A Level. Leiths
Food & Wine Certificate is also offered to girls in the Sixth
Form. Girls are prepared for GCSE, IGCSE, AS, A Level
and Pre-U examinations, with the vast majority of girls
going on to University or some other form of Higher Education.

Downe House is a Microsoft Showcase School and inno-
vates with digital learning in the curriculum. Microsoft Surface devices are being introduced and ICT skills are
developed across the years with all girls following a general
ICT course. All girls have their own Downe House email
address.

All girls in the Lower Fourth, aged 12, spend a term at the
School's House in France in the Dordogne, to study French
and increase their awareness of themselves as global citizens.

Careers Specialists give help to the girls in selecting their
careers and a Careers Resource Centre is available to all
ages.

There are many extra-curricular activities, including a
variety of musical instruments, Drama, Sub Aqua, Pottery,
Photography, Art, Craft, Singing, Speech & Drama Training, Cookery, Dance (Tap, Modern, Ballet, Hip Hop, Street).
There is a regular programme of varied weekend activities,
including The Duke of Edinburgh's Award scheme, which
develops leadership qualities, plus Young Enterprise which
offers an insight into business practice in the UK.

Fees per term (2018–2019). £12,510 for boarders and
£9,165 for Day Girls.

Admissions. Girls may enter the school at 11+, 12+ or 13+ after assessment, interview and Common Entrance. A few girls join the school at 14+ and also in the Sixth Form after interview and entrance test.

Application for entry should be made well in advance. Prospective parents are asked to make an appointment to visit the school and meet the Headmistress.

Scholarships. Scholarships are awarded to recognise girls with strong academic, musical, artistic, sporting or dramatic potential from a variety of backgrounds and who will benefit from the overall education offered by Downe House.

The School offers a number of Academic Scholarships at 11+, 12+, 13+ and for entry into the Sixth Form. Scholarships are also awarded in Music, Art and Sport (11+ and 13+) and Drama (13+ and 16+) and there are Headmistress's Awards for outstanding all-round performers.

Music Scholars receive free tuition in two instruments, which may include the voice, up to a maximum of 30 lessons per year. Exhibitioners will receive free tuition in one instrument, up to a maximum of 30 lessons per year.

Candidates who are successful in gaining an award, but require remission in fees in order to be able to take up their place may apply for an Academic, Art, Music, Sport or Drama means-tested Bursary, as appropriate.

Academic Awards. The Olive Willis 13+ Scholarships, 12+ and 11+ Downe House Scholarships are awarded on the results of examinations and interviews with the Headmistress, Head of Upper School and Head of Lower School, held each year in January. In addition to these major awards, Exhibitions may be awarded in each age group. Further Minor Awards for excellence in specific fields may be made if candidates of sufficient merit present themselves. Candidates sit papers in English, Mathematics, Science, French (12+ and 13+ only), a General Paper, plus Latin (optional).

Sixth Form Scholarships are year round and candidates sit papers in two subjects of their choice, together with a General Paper. Candidates will also be required to undertake an interview with the Headmistress and Head of Sixth Form.

Age of entry will normally be in line with general entry, i.e. 11+, 12+, 13+ and Sixth Form (16+). Candidates must be under 12, under 13 or under 14 on the 1st September following the examination. Girls sitting for entry to the Sixth Form must be in the final year of their GCSE studies or equivalent.

Music Awards will be made on the results of auditions and aural tests held at Downe House in February each year

Art Awards will be made on the results of a girl's portfolio and a practical test held at Downe House in June each year.

Drama Awards will be made on the results of a one-hour written paper and a one-hour practical examination held at Downe House in May/June each year.

Sports Awards are made in March each year. It is expected that potential candidates will be at the top level of their year group in a minimum of two major sports. Candidates will be invited to undertake a programme that will test general principles of fitness and skill acquisition. All candidates will also be assessed in swimming.

A number of *Headmistress's Awards* may be awarded, at the discretion of the Headmistress, to reward outstanding all-round performers.

For Music, Art, Sport and Drama awards junior candidates must be under 14 on the following 1st September of the year of entry. Potential award holders are required to reach a satisfactory standard in the Common Entrance examinations for their age group before taking up their Award. Senior candidates (i.e. those entering the Sixth Form) must achieve Grade B or above in seven IGCSE subjects before taking up their Award and at least an A/A* grade in the subjects they wish to pursue in the Sixth Form.

Bursaries. The School is able to award a small number of full means-tested Bursaries for girls to join the School at 11+, 12+ or 13+. Girls should be able to meet the entry requirements and benefit from a busy boarding environment.

Alumnae Bursaries are available for the daughters of alumnae if their parents are in need of financial assistance.

Charitable status. Downe House School is a Registered Charity, number 1015059. Its aim is the provision of a sound and broadly based education for girls, which will fit them for University Entrance and subsequently for a successful career in whatever field they choose.

Governors:
Chairman: Mr M J Kirk, MA
Mr S Creedy-Smith, BA, ACA
Lady Cunningham, BSc, FRCP
Mrs V Exelby, MA
Mr N Gold, FCA
Mrs J M Grant Peterkin, BA
Ms F Hazlitt
Mrs F Holmes
Mr Nicholas Hornby, BSc
Dr Christopher O'Kane, MA, MB BChir, MSc, DPhil
Mr Christopher Radford, BSc (*Chairman of Estates Sub-Committee*)
Mr Mark Ridley

Headmistress: Mrs E McKendrick, BA Liverpool, PGCE, FRSA

Deputy Head: Mrs A Bizior, BSc, PGCE, BEd University of South Africa
Academic Deputy: Mr M Hill, BA Hull, MA Reading, MEd Open, PGCE
Boarding Deputy: Mrs G Ford, BA Bristol, PGCE
Head of Sixth Form (Acting): Mrs P Toogood, BA, MSt, PGCE
Head of Upper School: Mrs Anna Dourountakis, BA Hons, HDE PG
Head of Lower School: Mrs J Gilpin Jones, LWCMD
Assistant Headmistress (Foundation): Mrs M Scott, BEd Brisbane
Finance Bursar: Mr C Cockburn, FCCA
Director of Information Systems: Mr D McClymont, PG Dip, MCITP EA
Director of HR: Mrs K Tuttle, MCIPD
Director of Estates, Property and Services: Mr A Heath
Director of Business Development: Mr H Morgan, LLB

Director of External Relations: Mrs S Taylor
Director of Operations: Mrs Y J Charlesworth, BSc Reading, PGCE (*also Head of Science*)
Director of Curriculum Administration: Mrs K Henson, BA, MA, PGCS, MEd

Heads of Department:
Art: Mrs S J Scott, BA Central England, PGCE
Biology: Miss C M Pugsley, BSc Warwick, PGCE
Business & Economics: Mrs Orla Cahill, BA
Higher Education and Global Initiatives: Mrs M Ahktar, BA, MA, PGCE, PG Cert
Chemistry: Mr A Reynolds, BSc Loughborough, PGCE
Classics: Mrs L Dakin, MA Cantab
Co-Curricular: Mr I Stuart
Design & Technology: Miss S Singh, HDE Natal, South Africa, QTS
Drama, Curriculum: Miss K Anger, BMus, GSMD, PGCE (*Acting HoD*)
Drama, Extra-Curricular: Mrs R Watson, BA, AVCM
English: Mrs J Harrington, BA, PGCE

Geography: Miss K Rawlinson, BSc Hons, MSc, PGCE
History: Mr W Lane, MA, PGCE
ICT: Mr G Bouwer
Learning Skills: Mrs P Bell, BA, RSA Dip SpLD, APC
Library: Ms L Scott-Picton, BA, MLib, PGCE, MCLIP
Mathematics: Mr R S Barnes, BSc East Anglia, PGCE
Modern Languages: Mrs J Basnett, BA Westminster, MA, PGCE
Music: Dr C Exon, BMus, PhD Birmingham, PGCE
Performing Arts: Miss K Grandi, BA, MA, PG Dip (*Acting HoD*)
Physical Education: Mrs L J M Rayne, BEd Hons
Physics: Mr M Rivers, MA, PGCE
PSHE: Mrs N Riddle, B PhysEd, Dip T
Religious Studies: Mr P Evans, BD London, MA London, PGCE
Science: Mrs Y J Charlesworth, BSc Reading, PGCE

Housemistresses/Housemaster:
Hermitage House: Mrs K Collingwood, BSc, PGCE
Hill House: Miss A Brown, BA Hons, PGCE
Darwin: Mrs F V Capps, CertEd Bedford College
Veyrines (France): Mrs D Scotland
Aisholt: Mrs J Boswell, MA, PGCE
Ancren Gate North: Mr A Treadaway, BA, MA
Ancren Gate South: Mrs S McClymont, LLB, PG Dip LPC
Holcombe: Mrs Mears-Smith, BA, PGCE FE, TEFL
Tedworth: Mrs S Barnard, MA
Willis House East: Mrs T Reeve, MA, PG Dip
Willis House West: Mrs V Ryan, BA Bangor, PGCE
York House North: Miss Ellen Clark, BA, QTS
York House South: Mrs C Walton-Walters, BSc Open, Cert Ed

Chaplain: Revd Anthea Platt
Nurse Manager: Ms G Palmer, BSc RGN, BSc RM

Downside School

Stratton-on-the-Fosse, Radstock, Bath, Somerset BA3 4RJ

Tel: 01761 235100
Fax: 01761 235105
email: reception@downside.co.uk
website: www.downside.co.uk

Downside School is one of England's oldest and most distinguished Catholic schools. It is an independent, full-boarding school for boys and girls aged 11–18. Founded in 1606 in Douai (in France), the School sits in a 500-acre estate at the foot of the Mendip Hills in Somerset, twelve miles south of the City of Bath. Voted as one of the 'Top 10 Most Beautiful Schools in the UK' by the Daily Telegraph.

Downside is a strong academic school with outstanding examination results. Everyone is encouraged to aspire beyond their expectations and the School has a thriving academic life with excellent admission rates to all the top UK universities. Importantly, Downside was also voted "Best for well-being" by The Week Independent Schools Guide in 2015. The happy atmosphere which pervades is remarked on by all visitors.

Academic. Strong intellectual traditions focusing on academic subjects, with a range of additional options to encourage independent learning and an enquiring mind. In 2017, pupils gained places to study Medicine and at the Royal Veterinary College, with 20% of pupils collecting a straight set of A*/A grades.

Boarding. 82% of Downside pupils are 7-day-a-week boarders and approximately 28% are international from all over Europe and worldwide. Weekends for boarders are busy with Saturday morning lessons, sports fixtures in the afternoon and a full programme of activities; film nights, theatre trips, cookery and quiz competitions to name but a few. Pupils are all invited to celebrate Mass in the Abbey Church on a Sunday morning.

Downside has six boarding houses: Powell, Isabella, Caverel, Barlow, Roberts and Smythe, with boarders and day pupils integrated together in all the houses. Junior boys join Powell House at 11, 12 & 13, before moving up to one of three senior boys' houses: Barlow, Roberts or Smythe, whilst girls join Caverel or Isabella House.

Each House has its own spirit, character and traditions. Pupils have friends across the Houses but avidly compete in inter-house games, drama, music and other activities.

Downside School is proud to provide 24/7 professional nursing care, with access to three GP surgeries on site each week.

Sport. Pupils compete in a range of high quality fixtures throughout the year in Rugby, Hockey, Netball, Cricket, Tennis, Cross-Country, Athletics and Football. Additional disciplines are offered as activities, ranging from Judo to Squash, and Zumba to Polo.

Downside School believes that physical activity plays an important role in every pupil's life. Sport for All is a central part of the school's philosophy as is the desire for every pupil to enjoy sport and achieve their own personal best. With all our facilities on campus pupils can also swim, use the gym and play tennis in their own time and for budding athletes a cross country run need never leave the estate.

Arts. You'll discover that Art, Drama, Music, and Design & Technology are very popular amongst Downside pupils, both at GCSE and A Level, and as additional activities. The department is open on Sunday afternoons for recreation or to catch up on work and our association with Hauser Wirth Somerset means that top quality art installations are on our doorstep.

Concerts are held in the magnificent Abbey Church throughout the year, with plays performed in our new Performing Arts Centre. We have an Artist-in-Residence who continually inspires the children, and the very latest equipment in our Design workshops: from 3D printers to an iMac suite.

Founded over a century ago, Downside's Schola Cantorum is the oldest Roman Catholic school choir in the UK. Formed of boys and girls, it gives concerts of large-scale sacred works throughout the year and has topped the charts with its CDs, The Abbey and Gregorian Moods. There are three Chamber Choirs at Downside, plus opportunities in orchestral, band and chamber music, with frequent concerts and recitals as well as a new recording studio for budding professionals.

Development. In the last few years, Downside has developed a brand-new Learning Support Centre, a new Performing Arts Centre, a refurbished Sports Hall and Swimming Pool complex, and a new Art and Design faculty. The Monastic Library, subject to a Lottery Grant to make its treasures available to a wider public, is now a wonderful new resource for serious historians and scholars studying at the School.

Alumni.
Tom Bethell (Journalist)
Rocco Forte (Hotelier)
Brion Gysin (Artist)
Jared Harris (Actor)
Christopher Jamison (Monk)
Emmanuel de Merode (Conservationist)
David Mlinaric (Designer)
William Nicholson (Writer)

Anthony Palliser (Artist)
John Pope-Hennessy (Art Historian)
Auberon Waugh (Journalist)
Adam Zamoyski (Historian)
Fees per term (2018–2019). Boarding £8,412–£11,287; Day £5,414–£6,417.

Scholarships are available for gifted and talented pupils in a range of areas. Please contact our Admissions Department for the latest assessment deadlines.

Charitable status. Downside School is a Registered Charity, number 1158507. Its purpose is to advance the cause of Catholic Education.

Prior of Downside Abbey, Chairman of Downside Abbey Trust: Dom Nicholas Wetz

Chairman of School Governors: A Aylward

Head Master: A R Hobbs, MA

Deputy Head Master: M Randall, BSc

Senior Leadership:
Director of Studies: D M Gibbons, BA
Director of Pastoral Care: Mrs C Murphy, BSc
Chief Executive (Downside Trust): S Treloar
Director of External Communications: Mrs J Vines

House Mistress of Caverel: Mrs B Bouchard, MA
House Mistress of Isabella: Mrs K Westlake, BA
House Master of Barlow: S J Potter, BA
House Master of Roberts: S Ottewell, BA
House Master of Smythe: J Storey, BA
House Master of Powell: J Dolman, BSc

School Chaplains: Dom James Hood, Dom Boniface Hill, Dom Anselm Brumwell, Mr Paul Andrewartha (*Lay Chaplain*)

Director of Music: J McNamara, MA
Director of Sport: R Jones, BA

Heads of Faculty:
Art & Design: N J Barrett, BEd
English: Mrs J Rainey, MA
Humanities: O G Simper, BA
Languages: R C Rawlins, MA
Mathematics: Miss S Moody, BSc
Science: P Rigby, BSc
Theology & RS: H F Walters, MA

Learning Support: Mrs C Storey

Head of Nursing: Miss M Pye

Registrar: Mrs I Hartnell
email: admissions@downside.co.uk

Dulwich College

Dulwich Common, London SE21 7LD
Tel: 020 8693 3601
Fax: 020 8693 6319
email: info@dulwich.org.uk
website: www.dulwich.org.uk
Twitter: @DulwichCollege
Facebook: @DulwichCollege

Motto: *Detur gloria soli Deo ~ Let Glory be given to God alone*

Dulwich College was founded in 1619 by Edward Alleyn, the Elizabethan actor, and is approaching its 400th anniversary.

The College is an academically selective, independent day and boarding school for boys aged 7–18; full and weekly boarding is available for boys aged 11–18. Situated in over 70 acres of grounds and playing fields, the campus is just 10 minutes by train from London Victoria. A Dulwich education ensures each pupil fulfils their academic potential whilst taking advantage of the wide range of sporting, cultural and adventurous activities on offer.

Boys move on to universities, medical and dental schools, music and art colleges. Almost all enter higher education, but an increasing number of boys are following vocational paths. Pupils are prepared for entry to the most competitive universities such as Oxford, Cambridge and Imperial, where a very good record of places is maintained each year.

The College's principal aims for all its boys are:
• to offer an appropriate academic challenge which enables each pupil to realise his potential;
• to create an environment which promotes an independent work ethic and encourages all boys to acquire a love of learning;
• to provide a wide range of sporting, cultural and adventurous activities for pupils to enjoy and through which they can learn to work cooperatively and to take a lead;
• to nurture a supportive community that encourages a sense of social responsibility and spiritual and personal development;
• to ensure that pupils from a broad variety of backgrounds can feel equally secure and valued;
• to offer boys and staff opportunities to benefit from and contribute to the College's international and UK educational partnerships.

Organisation. The College, comprising some 1,500 boys, has four specific schools: Junior School, Lower School, Middle School and Upper School. Each of these has its own Head who is responsible to the Master for that part of the College. Within each School there are Heads of Year and Form Tutors who have daily contact with boys in their care. These teams are responsible for overseeing the pastoral and academic welfare of the boys and they ensure that close links are fostered between parents and the College.

DUCKS. Dulwich College's Kindergarten and Infants' School is the only co-educational element of the College providing a secure foundation for future learning and development for children from 6 months to Year 2. Most children from DUCKS enter leading independent schools in south London, and many boys will pass the entrance examination for the College.

Day House system. A thriving Day House system offers boys the opportunity to take part in a wide range of competitive activities including art, chess, poetry, general knowledge, debating, drama and music. They can also compete in a number of sports throughout the academic year, including rugby, soccer, hockey, cricket and athletics.

Curriculum. In Years 7 and 8 all boys follow a broad and balanced curriculum, including all standard core subjects and French or Spanish, Chinese, Latin, Wellbeing, PE, Computing, Drama, DT, Art and Music. In Year 8, boys make a choice between Latin, Chinese or German; this reduces the number of languages studied to two, allowing boys the time to engage rigorously in their chosen languages and make significant progress. In Year 9 boys continue with the core subjects, Wellbeing and PE together with French or Spanish, and they choose a second language from German, Chinese, French, Spanish, Latin or Italian. This second language may be a continuation of languages they have previously studied, or they may start them from scratch. In Years 10 and 11 boys take between nine and 10 GCSE subjects, comprising English, English Literature, Mathematics, Biology, Chemistry, Physics and French or Spanish plus three optional subjects; they all continue with Wellbeing and PE. In the Upper School (Years 12 and 13), there is a free choice of three A Level subjects (four if they are studying Further Mathematics) and from 2017 every pupil will opt for an A Level 'Plus' option which is an in-house qualification that aims to provide enrichment, cross-curricular links and programmes that reflect the likely courses boys choose at university. Boys will also choose a 'Link' course in conjunction with James Allen's Girls' School that will provide breadth to their educational profile, including a regular lecture series and community service options. The concept of Free Learning (supra-curricular and other learning beyond the curriculum) is now fully embedded in the life of the College across all year groups.

Facilities. Over the years the College has developed its complex of buildings to meet the needs of boys' education in the twenty-first century, and this development continues.

The latest addition is The Laboratory, a new state-of-the-art building that brings together the twin cultures of Science and Art. There are 21 laboratories, three preparation rooms and the James Caird Hall, which houses the rescue boat of one of the College's most famous Old Alleynians, Sir Ernest Shackleton. There are five adaptable 'Informatics' suites with free-thinking spaces for creative learning and cross-curricular collaboration and a seminar room with full video-conferencing facilities. In addition there is a versatile 240-seat auditorium which is available to the whole Dulwich community for events and exhibitions and an outdoor piazza for recreation and performance.

Extensive IT facilities are available to all pupils. The IT network gives pupils and staff access to a wide range of centrally stored learning resources through the College's own virtual learning environment, 'MyDulwich'. Three separate libraries, all staffed by professional librarians, cater to the specific needs of different age groups. Exhibitions, drawn from the College archive, are regularly mounted in the Wodehouse Library.

The College has two separate dining areas which provide a wide choice of food, including a vegetarian option, on a cafeteria basis for both pupils and staff. The College also has its own shop, the Commissariat, where uniform, equipment and stationery can be purchased. The Richard Penny Medical Centre provides professional nursing care on a round-the-clock basis for boarders and day boys. The College Counsellor, based in the Medical Centre, provides confidential consultation for pupils and parents.

Sport is integral to life at Dulwich College both within the curriculum and as part of the wider co-curricular programme. There are over 70 acres of playing fields. The PE Centre includes a substantial sports hall and a modern indoor 25-metre swimming pool. The College owns a boathouse on the Thames, accommodating the thriving Boat Club, and an Outdoor Centre in the Brecon Beacons which is used for a variety of activities and residential courses. The sports programme provides a continuity and breadth of experience across the age range, with 24 different sports on offer, giving all boys the opportunity to reach their sporting potential.

Music and Drama. A professionally equipped, purpose-built Music School provides all pupils with the opportunity to study a musical instrument. More than 500 pupils receive individual tuition every week from 35 experienced specialist musicians, led by the Heads of Strings, Wind, Brass, Keyboard and Singing. The College Chapel Choir, an ancient foundation, leads regular services in the Foundation Chapel (Christ's Chapel) and also at other venues throughout the country. The Edward Alleyn Theatre is a fully rigged auditorium with a capacity of 250; over 50 events are staged annu-

ally and the facility includes rehearsal and teaching spaces, as well as dressing rooms.

Clubs and Societies. A wide variety of clubs and societies, many run by the boys themselves, take place during the lunch break and after school. These range from Lego for the younger boys to the Political Society which is responsible for inviting prominent public figures to speak. The College is particularly renowned for its Debating success that in 2016 culminated in a Year 12 boy captaining Team England to victory in the World Schools Debating Championships. The College encourages boys to take part in expeditions as well as many community-based activities which can include membership of the Combined Cadet Force, Scouts, the Duke of Edinburgh's Award scheme and Community Action. Academic, cultural and sporting excursions take place at various points throughout the school year.

Careers. Specialist careers staff, professional external advisors, dedicated IT facilities and an accredited library provide an up-to-date service assisting boys in planning higher education and careers. Boys and their parents attend the annual Courses and Careers Convention to consult with representatives from key employers, professional institutes and around 25 universities. Upper School boys receive guidance on how degree course choices might influence their future careers.

Boarding. There are three boarding houses in Dulwich College, all situated within or close to the campus. Each house has a Housemaster who is resident with his family. Boys in Years 7–13 live in Old Blew and The Orchard and boys in the Upper School live in Blew House and Ivyholme, where each boy has his own room with en-suite facilities. At present, there are around 140 boarders. Boarding at Dulwich is truly international with boys coming from all over the world and this adds to an atmosphere of cultural tolerance and intellectual curiosity.

ISI Inspection November 2014. ISI Inspectors awarded Dulwich College, Dulwich College Junior School and DUCKS 'Excellent' in every category, 'Exceptional' for 'the quality of pupils' achievements and learning' for the senior school – the only category for which this grading can be given – and 'Outstanding' for the EYFS (Kindergarten, Nursery and Reception).

Entry. Boys are admitted to the College as day boys, boarders or weekly boarders. Places are available at age 7, 11, 13 and 16. Casual vacancies occur from time to time at ages 8, 9, 10 and 12. At age 7 places are awarded on the basis of interview, report and practical assessment during the Lent Term. At age 11 places are awarded on the results of the Combined Entrance and Scholarship Examination held in the Lent Term. Candidates take papers in English and Mathematics and also a Verbal/Non-Verbal Reasoning test. At age 13 boys may take the College's own Entrance Examinations held in the Lent Term. Entrance is by examination and interview. At 16+ places are offered on the results from subject specific tests, interview and GCSE grades. Application should generally be in the year before desired date of entry. For further information please see the Admissions section on the College website. A non-refundable registration fee of £100 is charged for all applications and £200 for overseas applications.

Fees per term (2018–2019). Day £6,816 (includes lunch for Junior and Lower School pupils); Full Boarding £14,227; Weekly Boarding £13,339.

Scholarships and Bursaries. Over 35% of boys at Dulwich College are supported with financial awards. A significant number of academic scholarships are awarded each year up to one-third of the tuition fee. There are also scholarships for Music, Art and Sports. Scholarships can be enhanced by Bursaries in cases of financial need. A substantial number of Bursaries are awarded annually to new boys entering Year 3, Year 7 or Year 9 where parents are unable to pay the full tuition fee. Bursaries are means-tested and reviewed annually. All applicants will be considered on the basis of their performance in the entrance examination and interview. A Bursary and a Scholarship might be awarded together up to a maximum value of 100% of the school fees.

Old Alleynians. Founded in 1873, The Alleyn Club is a flourishing former pupils' association with over 10,000 Old Alleynian (OA) members living in more than 90 countries. The club's name acknowledges the founder, Edward Alleyn, actor, theatre manager and contemporary of William Shakespeare.

Charitable status. Dulwich College is a Registered Charity, number 1150064.

The Governing Body:
Chairman: The Rt Hon P J R Riddell, CBE, MA, FRHistS
Vice Chairman: Ms J Hill, MA [née Black]
Sir Brian Bender, KCB
Dr I Bishop, CBE, BEd, MA, LLD
Ms V Flind, BA
Mr R J Foster, BEd
Mr B Ghosh, BA, MA
Dr A H Köttering, BSc, MSc, DPhil
Mr D Parfitt
Professor R Parish, Commander dans L'Ordre des Palmes Academiques, BA, MA, DPhil
Mr T Pethybridge
Mr P M Thompson, RD, MB BS, FRCS [OA]
Mr G N C Ward, CBE, MA, FCA [OA]

Honorary International Advisor to the Governors:
His Excellency Khun Anand Panyarachun, Hon KBE, MA [OA]

Special Advisor to the Governors: Sir John H Riblat, FRICS, Hon FRIBA [OA]

[OA] *Old Alleynian*

Clerk to the Governors: Ms K Jones, LLB

Master of the College: Dr J A F Spence, BA Hons, PhD

Deputy Masters:
Mrs F M Angel, BA (*Pastoral*)
Mr D A P King, MA (*Academic*)
Dr C S B Pyke, MA, MMus, PhD (*External Relations*)
Mr I L H Scarisbrick, BSc (*Co-curricular*)

Chief Operating Officer: Mr S J Yiend, MA
Director of Finance: Mr N Prout, BA, ACA
Director of Communications: Ms J M Scott, MA, MBA
Director of Development: Mr M Jarrett, BA

Head of Upper School: Mr A J Threadgould, BSc
Head of Middle School: Dr N D Black, BA, PhD
Head of Lower School: Mr S Tanna, BA
Head of Junior School: Dr T G A Griffiths, PGCE, MA, MSc, DPhil
Head of DUCKS (*Kindergarten and Infants' School*): Mrs M Norris, BEd, ILMP, MEd

Registrar: Mrs S Betts
Archivist: Mrs C M Lucy, BA, MCLIP
Head of Academic Administration: Dr J Kinch, BA, BPhil, DPhil
Head of Outings & Expeditions: Mr S Croucher
Examinations Officer: Mr M Grantham-Hill, BSc
Staff Tutor: Mr P J Whibley, BA

Heads of Departments:
Art: Mrs S Mulholland, BA (*Director of Art & DT*)
Classics: Dr J-M Hulls, MPhil, PhD
Drama:
Mr P V Jolly, BA, DipRSA (*Director of Drama*)

Mrs K Norton-Smith, BA (*Head of Academic Drama*)
EAL: Miss S E Horsfield, BA
Economics: Mr N Fyfe, BA
English: Mr R Fisher, BA
Geography: Miss J K Woolley, BA
Higher Education & Careers:
Mr R F Sutton (*Director of University Admissions*)
Mrs E H Soare (*Head of Careers*)
History and Politics: Mr D Flower, BA
ICT:
Mr J D Cartwright, MA (*Head of Computing*)
Dr A C Storey, BA, MSc, PhD (*Director of ICT*)
Learning Support: Miss E Walters
Libraries:
Mr P J Fletcher, BA, DipLib, MCLIP (*Head of Libraries*)
Mr R Weaver, BA, MA, FSA Scot (*Keeper of the Fellows' Library*)
Lower & Junior School Science: Mr Graham Wilson, MPhys
Mathematics: Mr C J Ottewill, BA, MPhil
Modern Languages:
Mr R S Baylis, MA, MA (*Head of Modern Languages*)
Mr N Mair, BA (*Director of Languages*)
Chinese: Mr A M Stark, BA, DMS, MA
French: Mr J G Brown, BA
German: Mr W Dugdale, BA
Italian: Mrs J Briggs, BA
Spanish: Mr A Iltchev, BA
Music:
Mr R G Mayo, MA, MusB, FRCO (*Director of Music*)
Dr J Carnelley, BMus, MMus, ARCO (*Head of Academic Music*)
Physical Education:
Mr P C Greenaway, BSc (*Director of Sport*)
Mr M Burdekin, BA (*Head of Academic PE*)
Religion and Theology: Mr J H Fox, BA
Scholars and General and Liberal Studies: Dr N T Croally, MA, PhD [OA]
Science:
Dr R E McIlwaine, MChem, PGCE, PhD (*Director of Science*)
Biology: Dr P J Cue, BSc, PhD
Chemistry: Miss L V A Rand, MChem
Physics: Mr A Wheble

DUCKS (*Dulwich College Kindergarten and Infants' School*):
Mrs M Norris, BEd ILMP MEd (*Head of DUCKS*)
Miss S Donaldson, NNEB, MA (*Head of Kindergarten*)

Medical Centre Charge Nurse: Mrs C Baxter-Wilks, RN, BSc, MSc
College Counsellor: Ms J De Heger, BEd, Dip Art Therapy
Medical Officer: Dr R A Leonard, MBE, MA, MB, BChir, MRCGP, DRCOG
PA to the Master: Mrs M Wood
PA Governance & Finance: Ms S White

The High School of Dundee

Euclid Crescent, Dundee, Tayside DD1 1HU

Tel: 01382 202921
Fax: 01382 229822
email: enquiries@highschoolofdundee.org.uk
website: www.highschoolofdundee.org.uk
Twitter: @HSofDundee
Facebook: @highschoolofdundee

Motto: *Prestante Domino*

The present School traces its origins directly back to a 13th century foundation by the Abbot and Monks of Lindores. It received a Royal Charter in 1859. Various Acts of Parliament in the 19th Century were finally consolidated in an Order in Council constituting the High School of Dundee Scheme 1965, which was revised in 1987.

Admission. The School comprises three sections:

The Nursery – 67 pupils (age 3–5; pre-school and ante pre-school).

The Junior Years – 304 pupils (Primary 1 to Primary 7).

The Senior Years – 661 pupils (S1 to S6).

The normal stages of entry are Nursery, Primary 1 and S1. Entry to Primary 1 (age 4½ to 5½ years) is by interview held in January and to S1 (age 11 to 12 years) by an Entrance Assessment held in January. Where vacancies exist entrance is usually available at all other stages subject to satisfactory performance in an entrance assessment.

Bursaries. A number of means-tested bursaries are provided for entry to P6/7 and from S1 in the Senior Years, to help those who otherwise could not afford the fees.

Fees per term (2018–2019). Primary: £3,053 (P1 to P3), £3,199 (P4 to P5), £3,634 (P6 to P7); Secondary £4,333. Nursery varies according to the number of sessions selected.

Buildings. The six main school buildings are in the centre of the city and form an architectural feature of the area. Two excellent, extensive playing fields – Dalnacraig and Mayfield – are situated some 1½ miles to the east of the school. As well as grass pitches, the facilities include an international standard synthetic water-based hockey surface and a sand-dressed synthetic hockey pitch which is up to national standard. The school's Mayfield Sports Centre, comprising a state-of-the-art games hall, dance studio, gymnasium and fitness suite, is adjacent to the playing fields. The Nursery is also located at Mayfield. In 2013 the School acquired the former Head Post Office Building, located just yards from the city centre campus, and is currently in the midst of an ambitious project to transform this landmark building into a flagship centre of excellence for performing and visual arts, both for the school and for the wider community.

Curriculum. The Junior Years follow a wide-ranging primary curriculum. Subject specialists are employed in PE, ICT, Music, Science, Modern Languages, Art, Drama and Health and Food Technology.

In the Senior Years, after two years of a general curriculum, some specialisation takes place with pupils currently being prepared for the Scottish Qualifications Authority examinations at National 5, Higher and Advanced Higher which lead directly to university entrance. Results in public examinations are amongst the best in Scotland, with pupils regularly achieving the top marks nationally in individual subjects, and 90–95% of leavers enrolling at universities in the UK or abroad.

Co-Curricular Activities. Almost 100 co-curricular activities are offered. Sports teams compete at the highest levels and each year a number of pupils represent their country in a wide range of sports. Music plays an important part in the life of the school, with a large number of orchestras, bands, choirs and musical ensembles to choose from. Special tuition is provided in a wide variety of instruments.

There is a flourishing contingent of the Combined Cadet Force including a pipe band. Drama, Public Speaking and Debating, Chess and The Duke of Edinburgh's Award scheme are examples of the wide variety of activities available.

Charitable status. The Corporation of the High School of Dundee is a Registered Charity, number SC011522. The school is a charity to provide quality education for boys and girls.

The Board of Directors comprises:
Chairman, 2 ex officiis Directors, viz, The Lord Dean of Guild and The Parish Minister of Dundee. The Guildry of Dundee, the Nine Trades of Dundee, the Old Boys' Club and the Old Girls' Club and the Parents' Association each elect one Director. Six Directors are elected by Friends of the High School and up to 6 co-opted by the Board.

School Staff:

Rector: Dr J D Halliday, BA Hons, PhD

Deputy Rector: Mrs L A M Hudson, MA

Assistant Rector – Junior Years and Nursery: Mrs J Rose, BEd

Bursar: Miss J Henderson, BAcc, CA

Deputy Heads – Senior School:
Mr D A Brett, BSc
Mr N R Clarke, BSc, MSc
Mr D G Smith, BSc
Mrs S J Watson, MA

Deputy Heads – Junior Years:
Mr R Petrie, BA
Mrs C E Proudfoot, MA, DELL

Director of ICT: Mrs W Wilson, BSc

Junior Years:

Mrs L J Mooney, Dip CE, IE	Mrs K Goldie, BEd
	Mrs M R Leburn, MA
Mrs L Docherty, Dip CE	Miss J Wallace, BEd
Miss M Cardno, MA, CEEd	Mrs D Sager, MA
	Mrs F A Trotter, BSc
Mrs L Smith, BEd	Mrs L Duff, MA
Mrs A Davie, MEd	Miss H Brian, BEd
Mrs C Taylor, BSc	Mrs G Johnson, BEd
Mrs L Coupar, MA	Mr N W Joss, MA
Mrs C Reid, BEd	Mrs A Milne, MA
Mrs S Fish, BEd	Mrs C E Rankin, BA
Miss K A Reith, MEd, DELL	Mrs C E Proudfoot, MA, DELL
Miss L Carrie, MA, MPhil	Mr R Petrie, BA

Nursery:
Manager: Mrs S C Tosh, MA, PGCE

Mrs L C Yule, BA	Miss N V Whyte
Mrs D M Irving, BA	Mrs K Roberts
Miss A A Balfour	Miss H Robertson
Mrs C Stott	Miss J Wakeford

Senior School:
* *Head of Department*

English:

*Ms J V Cortazzi, BA, MA, MEd	Mr R W Welsh, MA
	Miss K H E Douglas, MA
Mr C Anderson, MA	
Ms J Fulton, MA	*Geography*:
Ms F H J Murray, MA	*Miss J L Stewart, BSc
Ms R A Hall, BA	Mr C R McAdam, MA
Mr D P Campbell, MA	Mrs S B Williams, MA
	Mrs R Lloyd, MA, MSc
Drama and Media Studies:	Mrs S J Watson, MA
*Mrs L M Drummond, Dip Drama	
	Philosophy and Religion:
	*A W Cummins, BD, Dip Min
History and Modern Studies:	
	Business Education:
*Mr G Fyall, BA, Dip Ed	*Mrs C A Laird-Portch, BA
Miss K McKie, MA	Mr N S Higgins, BSc
Ms L Hegan, MA	
Mrs L A Hudson, MA	*Classics*:
Mr C Melia, MA	*Mr E Faulkes, BA
	Ms A Lazani, BA, MA

Modern Languages:
*Mr N A MacKinnon, MA
Mrs I M McGrath, MA
Mrs J Brown, BA
Ms A Aguero, BA
Mr F M McAvinue, MA, MSc
Dr J D Halliday, BA, PhD
Mr J P Nolan, MA
Mrs D M Wedderburn, MA
Mrs Y Murdoch, MSc
Mrs L C Smith, MA

Mathematics:
*Mrs L A Craig, BSc
Mr N R Clarke, BSc, MSc
Mr R C Middleton, BSc
Miss D Macdonald, BSc
Dr P A Smith, BA, MEng, MA, PhD
Dr F Spiezia, MSc, PhD
Mr K M Hodgson, BSc, MSc
Mr P Moon, BSc

Chemistry:
*Dr P Taylor, PhD, BSc, MRSC, CChem
Mrs R J Broom, BSc
Mr D A Brett, BSc
Mr A S Downie, BSc
Dr E R T Robinson, MChem, PhD
Dr A K Pepper, MChem, PhD, FRSC

Biology:
*Dr E Duncanson, BSc, PhD
Dr M W Fotheringham, MA, PhD
Mr G M S Rodger, BSc
Mr R H Bunting, BSc

Physics:
*Mr J Darby, BSc
Dr D G Brown, BSc, PhD
Dr G MacKay, BSc, MSc, PhD

Technology:
*Mr F Walker, BSc
Mr D F Preston, MEd, BEd

Computing:
*Mr S McBride, BSc
Mr D G Smith, BSc
Mr A N Wilson, BA

Art and Design:
*Mr A Kerr, BA
Mrs M Angus, BA
Mrs A Ross, BDes
Mrs J Cura, MDes

Music:
*Dr L S Steuart Fothringham, MA, PhD, FRCO
Mr D G Love, Dip MusEd, DRSAMD
Ms G Simpson, Dip Mus, ALCM
Mr S Armstrong, DRSAMD

Mrs S Sneddon, LTCL, ALCM
Miss A Evans, BA, LTCL
Ms S Morgan, BMus
Mrs J Petrie, BA, CPGS
Mrs E M J Stevenson, MA
Mrs S Colgan, BEd, PG Dip, LRAM
Mr D W S Wilton, BA
Mr E J Tonner, BMus

Learning Skills:
*Mrs P A Maxwell, BEd, DPSE, Cert SpLD
Mrs J M Downie, MA, Cert SpLD
Mrs J Chalmers, DPE SIQ
Mrs L Duff, MA
Mrs P M Spowart, BEd
Mrs C McDonald, BEd

Physical Education:
*Mr E D Jack, BEd
Mr G R E Merry, BSc
Mr W Nicol
Mrs S McKenzie, BEd
Miss J McMullen, BSc
Mr I Strachan
Mr C K Allan, BSc
Mrs L S L Baxter, BEd
Mrs L Anderson, BEd (*Head of Hockey*)
Mr P J Godman (*Head of Rugby*)
Mr C D O'Donnell, BSc
Ms C Jones

Home Economics:
*Mrs L J Ross, MA
Mrs O Anderson, BSc

Library:
*Miss I McFarlane, MA, MSc
Mrs J S Hutton, MA

Guidance:
Mrs S J Watson, MA (*Deputy Head with responsibility for Guidance*)

Principal Teachers:
Mr R W Welsh, MA
Mrs P M Spowart, BEd
Mrs J Brown, BA
Mr C R McAdam, MA

Assistant Principal Teachers:
Mr C K Allan, BSc
Mrs L S L Baxter, BEd
Mr A S Downie, BSc
Mrs S B Williams, MA

Head of Careers:
Mr G M S Rodger, BSc

Outdoor Activities Coordinator:
Mr G M Ross, BA

Head of Academic Administration:
Mrs I M McGrath, MA

Eastbourne College

Old Wish Road, Eastbourne, East Sussex BN21 4JX

Tel:	Headmaster: 01323 452320
	Bursar: 01323 452300
email:	reception@eastbourne-college.co.uk
website:	www.eastbourne-college.co.uk
Twitter:	@EBCollegeLife
Facebook:	@EastbourneCollege
LinkedIn:	/eastbourne-college

Founded 1867; Incorporated 1911.

Eastbourne College recently completed Project 150, a £33 million state-of-the-art development for educating pupils 13–18. Set in the hub of the safe and increasingly lively seaside town of Eastbourne, and a stone's throw from the picturesque seascape of the South Downs National Park, pupils at the College enjoy the 'blue health' afforded to them by this inspiring environment. With its endless horizons and endless opportunities, the College achieves a healthy balance between school work, extra-curricular activity and socialising. Academic excellence is ingrained into the culture enabled by a caring and productive house system to which pupils feel they belong. Boasting a ten-year rolling average of 78% A*–B at A Level, Eastbourne College is an excellent choice for families who want to prepare their young adults effectively for all that life can throw at them.

The headmaster, Tom Lawson, believes that the most important aim is to produce good people whom other people want to be with. Furthermore, he is a proponent of the blue health that the school's location offers, adopting a healthy learning for the future approach. Since he began his headship, he has introduced a new boarding lodge which caters for day pupils with occasional boarding needs, an annual biathlon / steeplechase which encompasses the South Downs National Park, and has furthered the work of the Eastbourne Schools Partnership, a community outreach project that accounts for 14,000 local school children in the maintained sector. In July 2018, Mr Lawson and Head of Partnerships, Linda Salway, received the Education Business Awards Community Award, on behalf of Eastbourne College, for outstanding community partnering work.

Location. Only 70 miles from London, Eastbourne College is an educational community as opposed to an academic institution and provides an educational experience that is light years away from the world of London day schools. The College nestles at the foot of the South Downs, five minutes from the sea and a six-minute walk from the station where direct trains to Gatwick, Clapham and Victoria take 60, 80 and 90 minutes respectively.

A Superb Range of New Facilities for a Brighter Future. Eastbourne College is proud to announce completion of Project 150, a £33 million fabric enhancement that places the College at the forefront of learning environments in the UK. The ground-breaking, environmentally friendly, state-of-the-art development marks a pivotal point in the College's history. Employing a predominantly local workforce and utilising expert knowledge from local companies and subcontractors, Project 150 (P150) has delivered everything asked for and contributed to the ongoing enhancement of Eastbourne's Devonshire Quarter. Casting off into a sea of endless opportunities, the completion of P150 launches both an educational vessel and lights a bright beacon for children living in Eastbourne, London and the South East, and throughout the world. New facilities include:

- 32 state-of-the-art classrooms
- two technology suites

- cricket pavilion with live-stream video analysis
- dance studio with sprung floor and ceiling recess for ballet lifts and throws
- large Sport England compliant sports hall (5 badminton courts long) enabling year-round multi-sport training
- Sport England compliant six-lane 25m indoor swimming pool with full Swiss touchpad digital timing system
- fitness suite for elite and inclusive participation, comprising cardiovascular machines (skiing, rowing, running, spin bikes and cross-trainers), free weights and CrossFit area, sprint track, and stretching / Pilates area
- two glass-backed squash courts
- alfresco-feel dining hall for 600
- Tim's cafe, including comfy sofas, widescreen HD TV, full barista service and Wi-Fi for catching up on studies (ideal preparation for university and beyond)
- stunning entertainment and exhibition spaces

150 Years of Academic Excellence. Eastbourne College strikes an excellent balance between academic success, healthy pursuits and time to explore the moral compass. We are advocates of an education that produces confident and resilient young adults as subtle by-products of outstanding teaching, and house tutors who ensure pupils reach beyond their perceived potential. It is with good reason that Eastbourne College is one of the top independent day and boarding schools and can boast a ten-year rolling average of 78 per cent A*–B grades at A Level. In summer 2018, College pupils achieved exceptional A Level results with almost 40% of grades awarded at A* or A. College pupils take at least three subjects, all at the gold standard A Level or Cambridge Pre-U level, and many extend their learning achieving high grades in the popular extended project qualification (EPQ). These results ranked alongside the most selective schools in the country. As well as the consistently high academic results, the College ensures that all pupils receive the time they need to expand their contemporary knowledge and global perspective, while having access to an abundance of fun, inclusive social opportunities. Almost every boy and girl goes on to university, 70% to Russell Group universities and nearly 10%, on average, to Oxbridge. Scholarships are offered for Year 9 and Year 12 entry.

A Vast Array of Extra Opportunities for Pupils. Both sport and the arts are considered vital elements in the education of all pupils. Many boys and girls achieve excellence in sport at regional and national level, whilst others excel in the fields of music, drama, art and dance. The Birley Centre is home to a wide variety of workshops and master classes run by Glyndebourne Youth – just one of a number of projects that make up an official partnership with Glyndebourne. Ballet Rambert visits regularly for workshops. There is a very varied and popular Pro-arts Programme for students, parents and visitors alike. Strong Pastoral and Family-friendly Pastoral support at the College is renowned. Pupils and their families are valued in this educational community where strong relationships are nurtured and highly prized. In recognition of the pressures of modern family life day pupils may go home any time between 6.00 and 8.00 pm, with parental and school permission. Many pupils make use of the wide-reaching minibus routes available.

Admission. Boys and girls are generally admitted between the ages of 13 and 14 years in Year 9 or for the Sixth Form in Year 12 after GCSE examinations. A prospectus and application form may be obtained from the Admissions Officer. The website contains more information and parents and prospective pupils who wish to visit the school are welcomed. Early registration for a place is recommended, preferably a year in advance; a registration fee (£100) is charged and places are confirmed with a guaranteed place deposit (£750 for UK; £12,000 for overseas) within a year of entry. All pupils start in September, although exceptional cases are occasionally considered at other times.

Scholarships and Bursaries. At 13+, academic, art, drama, music and sports scholarships are offered. In line with most top independent schools, the great majority of awards given at the College are between 5% and 20% of the day or boarding fees but more may be offered in exceptional circumstances (up to a maximum of 50%). Applicants must be under 14 on 1 September in the year they are due to enter the College. At 16+, academic scholarships (including the Scoresby-Jackson Science Award and the Bernard Drake Award), art, drama, design and technology, music, and sports scholarships are offered to pupils who join the school in Year 12 after GCSEs. A 10% boarding discount is available to HM Forces and Diplomatic Service families.

Bursaries are awarded in appropriate circumstances. All are means tested according to the Charity Commission criteria.

Entry forms for scholarships can be obtained from The Registrar.

Fees per term (2018–2019). Boarding: £11,750 (Years 9–11), £11,885 (Sixth Form); Day: £7,710 (Years 9–11), £7,835 (Sixth Form). An additional supplement for overseas pupils of £160 per term applies. Fees include meals and most extras.

Preparatory School. The charitable bodies governing Eastbourne College and the independent prep school, St Andrew's Prep, amalgamated in February 2010 to become one charity. Collaboration between the two schools had always been extremely close but, until then, there had been no formal financial or governance links between them. This was a change of governance and not of the school. The schools continue to operate independently and St Andrew's prepares boys and girls for a variety of schools including the College.

The **Eastbournian Society** brings together all those with a College connection: parents of current and former pupils, current and former staff, Old Eastbournians, friends, neighbours and local businesses. In particular, strong links are maintained with former pupils who offer careers assistance to current pupils (there is a convention every year to support the careers and higher education programme). The Society provides a series of social events and career and business networking opportunities. It comprises also the College's fundraising activity, providing funds for bursaries and new developments.

The **Devonshire Society** (legacy club) meets annually.

Charitable status. Eastbourne College Incorporated is a Registered Charity, number 307071. It exists for the purpose of educating children.

Board of Governors:

President: His Grace The Duke of Devonshire, KCVO, CBE, DL

Vice-Presidents:
The Earl of Burlington
His Excellency Nasser Judeh, BSc
General The Lord Richards of Herstmonceux, GCB, CBE, DSO, DL
Mr D Winn, OBE, MInstM

Chairman: Mr P A J Broadley, MA Oxon, MSc, FCA
Vice-Chairman: Mr J P Watmough, LLB

Members:
Mr A J G Brown, BSc
Mr C M P Bush, MA Oxon
Mr J R E Compton, BSc, MRSC
Mrs A C Coxen, LLB
Mr R V Davidson-Houston, BA

Mr C M Davies, FRICS, ACIArb
Mrs N L Eckert, BA, PGCE
Mr N J P Elliott, BA
Mrs V J Henley, BA
Prof K Gull, CBE, DSc, FRS, FMEDSci, FRSB
Mrs C P Locher
Mr G Marsh, MA Oxon
Dr R A McNeilly, MBBS, DCH, MRCGP, DOccMed, MBA
Mr D L Meek, LLB, FCA
Mr J W S Piper, BA, MEd
Ms C Radwan, MA, MSc
Mrs M J Richards
Mr T S Richardson, FRICS
Mr A M Robinson, BA, ACA
Mr J H Ryley, BA, AMP
Mrs H J Toole, MBA
Ms J A Wheeldon, BA, FCA

In Attendance
Mr G A Anderson, HDE
Mr G E B Jones, BA, MEd
The Hon T N M Lawson, MA Oxon
Mr C W Symes, BSc, MEd, MCGI

College Chaplaincy:
Chaplain: Revd D J Merceron, BA Institute of Archaeology

Bursar and Clerk to the Board of Governors: Mrs C Meade, MA Cantab

Senior Management Team:

Headmaster: The Hon T N M Lawson, MA Christ Church Oxford

Second Master: Mr C W Symes, BSc, Med, MCGI, Edinburgh
Bursar to the Eastbourne College Charity: Mrs C Meade, MA Selwyn College Cambridge
Deputy Head (Academic): Mr J M Gilbert, BSc Cardiff, MBA, MRSC
Deputy Head (Co-curricular): Mr A T Lamb, MBE, BA University of New England NSW Australia, DipEd, DL
Deputy Head (Pastoral): Mrs G E Taylor-Hall, BA Liverpool
Development Director, Eastbournian Society: Mr D A Stewart
Director of Admissions: Ms E D Cheary, BSc Witwatersrand SA, MBA
Marketing and Communications Director to the Eastbourne College Charity: Mrs J S B Lowden, BA St Aidan's College Durham

Academic Departments and Personnel:

* *Head of Department*

Art:
*Mrs J L A Harriott
Ms E Z Greenwood (*also teaches photography*)
Ms J Lathbury
Mrs S A Martin (*i/c photography*)
Miss E Horridge (*also teaches photography*)

Biology:
*Miss V Woodham
Mr A Ahmed
Mrs R N Cooke
Mr P J Fellows
Mrs J F Lawson

Business:
*Mr M J McVeigh
Dr L S Flanagan
Mr T J Holgate
Mr O M Torri

Chemistry:
*Mr D C Miller
Mrs R N Cooke
Mr J M Gilbert
Revd D P Ibbotson
Miss H L Simmons
Mr A D Swift

Classics:
*Mr P J Canning
Mr H B Jourdain
Revd D J Merceron

Miss K L Morton
Mr I P Sands
Dr P S Taraskin

Dance:
Miss K A H Reid

Design and Technology:
*Mr M J Clover
Mr N J Clark
Mr S J Norris
Mr W L Trinder

Drama:
Director of Drama: Mrs C E A Sinnett
Miss E J Arnold
Mrs L J Jourdain
Mrs L A Salway

Economics:
*Mr J M Bathard-Smith
Mr T N M Lawson
Mr M J Pringle

English:
*Mrs J E Bathard-Smith
Miss P M H Squire (*2nd i/c Dept*)
Mrs L J Jourdain
Mr P H Lowden
Mrs L J C MacKenzie
Mr O K Marlow
Mrs A P M Tutt
Miss G S Woodroffe
Mr S P Young

English as an Additional Language:
*Miss K Briedenhann
Mrs G L Williams
Mrs H J Williams

Geography:
*Mr S Mason
Mr R K Hart
Mr A T Lamb
Mr W M Longden
Mrs L Price
Mr A O Wingfield Digby

History:
*Mr T J Spiers
Mr R H Bunce
Mr S A Gent
Miss L A Jackson
Mr J C Miller

Information and Communication Technology:
*Mr I R Shakespeare
Mrs M A Ambler

Learning Support:
*Mr A J Spraggon
Mrs E D Harter
Dr E B Miller
Mrs H J Williams

Mathematics:
*Mr J R Wooldridge
Mr S E Beal (*2nd i/c Dept*)
Mr P R Calvert
Mr O L Dennis
Mr J N Hooper
Mr L G Karunanayake
Miss J K Lusty
Mr I R Shakespeare
Mrs E M Sheridan
Mrs C Sinclair

Modern Languages:
*Mr E V Protin
Mr M Thelwall Jones (*2nd i/c Dept*)
Miss V E Burford
Mrs M J De La Torre
Ms A G Del Angel
Miss C Ponté
Mr D J Ruskin
Mr J Thornley
Mrs M C Tripp
Mrs G A Webb
Mrs E M Wingfield Digby

Music:
Director of Music: Mr D K Jordan
Assistant Director of Music: Mr A C Eadon
Head of Academic Music: Mr T G Laverack

Philosophy and Theology:
*Mr A P Wood
Miss C M Ball
Revd D J Merceron
Revd D J Peat
Mr A J Spraggon

Physical Education:
*Mrs J M Simmonds
Mr M T Harrison
Mrs J M Kirtley
Mrs G E Taylor-Hall
Mr O M Torri
Mrs A P M Tutt
Mrs C Whiddett-Adams

Physics:
*Mrs E J Livingstone Greer
Dr A Ball (*Senior Scientist*)
Mr D J Hodkinson
Mr A M Kuchta
Mr A T Roberts

Politics:
*Mr R H Bunce
Dr L S Flanagan
Mr A P Wood

PSHE:
*Mrs J M Kirtley

Textiles:
*Ms Z B Cosgrove
Mrs A Young

The Edinburgh Academy

42 Henderson Row, Edinburgh EH3 5BL

Tel:	0131 556 4603
	0131 624 4987 (Admissions)
Fax:	0131 624 4990
email:	enquiries@edinburghacademy.org.uk
	admissions@edinburghacademy.org.uk
website:	www.edinburghacademy.org.uk
Twitter:	@edinburghacad

The Edinburgh Academy is a co-educational day school for pupils aged 2 to 18 with a proud history and outward vision. Founded in 1824 with the aspiration to create a school where excellence could always be achieved, the School motto translates as 'Always Excel'. The Edinburgh Academy is built on strong traditions but is always seeking to innovate.

The Edinburgh Academy consists of a Nursery of 98 children, a Junior School of 390 children and a Senior School of 557. The School's size allows it to cater for the individual needs and ambitions of each child whilst high staff ratios means that at each stage it can tailor the teaching and pastoral care to the needs of each pupil, giving them the best possible chance to develop their unique talents. Through a rounded education Academy pupils enhance their social, emotional and spiritual capacities; equipping them for citizenship in a challenging and changing world. The attributes of an Academy Learner are that they are curious, creative, independent, collaborative and resilient.

Campus. A strength of the Academy is the split campus. This allows for purpose-built facilities and high-quality teaching at each age and stage through which all children can flourish.

Situated in Edinburgh's New Town since 1824, the Senior School is a stunning architectural blend of traditional and modern buildings. The most recent additions have been the splendid Science Centre (inspired by an alumnus of the school, mathematical physicist James Clerk Maxwell) and the Salvesan Performing Arts Centre.

The Junior School, Nursery and Playing Fields are on Arboretum Road: next to the world-renowned Royal Botanic Gardens. The recently opened McTavish Wing at the Junior School has created a new library, learning resource centre and four additional classrooms whilst the purpose-built Nursery provides a bright, functional and fun environment ensuring the best of opportunities for learning through play and experience both inside and out.

Academic. The Academy supports each child on their preferred education path and gets to know each individual extremely well in helping them to reach their personal goals and achieve to the best of their ability. The pre-14 curriculum offers flexibility; giving a very good grounding in basic skills whilst allowing pupils to progress through developing the critical higher order skills inherent in the best parts of 'A Curriculum for Excellence'. Older Senior School pupils present for exams in a wide range of subjects at National 5, Higher and Advanced Higher.

In keeping with the stated vision of producing children who are 'Grounded in Scotland, Ready for the World', the school takes pride in the fact that there are Academicals (alumni) around the globe who look back on their Academy education as their first crucial step on the ladder to success.

Class Sizes. Class sizes are kept relatively small to allow teachers to identify and nurture each child's strengths. In the Junior School the aim is to keep class sizes of around 22 children. In the Senior School, no teaching group is larger than 24 pupils, and most are substantially smaller.

Courses of Study. A very wide general curriculum is taught at the Edinburgh Academy between the ages of 2 and 14. Away from the valuable lessons taught by their class teacher, Nursery pupils receive specialist teaching in Science, PE, Modern European Languages and Music. In Junior School this is further complimented by Art and Mandarin (from Primary 5) whilst in Senior School specialist Latin, Drama and Design Technology are introduced. Maths is set from Primary 3 and all subjects are taught by Secondary School specialist teachers from Primary 7 (Geits).

Eight subjects are taken for National 5 (GCSE equivalent): English, Maths, a foreign language and a science must be taken and it is recommended that pupils complete the balance by adding either History or Geography, and one of Art, Music, Drama, PE or a technical subject.

In the final years of the Senior School the emphasis increasingly moves towards preparing young people for higher education and beyond. The penultimate year sees the breadth inherent in Scottish Highers followed by the greater depth of Advanced Highers. In Art and Music a two-year A Level course is offered in the belief that this is better suited to the needs of pupils looking to progress in those specialisms.

Physical Education. All Academy pupils are encouraged to stay active and healthy. Over 25 acres of sports pitches, including four all-weather surfaces, squash, tennis and fives courts and a sports centre, are coupled with top-class coaching to help them enjoy their chosen sports. Pupils can choose from a full range of winter and summer sports and teams represent the School in rugby, hockey, football, cricket, tennis, squash, badminton, fives, athletics, skiing, shooting, golf, shooting, sailing, swimming, cross country running, basketball, netball and dance.

In March of 2015 the Academy opened a brand new state-of-the-art Climbing and Bouldering Facility that is without doubt the best school arena of this type in the country.

Outdoor Education. The Edinburgh Academy has invested significantly in its recently established 'Spirit of Adventure Fund'. As well as the Climbing Wall this has allowed for the recruitment of both a Head of Outdoor Education and an Early Years Outdoor Learning specialist. This example of 'EA Innovation' means that all Academy children from the youngest in the Nursery to those completing their Gold Duke of Edinburgh's Award benefit from the resilience and character most easily developed in the outdoors.

Music, Drama, Art. The Creative Arts are an important part of Edinburgh Academy life and pupils are encouraged to take part from Junior School and beyond. Most pupils learn a musical instrument and are members of the various choirs, orchestras, bands and ensembles. All Junior School pupils take part in an annual drama production whilst the Senior School produces extremely high-quality performances at regular intervals throughout the year.

In Art, a large number of pupils take the A Level and the success rate for being accepted into Art College is very high. A number of students join the Academy each year with their primary objective being to study Fine Art. This is complemented in Design and Technology where there is a fully furnished Jewellery Studio. At the end of each year there is a major exhibition in these subjects where pupils' work is displayed and sold.

Extra-Curricular. The Academy recognises that significant learning takes place outside the formal classroom and believes in a balance between academic and co-curricular activities; offering a wide range of opportunities to participate and represent the Academy in sport, music and a variety of expressive and creative arts.

There is an extremely broad range of co-curricular activities available including Debating, Photography, Computing, Model United Nations, Modern Languages, Jazz, Politics, Scripture Union, Film Club, Bridge, Chess, Eco Group, Sailing, Cross Country, Climbing, Football and many, many more.

Combined Cadet Force and The Duke of Edinburgh's Award. All pupils over the age of 14 must participate in either the CCF (Army, RAF or Pipe Band sections) or The Duke of Edinburgh's Award scheme for a period of three terms after which further participation is voluntary. The CCF sections offer training in field craft, weapons handling, orienteering, drill and first aid and affords young people the opportunity to develop their leadership potential.

Fees per term (2018–2019). Nursery £2,246–£2,931. Junior School P1–P6 £2,811–£3,498. Senior School: £3,792 (Geits), £4,707 (2nds–7ths).

When 3 or more siblings are in attendance at the School (excluding Nursery) at the same time, a reduction of one-third of the tuition fees is made for each sibling after the first two.

The Academy is currently in partnership with Edinburgh City Council regarding Nursery Provision. For further details about the financial package available please contact Accounts on 0131 624 4916.

Scholarships and Bursaries. Means-tested Bursaries of up to 100% of fees are offered to pupils who are most able to benefit from an Edinburgh Academy education; irrespective of financial means. These are generally available to Senior School pupils.

A number of Scholarships (age 11+) are offered to candidates of very high ability either academically or in Art, Music or Sport. Examinations and assessments are held in January.

Admissions. The majority of new pupils join at the beginning of the Autumn Term in late August though some also join during the session. Other than for Nursery, all candidates for admission to the Edinburgh Academy must be assessed by the School and assessment days are held in November (Junior School P2–6) and January (P1 and Senior School). The Academy is always delighted to welcome families outwith this time. Initial enquiries should be made to the Admissions Registrar: Tel: 0131 624 4987; email: admissions@edinburghacademy.org.uk.

Edinburgh Academical Club. There is a strong former pupil community and the Club works hard to remain in contact with former pupils all over the world. They host events each year, both from a social and career perspective, and have established a career mentoring and internship service to help former pupils. Contact: Ms Eve Macdonald, Tel: 0131 624 4958, email: accies@edinburghacademy.org.uk.

Charitable Status. The Edinburgh Academy is a Registered Charity, number SC016999. It exists for the advancement of education and the contribution to the educational life of Scotland in its widest sense.

Court of Directors:

Chairman: M W Gregson, MBA, BSc

Extraordinary Directors:
Lord Cameron of Lochbroom, PC, FRSE
Professor J P Percy, CBE, LLD, CA
J H W Fairweather, MA
S A Mackintosh, MA, LLB, WS

Elected Directors:
B E Beveridge, LLB, Dip LP, NP (*Chair EA Foundation*)
Dr A E Gebbie, MB ChB, FRCOG, FFSRH, DCH
Dr B A Hacking, MA Hons, D Clin Psychol
G T Hartop
Dr A Huntingdon, BA, PhD, FSI

M McNeill, LLB, LLM, Dip LP
P H Miller, BLE, MRICS
C C R Robertson, MA
Sheriff Principal CAL Scott, QC
J F Smith, MA Hons, BSc Hons
V Khurana LLB, Dip LP, MB ChB, DRCOG, JCCC, MRCGP, DCCH
V Skene, MCIPD
P Dollman, BSc Hons
R A Fletcher
D J Knapman, BA, BSc, MPhil

Co-opted Members:
The Rector
The Headteacher of Junior School
The Senior Deputy Rector of the Senior School

Bursar and Clerk to the Court: G G Cartwright, MA CA

Rector: Mr Barry Welsh

Junior School Staff:
Head of the Junior School: Mr G A Calder, MA Hons, PGCE, Dip Ed Leadership
Deputy Head of the Junior School: Mrs L Htet Khin, LLB Hons
Deputy Head (Admissions and Early Years): Mrs L Paterson, DCE, INSC

Heads of Departments:
Support for Learning: Mrs P A Macnair, BA, MEd
Middle Years: Mrs B G G Robertson, BEd, DPSE
Upper Years: Mrs C A Petrie, BEd
Music: Mrs L A Russell, BEd Hons

Senior School Staff:
Senior Deputy Rector:
Deputy Rector (Director of Studies): Dr R Wightman, BSc, PhD
Deputy Rector (Pastoral and Personnel): Mr M Bryce, BSc
Deputy Rector (Learning and Teaching): Mrs C E Hancox, MA, PGCE,

Head of Sixth Form: Mrs F B Slavin, MA

Heads of Departments:
Art: Mr D L Prosser, BA
Biology: Mr A W MacPherson, BSc, MSc, PhD
Business Studies/Economics: Mr W J Turkington, BA
Careers: Mrs Y D Harley
Chemistry: (*to be appointed*)
Classics: Mr A K Tart, MA
Computing: Mr D G Stewart, BSc
Design & Technology: Miss S M Hennessy, BA, MA
Drama: Miss G D M Henderson, BA
English: Mr J R Meadows, BA
Geography: Dr D J Carr, BSc, PhD
History, Politics and Modern Studies: Mr J Lisher, BA Hons
Mathematics: Mr C A Brookman, BSc, PhD, GRSC, MInstP
Modern Languages: Mr Youssouf Kassime, PGCE Masters
Music: Dr P N Coad, MA, PhD, FRCO (*Director*)
Physical Education: Mr M J de G Allingham, MSc
Curricular PE: Mr M E Appleson, BA
Physics: Mr N Armstrong, MA, CPhys, MInstP
Religious Education: Mr H Jarrold, M Theol
Support for Learning: Mr C Gerrard, BSc Hons

Admissions Registrar: Mrs J Murray Brown
PA to the Rector: Mrs F Bell
PA to the Headteacher: Mrs T Maguire

Elizabeth College

**The Grange, St Peter Port, Guernsey, Channel Islands
GY1 2PY**

Tel: 01481 726544
Fax: 01481 714839
email: office@elizabethcollege.gg
website: www.elizabethcollege.gg
Twitter: @Eliz_Coll
Facebook: @ElizabethCollegeGuernsey

Motto: *Semper Eadem*

Elizabeth College was founded in 1563 by Queen Elizabeth I in order to provide education for boys seeking ordination in the Church of England. It is one of the original members of HMC and has Direct Grant status. It provides a broad education while maintaining the Christian aspirations of its Foundress. There are approximately 785 pupils in the College, of whom about 270 are in the Junior School. Girls are accepted into the Junior School. The Sixth Form is mixed through a partnership with nearby Ladies' College.

Buildings and Grounds. The Upper School (for pupils over 11 years) is situated in imposing buildings dating from 1829 which stand on a hill overlooking the town and harbour of St Peter Port. The classrooms and laboratories, all of which are equipped with appropriate modern teaching aids, the Hall, Sports Hall and Swimming Pool are accommodated on this site. Improvements in recent years have included a new Refectory, Performing Arts Suite, six new Mathematics classrooms and an additional classroom at the Junior School. There are two large games fields, one of which includes an artificial pitch for hockey. Elizabeth College Junior School comprises Beechwood, a prep school, and Acorn House, a pre-prep and nursery school. The Junior School has its own site some ten minutes' walk from Elizabeth College. It takes boys and girls from 7 to 11 years old. Acorn House accepts boys and girls from 4 to 7 years old and also has a pre-school facility for younger children.

Academic Curriculum. At Key Stage 3, boys follow a broad curriculum which is common to all, covering arts, sciences, creative and practical subjects. Information Technology is timetabled in all three years to develop the skills needed for the demands of GCSE and A Level courses. Opportunity is also afforded to boys to sample both Latin and a second Modern Foreign Language in addition to French. PSHEE (Wellbeing), RS, PE, Games and Drama are timetabled throughout. In Years 10 and 11 the aim is to produce a high level of achievement and choice at GCSE by offering flexibility wherever possible. Three separate sciences or Core and Additional Science are studied. At least one modern language should be taken, although more are available as options. English Literature is studied within the English teaching groups, but is not compulsory for all. Other GCSE options combine the traditional with the contemporary: Art, Business Studies, Ancient History, Computing, Drama, Graphics or Resistant Materials, History, Latin, Music and PE are currently offered. Alongside the GCSE courses PSHEE (Wellbeing) and PE/Games continue to be taught. The Sixth Form is run in partnership with The Ladies' College, with interchange of pupils between schools and shared teaching of many groups. The Sixth Form offers a very broad array of subjects across the two schools enabling a wide variety of choices, with subjects ranging from the traditional to the new, including Computing. Tutorial periods enable vocational, careers and pastoral guidance to be available.

Music. There is a lively extra-curricular music programme which includes the College Orchestra, Wind Ensemble and Brass Jazz Band, with numerous small ensembles running alongside these larger groups. There is a variety of choral groups, with the College choir making regular visits to France to sing in Cathedrals and at concerts. Individual instruction is available in instrumental and vocal studies, catering for a wide range of interests including piano, organ and traditional orchestral studies as well as contemporary and jazz styles. The Junior School has its own choirs, orchestra, recorder group and steel pan band. Each summer holiday the College hosts a week-long orchestral course when tuition is provided by eminent professionals to over two hundred and fifty boys and girls drawn from the islands, the UK and other parts of Europe.

Games. The sports fields cover some 20 acres. The Junior School has its own small playing field, and also has access to the facilities of the Upper School. The major College games are Association Football, Hockey and Cricket. Athletics, Badminton, Basketball, Cross-country Running, Fencing, Golf, Rugby Football, Sailing, Shooting, Squash and Swimming also flourish. Physical Education forms a regular part of the curriculum for all boys up to the end of Year 11. Some seniors specialise in Outdoor Pursuits as their Games option under the guidance of a fully qualified expert. Despite the size of the Island, plentiful opposition for sports fixtures is available. The College competes against other Island schools, has a traditional rivalry with Victoria College in Jersey, makes regular tours to the UK mainland and hosts return visits from UK schools.

Combined Cadet Force. This is voluntary and optional from Year 10, and is Tri-Service. Cadets travel regularly to the UK and beyond for proficiency training, camps, courses, qualifications and competitions, as well as adventurous training. Competition shooting forms a major part of the CCF and there is a long and distinguished record at Bisley. The CCF has an important role in providing Guards of Honour for Island ceremonial occasions.

Duke of Edinburgh's Award. Boys are encouraged to participate in this scheme. Both Bronze and Gold Awards are offered as extra-curricular activities. Bronze expedition work takes place locally in the Channel Islands whilst the expedition work necessary for the Gold Award takes place on the UK mainland during the Easter and Summer holidays.

Community Service. This is an alternative option to CCF for pupils in Year 10 and above. Pupils actively contribute to a wide range of service activities including sports leadership in primary schools, subject leadership in junior lessons and support of local charities.

Scouts. There is an active Elizabeth College Scout Group, whose headquarters are situated on the College Field. At the Junior School there is a Cub Scout Group.

Clubs and Societies. The College stresses the importance of extra-curricular activity. Among over thirty currently active clubs are those which foster Bell Ringing, Chess, Climbing, Debating, Design Technology, Fencing, Life Saving, Model Railways, Sailing, Shooting, Squash and War Gaming.

Pastoral Care. In the Upper School each year has a Head of Year assisted by four Tutors. Acorn and Beechwood have Form Tutors. All these staff provide pastoral care and academic guidance for their own sections of the College. They are supported by a Chaplain who conducts services in all three schools as well as preparing boys for Confirmation.

Parental Involvement. Parents are strongly encouraged to take an active part in their child's education. There are regular assessments and reports, parents' evenings, pastoral information evenings and parent workshops. Heads of Year keep in regular contact with parents through newsletters and email. The Heads of Year and pupils' tutors are always available to meet with parents to discuss any concerns.

Admission. The principal ages for admission into the school are 4, 7, 11, 13 and 16, but there are usually vacancies for entry at other ages. Entry is by means of assessment and/or interview which are adapted to the age of the applicant. There is a £110 non-refundable registration fee. Applications for entry should be addressed to the Principal.

Scholarships to the College. The Gibson Fleming Trust provides Awards on a means-tested basis for current pupils to support them in their involvement with extra-curricular activities.

Choral and Instrumental Scholarships. The Gibson Fleming Trust provides Choral and Instrumental Scholarships to current pupils. Details of the scholarships may be obtained from the Principal or Director of Music.

Scholarships to the Universities. The College Exhibitions, Scholarships and Prizes include the Queen's Exhibition, the Lord de Sausmarez Exhibition, the Mainguy Scholarship, the Mansell Exhibition and the Mignot Fund.

Travel. There are several flights each day from Southampton (half an hour), Gatwick (about three quarters of an hour) and Stansted (about one hour). There are also regular flights to the West Country and to Midlands and northern airports. There are frequent sailings to and from Portsmouth and Poole, which offer vehicle transportation.

Old Boys. The Honorary Secretary of the Old Elizabethan Association is Rupert Pleasant who may be contacted via www.oea.org.gg.

Fees per term (2018–2019). Acorn House (Pre-Prep): £3,450; Beechwood (Prep): £3,790; Upper School (11–18): £3,995.

Visitor: The Assistant Bishop of Winchester

Directors:
The Very Revd T Barker, Dean of Guernsey (*Chairman*)

M R Buchanan	L S Trott
Mrs A-M Collivet	Mrs K Ovenden
M R Thompson	S Sharman
S Falla	A Tautscher

Principal: Mrs J M Palmer, BA

Vice-Principal: R J W James, BA
Assistant Principal (*Teaching & Learning*): T I Addenbrooke, BEng, MSc, PhD
Assistant Principal (*Sixth Form*): C R W Cottam, MA, CT ABRSM
Assistant Principal (*Pupil Progress & Inspection Compliance*): Mrs P E Cross, BA, ARCM
Assistant Principal (*Pastoral & Wellbeing*): C D Eyton-Jones, BA Ed
Head of the Junior School: R I Fyfe, BA
Foundation & Marketing Director: Mrs D A Carruthers, BSc
Bursar & Clerk to the Directors: M F Spiller, MSc, BSSc, FCILT

Members of Teaching Staff:

E C Adams, BA	D J Costen, BA
B E H Aplin, BSc	G S Cousens, BA
Mrs S Benson, BA	Mrs G Dallin, BSc
Mrs E F Blazina, BA	P G Davis, BSc
Mrs N C Brown, BA	R M Davis, BA
Mrs C S Buchanan, BA	T R de Putron, BSc
M A M Buchanan, BA	Miss A C M Demongeot, BA, MA
I Burnett, BA	
R G Campbell, BSc, MSc	Mrs J-A Dittmar, BSc
A P Carey, BA, MA	T P Edge, BA, MA
Mrs E J Chamberlain, BSc, MEd	L R G Garland, BSc, MA
	M Garnett, BA
J J Conner, BSc	A J Good, BSc
Mrs P S Copeland, BA	Mrs M E Gordon, MA

M N Heaume, BSc	Mrs J B Odlin, BSc
G A Henshall, BA	Ms J M Pendleton, BA
S J Huxtable, MA	Mrs P J Read, MSci, MA
D R L Inderwick, BA, MA	J R D Rowson, BA
R G Le Sauvage, BSc	Miss M Schofield, BA
Mrs S Lee, Mgr	Miss R L Seymour, BSc
Ms E A Loveridge, BA	T C Slann, Dip NEBSS
D R Loweth, MA, MEd	Ms T L Smith, BA, MA
Mrs H M Mauger, BA	M A G Stephens, BA
R A Morris, BA	A G Stewart, BSc
S G D Morris, BSc	M W R Stokes, BA
A R Mulholland, BSc, MA	Ms S L A Tribe, BA
Mrs K A Norman, BA	Mrs S Zhou, BA, MA

Chaplain: The Revd P A Graysmith, BSc
Director of Music: Miss E D Willcocks, BMus, MA
Games and Physical Education: T P Eisenhuth, BPhysEd

Prep:
Deputy Head Pastoral: Mrs E Bott, BEd
Deputy Head Academic: Miss E J Brooker, BSc

Miss N Bourne, BEd	Mrs K Reed, BA
Mrs M Brady, BA	Mrs J Ricketts, BA
Mrs S Crittell, BA	P Sargent, BA
Mrs S Ellis	Mrs B Santi, BSc, MA
Mrs C Herve, BA	Mrs N Stevens, BEd
Mrs D M McLaughlin, BSc	R Sutton, BA
Mrs E Parkes, BEd	Mrs C Wray, BSc
Mrs A M Pollard, BEd	

Pre-Prep:
Deputy Head: Mrs J Atkinson, BEd

Mrs C Bowden, BA	Mrs J Hamilton, BA
Miss R Curtis, BA	Mrs E Jones, BA Ed
Mrs L Du Port, BEd	Mrs C Martel, BA Ed

Ellesmere College
A Woodard School

Ellesmere, Shropshire SY12 9AB

Tel:	01691 622321
Fax:	01691 623286
email:	hmsecretary@ellesmere.com
website:	www.ellesmere.com
Twitter:	@ellesmerecoll
Facebook:	@Ellesmere-College

Motto: *Pro Patria Dimicans*

Ellesmere College is a fully co-educational school set in the beautiful English countryside. Founded in 1884, the school offers students between the ages of 7 to 18 the chance to achieve success in both their studies and a wide range of activities, including music, art, sport and drama, in a happy, friendly atmosphere. We prepare students for their GCSEs, A Levels, BTEC and the International Baccalaureate as well as giving them the opportunity to enjoy a full and varied sports and social programme. Standing in its own stunning grounds covering more than 50 hectares, the school is conveniently located near the small, historic town of Ellesmere, and is less than 100 kilometres from both of England's second major cities, Manchester and Birmingham.

The College Building. The main school building contains three boys' Boarding and Day Houses, as well as a mixed 10–12 junior Boarding and Day House, accommodation for Housemasters and Housemistresses and/or Assistant Housemasters and Housemistresses, the Chapel and the Dining Hall. St Luke's Boarding House completes the main quadrangle. A 13–16 girls' Boarding and Day house has its own wing in the main building and was opened in response to demand in 1996. The girls' Sixth Form Boarding and Day House which accommodates girls in a combination of shared and single study bedrooms and dayrooms was completed in 1986. A Gymnasium, Big School (Assembly Hall) which houses the Schulze Organ, and three subject Departments are also located in the main building. September 2004 saw the opening of the College's new Sports Hall, which adds to facilities that include two other gymnasia, squash courts and Tennis Centre completed in 2017.

Additional wings contain the Library and Sixth Form Centre. Other subjects are taught in their own Departmental blocks close to the main building, and include Science Laboratories, a Modern Languages Department with a Language Laboratory, an Art School, a Design & Technology Centre, and a Business Studies Department with its own computer suite. A purpose-built Lower School for Years 3–8 was opened in 1999.

The House System. The Lower School (ages 7–13) has a competitive system based on 3 Houses. The Senior School has a competitive system based on 4 Houses all of which are co-educational and combine boarding and day pupils. Separate from the competitive Houses is the residential House system for living arrangements. There are 2 Girls' Houses, catering for age 13–16 and Sixth Form respectively; there are 4 Boys' Houses: two for age 13–16 and two Sixth Form Houses; there is also a Mixed House catering for boarders of ages 10–12.

Curriculum. In the first year in the Senior School a full range of fourteen subjects is studied, including Art, Design and Technology, Computing and Technical Drawing. This curriculum is designed to give all pupils a comprehensive introduction before focusing on their core elective subjects for GCSE. At GCSE all pupils take English, Mathematics, and either Dual Award Science or the three Sciences studied separately. Other subjects depend on individual aptitude and choice.

In the Sixth Form over 20 different academic subjects are available for study to A Level, BTEC Diploma or International Baccalaureate (IB) Diploma to prepare for University Entrance or entry to the Services and the Professions.

Music. The College has a very strong musical tradition and has been awarded Artsmark Platinum in recognition of the award-winning arts provision at the College. It possesses two of the finest organs in the country, including the internationally renowned St Mary Tyne Dock Schulze Organ. The Chapel Choir has a wide repertoire of Church Music. There is a Chamber Choir, Coro Lux, Big Band, a Choral Society, a Jazz Group and other ensembles, all of which give regular concerts. There are House Music Competitions every year, and the community Sinfonia Orchestra.

An annual programme of Celebrity Concerts brings distinguished musicians to the College.

The Music School is part of the College Arts Centre which provides first-class facilities, including 8 Practice Rooms, a Recording Studio, Teaching Rooms and a Studio Theatre designed for small concerts and seating 220 people.

Arts Centre. This purpose-built complex hosts Drama, Dance, Film, Music and Art Exhibitions. A programme is organised in which international artists in all these fields visit the Centre, which shares its facilities with the local community.

Careers. At all levels pupils are encouraged to seek advice from the College careers Masters and Mistresses as well as representatives from the Independent Schools Careers Organisation. A Careers Convention is held each year for pupils in Year 11. Students also take ESB (English Speaking Board), ILM (Institute of leadership & Management), SATS and mentoring programmes.

Games and Physical Education. Ellesmere has a long tradition of sporting excellence and has a total of 7 Sporting Academies in rugby, football, tennis, swimming, golf, cricket, and shooting. The sporting excellence is supported by the Rugby Academy programme (3 leavers turned professional in 2008), the Tennis Academy, and the joint College and Community Ellesmere College Titans Swimming Team. The Cricket Academy was launched in 2009, the Shooting Academy in 2010, Golf Academy in 2015 and the Football Academy in 2016. Ellesmere College also has a High Performance Hockey Programme with a pathway to international progression.

All members of the School are required to participate in a regular programme of games, though particular inclinations and aptitudes are taken fully into consideration. Facilities include two sports halls, floodlit multi-sports astroTurf pitches, a fitness centre, squash courts, a heated indoor swimming pool, indoor and outdoor shooting ranges, two high-tech gymnasia, a purpose-built LTA accredited indoor 4-court tennis centre, 6 floodlit all-weather tennis courts, a golf course, rugby pitches, all-weather hockey pitches, cricket squares, and an athletics track.

Ellesmere is superbly placed for outdoor pursuits. Easily accessible lakes, rivers and hills provide opportunities to develop talents and interests.

Sailing takes place on Whitemere. The School owns six boats and pupils are allowed to bring their own craft. Canoeing takes place on the Ellesmere canal and on local rivers such as the Dee and the Severn. Horse riding takes place at a local stable.

All pupils are expected to join one of the following: D of E (Duke of Edinburgh's Award), Outdoor Training Unit, CCF, Social Service. These activities occur on one full afternoon a week, but, in order to extend their activities, twice a year 3 days are set aside when all members of the School participate in 48-hour expeditions. In the Lent Term a single day is devoted to expeditions.

Admission. Boys and girls are admitted at all points of entry into the school. Entrance examinations are held in February for Lower School entry. Scholarships for Prep School candidates are held in May, while others take the Common Entrance Examination in June.

Scholarships and Bursaries. A wide range of Awards recognising a range of talents is available:

Academic: Available at 8+, 9+, 11+, 13+ and 16+ entry worth up to a maximum of 50% fee remission.

All-Rounder: Available at 11+, 13+ and 16+ entry worth up to a maximum of 25% fee remission.

Art: Available at 13+ and 16+ entry worth up to a maximum of 25% fee remission.

Drama: Available at 13+ and 16+ entry worth up to a maximum of 25% fee remission.

Music: Available at 8+, 9+, 11+, 13+ and 16+ entry. Scholarships are worth up to a maximum of 50% fee reduction and free tuition in two instruments. Exhibitions are worth up to a maximum of 25% fee reduction and free tuition in one instrument.

The *Schulze Organ Award* is reserved for Sixth Form candidates and is valued at 50% of fees.

Sports: Available at 13+ and 16+ entry and may be worth up to a maximum of 50% fee remission. (Awards below Sixth Form level are unlikely to exceed 25% fee reduction.)

In cases of need, all awards may be supplemented by means-tested bursaries.

There are reduced fees for children of the Clergy. Foundation and Regional awards are available for children of parents of limited means.

Fees per term (2018–2019). Upper School: Boarders £10,977, Weekly Boarders £7,908, Day £6,123. Lower School: Boarders £8,796, Weekly Boarders £7,500, Day

£3,735–£4,293. Fees are inclusive of general School charges.

Music lessons are given at a charge of £284 for ten lessons and individual tuition for dyslexic pupils also incurs an extra cost. A scheme of insurance is in force under which the School Fees may be insured for a small termly premium for any number of years and which enables a pupil to remain at Ellesmere to complete his/her education free of all board and tuition fees, if a parent dies before the pupil's School career is ended. There is also a School Fees Remission Scheme for insurance of fees in cases of absence through illness and of surgical and medical expenses. Arrangement can be made for a single advance payment of fees.

'Old Boys and Girls'. Former pupils of the school normally become members of the Old Ellesmerian Club, which in turn enables them to take part in a number of societies and activities. For further information contact: Olivia Beckett, External Relations Officer, Ellesmere College, Ellesmere, Shropshire, SY12 9AB.

Charitable status. Ellesmere College is a Registered Charity, number 1103049. It exists to provide education for children.

Founder: The Revd Nathaniel Woodard, DCL, then Dean of Manchester

Visitor: The Rt Revd The Lord Bishop of Lichfield

College Council:

D C Brewitt	C E Lillis
Mrs F M Christie	J A Mathias, FCA
The Reverend Canon B C	A L Morris
Clover	Mrs C S Newbold, BA
Mrs S Connor	Mrs R E Paterson
J S Hopkins	The Reverend M J Rylands
R A K Hoppins	M D T Sampson

Headmaster: B J Wignall, BA, MA, MCMI, FRSA

Deputy Head (*Pastoral*): Dr R Chatterjee, BSc, MSc, PhD, Cert SpLD
Deputy Head (*Academic*): Mrs S V Pritt-Roberts, BEd, MEd, NPQH
Head of Sixth Form: P A Wood, MA (*General Studies*)
Head of Middle School: Dr T Gareh BSc, MSc, PhD, CSci, CChem, MRSC
Head of Lower School: Mrs S Owen, BEd
Director of Activities: Mr C Davies, BA
Chaplain: The Revd Phillip Gration
Director of Finance: N Haworth, ACMA, BA
Director of Operations: M McCarthy, BSc, DMS

Teachers:
* *Head of Department*
† *Housemaster/mistress*

Ms C Allen, BA (**EAL*)
M Atheron
†J J Baggaley, BA
D Bottom, BA
M P Clewlow, BSc
Mrs J Chatterjee, BSc
Dr J K Collins, BSc, PhD (**Biology*)
T Coupe, BMus (**Music*)
J H Cowley, BSc, NPQH (**Mathematics*)
D W Crawford, MA, MSc, MPhil
K Curzon, BSc
Miss A C Darrant, BSc (**Physics*)
Mrs H L Davenport, BSc (**Physical Education*)
C R Davies, BA
Mrs J M Davies, BA
J Dilks, BA
†Mrs A Done, HD
Mrs J Evans

†Mrs Z Fisher
C Garratt, BA
Dr R Hansford, BSc
Mrs J M Hibbott, BA
Mrs V M Howle, BEd, Cert SpLD, Dip RSA
Mrs M E Hutchings, MA, MA (**Media Studies*)
W J Hutchings, BEd
J Haycock, BA
S Hutchon, BSc
Miss E A Killen, BEd
R J Macintosh, BSc
Miss J M Manion, BA, NPQH (**Support for Learning*)
†D J Morgan, BSc
Mrs S E Morgan, BEd
Miss K Marshall, BSc
S B Mullock, BA
A Murphy, BSc
Mrs J R Nicolson, MA
H B Orr, BD (**Religious Studies and Sociology*)
†G Owen, BEd
Mrs R Paul, BA
Mrs E Phillips, BSc
Mrs S Phillips, MA (**Art and Design Technology*)
S Prescott, BA
†I Roberts, BA
S Shakibi, BA (**Computer Science*)
Ms R Schubert, BA (*Director of Drama*)
P E Swainson, BSc (**Chemistry*)
Ms M J Tarrega, MA
Miss M Thomas, MA
Dr I G Tompkins, MA, BD, DPhil (**IB Coordinator*)
J Underhill, MA
Mrs R Waddams, BSc (**Geography*)
K Whitley, BA
S Welti, LTA Club Coach
Mrs C Westwood, BA (**MFL*)
I L Williams, BEd

Registrar: Ms K Randall, BSc

School Medical Officer: Dr E A M Greville, MBChB
Chaplain: Revd Phillip Gration

Eltham College

Grove Park Road, London SE9 4QF

Tel:	020 8857 1455
email:	mail@eltham-college.org.uk
website:	www.elthamcollege.london
Twitter:	@ElthamCollegeUK
Facebook:	@ElthamCollegeOfficial
LinkedIn:	/Old-Elthamians

Eltham College is a thriving independent day school for boys aged 7 to 18, with a co-educational Sixth Form. From September 2020 it will move to become fully co-educational when it begins to welcome both girls and boys at Year 3 and Year 7 entry points.

It is a highly successful and exciting school which aims to provide a broad and balanced education to both boys and girls that will prepare them for the modern world. The College is regularly found amongst the leading academic schools in the country and boasts many county and national players in a range of sports. The co-curricular programme is wide and diverse.

The school has a distinctive character, born out of its Christian heritage, and continues to focus on the care of the individual. Strong pastoral care and a relaxed and unpretentious atmosphere make the school a happy and vibrant place.

There is an ambitious programme of development and expansion as well as a strong emphasis on staff development. Many staff choose to stay; but equally others are prepared and trained for future promotion in leading HMC schools.

History. The College was founded in 1842 as the School for the Sons of Missionaries and it began life as a small boarding school catering for these children whose parents were serving overseas, famously including the Olympic athlete Eric Liddell. The College moved to its present extensive site in Mottingham in 1912, with just under 70 acres of playing fields surrounding an elegant 18th century mansion. The College has developed into a day school primarily for boys and has been admitting girls into the Sixth Form since 1980. Eltham College now numbers 910 students in total, with 240 boys in the associated on-site Junior School and 240 students in the co-educational Sixth Form.

Location. The College is fortunate to occupy a spacious and pleasant site with extensive playing fields in the London Borough of Bromley, adjacent to the boroughs of Royal Greenwich and Lewisham. The College has easy access to the Kent countryside and the M25, which is just 15 minutes away. There are frequent fast trains to London Bridge, Charing Cross and Victoria (15–20 minutes). The majority of students live locally but the catchment area is expanding and students are drawn also from Kent, Dulwich, Croydon and Docklands.

Facilities. The College, set in almost 70 acres of land, enjoys superb facilities which have been improved considerably in recent years, including the Gerald Moore Gallery, new Science laboratories, a floodlit all-weather AstroTurf pitch and an extended Dining Hall. A substantial new building to house Languages and Maths classrooms, as well as a Sixth Form centre, is under development due to open in 2019. Alongside this will be a new Medical and Well-being Centre.

Curriculum. The College has maintained its grammar school ethos and puts academic achievement as its first priority. The curriculum is broad and balanced, incorporating both traditional and modern elements: for example, all students in Year 7 study both Latin and Mandarin. All students study at least one Modern Language to GCSE, and separate Sciences are available to all. Most students take ten GCSEs and three or four A Levels, chosen from a wide range of subjects. Recent examination results placed Eltham amongst the top day schools in the country: at GCSE 97.5% of grades were A* to B and the vast majority of Sixth Formers start with straight A*/A profiles. A Level results are consistently around 85% A* to B. Almost all students get in to their first choice university with over 80% at Russell Group universities and more than 20% of the cohort studying either medicine or courses at Oxford and Cambridge.

Co-Curricular. We are equally proud of our co-curricular activities which provide an impressively wide range of opportunities while ensuring that academic potential is fulfilled. We have an enviable reputation in Sport, Music and Drama: the College has a number of international and Olympic standard sports coaches; the quality and range of Music compares favourably with specialist Music schools; and audiences are frequently treated to spectacular school productions in our purpose-built theatre.

The majority of students participate in the vast amount of clubs and societies available, including (to name but a few), The Duke of Edinburgh's Award, Debating Society, Chess, Japanese Club, Eco-Eltham, Rocket Club and Water Polo. We encourage students to help those less fortunate than them by participating in charity fundraising events and the Lower Sixth Formers take part in our Community Service scheme.

Trips and expeditions are a major feature of life at Eltham College. These range from the traditional UK visits to more ambitious overseas trips, which in recent years have included Norway, Nepal, Tanzania, Italy and China. Language trips and exchanges are encouraged. Sport, Drama and Music tours are frequent occurrences, and have included the USA, Australia and South Africa.

Admission. Students are mainly admitted at the ages of 11, 13 and 16 via our own entrance examination. The College is academically highly selective, with over three applicants for every place. Approximately half our students come from primary schools and half from the preparatory sector, and the College has an unusually wide social mix, thanks, in part, to our generous Bursary scheme, which provides financial assistance for those unable to afford the full fees. In the most deserving cases, remission of up to 100% of fees is available.

Scholarships. It is our aim to provide as much assistance with the fees as we can to attract the brightest and most talented students to the College. Scholarships and Bursaries (financial assistance) are available to all students applying to the Senior School and Sixth Form.

Scholarships of not more than 50% of fees are awarded on Academic performance at 11+, 13+ and 16+, Music Scholarships at 11+, 13+ and 16+, as well as Sport, Art and Drama at 11+ and 16+.

Bursaries. As befits a school founded for the sons of missionaries and a former Direct Grant School, many students receive financial support to attend. Bursaries are available up to 100% of fees subject to ISBA confidential means test. Community Scholarships (for 11+ boys from the immediate neighbourhood) are assessed on financial need.

Term of Entry. The College normally accepts students only for the beginning of the academic year in September but, if gaps in particular year groups occur, it is willing to interview and test at any point in the year with a view to immediate or subsequent entry.

Junior School. The Grange, a large house on the College estate was converted and extended and now accommodates about 240 day boys in classes of approximately 22. The form rooms are complemented with an Assembly Hall, Science Room, Music Room, and Art, Design and Technology Room. With an emphasis on English and Mathematics, the curriculum, which includes Mandarin as the main Modern Foreign Language along with French in Year 6, provides an excellent foundation.

Excellence is also pursued outside the classroom whether on the sports field, stage or concert hall. In recent years we have had rugby teams with 100% wins, trebles singing at world famous venues and actors earning hosts of awards at local festivals. The Junior School is managed by its own Master who is responsible to the Headmaster.

Admission is at the age of 7, though there may also be an opportunity for boys to enter at 8+, 9+ and 10+ if there are places available. There is no entrance test for boys from Eltham College Junior School wishing to enter into the Senior School. Recommendation for is made on the basis of a boy's performance during their time in the Junior School and on their potential to flourish in the Senior School. Almost all boys therefore progress seamlessly through to Eltham College Senior School. This transition provides an opportunity for 11 years of uninterrupted education in healthy surroundings.

Junior School applications should be made to the Registrar.

Fees per term (2018–2019). Senior School £5,925, Junior School £5,230. Lunch: £278.

Charitable status. Eltham College is a Registered Charity, number 1058438. It exists to provide education for boys and girls.

Governors:
The Governing Body comprises the Chairman and Vice Chair, ten Trust Governors and eight Nominated Governors representing the Baptist Missionary Society, the Council for World Mission, the United Reformed Church, the London Boroughs of Bexley and Bromley, the Parents (two representatives elected by the parental body) and the Staff Common Room (one representative elected by the Teaching Staff).

Chairman of the Board: Mr S Wells, RIBA

Headmaster: Mr G Sanderson, MA Oxon, FRSA

Bursar: Mrs S Roxby
Deputy Head (*Curriculum*): Mr J Martin
Deputy Head (*Pastoral*): Mrs A Massey
Director of Studies: Mr E Wright, MA

Senior School Teaching Staff:

Art:
Miss S Heraghty, BA (*Director of Art*)
Mrs M Franklin, MA (*Head of Well-being*)
Mrs A C E Richards, BA (*part-time*)

Biology:
Mrs C M Hobbs, BSc
Mrs N Colwell, BSc
Mr S Marlow, BSc
Ms M Pokorny, BSc
Mrs H C Clough, BSc (*part-time*)
Mrs J C Perry, BSc (*part-time*)

Chemistry:
Dr F Williams, BSc, PhD
Ms E Lucas, BSc, MA
Mr J Copley, MSci
Dr J N Hill, BSc
Mrs J C Perry, BSc

Classics:
Dr E Michalopoulou, BA, MA, PhD
Mr J Barnes, MA

Computing, ICT and Computer Science:
Mr T Collins, MSc, BEng
Ms R Alcraft, BSc
Mr J P Pringle, BSc (*Curriculum Coordinator*)

Design and Technology:
Mr M E L Gennari, BSc (*Head of Universities and Enrichment*)
Mr P J Wren, BSc, TEng

Drama:
Mrs K Robinson, BA, MA
Mrs S Mann, BA
Mr C Devellerez, BA, MA

Economics:
Mrs S Potter
Mr S G Milne, MA (*Head of Sixth Form*)
Mrs K Evans, BSc

English:
Mr T C Mitchell, BA
Miss V Barsby, BA
Miss A Budden, BA
Miss V K Edgar, BA (*Deputy Head of Lower School*)
Mr J Owen, MA (*Head of Academic Scholarship*)

Geography:
Mr P Angel, MA, BSc, NPQSL
Mr A D Beattie, MA
Mr J P Chesterton, BSc (*Deputy Head of Middle School*)
Mr N Morris, BA
Miss K Richard, BSc

Mr J Willatt, BSc (*Assistant Head – Co-curricular*)

Geology:
Mr P Angel, MA, BSc, NPQSL
Miss K Richard, BSc

History:
Dr A Davies, BA, MA, PhD
Mr D R Grinstead, BA (*Head of Chalmers*)
Mr M E R Chesterton, BA (*Head of Moffat*)

Mathematics:
Mrs N Bilsby, BSc, MA (*Deputy Head – Sixth Form*)
Mr J L Baldwin, BSc (*Master in charge of Cricket, Head of Livingstone and Assistant Head of Maths – Lower School*)
Mrs R E Bevington, BSc
Mr V Broncz, BSc
Mr J P Crowley, BEng
Ms R Gordon, BSc (*Assistant Head – Teaching and Learning*)
Mr A Hon (*Deputy Head of Sixth Form*)
Mr L Watts, BSc (*Assistant Head – Head of Middle School*)
Mrs S Wood, BSc (*part-time*)
Ma R Alcraft, BSc, MSc (*part-time*)

Modern Languages:
Mr D Boudon, L-ès-L
Mr J Houghton, MA (*Chaplain*)
Ma C Franz, MA (*Head of German*)
Ms E Paull (*Head of Spanish*)
Mr F Nieto Almada, MA
Mr F Meier, MA (*Assistant Head – Head of Lower School*)
Miss L Scarantino, BA (*Head of Modern Foreign Languages*)
Mrs B Martin, BA
Ms M Su, BA, MA (*Head of Mandarin Chinese*)

Music:
Mr P Showell, BMus (*Director of Music*)
Mr L Swadkin, BMus (*Head of Academic Music*)
Mr N R Miller, BA (*Musician-in-Residence*)
Miss D Gibbs, BA(*Mus*), PhD

Physics:
Mr A Hindocha, BSc
Mr A Chan, MEng
Dr M Cianciaruso, PhD
Mr J Crowley, BEng
Mr S Whittaker, MSc (*Head of Science*)
Mr E B Wright, MA (*Director of Studies*)

Politics:
Mr S Marlow, MA

Psychology:
Ms M M Pokorny, BSc
Mr G E Marshall, MA, MSc

Religious Studies:
Ms E G Haste, BA
Mr G E Marshall, MA, MSc
Mrs S Stileman, MA

Sport:
Mr J L Baldwin, BSc (*Master in charge of Cricket, Head of Livingstone and Assistant Head of Maths – Lower School*)
Mr A Brown, BSc (*Head of Sport Scholarship*)
Mr S D Howard, BSc (*Director of Rugby*)
Mr B King, BSc
Mr D Lespierre, BSc
Mr G Hammond, BSc
Mr A Thomas, BEd (*Activities and Transition Coordinator*)

Mr E T Thorogood, BSc (*Head of School Sports*)
Mr M Wilkins (*part-time*)

Learning Support:
Mrs C Georgulas

Library:
Mrs C M Roche, MiL
Mrs J Angel

Development Director: Mr S McGrahan, MSc
Registrar: Mrs C St Clair-Charles

Junior School:

Master: Mr E R Cavendish, MA

Deputy Master: Mrs V Meier, MA

Director of Studies: Mrs N Devon

Junior School Teaching Staff:
Mr H Mitchell-Morgan (*Form Tutor Year 3*)
Miss H L Reed, BSc (*Head of Computing, Form Tutor Year 3*)
Miss N L Tutchings, BEd (*Subject Leader PSHE, Form Tutor Year 4*)
Mr S Oliver, BSc (*Head of Mathematics, Form Tutor Year 5*)
Miss M S Johnson, BA (*Head of Design and Technology, Form Tutor Year 4*)
Mrs N J Chamberlain, BEd (*Learning Support Coordinator, Form Tutor Year 5, PTA Rep*)
Mr T Laubach, (*Head of Tranistion and RS*)
Mt I Wearmouth (*Head of Year 5 and 6*)
Mr W Schaper, BEd (*Head of Geography, Form Tutor Year 6*)
Mr N Dale, BA (*Head of Science, Form Tutor Year 5*)
Mr M O'Dwyer, BEd (*Head of Co-curricular*)
Mrs A Carey, BA (*Head of English, Form Tutor Year 6*)
Mr M Alexander, BA (*Head of Junior School Music*)
Mrs B Martin (*French Teacher*)
Mrs H Pan, (*Head of Junior School Mandarin*)

Emanuel School

Battersea Rise, London SW11 1HS

Tel: 020 8870 4171
Fax: 020 8877 1424
email: enquiries@emanuel.org.uk
website: www.emanuel.org.uk
Twitter: @Emanuel_School
Facebook: @EmanuelSchoolAlumni

Motto: *Pour bien désirer*

The School was founded in Westminster by Lady Anne Dacre in 1594, and moved to its present site on the north side of Wandsworth Common in 1883 as one of the five schools of the United Westminster Schools Foundation.

Emanuel is a fully co-educational day school. We have 924 pupils with over 200 in the sixth form.

Admission. Each September 48 pupils are admitted into Y6 (10+), 96 pupils into Y7 (11+) and 6 to 8 into Y9 (13+). There are also 10–20 external candidates admitted into the sixth form each year.

The entry criteria are latest school report, headteacher's reference and entrance examination, held at the school each year in January. Registration for all entry points for September 2020 closes in October 2019. Entry to the sixth form is by interview and tests held in the November before entry.

Prospective parents are warmly encouraged to visit the school and there are many opportunities to do so. Please see our website or telephone for details.

Fees per term (2018–2019). £6,194 covering tuition, some stationery, books and lunch. Extras charged are for individual instrumental tuition and some external visits and trips.

Site and buildings. Emanuel was founded in 1594. In 1883 it moved from Westminster to the present site in Wandsworth. The original Victorian building is the core of the school, with most of its classrooms, a fine library, theatre and a beautiful chapel. The new Dacre building opened in 2017, with outstanding art facilities, galleries and a film studio.

The school's playing fields adjoin the school buildings together with a sports hall, full-sized indoor swimming pool and fives courts. The school has a boathouse on the Thames by Barnes Bridge and further pitches at 'Blagdons' on the A3 near Raynes Park.

Scholarships and assistance with fees (bursaries) and exhibitions. There are academic and co-curricular scholarships available. Pupils may hold more than one scholarship. All types of scholarship can be topped up using school bursaries to a maximum of 100% of the school fee, depending on financial need.

Academic scholarships are awarded at 10+, 11+ and 13+ on the basis of outstanding performance in the school entrance examinations held in January. At 16+ academic scholarships are awarded to internal candidates on the basis of internal tests and to external candidates on the basis of their performance in the interviews and assessment tests.

Candidates applying for Music, Art, Drama and Sports scholarships must meet the required minimum standard in the entrance examinations (60%) before a scholarship can be awarded. Thereafter each department has specific criteria for their scholarship requirements. Please see our website for details: www.emanuel.org.uk

Exhibitions are awards of up to £1,000 on the basis of a pupil's high attainment in the entrance exams and scholarship assessments.

Bursaries are intended to help parents of pupils who can demonstrate financial need. Most bursaries are used to top up scholarships.

Full details of scholarships, exhibitions and bursaries can be found on the school website or by contacting the Admissions Secretary.

Organisation. There are two forms for pupils who join at Y6 (10+). Pupils joining at Y7 (11+) are placed into six forms. Primary responsibility for their care rests with the form teacher and the head of year, under the overall supervision of the Head of the Lower School, who deals with Years 6, 7 and 8. As all pupils move from Year 9 into Year 10 there is a regrouping along the lines of the subjects chosen for GCSE examinations. In the sixth form a tutor system operates.

Pupils are placed in houses when they join the school and they stay in these houses throughout their school career. Although originally intended as a means of fostering competition in games, these houses have developed over many years a strong community spirit.

For more details please ask for the school prospectus or go to the website.

Times. The normal school day runs from 8.25 am to 3.45 pm, but many activities extend into the late afternoon after school. Some school activities, especially sports fixtures, but also music and drama rehearsals, take place on Saturdays and Sundays.

Curriculum. Pupils are prepared for GCSEs and IGCSEs. There is a wide range of options with most pupils taking nine subjects.

Thereafter, in the sixth form, there is a further range of options from which pupils choose three or four A Level subjects leading to examination at the end of the upper sixth. Pupils also complete the extended project qualification (EPQ). Sixth form leavers go on to a variety of institutions, including Oxbridge and Russell Group universities, art colleges, music and drama conservatoires or universities overseas

Religious Education. There are two Chaplains who work in the school, whose general religious tenor is that of the Church of England. A daily service is held in the school chapel. Pupils in Years 6, 7, 8 and 9 receive one or two periods per week of religious education, which continues into Years 10, 11 and the sixth forms as a GCSE or A Level option.

The Arts. Emanuel has a long-standing tradition of excellence in Art, Music and Drama and all pupils are encouraged to participate in one or more of these activities. The school has a chapel choir and a chamber choir, an orchestra and ensemble groups and there are major concerts and a musical production each year.

There is a specialist suite of art rooms in the new Dacre building with facilities for all kinds of creative activity. A great deal of high quality work is displayed around the school and several pupils a year go on to foundation courses at art college.

Drama is taught throughout the school and there is a major school production every year, usually in the spring term, with many smaller-scale events during the year.

We have an annual arts festival in July with an art exhibition, summer serenade, performances by pupils and visitors and a series of talks by visiting speakers.

Games and Activities. Rugby, cricket and rowing are the main school games for the boys. For the girls the main activities are netball, cricket, hockey and rowing. Many other activities become available as a pupil moves up the school. Each pupil will have one games afternoon each week and other opportunities for physical education and swimming. The school has its own playing fields, sports hall, swimming pool, fives courts and boathouse on the Thames.

The Duke of Edinburgh's Award scheme is offered to pupils from Year 9 upwards. Community outreach is arranged for senior pupils and can involve hospital visiting or voluntary work in local primary schools, charity shops or our local hospice. More formal work experience is offered as part of an extensive careers and further education advice programme from Year 9 upwards. There is a very strong Young Enterprise programme in the lower sixth.

Careers. Careers and further education advice is readily available from an experienced team. There is an annual careers convention for the senior school when many representatives from the professions and commerce visit the school to talk about career options. All pupils become members of the Independent Schools Careers Organisation (included in the fees).

Old Emanuel Association. *Membership Secretary*: Mr Brian Cassidy.

Charitable status. Emanuel School (administered by the United Westminster Schools' Foundation) is a Registered Charity, number 309267. Its aims and objectives are for "the bringing up of children in virtue and good and laudable arts".

Governing Body:

Chairman: F R Abbott, BA
Vice Chairman: C F Scott

M Jaigirder, MA
Vice Admiral P Dunt, CB, DL, ADD
Alderman D Graves, MA
Ms M A D'Mello, BSc, MSc
Mrs M M Parsons, MA
Mrs S Sassoon, MA
The Very Revd V A Stock, OAM, Hon D Surrey, AKC, FRSA
Mrs J Sutcliffe, MA
J G M Wates, CBE

Clerk and Receiver: R W Blackwell, MA

Headmaster: Mr Robert Milne, BA

Deputy Head (Pastoral): Mr R Kothakota, MEd Buckingham
Deputy Head (Academic): Mrs J L Peters, MA Oxon
Deputy Head (Staffing and External Relations): Dr S J Wakefield, PhD King's College London
Assistant Head (Academic): Dr R M Evans, DPhil Oxon
Assistant Head, Co-Curricular: J P Layng, BSc Nottingham, MCIEA, MSB
Assistant Head, Teaching and Learning: Miss J A Johnson, MA Oxon
Head of Sixth Form: Ms K Bainbridge, MA King's College London
Head of Middle School: Mr S P Andrews, BA Swansea
Head of Lower School: Ms H C Windsor, BA Cardiff
Senior Chaplain: Revd R F Walker, BSc, BD Glasgow, ThM
Assistant Chaplain: The Revd S Labran, BA Leeds, MPhil Cantab

Teaching staff:
* Head of Department

Miss K Adams, MSc
Mr P Adams, MA (*Classics)
Mr S Andrews, BA
Mr R Arnott, BA
Ms K Bainbridge, MA
Mr J Barber, BA (*MFL, *French)
Mr R Bishop, MEng (*Mathematics)
Miss H Blaikie, BSc
Dr P Blum, BA, PhD (*Learning Support)
Mrs R Brown, MA Oxon (*Science, Chemistry)
Mrs E Burbidge, BA
Ms H Burnett, BA
Ms U Casais, BA
Ms R Chetwood, MA
Mr R Chuter, MA
Miss L Cleveland, BTh Oxon, MTh
Ms V Cojbasic, BSc
Ms R Cottone, MA
Miss H Coulson, BA (*Geography)
Mr C Csaky, BSc, MA Ed (*ICT)
Dr M Dancy, BSc, PhD
Mr W Davis, BA
Ms V Dittmer, BSc
Mr J Dunley, BA
Dr R Evans, DPhil Oxon
Mr N Fazaluddin, BSc
Miss C Fearnley, BA (*Drama)
Miss L Fitzgibbon, BSc
Mr W Ford, MA
Mr S Gaynor, BSc
Mr S Gregory, MA Oxon, ARCO (*Music)
Miss C Greenwood, MA
Mr N Guegan, MA
Mr T Gwynne, BSc
Mr J Hale, BA
Mr D Hand, BA

Mr W Hanson, BA (*Physical Education*)
Mr S Healy, BA
Miss J Henderson, BA
Mr M Hipperson, BA
Miss L Holden, LLB
Ms C Hoult, MA
Mr N House, MA
Mr H Jackson, BA (*German*)
Mr S James, BAEd
Miss J Johnson, MA Oxon (*English*)
Mr S Jones, MPhil (*History*)
Mr A Keddie, MA Oxon, ACIB
Mr R Kothakota, MEd
Mr P King, BSc
The Revd S Labran, BA, MPhil (*Religious Studies*)
Mr W Lai, MA, MEng Cantab
Mr J Layng, BSc, MCIEA, MSB
Mr A Leadbetter, BSc
Ms C Lepetre, Licence d'Anglais
Mrs R Lewis, MA
Mrs A Limon, BA
Ms S MacMillan, BA (*Art*)
Miss H Malik, BSc
Miss E McCloud, BA
Mr A McMahon, BA Oxon
Mr P McMahon, MA Cantab
Mr R Milne, BA (*Headmaster*)
Miss K Moore, BA
Mrs J Morrison-Bartlett, BSc
Miss E Moseley, BSc
Miss R Mott, BA
Mr H Nilsson, BA (*Politics*)
Dr S Parsons, MSc (*Physics*)
Miss D Patel, MA (*Biology*)
Mrs M Pattinson
Mrs J Peters, MA Oxon
Mrs S Potts, BMus
Mr R Price, BSc (*Design and Technology*)
Mr C Reed, BA
Mr E Rice, BA Cantab
Mrs S Riley, MBA (*Life Education*)
Mr M Roberts, BSc
Mr B Rogers, BSc
Mrs S Shaw, Dip SpLD
Mr M Shetzer, MA
Miss N Sidhu, BSc
Miss L Stoby, BA
Mr M Swift, MFA
Miss N Tawil, BA
Miss R Tendler, BA
Mr R Tong, LLB (*Business Studies & Economics*)
Dr S Wakefield, PhD
The Revd R Walker, ThM (*Chaplain*)
Mrs V Walton, BA Oxon
Mrs L Wilson, BSc (*Psychology*)
Miss H Windsor, BA
Mr R Worrell, BA
Miss C Yeomans, BSc
Ms A Zaratiegui, MA (*Spanish*)

Visiting Music Teachers:
Ms L Anstee, Mus Dip RAM
Mr F Baird, Dip TCL, ARCM
Mrs H Belsey, BMus
Mr A Boushell, BMus
Ms C Boushell, MMus, PG Dip, ArtDipOp RCM
Mrs Y Burova, BMus, GSMD
Mr H Cameron Penny, BMus
Mr F Crowther, BMus
Mr M Davis, BMus
Ms L Easton, BA

Mr B Havinden-Williams, BMus
Mr S Kinrade, BMus
Ms K Lauder, BMus RNCM
Mr M Livingstone, BA
Mr J McCredie, MMus, CertEd
Mr J Oldfield, MA, PG Dip, ArtDipOp
Mr G Philips, BMus, GSMD
Mr P Sharda, LLCM
Mr M Spiers, BMus
Dr F Tarli, MMus, PhD
Mr D Watts, BMus RNCM
Mr T Williams, MA, Dip ABRSM

Senior Librarian: Mr T Jones, BA, PG Dip
Assistant Librarian: Mr G Dibden
Director of Finance and Administration: Mr J Sharp, MA Cantab, ACA
Development Director: Mr J Clark, BA
Executive Assistant to the Headmaster: Miss C Procter, BA
Head of Admissions and Communications: Miss E Maclean, BSc
Marketing and Communications Coordinator: Miss B Gore, BA
Admissions Secretary: Ms D Shuttleworth

Epsom College

College Road, Epsom, Surrey KT17 4JQ

Tel:	01372 821004 (Headmaster)
	01372 821234 (Director of Admissions)
	01372 821133 (Bursar)
email:	admissions@epsomcollege.org.uk
website:	www.epsomcollege.org.uk
Twitter:	@EpsomCollegeUK
Facebook:	/Epsom-College

Motto: *Deo non Fortuna*

Founded in 1855, Epsom College is situated in 85 acres of parkland estate close to Epsom Downs and is only 15 miles from central London. Epsom is one of the most successful co-ed boarding and day schools for girls and boys aged 11–18.

In 2017, 86% of A Level examinations were graded A*–B, a record performance for the College. Likewise, GCSE results eclipsed previous years with over half of examinations awarded A*, and 78% graded A*–A.

Almost all leavers go on to degree courses, especially at the research-led universities. The Russell Group universities are particularly popular, with Bristol, Durham and Oxford and Cambridge strongly represented each year.

Boarding is central to the College with many of our boarders – both week and full boarders – living within 25 miles. The House system is central to our success, ensuring a strong sense of community and support. All pupils, whether day, weekly or full boarders, are placed within one of our 13 Houses. Year groups mix, and a strong sense of pride in the House, and care for fellow pupils of all ages is encouraged.

Numbers and Houses. The College has been fully co-educational from September 1996. There are just under 890 pupils in the School, around 60% are day pupils.

There are 343 in the Sixth Form. The College has 19% of pupils from overseas and a spread of 38 nationalities. The boy to girl ratio is 2:1 in the senior year groups and 1:1 in the Sixth Form and Lower School (Years 7 and 8).

There are 6 separate houses for girls: two boarding houses, Crawfurd and Wilson; three day houses, Murrell,

Raven and Rosebery; and a Sixth Form house, White, for both boarding and day girls.

The boys' boarding houses are: Fayrer, Forest, Granville and Holman. All boarding Sixth and Fifth Formers and Upper Fourth Formers have study-bedrooms in the modernised Houses.

In the Michaelmas Term there are two weekend exeats roughly halfway through each half of term, in addition to a two week half-term holiday. In each of the other two terms there is one exeat in the first half followed by a one week half-term holiday. Weekly boarders can go home every weekend.

The day boy Houses are: Carr, Propert and Robinson. Day boys and girls are full members of the School community and have lunch and tea in College. All members of the School, boarders and day, eat centrally in the Dining Room which makes for efficiency and strengthens the sense of community.

Pupils who are ill are looked after in the School Medical Centre which has a qualified sister always on duty. One of the two (one male, one female) School Doctors visits daily except Sundays.

Academic Work. In the Lower School the design of the curriculum follows a number of key principles: Skills for the future, learning to learn, well-being and 21st century education.

Middle Fourth (Year 9) pupils take English, Mathematics, Physics, Chemistry, Biology, Religious Studies, Drama, Geography, History, Art, Music, Information Technology and Design Technology. Normally two languages are studied, chosen from French, German, Spanish and Mandarin. The College will select two sets of pupils to study Latin from those who perform well on Latin papers at Scholarship and CE. The normal programme is to enter the Middle Fourth at the age of thirteen and take the main block of GCSEs at the end of the Fifth Form (Year 11). Almost everyone then enters the Sixth Form of approximately 325 pupils. Students will choose 3 principal subjects to study at A Level or Pre-U. These will then be enhanced by choices from the core curriculum where they can choose from: Internationalism, Research & Analysis or Core Skills. They will also benefit from a varied lecture programme and Epsom's award winning service programme. A wide range of A Level subjects are offered. Options in Business Management, Politics and Government, Photography and Economics are introduced to complement the broad range of subjects already available at GCSE. The courses are linear meaning all examinations are taken at the end of Upper Sixth.

There are excellent facilities for work in one's own study, in the main Library or one of the specialist Departmental Libraries. The school is fully networked and has the latest Wi-Fi router system, including all Houses, and has over 600 computers alongside a further 600 personal computer points, as well as digital projectors and electronic whiteboards used across the curriculum. There are five fully-equipped Information Technology rooms and Design Technology is housed in award-winning buildings, with state-of-the-art, industrial-standard CAD and CAM facilities.

Higher Education. Almost all students go on to university, with the occasional student choosing to follow another path, such as Art Foundation. In recent years, Medicine, Law, Engineering, Economics and Business degrees have proved particularly popular degree options, but Epsom students have been successful in gaining places on a broad variety of competitive courses. Approximately 70% of all pupils go to Russell Group or 1994 Group universities each year.

Careers. Careers education is offered from the first term at Epsom and is particularly well developed in the Sixth Form. Epsom has an experienced team of careers tutors with specialists in Medicine, Oxbridge Entrance, Engineering and American University Entrance. There is a well-stocked Careers Room attached to the Library, and much care is taken to assess a pupil's potential and aptitude and to provide proper guidance on careers. All pupils belong to Inspiring Futures and all Fifth Form pupils take careers aptitude tests through their Futurewise programme. There is a well-established work experience programme and a Careers Convention is organised each year for the Fifth Form and Lower Sixth. The College also hosts a GAP Year Fair.

The **Religious Teaching** and the Chapel Services follow the doctrines of the Church of England, but there are always pupils of other denominations and faiths. Multi-faith services take place regularly. There is a Senior Chaplain who works together with a visiting Rabbi and a Hindu priest to ensure a multi-faith approach. Muslim pupils attend prayers at the College.

Games and other Activities. Games contribute much to the general physical development of girls and boys at Epsom and the College has a strong tradition of high standards in many sports. The very large number of teams means that almost all pupils are able to represent the School each year. A wide range of sports is available: Rugby, Hockey, Netball, Cricket, Tennis, Athletics and Swimming, Squash (6 courts), Target Rifle Shooting (with an indoor range), Football, Cross-Country, Fencing, Golf, Badminton, Rounders, Basketball, Judo and Sailing. The Indoor Sports Centre, housing two sports halls, a fencing salle and climbing wall, was opened in 1989 by the Patron of Epsom College, Her Majesty The Queen.

The Target Rifle Team has a long history of excellence at Target Rifle Shooting, both small-bore and full-bore, and over the last 20 years has consistently been the premier rifle shooting school in the UK. The College Rifle team has won the National Championships – the Ashburton Shield – 14 times in the past 26 years and 15 times overall. The College holds the record for the highest number of Ashburton wins by a single school.

The CCF has Naval, Army and RAF Sections and pupils over the age of 14 are expected to join for 2 years when much time is spent on camping and expeditions. Older boys and girls may join instead The Duke of Edinburgh's Award scheme, while others are involved with the service programme in Epsom where they contribute to the community and take a leadership role in service projects.

The College ensures that all pupils take advantage of an extensive range of activities from Dance to Design Textiles.

Music, Art and Drama. There are three full-time Music teachers and a large staff of visiting music teachers. Over one-third of the pupils learn musical instruments and virtually any instrument can be taught, and many take singing lessons. There are four Choirs, a School Orchestra and seven major instrumental ensembles, including Big Band, Clarinet, Saxophone and Classical Guitar. Visits are arranged each term to concerts in London and elsewhere. The Music School has a Concert Hall and 18 practice rooms. Recent productions have included *The Coronation of Poppea, Sweeney Todd, Les Misérables, Jesus Christ Superstar and Cabaret.*

Art, which includes pottery, printing and sculpture as well as painting and drawing, is housed in a spacious building with 8 studios, a Library, an Exhibition Room and an Exhibition Hall. There are two full-time Art teachers and one part-time, and Art is studied up to GCSE and A Level.

There are several major Drama productions each year, from classical theatre to the modern musical, produced by a range of staff and pupils. These give boys and girls an opportunity to develop their talents and interests in Drama. In 2004 staff and pupils wrote their own show which was performed at the Royal Albert Hall, with over 1,000 performers, to mark the 150th Anniversary of the College.

Admission. Almost all pupils enter Epsom College in September. There are 3 entry levels: 11+, 13+ and 16+.

For those entering at 11+ candidates will be assessed for entry in January of Year 6. They will sit papers in English, Mathematics and verbal reasoning, and these tests will be supported by a short interview and a report from their current school.

For those entering at 13+ after reaching a satisfactory standard in the Common Entrance or Scholarship Examination or the Epsom College January Entry Test examination set specially for those who are not prepared for Common Entrance. All boys and girls will be expected to sit a Pre-Test Examination in their Year 6 of corresponding entry at 13+. If the required standard is achieved, a pupil will be offered a place for entry at 13+, conditional upon maintaining the same standards at the present school and they will also sit a test in the year of entry for setting purposes. Some enter the school later than this and there is always a direct entry into the Sixth Form, both for girls and boys.

A boy or girl may be registered at any age by sending in the registration form and fee. All enquiries should be sent to the Director of Admissions from whom a prospectus may be obtained.

Fees per term (2018–2019). Boarders £12,421; Weekly Boarders £11,283; Day Pupils £8,422. Lower School: Weekly boarders £8,154; Day pupils £6,255.

The fees are inclusive and cover the normal cost of a pupil's education. The main extras are for examination fees, private tuition and a pupil's personal expenses. Fees for day pupils include lunch and tea.

There is a College Store for the provision of uniform, clothing and other requirements.

Entrance Scholarships. Scholarships are available at 11+, 13+ and 16+ entry for excellence in academic study, the arts or sport.

Girls and boys holding awards invariably go on to contribute much to school life throughout their time at Epsom. The College community holds them in high regard.

Candidates may apply for more than one award. Scholarships and Exhibitions will only be awarded if candidates of sufficient merit present themselves.

If a Scholarship or Exhibition is not awarded on entry to the College in Year 7 or 9, there is a further opportunity to be promoted to the status of an award holder in Year 12 (Lower Sixth).

Bursaries. Over the past six years, Epsom has reduced the value of non means-tested Scholarships and Awards, which can be worth up to 10% a year. This has enabled us to double the bursary fund which is allocated to families with demonstrable financial need.

In turn this has helped us, with Educational Trust support, to widen our access to disadvantaged families. This is one of the College's declared aims in line with both Government and HMC guidance. Potential scholarship applicants are encouraged to seek extra financial support, if appropriate, by way of a means-tested Bursary. Application forms are available on request from the Bursar or Admissions Registrar.

Old Epsomians. The Old Epsomian Club promotes sporting activities, social gatherings and networking events among its former pupils, with eight international chapters and an online database. On leaving the College, all pupils automatically become lifelong members of the OE Club and they are invited back regularly for reunions, the OE Dinner and Founder's Day. They also receive several publications each year, including the OE magazine. Bursaries are available for the sons and daughters of OEs who wish to attend the College.

Charitable status. Epsom College is a Registered Charity, number 312046. It exists for the advancement of education.

Patron: Her Most Gracious Majesty The Queen
President: Lord McColl, CBE, MS, FRCS, FACS

Visitor: The Right Reverend The Lord Bishop of Guildford

Chairman: Dr A J Wells, MB BS, DRCOG, MRCGP
Vice-Chair: Mrs Karen Thomas, BM Soton, FRCS Orth
Treasurer: Mr A J Pianca, FCA
Dr J Bolton, MA, MB BChir, FRCPsych
Mrs F Boulton, BSc, MA
Dr H H Bowen-Perkins, LMSSA, MRCS Eng, LRCP Lond, MB BS
Mr K Budge, MA Oxon
Mr E Chandler, MA Cantab
Mrs B Dolbear, LLB
The Very Revd D Gwilliams, BA, MA
Mr J A Hay
Dr S Lipscomb, MA Oxon, MSt Oxon, DPhil Oxon
Mr D Mahoney, MA Cantab
Mr G B Pincus, MBE, MIPA
Mr P Stanford, BA
Dr A J Vallance-Owen, MBE, MBA, FRCS Edin
Mr C Watson, ACA

Bursar and Clerk to the Governing Body: Mrs S E Teasdale, BSc Lond, FCA

Headmaster: Mr J A Piggot, BA Cardiff, MA Liverpool

Second Master: Mr P J Williams, BSc Dunelm
Deputy Head Academic: Mr R Alton, MA Cantab
Director of Academic Operations: Mrs T Muller, MA Oxon
Assistant Head, Total Curriculum: Mr A J Bustard, BA Swansea
Assistant Head, Teaching Staff and Examinations: Mr W Keat, MA Lond
Assistant Head, Sixth Form: Mr N Russell, MA Liverpool
Assistant Head, Pupil Welfare: Mrs H E Keevil, BA Exeter
Head of Lower School: Mr Ed Lance, BSc Durham

Heads of Year:
Head of Sixth Form: Mr N Russell, MA Liverpool
Head of Lower Sixth: Mr M C Conway, MA Cantab
Head of Fifth Form: Ms T St Clair-Ford, BA Cantab, MA Chichester
Head of Upper Fourth: Mrs C C Winmill, MA Bordeaux
Head of Transition: Mrs F C Drinkall, BSc Loughborough
Head of Third Form: Mr R C G Young, BSc Bath

Headmaster's Office:
Headmaster's PA: Mrs C Beesley
Assistant to Headmaster's PA: Mrs M McDonald
Deputy Heads' Secretary: Mrs E Bauchop, Mrs S Lawrence

Admissions and Marketing Office:
Director of Admissions: Mrs C Kent
Director of Marketing: Mr M Tobin
Admissions Manager: Mr M Day, BEd Trent Polytechnic
Communications Manager: Ms L Kendall
Marketing & Events: Ms J Busby
Admissions Assistant: Mrs D Upot

Bursars Office:
Bursar's PA: Ms K Plimmer

Epsom College Education Trust and OE Club:
Director of Education Trust: Ms Karen Doyle, BA Warwick
Education Trust Coordinator: Mr C Collins
OE Club Secretary: Mrs S Croucher
Education Trust Administrator: Mrs C Mowbray

Examinations Office:
Database Administrator: Mrs N Elliott

The Royal Medical Foundation:
Administrator: Mr C Titman
RMF Caseworker: Mrs H Jones

Eton College

Windsor, Berkshire SL4 6DW

Tel: 01753 370611 (Admissions)
            01753 370100 (Head Master)
            01753 370540 (Bursar)
email: admissions@etoncollege.org.uk
website: www.etoncollege.com

Eton College is a full boarding school for boys with 1,320 pupils, situated next to the historic town of Windsor, Berkshire. It was founded in 1440 by King Henry VI with the purpose of educating 70 poor, but talented boys. The school's ethos is to take talented pupils with character and give them the skills to progress through life as happy, successful and socially responsible adults. Academic results are important but so too are the skills gained from co-curricular activities including music, drama, art, sports, CCF, outdoor education and the many different societies. At Eton the emphasis is on finding, nurturing and giving value to each pupil's unique talents.

Over one fifth of the boys at the school currently receive means-tested bursary support and there are also a number of scholarships available. See our website www.etoncollege.com for further details.

Recent Developments. Eton College's Head Master, Simon Henderson, joined in September 2015. Simon was previously at the helm of Bradfield College and has built a reputation as a progressive and innovative head. He knows Eton well having taught history here for eight years; four as head of department. Simon is a graduate of Brasenose College, Oxford and is married with a young family. The Lower Master (the senior Deputy Head) is Su Wijeratna, who joined from St Paul's Girls' School (where she was Deputy Head) in 2017. Su is Eton's first ever female Lower Master.

Centre for research and learning. The world of teaching and the way young people learn is set to be transformed through the advent of new technologies (including apps) and a better understanding of neuroscience. The Tony Little Centre for Research and Innovation in Learning was opened in May 2015, with the aim of putting Eton into the forefront of global teaching and learning development.

The centre works alongside schools and universities around the world to exchange ideas and share best practice, carry out research and analyse new developments – with the aim of continually improving our outstanding teaching and learning experience for our pupils, as well as society more widely.

Academic achievement. Academic excellence is central to Eton life, with the vast majority of our pupils going on to attend leading universities; an increasing number are also attending leading universities in the United States. Our pupils go on to study a range of subjects as undergraduates including the sciences (inc. medicine), humanities/English, modern languages and economics/business. Eton has its own dedicated Learning Support centre for boys with special educational needs or specific learning challenges, such as dyslexia or dyspraxia.

Sport plays a central role in school life, both within and outside the curriculum. There are nearly 30 different activities on offer, ranging from the more familiar football, rugby,

cricket and rowing to Eton's own unique sports – the Wall and Field Games.

We have a range of highly skilled professional coaches and masters leading our extensive games programme. Success on the field is important, and we have provision for elite athletes, but at Eton we consider the central ethos of sport – encouraging teamwork as well as leadership, dedication, respect, physical fitness and well-being, to be the real goal for our pupils.

The Arts. Over 1,300 music lessons are taught each week at The Music Schools by a staff of seven full-time masters and 70 specialist visiting teachers. Our facilities include a modern concert hall, orchestral rehearsal hall, recording studio, rock studio, numerous teaching and practice rooms, and a music library. There are two chapel choirs, a concert choir, a choral society, three orchestras, two concert bands, two big bands and a large number of smaller ensembles. Senior boys regularly put on their own concerts – a tradition initiated by Hubert Parry during his time as a boy at Eton. A number of music scholarships are available.

Eton's Director of Drama is actor and director Scott Handy, who is a former member of the RSC, with numerous film and television credits to his name. More than 20 theatrical productions are staged at the school each year, affording boys the opportunity to take part both onstage and behind the scenes; these opportunities have seen a number of former pupils forging very successful careers in the industry. The facilities include the 400-seater Farrer Theatre, a flexible auditorium with a scenic workshop, wardrobe, make-up studio and dressing rooms. The smaller Caccia Studio seats 100.

Our stunning Drawing Schools have opportunities for printmaking, computer graphics and digital photography, painting and drawing. There are also two purpose-built 3D studios with facilities for sculpture (in wood, metal, plaster) and ceramics. Regular exhibitions are staged and there is also an ambitious Artist in Residence programme. Art and design features in the curriculum but pupils are also encouraged to use The Drawing Schools in their free time.

Additional activities. Eton societies are extremely popular and there are a large number available (around 50 at any one time), covering a broad range of topics – from the Mountaineering Society to the Political Society, the Culinary Society to the Medical Society and the recently formed Tech Club and Investment Society.

Pupils are also encouraged to develop a sense of social responsibility and they give back in a number of ways, including volunteering with school children or the elderly and taking part in charity fundraising events, such as the annual Eton Community Fair.

Pastoral Care. The welfare of boys at Eton College is taken extremely seriously and a robust system is in place, specifically designed to enable staff to spot problems as early as possible. The house structure, tutor groups, our own health centre the Stephenson Centre for Wellbeing (housing an adolescent psychiatrist, two clinical psychologists and a counsellor) and the chaplaincy teams (with representatives of multiple faiths) all play a role within this system. Our pastoral care procedures are reviewed regularly by the Head Master, Lower Master and Deputy Head (Pastoral).

Admissions. The majority of pupils are admitted to the school aged 13. For entry up to and including 2019 registration is required by the age of 10 years and 6 months. For entry in 2020 and beyond registration is required by 30th June in UK School Year 5 (the academic year in which a boy reaches the age of 10); please note these are strict deadlines. There are scholarships for entry aged 13 – the academic King's Scholarship and the Music Scholarship – as well as means-tested bursaries. There are also a small number of

Sixth Form Scholarships and Sixth Form admissions available.

The Admissions process for entry up to and including 2019 consists of a report from the pupil's current school, an interview and a specially designed computer test. For entry in 2020 and beyond the process will also include the ISEB Common Pre-tests and an assessed group activity. A visit to the school either before registration or before assessment is recommended. Please contact the Admissions Team via www.etoncollege.com for further details.

Fees per term (2018–2019). £13,556.

Charitable status. Eton College is a Registered Charity, number 1139086.

Visitor: The Right Revd the Lord Bishop of Lincoln

Provost: The Lord Waldegrave of North Hill, PC, MA

Vice-Provost: Dr Andrew Gailey, CVO, MA, PhD

Fellows:
Professor Michael Proctor, MA, MMath, ScD, FRS, FRAS, FIMA (*Provost of King's College Cambridge, Senior Fellow*)
The Duchess of Wellington, OBE, BA
Professor Kim Nasmyth, PhD, FRS
Dr Caroline Moore, MA, PhD
Mr Hamish Forsyth, MA
Mr Mark Esiri, LLB, MBA
Sir George Leggatt, MA
Mr Thomas Seaman, MA, MBA
Sir Mark Lyall Grant, MA
Dame Helena Morrissey, MA

Honorary Fellows:
Sir Simon Robertson
Sir Eric Anderson, KT, MA, MLitt, DLitt, FRSE
Lady Smith, OBE, BA
Mr David Reid Scott, MA

Head Master: Mr Simon Henderson, MA

Lower Master: Mrs Susan Wijeratna, BA

Bursar: Miss Janet Walker, MA, FCA

Deputy Head (Pastoral): Mr David Gregg, BSc

Deputy Head (Academic): Mr Tom Hawkins, MA

Deputy Head (Co-Curricular): Mr Justin Nolan, MA

Director of Outreach & Partnership: Mr Tom Arbuthnott, MA, MPhil

Conduct: The Revd Stephen Gray, MA

Precentor: Mr Tim Johnson, MA

Clerk & Legal Advisor to Provost & Fellows: Ms Serena Hedley-Dent, MA

Buildings & Facilities Director: Mr Ian Mellor, BA, FRICS

HR Director: Miss Anna Tomlinson, BA, MSc

Finance Director: Mrs Catherine Taylor, BA, ACA

Director of Development: Miss Jane Hatch, BA, MBA

Heads of Departments:
Art: I Burke, MA
Classics: C J Smart, MA
Computing & Digital Education: J W F Stanforth, MA
Design & Technology: K R N Ross, BSc
Divinity: W I N Griffith, MA
Economics & Politics: P R K Bird, BA
English: B B Cooper, MA, MPhil, PhD
Geography: D E Anderson, BA, DPhil
History: D Yuravlivker, BA, MSc, PhD

Mathematic: J E Thorne, BSc
Modern Languages: J M Burrows, MA
Music: T J Johnson, MA
Options: A J Maynard, MA
Physical Education: P I Macleod, BEd, BA
The Sciences: K Frearson, MA

Head of Teaching & Learning: J M Noakes, MA
Head of Career Education: G D Fussey, BSc

Exeter School

Victoria Park Road, Exeter, Devon EX2 4NS

Tel:	01392 273679 (Headmaster/Registrar)
	01392 258712 (Bursar/Office)
Fax:	01392 498144
email:	admissions@exeterschool.org.uk
website:	www.exeterschool.org.uk
Twitter:	@ExeterSchoolUK

Motto: ΧΡΥΣΟΣ ΑΡΕΤΗΣ ΟΥΚ ΑΝΤΑΞΙΟΣ

Founded in 1633, Exeter School occupies a 25-acre site, located within a mile of the city centre, having moved from its original location in the High Street in 1880. Some of its well-designed buildings date from that time but many new buildings have been added over the past twenty years and the school now enjoys first-rate facilities on a very attractive open site.

The school is fully co-educational and offers education to boys and girls from 7 to 18. It has its own Junior School of around 200 pupils, nearly all of whom transfer to the Senior School at the age of 11. The Senior School has around 720 pupils, including a Sixth Form of 220. (*For further information about Exeter Junior School, see entry in IAPS section.*)

Exeter School is a well-run school with high all-round standards and very good academic results. It prides itself on strong cultural, sporting and extra curricular achievement. Its music is outstanding and there is a strong tradition of performance drawn from all age groups in the School. It offers a very wide range of sports and maintains consistently high standards especially in hockey, rugby and cricket. It is well placed for outdoor pursuits (e.g. Duke of Edinburgh's Award scheme and Ten Tors on Dartmoor) and has its own very large voluntary CCF unit. The School is closely involved with the life of the City of Exeter and its university and it has a substantial commitment to support the local community.

Buildings, Grounds and General Facilities. The Senior School block includes a large multi-purpose assembly hall, a library, a private study area, dining hall and Sixth Form Centre as well as many well-appointed classrooms. A major refurbishment of the former boarding accommodation to include a new Library and Study Centre was completed for September 2006. There are separate buildings on the site housing the Chapel, the Music School, the Science Centre, Art Studios, Drama Studio, Design and Technology Centre and Exonian Centre. The Science Centre provides 14 laboratories and there are four fully-equipped computer rooms. All departments have access to their own computers and the School has a wide, controlled access to the internet. In 2005 the school opened a new dance studio and a fitness suite to add to the existing sports facilities of a large modern well-equipped Sports Hall with its own squash courts and access to on-site floodlit all-weather sports arena, top-grade all-weather tennis/netball courts and a 25m indoor swimming pool, built in 2017. The playing fields, which are immediately adjacent to the School buildings are well kept and provide, in season, rugby, cricket, hockey, football, rounders and athletics areas. The Junior School, which was extended in 2017 to provide additional changing room facilities and an Art and Design studio, has access to all the Senior School facilities but is self-contained on the estate.

Admission. The majority of pupils enter the Junior School at 7 or 9 and the Senior School at 11 or 13. Admission is also possible at other ages where space allows and a significant number of pupils join at the age of 16 for Sixth Form Studies.

Entrance to the Junior School is by assessment in January. This includes a report from the child's previous school, classroom sessions in the company of other prospective pupils, and literacy and numeracy tasks.

Entrance examinations for the Senior School are held in January.

Assessment for entry to the Sixth Form at 16 is by interview and a report from the applicant's previous school. Dedicated interview days are held monthly from December to March each year and the entry requirement is a minimum of 3 A/7 and 3 B/6 grades at GCSE, including English and Mathematics, with normally an A/7 grade in the subjects chosen for study.

Registration Fee £100.

Fees per term (2018–2019). Junior School: £3,975 (includes lunch which is compulsory). Senior School: £4,410.

Sibling discount of 5% for the second child and 10% for the third or subsequent child attending concurrently.

Scholarships and Financial Awards. Entrance Scholarships and Exhibitions, in the form of an individual prize, are offered annually to pupils who excel in the school's entrance tests at 7+, 11+ and 13+. Music Scholarships and Exhibitions are offered at 13+ and 16+ following an audition and interview.

The School annually makes available a number of means-tested bursaries. These are for external candidates joining the School, who meet the academic entry requirements and whose parents could not afford to send them to Exeter School without financial assistance. As a general guide, gross parental income will need to be below £60,000 per annum to allow consideration for a bursary. In addition, there are also a number of free places for 11+ and 16+ candidates made possible by donations from local benefactors for able pupils whose parents require financial assistance.

Curriculum. In the first 3 years in the Senior School all pupils take English, History, Geography, a carousel of French, German, Spanish and Latin, Mathematics, IT, Physics, Chemistry, Biology, Art, Design Technology, Drama, Music and Religious and Physical Education. After this there is a wide choice of subjects at GCSE level, including English, one compulsory Modern Foreign Language, Mathematics, dual or triple award Science and 3 of the following: Latin, French, German, Spanish, Classical Civilisation, Religious Studies, History, Geography, Music, Drama, Art, Design and Technology, and Computer Science.

Pupils enter the Sixth Form choosing over 20 different subjects for A Level study and are prepared for university scholarships, university entrance and admission to other forms of further education or vocational training. Over 95% go on annually to Degree Courses.

Houses. There are ten Pupil Houses. Each is under the personal care of a Head of House and his/her deputy, with whom parents are invited to keep in touch on any matter affecting their child's general development and progress throughout the school.

Religion. All pupils attend Religious Education classes, which include Sixth Form discussion groups. Full time Chaplain.

Games. Rugby, Hockey, Cricket, Swimming, Athletics, Dance, Cross Country, Tennis, Badminton, Squash, Shooting, Basketball, Netball and Golf. Further activities are available for the Sixth Form, including Football and Multi-Gym sessions.

Community and other Service. All pupils learn to serve the community. Many choose to take part in Social Service, helping old people and the handicapped young. There is a voluntary CCF Contingent with thriving RN, Army and RAF Sections. The CCF offers a large variety of Outdoor Activities, including Adventure Training Camps, Ten Tors Expedition Training as well as specialist courses. Pupils are encouraged to participate in the Duke of Edinburgh's Award scheme.

Music. Pupils are taught Singing and Musical appreciation and are encouraged to learn to play Musical Instruments. More than one third of all pupils have individual lessons on at least one instrument. There are 4 Orchestras, a Choral Society which annually performs a major work in Exeter Cathedral and 4 Choirs, 3 jazz bands, and numerous smaller groups from string quartets to rock bands. There are over 30 visiting instrumental teachers. Over 20 public concerts are given each year. Recent Summer Music trips have included Salzburg and New York.

Drama. Drama is developed both within and outside the curriculum. The School Hall with its large and well-equipped stage provides for the dual purpose of studio workshop and the regular production of plays and musicals. The recently refurbished Drama Studio is used for smaller productions.

Art and Design. Art lessons are given to junior and senior forms. Apart from the formal disciplines of GCSE and A Level, which can be taken by those who choose, all pupils have opportunity for artistic expression in painting, print-making, photography and construction in many materials. All younger pupils learn to develop craft skills in wood, metal and plastic and to use them creatively in design work. Some then follow GCSE or A Level courses in Design and Technology. There is an annual art exhibition in July.

Expeditions. Throughout the school a large number of residential field trips and expeditions take place each year including a Third Form new pupils' Dartmoor weekend, various departmental excursions, several foreign exchanges and Duke of Edinburgh's Award expeditions. In recent summers, the school has run its own adventure trips to Namibia, Peru, Vietnam, the Himalayas and Cuba. There is a programme of major and minor sports tours.

Societies and Clubs. Pupils are encouraged to pursue their interests by joining one of the School Societies. Groups of enthusiasts can form new Societies or Clubs, but the following are at present available: Art, Badminton, Basketball, Chess, Choral Society, Computing, Dance, Drama, Electronics, Model Railway, MUN, Music, Politics, Shooting and Squash.

Social. Close contact is maintained with the City and the University. Association between members of the School and the wider society outside is fostered wherever opportunity offers.

The staff believe strongly in the value of association with parents, who are invited to meetings annually throughout their sons' or daughters' time at the School. A termly lecture by a visiting speaker is provided for parents. The Exeter School Parents' Association exists to promote closer relations between the School and its parents.

Careers. Careers education begins at the age of 13 and continues on a progressive programme until students leave the school. Careers evenings are held annually when pupils and their parents have the opportunity to consult representatives of the professions, industry and commerce. A work experience programme is organised for Year 11 pupils each summer, and a scheme of mock interviews with career professionals for pupils in the Sixth Form. A major Careers Convention is held at the school each Autumn for pupils from Years 9 to 13.

Honours. Pupils regularly gain admission to Oxford and Cambridge. The School encourages application to the leading universities, including the Russell and 1994 Groups.

Leading musicians have gained places at the Royal College of Music and the Royal Academy of Music.

Charitable status. Exeter School is a Registered Charity, number 1093080, and a Company Limited by Guarantee, registered in England, number 04470478. Registered Office: Victoria Park Road, Exeter, Devon EX2 4NS.

Patrons:
The Lord Lieutenant of the County of Devon
The Right Reverend the Lord Bishop of Exeter
The Right Worshipful the Lord Mayor of Exeter

Governors:
Appointed by the Devon County Council:
Ms R Vigers

Appointed by the Exeter City Council:
G J Prowse

Appointed by the Governors of St John's Hospital:
A C W King (*Chairman*) [OE]
Miss R Edbrooke, BEd

Representatives of the Universities of Exeter and Oxford:
Exeter: Professor S C Smart, BA, PhD
Oxford: Dr M C Grossel, MA, PhD

Co-opted Governors:
J D Gaisford, BSc, ACA (*Vice-Chairman*)
A P Burbanks, BA [OE]
K Cheney, BA
Mrs H Clark
Ms G A Hodgetts, BA, MSc (*Vice-Chairman*) [OE]
Professor A F Watkinson, MSc, FRCS
Brigadier S P Hodder, BSc [OE]
Ms C Gibaud, QC, MA
P Fisher, MA
R May, BA, MRICS

Headmaster: R Griffin, MA

Senior Deputy Headmaster: M J Hughes, MA
Deputy Head: Mrs N A Fairweather, BA
Deputy Head: G S Bone, BSc
Deputy Head: Dr J L Wilson, MPhys, DPhil

Assistant Staff:
* *Head of Department*
† *Housemaster/mistress*
§ *Part-time or Visiting*
[OE] *Old Exonian*

Art & Design:
*Mrs A J Escott, BA
*Mrs J H Rafferty-White, BA

Biology:
*Mrs J H Metcalf, MA
†P J C Boddington, BSc
Miss J M Booth, MSc
Mrs A C Johnson, BSc
Mrs K A Coe, BSc
Miss A Brookes, BSc [OE]

Chemistry:
*R F J Tear, BSc (*Director of Science*)
M K Chitnavis, BSc, CSci, FRSC (*Universities Adviser*)
Dr S P Smale, BSc, PhD (*CCF Contingent Commander*)

Miss K L Morley, BSc
§Mrs F J Tamblyn, BSc

Classical Subjects:
*Mrs S Shrubb, MA
N P L Keyes, MA
Mrs E K J Dunlop, MA, MPhil

Computer Science:
*Mrs A O Pinches, BEng
Mr G J McGrath, BSc

Design Technology:
*M J Rose, BSc
I R Lowles, BA

Drama:
*J S Brough, BSc
Mr C C Harknett, BA

Electronics:
*M E Schramm, BSc
D S Cortese, BSc, MSc

English:
*A S Dobson, MA
†Mrs J H Daybell, MA
†Mrs E K J Dunlop, MA, MPhil
†Mrs E A Whittall, BA, MA
Mrs K L Ridler-Murray, BA, MA
R O Evans, BA
E J Seaton-Jones, BA
Mr C C Harknett, BA

Geography:
*P M Hyde, BSc
†Mrs H M Sail, MA
Mrs N A Fairweather, BA (*Deputy Head*)
Mrs A Roff, BSc
J W J Bird, BSc, MA, MSc

History:
*G N Trelawny, BEd, MA
Mrs A-J Culley, BA, BSc
Ms J R Hodgetts, BA
Mrs M F Sheehan, BA

Languages:
*M F Latimer, MA, MSt
M C Wilcock, BEd
Mrs A M Francis, MA
§Mrs S C Wilson, BA
R A Charters, BA
Mrs D D S Masters, BA
Mrs R Alborough, BA

Mathematics:
*Mrs E V Cartwright, BSc
G R Willson, BSc
A J Reynolds, BSc
M J Hughes, MA (*Senior Deputy Headmaster*)
†Dr G J D Chapman, BSc, MSc, PhD
Mrs A J James, BSc
Mrs M McCluskey, MSc
S J Parry, BA
B M Hall, BA

Music:
*P Tamblyn, MA, MMus (*Director of Music*)
T P Brimelow, MA
Mrs T M Guthrie, BA
D Bowen, BEd
A Daldorph, BA
§A Gillett, ARCM
§P Painter, DipMusEd, Cert Ed
§B Moore, BA

Physical Education and Games:
*A C F Mason, BA (*Director of Sport*)
Mrs A J Marsh, BEd (*Head of Sixth Form*)
†E P M Jones, BSc
Miss R A Carter, BSc
§G Skinner, BEd
T N Ross, BSc
Miss D S Lunn, BSc
Miss C McIlwrath, BSc

Physics:
* D L N Tuohey, MSc
G S Bone, BSc (*Deputy Head*)
M E Schramm, BSc
Dr G B N Robb, MPhys, MSc, PhD
D I Trim, BSc
D S Cortese, BSc, MSc
Dr J L Wilson, MPhys, DPhil (*Deputy Head*)

Psychology:
Mrs C Gooddy, MSc
Mrs A M Godfroy, BA

Religious Studies:
*†M H R Porter, BA
†Mrs J M K Murrin, BA
Mrs A J Marsh, BEd
Revd T P Carson, MTh, MA (*Chaplain*)
Mrs C Gooddy, MSc

Social Studies:
*S K Mackintosh, BA (**Economics*)
*Mrs M F Sheehan, BA (**Politics*)
†R J Baker, BA
P Bell, MA

Learning Support:
§Mrs A Reeves, BSc
§Mrs S E Oliver, BEd

Junior School

Headmistress: Mrs S Marks, BSc, PGCE

Assistant Head: J S Wood, BA

Assistant Staff:
R Bland, BEd
G E L Ashman, BA [OE]
Mrs P A Goldsworthy, BA, LTCL
R J Pidwell, BA
Ms J A Barnes, MSc
Mrs C H Handley, BEd
Mrs L L Hardy, MA
Mrs R E Pettet, BA
Mrs K L Jones, BSc
Miss H D Robinson, BA
Mrs S S Morgan, BA
Miss K E Wright, BA

Bursar and Clerk to the Governors: M C M MacEacharn, FCA, BSc

Deputy Bursar and Company Secretary: Mrs G M Robins, BA, FCCA

Estates and Facilities Manager: C A Stewart

Director of Development and Alumni: Mrs R F H Magee, BA

Registrar: Miss S M Allen, BA

Headmaster's PA: Mrs K Leach

Bursar's PA: Mrs J W Furniss

Information Systems Manager: A D R Carter, BEng

Network Manager: P D Sprake, MCSA

Librarian: Mrs E G Taylor, BSc, DipLib

School Nurse: Mrs M R Sanders, RGN

Felsted School

Felsted, Dunmow, Essex CM6 3LL

Tel: 01371 822606 (Headmaster)
           01371 822605 (Admissions Registrar)
email: reception@felsted.org
website: www.felsted.org
Twitter: @felstedschool
Facebook: @felstedschool
LinkedIn: /Felsted Network

Founded in 1564 by Lord Richard Riche, Felsted educates boys and girls aged 4 to 18. Felsted is ideally situated in a picturesque North Essex village, close to both London and Cambridge, and within easy reach of Stansted and other international airports. Felsted is a Church of England foundation but welcomes pupils from all religious traditions and none. The Senior School, for 13 to 18 year olds, has around 560 pupils; the majority are boarders and weekend arrangements are flexible. The Preparatory School boasts 510 pupils, with a buoyant boarding house, home to full, weekly and flexible boarders.

Felsted seeks to develop the character of every student, to help prepare them for life beyond school. This is done through a broad and holistic education with strength in Music, Drama, Sport, The Arts, Leadership and Service. Felsted seeks to develop and stretch students academically, to be lifelong learners, well-rounded, aspirational and globally minded, with the skills to flourish beyond school, applying the principles of a growth mindset, to be the best they can be.

Felsted celebrated its 450th anniversary in 2014, and was honoured by a visit from Her Majesty The Queen.

The School is a Global Member of the Round Square Organisation offering international exchanges and collaboration, and offers both A Levels and the International Baccalaureate Diploma in the Sixth Form, plus the Extended Project Qualification (EPQ). The website hosts much information about the school plus many videos, including one called 'Boarding at Felsted'. Felsted had an Ofsted boarding and welfare inspection in 2011 and was rated 'outstanding' in every aspect, and also received an 'excellent' rating in all aspects in the Independent Schools Inspectorate inspection in 2013. The school passed with flying colours in a full compliance inspection across both the Preparatory and Senior Schools in 2016. Details are available on our website, and directly on the ISI website. Felsted was shortlisted for five TES Independent School Awards in 2018, including Boarding School of the Year.

The Houses. There are ten Houses at Felsted, a day house for boys, a day house for girls, three boarding houses for boys, three boarding houses for girls, an Upper Sixth House for boys and an Upper Sixth House for girls. Each House is under the direction of a resident Housemaster or Housemistress.

Each Boarding House is supported by a pastoral team comprising a resident Assistant House Parent, a matron responsible for overseeing the domestic arrangements, and several House tutors, a number of whom are resident.

The Curriculum. All pupils study English Language, English Literature, Mathematics and Sciences (Double or Triple Award) to GCSE and choose a further four subjects from the following: History, Geography, TEP (Theology, Ethics and Philosophy), French, German, Spanish, Latin, Classical Civilisation, Art and Design, Music, Drama, Triple Science, Design & Technology (Resistant Materials), Physical Education and Computer Science.

One of the options is expected to be a Modern Foreign Language and one is expected to be a Humanities subject. Pupils also study the Higher Project Qualification (HPQ).

In the Sixth Form pupils have a choice between A Levels and the International Baccalaureate Diploma.

Those studying A Levels normally choose three subjects to study along with an Extended Project Qualification (EPQ). The following subjects are offered: Art and Design, Business Studies, Classical Civilisation, Computer Science, Design Technology, Drama and Theatre Studies, Economics, English Literature, Geography, Government and Politics, History, History of Art, Latin, Mathematics, Further Mathematics, French, German, Spanish, Italian, Music (and Music Technology), Physical Education, Psychology, TEP (Theology, Ethics and Philosophy), and Sciences (Biology, Chemistry, Physics).

IB pupils study six subjects, one from each of the following categories: Language and Literature (English, German, Italian, Self-Study Language, Spanish and French), Language A (English, German, Italian, Self-Taught), Language (Other) (French, German, English, Spanish, Latin and Italian 'ab initio'), Humanities (Economics, Geography, History, Philosophy, Psychology), Sciences (Biology, Chemistry, Design Technology, Physics, Nature of Science, Sports Exercise and Health Science), Mathematics (Maths Analysis and Approaches or Maths Applications and Interpretation), The Arts/Elective (Music, Visual Arts, Biology, Economics, French B, Spanish ab initio). They also follow a course on the Theory of Knowledge, write an extended essay and are fully involved in the Creativity, Action and Service Programme.

Scholarships and Bursaries. Academic, Music, Drama, Art, Design/Technology/Engineering and Sports Scholarships are awarded annually for entry into Year 9, 10 and 12, up to the value of 20% of the fees.

The examinations for the Year 9 and 10 Scholarships take place in November and February and for the Sixth Form Scholarships in November.

Mary Skill Awards (named after a generous benefactor to the school), which recognise all-round ability or a specific ability in one area, are also available.

Means-tested Bursaries may be available to increase an award.

At least two Open Bursaries (100%) each year are available to those who might otherwise not be able to consider Felsted, due to financial circumstances.

Talented students in Design are also entered at 16+ for Arkwright Foundation Scholarships.

Scholarships are also awarded at 11+ at Felsted Preparatory School and these may be carried through to the Senior School.

Fee reductions are available for children of those serving in the Armed Services, or the Foreign Office.

Full details are available at www.felsted.org and from the Admissions Registrar.

Registration and entry. Boys' and girls' names can be registered at any time. Registration fee £125.

Before admission to Felsted pupils must pass the Common Entrance Examination or the Felsted Entrance Test, plus a Head Teacher's report and interview. For Sixth Form entry, a minimum of 32 points must be gained across their best six subjects at GCSE, with at least a 6 in the subjects to be studied at A Level or at Higher Level in the IB Diploma.

Fees per term (2018–2019). Senior School: Full Boarding (7 nights), £11,995 Weekly Boarding (5 nights) £11,130, Contemporary Boarding (3 nights) £9,670, Day £7,850. Preparatory School: Day £3,095–5,940, Weekly Boarding £7,750, Full Boarding £8,155.

Felsted Preparatory School, whose Head is a member of IAPS (The Independent Association of Prep Schools), shares the same governing body with Felsted School. It has its own campus, with 510 pupils aged 4 to 13. There is a dedicated teaching centre for 11–13 year-olds and a state-of-the-art Pre-Preparatory Department, which opened in 2011. (For further information, see entry in IAPS section.)

The Old Felstedian Society organises both social and sporting activities, plus networking opportunities across a variety of industries. The Old Felstedian Liaison Manager, Miss Selina Joslin, would be pleased to answer queries about the Alumni (ofs@felsted.org) and further information can be found via the school's website.

Charitable status. Felsted School is a Registered Charity, number 310870. The charity is based upon the Foundation established by Richard Lord Riche in 1564 with the objective of teaching and instructing children across a broad curriculum as ordained from time to time by its Trustees.

Governing Body:
Chair of Governors: John Davies, OBE

Peter Lee	Bruce Grindlay
Philip Hutley	Revd Nic Stuchfield
Bobbi Davy	Ann Carrington
James Nicholson	Robert Brown
Oliver Stocken, CBE	Geoffrey Boult
James Tibbitts	Julia Abel Smith
Jane Crouch	Mike Beale
William Sunnucks	

Bursar and Clerk to the Governors: Andrew Clayton MA

Headmaster: **Christopher Townsend**, BA

Bursar: Andrew Clayton, MA
Senior Deputy Head: George Masters, BA
Deputy Head (Wellbeing): Karen Megahey, BSc
Deputy Head (Academic): Sarah Capewell, MA
Director of Global Education: Daniel Emmerson, MA
Prep School Headmaster: Simon James, BA

† *Housemaster/mistress*

Art:
D J Smith, BA Durham (*Arts Coordinator*)
K J Ayettey, BA Nottingham Trent
A V Warner, BA Maidstone College of Art

Classics:
G C Allen, MA Oxford
E M McLaren, MA Cambridge (*Roberts Society Coordinator*)
S R Capewell, MA Edinburgh (*Deputy Head Academic*)
D A Rees, BA Nottingham

Computer Science:
T Oakley-Agar, BSc APU
C Croydon, MSc London (*Timetabler and Curriculum Coordinator*)
M W J Redding (*Head of ICT Services*)

Design and Technology:
M A Pitts, BEng Loughborough
H E Charlton-Ricks, BA Rochester
H K Pheloung, BA Northumbria

Drama:
M C Donaldson, BA Derby (*Director of Performing Arts*)
L Macey, BA Roehampton
L J Mann, BA Essex
J Stacey, BA Middlesex

Economics and Business Studies:
J E McArdle, BA Hertfordshire, MBA Coventry (*Director of Business, Economics & Enterprise Education*)
M Foster, BA Loughborough (*Economics*)

†M L McIlvenna, BA Brighton, MEd Cambridge
A T Mohindru, LLB Brunel
†S D Wilson, BA Humberside

English:
E L Predebon, MA Anglia Ruskin
Dr J S Alsop, PhD Exeter
C M James, BA Leeds (*Head of Project Qualifications*)
J C Johnson, BA Birmingham
A M Manzi-Davies, BA Exeter
R J Purdy, BA Essex (*PSHE, Director Co-Curriculum, MUN Coordinator*)
N M Sunshine-Harris, BA East London

Geography:
T P C Galvin, BSc St Andrews
K Moir-Smith, BA London
E K Rose, BA Durham
G R Stringer, BSc Durham

History & Politics:
R Pathak, BA Oxford
B R Maude-Barker, MA Cambridge
L M Scofield, BA Reading (*Director of Professional Guidance*)
Dr T Strange, PhD Manchester

History of Art:
M Atkinson-Wood, MA King's College, London, BA Cambridge (*Senior Scholarship Coordinator*)

Mathematics:
M J Campbell, MSc St Andrews
C Donaldson, BSc Reading
R L Feldman, MSc London (*Director of Reports and Reviews*)
J M Jevons, BA Nottingham
A Munns, MA Nottingham
L E A Stuchfield, BA Oxford

Modern Languages:
L Robertson, MA London (*French and German*)
A N Fazekas, MA Dresden (*German*)
F Sanchez del Rio, Licenciatura Cadiz (*Spanish, Editor of 'The Felstedian'*)
S Alvarez Alba Cortes Trinity Laban Conservatoire (*Spanish*)
R Grant, BA Leeds (*Spanish, Round Square Coordinator*)
J K Mallett, BA UCL (*French Magic Bus Coordinator*)
N F S O'Brien, MA Glasgow (*Spanish, EAL DSL*)
M Trucco, MA Turin (*Italian and French*)
N Lemm (*German Language Assistant*)
C Menet (*French Language Assistant*)
G Suarez Suarez (*Spanish Language Assistant*)

Music:
P G Bennett, AGSM Guildhall School of Music and Drama (*Director of Music*)
W J Warns, MA Cambridge, Dip ABRSM, FNCM, FGMS, FNFCM, MISM (*Head of Academic Music and Choirmaster & Organist*)
R A Thear, BA Leeds

Physical Education and Sport:
L Willis, BSc Durham (*Director of Girls' Sport & Head of Girls' Hockey*)
†S Barrett, BSc Sheffield Hallam
†B J Bury, BA Exeter
J E R Gallian (*Director of Cricket*)
†C S Knightley, BA UWIC (*Director of Sport*)
†A Le Chevalier, PGCE (*Director of Rugby*)
N J Lockhart, ECB3, EH2 (*Head of Grounds & Cricket Professional*)
R Marriott-Cox (*Director of Tennis*)
N J Phillips, BA Durham (*Head of Boys' Hockey*)

C E Rudd, BSc Cardiff
G Catchpole GRA
Z V Griffith GRA
C J Wukics, BSc Brunel GRA

Project Qualifications:
C M James, BA Leeds

PSHE:
R J Purdy, BA Essex (*English, Director of Diploma & Co-Curricular*)
K A Megahey, BSc Nottingham (*Deputy Head Wellbeing*)

Psychology:
V L Smith, BSc OU
M Cacace, BA Exeter (*Head of IB Core*)

Religious Studies:
B S Roberts Jones, BSc Kent MEd Cambridge
Revd N J Little, BA Middlesex (*Chaplain, i/c Charities*)
L M Keable, BA Bath Spa
G W S Masters, BA Durham (*Senior Deputy Head*)
L K Stefanini, BSc London School Economics, MA London (*Assistant Head Academic*)
L H Wigglesworth, BA Hull [maternity leave]

Science:
H J Mollison, BSc Hertfordshire (*Head of Science, Chemistry*)
L E Barden, BSc Bath (*Chemistry*)
K Farr, MSc Surrey (*Biology*)
D T Smith, BSc Newcastle Upon Tyne (*Physics*)
J Entwistle, BSc UAE (*Biology*)
†Dr S McGuire, BSc, MSc, PhD Manchester (*Chemistry & Biology*)
†C H Palmer, MA Cambridge (*Physics, Mathematics*)
A J A Pask, BSc York (*Chemistry*)
†B R Peart, BSc Durham (*Biology, i/c Christian Forum, Senior HM*)
A L F Simpson, BSc London (*Director of Assessment and Tracking*)
R Sloman, MSc Exeter
K L Woodhouse, BSc Birmingham (*Physics, Director of International Baccalaureate*)

Support for Learning:
J W Hipkin, BA Manchester QTS, MEd
S J Beale, BA Bristol
N J Johnson, CDip
E L Masters, MA Aberdeen
Dr P H Milner, BSc, PhD, CChem, MRSC Nottingham
†C M Phillips, MCILIP W London
†A L Salmon, BA Leicester MEd Middlesex
J C Turner Jones, BA Birmingham

EAL:
D K Guerrero, BA Middlesex Dip TEFLA
J A D Farrington, MA Writtle, QTLS

CCF:
C H Palmer, MA Cambridge (*CCF Contingent Commander*)
L W Jay

Duke of Edinburgh's Award & Educational Visits:
D L Whittock

Library:
N S Howorth, BA Edge Hill, Dip Lib, MCLIP

Houses and Housemasters/mistresses:

Boys' Houses:
Deacon's: Barny Bury
Elwyn's: Ben Peart
Gepp's: Luke McIlvenna

Montgomery's: Andrew Le Chevalier
Windsor's: Clifford Palmer

Girls' Houses:
Follyfield: Sonia Wilson
Garnetts: Sarah Barrett
Manor: Carolyn Phillips
Stocks': Anna Salmon
Thorne: Sufia McGuire

Director of Marketing: Mrs Sophy Walker
Admissions Registrar: Mrs Ruth Wyganowski
School Chaplain: Reverend Nigel Little
Medical Officer: Mrs Sally Staines

Fettes College

Carrington Road, Edinburgh EH4 1QX

Tel: +44 (0)131 311 6744
Fax: +44 (0)131 311 6714
email: admissions@fettes.com
website: www.fettes.com
Twitter: @Fettes_College
Facebook: @FettesCollegeFettesPrep

Motto: *Industria*

Founded in 1870 by Sir William Fettes and designed by David Bryce, Fettes College is uniquely situated in extensive grounds and woodland close to the heart of Edinburgh, and enjoys a reputation as one of the pre-eminent co-educational boarding schools in the UK. Fettes College has 766 pupils aged 7–18 (214 in the Prep School and 552 in The College), with 80% boarders and 20% day pupils in the Senior School and 30% boarders and 70% day pupils in the Prep School. Fettes students are drawn from all over the British Isles and from abroad and this diverse and healthy mix of backgrounds provides a richness that contributes to the stimulating, warm and energetic community that is Fettes College.

Fettes College has over 5,000 Old Fettesians who remain in touch with us for one very compelling reason: being educated at Fettes was one of the most important and beneficial aspects of their lives.

Fettes is where their confidence was built, horizons broadened, talents nurtured and lifelong friendships made, where they achieved exam success, broke sporting records, were inspired by teachers and learnt the skills which would equip them for later life.

Fettes is where they were enthused, praised and encouraged to work hard and achieve the very best they could, while being surrounded by like-minded peers and caring staff.

To this day, a Fettes education is an incredible start to life.

Situation and Buildings. Fettes stands in 80 acres of parkland close to the centre of Edinburgh. Being just 20 minutes' walk to the city centre, means that Fettes students can take full advantage of the wealth of cultural resources on offer in Scotland's Capital city such as galleries, museums and theatres. Students also have every opportunity to enjoy the majestic Scottish outdoors with a full programme of trips and experiences from hillwalking to canoeing, camping to white water rafting. Regular national and international school trips further broaden the experience Fettes students are offered.

Transportation links by road, rail and air are excellent.

Organisation. Each member of the School is the responsibility of a Housemaster or Housemistress. In the Senior School there are four Houses for boys, four for girls, and a co-ed Upper Sixth Form house. The Upper Sixth Form boarding house provides individual and twin study-bed-rooms with en-suite facilities for all boarders. There is a strong tutorial system for the encouragement and guidance of each pupil.

Aims. Our mission at Fettes is to develop broadly educated, confident and thoughtful individuals. The hopes and aspirations of each and every one of our students are of central importance to us, and the happy, purposeful environment of the College encourages the boys and girls to flourish and develop fully the skills and interests that they possess.

Curriculum. For GCSE all students take English, Mathematics, Physics, Chemistry and Biology. Students then choose four subjects from the following list: Art & Design, Computer Science, Classical Civilisation, Classical Greek, Drama, Economics, French, Geography, German, History, Latin, Mandarin, Music, PE and Spanish. Students must choose at least one modern foreign language.

Fettes offers a very broad range of subjects in the Sixth Form with students choosing either A Levels or International Baccalaureate, therefore allowing a choice of curriculum to best suit the needs of the individual student. Over 98% of pupils gain university entry with up to 15 students securing places at Oxford and Cambridge each year.

Careers. The School is a member of the Independent Schools Careers Organisation, and a team of Staff are responsible for providing specialist advice on careers and Higher Education and for developing links with industry and commerce. Fettes Community & Fettes Career Partnership was launched in 2014 providing business networking links between Old Fettesians, current parents, past parents, Fettes students and recent Fettes graduates.

Chapel. The College Chapel, situated in the heart of the School, is central to life at Fettes with the daily Chapel service forming the core of the moral and spiritual guidance offered at Fettes. Fettes has a strong Christian tradition but members of other faiths and those with no faith are warmly welcomed, and this is reflected in the tolerant and questioning character of the School.

Games. All students are involved in sports at least 3 afternoons per week. All major sports are offered at Fettes in fact there are very few sports you cannot pursue. Rugby, cricket, hockey, lacrosse, netball, athletics, tennis, squash, fives, swimming, badminton, fencing, basketball, volleyball are an example of what is on offer. Fettes College is very proud of the individual and team success at school and national levels across a range of sports including rugby, fencing, sailing and cross-country. Fettes College also has excellent sporting facilities including a purpose-built sports centre, all-weather pitches, indoor swimming pool, climbing wall, courts for fives and squash, shooting range and a separate specialist gym for Sixth Form pupils.

Other activities. There are 50+ societies, clubs and extra-curricular activities, and each pupil is encouraged to develop cultural interests. On Saturday evenings, in addition to lectures, plays and concerts, there are regular dances and discos, and committees of pupils, with the assistance of members of Staff, are responsible for planning and organising social events for different age groups.

Music. The College possesses a strong musical tradition, and many pupils receive instrumental tuition. In addition to the orchestras there are ensembles, a swing band, Chapel Choir and Concert Choir. A major concert is held at the end of every term. Standards are very high and the Chapel Choir has achieved notable success, being recorded by the BBC and performing by invitation at Westminster Abbey and St Paul's Cathedral.

Drama. Drama is lively and of a high standard. Each year the School Play and House plays offer great opportuni-

ties for large numbers of boys and girls to act and to participate in Lighting and Stage Management.

Art. The Art School is flourishing, and the standards of
pupil attainment are very high. Regular House art competitions and gallery display of current work occur.

**Combined Cadet Force, Duke of Edinburgh's Award,
Outside Service.** Pupils are members of the CCF for two
years and may choose to extend their service while they are
in the Sixth Form. Training is offered in Shooting, Vehicle
Engineering, Canoeing, Rock-Climbing, Skiing, Sub-Aqua
and Sailing.

In the Sixth Form many pupils pursue the Gold Standard
of the Duke of Edinburgh's Award scheme, and some 70
members of the School join the Outside Service Unit which
provides help for others in difficult circumstances and raises
funds for Charities.

Outdoor Activities. The School aims to make full use of
its proximity to the sea, the Dry Ski Slope, and the rivers and
mountains of Scotland. Outdoor activities are encouraged
for the enjoyment that they give and the valuable personal
qualities which they help to develop. A number of members
of Staff are experts in mountaineering, skiing and watersports, and all pupils have opportunities for receiving
instruction in camping, canoeing, sailing, hillwalking and
snow and rock climbing. There are regular expeditions
abroad.

Preparatory School. The Preparatory School for 214
boys and girls aged 7 to 13 is situated in the School grounds.
Boarders stay in the modern purpose-built Houses. Pupils in
the Prep School share the facilities of the senior school and
participate in the full range of activities enjoyed by the College as a whole. (*For further details see entry in IAPS section.*)

Admission. Personal interviews assess the promise of
each individual and determine those who will gain most
from a Fettes education. Entrance exams are also required
for entry. Pupils may join the Preparatory School at any
stage (7–13) with students normally joining the Senior
School at 13+, 14+ and 16+. Further details are available
from the Registrar.

Scholarships and Bursaries. All applicants can apply
for a means-tested bursary which can cover up to 100% of
the fees. There is a finite amount of funding available each
year and therefore not all applicants will be successful. Bursaries are awarded independently of any Scholarship or
Award. The process for applying for a bursary is completely
separate to the admissions process and must be done through
the Bursar's Office.

There is a wide range of Scholarships and Awards available at 13+ and/or 16+ including Academic, All-Rounder,
Sport, Music, Art and Piping. There is great kudos associated with being a scholar or award holder of The College.
Scholarships also attract reductions of up to 10% of the fees
while Awards can also attract reductions of up to 5% of the
fees unrelated to parents' financial circumstances.

Children of members of HM Forces qualify for a reduction in fees and Special Bursaries (Todd) are available for
descendants of Old Fettesians.

Past papers are available and further enquiries should be
made to the Registrar.

Fees per term (2018–2019). Senior School: Boarders
£11,600, Day Pupils £9,400. Prep School: Boarders £8,070,
Day Pupils £5,500. The fees cover all extras except books
and stationery, music lessons and subscriptions to voluntary
clubs and activities.

Registration Fee £100.

Old Fettesian Association. *Liaison*: Old Fettesian Association Office, Fettes College (Telephone +44 (0)131 311
6741).

Charitable status. The Fettes Trust is a Registered Charity, number SC017489. Fettes aims to provide a quality education at Junior and Senior level.

Chairman of Governors: I M Osborne

Senior Management Team:

Headmaster: **Mr Geoffrey Stanford**, MA, MBA

Deputy Head: Mrs H F Harrison, MA Cambridge
Assistant Headmaster & Director of Studies: A Shackleton,
MA Cambridge
Headmaster of the Preparatory School: A A Edwards, BA
London
Director of Teaching & Learning: A J Armstrong, MA St
Andrews
Assistant Director of Studies: L J Whyte, BSc PhD
Norwich
Head of Pastoral Care: Mrs C M Harrison, BA Cambridge
Head of PSE: Mrs S A Bruce, BSc St Andrews
Director of Digital Strategy: Mrs YEA Mitchell, BSc
Durham
Bursar: P J F Worlledge, BSc Bristol
Director of Marketing and PR: Mrs G G Gray, MA
Edinburgh
Director of Development: Ms N Pickavance, LLB
Aberdeen

Chaplain: Revd Dr A Clark, BA York, PhD St Andrews

Forest School

Snaresbrook, London E17 3PY

Tel:	020 8520 1744
Fax:	020 8520 3656
email:	info@forest.org.uk
website:	www.forest.org.uk
Twitter:	@ForestSchoolE17
Facebook:	@ForestSchoolE17

Motto: *In Pectore Robur*

Established in 1834, Forest School is London's only diamond structure school located at the edge of the capital's
largest open space, Epping Forest.

There are currently 1,438 pupils in the School (1,160
boys and girls in the Senior School, 278 boys and girls in the
Pre-Preparatory and Preparatory School). All pupils share
the main school campus and facilities such as the Chapel,
Dining Hall, Sports Hall, playing fields, Deaton Theatre and
the Martin Centre for Innovation. Sixth Form pupils enjoy
use of a dedicated Sixth Form Centre including collaborative IT work spaces, group study areas and a careers room.
The School site and playing fields cover 50 acres.

Diamond Structure. Boys and girls are taught in co-educational classes when they join Forest School in the Pre-
Prep, then in single-sex classes within the Prep School from
Y3. At 11, pupils join the Senior School and single-sex
teaching continues until the Sixth Form, where classes are
once again co-educational. Co-curricular activities are
largely co-educational although boys and girls follow different sports programmes.

While the existence of the diamond structure at Forest is
a result of evolution rather than initial design, the Forest
School of today regards the mix of single-sex and co-educational teaching as an educational model of which to be
proud, and thought and effort goes into making it a structure
that is very popular with both parents and pupils who enjoy
the best of both worlds – single-sex teaching in a co-educational school.

Curriculum. The Forest curriculum parallels the National Curriculum, although the School exercises its independence to enable teachers to exploit the high academic ability of the pupils. In Y7–Y9 a broad range of core subjects is taught, including Modern and Classical Languages, incorporating Mandarin Chinese, and the three Sciences. Options in Y9 include Computer Science, Ancient Greek and Food & Nutrition, as well as more traditional subjects. At GCSE, all pupils follow a core curriculum of English Language & Literature, a Modern Foreign Language, Maths and Science (separate or Double Award, according to preference) as well as a choice from around 15 optional subjects. A distinctive feature of the curriculum is that all pupils also submit work for the Higher Project Qualification (HPQ) – a research-based dissertation on a subject of the pupil's own choosing, following a taught course of critical thinking and project skills, assessed at GCSE level.

In the Sixth Form, pupils take the Forest Diploma. A Levels provide the core academic element and Sixth Formers can choose from 26 different A Level subjects, with most choosing three main subjects, examined at the end of the two-year course, and taught in small teaching groups of typically around ten to fifteen pupils. All Diploma pupils begin a course in Project Skills in Year 12 and will continue to produce an Extended Project Qualification (EPQ), which may take the form of a dissertation-style essay, or perhaps a 'creative artefact', like a film, composition or even a computer program.

The School places considerable emphasis on teaching the effective use of Information and Communications Technology. Every pupil in the Senior School is required to have with them a keyboard-enabled device in school, and all pupils are trained in the use of mobile devices as an appropriate tool for some learning tasks. All teachers incorporate digital materials and applications within their teaching, to a greater or lesser extent. Computer Science, with an emphasis on programming, is available from Y9 as an academic subject.

The curriculum is augmented by a wide range of popular academic co-curricular activities which supplement timetabled subjects. Lessons in Italian and Russian are offered, as well as opportunities to develop skills through Science and Maths competitions, societies and online courses.

Co-Curriculum. The School has a large Music Department with more than 50 visiting staff, teaching a wide range of instruments and voice. Regular concerts take place in school venues and outside including House Music and national competitions. Drama offers three major productions per year alongside House Drama competitions, and regular showings for curricular Drama. Art presents exhibitions and cross-curricular projects with English and other departments. Our PE department boasts a heritage of sporting excellence in a wide range of both mainstream and less conventional sports with pupils regularly selected at district, county and national level. Other activities include Forest's Combined Cadet Force, which is linked to the Royal Green Jackets, and The Duke of Edinburgh's Award scheme which offers Bronze, Silver and Gold levels with high completion rates at all stages. Pupils can choose anything from horse riding to chess, technology to debating, drama and a wide range of musical activities to some of the best sporting offerings. Pupils participate in a diverse programme of activities that encourage learning of physical, cultural and leadership skills throughout their time at Forest. The Forest Portfolio, which pupils begin in Year 7 and continue through to Sixth Form, is a journal of a pupil's co-curricular experiences and achievements at Forest; this includes encouraging them to become active members of the wider community through our Community Action initiative.

Games. The main games are association football, hockey, cricket, netball, athletics, basketball and swimming. The sporting facilities are extensive and include an all-weather astroturf facility, tennis and netball courts, indoor and outdoor cricket nets, gym, sports hall, two swimming pools, strength and conditioning suite, 5-a-side 3G and acres of sporting fields. Additional sports such as fencing, rowing, golf, squash, mountain biking, table tennis, badminton and water polo are also available.

Fees per term (2018–2019). Reception to Year 2: £4,365, Year 3: £4,656, Year 4 to 6: £5,009 Year 7 to 13: £6,227. Fee reductions are available for children of the Clergy.

Careers. Almost all pupils go on to universities to take degree courses, including approximately 10 each year to Oxford and Cambridge.

Admission – Preparatory School. In principle, pupils are assessed on the basis of:

4+ entry:

- A series of low-key activities which include: picture recognition, some letter recognition, following a pattern, knowing colours, counting, drawing, naming simple shapes, sequencing, listening to a story, playing and responding sensibly to the adults who are present

7+ entry:

- Initial assessments using the computer and a literacy task
- Upon selection for the second stage: creative writing, collaborative activities and reading test
- A written confidential report from the present school is also requested

Admissions – Senior School. In principle, pupils are assessed on the basis of:

11+ entry and 13+ entry:

- Performance in English and Mathematics examinations
- An interview with a senior member of staff
- A written confidential report from the present school

16+ entry:

- The entrance examination consists of a compulsory critical thinking paper and two GCSE-standard papers
- An interview with a senior member of staff
- Entry into the Forest Sixth Form requires at least three grade 7s or above; and at least three grade 6s or above; and at least grade 4 in English and Maths; and the required grade at I/GCSE in the qualifying subject/s required for their chosen courses.

Full GCSE grade requirements can be found on the School website: www.forest.org.uk. A written confidential report from the present school will also be requested.

Scholarships and Bursaries are available at 11+, 13+ and 16+ entry. The maximum non-means-tested fee remission awarded in respect of any one pupil is 50% of full fees, whether in one area of excellence or in a combination of one or more areas of excellence.

Bursaries are means-tested and are awarded in addition to Scholarships, up to and including the total remission of fees; in other words, a free place. Bursaries are only given in conjunction with a Scholarship.

11+ entry:

Up to the equivalent of 14 places may be given annually to pupils at 11+ following Scholarship assessment in January of the year of entry. This figure includes both Scholarships and Bursaries.

- Academic Scholarships
- Music Scholarships
- Sport Scholarships

13+ entry:

Up to the equivalent of 2 places may be given annually to internal and external applicants at 13+ following Scholarship assessment.

- Academic Scholarships
- Music Scholarships
- Sport Scholarships

16+ entry:

Scholarships are awarded for outstanding academic ability and exceptional attainment in Art, Drama, Music and Sport.

Up to the equivalent of six places may be given annually to both internal and new entrants to the Sixth Form.

For full details visit www.forest.org.uk.

Old Foresters Club. *President*: Nigel Herd, c/o Forest School.

Charitable status. Forest School, Essex is a Registered Charity, number 312677. The objective of the School is Education.

Governing Council:
Chairman of Governors: D Wilson, LLB
The Venerable Elwin Cockett, Archdeacon of West Ham
Mrs J Davies
W Fuller
G S Green, MA
Dr S Hadi, BSc Hons, MBBS, MRCOG
Mrs G Jenkinson, AGSM, Dip Ed
His Honour Judge W Kennedy
Mrs P Oates, BEd
Mr M Robinson

Leadership Team:

Warden: Mr M Cliff Hodges, BA University College Cardiff, MA University College London

Bursar and Clerk to the Governors: Mrs D E Coombs, BSc Cape Town, Hons B&A, MBA Stellenbosch

Deputy Warden: Mr G du Toit, MA King's College London

Head of Preparatory School: Mr J E R Sanderson, BMus Perf Hons Elder Conservatorium, BMus Adelaide, FRSA

Deputy Head Academic: Mr T Mahmoud, MA Heythrop College London

Deputy Head Pastoral and Designated Safeguarding Lead: Mr J H Kayne, BSc Nottingham Trent, NPQH

Deputy Head Co-Curricular: Mrs G van Praagh, BA American Academy of Dramatic Arts

Head of Sixth Form: Ms K Spencer Ellis, MA Christ Church Oxford

Head of Middle School: Miss H Dyke, BA Nottingham

Head of Lower School: Mrs L E Lechmere-Smith, BA Sheffield

Director of Outreach: Mrs A Kay, MA Institute of Education

Director of Marketing and Communications: Mrs J O'Keeffe, BA Sussex

Teaching Staff:
[P] *Prep School*

B D Adams, BSc Exeter (*Director of Sport*)
K C Adams, BA Exeter (*Head of Spanish*)
Y Adlan Disney, MA King's College London (*English*)
E J Adshead, BSc Birmingham (*Chemistry, Asst Head of Sixth Form – Forest Diploma*)

Y Ahmed, MA London (*History*)
A Amirthananthar, BSc Westfield College, Queen Mary London (*Chemistry, Head of CCF Army Contingent*)
F Anwar, BA Huddersfield (*Learning Support*)
C Appiah-Kusi, PhD Cambridge (*Chemistry*)
L P Arnold, BA Exeter [P] (*Art Subject Leader*)
T J Arnold, BSc Exeter [P] (*Head of Prep School Boys' Pastoral Care*)
P T S Aspery, BA Lady Margaret Hall Oxford (*Head of Physics*)
J Atwal, MSc Southampton (*Head of Government and Politics*)
L M Baber, MSc Harvard (*Biology, Head of House*)
L Bainbridge, BA Selwyn College Cambridge (*Geography*)
L D Barker, BA Brighton (*Head of Art and Design*)
T A Barlow, MA Birmingham (*English*)
C A Barras, BSc Loughborough (*Head of Girls' Games*)
G R Barton, BA University College London (*Mathematics*)
G M Bassett-Jones, BSc Manchester (*Biology*)
S Beasley, MA Surrey (*Mathematics*)
R Begom, MSc London School of Hygiene and Tropical Medicine London (*Biology*)
E L Bellieu, BSc Sheffield (*RS and Philosophy, Head of Projects*)
A N Bergès, Lic-es-Lettres Paris (*Modern Languages*)
H R Betteridge, BA Durham (*RS and Philosophy*)
L S Bishop, BSc London (*Food and Nutrition, Examinations Officer*)
L Bouzguenda, BSc Salford (*Biology, Head of House*)
R L Broom, BSc Aston (*Economics, Head of Economics and Business*)
M Broughton, BA Leeds Metropolitan (*PE and Games, Master i/c Football*)
C P A Browne, MA Institute of Education, London [P] (*Senior Deputy Head of Preparatory School*)
S L Campbell, BA Worcester [P] (*Coordinator Extra-Curricular Activities & RE Subject Leader*)
D Cawley, BSc Leeds (*Science*)
B Christopher, BA Oxford (*Graduate Teaching Assistant Performing Arts*)
K L Clark, BEd Homerton College Cambridge [P] (*Deputy Head Pastoral of Preparatory School*)
J Clements, BMus Guildhall School of Music and Drama [P] (*Head of PS Music*)
M Clifford, BSc Queen's Belfast (*Biology, Asst Head of Sixth Form – Higher Education*)
A J Clifton, BA Sussex (*Learning Support*)
H W Clough, BA Somerville College Oxford (*History*)
N Coghlan, BA Roehampton Institute (*Learning Support*)
H Cole, BA Wales (*Geography*)
P R Cooper, BSc Leeds Beckett (*PE and Games*)
H Corbett, MA Northampton (*Art and Textiles*)
P Cordón, BA Vigo Spain (*Spanish*)
J Davies, MA Leeds (*Modern Languages*)
M Dean, MBA Stellenbosch South Africa (*Economics and Business Studies, Asst Head of Sixth Form Careers*)
T Dewhurst, BA Emmanuel College Cambridge (*Mathematics*)
O Dhani, BSc City London (*Mathematics*)
S Dhanjal, BSc University College London (*Art and Design*)
J Diangangu, BA East London (*Graduate Assistant Teacher Sport*)
A Eckton, BSc Brunel (*Design and Technology*)
H Edwards, MA Edinburgh (*Classics*)
S Elgie, MA Royal Holloway London (*English*)
M A Ellis, MA Cambridge (*Religious Studies and Philosophy*)
P M Faulkner, MSc Edinburgh [P] (*Head of Pre-Preparatory School*)
S F Firek, PhD Portsmouth Polytechnic (*Head of Biology*)

M J L Fisher, BA St Andrews (*Physics*)

A E Foinette, MA Nottingham (*Classics*)

R Gao, MA London Metropolitan (*Mandarin Teacher*)

A Gillham, BA Queens' College Cambridge (*English*)

J L Gordon, BA Anglia Ruskin [P] (*Geography Subject Leader*)

A G Gould, MA Balliol College Oxford (*Head of Classics*)

F J Grace, BSc Sussex (*Chemistry, Head of CCF RAF Contingent*)

M Gray, MA Middlesex (*Design and Technology*)

T F Grayson, BSc Kent (*Chemistry*)

R Greasley, BEd Liverpool John Moores (*Design and Technology*)

E Greatorex, BA Swansea (*Geography*)

P Gunpath, HED Springfield College of Education (*Physics*)

K Hall, BA Nottingham (*RS and Philosophy, Head of House, Assistant Head of PSHEE*)

A Hargitt, MA Christ Church Oxford, MA Durham (*Classics*)

L J Harris, BSc Bournemouth (*Head of Food and Nutrition*)

S M Harris, MA East London (*School Counsellor*)

A Hartley-Mottram, BA Brighton [P] (*Physical Education*)

J E Hayes, BSc London Metropolitan (*Food and Nutrition, Head of House*)

C A Heath, BA Westfield College, Queen Mary London (*Head of French, Head of House*)

K J Hopkin, BA Durham [P] (*History Subject Leader*)

D Hordok, BA Liverpool (*Modern Languages*)

C Horner, BA Birmingham (*History*)

H Hughes, MA St Andrews (*History*)

J Hurst, MA Institute of Education (*Assistant Director of Music*)

M S Jalowiecki, BA Queen Mary London (*Computing*)

L Jamieson, BSc Sussex (*Mathematics*)

R K Jeffries, BA University College London (*Classics*)

S Kadir, PhD Bristol (*Classics*)

J J Kay, BA Leeds (*English, Head of House*)

R H Kay, MA Warwick (*History, Head of House, Head of PSHEE*)

A Kelly, BSc Surrey (*Physics*)

J R Kendall, BA East London [P]

M E Key, MSt Oxford, MA Warwick (*Head of History*)

V Kieu, MSc Cranfield Institute of Technology (*Computing*)

A Landi, MA City [P] (*Drama*)

A L Lawes, BA Newcastle (*Mathematics, Timetabler*)

R Lawrence, LLB Manchester [P]

I M Leitão, MSc Glamorgan (*Physics*)

A C C Lindsey, BSc Sheffield City Polytechnic (*Head of Computing*)

O E Ling, BA Westfield College, Queen Mary London (*Government and Politics, Head of House*)

R Lokier, BA Downing College Cambridge (*Head of MFL*)

B J D P Lumley, MA Leeds Metropolitan (*Head of Boys' Games, Head of House*)

R Mackie, MA, MEd Fitzwilliam College Cambridge (*Head of RS and History, Assistant Head of Projects*)

A Manlangit, BEd McGill [P] (*Head of Pre-Preparatory School Teaching and Learning*)

N Marie, BMus Edinburgh (*Music*)

G McCormick, MA Glasgow [P]

I A McGregor, MA Fitzwilliam College Cambridge, MA, Keele (*Director of Music*)

A J McIlwaine-Smart, MA Sidney Sussex College Cambridge (*Director of Drama*)

S Merali-Smith, MA Manchester (*Classics*)

C E Middleweek, BA Bristol [P] (*PSHE Subject Leader*)

H P R Miller, BA University College London (*Head of German, Head of House*)

J Miller, BA Exeter (*Modern Languages, Head of House*)

A Mills, MA King's College London (*Religious Studies and Philosophy*)

I Mirza, BSc Greenwich [P] (*ICT Subject Leader*)

S A Mitchell, BA Liverpool John Moores (*Art and Textiles*)

L C Moore, BA Anglia Ruskin (*Art and Textiles*)

L A R Morrell, BA Brighton (*Girls' PE and Games*)

E W Morris, BSc Cheltenham & Gloucester College of HE (*Head of Geography*)

G Morris, BA King's College London (*Religious Studies*)

S P Morris, BSc York (*Chemistry*)

G Moss, BA Worcester [P]

S Mozakka, BSc University College London (*Mathematics*)

Z A Munir, BA Westminster (*Economics and Business Studies*)

G Murphy, MA Melbourne (*English*)

L E Nash, BA University College London (*Modern Languages*)

Z H Nazir, BSc, DPhil Sussex (*Mathematics*)

E Newman, MA Sheffield (*History and Religious Studies*)

C L Nightingale, BA Corpus Christi College Cambridge (*Head of English*)

R Nolan, BA Anglia Ruskin (*Art and Textiles*)

C M Nortier, BSc Free State (*Mathematics, Director of Studies*)

W O'Brien, BA Bath (*Graduate Assistant Teacher Sport*)

J F O'Riordan, BA College of Marketing and Design, Dublin (*Design and Technology*)

S Pascual, BA Alicante (*Modern Languages*)

F M Pereira, MA Middlesex (*Art*)

E Perez, BA La Salle Catholic University (*Food and Nutrition*)

J Perham, BSc West of England (*PE and Games*)

P Peters, PhD Université Lille: Sciences (*Physics*)

B M J Phillips, BSc Cardiff Metropolitan (*PE, Head of House*)

M M Pickwick, BSc City of London Polytechnic [P] (*Learning Support*)

A Plumb, MEd Cambridge (*Biology*)

D R Potter, BA Birmingham, PG Dip Acting, Webber Douglas Academy (*Drama*)

J S Pryke, BA St John's College Cambridge [P] (*Head of Pre-Preparatory School Teaching and Learning*)

C M Ranger, PhD Essex (*English*)

D Rathod, MSci Imperial College London (*Mathematics*)

L Raymond, BA London College of Fashion (*Art and Textiles*)

B A Richardson, BSc Witwatersrand (*Mathematics*)

K J Ridley, MChem St Andrews (*Head of Chemistry*)

C Risk, BSc, BPhD Otago Dunedin NZ (*Girls' PE and Games*)

V J Robertson, BA Middlesex University (*Design and Technology*)

M Salamut, BArch Westminster, BSc Warwick (*Mathematics*)

E L Sandhu, BA Birmingham (*History*)

A Sanghera, BSc Birmingham (*Graduate Assistant Teacher Sport*)

J B Scott, BA Reading [P] (*Maths Subject Leader*)

K A Scott, BA Ulster [P] (*English Subject Leader*)

K Sergent, BA Université Lille 3 (*Modern Languages*)

J T Sloan, BA Royal Holloway London (*History, Head of House*)

E Smith, MPhil Oxford (*Religious Studies and Philosophy*)

J Spencer, MSc London School of Economics (*History*)

M H A Stern, PhD Kent (*English*)

E Stockwell, BMus Royal Holloway London (*Music*)

J Sundhu, BSc Manchester (*Mathematics*)

M J Taylor, MA Jesus College Oxford, MSc Manchester (*Head of Mathematics*)
C Thompson, BA Leeds (*Economics*)
Reverend P K Trathen, MA York (*Chaplain*)
D L Tubb, BEd I M Marsh College of PE Liverpool (*PE and Games*)
F H van Niekerk, BSc North West (*Geography*)
K Vidos, BSc Nottingham (*Biology, Junior Science Coordinator*)
J White, MA Institute of Education (*Head of Science*)
J A C Whitmee, BA Sheffield (*Geography*)
M Wright, BA Kent (*Head of Learning Support*)
J H Wyn-Thomas, MA Trinity College Cambridge (*English*)

F J Alvarez (*Spanish Language Assistant*)
D Blanco (*Y4 Teacher's Assistant*)
J Clifton (*Teacher's Assistant Reception*)
L Crisp (*Classroom Assistant*)
M Deboub (*Y5&6 Teacher's Assistant*)
H Fellowes (*Y3 Teacher's Assistant*)
D Groves (*Y1 Teacher's Assistant*)
G Henze (*German Language Assistant*)
K Kelsey (*Y2 Teacher's Assistant*)
F Matson (*Teacher's Assistant Reception*)
N Messalti (*French Language Assistant*)
S Sahins (*Y2 Teacher's Assistant*)
D Young (*Y1 Teacher's Assistant*)

Support Staff:

Admissions:
Assistant Registrar: Mrs D Carbonaro, BA Nottingham
Admissions Administrator: Mrs V Rooprai, BA Hertfordshire

Alumni
Alumni Manager: Mrs S Gautama, BA London

Bursar's Office:
Chief Accountant: Mr N Asghar, BA East London
Assistant Accountant: Mrs T Prior
Accounts Clerk: Mrs E Kearney
Assistant Accounts Clerk: Ms S Morl

Careers:
Careers Manager: Mrs S Coates, LLB Exeter

Co-Curriculum:
Co-Curriculum Manager: Mrs D Cleveland-Hurley
Vehicle Maintenance/Driver: Mr D Collett
Activities Administrator: Mrs A Lincoln
DofE Scheme Manager: Mr J Moore-Hurley
Sports Administrator: Ms N Okey
Music Administrator: Mrs S Roach
Technical Theatre Manager: Mr C Tindall
Events Manager: Mr S Zieba

Design:
Graphic Designer: Miss L Thomas-Dixon

Estates:
Estates Manager: Mr J Stalley
Estates Helpdesk Administrator: Miss A Townsend
Head of Maintenance: Mr C Blanchard
Carpenter/Joiner: Mr R Coles
Head Groundsman: Mr P Gleaves
School Porter: Mr S Grant
Assistant Groundsman: Mr D Mackenzie
General Maintenance: Mr D McFarlane

Exams Office:
Exams Officer: Mrs L S Bishop
Assistant Exams Officer: Mrs P Folta

Health, Safety and Compliance:
Health & Safety and Compliance Director: Mr W Bishop, Dip NEBOSH, Grad IOSH
Health & Safety and Compliance Assistant: Ms J Cassidy

HR Office:
HR Assistant: Miss M Lapes, BA, UEL, CIPD Level 5 Human Resource Management

Information and Technology:
Director of Information and Technology: Mr D Lundie, MBA Stellenbosch Business School
IT Services Manager: Mr G Triggs, MCSA, MCSE, MCDBA, ACE, IT Dip
IT Support Engineer: Mr M Allen
IT Support Engineer: Mr K Dearing, CCNA, CompTIA A+
IT Support Engineer: Mr D Daramola, BSc London, CCNA, CCNP
Junior IT Support Engineer: Miss A Hales
I & T Helpdesk Administrator: Ms J Perry
Head of e-Learning: Ms L Golding-Hann, BSc, UWE Bristol, PG Dip Hertfordshire
Database Manager: Mr I Gulma
Data Analyst: Ms Z Fookeer, BSc Westminster
Head of Reprographics: Mrs D Batley
Reprographics Designer: Miss J Uzice

Library:
Head Librarian: Mr A Black, LLB Cardiff, Dip Lib, MCLIP
Systems Librarian: Mr E Milford Dickson, MSc Simmons College Graduate School of Library & Information Science USA (*School Magazine Editor*)
Prep School Librarian: Mrs S Goring, BA East London
Library Assistant: Miss C Griffiths, BA Roehampton

Medical:
Matron: Mrs G Delaforce, RGN
Matron: Mrs S Dempsey, RGN

PAs:
PA to the Head of Prep School: Ms V Alexander
PA, Pastoral Office: Miss A Buck
PA to the Bursar: Mrs A Crawley
PA to the Deputy Head Academic: Mrs T Hogg
PA to Deputy Warden: Mrs A Patuto
PA to Deputy Head Pastoral: Miss D Tardioli
PA to the Warden: Miss S Woolston

Reception:
Receptionist: Mrs J Bell
Receptionist: Ms J Wilson

School Offices:
School Office Manager: Mrs K Wolstenholme
Deputy School Office Manager: Mrs E Ruiz Rull
School Office Assistant: Ms J Clarke
School Office Assistant: Mrs S Church
School Office Assistant: Mrs C Piquito
School Office Assistant: Miss J Prior
Prep School Office Manager: Mrs T Petherbridge
Sixth Form Secretary: Mrs D O'Brien
Sixth Form Administrator: Mrs E Campbell

Sylvestrian Leisure Centre:
Centre Manager: Miss L Cooper, BSc Wales, Bangor
Operations Manager/Fitness Manager: Mr J Wilson
Duty Manager: Mr E Palmer
Mr J Ballah, BSc London Metropolitan
Mr J Bennett, BSc West London
Holiday Activities Manager: Miss J Brown
Swimming Coordinator: Miss S Bellas
Receptionist: Miss M Stavri, Miss J Louisy
Recreation Assistant: Miss S Lesurf

Technicians:
Senior Technician: Mrs A Christou
Senior Science Technician: Mr T Bennett
Laboratory Technician: Mr A Christou
Laboratory Technician: Mrs C Ford
Laboratory Technician: Mrs S Hammond
DT Technician: Mrs K Panesar
Laboratory Technician: Mr E Saggers
Art Technician: Ms R Wojs
Food Technician: Mrs P Folta
Food Technician: Mrs S Santos

Chartwells Catering and Cleaning:
Manager: Mr S Moore
Head Chef: Mr D Leonard
Catering Manager: Mr B Carter
Assistant Manager: Mrs H Runacres
Deputy Manager: Mrs M Uzice
Catering Administrator: Mrs S Moore
Cleaning Supervisor: Mrs C Mensah

School Solicitor: Mr C F Newman, MA, LLM

Auditors: Haysmacintyre & Co

Co-Curriculum Staff:

Piano:
Ms J Trew, PRAM, LRAM, LTCL
Mr R J Hunter, BMus Hons
Mrs L Neugasimova
Ms Z Mather, AGSM
Piano & Organ: Mr J Waggott, MMus ARCO
Recorder: Mrs E Bloom, BMus Hons, PG Dip
Violin and Viola:
Mrs S Sheppard, LRAM
Mr M Trandafilovski, BMus, MMus, DMus
Mr R MacManus, BMus Hons, MMus
Mrs O Jennings, Dip Mus Lviv
'Cello: Miss A Manthorpe Saunders, MA RAM, BMus Hons, PG Dip
Double Bass & Bass Guitar: Mr A Storey, T1 Exceptional Talent
Flute, Piccolo & Piano: Mr K Bartels, BMus, LGSM [flute], LGSM [clarinet], LGSM [piano], LTCL, ARCO
Flute & Saxophone: Mr P Knights, BA Hons Jazz
Clarinet & Saxophone: Mr N Webb, GTCL, ARAM, Dip RAM
Saxophone: Mr J Arben, BA Oxon, MMus
Saxophone & Jazz Piano: Mr J Kemp, MA Oxon, LGSM, PG Dip
Oboe:
Mrs H McKean, LTCL, FTCL, ARCM
Miss R Berresford, BMus Hons GSMD, LGSMD, PG Dip Mus GSMD
Bassoon: Miss E Trigg, BMus Hons, PGNRCM, LRAM
French Horn: Mr J Thomas, MMus, BMus Hons
Trumpet & Cornet: Mr D Clewlow, BMus Hons
Trombone: Mr A White, BA RCM
Tuba: Mr C Barrett, BA RAM
Guitar:
Mr S Golding, Dip Arranging & Composition
Mrs G Cooney, BMus Hons, LRAM
Voice:
Miss H Meyerhoff, BMus Hons RNCM
Mr T McVeigh, DRSAMD
Miss S Young, BA Hons, PGCE, LTCL
Voice & Music Theatre: Miss G Oldman, BA Hons
Percussion: Mr J Davis, BA Jazz, MA
Orchestral Percussion: Mr G Boynton, Dip RCM, ARCM, Dip RCM PG
Harp: Mrs R Bartels, BMus, LRAM

Composition: Mr D S Bloom, MMus Dist RAM, BMus Hons, RCM, LRAM
Speech and Drama:
Miss G Brooks, AGSM, Dip Ed
Mr C Jenkinson, WDA Diploma in Acting
Miss N Michaelides, BA, ALA
Mr R Zagger ALAM
Dance:
Mrs F Tolland-Woodley, MRes, MA, AISTD
Miss N Saville, BA, AIDTA
Miss F Crosbie, BA
Miss J Noverre, BA, DDI

Combined Cadet Force:
Capt A Alexander (*Contingent Commander*)
Lt A Amirthananthar (*O/C Army Section*)
Plt Off F J Grace (*O/C RAF Section*)
Sgt H Hughes (*SSI*)
Plt Off P Peters (*RAF*)
Mr D Collett (*Drum Corps*)
Mr M Bassett-Jones (*Army*)
Mr A Mills
Miss H R Betteridge

Heads of Department:
Art and Design: Mr L D Barker
Biology: Dr S F Firek
Chemistry: Miss K Ridley
Classics: Mrs A G Gould
Computing: Mr A Lindsey
Drama: Mrs A J McIlwaine-Smart
Economics and Business: Ms R L Broome
English: Mrs C L Nightingale
Food Science: Miss L J Harris
French: Miss C A Heath
Geography: Mr E W Morris
German: Mrs H P R Miller
Government and Politics: Mrs J Atwal
History: Mr M E Key
Learning Support: Mrs M Wright
Mathematics: Mr M J Taylor
Modern Foreign Languages: Mr R Lokier
Music: Mr I A McGregor
Physical Education: Mr B D Adams
Physics: Mr P T S Aspery
Projects: Mrs E Bellieu
PSHEE: Mrs R H Kay
Religious Studies & Philosophy: Miss R Mackie
Science: Mrs J White
Spanish: Mrs K C Adams

Games:
Director of Sport: Mr B D Adams
Boys' School Games: Mr B J D P Lumley
Girls' School Games: Miss C A Barras
PS Sport: Mr T J Arnold
Athletics & Cross Country: Mr P Cooper
Basketball: Mr B M J Phillips
Badminton: Mrs A Amirthananthar
Cricket: Mr J F Perham
Football: Mr M L Broughton
Golf: Mr B D Adams
Boys' Hockey: Mr D Gilkes
Girls' Hockey: Miss C A Barras
Netball: Miss C Risk
Cycling: Mr R Greasley
Swimming: Mr M Bush

Houses & Housemasters/mistresses:

Boys' Houses:	Copeland's: Mrs H P R
Bishop's: Mr O E Ling	Miller
Doctor's: Mr B M J	Phillips

Guy's: Mr L Bouzguenda
Johnians: Mr J Miller
Miller's: Mr J J Kay
Poole's: Mr B J D P
Lumley

Girls' Houses:
Astell: Miss C A Heath

Baylis: Mrs J E Hayes
Eliot: Miss H Edwards
Franklin: Mrs R H Kay
Hepworth: Mrs K Hall
Kingsley: Ms L Baber
School: Mr J T Sloan

Framlingham College

Framlingham, Woodbridge, Suffolk IP13 9EY

Tel:	01728 723789
Fax:	01728 724546
email:	admissions@framcollege.co.uk
website:	www.framcollege.co.uk
Twitter:	@FramCollege
Facebook:	@framcollege
LinkedIn:	/framlingham-college

Motto: *Studio Sapientia Crescit*

Location. The school is situated close to the wonderful Suffolk Coast, in the historic market town of Framlingham, overlooking the Mere and Castle, and is served by good road and rail links to London, Cambridge, Colchester, Norwich and all the main London airports.

History. The School was founded in 1864 by public subscription as the Suffolk County Memorial to Prince Albert and was incorporated by Royal Charter.

Organisation. Mr Taylor became Headmaster in September 2009; he was formerly Lower Master (Deputy Head) at King's School in Canterbury. He now leads a school that has recently received an excellent ISI Inspection Report, which described the College as highly successful in meeting its stated aims and mission of providing a first-class, holistic education, in a safe and inspiring environment, accessible to a broad range of boys and girls. The Senior School numbers some 405 pupils of whom 250 are boarders. All students are accommodated in seven fully-integrated boarding and day houses: three for girls and four for boys.

Preparatory School. Framlingham College Prep School, located 4 miles away at Brandeston Hall, is a leading preparatory school for boys and girls aged 2–13. All students are prepared for the ISEB Common Entrance Examination. (*See entry in IAPS section.*)

Facilities. Framlingham has invested heavily in its facilities which includes the Headmaster Porter Theatre, a drama and music facility. Science, Technology and Art also enjoy purpose-built buildings. The sports facilities include an impressive array of outdoor pitches and grounds, a 9-hole golf course, plus two floodlit artificial hockey pitches and tennis/netball courts. The Sports Centre houses an indoor pool, gym, performance suite, spinning room, weights room and cardiovascular room. Pupils can benefit from the guidance of our strength and conditioning coaches, who create specialist programmes for our elite athletes and for injury rehabilitation. In September 2017, the Fowler Pavilion was opened. This fantastic facility overlooks the 1st XI cricket pitch and Inskips hockey pitch. The flourishing Sixth Form is 200 strong and students enjoy their own Centre, which overlooks the 1st XI cricket pitch and an attractive central concourse used extensively for informal gatherings. There are further plans to improve the warm and friendly boarding houses.

Curriculum. The College has a fine record in stretching the most able, while the 'value added' rating for those pupils who are not automatically destined to achieve A grades at GCSE and A Level stands among the very best in the country. This is reflected in the ISI Inspection report which describes the teaching and learning as '*excellent*'. The College offers a broad curriculum encompassing traditional subjects alongside 21st Century subjects such as Computer Science and Graphic Design. There is also the opportunity to take BTEC courses in the Sixth Form.

Co-Curricular Activities. Our academic success rates are mirrored by outstanding sporting achievements, commitment to the popular and extremely successful Duke of Edinburgh's Award scheme and the outward-bound work of the voluntary Combined Cadet Force. From the cut and thrust of the debating society there are visiting speakers and musical performances, charity competitions, formal house suppers and many cultural, educational and recreational visits. Whether it is choral or debating society, go-kart construction or drone flying, a round of golf on campus or trekking in Nepal, there is something for everyone.

Games. Framlingham College enjoys an enviable reputation for sport and fields a large number of teams. The major sports are rugby, hockey, cricket, athletics and tennis for boys, and hockey, netball, cricket, tennis and athletics for girls. The school regularly has pupils representing England at Hockey and Rugby. There is a wide range of other sporting opportunities, including squash, football, badminton, basketball, swimming, archery, shooting, volleyball and table tennis. The immaculately tended grounds include four rugby pitches, two floodlit artificial pitches, a golf course and one of the finest cricket squares in the East of England. The facilities also include a sports hall, indoor swimming pool, fitness centre, gym, squash courts, netball courts and tennis courts. Students benefit from Golf fixtures and practice at Aldeburgh Golf Club. Framlingham has been awarded MCC Foundation Hub status and features in the Top 100 Cricket Schools.

Music and Drama. Framlingham has a very strong choral tradition, and there is a wide range of orchestras and instrumental ensembles. In the past seven years, three pupils have reached the finals of BBC Radio 2 Chorister of the Year and one student has just been awarded a Scholarship to the Royal College of Music. The College's dramatic productions enjoy a very high reputation. The main productions each year generally include one musical, a major drama and a junior play. Every year a drama group takes part in the annual Edinburgh Fringe Festival.

Religion. The College has a strong Christian foundation, but students of all backgrounds are welcomed.

Admission. Common Entrance and interview form the normal means of entry to the College at 13+. Entrance at 16+ is normally on the basis of GCSE results and interview or testing, but special arrangements are made for overseas students who are not following the British Curriculum. Visits from interested parties are welcomed; please contact us to make an appointment.

Scholarships and Bursaries. Academic, Creative Arts (art, DT, drama, music and computer science) and Sports Scholarships are awarded at 11 +, 13+ and Sixth Form.

Successful candidates can be offered further assistance through bursaries in cases of proven financial need.

Special bursaries are available for the children of serving members of HM Forces.

Fees per term (2018–2019). Boarding £10,328, Day £6,641.50 (including lunch).

Charitable status. Albert Memorial College (Framlingham College) is a Registered Charity, number 1114383.

Chairman of Governors: Air Vice-Marshal T W Rimmer, CB, OBE, MA, FRAeS, FRGS, RAF Retd

Headmaster: **Mr P B Taylor**, BA Hons

Senior Deputy Head: Miss S M Wessels, BSc Hons, MEd

Deputy Head Academic: D G Ashton, BA Hons, Dip Ed
Deputy Head Co-Curricular: M D Robinson, MA, BEd Hons (*Head of History*)
Deputy Head Pastoral: T J Caston, BA Hons, MSc

Heads of Department:
Art: Mrs S Tansley, BA Hons, PGCE
Business Studies & Economics: M Milne, BA Hons, PGCE
Careers: Miss C Cranmer, BA Hons, PGCE, Dip Speech & Drama
Universities: R W Skitch, BSc, ACCEG, ACIB, PGCE
Computer Science: J Harrod, BA Hons, PGCE
Design & Technology: J Buxton, BA Hons, PGCE, MEd
Drama: Ms D Englert, BA Hons, PGCE, Dip Speech & Drama
ESL: Mrs K Cavalcanti, BEd Hons, RSA Dip EFL
English: L Goldsmith, BA Hons, MBA, PGCE
Geography: E Newman, BSc, PGCE
French: Mr B Dyer, BA Hons, PGCE, AST
Spanish: Mr J Sedeno, BA Hons
Learning Support: Mrs F Reagan, BA Hons
Mathematics: Mrs H McCartney, BA Hons, PGCE
Director of Music: Mrs L Bloore, Dip TCL, LTCL, PGCE
Psychology: Mrs J S Hobson, BA Hons, PGCE
Religious Studies & Philosophy: Dr P Giles, BD Hons, PGCE, MEd, PhD
Science: Dr D R Higgins, MA, PhD, PGCE
Director of Sport: N Gandy, BA Hons, PG Dip
PE: Chris Gange, BSc Hons, PGCE

Finance Director: N J Chaplin, BA Hons, FCCA
Operations Director: A L Payn, Chartered FCIPD
Development Director: M K Myers-Allen, BSc Hons, PGCE
Admissions Registrar: Miss E Rutterford, BA Hons
Headmaster's Personal Assistant: Mrs L Flack

Francis Holland School
Regent's Park

Ivor Place, London NW1 6XR

Tel: 020 7723 0176
Fax: 020 7706 1522
email: admin@fhs-nw1.org.uk
website: www.fhs-nw1.org.uk
Twitter: @FHSRegentsPark
Facebook: @FHSRegentsPark

Founded 1878.
There are 495 day girls and entry by examination and interview is normally at 11+, with a number joining at 16+ for the Sixth Form. The school was founded in 1878 and is affiliated to the Church of England, but girls of all Christian denominations and other faiths are accepted.

Curriculum. Girls are prepared for GCSE, A Levels, and for admission to Universities, and Colleges of Art and Music. Sport takes place in Regent's Park and full use is made of the museums, theatres and galleries in central London. Extra lessons are available including fencing, music, Speech and Drama, kickboxing, Mandarin Chinese, cookery, street dance, yoga and cheerleading. For the first five years, to GCSE, girls follow a broad curriculum and normally take 10 GCSE subjects. Careers advice is given from the third year, and all pupils receive individual guidance through to the Sixth Form. In the Sixth Form a wide choice of A Level subjects is combined with a general course of study, including the opportunity to take the Extended Project. All girls are expected to stay until the end of the A Level course.

Scholarships and Bursaries. We will consider awarding a bursary to girls who demonstrate the ability to succeed at Francis Holland, but whose parents might not have sufficient financial resources.

A bursary is a means-tested award and is determined by the family's financial circumstances, taking into account income, realisable assets and other relevant circumstances. The level of assistance provided will depend on individual circumstances, which will be reviewed annually. The number of bursaries awarded each year is at the discretion of the Governors and may vary.

Remission of a third of the fees is available to places offered to daughters of the clergy.

Fees per term (2018–2019). £6,680.

Situation. The school is situated just outside Regent's Park and is three minutes from Baker Street and Marylebone stations. Victoria and Hampstead buses pass the school.

Charitable status. The Francis Holland (Church of England) Schools Trust Limited is a Registered Charity, number 312745. It exists to provide high quality education for girls.

Patron: The Right Revd and Right Hon The Lord Bishop of London

Council of Governors:

Chairman: Mrs M Winckler, MA
Vice-Chairman: Mrs A Edelshain, BA, MBA, MCIPD
Mr R Backhouse, MA
Mr G Bennett, MA, ACA
Ms C Black, MC SI
Revd Dr M Bowie, BA, DPhil
Ms J Briggs, BA, MA, PGCE, Adv Dip CIPFA
Mr M Cuthbert, FRICS, BSc, MBA, Dip ProjMan
Mr D Dowley, MA, QC
Mr A Fincham, MA
Dr C Gwenlan, MSci, PhD
Dr M Harrison, BA
Mrs A O'Keeffe, BA
Professor J Parry, MA, PhD
Mr I Ramsay, BSc, FCA
Ms N de Renzo, MSc Bocconi
Lady R Robathan, BSc
Miss S Ross, BSc, FInstP
Dr H Spoudeas, MBBS, DRCOG, FRCPCH, FRCP, MD
Mr G Stead

Bursar: Mr G Wilmot, BA, ACA
Clerk to the Governors: Mrs G Shaw, BSc

Senior Leadership Team:

Headmaster: Mr C B Fillingham, MA King's College London

Senior Deputy Head: Ms A Slocombe, MA Cantab
Academic Deputy Head: Miss J Zugg, BSc Cape Town South Africa
Pastoral Deputy Head: Miss C Mahieu, BEd Sydney Australia
Assistant Head (Extra-Curricular): Mrs A Francisco, BA Sydney Australia
Assistant Head (Operations): Ms S Hack, BA Portsmouth, FRGS
Director of External Relations: Mrs V McKinley, BA London
Director of Information Services: Mr D Nanton, FInstLM, MBCS, AAPM, MCSE

Heads of Year:
Head of Year 7: Mr A Smith, BA York
Head of Year 8: Mrs S Bexon, BA King's College London
Head of Year 9: Mrs V Randle, BA Cantab

Head of Years 10 and 11: Mr H Clayton, BA Liverpool
Deputy Head of Years 10 and 11: Miss M Gustave, BA MA
   Montpellier
Head of Sixth Form: Mr N Gridelli, BA Bologna Italy
Deputy Head of Sixth Form: Dr F De Bono, PhD London

Teaching Staff:

* *Head of Department*

Art:
*Miss N Carew, BA National College of Art & Design,
   Dublin
Miss J Orr, BA NkU, MA Sussex
Miss H Gardner, BA Hons Nottingham
Mrs Rosie North, PG Dip RA [maternity leave]
Miss Louise Evans, BA Wimbledon College of Art

Classics:
*Mrs H Packford, BA Cantab, MA Birkbeck [maternity
   leave]
Ms E Simons, MA Cantab (*Acting Head of Dept*)
Mrs J Cohen, MA Oxon
Mrs V Randle, BA Cantab (*NQT and Oxbridge
   Coordinator*)
Mrs A Hillier, MA Cantab
Miss H Williams, MA Durham
Miss Z Cannell, BA Oxon

Economics:
*Miss A M Conway, MA St Andrews

English and Drama:
Head of Dept (English): Mrs L Parkes, BA Oxon
Head of Dept (Drama): Mrs H Simmons, MA Warwick,
   BA Keele
Ms E Williams, BA Leeds
Mrs N Foy, MA London
Dr F De Bono, PhD London (*Director of Higher Education
   and Deputy Head of Sixth Form*)
Mr A Smith, BA York
Mrs A Phillips, MA Oxon

Geography:
*Mrs J Dawes, MA UCL
Ms S Hack, BA Portsmouth FRGS (*Assistant Head*)
Miss E O'Neill, BSc St Andrews [maternity leave]
Miss K Voth, MA Cantab
Ms V Robin, BA Oxon

History and Politics:
*Mr P Glavin, BA Liverpool
Mr H Clayton, BA Liverpool
Mr D Bryson, MA Warwick
Miss L Quick, BA KCL

History of Art:
*Miss C MacDonnell, MA London
Mrs A Francisco, BA Sydney Australia

Information Technology:
*Miss V Rusu, BEd Alberta
Mrs M Anastasi, BSc Open University

Learning Enhancement:
*Mrs M Wynne, BA Dunedin New Zealand, RSA Dip of
   SLD UCL
Mr T Carew Hunt, MA UCL
Mrs J Lewey, ARCM
Mrs N Thompson, BA Liverpool, MA UCL

Librarian:
Mrs E Aves, BA Gloucestershire
Miss S Lawrence, BA Lancaster

Mathematics:
*Mrs C Thornhill, BSc Oxon

Miss N Murugan, BSc Heriot-Watt, MSc KCL
Miss R Le Roux, BSc Nottingham Trent, MSc Essex
Miss J Zugg, BSc Cape Town South Africa
Miss H Blazewicz, BSc Bristol
Mrs K Healy, BSc Queen's Belfast
Mrs T Hay, BSc Lycée Saint Louis
Mr O Bello, BSc KCL

Modern Languages:
Acting Head of Dept (MFL and Spanish): Mrs N Estima,
   MA KCL (*DofE Co-ordinator*)
Head of Dept (French): Miss A Spera, BA Pisa
Head of Dept (Italian): Mr N Gridelli, BA Bologna Italy
Head of Dept (German): Ms R Iksilara, BSc Athens, BA
   KCL, MA IoE London
Herr R Diesel, Technische Universitat Berlin
Miss M Gustave, MA Montpellier
Ms A Slocombe, MA Cantab (*Senior Deputy Head*)
Mrs F Boschi, AVCE
Ms A Diaz-Crespo, MA Cadiz
Mrs A McBurney, MA Cantab, MA KCL (*Exams Officer*)
Mr C B Fillingham, MA KCL (*Headmaster*)
Mrs W Hu, MA Central Saint Martins, MA UCL
Miss J Soyer, BA Université de Poitiers
Dr N El Akel, BA Université Charles-de-Gaulle, MA
   Université Charles-de-Gaulle, PhD KCL
Mrs E Warner, BA Bristol
Miss L Glas, MA Université Paul Valéry

Music:
*Mr R Patterson, MA Cantab, FRCO
Mr A Smith, BA York
Miss L Zarina, BMus Trinity Laban Conservatoire

Visiting Music:
Mr K Abbs, FTCL (*Clarinet/Saxophone*)
Miss E Bassett, MA LRAM (*Trombone*)
Miss A Bevan, ABRSM (*Flute*)
Ms K Bennett, MMus (*Flute*)
Miss T Clifford, MMus, PGDip (*Piano*)
Ms F Firth, LTCL (*Voice*)
Ms K Gillham, BA, MMus (*Piano*)
Miss C Graham, MMus (*Cello*)
Mr E Hackett, LRAM (*Percussion & Kit*)
Mrs C Hall, LRAM (*Voice*)
Miss J Harris, BMus (*Trumpet*)
Miss M Holmes, BA Cantab (*Voice*)
Mr O Lallemant, MA Cantab (*Organist*)
Ms C Marroni, MusB, MPerf (*Bassoon*)
Ms J Lewey, ARCM (*Theory*)
Mr D Parsons, ARCM (*Guitar*)
Miss C Parker, BMus (*Violin*)
Mr S Queen, MA Cantab (*Voice*)
Ms J Schloss, BMus Qld (*Piano*)
Miss E Woollard, BMus (*Oboe*)
Mrs M Ryan, MA CIT (*Violin*)

Also visiting teachers for:
musical instruments, aerobics, kick boxing, self-defence,
   pottery, cookery, fencing, yoga and Alexander
   Technique, according to demand.

Physical Education:
Director of Sport: Miss L Burroughs, BA Brighton
Miss J Tucker, BEd Queensland, Australia (*Educational
   Visits and Timetable Coordinator*)
Mrs K Lombard, BEd Canterbury, New Zealand (*Deputy
   Head of Careers*)
Miss C Mahieu, BEd Sydney, Australia (*Pastoral Deputy
   Head*)
Miss M Merrigan, BSc Loughborough (*Head of PSHE*)
Miss G Clydesdale-Huch, MA Otago, BSc Otago
   Polytechnic

Mrs B Percy, MA Buckingham, BA Royal Holloway

Psychology:
*Mrs A Packer, BSc University of the West of England
Dr J Rodgers, PhD Institute of Education, MA Birkbeck, BA Cantab

Religious Education:
*Mrs J Farthing, BA Bristol
Mrs S Bexon, BA King's College
Ms C Sivvery, BA Open University, BA Manchester

Speech and Drama:
Ms K Mount, BA Rose Bruford College
Miss M Leaf, BA Goldsmiths

Science:
*Mr D Ward, BSc Nottingham Trent, MA Open University (*Science*, *Physics*):
*Mr P Tiley, BSc Bristol (*Chemistry*):
Ms A Kadodia, NPQML, BSc Warwick (*Biology*)
Mrs R Grant, BSc Sheffield
Mr J Peters, BSc Swinburne
Miss B Shah, MSc Queen Mary's
Dr C MacTavish, DPhil MSc Toronto, BSc Guelph
Mr J Bossé, BSc BEd Moncton (*Director of Careers*)
Miss C Till, BSc St Andrews (*Pre-U Global Perspectives Coordinator*)
Miss E Hollender, MSc Durham (*Deputy Exams Officer*)

Non Teaching Staff:
PA to the Headmaster: Miss O Birkby, BA Bristol
Admissions Registrar: Mrs F Whitehead, LLB Sydney
School Secretary: Ms J Bhachu, MA World Sikh University
School Secretary: Ms A Broderick, BA Queen Mary
Display & Art Technician:Miss N Stowell, BA London
Art Technician: Mrs H Maund, BA Leeds College of Art
Systems Manager: Mr S Andrews
ICT Technician: Mr M Jaskiewicz
Database Manager: Mr B Yeboah, BA Hertfordshire
Examinations Officer: Mrs A McBurney, MA Cantab, MA KCL
Deputy Examinations Officer: Miss E Hollender, MSc Durham
Assistant Examinations Administrator: Mrs S Gurini
School Counsellor: Ms C Vincenti, UKCP reg, PgDip, ADEP, Regent's University, London
Church Co-ordinator: Mrs S Bexon, BA King's College
Development Manager: Mrs H Mumford, MA Edinburgh
Development Executive: Miss E Scouller, BA Falmouth
Senior Marketing and Design Executive: Miss L Pringle, BA Northumbria
Marketing Assistant: Mr L Powell, BA Birmingham
Alumni Relations Officer: Miss C Brazer, MSc Southbank
Resources: Mrs E Sheriffs
Gap Year Placement: Miss F Wright

Science Technicians:
Mrs G Unwin, BSc Greenwich
Mrs N Kazemi, BSc North London
Mrs M Shah, BA Tribhuwan University Nepal

Facilities Director: Mr S Vincent
Facilities Manager: Mr M Dempsey

Caretakers:
Mr C Alarcon Mejia
Mr J Saguiguit
Mr K Bright
Mr E Lemonaris

Catering Manager: Mr S King
School Counsellor: Ms C Vincenti, UKCP reg, PG Dip, ADEP, Regent's University London

Francis Holland School
Sloane Square

39 Graham Terrace, London SW1W 8JF
Tel: 020 7730 2971
Fax: 020 7823 4066
email: office@fhs-sw1.org.uk
website: www.fhs-sw1.org.uk
Twitter: @FHSSloaneSquare
Facebook: @FHSSloaneSquare

Founded 1881.

Numbers and age of entry. There are 520 Day Girls in the School and entry by the School's own examination is at 4+ for the Junior School (ages 4–11), 11+ for the Senior School (ages 11–18) (member of The North London Independent Girls Schools' Consortium) and 16+ for Sixth Form.

Curriculum and Aims. Excellent academic standards are achieved through the provision of a challenging academic curriculum and talented staff who encourage an enthusiasm for learning, intellectual curiosity and creativity. This allows our girls to thrive in a relaxed and happy environment where they are respected as individuals and able to fulfil their unique potential.

Junior School. There is a Junior Department attached to the school.

Religious Education. The school's foundation is Anglican but girls of other faiths are welcomed.

Physical Education. Hockey, Netball, Rounders, Health-related Fitness, Gymnastics, Athletics, Tennis and Swimming are taken. Senior girls have a choice of other activities as well including Boxercise, Aerobics, Parkour, Trampolining, Pilates, Yoga and Zumba.

Fees per term (2018–2019). £6,160–£6,970.

Scholarships and Bursaries. There are the following competitive awards each year:

11+ Academic scholarships and Music scholarships are available to the value of 5% of fees. 1 Art award is also available.

Sixth Form: Academic scholarships (internal and external) up to the value of 25% of fees, Music scholarships up to the value of 25% of fees, Drama scholarships up to the value of 25% of fees.

We will consider awarding a bursary to girls who demonstrate the ability to succeed at Francis Holland, but whose parents might not have sufficient financial resources. The level of assistance provided will depend on individual circumstances, which will be reviewed annually. The number of bursaries awarded each year is at the discretion of the Governors and may vary.

Remission of a third of the fees is available for places offered to daughters of the clergy.

Charitable status. The Francis Holland (Church of England) Schools Trust Limited is a Registered Charity, number 312745. It exists to provide high quality education for girls.

Patron: The Right Revd and Right Hon The Lord Bishop of London

Council of Governors:

Chairman: Mrs M Winckler, MA
Vice-Chairman: Mrs A Edelshain, BA, MBA, MCIPD
Mr R Backhouse, MA
Mr G Bennett, MA, ACA
Rev Dr M Bowie, BA, DPhil
Ms J Briggs, BA, MA, PGCE, Adv Dip CIPFA

Mr M Cuthbert, MBA, BSc, FRICS
Mrs N de Renzo, ACA
Mr D Dowley, MA, QC
Mr A Fincham, MA
Dr C Gwenlan, MSci, PhD
Dr M Harrison, BA
Mrs A O'Keeffe, BA
Professor J Parry, MA, PhD
Mr I Ramsay, BSc, FCA
Lady R Robathan, BSc
Miss S Ross, BSc, FInstP
Dr H Spoudeas, MBBS, DRCOG, FRCPCH, FRCP, MD
Mr G Stead

Chief Operating Officer: Mr G Wilmot, BA, ACA
Clerk to the Governors: Mrs G Shaw, BSc

Senior Leadership Team:

Headmistress: Mrs L Elphinstone, MA Cantab, FRSA
(*English*)

Deputy Head: Mr P Jeanes, BMus London, FRSA (*Music*)
Director of Studies: Mr R Cawley, MA BA Lancaster
(*Religious Studies*)
Director of Pastoral Care: Mrs J Piercy, BA London
(*History*)
Joint Head of Sixth Form: Mrs R Sawyer, MA Cantab
(*History*)
Joint Head of Sixth Form: Mrs J Banks, MA London, BA
Durham (*English/Debating*)
Director of Creative Enterprise: Mr N Dyson, BA
Southampton (*Geography*)
Head of Junior School: Ms C Spencer, MSc Sheffield, BSc
Leeds
Director of External Relations: Mrs V McKinley, BA
London
Director of Information Systems: Mr D Nanton, FInstLM

Senior School Staff – Full time:
Miss A Allen, BA Chichester (*Assistant Head of Lower
School, Physical Education*)
Miss J Arlington, BA Surrey (**Photography*, Art*)
Mr C Bartram, BA Portsmouth (**Biology*)
Miss E Boon, MA Oxon (**History*)
M. F Calvet, MPhil Grenoble, MA Perpignan, Diploma
Toulouse (**Modern Foreign Languages, French*)
Mr N Casselle, MSc London (**Psychology, Head of
Academic Mentoring*)
Miss C Clements, BSc Texas, BSc London (*Science
Assistant*)
Miss P Crawley, MA SOAS, BA Oxon (**Religious Studies*)
Miss H Davidson, BA Newcastle (*Music*)
Miss D Dumortier, MA Paris (*Second in Department MFL
French/Spanish, DoE Coordinator*)
Mr D Edes, BA Exeter (**Art*)
Mr A Fernandes, MA UCL, BA London (**English*)
Mr W Galloway, BA Nottingham (*Head of Outreach,
English*)
Miss M Geussens, MA Cantab (*EPQ and Oxbridge
Coordinator, English, History*)
Ms W Grimshaw, BA Manchester (*Head of Upper School
Years 10–11, History*)
Miss E Holley, BA Brighton (*Physical Education*)
Mr J Hunt, MSc Surrey, BSc Sheffield (*Director of Digital
Learning, Timetable & Data Manager, *Computing*)
Mrs S Hyde, PCE, BA London (**Economics*)
Miss L James, BA Leeds (*Mathematics*)
Miss D Kaleja, I and II Staatsexamen Hanover, BA London
(**German*)
Father M Kenny, MA London, BA Leeds (*Director of
Spiritual Care, Debating, Religious Studies*)
Miss S Lee, BMus London (*Music Dept Assistant*)

Mme A Lenec'h, Licence Rouen, MA Connecticut USA
(*Head of Lower School Years 7–9, French*)
Mr A Macdonald-Brown, BA Oxon (*English & Classics*)
Miss C Mackenzie, BSc London (**Geography*)
Dr T Marshall, PhD Edinburgh, BA Cantab (*Examinations
Officer, Biology, Chemistry*)
Mrs V Marshall, MA London, BSc Newcastle, AMBDA,
APC (*Senior SENCO*)
Miss M McLaren, BSc Glasgow (**Chemistry, *Science*)
Miss G Newsome, BA Bath (**Director of Sport*)
Miss D Ortega, MA London (**Spanish*)
Mrs I Ramage, MSc LSE, BA Moscow, BSc Open
University (*Assistant Head of Sixth Form, Mathematics*)
Miss A Rinck, MEd Manchester, BA Cantab (*Assistant
Head of Upper School, Stretch and Challenge
Coordinator, Biology, Chemistry*)
Mr M Rowlands-Roberts, BA Middlesex (**Drama*)
Mrs E Shevah, MA Brunel, BA Nottingham (*English,
Learning Support*)
Mr S Taylor, BSc Leeds (**Mathematics*)
Dr N Upcott, BSc, PhD Leeds (*Expedition Coordinator,
Physics)
Miss H Vickery, MA Cantab, LRAM, Dip RAM (**Music*)
Mrs L Wilkinson, BSc Samford (*Chemistry & Lower
School Science*)
Mrs J Wood, MA, BA Cantab (*Second in Department
Mathematics*)

Junior Staff – Full time:
Mrs J Amin, MEd Exeter, BA Durham
Miss E Bartlett, BA Oxford Brookes
Miss B Collins, MSc Leicester
Miss H Dixon, MA St Andrews
Miss L Farquhar
Miss A Feeney, BA Bedfordshire (*Head of Junior PE &
Games*)
Mr M Hamilton-Foyn, BSc Aberystwyth
Miss V Kay, BA Sheffield
Miss R Merolla, BA UCL (*Deputy Head of Junior School*)
Ms N Mikac
Miss S Parker, BSc Oxford Brookes
Miss H Pople, MA Portsmouth, BSc Portsmouth
Mrs K Rowland, BA Winchester (*Head of Junior School
Science & STEM Coordinator*)
Mr W Russell, MSc Bristol
Ms J Schott, BA Open
Miss C Smith, BA Oxford Brookes (*Deputy Head of Junior
School*)
Miss N van Kamp, MA Central Saint Martins

Staff – Part time:
Mr R Allan, BA UCL (*Geography*)
Mrs M Arnaud, MA Grenoble (*French*)
Dr L Bourne, BA Oxon MRCPath (*Chemistry*)
Mrs L Carr, MA London()BA Leeds (*French*) (*& Spanish*)
Ms S Carr-Gomm, MA London, BA UEA (**History of Art*)
Mrs A Christou, MA Middlesex, BA London (**Classics*)
[Maternity Cover]
Ms A Crawford RAD PDTD former soloist English
National Ballet (*Classical Ballet*)
Mr L Dare, BA Cantab (*STEM Coordinator, Physics*)
Ms P Edgeley, MA London (*Art*)Mrs R Floyd, BA Durham
(*Music*)
Mrs K Francis BEd Hertfordshire College (**Learning
Support*)
Dr S Hayes, PhD, MA, BA Exeter (*Classics*)
Mrs V Hitchen, FRAD, RBS, TTC Dip, RAD examiner
emeritus (*Classical Ballet*)
Mrs N Hogg, BA Bath (*Head of Senior PE*)
Ms T Jensen, MA Bristol (*Classics*) [Maternity Leave]

Miss D Kefalidi, BA London RBS Diploma of Dance Teaching Education Practice Ballet Administrator (*Classical Ballet*)
Ms H Lambert, BA London (*Classics*)
Mrs L Mapstone, BA California (*Careers*)
Mrs J Mesrie, BSc Leeds (*Art*) [Maternity Leave]
Ms S Osborne, BSc London (*Geography*)
Miss S Pope, BSc City University
Mrs C Price, BSc Durham (*Assistant Examinations Officer*)
Dr C Price, PhD Imperial & Cantab, MSc, BSc Imperial (*Physics*)
Ms A Riaz, BA Brighton (*Computing Studies*)
Miss G Robinson, BA Bath (*Actor in Residence, Drama*)
Mrs L Sanderson, MA Chester, BA London (*Drama*)
Mrs R Smallshaw, MA Estonia (*Accompanist Classical Ballet*)
Mrs R Smith, MA Cantab (*Classics*) [Maternity Leave]
Ms C Stansfield, MA Courtauld, BA Oxford (*Government and Politics*)
Mrs S Street, MA, BA Cantab, MA London (*English*)
Mrs S Townshend, MA Edinburgh (*Spanish & French*)
Miss L Woodman, BSc Kent (*Psychology*)

Staff – Visiting:
Mrs G Bailey-Smith (*Jazz Dance*)
Miss A Barlow, BA Bath (*Pottery*)
Ms J Benson, BA (*Singing*)
Miss C Constable, BMus, PG Perf Cert, MMus RCM, ABSM (*Cello and Piano*)
Miss B Corsi, LTCL, FTCL (*Clarinet, Recorder, Piano*)
Miss A Cviic, BA, PG Dip RCM (*Singing*)
Mr P Dalle (*French Club*)
Mrs D Ellin, BMus RSAMD (*Flute*)
Mr J Gee (*Bass*)
Mr S Gillot (*Organ*)
Mr J Godfrey, BMus, PG Dip RCM (*Percussion*)
Ms D Halpin, MMus, PG Dip Guildhall (*Singing*)
Mr R Johnson (*Fencing*)
Ms M Leaf, BA London (*Speech & Drama*)
Miss J Lister, MA Cantab (*Harp*)
Mr M Mason (*Cricket*)
Miss E Mazzon, MA Trieste (*Italian*)
Mr A McLean, BMus Edinburgh (*Trumpet*)
Ms M Y McNulty, BSc Brunel (*Mandarin*)
Mr D Schroyens, FTCL (*Piano*)
Miss V Smith, BMus RCM (*Violin*)
Mr J Sparks, BA, MA, FCCM (*Guitar*)
Mrs S Stewart, BMus, LRSM, PG Dip RCM (*Singing*)
Mr C Weale, BMus, PG Dip RCM (*Piano*)
Mr Y-S Yeo, BMus (*Piano*)

Support Staff:
Mrs T Bannister (*Reprographics & Resources*)
Miss S Bell, BA (*PA to the Head of Junior School*)
Miss C Brazer, BSc (*Alumni Relations Officer*)
Mr P da Costa, BSc (*Information Systems Manager*)
Miss E Devane (*Lab Technician*)
Miss K Drinkwater, BA (*Events Technician*)
Mrs H Farokhipoor, BSc (*Lab Technician*)
Mrs H Griffith-Payne, BA (*Office Manager*) [Maternity Leave]
Mrs G Hammond, MSc, BA (*Virtual Assistant*)
Mrs F Holland (*Registrar*)
Miss L Ivison, BA (*Librarian*)
Mrs N Kauders, BA (*Art Technician*)
Miss M Livingstone-Learmonth, BA (*Office Manager*) [Maternity Cover]
Miss A Martin (*French Language Assistant*)
Mrs H Mumford, MA (*Development Manager*)
Miss V Phillips (*PA to the Headmistress*)
Mr L Powell, BA (*Marketing Assistant*)
Miss L Pringle, BA (*Marketing & Design Executive*)

Mrs H Ramji (*Lab Technician*)
Dr P Richards, PhD, BA (*ICT Support Technician*)
Mrs C Robinson, BA (*Operations Manager*) [Maternity Leave]
Miss E Scouller, BA (*Development Executive*)
Miss C Solms (*School Secretary*)
Dr S Rankine, MB BS, DCH, DRCOG, DFFP, MRCGP (*School Doctor*)

Frensham Heights

Rowledge, Farnham, Surrey GU10 4EA

Tel: 01252 792561
email: admin@frensham-heights.org.uk
website: www.frensham.org
Twitter: @FrenshamHeights
Facebook: @frensham

Frensham Heights is a highly distinctive day and boarding school nestled in the beautiful Surrey Hills.

Founded in 1925, we welcome students from the age of 3 to 18 and we give them the tools to succeed in their education, helping them to extend their abilities and exceed their own expectations. We are located three miles from the beautiful Georgian market town of Farnham, 15 miles from the historic city of Guildford, about an hour from the centre of London and 30 and 50 miles respectively from Heathrow and Gatwick airports.

Ours is a culture that says come and be you and the beauty of Frensham lies in diversity.

Musicians learn alongside scientists, budding authors sit amongst future engineers. They discover a world of creative and academic subjects and each take away something different. Their own passion, their own strength and their own self-belief. We achieve exceptional academic standards, but our aim is to provide a really good robust academic environment alongside a much richer experience as well. We do have clear goals, but equally we want our students to be confident in themselves, because if you value who you are, you are more likely to be successful.

We're looking to the future. We want to prepare young people who are open-minded, who are not afraid to ask the difficult questions.

These are the young people who will go into companies with the right skill set to succeed in a workplace where many traditional careers may become obsolete. We want to face the challenges by encouraging our students to think, understand and ask the right questions. We also encourage our teachers to be open-minded, to take risks and to be creative in their teaching. Our students don't just go on to be dancers, doctors and engineers. They go on to follow a whole range of careers with a personal self-belief that helps them succeed. But more importantly they learn the skills, the future skills, to build a life not just a living.

With real adventure the unexpected will always happen and it is then that students discover their true strengths and exceed their personal limits.

Our Outdoor Education programme runs from Forest Classes for the youngest students, Duke of Edinburgh's Award challenges for older students through to overseas ventures, mountaineering and exploring for the Sixth Form. From 2018, our entire Year 9 class will travel together to the furthest reaches of Scotland to spend 2 to 3 weeks in a world miles away from their everyday life, no phones, no social pressures, just children remembering how to be children. Whatever the adventure, our aim is to ensure students enjoy the freedom to explore, investigate, experience and take small but significant risks that help them grow into curious and self-aware adults.

We welcome boarders from Year 7 upwards.

We offer full, weekly and, where space allows, flexi boarding. Alongside our many and varied extracurricular activities, boarders are offered shopping, theatre and cinema trips. Students can get to know and bond with the small dedicated staff teams and parents can feel confident that we know and look after their children. Our co-educational boarding houses are relaxed, warm, lively and supportive with boys and girls accommodated in separate areas but sharing comfortable common rooms where they can study and socialise.

Student numbers. 500 boys and girls aged 3 to 18 years. Average class size: 18.

Admissions. Children entering from Nursery to Year 6 have an assessment day, with older children called during a two-week period in February. Children entering the school at the age of 11+ and 13+ sit the Frensham Heights Entrance Examination, held in January. Entrance to the Sixth Form is by examination and interview with a minimum of six GCSE passes at Level 9–4 (minimum Level 6 in A Level subjects).

Curriculum. Most students take nine or ten GCSE subjects of which the compulsory elements are English Language and Literature, Mathematics and triple or double award Science. The top set take three separate sciences. Students then choose from Geography, History, Business Studies, a second modern language, Art, 3D Design, Dance, Design Technology, Drama, Music, or PE. Photography is taught to GCSE as an extracurricular activity and as part of the curriculum at A Level. There are 24 subjects to choose from at A Level. The AQA Extended Project Qualification is also offered for suitable candidates. PSME is taught throughout the school.

Academic Results. Examination results are very good. There is a strong Sixth Form.

Extracurricular Activities. All pupils are expected to take part in extracurricular activities. An extensive and varied selection of activities includes sports of all sorts, art, music, dance, drama, hobbies and clubs.

Religion. Frensham Heights is non-denominational and there are no religious services during the school day.

Dress. There is no uniform but students follow a dress code based on respect for others.

Welfare and Discipline. The school's discipline is firmly based on good relationships between staff and students and reflects the values of the school, including respect, tolerance, self-discipline, cooperation and creativity. Every student has a personal tutor. Senior pupils act as mentors to younger members of the school. The boarding house staff are supported by a school nurse and a part-time counsellor.

Learning Support. We are able to provide support for children with mild learning difficulties.

Overseas Students. The school admits a small number of boarders from overseas each year and provides tuition in English as a Second Language as part of their curriculum.

Fees per term (2018–2019). Nursery (EYFE Scheme): £19.50 (morning session, including lunch), £34 (afternoon session, including lunch), £37 full day; Reception £2,300; Years 1–2 £2,810; Year 3 £3,370; Year 4 £3,440; Years 5–6 £4,255; Years 7–8: £6,110 (day), £8,790 (boarding); Years 9–13: £6,410 (day), £9,890 (boarding); New Sixth Form Entrants: £6,810 (day), £10,270 (boarding).

Scholarships and Bursaries. Scholarships are awarded for Academic distinction or exceptional promise in Music, Art, Dance, Drama and Sport at 11+, 13+ and for Sixth Form entry. These do not have monetary value but they recognise and celebrate excellence. Scholars access dedicated Enrich-

ment activities. Bursaries are awarded on the basis of a means-tested assessment.

Charitable status. Frensham Heights Educational Trust is a Registered Charity, number 312052. It exists to provide high quality education for boys and girls.

Patrons:
Professor T Sherwood, MB, MA, FRCP, FRCR (*Emeritus Professor of Radiology, Cambridge, Fellow of Girton College*) [OF]
Mrs J Read, BA, FCIPD (*Semi-retired HR Consultant*) [OF]

Governors:
Chair: Mrs M Coltman, BA, LLB (*Group General Counsel and Company Secretary at Prudential plc*)
Vice Chair: Mr G Holden, MA, PGCE, CAPSE, FRSA (*Education Consultant and Former Head of Rendcomb College and Dover College*)
Treasurer: Mr W Bird, BA, MA, MBA, MBCS, FRAeS, MBE (*Consultant specialising in defence and commercial management programmes*)
Company Secretary and Clerk to the Governors: Eme Dean-Lewis, BSc, FCMA, MBA, CGMA
Mr M Lupton, MRCOG, MBBS, MA, Cert MEd, Dip MEd, MEd (*Consultant Physician*)
Mrs K Poulsom (*Managing Director of an Agricultural Contracting and Plant Hire Company*)
Mrs J Sullivan, RICS (*Chartered Surveyor*)
Mr P Ward, BEd (*Headmaster of Thomas's Preparatory School, Clapham*)
Mr Angus Carlill, MA (*Chartered Accountant*)
Mr R Fry, MA, MEng (*Technology consultant in life sciences research and development*)

[OF] *Old Frenshamian*

Head: Rick Clarke, BA, PGCE

Bursar & Clerk to Governors: Eme Dean-Lewis, BSc, FCMA, MBA, CGMA

Deputy Head: Becks Scullion, BSc, PGCE
Deputy Head (*Academic*): Laura Griffiths, BA

Heads of Schools:
Sixth Form: Peter Unitt, BSc, PGCE
Middle School: Andy Spink, BSc, QTS
Junior School: Nic Hoskins, BA, QTS

Heads of Department:

English:
Deirdre Gannon, BA, Dip Ed

Mathematics:
Russell Crew, BEng, PGCE

Science:
Nick Boon-Arnell, BSc, PGCE

Modern Foreign Languages:
Tim Seys, BA, PGCE (*Spanish/French*)

History:
Matthew Burns, BA, PGCE

Geography:
Nicola O'Donnell BA, MEd, PGCE

Economics & Business Studies & Sociology:
Hugh Robertson, BSc, PGCE, MBA

Psychology:
Hannah Manton, BSc, PGCE

IT:
James Clarke

PE & Games:
Joanne Dalziel, BSc, PGCE

Outdoor Education:
Linn Kathenes, BSc, PGCE

Art & Design:
Brendan Horstead, BA, PGCE

Dance:
Robert Keane

Drama:
Amanda Liddle, BA

Music:
James Casselton, BA, PGCE

Learning Support:
Beverley Wrigglesworth, OCR Level 5 Cert SpLD, OCR
    Level 7 Dip SpLD

PSME:
Kate Middleton, BA, PGCE

RE:
Karen McBride, BSc, PGCE

Boarding House Staff:

Becks Scullion (*Deputy Head, Director of Boarding*)

Hamilton House (*Years 7 to 9*):
Sian Owens (*Housemistress*)
Josh Edwards (*Deputy Housemaster*)

Main House (*Years 10 and 11*):
William Paskell (*Housemaster*)
David Lloyd (*Deputy Housemaster*)

Roberts House (*Sixth Form*):
Richard Arthur (*Housemaster*)
Dan Pullen (*Deputy Housemaster*)

Headmaster's Office:
Lindsey Boyce (*Head's PA*)

Admissions Registrar:
Sarah Windsor, BA (*Admissions Registrar*)

George Heriot's School

Lauriston Place, Edinburgh EH3 9EQ

Tel: 0131 229 7263
Fax: 0131 229 6363
email: enquiries@george-heriots.com
website: www.george-heriots.com

Motto: *I distribute chearfullie*

Heriot's Hospital was founded in 1628 to care for the fatherless children of Edinburgh. Today it is a fully co-educational day school.

The School is attractively situated in its own grounds close to the city centre and within easy walking distance of bus and rail terminals. A number of bus routes also service the School. Edinburgh Castle forms a magnificent backdrop, and Edinburgh's flourishing financial centre, the University of Edinburgh, the College of Art, the National Library and the Royal Scottish Museum are located close by.

The original building, described as a "bijou of Scottish Renaissance Architecture", has been carefully preserved and, as a historic monument, is open at certain times to the public during school holidays. The Chapel, Council Room and Quadrangle are particularly notable.

Over the years a succession of new buildings has provided the full complement of educational facilities. A state-of-the-art Sports Centre was opened in 2012. The School has excellent sports fields and facilities at Goldenacre and sole use of an outdoor centre in the Scottish Highlands.

Our aim is to introduce all our pupils to the broadest possible spectrum of academic, cultural and sporting interests and experiences, which will enable them to develop into articulate, self-reliant, hard-working and kind adults who play their full part in an ever-changing society. The School had a highly successful QUIPE inspection by HMISS in September 2016.

Heriot's has long enjoyed a reputation for academic excellence, with outstanding examination results and we value scholarship and effort. In the same spirit, every pupil is encouraged to participate in an extensive array of extra-curricular activities. We encourage participation and success in an unusually wide range of sports; the main sports are cricket, cross-country running, hockey, rowing, football, rugby and tennis but we also strongly encourage more minority sports.

We have an outstanding record in music, both choral and instrumental and in drama. Both Junior and Senior schools boast a huge range of clubs, with particular strength in our Debating Society, our Pipe Band, our Drama productions, The Duke of Edinburgh's Award and our Combined Cadet Force. The School proudly holds Gold level in UNICEF's Rights-Respecting Schools Award. There is a heavy emphasis throughout the School on charitable fundraising and community service including our award-winning S6 Voluntary Service programme.

The Nursery (32 children). The Nursery accommodates children in their pre-school year. It is part of the Early Years Department. Admission to the Nursery is open to all.

The Junior School (575 pupils). The Junior School follows a bespoke curriculum with a focus on academic rigour and solid subject content, particularly with regard to literacy, numeracy and science. Art, drama, modern languages, music, computing and all areas of physical education are taught by specialists. Philosophy is a key strength in the Junior School.

The Senior School (1028 pupils). For the first two years, a broad curriculum is followed. An unrivalled choice of subjects is available from S3 to S6 in preparation for Scottish Qualifications Authority examinations at every level. Most pupils stay on for our carefully designed Sixth Year and proceed to university or other forms of tertiary education.

Heriot's enjoys a reputation as a caring community. The greatest importance is given to pastoral care and a sophisticated careers advisory programme is in place. The Support for Learning Department provides invaluable help to many Junior School and Senior School pupils.

Admission: Admission (other than for Nursery) is by assessment or examination. Application for occasional places is welcome at any time, but for the main stages should normally be submitted by the end of November.

Fees per annum (2018–2019). Junior School: £8,349 (Nursery, P1 & P2), £10,134 (P3 to P7); Senior School: £12,522.

A limited number of Bursaries is available in Senior School and there are Scholarships for entry at S1. Fatherless and motherless children may qualify for free education and other benefits through the Foundation and James Hardie Bursaries. Full information is available from the Finance and Business Office on request.

Charitable status. George Heriot's Trust is a Registered Charity, number SC011463. It exists to provide education for children.

Governors of George Heriot's Trust:
Chairman: Mr A D Paton
Vice-Chairman: Prof M W J Strachan
Finance & Resources Convener: M A Simm
Education Convener: Dr P Sangster
Mr H Bruce-Gardyne
Mrs K Cherry
Mr I Herok
Mr V Lal
Mr A McGeough
Mr C Stott
Mr J Thomson
Mr A Urquhart

Principal: Mrs L M Franklin

PA to the Principal: Miss C Macleod

School Management Team:
Mrs J A Alexander (*Bursar*)
Miss S P Donnelly (*HR Manager*)
Mrs J J Easton (*Director of External Relations*)
Mr P A Fairclough (*Head of Senior School*)
Mr A G Morrison (*Head of Junior School*)
Mr A MacLachlan (*Estates Manager*)
Mrs K S O'Hagan (*Deputy Head of Junior School*)
Mr A Semmler (*Director of IT*)

Deputes, Senior School:
Mrs C W Binnie
Miss K A Macnab
Mr K J Ogilvie
Mr N J Seaton
Mr R H Simpson

Deputes, Junior School:
Mr C W McCloghry
Mrs K L Stevens
Mrs K L Reid

Chaplain: Mrs A G Maclean

Art:
*Mrs A J E Thomson
Mrs R E Billett
Mrs J R Coombs
Mrs C M Fraser
Ms N Garriock
Mrs S L Jamieson
Mrs C J McGirr

Biology:
*Ms A McKenzie
Mrs L J Anderson
Ms D Barnaby
Mrs A Macleod
Dr E Marshall
Mr A A N Ramage

Business Education:
*Mrs J R Arnott
Mr A J Armstrong
Mrs A Donaldson
Mrs C Gill
Mrs G Line
Mr J Payne

Chemistry:
*Mrs F Donaldson
Mr T E Beaven
Mrs J Blaikie
Miss E L Maclean
Mr J Wilson

Citizenship:
*Mrs G K Hay

Classics:
*Mr D Carnegie
Mr D R Underwood

Computing:
*Mr J T Scott
Ms J McColgan
Mr M P Hill
Mr A Semmler

Design & Technology:
*Mrs E Watson-Massey
Mr F Cross
Miss H L O'Boyle
Mr I Purves
Miss A D Williamson

Drama:
*Mrs M Berry
Mrs E R Mackie
Mr T R Timms

English:
*Mr K Simpson
Mr R Gray
Mrs G K Hay
Mr P J Lowe
Mrs M C Massie
Miss K H Morgan
Mr J R Muir
Dr A Neilson
Mr D J Stenabaugh

Geography:
*Mrs A Hughes

Miss R Hay
Mr K J Ogilvie
Mr A Ross
Mr E J Watson

History and Modern Studies:
*Mr M A McCabe
Miss M Buchanan
Mr T J Clancey
Ms A Connor
Miss M Duck
Mr C D Francis
Miss T Peters
Miss L P Robertson
Mr N J Seaton

Mathematics:
*Mr R G Kearsey
Mrs E Bleakley
Ms M B Deely
Mr G A Dickson
Mrs P E Hart
Miss K Henry
Mrs L C Hood
Mrs K Lydon
Miss F Moir

Modern Languages:
*Mr M G Grant
Miss M Altelarrea Llorente
Mrs C W Binnie
Miss C Boscher
Ms E Bottaro
Ms A E V Bruce
Mrs H Davies
Miss L Gibson
Ms J Murphy
Dr S T S Tonini
Ms G H Zhang

Music:
*Mr G C W Brownlee
Mrs J Buttars
Mrs S C Lovell

Junior School Teachers (*including Nursery*):
Miss M Anderson
Mrs V E J Clark
Mr G Cockburn
Mrs L Gilmour
Mrs G Happs
Mrs S Hoyte
Mrs B I S Hunt
Miss A K Jackson
Mr C Johnstone
Ms A Josiffe
Miss C Mackenzie
Mrs G McKinnon
Mrs R L McKinnon

Junior School Principal Teachers:
Miss S Gordon
Mrs R McKinnon
Miss L M Waddell

Learning Enhancement:
Miss J Attenborough
Ms H A Bassam
Miss K A Duncan
Mrs C Humphreys

Mr G D Maclagan
Mrs R S J Weir

PE/Games:
*Mr M J J Mallinson
Miss A L Brodie
Mr J A Davidson
Mr A D Easson
Mr E Harrison
Mr G Hills
Mrs N Kesterton
Mrs L Nelson
Mr L C Porteous
Mrs K F Rutherford
Mr R Stevenson

Philosophy and Religion:
*Mr J C Rodger-Phillips
Mrs L Beilby
Miss R Davies
Mr R H Simpson

Psychology:
Ms S A Regnart

Physics:
*Mr R M Bush
Dr F M Baumgartl
Mr E Dobbin
Mrs R D Mayo
Ms W C Morgan
Dr K Ward

Support for Learning:
*Mrs H A Staines
Mrs H R Fennell
Ms S G Gallacher
Mrs C Guy
Mrs S C Harrod
Mrs J Jackson
Miss N Knopfel
Mrs E J Speedy
Mr I J Smith
Mr D Thain

Ms A J McNeill
Miss L E Meikle
Mrs K H Noble
Miss H Oliver
Mrs G L Rogatchevskaia
Mr N J Ross
Mr E P Santer
Miss M J Smith
Mrs E S R B K Szczypka
Mr B Tyler
Mr R J Waters
Mr J Webster
Miss L J Wormald

Mrs H Murphy
Mrs L J Smith
Mrs S E Wilken
Mr I J S A Woolley

Giggleswick School

Giggleswick, Settle, North Yorkshire BD24 0DE

Tel: 01729 893000 Headmaster's Office
           01729 893012 Bursar's Office
Fax: 01729 893150
email: admissions@giggleswick.org.uk
website: www.giggleswick.org.uk
Twitter: @giggschool
Facebook: @GiggleswickSchool

Giggleswick School is based on the edge of the Yorkshire Dales National Park, offering affordable independent education and academic excellence for girls and boys aged 3 to 18. The school was awarded 'excellent' in an impressive six aspects of provision by the Independent Schools Inspectorate (ISI).

Located on the edge of the beautiful Yorkshire Dales National Park, the school sits within a 200-acre campus of stunning countryside, where you'll find 500 years of heritage, exceptional modern facilities and a happy, welcoming community.

350 boys and girls attend Giggleswick, either as full-time or flexi boarders or day pupils. It is a traditional British boarding school with 60% of pupils boarding, 17% of whom are from military families and 19% from the international community. The approach to education combines excellent academic achievement, ambition and strong self-belief, with a strong focus on personal development. The school's core values are participation, ambition and respect.

In 2018, the school achieved a 100% A Level pass rate with 36% achieving A*/A grades. At GCSE, 46% achieved A*/A grades and 71% A*–B.

However, life is about more than great grades at Giggleswick. The extended day and boarding ethos gives all pupils the chance to participate in any of over 70 co-curricular activities that encourage pupils to explore new horizons, challenge themselves and often achieve beyond their expectations. 50% of pupils take part in music lessons at Grade 6 or above with 120 pupils in drama productions. Average class sizes are 14 in Key Stage 3 and 4 and seven in Sixth Form.

All boarders live in one of seven boarding houses with a dedicated co-ed house for young boarders in Years 5 to 8. A multimillion pound investment in boarding facilities is currently in progress, which is shaping a new family-friendly model of boarding to create a modern home away from home with a real focus on community and wellbeing.

There are excellent sports coaches at all levels, superb facilities and regular programmed training sessions. Each year a number of pupils gain representative honours in a range of sports and a place on the Elite Sports Programme. This includes specialist coaching, mentoring, professional sports visits and strength and conditioning training.

Facilities include a floodlit AstroTurf, a brand new fitness centre, two indoor sports halls and an indoor swimming pool. The Outdoor Pursuits Department is staffed with seven mountain leaders and five rock climbing instructors, with a state-of-the-art indoor climbing facility as well as 34 crags within 10km of the school and the school's own mountain bike trail and shooting range.

Giggleswick's Art Department provides a lively and stimulating environment where pupils can explore and develop their creative skills. The department includes a resident ceramic artist, who works and teaches in the Department. There is a well-equipped ceramics studio, a vacuum silkscreen printing bed, plus facilities to make photo silkscreens, and a large etching press.

Drama takes place in the state-of-the-art Richard Whiteley Theatre, a 250-seat professional venue. There are opportunities to develop skills in stage management, sound and lighting as well as acting in productions such as Les Miserables.

In the music department there is a Head of Instrumental Music as well as a Head of Department and four full-time musicians. They are assisted by a team of 13 visiting teachers, and ensembles include the School Orchestra, Concert Band, Chapel Choir, Concert Choir, a Brass Ensemble and a String Quartet as well as a number of rock bands. Numerous performance opportunities are offered including trips abroad.

Giggleswick is not a selective school. The school has an equal opportunities policy and is happy to consider applications from any child so long as other entrance criteria are met. Various scholarships and bursaries are also available. Please visit http://www.giggleswick.org.uk/How-to-Apply-Senior for more information

The school is an hour's drive from Leeds, Manchester and The Lakes. It can be reached from the M6 or M1 motorways or by rail via Settle or Giggleswick stations. Overseas students fly to Leeds/Bradford or Manchester Airports.

Fees per term (2018–2019). The fees are fully inclusive. Senior School: Boarders: £7,850 (Years 7 & 8), £10,715 (Years 9–11), £11,250 (Sixth Form); 5-night flexi boarders: £7,535 (Years 7 & 8), £9,650 (Years 9–11), £10,180 (Sixth Form); 3-night flexi boarders: £7,105 (Years 7 & 8), £8,595 (Years 9–11), £9,125 (Sixth Form); Day Pupils: £5,195 Years 7 & 8), £6,475 (Years 9–11), £6,995 (Sixth Form).

Charitable status. Giggleswick School is a Registered Charity, number 1109826.

The Governing Body:
Chair: Mrs H J Hancock, MA, LVO
Vice-Chair: A R Mullins, BSc, MBA, ACA

Bursar & Clerk to the Governors: M Z Hodge, BA, CPFA

Headmaster: M M Turnbull, BA, MA

Deputy Head: A Simpson, BA, MSc

Senior Master: N A Gemmell, BA

Assistant Head (*Academic*): Miss A L Wood, MA

PA to the Headmaster: Mrs C A Jowett

Director of External Relations: Mrs J Paul

The Glasgow Academy

Colebrooke Street, Glasgow G12 8HE

Tel: 0141 334 8558
Fax: 0141 337 3473
email: enquiries@tga.org.uk
website: www.theglasgowacademy.org.uk

Motto: *Serva Fidem*

Founded in May 1845, The Glasgow Academy is the oldest continuously independent school in the west of Scotland. It has been co-educational since 1991, when it joined forces with Westbourne School for Girls. Mergers with Atholl Preparatory School in Milngavie (1999) and Dairsie House School in Newlands (2005) have given parents a choice of three locations for their children in the Nursery to Prep 4 age group, contributing to the school's enduring success as a school covering the whole of west central Scotland. Children from TGA Milngavie and TGA Newlands transfer to the main Academy site at Kelvinbridge at Prep 5. The school's affairs are managed by The Glasgow Academicals' War Memorial Trust, formed to commemorate the 327 former pupils killed in the war of 1914–18.

Organisation. The Preparatory School contains some 722 pupils (371 boys, 351 girls) between the ages of 3 and 11 and educates pupils from the earliest stages for the work of the Senior School. The Senior School contains 703 pupils (370 boys, 333 girls). They are prepared for the National Qualifications at National 5 level at the end of S4, Higher at the end of S5 and Advanced Higher or Higher at the end of S6. The Sixth Form provides courses in most subjects leading to presentation at Advanced Higher. Pupils are prepared for entrance to Oxford and Cambridge. The Academy has a history of successes at Oxford, Cambridge and the Scottish Universities. It aims to offer a unique combination of academic, musical, dramatic, sporting, co-curricular, social and outdoor education opportunities, backed up by high levels of pastoral care. There are numerous opportunities for children to develop leadership skills and take on responsibilities.

Buildings. The magnificent main building (1878) contains the Senior School library as its centrepiece and classrooms. Recent purpose-built facilities include a Music School (1994), Art and Design School (1998), Preparatory School (2008) and multiple award-winning Science centre, auditorium and hospitality/social area (2015). Two drama studios, a dance studio, rowing studio, medical centre and fitness area were also created in 2015. There are extensive sports facilities, including new astros, rugby/cricket pitches and a water-based hockey pitch. The school's Wi-Fi network covers the entire campus and supports pupils' own iPads, laptops, smart phones and tablets. Information technology is used to engage pupils and parents in the learning process.

Health and Wellbeing. The school places great importance on supporting pupils' health and wellbeing. Pupils are at the heart of this with an influential School Council meeting each week, with a HWB sub-committee working in partnership with staff to lead improvement in safeguarding, a regularly reviewed and evolving PSE curriculum, and provision of assemblies and guest speakers on a range of topics relevant to young people's lives. S6 pupils lead a school buddy system, including the delivery of digital awareness and online safety workshops to younger pupils and parents. The school website features information for parents on how to support their child's wellbeing.

Music and Drama. Music tuition is offered in a wide range of instruments by 21 tutors. There are Senior, Junior and Theatre Choirs, a Concert Band, Pipe Band, Brass Group, Percussion Ensemble, Orchestra and various Prep School groups. Concerts and large-scale drama productions take place regularly and are supplemented by plays mounted by smaller groups. There are music tours to places such as New York, Rome and Barcelona.

Societies and Activities. These range from Basketball, Chess, Debating and Public Speaking to Engineering, Fairtrade and Research clubs. Very large numbers of pupils undertake each section of the Duke of Edinburgh's Award and there is a thriving Young Enterprise group. Residential education is an integral part of the curriculum at various stages of both the Prep and Senior schools. These experiences augment the PSE programme by promoting team building and personal and social development through outdoor challenges.

Games. Teams represent the school in Hockey, Rugby, Cricket, Swimming, Golf, Tennis, Athletics, Rowing, Football, Shooting and Squash. Options include Badminton, Cross-Country running, Dance and Outdoor education.

Combined Cadet Force. The Academy has a strong voluntary contingent with RN, Army and RAF Sections.

Childcare outside school hours. The Academy provides care before and after school for its younger pupils. There is also provision for children between the ages of 3 and 12 through the holidays.

Entrance. Pupils may be registered at any age. The main entry points are (a) in the Preparatory School: age 3, 4 and 10; (b) in the Senior School: age 11 or 12 or for Sixth Form. Bursaries are available for P7–S6.

Fees per term (2018–2019). Preparatory School: P1 £2,782/£3,028, P2 £2,865/£3,117, P3–P4 £3,167/£3,401, P5 £3,401, P6–P7 £3,985. Senior School: S1–S2 £3,804, S3–S5 £4,128, S6 £4,128, (Autumn & Spring Terms), £3,367 (Summer Term).

Charitable status. The Glasgow Academy is a Registered Charity, number SC015638. It exists to provide education for girls and boys.

Chairman of Governors: Graham Scott, FCIBS

Nominated and Elected Governors:
Mrs C F Abercrombie, BAcc, CA
Jeremy Glen, LLB, Dip LP, NP
Mrs J Gotts, MA Hons
Mrs M Khnichich, BAcc, CA, CTA
Duncan Mackison
Professor Andrew Marshall, BA, MPhil
John Mason, BAcc, CA
Dr K Percival, MB ChB, MRCGP
Mrs A Salwan, LLB Hons, Dip LP, Ce MAP
Andrew Sime, BA
Andrew Waddell, MA, CA, ASIP

Secretary: T W Gemmill, LLB, NP

Rector: P J Brodie, MA Oxon, MA Management of Education, Canterbury Christ Church University College

Deputy Rector: M K Pearce, BA, Dunelm

Deputy Heads:
Dr M Gibson, BSc Edinburgh, PhD Edinburgh
Mrs K R Graham, BSc Newcastle-upon-Tyne, MEd Aberdeen
A N MacRae, BSc Strathclyde

Heads of Department:
English: Mrs A F Watters, MA St Andrews
Mathematics: Dr S Levine, BA City University New York, DPhil Oxford
Modern Languages: Mrs E B Holland, MA Glasgow
Biology: J Laycock, BSc Edinburgh
Chemistry: Dr C A Main, MSci Glasgow, PhD Glasgow
Physics: Mrs H McMillan, BSc Strathclyde
Art/Craft & Design: J M McNaught, BA Glasgow
Classics: S A A McKellar, MA Glasgow
Computing Science: Mrs J E McDonald, MA Glasgow
Drama: G E Waltham, MA Glasgow
Economics & Business Studies: Mrs S McKenzie, MA Glasgow, PG Dip Bus Admin Strathclyde
Food Technology: Ms C Dolan, BSc Manchester Metropolitan University
Geography: Mrs V Magowan, MA Glasgow
History & Modern Studies: S M Wood, MA St Andrews
Music: T E Mills, BMus Bangor
Physical Education/Sport: Mrs R Toft, BEd Heriot-Watt (*Director of Sport*)
M A Manson, BA Strathclyde (*Head of PE*)
Outdoor Education: Miss R Goolden, Mountain Instructor Certificate, Outdoor Education Diploma & National Governing Body Awards, Newbury College
Learning Support: Mrs A A Harvie, BA Strathclyde, PG Dip Ind Admin Glasgow Caledonian

Careers: A J McCaskey, MA Glasgow
Counsellor: Mrs A F Young, MA Glasgow, MRes
Strathclyde, PG Dip Psychodynamic Counselling
Garnethill Centre University of the West of Scotland,
BACP

Preparatory School:
Head: A Mathewson, BEd Strathclyde
Deputy Head: S Fairlie-Clarke, BSc Glasgow, PG Dip
Napier
Deputy Head: Miss L Smith, MA Glasgow

TGA Milngavie:
Head: Miss J McMorran, DCE, PG Dip, DipTEFL

TGA Newlands:
Head: Miss H J Logie, BEd Oxon

After-school Care:
After-school Care Manager: Mrs C Bremridge, BA
Childhood Practice Glasgow

Chaplains:
Revd D J M Carmichael, MA, BD
Revd A Frater, BA, BD
Revd R S M Fulton, BA Sheffield, BD Glasgow
Revd G Kirkwood, BSc, BD, PGCE
Revd S Matthews BD, MA

Combined Cadet Force:
Contingent Commander: Captain L Smith
SSI: Major C J Duff

Administration/Finance:
Bursar: Mrs L Brown, BAcc Glasgow, CA Institute of
Chartered Accountants of Scotland

Rector's PA: Mrs L Fletcher

Administration Manager: Miss I Kovacs, BA Strathclyde
School Secretary: Mrs A M Farr
Database Coordinator/Administration Secretary: Miss C A
Louis, BA Université Stendhal Grenoble 3, MA
Aberdeen

Development:
Director of External Relations and Development: S A
Dignall, BA Strathclyde

The High School of Glasgow

637 Crow Road, Glasgow G13 1PL

Tel: 0141 954 9628
email: rector@hsog.co.uk
website: www.highschoolofglasgow.co.uk
Twitter: @HSofG

Motto: *Sursum semper*

The High School of Glasgow is a vibrant, caring and
high-achieving co-educational day school, which has been
part of Glasgow's story since the 12th century and is the oldest continuous school in Scotland. Its present incarnation
came into being in 1976 following a merger involving the
Former Pupil Club of the High School, then a selective state
grammar school, and Drewsteignton School in Bearsden.

Buildings. The Senior School occupies modern purpose-
built buildings at Anniesland on the western outskirts of the
city immediately adjacent to twenty-three acres of playing
fields. The Junior School is in the extended and modernised
former Drewsteignton School buildings in Bearsden about
three miles away. New facilities opened during the last few
years include a purpose-built Science extension, a water-
based artificial pitch and 3G multi-sports area, a Junior

School extension, a Drama Studio, a Refectory, a Fitness
Centre, a Grandstand and an Information and Communications Technology building, and in 2017 a Health and Well-
being Centre.

Organisation. The School is a day school with about
1,000 boys and girls. The Junior School, which includes a
pre-school Kindergarten, has some 312 pupils (ages
3½–10). Primary 7 pupils are included in the Senior School
which has about 688 pupils (ages 11–18). A general curriculum is followed until the Third Year of the Senior School
when, with the Scottish Qualifications Authority examinations in view, a measure of choice is introduced. In Fifth
Year Higher examinations are taken and in Sixth Year
courses for Advanced Highers are offered. Whilst the majority of pupils are aiming for the Scottish universities, places
are regularly gained at Oxford, Cambridge and other
English universities.

Throughout the School, time is allocated to Art, Music,
Personal, Social and Health Education, Physical Education
and Religion and Philosophy. All pupils will also take
courses in Computing Studies, Drama and Health and Food
Technology at various stages in their school careers.

Games. The main sports are hockey, rugby, athletics,
cricket, tennis and swimming. Pupils participate in a wide
variety of other sports, including badminton, basketball, netball, football, volleyball, golf, cross-country running and
skiing.

Activities. Pupils are encouraged to participate in extra-
curricular activities. Clubs and societies include debating,
Scripture Union groups, computer, table tennis, chess, art,
bridge, chemistry, electronics, drama and film clubs. Pupils
take part in the Duke of Edinburgh's Award Scheme and the
Young Enterprise Scheme, and parties regularly go on tour.
There are choirs, orchestras, jazz and concert bands and a
pipe band and tuition in Instrumental Music is arranged as
requested. Each year there are several concerts and dramatic
productions. The Chamber Choir was BBC Songs of Praise
Senior School Choir of the Year 2013.

Admission. Entrance tests and interviews are held in January. The principal points of entry are at Kindergarten (age
3½–4), Junior 1 (age 5), Transitus (age 11) and First Year
(age 12) but pupils are taken in at other stages as vacancies
occur.

Fees per term (2018–2019). Junior School: £1,473–
£3,656; Senior School: £3,703–£4,256.

Bursaries. The School operates a Bursary Fund to give
assistance with fees in the Senior School in cases of need.

Former Pupils' Club. The Glasgow High School Club
Limited is the former pupils' association of the old and new
High Schools. Former pupils all over the world maintain an
interest in the life and work of the School. *Secretary*: Murdoch C Beaton, LLB.

Charitable status. The High School of Glasgow Limited
is a Registered Charity, number SC014768. It is a recognised educational charity.

Governing Body:
Honorary President: Lord Macfarlane of Bearsden, KT
Chair: B C Adair, TD, LLB
Mrs P Galloway, FCA
Dr M N Gupta, BSc Hons, MBChB, MD FRCP
A Horn, MA, LLB
E W Hugh, CA
S J MacAulay
C M Mackie, BSc
S C Miller, WS, LLB Hons, Dip L
Professor Sir V A Muscatelli, MA, PhD, FRSE, FRSA
Mr S Pengelley, BA

K M Revie, LLB Hons

Dr C M Stephen, MBChB, DGM

Mrs M A Stewart, LLB Hons, Dip LP, DFM

R G Wishart, FCMA

Rector: **J O'Neill**, MA Hons

Senior Deputy Rector: K J A Robertson, BSc

Deputy Rectors:
Ms S Gibson, BEd
I S Leighton, BSc
G J Robertson, MA, CA

Staff:
* *Head of Department*
† *House Staff*

English:
*P A Toner, MA
†P D C Ford, MA
Mrs R A Baynham, MA
Mrs S de Groot, MA
Mrs N Lawther, MA, MPhil
T Lyons, MA
Mrs J Muir, MA
Dr P Toal, PhD
Mrs M Noonan, BA (*Drama*)
Mrs A Viswanathan, MA (*Drama*)

Mathematics:
*S J Welsh, BEng
†Mrs C V M Anderson, BSc
†J G MacCorquodale, BSc
Mrs E Clark, BSc Hons
D K Hamilton, BSc, PhD
T A Lockyer, LLB
D R MacGregor, BSc
Mrs H S Mills, MEng
Mrs N Morrison, BSc
Mrs J B Armstrong, BSc

Computer Studies:
*Mrs S E Sterkenburg, BSc, PgC MLE
D D Muir, BSc
I R Purdie, BSc

Science:
N M E Dougall, BSc, MSc, (*Biology)
Mrs K S M O'Neil, BSc (*Chemistry)
Dr D R Went, MSc, PhD (*Physics)
J Campion, BSc
Miss G F Gardiner, BSc, PCert LAM
Dr M McKie, BSc, PhD
Mrs A E McNeil, BSc, MSc

Mrs M R Peek, MSc
Dr N J Penman, BSc, PhD
K J A Robertson, BSc
I J Smith, BSc

Modern Languages:
*N F Campbell, MA, LLB
†Mrs K J Bhatia, BA
†Miss M B Cranie, BA
†Mrs J M Horne, MA
Mrs K Evans, MA (*Careers)
Miss K Péron, MA
Mrs A M T Drapeau-Magee, L-ès-L, M-ès-L
A Fernandez Lucas
Mrs A Hilt, MA
Mrs V MacCorquodale, MA
Mrs L Muir, BA Hons

Classics:
*A H Milligan, MA
Mrs C Bell, MA
J Bullen, BA

Economics and Business Studies:
*T J Jensen, MEd, BComm
Mrs E A Milne, BA, MCIBS

Geography and Modern Studies:
*Miss N L Cowan, MA
K F FitzGerald, BSc
I S Leighton, BSc
Miss J A McAteer, BA
Mrs C McKeown, BA
Miss K Macpherson, MA
G J Robertson, MA, CA
Dr H Ross, MA

History:
*C MacKay, BA
†Miss N Sutherland, MA
Mrs G A C Lindsay, MA
Dr H Ross, MA

Art:
*Mrs C J Bell, BA
Miss N J Henderson, BDes
Mrs J Stewart, BA

Health and Food Technology:
*Miss K D Moore, BA
Mrs C Elsby, BA

Learning Support:
*Mrs R E Hamilton, BA, Dip SfL
Mrs N Morrison, BSc
Mrs R Owen, BEd

Music:
*Mrs S C Stuart, MA/Mus Oxon, MSt Oxon, PG Adv Dip RCM
L D Birch, BA, LRAM, DRSAMD
Miss G Daly, MMus, BMus, LRSM, ARIAM
B Docherty, DRSAM
R McKeown, DRSAMD
Mrs C N Mitchell, MMus, BMus

Junior School Staff:
Head Teacher: Miss H Fuller, BEd Hons
Mrs G Morrans, BEd (*Deputy Head*)
Ms L Boothroyd, BA Hons
Miss C E Carnall, BMus, MA (*Music*)
Mrs L Cowan, BEd Hons
B Docherty, DRSAM
Mrs A Dougherty, BA Hons
Mrs A Duncan, MA Hons
Mrs A M T Drapeau-Magee, L-ès-L, M-ès-L (*French*)
Mrs H M Eustace, BEd Hons
Mrs S A Foster, MA Hons
Mrs E Gibson, Bed
Mrs H Gill, BEd Hons
Mrs M J Gillan, DPE, Dip Sfl, ATQ
Miss K Hallam, BEd Hons
Mrs L A Lambie, BEd Hons
Ms D Lamont, MA Hons (*Principal Teacher*)
J McCarthy, BEd Hons
Mrs E J McConechy, BEd Hons
R McKeown, DRSAMD
Mrs J MacLaren, BEd, MA Cert (*Principal Teacher*)
Mrs C Mitchell, PGDE
Mrs M I Moreland, DCE, AEE
Miss K Péron, MA
Mrs M Pollock, BA Hons, PG Dip Mus, MMus (*Principal Teacher*)
Miss I Rashid, BA Hons
Mrs G Reid, MA (*Principal Teacher*)
Mrs C A Ritchie, DCE
Mrs P Rooney, MA, Dip SfL (*Principal Teacher*)
Miss R Saunders, BEd Hons
Miss A Taylor, MA Hons
Mrs S Ure, BEd, CEPE
Mrs R Young, SVQ4 Social Services

Bursar: Mrs J M Simpson, BAcc, CA

Rector's PA: Ms J Mackay

Mrs J Tierney, BMus
F Walker, BA, ARCO

Religion & Philosophy:
*C F Price, MTheol, MPhil
Mrs G A C Lindsay, MA

Physical Education:
*D N Barrett, BEd
Mrs A Cox, BEd (**Girls' PE*)
†S Leggat, BEd
K F FitzGerald, BSc
Ms S Gibson, BEd
F J Gillies, BSc
J McCarthy, BEd
A W Meikle, MA
Miss R Ward, BSc
Mrs H Cannon, BEd
Mrs S Dougan, BEd
Mrs M J Gillan, DPEMs J Hood, BEd
S Ingles, BEd
Mrs D McCluskey, BSc
J McConnell (*Rugby*)
Mrs S Mitchell, BEd
Mrs R Owen, BEd

Glenalmond College

Glenalmond, Perth, Perthshire PH1 3RY

Tel: 01738 842000
        Admissions Office: 01738 842144
Fax: 01738 842063
email: registrar@glenalmondcollege.co.uk
website: www.glenalmondcollege.co.uk
Twitter: @GlenalmondColl
Facebook: @GlenalmondCollege

Motto: *Floreat Glenalmond*

Glenalmond College, was founded by Mr W E Gladstone and others in 1841 and opened as a School in 1847.

The College is built on the south bank of the River Almond, from the north bank of which rise the Grampian mountains. It is about 50 miles north of Edinburgh and 8 miles from both Perth and Crieff.

The College Buildings, grouped round a cloistered quadrangle, comprise the Chapel, Hall, Library, houserooms and studies, study bedrooms, classrooms and laboratories. A separate block houses additional laboratories and a Theatre. A few metres away are the Art School and the Design and Technology Centre. Next to these are the Music practice rooms and a Concert Hall.

The Sports Complex consists of a cardiovascular training suite, a weights room and dance studio, an indoor sports hall and a heated indoor swimming pool and fitness suite.

The College also has a state-of-the-art Science Block and IT Resources Centre.

Houses. There are 5 houses for boys, and 3 for girls. Each house has accommodation for the resident Housemaster or Housemistress and their family. Senior boys and girls have study-bedrooms of their own.

Religion. The College has an Episcopalian foundation and has a splendid Chapel. However pupils from a wide range of ethnic, religious and cultural backgrounds are welcomed; the needs of other religious groups and recognised faiths will be observed and supported.

Admission. Boys and girls may be registered for admission at any time after birth and enter the College between the ages of 13 and 14 via the Common Entrance Examination or Entrance Scholarship papers. Pupils leaving Primary Schools may qualify by tests and examinations for junior entry at age 12. Girls and boys may also qualify for entry into the Lower Sixth, or at other points during their school career. Boarding and Day pupils are welcomed throughout the school.

For those applying from overseas, or whose first language is not English, we expect, as a minimum, an Intermediate standard of written and spoken English (IELTS Grade 4 or equivalent).

Curriculum. In the Second and Third Form (Years 8 and 9, S1 and S2) all pupils take a wide range of subjects including English, Mathematics, History, Geography, French, Spanish or German, Latin or Ancient Civilisation, Biology, Chemistry, Physics, Technology, Music, PSHCE, Drama, Art and ICT. In the Fourth and Fifth Forms pupils may choose three options from a wide range of subjects (including Latin and Greek), along with the core subjects of Mathematics, English Language and Literature, French and the three Sciences. Each pupil is guided by an academic tutor who meets regularly with their tutor group.

The Sixth Form curriculum is designed to allow pupils as wide a choice as possible with 25 A Level subjects being offered ranging from Business to History of Art and Physics to Politics. There are weekly lectures from outside speakers on social, economic and cultural subjects which foster academic excellence across the age ranges. The more able pupils are encouraged to join the William Bright Society which promotes cross year group discussion on relevant academic and moral issues.

Careers. Over 98% of pupils continue to university; a few go direct to professional careers, industry, the Services, etc. Around half of pupils go to Russell Group universities, with a good number gaining places at Oxbridge each year. Great emphasis is placed on careers guidance: careers talks, visits and advice along with a well-stocked careers room assist pupils in their choice. All pupils are encouraged to take psychometric careers aptitude tests at age 16.

The computer network extends to all parts of the campus. ICT is available in libraries and all classrooms, and all pupils have access to email and the internet within their Houses.

Art, Drama and Music. Music plays a central part in the life of the school: there is an Orchestra as well as smaller String, Woodwind and Brass Groups. A large Choir and Choral Society perform at the College, in Perth and in Edinburgh. A new Harrison and Harrison pipe organ supports Glenalmond's central Chapel tradition. The Concert Society arranges recitals and concerts at the College; frequent visits are made to concerts in Perth and elsewhere. There are currently two Pipe Bands.

The Drama and Art departments flourish, in conjunction with the well-established Design and Technology Centre. Both Art and Music as well as Design/Technology form part of the normal curriculum and can be taken at GCSE and A Level.

Sport and Recreation. Rugby (boys) and Hockey (girls) are played in the Michaelmas Term and there is a wide variety of activities to choose from in the Lent Term, including Lacrosse for girls and Hockey, Football and Cross-Country for boys, with Cricket, Athletics, Basketball, Shooting, Sailing, Tennis and Golf in Summer. Shooting on the Miniature Ranges takes place during the two winter terms. There is a large indoor heated Swimming Pool and pupils are also trained in personal survival and Lifesaving. Instruction in Sub-aqua and Canoeing is given. There are also Squash Courts, Tennis Courts, a nine-hole (James Braid designed) Golf Course, and a world-class water-based astroturf pitch for Hockey.

During the Summer, pupils have the opportunity to explore the hills and the neighbouring countryside. There is also a Sailing and Windsurfing Club which uses a neighbouring loch. Weekend camping expeditions are arranged to encourage self-reliance and initiative.

Glenshee is just over an hour away and there are opportunities for skiing in the Lent Term.

Combined Cadet Force. There is a contingent of the Combined Cadet Force which has strong links with the Armed Forces.

Army and Air sections, with a Pre-Service section for Junior Pupils, are organised on the basis of The Duke of Edinburgh's Award. Adventure and Leadership Training figure prominently.

Fees per term (2018–2019). £11,502 Senior Boarders; £11,613 Senior Boarding (non-EU); £7,501 Senior Day Pupils; £8,617 Junior Boarders (2nd Form); £8,700 Junior Boarders (2nd Form non-EU); £5,627 Junior Day.

Our school fees are as inclusive as possible, and cover all of the teaching, accommodation and living costs. They also cover the charges that are common to all pupils, such as the expenses of games, activities, membership of the CCF, use of the library, initial stationery pack, laundry and sewing.

Sibling discounts are available. Children of serving members of the Armed Forces and members of the Clergy receive an automatic 10% fee discount.

Term of Entry. Entry is normally in September. Entry in January or April can be considered where special circumstances exist.

Scholarships and Bursaries. Academic Scholarships and Exhibitions are awarded. Junior Scholarship candidates must be under 14 on 1 September of the year of entry. A short statement showing the scope of the examination will be forwarded on application, and copies of last year's papers may be obtained. Scholarship candidates will be examined at Glenalmond. The Entrance Scholarships Examinations are usually held in March for younger pupils and in November for entrants to the Sixth Form.

Music Scholarships may be available to entrants at 12+, 13+ or Sixth Form. Candidates will usually offer two instruments at least to Grade V. Promising string players and singers will be considered with great interest. Award holders receive free musical tuition.

An Organ Scholarship, Piping Awards and Art & Design Scholarships are also available. There are also Outstanding Talent Awards for Sport.

All-Rounder Awards are available to 13+ entrants only; candidates must demonstrate strength in at least two of the following areas: Drama, Sport, Music, Art.

All Awards can be increased in cases of need. A number of means-tested bursaries are available each year for up to 100% of fees. Applications should reach the Director of Finance no later than 1 February in the year of entry.

The Old Glenalmond Club. *OG Club Secretary*: David Sibbald.

Charitable status. Glenalmond College is a Registered Charity, number SC006123. It exists for the all-round education of Boys and Girls in the tranquillity of a rural setting.

Council:
*President of Council: The Primus of the Episcopal Church in Scotland, The Most Reverend Mark Strange, Bishop of Moray, Ross and Caithness
*Chairman of Council: N S K Booker, MA Hons [OG]
*Chairman of Committee of Council: K R Cochrane, CBE, BAcc, HonDSc, FRSE, CA
The Earl of Home, CVO, CBE
**D G Sibbald, BArch Hons, RIBA, FRIAS (*OG Club Secretary*)
J V Light, MA
**J Miller, BSc, MRICS
**J G Thom, LLB, Dip LP, NP, TEP [OG]
Prof A McCleery, MA, PhD
T J O Carmichael, BA, PGDE
Mrs L White, LLB
[*H Ouston, MA, PGCE, Dip Ed] [OG]
Ms A Miller, BA Hons, MSc, CFP
Mrs K Porter BSc, Dip HE Nursing
J Oliver (*OG Club Chairman*)
C Nicholson

* *Committee of Council*
[OG] *Old Glenalmond*

Interim Warden: H Ouston, MA, PGCE, Dip Ed

Sub-Warden: C G Henderson, BSc, PhD St Andrews
Deputy Head – Academic: Dr S N Kinge, BSc, PhD
Deputy Head – Teaching and Learning (Joint): G O'Neill, BSc Belfast, PGCE; Mrs J Davey, MA Edinburgh, PGCE
Deputy Head – Pastoral: Mrs S Sinclair, BSc Edinburgh, PGCE
Head of Admissions: M T Jeffers, BSc, PGCE
Chaplain: The Revd G W Dove, MA, MPhil, BD
Chief External Relations Officer: Dr C Fleming, BSc, PhD

Teaching Staff:
* *Head of Department*
† *Housemaster/mistress*

English:
*J Hathaway, BA, MA, PGCE
Miss V M Dryden, BA, PGDE
Miss L Kirk, RSAMD Glasgow, PGCE
Mrs L Swaile, MA, PGDE
Miss K Hynd, MA Dundee, PGDE
†E A J Phillips, MA, QTS

Mathematics:
*G G O'Neill, BSc, PGCE
M T Jeffers, BSc, PGCE
S P Erdal, BSc, PGCE
Mrs S Sinclair, BSc, PGCE
M A Orviss, MA Cantab, PGCE
Mrs S Smith, BSc, PGCE
Miss R Brown, BSc, PGCE

Classics:
*G W J Pounder, MA Oxon, PGCE
Miss R Masson, MA, MLitt

Modern Foreign Languages and EAL:
*Mrs J Davey, MA, PGCE
J A Gardner, BA, PGCE
Mrs S Baldwin, MA Cantab, PGCE
Mrs I Reynolds, MA
Dr C Murie, MA, PhD, PGCE
Mrs E Mundill, MA, Dip Lib, MCLIP, Cert TM, TESOL

Geography:
*T Mason, BSc, PGDE
S Smith, MA, PGDE
†C S Swaile, MA, PGCE
†M Gibson, BSc, PhD, PGCE, FRGS
R L Myers, BEd, BA

History and Politics:
*D Tolan, MA, PGDE
†Miss J H Kaye, MSc
R L Myers, BEd, BA
†G E Draper, BA, PGCE

Biology:
*A C Hughes, BSc, PGCE
C G Henderson, BSc, PhD, PGCE
Dr S Colby, BSc, PhD, PGCE
Mrs L Tosh, BSc, PGCE
Miss F McGregor, BSc, PGCE, PGDE

Chemistry:
*Dr T S Wilkinson, BSc, PhD, PGCE
S N Kinge, BSc, PhD
Mrs T T Hughes, BSc, PGCE
Mrs L Tosh, BSc, PGCE

Physics:
*R Benson, BSc, PGCE
S N Kinge, BSc, PhD
D M Smith, BSc, MEng, PGCE

Economics and Business:
*J C Robinson, BA, PGCE
†P J Golden, BSocSc, MA, PGCE
S P Erdal, BSc, PGCE, Dip Acc

Computer Science:
*Ms J MacDonald, BSc, MLitt, Dip Ed

Drama:
*Mrs E Moss, MA, BA, PGCE
*Miss L Kirk, RSAMD, PGCE (*Head of Drama and Performance*)
Miss E Grace, BA, Hull, PGCE

Music:
*T J W Ridley, GRSM, PhD, LRAM, FRSA
B J Elrick, LLB
Ms J Nicholson, BEd

Art and Design:
Miss E Meldrum, BA Hons, PGCE (*Acting Head of Art*)
Mrs M S F Willington-Piper, BA Hons, MSc
A McLean
C Moss, BA Hons, Bath Academy of Art, PGCE

History of Art:
*†Mrs C J R Butler, MA

Divinity and Religious Studies:
*Revd G W Dove, MA, MPhil, BD

Library and Archives:
Mrs E Mundill, MA, Dip Lib, MCLIP, Cert TM, TESOL

Design Technology:
*A A Purdie, BSc, BEd
Mrs G Crozier, BTecEd

Physical Education:
*G Smith
Miss C Bircher, BEd
Miss R Greenhalgh, BA
P Wilkinson BSc, PGCE
Miss R Cave, BSc
D Stott, CMI, MMI (*Hockey consultant*)

Learning Support:
*Mrs N Henderson, BSc, PGCE
Mrs L Critchley, Montessori Diploma
Mrs S Spiers, BA, PGCE

The Godolphin and Latymer School

Iffley Road, Hammersmith, London W6 0PG

Tel: 020 8741 1936; 020 8735 9595 (Bursar)
Fax: 020 8735 9520
email: office@godolphinandlatymer.com
website: www.godolphinandlatymer.com
Twitter: @GandLSchool
Facebook: @GandLSchool

Motto: *Francha Leale Toge*

Foundation. Godolphin and Latymer, originally a boys' school, became a girls' day school in 1905. It was aided by the London County Council from 1920 onwards and by the Inner London Education Authority when it received Voluntary Aided status after the 1944 Education Act. Rather than become part of a split-site Comprehensive school it reverted to Independent status in 1977.

Godolphin and Latymer is an independent day school for approx 800 girls, aged 11 to 18. The school stands in a six-acre site in Hammersmith, near Hammersmith Broadway and excellent public transport. The original Victorian building has been extended to include a pottery room, computing facilities, science and technology laboratories, art studios, a dark room and an ecology garden. The girls benefit from a recently renewed all-weather surface for hockey and tennis, as well as netball courts and a Sixth Form Centre. Since September 2006, the school has leased St John's Church and its Vicarage, both adjacent to the existing site. The Vicarage, renamed the Margaret Gray Building, provides additional classrooms. The Rudland Music School opened in the Autumn Term 2008 and the renovated church, The Bishop Centre, for the performing arts was completed in early Spring 2009. These state-of-the-art developments provide a range of teaching and performance spaces, recording studios and a music technology suite. The Bishop Centre provides an auditorium to seat over 800. In September 2015 a new Sports Complex, the Hampton Centre, was opened.

The Godolphin and Latymer School aims to provide a stimulating, enjoyable environment and to foster intellectual curiosity and independence. We strive for a love of learning and academic excellence, emphasising the development of the individual, within a happy, supportive community.

While girls are expected to show a strong commitment to their studies they are encouraged to participate in a range of extracurricular activities. We aim to develop the girls' self-respect, self-confidence and resilience, together with consideration and care for others so that they feel a sense of responsibility and are able to take on leadership roles within the school and the wider community.

Pastoral Care. The school has a close relationship with parents, and every member of the staff takes an interest in the girls' academic and social welfare. Each girl has a form teacher and a deputy form teacher and there is a Head of Lower School, Head of Middle School and a Head of Sixth Form, each with at least two deputies.

Curriculum. We offer a broad, balanced curriculum including appropriate education concerning personal, health, ethical economics and social issues. During the first three years Philosophy and Religion, English, French, Spanish or German, Mandarin, Latin, History, Geography, Mathematics, Physics, Chemistry, Biology, Food Preparation and Nutrition, Design Technology, Art, Music, Drama and Physical Education are studied. In Year 10 Italian, Greek, Classical Civilisation and PE and Drama become available. Computing is studied in Years 7 and 8, and Computer Science is now available at GCSE and A Level. Girls take ten subjects to GCSE.

In the Sixth Form there is a choice of curriculum between the Advanced Level and the International Baccalaureate Diploma. All subjects (except PE) offered to GCSE can be continued into the Sixth Form with the addition of Ancient History, Drama and Theatre Studies, Economics, Government and Politics and History of Art. Sixth Formers also undertake the Extended Project Qualification (AL) or Extended Essay and Theory of Knowledge (IB) and attend lectures given by outside speakers.

The Sixth Form. The Sixth Form facilities include a Common Room, Work Room and Terrace. The 210 girls in the Sixth Form play a leading role in the school, taking responsibility for many extracurricular activities, producing form plays and organising clubs. They undertake voluntary work and lead our Raising and Giving programme.

Higher Education and Careers Advice. A strong careers team offers advice to girls and parents. Our specialist room is well stocked with up-to-date literature and course information, and lectures and work shadowing are arranged. Almost all girls proceed to Higher Education degree courses (including an average of 15 a year to Oxford and Cambridge and around 13 to US Universities and Colleges).

The Creative Arts. Music and Drama flourish throughout the school. The Rudland Music School has outstanding facilities for music: 20 soundproofed rooms for individual or group work, a recording studio, ICT suite and two classrooms which open out into a very large rehearsal space for choirs and orchestras. There are four choirs, two orchestras and several small ensembles, and a joint orchestra. Individual music lessons are offered in many different instruments. Each year there is a pantomime, Year 10 and Sixth Form plays as well as the school productions. The refurbished church, known as The Bishop Centre, offers a superb performing arts space for music, drama and dance.

Physical Education is a vital part of a girl's development as an individual and as a team member. Younger girls play netball, hockey, tennis and rounders and have gymnastic and dance lessons. In the senior years there is a wider range of activities offered, including rowing and squash off site. A state-of-the-art Sport and Fitness Centre opened in September 2015 providing a Sports Hall, climbing wall, dance studio and fitness suite. Tennis/netball courts and an astroturf hockey pitch are also on site.

Extracurricular Activities. The many opportunities for extracurricular activities include the British Association of Young Scientists, Computing, Chess, Model United Nations, Debating, Creative Writing, Classics Club and the Duke of Edinburgh's Award scheme, as well as a wide range of sporting activities such as karate, fencing, rowing and trampolining.

Activities outside the School. We organise language exchanges to Germany and France and a musical exchange to Hamburg and Sixth Form work experience in Versailles and Berlin. There is also an exchange with a school in New York. Each year, Year 9 girls ski in the USA and there are study visits to Spain, Italy and France and History of Art visits to Paris, Bruges, Venice and Florence.

We take advantage of our London location by arranging visits to conferences, theatres, exhibitions and galleries. Field courses are an integral part of study in Biology and Geography.

Admission. Girls are normally admitted into Year 7 (First Year Entrance) or into our Sixth Form. Examinations for First Year entrance are held in January and for the Sixth Form in November. There are occasional vacancies in other years. Entry is on a competitive basis.

Fees per term (from January 2019). £7,205. Fees are liable to change each January. Private tuition in music and speech and drama are extra. Most girls have school lunch, but it is an option from Year 8.

Scholarships. Music scholarships are available on entry to Year 7 and in the Sixth Form and include free tuition in one instrument.

An Art scholarship is available in the Sixth Form.

All scholarships are worth up to 30% of fees and may be topped up by means-tested bursaries in cases of need. For all awards, candidates must satisfy the academic requirements of the school.

Bursaries. A number of school bursaries are available annually.

Uniform. Uniform is worn by girls up to and including Year 11.

Charitable status. The Godolphin and Latymer School is a Registered Charity, number 312699. It exists to provide education to girls aged 11 to 18.

Governors:
Chairman: Mrs A J S Paines, MA Cantab
Mr S Carney, JD Chicago Law School, BEc Harvard College
Ms J Collins, MA Edinburgh, ACCA
Mr S Davies, BA Oxon
Ms S Davies, BA Wimbledon College of Art, MA London
Professor Dame Julia Higgins, DBE, BA, DPhil Oxon
Mr T Howe, QC, MA Oxon, GDL City
Mrs G Kettaneh Priestley, BSc LSE, JD Harvard Law School, MPA Harvard Kennedy School
Mrs S Kinross, BA Exeter
Mr K Knibbs, MA Oxon
Mrs S Lane
Dr L Magrill, BSc Edinburgh, MCom Birmingham, PhD Bradford
Mrs D Rose, MA Cantab
Mr M Sanderson, MA Cantab

Mr O Waring, BA Oxon, LLB King's College London
Mrs E Watson, BA Exeter

Clerk to the Governors: Mrs Diana Lynch, BSc Kingston, FCCA

Staff:

Head Mistress: Dr Frances Ramsey, MA, DPhil Oxon

Senior Deputy Head (*Pastoral*), *Deputy Designated Safeguarding Lead*: Mrs A Paul, BA Durham
Deputy Head (*Curriculum and Academic Matters*): Dr S Harnett, MA DPhil Oxon

Senior Teachers:
Learning and Teaching and New Technologies: Dr C Badger, MSci PhD Cantab
School Organisation and Co-Curricular: Mr J Carroll, BSc Durham
Head of Sixth Form: Ms C Drennan, MA Oxon, MA East Anglia
Development Director: Miss J Hodgkins, BEd West Sussex Institute of Higher Education, MA Brunel
Staff Professional Development, Designated Safeguarding Lead: Ms A Triccas, BA MA London

Heads of Departments:

Art and Design:
Miss L Cooper, BA Staffordshire, MA Wimbledon School of Art

Classics:
Mrs L Duffett, BA Oxon, MA London

Computing:
Mrs G Oliver, MA Cantab

Design and Technology:
Ms M Martins, BA Leeds

Drama:
Ms S Adams, BEd Melbourne

Economics:
Mr A Shah, BA City of London Polytechnic, MEd Sheffield

English:
Mr J Bell, MA Cantab, MA Sussex

Geography:
Mr M Golland, BA London, MEd Cantab

History and Government and Politics:
Mrs A Armstrong, BA York
Dr B Snook, BA MPhil PhD Cantab

History of Art:
Ms C Osborne, BA Nottingham, MA Sussex

Individual Learning Needs:
Ms A Clark, BA Oxon

International Baccalaureate Coordinator:
Ms A Dubois, BA MA Le Littoral

Mathematics:
Mrs D Malone, MEng Oxon, MA KCL

Modern Foreign Languages:
Mrs C Corcoran, BA Orléans, MA Southampton

French:
Mrs C Corcoran, BA Orléans, MA Southampton

German:
Mrs U Fenton, MA Freiburg

Italian:
Miss L Padalino, BA Bologna

Mandarin:
Mrs S Whittaker, BA Durham

Spanish:
Miss H Matthews, BA Cantab

Music:
Miss L McAdam, MA Cantab

Philosophy & Religion:
Mr L Higgins, BA Nottingham, MEd Cantab

Physical Education:
Miss E Elfick, BEd Exeter

Science:
Ms G Andrade, BSc London, MA East London

Biology:
Miss T Dean, BSc Edinburgh

Chemistry:
Miss J Smart, BSc Birmingham

Physics:
Mr J McGrath, BSc Wales, MSc Cranfield

Speech & Drama:
Miss L Tricker, BEd CSSD, MSc London

Bursar: Mrs Diana Lynch, BSc Kingston, FCCA
Registrar: Mrs Felicity Lundberg
Higher Education and Careers: Mrs F Downham, BA Sheffield
Head Mistress's PA: Miss Victoria Stearns
School Doctor: Dr Samia Hassan, MBBS Imperial, MRCGP, DSFRH, PGCE
School Nurses:
Mrs Victoria Dickins, RN, BSc Clinical Practice, Dip SpLD Hornsby
Mrs Tessa Vardigans, RN, SpCPHN-SN

Godolphin School

Milford Hill, Salisbury SP1 2RA

Tel: 01722 430500
Fax: 01722 430501
email: admissions@godolphin.wilts.sch.uk
website: www.godolphin.org
Twitter: @GodolphinSchool

Motto: *Franc Ha Leal Eto Ge* (Frank and Loyal art though)

Inspiring Girls from 11–18 years, Godolphin is an independent boarding and day school offering flexi, weekly and full boarding. Founded by Elizabeth Godolphin in 1726, the school continues to honour its traditional values, whilst educating girls for the 21st Century. The school has 290 girls in the senior school, 100 in the Sixth Form. Godolphin Prep educates girls from 3–11 years. The school stands in 16 acres of landscaped grounds on the edge of the historic cathedral city of Salisbury, overlooking open countryside.

Curriculum. A strong academic life combines with thriving art, drama, music and sport. A five-studio art centre provides excellent art and design facilities, while the Blackledge Theatre provides a professional environment for drama and music performance. Sciences are taught within the well-equipped laboratories.

High academic standards (85% A* to B grades at A Level in 2018) are combined with a wide range of clubs, societies and weekend activities; also an outstanding programme of trips and expeditions. Activities include: Duke of Edinburgh's Award, Combined Cadet Force, community service, debating, creative writing, academic societies and wide ranging opportunities in art, drama, music and sport. 24 subjects are available at A Level, and virtually all students continue to higher education, most to universities, including Oxbridge; 92% of students go to their first-choice university and 63% gain places at a Russell Group University. There is considerable emphasis on Careers guidance, including an excellent work shadowing scheme.

Religious Instruction. Godolphin has strong affiliation with the Church of England, but religious instruction covers all major world faith.

Physical Education. Strong sporting record with pupils regularly selected for county and regional teams; also at national level. 22 sporting options include lacrosse, hockey, netball, tennis, athletics, swimming, gymnastics, dance, rounders and cross-country. Each girl is encouraged to find at least one sport she really enjoys during her time at Godolphin.

Entrance Examination. Godolphin's own assessment and interview at 11+ and Common Entrance Examination at 13+. Examination and interview at all other levels, including Sixth Form.

Scholarships and Bursaries. 11+ and 13+ for outstanding merit or promise in academic work, music, sport or art. Candidates for music awards should have attained at least Grade 4 at 11+ (Grade 6 at 13+) on one instrument. They are also expected to reach an acceptable academic standard.

Sixth Form Academic, Art, Drama, Music and Sports scholarships are also available.

Foundation Bursaries are available and the Old Godolphin Bursary is awarded by the Old Godolphin Association to the daughter of an Old Godolphin.

Fees per term (2018–2019). Senior School: Boarding £9,095–£10,675 (Full), £11,705–£12,075 (International); Day £6,325–£7,030.

Prep School: Boarding: £8,410 (Full), £8,870 (International), Day: £4,645 (Years 4–6), £3,690 (Year 3), £2,385 (Years 1–2), £2,375 (Reception).

Extra Subjects. Individual tuition in music, speech and drama, tennis, fencing, judo, EFL and learning support.

Old Godolphin Association. *Secretary*: Mrs Annie Burchmore, email: oga@godolphin.wilts.sch.uk.

Charitable status. The Godolphin School is a Registered Charity, number 309488. Its object is to provide and conduct in or near Salisbury a boarding and day school for girls.

Governing Body:
M J Nicholson (*Chairman*)

Mr J S Lipa	Mr R Franks
Mrs R Hawley	Mrs N Huggett
Revd I Woodward	Mrs A Burchmore
Mr G W Green	Mrs C Mannion-Watson
Dr R Griffiths	Dr Elizabeth Shaw
Mr J Kelly	Mr K Thompson
Mr J Booker	General N Pope
Mr A F R Boys	

Clerk to the Governors: Mrs J Wilson

Headmistress: Mrs Emma Hattersley, BA Dunelm

Deputy Head: Mr R Dain, MA Oxon
Academic Deputy: Mr G Budd, BA Hons Durham
Pastoral Deputy: Mrs J Price

Director of External Relations: Mrs M Rowney
Head of Admissions: Mrs C Florence

For a full Staff List please visit www.godolphin.org

Gordonstoun

Elgin, Moray IV30 5RF

Tel: +44 (0)1343 837837
email: admissions@gordonstoun.org.uk
            principalpa@gordonstoun.org.uk
website: www.gordonstoun.org.uk
Twitter: @gordonstoun
Facebook: @GordonstounSchool

Introduction. As well as preparing students for exams, Gordonstoun prepares them for life.

The school's uniquely broad curriculum encourages every individual to fulfil their potential academically and as human beings. The school motto is 'Plus est en vous' – There is more in you. At Gordonstoun, this sense of possibility is presented to its students, every single day.

'It wasn't until we saw the curriculum and the schedule of what they would be doing each day that we truly understood the difference between Gordonstoun and other schools.' Current parent.

Gordonstoun's location on a 200-acre woodland estate in the North of Scotland provides the background for its world-beating outdoor education. Expeditions to the Scottish Highlands or sail training on the School's 80ft boat are an integral part of school life.

Active engagement in service to the local community also comprises a core part of Gordonstoun's 'working week', further expanding the students' sense of personal and social responsibility and building self-esteem.

Gordonstoun follows the English GCSE and A Level curriculum. Every student's progress is carefully overseen by their tutor and they go on Universities, Colleges and Art Schools all over the world.

Gordonstoun students inhabit a community which is both balanced and internationally dynamic, living and learning alongside fellow students from across the social, cultural and geographical board. The school's seven day programme ensures that students are happily integrated and engaged.

The uniquely all-round education on offer at Gordonstoun provides its students with the chance to develop intellectually, emotionally, physically and spiritually because Gordonstoun understands that the broader the experience, the broader the mind.

The School. Gordonstoun is a co-educational boarding and day school for children aged 6–18. Our main entry points are at age 6 for the Junior School, age 13 for the Lower School (Years 9–11) and age 16 for the Sixth Form (Years 12 and 13), though students can be admitted into any year group if space allows. There are approximately 115 pupils in the Junior school and a further 410 in the Senior School. Gordonstoun prides itself on the international make-up of the student body with approximately one third from overseas, one third from Scotland and one third from the rest of the UK. Gordonstoun is a founding member of The Round Square Organisation and in Year 10 approximately 20 students each year participate in a term's exchange with other Round Square schools in countries such as New Zealand, Australia, Canada, South Africa, Germany, Denmark and the USA. A corresponding number of students from the recipient schools arrive at Gordonstoun each Spring Term.

Boarding. Gordonstoun is one of the few remaining full-boarding schools in the UK and nearly 90% of students in the Senior School are full boarders. This ensures that a full programme of activities is offered throughout weekends and Leave-out weekends. Day pupils join in with weekend activities. There are 8 boarding houses in the Senior School, all but one of which are all-through Houses for boys or girls aged 13–18. One House is for Sixth Form boys only.

Pastoral Care. Gordonstoun's commitment to the well-being, care and protection of every child and young person in our Junior and Senior Schools is paramount. In every aspect of the pastoral care and curriculum experience we endorse the national focus on 'getting it right for every child' and our commitment to ensuring our compliance with the Children and Young People's Act (Scotland) 2014 supports this focus. We place particular importance on ensuring that all students at Gordonstoun have their wellbeing carefully and sensitively managed. Any student joining the school is well cared for, and monitored throughout his or her education. Our systems are built around our pastoral aims, which closely reflect the Gordonstoun ethos and our aim of developing the whole person. This is achieved by an exceptional pastoral team, who devote boundless time, energy and expertise to developing, encouraging and advising students.

Curriculum. Year 9 students carry out a broad and balanced curriculum in both the core and non-core GCSE subjects. English, Maths, Core Languages (French/Spanish) and Physical Education are set independently of each other and students are streamed according to ability. For the remainder of the curriculum time students are assigned to one of four form sets. The form set will also be the class in which students are grouped together to carry out humanities and creative arts. A second language, chosen from French, Latin, German and Spanish is available as an option across the year.

Gordonstoun follows the English National Curriculum of GCSE and A Level examinations. There are a wide range of subjects available at both levels.

At GCSE students take the core subjects of English, Maths and Science with a choice of four optional subjects. Non-examinable subjects in the Core include International & Spiritual Citizenship – a course encompassing and enhancing Religious Studies and Personal & Social Education – and Physical Education.

In Year 12 most students choose three A Level subjects and an optional EPQ. Most non-English speaking students take their native language at A Level. The School offers a range of A Levels allowing students to choose the course that suits them. The School is continually looking to develop new opportunities for students so new courses may become available. In addition to academic subjects, students attend a weekly lecture and International and Spiritual Citizenship lessons where they explore what they believe and their role as an international citizen.

Gordonstoun has a wide support network for those students requiring Learning Support and there is the opportunity to receive one to one or small group teaching. We also offer lessons to prepare international students for IELTS (the International English Language Testing System) for entry into a British University and to acquire the skills they need to study in English in the Sixth Form and beyond.

Academic Results. 2018 was an excellent year for both GCSE and A Level results and we are very proud of our hard-working students. The A Level results converted into a strong year for university admissions with an overwhelming majority of applicants gaining a place at the university of their choice.

Destination of Leavers. Gordonstoun students are joining a range of universities this autumn including St Andrews, University College London, Newcastle, Edinburgh, Warwick and Exeter. Some students have chosen to continue their studies overseas including Georgetown (USA) and universities in Germany and Holland.

The class of 2018 left to study the usual diverse range of subjects from astrophysics to zoology and mechanical engineering to music. Three students left to study medicine.

Sport and Activities. The Gordonstoun Activities programme is carefully designed to enhance and enrich the experience and opportunities of the student body. Students are encouraged to maximise these opportunities by experiencing a wide range of activities whilst also pursuing their passions and strengths. There are many different activities available at Gordonstoun using both the School's facilities and facilities further afield. These activities range from the physical to the cerebral, from team to individual.

The School has competitive teams in rugby, football, hockey, basketball, cricket, tennis, athletics and squash for the boys; hockey, netball, tennis, athletics and squash for the girls; and mixed teams in golf and tennis. These teams participate in national competitions and players are regularly chosen to represent district and regional teams. There are also opportunities to compete in swimming galas, cross-country running, skiing, sailing and adventure races. There is a wide range of recreational sports available including: riding, target shooting, badminton, golf, aerobics, yoga, mountain biking, cycling, climbing, kayaking, orienteering and table tennis.

Cultural activities are designed to give the students opportunities to taste other areas of intellectual stimulation. They include: conversational French and Spanish; cooking, newspaper editing, Jazz dance, electronics, web design, arts, crafts, debating, film and digital art, drama, dance, chess and music practice.

The Performing Arts. Gordonstoun prides itself on the strength of its Performing Arts. Dance, Drama and Music are available to all students and there are regular collaborations between the three departments to produce major theatrical productions. A weekly Dance activity is available to all students and there is also an annual Dance Show, regular Shakespeare productions and an annual Theatre Festival. The School also routinely takes shows to the Edinburgh Fringe Festival. Music students are encouraged to become accustomed to performing in front of audiences large and small via a weekly series of relaxed lunchtime concerts as well as full-scale, formal musical events. Nearly half of the student body receives individual musical tuition in a wide range of instruments.

Outdoor Education and Sail Training. Gordonstoun's outdoor education and learning programmes of expeditions and adventure activities aim to provide experiences that encourage greater personal understanding within individual students. The programmes and sessions look to instil effective learning habits that develop confidence, resilience, tenacity and creativity into the core of all students. The School's fantastic location means that Gordonstoun can provide students with a structured and inspiring programme of mountain, river and sea-based wilderness expeditions. Gordonstoun uses a variety of beautiful and remote settings for Year Group, House, DofE and PE expeditions and journeys which allow students to learn more about and develop a respect for the natural environment while encouraging independence, resourcefulness and effective collaboration.

Sail training is an essential component of Gordonstoun's broader curriculum. It helps to develop teamwork and leadership skills, which complement personal challenge. All students undergo seamanship training in cutters at nearby Hopeman Harbour and on the Moray Firth where they learn basic skills in preparation for a voyage off the Scottish coast in the School's own 80-foot sail training vessel, Ocean Spirit of Moray. Year 8 pupils at the Junior School participate in a two day voyage, Year 10 students are on board for six days and Sixth Formers undertake a week-long Sail Training voyage. These experiences are unique in British mainstream education, combining the challenge of the sea with the development of interpersonal skills, teamwork and leadership. In the Sixth Form there are other opportunities to sail on Ocean Spirit during holiday periods, including participation in a Tall Ships Race or voyaging to the Svalbard Archipelago.

Services. Service at Gordonstoun is concerned with fostering and developing a sense of responsibility and a feeling of care towards all fellow beings. It builds on the experience of responsibility within the School community, transferring this to society at large. It involves each student demonstrating a willingness to give up his or her time and effort to benefit another individual or group without expecting return or reward and is an excellent way of fostering links with the local community and of increasing self-esteem. There are nine Services, each of which has a particular set of skills it requires or develops to put something back into the community. Many include training which leads to nationally recognised qualifications that will be useful beyond School life. The Services provide an opportunity to develop and use existing skills or a chance to learn new skills. Every student from Year 11 onwards is expected to take part in one of the services on offer at Gordonstoun.

Admissions. Gordonstoun will be different from any other school you have looked at or visited – of that we are totally convinced! We are also certain that if you can come and see us you will understand our confidence.

We do not hold Open Days as we like to tailor-make your visit and spend as much time with you as you wish. You are welcome to visit Gordonstoun at any time of the year and on any day apart from Sunday; you just need to arrange a mutually convenient time with us. We are happy to assist you with your travel plans and pick you up from Inverness or Aberdeen airports.

During your visit you will meet the Headmaster and senior staff and have a tour of the school with a student. Any information you can give us in advance about the interests of your child will help us to tailor your visit.

Entry to Gordonstoun is by interview and a report from the previous school. The norm for those wishing to enter at Year 12 is a minimum of 5 GCSEs (or equivalent) at grade 4 or above. Scholarships are available for entry to the Junior School (from Year 4), to Year 9 and to Year 12. Scholars are awarded a 10% fee reduction with any further bursary based on means-testing. Approximately one-third of our students receive support of up to 100%.

Please contact Fiona McWilliam or Emma Thorpe on admissions@gordonstoun.org.uk or +44 (0)1343 837829 and they will make all of the necessary arrangements for your visit.

Fees per term (2018–2019). Day fees range from £4,787 (Junior School) to £9,445 (Year 12 direct entry). Boarding fees range from £7,786 (Junior School) to £12,765 (Year 12 direct entry). Weekly boarding is available in the Junior School only.

Scholarships and Bursaries are available for entry to the Junior School, Lower School and Sixth Form. The range of Scholarships include: Academic, All-Round, Music and Art; additionally, Sport, Drama, IT and Design in the Sixth Form. The award is generally for 10% of the annual fee. Additional awards (fee reductions) may be available, based on means-testing. Further information on this is available from Gordonstoun's Finance Department.

Charitable status. Gordonstoun Schools Limited is a Registered Charity, number SC037867.

Chair of Governors: Dr Eve Poole

***Principal*: Lisa Kerr**

Headmaster: Titus Edge

Head of Junior School: Robert McVean

Deputy Head (*Pastoral Care*): Karen MacGregor

Deputy Head (Curriculum): Hayley Atkins

Head of Sixth Form: Suzy Morton

Year 11 Leader: Paul Chatwin

Year 10 Leader: Aidan Duffy

Year 9 Leader: Fiona Lawrence

Director of Admissions: Sabine Richards

Finance Director: Pamela Muir

Director of Gordonstoun International Summer School:
    Claire McGillivray

The Grange School

**Bradburns Lane, Hartford, Northwich, Cheshire
CW8 1LU**

Tel: 01606 539039
Fax: 01606 784581
email: office@grange.org.uk
website: www.grange.org.uk
Twitter: @GrangeHartford
Facebook: @grangeschoolhartford

   Motto: *E Glande Robur*

   The Grange was founded in 1933 as a Preparatory School, the Senior School opening in 1978. The School is co-educational, with 1,177 pupils from 4–18 years, and is situated in the village of Hartford, half an hour away from Chester and Manchester and eight miles from the M6 motorway.

   The Junior School (425 pupils). 1996 saw the opening of a brand new, purpose-built Junior School for children aged 4–11. In 2010 an additional extension was added incorporating a sports hall, Music Department, Science, Design Technology and Art rooms. These developments have brought together all the children of this age group on to one attractively landscaped eleven acre site which is within walking distance of the Senior School. The main teaching takes place in 21 large, self-contained classrooms on two floors, with the younger children located on the ground floor separated from the older children. The school has its own extensive playing fields and generous play areas while three large halls provide facilities for dining, teaching, sports and school productions. Rooms are provided for specialist teaching in Science, Art, Design Technology and a Music Department with no fewer than 6 individual music practice rooms. As well as a broad curriculum, junior pupils study ICT and a modern language; they have regular swimming lessons and compete in sport with other schools. Close attention is given to each child's progress with two parents' evenings each year. Children learn to use computers from Reception, there is a junior orchestra, and opportunities for private music and drama lessons. Extra-curricular activities are held both at lunchtimes and after school. Before and after school care is available from 7.30 am and until 5.45 pm during term time.

   The Senior School (727 pupils). The pupils benefit from excellent extra-curricular and study facilities. The Grange has never been a school to stand still. As a very young school in a lively and competitive market, we spent many of our early years in 'catching up', in terms of our facilities, with the more established schools around us. The physical development of both sites was a top priority at that time.

   In more recent years, while the quality of our provision inside our classrooms has been our major focus, we have still built several new buildings – The Grange Theatre, the Junior School sports hall, music and science extension and the pavilion on the seven acres of playing fields – which have greatly enhanced the life of our community, and demonstrate the quality we now aspire to as an established and successful institution.

   The Sixth Form facility, completed in September 2014, offers a two-storey, pavilion-style building, with a terrace and garden to the rear. Whilst still closely connected to the rest of the school, the Sixth Form Centre provides our senior students with unique and largely self-contained social facilities, careers room and seminar suites. The ground floor is largely given over to a substantial Common Room with room for over 200 and a café only open to Sixth Formers and staff.

   A new £6m Sports Centre is due to open in early 2019. The new high-level facility will include premier netball, badminton, football and basketball courts. Other facilities will include an area tailored for activities such as yoga, dance, gymnastics and aerobics, a dedicated area for rowing machines and free weights, climbing wall and bespoke classroom facilities. New changing and catering facilities have been incorporated into the design which promises to enhance the user-experience.

   Curriculum. In the Senior School, Years 1, 2 and 3 follow a broad curriculum with all Third Year pupils studying two modern languages. In the Third Year pupils continue to study English, Mathematics, Biology, Chemistry, Physics, History, Geography, Classical Civilisation or Latin, Religious Studies, Information Technology, PE/Games, two Modern Languages, and select three of five practical subjects. At the end of the Third Year pupils opt for nine GCSE subjects which must include Mathematics, English, at least one science and at least one modern language. Personal and Social Education is taught in Years 1 to 5.

   From the Third Year advice and assistance is available to all pupils on a wide range of career possibilities. The careers team arrange a biannual careers convention supplemented with regular visits and talks when advice is given by consultants from a variety of professions. There is a fully equipped careers room.

   Pastoral Care. The School provides a disciplined, caring and secure environment in which pupils may work and play without being subjected to harm or distress, in which they may develop their personalities to the full and enjoy their time at school. The Form Teacher is the key figure in each pupil's academic and pastoral welfare and is the first point of contact with parents. The Form Teacher is supported by Heads of Year and regular meetings are held to ensure that the pastoral needs of all our pupils are met. The system is enhanced by a Peer Support scheme which allows trained senior students to listen to younger pupils' concerns.

   House Activities. Each pupil is allocated to one of four Houses on entry to the school; siblings are allocated to the same House. A House Convener arranges meetings with Heads of House to discuss policy, procedure and House activities. These activities range from sporting competitions to an art and a literary competition. Each year the pupils produce their own play for the drama competition and their own repertoire for the music competition. The organisation of such activities is carried out by the pupils themselves with staff providing support and guidance. All pupils are actively encouraged to participate in the full range of activities in order to raise their self-esteem and to allow each to shine; they gain much from the experience. Junior, Intermediate and Senior House Assemblies are held on a weekly basis.

   Sixth Form and Higher Education. Students take four or five subjects plus General Studies to AS Level in the Lower Sixth. They continue with three or four of those subjects plus General Studies to A2 Level in the Upper Sixth. The subjects are chosen from an extensive range with 27 presently available. All Sixth Formers participate in Games lessons, where a wide choice of activities is provided. Supplementary courses provided include Information Technology, Application of Number and Communication and ab initio language courses.

Careers guidance is given considerable emphasis in the Grange Sixth. Each student is attached to a member of the careers team and linguists are given the opportunity to undertake their work experience abroad. Almost all the students progress to higher education, with around 15% going on each year to Oxford and Cambridge.

Sixth Formers are expected to play a leading role in school life. They also participate in the extensive programme of House activities as well as in the Duke of Edinburgh's Award scheme, outward bound courses, Young Enterprise, and the Engineering Council Award scheme.

All students are required to participate in the execution of duties around school and there is a Sixth Form Council, run by the Head Girl and Head Boy, to coordinate the various aspects of Sixth Form life.

Reporting to Parents. The School recognises that our pupils are best served when parents and the School work together and to this end we consider it important to report to parents fully and regularly. We encourage full discussion of the pupils' progress and well being. Each pupil receives at least two full reports per year. Each half term brings a progress report with academic grades and a profile of the pupil's extra-curricular involvement and pastoral welfare. There are two parents' evenings each year for all Junior School pupils and Years 1, 4 and Lower Sixth in the Senior School, and one for all other year groups. If parents have any concerns, they are encouraged to discuss these with the relevant staff at the earliest opportunity and the School will always contact parents and invite them to discuss issues should we feel it necessary.

Games. The School has 22 acres of sports fields across both schools, an all-weather sports area including a 60m athletics track and a low ropes course. The principal games are hockey, netball, rugby, rowing, football, cricket, cross country, athletics and tennis. There are four all-weather tennis courts as well as three badminton courts.

Art, Design, Drama, Music. In addition to timetabled lessons for these subjects there are numerous opportunities to participate in extra-curricular activities.

In the music department no less than 15 peripatetic teachers provide 420 private lessons a week. There are two orchestras, jazz, string, wind and saxophone ensembles, senior choir and choral society. Cantores Roborienses, the School's senior singing group, and the Chamber Orchestra perform at the many informal concerts held during the year and at numerous public events.

Considerable emphasis is placed on Drama in the school with two part-time and two full-time members of staff and pupils participate in a number of drama festivals with a high degree of first and second placings. Over 80 private Speech and Drama lessons take place each week, with all these pupils entering Trinity-Guildhall examinations, from Junior Preliminary to Grade 8. Regular school productions take place each year with frequent theatre trips.

Religion. The School is Christian based but pupils of all faiths or no faith are accepted as long as they are prepared to take a full part in the life of the School. Full School Assemblies take place twice a week.

Transport. Hartford is served by two main line stations, Manchester to Chester and Crewe to Liverpool. The majority of children travel to and from school by car or by one of the private buses which cover a 30-mile radius.

Admission. Reception by informal assessment at the end of January; Senior School by entrance assessment on the first Saturday in February; Sixth Form by interview and good GCSE results.

Pupils are also admitted at other ages as vacancies occur. Admission is gained by interview and test performance. Enquiries for admission are welcome at any time of the year and a copy of the school prospectus may be obtained by contacting the Admissions Registrar.

Open Morning. The School holds three Open Mornings in the Autumn term when prospective parents and pupils are welcome to see the facilities available and to talk to the pupils and staff. Appointments to view the school can be made at other times by contacting the Admissions Department.

Fees per term (from January 2019). Junior School: £2,867 (Reception & Year 1), £3,105 (Years 2–6); Senior School & Sixth Form £3,835.

Scholarships. Several scholarships are offered for entry to the Senior School for exceptional academic ability and music. A number of Sixth Form Scholarships are awarded for outstanding academic potential after an examination held at the end of spring term preceding Sixth Form entry.

Bursaries worth up to full fees and assessed according to means are available to new entrants to the Senior School.

Charitable status. The Grange School is a Registered Charity, number 525918. It exists to provide high quality education for boys and girls.

Governing Body:
Chairman: Mrs K Williams

Head: Mrs D Leonard, BEd, MEd

Senior School:

Deputy Head Pastoral: Mr R Oakes, BA
Deputy Head Academic: Mr A Crook, MA, MPhil
Assistant Head (Co-Curricular): Mrs H Eaton, BA
Assistant Head (Sixth Form): Mr J Walker, BA
Director of Finance and Operations: Mrs D Torjussen, BA Eng, ACA

PA to the Head: Mrs J Ward, BA
Bursar: Mrs L Foxley, ACA
Estates Manager: Mr C Lupton
Marketing Manager: Mr Kieran Seymour, BA
Admissions Registrar: Mrs H Ritchie, BA

Junior School:

Head of Junior School: Mr G Rands, BSc
Deputy Head Pastoral Care: Miss A Evans, BEd
Deputy Head Academic Development: Mr J Land, BEd

PA to the Headmaster/Admissions Registrar: Mrs N Pratt, BA

Gresham's School

Cromer Road, Holt, Norfolk NR25 6EA

Tel:	01263 714500
	01263 714614 (Admissions)
email:	admissions@greshams.com
website:	www.greshams.com
Twitter:	@Greshams_School
Facebook:	@greshamsschool

Motto: *All Worship Be To God Only*

The School was founded in 1555 by Sir John Gresham Kt and the endowments were placed by him under the management of the Fishmongers' Company.

There are 493 pupils in the Senior School, 285 boys and 208 girls, of whom 197 are in the Sixth Form and 290 are boarders.

The School is situated about 4 miles from the breathtaking north Norfolk coast, in one of the most beautiful parts of England. Gresham's enjoys a spacious setting of 200 acres including 50 acres of woodland. Numbered amongst its alumni are W H Auden, Benjamin Britten, Stephen Spender, Lord Reith, Ben Nicholson and Olivia Colman on the Arts side, Christopher Cockerell, inventor of the hovercraft, Ian Proctor, yacht designer, Sir Martin Wood, co-founder of Oxford Instruments, Sir James Dyson, inventor and, more recently, Tom and Ben Youngs, International rugby players. It offers excellence in a wide range of fields, from which pupils gain an outstanding, all-round education.

Gresham's is a Church of England foundation, which welcomes all religious denominations to the school. A 24-hour Health Centre provides a multi-disciplinary professional health service and access to a school counsellor.

In the Senior School, there are four boys' boarding houses and three girls' houses. Students joining in Year 9 share a small dormitory, while older pupils share study-bedrooms, and most Sixth Formers have their own room.

Curriculum. In their first year (Year 9), students study the complete curriculum, including exposure to the full set of sciences, humanities, creative subjects, IT and up to three languages. There is a comprehensive language tuition programme and pupils can select up to three language choices from French, Spanish, German, Latin, Mandarin and Japanese. The curriculum is designed to allow students to experience the full range of subjects prior to making their choices for their two year GCSE programme. For their GCSEs all students follow a compulsory curriculum of English, Mathematics, a language and either dual award or all three sciences, together with an option system allowing for up to a further four subject choices (including further languages) to be made. In Years 10 and 11, students study up to ten IGCSE and GCSE subjects, which enable them to keep open a wide diversity of career opportunities. It is possible to take Mathematics early and for top-set mathematicians to additionally sit AO Mathematics in Year 11. The flexibility built into our option system allows for a wide range of subject combinations.

Since September 2007, we have offered a one-year Pre IB course to a small number of students each year. This course is specifically designed to integrate overseas students into life at Gresham's and most students will gain approximately 8 full GCSEs as a result. The course offers the ideal preparation for the IB Diploma Programme and students follow an individually tailored curriculum centred on English Language, Mathematics, (usually) two sciences and two or three other option subjects.

Entry into the Sixth Form is dependent on students achieving a minimum of six GCSE passes at A* to B grade (9–6), to include passes in Mathematics and English. Students can opt either for A Levels or the IB Diploma. All students receive advice, information and guidance on academic choices and full support for university entrance.

For those students following the A Level course, three subjects are normally taken, though four or more are possible for very able students. All A Levels at Gresham's are now linear. Students are also encouraged to complete an Extended Essay on a subject and topic of their choice. A supplementary course is offered providing enhancement skills in advanced thinking techniques, numeracy, literacy and ICT skills.

For those students entering our IB Diploma, six subjects have to be taken, at least three at higher level and three at standard level. In addition, a Theory of Knowledge (TOK) course is taken, a Creativity, Action and Service (CAS) course followed and an Extended Essay (effectively a research project on a subject of the student's choosing) has to be written. This rigorous programme helps pupils become lifelong and independent learners and the IB qualification is recognised by universities throughout the world.

Pupils entering the Sixth Form receive continual and experienced support and guidance on the UCAS process to help them make realistic and informed decisions about their futures. Lower Sixth pupils are included in the Career and Course Bites sessions where they hear from visiting career professionals and university lecturers. They also participate in a number of careers events throughout the year.

A varied programme of enrichment is offered across the school. In Year 9, students select an area of specialism – academic, drama, art, music or sport. In Year 10, all pupils experience an academic enrichment carousel, which includes a stimulating Friday night lecture programme. Lower Sixth pupils also experience a successful well-being programme. There are many societies to take part in which are dedicated to English, the humanities, foreign languages, the sciences and philosophy. Wider scholarship is also nurtured through activities like debating, Model United Nations, and Electives.

Sport, Music and Drama. The School has abundant playing fields, astroturf pitches, tennis courts, as well as a swimming pool, gym, sports hall and its own indoor shooting range. The main sports are athletics, cricket, hockey, netball, rugby and tennis. Shooting, sailing, swimming, squash, badminton, football, cross-country and running are also very popular, and a number of former pupils have gone on to achieve international success in rugby, shooting, sailing and hockey.

There is a flourishing CCF contingent and Duke of Edinburgh's Award section and approximately 25 gold awards are achieved each year. The School has a talented choir, which performs regularly in East Anglia and travels overseas on its annual choir tour. Several of its members have recently sung in the National Youth Choirs of Great Britain. The school has its own theatre, outdoor amphitheatre in the woods and a state-of-the-art Music School which was opened in 2017. In 2018, a new Outdoor Activity Centre was opened which features a 28-metre climbing tower, 250-metre zip wire, low and high ropes and obstacle courses. Art and drama are also exceptionally strong with drama and theatre studies offered at GCSE, A Level and IB.

Entrance. Those entering at Year 9 from Preparatory Schools take Entrance Examinations in January. Gresham's Prep pupils take Year 8 exit examinations. Tests in Mathematics, English and a General Paper are given to those entering from independent schools and from the maintained sector. Candidates applying from overseas sit assessments in Mathematics and English.

Scholarships and Bursaries. The School is extremely grateful to benefactors, in particular, the Fishmongers' Company, for financing many of the awards below. Scholarships are offered to talented and dedicated students who show outstanding potential academically or in the fields of Art, Drama, Music or Sport.

Senior School: There are Academic scholarships available for entry into Year 9 and Year 12, as well as scholarships for those who are exceptional in Music, Art, Drama and Sport. Britten Instrumental Scholarships and Vocal, Organ and Instrumental Scholarships are available for talented musicians wishing to join Year 7, 9 and Year 12.

Year 9: Academic scholarships are worth up to 50% of the fees. Music, Art, Drama or Sport scholarships are worth up to 20% of the school fee. A means-tested bursary may also be awarded.

Sixth Form: Academic, Music, Art, Drama and Sport scholarships are worth up to 20% of the fee. Contact our Admissions Manager for further details at admissions@ greshams.com

Prep School: Academic scholarships are worth up to 50% of the fee for entry into Year 7, Music, Art, Drama and Sport scholarships are worth up to 10% of the fee. Contact Mrs Helen Dye at prep@greshams.com for further information.

Fees per term (2018–2019). Senior School: £11,660 (boarding), £8,140 (day).

These are inclusive fees; no extra charge is made for laundry, games, medical attention, etc, although some areas, such as individual music tuition, trips, English as a Second Language and learning support, attract extra charges.

Day pupils' meal charges are included in the fees.

Honours. In 2018, 92% of pupils achieved A*–C (or equivalent) grades at GCSE. At A Level pupils achieved an overall pass rate of 96% with 60% achieving A*–B grades. In the IB Diploma, the average point score was 34 points, 4 points above the worldwide average. We consistently send around 95% of our Upper Sixth leavers on to higher education, most of these going to their first-choice courses.

Gresham's Prep School is a flourishing boarding and day co-educational Prep school of 226 pupils within half a mile of the Senior School. Its Head is a member of IAPS. (*For further details see Gresham's Prep entry in the IAPS section.*) There is also a Nursery and Pre-Prep School of approximately 99 pupils.

The Old Greshamian Club. The Club is active on behalf of present and former members of the School and it can be contacted through its Alumni Manager, Mrs J Thomas-Howard, at Gresham's School.

Charitable status. Gresham's School is a Registered Charity, number 1105500. The School is a charitable trust for the purpose of educating children.

Chairman of Governors: Mr M Goff

Ex Officio Governor:
Mr D Robertson, Prime Warden of Fishmongers' Company

Governors:
Sir James Dyson, OM, CBE, FRS, FREng
Mr J fforde
Mr S Gorton
Mrs V Graham
Mr D Jones, MA Cantab
Mr J Maunder Taylor
The Rt Reverend Jonathan Meyrick, The Bishop of Lynn
Mrs A Dugdale
Mr G Able, MA Cantab
Mr A de Capell Brooke, MRICS, DL
Mr E Gould, MA Oxon
Mr P Marriage, MA Oxon
Mr J Morgan, LLB
Mr S Oldfield
Dr S Rubin, FRCPCH, FRCP
Mrs R Walwyn, BEd, MA, Cert Spec Ed

Headmaster: Mr D Robb, MA, MEd

Deputy Head – Academic: Mr T Hipperson, BA, MA, QTS, PGCE
Deputy Head – Pastoral: Mr W Chuter, BA
Bursar: Mr S Willis, MSc, BSc Hons, CDipAF
Director of Admissions & Marketing: Ms S V Wilson, BA, MCIM

Staff:

Director of Pastoral Care: Mrs J Flower, Dip Boarding Education
Housemasters/mistresses:
Farfield: Mr D Atkinson, BA Hons, PGCE
Oakeley: Mrs K Mousley, BA, PGCE
Woodlands: Mr F J V Retter, BA, PGCE
Howson's: Mr A Stromberg, BEng, MSc, AFRIN, PGCE

Tallis: Mr C Cox, BA, PGCE
Edinburgh: Dr E Fern, BA, MA, PhD, PGCE
Queens': Mrs V Seldon, BA, PGCE

Heads of Departments:
Academic Music: Mr E Coleman, BMus, MMus, ALCM, ARCO
Art, Design and Technology: Mr A Gray, BA, PGCE (*Director of Art*)
Biology: Mr T Philpott, BSc Hons, PGCE
Business Studies: Mr A Coventry, BA, PGCE
Chemistry: Mr M Kemp, BSc, PGCE
Classics: Mr W Chuter, BA
Computer Science: Mr W M Robinson, BSc Hons, CSIT
Drama: Miss B O'Brien, BA, PGCE
Economics: Mr P Detnon, BSc, PGCE
English: Mrs C van Hasselt, BA Hons, PGCE
ESL: Mrs S L Ellis-Retter, BA, PGCE
French: Mrs A Watt, BA, PGCE
Geography: Mr S Brown, BA, PGCE
German: Mr F J V Retter, BA, PGCE
History: Mr S A Kinder, BA, PGCE
History of Art: Mrs H Robinson, BA, MA
IT: Mr M Seldon, BA Hons, MA, PGCE (*Director of Studies & Director of IT*)
Japanese: Mr R West, MA, PGCE
Learning Support: Mrs S Gates, BA Hons, PGCE, QTS, OCR Dip SpLD, Cert TESOL
Mandarin: Dr C Greenfield BA, PGCE
Mathematics: Mr J R Thomson, BEng, PGCE
Music: Mr J Bowley, MA Cantab, ARCM PG (*Director of Music*)
Music Technology: Mr J G N Myers, DipHE, GSMD
Philosophy: Mr S B Gates, BA, MA, PGCE
Physical Education: Mr S Adams, BEd (*Director of Sport*)
Physics: Mr D Saker, BSc, MSc, PGCE
Psychology: Miss E Whittle, BA Hons, PGCE
Religious Studies and Philosophy: Mr S B Gates, BA, MA, PGCE (*Contingent Commander CCF*)
Spanish: Miss J Challis, BA, PGCE

School Chaplain: Revd B R Roberts, BD, DipTheol

Prep School:

Acting Head & Deputy Head (Academic): Mrs C Braithwaite, BA Ed Hons, QTS
Deputy Head: Mr J Hyatt, BA Hons QTS
Assistant Deputy Head, Staff and Events: Dr L Betts, MB BS, MS PGCE
Assistant Deputy Head, Academic: Mrs A Nash, BA, PGCE (*Gifted and Talented Coordinator*)
Senior Master: Mr N Thomas, BA Hons, PGCE

Housemasters/mistresses:
Crossways: Mrs K Fields, BEd
Crossways: Mr S Fields, BSc, QTS (*Head of Boarding*)
Kenwyn: Mrs A Horsley, BSc, QTS, PGCE
Kenwyn: Mr J Horsley, BA, PGCE

Heads of Departments:
Art: Mrs S Li-Rocchi, MA, BA Hons, PGCE
Boys' PE: Mr S C Worrall, BA, PGCE
Classics: Mrs S Vare, BA
Dance: Mrs K Edwards, MA, BA
Design Technology: Mr P M Laycock, BA Hons, BSc, PGCE
English & Drama: Miss V Harvey, BA Hons
French: Mrs E Ashcroft, BA, PGCE
Geography & History: Mrs S O'Leary, BA Hons
Girls' PE: Mrs A Horsley, BSc, PGCE
ICT: Mrs H E Witton, BSc Hons
Juniors: Kate Gill, BA, PGCE
Learning Support: Mrs J Fenn, MEd, Dip HD

Mathematics: Mr S Fields, BSc, QTS
Music: Miss L B Roberts, BA, ARCM, AGSM, Dip NCOS
(*Director of Music*)
Religious Studies, *Spanish*: Mrs A Nash, BA, PGCE
Science: Dr L Betts, MB BS, MS PGCE

Pre-Prep School:
Headmistress: Mrs S Hollingsworth, PGCE, QTS, BSc, DSL

Deputy Head: Mrs N Adams, BEd Hons
Miss B Court, BEd Hons (*Early Years Lead, Reception*)

Guildford High School – Senior School
United Learning

London Road, Guildford, Surrey GU1 1SJ

Tel: 01483 561440
email: guildford-admissions@guildfordhigh.co.uk
website: www.guildfordhigh.co.uk
Twitter: @guildfordhigh
Facebook: @GuildfordHigh

Age Range. Girls 11–18.
Number of pupils. 700.
Fees per term (2018–2019). £5,664. Fees exclude lunches. Textbooks and stationery are provided.

Guildford High School consistently boasts some of the best academic results in the country but we are proud to be a local school serving the local community since 1888. Located next to London Road train station our girls travel in from the surrounding towns and villages each morning and a successful train buddy scheme ensures our younger girls do not travel alone.

Awarded the leading Independent school in the country for pastoral care by The Week Magazine 2018, we believe that young people learn best when they are happy and with that in mind we have carefully created an environment in which girls feel safe to push their boundaries and challenge themselves. Our annual 'Well-being Week' is an established highlight of the school calendar and in previous years has featured yoga, circus skills, a silent disco and mindfulness. Our pastoral staff, led by our vibrant Deputy Head Pastoral, are second to none.

Creating an environment in which girls feels safe and valued allows them to throw themselves into their learning. Joining the Senior School in Year 7, girls will find themselves studying Current Affairs, Philosophy and Latin in addition to the more traditional subjects you would expect to find on the timetable. As they go through the school, subject options increase again and new subjects such as Greek are offered at GCSE and Psychology, Politics and Economics at A Level.

Homework is kept to a minimum at Guildford High School. In Years 7–9, our pupils spend no more than 1 hour per evening on homework and no homework needs to be handed in the next day. This allows time for extra-curricular activities to be enjoyed and new skills developed. Similarly, no homework is set for holidays – that's time for family visits, relaxing and enjoying hobbies.

Pupils joining us in Year 7 or for Sixth Form come from a huge number of schools throughout the local area and there is no one type of 'GHS girl'. We are a community of actors, musicians, artists, scientists, bookworms and sports women. In an environment that buzzes with creativity and rings with laughter, girls are unlimited in their belief in each other and

themselves. Our former pupils go on to achieve great things in all walks of life.

Facilities. Facilities include libraries, eleven well-equipped laboratories, whiteboards in every classroom, an Information Technology Centre, a Design Technology Centre, Art and Design Studios, a Food Technology Room, Music Rooms, Music Technology Studio, a Careers Room and Dining Hall. The school also opened a £5 million Sports Hall and indoor swimming pool in 2006, and a new Music Recital Hall in 2016.

Charitable status. Guildford High School Senior School is part of United Learning which comprises: UCST (a Company Limited by Guarantee, Registered in England, number 2780748, and a Registered Charity, number 1016538) and ULT (a Company Limited by Guarantee, Registered in England, number 4439859, and an Exempt Charity).

Governing Body: The Council of United Learning

Patron: The Most Revd and Rt Hon Justin Welby, Archbishop of Canterbury

Local Governing Body:
Mr Dan Perrett (*Chairman*)
Canon Robert Cotton
Mrs Anna Lise Gordon (*Child Protection Representative*)
Professor Ortwin Hess
Mr Robert Turnbull
Ms Zip Jila (*EYFS Representative*)
Mr John Rigg, FRICS
Miss Karen Braganza
Mr Mark Barlow
Mr Richard Webb

Headmistress: **Mrs Fiona J Boulton**, BSc Hons Cardiff, MA London

Deputy Heads:
Pastoral: Mrs Karen Laurie, BA Hons Leeds
Academic: Mr Duncan Peel, BA Hons Bristol, MA London
Co-curricular: Mr William Saunders, BA Hons Bristol, MA St Mary's Twickenham

Heads of Year:
Year 7: Mrs Wendy Bengoechea, BEd Hons Bath
Year 8: Mr Tom Helliwell, BSc Hons Southampton
Year 9: Mrs Emilie Forrest-Biggs, MA Downing College Cambridge
Year 10: Mrs Catherine Gilmore, BSc Hons Bath
Year 11: Mrs Sarah Glyn-Davies, BA Hons East Anglia
Lower Sixth: Mr William Forse, BSc Hons Southampton
Upper Sixth: Mr Daniel Martin, BA Hons Fitzwilliam College Cambridge, MA London
Director of Sixth Form: Miss Katrina Sloan, BA Hons Reading, MA Warwick
Head of Sixth Form: Miss Kathy Buckley, BA Hons Exeter
Assistant Heads of Sixth Form:
Mrs Anna Worthington, BSc Hons London
Mr Andrew Hadfield, MA MEd St Catharine's College Cambridge

Senior Teachers:
Pupil Progress: Mr Brad Russell, BEng Hons London
Digital Learning: Mr Martin Holtham, BA Hons St John's College Cambridge
Staff Development: Mrs Róisín Watters, BA Hons Ulster
Curriculum: Mrs Joanne Holt, BA Hons York, MA London

Heads of Department:

Art and Design: Mrs Susan Kew, BA Hons Kingston

Classics: Mr Andrew James, MA Worcester College Oxford

Computer Science: Mr Javier González Abia, BA Hons Valladolid Spain, BSc Hons Open University, BSc Cert Chartered Institute for IT

Critical Thinking: Dr Nicholas Harries, MPhus DPhil New College Oxford

Design & Technology:
Mrs Wendy Bengoechea, BEd Hons Bath (*Fashion and Textiles*)
Mr Christopher McGhee, BA Hons Loughborough (*Resistant Materials*)

Economics: Mrs Carol Jones, BA Hons Sheffield

English & Drama:
Miss Jemima Kettle, BA Hons Keble College Oxford (*English*)
Ms Ashley Fenton, BA Hons Aberystwyth (*Drama*)

Geography: Mrs Sharon Howitt, BA Hons Belfast

History: Mrs Ann Minear, BA Hons Exeter

Mathematics: Mrs Kate Denny, BSc Hons London

Modern Languages: Mrs Róisín Watters, BA Hons Ulster

Music: Mr Grayson Jones, BMus Hons Birmingham

Physical Education:
Mrs Keely Harper, BSc Hons Loughborough (*Director of Sport*)
Mrs Louise Stone, BEd Hons Bedford College (*Executive Director of Sport*)
Mrs Rachel Byrne, BEd Hons De Montfort (*Assistant Director of Sport*)

Politics: Mr David Cleaver, MSc Econ Swansea, MA Econ Manchester

Psychology: Mrs Carol Benson, BA Hons Manchester

Religious Studies: Mrs Julie Shopland, BA Hons Lampeter

Science: Miss Kimberley Walrond, BSc King's (*Head of Science and Physics*)
Miss Amy Dixon, BSc Hons Southampton (*Biology*)
Mr William Hack, BA Hons MSci Trinity Hall Cambridge (*Chemistry*)

Key Support Staff:
Mrs Helen Thompson (*PA to the Headmistress*)
Mrs Katherine Perricos (*Finance Manager*)
Mrs Susan Mooney (*HR Manager*)
Mrs Helen Moffat (*Director of Admissions*)

The Haberdashers' Aske's Boys' School

Butterfly Lane, Elstree, Hertfordshire WD6 3AF

Tel: 020 8266 1700
Fax: 020 8266 1800
email: office@habsboys.org.uk
website: www.habsboys.org.uk
Twitter: @habsboys
Facebook: @habsboys

Motto: *Serve and Obey*

The School was founded in 1690, endowed by an estate left in trust to the Haberdashers' Company by Robert Aske, Citizen of London and Liveryman of the Haberdashers' Company. In 1898 it was transferred from Hoxton to Hampstead and in 1961 to Aldenham Park, Elstree, Hertfordshire.

The aim of the School is the fullest possible development of the varied talents of every boy within it, and to this end a broad curriculum is provided, together with extensive facilities for the development of each boy's cultural, physical, personal and intellectual gifts. The School sets out to achieve high academic standards and sets equally high standards in cultural and other fields. In matters of behaviour a large degree of self-discipline is expected, and of mutual tolerance between members of the School community.

Organisation. The School, which is a day school, has 72 boys in the Pre-Prep (ages 5–7) and over 200 boys in the Preparatory School (ages 7–11), 300 in the Junior School (ages 11–13), 500 in the Senior School (ages 13–16) and over 300 in the Sixth Form (over 16). There are 6 Houses. The School regards pastoral care as important; all the Housemasters and Deputy Housemasters and Heads of Section have a large responsibility in this field but so also do House Tutors, the Senior Master and the Chaplain, as well as other members of the staff.

Forms. In the Pre-Prep School there are two forms in Years 1 and 2 with approximately 18 boys in each form. In the Preparatory School there are three forms in Years 3, 4, 5 and 6 each with about 18 boys. In the Senior School there are six forms in Years 7 and 8 with approximately 25 boys in each form. There are twelve forms in Year 9 each with about 14 boys. Years 10 and 11 are divided amongst eighteen forms each with 17–18 boys. The usual size of teaching groups in the Sixth Form is about 10–15.

Facilities. The School and its sister Girls' School, Haberdashers' Aske's School for Girls, enjoy the use of a campus of over 140 acres with extensive woodlands. The playing fields surround the buildings, which in the Boys' School include the following: Assembly Hall, Dining Hall, Sixth Form Common Room, Music Auditorium, special accommodation for Classics, English (including a Drama Room), History, Geography, Mathematics, Information Technology, Modern Languages including 2 Languages Laboratories, Music School, Science and Geography Centre with 19 laboratories and 8 classrooms, a Design Centre for Art, Craft and Technology, state-of-the-art Sports Centre, Gymnasium, Indoor Swimming Pool, two Artificial Grass Pitches and School Shop.

The Preparatory School is situated on the same campus in a new building of its own. (*For further details, see Preparatory School entry in IAPS section.*) The Pre-Prep is situated on its own nearby campus.

The Curriculum up to the age of 13 is common for all, with no streaming or setting except in Mathematics in Year 8. From the age of 11 in addition to the usual subjects it includes three separate Sciences and two foreign languages which are taught as a carousel to ensure all boys have sampled all languages before making informed choices. From the age of 13, subjects are taught in sets of mixed abilities. GCSE courses start in Year 10, when boys take ten subjects. In the Sixth Form students study four subjects to AS in the Lower Sixth, narrowing to three A2 subjects in the Upper Sixth. The School takes seriously its commitment to Enrichment and Enhancement; this non-examined part of the curriculum occupies 10% of the week in both Upper and Lower Sixth. Boys are entered for the GCE examination at A Level at the age of 18 and are prepared for entry to degree courses at Universities. The wide scope of the School's curriculum gives ample opportunity for all its boys whether preparing for University (overwhelmingly their primary interest), for a profession, for the services, or for commerce or industry. The University Applications and Careers Departments have their own modern facilities, and careers advice is readily available to parents and to boys.

Religious Education. The School is by tradition a Church of England school, but there are no religious barriers to entry and no quotas. It is part of the ethos of the School that all its members respect the deeply-held beliefs and faith of other members. The School Chaplain is available to, and holds responsibility for, all boys in the School of whatever faith. He prepares for Confirmation those who wish it, and there are weekly celebrations of Holy Communion and an annual Carol Service in St Albans Abbey. The morning assembly and class teaching, however, are non-denominational in character. Faith assemblies are held on Thursday mornings, and comprise separate meetings for Christians, Jews, Muslims, Hindus, Jains, Sikhs, Buddhists and Humanists.

Physical Education. A wide variety of sports is available, including Athletics, Badminton, Basketball, Cricket, Cross-Country Running, Fencing, Golf, Gymnastics, Hockey, Rugby, Football, Sailing, Squash, Shooting, Swimming, Tennis, Table Tennis and Water Polo. All boys are expected to take part in physical education unless exempt on medical grounds.

Out of School Activities. The extensive range includes a period of two hours on Friday afternoon when boys can choose one of a large variety of activities of a service nature. This includes Community Service, both on the School campus and among those who need help in the surrounding district. It also includes the Combined Cadet Force, which has Royal Navy, Army and Royal Air Force sections, and Adventure Training.

Music and Drama. Both have a prominent place in the School. The Music School has a Recital Hall and some twelve other rooms; 20 visiting instrumental teachers between them teach 500 instrumental pupils each week covering all the normal orchestral instruments together with Piano and Organ. There is a Choir of 250, and several orchestras. For Drama the facilities include a generously equipped stage and a separate Drama Room with its own lighting and stage equipment.

School Societies. School Societies and expeditionary activities in term time and holidays include Amnesty, Archery, Art, Badminton, Bridge, Canoeing, Chess, Choral, Classical, Crosstalk, Debating, Duke of Edinburgh's Award, Dramatics, English, Football, History, Jazz, Jewish Society, Life-saving, Life Drawing, Modern Languages, Mountaineering, Philosophical, Photography, Politics, Puzzles and Games, Rifle, Sailing, Science, Squash, Stamp Club, Windsurfing and many more.

Transport. There is a joint schools coach service providing an extensive network of routes and some 110 pick-up points, to enable boys and girls to attend the School from a wide area, and to remain for after-school activities.

Admission. Boys are admitted only at the beginning of the school year in September. They may be admitted at the age of 5 and may remain in the School until the end of the academic year in which the age of 19 is attained, subject to satisfactory progress at each stage of the course and to compliance with the School Rules currently in force. Each year approximately 36 boys are admitted at age 5, a further 18 boys at age 7, approximately 100 at age 11 and approximately 25 at age 13. There are competitive examinations including written and oral tests of intelligence, literacy and numeracy at the ages of 7 and 11, held in January for admission in the following September. Applicants aged 13 also take examinations at the beginning of January and are interviewed later in the month for entry in September. Registration Fee: £100

An Open Day for prospective parents is held each year early in October.

Scholarships and Bursaries. A number of Academic Scholarships are awarded annually to pupils entering the Senior School. A smaller number of Music Scholarships are

also awarded each year to candidates showing special promise in music.

A significant number of means-tested Governors' Bursaries are awarded at age 11+, valued from a few hundred pounds to full fees (and in some cases coach fares), depending upon financial need. Open equally to boys progressing from the Prep School and to those applying from other Schools.

Full details of all these awards are included in the prospectus available from the School Registrar who is happy to answer enquiries. Alternatively you can request a prospectus via the school's website: www.habsboys.org.uk.

Fees per term (2018–2019). Main School £6,782 exc lunch; Preparatory School (Years 3–6) £6,782 exc lunch; Pre-Preparatory (Years 1 & 2) £5,113 inc lunch.

Piano, Organ and Orchestral instruments (individual tuition) £225 per instrument; Orchestral classes £145; Aural classes £72; Instrument hire £35.

Honours. In 2018, 27 boys secured a place at Oxford or Cambridge.

Charitable status. The Haberdashers' Aske's Charity is a Registered Charity, number 313996. It exists to promote education.

The Governors:
Sheridan Swallow (*Master of The Haberdashers' Company*)
Mr Simon Cartmell, OBE (*Chairman of the Aske Board*)

Boys' School Committee:
Mrs M Chaundler, OBE (*Chairman of the Boys' School Committee*)

S Ajitsaria	J Gatehouse
R Gokhale	J Gregory
Professor L Goldman	C Clapper
T Jackson-Stops	H Gough
S Behr	D Peters
M Scribbins	

Girls' School Committee:
T Johnstone-Burt, CB, OBE (*Chairman of the Girls' School Committee*)

Dr Y Burne	R Ohrenstein
E Howarth	T Dolan
L Leigh	H Rosethorn
A Manz	J Myers
Dr J Maxton	

Clerk to the Governors: C M Bremner

Headmaster: A R Lock, MA

Head of the Prep and Pre-Prep Schools: M E Rossetti, MA
Senior Deputy Head: J Maguire, MSc
Deputy Head Pastoral: Mrs M J C Jones, BEd
Deputy Head Staff: Mrs C B Lyons, MA
Director of Finance and Operations: D S Thompson, BA

Head of the Sixth Form: R Amlot, MA
Head of the Middle School: G J Hall, BA Hons, BSc Hons, MBA
Head of the Junior School: Mrs D J Bardou, BA
Director of Admissions: Mrs K R Pollock, MA
Director of Co-curricular: A J Simm, BA
Director of Digital Development: V N Connolly, MPhil
Director of Foundation: R de H Llewellyn, MA
Director of ICT: I R Phillips, BSc
Director of Studies: Mrs K Shah, MPhil
Director of Teaching: J S Bown, BA

Heads of Department:
Academic Support: P G Milton, MSc
Art: Mrs K R Weber, BA
Careers: Mrs K Nash, BA

Classics: Dr C Joyce
Computing & ICT: I R Philips, BSc
Design & Technology: S Vincent, MA
Economics: M T Catley, BSc
English & Drama: I D Wheeler, BA
Examinations: Mrs A Thakar, BSc
Geography: Mrs S C Edwards, BSc
History: S P Clark, BA
Libraries & Archives: Mrs A Oatham, BA
Mathematics: A M Ward, BSc
Modern Languages: R J Thompson, BA
Music: R T Osmond, MA
Physical Education & Games:
Director of Sport: R J McIntosh, MEd
Head of PE: D H Kerry, BSc
Politics: S P Clark, BA
PSHEE: C R Bass, BA
Science: Dr G R Hobbs, PhD
Theology & Philosophy: A M Lawrence, BA
University Applications: Mrs J B Swallow, BA

Housemasters:
Calverts: P H Bartlett, MA
Hendersons: Dr C L Harrison, PhD
Joblings: J C Swallow, MA
Meadows: D C Taberner, MSc
Russells: T B W Hardman, BEd
Strouts: A F Metcalfe, BSc

Preparatory School:
Head: M A Rossetti, MA
Deputy Head (Academic): J J Evans, MA
Deputy Head (Pastoral): Mrs C M Griggs, Cert Ed Dip
Senior Teacher: Mrs H M R Pullen, BEd

House Leaders:
Andrews: Mrs K Bruce-Green, BEd
Davids: L Harrington, BA
Georges: Mrs S Adat, BA
Patricks: N Bowley, BSc

Phase Leaders:
Yr 3 & 4: G Thomas, BA
Yr 5 & 6: Dr C Lessons, PhD

Secretary: Mrs D Jones
Administrator: Mrs A Thomas
Head of Library: Mrs S Thomas

Pre-Preparatory School:
Head: Mrs V Peck, BSc
Secretary: Mrs R Hodis, BSc

Chaplain: The Revd M Brandon, MA, MTh

Support Staff:
PA to Headmaster: Mrs C Russell
PA to Senior Deputy Head: Mrs W Hunt
PA to Deputy Head (Staff): Miss J Woodham
PA to Deputy Head (Pastoral): Mrs S Muller
PA to Director of Finance and Operations: Mrs C Pluck
Admissions & Database Officer: Miss C Allison
Catering Manager: S Whybrew
Deputy Bursar: M Lewis
Estates Manager: R A Hamzat
Marketing & Communications Officer: J Suchak, BA
Finance Manager: M O'Donnell
Grounds Manager: J Lewis
HR Manager: Mrs R Titley
ICT Service Manager: R Patel
Pastoral & Co-curricular Secretary: Mrs S Goldberg
Payroll: Mrs L Meighan
Prep School Secretary: Mrs D Jones
School Counsellor: Ms L Nolte

School Nurses: Mrs G McGrath, RGN; Ms M McGrath, RGN
School Office Manager: Mrs S Vithlani
School Shop Manager: Mrs F Hogberg
Transport Manager: Ms R Caterer

Halliford School

Russell Road, Shepperton, Middlesex TW17 9HX

Tel: 01932 223593
Fax: 01932 229781
email: registrar@hallifordschool.co.uk
website: www.hallifordschool.co.uk

Halliford School was founded in 1921, moved to its present site in 1929. The Headmaster is a member of both HMC and the Society of Heads.

Facilities. Halliford School is situated on the Halliford bend of the River Thames. The old house, a graceful eighteenth century building, which stands in six acres of grounds, is the administrative centre of the school. Some 500 yards from the school gate there are six additional acres of sports fields. Over the years there has been a steady development programme, including a new 320-seat theatre, a refurbished kitchen and dining room, new classrooms and a new Science laboratory. In September 2005 a new Sports Hall with new changing facilities, Library and additional classrooms was opened. In September 2012 the Philip Cottam building was opened. This incorporates the Sixth Form, Art Studios, Music Centre and the Vibe Café. In 2018 the facilities were further developed including a professionally-designed Sixth Form Centre, IT suites and Science Laboratory.

Admission. There are approximately 400 pupils on roll with a three-form entry at Year 7 (approximately 60 pupils). There is a further entry at Year 9 and admission is possible into other Year Groups dependent on the availability of places. Entrance is by examination (English, Mathematics and Reasoning) and interview. Siblings are given priority as long as they can benefit from a sound academic education. This policy creates a strong feeling of a family community and helps reinforce the close partnership that exists with parents. Girls and Boys are admitted the Sixth Form on the basis of their GCSE predictions, a report from their current school and an interview.

Curriculum. In Years 7 to 9 pupils study the following subjects: English, Mathematics, two languages (French, German or Spanish), Latin/Classical Civilisation, Biology, Chemistry, Physics, History, Geography, Art, Drama, Music, Design and Technology, Computing, Religious Studies and Physical Education. In Years 10 and 11 (GCSE) there is a compulsory core of English Language and Literature, Mathematics (some also take Further Mathematics), a Modern Foreign Language (French, German or Spanish), and the three separate Sciences. Pupils choose a further three subjects: a second Modern Foreign Language, Latin, Classical Civilisation, History, Geography, Religious Studies, Art, Drama, Music, PE, Business Studies, Design Technology (either Resistant Materials or Graphic Products) or Computing Science.

In the Sixth Form some 25 subjects are available at A Level and all teaching is co-educational. Many pupils also complete an extended project.

Games. Rugby, Football, Cricket are the main games played at Halliford. Athletics, Basketball, Badminton, Volleyball and Golf are available, plus a number of other activities.

Pastoral Organisation. There are four Houses and pupils are tutored in House groups. Parents receive either a grade card or full report every half term. Tutors are always willing to see parents and the Headmaster can usually be seen at very short notice.

Out of School Activities. These include very successful Drama, Music and Art Departments.

There is a long list of clubs including Chess, Design, Computing, Film, Creative Writing, Modern Languages, Science and Art. In addition there are Senior and Junior Debating and Academic Societies and Inter-house Public Speaking and Unison Singing Competitions. The Duke of Edinburgh's Award is available as an additional activity.

School Council. Each Tutor group elects a representative to the School Council. This is not a cosmetic exercise and in recent times the School Council has effected real changes. Halliford believes that pupils do have good ideas which can be utilised for the well-being of the School as a whole.

Prospective Parents. The main school Open Day is held in October on a Saturday. Further Open Days are held in November, March and May during the school week. Also in October the school holds a Sixth Form Open Evening. Prospective parents are welcome at other times by appointment.

Fees per term (2018–2019). £5,320.

Scholarships and Bursaries. The School offers scholarships up to the value of 10% per annum of the annual tuition fees for entry at Year 7 and in the Sixth Form. The scholarships awarded are: Academic, Art, Drama, Music and Sport.

The school is also keen to help those who could not otherwise afford the fees and means-tested Bursaries are available on application.

Old Hallifordians. *Chairman*: Darren Allen.

Charitable status. Halliford School is a Registered Charity, number 312090. It exists to provide high-quality education.

Governors:

Chairman: Mr K Woodward	Mr A Hirst
Deputy Chairman: Mr C S Squire	Mrs P Horner
	Mr A Lenoel
Mrs N Cook	Mr N Maud
Mr M Crosby	Mr R Parsons
Mr R Davison	Professor J P Phillips
Mrs K Gulliver	Mr P Roberts
Mr B Harris	Dr M Sachania

Headmaster: **Mr James Davies**

Deputy Head (*Academic*): Mrs C Cotton
Deputy Head (*Pastoral*): Mr J Bown
Bursar: Mrs E Sanders
Senior Tutor: Mr J Carrington
Head of Sixth Form: Mr S Slocock

Hampton School

Hanworth Road, Hampton, Middlesex TW12 3HD

Tel:	020 8979 5526
Fax:	020 8783 4035
email:	headmaster@hamptonschool.org.uk
	admissions@hamptonschool.org.uk
website:	hamptonschool.org.uk

Motto: *Praestat opes sapientia*

Founded in the academic year of 1556/57 by Robert Hammond, a Hampton merchant, and re-established in 1612. From 1910 the School was administered by the local authority, latterly as a voluntary aided school, but in 1975 reverted to independent status.

Hampton is a day school of around 1,250 boys aged from 11 to 18, including a Sixth Form of about 340. The School achieves all-round excellence, encouraging academic ambition, personal responsibility and independent thinking in an energetic, happy and well-disciplined community. It aims to provide a challenging and stimulating education for boys of high academic promise from the widest possible variety of social backgrounds.

In the most recent ISI inspection (March 2016) Hampton was awarded the highest judgement possible in each individual category. The quality of pupils' achievements in academic and co-curricular areas is exceptional and the contribution of arrangements for pastoral care excellent. The School achieves excellence in the spiritual, moral, social and cultural development of pupils and meets its aim to provide a friendly and supportive environment. The teaching at the School is described as excellent and teachers display expert subject knowledge which is used to inspire and guide pupils. Many lessons have a real sense of scholarly collaboration between teachers and pupils, based on mutual respect and a shared love of learning. It was also noted that the curriculum is enriched by an extensive, varied range of co-curricular activities and strong links with the community. The inspection report confirmed the School's success in meeting its aim of producing mature, confident yet grounded young people who aim for personal success while supporting those around them.

Hampton is academically selective and virtually all boys go on to Russell Group or equivalent universities, with increasing numbers to American Ivy League Universities. Examination results in 2018 at A Level (90% A*, A and B grades) and GCSE (94% 9–7/ A*–A grades) were extremely strong: 82% of boys secured nine or more 9–7/A*–A) grades and 75% of grades were awarded at 9–8/A*. 91% boys gained places at Russell Group Universities or equivalent. The Sixth Form has a strong emphasis on deep academic enquiry, breadth of study, critical thinking and independent learning.

An annual exchange programme offers boys the chance to visit Spain, Germany, France, Italy and Russia as well as Asia, Africa and the Far East. Boys visit many other countries through academic and sporting initiatives and there is an extraordinary range of trips available.

The extensive co-curricular programme forms an essential part of the balanced education which Hampton provides. Music and drama are central to the character of the School and concerts, musicals and plays involve all age groups throughout the year. Over half the boys learn musical instruments and there are frequent music and choir tours abroad. A notable number of Organ and Choral Scholarships to Oxbridge colleges have been won over recent years.

Drama is included in the curriculum, in addition to regular School and Year group productions. There are major joint musical and drama productions regularly with neighbouring LEH. Recent highlights include *Anything Goes, West Side Story, Mack & Mabel, Jekyll & Hyde, Chicago, Les Misérables*, Shakespeare's *The Tempest*, Joseph Kesselring's *Arsenic and Old Lace*, Jez Butterworth's *Jerusalem* and *Oliver Twist*, a joint production with Waldegrave School for Girls.

Hampton has an outstanding reputation for sport and standards are very high indeed; many boys play at county and national level in a wide range of sports. Particular strengths are cricket, football, rowing, rugby, tennis and chess. Boys benefit from superb facilities and specialist coaching. Hampton has produced many schoolboy internationals in a wide range of sports and also Olympic rowers;

the School shares a nearby boathouse on the River Thames with LEH.

Integrity and social conscience are encouraged implicitly through the daily interaction of boys and teachers, as well as explicitly through School assemblies, PSHE lessons, extensive Charity, Environment and Community Service programmes, and long-standing links with the Hampton Safe Haven, now a government approved primary school in Malawi. The School was one of the two founding schools of the 'Mindfulness in Schools Project' promoting pupil well-being and emotional resilience.

Hampton School and LEH are served by 23 coach routes across south-west London, Surrey and Berkshire.

Buildings and Grounds. The School has been situated on its present site since 1939. Its premises and facilities for both academic work and co-curricular activity have been greatly improved and extended since 1975 when the School, formerly Hampton Grammar, reverted to independence.

Set within grounds of some 27 acres all facilities (with the exception of the Boat House) are on site including four rugby pitches, seven football pitches, six cricket squares and six hard tennis courts. Buildings include an Assembly Hall, Dining Hall, large multi-purpose Sports Hall, fully-equipped Library and specialist facilities for Art, Science, Technology, ICT and Languages.

The Millennium Boat House, located on the nearby River Thames and shared with LEH, was opened in 2000 by Sir Steve and Lady Redgrave and provides the focal point for the popular and highly successful Boat Club.

The magnificent Hammond Theatre provides exceptional facilities for the performing arts, doubling as a theatre and concert hall.

A rigorous development programme ensures that all boys continue to benefit from excellent facilities. A three-storey Atrium extension opened in September 2011, comprising 11 classrooms, a new Biology lab and a large display area and a state-of-the-art, all-weather 3G sports ground, opened in 2013, for football, rugby and recreational use. The 3G area is a unique facility for a school and has dual accreditation from FIFA and the Rugby Football Union. A new bespoke Sixth Form Study and Careers Centre will open in 2019.

Community. Community service forms an integral part of life at Hampton and the School's aim is for boys to leave as happy, educated and well-rounded young men with a sense of social responsibility and the desire to make the world a better place. The School has developed extensive partnerships both locally and internationally and enjoys particularly strong links with neighbouring Hampton High and LEH. These two schools participate in a wide range of activities with Hampton pupils including Drama and Music, Combined Cadet Force and the very popular visiting speakers '*Talk*!' programme. Strong links are also maintained with the numerous local state primary schools which provide around 60% of the First Year intake. Year 5 and Year 6 pupils from a number of local state primary schools attend teaching sessions in a range of subjects on Saturday mornings. The School also works in partnership with other local independent and state secondary schools offering GCSE revision courses and a range of academic and co-curricular activities. Senior pupils also visit Hampton High and Twickenham Academy each week providing peer mentoring for Mathematics.

In addition, Hampton School has a busy Community Service programme and also hosts many events for schools in Richmond Borough including Music and Science days. All members of the Lower Sixth undertake a placement in a local primary school as part of their Curriculum Enrichment Programme, working with young children on literacy, numeracy, computing and sport. Many boys in the Fourth Year and above volunteer their assistance in primary schools, residential homes for the elderly and local charities. Various joint activities are run with LEH, including an annual autumn tea party and a Christmas Party for local senior citizens and trips to LEGOLAND and the Discovery Centre for children with special needs. Several senior boys participate in holiday schemes for young people such as The Challenge. The Sixth Form Enrichment Programme is also run jointly with LEH.

Curriculum. Boys in the Lower School follow a wide curriculum, including Technology, Coding and Computing, Physics, Chemistry, Biology, a Modern Language (French, German or Spanish), Latin, Art, Drama and Religious Studies. Mandarin, Greek and Russian are optional subjects begun in the Third Year. In the Fourth and Fifth Years all boys continue to study, in addition to PE, Games and Mindfulness, the following: English Language, English Literature, a Modern Language, Mathematics and the three sciences for either GCSE or IGCSE. They choose three subjects from the following: Art, Ancient History, Computer Science, Drama, French, Geography, German, Greek, History, Latin, Mandarin, Music, Religious Studies, Russian, Spanish and Technology. Most of these GCSEs/IGCSEs are taken at the end of the Fifth Year. The most able mathematicians also take Additional Mathematics GCSE and then move on to AS Level study in the Fifth Year.

The Sixth Form offers a free choice of A and AS Level subjects, in addition to a wide range of courses delivered through the Curriculum Enrichment Programme, including Critical Thinking and Oracy. The Cambridge Pre-U is offered in addition to the standard A Level in Art, Physics, Chemistry, History, German, Mandarin, Mathematics and Philosophy. Additional teaching and preparation is provided for boys seeking entrance to highly-selective universities, including Oxford and Cambridge, to which around twenty-five to thirty boys are admitted each year. About fifty boys a year also opt for the Hampton Extended Project, a substantial piece of independent research of around 5,000 words.

Games. Sport and Physical Education are part of every boy's School week. A very large number of boys also take part in voluntary sport on Saturdays; fixtures, at a range of ability levels, are arranged for each age group. All boys are able to choose which sport to follow, with a wider range of options available to Sixth Form boys. In winter, the major games are Rugby, Association Football and Rowing; in summer, Cricket, Athletics and Rowing. Other sports include Tennis, Real Tennis, Fencing, Squash, Skiing, Windsurfing, Sailing, Climbing, Cycling and Swimming.

Careers. Each boy receives advice from the careers staff at those points when subject choices should be made. The School is a member of Inspiring Futures, who provide Morrisby testing and interviews as part of the Fifth Year advice programme. A Careers Convention is held annually and there are advice evenings for parents and pupils on Sixth Form choices and on university decision-making.

Pastoral Care. This is one of the strongest features of the School. A boy's Form Tutor is responsible in the first instance for his academic and pastoral welfare and progress. The work of Form Tutors is supported and coordinated by Assistant Heads of Year and Heads of Year under the direction of the Deputy Head (Pastoral). The School works in partnership with parents who are always welcome to discuss their son's development with any of these tutors; Parents' Evenings provide an opportunity to meet subject teachers. Year group Pastoral Forums provide parents with an opportunity to meet staff responsible for pupil welfare and to discuss a variety of pastoral issues. The School was one of the first in the country to develop a course in Mindfulness, which is delivered to all pupils in the Fourth Year as part of the taught curriculum. There is also an active Parents' Association.

Societies. The School's large CCF contingent, run jointly with LEH, and Hampton High School, comprises Army and RAF sections and has a programme which includes adventurous training, orienteering and gliding. The very active Adventure Society provides opportunities for kayaking, climbing, orienteering, camping and expeditions both in the UK and abroad. A very large number of boys regularly undertake The Duke of Edinburgh's Award – Gold, Silver and Bronze.

The Music Department fosters solo and ensemble performance as well as composition, and offers pupils an opportunity to perform in the School's orchestras, bands and choirs including National Choir of the Year Finalists and Voice Festival finalists, Voices of Lions. Singing is very popular and there are eight different choral groups. The Joint Choral Society, with the neighbouring LEH, gives a performance of a major choral work annually. There are numerous drama productions with at least one dramatic production each term, and also an annual musical. In all these activities, as in the Community Service work, the School enjoys close cooperation with LEH. Hampton is also an *All-Steinway* school.

A programme of visiting speakers, '*Talk*!', holds lunchtime and evening meetings and offers boys the opportunity to hear and question distinguished politicians, writers, academics and scientists.

There is also an extensive range of co-curricular societies, among which Chess, Debating, the Technology Club, Drone Club and the Creative Writing Society are particularly strong.

Admission. Boys are usually admitted to the School into the First Year (Year 7), Third Year (Year 9) and the Sixth Form. Approximately 130 boys join the First Year at 11+ each September and a further 60–70 join the Third Year at 13+. A small number join the Sixth Form each year.

Entry at 11+ is via the School's own entrance examination, which is held in the January of Year 6 and entry at 13+ is via the School's own Pre-test which candidates sit in the January of Year 6. A further Pre-test is held in Year 7 for those who sat the Year 6 Pre-test without gaining an offer, as well as to those who have not sat before.

Boys may also be admitted to fill occasional vacancies at other ages at the discretion of The Headmaster. Further details may be obtained from the Head of Admissions (Tel: 020 8979 9273).

Fees per term (2018–2019). £6,685 inclusive of books and stationery.

Scholarships and Bursaries. Scholarships (remitting up to 25%) are awarded for academic, musical, artistic and all-round merit at 11+ and 13+. Choral Scholarships, awarded in conjunction with the Chapel Royal, Hampton Court Palace, are also available at 11+ entry.

The School also has a Bursary Fund from which awards are made according to parental financial circumstances. A number of free places are also awarded each year.

The School's newly-dedicated charity, The Fitzwygram Foundation, was launched in March 2018. The Foundation provides funds to offer completely Free Places at Hampton to boys from all backgrounds.

Further details on all Awards may be obtained from the Admissions Office.

Hampton School Alumni. Hamptonians join a successful alumni network. The lifelong relationship with the School provides opportunities for mentoring and a programme of alumni events. The Alumni Office is located in the heart of the School and regularly welcomes Hamptonians back to their School.

Charitable status. Hampton School is a Registered Charity, number 1120005.

Governors:
Chairman: J S Perry, BA
Vice-Chairman: A H Munday, LLB, QC
Vice-Chairman: N J Spooner, BA
S A Bull, BSc, ACA
Mrs M Choueiri, BA, MBA
Mrs M Ellis, Cert Ed
L R Llewellyn, BSc, MMus, MBA, FCMA, FRSA
Revd B R Lovell, BEng Hons, BA Hons, MA
Mrs H A Lowe, BA Hons, LGSM
Mrs R Mercer, BA Hons, PGCE
A J Roberts, CBE, BA, FRSA, FColl
Air Vice Marshal [Retd] G Skinner, CBE, MSc, CEng, FIMechE, FILT, FRAeS
R M Walker, MA
R J K Washington, MA Oxon, MBA
L H Welch, BArch Hons, RIBA, RIAS
Ms A Yandle, MA Oxon

Clerk to the Governors: M A King, BSc

Senior Management Team:

Headmaster: Kevin Knibbs, MA Oxon

Deputy Heads:
Pippa Z S Message, BSc
Philip D Hills, MA Cantab, PhD
J Owen Morris, MA Cantab

Assistant Heads:
M A Nicholson, BA
N D Woods, MA, MEng

Bursar: Mike A King, BSc
Director of Studies: Alasdair N R McBay, BSc, MSc

Senior Tutors:
David R Clarke, BHum
D J Fendley, BEng
Ski Paraskos, MA Oxon
S Andrew Wilkinson, MA Oxon
Richard D Worrallo, MA Oxon

Departmental Staff:
* *Head of Department*
§ *Part-time*

Art:
*Karen A Williams, BA
Joel Baker, BA
Adrian J Bannister, MA
§Stephanie Kirby, BA
§Joanna Grace, MA
Jerry Blighton (*Technician*)

Biology:
*Phil H Langton, BSc, Dip Env Sci
Guy K Baker, MBiochem (*Head of Fifth Year*)
Victoria Barnes, MSc
Richard J Davieson, BSc
Sarah Hendry, PhD
Polly A Holmes, BSc (*Head of Upper Sixth*)
Katya L Martin, MA Oxon
Pippa Z S Message, BSc (*Deputy Head, Designated Safeguarding Officer*)
Katie Mimnagh, BMedSci
Harry Moore, BSc
Janice Green (*Senior Technician*)
Jenita Jeyarajan (*Technician*)

Chemistry:
*David Schofield, MA
Jo S Cooper, BSc
Neil J I Double, BSc (*Asst Head of Upper Sixth*)
Aidan Doyle, BSc

George Draganov, MSci
Polly A Holmes, BSc (*Head of Upper Sixth*)
J Francesca Knibbs, BSc
Jonathan Neville, MChem (*Asst Head of Fourth Year*)
Lelja Puljic, DPhil
Maria G Stuart, DPhil
Vijaya Mallula (*Technician*)
Gillian Winskell (*Technician*)
Andrew Deevey (*Assistant Technician*)
Claire Webb (*Assistant Technician*)

Classics:
*J Wesley Barber, MA Oxon
Gemma J Busby, BA
Samuel Hitchings, BA, MA
Tim J Leary, MLitt, PhD (*Keeper of the Archives*)
Alex Ziegler, MPhil
§Helen M Carmichael, BA, MA
§Alice H Jacobs, MA Cantab
Amy Winstock, BA

Computer Science:
*Gordon Clark, BSc
Chris Arnold, BA, DPhil
Alan Knifton, BSc
James Hope, BSc
Floriane Latulipe, MA
Tanya Scorer, BSc

Design Technology:
*Oliver Rokison, MEng
Mark Preston, BSc
Michael Richards, BSc
Joseph O Sarpong, BSc
Diane C Woodward, BSc
A [Tony] Barun (*Technician*)

Drama:
*Joanne James, MA (*Head of Drama*)
Ravi K Kothakota, BA (*Head of Fourth Year*)
Laura Moore, BA

Economics and Business Studies:
*§Ski Paraskos, MA Oxon (*Senior Tutor*)
Bharat Khanna, MA
Tom F Rigby, BA (*Head of Third Year, Charities Coordinator*)
§John D Slater, BA
Alice Thornton, MPhil

English:
*Catherine E Rigby, BA
Michael M Baker, MA
Tessa Bartholomew, BA (*Asst Head of Lower Sixth*)
Martha B Bedford, BA (*Asst Head of First Year*)
Oliver Ellsworth, BA (*Asst Head of Fourth Year*)
Toby Green, BA
Danielle Harris, BA
Louise A Teunissen, BA Oxon
Paul D Thomas, BA, MSc
§Helen V Booker, BA
§Alexandra C McLusky, BA
§Peter Smith, BA, MA

Geography:
*Barney S Bett, BA, MA
Charlotte Brown, BA
Thomas E Hill, BA (Head of First Year)
Rachael Kugele, MSc
James Odling, BSc
Dominic Saul, BSc
Harriet Slator, BA

History:
*Esther Arnott, BA
*Andy Lawrence, BA
David R Clarke, BHum (*Senior Tutor*)
Shelley Havord, MA
Kevin Knibbs, MA Oxon (*Headmaster*)
J Owen Morris, MA Cantab (*Deputy Head, Designated Safeguarding Lead*)
Jim Parrish, BA (*Head of Upper Sixth*)
Jennifer L Peattie, BA (*Head of First Year*)
Victoria M Smith, BA (*Head of Third Year*)
Sarah Willcox, MA
Richard D Worrallo, MA Oxon (*Senior Tutor Careers & UCAS, Talk!*)
§Jon Cook, MA
§Martin P Cross, BA
§Holly E Partridge
§Alan Thomas, BA

Information and Communications Technology:
*§Simi Kandola (*Director of IT*)
Bobby Moore (*IT Development & Project Manager*)
Harjit Singh (*Senior IT Technician*)
Terrence Brown (*Senior IT Technician*)
Nathan Jenkins (*IT Apprentice*)

Learning Support:
*Caroline Conway (*Head of Learning Support*)
§Susanne Harradine, CertEd, BDA Dip SpLDs, PG Dip Ed (*Specialist Teacher*)
§Nicola Day, BEd (*SpLD Teacher*)
§Sian Reeve, BA
Sylvia Garrido-Soriano, BA (*Academic Extension & Think! Co-ordinator KS3*)

Library:
*Karl Hemsley, MA

Mathematics:
*Joanna R Condon, MMath Oxon
Christopher G Aubrey, MA Oxon (*Head of Key Stage 4 Mathematics*)
Gareth Bailey, BSc
Ami Banerjee, BSc, MBA (*Head of Cricket*)
Rosamund Bradbury, MSc Cantab
Hannah Clarke, BSc (*Mathematics Entrance Coordinator*)
Michelle Costabile, MA
Daniel Griller, BA Cantab
James Hope, BSc
Aidan W Kershaw, BSc Cantab
Floriane D Latulipe, BSc
Jeremy J Lee, MA Cantab
Alasdair N R McBay, BSc, MSc (*Director of Studies*)
Daneila Mingham, MA
Christopher M Schurch, BSc
Verity Short, MA
Nick Stebbings, BEng
Michael Thornton, BA, MSci
Rohit R Trivedi, MA (*Key Stage 4 Maths Coordinator*)
Marta Watson-Evans, BSc
§Adrienne Burke, BA
§Mark Curtis, MSc Oxon, DPhil (*KS5 Coordinator*)
§Mei-Wah Field, BSc (*Head of SIMS*)

§Tim N Passmore, MEng
§Caroline Reyner, MSc

Modern Languages:
*Frederic Chaveneau, BA (*Head of Modern Languages &
    Head of French*)
Haig Agulian, BA
Thomas R Aucutt, BA (*Head of Spanish*)
Christopher J Blachford, BA
Marc Boardman, BA (*Asst Head of Fourth Year*)
Shirley A Buckley, BA
Francesca G Byrne, MA (*Asst Head of Second Year*)
Silvia Garrido-Soriano, BA (*Academic Extension and
    Think!, Coordinator for KS3*)
Charles Malston, BA (*Asst Head of Second Year*)
Natalie Noble, BA
Jill C Owen, BA (*Head of Second Year*)
Philipp Studt, BA, MA (*Asst Head of Third Year*)
Paddy G Turner, BA
Katya White, BA (*Russian*)
Katherine Willett, BA
Sophie C Yoxon, BA
Hong Zhang, MA (*Mandarin*)
§Margaret Chandler, MA
§Ms Maria Doncel-Cervantes, BA
§Ms Y Isaeva (*Russian Conversation*)
§Sophie E May, BA Oxon
§Augusta Samuel, BA
§Ludmilla Wilson, BA (*Russian Conversation*)
Joanne Iredale, BA, DipIM (*Languages Resources*)

Music:
*Iain C Donald, BA
Daniel E Roland, MusB
Elizabeth Esser, BA
Alex Fox, MA
Tony Green (*Performing Arts Administrator*)
§Miss J M Ainscough, LTCL, GTCL, FTCL, MMus FRCO
    (*Organ*)
§Mr J Akers, BMus (*Classical Guitar*)
§Mr T Barry, GGSM (*Percussion*)
§Mr K Christiane, DPLM (*Saxophone*)
§Mr C Clague, ARCM, BA (*Trumpet*)
§Miss J Clare, GRNCM (*Violin and Viola*)
§Mr P Dennis, RAM, LRAM (*Singing*)
§Miss J Estall, GTCL, FTCL, COS Dip Dist (*Clarinet,
    Head of Woodwind*)
§Mr D Horden, MMus, BMus (*Trombone*)
§Mr S Hvartchilkov, BMus, LRAM (*Classical Guitar*)
§Mrs J Jaggard, AGSM, NCOS Dip (*Oboe*)
§Mr J A Jones, GMus, ARCM (*Pianoforte, Head of
    Keyboard Studies*)
§Miss J Koster, GRNCM, PPRNCM (*Flute*)
§Mr T Law, BMus RCM, MMus GSMD (*Saxophone*)
§Mr D Nair, BMus (*Jazz Piano*)
§Mr A Pym, RGT (*Modern Guitar*)
§Mr M Schofield, GMus (*Violin & Viola*)
§Mr M Steward (*Modern Guitar*)
§Angharad Thomas (*Bassoon*)
§Miss Tshui Fei Lim, ARCM, LRAM (*Pianoforte*)
§Miss E van Ments, GMus RNCM, PG Dip PPRNCM
    (*Violin and Viola, Head of Strings*)
§Mr D Ward, AGSM (*Trumpet*)
§Miss S Whale, LRAM (*Cello*)
§Mr S Willmott (*Percussion*)

Personal, Health & Social Education:
*Jack H Talman, BA (*Head of Third Year*)
§Rebecca J Nicholson, MPhys Oxon (*Asst Head of PSHE*)

Physical Education and Games:
Carlos Mills (*Director of Sport*)

P [Billy] D Bolton, BSc (*Athletics*)
Andrew Beattie, BSc
David Burke (*Head of Football*)
David R Clarke, BHum (*Senior Tutor*)
Colin Greenaway (*Director of Rowing*)
Christian Hurst
Matthew K Sims, BSc (*Sports Rehabilitation & Asst Head
    of Second Year*)
Paul Taylor (*Outdoor Pursuits Specialist*)
Sean Thomson (*Director of Rugby*)
Joseph Cumberbatch (*Sports Assistant*)

Physics:
*Mark G Yates, PhD
Nick J Allen, MSc
Christopher P Arnold, BA, DPhil Oxon (*Asst Head of Fifth
    Year*)
Gordon H Clark, BSc (*Head of Computing Science*)
Dan J Fendley, BEng (*Induction Tutor, Designated
    Safeguarding Officer*)
Stephen Gray, BSc
Kathryn E Millar, BEng (*Head of Third Year*)
Christine Reilly, MSc
Leonard O Rouse, BSc
Michael Thornton, MSci
Amy White, BA, MA
Nicholas D Woods, BA, MEng Cantab (*Assistant Head*)
§Rebecca J Nicholson, MPhys Oxon (*Asst Head of PHSE*)
Christine Reilly, MSc
David A Hughes, HNC (*Senior Technician*)
Rebecca Galan (*Technician*)

Politics:
*Jenny A Field, MA
Robin Hardman, BA
Tom F Rigby, BA (*Assistant Head of Third Year, Charities
    Coordinator*)
Victoria M Smith, BA (*Head of Third Year*)
Richard D Worrallo, MA Oxon (*Senior Tutor Careers &
    UCAS, Talk!*)
§Martin P Cross, BA
§Holly Partridge, BA

Psychology:
*Alice Goodman, BSc (*Asst Head of Careers*)
Rachael O'Connor, BA

Religious Studies & Philosophy:
*Neal K Carrier, BA, MPhil, PhD (*Asst Head of UCAS,
    Talk!*)
Tom Jenkins, BA
Carlo Lori, BA Cantab
Mark A J Nicholson, BA (*Assistant Head*)
Gayle Russell, MPhil Oxon
Jack H Talman, BA (*Head of PSHE*)
S Andrew Wilkinson, MA Oxon (*Senior Tutor*)
§Judy A Perkins, BA, MA, MPhil

Combined Cadet Force:
Jeremy Schomberg (*Commanding Officer CCF Contingent*)

Administrative Staff:
Examinations Officer: Michelle Barnes
Headmaster's PA: Valerie Conroy
Head of Admissions & Marketing: Dorothy Jones, BA, Dip
    Mar
Deputy Admissions Manager: Caroline Elia
Admissions Assistant: Kathy Hadrill, Karen Saul, Mandy
    Phillips, Chanel Morris
School Nurse: Elizabeth Searle, Sue Webster

Harrow School

Harrow on the Hill, Middlesex HA1 3HP

Tel: +44 (0)20 8872 8000 (Enquiries)
          +44 (0)20 8872 8003 (Head Master)
          +44 (0)20 8872 8007 (Admissions)
          +44 (0)20 8872 8320 (Bursar)
Fax: +44 (0)20 8423 3112 (School)
email: harrow@harrowschool.org.uk
website: www.harrowschool.org.uk

Mottos: *Stet Fortuna Domus; Donorum dei dispensatio fidelis*

Harrow School is a full-boarding school for boys aged 13 to 18. It was founded in 1572, under a royal charter from Queen Elizabeth I, by a local landowning farmer, John Lyon, whose original intention was to provide 30 boys of the parish with a classical education. Today, the School's purpose is to prepare boys with diverse backgrounds and abilities for a life of learning, leadership, service and personal fulfilment; distinguished Old Harrovians include seven British prime ministers and the first prime minister of India, Pandit Nehru, as well as poets and writers as diverse as Byron, Sheridan and Richard Curtis. This statement of purpose is borne out through our various areas of activity: teaching that helps boys achieve their best academically, pastoral care that matures them both emotionally and spiritually, and an extra-curricular programme that develops their characters and interests. The School's 300 acres have a collegiate feel, its historical architecture complemented by modern buildings that meet its pupils' developing needs. Approximately 820 boys attend Harrow, from across the UK and further afield.

Academic. The A Level results of Harrow boys in the last two years have been the best in the School's history. This year, after some early marking reviews, the A* rate currently stands at more than 31%, while the A*A rate is above 64%. 28 boys achieved three or more A* or equivalent grades, and three-quarters achieved grades of ABB or better. At GCSE, numerical grades were awarded in ten of the 28 subjects taken by Harrovians, making comparisons with previous years more difficult. Overall, however, the proportion of grades awarded at 9, 8, 7, A* and A was more than 84% – a two percentage point increase on last year. Approximately one-third of the year group achieved nine or more A* grades, and more than half gained seven or more, typically from ten subjects.

Nineteen boys took up places at Oxford (12) and Cambridge (7). Other popular university destinations were Edinburgh (16), Exeter (13), UCL (13), Durham (10) and Newcastle (10). Eighteen boys will take up places at universities in the United States, including Yale, Stanford and Chicago. Overall, nearly a quarter of last year's applicants will take up places at universities ranked in the top ten in the world.

The Super-Curriculum. Beyond the examination syllabus, our Super-Curriculum focuses on the aspects of scholarship that are not formally assessed: habitual reading, independent research, reflection and debate. Central to this is the electives system, in which boys select a challenging off-syllabus course that is taught in small groups. These courses promote lateral thinking, problem-solving and the articulation of profound thought, while also allowing boys to lead their own learning. On virtually every night of the week, there are seminars and society meetings, and we are able to attract eminent speakers from all walks of life to enrich and broaden the boys' experience of academic and cultural life.

Boarding. Our leafy 300-acre estate contains 12 Boarding Houses. The buildings are quite individual, with their own gardens and facilities, helping to set each house apart. The Houses inspire fierce loyalty from the boys and old boys, who take pride in their own part of Harrow. House Masters and their families live in the houses, and are assisted by an Assistant House Master, Matron, Year Group Tutors and Health Education Tutors. In addition, the chaplaincy, full-time psychologist and pastoral support committee provide further layers of nurturing and support. Approximately 70 boys live in in each House. There are no dormitories: a boy shares his room with a boy of the same age for the first year or so, and thereafter has a room to himself. Every boy has a computer in his room and each house has common rooms and shared kitchens. All teachers live in the School. Typically, for the first two weekends of a term, all pupils are in the School. If they are able to, parents come and visit. On the third weekend – an exeat – all pupils go home or to friends; the weekend starts at 12 noon on Friday and ends at 9.00 pm on Sunday. The next two weekends are followed by a nine-day half term.

Sport. With afternoon games available in 32 sports, five times a week, sporting fixtures against other schools and the chance to compete regularly in House matches, boys are kept healthy and active. Under the expert guidance of some of the country's leading coaches, boys develop their skills, character and confidence. Through games such as rugby, soccer, cricket and Harrow football, they learn how to be team players. Equal emphasis is placed on the many individual sports offered here that cultivate resilience, self-discipline and enjoyment. Surrounded by acres of sports fields, AstroTurf pitches, a golf course, swimming pool, sports centre, tennis, rackets and fives courts, Harrow has a breadth of sporting opportunities. Our elite sportsmen have an impressive record of achieving excellent standards and some go on to enjoy successful, professional sporting careers. Unique occasions like the annual cricket match versus Eton at Lord's provide memorable highlights in the School year.

The Arts. The arts are an extremely important part of Harrow's packed calendar of activities. Whether it's learning a musical instrument, playing in orchestras and ensembles, singing in choirs or in houses, performing in plays or discovering beauty in fine art, sculpture and ceramics, the opportunity for creative expression at Harrow not only sets our boys on a lifetime of personal enrichment and enjoyment, but also teaches them to be more self-disciplined, attentive and better at planning and organising their busy lives. Boys who participate in the vast spectrum of Harrow's creative and performing arts also find that this involvement has a broader, more beneficial effect on their overall academic performance. By encouraging boys to perform in the highest-quality School and house concerts, plays and competitions, we see them finding their own voice and the confidence to express their individual creativity, regardless of innate talent.

After Harrow. Virtually all of our boys take up places at selective universities. Boys who are heading towards Oxbridge, Ivy League and other competitive institutions are given specific guidance and preparation from their House Masters and our dedicated Universities Team. Over the last three years, 67 boys have taken up places at the universities of Oxford and Cambridge. A total of 11 boys have taken up offers to study medicine over the last three years. Almost every boy goes onto university with three quarters of boys taking up places at Oxbridge, Ivy League or Russell Group universities in 2017. During the last three years, a total of 46 boys took up places at US universities. Out of these, 37% went to schools in the Ivy League, with three boys going to Harvard. Over the last three years, the most popular university destinations have been: Bristol (45); Edinburgh (42);

Oxford (40); Durham (31); Exeter (30); Newcastle (29); Cambridge (24); Imperial (20); KCL (17); UCL (17) and Manchester (16).

The Harrow Association, Harrow's Old Boys' Society, has a thriving membership of over 10,000. Tel: 020 8872 8200, email: ha@harrowschool.org.uk.

Admission. Boys are typically admitted for entry at 13 and a smaller number at 16. Visit http://www.harrow-school.org.uk/Admissions-Home for more information.

Fees per term (2018–2019). £13,350, including board, tuition, textbooks, a stationery allowance and laundry. For any subject requiring additional tuition, there is an extra charge.

Scholarships and bursaries. A large number of scholarships are awarded every year. Scholarships have a value of 5% of the fee and are held throughout a boy's time at Harrow, subject to satisfactory performance. Boys may apply for more than one of the different types of scholarship, which include Academic, Music, Art, Sport and Outstanding Talent. Scholarships can often be supplemented by a means-tested bursary of up to 100% for parents who might not otherwise be able to afford the fees.

Charitable status. The School is constituted as a Royal Charter Corporation known as The Keepers and Governors of the Possessions Revenues and Goods of the Free Grammar School of John Lyon, which is a Registered Charity, number 310033. The aims and objectives of the Charity are to provide education for the pupils at the two schools in the Foundation, Harrow School and The John Lyon School.

Visitors:
The Archbishop of Canterbury
The Bishop of London

Governors:
J P Batting, MA, FFA (*Chairman*)
R C W Odey, BA, FRHS (*Deputy Chairman*)
Professor D J Womersley, MA, PhD, FBA
C H St J Hoare, BA
K W B Gilbert, BA, FCA
E J H Gould, MA
M K Fosh, BA, MSI
Professor G Furniss, BA, PhD, FBA
Professor Sir D Wallace, CBE, FRS, FREng
The Hon R Orr-Ewing
Mrs S Whiddington, AB
Admiral Sir G M Zambellas, KCB, DSC, BSc, FRAeS
Professor P Binski, MA, PHD, FBA
C G T Stonehill, MA
Dr I Dove-Edwin, BSc, MDCM, MRCP
G W J Goodfellow, QC, MA, LLM
J M P D Stroyan, MA
Mrs M S Brounger, LLB
A C Goswell, BSc, MRICS
The Hon Andrew Butler, MA
D G P Eyton, FREng, FIOM³, FIOD
J C Faber, MA
A D Hart, ACA, FRSA
R T G Winter, BA, FCA

Clerk to the Governors: The Hon Andrew Millett, MA
Pemberton Greenish, 45 Cadogan Gardens, London SW3 2AQ

Interim Head Master: M L Mrowiec, MA
Head Master from April 2019: W M A Land, MA

Deputy Head Master: A K Metcalfe, MA, FRGS, CGeog

Senior Master and Director of Boarding: P J Bieneman, MA

Senior Tutor: A R McGregor, MA

Director of Studies: A J Chirnside, MA

Registrar: E R Sie, BSc, PhD, CChem

Academic and Universities Director: Dr M E P Gray, BA, MA, PhD

Bursar: N A Shryane, MBE, BA, MPhil

Head of Departments:
Astronomy: Dr C M Crowe
Director of Art: L W Hedges
Biology: N S Keylock
Chemistry: CE Penhale
Classics: Dr S M Kennedy
Computing: Dr C M Crowe
Design and Technology: T M Knight
Drama: A P Cross
Economics: C T Pollitt
English: L S Ashe
French: O Syrus
Geography: S M Sampson
German: H K Johnson
Politics: A Cook
History: A D Todd
History of Art: L W Hedges
ICT: Dr C D O'Mahony
Italian: H A Haldane
Mathematics: J M Ashton
Modern Languages: H K Johnson
Director of Music: D N Woodcock
Oriental Languages: R M Tremlett
Painting: S N Page
Photography: D R J Bell
Physical Education: B McKerchar
Russian: K A Fletcher
Spanish: A D J Turner
Theology and Philosophy: C E G Bailey

Houses & House Masters:
Bradbys: Dr D Earl
Druries: Mr M J M Ridgway
Elmfield: Mr A Campbell
Lyon's: Mr N J Marchant
Moretons: Mr R S Martin-Jenkins
Newlands: Mr E W Higgins
Rendalls: Mr S N Taylor
The Grove: Mr C S Tolman
The Head Master's: Dr S A Harrison
The Knoll: Dr C Owens
The Park: Mr B J D Shaw
West Acre: Dr J Roberts

Hereford Cathedral School

Old Deanery, The Cathedral Close, Hereford HR1 2NG

Tel:	01432 363522 (Senior School)
	01432 363511 (Junior School)
Fax:	01432 363525
email:	schoolsec@herefordcs.com (Senior School)
	enquiry@herefordcs.com (Junior School)
website:	www.herefordcs.com
Twitter:	@Herefordcs1
Facebook:	@HerefordCathedralSchool

Hereford Cathedral School is one of the oldest schools in the country, located in the beautiful surroundings of a Cathedral Close. A happy, inclusive school with a national reputation for music, sport and academic achievement, the School offers pupils a personalised education helping individuals to set their sights high and feel valued for who they are.

The School is thought to have been founded as a song school attached to Hereford Cathedral in Anglo-Saxon times. The first written reference of the School dates back to Bishop Gilbert's letter of 26 December 1384, appointing Richard of Cornwall as Headmaster.

It is a fully co-educational day school of 497 pupils aged 11–18.

Admission. Admission is usually at 11+, 13+ or 16+ (although arrangements can be made for children who wish to transfer to the Senior School at other ages, subject to the availability of places). Admission is subject to satisfactory performance in the Entrance Assessment (usually an exam) or satisfactory GCSE grades, interview and suitable references, and at the Headmaster's discretion.

Facilities. The School occupies many historic buildings and some later ones, all adapted for School use, as well as purpose-built facilities. On the main campus are, in addition to some of the main departments, eight science departments, a large music school, an Art, Design and Technology and Computer Centre (that gained Hereford's first RIBA award for architecture), the Gilbert Library and a refurbished Dining Hall. The Zimmerman Building provides 20,000 square feet of robust working space for Classics, Modern Languages, examination/functions hall, Geography and Drama departments and the Sixth Form Centre. An on-site gym and Sports Hall offers first-class facilities for badminton, five-a-side football, netball, and basketball and four sets of cricket nets. Rugby and outdoor cricket is held at the School's Wyeside sports ground, alongside the HCS rowing club.

Curriculum. Pupils are divided on entry at 11 into four forms (a maximum of 24 pupils per form) for academic and pastoral purposes. Below the Sixth Form, pupils take a broad range of subjects. Option choices are made at the end of the third year (Year 9).

In the Sixth Form pupils are prepared for A (AS/A2) Levels, for which there is a wide choice of subjects: Latin, Greek, English Literature/Language (Combined), English Literature, French, Philosophy and Ethics, Classical Civilisation, Spanish, Economics, History, Geography, Mathematics, Further Mathematics, Biology, Physics, Chemistry, Design and Technology, Fine Art, Textiles, Business Studies, Music, Drama and Theatre Studies and Physical Education. Almost all students go on to Higher Education degree courses and the vast majority to the university course of their choice.

Religious instruction throughout is in accordance with the doctrines of the Church of England. The School is privileged to have the daily use of Hereford Cathedral for Chapel.

Sports/Activities include Rugby, Cricket, Football, Badminton, Tennis, Hockey, Netball, Athletics, and Rowing. There is a CCF Group and a wide range of societies active within the School. The School is an Operating Authority for the Duke of Edinburgh's Award scheme. Drama flourishes, with several productions each year. The School has a national reputation in debating.

Music. The School is nationally recognised for its excellence in music. Over half the pupils receive tuition in the full range of orchestral instruments, piano, organ and classical guitar, and many take part in orchestras, choirs and chamber groups. There is a Senior Symphony Orchestra, Senior Wind Quintet, Junior and Senior String Quartet, a Jazz Ensemble, Senior Chamber Choir, award-winning Cantabile Girls' Choir, a Chapel Choir, a Junior Choir and many chamber music groups. The musical tradition is strengthened by the presence of the Cathedral Choristers (and former Cathedral choristers) in the School.

Fees per term (2018–2019). £4,627.

Extras. Lunches £160 per term, CCF £15 per term from Year 10; DoE from Bronze to Gold level costs to be confirmed; Instrumental Tuition £17.85 per lesson, Speech and Drama £13.75 per lesson, plus public examination fees; PTA £20 per family annually.

Scholarships. Academic (Dean's) Scholarships are awarded as a result of the Senior School Entrance and 11+ Scholarship Examination. Further Dean's Scholarships are also awarded at 13+ and 16+. Art and Drama Scholarships are available at 13+ and 16+ entry. Sports, Music and All-Rounder Scholarships are available at 11+, 13+ and 16+ entry. All Scholars are admitted to the Foundation by the Dean of Hereford each Autumn term.

Cathedral choristers are members of the School from entry. They are accepted from the age of eight as probationers following voice and educational tests held in May each year, and are educated initially at the Junior School. The Governors and the Chapter award choral scholarships jointly each year. A substantial reduction in tuition fees is available for Cathedral choristers.

Assisted Places (Bursaries). A number of means-tested bursaries (assisted places) are available each year to provide financial support to families who would not otherwise be able to support their child's education at the School.

Old Herefordian Club. *Alumni Coordinator*: Mrs Helen Pearson.

The Junior School. This is situated close by the main school. (*For details, please see Junior School IAPS entry*).

Charitable status. Hereford Cathedral School is a Registered Charity, number 518889, and a Company Limited by Guarantee, registered in Cardiff, number 2081261. Its aims and objectives are to promote the advancement of education.

Governing Body:
President: The Very Revd M Tavinor, Dean of Hereford, MA, MMus
Chairman: Rear Admiral P Wilcocks, CB, DSC, DL
C D Hitchiner, LLB, ACIS
A Teale, BSc, PGCE
Major L C Glover, BA
Mrs K Usher, DL
W Hanks, BDS Lond
S Borthwick
T Keyes, MA
The Right Revd A Magowan, BSc, Dip HE, MTh Oxon
Mr J Sheldon, MA Cantab, FCA, CFA
Mr J Preece, BSc, MRICS

Clerk to the Governors: R Pizii, MA, BSc

Headmaster: **P A Smith**, BSc

Deputy Head: B G Blyth, BA

Deputy Head (*Academic*): J P Stanley, MA, MBA

Assistant Head: M J Blackburn, BA

Head of Sixth Form: J R Terry, BSc

Heads of Department:
Art: C A Wilkes, BA
Biology: Mrs S V Phelps
Chemistry: Mrs A J Burdett, MSc
Classics: P Daley, BA MSt
Drama: Miss M M Lancaster, BA
Economics: M R Jackson, BA
English: B E Abbott, BA
Geography: Mrs R M Floyd, BSc
History: P A Wright, BA
Junior ICT: Mrs M J Cuthbert, BMus
Learning Support: Miss L R Stevens, BA, Cert SpLD
Mathematics: M Taylor, BSc, ARCM
Modern Languages: Mrs N J Teale, BA
Music: D R Evans, MA, GBSM
PE and Games: M J Blackburn, BA

Physics: Dr S J B Rhodes, BEng, PhD
Religious Studies: K E Scott, BA
Design and Technology: C J Howells, BA
Careers Adviser: Mrs M McCumisky, BA
OC CCF: Sqn Ldr A D Howell, RAFVR
Director of Finance and Resources: R Pizii, MA, BSc
Headmaster's PA: Mrs S Gurgul
Marketing Manager: Mrs L K Yates
Development Director: Mrs C M Morgan-Jones
Admissions Officer: Mrs S D A Fortey
Tel: 01432 363506, email: admissions@herefordcs.com
Examinations Officer: Dr D Summers
School Office Administrator: Mrs L G Harding

The Junior School
Headmaster: C Wright, BSc, MSc, PGCE
Deputy Headmaster: J M Debenham, BEd
Head of Pre-Prep: Mrs E Lord, Bed
Head of Nursery: Mrs J Windows, BA

Heads of Department:
English: C Roberts
Maths: Miss N Jeynes, BEd
Science: Dr I Barber, BSc
French: Miss C Lambert, BA
Humanities: T Brown, BA
Drama: Miss A Sutton, BA
ICT: T Hutchinson, BSc, CertEd
Art: Mrs K Gummerson, BA
Music: Miss R Toolan, BMus, PG Dip Perf Hons
PSHE: Mrs S Price, LLB, PGCE
Learning Development: Mrs T Denny, BSc
Boys Games: S Turpin, BA
Girls Games: Miss K A Davies, BEd
Gifted & Talented:

Headmaster's PA and Registrar: Mrs S Stick
School Secretary: Mrs A Phillips

Highgate School

North Road, London N6 4AY
Tel: 020 8340 1524 (Office)
           020 8347 3564 (Admissions)
email: office@highgateschool.org.uk
           admissions@highgateschool.org.uk
website: www.highgateschool.org.uk

Motto: *Altiora in votis*

Sir Roger Cholmeley's School at Highgate – to give us our full name – was founded by Sir Roger Cholmeley in 1565, and confirmed by Queen Elizabeth I. We are a co-educational day school with pupils from a diverse range of backgrounds across North London.

Our School has three principal aims: to be a place for learning and scholarship; to be an exemplar for the healthy life; and to be a reflective community.

We have 1,220 boys and girls in our Senior School. Our Junior School has around 400 boys and girls, aged 7 to 11, while our Pre-Preparatory School has some 150 boys and girls aged 3 to 7. We admit boys and girls at each entry point.

Situation and grounds. Our Senior School is situated in the heart of old Highgate village. This means Victorian buildings, like our Chapel, Central Hall classrooms and the Sir Martin Gilbert Library, sit alongside modern facilities such as Dyne House, with its 200-seat auditorium and dedicated recital space, our Art, Design and Technology Centre, the Charter Building for our English and Geography Depart-

ments, plus science laboratories and ICT suites. An extension to our Garner Building, providing two new science laboratories and three new modern languages classrooms, opened in 2014.

Highgate underground station, on the Northern line, is a short walk and there is easy access to our School by bus. It is four miles to central London (City or West End).

A few hundred yards along Hampstead Lane is more than twenty acres of School playing fields together with the Mallinson Sports Centre, indoor swimming pool and extensive sporting facilities, our dining hall, newly rebuilt Junior School (which opened in 2016), and Pre-Preparatory School. Hampstead Heath and Kenwood, the largest expanse of open country in London, are adjacent.

Pastoral care. The wellbeing of our pupils is of primary importance and at the heart of all we do. We organise pastoral care to ensure teachers know pupils and pupils know teachers and each other. For example, all our Junior School pupils belong to a class and to one of four houses. Their sense of belonging is encouraged through daily contact with a trusted teacher.

In our Senior School, Year 7 and 8 pupils are placed in a form group of around 20 to 22 pupils under a form tutor. Pupils are encouraged to take part in inter-form competitions and activities, and to contribute to our weekly assembly and tutorial programme.

On arrival in Year 9, each pupil is placed in one of our twelve houses. Each Head of House, assisted by tutors, monitors the progress and welfare of their house, and liaises with parents. Our house system establishes a basis for lasting friendship and each house creates its own identity through inter-house activities and competitions.

Academic curriculum. Pupils enter our Senior School at 11+ (Year 7). We have a further, limited, entry at 13+. There are eight forms in Years 7 and 8, and our curriculum is broad.

In Years 7 and 8, all follow a common timetable and experience a wide spectrum of academic disciplines: Mathematics, English, French, Latin, History, Geography, Religious Studies and Philosophy, Music, Art, Drama, Design Technology and Engineering, Information Technology, and Sport and Exercise.

Year 7 pupils also follow a General Science course that introduces scientific methods and investigations. In Year 8, they have lessons in the three separate sciences (Biology, Chemistry and Physics) and begin a second modern language from Spanish, Russian, German or Mandarin.

In Year 9, the same broad curriculum is followed. While all pupils continue with Latin, our best linguists are encouraged to follow a course that combines Latin with an introduction to classical Greek. By the time they start GCSEs, pupils have developed an appropriate pattern of work, both in class and out of school. Homework is an integral part of study.

In Year 10, all pupils start I/GCSE courses in Mathematics, English Language, English Literature, Physics, Chemistry and Biology, and at least one modern foreign language (French, German, Spanish, Russian or Mandarin). In addition, pupils take three additional subjects from: a second modern foreign language, Latin, Greek, Classical Civilisation, History, Geography, Religious Studies, Music, Art, Design Technology and Engineering, Computer Science, and Drama. Pupils take ten GCSEs or IGCSEs.

Year 10 pupils take non-examined courses in Religious Education (Applied Religious Ethics), Sport, and Physical Education, and a carousel of classes that includes ICT, and personal, social and health education. Year 11 pupils have sport, plus non-examined courses in Politics, Economics, Philosophy and Art History.

Our teachers are enthusiastic, experienced and well-qualified subject specialists. Our teacher to pupil ratio is about 1:9. Class sizes are generally in the low twenties in Years 7 to 9 and just under twenty in Years 10 and 11, although for some subjects they are smaller. In our Sixth Form, classes of 6 to 12 are usual.

Educational resources include a learning platform, HERO, which enables pupils to access materials and extension work. This complements an extensive intranet on a large information technology network, and parent and pupil portals. This use is guided by trained professionals, alongside facilities in our academic departments, which have specialist teaching rooms, equipment and, where appropriate, technicians, computers and libraries. Fieldwork and visits to galleries, museums, exhibitions and lectures are an integral part of our academic programme.

Highgate's sixth formers study four courses (A Level or Pre-U) in Year 12 and complete three or four full A Levels/Pre-Us by the end of Year 13. Each year, a growing number take four courses in Year 13. We offer individual advice on sixth form choices, and strive to ensure that every pupil has a programme of study that best suits their individual abilities and ambitions.

At present we offer the following A Level or Pre-U* courses: Ancient History, Art (Fine Art), Biology, Chemistry, Classical Civilization, Computer Science, Design Technology and Engineering, French*, Economics, English Literature*, Geography, German*, Greek, History, History of Art, Interdisciplinary Design*, Latin, Mandarin*, Mathematics, Further Mathematics, Music*, Philosophy*, Physics, Politics, Russian*, Spanish*, Theatre Studies, and Theology.

In addition, all sixth formers follow a one-year course in Critical Method in Year 12 and a one-term course in Critical Independence in Year 13. Many embark on the Extended Project Qualification during Year 12. Throughout our Sixth Form, emphasis is placed on working independently and developing advanced study skills. We provide common rooms, plus weekly sports afternoons for sixth formers.

Religion. Highgate has a Christian tradition but pupils from all faiths and denominations, or none, are welcome. Pupils attend either Chapel, Jewish Circle or Dyne House Assembly (for other faiths) once a week and there are weekly voluntary celebrations of Holy Communion. Choral Evensong is sung on some Sundays, at which parents are welcome.

Music, drama and art. Highgate music has a long and distinguished tradition. Many former pupils are now leading composers, conductors or performers. Our range of musical activities encourages the beginner or furthers the skills of the talented musician. State-of-the-art performance spaces for orchestral and chamber music, complete with computerised recording facilities, are in Dyne House.

We have the following instrumental ensembles: a senior and junior symphony orchestra, chamber orchestra, senior and junior woodwind ensembles, several jazz bands and a brass group. Three choirs provide music for Sunday Choral Evensongs, with a further three choirs covering a range of repertoires. There are four main concerts each year, one in a major London venue. Numerous chamber groups rehearse weekly and regular concerts are arranged, plus masterclasses, workshops and an annual house music competition.

Individual music lessons are available with specialist visiting teachers in all the main instruments and in singing. Certain orchestral instruments may be available to learn, for free, through a rare instrument scheme specifically aimed at beginners (at the discretion of our Director of Music).

Every encouragement is given to participation in drama, as actors, in stage management, or assisting with sound and lighting. Recent major productions have included *South Pacific*, *West Side Story*, A *Midsummer Night's Dream*, *Sweeney Todd*, *Les Misérables*, *The Trojan Women*, *The Bacchae*, *Medea*, *The Tempest*, and a promenade production of *A Christmas Carol*. Small-scale plays are staged most terms, some by younger pupils, and there is a biennial play in French. A separate drama studio provides additional rehearsal and performance space. Regular visits to the theatre are arranged.

Our excellent Art Department has facilities for painting, print-making, life drawing, sculpture, pottery, photography, and film-making. Whether taking part in formal classes or working in their free time, pupils are encouraged to explore ways of expressing ideas visually. Work is regularly exhibited, both in the department and around our School.

Sport and exercise. Highgate is exceptionally fortunate when it comes to sport. Our extensive playing fields are complemented by facilities at the Mallinson Sports Centre, by courts for squash, tennis and Eton Fives, by our all-weather pitch, by our cricket nets, and by our location next to Hampstead Heath.

Our sport and exercise curriculum aims to maximise participation, promote enjoyment and ensure progression. Sport (one afternoon per week) and Exercise (a double period in Years 7 to 10) are integrated to ensure pupils develop skills and strength relevant to the sport which, from Year 8, they choose. Sport offered includes team games of football, netball, hockey, cricket and rugby, plus the following: athletics, Eton Fives, swimming, tennis, water polo, triathlon, cross-country, rowing, climbing, fencing, golf, gymnastics, dance, kayaking, sailing and squash. Specialist coaches and teachers lead on the delivery of this innovative curriculum, which is complemented by early-morning, lunch-time and after-school training. We have a high performance programme, as well as a strength and conditioning programme that support our pupils' performance on their chosen sport pathways. A programme of tours take place annually, either to short- or long-haul destinations, including Barbados, Atlanta, Barcelona and Jersey.

Activities. We aim to provide as many opportunities as possible in which pupils develop qualities of self-reliance, endurance and leadership, in which pupils serve the community and in which pupils develop their interests and enthusiasms. We have a large number of societies and clubs, usually meeting over lunch or after school. Highgate is an operating authority for the Duke of Edinburgh's Award scheme, so many pupils gain the bronze award and, often, silver and gold awards. There is also a Community Service scheme and an Urban Survival award scheme.

Admission. Entry to our Junior School is normally at the age of 7. All candidates take an entrance examination in January, and a significant proportion are then interviewed in groups. Entry is the following September. Application forms are available on our website. For enquiries concerning admissions, please contact our Junior School Admissions Office.

For pupils joining our Senior School at 11, there are tests in December, and a significant proportion of candidates are then interviewed in January. Entry is the following September. There are a generally a few places for 13+ entry although these are limited and competition is high.

Pupils from other schools are admitted to our Sixth Form at Highgate, following an interview. Only occasionally are there vacancies at other levels. For enquiries concerning admissions, please contact our Head of Admissions, email: admissions@highgateschool.org.uk.

Fees per term (2018–2019). Senior School: £6,990; Junior School: £6,410; Pre-Preparatory School: £6,055 (Reception–Year 2), £3,020 (Nursery).

Fees include lunch (excluding Nursery), the use of books and stationery, future life membership of our Cholmeleian

Society, and compulsory fieldwork and day visits during curricular time.

Scholarships and bursaries.

Bursaries: Our Admissions Officer (Widening Access), email: admissions@highgateschool.org.uk, can provide information about the process for bursary applications and the number of bursaries held.

Scholarships: Academic scholarships are honorary and do not bring any remission of school fee. We do not award academic scholarships on the strength of the entrance tests alone. We believe we gain a more accurate picture of a child's academic ability after we have had an opportunity to see the quality of their work within our School. Therefore, we award academic scholarships at the beginning of Years 8, 9, 10 and 11, and again in our Sixth Form.

Music awards: We have music awards (scholarships and exhibitions) for pupils joining at 11+, by means of audition at the point of entry. Awards are also made to current Highgate pupils, at these points, where they have met the required standard. Music scholarships bring up to a maximum of 10% remission of the fee and free tuition on two instruments, provided tuition is by instrumental teachers employed at Highgate. For enquiries, please contact our Head of Admissions, email: admissions@highgateschool.org.uk or the Music Department, email: natasha.creed@highgateschool.org.uk.

Old Cholmeleian Society. All former Highgate pupils (OCs) are automatically members of The Cholmeleian Society, a group of over 6,000 alumni across the world. The Cholmeleian Society helps OCs keep in touch, and offers social events, networking, and university and careers mentoring. For enquiries, please contact our Development Office, email: oc@highgateschool.org.uk.

Charitable status. Sir Roger Cholmeley's School at Highgate is a registered charity, number 312765. The importance that we attach to our social responsibilities has become more focused but is not new, since the original objectives stated in our foundation are: "the advancement of education by the provision of a school in or near Highgate, the provision of incidental or ancillary educational activities, and the undertaking of associated activities for the benefit of the public." More detailed information can be found on our website.

Visitor: Her Majesty The Queen

Governors:
R M Rothenberg, MBE, BA, FCA, CTA, MAE (*Chairman*)
B Davidson, MD, FRCS (*Deputy Chairman*)
G Aitken, BA
A Buckley, MA
J Claughton, MA
J Coleman, MA, LLDip
M Danson, MA
R Langdale, QC, LLB, MPhil
K Little, MBBS, BSc
P Marshall, BSc, MRICS
K Panja, BA
A Patel, BA
J D Randall, BSc
P Rothwell, MA

Bursar and Secretary to the Foundation: J C Pheasant, BSc, LLDip, Barrister

Head: **A S Pettitt**, MA

Deputy Heads:
T J Lindsay, MA (*Principal Deputy Head*)
S M James, BA, MA (*Principal of the Junior School*)

J P R Newton, BA, MSc (*Deputy Head, Academic*)
L M Shelley, BA (*Pupils' Personal Development and Employability*)

Assistant Heads:
S N Brunskill, MA (*Head of Sixth Form, Pastoral*)
H Evans, BA (*Head of Middle School*)
C M Goldsworthy, BA (*Assistant Head, Communications*)
S A Pullan, LLB, MA (*Head of Lower School*)
G A Waller, MA (*Head of Sixth Form, Academic*)
J C Y Welch, BSc, MSc, PhD (*Assistant Head, Projects and Logistics*)
B S Weston, BSc, PhD, FSB, CBiol (*Assistant Head, Teaching and Learning*)

Heads of Department:
Art: C M Goldsworthy, BA
Biology: R J Lockhart, BA
Chemistry: I R Davies, MChem, PhD
Classics: H E Shepherd, MA
Computing: M A O'Connor, BA
Design Technology Engineering: A F Thomson, BSc
Drama and Theatre Studies: J E Fehr, BA
Economics: A C Burrows, BA
English: R J Hyam, BA
French: C C Hayes, L-es-L
Geography: B M Beloe, BSc
German: G D C Creagh, BA
History: B J Dabby, MA, MPhil, PhD
History of Art: J E J Jammers, MA, PhD
Learning Support: S M Bambrough, BA, MEd
Mandarin: Q W Wallis, BA
Mathematics: P F D Brownlee, BSc, MSt; J Wright, MMath
Modern Languages: J A J Watts, BA
Music: J P Murphy, GRNCM
Physics: A C Cheung, BA, MA, MSci, PhD
Politics: K B Shapiro, BA, MA
Religious and Philosophy: R Leigh, MA, MPhil, PhD
Russian: R J Newton, MA
Spanish: N Arosemena Manso, BA
Sport and Exercise: C L M Henderson, BEd; S Pride, BSc

Highgate Junior School
3 Bishopwood Road, London N6 4PL
Telephone: 020 8340 9193
Email: jsoffice@highgateschool.org.uk
Principal of the Junior School: S M James, BA, MA
(*For further details, see entry in IAPS section.*)

Highgate Pre-Preparatory School
7 Bishopswood Road, London N6 4PH
Telephone: 020 8340 9196
Email: pre-prep@highgateschool.org.uk

Hurstpierpoint College
A Woodard School

College Lane, Hurstpierpoint, West Sussex BN6 9JS

Tel: 01273 833636
Fax: 01273 835257
email: registrar@hppc.co.uk
website: www.hppc.co.uk
Twitter: @Hurst_College
Facebook: @HurstCollege

Motto: *Beati mundo corde*

Founded 1849 by Nathaniel Woodard, Canon of Manchester.

Hurstpierpoint College is a co-educational day and boarding school for boys and girls aged between 4 and 18 years. Pre-Prep, Prep and Senior Schools are linked by common values and a common academic and administrative framework, to provide a complete education. There are currently 434 boys and 370 girls. 50% of the pupils are boarders. The Preparatory School has a further 300 boys and girls and the Pre-Prep currently has 57 pupils.

The school is truly co-educational throughout and offers boarding for boys and girls in the Senior School. Boarding is a particularly popular option at the school with many day pupils and flexi boarders later opting to become weekly boarders. In their Upper Sixth year at Hurst, pupils join St John's House, a co-educational day and boarding house where, appropriately supervised, they enjoy greater freedom and are encouraged to further develop their independent learning skills in preparation for university.

Buildings and Facilities. At the heart of the school's large country campus lie the core school buildings and Chapel arranged around three attractive quadrangles built of traditional Sussex knapped flint. Key facilities nearby include three floodlit Astroturfs, art school, sports hall, music school, dance and drama studios, 250-seat theatre, indoor swimming pool and Medical Centre. Other facilities include a new Library and fully-equipped IT Centre. A new performing arts building is currently under construction. The extensive grounds are laid mainly to playing fields and include one of the largest and most attractive school cricket pitches in the country.

Chapel. As a Woodard School, Hurstpierpoint is a Christian foundation and underpinned by Christian values, although pupils of other faiths or of no faith are warmly welcomed. Pupils attend up to three assemblies during the week. The main Eucharist, which parents and friends are most welcome to attend, takes place early on Friday evenings, although there are also occasional Sunday services in addition to voluntary celebrations of the Holy Communion. Pupils who wish to do so are prepared in small classes for the annual Confirmation taken by one of the Bishops of the diocese.

Curriculum. The five-day academic week is structured to allow boys and girls to study a variety of subject options that can be adapted to suit their natural ability. The entry year (Shell) gives pupils the chance to experience most of our GCSE subjects before they choose their options. It involves the study of English, History, Geography, French, Spanish, Latin, Classical Greek, Mathematics, Physics, Chemistry, Biology, Religious Studies, Art, Design & Technology, Music, Dance, Drama, Physical Education and Computer Science. In the second (Remove) and in the third (Fifth) years the curriculum is split into two parts: core subjects (English, maths, three sciences, dance) and optional subjects such as Art & Design, Classical Greek, Computer Science, Drama, Humanities, Modern Foreign Languages, Design Technology, Latin.

Students entering the sixth form study A Levels with the majority selecting 3 subjects and some selecting 4 and all sixth form pupils take the EPQ as an extension of one of their A Level subjects. The subject choice is wide from: Art & Design, Business, Classical Civilisation, Classical Greek, Computer Science, Dance, Design & Technology, Drama & Theatre, Economics, English Literature, Geography, History, Latin, Maths and Further Maths, Modern Languages, Music, Music Technology, Physical Education, Politics, Psychology, Religious Studies, Sciences (Physics, Chemistry, Biology) and Sociology.

All pupils' work is overseen by academic tutors and we take particular care to ensure that university applications are properly targeted to suit the students' aspirations and talents.

Games. The School operates a "Sport for All" policy that seeks to place pupils in games most suited to their tastes and abilities. During the first two years they are expected to take part in at least some of the major sports but thereafter a greater element of choice occurs. The major sports are Rugby, Hockey, Cricket and Athletics for boys; Hockey, Netball, Athletics and Tennis for girls. Recent tours for major sports include Rugby (Italy), Netball (Barbados), Dubai (Cricket), South Africa (Hockey). In addition there are teams in Basketball, Cross Country, Football, Golf, Polo, Rounders, Shooting, Squash, Swimming, Triathlon, boys' Tennis, girls' Cricket and girls' Rugby. The Sports Hall and indoor Swimming Pool provide opportunities for many other pursuits such as Aerobics, Badminton, Equestrian, Fencing, Gymnastics, Power Walking, Weight Training and Water Polo, while the Outdoor Pursuits enable pupils to enjoy challenges such as Rock Climbing, Mountain Biking, Sailing, Kayaking and Canoeing.

Service Afternoons. On Wednesdays all pupils other than the Shell (Year 9) are expected to take part in The Duke of Edinburgh's Award activities alongside the Combined Cadet Force (Army, RN or RAF sections), Community Service or Environmental Conservation.

Music. There has always been a strong musical tradition at Hurstpierpoint with an orchestra and other more specialised ensembles. A large proportion of the pupils, currently 160, take individual instrumental lessons and give frequent recitals. The Chapel Choir plays a major part in regular worship and there are several other choral groups.

Drama. The Shakespeare Society is the oldest such school society in the country and organises an annual production and an annual musical. Drama covers a wide range and varies from major musicals to more modest House plays and pupil-directed productions. The 250-seat Bury Theatre also gives the more technically minded ample opportunity to develop stage management, lighting and sound skills.

Other Activities. The Thursday afternoon activity programme is for Shell and Remove pupils (Years 9 & 10) and includes Art, Climbing, Dance, Self-Defence, Car Maintenance, Girls' Football, Hurst Farm, Robotics, Japanese, LAMDA, Ningitsu, Shooting, Horse Riding, Polo, Karate, Golf Range, Squash, Clay Pigeon Shooting, Dinghy Sailing and Surfing alongside a variety of music clubs and literary clubs. Other activities also take place during the school week.

Hurst Johnian Club. In addition to providing facilities and events for Old Pupils, the Club also assists with careers and supports the current pupils in various ways, e.g. Gap Year travel fund and tour sponsorship contributions. Contact the Hon Secretary, c/o Hurstpierpoint College.

Fees per term (2018–2019). Senior School: Weekly Boarding £9,985–£9,885; Flexi Boarding £9,375–£9,275; Day £7,950–£7,850.

Scholarships and Bursaries. Awards available at 13+: Academic, 'Hurst' All-Rounder, Art, Dance, Drama, Music and 'Downs' Sports. Please note that candidates entering for awards other than Academic are not eligible to apply for All-Rounder awards. Such candidates will be considered for All-Rounder awards as part of their other applications. Awards available at 16+: Academic, Art, Drama, Music and 'Downs' Sports.

Academic Award examinations are held annually in May for 13+ candidates. Assessments for All-Rounder, Art, Drama and Sports Awards are held in February.

Music Award assessments are held in January of the year of entry for entrants to the Prep School and in February of the year of entry for entrants to the Senior School. Awards are offered with free musical tuition in two instruments. Informal auditions are encouraged and may be held at any time by arrangement with the Director of Music. The

Awards are given subject to satisfactory Scholarship or Common Entrance results or the College's own entry tests.

Art Scholarships: A folio of work is presented and there is an objective test as well as an interview.

Assessment for Sixth Form awards takes place in November of the year prior to entry.

Means-tested bursaries may be available to supplement awards.

Admission. For 13+ entry, pupils must be registered on the School's list and will sit the Common ISEB Pre-Test in Year 6. Offers are made subject to passing Common Entrance or Scholarship examinations. Entry from Hurst Prep school is by the College's own examinations. Entrants from maintained schools and from overseas undergo separate tests and interviews.

To matriculate into the sixth form at Hurst pupils require at least 4 Grade A or level 7 GCSEs. They should achieve an A or A* grade in the subjects they intend to sturdy and, where a pupils wishes to start a new subject which they have not studied before, they need to have achieved an A/A* in a GCSE subject closely related to it (i.e. for Economics, ideally a pupil should have an A/A* in Maths GCSE). Students should also have a minimum of a C grade or Level 5 at GCSE in Mathematics and English.

Please contact the Senior School Admissions Office for further information.

Preparatory School. *See entry in IAPS section.*

Charitable status. Hurstpierpoint College is a Registered Charity, number 1076498. It aims to provide a Christian education to boys and girls between the ages of four and eighteen in the three schools on the campus.

School Council:
Chairman: Mr A Jarvis, BEd, MA, FRSA (*Custos*)

Members:
Professor J P Bacon, MA, MSc, PhD
Dr S Brydie, MBBS, MD, MRCGP
Dr J A Chocqueel-Mangan, BEng, MSc, DBA, CEng, MIMechE, FRSA
Mrs L J Corbett, OBE
Mr R P Dean, BA, LLB Hons
Mr P M Dillon-Robinson, BA Hons, FCA, MBA
R J Ebdon, BSc Hons, MAPM, ICIOB, FRSA (*Vice Custos*)
Mrs F M Hampton
Mrs K M Mack, BA Hons, ACA
Mr K S Powell, FCA
Mr G A Rushton
Mr G J Taysom, BSc, FRSA

Headmaster: Mr Tim J Manly, BA Oriel College Oxon, MSc LSE

Head of Senior School: Mr Dominic W Mott, MA Queens' College Cantab
Head of Prep School: Mr Ian D Pattison, BSc Southampton
Deputy Head Pastoral: Mrs Caty E Jacques, BSc Surrey
Deputy Head Co-Curricular: Mr Tim F Q Leeper, BSc Edinburgh, CBiol, MIBiol
Deputy Head Academic: Mr Lloyd P Dannatt, MEng Imperial College London
Bursar: Mr Stephen A Holliday, BSc, ACIB, MAPM
Director of Operational Technology: Mr Dan M Higgins, BA, Cert Ed Loughborough
Director of Staff and Pupil Wellbeing: Mr Mike Lamb, BSc Nottingham, MA Edge Hill
Director of Professional Development and Performance: Mrs Michelle Zeidler, BEd Homerton College Cantab, MEd OU

Prep School Deputy Head: Mr Nick J Oakden, BA Wales, MEd Buckingham, NPQH

Directors:
Mr Liam J Agate, BA Sidney Sussex College Cantab (*Director of Academic Development*)
Mr Robert J Ashley, BA Manchester, MA Melbourne (*Director of Learner Development*)
Mrs Keramy J Austin, BSc Edinburgh, CChem FRSC CSci (*Director of Academic Administration*)
Mr Luke A Gasper, BA Dunelm (*Director of Drama*)
Mr Dan M Higgins, BA, Cert Ed Loughborough (*Director of Operational Technology*)
Mrs Caty E Jacques, BSc Surrey (*Director of PSHCEE*)
Mr Rob M Kift, BEd Madeley College of PE (*Director of Sport*)
Mr Mike Lamb, BSc Nottingham, MA Edge Hill (*Director of Staff and Pupil Wellbeing*)
Mrs Jan Leeper, BA University College London (*Director of Pastoral Care and Boarding, i/c Head of Careers*)
Mr Neil Matthews, BA St John's College Durham (*Director of Music*)
Mr Fred Simkins, GCGI, CVQO Surrey (*Director of Outdoor Education*)
Mrs Debbie K Stoneley, BEd London (*Director of Safeguarding*)
Mrs Michelle Zeidler, BEd Homerton College Cantab, MEd OU (*Director of Professional Development and Performance*)

Housemasters/Housemistresses:
Miss Jess G Coleman, MA St Andrews (*Wolf*)
Mr Nick Creed, BSc UWIC (*Crescent*)
Mr Andrew G Daville, MA Lady Margaret Hall Oxon (*St John's*)
Miss Jami A Edwards, BA Cardiff (*Fleur*)
Miss Tania C Fielden, BA Brighton (*Pelican*)
Mr Oliver J J Gospel, BEng Liverpool (*Eagle*)
Mrs Helena E Higgins, BA, Cert Ed Loughborough (*Phoenix*)
Mr Adam J Hopcroft, MEng Bath (*Red Cross*)
Mrs Sarah Hyman, BA Lancaster (*Martlet*)
Mrs Janina S Jedamzik, BA, MA Sussex (*St John's*)
Mr Duffy E Parry, MA Edinburgh (*Chevron*)
Mrs Alice S Paterson, BSc Edinburgh (*Shield*)
Mr Andrew J Smith, BA Warwick, MA Royal Holloway London (*Woodard*)
Mr David R Williams, BA Oxford Brookes (*Star*)
Mrs Fran Williams, BA, MA St Hugh's College Oxon (*Star*)

Heads of Years:
Rec–Year 2: Mrs Debbie Ross, BEd Brighton
Years 3–6: Mrs Alexandra E A Oakden, MA St Andrews
Year 7: Mrs Tracey-Ann Preen, BSc Southampton
Year 8: Ms Karen A Pattison, BA Wales
Shell: Mr Mike Lamb, BSc Nottingham, MA Edge Hill
Remove: Mr Owain J Jones, MA St Edmund Hall Oxon
Fifth Form: Miss Amy V Doonan, BA Cardiff, MSc Green Templeton College Oxon
Head of Sixth Form: Mrs Janina S Jedamzik, BA, MA Sussex
Assistant Heads of Sixth Form: Mr William G D Bradley, BA Essex; Mr Simon Hastilow, BSc Warwick

Teaching Staff – Heads of Department:

Art:
Mrs Amanda G Duke, BA Goldsmiths London (*Head of Department*)
Mrs Lucy A Lane, BA West Surrey College (*Head of Art Years 3–8*)

Business Studies:
Mr Liam J Agate, BA Sidney Sussex College Cantab (*Head of Department*)

Classics:
Miss Katherine S E Barker, MA Exeter College Oxon (*Head of Department Yrs 7–13*)

Computing:
Mr Steve J Crook, BSc East Anglia (*Head of Department*)

Dance:
Miss Nicola C Dominy, BA Surrey (*Head of Department Years 7–13*)

Design Technology:
Mr Kaeran D K MacDonald, BA Brunel (*Head of Department Years 7–13*)

Drama:
Mr Luke A Gasper, BA Dunelm (*Director of Drama*)
Mr Liam Harris, BA London (*Head of Academic Drama*)
Miss Rose E Hall–Smith, BEd Edinburgh, MA London (*Head of Drama Years 3–8*)

Economics:
Mr Liam J Agate, BA Sidney Sussex College Cantab (*Head of Department*)

English:
Mr Tom Smith, MA Pembroke College Cantab (*Head of Department*)
Mr Nick Fanthorpe, BA Trinity College Oxon (*Head of English Year 10*)
Ms Karen A Pattison, BA Wales (*Head of English Years 7&8*)
Mrs Sarah L Deelman, BSc Surrey (*Head of English Years 3–6*)
Mrs Debbie A Ross, BEd Brighton (*Head of Literacy Rec–Year 2*)

ESL:
Mrs Kay L B Goddard, MA The Queen's College Oxon (*Head of Department*)

Geography:
Mr Rob J Ashley, BA Manchester, MA Melbourne (*Head of Department*)
Miss Rebecca L Bownas, BSc East Anglia (*Head of Geography Years 9–11*)
Mr Tom B B Williams, BSc Manchester (*Head of Geography Years 3–8*)

Government and Politics:
Mr Brian T Schofield, BA Pembroke College Oxon (*Head of Department*)

History:
Miss Joanna C Clarke, BA Edinburgh (*Head of Department*)
Mrs Alexandra E A Oakden, MA St Andrews (*Head of*) (*History Years 3–8*)

Learning Support:
Mrs Jill C Silvey, BA Newcastle NSW (*Head of Department*)
Mrs Kate J Parker, BA Liverpool, MA London (*Head of Learning Support Rec–Year 8*)

Modern Foreign Languages:
Mrs Jessica B Smith, MA King's College Cantab (*Head of Minority Languages*)

French:
Mrs Grace I Butler, BA Birmingham (*Head of Department*)
Mrs Alison Filkins, BA Roehampton (*Head of French Years 3–8*)

Spanish:
Miss Hannah C K Prescott, BA, King's College London (*Assistant Head of Department*)
Mrs Alison Filkins, BA Roehampton (*Head of Spanish Years 3–8*)

Mathematics:
Mrs Leah J Mackinder, BSc Nottingham (*Head of Department*)
Mr Sam N Higazi, BSc Birmingham (*Head of Maths Years 9–11*)
Mr James S McIntyre, BA Exeter (*Head of Maths Years 7&8*)
Mrs Tracey–Ann Preen, BSc Southampton (*Head of Maths Years 3–6*)
Mrs Lauren S Johnson, BA Brighton (*Head of Numeracy Rec–Year2*)

Music:
Mr Neil Matthews, BA St John's College, Durham (*Director of Music*)
Mr Darren Jameson, GTCL Trinity College of Music, MA York, FTCL, LRSM (*Head of Academic Music*)
Mr Will Carroll, BSc Montreal (*Head of Music Technology*)
Mrs Claudette C Hastilow, BMus Trinity College of Music, MEd Homerton College Cantab (*Head of Music Rec–Year 8*)

PE & Sports Science:
Mr Steve J May, BSc Chichester (*Head of Department*)
Mr James Baldwin, BSc Exeter (*Head of Academic PE Years 3–8*)

Psychology:
Mr Simon P Poole, BEd Exeter, MBA EdMan Leicester (*Head of Department*)

Philosophy and Theology:
Mr Gareth T Richards, BA Exeter (*Head of Department*)
Mr Martin Clay, MBA OU (*Head of RS Years 3–8*)

Science:
Mr Peter A Browne, BSc Leeds & Sussex (*Head of Department*)
Mrs Lindsay A Moakes, BA Brighton (*Head of Science Years 3–6*)
Miss Ana Scandian, BA Chichester (*Head of Science, Rec–Year 2*)

Biology:
Mrs Natasha Coxon, BSc Grey College, Durham (*Head of Biology Years 12&13*)
Miss Siobhan O K McCrohan, BSc St Aidan's College, Durham (*Head of Biology Years 9–11*)
Mr Owain J Jones, MA St Edmund Hall Oxon (*Head of Biology Years 7&8*)

Chemistry:
Mr Peter A Browne, BSc Leeds & Sussex (*Head of Department*)
Mrs Sue Crickmore, MA Newnham College Cantab (*Head of Chemistry Years 12&13*)
Mrs Helen A Harper, MSc Wadham College Oxon (*Head of Chemistry Years 7&8*)

Physics:
Mrs Naomi C Smith, MPhys Leeds (*Head of Department*)
Miss Fallon Sheffield, BSc St Andrews (*Head of Physics Years 7&8, Physics Coordinator*)

Sociology:
Miss Rebecca L Bownas, BSc East Anglia (*Head of Department*)

Enrichment:
Mr Liam J Agate, BA Sidney Sussex College Cantab
(*Director of Academic Development*)

The Library:
Ms Dominique B Collins, MA UCL (*Head of Library*)
Mrs Trisha A Barrett, BA Birmingham, MA Chichester
(*Prep School Librarian*)

Outdoor Education:
Mr Fred Simkins, GCGI, CVQO Surrey (*Director of Outdoor Education*)
Miss Sarah K Turner, BA Northumbria (*Assistant Director of Outdoor Education*)
Combined Cadet Force:
Capt Mr Sam Amos, Contingent Commander

Sport:
Mr Rob M Kift, BEd Madeley College of PE (*Director of Sport*)
Mr Nick Creed, BSc UWIC (*Assistant Director of Sport, Boys*)
Mrs Rebecca J Jutson (*Assistant Director of Sport, Girls*)
Mrs Carol Adams, Diploma Colchester Institute (*Head of Girls Games Years 3–8*)
Mr James Baldwin (*Head of PE Years 3–8*)
Mr Dafydd J W Charles, BSc Sheffield (*Head of Hockey*)
Mr Ben M Dewey, BSc Northampton (*Head of Boys Games Years 3–8*)
Miss Carla Dilley, BA Brighton (*EYFS & KS1 PE*)
Miss Ellen M Franks (*Mistress i/c of Girls' Athletics & Head of Netball*)
Mrs Jean A Leak (*Head of Swimming Years 3–8*)
Mr Martin R Tigg (*Master i/c Tennis*)
Mrs Tina M Towler (*Sports Coach and Mistress i/c Girls' Cricket*)

Head of Admissions: Mrs D S Allison

Hymers College

Hymers Avenue, Hull, East Yorkshire HU3 1LW

Tel: 01482 343555
Fax: 01482 472854
email: enquiries@hymers.org
website: www.hymerscollege.co.uk
Twitter: @Hymers_College
Facebook: @HymersCollege

Hymers College in Hull was opened as a school for boys in 1893, when the Reverend John Hymers, Fellow of St John's College, Cambridge, and Rector of Brandesburton, left money in his Will, for a school to be built 'for the training of intelligence in whatever social rank of life it may be found among the vast and varied population of the town and port of Hull'. Although the school has remained true to its Founder's intentions, the catchment area now stretches across East Yorkshire and North Lincolnshire and the school became fully co-educational in 1989.

Number of Pupils. 930.

The Junior School has 168 pupils aged 8–11. There is a full range of academic, sporting, music and extra-curricular activities.

The Senior School has 576 pupils in Years 7–11 and the Sixth Form has 186 pupils.

Admission is by competitive examination at ages 8, 9 and 11, together with an interview with the Headteacher. Most pupils proceed at age eleven into the Senior School by an examination taken also by pupils from other schools. Almost all pupils qualify for the Sixth Form through GCSE results. Pupils from other schools are admitted to the Sixth Form on the basis of good GCSE results and interview with the Headmaster.

Pupils are prepared for the GCSE in a broad curriculum including music, business-related subjects, computer studies, technology and the arts.

There is a full range of courses leading to A Level examinations, and special preparation is given for Oxford and Cambridge entrance.

Facilities. The buildings consist of 35 classrooms, 11 specialist laboratories, a 30-booth language laboratory, extensive ICT facilities, audio-visual room, art rooms, theatre, Art/Design Technology Centre, a gymnasium and very large sports hall. A new Music Block opened in September 2014 providing a full range of music facilities including a Recital Hall, Rehearsal and Music Technology Rooms and a Recording Studio. The most recent addition is our award-winning Learning Resource Centre and we have recently refurbished both our Chemistry and Physics laboratories. The Junior School building contains 9 classrooms and specialist rooms for music, DT, art, ICT and science, along with a library, hall and changing rooms. The grounds, which extend over 40 acres, include an all-weather hockey pitch, 12 tennis courts and a swimming pool/sports centre.

Extracurricular Activities. All pupils are strongly encouraged to participate in the very wide range of extracurricular activities. The main school games are rugby, cricket, hockey, netball, tennis and athletics. There are also school teams in swimming and fencing. The school regularly competes at national level in these sports and provides members of county and national teams. Many pupils take part in The Duke of Edinburgh's Award scheme and the school has an impressive track record in Young Enterprise. Other clubs include ACF, chess, debating, photography, community service and journalism. Drama is particularly strong, with several productions a year. Music is a major school activity; there are three full orchestras, a large choir, and several chamber groups in each part of the school. Individual tuition is available in most instruments.

Fees per term (2018–2019). Senior School £3,786; Junior School £3,153–£3,330; Sixth Form £3,786. Hymers Bursaries are awarded at ages 8, 9, 11 and 16.

The Old Hymerians Association, c/o Alumni Relations Manager, Hymers College, Hull HU3 1LW.

Charitable status. Hymers College is a Registered Charity, number 529820-R. Its aims and objectives are education.

Governors:
Mr Michael de-V Roberts, FCA (*Chairman of Governors*)
Mr John M V Redman, BSc, FIDM, MIOD (*Vice Chairman*)
Mr Michael P Astell, BEng, MBA, FIMechE, CEng
Mr P Adrian B Beecroft, MA, MBA, FInstP
Professor P Glenn Burgess, MA, PhD Cantab, FRHistS
Mrs Tracey A Carruthers, RGN
Mr John F Connolly, BSc
Dr Georgina J Gateshill, BMedSci, BMBS
Mr Dominic A Gibbons, BSc, MRICS
Mr William H Gore, BSc, MSc, PhD, ACA
Mrs Glenda A Greendale
Mr Martin C S Hall, BSc
Mr Jonathan G Leafe
Mrs Elizabeth A Maliakal, LLB
Dr Ashok Pathak, MBBS, MAMS
Mr Christopher M Read, MA Oxon, MRICS
Mr John G Robinson, BA
Mrs Nicki Shipley, FCA
Mrs G V Vickerman, BSc, MSc, MRICS
Mrs Sameera Anwar West

Mr Jamie R Wheldon, LLB Hons, MRICS, ACI Arb
Mr Peter J E Wildsmith, LLB

Headmaster: Mr D C Elstone, MA Ed Mgt

Deputy Head (Management): Mr R Wright
Deputy Head (Pastoral): Mrs H Jackson

Head of Junior School: Mr P C Doyle, BSc

Teachers:
* *Head of Department*

Mr G Whitehead (*Art*)	Mr I Sanderson
Mr D Whittaker	Mrs M Humblet
Mr P Roberts (*Biology*)	Miss N Jack
Mr G Gibson	Ms S Daflon
Mrs H Jackson	Miss Herrera Garcia
Dr J Jarvis	Mrs L Sanderson (*Music*)
Dr R Pybus	Mrs C Cook
Mr G Prescott (*Chemistry*)	Mr R Quick
Dr J Martin	Miss M Pearson
Mr P Meadway	Mr J Shepherd
Mr J Hayes	Mr A Penny
Miss K Walker	Mr L Bartlett
Mr D Mills (*Design &*	Mrs M Armstrong
Technology)	Mrs M Riley
Mrs L Roberts	Mr M Couzin
Mr S Syson	Mr P Lusvardi
Miss N McLeod (*Drama*)	Mrs B Lewis
Miss R Clark	Mr W Hayton
Mr J Mutter (*Economics*	Mrs R England
& Business Studies)	Mrs W Johnston (*Sport*)
Mr N Exley	Mr S Walmsley (*PE*)
Mr M McTeare	Mr W Murray (*Hockey*)
Mrs R Elstone (*English*)	Mr B Skirving (*Rugby*)
Mr A Whittaker	Mr G Tipping
Mrs S Hickman	Mrs J Fillingham
Miss T Parker	Mr J Tapley
Miss M Caley	Mrs A Powell
Miss N Batch	Mrs K Wylde
(*Geography*)	Mr B Young (*Physics*)
Mrs C Copeland	Dr M Pickles
Mr D Elstone	Mr A Javed
Dr J Denton (*History*)	Mr A Stirk
Mr D Harrison	Dr J Denton (*Politics*)
Mr C Setterington	Mr R Summers (*PHSE*)
Dr A Smith	Mr C Gaynor-Smith (*RE*)
Mr P Cook (*Computer*	Mr G Hambleton
Science)	Mr P Doyle
Mr A Cadle	Mrs A Exley
Mr McPherson (*Latin*)	Mrs H Harrison
Mrs S Dickinson	Mrs Z Gillett
Mr E Tame (*Mathematics*)	Mrs H Griffith
Dr R Bennett	Mr A Taylor
Mr R Simpson	Mrs L Walmsley
Mr R Wright	Ms T Redhead
Mr D Hickman	Ms F Rix
Mr A Pailing	Mr R O'Hara
Miss A Dai	Mr A Copeland
Mrs C Ferry-Bolder	Mrs S Julian
Mr A Sanz Caro (*Modern*	Mr S McLoughlin
Languages)	Mr M Hodsdon

Ibstock Place School

Clarence Lane, London SW15 5PY
Tel: General Enquiries: 020 8876 9991
             Headmistress's PA: 020 8392 5802

Bursar's Office: 020 8392 5804
Registrar: 020 8392 5803
email: office@ibstockplaceschool.co.uk
website: www.ibstockplaceschool.co.uk

Age Range. 4–18 Co-educational.
Number in School. 962: 482 Boys, 480 Girls.

Ibstock Place School is located in spacious grounds of some eight acres adjacent to Richmond Park and with easy access to Putney, Barnes, Richmond and Hammersmith. The school offers a balanced education combining a traditional academic curriculum with an extensive range of co-curricular opportunities.

This co-educational school has grown and prospered with significant building development in recent years. A Sports Hall opened in 2008. New School, occupying Clarence Lane and Priory wings and comprising twenty-one classrooms, six laboratories and two computer suites, opened in 2011. Additional facilities include: a stunning purpose-built Library accommodated over two floors, a Music Technology studio, all-weather and sports pitches on the adjacent Lawrence House campus site, and a swimming pool. A Theatre, including flexible, state-of-the-art stage, fully-equipped Drama Studio and backstage facilities comprising Dressing Rooms, Green Room and Workshop opened in 2015. A new Refectory will open in 2019.

The Preparatory Department and the Senior School remain distinctive and are housed separately, so that each child benefits from a small-school ambience and the younger pupils gain from many of the facilities enjoyed by the Senior School. The Prep School, which incorporates Pre-Prep, provides a rich and stimulating environment, with a wide range of curricular activity carefully planned to realise each child's abilities and talents.

The Senior School, age 11–18, offers a full range of Arts, Humanities, Languages, Science and Technology subjects. All pupils follow a core curriculum which includes a requirement to study two languages at GCSE/IGCSE, along with many opportunities for enrichment. Co-curricular emphasis is placed on Music, Drama and Sports, and recent tours have taken pupils to China, Iceland, India, South Africa and the USA, as well as language and choral visits to European destinations closer to home. There is an outstanding programme of outdoor education, a wide range of after-school clubs, as well as The Duke of Edinburgh's Award scheme. All pupils are supported by a strong and effective pastoral system which operates through four houses. House Groups are vertically organised to engender companionship and aspiration.

A Level results in 2018 have placed our departing Sixth Form pupils within the front rank of British school leavers. A quarter of the cohort managed to achieve three A grades or better and in terms of the overall percentage of entries graded at A* or A, our pupils' performance surpassed the national figure by almost double. In the Extended Project Qualification, which is now a well-established feature of our Sixth Form curriculum, 84% of our entrants secured an A* or A.

Over recent years our leavers have proceeded to an impressive range of world-class institutions including Cambridge, Oxford, St Andrews, Imperial College, Durham, Lancaster, UCL, Warwick, Leeds, LSE, Bath and Exeter, and there is now barely a single Top 50 university in the UK which does not boast at least one Ibstonian undergraduate.

GCSE/IGCSE examination results in 2018 were record-breaking. With much being made this year of the increasing degree of difficulty following the reforms introduced to these public examinations, the IPS cohort achieved 56% of entries graded A* and 84% of entries graded at either A* or A (9–7) – an outstanding performance.

Entry to the Pre-Prep is by date of Registration and for subsequent years by assessment. There is no guaranteed transfer from the Prep School to the Senior School. All candidates for Senior School entry are interviewed and take examinations in Mathematics, English and Reasoning. A satisfactory report from the entrant's current school is also required.

Further information is available from the Registrar and Open Mornings and Evenings are held regularly through the year. Occasional places may arise from time to time (e.g. at 13+).

Fees per term (2018–2019). £5,430–£6,960 (including lunches).

Charitable status. Ibstock Place School is a Registered Charity, number 1145565.

Chairman of Governors: Richard Jackson, MA FRSA

Headmistress: **Mrs Anna Sylvester-Johnson**, BA Hons, PGCE

School Executive:
Deputy Headmaster: Mr Christopher Wolsey, MA Nottingham, MEd Buckingham
Senior Master: Mr Christopher Banfield, MA Leeds, MSc Open

The Senior Management Team:
Director of Operations/Head of PVI: Mr Russell Collins, BSc Hons Cape Town
Head of Sixth Form: Mr Kevin Darlington, MSc LSE
Master in Charge of Teaching and Learning: Mr Lee Faith, BSc London Metropolitan
Deputy Head of Sixth Form and PVI, Sutherland Tutor: Mrs Sophie Gillen, MA Oxon
Senior Tutor: Mr J-D Price, BSc Exeter

Head of Pre-Prep and Preparatory School: Miss Kate Bevan, MA Surrey

Immanuel College

Elstree Road, Bushey, Hertfordshire WD23 4EB

Tel: 020 8950 0604
Fax: 020 8950 8687
email: enquiries@immanuelcollege.co.uk
website: www.immanuelcollege.co.uk
Twitter: @ICBushey
Facebook: @ImmanuelCollegeUK

Motto: *Torah im Derech Eretz ~ Jewish learning leading to secular success*

Immanuel College is a selective, co-educational day school founded in 1990 by the late Chief Rabbi, Lord Jakobovits to fulfil his vision of a school affirming orthodox Jewish values and practice in the context of rigorous secular studies. The College aims at giving its pupils a first-class education that encourages them to connect Jewish and secular wisdom, to think independently and to exercise responsibility. Its ethos is characterised by attentiveness to individual pupils' progress, high academic achievement and the integration of Jewish and secular learning. There are both Jewish and non-Jewish teachers at the school, the common element being enthusiasm for their work and concern for their pupils. Its results at GCSE and A Level have been increasingly impressive in recent years. In 2018 78% of all GCSE entries were graded A or A* (7, 8, 9) and over 51% of A Levels were graded A or A*.

Age Range. 4–11 and 11–18. The Preparatory School opened in September 2011 and now includes Reception to Year 6 classes.

School Roll. There are 681 pupils on roll, of whom 323 are girls and 358 are boys. There are 101 pupils in the Sixth Form.

Buildings and Grounds. The College is situated in a tranquil 11-acre site dominated by Caldecote Towers, a Grade II listed 19th-century mansion. Facilities include the Joyce King Theatre, two suites of science laboratories, a fitness suite, a large all-weather surface for tennis and netball, cricket and football pitches, and grounds for field events and athletics. Professor Lord Winston opened a new multi-functional 8-classroom building in September 2010, and a further building for an enhanced Jewish Learning facility (Atar-Zwillenberg Beit K'nesset), additional classrooms and state-of-the-art laboratories was opened in November 2014 by Chief Rabbi Ephram Mervis. Dining room facilities were upgraded in 2017, along with a new 6th Form Art Studio and an expanded library. In 2018 a new Sixth Form classroom block has been opened, a completely refurbished computing suite has been installed and there have been further improvements to playgrounds and security features.

Admission (Senior School). Most boys and girls enter in September, though pupils are accepted in all three terms. Admission into the Senior School is on the basis of performance in the College's entrance examination and interview. The principal entry is at 11+, but the school considers pupils for admission at any point. A growing number of boys and girls join the College in the Sixth Form; offers of places are gained by entrance examinations and interview and are conditional upon GCSE results and suitability for A Level courses.

Admission (Preparatory School). Admission into Reception and Year 1 is on the basis of informal assessment consisting of a play session and a focus activity. For Year 2 there is a short Mathematics activity and a reading/writing task.

Fees per term (2018–2019). Senior School: £5,890; Lunch £310. Preparatory School: £3,330; Lunch £210.

Scholarships and Bursaries. Immanuel Jakobovits, Academic, Jewish Studies and Science Scholarships are awarded on a competitive basis to outstanding 11+ entrants. Exhibitions to the value of £2,000 per annum are awarded to pupils who show exceptional promise in Art and Music. Means-tested bursaries are awarded to a number of boys and girls from less affluent families who are academically and personally suited to the education the College provides.

Curriculum. The articles of the College's faith are that Jewish and secular learning shed light on one another, that the appreciation of each is deepened by study of the other, and that the life of the mind and spirit should not be compartmentalised but holistic. As such, the school offers a wide range of secular subjects, including English, Mathematics, Further Mathematics, Computing, Electronics and the Sciences, as well as Art and Design, Photography, Drama, Geography, History, French, Spanish, Modern Hebrew, Music, Personal, Social and Health Education and Physical Education. At A Level, additional subjects include Economics, Government & Politics, Media Studies and Psychology. Throughout a pupil's time at Immanuel, Jewish Studies forms part of the core curriculum. Jewish ethics, philosophy, history and religion and Israel Education are studied by way of close textual learning and through guest speakers and seminars, developing *Chochma* (wisdom) and well-founded Jewish identities. All members of the College have informal and formal opportunities to deepen their understanding of Jewish faith and practice with team members from the school's Jewish Study Centre, the Beit.

Pastoral Care. The College prides itself on attentiveness to the needs of individual pupils. The Pastoral Team includes Form Tutors and Heads of Section, who in Years 7 to 11 work under the direction of the Deputy Head for Pastoral Care and Pupil Progress. The Director of Sixth Form is in charge of a team of Form Tutors. Parental consultation evenings take place regularly. The School Council, which meets fortnightly with the Deputy Head for Pastoral Care and Pupil Progress, gives pupils the opportunity to express their views and make suggestions about further improving school life.

Religious Life. The College commemorates and celebrates landmarks in the Jewish and Israel calendar such as Purim, Chanukah, Succot and Yom Ha'atzmaut. Each January, on Holocaust Memorial Day, Lower Sixth Form students share the knowledge and insights that they have gained on their trip to Poland with pupils in the first five years of the Senior School. The College also commemorates Yom Hazikaron. Pupils attend morning and afternoon prayers on a daily basis.

The **Inclusion and Learning Support Department** supports teachers to help pupils become independent and successful learners. In addition to the programme followed by all pupils, the Department provides a range of tailored programmes to pupils whose learning needs are more specific. Pupils with a variety of learning profiles are thereby helped to develop confidence and to exceed their predictions and reach their potential.

Art, Music and Drama. The College enjoys a tradition of excellence in the visual arts (the annual Gottlieb Art Show being the highlight of the artistic year) and drama (recent school productions have included *Macbeth, An Inspector Calls, The Happiest Days of Your Life, Pygmalion, The Trojan Women, Twelfth Night, Three Sisters, Mary Poppins, My Fair Lady and Oliver*). There is a yearly Music Festival and the calendar includes a number of concerts and recitals involving soloists, ensembles and orchestra.

Games. The PE and Games staff involve pupils in activities that range from aerobics, golf, and trampolining to athletics, cricket, football, hockey, table tennis, netball, badminton and tennis. Over twenty sports clubs meet weekly. Physical Education may be studied for GCSE and A Level. Sports facilities include an all-weather surface and a fitness suite. The College has won trophies in many sporting competitions in recent years.

Enrichment activities. The many co-curricular activities on offer include opportunities for pupils to participate in leadership programmes, volunteering schemes, The Duke of Edinburgh's Award, public speaking, debating competitions and Young Enterprise. There are also clubs in areas such as philosophy, chess, art, STEM, military history, Jewish life and learning, world affairs and modern European languages.

Educational Journeys. In Year 7 pupils visit Amsterdam; in Year 8 they visit an outward bound centre in France; in Year 9 they spend three weeks in Israel; in Year 10 they visit Strasbourg and Madrid; and in the Lower Sixth they spend eight days in Poland. These experiences encourage pupils to understand themselves, bond with one another and comprehend the forces that have shaped contemporary Jewry. Photography students benefit from trips to foreign locations of great natural beauty.

Careers. The guidance provided by the College supports pupils in their research about choices beyond Immanuel. Through assemblies, the lower years are encouraged to start thinking about their own strengths and weaknesses and likes and dislikes which lead to discussions about future pathways. Even at this stage, any experience in the labour market is encouraged and supported. By the time GCSE subject choices need to be made, pupils are aware of the wider world around them and are closely monitored throughout the process. During Year 10 and Year 11, pupils make use of the weekly Careers Clinic, where they may collect information about relevant courses, one-day events and other opportunities to engage directly with people from specific areas of work. Year 11 pupils may also undertake testing by Cambridge Occupational Analysts and this, along with a personal interview after mock examinations, helps pupils and their parents to feel confident about making the right A Level choices. Pupils continue to enrol in career-specific courses and events throughout the Sixth Form, and all are welcomed to our Careers Fair.

Charitable status. Immanuel College is a Registered Charity, number 803179. It exists to combine academic excellence and Jewish tradition in a contemporary society.

The Board of Governors:
Mr Edward Misrahi, BA Econ Hons (*Co-Chairman*)
Professor Anthony Warrens, DM Oxon, PhD, FRCP, FRCPath, FEBS, FHEA (*Co-Chairman*)
Dr Daphna Atar-Zwillenberg, PhD
Mr Keith Barnett, BA Hons
Mrs Hannah Boyden, BA Hons
Mrs Lynda Dullop, BA Hons (*Director of Admissions and Operations*)
Mrs Valerie Eppel, BA Econ Hons, ACA (*Treasurer*)
Mrs Ruth Hoyland, BSc Hons (*Immanuel College Preparatory School*)
Mrs Annette Koslover, LLB Hons (*Designated Child Protection Governor*)
Mrs Erica Marks, BA Comb Hons, MBA (*Compliance*)
Ms Lucy Marks, MA
Mr Neal Menashe, CA SA
Mrs Michelle Sint, MA (*Jewish Life & Learning*)
Rabbi Eliezer Zobin, MA (*Principal*)

Rabbinic Advisor: Dayan Ivan Binstock, BSc Hons

Clerk to the Governors: Mr Antony Berkin, BA Hons, FCA (*Bursar*)

Secretary to the Governors: Mrs Elaine Essex (*Senior School Secretary, Head Master's Office*)

Head Master: Mr Gary Griffin, BA Soc Hons

Principal: Rabbi Eliezer Zobin, MA

Deputy Head, Pastoral Care and Pupil Progress: Mrs Beth Kerr, MSc, BSc Hons (*Designated Senior Person in charge of Child Protection*)

Deputy Head, Academic: Mr Barnaby Nemko, MSc, MA

Senior Leadership Team:
Mr Paul Abrahams, BA Hons (*Director of Academic Operations*)
Mr Danny Baigel, BA Hons (*Director of Jewish Education*)
Mr Antony Berkin, BA Hons, FCA (*Bursar*)
Mrs Lynda Dullop, BA Hons (*Director of Admissions and Operations*)
Mr Richard Felsenstein, BA Hons (*Assistant Head, Community & Communication*)
Mrs Jo Fleet, BA Hons (*Assistant Head, Personalisation, Transition 13–17 and Guidance*)
Mrs Alexis Gaffin, BEd Hons Cantab (*Head of Immanuel College Preparatory School*)
Ms Rachelle Hackenbroch, BA Hons (*Director of Human Resources*)
Mr Lee Rich, BA Hons (*Assistant Head, Teaching Quality and Pupil Learning*)
Mrs Sharron Shackell, BA Hons (*Assistant Head, Director of Sixth Form Studies*)

Assistant Masters and Mistresses:
* *Head of Department*

Art and Photography:
*Mrs Alison Ardeman, BA Hons
Miss Susan Ribeiro, BA Hons (*Deputy Head of Art, Marketing Executive*)
Mrs Dawn Goulde, BA Hons, MA
Mrs Bettina Jacobs, BA Hons
Mrs Lesley Peacock, BA Hons CertSocSci
Mrs Sara Dryburgh (*Art Technician*)
Mr Alex Poirier, BA Hons (*Photography and Media Technician*)
Mrs Hinda Golding (*Departmental Advisor*)

Business and Economics:
*Mr Ben Freedman, BSc Hons
Mrs Charlotte Lichman, BSc Hons (*Head of PSHEE*)

Computing:
*Mr Peter MacDonagh, MA, BSc Hons

Electronics:
*Ms Kirsti Cullen, BSc Hons

English:
*Mr Gordon Spitz, BA Hons, MA
Ms Naomi Amdurer, BA Hons (*Head of Middle School, Head of Charity & Social Action*)
Ms Laurel Endelman, BA Hons, MA (*Director of Academic Intervention*)
Mr Jonathan Kerridge-Phipps, MA (*Gifted & Talented Coordinator*)
Mrs Janine Lewinton, BA Hons (*Head of Inclusion and Learning Support*)
Mrs Anne Pattinson, BA Hons (*Assistant Head of English, Head of Upper School*)
Mr Greg Broad, MA Hons, RSA Dip TEFLA
Mrs Emma Longland, MA, BA Hons
Mrs Sarah Minde, BA Hons
Mr Ben Wolfin, BA Hons

Geography:
*Mr Lee Raby, BA Hons
Mrs Caroline Ezekiel, BSc Hons (*Key Stage Five Geography Coordinator*)
Miss Staycie Domzalski, MSc, BSc Hons

History, Government and Politics:
*Mr Geordie Raine, MA, BA Hons, BEd
Mr Barnaby Nemko, MSc, MA (*Deputy Head*: Academic)
Mr Richard Felsenstein, BA Hons (*Assistant Head, Community & Communication*)
Mr Lee Rich, BA Hons (*Assistant Head, Teaching Quality and Pupil Learning*)
Mrs Sharron Shackell, BA Hons (*Assistant Head, Director of Sixth Form Studies*)
Mrs Laura Hill, BA Hons (*i/c Government & Politics*)
Mr Liam Suter, BA Hons (*Coordinator of Enrichment, Oxbridge and Partnership*)

Jewish Education:
*Mr Danny Baigel, BA Hons (*Director of Jewish Education*)
Mr Richard Felsenstein, BA Hons (*Assistant Head, Community & Communication*)
Mr Aryeh Richman, BA Hons (*Key Stage Three Jewish Studies Coordinator, NQT Coordinator, Assistant Head of Middle School*)
Mrs Deborah Unsdorfer, BSc Hons (*Head of Lower School Jewish Studies*)
Mr Jonathan Atkins, BA Hons (*Key Stage Five Religious Studies Coordinator*)
Mr Michael Lewis, MA, BA Hons (*Jewish Enrichment Coordinator*)

Mr Bradley Conway, BA Hons
Mr Yitzy Hill, BTL
Mr David Shaw, MSc, BA Hons
Rabbi Eliezer Zobin, MA (*Principal*)
Ms Aviva Lyons, MA (*Head of Informal Education, promoting Israel Education*)
Miss Hannah Goldstein, MA (*Educational Operations Coordinator*)
Mr Marc Jacob, BA Hons (*Informal Jewish Educator*)
Mr Joseph Miller (*Informal Jewish Educator*)
Miss Talia Segal (*Informal Jewish Educator*)

Learning Support Department:
*Mrs Janine Lewinton, BA Hons (*Head of Inclusion and Learning Support*)
Mrs Vicky Arnold, BA Hons (*Assistant SENCO with responsibility for the Immanuel College Preparatory School*)
Ms Debby Benjamin
Mr Greg Broad, MA Hons, RSA Dip. TEFLA
Miss Amreen Rajulawalla, BA Hons
Mrs Rosalind Reindorp, BA Hons
Mrs Melisa Resnick, MPhil
Mrs Dawn Trober, SP LSA

Library and Independent Learning:
Mr Alex Coope, MA (*Independent Learning Coordinator*)
Mrs Laura Samuels (*Library Assistant*)

Mathematics:
*Ms Kalpana Patel, MBA, BA Hons
Mr Daniel Littlestone, MSc (*Second in Department, Head of GCSE Further Mathematics, Assistant Director of Studies*: Performance Data Management)
Mrs Orly Selouk, BEng Hons (*Key Stage Three Mathematics Advisor*)
Mrs Sara Wolman, BSc Hons (*Virtual and E Learning Coordinator*)
Mrs Ruth Davis, BA Hons (*Key Stage 5 Mathematics and Further Mathematics Coordinator*)
Mr Reza Anghaee, Msc, MA, BSc Hons
Mr Conrad Cohen, BSc Hons
Mr Peter Fleeman, BSc Hons
Dr Sapna Somani, MSc, BSc Hons
Mrs Rosina Abrahams, BSc Hons (*Mathematics Tutor*)

Media Studies:
*Mr Jonathan Meier, MA Oxon
Mrs Dawn Goulde, MBA, BA Hons

Modern Foreign Languages:
*Mrs Nicola Fahidi, BA Hons
Mr Paul Abrahams, BA Hons (*Director of Academic Operations*)
Ms Naomi Amdurer, BA Hons (*Head of Middle School, Head of Charity & Social Action*)
Ms Sarah Perlberg, BA Hons (*Head of French, Assistant Head of Upper School*)
Mrs Vardit Sadeh-Ginzburg, MA, BA Hons (*Head of Modern Hebrew*)
Mrs Lili Schonberg, BA Hons, BSc Ed Hons (*Head of Preparatory MFL*)
Mrs Claire Shooter, BA Hons (*Head of Spanish, Joint Head of Year 7 Girls*)
Mrs Deborah Clayden, BA Hons (*French and Spanish*)
Mrs Na'ama Fialkov, Montessori Certified (*Ivrit*)
Miss Dalia Freedman, BA Hons (*Spanish and French*)
Mrs Tamar Hershko, BA Hons (*Modern Hebrew*)

Performing Arts:
*Mrs Sara Green, BA Hons (*Head of Drama*) [maternity leave]
*Mr Stephen Levey, LLB Hons (*Head of Music*)

Mrs Joanna Fleet, BA Hons (*Assistant Head, Personalisation, Transition 13–17 and Guidance*)
Ms Lisa Freedman, BEd [maternity cover]
Mr Adam Gooch, BSc Hons

Peripatetic Teaching Staff:
Mrs Fella Berenblut, BA Hons (*French*)
Mrs Samantha Cooper, BA Hons (*Singing*)
Ms Helen Day, MA, BA Hons (*Mandarin*)
Mr Tomer Eden, UK Master (*Chess*)
Mr Adam Edgeworth, BA Hons (*Percussion*)
Mrs Danielle Farmer (*LAMDA and Ballet*)
Mr Lewis Fisher, BA Hons, ATCL (*Pianoforte*)
Mr Nicholas Garman, BA Hons (*Trumpet*)
Mrs Beth Greenfield, BA Hons (*Singing*)
Mr Richard Herdman, BA Hons (*Guitar & Guitar Ensemble Bass Guitar Acoustic/Electric*)
Ms Katie Jackson (*LAMDA*)
Mr Colin Lee, BSc Hons (*Chess*)
Mr Javier Moruno-Gilabert, BA Hons (*Spanish*)

Physical Education:
*Mr Philip Monaghan, BA Hons
Mrs Lorraine Conetta, BEd Hons (*Head of Girls' PE, Head of Immanuel College Preparatory School PE*)
Mrs Beth Kerr, MSc, BSc Hons (*Deputy Head, Pastoral Care & Pupil Progress*)
Mr Robert Hammond, BSc Hons (*Assistant Head of Sixth Form*)
Miss Lauren Burns, BA Hons
Mr Adam Gooch, BSc Hons
Ms Helen Lord, BSc Hons
Miss Emma Whyte, BSc Hons
Miss Emily Balsam (*Sports Assistant*)

Psychology:
*Mrs Helen Stephenson-Yankuba, BSc Hons
Mrs Melisa Resnick, MPhil

Science:
*Mr Felix Posner, BSc Hons (*Assistant Director of Studies, Timetable and Curriculum*)
Dr Ben Tabraham, MSci, PhD, BSc Hons (*Head of Chemistry*)
Mrs Vanessa McClafferty, BA Hons (*Head of Physics*)
Ms Kirsti Cullen, BSc Hons (*Head of Electronics*)
Ms Yewande Ajayi, BSc Hons, MSc
Mrs Julyanne Burgess, BSc Hons
Mrs Michelle Sacker, BSc Hons
Mr Robert Tunwell, BSc Hons (*Key Stage Three Science Coordinator*)
Mrs Camilla Turze, Bsc Hons
Mr Frank Walters, BSc Hons
Mr Ben Waterhouse, BA Hons
Mr Jonathan Fitzsimmons (*Senior Exam Invigilator, Assistant Science & Engineering Technician*)
Miss Sheena Murphy, BA Hons (*Senior Science Technician*)
Mr Muhummad Rahman, MSC, BSc Hons (*Science Technician*)

Immanuel College Preparatory School:
Mrs Alexis Gaffin, BEd Hons Cantab (*Head of Immanuel College Preparatory School, Designated Senior Person in Charge of Child Protection for Preparatory School including EYFS*)
Rabbi Moshe Braham, BSc Hons (*Deputy Head of Immanuel College Preparatory School, Director of Jewish Life and Learning*)
Ms Jacyn Fudge, BSc Hons (*Deputy Head of Immanuel College Preparatory School and Head of EYFS, Deputy Designated Senior Person in Charge of Child Protection for Preparatory School*)

Mrs Shelley Peysner, LLB Hons (*Preparatory School Administrator*)

Class Teachers:
Miss Laura Beer, BA Hons
Mrs Olivia Davies, BEd Hons [maternity cover]
Mrs Jill Ducasse, BEd Hons
Mrs Alison Gellman, BEd Hons
Mrs Lara Goldstein, BA Hons
Mrs Lucy Handelsman, BA Hons [maternity leave]
Mrs Louise Lewis, BEd Hons
Mrs Miriam Selby, MSc
Mr Jonathan Sumroy, BA Hons

Jewish Studies:
Mrs Rochel Levine
Miss Nechama Lieberman
Mrs Sarah Phillips

Modern Foreign Languages:
Mrs Lili Schonberg, BA Hons, BSc Ed Hons (*Head of Preparatory MFL*)

Music:
Mr Lewis Fisher, BA Hons, ATCL (*Pianoforte*)

Physical Education:
Mrs Lorraine Conetta, BEd Hons (*Head of Girls' PE, Head of Immanuel College Preparatory School PE*)

Teaching Assistants:
Mrs Gemma Buckland, BSc Hons
Mrs Niki Cotsen
Miss Samantha Eisner
Miss Claire Franks, BSc Hons
Mrs Naomi Goldberg, BA Hons
Mrs Nicole Greenwold, BA Hons
Miss Vanessa Lawee, BA Hons
Mrs Jane Marks
Mrs Sarah Phillips, Jewish Studies
Miss Lauren Sherman
Mrs Samantha Rosenthal

Breakfast Club Assistants:
Mrs Pam Young (*First Aid Officer*)
Mrs Annette Wright

Lunch Time/After School Assistants:
Mrs Hayley Goldman
Mrs Leila Peterman
Mrs Stephanie Posner

Safeguarding and Child Protection for Senior and Prep School:
Mrs Beth Kerr, MSc, BSc Hons (*Deputy Head (Pastoral Care & Pupil Progress) Designated Senior Person in Charge of Child Protection*)
Mrs Alexis Gaffin, BEd Hons Cantab (*Head of the Preparatory School, Designated Senior Person in Charge of Child Protection for Preparatory School including EYFS*)
Mrs Jo Fleet, BA Hons (*Assistant Head, Personalisation, Transition (13–17) and Guidance, Deputy Designated Senior Person in Charge of Child Protection for Senior School*)
Ms Jacyn Fudge, BSc Hons (*Deputy Head of Immanuel College Preparatory School and Head of EYFS, Deputy Designated Senior Person in Charge of Child Protection for Preparatory School*)
Mrs Janine Lewinton, BA Hons (*Head of Inclusion and Learning Support, Deputy Designated Senior Person in Charge of Child Protection*)

Support Staff (*Senior and Prep School*):

Administration:

Mrs Louise Cohen (*Administrative Assistant*)

Mrs Shelley Peysner, LLB Hons (*Preparatory School Administrator*)

Mrs Ann Stern (*Sixth Form Administrator*)

Mrs Lisa Fisher (*Administrative Assistant*)

Mrs Lesley Gold (*Administrative Assistant*)

Mrs Hayley Goldman (*Administrative Assistant*)

Mrs Debbie Myers, BA Hons (*Administrative Assistant*)

Admissions:

Mrs Lynda Dullop, BA Hons (*Director of Admissions and Operations*)

Mrs Celia Rabstein (*Admissions Coordinator*)

Bursary:

Mr Antony Berkin, BA Hons, FCA (*Bursar*)

Mr Davey Carmona (*Accounts Assistant Apprentice*)

Mr Navnit Popat (*Finance Officer*)

Mrs Helen Rowbottom (*Sales Ledger Administrator*)

Examinations:

Mrs Debbie Fitzsimmons (*External Examinations Administrator*)

Mr Jonathan Fitzsimmons (*Senior Exam Invigilator, Assistant Science & Engineering Technician*)

First Aid:

Mrs Pam Young (*First Aid Officer*)

Head Master's Office:

Mrs Simone Garfield (*PA to the Head Master and Deputy Heads*)

Mrs Elaine Essex (*Senior School Secretary*)

Miss Maureen O'Shea (*HR Administrator & Administrator in charge of Appointments*)

Miss Faye Westbrook, BA Hons (*Human Resources & Compliance Officer*)

Human Resources:

Ms Rachelle Hackenbroch, BA Hons (*Director of Human Resources*)

Miss Maureen O'Shea (*HR Administrator & Administrator in charge of Appointments*)

Miss Faye Westbrook, BA Hons (*Human Resources & Compliance Officer*)

IT:

Mr Ashley Shonpal, BA Hons (*IT and Communications Manager*)

Mr Pardeep Karwal (*IT Support Administrator*)

Mr Jonathan Hayward (*IT Technician*)

Marketing:

Miss Susan Ribeiro, BA Hons (*Deputy Head of Art, Marketing Executive*)

Mr Bailey Spencer (*Marketing Apprentice*)

Miss Malka Weissler (*Marketing Assistant*)

Pastoral Office:

Mrs Rochelle Freedman (*Head of Pupil Pastoral Office*)

Mrs Gemma Buckland (*Pastoral Administrator, Fridays only*)

Site Team:

Mr Gary Hanscomb (*Director of Estates*)

Mr Ronald Hanvey (*Senior Caretaker*)

Mr Luis Fidalgo (*Caretaker*)

Mr Mick Johnston (*Caretaker*)

Mr Ernest Rangarira Karumazondo (*Caretaker*)

Ipswich School

Henley Road, Ipswich, Suffolk IP1 3SG

Tel:	01473 408300
Fax:	01473 400058
email:	enquiries@ipswich.school
website:	www.ipswich.school
Twitter:	@ipswichschool

Motto: *Semper Eadem*

The School was founded in the fourteenth century by the Ipswich Merchant Guild of Corpus Christi. Its first Charter was granted by Henry VIII and this was confirmed by Queen Elizabeth I.

At Ipswich School we pride ourselves on a passion for learning, and the care and attention we give to our pupils. Through these we help our pupils to unlock their potential and develop their talents.

Ipswich School occupies an attractive site adjacent to Christchurch Park. The cricket field lies within the perimeter of the school buildings and a further two sports sites, Notcutts playing fields and Ipswich School Sports Centre (Rushmere) – with its three astroturf hockey pitches and six netball courts – are owned by the school locally.

There are 787 pupils in the Senior School (11–18), including 46 boarders. Of these, 222 boys and girls are in the Sixth Form. There are 264 pupils in the Preparatory School (2–11).

The Boarding House stands in its own grounds a short distance from the school. There is a choice of full, weekly and occasional boarding for pupils in the Senior School.

All academic subjects have been housed in new or refurbished rooms in the last few years and visitors comment on the quality of the buildings, which are grouped around one of the School's playing fields.

The Preparatory School is housed in purpose-built accommodation on an adjacent campus; it benefits from all the amenities of the Senior School including the Sports Hall, Swimming Pool, Performing Arts Centre and Playing Fields. (*For further details, see entry in IAPS section.*)

Admission. Entry to the Preparatory School after Nursery is by means of age and stage-appropriate assessments consisting of English, Mathematics, Non Verbal Reasoning and appropriate behaviour. At age 11, admission is by means of the Entrance Examination which is held at the end of January or early February. This consists of a Reasoning Test and papers in Mathematics and English. Practice papers are available and the examination is set to assess potential. At age 13, admission is by means of either the Common Entrance Examination in June or our own Entrance and Scholarship Examination in March. Admission to the Sixth Form for girls and boys from other schools is by attainment of the required grades at GCSE, a report from the previous Head and an interview in November. Application forms may be obtained from the Director of Admissions. A registration fee of £50 is payable (£25 for brothers or sisters).

Religious Education. There is religious education throughout the age range and weekly chapel services for different sections of the school; there are also occasional Chapel Services on Sundays and after School at which pupils and their parents are most welcome.

Careers. Computer analyses of interests and aptitudes complement carefully planned advice about GCSE, A Level choices, higher education and professional training. There is also a wide variety of talks, seminars and work experience options throughout the year.

Curriculum. In the Preparatory School pupils study English, Mathematics, Languages, Computing, History,

Geography, Religion, Science, Music, PE, Games, Art and Design Technology, PSHE and Outdoor Education.

Senior School pupils follow a common curriculum in the first two years with a choice between French and Spanish, plus Classical Civilisation in Year 7 and Latin in Year 8. German or Russian are introduced in Year 9. Mathematics is taken at IGCSE, one or more Modern Foreign Languages and separate Sciences are taken by all pupils to GCSE level. Apart from these compulsory subjects, pupils are examined in three other subjects chosen from French, Latin, History, Geography, German, Russian, Spanish, Drama, Design and Technology, Classical Civilisation, Art and Design, Computer Science, Philosophy, Religion and Ethics, and Music.

In the Sixth Form, A Level subjects are chosen from the following:

Mathematics, Further Mathematics, Physics, Chemistry, Biology, Latin, Classical Civilisation, Economics, Business Studies, Art, Design Technology, Music, History, Geography, English, French, German, Russian, Spanish, Psychology, PE, Philosophy, Religion and Ethics, and Theatre Studies.

In addition to their A Level studies, all Sixth Formers participate in an Enrichment Programme designed to complement and broaden the conventional curriculum. Students are also able to gain qualifications in a range of subjects such as ICT, Mandarin, Politics, Photography, Law and Spanish, and the Extended Project Qualification (EPQ).

Clubs, Trips and Activities. All are encouraged to participate in a variety of co-curricular activities which take place in lunchtimes, after school, at weekends and during the holidays. One afternoon a week is devoted to a host of community service activities, such as music and drama in the community, volunteering at local Primary schools and Special schools, journalism for internal publications, CCF (Army and RAF contingents) and a variety of sports and other pursuits. Sixth Formers may participate in the School's Leadership Programme at this time.

Drama in the school is particularly strong; continuous activity in this sphere maintains a succession of productions throughout the year, in all age groups. Productions in 2017–2018 included: *A Midsummer Night's Dream*, *She Stoops to Conquer* and *Peter Pan*.

Ipswich School's Britten Faculty of Music has an impressive reputation as a place where musicians thrive, finding unstinting support from expert staff. Opportunities abound for enjoyable music-making, including Symphony, Intermediate and Chamber Orchestras; Chapel Choir; Wolsey Consort; Show Choir; Choral Society; Intermediate String Ensemble and various Chamber Music Groups; Big Band, Stage Band and Sax Ensemble. We have an annual concert at Snape Maltings featuring ensembles from the Senior School and Prep School; our 2018 concert included John Rutter's *Gloria*, an arrangement of *Chitty Chitty Bang Bang* by Old Ipswichian Ben Parry and Rachmaninov's *Piano Concerto No. 2*. We have a popular annual music competition which culminates in a "Young Musician of the Year" final, and the Preparatory School runs its own Summer Strings course. Our annual Festival of Music brings world-renowned musicians into the school environment. Highlights of the 2018 Festival include violinist Jennifer Pipe and Alex Mendham and his Orchestra. Our state-of-the-art Music School was officially opened in March 2016 by Julian Lloyd Webber.

Duke of Edinburgh's Award. The School runs a successful Duke of Edinburgh's Award scheme. In 2018 we have a record 86 of our Year 10 pupils enter the Bronze Award. In 2018, there were also Silver expeditions to the Wye Valley and Gold expeditions to Southern Snowdonia. Some of our Gold candidates in 2018 participated in a community project in the mountains of Tajikistan, where they worked alongside their young Tajik guides in the Fann Mountains, whilst closer to home a number of our Bronze candidates undertook their volunteering in local primary schools.

Games. Our key aim is to support the development of individuals at every level, whatever their sport of choice. In line with the school's core values, our sports ethos centres around passion, potential and performance. We aim to develop an environment where athletes set realistic but challenging goals, are encouraged to be curious, creative and take risks, and are given opportunities to express themselves without fear of failure. Success is judged and celebrated not just on the outcome, but on the process and the spirit of sport. It is our goal that every pupil who participates in sport at School feels important, supported and has a sense of belonging to not just their team, but Ipswich Sport as a whole. The termly sports for boys are Rugby, Hockey and Cricket and for girls, Hockey, Netball and Cricket in the summer. These take place on our excellent Notcutts playing fields and our Sports Centre at Rushmere, which boasts 3 hybrid hockey pitches and 6 netball/tennis courts. In addition to termly sports pupils have the opportunity to be involved in a range of other sports including indoor hockey, athletics, golf, tennis, Eton fives, football, squash, sailing, badminton and swimming. Ipswich School has links with a number of external clubs and academies and we are proud of our range of sports touring opportunities on offer to our pupils.

Fees per term (2018–2019). Day: Senior School £5,193; Lower School £4,736; Preparatory School: £4,116 (Years 4–6), £4,328 (Year 3 inc lunch); Pre-Preparatory School (Reception, Years 1 & 2) £3,950 (inc lunch); Nursery (inc lunch): £34.56 (am/pm session), £65.36 (whole day).

Boarding (inclusive of tuition fees): Full Boarding: £10,057 (Years 9–13), £8,792 (Years 7 and 8); Weekly Boarding: £9,127 (Years 9–13), £8,134 (Years 7 and 8). Please note that we only accept full boarders in Year 7 and 8 under exceptional circumstances.

Scholarships. These are available for external candidates at Years 7, 9 and 12 entry.

Academic scholarships, known as Queen's Scholarships commemorating the Royal Charter granted to the School by Queen Elizabeth I in 1566, of up to half fees are awarded at Years 7 and 9 entry on the basis of examinations and an assessment visit. Art, Music and Sport scholarships are awarded at Year 7 entry. All-Rounder, Art and Music scholarships are awarded at Year 9 entry. Music and Art scholarships are awarded on the basis of excellence in these areas as demonstrated by audition or portfolio. Music auditions for promising instrumentalists entering Years 7 and 9 are held in January. Sport scholarships are awarded to pupils who will make a significant contribution to the quality of sport at the school.

Sixth Form Scholarships are awarded for academic excellence, for exceptional musical talent and for an all-rounder who will do well academically and contribute outstandingly in other areas of school life such as sport or drama. Academic Scholarships are awarded on the basis of school reports, predicted GCSE grades, interview, group activity and scholarship essay. Sixth Form Music scholarship auditions are held in November. A Sports scholarship is also available at 16. We also offer Arkwright Scholarships, which focus on Design Technology.

Awards may be supplemented by bursaries in cases of proven need.

Bursaries. These are available on a means-tested basis, up to full fee remission, for entry at 11, 13 and 16 years.

The Old Ipswichian Club. The alumni association for former pupils of Ipswich School. Annual dinners are held in London and Ipswich, and many less formal socials are held in a variety of venues each year. Sports gatherings are held for cricket, fives, golf, rugby and cross-country.

Charitable status. Ipswich School is a Registered Charity, number 310493. It exists for the purpose of educating children.

Visitor: Her Majesty The Queen

Governing Body:
H E Staunton, BA, FCA (*Chairman*)
N C Farthing, LLB, (*Vice Chairman*)
T Baxter
C D Brown, MA
W D Coe, BSc
The Revd Dr G M W Cook, MSc, PhD, FIBiol, FRSC
Mrs J Crame, BSc, ACA, PGCE
J S Davey, BA, MBA
Mrs E Garner, MEd, BA, PGCE
Dr O Goble, MBBS, DRCOG, DFFP, JCPTGP
Dr R E Gravell, PhD, BMEdSci, BSc, MRCSLT, MUKCP
E B Hyams, BScEng, ACGI, CDIPAF, MIET
C Oxborough, BSc, FCA
A C Seagers, BA
Rt Revd M A Seeley, MA, STM, Bishop of St
  Edmundsbury & Ipswich (*ex officio*)
M Taylor, BA, ACA
Dr R A Watts, MA Oxon, DM Oxon, FRCP
Dr T A H Wilkinson, MA, PhD
R P E Wilson, MA, ARCM

Headmaster: N J Weaver, BA, MA

Senior Deputy Head (*Pastoral*): Mrs A Cura, BSc
Deputy Head (*Academic*): T Allen, BSc
Head of Sixth Form: Mrs Z Austin, MA
Head of Middle School: A R Bradshaw, BA
Head of Lower School: B Cliff, MA
Chaplain: The Revd Holly Crompton-Battersby, BA, BTh

Heads of Houses:
J W Orbell, BSc
S J Blunden, BA
D J Beasant, BA
Mrs C J Ward, BSc
Ms A Caston, BSc
L Morgan, BSc

Heads of Department:
Art and Design: R J Parkin, BA
Biology: Mrs H Blee, BSc
Sixth Form Careers: A M Calver, BSc
Chemistry & Science: D J P Halford-Thompson, BSc
Classical Civilisation: Miss K Hutton, BA, MEd
Design Technology: M A J Molenaar, BEng
Drama: Mrs S Pitt, BA
Economics & Business Studies: E R Wilson, BEd
English: Ms N S Carter, BA
Geography: R G Welbourne, BA, FRGS
History: Mrs O E Tollemache, BA
Life Skills: S J Duncombe, BA
Mathematics: M J Core, BSc
Modern Languages: J A Thompson, MA
Music: Mrs B Steensma, BEd (*Acting Director of Music*)
Physical Education:
Mrs C J Chapman, BSc (*A Level PE*)
Mrs S M Carvell, BA (*Curriculum PE*)
Physics: S A Arthur, MSc, BEng
Psychology: P E Cline, MPhil
Philosophy, Religion & Ethics: Ms T Walker, MSci Ed

Head of Preparatory School: Mrs A H Childs, BA QTS,
  PGC PSE, DipEd, MA

Bursar: P Wranek, BSc, ACA

Director of Admissions: Mrs Y M Morton
Headmaster's PA: Mrs Y R Gills

James Allen's Girls' School (JAGS)

East Dulwich Grove, London SE22 8TE
Tel: 020 8693 1181
email: enquiries@jags.org.uk
website: www.jags.org.uk
Twitter: @JAGSschool
Facebook: @JAGSschool

The school was founded in 1741 and is the oldest independent girls' school in London.

JAGS is set in 22 acres of grounds in North Dulwich, with extensive playing fields and long-established Botany gardens. The school buildings include a brand new community music centre with purpose-built practice rooms, well-equipped modern library, 13 science laboratories, a purpose-built suite of language laboratories, 6 art rooms, 4 computer rooms, design technology workshops, swimming pool, floodlit artificial turf pitch, dance studio, sports hall with squash court, fitness studios and a climbing wall and a professionally-managed theatre. The Sixth Form Centre has its own tutorial rooms, common rooms and lecture theatre.

There is a five-form entry at 11 and JAGS senior school has approximately 800 pupils with 200 in the Sixth Form. About a third of girls come up from our junior department, James Allen's Preparatory School (qv) with about two-thirds entering from other preparatory and state primary schools.

Girls follow a broad curriculum with a wide choice of GCSE/IGCSE options, structured to ensure a balanced programme. A Level courses are available in all the usual subjects as well as Classical Civilisation, Greek, Latin, Russian, Spanish, Italian, Japanese, Economics, Philosophy, Physical Education, Politics, Music and Theatre Studies. Art is a particular strength throughout the school. The Pre-U English course is followed.

The extracurricular programme is a key part of the JAGS education. The excellent Prissian Theatre enables first-class, full-scale drama productions, while the active music department plays a central role, offering some 30 ensembles including 6 choirs, 4 orchestras, brass ensembles, wind ensembles plus jazz and big bands. A great variety of other interests is encouraged, from The Duke of Edinburgh's Award, debating, photography, and the Literary Society, to Politics and Amnesty International. Study visits to Russia, France, Germany, Italy, and Spain are regularly organised. The choirs, orchestras and sports teams also visit overseas. Community Action plays an important part in school life, and there are extensive partnership activities with other local schools and community groups.

Sports: Hockey, netball, football, aerobics, basketball, gymnastics, dance, tennis, rounders, swimming, athletics and self-defence are taught in the curriculum, with opportunities for yoga, fencing, rugby, badminton, sailing, ice skating and golf.

Individual lessons in Instrumental Music and Speech and Drama are available (fees on application).

Fees per term (2018–2019). £5,997.

Admission. Girls are mainly admitted at 11+ and also into the Sixth Form. Casual vacancies at other ages. Registration fee: £100.

Entrance Examination. Every candidate for admission will be required to pass a pre-selection assessment and an entrance examination. For details and method of admission, please visit www.jags.org.uk.

Scholarships and Bursaries. Up to twenty Academic Scholarships are awarded every year to girls of 11 years of age on entry to the School. There are also Scholarships on entry into the Sixth Form. Scholarships are awarded for academic ability, but are also available for Music, Sport and Art up to a potential value of £4,000 per annum. Music Scholarships are on the same basis as academic scholarships but also include instrument tuition. Candidates must satisfy the academic requirements of the school and pass an audition. All Scholarships are augmented by a means-tested element where there is need.

Following the demise of the Government Assisted Places Scheme, the School has introduced James Allen Bursaries to continue to enable talented girls from families of all backgrounds to enter JAGS. Fee support up to 100% is available and the average for all pupils receiving bursaries is well over 80% of fees covered.

Charitable status. James Allen's Girls' School is a Registered Charity, number 1124853 and exists for the purpose of educating girls.

Governors:
Mrs Frances Read, MA Cantab, FCA, MSI (*Chair*)
Mrs Alison Fleming, BA Hons, MA Ed, PGCE
Mrs Geraldine McAndrew, BA Hons Sussex, CQSW Herts
Dr Jane Marshall, MB BCh, BAO Hons, DCH, MRCP, MRCPsych & FRCPsych
Mr David Miller, MA, FCSI
Ms Helen Nixseaman, MA, FCA
Mrs Jane Onslow, MA
Dame Erica Pienaar, BA Hons, MBS, FRSA
Mr Simon Smith, BA Hons, Dip Arch, ARB, RIBA
The Hon Dr Rema Kaur Wasan, MA Cantab, MBBS Lon, MRCP, FRCR UK
Mr Nick Wood, MA

Director of Operations & Clerk to the Governors: Mrs Justine Addison, MA Northumbria

Headmistress: Mrs Sally-Anne Huang, MA Oxford, MSc

Deputy Head, Academic: Laurence Wesson, BSc Hons London (*Biology*)

Deputy Head, Pastoral: Samantha Payne, BA Hons Central St Martins (*Art*)

Assistant Head, Head of Extra & Co-Curricular Activities: Miss Fiona Murray, BEd Hons London (*PE*)

Assistant Head, Head of Schools Partnership: Mr Robert Wallace, MA Birmingham, MBA Nottingham (*DT*)

Assistant Head, Head of Teaching & Learning: Mrs Alice Mollinson, MA Hons Edinburgh

Assistant Head, Head of Sixth Form: Mr Matthew Weeks, MA Hons Oxford (*Geography*)

Assistant Head, Head of Years 10 and 11: Mrs Anna Jones, BA Hons Nottingham (*English*)

Assistant Head, Head of Years 7–9: Miss Rhona Muir, MA Oxford (*Philosophy, Politics and Economics*)

Head of Year 13: Dr Anna Parrish, BSc Hons Loughborough, PhD Exeter (*Chemistry*)
Head of Year 12: Miss Rachel Barnes, BA Hons Belfast (*Religious Studies*)
Head of Year 11: Mr Isaac Burrows, BSc Hons Bristol (*Biology*)
Head of Year 10: Miss Gina Thomson
Head of Year 9: Miss Nicki Roden, BSc Hons Bristol (*Biology*)

Head of Year 8: Mrs Luisa Alonso, BA Hons Durham (*Spanish*)
Head of Year 7: Mrs Marta Totten, MA Bergamo (*Italian*)

Art:
Ms Sarah Vanderpump, BA Newcastle (*Head of Art*)
Ms Rose Aidin, BA Hons East Anglia, MA London (*History of Art*)
Mr Andrew Carter, BA Hons, Central St Martins
Mrs Katharine Firth, BA Hons CNAA
Mrs Chantal Gilou, BA Hons Norwich
Ms Samantha Payne, BA Hons Central St Martins
Ms Irene Riddell, BA Hons Glasgow
Mr John Luttick (*Art Technician*)

Classics & Philosophy:
Miss Rachel Hyde, BA Hons Oxford (*Head of Classics*)
Mrs Rachel Marshall, MA Oxford (*Head of History of Art*)
Mrs Saltanat Hanif, BA Hons Cambridge
Mrs Sonia McGarr, BA Hons KCL
Dr Howard Peacock, BA Hons Oxon, MPhil London, PhD UCL

Drama:
Mrs Joanna Billington, BA Hons Middlesex (*Director of Drama*)
Rebecca Wilson, Director in Residence
Miss Emma Copland, Drama Teacher, BA Hons Belfast, MA Birmingham
Mrs Jessica Drucker, BA Hons Hull
Ms Louise Roberts, BA Hons Leeds
Mr Tim Crowther, BA Hons Mountview Academy of Theatre Arts, MA Goldsmiths
Mr Simon Jermond, BA Middlesex
Olivia Hutchinson, BA Hons Royal Central School of Speech and Drama
Miss Lindsey McDonald (*Performing Arts Assistant*)
Mrs Jordan Richardson-Smith (*Technical Theatre Manager*)

English:
Dr Matthew Edwards, BA Hons, PhD Bristol (*Head of English*)
Ms Katherine Bishop, BA Hons Cambridge
Ms Melanie Duignan, MA Manchester
Mrs Rachel Edwards, BA Hons Cambridge
Mrs Catherine Ferrar, MA Cambridge
Mrs Alison Holmes-Milner, BA Hons York
Mrs Anna Jones, BA Hons Nottingham
Miss Jane Quarmby, BA Hons Bristol
Miss Rachel Wilkinson, BA Hons Ulster
Ms Reesa Amadeo, MA King's College London (*EAL*)

Humanities:
Mrs Monica Buckley, MA Oxon (*Head of History & Politics*)
Mrs Amy Meachan, BSc UCL (*Head of Economics*)
Mrs Deborah Lewis, BA Hons Sheffield (*Head of Religious Studies*)
Mrs Emma Bailey, BA Hons Newcastle (*Head of Geography*)
Mrs Alice Mollison, MA Hons Edinburgh (*Geography*)
Ms Verity Aylward, BA Hons Leicester (*History & Politics*)
Miss Rachel Barnes, BA Hons Belfast (*Religious Studies*)
Mr Jonathan Chesterman, BA Hons King's College London (*Modern History*)
Mrs Rachel Duke, BA Hons King's College London (*Religion Philosophy and Ethics*)
Dr Mark Fowle, MA & BA Hons Sheffield, PhD Warwick (*History & Politics*)
Mrs Elizabeth Gerhardt, BA Hons London (*History & Politics*)

Mrs Imogen Mules, BSc Hons Leeds (*Geography*)
Mr Matthew Weeks, MA Hons Oxford (*Geography*)
Miss Rachel Wilson, BA Hons King's College London
  (*Geography*)
Dr Hannah Robinson, BA Hons Northwood (*Religious
  Studies*)
Mrs Julie Adabie, BTh Hons Westminster College
  (*Religious Studies*)
Ms Ceri Blunden, BA Hons York (*History*)
Mr Tom Cannon, BA Hons Nottingham Trent (*Economics*)
Mr Jon Davies, BA Hons Oxford (*History*)

Languages:
Ms Cristina Sanchez-Satoca, BA Hons Barcelona, MA
  London (*Head of Spanish, Head of Modern Languages*)
Mr Arvind Arora, Staatsexamen Germany (*Head of
  German*)
Mrs Giulia Marchini, Dottoressa Bari (*Head of Italian*)
Mrs Claire Gene, License LCA Paris (*Head of French*)
Mrs Laurence Arora, BA, MA & DEUG UCO (*French*)
Mrs Sally George, MA London, BA Hons London (*Head of
  Russian*)
Mrs Ksenia Wesson, BEd Hons Krasnoyarsk (*Russian*)
Mr Timothy Billington, BA Hons London (*German, ICT*)
Ms Georgina Legg, BA Hons Sussex (*French*)
Ms Lorna Macleod, MBA Warwick, BA Hons Bristol
  (*French*)
Ms Lola Merino, BSc Hons London (*Spanish*)
Mr Hiroshi Okura, BA Waseda (*Japanese*)
Mme Charline Reddihough, Licence-Maîtrise Strasbourg
  (*French*)
Mr Jerome Roussel, Licence France (*French*)
Mrs Marta Totten, BA Hons Bergamo (*Italian*)

Mathematics:
Mrs Natalie Plant, BSc Hons Bristol (*Head of
  Mathematics*)
Ms Sara Glover, BSc London
Ms Antonia Buccheri, BSc Hons Manchester
Mrs Olivia Hamidzadeh, BSc Hons Cardiff
Miss Jessica Higgit, BSc Cardiff
Mrs Jessica Millar, BSc Nottingham
Miss Rhona Muir, MA Oxford
Mr John Pattison, BSc Hons Newcastle, MA Lancaster
Mrs Lucy Rose, BSc Hull, BA Hons, MA London
Mrs Tracey Walton, MA Cantab
Mrs Catherine Winter, BSc Hons Bristol

Music:
Mr Peter Gritton, BA Hons Cambridge (*Director of Music*)
Mrs Samantha Clare-Hunt (*Music Coordinator*)
Miss Elinor Corp, BA Hons Bristol, MA (*Deputy Head of
  Music*)
Ms Kay Dickson, GRSM, Dip RCM London (*Head of
  Strings*)
Dr Jonathan Lee, BA Hons & MA Chichester, PhD Exeter
Mr Andrew Tait, MA Middlesex, MMus London
Mr Anthony Noonan (*Music Technician*)

PE:
Danielle Mugridge, BA Hons Chichester (*Head of PE*)
Mr Jonathan Baxter, BMus Middlesex, Academy of
  Contemporary Music (*Hockey*)
Miss Wendy Johnson, BEd Hons London
Mrs Leanne King, BSc St Mary's University College
  Ireland, PGCE Physical Education London Metropolitan
Miss Fiona Murray, BEd Hons London
Miss Gina Thomson, BA Hons Brighton
Ms Camilla Byron (*PE Technician*)

Science:
Miss Natalie Davidson, MChem Durham (*Head of
  Chemistry*)
Mrs Nicola Halewood, BSc Plymouth (*Head of Biology*)
Mr Andrew Hicklenton, BSc Hons Southampton (*Head of
  Physics*)
Mr Christopher Adams, BSc Hons KCL (*Physics*)
Mrs Deborah Bicknell, BSc Hons, Durham, MBA
  Nottingham (*Biology*)
Mr Isaac Burrows, BSc Hons Bristol (*Biology*)
Mr Stuart Byfield, BSc Hons London (*Biology*)
Miss Hedy Canessa, BSc Southampton (*Physics*)
Mr Paul Davies, BSc Hons Newcastle (*Physics*)
Mr Dominic Gillespie, BSc Manchester (*Physics*)
Miss Yihuan Huang, MSci Imperial College (*Chemistry*)
Ms Tasha Jovanovic-Callaghan, BSc Hons Former
  Yugoslavia (*Chemistry*)
Dr Anna Parrish, BSc Loughborough, PhD Exeter
  (*Chemistry*)
Mrs Andrée Roberts, BSc Hons London (*Microbiology*)
Miss Nicola Roden, BSc Hons Bristol (*Biology*)
Mr Laurence Wesson, BSc Hons London (*Biology*)
Ms Natasha Jovanovic-Callaghan, BSc Hons Belgrade
  (*Chemistry*)
Mrs Lucy Bond, BSc Hons Exeter (*Biology*)
Mr Matthew Stamp, BSc Hons KCL (*Pharmacology*)
Mrs Reema Hooks, MSci ICL (*Chemistry*)
Mrs Christine Bobrowicz, HNC Applied Biology (*Biology
  Technician*)
Miss Pamela Kettle, BTEC Science (*Science Technician*)
Mr Kevyn Knight, BSc Hons Thames Poly (*Chemistry
  Technician*)
Mr Mark Standing, BSc Hons Thames (*Physics
  Technician*)
Ms Elisabeth Temuena, BSc Hons Imperial (*Science
  Technician*)
Mrs Sylvia Thompson, HND Microbiology (*Biology
  Technician*)

Technology:
Miss Louise Cook, BA Hons Wolverhampton (*Head of
  Technology*)
Dr Bose Onifade, BSc Hons Birmingham (*Head of
  Computing*)
Ms Lara Brookes, BEng Hons London
Ms Paula McCormick, BA Hons London
Mr Robert Wallace, MA Birmingham, MBA Nottingham
Mr Andrew House (*Design & Technology Technician*)

SENCO:
Years 7 & 8: Mrs Joyce Hepher, BEd Hons, Dip SpLD,
  CCET, ACC
Years 9 – 13: Mrs Catherine Winter, BSc Hons Bristol
  (*Mathematics*)

IT Support:
Mr Daniel Szenasi-Holland, BA Hons Leeds
Mr Joe Williams
Mr Dominic Hurley-McBean

Librarians:
Mrs Elen Curran, BA Hons Reading, Dip Lib, MCLIP
Mrs Nel Yiend, BA Hons Exeter, ACILIP
Mrs Susan Stacey, BA Hons Manchester
Mrs Sue Stevens (*Library Assistant*)

Administration & Secretarial:
Mrs Elizabeth Allan, BSc Hons London (*Assistant to the
  Head of Sixth Form & Higher Education Coordinator*)
Mrs Christine Allen (*SLT Administrator*)
Mrs Helen Careswell, BSc Hons York (*PA to the
  Headmistress*)

Miss Henrietta Smith, BA Hons Warwick (*PA to the Director of Operations & Clerk to the Governors*)
Ms Joan Dwyer (*Trips Administrator*)
Mrs Buffy Handslip, BA Hons Leeds (*Assistant Registrar*) [Maternity Leave]
Mrs Tricia Jannaway, BA Hons Middlesex (*Acting Registrar*) [Maternity Cover]
Mrs Sejal Joshi, Dip Hons Gujarat, India (*Data Administrator*)
Mrs Henrietta Kiezun, BA Hons Keele (*Registrar*)
Mrs Meg Douglas (*Pupil Coordinator & Attendance Administrator*)
Ms Toni Smith (*Staff Resources Administrator*)
Miss Ayesha Ellis (*Sixth Form Administrator*)
Mrs Tina Robinson Rising (*PA to the Deputy Head, Pastoral*)

School Nurses:
Mrs Karen Cattanach, RGN
Mrs Helen Mandefield-Chang, RGN
Mrs Charlotte Thornton (*School Nurse*)

Bursary:
Mr Kevin Barry, ACA (*Financial Controller*)
Mr Nazir Badshah, BA Hons London (*School Accountant*)
Mrs Samantha Dock (*Finance Manager*)
Purchase Ledger Clerks: Mrs Sarah Hand and Miss Laura Rance

Human Resources & Finance:
Mrs Sabrina Deacon (*HR Manager*)
Mr Adrian Gibbs (*HR Assistant*)
Mr Nazir Badshah, BA Hon London (*School Accountant*)
Mrs Samantha Dock (*Finance Manager*)
Mrs Sarah Hand and Miss Laura Rance (*Purchase Ledger Clerks*)

Communications, Marketing and PR:
Mrs Jo Denham, BA Hons (*Marketing Manager*)
Miss Kate Cheshire (*Marketing Coordinator*)
Mr Joe Ridge, BA Hons York (*Marketing & Communications Coordinator*)

Reception:
Ms Lucy Geoghegan
Mrs Rebecca Goddard

Facilities & Estates Department:
Mr Simon Willoughby (*Facilities and Estates Manager*)
Mr Nar Sunar (*Residential Security Officer*)
Mr Buddhi Lal Gaha (*Security Officer*)
Mr Bert Kingsford (*Maintenance Assistant*)
Mr Dmitrijs Gorbacovs (*Multi Skilled Engineer*)

Schoolkeeping Department:
Mr Robert Thompson (*Head Schoolkeeper*)
Mr James Norris
Mr Michael Norris
Mr Luis Cagica
Mrs Christine Rousseaux
Mr Jim Stevens
Mr Keith Van Ackeren

Grounds Department:
Mr Peter Hammer (*Head Groundsman*)
Mr Jamie Adams (*Deputy Head Groundsman*)
Mrs Jennifer Morriss
Mr Ian Hanks (*Assistant Grounds Person*)

Botany Gardens Manager: Mr David Benson, BSc Hons Reading

Catering:
Mr Martin Benson (*Catering Manager*)
Mr Richard Thompson (*Head Chef*)

Pastoral:
Reverend Cecile Schnyder (*School Chaplain*)
Meg Douglas (*Pupil Attendance & Pastoral Support Administrator*)

Charity:
Reesa Amadeo Wolf, MA KCL, EAL (*Head of Community and Charity*)

The John Lyon School

Middle Road, Harrow-on-the-Hill, London HA2 0HN
Tel: 020 8515 9400
Fax: 020 8515 9455
email: admissions@johnlyon.org
website: www.johnlyon.org
Twitter: @JohnLyonHarrow
Facebook: @JohnLyonHarrow
LinkedIn: /johnlyonharrow

Motto: Stet Fortuna Domus

John Lyon is an academically selective independent boys' day school, based in Harrow-on-the-Hill in North West London.

Academic excellence is at the very heart of what the School achieves for the 600 boys who study there. Pupils gain a good grounding in all the major academic subjects. Dedicated teachers work to develop learning skills, creativity and the ability to apply their learning in all areas of life. Building on this platform, boys perform well from the point they join – whether at age 11, 13 or 16 – and achieve excellent results in public examinations at GCSE and A Level. Most students gain places at leading UK universities and then move on into the workplace in a huge and varied range of valued professions.

A John Lyon boy also gains from his time outside the classroom. In particular, there is a strong and growing reputation for Music, Art, Drama and Sport. Add to this an exciting Co-Curricular timetable focusing on each boy's sense of community, achievement and wellbeing, a range of more than 70 extra-curricular activities, and pastoral care that is second to none, John Lyon is a school designed to nurture high-achieving and happy boys.

Admission. John Lyon offers a broad education to pupils who aspire to achieve excellence in all they do. As such, the admissions procedure is designed both to reveal applicants' ability as well as to judge their potential. The School offers places to able young pupils who have a great attitude to learning combined with a desire to be the best that they can be.

Pupils typically join John Lyon in Years 7, 9 and the Lower Sixth, largely from a North West London catchment area including Harrow, Wembley, Stanmore, Pinner, Watford, Rickmansworth, Northwood, Ruislip, Hillingdon, Uxbridge, Ickenham, Northolt, Southall, Ealing, Acton, Edgware, Brent Cross, Finchley, Barnet, Camden, Westminster, Kensington & Chelsea, Hammersmith & Fulham, as well as other parts of Middlesex, Berkshire, Buckinghamshire and Hertfordshire.

The School prides itself in its welcoming and helpful approach to admissions, for boys at 11+, 13+ and at 16+ into the Sixth Form.

11+ selection is based on English and Mathematics examinations, participation in a group activity and an interview. 13+ selection includes examinations in English, Mathematics, French and Science, as well as an interview with the Head. 16+ entry is by interview and results at GCSE.

Curriculum. The Academic curriculum is at the very heart of everything at John Lyon. A School day is made up of six to eight periods, with lessons of either 40 or 60 minutes, depending on year group and subject. This well-structured curriculum means that lesson length is tailored to the requirements of that subject and year group. It also means that John Lyon is not an environment where bells mark the change of lessons.

Different year groups will follow different daily routines. Boys are taught the importance of self-management and good timekeeping, and are entrusted to move themselves around the School site quietly and efficiently.

Scholarships. All pupils who join at 11+ an 13+ will be considered for an Academic Scholarship. Their performance in the entrance examination, their school reference and their interview will all be taken into consideration. Sixth Form Scholarships are awarded dependent on GCSE results.

John Lyon also awards a small number of scholarships to candidates of outstanding ability and potential in Drama, Music and Sport. Scholarships normally provide for between £500 and £2,000 of the tuition fees each year.

Bursaries. John Lyon is committed to widening access for local families, enabling the children of those who could not otherwise afford the fees to benefit from an all-round independent school education. This corresponds to the original intention of John Lyon, who, when he founded Harrow School in 1572, stated that he wished to provide an education for children in the parish. Each year, the School makes available a proportion of means-tested bursaries to pupils who demonstrate exceptional talent and potential.

School Buildings. The School buildings are on the west side of Harrow-on-the-Hill and include a range of facilities. Additions and investment are regularly undertaken, according to a ten-year Estates Strategy. The main School buildings house the Science laboratories, Drama studios, Art studios, gallery and the Boyd Campbell Hall. The Music School has a 120-seater recital hall, a recording studio and eight individual practice studios. The Sports complex comprises a 25-metre indoor swimming pool, fitness studio and sports hall.

Games. A floodlit multi-use games area opened in 2016 allowing for all-weather Hockey and Tennis at the 25-acre Sudbury Playing Fields, a short distance from the main School site. There are four main cricket squares, seven football pitches, a challenge course, pavilion and archery range. In addition, the School can access the sporting facilities of Harrow School including Cricket nets, an Athletics track, a nine-hole Golf course, Tennis, Squash and Badminton courts.

The main Sports are Association Football and Hockey in the Autumn and Spring Terms, and Cricket, Athletics, Tennis and Swimming in the Summer Term, supported by Badminton, Basketball, Archery, Water Polo, Squash and other games. PE and Swimming are in the curriculum.

Co-Curricular Programme. On Friday afternoons at John Lyon all pupils put their Academic timetables to one side and participate in the School's broad, engaging and fascinating Co-Curricular Programme.

The Co-Curricular Programme offers something different to pupils beyond the classroom and is aimed at developing a sense of achievement, wellbeing and enjoyment, while gaining practical skills and engaging with the eight School Values.

During the Autumn and Spring Terms, boys in Years 7 and 8 engage in a bespoke carousel of activities before undertaking a larger project in Summer Term.

For boys in Years 9 to Upper Sixth, there is an hour of mandatory activities in Autumn and Spring Terms, followed by an hour of an activity of their choice selected from a large list of options. The Summer Term focuses on wider projects and preparation for exams and university for the older students.

Extra-Curricular Programme. John Lyon's Extra-Curricular Programme of sports practices, clubs and activities is a much-loved element of School life, aimed at encouraging curiosity, furthering knowledge and nurturing passions outside the timetable.

The Programme is second to none and allows every boy to flourish as an individual. The School believes that activities beyond the classroom are essential to balance the learning in class. They teach resilience, teamwork and leadership, and are seen by many as a distinguishing feature on a university application form and then on a CV. But above all, a well-rounded pupil is a happy pupil.

The School typically offers more than 50 clubs and societies every week (including the Duke of Edinburgh's Award and CCF) that provide a wealth of skills, experiences and opportunities to every pupil, as well as a host of sports practices, which change seasonally.

Charity and Community. The charitable ethos that has run through John Lyon since its founding in 1876 shows no sign of slowing, and this generation of pupils, like their predecessors, engage in numerous charitable and community projects, giving time and raising money for projects in Harrow and beyond.

John Lyon's public benefit objectives are to support the wider community through the sharing of expertise and facilities in sport, the arts and academia. The School has strong links with schools in the maintained sector, who regularly join events; facilities are used by local schools and community groups; pupils raise significant sums for local, national and international charities; access to a John Lyon education is widened through scholarship and bursary awards; and pupils are seen out in the community all year round, giving their time to local initiatives.

The School is part of the John Lyon Foundation, an educational foundation also consisting Harrow School and John Lyon's Charity. The Foundation aims to maximise the opportunities for children and young people by enabling them to realise their potential, broaden their horizons and ultimately enable them to experience and enjoy a better quality of life.

Careers. Specialist advice concerning entrance to Higher Education is given and there is a team of specialists in the Sixth Form Centre to offer guidance and support with UCAS, University choices and careers. Morrisby testing is undertaken.

Entry to University. 2018 University destinations include Oxford, Cambridge, KCL, UCL, LSE, Imperial, Durham, Manchester, Warwick, Bristol, Southampton and Exeter. 44 per cent of students went to a Russell Group University. One in five students went to the University of London.

The Lyonian Association. All boys on leaving the School from the Sixth Form become life members of the Association. The Association has shared use of the School's sports ground, and its own pavilion, at Sudbury Fields.

Fees per term (2018–2019). Years 7 to 11: £6,194 (including lunch); Sixth Form: £5,966 (lunch optional).

Charitable status. The Keepers and Governors of the Free Grammar School of John Lyon is a Registered Charity, number 310033. The purpose of the charity is the education of boys living within reach of Harrow between the ages of 11–18.

Governors:
Mr G Goodfellow, QC, MA, LLM (*Chairman*)
Mr J H Dunston, MA, ACIL, FRSA (*Deputy Chairman*)
[OL]
Professor J S Chadha, BSc Econ, MSc Econ [OL]

Mr R M Fox, LLB Hons [OL]
Mr G Stavrinidis, BSc Eng, MBA, DipM [OL]
Dr S Jollyman, MBChB, MRCGP
Mr I Kendrick, BEd Hons, MA
Mr D Tidmarsh, BSc Hons, PGCE
Mr J Graham, BSc Hons, MRICS [OL]
Mr L Halligan, MPhil Econ, BSc Hons [OL]
Mr N Enright, MA Oxon, MBA, NPQH, FRSA [OL]
Mrs M Beresford-Smart
Mr R Winter, CBE, FCA
Mr A Smith, BA, Dip RAM, ARAM
Mrs C Southgate, B Bus Acc, FCA

Clerk to the Board of Governors: The Hon Andrew C
   Millett, MA [OL]

[OL] *Old Lyonian*

Head: **Miss K E Haynes**, BA Warwick, MEd
   Birmingham, NPQH

Deputy Heads:
Mr J O M Pepperman, MA Cantab
Mr A J Sims, MA, MEng Cantab

Senior Teachers:
Mr D P Boylan, BEd Queen's Belfast (*Admissions*)
Mr T Lewis, MA, MEng Cantab (*Director of Studies*)
Mr I R Parker, BSc Loughborough (*Co-Curricular*)
Mr J C Rowe, MA UEA (*Head of Sixth Form*)
Mr A S Westlake, BA Southampton, BA Bristol, MA
   King's College London (*Staff*)

Kelvinside Academy

33 Kirklee Road, Glasgow G12 0SW

Tel: 0141 357 3376
Fax: 0141 357 5401
email: rector@kelvinsideacademy.org.uk
website: www.kelvinsideacademy.org.uk
Twitter: @KAGlasgow
Facebook: /KelvinsideAcademy

Motto: AIEN APIΣTEYEIN

The Academy was founded in 1878. Since May 1921, it
has been controlled by the Kelvinside Academy War Memorial Trust, which was formed in memory of the Academicals
who gave their lives in the War of 1914–18. The affairs of
the Trust are managed by a Board of Governors, mainly
composed of Academicals and parents.

Kelvinside Academy is a co-educational day school for
some 580 pupils, aged 3 to 18.

The main building is in neo-classical style and Grade A
listed but has been extensively modernised within. Further
buildings and extensions provide excellent facilities for all
subjects and interests, and are symptomatic of the school's
progressive approach. Recent additions include state-of-the-
art IT and multimedia suites, custom-built nursery, library
upgrade and sports pavilion.

Curriculum. Junior School pupils (from J1) benefit from
specialist input in Art, Music, PE and Modern Languages.
The Senior Prep (P7) year is a transitional year with a core
curriculum taught by the class teacher but science, languages, art, music and PE are delivered by secondary specialists. Computing is a core compulsory subject up to S4.

Senior 3 and 4 pupils follow eight National 4 or 5
courses, followed by Higher and Advanced Higher courses
in Senior 5 and 6.

Combined Cadet Force. The hugely popular CCF is
compulsory for one year in Senior 3. Pupils embark upon
The Duke of Edinburgh's Award scheme at this stage.

Games. Rugby and hockey are the principal team games
in the winter terms with athletics, tennis and cricket in the
summer. A range of additional sports and games, from football to basketball and dance, is offered.

Activities. A rich programme of extracurricular and
House activities contributes significantly to the broad educational experience enjoyed by all pupils.

The Expressive Arts. Music, drama, dance and the
visual arts have a central role in both the curriculum and the
co-curriculum.

Fees per term (2018–2019). Nursery £820–£3,060,
Junior School £2,665–£3,995, Senior School £3,995–
£4,220.

Admission. For Nursery and P1, children undergo an
informal assessment. For P2 to Senior 3, children sit an
entrance test and informal interview. For Senior 4 to Senior
6, entry is by interview, school report and exam results.

Bursaries. Financial support with fees (ranging from
10%–100%) is available to P7 and Senior School pupils.

Charitable status. The Kelvinside Academy War
Memorial Trust is a Registered Charity, number SC003962.
The purpose of the Trust is to run a combined primary and
secondary day school in memory of those former pupils of
the school who gave their lives in the war of 1914–18.

Board of Governors:
Mr D Wilson, BAcc, CA (*Chairman*)
Mr A Martin (*ex officio*)
Professor W Cushley, BSc, PhD, FSB
Mr C J Mackenzie, LLB, Dip LP, NP
Mrs A McDowall, LLB Hons, Dip LP
Mr H Ouston, MA
Mr A Palmer, BAcc, CA
Mrs J Rowand, FIRP
Mrs S Taylor
Mr D Morwood
Mrs J MacGeachy
Mrs N Hinde
Mr Mel Scott
Mrs S Taylor

Rector: **Mr I H Munro**

Deputy Rector: Mr D J Wyatt
Academic Deputy: Miss L A Thrippleton
Assistant Deputy: Mr J I Cuthbertson
Head of E-Learning and Professional Development: Mrs J
   Maclean
Head of Support for Learning: Mrs L Harkins

Head of Senior 6: Ms D Gallacher
Head of Senior 5: Mr C Simpson
Head of Senior 4: Mrs L Harkins
Head of Senior 3: Mr B FitzGerlad
Head of Senior 2: Miss M Orr
Head of Senior 1: Mrs F Kennedy

House Staff:
Buchanan: Mrs F Cafolla
Colquhoun: Mrs L FitzGerald
MacGregor: Mrs F Kennedy
Stewart: Miss L Preston

Enterprise Coordinator: Mrs J Shields

Faculty of Language (*English, Modern Languages*):
Mr D Miller (*Head of Faculty*)
Mrs A Mullan (*Deputy Head of Faculty*)
Mrs H Jephson
Mr D O'Neil

Miss M Orr
Miss L Preston
Ms D Gallacher
Mc C Winning

Faculty of Maths, Science and Technology (Maths, Physics,
Chemistry, Biology, Computing):
Mr M Smith (*Head of Faculty*)
Mrs L Hartley (*Deputy Head of Faculty*)
Mr S H Connor
Mr J Cuthbertson
Miss S Edmond
Mrs L C FitzGerald
Mr B FitzGerald
Mrs A Gess
Mr G Guile
Mr I Nicholson
Miss L Thrippleton
Mr C Watts
Mr K Mason

Faculty of Social and Business Studies (History,
Geography, Modern Studies, Business Subjects,
Religious Education):
Mrs J Clark (*Head of Faculty*)
Mr J Calder (*Deputy Head of Faculty*)
Mrs J Hannah
Miss D Laverick
Mrs N Mathews
Mrs B Meikle
Mr N Reid
Mrs J Shields
Mr C Simpson
Mr J Smith

Faculty of Expressive Arts (Art & Design, Music, Drama):
Mrs J Cunningham (*Head of Faculty, Director of Music*)
Mrs J Hardy (*Deputy Head of Faculty*)
Mirs C Campbell
Mrs A Gallie
Mrs S Gillan
Mrs A H M Schneeberger
Ms J Sampaio

Faculty of PE, Games & Extracurricular (Games, PE,
Outdoor Education, Extracurricular):
Mr D J Wilson (*Head of Faculty, Director of Games*)
Mrs F Cafolla
Mr C J Lawson
Mr G Mercer
Miss H Lang
Miss R Currie

Teachers of Senior Prep:
Mrs F Kennedy
Mrs C Milne
Mr N Armet

Support for Learning (SfL):
Mrs L Harkins (*Head of Department*)
Mrs N Anderson
Miss H MacLeod
Ms J Thomson (*ESOL*)

SQA Coordinator: Mrs C Campbell

Librarians:
Ms S Tipping
Ms S McLay

Duke of Edinburgh's Award Coordinator: Mr N Reid

Head of Junior School: Mrs L MacBeath

Junior School Class Teachers:
Junior 1A: Mrs L McColl, Mrs L Hill

Junior 2A: Mrs Henderson
Junior 3A: Mrs E Laird-Jones, Mrs L Hill
Junior 4A: Mrs S Rodger, Mrs G Roberson
Junior 5A: Mrs A Stevenson
Junior 5B: Mrs A McAllister
Junior 6A: Mrs S Paterson
Junior 6B: Mrs G Flanigan

Teachers with a specific remit:
Senior Teacher, Upper Primary: Mrs S Paterson
Senior Teacher, Early Years/Transition: Mrs L McColl
Senior Teacher, J2–J3: Mrs E Laird-Jones

Nursery Staff:
Head of Early Years Education: Mrs T Nugent
Nursery Head (Balgray): Miss P Argue
Nursery Head (Green Forest): Mrs J Hartley
Early Years Practitioner: Mrs J Pettigrew
Early Years Practitioner: Mrs G Stewart
Early Years Practitioner: Miss M McNeil
Early Years Practitioner: Miss D Mardon
Early Years Practitioner: Miss S Singleton
Early Years Practitioner: Miss E Sorensen
Early Years Practitioner: Miss M Farrell
Early Years Practitioner: Ms J Griffin
Apprentice EYP: Miss L Morrison
Apprentice EYP: Miss E Trainer
Support Worker: Ms K Laurie

Non-Teaching/Support Staff:
Bursar: Mr D Pocock
Finance Officer, Deputy Bursar: Mrs E Cummings
Registrar: Mrs L Andonovic
Secretary to the Bursar: Ms M Fraser
Finance Assistant: Mrs J Arthurs
Finance Administrator: Mrs P Chengeta, Mr G McKee,
Mrs P Smith
Director of Admissions and Communications: Mrs K L
Bottomley
Development Manager: Mrs E Solman
Marketing Officers: Mrs L Lawson
PA to the Rector: Miss A-M Cormack
School Receptionist/Secretary: Mrs C Craig, Mrs P
Lindsay, Mrs S Lander
Junior School Secretary: Mrs I Lindsay
School Nurse: Mrs L MacDonald, Mrs E Semple
ICT Systems Manager: Mr J Brindley
IT Technician: Mr E Longmore
Laboratory Technician: Mrs P McArthur
Learning Admin, SQA Coordinator, Classroom Assistant:
Catherine Campbell
After School Club Supervisor: Ms E Grant
After School Club Supervisor: Ms L Hickson
After School Club: Ms R Simpson
Classroom Assistant: Mrs J Park
After School Club Supervisor, Classroom Assistant: Miss A
M Gunn
CCF Head of Army Section: Mr J Ferguson
CCF School Staff Instructor: Mr D Reid
Facilities Manager: Mr C Shaw
Head Janitor: Mr D Anderson
Assistant Janitor: Mr S Lau
Head Groundsman: Mr C McFarlane
Assistant Groundsman: Mr B Fenton
Road Crossing Patrol Staff: Mr A Craig
Marketing Assistant: Miss E Dickson
Development Assistant: Miss E Cowan

Kent College

Canterbury, Kent CT2 9DT

Tel:	01227 763231
email:	registrarseniorschool@kentcollege.co.uk
website:	www.kentcollege.com
Twitter:	@kentcollegehm
Facebook:	@kentcollege
LinkedIn:	/Kent-College-Canterbury

Motto: *Lux tua via mea*

This outstanding boarding and day school is situated on the rural edge of the beautiful City of Canterbury. Students come to the school from the age of three through to eighteen. The majority of students live within an hour of the school. However, the school also has a strong and fully integrated boarding community of children from the age of seven; these children come from all over the world and add an exciting international aspect to the school. Academic, sporting and musical achievements are nationally acclaimed. Parents choose the school for its warm, friendly and welcoming nature where their children are encouraged to achieve all that they can, in a happy and supportive environment.

Facilities. The Junior and Senior schools occupy two independent sites. All of the six boarding houses are situated on site. Both of the schools are surrounded by extensive playing fields which are used throughout the school day. Modern classrooms and provision of laptops to senior school students, distinguishes Kent College as a market leader in education. Excellent sport, music and drama facilities are augmented by the highest level of teaching and coaching. The school also runs its own farm and equine unit.

Curriculum. The curriculum is aligned to the National Curriculum but a greater range of subjects is provided. It is not the aim to specialise in any one group of subjects but to provide a balanced curriculum which will give full opportunity for students to get a good grounding of general knowledge and later to develop particular talents to a high standard. We pride ourselves on being able to provide a personalised learning experience, where we can organise the curriculum to suit the child.

The International Baccalaureate is offered alongside A Levels in the Sixth Form with outstanding results in both.

Dyslexia Unit. The Dyslexia Support Centre is a haven of help for those amongst the school intake that need extra support. Students are taught all the mechanisms that they need to access the whole curriculum. Support remains a constant throughout the child's time here.

International Study Centre. Small group lessons and specific language assistance provide a useful platform for those students who arrive without an adequate level of English. These students are then integrated into the mainstream classes at a pace that suits them.

Pastoral Care. The school operates closely with each student and the student's parents to ensure that there is an open line of communication. Each student is individually supported by a strong team: house parents; year heads; tutors; teachers and peer mentors all of whom take a significant interest in looking after the needs of each individual.

Religion. As a Methodist school a strong Christian ethos purveys all that the school does. Students of all faiths and no faith are welcomed in the school.

Games and Activities. The school possesses 28 acres of playing fields and a floodlit all-weather hockey pitch. The major games for boys are Rugby, Hockey, Tennis, Cricket and Athletics and for girls Netball, Hockey, Tennis, Cricket, and Athletics. Hockey is a particular strength with teams regularly attaining National championship status. Representative honours are common occurrence in all sports. The boarding community enjoys full use of the facilities in the evening with regular activities in Basketball, Football and Fitness Training. Senior pupils take part in various forms of community service in the City and the school also has its own Duke of Edinburgh's Award group. There is a full range of optional school activities, including Art, Debating, Chess, Conservation, CDT and Photography. The School has its own farm and developing equine unit which provides countless opportunities for outdoor adventure and agricultural experiences.

Music and Drama. Music and drama play an important part in the life of the school.

There are four choirs, two orchestras, a jazz band, rock groups and a variety of other specialist ensembles and singing groups. Many concerts are given each year, including the annual Carol Service in Canterbury Cathedral. The last whole-school production was *Oklahoma*, which was a great success!

Admission. The usual ages of admission to the Senior School are 11, 13 and 16. Entrance Examinations usually take place in the Spring Term for admission the following September.

Fees per term (2018–2019). Day Pupils: £5,488–£6,105; Boarders: £8,412–£11,497 (full). International Study Centre: £1,350 extra.

Entrance Scholarships. The school awards academic, music, sport, drama and art scholarships to pupils for entry into Years 7, 9 and 12. Scholarships normally carry a value equivalent to a percentage remission of the tuition fees which would not exceed a maximum of 50% and would be at the discretion of the Head Master. Full particulars may be obtained from the Registrar.

Academic scholarships for Years 7 and 9 are awarded as a result of performance in our Entrance Test, usually held in the Spring Term, for entry the following September. Sixth Form academic scholarships are awarded on the basis of existing performance, a detailed report from the Head of Year or current school, and confirmation of high levels of performance in the final GCSEs. The school also offers specific scholarships for the International Baccalaureate.

Music/Drama GTX scholarships of up to half the tuition fee are offered in conjunction with the Entrance Test to candidates for entry into Years 7, 9 and 12. Free tuition on two instruments is offered to Music Scholars.

Sports GTX scholarships of up to half the tuition fee are awarded to pupils for entry into Years 7, 9 and 12. For Years 7 and 9 these will be awarded in the Spring Term in conjunction with the Entrance Test and on the basis of assessment at Kent College. For Year 12, Sports scholarships will be based on current performance and other assessment methods during the year. Scholars receive 1:1 coaching, physiotherapy support and enjoy a programme of nationally recognised motivational speakers.

Bursaries will be awarded in accordance with, and after consideration of, the financial circumstances of parents. Parents will be invited to complete a financial assessment form and the scale of bursary awarded will be based on the information provided and the financial criteria which the school applies to all bursary awards. All bursaries are reviewed annually.

In addition, the school operates an awards system for the children of HM Forces, NATO and War Graves Commission personnel, whereby the parents pay a set figure, normally 10% of the inclusive fee, plus the amount of Boarding School Allowance which they receive. The balance is treated as a Bursary Award.

Honours. Most school leavers go on to Russell Group and other top universities both in the UK and abroad. Each year a number of pupils secure offers of places at Oxford and Cambridge.

Charitable status. Kent College, Canterbury is part of the Methodist Independent Schools Trust, which is a Registered Charity, number 1142794. The School was founded to provide education within a supportive Christian environment.

Governors:
Chairman: Lorna Cocking, BA
Secretary to the Governors and Bursar: Mrs A C Hencher, AInstAM

Executive Head Master: Dr D J Lamper, EdD Hull, BMus, MA London, AKC

Senior School Head Master: J G Waltho, MA Oxon

Deputy Head: G Letley, BA Kent

Chaplain: Revd Dr P Glass, BA Leeds, MA Cantab, PhD Leeds

Director of Marketing and Admissions: Mrs Andrea Warden
Executive Head Master's PA: Miss M Lucas
Senior School Head Master's PA: Mrs K Simpson

Junior School Head Master: A J Carter, BEd
Junior School Head Master's PA: Miss Millie McCabe
(*See entry in IAPS section*)

Kimbolton School

Kimbolton, Huntingdon, Cambs PE28 0EA

Tel:	01480 860505
Fax:	01480 860386
email:	headmaster@kimbolton.cambs.sch.uk
website:	www.kimbolton.cambs.sch.uk
Twitter:	@KimboltonSchool
Facebook:	@KimboltonSchool

Motto: *Spes Durat Avorum*

The School was founded in 1600 and was awarded Direct Grant status as a boys' day and boarding school in 1945. Girls were first admitted in 1976. The Preparatory School (ages 4–11) and the Senior School are fully co-educational with day boys and girls (4–18) and boarding boys and girls (11–18). As a result of the withdrawal of the Direct Grant the School assumed fully independent status in 1978. There are around 300 pupils in the Prep School and 660 pupils in the Senior School. There is almost a 1:1 ratio of girls to boys.

Mission Statement. Kimbolton School creates a caring, challenging environment in which all pupils are encouraged to fulfil their potential and are given opportunities to flourish in a wide variety of curricular and extra-curricular interests.

It provides a close family environment where young people are educated to be tolerant, socially responsible and independent of mind, equipping them for our changing world. It is a community that challenges pupils to discover their talents, develop socially and excel.

Facilities. The Senior School facilities are situated in and around the main school building, Kimbolton Castle, once the home of Queen Katharine of Aragon and for three centuries the home of the Dukes of Manchester. Now, with its Vanbrugh front and Pellegrini murals, it is a building of considerable beauty and architectural importance. The former State Rooms are study areas for senior pupils and the Castle Chapel is used each day for prayers.

The Queen Katharine Building is a state-of-the-art teaching and learning centre, complete with a 120-seat multimedia lecture theatre. Its new two-storey Science and Maths wing, opened in September 2015, provides outstanding facilities including 12 new laboratories and a digital learning suite. The Lewis Hall caters for the performing arts and daily assemblies and provides modern theatre and concert facilities. The Design Technology Centre is up-to-date and well-equipped, as is the Music School.

A large sports complex, incorporating squash courts, gymnasium, sports hall, multi-gym and changing rooms stands in the Castle's parkland. Closer to the Castle itself, lie a modern Art Centre, Library and an indoor swimming pool. The School has two fine all-weather hockey pitches, one of which is floodlit.

Our separate girls' and boys' boarding houses stand adjacent to the grounds in the picturesque Kimbolton High Street. The boarding community is an important part of the School.

The Prep School is located to the west of Kimbolton village, at the opposite end of our 120 acres of parkland and playing fields. It has, on site, a dining hall, library, digital suite, assembly hall, music teaching and practice rooms, science laboratory, art and design technology room, and sports hall, as well as large, light and airy classrooms.

We are very much one school: the curricula of the Prep and Senior Schools are aligned, our warm caring ethos starts at Reception Year and continues through to the Upper Sixth; and some of our staff teach at both the Prep and Senior Schools.

Admission and Organisation. The Prep School admits children at 4+, 7+ and 9+ (as day pupils) with the expectation that they will complete their education in the Senior School. Entry at other ages is sometimes possible. Tests for entry at the Prep School are held in February. Entry into the Senior School at the age of 11 is open to boarders and day pupils; the Senior School Entrance examinations are also held in February. There are significant entries at 13+ usually by the Common Entrance Examination in June. Those not preparing for Common Entrance may sit the School's own 13+ examination in February. Entry into the Sixth Form is based on interview and GCSE/IGCSE results.

Arrangements can be made for overseas candidates to take the entrance examination at their own schools.

Pupils are accepted in September at the start of the academic year, but a few places may be available for entry in other terms.

The relationship between the Prep and Senior Schools is a close one and contributes to the strong 'family' atmosphere of the whole School. In the Senior School, there are four senior houses and one junior house. It is an important element of our pastoral care that boarding pupils and day pupils are together – there are no day houses. Housemasters/ Housemistresses, assisted by Tutors, look after the general well-being and progress of their charges.

Work and Curriculum. For the first two years in the Senior School there are four or five parallel forms; in each of the third, fourth and fifth years there are five or six smaller forms with sets for some subjects. Boys and girls entering at 13 join one of the Third Forms. An option scheme is introduced in the Fourth Form. In the Sixth Form specialisation occurs, and pupils will usually study three subjects from the following list: English Language and Literature; English Literature: History; Geography; French; Spanish; Maths; Further Maths; Physics; Chemistry; Biology; Music; Art (Fine Art); Art (Photography); Art (Critical and Contextual); Design Technology and Engineering; Drama and Theatre Studies; Physical Education; Economics; Business; Politics; and Philosophy, Religion and Ethics.

Each A Level has a 7th period of subject enrichment, allowing students to explore topics beyond the curriculum. To widen their interests and experience, all students also choose to take an Extension Course in subjects including Astronomy, Classics, Robotics, Cooking For Life, Creative Writing, Debating, Digital Media, Ethical Philosophy, Music Technology, Political Ideas, Psychology and World of Wine. All Sixth Formers follow a 'Preparing for Citizenship' series of lectures, seminars and debates. Almost all leavers gain places at the universities of their choice, with many heading to Oxbridge colleges and Russell Group universities

Religious Teaching. Our school is non-denominational with a Christian ethos and attracts children of all religions and none. Pupils attend Chapel once a week and have RS lessons each week in the First to Third Form. Other services are held in the School Chapel during each term for pupils and parents to attend. Sunday Services are held in the Chapel and occasionally the School worships in the Parish Church.

Sport and Activities. The School owns over 120 acres of land, more than 20 of which are laid out as playing fields. The major sports for boys are association football, hockey and cricket. For girls the main sports are hockey, netball and tennis. Other sports include athletics, gymnastics, dance, climbing, archery, swimming, golf, fitness training, rifle shooting, clay pigeon shooting, squash, badminton, rowing, basketball and rounders. Swimming is popular with before and after school sessions and numerous galas. Extensive use is also made by the sailing club of nearby Grafham Water, both for recreational sailing and inter-school matches. Canoeing is popular and each year a team competes in the highly demanding 125-mile Devizes–Westminster challenge. The equestrian club competes in around twenty fixtures during the course of the year. The aim is to find a sport that each pupil loves and will continue to enjoy long after leaving Kimbolton.

Music and Drama play an important part in the life of the School and almost half of the pupils take lessons in a great variety of instruments. There is a Choral Society, two orchestras, several bands and many ensemble groups. The School stages plays, musicals or concerts each term.

The School contingent of the CCF is a voluntary, keen and efficient body, divided into Navy, Army and RAF Sections with a national reputation for excellence; Community Service is an alternative. There is a successful Duke of Edinburgh's Award scheme with a growing number of participants.

There are many other activities and societies that meet on a regular basis, such as debating, public speaking, Young Enterprise, forensic science, photography, chess, robotics, motor vehicle engineering, bookworms, dance, beekeeping, gardening, modelling, pottery and philosophy.

All pupils are able to participate in the large number of trips in the UK and abroad.

Careers. Advice can be sought at any time by pupils or their parents from the Careers Staff, three of whom specialise in university entrance. There is a well-stocked Careers Room; the School is a member of Inspiring Futures and Fifth Formers take careers test in their Futurewise programme. An annual Careers Fair is held for Fourth to Sixth Formers.

Dress. The School colours are purple, black and white. Boys wear blazers and grey flannels (shorts until the final year in the Prep School). The girls' uniform includes a standard skirt, blouse and blazer. Sixth Formers wear a black suit.

Scholarships and Bursaries. A number of scholarships are awarded at 11+ and 13+ to candidates who perform with distinction in the Entrance Examination or in Common Entrance.

In addition, William Ingram Scholarships are awarded for 13+ entrants who excel at Music, Art or Games and Leadership.

Sixth Form Scholarships and Exhibitions are awarded to those who achieve outstanding results in GCSE.

There is a bursary scheme for deserving candidates aged 11 or over; bursaries may be awarded on their own or in addition to scholarships.

Fees per term (2018–2019). £3,290 (Lower Prep), £4,295 (Upper Prep), £5,265 (Senior Day), £8,760 (Senior Full Boarding), £7,975 (Senior Weekly Boarding). A 2% discount is applied if fees paid by termly direct debit.

The fees are inclusive of lunches and there is no charge for laundry, books, stationery and examination entries.

There is a reduction of 2½% in tuition fees when siblings attend at the same time.

Music Tuition Fee: £248–£290 per term for individual lessons. (Half a term's notice must be given in writing before a pupil discontinues music lessons.)

Old Kimboltonians Association. All correspondence to: Mrs H M Hopperton, Alumni Officer, OKA, Kimbolton School, Kimbolton, Huntingdon, Cambridgeshire PE28 0EA; email: alumni@kimbolton.cambs.sch.uk.

Charitable status. Kimbolton School Foundation is a Registered Charity, number 1098586.

Governing Body:
Mr C A Paull, MPhil, FCA (*Chairman*)
Mr J W Bridge, OBE, DL (*Vice Chairman*)
Mr P F R D Aylott, MA, MNI
Prof F Broughton Pipkin, MA, DPhil, FRCOG
Mrs S M Brereton
Mrs J L Doyle
Lady S E Duberly, DL
Mr P J Farrar
Cllr J A Gray
Cllr Mrs D Hellett
Dr T P Hynes, BA, MA, PhD
Mrs K E S Lancaster, MC Cantab, LPC/CPE
Ms B E Madson
Mr S J F Page, BA Hons, Cert Ed
Mr G K Peace
Mrs J L Rice
Mr D J Suckling
Mr G Yeandle

Headmaster: **Mr J Belbin**, BA, FRSA

PA to the Headmaster: Mrs J Nelson-Lucas

Senior School:

Senior Deputy Headmaster: Mr M J Eddon, BSc
Deputy Headmaster (Academic): Mr C J A Bates, BA, MA
Assistant Head (Extension & Enrichment): Mr J C Newsam, MA, MEd
Assistant Head (DSL): Mrs C A Stokes, BEd
Assistant Head (Staff): Mrs L A Hadden, BA
Director of Activities: Mr R E Knell, BA
Head of Sixth Form: Mr A J Bamford, MA

School Chaplain: Mr P J Crawford
Head of Careers: Mrs A J Bates, BA

Heads of Departments:
Art: Mrs L D Bamford, BA, MA
Design, Technology & Engineering: Mr K Spencer, BEd, MSc, MInstMI
Digital Learning: Mr M Reed, MEng
Drama: Mrs J C Webber, BA
Economics & Business Studies: Mr J R Saunders, BA

English: Mrs A E O'Donnell, MA
Food & Nutrition and Textiles: Mrs C E Bennett, BSc
French: Mr R E Knell, BA
Geography: Mr S Wilson, BA
History: Mr A J Bamford, MA
Maths: Mr A S Jessup, BSc, MA
Music: Mr D Gibbs, MA, FRCO
Physical Education: Mr M S Gilbert, BEd
Politics: Mr F W B Leadbetter, MA, BD, AKC, FRSA, FRHistS
Religious Studies: Mrs L Stone, BEd
Spanish: Mr J C Gomez, BA
Director of Science: Mr A Gray, BSc
Biology: Mr P M Gillam, MA
Chemistry: Mr E C Drysdale, BSc
Physics: Mr C A M Holmes, BSc, BA
Academic Support: Ms R Stewart, BEd
Outdoor Pursuits: Mr J Sweet, BA

Preparatory School:

Headmaster of Preparatory School: Mr J P Foley, BA
Senior Deputy Head (DSL): Mr O C Stokes, BEd, MEd
Deputy Head (Academic): Mrs R L Lambert, BEd
Head of Lower Prep: Mrs L K Collins, BA

Bursar & Clerk to the Governors: Mr E F P Valletta, MBIFM
Registrar: Mrs R White

King Edward VI School
Southampton

Wilton Road, Southampton, Hampshire SO15 5UQ

Tel: 023 8070 4561
Fax: 023 8070 5937
email: registrar@kes.hants.sch.uk
website: www.kes.hants.sch.uk

King Edward VI School was founded in 1553, under Letters Patent of King Edward VI, by the will of the Revd William Capon, Master of Jesus College, Cambridge, and Rector of St Mary's, Southampton. The original Royal Charter, bearing the date 4th June 1553, is preserved in the School. The first Head Master was appointed in 1554.

There are about 960 pupils in the School, of whom over 220 are in the Sixth Form.

Admission. An entrance examination is held in January for boys and girls seeking to enter the First Year at age 11 or the Third Year at age 13 that September. Applications from able under-age candidates will also be considered. Smaller numbers of entrants are accepted into the other school years if there is space, provided the applicants are of suitable academic ability. Students may also apply to join the Sixth Form. In order to qualify for entrance to the Sixth Form a student will normally be required to have grade B (or a 6) or above in six subjects at GCSE, including English Language and Mathematics, and A grades in the subjects to be studied at A Level.

Registration for entry may be made at any time on a form obtainable via the school website or from the Registrar, who can supply current information about fees, bursaries and scholarships.

Class sizes average 22; the average size of Sixth Form sets is 8.

Curriculum. All pupils follow a common course in the first two years: this includes French or German or Spanish with Latin or Classical Civilisation, Mathematics, Science and an Extended Studies programme. In years 3, 4 and 5 all

pupils study eight 'core' subjects to IGCSE: Biology, Chemistry, English Language, English Literature, a Modern Foreign Language, Mathematics, Religious Studies and Physics. In addition there is a range of 'option' subjects: Art, Computer Science, Design and Technology, Economics, French, Geography, German, History, Italian, Music, PE, Philosophy, Spanish, Sports Science and Theatre Studies. The syllabus leading to the IGCSE Examinations, in which most pupils take eleven subjects, is designed to avoid any premature specialisation. In the Sixth Form, students study four A Level subjects in the Lower Sixth and then at the end of this year choose to continue with all four or just to continue with three of the subjects. In addition, all have an afternoon of Games in both years and follow a Foundations Studies programme in both the Lower and Upper Sixth Year.

On entering the First Year, pupils join a form of about 22, with a Form Tutor responsible for their general welfare and progress. The other years are organised on a system of pastoral groups of about 16. Each group has its own Year Head. In addition there is a Head of Lower School who has general responsibility for the first three years; a Head of Upper School and a Director of the Sixth Form have similar responsibilities in their respective areas.

Our aim is to provide a congenial atmosphere and a disciplined environment in which able pupils can develop as individuals.

School Activities. 10% of a student's timetable is devoted to physical education as sport and games are regarded as forming an integral part of life at King Edward's. The major sports played in the three terms are rugby, hockey, cricket and tennis for boys; and netball, hockey, tennis and rounders for girls; other sporting activities include athletics, basketball, badminton, fencing, squash, swimming and a number of other games. The School has a large sports hall, a dance studio, and a fully equipped fitness studio and an all-weather pitch for Hockey and similar games which provides twelve Tennis Courts in Summer. There are a further 33 acres of off-site sports fields which include a second astro pitch and floodlit netball and tennis courts.

A considerable range of clubs and societies meets during lunchtime, after school, at weekends and in school holidays, catering for pupils of all ages and many differing tastes. All are encouraged to join some of these societies, in order to gain the greatest advantage from their time at the School.

In addition to a large number of sporting teams representing the School, there are such activities as charitable and community work, dance, drama, debating, chess, Duke of Edinburgh's Award scheme, International Expeditions, sailing and numerous superb musical opportunities. The School has flourishing choirs, as well as orchestras and a large number of smaller instrumental groups. We have a brand new bright and large Art department and vibrant and well-equipped Design and Technology premises. The studios and workshops are usually open during lunchtimes and after school. Over the past 6 years the whole school has been expanded and refurbished with modern classrooms and specialist rooms. We have recently built a fabulous new 400-seat theatre and in September 2018 we opened our new extended dining room.

Fees per term (2018–2019). £5,350. Fees can be reduced in appropriate cases by the award of Bursaries and Scholarships. Scholarships are available on entry at age 11, 13 and 16. Further Scholarships may be awarded during a pupil's career in the School. Some Scholarships are awarded for proficiency in the Creative Arts. Foundation Bursaries are available at age 11, 13 and into the Sixth Form.

Charitable status. King Edward VI School Southampton is a Registered Charity, number 1088030. The object of the Charity is to advance education and training in or near

Southampton or elsewhere, including the carrying on of school or schools or other educational establishments and ancillary or incidental educational or other associated activities for the benefit of the community.

Patron: The Lord Lieutenant for the County of Hampshire, Mr Nigel Atkinson

Governors:
Chair: A J Morgan, MA Oxon, FCA, ATII
B E Gay, BA
Vice-Chair: P W Brazier, BSc, FCIOB
Dr Y Binge, MB ChB
Dr R B Buchanan, FRCP, FRCR, MBBS
Councillor M Chaloner
Mrs M L Chant
J J Gray
Mrs S J Mancey
Miss J C May
M H Mayes, MA, MSc, MBA
J W J Mist, FCA
Dr J Mitchell, MA Cantab, MBBS, DRCOG, DCH
Mrs C G Musker
Councillor R Perry, BA
Mr A J Reid, MA Cantab, PGCE, NPQH
B W Richards
I H Rudland
Mrs W P Swinn
Dr A L Thomas, MA, PhD Cantab, CBiol, MRSB
Mrs J L Wadsworth
K St J Wiseman, MA Oxon

Bursar and Clerk to the Governors: Mr Ray Maher, BA Econ, ACA

Head: **Mr Julian Thould**, MA (*History*)

Senior Deputy Head: Mr Adrian Dellar, BSc (*Chemistry*)
Deputy Head (Academic): Dr Bruce Waymark, BA, MA Ed, PhD (*Geography*)
Assistant Head (Pastoral): Mr William Collinson, BA (*English*)
Assistant Head (Registrar): Mrs Emma Sheppard, BSc (*Chemistry*)
Assistant Head (Staff Development): Mr Stephen Hall, BSc (*Biology*)
Assistant Head (Co-Curriculum): Miss Hilary Smith, BSc (*Biology*)
Assistant Head (Co-Curriculum): Mrs Paula Burrows, MSc (*Physics*)
Assistant Head (Digital Strategy and ICT): Mr Bob Allen, BSc (*Computing*)

Director of Sixth Form: Mr Nick Culver, MA (*Economics*)
Head of Upper School: Dr Emma Thomas, BSc, PhD (*Chemistry*)
Head of Lower School: Mrs Lisa Henderson, BEd (*PE*)
Director of Student Guidance: Mrs Lem Millar, BSc (*Biology*)

Teaching Staff:
* Head of Department

Art:
*Mr Graham Piggott, BA
Miss Alex McGinn BA
Mrs Nicola Moxon, BA
Mr Ed Lewis, BA

Biology:
*Mr Simon Aellen, BSc
Mrs Josephine Barnes-Wardlaw, BSc
Mrs Laura Burnett, BSc
Miss Lucinda Downing, BSc (*Junior Science Coordinator*)
Mr Stephen Hall, BSc
Mr James Hyder, BSc
Miss Gemma McGregor, BSc
Mrs Lem Millar, BSc
Mr Mark Miller, MA, DPhil
Miss Hilary Smith, BSc
Miss Katrina Yerbury, BSc

Chemistry:
*Mr Richard Cross, BSc
Mrs Jan Collinson, MChem
Mrs Claire Costello-Kelly, BSc
Miss Lucinda Downing, BSc (*Junior Science Coordinator*)
Mr Adrian Dellar, BSc
Dr Stuart Gamblin, BSc, PhD
Dr Viv Green, MSc, PhD
Mrs Emma Sheppard, BSc

Classics:
*Mrs Jacqui Meredith, BA
Mr Stuart Ayers, BA
Mr Chris Giles, BA
Mr Julian Halls, BA
Miss Alice Rieuf, MA

Computing:
*Mr Peter Mapstone, BSc
Mr Bob Allen, BSc
Mr George Twum-Barima, BSc
Mr Mark Willis, BSc

Design & Technology:
*Mr Simon Barker, MA
Mr David Blow, BSc
Mrs Sarah Peterson, BSc
Mrs Helen Sheridan, BA
Miss Amelia Stone, BSc

Economics/Business Studies:
*Mr Paul Sheppard, BSc
Mr Nick Culver, MA
Mr Matthew Laverty, BA
Mrs Sue Quinn, BA

English:
*Dr Alistair Schofield, MA
Mrs Hannah Arnold, BA
Mr William Collinson, BA
Miss Emer Cullen, BA
Mrs Sam Evans, BA
Mrs Joanna Gunton, BA
Mrs Julia Hardwick, BA
Mr Peter Jennings, BA
Mrs Catherine Lane, BA
Mrs Ellen Rawson, MA
Mrs Janette Roy, BA

Geography:
*Miss Laura-Jane Grant, BA
Mr David Brown, BA
Mr Andy Gilbert, BA
Mr Geoff Havers, BSc
Ms Teresa King, BA
Mrs Alice Penfold, BA
Mrs Emily Walls, BA
Dr Bruce Waymark, BA, MA Ed, PhD

History:
*Mr Nick Diver, MA (*Head of Humanities*)
Miss Jacky Barron, BA
Mrs Shona Burt, BA
Mr Kevin Coundley, MA
Dr David Filtness, MA
Mrs Rosemary Potter, BA
Mr Julian Thould, MA

Mathematics:
*Mr Gerard Eyssens, BEd
Mrs Catherine Asiki, BA
Mr Simon Barley, MSc
Mr Peter Collins, BSc
Mr Richard Nichols, BSc
Miss Emma Ridley, BSc
Mr Paul Robinson, BEng
Mr Ian Rosenburg, BEd
Mr John Singleton, BSc
Mrs Jennifer Thimbleby, BSc
Mr Mark Willis, BSc
Mr Richard Wood, BEd

Modern Languages:
*Mr Kevin Jepson, MA (*Head of Modern Foreign Languages*)
Mrs Karen Clement, BA (*French*)
Mrs Elisa Ladislao, BA (*Spanish*)
Mr Stuart Ayers, BA
Mrs Emily Brown, BA
Mrs Rebecca Hall, BA (*German Coordinator*)
Mrs Hong Deng, MA
Mr Gavin Lawson, MA
Miss Victoria Pastor, MA
Miss Alice Rieuf, MA
Mrs Sophie Rugge-Price, MA
Mr Alastair Sinclair, MA

Music:
*Miss Charlotte Forsey, BMus, PG Dip (*Director of Music*)
Miss Irene Anderson, MA
Miss Stacey Barnett, BA
Mr James Belassie, MA
Mr StJohn de-Zilva, BA

PE:
*Mr Daniel Kent, BA (*Director of Sport*)
Mrs Jessica Ferrand, BA (*Deputy Director of Sport*)
Mr Matt Mixer, BSocSc (*Sports Science*)
Mr Calum Crichton, BA
Mrs Lisa Henderson, BEd
Mrs Clare Kelly, BA
Mrs Janis Kent, BA
Mr Alex Penn, BA
Mrs Hannah Penn, BA
Mr Lloyd Powell, BSc (*Performance & Fitness Coordinator*)
Mr Richard Wood, BEd (*Physical Education Coordinator*)

Psychology:
*Mrs Rachel Moody, BA
Mr Mark Miller, MA, MPhil
Miss Hilary Smith, BSc

Physics:
*Mr Rob Simm, BSc
Mrs Paula Burrows, MSc
Dr Helen Dean, BSc, PhD
Mr John Foyle, BSc
Mr Lawrence Herklots, BSc (*Head of Science*)
Mrs Maryam Mahdavi, BSc
Dr Magdalena Mayor, MSc, PhD
Mr Jamie Shadbolt, BA

RE:
*Mrs Helen Searles, MA
Mrs Rachael Kairis, BA
Mrs Catherine Lane, BA
Revd Julian Poppleton, BA, Dip RS
Mrs Janette Roy, BA
Mr Tim Tofts, MA, Dip Phil

Theatre Studies:
*Mr Dameon Garnett, BA (*Director of Drama*)
Mrs Hayleigh Hawker, BA
Mrs Lisa Gilmour, BA

Curriculum Support:
*Mr Stefan Smart, BA, MPhil
Mrs Georgina Dellar, BA
Mrs Susie Smart, BA
Mrs Jane Thould, BA

King Edward's School
Bath

North Road, Bath BA2 6HU

Tel: Senior School: 01225 464313
            Junior School: 01225 463218
            Pre-Prep School: 01225 421681
Fax: Senior School: 01225 481363
            Junior School: 01225 442178
            Pre-Prep School: 01225 428006
email: reception@kesbath.com
website: www.kesbath.com
Twitter: @KESBath
Facebook: @kesbath

As the city's former grammar school, founded in 1552, KES has a very healthy tradition of nurturing academic excellence and ambition, reflected these days in the School's outstanding results which consistently place us in the top five independent schools in the South West. The ethos of the School is one that encourages all pupils to play as hard as they work and to make the most of all the wonderful opportunities here, both in and out of the classroom, that enable them to grow and thrive within a supportive and caring framework. We set the bar high, but we also give our pupils all the tools that they need to reach those ambitious standards. We aim to foster talent in all its forms and to open doors to enquiry and discovery. Independent-mindedness and creative spirit are strong suits, but so too is the sense of community that seeks to respect and value all its members.

As a family of three schools, the Pre-Prep, Junior and Senior sections of King Edward's offer an inspiring and supportive environment for children age 3 to 18. Some join us just for the Sixth Form, many stay for their entire school career. All pupils are encouraged to be the best they can be and all are nurtured along the pathway to leading happy, fulfilled and successful lives at school and beyond.

ISI Inspection report. In 2015 the School was inspected by the ISI and was judged as 'excellent' across all eight aspects of school life under review including pastoral care and co-curricular provision. The report noted that "The success of the school lies in the strength of the ethos which permeates it from the EYFS to the sixth form. All three sections of the school encourage the pupils to strive for excellence and to achieve to the best of their ability in a stimulating environment so that they acquire a love of learning which goes beyond the formal curriculum."

Organisation. King Edward's is a co-educational day school. The School consists of a Senior School of 817 pupils, a Junior School of 196 pupils and Pre-Prep & Nursery of 107 pupils.

Facilities. The Senior School is situated on a 19-acre campus with stunning views across Bath. A further 17-acre site at nearby Bathampton is home to the School's playing fields and sports pavilion. Senior School buildings include the Wroughton Theatre, extensive laboratories for Biology, Chemistry, Physics and ICT and a Modern Foreign Languages suite. The newly refurbished Holbeche Centre includes a Sixth Form Centre with adjoining café, an extended Careers and Higher Education Centre, a refurbished Design Suite and Design Technology studios. There is also a modern Sports Hall, together with an artificial playing surface. One of the most iconic buildings on the site is the stunning Wessex Building: a three-storey, glass-fronted structure with a dining room and servery on the first floor, a multi-purpose second floor for assemblies, presentations, concerts and social gatherings, and a state-of-the-art Library on the ground floor. The Senior School has also just opened its newest facility, a purpose-built Drama Centre.

Admission. King Edward's Pre-Prep and Nursery is non-selective upon joining. Children can join the Nursery after they turn three. Thereafter, children progress to Reception and then on to Years 1 and 2. Space allowing, children are also welcomed throughout the academic year.

Junior School: Children joining from our own Pre-Prep do so via internal assessment. They do not sit an entrance examination. Pupils from other primary schools and preparatory schools are offered places based on assessment and interview. The main entry is in Year 3 but other vacancies may occur.

Senior School: All potential Year 7 pupils are interviewed and assessed via an entrance examination testing Verbal Reasoning, Mathematics and English. Older pupils may enter the Senior School, if and where places are available, by sitting an entrance examination appropriate to their age.

Pupils may also seek direct entry into the Sixth Form. Such pupils are expected to acquire a sound set of GCSE passes before transfer for advanced study. Applicants are interviewed and a reference is sought from their present schools.

Application forms and further information concerning entry are obtainable from the Registrar or available online. Open Days are held in the Autumn and Spring terms.

Fees per term (2018–2019). Pre-Prep £3,385, Junior School £3,750, Senior School £4,745–£4,825.

Scholarships. Scholarships are awarded in Year 7, either for academic excellence or for an outstanding special talent in art, drama, music and sport.

Bursaries. Income-related entrance Bursaries may be awarded to children entering Years 7 and 12, whose parents are unable to pay the full fee. A general Bursary fund is also available to assist parents during times of unforeseen family circumstances, when they may find themselves unable to fund full school fees. Further details are obtainable from the Bursar's office.

Senior School Curriculum. We start in Years 7 and 8 with a broad range of subjects, to which we add choice and greater range in Year 9. By the time pupils are choosing their GCSE options, they will have a clearer idea of their strengths and enthusiasms and be able to select the best range of subjects to go alongside the core subjects of English, Maths, all three sciences and a modern foreign language.

For A Level, further specialisation and greater focus on personal interest and academic strengths come into play as pupils look to their education and potential careers after life in the Sixth Form. We offer careers guidance and testing to support these fundamental choices and then UCAS and Higher Education guidance as they look to make the move to their chosen degree subject from the A Levels they will complete in Year 13.

No two pupils are the same and so we work to provide as much choice and flexibility as we can in our options schemes for Years 9, 10 and 12. All combinations are possible in principle and a broad mix of subjects is as supported as more traditional routes of sciences, languages or humanities.

Throughout, there is an underlying appreciation that pupils succeed best when taught interesting and engaging lessons by enthusiastic, specialist staff. We want our pupils to leave here with valuable study skills, having found their intellectual and academic passion and having fulfilled their potential in that area.

Music and Drama. There is a healthy musical tradition in the School, with over 20 instrumental and choral groups affording opportunities to explore differing musical styles. Partnerships with Bath Abbey and Bath Philharmonia Orchestra help to further extend the experience of our musicians and choirs.

King Edward's is known for producing exceptional theatrical work and is regarded as a centre of excellence for its creative and challenging performance work, the professional standards of its productions, and its consistently outstanding academic results. In addition to two big productions each year, the Senior School also offers inter-form competitions, Duologue performances, drama clubs, tech club and an end-of-year 'Spectacular'. The School has also recently introduced LAMDA exams and taken several shows to the Edinburgh Fringe.

Sport. Sport plays a significant role in the life of King Edward's School. The School enjoys a strong sporting tradition, where all pupils are encouraged to take an active role in the curricular and co-curricular opportunities available to them. Each pupil is encouraged to develop their potential, creating the opportunity to allow later involvement at recreational level or within a competitive environment. We aim to nurture teamwork, leadership, commitment and a passion for sport through the opportunities available to all pupils at KES. The major games are rugby, hockey, cricket and netball. Minor sports include athletics, cross-country, tennis, soccer, badminton, golf, dance, gymnastics, table tennis and trampolining.

School Societies and Activities. The School aims to challenge and stimulate all pupils by offering a wide range of activities and experiences beyond the classroom. The 2015 ISI Report found our extra-curricular provision to be "outstanding", and we truly believe that there is something for everyone from among the 100 clubs and societies running each year.

Outward bound opportunities include joining the School's CCF, founded in 1896, or taking part in the Duke of Edinburgh's Award scheme. The School also enters the Ten Tors Competition each year. Lunchtime clubs include Lego Robotics, KES Amnesty Club, the Socrates Debating Club and IFS Student Investor Club.

Pastoral Care The Deputy Head (Pastoral) coordinates the pastoral team. Every child has a Form Teacher who is at their foremost contact during daily life at school. Tutors work in teams managed by Heads of Year or Senior Tutors who are in turn assisted by Heads of Sector (Lower, Middle School and Sixth Form). The pastoral staff are ably supported by a School Nurse and Counsellor. The School prides itself on its family atmosphere and the excellent relationships between pupils of all ages and staff.

Honours. In 2018 pupils performed exceptionally in their A Levels: 28.4% at A*, 60.4% at A* or A and 79.2% at A* to B. At GCSE: 55.3% at A*9–8 and 78.8% at A* or A/9–7.

King Edward's Junior School and Pre-Prep and Nursery. For further details please see separate entries for the Junior School and Pre-Prep and Nursery under IAPS.

The Association of Old Edwardians of Bath. c/o The Development Office.

Charitable status. King Edward's School Bath is a Registered Charity, number 1115875. It is a charitable trust for the purpose of educating children.

Chairman of Governors: Mrs W Thomson, MEd, BEd Hons, LLCM TD

Headmaster: Mr M J Boden, MA (*French & German*)

Second Master: Mr M J Horrocks-Taylor, BSc, MEd (*Geography*)

Bursar and Clerk to the Governors: Mr J Webster, BSc, ACA

Deputy Head Academic: Mr T Burroughs, BA (*History & Politics*)

Deputy Head Pastoral: Ms C Losse, MA (*German & French*)

Assistant Heads:
Head of Middle School, Compliance: Mr A Bougeard, BSc (*Chemistry*)
Staff Development: Mrs P Bougeard, MA (*Spanish & French*)
Head of Lower School, Events: Mr D Chapman, BA (*Mathematics*)
Curriculum & Digital Strategy: Mr D Middlebrough, BA (*Mathematics*)
Head of Sixth Form: Mr P Simonds, BSc (*Geography*)
Co-curricular: Mr J Tidball, BSc (*Geography*)

Teaching Staff:
* *Head of Department*
¹ *Head of Year/Sixth Form Senior Tutor*
[..] *On leave*

¹Mr M Barber, BA (*Economics & Business Studies*)
Mr N Barnes, MA (*Chemistry, *Careers*)
Mrs H Bateman (*Learning Support*)
[Mrs S Bird, BA (**Drama/Theatre Studies*)]
Mr M Boden, MMus (*Music*)
Mr G Brown (*Physical Education & Games*)
Mrs C Bruton, BA (*English*)
Mr M Bull, MA (**Classics*)
[Mrs J Burchell, MA (*Classics*)]
¹Mr M Buswell, ME (**Religious Studies & Philosophy*)
Mr G Butterworth, BA (**Economics & Business Studies*)
Miss B Carr, BA (*Spanish & French*)
Mrs B Charlton (**Spanish*)
Mrs S Chubb, BA (*English*)
Miss A Cottingham, BA (*Religious Studies & Philosophy*)
Mrs S Cox, BSc (*Learning Support*)
Mr P Davies, BSc (*Mathematics*)
Mrs T Dawson, BSc (*Mathematics*)
Mrs L Dias, BSc (*Economics & Business Studies*)
Mr T Dore, BSc (*Biology*)
Mr R Drury, BA, LRAM (**Music*)
Mr M Evans, MMath (*Electronics*)
Mr P Feeney, MA (*Classics*)
Mr C Ferguson, BA (**German*)
Dr A Fewell, BSc, PhD (*Biology*)
Mr T Fisher, MA (*English*)
Ms O FitzGerald, BA (*Classics*)
Mrs R Flay (*Art & Photography*)
Mr J Garner-Richardson, BSc (*Chemistry & Biology*)
¹Mrs H Graham, MA (*History & Politics*)
Mrs E Grainger, BA (*French & Spanish*)
Dr C Gruzelier, MA, PhD (*Classics*)
Mrs L Gwilliam, BSc (**Physical Education & Games*)
Mr D Hacker (**Physical Education & Games*)
Mr M Harrison, BSc, MSc, CPhys, MInstP (*Physics*)
Miss C Hartley, BA (*English*)
Mr R Haynes, MA (**Physics*)
Mr J Holdaway, BEng (**Design & Technology*)
[Mr M Howarth (*Physical Education & Games*)]
Mrs F Hughes, MA (*Art & Photography*)
Miss S Hurst, BA (*Design & Technology*)

Mrs S Hutchings, BEd (*Mathematics*)
Mrs C Jones, BA (*German & French*)
Miss Z Kayacan, BA (**English*)
Mrs A Kean, BSc (*Biology*)
Mr J Kean, MA (*English*)
Mr L King, BA, MSc (*Physical Education & Games*)
Dr J Knight, BSc, PhD (**Geography*)
Mr T Laney, BSc (**Biology*)
Mr B Lang, BSc (*Physics*)
Mrs R Lang, BSc (*Mathematics*)
Mr D Lehmann, BSc (*Mathematics*)
Mr C Lilley, BSc (*Physical Education & Games*)
Mr S Lilley, BSc (*Physical Education & Games*)
¹Mrs C Livesey, BEd (*Academic Cover*)
Mr P Livesey, BEd (*Physical Education & Games*)
Mr S Lomon, BA (**History & Politics*)
[Mrs P Mason, BSc (*Biology & Chemistry*)]
Mr J Mawer, BSc (*Geography*)
Miss S McCrorie, MA (*Mathematics*)
Mr T Medhurst, BEd (**Information Technology*)
Miss L Miners MSc (*Chemistry*)
Miss S Moon, BA (*History*)
Mrs K Moreno, BA (*Physical Education & Games*)
¹Mrs A Munn, BA (**Learning Support*)
Ms C Nightingale MSc (*Psychology*)
Mr M Oehler, BSc (**Chemistry*)
Mr R Pagnamenta, MEng (**Mathematics*)
Mr M Pell, BA (**Art & Photography*)
Miss L Perris, BMus (*Music*)
Mr P Perry, BA (*English*)
Mr N Purcell, MA (*Design & Technology*)
¹Mrs S Richardson, MSc, MA (*Physics*)
Mrs A Salako, BA (*Economics & Business Studies*)
Mrs K Simonds, BSc (*Learning Support & Geography*)
Mr T Sneddon, BSc (*Mathematics*)
Ms S Stanford-Tuck, BSc Ed (*Biology*)
Mrs V Stevens-Craig, BA (*Drama/Theatre Studies*)
Mrs D Tamblyn, BEd (*Drama/Theatre Studies*)
Mr R Thomas, MA (*History & Politics, *HE/UCAS*)
Mrs R Trust, MA (*Acting Head of Drama/Theatre Studies*)
¹Mrs A Tse, BSc (*Biology*)
Mrs S Utton, BSc (**Psychology*)
Mr A Vass, MA (**French*)
¹Ms S Vernon, BA (*English*)
Dr L Wainer MSc, PhD (*Mathematics*)
Mr T West, BA (*ICT*)
Mrs J Wilcox, BSc (*Mathematics*)
Mr D Willison, BA (*Art*)
Dr M Wood, MA, PhD (*Religious Studies*)
Miss E Young, BEd (*Physical Education & Games*)

Examinations Officer: Mrs S Moles
School Chaplain: Revd Caroline O'Neill
School Librarian: Miss L Bowman, BA, MLS (*Head of PSHE*)
SSI KES CCF: CSgt P H Jones
Finance Manager & School Accountant: Mrs N Rowlands, AAT
Headmaster's PA: Ms L Wolfe, BA
School Secretary (Academic): Mrs K Tedstone
School Secretary (Pastoral): Mrs B Lascelles, BSc
School Receptionist: Mrs A Budgett
Registrar: Miss A Rashid
Admissions Administrator: Miss H Lane
Development Director: Ms K Teague, BA, MInstF Dip
Development Officer: Mrs C Davies, BA
Communications Officer: Mrs K Gentle, MA
Marketing Communications Officer: Mr G Goold, BA
Music Administrator: Mrs C Blau Davies
PE Administrator: Mrs R Worsdall, BA
School Nurse: Mrs C Morris, RGN

Junior School:
Head of Junior School: Mr G Taylor, BA Ed, NPQH
Deputy Head: Mr M Innes, BA, PGCE
Deputy Head (Pastoral): Mrs R Hardware, BEd
Miss L Atkinson, MEd, PGCE
Mrs R Barrett, MA Oxon, PGCE
Mr S Carr, BEd
Mr C Carter,. BEd
Miss L Chapman, MA, PGCE
Mr J Corp, BSc, PGCE
Mr D Cousins, BA
Mrs F Dore, BSc, PGCE
Mr N Gray, BA
Mrs E Heaney, BEd
Miss S Hurst, BA
Mrs C Hutchings, BMus, PGCE
Mrs A Jabarin, BA, PGCE
Mrs G Oliver, CertEd, ASM
Mrs E Pike, BA, PGCE
Mrs R Reid, LLB, PGCE, AMBDA
Mr J Roberts-Wray, BA, PGCE
Mr D Willison, BA
Miss A Young, BSc, PGCE

Junior School Administrator: Mrs V Gibbens

Pre-Prep School Staff:
Head of Pre-Prep & Nursery: Ms J Gilbert, BEd, NPQH
Deputy Head: Mrs D Bright, BA, QTS
Mr S Boydell, BA, PGCE, MEd, MRHistS, PGCert
Mrs H Blakey, BSc, PGCE
Mrs J Carter, BA
Miss S Cullen, PGCE, EYTS
Miss S Knight, MA, PGCE
Ms E Rocksborough-Smith, BA, PGCE
Ms L-M Williams, BSc, PGCE

Pre-Prep Administrator: Mrs A Foxall

King Edward's School
Birmingham

Edgbaston Park Road, Birmingham B15 2UA

Tel: 0121 472 1672
Fax: 0121 415 4327
email: admissions@kes.org.uk
website: www.kes.org.uk
Twitter: @KESBham
Facebook: @KESBham

Motto: *Domine, Salvum fac Regem*

King Edward's School, Birmingham, was founded in 1552 and occupied a position in the centre of the city until 1936 when it moved to its present 50-acre site in Edgbaston, surrounded by a golf course, lake and nature reserve and adjacent to the University. It is an independent day school with 874 boys aged 11 to 18. Approximately 50 boys in each year receive financial assistance with fees, from scholarships and the Assisted Places Scheme. The School belongs to the Foundation of the Schools of King Edward VI in Birmingham (two independent, six grammar schools and two academies), and its sister-school, King Edward VI High School for Girls, is on the same campus. Academically one of the leading schools in the country, King Edward's is also renowned for the scale of its provision and its excellence in sport, music, drama, outdoor pursuits and trips and expeditions.

Admission. Most boys enter the school at 11+, although a small number join at 13+. In addition, applications at 16+ to enter the Sixth Form are encouraged. At both 11+ and 13+ candidates take papers in Mathematics, English and Verbal Reasoning at a level appropriate to the National Curriculum. A large number of pupils are also interviewed as part of the admissions process. At 16+ entry is decided by interview, report from current Headteacher and predicted GCSE grades.

The names of candidates must be registered at the School before the closing date as stated on the School's website. A recent photograph must be produced when the name of a candidate is registered for the examination.

Term of Entry: Autumn term only.

Scholarships and Assisted Places. Approximately 25 academic scholarships varying in value from 5% to 50% of the fees are awarded each year. Most of these scholarships are awarded at 11+, but awards are also made to outstanding candidates at 16+ and, very occasionally, at 13+. Music scholarships are also available.

The Assisted Places Scheme offers means-tested support to up to 25 boys a year. The scheme targets primarily 11+ entrants but 16+ entrants are also eligible to apply.

Fees per term (2018–2019). £4,410.

Academic Success. The School's 2018 International Baccalaureate Diploma results were excellent, with an average point score of 37.9. 46% of the boys gained 40 points or above, the equivalent of more than four A*s at A Level. Almost all leavers go on to university, some after a gap year. 17 pupils gained places at Oxford and Cambridge. Additionally, 17 boys will study medicine.

At GCSE, 65% of results were graded A*/9/8 grades and 85% were A*/A/9–7. Furthermore, 26 boys achieved 10 A*s/9s/8s, 23 achieved 9 A*s/9s/8s, and 54 boys achieved only A*s/9s/8s and As/7s.

Curriculum. *Lower School*: The following subjects are studied by all boys to the end of the third year: English, Mathematics, French, Geography, History, Physics, Chemistry, Biology, (General Science in first year), Latin, Art, Design, Drama, Music, PE and Religious Studies. All boys study one of German, Spanish or Classical Greek in the third year and may take their choice to GCSE or IGCSE and beyond. In addition, boys are required to undertake familiarisation courses in Information Technology. In the Fourth and Fifth year, boys take 10 subjects. All boys must study Mathematics, English Language, English Literature, a Modern Foreign Language and at least two sciences, plus three or four other optional subjects at GCSE or IGCSE.

Sixth Form: Since September 2010, A Levels have been replaced entirely with the International Baccalaureate Diploma. The School believes that this diploma provides a more challenging and broad Sixth Form education with greater opportunity for independent learning and is a better preparation for university study and life thereafter.

The School's curriculum goes beyond preparation for examinations. For example, PE and games are compulsory for all and Friday afternoon is set aside for the entire school to pursue non-academic activities: Combined Cadet Force, Leadership, service in the community, outdoor pursuits, Art, Information Technology etc.

Music and Drama. The School has a very rich musical and dramatic life. Many of the musical groups and theatrical productions take place jointly with King Edward VI High School for Girls. There are over ten different musical groups and choirs. The School's Performing Arts Centre has main hall seating for up to 500 and excellent facilities for music and drama.

Games. Rugby, cricket, hockey, and water polo are the major team games in the School. However, many other games prosper including archery, athletics, badminton, basketball, chess, cross-country, cycling, fencing, golf, kayaking, squash, swimming, table tennis and tennis. The School has extensive playing fields for all these activities plus its own swimming pool, international-standard athletics track, sports hall, gymnasia and squash courts. In 2015 the School opened a new hockey pavilion and astro pitch, and a new sports centre is opening in the 2018–19 academic year.

Societies and Clubs. The School has a very wide range of clubs and societies including Christian Union, Islamic Society, Literary Society, History Society, Bookworms, Economics and Business Society, Senior and Junior Dramatic Societies, Art Society, Geographical Society, Debating Society, Mentoring Society, Mathematical Society, Modern Languages Society, Writers' Society, Lifeguarding, Chess Club, Model United Nations, Spectrum, School Chronicle and Hillwalking.

CCF, Outdoor Pursuits and Expeditions. The Royal Naval, RAF and Army Sections of the Combined Cadet Force are very popular amongst pupils. In addition, the KES Award and the Duke of Edinburgh's Award scheme have grown substantially in recent years, so that the majority of pupils in the third year gain the KES Award and about 20 each year gain the Gold Duke of Edinburgh's Award. All of this forms part of a strong tradition of trips and expeditions, ranging from cycling and caving and walking and skiing trips, to language trips to Europe to major expeditions to Ecuador and the Galapagos Islands, Guyana and Madagascar. There have also been very successful rugby tours to Australia, India, Canada, South Africa and China.

Forms and Houses. In the first five years, each form has an average of 24 pupils. In the Sixth Form, forms are on average 12 in number, and often comprise pupils together from the Lower and Upper Sixth. There is also a house system, comprising eight houses, which continues to provide an important element of pastoral support and competition in sport, music, drama, debating and general knowledge.

Charitable status. The Schools of King Edward VI in Birmingham is a Registered Charity, number 529051. The purpose of the Foundation is to educate children and young persons living in or around the City of Birmingham.

Governing Body:
Mr Tim Clarke (*Chairman*)

Dr B Adab	Mr I Metcalfe
Mr G Andronov	Mr C Parker
Mrs G Ball, OBE	Dr J Sherwood
Dr G Brodie	Mr S Southall
Mr P Burns	Mr G Thomas
Mrs J Hundle	Mr H Thomas
Mr B Lennon	Prof S West
Mr G Marsh	Dr I Yunas
Mr B Matthews	

Acting Chief Master: **Mr Keith Phillips**, BA

Acting Second Master: Mr R D Heathcote, BSc
Acting Deputy Head: Ms D E McMillan, BSc

Assistant Heads:
Mr H M Coverdale, BSc Econ
Mrs J K D'Arcy, BSc
Mr G J Watson, MA

Assistant Teachers:

Mr L W Evans, BA	Mr M J Monks, GRSM,
Mr J C S Burns, MA	Dip RCM
Mr L M Roll, BA	Mr R W James, BA
Mr E J Milton, BA	Mr S L Stacey, MA
Mr B M Spencer, BA	Mr T F Cross, BSc
Mrs G A Ostrowicz, BA	Mr D J Ash, MA
Mr C D Boardman, BSc	Mr J P Smith, BA
Mr S J Tinley, BSc	Mr P A Balkham, BA
Mrs C M L Duncombe, BA	Mr D M Witcombe, MSc
Mr J Porter, BSc	Mr I J Connor, BSc
	Mr R D Davies, BSc

Ms S-L Jones, BSc	Mr N A Shepherd, BSc
Dr J L Amann, BA, PhD	Mr G P J Browning, BA
Ms E K Sigston, BA	Mr J M Butler, BA
Mr P W L Golightly, BA	Ms A Havel, BA
Mr M J Bartlett, BA	Ms P K Higgins, BA
Mrs P J R Esnault, MA	Ms N B Lockhart-Mann,
Senora A Estevez, BA, MA	BA
Mr C A P Johnson, BA	Ms R Irani, BSc, MSc
Dr M R Follows, BSc, PhD	Mr A D Langlands, BSc
Dr D C Wong, BEng, PhD	Miss R V Morris
Ms L C Seamark	Mr N W Round
Mrs K S Charlesworth-	Mr A W J Petrie, BA
Jones, BA	Miss R A Smedley, BSc
Ms H A Ferguson, BSc,	Mr C R Turford, BA, MA
MSc	Dr A D Webb, MChem
Mrs G J Babb, BA, MA	Mr B A Coates, BSc
Mr T J Wareing, BA	Mr G Adams, BSc
Dr C Arico, MSc, PhD	Mr J M Benge-Abbott, BSc
Miss F C Lee, BA	Mr J W Brogden, BA
Dr M Romon Alonso, MSc,	Ms H E Falkner, BA, MA
PhD	Ms R Leaver, MEng
Mr J J W Fair, BSc	Mr A J Pearson, BA
Dr T S Miles, MSc, PhD	Miss C V Bayley, BA,
Mr P R Ollis, BSc, MA	MEd
Mr J M Pavey, BSc	Miss A Bishop, BA
Ms D K Poole, BA	Mrs R J Froggatt, BSc
Mr E J Aston, BSc	Mr G Macdonald, BSc
Mr T Burdett, BSc	Mr P D J Moore-Bridger,
Mr A M Dutch, BMus	BA
Dr J Fennell, BSc, PhD	Mr R D Orchard, BSc
Mrs C L Gillow, BA	Mr T G A Wyndham, BSc,
Dr S P Kulkarni, BSc,	MSc
MPhil, PhD	Mrs O Zamaniego, BA
Dr M D Leigh, MA, PhD	

Part-time Teachers:

Mr D C Dewar, BSc	Mr R J Deeley, MA
The Revd D H Raynor,	Mrs S L Behan, BSc
MA, MLitt	Mrs R D'Aquila, BA
Mrs G S Hudson, BEd	Ms B Dehame-Hare, MA
Mrs C R Bubb, BA	Ms C Shuker, BSc
Mrs H J Cochrane, BA	Dr M Slaski, BSc, MSc,
Mrs F M Atay, BA	PhD
Mrs E J Wareing, BA	Mrs K C Linehan, BA, MA
Mrs C Smith, BA, MA	

Librarian: Ms K A Fletcher-Burns, BA, MSc Econ

School Medical Officer: Dr M Forrest, MBChB, DRCOG, MRCGP

King Edward's Witley

Petworth Road, Godalming, Surrey GU8 5SG

Tel:	01428 686700
email:	admissions@kesw.org
website:	www.kesw.org
Twitter:	@KESWNews
Facebook:	@King-Edwards-School-Witley
LinkedIn:	/king-edward's-school-witley

King Edward's Witley was founded in 1553 by King Edward VI as Bridewell Royal Hospital. Originally housed at the Bridewell Palace, which was given under Royal Charter to the City of London, the School moved to Witley in 1867, simultaneously changing its name; it became co-educational again in 1952. The School is an independent boarding and day school for girls and boys aged 11–18. The School has 400 pupils; approximately 40% are day pupils. There are a substantial number of bursaries, currently around 75, available to help boys and girls whose home circumstances make a boarding style of education a particular need.

The School is situated in a 100-acre campus in an Area of Outstanding Natural Beauty in the Surrey countryside, approximately ten miles south of Guildford, with Heathrow and Gatwick international airports both within a 45-minute drive.

King Edward's Witley is steeped in history, but combines its traditional strengths with a modern outlook. The School prides itself on its ability to provide a school community that reflects the real world admitting pupils from a broad range of academic, social, economic and cultural backgrounds – 65% are English native speakers and 45 countries are represented. All children are nurtured to encourage independent thinking and a spirit of respect and understanding for others, resulting in a mature and well-rounded outlook on life and a commitment to upholding the strongest moral values.

King Edward's Witley is proud to be one of the first English boarding schools in the area to offer the IB Diploma Programme and has been offering the IB for 14 years. In 2018 72.6% achieved grade 7–5, the equivalent of A*, A & B grades at A Level. 41.6% achieved grade 7–6, the equivalent of A* and A grades at A Level. The average points obtained per pass was 32.4 (out of 45) and the average grade obtained per subject was 5.19 (out of 7). Three pupils scored 40+ points and the top points score was 44 (out of 45).

From 2015, King Edward's has also offered the new A Level course as an alternative to the IB, ensuring pupils have a choice of routes to secure a place at university. In 2018 10% of cohort averaged 149 UCAS points (A*AA or equivalent) and 25% of cohort averaged 130 UCAS points (ABB or equivalent).

In 2018 at GCSE 84% of pupils achieved 5 or more grades at A*–C including English Language and Mathematics. 45.5% of grades were A*–A (national average 21.3%); 92.6% of grades were A*–C (national average 65.3%).

The School also runs a one-year Pre Sixth Form course for overseas pupils, representing an opportunity to improve English language skills and trial both IB and A Level subjects on offer, allowing for more Sixth Form choices.

Renowned for its ability to nurture pupils so they excel in their academic studies, King Edward's Witley also provides a highly motivating and inspiring environment for children to equally thrive in other sporting / creative activities. The School has an excellent reputation for its welcoming community and the provision of high-quality pastoral care.

The 1st and 2nd Forms constitute the Lower School and are accommodated in Queen Mary House with shared communal facilities for boys and girls. From the 3rd Form upwards boys and girls live in seven modern, purpose-built paired houses where the accommodation and study areas are completely separate but everyone can come together in the shared communal facilities on the ground floor.

Facilities at the School are second to none and include a brand new state-of-the-art Business and Finance Centre, indoor swimming pool, gym, all-weather hockey and tennis playing fields and a central dining hall, which delivers an outstanding standard of catering. The School pioneered paired boarding houses with communal areas, where everyone can come together in their spare time to enjoy games, TV, music and conversation in the common rooms, kitchen, music and television rooms. For the Sixth Form, a lively common room, new Sixth Form prefects room, study area and careers library provide an environment for independent learning and recreation.

Admission. Children are normally admitted at 11+, 13+ and 16+ but if there is room they may be admitted at other times, and occasionally a child who should clearly be working alongside older children is admitted at 10+. Admission is by pre-testing or by the School's own entrance examination and interview taken normally in the January prior to entry.

Fees per term (2018–2019). Boarders: Lower School £10,270, Forms 3–5 £10,270, (Pre) Sixth Form £10,665, including all boarding and tuition fees, books and games equipment, and the provision of school uniform and games clothing.

Day Pupils: Lower School £5,120, Forms 3–5 £6,400, (Pre) Sixth Form £6,820, including meals and uniform. Individual music tuition in piano, organ, singing and all orchestral instruments is available.

Bursaries. Bursaries are available for both boarding and day pupils. The School has an endowment providing support for children whose circumstances make boarding a particular need. Awards are reviewed annually with regard to parental circumstances and to school fees. They may be given in conjunction with Local Education Authority grants or help from a charitable trust. The School has a dedicated Bursaries Officer who works with applicants to source the financial support needed to enable worthy candidates to join the School.

Scholarships. Academic, Art, Drama, DT, Music and Sports Scholarships are offered at 11+, 13+ or 16+ for entry to the Sixth Form. These awards will be up to a maximum of 30% of full fees but may be augmented in case of financial need. Children of serving members of the armed forces will be considered for a discount. There is a special IB Sixth Form Day scholarship available, awarding 100% of fees.

Charitable status. King Edward's Witley is a Registered Charity, number 311997. The Foundation exists to provide boarding education for families whose circumstances make boarding a particular need, though the excellent facilities and the high standards of academic achievement and pastoral care make it attractive also to any family looking for a modern and distinctive education.

Treasurer and Chairman of Governors: Mrs J Voisin, BA

Headmaster: **J Attwater**, MA

Senior Deputy Headmaster: S J Pugh, MA

Academic Staff:
* Head of Department
† Housemaster/mistress

G Ainge, BSc (*Science*)
Mrs S Antill, NatDip (*ICT*)
R Arch, MA (**Economics & Business Studies*)
B Arthey, BA (*Guitar*)
J Attwater, MA (*Headmaster, Religious Studies & Philosophy*)
Mrs V Attwater, BMus (*Music*)
Dr P Attwell, BSc, PhD (*Science*)
A Bardell (*Technician – Art & Photography*)
A Baynes, MA (**Modern Languages*)
M Bennett, BA (**History*)
Mrs A Butler (*School Office Administrator*)
Mrs S Butler, BA, MEd (**Learning Support and EAL*)
Miss T Butterworth, BMus (*Double Bass*)
T Campbell, BA (**Geography*)
Miss E Cattle, MA (**Classics*)
Dr P Cave, LRAM, GRSM, ARAM, PhD (*Piano*)
R Chadwick, Dip ABRSM (*Classical Guitar*)
Mrs Z Clarke, MA (*Deputy Head Academic, Classics, English*)
Mrs L Cleaves, BA, MA (**Drama*)
B Cochrane, BEng (*Science*)
Miss S Condy, BTh, MA (*†Elizabeth, Religious Studies & Philosophy*)
Miss T Cowell, BMus, MMus (*Brass*)

J G Culbert, BSc, Dip Comp Sc (*Science*, *Physics*)
R Davies, BSc, MLitt, MA (*Sixth Form, Mathematics*)
Miss J Dibb-Fuller, BSc (*Learning Support and EAL*)
Miss A Edwards, BA (*Graduate Assistant Teacher Art & Photography*)
Mrs S Ellison, BA, LRAM (*Bassoon*)
N Emsley, BSc, Dip Com (†*Grafton, Mathematics, Science, Theory of Knowledge and Critical Thinking*)
T Frazer, BA (*Graduate Assistant Teacher Music*)
D G Galbraith, BSc (*Chemistry*)
S Gardner (*Head of Lower School*, †*Queen Mary House, Drama, English, PSHE*)
Mrs K Gardner, Dip (†*Queen Mary House, Voice*)
A Guthrie (*Science Technician*)
Mrs H Hanley, BSc (*Geography, ICT*)
Mrs R Hallam, BSc (*Careers and Higher Education*)
Mrs E Harman, BSc (†*Ridley, Economics & Business Studies*)
Mrs J Harris, BA (*Library & Resources, Extended Essay Coordinator*)
Mrs L Harris-Jones, BA, MA, MBA, (*Religious Studies and Philosophy*, *Theory of Knowledge and Critical Thinking*)
M Harrison, BA (*Director of Co-Curriculum and Leadership, Modern Languages*)
G Haylock, BA (*Head of Football*)
P W Head, BEng, MPhil (*Mathematics*)
J Hennessey-Brown, ARCM, BMus (*Cello*)
Mrs A Hill, BSc (*Science Technician*)
Mrs R Hillage, PGCE, BA (*Learning Support and EAL*)
Mrs S J Hinde-Brown, BA (*Modern Languages*)
Mrs J A Hinton, BSc (*Modern Languages*)
Mrs G Holtham, BA (*Modern Languages*)
Mrs J Hooker (*Technician, Design & Technology Food and Textiles*)
Miss S Hughes, MChem (*Science*)
Ms U John, GMD, RNCM (*Violin and Viola*)
A N K Johnson, BSc, MSc (*Design & Technology Resistant Materials*)
J C Langan, BA, MEd Cantab (*Middle School, English*)
Mrs T Lambe, MSc (*Mathematics*)
D Laurence, BA (*Economics & Business Studies*)
Dr A Lennard, PhD, BSc (*ICT*)
G Lynch-Frahill, BSc, BEd, MEd (*History, Theory of Knowledge and Critical Thinking*)
Mrs J M Lyttle, BA (†*Queens', English & Drama*)
A Macmillan, BA (†*Wakefield, Design & Technology Resistant Materials*)
Mrs S Matthews, BSc, MSc (*Science Technician*)
Mrs A Meyer, BSc, BEd (*Mathematics, Assistant Head of Sixth Form, Pre Sixth Coordinator*)
Dr H Mir, PhD (*Mathematics*)
Mrs L Moore, BA (*Art & Photography*)
Mrs P V Nash, BEd (*Science*)
Miss S Patel, MA (*Artist in Residence*)
Mrs M Pevreall, BSc, MSc (*Biology*)
Mrs M Phillips, BA (*History*)
Mrs C Pitt, BA (*Art & Photography*)
S J Pugh, MA (*Senior Deputy Headmaster, Classics*)
Mrs H Pullen (*Girls' Sport Development*)
Mrs C Richards BMusEd (*Organist in Residence*)
C Robinson (*Technician, Design & Technology Resistant Materials*)
A Shaw, BSc (*Graduate Assistant Teacher PE and Sport*)
Mrs C Shouksmith, BA (*Art & Photography*)
A Sibacher, BSc (*Mathematics*)
B Simmonds, BMus, Dip ABRSM, LLB, MPerf (*Piano*)
A Skau, BA (*Language Assistant*)
Mrs N Skau, BSc (†*Tudor, PSHE, Modern Languages, Library & Resources*)
D Slater, BA (*English*)

S Sliwka, BMus, FRCO, LRSM (*Director of Music*)
Miss A Small, BSc (*Design & Technology Food & Textiles*)
Rev Dr D Standen, AKC, CTM, BA, PhD (*Classics, School Chaplain*)
D Standing, MA RAM (*Voice*)
Mrs H Thorpe, BA (*Geography*)
D Tobias, BA (†*Edward, English, Theory of Knowledge and Critical Thinking*)
Mrs J Todd (*Examinations Officer*)
S L Todd, BSc (*Examinations Officer*)
J Trinder, BA, MA (*Religious Studies & Philosophy*)
Mrs A Valentino, BA, MEd (*English*)
Mrs C van der Vijer, BA (*Language Assistant*)
Mrs B Waters, BEd (*Modern Languages*)
Mrs A Webster, BA (*Learning Support and EAL*)
Ms J Webster, BMus (*Flute*)
S Whittaker, BMus (*Percussion*)
H Wiggin, BMus, Grad Dip, MPerf (*Clarinet, Saxophone*)
Mrs K A Wilson, DipM, ACIM (*Economics & Business Studies*)
Mrs C Wickramasinghe De Silva, BA QTS (*Learning Support and EAL*)

Houses and Housemasters/Housemistresses:

Queen Mary House (*Junior Boys and Girls*): S Gardner and Mrs K Gardner
Senior Paired Houses:
Wakefield (*Boys*): A Macmillan and *Elizabeth* (*Girls*): Miss S Condy
Edward (*Boys*): D Tobias and *Tudor* (*Girls*): Mrs N Skau
Ridley (*Boys*): Mrs E Harman and *Queens'* (*Girls*): Mrs J Lyttle
Grafton (*Boys*): N Emsley

Director of Finance and Administration: A Lewis
Director of Admissions & Communications: J Benson
Head of Marketing: Miss N Dimmock
Development Director: Ms L Humphreys
PA to the Headmaster: Miss F Sumner

King Henry VIII School
(Part of the Coventry School Foundation)

Warwick Road, Coventry CV3 6AQ
Tel: 024 7627 1111
email: info@khviii.net
website: www.khviii.com
Twitter: @KHVIIISchool
Facebook: @KingHenryVIIISchool

Founded in 1545 by John Hales, Clerk of the Hanaper to the King, under Letters Patent of King Henry VIII, King Henry VIII School has a deserved reputation as one of the finest independent, co-educational day schools in the UK.

"Success, responsibility and enjoyment – these are our prime aims", states Jason Slack, Headmaster.

The school is represented on the Headmasters' Conference and on the Association of Governing Bodies of Independent Schools. The governing body is the Coventry School Foundation, on which are represented Sir Thomas White's Charity, the Coventry Church Charities, Coventry General Charities and Birmingham, Coventry, Oxford and Warwick Universities. There are also several co-opted Governors.

There are 414 boys and 326 girls in the Senior School, and 256 boys and 215 girls in the Prep School.

Facilities. The school moved to its present extensive site in a pleasant part of Coventry in 1885. The Governors have continually improved, extended and restored the buildings which are well equipped to cope with the demands of an up-to-date, relevant and challenging curriculum. The school has extensive playing fields, some of which are located on the main site. Other playing fields are five minutes away by minibus.

The Governors have committed themselves to a major building programme at the school. A new Prep School, Art facility, Sixth Form Centre and Sports Hall have recently been completed. Both Senior and Prep Schools have a first-rate computer network available to all pupils. A six-lane, 25m swimming pool (and fitness suite) opened in 2009. An Archive was opened in 2014 containing a timeline from 1545 to 2014 and original Tudor artefacts.

Curriculum. The curriculum is broad and balanced, integrating National Curriculum principles and practices where appropriate. The Senior School curriculum provides courses leading to the GCSE examinations and GCE AS and A Levels. Subjects available currently are Art, Biology, Business Studies, Chemistry, Classical Civilisation, Computing, Design and Food Technology, Drama and Theatre Studies, Economics, English, French, Geography, German, Greek, History, Information and Communication Technology, Latin, Law, Mathematics, Music, Photography, Psychology, Physics, Religious Studies and Spanish. Physical Education and Sport are also considered to be a vital part of the curriculum and are available as an AS and A2 Level option. All students follow a structured PSHE course.

Courses in Key Skills/Complementary Studies and Critical Thinking are offered in the Sixth Form. The Extended Project Qualification was introduced for Year 13 in 2012.

Examination results at all levels are excellent.

Games. Rugby, Hockey, Netball, Basketball, Cross-Country Running, Athletics, Rounders, Tennis, Cricket, Swimming, Golf, Orienteering and Fencing. Prep School games include Tag Rugby, Swimming, Soccer, Rounders, Athletics, Cricket and Cross-Country Running. In 1986 the largest artificial turf games area in the country was created, and refurbished in 2014, used mainly for hockey, but providing an additional 24 tennis courts in the summer. This facility is shared with Bablake School.

Extracurricular Activities. The School is noted for the excellence of its sport, music, drama, debating, public speaking and outdoor pursuits. All pupils are encouraged to make a contribution to the extracurricular life of the school. The School has close connections with many universities including Oxford and Cambridge.

Admission. Admission is via the School's own Entrance Examination, held annually in October for entrance the following September. The normal age of entry is 11, but there are additional intakes at other ages and also at Sixth Form level. All enquiries about admission to the school should be addressed to the Headmaster.

Scholarships. The Governors award annually a number (not fixed) of entrance bursaries and scholarships. Full details regarding financial assistance are available from the Headmaster at the school.

Old Coventrians Association. Email: alumni@khviii.net; website: www.khviii.com.

Fees per term (2018–2019). Senior School £3,898; Prep School £2,981–£3,087.

Prep School. The Prep School is based on two nearby sites and enjoys excellent facilities which include an Early Years Centre, a Library, ICT rooms with networked PCs, an Art and Design rooms, a Science room, Astroturf and Sports Hall and a Music room. Children are accepted by competitive examination from 7+ to 10+. The emphasis is on a broad education based upon the National Curriculum and children are prepared for the Entrance Examination for entry to the Senior School.

(*For further information about the Prep School, see entry in IAPS section.*)

Charitable status. Coventry School Foundation is a Registered Charity, number 528961. Its aim is to advance the education of boys and girls by the provision of a school or schools in or near the City of Coventry.

Chairman of Governors: Mrs Julia McNaney

Senior School

Headmaster: **Mr Jason Slack**, BSc, MA Ed

Deputy Heads:
Dr Michele Cuthbert, BSc, MEd, HDipEd, WITS
Mr Philip Dearden, MA Ed, BA
Mr Richard Sewell, PGCE, BA Hons

Teaching Staff:
Miss Lucy Ainsworth
Mr Naz Amlani, BSc
Mr Tom Andrews, BSc
Mr Conn Anson-O'Connell, BA
Miss Sarah Baker, BSc
Miss Marysia Bancroft, MA
Dr Steven Barge, BA
Mrs Michelle Bayne-Jardine, MA, MPhil, LLB
Mr Matthew Blake, MPhys
Mr Philip Bond, BA, PG Cert RE
Mrs Sally Bradley, BA
Miss Sally Burton, BA
Dr Helen Buttrick, MA, MSCi
Mr James Carlyle, BA
Mrs Anna Clegg, BA
Mrs Louise Collett, BA
Dr Rosalyn Coull, BMus, MMus, PhD
Mrs Carrie Dowding, BSc
Mr Jon Fitt, BSc
Miss Laura Garcia, BA
Miss Margot Griffiths, BSc
Mr Richard Harrington, MA
Dr Debbie Hayton, BSc
Mrs Anna Heathcote, BA
Mr John Henderson, BA
Mrs Julie Holland, BA
Dr Tim Honeywill, MMath
Mrs Linda Horton, MA
Mrs Kathryn Hunt, BSc
Mrs Merun Hussein, BA
Mr Peter Huxford, MA
Mrs Anna Jewell, BA
Mrs Joanne Jones, BEd
Mr Nicholas Jones, MA
Mrs Victoria Kaczur, BA
Mr Andrew Keeley, BTec App Biol
Mrs Aileen Lockey, MA, DipEd
Mr Alistair Kennedy, BA, BA Mus
Mr Duncan Lovell, LLB, MA
Mr Peter Manning, MA
Mrs Rachel Mason, BSc
Mrs Jaynita Mattu, BSc
Mr Craig McKee, BTEC NDip, BSc
Dr Mary McKenzie, MA
Mr Nick Meynell, BA
Mr John Miller, MA
Mrs Jenny Morris, MA
Miss Sarah Mould, BA
Mrs Cindy Neale, MA
Mr Robin Newton, BA, MA Cantab
Dr Donna Norman, BSc
Mr Francis O'Reilly, BA

Mrs Kerry Owens, BEd
Mrs Kulwinder Pabla, MSc
Mrs Denise Pandya, BMus
Mr Andrew Parker, BEd
Mr Guy Parker, BSc
Dr Adam Petherwick, BSc
Mr Rob Phillips, BA
Mrs Dolores Pittaway, BA, PG Dip
Mrs Jessica Proudlock, BA
Mrs Debra Quinn, BA
Mr Alastair Rendle, BEng
Dr Lynn Reynolds, BSc
Ms Sally Ridley, BA, MBA
Mr Paul Robbins, MEng
Mrs Lynne Roote, BSc
Miss Tajinder Sanghera, MA
Mrs Christine Spriggs, BSc
Miss Grace Spring, BA
Miss Sally Spruce
Mr Stuart Sweetman, MA
Mr Thomas Swinford
Mr Neil Tingle, BA
Mrs AJ Tracey, BSc
Mrs Kate Whitehead, BSc
Mrs Lisa Whiteman, Nat Dip Perf Arts, Higher Nat Dip
    Dance
Mr Chris Wilde, BA

Administrative Staff:
Director of Finance & Operations: Mrs Jacqui Hammond
School Administrator: Mrs Julie Low, HND
Headmaster's PA/Admissions Secretary: Mrs Amanda
    Skinner
Marketing Manager: Mrs Suzanne Jackson
Examinations Officer: Mrs Belinda Leslie, MBA
Careers Advisor: Mrs Sally Pike, BA, Dip Careers
    Guidance
Chaplain: Revd Alison Hogger-Gadsby, BA, Dip HE,
    Clerk in Holy Orders
School Nurse: Mrs Sarah Cadwallader, RGN
School Network Manager: Mr Tim Lees
Office Manager: Mrs Ravinder Bhuhi, BSc Hons, MSc
Sports Centre Manager: Mr Neil Beckett
Librarian: Ms Helen Cooper, LLB, PGCE
Alumni Relations Officer: Mrs Kathryn Goodfellow, BSc
    Hons

King Henry VIII Preparatory School

Head: Mrs Gill Bowser, BA Hons, NPQH
Deputy Head (Swallows): Miss Caroline Soan, GMus,
    PGCE
Deputy Head (Hales): Mrs Kate Price, BA Hons, PGCE
Assistant Head (Swallows): Mrs Kate Parkes, BA, PGCE
Assistant Head (Hales): Mrs Manisha Patel, MA, PGCE
Inclusion Leader: Mrs Claire Brindley, Bsc
School Business Manager: Mrs Christine Clough, Cert.
    School Business Management

Teaching Staff:
Mrs Rachel Avlonti, BEd
Ms Emma Barwell, BA
Miss Nicola Bawcutt, BMus, PGCE
Mr Greg Beaufoy, BSc
Mrs Sarah Brand, BEd
Miss Lynn Brown, BSc, PGCE
Mrs Nazan Cooper, BA, PGCE
Mrs Emma Curran, BEd
Mr Steve Dhaliwal, BEd, MSc
Mrs Justine Doe, PGCE
Mrs Lucy Duckers, BA, PGCE
Mrs Charlotte Ferguson, BA
Mrs Rachel Gallon, MA, PGCE

Mrs Sarah Gillett, BA
Miss Rebecca Green, BA
Mrs Julia Halstead, BA, PGCE
Mrs Helen Harvey, BA
Miss Danielle Jack, BA
Miss Shona Johnson, MA, PGCE
Mrs Rajwinder Lidder, BA
Miss Emily Manship, BSc, PGCE
Mr Philip McGrane, BSc, PGCE
Mrs Helen Mellor, BEd
Mrs Ruth Morris, BA, PGCE
Mr Neil Mosedale, BSc, PGCE
Mrs Kelly Osman, BA, PGCE
Mrs Sonja Parker, BEd
Mr Ken Pearson, BEd
Miss Jenna Sainsbury, BA, PGCE
Mr Phil Savage, BA, PGCE
Mrs Jill Sutherland, BA
Mrs Emma Tucker, Bed
Mr Jack Vaabel, PGCE
Mrs Sian Westmancoat, BA Ed
Mrs Helen Williamson, BSc
Miss Nicola Wood, BS, PGCE
Ms Kate Wozencroft, BEd Hons
Mrs Sophia Wright, BA, PGCE

Support Staff:
Admin Officer: Mrs Didi Parker
Admissions Officer: Mrs Kelly Harrison
HR & Finance Officer: Mrs Gillian Barge
IT Technician: Miss Abi Brown
Librarian: Mrs Anna Cowell
Medical Assistant (Swallows): Miss Dawn Cook
Nursery Manager: Mrs Sharon Doran
Nursery Nurse: Miss Lisa Adams
Nursery Nurse: Miss Fiona Allan-Smith
Receptionist: Mrs Suzanne Brannigan
Receptionist/Medical Assistant: Miss Christina Lawless
Receptionist: Mrs Sharon Bradley
Receptionist: Miss Nicola Baker
Site Services Assistant: Mr Simon Gulliver
*Specialist Sports Teaching Assistant & Holiday Sports
    Club Leader*: Mr Simeon Newland-Smith
Teaching Assistant: Mrs Naomi Draper
Teaching Assistant – HLTA/Thrive Practitioner: Mrs Krista
    Gayton
Teaching Assistant: Miss Emma Lawless
Teaching Assistant: Mrs Kimberley Lunn
Teaching Assistant: Mrs Hayley McTeigue
Teaching Assistant – HLTA: Mrs Helen Smith
Teaching Assistant: Mrs Anu Dudha
Teaching Assistant: Mrs Manminder Gill
Teaching Assistant: Mrs Kay Montgomery
Teaching Assistant – HLTA: Mrs Julie Reeve
Teaching Assistant – HLTA: Miss Jo Rothwell
*Teaching Assistant, Wraparound Play-worker & Holiday
    Club Play-worker*: Miss Shamim Suleman
Wraparound Play-worker & Holiday Club Play-worker:
    Miss Jade Clements
Wraparound Play-worker: Miss Sabina Parveen
Wraparound & Holiday Club Supervisor: Mrs Natasha
    Cagribay
*Wraparound Supervisor, Holiday Club Play-worker &
    Swimming Assistant*: Mrs Caroline Blincow

King William's College

Castletown, Isle of Man IM9 1TP

Tel: 01624 820400
email: admissions@kwc.im
website: www.kwc.im

Motto: *Assiduitate, non desidia*

King William's College owes its foundation to Dr Isaac Barrow, Bishop of Sodor and Man from 1663 to 1671, who established an Educational Trust in 1668. The funds of the Trust were augmented by public subscription and the College was opened in 1833 and named after King William IV, 'The Sailor King'.

In 1991, the College merged with the Isle of Man's other independent school, The Buchan School, Castletown, which had been founded by Lady Laura Buchan in 1875 to provide education for young ladies. The Buchan School has been reformed as the junior section of the College for boys and girls up to age 11. (*For further details of The Buchan School, see entry in IAPS section*).

The Isle of Man, being internally self-governing, has a very favourable tax structure and the independence of College would not be affected by changes in UK legislation.

The College is set in superb countryside on the edge of Castletown Bay and adjacent to Ronaldsway Airport. The Isle of Man is approximately 33 miles long and 13 miles wide and is an area of diverse and beautiful scenery. The Isle of Man is an unusually safe environment with a very low crime rate.

There are approximately 370 pupils at College and a further 160 pupils at the Preparatory School. There is also a Nursery School for 2 to 4 year olds on the Buchan site. Both King William's College and The Buchan School are fully co-educational.

Entry. New pupils are accepted at any time, but most begin at the start of the September Term. Boys and girls are admitted to the Preparatory School up to the age of 11 at which point transfer to King William's College is automatic. Entry to College, including Sixth Form level, is by Head's report and interview.

Further details and a prospectus may be obtained from the Admissions Office to which applications for entry should be made.

Organisation. The school is divided into three sections: Fourth Form (Years 7 & 8), Fifth Form (Years 9, 10 & 11) and Sixth Form (Years 12 & 13). Each section is led by a Head of Year, assisted by a team of tutors who monitor the academic progress and deal with all day-to-day matters relating to the pupils in their charge. In addition, all pupils are placed in one of three co-educational Houses for internal competitive purposes, which provides an important element of continuity throughout a pupil's career at the School.

Boarders. There are two houses: one for boys and the other for girls. The living and sleeping accommodation is arranged principally in study-bedrooms for senior pupils with junior pupils sharing with one other student. Each House has its own Houseparent who is responsible for the pastoral welfare of the pupils. He or she is assisted by two or three tutors, of whom at least two are resident.

Chapel. The College is a Church of England foundation but pupils of all denominations attend Chapel; the spirit of the services is distinctly ecumenical.

Curriculum. Pupils at both Schools follow the National Curriculum in its essentials.

The curriculum is designed to provide a broad, balanced and challenging form of study for all pupils. At 11–13 pupils take English, Mathematics, French and Spanish or Latin, Science, History, Geography, Design Technology, ICT, Art, Music, Drama, Religious Studies, Physical Education, PSHE. Pupils then go on to study typically 9 or 10 subjects at IGCSE/GCSE level from a wide number of options.

In the Sixth Form King William's College offers the **International Baccalaureate**. Students choose 6 subjects, normally 3 at higher level and 3 at standard level, which must include their first language, a second language, a science, a social science and Mathematics. In addition, students write an extended essay (a research piece of 4,000 words), follow a course in the Theory of Knowledge (practical philosophy) and spend the equivalent of one half day a week on some form of creative aesthetic activity or active community service (e.g. Duke of Edinburgh's Award fulfils this requirement).

Music and Drama. There are excellent facilities for Drama with House plays and at least one major school production each year, together with regular coaching in Speech and Drama. There are Junior and Senior Bands and Choirs, and a very flourishing Chapel Choir. The House Music competition is one of the many focal points of House activity.

Games. The College has a strong tradition and a fine reputation in the major games of rugby, hockey, netball and cricket. There are regular fixtures with Isle of Man schools and schools in other parts of the British Isles. Athletics, football, cross-country and swimming all flourish and there are both House and College competitions. Senior pupils may opt to play golf on the magnificent adjoining Castletown Golf Links or to sail as their major summer sport. There are approximately thirty acres of first class playing fields, an indoor heated swimming pool which is in use throughout the year, a miniature rifle range, a gymnasium for basketball and badminton, hard tennis courts, two squash courts and an all-weather pitch and outdoor cricket nets.

Other Activities. There is a wide range of societies and activities to complement academic life. The Duke of Edinburgh's Award Scheme flourishes and expeditions are undertaken regularly both on the Island and further afield. There is a thriving Combined Cadet Force and Social Services group. There are strong links with the Armed Services who help regularly with Cadet training. There are regular skiing trips, choir tours and educational trips to the UK and abroad.

Travel. King William's College is easily accessible from the UK and abroad. Some boarders come by sea from Heysham or Liverpool using the regular service to Douglas but the majority of boarding pupils and parents come by air from the British Isles and much further afield. There are direct flights to London, Belfast, Birmingham, Dublin, Liverpool, Manchester, Bristol and other UK cities. Boarding House staff are fully experienced in arranging international flights and younger pupils are met at the airport.

Health. The health of all pupils is in the care of the School Doctor. There is a sanatorium supervised by a qualified nursing staff and high standards of medical care are available at Noble's Hospital in Douglas.

Fees per term (2018–2019). Day: £5,600 (Years 7 & 8), £6,520 (Years 9–11), £7,450 (Years 12 & 13). Boarding Fee: £3,362 in addition to Day Fee.

A reduction of one-third of the fee for boarders and one half of the fee for day pupils is allowed for children of clergy holding a benefice or Bishop's licence and residing in the Isle of Man. There is a similar arrangement for children of Methodist Ministers.

A reduction of 15% is allowed for serving members of the Armed Forces of the Crown. Once a pupil is accepted, the reduction continues even though the parent may leave the Services.

A reduction is allowed for the second, third and fourth child.

Scholarships and Bursaries. Year 7 Academic Scholarships are offered up to the value of 20% of the current tuition fee and examinations take place in late January. There are papers in English and Mathematics and an interview.

Sixth Form Academic Scholarships are offered up to the value of 20% of the current tuition fee and examinations are normally held in November of the year prior to entry and February of the year of entry. There are papers in Mathematics, English, one other subject chosen by the candidate and an interview.

Drama, Golf, Music and Sports Awards to the value of 20% of the tuition fee are available to candidates entering either the Lower Fourth or the Lower Sixth Form who demonstrate exceptional talent or potential. Examinations and auditions take place by arrangement.

There is also a Bursary fund to support students if the financial circumstances of parents make this necessary.

Further details of all scholarships may be obtained from the Principal's Office and on the website.

Charitable status. King William's College is a Manx Registered Charity, number 615 and is operated as a Company limited by guarantee.

Visitor:
The Most Reverend and Right Hon Dr J Sentamu, Lord Archbishop of York

Council Members of Bishop Barrow's Foundation:
His Excellency Sir Richard Gozney, Lieutenant Governor of the Isle of Man (*Chairman of Council Members*)
[1]Professor R Barr, Chief Executive Officer, Department of Education and Children*
Mr S Billinghurst, BA Hons, ACA
[1]The Venerable A Brown, MA, Archdeacon of Man
[1]Mr A C Collister, CCTC
[1]Mr T W B Cullen, MBE, MA
The Lord Bishop, Rt Revd P Eagles
[1]Mrs E J Higgins, BSc, ACA
[1]Dr M J Hoy, MBE, MA, PhD
[1]Mr N H Wood, ACA, TEP

[1] *Also Trustee of Bishop Barrow's Charity*

Governors:
Mr N H Wood, ACA, TEP (*Chairman*)
Mr S Billinghurst, BA Hons, ACA
Mr A C Collister, CCTC
Mr P B Clucas, BA, BSc Hons
Mrs C Edmundson, BMus, MBA, PGCE, LRAM, ARCM
Mr M Grace, BSc Hons, MRICS
Mr P L Harwood, BSc Hons, FIA
Mrs E J Higgins, BSc, ACA
Dr L V Hulme, LRCP, MRCS
Miss S J Leahy, LLB, Dip LP
Mr R Raatgever, BCom, BAcc Hons, CA SA, ACA

Bursar and Clerk to the Governors: Mr J V Oatts, BA, MSc, Dip Surv

Principal: **J H Buchanan**, BA

Deputy Head Academic: Miss C L Broadbent, MA
Deputy Head Pastoral: Mr S L Corrie, BMus

* *Head of Department*
† *Housemaster/mistress*

Ms R Abbott, BA
Mr J M Allegro, BA
Mrs M Bailey-Barnes, BA
Mrs E J Ballantyne, BSc
Mrs A G Beesley, BA
Miss C R Beswick, MSci

Mrs K E Brew, BEng
Mr H Brindle, BA
Mrs A Z A Clarke, MA (**English*)
Mr S N Cope, BA (**Geography*)
Mr M C Crabtree, BSc (**Boys PE & Games*)
Mrs K M Brown, MPhys (**Physics*)
Mrs D J Currie, BA (**Religious Studies, History*)
Mr C Davidson, MA
Mr S M Daykin, BMus (*Director of Music*)
Miss E F Drane, BA
Mrs B Dunn, BEd (*Director of Sport*)
Mrs S M Ellson, MA
Miss C Ganzo Perez, BA
Ms M Gerbaut
Miss S Hathaway, BA
Miss F Heckel, MA (**French, *Modern Languages*)
Miss L Hewes (**Latin, Deputy Head of Sixth Form*)
Ms V Hope, BSc
Mr N A Howell-Evans, BA (*Head of Science*)
Mr E J Jeffers, BA (*Head of Boarding, †Colbourne House*)
Mrs S A Jeffers, BA
Mr S B Jelly (*Head of Fourth Form*)
Mr S P Kelly, BA (**Art*)
Miss A Kerr, MA
Mrs B Kneen, BSc (*Head of Fifth Form*)
Mr A Laiz-Rubio
Mr O Lloyd, BA
Mr D M C Matthews, BSc (**Mathematics*)
Mrs A L Morgans, BA Ed, BSc (*Head of Sixth Form*)
Dr P H Morgans, BSc, PhD (**Science, *Chemistry*)
Mrs J Munro, BA
Mrs G R Murphy, MCLIP (*Librarian*)
Mr R C Parry, BSc
Mrs S Parry, BA (*†School House*)
Mr R Riekert, BComm (**Economics*)
Mrs A M Schreiber, MA
Ms Z E Shimmin, BSc
Mrs C V Singleton, BA (**Drama*)
Mr C Smith, BA
Mr M C D Taylor, BA
Miss K K Teare, BSc
Mr A D Ulyett, BSc (**Biology, IB Coordinator*)
Mr P Verschueren, MSc
Mrs Z A Watterson
Ms M Westall, BSc
Miss E C Winstanley, BA
Mr J J Wood, MSc

Part-time Staff:
Miss J Busuttil, BA
Mrs J M Finch, MA
Miss B C Harkin, MA
Mrs P Howell Evans, BA
Mrs S A Ross, BEd
Mrs E Sinclair, BA
Reverend E J Scott, BA (*Chaplain*)

Principal's PA: Mrs J Bateson
Admissions Registrar: Mrs M Taggart
School Medical Officer: Dr Marijtje Drijfhout, MRCGP, DRCOG, DFFP, DPalMed, DOcMed

King's College School

Wimbledon Common, London SW19 4TT

Tel:	020 8255 5300 (Senior School)
	020 8255 5335 (Junior School)
Fax:	020 8255 5309 (Senior School)
	020 8255 5339 (Junior School)
email:	admissions@kcs.org.uk (Senior School)
	jsadmissions@kcs.org.uk (Junior School)
website:	www.kcs.org.uk
Twitter:	@KCSWimbledon
Facebook:	@kingscollegeschool

Motto: *Sancte et Sapienter*

King's College School was founded as the junior department of King's College in 1829. According to the resolutions adopted at the preliminary meeting of founders in 1828, "the system is to comprise religious and moral instruction, classical learning, history, modern languages, mathematics, natural philosophy, etc., and to be so conducted as to provide in the most effectual manner for the two great objects of education the communication of general knowledge, and specific preparation for particular professions". In 1897 it was removed from the Strand to its present spacious site on Wimbledon Common.

Organisation. King's College School is a day school. Boys only are admitted below the sixth form whilst the sixth form is co-educational. The school consists of a senior school of 975 pupils aged 11 to 18 and a junior school of 435 pupils aged 7 to 13 who are prepared for entry to the senior school. On entry to the senior school, pupils are placed in a house. Every pupil has a tutor who is responsible for their progress and welfare throughout their school career.

Admission. Entrance at 13+ to year 9 is via a pre-test which boys sit in year 6 followed by the CE or scholarship in year 8. Since September 2016, the senior school has admitted boys in year 7 after entrance tests in year 6. Candidates from King's College Junior School sit either the transfer examination or the scholarship examination. Places for girls and boys are available each year for entry to the sixth form. Preliminary enquiries about entry should be made to the admissions registrar. A non-refundable registration fee of £150 is charged.

Junior School. Entrance examinations, graded according to the ages of the pupils, are held in the January of the year of entry. Enquiries should be made to the junior school secretary. (*For further details of the junior school refer to entry in IAPS section.*)

Scholarships.

11+ Academic scholarships for entrance into the senior school. After the 11+ examinations and interviews, boys who have performed exceptionally well and shown the greatest promise and potential will be awarded scholarships. Rogers scholarships, which currently carry a £1,500 per annum reduction in fees, are named after one of the school's most successful and influential Head Masters: Herbert Lionel Rogers. Cayley scholarships, which currently carry a £750 per annum reduction in fees, are named after Arthur Cayley, an eminent mathematician and one of King's most notable old boys.

11+ Music scholarships: One or more scholarships currently worth up to £1,500 of the school tuition fee, plus free instrumental tuition on two instruments, may be awarded each year. It may also be possible to gain an exhibition, which is a smaller award. This will depend on the quality of the candidates each year. Suitable applicants will be invited to an audition, which takes place at a similar time to the

interviews, if they have also been invited back for an academic interview.

11+ Sport scholarships: One or more scholarships currently worth up to £1,500 of the school tuition fee may be available. It may also be possible to gain an exhibition, which is a smaller award. This will depend on the quality of the candidates each year. An assessment day is held before the entrance examinations take place in December of year 6.

13+ Academic scholarships: Up to 15 academic scholarships may be awarded. The number will vary according to the quality of the candidates. Candidates must be under 14 years of age on 1st September of the year in which they sit the examination. This is held at King's College School in early May. The maximum award for major scholarships is currently £1,500. Smaller awards will be fixed sums currently of £1,000, or £500. If a pupil is awarded two or more scholarships, the maximum fee remission is currently £2,000 pa. All additional financial benefits will be means tested, so that any award would be supplemented by fee remission of up to 100% inclusive of the scholarship.

13+ Art scholarships: One or more art scholarship and/or exhibition currently worth up to £1,500 of the school tuition fee per annum may be awarded annually to a boy of high artistic ability or potential. Selection will be by folio inspection and by invitation to a half-day of practical work in an informal and friendly atmosphere in the King's studios.

13+ Drama scholarships: One or more drama scholarships or exhibitions currently worth up to £1,500 of the school tuition fee per annum may be awarded annually. The school's intention is to offer awards to drama enthusiasts of outstanding ability and potential as performers, technicians or practitioners.

13+ Music scholarships: Three or more music scholarships or exhibitions currently worth up to £1,500 of the school tuition fee, in addition to free instrumental tuition on two instruments, may be awarded annually. The school's intention is to offer awards to instrumentalists of outstanding ability and potential. As a guideline, a boy of at least Grade 6 standard on his first instrument would be considered a promising candidate.

13+ Sport scholarships: One or more scholarships or exhibitions currently worth up to £1,500 of the school tuition fee per annum may be awarded annually to boys of exceptional ability or potential, determination and enthusiasm. Sports scholars should have exceptional talent in one or more sports, normally at least two. Candidates for all scholarships must be under 14 years of age on 1 September in the year of entry.

It is a condition of the award that the scholar achieves the King's pass mark in the common entrance examination, the King's scholarship examination or the transfer examination.

Sixth Form Academic scholarships: Rossetti and Fawcett scholarships which recognise academic performance in the entry examinations are available for boys and girls entering the Sixth Form.

Sixth Form Music scholarships: One or more music scholarships and exhibitions currently worth up to £1,500 may be awarded annually following auditions in November. The school also awards an organ scholarship. Recipients of these awards additionally receive free tuition on one or more instruments.

Sixth Form Drama scholarships: One or more drama scholarships or exhibitions currently worth up to £1,500 of the school tuition fee per annum may be awarded annually. The school's intention is to offer awards to drama enthusiasts of outstanding ability and potential as performers, technicians or practitioners. Selection takes place in the summer term of Year 11 through auditions and a workshop day.

Sixth Form Sport scholarships: We will consider awarding sports scholarships to sixth form entrants based on the pupil's track record and/or their impact in their first term at King's.

Bursaries: The school is making increasing provision for bursaries both from its own resources and as a result of the generosity of its many benefactors. The bursaries programme on offer at King's has allowed us to share some of the best schooling in the world with bright children, regardless of their parents' ability to pay, by giving them assistance with the fees. Anyone who wishes to apply for assistance with paying the fees will need to complete a bursary application which is requested as part of the online registration process. The bursary application must be completed and submitted by the published deadline which will always be before a candidate sits our entrance exams.

Fees per term (2018–2019). Senior school (year 9 onwards) £7,200; Lower school (years 7–8) £6,510; Junior school (years 5–8) £6,510; Junior school (years 3–4) £5,980.

The Curriculum – Junior School. The curriculum of the junior school is designed to lead naturally into that of the senior school in content and style. All boys within a year group follow the same timetable.

Transition, first and second forms (years 3, 4 and 5):

English; Mathematics; Science; History; Geography; Religious Studies; Music; Drama; Art; Technology (year 3 only); ICT; Personal, Social, Health and Economic Education (PSHEE); Think Tank (in years 3 and 4); French (from year 5); three double sessions of Physical Education and Games.

Third and remove forms (years 6, 7 and 8):

English; Mathematics; Science; French; Latin; Geography; Religious Studies; Music; Drama; Art; Design and Engineering; ICT; Personal, Social, Health and Economic Education (PSHEE); Physical Education and two afternoons of Games.

The Curriculum – Senior School. The lower and middle school curriculums offer a wide range of options which enable the maximum choice of subjects in the sixth form. A very wide range of subjects is available at GCSE and IGCSE (International GCSE). In the sixth form, pupils choose to study either A Levels or the International Baccalaureate diploma (IB).

Religious Education. King's is an Anglican foundation but welcomes pupils from all churches and faiths. The practice of other faiths is encouraged. The school has a Chaplaincy through which pupils are prepared for confirmation and there is a Chapel for voluntary worship and communion.

Music. There is a new state-of-the-art music school, with a 200-seat concert hall, which opened in the spring 2018. Four orchestras, three choirs and two wind bands, as well as various smaller groups and jazz groups, perform a number of major choral and orchestral works each year. There are regular performances at major London venues including Westminster Abbey, Cadogan Hall, St Paul's Cathedral and St John's Smith Square. Also, the choir and orchestra undertake international tours. Approximately 30% of the pupils have individual music lessons at the school.

Games. After an introduction to a range of games in the fourth form, pupils have a free choice of termly sports. The major sports are rugby, hockey, soccer and cricket and the games programme also includes athletics, badminton, basketball, cross-country running, fencing, fives, hockey, karate, rowing, sailing, shooting, squash, swimming, tennis and water polo. The school has its own indoor heated swimming pool. The sports hall has a floor area providing four badminton courts, as well as volley and basketball, indoor tennis and cricket nets, together with a fitness training room and four squash courts. There are two all-weather surfaces for hockey and tennis at the Kingsway ground. The school's boathouse is on the Tideway at Putney Bridge. An additional multi-function sports and swimming complex is due to open in 2019. It will provide a second six-court sports hall, a six lane, 25m swimming pool, aerobic areas, a strength and conditioning room and a large studio amongst other facilities.

School societies and activities. Every pupil is encouraged to take part in extracurricular activities. Societies meet in the two extended lunch breaks and after school. Friday school finishes early to allow pupils to participate in a range of activities such as the CCF and community service. The school runs an impressive outreach programme supporting a number of neighbouring state schools. There are active drama and debating societies, together with a wide range of other societies.

Honours. Places offered at Oxford and Cambridge for 2016: 57, 2017: 51, 2018: 44.

Charitable status. King's College School is a Registered Charity, number 310024. It exists to provide education for children.

Governing Body:
The Archbishop of Canterbury (*Visitor*)
The Rt Revd Christopher Chessun, Bishop of Southwark
  (*ex officio*)
Lord Deighton, KBE (*Chairman*)
G W James, MA (*Vice Chairman*)
S A Bennett, BA
S M Bourne, BSc, PGCE
O L Carlstrand, BSc, CEng, MICE
C G Hale, MA, LLM
S A B Hobbs, BA, PGCE
D G Ingram, MA
Sir Robert Jay, QC, BA
Professor D A Lievesley, CStat, AcSS, CBE
I A Macmillan, BSc, ACA, MBA
R J Parker, MA
J L Robinson, BA, PGCE, MEd
J G Sarpong, BSc, MBA
M D J Sharp, BA
G C Slimmon, MA, MBA
P J L Strafford, BA, MBA
D A Walls, BA

Bursar & Secretary to the Governing Body: Mrs A M
  Clarke, MA Oxon

Senior School Staff

Head Master: Mr A D Halls, MA, FRSA

Deputy Head: Miss M J Clarke, MA
Deputy Head: Mr J A Galloway, BA
Deputy Head: Ms J Lowson, MA
Deputy Head: Mr J A Short Ring, BA

Assistant Heads:
Mr M D Allen, MA (*Head of IB Diploma, HE Advice and
  Careers*)
Mr B M Baulf, MA (*Head of Teaching and Learning*)
Mr J S Gibson (*Head of Lower School*)
Mr K Gross, MA (*Director of Overseas Schools*)
Mr R J Mitchell, MA (*Head of Public Occasions*)
Mr H J Phillips (*Head of Sixth Form*)
Mr J H Renwick, MA (*Head of Middle School*)
Mr M P Stables, MA (*Director of Studies*)

Teaching Staff:
Mr M D Allen, MA (*Assistant Head, Head of IB Diploma*;
  Head of HE Advice & Careers)
Mrs A J Ansbro, MA (*Modern Languages*)
Mr M F Baggs, BA (*Director of Sport*)
Ms D J Barron, MA (*Director of Drama*)
Mr B M Baulf, BA (*Assistant Head, Head of Teaching and
  Learning*)
Mr G E Bennett, BA (*Deputy Head of IB, Classics*)
Miss R Bhattacharya, BA (*Mathematics*)

Mrs K L Bird, MA (*English*)

Ms J A L Blunden, MA (*English & UCAS Advisor*)

Dr I I F Boogaerts (*Deputy Head of IB, Chemistry*)

Mr S J Bradley, BEng (*Mathematics*)

Mr B L Bransfield, MA (*English*)

Mrs E S Britton, MSc (*Head of Psychology*)

Mr J D Broderick, MA (*Assistant Head of Layton House, Design Technology*)

Mr W J Byfield, MSc (*Biology*)

Dr J P D Cannon (*Head of English*)

Miss V R Casemore, MA (*Classics*)

Mr D I Cass, BA Deputy (*Head of English, Deputy Head of Staff Development*)

Mr G Cawley, BSc (*Head of Science*)

Miss B P Cerda Drago, BA (*Deputy Head of Modern Languages, Head of Spanish*)

Mr H Chapman, MA (*Modern Languages*)

Mrs L J Charlesworth, Dip SpLD (*Head of Learning Enrichment*)

Mr M V Christou, MA (*Head of Geography*)

Miss M J Clarke, MA (*Deputy Head Academic*)

Dr H M Cocksworth, MA (*Theology & Philosophy*)

Mr M J Cole, MEd (*Physics*)

Miss E C Collin, BA (*Head of Sixth Form Girls*) (*sabbatical*)

Dr S Coury (*Mathematics*)

Revd Dr J W Crossley (*Chaplain, Theology & Philosophy*)

Miss C F Crothers, BA (*English*)

Mrs S M Danaher, BA (*Head of Economics*)

Mr T J Davies, BA Hons, PGCE (*Director of Digital Learning, Theology & Philosophy*)

Miss R M Davis, BA (*Director of Staff Development*)

Miss A M Dawe, BSc (*Chemistry*)

Miss J L Duncombe, MPhys (*Physics*)

Mrs N L Edwards, BA (*Head of Girls' Games*)

Miss A V Eilert, MA (*English and Chinese*)

Mrs E J Elwell, BSc (*Psychology*)

Miss E J Emmott, BA (*Art*)

Mr R W Entwisle, MEng (*Design and Engineering*)

Mr S A Etienne, MA (*Deputy Head of French*)

Mr D S Fickling, MMath (*Mathematics*)

Mr W S Ford, BA (*Academic Music*)

Mr A J Foster, MA (*Physics*)

Mr J A Galloway, BA (*Deputy Head, Geography*)

Mr N J Gardner, MSc (*Biology*)

Miss E A Garnett, MA (*Classics*)

Mr J S Gibson, BA (*Assistant Head, Head of Lower School*)

Mr M P Gibson, BSc (*Head of Kingsley House*)

Mr J E Grabowski, BSc (*Acting Head of Biology, Head of Layton House*)

Mr K Gross, BEd (*Assistant Head, Director of Overseas Schools; Modern Languages*)

Mr A D Halls, MA (*Head Master, English*)

Miss O R Harman, BA (*English*)

Mr J A Harris, MEng (*Deputy Head of Sixth Form, Mathematics*)

Mr P A Hatch, MusB (*Director of Partnerships & Outreach, Assistant Director of Music*)

Dr A M Hayes (*Head of Chemistry*)

Mr A P Hedges, BSc (*Biology*)

Mr B T Hudson, BSc (*PE & Games*)

Mr J T Hyam, BA (*French*)

Miss J E James, BSc (*Mathematics*)

Mr E Josypenko, MSc (*Head of A Level Chemistry*)

Miss G A Joyce, BA (*Head of Art*)

Mr C Kandemir, BSc (*Economics*)

Mr L B D Kane, BSc (*Director of Co-Curricular Education & President of CR*)

Mr A L V Karski, BA (*Classics*)

Mr S C Kent, MA (*Chinese Mandarin, Assistant Head of Sixth Form and Senior UCAS Advisor*)

Miss M M E Kidwell, MA (*Spanish and French*)

Miss D Langenberg, BA (*Coordinator of International Links*)

Mr J G Lawrence, MA, MLitt (*History*)

Miss J M Lawton-Cook, BSc (*Head of Maclear House*)

Mrs H M Lindsey-Noble, BA (*Head of German*)

Dr P M Lloyd (*Deputy Head of IB & Chemistry*)

Mrs H E Marion, MA (*Economics*)

Miss C K McWhirter, BA (*Geography*)

Mr K Meng, BA (*Mathematics*)

Mr D Miller, BSc (*Head of Physics*)

Mr R J Mitchell, MA (*Assistant Head, Public Occasions; Chemistry*)

Mrs H M Mulcahy, BA (*Head of Modern Languages*)

Mrs E C Nicholl, BSc (*Mathematics*)

Mr S J Nye, BSc (*Head of Mathematics*)

Mrs A J Panaite, BSc (*Mathematics*)

Miss R C Peel, BA (*Modern Languages and Head of Major House*)

Mr D G Phillips, MA (*Director of Music*)

Mr H J Phillips, BSc (*Head of Sixth Form*)

Mr N Pollen, MA (*Art*)

Mrs K E Potts, MA (*Geography*)

Mr E J Prior, BA (*English*)

Miss C A Ramgoolam, MA (*Head of Exams, ICT and Computing and EVC*)

Miss N M Rarity, BA (*Classics*)

Mr B E F Reekes, BA (*Head of Cross Country*)

Mr T D Rendell, BA (*History*)

Mr J H Renwick, MA (*Assistant Head, Head of Middle School*)

Revd B W Rickards (*Assistant Chaplain*)

Mrs F A Ring, MA (*Head of History*)

Ms C O H Robinson, BA (*Modern Languages*)

Mr T P Rogers, BSc (*Head of Rugby*)

Mr J M A Ross, BA (*Modern Languages*)

Miss E J Sadler, BA CPT3A (*Learning Enrichment*)

Mr C P Sandels, MSc (*Physics*)

Mrs A L J Sandwell, BA (*Learning Enrichment*)

Ms M E Sanford, BSc (*Chemistry*)

Mr J R C Saxton, BA (*Modern Languages*)

Mr R S Shipperley, BA (*Geography*)

Mr J A Short Ring, BA (*Deputy Head, History*)

Mr G J A Simpson, BSc (*Economics*)

Mr T J Smedley, BMus (*Head of Strings*)

Miss L E L Spicer, MSc (*Head of Design & Engineering*)

Ms M A G Spottiswoode, MBA (*Physics*)

Dr T R Squires, BA (*Head of Alverstone House*)

Mr M Stables, MA (*Assistant Head, Director of Studies; Mathematics*)

Mr J M Stanley, BSc (*Head of Glenesk, Head of Safeguarding*)

Mr D Starrett, BA (*German, French*)

Mr M J Stenning, BSc (*Mathematics*)

Mr M A Stephenson, MA (*History*)

Dr A C Stewart (*Head of Biology*) [maternity leave]

Miss K E Sullivan, BSc (*Assistant Director of Studies*)

Mr A P Tep, BA (*Biology*)

Mr J G Thomas, BSc (*Biology*)

Mr D A Thomson, BA (*Deputy Director of Sport and Head of Football*)

Mrs A C Tingle, BA (*Learning Enrichment*)

Miss E R Tozzi, BA (*Assistant Head of Major House, Theology & Philosophy*)

Mr J L B Trapmore, MA (*English and Drama and Head of Curricular Drama*)

Mrs L Tremayne, BA (*French*)

Mr H R Trimble, BA (*English*)

Mr A M R Trosser, MSci, ARCS (*Mathematics*)

Mr S A Williams, BSc (*Deputy Head of Mathematics*)
Mrs S Williams, BCom (*Economics & Social Sciences*)
Mr W W Wilmot, BSc (*Assistant Head of Kingsley*)
Dr R A L Winchester (*Chemistry, Head of Rowing*)
Mrs S E Wiseman, MA (*History*)
Miss E J C Witney-Smith, BSc (*Biology*)
Mr A J Wood (*Head of Theology and Philosophy*)
Mrs J I Woodward, MA (*History*)
Mr S L C Young, BA (*Head of Classics*)
Dr S D B Zieleniewski, DPhil (*Physics*)

Junior School Staff

Headmaster: Dr G A Silverlock, BEd Hons, MLitt, PhD

Deputy Heads:
Mrs H J Morren, MA (*Pastoral*)
Mr D Jones, BA (*Academic*)

Assistant Head: Mr J E Hipkiss, BSc Hons (*Head of Communications & Head of Science*)

Head of Rushmere: Mrs C S Madge, BEd

Teaching Staff:
Mr R D Anderson, BComm (*Mathematics*)
Miss V J Attié, BA (*Head of Tudor House, Modern Languages*)
Mr A Baker, BEd (*Professional Tutor*)
Mr J J Barrington, BSc (*Head of Football*)
Miss C M Bitaud, BA (*Head of Years 7 & 8, Modern Languages, EAL*)
Mrs J C Blight, BEd (*Rushmere Teacher*)
Mr E J M Borton, BA (*Head of Geography*)
Mrs C Bourne, BEd (*Head of Years 5 & 6, English and Mathematics*)
Mr P K Brady, BA (*Head of Stuart House & Geography*)
Mr D Cheers, BEd (*Head of Rugby*)
Mr S F Connolly, BSc (*Head of Norman House, Rushmere Teacher*)
Ms T M Davies, BA (*Music*)
Mrs S J de Montfort, MA (*Rushmere Teacher*)
Miss E J Emmott, BA (*Art*)
Miss L S Gillard, MA, ATC (*Head of Art & Design*)
Mrs E E Gordon (*English*)
Mrs O M Hamilton, MA (*Head of Religious Studies*)
Mr M J Hortin, MA (*Head of Classics*)
Mrs S V D Howes, BA (*Head of Drama*)
Mrs A Huckerby, BA (*Rushmere Teacher*)
Miss S R Hunter, BSc (*Science*)
Mr N A Jay, BA (*French*)
Mrs J C Lewis, BA (*Rushmere Teacher*)
Mrs S J Martineau Walker, BA (*Art*)
Mr J K McAuslan (*Head of Windsor House, Mathematics*)
Mr R McCluskey, MA (*Head of PE & Games*)
Ms C McGregor, BA (*Head of English*)
Ms H F Montgomery-Massingberd, BA (*Head of French*)
Mrs R K Moore, BSc (*Senior Teacher Academic, Head of Mathematics*)
Mr I D Morris, BA (*History*)
Mr M L Nixon, BMus (*Head of Keyboard*)
Mrs S K Phillips, BEd (*Rushmere Teacher*)
Miss K Pilling, BBus (*Mathematics*)
Mrs R F A Rose, BSc (*Senior Teacher Public Occasions, Head of PSHEE*)
Mr P P Thomas, MA (*Head of ICT*)
Mrs A C Tingle, BA, Dip SpLD (*Learning Enrichment*)
Mrs S J Walker, BA (*Rushmere Teacher*)
Mr E T Watkins, BA (*Head of History*)
Mr R Weber (*Head of Music*)

Support Staff:
PA to the Head Master: Mrs S Carrett
Admissions Registrar: Ms S J W Dowling, BA
PA to Junior School Headmaster: Mrs S Richards

King's College, Taunton
A Woodard School

South Road, Taunton, Somerset TA1 3LA

Tel:	Headmaster: 01823 328210
	Reception: 01823 328200
Fax:	01823 328202
email:	admissions@kings-taunton.co.uk
website:	www.kings-taunton.co.uk
Twitter:	@KingsTaunton
Facebook:	@kingscollegetaunton

Motto: *Fortis et Fidelis*

A Woodard school, Canon Nathaniel Woodard renamed the school King's College in memory of King Alfred, when he bought it in 1879, but its historical links go back to the medieval grammar school which was founded by Bishop Fox of Winchester in 1522.

King's College, Taunton is an independent co-educational boarding and day school for 460 boys and girls aged 13–18 years.

Situated on the outskirts of Taunton, the county town of Somerset, on a splendid 100-acre site, King's College offers high academic standards, a friendly and caring day and boarding community, and has an enviable reputation for music, drama and sport. Kindness, consideration for others, honesty and self-discipline are the values which King's hopes will provide its pupils with the inner resources not just for school, but for life.

King's College, Taunton, delivers success at all ages whilst offering a friendly, happy and safe living and working environment. The school provides an extraordinary breadth of opportunities to pupils and has very high academic standards. As well as the school's academic success, pupils also enjoy the highest levels of achievement in sports, art, drama and music. The school won the 2007 BBC Songs of Praise Senior School Choir of the Year title, as well as the Rosslyn Park 7s Rugby Cup – a taste of the breadth of opportunity available to pupils.

King's College has produced a large number of Oxbridge entrants over the years and is well regarded by the top universities in the UK. Pupils can join the Third Form (Year 9) at 13, going on to take GCSE exams, or in the Sixth Form (Year 12) at 16 or 17 to study for A Levels. The school is blessed with highly-qualified and committed members of staff who see their role as ensuring the happiness and successful development of each individual member of the school community. The word community is very prominent at King's: Boarders and day pupils benefit from a strong Christian ethos: an environment where self-respect and kindness to others are highly-regarded qualities.

Admission. All entries are made through the Headmaster. Pupils normally enter at 13 years in the Michaelmas term and are admitted via Common Entrance or the Scholarship Examination.

The registration fee is £75.

Fees per term (2018–2019). Boarders £11,055, Day Pupils £7,460. The fees are inclusive of all extra charges of general application.

Scholarships. Scholarships are available to boys and girls going into the Third Form (13+) and Sixth Form. Major

Academic scholarships are awarded, as well as scholarships for Music, Drama, Art, DT and Sport.

Auditions for Music and Drama Scholarships and Awards are held in February (13+), and in November for Sixth Form.

Applicants for Art and Design & Technology Scholarships are invited to visit the school during the Lent term with a portfolio of work.

13+ Sports Scholarships are available for competition each February and Sixth Form Sports Scholarships are available in November.

Charitable status. Woodard Schools Taunton Ltd is a Registered Charity, number 1103346. King's College exists to provide high quality education for boys and girls aged 13–18.

Headmaster: **R R Biggs**, MA Rhodes Scholar Pembroke College Oxford, BSc Cape Town

Deputy Head (Pastoral): Mrs K L McSwiggan, BA Reading

Deputy Head (Academic): Mr J J B Lawford, MEd Open, BA Birmingham

Deputy Head (Co-Curricular): Mr C J Albery, BMus Exeter

Head of Sixth Form: Mr O R Ridley, BA York

Head of Boarding: Mr J H Griffiths, BTech Brunel

Director Finance & Operations: Mr S C Worthy, BA, MBA

Director of Admissions & Marketing: Mrs K J Rippin

Director of Development: Mr J J Mack

PA to the Headmaster: Mrs F Byrne

King's Ely

Old Palace, Palace Green, Ely, Cambridgeshire CB7 4EW

Tel:	01353 660701 (Principal's PA)
	01353 660707 (Head of Pupil Recruitment)
Fax:	01353 667485
	01353 660712 (Business Manager)
email:	admissions@kingsely.org
website:	www.kingsely.org
Twitter:	@kings_ely
Facebook:	@Kings-Ely

Energy, Courage, Integrity

An independent, co-educational school, with day and boarding facilities, offering a seamless education for students from 1 to 18. With over 1000 years of experience educating young people, King's Ely is a school that is innovative, challenging and inspiring. Boasting as its school chapel one of the world's finest cathedrals, with easy access to London, King's Ely offers a very special and very tranquil environment, with one of the best stretches of training river in the UK.

King's Ely is a school where education really is an adventure. Students of all ages are encouraged to take risks in their learning, pushing themselves beyond the boundaries of their expectations, discovering more about the world around them, and, in so doing, more about themselves. What makes us special is our determination to instil in the young people in our care a real enthusiasm for learning and a belief that drives us all, that all students can achieve if the teaching is approached in a way that suits the learning style of each stu-

dent. This is not easy necessarily; it is challenging, often uncomfortable, but King's Ely students know that they are well supported, that their teachers believe in them, and so they are willing to step out of their 'comfort zone' and take the very risks that will bring about high-level learning.

Our long and illustrious past provides a dynamic springboard to the future; our confidence is born of tradition, our aspirations reach for the stars.

Organisation. The school is fully co-educational from the ages of 1 to 18. The total roll is 985 and more than a quarter of pupils over the age of eight are boarders.

The school is divided into four parts: King's Ely Acremont, the Nursery and Pre-Prep for children aged 1 to 7 (Year 2). standing in its own grounds at Acremont House; King's Ely Junior for children aged 7–13 (Years 3–8); King's Ely Senior for students aged 13–16 (Years 9–11) and King's Ely Sixth Form for students aged 16–18 (Years 12–13).

Buildings. The Old Palace on Palace Green, home for centuries to the Bishops of Ely, serves as the entrance to the school, housing the Sixth Form Centre, the Head's Offices and Admissions, as well as the Development Office. The school still uses many of Ely's medieval monastic buildings – as boarding houses, as classrooms and as the dining hall. The 14th century Porta, the great gateway to the monastery, has been converted into a magnificent Senior School library. Other recent buildings show the continuing and substantial investment in modern facilities: the renovated Georgian villa that now houses the Nursery and Pre-Prep section of King's Acremont; a brand new Art School and Performance Studies block, housing the new Dance Studio and 'Black Box' Drama Studio; a Technology Centre; a senior Music School and Recital Hall and a self-contained, two-storey accommodation including seven classrooms and a science laboratory for Years 7 and 8.

King's Ely Acremont. At King's Ely Acremont, children thrive in a happy, safe environment where they feel secure and valued and quickly develop a sense of belonging. Children from 1 to 7 are encouraged to question, explore and have the confidence and security to take risks in their learning. A rich, creative curriculum sets the children on the road to becoming lifelong thinkers and learners. Courage and courtesy are valued, encouraged and celebrated publicly.

Children may start in King's Ely Nursery in the term in which they turn one. The Nursery is sessional and it is recommended children attend three sessions a week from the outset. However, flexibility to suit the needs of each individual child is important. As children progress through the Nursery, the number of sessions should increase to a minimum of five sessions per week. The children are very well prepared for a smooth transition into Reception through regular visits ensuring that they are very familiar with both staff and setting in the next stage of their journey through King's Ely. Please contact Admissions to discuss suitable sessions for your child.

Children start Reception in the September following their 4th birthday. Reception, Year 1 and Year 2 are all taught in Acremont House. Small class sizes, with a Teacher and Teaching Assistant in each, allow children to flourish, preparing them well for the transition to King's Ely Junior.

King's Ely Acremont offers working parents the option of an 8.00 am Breakfast Club, After School Care until 6.00 pm and Holiday Club.

King's Ely Junior. King's Ely Junior celebrates the many ways that students learn and is keen to embrace different learning styles. Students are encouraged to develop their autonomy as they mature and there is an expectation of an ever-increasing use of information literacy, technology and study skills during the students' time at King's Ely Junior. Individual responses, such as films being made for homework, or a computer generated response to a task are equally as welcome as a formal written piece of work. Students can be characterised by their flexibility of approach and it is seen as an important life skill for the next generation.

Ensuring that every student is challenged to fulfil their potential and encouraged along the way, requires that the progress of each student is measured and supported well at all times. Form Tutors shoulder this role on a day to day basis. However, each student has a Head of Year who monitors their work and considers how well they are progressing against our predictions. Weekly meetings ensure that speedy intervention is offered to support or extend students appropriately.

From Year 5 onwards, students are set for Maths and English. At this point the students are split between four sets of about 14. These groups are reviewed frequently by the subject teachers and the Head of Year and any adjustments to the sets are made by the Director of Studies, following discussion with parents. As students progress through the school more subjects are set, such as languages and Science. In Years 7 and 8, subjects are linked according to the English, Maths and Science or Language sets. Students are taught in four or five groups, depending on subject.

Every term is punctuated by a host of academic challenges that serve to inspire the pupils and encourage them to push the parameters of their learning. Examination results are high and the school prides itself on being at the forefront of developments in the educational world.

During the school day all children are divided among four co-educational Houses for pastoral and competitive purposes; each of these Houses is staffed by male and female members of the teaching staff. King's Ely Junior has one co-educational boarding house and one for the boy choristers of Ely Cathedral who are all pupils of King's Ely Junior. There is a wide range of extra-curricular opportunities both at lunch times and after school.

King's Ely Senior. The amount of academic choice that pupils can exercise grows as they move through the Senior School. Options in the Sixth Form are very flexible and the sets are often small. Up to GCSE (Year 11) there is a compulsory core of English, Mathematics, Religious Studies and Sciences. In addition, every pupil chooses up to four option subjects from: Art, Business Studies, Classical Civilisation, Design & Technology (Resistant Material Technology, Food and Nutrition), Drama, English as a Foreign Language, French, Geography, German, History, Latin, Music, Physical Education, Spanish. Inter-House competitions in disciplines such singing, Ely Scheme and debating are keenly participated in.

King's Ely International. At King's Ely International, students are welcomed from all over the world to engage with the unique community that is King's Ely. The aim is to ensure a smooth and successful transition into the vibrant environment of a UK boarding school, steeped in history but offering an innovative educational experience.

Although fully integrated with the main school, King's Ely International offers effective support academically for international students between the ages of 14 and 16 who may be studying for the first time in the UK. The one-year intensive GCSE course suits students who wish to complete their GCSEs in a year. The Pre-GCSE programme is for students between the ages of 14 and 15 who need support in their English. It is also a "stand-alone" course and may be seen as a sabbatical year, especially for European students who wish to return to their home countries after a year abroad improving their English.

Extra-Curricular Activities. Music, art, drama, outdoor pursuits, sports, practical hobbies and interests – all are catered for in a large range of lunchtime and after-hours activities.

The Ely Scheme. All pupils in Year 9 are introduced to the school's distinctive outdoor pursuits programme, the Ely Scheme, which provides a training in practical and personal skills and in teamwork, initiative and leadership. For some pupils it leads on to the Duke of Edinburgh's Award Scheme or to specialised activities such as climbing, kayaking or pioneering.

Art, Drama and Music. Music is strong, as one would expect in a school that is so closely linked to the cathedral. There is a full programme of performances for school and public audiences, and regular tours overseas. Nearly half of all pupils have personal tuition in a musical instrument; many learn two or even three. An outstanding Art School, opened in March 2010, inspires Fine Art, Sculpture, Photography and Textiles. All parts of the school present plays every year in addition to productions by year or ad hoc groups.

Games. The school's main sports are Rowing, Rugby, Football, Netball, Hockey and Cricket. Athletics, Badminton, Basketball, Tennis, Sailing, Squash, Swimming, Golf, Clay Pigeon Shooting and Horse Riding are also available. All pupils are encouraged to take part in team games, and there is a full programme of fixtures against other schools.

Religious Worship. The Junior and Senior Schools worship regularly in Ely Cathedral. Other services weekly are also in accordance with the principles of the Church of England. The Bishop conducts a confirmation service for pupils in the Lent Term. However, all denominations (or none) are warmly welcome.

Exeats. Boarders are granted weekend exeats on the written request of a parent or guardian. Weekly and flexi boarding are increasingly popular.

Admission. Registration forms can be obtained from the Admissions Department and a £100 (£150 for non-EU) fee is payable at first registration.

Admission to King's Ely Acremont is by interview.

Admission to King's Ely Junior is by interview and INCAs in English and Maths. There is also Lucid screening for dyslexia. King's Ely Junior entrance assessments are held in January prior to the following Michaelmas Term. Small groups of children are invited to attend assessments throughout January. Offers are made for the beginning of February.

Admission to King's Ely Senior at 13+ entrance is by the school's entrance examination consisting of English, Maths, Science and Lucid in late January.

Admission to Year 12 at 16+ is by interview with the Principal and predicted GCSE grades. The entry qualification for the Sixth Form is not less than six C grades with B grades in subjects selected for A Level. Twenty-seven AS/A2 Level subjects are offered in Years 12 and 13. Taster Days are held throughout November and December.

Pupils may enter the school at any time, depending on availability of space and assessment.

Scholarships and Exhibitions. Entrance Scholarships and Exhibitions up to a cumulative total of 10% of tuition fees are awarded for achievement and potential in academic work, music and sport, and 5% in art, design technology, drama.

A competitive examination is held in January each year and successful candidates enter Year 9 the following Michaelmas Term. These Scholarships will be continued until the end of Year 11, subject to satisfactory progress, after which an application for a Sixth Form Scholarship may be made.

King's Ely Senior:

Academic Scholarships are for the three years from Year 9 leading to the GCSE examinations and are made on the basis of a competitive examination set by the school in January. Successful candidates are also interviewed.

Music Scholarships are available for choral and/or instrumental excellence, including organ-playing, and may include free weekly tuition on two musical instruments. Candidates for entry into Year 9 are invited to the school for auditions in January.

All boy Choristers of Ely Cathedral are full boarders of King's Ely Junior and receive a choristership worth 50% of fees while they remain in the choir and a bursary worth 33% of fees on transfer to King's Ely Senior. Members of the Cathedral Girls' Choir are all boarders in King's Ely Senior and receive a bursary worth 33% of boarding fees. Additional means-tested funding may be available. Chorister auditions are held in February for boys who will be aged 8 and for girls who will be 13 by the following September.

Sports Awards for entry into Year 9 are open to boys and girls with potential for major county, regional or national representation or with all-round sporting excellence. Reports will be sought from the candidates' coach(es) and practical tests, if required, will be held at the school in January.

Art, Drama and Design Technology Exhibitions are available for entry into Year 9 and assessments are held in January.

Sixth Form:

Academic Scholarships are for the two years of the A Level course and are made following an examination in November and an interview with the Vice Principal (Academic) and Head of Sixth Form (Academic). Candidates should be on course for at least six A* or A passes at GCSE.

Music Scholarships are available for choral and/or instrumental excellence, including organ-playing, and may include free weekly tuition on two musical instruments. Candidates for entry into Year 12 are invited to the school for auditions in November.

Sports Awards, for entry into Year 12 are open to boys and girls with potential for major county, regional or national representation or with all-round sporting excellence. Reports will be sought from the candidates' coach(es) and practical tests, if required, will be held at the school in November.

Art, Drama and Design Technology Exhibitions are available for entry into Year 12 and assessments are held in November.

Full particulars of all awards are available on the King's Ely website.

Bursaries. Awards may be supplemented by a means-tested Bursary if there is genuine financial need. Bursary support may be available to new pupils over the age of 7 whose parents are unable to pay the full tuition fee.

Fees per term (2018–2019). King's Ely Acremont Nursery and Pre-Prep: Nursery places are booked by the session (morning or afternoon) and the day of the week; Daily rates range from £50–£60. The fee for Pre-Prep Reception to Year 2 is £3,359 per term (no boarding). Pre- and after-school care and holiday club are available at extra charge.

King's Ely Junior per term: Years 3 and 4: £4,744 (day); £7,564 (boarding); Years 5 to 8: £5,177 (day); £7,985 (boarding).

King's Ely Senior per term: Years 9 to 13: £7,153 (day); £10,355 (boarding).

Flexi boarding: It may be possible to offer overnight accommodation for day pupils on an occasional basis at a cost of £52 per night. The cost of extended flexi boarding will be quoted in advance upon application to Admissions. There is also an extensive bus service for day children and Ely station, on the main King's Cross to King's Lynn line, is just a 5-minute walk from school.

Concessions: A generous discount in fees is available from age 4 for children of clergy serving the Christian faith and boarders who are children of Services personnel in receipt of CEA and also for children of FCO employees. Sibling discount on the third child is available. Bursaries are available to those entering Year 7 or beyond.

Old Eleans. Former pupils receive news of the school and of their contemporaries and are invited annually to events.

Charitable status. The King's School, Ely is a Registered Charity, number 802427. Its aims and objectives are to offer excellence in education to day and boarding pupils.

Visitor: The Rt Revd S Conway, Bishop of Ely

Governors:
Chairman: Mr J Hayes
Vice-Chairman: Air Vice-Marshal C Bairsto, CBE, CMgr, FRAeS, FCMI, RAF [OE]
Chairman of Finance and General Purposes Committee: Mr D Day
Chairman of Education Committee: Mr P Cantwell
Chairman of Estate Committee: Mr G F Chase, FRICS, CArb, FRSA, FInstCPD
Chairman of Nominations Committee: Mr J Hayes
Chairman of Strategy, Development and Risk Committee: Mr J Hayes
Mr G Acheson
The Very Revd M Bonney, MA, The Dean of Ely
Mrs A East
Mrs A Kenna, MEd, LRAM
Mr M E Myers, MA
Mrs I Newport-Mangell
Sir J Paice
Mr J Peake (*elect*)
Prof M Proctor, FRS

[OE] *Old Elean*

Principal: **Mrs S E Freestone**, MEd, GRSM, LRAM, ARCM, FRSA

Head of Pupil Recruitment: Mrs J Formston, BA, PGCE
Head of Admissions: Mrs D Burton

King's High School

Smith Street, Warwick CV34 4HJ

Tel:	01926 494485
Fax:	01926 403089
email:	enquiries@kingshighwarwick.co.uk
website:	www.kingshighwarwick.co.uk

Situated in the heart of Warwick, King's High School is an independent day school for girls aged 11–18. Our school is a warm, lively community and we enjoy a reputation, of which we are rightly proud, both for academic success and the personal development of our girls. Our winning formula of encouraging excellence in academics, sport and the arts, along with lots of enrichment through our supra-curricular programme, has produced consistently excellent performance for King's High and allows our girls to flourish. This was reflected in our May 2017 ISI Report where we were judged 'Excellent' in all areas. We believe that our girls obtain the best of both worlds, one that is unique in our area, to be educated within a single-sex environment, whilst reaping co-educational benefits from our close links with nearby Warwick School, our brother school in the Foundation. This will be enhanced when, in 2019, King's High moves to our brand new, state-of-the-art school now being built on our Foundation's Myton Road campus.

The curriculum aims to give pupils as broad, engaging and rigorous an education as possible. All pupils study two modern languages and Latin and may choose three separate sciences for the IGCSE. There is an exceptionally wide choice of A Level subjects.

The excellence of the girls' achievements and the year-on-year excellent 'value added' was recognised in our recent ISI Inspection Report statement: *'Results in A level examinations and standard measures of progress indicate that pupils make excellent progress by the time they leave the school compared to the average for pupils of similar abilities.'* This success continues with our outstanding 2017 A Level and GCSE successes.

Extra-curricular and community activities flourish, with over 130 clubs and societies on offer. Most girls achieve the Duke of Edinburgh's Bronze Award and many continue to Silver and Gold. Girls distinguish themselves in sport, music, drama and the countless other activities on offer. We offer a unique, bespoke qualification, The King's High Baccalaureate, which reflects the depth and breadth of our supra-curricular and extra-curricular opportunities. The school organises many day, evening and residential trips to destinations at home and abroad and invites prestigious women, such as Dame Judi Dench, DBE and Professor Germaine Greer, to visit and speak.

King's High provides an enjoyable, safe and stimulating experience in which girls can grow into confident and secure young women, equipped to make choices as they progress through their education and enter the world, prepared for change and able to make a positive and generous contribution to society.

The Good Schools Guide review of 2018 stated: 'The girls are just lovely. What can you say? Who wouldn't want their daughters to be like this at 18? Confident but not arrogant; excited about their future but hugely loyal to their past; believing the world is theirs for moulding into something much fairer and better than has gone before; sure that they can do it, but knowing they will need support and networks and kindness and empathy to succeed'.

Admission. Girls are required to take an entrance examination and attend an interview.

Fees per term (2018–2019). Tuition £4,325. Music: Brass, Pianoforte, Strings, Woodwind, Guitar, Drums, Singing £231.50 for 10 lessons.

Financial Assistance. Academic and subject scholarships in Art, Drama, Music and Sport are available on entry at age 11. Application for a range of Sixth Form Scholarships is open to internal and external candidates for the Sixth Form. Means-tested Warwick Foundation Awards, up to the value of full fees, are also available on entry at 11+ and at Sixth Form.

Charitable status. King's High School is a part of the Warwick Independent Schools Foundation which is a Registered Charity, number 1088057. The aim of the charity is "to provide for children (3–18) of parents of all financial means – a high proportion of whom shall come from Warwick and its immediate surroundings, but subject to satisfying academic standards where required – education of academic, cultural and sporting standards which are the highest within their peer groups".

The Governing Body:
Chairman of the Warwick Independent Schools Foundation: [1]Mr D B Stevens, BA

Chairman of King's High School Committee: [1]Mrs G Low, MA Oxon

Foundation Governors:
[1]Mrs M B Ashe, BBusSc, PGDAcc CA SA
[1]Mrs S M Austin, BA, PGDPM, MCiPD

Mr J P Cavanagh, QC, MA Oxon, LLM Cantab
[1]Dr A D Cocker, BA, DPhil, MBA
Mr T Cox, LL The Lord Lieutenant of Warwickshire (*Ex-Officio*)
Mr A Firth, BSc, MBA
Mr C Gibbons, MBA, MSc, MEng, MAPM
Cllr Mrs M Grainger
Mr R Griffiths, BA, MBA, Solicitor
Mr N F Keegan, MA Oxon, FCA
Mr T Keyes, MA Oxon
[1]Mrs E J Lillyman, Cert Ed, NFF
Ms K Parr, LLB
[1]Mrs C Sawdon, BSc, JP
Mrs P A Snape, FCIPD
[1]Mr J N Wallis, BA, MSc, MRICS
Professor Griffin, BM BCh, MA, MPhil, FRCS

[1] *Member of the King's High School Committee*

Senior Executive Group, King's High & Warwick Prep:

***Head Master, King's High School*: Mr R Nicholson**, MA Pembroke College Oxford (*Chair*)

Headmistress, Warwick Preparatory School: Mrs H Dodsworth, BA QTS Warwick, NPQH
Deputy to the Head Master, Deputy Head Pastoral, King's High School: Mrs C Renton, BSc Leicester, MSc University College, London
Deputy Head Academic, King's High School: Dr S Burley, BA University College London, PhD Queen Mary College London, MPhil St Catherine's College Oxford
Development Director: Mr P Rothwell, BA St Chad's Durham, CFRE

Senior Management Team:
Head Master: Mr R Nicholson, MA Pembroke College Oxford
Deputy to the Head Master, Deputy Head Pastoral: Mrs C Renton, BSc Leicester, MSc University College, London
Deputy Head Academic: Dr S Burley, BA University College London, PhD Queen Mary College London, MPhil St Catherine's College Oxford
Director of Educational Innovation: Mrs J Parkinson-Mills, MSc Jesus College Cambridge
Director of Co-curricular Activities: Mrs S Didlick, BEd CNAA
Head of Key Stage 3 (*Years 7–9*): Mrs S Watson, MA Hertford College Oxford
Head of Key Stage 4 (*Years 10–11*): Miss C Tedd, BA Trinity College Oxford, MA Birkbeck College London
Head of Sixth Form: Mrs C Murphy, BA Royal Holloway London

Key Support Staff:
Mrs T Rutter (*Matron*)
Mrs E Wathen (*Senior Office Administrator*)
Mrs L Ashley (*Office Receptionist/Administrator*)
Mrs A Wheals (*Head's PA & Office Manager*)
Mrs G Worrall (*Registrar & Head of Admissions*)

Health:
§Mrs T Rutter, RGN, QARANC (*Matron*)
§Ms E Williams, BA Warwick (*Well-being Mentor*)

Members of Staff:

* *Head of Department*
§ *Part-time*

Art:
*Ms S Jordan, BA Wolverhampton
Mrs E Ashby, BA Kent (*Second in Department*)
Miss A Wright, BA Leeds College of Art (*Artist in Residence*)

Careers and Higher Education:
Mrs J A Coplestone-Crow, BA St Aidan's College Durham
(*Head of Higher Education*)
§Mrs A E Browning, BA King's College London (*Work Experience Coordinator*)
Miss C Gilbert, BA Liverpool John Moores (*KS3/4 Careers Coordinator*)
Ms S Ostrander, BSc Bristol (*Sixth Form Careers Coordinator*)
Dr P Seal, BA MPhil Bristol, DPhil Balliol College Oxford (*Head of Academic Enrichment & Research*)
Miss S Shaw, BSc Warwick (*Higher Education Advisor*)
Mrs K White, BA Exeter, MEd Homerton College Cambridge (*Higher Education Advisor*)

Classics:
*Mrs J A Coplestone-Crow, BA St Aidan's College Durham
Mrs L Shaw, BA Warwick, MA UWE (*Assistant to Head of Sixth Form & Head of House*)
Miss C Tedd, BA Trinity College Oxford, MA London (*Head of Key Stage 4*)

Computer Science:
*Mr S Reid, BA Anglia Polytechnic University
§Ms L Thomas, BSc Exeter, MSc Coventry

Design Technology:
*Mr N C Walker, BSc Brunel (*Duke of Edinburgh's Award Coordinator*)
§Mrs J Knight, BA Portsmouth

Drama:
*Miss C Price, BA Manchester (*Head of House & Staff Mentor*)
§Mrs J Wild, BA East Anglia (*New Staff Mentor*)
§Mrs T Bokota, BA Kingston (*Head of LAMDA*) [maternity cover]
§Mrs C Mackenzie, BA Sheffield, MA Derby RADA Dip (*Teacher of LAMDA*)
§Mrs S Marshall, BA GSMD, ADB Theatre Studies (*Teacher of LAMDA*) [maternity cover]
§Mrs F Mills, BA Leeds (*Head of LAMDA*) [maternity Leave]
§Mr J Partridge, BA Birmingham (*Teacher of LAMDA*) [maternity cover]

English:
*Miss R Bradbury, BA York, MA Leeds
Dr S Burley, BA University College London, PhD Queen Mary College London, MPhil St Catherine's College Oxford (*Deputy Head Academic*)
Mrs O Doughty, BA Exeter
Mrs F McClean, BA MA Durham, MSc Kellogg College Oxford
§Mrs C Richards, BA Exeter
Dr P Seal, BA MPhil Bristol, DPhil Balliol College Oxford (*Head of Academic Enrichment & Research*)
Mrs L Shaw, BA Warwick, MA UWE (*Assistant Head of Sixth Form & Head of House*)

Economics & Business Studies:
*Mr J W Wood, BA Nottingham, MSc Leicester
§Mrs A E Browning, BA King's College London (*Teacher of Business Studies*)

Food:
*S Didlick, BEd CNAA (*Director of Co-curricular Activities*)
Mrs D Gregory, BSc Birmingham (*Assistant to Head of KS3*)

Geography:
*Mrs K White, BA Exeter, MEd Homerton College Cambridge (*HE Advisor*)

§Mrs A E Browning, BA King's College London
Mrs R Cresswell, BA Georgia (*Coordinator of Pupils' Personal Development*)
§Mrs C Walker, BEd Chelsea School of Movement
Mrs S Watson, MA Hertford College Oxford (*Head of Key Stage 3*)

History & Politics:
*Mrs C Wellman, BA Warwick (*Head of House*)
Miss J Wightman, BA Durham
Dr G Gifford, MSc MA PhD Edinburgh
Mr C Grier, BA York

Mathematics:
*Mr A Wild, BSc Wales
Mr H Ashby, BEng CNAA (*Examinations Officer Assistant*)
Miss U Birbeck, BA Warwick (*Timetabling Assistant*)
§Mrs C Dempsey, BSc Durham
Mr P Garratt, BSc Nottingham
§Mr J McGuire, BA Coventry, Cert HE Open University
Miss S Shaw, BSc Warwick (*Higher Education Advisor*)
Mrs C Topping, BSc Wales, MSc Warwick

Modern Foreign Languages:
*Ms K Gibson, BA Salford (*Acting Head of Department & Head of French*)
Mrs N Lopez, BA Madrid (*Head of Spanish*)
Miss K Großer, BA Leipzig & Leeds MA Leipzig (*Head of German*) [maternity leave]
§Mrs V McRoberts, Licence MA University of Saint Etienne
§Mrs E Montiel, Licenciatura en Educación
Mrs C Murphy, BA Royal Holloway London (*Head of Sixth Form*)
§Miss D Pearce, BA King's College London [maternity leave]
§Mrs H Shirley, BA Exeter [maternity cover]
Miss R Yates, BA Newcastle (*Acting Head of German*) [maternity cover]
§Mrs H Brebner, MA Lady Margaret Hall Oxford (*German Assistant*)
§Mrs D Chastel Hammond, BA MA Birmingham City (*French Assistant*)
§Mrs M Esteban-Stephenson (*Spanish Assistant*)
§Mrs S Freton-Khatkar, BA Lille, MA Paris (*French Assistant*)
Lt Col J W Rutter [retired], MCGI (*French Assistant*)

Music:
*Mr A Laing, BA Christ's College Cambridge, DPS Birmingham Conservatoire (*Artistic Director Music, Head of Faculty*)
Miss A Griggs, BA Open University (*Director of Music, Warwick Preparatory School*)
Mr O G A Hancock, MA Jesus College Oxford, MMus Selwyn College Cambridge, FRCO (*Choral Director, King's High School; Director of Music, St Mary's Church Warwick*)
Miss K Potts, BMus MMus Royal College of Music (*King's High School*)
Dr H Smith, MA, BMus, PhD Birmingham (*Warwick Preparatory School*)
Mrs D Wallace, BMus Goldsmiths London, LRAM Royal Academy of Music, LTCL Trinity College (*Head of Academic Music, King's High School*)
§Mrs S Mann (*Music Administrator & Assistant to the Artistic Director Music*)

Personal Development:
PSHEE & Springboard, Create and Curiosity, Your Future
Mrs R Cresswell, BA Georgia (*Personal Development Coordinator*)

Dr P Carr, BA Girton College Cambridge, MA PhD
Lancaster
Mrs J A Coplestone-Crow, BA St Aidan's College,
Durham
Mrs S Didlick, BEd CNAA
Mrs J Knight, BA Portsmouth
Mrs C Murphy, BA Royal Holloway London (*Head of
Sixth Form*)
Mr R Nicholson, MA Pembroke College Oxford (*Head
Master*)
Ms S Ostrander, BSc Bristol
Mrs C Renton, BSc Leicester, MSc University College
London (*Deputy Head to Head Master & Deputy Head
Pastoral*)
Dr P Seal, BA MPhil Bristol, DPhil Balliol College Oxford
Mrs L Shaw, BA Warwick, MA University of the West of
England
Miss C Tedd, BA Trinity College Oxford, MA London
(*Head of Key Stage 4*)
Mrs S Watson, MA Hertford College Oxford

Physical Education
*Mrs S Parkinson-Mills, BSc Loughborough (*Director of
Sport, Head of Faculty*)
Ms V Sarson, BA Bristol (*Director of Sport, Warwick
Preparatory School*)
Mrs L Steinhaus, BSc Sheffield Hallam (*Second in
Department & Head of Year 7, King's High School*)
§Mrs K Bryce, BSc Brunel (*Pastoral Assistant to Key
Stage 4, King's High School*)
Miss E Callan, BSc Sheffield Hallam (*Graduate Sports
Assistant, King's High School*)
Miss V Carvell, BSc Cardiff Metropolitan University
(*Warwick Preparatory School*)
Mr A Proctor, BA University of Central Lancashire
(*Warwick Preparatory School*)
§Mrs K Riley, BA Exeter, MSc Chester (*Head of Academic
PE, King's High School*)
§Mrs C Walker, BEd Chelsea School of Movement

Psychology
*Ms S Ostrander, BSc Bristol
Mrs V Baker BSc Nottingham Trent

Religion & Philosophy:
*Dr P Carr, BA Girton College Cambridge, MA PhD
Lancaster
Dr G Gifford, MSc MA PhD Edinburgh
§Dr K Moody, BA Canterbury Christ Church, MA PhD
Lancaster

Science & Engineering:
*Mrs A Sims, MA Peterhouse Cambridge
§Mr J McGuire, BA Coventry, Cert HE Open University

Biology:
*Mr P McCorquodale, BSc Imperial College London
Mrs A Sims, MA Peterhouse Cambridge
Mrs V Baker, BSc Nottingham Trent
Mrs H Harrison, MEarthSci St Hugh's College Oxford
(*Assistant to the Head of Academic Enrichment &
Pastoral Assistant to the Head of Key Stage 4*)
Mrs A Paterson, MA Worcester College Oxford

Chemistry:
*Dr A Grist, BSc PhD Leicester
Mrs R Chapman, MA St Hilda's College Oxford (*Assistant
to the Director of Educational Innovation*)
Miss E Lees, BSc Leeds, MChem (*Assistant to Head of Key
Stage 3*)
Mrs J Parkinson-Mills, MSc Jesus College Cambridge
(*Duke of Edinburgh's Award Leader*)

Physics:
*Mrs J Scott, MPhys Hatfield College Durham, MA
Warwick [maternity leave]
Dr A Chamberlain, BSc PhD Warwick (*Acting Head of
Department & Academic Administrator*)
§Mrs K Clarke, BSc MSc Birmingham
Mr S Cleaver, BSc Manchester (*Assistant to Head of Sixth
Form*)
§Mr J McGuire, BA Coventry
Mr P McLeish, BSc Eng Cape Town [maternity cover]

Student Support:
*Mrs L Harris, BA Ed QTS Exeter, PG Cert Northampton
NASENCO (*Head of Learning Support*)

Boost Team:
§Mrs R Arun, BA MA Bangalore
§Mrs E Bolton, BSc Birmingham, MSc Open
§Mrs H Bottomley, BA Warwick
§Mrs R Brackley, BSc MSc Warwick
§Mrs N Fitch, BSc Wales
§Mrs S Parker, BA Birmingham
§Mrs C Townshend, BA East Anglia

Academic Enrichment:
*Dr P Seal, BA MPhil Bristol, DPhil Balliol College
Oxford (*Head of Department & EPQ/Research*)
Mrs M Harrison, MEarthSci St Hugh's College Oxford
(*Asst to the Head of Academic Enrichment & Pastoral
Asst to the Head of Key Stage 4*)
Ms R Giniunaite, MMath Warwick (*Graduate Seminar
Leader*)
Miss D Cugini, BA Emmanuel College Cambridge
(*Graduate Seminar Leader*)

Visiting Staff for Music:
Mrs K Alcock, BA
Miss F Barsby, BMus
Miss T Butterworth, BMus
Miss A Chalmers, AGSM
Mr G Dunn, BA, MMus
Mrs C Herbert, BMus
Mr N Hudson, FLCM, LGSMD
Mrs S M Irving, BEd Homerton College Cambridge,
MMus
Mrs R Jefferies, BA, MMus, ARCM
Mr N Jones
Miss K Lambeth, BMus, MMus
Mrs V Lee, BMus
Mr T Lindsay, BSc, Grad Dip Birmingham Conservatoire
Mrs J Mayne, BMus, PG Dip
Mrs S Meteyard, GBSM, ABSM
Ms C Mills BMus, LTCL, ABRSM, LRSM, ARCM
Miss B Morley, BA Coll
Mr G Prosser, HND
Miss S Saunders, BA
Dr H Smith, PhD, MA, BMus, Dip ABRSM
Mrs K Trethewey, BMus, PG Dip
Miss A H Whelan, DRSAMD
Mrs A Williams, LRAM, ARCM
Ms C Xi, BMus

Visiting Coach/Teachers for Activities:
Mr J Adam (*Strength & Conditioning*)
Mr M Beckett (*Duke of Edinburgh's Award*)
Mrs S Cartwright-Randle (*Badminton*)
Mr N Chapman [Warwick School] (*Fencing*)
Mrs Z Chen (*Mandarin*)
Mrs S Cleaver (*Netball*)
Mrs A Cooke SRN (*First Aid*)
Mrs L England (*Dance/Hip Hop*)
Mr P Fox (*Clay Pigeon Shooting*)
Miss I Gray (*Ballet*)

Mr P Helps [Warwick School] (*Clay Pigeon Shooting*)
Mr G Henderson (*Tennis*)
Mr A Hodskinson [Warwick School] (*Climbing Club*)
Mrs E Holding (*Hockey*)
Miss M Ingles (*Yoga & Contemporary Dance*)
Miss H McGrath (*Yoga*)
Mrs D Monnington (*PE & Junior Badminton/Rounders*)
Mr C Osborne (*Badminton*)
Mr P Pardoe (*Clay Pigeon Shooting*)
Mrs P Quinn (*Fitness*)
Mrs L Rodriguez (*Martial Arts*)
Mrs A Stanley (*Zumba*)
Mr A Wilson (*Duke of Edinburgh's Award*)
Mrs C Wilson (*Duke of Edinburgh's Award*)
Mrs M Yates [Warwick School] (*Lifesaving*)

Members of Non-Teaching Staff:

Administration:
§Mrs A Wheals (*Head's PA & Office Manager*)
§Mrs S Norton (*PA to Deputy Heads*)
Miss H Paddock, BA Lancaster (*Data Manager*)
§Mrs P Mullin, BA Birmingham (*Examinations Officer*)
§Mrs S Mann (*Music Administrator & Assistant to the Artistic Director (Music)*)
§Mrs E Wathen (*Senior Office Administrator*)
§Mrs C Gentles (*Staff Cover & Office Administrator*)
§Mrs L Prescott (*Administrative Assistant*)
§Mrs L Ashley (*Office Receptionist/Administrator*)

Marketing:
Ms N Dumbleton, BSc Nottingham Trent (*Head of Marketing*)
§Mrs E Guest (*Marketing Administrator*)
§Mrs D Shields, BA St Anne's College Oxford (*Marketing Assistant*)
§Ms E Tyreman, BSc Manchester (*Marketing Administrator*)

Admissions:
Mrs G Worrall (*Registrar & Head of Admissions*)
§Miss B Taylor (*Admissions Administrator*)

Development:
Mr P Rothwell, BA St Chads College Durham (*Development Director*)
§Miss L Bainbridge, BSc Birmingham (*Development & Landor Association Manager*)
Mrs P Beidas, BA MA Sheffield (*Development & Landor Association Administrator*)

The King's Hospital

Palmerstown, Dublin 20 D20 V256, Ireland

Tel: 00 353 1 643 6500 Reception
          00 353 1 643 6564 Admissions
Fax: 00 353 1 623 0349
email: khadmissions@thekingshospital.ie
website: www.kingshospital.ie
Twitter: @Kings_Hospital
Facebook: @thekingshospital
LinkedIn: /the-kings-hospital

Voluntary Church of Ireland (Anglican), co-educational, secondary school for boarders and day pupils aged 12–18 with 716 pupils, of whom 278 are boarders and 438 are day pupils. We try to maintain an equal balance of boys and girls.

The King's Hospital, one of the oldest boarding schools in Ireland, was founded in 1669 as The Hospital and Free School of King Charles II. In 1969 the School began the move from the centre of Dublin to its present, modern setting in spacious, scenic grounds of over 85 acres on the banks of the River Liffey in Palmerstown, yet remains only 15 minutes from Dublin International Airport. The King's Hospital attracts pupils from all over Ireland with approximately 10% from overseas.

The fundamental values of a Christian conscience, a sense of duty and loyalty and a love of learning are actively promoted.

The school offers five-day teaching programme with quality 5 and 7 day boarding options at extremely competitive rates. Our Saturday Programme of activities is designed to support the school curriculum and offer the pupil the opportunity to expand his/her knowledge base. Workshops in Web Designing and Coding, Extra English classes, Indoor Sports are a sample of the options available on Saturday mornings. The students also have organised social evenings, cultural trips and can join one of our many extracurricular clubs at the weekend.

The King's Hospital believes that every child should achieve his or her true potential intellectually and socially, through personal endeavour and the encouragement and support of our staff, parents and governors. Through our academic, pastoral and extracurricular programmes, we strive to develop core values of:

- a love of learning which makes all study a discovery and a joy, and which leads to standards of academic excellence appropriate to each child's ability;
- a Christian conscience and awareness which enables our pupils to develop a personal faith in God, to lead fulfilling lives which will enrich the communities in which they live, to uphold truth and show respect for others as well as for themselves, and to accept responsibility for their own actions;
- a sense of duty and loyalty which encourages participation in, and commitment to, every aspect of school life.

Academic. The school has an excellent academic record (97% progression to Higher Education in 2017), numbers that are not captured accurately in school league tables as they only count students who entered Irish Universities. In 2017 17% of our students took places in Universities in the UK, Europe and the US.

Most pupils pursue a 6 year course on entering the school at the age of 12. The first three years lead to the Junior Cycle Examination, followed by a Transition Year, and the final two years are devoted to the Irish Leaving Certificate Examination (equivalent to 4 A Levels) providing access to universities in the UK and throughout the World. The consistently high level of academic achievement is a reflection of the manner in which the School has always adapted to the ever-evolving education process and the ever-changing needs of its pupils by providing a comprehensive and progressive range of subjects, extensive specialist facilities and a highly qualified teaching staff.

The specialist facilities range from laboratories, workshops and computers to technical equipment and instruments, with Computer/PowerPoint facilities in all classrooms. A highly trained and well-equipped Special Needs department is available for both gifted children and those with learning difficulties. Media technology in the Harden Library provides access to national and international databases for project work as well as a computerised resource centre for information and guidance on careers. Tablets and laptops are available in classrooms for coursework that requires it.

Extracurricular. In addition to academic pursuits, The King's Hospital is renowned for its choice of recreational activities and offers a wide variety of sporting, music, drama and academic clubs and societies with unrivalled facilities. Students are encouraged to participate and all have the opportunity to represent the School at various levels in the activities of their choice.

An ultra-modern Sports Hall incorporating a fully-equipped fitness centre, a 25-metre indoor heated swimming pool and a floodlit astroturf pitch are among the outstanding facilities providing ample opportunity for Rugby, Hockey, Athletics, Swimming, Rowing, Cricket, Soccer, Basketball, Badminton and Tennis.

The promotion of cultural activities is catered for through Arts and Crafts, Choirs, Orchestras and Drama and Musical productions. A dedicated Performing Arts Centre is a recently built facility.

A diverse array of recreational activities is covered with clubs and societies, a Student Council, social work and European Studies, theatre and concert trips and trips abroad, both sporting and cultural.

Pastoral. Cooperation and mutual respect between pupils and staff, as well as a specified code of behaviour, are central to the daily life of the School. There are ten houses whose Housemaster or Housemistress has specific responsibility for the general welfare and development of students under his or her care. Peer mentoring in the form of Prefects and Mentors also provides a very supportive environment for the pupils. The diverse aspects of health education are included in the School's programme and 24 hour nursing care and a counsellor are available. Worship, according to the rites of the Church of Ireland and led by the resident Chaplain, is an integral part of daily life and pupils gain an understanding of and respect for all religious persuasions.

The Future. A vision for the future of the School is embodied in an ever-evolving School Strategic Plan and the Board of Governors is committed to implementing the development strategies within that plan. The School maintains its position as one of Ireland's leading educational institutions through this ambitious development programme. During 2018/19 all our boarding houses are being extensively refurbished and additional supervision staff accommodated. We have added a second hockey pitch and planning permission is being sought for the first phase of our Campus Master Plan, which will includes a STEAM Centre.

Fees per annum (2018–2019). Pupils with an Irish Passport: 5-Day Boarding €14,890, 7-day Boarding €16,795, Day (Irish resident only) €7,190. Pupils with a EU Passport: 7-Day Boarding €20,154. Pupils with Non-EU Passport €20,994.

Chairman of Governors: Mr Ken Peare

Headmaster: **Mark E Ronan**, MA Cantab

Deputy Head: Louise Marshall, BEd Hons QUB

Deputy Principal & Acting Head of Boarding: Cormac Ua Bruadair, BA UU, HDipEd TCD, HDipEdL NUI Maynooth

Assistant Heads:
Siobhán Daly, BA Mod, HDipEd TCD (*Academic Affairs*)
John Aiken, BA, HDipEd TCD (*Wellbeing*)
Kerrie O'Reilly, MA Hons UCD, BA Hons Brunel (*Arts, Culture & International Students*)

Chaplain: The Revd Canon Peter Campion, MPhil, MA, PGCE

Director of Sport: David Keelty

Head of Finance and Operations: Tony Kearney

Marketing & Admissions Manager: Síle Jio

Subject Coordinators:
Detta Brennan, Dip Fine Arts, Dip ADT (*Art*)
Corina Geraghty, BA Hons, HDip Ed WUT (*Mathematics*)

The Revd Canon Peter Campion, MPhil, MA, PGCE (*Religious Education*)
Jean Atkinson, BBS, HDipEd (*Business*)
Annabel Browne, BA, HDipEd (*Geography and CSPE*)
Glenda Ua Bruadair, BA, PGCE (*English*)
Janet Nelson, MSc, BA, HDipEd, DSEN (*Special Education Needs*)
John Huggard, BA, HDipEd (*History*)
Emma Ryan, BSc QTS (*Physical Education*)
Caroline Brady, BEd (*Home Economics*)
Dymphna Morris, BA, Dip Comp (*Information Technology*)
Michelle Murray, MEd Mgt, BA Special, HDipEd (*Irish*)
Patrick O'Shea, BTechEd (*Design and Communication Graphics*)
Cara O'Donoghue, BA Hons, HDipEd (*Modern Languages*)
Miriam Wright, BMus, HDipEd (*Music*)
Susan Tanner, BSc, HDipEd, HDCG (*Career Guidance and SPHE*)
Ciaran Whelan, BSc, HDipEd (*Science*)

Housemasters/Mistresses:
Caroline Brady, BEd Hons (*Mercer House*)
Rachelle Van Zyl, BComm Hons, HDipEd (*Grace House*)
Niall Mahon, BSc, HDipEd (*Ormonde House*)
Paul O'Donoghue BA, HDipEd, PGD (*Morgan House*)
Raymond McIlreavy, MEd, BA, HDipEd (*Bluecoat House Boys*)
Amy Fitzgerald, BA Hons, HDipEd (*Bluecoat House Girls*)
David Plummer, BSc, PGCE (*Ivory House Boys*)
Denise Farrelly, BA Hons, HDipEd (*Ivory House Girls*)
Alison Gill, BA Hons, PGCE (*Desmond House*)
Dean Maguire, BComm, HDipEd (*Stuart House*)
Noel Cunningham, MSc, BSc, HDipEnvirEng, HDipEd (*Blackhall House*)
Elizabeth Peoples (*Swift House*)
Yvonne Duggan, BComm, HDipEd NUI, BSc Hons (*Bluecoat House Day*)

Headmaster's PA: Lorraine Walker

The King's School
Canterbury

25 The Precincts, Canterbury, Kent CT1 2ES

Tel:	Reception: 01227 595501
	Bursar: 01227 595544
	Admissions: 01227 595579
Fax:	01227 766255
email:	headmaster@kings-school.co.uk
website:	www.kings-school.co.uk

St Augustine's foundation of a monastic school in Canterbury in 597 AD marks the origin of The King's School: hence, its claim to be the oldest school in the country. It was re-founded by King Henry VIII in 1541. More recently, a Junior School has been established on the former estate of Lord Milner outside the city. The close relationship with the Cathedral Foundation has been there throughout.

King's Scholars. Many schools cherish the notion that they are the oldest school in the country, but there is little doubt that there has been a school on the present World Heritage site of King's School, Canterbury since the Augustinian mission to England in 597 AD. The name of the school and its intimate relationship with the Cathedral community of the mother church of the Anglican Communion date from the Henrician settlement, as do the King's Scholars who, along with the Headmaster and the Senior Deputy Head, form part of the original Foundation of Christchurch, Canterbury. So much for the history, the King's Scholars continue to occupy buildings and be taught in classrooms that predate the Reformation. Besides their function in the Cathedral, the King's Scholars are at the heart of the vibrant and open-ended academic life of the school. Each year, some of the King's Scholars are on full means-tested bursaries, keeping alive the original vision of the school. The modern King's Scholar discovers a school which is fully co-educational, diverse in its catchment and intentions, as well as in tune with the wider life of the city of Canterbury and national/international context beyond its immediate compass.

Scholarships and Bursaries. Up to twenty King's Scholars and Exhibitioners are elected each year following competitive examinations and interviews in February. A further group of King's Scholars are added at the Sixth Form entrance stage (competitive examination and interviews in the November preceding entry). These academic awards have a meritocratic value of 10% of the fees, but the crucial thing is that they can be augmented by means-tested bursaries up to 100%. The extremely strong tradition of music at King's, both instrumental and choral, means that Music Scholarships (about 20 are awarded annually) are generously provided for. The school is particularly welcoming for those who have come on to King's from the choir schools of Cathedrals and Colleges. There are further Music Scholarships made for Sixth Form entry.

There are further Scholarships and Exhibitions at 13+ for exceptional ability in Art and Sport – the Gower Sports Scholarships named after the former England cricket captain – and the school also grants awards for DT, Drama and Dance.

Academic Life. The King's curriculum is distinct for its combination of striving for the very highest standards in the most appropriate Public Examinations (IGCSEs at the end of Year 10 for a few subjects, but mainly at the end of Year 11; A Levels and Pre-U courses in the Sixth Form) on the one hand, and the pursuit of learning and the development of the intellect for its own sake (self-standing courses, tutorials and lectures in the evenings and extended project qualifications, as well as independent research). The school puts particular emphasis on studying Mandarin, German and Russian, as well as 'new' subjects like Photography and Computer Science. A wide degree of choice of subject in the Sixth Form (Earth & Planetary Sciences and Philosophy, for example) is often an engine for academic success.

Some 20–25 offers of admission to Oxford and Cambridge are received each year.

All round vision. Christopher Marlowe, William Harvey and Thomas Linacre number amongst King's pupils and the pursuit of the Renaissance ideal still resonates in the contemporary school. The strongest encouragement is given to Music, Drama, Sport, CCF and the Visual Arts. This stems from belief in the value of these activities in themselves, but also since recreation and success in these fields leads to growth in self-confidence and better academic performance. Alongside these activities are opportunities to get involved in Partnership projects and pursue the Duke of Edinburgh's Award.

Numbers and Organisation. There are currently 886 pupils on the school roll, 432 boys and 444 girls, of whom 80% are boarders. There are 6 boys' boarding houses, 7 girls' boarding houses and 3 (mixed) day houses. To the east of the main school buildings in the Cathedral Precincts is St Augustine's, home to 5 boarding houses, the original Medieval Hall and magnificent school library. There are 2 major sites for sport, Birley's and Blore's, each with extensive sports facilities. Junior King's School, the prep school of King's, occupies a site on the River Stour, in Sturry, three miles from Canterbury. There are currently 376 pupils at Junior King's, 202 boys and 174 girls of whom 89 are boarders.

Admission. Application should be made to the Assistant Registrar. It is advisable to register pupils at an early age. Admission is normally through the Common Entrance Examination, the King's School entrance examination (for non-CE candidates) or, if academically appropriate, through the King's Scholarship Examination. The age of entry is about 13.

Fees per term (2018–2019). Senior School: £12,485 for boarders and £9,165 for day pupils. Junior School: £8,570 for boarders and £5,620–£6,245 for day pupils.

OKS (Old King's Scholars). *Coordinator*: Miss Hannah Pinney, OKS Association Office, Tel: 01227 595669; email: oks@kings-school.co.uk.

The King's Society exists for all parents, past and present. A termly programme of social and cultural events is open to all members and is published on the school website.

Charitable status. The King's School of the Cathedral Church of Canterbury is a Registered Charity, number 307942. It exists to provide education for boys and girls.

Visitor: The Lord Archbishop of Canterbury

Governors:
Chairman: The Very Revd Dr R A Willis, DL, DCL, DD, Dean of Canterbury Cathedral
Vice-Chairman: N S L Lyons, MA
Mrs E McKendrick, BA
Sir Roger De Haan
J D Tennant, MRICS
R C A Bagley, LLB
Miss F J Judd, QC
M W S Bax, FRICS
T M Steel, MA, DL
Dr M L Sutherland, BSc, MSc, PhD
Mrs C Swire, MA, Dip Cons BA
The Venerable J Kelly-Moore, BA, LLB, BD
Revd Canon Dr Tim Naish, MA, PhD
B Moorhead, DL

Clerk to the Governors: M R Taylor, FRSA

Governors Emeriti:
The Very Revd J A Simpson, OBE, MA, DD
The Lady Kingsdown, OBE, DCL

Headmaster: P J M Roberts, MA

Headmaster's PA: Miss C Dixon
Lattergate Office Administrator: Mrs L Hutchinson
Lattergate Receptionist: Miss C J M Finch & Mrs A Goodier

Senior Deputy Head: Mrs E A Worthington, MA

Deputy Head Academic: L G Bartlett, BA, MRSC
Deputy Head Pastoral: Miss T Lee, BA
Deputy Head Admissions and Marketing: I S MacEwen, MA

PA to Senior Deputy Head/Deputy Head Pastoral: Miss A L Tamblyn, BA
Academic Assistant: Mrs G V Hone, BSc Econ
Examinations Officer: Mrs L A Renault

Head of Sixth Form: A J Holland, BSc
Heads of Middle School: M W Browning, BA and Dr S T Hayes, MSci, PhD, MRSC
Head of Lower School: R T M Harrison
Head of Oxbridge: Dr R A B Johnson, MSc, PhD
Head of Extended Projects: Miss A K Fraser, MA, MPhil

Bursar: M R Taylor, FRSA

Capital Projects Director: L Dudas, BSc, Dip Surv, Associate RICS
Deputy Finance Bursar: D Rogers, ACCA
Human Resources Manager: J Hadlow, BA, Associate CIPD

Director of Development: Mrs K E Chernyshov, BA

Head of Marketing: K L Orwin, BA

Registrar: J W Outram, BA
Assistant Registrar: Mrs B Skilton

Senior Tutor: M J Miles, MA
University and Careers Adviser: Ms P D Williams, MA, DipCG

Senior Chaplain: The Revd L R F Collins, BD, AKC, MTh
Assistant Chaplain: The Revd M Robbins, BA, BTh

Librarian: Miss P K Rose, FDA, MA, PGCHE, ACLIP

Medical Officers:
Dr W Lloyd Hughes, MB BS
Dr T Crook, MB BS, MRCGP, DRCOG

* *Head of Department*
† *Housemaster/mistress*

Art:
Mrs G C Burrows, BA
*P K Cordeaux, BA
Mrs I A Dutton, BA
M McArdle, BA
Mrs J Taylor-Goodman, BA, MA
I S Wallace, BA
D K Willis, BA

Classics:
M W Browning, BA
Dr G M Longley, MA, DPhil
*Miss J Taylor, BA
Miss H L Warwicker, BA

Design & Technology:
M J Franks, BEd
*M J Rolison, BEd
G J Swindley, BSc

Drama:
*Mrs R J Beattie, BA, FRSA
Miss F R Mountjoy, BA
Miss A L Tamblyn, BA

Economics:
*S N Chester, BA
Mrs L A Horn, BSc
†R W Ninham, MA
A Rodriguez, MSc
M D Bell, BCOM, CIMA

English:
Dr H Barton, MA, PhD
Mrs L Carlyle, BA, DPhil
†Mrs J M Cook, BA
E J Flower, BA
*Dr A T H Latter, MA, PhD
A J W Lyons, BA, MA, FRSA
Mrs K J Newsholme, BA
Dr J P Wilper, BA, MLitt, PhD
†Mrs A L Young, MA

Geography:
A J Holland, BSc
†M E Lister, BSc, MSc
J A Lloyd, BSc
*R P Sanderson, BA
Mrs S J Sensecall, BSc
M C E Turner, BSc

History:
Miss C E Anderson, BA, MA
W M R Flint, MA
†G W H Harrison, MA
Miss A V Loveday, BA
*D J C Perkins, BA, MA, Dip Law, PhD
L J W Philipps, MA
Mrs E A Worthington, MA

History of Art:
Dr H Barton, MA, PhD
*D J Felton, BA, MA

ICT and Computing:
Mrs L M Cousins, BA
*A J Holland, BSc
B D M Katz, BA, MSc
Dr S Kerridge, BA, BSc, PhD
M C E Turner, BSc
*C P Wooldridge, BSc

Mathematics:
Mrs E R Bell, MSci
M O Cox, MA, MEng, Dip ITEC
M P H Dath, L-ès-ScM, M-ès-ScM
Mrs J J de Villiers, MA
J P E Dickson, BSc, MSc, RN
Dr R A B Johnson, MSc, PhD
Mrs J Gorman, BSc
B D M Katz, BA, MSc
Dr S Kerridge, BA, BSc, PhD
A McFall, BSc

*S P Ocock, BA
Dr K J Palmer, BSc, PhD
R C Stuart, BSc
R N Warnick, MA

Learning Support:
Mrs D J Ardley, BA
*Mrs P J Brown, BA, MA
Mrs S Burke, MA
Mrs C J Carrier, MA
Ms G R Moorcroft, BEd, MA
Mrs M L Orders, BA
Mrs C R Titterton, BA
Mrs J Wright
Mrs B Raffety
Mrs K Rothwell

Modern Languages:
†Mrs Z T Allen, MA
Miss L N Bernardo Otamendi, Lda, MPhil, MA
Mrs A Browne, LSc
Miss H C Davies, MA
*Mrs M B Garcés-Ramón, Lda
Mrs N Geoffroy, L-ès-ScEd
R T M Harrison, BA
†Mrs R E Heskins, BA
Dr J R Karolyi, BA, PhD
Mrs C L Kelly, MA, BEd
*Mrs L Liu, BA, MPhil
Miss J M Maréchal, BA, MSc
M J Miles, MA
Miss A M Pedraza Rascado, BA, MA
*B R Pennells, BA
Mrs L Waitt, MA Ed
Mrs L J Warnick, MA
Miss F Zanardi, MA

Music:
K Abbott, Dip RCM
*W Bersey, BMus
S J R Matthews, MA
A Pollock, MA
G R Swinford, BA
N G Todd, MA

Politics:
Mrs D J Ardley, BA
I S MacEwen, MA
*O T Moelwyn-Hughes, BA, LLB, MSt

Physical Education:
*Miss K V Batty, BSc
†M E Lister, BSc, MSc
*L W Portsmouth, BSc
R A L Singfield, BEd (*Sport)

Religious Studies and Philosophy:
Miss S I Barnard, MA, MPhil
Dr D Cardinal, MA, PhD
G R Cocksworth, BA, MA
The Revd L R F Collins, BD, AKC, MTh
Mrs C A Cox, BA, MPhil
Miss A K Fraser, MA, MPhil
Mrs C A Hayes, BA

E D Hearson, MA
*Miss T Lee, BA
J W Outram, BA
The Revd M Robbins, BA, BTh

Science:

Biology:
Ms K Budden, BSc
Dr H E Cunnold, BSc, PhD
J M Hutchings, BA
Mrs E H Lockwood, MA, BSc
Dr M A McVeigh, MSc, PhD
Miss S A Rajska, BSc
†M J W Smiley, MA
†M J Thornby, BSc
*S J Winrow-Campbell, BSc, MIBiol, CBiol

Chemistry:
L G Bartlett, BA, MRSC
R P Cook, BSc
Miss A R Donkin, MChem
*Dr S T Hayes, MSci, PhD, MRSC
L W Hynes, BSc PhD
Dr L E J Jones, MChem, PhD
D A Scott, BSc, MSc, MA Ed, MRSC (*Science)
†A S D Stennett, BSc
†Dr T J Waite, BSc, HND, PhD

Physics:
*Miss L M Comber BSc (*Science)
Mrs S K Dieu, BAppSc
F Elias, Ldo, PhD
Miss L M Kendrick, BSc
†Mrs E S Ladd, BEng
†M C Orders, BSc
D M Tanton, MA, MSc, DipD'I, PhD
J S Tutton, BEng

Earth & Planetary Sciences:
*M R Mawby, BSc

Houses and Housemasters/mistresses:

School House: A Vintner
The Grange: C Orders
Walpole: Mrs A L Young
Meister Omers: R W Ninham
Marlowe (day): G W H Harrison
Luxmoore: Ms L Cousins

Galpin's: Dr T J Waite
Linacre: M Lister
Tradescant: A S D Stennet
Broughton: Dr D McVeigh
Mitchinson's (day): Mrs E S Ladd
Jervis: Mrs R E Heskins
Harvey: Mrs J M Cook
Bailey (Sixth Form): Mrs E Bell
Carlyon (day): M J W Smiley
Kingsdown: Mrs C A Hayes

The Junior King's School
Milner Court, Sturry, Nr Canterbury, CT2 0AY.
Tel: 01227 714000
Headmistress: Mrs E J Karolyi, MA
(*For further details see King's Junior School entry in IAPS
section.*)

The King's School

Chester

Chester CH4 7QL

Tel:	01244 689500
Fax:	01244 689501
email:	info@kingschester.co.uk
website:	www.kingschester.co.uk

Motto: *Rex Dedit, Benedicat Deus*

The School was founded AD 1541 by King Henry VIII, in conjunction with the Cathedral Church of Chester. It was reorganised under the Endowed Schools Act in 1873, and by subsequent schemes of the Ministry of Education. The School is now Independent. The aim of the School is to prepare pupils for admission to Universities and the professions, and at the same time provide a liberal education.

Organisation. The School, which at present numbers 1100, consists of (i) an Infant School for pupils aged 4 to 7 years, (ii) a Junior School for pupils aged 7 to 11 years, and (iii) the Senior School. The Infant and Junior Schools are housed in separate buildings, but are run in collaboration with the Senior School. On entry to Shells (2nd year of the Senior School) pupils are placed in one of eight houses; every student has a tutor who oversees their progress and welfare throughout their school career.

Admission. Please refer to our admissions policy which outlines the criteria and selection process for entry: www.kingschester.co.uk/policies. Selection is by academic merit alone.

Academic. Departments are grouped into four Faculties whose Heads report to the Academic Deputy Head. The subjects offered for study in the Sixth Form are – on the Arts side: Art, Business, Classical Studies, Drama, Economics, English, English Language, French, Geography, German, History, Latin, Music, Philosophy, Politics, Religious Studies, Spanish; and on the Science side: Biology, Chemistry, Computing, Further Mathematics, Mathematics, Physics, Sports Science and Design Technology. It is possible to take most combinations of subjects in the Sixth Form.

Spiritual life. The School is part of the Cathedral Foundation and regularly holds its own services in the Cathedral. Spiritual assemblies are held regularly in school.

Music. Music is part of the general curriculum for all pupils up to the age of 14. After this music may be taken at GCSE and A Level. Private tuition in orchestral instruments, piano and organ is available. There are many musical ensembles and choral groups including the Schola Cantorum which leads the worship in Cathedral services.

Cadet Corps. There is a CCF contingent which gives pupils opportunities to develop leadership skills and to undertake adventurous training.

Outdoor Education. Opportunities are provided both within and outside the curriculum for outdoor education, and all pupils in each of the first three years of the senior school spend some days away at centres specialising in outdoor activities. In addition many pupils participate in the Duke of Edinburgh's Award Scheme at all levels.

Games. Football, Hockey, Netball, Rugby, Cricket, Rowing, Swimming, Badminton, Basketball, Athletics, Netball, Tennis, Squash, Golf, Rounders.

Buildings. Formerly situated adjacent to the Cathedral, the school moved into new buildings in 1960 situated in rural surroundings nearly 2 miles from the centre of Chester. Since then there has been an impressive programme of additional building development. These include the Wickson Library, a new Music School, the Vanbrugh Theatre and extensions to the Sixth Form Centre. In September 2014 the Junior School was extended to provide a new Junior School Library and Learning Centre, and in September 2015 a purpose-built Infant School was opened by the Duke of Westminster. A state-of-the-art Sports Centre is due to open in March 2019.

Alumni associations. Please see the website (www.kingschester.co.uk/kings-alumni) for details of OAKS (the Organisation for the Alumni of the King's School) and CAOKS (Chester Association of Old King's Scholars).

Fees per term (2018–2019). Tuition: Senior School £4,505, Junior School £3,454, Infants £3,050.

The School offers a small number of bursaries annually.

Scholarships. Academic scholarships of up to £500 are awarded to pupils during their early years in the Senior School. Scholars carry the title 'King's Scholar' throughout their time at the school.

Tenable in the Sixth Form: A number of scholarships are awarded to students on entry to the Sixth Form and during their Sixth form years. These include: (1) Keith Oates Scholarship: £1,000; (2) Investec Scholarship: £1,000; (3) King's School Parents' Association Scholarship: £500.

Tenable at Universities: (1) Old King's Scholars Exhibition: £750; (2) Robert Platt Exhibition: £500; (3) John Churton Exhibition: £500; (4) Haswell Exhibition: £500; (5) Finchett Maddock Exhibition: £500; (6) King's School Parents' Association: two exhibitions of £600.

Charitable status. The King's School, Chester is a Registered Charity, number 525934. The aim of the charity is to provide a sound education to all boys and girls who can benefit from it regardless of their economic and social background.

Governors:
D K Rowlands (*Chairman*)
R Arnold, BSc, ACA
Prof R Ashford, PhD, FCIM, FHEA, BEd
Prof J Billowes, MA, DPhil, FInstP
Mrs J Carr, BA, FCA
S Docking, BA
Mrs C A Edwards, MA
I O'Doherty, BE, MSc, MBA
G P Ramsbottom, BSc, MSc, MRICS
Mrs S J Verity, BSc
N H Wood, BSc, MRICS, IRRV

Clerk to the Governors: S P Cross, MSc, LLB

Headmaster: **G J Hartley**, MA Cantab, MSc

Senior Deputy Head: Dr J M Byrne, BA, MBA
Deputy Head (Academic): J E Millard, BA
Deputy Head (Pastoral): M J Harle, BSc

Head of Sixth Form: J P Carter, MA
Director of Studies: A J Dewbery, MA
Senior Tutor: R G Wheeler, BA
Director of Learning Support: Mrs S Glass, BA

Assistant staff:
* Head of Department
Art and Design:
*S Downey, BA (*Head of Faculty – Creative Arts & PE*)
Ms L Black, BA
Mrs A L Hollingworth, BA (*Assistant Head of Sixth Form*)

Biology:
*R H Jones, BSc, PhD
J A Dunn, MSc
R D J Elmore, BSc, MIBiol, CBS
Dr H C Faulkner, BSc, DPhil (*Head of Faculty – Science*)
L A Parkes, BSc, MSc (*Head of Dutton House*)

Chemistry:
*A Cook, BSc, PhD
Dr C A Gleave, BSc, PhD
M J Harle, BSc
Mrs J E Jepson, BSc
Dr J R Macnab, BSc, PhD
Mrs K L Russon, BSc

Classics:
*P R Wilcock MA
Mrs S H Gareh, BA, MA
M J P Punnett, MA

Design Technology:
*R J Curtis, BSc
Ms L Black, BA
Miss S J Champion, BA

Drama:
*Mrs C L Howdon, BA
Mrs J Williams, BA, MA

Economics & Business:
*S D Walton, BA, MSc
Miss E M Rowley, BSocSc
Mrs C A Rule, BA
G F Smith BA

English:
*R J Aldridge, BA, MBA
M A Boyd, BA
Mrs A C Leake, BA, MEd
Dr K F Mair, MA
Mrs A E Richards, BA (*Head of Walsh House*)
R G Wheeler, BA

Geography:
*M J Prestshaw, BSc MEd, MRes
Mrs R H Aldridge, BA (*Head of Enrichment*)
J A D Blackham, BA (*Head of Grosvenor House*)
Mrs A M McNabb, BA
Mrs K Jones, BA (*Assistant Director of Sport; Head*

History & Politics:
*P G Neal, BA
J P Carter, MA
Mrs G K Chadwick, BA
R J M Hensman, BA, MA, PhD
S Neal, BA (*Head of Faculty – Languages & Humanities*)

Information Technology:
*A Rahman, BEng
A J Dewbery, MA
Mrs E E Simpson, BA, MBA

Mathematics:
*Mrs C E Lanceley, BSc
S D Bibby, BSc
C J Canty, BSc
Mrs S Cooper, BSc
A J Dewbery, MA
Mrs A Ignata, BSc
Mrs C Plass, BSc
Mrs C N Ranson, BSc
Miss D Roberts, BSc
Mrs H E Sugarman, MMath

Modern Languages:
*Miss L E McCutcheon
M D Bircham, BA
Dr J M Byrne, BA, MBA
Miss K Donaldson, BA
Mrs C E Irvine, BA
Mrs M Rowley Williams, BA, MEd
Mrs R E Webb, BA (*Head of Gladstone House*)

Music:
*T M Harvey, BA, ARCO (*Director of Music*)
Ms D L Neal, BMus, MA (*Assistant Director of Music*)
Mrs V L S Latifa, BMus
J E Millard, BA

Personal & Social Education:
*M S Lee, MA

Philosophy & Theology:
*J R Rees, BA
M S Lee, MA (*Head of Werburgh House*)
Ms J E Rutberg, MA (*Head of Faculty – Social Sciences & Maths*)

Physical Education:
*R Lunn, BEd (*Director of Sport*)
*Mrs C Sumner, BA (*Head of Academic PE; Head of Lester-Smith House*)
of Fox House*)

R I D Hornby, BA (*Head of Bradbury House*)
B Horne, BSc (*Director of Football*)
Ms J Huck, BA
C Morris, BEd

Head of Junior School & Infant School: Mrs M A Ainsworth, LLB, MEd

Deputy Head (*Junior School*): A Griffiths, BA

Director of Studies (*Junior School*): T W Griffin, BA

Deputy Head (*Infant School*): Mrs J C Callaghan, BEd

Assistant Staff (*Junior School & Infant School*):
Miss J M Anderson, BA, CertEd
Mrs J Benson, BA
H J Duncalf, BEd
Miss H Fountain, BA
Mrs H George, MA
Miss J M L Hartley, BA
K A Hollingworth, BEd
Miss K Johnson, BA
Miss S Ley, BA
J B Melville, BEd
Mrs N C M Moffatt, BA
Mrs M D O'Leary, BA
D M O'Neil, BSc
Mrs S Parker BEd
Mrs D L Grove, BA
Miss K A Savage, BA
J N Spellman, BEd
Mrs N J Stevens, BMus
Mrs A Stevenson, BEd
Mrs N M Tomlinson, BA
Mrs S Tomlinson, BEd
Mrs K Williams, BEd

Visiting Music Teachers:
W Armstrong, BA, PGRNCM (*Oboe*)
Ms S Boryslawska, BA
S J Hall, BSc (*Bass Guitar*)
Mrs V L Ierston, LTCL (*Piano & Flute*)
G Macey, ATCL (*Woodwind*)
Ms S Marrs, FTCL (*Voice*)
N Middleton, BA (*Drums*)
Mrs R Mulholland, ARCM, LRAM (*Cello*)
D Ortiz, BMus (*Head of Brass*)
A Parker, MA (*Saxophone*)
M Reynolds BA (*Piano*)
Mrs J Richardson, CT ABRSM, ATCL (*Flute*)
S A Rushforth (*Head of Strings*)
T Wyss, ARCM, LRAM, LTCL (*Brass*)

Extra-Curricular Staff:
Director of Rowing: J A D Blackham, BA
Contingent Commander, CCF: Maj M S Lee, MA
Duke of Edinburgh's Award Coordinator: D A Brown
Educational Visits Coordinator: R I D Hornby, BA

Director of Finance & Operations: Mrs J H Beer, ACMA, CGMA, CIPS
Director of Human Resources: Mrs E R Davidson, BA, CIPD & Mrs A H Millard, BSc, MCIPD
Director of External Relations: Ms V M Titmuss, BA
Director of Development: Mrs E E Gwyther, BA
Director of ICT: J K Warne, BSc, MCSA
Admissions Manager: Mrs E R Sears, BA
Head Librarian & Archivist: Mrs R Harding, MA
Examinations Officer: R D J Elmore, BSc
School Nurse: Mrs L Jones, RN
Care Scheme Manager: Mrs R Probert

Headmaster's PA: Mrs A M E Wilson, BA

Physics:
*S Bosworth, MA, DPhil, FRAS
Ms H M Davies, BSc, MSc
N Heritage, MSc, PhD, MInstP, CPhys
B Horne, BSc
Mrs K L Scutter, BSc

The King's School
Macclesfield

Cumberland Street, Macclesfield, Cheshire SK10 1DA

Tel: 01625 260000
Fax: 01625 260022
email: mail@kingsmac.co.uk
website: www.kingsmac.co.uk

The King's School is the top performing independent school in Cheshire East for both GCSE and A Level results and is in The Telegraph Top 200 Independent Schools for exam results in 2014–2018.

Founded in 1502 and situated in rolling Cheshire countryside, King's offers an exciting academic education for boys and girls aged 3–18. It places an emphasis on excellent teaching and academic standards combined with an extensive range of extra-curricular activities and exceptional pastoral care. In its most recent ISI Inspection, King's was found to be 'excellent' in ALL aspects.

Number in School. Infants 3–7: 51 boys, 47 girls. Juniors 7–11: 121 boys, 100 girls. Boys (11–16) 400; Girls (11–16) 265. Sixth Form: 130 boys, 111 girls. Total: 1,225.

Organisation and Curriculum. The King's School is organised into four Divisions over two sites, about 1 mile apart. Each Division is run by a Principal, who is responsible for day-to-day organisation and welfare of pupils. Girls and boys from 3–18 enjoy the same broad range of opportunities.

The King's School has one Board of Governors and one Headmaster, plus a Senior Management Team, who manage the school.

King's aims include 'to challenge our pupils to aspire, work hard and achieve' and 'to develop lively and enquiring minds'. The curriculum is broad and rich throughout all year groups offering pupils of all ages choice and a range of experiences.

The School's most recent ISI Inspection Report (2015) graded King's as 'excellent' – the highest ranking – in all eight aspects. As well as teaching and pupils' achievements being excellent, so too is Pastoral care, which is a high priority within the school. The divisional structure is key to enabling each unit to be small and operate as a community. Coupled with the aim of 'fostering a friendly, polite and caring community', King's is definitely a happy place to be a pupil.

Students are assigned to a personal tutor responsible for a group of 10 or so pupils throughout their Sixth Form course. Any justifiable combination of available A Level subjects may be pursued, complemented by an IGCSE Global Perspectives (in Year 12), EPQ and Recreational Activity. Students choose from a wide range of options designed to extend their breadth of cultural interest and intellectual inquiry, whilst Recreational Activities are designed to encourage the positive use of leisure time and offers initial experience in sports and activities new to the individual. Pupils are also prepared for University Entrance Examinations where appropriate.

New campus. The King's school is currently building a new, £60m campus. All pupils will be relocated to the single, new campus in 2020. The state-of-the-art facilities will enhance the educational experience of all pupils, from 3–18 years old. The new site will include a dedicated Sports Centre containing a swimming pool, indoor cricket facilities, courts, a martial arts studio, gym and cafe.

Arts and Craft. Well-equipped art rooms and Design & Technology (DT) workshops are also available for use by the members of the Art Club, STEM Club, Textile Club and Craft societies outside the timetable.

Music. Over 400 pupils receive tuition in the full range of orchestral instruments, the Piano, Organ, Classical Guitar and Singing. An introductory tuition scheme enables all new entrants to assess their talent. There are three orchestras, a Concert-band, two Jazz bands, three Choirs and many ensembles, all of which provide regular performing experience. The Foundation Choir was the first BBC Songs of Praise Choir of the Year in 2003. Pupils regularly enter music profession in addition to those pursuing academic training.

Drama. Theatre Studies is an important creative option at GCSE and covers all aspects of the theatre. Great importance is attached to the regular school plays and musicals, which involve large numbers of pupils and enjoy a distinguished reputation. Pupils regularly take examinations and study for LAMDA qualifications in performance and public speaking.

Games. All pupils take part in games and athletic activity appropriate to the season. Junior School sports include Football, Cricket, Netball, Hockey, Tennis, Rounders, Rugby, Swimming, Athletics and a wide range of individual games. In the Senior School, boys' sports include Rugby, Hockey, Cross-Country, Squash, Badminton, Cricket, Tennis, Athletics and Basketball; the girls' sports include Hockey, Netball, Tennis, Football, Cross-Country, Volleyball, Cricket, Gym and Athletics. In addition there is a varied programme of sports in the Sixth Form, including activities such as Caving, Fell Running and Rock Climbing which are actively pursued by boys and girls.

Outdoor Pursuits. This is a thriving part of the school. There is a regular programme of activity weekends including canoeing, gorge scrambling, surfing, coasteering, etc. In addition, numerous expeditions are arranged in the many favourable areas near the school and also abroad. Sailing and Orienteering are popular and The Duke of Edinburgh's Award scheme attracts around 300 pupils each year. King's is one of the largest DofE authorising centres in the north of England.

Clubs and Societies. There is a wide range of other clubs catering for most interests and hobbies, ranging from Astronomy, Debating, Dance, Chess and Squash to Sailing, STEM Club, Equestrian Society, Electronics Club, Coding Club and Taekwondo.

Fees per term (2018–2019). Senior School and Sixth Form £4,330, Infants & Junior School £3,500.

Scholarships and Bursaries. Bursaries are available for entry at 11 and 16 years of age. In addition a number of Academic Scholarships are awarded based on performance in the Entrance Examination. Senior School Music Scholarships are available for instrument or singing. Academic, Music and Organ scholarships are also available in the Sixth Form. Funds are available to assist pupils attending courses and field trips and to help in cases of urgent need.

Admissions. Admission for the Infants is non-selective. Admission for the Juniors and Seniors is normally for September each year through competitive examination of age-appropriate Entrance papers. Girls and boys are admitted to the Sixth Form subject to academic attainment, interview and course requirement: a minimum of four grades 7 or above (A*/A) and two grades 6 or above (B) is standard. Further details of Admission arrangements are available on the website and upon request. Immediate admission, e.g. for new arrivals in the area, is possible.

Former Pupils' Association. Chairman: David Barratt; email: formerpupils@kingsmac.co.uk. An annual magazine and termly newsletter are provided to former pupils.

Visit the Website. The award-winning website is found at www.kingsmac.co.uk.

Charitable status. The King's School, Macclesfield is a Registered Charity, number 1137204. It exists for the education of boys and girls between the ages of 3 and 18.

Chairman of the Governors: Dr J Kennerley
Vice-Chair of Governors: J Sugden, MA, FIMechE, CEng

Senior Management Team:

Headmaster: Dr S Hyde, MA, DPhil

Deputy Headmaster (Academic): R Griffiths, MA Cantab
Director of External Relations: Mrs C Johnson, BSc, DipM
Director of Finance: Mr J M Spencer Pickup
Senior Teacher: Mrs R Roberts, BA, PGCE
Principal of Boys & Deputy Head: Mr P J Cooper, BSc
Principal of Girls: Mrs H L Broadley
Principal of Infants & Juniors: Mrs R Cookson, BA
Principal of Sixth Form: Mr R Davies, MA

Vice-Principal of Juniors: Mrs A Lea, BMus
Vice-Principal of Infants: Mrs E L Warburton, BEd

Heads of Departments:
Art & Design: Mrs D Inman, BA
Biology: Dr Patrick
Chemistry: Miss L C Watkins, BSc
Classics: A Mallin, BA
Design & Technology: J Nichols, BEd
Drama: D A Forbes, BA
Economics & Business Studies: J S MacGregor, MA
English: Mr R Kellett, BA, PGCE
Geography: A S Puddephatt, BA
Geology: Dr J A Fitzgerald, BSc, MSc, PhD
German: Mrs J Houghton, BA
History: Mr G Barker, MA, PGCE
Computing: Mr P Mackenzie, BSc
Learning Support: Mrs N S Davis, BA, Dip Psych, PG Cert
Modern Languages: I E Dalgleish, BA
Director of Music: I Crawford, BMus
Physical Education (Director of Sport): C S Thompson, BA, PGCE
Physics: Dr S J Hartnett, BSc, DPhil, PGCE
Psychology: Mrs C Bell, BSc, PGCE, MA Ed
Religion & Philosophy: R N Jackson, BA
Science: J Street, BSc, PGCE
Spanish: Mrs V Bartle

King's Rochester

Satis House, Boley Hill, Rochester, Kent ME1 1TE

Tel: 01634 888555
Fax: 01634 888505
email: admissions@kings-rochester.co.uk
website: www.kings-rochester.co.uk
Twitter: @Kings_Rochester
Facebook: @KingsRochester
LinkedIn: /king-s-school-rochester

The School traces its history to 604 AD, when St Justus, the first Bishop of Rochester, formed a school in connection with his Cathedral; it was reconstituted and endowed by Henry VIII as the King's School in 1541. The School has been fully co-educational since 1993.

The School is situated in the Cathedral Precinct of Rochester and sits in the shadow of the Castle on the bank of the River Medway; it enjoys the open spaces of the Esplanade, Vines and the Paddock, which is one of the School's playing fields. The Alps, a multi-sport playing field, is just 5 minutes from the School. Further up the road is the King's Rochester Sports Centre, which is home to 9 external tennis/

netball courts, a large gymnasium, a fitness gym, physio suite and changing rooms, in addition to the indoor swimming pool and playing fields already on the 1400 year-old school's town centre site.

The Main School dates from the mid-nineteenth century, but the School also has a number of fine listed buildings from the eighteenth century and considerable extensions of more recent date, including a Conference Centre and dining facility, a girls' boarding house, and a Pre-Prep building with Sports Hall and a modern, self-contained nursery.

The School numbers about 650 pupils, including a small but significant community of 70 boarders from the local area, London and overseas. The School is fully co-educational and divided into a Pre-Preparatory School of approximately 140 pupils (4–8 years), plus 33 in the nursery, a Preparatory School of approximately 200 pupils (8–13 years) and a Senior School of approximately 300 pupils (13–18 years); this provides 3 units of an intimate size, which are regarded as a single community working closely together. While catering for the whole of a pupil's career from 3 to 18, there is a large entry of pupils at 11, 13 and 16 who bring experience from other backgrounds, and enjoy the advantages of coming into a stable community with a strong family atmosphere.

The boarders, some of whom are weekly, play an important part in the life of the School. Although a small community, they are a large enough part of the School to make a very significant contribution of their own, and enjoy a more intimate atmosphere than is possible in a larger boarding environment.

King's is the Cathedral School. The Dean and Chapter are ex officio Governors, the Principal and King's Scholars are members of the Cathedral Foundation, and the Cathedral Choristers are members of the Preparatory School. The School uses the Cathedral for worship.

Work. In the Pre-Preparatory School, the pupils follow a four-year curriculum of Maths, Science, English, Religious Studies, Geography, History, Computing, Art and Craft, Design & Technology, Music, Physical Education and PSHEE. Daily spoken German lessons taught by native German teachers form part of the curriculum from the age of 4.

In the Preparatory School, the curriculum covers Art, Religious Studies, English, General Science, History, Geography, Mathematics, Computing, Latin, French, German, Spanish, Music, Drama, Physical Education, Design & Technology and PSHEE.

In the Senior School, the curriculum is as broad as possible to enable a wide choice of option subjects for the Fifth Form, including: Art, Classical Civilisation, Computer Science, Design and Technology, Drama, French, Geography, German, History, Latin, Music, Physical Education, Russian and Spanish. Games, CCF or TechSoc, and PSHEE are also on the curriculum.

In the Sixth Form, a wide range of A Level subjects are available and most pupils study three. Some pupils also take the Extended Project Qualification as additional study alongside their A Levels and sometimes a fourth A Level such as Further Mathematics.

All Sixth Formers who wish to, go on to university or other further education, and are encouraged to think carefully about their ultimate careers. Careers talks are given by outside speakers during the GCSE year, and the advice of specialist careers advisers and the careers teachers is available at all stages.

Activities. The School aims to develop pupils through a wide range of activities, both within the School programme and outside it.

There is a large CCF contingent, with Army, Navy and Air Force sections. Strong Service connections locally give particularly wide scope for CCF activities.

Pupils also undertake a variety of activities in Community Service and participate in the Duke of Edinburgh's Award scheme.

Out of School there is a range of over 25 school societies in all three parts of the School, and in the holidays there is a strong tradition of annual cultural and outdoor expeditions in this country and abroad for Preparatory and Senior School pupils.

Art, Drama and Music. The School sets great store by the Arts, and uses the comparative proximity to London to take pupils to art exhibitions, concerts and the theatre. The School stages major drama productions each year, recently *Into the Woods, Les Misérables, Sweeney Todd, Joseph and the Amazing Technicolor Dreamcoat* and *The Merchant of Venice* have been the main presentations. There is a strong musical tradition enhanced by visiting music staff, and pupils are encouraged to learn instruments. In addition to concerts in the School and the Cathedral, the Orchestra gives a number of outside performances each year, some by invitation. The choral tradition is strengthened by the presence of the Cathedral choristers in the School who regularly undertake overseas tours. Many pupils are in the national theatre and orchestra groups, the BBC Young Chorister of the Year 2016 was from King's Rochester.

Games. The boys' games are Rugby, Hockey, Football (Preparatory School), Cricket and Tennis and for girls' Hockey, Netball, Cricket and Tennis. Other team sport options are Rowing (from our River Medway boathouse), Athletics, Cross Country, Fencing and Swimming, and there are opportunities in addition for Squash, Badminton and Sailing. Physical Education is a regular part of the School curriculum and all pupils are required to take part in games. 80% represent the School competitively.

Religious Education and Worship. Although there is no denominational requirement for entry to the School, religious instruction is in accordance with the principles of the Church of England. All three parts of the School begin the day with an assembly or chapel service, some of which are held in the Cathedral.

Admission. Pupils can enter the School at any age from 3 to 18, although the main entry points are: 4+, 7/8+, 11+, 13+ and 16+. Entrance to the Senior School is either by Common Entrance at 13 or by the School's own examination for pupils who have not been prepared for Common Entrance.

Sixth Form entry is on the basis of interview and School report, together with satisfactory GCSE results (Pupils should attain a minimum of a grade 6 in the subjects they wish to study at A level).

Choristers. Choristerships are awarded to boys aged 8 and girls aged 10 following voice trials and a satisfactory performance in the Preparatory School Entrance Examination. Under normal circumstances, the choristership will continue until a boy transfers to the Senior School or until a boy or girl leaves the choir.

Scholarships and Bursaries. Scholarships are offered in the Senior School and Preparatory School in recognition of talent and commitment in the following categories:
- Academic 11+, 13+ and 16+ entry
- Music 11+, 13+ and 16+ entry
- Sport 11+, 13+ and 16+ entry

The following Scholarships are also available offering varying generous fee remission:
- Cathedral Choristership for boys aged 8 and girls aged 10
- Dame Susan Morden Choral Scholarship for boys aged 8
- Chesterfield Organ Scholarships 13+ and 16+ entry only
- The Peter Rogers' Music Scholarship for Senior School pupils

External candidates should liaise with the Registrar for details of entry assessment and process. Internal candidates should always discuss applications with the Head of the Preparatory or Senior School as relevant, prior to application. All Scholarships are reviewed annually and their continuation is subject to satisfactory progress being maintained.

Bursaries offer means-tested financial support to able pupils who would otherwise be unable to attend King's.
- They are only available to assist those in financial need
- They are available to current pupils whose financial circumstances have significantly changed
- They are generally only offered to external pupils in addition to a Scholarship Award and also on assessment of the mutual benefit to the child and the School

Fee Remissions. Children of Church of England ministers are given an annually means-tested reduction in tuition fees.

Children of Service Personnel are given a 20% reduction in tuition fees.

Where parents have three or more children at the school a reduction after the second child is given, amounting to 10% of the third child's tuition fees, 20% for the fourth child and 40% for the fifth and subsequent children.

Fees per term (2018–2019). Senior School: Boarders £10,530, Day Pupils £6,440. Preparatory School: Boarders £7,320, Day Pupils £4,395–£4,985 (inc lunch). Pre-Preparatory School (Day only): £3,385–£3,670 (inc lunch).

Charitable status. King's School, Rochester is a Registered Charity, number 1084266; it is a charitable trust for the purpose of educating children.

Patron: The Lord Bishop of Rochester, The Rt Revd James Langstaff

Governing Body:
Chairman of Governors: Ms J A Shicluna, MA Oxon
Vice-Chair of Governors: The Very Revd Dr P J Hesketh, PhD, BD, AKC
Assistant Vice-Chair of Governors: Mrs R A Rouse, MSc
Governors:
Mr B A Bell, BSc Hons, CIM Dip, FCIM
The Venerable S Burton-Jones, MA, BTh
Mr M J Chesterfield
Mr J K Daffarn, FRICS
Mr J Franklin, BA, Dip Teach, MA Ed
Mrs J Glew, BA Hons, CIMDIP, MA
Mr D R Graves, BA Hons, FCA
Dr R J Kennett, MBE
Mrs R A Olley, CEd
The Revd Canon R S Phillips, MA, MPhil
Mr P L Rothwell, LLB Hons
The Revd Canon M Rushton, MA Oxon, MA
Mr C R Shepherd, BSc, CEng, FICE, FRSA

Executive Board:

***Acting Principal of King's Rochester & Acting Headmaster of the Senior School*: Mr R P Overend**, BA, FTCL, ARCM, FRSA
Principal of King's Rochester & Headmaster of the Senior School from April 2019: Mr B P H Charles, BA, FRSA

Headmaster of the Preparatory School: Mr T Morgan, BMus Hons RCM, QTS
Headmistress of the Pre-Preparatory School: Mrs C E Openshaw, MA Ed, BEd Hons
Bursar and Clerk to the Governors: Ms D J Godwin, BA (*Hons*), CIMA

Senior School:

Acting Principal of King's Rochester & Acting Headmaster of the Senior School: Mr R P Overend, BA, FTCL, ARCM, FRSA
PA to the Principal: Mrs B J Avenell

Deputy Head (Academic): Miss N Steel, BSc
Deputy Head (Pastoral): Mr C H Page, BA
Deputy Head (Operations): Miss H L Catlett, MA
Chaplain: The Revd S J Padfield, MA

Heads of Department:
Art: Mr A J Robson, BA
Biology: Miss V Burgess, BSc
Chemistry: Mr M Mitchell, MChem
Classics: Mr S C Janssens, MA
Design & Technology: Mr S J Johnson, BEd
English: Mrs E M McCarthy, BA
French: Mrs A Warne, Maîtrise
Geography: Miss L Costelloe, BA
German & Russian: Mr B W Richter, BA
History: Mr S Fish, BA
ICT: Mr S Lea, BA
Mathematics: Mr P G Stevens, BSc
Music: Mr J Mountford, BA
Physics: Mrs E L Parren, BSc
Physical Education: Mrs A J Richter, BSc
Religious Studies: Mrs L A Rogers, BA
Sport: Mr M Hebden, BA

Registrar: Mrs S Webb
Librarian: Mrs X Guo, MA
CCF Contingent Commander: Major S Short

Preparatory School:
Headmaster: Mr T Morgan, BMus Hons RCM, QTS
Deputy Headmaster: Mr P N Medhurst, BA, MA

Pre-Preparatory School:
Headmistress: Mrs C E Openshaw, MA Ed
Deputy Headmistress: Mrs K Crozer, BEd
Honorary Pre-Preparatory School Lay Chaplain: Dr S
  Hesketh, MB BS, MRCGP, AKC, PRCOG, DCH,
  DFSRH

Music Department:
Director of Music: Mr J Mountford, BA
Preparatory School Director of Music & Head of Strings:
  Mrs J M Hines, BA
Head of Woodwind: Mr G Vinall, BA, LRAM
Cathedral Director of Music: Mr S Farrell, BMus Hons,
  ARCO, ARCM, PGCE

Medical Officer: Dr M Ojedokun, MB BS, MRCGP

The King's School
Worcester

5 College Green, Worcester WR1 2LL

Tel:	01905 721700 (School Office)
	01905 721721 (Bursar)
	01905 721742 (registrar)
Fax:	01905 721710
email:	info@ksw.org.uk
website:	www.ksw.org.uk
Twitter:	@KingsWorcester
Facebook:	@KingsWorcester

A Cathedral School appears to have existed at Worcester virtually continuously since the 7th century. In its present form, however, The King's School dates from its re-foundation by King Henry VIII in 1541, after the suppression of the Cathedral Priory and its school. In 1884 the School was reorganised as an Independent School and in 1944 the Cathedral Choir School was amalgamated with The King's School.

Today, the King's School Worcester is a foundation comprising two junior schools and a senior school – all three are co-educational day schools.

The School still occupies its original site south of the Cathedral. The buildings are grouped around College Green and the School Gardens. They range in date from the 14th century College Hall and Edgar Tower through the 17th and 18th century buildings surrounding College Green, to a range of modern, purpose-built accommodation, much of which has been constructed in the last twenty years. Capital projects including a new boat house, a new Sports and Performing Arts Centre and refurbishment of the Modern Languages Department and Dining Hall have been completed recently.

There are two Junior Schools. King's St Alban's stands in its own grounds on the edge of the main school site, offering education from age 4–11 with a purpose-built pre-prep department for girls and boys aged 4–7. King's Hawford is in a spacious rural setting just to the north of the city and offers education from age 2–11.

Numbers and Admission. The school is fully co-educational. King's St Alban's has 193 pupils. King's Hawford has 297 pupils. The Senior School has 890 pupils, including 265 in the Sixth Form.

Entrance to the school is by the Junior Entrance Test at 7, 8 or 9, or by the School's Examination at 11, 12 and 13. Boys and girls also join the School at Sixth Form level; this entry is by test, interview and GCSE results.

Term of Entry. Pupils are normally admitted annually in September.

Religion. The School has an historic connection with the Cathedral. Religious education, given in accordance with the Christian faith, is non-denominational. Pupils of all denominations and faiths are welcomed.

Curriculum. The School offers GCSE and A Level examinations in preparation for Higher Education. The curriculum is designed to give all pupils a general education and to postpone specialisation for as long as possible. Further details will be found in the Prospectus and on the School's website.

Games. The major sports are Rugby, Netball, Hockey, Football, Rowing and Cricket. Other sports include Tennis, Athletics, Cross Country, Badminton, Rounders, Fencing, Squash, Golf, Swimming, Sailing and Canoeing. PE and games are compulsory for all; a wide choice is offered to Sixth Formers. The school has been awarded the Sportsmark Gold award.

Other Activities. The school has a Choral Society and two other Choirs, 3 Orchestras and a Wind Band; there are at least 20 concerts each year. There are more than a dozen dramatic productions each year, including two or three major School plays, one of which is usually a Musical. The School takes part in The Duke of Edinburgh's Award scheme; there is a CCF and a Welfare and Community Service group. Young Enterprise companies in the Sixth Form are well subscribed and highly successful. A large number of societies and groups cater for a wide variety of other out-of-school activities and interests. The School has an Outdoor Activities Centre in the Black Mountains which is widely used both during the term and in the holidays. The Himalayan Club takes about 25 pupils on expeditions each year.

Scholarships and Bursaries. Both Music and Academic Scholarships are available at 11+, 13+ and 16+ in the Senior School, value up to one third of tuition fees. Academic scholarships at 11+ and 13 + are awarded on the basis of the Entrance Test and an interview; at 16+ on the basis of an aptitude test and interview, along with a report from the candidate's school.

Means-tested bursaries up to 100% of fees are available to academically-able candidates and can be combined with a scholarship. Full details are available from the Registrar.

Fees per term (2018–2019). Senior School £4,663; Junior Schools £2,336–£4,407.

Chorister Scholarships. Entry to the Choir is by means of Voice and Academic Tests which are held at various times throughout the year. A high vocal and musical standard is naturally required and boys must also have sufficient intellectual ability to hold their own in the Choir and the School. Boys should be 7–11 years old at the time of entry.

The **Prospectus** and information about Entrance Tests, Awards and Chorister Scholarships can be obtained from the Registrar at King's St Alban's.

Charitable status. The King's School Worcester is a Registered Charity, number 1098236. It exists to provide high quality education for boys and girls.

Visitor: The Lord Bishop of Worcester

The Governing Body:
Mr H B Carslake, BA, LLB (*Chairman*)
The Very Revd P G Atkinson, MA, FRSA (*Vice-Chairman*)
Mr M Atkins, MRICS
Revd Canon Dr Michael W Brierley
Professor M Clarke, CBE, MA, DL
Mr D Dale, MA, FCA
Mr J W R Goulding, MA Oxon
Mr D L Green, LLB
Mrs J H Jarvis, BA, MCIPD
Mr R S McClatchey, BA
Mrs C Pike, OBE, LLB Hons
Mrs P Preston, MA Oxon, DipM
Mr A E Reekes, MA, MRes, FRSA
Dr Leah Tether, BA Hons, MA, PhD Dunelm, SFHEA
Mr Andrew Underwood
Professor J Vickerman, BSc, PhD, DSc
Mr P Walker, MBE, BSc, MPhil, CEng, MIMMM

Clerk to the Governors and Bursar: Miss H L Jackson

Headmaster: Mr M G Armstrong, MA

Senior Deputy Head: Mr J Ricketts, BSc
Academic Deputy Head: Mr D S King, BSc
Deputy Head (Staff and Co-curricular): Miss A Oliver, MSc
Assistant Head (Pupil Development): Mrs Katie Beever, MA, CEng
Assistant Head (Pastoral): Mrs S Toland, BA

The King's Junior Schools:

King's St Alban's:
Tel: 01905 354906; email: ksa@ksw.org.uk

Head: Mr R A Chapman, BSc
Deputy Head: Mrs R Duke, BA
Academic Deputy Head: Mr N Mann, BA
Director of Studies: Mr D Braithwaite, BEd
Pre-Prep Coordinator: Mrs K Hadfield, BA

King's Hawford:
Tel: 01905 451292; Fax: 01905 756502;
email: hawford@ksw.org.uk

Head: Mr J M Turner, BEd, DipEd, ACP
Deputy Head: Mrs L Baxter, BSc
Deputy Head: Mr J Turvey, BA
Assistant Head: Mrs A Marshall-Walker, BA
Head of Lower School: Mrs C Knight, BEd
Head of Early Years: Miss A L Kingston, BA

Kingston Grammar School

London Road, Kingston-upon-Thames, Surrey KT2 6PY

Tel:	020 8546 5875
email:	enquiries@kgs.org.uk
website:	www.kgs.org.uk

Motto: *Bene agere ac laetari*

A school is believed to have existed in the Lovekyn Chantry Chapel since the fourteenth century. However, in 1561, Queen Elizabeth I, in response to a humble petition from the Burghers of Kingston, signed Letters Patent establishing the "Free Grammar School of Queen Elizabeth to endure for ever". In 1944 the School accepted Direct Grant Status and became fully independent in 1976. Two years later the School became co-educational, initially with girls in the Sixth Form, but in the following year joining in the First Year, to progress through the School. There are still close links with the Royal Borough of Kingston upon Thames, but no residential qualification for entry to the School. There are around 840 pupils and the proportion of boys to girls is approximately 54%–46%.

Buildings. Starting with the medieval Lovekyn Chapel, the site of Kingston Grammar School has been developed over 450 years. The refurbishment of the Fairfield Building has provided modern, energy-efficient classrooms and science laboratories. The Queen Elizabeth II building, opened by Her Majesty in 2005, has a Performing Arts Centre, a Music Technology Suite, Sixth Form Centre and classrooms. Pupils have access to an extensive networked computer system which they can access from home. The school is easily accessible by road and rail links to Kingston. The 22-acre sports ground includes an indoor sports pavilion, 4 cricket squares, 6 netball courts, 8 tennis courts, 6 cricket nets, 2 hockey pitches plus practice area, 4 football pitches, an Olympic gym and the KGS Boat House.

Entry to the School. Admission to the School at 11+ and 13+ is by examination and interview and at 16+ by examination, interview and GCSE results. Candidates sit the School's own examination papers; for 13+ and 16+ in November prior to year of entry and for 11+ in January of the year of entry. We also hold a 10+ deferred entry exam for candidates in Year 5 at primary school to enter in Year 7.

Term of Entry. Pupils enter in September. Occasional vacancies are considered.

Fees per term (2018–2019). £6,410; this covers all charges excluding public examination fees and lunch.

Scholarships and Bursaries. The Governors award scholarships (on merit) and means-tested bursaries to pupils entering the School at 11+, 13+ and 16+.

At age 11 the School offers Academic Scholarships that are awarded based on the results of a scholarship examination and interviews, which are by invitation only following the Entrance Examination.

Academic Scholarships are also awarded to entrants into Third Year, at the discretion of the Head Master following entrance examinations and interviews and, to the Sixth Form, following entrance examinations, interviews and successful GCSE results.

Music Scholarships, plus free tuition on one instrument, are available. Auditions are in January for candidates who are applying for entry at either 11+, 13+ or 16+.

Art Scholarships may be awarded at 11+, 13+ and 16+ following practical test, an interview and submission of a folder of work.

Design and Technology Scholarships may be awarded at 16+ following an interview and submission of a folder of work.

Sport Awards for candidates demonstrating outstanding sporting potential are available at 11+, 13+ and 16+, based on practical assessment.

Drama Scholarships are also available at 16+, based on auditions and an interview.

Curriculum. The academic curriculum through to GCSE emphasises a proper balance between varied disciplines and a range of intellectual experience, with all taking Maths, English, the three sciences and at least one modern foreign language as part of 10 IGCSE/GCSE subjects. Maths IGCSE may be taken early by the most able candidates. There is a Learning Support Department and mentoring for pupils with specific needs. A full Careers Programme is offered with support for university entry as well. Pupils are encouraged to view academic pursuit as a desirable end in itself, using a profiling process to develop their commitment to study. In the Sixth Form, students choose 4 A Level subjects in the Lower Sixth and normally continue with 3 into the Upper Sixth. In addition, students in the Lower Sixth undertake an academic enrichment programme, designed to develop the skills necessary to learn independently and to broaden their horizons. They are able to choose from courses such as the Extended Project Qualification (EPQ), MOOCS, OU courses or Critical Thinking. They also engage in community service. All Sixth Form students attend fortnightly lectures on wider social issues and international themes. Almost 100% of the Sixth Form elect to proceed to higher education, including Oxford and Cambridge, with a high proportion gaining entry to Russell Group institutions.

Care. A pupil's Form Tutor is responsible for welfare and progress. Heads of Year, supported by Senior Tutors, coordinate the work of form tutors. There is a full-time qualified nurse and a School Counsellor visits two days a week to support any pupils who have concerns in and out of school. Parents' meetings are held regularly and pupils receive two written reports per year, in addition to twice termly grade cards. Pastoral evenings are also held, where parents can discuss with each other and staff the difficulties and anxieties faced by young adults.

Games. The School's sports grounds are beautifully situated at Thames Ditton, by the River Thames opposite Hampton Court Palace. Kingston Grammar School prides itself on the large number of pupils who represent Great Britain in hockey and rowing.

Hockey (in both winter terms) and Rowing (all the year round) and cricket are main games with teams at all levels regularly competing in County, Regional and National Championships. The School also has representative sides in Football, Athletics, Tennis, Golf, Cross-Country and Netball, with an emphasis on sport for all and participation as well as on training for performance athletes.

Societies. The School is proud of its extensive co-curricular provision and its programme of House-based activities. A large number of School societies provides for the interests of pupils of all ages. They range from Chess and Debating, to Natural History and Young Enterprise. The Duke of Edinburgh's Award scheme is popular and overseas travel is a regular feature of many activities. The Music Department has a vigorous programme of concerts and tours, and a flourishing Drama Department provides a wealth of opportunity for pupils in all aspects of dramatic production.

Community Service. A large number of pupils are involved in over ten external organisations as a result of the Community Service Programme at KGS, including MENCAP, the Joel Community Project, Kingston Food Drive, local primary schools, Kingston Hospital, St Stephen's homeless shelter and Elmbridge Community Link. While older pupils are directly involved in the projects, younger pupils also support groups through activities that take place within school. Volunteering helps pupils to develop awareness and understanding of elements within society that frequently go unnoticed by young people. Although KGS already offers a wide range of activities to choose from, staff are also willing to help pupils find other projects. In addition, the School has a partnership with a school in Ghana; gap year students undertake periods of work experience at the school, whilst younger pupils are involved in fundraising activities and co-curricular links.

Combined Cadet Force. The CCF is divided into Army and RAF sections with a variety of activities ranging from night exercises and flying to outward bound and adventure training. Camps are held in school holidays and pupils attend courses in a range of subjects. This is an entirely voluntary activity which pupils may take up in the Third Year continuing until the end of the Upper Sixth.

Careers. The Careers Staff assist students with their options at all levels, are available at parents evenings and give advice on possible future careers. They are in close contact with employers in professions, commerce and industry through a strong alumni department. All Fifth Year pupils undertake a period of work experience after their GCSE examinations. All pupils undertake the Morrisby Profile at the end of Fourth Year to assist with career and study choices. An annual Careers Fair and other specialist careers seminars are offered during the academic year. Particular attention is given to the advice on entry to universities to which the majority of Sixth Formers go and students are encouraged to explore Apprenticeship routes as well.

Parents' and Staff Association. The Association exists to further the interests of the School in the broadest possible way and does much to strengthen the links between staff, parents and students. The Sherriff Club (rowing), The Hockey Society, Music Society, and Drama Society also support school activities.

KGS Friends (our Alumni Society) does much to foster a spirit of unity and cooperation. All pupils and their parents automatically join the Friends on leaving the School.

Honours. 6 to 12 students achieve places at Oxford and Cambridge each year.

Charitable status. Kingston Grammar School is a Registered Charity, number 1078461, and a Company Limited by Guarantee, registered in England, number 3883748. It exists to enable children to adapt their talents to meet the needs of an ever-changing world, whilst holding fast to the principles of self-reliance, a sense of responsibility and a determination to seize opportunity.

Governing Body:
R O'Dowd, BSc, RSA (*Chair*)
E A Kershaw, MA, MPhil (*Vice Chair*)
Mrs L Adam, BSc
M Annesley, BA, ACA
R W Brown, MA, ACMA
Mrs C Chevallier, MA, CIPD
D P D Combe, BA
Professor Mischa Dohler, PhD, FIEEE, FRSA
A D Evans, BSc, ACA
N Khandan-Nia, BSc
Ms F C Le Grys, MA
Mrs D Rose, MA Cantab
Mrs K Sonnemann, Dipl-Ing Architect TU Berlin RIBA

Head Master: **S R Lehec**, BA

Deputy Head Pastoral: Mrs V S Humphrey (*Geography*)
Deputy Head Academic: W Cooper, MPhil (*Religion & Philosophy*)
Assistant Head: Mrs D M Sherwood, BSc (*Geography*)
Assistant Head: Mr A J Beard, BA (*History*)
Assistant Head: Mrs A Lett, BSc (*Chemistry*)

Assistant Head: Ms A Williams, BSc (*Chemistry*)

Staff:
* *Head of Department*

Miss L S Andrews, BSc (*Mathematics*)
Mrs A Angell, BA (**History, Joint Head of Academic Monitoring*)
Mrs J Barkey, BA (*Art*)
Miss C Beckford, BA (*Design Technology*) [maternity leave]
M Behnoudnia, BSc (*Second in Physics, Assistant Head of Academic Scholars*)
T G Benson, MSci (*Physics, Head of STEAM*)
C Bequignon, MA (*French & German*)
Miss S J Boulton, MA (**Director of Drama*) [maternity leave]
Miss K A Brackley, BA (*English, Gibbon Society*)
N M Casasanto, BSc (*Chemistry*)
Mrs J Butcher, BA (*History & Politics*)
Miss S J Butler, BA (*PE*)
D G Buttanshaw, BEd (*Mathematics, Hockey*)
B Campbell, BA (*English*)
Miss S E Christie, BA (*Art*)
Mrs H L Cleaves, MA (*Librarian*)
Ms S Clifford, BSc (*Mathematics*)
Miss L Collison, BSc (*Mathematics*)
K Connor, MEng (*Second in Mathematics*)
M Cooney, BA (*Classics, Hockey*)
Mrs H B Cook, BSc (*Mathematics*)
Mrs S J Corcoran, BEd (*Learning Support)
Dr A Crampin, BSc, PhD (*Physics, Head of First Year*)
S R Crohill, BA (*Assistant Director of Drama*)
M Daly (*Hockey*)
J M Davies, MA (*History*)
T Deas, BA (**Boys' Hockey*)
I Deepchand, BSc (**Physics, Sixth Form Senior Tutor*)
Dr A Deters, MA, PhD (*English*)
Miss M Dew, BMus (*Music Trainee*)
Mrs S Dieu, BSc (*Physics, Rowing*)
J A Dyson, BA (*Art)
Mrs A L Edwards, MA (**Psychology, Joint Head of Academic Monitoring*)
M B Emmerton, MEng (*Maths Trainee*)
D Farr, BA (**Design Technology*)
A R Fitzgerald, MA (*Director of Careers & Universities*)
J-P Flavell, BA (*Biology*)
N S Forsyth, BSc (*Biology, Head of Wellbeing*)
O P Garner, BA (*French & Italian, Head of Fifth Year*)
Mrs P S Garside, BA, MA (*English)
R M Gee, BA (**Acting Director of Drama*)
M S Grant, BA, MA (*History, Head of Fourth Year*)
Ms Y Greaves, BSc (*ICT*)
Miss C M Hall, BSc (*Chemistry*)
J Halls, BA (*Design Technology*)
Miss A Henderson, BA (*History*)
Mrs R L Hetherington, BA (*Design Technology, Head of Fourth Year*) [maternity leave]
D C Hewitt, Graduate Dip in Tech Ed (*Design Technology*)
Miss A L Hicks, BSc (*Biology*)
A S House, MSc (*Geography)
Mrs H Hunt, BA (**Religion & Philosophy*)
Mrs C A Jones, BSc (*Mathematics, Head of Lower Sixth*)
Dr R Justice, PhD (*English*)
Miss J Kaur, BSc (*Geography*)
Dr K Kennedy, MSt (*History, Young Enterprise*)
Miss R Kerr, BA (*MFL*)
M Laflin, BA (**Director of Music*)
H R Lawrence, BSc (*Religion & Philosophy*)
Mrs N Maclean, BSc (*Director of Sport*)
Miss R M McBrien, MSc (*Mathematics*)

Miss B A McDonald, BA, MA (*Classics, Director of Sixth Form*)
Mrs L M Macfarlane, MSc (*Geography, Head of Third Year*)
S R Morris, BSc (*Mathematics, Deputy Director of Careers & Universities*)
Miss H M Naismith, MSc (*PE, **Girls' Hockey*)
Miss R Pastore, MA (*Spanish, Italian*)
Mrs K D Pinnock, BA (*French & Italian, Head of Community Service*)
Mrs A Plumridge, BSc (*Biology, Head of Second Year*)
Dr A J Reay, MChem, PhD (*Chemistry*)
Mrs E Pytel, BA (*Classics, Head of Academic Scholars*)
Mrs N A Reilly, MSci (*Mathematics*)
Miss N Reynolds, BA (*Spanish & French*)
Mrs L Rhys, BSc (*Mathematics*)
P J Ricketts, MA (**Economics, University Admissions Tests Tutor*)
Miss L Robinson, BA (*Drama, Hockey*)
Mrs M Robinson, BSc (*PSHE)
M J C Rodgers, BSc, MSc (**Biology, Golf Programme*)
Mrs T M Russell, Mag Phil (**Modern Foreign Languages*)
M D Scott, BA (*Religion & Philosophy*)
Miss R J Sharp, BA (*French & Spanish, Second in Modern Foreign Languages*)
P J Simmons, BSc (*PE Trainee Teacher, Rowing*)
J W Skeates, MA (*Mathematics)
J S Smith, BA, MPhil (*English*)
Dr L J Snook, MPhil, PhD (*Classics)
D A R Sorley, BA (**Politics, History, Professional Tutor*)
Mrs J Stapleton (*Netball)
Mrs P W E Stones, MA (*Second in English*)
S Symington, MSc (*Economics*)
J J Tierney, BMus (*Music*)
K Turner, BA (*German & French*)
Ms E K Varley, BA (*English, Head of Lower Sixth*) [maternity leave]
Mrs R Wakely, BA (*Art*)
C G Wenham, BA (*Second in Chemistry, Head of Upper Sixth*)
Miss O J Wigmore, BSc (*Geography, Duke of Edinburgh's Award Coordinator*)
Mrs C Williams, BA (**Religion & Philosophy*) [maternity leave]
Dr L H Winning, MChem, DPhil (*Chemistry)

Interim Bursar and Clerk to the Governors: Stephen Launchbury
Facilities Manager: J Farmer
Development Manager: Ms L Beatty
Head Master's PA: Mrs C Pink
Registrar: Miss K Riches
Head of Marketing: Mrs N Man [maternity leave]
Acting Head of Marketing: Ms E Elliott

Kingswood School

Lansdown, Bath BA1 5RG

Tel: 01225 734210
Fax: 01225 734305
email: admissions@kingswood.bath.sch.uk
website: www.kingswood.bath.sch.uk
Twitter: @KingswoodSchool
Facebook: @KingswoodSchool
LinkedIn: /kingswoodschool

Motto: *In via Recta Celeriter*

Kingswood is one of the UK's leading co-educational boarding and day schools. Founded in Bristol in 1748 by John Wesley, the School moved to its 200-acre site overlooking the World Heritage City of Bath in 1851.

Kingswood offers an inclusive boarding and day community that is free of pretension and balances academic rigour, strength in the arts and sport, traditional values and outstanding pastoral care with a forward-thinking, can-do approach. Pupils are encouraged to develop self-assurance and high levels of personal motivation. In this environment, pupils achieve astonishing successes as they constantly progress well beyond their natural potential.

There are 774 students in the Senior School (11–18) and 327 in the Prep School (9 months–11).

Site and facilities. Kingswood School is situated on a magnificent 200-acre site in Lansdown, Bath and is within easy reach of the M4 and M5 motorways, as well as having major rail and air links. The School sits alongside original Victorian buildings and a host of modern developments, including boarding houses, a theatre, a sports hall and a sixth form centre and dining area. As well as classroom and laboratory facilities, the School benefits from specialist centres for Computing, Technology, Art, Drama and Music. The School Chapel, the well-equipped Library and Resources Centre and the Dining Hall sit at the heart of the School, whilst each academic department benefits from its own well-resourced subject area. The seven boarding and day houses are located within the school campus; in addition to the sports hall, sporting facilities include a swimming pool, two floodlit astroturfs, extensive playing fields and a modern pavilion.

Curriculum. Kingswood encourages its students to develop lively, enquiring and well-informed minds. The very high level of attainment reached by the students both in external examinations and in wider areas of academic achievement has been commended by school inspectors. A broad and balanced curriculum is followed in the junior years, before decisions are made about greater specialisation in senior years. At Sixth Form level students take either three or four subjects from over twenty options, as well as participating in a programme of General Studies, and many pursue an Extended Project Qualification.

Organisation. Kingswood Prep School (*see entry in IAPS section*) caters for boarding and day pupils up to the age of 11. Most children move at age 11 to the Senior School, where they are joined by children from a wide variety of other feeder schools. Each year group comprises approximately 100 students, evenly split between boys and girls. For their first two years, both boarding and day students are in the co-educational junior house, meaning that they enjoy the atmosphere traditionally associated with a prep school whilst also benefiting from the range of senior school facilities, resources and teachers. From age 13, students are assigned to one of six senior houses (three for boys, three for girls). They remain in these houses for their five senior years. The Sixth Form has approximately 230 students and Sixth Formers also have their own specialist study and social centre.

Houses. Each of the seven houses has its own distinctive character. Emphasis is placed on providing exceptional pastoral care within a family atmosphere. Individual student progress and welfare is carefully monitored by tutors and senior house staff. Many staff live on the school campus and relationships between staff and students are warm and supportive. As part of an ongoing development of pastoral facilities, there has been considerable investment in the houses in recent years.

Sports and Games. The sporting and leisure activities programmes have over 100 activities with particular emphasis on Sport, Drama, Music, Art and outdoor pursuits. Kingswood has developed a tremendous reputation across all its main sports and is a competitive fixture for any school in any area. In our most recent ISI Inspection, the Kingswood co-curricular programme was rated as "excellent". We are passionate here at Kingswood that educating young people is not just about inspiring pupils academically but also giving them a really broad range of opportunities.

Health. The well-equipped School Medical Centre is under the supervision of a fully qualified resident Sister and the School Medical Officer.

Religious Activities. Kingswood welcomes pupils from all denominations. In addition to regular morning worship, there is a wide variety of guest speakers and the Christian Fellowship organises its own events. There are regular fundraising activities for charities and a Community Service programme. Every year a joint Methodist-Anglican Confirmation service is held and there are special services in Bath Abbey for the whole school Carol Service and for Commemoration Day.

Careers. From the earliest stage possible, students are encouraged to participate in all decisions affecting their future. Kingswood subscribes to the Independent Schools Careers Organisation and has links with local career guidance organisations. A programme of work experience is followed by all members of the Lower Sixth and is aimed at providing experience of the entire process of job application, interview and work itself. The School has established close links with local employers to make all this possible. A series of lectures and discussions with visiting employers is also organised and endorsed by the Head of Sixth Form.

Leavers. The vast majority of students choose to go to university, with over 90% securing places at their preferred choice in 2017. Over the past five years, an average of over 80% of A Level grades have been at A*–B, the grades required for entry to the Russell Group of leading universities. The growing number of students seeking apprenticeship or employment opportunities are also offered expert support with their applications.

Fees per term (2018–2019). £5,061 (day), £9,107–£10,909 (full boarding), £7,956–£9,856 (weekly boarding).

EAL teaching is provided for students who do not speak English as their first language – this is invoiced separately as required.

Entry Requirements. Entry at 11+ and 13+ is based on Kingswood's own entrance examination, a report from the candidate's current school and, where possible, a personal or group interview. Sixth Form entry is dependent on performance at interview, current school report and GCSE achievement, with a minimum requirement of 6 Grades A*–C, including at least 4 B grades. Individual subjects also have specific entry requirements, details of which are available on the school website. Approximately 25 places are available each year for entry at Sixth Form level.

Scholarships and Bursaries. Academic and Special Talent scholarships (up to a maximum of 25% of the basic fees) are available annually to day and boarding pupils entering Years 7, 9 and Lower Sixth. Special Talent scholarships are awarded for excellence in a particular field: Art, Drama, Music, Sport, Design Technology. John Wesley All-Rounder Awards are also available for boarders only.

Means-tested bursaries, worth up to 100% of fees, are available in Years 7, 9 and Lower Sixth, awarded annually at the discretion of the Headmaster and the Governors.

Very special provisions are made for the children of Methodist Ministers (up to 100% bursary assistance) and consideration may also be given to assist the sons and daughters of clergymen of other denominations, with a reduction in fees according to circumstances.

HM Forces families receive a reduction in boarding fees of up to 20% for each child.

Further details of scholarships and bursaries can be obtained from the school website: www.kingswood. bath.sch.uk.

Charitable status. Kingswood School is a Registered Charity, number 309148. Founded by John Wesley, it maintains its Methodist tradition in providing preparatory and secondary education.

Chairman of the Governing Body: Mr T G Westbrook

Clerk to the Governors & Bursar: Mr S Vickery

Headmaster: Mr S A Morris

Deputy Head Academic: Mr J M C Davies
Deputy Head Pastoral: Mr G D Opie
Chaplain: Revd D A Hull

Senior School Teaching Staff:
† *Senior Housestaff*
§ *Part-time staff*

Mrs H Aird (*Mandarin*)
Mr E T Allchorne (*Biology*)
§Miss S Andell (*French, Spanish*)
Miss A Arjona (*Spanish*)
Mr A Barton (*Director of Music*)
Miss N J Beale (*French, German*)
Miss S Belinger (*PE, Games*)
Miss C Brousse (*French*)
Ms N Taibi (*Head of French*)
Miss C Brousse (*French*)
Mr B N Brown (*Head of Design Technology*)
Mrs E E Brown (*Head of English, Gifted and Talented Tutor*)
Mr J O Brown (*Head of Boys' Games*)
§Mrs M L Brown (*Physics*)
Mr S T Brown (*Head of Art*)
Mr R E Burton (*Head of Physics*)
Mrs I Chamen (*Head of Learning Support*)
Mr J J Chua (*Mathematics, Resident Assistant Housemaster – Hall*)
Mr J Cope (*History*)
Mrs N L Curtis (*Head of Academic PE*)
Mrs S Dakin (*Head of Classics*)
Mr D M Darwin (*History and Politics*)
Mr J W Davies (*History and Politics, Director of Co-Curricular, Member of SMT*)
Ms B Dreher (*Head of EAL*)
†Mr R J Duke (*German, Boarding Housemaster of Westwood*)
Mr O East (*Design and Technology*)
Mr G D Edgell (*Head of Computer Science*)
Mrs C E Edwards (*Head of Psychology, Assistant Head of Sixth Form*)
Miss S V Elliott (*Art*)
Mrs S C Fountain (*Humanities*)
Miss A K Fox (*Mathematics*)
§Mrs E K Francis (*Music*)
Mrs J T Hallett (*Learning Support*)
†Mr D T Harding (*Drama & Theatre Studies, Senior Housemaster Hall*)
§Mrs S F Herlinger (*History and Politics, Assistant Head of Lower School*)
Mr P J Hollywell (*PE, Geography*)
Mrs A Holsgrove (*Learning Support*)
Mrs S Hopkin (*Head of Economics*)
Miss M G Huckle (*Music*)
Miss H J Hughes (*French, Spanish*)
Miss S A Jones (*English*)
Mrs A M Knights (*Mathematics*)
Mrs P Lam (*Mandarin*)

Mr P P G MacDonald (*Head of History and Politics, Outreach/Public Benefit Coordinator*)
§Mrs J L Mainwaring (*English*)
Mr R A Mansfield (*English*)
Mrs S J Marshall (*Religion, Philosophy & Ethics*)
Miss N Martin (*English*)
†§Mrs A K Matthews (*Geography, Senior Housemistress Summerhill*)
Mr J Matthews (*PE, Director of CPD*)
Mr T Moat (*Head of Geography*)
Miss A Moore (*English, Resident Assistant Housemistress, Fonthill*)
Miss N Moore (*English*)
Mrs C D Morris (*Head of German*)
§Mrs R H Murchison (*Mathematics*)
Mr W T Musgrove (*Physics*)
Mr G Musto (*Director of CPD, Member of SMT*)
Mrs C Nash (*Head of Drama and Theatre Studies*)
Mr G S Newbould (*History and Politics*)
Miss M Newman (*PE*)
Mrs J R Opie (*Head of Biology*)
§Mrs E Pasco (*French, Spanish, Head of Careers*)
Mrs M K Patterson (*Biology*)
†Miss U J Paver (*PE, Biology, Senior Housemistress School*)
Mr E C Peerless (*Physics, Head of Lower School Science*)
†Mr S D Pentreath (*Chemistry, Head of Lower School, Member of SMT*)
§Mrs A V J Phillips (*Classics*)
Ms J Reeman (*Mathematics*)
Mr T P Reeman (*Director of Sport*)
Miss N Robinson (*French, Spanish*)
§Miss B G Rolfe (*Head of PSHCE, Biology*)
†§Mrs C M Sergeant (*Computer Science, Senior Housemistress Fonthill*)
Mr J Shah (*Computer Science, Mathematics*)
Mrs V M Sim (*Head of Girls' Games*)
Mr M D Smith (*Mathematics*)
Mr M W Smith (*Head of Mathematics*)
§Mrs L Smyth (*Biology*)
†Mr S D Smyth (*Geography, Senior Housemaster Middle*)
Mr M S Snell (*Chemistry*) [maternity cover]
§Mrs J Solomon-Gardner (*Computer Science*)
Miss N J Sparks (*Chemistry*) [maternity leave]
Mr B Stuttard (*Geography*)
Miss K A Sutherland (*Librarian, Head of EPQ, Resident Assistant Housemistress – School*)
Ms N Taibi (*French*)
Mr M S Thatcher (*Head of Religion, Philosophy & Ethics and Critical Thinking*)
Mrs A Vaid (*Physics*)
Mr D Walker (*Head of Languages, Head of Spanish*)
§Mrs E L Ward (*Drama*)
Mr D C Webb (*Athletic Development Co-Coordinator*)
Mrs K W Whishaw (*Economics*)
†Mr J R White (*Mathematics, Senior Housemaster Upper*)
Mrs J-A Wilcock (*Chemistry*)
Miss H C Wilson (*Religious Studies, Activities Coordinator*)
Miss F Witting (*German*)
Dr J M Wood (*Head of Chemistry and Science*)
Mr C B Woodgate (*History and Politics, Head of Sixth Form, Member of SMT*)
Miss C E Wormald (*English*)
Miss A T Wright (*Psychology, Head of Boarding, Member of SMT*)

Head of Marketing & Communications: Mrs S Patten
Head of Admissions: Mrs D W Patterson
Director of Fundraising & Development: Mr G Papenfus

Kirkham Grammar School

Ribby Road, Kirkham, Preston, Lancashire PR4 2BH

Tel: 01772 684264
Fax: 01772 672747
email: info@kirkhamgrammar.co.uk
website: www.kirkhamgrammar.co.uk

Kirkham Grammar School, founded in 1549, is a co-educational independent School of 830 pupils aged between 3 and 18. The Senior School of 610 pupils, 65 of whom are boarders, incorporates a Sixth Form of 180, and the Junior School, for day pupils, has 220 on roll.

Kirkham Grammar School prides itself on developing well-balanced and confident young people, the vast majority of whom go on to University. As well as excellent academic results and a good Oxbridge entry record, the School introduces pupils to as wide a range as possible of cultural, sporting and creative activities and encourages them to participate in those which appeal to them. Great emphasis is placed on preparing pupils for life beyond university.

The School has a strong Christian ethos, with an emphasis on care for the individual, traditional family values, good manners and sound discipline.

It is a friendly close-knit community where staff and pupils work closely together, fostering leadership and self-discipline, and encouraging cheerful, friendly and supportive relationships within the framework of 'one family'.

Facilities. Occupying 30 acres of its own grounds, Kirkham Grammar School boasts some excellent facilities, which include a large multi-purpose hall, a superb floodlit all-weather pitch, a Sixth Form Centre, an outstanding Technology Centre and Languages Centre, and a magnificent Dining Complex. The School has built a Science Centre alongside a new extended classroom block incorporating interactive facilities and also a new PE Laboratory and Business Studies Classroom. Significant developments have also been made to both Music and Sport facilities.

Boarding. The School is a member of the Boarding Schools' Association. The refurbished Boarding House is pleasant and comfortable and is run by a House Parent (Academic), whose residence is attached to the boarding wing of the School. The House also has a team of full-time support staff and tutors.

Academic Programme. The courses lead to GCSE and A Level. In the first three years, the basic subjects studied are English, French, Mathematics, German, Spanish, Geography, History, Physics, Chemistry, Biology, Music, Art & Design, Drama, Computing, Design and Technology, Religion, Philosophy & Ethics and an enrichment programme including Philosophy. The first stage of specialisation takes place on entering the Fourth Year where the core subjects of English, Mathematics, Physics, Chemistry and Biology are taught in sets, and there is a further choice of subjects from four option blocks, which include: Art & Design, Computer Science, Design and Technology, Drama, Business Studies, French, Geography, German, History, Latin, Music, Physical Education, Religious Studies and Spanish.

In the Sixth Form, A Level subjects are chosen from the following: English Language and Literature, Maths, Further Maths, Biology, Chemistry, Physics, French, German, Latin, Spanish, Art & Design, Music, Design Technology, Geography, History, Psychology, Government & Politics, Drama, Religious Studies, Business Studies, Economics and Physical Education.

In addition many Sixth Formers voluntarily continue in the CCF and the Duke of Edinburgh's Award, Young Enterprise or Community Service. Extra tuition is provided for Oxbridge candidates. Students are also offered the opportunity to undertake an Extended Project Qualification (EPQ) alongside their A Levels. A comprehensive careers service is available.

Sport. There is a strong sporting tradition at Kirkham Grammar School and it ranks among the very best schools in the country for rugby and girls hockey. The other main sports played are cricket, athletics, tennis, netball, cross-country, badminton, squash, swimming, rounders, volleyball and basketball.

Music. There is a very active musical life at the School, with regular Concerts both at lunchtime and in the evening, providing a platform for the Orchestra, various ensembles and Soloists.

Co-Curricular Activities. An impressive range of co-curricular activities is offered by a School renowned for its sporting prowess, but with strength across the board in music, art and drama. There is a strong and popular Combined Cadet Force contingent, with Army and RAF sections, and a flourishing House System. A large number of societies cater for a wide range of interests including archery, astronomy, drama, debating, the very popular Duke of Edinburgh's Award scheme, chess, public speaking, badminton, climbing, science, young engineers, music and many others.

Admission to Senior School. Four Year entry. Pupils are usually admitted at 11 years old after passing the entrance examination held in February each year. Admissions to the School in other year groups, especially the Sixth Form, are possible. Day and Boarding applications should be made to the Registrar who will be glad to provide further details.

Fees per term (2018–2019). Day (excluding lunches): Senior School £3,875; Junior School £2,895; Pre-School: £250 (full week), £51.00 (full day).

These fees cover tuition, use of class, text and library books, school stationery, scientific equipment, games apparatus.

Senior School Boarding: £3,480 in addition to the Day fee. The boarding fee is discounted by 5% for children resident Monday to Friday (weekly boarders) and for children whose parents are current members of HM Forces.

Scholarships and Bursaries. The School offers an impressive number of Scholarships and Bursaries at 11+ and 16+. Further details are available from the Registrar.

Junior School (3–11 years). An integral part of the School under the same Board of Governors, the Junior School comprises a Pre-School, an Infant Department and a Junior Department, housed in splendid, purpose-built accommodation. The curriculum is organised in close consultation with the Senior School to ensure that education in its broadest sense is continuous and progressive from the age of 3 to 18.

The curriculum is broad but balanced. The core subjects – English, Maths, Science and ICT – are given priority as set in the National Curriculum. History, Geography, RE, Music, ICT, Design and Technology, Art, PSHE, PE and Games are studied as pure subjects and also as they relate to one another in a cross-curricular manner. In the Early Years we offer a fun, stimulating and caring environment, which follows the Early Years Foundation Stage Framework.

Application should be made direct to the Headmistress's PA from whom a separate prospectus may be obtained.

Old Kirkhamians Association. For further details contact the Secretary, Mr S P D Walmsley, via the School.

Charitable status. Kirkham Grammar School is a Registered Charity, number 1123869. The object of the Charity shall be the provision in or near Kirkham of a day and boarding school for boys and girls.

Chairman of Governors: Mrs L Wareing

Headmaster: **Mr D H Berry**, BA, NPQH

Senior Deputy Head: Mrs D C Parkinson, BSc, NPQH
Deputy Head (Operations): Mr M J Hancock, BEd, MA, MBA
Head of Sixth Form: Mr M P Melling, BA, MA Ed
Deputy Head (Pastoral): Mrs N Walter, BA

Heads of Year:
Sixth Form: Mr M P Melling, BA, MA Ed
Assistant Head of Sixth Form: Mrs J Stanbury, BA
Fifth Year: Mr S Duncan, BA
Fourth Year: Mr C Gaitatzis, BSc, MBA
Third Year: Mr D Gardner, BEng
Second Year: Mr G S Partington, BA
First Year: Mrs G R Latham, BA

Heads of Departments:
Art: Mr S P Gardiner, BA
Boys' Sport: Mr J P Roddam, BA
Business Studies & Economics: Mrs L E Hargreaves, BA
Biology: Ms P E Halloran, BSc
Chemistry: Dr A B Rollins, BSc, PhD
Design & Technology: Mr D Gardner, BEng
Drama: Mr E I Moore, BA
English: Mrs K C O'Flaherty, BA
Geography: Mr S R Whittle, MA Cantab
Girls' Sport: Mrs L D Osborne, BA
History: Mrs H L Atkinson, BA
Latin: Mrs S P Long, BA
Learning Support: Mrs B P Batty, BSc
Mathematics: Mr D R Carter, BSc
Modern Foreign Languages: Miss L E Vicquelin, BA
Director of Music: Miss J Z Crook, BMus
Physics: Miss C Courtney, BSc
Politics: Mr M P Melling, BA, MA Ed
Psychology: Mrs J Stanbury, BA
Religion, Philosophy & Ethics: Mrs L Bowles, BA

Houses & House Parents:
House Parent (Academic): Mr A E Trenhaile, BA, MEd
House Parent (Pastoral): Miss S Dunand-Clarke
Kirkham House: Mr M J Percy, BA
Fylde House: Mr S R Whittle, MA Cantab
School House: Mr J R Lyon, HND
Preston House: Mrs J M Glover, BEd

Bursar: Mrs C E Brown

Headmaster's PA: Mrs J Hunt
Registrar: Mr S P D Walmsley

Junior, Infant and Pre School:
Headmistress: Mrs A S Roberts, BEd
Deputy Headmistress: Mrs H Shuttleworth, GMus, RNCM
Assistant Head: Mr S Lewis, BA
Pre-School Manager: Mrs S Anyon, BTEC

Junior School Headmistress's PA: Miss J Stewart
School Secretary: Mrs A Taylor

Lancing College
A Woodard School

Lancing, West Sussex BN15 0RW

Tel: 01273 452213
Fax: 01273 464720
email: admissions@lancing.org.uk

website: www.lancingcollege.co.uk
Twitter: @lancingcollege
Facebook: @lancingcollege

Motto: *Beati mundo corde*

Founded in 1848 by the Revd Nathaniel Woodard, Lancing College is one of the first schools of the Woodard Foundation.

There are 590 pupils in the school, accommodated in ten houses.

Location. The school stands on a spur of the Downs, overlooking the sea to the south and the Weald to the north, in grounds of 550 acres, which include the College Farm.

By train, Lancing is 10 minutes from Brighton, 30 minutes from Gatwick Airport and 75 minutes from central London.

Buildings and Facilities. The main school buildings, faced with Sussex flint, are grouped around two quadrangles on the lines of an Oxford or Cambridge College.

The Chapel, open to visitors every day, has the largest rose window built since the Middle Ages.

The College has extensive laboratories, a purpose-built Music School, a Theatre with a full-time technical manager and a modern Design and Technology Centre with computerised design and engineering facilities. Alongside this, a strikingly modern Art School provides vast studio space and a photography suite. More recently a café has been created in the centre of the school for use by pupils and staff. There are over 350 private studies for boys and girls, many of which are study-bedrooms. There is a sports hall, indoor swimming pool and a miniature shooting range. Sporting facilities also include Squash, Tennis and Fives courts and an all-weather surface and full-sized AstroTurf hockey pitch. The College opened an Equestrian Centre in 2017, providing livery as well as additional centre horses for co-curricular activities.

Admission. Boys and girls are normally admitted at the beginning of the Autumn Term in their fourteenth year. Admission is made on the result of either the Entrance Scholarship, the Common Entrance Examination or by private testing. A registration fee of £100 is paid when a child's name is entered in the admission register. Entries should be made via the Registrar, who will assign a House, following as far as possible the wishes of the parents. After a pupil has joined the school, parents usually correspond with the Housemaster or Housemistress directly.

Sixth Form Entry. Applications for entry should be made to the Registrar one year prior to the year of entry. Testing takes place in November or by private arrangement.

Curriculum. Designed as far as possible to suit every pupil's potential with a wide range of subjects on offer including over 20 at A Level. Pupils work closely with academic staff and personal tutors to help them consider future options, entry to universities and to a wide range of professions. The College prides itself on the individual support available for pupils.

In a pupil's first three years the curriculum provides a broad, balanced education without premature specialisation. The total of subjects taken at GCSE is limited to about nine or ten, the object being to promote excellence in whatever is studied and to lay firm foundations for the Sixth Form years.

The following subjects are studied in the Senior School: English Language and Literature, Religious Studies, Mathematics, Physics, Chemistry, Biology, French, Spanish or German, Geography, History, Physical Education, Music, Art, Design and Technology, Photography, Latin or Classical Civilisation and Drama.

In the Sixth Form there is a choice of over 20 subjects which can be studied to A Level. A BTEC qualification is also available in Sport, and a Pre-U in Photography. Pupils are also encouraged to carry out an EPQ (Extended Project Qualification) to enhance their studies.

A close connection has been established with schools in Germany and Spain, with which individual and group exchanges are arranged.

Tutorial System. In addition to the Housemaster or Housemistress there are pastoral Tutors attached to each House who act as Academic Tutors to individual pupils. The Tutors' main functions are to supervise academic progress and to encourage general reading and worthwhile spare time activities. A pupil usually keeps the same Tutor until he or she moves into the Sixth Form, where this function is taken over by an Academic Tutor chosen from one of the specialist teachers.

Music and Art form an important part of the education of all pupils. There are orchestras, bands, ensembles and choirs. Organ and Choral awards to Oxford and Cambridge and Colleges of Music are frequently won. There is a full programme of extra-curricular **Drama**. The **Art School** and **Design & Technology Centre** provide for a wide range of technical and creative work.

Other Activities. Boys and girls in their first year are given the opportunity to sample the many activities on offer at the College. A well-organised extra-curricular programme is followed by pupils of all age groups and participation is strongly encouraged under the supervision of the Assistant Head, Co-curricular.

Several plays are produced each year and pupils are able to write and perform their own plays and to learn stagecraft.

In the Advent Term the main sports are Association Football for boys and Hockey for girls; in the Lent Term Football and Hockey for boys and Netball for girls. Squash, Fives, Badminton, Basketball, Volleyball, Cross Country and Shooting (the College has an indoor range) take place during both terms for boys and girls. Some Rugby is played in the Lent Term. Cricket, Tennis, Sailing, Athletics and Rounders take place in the Summer Term, and there is Swimming all year round in the College's indoor heated pool.

The College has a CCF contingent (with Army and RAF sections) and takes part in the Duke of Edinburgh's Award scheme. There is also a flourishing Outreach group, which works in the local community. Pupils help to run a small farm (including sheep, goats, pigs, alpacas and chickens) and participate in conservation projects under the supervision of the Farm Manager.

Links have been established with local industries and pupils are involved in business experience through the Young Enterprise scheme.

Careers and Higher Education. A number of the teaching staff share responsibility for careers advice and there is a well-equipped careers section in the Gwynne Library. Popular universities include Manchester, Bristol, Imperial College, UCL, LSE, and Sheffield; six to Oxbridge in 2018; several to other international universities. All members of the Fifth Form attend the annual Careers Symposium and most enrol in the Inspiring Futures Futurewise scheme. Lancing also offers the Sixth Form a new "Leaving Lancing" programme with activities to help pupils develop practical, team working and leadership skills.

Scholarships and Exhibitions. Candidates for the following awards must be under 14 years of age on 1st September in the year of the examination. The age of the candidate is taken into account in making awards. A candidate may enter for more than one type of award, and account may be taken of musical or artistic proficiency in a candidate for a non-musical award; but no one may hold more than one type of award, except in an honorary capacity.

A number of scholarships in Academic subjects, Art, Drama and Sport are offered every year, ranging in value up to a maximum 10 per cent of the annual school fee. In very exceptional cases, awards of up to 25 per cent are made.

A number of Music Scholarships ranging in value up to a maximum 10 per cent of the annual school fee (25 per cent in very exceptional cases). Scholarships may be offered to pupils from schools where the time for Music is less than in some others, and where a candidate may have less musical experience but greater potential.

One Professor W K Stanton Music Scholarship for a Chorister from Salisbury Cathedral School, or failing that any Cathedral School. A Stanton Exhibition may also be awarded.

The Peter Robinson Cricket Scholarship is awarded to an outstanding young cricketer at 13+ and 16+ entry.

A number of Ken Shearwood Awards, ranging in value up to a maximum 10 per cent of the annual school fee (25 per cent in very exceptional cases), are made to pupils of all-round ability and potential who have made outstanding contributions to their present schools.

Entry Forms for Academic, Art, Music, Drama, Sport and All-Rounder (Ken Shearwood) awards are obtainable from the Admissions Manager.

Sixth Form Awards: Scholarships are available for new entrants to the Sixth Form with special proficiency in Academic subjects, Art, Music, Drama and Sport. There is also one Organ Scholarship. The candidate's general ability to contribute to the life of a boarding school community will also be taken into account. A small number of Scholarships is also available internally on the strength of GCSE results.

The value of all Entrance Scholarships may be augmented by bursaries, according to parental circumstances.

Fees per term (2018–2019). Boarding £11,995; Day £8,190.

Further details about fees, including the scheme for payment in advance of a single composition fee to cover a pupil's education during his/her time in the School, are available from the Bursar.

Charitable status. Lancing College is a Registered Charity, number 1076483. It exists to provide education for boys and girls.

Governing Body:
The Provost and the Directors of Lancing College Ltd

Visitor: The Archbishop of Canterbury

Governors:
Chairman: Dr Harry Brünjes, BSc, MBBS, DRCOG, FEWI
Vice-Chairman: Mr Martin Slumbers, BSc, ACA [OL]
Mr David Austin, BSc
Baroness Cumberlege, CBE, DL
Mr C F Dennis BA, MA
Mrs Anne-Marie Edgell, LLB
Professor Michael Farthing
Dr Sally Godward
Mr T J P Hancock, MA Hons
Mrs Ena Harrop
Mr Justin Higgo [OL]
Ms Charlotte Houston, BSc, ACMA, CGMA [OL]
Ms Helen Hunter
Mr Henry Lawson, MA Cantab, MBA Harvard [OL]
Mr Richard Stapleton, FRICS (*Chairman of Estates Committee*)

[OL] *Former Pupil*

Head Master: D T Oliver, BA, MPhil

Bursar: M B Milling, CA
Senior Deputy Head: Mrs H R Dugdale, MA
Deputy Head: J R J Herbert, BA, PhD
Assistant Head (Pastoral): D S Connolly, BA, FRSA
Assistant Head (Academic): Mrs P S Faulkner, BSc

Registrar: A J Betts, BA, PhD
Head of Outdoor Learning: C P Foster, MA [OL]
Director of IT: A C Brown
Chaplain: The Revd R K Harrison, BA, MA
Director of External Relations and Communications: Mrs Diana Cree, BA, MBA, MRS, CIM
Foundation Director: Ms Catherine Reeve, BA [OL]

Common Room:
Miss K O J Allan, BSc Newcastle (*Mathematics*)
Mrs Karen Andrew, BA De Montfort, PGCE Bedford (*Head of Academic PE*)
Mr T S Auty, BA Norwich School of Art (*Photography, Art*)
Dr C N M Baldock, BA Cantab, PhD Yale (*History*)
Mr N D D Beeby, BA London, LGSMD (*Director of Drama and Dance*)
Mr G D Bird, BSc, MSc Wellington (*Psychology*)
Mrs K J Blundell, BA Photography Westminster, BA Textiles Chelsea College of Art and Design (*Head of Art*)
Mrs M Brookes, Referendarstudium 2, Münster (*German*)
Mr N A Brookes, BSc Manchester, MSc Newcastle (*Mathematics*)
Mrs L M Brünjes, BA Loughborough (*Head of Learning Support*)
Mr J J Bullen, BSc Bristol (*Head of Mathematics*)
Mrs E Campbell, MA Oxford, BTh South Africa (*Mathematics*)
Mr A M Chappell, BSc Durham (*Biology, Chemistry*)
Mr A R Coakes, BA Nottingham, MSc Brighton (*Design and Technology*)
Mr D J Collins, BSc Exeter (*Physics*)
Mr D S Connolly, BA Newcastle, AdDip Cantab, FRSA (*Assistant Head Pastoral*)
Mr G Costarella, BA L'Aquila (*Spanish, French*)
Mr D N Cox, MA Cantab, FRCO, FTCL, LRAM, ARCM (*Director of Music, Chapel*)
Mrs M J Creer, BA Swansea (*English*)
Mr C P E Crowe, BEd Sheffield Hallam (*Director of Sport*)
Mr D G Davies, BA Portsmouth, ALCM (*Head of Spanish, French*)
Mr S A Drozdov, BEd Russia (*Head of MFL, Head of German*)
Mr G A Drummond, BSc Bath (*Head of PSHE, Economics, Politics*)
Mrs H R Dugdale, MA Cantab (*Senior Deputy Head, English*)
Mr A M Durkan, MPhys Southampton (*Physics*)
Mr J R J East, BSc Manchester (*Mathematics*)
Ms K V Edwards, BA de Montfort (*Assistant Director of Sport*)
Ms M Espiga, BA Malaga (*Spanish*)
Mr C J Eustace, MA Cantab (*Assistant Head, Co-Curricular*)
Mrs P S Faulkner, BSc Edinburgh (*Assistant Head, Academic*; *Biology*)
Mr C P Foster, MA Oxford (*Head of Geography, Head of Outdoor Learning*)
Miss L J Freeland, BA Oxford, MPhil Cambridge (*English, Overseas Applications Coordinator*)
Mrs L Fryer, BA Newcastle (*Assistant Head of Languages, Spanish*)
Mrs R A Gardner, BSc Birmingham (*Head of Biology*)
Miss L J Gaukroger, BA, MPhil Kent (*Classics*)
Mr J A Grime, BSc Liverpool (*Geography*)
Mr D J Harman, BA Exeter, MA Sussex (*Head of English*)
The Revd R K Harrison, MA Oxford, BA Leeds (*Religious Studies, History*)
Mr D J Harvey, BSc Reading (*Biology*)
Mrs H L Harvey, BA Gloucestershire (*Mathematics*)

Dr J R J Herbert, BA, PhD Birmingham (*Deputy Head, English*)
Dr E P Keane, BA College of the Holy Cross, PhD Cambridge, MA New York (*Head of Politics, History*)
Dr D A Kerney, MA Cantab, PhD Sheffield, FRSA (*Head of History*)
Mrs C M Krause, BA Melbourne, MEd Buckingham (*History, RS*)
Mr C Langworthy, MusB, Dip ABRSM (*Assistant Director of Music*)
Miss R Lawrence, BA Exeter (*Art, Classics*)
Mrs S E Lawrence, BA Brighton (*Design and Technology*)
Mrs Q Liang, MA Sussex (*Chinese*)
Mrs K Lindfield, HND Northbrook College of Art and Design (*Art*)
Mrs R Loftin, BA Brighton (*Library Supervisor*)
Mrs S E Marchant, BA Brighton, MCLIP (*Librarian*)
Mr R J Maru, NCA Advanced Coach & ECB Level III (*Director of Cricket*)
Ms A McKane, MA Monash (*English*)
Mrs R J McNamara, BA Brunel, MA UCL (*Learning Support*)
Mr T J Meierdirk, BFA Illinois (*Head of Design and Technology*)
Mr R P Mew, MA, BA LitHum Oxford (*Head of Classics*)
Mr T A Miller, BSc Manchester (*Mathematics*)
Mr C M Mole, BSc Manchester (*PE*)
Mrs C R Mole, BA UCL (*Head of Economics and Business Studies*)
Dr I Morgan-Williams, GMus RNCM, DPhil Sussex (*Director of Music, School*)
Mr J Naughalty, BSc Cardiff Metropolitan (*Director of Hockey*)
Dr S R Norris, BSc, PhD Southampton (*Chemistry*)
Dr M S W Palmer, BA Sussex, PhD Edinburgh, MIL (*German, Italian*)
Mr N L Payne, BA London (*English*)
Mr K Perrault, Masters Nanterre Paris-Ouest la Défense (*French*)
Mrs M S Porter, MSc Southampton (*Physics*)
Dr G A Preston, BSc Portsmouth, PhD Southampton (*Head of Science, Physics*)
Dr A J H Reesink, MSc Utrecht, PhD Binghamton, New York (*Geography*)
Mr P C Richardson, MA Cantab, MA London (*Head of RS, History*)
Mrs H M Robinson, BSc Newcastle (*Chemistry*)
Mr M J H Smith, BA Durham (*RS, Classical Civilisation, English*)
Ms H A Stevenson, BLib Wales, MCLIP (*Assistant Librarian*)
Mr P W Tarbet, BSc Durham (*Mathematics*)
Mr G C Thomas, BEng Bristol, MInstP (*Head of Computing, Physics*)
Mr A W Tobias, BA York, MA Exeter (*Economics*)
Dr M E Walsh, DPhil Oxford, BSc Leeds (*Head of Chemistry*)
Mr E D Watson, BSc Hull (*Economics, Business Studies*)
Mrs R M Webber, MBA Lancaster, BSc York (*Biology*)
Mr A P Williamson, MA Oxford (*Chemistry*)

Houses & Housemasters/mistresses:

Boys:
Head's: Mr A M Chappell
Second's: Mr D J Harvey
School: Mr C M Mole
Gibbs': Mr M J H Smith
Teme: Mr J A Grime

Girls:
Field's: Mrs M J Creer
Handford: Ms A McKane
Manor: Mrs C M Krause
Sankey's: Mrs E Campbell

Co-ed
Saints': Mrs S E Lawrence
Head Master's Secretary: Mrs H L Betts, BSc
Admissions Manager: Mrs S L Linfield

School Medical Officers
Dr V Figuera, DM, MRCGP
Dr C Huckstep, MB BS, DRCOG, DCH
School Dental Officer: Mrs J M Edwards, BDS, DOrth,
    MOrth [Orthodontics only]
Health Centre Counsellor: Ms J Painter, BA Sussex, Dip
    Psychodynamic Counselling
Health Centre Manager: Mrs A Brennan, BA, RGN
Nursing Sisters: Mrs A Hill, RGN, BSc; Mrs C Johnson,
    RGN; Mrs G Johnston, RGN, BSc; Mrs J Line, RGN

Latymer Upper School

King Street, Hammersmith, London W6 9LR

Tel:	020 8629 2024
Fax:	020 8748 5212
email:	head@latymer-upper.org
website:	www.latymer-upper.org
Twitter:	@LatymerUpper
Facebook:	@latymerupper
LinkedIn:	/latymer-upper-school

The Latymer Foundation owes its origin to the will of Edward Latymer, dated 1624. It is a Day School of 1,231 pupils, of which 386 are in the Sixth Form. The School is fully co-educational with 51% girls and 49% boys. There are also 168 pupils in the co-educational Latymer Prep School which shares the same grounds. (*Please see entry in IAPS section.*)

Admission. This is by competitive examination and interview at 11. The 11+ examinations are held every year in January followed by interviews for selected candidates in late January/early February. Entry to the Sixth Form is based on interview in November of the year before entry and conditional offers at GCSE.

Details of Open Days and Entry are obtainable from the Registrar.

Preparatory School. Pupils sit the 11+ Entrance Exam for the Upper School from Latymer Prep School. (*For further details see entry in IAPS section.*)

Fees per term (2018–2019). £6,710.

Bursaries. A number of means-tested bursaries are awarded every year assessed on academic merit and family circumstances. These range from 25% of fees to full fees and are available at 11+ and 16+. Currently 18% of pupils are in receipt of fee assistance.

Scholarships. *11+ Entry*: Music Scholarships of varying amounts are offered, together with music awards of free tuition on two instruments. Scholarships will only be offered to candidates who are successful in the school's competitive entrance examination.

16+ Entry: Scholarships for Music, Drama, Art and Sport. Candidates who have satisfied the academic requirements will be invited to an interview and assessment in January.

Further details are available from the Director of Admissions (020 3004 0478; csh@latymer-upper.org).

Curriculum. A full range of academic subjects is offered at GCSE and A Level. Languages include Spanish, Mandarin, Latin, French, German, Greek and Italian (European Work Experience and exchanges are run every year). Science is taught as separate subjects by subject specialists from Year 7. Form sizes in the Lower School of around 22 and smaller teaching group sizes ensure the personal attention of staff. Our own World Perspectives Course, now UCAS accredited, comprising elements of Geography, History, RS, Politics, Philosophy, and Economics is enjoyed by Years 10 and 11.

Pastoral Care. The School has a strong tradition of excellent pastoral care led by the Deputy Head Pastoral. There are three Divisions (Lower School, Middle School, Sixth Form) and each Division is led by an Assistant Head. A Head of Year is responsible for the pupils in each year. Teams of Form Tutors deliver a coherent PSHE programme which promotes involvement in the community, charity work, and the personal, social and academic development of the Form.

Sixth Form. The large co-educational Sixth Form offers around thirty-five A Level choices; students opt to take three or four subjects at A Level including the very popular Extended Project. Students have the opportunity to undertake work experience in Paris or Berlin and receive extensive Careers and Higher Education guidance. All students expect to go on to University or Art College; 23 students went to Oxbridge in 2018 and 20 to Universities overseas. The Sixth Form has its own Common Room as well as a University and Careers Centre.

Music and Drama. These activities play a large part in the life of the School. The Latymer Arts Centre houses music practice rooms and a 300-seat Theatre in addition to increased facilities for Art. The Latymer Performing Arts Centre houses a 100-seat recital hall, music classrooms and more practice rooms and a dance/drama studio. There are several orchestras and bands and a number of major concerts each term, both here and in Central London venues. There are five major drama productions each year, and opportunities for all pupils to perform in events.

Science and Library. A state-of-the-art building, housing Science Laboratories, a Library, Sixth Form Study Common Room and Study Centre, opened in September 2010. All year groups have the use of these facilities.

Sport. The new Sports Centre – opened by Sir Steve Redgrave – features outstanding facilities including a 6-lane, 25m pool with an adjustable floor, a large sports hall, fitness suite and three studios all providing a full programme of indoor sporting activities and fitness training throughout the year.

The School has a Boat House on site with direct river access and on-site netball courts. The Wood Lane complex (a short coach drive away) features all-weather, floodlit playing surfaces including 4 rugby/football pitches, 3 cricket squares, a floodlit Astroturf for hockey, netball, football and tennis and a modern pavilion and changing rooms. Out of school hours the facilities are used for training by the England Rugby Team and visiting international teams.

The emphasis is on involvement, participation and choice. School teams enjoy great success in the major sports of rugby, football, netball, hockey, rowing, cricket and athletics; other sports such as karate, judo, dance, swimming, pilates and power walking for individual interests. The School maintains excellent fixture lists for all major sports.

Extra-Curricular Activities. There is a wide range of clubs and societies at lunch time and after school. In addition, every pupil has the opportunity to have residential experience and to take part in outdoor pursuits as part of the annual Activities Week. Fundraising by a very active Parents' Gild ensures that nobody is excluded from an activity for financial reasons. The Duke of Edinburgh's Award scheme flourishes with a number of students achieving the Gold Award each year.

Charitable status. The Latymer Foundation is a Registered Charity, number 312714. It exists to provide education for children.

Chairman of Governors: Ros Sweeting, LLB

Co-opted Governors:
Stephen Hodges, MA
Nicholas Jordan, MA
Tracey Scoffield, BA
Professor Jim Smith, MA, PhD, FRS, FRSA, FMedSci
James Priory, MA
Joanna Mackle, BA
Hugh Sloane, BSc, MPhil
Alex Plavsic, MA Oxon, FCA
Gubby Ayida, MA, FRCOG, DM
Charlie Wijeratna, BA
Annamarie Phelps, MA, CBE
Mark Brewer, BA

Ex officio Governor: The Reverend Simon Downham, LLB, DipMin, MA

Clerk to the Governors: Lucinda Evans

Head: David Goodhew, MA, FRSA Corpus Christi College Oxford

Deputy Heads:
Andrew Matthews, MA Sidney Sussex College Cambridge (*Academic*)
David Boyd, BA, MA (*Pastoral*)

Finance Director: Fiona I'Anson

Director of Development: Amanda Scott, MA

Assistant Heads:
Charlie Ben-Nathan, BA Exeter, MBA Middlesex (*Director of Studies*)
Rachel Collier, MA Corpus Christi College Oxford, MA Birkbeck London (*Sixth Form*)
Matt Chataway, BA, MA King's College London (*Middle School*)
Amy Sellars, BSc Cardiff (*Lower School*)

Prep School Principal: Andrea Rutterford, BEd

Director of Admissions: Catriona Sutherland-Hawes, MA

Heads of Year:
Mark Holmes, BA Bristol (*Head of Upper Sixth*)
Sam Adams, BA Birmingham, MA Surrey (*Head of Lower Sixth*)
Paul Goldsmith, BA Leeds, MBA Cass Business School, FRSA (*Head of Year 11*)
Rachel Monahan, BSc Birmingham (*Head of Year 10*)
Debbie Kendall, BA Leeds (*Head of Year 9*)
Katie Temple, BA Durham (*Head of Year 8*)
Gareth Cooper, BSc Port Elizabeth (*Head of Year 7*)

Heads of Departments:
Academic Mentoring: Jacqueline Heywood, BSc LSE, SENCO
Art & Design: David Mumby, BA Wolverhampton, PGCE Goldsmiths
Biology: Matt Reeve, BSc Newcastle
Chemistry: Ed Forbes, MChem Edinburgh
Classics: Marcel Lewis, BA Durham
Computing/IT: Edward Charlwood, BSc Aston
Director of Drama: Justin Joseph, BA London
Economics: Mark Wallace, BSc Birmingham
English: Jonathan Monk, BA Lady Margaret Hall Oxford

Geography: Michael Ashby, BA Middlesex, MSc King's College, FRGS, CGeog
History: Jonathan White, MA Selwyn College Cambridge
History of Art: Ruth Bell, BA Bristol, PG Dip Art Gallery/Museum Studies Manchester
Mathematics: Patrick MacMahon, MA Emmanuel College Cambridge, MSc Open University
Modern Languages: Cameron Palmer, BA, MA UCL Institute of Education
Director of Music: Tony Henwood, MA Exeter College Oxford, ARCO, FRSA
Physics: Alex Birchmore, MSci Nottingham
Politics: John Gilbert, MA Wadham College Oxford
Religious Studies & Philosophy: Keith Noakes, MA Corpus Christi College Cambridge, MA Manchester
Director of Sport: Tallan Gill, BA Manchester Metropolitan

The Grammar School at Leeds

Alwoodley Gates, Harrogate Road, Leeds LS17 8GS

Tel: 0113 229 1552
Fax: 0113 228 5111
email: enquiries@gsal.org.uk
website: www.gsal.org.uk
Twitter: @TheGSAL
Facebook: @TheGSAL
LinkedIn: /the-grammar-school-at-leeds

The Grammar School at Leeds is one of the UK's leading independent, co-educational schools. It enjoys the heritage of both Leeds Grammar School and Leeds Girls' High School with a lineage traceable back to 1552 with a long history of academic excellence. It benefits from a magnificent site on the outskirts of the north of Leeds.

We are committed to caring for our pupils as well as educating them. Our aim is to help them develop their individual abilities and talents within an ethic of teamwork, friendship and mutual respect.

We teach with pleasure and our pupils learn with enjoyment. That essentially sums up our mission. How well we accomplish it depends on much more than just excellent exam results. Our satisfaction lies in guiding children and young adults to become, quite simply, the best of their generation.

Structure. Pupils are taught using the structure that has come to be known as the 'diamond model'. Classes are fully co-educational from age three to eleven and again in the Sixth Form. Between the ages of eleven and sixteen, boys and girls are taught separately, but enjoy mixed extracurricular and pastoral activities. Pupils therefore have both the social benefits of co-education and the academic benefits of single-sex teaching in the adolescent years.

Junior School pupils progress to Senior School, in most cases automatically. Junior School begins with Year 3, Senior School Year 7 and Sixth Form Year 11.

Religion. The School has a Chaplain and its own Chaplaincy centre which serves as a focus for worship and pastoral care. Although an Anglican foundation, the School welcomes boys and girls of all faiths and separate meetings are held for Jewish, Muslim, Hindu and Sikh pupils.

Facilities. The Grammar School at Leeds occupies a modern, purpose-built site whose facilities are unrivalled anywhere in the country. They include:

• Specialist suites of teaching rooms for all subjects with the necessary support systems for each faculty.
• Centres for each section of the School, with generous common rooms, locker and cloakroom areas.

- A large assembly hall.
- A newly extended Junior School, having its own identity, specialist resources and operating an independent timetable.
- A library incorporating multimedia facilities.
- IT centre with three interlocking suites.
- A dedicated art, design and technology unit with computer aided design suite.
- Seventeen specialist science laboratories.
- A fully resourced music school.
- Theatre with fully-equipped lighting gantry.
- A new Food Technology Suite.
- Extensive playing fields with changing facilities and hospitality areas.
- A large indoor sports complex with 2 sports halls, climbing wall, squash courts, conditioning room, a 25m swimming pool of competition standard.
- Extensive grounds with pitches, tennis courts, athletics track.
- Large play and recreation areas for each section of the School.
- Refectory for breakfast, lunch and snacks.
- Provision for a wide variety of indoor and outdoor extra-curricular pursuits.
- Conservation areas.
- A versatile Chaplaincy Centre.
- A new Sixth Form Centre with its own cafeteria, study area and IT and leisure facilities.

Curriculum. Rose Court Nursery and Pre-Prep establishes the foundation for a long and rewarding education – pursuing a broad and balanced curriculum, which builds upon the natural aptitudes, learning skills and interests of each child, whilst enabling each to develop at his/her own pace. We use our own schemes of work, broadly based upon the early years of the National Curriculum, but refined by our own expertise and experience.

In the Junior School pupils concentrate upon the core subjects of English, Mathematics and Science. History, Geography, French/German, Religious Studies, Music, Art and Technology are also taught.

Pupils follow a broad curriculum, including two foreign languages in Years 7–9.

At the end of Year 11 pupils are presented for the GCSE examination.

In the Sixth Form students choose to study up to 4 A2 Level subjects and are encouraged to choose a broad range of subjects.

Games. Rugby, Football, Cricket, Athletics, Swimming, Tennis, Basketball, Badminton, Cross-Country, Volleyball, Hockey, Netball, Rounders, Squash, and Golf. There is a running track, swimming pool and a sports centre, including squash courts.

Other Activities. The School's many clubs and societies offer pupils the opportunity to participate in a wide range of out-of-school activities from Mountaineering and Skiing to Choral Singing, Dancing and Drama. There are regular tours and visits abroad and there are long-established exchanges with French and German schools.

The School has an extensive Arts Programme which covers music, film, drama, debating and creative art and includes visiting groups with national reputation as well as the students' own contributions.

The School provides a contingent of the CCF (Army & RAF sections), and has a Scout Troop, with Cub Pack and Venture Scout Unit. The School participates in the Duke of Edinburgh's Award scheme and Community Service is compulsory in the Sixth Form.

Admission. The entrance procedure takes place in the Spring term for entry the following September and is based upon an examination, an interview and school report. Very young boys and girls are assessed through a series of observed activities. The usual points of entry are 3+ for Nursery, 4+ for Reception, 7+ for Junior School and 11+ for Senior School, although applications can be made at any time for any age. Entry to the Sixth Form is based upon interview and report and the attainment of good GCSE grades.

Details of the entrance procedure together with copies of sample papers are available from the Headmaster's secretary.

Fees per term (2018–2019). Senior School £4,596; Junior School £3,432; Rose Court Nursery & Pre-Prep: £3,147 (full-time), £2,517.60 (4 days part-time), £1,888 (3 days part-time).

Bursaries. A number of means-tested bursaries (some full fee) are currently awarded each year to pupils entering the school at 11+ and 16+ (Sixth Form).

GSAL Alumni. This includes the Old Leodiensian Association – Leeds Grammar School and the Old Girls Club – Leeds Girls' High School. See Alumni section of school website, email: alumni@gsal.org.uk.

Charitable status. The Grammar School at Leeds is a Registered Charity, number 1048304. It exists for the advancement of education and training for boys and girls.

Governors:
Mr D P A Gravells, JP, MSc (*Chairman*)
Mr A M Martin, MA, FCA (*Vice Chairman*)
Mrs E E Bailey, BChD, LDS, RCS, DOrthRCS
Sir Stephen Brown, KCVO
Mr J Cross, BA Oxon, ACA
Mr M Curle, LLB, Chartered MCSI
Ms J A Harper, MBE, MA, Hon Fellow
Professor A Harrison Moore, MA Hons, AGMS Dip, PhD
Mrs D Kenny, BEd
Mrs C Lyons, BA Hons
Mrs J Semple, BSc, MSc
Mrs S A Solyom, BA, ACA
Mrs C Vilarrubi, BSc Hons, MSc, MBA, CPsychol
Mr A J Walsh, ACIB
Mr J Woodward, MA

Teaching Staff:

Principal & Chief Executive: Sue Woodroofe

Head of Junior School: Robert Lilley
Head of Rose Court (Pre-Prep): Jo Hall
Senior Deputy Head (Pastoral Care): Helen Stansfield
Vice Principal & Head of Senior School (Co-Curricular): Neal Parker
Deputy Head (Academic): Debbie Danks
Director of External Relations: Helen Clapham
Director of Finance: Steve Kingston

Director of Sixth Form: Paul Rushworth
Head of Student Development: Christine Jagger
Head of Upper Sixth: Pat Brotherton
Head of Lower Sixth: Sean Corcoran
Head of Year 11: Maria Collins
Head of Year 10: James Veitch
Head of Year 9: Carol Heatley
Head of Year 8: Rachel Hayward
Head of Year 7: Stephen Gibbin

Heads of Department:

Art: Stewart Kelly
Design & Technology: John Bagshaw
Biology: Lynne Gilbert

Chemistry:Geoffrey Huband
Classics: Martin Gibson
Drama: Roz Bendelow
Economics/Business Studies: Rob Stephenson
English: Laurel Rees
Food Technology: Yvonne Wilson
French: Nick Hele
Geography: Simon Knowles
German: Emma Whittaker
History: Keith Milne
ICT: Tim Street
Mathematics: Orla Weaver
Music: Niall Doherty
Physics: David Dee
Politics: Andrew Stodolny
Psychology: Alison Wilson
Religious Studies: Fiona Fishburn
Spanish: Rowan Reed-Purvis
Sport: Paul Morris

Admissions: Alice Gibbons
Principal's Secretary: Elaine Green

Leicester Grammar School

London Road, Great Glen, Leicester LE8 9FL

Tel: 0116 259 1900
email: admissions@leicestergrammar.org.uk
website: www.lgs-senior.org.uk
Twitter: @LGS_Senior
Facebook: @Leicester-Grammar-School
LinkedIn: /leicester-grammar-school

Leicester Grammar School was founded in 1981 as an independent, selective, co-educational day school to offer able children in the city and county a first-class academic education. Its founders sought to create a school which would maintain the standards and traditions of the city's former grammar schools lost through reorganisation and develop them to meet the demands of a rapidly changing environment. The School moved to a new state-of-the-art building on the south-east side of Leicester in September 2008.

There are 860 day pupils in the Senior School (393 girls, 467 boys), of whom 239 are in the Sixth Form. A further 385 pupils, aged 3–11, attend the Junior School.

Admission. An entrance examination is held in the Lent Term for boys and girls seeking to enter the Preparatory (10+) and Year 7 (11+) forms in the following September. Papers are taken in verbal reasoning, English and Mathematics. A pre-assessment day is held for all prospective Year 7 pupils on one of two dates in December. The pre-assessment day will involve group work investigating mathematical puzzles, science problems and a creative task. In addition, admission into Years 9 and 10 takes place at ages 13 and 14 and there is provision for direct entry into the Sixth Form, offers of a place being conditional upon the GCSE grades gained. The normal entry requirement to the Sixth Form is a minimum of three GCSEs at Grade 7 or better accompanied by a minimum of three further GCSEs at Grade 6 or better. Visitors are always welcome to make an appointment to see the school and meet the Headmaster. All applications are handled by the Head of Marketing & Admissions, from whom all Registration forms are obtainable. Candidates at all levels may be called for an interview.

Scholarships and Bursaries. The School offers a range of scholarships for pupils of outstanding academic, musical, sporting or artistic talent. These are awarded on the basis of examination and assessment. Awards cover entry at all ages from Year 7 including sixth form entrants.

The fee remission associated with scholarships is not means dependent and is usually worth no more than 5–10% of the termly fee.

Bursary support is available either for new applicants to the School or for existing pupils whose circumstances have changed. Bursaries are available only to pupils in Year 7 and above at Leicester Grammar School. Bursaries of up to 100% of the termly fee are available, subject to rigorous testing of financial need and limited by the overall bursaries budget.

Curriculum. Class sizes are about 20 to 24 in the first three years; the average size of a GCSE group is 19, of a Sixth Form group 12.

All pupils in the first three years (and those entering the preparatory form) follow a balanced curriculum covering the National Curriculum core and foundation subjects, Religious Studies and Latin (Classical Studies in the preparatory form). Classes are split into smaller groups for the creative and technological subjects, so that all pupils can gain practical experience, whether in the School's ICT suite or on its extensive range of musical instruments. From Year 8 the three science subjects, Biology, Chemistry and Physics, are taught separately. There is no streaming and setting occurs only for Mathematics and French from Year 8. In Year 9 an element of choice is introduced and pupils must opt from a choice of third languages and from a list of five creative subjects.

In Years 10 and 11 pupils prepare for GCSE or GCSE equivalent examinations in ten subjects, as well as doing PE/Games. All study a 'core' of three subjects: Mathematics and English Language and Literature. The range of 'options' includes Art, Biology, Chemistry, Classical Civilisation, Computing, Design and Technology, Drama, French, Geography, German, Greek, Religious Studies, History, Latin, Music, Physics, Spanish and PE. Students will normally follow at least two Science subjects and at least one Modern Foreign Language.

Students in the Sixth Form normally study 4 A Levels from a choice of 19 subjects, including Further Mathematics, Economics, Physical Education, Politics, Computing and Theatre Studies. There is no rigid division between arts and science sides. To ensure that breadth of education does not suffer, the majority of the Sixth Form complete an Extended Project. The school has an excellent record of success at public examinations and university admissions, including Oxbridge. The Careers Department is very active in giving help and advice to students.

School activities. A broad range and variety of activities complements the academic curriculum. Participation rates are high.

Music, drama and sport form an integral part of life at LGS. Every pupil in the First Year learns a musical instrument and a high proportion continue afterwards with private weekly lessons. The School Orchestra gives two major concerts a year, whilst a training orchestra, a jazz band, a dance band, recorder groups and various chamber ensembles explore other avenues. The School Choir is the resident choir for the Crown Court Services and tours regularly. Links are strong with the Leicestershire School of Music orchestras and several pupils play in national orchestras. Senior and junior drama clubs function throughout the year, a major play or musical and a junior play are staged regularly and house drama extends the opportunity to act to most pupils.

Games are seen as an important means not only of promoting health and fitness but also of inspiring self-confidence. Major winter games are hockey, netball and rugby and in summer athletics, cricket and tennis. Opportunities occur for individuals to follow their interest in badminton, basketball, squash, golf, table tennis, gymnastics, dance, sailing and cross-country running whilst swimming is an integral part of the PE programme. The School's own facilities are extensive and meet all modern standards for sport. Teams represent the School in the main games at all age groups and several students achieve recognition at county or even national level. The school is proud of the fact that it is one of only eight other schools to have been awarded the Sportsmark Gold with Distinction, for the quality of the delivery of sport within the school.

Societies and clubs complement these activities, ranging from chess to The Duke of Edinburgh's Award scheme, history and Lit Soc to model aeroplanes, debating to art, design and technology, for which the workshop and art rooms are usually open during lunchtimes and after school.

Religion. The school espouses the principles of the Church of England, teaching the Christian faith, its values and standards of personal conduct, but also prides itself on welcoming children of all faiths, who play a full part in the life of the community. Very strong links exist with Leicester Cathedral and there is a flourishing Guild of Servers and University of Leicester clergy participate in school life and prepare confirmation candidates.

Pastoral Care. Responsibility for a wide-ranging system of pastoral care and for the creation of the caring, friendly and disciplined environment, resides in eight Heads of Year, assisted by form teachers, personal tutors and a very active house system.

Junior School. Entry to the Junior School is by interview and, where appropriate, assessment at 3+, 4+, 7+ and into other school years, when places are available. Pupils are prepared for entry to the Senior School. A balanced curriculum is followed covering National Curriculum Key Stages 1 and 2 and beyond; French (from 5 years), classical studies and ICT are also taught. A wide range of activities complements the academic curriculum, with a strong stress on music and a rapidly growing games programme. The School is a Christian foundation and lays great emphasis upon the pastoral care of young children. (*See also Junior School entry in IAPS section.*)

Fees per term (2018–2019). Senior School £4,343; Junior School (Years 3–6) £3,745; Kinders to Year 2 £3,531.

Old Leicestrians Association. All correspondence to the OL Secretary, c/o the School.

Charitable status. Leicester Grammar School Trust is a Registered Charity, number 510809. Its aims and objectives are to promote and provide for the advancement of education and in connection therewith to conduct, carry on, acquire and develop in the United Kingdom or elsewhere a School or Schools to be run according to the principles of the Church of England for the education of students and children of either sex or both sexes.

Acting Headteachers:
Academic: **C S James**, MA Girton College Cambridge (*Director of Studies, Mathematics*)
Pastoral: **Mrs A M Ewington**, MA Nottingham, CBiol, MSB (*Biology*)

Assistant Head: Mrs CL Jess, MA Gonville & Caius College Cambridge (*Head of Year 10, French & Spanish*)
Assistant Head: R W S Kidd, BA, MA Ulster (*Head of English*)

Academic Staff:
Miss R E Adams, BA Italia Conti Academy (*Drama*)
Dr S W Ainge, BSc, PhD Newcastle, CChem, FRSC (*Head of Chemistry, Head of Science, School Organist*)
Miss E S Allcoat, BSc Bristol (*Physics, Senior House Coordinator, Head of House – Masters, Charities Coordinator*)
J P Allen, BA Dunelm (*Physical Education, Head of House – Vice Chancellors*)
T P Allen, BA Kent (*Head of Sixth Form, History*)
J M Barker, BMus, MMus Royal College of Music (*Director of Music*)
Miss R S Burfoot, BSc Birmingham (*Mathematics*)
W D Burns, BSc Edinburgh Napier (*Design, Engineering & Technology*)
Mrs A J Button, BA Loughborough (*Physical Education*)
Mrs C Calland, BA De Montfort (*Physical Education*)
Miss K A Campbell, BA Nottingham Trent (*Head of Design, Engineering & Technology*)
R T Campbell, MA Edgehill (*Head of Geography*)
Miss Z Carter, BSc Leicester (*Mathematics, Pastoral Liaison for International Students, Duke of Edinburgh's Award*)
Mrs C E Charles, BTh Selwyn College Cambridge (*Learning Support*)
Miss M J Clapham, BA Hons, MBA Ed, PGC SpLD Leicester, PGC SENCO Northampton, SpLD APC and TPC Patoss (*Head of Learning Support*)
Mrs P Clare, BSc Leicester, MSc Imperial College (*Biology*)
Miss J A Copley, BA Leeds (*History*)
P Cox, BSc Bangor (*Biology, Duke of Edinburgh's Award*)
Miss L Crampton, MEng Hull (*Design, Engineering & Technology, ICT, Staff Development Coordinator*)
Dr D M Crawford, MA, DPhil Jesus College Oxford, MEd Bristol, MA Ed OU, MSc OU (*Head of Mathematics*)
Mrs A J Davies, MA De Montfort (*Art*)
G D Davies, MEd, BSc De Montfort (*Head of PE and Games*)
Mrs A M Dewe, BA Warwick (*French*)
Mrs K R Douglas, BA Liverpool (*Italian*)
A N Duffield, BSc Cardiff, CBiol, MSB (*Head of Biology*)
H A Ellis, BSc Loughborough (*Physical Education*)
K Esmail, BA Portsmouth (*Economics, History, Head of PSD*)
Dr S L Ewers, BSc, PhD Bristol (*Biology*)
Mrs S M Faire, BSc Surrey (*Mathematics, Maths Learning Support*)
Dr C H Fearon, BSc Liverpool, PhD Birmingham (*Biology, AQA Baccalaureate EPQ Centre Coordinator for Enrichment Programme*)
Miss C L Feeney, BA Dunelm (*Physical Education*)
Ms J A M Ford, BA Newcastle (*Head of Religious Studies*)
Dr K L Fulton, BSc Dunelm, PhD Nottingham (*Biology*)
C I J Gilham, BA London (*Classics*)
Miss E Graff-Baker, MA The Queen's College Oxford (*Music*)
Dr J M Griffin, MA Fitzwilliam College Cambridge, PhD OU (*Deputy Head of English, Theatre Studies*)

N Grimadell, BSc Derby (*Design, Engineering & Technology*)

Mrs A L Harris, BA Essex, MA Loughborough (*Head of Drama*)

Miss S A Harris, BSc Nottingham (*Chemistry*)

Ms S Haywood, BEd Worcester College, BA OU (*Art, History of Art*)

Dr A Higginson, MPhil Essex (*Physics*)

Mrs M Higginson, BEd, MA Toronto (*English, Editor of Leicestrian*)

Mrs A J Hillier, BA Nottingham (*Religious Studies*)

Mrs V Hird, BA Leicester (*History*)

Mr R C Horton, BSc Loughborough (*Sports Graduate*)

Miss L Howd, BSc East Anglia (*Mathematics*)

C W Howe, BEd CNAA Crewe & Alsager College (*Director of Sport*)

Miss N Hughes, BA London (*English, Staff Induction & Teacher Training*)

J T Hunt, BA Reading (*Head of Sixth Form, English, AQA Baccalaureate & Extended Project Team Leader*)

Mrs J Hutchinson, BEd Durham, MA Ed OU (*Physical Education, i/c Academic PE, Mathematics*)

G Inchley, BSc Hull, MSc Bristol (*Deputy Head of Mathematics*)

R A Jacobs, BSc Leeds, BA Open University (*Mathematics*)

Dr A J Kendall, MA Wadham College Oxford, DPhil Linacre College Oxford (*Chemistry*)

Mrs R E Kendall, BA Dunelm, MA Goldsmiths (*English*)

A T King, MChem Loughborough (*Chemistry*)

Miss J L Knight, BA De Montfort (*Art*)

Mrs J Kungu, MSc Lancaster (*Geography*)

Mrs N L Laybourne, BSc Hons, MSc Loughborough (*Head of Year 7, Physical Education*)

Mrs S Lopez-Correia, MA Université de Picardie Jules Verne (*Head of Modern Languages*)

R L Longson, BA Aberystwyth, DipCG LGMB, Swanley, MCDI (*Head of Career Development*)

P J Lowe, BA Southampton (*Geography*)

Miss K L Macleod, BSc University College London (*Physics*)

Dr D W Maddock, BA Bristol Polytechnic, MA Leeds Polytechnic (*Head of Art*)

Sra I Manktelow, BSc Instituto Politécnico Nacional, Mexico (*Spanish*)

Sra P Matalobos, BA, MA Santiago dé Compestela (*Spanish Assistant*)

D McCann, BEd Leicester (*Physical Education*)

R J McLean, BA Lady Margaret Hall Oxford (*Head of Classics*)

Mrs M A McNally, BA Westminster (*Geography*)

Mrs A E McPherson, BA St Anne's College Oxford (*Deputy Director of Music*)

P Moore-Friis, BA De Montfort, PG Dip Oxford, CIM Dip (*Head of Economics, Young Enterprise Coordinator*)

Miss J Mould, BEd Bedford College of HE (*Head of Preparatory Department, Trips Coordinator*)

N Murray, BSc Imperial, MA London, MSc Sheffield Hallam (*Mathematics*)

Mrs E J Nelson, BA Northumbria (*German*)

Mrs E Nisbet, BEd Trent Polytechnic (*Food Technology*)

Mrs F Paton, DEUG and Licence Bordeaux (*French*)

Miss A M Patterson, BSc Sunderland Polytechnic (*Chemistry, Head of House – Duke's, Community Service Coordinator*)

A J Picknell, BA Manchester, MA London (*Head of History*)

D Pilbeam, MChem Nottingham (*Chemistry, Examinations Officer*)

Mrs K G Pollard, BSc Loughborough (*Mathematics*)

L Potter (*Head of Year 8, Physical Education*)

P M Pratt, MA Harvard (*Classics*)

Miss S H Proffitt, BA Bristol (*Classics and English*)

S J R Radford, BSc Sheffield (*Mathematics, Head of House – Judges*)

P T G Reeves, BSc Manchester (*Head of Physics*)

Mrs G M A Rodgers, MA Newnham College Cambridge (*English*)

Mrs M Sian, BA Middlesex (*Head of Computing*)

C I Silvester, BA Plymouth (*Art*)

Mrs S Stout, BSc Aston (*Deputy Head of Modern Languages*)

T A Thacker, Bed CNAA Crewe & Alsager College (*Head of Year 11, Physical Education*)

Mrs J Tompkins, BA Leicester (*Head of Year 9, Religious Studies*)

Dr A Vassilliou-Abson, BA Athens, MPhil, PhD Birmingham (*Classics, Critical Thinking*)

D R Willis, BSc CNAA Portsmouth Polytechnic (*Science*)

Ms Y Yau, BA De Montfort (*Extra-Curricular Mandarin Chinese*)

Dr S Yeomans, MA, PhD Loughborough Politics (*Head of Politics, School Council Link Teacher*)

Chaplain: Revd Liz Wilson

School Nurse: Mrs Julia Parsons, Dip HE Adult De Montfort, Dip HE Child Nottingham

Marketing & Admissions: Mrs Natalie Hunt, BA Nottingham Trent

Leighton Park School

Shinfield Road, Reading, Berkshire RG2 7ED

Tel:	0118 987 9600
Fax:	0118 987 9625
email:	admissions@leightonpark.com
website:	www.leightonpark.com
Twitter:	@LPSchool
Facebook:	@leightonparkschool
LinkedIn:	/leighton-park-school

At its core, a Leighton Park education focuses on the individual and the promise of choice. Our ethos informs an approach where students are able to follow their most impassioned interests, become active learners and strive to fulfil their potential.

Academic. Students benefit from an academically rigorous, broad and innovative curriculum. The sciences, mathematics and the creative arts, including music, film production and art, are particular strengths of the school. This strength in breadth enables a focus on creative problem-solving and interdisciplinary approaches, encouraging students to analyse and put forward solutions to today's complex challenges, often supported by the school's impressive partnerships with universities, industry and cultural organisations, such as Cisco and Pinewood Studios. The success of our approach is demonstrated by 94% of our Sixth Formers achieving places at their first-choice university last year.

Sixth Form. In Sixth Form, students can choose between the International Baccalaureate Diploma Programme (IB) and A Levels, and can opt to do four A Levels so that their choices are not limited so early in life. Among other accolades, the school is in the top five in the UK for small cohort IB results.

Hobbies and other activities. Our wrap-around provision, which welcomes day students from 7.20 am to 9.00 pm, offers all our pupils the time to discover and develop their greatest talents. The school's cross-cutting skills programmes position students for success in a fast-changing world, where many of today's jobs will not exist in 30 years' time. Central to the school's approach, we teach leadership, creative thinking and risk-taking, empowering students to be a force for good in the world and reflecting the school's Quaker ethos. The range of choice and the school's focus on the individual create a fun, supportive and nurturing programme.

Sports. Sport plays an important role in life at Leighton Park with many individual performers and teams reaching county and regional level in sports. The school's Advanced Performer Programme supports elite athletes. While the school does very well in traditional sports such as rugby, netball, cricket and hockey it also has strong teams in football, basketball and table tennis. The school is very supportive of individual talents and interests from equestrian sports to gymnastics. First-rate coaching and superb facilities ensure that talented and enthusiastic students can develop their sporting abilities to the full.

Music. Music and creative media is a particular strength at Leighton Park, reflected by the school's status as a Yamaha Education Partner – the only one in the UK. Students have so many opportunities to play or perform at Leighton Park: the Music Department is one of the busiest places in school, catering for all musical tastes from classical to jazz, indie to rock. Opportunities to perform include regular concerts and tours abroad.

Location and school life. The school is located in Reading, 25 minutes by train from central London and 30 minutes from Heathrow airport. The quiet moments and the calm atmosphere of our 60-acre park, encourage students to collect their thoughts and reflect within a caring community, providing high academic standards, excellent pastoral care and a rich and diverse co-curricular programme of activities. All of this, and the focus on mutual respect, create a stable, unique and sustainable environment where children can live, learn and grow.

Facilities. Leighton Park has the facilities you would expect of a leading independent school, including an impressive library, swimming pool and historic buildings. In recent times investments have been made to support the school's Science, Technology, Engineering, Arts and Maths focus, placing the creative arts at the heart of the traditional STEM approach. This includes modern science labs, a wonderful Design Technology centre and impressive mathematics facility. A brand new Music and Media Centre will provide fabulous music and creative media facilities for students, including a Live Lounge, music practice rooms and performance spaces. The school's innovative use of the latest teaching and learning technologies is supported by continuous investment in technology, including Google Classroom, Clever Touch screens in classrooms and personal Chromebooks.

Boarding. Leighton Park has a thriving boarding community, offering full, weekly and flexible options for students. Co-educational, the boarding houses are split roughly 50/50 boys and girls with each group having their own wings but sharing communal spaces. Students represent 32 countries, with strong UK representation. The five houses mix boarding and day students, creating vibrant communities, with day students welcome to stay until 9.00 pm to spend time with friends or have time and space to focus on their prep.

Housemasters and Housemistresses create homely environments supported by tutors and matrons, ensuring each student feels relaxed and comfortable. With a dedicated staff and plenty of opportunity to socialise with other students, each house is very much its own community.

Entry. Entry to the school includes consideration of school reports, tests in English, Maths, essay writing and an interview, with an additional English test where appropriate.

Pupils are normally admitted at one of three points: Year 7 (age 11); Year 9 (age 13), and the Sixth Form. Entry to the Sixth Form requires 5 GCSE passes or equivalent at Level 6 / Grade B or above. We also offer a Pre-Sixth course of 5 GCSEs in one year.

Fees per term (2018–2019). Full Boarding £9,507–£11,915; Weekly Boarding £8,121–£9,962; Day £5,873–£7,326.

Scholarships and Bursaries. Several Academic, Music, Drama, Art & Design and Sports Awards are made each year for entry in Year 7, Year 9 and the Sixth Form and are also available to existing pupils. Candidates may apply for any combination of scholarships, but can only receive the financial benefits of one (in the region of 10% of Day student fees). Bursaries may be available, in cases of financial hardship, to existing and prospective pupils. Bursaries are always means-tested and subject to annual review. Additional awards may be made by the David Lean Foundation.

Old Leightonians. Website: www.leightonpark.com/oldleightonians.

Charitable status. The Leighton Park Trust is a Registered Charity, number 309144. It exists to provide education for young people.

Governors:
David Isherwood (*Chairman*)

Sally Jayne Bonner	Simon Hollands
John Crosfield	Chris Houston
Eme Dean-Lewis	Bruce Johnson
Jan Digby	Helen Johnson
Caroline George	Martin Lloyd
Philip Griffin	Liza Phipps
David Hickok	Matt Winkless

Head: Matthew Judd, BA, PGCE

Deputy Head: Edward Falshaw, MA
Deputy Head (*Academic*): Karen Gracie-Langrick, MA

Bursar: Keith Eldridge, BA, FCA

Teaching Staff:
* *Head of Department*
§ *Part-time*
† *Housemaster*

Paulo Arruda, BSc, MSc (*Beliefs and Values*)
Adam Ball, BSc, QTS (*Chemistry)
Jeremy Belas, BSc, QTS (**Director of Sport*)
Ramona Bellinghausen, BA, QTS (**Modern Foreign Languages*)
Naomi Bonthrone, BA, QTS (*English*)
Simon Booth, MEng, PGCE, QTLS (*Physics)
Mark Budge, QTS, MEng (*Mathematics*)
Beth Butler, BA (*Dance*)
Tom Cartmill, BA, BSc (*English as a Second Language*)
Wai Chiu Wong, BSc (*Mathematics*)
Bridget Clarke, BSc (*Mathematics*)
Jon Clarke, BSc (*Physics*)
Maddie Cottam, MA (*Music*)
Harriet Custance, MA, BA (**English as a Second Language*)
Matthew Dawes, BA, QTS (*Economics)
Kate Donegan, BSc (*Biology*)
Richard Duckett, BA, PhD (*History, Politics*)
Beverley Eldridge, MBA, BA, QTS (§*Economics*)
Katie Evans, BA (*Resident Graduate, PE & Games*)
Eddie Falshaw, MA, BA (*History, Deputy Head*)
Kate Findlay, MA, BA (§*History*)
Anne Fitzsimons, PGCE (*Mathematics*)
Andrew Gallacher, BA (*Resident Graduate, PE & Games*)
Pablo Gorostidi Perez, MBA (*MFL*)

Karen Gracie-Langrick, MA, BA (*History, Deputy Head Academic Studies*)
Claire Gray, BA (*Individual Learning Centre*)
Claire Gray, Dip Dyslexia (*ILC*)
Tim Green, BSc (*Games, Head of Boys' Games*)
Claire Gulliver, BSc, PGCE (*Psychology*)
David Hammond, MSc, BSc, QTS (*§Biology*)
Nicky Hardy (*Assistant Head – Head of Pastoral Welfare & Safeguarding*)
Emilia Hicks, BSc (*Biology and Science*)
Alex Huyton-Fox, BSc (*PE and Games*)
Deborah Ince, BA, PGCE (*Art and Textiles*)
Rosanna Jahangard, QTS, PGCE, MA, BA (*English*)
Matthew Judd, BA, PGCE (*Head*)
Heidi Kenny, BSc (*Resident Graduate, PE & Games*)
Elaine King, BA (**Careers, Art, Games*)
Adél Kiss, BSc, BEd (**Mathematics*)
Eithne Laird, BSc, MSc, PGCE (**Geography, †Fryer House*)
Isabelle Lauzeral, MA, BA (*Modern Languages*)
Alex Leighton, MA, BA, PGCE (*English, Leader of Learning Technologies, †Field House*)
Robin Longworth, MA, BSc (*Geography, †Reckitt House*)
Zoe Macpherson, BA (*Graduate Teacher, Girls' Games*)
Jakki Marr, BEd (*Head of Girls' Games, †Field House*)
Peter Marshman, QTS, PGCE, MA (**Computer Science*)
Rachael Martin, BEd (*Individual Learning Centre, †Reckitt House*)
Mair Mayers, BSc (*§Mathematics*)
Sheila Metcalfe, MEng (*Mathematics*)
Chris Mitchell, BA (*§Assistant Director of Music and Media Arts Development*)
Ann Munday, BSc (*Mathematics, DofE Coordinator*)
Myles Nash, BA (*Design Technology, †School House, Head of Boarding*)
Lynne Parry, BA (*Individual Learning Centre*)
Helen Porter-Hughes, BSc, MSc (*ILC*)
Jonathan Porter-Hughes, BA, PGCE (*English, †School House*)
Jennifer Powlesland, BA (*English, Assistant Head – Head of Teaching and Learning*)
Tom Rawlings, BA, PGCE (**English*)
Martin Reeves MBA, BSc (*Acting Head of Geography*)
Patricia Robson, MA, BEd (*ILC*)
Ian Rowe, BSc (*Head of Individual Learning Centre, SENCO*)
Premnath Samyrao, MSc, MEd (*Mathematics*)
Rosemary Scales, BA, MA (**Director of Music*)
Peter Scoggins, BA, PGCE, QTS (**Drama*)
Caroline Semeyn, BA (*MFL*)
Nick Sexton, BSc (*Physics*)
Saima Shabir, DPhil, BSc, PGCE, QTS (*Chemistry*)
Mark Simmons, BEd (*PE, Games, Assistant Head – Senior Master & Head of Middle School*)
Gemma Sims, MSc, BSc (**Biology*)
Kelly Slade, BA (*Resident Graduate Theatre Arts Technology and Fryer*)
Alice Smith (*Individual Learning Centre*)
Graham Smith, BA (*Games, Geography, †Grove House*)
Mark Smith, BEng, BSc (**Design Technology*)
Adrian Stewart, BPrimEd (*Geography, Games, Assistant Head – Head of Fryer and Lower School*)
Rod Tait, QTS (*Physics*)
Shazia Taj, BA, MA, PGCE (**Beliefs and Values*)
Helen Taylor, BA, PGCE (*Science, Assistant Head – Head of Sixth Form, IB Coordinator*)
Sherilyn Wass, BSc, PhD (*§Chemistry*)
Mark Wood, BA, PGCE (**Art*)
Lan Worrall, MA, BA (**Mandarin Chinese*)
Damon Young, BA (*Drama, Theatre Studies, †Grove House*)

Registrar: Claire Elmer
Head's PA: Virginia Cashin
Librarian: Chris Routh, BA

The Leys

Trumpington Road, Cambridge CB2 7AD

Tel: 01223 508900
email: office@theleys.net
website: www.theleys.net
Twitter: @LeysCambridge
Facebook: @TheLeysSchoolCambridge

Motto: *In Fide Fiducia*

The Leys is situated half a mile from the centre of the university city of Cambridge, close to the River Cam and Grantchester Meadows. The School was founded in 1875 on the initiative of a group of leading Methodists to provide a liberal Christian education, establishing a tradition which has continued unbroken to this day. The School was incorporated as a Charitable Trust in 1878. All the buildings are grouped around the Main Field and lie within the estate originally acquired for the purpose; there is a second extensive playing field nearby.

The Leys is a friendly, caring and happy community, large enough to offer many opportunities, but not so large as to lose sight of the individual. The School is fully co-educational; of a total of over 560 pupils, 200 are in the Sixth Form. Girls and boys are accommodated in separate houses. 70% of the pupils are accommodated in the boarding houses, but all, including the 160 day pupils, are able to enjoy all the opportunities offered by boarding school life.

Buildings and Facilities. There is a continuing development programme involving all areas of the School. A state-of-the-art Music School was opened in 2005. There is an excellent Humanities Building with first-class facilities for Geography, History, Classics and Divinity together with a Museum and Archives Centre, and an award-winning Design Centre, which contains workshops (metal, plastic and wood), a 3D printing and laser cutting area, Art School, Ceramics Studio, Computer Centre, together with facilities for Design, Photography, Cookery and an Exhibition Centre. A Sports Hall and all-weather pitch were built in 1995. In 2008 the Sports Hall was extended to include a superb fitness suite and cricket pavilion, and a second Astroturf pitch was added. A new climbing wall was constructed in summer 2007. A major capital development has been added, which provides a new theatre, Assembly Hall, Drama and Dance Studios, Drama Department, School Café and three new Science Laboratories. This project, known as Great Hall, was completed in summer 2013. There are 40 acres of playing fields, an indoor heated swimming pool open all the year, a recently refurbished boat house on the Cam shared with King's, Selwyn and Churchill Colleges, and synthetic as well as grass tennis courts. A radical redesigning and refurbishment of all boarding houses began in summer 2006, with the aim of providing the most comfortable and homely of boarding facilities. To date six of the seven Senior Boarding Houses have been refurbished. The School Library underwent a major refurbishment in 2008.

Admission. Admission for girls and boys is mainly at 11+, 13+ and 16+. Entrance tests for 11+ and 13+ entry are held in the January prior to entry. Places in the Sixth Form are available for both girls and boys who have successfully completed their GCSE or equivalent courses elsewhere. Application for admission should be made to the Admissions Office in the first instance.

Scholarships. Scholarships are available for entry at 11+, 13+ and to the Sixth Form, valued at a maximum of 5% fee remission, which can be supplemented by means-tested bursaries up to a total concession of 100%.

Academic Scholarships are available for entry at 11+, 13+ and for entry to the Sixth Form at 16+. Scholarships are also available for entry at 13+ in Music, Art, Design Technology, Sport, Drama and all-rounders, and for entry to the Sixth Form at 16+ in Music, Art, Sport and Drama.

The School also participates in the Arkwright Scholarship Scheme, which is an external examination offering Scholarships for those wishing to take Design and Technology in the Sixth Form and who are aiming to read Engineering, Technology or other Design-related subjects in Higher Education.

The Scholarship Examinations at 11+ and 13+ take place in the Spring Term and the Sixth Form Scholarship Examination takes place in the November of the year prior to entry.

Bursary awards are made on a means-tested basis, and applications for bursaries must be made before entrance tests are taken.

Special awards for children of Methodist Ministers and members of HM Forces are available. Special consideration is given to the sons and daughters of Old Leysians.

Further particulars may be obtained from the Registrar.

Curriculum. The academic curriculum broadly conforms to the National Curriculum but is not restricted by it. Each pupil has an Academic tutor who, in conjunction with the Director of Studies and the Housemaster or Housemistress, works to tailor the pupil's programme to suit the needs of the individual wherever possible. Pupils follow a broad programme in the first three years (Years 7, 8 and 9). At the end of Year 9 they choose three from a wide range of options to add to the basic core of IGCSE English Language and Literature, separate Sciences and a Modern Foreign Language, and GCSE Mathematics and Religious Studies. The GCSE examinations are normally taken at the end of Year 11, but Religious Studies is taken by all pupils in Year 10.

In the Sixth Form, a similar option scheme operates with pupils choosing from a total of 25 subjects to take normally 3 A Levels in the Sixth Form. Double Maths (Maths and Further Maths) is regarded as one subject leading to two A Levels.

There is considerable flexibility of combinations possible at both levels, and choices are made after consultation between parents, tutors, careers staff and subject teachers. The most able pupils are given an enrichment programme under the guidance of the Director of Academic Development, including extension projects, visits to Gifted and Talented seminars, and seminars with Cambridge undergraduate or postgraduate students. In addition, departments organise extension groups and societies and the school has a thriving Debating Society and a Model United Nations group. The school runs its own Independent Research Project to help senior pupils develop independent study skills.

About 95% of the A Level candidates proceed to degree courses. A Reading Party for potential Oxford and Cambridge candidates is held during the Summer Term.

Personal and Social Education forms an integral part of the curriculum at all levels. In the Sixth Form this is supplemented by a year-long programme that draws on the cultural resources of Cambridge University and the city as a whole.

The Chapel. The School Chapel is at the heart of the community in every sense. From the time of its Methodist foundation The Leys has been firmly based on non-sectarian Christian principles. It welcomes boys and girls of all denominations and religions, encouraging them to see the relevance of a personal faith of their own. Religious Educa-

tion forms part of the curriculum. Preparation is also given for Church membership, and a combined confirmation service is held.

Physical Education. The physical education/games programme aims at introducing a wide variety of physical activities. Sports available are Rugby, Hockey, Cricket, Tennis, Athletics, Netball, Badminton, Basketball, Gymnastics, Golf, Rowing, Sailing, Dance, Shooting, Climbing, Squash, Swimming, Volleyball, Water Polo. Outdoor activities such as Camping, Orienteering, Canoeing, and Climbing are also encouraged through CCF and The Duke of Edinburgh's Award. PE is offered at GCSE and A Level. The School has close links with many Cambridge University Sports Clubs, with the Sixth Form competing in University Leagues.

Careers. In the Lower School, careers guidance forms part of the PSHE programme and is carried out by tutors and members of the Careers Department. Year 9 are supported in their option choices by tutors and Careers staff and are introduced to the Careers Library. Year 11 take the Preview Careers Selection Programme. It matches pupils' interests and abilities to appropriate career fields and is followed up by two individual interviews with career specialists. Year 11 pupils are also encouraged to participate in the Work Experience scheme. Support continues into the Sixth Form with all Lower Sixth being interviewed by Careers staff. An annual Careers Forum is organised in the Lent term, enabling pupils to investigate various career paths before embarking on their UCAS applications. Work experience is organised throughout the Sixth Form.

Societies. All are encouraged to participate in out-of-school activities of their choice. These range from Literary, Philosophical, Scientific, Mathematical, Languages, Debating, Music and Drama societies to any of the activities available in the Design Centre, which are available after School and at weekends. The life of the School is enriched by its proximity to Cambridge; distinguished visiting speakers are available, and pupils are encouraged to go to plays, concerts and lectures in the town. The programme of visiting speakers is largely run by the pupils themselves, overseen by a member of staff. A programme entitled the Cambridge Experience ensures that all Sixth Form pupils avail themselves of the cultural opportunities afforded by the school's location.

Combined Cadet Force. Except in special circumstances, pupils in Year 10 join the CCF (Army or Navy section) and also follow The Duke of Edinburgh's Award scheme. CCF camps take place annually. There is a miniature range, and a Rifle Club exists for small-bore shooting. The School is an authorised centre for the organisation of activities within The Duke of Edinburgh's Award scheme and pupils work towards the Bronze, Silver or Gold awards in the four sections: community service, expeditions, physical recreation and skills or hobbies.

Fees per term (2018–2019). Years 7 and 8: £8,000 Boarders; £5,300 Day Pupils. Years 9 to Sixth Form: £10,975 Boarders; £8,255 Home Boarders; £7,345 Day Pupils.

St Faith's Preparatory School is part of the same Foundation. It was founded in 1884 and acquired by the Governors of The Leys in 1938. There are 547 boys and girls, aged 4–13 years. The buildings, which include the Keynes Building opened in 2006 and a new Sports Hall opened in May 2011, stand in 10 acres of grounds. Full particulars may be obtained from the Headmaster of St Faith's, Mr N Helliwell, MA. (*For further details, see entry in IAPS section.*)

The Old Leysian Society. *Secretary*: J C Harding, MA, The Leys School, Cambridge CB2 7AD. Handbook and Directory, twenty-second edition, 2010.

Charitable status. The Leys and St Faith's Schools Foundation is a Registered Charity, number 1144035. It aims to enable boys and girls to develop fully their individual potential within a School community firmly based on Christian principles.

Governors:
Chairman: Sir Tony Brenton, KCMG
Mrs H Arthur, Cert Ed
R Ashby-Johnson, MA [OL]
M D Beazor, BA, FRSAHH
HH Judge Revd M A Bishop, MA [OL]
Mrs A M Brunner, BA
Miss J H E Burton, BA
M A Elliott, BSc [OL]
Mrs P M Graves, MA, Dip S W
B Haryott, BSc, FREng, CEng, FICE, FIStructE, FRSA, CRBCCC [OL]
R B Hewitson, LLB
Mrs E Hooley
C M Kidman, ACIOB [OL]
P R Lacey, MA, PGCE, FRSA
A S MacGregor BSc CertEd
Mrs M E Mackay, RGN
T C Moore [OL]
R Norfolk
Mrs J Plows, BA
Revd J M Pursehouse
R C Sadler, FRICS
A V Silverton, BSc, FCSI [OL]
D Unwin, MA, ACA [OL]
Dr R D H Walker, MA
R B Webster, FCA
R J Willmott, MCIOB

[OL] *Old Leysian*

Headmaster: M J Priestley, MA Oxon

Deputy Head: Mrs C E Mayo, MA Cantab

R Adamson, BSc, PhD
B A Barton, BA
A R C Batterham, BA
Miss C E Battison, BA
D R Bell, MA
A Bennett-Jones, BSc
Ms E Bonnaud, BA, MA
N R Born, MA
M A Brown, BSc
Miss S J Byrne, MA, PGCE
D Cassidy, BPhEd
Ms H S Clark BA
Ms L J Clark, BA
Miss L Corble, BA
Mrs K J Cox, BSc
P J Crosfield, BA
Mrs E R Culshaw, MA
T Dann, BSc
P M Davies, BSc
G J Deudney, BSc, BEd
D A Divito, BSc, MSc, PGCE
N J Dix-Pincott, BA, MA
R J Driscoll, BA, BEd
T P Dunn, BA, MSc, MEd Cantab, CPsychol, FRSA
Mrs C M Earl, BSc
W J Earl, BSc
Miss K E Eaves, MA
Miss H Edmondson, BA
M A Egan, BSc
A S Erby, BSc
J W Fawcett, BA, MA
D K Fernandes, BSc

R Fielden, MA, DPhil, PGCE
R Francis, MA, MEd
Revd C I A Fraser, BA, MA Ed, MCMI, PG Dip, FRSA
M C Gale, BEd
Miss G H Jefferies, BA
E M W George, BEd [OL]
Mrs J George, FIMLS
S G Hancock, BA, MA
A P Harmsworth, MA, FRAS
Ms J L Hebden, BA, MA
L D J Higgins, BA
R A D Hill, BA
Mrs A Hodges, BSc, RSA Cert SpLD
Ms C C Howe, BA
Mrs C L Howe, BSc, PhD
G K Howe, BSc, MSc, MA, MEd
R I Kaufman, BA
M J Kenworthy, BMus
Miss C A Knights, BA
Mrs A Lainchbury, BA, MCLIP
S N Leader, BA
Mrs C E Leigh, BA, MEd
Mrs G L Lester, MA, BA, Dip SpLD
M P J Lindsay, MSc
A C R Long, BA
Mrs C E Mayo, MA Cantab

R S McAlinden, BA
Ms S J McEwan, BA
Revd C J Meharry, BEd, BTh
S A Newlove, BSc, PhD
D J Nye, BSc
Ms E F Prosser, BSc
T L Reed, MA, MSc
Mrs L A Reyes, MA
N P Robinson, BSc, MBA, CEng
R T Roe MA PGCE

Mrs J A Samuel, BSc
Mrs J Schofield, BSc
Mrs J Stobbart, BA
B R Stuttard, BA
W P Unsworth, BSc, PhD
P R Wallace, BSc, MPhil, DPhil
A J Welby, BA
P White, BEd
Mrs C E Wiedermann, MA
Mrs H Williams, BA

[OL] *Old Leysian*

Housemasters and Housemistresses:
Barker House: Mr G J Deudney
Barrett House: Mr M C Gale
Bisseker House: Miss E F Prosser
Dale House: Miss C E Battison
East House: Mr. N. Dix-Pincott
Fen House: Mrs K J Cox
Granta House: Mrs H Williams
Moulton House: Miss A Macpherson
North A House: Mr B A Barton
School House: Mr J Fawcett
West House: Mr A C R Long

Director of Studies: P J Crosfield
Director of Pastoral Care: Mrs Helen Hynde
Senior Tutor: W R Davidson
Director of Wider Curriculum: W J Earl
Chaplain: Revd C J Meharry
Director of Sport: J G Clarke
Examinations Officer: Miss Anna Hunt
Head of Careers: N P Robinson
Head of Outdoor Education: R S McAlinden
Bursar: P D McKeown, BA
Finance Bursar: Mrs M Cooksey, FCCA
Bursar's PA: Ms Karen Barrett
Headmaster's PA: Ms Helen Hammond
Registrar: Ms Nathalie Edge-Partington
Deputy Registrar: E A Munro
Head of Marketing: Mrs A M Cox, CIM
Medical Officers:
Dr A J Stewart, MA, MB BCh, DRCOG, DCH, MRCGP, AFOM
Dr C Lea-Cox, BSc, MB BS, MRCGP, DCH, DFFP
Nursing Staff:
Sister M A Williams, SRN, SCM
Sister L Gate, RGN
Sister J Rhodes, RGN

Lincoln Minster School
Part of United Learning

The Prior Building, Upper Lindum Street, Lincoln, Lincolnshire LN2 5RW

Tel: 01522 551300
Fax: 01522 551310
email: admissions@lincolnminsterschool.co.uk
website: www.lincolnminsterschool.co.uk
Twitter: @MinsterSchool
Facebook: @LincolnMinsterSchool
LinkedIn: /Lincoln-Minster-School

Lincoln Minster School is an independent co-educational HMC day and boarding school for pupils aged 2–18 years. We aim to provide an inspirational all-round education which combines academic achievement with a wealth of co-curricular opportunities.

Structure and Organisation. Lincoln Minster School educates pupils from nursery to A Level over several sites in the heart of historic Lincoln close to the Cathedral and Castle.

A new £10 million Music Centre and Sports Hall, redeveloped and extended Preparatory School and refurbished boarding accommodation have augmented the School's facilities dramatically and are bolstering the School's growing reputation for excellence. With a new strategy to open its doors worldwide, the School is seeking to build on a growing national reputation to become a school of international renown, especially in the field of Music.

Inspired teaching, individual focus and small classes create an excellent learning environment. There is excellent pastoral care and award-winning careers provision designed to equip youngsters for life beyond the classroom. The Nursery and Early Years department attained 'outstanding' status in their current Ofsted inspection report, underlining the quality of provision across all areas.

Lincoln Minster School is a member of United Learning, which owns and manages independent schools and academies across England. There is no doubt that membership of a group of this size gives Lincoln Minster School strength and breadth of contact.

Curriculum. A full range of subjects is offered and the school is proud of its excellent track record of examination success.

The curriculum is supported by a wealth of trips, visits and activities, too numerous to list, plus a comprehensive sports programme to cater for all tastes.

Pupils of all ages are encouraged to develop intellectual curiosity, resilience and self-confidence.

Music. As the Choir School for Lincoln Cathedral, Lincoln Minster School provides for the all-round education of boy and girl choristers. About 70% of pupils receive individual instrument lessons. Music is a focal point of school life and opportunities for public performances abound.

Boarding. Weekly and termly boarding is offered. The large family of boarders is very much at the heart of the School. There are 3 boarding houses, all in close proximity to the School and within the beautiful conservation area of uphill Lincoln.

Admissions. Lincoln Minster School welcomes pupils of a wide range of ability and all faiths. Admission is by interview and report, and subject to availability of a place.

Chorister Auditions, open to boys and girls 7–10 years, are held in November and March. These are worth up to 50% of boarding and tuition fees. Other dates by arrangement. For further details apply to The Registrar.

Scholarships. Art, Sport, Drama and Academic Scholarships are available. Music Scholarships are available for entry into Y7, 9 and 12.

Fees per term (2018–2019). Day (including lunch): Nursery & Early Years £2,799 (all day), Pre-Prep £3,198, Prep £4,040, Seniors £4,608. Termly Boarding: £7,783 (Up to Y6), £9,022 (Y7–13), £10,350 (Overseas Boarders); Weekly/Flexi Boarding: £7,074 (Up to Y6), £8,179 (Y7–13).

Charitable status. Lincoln Minster School is part of United Learning which comprises: UCST (a Company Limited by Guarantee, Registered in England, number 2780748, and a Registered Charity, number 1016538) and ULT (a Company Limited by Guarantee, Registered in England, number 4439859, and an Exempt Charity).

Chair of Local Governing Body: Mrs Linda Heaver

Members:
Professor Matthew Cragoe
Dr Barry Devonald
Mr Steve Gelder
Mrs Cordelia McCartney
Mrs Lydia Rusling
Mrs Sharon Stone
Mr Alexander Thompson
Dr Elinor Vettraino
Mr Robin Wright (*Vice Chair*)

Senior Leadership Team:

Headmaster: **Mr Mark Wallace**, MBA

Deputy Head (*Academic*): Mr R Eastham, MEd, BSc Hons, PGCE
Deputy Head (*Director of Studies*): Mr S Grocott, BSc Hons, PGCE
Assistant Head (*Pastoral*): Mrs J Muir, BA Hons, PGCE
Assistant Head (*Co-Curricular and External Relations*): Mr I McGowan, MEd, BA Hons, PGCE
Head of Preparatory School: Mrs F Thomas, BEd Hons, NPQH
Head of Pre-Preparatory School: Mrs Victoria Whitworth, BSc Hons, QTS
Deputy Head of Preparatory School: Mr Mark Burton, BEd Hons
Bursar: Mr Tim Fenton

Heads of Department:
Mrs K Cook-James, BEd (*Learning Support*)
Mr N Boot, BA Hons, DipLaw, QTS (*History*)
Mrs R Hewitt, MEd, BA Hons, PGCE (*English*)
Mr J Cochrane, BSc, PGCE (*Mathematics*)
Mr C Freckelton, BSc Hons, GTP (*Food Science*)
Mr A Ganfornina, BA Hons, PGCE (*Modern Foreign Languages*)
Mrs A Gilbert, BSc Hons (*PE & Games*)
Mrs R Gladwin, BA Hons, PGCE (*Social Sciences*)
Mrs J Glenn-Batchelor, BA Hons, GTP (*Geography*)
Mr S King, BEng Hons, PGCE (*ICT*)
Mrs H Mason, BSc Hons, PGCE (*Science*)
Mrs N Hutchinson, MEd, BMus Hons, PGCE (*Music*)
Mrs C Servonat-Blanc, BA Hons, PGCE (*Art*, *Graphics & Photography*)
Miss A Tweedale, BA Hons, PGCE (*Business Studies*)
Mrs J Wafer, BA Hons, PGCE (*Drama*)

Executive Assistant to the Headmaster: Miss C Swallow
Registrar: Mrs A Stuffins
Examinations Officer: Mr J Hart, MSc, BSc Hons, PGCE

Lingfield College

St Piers Lane, Lingfield, Surrey RH7 6PH

Tel:	01342 832407
email:	office@lingfieldcollege.co.uk
website:	www.lingfieldcollege.co.uk
Twitter:	@LingfieldColl
Facebook:	@LingfieldCollege

Age Range. 2–18.
Number in School. 922.
Fees per term (2018–2019). £3,750–£5,104. Nursery according to sessions attended.
Situation. The School is located just outside the village of Lingfield on the Surrey, Sussex, Kent border. Lingfield station has a line to London Victoria via Hurst Green, Oxted and Woldingham and is 5 minutes' drive or ten minutes' walk. The School also operates an extensive bus service.

Entry. Senior School: at 11+ and 13+ by Entrance Examination and report from previous school. At 16+ by 6+ GCSEs results and school report.

Scholarships. Available to existing pupils from Year 4. To existing and external pupils at 11+ (Academic, Art, Drama, Music and Sport) and at 13+ (all those available at 11+). Means-tested Bursaries may also be available to Scholars. Scholarships are also available for the Sixth Form.

Academic. In Years 7–9, the pupils study the core subjects and a range of other options within the Lower School Curriculum. Pupils typically take 10 GCSEs which consist of English Language and Literature, Triple Science (although some may take Dual Science), at least one Language and 3 other subjects of their choice which include Computing, Media and Economics. IGCSEs are taken in the majority of subjects. The top Maths set takes Additional Maths as well as IGCSE Mathematics. 23 subjects are offered at A Level and many students also sit the Extended Project Qualification.

The School offers an extensive Scholars' Programme for its Academic Scholars and Award Holders. Seminars are held and special excursions planned as part of the Scholars' enrichment programme. Headmaster's Lectures are held every term. The School is dedicated to a progressive and innovative approach to learning and has invested heavily in digital learning (including a new Mac Suite and i-Pads plus an interactive lecture theatre), whilst valuing traditional methodology.

Pastoral. Pastorally, the School was considered 'outstanding' in its last inspection. Since then, improvements such as smaller tutor groups, more parent focus groups, regular school council and House meetings have further enhanced the feel of a forward-thinking, family-focused school. Communications between the Lingfield village community, staff, students and parents are both open and honest. The School also employs a part-time councillor to support and advise pupils where necessary.

Sport. The School has a sporting ethos of 'Opportunity, Participation and Excellence' and the students have access to a wide range of sporting activities which take place at lunchtime and after school. Students represent the School across a full range of sports at all levels and age groups, as well as participating in regional and national competitions. Hockey, netball and football form the core of major team sport representation in the autumn and spring terms whilst cricket, athletics, tennis and rounders provide the main options for the summer term.

The Rugby Club runs for both the autumn and spring terms and provides an option for those who want to play rugby to represent the School. Golf, equestrian, swimming, cross country, badminton, basketball and table tennis are some of the other competitive team sports available.

Pupils who hold Sport Scholarships benefit from the Elite Sports Mentoring Programme which helps aspiring young athletes fulfil their potential.

Co-curricular. The School has an extensive co-curricular programme with over 140 clubs on offer, taking place both at lunchtime and after school. The clubs vary from arts and crafts to sporting and practical activities and have been designed to assist pupils develop their hobbies, strengths and skills. There are numerous trips for the students to go on. These include departmental trips, languages exchanges and sports tours.

The Duke of Edinburgh's Award programme is particularly popular. More than 90% of pupils take the Bronze Award in Year 10 and about 40% of them proceed to the Silver and Gold Awards.

In the Sixth Form a wide programme of activities is arranged such as Zumba, Ballroom Dancing, Self Defence, Car Maintenance, Orienteering, Cooking, Youth Parliament, Debating, Public Speaking, Critical Thinking and Safe Driving Talks. In addition to this, an extensive range of outside speakers visits the School to hold seminars and lectures, offering pupils the chance to broaden their horizons.

Music. A substantial number of students subscribe to instrumental lessons and participate in the numerous ensembles available to them. The School maintains two orchestras, three choirs, a jazz band, ukulele group and various chamber ensembles, including String, Flute, Percussion, Woodwind and Brass Ensembles, which are run by a team of specialist instrumental tutors. As well as the main school concerts and productions, regular informal recitals are given.

Drama. The Drama Department offers a full range of theatrical experience to its actors and audiences alike. The Department explores challenging texts from the classics and from modern writers which push both the academic and performance boundaries of the students. All pupils are taught Drama in the Lower School and it is a popular and successful option at both GCSE and A Level. They are all accommodated in the School's newly extended and refurbished teaching suite which includes two fully equipped studio spaces, technical, costume and make-up workrooms as well as a specialist Speech and Drama room.

Religion. Lingfield transferred to a lay management in 1987. It maintains its Christian ethos and welcomes students and staff of all faiths, and of none. Its philosophy is based on a strong belief in the development of the whole person. The School has a tradition of providing a caring, friendly and disciplined environment.

Buildings. The School has experienced substantial redevelopment in the last 15 years. Recent improvements include a new Sports Hall, Drama Centre, Science Rooms and Art and Photography facilities. A state-of-the-art Sixth Form Centre was opened in September 2014, offering a university-style lecture theatre, modern, interactive classrooms, atrium coffee shop and student-designed common room. A new Performing Arts Centre opened in September 2017. There are 40 acres of grounds which include 4 football pitches, a floodlit astro and cricket nets.

Charitable status. Lingfield Notre Dame is a Registered Charity, number 295598. It exists to provide education.

Chair of Governors : Mrs S Rutherford

Headmaster: **Mr R W Bool**, BA Hons, MBA

Deputy Heads:
Mrs J Richards, MA
Mr D Snowden, MA

Assistant Heads:
Mr I Copeland, BSc Hons
Mrs A Folkard, BSc Hons
Mr S Casey, BA Hons

Heads of Departments:
Academic PE: Mr Joe Radmore, BA Hons
Art: Miss K Muir, MA, BA Hons
Boys' Games: Mr N Harrison, BA Hons, QTS
Chemistry: Mr Paul Rickard, BSc Hons
Computer Science: Mr B Monk, BSc Hons
Drama: Mr Josh McEwan, MA ,LGSM
Economics: Mr R Dewey, BA Hons
English: Mrs A Saunders, BA Hons
Food & Nutrition: Mrs S Jenn, BSc Hons
MFL, French: Mr R Appleton, BA Hons
Geography: Mrs A Greetham, MSc, BSc Hons
German: Mrs B Edwards, BA Hons
Girls' Games: Mrs L Nicol, BSc Hons
History: Miss S Allen, BA Hons
Learning Support: Mrs S Sevier, BA Hons
Mathematics: Mr M Maranzano, BSc Hons

Media: Mrs S House, BA Hons
Spanish: Mrs Carballo-Varela, MA
Physics: Mr C Fast, BEd, BSc
Psychology: Miss R Hase, BSc Hons
Religion and Philosophy: Mr A Gaunt, BA
Science, Biology: Mr J Grant, BSc Hons

Prep School:
Headmaster: Mr R W Bool, BA, MBA
Head of Prep School: Mrs J Shackel, BA Hons (*SENDCO*)
Head of Academic, Prep School: Mr James Walton, MEd,
    BA Hons QTS

Peripatetic Staff for:
Bassoon, Brass, Cello, Clarinet, Classical Guitar, Drums,
Flute, French Horn, Guitar, Harp, LAMDA, Oboe, Percussion, Piano, Saxophone, Trombone, Viola, Violin, Voice.

Finance Manager: Mrs A Brassett
Marketing Manager: Ms M Morgan
Registrar: Mrs M O'Neill
Headmaster's PA and Clerk to Governors: Mrs T Unwin
Prep School Head's PA: Mrs S Wood

Lomond School

**10 Stafford Street, Helensburgh, Argyll and Bute
G84 9JX**

Tel: 01436 672476
Fax: 01436 678320
email: admissions@lomondschool.com
website: www.lomondschool.com
Twitter: @LomondSchool
Facebook: @lomondschool

A superb quality of life. Lomond School is a co-educational independent school, for children aged 3 to 18 years, positioned in the elegant suburbs of the coastal town of Helensburgh located only 10 minutes from Loch Lomond and the Trossachs National Park. We make the most of our unique location by providing and encouraging participation in a wide range of opportunities for outdoor learning, sports and activities. Students can enjoy a superb quality of life in a beautiful and safe environment.

Personalised Education. At Lomond School we believe passionately that education should be about supporting our young people to develop and grow, both academically and personally, as rounded individuals with strong values who are ultimately prepared to embark confidently and successfully on their life beyond Lomond School.

We uphold this commitment with six **Guiding Principles** which are delivered throughout our curriculum and co-curriculum. These include: Internationalism; Environmentalism; Adventure; Leadership; Lifelong Learning and Service. To find out more visit our website at www.lomondschool.com.

Inclusive Ethos. Our focus is on preparing our students for their future by ensuring that they learn the skills necessary to be successful in the 21st century whilst developing the traditional values and qualities that they require to be responsible and active global citizens.

We provide small class sizes, an extensive programme of extra-curricular activities, attention to the individual and a strong record of academic achievement which opens the door to allow new experiences, skills and talents to be explored. All aspects of development are accorded importance, be they academic, musical, dramatic, sporting or in wider outdoor activities.

We were one of the first schools in the UK to integrate an ICT strategy which provides all our P6 to S6 students with their own personal iPad.

The Lomond Family. Our experienced pastoral care team ensures the welfare and onward progression of all of our students. Our young people are well known by staff and teachers and we see ourselves as a large family where any issues or problems are identified and dealt with promptly and effectively.

Extra-curricular and Outdoor Learning. Our location means that there is a particular emphasis on outdoor pursuits. The Duke of Edinburgh's Award is, without doubt, a significant feature and we have enjoyed great success carrying out expeditions both locally and abroad. Many of our trips and excursions revolve around our passion for the outdoors and have included trekking in Morocco, canoeing in Norway and skiing in Austria.

We also build many cultural and educational trips into the school year with visits to Paris, Berlin, Brussels and Iceland, as well as Hockey and Rugby tours to South Africa or more locally. We support and encourage our young people to make the most of the opportunities available, recognising both the immediate and long-term benefit of the personal development these experiences and activities can offer.

Living at Lomond. Our boarding facility adds a distinctive dimension to the school; the mix of cultures and backgrounds enriches our curriculum and co-curriculum, supporting all of our pupils to develop their global awareness and understanding.

Our infrastructure boasts a mix of modern, purpose-built structure and characterful listed buildings, which make for an inspirational setting for our young people. We continually invest in our facilities and take a cutting-edge approach to every new project we initiate.

Entry and Scholarships. Means-tested bursaries are available for entry between T2 and S6 with fee assistance ranging from 10% to 100% depending on circumstances. In addition, means-tested bursaries are available for services personnel with children who board at Lomond.

Lomond is a non-selective school. Part of our admission process, however, is an assessment in Mathematics and English for 11 to 18 year-olds. For younger pupils, placement in classes is the main requirement, whilst for senior pupils reports and examination results are given due weighting.

Fees per term (2018–2019). Tuition: £2,343 (Nursery, 5 full days, net of Local Council Funding), £2,880 (Junior 1–2), £3,360 (Junior 3–5), £3,660 (Transitus 1), £3,900 (Transitus 2), £3,990 (Senior School).

Boarding (inc Tuition Fees): £9,250.

A levy of £50 per pupil per term is payable along with tuition fees.

Charitable status. Lomond School Ltd is a Registered Charity, number SC007957. It exists to provide education for boys and girls.

Board of Governors:
Chair: Mr A J D Hope, LLB
Vice-Chair: Mr C Burnet, LLB, CA
Professor R Brown, BSc Hons, PhD
Mrs D Cook
Mr S Etchells, LLB
Mr D Girdwood
Mr A Hart
Mrs L Pender, BA, PGCE
Mrs A Stanley-Whyte, LLB

Staff:

Principal: **Mrs J Urquhart**, BSc Hons, PGCE, MEd

Academic Depute: Mrs C Chisholm, MA Hons, PGCE
Pastoral Depute: Mr A B H Minnis, MA Hons, PGCE,
    Cert PP
Head of Junior School: Mrs A Lawn, BSc Hons, PGCE
Bursar: Ms Anne Sheehan, BA, MSc, CSBM
Marketing: Mrs J Scullion and Mrs L Mathis
Admissions: Mrs J Dixon ACIM

* *Head of Department*

Subject Teachers – Secondary:

Art & Design:
*Mrs D Aitken, BA Hons, Cert Ed
Mrs L Jack, BA Hons, PGCE

Business Studies & Economics:
*Mrs K Ferguson, BA Hons, PGDE

Drama:
Miss S Gibbs MA PGDE

EFL:
Mrs J Robertson, BEd

English:
*Mrs E Kydd-Corr, BA, PGCE
Dr M Cotter-MacDonald, MA Hons, PhD, PGDE
Mrs M McKillop, MA Hons, MPhil, PGCE
Mrs C Chisholm, MA Hons, PGCE

Geography:
*Mrs N McKenzie, MA Hons, PGCE

Graphic Communication:
Mr J Stewart, BSc, PGDE

Health & Food Technology:
Mrs N Harwood, BSc Hons, PGCE, MEd

History and Modern Studies:
*Mrs S Guy, MA Hons, PGCE
Mr J Forrest BA Hons PGDE
Mr A B H Minnis, MA Hons, PGCE, Cert PP

Learning Support:
*Mr H Hunter, BA Hons, PGDE
Mrs S Bell, BEd, PGDE

Mathematics:
*Mr G Macleod, BSc Hons, MEd, CMath, CSci, FIMA,
    PGCE, Adv Dip Hist Oxon
Mrs E Cameron, BSc Hons, PGCE
Mrs L McGarry, BSc Hons, PGCE

Modern Languages:
*Mr A Greig, MA Hons, PGCE, PG Dip
Mr N Mackay, MA, BA/BEd Jt Hons
Ms I Skowronski, LLCE English, PGDE

Music:
*Mr D Fleming, BMus Hons, PGCE
Miss M-C Brown, BA Hons, PGDE

Physical Education:
*Mrs M G Taylor, BEd
Mr C Dunlop, BEd Hons
Mr S Louden, BA, MEd, PGCE
Miss F Arthur

RME:
Mrs C Greig, BA Jt Hons, PGCE, Dip Ed Tech

Science:
Biology:
*Mr T Chambers, BSc Hons, MSc, PGDE
Ms K Griffin, BSc, PGCE
Chemistry:
*Mr D L Dodson, BSc Hons, Cert Ed
Miss M Ward, BSc Hons, PGCE

Physics:
*Dr A MacBeath, BEng Hons, PhD, PGDE
Mr A Meikle, BSc Hons, MSc, PGCE

Careers Advisor:
Mr D L Dodson, BSc Hons, Cert Ed

School Nurse:
Mrs Lesley Serpell, RGN, MPH

Head of Junior School:
Mrs A Lawn, BSc Hons, PGCE

Class Teachers – Junior School and Transitus:

Class Teachers – Transitus:
Mrs C Greig, BA Jt Hons, PGCE, Dip Ed Tech
Mr S Collins, BMus, PGCE
Dr M Cotter-MacDonald, MA Hons, PhD, PGDE

Class Teachers – Clarendon
Mrs J Fullarton, BA Hons, PGCE
Mr J Grafton, BEd Hons
Mrs J Macleod, BEd Hons, MEd, Dip RSA, Dip APS, Dip
    Ed Lead, SQH
Mrs K Muggoch, MA Hons, PGDE
Mrs L LeGood, MA Hons, PGCE
Mrs S Bell, BEd PGDE

Nursery/Pre-School Group:
Head of Nursery: Mrs L Canero, BA, PGDE
Mrs J McArthur, SNNEB
Mrs G Thomas, HNC
Miss J Wardle
Mrs E Nelson
Mrs K Ross

Lord Wandsworth College

Long Sutton, Hook, Hampshire RG29 1TB
Tel: 01256 862201 (Main Office)
            01256 860348 (Headmaster)
            01256 860200 (Admissions)
email: info@lordwandsworth.org
website: www.lordwandsworth.org

Motto: *Vincit Perseverantia*

Lord Wandsworth College is a co-educational secondary
school for 620 pupils between the ages of 11 and 18.
Approximately 55% of the pupils are boarders, either full,
weekly or flexi.

Location and accessibility. The school occupies a magnificent rural setting on the North Hampshire/Surrey border
just five miles from Junction 5 of the M3 and only an hour
from London by road or rail.

History. Lord Wandsworth died in 1912 and left a large
sum of money for the foundation of a school. The College
that bears his name now occupies a 1,200 acre site. The Lord
Wandsworth Foundation awards a number of places annually to children who have lost the support of one or both parents through death, divorce or separation with priority to
those who have lost a parent through death.

Mission statement. LWC is a socially inclusive non-
denominational boarding and day Foundation school for
boys and girls. We focus on the needs of each individual,
while developing in each child a concern for others and a
love for and loyalty towards the school community. We
ensure that each pupil shapes their values and aspirations
within a stimulating and supportive environment, and strive
constantly to improve the quality of teaching and learning.
We aim to equip pupils with character attributes, passion,

resourcefulness, independence, skills, knowledge and qualifications so they can become the best possible version of themselves and make a great contribution to a changing world.

The outstanding features of the school are

- that almost all academic staff live on campus allowing them to provide a high level of pastoral care;
- that Character Education is imbedded into the curriculum and co-curriculum. By promoting Character Education, we believe we will give all pupils the best chance of realising their full potentials.
- that all pupils, whether full, weekly, flexi boarding or day, belong to one of the eight houses and are fully integrated into the social life of the school;
- that the school is purpose-built with an outstanding range of facilities for both academic and extracurricular activities;
- that the school is an unusually unpretentious, happy and caring community.

Curriculum. The aim of the curriculum is to provide a full and flexible range of subjects to fit the needs of each individual. The school's policy is to follow closely the National Curriculum.

Subjects taught to GCSE are: English (Language and Literature), French, Geography, Mathematics, History, Latin, Classical Civilisation, Drama, Physics, Chemistry, Biology, Spanish, German, Art, Music, Design & Technology, Computer Science and Religious Studies.

Most pupils continue into the Sixth Form where the subjects taught at A level are: English, History, Geography, Economics, Business Studies, Classical Civilisation, Music, Latin, French, Spanish, German, Government and Politics, Physics, Chemistry, Biology, Mathematics, Further Mathematics, Art, Design, Theatre Studies, PE, and Psychology. We also offer the EPQ and BTech Sport.

Games. The school lays great store by its games involvement and has a local and national reputation for many of its pursuits. The main boys' games are rugby, hockey and cricket and for girls hockey, netball and cricket. In addition swimming, athletics, tennis, football, golf, cross-country running and canoeing are all on offer.

Drama. Drama has a high profile and several shows are staged each year. There is a musical production every other year as well as showcases, reviews and workshops. Pupils are encouraged to participate in all fields of drama either acting, writing, set design, lighting, stage management, prop-making or sound.

Music. There is a large variety of instrumental ensembles, including a swing band, chamber and rock groups. Pupils sing in two choirs. Tuition is available in singing, all orchestral instruments, piano, percussion and guitar. Musicians regularly perform formally and informally both within school and at local venues.

Other activities. There is an extensive extracurricular programme. Some of the activities on offer are: Cookery, Chess, Community Service, Pottery, Drama clubs, Mountain Biking, Dance, Photography, Art clubs, Riding, Life-saving, Debating and Climbing.

The Duke of Edinburgh's Award scheme is thriving and the College has its own licence to run the scheme. There is an active CCF programme for Year 10 pupils and above which has an Army and Air Force Section.

Organisation. There is a two or three form entry at age 11. For the first two years all pupils are in the co-educational Junior House. At 13 there is another entry, mainly from children who have taken Common Entrance. All houses are in the charge of Houseparents assisted by a team of tutors and matrons.

Scholarships and Awards on offer are:

First Form (Year 7): Academic, Performing Arts (Music, Drama and Dance) and Sport.

Third Form (Year 9): Academic, Performing Arts (Music, Drama and Dance), Art, Sport and All-Rounder

Sixth Form (Year 12): Academic, Performing Arts (Music, Drama and Dance), Art, Sport and All-Rounder

Foundation Awards are available for children who have lost the support of one or both parents through death, divorce or separation.

Further details for all scholarships and awards may be obtained from the Admissions Office.

Fees per term (2018–2019). Senior Full Boarding £11,100, Senior Weekly Boarding £10,600, Senior Flexi Boarding £9,200, Senior Day £7,820, Junior Full Boarding £9,750, Junior Weekly Boarding £9,430, Junior Flexi Boarding £8,260, Junior Day £6,810.

Charitable status. Lord Wandsworth College is a Registered Charity, number 1143359. It exists to provide education for boys and girls.

Chairman of Governors: R J Hannington

The Governing Body consists of 12 governors.

***Headmaster*: Adam Williams**, MA

Senior Deputy Head: Alex Battison, MA
Deputy Head, Teaching and Learning: Stephen Badger, MA Cantab
Deputy Head, ISI Compliance, Inspection & Academic Systems: Jackie Davies, MA
Bursar: Richard Gammage, MSc, MA

Teaching Staff and Assistants:
† *Houseparent*

Vic Allan, BA (*Head of Performing Arts*)
Marie-France Allen (*French Assistant*)
Sharon Allmark, BA (*Careers & Higher Education*)
Chris Andrews, BA (*Computing, Head of Digital Strategy*)
Sarah Badger, MA (*Head of French and MFL*)
Pippa Battison, BA (*History*)
David Beven (*Sports Assistant, Head of Cricket*)
Sue Brown, MA (*Librarian*)
†Oliver Butterworth, BA (*Economics*)
Jennifer Cooper, BA (*English*)
Kazuko Copeman, (*Business Studies*)
Diane Crichton, BSc (*Chemistry & Head of 4th Form*)
†Kate Cuff, BA (*Drama*)
Rachel De La Cruz, MA (*Head of Spanish*)
Alice Greer, MA (*English*)
Lauren Griffin, BMus, MA (*Head of Music*)
Sally Dawson-Couper, MA (*Head of Mathematics, Assistant Deputy Head, Academic Systems*)
Natalie Eley, BSc (*Chemistry*)
Margaret Ellwood, MA (*Learning Support*)
Alison Fisher, BA (*EAL*)
Russell Fisher, BA (*Design and Technology*)
Max Gaulton, BEcon (*Mathematics*)
Elisabeth Greenaway, BSc (*Geography*)
Alex Hamilton, MA (*Head of Latin and Classics*)
Joely Harris, BA (*English*)
Esther Haydock, BSc (*Physics*)
Ben Hazell (*Sports Assistant*)
†James Hine, BA (*History*)
Oscar Hird, MA (*Latin and Classics*)
Holly Hunter-Wright, BA (*Art & Head of 3rd Form*)
†Chris Irvine, BSc (*Head of Physics*)
Nicole Jinadasa, BSc (*Chemistry*)
Richard Kimber, BEng (*Mathematics*)
Beverley Lane, BSc (*Mathematics*)
Andrew Lay, BSc (*Head of Economics*)
Sian Lewis, BSc (*Head of Psychology*)

Claire Liggins, BA (*Head of Design & Technology, Assistant Deputy Head, Pastoral*)
Jonathan Lilley, BA (*Head of History*)
Rebecca Lodge, BA (*Design and Technology*)
Jeni Loud, BSc (*Physics & Chemistry, Assistant Deputy Head, Teaching & Learning*)
Samantha Ludlow, BSc (*Geography*)
Audley Lumsden, BSc (*Physics*)
Pete Maidment, BA (*Chaplain*)
Kirsty Mason, DPhil (*Latin and Classics*)
Jessica McKinnon, BA (*German, Deputy Head of Co-Curriculum*)
Lucie McNabb, BA (*Head of German, Head of 5th Form*)
Chris Millington, BA (*ICT & Computer Science*)
†Jane Mitchell, BA (*German*)
Graham Mobbs, BA (*Head of Art*)
Vincent Murtagh, BSc, PhD (*Head of Chemistry*)
Gill Neighbour (*Head of 1st Form & PE*)
Jan Norgaard, BSc (*Head of Geography*)
Aaron Parker, (*Assistant Head of Music*)
Harriet Paskell, BSc (*Geography*)
Sanna Pollard, MA (*Biology*)
†Kay Price, BA (*History*)
†Robin Pyper, BSc (*PE*)
Chris Radmann, BA (*Head of English, Head of 6th Form*)
Lesley Radmann, BA (*English*)
James Rayner, BA (*Sports Assistant, Head of Rugby*)
Noel Reeson, BA (*French & Spanish*)
Tim Richardson, BA (*Head of PE & Co-Curriculum*)
Zoe Richardson, MA (*English*)
Judit Schlosser, MA (*Mathematics*)
Craig Scott, BSc (*Biology*)
Dan Scott, BA (*Spanish*)
Shatrugan Sookhun, DPhil (*Mathematics*)
Helen Shedden, BA (*English & EPQ*)
†Tom Shedden, BA (*History*)
Soma Singh, BA (*Head of Sport*)
Susan Stevens, BA (*Art*)
Eleanor Swingler (*Art*)
Richard Thorne, BA, MSc (*Head of Science*)
Jane Turner, BA (*Learning Support*)
Jonathan Turney, MA (*Head of Biology*)
Edward Walker, BSc (*Business Studies*)
Ian Watson, MEng (*Mathematics*)
Christian White, MA (*Head of Philosophy & Ethics*)
Cameron Wicks, BA (*Sports Assistant*)
David Widdowson, BSc (*Mathematics*)
Ian Williams, MA (*English*)
Colin Wiskin (*Ceramics*)
Yiaoou Williams, BSc (*Learning Support*)

Librarian: Sue Brown

Director of Admissions & Marketing: Mary Hicks

Medical Officers:
Dr R Assadourian, MB BS, BSc Hons, MRCGP, DRCOG, DFFP

Loretto School

Linkfield Road, Musselburgh, East Lothian EH21 7RE

Tel: School: 0131 653 4444
          Headmaster: 0131 653 4441
          Admissions: 0131 653 4455

Fax: School: 0131 653 4445
          Admissions: 0131 653 4401
email: admissions@loretto.com
website: www.loretto.com

A small School, big on heart, big on ambition

- Scotland's oldest boarding school, founded in 1827.
- An independent, private boarding and day school for girls and boys, from 0 to 18 years.
- Set in a safe, leafy, spacious, 85 acre campus in Musselburgh; the school enjoys all the advantages of its rural setting.
- Globally connected, with the convenience and opportunities of being just 9 kilometres / 6 miles from Edinburgh, its international airport, rail and road networks.
- Offering the traditional British / English curriculum of GCSEs and A Levels, and ranked in the top 7% of schools nationally for A Level.
- 97% of pupils enter the University of their choice, such as Oxford, Cambridge, St Andrews, and Durham.
- One of Scotland's leading schools: a small school, big on heart, and big on ambition.
- Welcoming 600 pupils, 400 in the Senior School, 200 in the Junior School and Nursery.
- Boarders (75% of Senior School pupils) reside in six Houses with all they need to feel at home and benefit from excellent pastoral care
- An excellent staff to pupil ratio (1:7)
- Every pupil is known personally, and can grow and develop wherever their interests lie.
- A distinctive emphasis on the full development of the individual in mind, body and spirit.
- Exceptional facilities, bespoke to learning and teaching, sport, drama, dance, art and music.
- A dedicated Sixth Form Centre
- Extensive Sports programme with specialised coaches in major sports including Cricket, Hockey, Lacrosse, Rugby and more
- An industry-leading Golf Academy with indoor and outdoor centres, providing every pupil with an unmatched opportunity to develop their talent.

Fees per term (2018–2019). Boarding: £7,445–£11,420; Flexi Boarding (3 nights p/w): £6,320–£9,485; Day (including meals): £5,600–£7,775.

Admission. Loretto School's Admissions procedure aims to ensure that boys and girls who join Loretto are able to be happy, successful and secure within its academic, cultural and pastoral environment, whether they are boarders or day pupils.

Applications are accepted for entry into most years in the School except Upper Sixth (Year 13).

The selection criteria include provision of satisfactory evidence, through the School's own age-appropriate assessment tests, of academic ability sufficient to access the School curriculum, and a satisfactory reference from the applicant's current school. Loretto is academically selective but also recognises the central value of co-curricular activities, and enthusiasm in these fields is expected and encouraged.

Scholarships and Bursaries. Academic, Art, Drama, Golf, Music, Piping and Sports Scholarships are available. Means-tested bursaries up to 105% are also available.

To find out more, please visit www.loretto.com or contact the Admissions Department, Tel: 0131 653 4455, email: admissions@loretto.com.

Loretto Junior School. Please see Loretto Junior School's entry in the IAPS section.

Chairman of Governors: Mr Peter McCutcheon

Headmaster: **Dr Graham R W Hawley**, BSc Hons, PGCE, PhD

Head of Junior School: Mr Andrew Dickenson

To view Loretto Senior School's Staff Directory, please visit www.loretto.com/staff-directory

Loughborough Grammar School

Burton Walks, Loughborough, Leicestershire LE11 2DU

Tel: 01509 233233
Fax: 01509 218436
email: grammar.admissions@lsf.org
website: www.lsf.org/grammar

Motto: *Vires acquirit eundo*

Loughborough Grammar School was founded in 1495 by Thomas Burton, Merchant of the Staple of Calais, though it is probable that the Trustees of the Town Charity were managing a free school well before that date. The School is itself part of a larger 'family' known as the Loughborough Schools Foundation. Situated in the spacious and attractive grounds surrounding the Grammar School are Loughborough High School for Girls (*see GSA entry*), and Fairfield Prep School, our co-educational preparatory school (*see IAPS entry*). Nearby is Loughborough Amherst School, a co-educational secondary school (*see ISA entry*). Links between all four schools are very strong.

There are just under 1,000 boys in the School, including 60 boarders.

The School moved to its present site of some 27 acres in 1852 and is situated away from the centre of the town in attractive grounds containing the beautiful avenues of trees known as Burton Walks. At its centre is a handsome Victorian College quadrangle. There has been an impressive development programme in recent years – a new Music department was opened in September 2006; a new state-of-the-art Chemistry building in September 2009; a refurbished and extended Biology building in September 2011; a new Physics building in September 2012 and a new Mathematics building and boarding provision in 2013, completing the Science Park.

Admission. Entry to the School is by the school's own examination at all levels and also by Common Entrance at 13+. Sixth Form entry is dependent on GCSE results and interview with the Headmaster and other senior staff.

Boarding Arrangements. Boys are admitted to Denton House at the age of 10 or over; Sixth Form boys are in School House. Termly and Weekly boarding is available.

Fees per term (2018–2019). Day £4,183 (includes books and stationery); Full Boarding £9,584 (includes laundry, board, medical attendance).

The School offers a 25% boarding fee remission to sons of HM Forces and sons of Clergy.

Scholarships and Bursaries. A number of Scholarships are offered, based on performance in the Entrance Examination. Sixth Form scholarships are based on GCSE results. Music Scholarships are also awarded at 11+, 13+ (Common Entrance), and 16+ (Sixth Form). There are also a number of bursaries, dependent on parental income.

Foundation Bursaries. School Assisted Places (up to 100% fee remission) are based on financial need and Entrance Examination performance. Such places are means-tested and an application for one requires the completion of a form declaring income and a home visit.

Religious Teaching. The School is non-denominational though there is a strong Christian tradition. The Chaplain teaches Religion and Philosophy but is available for boys at any convenient time. On Wednesdays, Boarders attend the School Chapel and, on request, are prepared for Confirmation by the Chaplain.

Curriculum. The aim of the School is to give a broad and balanced general education to GCSE with greater specialisation afterwards. In Year 6, boys follow a curriculum similar to that of their last year of junior school; subjects included are English, Mathematics, French, Art, Sciences, Drama, Design and Technology, Geography, IT, History, Music, PE, RE. In Year 7, all boys study English, Mathematics, Biology, Chemistry, Physics, French, History, Geography, Latin, and Music. Additionally, all boys have lessons in RE, PE, PSHE and Games. In Year 8, Design and Technology is introduced and, in addition to French, boys choose a second language from either German or Spanish, and the boys are taught separate sciences. In Year 9 pupils continue with both MFLs, and make some choices from their existing subjects as well as Ancient Greek and Drama.

In Years 10 and 11, for GCSE, boys study English Language and Literature, Mathematics, a modern Foreign Language, and at least two sciences. They also choose three subjects from an extensive options list. Some more able boys study a tenth subject.

The Sixth Form contains 300 boys. In Year 12, boys study 4 subjects to AS Level and in Year 13 they will take 3 or 4 of them to A2 Level. A wide range of subjects and combinations is available, along with General Studies, EPQ, Games and other activities. There are some joint teaching lessons with the Girls' High School.

Games. The School has an excellent First XI field and a junior field of over 13 acres within its precinct and within two miles are well-equipped playing fields extending to nearly 70 acres.

The School runs teams in Rugby, Soccer, Hockey, Cricket, Athletics, Tennis, Cross Country, Swimming, Badminton, Fencing and Squash. In addition, there is a Sailing and Canoe Club. The School prides itself in an array of Mind Sports, with teams in Bridge, Chess, Go and Chinese Chess.

Combined Cadet Force. There is an efficient and keen CCF of about 250 boys from Year 10 onwards, run on an optional basis, with 17 Officers, an SSI and a RQMS. Boys have the choice of joining the RAF, Army or Royal Navy Sections. The CCF complex is purpose-built with excellent facilities and many varied and Adventurous Training courses are available to members.

Scouts. There is a flourishing Scout Troop of 35 boys and 1 Scouter.

The Duke of Edinburgh's Award. Over 250 boys are actively involved in the scheme and each year a large number earn Gold, Silver and Bronze awards.

Music (of which much is joint with the Girls' High School) takes place in our award-winning Music department, which has "All-Steinway School" status, and instrumental ensembles involve all the schools in the Foundation. For boys at LGS, there are 4 Choirs and 26 instrumental ensembles, including 3 Orchestras, 2 Wind Bands, 2 Jazz Bands and nearly twenty smaller instrumental ensembles, which each rehearse weekly. Our top ensembles perform on the national stage regularly, including in the MfY Schools' Prom at the Royal Albert Hall (2017), and there are annual music tours for instrumental and vocal groups alike: recent tours have taken in Barcelona (2014), Truro (2015), Prague (2016) and Belgium (2017). Our sacred choirs sing services regularly at cathedrals around the UK, having performed in Southwell Minster, as well as Coventry, Birmingham, Leicester, Gloucester and Worcester Cathedrals in the past couple of years. We put on a large-scale concert each spring at De Montfort Hall, involving all Year 7 pupils and other choirs performing a choral masterpiece (Carmina Burana, Mozart's Requiem, Verdi's Requiem) with our symphony orchestra.

Drama. The School has a fine Studio/Theatre and all boys in Years 6, 7 and 8 participate in a dramatic production. After that, there are productions for other age groups in conjunction with the Girls' High School each term.

Careers. Careers advisors are available to inform boys on options for their futures, with special regard to University or Professional careers. The School is a member of the Independent Schools Careers Organisation.

Academic Successes. An average of 10 boys per year gain admission to Oxford and Cambridge, and over 98% each year begin degree courses at Universities.

The Loughburians Alumni Association. All former pupils of the Loughborough Schools Foundation have automatic free membership to the alumni association. All enquiries to loughburians@lsf.org.

Charitable status. Loughborough Schools Foundation is a Registered Charity, number 1081765, and a Company Limited by Guarantee, registered in England, number 4038033. Registered Office: 3 Burton Walks, Loughborough, Leicestershire LE11 2DU.

Governing Body:
Chairman: Mr G P Fothergill, BA

School Board Chairs:
Professor A Dodson, BSc Hons, PhD, DSc
Professor J Ketley, BSc Hons, PhD Bham, CBiol, MSB
Mrs G Richards, BA Hons, MEd, Hon EdD
Admiral Sir Trevor Soar, KCB, OBE, DEng Hon, FCMI

Co-optative Governors:
Mr P Alexander
Professor R Allison, BA PhD
Mrs E K Critchley, MA Oxon
Professor J Feather, MA, PhD, FRSA
Mrs M Gershlick
Lady Jennifer Gretton, DVCO, JP, LLD Hon, DUni Hon, Hon DLitt
Mr R Harrison, MA Cantab, Dip Arch RIBA
Mr P M Jackson, FIMI
Mr A D Jones, BA, FCA
Mrs R J E Limb, OBE, MA Cantab
Mr P Middleton, MA Oxon, BA Hons Oxon
Mrs A Murphy, MA
Mrs P O'Neill, MA Cantab
Mr P Snelling
Mr J Stone
Mrs L Webb, BSc Hons

Nominated Governor: Sister C Leydon

Ex-Officio Governors:
Dr A de Bono, MA, MB, FRCGP, FFOM (*Bursary Committee member*)
Dr P J B Hubner, MB, FRCP, DCH, FACC, FESC (*Bursary Committee member*)
Mr H M Pearson, DL, DUniv Hon, BA Econ (*Bursary Committee*)

Chief Operating Officer: J W Doherty, MIoD

Senior Leadership Team:

Headmaster: **Mr D J Byrne**, MA Cantab, MEd Trinity College Cambridge

Deputy Head: Dr T G Willmott, BSc, PhD London, MBA Leicester

Deputy Head Pastoral: Mrs H M Foster, BA Greenwich, MEd Buckingham

Deputy Head Academic: Mr W J Perry, BSc Warwick

Assistant Head Wellbeing & Learning: Mr R B Parish, BSc, MSc Bristol

Assistant Head Co-Curricular: Dr A D Waters, BSc Cambridge, PhD Bristol

Head of Sixth Form: Miss S H Jenkins, BA UCL

Director of Admissions/Marketing: Mr C J Feakes, BSc Leicester, MSc Leicester

Magdalen College School
Oxford

Cowley Place, Oxford OX4 1DZ
Tel: 01865 242191
Fax: 01865 240379
email: admissions@mcsoxford.org
website: www.mcsoxford.org

Motto: *Sicut Lilium*

Magdalen College School consists of 595 boys aged 7–16 with a co-educational Sixth Form of 320. Academic standards are amongst the highest in the country and there is a strong emphasis on study beyond the syllabus, especially in the Waynflete Studies programme. This allows Sixth Formers to develop a personal project, which is finally supervised by university academics. Almost all pupils go on to higher education with about a third each year progressing to Oxford or Cambridge. The school seeks to develop the individuality and interests of each pupil. There is a strong emphasis on extracurricular activity, with particularly proud traditions in sport, music and drama.

History. Founded by William of Waynflete, Magdalen College School opened in 1480, and rapidly acquired an international reputation. Early Masters included Thomas Wolsey, early pupils Richard Hooker, John Foxe, Thomas More and William Tyndale. The school, which from an early stage provided choristers for the College choir, was accommodated entirely in College until the late 19th Century, when expanding numbers led to the acquisition and erection of buildings on the other side of the Cherwell, opposite the University Botanical Gardens and adjacent to St Hilda's College. Today's school still occupies this picturesque site.

Buildings. The school buildings include a Chapel which also serves as a theatre, a library, classrooms, science laboratories, Music School, Sports Complex, Design and Technology Rooms and an art department. In June 2001, a £2m sports complex was opened and in 2005, the school opened its new Sir Basil Blackwell Library. In Autumn 2008 a new building was opened which houses a modern dining hall, the Art and Design department, Senior Common Room and reception area. In 2012, the Sports Hall was extended to incorporate a studio and additional classrooms, and a climbing wall was added. A new state-of-the-art Sixth Form Centre was completed in October 2017, including a cafeteria, study space and offices as well as the central social space.

Pastoral. From 7–11, boys are in form groups. Their Tutor is responsible for day-to-day care, pastoral welfare and academic progress. Boys from age 11 and Sixth Form girls are allocated to one of the six Houses. A Housemaster or Tutor in charge of each section is responsible for the pastoral and academic welfare of pupils in his or her Houseroom. The Heads of Departments, SENCO, Chaplain and Matron also play key roles in the pastoral organisation.

Organisation and Curriculum. All boys study a core of subjects to GCSE level, consisting of English, Maths, Science and at least one modern foreign language. In addition, there is a wide variety of options taken by pupils in their

GCSE years including Latin and Greek, Geography, German, Spanish, History, Computing and Art. There is no streaming and very little setting.

Pupils study four subjects in the Lower Sixth and sit rigorous internal exams in the Trinity Term. Pupils have the opportunity to focus on three subjects in the Upper Sixth, but a significant proportion sit four or even five A Levels. MCS has a busy curriculum in the Sixth Form; as well as their A Levels, all pupils complete an independent research project (Waynflete Studies), have Games sessions and take part in our Community Service Programme. The provision is further enriched by a Thinking Skills programme and by regular seminars and lectures delivered by members of the MCS community and visiting speakers.

Careers. Careers Aptitude Tests are offered to all boys in the Upper Fourth Form, and there is a regular programme of careers workshops with support programmes for specific careers, e.g. Medicine. Most pupils undertake a work experience placement at the end of the Fifth Form; an extensive programme offering entrepreneurship opportunities from Year 9 upwards is in development.

Sports and Societies. In addition to Physical Education, which is taught in the curriculum, games play a major part in the School. Major sports are rugby in the Michaelmas Term, hockey and rowing in Hilary, and cricket, rowing and tennis in the Trinity Term. Other sports include basketball, netball, football, fencing, cross-country, sailing and athletics. There are Army and Air Force sections of the CCF and a Community Service Organisation. Many pupils participate in the Duke of Edinburgh's Award scheme.

The main playing field, surrounded by the River Cherwell, adjoins the grounds of School House and covers 11 acres. The school also enjoys the daily use of the adjacent Christ Church playing fields and regularly uses a number of other university sporting and cultural facilities. In addition, the school has use of the Magdalen College sports fields one mile from the School. Rowing takes place on the Cherwell from the school grounds.

Music is extremely important in the school and there is a large Choral Society, a Madrigal Group, Senior and Junior Orchestras, a Jazz Band and other ensembles. Many pupils are involved in drama and there are several productions in the year, including performances at theatres around Oxford. There are many other societies and clubs covering cultural and recreational activities. The main school concert is held annually in the Sheldonian Theatre. The school is the founder and main sponsor of the Oxford Festival of the Arts, which features events throughout the City and pupils throughout the county take part.

Admissions. The main entry points are at 7, 11, 13 and 16. Around 25 boys are taken at 7, a further 15 or so at 8 and 9, and about 70 at the age of 11. Up to 25 boys are taken at 13. Around 60 boys and girls join the school directly into the Sixth Form.

Admission at ages 7, 8, 9 and 11 is by a School Entrance Examination held in January or February each year.

Admission at age 13 is by pre-test at 11 followed by the Common Entrance Examination for most candidates at preparatory schools and by a School Entrance Examination held in March each year for candidates at maintained schools.

Offers of Sixth Form places are made after interview, and are conditional on good GCSE grades.

Candidates can be registered at any age. Full particulars can be obtained from the Registrar.

Term of Entry. Pupils enter the school in September. Exceptionally, for example if parents move into the Oxford area, other arrangements can be made.

Fees per term (2018–2019). Day pupils: £6,159 (Years 5–13); £5,933 (Years 3 and 4). They are payable in advance and are inclusive of textbooks and stationery. The Registration Fee (non-returnable) is currently £100.

Scholarships, Exhibitions and Bursaries. Scholarships, Exhibitions and Governors' Presentation Awards are awarded at all points of entry.

Bursaries are available subject to testing of parental means and many bursaries are supported through alumni gifts.

At age 13, up to 16 Scholarships of up to £300 are awarded each year based on the results of a two-day scholarship examination in February. Candidates should be under 14 on the subsequent 1 September. Closing date for entries: 11 January.

Music, Art, Drama and Sports Scholarships are awarded each year on the results of assessments held in January (Music), February (Art and Drama) and November (Sports). Music award holders also receive free tuition in one instrument.

Further information can be obtained from the Registrar.

Choristerships. There are 16 Choristerships. Entry is by Voice Trial and candidates should normally be between the ages of 7 and 9. For a Chorister two-thirds of the tuition fee is remitted. All enquiries about Choristerships should be addressed to the *Informator Choristarum, Magdalen College, Oxford OX1 4AU*. Choristers normally continue at the school after their voices have broken. In deserving cases, further financial help may be available.

Honours. Almost all pupils go on to higher education when they leave – to Oxford, Cambridge and other universities.

Old Waynfletes. The school has an active alumni network which supports social and professional activities and fundraising projects. Representative Old Waynfletes of the 20th century include Olympic athlete and soldier, Noel Chavasse, VC and bar; bookseller Sir Basil Blackwell; Nobel Prize winner Sir Tim Hunt; composer Ivor Novello; educationalist Tom Wheare; theatre directors John Caird and Sam Mendes, and sports commentators Nigel Starmer Smith and Jim Rosenthal.

Contact: Waynflete Office, Magdalen College School, email: waynfleteoffice@mcsoxford.org.

Charitable status. Magdalen College School Oxford Limited is a Registered Charity, number 295785. Its aims and objectives are to promote and provide for the education of children.

Governors:
Dr P N Withers (*Chairman*)
Dr C A Benson
Ms P Cameron Watt
Professor C C Coussios
Mr T P Edwards
Mr A D James
Professor D H F E Kroening
Ms J Longworth
Professor S R MacKenzie
Ms J Phillips
Mr N P Record
Dr N Richardson
Dr R A Saldanha
Mr B A M Vessey
Mr C G Young

Master: **Miss Helen L Pike**, MA Oxon, MA Michigan, MA London

Usher: Mr T G Beaumont, MA (*History, Safeguarding Officer*)
Deputy Head (*Academic*): Mr B D White, BA (*Mathematics*)

Deputy Head (*Education Development*): Dr S R Crawford, BA, PhD (*Biology*)

Teaching Staff:
* *Head of Department/Subject*
Miss F J Amswych, BA (*Learning Support, SENCo*)
Mr S J Andrew, MSc, MPhil (*Mathematics*)
Ms S-J Arthurs, BSc (*Physics*)
Mr G C Atkin, BSc (*Rowing Professional*)
Miss J C Attia, MA (*French*)
Mr A J Awcock, BSc MA (*Head of Rugby*)
Mr A Baker-Munton, MA (*French and German*)
Mr D S Barr, BA, MA (*English*)
Dr D Bebbington, BSc, DPhil (*Chemistry*)
Dr C L Bell, BSc, MPhil, DPhil (*Chemistry*)
The Revd W W Bell, BA, BA (*Chaplain, Theology, English*)
Mr R S Bolton, BA (*Rugby Professional*)
Mr T D Booth, MA (*Geography, Assistant Timetabler*)
Mr C J Boyle, BA (*Cricket, PE, Games*)
Mr N D Brittain, BA (*French, German*)
Mr M R Burchett, BSc, MSc (*Junior School Sport*)
Dr J C Carter, MA, MSt, DPhil (*Head of U4th, *Theology*)
Miss E H Churcher, MA, LRSM (*Music*)
Mr B W Cole, MA (*Head of L4th *Classics*)
Mr A C Cooper, BA, MSc (*Mathematics, Director of Alumni Relations*)
Mr T P Cooper, BSc (*Head of Middle School, Mathematics*)
Mr J D Cullen, BA, MA (*Music*)
Mrs E J B Denhart, MA, MSc (*Physics*)
Mr A A Duncan (*Cricket Professional*)
Mr E T Dupée, BSc (*PE Coordinator*)
Mr A P Dymond, BA (*History*)
Mrs L D Earnshaw, MA (*Mathematics, Outreach Coordinator*)
Mr T J Elton, MMath (*Deputy Head of Mathematics*)
Mrs A J Eyres, BA (*Junior School*)
Mr B J Ford BSc (*PE and Games*)
Sra M-J Gago, BA (*Spanish*)
Mr M A Gardner, MA (*Mathematics*)
Mrs J L Gladstone, MA (*Biology*)
Dr M P H V Habsburg, MA, MLitt, PhD (*History*)
Mr C E Hack, MSc (*Physics*)
Mrs D Hackett, BEng (*Junior School*)
Dr R K Hamer, BA, DPhil (*Biology*)
Miss E S Haynes, BA, MPhil (*Classics*)
Ms A Hayton, BA, MPhil (*History, Politics*)
Mr R A Hemingway, BA (*Head of Lower School, History*)
Mrs S Herrmann-Sinai, MA (*German*)
Ms G E Hildick-Smith, MA (*English*)
Mrs H C Hinze, BA (*English*)
Mr N J Hinze, BA (*Chemistry*)
Mr W H Hlaing, BSc (*Design Technology*)
Mr D L Hodgkinson, MA (*Classics*)
Dr C Howell, BA, MA, DPhil (*Learning Support Coordinator, History*)
Mr T P Hunter, BA (*Art*)
Mr J O Jefferson-Loveday, BSc (*Geography*)
Mrs C J Kelly-Eldridge, BMus, MA (*Junior School*)
Mrs A C Kenyon, MA (*NQT Mentor, CSO, Classics*)
Dr A I Kostyanovsky, BA, PhD (*Deputy Head of Sixth Form, Waynflete Studies, Theology*)
Mrs C A Lewis, MA, MEng (*Mathematics*)
Mr P J McDonald, MA (*Director of Higher Education, Classics*)
Mrs M D McDonough, MA, MSt (*Junior School Librarian*)
Mrs L E Mehrabian BA (*EAL Coordinator*)
Miss N M Moloney, BA (*Junior School Music*)
Mrs L A Moylan, BA (*Spanish*)

Mr C E Newbury, BA (*Junior School Director of Studies, History*)
Srta A Nogales Torres, BA, MA, MA (*Spanish*)
Dr J J Older, BSc, PhD (*Chemistry*)
Mr J C P Otley, BA (*Art*)
Mr S Pahl, BSc (*Contingent Commander CCF, *DofE programme, Games*)
Dr J K Panton, MSc, MPhil, DPhil (*Head of Upper Sixth Form, *Politics, Philosophy*)
Mrs S L Panzer, BA (*Rowing, Mathematics*)
Mr T J Parker, MA (*Chemistry*)
Mrs H C Parry, BSc (*Chemistry*)
Dr C G Pearson, BSc, DPhil (*Head of Sixth Form, Biology, Deputy Safeguarding Officer*)
Mr M Penton, BA (*Surmaster, Head of 3rd Form, PE*)
Dr J C Petersen, BSc, PhD (*Physics*)
Miss J P A Pick, BSc (*Economics*)
Miss L W Pinching, BA (*English, Charities Coordinator*)
Mr J F Place, BA (*Chess*)
Mr A J Pott, BA (*Tutor to the Choristers*)
Mr T D Quayle, MA, MSt (*Head of Lower Sixth Form, Deputy Head of English*)
Mr R E Presley, MA (*Economics*)
Mrs F J Pritchard, BA (*Deputy Head of Sixth Form, Art*)
Mr T D Quayle, MA (*English*)
Mr G T Quiney, BA (*Art*)
Mr C J Reid, BSc, MLitt, MSc (*Physics*)
Miss K J Rooney, BSc (*Head of Lower Sixth, Biology*)
Mrs H Rutter, BA (*Art*)
Mr A J Scriven (*Cricket*)
Miss S Shortland, BA (*Head of Upper Sixth, Assistant Director of Music*)
Mr A C Shouler, MA, MSt (*English*)
Dr P A Shrimpton, MA, MEd, PhD (*Mathematics*)
Mr T E Skipwith, BSc (*Head of Junior School, Deputy Safeguarding Officer*)
Miss K M Smith, BSc (*Girls' Sport, *Tennis, PE, Games*)
Mr P D Smith, MA, LTCL (*Music*)
Mrs J A Soave, BA (*Junior School Learning Support*)
Mr T S Sobey, MMath (*Mathematics*)
Mr S A Spowart, BA (*Master of Boats*)
Mrs H R Stammers, BA (*Theology*)
Mrs B C Stanworth, BA (*Geography*)
Mrs E Stapleton, BHum (*Deputy Head of Junior School*)
Mr L A Stone, BEd, MSc (*Hockey, PE, Games*)
Mrs J A Taylor, BSc (*Geography*)
Mr J P Terry, BA, MSt (*Junior School English*)
Mr A D Thomas, MA (*Drama, History*)
Dr B P Thurston, BA, DPhil (*Modern Languages*)
Mrs C G Thurston, MA (*French*)
Mr D Tuck, BSc (*Tennis Professional*)
Mr J P Unwin, BA (*Philosophy, *Sailing*)
Mr T J M Vallance, MA (*Classics, Trips Coordinator*)
Mrs J M H Wade, BA (*Junior School*)
Mr P S Walter, MPhil (*Computing, Mathematics*)
Mr A G Watts, BSc (*Director of Sport*)
Mrs F O White, MA (*Biology*)
Mr T R Williams, BA (*Hockey Professional*)
Mrs C E Winstone, BA (*Junior School*)

Clerk to the Governors and Bursar: Mr J D Clarke, BA
PA to the Master: Mrs A Sweeney, BA
Registrar: Mrs B Mallett, MA
Director of the Waynflete Office: Mrs S J Baker, MA

Malvern College

College Road, Malvern, Worcestershire WR14 3DF

Tel: 01684 581 500
Fax: 01684 581 617
email: enquiries@malverncollege.org.uk
website: www.malverncollege.org.uk
Twitter: @malverncollege
Facebook: @MalvernCollege
LinkedIn: /malvern-college

Motto: *Sapiens qui prospicit ~ Wise is the one who looks ahead*

Malvern College was founded in 1865 and incorporated by Royal Charter in 1929. The College is co-educational for children aged 13 to 18. There are five girls' Houses and six boys' Houses, each of which accommodates boarding and day pupils. Malvern is a proper boarding school with the majority of its pupils in residence at weekends. It is associated with The Downs Malvern, a co-educational preparatory school for pupils aged 3 to 13 (*for further details, see IAPS entry*).

Malvern College is particularly fortunate in its location. Situated on the lower slopes of the Malvern Hills and close to the centre of Great Malvern, the main College campus commands striking views eastwards across the Severn Valley towards the Cotswolds.

The school is justly proud of its academic standards and the high level of pastoral care it provides. Malvern College received the highest quality rating possible with regard to the educational provision for pupils in the ISI Report in November 2017. In the Sixth Form about half study for the International Baccalaureate and half for A Levels: each course of study offers pupils a real choice of subjects. Facilities are excellent: a state-of-the-art science centre was opened in the College's 150th year and the campus based Rogers Theatre has recently undergone a complete refurbishment including the construction of a foyer and studio spaces as well as upgrading technical capabilities with state-of-the-art 'theatre tech'.

Curriculum. In the Foundation Year (Year 9), pupils study a wide range of subjects. In addition to English, Mathematics, all three Sciences, French, History, Religious Studies, Geography, Art, Drama, Design Technology and Music, nearly all pupils are introduced to Spanish and German and most study Latin. All pupils study Debating and web design as well as Physical Education. The object of this year (as in co-curricular activities) is to show pupils as much as possible of what the College has to offer. On entering the Remove (Year 10), pupils choose their GCSE or IGCSE subjects to be taken at the end of the Hundred (Year 11). The compulsory subjects are English, Mathematics, Biology, Chemistry, Physics and one Modern Foreign or Classical Language. Pupils also choose optional subjects from Art and Design, Classical Civilisation, Computer Science, Design Technology, Drama, Geography, French, German, History, Latin, Music, Photography, Physical Education, Religious Studies and Spanish. Greek is available for those who began it in the Foundation Year (Year 9). A Separate Sciences option enables pupils to extend the core Double Award Science to the three separate science IGCSEs. Pupils generally choose five options. Pupils decide on their choices in consultation with their Tutors, Housemasters/Housemistresses, Heads of Year and parents.

In the Sixth Form, there is a choice between A Levels and the International Baccalaureate. In the IB, combinations of the following subjects are offered: Visual Art, Biology, Chemistry, Business Management, Economics, English Literature, English Language and Literature, Environmental Systems and Societies, French, German, Geography, Greek, History, Italian, Latin, Mathematics, Further Mathematics, Music, Physics, Spanish, Technology, Philosophy and Sports, Health and Exercise Science. All pupils take the valuable Theory of Knowledge (ToK) Course. A Levels are available in all of the subjects listed above for the IB (except Environmental Systems and Societies, Philosophy and Italian) and also in Religious Studies, Classical Civilisation, Photography, Politics, Physical Education and Psychology. Most pupils take three subjects to A Level. Pupils studying A Levels also choose, in addition, one option from the Enrichment Programme, which includes the Extended Project, beginner Italian and Mathematics for Scientists.

Sport. Pupils are offered a range of sports throughout their time at Malvern College. Each term there is a focus on priority sports; for girls these are Hockey in the Autumn term, Netball in the Lent term and Cricket, Tennis and Athletics in the summer. In addition to these, regular fixtures are offered for girls in Football, Cricket, Badminton, Golf, Fives and Cross Country. The boys' priority sports are Rugby in the Autumn term, Football in the Lent term, and Cricket in the summer. In addition to these, regular fixtures are offered for boys in Hockey, Tennis, Badminton, Golf, Cross Country, Athletics, Squash, Rackets, Basketball and Fives.

The co-curricular activity programme provides an extensive range of physical activity for pupils to engage in to develop their health, fitness, confidence, leadership and social skills.

Exceptionally talented pupils are invited to join the Performance Pathway, which comprises specialist strength and conditioning sessions and offers support with lifestyle management and progression through their sport performance pathway. We foster strong links with clubs such as Worcestershire County Cricket Club, Worcester Warriors Rugby Club, Stourport Hockey Club, Malvern Town FC, Ledbury Swimming Club and Hucclecote Netball Club.

A state-of-the-art Sports Complex includes a 25m swimming pool, a double sports hall (eight badminton courts), a shooting range, squash courts, fitness studio, climbing wall and fitness suite. The Sports Complex has a Cricket Centre which is the official training venue for Worcestershire County Cricket Club. The College has two Rackets courts, which offer tournament standard Rackets facilities. In addition there are 10 hard court Tennis/Netball courts and Fives courts. In our extensive playing fields there is a Grandstand overlooking the athletics track, six football/rugby pitches, a water-based all-weather pitch and a sand-based AstroTurf which host regular local club fixtures as well as the Worcestershire Hockey Junior Development Centres as part of the England Hockey Performance Pathway. The Malvern Hills and Peachfield Common offer marvellously challenging terrain for the College's cross-country runners and mountain bikers.

Co-Curricular Activities. Pupils have the opportunity to take part in a range of activities such as sailing, trampolining, jewellery-making, volleyball, fencing, photography, golf, polo, cookery, speech & drama, mountain-biking, canoe-polo, kayaking, judo, silversmithing, archery, and yoga.

The College has a strong tradition of expedition training and outdoor pursuits, including rock-climbing, kayaking, paragliding, stand-up paddle boarding and mountaineering (summer and winter, UK and abroad). Opportunities exist for the use of the College's cottage in the Brecon Beacons. Annually expeditions go to Scotland and have also recently been to Iceland, the Alps, Malta, Namibia, Costa Rica, Ghana and Swaziland in the school holidays. Many of these activities are an integral part of the voluntary CCF (which has RM, Army and RAF sections) and The Duke of Edinburgh's Award scheme. There is also a flourishing Community Service Volunteering Organisation.

Music is strong at Malvern. Approximately 35% of pupils learn a musical instrument and there are eight musical ensembles including orchestras, concert band, jazz band and choirs. The well-equipped Music School (22 practice rooms, three large rehearsal rooms) includes a soundproofed practice pod for percussion and an IT suite. Attached to the Music School is St Edmund's Hall, a 150-seat recital hall with a fine Steinway piano. Pupils of all standards are encouraged both instrumentally and vocally, and regularly give performances (internal, locally and further afield). Inter-House competitions are held throughout the year. The Music department works collaboratively with the Drama department and the most recent productions were *Hairspray, Grease, Dido and Aeneas* and *Oh What a Lovely War*. The Elite Music Programme offers further opportunities for pupils to meet performers and composers in both the classical and contemporary realm, and to attend concerts and workshops.

Drama is a thriving creative force within the community of the school. Pupils are encouraged to play a full part in all aspects of theatre, whether as actor, theatre maker or technician. This might be through academic study at GCSE or A Level, participation in the many co-curricular productions staged each year, or the annual House Drama Competition. Recent productions staged in the College's Theatre include *The Great Gatsby, Henry V, The Sound of Music, Noughts and Crosses, The Odyssey, A Midsummer Night's Dream, South Pacific, Jane Eyre, Blue Stockings, Private Peaceful* and *Les Misérables School Edition*. Speech and Drama tuition is a popular option for many, with pupils receiving preparation for LAMDA examinations or local public speaking festivals. Regular attendance at the Malvern Theatres in town is complemented by visits to Stratford, London and Bristol.

Art. The purpose-built Art School has a focus on Fine Art and Photography. There are facilities for Painting, Drawing, Intaglio and Relief Printmaking, Photography and Digital Imaging. Pupils of all abilities develop a rich visual vocabulary in these media from the Foundation Year, enabling work to become increasingly fluent and sophisticated as they progress through the school. Pupils visit galleries and exhibitions in the UK as part of their course and the department organises regular overseas visits. The department is open during the evening and at weekends to enable pupils to develop their work. A rich co-curricular programme is offered in areas such as Life Drawing, Photography and Digital Imaging. The Elite Art Programme offers further opportunities for pupils to meet artists and designers, attend talks and workshops to extend and nurture their work. The standard of work produced is exceptionally high with a focus on technique, especially drawing, together with an informed understanding of others' art practice.

Design and Technology. There is a very well-equipped Design & Technology Centre which ensures that pupils have the opportunity to develop their design skills and material knowledge through practical project work in this exciting subject. Facilities include Fashion and Textiles, woodworking, metal working in small and large scale, Computer Aided Design and Manufacture including 3D Printing, CNC Lathes, Milling Machines, Laser cutters and routers.

Careers. Malvern College is a member of Inspiring Futures. In their GCSE year pupils take the Inspiring Futures 'Futurewise New Generation' online careers guidance tests which assess ability, personality, aptitude and interests. An in-depth interview with an experienced IF careers advisor helps pupils to make sensible and informed choices about their future. A Careers and Futures evening which takes place in March every year gives pupils the opportunity to learn from current parents and alumni about a variety of careers and pre- and post-university activities. All pupils in the Lower Sixth are encouraged to spend at least one week in the holidays on work experience. Pupils are given advice on choice of course at University (both UK and international) and help with their application (including interview and SAT preparation) by teachers in the Careers and Higher Education Department, and by their Sixth Form Tutor and Housemaster/Housemistress.

Pastoral Care. Housemasters and Housemistresses work closely with Tutors who share the responsibility for pupils' overall personal development and well-being. Members of the Sixth Form choose their own Tutor in collaboration with the Head of Sixth Form and Head of Lower School. The Pastoral Team meets regularly and comprises the Senior Deputy Head, Deputy Head: Pastoral as well as the Safeguarding Team, Heads of Year, Medical Centre and full-time Chaplain. The school prides itself on proactive pastoral care – staff and pupil 'Thrive Teams' meet weekly. There are well-developed Peer Mentoring and House Buddy systems and Heads of House and Chapel Prefects are trained in their roles to support younger pupils. Pupils also have access to school counsellors and Independent Listeners. Malvern hosts an annual Pastoral Care conference which has recently focused on topics such as mental health.

Health Care. There is a modern and well-equipped Medical Centre staffed 24 hours a day by Registered Nurses.

Coaches. During the school year there are three half-term holidays and about five leave-out weekends. On these occasions, school coaches are run to Guildford, London Paddington and Birmingham airport, according to demand. A coach service to Heathrow airport runs at the start of half term and the end of term.

Admission. Most pupils start school at Malvern between their thirteenth and fourteenth birthdays and may qualify for admission to the school by a satisfactory performance in the Common Entrance Examination or the annual Scholarship Examination. Pupils who wish to enter from schools which do not prepare pupils for Common Entrance are required to sit internal entrance examinations.

Pupils are also admitted to the Sixth Form at 16 on the basis of GCSEs/IGCSEs, interviews and entrance tests.

Application for admission should be made to the Registrar.

Scholarships. Malvern College offers a generous number of Scholarships and Exhibitions at 13+ each year, varying in value according to merit and financial circumstances up to 50% of the current fees. Scholarships and Exhibitions are offered for Academic potential, Art, Drama, Music, Sport and Design and Technology. Entries must be received three weeks before the assessment. For academic scholarships, Malvern College offers the Common Academic Scholarship Examination. Details and entry dates are available from the ISEB, the Preparatory School or Malvern College. There is also a range of scholarships available in the Sixth Form.

Further particulars may be obtained from the Registrar, Tel: 01684 581515, or email: registrar@malvern college.org.uk.

Fees per term (2018–2019). Senior School: Boarding: £12,709–£13,153; Day £8,485.

The Malvernian Society. On leaving, Malvernians retain contact with the College by joining the Malvernian Society. They also become members of the OM Club which organises various teams and a number of social functions. Secretary of the Malvernian Society: Paul Godsland (Tel: 01684 581517).

College Council:
Ten members of the Council may be nominated, one each by the Lords-Lieutenant of the Counties of Gloucestershire, Herefordshire and Worcestershire, by the Vice-Chancellors of the Universities of Oxford, Cambridge and Birmingham, by the Service Boards of the Navy, Army and Air Force, and by the Headmaster and Teaching Staff. Ten members are elected by the Governors, and between six and ten are appointed by the Council.

President and Visitor: The Lord Bishop of Worcester

Chairman: Mr R K Black [OM]
Vice Chairman: Miss S R Duff [EOG]
Treasurer: Mr C A P Leonard, JP

Mrs F P Bridge	Mr G E Jones
Mr P G Brough	Dr A M D Kennedy
Mr W J Burke III [OM]	Revd K U Madden
Mr P J Cartwright [OM]	Mr P C Nicholls [OM]
Professor K J Davey, OBE	Mrs L M Penrice
Mrs J Edwards-Clark, MVO [EOG]	Mrs S Raby-Smith
Mr N C S Engert [OM]	Mr D G Robertson
Ms C D Fairchild	Dr D C Sandbrook [OM]
Mr J P Foxall [OM]	Dr C W O Stoecker [OM]
Mr F R R Francis	Mr T D Straker, QC [OM]
Mr J M J Havard [OM]	Mr A F Trotman
Mr S M Hill	Mr B S Walker [OM]
Professor P B Jackson	Dr H M Wright

[OM] *Old Malvernian*
[EOG] *Ellerslie Old Girl*

Clerk to the Council & Bursar: Mr G R H Ralphs

Headmaster: Mr A R Clark, MA Cantab

Senior Deputy Head: Mrs S G Angus, MA
Deputy Head: *Pastoral*: Mr L A Faulkner, MA
Deputy Head: *Logistics*: Mrs R H Keys, MA
Deputy Head: *Academic*: Mr J A Gauci, BA

Heads of Department:
Design, Technology and Art: Mr D Stokes, MA
Drama: Mr K R C Packham, BA
Economics, Politics and Business Studies: Mr S C Holroyd, BA
English: Dr B M Wells, MA, PhD
Geography: Mr R Needham, BSc
History: Mr J C Herod, MA
Psychology: Mrs M E Stephen, BSc
Mathematics: Mr C Thomas, BEng
Modern Languages: Mr W Matthews, BA
Music: Mr J M Brown, BMus
Religious Studies: Mr D O'Keeffe, BA
Science: Dr N V Watson, BA, PhD
Sport: Mrs C A Hooper-West, BSc

Boarding Houses:
Mr M E A Hardinges, BSc (*School House*)
Mr A J Wharton, BTh (*No.1*)
Mr J J W E Major, BA (*No.2*)
Mrs F C Packham, BSc (*No.3*)
Mrs A I Sharp, BA (*No.4*)
Mr R W Howitt, BSc (*No.5*)
Mrs V E Young, BA (*No.6*)
Mr D J Eglin, BSc (*No.7*)
Mrs M J Nardone, LLB, MLitt (*No.8*)
Mr P Wickes, BSc (*No.9*)
Mrs E Brown, BA (*Ellerslie*)

Chaplain: The Revd D P Ibbotson, FdA, BSc
Registrar: Mr G Vosper-Brown

The Manchester Grammar School

Old Hall Lane, Manchester M13 0XT

Tel:	0161 224 7201
Fax:	0161 257 2446
email:	general@mgs.org
website:	www.mgs.org
Twitter:	@MGSMagic
LinkedIn:	/the-manchester-grammar-school

Motto: *Sapere Aude ~ Dare to be Wise*

The Manchester Grammar School was founded in 1515 to promote 'godliness and good learning' and it has endeavoured throughout its history to remain true to these principles, while adapting to changing times. It is now an independent boys' day school with around 1,500 pupils. Almost all leavers go on to university, and there is a strong tradition of boys progressing to Oxford and Cambridge (32 boys were offered places for entry in 2018) and other leading Russell Group universities. 33 pupils received university offers to study Medicine, Dentistry or Veterinary Science for 2018 entry. A number of pupils each year obtain offers from prestigious US universities. Over 150 qualified teaching staff provide all pupils with a broad, traditional and flexible curriculum; for example, boys may study up to five languages at GCSE, from a choice of Latin, Greek, French, German, Italian, Mandarin, Russian and Spanish. Arabic and Czech are available as part of the options programme in the Sixth Form. The School offers a vast and diverse range of co-curricular opportunities.

The tradition of offering places to clever pupils regardless of their background is maintained by MGS bursaries. Approximately 220 pupils in the school are fee-assisted. Our pupils come both from primary and preparatory schools and represent a wide variety of cultural, ethnic and religious backgrounds.

Registration and Entry. Entry to the Junior School is considered at age 7, 8, 9 and 10, subject to availability at any stage during the academic year. Junior School pupils progress automatically to the Senior School. Entry for most other boys joining the School is at age 11, although entry at other ages is considered, subject to availability and applicants for Sixth Form entry are particularly welcomed. At all levels the normal assessment for entry involves prospective pupils spending a day in School, being taught and assessed in small groups. Alongside these assessment days, there is an entrance exam for entry at age 11. Sixth Form entrants have to meet GCSE grade requirements. Further details are available from the Admissions Office.

Fees per term (2018–2019). £4,190 (£12,570 per year).

Bursaries. The School offers means-tested bursaries of up to 100%. There are currently approximately 220 boys in receipt of financial support from the School and the majority receive full-fee support (the average fee support is currently 91%). The School does not offer academic scholarships.

Junior School. The Junior School opened in September 2008 in award-winning accommodation. It admits boys from age 7 and currently has approximately 240 pupils. There is a strong focus in its curriculum on creativity, academic enrichment and skills-based learning. Specialist teachers from the Senior School contribute to the academic enrichment in Years 5 and 6.

Senior School Organisation and Curriculum. During the first two years the boys will study English, Mathematics, a modern foreign language (French, German, Russian, Spanish and Mandarin Chinese are offered), Classics (including Latin) History, Geography, General Science, Religious Studies, PSHE, Computing, Music, Art & Design,

Drama, PE, Swimming and Games. Greek, Italian and Electronics are introduced as options in Year 9; there is also the opportunity for pupils who have not already done so to take up languages offered in Year 7. In Year 10 pupils may opt to study for an AS Extended Project Qualification; Classical Civilisation is also offered. Pupils make IGCSE/GCSE choices towards the end of Year 9 and typically take ten subjects, including Mathematics, English, English Literature, a language and at least one science subject.

In the Sixth Form A Level, Pre-U and International A Level courses are offered, with each department selecting the course which offers the best preparation for university; in addition, all students participate in the School's own non-examined enrichment programme, which includes a philosophical and critical thinking course (Perspectives).

Pastoral Care. Each form in the school is looked after by a Tutor, who is responsible, with the appropriate senior members of staff, for the academic and general progress of each pupil. In the Senior School Tutors work with no more than 13 boys. Regular written reports are supplemented by Parents' Evenings. The School Medical Room is staffed by a part-time doctor and two full-time Nursing staff. The older pupils selected as prefects are encouraged to help younger pupils in running societies and other co-curricular activities.

Creative Arts. All pupils experience Music, Art & Design and Drama within the curriculum; in addition, each of these areas offers activities to large numbers of pupils during the lunch-hour and after school. There are choirs, orchestras and instrumental tuition; plays, drama workshops and musicals; clubs for art, pottery, and computer design. There are regular exhibitions and public performances both in school and in public venues. The School has a well-equipped theatre and drama studios, providing many opportunities for pupils both to perform and provide technical support for productions.

Sport. All boys take part in timetabled games and the school produces successful teams in most sports. A new sports hall opened in 2015; there are extensive playing fields, a gymnasium, indoor swimming pool, squash courts, tennis courts and fitness suite. The choice of sport increases with age, to include rowing, climbing and golf in addition to mainstream sports.

Outdoor Pursuits. The school has a long tradition of camping and trekking and there are numerous weekend and holiday excursions. The School is the largest centre for D of E in the North West. Mountain activity days are offered most weekends, free of charge. Four annual camps cater for the full age range and offer a wide choice of activities. In recent years expeditions have visited the Alps, the Pyrenees, Morocco and Scandinavia. The school has two centres in Cumbria and one in Derbyshire.

Foreign Visits. Many trips abroad are organised each year, providing enjoyable holidays of broad educational value. Destinations include France, Germany, Spain, Russia, Italy, Greece, Mexico, Argentina, Peru, Mexico, Egypt, Tunisia, South Africa, India and China.

Societies and Activities. There are over 200 clubs, societies and activities catering for a variety of interests, including Chess and Bridge Clubs, and a school newspaper produced by pupils. The School is active in charitable fundraising and has a very extensive community action programme, including projects in Manchester and Salford, as well as in Uganda.

Prizes and Scholarships. In addition to bursaries, funds are provided for grants to help deserving pupils with the expense of a range of co-curricular activities. Prizes are awarded in all subjects in the curriculum.

Old Mancunians' Association and MGS Parents' Society. The Old Boys' Association has many regional sections. There is an annual Old Boys' Dinner in Manchester.

The Development Office Secretary is Mrs Jane Graham who can be reached at the School.

The MGS Parents' Society has a membership of parents and friends and exists to support school activities and promote a programme of social events.

Charitable status. The Manchester Grammar School is a Registered Charity which provides Public Benefit. The aim of the School is to prepare able boys from the Manchester area, regardless of their financial background, to proceed to university and make a positive contribution to society in their adult life.

Co-optative Governors:

Professor T A Hinchliffe	J P Wainwright
J Kingsley	J Young
J Luca	E M Watkins, CBE
C Bolton (*Treasurer*)	(*Chairman*)

Professor D A Cardwell, The University of Cambridge
Dr J R W Prag, The University of Oxford
A Beardsworth
R Race

Ex officio Governors:
The Dean of Manchester
The Lord Mayor of Manchester

Bursar and Clerk to the Governors: Mrs G M Batchelor, BSc

High Master: M A Boulton, BEng, PhD

Deputy High Master: P A M Thompson, BA, DPhil, MA Ed
Academic Deputy Head: Mrs M A S Lowe, BA, MPhil, MEd
Pastoral Deputy Head: A N Smith, BA
Surmaster & Head of Co-Curriculum: J W Mangnall, MA
Head of Junior School: Mrs L A Hamilton, BEd
Head of Lower School: P W Freeman, BSc, MSc
Head of Middle School: S G Crawshaw, BSc, PhD
Head of Sixth Form: C P Thom, MA
Director of Development: S P Jones, BA
Assistant Head: S Foster, BA, MA
Proctor: S J Burch, BSc, PhD, MIBiol
Director of Admissions: D L Virr, BSc
Director of Studies: D Jeys, BSc, MA

Academic Staff:
* *Head of Department/Subject*
¹ *Language Assistant*
² *Teaching Assistant*

Art & Design:	*Chemistry*:
R E Berry	T Ahmed, BSc
K Davidson, BA, MA	I Airth, BSc
Mrs J Dobbs, BA, MA Ed	C Buckley, BSc
*Mrs L J Murphy, BA, MA	M Facchini, BSc, MSc
Miss S Taylor, BA	Dr S Graham, MSci, PhD
	Mrs H M Hughes, BSc
Biology:	Mrs T C James, BSc
*J Blair, BSc	*Miss F C Roberts, MChem
Dr S J Burch, BSc, PhD, MSB	G M Tinker, MEng
Dr S G Crawshaw, BSc, PhD	*Classics*:
P W Freeman, BSc, MSc	B S Edwards, MA
Dr E Loh, BSc, MSc, PhD	L D Hopkins, BA, MPhil, DPhil
Mrs N A Loughlin, BSc	*Miss C A Owens, BA, MA
Mrs C Morgan, BSc	X J Pollock, BA, MA, MPhil
M J Smedley, BSc, PhD	
Miss A Wicking, BA	C R Sykes, BA, MA MA Ed, DPhil
Dr P A M Thompson, BA,	

N G Williams, BA
Dr R G Williams, BA, DPhil

Computing:
*D E Millington, BSc, MSc
D Soon, BSc, MBA

Drama:
S Abbs, BA
Mrs K Hellier, BA
*M J Nichols, BA
Mrs J Sherratt, BA
K Tetley, BA

Economics:
*Miss H L Dangerfield, BA
A E Rigler, BA
J A Shirlin, BA

Electronics:
*D P Smith, MEng, PhD

English:
Mrs R E Adams, BA
Miss E C Appleton, BA, MA
R J L Geldard, BA, MA, MA
Mrs V E Horsfield, BA, MEd
Miss A Lloyd-Hughes, BA
C McCarthy, BA, MA
O N Nzelu, BA
F S Sugarman-Warner, BA
B Townsend, BA
S Van der Ouderaa, MA
*N Warrack, MA, MA
Miss J Welsh, BA, MA
Mrs L F Williamson, BA

General Science:
*D W Inglis, BSc, PhD
D L Virr, BSc

Geography:
F C G Baker, BA
M D Corbett, BSc
Mrs A Curry, BSc
Miss P J Higgins, BSc
S P Jones, BA, MBA
J W Mangnall, MA
M A Nowell, BSc
S P G Spratling, BA
*P J Wheeler, BSc

History:
*Mrs E Carter, MA
S R Garvey, BA
S F Carter, BA, MA
C L Pearson, MA, MA
A R T Hern, BA, MPhil, MPhil
D O Lacey, BA, MEd
Ms M A S Lowe, BA, MPhil
Dr S Orth, BA, MA, PhD
W B Pye, BA
A M Smith, MA
M G P Strother, MA, MPhil
D M Taylor, BA

Junior School:
Mrs C Ashurst, BA, MEd
Miss K V Atty, BA

Mrs D R Barnett, BEd
A G Bird, BSc
C E Boddington, BSc
Mrs L E Brunsden, BA
Mrs C Burke, BSc, MSc
Mrs S M Callaghan, BA
²Miss J S Claverly
G Clayton, BSc
Miss L Doyle, BEd
²Miss C Emslie
T Glennie, BA
*Mrs L A Hamilton, BEd
J S Howe, BA
²Miss N Jones
D A Laird, BA
Mrs T C Neild, BA
Miss I E Nuttall
²Mrs S Reed, BA
²Miss N Reynolds BSoc-Si
²Mrs J Robinson, BA
Mrs V Shingler, BA
Miss E J Thorpe, BSc
²Mrs V J Tierney
²W J van Zyl, BSc
Mrs Z L Ward, LLB

Learning Support:
*Mrs H Butchart, BA, LTCL
Mrs L Merlo, BA, MA
Miss H Sargeant, BA, MA

Mathematics:
Mrs J Allinson, BA, MA
Dr J J Burke, BSc, PhD
Mrs A E Carolan, BSc
A R Davies, BSc, MSc
Dr A C Hunter, BSc, MSc, PhD
D Jeys, BSc, MA
I Z Khan, BSc
S J Leigh, BEng
O W J Llewelyn-Smith, BSc
J L McMillan, BSc, MA
G J Morris, BSc
D V Naughton, MM, PhD
*T J Pattison, BSc, MIMA, CMath
S E Phillips, BMus
Dr H G Read, BSc, PhD
R T Watt, BSc
Mrs N M Williams, BSc, FRGS
J C Butterfield, MMath

Modern Languages:
E C F Cittanova, L-ès-L, M-ès-L, DEA
Mrs E R Dalton, L-ès-L
A P Dobson, BA, MA (*German*)
Miss E A Garnett, BA
*Mrs A V Hemsworth, BA (*Italian*)
*Miss A Jacinto, BA
Mrs S E Jones, BA
Mrs O Kelly-Saltaleggio, BA
Mrs R Lan, BA, MA
S Lu, BA
M Morato

Mrs D Minguito-Pantoja, BA
R J Neal, BA, MA, MEd
Mrs S J Paulson, BA
L M Rigby, BA
Mrs G Rrugeja
N J Sharples, BA, MA (*Spanish*)
C J Shaw, BA
Mrs L Speed, Mosc Dipl
P R Taylor, BA
C P Thom, MA
*Miss K J Tinslay, BA

Music:
G Blackwell
Mrs F A Bradley, BMus
Mrs H Butchart, BA, LTCL
*R M Carey, MA (*Director of Music*)
Miss E M Shercliff, BA (*Junior School Music*)

Physical Education:
T A Grainger, BSc
R F Jennings, BA
A Khares
J L Leggett, BA
M P Murtagh, BSc, MSc
M J Roe, BSc
S Swindells, RFU II, RFU III
M Watkinson

Medical Officer: Dr J L Burn, FRCP, FRCPCH
PA to the High Master: Lorraine Coen
Admissions Office Manager: Kath Heathcote

G Wilson
*M A Walmsley, BSc

Physics:
Dr M A Boulton BEng, PhD
Ms S M Hewett, BSc
Dr P Holt, BSc, DPhil
*S J F Hunt, MA
M Saghir, PhD
Dr D P Smith, MEng, PhD
Miss L Thewles, BSc
R W Morley, BSc, MA
S U Riley, BEng, PhD

Politics:
S Foster, BA, MA
*R N Kelly, BA, MA, MPhil
Dr E C Kilheeney, BA, MA

Religion & Philosophy:
Mrs L J Anderson, BA
*A Brower-Latz, BA, MD, PhD
M P A Coffey, MA
D Farr, MA
A Greggs, BA
J Kenny, BA, MA
A N Smith, BA
Mrs J A Whittell, MA Cantab

Marlborough College

Marlborough, Wiltshire SN8 1PA

Tel: Main Switchboard: 01672 892200
          The Master's Office: 01672 892400
          The Bursary: 01672 892390
          Admissions: 01672 892300
Fax: Main No: 01672 892207
          The Master's Office: 01672 892407
email: master@marlboroughcollege.org
          admissions@marlboroughcollege.org
website: www.marlboroughcollege.org
Twitter: @marlboroughcol

Founded 1843. Incorporated by Royal Charter.

The College is fully co-educational and there are 968 boys and girls in the 16 Houses of whom 935 full board. The usual age of entry is either 13 or 16.

Registration. For entry to the College at 13+ registrations are accepted no earlier than four years before entry. The College assesses the majority of applicants in the January of Year 6 and offers are made for approximately 75% of places. There is a second entry point in the January of Year 7 when approximately 20% of places will be offered. The final 5% of places will be offered in February of Year 8. All applicants to the College must meet our entry criteria and take either the Academic Scholarship or the Common Entrance examination. Please see our website for details of this policy: www.marlboroughcollege.org. The 13+ Scholarship examination is in March of the year of entry. Sixth Form entry and Scholarship examination is in the November before entry. Registrations for entry at 16+ must be made before the 1st of October in the year before entry.

Scholarships. All Awards enable those with a financial need to receive bursarial assistance with the fees. The degree of support given will be subject to a means test. Candidates for entry in the Shell (Year 9) must be under 14 on 1st September. The closing date for entries is late January of Year 8. There are up to 16 academic scholarships at 13+ and a further 22 Awards in Music, Art, Design and Sport. There are also William Morris All Rounder Awards based upon strengths in academic work, Sport, Art, Drama or Music. Up to 20 awards are made at Sixth Form entry. From time to time there are a number of other special categories of scholarship based upon parental occupation and particular abilities. The College offers a limited number of Foundation (Clergy) places and Armed Services closed scholarships.

A Scholarship Prospectus and copies of past papers may be obtained from the Admissions Office. Applications and enquiries about entries and scholarships should be addressed to The Director of Admissions, tel: 01672 892300; email: admissions@marlboroughcollege.org.

Academic. The College's curriculum follows and extends the National Curriculum to allow for a proper combination of breadth and specialisation. It is designed to stimulate, challenge and support all pupils and to ensure that they maximise their potential. There is a clear focus placed upon success in public examinations, where standards are very high, but the College prioritises pupil success at university and in their subsequent careers.

Almost all pupils go on to study at university either in the United Kingdom (around 85% annually to Russell Group universities) or, increasingly, overseas with destinations ranging from Europe to North America and beyond.

In the Lower School a wide-ranging curriculum is followed. Central to this is "Form", an innovative and unique humanities course which embraces English, History and Religious Studies. It gives pupils a sense of the history and evolution of human culture, and our place within it. It aims to develop the skills and habits of mind that will lead to success at the College and beyond – wide reading, critical analysis, synthesis and evaluation of ideas, the confidence to have a go and voice their opinions. Choices are made at the end of the Shell (Year 9) leading to 10 or 11 GCSEs and IGCSEs. In the Sixth Form, pupils choose from over 30 A Levels or Pre-Us, as well as having the option to take on the Extended Project (in which the College is a large and successful centre), further language options, or one or two Electives courses (with over 50 different courses on offer to date). The College does not offer AS examinations in any subject.

The curriculum is supported by an enormous range of academic extension and enrichment activities through societies, lectures, theatre trips, museum and gallery visits, debates, poetry readings, conferences, concerts, creating a full co-curriculum which recognises that qualifications alone do not produce an educated person.

Universities & Careers. Nearly all pupils who come to Marlborough go on into the Sixth Form and virtually all proceed to degree courses. The well-resourced Guidance Department is located at the heart of the College and assists Housemasters and Housemistresses in advising boys and girls and their parents about Sixth Form subject selection, higher education options, gap year projects, work experience and careers. Each year, a good number of pupils take up Oxbridge and medical places, and around 10% move on to universities overseas. The College is an ACT testing centre (for those considering North American universities).

Co-Curricular. Sports facilities are outstanding. There are two brand new floodlit AstroTurf pitches, acres of sports pitches, a tartan athletics track, a sports hall, 24 tennis courts and nine netball courts. The main sports for boys are rugby, hockey, cricket, football, athletics and tennis, and for girls, hockey, netball, tennis, lacrosse and athletics. Alternative sports include aerobics, badminton, basketball, beagling, clay pigeon shooting, fencing, fishing, fives, girls' cricket, golf, jiu jitsu, rackets, riding, rugby sevens, shooting, squash, swimming, water polo, watt biking and yoga. There are regular fixtures in many of these sports and several run sports tours and pre-season trips. Recent tours include cricket to Barbados, netball to Barbados, lacrosse to the USA and hockey to the Netherlands.

An Outdoor Activities Department offers the Gold and Silver Duke of Edinburgh's Award, canoeing, climbing, kayaking, mountain biking and sub-aqua. The annual Devizes to Westminster kayak race has become a feature of the Lent Term for up to 10 Upper School crews. There are numerous OA activities each Sunday in term-time in House groups and more adventurous trips further afield in the school holidays. Recent destinations include the Brecon Beacons, Snowdonia, Nepal, Peru, Iceland, Tanzania, Slovenia and Sweden. The Gold Duke of Edinburgh's Award Training, Practice and Assessed Expeditions take place in school holidays and half-terms.

The College's Combined Cadet Force is thriving. It is compulsory in Year 10 and optional thereafter. It provides excellent leadership training and there is a strong record of College pupils winning Sixth Form Army Scholarships. All year groups take part in Field Days or CCF Camps both in the UK and abroad; the Upper School cadets have visited the US Navy Seals in California on three occasions recently.

The College also offers a comprehensive Outreach Programme in the local community. The mantra "with privilege comes responsibility" is the underlying philosophy. Many of the pupils are involved with local primary schools, a special school, care homes for the elderly and charity shops. The College has a partnership with Swindon Academy which involves College staff and pupils providing academic support. Swindon Academy pupils also attend some themed residential weekends at the College. The Swindon Academy Year 7 and Year 8 pupils visit the College weekly.

The College has a large array of thriving academic and intellectual societies which complement and support the academic programme, attracting impressive speakers each term from across a broad section of disciplines.

There is a programme of Day Trips in term-time and Study Trips in the holidays, which support and enrich the academic curriculum. Recent examples include Geography to China and Tenerife, History of Art to Italy, Politics to Washington, Classics to Greece, English to Ireland and Physics to CERN. The Modern Languages Department runs a series of exchanges and trips to language schools in the target country.

Music. Music at Marlborough plays an essential part in the cultural life of the College.

Based in the state-of-the-art, purpose-built Henry Hony Centre, the Department is home to some 40 Music scholars and with over 55% of pupils taking instrumental lessons. The major groups are Chapel and Chamber Choir, Symphony Orchestra, Chamber Orchestra and Senior Wind Orchestra. Unique to Marlborough is the College's professional orchestra in partnership, London's Southbank Sinfonia.

Drama. Drama at Marlborough is all about collaboration, creative debate, experimentation and excellence. With many productions every year diversity of style is at the heart of what we offer; from contemporary productions of classical tragedy to musicals and farcical comedy. Independent productions give the opportunity for pupils to write, direct and produce, working alongside visiting practitioners and influenced by the wide range of touring productions that visit our three well-equipped theatres. Drama is offered as an option in the Shell (Year 9) and is popular thereafter.

Art and Design. The Art Department is an inspirational and engaging creative environment, where every pupil's individuality, visual literacy and potential to fully realise their artistic ambitions is highly valued. All pupils study Art in their first year and many go on to take the subject at GCSE or A Level. Pupils may specialise in Fine Art or Photography at A Level.

The purpose-built Art School houses painting, drawing, relief and intaglio printmaking studios, a photography darkroom, lecture room and an IT suite within the main building. In addition, there is a well-resourced art library. Two annex buildings accommodate ceramic workshops, a drawing studio, the Mount House Gallery and an Apple Mac digital editing and animation suite.

Design and Technology. Design & Technology is studied by all pupils in the Year 9. During this foundation year, pupils undertake a variety of design projects which encourages them to question and evaluate their design thinking. At the end of Year 9 pupils can opt to follow the GCSE OCR Design and Technology (9–1) specification.

In the Sixth Form pupils currently have the opportunity to study OCR Product Design at A Level, where they will undertake a range of more ambitious projects which match the needs of any promising young designer or engineer.

Fees per term (2018–2019). £12,605 Boarding.

The Marlburian Club. www.marlburianclub.org.

Charitable status. Marlborough College is a Registered Charity, number 309486 incorporated by Royal Charter to provide education.

Governors & Staff:

Visitor: The Most Revd The Lord Archbishop of Canterbury

Council:
President: The Rt Revd The Lord Bishop of Salisbury, BA, BD, MA, AKC, FKC, DCL
The Rt Hon The Lord Malloch-Brown, KCMG, PC, BA, MA (*Chairman*)
Lieutenant General Sir J G Lorimer, KCB, DSO, MBE, MA
J K Baker, BSc, FCA (*Chairman Finance Committee*)
The Revd Charlotte Bannister-Parker, BA, MA
Professor Sir J Bell, GBE, FRS, Hon FREng, PMedSci
S M W Bishop, BA
J P W Coleman, LLB
Mrs A Cooke, LLB
P Freeman, BA
Ms G Gopalan, BA
Ms S Hamilton-Fairley, MA
Dr Tracy Long, CBE, BA, MBA, Hon ARAM, APD, DBA
W Mills, BA
C H Pymont, QC, MA Bar
The Revd Rachel Weir, BA, LLB

International Council:
Y A M Tunku Ali Redhauddin ibni Tuanku Muhriz, BA, MC/MPA
T D P Kirkwood, MA

Master: **L J Moelwyn-Hughes**, MA, MEd

Second Master: W D L Nicholas, BEng, MSc
Deputy Master & Director of Corporate Resources: P N Bryan, BA, ACA
Deputy Head (Academic): E J Tolputt, MA, MEng
Deputy Head (Boarding): Lady Cayley, MA
Deputy Head (Co-Curriculum): Mrs D J Harris, MA
Director of Admissions: Mrs J Hodgson, BA

Assistant Staff:
* *Head of Department*
† *Housemasters/Housemistresses*
P R Adams, BEd (**Design and Technology*)
Miss A L Adderley, BA
B R Allen, MA
Miss N L Allen, BSc
M W Alleyne
N M Allott, BSc
D I Andrew, MA, MSci (**Economics & Business Studies*)
A J Arkwright, BA
D R Armitage, MA (†*B House*)
M Baldrey, BMus, FTCL
C E Barclay, BSc, FRAS, FRSA (*Director of the Observatory, Director of EPQ*)
J S M Birchall, BSc
T A Birkill, BSc (*Biology)
Miss S H Bingham, BA
M B Blossom, MA
A J Brown, MA (*Modern Languages)
Ms V R Brown, MA
Mrs R L T Bruce, BA
M P L Bush, BA
J P Carroll, BEd
D T Clark, MTheol (**Religious Studies*)
S C Clayton, BA
M Conlen, BSc (†*Cotton House*)
Mrs H A M Cox, BSc (†*Elmhurst*)
Ms M A D'Angelo, BA
Miss J Darby, BA, GMus
A H de Trafford, MA (*Spanish)
Miss V G M Delalleau, BA
Mrs I D Dennis, MA
S J Dennis, MBE, MSc
R G De Rosa, BSc (*Geography)
Dr G A Doyle, BSc, MSc, PhD, DIC, CChem, MRSC (*Science)
P T Dukes, FGSM, ARAM (**Artistic Director*)
Mr J J Duplock, MA
Mrs A J Finn, MSc (†*Morris House*)
Dr S D Flatres, MSci, PhD
C A Fraser, MA
[Mrs J L Fruci, BA]
Miss O Gallagher, BSc
B W Giles, MA
T P Gilmour (*Rugby)
A Gist, MA (*Form Coordinator*)
N O P Gordon, MA (*English)
M A Gow, BA (*Politics)
Miss O F Grimley, BSc
A J Hamilton, BA
C L Harrison, BSc (†*Summerfield*)
S R Hawthorn, BSc (*Designate* †*Preshute*)
Miss V D Herrenschmidt, BA
J A Hodgson, BSc
Mrs R F Horton, MA (**Director of Sport*)
Miss A F Hudson, BSc
Miss J C Isitt, BA
[Mrs R L Jerstice, BA]
H E B Jones, BA
P N Keighley, BEng
Mrs A L Keighley, BA
D Kenworthy, BA, MFA (*Drama)
T A Kiggell, MA
Mrs K J Kiggell, MA (†*Dancy House*)
G D M Lane, BSc (†*C3*)
Mrs J E Lane, BSc
J T W Lane, BA
Miss A C Langdale, MSc
T C M Lauze, BA, MBA (*Director of Teaching & Learning*)

Ms Q Li, MA (*Mandarin Chinese*)
Mrs D L Lilley, MA (†*Mill Mead*)
J F Lloyd, BA, MPhil (*Classics*)
M C J Loxton, MA
Mrs J L Luker, BSc (Acting *Psychology*)
J J Lyon Taylor, BSc (†*Littlefield*)
G I Macmillan, BA, (†*Turner House*)
D J Madden, BEng
Miss I C M Marks, MA
T G R Marvin, MA (†*Preshute*)
Mrs J McClean, BA (*Learning Support & Study Skills*)
Mrs J McFarland, BSc
Dr F S McKeown, BA, PhD, FRNS (*History of Art*)
M McNally, BSc
G J McSkimming, BSc (†*Barton Hill*)
Miss H L Meehan, BSc
B H Miller, BSc
W J Molyneux, BA
Mrs Y Momota
N J L Moore, MA
J V T Morell, MSc
P N Morley-Fletcher, MA (*French*)
C A F Moule, MA (*History*)
N Nelson-Piercy, BA (*Russian*)
J N Newman, BSc
E G Nobes, MA (*Careers*)
P J O'Sullivan, BA
Mrs C E Page, MA
J H Parnham, MA
Mrs C N Pembroke, BA (†*Ivy House*)
G R Playfair, MA (†*C2*)
Dr M J Ponsford, BA, PhD
Miss T C Rainer, MA (*German*)
M S Ramage
K J D Richards, MA
Dr L J Richards, BSc, PhD
Dr D G Roberts, MSc, PhD
Mrs E J Ross, MA
Dr E Ryder, BSc, PhD
Mrs M C Sandall, MA
R A Sandall, BCom, BA
Mrs R Scott, MA
H M H Scott, DRSAMD
Dr A D Sharp, BSc, PhD
M J Sharrad, BSc (*PE*)
G B Shearn, BSc (*ICT*)
Mrs S Shearn, BEd (†*New Court*)
C S Smith, BEng, MSc
Mrs E C Smith, BA
K G A Smith, BA
A O J Staines, BA (*Choirmaster*)
C O Stewart, MA
Dr J P Swift, BSc, PhD (†*C1*)
Ms R C Thomas, BA
H L R Tilney, BA (*Academic Scholarship & Leadership Programme*)
Mrs M Tollit, MA
R Tong (*Outdoor Activities*)
Miss C Toomer, GGSM
E F J Twohig, MA, MFA (*Art*)
Mrs C A Walsh, BSc (*Chemistry*)
C J Wheatland, MPhys
I A Wilkins, MFA
R D Willmett, BA
Mrs A T Woodford, BA (*Italian*, *Oxbridge Coordinator*)
Miss B L Woods, MSc
Mr J Wright, BSc

Senior Chaplain: The Revd T W G Novis, BA, Mdiv
Assistant Chaplain: Revd Dr J Blokland, MA, MSc, PhD

Medical Officer: Dr J Campbell, MBBS, DRCOG, DFFP, MRCGP
Librarian: J E Burton, BA
Master's Assistant: Mrs S Nicholas

Merchant Taylors' Boys' School
Crosby

186 Liverpool Road, Crosby, Liverpool L23 0QP

Tel: 0151 949 9366 (Admissions Office)
Fax: 0151 949 9300
email: infomtbs@merchanttaylors.com
website: www.merchanttaylors.com
Twitter: @MerchantsCrosby
Facebook: @merchanttaylorscrosby

Motto: *Concordia parvae res crescunt ~ Small things grow in harmony*

The Boys' School was founded in 1620 by John Harrison, citizen and Merchant Taylor of London. In 1878 the School was transferred to its present site where it is now housed beneath the iconic red brick clock tower.

The Senior Boys' School is attended by over 550 boys aged eleven to eighteen, 158 of whom are in the Sixth Form. There is also a Junior Boys' School with 160 boys aged between seven and eleven.

The school has a reputation for academic excellence and the majority of our leavers go on to study at Russell Group universities including Oxford and Cambridge. The emphasis throughout is very much on developing learners who are able to work independently and who have a genuine curiosity in their studies.

Curriculum. In the first three years of the Lower School boys study a wide variety of national curriculum subjects including separate sciences as well as the opportunity to pick up extra modern and ancient languages. They gradually specialise in the Middle School where there is the flexibility to study between 8 and 11 GCSEs including an accelerated IGCSE mathematics course. There is an additional timetabled Friday afternoon in Years 7–9 for enrichment activities. The Gifted and Talented extension programme offers practical lessons in beekeeping, skateboard design, shooting, fencing, ceramics, scuba diving and many others.

In the Sixth Form the following subjects are available at A Level: Mathematics, Further Mathematics, Physics, Chemistry, Biology, Latin, Greek, Classical Civilisation, English Language, English Literature, History, Geography, Economics, French, German, Spanish, Design and Technology, Art & Design, Music, Theatre Studies and Physical Education. In addition, students in the Sixth Form will have an opportunity to follow a course in General Studies.

Games. Facilities include a £5 million sports centre with climbing wall, fitness suite, sports hall and dance studio. There is a heated indoor swimming pool on site, extensive playing fields, cricket nets, a share of Northern Club's facilities and three tennis courts.

Games played are Rugby, Hockey, Cricket, Athletics, Rowing, Football, Swimming, Tennis and Cross-Country. All boys are encouraged to try at least one of the many games options available during their time at school.

School Societies. A wide range of activities and interests is covered by School Societies including a very enthusiastic and strong Debate Society.

Music and Drama. About 200 boys receive weekly instrumental tuition and there is a subsidised scheme for beginners on orchestral instruments. There is a School Choral Society, Junior School Choir, Concert Band, Swing

Band, a Chamber Orchestra along with various woodwind and brass ensembles. Boys regularly perform both in and out of School at a variety of events and are given many opportunities to perform publicly.

There are two full-time teachers, plus a team of visiting specialist instrument teachers. There are links in Music with our sister school, Merchant Taylors' Girls' School. There are also close links with the Girls' School in Drama, which now forms an integral part of the Senior School curriculum as well as being a major extracurricular activity.

Combined Cadet Force. The School has a voluntary contingent of the Combined Cadet Force with Royal Navy, Army and Royal Air Force Sections. Activities include mountaineering, camping, sailing, flying and shooting, and there is the opportunity to attend a variety of camps and courses, both in Great Britain and overseas. There are around 300 members of the CCF, many of whom are girls from our sister school.

Admission. Boys are admitted to the Junior School at age 7 and to the Senior School at 11 or at Sixth Form. Bursary Places are available at age 11 and Sixth Form.

Fees per term (2018–2019). Tuition: Senior School £3,798, Junior School £2,839.

Old Boys. There is an active Old Boys' Association (The Old Crosbeians) whose Secretary may be contacted via the School and from whom a handbook/register may be obtained (please email Mrs Lisa Connor in our Development Office if you wish to get in contact: l.connor@merchanttaylors.com). The OBA is a lively and sociable association which organises events up and down the country throughout the year.

Charitable status. The Merchant Taylors' Schools Crosby is a Registered Charity, number 1125485, and a Company Limited by Guarantee, registered in England, number 6654276. Registered Office: Liverpool Road, Crosby, Liverpool L23 0QP.

Governors:
Chairman: Mrs B Bell, CBE, LLB Hons, FCLIT, FSOE, FIMI, FIRTE
Mr J Cartwright, BSc
Mr C Cowling, BSc, FIA, FIMA, CSci, CMath
Mrs K Crewe-Read, BSc, PGCE
Mr D S Evans, LLB, MA Oxon
Dr Je A Fox, MBChB, DRCOG, MRCGP, FRCGP
Mrs S Gascoigne, BEd Hons
Miss A Gervasoni, MBA, BHSc Hons, ALMC, LLCM
Mr J Hepworth, MRICS
Ms L C Martin Wright, ONC, JP, DL
Mr S A Wilkinson, BA, FCA
Mr D Yip, MA, IoD

Clerk to the Governors & Director of Finance and Operations: Mrs Lynn Hill
Accounts: Mr D Norton

Headmaster: **Mr David Wickes**, MA Oxon

Deputy Headmasters:
Mr R A Simpson, MA, MCIEA, BA Hons, PGCE
Mr D Williams, BSc

PA to the Headmaster: Mrs B Hatton

Head of Sixth Form: Mr G Bonfante, BSc Hons, MA, PGCE
Head of Middle School: Mr R Yates, MSc, BSc Hons, PGCE
Head of Lower School: Mr N A Hunt, BA Hons
Assistant Headmaster Operations: Mr J B Green, MA, BA Hons
Director of Music: Mr D Holroyd, MA, GMus Hons RNCM, PPRNCM, ARCO

Emeritus Chaplain: Revd D A Smith, BA

Junior School:
Head: Mrs J E Thomas, BEd Hons, MEd, NPQH
Deputy Head, Pastoral: Mr D K J Youngson, BA Hons
Deputy Head, Academic: Mrs Y Bonfante, BEd Hons
PA to the Headmistress: Mrs A Hodson

Admissions: Mrs S Barrington

Merchant Taylors' School

Sandy Lodge, Northwood, Middlesex HA6 2HT
Tel: Head Master's PA: 01923 821850
            Reception: 01923 820644
            Admissions Officer: 01923 845514
            Bursar: 01923 825669
Fax: 01923 845522
email: info@mtsn.org.uk
website: www.mtsn.org.uk
Twitter: @MerchantTaylors
Facebook: @MerchantTaylors
LinkedIn: /merchanttaylorsschoolnorthwood

Motto: *Concordia parvae res crescunt*

The school has enjoyed a distinguished history since its foundation by the Merchant Taylors' Company in 1561. It was one of the nine original "Clarendon" public schools and its pupils have achieved distinction throughout its history. The school enjoys close links with the Company, which, to this day, constitutes its Governing Body. In 1933 the school moved from central London to its present superb, rural setting of 280 acres at Sandy Lodge, Northwood. We are within easy reach of parents in Buckinghamshire, Hertfordshire, Middlesex and North-West London by car, train or school coach service, as well as a mere half hour by tube from Baker Street.

Four distinct boys' day schools share the campus. The nursery school, pre-prep and prep cater for 330 boys from 3 to 13 years of age (the prep school shares some of its facilities with the senior school, but is a separate school in its own right), while the senior school has approximately 890 pupils from 11–18, with over 300 in the sixth form.

All pupils have an individual tutor who looks after them during their school career in small House tutor groups. They are encouraged to cultivate interests at which they can excel, to have confidence in their abilities and to gain self-knowledge as well as knowledge. The academic achievements of the school are first-rate and are achieved in a humane, civilised and unpressured atmosphere. We place a great emphasis on encouraging boys to organise many activities themselves and to take responsibility for others.

Admission. Entry to the senior school at 11+ and 13+ is by the School's own Entrance Examinations, together with an interview; for entry to the Prep school, see Merchant Taylors' Prep entry in the IAPS section. 16+ applications are invited after the publication of GCSE results. Applicants should have at least seven top grades at GCSE.

Term of entry. September unless there are very special circumstances.

Scholarships and Bursaries. There are no separate Scholarship papers in the Entrance Examinations. We make awards to boys who perform exceptionally well in these examinations and at a separate interview; we take into account information received from the boy's current school.

11+ entry: At least 5 major Academic Scholarships are awarded, each up to a maximum value of 50% of the School fee. Up to 5 minor Academic Scholarships each to the value of £200 per annum. Up to 2 All-Rounder scholarships, each up to a maximum value of 50% of the School fee. Scholarships for Sport, Art, Design Technology & Drama (a maximum of 2 per subject) each to the value of a £200 department programme and associated materials.

13+ entry: At least 5 major Academic Scholarships are awarded, each up to a maximum value of 50% of the School fee. Up to 12 minor Academic Scholarships each with a minimum value of £200 per annum. Up to 2 All-Rounder scholarships each up to a maximum value of 50% of the School fee. Up to 8 scholarships for Sport, Art, Design Technology & Drama (a maximum of 2 per subject) each to the value of a £200 department programme and associated materials.

16+ entry: Entrance Scholarships are available across the disciplines of Engineering; Bio-Medicine; Finance and Economics; Languages; Humanities; Creative Arts and Technology. Each up to a maximum value of 50% of the School fee. One bursary up to the value of the full School fee is available.

Music Scholarships: Four Music Scholarships (one of up to 25% of the School fee; one of up to 15% and two of up to 10%) awarded across 11+, 13+ and 16+. A Scholarship includes free instrumental and/or singing tuition on two instruments (or instrument and voice). Additional awards of free tuition may be made if there are boys of sufficient merit.

All Scholarships can be supplemented by means-tested bursaries should there be a proven need.

Bursaries: The School welcomes applications from parents whose sons would benefit from attending Merchant Taylors' School, and who will contribute strongly to the life of the community, but who require financial assistance. Means-tested bursarial support is available up to the value of 100% of the School fee; further details can be obtained from the Admissions Office.

Scholarships at Oxford and Cambridge Universities. At the end of their first undergraduate year, Old Boys are eligible for election to a maximum of three Sir Thomas White Scholarships at St John's College Oxford, a Matthew Hale Scholarship at The Queen's College Oxford and a Parkin & Stuart Scholarship for Science or Mathematics at Pembroke College Cambridge.

Curriculum and Organisation. The curriculum in years 7, 8 and 9 (Thirds, Upper Thirds and Fourths) is a broad one: Art and Design, Biology, Chemistry, Computing, Design Technology, Drama, English, French, Geography, History, Latin, Mathematics, Music, Physical Education, Physics, PSHCE, and Religious Studies. Greek, German, or Spanish are started when 13+ boys enter the school. All boys take nine or ten GCSEs, chosen from the subjects above. Boys are entered for IGCSEs and GCSEs. A student entering the Lower Sixth embarks upon a two-year course in which all boys initially study four subjects to A Level, with most certifying three and some four. An extensive choice of supercurricular options is available, including the EPQ, Thinking and Study skills and Careers Preparation.

Music. All orchestral and band instruments, piano, organ, percussion and guitar are taught to boys throughout the school. Choirs, orchestras, bands and chamber groups give frequent concerts throughout the year.

Games and Physical Education. Magnificent playing fields include over 55 acres dedicated to Rugby, Cricket, Soccer and Hockey. There are Fives, Squash and Tennis Courts; an athletics track and two floodlit, all-weather pitches. The Sports Hall accommodates four badminton courts, a multi-gym, a climbing wall, a fencing salle and indoor cricket nets. The school's lakes provide a marvellous facility for our Sailing Club, canoeing and windsurfing. Physical Education is compulsory for all pupils, and all pupils learn to swim. There is an indoor swimming pool and Water Polo is offered. Coaching in Fencing, Basketball,

Judo and Karate is excellent. MTS is one of only two schools in the country to host first-class cricket fixtures and is the home of Middlesex Youth Cricket.

Service Sections. The school has a Contingent of the Combined Cadet Force with RN, Army, and RAF Sections. The CCF includes girls from St Helen's School, Northwood. There is a Rifle Range for the use of the Contingent (and we send a team to Bisley every year). The Duke of Edinburgh's Award scheme allows boys to achieve Bronze, Silver and Gold Awards, and the Community Service programme provides an opportunity for a wide range of activities in the local area. All boys in Years 10 and 11 take part in the CCF, The Duke of Edinburgh's Award scheme or Community Service teams.

The school places great emphasis on charitable endeavour and the boys run a great many societies to support good causes. A special feature of the school's charity work is Phab, a week-long residential holiday for handicapped children held every Easter and organised by Sixth Form boys together with the girls of St Helen's School. The school also has a charitable partnership with two schools in India.

School Societies. A large number of societies cover a wide field of interests and activities.

Careers. There is an outstanding Careers Advisory Service, which organises annual Careers and Higher Education Conventions at the school and a range of work experience.

House and Tutorial Systems. The school is divided into eight Houses. Each House is under the care of a Head of House and a team of tutors, who are responsible for the pastoral care of boys in that House.

Fees per term (2018–2019). £8,278 (Autumn Term), £6,210 (both Spring Term & Summer Term); these cover not only tuition, games, and lunch but also a lifetime alumnus subscription (OMT). There is a non-refundable registration fee of £100; separate admission fee deposits are charged later.

Merchant Taylors' Prep, the Preparatory school to Merchant Taylors', adjoins the senior school.

(*For further details see Merchant Taylors' Prep entry in IAPS section.*)

Charitable status. Merchant Taylors' School Charitable Trust is a Registered Charity, number 1063740. It exists to provide a first-class all-round education for boys, irrespective of their background.

The Governors of the School:
Chairman: C P Hare

G B M H du Parc Braham	D Haria
R J Brooman	Mrs S Morgan
Dr J M Cox	A G Moss
A Eastwood	Mrs J Redman
Mrs L Gadd	D J Shah
Ms G Gardiner	R J Temmink
Lady P A Harding	Sir M Tomlinson

Head Master: **S J Everson**, MA

Bursar: I D Williams, MBA, CMgr, FCMI, MAPM, MCIL
Second Master: M C Husbands, MA
Senior Deputy Head (*Academic*): B J C Horan, MA
Senior Master: C R Evans-Evans, BA, MEd, NPQH
Registrar: J G Taylor, MA
Deputy Head, Information Services: Dr A R H Clarke, MA, DPhil
Development Director: N J Latham, LLB Law
Head of Upper School: R C Garvey, MA
Head of Middle School: Mrs L P Pruden-Lawson, MA
Head of Lower School: T W Jenkin, MA
Chaplain: Reverend J Fields

Assistant Staff:

Art & Design:
Ms I Lumsden, BA (*Head of Art and Design*)
Miss H C Blowes, BA
Ms T Hoch, MA
S N Leech, BA

Biology:
Mrs S N Stuteley, BSc (*Head of Biology*)
T C H Greenaway, BSc (*Assistant Head Staff and Pupil Well-Being and SCR President*)
Dr A Komissarova, PhD
B C Oxenham, BSc
Mrs L P Pruden-Lawson, MA (*Head of Middle School*)
B A Simpson, BSc

Careers:
Mrs H Armstrong, BA, PG Dip (*Head of Careers*)
Mrs K Richards, Associate CFA UK (*Careers Coordinator*)
Mrs M Thobani, Work Experience Coordinator

Chemistry:
M P Powell, MA (*Head of Chemistry*)
R I M Alexander, BSc (*Director of Hockey & Deputy Leader of Co-Curricular Activities*)
M S Hughes, BSc
Dr M M Lohr, PhD
Dr M Lomas, PhD
Mrs F A Rashid, BSc (*Head of Science*)
J R Talboys, BSc

Classics:
P D Harrison, MA (*Head of Classics & Deputy Director of Teaching & Learning*)
Miss M A Bergquist, BSc (*Joint Deputy Director of Communications*)
Mrs C D Fielding, BA (*Staff Tutor*)
E H Gazeley, BA
M C Husbands, MA (*Second Master*)

Computing:
G N Macleod, BA (*Head of Academic Computing*)
J E Firestone, MA (*Head of CCF and Outdoor Education*)
E E W Williams, MA

Design & Technology:
H J Hutchings, BA (*Head of Design Technology*)
N J Kyriacou, BEd
Miss H M Park, BSc
S J Reid, BSc
G A Wilson, BA

Drama and Theatre Studies:
Miss C L Clarke, BA (*Director of Drama*)

Economics & Politics:
D C Halliday BA (*Head of Economics*)
Dr M I Beacham, PhD (*Head of Andrewes House*)
A R Fraser, MSc
R C Garvey, MA (*Head of Upper School & Teacher of Religion & Philosophy*)
E P James, BA (*Head of Politics & Assistant Head of Upper School*)
H C O'Grady, BA

English:
M G Hilton-Dennis, BA (*Head of English*)
Mrs J M Cox, BA
Ms M J Fitzpatrick, BA (*Temporary Teacher of English*)
D A Gibbons, BA (*Head of Phab*)
T W Jenkin, MA (*Head of Lower School*)
J D Manley, MA (*Head of Mulcaster House*)
I J Mitchell, BA, BSc (*Head of Psychology*)
A J Richardson, BA

D G Robinson, BA
Mrs K Shockley, BA (*Second in English*) (*Family Leave*)
Ms L V Smith, MA (*Director of Teaching and Learning & SCR Representative – Governing Body*)
Miss E K Trafford, MA (*Second in English, Temporary*)
J H Tyler, MA (*Head of Spenser House*)

Geography:
J D Innes, BA (*Head of Geography*)
Miss N M Innes, BA (*Assistant Head of Lower School*)
Mrs E J Lemoine, BA (*Joint Deputy Director of Communications & Head of Clive House*)
Miss H J Maxfield, BA (*Assistant Head of Middle School*)
Mrs S A Riddleston, BA
R Simmonds, BSc (*Head of PSHCE*)
J M Tidmarsh, BSc

History:
M W S Hale, BA, MPhil (*Head of History*)
Mrs F E Blatchford Pace, BA (*Assistant Head of Lower School*)
M Flower, BA (*Head of White House*)
M T Herring, BA
B J C Horan, MA (*Senior Deputy Head, Academic*)
P A Hoyle, MSt
J G Taylor, MA (*Registrar*)

Information Services:
Dr A R H Clarke, MA, DPhil, CPhys, MInstP (*Deputy Head, Information Services*)
P Gregory, HND (*Technical Services Manager*)
J P Beck (*Senior Network Engineer*)
P A J G Gregory (*Network Engineer*)
J D Pope (*IT Assistant*)
I Rudling (*Webmaster*)

Learning Support:
Ms E J Sadler, BA, MEd (*Head of Learning Support*)
Mrs D N Desai, BSc (*Teaching Assistant*)
Mrs D D Kotecha, MSc (*Teaching Assistant*)
Miss I E Roberts, BA (*Specialist Teacher*)
Miss E M Whaley, BA (*Graduate Assistant*)

Library:
Mrs A J South, BSc, Dip Lib (*Senior Librarian*)
Mrs P J Jones, BA, PG Dip (*Part-time Library Assistant*)
Mrs R J L Millard, BA, MA (*Assistant Librarian*)

Mathematics:
A S Miller, BSc (*Head of Mathematics*)
A P Carroll BA
N J Cleaver, MSc
S J Coles, BSc
P Davidson-Reiber, MMathPhil
Mrs H E Ezomo, BA
M A Fothergill, BSc (*Head of Manor House*)
Mrs D C Gedalla, BA
Mrs S M Hale, BSc (*Assistant Head of Upper School*)
S F Hardman, BSc (*Second in Mathematics*)
Mrs G M Hazan, BA
Mrs N Manek, BA (*Examinations Officer*)
Mrs T A Omert, BEng (*Head of Charities and Community Service*)
S L Rowlands, BA
S G Starost, BA
Mrs N K Turton, BA (*Family Leave*)

Modern Foreign Languages:
R P Bailey, BA (*Head of Modern Foreign Languages*)
Mrs M C R Castro, BA (*Spanish*)
Miss R G Haye, Licence LCE (*French and Spanish*)
Ms V M Kotsuba MA (*French*)
Miss H E McCullough, BA (*German and French*)
M W Pacey, BEd (*Subject Leader for German*)

J M S Rippier, BA (*Director of Communications &
French*)
T P Rocher, L-ès-L (*French*)
Mrs C E Udell, MA (*German and French*)
F R Vignal, DipHE (*Subject Leader in French and Second
in MFL, French & Spanish*)

Music:
S J Couldridge, DipTCL (*Director of Music*)
R W Crowley, MSc (*Temporary Teacher of Music*)
Dr R L Couchman, PhD (*Head of Academic Music*)
(*Family Leave*)
Mrs J H Stubbs, MusB, ARCO, ALCM (*Assistant Director
of Music*)

Physical Education:
L D Foot, BSc (*Director of Sport*)
R I M Alexander, BSc (*Director of Hockey & Deputy
Leader Co-curricular Activities*)
Miss R A Caulfield, BA (*Assistant Head of Outdoor
Education*)
P J Davies, BSc (*Head of Sports Science*)
C R Evans-Evans, BA, MEd (*Senior Master*)
I McGowan, MSc (*Director of Cricket*)
A J Mills, BSc (*Director of Rugby & Head of Walter
House*)
M J Penny, BSc

Physics:
Mrs A Mayadeen, MPhys (*Head of Physics*)
Dr A R H Clarke, MA, DPhil, CPhys, MInstP (*Deputy
Head, Information Services*)
S J Day, BSc
D W Hivey, BA
C P Hull, BSc (*Assistant Head of Middle School*)
Miss K N Hustwitt, BSc
D J Spikings, BA, MEng (*Director of Studies*)

Psychology:
I J Mitchell, BA, BSc (*Head of Psychology*)

Religion & Philosophy:
I L Regan-Smith, MA (*Head of Religion & Philosophy*)
L J Charman, MA (*Head of Hilles House*)
M Flower, BA (*Head of White House*)
R C Garvey, MA (*Head of Upper School & Teacher of
Economics*)

School Counsellor:
Mrs P Llewellyn, BSc Hons, PG Dip
A Muller (*Temporary*)

Visiting Teachers:
J Atkins, Dip RAM (*Trumpet*)
G Boyd, Dip Mus (*Double Bass*)
S Byron, BMus Hons RCM (*Trombone*)
Miss S Clark, MA, LRSM, ARCM, Dip RCM, CTABRSM
(*Piano*)
Mrs N S Coleman, CertEd (*Flute*)
Mrs R Couldridge (*Violin*)
Miss K Cormican, GTCL, PDOT (*Violin*)
J Francis (*Saxophone & Clarinet*)
A Gathercole, GGSM (*Trumpet*)
B Halford (*Guitar*)
Ms N Hawkins, (*Guitar*)
D Hester, LTCL, Dip TCL (*Bassoon and Music
Technology*)
C Hooker, LRAM, ARAM (*Oboe*)
J Lawrence, BA (*Percussion*)
Mrs N Manington, BMus, LGSM (*Piano and Jazz Piano*)
Miss Z Matthews (*Viola*)
N Martin (*Percussion*)
Ms P O'Sullivan, BA (*Recorder*)
D Robb (*Clarinet*)

D Saunderson, GGSM (*Singing*)
Mrs M Stone, MMus (*Piano*)
Mrs N Tait, LRAM Hons (*Cello*)
R Wainwright (*Organ*)

Sports:

A Bruce (*Strength and Conditioning*)	J Jones (*Judo*)
J Burley (*Rugby – Performance Analyst*)	M Khalifa (*Squash*)
	N Lambert (*Rugby*)
G Calway (*Cricket*)	R Lawrence (*Rugby*)
A Cawthone (*Fives*)	N Li (*Table Tennis*)
A Cuthbert (*Cricket*)	P Loudon (*Hockey*)
S Dokic (*Athletics*)	D Manley (*Athletics*)
D Emms (*Tennis*)	A Morris (*Sports Psychologist*)
L Fazekas (*Fencing*)	
A French (*Watersports*)	R Nangia (*Scuba Diving*)
H Geall (*Scuba Diving Instructor*)	G Price (*Fives*)
	A Reay (*Rugby*)
S Galloway (*Cricket*)	G Summerfield (*Cricket*)
J Gibbons (*Rugby*)	A Thomas (*Cricket*)
L Gick (*Physiotherapist*)	D Thorpe (*Squash*)
M Irving (*Hockey*)	L Wooldridge (*Cricket*)

Head Master's PA: Mrs J Jolliff
Admissions Officer: G McCann
Bursar's Secretary: Mrs A Johnson

Merchant Taylors' Prep:
Head of School: Dr Karen McNerney, BSc Hons, PGCE,
MSc, EdD
Senior Deputy Head: Mr Antony McConnell, MA Hons,
PGCE, FHA
Deputy Head: Mr Andrew Crook, BA Hons, PGCE

Merchiston Castle School

Colinton, Edinburgh EH13 0PU

Tel:	0131 312 2200
	Headmaster: 0131 312 2203
	Admissions: 0131 312 2201
Fax:	0131 441 6060
email:	headmaster@merchiston.co.uk
website:	www.merchiston.co.uk
Twitter:	@MerchiNews
Facebook:	@MerchistonEdinburgh
LinkedIn:	/merchiston-castle-school

Motto: *Ready Ay Ready*

The School was established in 1833 and moved in 1930
from the centre of the city out to its present spacious and
attractive site, bordered by the Water of Leith and close to
the Pentland Hills.

There are 440 boys in the School, of whom 286 are
boarders.

Admission. The normal ages of entry are 7–14 and 16,
though from time to time there may be vacancies at other
ages. Entry at 7–12 is by entrance assessment, interview and
current school report; entry at 13 by the Common Entrance
or Merchiston entrance examinations and current school
report. Entry at 14 is by Merchiston entrance examinations.
Entry to the Sixth Form at 16 depends on a successful showing in GCSE or National 4 and National 5 examinations as
well as on interview and a school report. There are approximately 150 pupils in the Sixth Form. Entry is possible in all
three terms where vacancies permit.

A prospectus and further details may be obtained from
the Admissions Office. Prospective parents are encouraged

to visit the School. Information may be also found on our website: www.merchiston.co.uk.

Video Gallery. Please follow this link to view videos of Merchiston life: Merchiston Video Gallery.

Courses of study. In the Juniors the curriculum comprises English, English Literature, Mathematics, Biology, Chemistry, Physics, History, French, Latin, German, Spanish, Mandarin, Geography, Religious Studies, Art and Design, Music, PE, Electronics, Design and Technology, and Information Technology.

In the Middle School a 2-year course leading to GCSEs is followed, consisting of a core curriculum: English, English Literature, Mathematics, a foreign language (French, German, Spanish, Mandarin), IGCSE Biology, Chemistry and Physics, and a wide range of optional subjects, including History, a second foreign language, Electronics, Information Technology, Geography, Latin, Religious Studies (Philosophy and Ethics), Art and Design, Design and Technology, and Music. Many boys take 10 subjects.

In the Lower Sixth, most boys study 4 subjects at AS Level. In the Upper Sixth, boys study generally 3 subjects to A2. A Level options include English Literature, Mathematics, Further Mathematics, Biology, Chemistry, Physics, French, German, Spanish, History, Geography, Economics, Government and Politics, Classical Civilisation, Religious Studies, PE, Information Technology, Latin, Design and Technology, Electronics (AS only) and Art. Other languages at A Level (including Classical Greek, Italian and Russian) are available on request and at additional charge. In addition to his main subjects, each boy follows a General Studies course offering Moral and Social Studies and Careers Guidance. Classes are small throughout the School, and all subjects are set by ability. The School prepares boys for entry to Oxford and Cambridge.

The School makes provision for specialist ESOL teaching for International students, including an opportunity to study GCSE English in the Upper Sixth year.

In 2018, the A Level A*/A pass rate was 50% with 95% of pupils gaining entry to their first or second choice university.

Support for Learning Provision. Able boys with learning difficulties, including dyslexia, enjoy successful careers at Merchiston. Our aim is to enhance self-esteem through genuine praise. We encourage each pupil to find success in his area of strength, whether inside or outside the classroom. The objective is that all pupils have access to a wide and varied curriculum, and that, as a result, each discovers his own personal strengths and talents, and enjoys the resulting success. All are expected to follow mainstream GCSE courses.

Houses. Each of the boarding houses caters for a particular age group and the atmosphere and activities are tailored accordingly. The purpose-built Sixth Form boarding house opened in 2009 offering 126 en-suite bedrooms, with modern kitchens, a multi-gym and open plan social spaces with stunning views of Edinburgh and Fife. The Housemaster, Housemother and House Tutors pay special attention to the care of the individual and to the development of both his studies and interests.

Day boys. The life of day boys is fully integrated with that of the boarders.

Games. The principal games are rugby, played in the Autumn and Lent Terms, and in the Summer Term cricket and athletics. There is a large indoor heated swimming pool and a sports hall, and there are good facilities for other sports including tennis, football, squash, fives, shooting, sailing, skiing, basketball, golf, badminton and hockey. Merchiston prides itself on fostering the pursuit of excellence in a sport-for-all environment. The School is currently represented nationally and internationally in many sports,

such as athletics, cricket, golf, rugby and target shooting. We have also achieved Scottish honours in tennis, rugby and clay pigeon shooting in the last three years. The Tennis Academy is ranked number two World Tennis School, by the ISF World Schools Championship, 2017–19. The Golf Academy is the number two UK Ranking Golf School in the ISGA rankings 2017–18, with two members ranked in the top four UK Individual Junior Players, 2017. Merchiston is also proud to be the Scottish Schools' U18 Rugby Champions and in the Top 100 Schools for Cricket.

Music. Music plays an important part in the life of the School. Tuition is available in all keyboard and orchestral instruments; currently about fifty per cent of the School are learning a musical instrument, and two choirs flourish. There is also a School orchestra, a close harmony group, a jazz band and two pipe bands. The choir and instrumentalists frequently go on tour, e.g. to the USA, the Far East, and Europe.

Drama. There is at least one major drama production a term, jointly staged with our sister school, as well as frequent House plays or drama workshop productions in a well-equipped, purpose-built theatre.

Art, Craft, Design and Technology, and Ceramics. The Art and Design Centre offers scope both within the curriculum and in the pupils' free time for painting, pottery, metalwork, woodwork and design work. Courses in Computing and Electronics are also available both within the curriculum or in free time.

Societies. There is a wide variety of clubs, including chess, debating and electronics. Visits to theatres, concerts and exhibitions are a frequent part of a boy's life at Merchiston. The Enlightened Curriculum uses Edinburgh as a prime resource for cultural experiences for all age groups.

CCF. All boys join the CCF for a period of three terms, after which point participation is voluntary. This includes outward bound activities such as climbing, hillwalking, canoeing and camping. All senior boys at Merchiston also undertake a Bronze Duke of Edinburgh's Award expedition, with participation at Silver and Gold level on a purely voluntary basis.

The School is also very active in community service work.

Girls. The School does not take girls but has a special relationship as brother/sister school with St George's School for Girls, Edinburgh and Kilgraston School in Perthshire. This includes joint expeditions, concerts, tours, seminars, debating, drama, social events and study courses. Merchiston operates a joint fees scheme with St George's School for Girls; Kilgraston School and Queen Margaret's School, York.

Careers advice. An expert careers adviser supplements the advice of the Academic Leadership Team, Housemasters and Academic Tutors. In the LVI year, pupils attend timetabled lessons in Careers as part of the General Studies Programme of the Sixth Form, where they are also encouraged to take a Work Experience placement and to visit local universities in the month of June. When pupils start in the Shell, they undertake Cambridge Occupational Analysts (COA) Preview and Profile assessments. These assess each individual's interests and abilities in several key cognitive areas. In the Fifth Form each individual has a discussion with the Head of Careers, during which interests are explored and feedback from the COA assessments is given. The discussion is focused on career areas of interest – as identified by the individual and the COA feedback – and identifying areas to be investigated, as well as touching on potential A Level programmes. There is an annual HE & Careers Fair to which other local schools are invited.

Links with parents. There are regular parent/staff meetings and parents are fully briefed and consulted with regard to all academic and career decisions. There is also a parents' forum, which holds regular meetings.

Health. There is a medical centre in the charge of the School Nursing Sisters and the School Doctor visits regularly.

Fees per term (2018–2019). Junior School: Boarders £7,030, Day boys £5,010; Forms 2 and 3: Boarders £8,170, Day boys £5,660. Senior School (Forms 4 and above): Boarders £10,970, Day boys £8,070.

Sibling, Forces and Teaching Profession (means–tested) fee reductions are available.

Scholarships and Bursaries. Scholarships are offered for competition from 10+ up to 16, with an emphasis on 13+ entry from Prep Schools.

Junior (10+-12+): Academic, Music (including a Piping Exhibition), All-Rounder.

Senior & Sixth Form (13+, 14+, 16+): Academic, Music (including a Piping Exhibition), Sports, All-Rounder, Art & Design, Design & Technology.

Scholarships no longer carry an automatic fee concession.

Means-tested financial assistance: where parental income is not sufficient to allow the pupil to attend Merchiston, parents may apply for means-tested financial assistance, which may be up to 100% of the day or boarding fees.

Forces: 10% fee remission is available to the sons of serving members of HM Forces.

Trust Applications: The School can apply to charities on behalf of prospective candidates who can demonstrate financial need.

Old boys. The Secretary of The Merchistonian Club, c/o the School. Former pupils include: The Rt Hon Lord John MacGregor, MP; Sir Peter Burt, former Chief Executive, Bank of Scotland; The Rt Hon Lord Kenneth Osborne PC, longest-serving judge of the current Scottish bench; Air Marshal Sir John Baird, Surgeon General of the British Armed Forces between 1997 and 2000, International Rugby Union players: N G R Mair, W S Glen, I H P Laughland, A C W Boyle, A H W Boyle, Q Dunlop, G R T Baird, J Jeffrey, P Walton, C Joiner, B R S Eriksson, D W Hodge, N J Mayer, I A Fullarton, P J Godman, F J M Brown, Sam Hidalgo-Clyne.

Charitable status. Merchiston Castle School is a Registered Charity, number SC016580. It aims to give each boy in his way the capacity and confidence to live in an uncertain world and to make that life as rich as possible; more specifically, to encourage him to work hard and to take pride in achievement, to think independently, to face up to challenges, to accept responsibility, to show concern for others and the environment, and to develop wider skills and interests.

Governors:
G T G Baird, HND, FRAgS (*Chairman*)
D C M Moore, BSc, MPhil, PhD
G R T Baird
S P Abram
I McAteer
R W Nutton, MBBS, MD, FRCS
D R Whiteford, OBE, BSc, FRSA, ARAgS
R S Elliott
Mrs P Abrahams, OBE, MA
A Fraser, LLB, DIPLP, NP, WS
D E L Johnston, QC, MA, PhD, LLD, FRSE
W J J Clayton, MA
Dr A Connan, MBBS, MRCGP, FSRH, MIPM
Mrs P Axon, BEng (*Secretary to the Governors*)
M Gray, BA

Staff:

School Leadership Team:

Headmaster: J Anderson, BA Queen's Belfast

Senior Deputy Head: A W Johnston, MA Edinburgh
Bursar: Mrs P Axon, BEng Reading
Deputy Head Academic: S Campbell, BSc Glasgow
Deputy Head Co-Curricular: R A Charman, BA Canterbury
Deputy Head Pupil Support: Ms K A Fox, BA Hull, BA Cambridge
Head of Merchiston Juniors: Ms N G Waldron, BA Kent

Academic Leadership Team:
Deputy Head Academic: S Campbell, BSc Glasgow
Assistant Head Academic: D D J Cartwright, BSc PhD Edinburgh
Assistant Head Academic: F E Newham, MA Oxford

Pupil Support Leadership Team and Delegated Named Persons:
Deputy Head Pupil Support: Ms K A Fox, BA Hull, BA Cambridge
Assistant Head Pupil Support: F P J Main, BEd Edinburgh
Assistant Head Pupil Support: Mrs I Stewart, BEd Glasgow
Senior Deputy Head: A W Johnston, MA Edinburgh

Housemasters:
Laidlaw South: N M Lieberman, BSc Northumbria
Laidlaw North: D P Rowlands, MA Cambridge
Evans: R L McCorkell, BSc Edinburgh
Rogerson: P K Rossiter, MA Oxford
Chalmers East: N Lear, BSc MSc Loughborough
Chalmers West: W J Ogilvie-Jones, BSc Brunel
Pringle: Ms N G Waldron, BA Kent

Academic Departments:

Art & Design and Design & Technology:
*J M V Cordingley, MA London
Miss F M Blakeman, Dip Des Napier
*J D Loftus, BSc Robert Gordon
F P J Main, BEd Edinburgh
Mrs C L Nugent, BSc Northumbria, MEd PhD Edinburgh

Biology:
*Mrs H J Williams, MSc Glasgow
D M George, BSc Edinburgh
N M Lieberman, BSc Northumbria
R Lilley, BSc Durham, PhD Cardiff

Chemistry:
*R R Greenwood, MSci London
D D J Cartwright, BSc PhD Edinburgh
Miss C Meigh, MChem St Andrews
K G Pettigrew, BSc PhD Edinburgh

Classics:
*Mrs R J Fawthrop, BA Oxford
M R Hillier, MA Cambridge

Economics:
*C Robson, MA Edinburgh
W Donkin, BEd Cape Town

Electronics:
*R P Nicholls, BSc Durham
J D Loftus, BSc Robert Gordon

English:
*Mrs S J Binnie, MA Edinburgh
Ms G Cunningham, BA Stirling
Mr S Douglas, BA Belfast
J D Lugton, MA St Andrews
C C Mechie, MA Edinburgh, MA London, DPhil Oxford
Ms R West, BSc LSE London, MSc Edinburgh

Mrs A E Torrance, BA Exeter
P S Williams, BA Leicester

English as an Additional Language:
*Mrs S J Hardman, BA Sheffield
Miss J M Bowman, MA Aberdeen
S J Horrocks, MA Cambridge

Geography:
*Mrs T A S Bower, BA London, MSc Toronto, DPhil
   Oxford
S I Buchanan, BSc St Andrews
B J Hall, BSc Strathclyde
M Harkins, BA Stirling
M K Raikes, MA Manchester

History and Politics:
*S R Thompson, MA Edinburgh
F E Newham, MA Oxford
Mrs L McDiarmid, BA Warwick
J Troxler, BA Stirling, MEd Glasgow

ICT:
*D H Thomson, MA Glasgow
J B Bisset, MA MSc Aberdeen (*Director of ICT Services*)
Ms J E Moran, BSc Limerick

Mathematics:
*Ms F Vian, PhD Parma
S Campbell, BSc Glasgow
R A Charman, BA Canterbury
M Harkins, BA Stirling
R L McCorkell, BSc Edinburgh
Ms J E Moran, BSc Limerick
Miss R A Mullan, BSc Belfast
Miss N M Steen, MSci PhD Belfast
J C O Vaughan, BSc Edinburgh
Ms J R Vaughan, BA Newcastle

Modern Foreign Languages:
*Mrs M H Gray, MA Lyon
Miss J M Bowman, MA Aberdeen
F Calvo-Martin, BA Salamanca
Mrs J Chang, MA Bournemouth, BA BSc Taiyuan
S J Horrocks, MA Cambridge
Ms A Komischke, BA Passau
D P Rowlands, MA Cambridge

Music:
*S M Dennis, BMus Edinburgh

Personal, Social and Health Education:
*F P J Main, BEd Edinburgh
D W Blair, BSc Stirling
S I Buchanan, BSc St Andrews
Ms K A Fox, BA Hull, BA Cambridge
M Harkins, BA Stirling
C R Harrison, BSc Napier
M R Hillier, MA Cambridge
N M Lieberman, BSc Northumbria
R L McCorkell, BSc Edinburgh
W J Ogilvie-Jones, BSc Brunel
P K Rossiter, MA Oxford
D P Rowlands, MA Cambridge
Ms N G Waldron, BA Kent

Physical Education:
*C R Harrison, BSc Napier
D W Blair, BSc Stirling (*Assistant Director of Rugby*)
R C Deans, BSc Abertay (*Director of Rugby*)
N Lear, BSc MSc Loughborough
R D McCann, BSc Ulster (*Director of Sport*)
M K Raikes, MA Manchester (*Director of Junior Sport*)

Physics:
*R P Nicholls, BSc Durham (*Head of Science &
   Technology*)
C King, BSc Heriot-Watt
J Mayoh, MPhys St Andrews, PhD Cambridge
Miss S M Twyford, MSc Strathclyde, PhD Glasgow

Religious Studies:
*Revd N G D Blair, MA Edinburgh

Support for Learning:
*Mrs I Stewart, BEd Glasgow
Ms J R Vaughan, BA Newcastle
Mrs C Weaving, BSc Leeds

Pringle Centre:
Miss R E Foster, MA Aberdeen (*Leader of Pringle Centre*)
Ms N G Waldron, BA Kent (*Head of Merchiston Juniors*)
Ms J R Vaughan, BA Newcastle (*Deputy Head Academic –
   Juniors*)
M Harkins, BA Stirling
M K Raikes, MA Manchester
Mrs A E Torrance, BA Exeter

Accounts and Human Resources:
Mrs P Axon, BEng Reading (*Bursar*)
Ms A Lees, BSc Oxford (*Financial Controller*)
Mrs C McIntosh, HNC Stevenson (*Assistant Bursar*)
Mrs K M Morrison (*Purchase Ledger*)

Administration:
Mrs L Campion, BSc St Andrews, BM Napier (*Assistant
   Secretary, Headmaster's Office*)
Mrs E Firoozi (*Academic Secretary*)
Mrs G B Gibson (*Receptionist*)

Admissions:
Mrs K Wilson (*Director*)
Miss H Aitken, BA Napier (*Assistant*)

Chapel Team:
Revd N G D Blair, MA Edinburgh (*Leader of the
   Chaplaincy Team*)
S M Dennis, BMus Edinburgh
P K Rossiter, MA Oxford

Departmental Technical Assistants:
C A Brown, BSc Heriot-Watt (*Network Administrator*)
N P Burt (*Design & Technology*)
Ms I Ciani, MChem Padua, PhD Venice
A C MacNeill (*IT Network Manager*)
Mrs K Ryan, BSc Abertay (*Lab Technician*)
R Shepley, MChem Edinburgh (*Lab Technician*)

Development:
D Rider, MinstF Cert (*Director*)
Miss G Imrie, BA Napier (*Assistant*)
D I Pratt (*Assistant*)

Domestic and Catering Management Team:
Mrs A J Hanna (*General Manager*)
Mrs J Hogg (*Duty Manager*)
Ms K Macdonald (*Domestic Manager*)
A Ruscheniko (*Executive Chef*)
Miss A Slodownik (*Assistant Domestic Manager*)

Examinations:
T J Lawson, BA Sheffield, PhD Edinburgh, FSA Scot
   (*Examinations Officer*)
F E Newham, MA Oxford (*Assistant Examinations Officer*)

External Relations:
Mrs T I Gray, BA Napier (*Manager*)
Miss M C White, BA Stirling (*Assistant*)

Library:
Mrs J M Williams, BA Leicester (*Librarian*)

Ms REA Gibb, BSc OU

Medical Staff:
Mrs SA McLean, RSCN, RGN (*Senior Medical Sister*)
Mrs N Fallowfield, RGN (*School Nurse*)
Mrs J N Fisher, RGN (*School Nurse*)
Mrs D Marshall (*Medical Officer*)
Dr G Parry, MBChB, MRCGP, FRACGP, DiMM
Dr K Robertson, MBChB, BSc, MRCP, MRCPGP

Specialist Sports Coaches:
B Gentleman (*Athletics*)
K Sanford (*Basketball*)
A Evans (*Cricket*)
S Gilmour, MSc Edinburgh (*Cricket*)
A Murdoch (*Golf Academy Leader*)
K Mungall (*Golf*)
J Hay (*Squash*)
I M Noble, BSc Napier (*Strength & Conditioning*)
A Young (*Swimming*)
D Brewer (*Tennis Academy Leader*)
N Lundy, MA Sunderland (*Tennis Academy*)

Support Staff:
Ms S Allison, BA Edinburgh (*Housemother*)
Miss D Boys (*Data Manager*)
Mrs C Blair (*Housemother*)
Mrs F Blair, BSc Edinburgh, BA Queen Margaret's (*School Counsellor*)
G Campbell, MA Aberdeen (*Master i/c Pipe Bands*)
Mrs M Cordingley, BA Roehampton (*School Shop Manager*)
Mrs K Coyne, BA Glasgow (*Housemother*)
Major A D Ewing, BSc Napier (*School Staff Instructor to CCF*)
Mrs J A Ghazal (*Support Assistant Juniors*)
Mrs F Horrocks, BA South Africa (*School Exchange Shop*)
Miss K Johnston, BMus Edinburgh (*Graduate Music Assistant*)
B T Lothian (*Transport Manager, Health & Safety Coordinator*)
Mrs M Lucas, BA Edinburgh (*Masterchef*)
Mrs R MacLennan, BA Robert Gordon (*Housemother*)
Mrs D Marshall (*Housemother*)
Mrs A McGregor, BA Edinburgh (*Housemother*)
Mrs D Stewart (*Housemother*)

Visiting Instrumental Music Teachers:
Ms C Bain (*Upper Strings*)
Mrs R Banyuls-Bertomeu (*Saxophone*)
Miss J Beeston (*Upper Strings*)
Mrs L Bell (*Woodwind*)
Ms M C Bell (*Oboe/Bassoon*)
P A Chamberlain (*Accordion*)
Mrs C Clark (*Singing*)
B Davidson (*Piano*)
B Donaldson (*Bagpipes*)
G Hodge (*French Horn*)
Mrs J Jablonska-Edmonds (*Cello*)
C Macgregor (*Kit*)
G McDiarmid (*Guitar*)
A McGrattan (*Brass*)
A Mitchell (*Guitar*)
Mrs K M Nicholls (*Piano*)
Ms J Pearce (*Flute*)
A Rankin (*Percussion*)
J Walker (*Drums*)

Visiting Language Teachers:
Mrs J L McKinlay (*EAL Consultant*)
Mrs S Abdo (*Arabic*)
Mrs N Davidson (*Japanese*)
Mrs R Nazipova-Petherick (*Russian*)

Works Staff:
J M Boag (*Facilities Manager*)
B Begley (*Electrician*)
A Brooks (*Painter*)
A Campbell (*Joiner*)
B McLeish (*Joiner*)
R Russell (*Plumber*)
Mrs K Stables (*Secretary*)
S Thomson (*Painter*)
M Yan Hip (*Head Groundsman*)
S Chalmers (*Groundsman*)
J W Hutchison (*Groundsman*)
D A Stewart (*Groundsman*)

Mill Hill School

The Ridgeway, Mill Hill Village, London NW7 1QS
Tel: 020 8959 1176
Fax: 020 8201 0663
email: office@millhill.org.uk
            registrations@millhill.org.uk
website: millhill.org.uk
Twitter: @MillHillSenior
Facebook: @MillHillSenior

Overview. Part of the Mill Hill School Foundation which educates boys and girls aged 3–18 in North West London, Mill Hill School offers day, weekly and full boarding for pupils aged 13–18.

History. Mill Hill was founded by Samuel Favell (1760–1830) and Revd John Pye Smith (1774–1851) as a grammar school for the sons of Protestant dissenters and opened in 1807. The School became fully co-educational in September 1997.

Location. The School is situated in Mill Hill village, a conservation area, on the borders of Hertfordshire and Middlesex, approximately 10 miles from the centre of London. Set in 120 acres of parkland originally formed by the famous botanist Peter Collinson, the grounds provide a spacious setting for the academic buildings, boarding and day houses and offer extensive facilities for sports and activities.

Houses. There are 756 pupils in the School of whom 125 are boarders. Weekly and full boarding is available for entry at Year 9, Year 10 and Sixth Form. There are five boarding Houses and seven day Houses all of which have been recently refurbished. Day pupils take a full part in the activities of the School. Full boarders have a full range of activities and workshops on Saturday mornings. These sessions are optional to day and weekly boarding pupils.

Admission. Application may be made as early as parents wish. The majority of boys and girls enter at the age of 13 and candidates are selected on the basis of interviews, examinations and a Head's confidential reference.

Pre-testing is offered in Year 6 for unconditional places at Year 9 (13+ entry). For Year 6 track candidates, the test is a computer-based assessment of aptitude in Reading Comprehension, Verbal, Non-Verbal and Numerical Reasoning. Results are age-standardised, enabling us accurately to compare candidates born at different times of the year.

For the Year 8 track, the tests remain as traditional entrance examinations in English, Mathematics, Science and French, with Latin as an optional paper. Year 8 examinations assess against the Common Entrance syllabus in each subject, and act as our Academic Award examinations. Final Year 8 Track in Intake is for 2019 entry.

Scholarship candidates are identified through the entrance tests and candidates are called back for interviews on the basis of their scores. Single subject awards may be made. Awards are also made for Art, Music, Drama, Sports and Design Technology.

There are two other methods of entry:

(a) A limited number of places are available at 14+. Candidates are selected on the basis of interview, performance in the 14+ Entrance Examinations (English, Maths, Science and French) and a Head's confidential reference.

(b) Sixth Form Entry: Admission to the Sixth Form is based on an entry requirement of five GCSE passes, at least two at Grade A plus three at Grade B, together with at least C grades in Mathematics and English, or equivalent qualifications for overseas pupils. More detailed entry requirements for specific AS courses are given in the School's Sixth Form Curriculum Guide. Candidates unable to offer the number of subjects required (e.g. some overseas candidates) will be considered on their individual academic merit.

Selection is by interview at the School (there are no examinations) and by reference from the candidate's present school. Offers made are conditional on meeting the entry requirements detailed above. International candidates may be asked to complete entry tests in the subjects they wish to study in the Sixth Form and are interviewed either in person or by Skype. All pupils with English as a second language will be asked to sit an EAL paper. Scholarships are awarded on the basis of examinations and interviews in January.

Pastoral Care. Pastoral care is organised by House and individual House identities are a significant feature of Mill Hill. All of the Houses (including day Houses) have their own designated space including recreational facilities and areas for relaxation and/or study. In the School's most recent full ISI Inspection in 2012, the overall quality of pastoral care was rated as *Outstanding* and genuine pride is taken in maintaining and developing this aspect as a real strength of the School as a whole. Boarding was also rated as *Excellent* in all five categories.

The report also portrayed *teachers and tutors as knowing their pupils very well* and described *pupils' behaviour as showing a high degree of maturity*. The provision of boarding too was rated as *Excellent* and the School received particular praise for providing *a lively supportive and caring environment that allows boarders to grow in confidence, independence and sensitivity to the needs of others, in line with its aims.*

One of the principal features of the Mill Hill approach to pastoral care is the continuity of support and involvement offered by Housemasters/Housemistresses throughout a pupil's career at Mill Hill, aided by Tutors and House Parents who work within a House dealing with day-to-day matters for specific year groups.

Another particularly notable element of Mill Hill's pastoral care is the wide range of dynamic pupil councils which meet regularly covering areas as diverse as anti-bullying and mentoring, boarding, charity, environmental issues, food, Fourth Form (new Year 9 pupils), inter-faith and Sixth Form-specific issues. In addition there is a Full School Council which offers an opportunity for the pupils' voices to be heard on key whole-School issues.

Curriculum. The School's academic curriculum is broad, flexible and forward-looking and is designed to encourage among pupils intellectual curiosity, sound learning and a spirit of enquiry in the pursuit of academic excellence. It seeks to enable pupils to acquire core knowledge and skills in English, Mathematics, Science and a Modern Language and, in addition, to develop their own particular academic interests. It also incorporates a full programme of Personal, Social and Health Education, appropriate guidance and information for pupils on subject choices, higher education and careers. Detailed information on the curriculum for each Key Stage is set out in a series of three curriculum guides, which are available on the School website and from the Admissions Office.

Provision for Pupils with Special Educational Needs and/or Disabilities (SEND) and Learning Difficulties and/or Disabilities (LDD). The School provides those pupils who have a statement of educational need or a learning difficulty or disability support to meet their requirements and a suitably adapted curriculum, where this is appropriate. The Learning Support Department plays a key role in this work, seeking to identify, through screening and ongoing monitoring, the particular needs of individual pupils and putting in place strategies (and, where necessary, additional assistance) designed to help them fulfil their potential. Pupils who have a Special Educational Need and/or Disability may have their curriculum modified to take account of their particular needs, as appropriate. Where a pupil has a statement of Special Educational Needs, the requirements of the statement are closely followed in order to ensure that the School provides an effective and accessible educational experience. The progress of all pupils on the School's Learning Support Register is regularly reviewed and support is amended as appropriate.

Academic and Careers Guidance. Through the tutor system, presentations and information evenings, pupils are helped to make the best possible choices of GCSE and Sixth Form courses and to make well-informed and appropriate higher education choices. In the Sixth Form the School arranges visits to universities as well as presentations, workshops and information evenings. The School has a full-time Head of University and Post-School guidance and an active Careers Department which provides information and advice on possible future careers paths. Careers Education is included within the School's Personal, Social, Health and Religious Education programme and careers interviews are arranged for pupils in Year 11 and in the Lower Sixth, and also on request for other pupils. Careers guidance was rated as *Excellent* in the 2012 ISI inspection.

Support for pupils with English as an Additional Language. For pupils whose first language is not English, class or individual tuition in EAL is provided as appropriate, to enable them to maximise their academic opportunities and to enjoy all of the social and cultural aspects of life at the School. Some EAL pupils follow a modified curriculum in order to accommodate their needs, where this is appropriate. EAL pupils are prepared for IGCSE English as a Second Language, ideally in Year 10, and IELTS in Year 11 or the Lower Sixth, depending on the point at which they enter the School. Extra, individual, EAL tuition in addition to class lessons can be arranged if required.

Academic Enrichment. The School prides itself on offering a broad variety of opportunities for pupils to pursue their curiosity and extend their knowledge and skills outside the formal curriculum. There is a plethora of subject societies operating in both the Lower School (Years 9–11) and the Sixth Form. Academic departments enter pupils of all ages for external competitions such as essay prizes in Humanities and Classics, Olympiads in Science subjects and national debating competitions for Modern Languages. A number of current and past pupils have held Arkwright Engineering Scholarships. Sixth Formers can opt for the Extended Project Qualification. The School uses its proximity to Central London to take pupils to lectures, plays, concerts, exhibitions and seminar days. There is a wide variety of academically based trips on offer, such as: Modern Languages exchanges and study visits to many destinations in Europe; Art trips to New York and the Venice Biennale; Design Technology trip to the Centre for Alternative Technology in mid-Wales; Geography field trip to Iceland.

Art, Drama and Music. The Creative Arts have a long and successful tradition at Mill Hill and are a key part of the academic curriculum. In addition to achieving excellent results in public examinations, relevant academic departments have a high success rate in preparing students for further study in the Arts. For example, six of the School's eight A Level Art candidates in 2016 have gone on to Art-related degrees.

Alongside academic successes, there is a substantial and varied programme of co-curricular activities in these subjects. The Art Department offers facilities and expertise for pupils to develop their interest and skills in painting and drawing, alternative media, film, illustration, multimedia, photography (including digital photography), printmaking, sculpture, textiles, theatre design and video.

In addition to the very extensive range and number of drama performances relating to examination courses there is a biennial inter-House Drama festival, which alternates with the biennial inter-House Music Festival; both attract a high level of pupil participation. There is a regular programme of School plays, ranging from Shakespeare to musicals. The School's musical ensembles include an orchestra, wind band, string ensemble, jazz band, four choirs and numerous ad hoc pupil bands and chamber ensembles. Individual tuition in most instruments and in singing is available from high quality specialist teachers. There is an extensive programme of concerts, competitions and recitals throughout the year, some of which include recitals by professional performers.

Tours have included drama performances at the Edinburgh Festival and choir tours to New York and Paris, plus a Chapel Choir residency at Canterbury Cathedral.

Sport. Mill Hill School is renowned for its sporting excellence. Every pupil, regardless of physical ability, is encouraged to participate in both competitive and non-competitive sport. The major sports for the boys are Rugby, Hockey, Football and Cricket and for the girls are Hockey, Netball, Rounders and Tennis. Other opportunities include Athletics, Basketball, Cross Country, Eton Fives, Golf, Horse Riding, Soccer, and Swimming. For our most able pupils we run a fantastic sports scholarship scheme which aims to increase the breadth of sporting experience of our youngest pupils and is increasingly sport focused at the top end of the School. There are a range of awards and bursaries (including full bursaries) available for talented sporting pupils designed to supplement our home grown talent. The level of professional coaching skills is exceptional. In addition to the excellent full-time staff members, we benefit from having a team of external coaches; including Strength, Conditioning and Kicking coaches from Saracens RFC and Middlesex CC to professional coaches in Netball and Tennis. The School has a 25-metre indoor swimming pool, three Eton Fives Courts, a shooting range, an all-weather pitch and a Sports Hall including a refurbished Fitness Suite and a Free Weights Room. Mill Hill is the home to the London Golf Academy which benefits from our own Golf professional, an on-site short course facility, indoor golf coaching facilities as well as having a link and access to the amazing facilities at The Shire Golf Club. Finally, the pupils are given the opportunity of participating in overseas sports tours for all of the major and many of the minor sports at the School.

Co-curricular Activities. Year 9 pupils are introduced to the range of minor sports (as above) and aspects of adventure training. All pupils are also offered a range of other activities such as debating, drama, chess, jewellery-making and computing. In Year 10 the focus is 'teamwork and leadership'. Pupils choose from a number of options including the CCF (Army, Navy and RAF), a Sports Leaders programme and Business Enterprise. In addition, many Societies exist to cater for a variety of out-of-school interests.

Fees per term (2018–2019). Day (including lunch) £7,047, Full Boarding £11,239, Weekly Boarding £9,508. Fees include the games fee and the cost of most textbooks and stationery.

Scholarships and Bursaries. Scholarships, which attract a maximum of 10% fee remission, are available to pupils showing exceptional talent in a variety of areas both in the classroom and on the sports field. Academic, Music, Drama, Art, Design and Technology, and Sports Awards are available at 13+ and Academic Scholarships are available to candidates entering the Sixth Form. In addition to major Awards, there are a number of minor Awards or Exhibitions also on offer.

Bursaries are available for those entrants able to demonstrate a financial need. Parents will be asked to complete a detailed statement of their financial circumstances. Applicants for Bursaries will be selected in the normal way. There is provision for the award of full-fee Bursaries for entrants at all levels. It is possible for bursary funds to be used to top up Scholarship Awards. As with scholarship queries, the Head, Deputy Head (External Relations) or the Assistant Registrar are happy to offer advice.

There are also a number of special scholarships and bursaries available, further information of which is available on the School's website millhill.org.uk.

Charitable status. The Mill Hill School Foundation is a Registered Charity, number 1064758.

Court of Governors:
Interim Chair of Governors: Mr Elliot Lipton, BSc Hons, MBA, FRSA, FRICS
Professor Eric W F W Alton, MA, MBBS, MD, FRCP, FHEA, FERS, FMedSci
Mrs Charlotte Avery, MA Oxon
Mr Robin Burdell, FCMA
Mr David J Dickinson, Dip QS, FRICS
Mr Jamie Hornshaw, BEd Hons, MEd, NPQH
Mr Rudolf A Eliott Lockhart, MA, MPhil
Mrs Stephanie J Miller, BA
Mr Andrew Millet, BA, MBA, FCA
Ms Sophie Mortimer, BA
Mrs Mangal Patel, MBA
Mrs Sunena Stoneham, LLB Hons, LPC
Mr Andrew Welch, MA Oxon
Mrs Pamela Wilkes, BEd, FRSA

Head: Mrs Jane Sanchez, BSc

Deputy Head (Academic): Mr Alex Frazer, MA
Deputy Head (Pastoral): Mr J C Dickin, BA Ed, MPS

Interim Director of Operations and Finance: Mr Shaun Wilson, BA, MSc

Assistant Head (Teaching and Learning): Mr Luke Stubbles, MSci
Assistant Head (Academic Administration): Mr Jason Lewis, MA
Assistant Head (Sixth Form): Mr John Barron, BSc, MA
Assistant Head (Sport and Co-Curricular): Mr Tom Vercoe, BSc, MA

Head, Mill Hill International: Mrs Sarah Bellotti, BEd

Head, Belmont: Mr Leon Roberts, MA, PGCE

Head, Grimsdell: Mrs Kate Simon, BA, PGCE

Millfield

Street, Somerset BA16 0YD

Tel: 01458 442291
email: generaloffice@millfieldschool.com
website: millfieldschool.com
Twitter: @millfieldsenior
Facebook: @MillfieldSchool

The school was founded in 1935 by R J O Meyer with the philanthropic aim of using its resources to generate places for boys who were gifted but not wealthy. The school became co-educational in 1939. In 1945 Edgarley Hall was acquired and the junior pupils were transferred there. This is now Millfield Prep School. The school expanded through the 50s and 60s offering a more orthodox curriculum, although it was never a 'normal' public school. C R M Atkinson became Headmaster in 1971, and carried out a major building programme that established modern purpose-built facilities throughout the academic and recreational areas of the school, including a prize-winning Library and Resource Centre and a large Fine Arts Centre, completed in 1992, a year after his death. Further improvements to the campus include a purpose-built Mathematics Centre, and 500-seat Theatre and Dining Hall. Nine new boarding houses have been opened since 2003. A Design & Technology building with high-tech equipment was completed in 2005 and a Music School complex housing the 350-seat Johnson Concert Hall was completed in September 2006. New Science laboratories and a Science lecture theatre were completed in September 2009. The main part of the school is surrounded by over 100 acres, which includes an equestrian centre, stabling for 64 horses, a 50m Olympic swimming pool, a golf course and an indoor Tennis Centre.

The school is fully co-educational with 739 boys and 506 girls; there are 941 boarders.

Housing. There are 16 single-sex, Year 10 to Upper Sixth, boarding houses. Most Sixth Formers have their own rooms whilst younger pupils share either in pairs or fours. Since the launch of Nine at Millfield there are dedicated Year 9 boarding and day houses. All Year 9 houses lie in the heart of the campus and have a higher staff to pupil ratio to oversee every aspect of each pupil's well-being and academic progress. There are four day houses for Year 10 to Upper Sixth; they have their own base on site and may stay in the evenings to do supervised prep.

The Curriculum. The academic programme is consistent with the broad principles laid down in the National Curriculum pre-16. Thus those moving to Millfield from a wide range of independent preparatory and maintained secondary schools should find both common academic ground and unrivalled choice for GCSE, Vocational Courses, BTEC and AS/A2 Level. A five-year course in Personal and Social Education is also included within the curriculum.

All pupils entering Year 9 (at age 13), regardless of ability, study English, Mathematics, three Sciences, at least one language, Art, Design and Technology, ICT, Food and Nutrition, Geography, History, Religious Studies, Physical Education and Music. The pupil to teacher ratio is 6.5:1. Pupils have a structured co-curricular programme.

In Years 10 and 11 pupils follow courses leading to GCSEs in the core subjects of English, Mathematics, Science and a Modern Language. In addition, there is a wide choice of options: Art & Design, Business Studies, Chinese, Computing, Drama, Economics, Food & Nutrition, French, Geography, German, Greek, History, ICT, Italian, Latin, Music, Physical Education, Product Design, Religious Stud-

ies and Spanish. The Learning Support Centre provides individual support for all pupils in need of this.

At Sixth Form level, a wide range of subjects is on offer leading to AS and A2 qualifications. These include Accounting, Art, Biology, Business Studies, Chemistry, Chinese Mandarin, Drama, Economics, English Literature, French, Further Mathematics, Food & Nutrition, Geography, German, Politics, History, ICT, Italian, Latin, Mathematics, Media Studies, Music, Philosophy, Physical Education, Physics, Product Design, Psychology, Religious Studies and Spanish. Also on offer are the vocational courses of BTEC Business Studies and BTEC Enterprise and Entrepreneurship (both equivalent to a two A Level course), BTEC National Diploma in Art & Design (equivalent to a three A Level course), BTEC Diploma in Sport (equivalent to 2 A Level courses), Leiths Cookery Course and the British Horse Society Equine Excellence Pathway in Complete Horsemanship. Most pupils choose four AS Level subjects in the Lower Sixth and then take three of these to the full A Level in the Upper Sixth. Wider enrichment opportunities are available to all Sixth Formers. The curriculum offers breadth, depth and flexibility in course choice. Pupils are also prepared for STEP papers and Scholastic Aptitude tests for American Universities. English as an additional language (EAL) and Learning Support is available at all levels.

Every pupil is guided through his or her school career by a Group Tutor. Each Tutor cares for between 10 and 14 pupils within a House, taking a close personal interest in each and maintaining regular contact with parents on academic matters.

Sport and Activities. Millfield runs an unparalleled range of sports and activities to engage all pupils. Pupils in Years 9, 10 and 11 generally choose from one of the core games of the term, including athletics, basketball, cricket, dance, football, hockey, netball, riding, rugby and tennis depending on term and gender. In Sixth Form, the range extends to include all of the above plus archery, badminton, canoeing, chess, clay shooting, climbing, karate, sailing, skiing, squash, trampolining, triathlon, and various fitness activities such as aerobics, pilates and yoga. Throughout the School, pupils may also specialise in one of our high performing programmes including athletics, cricket, fencing, golf, modern pentathlon, squash, swimming and tennis.

In addition, pupils in Years 9, 10 and Lower Sixth take part in the school's Activities Programme where they can further broaden their experiences through a choice of more than 100 activities, ranging from athletics to robotics, British Military Fitness, film clubs, dissection, lacrosse, ceramics, falconry and The Duke of Edinburgh's Award.

Fees per term (2018–2019). Boarding £12,870, Day £8,535.

Scholarships and Bursaries. Scholarships of up to 15% are awarded for exceptional talent in Academic, All-rounder, Art, Drama, Dance, Design & Innovation, Music, Sport and Chess. A limited number of Headmaster's Scholarships of up to 50% are also available. Where parental resources are limited, these may be augmented by means-tested bursaries of up to 100%.

Charitable status. Millfield is a Registered Charity, number 310283. Its aim is to provide independent boarding and day education for boys and girls, and to maintain an extensive system of bursary aid to gifted pupils or those in financial need.

Governors:
Chair of Governors: R Rudd

W J Bushell	R Exley
R J R Clark	T Griffiths
Mrs C Cripps	K Griggs
S East	C Hirst

A Jackson
J Lever
J Maudslay
Mrs A Sexton
M A L Simon

T M Taylor
R P Thornton
P Warner
D S Williamson

Clerk to the Governors: Mrs R Summerhayes

Headmaster: **Gavin Horgan**, MA Oxon

Bursar: M Suddaby, MA Hons, PGCE, ACA
Deputy Head (Academic): F J Clough, BSc Hons, PhD, QTS
Deputy Head (Pastoral): Mrs K Weston, BSc, MSc, PGCE
Assistant Head (Teaching and Learning): Dr C Fiddes, BA Oxon, PhD
Assistant Head (Pastoral): A Collins, BA, Dip, QTS
Assistant Head (Co-Curriculum): E Jones, BSc
Assistant Head (Sixth Form): Ms C Bowring, BA Hons
Director of Sport: Dr S Drawer, MSc, PGCE, PhD
Registrar: J Postle, BA Hons, PGCE, FRSA
Head of Marketing: Mrs L Webb, BA Hons
Director of IT: G Henderson, BA Hons, MA

Heads of Department:
Art, Design & Technology: P Maxfield, BA Hons, PGCE
Biology: Mrs L McEwan, BSc
Chemistry: D Armour, BSc
Computing and ICT: M Shields, BSc Hons, PGCE
English as an Additional Language (EAL): H Winkley, MA
Economics and Accounting: A Shaw, MA Oxon, PGCE
English, Drama and Media: J C Baddock, BA Hons
Equine Studies: D Anholt, BHSI HT
Geography: Miss A Starling, BA Hons, PGCE
History: A Arbuckle, MA Cantab, PGCE
Food and Nutrition: P Reeves, BA Hons, DTLLS, MA
Languages: B Doherty, BA Hons, PGCE
Learning Support Centre: Ms J White, BSc Hons, MEd, QTS, PG Dip, MDG
Library: D Trevis, BA, MEd
Mathematics: T Bowley, MSc, BSc
Music: M Cook, MA Music Cantab, PGCE Secondary Music
Physical Education: S Maddock, BA Hons, MEd
Physics: J Hudson, MA Hons Cantab, PGCE
Religious Studies: T Churchill, BA Hons, MA, PGCE
Sciences: Mrs R Landrigan, BA Hons, MA Oxon, PGCE

Houses and Housemasters/Housemistresses:

Boarding Houses:
Abbey House: Mrs C Shelver
Acacia House: Miss J Moore
Butleigh: Mr B C Boyd
Etonhurst: Mr T P Akhurst
Holmcroft: Mr R Owlett
Joan's Kitchen: Mr M A Speyers
Keen's Elm: Mr and Mrs T Sawrey-Cookson
Kernick: Ms C Coutand-Moore
Kingweston: Mr D Askham
Martins: Ms C Garcia
Millfield: Mr A Kemp
Orchards: Mr S Robertson
Portway: Mrs C Trainor
Shapwick: Mr J A Mallett
St Anne's: Mr P Williams
Southfield: Ms T Allen
The Grange: Mr T B Kingsford
Walton: Mr J Lewis
Warner: Mrs C Rose

Day Houses, Boys:
Great: Mr J A Bishop
Mill: Mr G Catto

Day Houses, Girls:
Overleigh: Mrs A E S Brade
The Lakes: Mrs J Gray

Day House (Year 9 Girls & Boys):
Ivythorn: Mrs K Butt

Heads of Sport:
Athletics: A Richardson, BA Hons, IAAF Level 5 Elite coach
Tutor i/c Badminton: K Lloyd, BSc
Basketball: C Seeley
Chess: M Turner, MA, Grand Master
Director of Cricket: M Garaway, ECB Level 4 Coach
Cross Country: J Allen
Dance: K Leader
Director of Fencing: T Parris, BAF Advanced Coach
Football: T Akhurst, UEFA A
Director of Golf: K Nicholls, PGA/LET member
Director of Hockey: R Keates, HA Coach Level 2
Martial Arts: T Cheung, purple belt in Washinkai Karate and Kickboxing, blue belt in Shotokan karate
Director of Modern Pentathlon: T Parris, BAF Advanced Coach
Netball: J Culley
Director of Outdoor Activities: N Mortley
Polo: D O Anholt, BHSl, HT
Director of Riding: D O Anholt, BHSI, HT
Director of Rugby: J A Mallett, RFU Level 4
Skiing: M Patel, MBiolSci
Director of Squash: I Thomas, High Performance Coach
Director of Swimming: E Dale, BSc
Director of Tennis: K Warne-Holland, LTA Level 4 Senior Performance Coach
Trampolining: T Allen
Triathlon: P Guthrie, BTF Level 3 Cert Coaching

Monkton Combe School

Monkton Combe, Bath BA2 7HG

Tel: 01225 721102
Fax: 01225 721181
email: admissions@monkton.org.uk
website: www.monktoncombeschool.com
Twitter: @monkton
Facebook: @MonktonCombeSchool

Monkton Combe School, just a mile from the World Heritage City of Bath, is an independent, co-educational boarding and day school for pupils aged 2–18. We pride ourselves on our lively Christian ethos, excellent exam results and our strong pastoral care. At Monkton, we are setting standards for life; giving young people the qualities of character they need to become trusted employees, inspiring leaders and valued friends.

Situation. The Senior School faces south across the Valley, or Combe, from which the place takes its name, while the Pre-Prep and Prep School are at the top of the hill above with magnificent views over Avon and Wiltshire.

Organisation. The Pre-Prep and Prep (ages 2–13) and Senior School (ages 13–18) each have their own Heads and the Principal of the Senior School has overall responsibility for the two schools; they share the same Board of Governors and there are close links between them.

(*For further details see Monkton Preparatory entry in IAPS section.*)

Numbers. *Preparatory School*: There are 275 pupils of whom 40 board and 60 are in the Pre-Prep.

Senior School: There are 375 pupils (226 boys, 149 girls), of whom 208 are boarders. The Sixth Form has 159 pupils.

Admission. *Prep School.* For those entering the Prep at age 7 years through to 13 years, admission is by tests in English and Mathematics, a Reasoning Test, a reference from the candidate's current school and an interview.

Senior School. (a) For pupils entering the Senior School from a Prep school, the usual means is via abilities test data collected from the prep school (if available), or ability test (CAT4), and an assessment day based around wider learning aptitudes (creativity, collaboration, confidence, craftsmanship, communication, commitment and curiosity), taken during the course of Year 6. A school reference and report will also be sought. Offers will be conditional upon the candidate completing the Common Entrance courses at his/her school from whom a reference would be sought.

(b) For those entering the Senior School at age 14, admission is by an abilities test (CAT4), a reference from the candidate's current school and an interview.

(c) For entry into Year 12, candidates will usually sit an abilities test (CAT4), and attend an interview, where possible. A school reference will be sought and any place then offered is subject to pupils obtaining an average score of at least 6.5 in all of the GCSE subjects taken. Progression to Year 13 will depend upon a satisfactory performance throughout Year 12. Please note that to study certain A Level subjects, a minimum grade at GCSE in that subject may be a prerequisite. Pupils are normally expected to attain at least 2 D grades in Year 12 for entry into Year 13.

Sport facilities. The School has extensive playing fields, an AstroTurf all-weather playing area for Hockey and Tennis, Boathouses on the River Avon, 3 Netball Courts, 18 Tennis Courts, a covered Rifle Range, a Rowing Tank, 2 Squash Courts, a Sports Centre and a 25m indoor Swimming Centre and Fitness Centre.

Chapel. There is a full-time resident Anglican Head of Chaplaincy. A short service or assembly is held three times each week. There is a Confirmation Service each year. The pupils run a Christian Union, which is popular, and attended by 70–100 pupils each week.

Houses. The three boys' Houses and three girls' Houses are all under the care of Houseparents, who together with their tutorial teams of colleagues are responsible for the boys' and girls' general welfare.

Day Pupils are fully integrated into the boarding houses and the total life of the School and are encouraged but not obliged to stay until the end of evening prep. Senior pupils are given opportunities for responsibility as School or House Prefects during their Sixth Form careers.

Tutor System. Each pupil has a Tutor, normally a member of staff of his or her own choice, who keeps in touch with parents and provides guidance and advice over every aspect of School life and over making choices for the future.

Curriculum. Our aim is to provide a broadly based curriculum in the years leading to GCSE. Those who show particular ability in Mathematics may proceed to work more advanced than GCSE before the end of Year 11. Personal, Social and Health Education is included up to Year 12. In Year 10, pupils have two supervised study periods to develop the skills they will especially need when in the Sixth Form, but which ultimately underpin genuine success at GCSE as well.

In Year 9 all pupils study English, Mathematics and the Sciences with a foundation course normally comprising two Foreign Language, Art, Design Technology, Drama, Geography, History, Information Technology, Music, PE and Religious Studies. In addition, pupils develop study and research skills with a library period. In Years 10 and 11 all pupils take IGCSE English, Mathematics, and either Dual Award or Separate Sciences (Biology, Chemistry and Phys-

ics), and almost all choose at least one Modern Foreign Language (French, Spanish or Mandarin). Pupils choose three other subjects from Art, Business Studies, Design Technology, Drama, Geography, History, Latin, Music, Photography, Physical Education, and Religious Studies. English and Maths support is available as an option instead of a Modern Foreign Language for those with particular needs in these areas. Pupils with English as a Second Language receive lessons according to their level of English.

Most pupils stay on for two years in the Sixth Form. The subjects offered are broad and include 28 subject areas. All pupils take the Extended Project Qualification. Most pupils entering Year 12 study three subjects to full A Level. A notable feature of the Sixth Form programme is the wide variety of lectures and presentations delivered by visiting speakers prominent in their field.

Careers Advice and Staff/Parent Meetings. An experienced Careers Teacher works closely with Tutors in advising pupils. There is also a member of staff responsible for advice on higher education. Parents, Old Monktonians and local people are invited to help pupils in their thinking about careers. The School belongs to the Independent Schools Careers Organisation which arranges Aptitude and Interest tests. Annual staff/parent meetings are held at the School to discuss pupils' progress. Parents are of course always welcome at other times.

University Entrance. The great majority of leavers go on to degree courses at Universities and Colleges of Higher Education. Over 90% of leavers go to their first-choice university and many of our pupils go to the top universities in the country including Oxford, Cambridge, UCL, Edinburgh, Durham, Exeter and Warwick.

Games. Those with particular abilities are encouraged to aim for excellence, but we also believe that participation in regular games and exercise are important for all, helping to build a healthy lifestyle for the future and fostering leadership, teamwork and cooperation.

The major sports for boys are: in the Michaelmas Term, Rugby; in the Lent Term, Hockey or Rowing; in the Summer Term, Cricket, Rowing or Tennis.

The major sports for girls are: in the Michaelmas Term, Hockey; in the Lent Term, Netball or Rowing; in the Summer Term, Tennis or Rowing.

Other sports include: Athletics, Badminton, Basketball, Cross-Country, Football, Golf, Judo, Squash and Shooting.

CCF and Community Service. There are sections for all three Services, as well as Bronze and Gold Duke of Edinburgh's Award and car maintenance. There is also an active Community Service group.

Leisure Activities. Monkton encourages as many worthwhile leisure pursuits as possible. Between 35 and 40 different activities are offered. All the facilities of the School, including the Art and DT Departments, Music Rooms and ICT Centre are available to pupils during their free time. The Choir, Orchestra, Jazz band and other less formal music groups play an important part in the School's life and tuition is available in all orchestral instruments. There is a major School drama production in the Michaelmas and Lent Terms. The School is conveniently close to Bath and Bristol for taking parties to concerts and theatres. Some 30 clubs and societies figure on the School List, ranging from the Bridge Club to the Literary Society and the Christian Union. Bible Study groups meet weekly.

Health. The School Medical Officer visits regularly and all boarders are required to register with him. The Medical Centre on site is under the care of a fully qualified Sister and Assistant.

Catering. Catering is provided by an external company, offering nutritious home cooked meals everyday. All pupils take their meals in the Dining Hall, with a range of choices available in cafeteria service.

Dress. All required items can be purchased in the School Shop.

Scholarships and Bursaries. Scholarships are awarded on entry to the School for candidates at Year 3, Year 7, Year 9 and Year 12. The Principal reserves the right to award up to two Year 10 Scholarships at his discretion; no application for this award is required. Scholarships recognise the contribution to School life which is made by exceptional performers by raising the aspirations of other pupils, by stimulating greater achievement in their peers and by enabling higher levels of performance in collaborative activities such as music, drama and sport. All scholarships awarded are conditional on this continued contribution to the area of School life which is recognized in the award. In addition, all scholarships are awarded until the next scholarship round. Moreover, candidates for all awards are expected to achieve satisfactory standards in Common Entrance, GCSE exams or other entry tests.

Monkton Senior School seeks to give bursaries to pupils who would otherwise not be able to come to the School. Special consideration is given to the children of clergy and missionaries, in accordance with the School's charitable objectives. Where a bursary and a scholarship are awarded to the same pupil, the scholarship is subsumed into the bursary (assuming this is the larger of the two); the bursary will never be reduced below the level of the original scholarship. Where a bursary has already been awarded, the scholarship will not increase the bursary unless it is greater than the bursary.

Details of all awards can be obtained from the Registrar.

Fees per term (2018–2019). Senior: £9,830–£11,115 (boarders); £6,630–£6,970 (day pupils). Preparatory: £7,290–£8,230 (boarders); £3,920–£5,710 (day pupils). Pre-Prep: £3,245–£3,340.

Old Monktonian Club. No additional charge is made for pupils to become full Old Monktonians. Details from the Development Office at the School.

Charitable status. Monkton Combe School is a Registered Charity, number 1057185, and a Company Limited by Guarantee, registered in England, number 3228456. Its aims and objectives are to provide education for girls and boys combined with sound religious training on Protestant and Evangelical principles in accordance with the doctrines of The Church of England.

Governors:

Chair of Governors: Prof H Langton, RGN, RSCN, ACNT, RNT, BA Hons, MSc

Mr C J Alexander, BA Hons Oxon
Revd S Barnes, BA QTS Hons, MA, Cert BA
Mrs R Coates, BA Hons
Mr C B Fillingham, MA
Mrs E S K Hubbard, BA Hons
Mrs J J Perry, BPharm Hons, MRPharmS, Dip Clin Pharm
Mr R J Pringle, BSc Hons
Mr D Rosser, BSc Hons, MRICS
Mr E J J Shaw, BA Hons
Mrs M K Townsend, BSc Hons
Mr S B M Young, BA, FCA, ACA
Mr E Shaw

Executive Leadership Team:

Principal: Mr C J Wheeler, BA Durham, PGCE Bristol

Prep School Headmaster: Mr M Davis, BEd Hons

Head of Pre-Prep: Mrs C Winchcombe, BEd Hons, MA Ed

Bursar: Mr T Davies, BA, ACA, DChA

Director of External Relations: Mr T Reid, BA Hons

Monmouth School for Boys

Almshouse Street, Monmouth, Monmouthshire NP25 3XP

Tel: 01600 713143
Fax: 01600 772701
email: boys.enquiries@habsmonmouth.org
website: www.habsmonmouth.org
Twitter: @Habsmonmouth
Facebook: @Habsmonmouth

Motto: *Serve and Obey*

Monmouth School for Boys guides day and boarding pupils aged 11–18 through this crucial stage of their educational and emotional development. We provide a positive, constructive and inspiring single-sex community within which boys thrive and flourish.

The school was founded in 1614, by William Jones, a merchant of the City of London and a Liveryman of the Worshipful Company of Haberdashers, who was born near Monmouth and bequeathed a large sum of money to found a school and almshouses in the town.

The school has derived immense advantage from this unusual association with the City of London.

The school is controlled by a Board of Governors appointed variously by the Haberdashers' Company, the Universities of Oxford, Cambridge and Wales, and local representative bodies.

Through our unique Monmouth Model, our boys benefit from the invaluable interaction with Monmouth School for Girls, sharing many trips and expeditions, events and community projects.

Our boys' talents are nurtured and they make the most of the area's wonderful natural resources and the excellent facilities on offer for sports, culture and the arts.

Monmouth Schools Sixth Form brings day and boarding boys and girls together at this final stage of their educational journey with us, recognising their greater maturity and focus. We offer the benefits of single-sex pastoral care within a co-educational academic environment.

There are approximately 520 boys in the senior school, of whom 163 are boarders. Monmouth School Boys' Prep caters for 130 day boys aged 7 to 11, with boarding available at age 9. (*For further details see entry in IAPS section.*)

Facilities. The summer of 2017 has seen a £2m upgrade of boarding at Monmouth with a complete redevelopment of the largest house, Weirhead. Over the past decade, a new sports complex, a studio theatre, an all-weather pitch, a 500-seat theatre and a stunning sports pavilion have all been added to the suite of historic buildings. The William Jones Building (opened in 2014 to mark the 400th anniversary) provides excellent facilities in classrooms for maths, English and modern languages as well as a completely new reception and administration area. This move has allowed the school to release space to expand and further enhance the boarding accommodation.

Boarding. The boarding community forms the core of the school. Junior boarders (9–12 year olds) are accommodated in Chapel House for their first few years and benefit from the care of a dedicated house team who also provide an ambitious and popular programme of extra-curricular activities, tailored to the interests of the age group.

There are three senior boarding houses for boys between 13 and 18. The school has a flexible boarding policy which provides a considerable degree of freedom for families to make boarding arrangements which fit in with their lives, but which encourages boys to take full advantage of the many sporting, cultural and extra-curricular activities for which the school is renowned.

September 2011 saw the opening of Buchanan House, a sixth form boarding house with single study-bedrooms and en-suite facilities.

Admission. The main admission points are 7, 10, 11, 13 and 16, but other stages will be considered if places are available. Candidates aged 7 and 11 sit the school's own entrance tests. At 13, candidates take the Common Entrance Examination, the school's own Foundation Scholarship Examination or its 13+ examination. Entrants to the Sixth Form are accepted either after sitting the Sixth Form Scholarship Examination or on the basis of GCSE results (or equivalent).

Candidates from overseas are welcome. Those whose first language is not English take a preliminary test of proficiency in English before proceeding to the appropriate entrance test.

The school accepts pupils with Dyslexia or similar specific learning difficulties. They are taught in mainstream lessons and additional study support is available.

Curriculum. The curriculum is designed to provide both flexibility and breadth and to be in step with the National Curriculum without being constrained by it. Those in Forms I and II (Years 7 and 8) study a wide range of subjects including Latin, French and combined science. In Form III (Year 9) the three sciences are taught separately and pupils have the option of starting Greek.

Pupils normally take nine or ten GCSE subjects, four of which are of their own choosing.

We offer a Foundation 1 Year GCSE course in up to 6 GCSEs including English, maths and the three sciences.

The school is enriched by close cooperation with Monmouth School for Girls in many areas of school life, especially at Sixth Form level. From September 2018, co-educational teaching will be offered from a range of 26 A Level subjects along with an enrichment programme.

A particular feature of the curriculum is the extensive range of Modern Languages. French is taught at all levels and Spanish and German are available from Form III.

The Chapel. The school is an Anglican foundation and the Chapel plays an important part in its life. All pupils attend Chapel at least once each week and there is a weekly service for boarders. A varied programme of preachers is organised, including clergy and lay people of many denominations. The Bishop of Monmouth officiates at the annual Confirmation Service.

Games. The main sports are rugby, rowing, cricket and soccer. Many other sports are also available at a highly competitive level including athletics, cross-country running, golf, softball, squash and swimming. Several members of staff have international sporting honours and pupils regularly gain places to represent Wales in a variety of sports.

Activities. There is an extensive programme of activities throughout the school. Pupils in Form IV and above may join the CCF (Army and RAF sections) which enjoy excellent links with locally based regular and territorial forces. Community Service is a popular option and many boys participate in the Duke of Edinburgh's Award scheme. There is a very strong musical tradition with many pupils taking part in choirs, orchestras and bands which achieve high levels of success in competitions, and play to appreciative audiences locally and on the regular overseas tours which take place. Drama is also strong and good opportunities are provided for participation at all levels. A wide range of school Clubs and Societies further enriches the life of the school.

Fees per term (2018–2019). Day £5,272, Boarding £9,994–£10,687; Monmouth School Boys' Prep: Day £3,697, Boarding £6,760.

Scholarships and Bursaries. A number of Entrance Scholarships are awarded to day boys or boarders on the basis of performance in the Year 7 Entry Assessments (11+), on the Foundation Scholarship Examination (13+) held in the Lent Term, and the Sixth Form Scholarship Examination (16+) held in November. In cases of need, Scholarships may be augmented by a means-tested Bursary.

Music Scholarships and Exhibitions may be awarded at 11, 13 and 16 and carrying free instrumental tuition. Sixth Form organ or instrumental scholarships are also available.

Sports Awards are available to suitable candidates at 11, 13 and Sixth Form entry.

Headmaster's Awards are available for candidates who show all-round ability and potential.

The E F Bulmer Award is available to suitable Sixth Form candidates living in Herefordshire; awards range in value from 50% to 100% of the fees. A new Sixth Form Boarding Scholarship is available, which is means-tested and can cover up to 75% of the fees.

Family fee support, by way of a bursary, can provide up to 100% remission of fees, in certain circumstances.

Service Bursaries are available for the sons of serving members of HM Armed Forces, who are in receipt of the CEA and this guarantees that no more than the minimum 10% of fees is payable by parents.

Old Monmothians. Past members of the school are eligible to join the Old Monmothian Club which enjoys a close relationship with the school. The Membership Secretary is Roger Atkins, c/o Old Monmothians, Monmouth School for Boys, Almshouse Street, Monmouth NP25 3XP.

Charitable status. William Jones's Schools Foundation is a Registered Charity, number 525616. Its aims and objectives are to provide an all-round education for boys and girls at reasonable fees; also to carry out the Founder's intention that local boys qualifying for entry should not be prevented from attending the school by lack of funds.

Board of Governors:

Chairman of Governors and Acting Chairman of Monmouth School for Boys Committee: Mr A W Twiston-Davies

Mr P M Alderman[1] (*Safeguarding Governor, Monmouth School for Boys*)

Mr M H C Anderson

Mrs J Booth[1]

Professor R J Carwardine

Mrs S Clayton (*Safeguarding Governor, Monmouth School for Girls*)

Mr M E Davidson[1]

Mrs M K Henderson (*Boarding Governor*)

Dr J Kelly[1]

Mr M Kerrigan[1]

Mr N G H Manns (*Chairman, Monmouth School for Girls Committee*)

Mr R Miners

Mrs H Moriarty[1]

Mrs M Nordal[1]

Councillor R Roden[1]

Mrs R F Rose

Mrs L Russen

Mr N Waters[1]

[1] *Member of the Monmouth School for Boys Committee*

Clerk to the Governors: Mrs F Creasey, BCom, ACMA

Headmaster: Dr A J Daniel, BSc, MEd, PhD, PGCE

Second Master: Mr S H Dorman, MA, MPhil
Deputy Head (*Academic*): Mrs E R Gregory, BA, MEd
Head of Boarding: Mr D K Jones, BSc
Head of Sixth Form: Mr J Boiling, BA

Assistant Staff:
* *Head of Department*
† *Housemaster/Housemistress*

Mrs E A Aldridge, BSc
Mrs E R Arrand, BA (†*Severn House*)
Mrs S G Atherton, BA
Miss E K Barson, BSc, MSc (*Biology)
Mr J W Bateman, LLB
Mr J Boiling, BA
Mrs J R Cardenas, MSc, MA
Mr K D Chaplin, BSc
Mrs E R Cole, BSc
Mrs A H Copley, BEd, PGDipTOD
Miss J M Creak, BA
Mr P D Daley, BA, MStud
Dr J P Danks, BSc, DPhil (†*Dean House*)
Mr J Despontin, BSc, MSc
Mr S H Dorman, MA, MPhil
Dr E Evans, BSc, PhD
Dr H B Evans, BSc, MSc, PhD (*Mathematics)
Miss S L Fowler, BSc
Mr L M P Godfrey, BSc
Mr N J R Goodson, BSc
Miss S M Gorman, BSc
Miss L M J Goupil, BA, MA
Mr P M Griffin, BA (*Drama)
Mr J D Griffiths, BSc
Mrs J R Gunn, BA
Mrs D M Harding, BSc
Dr J M Harrison, BA, PhD (*History)
Mr A Hawley, BA (†*Town House*)
Mrs S M Holmes, BEd
Mr D G Hope, BA (†*Weirhead House*)
Mrs L A Hope (*ICT)
Mr R Howe, BA (†*Monmouth House*)
Mrs J A Johnston, MA
Mr A J Jones, BA (*Director of Sport*)
Dr D G Jones, MPhys, PhD (*Physics)
Mr D K Jones, BSc
Mr I J Lawrence, BSc, MSc (†*Buchanan House*)
Mr D F Lawson, BA, ARCO (*Director of Music and Organist*)
Mrs L E Lewis, BA
Mr M Lewis, BA (†*School House*)
Mrs L R Livingston, BA
Mr K J Madsen, BA (*Economics, †*Glendower House*)
Mrs R J Marsh, BSc
Mrs T L Matthews, BA
Ms S M Mone, BA (†*Chapel House*)
Mr D G Murray, MA
Mrs L C Parr, BEng, BSc
Mrs L Parsons, BA (*Modern Languages)
Mr A K Peace, BSc (†*New House*)
Mrs G S Peace, BA, MA (†*Tudor House*)
Mr M Peake, BA (*Art)
Mr D J Pearson, BSc
Mr R D Picken, BA (*English)
Mr A E Shakeshaft, BA
Mr G F Stentiford, BSc, MSc (*Geography)
Mr C N Stonier, BSc
Mr M J Tamplin, BSc (†*Hereford House*)
Mr P Vaughan-Smith, BA
Mr A J White, BA (**Design Technology*)
Mr R C Whiteman, BA (*Classics)
Mrs R Widdicks, BA (*Study Support)
Mr O T R Williams, BSc, MA

Mr P R Williams, BA
Miss S E L Williams, BA, MA (†*Wye House*)
Dr A J Winter, BSc, PhD (*Chemistry)
Mrs R L Wynne Lord, MA (**Religious Education*)

Chaplain: Revd C R Swartz, BA, MA

Monmouth School Boys' Prep

Head: Mr N D Shaw, BA
Deputy Head: Mrs K E Kirman, BSc

Mr A J Ahmad, BSc	Mr D G Murray, MA
Mrs L Davies, BA	Mr K J Shepherd, BA
Miss R Forester-Bennett, BA	Mrs A M Taylor, LRSC
	Mr Dr S R Wall, BSc, PhD
Mr K T L Fradd, BSc	Mr J D Walton, BMus
Mr P N Morris, BEd	Mrs E R Waters, BA

Foundation Bursar: Mrs T Norgrove, MBA

Medical Officer: Dr J Knowles

Monmouth School for Girls

Hereford Road, Monmouth NP25 5XT

Tel:	01600 711100
Fax:	01600 711233
email:	girls.enquiries@habsmonmouth.org
website:	www.habsmonmouth.org
Twitter:	@Habsmonmouth
Facebook:	@Habsmonmouth

Motto: Serve and Obey

Monmouth School for Girls is one of the five schools of the William Jones Foundation, arising from a bequest in 1614, and administered by the Worshipful Company of Haberdashers.

The school guides day and boarding pupils aged 11–18 through this crucial stage of their educational and emotional development.

There are 489 girls in the senior school, including a Sixth Form of 125. Pupils aged from 7–11 have their own preparatory school, Monmouth School Girls' Prep, which has 139 girls on site.

A thriving boarding community with accommodation on the school site includes a junior house and modern senior house with study-bedrooms and Augusta House, the Sixth Form boarding facility, with 47 en-suite bedrooms.

Our girls thrive and flourish within a positive, constructive and inspiring single-sex community, set in the outstanding natural beauty of the Wye Valley. Education is carefully planned to motivate girls; we deliver a broad choice of subjects, with teaching specifically tailored to their learning styles and subject choices free from any gender stereotyping.

Through our unique Monmouth Model, girls also benefit from the invaluable interaction with Monmouth School for Boys, sharing many trips and expeditions, events and community projects.

Understanding the pressures of adolescence, our focused approach prepares girls for Sixth Form, where they have the confidence to aim high in their specialist academic subjects and to fulfil their particular sporting, musical or artistic ambitions. Monmouth Schools Sixth Form brings day and boarding boys and girls together at this final stage of their educational journey with us, recognising their greater maturity and focus. We offer the benefits of single-sex pastoral care within a co-educational academic environment.

Monmouth girls develop a can-do attitude and make the most of the superb facilities on offer for sports, culture and the arts. Full use is made of the ample sports facilities: spacious playing fields, all-weather pitch, tennis courts, indoor swimming pool and sports hall. All are adjacent to the school.

Main sporting activities include lacrosse, netball, softball, rowing, fencing, hockey, dance and equestrian. Many girls play at County, National and International level. A newly established tennis academy makes the most of the impressive site.

A purpose-built Performing Arts Centre, housed over three floors, opened in Autumn 2018. This state-of-the-art facility has replaced the old gymnasium and is linked to the existing theatre at stage and hall level. A new home to the music department and with a dance and drama studio on the top floor, it features a recital hall with space for an audience of up to 150 people and includes a viewing gallery.

The school has a Chaplain and is a Christian foundation. Girls are encouraged to attend the places of worship of their own denomination.

We teach classics throughout the school. At examination level, we offer Latin at GCSE and A Level, and Classical Civilisation at A Level. Classical Greek is offered by request as an extra-curricular activity. The school excels in a variety of STEM programmes, gaining many accolades in 'The Big Bang' and ESSW competitions.

Almost all our pupils progress to Higher Education. With excellent careers advice, girls are aware of the scope of degree subjects. More than 65% of our girls gain places annually at Russell Group universities, including Oxford and Cambridge.

We encourage creative and practical work, especially music and drama. Girls frequently attend concerts, plays and exhibitions, and take an active interest in industry and management. Local businesses lend support to the school's Young Enterprise schemes.

Girls participate in the Duke of Edinburgh's Award scheme, Combined Cadet Force, overseas expeditions and community projects and many also belong to local voluntary organisations.

Fees per term (2018–2019). Senior School: Day £4,926, Boarding £9,644–£10,687. Prep Department: Day £3,697, Boarding £6,760.

Entry is usually at 7, 11, 13 or post GCSE, although occasionally other vacancies occur. Informal assessments for entry at 7+ to Monmouth School Girls' Prep are held in the Lent term. Entry to the senior school is by examination, interview and report from the current school. The interviews and entrance examinations are held for 11+ in January, 13+ in February/March (or Common Entrance Examination in June), and for 16+ in November.

Further information and copies of the prospectus are available from the Admissions Registrar, Mrs Karen Stafford-Smith; Tel: 01600 711104, email: girls.admissions@habsmonmouth.org

Scholarships and Bursaries. A number of academic scholarships are awarded at 11+, 13+ and 16+ to the best candidates on the basis of the school's entrance examination, interview and report from the current school. Music scholarships, also available at 11+, 13+ and 16+, are awarded on the basis of audition and interview held in the Lent term for 11+ and 13+ and the Michaelmas term for 16+.

Sport and Dance scholarships are available at 11+, 13+ and 16+ entry and are awarded on the basis of assessment and interview, held in the Lent term for 11+ and 13+, and Michaelmas term for 16+. Creative Arts (art and drama) scholarships are awarded following an assessment day held at the school in the Lent term for 13+ and the Michaelmas term for 16+.

Means-tested Bursaries and Assisted Places of up to 100% of fees are also available at all entry points. Please contact the Admissions Registrar (as above) for further information.

Old Girls' Association. Mrs Clare Anning, c/o Monmouth School for Girls, Monmouth. The OGA Annual General Meeting is held at the school on the second Saturday in November.

Charitable status. William Jones's Schools Foundation is a Registered Charity, number 525616. The object of the Foundation shall be the provision and conduct in or near Monmouth of a day and boarding school for boys and a day and boarding school for girls.

Board of Governors:
Chairman of Governors: Mr A W Twiston-Davies (*also Acting Chairman of Monmouth School for Boys Committee*)
Chairman of Monmouth School for Girls Committee: Mr N G H Manns[1]
Mr P M Alderman (*Safeguarding Governor, Monmouth School for Boys*)
Mr M H C Anderson[1]
Mrs J Booth
Professor R J Carwardine[1]
Mrs S Clayton[1] (*Safeguarding Governor, Monmouth School for Girls*)
Mr M E Davidson
Mrs M K Henderson[1] (*Boarding Governor*)
Dr J Kelly
Mr M Kerrigan
Mr M Metcalfe
Mr R Miners[1]
Mrs H Moriarty
Mrs M Nordal
Councillor R Roden
Mrs R F Rose[1]
Mrs L Russen[1]
Mr N Waters

[1] *Member of the Monmouth School for Girls Committee*

Clerk to the Governors: Mrs F Creasey, BCom, ACMA

Foundation Bursar: Mrs T Norgrove, MBA

***Acting Head*: Mr T Arrand, MA Oxon, PGCE Cantab**

Deputy Head: Mr T Arrand, MA Oxon, PGCE Cantab
Deputy Head (*Academic*): Mrs O E Davis, BSc Joint Hons Salford, MA Ed, PGCE York
Assistant Head (*Academic*): Mr D R Evans, BA Hons Coventry, MA Wales, PGCE Wales
Head of Sixth Form: Mrs R Rees, BA Hons Manchester, PGCE Bristol
Chaplain: Reverend C Swartz, BA Hons Trinity College, Connecticut, Anglican Ministry Training Cambridge, MA Cambridge

* *Head of Department*

Art:
Mr S Huson, BA, BA QTS, MA, SFHEA
Mr C Beer, BA Hons, PGCE UWIC

Business Studies:
*Miss M C Attrill, BTEC Dip Business Studies, Cert Ed UWCN

Careers:
*Mrs A Johnson, BA Hons History Bangor, Dip Careers Guidance

Classics:
*Mrs L Beech, BA Hons Birmingham, PGCE Cambridge
Dr C H Geisz, Licence BA France, MA Paris IV, DPhil
    Oxon

Computing & ICT:
*Mr J Childs, BEng Hons Wales, PGCE USW
Mrs L Partridge, BA Hons Wales
Drama & Theatre Studies:
*Ms J Knight, BA Hons Cardiff, MA Cardiff, PGCE UWE
Mr D Murray, MA Hons Aberdeen, PGACA RWCMD

Economics:
*Miss M C Attrill, BTEC Dip Business Studies, Cert Ed
    UWCN
Mr D R Evans, BA Hons Coventry, MA Wales, PGCE
    Wales

English:
*Mrs Z Harvey, BA Hons Wales, PGCE London
Mr J A Edwards, BA Hons, MA Warwick, PGCE Wales
Mrs C Griffiths, BA Hons London, PGCE Reading
Mrs J Harper, BSc Hons Aberystwyth, PGCE Aberystwyth
Mrs J Hastings, BA Hons Westfield College London, MSc
    LSE, PhD LSE, BA Hons Open Univ
Ms J Knight, BA Hons Cardiff, MA Cardiff, PGCE UWE
Ms S White, BA Hons UEA, PGCE Bristol
Geography:
*Mr N Meek, BA Hons Middlesex, MA Leicester, PGCE
    Wales, MEd Birmingham
Mr L Jones, BSc Hons Reading, PGCE Swansea, MA
    Worcester
Mrs J E Harper, BSc Hons, PGCE Aberystwyth

History:
*Mr M Seaton, BA Hons, PGCE Swansea
Mr P Grant, BA Hons Durham, BA Hons OU, PGCE
    Swansea

Mathematics:
*Mr A Skailes, BSc Southampton, PGCE St Martin's
    London
Dr S Lawlor, BSc Hons Dublin, PhD Leeds, PGCE UWIC
Mrs J E Morris, BSc Hons, PGCE Wales
Mrs V R Price, BSc Ed UWCN
Mrs A K Creed, BEng Surrey, PGCE Reading
Mrs C Skailes, BEng Southampton, PGCE Lancaster, PhD
    Reading

Modern Languages:
*Mrs H K Smail, MA Reading, PGCE Birmingham
    (*French*, *German*)
Mrs O E Davis, BSc Jt Hons Salford, MA, PGCE York
    (*Spanish*)
Mrs H English, BA Hons Michel de Montaigne Bordeaux
    III, PGCE Wales (*Spanish, French*)
Mrs C A Griffiths, BA Hons London, PGCE Reading
    (*German*)
Mrs A Hutchings, BA Hons Bath, PGCE UWIC (*French,
    German*)
Mrs R Rees, BA Hons Manchester, PGCE Bristol (*French,
    German*)
Mrs R Jenkins, MA Cardiff, PGCE (*Spanish*)
Mrs C Takeuchi, MA Bournemouth, PGCE Cardiff
    (*French*)
French Foreign Language Assistant: Mrs M Neumer
German Foreign Language Assistant: Mr R Faessler

Music:
*Mr D Harris, GRSM Hons, Dip RCM Advanced/
    Teachers, PGCE
Mrs R Friend, LRAM, LRAM TD
Mr M Steer, MA, BMus Cardiff

Personal and Social Education (*Confidence 4 Life*):
Miss J Johnson, BSc Hons OU, PGCE Carmarthen

Physical Education, Sport & Dance:
*Miss L Scott, BA Hons QTS PE Chichester (*Director of
    Sport, PE & Dance*)
Ms R V Parry, BA Hons, PGCE Bedford (*Dance*)
Mrs K A Callaghan, BA Hons Surrey (*Rowing*)
Mrs R Harris, BSc Hons UWIC, PGCE Exeter
Mrs C E Jones, BSc Hons Wolverhampton, MSc Wales,
    PGCE
Ms Z Pritchard, TCert RAD, Teaching Associate ISTD,
    Dip Dance Ed
Mrs S J Rossiter, BSc Hons South Bank, PGCE Wales
Miss C Lewis, BSc Hons Cardiff (*Netball*)
Mr R Fletcher (*Rowing Coach and Boatman*)

Psychology:
*Mrs K Smith, BSc Hons Bath Spa, Dip Teaching
Miss J Johnson, BSc Hons OU, PGCE Carmarthen

Ethics & Philosophy:
*Dr H Whatley, PhD King's College London, PGCE
    London, MA Humboldt University, Germany, BA Hons
Edinburgh
Mr T Arrand, MA Oxon, PGCE Cantab
Miss J Johnson, BSc OU, PGCE Carmarthen
Revd C Swartz, BA Hons Trinity College Connecticut,
    Anglican Ministry Training Cambridge, MA Cambridge
Mrs M Wilkes, BA Hons Cardiff, PGCE Carmarthen'

Science:
Miss L J Woodburn, BSc Hons, PGCE Glasgow (*Science
    & *Biology*)
Mrs D E Clarke, BSc Hons Newcastle, PGCE Durham
    (*Chemistry*)
Mr G Dunn, BSc Hons Bath, MSc Wales, PGCE Wales
    (*Physics*)
Mrs L C Arnold, BA Hons Oxford (*Physics*)
Mrs C Avila-Jones, BSc Hons Wales, PGCE UWIC
    (*Physics*)
Mrs C Levick, BA Hons Oxford, PGCE Bristol (*Biology*)
Mrs V Lyons, BSc Hons Cardiff, PGCE (*Biology*)
Mrs S P Marks, BSc Hons OU, PGCE Wales (*Chemistry*)
Mrs C Natt, BSc Hons Swansea, PGCE Worcester, MA Ed
    OU (*Biology*)
Dr D Watson, MChem Cardiff, PhD Cardiff (*Chemistry*)
Mrs C Skailes, BEng Southampton, PGCE Lancaster, PhD
    Reading

Speech & Drama:
Mrs A Baker, BPhil Warwick, Cert Ed
Mr D Murray, MA Hons Aberdeen, PGACA RWCMD
Mr A Shakeshaft, BA Hons Loughborough

Technology:
*Mr S McCluskey, BSc Hons Wales, PGCE Wales
Mrs K Lewis, BEng Hons, PGCE Wales
Mrs R Nieuwoudt, BSc Hons, PGCE Wales

Learning Support:
Mrs J Jefferies, BEd Liverpool, PGCE Gloucestershire
Mrs C Bown, CNAA Jt Hons, PGCE Exeter
Miss T May, BA Hons USW, MA & PGCE TESOL USW

Duke of Edinburgh's Award Coordinator:
*Mrs A Creed, BEng Surrey, PGCE Reading

Monmouth School Girls' Prep (*Preparatory Department*):
Headmistress: Mrs H J Phillips, BA, BEd Exeter
Deputy Head: Mr T Evans, BA Hons Aberystwyth, PGCE
    Cardiff
Mrs A Griffiths, BA Hons Bristol
Mrs S Latheron, BSc Hons Brighton, BSc OU, PGCE
    Bristol

Mrs L Partridge, BA Hons Wales
Mrs S Ridyard, BEd Hons CNAA, MA Ed Brighton
Mrs A Roskilly-Green, BA Hons Kent, PGCE Brighton
Dr T Murcott, BSc Hons York, PhD Bristol
Mrs S Beaumont, BA Hons Aberystwyth, PGCE Glos
Miss N Price, BEd Hons UWE
Mrs H Rees, BA Hons Cardiff, PGCE UWIC
Mr M Steer, MA, BMus Cardiff
Miss R Sanderson, Sports Coaching Oxford Brookes, PGCE Worcester

Learning Support for Monmouth School Girls' Prep:
Mrs A Copley, BHEd Kingston

Moreton Hall

Weston Rhyn, Oswestry, Shropshire SY11 3EW

Tel: 01691 773671
email: admin@moretonhall.com
website: www.moretonhall.org
Twitter: @moretonhall
Facebook: @moretonhall

One of the UK's highest achieving schools, Moreton Hall was founded in 1913 by Ellen Lloyd-Williams (Aunt Lil) in Oswestry and moved to its present location in 1920. In 1964, the school became an educational trust. Although the school is predominantly boarding, a number of day pupils are admitted each year.

Member of HMC, GSA, The Society of Heads, IAPS, AGBIS, and Inspiring Futures.

Admission. Moreton First is the preparatory school of Moreton Hall, sharing not only its extensive facilities but also a commitment to nurture and celebrate the talents of each child. Moreton First takes girls and boys from Transition (age 3) to Year 6 and offers a unique start to their education, ensuring academic rigour goes hand in hand with encouragement to achieve success in all creative and sporting fields.

Girls are admitted to Moreton Hall, normally in September at age 11 and 13, either by Common Entrance or by the School's entrance examination which is held at the end of January each year. This examination requires no knowledge of foreign languages and is designed to test potential ability rather than factual recall. This examination can be taken by pupils at 10+, with supplementary papers at 12 and 13. Candidates from preparatory schools may enter through Common Entrance if they so choose at ages 11, 12 and 13. Sixth Form entrance is by current school report and interview, and numbers are limited. All applications should be addressed to the Principal.

Though predominantly boarding, day girls are welcomed. Boys may board from the age of 8–11.

Scholarships and Bursaries. A number of Academic scholarships worth up to 10% of fees will be awarded to pupils at ages 11+, 12+, 13+ and 16+. Scholarships for Music, Drama, Art and for outstanding sporting talent are also available. Students may apply for more than one scholarship. Means-tested bursaries may be awarded up to the value of 100% of fees. The Bronwen Scholarship is available to girls entering the school in Years 5–8.

Fees per term (2018–2019). Boarders: £7,560 (Moreton First), £11,005 (Years 7 and 8), £11,625 (Years 9–13). Day pupils: £3,280–£4,630 (Moreton First), £8,850 (Years 7 and 8), £9,575 (Years 9–13).

Curriculum. Going well beyond the National Curriculum, some 20 subjects are available at GCSE, varying from traditional academic subjects such as Latin and the Sciences, to practical subjects such as Drama, Dance and Physical Education. Modern Languages available include French, German, Spanish, Mandarin Chinese and Russian. A Levels in History of Art, Social Biology, Business Studies and Theatre Studies extend the range of the curriculum. Information Technology is a compulsory subject up to Sixth Form, optional thereafter.

Examinations offered. GCSE, A Level, ABRSM, ESB (English Speaking Board). Over 95% of Upper Sixth go on to University.

Religious activities. Non-denominational. Weekday service, longer service on Sunday, visiting preacher.

Academic, Sporting and Extra-Curricular facilities. Moreton Hall is engaged in an ambitious development programme and has facilities of the highest quality designed to provide the right environment for the education of girls in the twenty-first century.

Younger girls are housed in the Stables building under the supervision of resident houseparents, assistants and matrons. The building is designed to create a family atmosphere with dormitories split into smaller units, close to common rooms, washrooms and staff accommodation.

As pupils progress up the school, the dormitories are gradually replaced by double and finally single study-bedrooms. The Sixth Form Houses provide single and double en-suite facilities. Here, within the structure of a boarding school, senior girls are given the necessary freedom to prepare for the next stage in their careers.

The Centenary Science Centre is a unique Medical Science Faculty. The Science Centre, Information Technology rooms and Art and Design Centre are housed within a short distance of the central classroom, careers and library complexes.

All classrooms, libraries and boarding houses are networked and all Sixth Formers have internet access from their study-bedrooms.

An exceptionally well-equipped Sports Centre comprising a sports hall and floodlit tennis courts along with a heated indoor swimming pool, nine-hole golf course, an all-weather surface, and playing fields are set in one hundred acres of beautiful parkland at the foot of the Berwyn hills. The school offers a wide range of sporting options including Lacrosse, Netball, Hockey, Cricket, Tennis and Athletics. Sailing and Riding are also popular.

The Musgrave Theatre, Outdoor Theatre and Music School stimulate theatrical and musical activities ranging from house plays, lunchtime shows and jazz evenings through to ambitious school plays and orchestral concerts. Great emphasis is placed on girls taking part in as wide a range of extra-curricular interests as possible. The school is developing a community theatre which will be a cultural hub for all of the surrounding areas. The ground has been broken and the Holroyd Community Theatre is planned for Autumn 2019.

The nationally acclaimed Moreton Enterprises offers the girls real business experience. Supervised by professional advisers but all run by the girls themselves, Moreton Enterprises consists of retail businesses on site with a turnover of £50,000.

Old Moretonian Association. Katy Tanner, c/o Moreton Hall.

Charitable status. Moreton Hall Educational Trust Limited is a Registered Charity, number 528409. It exists to provide a high quality education for girls.

Governing Body:
Chair: Mr Josh Dixey, MD, FRCP
Deputy Chair: Mrs K Neilson
Chair of Finance Committee: Mr A Stockdale
Dr L Boon, MB BS, LRCP, MRCS

Ms E J Flynn, MA Ed
Dr M Grant, BSc, PhD
Mr M Heath
Mr N Pursglove
Mrs S Tunstall
Mrs L Yule, BSc

Principal: **Mr J Forster**, BA, FRSA

Vice Principal: Mrs C Tilley, GRNCM, PPRNCM
Head of Senior School: Miss S Hughes, MTheol
Head of Moreton First: Mrs C Ford, MA, BSc
Director of Business Development: Mrs A Griffith, BA
Director of International Recruitment: Mrs V Eastman, MA

Morrison's Academy

Ferntower Road, Crieff, Perthshire PH7 3AN

Tel: 01764 653885
Fax: 01764 655411
email: principal@morrisonsacademy.org
website: www.morrisonsacademy.org
Twitter: @macmorrisons
Facebook: @morrisonsacademy

Motto: *Ad summa tendendum ~ Striving for the highest*

Morrison's Academy Boys' School was opened in 1860 with a Girls' Department in 1861, an arrangement which continued until 1889 when a separate school for Girls was opened within the ten acres of the original site. In 1979 these two schools were brought together to become the one Morrison's Academy. The original foundation was possible through the generosity of Thomas Mo(r)rison, a native of Muthill who became a builder in Edinburgh and who in 1813 executed a Trust Deed directing that the fee of the reversion of his estate should be used to found and erect 'an institution calculated to promote the interests of mankind, having particular regard to the Education of Youth and the diffusion of useful knowledge …a new institution which may bear my name and preserve the remembrance of my good intentions for the welfare and happiness of my fellow men'.

The School. Morrison's Academy is an integral part of the community in Crieff and comprises a 10-acre main campus supplemented by 45 acres of sports fields, main hall, after-school/holiday club and Nursery. The school provides education for 503 boys and girls from 3 to 18 years. The Nursery was recently inspected by HMIE and the Care Commission and received an outstanding report, where all areas received 'excellent' or 'very good' indicators.

The Primary School, housed in a separate building on the main campus, educates 193 pupils in small classes. Transfer between primary and secondary is helped by our Transitional Year (P7), which provides teaching in the primary school by a class teacher supplemented by lessons in the secondary school taught by subject specialists.

The Secondary School has 310 pupils studying towards Scottish Qualifications and entry to universities in Scotland, the rest of the UK and abroad. Academic expectations and achievements are high and small groups encourage individual learning and development. Over ninety-seven percent of our S6 go on to university.

Staff and pupils mix easily and the scale of the school allows for every individual to be known and valued by all.

Situation. Morrison's Academy is situated in the beautiful market town of Crieff on the edge of the Scottish Highlands in Perthshire. Strathearn is a beautiful area of mountains, rivers, lochs and rich agricultural land. Pupils attend from the local area and travel from Perth, Pitlochry, Dunkeld, Auchterarder, Stirling, Dunblane and Falkirk.

Curriculum. Pupils in Primary and lower Secondary follow broadly the Scottish 5–14 programme of study, leading in upper Secondary to National 5 and then to Higher and Advanced Higher National Qualifications. Emphasis is placed upon academic achievement, while the pupils are also always encouraged to develop broad skills and interests outside the classroom. Co-curricular activities are extensive and Morrison's Academy makes good use of its glorious location.

Houses. All pupils are placed in one of the four houses named after local families: Campbells, Drummonds, Grahams and Murrays. There is healthy, competitive rivalry between the houses and senior pupils are encouraged to take charge of teams for sporting, music, debating and other events.

Games and Activities. Morrison's Academy encourages pupils to participate in a wide range of co-curricular activities and sports. All pupils use the playing fields and facilities on the main campus or walk to the 45 acres of playing fields, including an artificial pitch for all-weather playing, and pavilions at Dallerie. There is also a new Strength and Conditioning Suite for pupils. Main sports are rugby, hockey, cricket, tennis and athletics. From upper primary fixtures against other schools take place, generally on Saturday mornings. Other sporting activities include soccer, basketball, netball, swimming, golf, weight training, sailing, short tennis, skiing, climbing, karate and more. To complement the sporting activities, pupils are active in The Duke of Edinburgh's Award Scheme, the Combined Cadet Force, drama, music, debating, chess, Pipe and Drum Band, environment group, Young Enterprise, charity fundraising, highland dancing and more. Pupils are challenged to make the most of their time and all within the wonderful environment of Perthshire.

Fees per term (2018–2019). Day: Primary £2,875–£4,095, Secondary £4,332.

The fees include tuition, textbooks, stationery, external examination fees, sports and curriculum-related travel.

Admission Procedure. Admission to the school is by entrance test and school report and/or exam results and entrance interview. The school's main entrance testing/interview days are at the beginning of February and beginning of May, although entrance testing can take place throughout the year as required.

For a prospectus pack and any queries please contact the Admissions Registrar on admissions@morrisons academy.org.

Scholarships and Bursaries. There are Academic Scholarships and Music Scholarships for TR (P7) and S1. Sports Scholarships are available from S2. There are also a number of Sixth Form Scholarships which are awarded after examination and interview in May. The awards, which carry a nominal financial value, recognise both achievement and potential. Means-tested Bursaries are also available.

Charitable status. Morrison's Academy is a Registered Charity, number SC000458. The school is a recognised charity providing education.

Board of Governors:
Chairman: Mr L C Johnston

Mr N Beech	Mr D Glen
Mr PJ Brodie	Mr A P Godfrey
Mrs L Butler	Mr G Martin
Mr D Cloy	Mrs J F Morrow
Mr P J H Cook	Cllr C Reid
Mrs K M Elwis	Mr J W Stewart

Clerk to Governors: Mrs C M Adams

Staff:

Rector: Mr G Warren

Depute Rector: Mr D Johnston
Assistant Rector: Mr P J Lovegrove
Assistant Rector: Miss A McCluskey
Bursar (Finance): Mrs M Speak
Bursar (HR/Facilities): Mrs M Butler
Head of Primary: Miss M Bulloch
Development Officer: Mrs C Dingwall
Head of Nursery: Mrs B Thomson

Teaching Staff:

Art & Design:
Ms P M O'Neill
Miss G D McLaren

Business Studies:
Mrs M Stirling

Computing & IT:
Mrs P Boal

English:
Mrs L McNaughton
Mrs T Lafferty
Ms G Marshall

Drama:
Miss K V Haddow

Geography:
Mr A Wylie
Mr R S Anderson

History/Modern Studies:
Mr M J Clayton
Mr P J Lovegrove
Mr D Johnston
Miss C M Cully

Home Economics:
K. McDougall

Mathematics:
Mr I K O Barnett
Mr A M Jack
Mrs J McConville

Modern Languages:
Mr E Coffey
Miss A McCluskey
Mrs J White
Mrs K Buick

Music:
Mrs M Leggatt (*Director of Music*)
Mrs S Smart

Physical Education:
Mr S G Weston (*Director of Sport*)
Mr L Howell
Mrs J C Lee
Miss E McCormick
Mrs D J McMillan

Science:
Mr J B Beedie
Mr R S Armstrong
Mr F Black
Mr M McKeever
Mrs S Steven

Primary:
Mrs L S Anderson
Mr I Barr
Mrs A Beavington
Mr G Chater
Mrs W Clark
Mrs G M Lauchlan
Mrs C Marchbank
Miss B Kemp
Mrs H Andrews
Mr M Bray
Ms NG Hargreaves

Nursery:
Mrs B Thomson (*Head of Nursery*)
Mrs C Senior
Mrs G Thomson
Mrs M Thomson
Mrs C Armstrong
Mrs C Mackay

Learning Support:
Mrs K Fetter
Mrs G Wilkie
Mrs C Armstrong

Mount Kelly

Parkwood Road, Tavistock, Devon PL19 0HZ

Tel:	01822 813193
Fax:	01822 813168
email:	admissions@mountkelly.com
website:	www.mountkelly.com
Twitter:	@Mount_Kelly
Facebook:	@MountKellyFoundation
LinkedIn:	/mount-kelly

Mount Kelly is a fully co-educational, Independent day and boarding school for children between the ages of 3 and 18. Mount Kelly was established in June 2014 following the merger of two neighbouring Schools, Kelly College (founded in 1877) and Mount House School (founded in 1881).

Mount Kelly combines academic excellence with an outstanding range of opportunities beyond the classroom and exceptional pastoral care. The School offers day, weekly and full boarding places, currently for over 590 pupils (259 at the Prep and 331 at the College). Boarding is available from the age of 7.

We have high expectations and this encourages our pupils to believe in themselves, to be inquisitive, to be resilient and to show ambition both in and out of the classroom. Our pupils feel happy and valued, which in turn gives them the confidence, social awareness and enthusiasm for lifelong learning needed to succeed in a fast changing world. Respect for tradition and an openness to innovation are valued and we encourage our pupils to work with and learn from each other, whilst also showing moral courage to stand up for what they believe in.

Children at Mount Kelly are nurtured, guided and inspired to develop their own skills and interests. Each pupil joins one of the School's Houses, which serves as a boarder's 'home from home' and a day pupil's working base. Boarders and day pupils are integrated throughout the School with small class sizes offering exceptional levels of individual focus. Each pupil is cared for by a Housemaster or Housemistress and assigned a dedicated tutor who oversees their academic, pastoral and co-curricular progress. This comprehensive tutoring system produces happy pupils who are confident, well-rounded and ambitious.

Site and Buildings. Mount Kelly is set in over 100 acres of green fields and woodland on the edge of Dartmoor National Park and on the outskirts of the historic town of Tavistock, Devon. The buildings comprise the School Chapel, Assembly Hall, Performing Arts Centre, Dining Hall, Library and ICT Centre, Art Studios, Technology workshops, Science Laboratories, Swimming Pools (50m, 25m indoor and 25m outdoor), Sports Hall, Gym, Climbing Wall, Fives and Squash Courts, floodlit All-Weather Pitches, Golf course, an Armoury and Rifle Range. The school has access to an on-site residential Adventure Centre, including a high-ropes course and trapeze jump. The School also has its own Trout and Salmon fishing.

Term of Entry. Pupils may be accepted at any stage in the school year from the nursery though to the Lower Sixth Form.

Scholarships. Each year, Mount Kelly makes available a number of scholarships and awards to pupils hoping to join us in Year 9 or the Sixth Form. Scholarships and awards are competitive on entry, and provide exceptional opportunities for able pupils. Awards may be given in the following disciplines: Academic, Art, DT, Music, Sport and Swimming.

Curriculum. The GCSE curriculum is flexible and aims to stretch each pupil appropriately. The core subjects are Mathematics, English (Language and Literature), Science and a Modern Foreign Language. The range of option subjects include Art & Design, Business Studies, Computing, Drama, DT, EAL, Geography, History, Latin, Music, Physical Education and PRE.

Pupils entering the Sixth Form need to possess 6 GCSE passes. Mount Kelly pupils study for 3 A Levels. A Level option subjects include Mathematics, Further Mathematics, English Literature, Biology, Physics, Chemistry, Fine Art, Photography, Business & Economics, Geography, History, ICT, Music, Physical Education, Product Design, Psychology, Religious Studies, Modern Foreign Languages and EPQ. All pupils in the Lower Sixth year receive tuition in Public Speaking.

Co-Curricular Activities. Mount Kelly has a strong commitment to co-curricular activities and the majority of College pupils are involved with the Combined Cadet Force, Duke of Edinburgh's Awards, the Devizes to Westminster International Canoe Race or the Ten Tors Challenge.

Academic staff, in collaboration with the on-site Adventure Centre, run the innovative Learning Outside the Classroom Programme. Children in the Pre-Prep attend a weekly Forest School activity and the Shackleton outdoor programme is run for 9 to 13 year olds.

All pupils are encouraged to explore new interests and to make the most of their spare time. Societies and Activities include LAMDA, Debating, Current Affairs, Drama, Choir, Orchestra, Ensembles, Chess, Computer Programming, Photography, Robotics, Chess, Fine Arts, Surfing and Textiles.

Sport. Mount Kelly has a strong sporting tradition, particularly known for its elite international swimming programme, and has produced more Olympians and Internationals than any other school of its size. Sports undertaken are Rugby, Hockey, Cricket, Tennis, Athletics, Swimming, Netball, Rounders, Climbing, Cross Country, Golf, Horse Riding and Fives, Squash, Basketball, Sailing, Surfing, Tennis, Football and Yoga.

Fees per term (2018–2019). Day Pupils £2,410 to £5,840 and Full boarding: £6,040 to £10,190.

Charitable status. The Mount Kelly Foundation is a Registered Charity, number 306716.

Chairman of the Governors: Dr Kevin Wilson

***Head Master and Principal of the Foundation*: Mr Mark Semmence**, BA, MA Warwick, MBA, PGCE

Principal Deputy Head: Mr Adam Reid, MSc, PGCE
Deputy Head (Academic): Mr James Dixon, MA, PGCE
Deputy Head (Pastoral): Mr Drew Bott, BA, PGCE
Head of Prep: Mr Dominic Floyd, BA, PGCE, QTS
Bursar and Clerk to the Governors: Mr Steven Webber, MA, FCMA, FCIS

Mount St Mary's College

College Road, Spinkhill, Nr Sheffield, Derbyshire
S21 3YL

Tel:	01246 433388
Fax:	01246 435511
email:	headmaster@msmcollege.com
website:	www.msmcollege.com
Twitter:	@MountSpinkhill

Motto: *Sine Macula*

Mount St Mary's College, a co-educational boarding and day school, and its preparatory school and nursery, Barlborough Hall, educate children from age 3 to 18 in the Jesuit tradition. Mount St Mary's is a member of BSA and CISC, the Governing Body is a member of AGBIS and the Headmaster is a member of HMC.

Mount St Mary's College was founded in 1842 by the Society of Jesus in order to provide an education for the country's growing Catholic population. The manor of Spinkhill in North East Derbyshire was the first home of the College, forming the nucleus of the present school. The Elizabethan manor of Barlborough Hall, 1¼ miles away, is the home of the Preparatory School to the College (*see also Barlborough Hall entry in IAPS section*).

Educating children since 1842, we have over a century of teaching and pastoral expertise as well as long-standing traditions that embed charm and character in school life. Boys and girls excel during their time with us, growing in knowledge, confidence, humility and aspiration.

We follow a traditionally robust GCSE and A Level curriculum and the quality and quantity of our music and sporting departments is immense. In addition, we offer a varied range of popular co-curricular opportunities Combined Cadet Force, fencing and Latin, to name but a few. Our teaching nursery ensures children are school-ready when they join Reception.

Numbers. College 360 (11–18); Preparatory School (3–11 years) 210. Boarders, Weekly Boarders and Day Pupils (girls and boys) are accepted at the College.

Aims. Mount St Mary's College is a Jesuit Catholic school inspired by the ideals of St Ignatius of Loyola. The College seeks to develop the whole person and encourages an appreciation of the needs of others both in the College community and the world at large. Mount St Mary's prepares its pupils for an active life commitment through the development of 'a faith that promotes justice'. The College seeks to produce young men and women for others. Pupils of other and no religious denominations are most welcome.

Special Features. Mount St Mary's College is well known for its family atmosphere. Pupils benefit from the close interest and encouragement which they receive throughout their time at the College and parental involvement is particularly encouraged. The strong emphasis on extra-curricular activities illustrates the Jesuit commitment to developing each pupil's individual talents in all areas – academic, spiritual, cultural and physical.

Location. Situated in beautiful private grounds in villages in north east Derbyshire, between Chesterfield, Worksop and Sheffield, the schools are easily accessible from Junction 30 of the M1. A fleet of school minibuses operates throughout the region.

Boarding. Full and flexi boarding options are available for pupils in Year 7 upwards. Boarders live in the boys' or girls' houses, under the care of a Resident Boarding Pastoral Leader and Senior Boarding Tutor, assisted by resident House Tutors. The majority of rooms are en-suite, with either 2–3 sharing or in single rooms. Boarders, both domestic and international, enjoy a full evening and weekend programme incorporating studies, the arts, sport and social time.

Curriculum. Pupils at Mount St Mary's are prepared for GCSEs, AS and A Levels, and University entrance. The curriculum for the first three years (ages 11–13) broadly follows National Curriculum at KS3 with opportunity to pursue a second foreign language and a range of creative arts subjects. The standard GCSE package is nine GCSEs, although more or less is negotiable according to ability; this includes a core of English, Mathematics, a foreign language and between one and three separate Sciences. Several subjects follow the IGCSE curriculum. Other subjects are chosen from a range of options. In the Sixth Form pupils follow AS Levels (usually four) in the Lower Sixth. The most able pupils can continue with four A Levels in the Upper Sixth, although many pupils will choose to focus on three subjects. The College also runs an "A Level Plus" programme to stretch the more able students. In keeping with the school's Ignatian ethos, all pupils follow a Religious Studies course at every stage in addition to a full programme of Games and Physical Education at every level. Specialist tuition is available in a variety of musical instruments and in speech and drama training. Assessment and monitoring of work is built into the tutorial system and there is a regular timetable of reports, pupil progress interviews and communication with parents. Academic excellence and breadth of knowledge are characteristics of Jesuit education and the curriculum is constantly reviewed to ensure that the widest opportunities are available to each pupil.

Religion. Mount St Mary's College is a distinctively Jesuit school, that welcomes children of all denominations to share its ethos. Ignatian principles inform the College's work in fostering a realistic knowledge, love and acceptance of self and of the world in which we live and this underpins our main objective: the formation of young men and young women for others. There are school masses, year masses and other liturgical celebrations regularly throughout the school year, as well as retreats and pilgrimages. The College enjoys close links with the Hallam Diocese and participates in the diocesan pilgrimage to Lourdes. Religious Education is a part of the curriculum to GCSE and either as an examination or non-examination option in the Sixth Form. The Arrupe programme provides opportunities for Sixth Formers to give service to the local community. The College maintains a strong link with Jesuit missions in different parts of the world, finding ways to further the work of the Society in this area. Pupils have the opportunity to be involved in gap year projects supported by the Jesuits. Pupils and their parents are expected to recognise and endorse the religious commitment of the College.

Sports. The College has extensive playing fields for rugby, hockey, cricket and football. Rugby, for which the College has a strong regional and national reputation, is the major boys' sport. Cricket facilities are excellent with all-weather practice wickets and indoor practice nets. The main girls' sport in the winter term is hockey, for which there is a floodlit all-weather hockey pitch. There is a full-time Level 4 Athletics Coach. Other sports include swimming, tennis, basketball, volleyball, badminton, shooting, netball and fencing.

Art, Drama and Music. There are many opportunities to be involved in the Arts within the school, both within the curriculum and as part of the extra-curricular activities. Within the Art and Design department pupils can study fine art, textiles, resistant materials within the workshop, and photography. On Saturday mornings activities are run involving sculpture, textiles, art and photography.

Music is particularly strong, and popular at all levels. Pupils are encouraged to take up a musical instrument, and can participate in a wide number of musical activities, ranging from three choirs and a barber shop group to symphony orchestra, concert band, jazz band and many ensembles. Drama is also strong in the College, and several Senior and Junior productions are put on every year. The music and drama departments collaborate to produce a whole-school musical.

Combined Cadet Force and other Extra-Curricular Activities. All pupils in Year 10 participate in the Combined Cadet Force, in the Army or RAF section. They can continue to be a member, if they choose, in Year 11 and the Sixth Form. The CCF gives opportunities for external leadership courses and adventure training and fulfilling Duke of Edinburgh's Award options. There are extensive opportunities for extra-curricular activities at lunchtime, after school and on Saturday mornings. Pupils can pursue interests in drama, music, sports, the Duke of Edinburgh's Award and many other clubs and societies.

Facilities. Facilities include a Sixth Form Centre, a Drama Studio, ICT suite of three fully-equipped rooms, Music School with practice rooms, Recital Hall and Music Studio, College Theatre, Library with ICT facilities, various pupil common rooms, Fitness Centre, heated indoor swimming pool, Sports Hall, Rifle Range, Outdoor Pursuits Centre, all-weather tennis courts and 30 acres of games fields. A grade A accredited athletics track was opened in 2007.

Admissions. Entry to the College at age 11 is via the College's entrance examination, taken early in the Spring term at the College. At 13+, pupils either sit the College entrance examination or Common Entrance exam through their prep schools. At other ages, pupils are accepted on the basis of school reports, with College entry tests as appropriate and in the Sixth Form, pupils are accepted on the basis of GCSE results, or their equivalent.

Private tours of the school take place all year round. The Headmaster, Dr Nicholas Cuddihy, extends a warm welcome to families to visit Mount St Mary's College or its Preparatory School. Call the Admissions team on 01246 433388 or email: admissions@msmcollege.com.

Fees per term (2018–2019). Full Boarders: £9,995 (Years 9–13), £7,635 (Years 7 and 8). Weekly Boarders: £8,005 (Years 9–13), £6,220 (Years 7 and 8). Day Pupils: £4,695 (Years 9–13), £4,085 (Years 7 and 8). Barlborough Hall: £3,595 (Years 5 and 6), £3,525 (Years 3 and 4), £2,645 (Years 1 and 2).

Scholarships. Academic scholarships are awarded at 11+, 13+ and Sixth Form on the basis of the College's Scholarship Examination papers. GCSE results also form an aspect of Scholarship awards at Sixth Form. Music and sports scholarships are also available and the College will be happy to provide further information on these. In keeping with the College's ethos, bursaries are awarded in cases of demonstrable need. The Old Mountaineers offer postgraduate scholarships to former pupils of the College and applications are considered annually for these. All scholarships take place early in the Spring Term at the College.

Charitable status. Mount St Mary's is a Registered Charity, number 1117998. The College was founded in 1842 to provide an education for children.

Governing Body:
Chairman: Fr Adrian Porter SJ

Executive Team:

Headmaster: Dr Nicholas Cuddihy, EdD Dublin, BRelSc, MSc

Headteacher, Barlborough Hall School: Mrs Karen Keeton

Deputy Head (Academic): Mr Christopher McAllister
Deputy Head (Pastoral): Mr Jack Murphy
Head of Higher Line: Dr Sarah Dewar-Watson
Head of Lower School: Mrs Jill Phinn
Head of Marketing, Development, Admissions: Mrs Victoria McAllister

Jesuit Community:
Fr Michael Beattie SJ, STL Rome, MA London (*Resident Jesuit Priest*)

New Hall School

The Avenue, Boreham, Chelmsford, Essex CM3 3HS

Tel: 01245 467588
Fax: 01245 464348
email: registrar@newhallschool.co.uk
website: www.newhallschool.co.uk
Twitter: @NewHallSchool
Facebook: @newhallschool

Pupil numbers. Senior Divisions (11–16): 643. Sixth Form (16–18): 202. Preparatory Divisions (3–11): 364. Day 942, Boarding 246.

Location. New Hall School benefits from a magnificent campus and stunning heritage setting, with a grade I listed main building part of a former Tudor palace occupied by King Henry VIII.

We aim to educate the whole person: academically, creatively and socially, in a community which also nurtures the spiritual dimensions of human life. All benefit from the outstanding facilities on offer within our stunning 85-acre campus.

New Hall is set in an idyllic and convenient location, just 25 minutes by train from London Stratford and within easy reach of all major airports. We offer a distinctive education of real quality that is designed to give students the best start in life.

Diamond Model. At New Hall, students are educated in co-educational classes up to age 11 and again at Sixth Form, however, from 11 to 16 they are taught in single-sex classes.

The main benefits of the 'diamond model' and five years of single-sex teaching derive from the ability to tailor pastoral and academic provision more sensitively and expertly to the needs of young people going through the physical, emotional and social upheaval of adolescence. Young teenagers are liberated from the negative peer pressure of having to perform in mixed classes.

Gender stereotyping of subjects is also removed. Girls and boys follow an identical curriculum and do not learn to perceive subjects as being more suited to either girls or boys.

Curriculum. New Hall Preparatory Divisions curriculum is enriched by specialist subject teachers for Mathematics, French, Information Technology, Latin, Drama, Music, Physical Education and Dance. Their expert knowledge and passion for their subjects greatly enhance the children's learning experience.

The extensive co-curricular activities on offer set New Hall Preparatory Divisions apart; from Philosophy and Latin, to Mandarin and Poetry, there is always something to do.

Creative subjects including Music, Drama, Dance, Art and Design Technology all form part of the mainstream academic curriculum, and also feature in activities offered outside normal lessons. We have three choirs, infant, junior and chamber, as well as a Preparatory Orchestra. Our pupils regularly perform at prestigious venues, which include the O2 Arena and the Royal Albert Hall.

The Senior Divisions curriculum is distinctive in its breadth and academic rigour. An imaginatively taught and well-balanced curriculum is appropriately tailored to the needs of the individual. The experienced and dedicated staff endeavour to bring out the best in everyone.

New Hall has its own Most Able and Talented programme, which is proven to add exceptional value at GCSE and A Level. We believe that giftedness can be created and that students' academic skills can be developed at ever higher levels if they are given intellectual challenges.

New Hall encourages able students to apply for Oxford or Cambridge universities. The school has a good track record of students winning Oxbridge places in a wide range of subjects, including sciences, arts, humanities and languages.

We are proud that our examination results are consistently among the best of any independent school in the area.

Co-Curriculum. Our co-curricular programme is designed to add breadth to the New Hall education, which enables us to develop the well-rounded young men and women of whom we can be proud.

Our educational philosophy is reflected in the extensive array of challenging co-curricular activities. Educational visits in the Senior Divisions to countries such as India and China, alongside our societies and clubs, create a stimulating environment for your son or daughter to develop his or her passions, learning and talents.

Through activities such as debating, Model United Nations and political philosophy, students can become independent thinkers with a broad and rich experience of social and academic life.

Our Ethos. Our Catholic foundation and ethos is central to all that we do, supported by the work of our lively Chaplaincy Team. At New Hall, a special value is placed on love and forgiveness, which encourage relationships based on trust, kindness, self-respect and care for those in need.

All students participate in our award-winning New Hall Voluntary Service (NHVS), where they gain confidence, leadership and team-working skills and a desire to serve others. They will develop a sense of charity and community that will remain with them beyond their years at New Hall.

Boarding. We have a thriving full boarding community and options for weekly or flexible boarding. The six boarding houses offer their members a strong sense of identity and opportunities to forge new friendships. There are dedicated boarding houses for younger boarders (age 7–11), for students in the senior division (age 11–15) and for Sixth Form (age 16–18).

Although each of our boarding houses has its own individuality, a common theme throughout is the exceptional pastoral care and dedication of the residential team. This is a significant strength of our school.

Music and Performing Arts. Our dedicated Performing Arts Centre and theatres allow students opportunities for group or individual performances, which develop talent and encourage confidence.

Music has a long and fine tradition at New Hall. There is a host of performing groups, including chamber choir, chapel choir, senior orchestra, strings academy and jazz band. Students can participate in the London Academy of Music and Dramatic Arts (LAMDA) programmes, which develop presentation and public speaking skills. Drama performances range from Shakespeare to modern plays and musicals. Dance is a particular strength, with the annual dance show attracting a cast of more than 200 girls and boys.

Students take part in regional and national festivals and competitions and groups regularly perform in major venues across Europe.

Sport. New Hall students are able to develop their team spirit and physical development through our rich programme of sporting opportunities.

Under the guidance of expert coaches, including former international sportsmen and women, New Hall balances first-class training for those with particular sporting talents, with an inclusive 'sport for all' approach.

Our elite sportsmen and women compete at county, regional and national levels, at which they have enjoyed individual team success.

Our facilities set us apart and the rich variety of sports on offer include rugby, hockey, netball, cricket, swimming, athletics, golf, skiing and tennis.

Fees per term (2018–2019). Senior Divisions: Day £6,182–£6,626; Weekly Boarding £8,193–£9,523; Full Boarding £9,074–£10,002.

Preparatory Divisions: Day: £2,426–£4,826; Boarding (from age 7): £6,587 (weekly), £7,117 (full).

Sixth Form: Day £6,626; Weekly Boarding £9,523; Full Boarding £10,227.

There is a Prompt Payment Discount of £100 per term in Years 1–13 (included in the Fees shown).

Entry requirements. Entrance examination, school report, and interview.

Scholarships and Bursaries. Scholarship candidates follow the normal entrance procedure and, dependent on the type of scholarship, a further assessment. All candidates for Year 7 entry are entered for the Academic Scholarship, which is awarded to the highest achieving student from the entrance examination results. Other scholarships at Year 7 entry 2013 are available in Drama, Music and Sport. There are also scholarships available for Catholic students. Similar scholarships are available for Year 9 entry. For Sixth Form entry, there are scholarship awards available based on GCSE examination results as well as an Open (all rounder) scholarship, Boarding scholarship and Special Talent Award.

Means-tested Bursaries (up to 100% remission of fees) are available to new and current students.

Further information on Admissions, Scholarships and Bursaries is available from the Registrar and on the school website.

Charitable status. New Hall School Trust is a Registered Charity, number 1110286. Its aim is the education of children within a Christian environment.

Chair of Governors: Dr Miriam Edelsten

Senior Leadership & Management Team:

Principal: **Mrs K Jeffrey**, MA Oxon, PGCE Surrey, BA Div PUM, MA Ed Mgt OU, NPQH

Deputy Principal: Mr A Fardell, BA Kent, LRAM
Vice Principal: Mr J Sidwell, BSc Loughborough, PGCE London
Vice Principal: Dr P Tiffen, BSc Warwick, PhD Cambridge, PGCE ARU
School Chaplain: Fr L Bennett, BA Leeds
Head of Sixth Form: Mr J Alderson, BA Manchester, PGCE Cantab
Head of Girls' and Boys' Divisions: Mrs S Minnis, BA Chelsea
Head of Preparatory Division: Mr A Moulton, BA SHU
Head of Pre-Prep Division: Mr R Field, MA Oxon, PGCE Nottingham
Director of Learning & Teaching: Dr S Foster, BA PhD Loughborough, PGCE Anglia Ruskin
Director of Learning & Teaching: Mr P Bray, BA MA Dunelm, GTP
Director of Learning & Teaching: Mrs A Hilder, BA Southampton, PGCE Bath
Head of Boarding: Mrs E Searle, BA ARU
Head of Finance: Mrs D Came, IPFA, IoD
Director of Admissions, Communications & Development: Mrs D Attridge, BA Sheffield
Executive Assistant, Clerk to Governors & Company Secretary: Mrs E Murphy
Estate Manager: Mr S Hall, BSc Essex, Dip RSA, Grad IOSH

Newcastle High School for Girls
GDST

Senior School:
Tankerville Terrace, Jesmond, Newcastle-upon-Tyne NE2 3BA

Tel: 0191 281 1768
email: seniorschooloffice@ncl.gdst.net

Junior School:
Chapman House, Sandyford, Newcastle-upon-Tyne NE2 1TA

Tel: 0191 285 1956

website: www.newcastlehigh.gdst.net
Twitter: @NewcastleHigh

Newcastle High School for Girls offers an unrivalled educational opportunity for girls of the North East of England. It provides an outstanding academic education, always putting girls first to make sure that every single one of them grows into a bold and independent young woman, ready to take on the world.

Newcastle High is part of the GDST (Girls' Day School Trust), the leading network of independent girls' schools in the UK which educates around 20,000 girls across the country. Its mission is to deliver an outstanding, forward-looking education, rooted in traditional values. As a charity that owns and runs 23 schools and two academies, it reinvests all its income in its schools. For further information about the Trust, see p. xxiii or visit www.gdst.net.

Pupil Numbers. 870: Senior School 570 (aged 11–18 years) of whom 200 are in the Sixth Form; Junior School 300 (aged 3–11 years).

Launched in September 2014, Newcastle High was formed by the merger of Central High and Church High and has quickly established itself as a leading School in the North East; not surprisingly so with the combined 250 years of experience brought from its two founding schools.

In keeping with its proud history, Newcastle High School for Girls is exciting and innovative. The ethos, environment and curriculum have all been designed to meet the demands of the 21st Century. It aims to develop outward looking and socially responsible girls who are equipped with the confidence and ability to be the person they want to be and to embrace the opportunities and challenges of adult life. At Newcastle High, girls excel academically, develop skills, build character and participate in a wide range of co-curricular and enrichment activities.

With academic rigour and excellence at its heart, the school curriculum benefits from cross-curricular planning and a focus on deep learning that spans the subject disciplines through open ended enquiry and independent research. Creativity flourishes across the whole curriculum and the pupils at the School are motivated and full of energy. There is outstanding provision for Sport, Music, Art, Dance and Drama and the girls have the opportunity to develop many new interests and skills through the varied co-curricular programme.

The School strongly believes that one of the main reasons why girls succeed is its impressive pastoral care system underpinned by strong pupil teacher relationships and a supportive and caring school community.

The facilities across the whole School are excellent and all girls are able to take full advantage of them. Situated at Chapman House, Sandyford Park, Newcastle upon Tyne, the Junior School provides the very best learning environment for girls. Set in five acres of grounds, and including a John Dobson designed mansion, Chapman House offers a piece of the countryside right in the heart of the city centre. Spacious classrooms have been furnished with excellent resources to support teaching and learning and the Early Years have direct access to a specific open-air learning environment. There is ample indoor and outdoor space to explore ideas, discover and think creatively. The grounds have recently been landscaped to include all-weather surfaces, outdoor classrooms, a story telling area, kitchen garden and bog garden – just some of the exciting features designed to bring learning to life.

Senior girls moved to brand new state-of-the-art Senior School facilities in September 2016. The multimillion pound development in Jesmond included the remodelling of a beautiful Victorian building and the construction of a new three-storey building to create an outstanding school for the 21st Century. Facilities include an impressive Performing Arts venue with professional-standard lighting and sound equipment; up-to-the-minute Science laboratories, Science Demonstration Area, and Rooftop Terrace; and a Learning Resources Centre. Every teaching room includes a large interactive touch screen to enable truly flexible and seamless teaching and learning to take place. An all-weather sports pitch and track has been in use from January 2017.

Curriculum. The Junior School follows an innovative and creative curriculum which is focused on extending the girls' learning by allowing them to explore topics and subjects in greater depth. It is enriched with Music Art, Drama and Dance to give the girls ample opportunity to express their creativity. Outdoor leaning is an important part of the curriculum and the Junior School is an accredited Forest School.

The Senior School curriculum is designed to provide girls with the skills, knowledge and understanding that they will need in the years to come. The curriculum is rich in the Arts and strong in Humanities, Sciences and Languages. Sport is for all. The breadth and depth of intellectual challenge is a strong feature. As well as subject specific lessons, the Newcastle High curriculum promotes a cross-curricular approach that enables girls to make more sense of their learning. Knowledge and skills in one subject area are used to reinforce learning in another.

In Sixth Form, intellectual challenge and a love of learning are at the centre and the girls can choose from a wide range of A Levels. In addition to their A Level studies, the girls take part in an enrichment programme designed to extend their studies and broaden their understanding. Most girls take an Extended Project Qualification on a topic of their choice.

Admissions. Junior School: by assessment and interview.

Senior School: by entrance examination, interview and school report.

Sixth Form: by GCSE results, interview and school report.

Fees per term (2018–2019). Senior School £4,341, Junior School £3,429, Nursery £2,803.

The fees cover the regular curriculum, non-residential curriculum trips, school books, games and swimming but not optional extra subjects or school meals.

Scholar and Exhibition Awards. A range of Academic Scholar Awards and Exhibition Awards in Dance, Music, Sport and Exceptional Prior Achievement was launched in September 2018 for entry into Year 7 in September 2019.

Bursaries. The GDST Bursaries Fund provides financial assistance in the Senior School to suitably qualified girls whose parents could not otherwise afford the fees to enter or remain in the School. Bursaries are available for girls entering Year 7 and Year 12.

Charitable status. Newcastle High School for Girls is part of The Girls' Day School Trust, which is a Registered Charity, number 306983.

Chair of Local Governors: Mrs P Alexander

Head: Mr M Tippett, MA Oxon, PGCE Cantab, NPQH

Deputy Head (Academic): Mrs A Hardie, MA Oxon, MEd Newcastle, PGCE Durham

Deputy Head (Pastoral): Mrs L Franks-Doyle, BA Hons Manchester, PGCE Newcastle

Director of Sixth Form: Mrs H Harrison, BA Hons Huddersfield, PGCE Newcastle

Head of Junior School: Miss A Charlton, BA Hons, PGCE Newcastle, NPQH

Director of Finance and Operations: Mr J Crosby, MEng Nottingham, Adv Dip Durham, FCA

Director of Marketing: Mrs J Graves, BA Hons Northumbria, FCIM

Newcastle-under-Lyme School

Mount Pleasant, Newcastle-under-Lyme, Staffordshire ST5 1DB

Tel: 01782 631197
Fax: 01782 632582
email: info@nuls.org.uk
website: www.nuls.org.uk
Twitter: @NuLSchoolUK
Facebook: @NewcastleunderLymeSchool

Newcastle-under-Lyme School, which attracts pupils from a large area of North Staffordshire, South Cheshire and North Shropshire, is a co-educational day school for 800 pupils aged 3–18. The present School was formed in 1981 through the amalgamation of Newcastle High School and the Orme Girls' School, two schools which were endowed as a single foundation in 1872 under an educational charity scheme for children in Newcastle-under-Lyme which has its roots in the 1600s. The two schools enjoyed a reputation for scholarship and for service to the community throughout North Staffordshire, a reputation which has continued with the formation of Newcastle-under-Lyme School. The School is also well known for its high standards in sport, music and drama, which play a major part in the co-curricular life of the School. The Junior School is adjacent to the Senior School and has some 300 pupils aged 3–11.

Buildings and Grounds. Set in 30 acres of grounds, the School is pleasantly situated on high ground in a quiet conservation area close to the centre of Newcastle-under-Lyme. The original buildings still form part of the School and extensions have been added from time to time. A fine dining hall was opened in one of the wings of the original building, part of the continuing programme of development and refurbishment which was begun when the School reverted to full independence in 1981. The Millennium Sixth Form Centre opened in March 2000 affording spacious new accommodation for senior students. The new Stinton building was opened in September 2014. The excellent sports facilities were further enhanced in Summer 2018 with a newly resurfaced all-weather hockey pitch and cricket nets. The library, lecture theatre, new and refurbished laboratories and the enhanced indoor social space and cafe have transformed the whole building. The School has a Language laboratory, workshops, a Music School, an Art and Design Centre, a gymnasium, and a Sports Centre which includes a sports hall, a fitness suite and an indoor swimming pool. Computers are accessible in subject areas and in four modern laboratories, where machines are linked on a network basis. There are also tennis and netball courts and extensive playing fields, providing athletic facilities and pitches for cricket, rugby and hockey, adjacent to the School.

Organisation. The School is organised in two sections: the Junior School – nursery (2004), pre-preparatory (2004) and preparatory (1982) – which has up to 300 pupils in the age range 3 to 11 and the Senior School of some 500 pupils, including the Sixth Form numbering more than 150 students.

Form Tutors and Heads of Year have particular responsibility for the pastoral welfare of the pupils in their charge.

Curriculum. A broad curriculum in the first five years has English (Language and Literature), Mathematics, Biology, Chemistry, and Physics as core subjects. All pupils also take a Modern Foreign Language, selected from French, Mandarin, German and Spanish, Latin, Greek, History, Geography, Religious Education, Music, Art, Food and Nutrition, Design and Technology, ICT, PE, Swimming and Games. Pupils have the option of taking Biology, Chemistry and Physics as a dual-award GCSE or as three separate GCSEs in Year 10 and Year 11.

Pupils take nine GCSEs and the great majority will proceed to take between three and four A Level subjects in the Lower Sixth Form. There may also be the possibility of taking the Extended Project Qualification.

Choices in the Sixth Form include A Level Business Studies, Psychology, Philosophy, Economics, British Government and Politics and Physical Education in addition to AS Levels in the subjects available at GCSE. Pupils access programmes for Oxford and Cambridge Entrance and Medicine, Dentistry, Veterinary Science applications.

Co-Curricular Activities. The main school games are Rugby, Cricket, Hockey, Athletics, Tennis and Cross-Country for the boys and Hockey, Athletics, Netball, Tennis and Rounders for the girls. Swimming, Water Polo, Life Saving and Synchronised Swimming, Water Polo and Life Saving also feature strongly and there are opportunities for Shooting, Squash, Aerobics, Basketball, Badminton, Golf and other physical activities in the Sixth Form.

There are also strong traditions in both Music and Drama and standards are very high. More than 200 pupils receive instrumental tuition and there are a number of concerts in each year with major performances being given in local churches and in the Victoria Hall in Hanley. There are several major drama productions each year including one each at Upper School and Lower School levels plus a whole-School production.

The flourishing Combined Cadet Force has naval, army and air-force sections and there is also a large Scout troop, which enrols both boys and girls. Pupils also participate in the Duke of Edinburgh's Award scheme with great success.

Clubs and Societies meet during the lunch hour and after school.

Careers. The School places much emphasis on the importance of careers guidance, both in the GCSE years and in the preparation for higher education.

Admissions. Entry to the Nursery is on a first-come first-served basis. Entry to the Junior School and Years 7, 8, 9 and 10 of the Senior School is by examination/assessment only. Pupils moving into the area may be considered for entry at any time.

Entry at Sixth Form level is by interview and GCSE qualifications.

Registration forms, and copies of the Prospectus, are available on request.

Scholarships and Bursaries. The offer of a number of prestigious Scholarships has recently been enhanced with a range available at Year 7 and Sixth Form entry. They include academic, sports and music Scholarships and Exhibitions.

Bursaries: A number of Bursaries are available for pupils applying for entry to the Senior School and Sixth Form. Bursaries offer assistance with School Fees, depending upon parental income.

Further details may be obtained from the Registrar.

Fees per term (2018–2019). Senior School £3,993; Junior School: Preparatory £3,263, Pre-Preparatory £2,907, Nursery £41.00 per day (£26.50 per morning, £23.50 per afternoon session).

Charitable status. Newcastle-under-Lyme School is a Registered Charity, number 1124463. The object of the Charity shall be the provision and conduct in or near Newcastle-under-Lyme of a day or a day and boarding school or schools for boys and girls.

Governing Body:

Chair of Governors: Mr D P Wallbank, BA
Vice Chair of Governors: Mrs K A Miller, BSc, ACA

Dr S Edmends
Mrs JA Grant
Mr IG MacDonald
Mr D Holland
Mr AJ McGowan
Mr GE Neyt
Ms F Tordoff
M R Warren

Headmaster: **Mr M Getty**, BA Hons, NPQH

Deputy Heads:
Mrs J A Simms, BA, MSc (*Pastoral*)
Mr I S Dicksee, BA, MA (*Academic*)

Head of Sixth Form: Mrs B A Godridge, BA

Finance Bursar: Mr A Cryer

Newcastle-under-Lyme Junior School:

Head: Mr NJ Vernon, BSc, MA
Deputy Head: Mr M J Erian, BA, MA

Nursery Manager: Mrs A Smith, NNEB, NEBS

Norwich High School

GDST

95 Newmarket Road, Norwich, Norfolk NR2 2HU

Tel:	01603 453265
Fax:	01603 259891
email:	admin@nor.gdst.net
website:	www.norwichhigh.gdst.net
Twitter:	@NorwichHigh
Facebook:	@NorwichHigh

Founded 1875.

Norwich High School is part of the GDST (Girls' Day School Trust). The GDST is the leading network of independent girls' schools in the UK. As a charity that owns and runs 23 schools and two academies, it reinvests all its income in its schools. For further information about the Trust, see p. xxiii or visit www.gdst.net.

Number of pupils. Senior School: about 450, aged 11–18 years, of whom about 100 are in the sixth form. Prep School: about 170, aged 3–11 years.

Norwich High School draws its pupils in almost equal numbers from the city of Norwich and the county of Norfolk. It stands in 13 acres of grounds on the main Newmarket Road, a mile-and-a-half from the city centre. The main buildings are attached to a distinguished Regency house, built in 1820. In addition, there is a prep school with many specialist rooms, an extended sixth form centre, music school, spacious sports hall, 25m indoor heated pool and a performing arts centre. There are playing fields around the school with an additional astroturf a short walk away, and a wide range of indoor and outdoor physical activities is offered, including netball, hockey, rowing, athletics, tennis, cricket, badminton, gymnastics and dance. The school holds the International Schools' Award, the Sportsmark Gold Award for its sporting achievements and Artsmark for creative subjects.

The school is a caring community and parent-friendly. We are open early for breakfast and late for tea. Girls may use the ICT and library facilities after school in the senior school; the prep school has its own after-school club. There is a minibus service from the surrounding areas in all directions, both before and after school.

Admission. All girls are assessed prior to entry. The normal ages of admission are 3, 7, 11 and 16. Occasional vacancies may occur at other ages.

Curriculum. The school has always been proud to provide a broad and rich education, preparing girls for admission to universities, professions, commerce and industry. A wide range of subjects is available, currently 25 at A Level and 24 at GCSE.

Information systems. A computer network is shared by all departments, including the laboratories, library, all teaching rooms, two computerised language laboratories, the sixth form IT suite as well as the two senior and two junior IT suites. All girls work towards the European Computer Driving Licence qualification in Years 8–9.

Careers education and advice. A carefully planned Careers Information Education and Guidance programme commences in Year 7. Virtually all sixth formers continue on to higher education and the school ensures that they have received comprehensive guidance and preparation. The school has devised an Inspiring Females programme which draws a wide variety of successful women into school to share their experiences and mentor the girls.

Co-curricular Activities. These are extensive, for infants through to seniors. Music, Sport and Drama are all strong features of the school. Large numbers of girls also participate in both the Duke of Edinburgh's Award and Young Enterprise schemes, rowing, equestrian, debating and chess clubs, Amnesty International, Christian Union, fencing and life saving, and over 40 other clubs and societies. The school has a rich services programme for girls in the upper school.

Many excellent residential and day trips are arranged each year, by various departments. These are finely tuned to the curriculum and cover a full range of activities.

Fees per term (2018–2019). Senior School £4,854, Prep School £3,687, Nursery £3,066.

The fees cover the regular curriculum, school books, stationery and other materials, games fixtures and swimming lessons, but not optional extra subjects or school meals. The fees for extra subjects, including individual music tuition, are shown in the prospectus.

Financial Assistance. The GDST has made available to the school a substantial number of scholarships and bursaries.

Bursaries are available on or after entry to the senior school and applications should be made to the Head in cases of financial need. All requests are considered in confidence. Bursaries are means tested and are intended to ensure the school remains accessible to bright girls who would profit from a GDST education, but who would be unable to enter the school without financial assistance.

Various **Scholarships**, including music scholarships, are available to internal or external candidates for entry at 11+ or to the sixth form.

Charitable status. Norwich High School is part of The Girls' Day School Trust, which is a Registered Charity, number 306983.

Chair of School Governors: Mrs R Randle, LLB Hons

Headmistress: **Mrs K von Malaisé**, MA Cantab

Deputy Head (Academic): Dr B Ashfield, MA Oxon, PhD

Deputy Head (Pastoral): Mrs H P Dolding, BEd De Montfort

Head of Prep School: Mr N Tiley-Nunn, BEd Canterbury

Director of Marketing and Communications: Mr R Nobes

Director of Finance and Operations: Mr M Singh, PG Dip

Registrar: Miss A Ready

Norwich School

70 The Close, Norwich, Norfolk NR1 4DD

Tel: 01603 728430
email: admissions@norwich-school.org.uk
website: www.norwich-school.org.uk

Motto: *Praemia virtutis honores*

Norwich School is a co-educational, independent day school for pupils aged four to eighteen. Currently there are 1152 pupils attending the school. Set in the Cathedral Close, Norwich School is a traditional, yet lively place where boys and girls enjoy a rounded and stimulating education. The school is characterised by strong, warm relationships and a profound appreciation of scholarship.

The school achieves exceptional results but we believe that an education for life is about more than statistics. Here we enjoy local character, beautiful surroundings and a remarkable history. Staff and pupils together create a supportive atmosphere and boys and girls benefit from specialised facilities and a broad curriculum.

Ethos. Learning and scholarship are at the heart of the broad education that Norwich School provides. Christian values – notably love and compassion for one another – underpin our activities and relationships.

Aims. Norwich School is committed to producing scholarly, reflective young people who are capable of handling difficult concepts and expressing profound thought; providing a rich, varied and broad education that develops the diverse talents of the boys and girls and equipping pupils for leadership and service.

Pastoral. The Senior School is organised by Houses. Pupils are allocated to a House upon joining the school, and stay with that House as they move up through the year groups. Many of a pupil's first and firmest friendships will be forged within the House.

Each of the eight Houses is managed by a housemaster – a senior member of staff who comes to know the pupils and their parents very well during their years of association with the House, and who brings compassion and continuity to a pupil's life. If a problem arises, the tutor will involve the housemaster in its resolution; they are familiar figures in the school who offer a blend of experience and encouragement.

Sixth Form. Life in the Sixth Form is a busy and rewarding experience, combining rigorous academic scholarship and commitment to a range of extra-curricular activities, as well as leadership and service roles. Our aim is to ensure that all pupils reach their potential and are able to apply for the university courses and career paths of their choice.

Extra-curricular activity. There are many areas of life beyond the classroom that serve to fulfil the aim of a broad and varied education. Encompassed within the programme are challenges, opportunities for service, group cooperation, team participation and leadership. All are seen as central to the educational experience of each school member.

It is hoped that every pupil will find something from the programme which will influence and stay with them far beyond their school days.

Bursaries. Norwich School sets aside generous funds to enable pupils to attend the school who would otherwise not be able to do so without financial help. Bursaries are available in the Senior School only.

All bursaries are means-tested and can result in a reduction in fees of up to 100%; there is a sliding scale based on family income and finances and resources of the school.

Scholarships. The school offers a range of awards for excellence in five areas: academic excellence (11+, 13+ & 16+), music (11+, 13+ & 16+), sport (11+, 13+ & 16+), drama (16+ only) and art & design (16+ only). A place on one of our scholarship programmes is made available to Senior School pupils with outstanding ability, potential and flair, which the school assesses by examination, interview, portfolio and audition, as appropriate.

Means tested financial support is also available to candidates applying for these awards.

Admission. The main points of entry are at ages 4, 7, 11, 13 and 16.

Fees per term (2018–2019). Senior School £5,404; Lower School (Years 3–6) £4,925; Lower School (Reception–Year 2) £3,666.

Old Norvicensians. All enquiries should be made to Mrs R Lightfoot, Norwich School, 71a The Close, Norwich NR1 4DD.

Charitable status. Norwich School is a Registered Charity, number 311280. It exists solely to provide education.

Governors:
Mr P J E Smith (*Chairman*)

Mr N Q Back	Professor R J Last
Dr S C Bamber	Mr A R M Little
Mr A R Burdon-Cooper	The Reverend Canon A
T J Gould (*Vice Chairman*)	Platten
Mr A R Grant	Mr I Reid
Mrs A J C Green	Mr J M D Schofield
The Very Reverend Dr J	Mr D W Talbot
Hedges	Dr A Wood
Mr C W Hoffman	Dr D F Wood
Mr P J Henderson	Mrs D Willmott
Mr J M Holme	Miss T J Yates
Ms D G M Jarrold	Professor K H Yeoman

Representative Governors:
A R Burdon-Cooper (*Worshipful Company of Dyers*)
J M Holme (*Worshipful Company of Dyers*)
The Very Reverend Dr J Hedges (*Dean and Chapter*)
Professor K H Yeoman (*University of East Anglia*)

Senior Team:

Head Master: Mr Steffan D A Griffiths, MA Oxon

Principal Deputy Head: Miss Lara E Pechard, BA, MA Southampton
Deputy Head (Director of Studies): Dr David N Farr, BA QMW London, PhD Cantab, FRHS
Deputy Head (Co-Curriculum): Dr Richard Clark, BSc, PhD Essex
Assistant Head (Teaching & Learning): Mr Paul A Todd, BA Cantab
Assistant Head (Head of Sixth Form): Mr Craig Hooper, BA Loughborough
Assistant Head (Admissions, Marketing & Outreach): Mrs Nicola J Hill, BSc UEA
Master of the Lower School: Mr John K Ingham, BA Warwick
Head of Fifth Form: Andrew M Rowlandson, BA, PG Cert Bus Admin Open, MCCT
Head of Fourth Form: Mrs Cheryl A Wood, BA University of South Africa, MCLIP, Chartered Librarian
Bursar & Clerk to the Governors: Mrs Mary W T Cherry, BEng Loughborough, ACMA, CGMA
Assistant Bursar: Mr Christopher J Williams, BSc UEA, GD Law UEA

Heads of Department and Pastoral Leads, Senior School:
Ms Kabrie E A Adams, BA (*Head of Academic Drama*)
Mr Richard P Allain, BMus (*Director of Music*)
Mr David P D Bateman, BSc (*Head of Politics, Housemaster – Valpy*)
Dr James Bendall, MChem, PhD (*Head of Chemistry*)
Mr Rod A Bunting (*Assistant Director of Sport*)
Mr Edward J G Cann BA (*Housemaster – Parker*)
Mrs Charlotte {Rosie} Cawkwell, BA (*Head of Religious Studies*)
Mr Jed L Cawkwell, BSc (*Head of Cricket*)
Revd Corin Child, BA, MA (*School Chaplain*)
Miss Holly M Cook, BA (*p/t Acting Head of Geography*)
Mr Joe P Cowan, BSc (*Director of Sport*)
Mr William H J Croston BA (*Head of Examination Centre, UCAS & Careers, p/t Head of German*)
Mr Andrew P Curtis, BA (*Housemaster – Seagrim*)
Mr Alex J Daalhuizen, BSc, MSc (*Head of Strength & Conditioning*)
Mr Andrew L Fisher, BA (*Integrated Curriculum Coordinator*)
Mr John C Fisher (*Senior Master*)
Mr Jonathan C Gent, BSc (*Head of Biology*)
Mr Alex E W Grant, BA, MA (*Head of History*)
Mr Toby M Grieves, BA (*Head of Rugby*)
Mr Iain M Grisewood, BA (*Housemaster – School*)
Mrs Katie T Grote (*Head of Classics*)
Dr Stewart Hall, BEng, PhD, MSc, BSc (*Head of Physics*)
Mr Graham A Hanlon, BSc (*Housemaster – Coke*)
Mrs Victoria L Hood, BA, MA (*p/t Head of German*)
Mr Matthew D Hopgood, MA (*Head of Geography*) [sabbatical]
Mr Alex D Jenkins, MA, BSc (*Head of Digital Learning*)
Dr Simon Kirby, BSc, PhD (*Head of Mathematics*)
Mr James P I Large, BSc (*Housemaster – Nelson*)
Miss Georgina McDonald-Bell, BA (*Head of Film*)
Ms Tracey M Mounter, BA (*Housemaster – Brooke*)
Mr Michael Mulligan, BA, MPhil (*Head of Philosophy*)
Mr Andrew Murray, MA (*Head of English*)
Mrs Catherine L Norton, BSc (*Assistant Director of Sport, Head of Sports Science*)
Mrs Lucy E D Parkhouse, MA (*Head of French*) [maternity leave]
Mrs Gillian R Parsons, MA (*SENDCo*)
Mr Ian R Passam, BA (*Head of Art & Design*)
Mrs Nicola C Robinson, BA (*Head of Spanish*)
Mr Richard Sims (*Housemaster – Repton*)
Mr Robert E Sorrell, BSc (*Head of Hockey*)
Mr James A Storey-Mason, BA (*Head of French*) [maternity cover]
Mrs Nikki L Swinborne, BA (*Head of Netball*) [maternity leave]
Miss Victoria J Turner, BA, MA (*p/t Acting Head of Geography*)
Mr Thomas P White, BA (*Head of Economics, Business & Enterprise*)

Senior Team, Lower School:
Master of the Lower School: Mr John K Ingham, BA Warwick
Head of Pre-Prep: Mrs Anita E Barclay, BA UEA
Principal Deputy Head: Mr Alexander Wilson, BSc, MSc Aberystwyth
Deputy Head – Academic: Mr Christopher M W Parsons, MEd, BSc Lancaster
Director of Co-Curricular: Mr Tim J Brook, MSc Plymouth
Assistant Head – Learning & Assessment: Miss Franziska N R Brugger, BA Bishop Grosseteste

Support Staff:
Head Master's PA: J Grapes, BA

Bursar's PA: R Peters
Principal Deputy Head's PA: K Smith
Registrar: H Sharples, BA
Chief Examinations Officer: M Brown, MA
Head of Welfare: Georgina Valpied, DipHE

Nottingham High School

Waverley Mount, Nottingham NG7 4ED

Tel:	0115 978 6056
Fax:	0115 979 2202
email:	info@nottinghamhigh.co.uk
	enquiries@nottinghamhigh.co.uk
website:	www.nottinghamhigh.co.uk
Twitter:	@NottsHigh
Facebook:	@nottshigh
LinkedIn:	/nottshigh

Motto: *Lauda Finem*

This School was founded in 1513 by Dame Agnes Mellers, widow of Richard Mellers, sometime Mayor of Nottingham. The first Charter was given by Henry VIII, and supplementary Charters were given by Philip and Mary, and by Queen Elizabeth. The School, which remains independent, is now administered under the terms of a scheme issued by the Charity Commissioners.

Organisation. There are 1,051 day pupils, of whom 276 are in the Infant and Junior School and 237 in the Sixth Form. Nearly all Junior School pupils go on to complete their education in the Senior School. (*For further details about the Infant and Junior School, see entry in IAPS section.*) From 2015 the school became co-educational in the Sixth Form and Infant school, followed by the other year groups from 2016.

Curriculum. The Senior School curriculum leads to examinations at GCSE in the normal range of subjects. The Sixth Form are prepared for AS and A Levels. The range of subjects is wide: Latin, Classical Civilisation, Drama, Modern Languages, English, History, Economics, Politics, Design Technology, Geography, Mathematics, Physics, Chemistry, Biology, Music, Art, Philosophy, Psychology, RS, Classical Greek, Music Technology.

Admission. Entrance Examinations and assessments are held in January each year. Applicants for the Infant School should be between the ages of 4 and 7 years, for the Junior School between the ages of 7 and 11 years, and for the Senior School/Sixth Form between 11 and 16 years on 1 September of the year of entry subject to places being available and a successful interview (entry to Sixth Form is also dependent upon a minimum of 5 As at GCSE).

Fees per term (2018–2019). Tuition: Senior School £4,955, Junior School £3,947, Lovell House Infant School £3,393.

Entrance Scholarships and Bursaries. The Entrance Examination for the Senior School is held in January each year for the award of Entrance Scholarships. Part-Scholarships of a fixed sum may be awarded based on exam performance. They are not linked to parental finances and will normally continue throughout a pupil's school career. Application does not have to be made for part-scholarships as these are awarded at the discretion of the Headmaster, subject to entrance examination performance and interview.

Nottingham High School also has its own means-tested Bursaries to be awarded to pupils entering the Senior School at age eleven. All Bursaries will be awarded at the Headmaster's discretion and will normally continue until a pupil leaves the School.

Games. The Playing Fields, covering 20 acres, are situated about a mile and a half from the School with excellent pavilion facilities. There are also indoor cricket nets at the school. The School games, in which all pupils are expected to take part unless medically exempted, are Rugby, Hockey, (together with Association Football in the Junior School) in the winter, and Cricket or Tennis and Athletics in the summer for boys. Girls play Hockey, Netball and Rounders in the winter and summer terms respectively. Other alternatives provided for seniors include Cross Country, Squash, Association Football (Sixth Form), Badminton, Golf, Shooting, and Basketball. Swimming (the School has its own 25m pool) forms part of the Physical Education programme.

Combined Cadet Force. The School maintains a contingent of the CCF based on voluntary recruitment and consisting of Navy, Army and Air Force sections. There is a small bore range, and the School enters teams for various national competitions.

Societies. Individual interests and hobbies are catered for by a wide range of Societies which meet in the lunch break or at the end of afternoon school. These include and are not limited to Drama, Modern Languages, Mathematics, Chemistry, Biology, English, Politics, Arts, Music and Debating Societies, the Chess Club, the Bridge Club, Christian Union, and the Scout Troop. Over 120 pupils a year participate in the Duke of Edinburgh's Award scheme. The Community Action Group and the Explorer Scouts are alternatives to this.

Music. Apart from elementary instruction in Music in the lower forms, and more advanced studies for GCSE and A Level, tuition is offered by 3 full-time and 18 part-time teachers in the full range of orchestral instruments. There are 2 School orchestras of 50 and 30 players, 2 Choirs, a concert band (wind) of 50, a Training Band and Big Band and choral and orchestral concerts are given each year. Four instrumental bursaries, covering fee tuition on one instrument, are available to pupils entering Year 7.

Honours. 12 Places at Oxford and Cambridge in 2018.

Charitable status. Nottingham High School is a Registered Charity, number 1104251. It exists to provide education for pupils between the ages of 4 and 18 years.

Governing Body:
The Lord Lieutenant of Nottinghamshire
The Lord Mayor of Nottingham
Two Representatives of the City Council
One Representative of the Nottinghamshire County Council
Four Representatives of the Universities
Eleven Co-optative Members

Chairman of the Governors: Mr David Wild

Headmaster: Mr Kevin Fear

Deputy Head (Academic): Mr Paul Spedding
Deputy Head (Pastoral): Miss Lisa Gritti
Assistant Head (Co-Curricular): Mr Kieron Heath
Assistant Head (Director of Studies): Dr Katharine Linton
Assistant Head (Teaching and Learning): Mrs Angharad Simpson
Assistant Head (Pastoral): Ms Michaela Smith
Head of Sixth Form: Mr David Gillett
Head of Infant & Junior School: Mrs Clare Bruce
Director of Finance and Estates: Mr Stuart Ramsey

Learning Support Coordinator: Mr Mark Glarvey

Headmaster's EA: Miss Rebecca Winch
Director of Finance & Estates: Mr Stuart Ramsey
Head of Marketing: Miss Sophie Turner
Head of Admissions and Partnership: Miss Rebecca Russ

Head, Infant and Junior School: Mrs Clare Bruce

Deputy Head (*Academic*): Miss Lucy Thorpe
Deputy Head (*Pastoral*): Mr Christian Cordy

Oakham School

Chapel Close, Oakham, Rutland LE15 6DT

Tel: 01572 758500
            Admissions: 01572 758758
Fax: 01572 758818
email: admissions@oakham.rutland.sch.uk
website: www.oakham.rutland.sch.uk
Twitter: @OakhamSch
LinkedIn: /oakhamschool

Motto: *Quasi Cursores Vitai Lampada Tradunt*

The possibilities for learning really are limitless at Oakham. As a large co-educational boarding and day school with 1,044 pupils (549 boys, 495 girls) aged 10–18 and a boarder to day pupil ratio of 1:1, we are proud to be able to offer a truly staggering range of experiences, activities and opportunities.

Whilst academic excellence lies at the heart of everything we do, our focus goes far beyond helping our students to achieve outstanding examination results. The Arts flourish and we have an enviable reputation for excellent coaching in a variety of sports. Activities are also an integral part of life beyond the classroom.

Oakham is an exceptionally caring community. Our unique House structure ensures we nurture all aspects of our pupils' well-being throughout their Oakham journey; students are surrounded by staff who are expertly trained to both support their needs and to challenge them to become independent, thoughtful, and responsible young adults.

Oakham is well known and loved for being a friendly and unpretentious school. Whilst we are proud of our 400-year heritage, our priority is always to be at the forefront of educational developments. We were one of the first independent schools to move to co-education in 1971 and we were also one of the first schools to introduce the IB Diploma, alongside A Levels. We continue to look to the future and our focus now, in today's digital world, is on effectively teaching students Information Literacy.

Facilities. Oakham's facilities include one of the best school libraries in the country, state-of-the-art Science and Design Technology facilities, an art gallery, a new Faculty of Social Sciences, a theatre, and a music school. The sports facilities are extensive with 40 acres of superbly maintained fields, all-weather pitches for hockey and tennis, a sports complex with an indoor swimming pool, squash courts, fives courts and fitness centre, and access to nearby Rutland Water for sailing and Luffenham Heath for golf. The sports hall has recently undergone an extensive programme of refurbishment, which includes a viewing gallery for parents to enjoy the sport in action on our world-renowned pitches. A state-of-the-art Medical and Pastoral Centre opened in 2017.

Organisation and Curriculum. Oakham has 16 houses: four in the Lower School (ages 10–13), 10 in the Middle/Upper School (ages 13–17), and two houses for final year girls and boys, where they can concentrate more closely on their studies and enjoy increased freedom in preparation for university. The Housemaster or Housemistress is responsible for pastoral support. Each pupil has a tutor, who is responsible for pupils' personal and academic development, and for keeping a balance between academic, creative and social activities.

The curriculum is tailored so that an education at Oakham develops the potential of all our pupils, opening up academic and commercial opportunities around the world. The Lower School offers a unique and exciting programme combining the full range of traditional subjects with the development of essential learning habits. In the Middle School, pupils can choose their GCSEs and IGCSEs from a comprehensive range of subjects. In the Upper School Oakham is unusual in offering a choice between A Levels or the highly-regarded IB Diploma Programme.

GCSE/IGCSE: All pupils take English Language, English Literature, Dual-Award Science (which comprises Biology, Chemistry and Physics), with the possibility of studying separate Sciences, and Mathematics. They also choose from History, Geography, Religion and Philosophy, French, Spanish, German, Drama or Music and a variety of Creative Arts subjects (Fine Art – Painting and Mixed Media, Textile Design or Sculpture, Design Technology or Electronics. Other academic options include: Citizenship, Classical Civilisation, Computer Science, Creative iMedia, Greek, Latin and Sport Science. We expose pupils to a rich cultural environment, providing an exciting programme of projects and visits to enhance learning beyond the classroom and the exam syllabus.

16+: Upper School pupils may opt either for A Levels and equivalent stand-alone qualifications or the International Baccalaureate Diploma. A Level subjects on offer include: Art: Critical and Contextual Studies, Art, Biology, Business (A Level and BTEC), Chemistry, Classical Civilisation, Design Technology, Economics, English Literature, French, Geography, German, Classical Greek, History, Italian, Latin, Mathematics, Further Mathematics, Music (Cambridge Pre-U), Philosophy and Theology (Cambridge Pre-U), Physics, Politics, Spanish, Sport Science (A Level and BTEC), Theatre Studies. The International Baccalaureate Diploma Programme offers a similar range, but students study six subjects: three subjects are studied at Higher Level and three at Standard Level. Additionally, all students take the three Core Elements of the Diploma: Theory of Knowledge, the Extended Essay and a programme of Creativity, Activity and Service.

Music. Around half of all pupils play in musical ensembles, choirs, bands, orchestras, and musical theatre productions. Over 60 concerts each year present a wide variety of performing opportunities both in and out of School, as well as international tours. Pupils are regularly selected for national youth ensembles and the School Chamber Choir were finalists in the BBC 'Songs of Praise' School Choir of the Year Competition in 2016.

Drama plays an important part in the life of the School with five major productions each year. A majority of pupils at all levels takes part in at least one dramatic production a year.

Art, Design and Technology. The Richard Bull Centre and the state-of-the-art Jerwood School of Design together offer an extensive array of creative and Design Technology opportunities, including painting, pottery, sculpture, textiles, print-making, photography, computer-aided design and electronics, working in wood, metal and plastics. Pupils regularly compete for and win nationally recognised awards and scholarships, such as the Arkwright Scholarship.

Sport and Activities. Our major sports are rugby, hockey, cricket, athletics, netball and tennis. Some 30 other sports options are also offered. A typical year will see over 100 pupils progress to the national finals in 10 different sports. Oakham is proud to be a well-recognised training ground for national squads.

We offer a comprehensive activities programme (over 125 on offer) and each week pupils follow an activity (or hobby) and, from the Middle School upwards, a Service

Option. They can try something new or pursue an existing passion. Our Service Options develop skills and values for life. Pupils choose from an extensive volunteering programme, the Combined Cadet Force or the Duke of Edinburgh's Award.

Entry. Normal entry points are 10+, 11+, 13+ and 16+. Pupils are accepted mainly in September at the start of the academic year. Full admissions information is available from the Registrar.

Scholarships and Bursaries. The following scholarships are available: Academic and Music (11+, 13+ and 16+), All-rounder (13+), Art, Design and Technology, Drama and Sport (13+ and 16+). The basic value of a scholarship is up to 10% (academic up to 20%) and top-up means-tested support may be available. For further information including bursaries please request an information booklet from the Registrar, Tel: 01572 758758.

Fees per term (2018–2019). Lower School (age 10–13): £8,535–£9,150 (full boarding), £6,715–£8,690 (transitional boarding: 2 to 5 nights), £5,635–£6,065 (day).

Middle and Upper Schools (age 13+): £11,220 (full boarding), £10,660 (flexi boarding: up to 5 nights), £6,845 (day).

Honours 2018. Overall 46% of all exams taken at A Level, Pre-U, BTEC or in the IB Diploma were awarded A* or A or equivalent. At A Level/Pre-U/BTEC 37 students gained straight A*/A grades or equivalent. In the IB Diploma our average point score was 35, compared with the worldwide average of 30. Three students achieved 44, out of a maximum of 45 points – a feat achieved by only 1% of students worldwide. Over a quarter gained 38 or more points (equivalent to A*, A*, A at A Level. At GCSE of all the new graded (9–1) GCSE exams, over a quarter were awarded the new, harder to attain, grade 9, compared to around 4% nationally. 61% of pupils achieved A*/A grades with 31 pupils gaining straight A*/As. 97% of leavers went to university; 7 students gained places at Oxbridge; 4 students left to study Medicine.

Charitable status. Oakham School is a Registered Charity, number 1131425, and a Company Limited by Guarantee, registered in England and Wales, number 06924216. Registered Office: Chapel Close, Market Place, Oakham, Rutland LE15 6DT. It exists for the purpose of education.

Headmaster: **N M Lashbrook**, BA

Director of Operations and Strategic Planning: S Piggott, MA, MBA
Senior Deputy Head: Mrs L M North, BA
Deputy Head (*Pastoral and Co-curricular*): Mrs S J Gomm, BSc
Deputy Head (*Academic*): D A Harrow, MA

Senior Members of Staff:
Head of Upper School: Mrs S Lorenz-Weir, MA
Head of Middle School: J H Robinson, BA
Head of Lower School: A Morris, BEd
Director Teaching and Learning: J M Andrews, BA
Senior Housemistress: Mrs C Latham, BEd
Registrar: N S Paddock, BSocSc
Marketing Director: Mrs S Rowntree
Development Director: Ms A E Bentley

Heads of Department:
Activities: A V Petit, MA, MBA
Careers: Mrs P C Gibbs, BSc, MBA
Computer Science: M D Crofts, BSc
Creative Arts: Ms E Brass, MA
English: G B Austen, BA, MPhil, MA Oxon
Geography: H A Collison, BSc, MPhil
History: J N J Roberts, MA
Languages: E J Milner, MA
Learning Support: Mrs C D Hill, MA, Dip SpLD
Mathematics: Mrs W Singhal, BSc
Music: P Davis, MA, ARCO
Religion and Philosophy: Mrs M J Fairley, BA
Social Sciences: P Nutter, BA
Science: Dr J A Chilton
Sport: I Simpson, BSc

Chaplain: The Revd T F Tregunno, MTh

Housemasters/Housemistresses:

Lower School:
Ancaster: Mrs A Petit, LLB
Lincoln: Mrs M P Northcott, BA
Peterborough: M M Fairweather, MA
Sargants: A S Denman, BA

Middle School:
Barrow: N P Favill, BA
Buchanans: Mrs C L Latham, BEd
Chapmans: D W Bonanno, BA
Clipsham: T Dixon-Dale, BA
Gunthorpe: Mrs Lydia Dunbavand, BSc
Hambleton: Mrs S M Healey, BSc
Haywoods: G Gelderbloom, HDE Dip RSA
Rushebrookes: Mrs K M Hegarty, MA
Stevens: Mrs E Roe, BEng
Wharflands: J J Cure, BA

Upper School:
Round House: Mrs E L Durston, BSc
School House: D M Taylor, BA

Oldham Hulme Grammar School

Chamber Road, Oldham, Lancs OL8 4BX

Tel: 0161 624 4497
email: admin@ohgs.co.uk
website: www.ohgs.co.uk
Twitter: @OhgsPrincipal
Facebook: @OldhamHulmeGrammarSchool

Motto: *Fide sed cui Vide*

The school, founded in 1611, was reconstituted in the 19th century under the Endowed Schools Act. The main buildings of Oldham Hulme Grammar School were opened in 1895 on a commanding south-west facing site overlooking the city of Manchester.

The Oldham Hulme family of schools is renowned for delivering outstanding levels of education at each stage of a child's development. With unbeatable standards and outstanding achievements, the schools cater for boys and girls aged three to 18 and offer a caring, orderly and academically stimulating environment.

At the age of 3 school life begins in the Nursery which has recently moved into new modern premises. Confidence is then built throughout the infant, junior and secondary years and great care is taken in the sixth form to create extremely capable, well-balanced young adults.

The schools' primary aim is to provide a caring, friendly and lively school environment that fosters a desire to learn and at all times, pupils are encouraged to think and work independently. With a reputation for academic excellence and outstanding extra-curricular activities, pupils benefit from the right environment which enables them to achieve their full potential in life so that they go on to become successful, happy and confident young men and women.

Oldham Hulme Grammar School values academic achievement and standards are high. Consequently there is an excellent record of examination success at GCSE and A Level. Pupils are taught within small classes by a team of dedicated, well-qualified staff.

The schools also offer an excellent pastoral care system which guides and supports pupils, promoting their personal development within the wider school community.

The comprehensive careers education programme on offer widens each pupil's understanding of the opportunities available in the changing world of work, while equipping them with the skills to manage their future career.

A stimulating range of extracurricular activities provides opportunities for fun, challenge, initiative, leadership and service, while activities within the wider community encourage active involvement and promote a genuine concern for the needs for others.

Fees per term (2018–2019). Nursery, Infants and Juniors £2,740; Senior School and Sixth Form £3,745; International Students £16,500 per annum payable in advance.

A number of bursaries are awarded annually to pupils entering at the ages of 11 and 16. These awards are based on parental income and academic ability and will remain in place for the time in school subject to satisfactory progress by the pupil.

Charitable status. The Oldham Hulme Grammar School is a Registered Charity, number 526636. It exists to provide a balanced academic education for pupils aged 3 to 18.

Patron: The Lord Clitheroe of Downham

Governors:
Chairman: Mr V A K Srivastava, LLB Hons (*Chairman of the Finance and General Purposes Committee*)

Vice Chairman: Mrs A Richards, BSc (*Child Protection Governor*)
Hon Treasurer: Mr D M Meredith, CCB

Elected Governors:
Mr J Greenwood
Mr R S Illingworth, BSc
Mr R Lobley, MRICS (*Chairman of the Health & Safety Committee*)
Mr I G R Mills
Mr A Milnes, BA Hons, FCA (*Chairman of the Audit Committee*)
Mr K Sanders
Mrs V Stocker, LLB
Mr J Williams

Representative Governors, Metropolitan Borough of Oldham:
Mr Z Chauhan
Mr J Sutcliffe

Principal: C J D Mairs, MA Edinburgh

Deputy Principal – Pastoral: J C Budding, BEd Sheffield Hallam
Deputy Principal – Academic: N G H James, MA York
Deputy Principal – External Relations: D J Dalziel, BSc London, PG Dip Leeds

S P Adamson, MA Manchester (*English, Duke of Edinburgh's Award, Careers, Head of Booth/Platt House*)
D Aston, BA Birmingham City (*Head of Design Technology*)
W L M Atkins, BSc Keele (*Head of Biology, CCF*)
Mrs C Bailey, MSc Leicester (*EAL Coordinator*)
Dr P M Beagon, MA, DPhil Oxford (*Head of Classics*)
D Berry, BSc Huddersfield (*Head of Psychology*)
Mrs N Bibi, BSc Manchester (*Mathematics*)
Miss J C Brown, BA Liverpool (*Physical Education*)
Miss L E Bowden, BSc Manchester (*Biology, Head of Year 7*)
N P Buckley, BA Sheffield (*Business Studies and Economics, Head of Year 8*)
N J Chesterton, BA Leeds (*Physical Education and Games, Head of Assheton House*)
T M J Cotton, BEd Manchester Metropolitan (*Design Technology*)
Ms L J Cowan, MA Dundee (*History, Duke of Edinburgh's Award, Head of Year 9*)
Mrs N L Cross, BSc Manchester (*Mathematics, Duke of Edinburgh's Award*)
L Dainty, BSc Manchester (*Geography*)
L J Downie, MA Sheffield (*Mathematics*)
M N Dowthwaite, BA Manchester (*Head of History and Politics, School Functions Officer*)
Miss C W Duffy, BA, MPhil Aberystwyth (*History*)
Mrs S Eckhardt, BA Salford (*Head of Drama*)
Mrs C A Eliot, BA Heriot-Watt (*Head of Textiles, PSHE Coordinator*)
O M Gandolfi, BSc Bangor (*Biology, Duke of Edinburgh's Award, Head of Year 10*)
Mrs H Garside, BA North Wales (*Modern Languages*)
M J A Grant, MA Newcastle (*Modern Languages, Head of Hulme House*)
Miss J V Graystock, BA Liverpool (*Head of Art*)
J J W Gumpert, MA Cambridge (*Head of Religious Studies*)
Mrs E Harris, BA Liverpool (*Physical Education*)
A P Henson, BSc Loughborough (*PE*)
J R Hesten, BA Manchester (*Physics*)

Mrs A H Howarth, BEd, Manchester Metropolitan, PG Dip, Dip SEN, PG Cert SpLD AMBDA, SpLD APC Patoss (*Head of Learning Support*)

Mrs D Howarth, BSc Manchester Metropolitan (*Head of Home Economics*)

A H B Hurst, BA Manchester Metropolitan (*Head of Physical Education*)

Mrs C J Jones, BA Manchester (*English*)

M C Jones, MPhys Manchester (*Head of Physics*)

Mrs T A Kershaw, BA Salford (*Head of Modern Languages*)

Miss J P Knighton, BEd Leeds Metropolitan (*Head of Physical Education*)

Mrs J A Lamb, BSc Liverpool (*Head of Mathematics*)

P Langdon, BEd Manchester Metropolitan (*Computer Science*)

Miss L Lavin, BSc Manchester Metropolitan (*Biology, Peer Mentoring Coordinator*)

Mrs J Leach, BA Hull (*English*)

T A Leng, BA Leeds (*History, Teacher i/c Politics, i/c Newsletter*)

Mrs A Longley, MA Manchester (*Economics, Business Studies, Head of Year 6th Form*)

Mrs D Maders, BSc Leeds, MRSC (*Head of Chemistry*)

Mrs L Manton-Howard, BSc Leeds (*Mathematics*)

A H Marshall, BSc Hull (*Geography, Director of Pastoral Care, Head of Year 11*)

Miss G McCarrick, BSc, Manchester Metropolitan (*Geography*)

Mrs J McCarthy, MA, PG Dip Liverpool (*Art, Design Technology*)

Dr C R Millington, BSc, DPhil, MEd Durham, Oxford, Cambridge (*Chemistry*)

Ms E Mills, BA Manchester (*Head of English*)

S J Murray, BMus Manchester (*Music*)

S Norbury, BSc Liverpool John Moores (*Head of Computer Science*)

Mrs H M North, BSc Liverpool (*Chemistry*)

A Peacocke, BA Glamorgan (*Head of Geography*)

Miss R Peters, BA Edge Hill (*Computer Science*)

Miss H R Plews, BA Liverpool, MPhil Cantab (*Classics, Head of Lees House, Academic Tutor 6th Form*)

S G Rawlings, BEng Aston (*Mathematics, Physics, Head of Year 6th Form*)

D R A Rees, BSc Bradford (*Head of Business Studies and Economics*)

M Richmond, BSc Leeds (*Mathematics, Master i/c Football*)

D G Robertson, BMus Aberdeen, ALCM (*Director of Music*)

Mrs A G Robinson, BSc Romania, MSc Manchester (*Physics*)

Miss M F Robles, BA Manchester Met (*Languages*)

Miss S E Shepherd, BA London (*i/c French*)

Mrs K Stansfield, MA Sheffield (*English*)

Mrs J Travis, DipM (*Head of Careers, Food Technology*)

Mrs A Turner, Cert Ed Leeds (*Chemistry*)

M Turner, BEd Leicester (*Mathematics*)

Miss R L Turner, BSc Loughborough (*Mathematics, Duke of Edinburgh's Award Manager*)

Mrs S Webber, BSc University College London (*Mathematics*)

Mrs J C Wood, BA Leeds (*Religious Studies, Director of Pastoral Care, Head of Year 11*)

Nursery, Infants & Juniors:

Head of Nursery and Infants: Miss C Barnett, BA Edge Hill

Deputy Head of Nursery and Infants: Mrs A A Summers, MA Manchester Metropolitan

Head of Juniors: Mrs R Knott, BA, Surrey

Deputy Head of Juniors Upper KS2: M G Cowley, BSc Stirling

Deputy Head of Juniors Lower KS2: A Booth, BA Birmingham City

Miss L Lavin, BSc Manchester Metropolitan (*Science Coordinator*)

Mrs R L Christo, BEd Birmingham (*Literacy Coordinator*)

P S Coulson, BSc Edge Hill College (*ICT Coordinator*)

S Davies, BA Edge Hill University (*PSHE Coordinator*)

Mrs S Dockerty BA Huddersfield

Miss G A Fulford-Brown, BA Manchester Metropolitan

Miss C Goodwin, BA Manchester Metropolitan

A J Halliwell, BEd Manchester, CertEd Manchester

Mrs J Milnes, MA Edinburgh

Miss A Rees, EY QTS Edge Hill

Mrs H Russell, BA York, CSLPS OU, HLTA, QTS

Miss M Wall, BA Manchester/Lancaster

Mrs E White, BA Durham

Mrs H A Whitwam, BA Bradford College (*PSHE Coordinator*)

Visiting Music Teachers:

Miss C Babington, BMus, PG Dip, MMus RNCM, MusM VU Manc (*Cello*)

D Browne, GRNCM (*Cello*)

Miss A Cooper, GGSM (*Oboe & Bassoon*)

Mrs V Eastham, MA, FTCL, LRSM (*Piano*)

Ms S Gibbon, GRNCM (*Violin*)

K Heggie, GRNCM (*Guitar*)

Mrs M Hulme, BSc, LTCL (*Violin*)

Mrs J Kent, CT, ABRSM (*Brass*)

Miss G Murray, BMus RAM, PG Dip TCL (*Singing*)

O Patrick, BMus RCM (*Percussion*)

Miss J Puckey, BMus (*Clarinet & Saxophone*)

Mrs S Walker, GRSM, PPRCM (*Flute*)

Bursar and Clerk to the Governors: I Martin, BSc, FCA, FCMA

Admissions Manager: Miss A Fenton

Fundraising Director: Mrs B Fisher

The Oratory School

Woodcote, Reading, South Oxfordshire RG8 0PJ

Tel: 01491 683500
Fax: 01491 680020
email: enquiries@oratory.co.uk
website: www.oratory.co.uk

Motto: *Cor ad cor loquitur*

The Oratory School was founded in 1859, by Blessed John Henry Newman. It is currently an independent school for boys aged 11 to 18 offering an all-round education that is second to none. The school is pleased to announce that it will become a co-educational school, welcoming girls alongside boys from September 2020 at 11+, 13+ and 16+.

The School is situated in an area of outstanding natural beauty in grounds of approximately 100 acres, in South Oxfordshire, yet is within easy travelling distance of London, major motorways and airports.

The Oratory has high academic standards, however we believe that an education is about more than statistics. The school has a clear vision to ensure that each pupil flourishes and fulfils their maximum potential both in and far beyond the classroom. To this end a wide variety of co-curricular activities enrich the pupils' learning and all pupils get the opportunity to develop their specific talents to the full. The

Oratory is not a large school and this enables each and every boy to be known, valued and stretched as an individual within our nurturing community. The Oratory has an inclusive community atmosphere which nurtures confidence, self-expression and a desire to learn and grow. Our value-added results at A Level place the school in the top 3% of schools nationally.

Organisation. Five Senior Houses and one Junior House, St Philip House, both day and boarding. There are currently 240 pupils: 120 boarding, 110 day boys and 10 occasional boarding.

Health. The school's Medical Centre is permanently staffed during term time by a team of five Registered Nurses and a duty nurse is present night and day.

Admission. Pupils enter at 13+ through the Scholarship or Common Entrance Examinations, or at 11+ by entrance exam. Pupils also enter in the Sixth Form and in other year groups subject to availability. Pupils wishing to enter at 13+ are required to complete the ISEB Pre-test in Year 7 at the current Prep School.

Academic. Pupils are prepared for GCSEs and A Levels. A rich and varied curriculum is offered to all pupils. All academic subjects are taught in small classes by specialist teachers. The school is in the top 3% of schools nationally for value added results at A Level.

Religious Education. The school is a Catholic school which welcomes pupils of all faiths or none. There is a Resident Chaplain who looks after the needs of both pupils and staff.

Games. In addition to the main games – Rugby, Football, Cricket, Shooting and Rowing – boys take part in Athletics, Cross-Country Running, Swimming, Tennis, Badminton, Basketball, Squash, Golf, and Real Tennis. There is a nine-hole golf course on the 100-acre site and a four-lane indoor shooting range. Major girls' sports will be introduced in 2020 such as hockey, netball and dance as part of the PE curriculum.

Leadership. There is a flourishing contingent of the CCF which includes Army, RN, RAF, REME, Signals, and Adventure Training. The Duke of Edinburgh's Award scheme is popular with the gold expedition going to various locations in the UK and overseas.

Extracurricular activities. There are frequent theatre outings, visits to museums and art galleries, careers visits, as well as talks and lectures given in the School by visiting speakers. Co-curricular enrichment activities take place three or four times every week, with over 50 diverse activities to choose from, encouraging our pupils to try new things.

Optional Extras. Instrumental Music, coaching in Real Tennis, Lawn Tennis, Squash and Golf.

Careers Guidance. The Head of Sixth Form provides guidance for pupils in their choice of future occupation. There is also a Head of Careers who organises speakers and a Careers Fair.

Fees per term (2018–2019). Boarders: £11,433 (Junior House £7,565); Day Boys: £8,322 (Junior House £5,639).

The fees include board, tuition, consolidated extras, and games. Optional insurance schemes are in operation. A full term's notice of withdrawal is required; failing such notice a term's fees are payable. There may be a reduction for younger siblings and children of old boys. Means-tested Bursaries are also offered.

Scholarships. A number of Academic Scholarships and Exhibitions, and Awards in Music, Art, DT, Drama and Sport, are offered. Awards are of varying values. Music awards include free music tuition in two disciplines. All-rounder awards are made on the recommendation and reports from a pupil's current Headteacher. Sixth Form Scholarships are also available.

The Preparatory School is situated in grounds of 45 acres on the same ridge of the Chilterns, about 2 miles from the Senior School. This is co-educational. (*For further details, see entry in IAPS section.*)

The Oratory School Society. The Society has been set up to offer lifelong support and fellowship to all Old Oratorians and to further the interests of The Oratory and The Oratory Preparatory School while maintaining close links with former pupils and staff. Chairman: David Connolly.

Charitable status. The Oratory Schools Association is a Registered Charity, number 309112. It is a charitable trust dedicated to continuing the aims of its Founder, Blessed John Henry Newman.

President: The Rt Hon Lord Judge, MA Cantab, PC

Vice-Presidents:
Rt Revd R J Byrne, BD, AKC, Cong Orat
J J Eyston Esq, MA Cantab, FRICS, KSG
His Eminence Cardinal Vincent Nichols, MA, STL, PhL, MEd

Chairman: M W Stillwell Esq
Vice-Chairman: C J Sehmer Esq, FCA

The Governors:
M J Berkeley Esq, JP, BSc, BA, IMC, MCSI
B F H Bettesworth Esq, FRICS, ACIArb
Mrs M A Cochrane
Mrs M E Edwards
Professor P W Evans, MA Cantab, PhD
F J Fitzherbert-Brockholes Esq, MA Oxon
M H R Hasslacher Esq
Dr C B T Hill Williams, DL, MA, FRGS, FRSA
Very Revd D B Seward, MA Oxon, Cong Orat
Mr N J Tanner Esq, MSc
Colonel C R Sutherland, MA, GCGI PSC[J]
J R B Hobbs Esq, BA

Clerk to the Governors & Bursar: M W Halsall, MBA, FCMI

Head Master: J J Smith, BA, MEd, PGCE

Deputy Head Academic: M Syddall, MA Oxon, MSt (*Classics*)
Deputy Head Pastoral: M B Fogg, BA (*Theology*)
Chaplain: Revd K E MacNab, BA, MA (*Religious Education*)
Bursar: M W Halsall, MBA, FCMI
Director of Admissions and External Relations: R A Craven, BSc

Academic Staff:
* *Head of Department*
† *Housemaster/Housemother*
§ *Part-time*

J Aldridge, BSc (*Mathematics*, †*St John*)
C J Arnold (*Geography*)
M O Belassie-McCourt (*English*)
J Berkley, BA, MA (*French, Italian*, **Languages*)
J R Bonnett, BA (**Drama*)
S Bosher, BSc, Dip Des (*Design and Technology, CCF*, †*Faber*)
S A Bowles, BSc, PhD (*Chemistry*)
P W Brown, BSc (*Physics*)
S P S Burrows, BA (**Director of Music, Head of 6th Form*)
T F Burton (**Director of Rowing*)
P J Chaundy, BA (**Director of Art & Design*)
C Coombe, BA, MA, PhD (**Classics*)
C A M Curran (*Acting Head of English*)
T N Danks, BSc, PhD (**Chemistry*)
A P Dulston, BA (*Religious Education*)

E Dunckley (*English*)
P J Easton, BSc (*Biology*)
Revd D J Elliot, MA (**Theology*)
M R Fec, BA (*History*, †*Norris*)
R C Fec, MA (*Classics*)
J R Fenn, BSc (*Mathematics*)
V Fogg (**EAL*)
R J Ford (**Mathematics*)
A M Gemmill (*Biology, Deputy DSL, Head of PHSE*)
E Giles (*Curriculum Support*)
S P Hanna (*Art*)
M D Hennessy, BA (**History*)
D S Jezzard, BA, MA (*Modern Languages*)
N C Jones, BA, ARCO (*Music, *Examinations Officer*)
I P Jordan, BEd (*Physical Education, Mathematics,*
    †*FitzAlan*)
W J Keeling (**Physics*)
N Kemp (*Business Studies*, †*St John*)
Mrs S D Kenyon, BSc Hons, PGCE, QTS (**Biology*)
Mrs K S Lambert, BA (*Curriculum Support*)
G J M Lennartsson, MSc (*Mathematics*)
J Lewis, BA (*EAL*)
K K Maan, BSc (*Curriculum Support*)
S Mangaonkar, MA (*Art*)
R A O'Sullivan, BA (**Digital Learning*)
P E Poynter, BA (**Geography*)
C Sharrock, BA, MA (**English*)
S C B Tomlinson, BSc (**Director of Games*)
Mrs A D T Tuite-Dalton (*§French*)
C Watson, BA (*Junior Humanities*, †*St Philip House*)
V Watson, BEd (*PE*, †*St Philip House*)

Music Staff:
C Caiger (*Guitar*)
T D Carleston (*Singing*)
J Donnelly (*Drums, Percussion*)
Mrs S Ellison, BA, LRAM (*Oboe and Piano*)
Mrs S L Dytor, ARCM (*Violin*)
G Howarth, BSc, MA (*Brass*)
C C King, FRICS (*Drums & Percussion*)
M Knowles, AGSM (*Brass*)
Miss E V Krivenko, MMus Dip (*Piano*)
Miss R Watson, BA (*Cello*)
Mrs K E Laughton, BA (*Saxophone, Flute*)
Miss E L Mallett, BA (*Singing*)
Ben Giddens, BA, ARCO (*Organ*)
G Williams, FTCL, FLCM, LRAM, ARCM (*Bassoon*)

School Health Centre:
Dr A Goode (*Medical Officer*)
Mrs C McSoley, RGN (*Practice Manager*)
Mrs S Atkins, RGN
Mrs N L Barker, RGN
Mrs J Gregory, RGN
Mrs E Herbert, RGN
Mrs K Jarema, RGN
Mrs H Pirouet, RGN

Non-Teaching Staff:
Mrs J Armstrong (*SIMS Administrator*)
Mrs N Baker (*HR Advisor*)
Mrs T Barnsley (*PA to the Bursar*)
Mrs A Browning (*Secretary*)
T R Brittan, MCSA, CEH (*Network Manager*)
C J Lawman (*ICT Technician*)
Mrs C Macnab (*Librarian*)
Mrs J F Martin (*Registrar*)
Mrs N Moran (*PA to the Head Master*)
Mrs G Munoz (*§Reception*)
Mrs D Nash, MA (*§Archivist & Alumni*)
Mrs C Nicholl (*Bursary Assistant*)
Mrs A O'Connor (*Marketing Executive*)

A Rajan (*Finance Manager*)
Mrs R S Rawlings (*Head of Development & Alumni
    Relations*)
M Sixsmith, BSc, MPhil (*§Computer Services*)
Mrs D Smith (*Admissions Assistant*)
Mrs H M Shuttleworth (*HR Administrator*)
R Squizzoni (*Estates Manager*)
Mrs A Stanek (*Payroll Manager*)
Mrs K Warren (*§Secretary*)
Mrs R Watson (*Bursary Assistant*)
Mrs M Weekly (*Reception*)

Sports Centre Staff:
M Seigneur (*Professional Real Tennis*)
A Shotter (*Sports Centre Assistant*)
K Brouard (*Sports Centre Assistant*)
N Brouard (*Sports Centre Administrator*)
F White (*Swimming Coach*)

Oundle School

Oundle, Peterborough, Northamptonshire PE8 4GH

Tel: 01832 277122 (Reception)
          01832 277125 (Admissions Office)
email: admissions@oundleschool.org.uk
website: www.oundleschool.org.uk

Motto: *God Grant Grace*

Oundle School originated from the bequest of Sir William Laxton, a native of Oundle, to the Grocers' Company in 1556. The School was established with the object of providing a liberal education in accordance with the principles of the Church of England. The aims of the School are: to promote excellence and allow pupils to reach their full academic and intellectual potential; to develop independence and team players who will contribute to the community; to develop strong values, encourage involvement and an understanding of adult life, and prepare pupils for life beyond Oundle; to provide a full-boarding programme such that its excellence is recognised worldwide.

Oundle became fully co-educational in September 1990. Its buildings, dating from the 17th to the 21st centuries, are dispersed throughout the attractive market town of Oundle, giving the School a distinctive and unique charm. Oundle is the third largest independent boarding and day school in England, with national boarders coming from over 120 feeder schools all over the UK. 19% of pupils come from over 34 overseas countries. Laxton Junior School, a co-ed day School in Oundle for pupils aged 4–11, also comes under the Corporation of Oundle School.

Number of pupils (2017–2018). 847 boarders and 267 day pupils.

Admission. Main entry is at 11+, 13+ and 16+ with a small number of places available at other stages, including boarding places at 12+. Most pupils sit the June Common Entrance Examination or the Oundle Scholarship Examination at thirteen before joining in September. Those joining the School at eleven sit a written examination in January before entry in September, with papers in English, Mathematics, Science and a Cognitive Ability Test.

Facilities. Academic departments are situated in the Cloisters, the Needham building, the Adamson Centre, the Gascoigne building, Old Dryden and SciTec, Oundle's impressive home of science. In September 2016, a second phase of SciTec opened, with enhanced Design, Technology and Engineering facilities and a new purpose-built Mathematics department, bringing together the STEM subjects and embracing developments in new fields such as nanotechnology and mechatronics. The teaching areas are very well equipped; the Information Technology Centre includes two fully-equipped computer rooms and there are 'cluster networks' around the School. Thin Client terminals are located for each boarder in the Houses. Electronic whiteboards and computer-driven projectors feature in most teaching rooms. The Adamson Centre for Modern Languages opened in September 2013 and is equipped with two state-of-the-art language laboratories, six language assistant pods, fourteen teaching rooms and an International Suite.

Art, Music, Drama and Design and Technology are all very strong and well provided for. The Art Studios are large, airy and well equipped and the department includes the Yarrow Gallery. Facilities in Music include the Frobenius Organ and an electronic Music Studio. The Drama Department is centred on the Rudolph Stahl Theatre, a cleverly converted chapel in the middle of the town, where numerous productions of both the School and visiting companies take place.

The Chapel was built as a memorial shortly after the Great War and its East windows, designed by John Piper, were installed in 1956. Thirty-two stained glass windows by Mark Angus, added in 2005, compliment Piper's original vision. Religious instruction accords with the Church of England, but other faiths are welcomed.

The School is part way through a major development that has to date resulted in the opening of JM Mills Cricket Pavilion, two additional astroturf pitches, athletics track and forty new cricket nets. The next phase of the development will bring an impressive sports centre which will house a 50m pool, an 8-court sports hall, a fitness suite, dance studios and externally a new athletics facility.

Oundle has sixteen houses: eight boys' boarding houses, five girls' houses, a junior boarding house, junior day house and senior day house. A continuous cycle of renovation and refurbishment is in operation. Each house has its own distinct community, with in-house dining a hallmark of the School's character.

Academic Curriculum. Third Formers (Year 9) take a general course consisting of English, Mathematics, French, Latin, Physics, Chemistry, Biology, History, Geography, Religious Studies, Art, Design and Technology, PE, Music, Drama, Computing, and German or Spanish or Chinese or Greek. A unique 'Trivium' course introduces pupils to ideas, culture and pursuit of knowledge outside a prescribed syllabus. The First and Second Form curriculum is similar.

The traditional importance of Science and Technology is still maintained, with all pupils being taught the three Sciences to IGCSE level (both Triple Award and Dual Award on offer) and all Third Formers spending time in both the Art and the Design and Technology Departments. Computing and Microelectronics are available at all levels.

Pupils take English, Mathematics and the three Sciences as the core of their GCSE/IGCSE curriculum and choose a further five subjects from Arabic, Art, Chinese, Classical Greek, Computing, Design Technology, Drama, Electronics, French, Geography, German, History, Italian, Latin, Music, Physical Education, Religious Studies, Russian, and Spanish. Almost every pupil studies at least one modern foreign language (seven are timetabled), many study two or more.

In the Sixth Form, pupils choose four subjects from Art, Biology, Chemistry, Chinese, Classical Civilisation, Classical Greek, Computing, Design, Engineering and Technology, Economics, Electronics, Literature in English, French, Geography, German, Government and Politics, History, History of Art, Italian, Latin, Mathematics, Further Mathematics, Music, Philosophy and Theology, Physical Education, Physics, Psychology, Spanish and Theatre Studies. Of these, Chemistry, Chinese, Literature in English, German, History, History of Art, Italian, Physics and Spanish are assessed by the linear Cambridge Pre-U qualification; other subjects are assessed as A Levels.

Studies in the Sixth Form are enhanced by an extension block, in which is available the School's bespoke *Quadrivium* course – which is a selection of different courses divided into four topics looking at a central theme, and other options, such as one-year *ab initio* courses in Italian and Russian, Music Technology, preparation for Music Diplomas, and Projects. The last of these leads to AQA Extended Project Qualification.

Honours. 99% of Upper Sixth Former pupils go on to higher education at good universities; in 2018 eighteen pupils secured places at Oxford and Cambridge.

Sport. The main School sports are Rugby, Hockey, Cricket, Rowing, Netball and Tennis, but others available include Aerobics, Athletics, Badminton, Clay Shooting, Cross Country, Cycling, Fencing, Fives, Golf, Horse Riding, Sailing, Shooting, Soccer, Squash, Swimming and Volleyball.

Activities. A full range of activities take place which are an integral part of the wider school curriculum. Events in Drama and Music feature prominently in the School calendar, and Art Exhibitions are held regularly in the Yarrow Gallery. A large number of Societies meet on a regular basis. Links have been established with schools in France, Germany, Spain, Hungary, the Czech Republic, Russia, China, America and Australia, with annual Exchanges taking place. Pupils are able to participate in the very large number of expeditions and trips in the UK and abroad. There is a flourishing CCF comprising Army, Navy, RAF, Fire and Adventure Training sections and a thriving Duke of Edinburgh's Award scheme is in operation. Community Action plays an important part in school life and contributes significantly to the wider community. Much time and energy are devoted to fundraising activities in support of national charities, international aid programmes and holidays run at Oundle for MENCAP and inner-city children.

Entrance Scholarships. An extensive series of entrance scholarships is offered each year.

Scholarships at 13+:

Fifteen Academic scholarships. A qualifying examination takes place in January, with final papers in May.

Twelve General (All-Rounder) scholarships. Assessment in March.

Ten Music scholarships, including One Junior Organ Scholarship. Free tuition provided in all specified instruments, Audition and interview in January.

One Drama scholarship. Audition and interview in March.

Two Art scholarships. Assessment and interview in May.

Two Design and Engineering scholarships. Examination and interview in May.

Five Sports scholarships. Assessment and interview in November.

Scholarships at 11+:

Four Junior Academic scholarships for entry to The Berrystead or Laxton. Examination in January.

Two Junior Music scholarships. Free tuition provided in all specified instruments. Audition and interview in January.

Scholarships at 16+:

Two Academic scholarships. Examination in November.

One Music scholarship. Free tuition provided in all specified instruments. Audition and interview in November.

One Art scholarship. Examination and interview in November.

One Design and Engineering scholarship. Examination and interview in November.

Three Sport scholarships. Examination and interview in November.

Further details of all awards may be obtained from the Registrar (Tel: 01832 277125, email: admissions@oundle school.org.uk) or the Assistant to the Deputy Head Admissions (Tel: 01832 277116, email: hev@oundle school.org.uk).

Bursaries. Financial help towards the payment of fees in cases of proven need is available in some instances. This assistance is available in the form of bursaries which vary in size according to circumstance; some may be as high as 100%. Bursaries are not dependent on scholastic merit but are awarded to pupils who are likely to gain most from an Oundle education and who will contribute fully to the life of the School. The pupils in question must satisfy the School's academic entry requirements and continue to work to capacity as they progress through the School. Parents who feel that they may need the support of a bursary are encouraged to discuss the matter with the School well in advance of the child's due date of entry. Decisions regarding bursary assistance are made approximately two years ahead of entry. Judgements are dependent on a supporting reference from a candidate's previous school, an informal interview and on scrutiny of the family's financial circumstances.

Fees per term (2018–2019). Boarders: Berrystead Year 1 £9,295; Berrystead Year 2 £10,785; Years 3–7 £12,230.

Day Pupils: Year 1 £5,960; Year 2 £6,910, Years 3–7 £7,935.

Details of extras are given in the School prospectus. The registration fee is £250.

Laxton Junior School caters for 4 to 11 year old boys and girls and has 250 pupils on roll. (*For further details, see entry in IAPS section.*)

Charitable status. Oundle School is a Registered Charity, number 309921.

Governing Body:
[1]Mr R H Ringrose (*Chairman*) [OO]
Mr D A Hutchinson (*Vice Chairman*) [OO]
Mr C J Bartram [OO]
Mr J H Cartwright [OO]
Mr H Claydon
Ms K Hall
Mr K I Hodgson [OO]
Mrs J C Kibbey
Mrs R Lawes
[1]Mr C G McAndrew
Mrs D McGregor
Mr M C B Spens
[1]Mr T W Stubbs

Ex Officio:
[1]Mr J N Whitmore, Master
[1]Mr R W Uloth, Second Warden
[1]Mr T Coleridge, Third Warden
Mr D Toriati, OBE (*Bursar and Secretary*)

[1] *Member of the Court of the Grocers' Company*
[OO] *Old Oundelian*

The Staff:

The Head: Mrs S Kerr-Dineen, MA

Deputy Head: Mrs D L Watt, MA
Deputy Head Academic: I C Smith, MSc
Deputy Head Admissions: A B Burrows, MA Ed, BSc
Deputy Head Co-Curriculum: M A Shewin, MA
Deputy Head Pastoral: Mrs A E Meisner, BA
Senior Chaplain: Revd B J Cunningham, MA

Admissions:
Deputy Head Admissions: A B Burrows, MA Ed, BSc
Registrar: G Phillips, BA
Registrar Elect: A E Bounds, MA

Head of Laxton: Mrs V Gascoine, BEd
Head of International Admissions: Ms C M Redding, BA, Dip Ed, MA, Cert TESOL

Bursary:
Bursar: D J Toriati, MA
Director of Estates: R M C Tremellen, BSc, AIMBM
Head of Finance: P Lamb, ACMA

Director of Safeguarding: B A S Raudnitz, BA
Director of Professional Development: Mrs J T Coles, BA
Director of IT: Mrs L Waide
Director of Development: M J Dear, BTh, GDL, FInstPa
Director of Communications: Mrs R J Makhzangi, BA

Houses and Housemasters/Housemistresses:
Bramston: P A Liston
Crosby: A C Mansergh
Dryden: Ms K A Francis
Fisher: A J Brighton
Grafton: W W Gough
Kirkeby: Mrs J L L Banerjee
Laundimer: J R Hammond-Chambers
Laxton: Mrs V Gascoine
New House: Ms C A Rees
Sanderson: Mrs S L Ratchford
School House: A E Langsdale
Scott House: Mrs F L Quiddington
Sidney: Dr C J Quiddington
St Anthony: P J Kemp
Wyatt: Dr N M Mola
The Berrystead: Mme S Fonteneau

Medical Officers:
Dr M J Richardson, BSc, MBChB, MRCGP, DRCOG
Dr K Newell, MBChB, MRCGP, DRCOG

* *Head of Department*

Art:
*J D Oddie, BA, FRSA
Ms K A Hannant, MA
Mrs C L B Dent
T R J MacDougall, MA

Classics:
Mrs M P R James, MA
Mrs D L Watt, MA
N J Aubury, MA
T J Morrison, MA
Ms C L Westran, MA
Miss R L Hodgson, BA
Miss C I Harrington, MA
*Miss A M Harmer, MA
Miss S M Oade, DPhil
P A Liston, MA

Computing:
*R I Cunniffe, BSc
D S Barnes (*Head of Digital Strategy for Education*)
Miss A M Strachan, BSc
C H Bradnam, BEng

Design Engineering and Technology:
D Vincent, Capet Technology, MEd
O Jervis, C&G MecEng H03 H25
R Johnson, C&G 381/3 620/3,4
B J Rutter, DMS, HND
R H Lowndes, BSc, MEng
Mrs R L Lowndes, BSc
*J M Baker, BA

Drama:
Ms K A Francis, BA
*M Burlington, BA, MA
Miss N M Jones, MA (*Director of the Stahl*)

Economics:
A P Ireson, MA, DipFM
J Röhrborn, MA
Mrs F L Quiddington, BEcon, MT
*S J Janes, BA
Miss J A Kaur, MSc

*Educational Support (EFL, Specific Learning Difficulties
    and Study Assistance)*:
Ms C M Redding, BA, Dip Ed, MA, Cert TESOL
*Mrs A M J Taylor, MA, Dip RSA
Mrs A Larter, BA
Mrs Z J Thomas, BA (*EAL Coordinator*)
Mrs H J Whitehurst, MA, APC SpLD

English:
Ms M K Smedley, BA
N J T Wood, MA
Mrs J T Coles, BA
A D Martens, BA
B A S Raudnitz, BA
A J Sherwin, MA
Mrs H Wells, BA, MA, Liveryman of the Worshipful
    Company of Turners, Freeman of the City of London
Mrs H K Hopper, MA
*Mr R J Smith, BA
Mrs A J Gould, MA
Mrs E M A Talbot, BA

Examinations:
A P Ireson, MA, DipFM
D B Meisner, BA, MSc, PhD
J Röhrborn, MA
R A Barnes, PhD

Geography:
Mrs M S Turner, BA, MBA
J R Hammond-Chambers, MA
Mrs J L L Banerjee, BSc, MEd
*Mrs M T Chapman, MEd
P G Pitcher, BSc
A C Mansergh, MA

Government and Politics:
*D W Hine, MA
L C O MacKenzie, PhD
C T Standley, PhD

History:
I D Clark, BA
A J Brighton, BA
P J Kemp, MA
Mrs T E Harris, BA
*J M Allard, MA
J P Crawley, MA
W S Robinson, MPhil
C T Standley, PhD
A E Bounds, MA

Mathematics:
A P Ireson, MA, DipFM
D A Turner, BSc
R Atkins, BSc
N D Turnbull, BA
D B Meisner, BA, MSc, PhD
D P Raftery, BSc
*S G Dale, MEng
M A Blessett, MA
M M Sanderson, BSc, LRSM
S D Coates, BSc
R G Montgomery, MSc
Miss A M Strachan, BSc
R G B Macdonald, PhD
Ms L Man, MSc

Mrs A L Lunch, MSc
NV Salvi, MA

Modern Languages:
N M Mola, MA, PhD
B Béjoint, L-ès-L
J Röhrborn, MA
Mme S Fonteneau, L-ès-L, MA
Mme G M Skinner, L-ès-FLE, L-ès-LCE
T D Watson, MA (*Italian*)
*Mrs S J Davidson, MA, MEd
Mrs L M Brighton, MEd
S Jessop, BA (*French*)
R F Charters
Ms K Paone, LDML
W D Gunson, BA, LLB Hons, MPhil
Miss M Viruete Navarro, MA (*Spanish*)
Miss E J Wagstaffe, MEd (*German*)
Miss R A Blacknell, BA
Miss C H Hignett, BA
Mrs A C P Hurley, MA (*Chinese*)
Miss A Ford, MA (*Arabic*)
A O'Grady (*French Assistant*)
T Verite (*French Assistant*)
Q Berthemely (*French Assistant*)
A Chambazi (*French Assistant*)
B Hänert (*German Assistant*)
Mrs A L Charters (*Spanish Assistant*)
S de la Fuente (*Spanish Assistant*)

Music:
Director of Music: *Q P Thomas, MA, MMus, MA, ARCO
Head of Academic Music: J C Arkell, MA, FRCO, FTCL,
    FLCM, FGMS, FRSA, FCIEA
Academic Music Teacher: Mrs S L Ratchford, BA
Head of Brass: Mrs A S Hudson, GRNCM, PPRNCM
Head of Keyboard: A Hone, BMus, ARCM, ARCO
Head of Strings: A P Gibbon, GRNCM
Head of Woodwind: J H Broun, MMUS, PPRNCM
    [chamber], BMUS, PPRNCM [solo]
Music Studios Manager: C J Pettitt
Choirmaster: H Dustagheer

Physical Education:
Miss R S Goatly, BA (*Head of Athletics*)
Mrs L M Brighton, MEd (*Junior Girls Sports Coordinator*)
Mr B Grenfell (*Head of Health and Fitness*)
*R A J Finch, MSc (*Asst Director of Sport*)
D J Grewcock, BA (*Director of Sport*)
M P Walker, BA (*Head of Rowing*)

Sports Fellows:
R Bennett, S Compton, C Curuth, S Elridge, V Patel, F
    Scutt

Psychology:
S R Heath, MSc
Mrs S A L Ried, BSc
Mrs A L Barker, BSc

Theology, Philosophy and Religion:
Mrs V Gascoine, BEd
Mrs A E Meisner, BA
*B T Deane, BA, MA
Revd B J Cunningham, MA
Mrs C A Deane, BA
Miss H A Dawes, BA
Revd M E A Coulter

Science and Technology:
Head of Science:
*O E A Peck BSc (*Head of Biology*)

Biology:
A E Langsdale, BSc, MSc

Dr P J Rowe, DPhil
W W Gough, BSc
S K Burman-Roy, MA
Miss E A C Byatt, BA
Miss K M Morris, MSc

Chemistry:
R F Hammond, BSc
M J Bessent, MChem, PhD
C J Quiddington, MChem, PhD
Miss T A Dorman, MChem
*J H Peverley, MA
I C Smith, MSc
Miss E K Furber, MChem

Physics:
M N Wells, MA
A B Burrows, MA Ed, BSc
Mrs L E Kirk, BSc
Mrs T E Raftery, BSc
H Roberts, BSc, MSc, CPhys, MInstP
*D J Talbot, MPhys
Ms C A Rees, MSc
Mrs S J Waring, BEng
L V S Bezerra (*Fellow*)

Science Technicians:
Biology:
K Richards, C McKinnon, C Leo
Chemistry:
A Wilding, P Ayling, M James
Physics:
R Loades, M Seymour, H Orange

Cripps Library:
*Ms L Giurlando, BA, MSc, MCLIP
Mrs S Marsden, BA
Mrs A Money, BA
Mrs R Cook, BA

Pangbourne College

Pangbourne, Reading, Berkshire RG8 8LA

Tel: 0118 984 2101
email: admissions@pangbourne.com
website: www.pangbourne.com
Twitter: @PangColl
Facebook: @pangbournecollege
LinkedIn: /pangbourne-college

Motto: *Fortiter ac Fideliter*

Pangbourne College was founded in 1917 by Sir Thomas Devitt of the Devitt & Moore Company to train boys for a career at sea. It is now a modern, friendly boarding and day school for approximately 430 boys and girls aged 11 to 18. The College offers sound academic results, first-class sports coaching and an excellent pastoral structure prioritising the happiness and well-being of the individual. It celebrated its centenary in September 2017.

Location and Facilities. Set in 230 acres of grounds designated an Area of Outstanding Natural Beauty, a mile from Pangbourne village and neighbouring the town of Reading, the College combines a rural environment with easy access to London and Heathrow. The extensive school facilities include the Falkland Islands Memorial Chapel opened in March 2000, two modern girls' boarding houses, a drama studio, ICT suite and music hall. The modern, excellently equipped Sports Hall, floodlit Astroturf hockey pitch, spacious playing fields and boathouse on the River Thames provide sporting facilities of a professional standard. Boarding and day pupils are integrated across the seven boarding houses. Senior pupils share study-bedrooms and most have single rooms in the Sixth Form. Meals are taken in a central dining hall although the boarding houses contain kitchens too. Most academic staff live on the campus in College houses and there is an extremely strong community spirit.

Junior House. The Junior House, Dunbar, offers excellent, purpose-built accommodation and common room areas for 11 and 12-year-old pupils in the heart of the College. Fully integrated into the academic, cultural and social life, Dunbar pupils enjoy full use of all the senior school's facilities and its specialist teaching. Pupils transfer automatically to the senior school without further examination.

Academic Study. Pupils aged 11–16 follow a broad curriculum which reflects, but is not determined by, the National Curriculum. This covers all of the core and foundation subjects of the National Curriculum: English, Mathematics, Science, French, German, History, Geography, Design Technology (DT), Religious Studies, Personal, Social, Health and Citizenship Education (PSHCE), Art, Music, Drama, Physical Education (PE) and Computer Science. Pupils in Forms 1–3 are assessed by the College's own assessment and reporting system. A Learning Support Department, staffed by specialist qualified teachers, is available to help.

In the Sixth Form, students follow the A Level programme with 21 subject options on offer alongside two-year BTECs in DT, Music and Sport. Sixth Form class sizes are typically between 8 and 12 and each student works with a Tutor, a Housemaster/Housemistress and the Head of Sixth Form to help them successfully navigate their way through their academic study.

Although the College's primary focus is the pursuit of academic excellence, it does nonetheless cater for a wide spectrum of abilities. Pupils are given considerable opportunities to discover and develop additional skills and talents through the extensive Music, Art, Sport, Drama and leadership programmes.

Careers. The Head of Sixth Form and Head of Careers work closely with the individual's Tutor to ensure that wise, informed choices are made. Whilst many students go on to Russell Group universities and a few to Oxford and Cambridge, the College champions as equals and provides guidance for the minority of students who do choose to take the vocational route.

Games. For a small school, Pangbourne has an outstanding reputation for sport and thrives at Regional and National level in several games. The College has had many successes at Henley Royal Regatta and competes at a high level in rugby, consistently making good progress in the Berkshire Cup and national NatWest competitions. The hockey club regularly produce County players and have recently finished fourth in the National Hockey Championships. Pangbourne Equestrian provides professional and dedicated riding training which helped to produce a winners medal in the 1m Showjumping event at the NSEA County Championships in 2018. Other sports and activities offered include cricket, netball, tennis, football, athletics, golf, sailing and basketball. Pupils have regular access to the College's gym which is supervised by a member of the sporting faculty.

Adventure Training. Led by the Head of Adventure Training and Duke of Edinburgh's Award Coordinator, the College provides an extensive range of activities designed to foster teamwork, leadership and communication skills. There is a full programme of adventure training built into the curriculum from Form 1, with weekend and holiday expeditions. As well as the opportunity to take part in a major expedition abroad every two years, pupils have regular, supervised access to the College's on-site high and low ropes course.

The Combined Cadet Force (CCF) programme at Pangbourne allows students to split into Army, Royal Navy and Royal Marine Sections, with each providing tailored exercises and expeditions. Despite being mandatory only in Form 4, many of Pangbourne's pupils currently take part in the CCF.

All Form 3 pupils are entered for the Bronze Duke of Edinburgh's Award with many moving on to the Silver and Gold programmes.

Music and Drama. Pangbourne has a long tradition of excellence in Music and Drama. The Nancye Harding Recital Hall has provided the College with its own recital hall, music technology facilities and extensive rehearsal space, adding further performance space to the existing Chapel and school hall. The hall and wider Music Centre – which was opened in 2012 – houses the College's Steinway pianos, which gives Pangbourne its prestigious All-Steinway School status. There is also the opportunity to perform with the College choirs, Choral Society, Orchestra, Jazz Band and Marching Band, and the many professional musicians working around the College, including the Head of Instrumental Music, allowing students to pursue individual musical excellence.

Enrichment. The Enrichment programme is a dedicated time in the afternoon put aside for students and teachers to explore their interests and passions. Under the broad Enrichment banner rests a multitude of activities, clubs and societies, from academic support and extra language tuition to clay pigeon shooting and sailing clubs.

Admission. Children normally enter the Junior House, Dunbar, at 11+ through an interview and the College entrance examination. They are joined by more boys and girls at age 13+ through the Common Entrance or Scholarship Examinations. Sixth Form entry is based on interview, a satisfactory report from the previous school and good GCSE examination results. A prospectus and registration form may be obtained from the Registrar, Mrs Jane Herold, who is always pleased to arrange visits to the College.

Scholarships and Bursaries. Scholarships and Awards of up to 10% of fees may be offered at 11+, 13+ and 16+ for excellence in the academic, music, drama, art, technology and sporting spheres. Means-tested Bursaries are also available.

Scholarship and Exhibition assessments are set and held at the College in January and February of the year of entry. All candidates applying for an award – academic or practical – must be registered and fulfil the standard entry requirements of the College.

Academic: Scholarships or Exhibitions may be offered at 11+, 13+ and 16+, and are the most important scholastic awards made by the College. They are based on academic merit in a range of subjects and the potential to produce an outstanding performance at GCSE and A Level.

Art: Scholarships of up to 10% of fees may be offered at 13+ and 16+. Candidates must present a portfolio of work completed over the previous two years and attend an interview.

Drama: Scholarships may be offered at 13+ and 16+. Candidates are invited to attend an audition consisting of two prepared monologues, an improvised piece and sight reading.

Music: Several Music Scholarships or Exhibitions of up to the value of 10% of College fees are available at 11+, 13+ and 16+. For consideration, candidates should be approximately Grade 3 at 11+ entry, Grade 5 at 13+ entry and Grade 7 at 16+ entry on their main instrument. A second instrument or experience as a chorister is an advantage. Awards normally carry free tuition on two instruments.

Sports: Scholarships or Exhibitions may be offered at 11+, 13+ and 16+ to candidates who have the sporting potential to be a significant member of the College's first teams, in one or more of the College's major sports, and the ability to compete at County or higher representative level.

Technology: Scholarships may be offered at 13+. Candidates are expected to design and make an item out of scrap materials and be prepared to discuss their work at interview.

Please contact the Registrar, email: admissions@pangbourne.com or visit https://www.pangbourne.com/prospective-families/admissions/fees-scholarships-and-bursaries for more information.

Fees per term (2018–2019). At age 11 and 12: Boarders £8,290; Weekly Boarder £7,670; Part Boarders £7,390; Day Pupils £5,885. At 13 and above: Boarders £11,730; Weekly Boarder £10,850; Part Boarders £10,435; Day Pupils £8,295.

Charitable status. Pangbourne College Limited is a Registered Charity, number 309096. The objective is to provide an excellent all-round education for boys and girls between the ages of 11 and 18.

Governing Body:
Chairman: Rear Admiral R C Lane-Nott, CB
Vice-Chairman: Revd A T Bond

Headmaster: Mr T J C Garnier

Senior Deputy Head and Deputy Head Academic: Mr W Williams

Deputy Head Co-Curricular: Mr R Bancroft

Deputy Head Pastoral: Mrs C Bond

Bursar: Mr N Walne

The Perse Upper School

Hills Road, Cambridge CB2 8QF

Tel:	01223 403800
Fax:	01223 403810
email:	office@perse.co.uk
website:	www.perse.co.uk

The Perse School is Cambridge's oldest secondary school, founded in 1615 by Dr Stephen Perse, a Fellow of Gonville and Caius College. The school still maintains close links with both Gonville and Caius and with Cambridge University.

The Perse Upper School is a co-educational independent day school for pupils aged 11–18.

Ethos. A Perse education is an adventure, full of curiosity, discovery and challenge. Students come from a wide range of social and economic backgrounds thanks to the School's significant bursary programme and a commitment to keeping fee rises low. The School's values are: intellectual curiosity and scholarship, endeavour, breadth and balance, and valuing one another and the environment. The School encourages all pupils and staff *"To love learning and strive for the greater good."*

History. The School remains true to its historic roots, with close links to the University of Cambridge and a £1 million a year means-tested bursary programme that supports more than 120 pupils.

Admission. There are approximately 1180 students in the Upper, including 355 in the Sixth Form. The main entry points are Year 7, Year 9 and the Lower Sixth. For Years 7 and 9 candidates are examined in maths, English and verbal reasoning, and undertake a short humanities video/questions exercise. Sixth Form applicants sit entrance tests and offers are conditional on I/GCSE results.

Facilities. The Perse has invested more than £40 million in new facilities over the last decade. The Upper occupies an attractive 27 acre green field site with extensive playing fields and recreational areas. The School benefits from easy access to world-class facilities. Pupils enjoy high specification science labs and classrooms; a purpose built sports centre; on-site sports fields and all weather surfaces; a music centre including a rehearsal hall; art studios and a gallery; a lecture theatre; and an outdoor pursuits centre, climbing wall and shooting range. There is a 20,000 volume library and high-speed wired and wireless networks to ensure ready access to online learning resources. In 2018 the Peter Hall Performing Arts Centre opened.

Academic excellence. Perse pupils learn in a purposeful and supportive environment where they are taught to think independently and to make sense of a diverse and complex world. The School achieves some of the best A Level and Pre-U results of any co-educational school in the country, regularly appearing in the top 10 schools nationally. In 2018, 84% of entries were awarded A*–A at A Level. At GCSE, 80% of entries were awarded A* or 9/8 with A*–A at 94%. Pupils regularly excel in science and maths olympiads, economics and business challenges, drama and poetry contests and essay and fiction writing competitions.

Rounded education. There is a buzz about daily life at The Perse. There are more than 100 clubs and societies on offer. The School was awarded the Pro Corda Special Award for Schools for outstanding contribution to chamber music making. Nearly 500 pupils at the Upper School are involved in 68 ensembles and a typical year will see around 50–60 separate performance opportunities. There are at least eight drama productions each year. The main sports are cricket, hockey, netball, rugby, tennis, athletics and rounders. There is an extensive fixtures list; the School fields more than 160 teams in 30 different sports and regularly enjoys regional and national success. More than 400 pupils are involved in the Perse Exploration Society, learning outdoor skills as well as life skills such as team working and resilience. Other popular outdoor pursuits include adventure racing, shooting, the Combined Cadet Force and the Duke of Edinburgh's Award programme.

Supportive community. The Upper is a happy school where pupils feel safe, secure and supported. The School works hard to strike the right balance of work and play, comfort and challenge, instruction and discovery, rules and common sense, and guidance and independence. Each student has a pastoral tutor who monitors their progress and there are peer listeners, form prefects and a system of heads of year, heads of section, senior tutors and school counsellors. The Perse has a very active programme of charitable fundraising and outreach, and pupils have the chance to become involved in the wider community. Perse pupils work with children from local primary schools, teach the older generation digital skills, and volunteer in developing countries.

Global perspective. The Perse has strong international links including foreign language and cultural exchanges, a partnership with Christel House (a charity that educates some of the world's poorest children) and membership of the SAGE global alliance of leading schools. Pupils regularly travel overseas and increasingly collaborate remotely through the latest technology.

Fees per term (2018–2019). £6,044 for Years 7–8 including lunch and £5,774 for Year 9 and above excluding lunch.

Bursaries and scholarships. Means-tested bursaries are available, ranging from 5% to 100% of annual tuition fees. At Year 7 and Year 9 the School offers a small number of academic and music scholarships to pupils of exceptional merit. Sixth formers are able to apply for a maximum of two scholarships. All sixth form applicants who sit our entrance tests are automatically considered for an academic scholarship and general scholarship.

The Perse Prep is a co-educational preparatory school for pupils aged between 7 and 11. Tel: 01223 403920; email: prephm@perse.co.uk. (*See The Perse Prep School entry in IAPS section.*)

The Perse Pelican Nursery and Pre-Prep is for children aged 3 to 7. Tel: 01223 403940; email: pelicanschoolsec@perse.co.uk. (*See The Perse Pelican Nursery and Pre-Prep entry in IAPS section.*)

Alumni. Tel: 01223 403 836; email: development@perse.co.uk.

Charitable status. The Perse School is a charitable company limited by guarantee (company number 5977683, registered charity number 1120654) registered in England and Wales whose registered office is situated at The Perse School, Hills Road, Cambridge CB2 8QF.

Governing Body:

Representing Gonville & Caius College:
Dr A M Bunyan, BA, PhD
Dr E M Harper, BA, MA Cantab, PhD

Representing Trinity College:
Dr L Merrett, MA, PhD

Co-opted:
H Bettinson, MA, PhD
KA Davies, MA, FCA
W M R Dawkins, BA
I G Galbraith, MA
S W Graves, BSc, MBA [OP]
C P Hancock, QC, MA, LLM
S D Lebus, MA
R C StH Mason, BSc, MBBS, MRCP, MBA
G J Proudfoot, MA
S C Roberts, MA
D M Shave, MA, MBACP
B P Smith, MA, CPFA, FCIHT
S L Steele, CTA
C J Stenner LLB (*Vice Chairman*)
Sir David Wright, GCMG, LVO, MA, Hon LLD (*Chairman*)

Bursar & Clerk to the Governors: A Shakespeare

Head: E C Elliott

Senior Deputy Head (*Staff*): D R Cross

Deputy Head (*Pupils*): E W Wiseman

Deputy Head (*Teaching and Learning*): T Khimyak

Deputy Head (*Curriculum and Operations*): G Richards

Deputy Head (*Extra-curricular*): S A Richardson

Assistant Head (*Welfare and Admissions*): G F Hague

Plymouth College

Ford Park, Plymouth, Devon PL4 6RN

Tel: 01752 505100 (School Office)
01752 505104 (Headmaster)

01752 505107 (Finance Director)
01752 505115 (Admissions)
email: mail@plymouthcollege.com
             slambie@plymouthcollege.com
             accounts@plymouthcollege.com
website: www.plymouthcollege.com
Twitter: @plymouthcolleg
Facebook: @PlymouthCollege

Plymouth College, based in the maritime city of Plymouth with the moorland, countryside and coastal landscapes of Devon and Cornwall close to hand, has been at the forefront of education in South West England since its foundation in 1877. It amalgamated in 1896 with Mannamead School for boys in Plymouth, founded in 1854. The School became fully co-educational in 1995 and in 2004 merged with St Dunstan's Abbey for Girls.

Numbers. Currently there are 500 pupils in the school (160 in the Sixth Form) and of these 215 are girls.

Buildings. The Senior School stands on high ground in Plymouth. The buildings include Science Laboratories, Art and Craft rooms including extensive facilities for photography and print-making, the Dining Hall, an Assembly Hall in which concerts and plays are performed as well as a well-equipped Design and Technology Block. The grounds in Ford Park include a rifle range and an indoor, 25m heated swimming pool. Playing fields at Ford Park are supplemented by two other fields close by. There is an on-site astro surface and the school has use of a full-size astro for hockey nearby. In 2004 a hospitality suite and Music School opened and in 2011 two new boarding houses were established. The Boarding Houses have undergone a two-year refurbishment programme since 2016. For the Sixth Form there is a dedicated Sixth Form Centre with its own Bistro and 2016 saw the opening of the Michael Ball Drama Studio, opened by its namesake who is an old boy of the school, and another old boy, Tom Daley, opened the new Strength & Conditioning Gym in 2018. There is also an outdoor education centre located on Dartmoor.

The Preparatory School, for pupils 3–11, is on its own site, The Millfields, and is approximately a mile from the Senior School. It has its own playing field and well-equipped sports hall.

Organisation. Below the Sixth Form, pupils are set in some areas so that pupils may proceed at a pace best suited to their abilities. Pupils are organised in 4 Houses and participation in house events is actively encouraged. Each pupil is under the supervision of a Tutor and Head of Year who report to the Assistant Head. In Years 7–10 Form Prefects are appointed. Every pupil is expected to play a full part in games and other school activities outside the classroom. Pupils in Years 10 and above also take part in our enrichment programme which includes The Duke of Edinburgh's Award, CCF (all 3 sections), Sports Leaders Award and a wide range of other activities. All pupils take part in a PSHEE programme, with careers advice starting in Year 7. English (Language and Literature), a Modern Language, Mathematics, Physics, Chemistry and Biology are taken by all to GCSE. Normally three more are chosen by the pupils

Sixth Form. The Sixth Form is based on tutor groups with approx. twelve pupils in each group. Pupils usually study three subjects at A Level, with four being studied in exceptional circumstances. In addition, our Sports Baccalaureate is an alternative to A Levels and includes a BTEC in Sport & Outdoor Education as well as qualifications in other sporting and outdoor activity areas. Tutors keep a pastoral and academic watch on the pupils' performance, feeding information to the Head and Assistant Heads of Sixth Form.

Sixth Formers are well prepared for universities and careers both in the UK and overseas, including scholarship advice for the US, with detailed university advice starting in Year 9.

Games. Rugby, Football, Cricket, Hockey, Netball and Swimming are the major sports. There is also Athletics, Badminton, Basketball, Cross-Country Running, Fencing, Modern Pentathlon, Sailing, Shooting and Tennis. Games are compulsory but more senior pupils have a wide range of options available to them.

School Activities. Pupils take part in a very good range of activities. There is a contingent of the CCF with Navy, Army and Air Force Sections. There is also The Duke of Edinburgh's Award scheme and adventure training as well as participation in Ten Tors each year. Pupils in Year 10 participate in a Sports Leaders scheme with local primary schools. A number of overseas expeditions are also organised each year. School Societies cover a range of activities from Mountain Biking to Young Enterprise. There is also a very good and active Outdoor Education department which offers pupils opportunities in such activities as Bushcraft, Caving and Kayaking.

Music & Performing Arts. There is an excellent school choir that sings at all major school events, concerts, and church services throughout the school year. The school orchestra, like the choir, provides music at school events and concerts. In addition to these groups the school has various small ensembles that are run by the visiting specialist instrumental teachers. The school has a thriving house drama and music competition that attracts whole school support. As well as the formal/organized music making there are innumerable student-led bands that help to ensure that the music department is a vibrant environment. Tuition is provided on all orchestral instruments, including percussion. Voice, piano, organ and all types of guitar lessons are also available. Speech and drama lessons (LAMDA) are offered to all students. The music and drama departments work together on large-scale productions. The drama department offers drama clubs to all year groups. Both departments work with a number of visiting performers/practitioners throughout the year; these are usually focused on specific year groups or examination groups. There are annual music and drama scholarships and instrumental exhibitions.

Boarders. With pupils from all over the world, the boarding houses are run by an enthusiastic, experienced and friendly team who are responsible for all aspects of boarders' welfare. There is also a good mix of activities at the weekends including ten-pin bowling, ice skating, beach visits, cinema trips, surfing, moorland walking and horse riding.

The Boarding Houses are situated on the senior school campus: one for boys, one for girls (approximately 50 in each) and three smaller Sixth Form houses. They are located close to the school field and are equipped with small dormitories, common rooms, sickroom and games rooms. Meals are taken in the Dining Hall, supplied by a modern, well-equipped kitchen.

Admission. Admission to the Senior School is normally based on the College Entrance Examination for boys and girls over 10½ and under 12 on 31 August of the year of entry, but it is also possible to enter at 13 via the Common Entrance Examination or a Year 9 Scholarship/Entrance test. Occasional vacancies are available at other ages. Admission to the Preparatory School is from the age of 3+. For admission to both senior and prep schools, application forms may be obtained from the Registrar, email: admissions@ plymouthcollege.com.

Scholarships and Bursaries. For pupils entering at 11 there are 2 Major Scholarships (50% of fees p.a.) and 3 Ordinary Scholarships (one-third of the fees p.a.). Two of these awards are restricted to pupils coming from Plymouth College Preparatory School. There are also smaller awards for Art, Music, Drama and Sport and on occasion All-Round awards are given. Awards are made on the basis of the Entrance Examination.

At 13+ there is one Major and one Ordinary Scholarship and these are awarded on a Scholarship Examination.

For those entering the Sixth Form two further awards are made based on interview and GCSE results.

There are eight Scholarships and Awards for Art, Music, Drama and Sport. Four of these are awarded at 13 and four to Sixth Form entrants. The value of these awards is up to one-third of the fees.

Bursaries of up to half fees are available.

Further information from the Admissions department.

Fees per term (2018–2019). Infant Department: Kindergarten £2,560, Reception £2,665, Years 1 & 2 £3,150. Junior Department: Years 3–4 £3,380, Years 5–6 £3,535.

Senior School: Day: Years 7–8 £4,585, Years 9–11 £5,225, Sixth Form £5,430. Boarding: Years 7–8 £9,145, Years 9–11 £9,995, Sixth Form £10,480. Weekly Boarding: Years 7–8 £7,300, Years 9–11 £7,940, Sixth Form £8,145. Occasional boarding is available at £50 per night up to a maximum of 14 nights per academic year.

These fees include stationery and games. Music lessons and lunches are extra.

Armed Forces and sibling discounts are available.

Charitable status. Plymouth College is a Registered Charity, number 1105544. Its aim is to provide private education for boys and girls.

Governing Body:
Chair: Mr David Woodgate, BSc, MBA
Vice-Chair: Dr Penny Atkinson, MBChB, MRCGP, Dip SEM
Mr Adrian Brett, BSc, MInst RE
Mrs Sam Coutinho
Mrs Kelly Davis, FHEA, MEd, PGCE, BSc
Professor David Huntley, BA, MA, PhD
Mrs Clare Hammond, BSc Econ
Mr Peter Lowson, FCA
Mr Chris Morton, BSc, MA, FRICS
Mrs Alison Mills, ACIS, MCIPD
Dr Sue Thorpe
Dr Andrew Williams, BSc Hons, MSc, PhD

Clerk to the Governors: Mrs S Wills, MEng, ACA (*Senior & Preparatory School*)

Headmaster: Mr Jonathan Standen, BA Nottingham, NPQH

Deputy Head: Mrs J Hayward, MA Downing College Cambridge

Assistant Head: Mr C S Irish, BSc Birmingham

Teaching Staff:
Mr E Agobiani, LLB Leicester
Miss P J Anderson, MA Emmanuel College Cambridge (*Head of Classics*)
Miss N K Baker, BA Exeter, MA Exeter (*Head of History*)
Mr M Bennett, BA Exeter
Mrs A C Blunden-Currie, BA Exeter
Mrs S Blunden-Currie, BA Stirling (*Head of English*)
Mr K C Boots, BA Wales, MEd Exeter, AMBDA
Mrs P M Brockbank, Cert Ed
Mr M Byrne, BSc Loughborough (*Head of Boarding & Director of Cricket*)
Mr A R Carr, MA St Andrews (*Head of Sixth Form*)
Mr C Chilcott (*OED Tutor*)
Mrs A-L Chubb, BA Wolverhampton (*Head of Year 8*)

Mrs R L Connor, BA Nottingham (*Head of MFL & EAL Faculty*)
Mr R L Edwards, BA Wales (*Director of Rugby*)
Mrs B Field, BSc York (*Head of Chemistry*)
Mrs N E Glasgow, BA Aberystwyth
Mr J P Gregory, BA Birmingham (*Head of Economics & Business Studies*)
Dr A Green, BA Exeter
Mrs A E Green, BSc Nottingham
Mr D Green, BA Dartington College of Arts (*Head of Music & Performing Arts*)
P J Grey, BSc Open, AMInstP (*Head of Academic Progress*)
Mr D R Hawken, PG Dip, BMus Hons, Dip ABRSM Royal Welsh College of Music & Drama (*Head of Year 10*)
Dr A Hawker, BSc Plymouth, PhD
Ms J Herod, BA Nottingham, MSc East London (*Head of SEN / Educational Psychologist*)
Mrs C Herroro-Shaw, BA Middlesex
Miss N S L Husband, BA Queen Margaret
Mr D A Jones, BSc Birmingham (*Head of Mathematics*)
Dr S Jordan, PhD Dundee
Mrs N Lilley, BA Nottingham Trent
Mrs N Lisney, BA Plymouth (*Head of Design Technology*)
Mr G J Llewellyn-Rees, BEng Brunel, MEng Heriot-Watt, MBA Imperial College
Mr D J Martin, BA Warwick (*Head of Religious Studies*)
Mrs P M Martin, BA Southampton
Mr C Mayne, BSc Southampton
Dr A Miller, BSc PhD Bristol, CChem, MRSC, CPhys, MInstP (*Head of Computer Science*)
Miss I Moore, BEd St Mark & St John
Mrs R Moore (*Head of Lower School*)
Mr P M Mutlow, BA Durham (*Director of Sport*)
Mr C G Nicol, Dip Duncan of Jordanstone College of Art (*Head of Art*)
Dr A Norris, BSc Liverpool, PhD
Miss L M Odendaal, BA Stellenbosch
Mrs N Paice, BA St Mark & St John (*Head of Geography*)
Mr D P Prideaux, BSc Bristol (*Head of Biology*)
Mr P J Randall, BA Oxford Brookes (*Head of French & Spanish*)
Mr O Rees (*OED Manager*)
Mrs C Riley-Harling, BSc St Mark & St John
Miss L M Russo, MSci Imperial College
Miss A Savage, BSc Exeter (*Head of Psychology*)
Miss C P Sherratt, BSc Plymouth
Mrs L E Smith, BSc Exeter
Mrs S Sullivan, BA Glasgow School of Art
Mr A G Summons, BSc MSc Exeter (*Head of Year 11*)
Dr C Taylor, BSc Bath, PhD Bath
Mr M P Tippetts, BA Exeter
Miss E D Tremaine, BEd De Montfort (*Head of PE*)
Miss F Venon, Licence D'Anglais Universitie de St Etienne, Maîtrise (*Acting Head of Year 7*)
Mr M P Wesley, BSc Nottingham Trent
Mrs V J Willden, BA Plymouth (*Head of Year 9*)
Miss E Williams, BA Greenwich
Mr R P Wilson, BEng University College London
Mrs E Wright, BA University College London

Preparatory School:
Plymouth College Preparatory School
St Dunstan's Abbey
The Millfields
Plymouth PL1 3JL

Headmaster: Mr C D M Gatherer, BA

Pocklington School

**West Green, Pocklington, York, East Yorkshire
YO42 2NJ**

Tel: 01759 321200
Fax: 01759 306366
email: enquiry@pocklingtonschool.com
website: www.pocklingtonschool.com
Twitter: @PockSchool
Facebook: @PocklingtonSchool
LinkedIn: /pocklington-school

Inspired for Life

Pocklington is a thriving independent school, 12 miles east of York, providing outstanding day and boarding education from 3–18 years. Pocklington School delivers an excellent all-round education and a vibrant co-curricular life within a supportive and caring community, all founded on a 500-year tradition.

Set in a safe and picturesque rural setting, we are renowned for our emphasis on pastoral care, with a focus on the individual, which produces confident, resourceful and capable young adults.

Highly-skilled staff encourage an enthusiasm for learning and independent thought, helping pupils develop into motivated adults who are valued members of society.

Pocklington School was founded in 1514 and has remained true to its strong tradition of encouraging pupils to have the courage to take chances with learning and always remain true to themselves. Our motto Virtute et Veritate: With Courage and With Truth, reflects this.

Number of Pupils (2018–19). There are 540 pupils at Pocklington School (ages 11–18) and 220 pupils at Pocklington Prep School (ages 3–11). These numbers include 100 boarders aged 7–18.

Pocklington Prep School is on the same site as the Senior School. (*For further details, see entry in IAPS section.*)

Curriculum. Pocklington's curriculum has been developed to motivate and stretch pupils. Following foundations at Pocklington Prep School and in the Lower School at Pocklington, there are wide-ranging options in Year 9 and GCSE. In Sixth Form, A Level subjects offer a diverse selection of subjects and combinations. In addition, students can select from a range of enrichment qualifications, including BTEC courses. There is excellent careers and university advice.

Music, drama and art thrive, as do sport, outdoor education, community service and CCF. The main sports are rugby, hockey, cricket, athletics and tennis for boys and hockey, netball, tennis, athletics and rounders for girls. There is also a a wide range of other sports including archery, lacrosse, squash, table tennis, judo and swimming available.

Numerous co-curricular activities take place every day until 5.00 pm, and each pupil is encouraged to pursue their own interests to help develop the depth of character and self-awareness to tackle life's challenges on their own terms.

Location, Campus and Facilities. The school is set on a 50-acre rural site on the edge of Pocklington, a small, friendly market town. Emphasis is given to the importance of personal achievement in an attractive, high-quality learning environment with excellent facilities, which include a 300-seat theatre, an indoor sports hall, conditioning room and swimming pool, plus 21 acres of grass sports pitches and two full-sized synthetic pitches.

We employ the best educational tools and appropriate new technology facilities to ensure youngsters are enthused and inspired by the world of knowledge available to them.

The flexibility of learning platforms and the individual approach allows each pupil to progress at his or her pace, boosting their confidence and self-esteem so they often exceed their expectations.

Our new £3m Art and Design Technology Centre, which opened in Autumn 2017, has every facility to encourage the pursuit of traditional arts and crafts, as well as provide cutting-edge equipment for digital and computer design, and manufacturing technology. The innovation and cross-fertilisation of ideas the Centre promotes are increasingly valued in society today.

Sixth Form facilities include spacious communal areas, a study centre, and comprehensive library. Students are encouraged to work both collaboratively and independently as they begin to make the transition to university study and/or workplace success.

Boarding. Full, flexible and casual boarding options are available, in boarding houses which create a home from home for both domestic and international students. A flexible range of boarding opportunities allows students to create a balanced programme which not only fulfils their academic objectives, but also leaves time to explore new sporting, cultural and vocational activities to develop individual skills and strengths.

Admission. Progress into Year 7 is automatic for pupils who have attended Pocklington Prep School, provided there are no concerns about a child's behaviour or ability, which have previously been communicated to parents prior to the date of the entrance assessment. New entry to the School in Years 7–9 is subject to vacancy and to a satisfactory entrance exam result and school report. Interviews may also be held. Year 9 applicants sit either a Senior School entrance exam or Common Entrance. For Sixth Form applicants, an offer of a place is made subject to GCSE performance and school report. GCSE grades should include 4 B grades or grade 6, and 2 C grades or grade 4. Subject to these entry criteria, the school seeks to admit candidates who will benefit from what it has to offer and whom it will be able to support. Children with mild learning difficulties can be supported, as can those who will in due course seek entry to the most demanding university courses.

Scholarships and Bursaries. Three academic scholarships up to the value of 10% of the annual day fee and three exhibitions up to the value of 5% of the annual day fee are offered to entrants in each First Year and Third Year. Two further academic scholarships up to 10% of the annual day fee and two exhibitions up to the value of 5% of the annual day fee are offered to Sixth Form entrants. Means-tested Sixth Form bursaries providing up to 100% of annual day fees are also available. Pocklington School awards a maximum of six music scholarships annually, with three specifically intended for students joining the school at 13+, each valued at 5% of the annual day fee.

Awards are available to internal and external candidates. Tenure of all awards is for the duration of the pupil's time at Pocklington School subject to satisfactory performance and behaviour.

Fees per term (2018–2019). Day £4,873, Boarding £9,497, 5-Day Boarding £8,735, Extended Day Pupil (1–5 nights per week) £197–£923.

Charitable status. The Pocklington School Foundation is a Registered Charity, number 529834.

Chair of Governors: Mr T A Stephenson, MA, FCA

Headmaster: Mr T Seth, MA Cantab

Head of Pocklington Prep School: Mr I D Wright, BSc Hons, PGCE, NPQH

The Portsmouth Grammar School

High Street, Portsmouth, Hants PO1 2LN

Tel: 023 9236 0036
Fax: 023 9236 4256
email: admissions@pgs.org.uk
website: www.pgs.org.uk
Twitter: @PGS_1732
Facebook: @ThePortsmouthGrammarSchool

Motto: *Praemia Virtutis Honores*

The Portsmouth Grammar School is a happy and vibrant independent school located in the historic heart of Portsmouth and only a few minutes' walk from the Solent.

The support our pupils experience at PGS and the challenges they encounter have a shared purpose: that each individual should be happy and successful, in that order. In the spirit of our founder, Dr William Smith, we seek to provide excellence in all areas of school life and encourage our girls and boys to think not only about where they will be at 18 but where they aspire to be at 25. Portsmouth is, after all, a city concerned with destinations.

The Portsmouth Grammar School is a fully co-educational school which assumed full independent status in 1976. There are 1,143 pupils in the Senior School and 357 pupils in the Junior School. There are no boarders.

The Nursery School offers outstanding care and education for boys and girls from 2½ to 4 years old in a safe and stimulating environment. Currently there are 56 children in the Nursery.

The Junior School for boys and girls aged 4–11, is a thriving, dynamic and popular school, committed to giving pupils the best possible start to their educational lives. Juniors benefit greatly from an increase in specialist teaching and from learning in subject-specific rooms. This allows the school to immerse pupils in a stimulating and connected curriculum that combines the learning of skills and knowledge with an understanding and ability of how best to apply them. The main ages of entry are 4 and 7 however there are places available for intermediate entry. (*For further details see entry in IAPS section.*)

Since September 2015, pupils in the Junior School no longer sit the 11+ entrance assessments for entry in to the Senior School. The Headmaster of the Junior School will recommend entry to the Senior School following its programme of continuous assessment.

Senior School. Admission is by the School's Entrance Assessment at 11+ and at 13+. Entrants at 13 are usually pre-tested at 11 to accommodate high demand for places. Pupils are admitted at other ages, should vacancies occur, subject to assessments and satisfactory reports from previous schools. Admission to the Sixth Form, which numbers 352, is subject to satisfactory standard at GCSE and interview.

Curriculum. Pupils are educated for life as well as for academic achievements through initiatives such as The Portsmouth Curriculum in Year 7 and the wide-ranging General Studies Programme in the Sixth Form. After GCSE, pupils enter the Sixth Form, which seeks to prepare pupils for the challenges of university education and subsequent competitive employment. Pupils have the choice of either studying for the International Baccalaureate Diploma or A Levels. A Level subjects include: Art, Biology, Business Studies, Chemistry, Classical Civilisation, Design and Technology, Drama, Economics, Electronics, English Literature, French, Geography, German, Government and Politics, Greek, History, Italian, Latin, Mathematics, Further Mathematics, Music, Physical Education, Psychology, Religious Studies and Spanish. The General Studies Programme is mainly taught by outside professionals and is aimed at widening personal and academic horizons as well as offering some further academic opportunities. The Sixth Form prepares candidates for entry to Higher Education, and the Universities and Careers Department provides excellent support with UCAS applications and close relations with various forms of employment.

Religion. The Portsmouth Grammar is the Cathedral school. However, Religious Instruction, given in accordance with the principles of the Christian faith, remains, in accordance with a long tradition of latitudinarianism, non-denominational. The School has a Chaplain.

Pastoral Care. Pastoral Care is of paramount importance. On entry to the school pupils are allocated to one of four Houses. Heads of House and their House Tutors are responsible for the pastoral and academic welfare of all pupils, supported by Heads of Year, and provide a focal point for communication between teaching staff and parents. Particular emphasis is placed on the triangular relationship between pupil, parents and teaching staff, including a programme of telephone calls from tutors to new parents in which all senior staff and the Headmaster have a monitoring role.

Games. Rugby football, netball and hockey are the main games in Winter and Spring, cricket, tennis, athletics and rounders in the Summer. Cross-country running, squash, judo, badminton, gymnastics, basketball, aerobics, swimming and sailing are also available. The School has enjoyed national success in recent years in sports such as football, hockey, netball, athletics, cricket and rounders.

The Co-Curriculum. There are significant opportunities for co-curricular involvement at the school. Music, Sport, Drama, CCF and Outdoor Pursuits including Ten Tors and participation in the Duke of Edinburgh's Award scheme, play a huge role in the development of pupils and provide them with a diverse and popular range of activities. Service to the local community and charity work is also an important feature of the school's ethos. Many clubs and societies cater for a considerable range of co-curricular interests from the Model United Nations to Wildlife Club. Numerous expeditions, holiday activities and trips are actively encouraged and include many foreign tours for sports teams and music ensembles. The School has a flourishing exchange scheme with French, German and Spanish schools. Sports teams have recently gone on tour to Singapore, Malaysia and South Africa. Recent expeditions have seen pupils travel to Madagascar, Uganda, Cambodia, Argentina and Cuba.

Fees per term (2018–2019). Senior School £5,317; Junior School £3,411–£3,784. (Fees quoted include direct debit discount.)

Scholarships and Bursaries. An extensive programme of scholarships and means-tested bursaries is offered in the Senior School from 11–18 years and we are extremely grateful to all those, whose generosity makes it possible for a growing number of pupils to join PGS each year regardless of their financial situation.

Scholarships are non means-tested and awarded to recognise exceptional academic or co-curricular ability. Where appropriate, these awards may be augmented by a bursary.

Bursaries are entirely means-tested and reflect the outstanding academic potential of an individual pupil regardless of ability to afford the school's fees.

All candidates are automatically considered for academic scholarships at 11+, 13+ and 16+.

Additionally, scholarships can also be awarded for excellence in Art, Drama, Music and Sport at 13+ and 16+. Existing PGS pupils may also apply for consideration for these awards once they become eligible during their time at the school.

Full details of all scholarships and bursaries are available on the School's website.

Buildings. The School is located within the historic quarter of Portsmouth. The Grade II listed buildings of the Junior and Senior School sit comfortably next to modern developments such as the Bristow-Clavell Science Centre which opened in 2010, and the Sixth Form Centre which opened in September 2014. Construction of a new Performing Arts Centre is due to start in 2019. The School sports facilities are located at the Hilsea Playing Fields and include an all-weather pitch and Sports Pavilion.

Honours. In 2018 four pupils took up places at Oxbridge. Over 90% of pupils achieved places at their choice of university subjects going on to be studied including Computer Science with Games Engineering, Anthropology, Criminology, Product Design, Law and Natural Sciences. Seven pupils have places to study medicine or veterinary science and twelve are going on to read engineering courses. Sportsmen include England Cricket Captain Wally Hammond, Athletics International Roger Black, and Paralympian Ross Morrison. Military distinction in abundance, including 3 VCs (one the first VC submariner), several Admirals, Generals and Air Marshals. Medicine is also a continuing theme – from pioneer ophthalmologist James Ware to Viagra researcher Ian Osterloh. Arts are well and diversely represented: dramatist Simon Gray, poet Christopher Logue, novelist James Clavell, film director James Bobin, Sky News entertainment reporter Joe Michalczuk, cathedral organist Christopher Walsh, and pop singer Paul Jones. Civil Servants, Judges and barristers galore, plus entrepreneur industrialist Alan Bristow.

Old Portmuthian Club. This maintains links with former pupils not least by holding reunions in Portsmouth, London and Oxford, and is enhanced by its relationship with the School's Development Office.

Charitable status. The Portsmouth Grammar School is a Registered Charity, number 1063732. It exists to provide education for boys and girls.

Governing Body:
Chairman: Mr W J B Cha, BA
Vice Chairman: Mrs M Scott, BSc
Mr M R Coffin, BA Econ, FCA
Mr N D Latham, CBE, MSc, CEng, FIMarEST, MIMechE
Mr P Parkinson, BA Hons, Dip Arch Dist Thes
Mrs A Stanford
Dr M C Grossel, BSc, MA, PhD
Mrs K Bishop, BA
The Revd Canon Dr Edmund Newey
Mr Howard Tuckett
S Gingell, MSc, DIPSW
His Honour Judge Lodder, QC, LLB
The Revd Canon E Newey, MA, PhD
Mr J Nicholls, BA, ACA, FCT
Dr S Ross, MB ChB, MRCGP

Senior Team:

Head: Dr A K Cotton, BA, MSt, DPhil, MA Ed

Second Master: Mr B P H Charles, BA, FRSA
Deputy Head (Academic): Mr B C T Goad, BSc
Deputy Head (Co-curriculum and External Relations): Mr C J Hamlet, MA
Assistant Head (Sixth Form): Mr L F Rees, BA
Assistant Head (Teaching and Learning): Dr G T Purves, MPhys, PhD
Assistant Head (Head of Middle School): Mrs J Jackson, BSc
Assistant Head (Head of Upper School): Miss F E A Bush, BA
Bursar: Mr S R Merriam, BSc, CDir, FLoD

Senior School:
‡ *Senior Teacher*
§ *Part-time*

Mr J M I Addyman, BSc (*Mathematics, KS3 Mathematics Coordinator*)
Mr D P Ager, BSc, MSc (*Mathematics, Timetabler*)
Mr L A Ansell, BSc, MA (*Design & Technology*)
Mrs L C Ashdown, MA (*Mathematics, Second in Department*)
Mr J D Baker, BSc (*§Mathematics*)
Mrs E E Bell, BA (*English, KS3 English Coordinator*)
Mrs M C Bodman-Flack, BA (*Head of Design & Technology*)
Ms A E Bolton, BA, MA (*Classics*)
Mr G Brown, FLCM, LLCM TD, ALCM (*Head of Brass*)
Ms S H Brunner, MA (*§English, Deputy Head of Sixth Form and Head of Ignite!*)
Miss L V Burden, BA, MA (*Head of English*)
‡Mr J E Burkinshaw, BA (*English, Head of Careers and Universities*)
Mrs S A Burkinshaw, BA (*§English*)
Miss L J Burton, MA (*Geography and Geology*)
Mrs A S Casillas-Cross, BA, MA (*History, CAS Coordinator, Deputy Head of Smith House*)
Miss A J Chaplin, BA (*Head of Athletics*)
Miss E F Chilcott, BSc (*Biology*)
Mrs K E Clark, BSc, MSc (*Biology and Chemistry*)
Miss I M Clark, BA (*Head of Netball*)
Mrs A M L Clarke, MA (*§Classics*)
Mrs R H Clay, BA (*History, Head of Whitcombe House*)
Miss R L Close, BSc (*Economics and Business*)
Mr N E Colburn, BA (*§Economics and Business*) [Maternity Cover]
Miss K M Corney, MA (*§History*) [Maternity Cover]
Mr J A Cotton, BA, MA (*Assistant Director of Music*)
Mrs A Cross, BTh, MA (*Philosophy and Religious Studies, Deputy Head of Careers and Universities*)
Ms D J Curteis, MA Ed, FDE SNE LD, APC SpLD AMBDA (*Head of Learning Support*)
Mr S J Curwood, BEd (*Head of Cricket, Head of Rounders, Deputy Head of Latter House*)
Mr S J Dean, BEd (*Mathematics*)
Mr S G Disley, BSc (*Physics*)
‡Mr D T Doyle, BA (*Modern Languages, Head of Latter House*)
Mrs M G Dray, BA, HDipEd (*Learning Support*)
Mr J J Elphick-Smith, BA, MA (*English*) [Maternity Cover]
Mrs L C Erricker, BA (*§History and Politics, Deputy Head of Smith House*) [Maternity Cover]
Mrs M Fake, BSc (*Head of Physics*)
Mr P R Fisher, BA (*§Economics and Business*)
Ms R H Fry, BEd (*Learning Support*)
Mr P M Gamble, BA (*Head of French*)
Mr W P Gammon, BA (*PE and Games, Assistant Head of Hockey, Coordinator of House Sport*)
Mr J R C Gillies, BSc (*Mathematics, Head of Grant House*)
Mrs C A Gozalbez-Guerola, BA (*§Modern Languages*)
Mrs K I Greenslade, BSc (*§PE and Games*)
Miss P A Hardisty, BSc, MA (*Biology, Coordinator of Pupil Councils*)
‡Mr S J Harris, MA (*Chemistry, Surmaster, CCF Contingent Commander, DofE Manager*)
Ms B C Hart, MA (*English, Deputy Head of Whitcombe House*)
Mr S D Hawkswell, BA (*Head of Tennis, Head of Barton House*)
Miss S Heath, BMus (*Head of Academic Music*)
Mr G R J Hemmings, MA (*Director of Music*)
Mr J K Herbert, BSc (*Physics*)

Dr M R Howson, BSc, PhD, CChem, MRSC (*Head of Chemistry, Head of Science*)

Revd S C Hunt, BA (*Philosophy and Religious Studies, School Chaplain*)

Mrs J Ingamells, ARCM (*Head of Strings*)

Miss K A Jones, BA (*History*)

Miss K Kingsley GRSM, LRAM (§*Music*)

Mrs T A Knott, BSc, MSc (§*Geography and Geology*)

Mrs E M Kirby, MA (§*English*)

Mrs P I Langtry, BA (*Modern Languages*)

Mr S D Lavery, BSc, MSc (*PE and Games, Head of Athletic Development and Cricket Performance*)

Mr A D Leach, BSc (*Head of Hockey*)

Mr D D Lee, BSc (*Mathematics and Computing*)

‡Mr S Lemieux, MA (*Head of History and Politics*)

Ms S Leslie, BA, MA (*Interim Head of Learning Support*)

‡Miss H V Linnett, BSc (§*PE and Games, Deputy Head of Sixth Form*)

‡Mr B P Lister, BA (*Head of Classics*)

Mrs F E Lyon, MChem (*Physics, Coordinator of Physical Science, Bronze DofE Coordinator*)

Mr D J E Lyons, BA, MSc (*Head of Rugby*)

Mr S L McAll, BSc (*Biology*)

Mr S A McLean, BSc (*Physics*)

Mr T A MacFarlane, BSc (*Mathematics*)

Miss C A Martin, BA (*Drama, Head of Summers House*)

Mr A S Milford, BA (*History and Politics, Second in Department, Deputy Head of Sixth Form*) [Maternity Cover]

‡Mrs J L K Morgan, BA (*Philosophy and Religious Studies, Head of Pastoral Curriculum*)

Mr J H Murphy, BA (*Head of German*)

Mrs R L Nash, BSc (*Mathematics, Deputy Head of Upper School, Silver DofE Coordinator*)

Ms F J Nicholson, BSc, MPH (§*Geography*)

Mr J J O'Meara, BA (*German*)

Dr P A O'Neil, BSc, PhD (*Chemistry*)

Mr S Page, BA (§*Modern Languages*)

Mrs S E Palmer, BA, Dip SpLD (§*Learning Support*)

Mr R A Peebles, BA (*Head of Art*)

Mr A W Powell, BA (*Interim Head of Psychology, Coordinator of Aspirant Medics*)

Mrs K C Rees, BSc (§*Design & Technology*)

Mr M P Richardson, BA, MA (*English*)

‡Dr R J I Richmond, MA, PhD (*Head of Philosophy and Religious Studies*)

Mr J F Robinson, LLB (*Director of Drama*)

Mr D P Rogers, BSc (*Biology*)

Mrs A V Russell, BSc (*Chemistry, Coordinator of Internal Examinations*)

Mr G J Ryan, BSc (*Biology, Deputy Head of Upper School*)

Miss K Sanders, BA (*Economics and Business, Head of Hawkey House*)

Mrs H E Sands, BSc (*Geography and Geology*)

Mr A J Seddon, BSc (*PE and Games, Head of Eastwood House*)

Mrs E E Seddon, BSc (*PE & Games, Head of Hawkey House*) [Maternity Cover]

Mrs C D E Smith, BSc (*Chemistry*)

Ms L A M Smith, BA (*Philosophy and Religious Studies, Deputy Head of Middle School*)

Dr M J Smith, MChem, DPhil (*Chemistry, Second in Department*)

Mrs S Smith, BSc, MA (§*Mathematics, Deputy Head of Examinations*)

Mr T Spreafico, BA (*Economics and Business*)

Mr H C Stayte, BA (*Head of Digital Learning*)

Dr P G Stephenson, BSc, PhD (*Head of Biology*)

Miss E F Stretch, BA (*Director in Residence*)

Mr R E Stewart, BSc (*Director of Sport*)

Miss S L Stewart, BSc (*Head of Geography and Geology, Coordinator of ITT*)

‡Mr O G Stone, BA (*Head of Modern Languages*)

Miss L Szmid, BA (*Drama*)

‡Mr S C Taylor, MA (*Classics, Director of IB*)

Miss K G Thomas, MA (*Mathematics*)

Dr N Thomas, BSc, PhD (*Biology*)

Mrs R J Thomas-Snell, BA (*Second in English, Head of English*) [Maternity Cover]

Mr G T de Trafford, BA, MA (*Physics, Head of Smith House*)

Mrs S Tredwell, MA (§*Modern Languages*)

Mrs J L Tweddle, BSc (*Head of Physical Education*)

Mrs J M H Tyldesley, BSc (§*Biology*)

Mr V Valera-Ramiro, BA (*Modern Languages*)

‡Mr N G Waters, BA (*Modern Languages*)

Mrs W Whitaker, CertEd (*Design & Technology*)

Mrs D J Willcocks, BA, AKC (§*Modern Languages*)

Mr S P H Willcocks, BA (*Art*)

Mrs L A Williams, BA (*Art*)

Mr C M Williamson, MA, MSci (*Chemistry, Deputy Head of Grant House*)

Mr I C Wilson, MA (§*Mathematics*)

Mr J Winship, BEd (*Design & Technology*)

Mrs K E Winship, BA (*Head of Mathematics*)

Ms A J Wood, BA (*Head of Psychology*)

Mrs M J Worley, BA, MSc (*Head of Economics and Business*)

Ms R L Yates, BA, MBA (*Economics and Business*) [Maternity Cover]

Modern Languages Assistants:
§Mme E Doize
§Mrs M Chapero, BA
§Frau N Bühler
§Mrs M Ciraldo

Cathedral Organist and Master of the Choristers:
Mr S Gunga, BA, MMus, ARCO
Dr D J C Price, HonD Mus, GMus TCL, FGCM, Hon FASC

GAP Student Staff:
Mr P Ashdown
Mr E Clarke
Mr P Ellis
Mr J Furniss-Roe
Mr J Martin
Miss A Palethorpe
Mr O Wilson

Technical Support Staff:

Science Technicians:
§Mrs J Corke
Dr L Gray, PhD
Mr I Lowther, BSc
Miss Z Munday, MSc
Mrs C Rollins
Mrs M Smith, BSc
§Mrs F Truluck-Crocker, BSc

Theatre Technician: Mr L Tench, BA

Languages Technician: §Mr K Hodgson

Art Technician: Mr N Llewellyn-Thomas

Design & Technology: Mr D J MacDonald

Learning Support:
Learning Support Administrator: §Mrs T P Tredray, BA, ACMA, MBA
Higher Level Teaching Assistant: Mrs E Hunt, BA
Learning Support Teaching Assistant: Miss T Ellison

Visiting LAMDA Speech and Drama Staff:

Visiting Drama Staff:
Ms J de Jongh, ALCM, Dip GSA
Ms G Meadows, BEd

Cover Staff/Invigilators:
§Mrs H J Brine-Howe, BA
§Mrs A Waters, BA, Dip HE
§Mrs N A Watson BA

Examinations Office:
Assistant Head of Examinations: §Mrs D Valentine, BA

Junior School and Nursery

Head of the Junior School Mr P S Hopkinson, BA, PGCE
Deputy Head Mr J Ashcroft, BSc, PGCE

Assistant Heads:
Mrs P Giles, BA, PGCE (*Assistant Head Co-curriculum;
    Head of Years 5 & 6*)
Mr C Williams, BA, QTS (*Assistant Head Academic*)
Head of Nursery: Mrs K Moore, BA QTS

Academic Staff:
Mrs J M Albuery, BEd (*PRS Leader*)
Mrs L Atkinson, BSc, PGCE
Mrs A Ayres, BA, PGCE (*Writing Leader, Years 1–4*)
Mr G Brown, FLCM, LLCM TD, ALCM (*Head of Brass*)
Mrs J Budgen, BSc, PGCE (*Geography Leader, Years 1–4*)
Mrs S Carlin, BA, PGCE (*Reception Leader*)
Miss E Carter, BA QTS (*History Leader, Years 1–4*)
Mr A Chappell, BA QTS (*Director of Sport & Physical
    Education*)
Mrs L Curtis, BA, PGCE (*Director of Drama*)
Miss A Davies (*Games*)
Mrs L Dean, BA, PGCE (*Year 6 Leader; English Leader,
    Years 5 & 6; UJS Librarian*)
Mr C Ellis, BSc, QTS (*Resources Leader; Digital Learning
    Leader*)
Mrs R Evans, BA, QTS (*Senior Teacher, Head of Lower
    Juniors; House Leader, Juniors; PSHE Leader, Juniors*)
Mrs V Francis, BA, QTS (*Year 1 Leader; Computing
    Leader, Infants*)
Mrs J E Ingamells, ARCM (*Head of Strings*)
Mr M Le-Clercq (*PE & Games*)
Mr S Le-Clercq (*Games*)
Mr E Lydall, BA QTS, PGCE, MA (*Games*)
Mrs E Lydall, BA, PGCE (*Head of Girls' Games*)
Miss J McFadzean, BA, QTS (*PE & Games*)
Mrs K Martin, BA, GTP (*Design Technology Leader,
    Juniors*)
Mrs J L Millward, BEd (*Senior Teacher, Head of Infants;
    Reading Leader, Years 1–4; PSHE Leader, Infants*)
Mrs F Nash, BEd (*Assistant Director of Music*)
Mrs J Neilson, BA, MA, PGCE (*Year 3 Leader; Able,
    Gifted & Talented Leader*)
Mrs K Park, BA, PGCE
Mrs E Peskett, GGSM, PG Dip, RNCM (*violin*)
Mrs A Porter, BEd, Cert SpLD (*Learning Support*)
Mrs S Powlesland, BA, PGCE (*French Leader, Juniors*)
Mrs M Price, BEd
Mrs A Reader, BA, QTS (*Year 5 Leader; Maths Leader,
    Years 5 & 6; SMSCD Leader, Juniors*)
Mrs C S Sayers, BEd
Mrs P Sellars, BA, QTS (*Year 2 Leader, Maths Leader,
    Years 1–4*)
Mrs E G Sharrock, BMus Perf, LRAM ('*cello, String
    Scheme*)
Mrs V Shoebridge, BA, PGCE (*Science Leader, Year 1–4*)
Mrs P Spodzieja [Crysell], MMus, PG Dip
Mrs T Squire, BA, PGCE, SpLD (*Learning Support
    Coordinator*)

Mrs L Summerskill, BEd (*Art Leader, Juniors*)
Mr S Sykes, BA, QTS (*Geography & History Leader,
    Years 5 & 6*)
Mrs N R Townsend, BA, QTS Dance and Education (*Year
    4 Leader; Dance Leader, Juniors*)
Mrs S Trinkwon, PGCPP, BL, PGCE
Mrs S P Tyacke, BEd (*House Leader, Infants; Art Leader,
    Infants*)
Mrs S Webb, BA, PGCE (*Design Technology & Food &
    Nutrition Leader, Infants*)
Mr I Webber, BA Ed (*Director of Music*)
Mrs L Younger, BSc, PGCE

Assistants in The Junior School:

Miss K Bradley	Mrs S Jennings
Mrs K Broster	Mrs M Millerchip
Mrs S Buckett	Mrs K Moffitt
Miss H Green	Mrs J Northey
Mrs K Hinks	Mrs S Paterson
Mrs B Holloway	Mrs C Shahran
Mrs M Hopkinson	Mrs L Staley
Mrs N Hutton	Mrs C White
Mrs C Iliffe	Miss J Woodcock

Gap Year Assistants:
Miss Elizabeth Jones
Miss Megan Kennell
Mr Edan Moorhouse

Assistants in the Nursery:
Ms R Adderley (*Holiday Care Leader*)
Mrs R Cameron
Miss J Colley
Miss C Girling
Mrs W Heyes (*Nursery Administrator*)
Mrs S Hillier
Miss M Jarvis
Mrs S Johnson
Mrs S Newton (*Curriculum Leader*)
Mrs N Poland
Ms C Porter
Mrs M Sandford (*Toddler Group Leader*)
Mrs G Skingsley
Mrs S Smy
Mrs M Stone
Ms J Todman
Mrs S Wahid

Visiting Music Staff:
Mr R Blanken, GRNCM, ARCM (*performance, clarinet
    and saxophone*)
Miss L Cronin, MA (*voice*)
Mr M Davis, LTCL (*trombone*)
Mr K Dredge (*drumkit*)
Miss H Fenton, BA Hons, PGCE (*piano*)
Mrs J Flatman, BA Hons, LRSM, PGCE (*clarinet and
    recorder*)
Mrs T Foster (*piano*)
Mr M Frampton, LLB (*double bass*)
Canon Peter Gould, GRSM, FRCO, ARAM, LRAM,
    ARCM, Hon MMus, Hon FGCM, ARSCM (*organ*)
Mrs B Holton (*French horn*)
Mr N Ingamells (*bassoon and saxophone*)
Miss K Kingsley, GRSM, LRAM (*Head of Keyboard
    Studies*)
Mr A Mendoza, BA Mexico, ACS Holland (*percussion*)
Mrs R Musgrave (*voice*)
Mr I Naylor (*trumpet*)
Mrs L Peskett, GGSM, PG Dip RNCN (*violin*)
Mrs A Saunders, BA Hons (*classical guitar and piano*)
Mrs S Towner, ARCM (*cello*)
Mrs C Wall, MMus, FTCL, FLCM, LRAM (*flute*)
Ms P M Wilcockson, GGSM, PGCE (*piano and flute*)

Visiting Speech and Drama Staff:
Mrs J de Jongh, ALCM, Dip GSA

Princethorpe College

Princethorpe, Rugby, Warwickshire CV23 9PX

Tel: 01926 634200
Fax: 01926 633365
email: post@princethorpe.co.uk
website: www.princethorpe.co.uk
Twitter: @PrincethorpeCol
Facebook: @princethorpecollege

Princethorpe College is a Catholic, co-educational, HMC independent day school and welcomes members of all faiths and backgrounds. The school was founded as a boys' school in 1957 in Leamington Spa by the congregation of the Missionaries of the Sacred Heart (MSC), moving to its present site, a former Benedictine monastery, in 1966. The College became co-educational in 1996, and in September 2001 formed a partnership with Crackley Hall School in Kenilworth in order to provide continuous education from 2 to 18 years. A further merger took place in September 2016 with the Crescent School, Rugby. All schools are members of an independent trust – The Princethorpe Foundation.

Number in School. The school has around 900 day pupils from 11 to 18 years with some 200 in the Sixth Form. An extensive network of private coaches transports pupils from a wide area.

Aims. The College provides a caring, Christian environment for children where their needs can be met and their talents, confidence and self-esteem developed. There is a healthy balance between freedom and structure and an emphasis on self-discipline through responsibility and trust, which develops confidence and independence.

The College draws on a rich tradition of Catholic teaching and the spirituality of the Missionaries of the Sacred Heart, whose ethos is central to its character. In welcoming families of a variety of faiths and none, the school community is a living example of ecumenism. The College motto, *Christus Regnet* – let Christ reign – is a reminder of Christ's love, service, forgiveness and generosity of spirit.

Academic. A broad-based, stimulating curriculum satisfies a wide range of ability and fosters a love of learning. A favourable pupil to teacher ratio, permitting personal attention, contributes to impressive value-added achievements. High fliers are stretched and provided with intellectually challenging assignments through our da Vinci Programme, ensuring that they achieve at the highest possible levels. The curriculum is well supported by a magnificent library and ICT. Qualified specialists give tuition to pupils with special educational needs.

Pupils in Years 7 to 9 have a broad-based curriculum which avoids early specialisation and usually go on to take nine or ten GCSEs.

Supervised homework and free extended day are offered until 6.00 pm.

The Sixth Form. Students in the Sixth Form are prepared for A Level examinations after which the vast majority proceed to university. The Head of Sixth Form and the team of tutors monitor the academic progress of Sixth Formers through regular discussions with the students and their teachers. Visits to university Open Days, together with professional careers advice enables students to make the best choices about their next stage of education.

Our Sixth Form enrichment programme puts a strong emphasis on the acquisition of key skills and the education of the whole person. Sixth Formers are offered residential outward bound courses, training programmes and retreats which provide an opportunity for reflection and exploration, to develop a mature and balanced perspective. Guest lecturers, debates and trips all enhance Sixth Form life.

All Sixth Formers enjoy privileges and have the responsibilities of leadership and example; certain members are elected to perform prefectorial duties. Prefects attend a leadership course and learn valuable management skills. They organise activities for younger pupils and chair the School Council, which offers a forum for lively discussion and gives the students an influential voice in the running of the College. The House Captains have a pivotal role in the organisation of inter-house events.

Princethorpe Diploma. Open to all Sixth Form students the innovative Princethorpe Diploma brings together six components (work experience, community and ethos, service to others, extra-curricular, academic studies and attendance and punctuality) that we believe are critical in today's world, helping our students leave us as mature, confident, resilient, well-rounded young adults, with a strong set of moral values to guide them through adult life.

Careers. The Careers Advice Programme commences in Year 9 and regular tutorials are held concentrating on option subject choices and developing careers awareness. Interview technique is developed and students are assisted with work experience placements which are undertaken at the end of Year 10 and Lower Sixth. The College also holds a biennial Careers Fair for pupils in Year 10 to Sixth Form and their parents.

Art & Design. A feature which immediately strikes all visitors to the College is the outstanding display of canvases. Superb examination results and successes in national competitions are commonplace. The study of drawing, painting, graphics and ceramics are central and they are enhanced by using the work of great artists as stimulus material.

Technology includes Food, Graphics, Resistant Materials, Textiles and Electronics. Pupils can work with a variety of materials, realising their technical designs in the well-resourced workshops, which includes CAD/CAM facilities.

Music and Drama. Music is studied by all pupils in their first three years and as an option at GCSE and A Level. The College choir gives regular performances and tours. Many pupils learn instruments and are encouraged to join the orchestra. Peripatetic staff offer tuition in most instruments. There is a state-of-the-art studio with digital recording facilities for Music Technology and there is an acclaimed Binns organ in the magnificent Chapel built by Peter Paul Pugin.

The College has a newly refurbished theatre and regular productions are staged including musicals and revues. Productions involve a large number of pupils and staff and provide an excellent way for pupils of different years to get to know each other. There are thriving Dance and Drama Clubs. Theatre Studies is offered in the Sixth Form.

Physical Education. All pupils participate in games and Physical Education classes. Physical Education can also be studied as an examination subject at GCSE and A Level as can a BTEC in Physical Education. The major sports are rugby, netball, hockey, cricket, rounders, tennis and athletics; they are run in tandem with badminton, soccer, squash, basketball and trampolining.

The Sports Centre has a sports hall, fitness gym and a climbing wall. Extensive outdoor facilities include an internationally recognised cross-country course, floodlit all-weather pitch, tennis courts and over sixty acres of games pitches.

Sports Clubs include Rugby, Football, Hockey, Netball, Climbing Wall, Badminton, Archery, Golf, Fitness, Running, Trampolining, Cycling, Athletics, Rounders and Tennis.

Co-curricular Activities. There is always a wide range of clubs, societies and activities such as Art, Beekeeping, Bell-ringing, Book Club, Brass Group, Bridge, Chamber Music, Chess, Choir, Computing, Cookery, Craft, Creative Writing, Dance, Darts, Debating, Drama, Electric Car Club, Green Team, History, Jazz Band, Mindfulness, MFL – French, Spanish and German, Orchestra, Photography, Psychology, Robotics, School of Rock, Science, String Group, Textiles, Wind Band, Young Designers, Youth Chaplaincy and Youth St Vincent de Paul. The Duke of Edinburgh's Award, World Challenge, Camps International and Outward Bound courses are also offered. The Arts Society provides a cultural programme of lectures, poetry evenings, music recitals and play readings.

Admissions. Admission is by examination, in November, for entry the following September, generally at 11 and 13 and at other ages as space allows. Students from other schools join the Sixth Form after their GCSE courses.

Scholarships. There is a variety of Scholarships available for particularly able or talented candidates ranging from Academic, Art and Music to All-Rounder. Additionally, for the Sixth Form there are Academic, Art, Music, Organ and Sports Scholarships available. Scholarships to a maximum reduction of 50% of tuition fees are on offer.

Academic Scholarships: Candidates applying for entry in Years 7, 8, 9 and 10 will be considered automatically for an academic scholarship when taking the Entrance Examination.

All Rounder Scholarships: Sometimes there are students who are both academically able and gifted in a variety of areas and the most outstanding of these can be awarded an All Rounder Scholarship. Supportive evidence is required, such as references from team coaches or activity leaders.

Art Scholarships: Candidates must submit a portfolio and attend an Art Scholarship day. Further details and an Art Scholarship application form are available from the Registrar.

Music Scholarships – Instrumental and Choral: Candidates must attend an audition. Further details and a Music Scholarship application form are available from the Registrar.

Sixth Form Academic Scholarships: Sixth Form Academic Scholarships are open to all external candidates who are expected achieve 9–7 grades at GCSE. Applicants will be invited to the Academic Scholarships Day where they will sit a Verbal Reasoning examination and have an interview with the Headmaster. More details are available from the Registrar.

Sixth Form Sport Scholarships: Senior Sport Scholarships may be awarded to internal or external candidates entering the Sixth Form. Full details are available from the Registrar.

Sixth Form Music – Instrumental, Choral and Organ Scholarships: Candidates must attend an audition. Full details are available from the Registrar. In the Sixth Form there is also an Organ Scholarship of up to 50% of tuition fees available to candidates who have a high level of ability and are committed and enthusiastic performers. Again details are available from the Registrar.

Fees per term (2018–2019). £4,231 excluding transport and meals. Instrumental tuition, external examinations and some targeted support for those with learning needs are charged as extras.

Charitable status. The Princethorpe Foundation is a Registered Charity, number 1087124. It exists solely for the education of children.

Governing Body:
Chair of Trustees Mrs Elizabeth Griffin, BSc, PGCE, CTC

Trustees:
Quintin Cornforth, BSc
Mike Fletcher BSc
Charlie Jenkinson, BA, CIPS, MILT
Mrs Elizabeth Kenward, BA, PGCE, CTC
Mrs Cecilia Lane
Mrs Pat Lines, Cert Ed
Mrs Caroline McGrory, MA Oxon, Jurisprudence, LPC
Ms Teresa McNamara, BPhil, Cert Ed, CTC
Colin Russell, IEng, ACIBSE, MBA
Kieron Shaw, MBE, MSc, FCIS
Commodore Bernard Warner

Staff:

Headmaster: Ed Hester, MA Oxon, PGCE (*Mathematics*)

Deputy Head – Pastoral: Mrs Beth Sharpe, BSc, PGCE (*Design and Technology*)
Deputy Head – Academic: Dr Michael Reddish, LLB, LLM Harvard, PhD, PGCHE (*Law*)
Assistant Head – Co-curricular: Greg Hunter, BEng, Grad Dip Ed (*Physics*)
Assistant Head – Development: Alex Darkes, BEd
Assistant Head – Director of Digital Strategy: Andy Compton, BA, PGCE, MA (*Modern Languages*)
Assistant Head – Teaching and Learning: Dr Liz Pyne, BA, MA, PGCE, PhD (*History*)
Assistant Head – Marketing, Admissions and Communications and Old Princethorpians Secretary: Mrs Melanie Butler, BA
Head of Sixth Form: Mr Ben Collie, BSc (*Biology*)
Foundation Bursar, Company Secretary and Clerk to the Trustees: Eddie Tolcher, BA, ACIB, MCMI, TechIOSH

Art:
Paul Hubball, BA, PGCE (*Head of Art; also Head of Photography*)
Mrs Rebecca Blunsom-Washbrook, BA, GTP (*also Photography*)
Ms Catherine Gregg, BA, PGCE (*also Design and Technology*)
Mrs Susan Harris, BA, PGCE (*Head of Transition and Induction*)

Careers:
Mrs Jacqui Quinney, BA, PGCE (*Head of Careers*)
Mrs Kerry Low, BA, Dip CG (*Careers Adviser*)
Mike Taylor, BA, PGCE (*Head of Geography; Work Experience*)

Classics:
Mrs Rachel Taylor, BA, QTS (*Joint Head of Classics*)
Dr Melinda Palmer, MA, DPhil Oxon, QTS (*Joint Head of Classics*)

Computer Science:
Adam Depledge, BSc (*Head of Computer Science; also CoRE Programme*)
Mrs Jan Ryalls, BSc, PGCE

CoRE Programme:
Mrs Anne Allen, BSc, PGCE (*Assistant Head of Sixth Form; also Geography*)
Adam Depledge, BSc (*Head of Computer Science*)
Mrs Louise Harrison, BSc, PGCE (*Head of Academic PE*)
Roderick Isaacs, MA Cantab, MA, CertEd (*Assistant Head of Sixth Form; also Religious Studies and Games*)
Kieran McCullough, BA, PGCE (*Director of Ethos; also Religious Studies and Games*)
Mrs Helen Pascoe-Williams, BA, PGCE (*Leader of Learning, Innovation and Character Development; da Vinci Coordinator*)
Adam Rickart, BSc, PGCE (*Head of Psychology and Sociology*)

Design and Technology:
Paul Scopes, BEd, AST (*Head of Design and Technology*)
Ms Catherine Gregg, BA, PGCE (*Also Art*)
Matt Parsons, BA, PGCE (*TA Coordinator*)
Mrs Miranda Porter, BSc, PGCE
Ms Jacqui Scott, BSc, PGCE
Mrs Beth Sharpe, BEd, PGCE (*Deputy Head – Pastoral and Designated Safeguarding Lead*)

Drama and Theatre Studies:
Ms Aileen Cefaliello, BA, PGCE (*Joint Head of Drama and Theatre Studies; also English*)
Miss Vicky Roberts, BA, PGCE (*Joint Head of Drama and Theatre Studies*) [maternity leave]
Mrs Celia Scott, BA, ALA Associate

Visiting (Drama) LAMDA Staff:
Mrs Katherine Buckingham-Underhill, LAMDA
Mrs Chris Carpenter, LAMDA
Ms Fiona McCreath BA, ATCL (*also visiting Music Staff*)
Mrs Mary McDonald, LAMDA

Economics and Business:
Mrs Elizabeth Gane, BA, PGCE (*Head of Economics and Business*)
Mrs Helen Barker, BA, PGCE (*also Geography*)
Mrs Louise Fielding, BA, PGCE
Kenny Owen, BSc (*Head of Austin House; also Games*)

English:
Chris Kerrigan, BA, MA, PGCE (*Head of English*)
Ms Michelle Baker, BA Oxon, PGCE
Mrs Nicola Borman, BA, MA, PGCE, Post Grad Cert in Special Learning Difficulties
Mrs Lisa Challinor, BA, PGCE (*Head of Benet House*)
Miss Rachael Mack, BA (*also Hockey Coach*)
Mrs Fiona Moon, BA, PG Cert Dyslexia and Literacy (*Second in Department; also Special Educational Needs*)
Mrs Jessica Newborough, BA, PGCE (*House Activities Leader*)
Mrs Helen Pascoe-Williams, BA, PGCE (*Leader of Learning, Innovation and Character Development; also da Vinci Coordinator and CoRE Programme*)
Jonathan Washington, MA

Geography:
Mike Taylor, BA, PGCE (*Head of Geography; also Careers – Work Experience*)
Mrs Anne Allen, BSc, PGCE (*Assistant Head of Sixth Form; also CoRE Programme*)
Mrs Helen Baker, BA (*also Economics and Business*)
Stewart Dear, BSc, QTS (*also Games*)
Mrs Sarah Evans, BSc, PGCE

History:
Peter Bucknall, BA, MA (*Head of History; also Head of Rugby*)
Mrs Felicity Coulson, GMus, PGCE (*Peripatetic and Exam Coordinator for Music; History*)
Mrs Katharine Darwood-Bredin, BSc (*Head of Politics; House Activities Coordinator for More; also Games*)
Mrs Tracey Hester, BA Oxon, PGCE
Miss Julia Lindsay, BA, MA, PGCE (*House Activities Coordinator for Fisher; also Politics and Games*)
Dr Liz Pyne, BA, MA, PGCE, PhD (*Assistant Head – Teaching and Learning*)

Law:
Dr Michael Reddish, LLB, LLM, PhD, PGCHE (*Assistant Head – Director of Studies*)
Ms Loretta Jones, BA, PGCE, CPE

Mathematics:
Tomi Owens, MA Cambs, MSc, PGCE (*Head of Mathematics*)

Mrs Karen Bannister, BSc, PGCE
Mrs Christina Baxter, BSc, QTS
Mrs Rachael Beasley, BA, PGCE (*maternity cover*)
Mrs Clare Callaghan, BSc, PGCE (*also Special Educational Needs*)
Mrs Tanya Cowan, BSc, PGCE
Ed Hester, MA Oxon, PGCE (*Headmaster*)
Ms Helen Lewis, BA
Mrs Sharon McBride, BSc, PGCE, ALCM (*KS5 Mathematics Coordinator*)
Ms Davinya Munford, BSc, PGCE
William Uglow, BSc, MA, Dip ABRSM (*KS3 Mathematics Coordinator*)

Modern Languages:
Mrs Stella Keenan, MA, PGCE (*Head of Modern Languages; Spanish Subject Leader and French*)
Mrs Lourdes Camargo-Mantas (*Spanish Assistant*)
Andy Compton, BA, MA, PGCE (*Assistant Head – Director of Digital Strategy*)
Mrs Finola Coy, BA, PGCE, QTS (*German*)
Mrs Suzanne Ellis, BA, PGCE, Cert TESOL (*French Subject Leader; also Second in Department; German*)
Miss Anna Fennell-McLoughlin, BA, PGCE [maternity cover]
Mrs Bérénice Galano, Licence LLCE Anglais (*French and Spanish*)
Mrs Mariana Hunton, MA (*Cambs*), QTS (*Spanish and French*)
Mrs Katherine Parsons, BA, MA, PGCE (*Spanish*)
Miss Charlotte Verleure (*French; French Assistant; House Activities Coordinator for Austin*)

Music:
Gil Cowlishaw, BMus (*Director of Music*)
Mrs Alison Wakeley, BMus, MMus, PGCE

Visiting Music Staff:
Mrs Patricia Bach, BA, PGCE (*Flute*)
Mrs Felicity Coulson, GMus PGCE (*Peripatetic and Exam Coordinator for Music; also History; Flute, Oboe, Clarinet and Saxophone*)
Tom Durham, BMus (*Guitar*)
Mrs Jane Ebbon, BA, PGCE (*Saxophone, Clarinet and Double Reeds*)
Miss Jodie Fisher, ATCL (*Brass*)
Andrew Hughes, ABSM (*Violin and Viola*)
Mrs Joanna Kunda-Jedynak, MA (*Vocal Studies*)
Ms Fiona McCreath, BA, ATCL (*Vocal Studies*)
Adrian Moore, BA, ARCO (*Organ and Piano*)
Matthew Prior, BMus (*Classical and Electric Guitar*)
Mrs Abigail Rhodes, MA Oxon, LLCM, FLCM, ADPA (*Vocal Studies*)
Alan Wickett (*Drum Kit and Percussion*)

Photography:
Paul Hubball, BA, PGCE (*Head of Photography; also Head of Art*)
Mrs Rebecca Blunsom-Washbrook, BA, GTP (*also Art*)

Physical Education and Games:
Neil McCollin, BA, QTS (*Foundation Director of Sport; also Coordinator of Elite Sports Programme*)
Will Bower, BSc, Post Grad Dip with QTS (*Head of Outdoor Education*)
Miss Holly Brookes (*Trampoline Coach*)
Peter Bucknall, BA, MA (*Head of Rugby; Head of History*)
Ms Hannah Carminati, BSc, QTS (*House Activities Coordinator for Benet; also Primary School Sport Liaison*)
Ms Suzanne Cox, MSc (*Trampoline Coach*)

Mrs Katharine Darwood-Bredin, BSc, GTP (*Head of Politics; House Activities Coordinator for More and History*)

Stewart Dear, BSc, QTS (*also Geography*)

Stuart Friswell (*Rugby Coach*)

Mrs Louise Harrison, BSc, PGCE (*Head of Academic PE and CoRE Programme*)

Ross Holtom, BA (*in charge of BTEC Sport*)

Rod Isaacs, MA (*Cantab*), MA, Cert Ed (*Assistant Head of Sixth Form; also CoRE Programme and Religious Studies*)

Miss Jen Law, BSc, PGCE (*Head of Girls' Games*)

Mrs Julia Lindsay, BA, MA, PGCE (*House Activities Coordinator for Fisher; also History and Politics*)

Mrs Chris McCullough, BA, QTS, SpLD Cert (*Head of Fisher; also Special Educational Needs*) Deputy Designated Safeguarding Lead

Kieran McCullough, BA, PGCE (*Director of Ethos; also CoRE Programme and Religious Studies*)

Miss Rachael Mack, BA, QTS (*Hockey Coach; also English*)

Miss Emma Nobes, (*Games Coach*)

Kenny Owen, BSc (*Head of Austin House; also Economics and Business*)

Mike Turns, BSc, PGCE

Cyprian Vella, BA, MA, PGCE (*Assistant Head of Sixth Form; Oxbridge Coordinator; also Religious Studies*)

Paul Whitehead (*Hockey Coach*)

Politics

Mrs Katharine Darwood-Bredin, BSc, GTP (*Head of Politics; House Activities Coordinator for More; also History and Games*)

Mrs Julia Lindsay, BA, MA, PGCE (*House Activities Coordinator for Fisher; also History and Games*)

Psychology and Sociology:

Adam Rickart, BSc, PGCE (*Head of Psychology and Sociology; also CoRE Programme*)

Ms Jo Powell, BA, PGCE

Mrs Fionnuala Schofield, BSc (*Real Time Coordinator; CPD Lead*)

Mrs Clare White, BSc, PGCE (*also Science*)

Religious Studies:

Ian Lane, BA, PGCE (*Head of Religious Studies*)

Rod Isaacs, MA Cantab, MA, CertEd (*Assistant Head of Sixth Form; also CoRE Programme*)

Kieran McCullough, BA, PGCE (*Director of Ethos; also CoRE Programme and Games*)

Miss Alex Philpot, BA, QTS

Cyprian Vella, BA, MA, PGCE (*Assistant Head of Sixth Form; Oxbridge Coordinator; also Games*)

Special Educational Needs Department:

Ms Lorna Prestage, BSc, PGCE (*Special Educational Needs Coordinator*)

Ms Kat Brittain (*Learning Support Assistant*)

Mrs Clare Callaghan, BSc, PGCE (*SEN Mathematics Support; also Mathematics*)

Mrs Caroline Hardware (*Learning Support Assistant*)

Mrs Holly Hinks, BSc (*Learning Support Teacher*)

Mrs Anna Jelec, MEd (*Learning Support Teacher*)

Mrs Amanda Kelly (*Learning Support Assistant*)

Mrs Chris McCullough, BA, QTS (*Head of Fisher; also Academic PE and Deputy Designated Safeguarding Lead*)

Mrs Fiona Moon, BA, PG Cert Dyslexia and Literacy (*also English*)

Mrs Lee O'Gorman (*SEN Teaching Assistant*)

The Sciences:

Miss Emma Cooper, BSc, PGCE (*Head of Science; Head of Chemistry*)

Dr Digby Carrington-Howell, BSc, MA Ed, EdD, PGCE, NPQH (*Biology*)

Ben Collie, BSc (*Biology*)

Greg Hunter, BE, Grad Dip Ed (*Assistant Head – Co-curricular; Physics*)

Simon Robertson, BSc, PGCE (*Head of More House; Biology*)

Mrs Sophie Rose, BSc, PGCE (*Physics*)

Mrs Sarah Sephton, BEng, PGCE (*Head of Physics*)

Mrs Joanne Smith, MChem, PGCE (*Chemistry*)

Rob Southern, BSc, PGCE (*Physics*)

Mrs Catherine Warne, BSc, PGCE (*Head of Biology*)

Mrs Clare White, BSc, PGCE (*Science; also Psychology and Sociology*)

Dan White, BSc, PGCE (*Biology and Chemistry*)

Steve White BSc, PGCE (*Chemistry*)

Ms Francesca Wright, BSc, PGCE (*Chemistry and Biology*)

Prior Park College

Ralph Allen Drive, Bath BA2 5AH

Tel: 01225 835353
email: info@priorparkschools.com
website: www.priorparkschools.com
Twitter: @priorpark
Facebook: @prior.park.37

Motto: *Deo Duce, Deo Luce*

Prior Park College is a fully co-educational Catholic Boarding and Day School. Founded in 1830 by Bishop Baines, it was under the control of the Bishops of Clifton until 1924, when it passed to the Congregation of Christian Brothers. Since 1981, Prior Park has been under lay management and has more than doubled in size. Prior Park is a friendly, thriving community of around 600 pupils, with a strong boarding community, excellent academic standards and a strong devotion to educating the whole person.

The College is housed in magnificent Palladian architecture, built by John Wood for Ralph Allen, with glorious views of the World Heritage City of Bath. The 57-acre site combines an elegant setting for boarding and day education with access to Bath and its numerous cultural attractions. Proximity to the M4 and M5 motorways places the College within easy reach of London, the Midlands, the South-West and Wales. Good rail links and proximity to Bristol, Heathrow and Gatwick international airports allow easy transfer for our international students.

Structure of the School. Prior Park is a friendly, thriving community of approximately 600 pupils made up from approximately 440 day and up to 160 boarders. Full, weekly and flexi boarding is available for ages 11–18.

Objects of the College. The College provides an outstanding education, within the framework of a caring, Catholic community which warmly welcomes members of other denominations. Our A Level and GCSE results are consistently excellent, with our EPQ (Extended Project Qualification) results among the best in the country. Our resident Lay Chaplain serves the needs of the whole community and great importance is attached to the commitment of all staff to the ethos of the school. Pastoral care is perceived by the current parent body to be outstanding and great efforts are made to ensure that all pupils are nurtured and supported.

Buildings and Grounds. Ranked by the Oxford Royale Academy as the UK's most beautiful boarding school. The Houses, Administration and College Chapel are to be found in the fine 18th century architecture grouped around Ralph Allen's celebrated Palladian Mansion. A major programme of modernisation has enhanced the accommodation for residential staff and their families, and added to the attractive environment for the residential community. A major refurbishment programme of boys' and girls' boarding accommodation has provided comfortable study-bedrooms, quiet areas and recreational rooms. A rolling programme of refurbishment continues, including a new Sixth Form Centre in September 2015, a new multimillion pound Sports Centre in November 2015, a new D&T Sixth Form workshop and new all-weather pitch in September 2017.

Curriculum. The academic curriculum conforms to and goes beyond the requirements of the National Curriculum. Core subjects to GCSE are Mathematics, English, the Sciences, a Modern Language and Religious Studies. The curriculum in Year 7–9 is broad. Great care is taken to ensure that careful guidance is given to pupils in Year 9 and Year 11 when GCSE and A Level choices are being made. The Deputy Head Academic, Deputy Head Pupil Progress and the House staff work with pupils and their parents to tailor a programme which reflects the strength and interests of the individual. The majority of pupils will study ten GCSE subjects. In Sixth Form students mostly take three A Level subjects plus another qualification, e.g. an Extended Project Qualification (EPQ).

Music. The College has a highly-deserved reputation for musical excellence. Two chapel choirs provide high quality music for the weekly sung Mass in the glorious surroundings of the Chapel of Our Lady of the Snows. The John Wood Chapel, within Prior Park Mansion, offers a further concert and rehearsal venue for the many musicians in the school.

The Music Department, also in the Mansion, houses a recording studio and teaching and practice rooms. Around half the pupils learn a musical instrument and there are several thriving orchestras, chamber groups and bands, as well as a large and ambitious Choral Society, annual competitions and festivals. Many Prior Park musicians have gone on to Oxbridge. Other graduates go to major conservatoires and play in NYO, NCO, etc.

Performing Arts. The students stage around fifteen drama productions a year. Recent performances include: Hedda Gabler, Hamlet, Daisy Pulls It Off, The Crucible. The Julian Slade Theatre is a wonderful setting for this extensive and diverse performing arts programme. It has been extended to provide a Dance Studio and further teaching and technical support areas. There is also a full-time theatre technician.

Physical Education and Games. Physical Education is included in the curriculum. Games are an important part of school life. Main school games are Rugby, Hockey, Cricket, Netball and Tennis. Provision is made for Swimming, Badminton, Cross-Country, Football, Basketball, Table Tennis, Fencing, Athletics.

Activities Programme. The Daily Activities Programme features over 60 activities ranging from Sci-Fi club to Fencing. Students are required to choose one activity per week and the choice can vary each term.

The voluntary Combined Cadet Force includes Navy and Army Sections. Adventure training takes place both in the UK and overseas. Cadets are encouraged to participate in the Service and Contingent Camps and Courses.

The Duke of Edinburgh's Award scheme operates at Bronze and Gold Award level. Participants work on the four sections: volunteering, skills, physical, and expeditions; plus a residential project section at Gold Award level.

Saturday Active is a programme of courses that take place every Saturday morning. There are over 25 courses to choose from from Sailing to Street Dance.

Boarders and day pupils alike participate in a wide range of activities after school. Public speaking and debating thrive. All younger full-time boarders take part in Saturday Active.

Careers. Our careers guidance programme combines the traditional strength of the House system with the benefits of a specialised central careers department. Every pupil receives individual guidance through the five years from Form 4 (Year 9) to Upper Sixth, with particular support at the three critical stages of choice for GCSE, A Level, and university entrance. At the same time, professional careers advice is available from our independent Careers Advisor, who provides objective information and guidance.

Admission. Main points of admission are at 11+, 13+ and 16+ but pupils may transfer into the College at 12 and 14 if places are available. Early registrations are encouraged. Prospective families are encouraged to visit the College on Open Days or by arranging an individual visit.

Entrance and scholarship examinations for 11+ and 13+ take place in October and November prior to entry in September. 16+ scholarship examinations and interviews take place in November. Please contact the Registrar, admissions@priorparkschools.com, for the relevant entrance/scholarship admission booklet.

Scholarships and Bursaries. Academic Scholarships are available at 11+, 13+ and 16+. Creative Design, All-Rounder, Drama, Music and Sporting Excellence awards are available at 11+, 13+ and 16+. All awards carry with them a fee remission.

Bursaries are available, including HM Forces Bursaries of up to 20% of fees. The Bursar is pleased to discuss individual cases. Sibling discounts apply.

Fees per term (2018–2019). Boarding £10,315, International Boarding £10,700, Weekly Boarding £8,500; Junior Full Boarding (ages 11–13) £7,835, Junior Weekly Boarding £6,915. Day 16+ £5,665; Day 13+ £5,585; Day 11+ £5,000.

The Paragon School, Bath – Junior School of Prior Park College. The Paragon School is part of Prior Park Educational Trust. Housed in an impressive Georgian mansion, the co-educational school for 3–11 years is set in beautiful wooded grounds, only a few minutes drive from Prior Park College. A broad and balanced curriculum is delivered within a happy, caring environment.

Headmaster: Mr Andrew Harvey, BA Hons
For further details, see entry in IAPS section.

Prior Park School, Gibraltar. Opened in September 2016, Prior Park School is the first Independent co-educational senior school in Gibraltar for children 12–18 years.

Headmaster: Mr Peter Watts, BSc, CPhys
For further details please visit the website www. priorparkschools.com

Charitable status. Prior Park Educational Trust is a Registered Charity, number 281242.

President:
Sister J Livesey, CJ, MA Cantab

Patrons:
The Rt Revd D R Lang, BA, Bishop of Clifton
Miss J Bisgood, CBE
Mr C J B Davy, CB
Mr D R Hayes
Mr F J F Lyons, KSG
Sir Cameron Mackintosh
The Rt Hon the Lord Patten of Barnes, CH, PC
The Revd Monsignor Canon R J Twomey, VF
Commodore C B York, FCMI, Royal Navy

Governors:
Mr A M H King (*Chair of Governors*)
Mr A Bury, MBA, BSc Hons

Mr S Eliot, MA Cantab
Mrs N Freeman, BA Hons, MA, PGCE
Dr J Haworth, MBS, MSc
Mr J Jarvis, LLB Hons, BVC, Barrister at Law
Mrs A Lloyd, MA Ed, Cert Ed, LGSM
Mr P S J O'Donoghue, MA, FCA
Mrs N Pearson, BA Hons, PGCE
Rear Admiral N J Raby, OBE, MSc
Revd Prebendary N Rawlinson, MA, MB BChir, FRCS,
    FRCEM, Cert Pall Med, Dip Th
Ms A Shepherd, MBE, BA Hons
Mr J Shinkwin, MA Oxon, PGCE
Mrs J Singleton, BA Hons, Dip TEFL
Mr J Webster, BA, BArch, MCD, RIBA, MRTPI

Headmaster: **Mr James Murphy-O'Connor**, MA Oxon

Senior Deputy Head: Miss C Cummins, MA Oxon
Deputy Head Academic: Mrs L Stotesbury, MA Cantab
Deputy Head Pupil Progress: Mrs S Forshaw, BSc Hons
Deputy Head Operations: Mrs L Blake, BA Hons
Deputy Head Pastoral: Mr S Cane-Hardy, BA

Heads of Departments:
Art: Ms S Seville, BA Hons, BA Fine Art
Biology: Dr R Trott, BSc, PhD Newcastle & Bristol
Chemistry: Mr K Chard, BSc Leeds
Classics: Mrs S Hearn, BA Oxon
Design & Technology: Mr R Faulkner, BSc Nottingham
Digital Learning & Computing: Mr M Minghella, BA Hons
Drama & Theatre Studies: Mr D Langley, BA Manchester
Economics and Business: Mr M Jones
English: Dr K McGowran, BA, MA, PhD Hull
English as an Additional Language (*EAL*): Mr P Stroud,
    BA UCL, MSc Surrey
Geography: Mr S Burt, BSc Reading
History: Mr C Bartlett, BA
Learning Development Programme (*LDP*): Mrs K Mason,
    BA Hons, MA
Library: Mrs L Mallott, BA, MA Lancaster
Mathematics: Mrs J Jones, BSc Belfast
Modern Languages: Mr J George, BA
Music: Mr R Robertson, MA Cantab, ARCO
Physical Education & Sports Science: Mr R Gwilliam, BA
    Hons Cardiff
Physics: Mr C Gamble, MSci
Psychology: Mrs R Bird, MA, Dip Psych
Theology and Philosophy: Mr T Maxwell, BA London

Visiting Music Staff for Acoustic/Electric Guitar, Bass
    Guitar, Bassoon, Cello, Clarinet, Drums, Flute, Oboe,
    Piano, Saxophone, Trumpet, Violin, Viola, Voice.

Foundation Executive Personal Assistant: Ms D Miller
College Executive & Headmaster's PA: Miss E Wickham
Registrar: Mrs Vicki Quinn
Lay Chaplain: Miss Sarah Adams
Director of Development: Mr Declan Rainey

Queen Anne's School

6 Henley Road, Caversham, Berkshire RG4 6DX
Tel: 0118 918 7300
Fax: 0118 918 7310
email: office@qas.org.uk
website: www.qas.org.uk

Twitter: @QASCaversham
Facebook: @QASCaversham
LinkedIn: /QASCaversham

Queen Anne's is an independent boarding and day school
for girls with over 460 pupils aged 11 to 18 years. High aspirations combined with a positive approach to learning creates an environment where girls can grow into motivated,
decisive and self-assured individuals. We are renowned for
academic success alongside a rich programme of extra-curricular opportunities and excellence in the arts, drama,
music and sport.

We are a Church of England School and part of The Grey
Coat Hospital Foundation, Westminster, London. Located in
Caversham, Berkshire, the school is situated to the north of
Reading near Henley-on-Thames and is just over 40 minutes
from London. School transport is available throughout the
local area; a coach service runs every Friday and Monday to
London.

Queen Anne's was recently rated 'excellent' by the Independent Schools Inspectorate for both its academic achievements and personal development. The 2017 inspection,
carried out over two days in March, found that: 'Queen
Anne's School pupils are educated to a high level in accordance with the school's aim to promote excellence in all
areas of education.'

At the heart of our success is the 'human' aspect of
boarding and our excellent pastoral care. We pride ourselves
that Queen Anne's girls find their boarding experience fun
and their happiness is our top priority. The 24-hour nature of
school life means that members of staff are always on hand
to offer support and advice.

Queen Anne's TES award winning Sixth Form Centre,
The Space, provides girls with the perfect stepping stone to
university, promoting independent and collaborative study
in a creative environment. The building won the award for
'outstanding post-16 innovative provision' and was
designed to fulfil the philosophy behind the school's Brain-
CanDo educational neuroscience project. Alongside a modern restaurant for all pupils and staff, The Space is home to
the Digital Learning Space, a new digital library featuring
innovative learning pods as well as themed breakout rooms,
designed by the students themselves, and digitally enhanced
seminar and teaching rooms to facilitate collaborative learning.

The best way to find out about Queen Anne's is to talk to
those at the heart of our community – our pupils! Our website www.qas.org.uk contains images, videos and narratives
drawn from their experiences. We look forward to welcoming you to Queen Anne's!

Pastoral organisation. Queen Anne's has an excellent
reputation for pastoral care. Girls can attend Queen Anne's
daily or on a full, weekly, flexi or occasional boarding basis
according to individual family needs. Each girl, whether day
or boarding, belongs to a House and the House system is
integral to our academic and pastoral care.

The staff believe that students perform best when they are
happy and secure, and Queen Anne's has effective pastoral
systems in place to ensure this. The support network
includes Housemistresses and the House Pastoral Team,
Academic Staff and Tutors, and Heads of Year.

Curriculum. All girls follow a broad and varied curriculum up to GCSE. Separate subject sciences are taught, as
well as Dual Award; mathematics and music follow IGCSE;
Spanish, German or Mandarin may be taken from Year 9;
Latin is studied from Year 7. Music, art and drama form part
of the girls' timetable until the end of Year 9. Information
technology is taught throughout the school. A wide range of
A Level subjects is offered. A programme of personal,
social and health education is followed by all girls.

Careers. Girls go on to Higher Education courses at many top universities in the UK and overseas and also take up places on Apprenticeship schemes, including Ernst & Young and Coca-Cola.

Co-curricular activities. Queen Anne's is reputed for many of its achievements. It offers a full extra-curricular programme and excellent opportunities for sport, including tennis, lacrosse, 'rock' climbing and rowing on the nearby Thames. Music, drama and art are very strong. The Duke of Edinburgh's Award, Young Enterprise, public speaking and debating (National and International finalists), photography, dance, riding, socials and many more activities are available. A full programme of optional activities is available on Saturday mornings for pupils and parents.

Admission. Girls are admitted at 11+, 13+ and at Sixth Form by Queen Anne's Entrance Examination or by Common Entrance. Sixth Form places are offered on the basis of GCSE results. For further information please contact the Registrar.

Scholarships are offered for entry at 11+, 13+ and 16+ and are awarded for excellence in one or more fields of the life of the school. Awards may be made in respect of Academic Excellence, All-Round Contribution, Art, Drama, Music or Sport.

Fees per term (2018–2019). Full Boarding £11,860; Flexi Boarding £10,690–£11,270; Day pupils £8,045.

Charitable status. Queen Anne's School is part of The Grey Coat Hospital Foundation, which is a Registered Charity, number 312700.

Governing Body: The Grey Coat Hospital Foundation

Chairman: Mr J M Noakes, MA
Vice Chairman: Ms S A Thewlis, BA, MML

Board Members:
The Revd M R Birch, BVSc, MA
Mr C Booth, BA, FRSA, FCIPR
Mrs C Gray, BA
Ms A Kiem, MA, BMath, DipEd
Ms K Parsons, BA, MA, ACT
Mr R F Penfold, MBE
Mr M Sharrock
Mrs V S Simmons, MA
Mr D Taylor, MA, FRSA
Mrs L Troake, BA

Clerk: Mr R W Blackwell, MA

Headmistress: **Mrs Julia Harrington**, BA Exeter, PGCE, NPQH, Dip Counselling

Deputy Head – Pastoral: Mrs Lindsey Bryant, BSc Nottingham, PGCE Hertfordshire, MEd Cambridge
Deputy Head – Academic: Mr Mark Richards, BMus Wales, MMus King's College London, Research Fellowship Cardiff, FRSA
Director of Sixth Form: Mr Ben Stephenson, BSc Warwick, MSc Loughborough, GTP
Director of Teaching and Learning: Mrs Gill Little, BSc St Andrews, PGCE Cantab
Director of Finance and Administration: Mr Edward Hellings, BA, ACA
Head of Lower School: Mrs Linda McGrenary, BEd Strathclyde
Head of Middle School: Mr Daniel Boyes, BA MA Oxford, PGCE Cambridge, Dip Theology and Political Studies Oxford

Heads of Departments:
Art & Design: Ms Sarah Beales, MA Norwich, PGCE London

Classics: Mrs Sandra Smith, BA London, MA USA, Cert Archaeology London, PTLLS WEA
Drama: Mr Rhodri Punter, BA Wales
Economics & Enterprise: Mrs Anne Tynan, BA Manchester
English: Mrs Anna Spellman, BA, PGCE Reading
EAL: Ms Lesley McNeil, MEd Exeter, TESOL
Geography: Miss Joanne Clarke, MA Reading
History: Dr Juliet Ingram, PhD MA BA Warwick, PGCE (*Reading*)
Information Technology: Mr Thomas Lange, Dipl-Ing FH, BEng Germany
Mathematics: Mr Derek Bottomley, BSc Leeds, PGCE Oxford
Modern Languages: Mr Antoine Rogeon, License of English France, Masters France, QTS Reading
Principal Director of Music: Mr John Padley, BMus London, LTC, ACPID, FRSA
Psychology: Dr Amy Fancourt, BSc Durham, MSc London, PhD Goldsmiths London
Science: Mrs Sarah Eagle, BSc, PGCE Southampton
Director of Sport: Mrs Nicola Burley, BA North Staffs, PGCE Exeter

Queen Elizabeth's Hospital (QEH)

Berkeley Place, Clifton, Bristol BS8 1JX

Tel: 0117 930 3040
email: headmaster@qehbristol.co.uk
            office@qehbristol.co.uk
website: www.qehbristol.co.uk

Motto: *Dum tempus habemus operemur bonum*

Patron: Her Majesty The Queen

By his Will dated 10 April 1586, John Carr, a Bristol merchant, founded Queen Elizabeth's Hospital, a bluecoat school in Bristol on the lines of Christ's Hospital which was already flourishing in London. The Charter was granted to the School by Queen Elizabeth I in 1590. Originally composed entirely of boarders, the School continued so until 1920 when foundation day boys were admitted. Direct Grant status was accorded in 1945. The School is now independent and day only and, as of September 2017, has a co-educational Sixth Form.

Admission. There are 597 boys in the Senior School, ranging in age from 11 to 18. Entrance examinations for both Year 7 and Year 9 applicants are held in January each year; Sixth Form and other Years by arrangement. From September 2017, girls are able to join the QEH Sixth Form.

Term of Entry. Usually September.

Entrance Scholarships. A significant number of scholarships are offered at Year 7, Year 9 and Sixth Form. These are awarded purely on academic merit for outstanding achievement in the entrance procedures and may also carry with them generous assistance for applicants whose parents' means are limited. Sixth Form Scholarships are available for Maths, Science, Languages (Ancient and Modern), Literature, Art and Social Sciences, Art, Drama and Music.

Academic, Music and Sports scholarships are available at Year 7 and Year 9.

Assisted Places. There are many School assisted places available. The School has a substantial foundation income and is able to give generous support to parents whose means are limited.

Buildings. The School was originally close by the City Centre but moved to new premises on Brandon Hill in 1847. A major building and improvement programme has included the building of the QEH Theatre (1990), refurbishment of the Art School (2000), new Mathematics rooms and heavy investment in ICT (2004). An 80-strong Junior School opened in 2007 (increasing to over 100 in 2012) along with a new Sixth Form Centre. In 2008 a multimillion pound development programme, in conjunction with Bristol City Football Club, saw new football pitches on 23 acres at the Sports Ground at Failand. A new £3 million Science and Art Building was opened in October 2016 and there are future development plans which include improvements to Music and Art facilities and other areas of the school. An expanded Sixth Form Centre opened in September 2017.

Curriculum. Students are prepared for the GCSE (IGCSE in Mathematics and English) and GCE A Level, and for university entrance. The usual school subjects are offered at GCSE level, and the A-Level subjects are: English Literature, English Language, Drama, Economics, Latin, Greek, Classical Civilisation, History, Geography, French, German, Spanish, Art, Music, Mathematics, Further Mathematics, Music Technology, Physics, Chemistry, Biology, PE and Sport, Business Studies, ICT, Ethics and Philosophy, Government & Politics and Psychology.

Music & Drama. There is a School Orchestra, Choir, Jazz Band, Brass Group, and Wind Band among the twenty or so ensembles. Music is included in the timetable for all the junior forms. GCSE and A Level music is part of the School curriculum, and tuition is arranged for a wide range of instruments. The Choir and Instrumentalists perform regularly and also undertake joint ventures with other schools in Bristol. Drama flourishes and the school has its own high-tech purpose-built theatre which seats 220.

Art. The Department is well equipped and offers ceramics, screen printing, photography and computer imaging.

Religious Studies. The School is a Christian one which welcomes students of all faiths, or none. Religious Studies is part of the curriculum and students attend two services a year in Bristol Cathedral.

Games. Rugby, Football, Athletics, Cricket, Swimming, Tennis, Hockey, Netball, Badminton, Sailing, Squash, Fencing, Judo, Climbing and Mountain Biking. A large number of students also participate in The Duke of Edinburgh's Award and Ten Tors.

Dress. Boys wear either grey trousers and a blazer or a plain dark suit. Sixth Form girls wear smart business dress. Traditional bluecoat uniform is worn by some for special occasions.

General. All parents are encouraged to join the Friends of Queen Elizabeth's Hospital, a society whose aim is to promote a close relationship between parents and staff and to further the welfare of the School. There is a flourishing Old Elizabethans' Society, which holds regular meetings and circulates a newsletter. A panel of former pupils, formed from all professions, and working with the Head of Careers, is available to give advice on careers to students.

The School has long been known in Bristol as 'The City School' and its links with the Lord Mayor and Corporation are strong. Students read the lessons and sing in the Lord Mayor's Chapel, and groups are in attendance for such occasions as Mayor-making and Council Prayers.

The central position of the School, close to the University, the Art Gallery and Museum, the Central Library, the Bristol Old Vic and the Colston Hall, affords ready access to a wide range of cultural facilities which students are encouraged to use.

Junior School. 100 Boys aged 7–11. (*For further details see QEH Junior School entry in IAPS section.*)

Fees per term (2018–2019). Senior School £4,802, Junior School £3,218. Fees include text and exercise books, and essential educational trips but do not include public examination fees or lunches (which are £3.70 per day).

Charitable status. Queen Elizabeth's Hospital is a Registered Charity, number 1104871, and a Company Limited by Guarantee, number 5164477. Queen Elizabeth's Hospital has existed since 1590 to provide a first class education.

Governing Body:
D A Smart, BSc, FCA (*Chairman*)
P A Keen, SCIB (*Vice-Chairman*)

Mrs C Bateson, MA, BA Hons	Mrs S Cosgrove, BSc
Ms S Blanks, MSc	T Davis, BSc, MRICS
J Buchanan, LLB Hons, CTA	R J Hill, LLB Hons, TEP
	K Riley, BA Hons, MA
E Corrigan, BA, FCS, MAE	C Woodford, FRICS, BSc Hons

Bursar: R N Cook, FCA

Headmaster: S W Holliday, MA

Deputy Head (Academic & Pastoral): J Martin, MA
Assistant Head (Staff Development): C Brotherton, BA
Assistant Head (Operations): W R Ellis, BSc
Assistant Head (Sixth Form): Mr R Porter, MA
Head of Marketing and Communications: E A Down, BSSoc, LLB

S Albon, BSc	Dr J Jönsson, MSc, PhD
Mrs S K Allen, BSc	P E Joslin, BEd
P M Amor, BA	J Kelly, BSc
T Appleby, BA	Mrs S J King, MA
B Bohane, BA	P J Kirby, BA
Ms H Bosson, BSc	H L Kyle, BSc, PhD
Miss J Bowkett, BSc	Miss L Leone, BA
A E Calder, BA	Ms S Maltin, BA
D J Chalmers, BSc	Mrs H Mann, MA
A C Clements, BSc	Miss L Mantle, BA, MA
Ms R Coleman, MA	R Martineau, MEng
Mrs E Conquest, BA	Mrs A Masom, BA
C B Conquest, BEd	Mrs M McGowan, BA
P A Davies, BSc	Ms V Mico, BSc
Mrs M M Dimes, BSc	C Miller, BSc
T J Dunn, BSc	S Mitchell, BSc
M Dutton, BEd, MA, EdD	P C Moore, BEd
Miss N Dyer, BA	Mrs S Moritz, BA
Miss L Fenner, BA	S J Munnion, BA
Mrs C Gardner, BA	Mrs A Pegg, BA
E M Gent, BA	W G Plowden, BA
Mrs D Guthrie, BSc	N Pursall, BA
R J Harris, BA	C Ryan, BSc
S A Harris, BSc	Mrs L Shaw, BA
T Harrison, BA	Mrs H Shields, BA
D T Hawkes, BSc	M Sloan, BSc
Mrs P Hockenhull, BA	Mrs R Steven, BA
S Hofkes, BMus, PG Dip	A W H Swithinbank, BA
Mrs N Holcombe, BA	Ms E Taylor, BSc, MSc
A R Hughes, BA	Z Verry, BA
Ms K Izzard, BSc	Mrs F Waite-Taylor, BA
A Jarvis, BA	R J Waldron, BA
P M Jones, BA	

Junior School:
Headteacher: D M Kendall, BA

Visiting Teachers:
J Bacon, MMus
P Barrett, BA, PG Dip
Mrs D Dickerson, Dip LCM, Dip ABRSM, Dip ESA
K Figes, LGSM, PG Dip
R Grist, BA Hons, BMus Hons
Mrs A Howell, BMus, FRCO, LGSM, BA
Miss C Lindley, BA
N Malcolm

B Mullan, BMus
A Purnell, BMus Hons RWCMD
G Robinson, BMus
N Shipman, BMus, LGSMD
A Stewart, BMus
Miss L Tanner, BMus, MMus, PG Dip
R J Webb, BMus Hons
J Whitfield, BMus

Chaplain: The Revd S B Taylor, BA
Headmaster's Secretary: Mrs E Davies
Admissions Registrar: Mrs C Matthews
Librarian: Mrs A Robbins

Queen's College
Taunton

Trull Road, Taunton, Somerset TA1 4QS

Tel: 01823 340830 Admissions
email: admissions@queenscollege.org.uk
website: www.queenscollege.org.uk
Twitter: @QueensTaunton
Facebook: @queenstaunton

Motto: *Non scholae sed vitae discimus ~ We learn not for school but for life*

Introduction. Queen's College – one of the South West's leading independent day and boarding co-educational schools – is celebrating its 175th anniversary this year in 2018.

Queen's has a well-deserved reputation for the quality of its teaching and all pupils are cared for in small tutor groups. Pastoral care is outstanding. The staff work tirelessly to encourage students to develop their personal skills and abilities. Class sizes are small and the atmosphere is friendly and supportive – students are happy and motivated here.

The boarding community is strong with excellent houseparents, full activities programme and lots of support. Communication and relationships with parents are valued and all are included in the wider Queen's family.

Queen's is very strong in sport, in particular hockey, rugby, athletics and swimming. It also has an outstanding reputation for the visual and performing arts and the School currently has some outstanding musicians in the National Youth Orchestra.

Queen's operates a strong co-curricular programme including a wide variety of performing arts, sports, arts and outdoor pursuits and considerable emphasis is placed on participation in The Duke of Edinburgh's Award scheme. All students take Bronze, many go on to Silver and to date, over 300 Sixth Form students have achieved their Gold Awards. Queen's hosts its own Model United Nations conference and is a centre of excellence in the South West.

Number of Pupils. The Queen's College Nursery, Pre-Prep, Junior and Senior Schools are based on the same site with some facilities shared: continuity of education is assured. The Senior School (11 to 18 years) has 495 pupils of whom 203 are boarders. The Junior School and Pre-Prep (4 to 11 years) has 175 pupils, with a junior boarding house. The full College complement is an excellent size of 670 meaning that there are enough pupils for good friendship groups, team sports and school plays but it is still personal enough so that the Head Teacher knows every pupil. A happy, friendly, family school which doesn't stand on ceremony.

Situation and Buildings. Queen's College was founded in 1843 within Taunton's Castle walls but was relocated to the south western outskirts of Taunton three years later when the present main school buildings were constructed. It is in an excellent situation with fine views of the Quantock and Blackdown Hills, within easy reach of Exmoor and Dartmoor, just a short distance from Taunton town centre, easily accessible by road or rail, junction 25 of M5 is 2 miles away and serviced by Heathrow, Bristol International and Exeter Airports.

The 1846 original Grade II* listed building contained a School House, the School Hall and a Dining Room. Later a Junior School was added, an indoor heated Swimming Pool and a Music Department. Over the past 20 years there has been an extensive building programme which has included: nine classrooms for the Junior school, applied science, technology centre, new changing rooms, day girl and day boy accommodation, enlargement and modernisation of girl and boy boarding houses, school hall for the Junior school, new music school, concert/assembly hall for the Senior school, and a sixth form centre. Latest additions are a new Art & Drama building; Leisure and Performing Arts Centres; a new Science Block and major expansion of Pre-Prep facilities. Recently, a state-of-the-art Sixth Form Centre has provided an excellent interim between school and university, equipped with multimedia, social spaces, collaborative and quiet study areas. Other additions have included a new Medical Centre, new Languages Centre and new boarding wing with top-quality boarding accommodation. Definitely a school on the up which is modern in its outlook and does not rest on its laurels.

Organisation. There are two day boy houses and two day girl houses and each has a House Parent and set of Tutors for each year group. The boarding set-up is superb with some really committed House Parents who offer a combination of stability and fun. There are two boys' boarding houses and one large girls' boarding house and House Parents are supplemented by a resident Assistant House Master/Mistress. Tutors are attached to each house and are responsible for academic progress. They guide each student through GCSE and A Level choices, in conjunction with the Head Teacher, Deputy Head and Head of Sixth Form. In the Sixth Form students are able to choose their tutor, who will advise them on university selection and choices of career and the academic, careers and social programmes are excellent.

Curriculum. Pupils in the first three years of Senior School follow the national curriculum providing them with a sound base in the arts, sciences, humanities and technology based subjects as well as games and PSHME. They are streamed and taught as a form for most subjects and are set for mathematics, English and French. At GCSE there is a common core of English language and literature, mathematics, three sciences and a modern foreign language. Pupils then choose three option subjects.

In the Lower Sixth pupils usually choose three A Level subjects and the Extended Project Qualification. Throughout the Sixth Form some periods of curriculum time are devoted to a General Studies course which includes RE, PSHME and key skills and significant emphasis is placed on gaining good leadership, organisation and communication skills.

Co-Curriculum. In addition to games, music and drama, pupils are encouraged to participate in a range of activities including Model United Nations – a real strength at Queen's, debating, public speaking, general knowledge quizzes, ICT, chess, photography, robotic design, electronics and cookery. There are also a number of academic societies. Outdoor pursuits such as canoeing, mountain bike riding and rock climbing are popular and participation in The Duke of Edinburgh's Award scheme is a particular feature with a stunning 300 Queen's College pupils having now achieved their Gold Award.

Music. Queen's is the only school in the UK to have its own professional Orchestra-in-Residence, the Southern Sinfonia.

The Music staff provide teaching for keyboard, strings, brass, woodwind, percussion and singing among others. The purpose-built Music Department comprises classroom, six large teaching rooms, five practice rooms, electronic studio for keyboard studies, audio studio for computer-based composition (GCSE and A Level).

The Music Department also uses the beautiful Old Music Room and Performing Arts Centre in the main building for rehearsals and small concerts as well as the stunning Queen's Hall with its 570-seat multi-purpose auditorium, two-manual pipe organ and Steinway Concert Grand Piano.

Musical organisations include a variety of choirs, orchestra, wind band and swing band.

There is also a wide variety of small ensembles and chamber groups for strings, brass, woodwind with or without piano. A number of concerts are staged each year. Opportunities are available to help prepare for the National Youth Orchestra, Somerset Orchestra and Guildhall.

Drama. The provision for performing arts at Queen's is outstanding. The programme is extremely active throughout the College with the Senior School Drama department providing courses from Year 7 to Year 13. The department aims to involve all those wishing to develop their co-curricular and academic interests and sends many students on to drama school. A number of students have attended the National Musical Youth Theatre over recent years. Over seven different types of dance are studied ranging from ballet and tap to hip hop and jazz with a large-scale dance production and professional dancers coming in to give workshops. The school also runs an annual professional arts festival with performers and artists from all over the UK, also open to the general public.

In the Senior School, productions take place once a term. There are both Senior and Pre-Prep productions at the end of the Autumn Term, a major Dance Show at the end of the Spring Term, and Middle School and Junior plays at the end of the Summer term. Major productions and concerts take place in the Queen's Hall, drama and comedy in the Drama Studio and the Performing Arts Centre and Old Music Room stages smaller scale concerts and readings.

PE/Games. The playing fields are both extensive and adaptable and sport is strong at the school – in particular hockey, swimming, cross country, athletics and riding. However all abilities are welcomed.

In the Autumn Term the grass area provides seven rugby pitches which are also used for sevens in the Spring term.

In the Summer there are five cricket squares, a 400-metre athletics track and numerous rounders pitches.

The three AstroTurf pitches are used frequently – daily for hockey in the Autumn and Spring Terms – and are of such quality that Queen's has often been called upon to host County hockey tournaments. The hockey academy has produced a number of international players. The pitches are converted to tennis courts in the Summer, giving a total of 30 courts.

The hard court surface in the middle of the field is used for netball in the Spring term and for tennis in the Autumn and Summer terms.

The Sports Hall is used for gymnastics, basketball, badminton, volleyball, indoor hockey, football and indoor tennis. There is also a fully-equipped fitness centre adjoining the Sports Hall. Within the complex is an indoor heated pool that is used at various times for swimming from Pre-Prep through to Sixth Form lessons. Team swimming, canoeing, canoe polo and sub aqua are regular activities throughout the year.

Admission. Education at Queen's starts on entry to the Highgrove Nursery. The majority of pupils join the Pre-Preparatory school from the age of 4 years. Junior School pupils start at age 7. Entrance to the Senior School is by examination and those who are successful in gaining places to the Junior School transfer to the Senior School at the age of 11. There are places for boys and girls from primary schools at the age of 11 based on entry tests in Maths, English and verbal reasoning. There are places for boys and girls at the age of 13 from Preparatory schools also with entrance examinations and a number enter the Sixth Form direct on GCSE Level results.

Scholarships. 11+ scholarships are awarded in January, 13+ in February and Sixth Form in November. Full details are available upon application.

Fees per term (2018–2019). Pre-Prep £2,150–£2,210 (day pupils only); Junior Day Pupils £2,630–£4,330; Junior Boarders £4,885–£7,350; Junior Overseas Boarders £6,350–£8,890; Senior Day Pupils £5,100–£6,150; Senior Boarders £8,665–£10,660; Senior Overseas Boarders £10,360–£12,490. The fees are inclusive of most books and stationery, but exclude external examination charges.

Charitable status. Queen's College is a member of the Methodist Independent Schools Trust, which is a Registered Charity, number 1142794, and a Company, number 7649422.

Governors:
Chairman: Mr Mark Edwards
Vice Chairman: Mr Michael F Powell, BSc, FRICS, FAAV
Mrs Rachel Davies
Mrs Kate Gardner, LLB
Mr Michael Gough, FCMA, CGMA
Sir Nicholas Harvey
Mr Paul M Hughes, BSc, ACIB
Mr J David Jones, LLB
Professor Geraint Jones
Brig Thomas H Lang, QVRM, RD, FRICS, DL
Mr David Savill, LLB, FCA
Revd Graham Thompson
Mrs Janet Walden

College Leadership Group:

Head Teacher: Dr L Earps

Junior School Headmistress: Mrs T Khodabandehloo
Bursar: Mr A Stevenson
Deputy Head (Welfare): Mr A Free
Deputy Head (Teaching & Learning): Mr S Green
Director Outreach & Partnerships: Mrs J Evans

Senior School Management Team:
Head Teacher: Dr L Earps
Deputy Head (Welfare): Mr A Free
Deputy Head (Teaching and Learning): Mr S Green
Director of Studies: Mrs P Pawley
Head of Boarding: Mr J Shepherd

Senior Academic Staff:

* *Head of Department*

Art:
Miss L Burgoyne
*Mrs R Cade
Mrs S Spall

Biology:
Miss C Harrison (& *Head of PSHME*)
*Mrs L Henden (*Head of Science*)
Mr J Shepherd (*Head of Boarding*)
Mr S West
Mr A Williams (& *Chemistry and Physics*)

Business, Economics and Politics:
Mr M Aldridge (*& Sociology and History*)
Ms S Brown
*Mrs A Rust
Mr A Suppiah (*& Director of Cricket*)

Chemistry:
*Mr I Henden
Mr T Jolliff
Mr A Palmer

English:
Mrs J Brierley (& Drama*)
Mrs R Copeland
Miss D Manners (*& Drama*)
Ms Y Mount
Mrs S Wilde (*Head of Sixth Form*)

EAL:
Mrs M Armanasco
Mrs H Goodall
Mrs G Mainstone
*Mrs V Orme-Dawson
Mrs K Williams

Geography:
Mr P De Jaeger
*Mr M Neenan

History:
*Mrs M Allan [maternity leave]
Miss D Ashman
Dr Simon Cosgrove (*temporary*)

Languages:
Mr J Bird (*& EAL*)
Mrs S Brownlee
Mrs M Donaldson
Mrs D Greenow
*Miss A McGreal
Mrs L Schofield (*Head of Spanish*)
Mr M Wager
Mrs K Webber

Learning Development:
Mrs K Bloxham
Mrs A Brothwood
Mrs A Free
*Mrs R Jones

Mathematics:
Mr R Bowden
Mrs H Drummond (*& Geography*)
*Mr A Exley
Mr P Gibson
Miss J Hill
Mr C Monks
Mrs C Newsome
Mrs P Pawley (*Director of Studies*)

Music:
*Mr E Jenkins
Miss C Wills

Performing Arts:
Mrs J Evans (*Director Outreach and Partnerships*)
*Mr S Evans

Philosophy:
Mr S Green (*Deputy Head T&L*)
*Mr A Hamilton

Physical Education:
Miss R Booton
*Mr S Copeland (*Director of Sport*)
Mr A Free (*Deputy Head Welfare*)
Mr D Gibson (*Head of Hockey*)

Mrs E Halls (*Head of Girls' Games*)
Mr J Lintott
Mr P Mann
Mr J Roberts

Physics:
Dr D Haggerston
Ms T Newns
*Mr N O'Donnell
Miss S Robertson (*temporary*)

Psychology:
*Mrs C Barker

Religious Studies:
*Mrs A Houghton-Barnes

Technology:
Mr J Laney (*Computing*)
*Mrs Y Mackey (*Food & Nutrition*)
Mr M Taylor (*DT*)
Mr G Wilson (*DT & Computing*)

PA to the Head Teacher: Mrs Pam Chapman
Admissions Manager: Mrs Jo Chester
Academic Administrator: Miss Judith Poole

Junior School Management Team:
Headmistress: Mrs Tracey Khodabandehloo
Deputy Head, Director of Sport: Mr Dick Wilde
Curriculum Director: Mrs Teri Underwood
Head of Pre-Prep: Miss Samantha Horner
Head of Nursery: Miss Elizabeth Hayes

PA to the Headmistress: Mrs Julie Cameron
School Administrator: Mrs Sarah Musgrave
School Chaplain: Mr Tim Aldridge

Mrs Linda Alcock (*Year 6 Form Teacher, Head of French*)
Mr Doug Baker (*Year 5 Form Teacher, Games, Boarding Houseparent*)
Miss Henrietta Cash (*Year 3 Form Teacher*)
Mr Sam Chislett (*Year 6 Form Teacher, Head of Computing*)
Mr Andy Clark (*Head of Science, Senior School Boarding Houseparent*)
Mrs Fiona Douglas (*Support Assistant*)
Mr Phil Dudman (*Head of Art and Design Technology*)
Mrs Lucy Gardner (*Year 6 Form Teacher, PE, Head of Games*)
Mrs Laura Gent (*Games*)
Mrs Pat Fox (*Year 5 Form Teacher, Mathematics and English, Library*)
Mr Matthew Kirby (*Speech*)
Mr Phil Mann (*Games*)
Mrs Shirley Neale (*Head of Learning Development*)
Mrs Rebecca Oliver (*Mathematics and English*)
Mr Andrew Owen (*English, Head of History*)
Miss Pamela Rosie (*Drama*)
Miss Sarah Scutt (*Director of Music*)
Mrs Candice Thompson-Gardiner (*Year 4 Form Teacher, Library and Mental Health*)
Mrs Anne Wade (*Year 3 Form Teacher, Head of Religious Studies*)
Mrs Sharon Wilde (*Games*)
Miss Nikki Williams (*Year 4 Form Teacher, Head of Mathematics*)

Miss Samantha Horner (*Head of Pre-Prep, Year 1 Teacher and PSHE and Computing Coordinator*)
Mrs Helen Hitchin (*Deputy Head of Pre-Prep, Year 2 Teacher, Music and Mathematics Coordinator*)
Mrs Charlotte Baker (*Year 1 Teacher [job share] and RS Coordinator*)

Mrs Rebecca Milby (*Year 1 Teacher, Forest School and Science Coordinator*)

Mrs Clare Hood (*Reception Teacher [job share], English Coordinator*)

Mrs Jill Fear (*Reception Teacher [job share], Art and Design Technology Coordinator*)

Mrs Gill Harrison (*SENCO and Learning Development Teacher*)

Miss Elizabeth Hayes (*Head of Nursery Education*)
Miss Christina Hardwick (*Senior Nursery Practitioner*)
Mrs Kirsty Goss (*Nursery Practitioner*)
Mrs Jane Brown (*Nursery Practitioner*)
Mrs Charlotte Jenkins (*Nursery Practitioner*)
Mrs Clare Hammond (*Nursery Bank Staff*)
Mrs Johanna Harper-Grainger (*Nursery Bank Staff*)

Queenswood School

Shepherd's Way, Brookmans Park, Hatfield, Hertfordshire AL9 6NS

Tel: 01707 602500
Fax: 01707 602597
email: admissions@queenswood.org
website: www.queenswood.org
Twitter: @QueenswoodSch
Facebook: @Queenswood-School-Hertfordshire-UK

Motto: 'In Hortis Reginæ' – 'In the Queen's Gardens'.

The School was founded in 1894 in Clapham Park, London. It moved to its current site in Hertfordshire in 1925.

Queenswood is a progressive boarding and day school for around 430 girls, aged between 11 and 18, where boarders make up half of the School. An all-round education focuses on equipping the girls with all the life skills required of women in the 21st century. Within a caring and supportive framework, the girls enjoy a dynamic academic curriculum, supported by a diverse and exciting co-curricular programme.

It is a warm and friendly community where everybody knows each other. Girls thrive within a nurturing House structure tailored to meet their needs as they progress from the Lower School, through the Middle School, and on into the Sixth Form. Day girls are fully integrated within the Houses, are able to enjoy all the facilities and opportunities available to the boarders, but choose to go home at night after a packed school day. There is a flexible approach to boarding to meet the varying needs of individual families; girls may choose to flexi board for 1, 2 or 3 nights, weekly board or be full boarders. They can also flexi board for ad hoc nights.

Queenswood is proud to be an international community with an outward-looking approach; overseas girls make up around 20% of the pupils. We welcome girls of all faiths and none, recognise and support an individual's adherence to her own faith, but expect all girls to embrace the School's broad spiritual ethos.

The girls are ambitious high achievers, winning places at the top universities both at home and abroad prior to embarking upon a range of exciting careers. The School is, however, resolutely neither an academic hothouse nor overly selective. Individual talent also flourishes in sport and the creative and performing arts. The extensive co-curricular programme helps develop the girls' soft skills in a wide variety of ways and significantly contributes to their excellent academic results. As important as individual achievement is the development of a sense of responsibility for each other and the world in which they live.

Queenswood girls are thoughtful young people with a secure set of values and self-confidence.

The beautiful Queenswood estate provides the perfect educational environment. Being just 25 minutes from central London, it also has the advantage of easy access to the cultural richness of the capital. At the same time, its proximity to major international airports provides ease of travel for both our overseas girls and for those participating in the School's foreign exchange and visit programmes.

Curriculum. With over twenty-five subjects in the curriculum and more than ninety co-curricular activities available, girls have every opportunity to discover their strengths and to become exceptional learners and leaders. We offer a holistic educational experience which supports and encourages intellectual, physical, moral and spiritual development.

Spiritual Life. Queenswood encourages intellectual curiosity of which the spiritual dimension is an important part. Girls are therefore welcome to discuss their thoughts, feelings and faith in an open and supportive context. Since true education is holistic it includes spiritual and moral development. All pupils of the School, whatever their religion, are encouraged to explore and develop their own faith in an atmosphere of tolerance.

Boarding. We strongly believe that fun and friendship should be the foundation of our boarding community. So, we invite you to enter a world where your daughter will be able to embrace diversity, firmly establish her independence while still fostering a sense of care and concern for the community, sample more to achieve more and certainly make friends for life.

Lower School. Our ultimate aim in the Lower School is to help girls to become independent students with enthusiasm for learning and the ambition to develop their skills and qualities to their fullest extent. Beyond the classroom, there is a wealth of opportunities for younger girls to enrich their education. These include a wide range of over 90 co-curricular clubs and activities and a diverse programme of House outings and excursions.

Entry. Entrance to Queenswood is by examination (Common Entrance Exam or Queenswood's papers), interview and a report from the pupil's current Headteacher.

Scholarships. Academic, art, dance, drama, music, sports and tennis scholarships (honorary) are available at 11+, 13+, and Sixth Form entry. Bursaries are means-tested and reviewed annually.

Fees per term (2018–2019). Day: Sixth Form £8,275; Years 9–11 £8,125; Years 7–8 £6,975. Boarders: Sixth Form: Flexi boarding (1–3 nights) £8,825–£9,725, Weekly boarding £10,345, Full boarding £11,250; Years 9–11: Flexi boarding (1–3 nights) £8,675–£9,575, Weekly boarding £10,195, Full boarding £10,900; Years 7–8: Flexi boarding (1–3 nights) £7,175–£7,505, Weekly boarding £7,785, Full boarding £7,995.

Old Queenswoodians' Association (OQA) with 4,000+ members and an active young membership that support current Queenswoodians after their time at School has come to an end.

Charitable status. Queenswood School Limited is a Registered Charity, number 311060, which exists to provide high-quality education for girls.

Governors:
Chairman: Mr E M Sautter, MA
Vice-Chairman: Mr H J De Sausmarez, BA Hons, FCIS
Mr R Baines, BSc Hons, CIMA, CEng, MICE
Reverend David M Chapman
Mr T C Garnham, BSc Hons
Miss K Harvey, LLB Hons, PGL Dip, LLM (*Old Queenswoodian Representative*)
Dr O McGuinness, BSc Hons, MBBS, FRCP

Mr S Morris, MA, PGCE, NPQH
Mrs N Penny
Mr A D Poppleton, BEng, AKC, FIET, FBSC
Reverend T Swindell, BA Hons, BSc Hons, FCA
Mrs P M Wrinch

Principal: **Mrs J Cameron**, BSc Hons Surrey, PGCE

Bursar and Clerk to the Governors: Mr I Williams, BEng Hons RMCS Shrivenham, CEng
Director of External Relations: Mrs D Cresswell, BA Hons York, DipM
Deputy Head Academic: Mr I Sheldon, MChem Oxon, PGCE, MRSC
Deputy Head Pastoral: Mrs A Wakefield, BMus Hons Sheffield
Assistant Head, Pupils: Mrs H Mackay, BA Hons Yale, MA London, PGCE
Assistant Head, Pupil Data, Teaching and Learning: Mr S Daughton, BA Hons, PGCE, MRHS, MA London
Head of Sixth Form: Mr P Merrell, BA Hons UCL, MPhil Birmingham, PGCE
Head of PR, Digital and Print: Mr N Kelley, BA Hons Oxon

Head of Boarding: Ms S Hurndall-Waldron

Art and Design: Mrs L Wagstaffe
Classics: Mrs C Tarrega, BA Hons, MIL, QTS
Dance: Miss K Lasocski [Maternity Cover]
Design & Technology: Miss L Tillotson, BA Hons Lancashire, PGCE
Drama: Mrs A Kelley, BA Hons Wales, MA Portsmouth
Economics & Business Studies: Mr S Lovell, BA Hons Southampton, PGCE
EAL: Ms D Eastwood, BA Hons Leeds, TESOL
English: Mrs R New, BA Hons Lancaster, CTEFL
Geography: Mrs E Barnard, BA Hons Manchester, PGCE
History: Mrs J Curtin, BA Hons Queen's Belfast, MA, PGCE & Mrs S Scriven, BA Hons Hertfordshire, PGCE
History of Art: Dr W Bird, BA Hons Leicester, PGCE, PhD Reading
Languages: Mrs L Law, BA Hons Middlesex, PGCE
Personalised Learning: Mrs N Grant-Stevenson, BSc Hons Nottingham, MEd Belfast, MSc, PGCE
Mathematics: Mrs M Bromfield, BA, MA Oxon, PGCE
Music: Mr J Dobson, Prof Cert Hons RAM, LRAM
Physical Education: Mrs J Wakeley, BEd Hons London
Practical Cookery: Mrs J Lee
Religious Studies: Mrs B Gillon, BA Hons, MPhil King's College London
Science: Ms C Smith

Radley College

Abingdon, Oxfordshire OX14 2HR

Tel:	01235 543127 (Warden)
	01235 543122 (Bursar)
	01235 543174 (Admissions)
	01235 543000 (General Enquiries)
email:	warden@radley.org.uk
website:	www.radley.org.uk

Motto: *Sicut Serpentes, sicut Columbae*

St Peter's College, Radley, was founded by the Reverend William Sewell, Fellow of Exeter College, Oxford, to provide an independent school education on the principles of the Church of England. It was opened on 9 June 1847 and incorporated by Royal Charter in 1890. It stands in a park of some 700 acres.

General Arrangements. There are 690 boys in the school, all of whom board. On admission, boys enter one of the 10 houses known as Socials. All are close together within the grounds. All meals are served in Hall on a cafeteria system. There is a daily Chapel Service for all boys.

Admission. The 13+ admissions process for 2019 onwards will be held when boys are in Year 6. Boys will be assessed using the ISEB Common Pre-Test, a current school report and an interview with the Warden or Senior Master at Radley. Those who have registered early on the Radley List (generally before a boy is 3 years old) will go through this process in the Michaelmas Term of Year 6 with offers being made on 1st March of Year 6. Those who have not registered, or who are on the waiting list, go through the same assessments from 1st November to end of March in Year 6, with offers being made by May of Year 6. This process is called Open Entry. Offers will be unconditional, but boys are required to sit 13+ Common Entrance (or Maths and English exams for those abroad) and Radley reserves the right to refuse entry in exceptional circumstances. Any 2017 or 2018 candidates can apply to Radley through the scholarship process.

A few places are sometimes available for Sixth Form entry: details are available on our website.

Scholarships and Bursaries. Up to twelve Academic Scholarships and Exhibitions are awarded each year. In addition Music, Sport, Drama and Art Awards are offered. All awards may be supplemented by a means-tested bursary. Details of all awards are available from our website or the Registrar, admissions@radley.org.uk. Further means-tested bursaries (funded places) of up to 100% of the fees are available for boys who would otherwise be unable to afford to come to Radley.

Music: On average five Instrumental Scholarships and several Exhibitions are offered annually with free tuition.

Sport: At least five sport awards are offered annually.

Drama: Around two awards will be offered annually.

Art: Around two awards will be offered annually.

Work. In the Shells, Removes and Fifth Form a broad curriculum is followed. There is some choice at GCSE with boys generally taking nine or ten subjects.

In the Sixth Form a boy can specialise in a combination of Classics, French, Spanish, German, Theatre Studies, English, History, Religious Studies, Geography, Geology, Biology, Chemistry, Physics, Mathematics, Economics, Politics, Economics and Business, Music, Art or Design, leading to AS/A2 examinations.

Careers. Advice and assistance is available to all boys on a wide range of career possibilities through the Director of Careers. The School is a member of Inspiring Futures and close connections are maintained with the professions, with firms, with the services and with Old Radleians. Visits and talks by experts in these fields are a special feature.

Games. In the Michaelmas Term rugby football is the major school game. In the other two terms the 'wet-bobs' row; the 'dry-bobs' play hockey (the major game) and soccer in the Lent Term, cricket (the major game), athletics and tennis in the Summer. There are also numerous minor sports which involve boys in competition with other schools. The playing fields are close to the main buildings.

The College has its own boathouse, and the use of a stretch of the River Thames between Sandford and Abingdon. The VIIIs compete in regattas and Head of the River races.

There are three all-weather hockey pitches, an athletics track, five squash courts, a Real Tennis court, a rackets court, two covered Fives courts, 20 hard tennis courts and a 9-hole golf course. There is a large, well-equipped gymnasium and an indoor, heated swimming pool attached to a multi-purpose sports hall and a state-of-the-art rowing tank.

CCF and Duke of Edinburgh's Award. All boys, in their fourth term, join the Radley College Contingent, Combined Cadet Force (Army, Navy and Air sections). They work for the Proficiency examination, which takes three terms. When they have passed Proficiency and done a week's Corps Camp in the holidays they either stay on in a special section for further training or join one of the many Community Action Projects on offer. There is a thriving Duke of Edinburgh's Award scheme.

Fees per term (2018–2019). £12,775 (inclusive of medical attendance). There is available a system of insurance against loss of fees caused by illness, accident, or infection. Particulars can be obtained from the Bursar.

Charitable status. St Peter's College, Radley is a Registered Charity, number 309243. It exists for the purpose of the education of youth in general knowledge and literature and particularly and especially in the doctrines and principles of the Church of England.

Visitor: The Rt Revd The Lord Bishop of Oxford

Council:
Chairman: M E Hodgson, MA, FRICS
Vice-Chairman: D C S Smellie, MA

N J Henderson, MA, FRCS	Sir A C Mayfield, MBA
T O Seymour, MA	Sir J Holmes
M J W Rushton, MA	R N L Huntingford
Mrs D J Pluck, FCA	P E F Watson, FRGS
G A Kaye, BSc	Mrs E J Martineau, FRGS
Mrs E McKendrick, BA	H J R Willis, MA
W S H Laidlaw, MA	S J B Shaw
T M Durie, BA, ACA, FSI	Ms L Nixon
J C Bridcut, MA	Revd Dr S Hampton
R H Warner, MA, ACA	

Warden: J S Moule, MA

Sub Warden: B J Holden, MA, BTech
Academic Director: S R Rathbone, MA, MA

Senior Masters:
H D Hammond, BSc
R D Shaw, MA
N Murphy MA

Under Masters:
D C K Edwards, MA
R M C Greed, BSc

Teaching Staff:

G Wiseman, BA	†G H S May, MA (*H Social*)
P W Gamble, MA	
I P Ellis, BA, Dip RA Schls	†G R King, BA (*G Social*)
S Barlass, BA	D J Pullen, BSc
C M Bedford, BA, PhD	R K McMahon, MA, MPhil, DPhil
I S Yorston, MA	
W O C Matthews, BA	J E Gearing, BA
†T R G Ryder, BA, MFA (*A Social*)	Mrs G C Porter, MA, MSc
	†O H Langton, MA (*J Social*)
J M Sparks, BSc	
M R Jewell, BA	Ms E E N Danis, BA
R Johnson, BSc	†S R Giddens, BSc, MSc, PhD (*C Social*)
J R W Beasley, MA	
I K Campbell, BA	†T C Lawson, BA (*E Social*)
Mrs M C Hart, BA	
B R Knox, BEd	†C E Scott-Malden, BA, MA (*B Social*)
P M Fernandez, MA	
D W S Roques, MA	A D Cunningham, MA, PhD
K A Mosedale, MA, MSc	
Mrs K J Knox, BA	P J Miron, BSc, DPhil
†H Crump, LLB, BA (*D Social*)	M P Hills, MMath
	E O Holt, BA
S H Dalrymple, BA	†C A San Jose, BA (*F Social*)
K Halliday, BSc, PhD	

J W Schofield, BA, MSc	L Clogher
D L Cox, MMath	Miss L Taft
Mrs K C Ison, BA	J Gaunt
Ms L E Nott, BA	Mrs E Ellis
M G Noone, MA	J Sheldrake
R D Woodling, MChem	S Townsend
S J Perkins, BSc	R Burns, BA
M E Walker, BA, MA, PhD	Ms V Buse, BA
Ms M M Rodriguez	P W G Ford, BA
M C F Brown, BA	A J Hibbs, MPhys
Miss L P Gregory, BA	B T Knowles, BA
R E P Hughes, BSc	Ms S Milanova, MPhil
T C H Norton, MA	N J Pilborough, BA
Mrs L R I Smart, BA	L Ryan
Mrs C E Piller	O D Wills, MEng
M G D Glendon-Doyle, BA (*K Social*)	J A D Wilson, MChem
	O W Choroba, MPhil, PhD
K W S Willis-Stovold, BSc	A M H Hakimi, BSc, MPhil
Miss M Hurley, BA	Ms E Hardman Lea, BA
Mrs C E Piller	Ms A Little, BA Hons
P Asbury, BA	C R Mason, MMath Hons
S R Molyneux, BA	J C Nye
A F C Nash, BA	A P Pancrazi, Lycee
A C N Norman, MSc	J E Popplestone, BSc Hons
D Scott, BA	M I Rumbold, BA
Mrs R Tufnell, BA	P R Summers, MA Hons
C McKegney	D P Mathieson, BA Music

Chaplain: The Revd D Wilson, BSc, BA, MLitt, PhD
Assistant Chaplain: The Revd P J Taylor, MA, BTh
Librarian: Ms A K Muhlberg

Music:
Precentor: S J Gladstone
A J A Williams, MMus, Dip RAM, GRSM, LRAM
Miss S-L Naylor, MA
T M Morris, MA, DPhil, FRCO

There are 36 peripatetic music staff.

Bursar and Secretary: A Ashton, MA, ACIB
Medical Officer: Dr J N B Moore, BSc, MB BS, DRCOG, MRCGP
Development Director: Mrs Philippa Roberts
Registrar: Mrs V M G Hammond

Ratcliffe College

Fosse Way, Ratcliffe on the Wreake, Leicester, Leicestershire LE7 4SG

Tel:	01509 817000 School Office
	01509 817072/817031 Registrar
Fax:	01509 817004
email:	enquiries@ratcliffecollege.com
website:	www.ratcliffecollege.com
Twitter:	@RatcliffeColl
	@RColPrepSchool
	@RatcliffeSport
Facebook:	@RatcliffeCollege

Motto: '*Legis Plenitudo Charitas*'

Ratcliffe College is a co-educational Catholic day and boarding school. The School was founded in 1844 and opened in 1847; the original buildings, designed by the famous architect of the Houses of Parliament, Augustus Pugin, were erected with funds provided by Lady Mary Arundel of Wardour, who also bequeathed money for subsequent extensions.

Age Range. 3–18.

Number of Pupils. 849: 403 girls, 446 boys. Sixth Form 156; Boarders 111.

Aims. The vision of the College is to educate young people in the spirit of the Gospel and the traditions of the Catholic Church, seeking to nurture the God-given talents and potential of each individual, so that each one may become a confident, responsible and useful member of society. Whilst Ratcliffe is a Catholic school, it welcomes children of other denominations and faiths, whose parents feel they can share in and benefit from the School's ideals and environment.

Location. Ratcliffe College is set in over 200 acres of rolling parkland on the A46, seven miles north of Leicester. It is easily accessible by road and benefits from being free of congestion at peak times. The M1/M6 motorways, main line railway stations and airports of Birmingham and East Midlands are all within easy travelling distance. For day pupils, school buses operate daily from Leicester, Loughborough and Nottingham.

Site and Buildings. The main Senior School buildings surround a beautiful Pugin-designed quadrangle and contain the Administration offices, Chapel, Refectory, Library, Medical Centre, Media Rooms and pastoral areas, together with a number of subject departmental areas. In addition, there is a Music Department with Concert Hall; a fully-appointed Theatre; and a Science Centre with additional classrooms for Food Science. Sporting facilities include extensive playing fields, synthetic athletics track and two floodlit all-weather hockey pitches; the state-of-the-art Sports Centre comprises swimming pool and sports hall with a modern fitness suite and squash courts. A complex of recently refurbished buildings nearby provides departmental bases for Geography, Modern Languages and Mathematics. Modernised Boys' and Girls' boarding accommodation is situated on the upper floor of the main building, in separate wings, with individual study bedrooms for older students.

The Rosmini Sixth Form Centre, named after Blessed Antonio Rosmini, the founder of the Rosminian Order and the College, has an upper floor wholly dedicated to independent academic study with full IT accessibility, and ground floor areas providing for social and extracurricular usage. The Centre provides a flagship modern setting for Sixth Form study.

In 2014, the College invested £4.5 million opening a purpose-built Preparatory School building on the school site. The Prep School has twelve classrooms located over two floors, as well as a dedicated technology and languages centre, art, science and food science laboratory, library, central assembly hall and music room for the young pupils. It has been developed to be sympathetic to the original Pugin College.

The Nursery is adjacent to the Prep School in purpose-built accommodation.

Organisation. The College is divided into 2 sections: Senior School (11–18 year olds) and Preparatory School (3–11 year olds, including the Nursery for 3–5 year olds). The sections are closely integrated, allowing continuity of education from 3 to 18. Boarding girls and boys are accommodated in separate wings within the main Senior School building, under the supervision of the resident Senior Housemistress and Housemaster, together with their Assistants. There is a strong emphasis on pastoral care for all pupils. The teacher to pupil ratio in the Senior School is 1:10 (the ratio in the Sixth Form is much lower).

Curriculum. In the Nursery, the emphasis is on early Literacy, Numeracy and the development of personal and social skills, all of which contribute to a child's knowledge, understanding and skills in other areas of learning. Programmes of study are based on the Early Years Foundation Stage Curriculum, but extend well beyond these guidelines to develop a child's interests, talents, outlook and general knowledge and understanding of the world.

The Prep School offers small class sizes, well-resourced classrooms, a clear focus on the National Curriculum, an extended school day and a varied extracurricular activities programme. The curriculum is broad and balanced including extensive provision for Drama, Music, Modern Foreign Languages, Physical Education and Latin, taught by specialist teachers. Each classroom has the most up-to-date teaching and learning resources, with specialist classrooms for Art, Music, Science, Food Technology, ICT and Performing Arts. As the children move into Year 6, approximately half their timetable is taught by Senior School specialists. This enables the highest academic standards at the end of Key Stage 2, which means that all pupils move very happily into Year 7.

In the Senior School a broad and balanced curriculum is followed, which aims to identify and provide for individual needs. Most students take at least nine GCSEs. Core subjects consist of English Language, Mathematics, Religious Studies, a Modern Foreign Language and Science (Core and Additional or Triple Award). This is augmented by up to three further option subjects.

In the Sixth Form, students study 3 A Levels; some are studying 4. During the autumn term of Year 12, the large majority of students will then decide which three of these subjects they wish to continue to A Level, perhaps with an Extended Project Qualification (EPQ) to be completed in Year 12. In addition, students may opt to study the EPQ and the European Computer Driving Licence (ECDL) Level 3 along with two A Level subjects. To ensure a balanced programme, Games lessons and the Enrichment Programme are also part of the curriculum.

Games. The playing fields, which surround the College buildings, cover 200 acres. All pupils participate in Games, including Cricket, Hockey, Rugby, Tennis and Athletics for boys, and Hockey, Netball, Rounders, Tennis and Athletics for girls.

Co-Curricular Activities. Pupils' talents and interests are developed through an extensive programme of activities on weekdays and at weekends. As well as many sporting opportunities, 25% of pupils learn a musical instrument; there are many musical groups, including brass ensemble, orchestra and choirs; all Year 4 pupils have free year-round orchestral instrumental tuition. Many pupils are involved in school productions and film-making, and other media activities are popular. The Combined Cadet Force and The Duke of Edinburgh's Award both flourish. Students are encouraged to be caring and to have consideration for others through Chaplaincy groups and Voluntary Service activities.

Admissions.

Prep School (Nursery 3–5 year olds): Children spend the morning in the Nursery and are informally assessed during this time.

Prep School (Years 1–6, 5–11 year olds): Children spend a half day in School and, during this time, take assessments in English and Mathematics. Entry is normally at Year 3 and Year 5 (when additional classes of 18 pupils are admitted), but a small number of places may be available for entry to other year groups if there are vacancies.

Senior School (11–16 year olds): Entry is normally at age 11+ and 13+ (when an additional form of entry is admitted), but a small number of places may be available for entry to other years if there are vacancies.

11+, 12+, 13+ and 14+ Entrance Examinations are held on a Saturday morning in the first half of the spring term, prior to entry in September. Papers are set in English and Mathematics, and Science, for some year groups. Students also have an informal meeting with a member of the Leadership Team.

Sixth Form (16–18 year olds): All applicants are interviewed and entry is also based on successful performance in GCSE (or equivalent) examinations. Applicants should obtain at least 6 good passes at GCSE, including Mathematics and English. For any subject to be studied in the Sixth Form, applicants should have at least GCSE grade 6 in that subject or a related subject. GCSE grade 7 or higher is normally required to study the following subjects in the Sixth Form: Mathematics, Sciences, Languages and English Literature. Specimen English and Mathematics papers for entry into Years 7–10 are available on request from the Registrar.

Students with a Specific Learning Difficulty, who have evidence within a professional assessor report, are allowed extra time. Acceptable evidence will be in the form of an Educational Psychologist or Specialist Assessor report which clearly indicates speed scores for reading, writing or cognitive processing falling below SS85. Medical reports will also be considered. Such reports will need to be current, i.e. they will have been completed within two years of the Entrance Examinations.

Non-Native Speakers of English from Overseas: It is strongly recommended that overseas applicants should provide an IELTS or Cambridge Assessment English examination certificate to confirm their ability in English language. However, applicants for entry to Years 9 and 10 do have the option of sitting our own English examinations, but will have to provide an IELTS or Cambridge Assessment English examination at the end of their first academic year in order to progress through the School.

Students may also be tested in subjects such as Mathematics and Science.

Overseas applicants are also interviewed via Skype, if a personal visit to the School cannot be arranged.

Scholarships and Bursaries. Ratcliffe College offers a wide range of scholarships to recognise academic, sporting, musical, dramatic and artistic talent amongst applicants for the Senior School.

Each scholarship is worth up to 50% off the fees. Points at which scholarships are offered are Years 7 and 12.

Bursaries are available on entry to Years 7 and 12, for up to 80% of a student's School Fee and in exceptional circumstances up to 100%. All awards are subject to parental means-testing. Sixth Form Talent Bursaries are also available in Sport, Music, Drama, Art and Design. For further details, please contact the Registrar.

Fees per term (2018–2019). UK Students: Full Boarding (Years 7–13) £8,653; Weekly Boarding (Years 9–13) £7,713; Weekly Boarding (Years 7–8) £6,892. Boarding fees include the full cost of the programme of boarding weekend trips throughout the year.

Overseas Students: Full Boarding £10,258. Boarding fees include the full cost of the programme of boarding weekend trips throughout the year. Boarding fees include the cost of additional teaching of English as a Foreign Language with a minimum of 10 one-hour sessions per term.

Day: £3,115–£3,514 (Nursery aged 3–5); £3,514–£3,967 (Years 1–5); £4,581–£5,429 (Years 6–13).

Fees are subject to such termly increase as may prove necessary. Additional charges are made for: private Music lessons at £240 per term for 10 half-hour sessions (for individual tuition for each instrument); Where additional teaching of Learning Skills is required and agreed with parents, this will be charged at £45 per lesson. There is a non-refundable registration fee of £99 (£125 overseas) On acceptance of an offer, a deposit of £1,000 (£500 refunded during the second term) for students entering Ratcliffe College from the UK and of £5,000 (£3,000 refunded during the second term) for students from overseas, is payable on entry to the Preparatory School and Senior School. A deposit is not payable on entry to the Nursery, but will be required when the

child moves to the Preparatory School. The deposit is not refundable if the student subsequently fails to take up the place. As fees are payable termly in advance, the deposit will be held until the student leaves and may be used to offset charges incurred during the final term. Any balance remaining will be refunded at that time.

Charitable status. Ratcliffe College is a Registered Charity, number 1115975, for the education of children.

Governing Body:
Consists of two members of the Board of Directors of the Company Limited by Guarantee which owns the College (Ratcliffe College Ltd), together with up to 10 additional governors, appointed by the Directors, who hold office for a period.

Governors:
Mr Louis Massarella (*Chairman of Governors, Current Parent and Past Pupil*)
Mr Enzo Lallo (*Vice-Chair of Governors, Current Parent*)

Mrs T Gamble	Dr M Riley
Miss B Lavin	Fr P Sainter
Mrs L Marsden	Mr G Sharpe
Mr A Mee	Mr M Stokes
Mr P Mulvihill	Mr M Traynor

Senior Leadership Team:

***Headmaster:* Mr J P Reddin**, BSc, MSc, NPQH

Senior Deputy Head: Mr K Ryce, BA, MSc
Deputy Head Pastoral (*Senior School*): Mr C Donegan, BSc, MA
Director of Finance: Mr D Robson, Bcom Acc, ACA
Head of Preparatory School: Father C Cann, MA, MA Oxon, Cert Theol
Development Officer: Mr A Yell, BSc
Assistant Head, Head of Sixth Form: Mr J Neville, MPhil, MA
Assistant Head Academic: Ms J Davis, BA, MSc
Head of Boarding, Senior Girls' Housemistress: Mrs J Leite, BA, MA
Deputy Head, Preparatory School: Mrs J Cartwright, BA [maternity leave]
Acting Deputy Head, Music (*Preparatory School*): Mrs M Markham, BA [maternity cover]
Father President: Father P Sainter

Teaching Staff:
* *Head of Department*
Mr S Anagnostaras, BA, MA (**Latin*)
Mrs L Arnold, BSc, MPhil (*Information Communication Technology*)
Miss R Argo, BMus (*Music*)
Miss E Ault, MSc (*Physics*)
Miss E Bakewell, BA (*Physical Education*)
Mr W Ballard, BSc, MA (**Chemistry*)
Mr M Balmbra, BSc (*Physical Education, Geography, OC CCF*)
Mrs A Batten, BSc (*Learning Support Assistant*)
Miss S BEddoes, BA (*Languages*)
Mr M Benjamin, BA (*English and Head of Public Speaking and Debate*)
Mrs C Bennett, BA (**Media Studies, English*)
Mr D Berry, BA (**Art and Design*)
Mr J Box, BA, MA (*EAL*)
Mrs K Burton, BA (**Food Science and Nutrition*)
Mr J Cantrill, BA (**History*)
Miss M Casas-Ojeda, BA, MA (*Spanish*)
Mrs C Caven-Henrys, AISTD, Dip LCCD (*Drama, Dance*)
Ms P Charvong, BA, MA (*EAL*)
Mr A Chorley, MSc (**Science*)

Mrs S Clarke, BA (*Mathematics*)

Mrs J Cluley, BEd (**Special Educational Needs Coordinator*)

Mrs C Cole, MA (*Mathematics*)

Miss A Corbinzolu, BA (*Religious Studies*)

Mrs A Crebbin, DEUG (*French and Spanish*)

Mrs S Cushing, BA (**Languages*)

Mrs D Darlington, BSc (*Science*)

Mr M Darlington, BSc (*Curriculum Director, Physics*)

Mrs L Davids, BSc (*Learning Support, English*)

Mrs A Dungey, BSc (*Science, Food Technology*)

Mr A Dziemianko, BSc (*Geography*)

Mr P Enoux, BA (*Preparatory School*)

Mr W Faulconbridge, BSc (*Head of Preparatory School Sport*)

Mr A Ferrari, BSc (*Preparatory School*)

Mr J Finn, BA (*Preparatory School*)

Miss D Gatt, BSc (*Biology*)

Miss L Gentle, BSc (*Physical Education, Head of Girls' Netball*)

Mrs N Gilchrist, BEd (*Preparatory School*)

Mr P Gilchrist, BSc (*Senior Boys' Housemaster*)

Mrs D Grant, BEd (*Preparatory School*)

Miss R Green, BSc (*Head of Nursery*)

Mr B Hibbert, BSc (*Computer Science, Information Communication Technology*)

Mr G Higham, BSc (**Mathematics*)

Miss V Hobbs, BA (*English*)

Mrs S Hussain, Level III (*Learning Support Assistant*)

Miss C Jeyes, NNEB (*Early Years Practitioner, Nursery*)

Mr C Jones, BA, MA (*Business/Economics*)

Mr M Jones, BSc (*Head of Year 11, *Information Communication Technology*)

Dr S Jones, PhD (*Mathematics*)

Mr M Kaye, BA (*Physical Education, History*)

Mr A Kellighan, BA, MA (*Religious Studies*)

Mr D Kent, BA (*Preparatory School*)

Dr S Kyle-Ferguson, PhD (*Biology*)

Mr M Lambert, BSc (**Geography*)

Dr C Latham, BSc, MSc, PhD (*Learning Support Preparatory School*)

Miss C Llewelyn, BA (*Preparatory School*)

Mr M Lucas, BSc (**Academic PE*)

Mrs M Markham, BA (*Music, Preparatory School*)

Mr E McCall, BMus, MMus (**Music*)

Miss A McKenna, MA (*English*)

Mr P McCrindell, BA (*Head of Year 11, Languages*)

Mr P Michel, BA (*Lay Chaplain*)

Mrs A Mullan, BA (*Languages*) [maternity cover]

Mrs J Munton, BA (**Drama*)

Mrs S Neuberg, BA (*Nursery*)

Mr M Newman, BA (*Head of Year 13, History*)

Mrs K Noble, BA, MA (*EAL*)

Mrs Y O'Connor, BA, MEd (*Religious Studies*)

Mrs S Owen, BA (*Early Years Practitioner*) [maternity leave]

Mr B Plummer, BSc (*Preparatory School*)

Mrs J Reddin, BA (*French*)

Mrs M Reeves, BA, MSc (*EAL, English*)

Mr P Rogers, BA (*Head of Year 8, Design and Technology*)

Ms E Sellars, BSc (*Mathematics*)

Mr A Seth, BSc (**Design and Technology*)

Mrs A-M Slater, BA, MA (*EAL*)

Mr M Sleath, BSc (*Mathematics*)

Mrs H Smith, BSc (*Mathematics*)

Mrs P Smith, BA (*Religious Studies*)

Ms G Southwell, BSc (*Preparatory School*)

Mr P Spencer, ACIB (*Head of Year 12, *Business/ Economics*)

Miss T Spencer, BA (**PSHCE, Business Studies, Careers Coordinator*)

Miss A Stafford, BSc (*Director of Sport*)

Miss B Stanley, BSc (*Preparatory School, Boarding Assistant*)

Dr L Stannard, BA, MA, PhD (**English*)

Dr S Standen, BSc, PhD (*Science*)

Mr S Thorpe, BSc (*Head of Year 10, Biology*)

Mr P Trotter CChem, MRSc (*Science*)

Mr D Turner, BEd (*Preparatory School, Assistant Boys' Housemaster*)

Miss K Vickers, BMus (*Music*)

Mrs E Walker, BA (*PGCE (Nursery)*)

Mr N Walsh, LLB (**Religious Studies*)

Mrs E Waters, BEd (*Learning Support*)

Mrs L Watson, BA (*Nursery*)

Mrs L Wetton, BSc (*Preparatory School*)

Mrs L Whieldon, BA (*English*)

Mrs M Williams, BA (*Librarian*)

Mr E Woodcock, BA, MSc (*Head of Year 7, Physical Education*)

Miss A Wright, BA (*Art and Design*)

Sports Coaches:

Mr N Back	Mr K Marshall
Mr G Dawe	Mr D Moolman
Mr L Deacon	Mr J Nightingale
Miss E Durr	Miss N Panagarry
Miss E Godwin	Mr O Rogerson
Miss O Gilchrist	Mrs A Taylor
Miss H Joseph	Mr N Taylor
Mr G Laird-Craig	

Peripatetic Music Staff:

Mr P Bennett	Mr G Henderson
Dr M Bonshor	Mrs C Lee
Mr J Boyd	Mr B Matthews
Mrs S Cheeseman	Miss R Reedman
Mr C Earp	Mrs K Thompson (*Music Admin*)
Mrs S Forrester	
Ms S Hall	

LAMDA Teachers:

Mrs M Johnson

Mrs G Courtney

Miss S Green

CCF:

Major M Balmbra (*CCF OC*)

Mr M Edwards (*CCF SSI*)

Mrs H Grant (*CCF RAF OC*)

Mrs A Batten (*RAF OC*)

Graduate Sports Assistants:

Miss T Keast

Miss C McLoughlin

Mr M Bobath

Mr M Laycock

Languages Assistants:

Miss D Carlotti (*French*)

Mr H Münsch, BA, MA (*German*)

Mrs W Zagoza de Vale, Level III (*Spanish*)

Teaching Assistants (Preparatory School):

Miss C Croxall, Level III

Mrs R Deacon

Mrs L Finn, NVQ III

Mrs D Hately

Miss E Lacey, Level III (*Nursery*)

Mrs A Leake, NVQ II

Mrs R Muse, NVQ III (*Nursery*)

Mrs P McCall (*Nursery*)

Mrs S Wereszczynski
Mrs J Yapa, BA
Mrs N Zimmerman, Cert Ed

Ratcliffe Development:
Mr A Yell (*Development Director*)
Mrs L Liston (*Foundation Manager*)

Reading Blue Coat School

Holme Park, Sonning, Berks RG4 6SU
Tel: 0118 944 1005
Fax: 0118 944 2690
email: reception@rbcs.org.uk
website: www.rbcs.org.uk
Twitter: @ReadingBlues
Facebook: @ReadingBlueCoatl

The School was founded in 1646 by Richard Aldworth, a merchant of London and Reading, and a Governor of Christ's Hospital. There are 760 pupils (aged 11–18) including a co-educational Sixth Form.

Aims. The School aims to provide a stimulating and friendly atmosphere in which each pupil can realise his or her full intellectual, physical and creative potential. Pupils are encouraged to be self-reliant and adaptable and we hope that they will learn the basis of good citizenship founded on honesty, fairness and understanding of the needs of others.

The School is a Church of England Foundation, and emphasis is placed on Christian values and standards.

Buildings. The School is set in an attractive 46-acre site by the banks of the Thames in the village of Sonning. School House, originally built in the eighteenth century and extensively remodelled in the Victorian era, stands at the heart of the School. The School's facilities have undergone a continuous programme of improvement over the last decade, including a new IT Centre, a new Design Technology Centre, improvements to the school's entrance and dropoff/pickup area, a new geology and psychology block, a 23-classroom teaching facility, a cricket pavilion, improvements to the swimming pool and a boathouse on the banks of the Thames. The School has recently expanded its facilities for the Sixth Form and has plans for further development.

Curriculum. In Years 7 to 9, pupils study a broad range of subjects, including Classics, two modern foreign languages and Religious Studies. In Years 10 and 11, pupils follow courses in Mathematics and Science and also opt to complete four further courses in a wide range of additional subjects, such as History, Geography, Geology and Physical Education, with a modern foreign language being compulsory. A wide range of subjects is offered at A Level, including subjects such as Psychology, Economics, Business, Government and Politics, and Drama and Theatre Studies, with nearly every pupil going on to university, including Oxford and Cambridge.

Sixth Form. The co-educational Sixth Form Centre accommodates more than 250 students. Girls are fully integrated into all activities. In addition to A Level courses, all Sixth Formers follow a compulsory enrichment programme.

Games and Activities. A wide range of sports and activities is offered within the curriculum and regular school fixtures for all year groups are arranged. Full advantage is taken of the River Thames and Rowing is a popular sport for both boys and girls. The main boys' games are Rugby in the Autumn Term, Football in the Spring Term, and Cricket and Athletics in the Summer Term. Girls play Netball, Rounders and Hockey. Other sporting activities include Basketball,

Tennis, Golf, Table Tennis, Climbing, Swimming, Lacrosse, Archery, Cross Country, Badminton, Mountain Biking, Yoga and Sailing.

The Cadet Force includes Army, RAF and RN Sections. Camping and adventure training activities take place during holidays and at weekends. There is a wide range in the Activities Programme, which includes The Duke of Edinburgh's Award, overseas expeditions, community service and sports leadership.

Music and Drama enjoy a high profile in the life of the School. Well over a third of the pupils receive individual instrumental lessons and pupils are encouraged to join in activities such as the Choir, Chamber Choir, Piano Trio, String Ensemble, Concert Band, Saxophone Group, Brass Group, Swing Band, Wind Band, Junior Strings, Treble Choir, Rock Bands and Senior Brass Group. Concerts, plays and musicals are presented regularly.

Admissions. The two main points of entry in September are at 11+ and 16+. 11+ entry is by entrance examination taken the previous January. Entry at other levels is by examination and interview and is subject to vacancies. Entry to the Sixth Form for girls and boys is by assessment, interview and GCSE results.

Scholarships and Bursaries. The Foundation makes provision for awards of scholarships and bursaries, including academic, music, sport and art awards, based on merit and need. Foundation Scholarships up to 100% of fees are available according to financial need.

Fees per term (2018–2019). £5,565.

Charitable status. Reading Blue Coat School is a Registered Charity, number 1087839. Its aim is the provision of secondary education for pupils aged 11 to 18.

Chairman of Governors: P Bertram

***Headmaster*: J R Elzinga**, BA, MSt

Second Master: P J Thomas, BSc Hons, GTP (*Geology, Geography*)
Deputy Head, Academic: R Tidbury, MSc Hons, PGCE (*Mathematics*)
Deputy Head, Staff: Dr K J Magill, MPhil, BA, PGCE, PhD, FCCT (*Religious Studies*)
Deputy Head, Pastoral: P D Wise, MEd, BSc Hons, PGCE (*Geography*)
Bursar: S A Jackson, BSc, MBA
Director of Marketing and Admissions: Mrs J Jarrett
Director of Development: Mrs V E Fangen-Hall, BA Hons

* *Head of Department*

M J Baker, BA Hons, PGCE (*Geography)
Mrs C E Bamforth, MA, PGCE (*Biology*)
S D Bateman, BA (*Business, Economics*)
Mrs K E Bayliss, BA (*Business, *Economics)
Miss S Beaveridge, BA, QTS (*English*)
Mrs L J Bennett, BEd Hons (*Religious Studies*)
Mrs S E Berry, BA, PGCE, Dip SpLD, AMBDA (**Learning Support, French*)
T Blackburn, BA Hons, MPhil (*Religious Studies*)
C Bond (*Drama*)
J Bowler, BA Hons, PGCE, LTCL, ARCM (**Director of Music, Performance Studies/Drama and Theatre*)
B J Clark, BA Hons, MSt, PGCE (**Religious Studies*)
E J Clark, BA Hons, QTS (*Mathematics*)
Mrs M A Clews, BA, PGCE, PG Cert (**Psychology, Classics*)
Mrs N Coccia-Clark, BA Hons, MA (*Drama)
A W Colville, BSc Hons, BSc (*Biology)
S J Cook, CertEd, BA (*Physical Education*)
Mrs R L Crossland, MESci, PGCE (*Geology*)
Mrs C Dance, BA Ed Hons (*Mathematics*, **Girls' Games*)

J C Dance, BA Hons (*Sport and Physical Education*)

Mrs A M Dewar, BA Hons, PGCE (*French, German, Spanish*)

Dr S M Dimmick, BSc, DipEd, MSc, PhD (*Biology*)

R N Ennis, BA, PGCE (*Art*)

Mrs G R Finucane, BSc, MSc (*Geology, Geography*)

Mrs J L Forward, BSc (*Mathematics, Physics*)

A J French, BA Hons, PG Dip (*Head of Rowing*)

W E Gilbertson, MEng (*Mathematics, Physics*)

D Hales-Beck, BA Hons, PGCE (*Drama, English*)

K Hartland, BSc, QTS (*Chemistry*)

Mrs S A Head, MA (*Modern Foreign Languages, German, French*)

Miss C A Holliday, BA, PGCE (*German, French*)

M J Jerstice, BSc, PGCE (**Integrated Science, *Chemistry*)

L B Johnson, BA Hons, PG Law Diploma (**Government and Politics*)

K Karadimos, BA, BA Hons, PG Dip, PGCE (*Business, Economics*)

Ms B Kaur, BSc, PGCE (*Psychology*)

Mrs G M Kelly, BA Hons, PGCE (*Religious Studies, French*)

Mrs R Kennedy-George, MA, MPhil, PGCE (*English*)

S A Lambert, BA Hons, QTS (**Classics & Latin*)

Dr S R Langdon, MChem, PGCE, PhD (*Chemistry*)

J Leigh, BA Hons, MA (*History*)

A J Maddocks, BA Hons (**French, German*)

Mrs T A McConalogue, BEd (*Mathematics*)

S R McFaul, MEng, PGCE (*Mathematics, Physics*)

H J McGough, BSc Hons (**Design Technology*)

Mrs I A McGough, BA, PGCE (*Design Technology*)

A G McMahon, BMus, LTCL (*Music Technology*)

R Meehan, BA Hons, BA Hons, PGCE (**Music*)

R E Mellows, BEng (*Physics*)

Mrs G Mitchell, BA Hons, PGCE (*Information Technology, Religious Studies*)

W E Mitchell, BA Hons, PGCE (*Geography*)

W Nash-Wortham, BA Hons, PGCE (*Business, Economics, *Careers*)

G E Morton, BA Hons, PGCE (*English*)

Mrs H J Oliver, BA Hons, PGCE (*French*)

Dr B T Pennington, MSci, BA, PhD (*Geography*)

M J Pink, BA Hons, MSc (*Psychology, Sport and Physical Education*)

Miss G Plowman, BA Hons (*History*)

Mrs H E Rancombe, BSc Hons, PGCE (*Psychology, Biology*)

Mrs A J Redley, BA Hons (*English*)

Mrs C Rule, BA Hons, OCR SpLD Diploma (*Learning Support*)

D L Salmon, MA, Computing Dip, PGCE (*Physics, Electronics*)

Dr F B Santos, BSc, MSc, PhD (*Chemistry*)

D H R Selvester, BA, PGCE (*Design Technology*)

T E Seward, MSc (*Sport and Physical Education*)

B J Shuler, BEng, MEd (**Physics*)

R I Shuttleworth, BSc Hons, PGCE (**Mathematics*)

J R Slack, BSc Hons, PGCE (*Mathematics*)

Mrs J P Smith, BSc Hons, PGCE (*Physics*)

R P Starr, BA Hons, PGCE (*Spanish, French*)

Revd J A Stephenson, B Th, BSc Hons (*Psychology, Chaplain*)

M J Stewart, BA Hons, MA, PGCE (**English, Drama*)

Mrs A D Tapley, BSc Hons (*Biology*)

Miss A R Thomas, BSc, PGCE (*Mathematics*)

Ms C R Thomas, MA, PGCE (*History, Government and Politics*)

Miss J L Thompson, BA, PGCE (*Geography*)

The Revd K L Toogood, BSc Hons, PGCE, BA Hons (*Mathematics, Associate Chaplain*)

Miss B A Truman, BA Hons, MA, PGCE (*English, French, Film Studies*)

Miss T van der Werff, MA, PGCE (**History*)

W Voice, BA Hons, PGCE (*Information Technology*)

T C Walford, BSc, PGCE (*Information Technology*)

R J Wallis, BA, PGCE (**Art*)

N J Warde, BSc, PGCE (*Biology*)

Mrs N Watmough-Starkie, BMus Hons, PGCE (*Music*)

G A Wilson, BSc (**Sport and Physical Education*)

S Yates, BSc Hons, PGCE (**Information Technology*)

R W Yue, MSc, BSc, PGCE (*Mathematics*)

Mrs J F Zambon, BA Hons, PGCE (**Spanish*)

Headmaster's Secretary: Mrs K Abbott
Librarian: Miss C Knight, BA Hons, MA, PG LIS
School Nurse: Mrs G F Montgomery, RGN
Sports Centre Manager: R D Cook
Archivist: P J van Went, MA, CertEd

Reed's School

Sandy Lane, Cobham, Surrey KT11 2ES

Tel: 01932 869001
email: admissions@reeds.surrey.sch.uk
website: www.reeds.surrey.sch.uk
Twitter: @ReedsSchool
Facebook: @ReedsSchool

Reed's School is an HMC boarding and day school for boys from 11 to 18 with girls in the Sixth Form. It was founded by Andrew Reed in 1813 primarily for children whose fathers had died. In 1958 the School expanded to take fee payers and girls became eligible for entry in the 1980s. The Foundation is still at the heart of the school and bursaries are given to around 10% of the pupils who have lost the support of one or both parents, based on certain criteria. Each case is considered on an individual basis with the child's best interests at the centre of the discussions. The School is situated in Cobham, Surrey in 40 acres of heath and woodland. It can be reached in 30 minutes by train from Waterloo and is within half an hour's drive of both Heathrow and Gatwick Airports.

The original buildings have been extensively added to in the last 15 years to provide excellent academic facilities, a new Music School, Lecture Theatre and an Indoor Tennis Centre along with the most recent addition, an Indoor Cricket Centre. The FutureTech building is a vision for Science, Technology, Engineering and Mathematics (STEM) and a programme which involves Reed's School pupils, teachers and a wider community including other educational institutions and commercial organisations. A full refurbishment of the Sixth Form House is under way and will be fully completed by 2018/19.

There are 700 pupils with entry points at 11, 13 and 16. Admission at the age of 11 is based on the School's own entrance examinations; admission at the age of 13 is normally by the Common Entrance examination, with a pre-test in Year 6. There is admission into the Sixth Form for boys and girls via an entrance test sat in the November of Year 11.

Pupils are prepared for GCSE/IGCSEs and A Levels, and virtually 100% of Upper Sixth leavers go on to good universities. There is a wide range of extracurricular activities which are a particular strength of the School. There is also a broad range of Inter-House competitions.

Drama is central to the cultural life at Reed's; it has a reputation for putting on outstanding productions in a variety of styles. There is an impressive number staged each year, with pupils in all year groups given the chance to perform, be involved as a stage technician or as a member of the audience.

Music occupies a central role in daily life at Reed's and the school enjoys an enviable musical reputation, both locally and further afield. From many services in the beautiful Chapel to performances throughout the year to the full orchestra, many instrumental ensembles and individual lessons, the department is a vibrant and flourishing one.

Sport is exceptionally strong. Rugby, Cricket and Hockey are the major sports with additional sports of Athletics, Swimming, Squash, Netball and Basketball with specialised Academies for Tennis, Skiing and Golf.

The School has its own Combined Cadet Force with RAF and Army sections. The Duke of Edinburgh's Award can also be undertaken at Bronze, Silver and Gold levels.

Religious instruction, which promotes religious tolerance, is in accordance with the principles of the Church of England. An annual Confirmation Service is held in the School Chapel for which pupils are prepared by the Chaplain. Pupils of all denominations are accepted into the School and are expected to attend chapel.

The National Curriculum is broadly followed in Years 7 to 9 and early specialisation is avoided. There is a Careers Team which advises pupils and arranges suitable visits and interviews and gives advice on University degree courses. The main responsibility for each pupil is undertaken by his or her Housemaster, supported by a Tutor. The health of the pupils is in the care of a team of nurses in the Medical Centre.

Fees per term (2018–2019). Day Pupils (including meals): £6,580 (Years 7 & 8), £8,225 (Years 9–13). Boarders: £8,770 (Years 7 & 8), £10,600 (Years 9–13). All boarders may exercise a weekly boarding option. There are no compulsory extras.

Scholarships and Bursaries. Academic Scholarships are offered each year at age 11, 13 and 16. Scholarships may be awarded for Music, Drama, Art and Sport at age 11, 13 or 16. Design & Technology scholarships are available at age 13 or 16. Headmaster's Awards may be given to candidates who offer a high performance in more than one area.

As mentioned, a number of Foundation awards are made each year to boys and girls who have lost one or both parents, or whose parents are divorced or separated or whose home life is for some special reason either unhappy or unsatisfactory. The awards, which are means tested, vary according to circumstances.

All applications should be made to the Registrar.

Charitable status. The London Orphan Asylum (Reed's School) is a Registered Charity, number 312008.

Patron: Her Majesty The Queen

Presidents:
Viscount Bridgeman
P B Mitford-Slade, OBE
G M Nissen, CBE
I Plenderleith, CBE

Governors:
Mike Wheeler, CBE (*Chair*)

Marcus Baker	Steve Poole
David Barnett	Hugh Priestley
David Blomfield	Karen Richardson
Mandy Donald	Martin Robinson
James Fulton	Benn Shepherd
Dr Alison Mclean	John Simpson
Lucinda Napier	Ron Stewart
Diana Peacock	Nigel Taunt

Bursar & Secretary to the Governors: Mrs L Hurford, BSc, ACMA

Headmaster: **M W Hoskins**, BA, MA

Deputy Head (Academic): D J Atkins, BA, MA
Deputy Head (Pastoral): A R Balls, BEd
Senior Master: I A Clapp, BEd
Development Director: Mrs K Bartram, BA
Assistant Head (Teaching & Learning): Ms C F St Gallay, BA
Assistant Head (Sixth Form): †L G Michael, BA (*Media Studies*)
Assistant Head (Middle School): L Pytel, BA
Assistant Head (Academic Tracking): J S Ross, MA (*Geography*)
Assistant Head (Curriculum): D Thompson, BSc (*Physics*, *Science*)
Chaplain: The Revd A Winter, BSc, BD

Assistant Staff:
* Head of Department
† Housemaster

Ms M-P Ahanda
†J E Allison, BSc
J M Anderson, BA
Ms L Ashby, BA (*Spanish*)
Mrs L Balls, BA (*Girls' Sport*)
J O Bishop, BA
†A J Blackman, MA
Miss L Blair, BSc
Mr A Braithwaite, BSc
Ms J A Brewster, BSc
Mr L Buckingham, BSc
Mrs S E Butler, MA (*Academic Music*) [maternity leave]
I B Carnegie, MA (*Director of Music*)
J E Clatworthy, MA
C E Cole, BA (*Printing*)
Mrs C C Cook, BA
Miss F L Cramoisan, MA
A J Davey, BA
P P Davies, MA
Miss A Di Mond, BSc
J K Ditchburn, BA
†J B Douthwaite, BA
M R Dunn, HND
B J Edwards, BA (*Sport*, *Physical Education*)
M Farmer, BA
J M Finnerty, BSocSci
Ms M Fitzgerald, BA (*Librarian*)
Mrs M Francis, BA (*CPHSE*)
Mrs K D Goden, BSc [maternity leave]
T D Ha, BSc
†B J Haining, BSc
Mrs R F Harris, MA
†G S Hart, HEd (*Digital Learning*)
J G Hart, BA
Ms S M Hashmi-Lewis, BSc
C J Hawley, BA (*Chemistry*)
Miss R Hood, BSc
Miss S L Hughes, BSc
Miss A M Jiménez, BA
Miss A N Johnson, MA (*Art*)
Mrs D L Kane, BSc (*Head of Girls*)
F Kerr-Dineen, BA
Miss L King, BA
Mrs J A Lawrence, BA
D Leckie, BSc
Ms E McGhee, BA (*Learning Support*)
Miss E McMahon, BSc
K T Medlycott
P L Millington, BSc (*Design Technology*)
Mrs T A Millington, BEd
Miss K Morland, MA (*Head of Scholars*, *Classics*)

†J W Norman, BA
C J Osgood, MA
A R Pascoots
Mrs L Paterson, BSc (*Biology*)
W Pope, BSc
Miss M K Rai, BSc
Miss L Raymond, BA
Miss Z H Rice, BA
Miss F Roberts, BA
P W Rockett, BSc
T Rushbrooke, BSc
Mrs H T Salford, BA (*French*)
C Sandison-Smith, MA (*German*)
T P Silk, BA (*Drama*)
G S Stuckey, BSc
Mrs R L Sullivan, BA
E M Swift, BA (*Religious Studies*)
A R Talbot, BEd
T H Tam, BSc, PhD
A M Thompson, BSc, PhD
C S Thomson, BA
Mrs A Trehearn, BA (*English*)
M C Vernon, BSc
Mrs V Wakefield, BSc
A J Waller, BA (*History*)
J M Wallis, MEng
T A Webb, BA
S D Whiteley, BA (*Economics & Business Studies*)
R D Willey, GLCM
J Wright, BSc (*Mathematics*)

Headmaster's Secretary: Mrs V Cox
Registrar: Mrs R Morris
Assistant Registrar: Ms R Verity
Foundation Manager (*Pastoral*): Mrs R de Fraga Gomes
Foundation Manager (*Relations*): Mrs C Lewis

Development & Marketing Director: Mrs K Bartram
Assistant Marketing Director: Mrs A M Atkins
Assistant Alumni Director: Mrs S Matthews
Outreach & Events Manager: E Whiffin
Development & Alumni Officer: Miss L Sadler

Reigate Grammar School

Reigate Road, Reigate, Surrey RH2 0QS

Tel: 01737 222231
Fax: 01737 224201
email: info@reigategrammar.org
            admissions@reigategrammar.org
website: www.reigategrammar.org
Twitter: @ReigateGrammar
Facebook: @ReigateGrammarSchool

Reigate Grammar School is a co-educational day school for pupils aged 11 to 18.

The school was founded in 1675 as a free school for boys. It became an independent grammar school during the nineteenth century, but after the 1944 Education Act it came under the control of Surrey County Council. On the abolition of the direct grant in 1976, Reigate Grammar School reverted to independent status. At the same time girls were admitted for the first time, initially in the Sixth Form only, but throughout the school from 1993. The school now numbers 1000 pupils, of whom 260 are in the Sixth Form. In September 2003, the school merged with Reigate St Mary's Preparatory and Choir School (*see entry in IAPS section*), which provides education to 350 boys and girls aged from

rising 3 to 11. In 2017 Chinthurst Preparatory School joined the RGS group of schools (*see entry in IAPS section*).

The school is situated in the historic market town of Reigate, just outside the M25 yet with easy transport links into London, Surrey and Sussex. Pupils come from a wide geographical area and from across the social spectrum, thanks to the school's own bursary programme, and to the generous support of the Peter Harrison Foundation which provides substantial financial support each year. Around 50% of pupils come from primary schools, the remainder coming from the preparatory sector.

The Governors have invested considerable sums in new buildings in recent years. New laboratories and classrooms were completed in 2014; a new centre of learning incorporating a state-of-the-art library and Sixth Form Centre opened in 2017; and a new Sports Hall is currently in development. In addition to the main school site, the sports ground at Hartswood, two miles from the school, provides some 32 acres of playing fields and the RGS Hockey Centre with world-class floodlit all-weather pitches which opened in 2014.

Organisation. The school is divided into three sections: Lower School (First and Second Forms: Years 7–8), Upper School (Third, Fourth and Fifth Forms: Years 9–11), and Sixth Form (Years 12–13). The welfare of pupils is overseen by the Heads of Section and Heads of Year. The school has a House system.

Curriculum. The range of subjects on offer is traditional in the early years, but allowing for a broadening of options in the Sixth Form. Prior to GCSE all pupils study a core curriculum of Mathematics, English, Science, Modern Languages (French, German or Spanish), Latin, History, Geography, Religious Studies, ICT, Art, Design Technology, Food, Music, Drama, PE and Games. The three-year GCSE programme starts in the Third Form (Year 9) and most pupils take ten GCSEs or IGCSEs, chosen from the above, with the added options of Sports Studies and Greek. Both Dual Award Science and the separate sciences are offered.

Most pupils stay on into the Sixth Form and take three subjects to A Level. Subjects available include all of the above, with the added options of Economics, Politics, Psychology and Philosophy and Ethics. Further details are available on the website.

Extracurricular activities. Reigate Grammar School has a strong tradition of excellence in a wide variety of extracurricular activities, including an enviable reputation in sport, music and drama; large numbers of pupils participate in the Combined Cadet Force and in The Duke of Edinburgh's Award. The school raises a significant amount of money each year for local and national charities. The main sports are rugby, hockey and cricket for boys; and hockey, netball and rounders for girls, but other sports on offer include athletics, badminton, basketball, gymnastics, football, squash, swimming and tennis. There is a plethora of musical groups which rehearse regularly, including orchestras, a Swing Band, several choirs and numerous ensembles. There are frequent concerts at school and at local and national prestigious venues as well as overseas tours. The Drama department presents at least one major production each term, sometimes in collaboration with the music department, and is frequently represented in the local and national arena.

Admissions. Pupils are normally admitted to the School at 11+, 13+ or 16+, although vacancies occasionally occur at other ages. There is a registration fee of £100. All candidates are required to sit an entrance examination and attend an interview (normally in January or November). All enquiries concerning admission to the school should, in the first instance, be addressed to the Admissions Secretary.

Fees per term (2018–2019). Years 7–8 £6,200; Years 9–13 £6,240. Sibling discounts are available.

Scholarships and Bursaries. The school offers a wide range of scholarships and bursaries.

Scholarships are awarded at 11+, 13+ and 16+ for academic excellence and for talented students in music, sport, art and drama. Bursaries, which are means tested and are aimed at enabling parents who might not otherwise be able to consider a Reigate Grammar School education, may also be available. Applicants living in the Borough of Reigate and Banstead may be eligible for a Harrison Scholarship, which is means tested and made available through the generosity of the Peter Harrison Foundation. Further information is available on the school website or by application to the Admissions Secretary.

Junior School. Reigate St Mary's Preparatory and Choir School (*see entry in IAPS section*) is the junior and nursery school of Reigate Grammar School. It numbers approximately 350 pupils aged 3 to 11 and is one of the few choir schools in the country not attached to a cathedral or college.

Charitable status. Reigate Grammar School is a Registered Charity, number 1081898. Its aim is to provide high-quality education for boys and girls.

Governing Body:
Chairman: Mr J Dean

Mr M Benton	Mr L Herbert
Mr C Cobain	Mrs M Hulme
Mr D Cole	Mr R Newstead
Mr B Day	Mr M O'Dwyer
Mr C Dixon	Miss L Page
Mrs M Edmunds	Professor S Sayce
Mr E Elsey	Mr N Weber

Headmaster: S A Fenton, MA Oxford, MEd Oxford

Senior Deputy Head: Mrs M A Collins, BEng Bristol
Deputy Head: Miss S J Arthur, BA Durham
Deputy Head: Dr B P Stones, BSc, PhD Edinburgh

Assistant Head: A J Boothroyd, BSc Bradford
Assistant Head: N M Buchanan, BSc Edinburgh
Assistant Head: Mrs A L Crook, BSc Edinburgh, MSc Bristol
Assistant Head: H T Jones, BA Durham, MSt Oxford
Assistant Head: Mrs C H Lawson, BA Liverpool

Head of Lower Sixth Form: R T James, BSc Bristol
Head of Upper Sixth Form: Miss C Green, BA East Anglia
Deputy Head of Sixth Form: Mrs L C N Budden, MA Edinburgh, MA Queen Mary

Head of Fifth Form: Miss T Williams, BA Holloway
Head of Fourth Form: M H Hetherington, BA Nottingham
Head of Third Form: Mrs K Scaglione, BA Keele
Head of Second Form: Mrs S L Leck, MA Cambridge
Head of First Form: Mrs E J Mitchell, BEd Exeter

Chaplain: Rev P M Jackson, BA Cheltenham, BA Bristol
Bursar & Clerk to the Governors: S P Douty, FCMA
Head of Foundation and Business Development: S Davey, MA

Heads of House:
Head of House System: Mrs C L Cline, BSc St Mary's
Bird: Mrs A Fullalove, BA South Caroline, MA Queen's Belfast
Cranston: J M C Leck, BA East Anglia
Hodgson: Miss S Shah, Mpharm King's
Williamson: Mr M O'Donnell, BSc Kent

Teaching Staff:
A list of teaching staff is available on the website.

PA to the Headmaster: Mrs B G Eustace

Rendcomb College

Rendcomb, Cirencester, Gloucestershire GL7 7HA

Tel:	01285 832306
Fax:	01285 831331
email:	admissions@rendcombcollege.org.uk
website:	www.rendcombcollege.org.uk
Twitter:	@RendcombCollege
Facebook:	@Rendcombcollege
LinkedIn:	/rendcomb-college

Rendcomb College is a co-educational, independent day and boarding school for children aged 3 to 18 in the heart of the Cotswolds, UK. The College was founded in 1920 by Noel Wills and is set within a stunning 230-acre parkland estate which is equidistant from Cheltenham and Cirencester.

Our Mission. Our mission is to develop thoughtful, adventurous and academically ambitious young people who are lifelong learners. We aim to prepare them with the character and skills to succeed in the ever-changing world after school. Our pupils have the freedom to experience, explore and enquire about the world around them. We aim to encourage independence and tolerance in a safe, caring community and magnificent natural environment.

To achieve this we will:

- Promote a growth mindset, where abilities can be developed through dedication and hard work;
- Provide a co-curriculum that will challenge and support character development, leadership and teamwork;
- Encourage individualism, creativity and contribution to a nurturing and collaborative community;
- Engender physical, spiritual and mental wellbeing through a strong pastoral system;
- Prepare pupils for a life beyond school;
- Develop an appreciation for and responsible attitude towards their environment and surroundings.

Admission. Pupils join the Junior School from Nursery or Reception or join the Senior School at age 11, 13 or 16. The entrance examination at 11 is taken at Rendcomb and comprises three papers: English, Mathematics and Verbal Reasoning. At 13, pupils are admitted by Common Entrance or Rendcomb Examination and at 16 by interview, school reports and GCSE results.

Curriculum. Rendcomb College's curriculum extends well beyond the confines of the classroom and the core teaching day. Our small size in both the Junior and Senior schools enables all students to participate in a number of sports, in addition to a wide range of activities which begin after the end of formal lessons each day. Our philosophy is to consider these to be co-curricular, aimed at combining with the academic elements to genuinely develop the whole person and ensure that we provide a fully-rounded education.

University Entrance. In the last three years, leavers have gone on to a number of prestigious universities including Oxford, Bath, Exeter, Nottingham, Birmingham, Royal Holloway, Durham and Swansea. One student has received an academic scholarship to study Applied Medical Science at Swansea University.

Houses. Both Day pupils and Boarders share the same Houses, enabling strong friendships and comradery to flourish among all pupils throughout the College.

Pupils can board when they join the Senior School in Year 7 through to Sixth Form. From Year 10 upwards, all Boarders have their own modern, comfortable study bedrooms which can be personalised, whilst the younger pupils share dormitories with two or three other students.

Our boarding is very flexible, especially at weekends; from Saturday teatime onwards, Boarders choose to stay at school to work, relax or join in family life at home. There are beds for Day pupils too if they wish to try boarding, or if they need to stay over.

From September 2019, the Year 7–9 house, Godman, will be co-educational following refurbishment and extension. In Years 10 and 11, pupils are split by gender until they reach Sixth Form when they join the co-educational Park House.

Boarders' weekends are full, busy and purposeful through the provision of an extensive programme of activities run by our Boarding Activities Coordinator.

The four Houses at Rendcomb College are located on the school's campus and within easy reach of classrooms and sports facilities. Each with their own character and style, the Houses offer an ideal setting for all pupils to thrive and develop under the guidance of the Houseparents and their pastoral and domestic teams.

Bursaries. A number of contributory bursaries are awarded in keeping with the original charitable aims of the College's Founder. The amount of the bursary award is not influenced by the level of the child's academic ability but by the extent of need and each case is assessed on its own merits with awards being made accordingly.

Scholarships. A number of Scholarships (Academic, Art, Music, Drama and Sport) are awarded each year at Year 7, 9 and 12 with additional Scholarships awarded in Year 3. Scholarships are based on the assessment of a pupil's potential and the value that we believe they will add to the life of our school. We also award the Noel Wills Scholarship and the Rendcomb Scholarship at Year 7.

As we approach our 100th birthday in 2020, we have launched a number of 100% fully-funded scholarships for entry into Year 4 and Year 12 in September 2019.

Fees per term (2018–2019). Senior School: Boarding £7,250–£10,500, Day £5,305–£7,775. Junior School: Day £2,010–£3,865. We accept the Government's 30 hours scheme in Nursery and Reception for qualifying families.

Charitable status. Rendcomb College is a Registered Charity, number 1115884.

Chairman of Governors: Sir Francis Richards, KCMG, CVO, DL

Head of College: **Mr Rob Jones**, BA, MEd

Head of Juniors: Mr Gavin Roberts, BA, PGCE

Bursar: Mrs E Sharman, BSc

Registrar: Miss E Townsend, BA

Repton School

Repton, Derbyshire DE65 6FH

Tel:	01283 559222 (Registrar)
	01283 559200 (School)
email:	registrar@repton.org.uk
website:	www.repton.org.uk
Twitter:	@ReptonSchool

Situated in the heart of England, Repton School has been home to a spiritual community for over 800 years and the inspiring buildings of the 12th century Priory remain at the centre of our life together today.

Over its 450 years Repton has established a strong tradition of distinguished alumni in public life, sport and the arts including Roald Dahl, Archbishop Michael Ramsey, C B Fry, Graeme Garden, and most recently GB hockey gold medallists Georgie Twigg MBE and Shona McCallin MBE.

The 21st century Repton is a fully co-educational school with a strong boarding ethos and is home to around 650 pupils. Individuality flourishes within the context of a real community and every Reptonian is encouraged to discover those areas in which he or she can excel, and to prepare for the world of possibilities that lie beyond the Arch. Repton's Values are that of Wholeness, Truth, Excellence and Respect. The School's aim is that every Reptonian should develop into a confident individual and a person of integrity.

Admission. Pupils are admitted at 13+ (Year 9), 14+ (Year 10) and 16+ (Year 12). Application for admission should be made to the Registrar. There is a registration fee of £100 and 10% deposit of the first term's boarding fee for both day and boarding pupils, payable on acceptance of a place and refunded against the final school bill. 13+ candidates will normally have passed Common Entrance at their preparatory schools, but there is also an entrance examination for candidates not being prepared for CE in November of their Year 8.

Fees per term (2018–2019). Boarders £11,904; Day pupils £8,831. Some additional expenses (for books, stationery, pocket money, etc) will be incurred.

There is a Bursary Fund from which grants in the form of remissions from full fees may in certain circumstances be made. No remission of fees can be made on account of absence.

Scholarships and Bursaries. A number of scholarships and exhibitions are offered annually, at 13+ and 16+, though in exceptional circumstances candidates may be considered for awards at other entry points. The value of any award may be increased where need is shown.

Entrance Scholarships at 13+: The examination for non-academic awards is held at Repton in January for entry the following September, and the examination for academic awards is held at Repton in May for entry the following September. Candidates must be under 14 on 1 September in the year of the examination.

The *Repton Scholarship* is an academic award available to pupils in Year 8 prior to entry to Repton School in Year 9. It rewards academic excellence and a commitment to academic progress, enrichment and a lifelong process of learning. Further details are available on the school's website.

16+ Scholarships: The examination for both academic and non-academic awards takes place in November for entry the following September. A number of awards are available for pupils joining Repton from both the maintained and independent sectors.

Music Scholarships and Exhibitions are awarded at 13+ and 16+. Examinations take place in November (16+) and January (13+). An open day for potential music scholars is held in September.

Drama Scholarships and Exhibitions are also offered at 13+ with auditions and interviews taking place in January.

Art Scholarships and Exhibitions are offered at 13+ and 16+. Examinations take place in November (16+) and January (13+). Candidates will be assessed by examination, interview and an assessment of their portfolio.

Design and Technology (DT) Scholarships and Exhibitions are offered at 13+ and 16+. Examinations take place in November (16+) and January (13+). Candidates will be asked to complete a practical session and interview and to provide a folder of work for assessment.

Sports Scholarships and Exhibitions are offered at 13+ and 16+, to pupils of exceptional talent. Assessments are held by arrangement with the Director of Sport in January.

C B Fry All Rounder Award: awards worth up to 20% of the Repton boarding fee may be offered at 13+ to candidates exhibiting outstanding all-round leadership potential. Assessments take place in February or March when candidates are in Year 7.

Bursaries may be available to those who would not otherwise be able to attend an independent school. These may, in appropriate circumstances, be used to supplement Academic or non-academic awards. Means-tested bursaries are also available to Forces families.

Curriculum. Pupils in B Block (Year 9) have a broad and balanced curriculum. Pupils study: Biology, Chemistry, Classics (either Latin or Classical Civilisation), English, Ethical and Religious Studies, French, Geography, History, Information and Communication Technology (ICT), Mathematics, Physical Education and Physics. Pupils study German or Spanish as a second modern foreign language. There is also a timetabled programme of creative lessons: all pupils study both Design Technology and Art and most pupils will study two of Music, Drama and ICT (creative applications).

Pupils in A/O Blocks (Years 10/11) study a combination of core and optional subjects. All pupils study English, English Literature, Mathematics, Biology, Chemistry and Physics (leading either to three GCSEs in separate sciences for the more able students or two GCSEs in Science). The vast majority of pupils also take a modern foreign language (French, German or Spanish) as a core GCSE. In A Block, all pupils receive one lesson in ICT and one lesson in PSHCE per week. Pupils choose three subjects as optional subjects from the following list: Art, Business, Classical Civilisation, Classical Greek with Latin ("Gratin"), Design Technology, Drama, French (for dual linguists), Geography, History, Latin, Music, Physical Education and Religious Studies. Art and Music may also be taken "off the timetable" to provide pupils with the choice of a fourth optional subject. Specialised learning support lessons and lessons in EAL are taught as an alternative to the core modern foreign language. The top set in Mathematics takes the GCSE at the end of A Block and then studies a more advanced course in O Block.

In the Sixth Form (Years 12/13), the following subjects are available as a full A Level over two years: Art, Biology, Business, Chemistry, Classical Civilisation, Design Technology, Drama and Theatre, Economics, English Literature, French, Geography, German, Politics, History, Latin, Mathematics, Further Mathematics, Music, Photography, Physical Education, Physics, Religious Studies, Spanish and Textiles. Computer Science is available as an AS Level only over two years.

All pupils choose four subjects at the start of the Lower Sixth. During the Lent term of the Lower Sixth, each pupil decides his or her final academic programme for the remainder of the Sixth Form. A pupil may opt to drop one subject and continue with three subjects to A Level or to continue with all four subjects.

In the Lower Sixth, most pupils take "Extend and Enlighten", a course designed by the School to expand awareness of the world beyond the academic subjects that the pupils are studying.

In the Upper Sixth, there is a timetabled lecture programme where pupils have the opportunity to hear distinguished speakers talk on a wide variety of subjects.

Potential Oxbridge candidates are identified by the end of their second term in the Sixth Form and prepared for interview.

Chapel services are those of the Church of England and boarders are expected to attend a service every Sunday unless specially excused. A Confirmation is held each year.

Other activities. Every opportunity and encouragement is given to pupils to develop their creative interests in Art, Music, Drama and Design Technology. Facilities include dedicated Art, Drama and Music Schools, newly renovated Theatre, Studio Theatre and Textiles Studio. There are numerous School societies, covering a wide variety of interests. The Repton Diploma is a formal award recognising a Sixth Former's contribution to an all-round education and the Cross-Curricular Excellence Programme is a substantial programme whereby academic subjects collaborate with real world projects.

Games and sports. Football, hockey (three astroturf pitches – 2 water-based, 1 sand), cricket, netball, rugby, squash, tennis (2 indoor courts and 14 hard courts), cross-country, athletics, sailing, climbing, canoeing, swimming, fencing, golf and horse riding. Superb facilities are provided for physical education including a multi-purpose sports hall, strength and conditioning suite, gymnasium and indoor swimming pool. A complete redevelopment of the Sports Centre site is due for completion in 2019.

Combined Cadet Force. The School maintains a contingent of the Combined Cadet Force and every pupil is a member in Year 10. Subsequently pupils may remain in the CCF to take part in The Duke of Edinburgh's Award scheme or specialise as instructors. Sixth Formers have the additional choice of Community Service.

Houses. All pupils belong to a House, which is their home in the School, where they eat all meals, and is at the heart of their life at Repton. The Housemaster or Housemistress, who has overall responsibility for an individual pupil's work and development, lives in the House with his/her own family and is supported by a resident Matron and team of Tutors. Day pupils are fully integrated into house life.

Repton Preparatory School and Pre-Preparatory School at Foremarke Hall are approximately 1½ miles from the main school and house around 70 boarders and 390 pre-prep and prep day boys and girls. Pupils are taken from age 3 and prepared for entrance to Repton and other schools. Academic Scholarship examinations take place in January.

Further information may be obtained from The Headmaster, Foremarke Hall, Milton, Derbyshire DE65 6EJ. (*See Foremarke Hall's entry in IAPS section.*)

Charitable status. Repton School is a Registered Charity, number 1093166. It exists to provide high quality education for boys and girls.

Chairman of Governors: Sir Henry Every Bt

Headmaster: W M A Land, MA Trinity College Cambridge
Headmaster from April 2019: Mr M Semmence, MA Warwick

Second Master: Mrs S A B Tennant, MA late Scholar of Somerville College Oxford
Deputy Head (Academic): T C Owen, MA late Exhibitioner of St Edmund Hall Oxford
Deputy Head (Pastoral): J G Golding, BA King's College London
Senior Tutor: Mrs C E Goodhead, BSc Sheffield
Surmaster: A J Smith, BSc Loughborough
Director of Admissions: T J Collins, BA Exeter
Chaplain: The Revd Fr N C Robert, MA AKC Homerton College Cambridge

Heads of Department:
Classics: R G Embery, BA Durham
Modern Languages: Mrs C R Watson, MA Pembroke College Oxford
English: Miss K J Campbell, MA St Andrews
Drama: Miss K Chandley, BA Birmingham
History: Dr N F Pitts, BA, PhD Leeds
Government & Politics: Mrs A F Parish, BA Durham
Geography: Mrs L E Wilbraham, BA Queen Mary London
Economics: D A Exley, BSc York
Business: Mrs M K Court, BA Durham
Mathematics: P V Goodhead, MA late Scholar of Pembroke College Oxford

Ethical & Religious Studies: Mrs A V E Saunders, BA Leeds
Physics: Mrs H C Pettit, MA Imperial College London
Biology: Dr S M Ingleston-Orme, BSc, PhD Nottingham
Chemistry: R G Dexter, BSc Royal Holloway
Director of Music: O M Walker, BA Keble College Oxford
Director of Art: I J Whitfield, MA Royal College of Art
Design and Technology: Miss G L Hill, BA Nottingham Trent
Sport: I M Pollock, BEd Exeter

Boys' Boarding Houses:
The Cross: M R Wilson
Latham House: M W T Hunt
New House: J D Wilton
The Orchard: M M Carrington
The Priory: N F Pitts
School House: T H Naylor

Girls' Boarding Houses:
The Abbey: Mrs L E C Bispham
The Garden: Ms S J Lees
Field House: P J Griffiths
The Mitre: Mrs C J Jenkinson

Bursar: C P Bilson, MA, MBA Jesus College Cambridge
Registrar: Miss J Shone
Headmaster's Secretary: Miss J J Taylor

RGS Worcester

Upper Tything, Worcester WR1 1HP

Tel: 01905 613391
Fax: 01905 726892
email: office@rgsw.org.uk
website: www.rgsw.org.uk
Twitter: @RGSWorcester
Facebook: @rgsw.org.uk

School Aims. The aim of the family of RGS Worcester schools is to provide an excellent all round education for children aged 2–18 years, supporting them in their passage to adulthood by developing character, intellect, physical and emotional well-being and cultural understanding within a supportive community.

The School and its staff aim to cultivate an ethos in which each pupil is cared for individually, valued equally and achieves their potential.

RGS Worcester sets out to achieve these aims by:

- Encouraging the growth of intellectual curiosity, creativity and a positive attitude to learning, including the preparation of each child for life through a broad, coherent and balanced curriculum, the use of digital technology to enhance teaching and learning, and educational and enrichment opportunities

- Developing in every child quiet self-confidence, aspiration, responsibility, resilience, spiritual values and a personal moral code, leading to the highest standards of behaviour, consideration for others, tolerance and understanding of other cultures, awareness of British values, and pride in, and loyalty to, the School community

- Offering a wide range of co-curricular activities through which children can develop their social, sporting and cultural interests, explore and enhance their leadership skills and learn the importance of working together

- Providing well-qualified and able staff who are highly committed to delivering excellent teaching, enabling pupils to enjoy learning and achieve to their full potential

- Promoting opportunities for higher education and career options, and creating an awareness of the world beyond the School and a sense of service to the local and wider community

- Pursuing positive relationships with parents through open communication and opportunities to attend school events

It is hoped that, by our schools fulfilling these aims, our pupils will leave RGS Worcester as flexible, independent thinkers, who have quiet self-confidence, treat others with respect and kindness, and go on to make a very positive contribution to the community and to society as a whole.

History. The Royal Grammar School Worcester was founded ante 1291, received its Elizabethan Charter in 1561 and was granted its 'Royal' title by Queen Victoria in 1869. The Alice Ottley School was founded in 1883 as Worcester High School for Girls. The two schools merged to form RGS Worcester & The Alice Ottley School in September 2007 and was renamed RGS Worcester in September 2009.

Location and Buildings. The Senior School is situated a few minutes' walk from the centre of the City and is convenient for rail and bus stations. The Headmaster's office is housed in the Grade II* listed Britannia House, and there are several other historic buildings on the site, including the RGS Main Block, dating from 1868. Educational facilities are outstanding: there are two Sports Halls, specialist Art, IT, Technology and Textiles rooms, a Theatre, Library, Science Block, Music Technology room, and a Lecture Theatre, as well as several assembly halls. The playing fields and boathouse are close by and the School has good use of the local swimming pool. A full-size, floodlit all-weather pitch was opened in 2007 and a state-of-the-art fitness centre in 2008. A new Dance Studio plus changing facilities, two new Science Laboratories and a Digital Language Laboratory were also completed in 2008.

There are two co-educational Preparatory Schools. RGS The Grange (*see IAPS entry*) is set in 48 acres of grounds to the north of the city and has a 16-classroom, £4.5 million extension to complement the original Victorian building that houses the Pre-Prep. RGS Springfield (*see IAPS entry*) is housed in a beautiful Georgian building in the centre of the nearby Britannia Square, close to the city centre. It is secluded and secure, and benefits from its close proximity to the Senior School.

Organisation. The Senior School population is c768 (349 girls and 419 boys). The Senior School is divided into three sections – Lower (Years Seven and Eight), Middle (Years Nine and Ten) and Sixth Form – with an Assistant Head responsible for each. The basic unit is the form, and the form tutor, under the Head of Year, is responsible for all day to day matters relating to the pupils in their charge. In addition all pupils are placed in Houses which exist mainly for internal competitive purposes, but which do provide an important element of continuity throughout a pupil's career at the School. Both Preparatory Schools admit pupils from the age of two, and most proceed to the Senior School at the age of eleven, into Year Seven. RGS The Grange and RGS Springfield are both well known for the high standard of their pastoral care and for stretching the brightest children. Learning Support is particularly well organised.

Curriculum. Pupils follow a common curriculum for the first three years in the Senior School which includes the usual academic subjects, plus IT, Design Technology, Music, Drama and PE. The GCSE option arrangements (Years Ten and Eleven) allow a wide choice, subject to final selection, giving a balanced curriculum which does not prejudice subsequent career decisions. Normally nine to ten subjects are studied: IGCSE English, Mathematics, a Modern Foreign Language and Sciences being setted and compulsory, plus three from French, German, Latin, Spanish, Geography, History, RE, Drama, Art, Music, Textiles, Design

Technology. Most members of the Sixth Form study four subjects to AS Level and at least three to A2 Level. In addition to those subjects studied at GCSE Level, PE, Classical Civilisation, Business Studies, Economics and Politics may be taken up. The Digital Learning Programme was launched in September 2014, which saw iPads become an integral part of the teaching and learning experience.

Careers. The School is a member of Inspiring Futures; the award-winning careers service is readily available and the Head of Careers is responsible for ensuring that all pupils receive basic careers education, and subsequently, access to all the necessary information and experience on which a sound decision may be made regarding future career and Further or Higher Education.

Physical Activities. The School aims to satisfy a wide range of sporting interests and abilities. For boys, Rugby Football, Association Football, Cricket and Athletics are the main activities. Girls take Netball and Hockey in the winter and spring, and Athletics, Tennis and Rounders during the summer Term. Cross-Country Running and Rowing have a full programme of fixtures. A wide range of other activities share priority in the Sports Halls throughout the year, and high-quality cricket coaching is given throughout the winter months.

Outdoor Pursuits. Combined Cadet Force and The Duke of Edinburgh's Award scheme: all pupils may choose to join one or the other at the end of Year Nine. The strong CCF comprises Royal Navy, Army and Air Force sections. Good opportunities exist for attachments to regular units in UK and abroad, for flying training, for leadership training and for Adventure Training. Those who choose The Duke of Edinburgh's Award scheme may work for the Bronze, Silver and Gold Awards, and undertake adventure training and community service.

Other Activities. There is a wide range of clubs and societies. All Lower School pupils receive drama lessons as part of the curriculum and school productions take place each term. School music is also strong: in particular, there is a fine organ, a Big Band, several brass ensembles, two choirs, several smaller vocal ensembles and a very popular Jazz Band. The School fosters a range of international links including regular exchanges with schools in France, Germany, Spain, China and the USA. The School has strong links with schools in the developing world via the World Challenge Organisation, and the school community raises large sums for a range of local, national and international charities every year.

September Admission. This is by examination held in January, mainly at 11+ but also at 12+ and 13+. Pupils are also admitted into the Sixth Form on the basis of a test, interview and GCSE results. Exceptionally, pupils may also be examined and admitted at any time of the year. Admission to the Preparatory Schools is by assessment from age 6+ and by classroom visit before this age.

Fees per term (2018–2019). £4,360.

Scholarships and Bursaries. Scholarships are offered for academic achievement as well as for music, art, design, textiles, drama and sport of up to 50% remission of fees. Bursaries of up to 100% are also available according to parental means and academic potential. Further details can be obtained from the Registrars at the schools.

Charitable status. RGS Worcester is a Registered Charity, number 1120644. The aim of the charity is the education of boys and girls.

Board of Governors:
Chairman: Mr Quentin Poole
Vice Chair: Mrs R F Ham

Mrs L Cook	Sir R G Fry CBE
Mr N Fairlie	H Kimberley
Ms K Meredith	Dr E Robinson
Mrs S Mills	A Greenaway
J G Peters	P Lee
B W Radford	

Director of Finance & Operations and Clerk to the Governors: I T Roberts, OBE, MA

Headmaster: J D C Pitt, MA

Senior Deputy Head : Mr Lloyd Beecham

Deputy Head Academic : Ms Rebecca Roberts Gawen

Assistant Heads:
Dr L J Andrew BSc, PhD (*Pastoral*)
T Rounds, BA (*Co-curricular*)
R J Houchin, BA (*Academic*)

Preparatory School: RGS The Grange

Headmaster: G W Hughes, BEd Hons

Deputy Head (Academic): Mrs S Atkinson, BEd
Deputy Head (Pastoral): Mrs W Wreghitt, BA
Assistant Head (Co-Curricular): D Bousfield, BA

Preparatory School: RGS Springfield

Headmistress: Mrs L Brown, BA

Deputy Head: Mr Ian Griffin, BEd

Robert Gordon's College

Schoolhill, Aberdeen AB10 1FE

Tel:	01224 646346
Fax:	01224 630301
email:	enquiries@rgc.aberdeen.sch.uk
website:	www.rgc.aberdeen.sch.uk
Twitter:	@robertgordons
Facebook:	@robertgordonscollege
LinkedIn:	/robertgordonscollege

Motto: 'Omni nunc arte magistra'

An HMC independent co-educational nursery and day school in the heart of Aberdeen for children aged 3–18 years.

Our pupils' success is built on a strong sense of who they are, what they can achieve, and what it feels like to be part of a happy and purposeful school community. Our school motto translates as 'Be the Best You Can Be'. Every individual child deserves this ambition; Robert Gordon's College is a school which will prepare your child for a life where ambition, success and confidence are rooted in security, happiness and a sense of who they are.

Robert Gordon's College is home to the largest school teaching centre for science education in Britain – The Wood Foundation Centre for Science and Technology alongside The Craig Centre for Performing Arts, a new performance and digital recording venue. We look towards the creation of a new indoor sports facility to complement our on-site swimming pool at Schoolhill and our renowned sports grounds at Countesswells. Our ambitious plans demonstrate our commitment to our pupils and their future locally, nationally and internationally.

History. Robert Gordon was a merchant from Aberdeen who spent much of his life based in Poland. On retiring to Aberdeen, he left his fortune to found a 'Hospital' for boys' accommodation and education. The school opened in 1750. In 1881, the 'Hospital' was reconstituted as a day school under the name of 'Robert Gordon's College'. It continued to attract support from benefactors. In 1909 its charitable constitution changed to allow the development of adult education, a move which developed in the course of time into the Robert Gordon University. The next major change in the nature of the school was in 1989 when girls were admitted. Robert Gordon's College is now a co-educational day school in the Scottish tradition, which remains true to the charitable and educational principles on which it was founded by Robert Gordon over 250 years ago.

Number of Pupils. Nursery (age 3–5): 37 children; Junior School (Primary Classes 1–7): 476 pupils; Senior School (Secondary Forms 1–6): 1094 pupils.

Admission. The main entry points are Primary 1, Primary 6 and Secondary 1. Entry to Primary 1 (age 4½–5½ years) is by interview held in January/February, and to Primary 6 (age 9½–10½ years) by Entrance Test held in January.

Entry to Secondary 1 is by an Entrance Examination held in January.

Entry at other stages depends upon vacancies arising, and the offer of a place is subject to satisfactory performance in an Entrance Test and interview.

Fees per annum (2018–2019).
Nursery full day: £10,020 (incl lunch)
Nursery part time (half day): £5,220 (incl lunch)
Primary 1: £8,435 (excl lunch) £8,905 (incl lunch)
Primary 2: £8,435 (excl lunch) £8,925 (incl lunch)
Primary 3: £11,460 (excl lunch) £11,950 (incl lunch)
Primary 4–7: £11,460 (excl lunch) £12,080 (incl lunch)
Secondary: £13,130 (excl lunch)

Bursaries. Robert Gordon's College offers free places and reduced fee places to pupils every year for entry in to Secondary 1. These Bursaries are awarded after jointly assessing financial need and academic merit. Burnett Scholarships offer up to half-fee discounts to pupils of outstanding talent in academic subjects, in music, or in sport and are available to pupils currently in Fourth or Fifth Year at other schools.

Buildings. The centre block was erected in 1732, but there have been many modern additions. In 2016 The Wood Foundation Centre for Science and Technology and the Craig Centre for Performing Arts was officially opened by HRH The Princess Royal. The Wood Foundation Centre for Science and Technology is the largest school teaching centre for Science and Technology in the UK. The College is fully equipped with an Assembly Hall, Library, Laboratories, Art Rooms, Computing areas and Workshops. There are two Gymnasia and a Swimming Pool on site at the School. Countesswells Sports Fields was opened in 1992 on a 39-acre site three miles from the school incorporating first-class accommodation and facilities, including a water-based hockey pitch and an astroturf all-weather sports surface. A five-storey teaching block, incorporating a Dining Hall, was opened in 1994, and a new Library and Information Centre in 2000. A new Junior School building opened in Spring 2009, with newly located and renovated Senior classrooms following in Summer 2009.

Curriculum. In the Junior School the usual subjects of the primary curriculum are covered, with specialist teachers in Art, Drama, French, Music, Physical Education, Digital Education and Science. In the Senior School S1–S2 builds on the primary curriculum and as a foundation to the S3–S4 curriculum based on CfE principles. S3–S4 study eight National 5 subjects; S5–S6 Higher Grade and Advanced Higher. S6 pupils have Higher courses particular to them and specifically designed Enhancement courses. The vast majority of pupils go on to Higher Education once they leave school.

Games. Rugby, Hockey, Cricket, Netball, Tennis, Athletics, Cross-Country Running. A wide range of other sports is offered, including Triathlon, Badminton, Basketball, Volleyball, Golf, Squash, Skiing, Swimming, Hillwalking, Kayaking and Mountain Biking.

Extra-Curricular Activities. There is a strong Combined Cadet Force (Army, RAF and Pipe Band). The Choirs, Concert Band and Orchestras play a prominent part in the life of the School, as do Literary and Debating Societies who meet weekly, and dramatic societies, which present a variety of performances. Many other clubs and societies flourish, making over 120. A very large proportion of pupils undertake The Duke of Edinburgh's Award from S3 upwards.

Charitable status. Robert Gordon's College is a Registered Charity, number SC000123. It exists to provide education for boys and girls.

Chairman of Governors: Professor James Hutchison

Head of College: Simon Mills, MA, BA

Head of Junior School: Sarah Webb, BEd
Deputy Head of Junior School: Sally-Ann Johnson, BEd, MEd
Deputy Head of Junior School: Varie MacLeod, BEd
Head of Senior School: Michael S Elder, MA
Deputy Head (S1–S2): Stefan Horsman, MA, BA
Deputy Head (S3–S4): Anne Watson, BA
Deputy Head (S5 & Curriculum): Claire Cowie, MA, MLitt
Deputy Head (S6 & Pastoral): Robin Fish, MA
Director of Finance: Andrew W Lowden, MA, CA
Director of Development, Marketing and Admissions: Laura Presslie, BA
Director of ICT: David Stone, BSc, MSc

Roedean School

Roedean Way, Brighton, East Sussex BN2 5RQ

Tel: 01273 667500; Admissions: 01273 667626
email: info@roedean.co.uk
website: www.roedean.co.uk
Twitter: @RoedeanSchool
Facebook: @RoedeanSchool

Introduction. Roedean is a day, flexi, weekly and full boarding school for 620 girls aged 11–18. The school has grown from 360 girls in the last four years, and, due to increased demand from UK parents, it now has a four-form entry into Year 7. In 2016, the school received an outstanding ISI Inspection report, awarded 'excellent' in every category, and the girls also achieved the school's best-ever A Level and GCSE grades that year.

The three Lawrence sisters founded Roedean in Brighton in 1885 and the school was Incorporated by Royal Charter in 1938. Their original aims were to give due emphasis to physical and outdoor education, to encourage independence and self-reliance, 'to give as much liberty as can be granted with safety' and to supply a sound intellectual training.

Today the school community is made up of 40 different nationalities and remains committed to the founders' emphasis on independent learning and the development of self-confidence in readiness for professional life. The school buildings are set on a spacious, yet safe, 45-acre site surrounded by a further 70 acres of farmland. The campus looks out over the English Channel.

Philosophy. The Roedean philosophy is strongly focused on a holistic education, with success in all areas of school life complementing each other. Pupils are encouraged to challenge themselves and everything around them, and to be self-reliant, to explore their talents, to strive for excellence, to develop their intellectual curiosity, to lead as well as to be part of a team, and to appreciate cultural diversity. A girl educated at Roedean will have respect for herself and others, be qualified to enjoy a fulfilling career and feel confident she has the skills to balance her personal and professional life – our aim is that she will be creative, engaged, compassionate, independent, and curious, and she will have the space to grow up at her own pace.

The boarding approach is ideally suited to the school's holistic philosophy as it provides a rich and balanced programme of learning and activities in a structured yet informal environment. Day girls benefit from this ethos as they are well integrated into the House system. The single-sex environment has particular advantages for girls: it prevents stereotyping, raises expectations, and develops self-confidence by offering ample opportunities for leadership and responsibility.

Curriculum. Girls are given a structured grounding in basic skills and offered a very broad programme of knowledge and experience. Subject specialists work together in a coordinated approach to achieve maximum reinforcement and continuity across 30 subjects. The benefits of traditional subjects, including Latin, are balanced by Psychology, Russian, and Philosophy. Girls in KS3 take part in an academic enrichment programme called HHH (Heads, Hands, and Hearts), which includes self-defence, cookery, and Sign Language, among others. Class sizes are consistently small, ranging between 14 and 21 girls in the Lower School, with smaller groups in the Sixth Form.

Each girl's GCSE programme is individually tailored to provide a broad, balanced education and to ensure that requirements for higher education are met. The girls are strongly encouraged to undertake an independent academic project, with the support of specialist, in order to allow them to pursue their passions.

The strong Sixth Form offers an extensive range and combination of A Levels, covering over 20 subjects. Over time, the school has developed a strong link with the University of Sussex, enabling the most able Sixth Form mathematicians to study undergraduate geometry alongside their A Level courses.

Results in public examinations were excellent in 2018, with 23.3% of A2 grades awarded A* and 53.7% at A* and A. STEM is a particular strength of the School, and 37% of last year's leavers are now studying STEM subjects at university. At GCSE, 48.2% of examinations were awarded A* grades and 22.6% were awarded the new elite Grade 9.

Co-curricular Activities and Physical Education. The range of music, art and design, speech, debating, drama and dance opportunities within the curriculum are further supported by optional private tuition and club activities. The school is particularly strong in the performing arts: music (choirs and orchestras), drama, and dance.

The school has an excellent record in The Duke of Edinburgh's Award and Young Enterprise Business Scheme which offer girls opportunities to develop a spirit of discovery and independence and encourage links with the wider community.

The School has this year opened a floodlit all-weather pitch on site, along with new netball and tennis courts, and this facility will transform sporting opportunities at Roedean. Netball, hockey, tennis, swimming, athletics, cricket and rounders are the principal sports, with sailing, lacrosse, football, badminton, basketball, volleyball, squash, trampoline, gymnastics, fencing, golf, scuba diving and karate also available. Inter-school fixtures are part of all the major sport programmes and girls are encouraged to enter local, county and national tournaments.

Boarding. The House system provides the supportive and caring environment necessary for each girl, boarder or day, to flourish as an individual and a member of the community.

The four main Houses (for girls 11 to 16) and the separate Sixth Form Houses, Keswick and Lawrence, each have a dedicated team of staff in close contact with parents. Facilities range from bedrooms shared by 2 or 3 younger girls to university-style study-bedrooms for Sixth Formers. The girls in the four main houses are composed of a mixture of boarding and day students up to Year 11.

Continuity of individual guidance and care is ensured by the school's tutorial system. Tutors monitor each girl's academic progress and involvement in extracurricular activities and liaise with House staff on a regular basis to maintain a balanced, realistic timetable which meets each individual's needs and abilities.

Health. The School Health Centre is run by a Registered General Nurse who is assisted by a team of similarly qualified nurses. A doctor visits the School and holds clinics regularly each week. She is "on call" in case of an emergency. There is also a Counsellor who runs sessions in school each week.

Religion. The School welcomes students of all faiths, or none. Arrangements are made for Anglicans to be prepared for Confirmation, for Roman Catholics to attend Sunday Mass locally, and for Jewish girls to receive instruction.

Facilities. All subjects are taught in specialist rooms, and students have Wi-Fi access throughout the school to support their studies. There is a main library and resources' centre to support individual study. There are two art studios adjacent to a Design & Technology Centre, a multimedia Language Centre, a Performing Arts complex (including a theatre which seats 320 people, dance studios, music suite) and a Science wing with nine laboratories for Biology, Chemistry and Physics. A multi-purpose sports hall with gym, heated indoor pool, 13 newly-refurbished hard tennis and netball courts, squash courts, ample playing fields, including the new all-weather pitch, support the PE/Sports programme. The School is proud that Rio Olympic Gold Medallists Kate and Helen Richardson-Walsh are Roedean's Sports Ambassadors.

School Year and Leave Out. There are three terms, beginning in September, January and April. The summer holidays last eight weeks and Christmas/Easter up to four weeks each. Girls go home for half term and there are two weekend exeats each term. All boarders are free to go home at weekends and weekly boarders are escorted back to London on the train. The school provides a full boarding programme, but there is considerable flexibility to accommodate the individual needs of families.

Admission. Entry at 11+, 12+, 13+ and 16+ is through Roedean Entrance Examination papers in English, Maths, and Non-Verbal Reasoning, which can be taken at any time up to two terms before entry. A good number of suitably qualified girls are admitted each year to the Sixth Form.

Scholarships and Bursaries. Academic, Art, Dance, Drama, Music, and Sport scholarships (worth up to 10% of fees) and exhibitions (worth up to 5% of fees) are available for girls entering Year 7, Year 9, and the Sixth Form.

Junior Scholarship examinations are held in January; Sixth Form Scholarship examinations are held in November.

Means-tested Bursaries are available. Details of scholarships and bursaries may be obtained from the Registrar.

Fees per term (2018–2019). Full Boarders £10,620–£12,855; Weekly Boarders (5 days) £9,690–£10,805; Flexi Boarders (3 days) £7,880–£9,530; Day Girls £5,480–£7,165. For girls entering the Sixth Form from other schools, there is an additional supplement of £1,380 per term (boarding). Parents who wish to pay a single composition fee should apply to the Director, Finance and Administration.

Extra fees are charged for individual tuition in musical instruments, speech training, ballet and some athletic activities.

For further details please contact the Registrar.

Charitable status. Roedean School is a Registered Charity, number 307063. It exists to provide quality education for girls.

President:
Lady Patten of Barnes, BA [OR]

Vice-Presidents:
Mrs S M Fowler-Watt, RGN [OR]
Dr J M Peacey, MB BS, MRCGP [OR]

Chair of Council:
Mr R Sanders, OBE

Vice-Chairman of Council:
Ms A-M Martin, MBE, BSc, MSc

Council:
Ms J Barnard-Langston, BA, MA, Dip Couns, JP
Mrs K Cowell, BEd, MBA [OR]
Mrs J Clark
Dr A Edwards, MA Oxon, FRCP
Dr H Fajemirokun, MA Oxon, PhD
Mr S Hepher
Miss V Jenkins
Mrs C Nightingale, BA, MBA [OR]
Ms C Oram, MA Cantab, ACIB Dip Trans
Mrs T Outhwaite, BA, PG Dip [OR]
Ms D Patman, FRICS
Mr A J Pianca, FCA
Dr G Savage, MA Cantab, PhD, FRSA
Mrs V Smiley, BA [OR]

[OR] *Old Roedeanian*

Clerk: Mr J Fawcett-Ellis, LLB, LLM, MBA Oxon

ORA President: Ms Virginia Stephen

Staff:

Headmaster: Mr O Blond, BA Essex

Head of School: Miss T Keller, BSc Manchester, PGCE, NPQH
Senior Deputy Head, Pastoral: Mr R Chamberlain
Deputy Head, Academic: Dr J Hobbs, BA Leeds, PhD King's, PGCE
Director of Finance and Administration: Mr R Poffley, BA Sussex, FCCA

Head of Key Stage 3: Mrs K Newman
Head of Key Stage 4: Mrs D Robins, BA Brighton, QTS Brighton
Head of Sixth Form: Miss C Carragher, BSc Southampton, PGCE
Director of Sixth Form: Dr G Hannan, PhD London, MA, PGCE with QTS Durham
Director of Partnerships, Enrichment, and Events: Dr R Barrand, BA Durham, PhD Leeds, PGCE
Senior Boarding Mistress: Mrs J Chandler, BEd Sussex
Senior Boarding Mistress: Mrs O Waller, BA Manchester, PGCE QTS
Assistant Head, Co-Curricular and Scholarships: Ms H Boobis, MA Cantab, BA Cantab, MEd Open, PGCE

Heads of Department:
Art: Ms Sarah Strachan, BA Kingston, PGCE Cambridge
Classics: Miss Claudia Hindle, MA St Andrews, MEd Cambridge, PGCE
Dance: Miss S Abaza, BA Chichester
Design Technology: Miss E Griffiths-Moore, BA Edinburgh, PGCE Brighton

Drama: Mrs C Rigby, BA, MA Rose Bruford College of Speech & Drama
Economics: Mr P Clingan
English: Mr D Woodhouse, BA Anglia, MA Sussex, PGCE Brighton
Geography: Mr J Sheriff
History: Mrs S Black
ICT & Business Studies: Mr B Rous
Learning Support: Mrs M Muggeridge
Mathematics: Mr D Orys, BSc London, PGCE Sussex
Modern Languages: Mr J Sampieri, MA France, PGCE Kingston
Music: Miss V Fewkes, BA Bath, PGCE
Personal & Social Education (*PSHE*): Mr R Chamberlain
Philosophy & Religious Studies: Ms Edith Earl, BA Oxford, QTS
Physical Education: Mr A Carter
Psychology: Mr P Harrison
Science: Mr M Ebden
Biology: Miss P Harrison, BSc Durham, MSc London, PGCE
Chemistry: Ms F Walker
Physics: Mr J Higginson, MEng Newcastle, MSc, PGCE Lancaster

Director of Admissions: Mrs D Banham

Rossall School

Fleetwood, Lancashire FY7 8JW

Tel: 01253 774201
Fax: 01253 772052
email: admissions@rossall.org.uk
website: www.rossall.org.uk
Twitter: @RossallSchool
Facebook: @RossallSchoolUK
LinkedIn: /RossallSchool

Motto: '*Mens agitat molem*'

Rossall has been described by the Good Schools Guide as 'a warm, inclusive and remarkably happy place to be'.

Set on an historic 160-acre campus on the picturesque Lancashire coastline, Rossall is one of the country's leading independent co-educational boarding and day schools, where boys and girls aged 2–18 are nurtured in a safe, secure and supportive environment.

With a history dating back to 1844, Rossall combines a traditional British education with a modern approach which focuses on developing the whole child.

With nearly fifty different nationalities living and learning together, Rossall is a truly global village. The combination of UK day students and students from right across the world creates an exciting international dimension and an appreciation of diverse cultures, religions and politics.

Academic Curriculum. Rossall delivers a broad and balanced curriculum with the principles of the International Baccalaureate learner profile at its heart. At Nursery level, Rossall follows the Early Years Foundation Stage (EYFS) learning goals. From the age of 3 to 11, Rossall offers the IB Primary Years Programme (PYP).

At age 16, students sit GCSE and IGCSE examinations, then have the option to choose either the IB or A Level route in the Sixth Form. The IB principles run through Rossall's teaching and learning in every phase of the school and underpin a dynamic and enjoyable yet rigorous learning experience.

All subjects are equally valued at Rossall, giving students the freedom to experience a broad and balanced portfolio of learning up to the age of 16 so they can make informed choices about their Sixth Form studies.

Facilities. Rossall's generous facilities support the aims for teaching and learning excellence. From the dedicated Science building and state-of-the-art Design Technology workshops to the bright, spacious art studios complete with a computer-rich Graphics suite, Rossall provides every student with the space and resources to pursue their academic studies and outside interests.

For those with musical ambitions, the Beecham Music School, with its own practice organ, orchestra rehearsal room and Sibelius suite, offers students the opportunity to develop their skills, whilst our theatres, performance and exhibition spaces provide budding singers, actors and artists with the chance to explore their talents.

With the recent renovation of the Sixth Form study room (based on designs created by the students themselves) and the opening of a new kitchen classroom to support the development of Food Studies skills, Rossall is a school which is constantly evolving to meet the needs of its students as well as the curriculum.

Beyond the classroom, the spacious 160-acre campus has extensive sports and recreation facilities, including a golf academy – complete with GC2 simulator and putting green, a 25-metre indoor heated swimming pool, squash courts, tennis courts, fives courts, a modern all-weather sports pitch, a multi-use games area, two indoor sports halls, extensive sports pitches and a fitness room. In 2016, Rossall teamed up with League One football club, Fleetwood Town FC, to offer a Football Academy.

Rossall also has its own beach, which is put to good use for our own exclusive sport of Ross Hockey, and is proud to be one of the few schools in the country with an on-site Astronomy Centre.

The House System. For younger pupils (aged 7–13), Anchor House, our dedicated Junior Boarding House, has a home-from-home family atmosphere.

Anchor House is full of fun and laughter; from baking in the kitchen to celebrating a birthday or taking part in one of our many house trips, there's always something to do and someone to do it with. As well as a varied activities programme, all of the house staff are committed to developing and supporting all students with their academic needs, ensuring that all of our children succeed and reach their maximum potential.

There are seven Houses for Senior boarders: three for girls (Rose, Wren and Dolphin) and four for boys (Maltese Cross, Mitre Fleur de Lys, Spread Eagle and Pelican).

All Houses have triple, double and single bedrooms, a common room, a large games room, a kitchen for snacks and weekend baking and a library with computer workstations and internet access.

While each House has its own unique history and personality, all foster an environment in which boarders are encouraged to achieve their true potential and develop valuable skills and qualities such as communication, teamwork, leadership, empathy and cultural understanding.

Religious Instruction. Rossall was founded as 'the Northern Church of England School' and Chapel remains central to the well-being of the community. Pupils of all faiths are encouraged to share in this community, and the School has its own Chaplaincy with resident Chaplain.

Games. 45 acres of playing field and a gymnasium, a newly-built golf academy, floodlit Astroturf, multi-use games area, and indoor 25-metre swimming pool, along with squash, tennis, and fives courts allow all pupils to pursue a sporting interest. The boys mainly play rugby, hockey, cricket, football and basketball, with the girls playing hockey, netball, rounders and tennis. All pupils are taught to play the unique game of RossHockey on the sandy beach

owned by the School. The new Golf Academy boasts state-of-the-art technology, and with close links to major golf clubs, including Royal Birkdale and Royal Lytham and St Annes, students have the opportunity play at some of the most prestigious golf clubs in the world. There are full programmes of competitive fixtures against other schools and clubs. House matches occur in all major games, including football, cross country in the Lent Term. Archery, athletics, shooting, horse riding and many other activities are offered.

The CCF. Rossall's CCF contingent is the oldest in the country. Currently, most of Years 8 and 9 are in either the Army, Navy or Air Force sections. The school has a shooting range, keeps boats on the Wyre and there is the opportunity to fly at RAF Woodvale.

Activities and Clubs. Rossall is pleased to offer their biggest selection of extra-curricular activities to date.

Through our Activities Programme, Rossall students have the opportunity to learn new skills, socialise with other students and, most importantly, have fun.

The School encourages its students to try new activities, to help them broaden their horizons, so that they can meet the challenges of the wider world.

The extensive range of clubs we offer at Rossall include: Debating Club, Scuba Diving, The Duke of Edinburgh's Award, Robotics and Electronics, Creative Writing, Volleyball, Choir, International Cookery, Hockey, Photoshop and Creative Graphics, Knitting, Rugby, Ceramics, Basketball, Orchestra, and Climbing.

Admission. Any term in the year for boys and girls aged 7+ and 13+, September preferably at 16+ or 17+. All applications for entrance should be made to the Admissions Team. On registration, a fee of £50 will be charged to UK applicants and £175 to international students.

Fees per term (2018–2019). Day £2,680–£4,360; Full Boarding £6,870–£12,450; Weekly Boarding £4,620–£7,510.

Scholarships and Bursaries. Scholarships are offered for academic, music, art, drama, sport and all-round achievement. Scholarships are awarded solely on merit and range in value. In exceptional circumstances, the special Trapnell Scholarship for excellence in Maths and Science may award up to 100% fee remission.

A number of clerical bursaries are awarded on a means test to sons of Clergy who can sustain a proportion of the Fees themselves but who need extra help. Bursaries are also available to families from the British Armed Forces.

All enquiries about Scholarships and Bursaries and other awards should be addressed to the Admissions Team.

Rossall Junior School. Rossall has its own Junior School for children aged 7–11 situated within the same grounds. There is also a Nursery and Infants School for day boys and girls aged 2–7.

Access. Motorway: 15 minutes from M55 (spur off M6). Railway: Blackpool North (6 miles). Air: Manchester International Airport (55 miles by road).

Alumni. A network of Old Rossallians is managed by Julie Barkhuizen, Alumni Relations Manager at the school.

The Rossallian Club. This club for former pupils keeps a record of more than 5,000 members and coordinates the activities of eight Branches. A Newsletter is published twice each year.

Charitable Status. The Corporation of Rossall School is a Registered Charity, number 526685.

Governors:
Chairman: Mr Chris Holt, BSc, MBA, ACMA
Vice Chair: Mr S J Fisher, MA
Mr M J Reece, MA
Mr J F Parr
Mrs C M Preston, BSc, ARICS
Mr M Craven, MA In
Dr H O Fajemirokun
Mr C Littler, FCA
Mr M R Mosley, MA
Mr N K Ward, BSc
Dr D M Elliott, BSc MBChB
Mrs L Croston, BSc, PGCE, ALCM
Mrs M Smith, MSc, FFA, MInstF Dip, JP
Mrs K Thomas, MIFST, BSc, RSci
Mr D H Ewart, BA, PGCE, MA, DMS
Mr R A Wilson, MA
The Revd G Ashton, BA
The Revd Canon J M Hall, MA

Secretary to the Corporation and Council: Mr B E Clark, MBE

Head: Mr Jeremy Quartermain, BA, MA, MPhil

Deputy Head: Mr Robert Robinson, BA Hons, PGCE, MA
Bursar: Mrs Emma Sanderson, PGCE, MA Hons, MBA
Deputy Head (Academic): Mrs Gillian Pryor, BSc Hons, PGCE
Head of Dragon, Juniors, Infants & Nursery: Mrs Katie Lee, MA, CPP, Cert Ed
Head of EAL: Mrs Cheryl Wolstencroft, MEd TESOL, BA Hons
Head of Sixth Form: Mr Mark Bradley, BSc Hons, PGCE
Senior Master: Mr Mark Pryor, BSc Hons, PGCE

Heads of Departments:

Art: Miss Laura Heap
Business Studies: Mr Graham Wallace, MA, BEd, HND
Economics: Mrs Elizabeth Almond, BA, MA, PGCE
English: Miss Bethan Jones, BA, PGCE
Mathematics: Mr Philip Butterworth, BSc Hons
Modern Foreign Languages: Mrs Isabelle Wallace, BA Hons, MA, PGCE
EAL: Mrs Cheryl Wolstencroft, MEd TESOL, BA Hons
Director of Music: Miss Margaret Young, BA Hons, LTCL, LRSM
Science and Chemistry: Mr Ky Hutchinson
Physics: Ms Jane Mercer, BSc, PGCE
Biology: Mrs Alison Forster, BSc Hons, PGCE
Geography: Mr Anthony Fairhurst, BA Hons, PGCE
History: Mr Michael Holder-Williams
ICT: Mrs Ioana Kada, BA, MA
Physical Education (Academic): Mrs Emma Williams, BSc, PGCE
Director of Sport: Mr Jack Cropper, BA, MA
Design & Technology: Mr Lee Hodgetts, BA Hons
Religious Studies, Philosophy and Ethics: Mrs Francesca Saponiere, BA, PGCE
Psychology: Miss Nik Holmes, BSc Hons, MSc, MBPsS, Unicert TEFL, LTCL, Dip TESOL
Learning Support: Mrs Siobhan Edge, BA Ed Hons

Houses/Houseparents:
Anchor House: Mr Lee & Mrs Helen Gair
Dolphin House: Miss Amy Campbell
Maltese Cross House: Mr Graham & Mrs Isabelle Wallace
Mitre Fleur de Lys House: Mr Krishnan Pillai
Pelican House: Mr Anthony Fairhurst
Rose House: Mr Tim & Mrs Adele Fletcher
Spread Eagle House: Mr Gerrie de Beer
Wren House: Mrs Emma Williams

Instrumental Music Teachers for:
Brass, Flute, Guitar, Composition, Piano, Organ, Clarinet, Saxophone, Violin, Voice, Percussion

Director of Admissions, Marketing and Communications: Mrs Lucy Barnwell
International Registrar: Mrs Nicola Jackson
UK Registrar: Ms Gillian Leggett
Careers: Mr Jonathon Holland
IB Coordinator: Dr Doris Dohmen, DPhil, PGCE
Examinations Officer: Mr Ron Asher, BSc, PGCE
Librarian: Mrs Beth Simmons, BA Hons
Marketing Manager: Mrs Nancy Fielden
Medical Officer: Dr Smythe

Rougemont School

Llantarnam Hall, Malpas Road, Newport, South Wales NP20 6QB

Tel:	01633 820800
Fax:	01633 855598
email:	registrar@rsch.co.uk
website:	www.rougemontschool.co.uk
Twitter:	@rougemontschool
Facebook:	@Rougemont-School

Rougemont was founded in a house of that name immediately after the First World War as a co-educational day school taking children through to grammar school entrance at 11. It moved to Nant Coch House just after the Second World War and grew to about 200 pupils.

In 1974 the school was re-founded as a Charitable Trust. Since then it has bought extensive new buildings and has approximately 550 pupils on roll in the Preparatory School (Infant Department – Nursery to Year 2 and Junior Department – Years 3–6) and Senior School (Years 7–13).

The Preparatory Junior Department and Senior School moved to a new site at Llantarnam Hall, a large Victorian mansion set in 50 acres of grounds, between 1992 and 1995, with the Infant Department joining them in April 2004. The grounds have been landscaped to provide playing fields and an extensive building programme has taken place on the site. During 1998 a Liberal Arts area including Sports Hall, Music suite and Drama Studio was completed. In 1999 a new classroom block and library was completed and in 2000 additional classrooms together with Art studio were built. New Science and Technology buildings were completed in 2009.

Admission to the Preparatory and Senior Schools is by interview and assessments. Entry to the Sixth Form is dependent on GCSE results.

The following paragraphs refer to the Senior School although peripatetic specialists work in both and there is some interchange of teachers.

Curriculum. Pupils follow a wide syllabus to age 14. For the two years to GCSE pupils normally study ten subjects of which English Language and Literature, Mathematics and Numeracy, a language, science and a humanities subject are normally compulsory. 18 subjects are available.

Sixth Form. 19 AS/A2 Levels are available. Sixth Form pupils have their own common room and study area. Sixth Form pupils can also take part in a range of extracurricular activities and games.

Religion. Rougemont School has no direct affiliation to a Christian Church or denomination. However, the religious instruction, corporate worship and moral value system of the School is based on that of the broad tradition of the mainstream Christian Churches.

Careers. The School belongs to the Independent Schools Careers Organisation. The Senior teachers advise on all aspects of further education and careers.

Music. In addition to specialist teachers of music a large number of peripatetic teachers cover the range of orchestral instruments. There are choirs and instrumental ensembles for all ages.

Drama. In addition to the Infant Department's Spring Festival and the Senior School Eisteddfod, two major plays and two musical events take place each year.

Elocution and Dance. Visiting staff hold weekly classes for LADA courses, ballet and modern dance.

Sport. The School has developed a high standard of performance in most major sports. There is a wide fixtures programme for both boys and girls, as well as the opportunity to participate in numerous coaching courses.

Clubs. A wide variety of extracurricular activities and clubs are available at lunch time and after school, as is supervised prep.

The Duke of Edinburgh's Award. This is a very successful activity within the school and over 60 pupils have gained the Gold Award in the last twenty years.

Fees per term (2018–2019). Preparatory School: Infant Department £2,415–£3,045, Junior Department £3,471; Senior School: £4,017–£4,512.

Scholarships. A new Scholarship Programme, encompassing non-Academic as well as Academic Scholarships, was introduced in September 2018. The awards amount to between 10–25% of the school fees and are available for entry to Years 5, 7, 9 and Sixth Form. A limited number of means-tested bursaries are offered from Year 7 upwards.

Further information. A prospectus and other details are available from the Registrar (Tel: 01633 820800, email: registrar@rsch.co.uk).

Charitable status. Rougemont School is a Registered Charity, number 532341. It exists to provide education for boys and girls.

President: Mr I S Burge

Governors:
Chair: Mrs S Desai, BPharm, MRPharmS
Vice-Chair: Mrs A C Thomas, JP, SRN, SCM
Mr I G Short
Mrs J Clark, BA, PGCE
Miss J Sollis, BA, AKC
Mr M Tebbutt
Prof D Fone, MB BS, MD, FFPH, FRGS, MRCGP, DCH, DRCOG
Mr I Hoppe
Mr H Clark
Mr R Green, BSc, BArch, ARB, RIBA
Mr M Cordner
Mr P Harris
Mrs C McNamara

Headmaster: Mr R Carnevale, MA Ed, BSc, PGCE

* *Head of Department*
§ *Part-time*

Head of Preparatory School: Mrs L Pritchard, BA, PGCE
Deputy Head of Senior School: Mrs S Archer, BSc, PGCE (*Biology*)
Director of Staffing: Mrs S Roberts, BSc, PGCE (*Mathematics*)
Assistant Head (*Academic*): Mrs P Rogers, MA Ed, BSc, PGCE (*Director of Studies, Geography, ICT Coordinator*)
Director of Co-Curriculum: Mr A Rees, BA, PGCE (*Physical Education, Head of Years 10 and 11, DofE*)

Academic Registrar: Mr M James, MA Ed, BEd, BA, BSc, CBiol, MIBiol, Cert Maths Open (*Biology*)
Business Manager: Mr A Knight, ACA
Facilities Manager: Mr A Watts

Senior School:
Mrs L Bateman, BA, PGCE (*Art)
Mr K Bell, BA, PGCE (*Director of Sport*)
Mrs K Benson-Dugdale, BMus, MA, QTS, PGEM (*Higher Education Advisor*, *Music)
Mrs S Boon, BA, PGCE (*Art, DT*)
Mr M Bowman, BSc, PGCE (*Mathematics)
Dr S Brown, BA, BSc, PhD, PGCE (*Senior Laboratory Technician*)
Ms A Clason-Thomas, BA, MA, PGCE (*Learning Resources Manager, French, English*)
Mrs K Clegg (*Learning Development Centre*)
Mr D Cobb, BSc, PGCE, Cert Maths Open (*Biology)
Mrs L DeCruz, BA, PGCE (**Religious Studies*)
Miss C Dugdale, BA, PGCE (§*PE, Religious Studies*)
Mrs K Elms, BA, PGCE (*English, Film Studies*)
Mrs S Elson, LLB (§*Latin*)
Mrs E Ferrand, BEd (*Mathematics*)
Mrs H Garratt, BSc, PGCE (§*Physical Education, DofE*)
Mrs R Garrod, BA, PGCE (§*History*)
Mrs J Goodwin, BSc (**Physics, Head of Pupil Performance Y8–Y11*)
Mr J Hardwick, BSc, PGCE (*Biology, Science, Careers*)
Mrs K Hughes, BSc, PGCE (*Geography)
Miss R Hayes, BA, PGCE (*Head of Design & Technology, DofE*)
Miss J Jones, BA, PGCE (*English)
Mrs A Jenkins, BSc (*Chemistry, Physics*)
Mr M Jenkins, MA Cantab, PGCE (*History)
Mrs C Langford, BSc, PGCE (*KS3 and KS4 Coordinator for Chemistry*)
Mrs J Livings, BEd, PG Dip Dys and Literacy, AMBDA, SpLD Assessor (*Learning Development Centre*)
Mr P McMahon, MSc, BSc, QTS (**Computing and IT, Mathematics*)
Miss A Mintowt-Czyz, BA, PGCE (*English*)
Mrs D Moore, BA, PGCE (*Drama)
Mrs D Morgan, BA, PGCE (*French*)
Mrs S Munro, DEUG, Licence, PGCE (**French, Year 7 Pupil Progress Coordinator*)
Miss C Owen, BA, PGCE (**Business Studies, IT, House Tutor*)
Miss K Page, BSc, PGCE (*Physical Education, House Tutor*)
Mrs D Parry (*Learning Development Centre*)
Mr E Price, BSc, PGCE (*Mathematics*)
Mr W Price, BA, PGCE (*Head of Spanish*)
Mr A Richards, BSc, PGCE (*Mathematics, KS3 Coordinator for Mathematics*)
Mr M Savery, BA, PGCE (**Economics, Spanish*)
Mr H Singer, MA Ed, BA, PGCE (*Head of KS3, Design & Technology*)
Mrs L Singer, BSc, PGCE (§*Physical Education*)
Miss A Sutton, MA(*Ed*), PGCE, BA, PG Dip SpLD (**Learning Development Centre*)
Mrs L Thickins, BA, PGCE (*English, Film Studies*)
Mrs T van der Linde, MA Ed, BSc, PGCE (**Chemistry, Head of Sixth Form*)

Preparatory School, Junior Department:
Miss L Hallas, BA, PGCE (*Deputy Head of Prep School, English, History*)
Mr A Bevan, BA, PGCE (*Director of Staffing, Prep School, Junior Department Class Teacher*)
Mrs R Carroll, BA, PGCE (*Director of Creative Curriculum in Prep School, Junior Department Class Teacher, Able and Talented Coordinator*)

Mr C Dobbins, BMus, DipMus, LRSM, PGCE (*Music, Games*)

Mrs S Elson, LLB (*History, Religious Studies*)

Mrs K Galloway, KS2 (*Teaching and Learning Assistant*)

Mrs R Payne, NNEB (*Teaching and Learning Assistant*)

Mr A Pritchard, BSc, PGCE (*Mathematics*)

Mrs C Poore, BEd (*Science, Geography*)

Mr S Rowlands, BA, QTS (*Junior Department Class Teacher, House Tutor*)

Mrs L Singer, MA Ed, BSc, PGCE (*Junior Department Class Teacher, PE*)

Mrs L Watson, BA, PGCE (*Junior Department Class Teacher*)

Mrs K Williams, BEd (*Junior Department Class Teacher*)

Preparatory School, Infant Department:

Mrs H Ashill, NNEB (*Teaching and Learning Assistant*)

Mrs Z Bennett, NNEB (*Teaching and Learning Assistant*)

Mrs A Burridge, BSc, PGCE (*Infant Department Class Teacher*)

Mr C Dobbins, BMus, DipMus, LRSM, PGCE (*Music*)

Mrs S Hotchkiss, BA, QTS (*Deputy Head, Class Teacher*)

Miss C Leaves, BA, QTS (*Infant Department Class Teacher*)

Mrs T Mountford, BEd (*Infant Department Class Teacher*)

Mrs N Noor, BA, PGCE (*Class Teacher, Curriculum Director, Infants*)

Preparatory School, Rougemont Nursery:

Mrs J Forouzan, NNEB (*Nursery Teacher*)

Mrs A Exley (*Teaching and Learning Assistant*)

Mrs E Mian, NNEB (*Teaching and Learning Assistant*)

Miss C Smith (*Teaching and Learning Assistant*)

Registrar: Mrs N Bates

Royal Grammar School
Guildford

High Street, Guildford, Surrey GU1 3BB

Tel:	Headmaster: 01483 880608
	School Office: 01483 880600
Fax:	01483 306127
email:	office@rgsg.co.uk
website:	www.rgsg.co.uk
Twitter:	@RGSGuildford
Facebook:	@RGSGuildford

Located in the centre of the historic town of Guildford, the RGS is an independent day school for around 950 boys aged 11 to 18, some 270 of whom are in the Sixth Form. As a flagship for boys' education, the School has a national reputation for academic excellence but also prides itself on its traditional values of decency and respect, supported by outstanding pastoral care. RGS boys have the opportunity to experience the widest range of enriching activities providing them with a broad and balanced education. Academic excellence is at the very heart of the School's philosophy. The RGS aims to encourage the growth of intellectual curiosity and creativity and to inculcate a life-long love of learning in the boys. The RGS is consistently one of the top five boys' schools in the country at both A Level and GCSE, and is extremely proud of its Oxbridge record; in the last decade 346 offers have been made including 31 offers in the recent round of admissions.

Buildings and Facilities. The Tudor buildings in Guildford's High Street have been at the very heart of the RGS for over five centuries. The School was founded by Robert Beckingham in 1509 and established by King Edward VI's Charter of 1552, which decreed that there should be "...one Grammar School in Guildford ...for the Education, Institution and Instruction of Boys and Youths in Grammar at all future times for ever to endure". Among the first in the country to be purpose-built, the original buildings contain a remarkable Chained Library, which is now the Headmaster's Study. The School enjoys facilities appropriate to education in the 21st century, including a state-of-the-art Music School, Art School, purpose-built Sixth Form Centre, Sports Hall and the recently-opened John Brown Building which houses the innovative Design and Technology centre. The Sports Ground at Bradstone Brook provides twenty acres of pitches, tennis courts and a recently refurbished pavilion. The School also benefits from the use of nationally renowned sports facilities in the immediate proximity, including Surrey Sports Park.

Curriculum. The school day is from 8.45 am to 4.00 pm; there are no lessons on Saturdays. Many co-curricular activities and clubs take place after school, however. In the first three years (Years 7, 8 and 9 nationally), all boys follow a common curriculum embodying the programmes of study for Key Stage 3 of the National Curriculum. The subjects studied are English, French or Spanish, Geography, History, Latin, Maths, Information Technology, RE, PE, Art, Music, Drama, Design and Technology, and Science. In the Second Form, the boys study the separate sciences and in the Third Form all boys choose between Spanish, German and Greek as an additional language.

GCSEs and IGCSEs are offered with boys taking ten subjects out of the 17 available. At GCSE there is a range of ancient and modern languages including Ancient Greek and Latin, as well as French, Spanish and German. There is the opportunity to study Arabic, Mandarin, Japanese and Russian off timetable.

All Sixth Form boys take four subjects in the Lower Sixth Form and then three or four at A Level; over twenty A Level subjects are offered. A broad curriculum also includes the Independent Learning Assignment and a General Studies programme organised in conjunction with Guildford High School.

Religion. The ethos of the RGS is firmly based on traditional Christian principles and the School has strong links with Holy Trinity Church in the centre of the town and Guildford Cathedral; however, as a non-denominational school, boys from all faiths are welcomed. A diverse, stimulating assembly programme provides the opportunity for collective worship and broadens the boys' horizons while establishing a tolerant set of values. Religious Education lessons, which are an integral part of the School's curriculum, further contribute to developing each individual's moral compass.

Pastoral Care. Respect, tolerance and understanding of others characterise daily life at the RGS and the very strong rapport between boys and teachers makes for a vibrant environment. The boys establish lasting relationships within the year group; in addition, the house system, mentoring, and role of all senior boys as prefects ensure friendships are forged throughout the School. The outstanding pastoral care on offer from dedicated form tutors, heads of year and personal tutors, all overseen by the Deputy Head (Pupils), enables the boys to thrive in a mutually supportive environment where every boy can flourish as an individual.

Co-curricular Activities. The exceptional range of co-curricular activities offered is one of the greatest strengths of the School; there are currently over seventy societies at the RGS. These range from air rifle, chess, christian union, drama, Model United Nations, music, philosophy, squash to Young Enterprise. Boys have the opportunity to take Bronze, Silver and Gold Duke of Edinburgh's Award through the Combined Cadet Force, Scouts or Outdoor Pursuits. Over 30% of students learn a musical instrument and they can join a variety of instrumental groups including Big Band, School Orchestra, Choir and a strong Choral Society. There are many opportunities for boys throughout the School to get involved in drama productions, both for the School and their house.

Games. The School's principal games are rugby, hockey and cricket, although as boys move up the School their sporting options widen considerably. Sports available include athletics, badminton, basketball, cross-country running, fencing, football, golf, sailing, shooting, swimming and tennis. Professional coaching and outstanding facilities develop the skill levels of boys of all abilities; the School takes pride in providing competitive sport and opportunities for all while also nurturing the very best of sporting talent. The School currently has a significant number of boys who are competing for county, national and international honours.

Admission. Boys may be considered for entry to the RGS at any age between 11 and 18. The usual ages of entry, however, are at 11, 13 and 16 into the Sixth Form. Applicants at 11 take the School's entrance examination in the January before the year of entry; those for 13+ entry take the Common Entrance examination or Scholarship papers after 11+ assessment. New boys are admitted in September of each year. The Headmaster is pleased to meet parents, arrange for them to see the School, and discuss the possibility of their son's entry to the School. Appointments may be made through the Head of Admissions (Registrar and Marketing), who can supply a hard copy of the School's prospectus; it is also available on the RGS website.

Fees per term (2018–2019). £6,095 (plus £285 for lunches, which are compulsory for First and Second Forms) inclusive of all tuition, stationery and loan of necessary books.

Scholarships. Scholarships of up to 20% fee remission are awarded in recognition of outstanding academic merit. For boys entering the First Form at 11 there is a competitive examination in English and Mathematics, held in January. For boys entering the Third Form at 13 there is a two-day examination covering all Common Entrance subjects, held in March. The top scholar of a year group is designated the King's Scholar.

Music scholarships of up to 20% fee remission are available at 11 and 13. It is hoped that a King's Scholarship can be awarded each year to a boy of outstanding musical potential.

One Art Scholarship and one Sports Scholarship of 10% fee remission at 13+ is available annually.

Full details of Scholarships and Bursaries are available from the Head of Admissions (Registrar and Marketing).

Charitable status. RGS and Lanesborough is Registered Charity, number 1177353 and a Company Limited by Guarantee, incorporated in England and Wales, number 10874615. Registered Office: High Street, Guildford, GU1 3BB.

Governing Body:
Chairman: Mrs S K Creedy, MA
Vice-Chairman: His Honour Judge C Critchlow, LLB, DL
Mr C D Barnett, MA
Mrs C F Cobley, MCIPD
The Revd Canon RL Cotton, MA, DipTh
Mr D J Counsell, FCA [OG]
The Earl of Onslow, High Steward of Guildford
Mr J D Fairley, BA
Mr P Fell, BA, FCA
Mr S G S Gimson, MSc
Cllr Mrs J Jordan, BA
Dr L S K Linton, MA, MB ChB, MRCP

The Mayor of Guildford
Dr H J Pearson, OBE, MA, PhD, CMath, FIMA
Mr P G Peel, FCA
Professor S Price, MSc, PhD, FBTS, ERT, FHEA
Mr C T Shorter, CEng, MIStructE, FConsE, FFB
Mrs J Stott, BSc
Mrs H Styche-Patel, BSc, MBA
Mr N E J Vineall, QC, MA Cantab and Pittsburgh [OG]

[OG] *Old Guildfordian*

Chief Operating Officer: Mr R A Ukiah, MA
Bursar and Clerk to the Governors: Mrs C M Perceval, BA

Headmaster: Dr J M Cox, BSc, PhD (*Biology*)

Deputy Head (*School Development*): Mr G T Williams, MA (*History*)
Deputy Head (*Pupils*): Mr A U Woodman, BSc, MA (*Biology*)
Director of Studies, Careers and Higher Education: Mr P J Dunscombe, BSc (*Mathematics*)
Senior Master: Mr J W Pressley, MA (*Classics*)

Assistant Head (*Learning*): Miss N S Goul-Wheeker, MA (*Classics*)
Assistant Head (*Partnerships*): Mr T W Shimell, MChem (*Chemistry*)
Assistant Head (*Teaching*): Mr H R Wiggins, MA (*History*)
Assistant Head (*Operations*) : Mr N E Wild, BA (*Religion and Philosophy*)
Assistant Head (*Co-curricular*): Mr S J H Yetman, BSc

* *Head of Department*

Art:
*Mr A M J Curtis, MA
Mr A N Rozier, BA
Mrs R F Shepherd, BA
Mr K A Trim, BA

Biology:
*Dr E J Hudson, MA, MSc, PhD
Mrs J C Crouch, BSc
Mr A H Dubois, BSc
Mr J J Richards, BSc [OG]
Mrs J S Thorpe, BSc
Mrs K Walker, BSc

Chemistry:
*Mr W-S Lau, MChem, MRSC
Mr S W Armstrong, MA
Dr E T Batchelar, MChem, DPhil
Dr J L Bodmer, BSc, PhD, MBA
Dr J S Braithwaite, BSc, PhD
Dr L A Whall, BA, PhD

Classics:
*Mr E K D Bush, MA
Miss G R A Bell, BA
Mrs S E Besly-Quick, BA
Mrs S Cooper, BA
Mr P G Nathan, BA, LIB
Mr D J Woolcott, BA

Design & Technology:
*Mr J B Kelly, BA, MA, MA RCA
Mr M Bailey, BSc [OG]
Mr D M Hoyle, BEng
Mr K A Trim, BA

Drama:
*Ms N C McClean, BA, MA
Miss S J Cox, BA

Economics:
*Mr D S J Wright, BA
Mrs P A Brooks, MBA
Mr N W Gough, BSc, MSc
Mr R E Presley, MA
Dr J M Wisson, BSc, MPhil, DPhil

English:
*Mr A F E Quenault, BA, MA, MA
Mr D Amis, BA
Ms C J Clarkson, BA
Mrs H M Curtis, BA
Mr J Dunne, BA, MA
Dr E A McEwan, BA, MA, PhD
Miss E J Newton, BA, MA
The Revd J P Whittaker, MA

Geography:
*Mrs R G Waters, MA
Miss G M Clements, BA
Mr W D Cowx, BSc, MSc
Mr T E Fishpool, BA
Mr E G Pearson, MA
Mr R E J Seymour, BEd, FRGS
Mr J C Witts, BSc

History:
*Mr J A R Bass, BA, MA
Mr A C Dodd, BA, MA [OG]
Miss C E Hayes, BA

Mr D N Holliday, BA
Mr T J J Owens, BA
  (*Politics*)
Mr A J Shakeri, BA
Mr W H N Spouge, BA,
  MA

Mathematics:
*Mr S G Black, MMath
Mr J A Casale, BSc, MBA
Mr S L Dennett, BSc
Mr C George, BSc
Mr A R Gyford, MSci
Mr M R Jenkins, BSc
Mr A W J Jessett, MMath
Mr A B Kirkland, BSc
Dr A A Page, BA, MSci,
  PhD
Mrs S J Perrett, BA
Mr N C Pinhey, BSc
Miss H C Ward, MA
Mrs D B Webster, BA
Mrs C A Wellard, BSc
Mrs F M Wimblett, BSc

Modern Languages:
*Ms A V E Tournier, Lic
Mr S J Baker, BA
Mr M P Clarke, MA
Dr M M Creagh, BA, MSc,
  PhD
Mr P J Hosier, BA, MEd
Mr R J A Lemaire, BA
Mr A R Lowe, BA
Mr J Marchiafava, Lic
Miss M-L McCarter, Lic,
  MA
Mrs R J Rathmell, BA
Mrs C E Smith, BA
Miss G E Spencer, BA
Mrs N Wilson, BA
Mr R G Yardley, MA, MEd

Music:
*Mr P H White, MA
  (*Director of Music*)

Head of Admissions (*Registrar and Marketing*): Mrs K L
  Sweet, BA, MCIPD

Mr D H Chambers, BMus,
  PCASS
Miss J Newman, AGSM,
  CRD
Mr S J Orchard, BMus,
  MMus
Dr E R Thackrey, BMus,
  MMus, PhD

Physical Education:
* Mr G D G Cover, BSc
  (*Director of Sport*)
Mr R C Black, BSc
  (*Cricket*)
Mr B Dudley, BSc (*Rugby*)
Mr J D N Lythgoe, BSc
Mr C R Mullon, BSc
  (*Hockey*)
Mr T M Vickers, BA
Mr I Wilkes, BEd

Physics:
*Mr J P Hood, MA, MSci
Mr C S Bradford, MPhys
Mr M A Burbidge, BSc,
  BA
Dr A P Calverley, MSci,
  PhD, FRAS
Mr L M Holland, BSc
Mrs N L Odhams, MA,
  MEng
Dr D Patel, BSc, PhD
Mrs D Whitehead, BTech,
  Rsci

Religion and Philosophy:
*Mr R B Meadowcroft,
  BA, MA
Miss F A Bains, BA
Mrs L Griffiths, BA
Mr S T Herman-Wilson,
  BA
Mr K Tayar, BA [OG]

Royal Grammar School
Newcastle upon Tyne

Eskdale Terrace, Newcastle-upon-Tyne NE2 4DX

Tel: 0191 281 5711
email: admissions@rgs.newcastle.sch.uk
website: www.rgs.newcastle.sch.uk

The Royal Grammar School was founded and endowed in 1545 by Thomas Horsley, and by virtue of a Charter granted in 1600 by Queen Elizabeth it became 'the Free Grammar School of Queen Elizabeth in Newcastle upon Tyne'. For over 450 years and on six different sites the School has been of major educational importance in Newcastle and in the North East as a whole. It has valued its close links with the city and region, and its Governing Body consists largely of representatives of important companies, Local Authorities and Universities.

The School benefits from its central position, being within easy walking distance of the Civic and City Centres

and of Newcastle's two Universities, and linked with the whole region by easily accessible rail, bus and metro services.

The School is a Day School and moved towards full co-education in 2006 with places being allocated to boys and girls at all entry points (7+, 9+, 11+, 16+). There are about 1320 students, including 1065 in the Senior School (age 11–18) and 255 in the Junior School (age 7–11).

Curriculum. The aim of the curriculum up to Year 11 is to offer a general education, culminating in GCSE in a wide range of subjects. All students study English (Language and Literature), a Modern Language (French, German or Spanish), Mathematics, Biology, Physics and Chemistry to this level and three further examination subjects are taken at GCSE level from Ancient History, Art, Economics, Geography, German, Greek, History, Latin, Music, Spanish, Engineering Design & Technology and Drama. Additionally there is a programme of Art, Drama, Music and Technology for all in Years 7 to 9.

Sixth Formers will normally choose three A Level subjects. In addition, students will be required to select either a fourth A Level or a combination of two complementary courses from EPQ, two-year AS subject or non-examined subject. The range of A Level subjects is currently: Ancient History, Art, Biology, Chemistry, Computing, Engineering Design Technology, Economics, English, Film Studies, French, Geography, German, Greek, History, Latin, Mathematics, Further Mathematics, Music, Philosophy, Physics, Physical Education, Politics, Psychology, Spanish and Theatre Studies. There is also a compulsory series of lectures and talks/workshops designed to provide cultural and personal broadening and development.

Almost all Sixth Formers go on to University, and success in gaining entry at Oxford and Cambridge, and medical schools, has been an outstanding feature of the school's record.

Physical Education. All students are required to take part in a Physical Education programme which, up to Year 10, includes Rugby, Football, Cross-Country, Cricket, Athletics, Gymnastics, Hockey, Netball, Tennis, Rounders, Swimming. At the upper end of the School a wider range of activities is offered: in addition to the above students may opt for Badminton, Basketball, Climbing, Fencing, Fitness training, Karate, Orienteering, Squash, Tennis, Table Tennis, Volleyball and Dance. A wide range of activities is available to all through voluntary membership of various Sports Clubs.

Activities. Art, Drama and Music are strong features in the life of the School, all of them overflowing from scheduled lessons into spare-time activity. There is a large number of wide-ranging music groups and ensembles from choirs and orchestras to bands, jazz ensembles and rock groups. There are several productions in the theatre each term. Numerous societies meet in the lunch-break or after school, some linked with school work but many developing from private enthusiasms. There is a thriving Duke of Edinburgh's Award scheme. There is an entirely voluntary Combined Cadet Force Contingent. Annual overseas visits include ski-parties, sporting tours, Classics trips, visits to art galleries and to the battlefields of World War I.

Supervision and Pastoral Care. Each student is within the care of (a) Form Supervisor and (b) Tutor. The latter will normally be associated with the student throughout their school career, and the aim is to forge a personal link with students and their families.

The Careers programme begins in Year 9; in Year 11 and the Sixth Form every possible care is taken to advise each student individually about Careers and Higher Education.

The School's Medical Officers are available regularly for consultation; there are also male and female School Counsellors.

Buildings. Some of the School's buildings date from 1907 and are described by Pevsner as "friendly neo-Early-Georgian". Recent years have seen many developments and improvements, including the opening in February 1996 of a new Sports Centre, a new Science and Technology Centre which opened in 1997, and new Maths and ICT departments in 1998. A new Junior School extension opened in 2005 and a Performing Arts Centre opened in 2006. A new 6-lane, 25m swimming pool was completed in August 2015 as part of an additional sports complex which includes a second sports hall, a dance and fitness suite and new indoor and outdoor changing facilities. Currently under construction is a new library, a suite of rooms for Art, Maths, Science, Engineering Design Technology, and a home for the new Digital Technology and Computing Department. Similarly, a new Pastoral Centre will link this new building with the rest of the School – the building work is due for completion by July 2019.

Junior School. Years 3 and 4 of the Junior School are separately housed in Lambton Road opposite the Senior School playing fields. Years 5 and 6 are housed in a new extension on the main school site. Junior School students use the Sports Centre, Swimming Pool, games fields and dining hall. English and Mathematics are taught by Form Teachers, while History, Geography, French, Science, Religious Education, Music, Art and Physical Activities are taken by specialists.

Entrance. Entry is by examination. Application forms are available from the Admissions Secretary.

Junior School at 7+ and 9+. Prospective students attend Assessment Days held in November (9+) and January (7+) when they take part in a number of activities and sit a number of short tests. A reference is sought from previous/current school.

Senior School at 11+. The Senior School examination is held each January for prospective students who will be 11 on 1 September of the year in which entry is desired. Applications by 15 December (later application at School's discretion). A reference is sought from previous/current school.

Sixth Form at 16+. Applicants are considered for direct entry to the Sixth Form if their GCSE results are likely to form an adequate basis. A reference is sought from the previous/current school, prior to interview.

Each year a small number of places may be available at entry points other than the main ones listed. Please contact the Admissions Secretary for details.

Term of Entry. Autumn, although a small number of places may become available throughout the year.

Fees per term (2018–2019). Senior School £4,388, Junior School £3,696.

Bursaries. Some bursaries, awarded on the basis of parental income, are offered. Details are available from the Bursar.

Charitable status. The Newcastle upon Tyne Royal Grammar School is a Registered Charity, number 1114424.

Governing Body:

Co-opted Governors:
Chairman: Mrs J Drummond, BA, MA
Vice-Chairman: Mr I R Simpson, BA, MA
Mr P A Campbell, MA, DBA, FRSA
Ms N C D'Cruz, LLB
Dr I O Evbuomwan, MBBS, MD, FRCOG
Mr R H Fell, FRICS
Mr A Fletcher, LLB
Ms A Gupta, LLB

Ms T Hartley, MRICS, BSc, MSc, MBA
Mr A Lamb, BA, CA
Ms S Milligan, LLB
Mrs C S E Murphy, BSc
Mr T Murphy
Ms C Stonehouse
Ms S Woodroofe, BA, NPQH, MEd

Nominated Governors:
Professor M Haniffa, BSc, MBBCh, MRCP, PhD
Professor S Hambleton BA, BM, BCh, MRCPCH, DPhil
Councillor T Thorne, BA

Clerk to the Governors and Bursar: Dr M J Pitkethly, CEng, FIMMM, BSc, PhD

Headmaster: Mr J C Fern, MA

Deputy Head: Mr A A Bird, BMus, MEd, LRAM, FCCT

Assistant Staff:
* *Head of Department*
§ *Part-time*

Art:
*Mr G P Mason, BA
Miss H C Bray, BA, MA
Mr P Edwards, BA
Mrs C Egan-Fowler, BEd
Mrs K Nowicki, BA (*Head of Year 7*)
Mrs L E Thompson, BA

Biology:
*Mr P J Heath, BSc
Dr M H Bell, BSc, PhD
Mrs J A Malpas, BSc
Dr C J Murgatroyd, BSc, DPhil
Mr L Shepherd, BA
§Mrs S F Hutchinson, BSc
§Mr C J H Wancke, BSc

Chemistry:
Dr A J Pulham, BA, DPhil (*Science*)
*Dr E A Smith, BSc, PhD
Dr J L Greenhalgh, BSc, PhD
Mrs C J Hutton-Stott, BSc
Mr T Kelso, BSc (*Head of Year 12*)
Mrs N Wright, BSc (*Head of EPQ*)
§Dr R Campbell, BSc, PhD
§Mrs S L Coates, MSc
§Mrs M C Slack, BSc
§Mr R W Wiggins, BSc

Classics:
*Mrs V C Mee, BA, MA
Mr S M F Belfield, MA
Mrs P R Coningham, BA, MA
Dr L E Hope, PhD, MA, BA
Dr D A MacLennan, BA, MA
Miss P L Whitworth, BA

Digital Technology and Computer Science:
*Mr C J Wilde, BA

Economics/Politics:
*Mr J D Neil, MPhil

Mrs L E Davison, MA, BA
Mr R C M Loxley, BSc, MEd (*Director of Studies*)
Mr P Shelley, BA, MSc
Mr M J Smalley, BA
§Mr S O'Dwyer, BA

English:
*Dr S J Barker, BA, PhD
Miss S G Davison, BA
Mr L J Gilbert, BA
Dr C Goulding, BA, MLitt, PhD
Mrs K J Keown, BA
Mr A R D King, BA, MA
Dr S C Masters, BA, MA, PhD (*Film Studies*)
§Mrs L A Stadward, BA, MA

Geography:
*Mr D A Wilson, BSc
Mr M G Downie, BA (*Head of Careers*)
Mrs R J L Laws, MA (*Assistant Head of Careers*)
Miss S J Longville, BA (*Head of Year 11*)
Miss Z C Morrow, BSc, MA

History:
*Mr D Tyreman, MA
Mr O L Edwards, BA (*Oxbridge Coordinator*)
Mr D C Greenhalgh, BA, MA (*Head of Year 8*)
Dr E S Matthews, MA, PhD
Mr S E Tilbrook, BA
§Mrs A J Palmer, MA

Mathematics:
*Mr J A Smith, BSc
Dr J Argyle, BSc, MSc, PhD
Ms L Atkinson, BA, MA
Mr H M W Bingham, BA
Mr A Delvin, BSc, MSc
Mr G D Dunn, BSc

Mrs J Gwillim, BSc

Dr P M Heptinstall, BSc, PhD

Mr D A Jardine, BSc

Mr T E Keenan, BSc, MSc (*Head of Sixth Form*)

Mr M J Poole, BSc

Mr H Rashid, BSc, MSc

Mr A Snedden, BSc

Miss R M Watterson, BSc

§Mr A Pearson, BSc, MEd

Modern Languages:

*Miss K E Sykes, BA

Mr M S Bailie, BA, MA (*Head of Year 10*)

Miss S Demoulin, DEUG (**French*)

Senora B Membrado-Dolz (**Spanish*)

Mrs D Williams, BA (**German*)

Miss J Budd, BA (*Head of Year 13*)

Mrs C L Diaz-Crossley, BA

Mr T Harman, BA

Miss E L Hayes, BA

Mr M Metcalf, BA, MPhil (*Head of Year 9*)

Mrs C Towns, Staatsexamen

Music & Performing Arts:

*Z Fazlic, BA (*Director*)

Miss S L Bolt, BA

Mrs K Clappison, MA (*Head of Junior School Music*)

Mr T Walters, BA

§Mrs R A Shaw-Kew, BA

Pastoral:

Mrs S J Baillie, BA (*Pastoral Director*)

Ms A E Lee, MSc, BA (*Director of Student Progress*)

Junior School:

Mr R J Craig, BEd (*Headmaster*)

Mr J N Miller, BA (*Deputy Head*)

Dr A J Spencer, BSc, PhD (*Deputy Head*)

Mrs E J Barlow, BSc

Mrs C Baker, BA

Miss H Close, BSc

Mr A Cragg, BA

Mrs C M Cree, BSc

Mr T G Lloyd, BA

Miss S J McCulloch, BA

Miss M A Noble, BA

Mr J A Pollock, CertEd

Miss R S Scott, BA

Mrs L M Stairmand, BA

Miss P Sunderland, BSc

Mrs R S Towers, MEd

Mrs K Wall, BA

Ms A J Whitney, BA

Miss L R B Wood, BA, MA

§Mrs C A M O'Hanlon, BA

School Medical Officer: Dr R Pedlow

Admissions Officer: Mrs A Perry

Philosophy and Religion:

Dr M B A Read, MA, MPhil, PhD (*North American Universities Coordinator*)

Physical Education:

*Mrs A J Ponton, BSc

Mr H R T Chadwick, BSc (*Deputy Director*)

Miss H J Atkinson, BA

Mr A G Brown, BSc

Miss O Chapman, BA

Mr F Dickinson, BEd

Miss J Harrison, BSc

Miss A Lill, BSc

Mr A E Watt, BA

Mr J A Wood, BA

§Mr R V MacKay, BSc

Physics:

*Mr E T Rispin, BSc

Mr J L Camm, BSc

Dr R M Houchin, MSci, PhD

Miss B Milburn, BSc (*Careers Coordinator*)

Mr P Wilson, BSc, MSc

§Mrs P M Gill, BEng

PSHE:

Mrs K E J Hammill, BA

Psychology:

Dr C M Bone, PhD, BSc (*Complementary Studies*)

Miss K A Jacques, BSc

Engineering, Design & Technology:

*Mr P M Warne, MEng

Mr M Lowe, BA

Mrs C A Pipes, BA

§Miss R Harvey, MFA, BA

Royal Hospital School

Holbrook, Ipswich, Suffolk IP9 2RX

Tel: 01473 326200
Fax: 01473 326213
email: admissions@royalhospitalschool.org
reception@royalhospitalschool.org
website: www.royalhospitalschool.org
Twitter: @RHSSuffolk
Facebook: @RoyalHospitalSchool
LinkedIn: /Royal-Hospital-School

The Royal Hospital School was founded in 1712 in Greenwich, London, to 'improve navigation' through education and, as it prepared boys for a life at sea, many went on to become explorers and pioneers of their time. The School is immensely proud of these historic links and discovery, exploration and challenge continue to shape its ethos. The traditional values of loyalty, commitment, courage, respect, service and integrity have underpinned the School's core aims and philosophy from the very beginning. 300 years later, they are still as relevant to the education it provides as they were then. Today the School is set in 200 acres of Suffolk countryside overlooking the Stour Estuary and it is a co-educational HMC boarding and day school for 750 pupils providing a full and broad education, fit for the modern world. It aims to inspire its pupils to have the courage and commitment to be ambitious for their futures, whichever path they choose, challenging pupils of all academic abilities, steering them to look beyond the moment, and beyond the confines of the classroom, and to approach life with an open and receptive mind.

House System. 65% of pupils board and there is a strong diamond-shaped House System. An ongoing programme of refurbishment and development provides superb facilities and accommodation for both boarders and day pupils.

Pupils joining the School at 11+ are accommodated in the Junior House purpose-built with 4/6-bedded rooms and facilities, routines and pastoral care that assist the transition between junior and senior school. Weekly boarding and the opportunity to stay overnight on an ad hoc basis are available.

At Year 8 (13+) pupils join one of nine Senior Houses. Two are co-educational day houses and one is a boys' day house with flexi boarding facilities enabling the boys to board up to 3 nights per week. There are also 3 boys' and 3 girls' Senior Boarding Houses which are each home to approximately 60 full and weekly boarders. Boarders in Years 8 and 9 share rooms with up to four other pupils and older pupils have double or single studies with en-suite facilities.

In the Upper Sixth both boarding and day boys and girls join Nelson House, where they learn to live more independently in preparation for university.

Curriculum and Academic Development. The School's curriculum shadows the National Curriculum Key Stages 3 and 4. On joining the School, pupils are placed in forms on the basis of assessed ability from entrance testing or at 13+ the results of Common Entrance examinations. The School subscribes to the Durham University Value Added Measuring Scheme at all levels, allowing tutors to map pupil progress. In core subjects setting takes place from the outset and at GCSE level setting occurs in all core curriculum subjects. There are 66 x 55 min periods over a two weekly timetable.

Lower School (Years 7–8): The subjects studied are English, mathematics, science (biology, physics and chemistry), modern foreign languages (French, Spanish and German), Latin, geography, history, design technology, art, drama, IT (Information Technology), music, religious studies, RHS Compass (digital literacy, Personal, Social and Health Education, thinking and study skills) and PE. There are four forms in Years 7 and 8 and the average class size is 18 pupils. Homework is set daily and completed within supervised sessions during the working day by both boarders and day pupils. All junior pupils must take part in at least three co-curricular activities after lessons.

Middle School (Years 9–11): The subjects studied in Year 9 are the same as in the Lower School and a further intake of pupils from prep schools means that there is an additional class. GCSE courses start in Year 10 and most pupils will study 10 subjects including English language and literature, mathematics, a modern foreign language, physics, chemistry, biology (either as three separate sciences or as the dual award) as the core subjects and four options from science (if taking separate sciences), history, geography, PE (Physical Education and Sports Science), French, German, Spanish, media studies, religious studies, art, music, theatre studies, design technology and business studies.

Sixth Form (Years 12 and 13): Pupils choose three from 27 A Level subjects. Subject choice depends upon average point scores at GCSE and grades gained in specific subjects. As well as three A Level subjects, pupils must choose one from a range of academic Elective subjects which can range from an Extended Project Qualification to a BTEC Level 2 First Award in Information and Creative Technology. RHS+ provides sessions on careers, managing finances, cooking on a budget, digital effectiveness and safety and coping with stress and mindfulness. RHSXtra runs a series of talks and seminars on topics aimed at broadening horizons and inspiring curiosity. Around 90% of pupils go to the University or Higher Education institution of their choice and approximately 50% to Russell Group and other top-class universities. An increasing number of pupils are gaining places on Higher Degree Apprenticeship schemes with leading corporations.

Pupil progress is formally monitored by means of at least two assessments or reports per term which grade the academic performance of the pupil against their target or challenge grades. Every pupil has a personal tutor and bi-weekly tutorial meetings are an opportunity to deal with any problems and check on progress.

All pupils have access to iPads, a suite of mobile learning apps and Wi-Fi throughout the site. Additional networked computers are available in Boarding or Day Houses as well as in computer suites around the school. Mobile learning is embraced by the teaching staff with the aim of enhancing teaching and learning.

Through high quality, enthusiastic teaching, excellent resources and dedicated tutorial support, every pupil is encouraged to aim high and achieve his or her personal best. The most able pupils' potential is realised through the mentoring of scholars, the Stretch and Challenge scheme and Oxbridge preparation.

Sport and Leisure. Facilities include ninety-six acres of playing fields, a golf course, shooting range, sports hall, fitness suite, gym, climbing wall, large heated indoor swimming pool, squash courts, tennis and netball courts and an all-weather sports surface.

The School has a strong sailing tradition and all pupils joining in Year 7 receive sailing instruction to RYA Level 2. Through the School's RYA-accredited Sailing Academy, pupils have access to a fleet of 40 racing dinghies on adjacent Alton Water Reservoir, as well as traditional Cornish Shrimpers on the River Stour and Orwell. The School is widely known as one of the top in the country for both fleet and team sailing and offers an elite training programme for those wishing to follow Olympic pathway.

The recently launched Graham Napier Cricket Academy aims to provide a centre of cricketing excellence developing aspiring young cricketers to reach their full potential and promoting participation by girls and boys at all levels and ages.

The other main sports are rugby, hockey, netball, kayaking, athletics, cross country, climbing, basketball, football, tennis, riding and swimming. The swimming pool also offers opportunities for kayak-polo, life-saving training and sub-aqua.

Music and Drama. The School has a particularly strong musical tradition and the state-of-the-art Music School provides a recital hall, specialist rooms, recording studio, technical suite and "rock room". Almost half the pupils in the School are involved in music on a regular basis. The Chapel is of cathedral proportions and has one of the finest organs in Europe, much used by pupils as well as professional performers. Peripatetic teachers offer tuition in a wide range of instruments and the choir and chamber choir perform both nationally and internationally. As well as drama in the curriculum and LAMDA classes, productions are often combined with the music department for whole-school performances and there is a full programme of plays, competitions and festivals each year.

CCF and Community Service. All pupils participate in the Combined Cadet Force in Years 9 and 10 and are able to choose between Army, Navy, RAF and Royal Marine sections. The emphasis is on adventure training and personal development. More than 300 pupils take part in The Duke of Edinburgh's Award scheme and 100 of these to Gold Award. The Community Action Team promotes the School's social responsibility and is actively involved in a wide range of charitable activities in the local community.

Religion. The core values of the School are based on the Christian faith but pupils from a variety of religions and cultural backgrounds attend the School and all beliefs are respected. The magnificent Chapel, that holds over 1,000 people, is the spiritual hub of school life and the whole community gathers there most mornings for worship.

Admission. Entry to the School is normally at 11, 13 and 16 years. Pupils are asked to sit an entrance examination, comprising papers in English, mathematics and verbal reasoning, in the January prior to the September of the year of entry unless following Common Entrance for entry in Year 9. Entry into the Sixth Form is subject to a minimum average GCSE point score and specific grades in chosen A Level subjects. Entry is also subject to an interview and satisfactory reference from the pupil's current school.

Fees per term (2018–2019). Full Boarding: £8,430 (Years 7 and 8), £10,865 (Years 9–13). Weekly Boarding: £8,030 (Years 7 and 8), £9,970 (Years 9–13). Day: £5,230 (Years 7 and 8), £5,830 (Years 9–13). 3 Night Boarders: £7,070 (Years 7 and 8), £8,395 (Years 9–13). Discounts are available for services families eligible for the MOD Continuity of Education Allowance (CEA) and siblings where three or more children are in the School at any time.

Scholarships, Exhibitions and Awards are awarded annually for academic excellence, musical talent, drama, art, sport and sailing. All scholarship candidates are required to sit the School entrance examination (unless taking Common Entrance or GCSE examinations), have an interview and undergo an assessment in their relevant field. Full details from the Admissions Office, Tel: 01473 326136 or email: admissions@royalhospitalschool.org.

Bursaries. Pupils in receipt of a scholarship or award are eligible to apply for additional assistance by way of a means-tested bursary, should the financial circumstances of the family necessitate it. The School's parent charity, Greenwich Hospital, can award generous means-tested bursaries to the children of seafarers, particularly serving or retired Naval or Royal Marines personnel.

Charitable status. The Royal Hospital School is owned by Greenwich Hospital which is a Crown Charity.

Director, Greenwich Hospital: Mr H Player

Governors:
Chair of Governors: Mr H C T Strutt

Mr J Agar	Mr J Lynas
Mr N Bevington	Dr P Marshall
Mrs V Bidwell	Prof N Norris
Mr J Gamp	Mr P Smith
Mr T P J Hill, QC	Capt A Tate, RN Retd
Mr A Kerr	Mr P Winter

Senior Management Team:

Headmaster: **Mr Simon Lockyer**, BSc, MEd

Director of Finance and Operations (*Bursar*): Mr A McNiff, LLB, FCA, FCILT
Second Master: Mr S J Dixon, MA
Deputy Head (*Pastoral*): Mrs Z S King, BSc
Deputy Head (*Academic*): Mrs C A Stevens, BSc
Assistant Head (*Co-Curricular*): Mr C A Rennison, BSc
Assistant Head (*Pastoral*): Mr L M Corbould, BSc
Director of Communications: Mrs S Braybrooke, BA
Head of Sixth Form & Careers: Mr C Graham, BSc

Chaplain: Revd J W P McConnell, BEd, MA, BD, DASE

Head of Middle School: Mr A Wynn, BSc
Higher Education Coordinator: Mr C D Barker, MA
Head of Digital Learning: Mr H Mackenzie, BA
Examinations Officer: Mr A J Loveland, ACGI, MA

Heads of Department:
Art: Mrs H Barber, BA
Biology: Mr B A Raybould, BSc
Business and Economics: Mr T B Brightwell, BA
Chemistry: Mr M R J Ashworth, BSc
Classics: Miss H S Batten, BA
Head of Cricket: Mr P M Cohen, BA
Director of Graham Napier Cricket Academy: Mr G Napier
Design Technology: Mr O Millington, BA
Drama: Mr D Kerr, BA
English: Ms J L Stone, BA
English as an Additional Language: Mr D P Coleman, BA
Film & Media Studies: Mr M Vickers, BA
French: Mrs J Routledge, BA
Geography: Miss H Izod, BSc
German: Mrs N J Mann, MA
History and Politics: Mr R S Watson-Davis, BA
Learning Support: Mrs E Burge, MA
Librarian: Miss R Gitsham, BA
Mathematics: Mr K J Reid, MSc
Director of Music: Mr W Saunders, BMus, ARCO
Bandmaster: Mr R Harvey, BMus
Head of Academic Music: Mr E C Allen, BA
Science: Mr T Ellis-Peckham, BSc
Director of Sport: Mr D P Hardman, BA
Head of Academic PE: Mrs S J Williams, MA, BEd
Physics: Dr M R Gibbs, BSc
Psychology: Mrs M R Price, BA
Religious Studies: Mrs K O'Callaghan, MA
Director of Sailing: Mr E Sibson, MSc
Spanish: Mr R G Encinas, BA

Health Centre Sister: Sister D Sweeney, RGN
Head of Ceremonial: Lt Cdr Retd N Griffiths QGM
CCF Contingent Commander: Maj J F Pooley, BEd
CCF School Staff Instructor: WO1 [RSM] K Weaver

Duke of Edinburgh's Award: Sgt P Ryan

Registrar: Mrs K Evers, BA

The Royal Masonic School for Girls

Rickmansworth Park, Rickmansworth, Herts WD3 4HF

Tel:	01923 773168
Fax:	01923 896729
email:	enquiries@royalmasonic.herts.sch.uk
website:	www.rmsforgirls.org.uk
Twitter:	@RMSforGirls
Facebook:	@RMSforGirls
LinkedIn:	/the-royal-masonic-school-for-girls

There are 972 pupils in school, of whom 234 are in Cadogan House (Pre-Prep and Prep Department) and 64 are in Ruspini House, our co-ed Pre-School. There are 158 girls in the Sixth Form. Around 95 of the current school population are boarders and day girls and boarders are fully integrated through the Houses.

Premises and Facilities. Founded in 1788, the School came to Rickmansworth in 1934. It stands in over 150 acres of parkland on an attractive site overlooking the valley of the River Chess. The buildings are spacious and well-appointed. They include excellent ICT facilities, a well-equipped Science building, a Planetarium, a Chapel and Resource Centre of exceptional beauty.

The Sports Hall is equipped to the highest international standards. There is a heated indoor swimming pool, 12 tennis courts, four squash courts and superb playing fields. In 2015 the School opened its brand new All-Weather Pitch, funded by the Campaign for Excellence. The School has been awarded Sportsmark status. Work is currently under way for a new Performing Arts Faculty building, which is due to open later in the academic year 2018/19.

Location. Central London is 15 miles to the south and Amersham is just north of the town. The M25 is one mile from the school and links it to London (Heathrow) – 30 minutes, London (Gatwick) – 50 minutes, and Luton Airport – 30 minutes. London Underground services (Metropolitan Line) and British Rail from Marylebone enable Central London to be reached by train in 30 minutes.

General Curriculum and Aims. The first three years of Senior School provide a broad general education which fulfils the requirements of the National Curriculum and reaches beyond it. As well as the traditional academic subjects of English, Mathematics, Science, History, Geography and Religious Studies, girls study Design Technology, Information Technology, Home Economics, Art & Textiles, Performing Arts, Physical Education and Life Skills. Language Studies begin with French or Spanish and Latin. In Year 8 German and Mandarin are also offered.

GCSE options are chosen from among all the subjects taught in Years 7 to 9 and new possibilities, such as Child Development, Performing Arts, Drama and Business are introduced at this stage. Most pupils take nine or ten GCSE subjects and girls are guided in their choices by subject teachers, in full consultation with parents. Triple Science is available.

The Sixth Form. The School offers a wide range of A Level subjects in flexible combinations. Politics, Economics, Performance Studies, Classical Civilisation, Photography, Sociology and Psychology are all new additions to the curriculum at this stage. There are also practical and vocational courses leading to qualifications in Performing or Production Arts, Business and Health and Social Care. Virtually all Sixth Formers go on to higher education.

Religion. Girls of all faiths and none are welcome. School assemblies are traditional and inclusive in nature and Chapel Services for boarders are held according to the rites of the Church of England.

Health. The School Doctor attends the Health Centre regularly. There are two Nursing Sisters and a Medical Assistant.

Admission. Applications should be made to Mrs Gail Braiden, the Registrar (admissions@royalmasonic .herts.sch.uk). The School sets its own entrance examinations at all levels. New boarding and day pupils are accepted into the Sixth Form where there are wide-ranging opportunities for girls of all abilities.

Scholarships and Bursaries. Scholarships are offered by the School to encourage and reward excellence. Scholarships are awarded in recognition of outstanding achievement, or promise in a particular sphere, and involve financial support, not exceeding 25% of the annual fee.

A number of scholarships are available at 11+, 13+ and 16+, and some means-tested bursaries. The former are for open competition; the latter are restricted to certain categories of pupils in need. A scholarship and bursary could run concurrently in the case of a scholar who needed financial assistance.

At 11+: Awards are given in recognition of excellence with regard to academic achievement in the entrance examination, Sport, All-Rounder potential and Music.

At 16+: Awards are given for academic excellence, Music, Art, Sport and Performing Arts.

Bursaries enable suitable girls whose parents could not otherwise afford the fees to benefit from an education at The Royal Masonic School for Girls. Bursaries are awards made to girls who reach the School's required standards but who require financial assistance to take up a place. These awards are subject to means-testing, under a standard formula widely used within the independent sector, at the time the offer is made and biennially thereafter. The number of awards made in any one year will vary according to the quality and circumstances of candidates and the availability of funds.

Fees per term (2018–2019). Senior School: Full Boarders £9,945; Weekly Boarders £9,165; Day Pupils £5,825.

Cadogan House: Full Boarders: £7,075 (Years 3–6); Weekly Boarders: £6,705 (Years 3–6); Day Pupils: £3,825 (Reception, Years 1 and 2), £4,430 (Years 3–6). Ruspini House Pre-School (boys and girls aged 2–4): please visit our website for range of fees.

Charitable status. The Royal Masonic School Limited is a Registered Charity, number 276784. Its aims are the advancement of education.

Board of Governors:
Professor John Brewer (*Chairman*)
Mr K S Carmichael, CBE (*Honorary Life President*)

Mr S Brew	Mr C Heywood
Mrs P Dyke	Mr J Knopp
Mr D Ellis, OBE	Mrs F Richards
Mr K Emmerson	Mr N Springer
Mr J Flecker	Mr S Staite
Ms A Gray	

Head: **Mr K Carson**, MPhil Cantab, PGCE

Bursar: Mrs D Robinson, BSc Hons Bristol, ACA

Deputy Heads:
Miss R Bailey, BSc Hons York, PGCE, NPQH
Mrs C Bomford, MA Greenwich, BA Manchester, PGCE

Assistant Head: Mr D Cox, BEng Brunel, PGCE, NPQH

Head of Sixth Form: Mrs C Freeman, BSc Dunelm, PGCE

Senior Teacher: Mrs R L C Bloomfield-Proud, MA London, BA Leeds, PGCE

Chaplain: Reverend John Quill

Housemistresses:
Connaught: Miss K Batty (*Head of Boarding*)
Harris House: Mrs D Dwyer
Zetland House: Mrs R Dobson

Heads of Year:
Miss H S Stanley, BEd Liverpool (*Year 7*)
Mrs S Baron MA UCL, BA Nottingham, PGCE (*Year 8*)
Miss K Cook, BSc Reading, PGCE (*Year 9*)
Miss J Simmonite, BA Loughborough, PGCE (*Year 10*)
Mrs D E Heaffey, BA Middlesex, PGCE (*Year 11*)
Mrs C Freeman, BSc Dunelm, PGCE (*Sixth Form*)

Heads of Departments:
Art: Mrs M Nichols, BA Manchester Metropolitan, PGCE
Business Studies and Economics:Mrs V-A Bannister, MCom, MBA Dublin
Computing: Mr N Lilley BSc Leeds Metropolitan
Design Technology: Miss M Dines, BA Bucks
English: Mrs C Gardner, MA Open, LLB Leicester, PGCE
Food and Nutrition: Mrs H Clivaz, BSc Oxford, PGCE
Geography: Mrs J Walker, BSc London, PGCE
History: Mr F Grogan, BA York
Latin & Classical Civilisation: Mr N M Young, MA Oxon, MCIBS
Learning Support: Mrs A Ralph, BSc Lancaster
Mathematics: Mrs S Cubbon, MSc London, PGCE
Modern Languages: Mr J Piqueiras, BA Spain, PGCE Spain
Performing Arts: Mr D Hyde, BMus Birmingham, ALCM
Physical Education: Mrs L Cooper, BSc Loughborough, PGCE
Psychology: Mrs S Reeve, MSc London
Religious Studies: Mrs S Elder, BA Durham, PGCE
Science: Mrs N Timoney, MSc Warwick, PGCE
Textiles: Mrs G Coffey, BA Kent, PGCE

Cadogan House:
Head: Mr I Connors, BA Hons, NPQH
Deputy Head: Mrs A Brown, BA Reading

Ruspini House:
Head: Mrs V Greig

Visiting Music Teachers for bassoon, brass, cello, clarinet, drum kit, flute, guitar, oboe, organ, percussion, piano, saxophone, singing, steel pans, viola, violin.

Peripatetic Staff for Dance, Learning Support, Speech and Drama, EAL.

School Doctors: Dr C Orsi, Dr C Quinn
Personal Assistant to the Headmaster: Mrs S Clifford
Registrar: Mrs G Braiden

Royal Russell School

Coombe Lane, Croydon, Surrey CR9 5BX

Tel:	020 8657 4433
Fax:	020 8657 0207
email:	headmaster@royalrussell.co.uk
website:	www.royalrussell.co.uk
Twitter:	@Royal_Russell
Facebook:	@RoyalRussellSchool
LinkedIn:	/royal-russell-school

Motto: *Non Sibi Sed Omnibus*

Royal Russell School is an exceptional co-educational boarding and day school, for children aged 3 to 18 years, founded in 1853. Set in 110 acres of woodland, it enjoys excellent access to London, the South, and the airports at Gatwick and Heathrow.

Her Majesty The Queen is Patron of the School.

Number in School. There are 1076 pupils in the school: 750 pupils in the Senior School, of whom 229 are in the Sixth Form, and 326 in the Junior School. In the Senior School there are 148 boarders and 602 day pupils; of these 445 are boys and 305 are girls. In the Junior School there are 179 boys and 147 girls, all day pupils.

Admission. Most pupils enter the school in the Autumn term at the age of 3+, 11, 13 or 16. Space permitting, pupils may be considered and admitted at other ages, and there is a direct entry into the Sixth Form for eligible pupils.

Religion. The school's religious affiliation is to the Church of England but pupils of all persuasions are welcome. Our approach to daily life is founded on Christian principles and we maintain an atmosphere of mutual respect and understanding.

The resident Chaplain is responsible for the conduct of all services and the teaching of Religious Education throughout the school. Weekly Chapel assemblies allow a brief act of worship and an opportunity to share thoughts and ideas. The Sunday service is compulsory for those boarding at school, and the voluntary Eucharist is specifically for those with a Christian commitment. Enquiries regarding Confirmation to the Church of England are encouraged.

Curriculum. The keynote of curriculum organisation is flexibility and there is close alignment with the requirements of the National Curriculum. All pupils follow a curriculum designed to provide a sound foundation across a broad range of subjects. Equipped with this experience, pupils are helped in selecting their GCSE examination subjects from a wide range. Great care is taken to achieve balance in each pupil's timetable and to ensure that an appropriate number of subjects is studied.

A high proportion of pupils continue to the Sixth Form where, typically, three or four subjects are studied. At present A Level courses are available in Mathematics, Further Mathematics, Computing, History, Geography, Geology, Physics, Chemistry, Biology, English, Business Studies, Economics, Politics, French, Spanish, German, Drama and Theatre Arts, Media Studies, Art and Design, Photography, Design and Technology, Psychology and Music. There is also a CamTech Level 3 in Sport Science available.

It is our expectation that all pupils will leave the Sixth Form to go on to higher education and we regularly secure places at Oxford and Cambridge and Durham Group universities for our strongest pupils.

Facilities. The School lies in 110 acres of stunning private grounds providing excellent academic and sporting facilities for all age groups.

There are three Boarding/Day Houses and six Day Houses. A new boys' Day and Boarding House opened in September 2017 and a brand new girls' house will open in September 2020. A well-resourced School Library and Sixth Form Study Centre. Recent refurbishment has provided a stunning new Day and Boarding House for 80 pupils, refurbished classroom suite, spacious areas for Art, Design Technology, Food Science and Photography along with a new Media Studies Suite. A new sport pitch development has further enhanced our impressive sports facilities, providing a floodlit all-weather pitch, multi-use games area, new natural turf areas for cricket, athletics and football and resurfaced and extended netball courts. These are in addition to our Sports Hall and indoor swimming pool.

Our Science building extension will open in September 2019 with very well-equipped laboratories.

An outstanding purpose-built Music and Performing Arts building was opened in December 2010 along with new dining rooms, kitchen, servery and Café facility.

Careers. The Head of Careers coordinates careers advice, giving individual counselling and helping with all university applications. A Careers fair is held annually. The School is a member of the Career Development Institute whose services are available to all pupils. Towards the end of the Summer Term, work experience placements are organised for those who have completed GCSE examinations, and members of the Lower Sixth participate in organised visits to universities and colleges.

Organisation. The Senior School is divided into nine Houses, two Boarding/Day and three day for boys, one Boarding/Day and three day for girls. Each House has its own premises, Housemaster or Housemistress and Assistant House Tutors. It is expected that all pupils should be able and encouraged to participate as fully as possible in the co-curricular life of the school, becoming involved in evening and weekend activities irrespective of their status as a Boarder or Day pupil. Supervised homework sessions and drop-in subject clinics are provided for day pupils participating in evening activities and they attend supper with the boarders. Tutors play a vital pastoral and academic role, monitoring overall progress and development.

Games. Popular sports are hockey, cricket, football, netball, tennis, swimming and athletics. Badminton, basketball, table tennis, trampolining and volleyball are also played.

Music, Drama and Art. Music in the Senior School is in the hands of the Director of Music whilst the Assistant Director of Music concentrates on the Junior School. They are assisted by a large number of visiting teachers. There is a Senior School Orchestra and wind, brass, jazz, swing and string ensembles. Choral Society, Chapel Choir, Barbershop and Junior School Choir and Orchestra meet and perform regularly.

Drama is taught as part of the Creative Studies programme in the senior school and is available at GCSE and A Level where pupils make use of our Drama Studio, Auditorium and Technical Room.

In Art and Design, instruction is offered in a wide range of artistic techniques using a variety of materials – paint, ink, screen printing, ceramics and pottery.

Clubs and Activities. Senior School pupils choose from a programme of over 60 regular activities, with a participation rate of over 98%. Many activities are open to pupils in both Senior and Junior Schools, and the annual House Activities Cup is keenly contested by pupils in all year groups. The school's involvement in the Model United Nations programme is unique in this country, with our annual International MUN conference each October, attracting over 500 student delegates from all over the world. There is a flourishing voluntary Combined Cadet Force unit and Duke of Edinburgh's Award scheme, the Theatre Society takes advantage of the school's proximity to London's West End, and the annual ski trip is always over-subscribed.

Junior School. The aim in the Junior School is to instil a lifelong love of learning with a strong academic focus and extensive range of clubs and activities. A Breakfast Club and after-school care is available. The majority of children progress to the Senior School. The Junior and Early Years Section provides a happy, secure and purposeful environment. (*For full details please see our entry in the IAPS section.*)

Scholarships. A number of scholarships are available each year to pupils aged 11+ to 13+ who show particular promise and talent academically, in music, drama, art or sport. Sixth Form scholarships are also awarded annually.

For further details or an appointment to visit the school apply to the Headmaster.

Fees per term (2018–2019). Senior School: Boarders £12,175 (Years 7–13), Day £6,160 (inclusive of lunch and supper). Junior School: Years 5–6 £4,740 (inclusive of lunch, after-school clubs and supper), Years 3–4 £4,555 (inclusive of lunch, after-school clubs and supper), Reception–Year 2 £3,720 (inclusive of lunch), Nursery £2,240–£3,720.

Charitable status. Russell School Trust is a Registered Charity, number 271907. It exists solely for the education of boys and girls.

Patron: Her Majesty The Queen
Board of Governors and Trustees:

Chairman: Mr A Merriman

Mr S Kolesar	The Hon Sir Philip Moor
Dr A Fernandes	Mrs L Jessup
Mrs J Burton	Mr J D Lacey
Mr J Penny	Mr A Lorie
Mrs A Martin	Mr R Mathur

Senior School:

Headmaster: Mr Christopher Hutchinson, BMet, FRSA

Director of International Relations: Mr Graham Moseley, BEd Hons, MA
Deputy Head (Performance and Operations): Mr David Selby, BA Hons
Deputy Head (Pastoral and Designated Safeguarding Lead): Mrs Nathalie Hart, Licence D'Histoire, PDC
Deputy Head (Academic): Mr Daniel Botting, MSc, MA
Head of Sixth Form: Mrs Sandra Culbert, BEd Hons, MA, MA Ed Man, Dip M, ACCEG (*Careers*)

Teaching Staff:
Miss Sophia Ahmad, BA Hons
Ms Cathi Allison, BEd Hons, MA, NPQH, NCSL, CIEA (*English*)
Mr Carl Bailey (*Academic PE*)
Ms Deborah Baldwin, BA Hons, QTC (*Art*)
Mr John Baron, BSc Hons (*Admin and Activities Manager*)
Mrs Joanne Barton, BSc Hons (*Head of Biology*)
Mr Johnnie Blows (*Media Instructor/Technician*)
Mr Richard Brennan, BSc, MSc, BACR (*Head of Sports Science*)
Miss Stephanie Brennan, BSc Hons (*Head of Hockey*)
Mr Matthew Bubb, BA, UEFA License (*Postgraduate Sports Coach*)
Mr Jose Bueno, BSc Hons (*Modern Languages*)
Mr Michael Callow, MA Cantab (*Mathematics*)
Miss Sandrine Calvet, BA, MA FLE (*French*) (*Modern Languages*)
Miss Sarah Clarke, BEng (*Physics*)
Mrs Mary Colyer (*Librarian*)
Miss Alba Conde del Rio, BA Hons, MA (*Modern Languages*)
Mrs Alex Cook, BA Hons (*Science Technician*)
Mr Peter Cook, BSc Hons (*Mathematics*)
Mrs Victoria Corcoran, Cert Ed, MA (*Food Technology*)
Ms Elayine Cripps, Cert Ed (*Head of Drama*)
Mrs Melanie Davenport, BA Hons (*Drama*)
Mr John Davies, BSc Hons (*Head of Boys' PE*)
Mrs Saira Dean, BSc Hons (*Mathematics*)
Mr Colin Dear, BA Hons (*Head of Media Studies*)
Mr Dominic Dureau, BA Hons, MA (*English*)
Miss Louise Dye, BA Hons, PGCE (*Business Studies & Economics*)
Mr Jonathan Edwards (*Drama Technician*)
Mrs Kate El-Asmar, BA Hons (*English and Literacy Support*)
Mr Paul Endersby, BSc Hons (*Head of Science*)
Mrs Lynne Faulkner, BA Hons (*Business Studies & IT*)

Mrs Lisa Ford, BA Hons (*Music*)
Mr David Grindrod, BSc, MSc (*Geography*)
Mrs Helen Hadjam, BCom Hons (*Head of Economics*)
Mrs Jennifer Harris (*Library Assistant*)
Miss Katie Henderson, BSc Hons (*Sports Coach*)
Mrs Denise Hinson (*Design & Technology Technician*)
Mr Ed Hutchinson, BA Hons (*Head of History*)
Mr Mark Simmons (*Head of Football*)
Mrs Marion Januszewski (*Senior Science Technician*)
Mr David Jewiss, BEd Hons (*PE*)
Mrs Radha Kanji, BSc, MEd (*Head of Chemistry*)
Mr Andrew Kay, BA Hons (*Head of Design and Technology*)
Mr Simon Keable-Elliott, BA Hons (*Politics & Business Studies*)
Revd Henry Kirk, BA, BD Hons, MA, Dip Hist Art (*Head of Religious Studies*)
Miss Cassandra Lands, MA, PGCE (*Art*)
Mr Colin Leggatt, RAF VR T (*Contingent Commander CCF*)
Mrs Susan Lower, BA Hons, MSc (*Head of Support for Learning*)
Mr Jordi Major, BA Hons (*Head of Food Technology*)
Mrs Anne Mawer, MA, BA Hons (*Head of Modern Languages*)
Mr Alan McKenna, BSc Hons (*Head of Chemistry*)
Mrs Stephanie Milton-Thompson, BSc Hons (*Science*)
Mr Philip Millward, MA Hons, FRCO (*Head of Music*)
Miss Geeta Missan, BSc Hons, BA Hons (*Head of Spanish*)
Miss Kate Moore, BA, PGCE (*English*)
Mrs Lauren Morris, BSc Hons (*Mathematics*)
Mr Martin Muchall, MA, BA Hons (*Religious Studies*)
Mrs Karen Muldoon (*Drama Support Assistant*)
Miss Karen Palenski, BA Hons, MA (*Modern Languages*)
Mr Martin Parham, BSc, PhD (*Head of Geography*)
Mr Gunvantrai Parmar, Cert Ed/Dip Ed CDT & IT (*Design and Technology*)
Ms Tamsin Pearson, BA Hons (*Art & Design*)
Mrs Donna Pepperdine, BA Hons (*English*)
Miss Ruth Pringle, BA Hons (*English*)
Mr Mayuran Rajgobal, BEng QTS (*Mathematics*)
Mr Nigel Rocca, BA Hons (*Head of Business Studies*)
Miss Celia Roe, BSc Hons, RSA Dip, TEFL (*EFL & Spanish*)
Mrs Claire Rosser, BSc, MSc (*Science*)
Mrs Michelle Saunders (*Food Technology/Art & Design Technician*)
Miss Olesia Sava, BA, MA (*English, EFL & Modern Languages*)
Miss Malica Scott, BA Hons (*Geography*)
Mrs Lindsay Smith, BSc Hons, MA (*Mathematics*)
Mr Michael Stanley, BA Hons, MBA (*Head of Mathematics*)
Mr Alexander Stathopoulos, BSc Hons (*Head of Computing*)
Mr Alexander Sternfeld, MA, TESOL, Delta, BSc Hons (*Head of EAL*)
Miss Helen Stevens, MA (*Head of English*)
Mrs Susan Strutt, BSc Hons (*Biology*)
Mr Martin Tanner, BSc Hons, MA (*Head of Geology*)
Mr Adam Tansley, BSc Hons (*Mathematics*)
Mr Greg Thurstans, BSc Hons (*Director of Sport*)
Mrs Maria Wade, BA Hons (*Modern Languages*)
Miss Catherine Walton, BSc Hons (*Computer Science*)
Miss Charlotte Wheeler-Quinnell, BSc QTS (*Head of Psychology*)
Miss Karen Whitehead, BSc, PGCE (*Biology*)
Miss Tiffany Wood, BA Hons
Ms Julie Wong, BSc, PGCE (*Mathematics*)
Miss Michele Worsfold, MSc, MA Hons (*History*)
Miss Jemma Young, BA, PGCE (*History*)

School Counsellor:
Ms J Bovingdon, BA Surrey, Dip HE, MBACP Accred,
   UKRCP Registered

Houses and House staff:

Boarding:
Cambridge: Mr A McKenna
Oxford: Mr C Dear
Queen's: Miss M Davenport

Day:
Buchanan: Mrs D Pepperdine
Keable: Mr E Hutchinson
Madden: Mr A Stathopoulos
Reade: Mrs E Cripps
St Andrews: Mr A Tansley
Hollenden: Mrs S Strutt

Junior School:
Headmaster: Mr James Thompson, BA QTS
Deputy Head: Mrs Ruth Bannon
Deputy Head: Mrs Sarah Pain, BSc, PGCE, MA Ed Mgt
Assistant Head: Mr Varun Footring

Mrs Emma Austin, BA Hons
Miss Hannah Bisdee, BA Hons, PGCE
Mrs Abigail Cummings, BA Hons, PGCE
Mr James Davis, BSc
Miss Henriette Dijksterhuis, MSc, BA
Mrs Danielle Footring, BA Hons, PGCE
Miss Siobhan Fox, GTCL, LTCL (*Head of Music*)
Miss Bethan Frisby, BA Hons
Mrs Julia Green, BSc, PGCE
Mr John Janowski, BSc Hons
Mrs Caroline King, BSc Hons, PGCE
Mr Mark Lloyd BSc, PGCE (*Boys' PE*)
Mrs Laura Lloyd, BA (*Girls' PE*)
Mr Chris Lottering, BEd (*Science*)
Miss Holly Luke, BA Hons, PGCE
Mrs Judy Moseley, CertEd
Mrs Alys Netherway, BSc, PGCE
Miss Cheryl Parry, BEd Hons
Mrs Jozie Quinn, BEd Hons
Miss Aimee Rance, BA Hons, PGCE (*Head of Modern
   Foreign Languages*)
Mrs Fizza Rizvi, MA, PGCE
Miss Natasha Rogers, BA Hons
Miss Stephanie Scanlon, BA Hons, PGCE
Mrs Lucy Summer-Spriggs, BA Hons, PGCE
Mrs Louise Taylor, BSc
Miss Melanie Thompson, BSc Hons, PGCE
Mr Steve Urie, BA, PGCE, QTS
Mrs Ceri Warner, BA Hons, PGCE
Mrs Sue Wilson, BEd, MA

Teaching Assistants:
Mrs Teresa Bridgewater, CACHE Level 3 Dip Pre-School
   Practice
Mrs Lynne Bruce, NNEB, CCE
Mrs Adele Cane, Level 3 Dip
Mrs Susan Haig, NVQ Teaching & Learning L3
Mrs Yayoi Ikeda, Level 3 Dip, Adv Level Apprenticeship
Mrs Nicola Jordan, OCR Level 3 NVQ
Mrs Sharmaine Nemar, NVQ Early Years L2, Level 3 Dip,
   Adv Level Apprenticeship
Mrs Karen Parsons, NNEB
Mrs Kelly Payne, CACHE Level 2 NVQ
Miss Claudine Pettitt, Level 3 NVQ
Mrs Claire Tree, Level 2 NVQ
Mrs Janette Vallance, Level 3 Dip
Miss Emilie Webber, Early Years Foundation Degree
Mrs Anne Willis, CACHE Level 3 Dip Pre-School Practice

Director of Operations & Clerk to the Governors: Mr Neil
   Cufley
Admissions Registrar: Mrs Michele Stone
Marketing Manager: Mrs Ciara Campbell

The Royal School Dungannon

**2 Ranfurly Road, Dungannon BT71 6EG, Northern
Ireland**
Tel: 028 8772 2710
Fax: 028 8775 2845 Headmaster
              028 8775 2506 Bursar
email: info@rsd.dungannon.ni.sch.uk
website: www.royaldungannon.com
Twitter: @RoyalDungannon

Motto: *Perseverando* (*Excellence through Perseverance*)

In 1608 James I made an order in Privy Council establishing six Royal Schools in Ulster of which Dungannon became, in 1614, the first to admit pupils. In 1983 plans were first drawn up to incorporate the neighbouring girls' grammar school and to use both campuses' excellent facilities for co-educational purposes. This development came to fruition in 1986. A £9 million building and refurbishment programme began in 2000 and was completed in 2003, providing very high-tech specialist accommodation in science, technology and IT. In 2007 an international standard Astro-turf hockey pitch was completed with flood lighting and four new all-weather tennis courts were opened. Annual investment by Governors in the school's infrastructure has continued allowing RSD staff and pupils to enjoy excellent facilities.

For nearly four centuries the Royal School has aimed at providing an education which enables its pupils to achieve the highest possible standards of academic excellence and at developing each pupil into a mature, well-balanced and responsible adult, well-equipped for the demands of a highly complex and technological world.

There are four Houses which foster the competitive instincts and idiosyncrasies of young people. Pastorally, each year is supervised by a Head of Year who guides his/her pupils throughout the child's career in a caring school environment.

The Boarding Department provides accommodation for 54 Boarders with the Girls and Boys housed in separate wings of the modernised Old School building dating from 1789. The recently refurbished facilities include a new kitchen/dining area, recreation area with flat screen TV and games console, new furniture in all dormitories and fully regulated wireless internet throughout. There are a number of staff who assist in the Boarding Department, including a Head of Boarding, a team of seven resident teaching staff, a team of 5 day and evening matrons, and a large number of support staff. These staff all work together to ensure that high standards of care and support are maintained. The School is also serviced by a team of local doctors and dentists who support the Boarders. A major hospital is less than 30 minutes from the campus.

The extensive buildings are a mixture of ancient and modern, with recently opened technology and science accommodation. Eight well-equipped Science Laboratories, Audio/Visual Room, two Libraries, Sixth Form Centre and Study Rooms, Technology, two Music and Art Studios and two Information Technology Suites are supplemented by a Boarding Department housed in well-appointed accommodation which has been completely renovated in the recent times. Boarders are able to make use of a wide range of facilities such as Sports Hall, Computer Laboratory, Multi-gym, Badminton Courts, Television Lounges, satellite TV, high-speed broadband (including Skype) and nearby facilities such as the local swimming pool and extensive parkland walks. Situated in its own spacious grounds in a quiet residential area of this rural town, the School is linked directly by motorway to Belfast (40 minutes), two airports, cross-Channel ferries and railway stations.

The establishment of good study skills and practices is considered to be of crucial importance. The size of the School ensures that no child is overlooked in any way.

At A Level new subjects are offered such as Economics and, in collaboration with partner schools, Media Studies, Politics, Psychology and Business Studies.

Pupils are prepared for GCSE and A Levels under all the major UK Examination Boards and there is a tradition of Oxbridge successes as well as a high rate of entry to the University of Ulster, Queen's University Belfast and other leading British Universities. In most years around 95% of the Upper Sixth Form proceed to Higher Education. The School's overseas students typically choose to enrol both at UK universities and universities in their home country.

Many co-curricular pursuits are encouraged during lunchtime or after school, such as Choir, Orchestra, Duke of Edinburgh's Award scheme, Chess, Charities, Debating, Public Speaking and many more.

Alongside the School's academic achievements in both Arts and Sciences may be placed its record in the sporting world: in Rugby, Hockey, Cricket, Badminton, Shooting, Table Tennis and Tennis.

Fees per annum (2018–2019). Day: £150. 7-Day Boarding: £19,050 (non-EU passport holders), £10,650 (EU passport holders). 5-Day Boarding: £16,200 (non-EU passport holders), £7,950 (EU passport holders).

Charitable status. The Royal School Dungannon is a Registered Charity, number XN46588 A. It was established by Royal Charter in 1608 for the purpose of education.

Board of Governors:
Chairman: Dr G Walsh, BEd, PhD, ALCH, FHEA
Vice Chairman: Ven A J Forster, BA, BTh

Members:
Mrs J Anderson, BA Hons, MCIPD
Mrs K Bain, BEd
K Black, BEd
Mrs T Boyd
D N Browne, MIB, MIMgt
Mrs W Chambers, BSc, MEd, PGCE, DipIT
R J Clingan, BSc, MEd, PGCE, PQH NI
Dr B A Curran, BA, MA, PhD, PGCE
J C M Eddie
R Eitel
Mrs R Emerson, BSc, CSP
The Very Revd K R J Hall, MPhil
Mrs Y Halliday, BEd Hons
Mrs E Harkness, BL
Lord Maginnis of Drumglass, PC
Dr D Maguire, BDS
Mrs L McDonald
K McGuinness, BSc, PGCE
N H McLean, LLB, MBA
Dr H G McNeill, BA, MB, FFARCSW
Dr P G Steen, PhD, BSc, CPhys, MInstP
Revd A S Thompson, MA, BD
Mrs J Williamson, BA, MSc, PGCE, CPsychol AEP, HPCP
J G Willis LLb
I A Wilson, BSc, PGCE
Mrs G Leonard
R Patton, BA

Secretary to the Governors: The Headmaster

Headmaster: **Dr D A Burnett**, BA, PhD, NPQH

Teaching Staff:
* *Head of Department*
[1] *Head of Year*
[2] *Head of House*

Deputy Head: R J Clingan, BSc, MEd, PGCE, PQH NI

Senior Teacher: *G R Black, BSc, PGCE
Senior Teacher: *[1]Miss A E Chestnutt, BSc, MEd, PGCE
Senior Teacher: [1]Mrs C L Kerr, BA, MEd, PGCE

Head of Boarding: Mrs C J Mawhinney, BEd

Mrs A Best, BA, PGCE
A D Boyd, BMus Hons, PGCE, ALCM
*N J Canning, BEng, PGCE
*R E Chambers, BSc, PGCE
*Mrs W Y Chambers, BSc, MEd, PGCE, Dip IT
*[1]Mrs M E Clingan, BA, ATD
Miss S A Colgan, BSc, PGCE
*S J Cuddy, BMus, PGCE
Mrs A Gilkinson, MSc, PGCE
Mrs G S Glenn, BSc, PGCE
Miss A K Gorman, BEd
[1]J R Graham, BA, MSc, PGCE
*Mrs R L Hampton, BSc, PGCE
*J W Hunniford, BA, MA, PGCE
*Mrs S J Jackson, BA, MEd, PGCE
*[1]P S Kerr, BA, MSc, PGCE
[1]G S R Lucas, BSc, PGCE
[2]Mrs P L Matthews, BEd, PGCE
*[2]G W McClintock, BSc, PGCE
Miss D McCombe, BSc, PGCE
Mrs C E McMcCormick, BA, PGCE
Mrs S J McCullough, BA, PGCE
M McDowell, BA, MA, PGCE
*K McGuinness, BSc, PGCE
Mrs L McGurk, BSc, PGCE
*[1]Mrs P McMullan, BEd, PGCTEd
*Miss H Montgomery, BSc, PGCE
*P G Moore, MA, PGCE, GC, TEFL
*Ms A M Prescott, BEd, MEd
*[2]A S Ritchie, BSc, PGCE
*[2]Mrs D Robb, BSc, PGCE
Mrs J Stewart, BSc Hons, PGCE, DIS
Mrs E V Stitt, BA, PGCE
*Mrs A R Straghan, BSc Econ, PGCE
A T Turner, BSc, PGCE
[1]G T Watterson, MSc, PGCE
J W Willis, BEd
I A Wilson, BSc, PGCE

Chaplain: Ven A J Forster, BA, BTh

Administrative Staff:
Bursar: Mr D Wheeler, BSc Econ, FCA
Headmaster's Secretary: Mrs A Cullen

Matrons:
Mrs M Willis, SRN (*Day*)
Mrs M McNeill (*Evening*)
Ms M Campbell (*Evening*)

Rugby School

Rugby, Warwickshire CV22 5EH

Tel: 01788 556216 (Head Master)
            01788 556260 (COO)
            01788 556274 (Admissions Registrar)
Fax: 01788 556277 (Admissions Registrar)
email: head@rugbyschool.net (Head Master)
            bursary@rugbyschool.net (COO)
            admissions@rugbyschool.net (Admissions
            Registrar)
website: www.rugbyschool.co.uk

'The mantra here is the whole person is the whole point. To which we'd add that, at Rugby, you get the whole nine yards.' (Tatler Schools Guide 2017).

'Rugby puts an enormous amount of time and effort into its pastoral care' (Good Schools Guide)

Ethos. Rugby School pupils flourish in a supportive and spiritually aware community which challenges learners, develops resilience and encourages intellectual risk-taking. We foster academic excellence, nurture individual talents and ignite that spark enabling our students to develop a life-long love of learning, while achieving outstanding results.

Head Master, Peter Green, has a great passion for every area of School life at Rugby and his aim is for children to love being pupils here.

"There is a strong and genuine sense that this is a school of obligation, not privilege," he says. "A great education is so much more than a focus on academic excellence – children need resilience to face the challenges our fast-changing world throws at them. Rugby children aren't afraid to fail, we teach them how to recover, to move on, to make the very best of all the skills they have."

Rugby's greatest Head Master, Dr Thomas Arnold, knew that education is all about transforming lives and should clearly focus on the three areas of academic ability, moral principal and 'gentlemanly' conduct.

Excellence is celebrated here, but nobody is ever on the bench, every pupil is equally important – a good illustration is our 32 netball teams – everyone is included.

Our mantra is 'The Whole Person is the Whole Point'. Yes our pupils are achieving the best academic results in Rugby's history and overtaking our peer groups, but that is just one part of the whole story.

It's an exciting time; our 3Rs: restlessness, reflection and rigour are shared by our staff and pupils; we have a team united in their desire for growth and development. The momentum is palpable. This is why we are the leading co-educational boarding school in the country.

Number of pupils (2018–2019). 802 (45% girls and 55% boys).

Location. Enjoying a central location just 48 minutes by train from London and close to the M6, M1 and Birmingham Airport, Rugby School offers the best of all worlds – a leafy green 150-acre campus of the edge of the countryside but still part of the town.

Facilities. A rich, cultural heritage runs through the core of the School with many buildings of architectural distinction from the impressive Chapel to the splendid Temple Speech Room. Step away from the town and pupils enter another world of ancient cloisters and elegant quads punctuated by swathes of green.

The facilities are, however, state-of-the-art including a purpose-built Modern Languages building, an impressive Science Centre, a Design Centre featuring The Lewis Gallery with its dedicated art and exhibition space, a Media Centre with professional TV Studio and most recently, a huge new sixth form centre for A Level only subjects, complete with a debating chamber modelled on the House of Commons.

The Music Schools have recently been extended and refurbished to include 40 teaching/practice rooms, technology classrooms, recording studio and a small concert hall. Pupils regularly get to play with the School's professional orchestra.

Sports facilities are equally impressive including a modern Sports Centre, with its 25m pool, fitness suite and courts, three new astroturf hockey pitches, soccer and rugby fields and hard courts for tennis and netball. Our polo fields mark the boundary of this wide-reaching campus. Sport at Rugby includes Athletics, Badminton, Basketball, Cricket, Cross-country, Fencing, Fives, Football, Golf, Gymnastics, Hockey, Netball, Polo, Rackets, Rugby, Sailing, Squash, Swimming and Tennis. Every pupil has access to professional sports coaching and conditioning.

Boarding Houses. The House structure at Rugby is central to our strong sense of community. Ideas flourish best where they were originated and it was Dr Arnold who initiated the boarding house system to ensure exceptional pastoral care and provide the ideal social environment in which young people could thrive.

Much copied but never bettered, Rugby's 200 years of 'House' experience has resulted in a genuine and uncompromised care plan which supports every single student.

There are now 15 Houses at Rugby, each with their own unique character, in different locations and of varying sizes, but all offering a true home away from home, a real family to which every pupil belongs and is rightly proud of.

The ethos at Rugby that the whole person is the whole point is undeniably apparent within this perfected and seamless House structure. The role of Housemaster or mistress as head of the 'family' is to create and maintain a happy and balanced home with the able support of their deputy and the Matron, who importantly are all resident. Totally committed to the well-being of their young people, this nucleus of staff provides 24-hour care that is second to none.

Academic. *GCSE*: All the usual subjects are offered as well as Computing, German, Spanish, Latin, Greek, Design, Art and Music, PE, Theatre Studies and Religious Studies.

A Level/Pre-U: A Level is offered in all the GCSE subjects as well as in Business Studies, Economics, Graphics, History of Art, Textiles and Politics. The option of following Pre-U courses is available in Chemistry, Art and Design, Modern Foreign Languages, Mathematics and Physics. All pupils have the opportunity to pursue an Extended Project and all go on to Higher Education with around 10 per cent receiving Oxbridge offers.

A diverse programme of academic enrichment is an integral part of a Rugby education with all pupils attending at least three clubs and societies each week. Academic societies, many of which are pupil driven, invite a wide range of eminent figures to the School – speakers have included Rowan Williams, Ambassador Frank Wisner, Anthony Horowitz and Dame Tanni Grey-Thompson.

Spiritual Life. A well-balanced individual needs a sense of spiritual awareness along with academic achievement and physical ability. The experience of holiness, an understanding of right and wrong, and respect for the worth of each human being; these things are the invisible glue holding our community together. These values are learned in every part of our lives, but the School Chapel and the activities connected with it are a particular focus for our spiritual development.

The Chaplains get to know the boys and girls by sharing meals, visiting the Houses and involving themselves with all the School's activities. They also share the teaching of the younger pupils, giving them regular contact with the entire Lower School.

Co-curricular. Being part of Rugby's thriving community is exciting, inclusive and full of possibilities. Our teachers are as keen to devise fascinating clubs and activities to engage and feed inquiring minds as the pupils are to sign up for them. A good co-curricular programme is not about simply filling 'spare' time or bolt-ons to existing subjects, but more about creating enriching experiences that ignite a spark, lead to another question or nurture a quiet confidence.

It's the chance to try something new, to challenge body and mind, to follow the 'what-if', to try, perhaps to decide it's not for you, but to be encouraged to explore another path.

There are always many options here and the doors are open to as much as any pupil may like to fit in. The energy is inspiring, the approach inclusive and the emphasis is on enjoying life, because at Rugby, the whole person is the whole point.

There are some incredible trips organised annually – 2016 included a girls' hockey and netball tour to New Zealand and Singapore, and a boys' rugby tour to Japan. 2017 featured a World Challenge programme to Madagascar, a cricket tour to Dubai and a Philosophy expedition to Northern India.

Admission. At 11+ local boys and girls may be assessed for entry into Year 9 as day pupils. At 13+: offers of boarding places on the basis of previous school's report and interviews during Year 7, subject to CE at average 55% at least, or the School's own Maths and English tests, or scholarship entry.

At 16+: offers of places for boarders and day pupils on the basis of previous school's report, interview and written entrance tests during Year 11, subject to at least three A (or 7) grades and three B (or 6) grades or above (including English and Mathematics, and in the subjects chosen for A Level if applicable) at GCSE.

Scholarships. Our scholarship provision is designed to attract boys and girls of outstanding talent and skill in a variety of fields. We value scholarship of all sorts. Through the excellence of our academic provision and of our facilities we aim to foster high achievement at all levels and to challenge expectations. The interplay of teaching and learning, and the experiences to be gained from being part of a rich and diverse community, encourage all pupils to develop their talents and to emerge as confident, well-rounded individuals.

13+ (Year 9) Academic Scholarships: Examinations are held in February of Year 8.

16+ (Year 12) Academic Scholarships: Scholarship interviews are held in mid-November of Year 11. Candidates must first take the Sixth Form Entrance Examination and those showing scholarship potential will be called for Scholarship interviews.

Music Scholarships: Awarded each year at 13+ and 16+. At 13+ with assessment auditions held at Rugby School in late January of the year of entry. At 16+ the audition is held in November as part of the 16+ entrance procedure.

Art Scholarships: Awarded each year at 13+ and at 16+. At 13+ the assessment takes place in March of Year 8. At 16+, it is in November as part of the 16+ entrance procedure.

Design and Technology Scholarships: Awarded each year at 13+ and at 16+. At 13+ the assessment takes place in March of Year 8. At 16+ it is in November as part of the 16+ entrance procedure.

Sports Scholarships: At 13+ and 16+ for candidates with outstanding ability or potential in the major team games for boys (rugby, hockey, cricket and tennis) or girls (hockey, netball and tennis). At 13+ the assessment takes place in October of Year 8. At 16+ it is in October of Year 11.

Drama Scholarships: A number of Drama Scholarships are awarded each year at 13+ and 16+ to candidates with outstanding acting ability or potential. At 16+ there are also scholarships for technical ability in drama. At 13+ the assessment takes place in October of Year 8. At 16+ it is in October of Year 11.

Computing Scholarships: Awarded each year at 13+ and 16+. At 13+ the assessment takes place in May of Year 8. At 16+ it is in November as part of the 16+ entrance procedure.

Foundation Awards: Several Foundation Awards are made annually to day boy and day girl candidates at 13+ and 16+. These candidates must live within a radius of 10 miles from the Rugby Clock Tower – excluding the city of Coventry.

Awards and Augmentation: The value of a Scholarship Award or a Foundation Award (including more than one award) is a maximum fee concession of 10%. Support can be augmented up to 100% of the day fees subject to means assessment.

The Arnold Foundation aims to raise funds through charitable donations to support the education of talented boys and girls whose families would not be able to fund boarding school fees. Funds are available for several awards for entry to the sixth form and at 13+. Pupils offered a place through this scheme may be awarded up to 100% of the full boarding fee plus extras. The final selection is through interviews. Candidates are expected to pass the School's normal entrance requirements. Initial enquiries should be made via the Admissions Office

For further information and details of all Scholarships, Foundation Awards and the Arnold Foundation please contact the Admissions Registrar, Tel: 01788 556274, email: admissions@rugbyschool.co.uk.

Fees per term (2018–2019). The consolidated termly fee for boys and girls: £11,920 (boarding), £7,479 (day). Optional charge for instrumental or singing tuition: £331.

Further Information. Log on to www.rugbyschool. co.uk. Enquiries and applications should be made in the first instance to the Registrar.

Charitable status. The Governing Body of Rugby School is a Registered Charity, number 528752. It exists to provide education for young people.

Governing Body:
Mrs L J Holmes, BA (*Chairman*)
R C A Hingley, MA (*Deputy Chairman*)
The Rt Revd the Lord Bishop of Birmingham, D A
   Urquhart, KCMG
D J Bennett, MA
Prof C J Howe, ScD
S Lebus, MA
B J O'Brien, LLB
P Smulders, BA, MBA
Ms C J Marten, MA
Ms G Woodward, BA
Mrs J Eastwood, BA
Mrs H Jackson, BSc
G V Lloyd-Jones
J R Moreland, MA
A D Thomas, FCCA, CTA Fellow, ATT Fellow
Lieutenant General T Radford, CB, DSO, OBE
R J A Elmhirst, LLB

Chief Operating Officer and Clerk to the Governing Body:
   P A Nicholls, MA, FCA

Medical Officer: Dr S Brown, MA, MB, ChB, LLB, LLM,
   DCH, DRCOG, DFSRH, FRCGP

Head Master: P R A Green, MA, PGCE

Deputy Head: Dr N G Hampton, MA, PhD, PGCE

Deputy Heads:
Mrs S A Rosser, BEd (*Pastoral*)
G Parker-Jones, MA, PGCE (*Academic*)

Assistant Head (*Upper School*): Dr J D Muston, MA, MPhil, DPhil
Assistant Head (*Middle School*): E S Davies, BA, MSc, PGCE
Assistant Head (*Co-Curricular*): Mrs L M Hampton, BEd, MSc

Admissions Registrar: H G Steele-Bodger, MA

Assistant Teaching Staff:

Chaplaincy:
The Revd R M Horner, BSc (*Chaplain*)
Miss L Greatwood, BSc, DipMin, PGCE
D R Shaw, MA, PGCE

Classics:
A E L Thomson, MA (*Head of Department*)
Dr F B Chesterton, BA, MA, PhD
T J Day, BA, PGCE
Miss S R Harris, BA, MSt
Dr L B T Houghton, MA, MPhil, PhD, FSA

Design:
P A Byrne, BA (*Director of Design Faculty, Head of D&T*)
J Ryan, BA, BTech, PGCE, MFA (*Head of Art*)
Mrs A Bradbury, Dip AD (*Art, Photography, Graphics*)
Miss A K Janulewicz, BA, PGCE (*D&T*)
Miss H Kaur, BA, PGCE (*Art*)
Mrs S E Phillips, BA, QTS (*Art, Ceramics*)
B J Welch, BEng, PGCE (*D&T*)

Economics and Business Studies:
C J Fisher, BA (*Head of Department*)
A M Burge, BSc
Miss H Burrows, BA
H M Lam, BA
B M Marcas, MSc, PGCE
O W Wright, BSc

English:
T Eyre-Maunsell, MA, PGCE (*Head of Department*)
Mrs E M Beesley, MA
E Jaspers, BA, PGCE, QTS
A J Naylor, BA, PGCE
Ms A Scott-Martin, MA, MA, PGCE
A N Smith, MA, PGCE
Dr J A Sutcliffe, PhD
Dr J S Whitehead, MA, MPhil, PhD, FRSA

Geography:
R Ghosh, BSc, PGCE (*Head of Department*)
Mrs E Bernstein, BA, MPhil, PGCE
J C Evans, BA, PGCE
Dr L E Milner, MA, MSc, PhD
Mrs S A Rosser, BEd
L D Shepherd, BSc, PGCE
D Westcott, BSc, MSc

History:
Dr T D Guard, MA, MSt, DPhil, PGCE (*Head of Department*)
E S Davies, BA, MSc, PGCE
Miss K Hollings, BA
Mrs M H Mahalski, MA, GDL, LPC, PGCE
Dr J D Muston, MA, MPhil, DPhil
Mrs A Naylor, BA, PGCE
G Parker-Jones, MA, PGCE
O Schortz, BA, MSc
W Swain, BA, MLitt

Information Technology:
T E Rennoldson, BSc, PGCE (*Head of Department*)
Mrs L A Bell, BEng

Learning Development:
Mrs L J E Stevenson, LLB, Dip SpLD, Adv Dip, CPT3A (*Head of Learning Development*)
Mrs A L Cunningham-Batt, MA, OCR Cert SpLD
Mrs F J Fleming, MA, Cert TESOL, Adv Dip
Mrs B Green, MA, MEd, PGCE

Mathematics:
Miss R J Force, BSc (*Head of Department*)
I S Tipler, BSc, PGCE (*Second in Department*)
M R Baker, BA, PGCE
P K Bell, MA, Msc, PGCE
N Jones, MEng
B L Lane, MA, MSc, PGCE
Mrs S C McGuirk, BEng, PGCE, NPQML
W Murphy, MSc
B J Rigg, MA, ACA
D R Shaw, MA, PGCE
A J Siggers, BSc
Miss K Warwick, MA, BSc, PG DipEd

Modern Languages:
C M Brown, BA (*Head of Department*)
Dr A C Leamon, BA, MA, PhD (*Head of French*)
Mrs C A O'Mahoney, BA (*Head of Spanish*)
Mrs W J Corvi, BEd, PGCE
S Foulds, BA, PGCE
Miss J Holroyd, BA, PGCE
Dr B Parolin, BA, MA, PhD, PGCE
Ms C Piquard, MA
Ms B S Sanchez-Alonso, BA, BA, PGCE
Dr J C Smith, MA, DPhil, PGCE

Music:
R J Tanner, MA, FRCO, ARAM, Hon FGCM (*Director of Music*)
S Ferris, BMus, AKC (*Assistant Director of Music*)
A R Davey, LTCL (*Head of Contemporary Music*)
J T Oxley, MA, ARCM (*Head of Singing*)
Miss R Taylor, MA, LRAM (*Acting Head of Keyboard*)
J A Williams, MA, BA, Dip ABRSM, PGCE (*Head of Academic Music*)
Miss V Brandwood, BMus, PGCE

Philosophy and Theology:
D J McLean, BA, MA (*Head of Department*)
Mrs A L Parker-Jones, MA, PGCE
Revd R M Horner, BSc
Miss L J Greatwood, BSc, Dip Min, PGCE

Physical Education:
F J Hemming-Allen, BEd, MEd (*Head of PE*)
Mrs D L Skene, BSc, PGCE (*Director of Sport*)
Mrs L M Hampton, MSc, BEd
Miss E M Watton, BA, PGCE

Politics and International Relations:
P Teeton, BA, MA (*Head of Department*)
Mrs E Bernstein, BA, MPhil, PGCE
E E Trelinski, MA

Science:
Dr M A Thompson, BSc, PhD, PGCE (*Head of Science*)
Dr G C E Joyce, BSc, PhD, PGCE (*Head of Biology*)
T M White, BSc, PGCE (*Head of Chemistry*)
Dr A G Davies, BSc, PhD, PGCE (*Head of Physics*)
Dr S R Belding, MChem, DPhil
Miss O Cairns, BSc
R Dhanda, BSc
N A Fisher, BSc, MSc, MA, FInstP, PGCE
M Forth, MA, MChem, PGCE

O Gardner, MSci, MA, PGCE
Miss L J Greatwood, BSc, DipMin, PGCE
Dr N G Hampton, MA, PhD, PGCE
Dr M C Jones, MA, MSc, PhD, PGCE
R B McGuirk, BSc, MSc, PGCE
M A Monteith, BSc, PGCE
Dr N J Morse, BSc, PhD, CChem, FRSC
R Parker, BSc, PGCE
Mrs E A Robinson, BSc, PGCE, MEd
S P Robinson, BSc, PGCE, MRes
Mrs E L Sale, BSc, PGCE
G Toth, MSc, PGCE

Theatre Studies & Performing Arts:
Dr T D Coker, BA, MMus, MPhil, PhD (*Artistic Director*)
A K Chessell, BA, MSc, PGCE
Dr S L Hancox, BA, MA, PhD

Careers and Higher Education:
Mrs D J Horner, BA (*Head of Department*)
Ms L Waweru, BPhilEd, PQCG
Mrs J A Higgins

PSHE Education:
Miss L J Greatwood, BSc, Dip Min, PGCE (*Head of Department*)

Sport:
Mrs D L Skene, BSc, PGCE (*Director of Sport*)
M Bayley, BSc (*Director of Rugby*)
M J Powell (*Director of Cricket*)
J M Stedman, BA (*Director of Hockey*)
N T Atley, MSc (*Strength & Conditioning Coach*)
Mrs A Canning (*Netball Development Officer*)
S. Pointon, BSc, MSc (*XV Coach, Sports Performance Analyst*)
P J Rosser, BA (*Rackets Professional*)
J Taylor, BSc (*Tennis Development Officer*)

Houses and Housemasters/mistresses:

Boarding Houses (boys):
Cotton: Mr Ed Trelinski
Kilbracken: Mr Saul Foulds
Michell: Mr Tim Day
School Field: Mr Mindy Dhanda
School House: Mr Peter Bell
Sheriff: Mr Maurice Monteith
Whitelaw: Mr Chris Evans

Day Boy House:
Town: Mr Andrew Chessell

Boarding Houses (girls):
Bradley: Mrs Liz Sale
Dean: Dr Leanne Milner
Griffin: Mrs Liz Robinson
Rupert Brooke: Miss Katie Hollings
Stanley (*Sixth Form only*): Mrs Lara Hampton
Tudor: Mrs Debbie Horner

Day Girl House:
Southfield: Mrs Lizzie Beesley

Director of Development: Mrs K Wilson, BA

Ryde School with Upper Chine

Queen's Road, Ryde, Isle of Wight PO33 3BE
Tel: 01983 562229
Fax: 01983 564714
email: school.office@rydeschool.net
website: www.rydeschool.org.uk
Twitter: @rydeschool
Facebook: @rydeschool2013

Motto: '*Ut Prosim*'

Ryde School with Upper Chine is a day and boarding school providing education for boys and girls aged two and a half to eighteen. It is situated on the Isle of Wight. Ryde School was founded in 1921 to provide a Christian education for boys. In 1992 the School opened Fiveways, which caters for pupils in the Nursery, Reception and Years 1 and 2. Upper Chine was founded as a Girls' School in Shanklin on the Isle of Wight in 1914. The two schools merged in 1994 to form Ryde School with Upper Chine and in 1996 the School took over Bembridge School. As a result of these acquisitions and mergers the School is now fully co-educational. Boarding provision is situated on a coastal site of 117 acres in nearby Bembridge and in a newly-opened boarding house for 10 Sixth Formers in Ryde itself.

Situation and Buildings. The School stands in its own grounds of 17 acres in Ryde with stunning views over the Solent and is easily accessible from all parts of the Island and the near mainland. It is within walking distance of the terminals which link Ryde to Portsmouth by hovercraft (10 minutes) or catamaran (25 minutes) and a number of pupils travel daily from the mainland. In recent years there have been many additions to the School buildings. The School now enjoys up-to-date and extensive facilities. New Art and CDT departments opened in 2011 in the award-winning Bembridge Building and eight science labs have been recently fully refurbished and a new Health and Well-being Centre has been created.

Organisation and Curriculum. The School aims to provide a secure and nurturing environment from which pupils gain the ambition, courage and values to face the world. It enjoys an enviable reputation on the Island for high standards both inside and outside the classroom.

In the Junior School strong emphasis is placed on core skills, proficiency in reading, writing and number work. Pupils are prepared for entry into the Senior School, and, following a recommendation from the Head of the Junior School, they are offered places in the Senior School at the age of 11. All pupils in the Junior School get the opportunity to sail and engage in outdoor learning.

The programme of work in the Senior School is designed to provide a broad but challenging education up to the end of Year 11 with all pupils working towards the EBac. The subjects taught to IGCSE/GCSE level are English Language and Literature, Mathematics, Physics, Chemistry, Biology, French, German, Latin, Mandarin, Spanish, ESL, Geography, History, Religious Education, Business Studies, Art, Music, Physical Education, Drama, Computer Science and Design Technology. All pupils select an Elective subject from: Global Perspectives, Arts Award, Science CREST Award, Informatics or additional English and Maths. All pupils also follow a programme of Personal Development (PD) and Games.

In the Sixth Form pupils choose between three routes: the IB Diploma, 'A Level Plus' (3 A Levels plus various enrichment and extension options) and the IBCP (An IB certificate that combines academic courses alongside vocational qualifications in one of Business & Finance, Engineering, Art &

Design or Sport). In addition, pupils are encouraged to take the Extended Project Qualification, designed to add breadth to their academic studies. Courses lead to entrance to universities, the Services, industry and the professions. The Careers Department provides advice and guidance to all pupils who go to a variety of universities and careers, including Oxbridge, Medical Schools and other Russell Group Universities

Tutorial System. Each pupil has a tutor who is responsible for his or her academic and personal progress and general pastoral welfare. The tutorial system encourages close contact with parents, which is further reinforced by parents' meetings which are held at regular intervals and a parent portal. The School aims to maintain sound discipline and good manners within a traditionally friendly atmosphere and encourages pupils to live up to the School motto "Ut Prosim".

Games. The main games in the Senior School are hockey, sailing and athletics, with rugby and cricket for the boys, and netball and rounders for the girls. In the Junior School, football is also played. Other games include basketball, squash, golf, swimming, rowing and tennis. Regular matches are arranged at all levels against teams both on the Island and the mainland. There are growing opportunities for sailing and the School keeps some sailing dinghies at Seaview Yacht Club.

Music and Drama. The Music Department incorporates practice and teaching facilities and a well-equipped recording studio. The School has a flourishing choral tradition, with opportunities for participation in a variety of choirs and instrumental groups. Concerts and musical plays are performed in both Senior and Junior Schools, and concert tours abroad have taken place in recent years. Full-length plays are produced each year by both Senior and Junior Schools, and special attention is given in the English lessons of the younger forms to speaking, lecturing and acting. Musical Theatre is a particular strength. The School has its own theatre and studio theatre and a School Poet.

Activities. There are many societies which cater for a wide range of individual interests. The School has a contingent of the Combined Cadet Force with Royal Navy and Royal Air Force sections. Sailing, canoeing, gliding, and other forms of venture training are strongly encouraged. There is a flourishing Duke of Edinburgh's Award scheme; last year 88 pupils took part with 11 receiving their Gold Awards. Holiday visits and expeditions are regularly arranged, and there are opportunities for exchange visits with schools on the continent.

Boarding. Boarding for both boys and girls is available for pupils on the Bembridge Campus which offers approximately one hundred acres of playing fields and woodland in a beautiful setting overlooking Whitecliff Bay and Culver Cliff, some six miles from Ryde. Transport is provided to and from Ryde for the school day. A new boarding house for up to ten Upper Sixth Formers has recently opened in Ryde.

Fees per term (from January 2019). Tuition: Foundation Stage – please see School website; Pre-Prep £2,545–£3,520; Junior School £4,265; Senior School £4,410.

Boarding (excluding tuition): Senior School: £5,310 (full), £4,260 (weekly).

Rates for payment by Direct Debit.

Scholarships and Bursaries. Scholarships may be awarded on merit to external or internal candidates for entry at 9+, 11+, 13+ and 16+. All scholarships may be supplemented by bursaries, which are means-tested.

Charitable status. Ryde School is a Registered Charity, number 307409. The aims and objectives of the Charity are the education of boys and girls.

Governors:
Chairman: Mr C Lees
Vice-Chairman: Dr M Legg
Hereditary Governor: Mr A McIsaac
Chair of Finance & General Purposes Committee: Mr N Wakefield
Chair of Education Committee: Mr S Drew
Mrs J Bland (*Inspection*)
Mr A Crawford
Ms C Doerries, QC
Mrs D Haig-Thomas
Mrs A Harvey
Mrs Caroline Jacobs (*Safeguarding responsibility*)
Mrs J Wallace-Dutton
Mr P Weeks (*Health and Safety Committee*)
Dr Michael Wilson

Clerk to the Governors: Mr P C Taylor

Headmaster: Mr M A Waldron, MA Cantab, MEd

Deputy Head (Academic): Mr P R Moore, MA
Deputy Head: Mr B Sandford-Smith, BSc, MEd
Head of Junior School: Mrs L M Dennis, BEd
Head of Fiveways: Mrs E Willetts BA
Bursar: Mr J A F Marren, BSc
Director of Boarding: Mrs L Nestor-Powell, BSc
Second Master: Mr K J Dubbins, BEd
IB Coordinator: Miss K Gallop
Head of Sixth Form: Mr M J Windsor, BSc
Head of Pastoral Care: Miss C B Vince, BA

Senior Teachers:
Mr S R Baxter, BA (*Careers, Skills and Lifelong Learning*)
Mr D P C Blewitt, MSc (*Director of Studies*)
Mr A Graham, BA (*Mathematics*)

§ *Part-time*

Senior School:
Mr M Alderton, MPhys (*Head of Year 8, Physics*)
Ms Alma Alonso (*Languages*)
Mr H Bagnall (*Head of Round Square, Science, Mathematics, Sport*)
Mrs P Ball (*English, Silver Duke of Edinburgh's Award*)
Mr S Baxter (*Head of Careers, Skills & Lifelong Learning, Art, IBC, TOK*)
Mrs Bayley (*Head of Learning Support, Economics*)
Ms K E Bishop, BSc, BA Hons (*Head of Psychology, Science*)
Mr D P C Blewitt, MSc (*Director of Studies, Mathematics*)
Mrs S Blewitt (*Head of Year 9, Languages*)
§Miss S Broyé, BA, MA (*Languages*)
§Mrs J Bryant (*SEN, ESL*)
Mr T Bull, BA (*Head of Academic Drama, i/c Global Rock*)
Mrs M E Burgess, BSc (*Head of Social Sciences, Geography*)
Mr D Buyanov-Taylor (*Mathematics, Physics*)
§Mrs L Chalmers (*Religious Studies, Library*)
Mr M G Chalmers, BSc (*Head of Chemistry*)
Mr J C Comben, BA (*Head of History, Bronze Duke of Edinburgh's Award*)
Miss O E Crean, MA (*Head of Art, Head of Chine*)
§Mrs M Danaford (*Design Technology*)
Miss J Drabble, BA (*Head of Seaford, Head of Geography, Gold Duke of Edinburgh's Award*)
Miss A Drinkwater, BEd, MA (*Head of Games, Head of Netball and Athletics, PE*)
Mr K J Dubbins, BEd (*Second Master, Biology, PD for Years 9 to 11*)
§Ms J A Dyer, BA (*Head of Spanish, Languages*)
Mr H Edwards (*Head of Hockey, PE*)
Mrs N Fowke (*Science*)

Ms L Goodwin (*Latin, Drama, EPQ Coordinator*)
Mr A M Graham, BA, HNTD (*Mathematics, Senior Teacher*)
Mrs T A Hall, BA (*Director of Languages*)
Mrs H Hankey (*Director of Music*)
Mrs K Hayter (*History, Politics*)
Mr N Herbert (*Economics, Mathematics*)
Mr O Herbert (*Head of Rugby, PE*)
Mr L Ilott (*Head of PE, Bembridge Housemaster*)
Mr A Johnston, BA (*Head of ICT*)
Ms E C Jones, BA (*English*)
Mr N Jones (*Physics, Science*)
Miss E Kirkby (*Art*)
Miss A Lengersdorf, BA (*Languages*)
§Mrs C Manser (*Head of Economics & Business Studies, Head of Sailing*)
§Ms H McComb, BA, TEFL Dip (*Languages*)
Mr S M Mead, BEd (*Chemistry*)
Mr P R Moore, MA (*Deputy DSL, Deputy Head Academic, Mathematics, Science*)
Mrs A Nestor-Powell (*Assistant DSL, Director of Boarding, Business, Sport*)
Ms A J Newman, BA Hons (*IB TOK Coordinator, Head of Year 10, Mandarin*)
Mrs L E O'Sullivan, BSc Ed (*Head of Trinity, Mathematics*)
Mr P Pavlou (*Head of Mathematics*)
§Mrs J Ratcliff, BA (*Art*)
Ms M Rolf (*English*)
Ms C Rose (*Design Technology*)
Mr B Sandford-Smith, BSc, MEd (*Deputy Head, Psychology*)
Mr J B Savage (*Head of Year 11, Head of Design Technology*)
Dr G R Speller, BSc, MPhil, PhD Cantab (*Head of Science, PSB Coordinator, PD for Years 7&8*)
Miss G S Stenning, BA (*Head of English*)
Mr P J Stott, BA (*Head of Politics, Coordinator Challenge & Enrichment, Archivist*)
Mr P G Swann, BSc (*Head of Physics*)
Ms K Thomas (*Geography*)
Mr C G S Trevallion, BSc (*Head of Biology, Duke of Edinburgh's Award*)
Ms M Turner (*Languages*)
Mrs R F Tweddle, GTCL, LTCL (*Choir Director, Head of Academic Music*)
Miss C Vince, BA (*DSL, Head of Pastoral Care, English*)
Mrs L L Waldron, BA Hons, MA Ed (*Mathematics*)
Mr M A Waldron, MA Cantab, MEd (*Head Master, Politics*)
§Mr J Willetts BSc Econ (*Head of Religious Studies, Economics*)
§Mrs J J Whillier, BSc QTS (*Mathematics, Science*)
Mr M Whillier, BSc (*Head of Year 7, Chemistry*)
$Miss N Wilson (*English, Spinnaker Housemistress, EE Coordinator*)
Mr M J Windsor, BSc (*Head of Sixth Form, Geography*)
Mr A Woodward (*Cricket Professional*)
Mr C Youlten (*Head of Performance, Drama*)
Mrs W Youlten (*English, PGCE Coordinator*)
Ms H Young (*Head of Hanover, Head of Rounders, Chemistry*)

Junior School:

Head: Mrs L Dennis, BEd
Director of Studies: Mrs G Elsom, BEd
Senior Teacher: Mr E Marsden, BSc (*DSL*)

Mrs M Bawdon	Mr A Gallerwood, BA
Ms E Boxell	Mrs G Gallerwood, BA
Mrs S Burgess, BA	Mrs D Grubb

Mrs J Jeffery	Ms R Shaw
Mr J Mathrick, BSc	Mrs T Simons
Mr J McGouran, BA	Mrs H Vann, BA

'FIVEWAYS' Nursery and Pre-Prep:

Head: Mrs E Willetts (*DSL*)

Miss K Clarke, NNEB	Miss V Lovell, BEd Hons
Mrs F Curtis, MA, EYPS	Ms O Newnham
Ms P Evans	Miss N Noott, BA Hons
Mrs S Griffiths, BTech, NN	Mrs P Ong, DPP
Mrs S Lea, NTD	Ms G Owen
Ms G Mallinson	Mrs T Simons, BEd
Mrs G Marsden	Miss A Townson, NVQ3

St Albans High School for Girls

3 Townsend Avenue, St Albans, Hertfordshire AL1 3SJ

Tel:	01727 853800
Fax:	01727 792516
email:	admissions@stahs.org.uk
website:	www.stahs.org.uk
Twitter:	@STAHS
Facebook:	@stalbanshighschoolforgirls

Motto: *The fear of the Lord is the beginning of wisdom*

St Albans High School for Girls is a selective, independent day school for girls aged 4–18 years. It is uniquely placed in being able to offer all the advantages of a continuous education in two very different settings; the Prep School is based in the picturesque village of Wheathampstead whilst the Senior School enjoys a more urban setting in the heart of the historic City of St Albans.

Mission. Fostering scholarship and integrity, the High School provides inspirational opportunities and strong support to develop a lifelong love of learning and respect for others.

Aims.
- Scholarship: to offer an education for girls, which promotes intellectual confidence, curiosity and the joy of learning.
- Adventure: to build an outward looking community through local, national and international curricular and co-curricular programmes.
- Integrity: to sustain a community in which every girl feels supported, confident and ready to shape society in a school which builds a strong ethic of service and responsible citizenship.

Academically curious, girls here have high expectations of themselves; results are exceptional and learning fun, with the majority of girls going on to their first-choice university.

Excellent facilities for all subjects include the Jubilee Centre – a Performing Arts Centre and Art & Technology block; a Music School and a newly refurbished and expanded Science block. Girls are encouraged to embrace broad horizons through participation in an extensive programme of co-curricular activities and a wealth of wide educational opportunities. Sport and music feature strongly, as do an impressive selection of clubs and societies.

Outstanding pastoral care, based on a thriving house system, ensures that girls flourish with firm support around them. They are encouraged to feel valued for their contributions to the life of our outward-looking community. Inter-house sporting, drama and public speaking competitions are held throughout the year.

We are experts in girls' education and believe that they learn best in an all-girls environment. Our aim is that they leave the school as strong, resourceful young women, equipped with the skills of independent learning and enriched by the friendships they have made here.

Enjoying the benefits of membership of the GSA and the HMC, which support the country's leading independent schools, the school is embarking on an exciting new phase under the leadership of Mrs Jenny Brown who took up post in September 2014.

Fees per term (2018–2019). Reception (age 4) £4,930 (inc Lunch); Years 1 and 2 (age 5–6) £5,200 (inc Lunch); Years 3–6 (age 7–11) £5,200 (exc Lunch); Senior School £6,265 (exc Lunch).

Private music lessons, special tennis coaching, school lunch (from Year 3) and daily school coaches are all optional extras.

Scholarships. Academic and Music Scholarships are awarded annually at entry to Year 7 and Sixth Form. In addition to these, scholarships are also available for both internal and external candidates on entry to Sixth Form in Art/DT, Drama & Theatre Studies, and Sport. Fees Assistance up to 100% may be awarded in cases of hardship.

Admission. Pupils are normally admitted in September at 4+, 6+ and 7+ to the Prep School and at 11+ and 16+ to the Senior School. However, applications for places occasionally available in other year groups are welcome. Girls are expected to have at least 5 GCSE subjects at A grade or above, and an A or A* in the subject to be taken at A Level. However, entry is subject to interview, and there may be flexibility in the number of A grades required.

Open Events 2018.

Prep School Open Morning – Friday 5th October, 9.30 am – 12.00 pm

Prep School Snapshot Morning – Friday 9th November, 10.00 am – 12.00 pm

Senior School Open Morning – Saturday 13th October, 9.30 am – 12.00 pm

Snapshot Session – Wednesday 7th November, 9.15 am – 10.45 am

Charitable status. St Albans High School for Girls is a Registered Charity, number 311065. It exists to provide an education for girls "in accordance with the principles of the Church of England".

Visitor: The Right Reverend The Lord Bishop of St Albans

Council:
Mr D Alterman, MA Oxon
Mr P Brewster
Mrs C Callegari, BA Hons, CertEd
Mrs Moira Darlington, MA Oxon, PGCE
Mr N Enright, MA Oxon, MBA, FRSA, NPQH
Mr T Gardam, MA Cantab
Ms E de Galleani, BA Hons
Mrs H Greatrex, BA, MSc Hons ACA (*Chair*)
Miss D Henderson, MA Cantab, MA
The Very Revd Dr Jeffrey John, MA Oxon, DPhil Oxon
Mr M Keen, MA Oxon, MBA
Mr B Kettle, FRICS, MCIArb, MAE
Dr Felicia Kirk, BA, MA, PhD
Mr S Martin, MA Oxon
Miss R Musgrave, MA, MA
Mr D Roe, BSc Hons, MRICS
Mr J Thomson, CA
Mr R Ward

Headmistress: Mrs J Brown, MA Oxon

Senior Leadership Team:
Mr F Campbell, BSc Glasgow, FCMA (*Bursar & Clerk to the Governors*)
Mrs J Taylor, MA Cantab (*Senior Deputy Head*)

Ms J Healy, MA Oxon, MPhil Trinity (*Deputy Head Strategy & Communications*)
Mrs K Gorman, BA Birmingham, MEd Cantab (*Deputy Head Curriculum*)
Mr N Hamshaw, MMath Oxon (*Deputy Head Academic*)
Mr A Oulton, MSt Oxford, BA Oxford (*Assistant Head, Director of Sixth Form*)
Mrs J Rowe, BEd Durham (*Head of the Prep School*)

Senior Management Team:
Mrs J Douglas, BA Durham (*Senior Housemistress*)
Mrs R Frost, MA Ed, BA Open, BEd Dundee (*Senior Teacher*)
Mrs R Colman (*Registrar*)
Miss L Hicks, BSc Durham (*Director of Co-Curriculum, Duke of Edinburgh's Award Manager*)
Mrs G Lusby, FCIPD (*HR Manager*)
Mrs Helen Monighan, BA Durham (*Acting Director of Higher Education & Careers*)
Mr S Ramsbottom, BSc Reading (*Director of Professional Development*)
Ms A Greenfield, MSt Oxford, MA UCL (*Teacher of English, Secondment to SMT*)

Senior School Teaching Staff:
§ *Part-time*

Art:
Mr S McGuinness, BA Manchester Polytechnic (*Head of Art*)
Mrs S Brown, MA Manchester (*Assistant Head of Sixth Form*)
Miss R Marsh, BA Southampton
Miss C Weaver, BA Reading (*Bronze Duke of Edinburgh's Award Deputy*)

Classical Civilisation:
Dr J Powell, BA Cambridge, MA, PhD Durham (*Head of Classics*)
Miss A Fox, BA Oxon, MSt Oxon
Miss H Morrison, BA Oxon, MA Oxon

Drama:
Mrs Holly Whymark, BA Hull (*Director of Drama*)
Mrs Anna Bullen, BA Wales Aberystwyth (*Head of Academic Drama*)
§Mrs Alexandra Birkett, BA Glamorgan
§Mrs Zoe Briggs, BA Durham, MA King's College London (*Teacher i/c of Perspectives*)

Design & Technology:
Mrs G Davies, MSc Wales (*Head of Design & Technology, Young Enterprise Coordinator*)
Mrs W Emes, MSc Reading
§Mr N Chandler
§Ms J Cooper, BEd Cantab
Mr D Fitzgibbons, BSc De Montfort
§Mrs A Wigg, BSc Sheffield
§Mrs E Wadey, BA Winchester

Economics:
§Mr J Stanford, BA York (*Head of Economics*)

English:
Mr E Monaghan, BA Oxon, BA Birmingham (*Head of English, Debating Coordinator*)
§Mrs Zoe Briggs, BA Durham, MA King's College London (*Teacher i/c of Perspectives*)
Mrs J Douglas, BA Durham (*Senior Housemistress*)
§Mrs H Foster, BA Oxon, MSc LSE
Ms A Greenfield, MSt Oxford, MA UCL (*EPQ Supervisor*)
Ms J Healy, BA Oxon, MPhil Trinity (*Deputy Head Strategy & Communications*)
Mrs J Powell, BA Durham

Mrs P Ray, BA Leeds
§Ms P Willmott, BA London

Geography:
Mrs K Thomson, BSc London (*Head of Geography*)
Miss E King, BSc Durham
§Mrs A Macdonald, BA Cantab

History and Government & Politics:
Mr S Mew, MA Essex (*Head of the Politics & History Dept*)
Mrs S Darbar, MA Cantab (*Head of History, Debating & Public Speaking*)
Mr R Hillebrand, MA Oxon (*More Able/Oxbridge Coordinator*)
§Mrs S Jenkins, BA York, MA York
§Mrs C Kordel, BA Warwick
Mrs E Schaffer, BA Nottingham
Mrs J Taylor, MA Cantab (*Senior Deputy Head*)

ICCT:
Mr A Byfield, BSc Hertfordshire (*Acting Head of ICCT & Computer Science*)
§Mrs C Wright, BA Anglia Ruskin
Mrs L Jin, MSc Oxford, BSc Canada

Mathematics:
Miss K Sumner, BSc Warwick (*Head of Mathematics, Deputy Timetabler*)
Mrs R Frost, MA Ed, BA Open, BEd Dundee (*Senior Teacher*)
Mrs J Grimmette, MA Cantab
Mr N Hamshaw, MMath Oxon (*Deputy Head Academic*)
§Mrs V Jacques, MA Oxon
§Mrs S Khan, BSc UCL
§Mrs D Lewis, MA Oxon, MPhil Cantab
Mrs J Major, MA Cantab
Mrs V Parton, MA Hertfordshire, BSc York (*Head of Careers*)
Miss S Spanos, BSc UCL

Modern Foreign Languages:
Mrs K Guille, MA Bath, BA Birmingham (*Head of Modern Languages*)
Miss A Burgess, MA Cantab (*Head of French*)
§Mrs E Crowther, BA UCL
Miss M C Foster, BA Manchester, MEd Hertfordshire (*Head of Spanish, EPQ Centre Coordinator, Silver Duke of Edinburgh's Award Coordinator*)
Mrs Rachel Gupta, BA Bristol (*Head of German*)
Miss S Jost, MA Université de Lausanne
§Mrs E Kelly (*Cover Supervisor*)
§Mrs H Monighan, BA Durham
Mrs S Pearse, BA Durham
Mrs K Trenor, BA Sheffield
Miss R Williams, BA Cardiff, BSc Buckingham

Sra V Gonzales-Lorente (*Spanish Assistant*)
Frau Annette Lietz (*German Assistant*)
Mlle Z Lignel (*French Assistant*)

Music:
Miss E Price, BA King's College London (*Director of Music*)
Mrs C Turkington, BMus Ed Cape Town (*Head of Academic Music*)
§Mr P Dutton, BMus Guildhall
§Ms J Rowley Jones, MusB Manchester
Mr R Simons, BMus Scotland

Physical Education:
Miss K Eddison, MA Birmingham (*Director of Sport*)
Miss A Hedley, BEd Edinburgh (*Head of Netball & Tennis*)
§Mrs Elizabeth Davies, BA Warwick

§Mrs M Galea, BEd Exeter
§Mrs E Gray-Brown, BA Brighton
Miss R Griffiths, BSc West of England, MSc Loughborough (*Development of Pupil Leadership, Head of Athletics*)
Mrs E Greenall, BSc Birmingham (*Head of Lacrosse*)
Mrs R Hepworth, BA Leeds (*Head of Aesthetics*)
§Mrs S Oakey, BEd Leeds
§Mrs D Whiting, BSc De Montfort
Miss M Mercedes
Mr S McDermott (*Lacrosse Coach, Head of Swimming*)

Religious Studies:
Mrs H Harper, BA/MA Leeds (*Head of Religious Studies, Debating & Public Speaking*)
Miss J Broman, BA Birmingham
Mr A Oulton, MSt Oxford, BA Oxford
§Mrs M Patel, BA Aberystwyth

Science:
Mr D Thomson, BSc Edinburgh (*Head of Science*)
Dr S Legg, DPhil Oxon (*Head of Chemistry*)
Ms J Scott, MA Oxon (*Head of Biology*)
Miss S Day, MChem Oxon
Miss L Hicks, BSc Durham
Miss S Hull, BSc Loughborough
Mrs A Jallport, MA Institute of Education, BSc Hertfordshire
§Miss H McSherry, BSc Plymouth (*Head of PSHEE*)
Miss E Marsden, BSc UCL, MSc Sussex
Dr T Seaby, PhD, MRes, Msci, Imperial College (*EPQ Supervisor*)
Mrs S Stewart, BSc Leicester
Mr A Tickner, MSci Durham, MA East Anglia (*Head of Physics*)
Dr P Wallis, PhD, BSc University of Sussex
§Mrs A Winters, BSc Southampton
§Dr A Winder, MSc Manchester, DPhil Oxon, MA Oxon
§Dr S Stocks, PhD Cambridge, MA Cambridge

Learning Support:
Mrs T Corbett, SENCO Hertfordshire, BA Humberside (*Head of Learning Support SEND*)

Library Assistant:

Pastoral:
Revd D FitzGerald Clark, BA Rhode Island, M of Divinity GTS, NYC (*Chaplain*)
Mrs J Douglas, BA Durham (*Senior Housemistress*)
Mrs S Brown, MA Manchester (*Assistant Head of Sixth Form*)
Mrs K Trenor, BA Sheffield (*Julian Housemistress*)
Miss J Broman, BA Birmingham (*Assistant Julian Housemistress*)
Mrs S Stewart, BSc Leicester (*Mandeville Housemistress*)
Mrs E Schaffer, BA Nottingham (*Paris Housemistress*)
Miss S Day, MChem Oxon (*Assistant Paris Housemistress*)
Miss S Jost, MA Université de Lausanne (*Verulam Housemistress*)
Miss A Fox, BA Oxon, Mst Oxon (*Assistant Verulam Housemistress*)
Mrs H McSherry, BSc Plymouth (*Head of PSHEE*)

Senior School Support Staff:

Library
Mrs J Foster, BA North London Polytechnic, CILIP (*Senior School Librarian*)
§Mrs C Brailsford, MA Loughborough, BA Leicester (*Sixth Form Librarian*)
§Mrs Wendy Klein

Mrs E Kelly, BA Exeter (*Cover Supervisor*)

Administrative Staff:
Mrs R Simpson (*PA to Headmistress*)
Mrs L Carro
Mrs V Dawson
Mrs C Folling (*Examinations Officer*)
Ms D Galloway
Mrs D Helm
Mrs L Jennings
§Mrs M Mackenzie
Mrs L Mailing
Mrs H Paustian
§Mrs L Wakefield
§Miss S Edwards

Association:
§Mrs L Lord

Bursary:
Mr F Campbell (*Bursar & Clerk to the Governors*)
§Mrs C Anderson
§Mrs P Babbage
Mrs F Clarke (*Compliance Manager*)
Mr M Langley
§Mrs S Lofts
§Mrs J Ward

Domestic Bursary:
Mr P Crossey (*Director of Hospitality & Services*)
Mr D Almond
Mrs J Barker
Mrs A Bartley
Mrs M Browne
Mr P Cook
Mr D Cruddas
Mrs F Evison
§Mrs K Harper
Ms T Hart
§Ms N Dellemann
Mrs S Draycott
Miss J Driscoll (*Chef, Manager*)
Mrs S Horne
Mrs V King
Miss S Kirwan
Mrs M Payne
Mr A Mojzesz
Mrs S Moody
§Mrs C Parsons
Mrs J Patel
Mrs A Paul
Mrs S Pedder
Miss C Rawlinson
§Mrs E Scutt
Mrs A Thomas

Visiting Speech & Drama Teachers:
Mrs L Ashton, BA, PCert LAM (*Speech and Drama*)
Miss Lauren Cesena (*Speech and Drama*)
Ms R Woodward (*Speech and Drama*)

Visiting Music Teachers:
Mr E Alton, MA, BA York (*Guitar*)
Mrs K Bradley, LRAM (*Violin, Viola*)
Mrs P Burgess, BSc Middlesex, Dip ABRSM, ALCM (*Piano*)
Miss R Edmonds, GRSM, PG Dip UCLA (*Bassoon, Flute*)

Human Resources:
Mrs G Lusby (*HR Manager*)
Mrs J Twine
Mrs T Williams

IT:
Mr B Tavakoli (*Head of IT Services*)
Mr L Miles
Mr P Abbott
§Mrs C Ametrano
Mr K Corcoran
Mr A Fuller
Mr M Kret
Mr G Willis

Marketing and Admissions:
Mrs R Mason (*Registrar*)
§Mrs L Barnes (*Development Manager*)
Miss C Hardy
Miss N Begley
§Miss S O'Reilly
Mrs S Woodward

Maintenance:
Mr P Owen (*Estates Manager*)
Mr M Downes
Mr S Brady
Mr N Martin
Mr J O'Donovan
Mr P Vitek

School Medical Staff:
Dr L Wasson, MBCHb Cape Town (*School Medical Officer*)
§Mrs K Juviler-Bacon, Registered member of BAAT (*School Counsellor*)
§Mr M Schofield, MA Cambridge (*School Counsellor*)
§Mrs K Janes, RGN Bucks College of Nursing/Midwifery
§Mrs S Olney, BSc Children's Nursing

Technicians:
Mrs K Burchmore
Mr D Fox
Mrs A Hodsden
§Mrs A Kellard
§Mr T Morris
§Mrs N Phillips
Miss R Randall
Mrs L Vardon
Miss A Zabecka

Ms L Hayter, BMus PG Dip RCM (*Oboe*)
Mr R Hodge (*Conductor in Residence*)
Mrs C Heller-Jones, BMus, PGCE, PG Cert GSM (*Singing*)
Mr J Holling, Dip TCL, LTCL (*Percussion*)
Miss P Jeppesen, PG Dip GSM (*Violin*)
Mr S Jones, GTCL, LTCL, MTC (*Singing*)
Mrs L Lythgoe-Bathurst (*Bassoon & Teneroon*)
Miss F Meakins (*Harp*)
Mr E Morgan, RAM (*French Horn*)
Miss F Nisbett (*Cello, Piano, Double Bass*)
Mr M Onissi, LTCL (*Saxophone, Flute*)
Ms G Pevy, LTCL, FTCL (*Recorder, Piano*)
Mr J Pippen (*Brass*)
Mrs H Shabetai, BMus (*Piano*)
Mr W Smith, Trinity BMus, PG Dip (*Brass*)
Mrs H Templeton BA York (*Singing*)
Miss A Tysall, BMus (*Piano*)
Ms R Woodward (*Oboe*)

Visiting PE Teachers:
Mr L Allen (*Golf*)
Ms B Amos (*Tennis*)
Mrs W Burdett (*Gymnastics*)
Mrs E Coles (*Karate*)
Mr K Coles (*Karate*)
Mr T Dyball (*Tennis*)
Miss M Godfrey-Evans (*Tennis*)
Mr J Grant-Bailey (*Tennis*)
Ms J Hoare (*Swimming*)
Mr D Lawlor (*Tennis*)
Mr S Mardle (*Football*)
Miss N Marshall (*Ballet*)
Mrs J McKeating (*Netball*)
Mrs P Moxham (*Trampolining, Gymnastics*)
Miss G Nash (*Ballet*)
Mrs C Peers (*Yoga*)
Ms T Powell (*Fitness*)
Miss E Shortt (*Zumba*)
Mr J Simpson (*Tennis*)
Ms S Stephens (*Swimming*)
Mrs J Stokes (*Tennis*)
Mr A Trevillion (*Fitness*)
Mrs D Szokolovics (*Fencing*)
Mrs L Warne (*Pilates*)

Prep School Teaching Staff:

Mrs J Rowe, BEd Durham (*Head of the Prep School*)
Mrs L Perry, BSc Liverpool (*Deputy Head, Pastoral and Co-curriculum, Prep School; Science Coordinator*)
Mr M Vandewalle, BSc Middlesex (*Deputy Head, Prep School*)
Mrs E Courtney-Magee, BEd Reading (*Head of Pre-Prep*)
Miss H Ennett, BEd Limerick (*Curriculum Development Lead*)
Miss H Watts, MA RAM, BMus GSMD (*Director of Music*)
Mrs L Still, BA Exeter (*Director of Sport*)
§Miss C Allin, Licence LLCE (*French Coordinator*)
Mrs A Brady, BEd Leeds
Mrs C Caruso, BA Manchester (*Art Coordinator*)
Miss S Clay, BA Cambridge, MA Cambridge
Miss L Fidgeon, BSc Royal Holloway (*SEN Support*)
§Mrs A Fletcher, BSc Bath
Mr S Gajendra (*Maths Specialist*)
§Mrs M Gold, Dip Glasgow (*SEND Leader*)
Miss E Grant, BEd Hertfordshire (*Drama Support*)
§Mrs W Job, BEd Brighton
Mr D Jones, BA Warwick
§Mrs R Kerry, BA Chichester
Miss M McClean, BEd Hertfordshire (*Maths Coordinator*)
Mrs S Millac, BSc London (*ICT Coordinator, eLearning Coordinator*)
Mrs S Munday (*Librarian*)
Miss A Northen, BA Roehampton (*PSHEE Coordinator*)
Mrs C Petronella-Thakarer, BA Royal Holloway
Mrs A Rogers, MA Sheffield, BSc Sheffield (*English Coordinator*)
Mrs P Ross, BA Bedfordshire

Miss T Skuse, BSc Manchester (*RE Coordinator*)
Mrs L Storey, BA Birmingham (*DT Coordinator*)

Prep School Support Staff:

Administrative Staff:
Mrs C Gibbs (*PA to Head of the Prep School*)
Mrs J Brooks (*Receptionist*)
Mr A Kendall (*Officer Manager*)
Mrs A James (*Admissions Coordinator*)
Mrs N Thurston (*HR Advisor*)

Miss E Daley
Mrs A Di-Lieto, BA Hull, NVQ3+
Mrs J Englebright
Mrs S Holmwood, BA Manchester
Ms S Llewellyn
Mr D Mitchelmore
Mrs E Osborne, BA Open
Miss J Pegram

Nurse:
§Mrs MJ Regan-Vickers, RGN

Teaching Assistants:
Miss R Barnett
Mr T Cooke

Forest School:
§Miss B Dale (*Forest School Leader*)
§Mrs J Connelly-Owen (*Toddler Forest School Assistant*)

St Albans School

Abbey Gateway, St Albans, Herts AL3 4HB

Tel: 01727 855521
Fax: 01727 843447
email: hm@st-albans-school.org.uk
website: www.st-albans.herts.sch.uk
Twitter: @SASHerts
Facebook: @stalbansschoolherts

The origins of the School date back, according to tradition, to the monastic foundation of 948, and there is firm evidence of an established and flourishing school soon after the Conquest. Following the Dissolution, the last abbot, Richard Boreman, sought a private Act of Parliament to establish a Free School. Charters, granted to the Town Corporation by Edward VI and Elizabeth I, together with endowments by Sir Nicholas Bacon from the sale of wine licences, secured the School's continuance.

St Albans School is a day school of 850 pupils which, having been part of the Direct Grant System for many years, reverted to full independence. Girls have been admitted into the Sixth Form since 1991. The School's atmosphere and ethos derive from its long tradition and its geographical position near the city centre of St Albans in close proximity to the Abbey and overlooking the site of the Roman City of Verulamium. Whilst maintaining a high standard of academic achievement, the School aims to foster the development of talent and responsibility, along with the fulfilment of individual potential.

Buildings. For more than three centuries, the School was located in the Lady Chapel of the Abbey. It moved in 1871 into the Monastery Gatehouse, a building of considerable historic and architectural interest, where teaching still continues. There were extensive additions made to the campus during the twentieth century, which in recent years has been extended significantly by the purchase of a very large building on an adjacent site and its conversion to a superb Art school, Sixth Form Centre and a suite of classrooms and the building of a Sports Centre.

Work is now under way to construct a new Mathematics and CCF building, which, as well as significantly improving the home of the School's ever-popular CCF unit, will provide the Maths Department with a new building worthy of its outstanding results. The new building will house a brand new CCF shooting range and office space on the lower ground floor, and a bespoke two-storey Maths Faculty on the upper ground and first floors and will open in January 2020.

The School has close historical and musical ties with the Cathedral and Abbey Church of St Alban. By permission of the Dean, morning prayers take place twice weekly in the nave, where the School Choir sings regularly and an annual oratorio is performed in collaboration with St Albans High School for Girls.

Admission. The majority of boys enter at the age of 11 or 13, as well as into the Sixth Form at 16, when girls are also admitted; candidates are accepted occasionally at other ages. For the main entry at 11, an examination in basic subjects is held at the School each year in January, and parents of interested candidates can find all information on the School's website, along with online registration. Most candidates at 13 enter through the Common Entrance examination, and conditional offers of places are normally made about one year before entry, following a preliminary assessment. Ideally, parents should apply to the School at least 2 years in advance for entry at 13.

Pupils are admitted only at the start of the Autumn Term unless there are exceptional circumstances.

Enquiries about entry should be addressed to the Registrar.

Fees per term (2018–2019). £6,200.

Bursaries and Scholarships. Assistance with tuition fees may be available in cases of proven need from the School's own endowments. Such Bursaries are conditional upon an annual means test and will be awarded according to a balance of merit and need.

Numerous scholarships are awarded on academic merit at each age of entry. Scholarships in Art, Music and Sport are offered to existing pupils or new entrants at 13+ who show exceptional talent. Choral Scholarships are offered only at 11+.

Curriculum. The curriculum for the first three years is largely a common one and covers a wide range. All boys study three sciences and two languages, and devote some part of their timetable to Art, Drama, Music, ICT and CDT. Mathematics IGCSE is taken in the January of the Fifth Form (Y11), and in the Fourth and Fifth Forms a system of compulsory subjects and options leads in most cases to the taking of at least a further nine GCSEs or IGCSEs. In the Sixth Form, pupils are expected to study four subjects in the Lower Sixth, with 3 of these being continued into the Upper Sixth. In addition, all will take study modules in General Studies and Critical Thinking, part of the Enrichment course, and will embark on an Extended Project. The choice is wide, and the flexibility of the timetable makes it possible for almost any combination of available subjects to be offered. Virtually all Sixth Form leavers go on to universities or other forms of higher education, with the vast majority going to Russell Group universities, as well as Oxford or Cambridge.

Out-of-school activities cover a wide range and there are clubs and societies to cater for most interests. Several of these are run in conjunction with other schools. Musical activities are many and varied and include regular concerts and recitals by the School Choir, Choral Society and ensembles and by professional artists. Plays are produced three or four times a year either in the New Hall, the Drama Centre Studio, the English Centre Studio Theatre or in the Open-air Theatre, and there is ample opportunity for creative work in the Art school and the Design Technology Centre. There is a strong contingent of the CCF with sections representing the Army and RAF. Many pupils join the Duke of Edinburgh's Award scheme and do various forms of social service and conservation work in and around the city of St Albans. The School owns a Field Centre in Wales which is used for research and recreation in holidays, as part of the Lower School curriculum and as a base for field studies and reading parties.

Games. The School competes at a high level in Rugby Football, Hockey, Cross-country, Cricket, Tennis, Athletics, Netball and Lacrosse, in addition to a range of other sports including Association Football, Squash, Shooting, Sailing, Swimming, Orienteering, Basketball, Golf and Table Tennis. The School's Sports Centre offers a swimming pool, sports hall, fitness centre, dance studio and climbing wall. The School also owns a working 400-acre farm within 3 miles of the school, where the Woollam Playing Fields are located, comprising of an Astroturf all-weather pitch and a superb state-of-the-art pavilion. A video of Woollams' facilities can be viewed on the School's website. There are good links with Saracens RUFC, whose training is based at the Woollam Grounds.

The playing fields are within easy reach of the School, and the spacious and pleasant lawns on the School site, stretching down to the River Ver, give access to the open-air theatre, tennis courts and shooting range.

Old Albanian Club and the St Albans School Foundation. Information may be obtained from the Development Director, Mrs Kate Gray, at the School address or email: development@st-albans.herts.sch.uk.

Charitable status. St Albans School is Registered Charity, number 1092932, and a Company Limited by Guarantee, number 4400125. The aims and objectives are to provide an excellent education whereby pupils can achieve the highest standard of academic success, according to ability, and develop their character and personality so as to become caring and self-disciplined adults.

Visitor: The Rt Revd The Lord Bishop of St Albans

Governors:
Chairman: Mr S P Eames
Vice Chair: Miss L M Ainsworth, MA Oxon
Mr P G Brown
Lt Col M W S Cawthorne, RM [retd]
Mr A L Dalwood, BSc, BA Cantab, ASIP, CFA UK
Mr D K Foster, FCA
Sir R A Gardner
Ms A Hurst
Mr R R Lucas, BEng
Prof J P Luzio, FMedSci
Mr S Majumdar, BA
Mr C McIntyre, BA
Mr N C Moore, LLB, MA, CNAA
Dr M Pegg, MB BS, BSc, FRCA, LLM
Ms C Pomfret, MA Oxon, ACA
Mr M E Punt, MA, MSc
Mr A Woodgate, BA, MRICS

Advisory Council:
The Mayor of St Albans
The Dean of St Albans
The President of the Old Albanian Club
Prof R J C Munton, BA, PhD, ACSS
Mr C Oglethorpe
Mr P M Rattle, BA
Mr L Sinclair, BSc, MRICS
Mrs J Tasker, FCCA
Mr B C Walker, BA, PGCE, CELTA
His Honour Judge Wilding

Bursar and Clerk to the Governors: Mr R J Hepper, MA, FCA

Staff:

Headmaster: Mr J W J Gillespie, MA Cantab, FRSA

Second Master: Ms M Jones, BSc

Deputy Head Academic: Mr M E Davies, MA

Senior Master: Mr P W Taylor, BEd

Heads of Sixth Form:
Mr G J Walker, MA, FRSA
Dr R G Hacksley, BA

Head of Middle School: Miss R J Baxter, BA

Assistant Head – Co-Curricular and Head of Third Form:
Mr G S Burger, HDip Ed SA

Head of Lower School: Mr D Swanson, Dip RADA

Assistant Head – Teaching and Learning: Mrs V J Saunders, MEd, BA, BSc

Director of Marketing, Admissions and Communications:
Ms A J Crombie, BA

* *Head of Department or Faculty*

Art:
*Mrs S J Forbes-Whitehead, BA
Ms K K Lillian, MA

Classics:
*Mrs V L Ginsburg, BA
Mr E J L Baker, MA
Mr M E Davies, MA
Mr D M Rowland, MA (*Deputy Head of Middle School*)

Computing:
*Ms R A D'Cruz, MSc
Mr C P A Gould, BSc (*Director of e-learning*)

Design & Technology:
*Mr D J Phillips, BA
Mr O S Omoyeni, BA
Mr P W Taylor, BEd (*Deputy Designated Safeguarding Lead*)

Drama:
*Ms L J Hanneghan-Birt, BA
Miss R O Olaleye, BA
Mr D Swanson, Dip RADA (*Designated Safeguarding Lead*)

Economics:
*Mr G D Nichols, BA (*Gold D of E Coordinator*)
Mrs L A Bonner, MA
Mr J Fabinger, BA
Mr A Rowley, BA
Mr N P Webb, BSc

English:
*Mr J D Hughes, BA
Miss R J Baxter, BA
Dr M C Brereton, MA (*Deputy Head of Sixth Form*)
Mr N J Cassidy, BA (*Head of Publications*)
Miss E C Crowe, MSt
Dr R G Hacksley, BA
Mr A K Jolly, BA (*Academic Librarian*)
Miss S K Routledge, MA

Geography:
*Miss C E Whittle, MA
Ms L H M Andrews, BSc (*Deputy Head of Lower School, Deputy Designated Safeguarding Lead*)
Mr J P Hickman, BSc
Mr C C Johnston, MA, FRGS (*Deputy Head of Middle School*)

History:
*Miss E L Milton, MA
Mr A C Alcoe, MA (*Head of Government & Politics*)
Mr D J Forbes-Whitehead, BA (*Housemaster of Hampson*)
Mrs A J Gregory, BA

Mr P Middleton, MA
Mrs V J Saunders, MEd, BA
Mr G J Walker, MA, FRSA
Mrs M Webb, MA

Mathematics:
*Mr L V Robinson, BSc
Mr C D Bradnam, BEng
Mr G S Burger, HDip Ed SA, MEd
Mr P R Byrom, MSc
Mr I Charlesworth, MA
Mr C J Ellegard, BSc, Dip Eng Auckland
Mrs T J Gott, BSc, ARCS (*Deputy Head of Sixth Form*)
Miss Z E Harris, BA
Miss J Higgins, BSc, ARCM
Mrs K E Penfold, BSc
Mrs H J Robertson, BEng (*Deputy Head of Third Form*)
Miss E C Russell, BA
Dr J H Saunders, MA Cantab, PG Dip GSMD (*Data and Curriculum Manager*)
Dr D M Young, MSc

Modern Languages:
*Mr J R Russ, BA (*Head of French*)
Mr K J Squibb, BA (*Head of German*)
Mr R S Shaw, BA (*Head of Spanish*)
Miss C Bowie, BA
Mrs C E Coudert, BA
Dr J P Dray, MA (*Head of Oxbridge Applications*)
Ms A Marcos Garcia, Licenciada en Economia, MBA
Mrs G Renz, MA, MPhil
Ms J L Shen, MA
Mrs D P L McGorrian, BA (*French Assistant*)
Mrs P Gamble (*German Assistant*)
Mrs M Tamaral-Ramirez, BA (*Spanish Assistant*)

Music:
*Mr M R Stout, BMus (*Director of Music*)
Mr T H Young, MA, PG Dip (*Head of Academic Music*)
Mr P F G Craig, BMus (*Percussion*)
Mrs A Ritou-Marioraki, MA

Visiting Staff:
Mr P A Bainbridge, Dip RCM ARCM (*Brass*)
Mr J Bennett, BA, Cert HE (*Percussion*)
Mr D Bentley, GGSM (*Brass*)
Ms R Edmonds, GRSM, ARCM (*Bassoon*)
Mr M Greyling (*Organ*)
Ms L Hayter, BMus, PG Dip (*Oboe*)
Ms C Ireland, BMus (*Recorder*)
Mr S Jones, GTCL, LTCL, MTC (*Singing*)
Miss A Le Hair, BMus, Dip RCM Teachers, ISM Fellow (*Piano*)
Mr A Lucas, BMus, GRSM, FRCO, LRAM, ARCM, Hon FGCM (*Organ*)
Ms V Parker, LTCL, FTCL, Dip TCL, ARCM (*Clarinet*)
Ms M Parsons-Gurr, BMus, MPerf (*Cello*)
Mr O Roberts (*Electric Guitar*)
Miss J E Simmons, BMus (*Saxophone*)
Mrs Z Smith, BMus, GRNCM, PPRCNM (*Flute*)
Ms J Trentham, GLCM, LLCM, TD (*Strings*)
Mr N Woodhouse, FLCM, LTCL, LLCM, ALCM (*Guitar*)
Mr M Woodward, BMus (*Piano*)
Ms C Wright, LLCM, GLCM, LRAM, Cert Adv Studies RAM (*Double Bass*)

PE:
*Mr M J Langston, BSc (*Director of Sport, Head of Academic PE*)
Mr J R White, BSc (*Assistant Director of Sport*)
Miss V L Sandell, BSc (*Head of Girls' Games*)
Mr K P P Bracken, LLB
Mr R D Daurge, BSc (*Head of Marsh*)

Mr M C Ilott
Mr D G Odgers, HDip Ed SA
Mr T R Smith, BSc
Mr J F Walmsley, BSc

Religious Studies/Philosophy:
*Mrs C A Malacrida, MA
Ms R C Birch, BA
Mr T O Eames-Jones, BA (*Head of PSHE, Acting Head of RS*)
The Revd Dr C D Pines, MB BS, MA (*Deputy Head of Sixth Form*)
Mr J Qasim, BA

Science:
*Dr M J Guy, MSc (*Head of Physics*)
Dr K A Agyei-Owusu, MSc (*Head of Chemistry*)
Mr R J Lockhart, MA Cantab, MRSB (*Head of Biology*)
Dr F Bár, Dipl Math
Ms K L Bradley, MChem
Ms T E A Cheney, MSc
Dr J E Eastmond, MA Cantab
Dr L F Gray, BSc (*Housemaster of Hawking*)
Miss L J Hickey, BSc
Dr S A Hughes, BSc
Mrs J M Jex, BSc
Ms M Jones, BSc (*Deputy Designated Safeguarding Lead*)
Mrs V C McClafferty, BA
Mrs P M Mills, MA
Mrs L I Murphy, BA SA
Mr D S Russell, MChem
Dr I M Shillcock, BSc (*Housemaster of Renfrew*)
Mr G L Smithson, BSc
Mr G Spencer, BSc
Dr R E Tanner, BSc (*Director of Cross-Curricular Learning*)
Mr J W E Turley, BSc
Mr G W Tyley, MA

Chaplain: The Revd Dr C D Pines, MB BS, MA

Public Examinations:
Mr C J Ellegard, BSc, Dip Eng
Mrs N M Gull
Mrs T J Gott, BSc, ARCS

Learning Support:
*Mrs R E Taylor, MSc
Mr A J Bateman, BA
Mrs W Davies, BA

Marketing, Admissions and Communications Office:
Ms A J Crombie, BA (*Director of Marketing, Admissions and Communications*)
Ms M Davey, BA (*Registrar*)
Ms R C A Hawkes, BA (*Marketing and Communications Manager*)
Ms T Selwyn, BCompt, CA SA (*Admissions Assistant*)

Development Office:
Mrs K Gray, BSc (*Development Director*)
Mr C J Harbour, BA (*Development and Alumni Relations Manager*)
Miss S L Osborne, MA (*Alumni Relations and Development Assistant*)

Librarians:
*Dr H McCabe, BA, MLIS
Mrs S Feyisetan, BSc
Mrs J Vance, BA

Graduate Assistants:
Mr D C Learoyd, BSc
Mr J E Ridley, BSc

Medical Officer:
Dr T Jollyman, MB ChB, MRCGP, DCH, DRCOG

School Nurses:
Mrs V Blackman, RGN
Mrs S M Green, RGN, RSCN
Mrs C Russell, RGN, DN

Combined Cadet Force:
OC CCF: Major K J Everitt (*D of E Coordinator*)
SSI CCF: WO1 Mr W J Wilson

St Aloysius' College

45 Hill Street, Glasgow G3 6RJ

Tel: 0141 332 3190
email: mail@staloysius.org
website: www.staloysius.org
Twitter: @StAlsGlasgow
Facebook: @StAlsGlasgow
LinkedIn: /st-aloysius'-college

Motto: *ad majora natus sum* (I was born for greater things).

Founded in 1859, St Aloysius' College is a Catholic school for boys and girls aged 3 to 18. The school is fully co-educational at all stages (Kindergarten to S6) with a roll drawn from a wide catchment area in and around Glasgow.

As Scotland's only Jesuit school, St Aloysius' College shares in a tradition of educational excellence which is almost 500 years old. It is part of a worldwide network of schools and universities whose mission is the "*Improvement in living and learning for the greater glory of God and the common good*" (*St Ignatius Loyola*).

The College creates an environment which is underpinned by mutual respect, friendship and care for others. It prides itself on upholding a clear set of religious, moral and spiritual values.

Five Jesuit values underpin life at the College: Delight in Learning, Personal Excellence, Make a Difference, Care and Respect, and Faith and Values.

Great importance is placed upon educating the whole person, with pupils encouraged to develop confidence, leadership and teamwork through sport, outdoor activity, music, drama, and many other activities.

Buildings. St Aloysius' College is located in the historic Garnethill area of central Glasgow with additional facilities in Millerston. The College's main Garnethill campus is made up of a number of school buildings and is well served by public transport.

The College campus is varied, providing examples of both award-winning modern architecture and construction, as well as historic listed buildings. The original Jesuit residence, now part of the school, is a listed building, as is The Mount where Art and Music are taught, and the magnificent St Aloysius' Church which the College uses regularly.

Two further additions to the St Aloysius' College campus, The Junior School and The Clavius Building used for Maths, Science and Computing, have attracted widespread critical acclaim. Not only have the buildings been the subject of great praise, but they have won many architectural awards, including the Best New Building in Scotland 2004.

The Kindergarten building is located beside the Junior School and is the ideal place for younger pupils to learn and play.

The most recent building for 2017 is the brand new, state-of-the-art sports complex situated adjacent to the original College building. It comprises a large games hall, dance studio, cardio and weights room, viewing gallery and a café.

Curriculum. The Junior School and lower years of the Senior School follow internally devised courses which are suitable for academically able children. All Junior School pupils study specialist subjects such as science, art, music, IT and languages from Kindergarten and P1. National 5 is taken at the end of S4 and pupils take five Highers in S5. A wide range of Advanced Highers and other courses are available in S6.

Music and the Arts. At St Aloysius' College, pupils are taught the art of self-expression through the development of the imaginative, the affective and the creative. These three elements of Jesuit education are essential to the formation of the whole person. Art is taught from Junior School by specialist teachers and there is an established music department with instrumental lessons from P3, orchestras, and the unique Schola Choral Programme.

Sport and Outdoor Education. St Aloysius' College offers an outstanding programme of sport and physical education. Rugby and Hockey remain the College's principal sports from P6 to U18 level. Cross-country and athletics are also offered at all levels, whilst Senior School pupils have the opportunity to represent the college in basketball, football and swimming.

The College also offers opportunities to learn wider Outdoor Education and pupils have enjoyed great success in the Duke of Edinburgh's Award programme.

Co-Curricular. As well as Music and the Arts and Sport, St Aloysius' College has an extensive co-curricular programme designed to encourage personal excellence and a delight in learning. This begins at Junior School, where children can participate in the likes of STEM club, and continues in Senior School where pupils are involved in Public Speaking and Justice and Peace to name but a few.

Admission. Entrance assessments are held in January and informal meetings with parents form part of the application process at all stages. Pupils from Primary 4 upwards will also be asked to send in a 'Your Green Blazer Story' as part of their application.

Fees per annum (2018–2019). £7,263–£12,825.

Bursaries are available on consideration of parents' income.

Charitable status. St Aloysius' College is a Registered Charity, number SC042545.

Board of Governors:
Fr Damian Howard SJ (*College President*)
Mr John Hylands (*Chairman of Governors*)
Dr Isabelle Cullen
Mr Kevin Doherty
Dr John Halliday
Mr Greg Hannah
Mr Joseph Hughes
Mr Nigel Kelly
Ms Joan Kerr
Fr Dermot Preston SJ
Mr Matthew Reilly
Mr Mike Smith
Prof Jane Stuart-Smith
Mrs Angela Vickers

Bursar and Clerk to the Board: Mrs Kathleen Sweeney, FCCA

Head Master: Mr Matthew Bartlett, MA, PGCE, NPQH

Head of Junior School: Dr Aileen Brady, BSc Hons, PhD

Senior Depute Head (*Pastoral*): Mrs Isabelle Erskine, BSc

Depute Head (Academic Leadership): Dr Calum Kilgour, BSc Hons, PhD

PA to the Head Master: Mrs Monica Harper

St Bede's College

Alexandra Park, Manchester M16 8HX

Tel:	0161 226 3323 (Senior School)
	0161 226 7156 (Preparatory School)
Fax:	0161 226 3813 (Senior School)
	0161 227 0487 (Preparatory School)
email:	headmaster@stbedescollege.co.uk
	enquiries@stbedescollege.co.uk
	prepschool@stbedescollege.co.uk
	admissions@stbedescollege.co.uk
website:	www.sbcm.co.uk
Twitter:	@StBedesCollege
Facebook:	@St-Bedes-College-Manchester
LinkedIn:	/Bedian-Alumni

Motto: '*Nunquam otio torpebat*'

St Bede's is a Catholic HMC Independent Co-educational Grammar School welcoming Catholic and non-Catholic children from Nursery to Sixth Form. We are celebrating over 140 years of history set in a magnificent Grade II listed building in the heart of Manchester.

The College is widely recognised for the calibre of its students who leave as well-rounded, polite and articulate young adults who are academically successful and ready to meet the demands of life at university and beyond. Each year there are one hundred coveted places available ensuring each student is guaranteed individual attention and personalised support.

We believe passionately in the importance of traditional family values and in encouraging every pupil to develop genuine friendships. Each child in the College is known and valued in a community where there are no barriers to learning. Whilst academic success is a high priority, focus on developing lifelong learning is of greater significance. Ultimately we want to develop young men and women who are constructive and compassionate members of our society.

Admission. Children may join the College at different stages in their academic journey, where children can enjoy an all-through education, joining our co-educational Nursery for 3 year olds before moving up to our co-educational Prep School. and then on to the main College. It is assumed that all Prep pupils will transfer automatically into the Senior part of the College.

The College Entrance Examination for external candidates wishing to join the College at 11+ takes place in January each year. Details of the examination may be obtained from our Admissions Manager, Helen Taylor, email: admissions@stbedescollege.co.uk. There is also direct entry to the Sixth Form. Interviews are held from the beginning of the Easter Term.

Curriculum. Curriculum provision is constantly monitored to ensure the best possible educational provision for all students.

The Lower School curriculum offers the core subjects of English, Mathematics, Sciences and RE together with Latin, Computer Science, Technology, History, Geography and PE/Games and tutor time. In the Middle School four subjects are chosen from French, German, Spanish, Latin, Classical Civilisation, Economics, Business, Computer Science, Design & Technology, Art and Music for a one-year course to further enhance GCSE options.

At GCSE/IGCSE, ten subjects are taken in varied combinations supported by a programme of academic enrichment.

Students must achieve 7 GCSE passes (grades 9–4) to be admitted to the Sixth Form. At A Level approximately 23 different subjects are currently on offer. Four subjects are studied to AS Level, with the majority reducing to three A2 Levels in Year 13. Many students opt to study the increasingly popular Extended Project Qualification. Flexibility ensures that any desired combination of subjects can be offered.

A strong learning support department ensures that all pupils fulfill their educational potential.

Co-Curriculum. There is an extensive weekly programme of extra-curricular provision that complements learning from outside the classroom and all pupils are encouraged to try new activities or extend their leadership by organising new ones for their peers.

Our goal is to develop wider skills for lifelong learning as well as helping to prepare students for the major ideas, innovations and challenges that they face in a rapidly-changing society. Bedians are confident in their ability to make a difference once they have left the College fully prepared for top universities and the world of work.

Fees per term (2018–2019). Senior School £3,775, Prep School £2,692.

Charitable status. St Bede's College Limited is a Registered Charity, number 700808. Its aims and objectives are the advancement and provision of education on behalf of St Bede's College.

Governors:
Chair: Mrs Z Kwiatkowska, BA Hons
Mrs R Kennedy
Revd P Daly, PhB, STL
Mr T Walsh, LLB Hons, PG Dip Law
Mrs Clare Hopton
Mr David Frost

Clerk to Governors: Mr M Lynch, ACMA

Headmaster: Mr L d'Arcy, MChem Oxon

Senior Deputy Head: Mrs S Pike, BSc
Director of Studies: Dr A Dando, BSc, PhD
Assistant Head (CFA): Mrs T Davie, BSc, MSc
Bursar: Mr M Lynch, ACMA
Head of Sixth Form: Mrs M A Gallagher, BSc
Senior Master: Mr B V Peden, MA

Heads of Faculty:
Mr S Bargery, BSc (*Mathematics and Enterprise*)
Mrs M Reid, MA (*World Languages*)
Mr D Parkes, BA (*Humanities*)
Mrs S Pike, BSc (*Science*) [Interim HoF]
Miss A Smith, BMus (*Performing Arts*)
Mr D Mukalt, BA (*Sport*)

Sixth Form Pastoral Team:
Mrs M A Gallagher, BSc (*Head of Sixth Form & Transition*)
Mr M Gallagher, BBus, BEd (*Assistant Head of Sixth Form, Pastoral*)
Mrs R Lockett, BA (*Assistant Head of Sixth Form, UCAS & Careers*)

Assistant Staff:
* *Subject Leader*

Art:
*Mrs H Park, BA Hons
Mrs S Dittman, BA
Mr H Peers, BA

Business/Economics:
*Mrs J Hatton, BA
Mrs M Corbett, BA
Mr M Gallagher, BBus, BEd (*Director of Co-Curricular*)

Classics:
Mr G Yates, MA (*Assistant Head of Siena House*)

Performing Arts and Drama:
Miss A Smith, BMus (*Head of Faculty*)
*Mrs N Alderson, MA

English:
*Mrs C Boylan, BA (*Assistant Head of Upper Fifth*)
Mrs N Alderson, BA (*Head of Siena House*)
Mrs K Barber, BA
Mr A Hughes, MA
Dr A McMonagle, PhD
Mr B Peden, MA (*Senior Master*)
Mrs S Sullivan, BA
Mrs A Vyce, MA (*Head of Lower Seniors*)

Geography:
*Mr D Parkes, BA
Miss C Livesey BA
Mrs C Smith, BA
Mrs M Vidouris, BA (*Leader in Learning Difficulties &
    Disabilities*)

Geology:
*Mr M Parker, BSc (*Assistant Head of Upper Seniors*)

History:
*Mr A Power, BA
Mr M Lee, BA
Mr T Wilson, BA

Computer Science:
*Mrs C Earles, MSc, BITM

Mathematics:
*Mr C Wright, BSc (*Assistant Head of Magdalene House*)
Mr S Bargery, BSc (*Assistant Head of Upper Seniors*)
Mrs C Brewer, BA
Dr A Dando, BSc, PhD (*Director of Studies*)
Mrs T Davie, BSc, MSc (*Assistant Head CFA*)
Mr D McCotter, BSc
Miss C Murray, BSc
Mr J Parkinson-Jones, MMath (*Head of Campion House*)
Miss E Williams, BSc Hons

Modern Languages:
*Mrs M Reid, MA (*Head of Faculty*)
Mrs M B Girolami, BA (*Head of Upper Seniors*)
Mrs I Morillo, Licenciatura en Filología
Mr J Gerardo, MA
Mrs A Welch, BA (*Assistant Head of Bosco House*)

Music:
*Mr A Davies, BMus (*Head of Bosco House*)

PE:
*Mr D Mukalt, BA (*Director of Sport*)
Mrs N McCormick, BEd (*Head of Magdalene House*)
Mrs N Lavorini, BEd
Mr L Mitchell, BA (*Assistant Head Lower Seniors*)
Miss C Whitney, BA (*Assistant Head CFA*)

Politics:
*Mrs R Lockett, BA (*UCAS*)

Religion:
*Mr T Sanders, BA Hons
Mr M Bishop, BA Hons
Mrs M A Gallagher, BSc
Mrs E Meakin, BA

Science:
Physics:
*Mrs C Aspinall, BSc
Mr A Coyle, BSc
Mrs K Michael, MA (*Interim Head of Science*)
Chemistry:
*Mrs R Prince, BSc
Mrs S Ball, BSc
Mrs S Pike, BSc (*Senior Deputy Head*)
Mr S Hepburn, MA
Biology:
*Miss C Hennity, BSc
Dr S Powell, BSc, PhD
Ms N Kober, BSc Hons

Technology:
*Mr A Hennigan, BEd
Mrs M Collins, BEd
Mr S Fallon, BEd (*Director of Marketing*)
Miss S Manning, MA

EAL:
Mrs S Alexopoulou, BEd, TEFL

Preparatory School:
Head of Prep: Mrs C Hunt, BEd

Examinations Officer: Mrs P Mataskova
College Nurse: Mrs K Taylor, RSCN
Headmaster's PA: Mrs B McGoff

St Benedict's School

54 Eaton Rise, Ealing, London W5 2ES

Tel: 020 8862 2000 (School Office)
            020 8862 2010 (Headmaster's Office)
            020 8862 2254 (Admissions)
            020 8862 2183 (Finance Director)
email: enquiries@stbenedicts.org.uk
            admissions@stbenedicts.org.uk (Admissions)
website: www.stbenedicts.org.uk
Twitter: @stbenedicts
Facebook: @StBenedictsSchool
LinkedIn: /st-benedicts-school

Motto: *a minimis incipe*

St Benedict's is London's leading independent Catholic co-educational school, situated in leafy Ealing. The School is a successful blend of the traditional and the progressive; proud of its heritage but also forward thinking and innovative. A seamless education which can begin at the age of 3 and continue through to the Sixth Form, in a caring, happy community, enables our pupils to thrive.

St Benedict's has strong academic standards, with considerable ambition for future academic success. Inspirational teaching, tutorial guidance and exceptional pastoral care are at the heart of the education we offer, allowing children to develop their full potential.

The Junior School and Nursery provide a supportive and vibrant environment in which to learn. Sharing excellent facilities with the Senior School and a programme of cross-curricular activities help ease the transition at 11+ to the Senior School, which is on the same site.

At St Benedict's, there is a vital focus on personal development, and our outstanding co-curricular programme helps pupils to thrive by enabling them to find and develop their unique gifts and talents. St Benedict's has a distinguished sporting tradition, and Music and Drama are both excellent, with a strong choral tradition and termly drama productions.

We encourage principled leadership, resilience and character in our pupils, and promote the Christian values of integrity, fairness and generosity to others. This is a hallmark of the School and there could be no better way of equipping young people for the future.

Recent developments include a new Nursery and Pre-Prep Department (September 2017), providing our youngest pupils with a first-rate learning environment. This is in addition to a new Sixth Form Centre and Art Department.

St Benedict's School is unique. Come and visit, and see what we have to offer.

Fees per term (2018–2019). Senior School £5,615, Junior School £4,810, Pre-Prep £4,330, Nursery £2,885–£5,340.

Charitable status. St Benedict's School Ealing is a Registered Charity, number 1148512, and a Charitable Company Limited by Guarantee, registration number 8093330.

Governing Body: The Governing Board of St Benedict's School

Headmaster: Mr Andrew Johnson, BA

Deputy Heads:
Mr L Ramsden, BA, MSt
Ms F Allen, MSc

Finance Director: Mrs C Bedwin, BSc

Headmaster's PA: Mrs R Wynne

Registrar: Mrs L Pepper

Old Priorian Association: Mrs T George, Development Director

St Columba's College

Whitechurch, Dublin 16 D16CH92, Ireland

Tel:	00 353 1 490 6791 (Reception)
	00 353 1 493 2860 (Bursar's Office)
Fax:	00 353 1 493 6655
email:	admin@stcolumbas.ie
website:	www.stcolumbas.ie

Motto: '*Prudentes Sicut Serpentes et Simplices Sicut Columbae*'

St Columba's College was founded in 1843 and in 1913 it was incorporated by Royal Charter. As a Church of Ireland foundation, the chapel plays a central part in the life of the school.

The College is a co-educational boarding school of 330, with a number of day pupils. It offers seven day a week boarding, with school on Saturday mornings, which is unusual in Ireland. Situated on the slopes of the Dublin Mountains, the College is about 7 miles south of the city overlooking Dublin Bay, in an estate of 138 acres, which includes a 9-hole golf course and a deer park.

While the school prides itself on its enviable academic reputation, at its heart is a village community where every child is cared for, nurtured and equipped to find their own place in the world. Many of the staff live on site contributing to the atmosphere of "a home away from home". Its dedication to the best in pastoral care was highly praised by the Boarding Schools' Association after a visit in 2017. Opportunities abound with six afternoons of sport a week, drama, music, debating, public speaking and performing in front of peers and visitors. From the Warden (headmaster) downwards there is an emphasis on the spirit of servant leadership both within and beyond the College.

The College is proud of its heritage as one of the oldest schools in Ireland, while constantly matching itself to the needs of the 21st century. It boasts newly refurbished state-of-the-art science labs and the building of a social centre in the heart of the school will commence in 2019. There are also plans for another boarding house.

With excellent academic standards, the College sends pupils both to top Irish and UK universities, but also to Ivy League Colleges in the US and universities throughout Europe.

Admission. Application for admission should be made to the Warden. There is a registration fee of €150. There are two junior Houses for entrants between the ages of 11 and 13 years. An assessment day is held for 11/12 year old entrants in October prior to the year of entry. Entry is determined by a number of factors, including family association, geographical spread (including Northern Ireland, the UK and overseas), date of registration and an understanding of the values which underpin the College. Entrants from Preparatory Schools take the Common Entrance Examination. Admission may also be made at 16–17 years.

Curriculum. In the Upper School, a wide choice of subjects and a large number of courses are available for the Irish Leaving Certificate. This examination keeps many options open for third-level colleges. It is the qualifying examination for entry to Irish universities and is acceptable to the faculties of all British universities and further afield. The Irish Junior Certificate is taken in the third form. A compulsory Transition Year programme follows the Junior Certificate.

Religious Teaching. Chapel services are held daily for the whole school. Religious instruction is based upon the liturgy and doctrine of the Church of Ireland. Boys and girls of other denominations and faiths are included and welcome.

Other Activities. Music, Art, Pottery and Technical Graphics (which are part of the curriculum in the Lower School), Design and Communication Graphics (part of the curriculum offered in the Upper School) and Drama, Debating, Photography, Computers and various other clubs and societies function at all levels.

Games and Pursuits. Rugby, Hockey, Cricket, Athletics, Cross-country Running, Tennis, Badminton, Basketball, Golf, Swimming, Hillwalking, Polocrosse, Sailing, Archery and Aerobics. The proximity to the Dublin Hills creates wonderful opportunity for outward bound activities.

Fees per term (2018–2019). Day Pupils €2,747, Day Boarding €3,642 Full Boarding €6,521–€9,392.

The above fees are expressed in Euros. Fees may be paid in the Sterling equivalent.

Entrance Scholarships. Junior and senior awards are made at age 12 (entry to Form I), 15 (entry to Form IV) and 16 (entry to Form V). Entrance exhibitions are often awarded to candidates for entry to Form II through the Common Entrance Examination. Generous discounts are available for the sons and daughters of the Clergy of the Church of Ireland. Old Columban and sibling discounts are also available. Details on request.

Leaving Scholarship. Norman Scholarships, for three years or more at all university colleges in Britain, Ireland and elsewhere are open to the sons and daughters of Clergy of the Church of Ireland.

St Columba's Former Pupils' Society. Old Columban Society. *Hon Secretary*: G Brooks, St Columba's College.

Charitable status. St Columba's College is a Registered Charity, number 4024. Its aims and objectives are the provision of Secondary Education facilities.

Visitor: The Most Revd Dr Richard Clarke, Archbishop of Armagh and Primate of All Ireland

Fellows:
G Caldwell, BBS (*Chairman*)
T Banotti, MA
M Gleeson, MA, MSc
The Most Reverend M Jackson, MA, PhD
J R P Wardell, MA, ACA
R Johnson, BA
M H T de la Poer Beresford, MLitt
A W McPhail, MA
D J Reade
C Carroll, BA
J Bulbulia, BA, HDip Psych, Barrister at Law
T Petch
W I Fraser, MB, DMRT, FFRRCSI (*Chairperson of the Board of Management*)
M Herbst, MEng
A F F Cox, BA, MA Ed Mgt, HDipEd
S Love, BA, MMII
N Lyons, MA
V Atkins, MA

Warden: M Boobbyer, BA, PGCE

Sub-Warden: J M Girdham, BA, HDipEd

Bursar: Mrs S Gibbs, MA, MSc, HDipEd

Assistant Staff:
* *Head of Department*
† *Housemaster/mistress*

J R Brett, MA, MSt, HDipEd (**Latin, Senior Tutor, Librarian*)
Mrs A Morris, BA, HDipEd (*Director of Girls' Boarding*)
B A Redmond, BTech, HDip SGC, DipID (**Technical Graphics*)
L Canning, BA, HDipEd (*Director of Sport, English, †Stackallan*)
Miss A E Maybury, BA, HDipEd (*Irish, *SPHE, Deputy Liaison for Child Protection*)
Ms A Kilfeather, BA, HDipEd (*French, Spanish*)
P G McCarthy, MA NUI, HDipEd (**Business Studies, *Classical Studies, Transition Year Coordinator, House Tutor Gwynn*)
Ms S McEneaney, BA, PGCE (**Learning Support, Asst† Beresford*)
Dr M Singleton, MSc, PhD, HDipEd, Dip EdMan (*Registrar, Director of Studies, *Physics and Mathematics*)
Mrs G Malone-Brady, MA Mus, LRAM, ARCM, LRSM (*Director of Music*)
Mrs D Sherwood (*Learning Support, †Iona*)
D Higgins, MA, MEd, HDipEd (*Head of Pastoral Care, Designated Liaison Child Protection, Mathematics*)
Miss D Cullen, BEd Art and Design (*Art, †Beresford*)
P Cron, BA, NDip CMA, GDEd (*†Gwynn, RE, Business, Economics*)
R Swift, BA, HDipEd (**CSPE, Classical Studies, †Glen*)
Ms K Hennessey, BSc (*Biology, Physics and Astronomy*)
S G Crombie, BSc (*Director of ICT, House Tutor Glen*)
H Jones, BSc Ed, PG Dip GC (**Agricultural Science, Biology, Asst† Gwynn*)
Mrs S-J Johnson, BEd, BTEC ND (**Sports Coordinator, PE, Geography*)
B Finn, MA, HDipEd (**History, Asst† Glen*)
E Jameson, MA, HDipEd (*English*)
M O'Shaughnessy, MA (**Modern Languages, Asst† Stackallan*)
Ms J Robinson, BA, HDipEd (*Mathematics, †Hollypark*)
W E Gibbs (*Asst† Tibradden*)
[T Clarke, BA, PG DipEd (*French, Music, Irish, Asst† Gwynn*)]
[Ms K Smith, BA, PG DipEd (*English*)]

Mrs H Kavanagh (*Learning Support*)
T de Brit, BSc, PhD, HDipEd (**Geology, IT Administrator*)
Ms J Pyz, MA, PhD (*Asst† Iona*)
G Dean (*House Tutor Stackallan*)
S Duffy, BSc, MTeach, PGCE (**Geography, Asst† Glen*)
P Stevenson, BA, PGDE (*Geography, House Tutor Tibradden*)
The Revd D Owen, BSc, BTh (*Chaplain, *Religious Education*)
Ms A Thompson, BSc (*House Tutor Beresford*)
M O'Toole (*Learning Support*)
Mrs S Owen BSc (*Nursing*), RGN (*Guidance*)
E Duggan, MA, PGCE (*History, English*)
L Harrahill, BScEd (*Biology, Chemistry, Science, Asst† Hollypark*)
Mrs L Carey, BSc, MSc, PGDE (*Economics, Business Studies*)
E McDonald, BSc, PG DipEd (*House Tutor Glen, Mathematics*)
L Rice, BSc, PhD (*Asst† Iona, Chemistry and Science*)
L Lynch, BA, MEd (*House Tutor Hollypark, Irish*)
K Ryan, MA, PG DipEd, PDip SPInEd (*House Tutor Stackallan, Learning Support*)
C de Fréin, MA, CAPES (*House Tutor Hollypark, French*)
J Harkin, BEng, MSc, PME (*House Tutor Hollypark, Mathematics and Applied Mathematics*)
C Horgan, BA, PME (*House Tutor Glen, Art and SPHE*)
J Morley, BA, PGDE (*English*)
L Carey, MSc, BBS, PG DipEd (*Economics and Business Studies*)
P Pirrone, MA (*French*)
P Tice, BA (*House Tutor Stackallan*)
J Kent-Sutton, MA, PG Dip ILS, MCLIP (*Librarian*)
A Grundy, MA Mus, Hon VCM, FTCL, LRSM, ALCM (*Guitar*)
K Snowe, BA, ALCM (*Piano*)
T Lawlor, ALCM (*Guitar*)
A Murnaghan (*Cello, Theory*)
E Shannon, MA Mus (*Singing*)
M Buicke, BA Mus (*Singing*)
D Hatch, BMus (*Clarinet, Saxophone*)
R Scarlett (*Percussion*)
M O'Reilly (*Flute*)
R Sheldrick (*Brass*)
F Curtis (*Singing, Piano*)
C Eszter (*Violin*)

PA to the Warden: Ms E Bainton
Admissions: Mrs Amanda Morris, BA, HDipEd
Reception: Ms L Wynne
Finance Manager: Ms C McLerie, MATI
Accounts Assistant: Ms K Keane
Development Manager: Mrs S Young
Events and Marketing: Mrs C Boobbyer, BA Oxon, PGCE
Medical Officer: Dr A Khourie
Infirmary Sister: Ms A Getty, RCN, RGN
School Nurses:
Mrs R Cron, RGN, RM
Ms N Murphy, RCN, RGN
Mrs J Williams, RGN, BNS, RSCN

St Columba's College

King Harry Lane, St Albans, Hertfordshire AL3 4AW

Tel: 01727 855185
Fax: 01727 892024
email: admissions@stcolumbascollege.org
website: www.stcolumbascollege.org

Motto: '*Cor ad Cor Loquitur*'

St Columba's College was founded in 1939, and has been a school in the tradition of the Brothers of the Sacred Heart (United States) since 1955. It is a Catholic, selective boys' school, with a little over half of its pupils coming from other denominations and faiths. The predominantly lay staff works together with pupils and parents to provide a Christian education based on traditional values, balancing a friendly community with sound discipline and academic rigour.

St Columba's College stands in its own grounds overlooking the picturesque vale of St Albans and the Roman settlement of Verulamium. In the last few years extensive improvements have been made to Science, English and Drama, Sixth Form and Preparatory facilities, and a major building development at the heart of the College was completed in September 2013.

Entry. St Columba's College admits boys from 4–18. Currently there are 235 boys in the Preparatory School, aged 4–11, and 585 boys in the Senior School, aged 11–18. The main entry for the Senior School is at 11, by entrance test and interview, with a smaller group being offered deferred entry at 13+.

Scholarships. Academic Scholarships are awarded at 11, 13 and for the Sixth Form. Additionally, the College offers two Music Scholarships each year and means-tested Coindre Bursaries.

The Curriculum. This is kept as broad as possible up to GCSE, pupils usually taking 9/11 subjects from the traditional range of Arts and Science options. There are 21 A Level subjects for pupils to choose from. Sixth Form education is complemented by an enrichment course which prepares students for extra qualifications including the Extended Project, ICT and Personal Finance. Almost all of the Sixth Form students go on to universities, including Oxford and Cambridge.

Careers. A full-time Head of Careers and Higher Education works from a fully-equipped Careers Centre to ensure that all students receive high-quality guidance in order to make informed decisions about subject choices and university courses with subsequent career options in mind.

Pastoral Care. St Columba's is a Catholic foundation welcoming students from all traditions. The spiritual and moral well-being of our pupils is a matter of primary importance for all of our staff, the majority being tutors. The six Housemasters and their teams are supported by a Ministry Team. Relations between the College and parents are open – a strength of the Foundation – and they are in regular contact with each other in monitoring the progress of the boys. The College seeks to nurture the academic and personal talents of each individual.

Sport. All boys participate, and the College has a strong sporting reputation. A rich variety of sports is available, including Rugby, Basketball, Football, Tennis, Cricket, Athletics, Swimming and Cross Country. For Sixth Form boys, not selected for the major sports, an even wider range of activities is available. Facilities include a large gymnasium and sports field on site. The Sports Department makes extensive use of soccer and rugby pitches, an athletics track, swimming pool and a golf course which are all immediately adjacent to the College site.

Extended and Extra-Curricular Activities. The College offers a mix of activities both at lunch-time and after school. These include sports clubs such as; rugby, football, basketball, cricket and athletics, drama, art, chess, computing, Young Enterprise and many others, as well as a variety of academic and social clubs. There is a number of music ensembles, including a choir, orchestra and jazz band and four choirs of handbell ringers.

CCF. The Combined Cadet Force includes an Army and an RAF section and an SSI (School Staff Instructor) is employed by the College. The Duke of Edinburgh's Award scheme comes under the same management.

Preparatory School. The Preparatory School is on the same site as the Senior School and shares many of its facilities. The College has a strong family atmosphere, providing a secure and purposeful environment in which expectations are high. It admits boys only, by assessment, into the Lower Prep and Upper Prep phases. In their final year, most Preparatory School pupils are offered unconditional places at St Columba's College Senior School, following recommendations by Prep School staff.

(*See also St Columba's College Preparatory School entry in IAPS section.*)

Fees per term (2018–2019). Senior School £5,233, Prep 4–6 £4,519, Prep 3 £4,097, Reception–Prep 2 £3,494.

Charitable status. St Columba's College is a Registered Charity, number 1088480. It exists to provide a well-rounded Catholic education for pupils from 4–18 years of age.

Governors:
Chairman: Mrs J Harrison, BEd
Vice Chair:

Trustee and Dean of the College: Brother Daniel St Jacques SC, BA, PGF HG Dip Counselling, MBACP

Bursar and Clerk to the Governors: Mr Paul Daly, BA, FCIS

Headmaster: Mr David Buxton, BA, MTh, MA

Deputy Head: Mrs K Marson, MA
Academic Deputy Head: Mr I Devereux, BEd
Head of Sixth Form: Mr R McCann, BA
Assistant Head: Mrs L Cronin, MA Cantab
Assistant Head : Mr J Tatham, BA
Head of Preparatory School: Mrs R Loveman, BSc
Prep Pastoral Deputy: Mr K Boland, BA
Prep Academic Deputy: Mr M Ioannou, BEd

Heads of House:
Charles: Mr S Murphy, BSc
Guertin: Miss C Treacy, BA
Joseph: Mr K. Brown, MusB
Martin: Mr A Lowles, BA
McClancy: Mr M Livesey, BSc
Stanislaus: Mrs R Paterson, BA

Heads of Department/Subject Leaders:
Art: Mrs K Seagrave, BA
Biology: Mrs M Mester, BSc
Careers: Mr P Kelly, BA
Chemistry: Ms R Tuckwell, BSc
Classics: Mr S Graves, BA Cantab
Design Technology: Mr B Barnett, BA
Economics & Business Studies: Mrs A D'Arcy, BA and Miss K Fitch, BSc
English & Drama: Mr B Morris, BA
Geography: Miss A Ellis-Jones, BSc
History: Mr K Roberts, MA

Information & Communications Technology: Mr M Nyman, BA
Learning Support: Mrs N Taylor Imrie, BSc, OCR Dip SpLD
Library/Media: Mrs S Mathieson, Dip Lib
Mathematics: Mrs K Parsons, BSc
Modern Foreign Languages: Mr R Childs, BA
French: Ms S Jasieczek, BA
Spanish: Mr R Childs, BA
Music: Mr S McCall, BA
Director of Sport: Mr E Lowe, BSc
Politics: Mr R McKenzie, BA
Religious Education: Ms E McCarthy, BA
Science & Physics: Dr R Clarke, DPhil (*Physics SL*)
Sociology: Mr N Hogan, BA

Administration:
Marketing and Admissions: Mrs N McLeod, MBA
Headmaster's PA: Mrs R Coakley
Head of Prep's PA: Mrs C Tominey

St Columba's School

Duchal Road, Kilmacolm, Inverclyde PA13 4AU

Tel: 01505 872238
Fax: 01505 873995
email: secretary@st-columbas.org

Junior School:
Knockbuckle Road, Kilmacolm, Inverclyde PA13 4EQ

Tel: 01505 872768
email: juniorsecretary@st-columbas.org

website: www.st-columbas.org

Motto: *Orare Laborare Literisque Studere*

Founded in 1897, St Columba's School is a non-denominational day school for boys and girls aged 3–18 years and is renowned for its first-class education and academic excellence. Situated at the heart of Kilmacolm, yet within easy reach of the city of Glasgow and the surrounding areas, it is a forward-looking, vibrant and dynamic school.

The first thing you notice at St Columba's is the warm welcome and the strong sense of community. This is in part the result of its size where teachers know each pupil by name. Indeed, considerable effort is made to create an environment which allows the School to identify and nurture the unique talents and skills of each pupil, and encourage each one of them to realise their full potential, grow and flourish.

St Columba's success is evident not only in its excellent academic results, regularly placing St Columba's as one of the highest-achieving schools nationally, but in the impressive young people you will meet in a classroom, at an international debate, or on a rugby field: they are polite, articulate and quietly self-assured. The School combines the pursuit of academic excellence with a range of opportunity and challenge to develop self-confident and independent young people who have a strong sense of community and who will become responsible and reflective future leaders. High-quality teaching, a strong sense of belonging and the space for pupils to grow and achieve their full potential is what St Columba's offers. The School currently holds Investor in People status at Gold level and is the first school in Scotland to be awarded the Queen's Award for Voluntary Service.

St Columba's offers wraparound care from 7.30 am to 6.00 pm, financial assistance and a dedicated coach service.

Facilities. Our school campus sits within the heart of the village of Kilmacolm and easy travelling distance of Glasgow. Junior School is nestled in a woodland setting filled with light and colour and caters for our children in Early Years to Junior 6. Senior School is located a third of a mile from Junior School and caters for pupils in Transitus (J7) to Senior SVI.

Over the last 3 years we have invested £7 million to provide the Girdwood Building at Senior School that houses Transitus, English, Languages, Pastoral Care Suite, a Library and 13 classrooms, revamped our 6 science laboratories and landscaped our Junior School grounds. We are about to open a modern Health and Well-Being Centre. This new resource at the heart of the school reflects the values of St Columba's School where we recognise that for children to flourish and for staff to support them, health and wellbeing is paramount.

Sports facilities include: gym area for gymnastics and dance, large purpose-built sports hall including fitness suite, all-weather floodlit hockey/tennis ground, access to three rugby pitches and a large playing field used for athletics and cross-country running.

Curriculum. St Columba's School follows the Scottish Curriculum at all stages. Junior School pupils are taught French, music, drama and PE by specialist staff. Transitus (P7) is a transitional year with core curriculum taught by the class teacher and science, languages, art, music and PE delivered by specialist secondary teachers. Pupils in Senior IV are presented for National 5 examinations followed by Higher Grade and Advanced Higher Grade examinations in Senior V and Senior VI.

Games. Rugby, hockey, tennis, athletics, badminton, gymnastics, swimming, volleyball, basketball, soccer, dance (girls), orienteering. Optional: netball, squash, cricket, golf, skiing/snowboarding, curling, street dance, weight-training.

Extra-Curricular. Throughout the whole school there are approximately 60 clubs and societies. They range from athletics and orchestra, gardening and science, STEM and enterprise, debating and history film, through to coding and philosophy covering most letters of the alphabet. There is truly something for every child. Individual tuition in a wide range of instruments is available. Public performances and school shows are arranged on a regular basis.

We offer a range of nationally recognised, progressive outdoor education awards which allow pupils to develop resilience and the ability to problem solve; and learn to work as part of a team in some of Scotland's most beautiful locations – Duke of Edinburgh's Award, National Navigation Award Scheme, British Canoeing and the John Muir Award. We are proud to be sector leaders running one of the most successful DofE Award programmes in Scotland, with 76% of our Gold participants going on to achieve their award. Mini Duke and Junior Duke Awards are also offered to children in Junior 2–6.

There is a very strong tradition of fundraising for charity and community service within the School.

St Columba's has strong links with schools in France and Canada.

Organisation. The school is organised into four Houses for both pastoral and competitive purposes. Each house has a Head of House as well as pupil Captain and Vice-Captain. Career guidance is supported by Inspiring Futures.

Admission. Entry to St Columba's is by a combination of entry test, interview and, where applicable, a report from the applicant's previous school. Open events are held in November and entrance tests are held in January. The main entry points are Early Years, Junior 1 and Transitus, however, pupils are taken in at other stages as places become available.

Fees per annum (2018–2019). Early Years £3,080, J1 & J2 £8,780, J3 £9,620, J4 £10,220, J5 & J6 £10,750, Transitus–Senior V £12,095.

A number of bursary places, ranging from 10–100% of fees are available.

Charitable status. St Columba's School is a Registered Charity, number SC012598. It exists to provide education for pupils.

Governing Body:

Honorary President: Mr Guy Clark, Lord Lieutenant of Renfrewshire

Honorary Vice-Presidents:
Dr Helen M Laird, OBE, MA, PhD, DL
Ron Kennedy, TD, FCCII

Board of Directors:
Calum Paterson, BA, MBA, FRSE, CA (*Chairman*)
Dr Aileen Findlay, BSc, MBChB, MRCGP (*Deputy Chairman*)
Sue Bomphray, BSc
Hugh Currie, BSc, CEng, MICE, DL
Roddy Davidson, MA, MBA, ASIP
J N David Gray, BA
Jo Halliday, BSocSc
Katharine Hardie, LLB, DLP
Kenneth Wilson, MA, CA
Paul Yacoubian, BAcc, CA

Rector: **Mrs Andrea Angus**, BSc Edinburgh

Head of Junior School: Mrs A Duncan, MA St Andrews, Dip EdMan, SQH

Senior Depute Rector: Mrs V Reilly, MA Edinburgh

Depute Rector: Mr M J McLaughlin, MA Greenwich, BA Thames

Depute Rector: Ms A Berry, BA MRes Kent, MEd Buckingham

Depute Head of Junior School: Mrs J Andrews, BA King Alfred's, MA Ed Open

Depute Head of Junior School: Mr A McKay BEd Strathclyde

Registrar: Mr G Smith, MA Glasgow, MEd West of Scotland

Rector's PA: Mrs Moira McWhirter

Heads of House:
Strathgryffe: Mrs A Moran, MA Glasgow [Mrs N Smith, MA Glasgow]
Kilallan: Dr L Hay, BSc Aberdeen, PhD Strathclyde
Craigmarloch: Miss C Patterson, BMus RSAMD
Duchal and Head of Guidance: Mr A Tait, BA Stirling, BEd Edinburgh

Senior School Teaching Staff:
* *Head of Faculty*
‡ *Chartered Teacher*

Ancient & Modern Languages:
*Ms L Rodger, MA Edinburgh
Mrs V Reilly, MA Edinburgh
Mrs J Hepburn, MA Glasgow
Mrs P Kennedy, MA Glasgow
Mr T Ingham, MA St Andrews
Mr G Paterson, MA Glasgow
Mrs D Staber, MA Munich

Design – Art & Design:
*Mrs I Hemphill, DA Edinburgh
Mrs M R Robinson, BA Glasgow School of Art

Design – Technology:
*Mr A Morrison, BEd Strathclyde
Mr T Boag, DipTechEd Jordanhill

English:
*Mr G McNicol, BA Hertfordshire
Ms A Berry, BA MRes Kent, MEd Buckingham
Ms K Brash, MPhil Queensland, MA Glasgow
Mrs V Kennedy, BA Stirling
Mrs A Moran, MA Glasgow
‡Mr G Smith, MA Glasgow, MEd West of Scotland
Mr M J McLaughlin, MA Greenwich, BA Thames

Humanities:
*‡Mr R Arbuckle, MA Dundee
Ms F Fowler, BSc Glasgow
Dr C Gilmour, BA, PhD Stirling
Mrs A Gillen, MA Glasgow
Mrs J Kincaid, BA Paisley
Mrs R Kerr, MA Glasgow
Ms Z Shaw, BA Glasgow Caledonian
Mr G McConnell, MA Glasgow

Mathematics & ICT:
*Mrs F I Bruce, BSc Glasgow
Mrs E Brunton, MA Glasgow
Mrs F Houston, BSc Strathclyde
Mr A Walkey, BSc, MSc Glasgow
Mrs N Gardner, BA, MPA Indiana
Mrs B Mackenzie, MA Glasgow

Music:
*Ms Y Carey, Dip Mus Glasgow
Mrs K Fleming, BA RSAMD
Miss C Patterson, BMus RSAMD
Mrs A Sutherland, Dip Ed Mus, LTCL

Outdoor Education:
*Mr G McConnell, MA Glasgow
Mr G Smith, MA Glasgow, MEd West of Scotland

Physical Education:
*Mr E Milligan, BEd Edinburgh
Mrs L Carlton, BEd Edinburgh
Mrs J Bellew, BEd Dunfermline College
Mr A Tait, BA Stirling, BEd Edinburgh
Miss F Ramsay, BSc Stirling
Mr L Brims, BSc Stirling
Mrs S McGlennon, BA Strathclyde
Miss N Harkness, BSc Northumbria

Science:
Biology & Psychology:
*Mrs E Wilson, BSc Paisley
Mrs P Nicoll, BEd St Andrew's College, Dip for Med
Dr L Hay, BSc Aberdeen, PhD Strathclyde
Mrs L McCarthy, MA MPhil Glasgow
Chemistry:
*Mrs T Munro, BSc Paisley, Dip Comp Jordanhill, SQH
Ms L Robertson, BSc Strathclyde, Dip IT Paisley
Physics:
*Dr I Moore, MEng, PhD Glasgow
Miss J Boyle, MSc Glasgow

Transitus:
*Mr A McKay, BEd Strathclyde
Mrs G Hall, MA Cantab

Junior School Teaching Staff:
Mrs G Annetts, BA RSAMD
Miss C Bertram, BEd Glasgow
Mr F Campbell, BA Strathclyde
Miss A Kelly, BEd Strathclyde
Miss Hannah, BA Strathclyde
Mrs G Henderson, BA Paisley
Miss Hopkins, BA Northumbria
Mrs H Manceau, MA Glasgow
Mrs G Maxwell, BEd Dundee
Mrs K Fleming, BA RSAMD

Mrs R Porter, BEd Strathclyde, Cert LS Glasgow
Mrs J Wolfe, DipEd Jordanhill
Miss R Cannon, MA Aberdeen
Mrs U Smillie, BEd St Andrew's College Bearsden

Early Years Manager/Principal Teacher: Mrs E Corbett,
    BEd Jordanhill

Support for Learning Staff:
Mrs L Reid, BSc Caledonian, Dip ASN Edinburgh
Mrs H Davies, BA QTS Warwick

St Dunstan's College

Stanstead Road, London SE6 4TY

Tel: 020 8516 7200
email: info@sdmail.org.uk
            admissions@sdmail.org.uk
website: www.stdunstans.org.uk
Twitter: @StDunstansColl
Facebook: @StDunstansColl

Motto: '*Albam Exorna*'

The College was founded in the 15th Century in the Parish of St Dunstan-in-the-East, part of the Tower Ward of the City of London. In 1888 the school was re-founded in Catford, South East London. It became co-educational in 1994.

Buildings. The College is located in mainly Victorian buildings on a 15-acre site three minutes' walk from Catford and Catford Bridge railway stations. Facilities include an imposing Great Hall, a well-equipped Learning Resource Centre, a drama studio, three state-of-the-art ICT suites and refurbished chemistry laboratories. To complement extensive playing fields on site, St Dunstan's has a sports hall, fully-equipped fitness rooms, floodlit netball/tennis courts, rugby fives courts and an indoor swimming pool, along with a 20-acre sports facility on nearby Canadian Avenue called the Jubilee Ground. This site provides playing fields, multi-use games areas, a gym, dance studio and function rooms, further enhancing the sporting and other facilities available to its pupils and the wider community. A new Wellness Centre for physical and mental first aid, counselling, chaplaincy and peer mentoring is now complete, and there are plans to build a new Junior School, STEM Centre and Sixth Form Hub.

Organisation and Curriculum. The College educates boys and girls from the ages of 3 to 18. The Junior School comprises a nursery class for 20 children (3+), a Pre-Prep Department for 120 children aged 4–7 and a Prep Department of 160 children aged 7–11.

In the Junior School great emphasis is placed on letting children learn in a friendly, caring and stimulating environment. Pupils study a broad curriculum and participate in a wide variety of extra-curricular activities. The Head of the Junior School is a member of IAPS (*see entry in IAPS section*).

The Senior School, with a total of 620 pupils, comprises Key Stage 3 (Years 7–9), Key Stage 4 (Years 10 and 11) and Key Stage 5 (Years 12 and 13). A considerable choice of subjects is on offer – Art & Design, Biology, Business Studies, Chemistry, Classical Civilisation, Computing Science, Design & Technology, Economics, English, Drama, Geography, History, Latin, Mathematics, Modern Foreign Languages, Music, Philosophy, Religion and Ethics, Physical Education and Physics, along with Personal, Social and Health Education (PSHE).

The College is a vibrant, academic community with a friendly atmosphere. It values cultural diversity and has a reputation for high academic standards and excellent pastoral care. This continues into the Sixth Form where students are supported to achieve outstanding academic results (84% A*–B in 2018), whilst developing each individual's distinctive talents and skills. This philosophy has been the basis for the College's flagship St Dunstan's Diploma programme – a flexible, innovative and exciting programme designed to inspire, challenge and assist all Sixth Formers achieve their unique ambitions and potential.

Pupils have the opportunity to join a very wide range of co-curricular activities through its Forder Programme. This allows all pupils to immerse themselves in creative, active and service activities along with opportunities to develop leadership skills and a greater understanding of the wider world for the older year groups.

Combined Cadet Force. The CCF is extremely popular and comprises the Royal Navy Section, the Army Section and the Corps of Drums. Typically, cadets join the CCF in Year 9 and by Year 11 become responsible for training younger cadets. The activities undertaken are designed to develop qualities of leadership, resourcefulness, self-reliance, responsibility, confidence and a sense of community service.

Community Service. The College has a strong tradition of Service and involvement with the local community. Pupils from Year 9 upwards form a Community Service group that provides various types of help and support to the local community.

Drama. There are opportunities for pupils to be involved in drama productions to suit all ages and abilities. These range from small scale informal performance to larger whole College musicals. Pupils can study towards and be entered for LAMDA examinations. The College hosts an annual week-long Arts Festival in the summer.

Duke of Edinburgh's Award scheme. The College has very strong numbers of pupils involved at all Award levels.

Music. Pupils from all parts of the school participate in a variety of choirs, orchestras and instrumental ensembles. There is an annual Choral & Orchestral Concert for the whole College at St Pancras Church.

Sport. The chief sports are cricket, hockey, netball, rounders, rugby, soccer and swimming. Pupils also have opportunities to take part in cross-country running, fives, tennis, basketball, badminton, sailing, golf and fitness training.

Entrance. The main entrance points are at the age of 3, 4, 7, 11 or 16. Admission to the College is competitive in all years with the exception of the Nursery, and depends on academic ability and the demonstration of potential. At 11+ an Entrance Examination is held annually in January.

Entrance Scholarships. Scholarships are offered for academic merit and also for excellence in Music, Sport, Art & Design and Drama. Means-tested bursaries are available.

Fees per term (2018–2019). The consolidated fees (including lunch) are: Nursery £3,377; Junior School £4,304–£5,423; Senior School £5,732.

Old Dunstonian Association. The ODA has 4,000 members. All pupils subscribe to the ODA while at school and automatically become life members when they leave.

The Friends of St Dunstan's. This parent–school association works to support the educational, social and extra-curricular activities of the school for the benefit of all pupils. All parents are automatically members of the Friends of St Dunstan's.

Charitable status. St Dunstan's Educational Foundation is a Registered Charity, number 312747.

Governors:
Chairman: P L Coling, Esq, FRICS [OD]
Deputy Chairman: I Davenport, Esq
Mrs S Ahmed, BSc, PGCE, NPQH

Mrs V Alexander
Dr Y Burne, OBE JP
Ms J Clements, OBE
I Davenport, Esq
P Durgan, Esq
Mrs L Kiernan, MA, DipEd
Professor P Leonard, BSc Hons, FSRP, CRADP, CBiol,
    FSB, CSCI, CMARSCI, FI MAREST, FRPSL, FLS
K L Marshall, Esq, RD, FICS, ACII
D Probert, BA Hons, MBA
Miss D Robertshaw, BSc Hons, RGN, RSCN Dip Nursing
    Education
S Rahman, Esq
N Sheera, Esq, MA, MBA

[OD] Old Dunstonian

Clerk to the Governors and Bursar: Mrs C Wilkins

Senior School Academic Staff:

Headmaster: **Mr Nicholas Hewlett**, BSc

Deputy Head (Academic): A Johnson, BA
Deputy Head Pastoral: Mrs A Waite, BSc
Assistant Head – Head of Sixth Form: Mrs J McLellan, BA
Assistant Head – Head of Middle School: P O'Dwyer,
Assistant Head – Head of Lower School: Mrs G L Davies,
    BSc

* Head of Department

*Mrs J Anderson, BSc	Miss H Hughes, BA
J Apweiler, BSc	*Miss A Jordon, BSc
G Armstrong, BSc	Miss A Karmock-Golds,
Mrs J Atkinson, GRSM,	BA
NCOS	Miss S Kervella, MA
R Austin, BSc	O Knell, BSc
Mrs H S Baptiste, BSc	Mrs E Latham
J Bell, BA	*J Lavery, BA
Mrs C Bird, BA	*Miss F Low
Miss E Bocarro, BSc	*M McClune
S Bowering, BA	Miss C Marr
M Bradley, BA	Ms K Melhorn, BA
*Ms R E Butryn, MA	P O'Dwyer, MA
*Mrs J Byrne, MA	*D Oldfield, BA
*Ms M M Callaghan, BA	Mrs S Otley, BA
*Miss G Charleton, BA	Miss E Partridge, BSc
Miss Z Chen	Miss S Penny, BA
Ms K Collard	*G S Phillips, BSc, MSc
C Cox, BSc	*D Preece, PhD
Mrs G L Davies, BSc	*C Rawley
R W Davies, BA	Ms J Rice, BA
P Dawson, BA	Ms N Rich, BA
Miss S Dosanjh, BA	T Scambler, BA
Mrs S Drury, BSc	*D Sharples, BA
Miss F Du Sauzay, BA	G Stewart, BA
J P H Elmes, MA	*S Thompson
Miss A Esposito, BA	Miss W Y Tseng, BA
*B Ford, BSc	Dr C Vicenik
Ms A Gomez-Ramos, BA	*F Villatoro
*D Gower, BSc	*Miss D M Warren, BEng
R Gregg	*Miss R Watkins, BSc
Mrs L Hartwell, BSc	D J Webb, BA
R A Hill, BSc	Mrs J V Williams, BEd
J Holmes, BA	*M Woodward, BA
*T Hofmeyr, MA	

PA to the Headmaster: Mrs V Hearn
Director of Marketing, Admissions and Development: Mrs I
    Blake-James
Head of Admissions: Miss K Spooner
Head of Marketing: Mr J-L Squibb
College Chaplain: Revd C Boswell
Junior School Secretary/Registrar: Miss D Jackson

St Edmund's College

Old Hall Green, Ware, Hertfordshire SG11 1DS

Tel:	01920 824247
email:	admissions@stedmundscollege.org
website:	www.stedmundscollege.org
Twitter:	@StEdmundsWare
Facebook:	@stedmundscollege.org

Motto: '*Avita Pro Fide*'

St Edmund's College, England's oldest Catholic school,
is a leading Independent day and boarding, co-educational
Catholic School for boys and girls aged 3–18. From the
Nursery to the Sixth Form St Edmund's College offers an
education that challenges and stimulates, developing the
whole person in the intellectual, physical, emotional and
spiritual areas of life; the richness of our extracurricular provision and our high academic standards are testament to the
College's success and popularity.

Located on a beautiful site in rural East Hertfordshire,
only 40 minutes to London by train, St Edmund's has outstanding transport links to the surrounding area and makes
full use of the excellent facilities on its 450-acre site including floodlit astroturf pitches and and indoor swimming pool.

Scholarships are available at 7+, 11+ and 16+ and we
welcome applications for entry to all years if places are
available. St Edmund's welcomes students from all faiths
who support our ethos.

Admission. Students are mainly admitted at the ages of
11, 13 and 16, although entry is always considered at other
ages if there are spaces available.

Scholarships. The College offers the following scholarships:

St Edmund's College 11+ Scholarships:

Douay Academic Scholarships are decided by the mark
in the 11+ Entrance Exam, the school report, the confidential school report and the interview with the Headmaster.

Old Hall Academic Scholarships are restricted to Catholic students who are in a Catholic school (and have been for
the last two years). As above, this award is decided by the
mark in the 11+ entrance exam, the school report, the confidential school report and the interview with the Headmaster
or Registrar.

All Rounder Scholarships are decided by interview,
school report, confidential report and mark in the Entrance
Exam. For this award, the child will be competent academically and also be able to make a substantial contribution to
other areas of life at St Edmund's. This will be as agreed
with the Headmaster but contributions might be to one or
more aspects, such as drama, music, technology, the Catholic life of the College, specialised sports or outdoor pursuits.

Art Scholarships are decided by examination of a portfolio and a test. Scholars are required to make a significant
contribution to the artistic life of the College.

Music Scholarships are decided by audition and include
the provision of free tuition in two instruments. Scholars
will normally be required to play two instruments with at
least one to a high standard (voice can be counted as one
instrument).

Music Exhibitions may also be awarded which give free
tuition in either one or two instruments. Those in receipt of
Music Scholarships and Exhibitions are required to make a
significant and sustained contribution to the musical life of
the College.

Sport Scholarships are decided by open competition and
references from sport clubs or teachers where the child is
already involved in sport at a very high level for example

County level. Scholars will be expected to play a full and sustained role in the sporting life of the College.

The closing date for Year 7 scholarship applications is in November for entry the following September.

Sixth Form Scholarships:

At 16+, the Cardinal Allen Academic Scholarships are decided by open competition using the results of specially set scholarship examinations, interview and previous school reports. Candidates for these scholarships would be expected to achieve all A/A* grades in their GCSEs. Music, Sport and Art scholarships may also be offered through competitive test.

The closing date for Year 12 scholarship applications is in early November for entry the following September.

Bursaries. We also offer a limited number of means-tested Bursaries at 11+, of up to 100% of fees. The closing date is in November.

Further details are available from the Admissions Office on 01920 824247.

Fees per term (2018–2019). College: Day Pupils: £5,502–£5,935; Weekly Boarders: £7,820–£8,940; Full Boarders: £8,985–£10,305.

There are reductions for siblings and for sons and daughters of serving members of the Armed Forces.

Curriculum. All pupils follow the National Curriculum. At the end of Year 11, pupils take GCSE examinations in all courses that they have followed, usually more than is required by the National Curriculum.

In Rhetoric (Sixth Form) students study A Levels and the majority leave St Edmund's to progress to Russell Group universities including some to Oxford and Cambridge.

Religious Instruction. St Edmund's is a College for all those who appreciate the values of a Catholic Education. All students receive instruction in Christian doctrine and practice from lay teachers. Importance is attached to the liturgical life of the College and the practical expression of faith. All faiths and denominations are welcomed.

Sport. Great importance is attached to sport and physical education throughout the College. All pupils are required to participate in a variety of sports. The major sports for boys are rugby, football, cricket and athletics, while for girls they are hockey, netball, rounders and athletics. The other sports available are cross-country, tennis, swimming, basketball and badminton. A floodlit astroturf pitch, large sports hall, indoor swimming pool, tennis courts, fitness room, new outdoor astroturf cricket nets together with 450 acres of grounds provide excellent facilities.

Extracurricular Activities. At St Edmund's we believe our responsibility reaches far beyond the academic success of our students. We have a commitment to the whole person, which is reflected in the broad range of activities on offer to everyone and we wish to encourage the notion that success can be achieved in many ways, not just in the classroom.

Each day between 3.30 pm and 4.30 pm, time is set aside for students to pursue an interest or activity. Wednesday afternoons are also dedicated to our activities programme.

The CCF (RAF and Army sections), Community Service and The Duke of Edinburgh's Award play a prominent part in developing a self-reliant and confident individual.

Careers. There is a Careers teacher and Careers Library. Careers advice is available to pupils from the age of 13. There are regular careers lectures and visits to industry and Universities.

Prep School. St Edmund's also includes a Prep situated on the same estate. It consists of a Nursery, Infants and Junior School for pupils from age 3 to 11, which feeds into the Senior School at 11. The pupils are able to make use of many of the amenities of the Senior School such as the Refectory, Chapel, Swimming Pool and Sports Hall. There is no boarding at the Prep School.

(For further details, see entry in IAPS section.)

Charitable status. St Edmund's College is a Registered Charity, number 311073. It aims to provide a Catholic Education for students of all faiths between the ages of 3 and 18.

President & Patron: His Eminence Cardinal Vincent Nichols, Archbishop of Westminster

Governors:
Mr Patrick Mitton (*Chair of Governors*)
Mrs Jane Ranzetta (*Deputy Chair of Governors and Chair of Academic Sub-Committee*)
Mrs Madeline Roberts (*Chair of Finance Sub-Committee*)
Mr John Bryant (*Chair of Prep School Sub-Committee*)
Fr Mark Langham (*Chair of PR & Marketing Sub-Committee*)
Mr Stephen Grounds
Fr Alban McCoy
Mr Paul Raynes

Senior Leadership Team:

[1]*Headmaster, DSM Child Protection*: **Mr P Durán**, BA MA London

[1]*Head of Prep School*: Mr S Cartwright, BSc Surrey

[1]*Bursar*: Mr B Tomlinson, BA Hons London, ACMA

[1]*Senior Teacher in Charge of Religious Life*, *Charities Coordinator*: Mrs P Peirce, BD AKC London

[1]*Senior Deputy Head*: Mrs K MacDonald, BA Hons, PGCE, PQH NI Belfast

[1]*Deputy Head Pastoral, Registrar*: Mr A D Petty, BA Wales, MSc Herts, PGCE Cantab, FRSA

Assistant Head (Community Life), Deputy DSL Child Protection: Mrs L Dunhill, BSc Hons, PGCE Nottingham

Assistant Head (Pastoral), DSL Child Protection: Mr G West, BSc East Anglia

Assistant Head (Teaching and Learning): Mrs C Noble, BA Hons Exeter, PGCE Canterbury

Assistant Head Academic (Timetable, Curriculum & Data): Mrs R A K West, BEd Exeter

Assistant Head of St Edmund's Prep: Mr G Duddy, BEd Wales (*Year 5, RE, Activities*)

Deputy Head of St Edmund's Prep, DSL Child Protection: Dr F J F McLauchlan, MA PhD Cantab (*Director of Music and Performing Arts*)

Director of External Relations: Mrs M Burke

Human Resources Directors:
Mrs H Duffy, LLB Hull, PGDL
Mrs L Nice, BA Hons Herts

Priest in Residence: Revd Father P H Lyness, MA Rhodes

Technical Projects Director: Mr S Winfield, MCSE

[1] *Core Leadership Team*

St Edmund's College Teaching Staff:
* *Head of Department*

Art, Design and Technology:
*Miss A M Healy, BA Luton
Mrs J Armitage, BA Hons CSM PGCE Middlesex
Mrs S Applegate, MA, BA, PGCE Herts (*Lead Art Teacher*)
Mrs K Moore, BA Hons, PGCE Cardiff [Maternity Leave]

Mrs D Stringer, BA Hons, PGCE Surrey
Mrs J Daly, BSc Strathclyde, MFC

Business Studies and Economics:
*Mr C Upton, BA Hons Durham, PGCE Sunderland,
  PGDM Open
Mr W Fulford-Brown, BA Hons Leeds Beckett, PGCE
  Nottingham
Mr F Mandizha, BA Hons Herts, PGCE UCL
Ms L Sargent, MA Edge Hill, BSc Brunel

Drama:
*Mrs N Schiff, MA Herts, BA Plymouth, PGCE Reading

English:
*Mrs P Ager, BA Hons Middlesex, PGCE Anglia
Mrs S Appleford, BA Hons Wales, PGCE Cantab
Mrs K Evans, BA Hons Cantab, PGCE Cantab
Mr J Hayes, MA Oxon
Mrs M McCann, BA London, MA Birkbeck
Miss J McCarthy, BA Hons Lancaster, PGCE Westminster
  (*Duke of Edinburgh's Award Coordinator*)
Mrs P O'Neill, BA Roehampton

Geography:
*Ms Elizabeth Tucker, BA Hons Leeds, PGCE London
Mrs C McNiece, BA Hons Belfast, PGCE Dunelm
Mrs N Pitman, BA Hons Wales, PGCE Bath
Mrs T York, BSc Hons Wales, MA Canterbury, PGCE IOE

History:
*Mr J R Stypinski, BA York
Mr D Brett, MA Hons St Andrews, PGCE Leeds (*Head of
  Poynter House*)
Mrs C McNiece, BA Hons Belfast, PGCE Dunelm
Mr A D Petty, BA Wales, MSc Herts, PGCE Cantab,
  FRSA (*Deputy Head Pastoral, Registrar*)
Miss C Regan, MA Glasgow, PGCE Glasgow (*CAS
  Coordinator*)

Information Technology:
Director of ICT, Computing and E-learning: Mr K R Fry,
  BSc Brunel, MSc Herts, PGCE Exeter
Mr M Arif, MSc Middlesex, BSc Hons Pakistan
Mr B Kovacevic, BSc Middlesex, BSc Croatia

International Department:
Director of Summer School: Mr L Hawkes, MEd Open, BA
  Hons Open, PGCFSE Open
Head of EAL: Miss G Fanning, MA York, BA Hons Open

Languages:
*Ms L Hill, BA Sussex, PGCE Reading
Miss A Dunning, BA Bath (*Head of Talbot House and
  Head of German*)
Mrs E Franco, MA Leon (*Head of Spanish*)
Mrs Fleur Harvey-Keenan, BA Hons Durham, PGCE
  Nottingham (*Head of French*)
Mr C Holt, BA Reading
Mrs K MacDonald, BA Hons, PGCE, PQH NI Belfast
  (*Senior Deputy Head*)
Miss S Rinaldi (*Head of Italian and Latin*)
Miss M C Simon, Licence Bordeaux (*Head of Elements*)
Language Assistants:
Spanish: Ildefonso Soler Garcia
French: Marie Schepens
German: Franziska Renn

Mathematics:
*Mrs H Fraser, BSc, PGCE East Anglia [Maternity Leave]
Mr M Arif, MSc Middlesex, BSc Hons Pakistan
Dr L Banahan, BSc PhD PGD Dublin (*Second in
  Department*)
Mrs L Brown, BA Pretoria, PGCE South Africa
Mrs L Dunhill, BSc Hons, PGCE Nottingham

Mr N Harding, BA Hons Middlesex, PGCE Bath (*Activities
  Coordinator*)
Mr J Hounsell, BSc BCA Wellington, NZ (*Head of
  Mathematics*) [Maternity Cover]
Mr S Mohana, BEd MSc Bangalore
Mr G Sargent, MA Cantab, PGCE Greenwich
Mr G West, BSc East Anglia
Mrs R A K West, BEd Exeter (*Assistant Head Academic
  Timetable, Curriculum & Data*)

Media Studies:
*Mr L Woodward, BA Hons Bournemouth (*Head of
  Douglass House*)

Music:
Head of Music Academic: Mrs C Noble, BA Hons Exeter,
  PGCE Canterbury (*Assistant Head Academic Teaching
  and Learning*)
Head of Music Performance: Mrs K L Salter-Kay, GTCL,
  LTCL, ALCM
Mr C Benham, BA Colchester

Physical Education:
Miss A Hebdon, BA Hons Brunel (*Head of Girls' Games
  Head of Pole House*)
Mr A Cunnah, BA Brighton (*Head of Boys' Games Head of
  Challoner House*)
Mr K D Jones, BA Greenwich (*Head of PE*)
Mr O Plummer, BSc Hons Bristol
Miss E Wilkins, BA Hons Canterbury
Sports Coach: Neil Kimsey
Graduate GAP Assistants: Rhydian Stokes, James Adams

Psychology:
*Mr N Eliasson, MA Birmingham, PGCE Canterbury, BSc
  Hertfordshire
Mrs M Inglessis, BA Dunelm, MA Kent, PGCE London
  (*Teacher in charge of Staff Development*)

Religious Studies:
*Miss A Moloney, BA Hons Surrey, PGCE Roehampton
Mr D D'Cruz, BA India, BA Middlesex, PGCE Surrey
Mrs M Inglessis, BA Dunelm, MA Kent, PGCE London
  (*Teacher in charge of Staff Development*)
Mrs P Peirce, BD AKC London (*Senior Teacher in Charge
  of Religious Life & Charities Coordinator*)
Mr B Powell, BA Australian Catholic Bachelor of Teaching
  New England, Australia (*PHSE Coordinator, Co-
  Director Rhetoric*)
Miss J-A Murphy, BA Hons Liverpool
Mr A J D Robinson, BEd Exeter (*Head of Boys' Boarding
  – Allen Hall*)

Religious Volunteer: Brother Andrej Makovnik

Science:
*Miss M Towns, BSc UWE Bristol, PGCE London (*Head
  of Science EVC Coordinator*)
Mr N Cairns, MSc Dunelm (*Director of Key Stage 3*)
Mr R Chapman, BSc UWE Bristol, PGCE Aberystwyth
Mr M Connor, BSc Nottingham, PGCE Herts (*Director of
  Key Stage 4*)
Dr J Eves, BSc Berkeley USA, MSc PhD Dublin (*Gifted
  and Talented Coordinator*)
Dr J Heslin, BSc Canterbury, PhD Imperial College Grad
  IPM Middlesex PGCE Herts
Mrs V Jauncey, BSc Durham, PGCE Cantab
Mrs D Mallabone, BSc, PGCE Southampton (*Director of
  Key Stage 3*)
Ms J Marrinan, MA Open, BSc Hons London (*Co-Director
  of Rhetoric*)
Mr D Webster, BEng, PGCE Science (*Director of Key
  Stage 5*)

Cardinal Hume Centre, Learning Support:
*Mrs S Nicholson, BA Hons Manchester, PGCE Lancaster
Mrs L Barley (*SEN Assistant*)
Mrs M Sargent, NVQ3 (*SEN Assistant*)
Mrs N Wells (*SEN Teacher*)

Careers:
Ms J Marrinan, MA Open, BSc Hons London (*Co-Director of Rhetoric*)
Mr B Powell, BA Australian Catholic Bachelor of Teaching New England, Australia (*PHSE Coordinator, Co-Director of Rhetoric*)

Librarian: Mrs J Tyne, BA Newcastle-Upon-Tyne, MCLIP

St Edmund's Prep School

Head of St Edmund's Prep: Mr S Cartwright, BSc Hons Surrey

Deputy Head of St Edmund's Prep, DSL Child Protection: Dr F J F McLauchlan, MA PhD Cantab
Assistant Head of St Edmund's Prep: Mr G Duddy, BEd Wales (*Year 5, RE, Activities*)
Head of EYFS, Deputy DSL Child Protection: Mrs V Penfold, BA London Metropolitan

St Edmund's Prep School Teaching Staff:

Nursery & Reception:
Mrs K Purves, BA Birmingham, EYFS Herts (*Nursey Teacher, Library*)
Mrs P Jones, BA Hons Middlesex
Mrs V Penfold, BA London Metropolitan (*Reception Teacher, Head of EYFS*)

Years 1–6:
Mrs G Boulter, Diplôme Universitaire de Technologie France (*French & Humanities*)
Mrs A Chick, BA Hons Bristol, PGCE Bristol (*Prep Learning Support Manager*)
Mrs E Worton, BA Hons London, Cert Ed London (*Year 4, Maths*)
Mrs N Crick, BA Twickenham Year 6, Assessment
Mrs A Cutler, BA Leeds (*Year 4, English*)
Mr G Duddy, BEd Wales (*Year 5, RE, Activities*)
Mrs H Fox (*Prep Drama Teacher*)
Mr G Goodfellow, BA Northampton (*Year 5/6 Maths, PE/Games, Director of Sport Prep*)
Miss A Hewlett, BEd Herts (*Year 3, Science*)
Mrs Z Kirton, BSc Hons Derby, MSc London, QTS Herts (*Year 1, Head of Pre-Prep*)
Mrs C Mitton, BEd Cantab (*Year 5*)
Mrs M Murphy, BEd Hons Surrey (*Form 6*)
Mrs E Roper, BA Surrey (*Art*)
Mrs A Sayer, BA Hons Bournemouth, PGCE Greenwich (*Year 5, English*)
Miss K Simpson, BA Bradford (*Year 2, PSHE*)
Miss J Warnes, BA Hons Canterbury
Miss R Woodhead, BSc Gloucestershire, PGCE Roehampton

Nursery and Teaching Assistants:
Mrs I Antoniou
Miss C Dee (*Art, Tea-time Club Worker*) [Maternity Leave]
Mrs A Drabwell, Swiss Level 2, NVQ Level 3, ASA Level 1 Swim Coach)
Mrs E Gifford (*Midday Supervisor*)
Mrs S Goodfellow, NNEB
Mrs H Habergham, BA Hons York St John (*Tea-time Club Leader*)
Miss L Ingrao, NVQ Level 3 (*Nursery Nurse & Tea-time Leader*)
Miss S Jones (*Teaching Assistant*)

Miss Y Kemal, BA Hons Nottingham (*Midday Supervisor, Tea-time Club Leader*)
Mrs L Simson (*Breakfast Club Leader, Midday Supervisor*)
Mrs S Smith

Technician: Mr C Hull

Swimming Coach: Mrs L Short, Royal Life Saving Society UK – National Rescue Award for Swimming Teachers and Coaches

Administration & Secretarial Support:
Prep School Secretary: Mrs T Leader
Prep School Admin Assistants: Mrs T Dickinson, Mrs C Land

St Edmund's School Canterbury

Canterbury, Kent CT2 8HU

Tel:	01227 475601 (Admissions)
	01227 475600 (General Enquiries)
email:	admissions@stedmunds.org.uk
website:	www.stedmunds.org.uk
Twitter:	@stedscanterbury
Facebook:	@StEdsCanterbury

Motto: '*Fungar Vice Cotis*'

St Edmund's is an independent, co-educational day and boarding school for pupils aged between 3 and 18 years, comprising the Pre-Prep, Junior and Senior Schools. Its aim is to provide varied opportunities for academic, sporting, artistic, musical and dramatic achievement. The school has excellent teaching facilities and numerous options for extra-curricular activities.

First established in 1749 as the Clergy Orphan School in Yorkshire, the School later moved to London and settled in its present location in 1855. The School's commitment to its origins endures, as does its Christian ethos. However, the School welcomes pupils from all backgrounds and places a particularly strong emphasis on pastoral care.

St Edmund's is situated on a beautiful site at the top of St Thomas Hill, adjacent to the University of Kent and over-looking the historic city of Canterbury. It is within easy reach of the towns of East Kent, and is just over an hour from London. The proximity to London's airports, the Channel ports and Eurostar stations at Ashford and Ebbsfleet gives international pupils convenient access to the School.

The school is owned by St Edmund's School Canterbury, a charitable company limited by guarantee, registered in England and Wales.

St Edmund's is a distinctive and historic boarding and day co-educational school where a family atmosphere is fostered, individuals are valued, the spiritual element is explored, and pupils enjoy a rich academic and cultural experience. We are committed to producing happy and successful pupils who can access a high quality education, while enjoying a wealth of stimulating and exciting extra-curricular activity. Set within a beautiful and extensive green field site affording spectacular views of the city and Cathedral of Canterbury, St Edmund's not only enjoys a stunning location, but also offers a happy, vibrant and creative environment within a supportive community.

The school offers a nurturing, yet challenging, environment where an emphasis is placed upon academic rigour and extracurricular involvement. Its extracurricular provision is broad, but also encourages excellence in each individual area. Its tradition of housing and educating the Choristers of

Canterbury Cathedral brings much to the richness and diversity of our community.

Academic standards are set high. Its dedicated and talented teaching and support staff work alongside pupils to encourage them to develop into caring, resourceful and confident young men and women who are well equipped to tackle the demands of the modern world.

Organisation. The Pre-Prep, Junior and Senior Schools are on the same site and are closely integrated, using the same Chapel, music and art facilities, theatre, dining hall, science laboratories, sports facilities, and so on. However, for practical day-to-day purposes the Junior School is under the control of the Head of the Junior School and the Pre-Prep under the Head of Pre-Prep. St Edmund's derives much of its strength and its capacity to work efficiently and economically from its close-knit structure.

The Senior School is divided into four Houses: Baker, Wagner, Warneford and Watson, the respective Housemasters each being assisted by a team of Deputies and Tutors.

The Chapel. All pupils attend at least two of the morning services a week. Confirmation is conducted annually by the Archbishop of Canterbury (as Patron of the School) or by the Bishop of Dover acting on his behalf; the candidates are prepared by the School Chaplain. The School Carol Service is held in Canterbury Cathedral, by kind permission of the Dean and Chapter.

Buildings and Facilities. Over the past twenty years there have been extensive additions to and modernisation of the school's buildings and facilities: a new Junior School building; a purpose-built music school; a new Sixth Form Centre; the main hall with tiered auditorium and exhibition area; the sports hall; the technology department; additional classrooms and major extensions to science, art, IT and the Pre-Prep School; as well as the conversion of all Senior School boarding accommodation to study-bedrooms and refurbishment of Junior boarding premises. Recent additions include: phase one of the Academic Hub with 8 classrooms; new recreational facilities for Senior School boarders; a refurbished theatre and library; an AstroTurf pitch; a new medical centre; upgrading of classrooms, boarding and House facilities.

Academic Organisation. At St Edmund's, the academic expectations are high. The breadth and balance of the academic programme exceeds the requirements of the National Curriculum and pupils begin to be grouped by ability while they are in Junior School. This approach encourages children to apply their talents and aptitudes with diligence and perseverance. Comprehensive reports are sent regularly throughout the school year. A system of interim reports, as well as regular parents' meetings, ensures close communication with parents.

Pre-Prep School: The Pre-Prep School has its own classroom buildings and playground, creating a warm, secure and friendly learning environment in which pupils can develop to the full. The happy and purposeful atmosphere helps pupils develop their confidence.

The School has a wide range of excellent activities and teaches a broad-based curriculum that emphasises academic development as well as art, music, drama and sport. The teachers have many years' experience of working with Early Years' children and the small classes allow staff to focus on the needs of every pupil.

Junior School: The aim of the Junior School is to produce independent learners who are confident and motivated. In Forms 3 to 5, the National Curriculum is broadly followed and, while placing particular emphasis on English, Maths and Science, there is also focus on subjects such as Art, French, Geography, History, Information Technology, Latin and Music. Subject specialists teach Forms 6 to 8, helping to prepare pupils for Senior School. Music (from Form 3),

Drama, Technology and Art (from Form 6) and Science (from Form 7) is taught in specialist facilities.

The House system gives older pupils the opportunity to experience the skills of organisation, cooperation and leadership, by helping and encouraging younger members of their Houses and assisting with the organisation of House teams and events. Taking on more responsibility and developing greater initiative is valuable in smoothing their passage to Senior School.

Choristers: The 25 choristers of Canterbury Cathedral are all members of the Junior School. They board in the Choir House (in the Cathedral Precincts) in the care of Houseparents appointed by the school. All their choral training is undertaken in the Cathedral by the Master of Choristers and Cathedral Organist; the remainder of their education takes place at St Edmund's.

Senior School: In the first year of the Senior School (Year 9) pupils follow a core curriculum in English, Mathematics, French, Physics, Chemistry, Biology, History, Geography, Art, Music, Information Technology, Religious Education, PSHEE, Physical Education, and Technology. Drama, Spanish and Latin are options.

GCSE core subjects are: English, English Literature, French, Mathematics and the three (separate) Sciences. Options include Latin, Spanish, Arabic, Greek, History, Geography, Art (Ceramics), Art and Design, Technology: Food Technology, Product Design, Computer Science, Music, Drama, Dance, Physical Education and Religious Studies.

The following subjects are offered for A Level examinations: Art, Biology, Business Studies, Ceramics, Chemistry, Classical Civilisation, Design and Technology, Economics, English Literature, Film Studies, French, Geography, Government and Politics, History, Mathematics and Further Mathematics, Music, Music Technology, Photography, Physics, Psychology and Theatre Studies. In addition to their A Level choices, Lower Sixth pupils have the option to undertake an EPQ (Extended Project Qualification) and the Leiths Academy Diploma.

Careers and Higher Education. The School is affiliated to the Independent Schools Careers Organisation and the Careers Research and Advisory Centre. Pupils have the opportunity to undergo careers aptitude testing in the GCSE year, and all pupils are assisted in finding a placement for a week or more of work experience in the GCSE year. The careers and higher education staff give all possible help in the finding of suitable careers and in selecting appropriate universities and colleges of further education. Most A Level candidates go on to degree courses after leaving school; others join Art or Music conservatoires.

Music. Music is woven into the fabric of school life at St Edmund's, reinforced by the presence of the Canterbury Cathedral Choristers. In the purpose-built Music School, specialist teachers give lessons to pupils from Pre-Prep through to the Sixth Form. Pupils of all ages participate in numerous musical ensembles which cater for a range of vocal and instrumental abilities. As a result, there is an exceptional practical examination record, with more than 80% of entrants achieving Distinction or Merit. Over twenty-five concerts and performances take place each year, from small lunchtime recitals in the Recital Hall to large gala concerts in Canterbury Cathedral. The school acts as a focus for musical excellence for children throughout East Kent and enjoys a creative partnership with the Tippett Quartet.

Performing Arts. Dramatic performance is included in the curriculum from the earliest years. Every term, the Pre-Prep School holds thematic drama workshops. Pupils in Junior and Senior Schools participate in school plays and other performances with vitality and enthusiasm, as an outlet for expressing their talents in acting, dancing, singing, music, choreography and technical production. The consistently outstanding GCSE and A Level results are testament to the emphasis placed on drama within the curriculum and school life in general.

Art. The emphasis St Edmund's places on creative subjects means that art is embedded in the curriculum across the three Schools. Pupils studying Art and Design enjoy excellent facilities and teaching. Drawing, painting, print-making, photography (traditional and digital), sculpture and ceramics are offered to pupils in the Junior and Senior Schools.

Sport. Association football, hockey, cricket, athletics, tennis, squash and (for girls) netball and rounders are the principal sports but there are opportunities for many other forms of exercise, including cross-country running, indoor rowing, golf, badminton, basketball, volleyball, swimming and gym-based fitness training. There is an astroturf pitch and large playing fields that adjoin the school buildings. There is an open-air heated swimming pool. The sports hall is well-equipped. There are eight tennis courts (both hard and grass), a compact golf course and a rifle range.

Activities. For those in the first four years of Senior School one afternoon a week is given over specifically to a broad range of activities. A number involve helping the local community, while other pupils learn new skills, e.g. archaeology, broadcasting, Eco-Schools, Japanese language and culture, kite making, literary and debating societies, photography, Rotary Interact and yoga.

In the second year all Senior School pupils join the Combined Cadet Force, a highly successful unit commanded by a member of the teaching staff and administered by an ex-soldier. There is an annual camp in the summer and an adventurous training camp at Easter, attendance at which is voluntary. Cadets may remain in the CCF for the duration of their school career if they wish, and are encouraged to do so if contemplating a career in the armed forces.

Pupils may also participate in The Duke of Edinburgh's Award scheme and the British Association of Young Scientists. There are regular field trips, choir and music tours, sports tours and many other one-off trips.

In Junior School, too, there is a diverse range of extracurricular activities, many of which draw on the school's excellent facilities for sport, music and drama. There is a Year 8 outdoor activities week in Spain, an annual sports tour and skiing trip.

Health. The School Medical Centre is staffed by state registered nurses and provides medical care at all times. The health of the pupils is supervised by a senior local general practitioner under the NHS. A counselling service is available.

St Edmund's Festival of the Arts. Established in 2017, the Festival was planned and delivered with a clear and single aim: to celebrate the fantastic talents of young people by bringing to Canterbury an event as new and fresh as it was creative and innovative with a line-up of world-class artists. To date guest artists have included Freddy Kempf, Tasmin Little, Jess Gillam and has become a fixture in the Canterbury arts calendar.

Admission. *Pre-Prep School*: Entry at any age from 3–7. Once registered, children are invited to visit the School for informal assessment.

Junior School: Entry at any age from 7–12. Candidates will sit entrance tests and all prospective pupils will be interviewed or attend an assessment day.

Choristers: St Edmund's is the school of the Canterbury Cathedral choristers. For details of the voice trials please contact the Junior School Secretary.

Senior School: Entry at 13 from preparatory schools is through the Common Entrance Examination. Candidates

from other schools will be tested appropriately or sit the School's own entrance tests. There is also a large entry of pupils into the Sixth Form, usually on the basis of interview and GCSE grade estimates from their present school.

Fees per term (2018–2019). Senior School: Boarders £11,656; Weekly Boarders £10,865; Day pupils £6,822. Junior School: Boarders £8,876, Weekly Boarders £8,089, Choristers £7,809, Day pupils £5,032–£5,198. Pre-Prep: £3,130–£3,618, Nursery £2,549.

Music fees: £263.65 per term. Extras have been kept to the minimum.

Entrance Scholarships. Competitive scholarships of up to 25% of tuition fees are offered in academic achievement, music, drama and sport at 11+, 13+ and 16+. In addition, art scholarships are available at 13+ and 16+. At the discretion of the Head an All-Rounder scholarship may be made to a candidate whose combination of talents merits an award. Such a candidate will have sat the academic scholarship paper and been assessed for a scholarship in at least one other discipline.

Bursaries and Fee Concessions. Originally founded to provide a free education for the fatherless sons of the clergy of the Church of England and the Church of Wales, St Edmund's now accepts applications from boys and girls for Foundationer status. Bursaries to provide a temporary (no more than 12 months) cushion are granted on a means-tested basis to existing pupils. Fee concessions, also means-tested, can be provided to the children of the clergy, members of the armed forces and to the third and subsequent children of the same family in the school at the same time.

Charitable status. St Edmund's School Canterbury is a Registered Charity, number 1056382. It exists to educate the children in its care.

Patron: The Lord Archbishop of Canterbury

Governors:
Chairman: Air Marshal C M Nickols, CB, CBE, MA, FRAeS
Dr M Carnegie, MB BS
Dr P Eichorn, MD
Mr C Harbridge, FRICS
Mrs N Leatherbarrow, BSc, MBA
The Revd Canon Dr T J N Naish, BA, MA, PhD
Dr L Naylor, BSc, PhD
Mr Q L Roper, BA Hons, MA, NPQH
His Honour Judge P St John-Stevens
Mr S M Sutton, BA, FCA
Councillor P A Todd

Head: Mr E G O'Connor, MA Cantab, MPhil Oxon, MEd Cantab

Head of The Junior School: Dr E L Margrett, BA Hons Bristol, MA London, EdD Sussex, CCRS Roehampton, PGCE London

Head of The Pre-Prep School: Mrs J E P Exley, BEd Hons CCCU

Chaplain: The Revd M S Bennett, MusB Hons Canterbury NZ , BA Hons CCCU

Bursar: Mr N C Scott-Kilvert, FCCA

Senior Deputy Head Pastoral: Mrs C J Shearer, BA Bangor, PCGE Leeds

Deputy Head Academic: Ms A E Bensberg, BSc LSE, MA UCL, CELTA Cantab, Dip SpLD Northampton, APC

Assistant Head Co-Curricular: Mr L A Millard, BSc Loughborough, PGCE

Director of Studies: Mr R N Comfort, BSc Hons Wales

Heads of Departments:
[1] *Department serving both Senior & Junior Schools*

Additional Educational Needs:
Mrs L K Blench, BA Hull, PGCE CCCU

[1]*Art*:
Mrs A A Slater-Williams, BA Hons Glasgow School of
   Art, PGCE (*Director*)

Business Studies and Economics:
Mr R N Comfort, BSc Hons Wales

Computer Science:
Mr S K Wood, BEng, MSc Kent, GTP CCCU

Design and Technology:
Ms M Florence, BTec, BA Hons

[1]*Drama and Theatre Studies*:
Mr M Sell, NCDT Acc Diploma ALRA, PGCE (*Director*)

English:
Mr M J Whitman, BA Hons Nottingham Trent, MA Nott,
   PGCE

EAL:
Mrs H E Copland, TESOL Trinity College

Film Studies:
Dr M G Caiazza, BA MSMC, MA Kent, PGCE, PhD Kent

Geography:
Mrs V H Burton, BSc Hons Newcastle, PGCE

History/Government and Politics:
Mr D J Morrissey, BA Hons, MSc Keele, PGCE

Latin:
Mrs A I Heavens, MA Hons St Andrews, PGCE

[1]*Mathematics*:
Dr E R Jones, BSc Wales, MSc Liverpool, PhD Wales

Modern Languages:
Mrs D F Micheloud, BA Hons Kent, MA Fribourg, Dip
   MG (*MFL and French*)

[1]*Music*:
Mr S J Payne, BA Hons, MA, ARCM, LTCL, ARCO,
   PGCE (*Director*)

Personal, Social and Health Education:
Mr J M Clapp, BSc Hons, MA Reading (*Coordinator*)

[1]*Physical Education*:
Mrs H M Millard

Religious Studies:
Mrs V A Gunn, BA OU, BA Kent, MA Kent, GTP RMGS

[1]*Science*:
Dr G L Jones, MBChB Hons Birmingham, PGCE Warwick

Biology:
Dr G L Jones, MBChB Hons Birmingham, PGCE Warwick

Chemistry:
Dr E Fernández-Iglesias, LCQ Oviedo, Spain, PhD Exon,
   PGCE CCCU

Physics:
Dr J C Horn, BSc Hons, PhD Leeds

Additional Responsibilities:
Contingent Commander CCF: Major A R Jones
Editor of The Chronicle: Mr M J Whitman, BA Hons
   Nottingham Trent, MA Nott, PGCE
Head of Careers: Mrs M Judi-Sprinks, BA Hons Kent, Cert
   TEFL
Head of Progression: Dr C F Sotillo, MA, PhD Edinburgh
President of Common Room: Ms M Florence, BTec, BA
   Hons

Public Examinations Officer: Dr C F Sotillo, MA, PhD
   Edinburgh
Sixth Form Academic Enrichment and UCAS Coordinator:
   Dr C F Sotillo, MA, PhD Edinburgh
Work Experience Coordinator: Ms S A Scally

Junior School:

Head: Dr E L Margrett, BA Hons Bristol, MA London,
   EdD Sussex, CCRS Roehampton, PGCE London
Deputy Head: Dr H E Goodwin, BA Durham, MA London,
   PhD Middlesex, PGCE Goldsmiths (*Mathematics*)
Director of Studies: Mr M S Christodoulou-Jones, BSc
   Hons Bristol, PGCE CCCU (*Mathematics, Head of
   Computing, Director of JS ICT*)
Head of Junior School Co-curricular: Mr A J McKean,
   BA/BSc CCCU, PGCE (*Head of Geography, Head of
   PSHE*)
Senior Master: Mr T Hooley, MA Cantab (*Head of Latin,
   Teacher of History*)
Head of Lower School: Mrs A J Swatman, BEd Hons Kent
   (*Form 3*)

Support Staff:
Senior School Librarian: Ms S A Scally
Medical Officer: Dr J Thompson
Head's PA: Ms E Ottaway, BA Hons Essex
Junior School Secretary: Mrs Y King
Head of Admissions: Mrs A Strong

(*Please refer to the school website for full staff list*)

St Edward's, Oxford

Woodstock Road, Oxford OX2 7NN

Tel:	Warden: 01865 319323
	Bursar: 01865 319321
	Registrar: 01865 319200
Fax:	01865 319242
email:	registrar@stedwardsoxford.org
website:	www.stedwardsoxford.org
Twitter:	@TeddiesOxford
Facebook:	@TeddiesOxford

Motto: '*Pietas Parentum*'

St Edward's was founded in 1863 by the Revd Thomas
Chamberlain to educate the sons of middle class clergy in
the Anglican tradition. The somewhat cramped original
premises in the centre of Oxford soon proved inadequate for
the growing School, so the decision was taken in 1873 to
move to what were then the farmlands of Summertown.
Today, the School sits on a vast 100-acre estate complete
with riverside boat house, pitches, courts, sports centre, elegant Quad, golf course and canalside towpath – yet is only a
2-minute walk from the busy urban village of Summertown
and less than a mile from the centre of Oxford, a city world
famous for education and culture. The School has around
700 pupils, 85% of whom board, and 40% of whom are
girls. Pupils live in one of 13 houses (five for girls, seven for
boys, and an emerging co-ed house) and, in addition to having the run of extensive playing fields, benefit from access
to the Nuffield Health Fitness & Wellbeing Gym (owned by
the school but managed by Nuffield), the North Wall Arts
Centre, the new Ogston Music School and all the amenities
of a lively international city.

Ethos. The St Edward's ethos is underpinned by a firm
emphasis on the far-reaching benefits of participation and
engagement. We ask each of our pupils to engage in their
academic work with real belief – in themselves and in their
ability to achieve – and we encourage all pupils to take

advantage of the many opportunities on offer to them at Teddies. An important touchstone for the St Edward's educational ethos is the conviction that those pupils who derive joy and satisfaction from a wide range of activities outside the classroom are those who go on to perform exceptionally well in their academic work.

Pastoral Care. The comprehensive pastoral care system at St Edward's has long been regarded as one of the school's great strengths – a point highlighted by successive ISI reports. The system is underpinned by a highly-effective network of relationships offering distinct but interwoven levels of care. Each pupil sits at the centre of his or her network, surrounded by a range of people who can offer guidance and support. The Housemaster or Housemistress is a vital member of this web of care and in this role they are supported by an Assistant HM and a Matron. Also key are Tutors who monitor the academic and pastoral life of six to 10 pupils, meeting with them regularly to offer advice as necessary. Within the school community, Sixth Formers are trained to offer a peer listening service and a great many other leadership and support roles; the Head Boy and Girl meet regularly with senior staff to raise any areas of concern.

Academic Work. Academically, it would be hard to overstate the importance to St Edward's of being in Oxford, within easy reach of the stimulating academic life of the university. Academic endeavour lies at the heart of the School; pupils are expected to work consistently hard, to take responsibility for their own learning and to engage actively in the myriad opportunities open to them for broadening their intellectual horizons. The school offers GCSE (IGCSE in most subjects), A Level with the Extended Project and the IB Diploma. The Sixth Form community is split 40/60 between A Levels and the IB. Alongside these qualifications, the School offers its own bespoke courses: the Shell Curriculum in the first year teaches the skills necessary for successful study, the Warden's Project in the Fourth Form introduces the idea of an independent research project and the Taught Skills Course in the Lower Sixth teaches such vital topics as critical thinking, presentation and precis-writing. The Learning Development Department supports pupils who are mildly dyslexic or dyscalculic.

In 2018, 81% of Sixth Form grades were A*–B or Levels 7–5 (A Level or the IB Diploma). 58% of GCSE grades were A*/A. On average, some 80% of sixth form leavers take up places at Russell Group or equally prestigious universities, including Oxford and Cambridge and, increasingly, pupils look to study overseas. In recent years, pupils have gone on to study at US and Canadian universities, including Brown, Rhode Island; Columbia, New York; Dartmouth, New Hampshire; Georgetown, Washington; Berkeley, California; and McGill, Montreal. Pupils have also been successful in their applications to universities in Hong Kong and Japan, and to universities in a number of European cities including Dublin, Amsterdam, Leiden and Madrid.

To extend academic opportunities for all pupils, outstanding university-level facilities are currently under construction at the heart of the School in the Quad. A new Library and Study Centre, purpose built for a modern education, will open in 2020 alongside a stunning new Hall.

Higher Education and Careers. The new Careers Education Department is firmly rooted in the real world of work. Our Head of Careers, a former Head Hunter with first-hand knowledge of a wide range of industries, runs a structured programme. Every Fifth Former benefits from a termly, compulsory careers session to help them identify and secure the most relevant work experience placements. Informal careers receptions are organised each year covering everything from financial services, law, engineering and fashion to marketing services, manufacturing and design.

Higher Education advice is highly personalised and quite exceptional. The new Shell Curriculum is designed to feed directly into pupils' career planning by explicitly teaching the skills required for today's workplace: research, self-regulation, innovative thinking, presentation, collaboration and teamwork. Pupils are given every assistance in choosing the right course of further study and in preparing a strong application, including visits by representatives of UK and US universities, mock interviews and personal statement workshops. Tailored advice is given to Oxbridge and Ivy League candidates, to those aiming for highly-competitive courses, such as Medicine or Veterinary Science, and to those looking to study overseas.

Music, Drama and the Arts. The cutting-edge programming of the award-winning North Wall Arts Centre enriches the cultural life of both the School and the wider community, placing St Edward's at the forefront of developments in arts education. As a result, the arts are highly valued and enormously successful at St Edward's. The Drama Department is flourishing: main school productions, including musicals, are complemented by devised pieces, House plays, Shell plays and a Speech and Drama programme. The Art Department is strong and vibrant, benefiting from recently enhanced facilities and a stream of visiting exhibitions to The North Wall. The Dance programme is extensive, with over 30 classes every week – covering styles from ballet to hip hop – generating a range of material for the dance shows. The Music Department, now housed in the elegant, high-specification Ogston Music School, delivers about 500 lessons every week, taught by a team of 40 visiting specialists. The main school groups include the Orchestra, Chamber Orchestra, Chapel Choir, Chamber Choir, St Edward's Singers (a choir for the School and the local community), Concert Band, Big Band, Jazz Band and various Chamber Music groups. There are around 60 concerts a year, in School and further afield, with occasional foreign tours.

Sport, Games and Activities. A wide variety of sports, games and activities is on offer. We compete at the highest level in several sports and can boast of county and national representatives. We encourage all our pupils to participate and to enjoy playing at all levels. We have fielded as many as 27 teams on one day – over 400 children representing the school. These sports, games and activities include rugby, football, hockey, cricket, rowing, athletics, netball, squash, tennis, swimming, cross-country running, sailing, golf, football, canoeing, ceramics, theatre crew, filmmaking, debating, investment, textiles, cycle maintenance, volunteering, charitable challenges, community service – and much more. We operate a Combined Cadet Force with Navy, Army and RAF sections, and offer The Duke of Edinburgh's Award.

Admission to the School. Registration forms may be downloaded from the website or obtained from the Registrar. There is a registration fee of £100. Applicants applying from a Prep School are asked to sit the ISEB Common Pre-Tests in the autumn of Year 7. Separate arrangements are made for registered pupils not coming through the Prep School route. Place offers conditional on a satisfactory school report, performance at interview and in the Common Entrance Examinations, or our own 13+ entrance examinations, are made 18 months prior to entry. Lower Sixth interviews, scholarship and entrance examinations are held in November prior to entry; place offers in the Sixth Form are subject to good performance at GCSE (at least six A*–B grades, or six grade 6s or above in the new numerical system) and a satisfactory report from the previous school.

Scholarships. Academic, Music, Art, Dance, Drama and Sports Scholarships are available at both 13+ and 16+ entry. All-Rounder and Design Technology Scholarships are available at 13+ only.

Academic, Music, Sports and All-Rounder Scholarships, both for entrants at 13+ (into Year 9) and 16+ (into Year 12), can be increased via means-testing up to a total of 100% fee reduction. There is no means-tested fee support available for Dance, Drama, Art or Design Technology Scholarships.

Academic: Up to fifteen scholarships and exhibitions are available each year. 16+ academic scholarships take place in the November prior to entry in the September, 13+ academic scholarships take place in the March prior to entry.

Music scholarships: Most candidates perform on two instruments, and many offer singing as one of these options. Composition can also be considered. We look for potential rather than attainment to date, although the minimum standard required is about grade 5 for 13+ and grade 8 for 16+.

Dance and Drama scholarships: Candidates for both these awards will be expected to demonstrate considerable natural ability and should be able to confirm that they have begun to reach high standards on the stage.

Music, Dance and Drama 13+ scholarships take place in the January/February prior to entry, 16+ in the November prior to entry.

Art scholarships: Candidates must submit a portfolio of work prior to the assessment. On the day of the award they will be asked to complete an observational drawing task. 13+ scholarships take place in the January/February prior to entry, 16+ in the November prior to entry.

Sport scholarships for both 13+ and 16+ entry take place in the November prior to entry. Candidates will show considerable natural ability in at least one sport.

All-Rounder awards are available at 13+ only. Candidates must be academically sound, expecting to obtain over 65% at Common Entrance, show strong leadership qualities and be able to demonstrate considerable talent in two of the following areas: art, design technology, music, dance, sport or drama. The All-Rounder Award takes place in the February prior to entry.

Bursaries. The School may offer bursaries for children of clergy at the Warden's discretion.

Fees per term (2018–2019). Boarding £12,615; Day £10,095.

Charitable status. St Edward's, Oxford is a Registered Charity, number 309681. The aims and objectives of the school are to provide an outstanding education to pupils between the ages of 13–18 in order to prepare them for happy, fulfilled and productive adult lives.

Visitor:
The Rt Revd The Lord Bishop of Oxford

Governing Body:
Chris Jones, MA. FRSA [OSE] (*Chairman*)
Caroline Baggs, BSc
Georgina Dennis, MA [OSE]
Professor Louise Fawcett-Posada, MA, DPhil
George Fenton [OSE]
David Jackson, LLB
Kenneth MacRitchie, MA, BD, LLB
The Very Revd Professor Martyn Percy, BA, MEd, PhD
Michael Roulston, MBE, BPhil, MEd
Mike Stanfield [OSE]
Oliver Watson, BA [OSE]

[OSE] *Former Pupil*

Warden: Stephen Jones, BA, MSc, MLitt, FRSA

Bursar: Stephen Withers Green, MA, ACA

Sub-Warden: Tony Darby, BA

Deputy Head Academic: Matthew Albrighton, MA
Deputy Head Pastoral: James Cope, MA

Assistant Head Academic: Nicola Hunter, BA

Assistant Head Academic: Margaret Lloyd, BSc
Assistant Head Pastoral: Rachel Bellamy, MA
Registrar: Nicola Jones, BEd

Assistant Head Co-Curricular: Nick Coram-Wright, MA
Assistant Head Co-Curricular: Judy Young, BSc

Teaching Staff:
* *Head of Department*

Art:
*Adam Hahn, BA
Jane Bowen, BA
Philip Jolley, BA, BEd
Peter Lloyd-Jones, Dip FA
Nicholas Permain, BA
Lorraine Turley, BA
Instructor: Richard Siddons
Technician: Sharon Keen

Classics:
*Mark Taylor, BA
Edmund Hunt, MA
Flora Nelson, BA, MSt.
Simon Palferman, BA, MPhil
Matthew Parker, MA, MSc
James Sinclair, BA
Paolo Torri, MA, PhD

Design & Technology:
*Oliver Barstow, MEng
Laura French, BSc
Susan Holland, BSc
Ben Pyper, Dip AD
Andrew Rush, MSc
Technicians:
Stuart Giles
Lucian Taylor

Drama:
*David Aldred, BA
Katrina Eden, MA
Lauren Mackrell, BA

Economics:
*Emily Moss, MA
Tony Darby, BA
David Finamore, BSc
Yvette Ramadharsingh, BSc

English:
*Jason Clapham, MA, MSc
Lauren Bray, MA
Charles Davies, MA
Catherine Greves, BA
Nicola Hunter, BA
Fergus Livingstone, MA
Millie Pumfrey, MA
Chloe Riddle, BA
Simon Roche, BA
Edward Scates, MA

Geography:
*Hugh Stephens, MA
Matt Albrighton, MA
James Cope, MA
Garrett Nagle, MA, DPhil
Matt Strachan, BA
Fred Tao, MSc

History:
*Jonathan Lambe, BA
Elizabeth Boast, BA
Anna Fielding, BA

Peter Swainson, BA
Huw Thomas, LLB, MEd
Fiona Wickens, MA

History of Art:
*Nicola Hunter, BA
Charlotte Schofield, MA

Learning Development:
*Debra Clayphan, BA, MSc
Joanna Sephton, BA

Mathematics:
*Ashley Currie, MPhys
Sophie Barnes, BSc
Henry Chitsenga, BSc
David del Strother, MSc
Naomi George, BSc
Andrew Grounds, BA, MSc
Jonathan Ingram, MMath
Catherine James, BSc
Stephen Jones, BA, MSc, MLitt, FRSA
Margaret Lloyd, BSc
Anneli Ruele, BA
John Simpson, BEng
Jonathan Taylor, BSc
John Wiggins, MA

Modern Languages:
*Marie-Laure Delvallée, Licence d'Anglais (*French*)
Denise Kohlhepp, MA (*German*)
Jamie Davies, BA (*Spanish*)
Suzanne Arbuthnot, BA
Stuart Bartholomew, MA
Solana Cabello Malfetano, BA
David Caro, BA
Katherine Cole, BA
Nick Coram-Wright, MA
Robert Cottrell, BA
Ann-Laure Davies, MA
Paula Diaz Rogado, BA
Linda Raabe-Marjot, BA
Nicoletta Simborowski, MA
Paolo Torri, MA, PhD
Technician: Lucy Bentley

Language Assistants:
Aline Gay (*French*)
Anna-Lisa Vorbrugg (*German*)
Safae Samadi El Edrissi (*Spanish*)

Music:
*Alex Tester, MA (*Director of Music*)

Lawrence Tao (*Head of Academic Music*)

Neville Creed, MA (*Director of Cultural Activities*)

Gabriele Damiani, BMus, GSMD, ARCO

Richard Powell, GRSM, IRAM, ARCM

PHSE:

Debra Clayphan, BA, MSc (*Head of Pupil Wellbeing*)

Eve Singfield

Psychology:
*Annabelle Rose, BA
Rachel Bellamy, MA
Nic Bond, BSc
Adam Moffatt, BA

Politics:
*Jonathan Thomson, BA
Ariadne Tsenina, BA

Sciences:

Biology:
*Richard Storey, BSc
Lucy Baddeley, MA
Louise Bowen, BSc, PhD
Andrew Davis, BSc, PhD, FRGS
Alistair Marjot, BA
Rebecca James, BSc
Alastair Summers, BSc
Alexander Waring, BSc
Technicians:
Beata Kolodziej
Gail Benson

Graduate Assistants:
Jodie Atkins, BA
Amy Chang, BA
Ross Simmonds, BA
Jack Fairbrother, BSc

Houses and Housemasters/Housemistresses:
Cowell's: Simon Palferman
Sing's: Matthew Parker
Field House: Mark Hanslip
Macnamara's: Kate Newson
Apsley: Oliver Richards
Tilly's: Andrew Grounds
Segar's: Simon Roche
Kendall: Philip Waghorn
Oakthorpe: Elizabeth Boast
Corfe: Eve Singfield
Avenue: Yvette Ramadharsingh
Jubilee: Charles Davies
Cooper Lodge: Fergus Livingstone

Chaplain: Revd Ernest Lennon, MA
Examinations Officer: John Simpson, BEng
Careers Education: James Vaughan-Fowler

Medical Officers:
Dr Matthew Cheetham
Dr Lynsey Bennett

Chemistry:
Matthew Fletcher, MA, PhD, MRSC
Phaedra Gowen, BSc
Monica Islam, BSc
Natalie McDaid, MChem
Oliver Richards, MA
Beth Watts, BSc, PhD
Technician: Judy Roberts/ Liz May

Environmental Science:
*Andrew Davis, BSc, PhD, FRGS
Garrett Nagle, MA, DPhil

Physics:
*Matthew Rigby, MPhys, DPhil
Tom Holdsworth, BEng
Heather Murphy, BSc
Jem Pearson, MA, DPhil
Philip Waghorn, MSc
Judy Young, BSc
Technician: Graham Quelch

Sports Science:
*Becky Drury, BSc
Rachel Bellamy, MA
Nicholas Bond, BA
Robert Craze, BSc
Mark Hanslip, BEd
Kate Newson, BA

Theology, Philosophy & Ethics:
*Philip Mallaband, MA, PhD
Michael Bunch, BA, MEd
Ernest Lennon, MA
Jonathan Thomson, BA
Tom Wyatt, BA

St George's College, Weybridge

Weybridge Road, Weybridge, Surrey KT15 2QS

Tel: 01932 839300
Fax: 01932 839301
email: contact@stgeorgesweybridge.com
website: www.stgeorgesweybridge.com
Twitter: @sgweybridge
Facebook: @stgeorgescollegeuk

Motto: *Amore et Labore*

Founded by the Josephite Community in 1869 in Croydon, the College moved in 1884 to its present attractive grounds of 100 acres on Woburn Hill, Weybridge. Within its particular family orientated ethos, the College seeks to encourage a wide, balanced Christian education in the Catholic tradition encouraging excellence and achievement across a broad spectrum of academic, sporting and extra-curricular activities. Almost all pupils move on to higher education, the vast majority gaining places at Russell Group universities, including Oxford and Cambridge.

The College is co-educational throughout the school and there are approximately 940 girls and boys.

Admissions. Entry is normally at age 11 (First Year), 13 (Third Year) or 16 (Sixth Form). Students are accepted in September each year. Entry is also possible during an academic year if a place is available.

Admissions details may be obtained from the Admissions Department.

Entrance Scholarships. Academic Scholarships are awarded at 11, 13 and for the Sixth Form. Additionally, at age 11 Music, Art and Sports scholarships are offered and at 13 and 16 Music, Drama, Sport and Art Scholarships are offered.

Details of the number of scholarships at each year group, process for application and guidance on expected standards are to be found on our website under the Admissions section. Scholarships are awarded equally to boys and girls and a certain number are allocated to Junior School candidates each year.

Bursaries. The College provides short-term financial assistance for existing families who find themselves in difficult financial circumstances. Further information is available from the Bursar.

Assisted Places Scheme. St George's offers financial assistance of up to 100% relief on fees via its means-tested Assisted Places Scheme. The scheme allows families who would not normally be able to consider the independent sector to seek a St George's education for their academically able son or daughter. Places are awarded from the age of seven at the Junior School and 11 at the College. As with all applications, children will need to reach the academic entry standards required at both schools.

Facilities. Our state-of-the-art Sixth Form building provides group and silent study rooms, social space, five History and five Geography classrooms, staff offices and meeting areas. Refurbishment over the past three years has provided modern facilities for Music, Languages, English, Mathematics, Theatre and Technology. There is an extensive Arts Centre, an impressive Library and a large indoor Sports Hall with an adjacent fitness training room. The College has 19 tennis courts, including three international standard grass courts, clay courts and an impressive four-court Indoor Tennis Centre. In addition, there are floodlit netball courts, an all-weather athletics track and two astroturf hockey pitches. The College Boat Club is situated nearby on the Thames. Building work is currently under way on a world-class

Activity Centre, which is due to be completed in time to mark the school's 150 anniversary in 2019.

The Curriculum. This is kept as broad as possible up to GCSE, with a balance between Arts and Science subjects. Students usually take a maximum of 10 GCSEs, A Level candidates may choose from over 20 subjects. The vast majority of the Sixth Form go on to Russell Group universities including Oxford and Cambridge.

Careers. Guidance is given throughout a student's career but particularly in making GCSE, A Level and university choices. The Careers Coordinator has a modern well stocked Careers Room and makes effective use of testing, portfolios, work experience, trial interviews, Challenge of Industry days and computer software.

Art. The Art Department attracts large numbers of students at GCSE and A Level who achieve consistently high results in public examinations. A large proportion of A Level candidates successfully apply to Art Colleges, often each receiving several offers in this highly competitive field.

Music. Music plays a vital part in school life. There is a wide range of music-making encompassing early music, madrigal groups, jazz, rock, African Drumming as well as more traditional ensembles, orchestras and wind bands. The choir and orchestra give regular performances (including radio broadcasts), and tour Europe annually. Tuition is available on all orchestral instruments from a team of 36 visiting specialists who teach over 400 students each week. Students play in youth orchestras and have gained scholarships to the major conservatoires.

Responsibility and Service. Many girls and boys are engaged in the care for elderly people at home or in care homes, as well as those with physical or mental disabilities. Each Easter and Summer, groups of Sixth Formers accompany people with disabilities on visits to Lourdes. Students find these activities a rewarding exercise in Christian service. The Prefect system and the mentor system offer positions of responsibility to the oldest students. The Duke of Edinburgh's Award scheme is encouraged and there is a flourishing College Council.

Pastoral Care. The spiritual, moral and academic wellbeing of the students is the concern of every member of staff at the College. Nearly all staff act as Group Tutors with particular responsibility for the daily care of their students and for forging links with parents. Each Year Group is led by a Head of Year, and the Chaplain has a general pastoral role. All groups have a day of retreat away each year. The College also has four Houses to which the students are affiliated and all students have one period per week as part of their PSE programme.

Extracurricular Activities. A very wide range of clubs and societies take place both at lunchtime and after school. In addition to music and sport, a broad range of interests is catered for such as the Science Club, Cookery, Young Enterprise, Philosophy and Model Clubs.

Sport. All students participate and there is a variety of sports: rugby, hockey, netball, cricket, tennis, rowing, and rounders, plus a wide range of other activities such as golf, athletics, badminton, basketball and cross country. Each student has the opportunity to develop his or her own talents in small coaching groups. The College has its own boat house on the Thames, 19 tennis courts (including four indoor), two floodlit artificial pitches with viewing stand, floodlit netball courts, six artificial cricket nets, one main pavilion and two smaller cricket pavilions, eight rugby pitches. The College has access to the Junior School heated outdoor swimming pool. Attendance at national hockey finals is an annual event and the College hosts a very popular Under 18 Hockey Sixes every year. International honours have recently been gained in hockey, cricket, rowing and tennis.

Junior School. St George's Junior School is located nearby in Thames Street, Weybridge, and is co-educational, catering for boys and girls from 3 to 11.

(*For further details, please see Junior School entry in IAPS section.*)

Fees per term (2018–2019). First and Second Years £5,615; Third Year to Upper Sixth Form £6,395. Lunches (compulsory for First and Second Years) £315.

Charitable status. St George's College Weybridge is a Registered Charity, number 1017853, and a Company Limited by Guarantee. The aims and objectives of the Charity are the Christian education of young people.

Governing Body:
Chairman: Mr M Davie

Mr D Anderson	Mr J Lewin
Mr D Bicarregui	Ms I McCormick
Ms S Conrad	Ms A Muggeridge
Mrs D Ewart	Rev W M Muir, CJ
Mr J Hood	Mrs K Patterson
Mr C Jansen	Mr C Prescott

Clerk to the Governors and Bursar: Mr G Cole

Headmistress: Mrs R C F Owens, MA Oxon, PGCE, NPQH

Deputy Head Academic: Ms F M May, MA, BA, PGCE (*English*)
Deputy Head Pastoral: Miss S L Hall, BSc, PGCE (*Geography*)
Deputy Head Staff: Mr D Wright, MA, BA, PGCE (*History and Politics*)

Assistant Head Reporting: Mr J E Davies, BA, PGCE (*Geography*)
Assistant Head Timetabling: Mr P J Robinson, BEng, PGCE (*Mathematics*)
Assistant Head Sixth Form: Mrs M D Smith, BA Hons, PGCE (*History*)
Assistant Head Pastoral: Mrs T A Hall, BSc, MSc, PGCE

College Chaplain: Fr Martin Ashcroft CJ, MA, MA, STB, BPhil, BA, CertEd
Assistant Chaplain: Miss J Barnett
Assistant Chaplain: Miss A M Colantuoni, BE, MA

Miss S Arif, BSc Hons, MEd, PGCE (*Head of Mathematics*)
Mr M J Barham, BA Hons, PGCE (*Head of History*)
Mr A Barton, BA Hons, PGCE (*Head of 4th Year, Music*)
Mrs L Y Batten, BA Hons French & German, PGCE (*Languages*)
Ms P Berai, BA Hons, PGCE (*Geography*)
Dr J A Baur, BSc, MSc, MPhil, PhD (*Chemistry*)
Mrs M Bigwood, BSc, HDE (*Mathematics*)
Ms S Bird, BA Hons, NPQML, PGCE (*Geography*)
Mr N M Bissessar, BA Hons (*Drama*)
Mr G D Boyes, BSc, GTP (*Head of Geography*)
Mr D J Bradford, BHum, PGCE (*Mathematics*)
Mrs E M Brambell, BA Hons, PGCE (*Religious Studies*)
Mr M Bryant, BSc Hons, PGCE (*Biology*)
Ms C A Butler, BA, PGCE (*Art*)
Mrs S Carpenter, BA Hons, PGCE (*Languages, i/c Latin*)
Mr P Callaghan, BSc, PGCE (*Computing*)
Mr O J Clayson (*PE/Games; Head of Cricket*)
Miss V M Clayton, BA, PGCE (*Government and Politics*)
Mr A Cornick, BA Hons, PGCE (*Director of Sport*)
Mr M J Cullen, BSc, PGCE (*Economics & Business Studies*)
Mr J M Cunningham, BA, PGCE (*Religious Studies, i/c D of E*)
Mr D P Danaher, MTL, BA, PGCE (*Head of Economics & Business Studies*)

Mr T Deive, BA, PGCE (*Head of Languages*)
Ms S Devonshire, BA Hons, PGCE (*Languages*)
Mrs E L Doyle, BSc, PGCE (*Biology*)
Mrs V G Emad, BA Hons, PGCE (*Art*)
Mr I C Facey, BSc Hons, QTS (*Technology*)
Mr J V Fialho, BA, PGCE (*English*)
Mrs N D Flash, BSc, PGCE (*Science*)
Mrs E Fox, MA, MSc, QTS (*Biology*)
Mr N J Galanis (*Languages, i/c French*)
Miss N Gavin, BA Hons, PGCE (*History & Politics*)
Mrs L E Gibson, BSc, PGCE (*Head of Girls' Games,
    Acting Director of Sport*)
Ms S E Goodfellow, MA Oxon, BA Hons, PGCE (*Head of
    Chemistry*)
Mr A D Gradon, BSc, QTS (*Mathematics*)
Mr A J Graham, BSc Hons, PGCE (*Chemistry/Science*)
Mrs C F Grant, BA Hons, PGCE (*History and Politics*)
Dr F Grant, PhD, BSc, MA, PGCE (*Mathematics*)
Mr P J Graves, BSc, PGCE (*Languages, Head of Activities*)
Mr D A Green, BSc Hons, GTP (*Biology, Head of U6th*)
Ms G Hagiu, BSc, QTS (*Physics*)
Mrs G Hale, Deug LL France (*Languages*)
Mrs L Hamer, BSc, MA, QTS (*Geography*)
Mrs L C Hanlan BA, PGCE (*Languages*)
Miss T Haynes, BSc (*PE & Games*)
Mr P Hortor, BA Hons, QTS (*Physics*)
Miss N I Houston, BA Hons, PGCE (*Religious Studies,
    Head of 5th Year*)
Mr A Hudson, BA, PGCE (*Mathematics*)
Mr M S Hughes, MA, BA (*Head of Boys' Hockey*)
Miss C Hulf, BA Hons, MA, GTP Cert Ed (*Rowing Coach*)
Miss H Hunt, BSc, PGCE (*Biology*)
Ms M Hurlin, BA Hons, PGCE (*English*)
Mrs A S Huysamen, BA Hons Design, PGCE Art & Design
    (*Art*)
Mr B Johnston, RFU Level 3 Coaching Rugby Union
    (*Head of Rugby*)
Mr M Karim, BSc, PGCE (*Mathematics*)
Mr D Keightley, BA Hons QTS (*PE*)
Mrs S M Knights, BSc, PGCE (*Geography, Head of
    Careers*)
Mr M P Lakin, MA, BA, PGCE (*English*)
Miss M T Lane, BA Hons History, PGCE (*Head of
    Religious Studies*)
Mr R J Lawrence, BA, PGCE (*English*)
Mrs E Libbey, BA Hons, PGCE (*Biology*)
Mr J G Martin, BA, PGCE (*Economics & Business Studies*)
Mr T A McIlwaine, BA Hons, PGCE (*Head of Art*)
Ms T E Medhurst, BA Hons, PGCE, Dip Dyslexia
    (*Academic Support*)
Mr N Morgan, BA Hons, MPhil, PGCE (*Languages*)
Miss S J Napier, BA, PGCE (*Geography*)
Mrs J Nash, BSocSc (*Economics*)
Mr M Parnham, BEd Hons, CertEd (*Head of Technology*)
Mr B J Peake, BSc, PGCE (*Physics*)
Dr J Perz, PhD, MSc, BSc, PGCE (*Mathematics*)
Miss S G Peters, BA Hons, QTS (*History & Politics*)
Miss H M Pothecary, BA Hons, PGCE (*Mathematics*)
Miss R A Potter, BSc Hons, PGCE (*Biology*)
Mr R Quesnel, MA, BA Hons, Agregation de Musique
    (*Director of Music*)
Mr N Raftery, MSc, BEng Hons, GTP (*Physics*)
Ms R A Razzak, BA Hons, PGCE (*Art*)
Mr O Richards, BSc, PGCE (*Chemistry*)
Mr I Richardson, BA Hons, PGCE (*Head of Computing*)
Ms T Robertson, BA Hons, PGCE (*English*)
Mr M A Schofield, MA (*Director of Drama*)
Mrs I A Seymour, BSc, MSc, GTP (*Mathematics*)
Ms N Shedden, BSc Hons, PGCE (*Chemistry*)
Mr D I Shingles, BSc Hons, PGCE (*Head of Girls'
    Hockey*)

Mr M T Stather, BSc Hons, PGCE (*Head of Biology*)
Mrs M Strachan, BSc Hons Computer Science, PGCE
    (*Mathematics*)
Mr C Tapscott, BA Hons, PGCE (*History*)
Mr M F Tierney, MChem, PGCE (*Head of L6th,
    Chemistry*)
Mr M P Tiley, MA (*History*)
Mrs S H Turner, MA, BA, PGCE (*Religious Studies,
    Extension Programme Coordinator*)
Mr O J Vella, MMath, MSc, PGCE (*Mathematics*)
Ms A von Kuhlberg, MA, BA Hons, QTS (*Classics*)
Mr N Waight, BA Hons, PGCE (*English, PSHE
    Coordinator*)
Mr G P Walters, BSc (*Biology, i/c Rowing, Head of Petre
    House*)
Miss J A Ward, MA, BA (*English*)
Mr J T Ward (*Head Tennis Coach*)
Miss K B Wardil, BA Hons, PGCE (*Music*)
Mrs J B Weaver, BA Hons, PGCE (*Food Technology*)
Mrs K Wilkinson, BSc, PGCE (*Physics*)
Mrs E L Williams, BA Hons, PGCE, GTP Art (*Art*)
Mrs L L Willis, BA Hons, PGCE (*Drama, Head of 1st
    Year*)
Miss L M Willis, BA, PGCE (*Languages*)
Ms S J Wragg, DPhil, MPhil, BA (*English*)
Mr O Yanez Vila, BA Hons, PGCE (*Religious Studies*)
Miss C N Yeoman, BA (*PE/Games*)

Librarian: Mrs I Monem
Head of Marketing and Admissions: Mrs E Wood
Headmistress's PA: Miss P Bell
Admissions Manager: Mrs D Palmer-Smith
Matron: Mrs C Jones

St Helen & St Katharine

Faringdon Road, Abingdon, Oxon OX14 1BE

Tel: 01235 520173
Fax: 01235 532934
email: admission@shsk.org.uk
website: www.shsk.org.uk
Twitter: @SHSKSchool
Facebook: @StHelenStKatharine

Founded in 1903, St Helen and St Katharine is an independent day school for girls in Abingdon, six miles south of
Oxford. Our 734 students study in a campus-style environment of beautiful Victorian and modern buildings, set in 22
acres of grounds.

St Helen's is a school for bright girls with enquiring
minds, a place where success is celebrated but not revered.
We recognise that every girl is different and will bring to her
school a unique combination of interests, abilities and aspirations. Our aim is to ensure that every student achieves success as she defines it, so that she can believe in herself, her
talents and abilities, and feel prepared and equipped for life
beyond school.

Academic. Our outstanding academic record makes us
one of the leading girls' schools in the country. In each of
the four school sections – Junior Department, Lower
School, Middle School and Sixth Form – stimulating and
challenging teaching reaches beyond the curriculum,
enabling our students to become effective and independent
learners. The curriculum offers a broad range of subjects
including separate sciences, four modern languages, Latin,
Greek and the expressive arts. An extensive range of opportunities for academic enrichment beyond lessons is offered,
such as attending lectures and conferences outside school,

visiting specialist speakers, discussion dinners and Oxbridge preparation.

Academic life in Sixth Form is about individual choice and learning beyond the ordinary business of a curriculum. Every student will choose three or four A Levels as the core of their academic work, some taught jointly with Abingdon School. Students can then add a St Katharine's Study award option – which includes the Extended Project Qualification, Global Perspectives (Camb), Arabic and coding – to suit their own academic interests. Success in A Levels enables leavers to secure places on their chosen courses at top UK universities, including a significant number who advance to Oxford and Cambridge.

Results in I/GCSE and A Level examinations are consistently outstanding; in 2018 93.6% of A Level grades were A*–B, and 98.1% of I/GCSE grades were A*–B/9–6.

Pastoral. Form Tutors and Support Tutors are at the heart of the pastoral system and the Director of Students, Heads of Section, Health Centre and counsellors all play a role in supporting students, making the pastoral network strong and accessible. We give students the space to explore their individuality in an environment which is big enough to celebrate a wide range of personalities and interests but small enough to know, to care and to spot when someone is having a good or bad day. Every member of the school community is part of our students' journey, from the smiling catering staff serving our award-winning food at lunchtime to our most lovable of school dogs.

Beyond. Our broad and varied extracurricular programme of 100+ clubs and activities plays a central role within school life. We actively encourage students to give new things a go – they can participate purely for fun or follow their strengths and excel through selective teams and groups, music and drama productions. From fencing and photography to philosophy and Mandarin, as well as activities such as the Duke of Edinburgh's Award and Young Enterprise, there are always opportunities to explore and extend interests, to make friends across age groups and, through personal achievement, to build confidence and self-belief.

Admissions. Students are admitted to the Junior Department at either 9+ or 10+ and to the senior school at 11+, 13+ and 16+. It may be possible to admit students into other years; enquiries should be made to the Admissions Office.

Scholarships. These are awarded to recognise excellence, ability and potential in one or more academic or extracurricular area. We offer a range of scholarships at 11+, 13+ and 16+ for academic ability, art, drama, music, sport and an all-rounder award.

Bursaries. If a student has the ability, imagination and drive to grasp the opportunities on offer at St Helen's, we would like to offer her that chance, regardless of the limitations of financial circumstance. The School offers means-tested bursaries up to 100% of fees from Year 7.

Fees per term (2018–2019). £5,490.

Charitable status. The School of St Helen and St Katharine Trust is a Registered Charity, number 286892. The Trust was established to promote and provide for the advancement of education of children in the United Kingdom and elsewhere; such education to be designed to give a sound Christian and moral basis to all students.

Governors:
Chair of Governors: Mr Kevan Leggett

Mrs Pauline Cakebread	Mrs Hazel Knott
Ms Sally Dicketts	Mr Dave Lea
Mr Adrian Dray	Mrs Joanne Loveridge
Mr Piers Heyworth	Mrs Jenny Mitchell
Mrs Rebecca Kashti	Mr Stephen Ramkaran

Clerk to the Governors: Mrs Fiona Jennings

Staff:

Leadership Team:

Headmistress: Mrs R Dougall, MA London, BA Bristol

Deputy Headmistress: Mrs B Stubley, MA Greenwich, BA Kent

Bursar: Mr D Eley, BSc London

Assistant Head, Director of Students: Mrs E Bedford, MA Oxford Brookes, BA Durham

Assistant Head, Director of Staff and IT: Mr J Hunt, MA St Andrews

Director of Communications and Marketing: Ms L Askgaard, MA Southern Denmark

Head of Sixth Form: Miss H Doherty, MA Warwick, BSc London

Senior Management Team:
Director of Studies: Mr C Morris, MA Oxon
Head of Middle School: Mrs H Nash, BA Southampton
Head of Lower School: Mrs K Taylor, BA Wales
Head of Junior Department (*Year 5 and 6*): Mrs N Bass, BSc Nottingham

Heads of Department:

Art, Design and Technology:
Ms J McDonald, MA Royal College of Art, BA Exeter College

Classics:
Miss D Spain, MA Oxon

Computer Science:
Mrs L Stringer, BSc East Anglia, PG Diploma

Drama:
Miss K Grandi, MA London, BA Bristol

English:
Mr J Muir, MLitt, MA St Andrews

Food and Nutrition:
Mrs B Alpers, BCApSc New Zealand

Geography:
Miss H Spencer, MA Cantab

History:
Miss D Smith, BA Durham

Mathematics:
Miss C Clarke, MSc, BA Exeter

Modern Languages:
Mrs L Probert, BA Bath

Music:
Ms H Rakowski, BA, MA Oxon

Physical Education:
Mrs L Turner, BSc Brunel

Politics, Economics and Pre-U:
Dr L Gribble, MA Münster, DPhil Oxon

Psychology:
Mrs K Collett, BSc Worcester

Religion, Philosophy and Ethics:
Ms K Meuleman, BEd Eeklo, Belgium, PG Worcester

Science:
Biology:
Mrs R James, BSc Bristol, MSc Oxon
Chemistry:
Dr G Smith, MChem St Andrews, PhD Cantab
Physics:
Mrs J Edwards, BSc Nottingham

St Lawrence College

Ramsgate, Kent CT11 7AE

Tel:	01843 572900 (Principal)
	01843 572912 (Junior School)
	01843 808080 (Bursar and General Office)
	01843 572931 (Registrar)
email:	principal@slcuk.com (Principal)
	jsoffice@slcuk.com (Junior School)
	bursar@slcuk.com (Bursar and General Office)
	admissions@slcuk.com (Registrar)
website:	www.slcuk.com
Twitter:	@slcMain
Facebook:	@slcukofficial

Co-educational, Day: age 3–18 years, Boarding: age 7–18 years.

Number of Pupils. Senior School: 453: 262 boys (118 boarders, 144 day), 191 girls (71 boarders, 120 day).

Junior School: 12 boarders, 188 day pupils (of whom 14 attend the Nursery).

Educating children from the age of 3 to 18 years, this safe and caring school is set in over 45 acres of spacious, stunning grounds which house beautiful old architecture combined with new modern builds and facilities. Founded in 1879, it is home to just over 650 day and boarding pupils from local, UK and international families and welcomes boarders from 7 years of age.

A medium-sized school – small enough to ensure that individual pupils receive the attention and care they require, but large enough to provide outstanding facilities – and with something of a reputation for punching well above its weight in school competitions!

Academic. St Lawrence has a long record of providing an excellent academic education within a supportive community, but is also modern in its outlook and very well suited to preparing pupils for a rapidly changing world. Class sizes are small and pastoral support is strong. Academic standards are high and impressive results are achieved across all years in the school. An extensive choice of GCSEs and A Levels are offered, with an excellent success rate of pupils going on to their first-choice university, including Oxbridge.

Boarding. Boarding pupils enjoy a 'home from home' experience, both in terms of comfort and atmosphere. In recent years, a massive programme of investment has created some truly remarkable facilities for boarders. All senior boarders are housed in single or double rooms with en-suite facilities and younger boarders are placed in rooms of between two and five pupils with modern streamlined en-suite bathrooms.

Facilities & Extracurricular. Continued investment saw a new Science, Art and Design Centre opened in May 2018. Sporting facilities are exceptional and expert coaching is provided at all levels in a variety of disciplines including hockey, rugby, netball and cricket. There is an olympic-standard waterbase hockey pitch and the Sports Centre houses a fitness suite, squash courts, climbing wall, dance studio and a large sports hall for badminton, basketball, etc. Music and drama flourish, enhanced by a 500-seat Theatre. Alongside the traditional chapel and library sits the school's modern coffee shop and boarders are able to use all of the facilities in the evenings and at weekends. All pupils benefit from an extensive activities programme which includes the CCF (Combined Cadet Force) and the Duke of Edinburgh's Award scheme, as well as chess, archery, golf, fencing, horse riding, table tennis, musical theatre, and many more activities.

Location. The school is set in a safe, self-contained campus situated within easy walking distance of the historic seaside town of Ramsgate. It has excellent transport links to the continent, being near both Dover and the Channel Tunnel. London is only 75 minutes away by high-speed rail link to St Pancras International. Both Gatwick and Heathrow are under 2 hours away.

Exam Results. Outstanding results are achieved by the most academic students who progress to top universities. The school is also regarded as a centre of excellence for 'value added'; students who need additional support perform well beyond expectation.

2018 GCSE results: A*–C grades in Maths and English: 82.4%; A*/A grades: 37%

2018 A Level results: A*–B grades: 40%; A*/A grades: 18%

Admissions. At 11+ admissions are based on an Interview with the Principal. A copy of a recent school report will also be required. Testing will be carried out where appropriate.

At 13+ the offer of a place will be dependent on the Common Entrance Examination, GCSE predictions and/or an assessment of a recent school report.

At 16+ the offer of a place will be dependent on a minimum of 5 GCSEs passes.

EU and Overseas Students will be admitted on the basis of current performance, references and a short language test as interviews are not always possible. Our special EFL centre will assess and integrate overseas pupils into the curriculum by offering a range of English teaching options, including an intensive English course.

Fees per term (2018–2019). Boarders £9,995–£11,945, Day £5,000–£5,333. Fees are due and payable before the commencement of the relevant school term. St Lawrence College offers generous sibling allowances.

Individual Private Tuition: £55 per hour. Individual Instrumental Music: £40 per hour.

Bursaries. Parents in HM Forces pay the MOD CEA (Continuity of Education Allowance) plus 10% of our main boarding and tuition fees. Bursaries are awarded annually to pupils in need of financial assistance and who are likely to make a positive contribution to the life of the school. Bursaries may be awarded to new or existing pupils of the College and pupils who have been awarded a scholarship which requires supplementing. Parents may apply to the Governors' Bursary Committee for assistance and will be required to complete a confidential grant application form. Bursaries are means tested.

Scholarships. Scholarships can be offered in Years 7–11 for outstanding academic ability, art, drama, music or sports disciplines, worth up to 25% of fees. Sixth Form scholarships are also available.

Charitable status. The Corporation of St Lawrence College is a Registered Charity, number 307921. It exists to provide education for children.

The Council:

President: C Laing

Vice-Presidents:
The Baroness Cox, BSc, MSc, FRCN
Sir Martin Laing, CBE, MA, FRICS [OL]
G H Mungeam, MA, DPhil
S Webley, MA
The Revd Canon Nigel M Walker
B J W Isaac [OL]
Dr C H R Niven, OBE, MA, Dip Ed, FRSA
M Iliff, MSc [OL]

Chairman: D W Taylor, MA Oxon, PGCE, FRSA

Members:
G E Page
J B Guyatt, MA
A G Burgess, TCNFF, ACP
J H Tapp, BSc
N G Marchant [OL]
T L Townsend, LLB [OL]
M J Bolton, MBE, BA
J Laslett, BA Hons, FCMA [OL]
Rev G Warren, RN Hon, DMin Oxon
J Challender, BEd, MA
Rev S Rae, PG Dip, BA Hons
G Carter, FRICS, FCABE
G Sanderson

[OL] *Old Lawrentian*

Clerk to the Governors and Bursar: J A Connelly, MA,
    MBA, BEng, CEng, MIET

Principal: **A Spencer**, MA Oxon, ACA

Deputy Head (*Pastoral*): D Jackson, BA Durham
Deputy Head (*Academic*): W M Scott, BSc St Andrews
Registrar: Dr D M Smith, BA Hons Wales, PGCE
    Cambridge, MPhil Cambridge, MA Bath, PhD London
Chaplain: Revd P R Russell, BA, Dip Theo Min, PG Dip
    OM, CCCU (*Religious Studies*)
Assistant Head, 6th Form: E Matthews BA West of
    England (*Drama*)

Heads of Department:
A E Bailey, BEd London, MA Sussex (*Head of PSHE*)
Dr K E Barwell, PhD Kent, BSc Kent (*Head of Chemistry*)
J D J Bowyer, MusB Hons Manchester, PGCE (*Director of
    Music*)
D Brooks, BSc Kent (*Head of Mathematics*)
C Brown, BA Exeter (*Head of Economics and Business
    Studies*)
S J Clark, BEd Hons De Montfort (*Head of Academic PE*)
S Fraczek, BA Cambridge, MA Durham (*Head of English*)
R J Higgins, BSc Manchester (*Head of Modern Languages*)
N Hodge, BA Hons Birmingham City, PGCE (*Head of Art*)
A J Izzard, BA Chichester (*Director of Sport*)
S F King, BA RSA/Cambridge (*Head of EAL*)
E Kouthouri, BSc N&C Univ, Athens (*Head of Science,
    Head of Physics*)
T Moulton, BA Leeds (*Head of History, Universities &
    Careers*)
K B Parker, BA Hons Manchester Poly (*Head of Design
    Technology*)
E L Pegden, BSc Greenwich (*Head of Chemistry*)
J M Rawbone, BA Leeds, PG Dip Aspergers Sheffield
    Hallam (*Head of AEN*) [OL]
J E Van-Ebo, BA CCCU, MA CCCU (*Head of Religious
    Studies*)
N Watts, BA Hons Brighton, QTS (*Head of Geography*)
R B Wilkening, BA London, MA Kent (*Head of ICT*) [OL]
E J Young, BA Chichester (*Head of Drama*)

Houses and Housemasters/mistresses:
Bellerby: A Izzard
Clifford: A N Humphrys, BA Westminster
Deacon: G O Jones
Laing: F E Jackson, BA Leeds
Lodge: S Palacios, BMus CCCU, MMus CCCU
Newlands: N J Watts, BA Brighton
Tower: E L Pegden, BSc Greenwich
Kirby: C E Sharp, MEng Sheffield [OL]

Junior School
Head: Mrs E Rowe, BA Hons, PGCE

St Leonards School

St Andrews, Fife KY16 9QJ

Tel: 01334 472126
Fax: 01334 476152
email: contact@stleonards-fife.org
website: www.stleonards-fife.org
Twitter: @StLeonards_Head
Facebook: @stleonardsschool

Motto: *Ad Vitam*

Situated in the heart of idyllic St Andrews, St Leonards offers co-educational boarding and day education for ages five to 18, combining academic achievement and opportunity with an inspirational atmosphere.

There are approximately 535 pupils in the School, with an equal number of boys and girls and around 120 boarders.

Ethos. Founded in 1877, St Leonards aims to prepare young people for the challenges of life ahead and to provide them with the skills and abilities that will enable them to step into the world with confidence and integrity. We offer a broad, rigorous education and exceptional opportunities, while instilling confidence, responsibility and independence.

Location and Campus. St Leonards combines a beautiful, historic campus with the cultural and academic buzz that comes from being in the heart of the university town of St Andrews.

The School is situated in a picturesque and secure self-contained campus within the medieval walls of the former St Andrews Abbey. Our campus has served as a place of learning since the 16th century and contains several buildings of historical significance, including our library, a building once used by Mary Queen of Scots as lodgings.

Students at St Leonards have sandy beaches, historic landmarks and world-famous golf courses on their doorstep, as well as the friendly town of St Andrews itself, in which our pupils are made to feel very much part of the community.

St Andrews is just 45 minutes from Edinburgh and just 20 minutes from Dundee (a one-hour flight from London).

Curriculum. St Leonards is the only school in Scotland to have an all-International Baccalaureate Diploma Sixth Form. St Leonards has been ranked by the Sunday Times as the Top Independent School in Scotland for IB/A Level Results for three years in a row.

The Senior School (Years 8–11) prepares boys and girls for GCSEs – typically around ten.

The Junior School (Years 1–7) follows the International Baccalaureate Primary Years Programme, delivering a seamless and coherent transition into the Senior School.

University Link. The School has close links with the University of St Andrews and each year appoints an Associate Researcher, a postgraduate student who provides a link for the pupils to the research community at the University. St Leonards students also have access to the University Library and regularly attend special lectures.

Sport, Drama, Art and Music. Students regularly enjoy success on the playing field in sports including rugby, lacrosse, hockey, tennis and football. They are encouraged to make the most of living just a few hundred yards from the most famous golf links in the world. The School has a strong relationship with SALJGA (St Andrews Links Junior Golf Association), as well as its very own world-class three-tier school Golf Programme.

All pupils have the opportunity to learn a wide variety of musical instruments, leading to ABRSM recognition.

Drama students have the chance to take part in a number of professional quality productions, which are staged both in School and at the neighbouring Byre Theatre. Art students at St Leonards show off their inspiring work every year in an exhibition that is open to the public.

Co-Curricular. There is an extensive range of activities in which students can take part, including Duke of Edinburgh's Award expeditions, falconry classes, rock climbing, skiing and debating. Foreign trips are organised throughout the school year, with recent destinations including New York, Rome, the Italian Alps and Dresden. Community awareness is important at St Leonards and in the past few years our pupils have raised over £30,000 for charity.

Boarding. The School excels in its boarding provision. Thanks to an ambitious £3m refurbishment programme, students live in modern, stylish comfort in a country house setting. According to a Care Commission inspection report, St Leonards offers its boarding pupils, "an outstanding, Scottish, boarding experience", with the quality of care and support and the quality of the environment rated as "excellent". Full, flexi and weekly boarding options are available from the age of 11.

Fees per term (2018–2019). Junior School: £2,900 (Years 1–3), £3,469 (Years 4–5), £3,889 (Years 6–7) Boarding £7,582 (Years 6–7). Senior School and Sixth Form: Day £4,736; Boarding £7,582 (Year 8), £11,551 (Years 9–13).

Admission. Applications can be considered for any year group, at any time during the School year. Bursary support may be given, based on need. Full details are available from the Registrar.

Charitable status. St Leonards School is a Registered Charity, number SC010904.

Members of Council:
Chair: Prof Verity Brown, FRSE
Mrs Victoria Collison-Owen, MA
Mr Ken Dalton, BSc Hons, CEng
Mr Paul Dollman, BSc Hons, CA
Mr Neil Donaldson, MSc
Mrs Laura Jacks, JD
Mr Alistair J Lang, BLE Hons, LLB, Dip LP
Col Martin Passmore, MA, GCGI, FRSA
Mr Philip Petersen, BSc, MBA
Mrs Heidi Purvis, BA, PGCE
Mr Sandy Richardson, MA, MBA, FRRSA
Mrs Fenella Taylor, BA Hons
Mrs Clare Wade
Ms Charlie Wilson, BSc, FCCA

Academic Staff:

Headmaster: **Michael Carslaw**, BSc Hons Newcastle, MBA Nottingham, PhD London

Deputy Headmaster & Deputy Head Pastoral: Geoffrey Jackson-Hutt, BSc Hons, PhD Southampton
Deputy Head Academic: Dawn Pemberton-Hislop, BA Hons Sheffield, MBA Keele
Head of Sixth Form: Aileen Rees, MA Hons Cambridge
Diploma Curriculum Coordinator: Ben Seymour, BSc Hons UEA Norwich
Head of Year 10 & Pre IB: Andrew Durward, BEd Hons Edinburgh
Head of Years 8 & 9: Dan Barlow, MA Hons St Andrews
Middle Years Programme Coordinator: Kathryn McGregor, BA Hons Southampton

Art & Design:
Donna Rae, MA Glasgow, BFA Chicago
Margaret Behrens, BA Hons Edinburgh, Dip PG Edinburgh
Lisa Donald, BEd Manchester
Linda Jackson, BA Hons DJCA Dundee

Karen Wowk, MA Hons St Andrews
William Clark, MA Winchester, BA Hons Dundee

Classics:
Andrew Lang, MA Hons St Andrews
Tina Lang, BA Hons Sheffield, PhD St Andrews

Economics:
John Lambert, MA Hons Dundee
Paula Prudencio-Aponte, BSc Bolivia, PG Dip St Andrews, MSc Manchester

English:
Alfonso Iannone, MA Hons Edinburgh, PG Dip Edinburgh
Rupert Crisswell, BA York, MEd Cambridge
Katherine Gilbertson, MA Hons St Andrews [maternity leave]
Nicola Greener, BA Hons Newcastle, PG Dip Newcastle
Denise Johnston, BA Hons Cardiff
Mick Kitson, BA Hons Newcastle [maternity cover]
Vanessa Samuel, BA Hons Cambridge

Geography:
Amy Henderson, MA Hons Dundee

History & Politics:
Jam Fulton, BA Hons Sitrling, MA Hons Durham
Lorna Greenwood, MA Hons Edinburgh, Cert Ed Studies London

Learning Support:
Gillian Greenwood, MA Hons Cambridge
Lisa Donald, BEd Manchester
Ann Stephens, BEd Dundee

Library:
Angela Tawse, MA St Andrews, PG Dip St Andrews, MA UCL, MCLIP

Mathematics:
Russell Hall, BSc Hons St Andrews
Jonathan Edwards, BEd Hons Wales
Bryce Graham, BA Hons Open, BSc Glasgow
Paul McDonald, BSc Open, MSc Napier
Kristina Struck, State Exam MA Berlin
Louise Toye, BSc Hons St Andrews

Modern Languages:
Irene Kretschmann, BA Bonn
Rie Adya BA MA Rissho, MPhil PhD Delhi
Susana Aranzana-Gonzalez, BA, MA, CAP Valladolid
Yulia Barlow, BA Yaroslavl, MA Hons St Andrews
Tania Bermejo-Vanquez, BA Granada
Anne Bavaj, First State Examination MA Bonn, Second State Examination Aachen
Anna Beck, BA Columbia, MBA Cornell
Barbara Beedham, BSc Hons Salford
Dawn Cremonese, MA Hons St Andrews, MA, TESOL Leicester
Marion Donlon, MA Hons St Andrews
Nora Gannon, Masters History of Law Aix-Marseilles
Elena Germanino, MA Torino, BA Torino
Kathryn McGregor, BA Hons Southampton
Ronan McLaughlin
Rasa Ruseckiene, MA Hons Vilinus, PhD Moscow
Sheena Russo
Christina Steele, MA Hons St Andrews
Haiyan Wang, BA MA Sichuan, Chengdu, MSc Dundee

Music:
Fiona Love, BMus Hons Glasgow
Marjorie Cleghorn, LGSM Napier (*Music School Secretary*)
Robin Bell, BMus Glasgow, ARCO London, ARSCM Salisbury, PGCSE Edinburgh, Cert TESOL Edinburgh
Douglas Clark, Dip Mus Ed RSAMD

Kenneth Cormack, BMus Hons RCS
Martin Dibbs, MA, MLitt, PhD St Andrews, DMS ARMC
Marie Downes, BA Hons Sussex
Winston Emmerson, BSc Hons Rhodes, MSc, PhD UPE
Stuart Foggo
Joseph Fleetwood, BA Hons RSAMD, PG Dip RCM,
    MMus RSAMD
Ruth Irons, GDJ St Andrews, MA Hons Oxford
Jessica Long, MA Hons St Andrews, Dip ABRSM, PG Dip
    RCS
Dorothy McCabe, GRSM, ARCM, ATCL, Cert Ed London
Melanie O'Brien, Dip TCL TCM London, ALCM, LLCM
    Napier
Megan Read, MA Glasgow, PG Dip Mus RSAMD
Suzannah Rice, BA Hons Southampton
Lynne Ruark, DRSAM, LRAM, Glasgow, CertEd
    Edinburgh
Toni Russell, BA Hons Applied Music Strathclyde
Paul Shiells, BEd Hons Aberdeen
Sally Shiells, BEd Hons Aberdeen, MMus Aberdeen

Physical Education:
Mark Baxter, BEd Hons Edinburgh
Fintan Bonner, BA Ireland
Louise Carroll BEd Hons Edinburgh
Rosie Dawson, BA Hons Bangor
Paula Geatons, BEd Hons Edinburgh
Neil Hislop BEd Hons Jordanhill
Neil Ronaldson Dip PE Jordanhill
Andrew Turnbull, BSc Napier

Psychology:
Lin McLean, PhD St Andrews, BSc Hons Open, MEd
    Sheffield, CPsychol

Religious Studies:
Susannah Adrain, MA Hons Dundee

Science:
Sophie Pollard, BSc Hons Plymouth, MSRC
Patrick Smith, BSc Glasgow
Rachel Deegan, BA Oxford [maternity leave]
Catherine Dunn, BSc Hons, PhD St Andrews
Sophie Pollard, BSc Hons Plymouth
Mary Kennovin, BSc Hons Portsmouth Polytechnic, PhD
    St Andrews
Charlotte Kirby, BSc Hons St Andrews
Robert MacGregor, BSc Hons Edinburgh
Craig Martin, BSc Hons St Andrews
Anna Radons-Harris, BSc Hons Lancaster
Gillian Wilson, BSc Glasgow
Mark Arnold, HNC Dundee
Alison Hill, MSc Glasgow, BSc Hons Aberdeen PhD
    Belfast

Theatre:
Nichola McQuade-Powerll, BEd Hons London
Elizabeth Dunsmuir, DipPE
Laura Stewart, MA Hons Kent

St Leonards Junior School:

Headmistress: Ms Eve Moran, BA Hons Hull

Senior Staff:
Julianne Pennycook, BEd Hons Jordanhill (*Deputy*)

Nicola Arkwright, BEd Hons Coventry
Marina Barclay, PDA (*Classroom Assistant*)
Duncan Barrable, BCOM South Australia, GDTO South
    Australian (*Head of Outdoor Learning*)
Ailsa Beebee, BEd Dundee
Claire Boissiere, MA Hons Dundee (*Lower School
    Coordinator*)

Diane Cormack, BSc Hons St Andrews (*Mathematics &
    Science Coordinator*)
Valerie Donald, MA Hons St Andrews
Martin Donlon, MA Hons St Andrews
Anna Fisher, MA Hons Dundee
Teresa Flynn, MA Hons Edinburgh
Annabel Lindsay, BA Hons Oxford Brookes
Kathleen McKimmon, BCom Edinburgh
Adele Neave, BSc Hons Glasgow School of Art
Nicola Nejman, MA Hons St Andrews
Billie Paterson Herd, NC Childcare & Education
Caroline Soutar
Laura Stewart, MA Hons Kent

Bursar: Gerald Brown, BSc Dist Heriot-Watt, Dip H-WU,
    FCMI
Registrar: Caroline Routledge, BSc Hons Glamorgan, PhD
    Cardiff

St Mary's School Ascot

St Mary's Road, Ascot, Berks SL5 9JF

Tel: 01344 296600 (Main Switchboard)
            01344 296614 (Admissions)
email: admissions@st-marys-ascot.co.uk
website: www.st-marys-ascot.co.uk

St Mary's School Ascot is a Roman Catholic boarding
school founded by the Religious of the Institute of the
Blessed Virgin Mary. St Mary's today is a self-governing,
self-financing school.

Founded in 1885, the school is set in 55 acres within easy
reach of London and Heathrow and close to the M4, M3 and
M25 motorways.

Numbers on roll. Boarders 363, Day pupils 23.

Age range. 11–18.

Method of Entry. 11+ and 13+ School's own examination and interview. There is a small entry at Sixth Form.

Scholarships and Bursaries. At 11+ and 13+ there are
three Academic Scholarships available worth up to 5% of
the fees.

At 16+ there is one Academic Scholarship available
worth up to 5% of the fees and the Sixth Form Science
Scholarship worth up to 5% of the fees.

One Music Scholarship worth 5% of the fees and free of
charge musical instrument or vocal tuition for up to three
30-minute lessons per week is awarded annually to a pupil
entering the School at 11+ or 13+. Candidates must have
qualified to at least Grade V on the first study instrument at
the time of application.

One Art Scholarship worth up to 5% of the fees is
awarded annually to a pupil entering the School at 11+, 13+
or 16+.

One All-Rounder Scholarship is is awarded annually to a
pupil entering the School at 11+ and another at 13+.

One Sports Scholarship worth up to 5% of the fees is
awarded annually to a pupil entering the School at 13+.

Means-tested Bursaries are available.

Fees per term (2018–2019). Boarders £12,930, Day
pupils £9,210.

Curriculum. All pupils follow a broad curriculum to
GCSE including Religious Education, English, History,
Geography, Maths, Biology, Physics, Chemistry, French,
German, Italian, Spanish, Latin, Music, Drama, Art and
Design, Computer Science and Physical Education. Tuition
is also available in Piano, most String and Wind Instru-
ments, Ballet, Tap Dancing, Speech and Drama, Ceramics
and Craft activities, Tennis, Photography.

All pupils are prepared for GCSE at 16+ and typically take 10 subjects.

Sixth Formers have a choice of 25 A Level subjects and normally study 4 subjects. Interview, CV and course choice preparation is offered to all Upper Sixth including Oxbridge candidates. They are encouraged to undertake some of the many extra activities on offer and develop skills outside their A Level curriculum. Sixth Formers also have their own tutor who liaises closely with the Careers Specialist. Careers advice forms an integral part of the curriculum. This is supported by work experience, work shadowing placements and talks from external speakers, including Ascot Alumnae. The majority of Sixth Formers go on to university, and preparation is offered to Oxbridge candidates.

The School is a member of Inspiring Futures, which provides careers information, advice and guidance.

Religious Education is an integral part of the curriculum and the chapel holds a central position in the life of the school.

Sport. A varied programme is offered depending on age group. It includes Netball, Hockey, Gym, Swimming, Rounders, Tennis, Squash, Badminton and Athletics.

Purpose-built sports complex with sports hall, dance studio, squash courts and fitness suite. A floodlit 400m athletics track and hockey pitch provides a year-round, all-weather sports facility.

Drama. Performing Arts Centre which includes a flexible auditorium with lighting catwalks and control room with teaching facilities, fully-equipped drama studio and make-up and dressing rooms.

Art, Drama, Music, Science, Modern Languages and English. Specialist buildings are provided for all of these subjects and all pupils are encouraged to develop their musical, artistic, scientific and linguistic skills.

Libraries. The senior and junior libraries form the academic heart of the school. The senior library was built to meet the specific needs of Year 11 and Sixth Form girls and includes seminar rooms, which are used for teaching and careers advice.

Other Activities. Senior pupils are encouraged to participate in Community Service Projects, and those interested may enter The Duke of Edinburgh's Award scheme. There is a wide range of club activities for all ages, and, as a termly boarding school, generous provision is made for evening and weekend activities.

Charitable status. St Mary's School Ascot is a Registered Charity, number 290286. Its aim is to provide an excellent education in a Christian atmosphere.

Board of Governors:
Chairman: The Hon Mr M Hunt

Mrs A Ayton	Professor R Parish
Mrs C Colacicchi	The Revd Dr D Power, BA,
Miss J Ebner	BDSTL
Mr P Gaynor	
Mr E Horswell	Sr M Robinson
Mr P McKenna	Mr V Thompson
Mr G Moore	Ms C Vaughan

Council:
Chairman: Mr G van Cutsem, FRICS

Mr M Armour	The Lord Hemphill
Mr N Davidson	Baroness S Hogg, MA
Mr P Davis	The Hon Mrs O Polizzi

Senior Management Team:

Headmistress: Mrs M Breen, BSc Exeter, MSc Manchester

Headmistress Elect: Mrs D Staunton, BA York, MA York, PGCE

Senior Deputy Headmistress: Mrs V Barker, BSc Reading, PGCE

Bursar: Mr G Brand, BA Leeds

Academic Deputy Head: Mrs B Breedon, BEd Queen's Belfast, MSc Ulster

Pastoral Deputy Headmistress: Mrs C Ellott, BA Oxon, MA London, PGCE

Director of External Communications: Mr C Ellott, LLB UCL, BA OU, PGCE

Director of Sixth Form: Dr G Williams, BA MA Cambridge, EdD Cardiff

Support Staff:

Mrs R Brand (*Chapel Housekeeper/Resources Assistant*)
Mrs J Carrington (*Catering Manager*)
Mr T Clark (*Estate Manager*)
Mrs P Dewes, BA Leeds (*Development Director and Assistant to the Headmistress*)
Mrs D Fossey (*Housekeeper and Lettings Manager*)
Mrs F Green (*School Secretary*)
Mrs C Holland (*Assistant Registrar*)
Mrs S Hughes (*PA to the Bursar*)
Mrs R Johnson (*Estate Manager's Administrator*)
Mrs C Leneghan (*Alumnae Director*)
Mrs N MacRobbie, LLB Southampton (*Recruitment Administrator*)
Mrs E Mari Sanmillan (*Accounts Assistant*)
Mrs E May (*Accountant*)
Ms C Morgan-Tolworthy (*Accounts Assistant*)
Mrs C Radford (*Reprographics/Resources*)
Mrs C Sitta, Lic Phil I Zürich (*Administrative Assistant to the Senior Deputy Head*)
Mrs V West (*Administrative Assistant to the Academic Deputy Head*)
Mrs S Young (*Registrar*)

Reception Staff:

Mrs S Hickmott (*Receptionist*)
Mrs S Austin (*Saturday Receptionist*)
Mrs F Green (*School Secretary/Receptionist*)
Mrs A Hoolan (*Friday and Weekend Evening Receptionist*)
Mrs L Peacock (*Sunday Receptionist*)
Mrs C Roberts (*Evening Receptionist*)
Mr S Jackson (*Night Porter*)
Mr G Watts (*Night Porter*)

Heads of House:

Mary Ward: Mrs K Jenkinson, BSc Nottingham, MA London, PGCE
Babthorpe: Mrs H West, BA Surrey, PGCE
Bedingfeld: Mr T Parsons, MA York and Mrs K Parsons, BA York, MA Warwick
Poyntz: Ms R Toner, BA Cantab, MA London, PGCE
Rookwood: Mrs H Jansen, BEd Central School of Speech & Drama
Wigmore: Mrs V Hutchinson, BA Cork, Dip CompSc, DipEd HDGC and Mr N Hutchinson, GBSM, ARCO, ARCM, LTCL

Sixth Form:

Dr G Williams, BA MA Cambridge, EdD Cardiff (*Director of Sixth Form*)
Mrs B Chandler, LLB Southampton (*Administrative Assistant to the Director of Sixth Form*)
Mrs E Crean (*US Universities Advisor*)
Mr D Hillman, BA Oxon, MSc London (*Oxbridge Coordinator*)
Mrs H Williams, BA Cantab (*Administrative Assistant to the Director of Sixth Form*)

Pastoral and Residential Staff:

Mrs C Marchant, BA CCAT, PGCE (*Senior Boarding Mistress*)

The Revd Dr D Power (*School Chaplain*)
Mrs M McGeown, RGN SCM (*School Nurse*)
Mrs P Perera, RGN RM (*School Nurse*)
Mrs L Steele-Perkins, RGN RM (*p/t School Nurse*)
Dr G Tasker, MBRBS, DRCOG, MRCGP, DHC (*School Doctor*)
Mrs J Anderson
Mrs S Blackman
Miss J Bowen
Mrs B Green
Miss K Horwood, BA Plymouth, FRGS (*Deputy Senior Boarding Mistress*)
Ms R Kelly
Mrs S Malyon, CertEd, MA Ed
Miss D Nairne
Miss V Shipley
Miss V Swire
Miss S Tate

Graduate Assistants:
Miss E Came, BSC Cardiff Metropolitan
Miss F Davies, BA Oxford
Miss R Nelson-Owens, BA UCL, PGCE
Miss M Stépanian, BA , Dijon, PGCE
Miss H Waters, BA , York
Miss N Williams, BMus, Royal Holloway

Cover Staff:
Ms H Broad, BA South Bank (*Cover Supervisor/ Department Administrator*)
Mrs A Heath (*Cover/Lunch Supervisor*)
Mrs S McLachlan (*Cover/Lunch Supervisor*)
Mrs E White (*Cover Supervisor/Department Administrator*)

Academic Departments:

Art and Design:
Miss C Atwill, BA Loughborough, PGCE (*Head of Department*)
Miss L Clarke, BA Plymouth
Miss L Green, BA De Montfort, Reigate College of Art & Design, PGCE (*Art and Design*)
Mrs A Harle, BA Cardiff, PGCE
Mrs X Harrison, BA Wales, PGCE (*Ceramics*)
Mrs E Klein
Mrs G Neville, BA Coventry, MA Edinburgh (*Photography*)
Miss L Dawson (*Art Technician*)

Classics:
Mrs L Povey, BA Nottingham, MPhil London (*Head of Department*)
Mr M Clennett, BA Oxon, MA King's College London, PGCE
Mrs A Golding, BA Bristol, PGCE
Ms I Inskip, BA Oxford, PGCE
Miss Z Lackovic, MEd Zagreb, MA King's College London, QTS

Drama:
Miss A Lynch, Mountview Academy (*Director of Drama*)
Mr M Barker (*Rose Theatre Manager*)
Mr S Brownett, BA Southampton, MA UCL, PGCE
Mr C Dexter, Dip ALRA (*Assistant Drama Technician*)
Mrs C Ellott, BA Oxon, MA London, PGCE
Mrs H Jansen, BEd Central School of Speech & Drama

Economics & Politics:
Mrs E Crean, BA Cork
Mr D Hillman, BA Oxon, MSc London
Mr P Smith, BA Wales, MA Warwick, PGCE
Mr I Walker, BA Liverpool JM
Dr G Williams, BA MA Cambridge, EdD Cardiff

English:
Mrs L Waltho, BA, MLitt Newcastle (*Head of Department*)
Mrs K Anderson, BA Massachusetts, PGCE
Mr C Ellott, LLB UCL, BA OU, PGCE
Miss F McDermott, BA Cantab, PGCE
Mr T Parsons, MA York (*History of Art*)
Dr D Richards, BA MA PhD King's College London, PGCE
Mrs D Staunton, BA York, MA York, PGCE
Mrs M Vandenberg, BA London, PGCE

Food Technology:
Ms J Sherrard-Smith, BSc Westminster, PGCE
Mrs S Malyon, Cert Ed Gloucs, MA Ed OU

Geography:
Miss S Watson, BSc Reading, PGCE
Miss L Pitt, BSc Bath Spa, PGCE
Mrs H Tarasewicz, BA Cantab, MA Cantab

History:
Mr P Smith, BA Swansea, MA Warwick, PGCE
Miss J Brown, BA, MA Roehampton
Miss R Evans, BA Durham, PGCE
Mr D Hillman, BA Oxon, MSc London, PGCE

History of Art:
Miss H Oakden, BA Manchester, MA Courtauld (*Head of Department*)
Mr T Parsons, MA York

ICT & Computing:
Ms B Hudson-Reed, BA Natal Univ, HDE, FDE (*Head of Department*)
Mrs V Hutchinson, BA Cork, DipComSc, DipEd, HDGC
Miss V Parsons, BSc Portsmouth
Mr R Wakeford
Mr A West, BA UWE Bristol (*Network Services Manager*)
Mr A Luther (*Network Services Supervisor*)
Miss N Arnold (*Network Services Technician*)
Mr T Nicholson (*Network Service Engineer*)
Mr M Shrestha, BSc Surrey (*Junior Systems Developer*)

Mathematics:
Mr S Wilson, BSc Royal Holloway, QTS (*Head of Department*)
Mrs V Barker, BSc Reading, PGCE
Mrs B Breedon, BEd Queen's Belfast, BSc Ulster
Mrs A Cimoli, PhD Pisa, PGCE
Miss C Hicks, BSc Royal Holloway, PGCE
Mrs K Jenkinson, BSc Nottingham, MA London, PGCE
Mrs J Love, BA Sussex, PGCE
Miss S McCarthy-Brown, BSc Cardiff, QTS
Mrs G Miles, BSc London, PGCE
Mrs S Mwanje, BSc Makerere, MSc Hertfordshire, PGCE
Miss C Rutherford, BSc Loughborough, PGCE
Dr R Torcal Serrano, PhD Surrey, PGCE
Mr S Wilson, BSc London, QTS

Modern Languages:
Mme E Cook, DEUG Licence Toulouse, Adv Dip English Studies, PGCE (*Head of Department, French*)
Miss N Bourguilleau, Licence Maitrice Nantes, PGCE (*French*)
Mrs R Cabrera, Lic en traducción Granada and GTP, Cilt and Leeds Univ (*Spanish*)
Miss E Caretti, MA Milan, PGCE (*Italian*)
Mrs S Chasemore (*German Assistant*)
Ms T Correa-Sanchez, BA Salamanca (*Spanish*)
Miss S Doyotte, DEUG Nancy, PGCE (*French*)
Mrs L Harrison, BA Oxford, MA Oxon, PGCE (*French*)
Mlle M Hervi, Licence Maîtrise Rennes, PGCE (*French*)
Mrs M Kuo (*Mandarin*)
Mrs C Marchant, BA CCAT, PGCE (*French & Italian*)

Mrs S Webb, BA Cantab, PGCE (*German*)

Music:
Mrs A Rees, BA Surrey, MMus Royal Holloway, PGCE (*Director of Music*)
Mrs L Flockhart (*Secretary*)
Mr N Hutchinson, ARCO, ARCM, GBSM, LTCL
Mr J Rees, ARCM
Miss J Statham (*Music Assistant*)

Physical Education & Sport:
Miss G Eamer, BSc Coventry, PGCE (*Head of Department*)
Mr A Bennett, BSc St Mary's (*Head of Tennis*)
Mrs A Blakeway, BSc Birmingham
Miss S Bruce (*Sports Assistant*)
Mr B Challenger
Mrs J Freeme, BEd Johannesburg, PGCE
Miss A Haylett, Dip Sports Psychology, Newcastle College
Mr R Huysamen, BSc Stellenbosch, PGCE
Mrs L Lock, BSc Worcester, PGCE
Miss H Lovett (*Sports Assistant*)
Mrs J Obertell (*Department Administrator*)
Miss A Povey (*Lifeguard*)
Miss C Routledge (*Lifeguard*)
Miss S Windle, BSc, PGCE De Montfort
Mrs A Wright, BA OU, CertEd Chelsea College

Religious Studies:
Mr J Ware, BA Oxford, MA Oxford, PGCE (*Head of Department*)
Mr A Croft, BA King's College
Mr P Golden, BA Stirling, MA London, PGCE
Ms R Toner, BA Cantab, MA London, PGCE
Mrs M Vandenberg, BA London, PGCE
Mrs H West, BA Surrey, PGCE

Science:
Mr S Barker, BSc Bangor, PGCE (*Head of Department, Biology*)
Miss L Atkinson, MSc UCL, PGCE (*Chemistry*)
Mrs M Breen, BSc Exeter, MSc Manchester (*Physics*)
Mr R Dibsdall, BSc Exeter, MSc Exeter, PGCE (*Biology*)
Mrs A Finlay, BSc Anglia Ruskin, PGCE (*Biology*)
Mrs C George, BSc Durham, MA Nottingham, PGCE (*Biology*)
Mrs C Hutchings, BSc Oxon (*Physics*)
Dr D Lampus, MSci Cagliari, PhD Nottingham, PGCE (*Chemistry*)
Mrs A Lyne, BSc Milan, MSc Loughborough, PGCE (*Chemistry*)
Mr D May, BA Manchester, PGCE (*Physics*)
Mr D Riding, MPhys Sheffield, PGCE (*Physics*)
Mrs S Senior, BSc Durham, PGCE (*Physics*)
Mrs J Ford, ONC and HNC Med Lab Sciences (*Senior Technician*)
Mrs S Howard, BSc UMIST, MSc UMIST (*Technician*)
Mrs K Sidhu, BSc Wolverhampton (*Technician*)

Special Needs:
Mrs B Breedon, BEd Queen's Belfast, BSC Ulster (*Most Able Coordinator*)
Mrs A Bingham, BA Durham, PGCE (*Learning Support Teacher*)
Mrs M Vandenberg, BA London, PGCE (*SENCO*)
Dr G Williams, BA MA Cambridge, EdD Cardiff (*Academies Coordinator*)

Careers:
Dr G Williams, BA MA Cambridge, EdD Cardiff
Mrs B Chandler, LLB Southampton

Duke of Edinburgh's Award Scheme:
Mrs A Wright, BA OU, CertEd Chelsea College (*Coordinator*)
Mr P Edmunds, CertEd, MA Oxford Brookes
Mr N Jones, BSc Wales, MSc Wales, PGCE
Mrs F Kenden, CertEd ML
Mrs M Vandenberg, BA London, PGCE (*Administrator*)

Exam Office:
Mrs E White (*Examinations Officer*)
Mlle V Feuillet, DEUG Licence Maîtrise Sorbonne, PGCE
Mrs C Davidson (*Invigilator*)
Mr P Gallagher (*Invigilator*)
Mr N Hoad (*Invigilator*)
Mrs A Nash (*Invigilator*)

Skills for Life:
Mrs S Malyon, CertEd Gloucs, MA OU

Independent Listener:
Mrs M Jemmett, HE Dip Counselling

St Mary's Calne

Curzon Street, Calne, Wiltshire SN11 0DF

Tel: 01249 857200
Fax: 01249 857207
email: admissions@stmaryscalne.org
website: www.stmaryscalne.org
Twitter: @StMarysCalne
Facebook: @stmaryscalne
LinkedIn: www.cgacalne.org/linkedin

St Mary's Calne is a boarding and day school of around 365 girls aged 11–18. Around 80% of the girls board and it is a rich boarding life, with all girls taking part in the full curriculum and extra-curricular activities on offer. Situated two hours west of London, escorted travel is provided to and from London and airports at all holidays and exeats.

St Mary's is committed to providing a broad and fulfilling education that will challenge and inspire its pupils, as well as helping them to achieve excellent public examination results. All girls go on to higher education; the majority are awarded places at their first-choice university and a good number go on to Oxbridge every year. A new, purpose-built Sixth Form Centre, a tailor-made lecture programme, a Women in Corporate Culture Conference, debating competitions, careers advice, leadership roles and much more prepare the girls for university and beyond.

Pastoral Care. The school, which has a strong Sixth Form (120+ girls) is renowned for its outstanding pastoral care. Every girl is known and cared for as an individual and has a Tutor to support and guide her through every aspect of school life, from organisational skills and subject choices through to university application. St Mary's organises boarding specifically on the criteria of age. Within the seven residential Houses girls live with their own age group. This offers the maximum opportunity to establish firm friendships and fellowship across the year group which will last throughout school and beyond. Girls are therefore cared for by Housemistresses who are particularly aware of the needs of their charges' own individual age group.

Extra-Curricular Activities. Outside the classroom, there is a wide range of extra-curricular activities, clubs and societies. St Mary's opened a new £2.55 million Sports Complex in May 2018 and there have been many individual and team successes in sport. Large numbers of girls play lacrosse at County level, with many going on to play for the South West and National Teams. Girls compete in Athletics at County, Area and National level and we have a number of

International Equestrians. The St Mary's Calne Tennis Academy (SMCTA) offers a structured programme of tennis at all levels, from beginners up to our elite players. As well as the mainstream sports, girls also compete in fencing and ski racing and participate in many other clubs, such as golf and archery.

All girls work for the Bronze Duke of Edinburgh's Award with large numbers going on to higher levels. 80% of girls play musical instruments and take part in a wide variety of ensembles, including the award-winning Chamber Choir. Drama productions transfer to the London stage and the Edinburgh Festival Fringe and the department boasts a unique relationship with RADA. We have a dynamic Art Department and every three years we host an exhibition in London, with exhibits from former and current girls; the 2018 exhibition 'A Sense of Place' takes place in Mall Galleries in November.

St Mary's offers a holistic education and the girls benefit from trips which enrich this experience. Recent expeditions have included a Classics Trip to Rome, a French Trip to Samoens and a Music Tour to Poland. The girls are also involved in several projects working with charities; this year they have been fundraising to support the OSCAR Foundation's girls' educational and football tour of the UK (OSCAR is a not for profit organisation based in Mumbai, which uses football as the tool to encourage underprivileged girls and boys to go to school).

St Mary's girls play an important part in the local community; a number of our Sixth Form take part in a mentoring programme with a nearby specialist school for children with learning difficulties. The girls also perform regularly in the local community, in both local churches and in a nearby residential home for the elderly, as well as participating in the annual Calne Music & Arts Festival.

Fees per term (2018–2019). Boarding £12,975, Day £9,675.

Scholarships and Bursaries. Scholarships available at 11+, 13+ and 16+ entry are: Academic, Art, Choral, Drama, Music and Sport. A Bodinnar All-Rounder Scholarship is also available at 13+. For further details, please contact the Admissions Department: admissions@stmaryscalne.org

One Foundation Scholarship is available annually at 11+ and one at Sixth Form to particularly gifted and talented pupils from the state education sector who, for reasons of financial restriction, might otherwise be prevented from applying to the school. Foundation Scholarships are means-tested and could be worth up to 100% of the fees.

All awards are retained to the end of Sixth Form and are reviewed at regular intervals. Candidates who are successful in gaining an award, but require greater remission in fees in order to be able to take up their place may apply for a means-tested Bursary. HM Forces discounts are available.

Charitable status. St Mary's School (Calne) is a Registered Charity, number 309482 and exists for the education of children.

Chairman of Governors: Mr S Adde [Chairman Elect – in post from 17th November 2018]

Headmistress: Dr Felicia Kirk, BA University of Maryland, MA Brown University, PhD Brown University

Deputy Head: Mrs D Harrison, MA Cantab

Senior Mistress: Mrs A Davies-Potter, BSc Hertfordshire, MEd Bristol, PGCE

Director of Teaching & Learning: Mr M Smyth, BSc Newcastle, PGCE Cambridge, PG Dip Oxon

Director of Development: Mrs C Depla, MA St Andrews

School Chaplain: The Reverend J Beach, BSc Essex, BA Bristol, MTh Cardiff

Bursar: Mr D Boswell, BEd Cambridge, Fellow of Institute of Leadership & Management

St Mary's College

Everest Road, Crosby, Merseyside L23 5TW

Tel:	0151 924 3926
Fax:	0151 932 0363
email:	office@stmarys.lpool.sch.uk
website:	www.stmarys.ac
Twitter:	@stmarys_college
Facebook:	@stmaryscollegecrosby

Motto: '*Fidem Vita Fateri*'

St Mary's College is an Independent Catholic School for boys and girls of all faiths aged 0–18, rated 'Excellent' in all areas by the Independent Schools Inspectorate (ISI). We are a thriving community which places a high value on outstanding academic achievement and all-round personal development. Our school is built on strong values which emphasise the importance of caring for others and striving for excellence in all we do. Boys and girls can start at our Bright Sparks & Early Years department (0–4 years) soon after birth and progress to our Preparatory School (4–11 years) before moving on to the College (11–18 years), where typically they achieve up to 100% pass rates at both GCSE and A Level. Our rich programme of extracurricular activities equips our pupils with the skills and values which will guide and support them throughout their lives. Scholarships and bursaries are available.

Numbers. There are 414 pupils in the Senior School and 131 in the Preparatory School. There are no boarders.

Preparatory School. Open to boys and girls up to the age of 11. There is an Early Years Unit (0–4) comprising baby unit and kindergarten. Pupils are admitted to the Preparatory School after an interview at 4, 5 and 6 years of age and by informal assessment during a day visit.

The Prep School has a strong family atmosphere, providing a secure and lively environment in which expectations are high. The school takes what is best from the National Curriculum and follows an enhanced programme with greater emphasis on the 3 Rs and fostering self-discipline.

Sciences play an important part in the curriculum. Sport and Music are particularly strong. Tutoring in a wide range of musical instruments is provided. French and Spanish are taught in small groups from Reception.

The Head of the Preparatory School, Mr J Webster, will be pleased to meet you and show you round.

Senior School. Fully co-educational, the Senior School admits pupils at 11 both from the Prep and from primary schools over a wide area. An Entrance Examination is held in January each year. Generally speaking, pupils must be between the ages of 10½ and 12 on 1st September of the year in which they wish to enter the School. Sixth Form entry and entry into other year groups is also possible if places are available. A Registration Fee of £40 is payable with the form of application for admission.

The **Curriculum in the Senior School** includes English Language and Literature, French, German, Spanish, History, Geography, Classical Studies, Latin, Physics, Chemistry, Biology, Mathematics, Information Technology, Art, Music, Drama, Design and Technology and Physical Education. A broad curriculum of 14 subjects is followed for the first 3 years. In the Fourth and Fifth Years, pupils normally take 10 subjects at GCSE, including either single Sciences or Core plus Additional Science, and all pupils study for GCSE Religious Studies and an ICT qualification. In the Sixth Form there are Advanced courses in all the subjects mentioned above. Business Studies, Psychology, and Further Maths may also be taken at A Level. All Sixth Form students take three A Level subjects plus the Extended Project Qualification (EPQ).

St Mary's is a pioneer school on Merseyside in the inclusion of **orchestral music** as a normal feature of the School curriculum. All pupils are given the opportunity to play an orchestral instrument. The School Band and Orchestra give an annual Concert in the Liverpool Philharmonic Hall, win regional contests and undertake tours abroad.

Religious Education. Religious Education is a core subject through to GCSE. Religious Education in the Sixth Form is integrated through Outreach Work in the community.

Careers. The College works in partnership with the Independent Schools Careers Organisation. Arrangements are made each year for interviews for Fifth Formers to which parents are invited. Sixth Formers are interviewed several times to help them choose appropriate courses at University or in Higher Education. Advice is given to Third Year pupils in choosing options.

Games. Games periods provide opportunities for Rugby, Cricket, Football, Hockey, Netball, Squash, Golf, Cross-Country, Tennis and Basketball. The main games for girls are Netball and Hockey. There is an adjacent modern Sports Centre.

Activities. Some 40 extracurricular activities and societies are available, including The Duke of Edinburgh's Award scheme.

Combined Cadet Force. There is a very active Combined Cadet Force which contains Army and Air Force sections. Membership of the Combined Cadet Force is voluntary.

Fees per term (2018–2019). Senior School £3,720.33; Preparatory School £2,524.

Open Academic Scholarships. There are up to six Open Scholarships based on performance in the College Entrance Examination, worth up to half fees. The awards are based on academic merit alone and are currently irrespective of income.

There are also School Assisted Places, known as Edmund Rice Scholarships, at 11+. These are income-related and are open to pupils whose parents' joint income would have brought them within the Government scheme.

Further scholarships are available in Art, Music and Sport and these must be applied for separately.

Sixth Form Scholarships. Edmund Rice Scholarships (worth approximately 10% of fees) are available on merit, and are awarded on the basis of a Scholarship Examination in January.

Charitable status. St Mary's College Crosby Trust Limited is a Registered Charity, number 1110311. The aims and objectives of the Charity are to advance religious and other charitable works.

Governors:
Mrs S Ward, FCMA, BSc (*Chair of Governors*)
Mr M McKenna, LLB Hons (*Deputy Chair*)
Mr C Cleugh
Mrs A Daniels, MA, PGCE
Mr A Duncan, BA Hons, MBA
Mrs L Martindale, MA, BEd Hons
Mrs P Old, LLB
Mrs H Thompson, ACA, BSc
Mr K Williams
Mr C Wright, BSc Hons, MRSC, MIoD
Mr J Wright, BA, MA Oxon, MBA

Principal: **Mr M Kennedy**, BSc, MA, NPQH, CChem, MRSC

Vice Principal: Mrs J Thomas, BSc

Senior Leadership Team:
Mrs S Bartolo, BEd (*Head of Lower School, Learning Support Coordinator*)
Mr P Duffy, MPhil (*Head of Sixth Form, *Religious Studies*)
Miss A Fletcher (*Business Director*)
Mr J Quint, BA Hons, PG Cert (*Director of Marketing, Admissions & Development*)
Mr N Rothnie, MA (*Extended Learning Coordinator, *History*)

Teachers:
* *Head of Department*

Miss N Addy, BSc (**Biology*)
Mr J Armstrong, BA
Miss L Brace, BSc
Mr A Byers, BA (**Music*)
Mrs L Clark, BSc (**Chemistry*)
Mr P Devine, BSc
Mrs K Fallon, BA
Mrs E Ford, BA
Dr A Giafis, PhD (**Mathematics*)
Mr T Hammersley, MSc (**Psychology*)
Mrs C Hearty, BEd
M Ireland, BEng, MSc (**Design & Technology*)
Mrs N Moore (**Classics & Latin*)
Miss L Newman, BA
Miss H Orrett, BA
Mr M Prescott, BA, MA
Miss M Roberts, BA (**Art*)
Mr P Ravenscroft, BA (**English*)
Mr I Rhead, BSc
Mrs J Savage, BA (**Geography*)
Miss J Simpson, BA (**Business Studies*)
Mrs A Smith, BA
Mr A Stagogiannis, BA (**Modern Foreign Languages*)
Miss N Sykes, BSc, BA (**Physics*)
Dr J Thorne, PhD
Mrs S Townsley, BSc (**Girls' PE*)
Mr N Vagianos, BSc, MBA (**Information Technology*)
Mr D Williams, BA (**Boys' PE*)

Preparatory Department:
Headmaster: Mr J Webster, BA

Teachers:
Miss J Battisti, BSc
Mrs J Booth, BEd
Mr D Cooke, BA
Mrs K Gallagher, BA
Miss V Johnson, BA
Mrs S Murray, BA
Miss P Walton, BA

Mr A Chow

Claremont House:
Head of Early Years: Mrs A Haigh, BEd
Mrs A Fielding, NNEB
Miss R Malone, NNEB

St Paul's School

Lonsdale Road, Barnes, London SW13 9JT

Tel: 020 8748 9162
Fax: 020 8746 5353
email: reception@stpaulsschool.org.uk
website: www.stpaulsschool.org.uk

Twitter: @StPaulsSchool
Facebook: @StPaulsSchool1509
LinkedIn: /St-Paul's-School

Motto: '*Fide et literis*'

St Paul's School is one of the UK's leading independent schools, offering an outstanding all-round education for some of the brightest boys in the country.

Founded by John Colet, Dean of St Paul's Cathedral, in 1509 to educate boys "from all nations and countries indifferently," regardless of race, creed or social background, St Paul's School remains committed to his vision today.

Erasmus, the greatest scholar of the northern Renaissance, advised Colet in the original planning of St Paul's School and wrote textbooks for the School's use. Today, a sense of scholarship, a commitment to all-round excellence and a culture of venturing beyond the syllabus continues to pervade life at St Paul's, which is known for its inspirational and responsive teaching, and outstanding academic results.

University Destinations. The most recent year for which the School has a full list of the destinations of St Paul's leavers is 2017 since many pupils take a GAP year and apply to university after taking their A Levels.

For the 2017 leavers, totalling 200, 198 pupils opted to attend and took up places at universities. Out of these, 166 went to universities in the UK and 32 to universities abroad including 30 to the USA.

Of those staying in the UK, 95% (158) went on to Russell group universities, with 37% (61 pupils) entering Oxford or Cambridge.

Of those going abroad, 30 have chosen to study in the USA at Ivy League or equivalent universities; two have chosen to study in Canada.

Forty-six percent (90 out of 198) of university-bound pupils who left in 2017 are studying at universities ranked within the top 10 in the QS 2017 World University Rankings. Fifty-seven percent (112 out of 198) of pupils who left in 2017 who went to university are studying at universities ranked within the top 20 in the QS 2017 World University Rankings.

Admission. Application for Admission to St Paul's is made via online application form on the School's website. 13+ candidates can register when they are in Year 5. In the autumn term of Year 6, three years before entry, they must take the ISEB Common Online Pre-Test. The results of this, together with a detailed report from their current school, will be used to select candidates for interview. Following the interview, boys may be offered a Main List place which is conditional upon continued good conduct and academic progress at their existing school, including an unreserved reference of support from their Head Teacher in Year 8.

There is a registration fee of £175.

For 16+ applications should be made one year in advance. Further details can be found on the School's website. No registration fee is required at the time of applying. Successful applications will pay the fee when accepting their place.

A Deposit of £2,800 is required when a parent accepts the offer of a place for his son after interview. The Deposit will be returnable only if the boy fails to reach the necessary standard prior to entry or when the final account has been cleared after the boy leaves St Paul's.

Fees per term (2018–2019). The Basic Fee for St Paul's is £8,344 and £6,670 for St Paul's Juniors. This covers tuition, games, loan books, stationery, libraries, medical inspection, a careers aptitude test in the GCSE year, certain School publications and lunch, which all boys are required to attend. Charges are made for the purchase of some books (which become the personal property of boys) and public examination fees.

There are facilities for up to 35 boarders (ages 13 to 18) and boarding is flexible allowing boys to go home at weekends as they wish. The Boarding Fee is £12,537 per term. Boys joining at age 13 can only be weekly boarders and must return to a family member or approved guardian at weekends. Boys joining at age 16 can be full boarders.

Bursaries. St Paul's takes pride in giving the best possible education to talented boys, irrespective of their family's financial circumstances. Each year there are funds available for free and subsidised places for those with a household income below £120,000. Bursaries are means-tested each year and may change as a family's financial situation improves or deteriorates. More information can be obtained from the School's website.

Scholarships. A number of Scholarships are available to boys who have completed the application process and have been offered a place at the School.

Foundation Scholarships: A few Foundation Scholarships may be awarded to 11-year-old boys in St Paul's Juniors on the basis of examinations. The Scholarship Examination for St Paul's is held in May. Candidates must be under 14 on 1 September. There are 153 Scholars at any given time and about 30 vacancies arise each year. All new Academic Scholarships are honorary and carry an award of £60 per annum.

Music: A number of Music Scholarships and Exhibitions may be awarded at St Paul's each year. Auditions take place at the end of January/beginning of February. Candidates must be under 14 on 1 September following the audition and all boys must be registered for entry to St Paul's to apply for music awards. Candidates are normally expected to have attained at least Grade 6 standard on their principal study, but this is just a guide.

The Sharp Music Exhibition Award and the Dennis Brain Memorial Exhibition are awarded from time to time to a boy entering St Paul's for his A Level years.

Full particulars are available from the Director of Music.

Art: One or more South Square Art Scholarships are available each year to boys who have taken GCSE to assist them in following a career in practical art. These scholarships can be awarded for the candidate's A Level course at St Paul's.

Arkwright Scholarships: The School is a member of the Arkwright Scholarship Scheme which offers financial assistance to sixth-formers who intend to pursue a career in Engineering, Technology, or other Design-related subjects.

Leaving Scholarships or Awards. A number of Prize Grants and Exhibitions (including the Lord Campden's exhibitions, founded in 1625 by Baptist Hicks, Viscount Campden) are given by the Governors every year to boys proceeding to Oxford or Cambridge or to any other place of further education.

Curriculum. All boys follow a broadly based course up to IGCSE/GCSE. Thereafter in Y12 & Y13, A Level and Pre-U subjects are so arranged that boys can combine a wide range of Arts and Science subjects if they so wish. In Y12, nearly all boys take four subjects and may also undertake an Extended Project, followed by three or four subjects in Y13. Subjects are all taken in a linear way and there are no public exams in Y12.

Games. Physical Activities offered include: Aikido, Athletics, Badminton, Basketball, Cricket, Cross-Country, Fencing, Fives, Futsal, Golf, Judo, Rackets, Rowing, Rugby, Rugby Sevens, Sculling, Soccer, Squash, Swimming, Tennis, Table Tennis, Ultimate Frisby and Water Polo. In addition, Climbing, Cycling and Sailing take place off site. The School has its own Swimming Pool, Fencing Salle, Tennis, Squash, Fives and Rackets Courts, Dojo, Fitness Centre and its own Boat House. The Sports Centre also comprises a Main Hall and Gymnasium. The Sports Hall is equipped for Tennis, Badminton, Basketball and has five indoor Cricket nets.

Music. All boys are taught music in the classroom in the first year. In subsequent years, GCSE is taught as a two-year course, and A Level taught in the final two years. Additional tuition is available in piano, organ, all the standard orchestral instruments, jazz, music theory and aural. There are a wide range of ensemble activities – chamber music, jazz and big band, two full orchestras, two training orchestras and several choral/vocal groups. The music school contains a professional standard concert venue, the Wathen Hall, several rehearsal rooms, two large teaching rooms and a music technology suite. There are regular concerts and recitals, as well as music competitions, musicals and external engagements, workshops and festivals.

School Societies. There is a wide choice of more than 30 Societies, including Musical, Artistic and Dramatic activities, Debating, Historical and Scientific Societies, Politics and Economics, Bridge, Chess, Natural History, Photography, European Society, a Christian Union and Social Service.

St Paul's Juniors adjoins the School. (*For details see entry in IAPS section.*)

Charitable status. St Paul's School is a Registered Charity, number 1119619. The object of the charity is to promote the education of boys in Greater London.

Governors:
Chairman: Johnny Robertson, BSc
Deputy Chairman: Alistair Summers, BSc, MSc

Appointed by the Mercers' Company:
Sarah Barker, LLB
Nicola Doyle, BEd
Adam Fenwick, MA
Sir Simon Fraser GCMG
Lord Grabiner QC
Professor Rose Luckin, BA, DPhil
Alison Macleod, BSc, MA (*Safeguarding Governor*)
Alison Palmer BSc
Earl St Aldwyn, MA
Ben Thomas, MA
Chris Vermont, MA

Clerk to the Governors: Elizabeth Wilkinson

St Paul's Teaching Staff:

High Master: Prof Mark Bailey, BA Dunelm, PhD Cantab

Surmaster – Head of Senior School: Richard Girvan, MA, MEng Cantab
Deputy Head – Academic: James Gazet, MA Cantab
Deputy Head – Pastoral: Nick Watkins, MA Oxon
Deputy Head – Co-Curricular: Thomas Killick, MA, PhD Cantab
Director of Admissions: Andy Mayfield, BSc Manc, MSc, DPhil Oxon
Director of Assessment And Data: Simon Holmes, MPhys, DPhil Oxon
Director of Outreach and Academic Partnerships: Stuart Block MA Cantab
Director of Teaching & Learning: Simon Hollands, MA Dunelm
Director of Wellbeing & Mental Health: Samuel Madden, BA Exon, MA LSE

Undermasters:
Caroline Gill, MA Cantab (*4th Form*)
Glenn Harrison, BSc Brun (*5th Form*)
James Gilks, MSc, PhD Nott (*6th Form*)

Naomi McLaughlin, BA Card (*L8th Form*)
Andrew Sykes, MA Oxon, MSc London (*U8th Form*)

Head of Faculty – Creative and Performing Arts: Edward Williams, MA Cantab
Head of Faculty – Humanities: Graham Seel, MA St And
Head of Faculty – Languages: Douglas Perrin, MA Cantab
Head of Faculty – Science, Technology, Engineering, ICT & Computing: Camille Shammas, BSc Sheff, PhD Bris
Director of Extended Project Qualifications (EPQs): Thomas Weller, MSc, PhD Lond

Art:
Michael Grant, BA Goldsmiths, MA RCA, PGCE Goldsmiths (*Director of Art*)
Tom Flint, BA Leeds Met, MA London
Penny Holmes, BA, UED Natal
Michael Page, BA UCL, MA Royal College of Art
Erasmia Stravoravdi, MA Oxon, PG Dip RA
Ian Tiley, MA Newc, ATC London
Jonathan Williams, BA Wolv, MA RCA

Biology:
Jonathan Bennett, BA, DPhil Oxon, MSc Edin (*Head of Biology*)
Ben Burrows, BSc, MSc Canterbury, NZ
Sarah Field, BSc Edin, DPhil Oxon (*President of the Boat Club*)
William Kricka, BSc UEA, PhD TCD
Alexander Langley, MA, PhD Cantab (*Assistant Housemaster*)
Martyn Powell, BSc Sur, PhD Rdg (*PSHE and Citizenship Assistant Coordinator*)
Sam Roberts, MA Oxon (*Head of Voluntary Service*)
Camille Shammas, BSc Sheff, PhD Bris

Careers and Universities:
Neville Sanderson, BA, MA Lond (*Head of Careers and Universities also History*)
Carol Graham, BSFS, MAAS, MA Georgetown (*Head of US Universities*)

Chemistry:
Matthew Smith, MChem Oxon (*Head of Chemistry*)
Martin Fitzpatrick, BSc, PhD UCD (*Examinations Officer*)
Ann Jefferey, BSc Soton
Richard Jones, BEng, MSc, MRes, PhD, PGCE Newc
Tom Lowes, MChem Oxon
Janet Mitchell, BSc Bris, MSc Open
Thomas Orr, MChem Newc
Suzanne Squire, MSci Imp Lond

Classics:
Simon May, MA Cantab (*Head of Classics*)
Douglas Cairns, MA Glas
James Harrison, MA Oxon (*PSHE and Citizenship Coordinator*)
Hannah Mervis, BA Oxon
Robert Taylor, MA, MLitt St And (*Head of Charities*)
Katharine Waterfield, BA, MPhil Oxon
Alex Wilson, BA Exon (*Associate Director, Pauline Relations*)
Sarah Burges Watson, BA Cantab, MA Penn, PhD Harvard

Computing:
Chris Harrison, MSc, PhD Lond (*Head of Computing*)
Vincent Ting, BSc Lond, MSC KUL

Drama:
Christian Anthony, BA, MA Lond (*Director of Drama also English*)
Alex Kerr, MA Edin (*Head of Drama and Theatre Studies*)

Economics:
Samuel Schmitt, BSc Bris (*Head of Economics*)

Jack Allen, BA Oxon
Thomas Passmore, BA Dunelm (*Boarding Housemaster*)
Rebecca McGreevy, MA Edin

Engineering:
Katie Douglass, BA Open (*Director of Engineering & ICT*)
Edward Bailey, BSc Harper Adams, MSc Oxf Brookes
Dominic Boydell, BEng Hons South Bank, PGCE
　Greenwich, MSc Staff
David Emery (*Electronics Technician*)
Tomi Herceg, BSc Prince, PhD Lond (*Assistant
　Housemaster*)
Stephen Patterson, MSc, PhD Lond

English:
Tristram Hager, MA Cantab (*Head of English*)
Andrew Broughton, MA Cantab
Matthew Gardner, MA Oxon, MA Manc
Nicholas Kemp, BA Oxon, MPhil Cantab
Judith McLaren, MA Cantab, MA Westmin
Naomi McLaughlin BA Cardiff
Hannah Warner, BA Camb, MA Durh

Geography:
Alexander Isaac, MSc Bris, MA Lond (*Head of
　Geography*)
Rhiannon Cogbill, BA Cantab, MPhil Cantab
Linda Johnson, BA, MSc Rhodes
Nicholas Troen, MA Oxon, MSc LSE (*Head of
　Entrepreneurship*)

History:
Aaron Watts, MA Cantab, PGCE Buck, LLM Birkbeck
　College (*Head of History*)
Edward Beesley, BA Wales, PhD Bris
Suzanne Mackenzie, BSc Brun, MA Lond, OLY
Nick Watkins, BA Oxon (*Director of Pastoral Care and
　Boarding*)
Nathaniel Weisberg, BA Cantab

Learning Support:
Helena Howard, MA Oxon (*Head of Learning Support*)
Caroline Nolan, BA, PGCE Liv (*Learning Support
　Teacher*)

Mathematics:
Andrew Ashworth Jones, BSc PNL (*Head of Mathematics*)
Sebastian Allon, BSc Bris
Richard Baxter, BSc, PhD Queen's Belfast
Robert Breslin, MMath Sheff
Luis Cereceda, MPhys Warw, MSc Oxon, PhD Lond
Paul Charlton, BEng Nott (*Head of Junior Mathematics*)
Kerilynne Cloete, BSocSci Cape Town
Adrian Hemery, MMath Cantab, MSc, PhD Lough
Samuel Hewitt, BA, MMath Cantab
Thomas Lyster, BA Dunelm, MSc London
Ian McDonnell, MA, MEng, PhD, PGCE Warw
Alex Milne, MSc Imp Lond, MA Cantab
Tim Morland, MA Oxon
James Ramsden, BSc Dunelm
Amrita Shravat, BSc Lond, DPhil Oxon
Zhivko Stoyanov, Msc Sofia, PhD Bath
Owen Toller, MA Cantab

Modern Foreign Languages:
Peter Davies, MA Lond (*Head of Spanish*)
David Hempstead, BA, MPhil Bath (*Head of French*)
Douglas Perrin, MA Cantab (*Head of German*)
Alexander Tofts, BA Dunelm (*Head of Italian & ML
　Coordinator*)
Paul Collinson, MA Oxon
Eliza James, BA Manc
Amy Grogan, BA Bris
Rebecca Kemal-ur-Rahim, BA UCL

Larissa Lapaire, BA UCL, MA Lond
Guy Larlham, BA Newc

Music:
Mark Wilderspin, MA Oxon, MMus RCM (*Director of
　Music*)
Thomas Evans, BA, MPhil Cantab, PhD KCL (*Assistant
　Director of Music*)
Will Fairbairn, BA Cantab

Physics:
Michael Jacoby, BSc Bris, MA Cantab (*Head of Physics*)
Ryan Buckingham, MPhys Oxon, DPhil Oxon
Chongyu Qin, MA, MSc, Cantab
Benjamin Still, BSc Leic, PhD, PCHE Sheff, PGCE Buck
Joseph Swartzentruber, BA Cantab
Luke Warriner, BSc Warw (*Head of Football*)
Thomas Weller, MSci UCL PhD UCL (*Director of EPQs*)

Politics:
Rohan Edwards, MA Oxon, MSc Birkbeck (*Head of
　Politics*)

Sport & Physical Education:
Nigel Briers, BEd Lond (*Director of Sport, Head of
　Cricket*)
James Blurton, BSc St Mary's (*Assistant Director of Sport,
　Head of Physical Education & Head of Rugby*)
Ryan Blake (*Head of Strength and Conditioning*)
Abby Johnson (*Assistant Director of Rowing*)
Andy Maguire (*Head of Athletics, Head of Basketball*)
Gary O'Brien (*Head of Tennis, Sports Centre Manager*)
Roxana Roman (*Head of Aquatics*)
Steve Tulley (*Head of Rackets*)

Theology & Philosophy:
Rufus Duits, MPhil Cantab PhD UCL (*Head of Theology
　and Philosophy*)
Jade Ramsay Overall , BA Lond
Daniel Brigham, BA, MA York, PhD Cantab
Philip Gaydon, BA, MA, PhD Warw

St Paul's Juniors Teaching Staff:

Head of St Paul's Juniors: Maxine Shaw, BSc London,
　PGCE Hull, PG Dip Brunel, NPQH

Senior Deputy Head: Carol Hawkins, BA Birmingham,
　PGCE Manchester, PG Dip Ed Mgt Surrey, NPQH (*also
　History*)
Pastoral Deputy Head: Alex Matthews, BA, MA Oxon,
　PGCE, MA Ed Chich (*also Geography*)
Director of Studies: Jayne Gordon, BA Wales, PGCE Oxon
　(*also History*)
Head of Third Years: Alexander James, BSc Open, QTS
　Hertfordshire (*also Science*)
Head of Second Years: Pippa Kershaw, BA Oxon QTS
Head of First Years: Alistair Wilkinson, BA UCL, MA
　Warwick

[1] *teaches at St Paul's and St Paul's Juniors*

Art:
Neil Groom, BFA DipT Christchurch, NZ (*Director of Art*)
Jakob Rowlinson, BA Oxon
Joe Simpson, BA Leeds

Classics:
Emily Evans, BA Manchester, MA Royal Holloway, PGCE
　KCL (*Head of Classics*)
Sian Gill, BA Warwick, PGCE KCL
Georgina Tomaszewska, BA Oxon, MA Goldsmiths

Computing:
[1]Roisin Flanagan, BSc, PGCE Brighton (*Director of
　Computing*)
Ibe Akoh, BSc, MSc Exeter, PGCE Buckingham

Drama:
[1]Jonathan Boustead, BA Cumbria, MA York (*Director of Drama*)
Briony Bower N Dip Performing Arts Brooksby Melton College

English:
[1]Jemima Waller, MA Cantab, PGCE Inst Ed, Dip Education Birkbeck, Dip Law City (*Head of English*)
Louise Coghlan, BA Leeds, MA Roeh
Tiffany Masters, BA Centre Universitaire Hotel-Dieu Le Comte, PGCE Bath
Josephine Wielebinska, BA, PGCE Manchester (*also Geography*)

First Year:
Amanda Bodley, BSc Bristol, PG Dip Law College of Law, PGCE Roehampton
Rory McNish, MA Edinburgh, PGCE Edinburgh
Laura Moss, BA York, PGCE UCL
Tom Taylor, BSc PGCE Dunelm (*Head of PSHE & Citizenship*)
Camilla Waterworth, BA Newcastle, PGCE Roehampton
Danielle Dawson, BSc City of London, PGCE London

French:
Valerie Nolk, LèsL Sorbonne Institut Britannique de Paris (*Head of French, Archivist*)
Catherine Lê, BA Centre Universitaire Hotel-Dieu Le Comte, PGCE Bath
Patrice Reutenauer, LèsL Strasbourg, PGCE Brunel

Geography:
Gwyn Page, BA Southampton, PGCE Buckingham (*Head of Geography*)
James Brooks, BSc Cardiff, PGCE Buckingham
[1]Rhiannon Cogbill, BA Cantab, MPhil Cantab

History:
[1]Simon Motz, MA Oxon, PGCE London (*Head of History, Timetabler*)

Junior Engineering:
Sally Hamma, BSc Huddersfield, PGCE Goldsmiths (*Head of Junior Engineering*)
Ruth Afonso, BA Leeds, PGCE Nottingham Trent
Edward Bailey, BSc Harper Adams, MSc Oxford Brookes
[1]Dominic Boydell, BEng South Bank, MSc Staffs
[1]Katie Douglass, BA Open

Learning Support:
Iona Mitchell, MA Open, BSc Edinburgh, PGCE, AMBDA (*Head of Learning Support*)

Lower First Year:
Anna Boden, BA London, MSc Bath, PGCE Worcester (*Head of Lower First Year*)
Andrea Bartlett, BEd London
Josie Johnson, BA York

Mathematics:
George Tsaknakis, BSc Ed Exeter (*Head of Mathe*)matics
Samuel Bailey, BA Oxford Brookes
Benedict Rowan, MA Oxon, PGCE IOE Lond
Daniel Kugananthan, BSc Univ Tech Sydney, MA Univ Western Sydney

Music:
Andrew Casterton, BMus Leeds, MA Nott (*Director of Music*)
Robert Corrigan, BA Mus Leeds, PGCE Reading (*Assistant Director of Music*)

Science:
Michael McRill, BTech Brunel, PhD N Wales, PGCE Keele, MRSB, CBiol, NPQH (*Head of Science*)

David Alsop, BSc Newcastle, PGCE Sunderland
George Herbert, BSc Bristol, PGCE Oxon
Jennifer Kinrade, BSc Glasgow, PGCE Oxon (*Assistant Director of Studies*)

Theology and Philosophy:
Sophie Walton, BA Oxon GDL Oxford Brookes LPC BPP Law Sch,, QTS UCL (*Head of Theology & Philosophy*)

Sport:
Daniel Stewart, BA UWE QTS (*Director of Sport, Head of Cricket*)
Simon Cattermole, BA Exon (*Assistant Director of Games*)
Kiyo Jason (*PE and Field Games Coach*)
Saqib Malik (*Field Games Coach*)
Matthew Young, BA Reading, PG Dip Law QTS (*Head of Football*)

St Peter's School, York

Clifton, York YO30 6AB

Tel:	01904 527300
Fax:	01904 527302
email:	enquiries@stpetersyork.org.uk
website:	www.stpetersyork.org.uk
Twitter:	@stpetersyork
Facebook:	@stpetersschoolyork

Motto: Super antiquas vias

Founded in 627AD, St Peter's is one of the world's oldest schools. It provides outstanding boarding and day education for boys and girls from 13 to 18. Pupils at St Peter's School achieve some of the best grades in the North of England at GCSE and A Level. Its Prep School, St Olave's, admits boarding and day boys and girls from 8 to 13 and Clifton School and Nursery admits day girls and boys from 3 to 8.

St Peter's is a co-educational boarding and day school with 571 boys and girls aged 13–18. There are 138 boarders housed in four boarding houses, and all day pupils are assigned to a day house, all of which are on the campus. St Peter's offers full boarding.

Buildings & Facilities. The School occupies an impressive 47-acre site just a few minutes' walk from the historic centre of York. Playing fields stretch down to the River Ouse and the School boat house, and the sports facilities are further supplemented by three sports halls, a fitness suite, an astro pitch and a 25m 6-lane swimming pool.

There are three performance spaces of varying capacities, a music school, an outstanding art school with its own exhibition gallery and an extensive library. The school's sports pitches have been recognised for their excellence by the Institute of Groundsmanship, and construction is currently under way for a new Maths and Modern Foreign Languages block, due to be ready in September 2018.

Entrance. Pupils are admitted through the School's entrance examinations held at the end of January for 13+ and in mid-November for 16+. The School is oversubscribed and application before the entrance exam is strongly recommended.

Scholarships and Bursaries. Honorary scholarships are awarded to those performing extremely well in the entrance examination.

Various music awards covering a proportion of the fees and free tuition on up to three musical instruments are available for entrants at 13+ or Sixth Form. Interviews and auditions for these awards are held in January or February.

Help with Fees is available at 13+ and 16+. Full particulars on Help with Fees and scholarships are available from the Admissions Officer, Mrs Gillian Daniells, Tel: 01904 527305 or email: g.daniells@stpetersyork.org.uk.

Curriculum. St Peter's offers a very broad middle school curriculum including Music, PE, Art, Design & Technology, Community Action and courses in personal and social education, among many others.

Nearly all pupils proceed into the Sixth Form, and A Level courses are available in all subjects studied for IGCSE/GCSE, and in Economics, Politics, Business Studies, Further Mathematics and PE.

Academic and pastoral care. A comprehensive house and tutorial system with interim assessments and reports during the term ensure the close scrutiny by all the teaching staff of pupils' academic and general development.

Religious education and worship. Religious Studies are part of the curriculum, and Chapel is seen as an opportunity for pupils to be made aware of the School's Christian heritage.

Careers and university entrance. The School is an 'all-in' member of the Independent Schools Careers Organisation. Careers staff are available for consultation, maintaining an extensive library relating to careers and higher education and organising a full programme of events for the Sixth Form. In 2015 the School's Careers Department was accredited by Career Mark, 'The mark of Quality for Careers Education and Guidance'.

Games and Physical Education. Physical education is a significant part of the curriculum. There is an extensive games programme and excellent sports facilities. Rugby, netball, hockey, cricket and rowing are major sports, and many other options including swimming, athletics, cross country, basketball, squash, badminton, tennis, fencing, golf, mountain biking, trampoline, fitness and weight training are available.

Combined Cadet Force. A flourishing and voluntary CCF contingent, with army and air sections, allows the pursuit of many activities including a full programme of camps, expeditions and courses.

The Duke of Edinburgh's Award is also on offer with expedition training for all levels as part of the activities programme and 150 pupils are currently participating.

Music. Musical ability is encouraged throughout the School. There is an orchestra, bands, choirs, choral society, Barbershop and Barbieshop groups and numerous smaller activities. Concerts and tours abroad are a regular feature of the school year. Tuition in all instruments is provided, and music is offered at GCSE and A Level.

Art. Drawing, painting, print-making, ceramics and sculpture may all be taken up both in and out of school hours in an outstanding department.

Drama. The School has three performance spaces: the Memorial Hall, the Shepherd Hall and the smaller, more flexible Drama Centre. There are various productions through the year giving opportunities for acting and backstage skills.

Clubs and societies. Many societies flourish including chess, debating, Radio 627 and numerous others. The Community Action programme has over 100 regular participants.

Travel and expeditions. Recent opportunities for trips and tours have included skiing trips, Classics trips to Greece, trekking in Morocco, a Rugby tour to Canada and the USA, among many others.

The Friends of St Peter's. Parents are encouraged to join the Friends, a society whose aim is to promote a close relationship between parents and staff.

Fees per term (2018–2019). Full Boarding £10,010, Non-EU Full Boarding £10,760, Day £6,025. Tuition fees include the costs of stationery and textbooks. There are no compulsory extras except for examination fees. Lunches are included in day fees.

Further information. Prospectuses are available on request: tel: 01904 527305, email: enquiries@stpeters york.org.uk, or via the website: www.stpetersyork.org.uk.

(*See also entries for St Olave's School and Clifton School and Nursery in IAPS section.*)

Charitable status. St Peter's School, York, is a Registered Charity, number 1141329.

Visitor: The Rt Honorable the Lord Archbishop of York

Board of Governors:
Chairman: Mr W Woolley
Vice Chair: Mr J E Burdass
Vice Chair: Revd Canon Dr C Collingwood

Members of the Board

Mrs C Bailey	Miss S L Palmer
Dr D M Haywood	Mr A Taylor
Mr P B Hilling	Mr S Town
Ms P Kaur	Mr P Widdicombe
Dr A Lees	Mrs C Bailey
Professor M D Matravers	

Clerk to the Board: Ms Sara Esler

Head Master: Mr J M P Walker, MA Oxford, MA London

Senior Deputy Head: Mr A J Dunn, MA, DPhil Oxon

Deputy Head: Mrs J R Wright, BA, PGCE

Academic Deputy: Mr D H Gillies, BA, MSc

Heads of Departments:
Art: Mrs C Chisholm, BA Hons
Biology: Mrs S E Mckie, BSc, PGCE
Careers: Mrs J Loftus, BSc
Chemistry: Mr G Smith, BSc
Classics: Mr E Noy-Scott, BA, PGCE
Design and Technology: Mr P Cooper, BSc, QTS
Drama: Miss H K Lindley, BA, PGCE
Economics/Business Studies: Mr B D White, BA, PGCE
English: Mrs E Mallard, MA
Geography: Miss E C Ullstein, BSc
Government & Politics: Mr B Fuller, BA, PGCE
History: Mr R J Trevett, MA
Mathematics: Mr D J Spencer, BSc
Modern Languages: Mr M J Duffy, BA
Director of Music: Mr P Miles-Kingston, MA, LRAM, QTS
Director of Sport: Mr S J Williams, BEd
Physics: Mr M Edwards, MA Ed, BSc, MInstP
Religious Studies: Mr C D Bembridge, BTh, PGCE
Science: Mr M Edwards, MA Ed, BSc, MInstP

All other St Peter's academic staff are listed on the school website.

Administrative Staff:
Bursar: Mr R M Schofield, FCA
Director of External Relations: Miss H E M Hamilton, MA, ACIM
Head Master's PA: Miss J Warner, MA
Admissions Officer: Mrs G Daniells

The Prep School – St Olave's
Master: Mr A I Falconer, BA, MBA
Master's Secretary: Mrs C Murgatroyd

Deputy Head: Mr M C Ferguson, HDE
Senior Master: Mr C W R Lawrence, BEd, MIBiol
Director of Teaching & Learning: Mrs C Lees, BEd
Chaplain: Mr J Dodsworth, BA, MA

All other St Olave's academic staff are listed on the school website.

Clifton School and Nursery
Head: Mr P C Hardy, BA, PGCE
Head's Secretary: Mrs C Fattorini

Deputy Head: Mrs A Clarke

All other Clifton School and Nursery academic staff are listed on the school website.

Seaford College

Lavington Park, Petworth, West Sussex GU28 0NB

Tel: 01798 867392
Fax: 01798 867606
email: info@seaford.org
website: www.seaford.org

Motto: *Ad Alta – To The Heights*

The College was founded in 1884 at Seaford in East Sussex and moved to Lavington Park at the foot of the South Downs in 1946 in West Sussex. The picturesque grounds cover some 400 acres and include extensive sports facilities. The campus includes a Prep School for pupils aged 6–13 (*see IAPS entry*), outstanding Performing Arts Centre and Sports Hall, a superb Art and Design department, a Sixth Form Centre, purpose-built boarding houses, a state-of-the-art Mathematics, Science and Music School.

Seaford is controlled by an independent non-profit making Charitable Trust approved by the Department for Education and the Charity Commissioners, and is administered by the College Board of Governors.

Pupils. Seaford College offers day and boarding facilities, with options of full, weekly and flexi boarding. There are over 750 pupils at the College with 200 in the Sixth form. There are two boys houses, a girls house, a junior house and two Sixth Form boarding houses.

Aims. Seaford College's aim is to bring out the best of each individual, by helping every pupil to reach their full potential and to achieve personal bests both inside and outside the classroom. The aim is to enable pupils to leave the College feeling confident in their own abilities and able to contribute in the external world.

Academic. The Prep School (incorporating Years 2–8) offers a wide-ranging curriculum, which includes the core subjects of English, Mathematics, Science, Spanish, French and Information Technology, as well as Geography, History, Art, Music, DT, Sport, Forest School and PSHCE.

Years 10 and 11 lead up to the GCSE examinations. Students study the core subjects of English Literature, English Language, Mathematics and Science and then choose four other syllabuses to follow from a comprehensive list of subjects, which include: Art, Business Studies, Computing, Drama, Design and Technology, Geography, French, History, Music, Physical Education, Religious Studies and Spanish.

The A Level subject list is comprehensive. In the Lower Sixth, pupils choose up to four subjects to study but may choose to drop one subject after the first term, then continue with three subjects through to A Level. Over and above this in their first year students may undertake The Duke of Edinburgh's Silver/Gold Award. In the Upper Sixth students concentrate on their three A Level subjects or BTEC courses in Business, Sport, Countryside Management or Hospitality.

Music is an important part of life at Seaford and the Music School offers the latest in recording and performing facilities. The College boasts an internationally-renowned College Chapel Choir, who have sung on tour with Gary Barlow and have performed many concerts for charity. The College also has an orchestra and offers lessons for all instruments. Music can be studied at GCSE and A Level.

Sports. With superb facilities available in the grounds and staff that have coached and played at international level, the College has a reputation for sporting excellence. Facilities include: eight rugby pitches, eight tennis courts, three cricket pitches, a water-based all-weather hockey pitch, enclosed swimming pool, a large indoor sports hall that allows tennis and hockey to be played all year round, and a 9-hole golf course and driving range.

Art. The College has an excellent Art department, which allows students to exercise their talents to the fullest extent in every aspect of art and design, whether it is ceramics, textiles, fine art, animation, or any other medium they wish to use. Many pupils from Seaford go on to study at design school and work for design and fashion houses or advertising companies. Students display their work throughout the year in the department's large gallery.

Combined Cadet Force. The College has strong ties with the Military and has a very well supported Combined Cadet Force, with each wing of the armed forces well represented. Weekend exercises and training are a regular feature in the College calendar and include adventure training, canoeing, climbing, sailing and camping.

Admission. Entry at age 7 consists of a visit to the school, possible trial day and assessment. Entry at age 10, 11 and 13 is determined by cognitive ability testing and references. 13+ pupils will still be expected to take the Common Entrance Examination. Sixth Form entry is dependent upon GCSE results, Trial Day and interview. Pupils are required to have at least 45 points at GCSE (=9 C grades) and these should include English and Mathematics. Pupils may enter the school without one of these subjects on condition they retake. Overseas students are required to take an oral and written examination to determine level of comprehension in English.

Scholarships and Bursaries. Academic, Music, Art, Design Technology and Sports scholarships may be awarded to boys and girls entering the prep and senior school at 11+, 13+ and 16+. These scholarships are worth a fixed value of £500 per annum. Scholarship examinations take place in February of the year of entry.

Bursaries are available on a means-tested basis. A potential scholarship recipient in need of further financial assistance may apply for a means-tested bursary.

Sibling and Forces discounts are also available. Please contact the Admissions Secretary for more details.

Fees per term (2018–2019). Years 9–13: £11,030 (Full Boarding), £9,660 (Weekly Boarding), £7,130 (Day). Years 7 & 8: £7,590 (Weekly Boarding), £5,710 (Day). £7,170 (Year 6 Weekly Boarding), £3,440–£5,250 (Years 2–6 Day).

Extras. Drama, Clay Pigeon Shooting, Fencing, Duke of Edinburgh's Award, Golf, Sailing, Kayaking, Museum & Theatre trips, Creative Writing, Drone Club, Debating Club, Rock Climbing, etc.

Charitable status. Seaford College is a Registered Charity, number 277439. It exists to provide education for children.

Governing Body:
R Venables Kyrke (*Chairman*)
Mrs S Sayer, CBE (*Vice Chair*)

R Norton	H A Phillips
J Cooper	A Hayes
Mrs E Lawrence	J Scrase
N Karonias	S Kowszun
J R Hall	

Headmaster: J P Green, BA Hons, PGCE

Academic Deputy Head: Mrs B Jinks, BA Jt Hons, MA, NPQH
Deputy Head (*Middle School*): J A Passam, BA, FRSA
Deputy Head (*Sixth Form*): W Yates, BSc Ed
Prep School Head: A Brown, BE
Deputy Head Prep School: J Harte, BSc

Teaching Staff:
* *Head of Department*

Art & Design:
*A G Grantham-Smith, BA, PG Dip ArtEd
Mrs K Grantham-Smith, BA (*Photography*)
Mrs H Hatton, BA (*Ceramics*)
A Kirkton, BA Hons

Business Studies:
M Pitteway, BComm Hons

Classics:
T Farmer, BA

Computing
D Crook, BA
Ms S Byrne, BA

Design Technology:
*D Shaw, BEd
Miss A Prince-Iles, BA Hons, PGCE
P Harker, MDes Hons

Drama:
*Dr J Askew, BA Hons

EAL:
Ms Y Clarke, CELTA, BA Hons

Economics:
*E Reynolds, BA
K Naylor, BA

English:
*Ms H Johnson, BA Hons
J Doy, BA Oxford, PGCE
Mrs S Hollis, BA
Mrs S Roberts, BA Hons, PGCE
Mrs P White, BA, PG Dip SpLD
Mrs A Doy, BA, PGCE
G Vernon, BA, MA
R Morgan, BA Cambridge

Food Technology:
Mrs A Wilkins Shaw, BSc Hons, PGCE

Geography:
*N Q Angier, BSc, MA
J Hart, BA, PGCE
J Follows, BA Hons, PGCE
Miss E LeBarthe, BSc Hons
Miss S Evan, BA

History:
*J Gisby, BA Hons, PGCE
Miss M Beard, BA Hons
D Falvey, BA

Learning Support:
*Mrs P A Angier, BA, Dip CG, Dip SpLD
N Foster, BA, Hornsby Dip SpLD
Mrs M Gilbert, BA Hons, PGCE, OCR SpLD
Ms A Jensen, Dip SpLD
Mrs L Ferris, OCR SpLD
Mrs H Russell, BA, OCR Cert SpLD
Mrs E Jones, CE
Ms S George
Mrs B Vernon

Mathematics:
*S Kettlewell, BA
Mrs B Jinks, MA, BA, NPQH
Dr N Pothecary, PhD, BA
J Percival, BA, PGCE
Mrs J Percival, BSc, PGCE
D Lockyer, BSc, PGCE
Mrs E Bloem, BA
Miss N Phillips, BA

Modern Languages:
*Ms A Loten, BA Hons, PGCE
Ms H Martin, PGCE (*French*)
Mrs J Lingford, BA Hons, PGCE
Miss M Molinero Quiralte
Miss J Stroudley, BA, PGCE
J Jones, BA
Miss C Apps, BA

Music:
*J Weaver
Mrs J Hawkins, PGCE, BMus
Mrs S Reynolds, BA Hons (*Choirmaster*)
Tim Sheinman, BA, MA

Physical Education:
*L Doubler, BA
J Thompson, BA Hons, PGCE
Miss E Teague, BA Hons QTS
Mrs D Strange (*Coach*)
J Halsey (*Golf Professional*)
D Barnes, BA, PGCE
Mrs G Hegarty, BA Ed, PGCE
Mrs L Cook, BA Hons
D Joseph, QTS PE
C Adams (*Head of Cricket*)
J Bird (*Head of Tennis*)
C Greenway (*Head of Hockey*)

Psychology:
Mrs A Yates, BS, PGCE

Religious Studies:
Mrs L Stitt, BA Hons

Science:
*S D'Agar, BSc Hons, PGCE
Mrs G Pasteiner, BSc (*Biology*)
E Barkham, MA Hons
Ms K Bloomer, BSc Hons, PGCE
G Barham, BSc Hons, PGCE
Dr N Street, PhD, MBA, PGCE
A Plewes, BSc Hons, PGCE
P Whelpton, BA
Mrs H Harris, BA

KS2 Teachers:
Mrs A Hobbs, BA
Mrs S Lewis, BEd Hons
Mrs H Stevens, BA Hons
Mrs F Jones, CertEd
Mrs S Page, GRSM, LRAM, PGCE (*KS2 Music, PSE*)
Mrs M Mitchinson, BA, PGCE

Exams:
Mrs L Goddard

CCF:
A Plewes, BSc Hons, PGCE
K Lomas

Chaplain: (*to be appointed*)
Finance Manager: A Golding
Facilities Manager: G Burt
IT Systems Manager: G Bell
Marketing Manager: S Twigger

Headmaster's Secretary: Mrs A Thornley
Admissions Secretary: Mrs J Mackay-Smith

Sevenoaks School

High Street, Sevenoaks, Kent TN13 1HU

Tel: 01732 455133
Fax: 01732 456143
email: regist@sevenoaksschool.org
            admin@sevenoaksschool.org
website: www.sevenoaksschool.org
Twitter: @SevenoaksSchool
Facebook: @SevenoaksSchoolUK
LinkedIn: /sevenoaks-school

Motto: *Servire Deo Regnari Est*

Sevenoaks is one of the top schools in the UK, providing an outstanding modern education. It was The Sunday Times Independent Secondary School of the Year 2018.

Founded in 1432, Sevenoaks School is a co-educational day and boarding school for pupils aged 11–18. Alongside academic excellence, it offers strong pastoral care, co-curricular breadth, innovative thinking, and an inclusive global dimension inspired by the International Baccalaureate.

In 2017 Sevenoaks was the top UK fully co-educational IB school in the Education Advisers Ltd rankings. In 2015, Sevenoaks was the highest performing fully co-educational school in the Sunday Times Parent Power list of the top 50 fee-paying schools for the IB. In 2013 the Independent Schools Inspectorate (ISI) awarded Sevenoaks School the rare accolade of 'Exceptional' for its students' achievement.

Around one-third of the students board. There are seven boarding houses catering for ages 13–18, with accommodation ranging from a charming Queen Anne house to modern, purpose-built facilities. Our two single-sex Sixth Form houses (16–18) particularly welcome international students joining the school for the Sixth Form.

Sevenoaks has a reputation for exploring new ideas. The school has taught the International Baccalaureate since 1978 and was the first HMC school to offer the IB Diploma Programme exclusively. More recently, Sevenoaks was among the first schools in the UK to devise its own externally accredited qualification, the Sevenoaks School Certificate (SSC), which is taken at the end of Year 11 and is fully recognised by UCAS. A wide range of subjects is offered at GCSE, IGCSE and SSC, with setting in core subjects. In the Sixth Form all pupils study the IB Diploma Programme – a rigorous two-year diploma designed to provide a broad and balanced education. It is a well-respected qualification among universities and employers worldwide. Academic results in the school are excellent, with an average IB Diploma score of 39.6 points in 2018 (ten points above the world average) and 17 students achieving the maximum score of 45 points. Virtually every student goes on to one of the best universities. In 2018, nearly 80 per cent took up a place at one of the leading UK universities, while 13 per cent accepted places at top US, Canadian, European and other international universities.

There is a strong emphasis on the co-curriculum, from sport to music, drama and art. Pupils are regularly selected for regional and national orchestras and choirs, the NYT, and compete at county, national and international level in a number of sports. A variety of clubs and societies provide opportunities for all pupils to find and develop their interests. Sevenoaks was one of the first UK schools to incorporate voluntary service as a compulsory element of the co-curriculum, pioneering a local Voluntary Service Unit in the 1960s and continuing with a strong service programme

today. There is also a CCF, an emerging programme of social impact entrepreneurship and strong involvement in The Duke of Edinburgh's Award scheme, with Gold expeditions abroad as well as in the UK.

In 2017 the school launched its Middle School Diploma for Year 9, which records pupils' academic and co-curricular achievements in creativity, action and service as well as in the enriching Sevenoaks Core courses, Ten Ideas That Changed the World and Critical Perspectives.

There are lessons and sport for all pupils on Saturdays and a full programme of activities for boarders on Sundays.

The facilities are first-class. In 2018 a state-of-the-art science and technology centre opened, uniting the four core fields of science, with an innovative new Sixth Form Global Study Centre alongside, providing the school's first dedicated space for the IB and higher education. Other recent developments include a sports centre providing outstanding facilities and an award-winning, world-class performing arts centre.

Admission. The main points of entry to the school are at 11, 13 and 16 years. A small number are admitted at other levels. At 11+, pupils are admitted on the basis of a competitive examination held in January, an interview and school report. At 13+, candidates take part in an assessment process in the May of their Year 7. A reference from their current school is also required. Candidates studying at a UK preparatory school will then take either the school's academic scholarship examinations in the May of Year 8 or the Common Entrance examinations in the June of Year 8. At 16+ students are admitted into the Sixth Form based on their performance in interview and academic entrance tests, and on the strength of their current school reports. There are boarding and day places for boys and girls at all ages. All applications for entry should be addressed to the Director of Admissions (regist@sevenoaksschool.org).

Fees per term (2018–2019). Boarders £12,432; Day Pupils £7,785 (including lunch). Fees for pupils entering directly into the Sixth Form are £13,488 (boarding) and £8,841 (day).

Scholarships and Bursaries. Up to 50 awards are available at 11+, 13+ and 16+ for outstanding academic ability or promise, as well as outstanding ability in music, sport, art and drama.

Scholarships are awarded to the value of £1,000 or 10% of the day fee.

Applicants are invited to apply for 11+ scholarships on the basis of performance in entrance tests and interviews, and for music scholarships when confirming their application. For 13+ awards, candidates may be invited to take part in the Academic Scholarship exams, or those who attend a UK prep school may be put forward by their school. Internal candidates may apply for co-curricular scholarships.

Sixth Form academic scholarships are offered on the basis of performance in entrance tests and interviews. Applications for Sixth Form Art, Music, Drama and Sport scholarships should be made by expressing an interest during the application procedure.

Means-tested bursaries are available for pupils who could not otherwise afford the fees. Priority is given to local candidates. Scholarships may be augmented by bursaries in cases of financial need.

Charitable status. Sevenoaks School is a Registered Charity, number 1101358. Its aims and objectives are the education of school children.

Governing Body:
Chairman: R N H Gould, BA
Vice-Chairman: Mrs S Dunnett, BA

Governors:
Ms A Beckett, MBA, MA
A Boulton, MA
Mrs S Carr, BA
Lord Colgrain, MA
I Doherty, MA
Mrs E Ecclestone, LLb, Dip LP
C Gill
Prof S Iversen
J London, LLM
N May, MA, MSc
D M Phillips, BA, ACA
P Shirke, MBA
Dr A Timms
Prof I Wilson

Bursar and Clerk to the Governors: Mrs G Jones, BA,
   ACA

Academic Staff:

Head: Mrs C L Ricks, MA, DPhil

Senior Deputy Head: Miss T M Homewood, BSc, MA
Deputy Head (Pastoral): Miss H P Tebay, MA
Deputy Head (Academic): T R Jones, BA, MA
Deputy Head (Co-curriculum): A P Rainbow, BA, MA,
   PhD
Director of Administration: Miss A A Franks, MA
Director of Admissions: Mrs A M Stuart, BSc, MEd
Director of Development: M D Joyce, BA
Director of Institute for Teaching & Learning: M P
   Beverley, BA, MA
*Director of Institute for Higher Education and Professional
   Insight*: Mrs W J Heydorn, MA
Director of Information Systems: Mrs S J Williamson, BA,
   MSc
Director of Innovation & Outreach: G A Lawrie, BSc
Director of Curriculum: M P Beverley, BA, MA
Director of International Baccalaureate: N T Haworth, BA
Head of Sixth Form Admissions: Ms L A Dolan, BA
Head of Boarding: Mrs N J Haworth, MA
Head of Sixth Form: M T Edwards, BA, MPhil, PhD
Head of Middle School: Miss R L McQuillin, MA
Head of Lower School: P G de May, BA

Assistant Teachers:
* *Head of Department*
† *Housemaster/mistress*

Miss N L Atkinson, BSc (*Technology*)
†Mrs E M Bassett, BA (*Chemistry*)
P R Bassett, MA (*Mathematics*)
J H Beck, BA, MA (**Philosophy*)
A P Bishop, BSc, MSc (*Chemistry*)
Miss F J Bolton, BSc, MSc (*Mathematics*)
Miss H M Bonsall, BSc (*Biology*)
Mrs R L Brown, BA (**Technology*)
I C Campbell, BSc (**Psychology*)
Mrs R Campbell, BA (*English*)
M R Capelo, BSc (**Modern Languages, Spanish*)
J Cheetham, BA (*English*)
Miss C-Y Chiang, BSc (*Mandarin*)
Mrs E Coddington, BA (**German, Japanese*)
Mrs C H Collier, BA (*Classics*)
Miss M T Connolly, BSc (*Physics*)
†S A J Coquelin, MA (*French*)
J D Cullen, BSc, MSc (*Physical Education*)
T J Danby, BSc (*Geography*)
A G Day, MA (*Economics*)
Miss E B Delpech, BA (*Art*)
J H Dickinson, MPhys (*Physics*)
J Drury, MA (**Russian*)
Mrs C Duran-Oreiro, DegEd (*Spanish*)

Miss A M Durnford, BA (*English*)
†Mrs C E Dyer, BA (*French, German, LS*)
C H J Dyer, BA (**Music*)
†Mrs T G Edwards, MChem (*Chemistry*)
J C Emmitt, BA (**Physical Education*)
P L Eversfield, MA (**Economics*)
Mrs S C Eversfield, BA (*English*)
Miss N M Fayaud, MA (*French*)
T J K Findley, MSc, PhD (*Chemistry*)
Mrs V J FitzGerald, BA (*History*)
I A Fletcher, BSc (*Chemistry, *Service*)
P Freeman-Jones, BA (*Mathematics*)
Mrs C E Glanville, BA, MA (*Higher Education, English*)
R C Glass, MSci (*Mathematics*)
Mrs N A Glover, BSc (*Mathematics*)
Mrs S E Golding, BA (*Mathematics*)
J W Grant, BA (*Drama, Literature & Performance*)
D C Hall, MA, MPhil (*History*)
S A Hall, BSc (*Psychology*)
C M Harbinson, BA, MA (*English*)
Mrs P O Hargreaves, BA (**PSHE, Drama*)
Miss E R Harris, BSc (*Geography*)
J Harris, BA (*Geography*)
P Harvey, BA, MA (*Drama, English*)
Miss E Hastings, BA, MA (**French*)
M K Heighway, BA (*Music*)
G E Henry, BA, MA (**Drama*)
Mrs C J Henshaw, BA (**English*)
Miss A Hill, BSc (*Mathematics*)
S Holden, BEd (*Physical Education*)
G Howden, BSc, MA (**Mathematics*)
P J Hulston, BSc (*Economics*)
H J Jarvis, BA (*Physical Education*)
R M Jones, BSc (*Technology*)
Mrs E A Joseph, BA (*Physical Education*)
Mrs J L Kiggell, MA, ARCM, AMus, TCL (**Instrumental
   & Vocal Studies*)
L C Kiggell, MBA (*Economics*)
E Kirby, BSc (*Biology*)
N Kunaratnam, BA, MA (**Theory of Knowledge, French*)
Miss H Lacroix, BA (*French*)
J S Lee, BSc, MPhil (*Biology*)
P C Lilley, BA, MA (*Geography*)
R D Lyle, BA, MA (*English*)
T MacBain, BA (*History*)
Mrs A Mack, BA, MA (**History*)
J Magaz Gutiérrez, BA, MA (*Spanish*)
C R Martin, MA, PhD (**Science, *Chemistry*)
S B Mavroleon, BSc (*Physics*)
Mrs A J Maynard, BA (**Head of Learning Support,
   French*)
H A McCormick, BA, MPhil, DPhil (*History, Economics*)
Mrs K A Mylod, BSc (*Biology*)
Miss A E Nairn, BHPE (*Physical Education*)
K T Niklas, BA, MA (*Drama*)
G Oberti Oddi, BA, MA (**Spanish*)
C W Openshaw, BA (**Art*)
Mrs D Orme, BSc, MSc, PhD (*Mathematics*)
M Otero Knott, MA, MLitt, PhD (**Philosophy*)
†S M Owen, MA, PhD (*Chemistry*)
S Palmer, BA, BSc (*Music*)
P E Parham, MSci, MSc, PhD (*Mathematics*)
M Parsons, BA, PhD (*Chemistry*)
C D Potts, BA, MPerf (*Music*)
Miss O C Power, BA (**Systems of Belief, Theory of
   Knowledge*)
R Rands-Webb, MA (*Spanish, French*)
Mrs J E Redding, BA (**Entrepreneurship*)
D W Roche, BEng, MRes, DPhil (*Physics*)
Miss E S Schaefer, BA, MA (*French*)
Ms L U Seetharaman, BA, MA (*English*)

S J Sharp, BSc, PhD (*Physics*)
A Shelley, BA (*English*)
A C Smith, BComm (*Economics*)
Miss C M Smith, BSc (*Physical Education*)
E Spindler, BA, DPhil (*History*)
Miss O Springer, MA (*German*)
Ms N Y Strabić, MMath, PhD (*Mathematics*)
Mrs C S Tate, BA (*Classics*)
J L Tate, BSc (**Physics*)
C P Taylor, MA (**Classics*)
A W Thomas, BSc (*Technology*)
P R Thompson, BA, MA (**Geography*)
Miss A W White, BA (*Mathematics*)
Mrs G P Williams, BSc, PhD (*Mathematics*)
†G J Willis, BA (*Geography*)
A G Wilson, MA (*English*)
J L Witton, BSc (*Biology*)
Mrs N Yang, BSc, PhD (*Mathematics*)
Miss Y Yin, BS, MSc (**Mandarin*)

Part-time Staff:
Ms A Ashwell, MusB, MMus (*Instrumental and Vocal Studies*)
O C Barratt, BA (*Art*)
S Carr, MA (*Classics*)
A J Cornah, LLB, MSc (**Sailing*)
Mrs E M Cummins, BA (*Girls' Games*)
Miss A E Downton, BA (*Spanish*)
Mrs S K Harvey, MA (*Higher Education*)
Mrs J Hendry, Dip RSAM, ARCM (*Music*)
Mrs A M Hulston, BA (*English as an Additional Language*)
Mrs E Kelly (*Russian*)
Mrs S L Lawley, BA (*History*)
Miss G P Low, BA (*Artist in Residence*)
Mrs S J MacLeay, MA (*Geography*)
Mrs A Marr-Johnson, BA (*English*)
Mrs H de May, BA (*Classics*)
D Merewether (*Photography*)
A C Mitchell, BA (*Film, Video*)
Mrs C E Nicholson, BA (*Physical Education*)
Miss S Rahman, BA (*English*)
Mrs H Smith, BA (*Learning Support*)
Mrs A Symons, MSc (*Italian*)
Mrs A J Turner, BSc, MRes (*Biology*)
T T Wey, MA (**Keyboard*)
Mrs A Williams-Walker, BSc (*Mathematics*)

Head of Library: Ms C Woodhouse
Head's PA: Mrs M Thomas

Sherborne Girls

Bradford Road, Sherborne, Dorset DT9 3QN

Tel:	Admissions: 01935 818224
	School: 01935 812245
	Bursar: 01935 818206
Fax:	01935 389445
email:	registrar@sherborne.com
website:	www.sherborne.com
Twitter:	@sherbornegirls
Facebook:	@sherbornegirls
LinkedIn:	/Sherborne-Girls

Sherborne Girls, founded in 1899, provides an outstanding education for 11 to 18 year olds in the beautiful county of Dorset and is proud of its co-curricular programme and exceptional pastoral care. Girls are welcomed at 11+, 12+, 13+ and into the Sixth Form. There are 480 girls: 430 boarders, 50 day girls. The International Baccalaureate Diploma is offered in addition to A Levels, which provides education tailored to each girl's needs. A close relationship with Sherborne School allows co-ed opportunities including music, drama, activities, clubs and societies and social occasions. The schools have the same term dates.

Terms. Three terms of approximately 12 weeks each. Christmas holidays 3 weeks; Easter holidays 3 weeks; Summer holidays 9 weeks. Term dates are in common with those of Sherborne School.

Admission. Common Entrance Examination to Independent Schools. Scholarship Examinations and interviews. The School's own entrance examinations where Common Entrance is not possible. Girls should be registered in advance and reports will be requested from their current school. Pre-assessment for 13+ entry takes place 18 months before entry. For entry into the Sixth Form girls are required to gain 5 good passes in relevant subjects. See the "entry at 16+" page on the website for more details regarding the GCSE points.

Registration fee £200. A deposit of £2,000 is required before entry (a term's fees for overseas pupils) and credited to the last term's bill.

Scholarships and Bursaries. Academic Scholarships are offered at 11+, 13+ and 16+ annually as a result of examination and interview. There are also scholarships offered for outstanding promise in Music, Art, Drama and Sport. All examinations are held in January and February apart from Sixth Form in November. Scholarship awards are made on merit with a maximum merit award of £3,000. Scholarships may be combined with means-tested bursaries which can raise considerably the effective amount of an award. Bursarial support (up to 100%) may be available in cases of demonstrable need.

Music Awards (Junior and 16+): Scholarships of up to £3,000 with free music tuition for up to three lessons per week. Music Exhibitions offer free music tuition for up to three lessons per week.

Art Scholarships (Junior and 16+): Awards of up to £3,000. Candidates will be required to bring a portfolio with them and would be asked to do some work in the Art Department whilst they are here.

Sport Scholarships (Junior and 16+): Awards of up to £3,000. Candidates will offer one or more sports, preferably reaching county standard or higher.

Drama Awards (13+): Scholarships of up to £3,000 with free drama tuition for one lesson per week. Drama Exhibitions offer free drama tuition for one lesson per week.

All-Rounder Award (Junior): Awards of up to 15% of the current fees. All-Rounder Awards take into account ability in two areas of activity outside the classroom (art, drama, music and sport) as well as academic potential.

Fees per term (2018–2019). 13+: boarders £11,960, day boarders* £9,145, day girls £7,095. 11+: boarders £9,640, day girls £7,095 *Day boarders are girls who wish to stay overnight on the odd occasion and for whom a bed space will be made available on request.

Houses. There are five houses for 13–17 year olds and one Upper Sixth house. 11 and 12 year old girls spend their first two years together in Aldhelmsted West house.

Religion. The School has a Church of England foundation, but it values the presence and contribution of members of all the Christian traditions and of other faiths. Regular services are held in the Abbey, some jointly with Sherborne School.

Examinations. Girls are prepared for I/GCSE, A Levels and the International Baccalaureate Diploma. There is a wide choice of subjects to be studied.

Games. Hockey and Lacrosse/Netball are played in the Michaelmas and Lent terms and Tennis, Rounders and Athletics during the Trinity term. Oxley Sports Centre in partnership with Sherborne Girls contains a 25m pool and state-of-the-art fitness suite. There are Squash Courts, floodlit Astroturf, Sports Hall, Dance Studio and Climbing Wall. Riding, Badminton, Cross-Country Running, Golf, Aerobics, Judo, Sailing, Trampolining are some of the alternative games.

Sherborne Old Girls. All enquiries should be made to Mrs Fiona James at the School, Tel: 01935 818329.

Prospective parents and their daughters are invited to the school for Tour Mornings (approximately monthly during term time), or private visits by appointment. Please visit the school's website or telephone Admissions on 01935 818224 for further details.

Charitable status. Sherborne School for Girls is a Registered Charity, number 307427. It exists to provide education for girls in a boarding environment.

Council:
Chairman: Mr R Strang
Vice Chairs: Lady Plaxy Arthur
Members:

Ms J Blanch	Mrs L Hall
Mrs K Brock	Mrs A Harris
Mrs I Burke	Mr R A L Leach
Dr S Connors	Mr P Pilkington
Mr I Davenport	Mr R Price
Lt Gen Sir Robert Fry	Mrs A L M Simon
Mr W J A Gordon	Mr P Ward
The Rt Revd Karen	Mrs M Wingfield Digby
Gorham	Mr N Wordie

Clerk to the Council: Mrs F Clapp

Senior and Pastoral Staff:

Headmistress: Dr Ruth Sullivan, BSc, PGCE Edinburgh, MSc, PhD London School of Hygiene and Tropical Medicine

Bursar: Mrs Fiona Clapp, MBA, BSc Hons Londons PGCE
Deputy Head Teaching and Learning: Mrs Louise Orton, BSc Swansea, PGCE
Deputy Head Pastoral and Planning: Mr Ben Gudgeon, MA, BA, AMusTCL, FRSA
Head of Sixth Form: Mrs Florence Corran, MPhil Oxford
Director of Boarding: Miss Bex Brown
Director of Development and Marketing: Mrs Katherine Massey, BA Hons Oxford Brookes

Chaplain: Revd Katie Windle, BA Durham, MA Nottingham, PGCE, Dip MM Nottingham

Housemistresses of Boarding Houses:
Aldhelmsted East: Mrs D Miller, BEd Manchester
Aldhelmsted West: Miss H McIlvean, BSA Dip
Dun Holme: Mr R Garnsworthy, BE Australia and Mrs H Garnsworthy
Wingfield Digby: Mr O McManus, BA Hons Nottingham, PGCE and Mrs K McManus, BA Hons Bournemouth, PCE
Reader Harris: Mr J Hammond, BEd Hons Gloucester & Mrs S Hammond, BEd Wellington NZ
Kenelm: Mrs F Barnes, BSc Lancaster, PGCE
Mulliner: Miss C Howell Evans, BSc Hons Dunelm, PGCE

Staff:
* Head of Department

Art, Design and Food Technology:
*Mrs C Mason, BA Reading, MA, PCE
Mrs A D Heron Watkins, BA Southampton
Miss T Farris, Leiths, BSc Texas

Ms P Ellis, MA London, BA Courtauld Institute London
Mr J Casely, BA Hons, MPhil Birmingham
Miss F Bugg, BA Hons, PGCE
Mrs A Diggle Perry, BA Hons Middx, PGCE
Mr N Wright, BA, MA, PGCE
Mrs D Miller, BEd Hons
Miss E Smith, BA Hons, PGCE

Classics:
Mrs R M Allen, BA Birmingham
Miss S Haslam, MA Cantab, PGCE

Drama and Theatre Studies:
*Miss E Nurse, BA Manchester, PGCE
Mrs R Johnson, BA CSSD London
Miss S Skowronska, BA Hons Leeds

English:
Mrs L Troup, BA Hons London, PGCE
Ms K Chapman, BEd Southampton
Mr J Hammond, BEd Hons Gloucester
Mrs J Ward, BA OU, Dip SpLD, TESL Toronto, AMI Toronto, PGCE
Mr S P Wood, BA Oxon, PGCE
Mrs F Corran, MA Oxon, MPhil Oxon
Miss L Suttle, BA Birmingham
Mr O McManus, BA Hons Nottingham, PGCE
Mr R Barnes, LLB Hons Liverpool, MEd, PGCE

Geography, Economics and Business Studies:
*Mrs E Morray-Jones, BSc Surrey
Mrs C Morgan, BSc Wales, PGCE
Mrs F Barnes, BSc Hons Lancaster, PGCE
Miss L Mullins, BA Hons Loughborough, PGCE Durham
Mr D Banks, BSc Cardiff, PGCE
Mrs K Creswell, MA Edinburgh
Mrs E Wimhurst, MBA Bournemouth, PGCE

History:
*Mrs S Elliot, BA Hons Reading
Mrs S Francis, MA Oxon
Ms S Haslam, MA Cantab, PGCE
Mrs K Scorer, MA Oxon, PGCE

ICT:
Mr O McManus, BA Hons Nottingham Trent, PGCE

Mathematics:
*Mr P Utting, BSc Hons Warwick, PGCE Birmingham
Mrs L Orton, BSc Hons Swansea, PGCE
Miss J Davidson, BSc UMIST, PGCE
Mrs J Edmondson, BSc, MA
Dr A Moore, BEng, PhD Bristol, MA Nottingham
Mr S Payne, BSc Kent, PGCE
Dr G Collins, MMath Durham

Modern Languages:
*Miss M Gorbat, BA Oxford, DTLLS, PGCE
Mme M-D Bonelli-Bean, Licence LLCE Paris
Mrs G Carvia-Ruiz, PGCE
Mrs P J Fieldhouse, MA London, BA Rhodes, PGCE
Senora Lopez, BA Castellon
Mr J Reed, BA Hons London, MA Hong Kong, PGCE London

Music:
*Mr J M Jenkins, BA Dunelm, ARCO
Mr S Clarkson, BMus Edinburgh, FRCO, ARCM
Mr B Gudgeon, MA, BA, AMusTCL
Miss A Manero, BMus, PG Dip, MMus
Mrs J Nelson, MEd, Dip RAM, LRAM, RAM
Miss C Win Morgan, BMus Manchester, Dip RAM, LRAM
30 visiting teachers

Musical tuition in:

Flute, Clarinet, Saxophone, Percussion, Singing, Alexander Technique, Oboe, Bass/Electric/Classical Guitar, Baroque Recorder, Brass, Violin/Viola, Cello, Piano and Harp.

Physical Education:

Mrs J Dart, BSc Hons Oxford Brookes
Mr M Spivey, BAS Australia
Mrs N Matthias, BEd
Mr R Garnsworthy, BE Australia
Mrs E Spivey, BA Exeter
Miss S Walls, BEd
Mr J Bell, BA, Plymouth
Mr T Clarke, BSc Surrey, PGCE
Miss H Greenway, BSc Hons St Marks and St Johns, PGCE
Mr N Hind, BSc Hons Brighton

Religious Studies:

*Mrs G Burchell, BA Hons Middlesex, PGCE
Mr S D Loxton, PhD Seattle, BEd Sussex, MPhil Hull
Mrs S Hammond, BEd Wellington, NZ
Mrs M Tillyer, BA, PGCE

EAL and Learning Support:

Ms S Aristotlous, MEd, TEFL
Mrs L Broadbent, MA Edinburgh
Dr J Ivimey-Cook, BSc, PhD, PGCE
Mrs J Trew
Mrs J Birley, BA Hons OU, PGC TA DLHE
Mrs P Cole, BEd Exeter, Dip SpLD, Cert Ed
Mrs P Golovchenko, Cert Ed Southlands, OCR Dip SpLD
Mrs J Ward, MSc, BA, SpLD Dip, TESL, AMI, PGCE

Sciences:

*Mr A Angelosanto, BSc, PGCE
Mr T Connolly, BSc Kent, PGCE
Miss P Abbott, BSc Southampton
Mr M Crabtree, BSc, LRPS, PGCE
Mrs F Clapp, MBA, BSc London, PGCE
Miss R Brown, BSc London, PGCE
Mrs A Cochrane, BSc Nottingham
Dr J Hopper, BSc Birmingham, PhD London, PGCE
Miss C Howell Evans, BSc Hons, PGCE
Miss J Clarke, BSc Loughborough
Mr J Blake, BA Hons Oxon, PGCE
Mr James Grierson, MA Hons Oxon, PGCE

Sanatorium Sister: Mrs A Watson, RGN
Registrar: Mrs J Hinks
Librarian and Learning Resource Manager: Mrs J Watts, BA Hons
Head of Higher Education and Careers: Mrs P Utting, BA Hons Portsmouth
Headmistress's PA: Mrs J Horton
Outdoor Activities Instructor: Mrs J Dart, BSc Hons Oxford Brookes

Sherborne School

Abbey Road, Sherborne, Dorset DT9 3AP

Tel:	01935 812249
	01935 810403 (Admissions)
Fax:	01935 810426
email:	admissions@sherborne.org
website:	www.sherborne.org
Twitter:	@SherborneSchool
Facebook:	@SherborneBoysSchool

Royal Arms of Edward VI: *Dieu et mon droit.*

The origins of Sherborne School date back to the eighth century, when a tradition of education at Sherborne was begun by St Aldhelm. The School was linked with the Benedictine Abbey, the earliest known Master was Thomas Copeland in 1437. Edward VI refounded the School in 1550. The present School stands on land which once belonged to the Monastery. The Library, Chapel, and Headmaster's offices which adjoin the Abbey Church, are modifications of the original buildings of the Abbey.

Situation. The School lies in the attractive Abbey town of Sherborne. By train, Salisbury is forty minutes away, London and Heathrow two hours.

Organisation. There are about 550 boarders and 50 day boys, accommodated in eight houses, all of which are within easy walking distance of the main school.

Admission. Entry is either at 13+ (Year 9) or 16+ (Sixth Form) with a small number of places available at 14+ (Year 10) Assessment days take place for 13+ entry when pupils are in year 7. Pupils may then sit scholarship examinations or Common Entrance in year 8. Other entrance tests take place throughout the year of enrolment.

Parents who would like to enter their sons for the School or have any queries, should contact the Director of Admissions.

Visits. Visits can be arranged at any time of the year by contacting the Admissions Office, Tel: 01935 810403.

Scholarships and Exhibitions. Sherborne offers a wide range of scholarships and exhibitions at 13+ entry: Academic (February); Music (January); Art, Design & Technology, Drama, Sport (February), All Rounder (February). Sixth Form Academic and Sports Exhibitions are also offered annually.

Open Scholarships: For 13+ entry, a number of Scholarships of up to 20% of fees (the top scholarship being the Alexander Ross Wallace Scholarship) and up to eight Exhibitions of up to 10% of fees may be awarded. In awarding one of these Exhibitions regard will be paid to special proficiency in a particular subject.

In addition Awards are available to those who are able to demonstrate outstanding ability in one of the following areas: Art, Design & Technology, Music, Drama and Sport.

A number of Music Awards are available at 13+. In addition one Marion Packer Scholarship of £600 pa for an outstanding performance on the piano may be offered. Those given Awards receive free instrumental tuition.

A number of all-rounder awards are available for pupils showing talent and passion across a range of disciplines.

Closed Awards: Raban Exhibition of 10% of fees for the sons of serving or ex-service officers; a Nutting Exhibition of 10% of fees for sons of RN Officers.

The maximum value of any award is 20% of the fees but this may be supplemented by bursarial assistance in cases of financial need.

Further details of all awards are available from the Director of Admissions.

Sixth Form Entry. Places are available for boys who wish to join the Sixth Form to study A Levels for two years. Scholarship and entrance examinations take place by arrangement with the Director of Admissions. There are up to two scholarships offered annually. Also available, for good A Level candidates, is the Arkwright Scholarship for Technology. Offers of Sixth Form places are dependent on satisfactory performance in GCSE examinations.

Curriculum. All pupils follow a broadly based curriculum for their first three years to GCSE. In the Sixth Form boys study at least three A Levels drawn from a wide choice of available courses. There is also a diverse and stretching enrichment programme as a part of the compulsory curriculum. Opportunities for research projects are available to broaden the scope of pupils' studies. Some of the courses for A Level are run jointly with Sherborne Girls.

Careers and Universities. The Careers Department has an enviable reputation. Boys experience work shadowing programmes in the fifth and lower sixth forms – these are followed by careers conventions, university visits, parents' forums and lessons in interview techniques. There is an encyclopaedic, fully computerised Careers Room with regularly updated contacts with those at university and at work. The department has visited all universities and places of higher education. Virtually all leavers go on to university.

Pastoral Care. The boys in each house are in the care of a Housemaster and his wife, a resident tutor and a resident matron. In addition a team of tutors assists the Housemaster in the running of the House and boys have many avenues of support and advice available to them. The School Chaplain also plays a major role and will talk with a boy whenever required. A School Counsellor is available.

Tutor. Each boy has a personal Tutor who not only monitors his academic progress but provides a useful contact point for parents.

Religion. The weekly pattern of Christian services in the school Chapel or Sherborne Abbey underpin the spiritual rhythm of the school. There is a wide variety of voluntary Christian groups and services including a Friday night candlelit Eucharist which is well attended. Boys can be prepared for Confirmation into the Church of England and the Roman Catholic Church. Theology is taught throughout the school and boys can opt for a GCSE Religious Studies course and a Philosophy and Ethics A Level course.

Community Service. Boys take part in a busy programme aimed at encouraging a sense of responsibility towards the local community. Entertainment, fundraising, clubs and assistance are organised for the young and elderly in and around Sherborne.

Art. The Art School is a dynamic and highly successful department achieving outstanding academic results at all levels. The core disciplines are based around the study of Fine Art, which enables students to approach a broad curriculum encompassing an eclectic mix of approaches such as painting, photography, 3D, digital media, printing and performance.

Design and Technology. In recent years the Design and Technology Department has been through a programme of complete refurbishment. The subject is taught from year nine right through to A Level and pupils can go on to higher education courses in Product and Aeronautical Design, Architecture and Engineering. The department has developed links with local industries where pupils can see CAD/CAM production, commercial furniture design and precision casting in process. It runs afternoon activities and is open on both Saturdays and Sundays.

Music. There is a strong music tradition in the School – over 400 music lessons take place every week. There are two full orchestras, various chamber music groups, many different types of jazz band, a brass group, a swing band, Chapel choir and a choral society, not to mention rock bands. Many of these groups tour both home and abroad. Numerous concerts, recitals and musical productions are held throughout the year. Lunch time concerts take place every Friday. Regular subscription concerts are given by visiting professional musicians.

Drama. Drama productions of all kinds are a major feature of school life, from large scale musicals to classical drama, substantial modern works and fringe performances, many staged with Sherborne Girls. The sophisticated technical resources of the Powell Theatre attract programmes from professional touring companies. The newly instated, state-of-the-art drama studios underpin the school's ambition for this important part of the pupils' learning.

Information Technology. The school has a fast wireless network that is available throughout the school, including in boarding houses. Safe filtering systems and time restrictions are in place to protect pupils. Pupils are encouraged to connect their own devices to the network, but there are also a large number of fixed terminal computers, including six major computer suites around the school. The school is embracing new technologies and runs a sophisticated Virtual Learning Environment to support pupils' learning away from the classroom.

Sports. There are over fifty acres of sports fields, where, at any one time, seventeen various games or matches can take place. Other facilities include two AstroTurf pitches, twenty tennis courts, Rugby fives courts and a shooting range. Within the School's sports centre there is a sports hall, a twenty-five metre swimming pool, a fitness suite and squash courts. A wide variety of sports and activities are offered including athletics, badminton, basketball, canoeing, cricket, cross-country, fencing, fives, golf, hockey, polo, riding, rugby, sailing, shooting, soccer, sub-aqua, swimming and tennis.

Societies and Activities. In addition to a full sporting, music and drama programme, numerous academic societies meet regularly throughout the term. Other activities and clubs take place on Wednesday afternoons and whenever time allows. They include: bridge, chess, computing, debating, photography, dining, life drawing, cooking for university, film making, community service, speech and drama and United Nations.

The school has a strong tradition of outdoor education and, in addition to The Duke of Edinburgh's Award scheme, there are walking, climbing, kayaking and sailing trips. These are local or further afield in Scotland, the Lake District, Wales, Exmoor, Dartmoor and occasionally abroad. Boys also take part in the annual Ten Tors Challenge.

Membership of the Combined Cadet Force is voluntary and the Army, Royal Navy and Royal Marine sections attract about 150 boys each year. A large number of trips and camps are arranged during the term time and the holidays.

Old Shirburnian Society. Mr John Harden, Secretary, tel: 01935 810557, email: OSS@sherborne.org.

Girls' Schools. There is close liaison with the neighbouring girls' schools, which allows us to offer many of the real benefits of co-education with all the advantages of a single-sex secondary education. As well as the Joint Sixth Form academic courses with Sherborne Girls, drama, music and social activities are arranged throughout the year.

Fees per term (2018–2019). Boarders: £12,500; Day Boys: £10,125.

Charitable status. Sherborne School is a Registered Charity, number 1081228, and a Company Limited by Guarantee, registered in England and Wales, number 4002575. Its aim and objectives are to supply a liberal education in accordance with the principles of the Church of England.

Governors of the School:

Chairman: R S Fidgen Esq, FRICS
Vice-Chairman: G A Hudson Esq, MA

Ex officio:
Her Majesty's Lord Lieutenant for the County of Dorset's nominated representative, R Lucas-Rowe Esq, DL
The Rector of Sherborne, The Revd Canon E J Woods, DL, MA

Co-opted:
M L French Esq, FCA
R A L Leach Esq, MA
G Marsh Esq, MA, Cert Ed
Mrs I Burke, MB, BS, MRCGP
A Charlton Esq, CMG, CVO

Mrs V Cotter, LLB Hons, LLM
Mrs G Staley, BSc, MSc, CMIOSH
Mrs A C Lane, BA, FCA
R-J Temmink Esq, QC
R H W Robson Esq
M T Wilson Esq, BSc, QTS
Dr M Jonas Esq, MBBS, FRCA, FFICM
Mrs E Stallard, JP
Lt Gen D Leakey, CMG, CVO, CBE, MA Cantab

Staff Nominated: M J Whittell Esq, MA, MSc

Bursar and Clerk to the Governors: Mrs L A Robins, BSc, MRICS

Headmaster and CEO: D A Luckett, BA, DPhil, FRSA, FHA

Senior Deputy Head: M I Jamieson, BA
Deputy Head (Academic): T W Filtness, BA, MA, PhD
Assistant Head (Academic): Miss K L Millar, BA
Assistant Head (Co-curricular): H F Tatham, MA
Assistant Head (Sixth Form): T j Rimmer, BSc

Housemasters:
Abbey House: M J McGinty, AKC, BA, MSc (Tel: 01935 810561)
Abbeylands: S J Clayton, CertEd PE, Dip Sp Psy & Mrs V A Clayton, BA, MEd, MCLIP (Tel: 01935 810570)
The Digby: R C Le Poidevin, BA, MA, MSc (Tel: 01935 810170)
The Green: S K Byrne, BA (Tel: 01935 810440)
Harper House: J J B Wadham, BSc, PhD (Tel: 01935 812128)
Lyon House: B P Sunderland, BEng (Tel: 01935 810970)
School House: K G Jackson, BA (Tel: 01935 810411)
Wallace House: A D Nurton, BA (Tel: 01935 810980)

Director of Admissions: Mrs V Hicks
Admissions Officer: Miss A Wareham

Staff:
* *Head of Department/Subject*

Art:
*J E Wright, BA, MA
Mrs E S Drake, BA
M C Bone, BA
Miss K R Connelly, BA
Ms V L Fraser, BA
O Senneck, BA

Biology:
*J-P A Manning, BMSc, PhD, MEd
D J Ridgway, Bsc
T W Filtness, BA, MA, PhD
G R Harwood, BSc
Miss E L Southall, BSc, MSc
J J B Wadham, BSc, PhD

Chemistry:
*W E Buckley, BSc
N C Scorer, MChem
D A Watson, BSc
Mrs R C Utting, BSc

Classics:
*S A Heath, BA
P J Garland, BA, MA
N J Hall, BA
S Tremewan, BA, PhD

Design and Technology:
*P R Chillingworth, BA

J W R Walker, BA

Drama:
*I C C Reade, BA
Mrs V A Clayton, BA, MEd, MCLIP
Ms B Darnley, BA
Miss R K Thomas, BA

Economics and Business Studies:
*R T B Harris, BA, MBA
P C Bedford, BA
A R Duncan, BA
M C Ewart-Smith, MBA, MInstCEng
C M O'Donnell, BA
N J Robinson, BA

English:
*Mrs R E C de Pelet, MA
M J Brooke, MA
Miss H L Cant, BA
M P O'Connor, BA, Cert SpLD
T W Payne, BA
G T W Robinson, BA
J L Winter, MA

Geography:
*J P A Wilson, BSc
A M Hatch, BA
Miss K L Millar, BA

M Ollis, BA
T J Rimmer, BSc

Government and Politics:
*R C Le Poidevin, MA, MA, MSc
M J McGinty, AKC, BA, MSc

History:
*G D R Reynolds, MA
J P Crouch, BA
M J McGinty, AKC, BA, MSc
Ms A E Pearson, BA, MA
M I Jamieson, BA
B L Wild, MA, PhD, FRHistS

Learning Support:
*Mrs C J Carrier, BA
Mrs E J H Ashton, BBA, Dip SpLD
Mrs H M Bajorat, BA
M P O'Connor, BA, Cert SpLD
Mrs S G Ollis, BA
Mrs S M L Reade, BSc, UNESP

Mathematics:
*S-C Lim, MSc,
Miss A E R Civardi, BSc
T A J Dawson, BSc, Dip Stats, MA
Miss K L Evans, BSc
N A Henderson, BSc, MBA
Mrs S K Mertens, BA, MA, MSc, PhD
A C Morgan, BSc, MSc, FRSA
P C Spencer, BSc, PhD
Miss C M Standen, MA, FCA
B P Sunderland, BEng
Mrs C L Tatham, BSc

Modern Languages:
*Mrs J R Thurman, BA
Miss E A Bailon-Artal, MA

Medical Officers:
C P Cleaver, MBChB, MRCGP
K Dixon, MBBS, MRCGP, DFFP
I A Latham, MBBS, MRCGP, DFFP

Nurse Manager: Mrs M Hutchings, RGN
Sports and Uniform Shop: Mrs M Reade

S K Byrne, BA
Mrs C E Greenrod, BA, Cert TEFL (*Head of EAL*)
Miss F I James, BA, MA, MSc
Mrs L Liu-Plant
B Lucas, BA
P A Morrow, BA, MA (*Head of Spanish*)
A D Nurton, BA
A R Oates, BA, MLitt (*Head of French*)
Miss N C Ritty, BA
T J Scott, BA
Mrs J M Slade, BA

Music:
*J E C Henderson, MA
B J Davey, GRSM, LRAM
M D Lehnert, BA, MMus
E J Park, BA, MPhil

Physical Education:
*R P McGuire, BA, MPhil
D A R Guy, BA (*Director of Sport*)
S J Clayton, Cert Ed PE, Dip Sp Psy
C Smith, BA

Physics:
*M D Thurman, BSc
R A Brown, MPhys, PhD (*Head of Science*)
J J Kimber, BSc
D J Murray, BSC
J G Willetts, MA, CPhys, MInstP, MBCS

PSHE:
*D J Murray, BSc

Theology:
*J A Crawford, MA
Mrs N L J Bowerman, BA
Revd D Campbell, MTh, CECM, MTh, DMin
K G Jackson, BA
H F Tatham, MA

Shiplake College

Henley-on-Thames, Oxon RG9 4BW

Tel:	0118 940 2455
email:	registrar@shiplake.org.uk
website:	www.shiplake.org.uk
Twitter:	@ShiplakeCollege
Facebook:	@shiplakecollege

Motto: '*Exemplum docet*' (Example teaches)

Shiplake College is an independent boarding and day school for almost 500 pupils (boys aged 11 to 18 and girls aged 16 to 18), based in inspirational Oxfordshire countryside.

Ethos. Whilst Shiplake College has evolved and moved forward since its founding in 1959, many principles remain the same. We ensure that every pupil is challenged and supported according to their need and ability, providing an education that is tailored to the individual. We firmly believe that in addition to a solid academic grounding, sporting, social and cultural achievements are vital to a pupil's long-term development. Shiplake offers a wide range of challenging enrichment activities to ensure an all-round education.

Academic. We aim to admit a well-balanced intake of pupils with a variety of skills and talents. Pupils are selected on his or her potential to make the most of the opportunities that Shiplake can offer and the value we can add to their education. We are proud of our superb value-added results. At Shiplake, teaching and learning concentrates on delivering excellent teaching through small classes and individual attention with a supportive but stimulating environment.

Pastoral Care. Shiplake College is renowned for delivering outstanding pastoral care – a reputation that has been built and maintained over a sustained period of time, largely due to the belief in a holistic approach to education. Houses are a huge part of the Shiplake community. Each house is run by a Housemaster who is supported by a strong team of staff including the House Matron, House Tutor, Visiting Tutors, the Medical Staff and the Chaplain. The houses provide excellent support for the pupils in addition to ensuring a comfortable, homely environment for pupils to study or relax. There is a strong house spirit in evidence with competitions organised for arts, games and academic progress.

Boys joining at 11+ enter the Lower School which houses Years 7 and 8. From Year 9 all pupils become a member of one five houses. Both day and boarding girls join Gilson House, the purpose-built girls' house, but are attached to one of the boys' houses for social purposes, duties and inter-house competitions. The Upper Sixth boys enjoy the separate facilities of College House which helps establish independence before the move to university or a career.

Knowing our pupils well enables us to ensure that they get the best from their education at Shiplake. We know that every pupil is different and we aim to tailor the support and guidance they receive to suit their individual needs.

As a Christian School there is an extensive programme of worship, very often provided in the neighbouring Parish Church. The Chaplain, whose role is purely pastoral, is always available to any member of the College community. Shiplake also welcomes pupils of other faiths.

Boarding. Boarding is an integral part of life at Shiplake. Full, weekly, flexi boarding and overnight stays (all available from Year 7) allow pupils to fully benefit from all the academic and co-curricular opportunities that we offer. 150 weekly and full boarders enjoy a busy weekend and evening programme, which covers a mixture of cultural, social and sporting trips and activities. International pupils, including a balance of British and non-British students resident abroad, represent approximately 5% of the current school population.

Location. The College is situated in 45 acres of beautiful Oxfordshire countryside, just two miles upstream of the world famous Henley Royal Regatta town of Henley-on-Thames.

Although pupils love the acres of sports pitches and the country trails, parents appreciate the fact that Shiplake is conveniently placed for access to the M4 and M40 and the railway stations at Henley and Reading. This idyllic countryside location is just an hour from London and within easy reach of Heathrow and Gatwick airports.

Facilities. Shiplake House, built in 1889 as a family home, is at the heart of the school. The College is fortunate to have the use of the twelfth-century Parish Church for assemblies and worship. In addition to the main school buildings, Shiplake boasts a range of facilities including the innovative 'Thinking Space', Lecture Theatre, Recording Studio, Tithe Barn Theatre, Sports Hall, Fitness Suite and award-winning Sports Fields. The boathouses are a short walk from the main buildings, allowing direct access to the Thames.

Academic Structure. Boys entering the College in Year 7 follow the specially designed curriculum for Years 7 and 8 before moving on to the Upper School. Boys enjoy the broad and balanced Year 9 curriculum which provides a strong foundation for GCSE. Sixth Form pupils select three subjects from a choice of twenty-two and also complete the EPQ or CoPE qualification.

Learning Development. Shiplake has a dedicated Learning Development Department to provide tailored additional help for both those who are academically gifted and those who find certain subject areas difficult to access. The purpose-built Department is situated in the revolutionary John Turner Building, and provides a first-class environment for pupils to receive additional support, to improve pupils' confidence and self-esteem and equip them with the necessary skills. Pupils are able to approach their subject teachers for additional support whenever necessary.

Sport. Sport is an integral part of life at Shiplake College. Our extensive site on the banks of the River Thames makes Shiplake an ideal location for pupils who love sport. The College has an excellent sporting reputation and most pupils take part in a sporting activity every day. The College enjoys direct access to the river and boathouses, hockey, cricket and rugby pitches, tennis courts, squash courts and an outdoor swimming pool. The sports hall offers a variety of indoor sports, a weight-training gym and a fitness room.

Almost all boys play rugby in the autumn term. In the spring term boys play hockey, football or row, and in the summer term there is the choice of cricket, tennis or rowing. The girls enjoy hockey, netball, rounders, tennis and rowing. Basketball, badminton, judo, yoga, cross-country running and athletics provide additional activities to develop skills and fitness.

For a small school, Shiplake has a remarkable number of crews and teams taking part in events and competitions with national success. There have been a number of overseas tours involving the rugby, cricket, hockey and rowing clubs.

Music, Art and Drama. The College has a thriving mixture of Arts activities and performances and all pupils are encouraged to enjoy the Arts. The annual House Music Competition ensures that every pupil in the school is involved in preparing for a performance and every term there is at least one concert for pupils to demonstrate the progress they have made. The Drama Department provides a range of opportunities for the theatrically inclined, to explore and experiment with the subject beyond the constraints of the curriculum.

Activities. Two afternoons are dedicated to a Co-Curricular programme where pupils choose from a wide range of activities including art, ballroom dancing, cookery, debating, Japanese and canoeing. The College has a thriving Combined Cadet Force with Air Force, Army and Navy sections. Pupils take part in community service activities and the school has links to a Kenyan School for which fundraising activities are regularly undertaken. The College also runs a Duke of Edinburgh's Award scheme with a number of pupils each year collecting Gold Awards.

Careers. There is an experienced Careers Adviser and particular attention is paid to the choice of university and career from Year 11 onwards. The School is a member of Inspiring Futures.

Admission. The Registrar is the first point of contact for all admissions enquiries. Boys are admitted at 11+ into Year 7 and at 13+ into Year 9. There is an intake into the Sixth Form for boys and girls. Places are offered following an assessment day. Please contact the Registrar for further details. Occasional places arise in other years.

Scholarships. Means-tested scholarships and bursaries are offered for academic excellence and to outstanding sportsmen, artists, actors or musicians at Year 7, Year 9 and in the Sixth Form.

Fees per term (2018–2019). Full Boarders £11,025; Weekly Boarders: Years 9–13 (6 nights) £10,340, Years 7 & 8 (4 nights) £8,270; Flexi Boarding (2 nights): Years 9–13 £8,475, Years 7 & 8 £6,965; Day: Years 7 & 8 £5,900, Years 9–13 £7,410.

Alumni. The Old Viking Society has an annual programme of sporting and social events. The Society produces an annual magazine for Old Vikings, as well as frequent e-newsletters.

Charitable status. Shiplake College is a Registered Charity, number 309651. It exists to provide education for children.

Chairman of Governors: The Rt Hon T J C Eggar
Vice-Chairman of Governors: M G E Mackenzie-
    Charrington

Headmaster: **A G S Davies**

Bursar and Clerk to the Governors: J Ralfs
Deputy Headmaster (Academic): P Jones
Deputy Headmaster (Pastoral): N Brown
Assistant Head (Sixth Form): R Curtis
Assistant Head (Academic Studies): R Ebbage
Assistant Head (Co-Curricular): A Hunt
*Assistant Head (Staff Development and Community
    Outreach)*: A Dix
Director of Sport: M Griffiths
Director of Learning Development: Mrs A Higgins

Shrewsbury School

The Schools, Shrewsbury, Shropshire SY3 7BA

Tel: 01743 280500 (Switchboard)
            01743 280525 (Headmaster)
            01743 280820 (Bursar)
            01743 280552 (Director of Admissions)
Fax: 01743 243107 (Reception)
            01743 280559 (Admissions)
            01743 272094 (Bursary)
email: admissions@shrewsbury.org.uk
website: www.shrewsbury.org.uk
Twitter: @ShrewsSchool

Motto: '*Intus si recte, ne labora*'

Shrewsbury School was founded by King Edward VI in 1552 and augmented by Queen Elizabeth in 1571. In 1882 it moved from the centre of the town to its present site overlooking the town and the River Severn.

Number in School. There are 789 pupils in the School (618 boarding and 171 day).

Admission. Most admissions are in September. Girls and boys are admitted at 13 or (direct to the Sixth Form) at 16. Registration forms and other information can be obtained from the Admissions Office. The registration fee, which is non-returnable, is £100.

Entry at 13: Pupils usually take the Common Entrance Examination or the Scholarship Examination in the term preceding that in which they wish to come. The School has

its own entrance test for pupils who have not followed the Common Entrance syllabus.

Sixth Form Entry: Direct entry into the Sixth Form depends on examination at Shrewsbury, an interview, and a favourable report from the applicant's present school.

Scholarships. Shrewsbury School has had a tradition, since its founding Charter in 1552, of making generous scholarship awards. Scholarships fall into various categories – Academic, Music, Art, Drama, Design & Technology, Sport and All-Rounder. Awards are made either to pupils under the age of 14 joining the school in the Third Form, or to those entering the school at Sixth Form level.

Buildings. The school operates a rolling programme of refurbishment for all boarding houses. Similarly, large-scale refurbishment of the teaching accommodation is currently under way. All classrooms are professionally equipped to a very high standard. A Music School, including an auditorium and a large ensemble room, was opened in February 2001, a cricket academy and a new house (now accommodating day and boarding girls) opened in 2006, a new swimming pool opened in 2007, a new sixth form centre was completed in 2008, and two further houses for girls opened in September 2011 and September 2014 respectively. A new, 19-classroom academic block opened in October 2015 and a Design and Technology Centre was opened in 2016. A fourth girls' house was opened in September 2017.

The Moser Library houses the School Library, the Moser collection of watercolours, and the Ancient Library, which contains medieval manuscripts and early printed books.

Courses of Study. All pupils follow a general course as far as GCSE (or IGCSE) examinations. In the Sixth Form, pupils study either three or four subjects leading to A Level (or Pre-U) qualifications. Many also complete an Extended Project or follow the Pre-U Global Perspectives course.

Games. Rowing, Cricket, Association Football, Swimming, Lacrosse, Hockey, Netball, Cross-Country, Eton Fives and Rugby. The School has its own indoor Swimming Pool, Gymnasium, Multi-gym, Miniature Rifle Range, all-weather playing surface, Tennis Courts, Squash Courts and Fives Courts. The River Severn flows just below the Main School Building and the Boat House is within the school grounds.

Activities. Pupils are offered a considerable range of outdoor activities via the Combined Cadet Force, leadership courses and the Duke of Edinburgh's Award scheme. The programme of activities and opportunities continues to broaden as a pupil moves up the School.

Art and Design. Art and Design are taught to all pupils in their first year. For those not doing GCSE or A Level courses they subsequently become activities followed mainly, but not exclusively, out of school hours. The Art and Design Technology centres are available seven days a week. The Design Technology department offers the chance of advanced design work and of creative work in a variety of materials.

Societies. These range from Literary, Political, Debating, Drama and Language societies to those catering for practical skills. Hillwalkers and Mountaineers make use of the unspoilt country on the doorstep and of the Welsh hills.

Music. Teaching is available in any orchestral instrument, as well as the Piano and Organ. The charge for this is £22.50 per 40 minute lesson for all instruments. Regular Choral, Orchestral and Chamber Concerts both at the school and elsewhere (e.g. Cadogan Hall, St John's, Smith Square; Birmingham Town Hall) are given by the pupils. In addition concerts are given during the winter months by distinguished visiting artists.

Drama. Drama is a major feature of school life, with two school plays and a range of house plays every year, together with regular accolades at the Edinburgh Fringe.

Field Study Centre. Shrewsbury owns a farmhouse in Snowdonia, which is used at weekends throughout the year as a base for expeditions.

Careers. There is Careers Adviser and a Higher Education Adviser. Pupils receive a programme of Careers guidance throughout the school.

Community Service. In association with other schools in the town, pupils play an active part in caring for the old and needy in the Shrewsbury area.

Shrewsbury House. Founded in Liverpool as a Club for boys in 1903, it was rebuilt as a Community Centre in association with the Local Authority and the Diocese in 1974. There is residential accommodation in the Centre and groups of pupils from the School have the opportunity to go there on study courses.

Shrewsbury International Schools. The school has close links with Shrewsbury International School in Bangkok. Teaching and pupil exchanges take place between the two schools, and Governors of Shrewsbury School serve on the board of management of the International School. Shrewsbury International School Hong Kong opened its doors to primary school children in September 2018.

Fees per term (2018–2019). Boarders: £12,090–£13,040 including tuition, board and ordinary School expenses. There are no other obligatory extras, apart from stationery. Day Pupils: £8,295–£8,745.

Application for reduced fees may be made to the Governors through the Headmaster.

Old Pupils' Society. Most pupils leaving the school join the Salopian Club, The Schools, Shrewsbury SY3 7BA; email: oldsalopian@shrewsbury.org.uk.

Charitable status. Shrewsbury School is a Registered Charity, number 528413. It exists to provide secondary education.

Governing Body:

Chairman: T H P Haynes, MA

Vice-Chairs:
Mrs Lyndsey O'Loughlin, LLB
P StJ Worth, FCA

S R Baker, BSc, FCA, CF
Cllr T H Biggins, MA
R C Boys-Stones, BSc, FCA
D C Chance, MBA
J R Clark, MA
Sir Peter Davis, LLD Hons
Prof C Dobson, FRS
Mrs D Flint, DL
Dr Fiona Hay, MA, BM, BCh, DRCOG, MRCGP, DFFP, MSc PallMed
Mrs C Howarth, LLB, MA
W R O Hunter, QC
Prof A J McCarthy, BSc, PhD
J M H Moir, BA, MBA
Cllr C M Motley, BA
Mrs G Walters, BBLS
G C Woods MA

Headmaster: **N L Winkley**, MA, MEd

Bursar and Clerk to the Governors: M J Ware, MA, ACA
Second Master: M J Tonks, BA
Senior Master and Director of Admissions: M J Cropper, MA
Deputy Head (Academic): M H Walters, MA
Deputy Head (Pastoral): Ms A R Peak, BA
Deputy Head (Co-Curricular): P J Middleton, BA
Director of Teaching & Learning: S H Cowper, MA
Director of Shrewsbury School Foundation: J G E Rolfe

Assistant Masters/Mistresses:
* *Head of Faculty*
† *Housemaster/Housemistress*

Mrs R W Adams, BEc, BEd
Revd A C V Aldous, BA (*Assistant Chaplain*)
Mrs G Ansell (*Director of Internationalism*)
J C Armstrong, BA
A S Barnard, BA (†*Port Hill – day boys*)
M W D Barrett, BSc (†*Rigg's Hall*)
R Barrett, MSc, PhD
G StJ F Bell, BA
M C Bird, BA (†*School House*)
Mrs N J Bradburne, BA (*Head of Girls' Games*)
A D Briggs, BSc, PhD (*Science)
Miss H R Brown, MA (**Director of Drama*)
J R Burke, BSc
Mrs L A Caddel, BA (*Art)
R A J Case, BSc, PhD (†*Radbrook – day boys*)
O J Chipperton, BA
M D H Clark, MA
C E Cook, MA
S K P Cooley, MEng
Miss L J Cooper, BA
T A C Corbett, BSc (*Chemistry)
Mrs A J Crump, BSc (†*Emma Darwin Hall*)
N P David, BSc
Miss G M Davies, BSc
Mrs J M M Davies, BSc
Mrs L J Drew, BA
M S Elliot, MA, PhD
R F Evans, BSc
H A S M Exham, BSc (*Head of Digital Learning*)
H P Farmer, BA (*Director of Welfare*)
R T Fitton, MEng
P G Fitzgerald, MA (*Classics)
Mrs S Fletcher, BSc
S A A Fox, BA
J R Fraser-Andrews, MA
J Gabbitas, BA MA
S C Griffiths, BA (†*Ingram's Hall*)
M H Hansen, BSc
M J Harding, BA
S M Harrison, BA, MA
I P Haworth, MA
Ms P E Henderson, BA (*Spanish)
Miss E C Higgins, BA
R T Hudson, MA (†*Churchill's Hall*)
W A Hughes, BA (†*Ridgemount*)
M A C Humphreys, MA
A T Hundermark, BSc (**Director of Rowing*)
M D B Johnson, BSc, BA (†*Oldham's Hall*)
D M Joyce, Dip RCM, ARCM
P A Kaye, BEng (*Educational ICT)
C W Kealy, BComm (*Business Studies)
Mrs E J Kelly, BA (**Head of Curriculum Physical Education*)
Revd A F C Keulemans, BSc (*Chaplain*)
M A Kirk, BSc (*Physics)
Mrs V L Kirk, BSc
Mrs S G Latcham, BA
D A Law, BA, MA, PhD
Mrs K Leslie, BA (*English)
Mrs A Livingstone, MA
K M Lloyd, BA (**Design & Technology*)
J V Lucas, LLB, BSc (*Head of Third Form*)
H G Mackridge, MA (*History)
A E Mason, BA, MMus (*Director of the Chapel Choir*)
Mrs J A Matthews, BSc
F Matthews-Bird, BSc PhD
Miss H M Y May, AB (*Head of Middle School*)

Mrs M L McKenzie, BMus, MMus, LTCL (*Head of Wind, Brass and Percussion*)

P A Merricks-Murgatroyd, BA (**Economics*)

Miss E D Micklewright, BA

Mrs K V Mitchell, MA, Dip Ed, APC, AMBDA (**Learning Support*)

J F Moore, BA, LRAM (**Director of Music*)

T S Morgan, BSc, PhD (**Biology*)

A P Morris, BA

A J Murfin, BSc (**Director of Sport*)

D A G Nicholas, BA (†*Severn Hill*)

Mrs D B Nightingale, BMus, LTCL, ACCEG (*Careers Adviser*)

C L O'Rooke, MA

C W Oakley, MMath, DPhil

J L Pattenden, MA, DPhil (†*Moser's Hall*)

P Pattenden, MA, DPhil, CPhys, MInstP

I W Payne, BSc (**Mathematics*)

H R W Peach, BA (**German*)

T P Percival, MA (*Higher Education Adviser*)

D Portier, BA, MA (*Head of Sixth Form*)

Mrs N M Pritchard, BA (†*Mary Sidney Hall*)

W R Reynolds, BSc

D M Roberts, BSc, MEd

O J Russell, MPhil (**Geography*)

C M Samworth, BSc, PhD

Mrs A Z Schmaller-Russell, BA, PG Dip

M Schofield, BSc

A Shantry (*Cricket Professional*)

Mrs S L M Shantry, BSc

W M Simper, BSc

A Smiter, BSc

Mrs L R Temple, BA

T D J Warburg, MA

Miss R B Weatherstone, BA

N J Welch, BSc

Miss E J Wheeler, MA (**Philosophy and Theology*)

T C Whitehead, BA (**French*)

S P Wilderspin (*Master i/c Football*)

Ms S E Williams, MChem

Mrs C H L Wilson, BA (†*The Grove*)

R M Wilson, MEng Hons

Miss R Witcombe, BSc

Miss G Y Y Woo, MSc

D M Wray, MA

J M Yule, BA

N N Zafar, BA MA

Visiting French Fellow: Miss J Fournis, MA

Visiting Hispanic Fellow: Miss M G Martinez, BA

School Doctors:
The General Practitioner Team, Mytton Oak Surgery, Racecourse Lane, Shrewsbury

Dental Adviser: R J Gatenby, BDS, DGDP, RCS

Headmaster's Personal Assistant: Mrs E J Gibbs

Solihull School

Warwick Road, Solihull, West Midlands B91 3DJ

Tel: 0121 705 0958 (Headmaster)
          0121 705 4273 (Admissions)
          0121 705 0883 (Bursar)
Fax: 0121 711 4439
email: admin@solsch.org.uk

website: www.solsch.org.uk
Twitter: @solsch1560
Facebook: @SolihullSchool
LinkedIn: /SolihullSchool

Motto: '*Perseverantia*'

Solihull School was founded in 1560 with the income from the chantry chapels of the parish of Solihull. The school is particularly proud of the richness and diversity of the education that it provides. The school has always been closely involved with the community, making its sporting and theatrical facilities available for local schools.

Organisation. The school now provides education for over 1000 day pupils aged between 7 and 18. The Junior School, which occupies its own separate building on the site and has its own Headmaster, has more than 240 pupils aged from 7 to 11. In the Senior School there are approximately 570 pupils from Year 7 to Year 11 and around 260 pupils in the Sixth Form. In 1973 girls were accepted into the Sixth Form. In September 2005 the school became fully co-educational.

Site and Facilities. The school moved to its present site in 1882 and the original school building, School House, survives. The site now comprises over 50 acres of buildings and playing fields, which enable all teaching, games and activities to take place on the one site. In the last decade there has been a very substantial building programme. This programme originally involved the extension of the Science Department and Design and Technology Centre, the laying of an Astroturf pitch and three squash courts, and the substantial redevelopment of School House. In 2002 a new hall/theatre, the Bushell Hall, was built, which can accommodate a theatre audience of 600 and an assembly for 1000. At the same time, the old hall was transformed into a library and IT rooms. In 2003, a new pavilion, the Alan Lee Pavilion, was completed. In September 2005 a new teaching area, the George Hill Building, was unveiled to provide 16 new classrooms and an extensive social space. The Junior School, which has grown considerably in recent years, has been extended and entirely refurbished. A new music school was unveiled in September 2009 – The David Turnbull Music School. In September 2015 a new four-floor, state-of-the-art Sixth Form Centre, the Cooper Building opened. It was designed to transform the Sixth Form teaching and learning and incorporating the latest multimedia technology. A second Astroturf pitch was also completed in 2017. Throughout the school there are excellent IT facilities for staff and pupils.

Curriculum. In the Junior School particular emphasis is placed on establishing high standards in core subjects and key skills that permeate the children's learning across the curriculum. The Junior School has specialist teaching rooms for Art, Design and Technology, ICT, Music and Science and benefits from the additional facilities it shares with the Senior School on the same 55-acre campus.

At the beginning of the Senior School, all pupils take at least one year of Latin and Spanish. In the second year French and German are optional subjects. English Language and Literature, Mathematics, a Modern Foreign Language, Physics, Chemistry and Biology remain compulsory subjects to GCSE. Three other subjects are chosen from a wide range of options.

The size of the Sixth Form enables the school to offer a very wide range of subjects and combinations. These subjects are Art and Design – Fine Art, Biology, Business, Chemistry, Classical Civilisation, Design & Technology, Drama & Theatre Studies, Economics, English Literature, French, Geography, German, History, Latin, Mathematics (and Further Mathematics), Music, Photography, Physical Education, Physics, Politics, Psychology, Religious Studies

(Philosophy and Ethics) and Spanish. There is also a substantial programme of Enrichment for all pupils in the Sixth Form, ranging from Mandarin Chinese to Cookery.

Academic Success. In 2018 we recorded another great year of A Level results – 80 per cent of all grades were A* to B. At GCSE, 91% per cent of pupils were awarded grades 9 to 5 (A* to B) in 2018 and 46 pupils achieved an incredible 8 or more A* to A grades.

Games. Games are an integral part of the school curriculum and all pupils in the school are involved. PE is compulsory until Year 11 and all pupils in the school have a games afternoon. The school has a very strong tradition in the major team games for both boys and girls, but also offers a very wide range of other options. The principal team games are rugby, cricket, hockey (for both boys and girls) and netball. The Junior School pupils play football in addition to these sports. The school also has teams in tennis, athletics, swimming, clay-pigeon shooting, cross-country, badminton, basketball and fencing to name but a few. In recent years the school has organised very extensive tours for pupils of differing ages: in 2018 our senior rugby team toured Singapore and New Zealand, and our senior girls' netball and hockey teams visited Singapore and Malaysia. Individual and team national success is a regular feature of Solihull sporting life.

Music and Drama. The school has a very strong tradition in music and drama, which has been enhanced since the building of the Bushell Hall and the David Turnbull Music School. Over a third of all pupils learn a musical instrument and there are over 25 different musical groups in the Senior School. This ranges from orchestras, bands and choirs to piano, string and wind ensembles. Several of these groups are very successful in competition at local festivals. There are many opportunities for pupils to perform at concerts, both formal and informal, throughout the year. A busy programme of masterclasses is given by visiting professional musicians. There is also an excellent Chapel Choir that performs during the school week and at the chapel services each Sunday. Each term the choir sings Evensong in a cathedral (including an annual visit to St Paul's in London) and performs on BBC Radio 4's Daily Service. In 2015 the school joined the Steinway Initiative, purchasing three new Steinway grand pianos.

The drama and music departments come together each year for the staging of an ambitious musical, which always involves a large number of pupils. There are two major dramatic performances each year: a school musical (Spamalot 2014, Les Misérables 2015, Carousel 2016, Tommy 2017) and a school play (His Dark Materials [Parts 1 & 2] 2015 & 2016, Fuente Ovejuna 2018). In addition, there are several smaller productions in the course of the year.

Outdoor Pursuits. Outdoor pursuits play a major part in the school's life. In the Third Form pupils take part in an outdoor activities programme called Terriers. In the Shell Form every pupil spends a week at the school's mountain cottage in Snowdonia. From the Shell Form pupils are able to participate in the CCF, which has an Army and an RAF section, and from the end of the Fourth Form, they can pursue the Duke of Edinburgh's Award scheme. There are approximately 80 pupils in the CCF and 160 are involved at different stages of the Duke of Edinburgh's Award scheme. The school has a popular Mountain Club and organises biennial major expeditions: Cambodia in 2013, Ladakh India in 2015 and Alaska in 2017.

Admissions. Pupils are accepted into the Junior School through examination at 7+, 8+, 9+ and 10+, although the majority of pupils enter at 7+. Pupils joining the Junior School in Years 3, 4 or 5 (in most cases) have their places in the Senior School confirmed by the end of the Christmas Term of Year 5. The major point of entry is at 11+ (Year 7). Places are awarded on the basis of written exams in English

and Mathematics and, in some cases, an interview. Some pupils are also accepted to enter the school at 12+, 13+ and 14+. A substantial number of pupils enter the school at Sixth Form level. Offers for admission to the Sixth Form are made on the basis of an interview, predicted GCSE grades and a personal profile. Such offers are conditional on receiving a pupil's school report which should indicate high levels of effort and attainment, excellent conduct and a positive attitude to school life plus achieving a minimum of 2 grade 7s and 4 grade 5s at GCSE, normally including grade 5 in Mathematics and English. For further Mathematics, a grade 8 in GCSE Mathematics is required. For Biology, Chemistry, Mathematics, Physics or a Modern Foreign Language a grade 7 in the subject is required. For all other subjects a grade 6 in the appropriate facilitating subject for each subject is required; however, a grade 7 is recommended.

The dates for entrance examinations and the Sixth Form scholarship examinations are available on the school website.

Fees per term (2018–2019). Tuition: Senior School £4,299–£4,331, Junior School £3,497–£3,657. Lunch charges per day: £3.45 Junior School, £3.90 Senior School. There are few obligatory extras.

Scholarships and Assisted Places. The school offers approximately 25 academic scholarship awards at 11+ and 13+ and around 30 at Sixth Form. The number of awards and their value is at the discretion of the Headmaster. There are also Sport, Art, Music, Choral and Organ Scholarships which are awarded at 11+, 13+ and Sixth Form. These are awarded based on a musical, art or sporting assessment. Sixth Form Academic scholarships are available in all A Level subjects on the basis of examination and interview.

In addition to scholarships, means-tested Assisted Places are available to offer opportunities to able pupils with financial needs. Applicants for such assistance are considered at Senior School and Sixth Form entry.

Children of the clergy are offered a 50% fee remission.

Old Silhillians Association. The aim of the Old Silhillians is to support and maintain links with the school. They also have their own clubhouse and extensive sports facilities. Website: www.silhillians.net; email: osa@silhillians.net.

Charitable status. Solihull School is a Registered Charity, number 1120597. It exists to provide high-quality education for pupils between 7 and 18 years old.

Chairman of the Governors: Mr Mark Hopton, FCA

Bursar and Clerk to the Governors: Mr Richard Bate, MA Cantab, ACMA

Headmaster: Mr David Lloyd, BSc

Senior Deputy Headmaster: Mr Sean Morgan, BA

Deputy Headmaster (Academic): Mr David Morgan, BA, MA

Deputy Head (Teaching & Learning): Ms Daniele Harford-Fox, BA

Assistant Headteacher (Pastoral Care): Mrs Lisa Fair, BA, MA

Assistant Headteacher (Co-Curricular): Mrs Hannah Fair, BA, MA

Assistant Headteacher (ICT): Mr Dave Reardon, BSc

Head of Sixth Form: Mr Thomas Emmet, BSc
Head of the Middle School: Miss Natasha Evans, BA, MA
Head of the Lower School: Mr Owen Bate, BSc
Head of the Junior School: Mr Mark Penney, BA

Assistant Staff:
* *Head of Department*

Mr Gareth Affleck, BA (*History*)
Miss Rachel Airdrie, BA
Mr Oliver Anderton, BSc
Mrs Nicola Atkins, BEd
Dr Richard Atkinson, BA, DPhil Oxon
Mr Matthew Babb, BSc
Mrs Katie Baden, BSc
Mr Owen Bate, BSc
Mrs Jennifer Bernamont, BSc
Mr Mark Bishop, MSc (*Mathematics*)
Mrs Claire Black, BA
Mr Mark Briggs, BSc
Mr Darryl Brotherhood, BSc
Mr David Brough, BSc
Mrs Julie Brown, BA, MA
Mrs Lindsay Browning, BA
Miss Tracy Bryan, BA
Mrs Denise Buckle, BSc
Ms Libby Campbell, BA
Mr Samuel Chillcott, MSci, MEng (*Physics*)
Miss Joanne Collier, BSc
Mr Neal Corbett, BA (*Design Technology*)
Mr Martin Covill, BSc
Mr Geddes Cureton, BSc
Mrs Hannah Davidson, BSc
Mr Mark Davies, BEng
Mrs Pelvinder Deu, BSc
Mrs Nicola Dickerson, BA
Mr Andrew Dowsett, BA (*German*)
Mr Thomas Emmet, BSc (*Psychology*)
Mrs Hannah Fair, BA, MA
Mrs Lisa Fair, BA, MA
Mrs Suzannah Farnan, BSc
Mr Francisco Fernandez-Valverde
Dr Sian Foster, MA, MPhil, DPhil, MBA
Mrs Joanne Francis, BA, MPhil
Mr Michael Gledhill, BA, LLB
Mrs Corinne Goodman, BSc (*Chemistry*)
Mrs Kate Griffiths, BSc
Mrs Helen Hallworth, BSc
Mr James Hammond, MA (*Drama*)
Mr Stuart Hart, BA, MPhil (*English*)
Mr Stephen Hifle, QTS
Mrs Janet Humphreys, BEd Cantab
Mrs Eleanor Hurst, BA, Cert SpLD (*Learning Support*)
Revd Canon Andrew Hutchinson, BA, MEd
Mr Gareth James, BA
Dr Richard Jennings, BSc, PhD
Mrs Joanna Johnson, BA, MPhil (*Classics*)
Mr Andrew Jones, BSc (*Science*)
Mr Michael Jones, MA, BA
Mr Tim Kermode, MA (*Director of Music*)
Mrs Ruth Lancaster, BSc
Mr Nick Leonard, BEd
Dr Michela Luiselli, BA, PhD
Miss Lydia Lynch, BSc
Mr Andrew Macarthur, MSc
Mr Darren Maddy
Mrs Jane Mander, BA
Mrs Hanlie Martens, MA
Mr Philip May, BSc
Mr Chris Mayer
Mrs Wendy Meigh, BEd
Mrs Hayley Middleton, BEng, BCom
Mr Stephen Mitchell, BSc
Mrs Clare Mollison, BA
Mr Paul Morgan, BA (*MFL*)
Mrs Rachel Morgan, BEd

Miss Saranne Moule, BSc
Mrs Ulrike Mynette, MA
Miss Rebecca Noon
Mrs Dawn Parker, BSc (*Biology*)
Mr Owen Parsons, MSci
Dr Mary Partridge, BA Oxon, MA, PhD
Mrs Zoe Patching-Jones, BA
Mrs Vanessa Patel, BA
Mrs Donna Penney, BSc
Mr Simon Phillips, BA (*Music*)
Mr Alex Poole, BSc
Mr David Rice, BA, MA
Miss Stephanie Roberts, BA, MA
Mrs Alex Roll, BA (*Geography*)
Mrs Pilar Roman-Blythe, MA
Miss Luisa Rosina, BMus, PG Dip, Junior Fellow
Mrs Beatrice Rossay-Gilson (*French*)
Dr Amy Routledge, PhD
Miss Laura Rutherford, MA Cantab, MEd (*Religious Studies*)
Dr Szymon Sawicki, BA Cantab, MSc, PhD
Mrs Jane Sixsmith, MA & Honorary Doctorate
Mrs Helen Smith
Mr Michael Smith, BSc
Miss Rebecca Smith, BSc
Mrs Julie Spraggett, BMus
Mrs Laura Spratley, BA
Dr Peter Spratley, BA, MA
Mr Dan Super, BA
Mrs Lucy Super, BA
Miss Amy Thacker, BA
Mrs Sharron Thomas, BSc
Mr Steve Thompson, BSc (*Director of Sport*)
Mrs Donna Trim, BA (*Art*)
Miss Gabrielle Wallbank, BSc
Mrs Danielle Wana, BA (*Girls Games*)
Miss Francesca Wernham, BA
Mrs Ruth Whaley, MA
Mrs Lydia Wolsey, BA
Mr Liam Worth, BA, MA
Miss Zhe Zhou, BSc, MSc

Careers: Mrs Rhian Chillcott, MA

Marketing Manager: Miss Sophie Lodge, BA

OC CCF: Major Nick Leonard
SSI: WO2 Philip Dean, MBE

Medical Officer: Dr Sunil Kotecha, MBChB, FRCGP, MSc
Senior Nurse: Mrs Sarah Serle, RGN
School Nurse: Mrs Helen King, RGN

Headmaster's PA: Mrs Lisa McGann
Admissions Registar: Mrs Nicolette Mullan
Bursar's PA: Ms Suzanne Baldwin
Librarian: Mrs Alison Vaughan, BA

Stamford School

Southfields House, St Paul's Street, Stamford, Lincolnshire PE9 2BQ

Tel: 01780 750300
Fax: 01780 750336
email: headss@ses.lincs.sch.uk
website: www.ses.lincs.sch.uk
Twitter: @SpedeNews
Facebook: @stamfordendowedschools

Motto: *Christe me spede*

Founded by William Radcliffe, of Stamford, 1532.

Introduction. Stamford School is one of three schools within the overall Stamford Endowed Schools Educational Charity, along with Stamford High School (girls) and Stamford Junior School, the co-educational junior school.

Buildings and Grounds. Stamford School dates its foundation to 1532. The grounds include the site of the Hall occupied by secessionists from Brasenose Hall, Oxford, in the early 14th century. The oldest surviving building is the School Chapel, which was formerly part of St Paul's Church, but which from 1548 until restoration in 1929 was used as a schoolroom. Extensive additions to the School continued to be made throughout the nineteenth and twentieth centuries. In 1956 the Old Stamfordians gave the School a swimming pool as a war memorial. The science school was built in 1957 and extended in 1973 when a new dining hall and kitchens also came into use. These were subsequently completely redesigned and upgraded in 2003. A music school was built in 1977 and extended in 1984. A further extensive development programme was begun in 1980 and included the building of one new senior boarding house (Browne), opened in 1981, and extensive and comparable provision in the other (Byard). Development works in 2009 saw the creation of a new Research and Learning Centre in the School House building, providing a library, study space and additional IT facilities. The Sixth Form Common Room is now located in a newly-renovated section of Brasenose House, containing quiet study areas, IT and recreation facilities. A glass atrium linking School House and the Hall has been erected, providing a new focal point for the School in a unique architectural style. The Science rooms were also upgraded. A new Sports Centre, which includes a fitness suite, gymnasium and 25m swimming pool, has recently been completed and forms a central part of the curricular and extracurricular sports provision. The old gymnasium will now be renovated to become a state-of-the-art Performing Arts Centre.

School Structure and Curriculum. The school consists of around 680 boys divided into Lower School (11–14), Middle School (14–16) and Sixth Form. The Heads of each section, with their assistants and Form Tutors monitor the academic progress of each boy and manage the pastoral arrangements.

The National Curriculum is broadly followed but much more is added to the curriculum to make it stimulating and rewarding. Information Technology, Art & Design and Design Technology form an integral part of the curriculum and from Year 8 boys may begin German, Spanish or Russian. All boys are prepared for a complete range of GCSE examinations; the great majority of them continue into the Sixth Form and then on to higher education.

In the Sixth Form of about 190 boys (and 190 girls) the timetable is so arranged that a wide range of combinations of subjects is possible. In partnership with Stamford High School all Sixth Form students can choose from the full range of 27 subjects available across the two schools.

Activities. Art, Music, Drama, Games and Physical Education form part of the normal curriculum. There is a choral society, an orchestra, a band and a jazz band, and a chapel choir. The musical activities of the school are combined with those of the High School under the overall responsibility of the Director of Music for the Endowed Schools. The school maintains RN, Army and RAF sections of the CCF and there is a rifle club. A large number of boys are engaged at all levels of The Duke of Edinburgh's Award scheme.

The school plays rugby, football, hockey, cricket, tennis, golf. The athletics and swimming sports and matches are held in the summer term. In winter there is also badminton, cross-country running and basketball. There are squash courts and a full-sized, floodlit Astroturf hockey pitch.

There are many school clubs and societies and a thriving weekend activity programme.

Close links are maintained with the local community. The school welcomes performances in the hall by the music societies of the town and uses the excellent local theatre in Stamford Arts Centre for some of its plays.

Careers. The school is a member of Inspiring Futures and has a team of careers staff. There is an extensive new careers library, computer room and interview rooms.

House Structure. Boarding: Byard House; St Paul's; Browne House.

Weekly and three-night boarding are available, as well as full boarding.

Competition in games, music and other activities are organised within a house system. Housemasters with their assistants monitor boys' commitments to the wider curriculum and act as counsellors when boys need to turn to someone outside the formal pastoral and disciplinary system.

Admission. Registration Fee £100; Acceptance Fee £250.

The main point of entry is at age 11, but boys are considered at any age. A number join at age 13 or directly into the sixth form. Application forms for admission may be obtained from the school office. The school's entrance examinations take place in late January, but arrangements may be made to test applicants at other times. Entry into the sixth form is considered at any time. Boys who enter through the Stamford Junior School progress automatically on to Stamford School at age 11 without having to take further entrance tests.

Fees per annum (2018–2019). Day £15,318; Full Boarding £28,446; Weekly Boarding £24,801; 3-Night Boarding £21,552.

These fees include stationery, textbooks and games. School lunches for day boys are an additional charge.

Scholarships and Bursaries. The Schools offer a range of scholarships for pupils entering into years 7, 9 and 12 (Sixth Form). Scholarships are less common for pupils entering into other years but may at times be available. There are scholarships for Academic, Music, Art, Sports and All-Rounder performance. Means-tested bursaries can be applied for by families of pupils who would otherwise not be able to benefit from a Stamford education. Please see our website for full details.

Charitable status. As part of the Stamford Endowed Schools, Stamford School is a Registered Charity, number 527618.

Chairman of the Governing Body: Dr Michael Dronfield

***Principal of the Stamford Endowed Schools*: William Phelan**

Vice-Principal, Head: Nicholas Gallop

Deputy Head: William Chadwick
Director of Studies: Harvey Hewlett
Head of Sixth Form: Geoffrey Brown
SES Chaplain: The Revd Mark Goodman

Teaching Staff:
Justin Backhouse (*Maths*)
Lorna Blissett (*Deputy Head of English*)
Michael Blissett (*Head of Classics*)
Edmund Board (*Maths*)
Christopher Brace (*Head of Physics*)
Pierre Braud (*Head of French*)
Richard Brewster (*Head of Geography*)
Emma Calvert (*Biology*)
Martin Caseley (*English*)
Kenneth Chapman (*Senior Master Staff*)
Annette Chauvaux (*Head of German*)

Helen Chew (*EAL Teacher*)
Charlotte Clifton (*Religious Studies*)
Alexandra Colley (*History*)
David Colley (*PE*)
Anne Corrigan (*Speech and Drama*)
Jack Cropper (*Head of Hockey*)
Anneke Davies (*Head of Drama*)
Amber Dewey (*Drama*)
Rupert Dexter (*History*)
Dion Di Cataldo (*PE*)
Charles Esson (*PE*)
Julia Fox (*Deputy Head of 6th Form*)
David Gloucester (*History*)
Amy Halliday (*Business Studies*)
Faye Harrison (*Head of Religious Studies*)
Dean Headley (*Cricket*)
Richard Henry (*English*)
Eleanor Herdale (*Head of Economics*)
Carrie Hill (*Drama*)
Ashley Hilton (*Biology*)
Jonathan Hodgson (*Senior Master Co curricular*)
Michael Holdsworth (*DT*)
Annabelle Holland (*Head of Art*)
Peter Jones (*Head of Chemistry*)
Timothy Jones (*Chemistry*)
Samuel Jordan (*Physics*)
Louise Kemp (*Head of English*)
Austin Kersey (*Head of PE*)
Jamie Laird (*Physics*)
David Laventure (*Director of Sports*)
Karen Leetch (*English*)
Sarah Macaulay (*Head of Business Studies*)
Suzanne MacCarthy (*Business Studies*)
Susan Manning (*Head of Maths*)
Constanza Marquez-Godoy (*Spanish*)
Felicity McClarty (*French*)
Lisa McKenna (*Art*)
Kendal Mills (*Senior Master Pastoral*)
Malcolm Milner (*DT*)
James Mitchell (*Geography*)
Hannah Moody (*Geography*)
Brendan Morris (*Geography*)
Kieran Nally (*Maths*)
Alister Pike (*History*)
Catherine Pike (*Head of Spanish*)
Roxana Popa (*MFL*)
Nicholas Porteus (*Head of Science*)
Andrew Ramsey (*Geography*)
James Rushton (*Drama*)
Bryan Russell (*Maths*)
Bonita Smart (*Chemistry*)
Edward Smith (*Director of Outdoor Education*)
Daniel Stamp (*Head of History*)
Amanda Steven (*Maths*)
Rachel Tomlinson (*Art*)
David Tuck (*Head of Politics*)
Leigh Ware (*Biology*)
Victoria Washbrooke (*Biology*)
Mark Webb (*Maths*)
Gary Whitehouse (*Head of Learning Support*)
Paola Wigmore (*Speech and Drama*)
David Williams (*PE*)
Katherine Woodward (*Chemistry*)
Caroline Wray (*Head of MFL*)

SES Music Department:
Giles Turner (*Director of Music*)
Duncan McIlrae (*Assistant Director of Music*)
Stephen Chandley (*Head of Brass*)
Daniel Leetch (*Head of Strings*)

Visiting Music Staff:
Steven Andrews (*Drum Kit, Percussion*)
Jonathan Aughton (*Flute*)
Margaret Bennett (*Singing*)
Karen Bentley (*Cello, Double Bass*)
Tatiana Boison (*Pianoforte*)
Susan Bond (*Singing*)
David Brown (*Clarinet*)
Alexander Crutchley (*Lower Brass*)
Julie Dustan (*Flute*)
Frances Gill (*Saxophone*)
Nicholas Gray (*Electric Guitar*)
Nan Ingrams
Sarah Latham (*Violin, Viola*)
Alexander MacDonald (*Classic Pianoforte*)
Margaret Maclennan (*Pianoforte*)
Anne McCrae (*Bassoon, Pianoforte*)
Elizabeth Murphy (*Violin, Pianoforte*)
Janet Roberts (*Cello*)
Kieran O'Riordan (*Percussion*)
Elizabeth Taylor, BA (*Violin, Viola*)
Nicholas Taylor
Eleanor Turner (*Harp*)
Lynn Williamson, LTCC (*Pianoforte*)

Medical Officer: C S Mann, MBChB, BSc

The Stephen Perse Foundation

Union Road, Cambridge, Cambridgeshire CB2 1HF
Tel: 01223 454700
email: office@stephenperse.com
website: www.stephenperse.com
Twitter: @SPFSchools
Facebook: @stephenpersefoundation
LinkedIn: /stephen-perse-foundation

We are a family of schools in Cambridge, Madingley and Saffron Walden educating boys and girls aged 3 to 18.

By recognising our pupils as individuals – with unique hopes, talents and ambitions – we unlock their true potential.

We enjoy learning for its own sake. Our teachers ignite curiosity, encourage critical thinking and creativity. By learning to think for themselves our pupils go on to achieve exceptional results. But for us, education is not just about grades. It is about strength of character, a sense of social responsibility, learning to innovate, communicate and collaborate.

Education needs to prepare youngsters for life beyond tests, exams and certificates. Our pupils gain an exceptional skill set, one that prepares them for life in tomorrow's world. They leave us ready to make their mark and achieve their dreams.

Our history. Founded in 1881 as the Perse School for Girls, our history is part of Cambridge's rich academic past. Since evolving into the Stephen Perse Foundation in 2001, we have grown significantly, opening our doors to boys as well as girls and providing a complete educational pathway to inspire and guide young learners from the age of 3 to 18.

In 2008, we successfully set up a co-educational 6th Form College; in 2010 we acquired Madingley Pre-Prep; in 2011 we established a City Pre-Prep in Cambridge; in 2013 we merged with Dame Bradbury's School in Saffron Walden; and in 2014 we introduced the diamond model co-educational community into our Junior School, followed by our Senior School in 2017.

Our outstanding leadership and strategic vision has been acknowledged through awards and accolades including, in

2014, being named both Independent School of the Year at the TES Independent School Awards and taking home an award for Outstanding Strategic Initiative.

Their future. Today's young learners will go on to shape tomorrow's world. We believe that is our responsibility as teachers and parents to equip them with the tools they need to make their mark, whatever future they choose.

Through our forward-thinking vision for education and our creative curriculum, we foster a global outlook, digital citizenship, individuality and independent thought – empowering our pupils to succeed in tomorrow's world and the workplace of the future.

As well as being committed to academic excellence, we understand the importance of an education which values the immeasurable as well as the measurable. Our distinctive Learning Wheel illustrates our forward-thinking approach to education, putting our learners at its core.

As you may expect, we offer great facilities and one-to-one attention from brilliant teachers. What makes us different is the way we encourage young people to think: independently, analytically, logically, creatively and imaginatively – in an unusually friendly, relaxed atmosphere.

As an Apple Distinguished School, we are now leading the digital learning revolution, with our pupils using iPads as virtual satchels and unlocking new ways to learn and collaborate.

Dynamic and inspiring learning spaces are an important piece of our toolkit. We make use of Cambridge as our campus and enjoy first class facilities within our schools. We have most recently completed a transformational building project on our Senior School site in the heart of Cambridge, enjoyed by students across all our schools: a five-storey building with a rooftop sports pitch (the first of its kind in Cambridge), a Sport England standard four-court sports hall, activity space with viewing area, ten classrooms and an additional learning hub.

Admissions. Our pupils and students are as mixed as any group of young people – but they all have bright, enquiring minds, whether they're artistic or academic, sporty or in need of educational support.

There are many entry points across our schools, ranging from 3 to 18. Please see our website for details, dates and FAQs. We hold our own entrance tests and interviews, held annually, usually in January for a September start. Entry is available outside of these testing dates if places allow; please contact the relevant school if you would like more information.

Boarding will be available for our 6th Form students only from September 2019.

Scholarships, Exhibitions and Bursaries. Academic Scholarships and Music awards are available in the Senior School. 6th Form Scholarships are awarded on academic merit based on written papers and interviews. 6th Form Music and Art Scholarships are also offered. Bursaries are available for pupils throughout the Foundation. Information about these may be obtained from the Bursary.

Diamond Model. Focusing too much on testing fails to take account of the importance of inspiring children to believe in themselves and to believe they can dream. To make this possible we create small communities of learners. That's where the best pastoral support, teaching and guidance happens. Our commitment to this is absolute. We have introduced a diamond system because we believe for certain subjects, and at certain ages, boys and girls learn better in single-sex classes. Pupils from 9 to 16 will have single-sex classes for core subjects like English, Maths and Sciences. It's a 21st century version of single-sex education – the single-sex education that's right for the future.

Pastoral Care. We place a great emphasis on pastoral care and the well-being of all our students. Established pastoral structures support the students and foster personal development, responsibility and informed choices. Subject teachers and year staff care for the academic progress and individual welfare of each student.

All schools tell you they're wonderful but the only way to know if they're right for you is to see for yourself. At the Stephen Perse Foundation you'll find pupils and students who bubble with enthusiasm, teachers who love what they do and a place where young people blossom and have amazingly good fun. They'll be delighted to show you what being here is really like.

Results. Our students achieve top results and go on to study at world-leading universities. Just as importantly, they are encouraged to pursue their dreams and follow the path that's right for them. Over the past 5 years; 87% of all GCSE grades have been A* or A, 68% of A Level grades have A* or A, and 80% of International Baccalaureate (IB) grades were Level 6 or 7.

Our leaver destinations represent the best, most exciting opportunities the world has to offer. In 2018, this included History at Oxford, Chemistry with Molecular Physics at Imperial College London, and Liberal Arts and Sciences at University College Maastricht.

Fees per term (2018–2019). Stephen Perse Pre-Prep (Cambridge and Madingley) £4,000; Stephen Perse Junior School £5,050; Dame Bradbury's School £2,850–£4,600; Stephen Perse Senior School £5,850; Stephen Perse 6th Form College £5,610.

Extras: Individual music lessons in most instruments, speech and drama.

Charitable status. The Stephen Perse Foundation is a Registered Charity, number 1120608, and a Company Limited by Guarantee, number 6113565.

Governors:
Mr J Dix (*Chairman*)

Dr C Barlow	Mrs K Ollerenshaw
Dr V Christou	Mrs A Powell
Dr M Ellefson	Dr H Shercliff
Prof R Foale	Dr J Tasioulas
Mr D Gill	Dr A Thomas
Prof C Jiggins	Mr Sven Töpel
Dr G Johnson	Mr D Walker
Dr D Needham	

Principal: **Miss P M Kelleher**, MA Oxon, MA Sussex

Bursar: Mrs J Neild, BSc Southampton

Vice Principal (11–18): Miss N Atkins, BA Hons Nottingham

Vice Principal (3–11): Mrs T Handford, MA

Head of Senior School: Mr D Walker, BSc Hons Bristol

Head of Junior School: Miss K Milne, BEd Hons Cantab

Head of Pre-Prep: Mrs S Holyoake, BA Hons Cantab

Stockport Grammar School

Buxton Road, Stockport, Cheshire SK2 7AF

Tel:	0161 456 9000 Senior School
	0161 419 2405 Junior School
Fax:	0161 419 2407
email:	sgs@stockportgrammar.co.uk
website:	www.stockportgrammar.co.uk

Twitter: @stockportgs
Facebook: @stockportgrammar
LinkedIn: /Stockport-Grammar-School-Alumni

Motto: *Vincit qui patitur*

Founded in 1487, Stockport Grammar School is one of England's oldest schools. The founder, Sir Edmond Shaa, was a goldsmith, 200th Lord Mayor of London and Court Jeweller to three Kings of England. The School's rich history and traditions are celebrated in the annual Founder's Day Service in Stockport.

A co-educational day school, Stockport Grammar School is non-denominational and welcomes pupils from all faiths and cultures. Almost all leavers go on into Higher Education, including many to Oxbridge. Although academic performance is formidable, it is not the be-all and end-all of life at Stockport Grammar School.

Stockport Grammar School aims to provide the best all round education to enable pupils to fulfil their potential in a friendly and supportive atmosphere. The backbone of the school is academic excellence, with a clear framework of discipline within which every activity is pursued to the highest level. Entry is at 3, 4, 7, 11 and 16, but vacancies may occur at other stages. There are over 1,400 pupils aged 3–18 years, with 350+ in the Junior School and over 250 in the Sixth Form.

The Senior School. Admission at age 11 is by competitive entrance examination. This is held in January, for admission in the following September. There are several open events: see website for details. Occasional vacancies are considered on an individual basis and a few places are available in the Sixth Form each year. Visitors are always welcome to make an appointment to see the school.

Curriculum. The emphasis is on how to learn. The GCSE philosophies are introduced in the first three years as part of a broad general education. The sciences are taught as separate subjects and all pupils study Latin, French and German.

On entering the fourth year, at the age of 14, pupils retain a core of subjects but also make choices, so that individual aptitudes can be fully developed. GCSE examinations are taken in the fifth year. In 2018, 93.9% of GCSE entries gained an A* – C. On entering the Sixth Form, pupils begin with four subjects. The pass rate at A Level was 99.3% in 2018, with 79.4% of all entries gaining A* to B and 51.7% of entries at A* or A.

Art. A high standard is set and achieved. There are facilities for all aspects of two-dimensional work and textiles, plus a fully equipped ceramics area and a sculpture court. There are regular exhibitions in School and pupils' work is displayed annually at The Lowry.

Music. The curriculum provides a well-structured musical education for all pupils for the first three years. GCSE and Advanced Level are offered for those who aspire to a musical career as well as for proficient amateurs. Three main areas of musical ensemble – choirs, orchestras and wind bands – are at the centre of activities with opportunities open from First Year to Sixth Form. Emphasis is on determination, commitment and a sense of team work. All ensembles are encouraged to reach the highest standards.

Drama. A particularly strong tradition has been fostered over many years and regular productions involve all year groups. There are drama clubs, trips to local theatre groups and workshops in school.

Physical Education. The Physical Education curriculum is diverse, with activities including aerobics, ball skills, badminton, basketball, dance, gymnastics, health-related fitness, squash, swimming and volleyball. The main winter games for boys are rugby and football, and for the girls hockey and netball. In the summer, boys concentrate on cricket and athletics, whilst the girls focus their attention on tennis, athletics and rounders. Extracurricular clubs provide further sporting opportunities including archery, climbing and fencing. Up to 400 pupils represent the school at Saturday fixtures and the teams have an excellent reputation, gaining success in regional and national competitions. Almost fifty pupils have represented their country, region or county in the last year.

Information Technology. Dedicated Computer Suites accommodate full classes. All pupils have their own password and email address, and are able to use the Internet for research. The rooms are available to everyone as a computer resource at lunchtimes and after school. Information Technology skills are taught as part of the curriculum and academic departments incorporate the use of computers and interactive whiteboards into their everyday lessons. The subject is also available as a GCSE option.

Houses. Every pupil is a member of one of the four Houses, each led by two Heads of House staff assisted by a team of senior pupils. The Houses organise and compete in a wide range of sporting and non-sporting activities.

Clubs and Societies. The School has many active clubs and societies covering a wide variety of extracurricular interests, for example, debating, where Fifth and Sixth Formers have the opportunity to participate in up to four Model United Nations Assemblies around the world each year.

Development. In the summer of 2012 the School completed a major project providing new classroom accommodation on the Woodsmoor site for History, Classics, English, Economics, Business Studies and Psychology.

Visits. Well-established language exchange visits are made every year to France, Germany and Spain in addition to hillwalking, camping, mountaineering, skiing, sailing and cultural trips.

Assembly. Formal morning assemblies are held for all pupils; there are separate Jewish, Hindu and Muslim assemblies. House assemblies, which sometimes include Junior School pupils, are on Wednesdays; the Sixth Form have an additional weekly assembly.

Pastoral Care. Form Tutors get to know each pupil in the form individually, and are supported by Year Heads, by the Head of Lower School (years 1 to 3), the Head of Middle School (years 4 and 5), the Head of Sixth Form and the Deputy Head (Pastoral).

Discipline. This is positive and enabling. Much importance is attached to appearance and to uniform, which is worn throughout the school.

Fees per term (2018–2019). Senior School £3,900; Junior School £3,009.

Bursary Scheme. The School's own Bursary Scheme aims to provide financial assistance on a means-tested basis to families who have chosen a Stockport Grammar School education for their children. Details available from the Bursar.

Stockport Grammar Junior School. (*See also entry in IAPS section.*) With its own Headmaster and Staff it has separate buildings and a playing field on the same site. The Junior School has boys and girls between the ages of 3 and 11 years.

Boys and girls join the Nursery when they are three. In its own building and with a designated play area, the Nursery is very well resourced. The children are looked after by qualified and experienced staff.

Entrance is by observed play at the age of 4 years into two Reception forms, and by assessment in February for an additional form at the age of 7. All pupils are prepared for the Entrance Examination to the Senior School at the age of 11.

The Junior School buildings provide special facilities for Art, Technology, Music and Computing. The winter games are soccer, rugby, hockey and netball, with cricket and rounders in the summer. There are swimming lessons every week; other activities include the gym club, life saving, athletics and chess. There are clubs running each lunchtime and after school for both infants and juniors. Matches are played every Saturday against other schools in the major sports. Many pupils have instrumental music lessons and there is an orchestra, band, recorder group and a choir. The musical, held in May each year, is a very popular event in which all pupils participate. Visits are made annually to the Lake District in May. Short annual residential visits, are introduced from age 7.

Charitable status. Stockport Grammar School is a Registered Charity, number 1120199. It exists to advance education by the provision and conduct, in or near Stockport, of a school for boys and girls.

Patron: The Prime Warden of the Worshipful Company of Goldsmiths

Governing Body:
C Dunn, MA (*Chairman*)
P A Cuddy, BA (*Vice-Chairman*)
P J Britton, MBE, MA
A P Carr, MA
Miss S E Carroll, BA
P L Giblin, MA, MEd (*Teaching Staff*)
Mrs S Lansbury, LLB
J M R Lee, BA, MBA, DipM
P Milner, BA
Dr E M Morris, MBChB, DCH
Mrs C S Muscutt, BA
J A Shackleton, BA
A C Simpson, BSc, ACA

Clerk to the Governors and Bursar: C J Watson, MA

Headmaster: P M Owen, MA, PhD Cantab

Senior Deputy Headmistress – Academic: Mrs D L Harris, BSc
Deputy Headmistress – Pastoral: Mrs J White, BA
Deputy Headmaster – Staffing & Co-Curricular: E B S Bowles, MEng, MSc
Head of Lower School: Mrs H R Lawson, MA
Head of Middle School: Mrs J L Smith, BA
Head of Sixth Form: D J Stone, BA, MEd

Assistant Masters and Mistresses:
* *Head of Department*

Art:
*R A Davies, BA, MA
Miss R J Upton, BA

Biology:
J M Davies, BA
Miss K L Chandler, BSc
*P J Grant, BSc
Mrs E Niven, BSc
Mrs A R Reid, BSc
Mrs J White, BA
Mrs M Whitton, BSc
Mrs L J Withers, BA

Chemistry:
Miss J Berry, BSc
Mrs K L Britton, BSc
E Eeckelaers, BSc, MA
*Mrs A L Glarvey, MChem, PhD
Mrs R F Grey, MChem
R D Heyes, BSc

W Krywonos, BSc, MSc, PhD

Classics:
Miss L E McAllister, BA
*A C Thorley, BA
P A Urwin, BA
Mrs E Zanda, BA, PhD

Drama:
Mrs A K Moffatt, BA

Business & Economics:
Mrs S J Balfour, BA, Dipl
*Miss L Curl, BA, MA
A Phillips, BA

English:
Mrs R V Cross, BA
*Mrs G A Cope, BA
A J O Johnson, BA
R J Jones, BA
Mrs H R Lawson, MA

Miss E MacDonald, BA, MA
Mrs S L Moore, BA
Mrs A Mullholland, BA
Mr M Sallabank, BA
Mrs E E Suttle, BA, MEd

French:
Mrs S L Belshaw, BA
*Miss S M Gibson, BA
D Lorentz, BA, MA, DEA
Miss C L Stevenson, BA
J D Wilson, BA

Geography:
*A Cooke, BSc
Mrs H J Crowley, BSc
Mrs G N Miles, BA
Miss K E Owen, BSc, MA, PhD
Miss J Perkins, BSc
Mrs J L Smith, BA

German:
Mrs T Kampelmann, MA, PhD
Mrs L M Morgan, BA

History:
Mrs H R Ashton, BA
Mrs K J Chesterton, BA, MA
Ms C F Griffiths, BA, MA
S A Moore, BA
*S J D Smith, BA, PhD
D J Stone, BA

Information Technology:
N S Clarke, BA
*M J Flaherty, BSc

Life Studies:
*A G Ehegartner, BA
Miss H M Morgan, BA

Mathematics:
Mrs M Evans, BA
*G D Frankland, BSc
M Hamilton, MSc, PhD
Mrs D L Harris, BSc
Miss M E Higgins, BSc
Mrs L Lammas, BA
Mrs A S Larkin, BSc
Mrs C L Marshall, BSc, MSc

Miss C A Mills, BSc
K F J Prudham, BSc
Mrs R Reevell, BSc
Mrs R C Taylor, BSc

Music:
*M G Dow, MA, ALCM
P J Kennedy, BMus, MA
Mrs J Matthews, BA
Mrs E N Short, MA, LLCM

Philosophy/RS:
D Breffit, BA
Revd L E Leaver, MA, BTh
*J Swann, BA, MA

Physics:
Miss A Curtis, MEng
Mrs Z Dawson, MSc
*Mrs H M Fenton, BSc
Mrs C M Hird, BSc
I Killey, BSc, BEng
Miss R H Moore, MSc
P M Owen, MA, PhD
C Shaw, BSc

Physical Education:
R Bowden, BA
E H Corbett, BA
Mrs L E Goddard, BSc
A S Hanson, BEd
Mrs J Maskery, BEd
Mrs K Wilkinson, BA
Miss S Withington, BEd
*C J Wright, BA

Psychology:
*Miss H K Barton, BSc
T J Buxton-Cope, BSc

Spanish:
Miss K A M Psaila, BA
Mrs K Christmann, MA

Technology:
Miss S Hodkinson, BSc
Mrs H Oddy
Mrs H Tadman, BEng
Mrs Z A Vernon, BEd
G M Whitby, BSc
*N Young, MA

Learning Support:
Mrs S Boardman, BA
Mrs D H Meers, BA, MEd

School Chaplain: Revd L E Leaver, MA, BTh
Director of Music: M G Dow, BA, MA
Director of External Relations: Mrs R M Horsford, BA
Headmaster's Secretary: Mrs J E Baker
Admissions Officer: Mrs M Connor
Librarian: Ms J Pazos Galindo, BA, MA
School Nurse: Mrs P Ward, RGN, DipHE

Junior School

Headmaster: T Wheeler, BA, MA

Assistant Masters and Mistresses:
Mrs C Bailey, BA
Miss H Baker, BEd
Mrs S Barrowman, BA, MSc
Mrs H Carroll, BEd
Mrs L Carr, BA
Mrs R Cole, BA

Miss S Coleman
Mrs C Hampson, BA
Mrs L Hudson, BA
Mrs N Hurst, BEd
Mrs V Hutchinson, BA
Miss C Jeans, BA
Mrs N Jones, BA

Miss S Knowles, BSc
D Makinson, HNC Eng
S Milnes, BA
Mrs C M Nichols, BEd
Mrs J Noble, BA, PG Dip, AMBDA
Miss J Pepper, BA, ASA
Miss E Ripley, BA
Mrs K Roberts, BEd, MA

Mrs C Smith, BA
Mrs A Sullivan, BEd
Mrs J Swales, BA, ALCM
A Taylor, BSc
Mrs L Turner, BEd
Mrs K Wells, BA
Mrs S Westaway, BSc
Mrs C Woodrow, BA

Nursery Manager: Miss C Peake, BTEC, HND Ed
Headmaster's Secretary: Mrs B Cheyne

Stonyhurst College

Stonyhurst, Clitheroe, Lancashire BB7 9PZ

Tel: 01254 827073 (Admissions)
Fax: 01254 827135 (Admissions)
email: admissions@stonyhurst.ac.uk
                smhadmissions@stonyhurst.ac.uk
                internationaladmissions@stonyhurst.ac.uk
website: www.stonyhurst.ac.uk
Twitter: @Stonyhurst
Facebook: @stonyhurstcollege

Motto: Quant je puis – As much as I can

Stonyhurst College, together with its preparatory school Stonyhurst St Mary's Hall, is the UK's leading independent co-educational day and boarding Catholic school for 3–18 year olds. It is the oldest continuously active Jesuit school in the world and in 2018 it celebrates its 425th anniversary.

Stonyhurst pupils are encouraged to involve themselves fully in the opportunities offered to them. Living in a supportive and diverse community, they are helped to develop those qualities of character that will distinguish them in later life as men and women for others. As an Ignatian school, Stonyhurst provides a foundation for such a life through an education that nurtures individuality and encourages generosity. It is a springboard to a life of purpose.

There are 470 pupils at Stonyhurst College (13–18 years), including 297 boarders, plus an additional 279 pupils at Stonyhurst St Mary's Hall (3–13 years).

Academic. The school has an outstanding academic record, with many pupils going on to top universities in the UK, Europe and around the world. Teaching at Stonyhurst centres on the individual and encourages pupils to study independently and to think for themselves. All pupils have a personal tutor. An effective learning support department enables those with special educational needs to achieve their best.

The sixth form offers a choice of three study routes – A Level, International Baccalaureate Diploma or the IB Career Related Programme. Pupils receive a wealth of support to guide them through their chosen courses and to assist them with their university application.

The College houses the oldest museum collection in the English speaking world, dating back to 1609. The Collections focus on religious history and come from all over the world. Objects from the Collections, including a First Folio of Shakespeare, a natural history collection and medieval manuscripts, are used as a learning resource for students.

Pastoral care. The happiness and wellbeing of students is a top priority at Stonyhurst.

Each year group (known as a Playroom) has its own Head of Playroom, who has an overview of each student's complete experience at Stonyhurst. From academic performance to pastoral issues, the Head of Playroom stays with their year group for the duration of its time at the College, building a solid understanding of each individual.

There is also a team of pastoral staff, headed up by experienced Pastoral Heads. This team is dedicated to ensuring that Stonyhurst is a safe, positive and vibrant community where every individual student feels at home and secure.

Music and the arts. The creative life of the College is rich and varied, offering many opportunities to learn, perform and compete across music, art, drama and dance.

Sport and recreation. Sport plays an important part in the life of Stonyhurst; the College is represented in local and national fixtures, and international tours take Stonyhurst pupils all over the world. The main team games are rugby, hockey, cricket, netball, athletics and football.

Additional sports include tennis, cross-country running, gymnastics, basketball, and swimming. The school has world-class facilities, including an indoor swimming pool, a fitness suite, a nine-hole golf course, all-weather pitch, and indoor and outdoor tennis courts. The Duke of Edinburgh's Award scheme is extremely successful too, as is the Combined Cadet Force. Over 100 different activities are offered each week.

Spiritual. As a community Stonyhurst seeks to do everything to the greater glory of God. Pupils are encouraged to think beyond themselves and to do all that they can for others. In addition to young Catholics, the College welcomes young people who belong to other Christian traditions and other faiths.

Location. Stonyhurst is set in a magnificent Grade I listed building in a beautiful rural setting in Lancashire's Ribble Valley. Manchester Airport is just over an hour away and there are excellent rail and motorway links to London and all parts of the UK.

Scholarships and bursaries. Stonyhurst Scholarships are won on the basis of merit and are available to both boarding and day pupils. The number and size of scholarships is at the discretion of the Headmaster. The bestowal of any scholarship carries with it privilege and responsibility. Every scholar is expected to set an example to other pupils in their conduct and approach to study, and to participate fully in the life of Stonyhurst.

The allocation of a bursary is not linked to a scholarship application, but a good performance in the scholarship examinations will make a significant positive contribution to a bursarial application. All external scholarship candidates need to have registered for a place at Stonyhurst.

Scholarships are available for academic excellence, art, music and sport. In addition, two further awards are available: the All-Rounder award and the St Francis Xavier award.

Fees per term (2018–2019). Full boarding £11,600–£12,100; weekly boarding £9,950, day students £6,650.

Admission. Enquiries about admission should be addressed to the admissions team – please telephone 01254 827073 or email admissions@stonyhurst.ac.uk.

Charitable status. Stonyhurst College is a Registered Charity, number 230165. The Charity for RC Purposes exists to provide a quality boarding and day education for boys and girls.

Chairman of Governors: Mr Anthony Chitnis

Headmaster: Mr John Browne, MA

Second Master: Mr Matthew Mostyn, BA, MA Ed
Deputy Head (Pastoral): Mr Patrick MacBeth, BA
Deputy Head: Mr Neil Hodgson, BSc
Deputy Head (Learning): Mr Vincent Sharples, BA
Director of Studies: Mrs Lorraine Wright, BA
Director of IB: Mrs Debra Kirkby, BSc

College Chaplains:
Fr T Curtis SJ
Miss C Hanley, MA (*Lay Chaplain*)

Stonyhurst St Mary's Hall:
Stonyhurst Preparatory School
Boys and Girls aged 3–13
(*see entry in IAPS section*)

Headmaster: Mr Ian Murphy, BA

Stowe School

Stowe, Buckingham, Bucks MK18 5EH

Tel: 01280 818000
Fax: 01280 818181
email: enquiries@stowe.co.uk
website: www.stowe.co.uk
Twitter: @stowemail
Facebook: @stoweschool

Motto: '*Persto et Praesto*'

Stowe provides an all-round education of the highest standard, supporting Stoics in their passage to adulthood by developing individual talents, intellectual curiosity and a lasting sense of moral, social and spiritual responsibility. Confidence and tolerance of others flourish in a close community. The School provides a caring environment which promotes academic excellence, sporting prowess and artistic and musical creativity. Through teaching of the highest calibre, Stoics are encouraged to think for themselves, challenge conventional orthodoxies and pursue their own enthusiasms. Stoics acquire skills that enable them to live happily, work successfully and thrive in their future lives.

Stowe is a country boarding school with boys and girls from 13 to 18. The School roll is 815, comprising 700 boarders and 115 day pupils. Pupils are also accepted each year for 2-year A Level courses.

Houses. There are eight Boys' and four Girls' Houses, six of which are within the main building or attached to it and six at a short distance from it. In 2014 a new Sixth Form House, West, opened for boys and girls, and in 2019 two new Days Houses, Cheshire and Winton, will open.

The Curriculum allows pupils to enjoy a wide variety of subjects before they settle down to work for their (nine or ten) GCSEs taken in the Fifth Form. A flexible Options system operates at this stage. Most boys and girls will go on to take 4 A Levels. Throughout the School, boys and girls have a Tutor to look after their academic welfare and advise them on higher education. In the Lower School all pupils take the Vanguard Programme which is designed as a vehicle to help pupils develop an understanding of how learning happens and how challenge (and also failure) is essential to achieving progress. There is also a course in Visual Education for boys and girls in their first year at Stowe. It promotes an understanding of Stowe's architecture and landscape gardens in particular and the built environment in general.

Art, Design and Information Technology. All pupils are introduced to these subjects in their first year at Stowe. Art and Design are popular both for those pursuing hobbies and for those studying for formal examinations. Traditional skills are covered alongside more modern techniques such as computer-aided design and desktop publishing.

Music and Drama flourish as important and integral parts of the School's activities both within and outside the formal curriculum. There is plenty of scope to get involved in the School Orchestras, Jazz Band, Clarinet Quartet, Choirs, School plays, House plays and House entertainments. The timetable is sufficiently flexible to allow special arrangements to be made for outstanding musicians to study outside school. Drama Clubs and Theatre Studies groups have a fully-equipped theatre at their disposal. The refurbishment of the Theatre and classrooms, alongside a brand new Music School, allows these creative arts to flourish.

Careers Guidance. Pupils are provided with a variety of opportunities which allows them to make sound career decisions. Seminars, Gap Year advice and an interview training programme are all offered. The Careers Centre is extremely well-resourced, with a suite of computers and appropriate software, DVD facilities and a wealth of literature. Every encouragement is given to pupils to make regular visits to the Centre at Stowe and parents are always welcome to attend Careers events and to spend time using the available resources.

Religion. The School's foundation is to provide education in accordance with the principles of the Church of England and this is reflected in its chapel services on Sundays. Pupils of other faiths and other Christian Churches are welcomed and in some cases separate arrangements are made for them on Sundays. Every pupil attends the chapel services on weekdays.

Games. The key sports for boys are rugby, hockey and cricket, and for girls, hockey, lacrosse and tennis. The other main sports range from badminton, basketball, cross country, football, Eton Fives, fencing, golf, netball, squash, swimming and water polo in the winter to athletics, golf, polo, rowing, sailing and swimming in the summer; there are inter-school fixtures in most of these sports.

The School enters national competitions in many sports and encourages pupils to challenge for representative honours. The School has a heated 6-lane 25m indoor swimming pool with electronic timing system, a sports hall, squash courts, Eton Fives courts, a weight training/fitness room and two floodlit Astroturf pitches which also provide 24 tennis courts in the summer. There are also hard tennis courts available all the year round, plus outdoor netball and basketball facilities, an 8-lane sandwich surface athletics track, an indoor shooting range, a clay-pigeon shooting tower, a nine-hole golf course where the National Prep Schools (IAPS) annual tournament is played, and extensive playing fields for rugby, hockey, football, cricket and lacrosse. Sculling, canoeing, sailing and fishing take place on a lake within the Landscape Gardens as well as at Northampton Rowing Club and Glebe Lake, Calvert. The School opened its Equestrian Centre in 2012 and enters local and regional competitions.

Other Activities. Pupils complement their games programme with a broad variety of extra-curricular activities, including clubs and societies. There is a full weekend programme of events and activities. Stowe's grounds lend themselves to outdoor pursuits such as fishing and clay pigeon shooting, and the School has its own pack of beagles. On Mondays a special activities programme is based on Service at Stowe and at the heart of this is the Combined Cadet Force with all three service arms, the Duke of Edinburgh's Award scheme, Community Service (in the neighbourhood) and Leadership skills.

Fees per term (2018–2019). Boarders £12,220, Day In Boarding Pupils £8,785, *Day House Pupils £6,330 (*indicative fee based on 18/19 fee for Day House entry in 2019) payable before the commencement of the School term to which they relate. A deposit is payable when Parents accept the offer of a place. This deposit is repaid by means of a credit to the final payment of fees or other sums due to the school on leaving.

Scholarships and Bursaries. A range of Scholarships and Exhibitions, up to the value of 25% of the School fees, is awarded annually. Scholarships may be supplemented by means-tested bursaries, with a limited number of fully-funded places, where there is proven financial need.

Academic Scholarships up to the value of 25% of the School fees are available for pupils at age 13+ entering Stowe's Third Form, and are awarded to gifted children already following the ISEB Common Academic Scholarship syllabus at their Preparatory School.

Stephan Scholarships are awarded to academically bright pupils from independent or state schools which do not follow the ISEB Common Academic Scholarship syllabus.

Academic Scholarships are also available to pupils wishing to join the School in the Lower Sixth Form after GCSE at 16+. Competitive Entry Examinations are held in the November of the candidate's GCSE year consisting of a Verbal Reasoning paper, two subject papers related to their AS Level choices, and an interview. Successful Scholarship candidates would normally be expected to gain A* and A grades in all their subjects at GCSE.

Music Scholarships: Candidates at age 13 should be at least Grade Five standard on at least one instrument and preferably nearer Grade Six. An Exhibitioner may be around Grade Four standard. Candidates at age 16 should be the equivalent standard of Grade Six or above on one instrument and be of a good standard on a second instrument or voice. A candidate gaining a Minor Scholarship of up to 10% or an Exhibition may be around Grade Five standard.

Some *Art and Design & Technology Scholarships and Exhibitions* are available for pupils entering Stowe at age 13 or 16, and are offered to candidates who submit evidence of outstanding ability and a strong interest in these areas.

Sixth Form Arkwright Scholarships: Stowe is affiliated to the Arkwright Scholarships Trust which provides a number of scholarships available to students, both internal and external, who will be studying Maths and Design and Technology in the Sixth Form and intend to read Engineering, Technology or another Design-related subject at university.

Sports Scholarships and Exhibitions may be awarded to exceptional candidates at 13+ and 16+ showing outstanding potential in at least one of Stowe's key sports: hockey, lacrosse, netball or tennis for girls and rugby, hockey or cricket for boys.

Roxburgh (All-Rounder) Scholarships at 13+ and 16+ are intended to enable any boy or girl of outstanding all-round ability and leadership potential to benefit from Stowe's unrivalled environment to develop fully his or her talents. In addition to strong academic potential, which will be demonstrated in Stowe's Entry Examinations, candidates would be expected to demonstrate a high level of ability in at least one of the following: sport, music, art and drama.

Full details may be obtained from The Registrar.

Admissions. Boys and girls can be registered at any age. Full details can be obtained from the Admissions Department, who will supply entry forms. The School is always prepared to consider applications from pupils to enter the School at 14 if places are available. The date of birth should be stated and it should be noted that boys and girls are normally admitted between their 13th and 14th birthdays.

The Old Stoic Society. Director: Anna Semler. Old Stoic Society Office: Tel 01280 818252, email oldstoic@stowe.co.uk.

Charitable status. Stowe School Limited is a Registered Charity, number 310639. The primary objects of the charity, as set out in its Memorandum and Articles of Association, are to acquire Stowe House, which was achieved in 1923, and to provide education in accordance with the principles of the Church of England.

Visitor: The Rt Revd The Lord Bishop of Oxford

Governing Body:
Simon C Creedy Smith, BA, ACA (*Chairman*) [OS]
The Revd Peter Ackroyd

John R C Arkwright, FRICS [OS]
Jonathan M A Bewes, BA, FCA [OS]
Ms Julie C Brunskill, BSc, MRICS
Admiral Sir James Burnell-Nugent, KCB, CBE, MA Cantab [OS]
David Carr, MA Cantab [OS]
David W Cheyne, MA Cantab (*Vice Chairman*) [OS]
Ms Juliet C Colman, BA, Dip Arch, RIBA, SCA
Professor Guy Goodwin, BA, DPhil, FMedSci, FRCPsych
Mrs Joanne Hastie-Smith
David Hudson, MA Cantab
Mrs Andrea Johnson, BSc, PGCE
Robert A Lankester, MA Cantab
Mrs Catriona Lloyd, MA Cantab
Mrs Elizabeth Phillips, OBE, BA, MA, AKC
Mrs Vanessa Stanley, BEng, MEd, AdvCertEdMgmt, NPQH
Lady Stringer, BSc, MB BS, LRCP, MRCS
Christopher J Tate, BA, MIMC [OS]
Jonathon Hall, FIDM (*Chairman of the Old Stoic Society*) [OS]
Michael B M Porter, BA, MSc (*Secretary to the Governors*)

[OS] *Old Stoic*

Administrator to the Governors: Annabel Lovelock

Headmaster: A K Wallersteiner, MA, PhD

Senior Master: C C Robinson, MA, MPhil
Deputy Head, Academic: Dr J Potter, BA, MPhil, DPhil
Deputy Head, Pastoral: J H W Peppiatt, BA, MA
Deputy Head, Senior Master: M D G Wellington, BSc
Director of Admissions & Marketing: Mrs V M Roddy, BA, BSc, MSc

Assistant Staff:
* *Head of Department*

Art:
*D Scott, BA, MA
C J Grimble, BA
J Nicholl, BA
Miss Cheryl Syrett, BA

Biology:
*Mrs L M Carter, BSc
Mrs N Blake, BSc
Mrs P Bond, BSc
Dr M Lakin, BSc, DPhil
M A Righton, MA

Business Studies & Economics:
*A Ashfield, MA
R B Corthine, MA
P John, BSc
G West, MBA, LLM, DBA

Chemistry:
*Dr A Waine, MA, MSc, PhD
R G Johnson, BSc, MA
Mrs K M McMahon, BSc
J M Tearle, BA
M Teasdale, MChem

Classics:
*J M Murnane, MA
J A Smith, BA

Computing:
*A Gupta, BA, BSc, MA
N J Mellor, BA, MSc
Dr R Pawson, BSc, PhD

Design & Technology:
*M K Quinn, BSc
C Lloyd, BSc
C Peratopoullos, BEd
M D G Wellington, BSc

Drama & Theatre Studies:
*Ms R E Clark, BA
N D Bayley, Dip Acting & Theatre
Mrs C Dore, BA
Mrs L I Miller, BA, MA
Miss L Wiseman, BA

EAL:
*Mrs J Y Johnson, BA, MA

English:
*Ms S A H Puranik, BA, MPhil
Mrs E J Ackroyd, BA
J M Cook, BA, MSc
Ms H J Eisenhut, BA
F J B Parnaby, BA, MA
J W H Peppiatt, MA
Mrs S Rickner, BA
J F Smith, BA, MA, PhD

Games Coaching:
*C Sutton, BA, MEd
I Michael, BEd
Mrs C Davis (*Swimming*)
Mrs J M Duckett, BEd (*Lacrosse*)
A Hughes (*Rugby*)
J A Knott (*Cricket, Hockey*)

J S Skinner (*Tennis*)

Geography:
*Mrs S A Murnane, MA
Mrs S L Akam, BA
T Burch, BA
Mrs L C Campbell, BA
L Copley, BA
P J Deakin, BSc
T Elwell, BA

History:
*P Griffin, BA
G Cuddy, BA
Dr J Potter, BA, MPhil, PhD
Ms F Shah, BA
Miss R Stafford-Smith, BA
H J L Swayne, BA

History of Art:
*A Estorick, MA
C C Robinson, MA, MPhil

Library:
Mrs L Foden

Mathematics:
*M B Møller, BA
Dr C Adkins, PhD
Ms V A Green, BSc, CertEd
M Johnson, BA, MSc
S Karakus, BSc
Mrs M Matthews, BSc
L Murphy, AB Harvard
Miss S Penryhn-Lowe, BSc

Modern Languages:
*Mrs T L Jones, BA
Mrs H Browne, BA
S G Dobson, MA
G D Jones, BA
G R Moffat, BA
Mrs M L D Peña, BA
Mrs A P A Savage, BA
Mrs A R G Tearle, MA

Houses and Housemasters/mistresses:

Boys' Houses:
Bruce House: P Arnold
Temple House: B J Hart
Grenville House: A Hughes
Chandos House: P J Deakin
Cobham House: R Corthine
Chatham House: L Copley
Grafton House: G R Moffat
Walpole House: G D Jones

Girls' Houses:
Nugent House: Mrs J M Duckett
Lyttelton House: Ms V Green
Queen's House: Mrs S Rickner & M P Rickner
Stanhope House: Mrs L M Carter

Sixth Form House:
West House: Mr R Johnson & Mrs J Johnson

Day Houses
Cheshire: Mrs S Sutton
Winton: J Peppiatt

Medical Officer: Dr Ben Burgess, MBBChir, MA Cantab, MRCS Eng, MRCGP, DRCOG

Director of Development: C Dudgeon

Music:
*C Greene, MA, MPerf
B C Andrew, BMus
N C Gibbon, BSc
M R H Nottage
J Speakman, BA
B Weston, BA
C Windass, ABSM, GBSM

Philosophy and Religion:
*C S Bray, BA, BPhil
Dr P Dennis, BA, MA, PhD
Miss F Holloway, BA
C Lomax, BA
M P Rickner, BA

Physics:
*C W Donoghue, BSc
J Davis, BSc
B Hart, BEng
S Rose, BEng
P A Thompson, BSc
Dr T Yates, MPhys, PhD

PSHE:
*E Huxley-Capurro

Politics:
*S Cole, BA
J P Floyd, MA
Miss H Nelson, BA
Miss F Shah, BA

Skills Development:
*Mrs S Carter, BA, MA, MEd
Mrs E N Hughes, BA
Mrs S Rawlins, HLTA, Dip ADHD

Sports Science:
*A Jackson, BSc
P R Arnold, BSc
Mrs J M Duckett, BEd
I Michael, BEd
R C Sutton, BA
Mrs S E Sutton, BA

Director of Finance: M Greaves
Director of Operations: M Kerrigan

Strathallan School

Forgandenny, Perth, Perthshire PH2 9EG

Tel:	01738 812546
Fax:	01738 812549
email:	admissions@strathallan.co.uk
website:	www.strathallan.co.uk
Twitter:	@StrathallanSch
Facebook:	@strathallanschool

Motto: '*Labor Omnia Vincit*'

Harry Riley founded Strathallan in 1913 with the ambition to create a school where there would be opportunities for every pupil to excel, and the vision is one held true today.

The School is fully co-educational and numbers 520 pupils, of whom 200 are day pupils and 320 are boarders.

Situation. Strathallan School is located 6 miles south of Perth in the village of Forgandenny. It occupies an idyllic rural location, situated in 150 acres of richly wooded estate on the northern slopes of the Ochils and overlooking the Earn valley. At the same time, Strathallan is within easy reach of the international airports – Edinburgh (35 minutes) and Glasgow (1 hour).

At the centre of the School is the main building which dates from the 18th century and was formerly a country house and home of the Ruthven family. The School continues to invest in outstanding facilities. These include modern laboratories, a Theatre, Computer Centre, Library, Design Technology Centre, Sports Hall, Fitness and Weight Training Room, 2 Floodlit Synthetic Hockey Pitches, Indoor Multi-Sports Facility, Dance and Drama Studio, Medical Centre, Art School and newly refurbished Boarding Houses. All boarding houses have been built within the last thirty years with modern facilities and a single study-bedroom for every boarder in their last four years.

Aims. At the heart of the School's philosophy is the commitment to provide opportunities for all to excel and to help pupils make the most of their abilities within the framework of a caring environment.

Organisation. The School is primarily a boarding school yet also takes day pupils who are integrated into the boarding houses. There are four Senior boys' houses (Ruthven, Nicol, Freeland and Simpson). There are three girls' houses (Woodlands, Thornbank and Glenbrae). All boarding houses have their own resident Housemaster or Housemistress, assisted by House Tutors and a Matron. Boys have single study-bedrooms from the Fourth Form and girls have single study-bedrooms from the Third Form.

The Junior School, Riley House, is designed to cater for boys and girls wishing to enter the School at age nine. Riley is run by a resident Housemistress, assisted by tutors, two of whom are resident, and a resident Matron. After Riley, pupils move directly to one of the Senior houses. Riley is situated within its own area of the campus, yet also enjoys the facilities of the main School. It has its own common room, library, dormitories and music practice rooms.

The whole School dines centrally and there is a wide choice of hot and cold meals as well as vegetarian options. All boarding houses have small kitchens for the preparation of light snacks.

Religion. Strathallan has a Chapel and a resident Chaplain who is responsible for religious studies throughout the School.

Curriculum. Two of the keys to academic success are an ethos of continuous improvement and support from high quality, passionate teachers, and we pride ourselves on providing just such a learning environment. In addition, all pupils receive support from a tutor linked to their house and there is a full time Careers Advisor to help with opportunities available beyond school.

Junior. Boys and girls entering Riley House follow a course designed for the transition between their previous school and joining the senior part of Strathallan School at the age of 13. The following wide range of subjects is taught: Art, Computing, Design Technology, Drama, English, French, Geography, History, Latin, Maths, Music, PE, Personal and Social Development, Religious Education and Science. Courses are generally based on English Key Stages Two and Three.

The aim is to ensure pupils have an appropriate basis in the core subjects to move on to further study whilst also providing experience in specialist areas taught by subject experts. Teachers are careful to take account of ability and previous learning, guaranteeing each pupil works at an appropriate level for them and progresses at the right pace.

Third Form. Pupils in the Third Form participate in the following wide range of subjects: Art, Biology, Chemistry, Computing, Design & Technology, Drama, English, French, Geography, German and Spanish, History, Latin, Mathematics, PE, Physics and Religious Education. They are given a grounding in the skills necessary to pursue the subjects in the future should they wish, and an experience which is worthwhile in itself. All subjects are taught by specialists.

Fourth Form and the start of GCSE study. The two year GCSE course begins in the Fourth Form. All pupils study English, Mathematics, at least one Modern Language and the three Sciences. In addition, each pupil studies History or Geography (and can study both), plus two other subjects from an extensive choice. The aim is to ensure that pupils keep their options open, pursue a well-rounded curriculum, and establish a good basis for Sixth Form study.

Pupils are supported in their study not only by the individual teachers and the Heads of Department but also by a tutor who is linked to their house. A system of Merits and Distinctions rewards both individual pieces of outstanding work and continuous hard work and achievement. It is a central aim of the academic programme that pupils' efforts and achievements are recognised.

Sixth Form. Nearly all pupils stay on into the Sixth Form where the normal entry requirement is five passes at grade C or above at GCSE level. It is a special feature of Strathallan's Sixth Form that there is the flexibility to choose either A Levels or Scottish Highers. The choice is determined by the needs of the individual pupil. There is a wide range of subjects, including: Art, Biology, Business Management, Business Studies, Chemistry, Classical Civilisation, Computing, Design & Technology, Drama, Economics, English, French, Geography, German, History, Latin, Mathematics, Music, RMPS, Physical Education, Physics and Spanish.

The formal academic curriculum is supplemented by an extension programme of talks, visits and exchanges. We have well-established links with continental schools, and visits to theatres, galleries, courses and conferences in the UK and abroad often take place. Extracurricular activities and societies complement academic study and enhances pupils' interest in learning and discussion through activity beyond the classroom.

Each pupil is allocated a tutor who is a member of the academic staff and one of the duty staff of the boarding house. The tutor monitors pupils' academic and social progress and is responsible for discussing their regular reports with them.

Games. The main School games are rugby, cricket, hockey, netball, athletics and tennis, and standards are high. Other sports include skiing, squash, rounders, football, fencing, judo, badminton, table tennis, basketball, swimming, golf, horse riding and cross-country running in all of which national and regional success have been achieved in recent years.

Strathallan has two squash courts, 15 hard tennis courts, three netball courts, two floodlit synthetic pitches, a heated indoor swimming pool, sports hall, gymnasium and a fitness and weight training room. The sports hall comprises a basketball court, three badminton courts, a rock climbing wall as well as facilities for six-a-side hockey and indoor cricket coaching. Sailing, canoeing and skiing are recognised pastimes, and pupils participate in School ski days in the Spring term. Strathallan also has its own nine-hole golf course as well as Tennis and Shooting Academies.

Activities. All pupils are encouraged to take part in a range of activities for which time is set aside each day. There are over 50 weekly activities to choose from including dance, drama, pottery, chess, photography, first aid, lifeguarding, judo, horse riding, shooting (both clay pigeon and small bore) and fishing. There are also many societies and a programme of external speakers who visit the School. Pupils also work towards awards under The Duke of Edinburgh's Award scheme and are encouraged to take part in community service.

Music. The Music department has its own concert room, editing suite, keyboard room and classrooms, together with a number of individual practice rooms. Music may be taken at GCSE, Higher and AS/A2 Level. There are choirs, traditional music ensembles, jazz band, wind band, an orchestra, folk bands and rock bands. A house music competition takes place annually and there are regular concerts throughout the term. Individual tuition is available for virtually all instruments. The School has three Pipe Bands, including one for the Junior School, and a full-time Piping Instructor.

Art. Art is recognised as an important part of the School's activities and there are opportunities to study the subject at GCSE and AS/A2 Level. Pupils benefit from regular art trips abroad and have the opportunity to exhibit their work both locally and further afield. A purpose-built Art School features facilities for ceramics, sculpture and printmaking. National awards reflect pupils' achievements in this area.

Drama. Drama thrives throughout the School and the department makes full use of the Theatre as well as the purpose-built Dance and Drama Studio. There are junior and senior performances each year and pupils are encouraged to become involved in all aspects of production. The School also provides tuition in public and verse speaking and pupils regularly win trophies at the local festivals. There is also an annual Musical and pupils enter musical theatre exams.

Combined Cadet Force. There is a large voluntary contingent of the Combined Cadet Force with Navy, Army and Marines Sections.

Careers. Careers guidance begins in the Third Form. The Careers Adviser maintains close links with universities and colleges and regularly visits industrial firms. We have exchange programmes with schools in Australia, New Zealand and South Africa. There is a dedicated Careers Library, well-stocked with prospectuses, reference books and in-house magazines. Strathallan is a member of the Independent Schools Careers Organisation, a representative of which visits regularly and of the Scottish Council for Development and Industry.

All pupils have the opportunity to gain work experience in the Fifth Form, after their GCSEs. There is also a GAP year programme which provides placements for pupils to work overseas prior to going to university. Strathallan is developing particularly strong links with charities in Kenya.

Pastoral Care. At Strathallan, there is a strong emphasis on pastoral care. The School has drawn up its own welfare guidelines in consultation with parents, governors and Perth and Kinross Social Work Department.

Health Centre. Strathallan has its own purpose-built Health Centre with consulting and treatment rooms. There are nursing staff at the Centre and the School's Medical Officers visit four times a week. Physiotherapy, chiropody, and relaxation also take place in the Centre during term time.

Entrance. Junior Entrance – Boys and girls are admitted to the Junior School (Riley House) at either age 9, 10, 11 or 12. An Entrance Day (including those sitting scholarship examinations in January) is held in early Spring each year for those who are available. Entry is based on a satisfactory school report and assessments in Maths and English.

Entry to the Senior School – Candidates for entry into the Senior School at age 13 may enter via the Open Scholarship examination in February, Common Entrance or a satisfactory school report.

Sixth Form – Boys and girls may also enter at Sixth Form level, either via the Sixth Form scholarship examination in November or on the basis of a satisfactory school report and GCSE/Standard Grade results.

Scholarships. Awards are made on the basis of competitive examination/assessment. Bursary help is available to supplement awards for outstanding candidates on a financial need basis.

Awards are available in the following categories to candidates entering the school at three levels:

Junior School: Academic and Music/Choral/Performing Arts/Piping/Drumming, Drama and Sport. Candidates should be under 13 years old on 1 September in the year of entry. Scholarship Examination: January.

Third Form: Academic, Music/Choral/Piping/Drumming, Art, Design Technology, Drama and Sports. Candidates should be under 14 years old on 1 September in the year of entry. Scholarship Examination: February.

Sixth Form: Academic, Music/Choral/Piping/Drumming, Art, Design Technology/Arkwright, Drama and Sports. Candidates should be under 17 years old on 1 September in the year of entry. Scholarship Examination: November.

Further information is available on the School's website, www.strathallan.co.uk, or from The Admissions Office, Tel: 01738 815003, email: admissions@strathallan.co.uk.

Bursaries. Bursaries are awarded dependent on financial circumstances and are available to pupils who have qualified for entry through exam or school report or both. It is not necessary for successful candidates for bursaries to have achieved scholarship standard but it may be possible to add a bursary award to a scholarship to enable a pupil to come to Strathallan.

Fees per term (2018–2019). Junior School (Riley House): £7,850 (boarding), £4,900 (day). Senior School: £11,000 (boarding), £7,470 (day).

Prospectus. Up-to-date information is included in the prospectus which can be obtained by contacting the Admissions Office or via the School's website.

Charitable status. Strathallan School is a Registered Charity, number SC008903, dedicated to Education.

Board of Governors:

Chairman: Mr R K Linton, LLB, NP
Deputy Chairman: Professor J S Cachia, BSc, MBChB, MD, FRCGP, DRCOG, FRCPE
Mr J G Barrack
Mr N M Campbell

Dr J Crang, BA, PGCE, PhD, FRHist, FRSA
Prof A R Denison, PFHEA, FAcadMEd, FRCR, FRCP, MRad, DipMEd
Mr K C Dinsmore, BA, LLB, Dip LP
Mr S Fairbairn, MA, LLB, Dip LP NP
Mr D Gillanders
Mr M Griffiths, LLB Hons, CA
Mr R G A Hall, BArch, Dip Arch, RIAS, RIBA
Mr S J Hay, BA, MBA, MSc
Professor T Hoey, MA, PhD, Hon FRSGS
Mr J Leiper, CA, BA
Mrs C Miller, MA Hons
Mrs P A Milne, BA, MBA, MCIPD
Mr A Sinclair, BSc
Mrs G M Wilson, MA, PGCE

Headmaster: **Mr M Lauder**, MA

Assistant Staff:

Mrs T Ailinger, Staatsexamen, Cert TESOL
Mr Y Banda, BSc, PGCE
Mr D J Barnes, BSc, PGCE, PGCG, FRGS (*Deputy Head Pastoral*)
Mr G J Batterham, BSc, PGCE (*Simpson House*)
Mr M Bergin, BSc, PGCE
Mr D E Billing, MA, PGCE (*Nicol House*)
Mrs D Billing, MA, PGCE
Dr K E M Blackie, PhD, PGDE, BSc
Miss C Brownbridge, BA, PG Dip, PGDE
Mr F Burnett, BSc, PGDE
Miss E de Celis Lucas, BA, CAP
Dr A N Collins, BSc, BA, PhD
Dr B Cooper, BSc, PhD, PGCE
Mrs M-L Crane, BA, PGCE
Mrs L E Davies, BA, PGCE
Mr S Dick, BEd
Dr S B Downhill, BA, MSc, PhD, PGCE, FRGS
Mr S Drover, BSc, PGCE
Mrs E C Duncan, MA, PGCE
Mr A L M Dunn, MA, PGCE
Dr S R Ferguson, MA, PhD, MSc, PGCE
Mrs S E Fleming, BEd
Mr N P Gallier, MBE, MA, MSc, PGCE
Mr G N Gardiner, BSc, PGCE
Mr D R Giles, BA QTS, Cert PP
Mr M Gooch, BA GTS
Mrs S E Halley, BSc, PGDE
Mr S Hamill, BA (*Deputy Head Academic*)
Mr N A Hamilton, BMus
Mr B A Heaney, BSc, Dip Ed (*Freeland House*)
Mr A D Henderson, UKCC
Mr M Henderson-Sowerby, BSc, PGCE
Mr D M Higginbottom, MA, PGCE
Mrs J Higginbottom, MA, PGCE
Mrs R Hodson, MA, PGCE, MSc
Mrs C G Howett, BA, Dip Ed
Miss H Jassim, BSc, PGDE
Mr E Kalman, BSc, MPhil
Mr P J S Keir, BEd, Cert SpLD
Mr L Kent, BSc, PGCE (*Thornbank House*)
Mr E G Kennedy, BA, PGCE
Mrs E C Lalani, BEd, Dip Man (*Riley House*)
Miss C Laurie, BSc, PGCE
Mr E Lee, MA, PGCE
Mrs F MacBain, MA
Mr I McGowan, BCom Dip Teaching (*Ruthven House*)
Miss S Mackay, BA, MSc, PGCE
Mr K McKinney, BSc, BEd
Dr I Mitchell, BSc, PhD
Mr S Mitchell, BSc, PGCE
Miss J L Morrison, BTechEd
Mr C Muirhead, BA

Mr R Newham, BSc, PGDE
Mr T Ogilvie, LTA CC
Mr G S R Robertson, BA, DMS
Mr S W Robertson, MA, BSc, PGCE
Dr J D Salisbury, MA, PhD, PGCE
Mrs L Salisbury, BA, Dip Ed, PGCE, ALCM
Mrs C A Sim Sayce, BMus, PGCE
Miss A Sime, BEd (*Director of Sport*)
Mr J Storer, BEd, MA
Mr A C W Streatfeild-James, MA, PGCE (*Director of Studies*)
Mrs K L Streatfeild-James, BA, PGCE, Dip SpLD
Mrs R C W Stuart, MA, PGDE
Mrs J A Summersgill, BSc, PGCE
Mrs A J Tod, MA, PGCE
Mr M R A J B Tod, BSc, PG Dip
Mr P M Vallot, BSc
A Watt, BComm, BComm, HDE
Mrs L Waugh, BA, PGDE
Ms K Wilson, BSc, PGCE (*Glenbrae House*)
Dr I Woodman, MA, MLitt, PhD, PGCE
Mr C Wiles, BA
Revd J Wylie, BSc, BD, MTh
Mr D Yeaman, MChem, PGDE
T Zhou, MSc, PhD

Bursar and Clerk to the Governors: Mr A C Glasgow, MBE, BEng, MSc, CEng

Director of External Relations: Ms F Duncan
Marketing Manager: Mrs C Bath
External Relations: Mrs A Wilson
Communications Executive: Ms F Wild

Medical Officers:
Dr A M Lewis, MBChB, MRCGP
Dr L D Burnett, MBChB, BSc, DRCOG, MRCGP

Sutton Valence School

Sutton Valence, Maidstone, Kent ME17 3HL

Tel: 01622 845200
Fax: 01622 844103
email: enquiries@svs.org.uk
website: www.svs.org.uk
Facebook: @SuttonValenceSchoolKent

Motto: *My Trust is in God alone*

Founded in 1576 by William Lambe, Sutton Valence School has over 425 years of proud history. Today the School is co-educational and includes a preparatory school on a neighbouring site. Both schools are situated on the slopes of a high ridge with unequalled views over the Weald of Kent in the historic, beautiful and safe village of Sutton Valence.

Our greatest strength is our community. The relationships we enjoy between staff, pupils and parents allow us to craft an educational journey that is individually suited to every pupil. During a family's association with the School we hope they will feel involved, listened to and informed.

Through the high expectations and standards we set, all our young people are encouraged and helped to go further than they had thought possible in their academic, co-curricular, community and leadership journeys. We want them to become confident, civilised, tolerant and open-minded individuals who possess a love of learning and a strong sense of self-discipline along with a set of values reflecting our principles as a Christian Foundation.

Ethos. A community where each cares for all and individuality is cherished.

Sutton Valence is an educational community whose philosophy embraces a breadth of challenges. Through a diverse curriculum and a wide range of activities we cultivate an appreciation of academic excellence, responsibility, leadership, kindness and friendship amongst our pupils. All members of the School develop a sense of spiritual, moral and ethical awareness and, in so doing, come to appreciate their own place in the world.

At Sutton Valence every person is valued as an individual with their own distinct sense of worth and potential. Each member of the community has abilities, talents and skills unique to them. Our School strives to provide the seedbed to allow these gifts and talents to grow, develop and ultimately flourish.

Our community is founded on the principles of trust, tolerance and openness. As such, we expect all at Sutton Valence to treat each other with respect, humanity and care. Individuals therefore are obliged to recognise that the differences between us make us collectively stronger. It is essential that we understand, appreciate and celebrate the diversity of backgrounds, world views and attitudes expressed by those in our community.

At the foundation of our community is the expectation that every student will achieve their potential. Our commitment is to strive for excellence as pupils and teachers. To achieve this it is essential that every member of the School strives to give of their very best in all that they do.

Results. Sutton Valence School has an inclusive intake, however, our academic strength lies in enabling our students to achieve beyond their benchmarked potential, whatever their ability. On average, our students will gain results at A Level that outperform their predicted grade on entry to the School by 0.5 of a grade per subject. As measured by Durham University's Centre for Evaluation and Monitoring, which has a thirty-year history of computing these statistics, this year Sutton Valence is in the top 10% of schools for adding academic value (amongst those participating). That means that children at Sutton Valence do significantly better in their exams than they would do in 90% of other schools, nationally.

It is the combination of outstanding teaching and consistent effort by our students that brings these enviable results. For example, this year our top set students (many of whom did not pass the 11+) achieved 98% A* to B grades at A Level. Overall, our A Level results in recent years are similar to, or better than, those of the highly selective Kent grammar schools.

Curriculum. The academic curriculum is innovative and aims to achieve a balance between the needs of the individual and demands of society, industry, the universities and the professions. Classes are small and the graduate teaching staff to pupil ratio is 1:9.

Our First and Second Forms (Years 7 and 8) follow our innovative, challenging and stimulating Junior Curriculum, which has academic excellence at its heart and continues to promote our pupils' love of learning by emphasising the Sutton Valence Learning Habits of Being, Thinking, Doing and Relating. We also ensure that the fundamental study skills required for success are mastered so that our pupils can move on fully prepared to excel at GCSE and beyond. These pupils also pursue our excellent Junior Leadership programme which promotes those essential skills required in addition to academic study for them to become truly successful and make the most of all that is on offer; leading others, team membership, organisation, time-management and perseverance, as examples. In addition they each produce a Junior Portfolio which records their achievements over the two years and 'graduate' in readiness to join the Senior

School with the award of the Sutton Valence School Junior Curriculum.

Many pupils join us in the Third Form from other schools. In this Form we concentrate even more on developing a high level of competence in the essential numeracy, literacy and ICT skills, across all subjects, in targeted-ability groups, with the most able often undertaking extension programmes, in preparation for GCSEs in Core (English, Mathematics, Sciences, Humanities and Languages) and Option (Music, DT, Art, Drama, HE and PE) subjects, which are then studied in the Fourth and Fifth Forms. Every pupil is set 'Target Agreed Grades' (TAGs) in discussion with their teachers and their attainment and effort level in relation to their TAGs is reviewed half-termly. These grades are benchmarked against the performance of pupils of similar ability in other independent schools. Our aim is that Sutton Valence pupils will aspire to and achieve highly ambitious outcomes relative to their ability profile and thus amply fulfil their true potential. They are also heavily involved in our extensive co-curricular programme.

In Fourth and Fifth Form (Years 10 and 11) pupils usually study nine or ten subjects to GCSE level. These are divided between the core – English and English Literature, Mathematics, a Modern Language (French, Spanish, German), Science, Religious Studies, PSHE and ICT – and option groups. Each group contains a number of subjects, offering a choice which allows every pupil to achieve a balanced education whilst, at the same time, providing the opportunity to concentrate on his or her strengths. Subjects on offer are History, Geography, Drama, Business Studies, a second Language, DT, Home Economics, Art, Music, iMedia and PE.

Sixth Form Pupils, either progressing from our Fifth Form or joining us from elsewhere, pursue an A Level course in three or four carefully-chosen subjects, along with individual research in a specialist topic in preparation for submission of an extended project qualification (EPQ) or the BTEC Level 3 in Uniformed Public Service, which counts for university entry. As in the younger years, all pupils work towards ambitious TAGs based on Durham University's independent school benchmarking system. In recent years, our pupils have significantly outperformed these national expectations, achieving strong positive value added results which show that there is something special happening here relative to similar institutions. They can also expect to receive plenty of individual support and expert, bespoke, advice on appropriate Higher Education applications, interview practice, CV writing and careers in general. In addition there are numerous opportunities to be fully involved in wider School life and take on positions of leadership. The vast majority will continue their academic journey at university level, although employment-based training routes are becoming an increasingly popular option for some.

Potential Oxbridge candidates are identified in the Lower Sixth year and suitable tuition is arranged.

Choice of Subjects: Separate booklets on GCSE and A Level options are available.

Setting, Promotion, Reporting. In First to Fifth Form Mathematics and French are setted. In First to Third Form a top group is selected.

The minimum qualification for entry into the Sixth Form is normally considered to be five B grade passes at GCSE Level, or the equivalent for overseas students.

Academic progress is monitored by tutors and at regular intervals throughout the term every pupil is graded for achievement and effort in every subject for their classwork and for effort in their prep. Parents are invited to a 'monitoring morning' at every half term to discuss their child's progress and to set targets for improvement next half term, if required. At the end of term full subject reports are written on all pupils. Promotion between sets is always possible.

ICT (iMedia). In addition to well-equipped computer suites the School has developed a sophisticated campus-wide network with its own intranet and online systems of communication with parents.

The school network serves the whole site providing open access for pupils in the computer rooms and throughout the school via a Microsoft Windows-based system working on industry-standard software. The library stocks many CD ROMs and there is a CAD system in Design and Technology. Access to the network is available to pupils in their own rooms in boarding houses.

Higher Education and Careers. Sutton Valence has a modern and well-equipped Sixth Form Centre which incorporates a careers library and the latest technologies to help in degree and career selection.

Every pupil sits a series of aptitude and ability tests during the two years prior to GCSE. This is followed by a thorough interview with trained members of staff in conjunction with the Kent Careers Service, when suggestions are made for Sixth Form academic courses and possible degrees or careers are explored.

In the Sixth Form further interviews are conducted, the Higher Education Coordinator gives advice on university and college applications and a range of career lectures and visits are laid on, including trips to Oxford and Cambridge universities.

Music. Music plays a very important part in the life of the school, and we have a deservedly fine reputation for the quality and range of our music-making. The music school contains a concert hall, five teaching rooms, ten practice rooms and an ensemble room.

Approximately 40% of the pupils learn a musical instrument or have singing lessons; there are four choirs, an orchestra, wind band, string group, jazz band, and a very full programme of concerts. Music tours to Europe are arranged, and the Music Society organises a programme of distinguished visiting performers every year.

Drama. As with Music, Drama is central to the life of the school and the creative expression of our students. Every year there will be a number of productions, in addition to theatre workshops and reviews. Drama scholars and others also receive one-to-one drama coaching lessons in preparation for LAMDA exams. The Baughan Theatre provides an adaptable venue seating up to 250 for drama, music and lectures, along with rehearsal rooms, technical gantry and scene dock.

Sport and Physical Education. Sutton Valence has a deserved reputation as a strong sporting school, competing in seventeen sports. On average, forty pupils will have representative honours at County, Regional and National levels in the main sports as well as in other disciplines. On a typical Saturday afternoon, half the school will be engaged in matches.

The Talented Athlete Group (TAG), which includes sports scholars, helps those students, both inside and outside of Sutton Valence, who are performing at a very high level (county and beyond). Once identified, the student will have regular meetings with their coach, either as a group or individually, where aims and objectives will be set and a variety of subjects will be covered. Individual strength and conditioning programmes and sessions are offered for all senior teams and are monitored by professionally qualified staff.

Our 100-acre site has one of the best cricket squares in Kent, two floodlit Astroturf pitches for hockey, a six-lane indoor swimming pool, tennis, netball and squash courts, a sports hall encompassing a full-size indoor hockey pitch, sprung-floor cricket nets and fitness suite, six golf practice holes and a floodlit all-weather running track. In all, there is a tremendous range of choice for both boys and girls, all of whom will have timetabled sport on at least two days every week and could be involved in a sporting activity every day, if they wished. Additional sports, such as football, judo, dance, horse riding, badminton, basketball, fives and fencing are offered through our activities programme.

Pastoral System. The School is arranged vertically in houses, with the Juniors (Years 7 and 8) in a separate house. Each House has a Housemaster or Housemistress and is divided into Tutor Groups containing pupils from each year and from day and boarding. Pupils meet with their Tutor every day and this allows their progress to be monitored, as well as giving pupils an opportunity to seek guidance. In addition to monitoring academic progress, tutors help pupils develop their potential through the Personal, Social and Health Education (PSHE) programme.

The School is a Christian foundation, however, our values are very much based on openness, tolerance and inclusivity. As such, we welcome students from all faith backgrounds, as well as those families who have no faith commitment.

Community Service, CCF and Duke of Edinburgh's Award. The CCF provides an organisation within Sutton Valence School which enables boys and girls to develop self-discipline, responsibility, self-reliance, resourcefulness, endurance, perseverance, a sense of service to the community and leadership. It complements the academic and other co-curricular aims of the School in preparing our pupils for adult life. All the three service elements of Army, Navy and RAF are offered. Pupils may join in the Third Form (Year 9) and CCF is also one of the option choices in the Fourth Form (Year 10). Cadets are encouraged to join the Duke of Edinburgh's Award scheme where there is the opportunity for planning and undertaking expeditions. Sutton Valence School CCF is affiliated to the Princess of Wales's Royal Regiment.

The Duke of Edinburgh's Award scheme is, similarly, well supported with, on average, 18 Gold Awards being achieved each year. Others participate in Community Service activities whereby pupils visit local primary schools, old people's homes, hospitals, undertake charity work and help out with local conservation projects.

Clubs and Activities. Time is specifically set aside each week for clubs and activities. Every pupil spends time pursuing his or her own special interests, and with up to forty clubs or activities from which to choose, the range and scope is very wide. In addition, various school societies and some other activities take place out of school hours, for example the Kingdon Society for Academic Scholars.

Scholarships and Bursaries. Academic, Art, Design Technology, Music, Sport and Drama Scholarships are awarded at 11+, 13+ and Sixth Form entry. Candidates may apply for a maximum of two non-academic scholarships.

The Westminster Scholarship supports well-motivated and able pupils who enter Sutton Valence School at Sixth Form level and who are expected to achieve 5 A* grade passes at GCSE.

Bursaries are awarded according to financial need at the discretion of the Scholarship and Bursaries Committee, and are reviewed annually. Forces bursaries are available.

Further details may be obtained from the Admissions Officer.

Fees per term (2018–2019). Senior Boarding (in addition to Tuition): £3,980 (Full), £3,200 (5 nights pw), £2,615 (4 nights pw), £2,070 (3 nights pw). Junior Boarding (in addition to Tuition): £3,170 (Full), £2,765 (5 nights pw), £2,340 (4 nights pw), £1,850 (3 nights pw). Tuition: Junior £5,465–£6,210, Senior £7,135. Lunch for Day pupils and occasional boarders: £290.

Instrumental Music: £265 per term (10 lessons).

Extras: Stationery and clothing are charged for as supplied. A small charge is also made for entry at each stage to The Duke of Edinburgh's Award scheme. Any other extras are those expenses personal to the individual. We have a series of bus routes available to families from areas across Kent costing up to £300 per term. Further details of routes can be obtained on request.

Charitable status. United Westminster Schools Foundation is a Registered Charity, number 309267. Its aims are to promote education through its two independent schools and one state comprehensive school.

Visitor: The Lord Archbishop of Canterbury

Clerk: R W Blackwell, MA

Governing Body
Lady Vallance, JP, MA, MSc, PhD, FRSA, FCGI (*Chairman*)
Mrs H J Brunt, BSc, Dip Arch
Mrs J D Davies, BSc
A J Hutchinson, MA Cantab
S C James, BA
R J Lennard
T D Page
P P Sherrington, LLB, LLM, FCI Arb
The Reverend Canon D J Stanton, MTheol, MA
Mrs G Swaine, BSc Hons, MEd
E L Watts, OBE, BA, FRSA

Headmaster: B C W Grindlay, MA Cantab, MusB, FRCO CHM

Deputy Headmaster: J J Farrell, MA Cantab, MEd Buckingham (*History*)
Academic Deputy Head: Mrs R K Ball, BA Wales Lampeter (*English, Media Studies*)
Assistant Head: D R Sansom, BSc Wales Swansea (*Geography*)
Assistant Head: Mrs S Rose, BEd Bishop Otter College (*Designated Safeguarding Lead, English*)
Bursar: S R Fowle

† *Boarding Housemaster or Housemistress*
‡ *Day Housemaster or Housemistress*

Academic Staff:
Miss A K L Akehurst, BA Oxon (*MFL*)
Mrs K L Andersen, CertEd Elizabeth Gaskell College (*Home Economics*)
Miss C E Barden, BA Kent (*Mathematics*)
Mrs K M Buckland, BA Wolverhampton (*Assistant Director of Drama*)
‡Miss L J Burden, BA Anglia, BSc OU, Dip Hyp (*Head of Psychology, Community Service, Head of PSHE*)
‡R H Carr, BA St Johns College Durham (*History, Games, Head of the Juniors and Prep School Liaison*)
D E Clarke, BSc, CBiol, MSB Bristol (*Photography*)
‡T P Cope, MEng Loughborough (*Mathematics, CO RAF*)
†C M Davenport, BA Keele (*English*)
G A Davies, BA Wales Lampeter (*Chaplain, Religious Studies*)
†Mrs S H de Castro Franco, BA Manchester (*Head of MFL*)
J D Downs, MSc Birbeck College London, BA Essex (*Head of Geography*)
L Ellmers, BA Oxon (*Head of Spanish, MFL*)
A H Evans, BA Cantab (*Geography*)
B E Fewson, BA Hull (*Director of Drama*)
D Frost, BSc Wolverhampton (*Head of Learning Support*)
F Gergely, PhD Constantine the Philosopher University, Slovakia (*Mathematics*)
Mrs F M Gosden, BA Rhodes (*English*)

Miss L Gray, BA Bangor (*Religious Studies, Junior Leadership Coordinator*)

Dr E J Grindlay, MA Cantab (*Head of English, Head of Academic Scholars*)

Miss M A Halleron, BSc Leeds (*Head of Physics*)

Miss P L Hallett, BA Brighton (*Head of Academic PE, Head of Tennis and Rounders*)

A P Hammersley, BSc York (*Biology*)

Mrs L Harris, BA King's College London (*Learning Support*)

Mrs E Head, MA Dundee (*Learning Support*)

Mrs J Head, BA Canterbury Christ Church (*Learning Support*)

†S J Head, MSci Bristol (*Chemistry and Head of Boarding*)

J Henderson, BSc Leeds Beckett (*Head of Hockey, Games*)

Dr L A Henshaw, PhD King's College London, BSc Royal Veterinary College (*Physics*)

Mrs H E Heurtevent, BA Caen, DEUG I and II Université Catholique, Angers (*MFL*)

Dr S P Hiscocks, BSc Essex, MA King's College London, CChem, FRSC, CSciTeach (*Head of Chemistry*)

D W Holmes, LRAM, Prof Cert Royal Academy of Music (*Head of Strings*)

P J Horley, BA College of Ripon and York St John, PG Dip RNCM, ARCO, ATCL, ALCM (*Director of Music*)

Mrs R Howard, BA Bristol (*MFL*)

M D Howell, BSc Worcester (*Director of Sport, Head of Rugby*)

†M B James, MEd Macquarie Sydney, Grad Dip Ec New England University Australia (*Head of Business Studies and Economics*)

Miss H R Jelfs, BA Brighton (*Head of Girls' Cricket and Teacher of Academic PE*)

‡M A Jones, BSc East Anglia (*Geography*)

Mrs C J Kitchen, BEng Bradford, MSc Birmingham, BSc OU (*Mathematics, Timetabler and Academic Data Coordinator, D of E Coordinator*)

M R Latham, BSc St Mary's (*Games*)

Mrs E J Lesourd, MSc, BA Loughborough (*DT and Art*)

Mrs W M Loy, MSci Durham, MSc Birmingham (*Physics*)

Miss J A Manning, BA Kent, PG Diploma Dyslexia and Literacy York (*Head of ESL, French*)

‡Miss K J McConnachie, BSc Birmingham (*Academic PE, Games, Head of Netball*)

Mr P S Mayes, BA Greenwich (*Head of Design Technology*)

G J Millbery, BA Wales Lampeter (*Director of ICT, Contingent Commander CCF, Assistant D of E Coordinator*)

Mrs L A Mitchell-Nanson, BSc Kent (*Assistant Head of Mathematics*)

Miss E J Oliver, BSc Bangor (*Biology*)

Mrs B Palmer, MA Canterbury Christ Church (*ICT*)

A J F Penfold, BA Surrey (*Head of Religious Studies*)

R W J Plowden, MA Wales, BA Newcastle (*History*)

Mrs F H Porter, BA Leeds, MA Ed Canterbury Christ Church (*English, Head of Sixth Form*)

Miss S Pritchard, BA Greenwich (*Business Studies and Economics*)

Miss Z Radford, BSc Swansea (*Head of Biology*)

Miss E J Schofield, BA University of the Arts (*Art and Photography*)

Mr T B Sealy, BA Glamorgan (*Media Studies, English*)

Mrs A P Simpson, BSc London, PG Cert Dyslexia, PG Cert Educational Testing (*SEN*)

J D Soman, BA Oxford (*Assistant Director of Music*)

Mrs A J Sunde, BA Sheffield (*Head of History*)

Mrs N R Sutton, BA Canterbury Christchurch NZ (*Art*)

M J Thompson, BA Wolverhampton (*Head of Art*)

T S Waterworth, BSc Loughborough (*Geography*)

G A Wellings, BSc Plymouth (*Head of Mathematics*)

V Wells (*Head of Cricket, Games*)

Mrs C Westlake, BA Sussex (*Assistant Head of English*)

C J Westlake, BSc Glamorgan (*Mathematics*)

Mrs H M Wood, MSc BSc Hull (*Chemistry, CO Navy*)

J Zane, MA City University, BA Exeter (*Head of Media Studies, Drama*)

Boarding Support Staff:
St Margaret's House: Mrs B Sparrowhawk (*Matron*)
Sutton House: Mrs E Agu Benson (*Matron*)
Westminster House: Mrs D Aitken (*Matron*)

Administrative and Teaching Support Staff:
Assistant Bursar: Mrs D Van Leeuwen
Estates Bursar: Mrs J Vicary
Headmaster's PA: Mrs S O'Connell
Director of Marketing and Admissions: Mrs K Williams
Alumni Relations and Development Manager: W Radford
Admissions Officer: Mrs K Webster

Preparatory School:
Head: Miss C L Corkran, MEd, BEd Hons Cantab
Deputy Head: J Watkins, BSc Hons, PGCE Primary
Head of Pre-Prep: Miss P McCarmick, MA, BSc QTS, AMBDA
Director of Studies: Mrs R Harrison, BEd Hons

Head's Secretary: Mrs A Leckie
Admissions: Miss A Betts

Tonbridge School

Tonbridge, Kent TN9 1JP

Tel: 01732 365555
Fax: 01732 363424
email: hmsec@tonbridge-school.org
website: www.tonbridge-school.co.uk
Twitter: @TonbridgeUK
Facebook: @tonbridgeUK

Motto: '*Deus dat incrementum*'

Tonbridge School was founded in 1553 by Sir Andrew Judde, under Letters Patent of King Edward VI.

Tonbridge is an all-boys, 13–18, boarding and day school. 780 boys from a variety of backgrounds are offered an education remarkable both for its breadth of opportunity and the exceptional standards routinely achieved in all areas of school life.

The school aims to provide a caring and enlightened environment in which the talents of each individual flourish. We encourage boys to be creative, tolerant and to strive for academic, sporting and cultural excellence. Respect for tradition and an openness to innovation are equally valued. A well-established house system at the heart of the school fosters a strong sense of belonging. We want boys to enjoy their time here, but also to be made aware of their social and moral responsibilities. Ideally, Tonbridgians should enter into the adult world with the knowledge and self-belief to fulfil their own potential and, in many cases, to become leaders in their chosen field. Equally, we hope to foster a life-long empathy for the needs and views of others.

Over the past ten years, more than 98% of all Tonbridge boys have been successful at gaining a place at leading universities, including Oxford and Cambridge. Other popular destinations include Durham, Bristol, Bath, Exeter, London School of Economics and Imperial.

Visitors to Tonbridge are always welcome and full information about the school is available on our website: www.tonbridge-school.co.uk.

Location. Tonbridge School is just off the M25, on the edge of the Kent / Surrey / Sussex borders and attracts families from all over southern England and beyond. It lies in about 150 acres of land on the edge of the town of Tonbridge, and thus provides a good balance between town and country living.

Admissions. The majority of boys join the school at the age of 13, having gained admission through the Common Entrance Examination or the school's own Scholarship Examination (held in early May). About 145 boys are admitted at the age of 13 each year. An additional 20 places are available for entry to the Sixth Form at the age of 16. We also have up to 6 places for boys aged 14 (Year 10).

Registration for a boy at 13+ entry should be made, preferably, not later than three years before the date of intended entry. Boys will then be asked to complete the ISEB pre-test and to visit Tonbridge for an assessment afternoon, usually during the Autumn Term of Year 6. The information collected from these occasions, in conjunction with the current school Head's report, will determine whether the offer of an unconditional or provisional place may be made. Those receiving an unconditional offer will be required to complete no further assessment (although Tonbridge are pleased to receive and mark Common Entrance papers from those who wish to take these). Those receiving a provisional offer will be invited to take a further assessment (in maths and English) during the Summer Term of Year 7, after which a provisional offer may be converted to an unconditional offer.

Later registration for Year 9 entry is possible during Year 7, with such candidates following a modified entrance procedure. Details of this procedure can be found on our website or obtained from the Admissions Office: Tel: 01732 304297; email: admissions@tonbridge-school.org.

Applications for 14+ and Sixth Form entry are best made by 1 September a year before entry, but may be considered later. Admission at 14+ is gained via our own maths and English exams. Boys sitting for entry at 16+ will take papers in the 4 subjects they wish to study in the sixth form.

Parents wishing to send their sons to Tonbridge should apply to the Director of Admissions for a copy of the Prospectus, which gives full details of the registration procedure. Information is also available on the website: www.tonbridge-school.co.uk.

Scholarships and Bursaries. Some 45 scholarships are offered each year to boys in Year 6 (the Junior Foundation Scholarship) or in Year 8.

Up to 10 Junior Foundation Scholarships are available to candidates in Year 6 who are attending a state primary school or to those attending a prep school, but who would require financial support in order to attend Tonbridge. Candidates should register by 1 October during Year 6 and will be invited to attend an assessment afternoon in November, with the stronger candidates returning to take tests in maths and English in February. Such scholarships, which are confirmed in Year 6, may provide financial support of up to 100% to allow attendance at prep school for Years 7 and 8, as well as at Tonbridge from Year 9.

In Year 8, up to a further 21 Academic Scholarships are awarded (by examination in early May) as well as 10 or more Music Scholarships (for which auditions are held in early February), up to 10 Art, Drama or Technology Scholarships (assessed in early February) and up to 4 Cowdrey Scholarships, for sporting ability and sportsmanship (also assessed in early February). The award of any scholarship allows eligibility for means tested support of any amount up to the full school fee.

Entry forms and full particulars of all Scholarships and Foundation Awards may be obtained from the Admis-

sions Secretary; Tel: 01732 304297; email: admissions@tonbridge-school.org.

Fees per term (2018–2019). £13,482 for a boarding place and £10,114 for a day place.

Charitable status. Tonbridge School is a Registered Charity, number 1097977. It exists solely to provide education for boys.

Governors:
R J Elliott (*Chairman*)

T M Attenborough	G M Rochussen
D P Devitt	Dr M S Spurr, DPhil
M Dobbs	Dr G E Taggart
R J Elliott	Mr J Thompson
Mrs S Huang	Mrs K Wheadon
A Mayer	Mr G White
Mrs J Naismith	The Earl of Woolton

Clerk to the Governors: Major General A Kennett, CBE

Headmaster: J E Priory, MA Oxon

Second Master: Dr P H Williams, PhD
Director of Studies: J C Pearson, MA
Director of Teaching and Learning: M J Weatheritt, MA
Director of Admissions and Marketing: A J Leale, BA
Bursar: A C Moore, MA, MBA, INSEAD
Upper Master: J R Bleakley, BA
Lower Master: Miss J H Green, BA
Tonbridge Society Director: A R Whittall, MA

Assistant Staff:
* *Head of Department/Subject*

Art:
*F J Andrews, MA, BA
T W Duncan, BA
Mrs E R Glass, MA
Mrs B L Waugh, BFA
Artist-in-Residence: Mrs J de Pear, MA
Art Librarian: Mrs M P Dennington
Art Technician: Mrs J M Brent

Classics:
*Dr J A Burbidge, BA, MSt, DPhil
J A Nicholls, MA
Miss C C Read, BA
A P Schweitzer, MA
R J M Stephen, MA
L F Walsh, BMus

Design Technology and Engineering:
*R L Day, BSc
W D F Biddle, BSc
Dr A O Cooke, MEng, DPhil
J M Woodrow, BA
Engineering Associate: R D Knight, BSc
Technology Technicians: R Davies; O Longson
Teaching Assistant: C Martin
SCAD Intern: F Zeledon, BA

Digital Creativity:
*P J Huxley, BSc
Technology Tutors: D P Love MIET, C D Walker

Media Tutor: Mrs E R Sim, BA, MPhil

Divinity:
*J C F Dobson, MA
R Burnett, MA
S J Dungate, BA
P J North, MA, BA
A G Oxburgh, BA
The Revd D A Peters, MA
R T Scarratt, BA
Dr H J M Swales, MA, MPhil

Drama:
*G D Bruce, MA
R J Hartley, MA
L Thornbury, Dip Drama

English:
*N J Waywell, BA
J R Bleakley, BA
P S D Carpenter, MA
D Cooper, MA, BA
A J Edwards, MA
R H Evans, MA
S A Farmer, MA
R J Hartley, MA
Mrs S Pinto del Rio, BA
Dr J D Shafer, PhD, MA, BSc

Geography:
*C M Battarbee, BA
C M Henshall, BA
G P Gales, BEd
Miss J H Green, BA
Mrs J M Watson-Reynolds, MA, BA

History:
*Miss M L Robinson, MA

D Cooper, MA
Mrs F C Dix Perkin, MA
J C Harber, MA
Miss M A Lhroob, BA,
    MLitt
R W G Oliver, MA
N R V Rendall, BA
Dr C D Thompson, BA,
    MPhil, PhD

Mathematics:
*Dr I R H Jackson, MA,
    PhD
T G Fewster, BSc
R J Freeman, MA
K A Froggatt, MA
Miss J A D Gent, BA
Dr J D King, MA, PhD
M J Lawson, BA
N J Lord, MA
V Myslov, BA
Dr A A Reid, MChem,
    PhD, AFHEA
A P Schweitzer, MA
S J Seldon, MA, MEng
Dr Z Wang, MMath, PhD

Modern Languages:
*L Fuentes, BA
W H C Law, BA (*French*)
S Kerr (*German*)
L Fuentes, BA (*Spanish*)
X J Wu, MA (*Mandarin
    Chinese*)
Mrs C Clugston, MA
    (*EAL*)
R D Hoare, MA
    (*International
    Coordinator*)
Miss D M McDermot, MA
L S McDonald, MA
J A Nicholls, MA
A B F Pruvost, BA
J A Storey-Mason, BA
Mrs R Thomson, BA,
    DipHE, TESOL
C E Wright, BA
Mrs X Yu, BA

Music:
*M A Forkgen, MA,
    ARCO (*Director of
    Music*)
J R P Thomas, MA, FRCO
    (*Head of Academic
    Music & Choirmaster*)
A E L Pearson, BMus,
    ARCM, LRAM (*Strings*)
D L Williams, GRSM,
    ARCM, LRAM (*Piano*)
S J Hargreaves, MA, MEd
L F Walsh, BMus

Physical Education:
*Director of Sport and Head
    of PE*: C D Morgan, BSc

Houses & Housemasters:

Boarding:
School House: R Burnett
Judde House: A G McGilchrist
Park House: A T Sampson
Hill Side: P J North

*Assistant Director of Sport
    & Hockey Coach*: Mrs L
    Maasdorp

Science:
*Dr W J Burnett, BSc, PhD
*P G Deakin, MEng, BA
    (*Physics*)
G M Barnes, BSc
Dr A O Cooke, MEng,
    DPhil
R L Fleming, MA, MInstP
R J Freeman, MA, BSc
A G McGilchrist, MA
Dr D S Pinker, PhD, MSci
C T E Powell, BSc, MRes
M J Weatheritt, BSc, MA
*I A Roslan, MChem
    (*Chemistry*)
J A Fisher, BSc
M J Clugston, MA, DPhil
D P Dickinson, MChem
G C Fisher, BSc, MA
Dr C R Lawrence, MA,
    PhD
J F Painter, MA, MSc
J C Pearson, MA
Dr S X Sneddon, PhD, BSc
*H M Grant, MA
    (*Biology*)
Dr M R Ackroyd, BSc,
    PhD
Dr W J Burnett, BSc, PhD
P M Ridd, MA
A T Sampson, BSc
C J C Swainson, MA
Dr P H Williams, PhD

Social Science:
J Blake, BA, MSc
    (*Economics and
    Business*)
Miss K E Moxon, MA
    (*Politics*)
T J Ansdell, BSc
C M Ashurst, BA
A J Leale, BA
Miss M A Lhroob, BA,
    MLit
P J North, MA, BA
N R V Rendall, BA
Dr J D W Richards, MA,
    PhD
A J Sixsmith, BA

Director of ICT Services:
C J Scott, BA

*University Entrance and
    Careers*:
Mrs A Rogers, BA

Learning Strategies:
Mrs H F McLintock, BA
Mrs N M Gerard, BA

Parkside: Dr C D Thompson
Ferox Hall: J A Fisher
Manor House: C J C Swainson

Day:
Welldon House: R H Evans
Smythe House: C M Henshall
Whitworth House: W D F Biddle
Cowdrey House: J C Harber
Oakeshott House: G M Barnes

Administration:
Librarian: Mrs H Precious, BA, MSc, MCLIP
Headmaster's PA: Mrs J T Bishop
Admissions Secretaries:
Miss R G Hearnden (*Senior Admissions Officer*)
Mrs V C Larmour (*Admissions Officer Lower Sixth Entry*)
Mrs R Griffiths (*Admissions Officer Pre-testing*)
Examinations Officer: Miss B J Shepherd
PA to the Second Master & School Administrator: Miss E J
    Day
Music Dept Administrator: Mrs J Marsh

Trinity School
Croydon

Shirley Park, Croydon CR9 7AT

Tel: 020 8656 9541
Fax: 020 8655 0522
email: admissions@trinity.croydon.sch.uk
website: www.trinity-school.org
Twitter: @TrinityCroydon
Facebook: @Trinity-School
LinkedIn: /Trinity-School

Motto: '*Vincit qui Patitur*'

The School was founded by Archbishop John Whitgift in
1596. The full title of the school is Trinity School of John
Whitgift.

One of the three governed by the Whitgift Foundation,
the School is an Independent Day School for boys aged
10–18 with a co-educational Sixth Form. The School aims
to give a wide education to students of academic promise,
irrespective of their parents' income.

Buildings and Grounds. Trinity School has been in its
present position since 1965, when it moved out from the
middle of Croydon (its old site is now the Whitgift Centre)
to a completely new complex of buildings and playing fields
on the site of the Shirley Park Hotel. The grounds are some
27 acres in extent, and a feeling of openness is increased by
the surrounding Shirley Park Golf Club and the extensive
views to the south up to the Addington Hills. There are additional playing fields in Sandilands, ten minutes' walk from
the School.

The resources of the Whitgift Foundation enable the
School to provide outstanding facilities. All departments
have excellent and fully equipped teaching areas.

Admission. The main ages of admission are at 10, 11 and
13. Entry is by competitive examination and interview. A
reference from the feeder school will also be required. The
School attracts applications from over 150 schools, with
approximately 60% entering from state primaries. Entries of
boys and girls into the Sixth Form are also welcomed.

Fees per term (2018–2019). £5,816 covering tuition,
books, stationery and games.

Bursaries. Whitgift Foundation Bursaries (means-tested)
are available providing exceptionally generous help with
fees.

Scholarships. Academic, Art, Design Technology, Drama, Music and Sport Scholarships are available annually to boys applying for entry at 10+, 11+ or 13+. Boys must be the relevant age on 1 September of the year of entry. Awards are based on the results of the Entrance Examination, interview and current school reference. They are awarded without regard to parental income and are worth a percentage (maximum 50%) of the school fees throughout a pupil's career.

Academic, Art, Music and Sport Scholarships are also available for entry to the Sixth Form, based on GCSE results.

Scholarships may be supplemented up to the value of full fees if there is financial need.

Music Scholarships of up to 50% fee remission include free tuition in two instruments. Applicants are required to play two pieces on principal instrument and show academic potential in the Entrance Examination. Awards are available for all instruments and singing ability can be taken into consideration. Further details from the Director of Music.

Organisation and Counselling. The School is divided into the Lower School (National Curriculum Years 6–9) and the Upper School (Years 10–13). The Pastoral Leader in charge of each section works with the team of Form Tutors to encourage the academic and personal development of each boy. There is frequent formal and informal contact with parents.

A counselling service is provided to pupils as part of the pastoral provision and a fully qualified School Counsellor is on hand to help students with their individual needs. Pupils can refer themselves to the Counsellor or they may be referred by staff.

There is a structured and thorough Careers service, which advises boys at all levels of the School and arranges work experience and work shadowing.

While the academic curriculum is taught from Monday to Friday, there is a very active programme of sports fixtures and other activities at the weekend, and all boys are expected to put their commitment to the School before other activities.

Curriculum and Staffing. The School is generously staffed with well qualified specialists. The organisation of the teaching programme is traditionally departmental based. The syllabus is designed to reflect the general spirit of the National Curriculum while allowing a suitable degree of specialisation in the Upper School.

The normal pattern is for pupils to take 9 or 10 GCSE subjects, and to proceed to the Sixth Form to study an appropriate mixture of AS and A2 level subjects, complemented by a wide-ranging General Studies programme, before proceeding to university.

Games and Activities. The main school games are Rugby, Football, Hockey, Cricket and Athletics, with the addition of Netball for girls in the Sixth Form. Many other sports become options as a boy progresses up the School. Games are timetabled, each pupil having one games afternoon a week.

At the appropriate stage, most boys take part in one or more of the following activities: Community Service, CCF, Duke of Edinburgh's Award scheme, Outdoor Activities. There are many organised expeditions during the holidays.

Music. Music at Trinity has an international reputation, and every year Trinity Boys Choir is involved in a varied programme of demanding professional work. The Choir has performed at the BBC Proms for the past seven years and sings at the Royal Opera House, the English National Opera, Glyndebourne or Garsington 3–4 times each year. Recently the choristers have travelled to Vienna, Brussels, Venice, Dusseldorf and Wachock Abbey, Poland. They also appear regularly on radio and television. Trinity Choristers, who specialise in religious music, hold an annual residential Easter Course at a British cathedral. Choral Scholarships are awarded annually and enable boys to receive additional professional voice training without charge.

Many boys learn at least one musical instrument, and a large visiting music staff teach all orchestral instruments, piano, organ and classical guitar. There are numerous orchestras, bands and other instrumental groups for which boys are selected according to their ability. Musicians recently travelled to Canada and instrumentalists are regular finalists in the Pro Corda National Chamber Music competition.

Drama. There are two excellently equipped stages in the school and a lively and developing programme of formal and informal productions directed by pupils, staff and members of the Old Boys Theatre Company. Drama forms part of the formal curriculum in Years 6–9 and can be studied for GCSE and A Level.

Art and Design Technology. As well as the formal curriculum, which has led to 70% of the School taking a GCSE in art or design technology, pupils are encouraged to make use of the excellent facilities to develop their own interests.

Charitable status. The Whitgift Foundation is a Registered Charity, number 312612. The Foundation now comprises the Whitgift Almshouse Charity for the care of the elderly and the Education Charity which administers three schools.

Visitor: His Grace The Archbishop of Canterbury

Chairman of the Court of Governors: Mr C J Houlding
Court Governors:
The Bishop of Croydon, the Rt Revd Jonathan Clark
Mr C J Houlding
Mr G H Wright, TD, DL, PPCIOB
Mr I Harley, MA, FCA, FCIB
Mr D Mead, MBE, FCCA
Dr A Mehta FRCP
Mr D C Hudson, MA
Viscountess Stansgate, OBE, MA
Mrs P Davies, BSc, MEd
Mr A Patel, ACA, MSc
Mr M Proudfoot, MA, MLitt
Mr D Sutton, JP, FRICS
Mr D Seymour, CB

School Committee:
Chairman of Trinity School Committee: Mr D Seymour
Viscountess Stansgate, OBE
Mr A Crispin
Mr J Crozier
Mrs P Davies
Mr D Hudson
Mr S Jetha
Mr W Jones
Dr B MacEvoy
Mr D Mead, MBE
Mr T Perrin
Mr P Petty
Revd Canon Dr Andrew Bishop

Chief Executive: M C Corney

Headmaster: A J S Kennedy, MA

Deputy Headmaster: Mr E A du Toit, MA London
  (*Economics*)
Deputy Head, Pastoral: Miss S Ward, BSc Birmingham
  (*Psychology, Designated Safeguarding Lead*)
Director of Studies: Mr N H Denman, MA Oxford
  (*Mathematics*)
Head of Lower and Middle Schools: Mr S Powell, BSc
  Durham, MEd Cambridge (*Geography*)

Head of Sixth Form: Ms A M Geldeard, BA MA Cambridge (*English*)
Director of Teaching & Learning: Mr A J Corstorphine, MPhil Cambridge (*Classics, German*)
Director of Co-Curricular Activities: Mr J G Timm, BA Cambridge (*History, Politics*)
Bursar: Mrs J Stanley, BA, CCAT, ACA

* Head of Department

Mr M I Aldridge, BEd London (*Design Technology, Head of Upper Sixth*)
Mr S R Allison, BA Durham (*Spanish**)
Mr M Asbury, BSc Bath (*Mathematics, Internal Exams**)
Dr M S Asquith, BA, MA, PhD London (*English*)
Mr H Baggs, MSc UCL (*Maths*)
Ms D S Bala, BDS Chennai (*Biology*)
Miss R C Bainbridge, MA Durham (*Maths*)
Ms N M Beaumont, MA, MSc Oxford (*Mathematics**)
Mr L D Benedict, BA Bristol (*English, Head of Fourth Year*)
Mr O J Benjamin, BA Durham (*German, Spanish*)
Mrs I M Bennett, BEd Leeds Beckett (*Biology*)
Ms H A Benzinski, BSc London (*Mathematics, DofE Coordinator*)
Mr G C Beresford-Miller, BA Rhodes (*Physical Education, Clubs and Societies Coordinator*)
Mrs K A Beresford-Miller, BA King's College London (*Religious Studies**)
Mr R M Biggs, BSc Cardiff (*DT*)
Mr P J Blanchard, BSc, MBA Exeter, Warwick (*Chemistry*)
Mrs N Blamire-Marin, BA Granada (*Lectora, Spanish*)
Miss V J Boorman, BA King's College London (*Classics*)
Mrs M Bromberg, MSc Imperial (*Chemistry, Biology*)
Mr T M Brooks, BA Leeds (*Physical Education*)
Ms C Burke, BSc, MSc University College Dublin
Mrs S I Cater, BA King's College London, MPhil Queensland (*English, Drama, Assistant Head of Year, Sixth Form*)
Mr C S Chambers, BA Cambridge (*Drama Productions**)
Mr T W Chesters, BSc Strathclyde (*Design Technology, Assistant Director of Studies, Head of Information Management*)
Mr S W Christian, BA Liverpool (*French, Spanish*)
Mr R Collins, BSc, MSc Goldsmiths (*Psychology*)
Mr W A Woma, BA Leeds (*Art*)
Mr D W G Currigan, BA Chelsea, MA Kingston (*Design Technology**)
Mr T J Desbos, LCE Lille (*French*)
Mr F K Doepel, BSc Lancaster (*Economics and Business**)
Mr A B Doyle, MA, MA Glasgow, Open (*English**)
Mrs R Doyle, BEd Glasgow (*SEN Teacher*)
Mr T D Drake, BSc St Mary's Twickenham, MSc Roehampton (*Junior Science*)
Ms P Eberlin, BA Durham (*French*)
Mr M A Edwards, BSc Loughborough (*Physical Education**)
Miss J S Eminsang, BA Manchester (*Mathematics, Head of Junior Maths*)
Miss T Escacena, BA Seville (*Spanish*)
Mr N S Evans, BA Nottingham (*History, Politics*)
Mr R E Evans, Dip Perf Royal College of Music (*Head of Piano*)
Mr L M Flanagan, BA Cambridge (*Physics**)
Mrs A A Fulker, BA Oxford Brookes (*Art, Head of Personal Development*)
Mr F J Gabbitass, BA Bath (*Physical Education*)
Mr M J Gee, BSc Lougborough (*Maths*)
Mr N A Giles, BA Liverpool John Moores (*Head of Hockey*)
Mrs M K Gillett, BEng Kingston, DPhil Sussex (*SEN Teacher*)

Mr R J Gorrie, BA Oxford (*Music*)
Mr R M Greenberg, MA Oxford (*Biology*)
Mr T Heath, BSc Sheffield, MSc Bristol (*Biology, Junior Science*)
Miss R E Hodder, BA SOAS London (*History*)
Mr S M Hodge, BA Exeter (*Religious Studies*)
Mr R M Holdsworth, BA, MA Oxford (*Music**)
Mr L Husnu, BA East Anglia (*Director of Drama**)
Mr O J Hutchings, BA, MA York (*History, Politics & in Charge of Politics*)
Miss S J Justin, BA Reading (*Economics & Business Studies*)
Mrs D E M Kemp, BA Southampton, MA Institute of Education (*English*)
Mr I Kench, BSc Loughborough, MSc Oxford (*Geography, Physical Education, Director of Rugby, Head of Sports Development**)
Mr S D King, BA Manchester Metropolitan (*Physical Education, Head of Junior Year, Head of Aquatics*)
Ms P-S Lin, BA Taiwan, MA UCL (*Chinese**)
Ms A Long, Physical Education)
Mrs C D Lowry, BA Oxford (*Religious Studies, Drama*)
Mr D J P Lydon, BA, MA Dublin (*English*)
Mr A E Magee, MA St Andrews (*English*)
Miss K J Manisier, MSc Imperial (*Physics*)
Dr M Mariani, BSc Kent, PhD UCL (*Physics*)
Mr P Mazur, BA Wales, MA London (*Drama, Contingent Commander CCF*)
Mrs S J McDonald, MA St Andrews (*Head of Learning Support*)
Mr S A McIntosh, MA Oxford (*German**)
Mrs K Molteni, BA Hull (*History*)
Mr R D Moralee, BSc Johannesburg (*Biology**)
Mr S Munday, BA West of England (*Geography*)
Mr P D Murphy, BA Cambridge (*History*)
Mr J C Munnery, BSc Nottingham (*Geography*)
Mr S Orungbamade, BEd Nigeria (*Economics and Business*)
Mr S D Page, BSc Sussex (*Computer Science*)
Miss C A Parkinson, BSc Sussex, MSc UCL (*Psychology*, Science*)
Mr B J Patel, MA Cambridge (*Mathematics, Physics*)
Mr B Patel, MSc UCL (*Mathematics*)
Mr J A Paterson, BA Cambridge (*Classics*)
Mr C P Persinaru, Dip RAM, LRAM (*Music, Head of Strings*)
Mrs R J Petty, MA Oxford (*English, Drama, Deputy Designated Safeguarding Lead*)
Mrs X L Phasey, MA Schiller, International (*Chinese*)
Mrs A Prestney, BA Durham (*Geography*)
Mr J E Pietersen, BA Cambridge (*History, Politics, Head of Second Year*)
Mr D K Price, BA Wimbledon College of Art (*Design Technology, Director of Admissions*)
Dr A A Randolph, MA Oxford, PhD Nottingham (*Maths*)
Mrs S J Rapoport, BEd Twickenham (*Academic Mentor*)
Mrs L Regan, BMus, LRAM (*Music*)
Mr A Reza, BEng Queen Mary London (*Physics*)
Mr M D Richbell, BSc Liverpool (*Director of Sport**)
Mr P J Roberts, BSc Bath (*Physical Education, Economics & Business*)
Dr D P Robinson, MA, DPhil Oxford (*Chemistry*)
Dr K R Rogers, BSc Cardiff, PhD London (*Chemistry**)
Mr C P Ruck, BSc Southampton (*Geography**)
Dr J N Rush, Ba, PhD, MPhil Cambridge (*English*)
Mr M P Ryan, BA Oxford (*English, Teacher Development, EPQ Coordinator*)
Mr R M Salmanpour, BSc London (*Chemistry*)
Mrs V C Salin, MA Rouen, Northumbria (*French**)
Mr S D Schofield, BSc Worcester (*Physical Education, Head of Cricket, Cricket Academy*)

Mr L Signorelli, BSc Bath (*Economics*)

Mr A E Smith, BA York, MA, MSc London (*Religious Studies*)

Mr J J Snelling, BSc Swansea, MA London, CGeog (*Geography, Head of Staff Development*)

Ms J L Snowdon, BA Epsom (*Art*)

Mr G Spreng, MA Glasgow (*History**)

Mrs F M Stedman, BA Leeds, MA Bristol (*Religious Studies*)

Mrs B J Steven, BA Cape Town (*English, EAL*)

Ms T Stevens-Lewis, BA, MA Goldsmiths (*Art, i/c Photography*)

Mr J E Stone, BA Cambridge (*Classics**)

Ms C S Story, BA Durham (*English*)

Mr T M Strange, BA, MA Goldsmiths (*Art**)

Ms E M Suarez, BA Juan Carlos 1, Rey de Espana (*Lectora, Spanish and French*)

Miss A Sukiennik, BA, MA Paris X (*Lectrice, French*)

Mr D J Swinson, MA, FRCO, ARCM, LRAM, Cambridge (*Director of Music**)

Mrs S Z Taylor, BSc Exeter (*Mathematics, Professional Coordinating Mentor*)

Mr W S Tucker, BSc Exeter (*Head of Science**, Physics*)

Mrs T A Upton, BSc Warwick (*Mathematics*)

Miss S T Van Dal, BA, MA Cambridge, UCL (*Classics*)

Mr R van Graan, BA Canterbury Christ Church (*Director of Digital Strategy**)

Miss R M Walker, BMus Birmingham Conservatoire (*Music, Head of Lower School Music*)

Mrs Q Wang, BA Henan Institute of Finance (*Chinese*)

Mrs C E Webb, BSc Bath (*Maths*)

Miss H C Whiteford, BSc Durham (*Religious Studies, Head of Third Year*)

Mr R J Wickes, BSc Warwick (*Mathematics*)

Mrs C-J Wilkinson, BSc Glasgow (*Biology*)

Mr F R Wilson, BSc Southampton (*Chemistry*)

Miss J Wiskow, MA Wuppertal, Berlin (*German, Girls' Games**)

Admissions Registrar: Mrs P S Meyer

Sixth Form Admissions: Ms S Redican

Headmaster's Secretary: Mrs K Walsh

Truro School

Trennick Lane, Truro, Cornwall TR1 1TH

Tel: 01872 272763
email: enquiries@truroschool.com
website: www.truroschool.com

Motto: *Esse quam videri*

Truro School was founded in 1880 by Cornish Methodists. In 1904 it came under the control of the Methodist Independent Schools Trust (MIST) and is now administered by a Board of Governors appointed by the Methodist Conference. Although pupils come from all parts of the country and abroad, the roots of the school are firmly in Cornwall and it is the only HMC school in the county.

The religious instruction and worship are undenominational though the school is conscious of its Methodist origins.

There are 760 pupils (450 boys, 310 girls; 683 day, 77 boarders) in the Senior School (age 11+ and above). There are another 250 pupils in the Preparatory School, where boys and girls may start in the Nursery at the age of 3.

The school is fully co-educational throughout and there is a strong Sixth Form of some 200 pupils.

Boarding. At the Senior School girl boarders live in Malvern (Sixth Form and 5th Year) and Pentreve; boy boarders (4th–U6th) live in Trennick House; boy boarders (1st–3rd) live in Poltisco House. All are supervised by resident teaching staff and families. Pupils eat in the central dining room with a cafeteria system. There is a School Medical Centre on site.

Campus and Buildings. The *Prep School* campus is built around a country house acquired by the school in the 30s. It has an indoor heated swimming pool, a large assembly hall and extensive areas for science, modern languages, computing, art and crafts, as well as a modern sports hall. A new Dining Hall was opened in 2013. The Pre-Prep is housed in a purpose-built unit, with a new extension opened in September 2009.

The *Senior School* occupies an outstanding site overlooking the Cathedral city and the Fal Estuary; it is only five minutes from the centre of the city but the playing fields reach into the open countryside. The school is excellently equipped. There is a first-class Library, extensive science laboratories, excellent Technology and Art facilities, a computer centre, music school, Sixth Form centre, a Sixth Form cafeteria and a range of classroom blocks. The fine block containing the Burrell Theatre, six classrooms and a drama centre has been extended to provide a Modern Languages Centre in The Wilkes Building. An attractive and newly-refurbished chapel provides a focus for the life of the school. A new Dining Hall and social area opened in November 2009. The Sir Ben Ainslie Sports Centre, completed for September 2013, provides an eight-court multi-use sports hall, two county standard glass-backed squash courts with viewing gallery, large fitness suite with a range of aerobic, strength and conditioning equipment, a multi-purpose dance and exercise studio with a sprung wooden floor, adding to the existing excellent facilities of 25m swimming pool, cricket nets, tennis courts, 40 acres of pitches and cricket pavilion. Following a link with Truro Fencing Club in September 2014 the school has its own designated Fencing Salle. In September 2018 the School opened its new Cookery School, in association with Leiths of London – a state-of-the-art 10-bay facility for co-curricular cookery and delivery of the Leiths Introductory Certificate to Food and Wine during the Sixth Form.

Organisation and Curriculum. Our academic programme up to GCSE provides a balance between the three Sciences, Humanities, Creative Arts and Modern Languages. In the 1st to 3rd Year, pupils study English, Mathematics, Biology, Chemistry and Physics, French and German, Geography, History, Religious Studies, Art, Design & Technology, Drama, ICT and Music. Spanish is optional from 3rd Year. All pupils have PE as well as Games each week. Every pupil in the 1st Year is taught touch typing, and ICT lessons culminate in a City & Guilds certified qualification by the end of the 3rd Year.

At GCSE the norm is to study ten subjects at full GCSE. Compulsory subjects are English Language, English Literature, Mathematics, Religious Studies, Double Award or Triple Award Science; the options include French, German, Spanish, Geography, History, Art and Design, Design and Technology, Music, Drama, Computer Science, PE and Geology.

Sixth Formers usually study for four AS Levels in the Lower Sixth and these include the same subjects as at GCSE, but with the introduction of Further Mathematics, Religious Studies (with Philosophy and Ethics), Economics, Business Studies, Psychology and the Extended Project Qualification. Our Extension Studies programme includes modules on Photography, Philosophy and Film Studies. As part of this we provide advice on careers and university applications, with a specialised programme for potential

Medics, Dentists and Vets. The Community Sports Leadership Award is a popular option for the Upper Sixth. Three subjects will be most commonly continued into the Upper Sixth at A Level and the vast majority of Sixth Formers go on to further education when they leave. From September 2018 we offer the five-term Leiths Introductory Certificate which carries UCAS points.

Out-of-School Activities. Extracurricular life is rich and varied. There is a choir, school orchestra, a jazz group, a brass band and many other ensembles. Facilities such as the ceramics room, the art room and the technical block are available to pupils in their spare time. A huge variety of activities includes fencing, squash, sailing, golf, basketball, debating, surfing, and many others. Many boys and girls take part in the Ten Tors Expedition, an exceptional number are engaged in the Duke of Edinburgh's Award scheme, as well as local Community Service.

Games. All the major team games are played. Badminton, cross-country, hockey, netball, squash and tennis are available throughout most of the year. Rugby and Girls Hockey are played in the Winter Term and Soccer and Netball in the Spring Term. In the summer, cricket, athletics and tennis are the major sports. The covered pool is heated.

Admissions. Truro School was once a Direct Grant Grammar School and most pupils join at the age of 11. There are vacancies for entry at other ages, particularly at 13 and 16.

Scholarships and Bursaries. Scholarships are available and the School offers a small number of means-tested bursaries up to the value of full fees. Truro School has linked with Truro Cathedral to offer chorister scholarships for girls (ages 13–18) and boys (ages 7–13).

Fees per term (2018–2019). Senior School: International Boarders £10,205, Boarders £9,355; Weekly Boarders £8.040; Day Pupils (including lunch): £4,690. Prep (including lunch): £4,170 (Years 3–4), £4,330 (Years 5–6). Pre-Prep (including lunch): £2,965 (Nursery and Reception), £3,115 (Years 1 and 2).

Academic results. A number of pupils proceed to Oxbridge every year, along with overseas universities including, in 2016, MIT. Around 95% of the Sixth Form proceed to degree courses. The 2018 A Level pass rate was 99.7%, with 69% at A* to B grades. At GCSE in 2018 over 57% were at grades A*/A, 9–7 and 20% at grade 9.

Former Pupils' Association. There is a strong Former Pupils' Association and it has its own webalumnus. The "Friends of Truro School" involves parents, staff, old pupils and friends of the school in social events and fundraising.

Charitable status. Truro School is part of the Methodist Independent Schools Trust, which is a registered Charity, number 1142794.

Visitor: The President of the Methodist Conference

Administrative Governors:
Chairman: K Conchie, BA Hons
R R Cowie, FCA
Mrs C Arter, BA Hons, RN, RNT, PGCE, FHEA, JP
N Ashcroft, MBE
T Corby
W Dexter, BSc, ACA
B Dolan, LLb Hons
Mrs E Garner, BA Hons, MEd
R Griffin, MA
Revd Dr J Harrod, BSc, MA, PhD, FHEA
Dr R Kirby
A Luck
M MacDonald
P Stethridge, CEng, FICE, FIHT
Mrs H Sullivan, MA
R Thomas, BSc, MRICS

Revd Canon S Wild, MA
Dr J Williams, BSc Hons, MBBS

Headmaster: **A Gordon-Brown**, BCom Hons, MSc, QTS

Deputy Heads:
Mrs E Ellison, BSc
Dr S K Pope, BSc, PhD

Chaplain: A de Gruchy, MTheol

Boarding House Staff:
Mrs S Mulready, BA (*Malvern*)
T Copeland, BA (*Trennick*)
A D Lawrence, Cert Ed (*Poltisco*)
Ms K Broadhurst (*Pentreve*)

Heads of Year:
R Williamson, MA (*Head of Sixth Form*)
Mrs L R Jupp, BA (*Deputy Head of Sixth Form*)
Miss J R Egar, BA (*5th Year*)
G D Hooper, PGCE (*4th Year*)
R T Picton, MPhys (*3rd Year*)
Miss M E Macleod, BSc (*2nd Year*)
Mrs C McCabe, BSc (*1st Year*)

Heads of Department:
D Meads, BA (*Art*)
Miss S E Finnegan, BSc (*Biology*)
Dr A Brogden, MChem, PhD (*Chemistry*)
B Oldfield, BA (*Drama*)
C Baker, BSc (*Design and Technology*)
J Whatley, BSc (*Economics, Business Studies and Politics*)
Mrs A L Selvey BA, MA (*English*)
Mrs J Wormald, BSc (*Geography*)
Ms J Hope, BSc (*Geology*)
Dr M H Spring, MA, PhD (*History*)
S J McCabe, MA (*Mathematics*)
D A O'Neil, BA (*Modern Languages*)
M D Palmer, BMus, FRCO, LRAM (*Music*)
D J Sanderson (*Director of Sport*)
A L Laity, BSc (*Physics*)
Mrs E L Mitchell, BA, MEd (*Religious Education*)

Truro School Preparatory School
(*see entry in IAPS section*)

Head: Ms S Patterson, BEd
Deputy Head: A MacQuarrie, BEd

Bursar: Mr P Kerkin

University College School

Frognal, Hampstead, London NW3 6XH
Tel:	020 7435 2215
Fax:	020 7433 2111
email:	seniorschool@ucs.org.uk
website:	www.ucs.org.uk
Twitter:	@UCSHampstead

University College School is a leading London day school providing places for approximately 500 boys aged 11–16, with a co-educational Sixth Form of approximately 300 places. UCS admitted its first cohort of girls into the Sixth Form in September 2008 and around 50 girls will join UCS each year.

University College School was founded in Gower Street in 1830 as part of University College, London and moved to its current location in Hampstead in 1907. The UCS Foundation comprises three separate schools offering education to children at each stage of their development from the ages of 3–18, founded to promote the Benthamite principles of liberal scholarship and education. Intellectual curiosity, breadth of study and independence of mind combine to achieve academic excellence; they are not subordinate to it.

Selecting children with no regard to race or creed, UCS fosters in them a sense of community alongside a tolerance of and a respect for the individual. By offering the fullest range of opportunities for personal and for group endeavour, it teaches the value of commitment and the joy of achievement. It is a place of study, but also of self-discovery and self-expression; a school that places equal value on learning with others as on learning from others.

Admission. UCS Pre-Prep accepts boys at the age of 4 to join Reception. Boys join the Junior Branch at the age of 7 and the Senior School at the ages of 11 and 13. We invite both boys and girls to apply at 16 for places in our Sixth Form. We always advise parents to check the admissions pages on the UCS website for the most up-to-date information. Please note that all applications, whether to the Pre-Prep, the Junior Branch or the Senior School, are now made online through the website.

Curriculum. The UCS curriculum is designed to match the educational needs of pupils at all stages of their development. At the Pre-Prep, the mix of formal and informal learning develops independent and enquiring thinkers. At the Junior Branch, whilst the emphasis is on breadth, boys are also prepared for Key Stage 2 Tests in English, Maths and Science.

The Lower School: In the first years at the Senior School boys aged 11–13 follow a broad, common curriculum founded on the best features of the National Curriculum but enriched to develop a love of learning and positive study skills. These traits enable our pupils to develop their own academic specialisms as they go up through the school, whilst also ensuring that they receive a rounded academic education.

Mathematics is taught in banded groups related to boys' ability and progress. French is taught in sets to allow for those who have not studied the language previously. There is otherwise no streaming and subjects are studied within form groups. Homework is set each day, and usually takes between 45 minutes and one hour.

The Middle School. The curriculum is deliberately broad, in order to provide a suitable basis for further study leading to GCSE and Sixth Form courses. Pupils are divided into sets in Mathematics according to ability. More time is devoted to Science and boys may take up a further Classical or Modern Language (Greek, German, Spanish or Mandarin). In addition boys choose one option from Music, Drama and Computing. PSHE continues in Year 9 in the classroom and in the following two years, through a programme of presentations, discussions and visits from outside speakers. Homework tasks include a wider range of topics and activities than before.

For the two years leading to GCSE, boys continue with English and Mathematics. They may then choose freely a further seven subjects with the only proviso that, to maintain a sufficient breadth to their studies, they must include at least one Modern Language from those they have previously studied and at least one science subject. Boys in the top two Mathematics sets also take the Additional Mathematics qualification alongside their GCSE.

The GCSE subjects offered are: Biology, Physics, Chemistry, French, German, Spanish, Mandarin, Latin, Greek, History, Geography, Art, Design and Technology, Drama, Music, and Computing.

The Sixth Form. Pupils may study any combination of four subjects in the Transitus (Year 12) and may freely mix Arts and Science subjects if they wish. Careful guidance is provided to ensure that the course upon which they embark will provide an appropriate basis for an application to the Higher Education course and institution of the individual pupil's choice. After one year of study, pupils may continue with three or four subjects in the Sixth Form (Year 13). Sixth Form sets normally include 8–10 pupils who, in preparation for Higher Education, are encouraged to take greater personal responsibility for study.

The A Level/Pre-U subjects available are: English, Mathematics, Further Mathematics, Biology, Physics, Chemistry, French, German, Spanish, Mandarin, Latin, Greek, History, Geography, Economics, Politics, Philosophy, Psychology, Drama and Theatre Studies, Computing, Design and Technology, Art, Music and History of Art.

Pastoral Care. We regard the personal, emotional and moral development of our pupils as a major priority at every single stage of the education that we offer. The aim of our pastoral system is to encourage pupils to develop their own identities and to express them with a proper regard for the feelings and sensitivities of others. Pupils are encouraged from an early age to develop a sense of responsibility for their own behaviour. Much stress is laid upon tolerance of and respect for one another. Considerable effort is made to build a sense of community within the school. To this end, three days a week the school starts with a whole school, deme or year assembly of a non-denominational character. Pupils and their parents know the identity and the responsibilities of the members of staff concerned for their care. Parents are involved as fully as possible in pastoral matters and will always be informed and consulted.

Careers. Pupils are guided by means of interviews and tests towards careers appropriate to their gifts and personalities. Pupils are given opportunities to attend holiday courses directed towards specific careers. Also, visiting speakers are invited to the School and there are frequent Careers events. There is a full Careers Library and a comprehensive programme of Work Experience. The Parents' Guild and Old Gowers' Club (alumni organisation) also provide advice and support.

Physical Education and Games. The state-of-the-art Sir Roger Bannister sports complex opened in December 2006. The pupils have periods of Physical Education within their normal timetable in the sports complex. The School playing fields cover 27 acres and are situated a mile away in West Hampstead. In addition to grass surfaces, there is a large all-weather pitch and two pavilions. A new double pavilion is due to open in the spring of 2019 and the fields are currently undergoing major levelling and drainage works which are also due for completion in 2019. The major sports for Lower and Middle school boys are Rugby, Football, Hockey and Cricket with increased choices from Year 9. The School has its own Tennis and Fives courts at Frognal, together with an indoor heated Swimming Pool. Other sports include Fencing, Athletics, Squash, Badminton, Basketball, Fives and outdoor pursuits. For sixth form boys and girls there is a wide choice of indoor and outdoor sports.

Music and Drama. There is a strong musical tradition at UCS and many pupils play in the Orchestras, Wind Band and a great variety of groups and ensembles. Choral music is equally strong and Jazz is a particular feature. Instrumental tuition is given in the Music School, opened in 1995, and this and Ensemble Groups are arranged by the Director of Music. The School's Lund Theatre, opened in 1974, is the venue for a range of Drama from major productions to experimental plays, mime and revue. An open-air theatre was completed in 1994. A regular programme of evening events is arranged for the Autumn and Spring terms.

Other School Societies. These cover a wide range of academic interests and leisure pursuits, including the Duke of Edinburgh's Award scheme. There is a very active Community Action Programme, which works in the local community and there are regular fundraising initiatives for both local and national charities.

Development Programme. The Foundation completed the final phase of an ambitious programme of redevelopment in 2008. A state-of-the-art Indoor Sports Centre opened in late 2006, comprising Sports Hall, Swimming Pool, Fitness Centre and Health Club. The new Jeremy Bentham Building houses Modern Languages and Art & Design Technology and opened in October 2007. There was extensive refurbishment and reorganisation of classrooms, indoor and outdoor play spaces, administrative areas of the School and Sixth Form Centre. An extensive refurbishment of the library took place during the autumn of 2018 and in November it was reopened as the AKO Centre – a place for innovative learning and teaching. A fundraising appeal helped to achieve these improvements and enabled the School to double the provision of fee assistance.

Fees per term (2018–2019). Senior School: £6,776; Junior Branch: £6,263. This excludes fees payable in respect of music and other private lessons, and books.

Scholarships and Bursaries. UCS is firmly committed to promoting and increasing access to our unique education through fee assistance. From its beginning in 1830 UCS has had at its core a commitment to access, with a pledge that religion should be no bar to entry. In the 21st century, we add a further commitment – that the education we provide will not be restricted solely to those who can afford it and each year we commit £1.2 million to bursary support. We offer bursaries of up to 100% and UCS consistently ranks at the top of independent schools in London for the number of 100% bursaries awarded each year. The School also offers music scholarships which award the holder a reduction in the annual school fees of between 10% and, in exceptional cases, 50%. The precise value will depend upon the standard of applicants and the competition in any one year. Music scholarships entitle the holder to free instrumental tuition at school on an instrument (including voice) of the candidate's choice, which will remain in place throughout a pupil's time at UCS Senior School.

Old Pupils' Society (Old Gowers). The School maintains an active register of former pupils and plans events throughout the year.

Charitable status. University College School, Hampstead is a Registered Charity, number 312748. Its aims and objectives are the provision of the widest opportunities for learning and development of students without the imposition of tests and doctrinal conformity but within a balanced and coherent view of educational needs and obligations.

Governors:
Chairman: Mr S D Lewis, OBE, MA
Dr Y Amin, BSc, MB ChB, DA, FRCAMs
Ms L Bingham, OBE, MIPA, MABRP, DBA
Mr R Bondy [OG]
Mr R A S Datnow, BA, MA, Dip LP
Mr S Grodzinski, QC [OG]
Mr R Gullifer, MA
Dr S Rana, BA, MSc, PhD
Mr E Riche, BSc, MBA
Professor P Sands, QC [OG]
Mrs S L Soskin
Councillor G Spinella
Mr C Spooner, BA, MA
Professor C Tyerman, MA, DPhil Oxford, FRHistS

[OG] *Old Gower*

Senior School:

Headmaster: M J Beard, MA, MEd

Vice Master: C M Reynolds, BSc, MSc, FSS

Deputy Head (Academic): M T English, BA, MA
Deputy Head (Pastoral): A R Wilkes, BA

Assistant Head: R H Chapman, BSc
Assistant Head: E D Roberts, MSci
Assistant Head: P S Miller, BSc
Assistant Head: S A P FitzGerald, BA

Deme Wardens:
Baxters: S C Walton, MusB
Black Hawkins: J R L Orchard, MA
Evans: T J Allen, BA
Flooks: J P Cooke, BA
Olders: M Foster, BSc
Underwoods: A H Isaac, BA, MA

Sixth Form:
Head of Sixth Form: R H Chapman, BSc
Deputy Heads of Sixth Form:
H A Levy, MA
A D Hurst, BSc
R C Johnson, BA

Lower School Wardens:
Head of Lower School: E A Barnish, BA, MA
Entry: E R Orlans, BA, MA
Shell: O Bienias, BA

Senior School Heads of Departments/Subjects:

Art: Mr L A Farago, BA
Art History: Mr A M Mee, MA
Biology: Mrs K R Ward, BSc
Chemistry: Dr S K Hoyle, MSci, PhD
Classics: Mr D J Woodhead, BA
Director of Drama: Ms R H Baxter, BA, MA
Design & Technology: Mrs S L Slater, BA
Economics: Mr D G Hall, BA
English: Ms L C Birchenough, BA
Geography: Mr M B Murphy, BA
History & Politics:
Mr A G Vaughan, BA (*Head of History & Politics*)
Mr N Hillyard, BA, MA (*Head of Politics*)
Learning Support: Ms S K Thale, BA, MA
Mathematics & Computer Science:
Mr M Bullock, BSc (*Head of Mathematics*)
Mr S A Cork, BA (*Coordinator of Computer Science*)
Modern Languages:
Mr T P Underwood, BA (*Head of Modern Languages*)
Dr H L Laurenson, BA, PhD (*Head of Spanish*)
Mrs H Wiedermann, BA (*Head of French*)
Music:
Mr C R Dawe, BA, MA, MMus (*Director of Music*)
Mr I C Gibson, MA (*Head of Academic Music*)
Philosophy: Dr K S Viswanathan, BSc, MA, PhD
Physical Education: Mr E P Sawtell, BA (*Director of Sport*)
Physics: Mr A Westwood, BSc
Psychology: Mrs C E Hawes, BSc, MSc

Junior Branch:
Headmaster: Mr L Hayward, MA
Deputy Head (Curriculum): Mr M A Albini, MA, BSc
Deputy Head (Pastoral): Mr D J Edwards, BA

Pre-Prep:
Headmistress: Dr Z Dunn, BEd, PhD, NPQH
Deputy Head (Head of EYFS): Miss N Watt

Uppingham School

Uppingham, Rutland LE15 9QE

Tel:	01572 822216
Fax:	01572 822332 (Headmaster)
	01572 821872 (Bursar)
email:	admissions@uppingham.co.uk
website:	www.uppingham.co.uk

Uppingham School's foundation dates from 1584, the year in which Archdeacon Robert Johnson, a local puritan rector, obtained a grant by Letters Patent from Queen Elizabeth I to found a free grammar school for the male children of poor parents. The boys were to learn Hebrew, Latin and Greek. In 1853 this small local school was transformed into one of the foremost public schools of its time by the remarkable educational thinker and headmaster, Edward Thring. His pioneering pastoral ideas and belief in the values of an all-round education shaped the School then and continue to define it now. Small, family-like boarding houses that offer children individual privacy; an all-round education that caters for a broad range of pupils, and inspiring surroundings in which children are happy and learn better – all of these lie at the heart of Uppingham's identity.

Uppingham is a fully boarding school for boys and girls aged 13–18. There are around 795 pupils in the School, of which some 350 are in the Sixth Form. Girls have been accepted into the Sixth Form since 1975, at 13+ since 2001, and now make up 41% of all pupils. Around 17% of the School's pupils are foreign nationals, mainly from the European Union, Eastern Europe and South East Asia.

Uppingham is a Christian Foundation, and the whole School meets in the Chapel five days a week. The quality and volume of the congregational singing is legendary. Some pupils are members of other faiths, and every consideration is given to their needs. Pupils are prepared for Confirmation every year.

Situation. Uppingham is a small market town set in the beautiful Rutland countryside. It is about 100 miles north of London, roughly equidistant from the M1 and A1/M11, and midway between Leicester and Peterborough on the A47. The A14 link road makes connections with the Midlands and East Anglia easier and faster. It is served by Kettering, Oakham, Corby, Peterborough and Leicester train stations, and by Stansted, Luton, Birmingham and East Midlands airports.

The Buildings. At the heart of the School are the impressive buildings of the main quadrangle: the Victorian School Room and Chapel designed by the architect of the Law Courts in the Strand, George Edmund Street, the Library housed in a beautiful building dating from 1592, the Memorial Hall and the fine classroom blocks where the Humanities are based. The three Music Schools on this campus reflect the vitality of a musical tradition dating back to 1855. Edward Thring appointed the first Director of Music in any English public school. Nearby are the central Buttery, the Language Centre and the Sixth Form Centre.

At the western end of the town lies the Western Quad, the School's inspiring architectural vision of a space that unites Arts, Sciences, Theatre and Sport, and winner of several Royal Institute of British Architects National Awards in 2015. The magnificent Science Centre contains 17 laboratories (including an environmental studies lab, outdoor classroom and project room), a lecture theatre, library, offices and meeting rooms. There is also a giant working model of Foucault's Pendulum, reminding pupils and staff that despite the burdens of prep and marking, the earth continues to rotate. The Leonardo Centre for Art and Design looks across an open space studded with contemporary sculpture, and to the east sits the 300-seat Theatre with adjoining Drama Studio, workshops and Theatre Studies classrooms. To the north, overlooking an expanse of playing fields, lies the Sports Centre, opened by Lord Coe in 2011, its contemporary design complementing the central quad.

Academic Matters. Whilst the School is noted for its strong commitment to all-round education, the depth of its pastoral care and wealth of facilities, academic study is the priority. Pupils move around the School campus during the working day, and the 55-minute lessons encourage detailed and developed learning. A staff to pupil ratio of almost 1:7 caters for a wide range and ensures all subjects enjoy small class sizes.

Until GCSE, specialisation is minimal and pupils are taught in sets for most subjects. Most take a minimum of nine GCSE/IGCSE subjects. Members of the Sixth Form study three subjects alongside a curriculum enriched by lectures and a variety of extracurricular activities. Extended Project Qualifications (EPQ) are also offered.

In 2018, 55% of all A Levels and 71% of all GCSEs were A*/A grades or equivalent; 80% of A Levels were A*–B. More than a third of the A Level candidates achieved at least three A grades. At GCSE 50% of the year group gained at least 8 A*/A grades and the A*–C pass rate was 99%.

Each pupil's progress is monitored by a Tutor and the Housemaster or Housemistress – there are regular reviews of academic progress, in addition to pastoral reports.

At all stages of a pupil's career the Housemaster/Housemistress and Tutor is in regular contact with parents. Parent-teacher meetings take place annually for all year groups, and additional meetings are held to discuss options and higher education.

Nearly all pupils go on to further education. Parents and pupils may call on the School's Higher Education and Careers advisers and the professional services of Cambridge Occupational Analysts. Visiting speakers from universities and careers are featured throughout the year, and the School offers advice on GAP year planning.

Pupils have access to a beautiful, well-stocked central Library, the Science Library and other specialist libraries for most subject departments. For those with learning difficulties the School has trained staff to help with special education needs.

Beyond the Curriculum. Around 40 clubs and societies flourish within the School with a further 30 areas of activity on offer. Pupils can take bronze, silver and gold Duke of Edinburgh's Award. In the Fourth Form, one afternoon a week is spent on our 'creative carousel' which gives pupils the opportunity to rotate around the music, art, DT or drama departments. In subsequent years, options include joining the long-established CCF, or getting involved in the 'Making a Difference' programme such as visiting the elderly, assisting in local primary schools, Riding for the Disabled and other charity work.

Music. Uppingham has always had a very distinguished reputation for music, being the first school to put music on its curriculum for all pupils. More than 50% of pupils learn an instrument, and a busy programme of weekly public recitals, house and year group concerts, and performances in the UK and abroad offer pupils of all abilities regular chances to perform. 45 visiting staff and 9 full-time staff enable pupils to receive conservatoire-style tuition at the school.

The Paul David Music School is an inspirational centre for learning and rehearsal, with cutting-edge music technology suites and a 120-seat recital room. The School has an outstanding Chapel Choir, accomplished orchestras and national prize-winning chamber groups, a slick and polished

Jazz Orchestra, and a thriving Alternative Music Society promoting rock concerts.

The School has produced international opera singers, members of world renowned choral groups such as The Sixteen and rock bands such as Busted and McFly, several Oxbridge organ scholars and numerous choral scholars, and these distinguished results also extend to national Conservatoires.

Further enquiries may be made directly to the Director of Music (01572 820696).

Sports and Games. Uppingham has a strong tradition of sporting excellence, and pupils have gained county and national honours in a variety of sports. Sports on offer include rugby, hockey, cricket, tennis and athletics plus squash, badminton, swimming, football, sailing, aerobics and dance.

There is a full programme of formal house matches across all sports, providing an opportunity for all pupils to contribute within a team environment. The able are stretched and the very able are offered a high level of coaching from experienced coaches/professionals in all major sports, often going on to represent club, academy, county, regional or national teams.

The magnificent Sports Centre includes a sports hall, six-lane 25m swimming pool, fitness studio, gym, squash courts and dance studios. There are more than 65 acres of playing fields, three Astroturf surfaces (one floodlit), tennis, netball and fives courts, a shooting range and climbing wall. All these facilities are open seven days a week under the guidance of the Sports Centre manager and appointed staff.

The Leonardo Centre. The striking design of the Art, Design and Technology Centre by Piers Gough CBE (a past pupil of the School) allows the broad range of creative activities taking place in its single glass-fronted open-plan space to interact and stimulate each other. The Centre houses a fine art and printing space (with 3D printing), studios for design (including CAD design), ceramics, sculpture, photography and workshops primarily for wood, metal and plastic, and teaching rooms. The Warwick Metcalfe Gallery displays the work of pupils, staff and visiting artists. The Centre is manned and open to all pupils seven days a week as a creative, inspiring environment.

Drama. Uppingham Theatre is a flourishing professionally equipped 300-seat theatre, with a stylish adjoining Drama complex with an 80-seat 'black box' studio, workshops, classrooms and offices. Major school productions open to all pupils are staged annually, ranging from big musicals such as *Calamity Jane* and *Miss Saigon* to opera and plays such as *The Crucible* and *Dido and Aeneas,* and Shakespeare. There are Junior Drama Society productions, joint boarding-house productions, and pupils are an integral part of the running of the theatre. The theatre presents a varied programme of professional productions, including drama, music, children's theatre and comedy, and plays a significant role in the cultural life of the school and the local community. Drama and Theatre is also taught at GCSE and A Level.

Boarding and Pastoral. There are fifteen boarding houses dotted around the town and School estate: nine for boys, one for Sixth Form girls and five for 13–18 year old girls. Houses are small, most being home to around 50 children, 45 in the case of the Sixth Form girls' house. All pupils eat their meals in their own house dining room, and are joined at lunch by teaching and non-teaching staff.

All boys have their own private study upon arrival and, by their third year their own study-bedroom or share with one other. All girls entering at 13 share a room with up to three other girls and also have their own study area. In their second and third years girls have bed-sitting rooms, usually shared with one other. All Sixth Form girls have individual study-bedrooms.

Much of the non-teaching life of the School is organised around the houses and they inspire strong loyalties. In addition to excursions and social events, there is a long-standing tradition of inter-house competitions (House Challenge, singing, debating and sports), house concerts, and some ambitious drama productions.

Pupils are supported by a wide-ranging pastoral network. The Housemasters and Housemistresses are resident, and lead a team of at least five tutors, including a Deputy Housemaster/Housemistress. Assigned to particular pupils, tutors help to monitor academic progress and social development. Some male staff are tutors in girls' houses, and vice-versa. Each house is supported by an experienced matron providing medical support and supporting the pastoral care of the pupils. Any pupil may use the services of a professional psychologist or the School's qualified counsellor. The School's Medical Centre is open 24 hours a day, with qualified medical staff in attendance.

Technological Environment. Uppingham provides outstanding technology facilities for pupils in both academic and boarding areas. A complex IT infrastructure is maintained by an in-house team of eight IT experts, who ensure a fruitful and safe relationship with Cyberspace. Resources include the online Encyclopedia Britannica and JSTOR, an online collection of over 1,000 academic journals and one of the most trusted sources of academic content on the world wide web. The School also generates a wide variety of course-specific online media.

In the classroom academic departments have the tools to ensure that technology complements teaching and learning, from the Modern Languages Laboratory to the Music Technology Department's digital music suite.

Admission. Most pupils are admitted to Uppingham in the September following their thirteenth birthday. Prospective pupils and their parents usually visit the School at least three years prior to entry. If not already registered, prospective pupils should register then. Two years before entry all registered pupils are given pre-tests and interviews at Uppingham. All applications must be supported by a satisfactory reference from their current school. The Headmaster offers places to successful candidates after this process has concluded. Parents then complete and return an Acceptance Form together with an entrance deposit. Receipt of the entrance deposit guarantees a place in the School subject to the pupil qualifying for admission. In completing the Acceptance Form parents also confirm that Uppingham is their first choice of school.

The final offer of a place in the School is conditional upon the pupil qualifying academically (see below), and on his or her record of conduct.

There are three possible ways of qualifying academically:

- via the Common Entrance Examination (for which the qualifying standard is an average of 55% in the compulsory papers);
- via the Common Academic Scholarship Examination;
- in the case of pupils who have not prepared for the Common Entrance Examination, by means of a report from the Head Teacher of their present school and further tests and interviews at Uppingham.

To continue into the Sixth Form the minimum grade requirement is three 7s and three 6s at GCSE. It is recommended that pupils have at least 7 at GCSE in the subject they wish to continue at A Level. In some subject (Mathematics, the Sciences and MFL) an 8 or 9 grade is required.

There are a limited number of places available for boys and girls for entry into the Sixth Form. Pupils may register an interest in Sixth Form entry to Uppingham at any time and formal registration should be completed by the end of

September, eleven months prior to entry. The test, interview and offer procedures take place in October and November ten months before entry. Admission at this level is dependent on tests and interviews at Uppingham, and then achieving at least three 7s and three 6s at GCSE (or equivalent), excluding short course GCSEs. It is recommended that pupils have at least 7 at GCSE in the subject they wish to continue at A Level. In some subject (Mathematics, the Sciences and MFL) an 8 or 9 grade is required.

Enquiries and requests for information about admissions should be addressed to the Assistant Registrar (01572 820611).

Scholarships and Bursaries. Boys and girls may apply for Academic (ISEB Common Scholarship), Art/Design & Technology, Music, Sport and Thring (All-Rounder) Scholarships for entry at 13+. Exams are held in the February/March preceding entry, the deadline for entry being typically the end of December.

At 16+, Academic, Science, Art/Design & Technology, Sport and Music Scholarships are awarded in the November preceding entry. The deadline for entry is typically the end of September.

A number of music exhibitions granting free tuition on all instruments may also be awarded.

Where a family's financial means leaves them unable to afford a place at Uppingham they may be eligible to receive support via a means-tested bursary. All candidates seeking a bursary should be registered with the School and need to fulfil the same entrance criteria as described above.

Details of all scholarships and bursaries may be obtained from the Admissions Office (01572 820611).

Fees per term (2018–2019). Boarding £12,530; Day £8,771. There is a scheme for paying fees in advance; further details may be obtained from the Deputy Bursar (01572 820627).

Former Pupils. The Uppingham Association was founded in 1911 to maintain the link between OUs and the School. All pupils may become life members when they leave and a database of their names, addresses, school and career details is maintained at the School by the OU Administrator. In addition to a range of OU events that are organised each year for members, a magazine is published annually, which contains news about OUs and activities at the School, and all members are encouraged to make full use of the OU Website. Enquiries may be made directly to the Secretary to the Uppingham Association (01572 820616).

Charitable status. Uppingham School is a charitable company limited by guarantee registered in England and Wales. Company Number 8013826. Registered Charity Number 1147280. Registered Office: High Street West, Uppingham, Rutland LE15 9QD.

The Governing Body:

Chairman: Ms B M Matthews, MBE, BSc, FRSA [OU]
Vice-Chairmen:
Dr P Chadwick, MA, MA, FRSA
R J Tice BSc [OU]

The Rt Revd Donald Allister, MA, Bishop of Peterborough
The Very Revd Christopher Dalliston, Dean of Peterborough
Dr S Furness LL, Lord Lieutenant of Rutland
R Peel Esq, BSc, FRSA
D P J Ross Esq [OU]
A J D Locke Esq, MA [OU]
Dr S Goss, MA, DPhil
R N J S Price Esq
Dr D Thornton, MA, PhD, FSA, FRHistSoc
Ms S A Humphrey, LLB
The Rt Hon Sir Alan Duncan, MP

C F Ewbank
Professor J Scott
D Wallis, BA [OU]

[OU] *Old Uppinghamian*

Bursar/Finance Director, Clerk to the Trustees: S C Taylor, MA, ACA

Headmaster: **Dr R J Maloney**, MTheol St Andrews, MA, PhD King's College London

Senior Deputy Head: K M Wilding, BA
Deputy Head Academic: B Cooper, MA
Registrar: C S Bostock, MA, MSc
Chaplain: The Revd Dr J B J Saunders, BA, PhD
Assistant Head: Co-Curricular: Miss S E Delaney, BA
Assistant Head: Pastoral: T C Hicks, MA
Assistant Head: Teacher Development, Miss R R Trafford, MA, MA Ed

Assistant Staff:
* *Head of Department*
† *Housemaster/mistress*
§ *Part time*

Art, Design & Technology:
A J Halliwell, BA
H J Harrison, BA
*S N Jarvis, BA
Miss E K Rieveley, MA
C P Simmons, BSc
Miss E J Stokes, BA

Biology:
*Dr C L Pemberton, BSc, PhD
C R Birch, BSc
†N K de Wet, BSc, CBiol, MIBiol
Miss L E Hourston, BSc
Miss A Rajput, BSc
N Vastenavondt, BSc, MSc

Chemistry:
*C R Birch, BSc
Dr A J Dawes, MChem, MA, PhD
*Dr L F Dudin, MSc, PhD (*Head of Science*)
C L Howe, HDE
A Kowhan, BSc

Classics:
*Mrs C A Drinkwater, MA
Mrs S J Beresford, BA
†S G Dewhurst, BA
†Mrs A M Howe, MA, MPhil
Dr D C Oliver, PhD, MSc
†G S Tetlow, MA

Economics & Business:
*G R Matthews, BSc
N De Luca, MBA
T G Howe, MA
D P Lovering, BSc
T G MacCarthy, BA
T Oakley, BA

English:
*Dr J C Methven, DPhil, MPhil, MA
†A C Boyd-Williams, BA
Mrs J S Broughton, MA, Dip RSA SpLD

Miss S E Delaney, BA, BA
N G Fletcher, BA
T C Hicks, MA
Miss C M Mungavin, BA
Mrs H P Otter, BA, MA
Dr S E Raudnitz, MA, PhD
Mrs N L Reihill, MA

Geography:
*T P Davies, BSc
†Mrs C C Breakwell, BSc, MSc
†A N Huxter, BSc
§Mrs S J Kowhan, BA
R J O'Donoghue, BA
†Mrs K L Robinson BSc
Miss R R Trafford, MA, MA Ed
K M Wilding, BA

History:
*M J Patterson, BA
†J S Birch, MA
S J Hosking, BA
B M Kirby, MA
J Leang, BA, MA
T P Prior, BA, MA
†J A Reddy, BA

History of Art:
*D S R Kirk, BA
§Dr E E Wilce, MA, PhD

Information Technology:
*Miss S E L Webster, BSc

Learning Support:
*Mrs L Howe, BA
Mrs J S Broughton, MA, Dip RSA SpLD
§Mrs A M Merrett, BA
§Mrs K L Tetlow, BA
§Mrs J A Wilding, BSc

Life Skills:
T C Hicks, MA

Mathematics:
*Mrs M J Melville-Coman, BSc

†Mrs L J Allen, BSc, MBCS
Miss C L Finch-Wale, MMath
P Gomm, BSc
Mrs K F Hanrahan, BSc
Miss H L MacLean, BSc
A S M Moosajee, BSc
N C Newell, BSc
P J Nicholls, BSc
A D Parker, BSc

Modern Languages:
*Mrs M A B Davies, BA (*Spanish, Head of Modern Languages*)
*T R Worthington, BA (*Acting Head of French*)
*Miss C Zhang, BA, MA (*Mandarin*)
A D Burbidge, MA
†Mrs K S Boyd-Williams, MA
M R Broughton, MA
†Mrs H M Johnstone, BA
Miss M Kissane, BA
Mrs J E Newcombe, BEd
Miss M Sainte-Croix, BA
R M B Wilkinson, MA

Music:
*P M Clements, MA, FRCO (*Academic Music*)
*A A Ffrench, MA, AGSM, PG Dip GSMD (*Music Technology*)
B G Gill, BMus
Mrs C A Griffiths, GMus
R J Smith, BMus, PG Dip
S A Smith, BA, PPRNCM
§W F J Smith

Visiting Music Staff:
Miss I M Adams, GRSM (*Viola*)
S Andrews (*Drums*)
M Ashford, GRSM (*Guitar*)
A Ashwin, BMus, LRSM (*Singing*)
S Baker, BMus (*Trombone*)
Mrs T Boison, MA (*Piano*)
G Boynton, Dip RCM (*Percussion*)
Mrs M Braithwaite BA (*Singing*)
Mrs J Burgess, BMus, LGSM (*Oboe*)
Dr J T Byron, BA, MA, PhD (*Piano*)
Mrs L Clements, BA (*Flute*)
Mrs J A Dawson, GRSM, LRAM (*Piano*)
D P Ferris (*Piano*)
Mrs L H Ffrench, GRSM, LRAM (*Piano*)
N M France, GMus (*Drums*)
Mrs N J Gibbons, MMus, MPhil, LRAM, LRSM (*Piano*)
T M Gunnell (*Percussion*)
Mrs C J Gunningham, BA, MSTAT (*Alexander Technique*)
I Hildreth (*Bagpipes*)
Miss E S Hodgkinson, BMus, LRAM (*Piano*)
A J Kennedy (*Singing*)
K Learmouth, ALCM, FRSA (*Classic Guitar*)
Ms R R E Leyton-Smith, MA, Adv PG Dip RCM (*Cello*)
Mrs C Li, BMus, LRAM (*Flute*)
G K Lumbers, BMus (*Saxophone*)
Miss J A Moffat, DipRCM (*Singing*)
S P Morris, BMus (*Clarinet, Saxophone*)

Miss J Stevens, GGSM, MA
A P Webster, GGSM, PDOT

Philosophy and Religious Studies:
*P M Shacklady, BA
H D P Burling, BA, MPhil
B Cooper, MA
†R C Hegarty, MA
Dr R J Maloney, MTheol, MA, PhD
The Revd Dr J B J Saunders, BA, PhD
J E Taylor

Physical Education:
*Mrs S M Singlehurst, BEd, MSc
†D J Bartley
§J M Baker, BSc
C J Dossett, BSc (*Director of Sport*)
K G Johnstone, BEd
Mrs K L Maloney-Smith, BSc

Physics:
*Dr D D Boyce, PhD, CPhys, MPhys
W S Allen, BEd
C L Howe, HDE
G S Wright, BSc

Politics:
*R Hardman
†T Makhzangi, BA
†T G Howe, MA, MSt, MBA

Drama and Theatre:
*J Holroyd, BA
Miss S E Delaney, BA, BA
Miss C J Rayner, BA

Mrs V F Morris, AGSM, LRAM (*Clarinet, Saxophone*)
A J Pike, BA (*Music Technology*)
D N Price, LRAM (*Trumpet*)
Mrs A M Reynolds, MusB, GRNCM (*Piano*)
S Roberts, BMus (*Tuba*)
C Rutherford (*Horn*)
Mrs Y S Sandison, PPRNCM (*Singing*)
N Scott-Burt, BA, MMus, PhD, LRAM, ARCO (*Jazz Piano, Organ & Composition*)
A E Smith (*Alexander Technique*)
Miss C Tanner, BMus, LRAM (*Bassoon*)
Mrs E Turner (*Harp*)
J P Turville, MA, MMus, LLCM (*Piano*)
P N Warburton, GBSM, ABSM (*Violin*)
Ms P Waterfield, ARCM, MSTAT (*Alexander Technique*)
T J Williams, MA (*Singing*)
Mrs V D Williamson, GMus, RNCM, PPRNCM, LRAM (*Singing*)
Miss R K L Woolley, BMus, MMus (*Violin*)
Miss S J Wright (*Double Bass*)

Houses and Housemasters/mistresses:
Brooklands: Nick de Wet
Constables (*Girls*): Tyrone and Alex Howe
[*Fairfield* (*Girls*): Kate Robinson]
Fairfield (*Girls*) *Acting Housemistress*: Katharine Gaine
Farleigh: James Birch
Fircroft: Jim Reddy
Highfield: Richard Hegarty
Johnson's (*Girls*): Lesley Allen
The Lodge (*Girls*): Alex and Kate Boyd-Williams
Lorne House: Andrew Huxter
Meadhurst: Sam Dewhurst
New House (*Girls*): Christina Breakwell
Samworths' (*Girls*): Helen Johnstone
School House: Simon Tetlow
West Bank: David Bartley
West Deyne: Toby Makhzangi

Victoria College
Jersey

Mont Millais, Jersey, Channel Islands JE1 4HT

Tel: 01534 638200
Fax: 01534 727448
email: admin@vcj.sch.je
website: www.victoriacollege.je
Twitter: @VictoriaCollege
Facebook: @VictoriaCollegeJersey

Motto: *Amat Victoria Curam*

The College was founded in commemoration of a visit of Her Majesty Queen Victoria to the Island and opened in 1852. It bears the Arms of Jersey and the visitor is Her Majesty The Queen.

There are currently 656 boys in College, 277 in the Preparatory School and 99 in the Pre-Prep.

The College is situated in extensive grounds above St Helier and looks south over the Bay of St Aubin.

The fine building of 1852 with its Great Hall, de Quetteville Library and administrative areas is set at the centre of new teaching accommodation including classrooms, a music centre, an extensive Science suite opened by Her Royal Highness The Princess Royal, a Sixth Form centre, Art and Design Technology suite, computer suites and the Howard Davis Theatre refurbished in 1996. A suite of 4 new English classrooms were finished in 2014 along with a new modern Sixth Form Centre and new Houserooms in 2015.

College Field is adjacent to the main buildings and includes an all-weather hockey pitch.

Located in the grounds is a 25-yard shooting range, squash courts and CCF Headquarters. A multimillion pound sports complex with swimming pool was opened in 2003.

Education. There is an emphasis on academic success; nearly all boys go on to University in the UK. The curriculum conforms to the requirements of the National Curriculum. At GCSE, boys study English, Mathematics, Religious Education, French, Spanish, History, Drama, Geography, Biology, Chemistry, Physics, Music, Art and ICT.

In addition, boys select from optional subjects those which best suit their natural talents, the choice being guided by teaching staff in consultation with students and parents.

Boys may study three A Level subjects suited to their objectives and abilities. Enrichment skills are developed through the CCF, The Duke of Edinburgh's Award and wide-ranging co-curricular programmes.

In all year groups, there are opportunities for voluntary work, Music and the Arts, and these, with other subjects, are also encouraged by numerous School Societies.

Prizes. Her Majesty The Queen gives three Gold Medals annually for Science, Modern Languages and Mathematics as well as two Prizes for English History. The States of Jersey offers a Gold Medal and a Silver Medal annually for French. There is an award given to the boy achieving the top score in the Year 7 end-of-year examinations called the St Mannelier & St Anastase Gold Medal.

Physical Education and Games. The College places strong emphasis on sport and each year there are sports tours to the United Kingdom and abroad.

Winter games include Association Football, Rugby, Hockey and Squash. Summer games include Cricket, Swimming, Shooting, Tennis and Athletics.

Matches are played against Elizabeth College, Guernsey and numerous English Independent Senior Schools.

The College has an excellent CCF Contingent with an establishment of 90 in the Army Section, 60 in the RAF Section and 60 in the RN Section. It is commanded by Sqn Ldr S Blackmore.

Admission. The age of admission is 11 years though boys are considered for entry at all ages. Entrants must pass the College Entrance Examination.

Fees per term (2018–2019). £1,916. A grant is payable by the States of Jersey to supplement fees.

Preparatory School. The College has its own Preparatory School which stands in the College grounds. Boys progress to the College at the age of 11. (*For further details see entry in IAPS section*).

Leaving Scholarships. There are a number of Scholarships (of varying amounts). The Queen's Exhibition is tenable for three years at certain Universities; the Wimble Scholarship, the Sayers Scholarships and the De Lancey and De La Hanty Scholarship, tenable at British Universities, and the Rayner Exhibitions are recent additions to the rich endowment of Scholarships enjoyed by the College for its students.

Visitor: Her Majesty The Queen

Governing Body:
Chairman: B Watt

Vice Chairman: D Doyle	Y Kusumo
J Giles	T Smith
N Cawley	A Hossard
P Willing	A Watkins
M Gödel	G Hughes
K Slater	D Pateman
S Gibson	G Lumley

Headmaster: **Alun D Watkins**, BEd Hons, MEd Oxon

Deputy Headmaster: Gareth Hughes, BA Hons, MSc Oxon, MPhil, PhD Cantab, FRGS
Assistant Head (*Academic*): Patrick Crossley, BTh, MA Cantab, MEd
Assistant Head (*Pastoral*): Mark Gosling, BA Hons
Bursar: Carolyn Ferguson
Marketing & Communications Director: Tracy Mourant

Assistant Staff:
Marianne Adams, BA Hons
Kieran Akers, BA Hons
Gabrielle Armstrong, BA Hons
Keith Baker, BSc Hons
Lee Batchford, BSc Hons
Gareth C Bloor, BD, MA
Jacky Bryan, BA Hons
Brendan Carolan, BA Hons
Samuel Coe, BSc Hons
Steven Cooke, PhD, BEng
David Cox, BA, BEd
Joseph Crill, BSc Hons
Nicole Edgecombe, MA, BA Hons
Elise Falla, BA Hons
Thomas Fallon, BA Hons
William Gorman, BA Hons
Anthony Griffin, BA Hons
Samuel Habin, MPharmacol
Cristina Herrera-Martin, BA Hons
Ria Hill, BA Hons
Angela Matthews, BSc Hons
Kathryn Mawdsley, BA Hons
David McNally, BSc Hons
Denise Montgomery, BA Hons
Michel Morel
Rebecca Moon, BSc Hons
Francis Murton, BMus, LRAM, LTCL, ARCO, ACIEA
Lucy Ogg, BA Hons, LTCC
Aaron O'Hare, BSc Hons
Emma O'Prey, BEd Hons
Karen Palfreyman, BA Hons, MA
Ozzy Parkes, BA Hons
David Payne, MA
Monica Perestrelo
Richard Picot, BSc
Parmjeet Plummer, BA Hons
Orla Priestley, BSc, MSc
Majella Raindle, BSc Ed, MSc
Jefferson Randles, BA Hons
Jane Richardson, BSc, PhD
Steven Roberts, BA Hons, MA, PhD
Anna Robinson, BA Hons
Jennifer Roussel, BA Hons, M-ès-Lettres
Andrew Royle, BSc
Helen Ryan, BSc Hons, BA Hons
Rachel Smith, BA Hons
Matthew Smith, BA
Michelle Smith
Thomas Smith, BEng Hons
Julie Spencer, MA
Dierdre Twomey, BSc
Olivia Varney, BA Hons
Valerie Videt, Lic-ès-Lettres
Susan Watkins, BEd Hons
Robbie Webbe, MPhys
Carys Williams, BEng Hons
Matthew Widdop, MChem, MRSC

Preparatory School
Headteacher: Dan Pateman, BA Hons

Warminster School

Church Street, Warminster, Wiltshire BA12 8PJ

Tel: 01985 210100 (Senior School)
             01985 224800 (Prep School)
email: admissions@warminsterschool.org.uk
website: www.warminsterschool.org.uk
Twitter: @Warminster1707
Facebook: @WarminsterSchool
LinkedIn: /WarminsterSchool

The original boys' school was founded in 1707 by the first Viscount Weymouth, an ancestor of the present Marquess of Bath. It became an Independent Educational Trust in 1973 formed by the amalgamation of the Lord Weymouth School with the long-established local girls' school, St Monica's, founded in 1874. The School is a Limited Company whose Directors are Trustees elected by and from within the Board of Governors which is in membership of the Association of Governing Bodies of Independent Schools. The Headmaster is a member of both HMC (Headmasters' and Headmistresses' Conference) and The Society of Heads.

The School is a co-educational boarding and day school numbering some 550 pupils (140 in the Sixth Form) from 3 to 18, of whom around 200 are boarders. The Prep School of 140 pupils works in close cooperation with the Senior School and enjoys many of the same facilities. (*For further details see Warminster Prep School entry in IAPS section.*)

The School is situated along the western periphery of the town, looking out over open countryside, while its buildings are linked by extensive gardens and playing fields.

It is easily accessible by rail (via Warminster or Westbury) from London, Heathrow, the South Coast and the West, and by road (via the M3, M4 and M5).

Aims and Philosophy. The Warminster education aims to encourage each boy and girl to fulfil their academic potential and to promote intellectual curiosity and a love of learning. In addition, the School provides a secure and supportive pastoral environment, with an emphasis on character, values, leadership and service. The School believes in an all-round education and offers a wide range of co-curricular opportunities and experiences; it fosters a culture of enthusiasm, optimism and participation. A Warminster education prepares the pupils for life beyond school, at university and in the world of work. We are a community in which each boy and girl is valued and nurtured on the basis of who they are, whatever their year group, gender, natural gifts or background. *It is a preparation for life.*

Buildings. As befits a school with a long history, there is a wide variety of historic buildings. The History department, for example, teaches in the School's oldest building, School House, which was founded by Viscount Weymouth in 1707. The school boasts one of the oldest working Fives courts in England.

A multimillion pound development programme has taken place in recent years and has included completion of the Thomas Arnold Hall – a fantastic new multi-purpose space, a state-of-the-art science centre, new library, design technology centre as well as additional boarding facilities. Existing boarding accommodation has been extensively refurbished.

Boarders are cared for by Housemasters or Housemistresses, Resident Tutors and Matrons. Pupils typically enjoy single study-bedrooms in the Sixth Form.

Curriculum. In the first three years of the Senior School, all pupils follow a broad curriculum and GCSE pupils study a full and varied range of subjects. All pupils are involved in PE and Games, and Health and Social Education, as well as a comprehensive programme of Careers advice.

In the Sixth Form greater individual freedom and responsibility are encouraged. Sixth Formers are offered a choice between studying A Levels, the International Baccalaureate Diploma and the IB Career Related Programme, which is an increasingly popular choice for many of our pupils with others joining the Sixth Form from elsewhere to follow our successful IB programmes. The first school in the South-West to offer the IB Diploma, our IB results have placed us each year within the top thirty UK IB schools. Although the vast majority of pupils will be aiming for University, with over 95% winning places at leading institutions including Oxford and Cambridge, some will pursue gap years or enter business or the Armed Services directly. The overall pupil to staff ratio is under 10:1. Pupils receive an exceptional amount of individual attention and are encouraged to realise their full potential in as many areas as possible. There is an extensive tutorial system and a strong sense of the importance of the individual within the community. The school is at the forefront of developing 'personal, learning and thinking skills' both through the tutorial system and also via its academic and its rich co-curricular programme. A small learning support unit is staffed by expert and dedicated specialists.

Activities. A very wide range of activities is on offer, and pupils are encouraged to involve themselves fully. The School has a strong tradition of drama, and musical activities, including choir, orchestra and jazz band, are a real strength. There are currently over 40 hobby activities available and Forest School.

The School enjoys close links with the Armed Services, and the CCF, though voluntary, is traditionally strong. There is also a large involvement in The Duke of Edinburgh's Award scheme, whilst a number of pupils are actively engaged in Community Service in Warminster and the local area.

Games. Sports offered include Rugby, Hockey, Cricket, Tennis, Athletics, Netball, Rounders, Swimming, Cross-Country Running, Basketball, Squash, Badminton, and Volleyball.

There is a spacious Sports Hall with recently renovated squash courts, hard tennis courts, heated swimming pool, an Astroturf all-weather pitch and an indoor shooting range. Pupils have access to the local Golf Club and Riding Stables.

Admission. Pupils are admitted to the Prep School from the age of 3. Boarders are admitted from the age of 7. Pupils who enter after the age of 8 will be required to sit the Warminster School entrance examinations relative to the proposed year of entry. A report from the Head of a pupil's present school will be requested. Older pupils who qualify by good GCSE results and school report may be admitted directly to the Sixth Form. Scholarships are available for entry at 7+, 9+, 11+, 13+ and 16+. Examinations for Scholarships are held annually. Details may be obtained from the Head of Admissions.

Progress throughout the School, including the transfer from the Prep to the Senior School, is not automatic but will be based on the School's assessment of each student's ability at key points and will always be dependent on the pupil's continued commitment and progress in all areas of activity.

Great care is taken to consider individual needs and circumstances. The School provides a Special Support Facility for pupils who are dyslexic, or who have other similar needs. Parents of such pupils should ask to meet the Head of Learning Support.

Please telephone the School (01985 210160) to arrange a visit, and to meet the Headmaster or the Head of the Prep School.

A Registration Fee of £100 is payable and, upon the acceptance of a place, a guarantee fee of £500 for UK based parents and £1,000 for overseas based parents, credited to the final account, will be payable.

Fees per term (2018–2019). Day: Prep School £2,550–£4,080; Year 7 to Sixth Form £5,110. Boarding: Prep School £7,205; Years 7 to Sixth Form £10,195–£10,880.

Fees are as inclusive as possible, covering meals, stationery and textbooks. The Bursar welcomes consultation with parents over fees, insurance and capital payment schemes. As the School is an Independent Educational Trust, any financial surplus is used exclusively for the further improvement of the School. Fees are kept to the minimum required to run the School effectively, employ first-rate staff and keep the facilities and resources up to the level expected by parents.

Charitable status. Warminster School is a Registered Charity, number 1042204. It exists to promote the education of boys and girls.

Patrons:
The Revd Canon E J Townroe
Mrs D P Goodger
Mr R C Southwell, QC
The Rt Revd the Bishop of Salisbury
The Marquess of Bath

Chairman of Governors: The Right Hon Sir David Latham, QC

Staff:

Headmaster: Mark Mortimer, MBA, BA

Deputy Head: Rick Clarke, BA Hons, PGCE
Deputy Head (Academic): Mark Sully, BSc, PGCE
Head of Co-Curricular: Mrs Terri Wilcox, CertEd
Head of Sixth Form: Dr Thomas Horler-Underwood, BA, MPhil, PhD, PG Cert
Head of Middle School: Ms Nia Davies, BSc Hons, PGCE
Head of Lower School: Simon Rossiter, MSc, PGCE, CCRS
Examinations Officer: Dr Mark Martin, BSc Hons, PhD, PGCE, MIBiol

Heads of Department:
Art: Mrs Louisa Clayton, MA, PGCE
Business Studies & Economics: Adam Jacobs, BA, PGCE
D&T: Simon Rossiter, MSc, PGCE, CCRS
Drama: Mrs Emily Harris, MA, BA
EAL: Mrs Sarah Shanks, BA Hons, PGCE, RSA Dip TEFL
English: Miss Eleanor Mears, BA, PGCE
Geography: Harry Phillips, BSc
History: Mrs Juliette Walker, BA, QTS
Learning Support: Mrs Alison Hicks, BA Hons, Cert SpLD, Hornsby Cert
Mathematics: Austin Hill, BA, PGCE, CertEd
Modern Languages: Mrs Nicola Rogers, BA, PGCE
Director of Music: Mrs Caroline Robinson, BA, PGCE
RS: Matthew Harris, MA Oxon, MPhil, MEd, PGCE
Science: Dr David Hankey, BSc, PhD, MRSC
Director of Sports: Mr Tom Morison, BEd

There are 30 other full-time and part-time staff.

House Staff:
Mr William Vaughan (*St Boniface*)
Miss Barbarra Mitterrutzner (*Stratton House*)
Mr Malcolm Miller (*St Denys*)
Mr Jonathan Mercer (*Old Vicarage*)
Mrs Lisa Crinion (*Ivy House*)
Mrs Samantha Young, RGN (*School Nursing Sister*)

Bursar & Clerk to the Governors: Mrs Alison C Martin, MBA, FMAAT
Head of Admissions: Miss Fiona Beach-MacGeagh

Warwick School

Myton Road, Warwick CV34 6PP

Tel: 01926 776400
email: enquiries@warwickschool.org
website: www.warwickschool.org
Twitter: @warwickschool
Facebook: @OfficialWarwickSchool

Motto: '*Altiora Peto*'

Warwick School has a very long and rich history stretching back reputedly to 914, making it one of the oldest schools in the country.

A leading independent day and boarding school for boys aged 7–18, set in 50 acres, Warwick School is adjacent to the River Avon, within Warwick town. The school is proud of its outstanding facilities and Warwick Hall is one of the largest and most impressive performance venues in the region.

We aim to develop responsible, resilient and compassionate young men of character, equipped to succeed in a changing world.

High academic expectations and achievements, together with outstanding pastoral care and exceptional co-curricular provision make Warwick School a wonderful place to be educated.

Admission is by entrance examination set by the School. Entry to Junior School is at ages 7, 8 and 9. Entry to Senior School is at 11, 12, 13 and 16. The assessment at 11+ and 12+ includes English, Mathematics and a computer-based ability test (for 11+) or verbal reasoning (for 12+). The assessment at 13+ includes English, Mathematics, MFL, Science and VR. Sixth Form entry requires a minimum of three A and five B grades (or equivalent) at GCSE.

Curriculum. The aim of the school is to provide a broadly based education which allows pupils to achieve academic excellence. All pupils are encouraged to develop their individual talents to the full and to accept responsibility for themselves and others.

In the Junior School the curriculum aims to give a firm grounding in the National Curriculum foundation subjects English, Mathematics and Science. A range of other subjects including History, Geography, Design and Technology, French, Computing and Religious Education are taught throughout the school by specialist subject teachers. French is taught throughout as is Art, Drama, Music and Physical Education.

In the Senior School the curriculum offers a range of options but there is a core curriculum of English, Mathematics, Physics, Chemistry, Biology and Languages up to GCSE. Virtually all boys continue into the Sixth Form where three subjects are studied, with a fourth subject for the academically more able. The curriculum is designed to give all boys a broad general education and to postpone any specialisation for as long as possible.

Games and other activities. Active interest in out of school activities is much encouraged. Winter games are rugby, hockey, cross-country and swimming. These are played in the Michaelmas and Lent terms and our national reputation is strong throughout. Summer games are cricket, tennis and athletics. Badminton, basketball, clay pigeon shooting, golf and squash are played throughout the year. There are fine sporting facilities in the Halse Sports Pavilion, including a 25m 6-lane pool, squash courts, state-of-the-art rock climbing wall, fitness suite and sports hall. There are usually some 90 different clubs and societies active in school life.

Religious teaching. The Chapel Services and teaching are according to the Church of England, but there are always pupils of other denominations and race and for these other arrangements may be made.

Boarding. Senior School boys (from Year 9) may be weekly or full boarders. Flexi boarding can sometimes be arranged for day boys to accommodate short term requirements. There is also an opportunity for an extended day facility.

Fees per term (2018–2019). Senior School Tuition: £4,398; Boarding (in addition to Tuition): £5,188 (full); £4,563 (weekly). Junior School Tuition: £3,727–£4,183.

Scholarships. *Governors Scholarships* (11+, 12+, 13+, 16+) are available to reward academic excellence and talent. Scholarships are awarded up to the value of 20% of fees based on the results of the entrance examination and interview. For existing Sixth Formers, the scholarships are awarded based on GCSE results and school reports.

James Barr Science Scholarships worth £750 a year are available in the Sixth Form. There are two Natural Sciences scholarships for those studying the Sciences and two Pure Science and Engineering scholarships for those studying Mathematics and Physics.

Governors Music Scholarships at 11+, 13+ and 16+ are awarded up to the value of 20% of fees based on musical ability and potential with a high level of achievement in the entrance examination.

Two *Choral Scholarships*, each to the value of £1,650 per annum, may be awarded each year to boys aged between 7 and 11 years on 1st September, who are either entering or who are in attendance at Warwick Junior School and the Choir of St Mary's Church, Warwick.

Further details from the Admissions Team, Tel: 01926 776414, email: admissions@warwickschool.org.

Charitable status. Warwick Independent Schools Foundation is a Registered Charity, number 1088057. It exists to provide quality education for boys.

Foundation Secretary: Mr S T Jones

Chairman of the Governors: Mr A C Firth

Head Master: Dr D Smith, MA, PhD

Deputy Headmaster: Mr J Barker, BA
Deputy Head, Academic: Dr S R Chapman, BA, PhD
Deputy Head, Teaching & Learning: Mrs K Wyatt, BA
Assistant Head, Academic: Mr D Seal, BSc

Junior School:
Headmaster: Mr A C Hymer, BA, MA Ed, NPQH
Deputy Headmaster: Mr T Wurr, BA

School Chaplain: The Revd Dr Alycia Timmis, MA, PhD

Wellingborough School

London Road, Wellingborough, Northamptonshire NN8 2BX

Tel: 01933 222427
email: admissions@wellingboroughschool.org
website: www.wellingboroughschool.org
Twitter: @WboroSchool
Facebook: @WboroSchool

Motto: *Salus in Arduis*

Wellingborough School was founded in the period between 1548 and 1576, and has been in continuous existence since 1595. The School moved to its present site in 1881.

The School is a co-educational school for boys and girls from the age of 3 to 18. The School is firmly wedded to Christian principles, to equality of opportunity and the enrichment of individuals in the community. The School is divided into a Pre-Preparatory School (age 3–8: 124 pupils), the Preparatory School (age 8–13: 306 pupils), and the Senior School (age 13–18: 389 pupils).

Wellingborough is situated 63 miles from London, 10 miles east of Northampton. Close to the main railway line from St Pancras to Leicester and Sheffield, it is served by an excellent network of motorways and dual carriageways connecting the A1, A14 and the M1.

Buildings and Organisation. The School occupies a fine site on the south of the town, and stands in its own grounds of 45 acres. In the Senior School there are five boys' houses and three girls' houses, organised on boarding house lines. Each house has about 45 pupils. The Sixth Form has approximately 140 pupils, 90% of whom go directly to higher education.

Direct admission at 13+ for boys and girls is by means of entry tests and interview or by transfer from Wellingborough Preparatory School. Direct entry into the Sixth Form is on the basis of an interview, school report and likely GCSE results confirmed before entry. There is a 'Headstart' course after the GCSE exams in Year 11, which lasts around a week and to which all prospective Sixth Formers are invited.

The Preparatory School, while sharing some of the facilities of the Senior School, has its own buildings and classrooms on the east side of the campus. In recent years work has been completed on a large new library, incorporating a computer research area, fiction and non-fiction working areas, classroom and science laboratory, with up-to-date facilities and IT throughout. The Pre-Preparatory School occupies its own modern purpose-built buildings which have been substantially refurbished and extended.

The main buildings include a Study Centre, Library, Assembly Hall, Careers Room, Chapel, and three classroom blocks. There is a Design Technology centre, Music School, Modern Foreign Languages Centre, Sports Hall, Art Building and central Dining Hall.

Religion. The School welcomes pupils and families of all faiths or none. Pupils attend a weekly Chapel service and there are some Sunday services in term time, which are Christian in content but aimed at a wide congregation.

Curriculum. In the Pre-Preparatory School and the Preparatory School the curriculum is an enriched version of the National Curriculum. French, Latin and Spanish are also taught in the Preparatory School.

In the first year of the Senior School, pupils follow a core curriculum in English, Mathematics, a Modern Foreign Language, Chemistry, Biology, History, Geography, Design Technology, Art, Music, RS and PE. The study of a second Modern Foreign Language and Latin for those with some foundation are both options in this year. GCSE courses are offered in English, English Literature, Modern Foreign Language, Mathematics, Biology, Chemistry and Physics. Options include Latin, Spanish as a second Modern Foreign Language, History, Geography, Art, Photography, Design Technology, Music, Drama, PE, Computer Science and Religious Studies.

The following subjects are offered for A Level examination: Art and Design, Biology, Business, Chemistry, Design Technology, Drama, Economics, English Language, English Literature, French, Spanish, Geography, History, Latin, Mathematics and Further Mathematics, Music, PE, Physics, Politics, Psychology and Religious Studies.

Music, Drama, Art, Design. The Music School contains a central teaching hall, a second newly refurbished teaching room and several practice rooms. Professional tuition is given on all instruments and there are chapel and concert choirs, junior and senior bands and a school orchestra.

Concerts, small drama productions and lectures are held in the Senior School Hall. The annual Senior School drama production is held at the Castle Theatre in Wellingborough and the school has a new drama suite in the 'Pod'. The Richard Gent Design Centre offers workshops and studies for Design Technology and ceramics. The highly successful Art Department has its own dedicated building. Pupils are encouraged to make full use of these facilities in their spare time.

Sport. The playing fields, over 40 acres in extent, are used for the main boys' sports of rugby, soccer and cricket, and hockey and netball for girls; cross country, athletics, and tennis are also highly popular. The school site also boasts a nine-hole golf course, two astroturf pitches, five all-weather tennis courts, two squash courts, shooting range and Sports Hall. The latter has four badminton courts, indoor cricket nets and facilities for fencing, table tennis, basketball and a dedicated fitness suite.

Other Activities. After their first term in the Senior School all pupils join the Combined Cadet Force (Royal Navy, Army, Marines or RAF Section); this is compulsory until Easter of Year 10. Training is given in field craft, first aid, map reading and orienteering with opportunities to participate in training exercises at weekends. There is an annual CCF camp as well as specialist RAF and Marine camps and other opportunities include both indoor and open range shooting, canoeing and sailing. The Duke of Edinburgh's Award scheme is also a very popular option for Year 9 upwards; we offer Bronze, Silver and Gold in three modes of transport; walking, canoe and cycling.

A wide range of co-curricular interests is available through various societies and clubs. Pupils may also take part in local community service work.

Careers. Guidance is available to all pupils on further education and careers prospects through the Head of Careers and other members of staff. The School is a member of the Independent Schools Careers Organisation.

Scholarships. Scholarships are offered to external candidates for entry at 11+, 13+ and 16+. These Scholarships are awarded in the following subjects; Academia, Music, Drama, Art and Sports. Applications are required by the end of November and examinations take place in November and January.

Further details and application forms for all the above may be obtained from the Admissions Officers.

Bursaries. Bursaries are available, on a means-tested basis (subject to annual review), to support those pupils who would benefit from a Wellingborough education but whose families are unable to afford the full fees. All Bursaries are academically-scored first, *then* means-tested with priority going to those most-academically gifted *and* requiring financial assistance. Bursaries may also be available to augment Scholarships.

Further details and application forms for all the above may be obtained from the Admissions Officers.

Fees per term (2018–2019). Senior School: £5,330 (Years 9–13); Preparatory School: £5,085 (Years 7 & 8), £4,870 (Years 4, 5 & 6); Pre-Preparatory School: £3,275 (Years 2 & 3), £3,140 (Nursery, Reception & Year 1). Fees include most extras apart from instrumental lessons (termly payment) and optional overseas trips.

Admission. All applications should be made to the Admissions Office.

Term of Entry. New pupils are accepted at the beginning of any term. The largest entry is in September each year.

Old Wellingburian Club. All former pupils who have spent at least one year in the School are eligible for membership. Correspondence should be addressed to the OW Club Secretary at the School.

Charitable status. Wellingborough School is a Registered Charity, number 1101485.

Governors:

Dr J K Cox, MA, MB, BChir, BA, MBCS (*Chairman*)
Mrs A Coles, MA (*Deputy Chairman*)
T Baldry, Esq, FCA
I M Cantelo, Esq
J J Higgins, Esq
Mrs D A Line, BA, CA
S M Marriott, Esq (*Representative Governor of the OW Club*)
Mrs L Pape
R H Thakrar, Esq, BSc Hons, MBCS
P R Tyldesley, Esq, BA, ARICS
D A Waller, Esq, MA
C A Westley, Esq

Senior School:

Headmaster: A N Holman, MA Cantab, MEd

Bursar & Head of Finance: C J P Evans, BA Durham
Deputy Head Academic: S M Barnhurst, BSc Salford, MA Northampton (*Physics*)
Deputy Head Pastoral: Q Wiseman, BA Newcastle, PGCE London, BSA Roehampton (*Geography*)
Master i/c Sixth Form Academic Progress: J R Gray, BSc Bangor (*Biology*)
Assistant Head Co-Curricular: L J McAuley, BSc Glasgow (*Mathematics*)
Director of Learning & Teaching: S R Medd, BSc Durham, PGCE Cambridge (*Geography*)

[1] *also teaches in Preparatory School*

Housemasters/Housemistresses:
Fryer's House: [1]S M Curley, BA De Montfort (*English, Latin, EPQ Coordinator*)
Garne's House: [1]D A Coombes, BA Liverpool John Moores (*Design Technology*)
Platt's House: T J Fourie, MSc Port Elizabeth SA (*Mathematics*)
Cripps' House: [1]K C M Hargreaves, Rose Bruford College of Speech & Drama
Parker Steyne's: [1]G E Houghton, BA Durham (*PE/Games*)
Marsh House: C S Irvin, BSc Loughborough (*Head of Academic PE*)
Nevill House: J M Livingstone, BA Queen's Belfast (*Geography*)
Weymouth House: H M Pattison, BSc King's College London (*Head of Biology*)

Teaching Staff:
H C Arimoro, BA Durham (*Psychology*)
J H Austin, BSc Oxford Brookes (*PE and Geography*)
M Baddeley, BSc of York (*Head of Mathematics*)
S J Baxby, BA Northampton (*Head of Business Studies*)
[1]F J Burgess, BEd Exeter (*Head of PSHCE, PE/Games*)
C S Codner, BA Liverpool (*Head of Geography*)
K M Cook, BSc Wolverhampton (*Chemistry*)
[1]S L Egan, BEng Leicester (*Head of Design Technology*)
C Y Elwyn, Baccalaureat Lycee Nationalise Mixte, Diploma Languages I C (*French, Latin*)
P J Farley, BA York, MA Liverpool (*History and Politics*)
A R Gamble, BA St Edmund Hall Oxford (*Head of English*)
J C Hennessy, BA Leicester Polytechnic (*Head of Art*)
R Hill, BSc Manchester (*Head of Physics*)
[1]L M Hilton, BSc Loughborough (*Director of Sport*)
H L Hodgson, BEng Liverpool (*Mathematics*)
[1]A S Holley, BA Birmingham (*Head of Classics*)

C E M Horry, BA Kent (*Art, Chair of Senior School Council*)

K M Kelly, BA, MA Oxford (*Head of Religious Studies*)

K R Kenney, BA Birmingham (*English*)

S J Kielty, BA Wales, MA Warwick (*Head of History*)

R J Lamberton, BA, Lancaster (*English*)

[1]B Lavin Campo, Licenciado en Filosofia y Letras Valladolid, Spain (*Spanish*)

B Lawson, BSc Loughborough (*Mathematics*)

S D Lawson, BA, PGC-SEN Coordination Northampton, QTS Leicester (*Head of Learning Support*)

K M Loak-Crisp, PhD Aston (*Chemistry*)

K Meagan, FA Coaching Certificate, FA Coaching License and UEFA "B" Award (*PE/Games*)

A S Monaghan, BSc Dundee, PhD Cambridge (*Acting Head of Chemistry*)

C J Owen, BA Exeter (*Modern Foreign Languages*)

P J Phillips, BSc Portsmouth Polytechnic, PhD Warwick (*Physics*)

J A Ramsden, BA, Sheffield (*History, Politics*)

S S Rich, BSc Durham (*Head of Chemistry*)

G M Rodgers, MA Newnham College Cambridge (*English*)

[1]I Runnells, BA Northampton, LTCL, LLCM, ARCO (*Head of Music*)

G Scott, BA Leicester (*Business Studies*)

J F Selby, BA Leicester (*History*)

[1]C Stroud, Licence ès Lettres Sorbonne Nouvelle Paris (*Head of Modern Foreign Languages*)

P B Waugh, BEd Manchester Metropolitan (*Head of IT*)

A D Woodward, BSc City (*Head of Economics*)

C L Woodward, BA Surrey Institute of Art & Design (*Art, Photography*)

Preparatory School:

Headmistress: K Owen, BSc Exeter (*English, Mathematics, PSHE*)

Deputy Head, Curriculum: A I Fordham, BSc Oxford Brookes, MRes Open, PhD Open (*Head of Geography*)

Deputy Head, Pastoral: C Petrie, BSc Loughborough (*PSHE, Games*)

Pastoral Coordinator: J B Rowley-Burns, BSc Greenwich (*Head of Mathematics*)

Club Presidents:

Tigers: S C Allan, MA Cardiff (*Form Tutor 8SA, English, Games*)

Bears: P W Dennis, BA Oxford Brookes (*Form Tutor 8PD, History, Games*)

Panthers: W Richardson, BEd Leicester (*Form Tutor 8WR, Mathematics, Games*)

Wolves: B J Russell, Fd BSc Northampton (*Form Tutor 8BJR, Mathematics, Games*)

Jaguars: C L Whitaker, BA Brighton (*Form Tutor 8CLW, Geography, PE, Games*)

Lions: S J Whitby, BEng Kingston (*Form Tutor 8SJW, DT, Games*)

Teaching Staff:

H J Clark, BA Chester (*Form Tutor 6HC, French, Spanish*)

J Dean, BSc De Montfort (*Head of Sport and PE*)

F J Drye, BA Wales (*Form Tutor 5FD, Head of English, Life Skills*)

J Ferguson, BSc Northumbria (*Form Tutor 5JF, Science, Games*)

K W Leutfeld, BMus GSMD, MA Inst Ed (*Head of Music*)

J James, BA Queens of Belfast (*Head of Modern Foreign Languages*)

C L McDougall, BSc Brighton (*Form Tutor 4CM, English, Mathematics, Geography, Drama, RS, Life Skills*)

B McKenna, BSc Ulster, MSc Queen's Belfast (*Form Tutor 7BM, ICT, Mathematics*)

L McMillan, BSc Leeds Polytechnic (*Science*)

J Petrie, BA Hons Bournemouth (*Form Tutor 5JP, History, RS, English*)

C W Pickett, BCS Auckland University of Technology (*Head of History*)

R Roberts, BEd Chester (*Form Tutor 6RR, Head of Art*)

A J Simmons, BA Stirling (*Form Tutor 4AS, Year 4 Coordinator, Mathematics, English, Science*)

A J Staughton, BA Leeds Polytechnic (*Form Tutor 7AJS, Head of Science*)

L Williams, BA Bath, MSc Brunel (*Form Tutor 6LW, PE, Geography, Games*)

Pre-Preparatory School:

Headmistress: J M Everett, MA, BEd London

Assistant Head (*Curriculum*): D C Popplewell, BA Warwick (*Year 3*)

Assistant Head (*Pastoral*): R M Girling, BEd Cambridge (*Year 3*)

M Gutteridge, NNEB Southfields College (*Head of Nursery*)

Teaching Staff:

S Barber, FDLT Northampton (*PE/Games*)

J E M Espin, BA New Hall Cambridge (*Year 1*)

S Garfirth, Dip RCM, ALCM, Royal College of Music (*Year 3 Music*)

L Gillard, BA Northampton (*Year 1*)

D Herbert, NVQ Early Years Care & Education Level 3 (*Nursery*)

E Jakeman, BEd Worcester College (*Reception, Year 2, Year 3*)

S A Jamieson, BA Northampton (*Year 2, Year 3*)

M Mannion, HLTA Northampton (*ICT*)

J Mellor, BEd Kingston (*Reception*)

K Wood, BA East Anglia (*Year 2*)

C H Waite, BEd Ripon & York St John (*Year 2*)

Wellington College

Duke's Ride, Crowthorne, Berkshire RG45 7PU

Tel:	The Master: 01344 444101
	Director of Admissions: 01344 444013
	Group Finance Director & Bursar: 01344 444020
	Reception: 01344 444000
email:	info@wellingtoncollege.org.uk
website:	www.wellingtoncollege.org.uk
Twitter:	@WellingtonUK
Facebook:	@WellingtonCollege

Wellington College, founded in 1853, is arguably the UK's leading co-educational boarding and day school. Its pupils develop a unique identity inspired by intellectual curiosity, true independence, a generous and far-reaching inclusivity and the courage to be properly and unselfishly individual. Wellington's commitment to a properly holistic education ensures the College is celebrated for its achievements both in and out of the classroom: in particular its sporting, artistic and dramatic provision are second to none. Wellington has an extensive Service and Global Citizenship programme. The aim is for all pupils to understand that serving and caring for others brings the highest rewards in life and the greatest likelihood of long term happiness and fulfilment.

Stellar examination results, outstanding provision across all co-curricular areas, a raft of national accolades, and an exclusively 'excellent' 2014 ISI inspection report, place the College firmly among the Premier League of independent schools.

Organisation. There are approximately 1,040 pupils, with 640 boys and 400 girls, spread across all age groups. All pupils belong to one of seventeen Houses, seven of which are located in the main College buildings and ten in the grounds. Fifteen of the Houses accommodate the 80%+ who board at Wellington as well as a handful of day pupils. There are also two specific day Houses, one each for girls and for boys. 13+ boarders share rooms in their first year, and may do so in a second or third year, but then move on to their own room. There is a central dining hall with modern kitchens and serveries. Meals are taken here on a cafeteria basis by most of the pupils although some Houses outside the main buildings have their own dining facilities. The V&A café is also open during school hours for drinks and snacks. The school has its own Medical Officer and a 9-bed Health Centre constantly staffed by fully-qualified nurses. All Houses have their own tutors, House Matrons and domestic team, which are led by the Housemaster or Housemistress.

Academic. Wellingtonians study GCSEs, followed by the IB Diploma or A Levels and, whichever route they take, results are superb: in 2018, 89% of grades at A Level were A*–B; the IB Diploma average was 39.3 with 51% of students scoring 40 points or more. GCSE results were equally strong with over 60% achieving A* in unreformed subjects, while 20% secured 9s in the reformed subjects. The College is currently celebrating record Oxbridge success with 100 Wellingtonians being offered places over the past four years, while over 20 move on each year to American universities, including several to Ivy League universities.

Sport. The College has an outstanding reputation in sport and 31 different activities are offered. National team and individual success this year came in Athletics, Basketball, Cricket, Hockey, Equestrian, Golf, Gymnastics, Kickboxing, Modern Pentathlon, Rackets, Real Tennis, Shooting, Rugby, Skiing, Swimming and Triathlon; a staggering number of individuals gained National or International honours across 16 different sports. A relay team swam the English Channel for the fifth year in a row.

Performing Arts. Performing Arts are equally strong. Music and Drama are stunning, with nearly two-thirds of pupils taking lessons in musical instruments or LAMDA. Recent achievements include: the Orchestra playing at St John's, Smith Square, the Choir tour to Spain, the Singer-Songwriter tour to Nashville, an annual musical (this year was *Cats*), contemporary Shakespeare productions and imaginative and inclusive junior plays. Dance enjoys a purpose-designed studio and two spectacular shows each year play to packed houses. It was no surprise that Wellington was awarded Artsmark Gold by the Arts Council. Clubs and societies range from Amnesty International to the fully co-ed Field Gun team, from WTV (Wellington's own television company) and its pupil-run radio station, DukeBox to a full range of more traditional pastimes such as Photography, Cooking and Model United Nations. Wellington's spectacular new 900-seater Performing Arts Centre opened in 2018.

Leadership, service to others and developing an international outlook are also central to the College's core values which is why co-curricular activities include CCF, Duke of Edinburgh's Award, and a pioneering Global Social Leaders scheme, in which pupils learn to create and run innovative social action projects, tackling local and global issues.

Admission to the School. Most pupils enter the school in September when they are between 13 and 14 years of age. There are occasionally places available for pupils at 14+. Around 40 pupils also join the College for the Sixth Form. Registration (with £300 fee) is online. Those registered for 13+ entry (by the end of Year 5) sit the ISEB Common Pre-Test in the Michaelmas term of Year 6 and, if sufficiently strong academically or in other areas (e.g. sport, music), are invited for an assessment day (usually in the Lent term of Year 6). Those who are successful are then offered a conditional place subject to satisfactory results in Scholarship, Common Entrance or other entry exams. A Waiting List also operates. Where appropriate, an overseas deposit is also payable.

Scholarships. Detailed information about the Scholarships available on entry at age 13+ or 16+ can be found on our website. This detailed information explains aspects such as application, requirement, examinations, assessments, timetable and tenure. Scholarships are entrance awards intended to recognise talented children who have shown great promise in certain disciplines, but they do not carry any financial benefit in terms of fee reduction.

Wellington offers Entrance Scholarships at 13+ in Academics and Music, usually administered around six to eight months before a pupil enters Wellington. Scholarships in other areas (Art, Drama, Dance, Design Engineering and Sport) are offered at the end of Year 9 after a full year at Wellington. However, students are invited to participate in Inspire days in these areas during Year 8 as an initial stage in the Scholarship process.

For entry at 16+ Scholarships are awarded in all of the above areas as part of the full application process.

As well as it being a great honour and accolade, pupils awarded scholarships upon entry to the College, and those awarded at the end of Year 9, are expected to be leaders and role models within their field of interest. They will also take part in a programme of extension activities and opportunities appropriate to their particular area of talent. Music scholars, for example, attend regular masterclasses with visiting professionals and Academic award holders partake in an extension programme of study designed by our Head of Scholarship.

Bursaries. Widening access to Wellington is at the heart of the Governors' and Master's vision for the future of the College. All financial aid in terms of fee reduction is therefore awarded via a means-testing procedure (details from the Bursar's Office). Our aim is to enable an increasing number of families, who otherwise would not be able to afford the fees at Wellington, to send their son or daughter to the College. Means-tested bursaries may be up to 100% of College fees, depending on individual family circumstances.

Foundation Places. Very generous remission, including free places based on means-testing, are available for the sons and daughters of deceased military servicemen and servicewomen and of others who have died in acts of selfless bravery, subject to entry requirement and according to the rules of the Foundation. Further details are available from the Bursar's Office.

Fees per term (2018–2019). Boarders £13,250, Day (in boarding House) £11,120, Day £9,680. Separate charges totalling £322.50 per instrument are made for musical tuition (10 lessons). The school runs an attractive fees in advance scheme for parents with capital sums available.

The Wellington Community. Our role is to build a supportive, global professional and social network of students, Old Wellingtonians, parents (current and past), staff and partner schools. We deliver a diverse programme of engagement events and offer careers support, guidance and mentoring opportunities by drawing on our incredible resources within the Community; we truly champion the diverse skill sets our unique Community has to offer. We also run Wellington College's own networking website, Wellington Connect, where all members of our Wellington Community can share expertise, find (or offer) mentoring opportunities, and make connections with friends past and present. To find out more please email the Wellington Community office on community@wellingtoncollege.org.uk or go to the Welling-

ton Community website www.wellycom.net or sign up to
Wellington Connect at www.wellingtonconnect.co.uk

The Wellington Group. A significant feature of Wellington is its outward-looking, expansive approach to education. Wellington Colleges Shanghai, Hangzhou, Tianjin and Bangkok, the Wellington Academies in Wiltshire and Eagle House prep school all provide our pupils with meaningful opportunities for partnership and service within the national and international communities. This, combined with our Teaching School initiative, Leadership Institute, ISSP programme and extensive lectures and conference programme, which culminates in the annual Festival of Education, reflects our commitment to lifelong learning and to leading educational debate in the country.

Further information including details of Visitors Days can be found on the website, and the Admissions Office can be contacted on 01344 444013.

Charitable status. Wellington College is a Registered Charity, number 309093. It exists to provide education for boys and girls aged 13–18.

Visitor: Her Majesty The Queen

President: HRH The Duke of Kent, KG, GCMG, GCVO, ADC, DL

Vice-President & Chairman of Governors: Mr Peter Mallinson, BA, MBA

Ex officio Governors:
The Archbishop of Canterbury, MA, BA, DipMin
Arthur Charles Valerian Wellesley, 9th Duke of Wellington, MA, Hon DLitt, OBE, DL

Governors:
Professor Peter Frankopan, MA, DPhil, FRSA
Robert Perrins, BSc, ACA
Howard Veary, BA, FCA
The Rt Hon The Lord Strathclyde, CH
Ron Dennis, CBE
Edward Chaplin, CMG, OBE
Duncan Ritchie, FCA
Nigel Howard-Jones
Mrs Felicity Kirk, LLB
Ms Virginia Rhodes, BA Hons
Mrs Gabriela Galceran Ball
John Claughton, MA
William Jackson, MA
Ms Helen Stevenson, MA
Mrs Jill May, BA
Mr Mark Milliken-Smith, QC

Master: Julian Thomas, BSc Hons, MBA, FRSA

Second Master: Robin Dyer, BA
Director of Admissions: Ed Venables, BA
Deputy Head (Academic): Matt Oakman, BA
Deputy Head (Co-curricular): Mrs Cressida Henderson, BA
Deputy Head (Communications): Miss Rosie McColl
Deputy Head (Educational Developments & Partnerships): Iain Henderson, BA
Deputy Head (Pastoral & Wellbeing); Second Master Elect: James Dahl, MA
Deputy Head (Teaching Staff Performance & Development): Mrs Katy Granville-Chapman, BA, MSc

Assistant Staff:
* *Head of Department/Year*
† *Housemaster/mistress*

Art:
*Mrs Alice Carpenter, BA
Miss Sally-Anne Burt, BA
Mrs Bethan Carr, BA

Ms Amy Flanagan, BA
Miss Rachel Humphries, BA
Jonathan Nickisson-Richards, MFA, BA Hons
Adam Rattray, BA (*Art History*)
James Trundle, BSc, BFA

Biology:
*Dr Harry Wright, BSc, PhD
†Mrs Kate Harrison, BA
Sam Laing, MSc
Dr Elizabeth Lambert, BSc, PhD
Svend Larsen, BSc, MEd
†Nicholas Light, MA, MSc
Mrs Delyth Lynch, BSc
Mrs Miranda Patterson, BSc (**Director of Science, Technology & Engineering*)
Mrs Emma Poynter, BSc

Chemistry:
*Dr Caroline Evans, BA, PhD
Miss Heather Andrews, MChem
Miss Charlotte Barrett Denonain, BA
Dr Christopher Davison, PhD
†Mrs Rachel Loaring, BSc
Jack McGarey, MChem
Dr Julian O'Loughlin, MSc, PhD (*Director of Digital Learning*)
Stephen Simkin, BSc
David Wilson, MA

Classics:
*Simon Allcock, MA
Dr Rob Cromarty, MA, PhD
Dr Matthew Johncock, MA, PhD
Dr Emma Ramsey, BA, MA, PhD
Miss Caitlin Spencer, BA
Miss Becky Todd, BA

Computer Science:
*Jonathan Hooper, LLB, PG Dip
Paul Jennings, BSc

Dance:
*Mrs Caroline Kenworthy, BA
*Mrs Clare Cooke

Design, Engineering & Technology:
*James Inglis, BEng
Mark Ellwood, BEd
Martin Thomas, BEng Hons, PhD
Sam Wilson, BSc

Drama:
*Miss Jo Brayton, BA
Mrs Katie Hamilton, BA (*LAMDA*)
Alexander Mancuso, BA
Jim Russell, BA

Economics:
*Dushy Clarke, BA, MSc
Mrs Emmie Bidston, BA
Mrs Amanda Campion, MA
Chris Ewart, MA (*Careers)
Simon Roundell, MA
†Iain J Sutcliffe, MA, MBA
Mrs Julia Sutcliffe, BA (*Middle School)
John Whitworth, BA

English:
*Ms Estella Gutulan, BA
Ms Denise Brown, MA
John Craig, MA
Miss Sarah Donarski, BA
Tim Grant, MA
Tim Head, BA

Carl Hendrick, MA
Miss Rachael Kirby, BA
Dr Ruth Lexton, BA, MPhil, PhD
Miss Erynn Oliver, MA
Miss Kirsty Tyrrell, BA
Mrs Jo Wayman, BA
†Tom Wayman, BA, MPhil

Geography:
*Timothy Rothwell, MA
Jim Dewes, MA
Christopher Foyle, BA
Jack Murray, BA
Miss Alice Taylor, BA

History:
*Ben Lewsley, BA
Dr Victoria Gardner, BA, MLitt, DPhil
†Sam Gutteridge, MA
Philip Joy, MA
Tristan Macleod, BA
Matthew Pattie, MA
Miss Lucy Robb, MA

Mathematics:
*Aidan Sproat, MA
Richard Atherton, BSc, MPhil (*IB*)
Nick Carpenter, BSc
†Mike Cawdron, BSc
†Alexis Christodoulou, MA
Paul Cootes, MA, MSc (*3rd Form*)
Miss Clare Edwards, BA
Miss Helen Gray, BSc
Bob Jones, BSc
Edward Jones, BA, MSc
Kyle McDonald, BSc
John Rawlinson, BSc
Qasim Sayed, MPhys, MEd
Ms Jessica Van Driesen, MA
George Wells, BA
Ben White, MEng
†Jonathan White, BA

Modern Languages:
*Dr Rachelle Kirkham, MA, PhD
†Miss Sarah Brookes
Mrs Sandrine Duff, MA
†David Edwards, BA
Ms Aurora Gomez, BA
†Mrs Polly Gutteridge, MA
†Mrs Sophie Jobson, Lic d'Anglais, Dip d'Étude IFI
Mrs Katie Johnston, BA, MMus
Simon Kirkham, BA (*German*)
Miss Charlotte Le Bihan, Double Licence, Provence
   (*French*)
Mrs Ningning Ma, MA
Allan McPherson, MA, MSc
Charles Oliphant-Callum, MA
†Sam Owen, BA
Oliver Peat, BA
Mrs Yunyun Tang, MA
Mrs Catherine Willis-Phillips, BA (*Spanish*)
Alexander Young, BA
Mrs Camilla Young, BA

Music:
*Simon Williamson, MA, FRCO (*Director of Music &
   Arts*)
Nick Burrage, BA
George de Voil, BA
Sean Farrell, BA
Mrs Libby Fisher, BA
Jonathan Heeley, MMus

Mrs Susanne Henwood, GRSM Hons, LRAM, ALCM
Jeff Oakes, ARCM

Philosophy & Religion:
*Tom Kirby, BA, MSt
James Ellis, BA
Mrs Jessica Goves, BA
Dr James Tapley, BSc, MA, PhD (*Theory of Knowledge*)
Dr Guy Williams, MA, DPhil (*Upper School*)

Physical Education:
*Steve Shortland, BEd, MSc (*Director of Sport*)
Murray Barratt, BA
Ms Adele Brown, BEd
Mrs Jane Grillo, BEd (*PE*)
†Phillip Mann, BSc
Dan Pratt, MSc
Mrs Kate Pratt, BSc
†Charlie Sutton, BA
Ryan Tulley, BA, BSc

Physics:
*Adam Hicks, MEng
Edward Bull, MSci
Mrs Tamara Christodoulou, BA
Ian Frayne, BSc
Dr Will Heathcote, MPhys, DPhil
Tim Holmes, MSc
Dr Dane Tice, BA, DPhil
Mike Yuan, BA, MSc

Politics:
*Dibran Zeqiri, BA, MSc
Dr Anthony Coates, BA, MA, PhD
Daniel Richards, BA Hons

Psychology:
Miss Sophia Candappa, BSc
†Keith Reesby, MSc

Wellbeing:
*Ian Morris, BA
Gareth Carr

Academic Support:
*Mrs Kam Opie, BA, MA
†Dan Clements
Mrs Debbie Hathaway, BSc
Ms Sarah Thurston, BSc Hons, MBA
Mrs Ginette Vonchek, BEd, Cert TEFL, Cert IELTS (*EAL*)

plus 50 visiting instrumental teachers

Houses and Housemasters/mistresses:
Anglesey: Mrs Rachel Loaring
Apsley: Alexis Christodoulou
Benson: Dan Clements
Beresford: Keith Reesby
Blücher: Sam Owen
Combermere: Miss Sarah Brookes
Hardinge: Mrs Sophie Jobson
Hill: Phillip Mann
Hopetoun: Mrs Polly Gutteridge and Sam Gutteridge
Lynedoch: Mike Cawdron
Murray: Iain Sutcliffe
Orange: Tom Wayman
Picton: David Edwards
Raglan: Nicholas Light
Stanley: Charlie Sutton
Talbot: Jonathan White
Wellesley: Mrs Kate Harrison

CC CCF: Ian Frayne, BSc
Group Finance Director & Bursar: Stephen Crouch, BA,
   ACA
Director of Finance: Paul Thompson, MA, ACMA

Works & Estates Bursar: Malcolm Callender, MBA, FCMI, MCGI, MinstRE

Head of the Wellington Community: Murray Lindo, BA, MA, MSc, CIPD

Legal & Compliance Director: Mrs Katherine Baker, MA

Operations Bursar: Brian Cannon, MSyl, MCGI

Medical Officer: Dr Anant Sachdev, MB ChB, CFP, D Pall Med

Health Centre Sister: Mrs Bev Gilbert

Registrar: Mrs Louise Peate, BSc

EA to the Master: Mrs Angela Reed

PA to the Second Master: Ms Emma Davies

Bursary Assistant: Mrs Lisa Thompson

Wellington School

South St, Wellington, Somerset TA21 8NT

Tel: 01823 668800
Fax: 01823 668844
email: admissions@wellington-school.org.uk
website: www.wellington-school.org.uk
Twitter: @wellingtonsch1
Facebook: @WellingtonSchool

Motto: *Nisi dominus frustra*

Founded in 1837, Wellington School is a co-educational, academically selective school providing a friendly, disciplined environment and a wide range of co-curricular opportunities.

Situation. Located on the southern edge of Wellington, at the foot of the Blackdown Hills, this fully co-educational School is equidistant from Tiverton Parkway and Taunton Railway Stations. The M5 approach road (Junction 26) is within a mile. Currently there are 600 pupils in the Lower and Upper Schools (11–18 years), of whom 20% board.

Buildings. The School has witnessed an extensive building programme over recent years with a state-of-the-art study centre in the Duke's Building, brand new floodlit all-weather hockey pitch and refurbished cafe.

The John Kendall-Carpenter Science Centre has state-of-the-art laboratories and lecture theatre, a multimillion pound sports complex, a purpose-built Prep School and a new classroom block and examination hall. Major improvements to Performing Arts facilities, including a new foyer and theatre space, were completed in 2010. In 2017 a new junior girls' boarding house with en-suite rooms was opened.

Grounds. There are 35 acres of playing fields as well as a new floodlit all-weather hockey pitch, squash courts, an indoor swimming pool and a climbing wall.

Houses. There are separate Day Houses for boys and girls in Upper and Lower School, with many inter-house competitions. In addition, there are 5 boarding houses in total.

There is a central Dining Hall and all meals are served on a cafeteria basis. The School also has its own well equipped laundry.

There is a fully equipped Health Centre, with a trained staff under the direction of the School Medical Officer.

Academic Organisation. The School is divided into the Upper School (Year 9–Sixth Form) and the Lower School (Years 7 and 8). The Prep School (Nursery–Year 6) is on a separate, adjoining campus.

Most pupils enter the School at Year 7, 9 or 12. The curriculum in Years 7, 8 and 9 is designed to allow pupils to develop the skills needed to succeed at GCSE and features a good range of practical and more academic subjects including Latin. At GCSE all pupils study English, English Literature and Mathematics as well as a Modern Foreign Language and a further five or six subjects. Pupils have a free choice of studying three sciences separately or as Dual Award Science. The Mathematics and Science courses lead to IGCSE qualifications. The most able mathematicians take IGCSE at the end of Year 10 before taking Additional Mathematics in Year 11. Students have a free choice from a wide range of subjects in the Sixth Form as well as the Extended Project Qualification. A system of grades every term and tutor groups ensure that academic monitoring of pupils is supportive and effective.

Religious Education is part of the curriculum in the Lower School and is an option that at GCSE and A Level. The School is Christian in tradition and there is a short Act of Worship in the School Chapel on each weekday with a longer Sunday service. The content and form of these services are based on contemporary Anglican procedures. Attendance is expected although sensitivity is shown towards pupils of other faiths for whom alternative provision can be made.

Music. Tuition is available on all orchestral instruments, as well as piano, organ, drum kit and percussion, classical and electric guitars and voice. The department consists of 2 full-time, 1 part-time and 25 specialist instrumental staff. The School is an All Steinway School and facilities include a fine Steinway model D Concert Grand Piano. There is a large Rodgers Digital Organ in the Chapel. Some 30 ensembles rehearse each week, giving plentiful opportunities to performers of all ages and all instruments. The department currently runs 7 choirs of various kinds and styles from the renowned Chapel Choir to the lighter sounds of Girlforce9. Concerts of all kinds take place throughout each term and the Wellington Professional Concerts Series bring world class musicians to the School to give recitals and masterclasses. Pupils are entered for ABRSM, Trinity Guildhall and Rockschool exams each term.

Physical Education and Games. New Sport and Wellbeing Department in 2016 with all pupils playing games regularly, unless exempt for medical reasons. Wellbeing, which is also part of the curriculum for Years 7 to 11, takes place in the Sports Complex and includes nutrition, psychology and mental health alongside activities such as judo, zumba and body-pump with the aim of embedding physical activity as part of a healthy lifestyle. All pupils learn to swim and are given the opportunity to take part in as many sports as possible. In the winter term, rugby and hockey are the main sports; in the spring term hockey, netball and cross-country running; in the summer term athletics, girls and boys cricket, tennis and swimming. Team practices take place throughout the week with matches on Saturday afternoons. The Sports Complex houses a purpose-built fencing salle.

Out of School and CCF Activities. All pupils from Year 10 upwards either join the large CCF contingent, with army, naval and RAF sections, or are engaged in volunteering activities on a weekly basis, ranging from community services and conservation, to music, art and creative activities such as producing school radio podcasts. Outdoor Education, both within the CCF and as part of the School's flourishing programme to introduce all students from Year 7 upwards, includes camping trips, Duke of Edinburgh's Award and climbing and caving clubs are very popular, with many trips organised for all year groups. The CCF also has a highly respected Corps of Drums, which frequently features in local ceremonial events. Societies, in addition to the above, include art, chess and drama at various levels, STEM, computing and others.

Careers. A careers and higher education coordinator offers a guidance service including visits to and from employers and universities, a careers speed-dating event, careers talks, a careers networking dinner and careers fair with local schools.

Entry. Entrance exam for Year 7, 9 and Sixth Form. There is a registration fee of £50 for all pupils and a refundable deposit of £400.

Scholarships and Bursaries. A number of academic and sport, drama and art and design scholarships are offered each year for entry at 11+ and 13+. Music scholarships are awarded for entry at 11+, 13+ and above. Awards may be increased by an income-related bursary. A small number of awards are offered for the Sixth Form.

Fees per term (2018–2019). Boarders £9,630–£10,270, Weekly Boarders £7,710–£8,035, International Boarders £9,905–£10,575. Fees include tuition, board, laundry, medical attention and Health Centre and books. Day pupils £4,515–£5,075 (excluding lunch).

Extras. Apart from purely personal expenses, the termly extras are private music lessons from £235 to £290; EAL lessons at various rates depending on need.

Charitable status. Wellington School is a Registered Charity, number 1161447. It aims to provide a happy, caring co-educational day and boarding community, where pupils are provided with the opportunity of making best use of their academic experience and the School enrichment activities, in order to enhance their overall preparation for life after the age of eighteen.

Governing Body:

Chairman: Mrs A Govey, MSc
Joint Vice Chairmen: Mr J Hester and Mrs A Wilson
Prof L la Velle
Dr D Lungley
Mr R Palfrey
Cllr V Stock-Williams
Mr P Tait
Mrs S Vigus-Hollingsworth
Mrs L Wyeth
Mr J Vick

Headmaster: **Mr H W F Price**, MA Oxon

Academic Deputy Head: Dr H Barker, BA Hons, PhD
Deputy Head (*Pastoral*): Mr R MacNeary, BA Hons, MA
Deputy Head (*Co-curricular and IT Strategy*): Mr A Anderson, BA Hons, PGCE
Head of Sixth Form: Mr D Millington, BA, MSc, PGCE
Head of Lower School: Mrs V Richardson, BSc, PGCE
Head of Upper School: Mrs S A Dean, BA, PGCE
Head of Boarding: Mr S James, BA

Academic Staff:
Mr A Anderson, BA, PGCE
Mr C A Askew, BA, PGCE
Mrs K Bishop, BA Hons, MA, PGCE
Mr P J Buckingham, MA, PGCE
Dr L Burgos-Leonagoitia, BA, PhD
Mr C Carruthers, BA, MA, PGCE
Mr A R Carson, BSc, PGCE
Mr J Caulfield, BA, QTS
Mr M Charlton, MA, PGCE
Mrs N Clewes, BEng Hons, PGCE
Mr D A Colclough, BSc, PGCE
Mr M Cole, BEng Hons, PGCE
Miss M Collins, BA, MA, PGCE
Mrs J Cooling, BSc Hons, PGCE
Mr S Costello, BA Hons, PGCE
Mrs V Daley, BSc, PGCE
Mrs C Davies, BA, PGCE
Mrs S A Dean, BSc, PGCE
Mr M E Downes, BSc, PGCE
Mrs S D'Rozario BA, MA, PGCE

Mr G Durston, BSc Hons
Mr T Fasham, BSc, PGCE
Mrs C Foster, BA Hons
Dr P T Galley, BSc, DIC, PhD, PGCE
Mr W Garrett, BA, PGCE
Mr E Grey, BSc Hons, PGCE, Prof GCE
Mrs S Harrod-Booth, BEng, PGCE, MA
Mr C Hamilton, MChem, ACA, PGCE
Mrs I Hare, BA Hons, PGCE
Miss F E Hobday, MA
Dr K A Hodson, BA, MA
Mr G Horner, BA
Mr B House, BSc
Miss M Jago, BA
Mr S W James, BA, PGCE
Dr A R Jolliffe, BA, MA, DPhil
Mr S Jones, BSc, PGCE
Mrs T Kaya, BA, TESOL
Mr P Lawrence
Mr J-M Legg, BA, PGCE
Mr J Leonard, BA
Mrs L E Leonard, BA
Mrs L MacAlister, BA Hons
Miss R L Marsden, BA, PGCE
Mr R Marsh, BA, PGCE
Mrs E McCormack, BSc, PGCE
Dr G Meredith, BSc, PhD, PGSC
Miss S Middleton, BA, PGCE
Mr D Millington, BA, MSc, PGCE
Mr A Moy, BSc Hons, PGCE
Mr R Newsome, BA
Mrs M Payne, BA Hons, BTEC, PGCE
Mr A Phillips, BSc, PGCE
Mr N Renyard, MSc, BA, PGCE
Miss H Richards, BSc Hons, QTS
Mrs V K Richardson, BSc, PGCE
Mrs T Robertson, BA Hons, MPhil, PGCE
Mr C J Sampson, BMus
Mrs A Sands, MA Hons, PGCE
Miss K Sass, BA Hons, PGCE
Mr A C Shaw, BA, MSci, PGCE, LCGI
Mrs R Shaw, LTCL, GTCL
Mr K Smaldon, BA, PGCE
Mr N S Smith, BSc, PGCE
Mr R E Stevens, BSocSc, PGCE
Mrs L Tabb, BSc, PGCE
Miss H Tarver, MEng, PGCE
Miss A Tatham, BSc, PGCE
Miss S F L Toase, BSc, MSB, CBiol, PGCE
Mr A J Trewhella, BA, ARCO
Mr A Wilson, BA

Bursar: Mr T D Williams, BA, FCCA
Registrar: Mrs R Debenham, BA, FCIPD
Medical Officer: Dr R Yates

Wells Cathedral School

The Liberty, Wells, Somerset BA5 2ST

Tel:	01749 834200
Fax:	01749 834201
email:	admissions@wells.cathedral.school
website:	www.wells-cathedral-school.com

In 909AD there was a Cathedral School in Wells providing education for choir boys. Today, Wells Cathedral School is fully co-educational. Its spirit is a passion for learning and life; its dream an inspiring education set in a musically alive and beautiful environment as a brilliant foundation for life; and its focus, inspiring success.

There is a senior and junior school with 760 boys and girls aged from 2 to 18. Boarders number 300, whilst the remainder are day pupils. Once accepted, a child normally remains in the school without further Entrance Examination until the age of 18+.

Fees per term (2018–2019). Sixth Form (Years 12–13): Boarders £10,488, Day £6,267. Upper School (Years 10–11): Boarders £10,255, Day £6,124. Lower School (Years 7–9): Boarders £9,874, Day £5,919. Junior School (Years 3–6): Boarders £8,679; Day £5,125; Pre-Prep £3,406; Reception £2,547. Nursery: Morning with lunch £19; Afternoon with lunch £23; Afternoon £19; All day with lunch £33.

Scholarships and Bursaries. Scholarships and academic awards are made at 11+, 13+ and 14+ to those who show outstanding ability in the Entrance Assessment Tests held in late January at the school. Specialist gifts or aptitudes (e.g. sport, drama, art) are also considered. Sixth form academic, sporting, creative and all-rounder awards are made following the scholarship assessment day in November. Awards are given on the basis of performance in the assessment, rigorous interview, predicted GCSE results and a confidential reference from the applicant's current school. The value of the awards will depend on individual financial circumstances.

Means-tested specialist mathematics awards are available at 11+ for outstandingly gifted mathematicians.

A number of music awards are available depending upon the standard and quality of applicants and individual financial circumstances. Music auditions are held three times a year.

In addition, the school is one of only four in England designated by the Department for Education providing specialist musical education. The DfE therefore provides generous assistance (up to 100% of fees) with tuition, boarding and music fees for up to 78 gifted musicians, grants being linked to parental income, under the DfE Music & Dance Scheme.

Cathedral choristerships and bursaries, which can provide up to 25% of boarding and tuition fees, are awarded annually to boys between the ages of 8 and 10. Choral trials and academic entrance tests take place in January. Special arrangements can be made for children from overseas. School bursaries to the value of 10% of tuition fees are available for girl choristers. Supplementary means-tested bursaries are also available.

Ex-chorister bursaries: On ceasing to be a chorister, boys and girls are eligible for an ex-chorister bursary up to the value of 8% of tuition or boarding fees.

For further details of awards contact the Admissions team, Tel: 01749 834213, email: admissions@wells.cathedral.school.

Situations and Buildings. The mediaeval city of Wells, with its famous Cathedral and a population of only 10,500, is the smallest city in England. It is just over 20 miles from Bath and Bristol where there is a good rail service, and easily accessed from the M4 and M5 motorways. Bristol International Airport is a 40-minute drive away. The school occupies all but one of the canonical houses in The Liberty, keeping its mediaeval and 18th century atmosphere whilst providing for the needs of modern boarding education. There are modern classrooms and science laboratories built amongst walled gardens. A sports hall provides indoor facilities for tennis, badminton, cricket, basketball, volleyball, hockey, five-a-side football, climbing and multi-gym. There are theatrical and concert facilities, including a brand new award-winning concert hall, a music technology centre, a computer studies centre, art, design and technology department, drama studio, dance studio, library, sixth form centre,

25-metre covered swimming pool, tennis and netball courts, brand new astroturf pitch, three sports fields and an all-weather hard play area.

There are nine boarding houses, one for junior boarders, one for sixth form boarders and a further seven in the senior school, three for boys and four for girls, the most senior pupils having study-bedrooms. The aim is to give security to the younger and to develop a sense of responsibility in the older.

Organisation and Curriculum. Despite its national and international reputation, the school has retained close links with the local community, and its fundamental aim is to provide all its pupils with an education consistent with the broad principles of Christianity. More specifically, the school aims to be a well-regulated community in which pupils may learn to live in harmony and mutual respect with each other and with the adults who care for them. The curriculum has been designed to enable all children who gain entry to the school to develop fully all their abilities, and to take their place in due course in tertiary education and the adult community of work and leisure. Forms are limited to a maximum of 25; average class sizes are typically less than this.

The emphasis is on setting by ability in particular subjects rather than streaming. There is every attempt to avoid early specialisation. There is a sixth form of some 200 taking A Level courses in all major academic subjects.

The majority of pupils take up places at Russell Group Universities, with about 5–6 places regularly offered by Oxford and Cambridge; whilst musicians are regularly awarded scholarships to the top music colleges each year.

Societies. There is a wide range of indoor and outdoor activities in which pupils must participate, although the choice is theirs. Outdoor education is an important part of the curriculum. Besides a Combined Cadet Force with Army, Navy and RAF sections and a Duke of Edinburgh's Award scheme, activities as diverse as photography, sailing and golf are also on offer. Ballet and riding lessons can also be arranged.

Music. The school is one of four in England designated and grant-aided by the Department for Education (DfE) to provide special education for gifted young musicians, who are given substantial financial assistance. Wells is unique in that both specialist and non-specialist musicians are able to develop their aptitudes within a normal school environment. These talents are widely acknowledged by audiences at concerts given by pupils from Wells throughout the world.

There are over 200 talented pupils following specially devised timetables which combine advanced instrumental tuition and ensemble work with academic opportunity. More than half of the school learns at least one musical instrument. Violin and cello is taught to all children in the pre-prep as part of the curriculum. Pupils receive the highest quality teaching, often leading to music conservatoires and a career in music. Central to specialist music training are the opportunities to perform in public and there is a full concert diary. There are also regular concerts by the many ensembles in the school.

The Wellensian Association. Old Wellensians, Wells Cathedral School, Wells, Somerset BA5 2ST.

Charitable status. Wells Cathedral School Limited is a Registered Charity, number 310212. It is a charitable trust for the purpose of promoting the cause of education in accordance with the doctrine of the Church of England.

Patron: HRH The Prince of Wales

Governors:
Chairman: The Very Revd Dr John Davies, DL
The Revd Canon Andrew Featherstone, MA
The Reverend Canon Nicholas Jepson-Biddle, BA, MA

Prebendary Helen Ball, OBE
Prebendary Barbara Bates, BA, MA, FRSA
Mr David Brown, OBE, MA
Mr Tim Lewis, BA, FCA
Mr Jonathan Vaughan, Dip RCM Perf, Dip RCM Teach

Headmaster: **Alastair Tighe**, MA

Senior School Head: Dr Andrew Kemp, BA, MA, PGCE
 (*Mathematics*)
Assistant Head (Pastoral Care & Co-Curriculum): Andrew
 Mayhew, BSc (*Mathematics, Football*)
Assistant Head for Digital Strategy: Simon Balderson
 (*Head of Computing*)
Director of Music: Mark Stringer

Senior School

Teaching Staff:
Claudia Alabiso (*Modern Foreign Languages*)
Alison Armstrong, BMus, LRAM, PGCE (*Head of
 Academic Music*)
Martin Ashton, BA, PGCE (*English, Media Studies,
 Housemaster Cedars*)
Jonathan Barnard, BSc Hons, PGCE (*Physics*)
Jeremy Boot, BA, FRGS (*Head Geography, Cricket*)
Neil Bowen, BA, PGCE (*Head of English Faculty*)
Anna Brown (*Head of PSHE*)
John Byrne, Dip Moscow Cons, GRNCM (*Head of
 Keyboard*)
Nicola Connock, BSc, PGCE (*Head of Mathematics
 Operations*)
Jack Coward (*Music*)
Sarah Cowell, BA Hons, CTEFLA (*EAL*)
Andrew Davies, BA, PGCE (*Religion, Philosophy &
 Ethics, Cross country*)
Shelley Deans, MA (*Expressive Arts*)
Paul Denegri, FTCL, LTCL, Hon ARAM (*Head of Brass*)
Jules Desmarchelier, PGCE (*Head of Modern Foreign
 Languages*)
Christopher Eldridge (*Head of History*)
Stuart Elks (*CCF Contingent Commander, Outdoor
 Education and Duke of Edinburgh's Award Coordinator,
 Houseparent Shrewsbury*)
Mandy Fielding, BSc, PGCE, Cert SEN, Dip SpLD (*Head
 of Food Technology*)
Christopher Finch, MA, BMus Hons, LRSM, Dip ABRSM
 (*Head of Music Operations, Head of Vocal Studies*)
Janice Gearon, BA, MA, PGCE (*English*)
Penny Hall (*Religion, Philosophy & Ethics, Learning
 Support*)
Dominic Hansom, BMus, LRSM, ARCM (*Head of
 Accompaniment*)
Stephen Harvey (*Private Learning Coordinator*)
Ken Humphreys, BSc, PGCE (*Chemistry*)
Margaret Humphreys, BA, PGCE, AMBDA (*Modern
 languages French, German, Learning Support*)
Teresa Jarman, BA, QTS (*Economics & Business*)
Lisa Jarvis (*PE & Sport*)
Marcus Laing, MA, PGCE (*Head of Economics &
 Business*)
Ed Leaker (*Head of Woodwind*)
Catherine Lord, ARCM, Juilliard Diploma (*Senior Violin*)
James Mayes (*History, Classics, Latin and Head of
 Hockey*)
James Moretti (*Mathematics*)
Robin Murdoch, BA, MA, PGCE (*Mathematics*)
Dr Hilary Murphy, MA, BMus, LRAM, PhD, PGCE (*Head
 of Creative Arts Faculty, Academic Music*)
Eliana Nelson, BA Hons, QTS, CertEd (*Graphics,
 Photography*)
Jayne Obradovic, LTCL (*Head of Percussion*)
Keith Orchard, BSc (*Science, Physics*)

Kenneth Padgett, BSc (*Head of Science Faculty, Head of
 Biology, Ten Tors*)
Susie Petvin-Jameson, BSc, PGCE, CSci, FIMA, FCIEA
 (*Director of Specialist Mathematics*)
Lawrence Plum, BA Hons, AKC, PGCE (*Head of Classics,
 CCF*)
Gemma Pritchard, BSc, PGCE (*Sport*)
Jenna Rowland (*Head of Psychology*)
Rebecca Redman (*Housemistress Haversham, Religion,
 Philosophy & Ethics, Geography, CCF*)
David Rowley, BSc, PGCE (*Geography, Geology, Head of
 Year 7 & 8*)
Sally Rowley, BA Hons, PGCE (*English, Head of 6th
 Form*)
Dr Janette Shepherd, BSc, PhD (*Biology, Housemistress
 Edwards*)
Ellie Smith (*Head of Religion, Philosophy and Ethics*)
Matthew Souter, AGSM, Hon ARAM (*Strings*)
Linzi Stockdale Bridson, BA, PGCE (*Head of Art &
 Design, Graphics and Photography, Lower School
 skiing*)
Mark Stringer (*Director of Music*)
Ben Taylor, MA, PGCE (*Higher Education and Careers
 Advisor, French, Italian, NQT Supervisor*)
Damian Todres (*Head of Drama & Theatre Studies*)
Laurence Whitehead, BA, MA, GGSMD, PGCE
Lara Williams (*English*)

Junior School

Head of Junior School: Julie Barrow, BEd (*PSHE
 Coordinator*)
Deputy Head: Karl Gibson, Dip Teach, BEd (*Science
 Coordinator*)

Rebecca Allen, BSc, QTS (*EYFS Teacher*)
Steve Bratt, BEd (*Head of Sport & PE*)
Kate Dennis, BEd (*KS2*)
Jill Edmonds, BSc, ALCM (*Head of Music*)
Kelly Fairey, BEd (*PP teacher*)
Valerie Hancock (*Early Years*)
Kateley Kinnersley (*KS1*)
Charlotte Leatherby (*Junior School Teacher*)
Emma Morley, BEd (*Teacher*)
Fiona Shaw (*KS1*)
Emily Spencer (*Junior School Teacher*)
Lesley Wanklyn (*Junior School Teacher*)
Jonathan Ward, BSc, PGCE (*Mathematics Coordinator*)
Rosie Warner, BA QTS (*History Coordinator*)

Bursar and Clerk to the Governors: P Knell
Admissions Registrar: J Prestige
Head's PA: Mrs C Edwards
Publicity Manager: Mrs K Chantrey, BSc Hons
School Doctor: Dr C Bridson, MB BS, MRCGP, DipOCC,
 MED

West Buckland School

Barnstaple, Devon EX32 0SX

Tel:	01598 760000
Fax:	01598 760546
email:	headmaster@westbuckland.com
website:	www.westbuckland.com
Twitter:	@westbuckland
Facebook:	@wbsdevon
LinkedIn:	/westbuckland

Motto: '*Read and Reap*'

West Buckland School is an independent day and boarding school set in 90 acres of beautiful North Devon countryside in the South West of England. Founded in 1858, the school has always stressed the importance of all-round character development alongside good academic achievement. Our size allows pupils to receive plenty of individual care and attention to their needs and talents.

West Buckland Preparatory School educates children between the ages of three and eleven. There is strong cooperation and support between the schools which share the same grounds, so making the transition as easy as possible.

West Buckland is fully co-educational.

Situation. The School stands in 90 acres of beautiful North Devon countryside on the edge of Exmoor. Barnstaple is 10 miles away and the M5 motorway can be reached in 35 minutes. Boarders arriving by train at Exeter station are met by coaches.

Buildings and Grounds. The central range of buildings, dating from 1861, still forms the focus of the school, and now includes a performing arts centre. Other developments include a Sixth Form Centre, Mathematics and Physics Centre, boarding houses for boys and girls, a Preparatory School classroom block and the ICT Centre. The campus offers outstanding sports facilities, including a 9-hole golf course, an indoor heated 25-metre swimming pool, and an Astroturf hockey pitch. The Jonathan Edwards Sports Centre opened in 2008 and the award-winning 150 Building for Art, Design Technology and a Theatre opened in 2010. A new study centre for all senior school pupils and a co-educational Sixth Form boarding house with single en-suite bedrooms opened in 2015.

Admission. Boys and girls are admitted as boarders or day pupils. The present number of pupils is: 120 boarding, 502 day.

Entrance to the Preparatory School is by interview and assessment of school reports. Entry to the Senior School is by assessment or to the Sixth Form upon interview, GCSE results and school report.

Fees per term (2018–2019). Senior: Full Boarding £8,115–£10,240, Flexi/Weekly Boarding £1,040 (4 nights), Day £5,020. Preparatory: Day £2,690–£4,085. Nursery: Government-funded places under Early Years Entitlement are available up to 15 hours per week during term time. £4.00 per hour thereafter.

Scholarships and Bursaries. A number of scholarships are awarded for entry at 11+ or 16+ (value at the discretion of the Headmaster). Candidates must be under 12, or 17 years of age on 1st September following the assessments which take place between November and January.

Academic Scholarships at 11+ are based on results of entrance assessment in November and January for entry the following September.

Assessment for Academic Awards at 16+ are in November – see our website for details.

Music and Art scholarships are available for entry at 11+ and Sports scholarships at 11+ and 16+. Details and deadlines are available on our website.

With the support of the West Buckland School Foundation, means-tested bursaries are available for boarders and day students at all ages.

Curriculum. In the Preparatory School the main emphasis is upon well-founded confidence in English and Mathematics, within a broad balance of subjects that adds modern languages to the national curriculum. Particular attention is given to the development of sporting, artistic and musical talents.

In the Senior School breadth is complemented by specialisation. All students study the three separate sciences from Year 7, while both French and Spanish are the principal languages offered from Year 7. Our flexible options arrangements at GCSE respond to students' individual strengths and preferences. A wide range of A Level subjects is offered to sixth formers whose results uphold the high academic standards of the School.

Careers. The Careers Staff advise all pupils upon the openings and requirements for different careers. They make full use of the facilities offered by Connexions.

Games, The Performing Arts and other activities. One of the most impressive features of life at West Buckland is the quality and range of extracurricular activities, with a high level of involvement from pupils and staff.

The school has a strong sporting tradition. Rugby, hockey, cricket, netball, tennis, athletics, swimming, cross-country, squash, golf, shooting, badminton, basketball and many other sports offer opportunities for inter-school and inter-house competition and for recreation.

About a third of all pupils receive instrumental and singing tuition from specialist teachers. The wide range of choirs and instrumental groups give concerts at least once a week throughout the year. Drama is strength of the school with productions of many kinds throughout the year. The Performing Arts are complemented by the exceptional facilities provided by the school's award-winning 150 Building which houses an impressive studio theatre.

Music. Over 120 members of the school receive instrumental tuition on all instruments. They are encouraged to perform in concerts, in choirs and instrumental groups. Music Technology is also a strong feature of the department's work.

Outdoor Education. Much use is made of the proximity of Exmoor and the coast for climbing, kayaking, mountain biking, surfing and other adventurous activities. All pupils receive instruction in camp craft, first aid and map reading. The Combined Cadet Force has Army and Royal Air Force sections, and offers a range of challenging pursuits. Our students succeed at all levels in The Duke of Edinburgh's Award scheme each year, and there is a regular programme of expeditions in this country and overseas.

Religion. The tradition is Anglican but the school welcomes children from all denominations and faiths – or none. Services of worship are held on a regular basis at East Buckland Church.

Attitudes and values. The School sets out to be a friendly and purposeful community in which happiness and a sense of security are the foundation on which young lives are built. At all levels members of the school are asked to lead a disciplined way of life, to show consideration for others, to be willing to be challenged and to recognise that the success of the individual and the success of the group are inextricably linked.

Charitable status. West Buckland School is a Registered Charity, number 1167545. Its purpose is the education of boys and girls from 3 to 18.

The Governing Body:

Patron: P D Orchard-Lisle, CBE, TD, DL LLD [hc], DSc [hc], MA, FRICS

President: The Countess of Arran, MBE, DL

Vice Presidents:
Lady Gass, JP, MA
W H G Geen

Chairman: J M H Light, LLB

Vice Chairmen:
Mrs L Cairns, BA Joint Hons

Governors:
A Boggis, MA, PGCE

Dr R J Fisher-Smith, BA, MA, PGCE, PhD
Mr J Hall
R A Ingram, MA, PGCE
A Jackson
N Kingdon, BDS, MOrthRCS
J Palk
Mrs M A Read, BA Hons
Mrs S C E Salvidant, BEd Hons
P Stucley, BA Hons
K Underwood
Mr J Wilson
Mrs N J Wild, BA Hons, MRICS
Mr G C James
Mr I Blewett

Headmaster: **Mr Phillip Stapleton**, BSc, MA Durham, MBA, PGCE, MRSC

Deputy Head: D M Hymer, BSc University College London

Director of Studies: C J Burrows, MA Exeter College Oxford

Deputy Head Pastoral: Mrs C Pettingell

Headmaster, Preparatory School: N Robinson, MSc

Bursar: B Login, MA, MBA, FCIS, MBIFM

Head of Sixth Form & Careers: Mr M Brimson

Day Houses & Housemasters/mistresses:
Brereton House: Dr E N D Grew, PhD Exeter
Courtenay House: C J Allin, BA Leicester
Fortescue House: Ms K Venner, BSc Loughborough
Grenville House: Mrs R L Thompson, BA Aberystwyth

Boarding:
Head of Boarding: Mr M F Robinson

Houseparents:

Parker's (Sixth Form):
Mrs M Robinson
Mrs A Booker
J Conlon

Boyer (Boys):
S Morrison
Mrs K Turner

Bamfylde (Girls):
Ms K Bondy
Mrs A Melchior

Admissions Manager: Mrs M Tennant
Headmaster's PA: Mrs S Small
Librarian: Miss L Warrillow
Medical Officer: Dr C A Gibb, BMed, BM, DA, MRCGP, DRCOG, DPD

Westminster School

17 Dean's Yard, Westminster, London SW1P 3PB

Tel: 020 7963 1042 (Head Master)
          020 7963 1003 (Registrar)
          020 7963 1000 (Other enquiries)
          020 7821 5788 (Westminster Under School)
Fax: 020 7963 1002
email: registrar@westminster.org.uk
website: www.westminster.org.uk
Twitter: @wschool

Motto: '*Dat Deus Incrementum*'

Westminster School is a Boarding and Day School which is co-educational in the Sixth Form. The present number of boys and girls is 760.

The School traces its origins to the school that was attached to the Benedictine Abbey at Westminster. Queen Elizabeth I re-founded the School in 1560 as part of the College of St Peter at Westminster.

The Queen's Scholars. An examination (The Challenge) is held annually to elect The Queen's Scholars who board in College, one of our 6 boarding houses. There are a total of 48 Queen's Scholars, with 12 chosen every year: eight boys at age 13 and four girls at age 16. The fee for a Queen's Scholar is set at half way between 50% of the boarding fee and the day fee. Boys who do not wish to board may be candidates for the title of Honorary Scholar. Up to 5 exhibitions may be awarded each year to those who narrowly miss being offered a scholarship. Boys, who must be under 14 on 1st September of their year of entry, sit The Challenge at Westminster School in late April or early May. The examination consists of papers in Mathematics, English, French, Science, Latin, History, Geography and an optional Greek paper. A scholarship, which is not means-tested, is normally tenable for 5 years.

Application forms and past papers may be obtained from The Admissions Administrator (13+ Entry) (tel: 020 7963 1003, email: registrar@westminster.org.uk).

The value of a scholarship may be supplemented by a bursary (remission of the fees) up to a maximum of 100% if there is proven financial need. Parents who wish to apply for financial assistance should request a Bursary Application Form from the Registrar.

Music Scholarships. Up to eight 13+ and four 16+ music scholarships worth 10% of the day fee may be awarded annually These may be supplemented by additional means-tested bursaries to a maximum of the full fees. There are also several Music Exhibitions which provide for free music tuition on two instruments.

Applications for 13+ close on 1st December and the auditions take place in late January. Candidates, who must be under 14 years of age on the following 1st September, must subsequently take either the Common Entrance or gain admission through the Scholarship Examination, The Challenge.

Applications for 16+ close on 5 October and the auditions take place in late November at the same time as the academic entry interviews. The Dean and Chapter of Westminster Abbey also kindly support a 16+ Henry Purcell Organ Scholarship at Westminster School worth 10% of the current day fees.

The Director of Music is happy to give informal advice to potential candidates and it is recommended that an informal audition is arranged before submitting an application. Please contact the Music Administrator on 020 7963 1017.

Music Scholarships are also available at Westminster Under School at 11+.

For further information on all Scholarships, please contact the Registrar.

Bursaries. Westminster School has made it possible, since its first foundation, for academically able pupils to attend the School who would not otherwise have been able to do so without financial support. Bursaries (remission of fees) up to a maximum of 100% are available and are awarded according to individual need following a full financial assessment, which may include a home visit, to pupils who gain a place on academic merit. Bursaries are awarded at 13 + and 16+ entry to Westminster School and at 11+ entry to Westminster Under School. All bursaries continue until a pupil leaves the School at 18, although they may be adjusted up or down if financial circumstances change.

Parents who wish to apply for financial assistance should request a Bursary Application Form from the Registrar at Westminster School (tel: 020 7963 1003) or Westminster Under School (tel: 020 7821 5788).

Admission. The two main points of admission are 13+ (boys only) and 16+ (girls and boys). Parents should register their sons for 13+ entry by the start of Year 6 – the academic year of a child's 11th birthday. In the Autumn Term of Year 6, the boy will take the ISEB Common Pre-Tests in Mathematics, English and Verbal and Non-Verbal Reasoning. Selected boys will be invited to Westminster School for interview during the Spring Term. On the basis of the candidate's test results, the interview and a report from his present school a decision will be made whether to offer an unconditional place. This unconditional offer is on the expectation of continued good conduct and academic progress at their existing prep school, including an unreserved reference of support from their school in year 8. Candidates who are not offered an unconditional place may be placed on a waiting list and they may sometimes be invited to sit further tests at the end of year 7. Registration for 16+ entry opens in the summer a year before entry. Entry is by competitive examination and interview at the School in November. Candidates choose four entry examination subjects, usually the four subjects they plan to take for A Level. For further information about entry at 13+ or 16+ or to arrange a visit to the School please telephone 020 7963 1003. Please see the school's website www.westminster.org.uk for details of open days.

Fees per term (2018–2019). Boarding: £13,084, £7,800 (Queen's Scholars). Day Pupils (inclusive of lunch): £9,058, £9,903 (entry at Sixth Form).

Preparatory Department (Day Boys only). The Under School has 286 pupils; entry is at 7, 8 and 11. All enquiries should be addressed to the Master (Mr M O'Donnell), Westminster Under School, Adrian House, 27 Vincent Square, London SW1P 2NN (tel: 020 7821 5788).

(*For further details, see entry in IAPS section.*)

Charitable status. St Peter's College (otherwise known as Westminster School) is a Registered Charity, number 312728. The school was established under Royal Charter for the provision of education.

Visitor: Her Majesty The Queen

Governing Body:
Chairman: The Dean of Westminster, The Very Reverend Dr John Hall (*Chairman*)
The Dean of Christ Church, The Very Reverend Professor Martyn Percy
The Master of Trinity, Sir Gregory Winter, CBE, FRS
The Reverend Canon Jane Sinclair, MA, BA
The Reverend Canon David Stanton
Professor Maggie Dallman, OBE
Mr Michael Baughan [OW]
Mr Christopher Foster [OW]
Dr Priscilla Chadwick, MA, FRSA
Professor Sir Christopher Edwards, MD, FRCP, FRCPEd, FRSE, FMedSci, HonDSc
Dr Alan Borg, CBE, FSA [OW]
Sir Peter Ogden
Mr Richard Neville-Rolfe, MA [OW]
Dame Judith Mayhew Jonas DBE
Mr Mark Batten [OW]
Ms Joanna Reesby
Mrs Ina De [OW]
Mr Edward Cartwright [OW]
Mr Tony Little, FRSA
Ms Emily Reid [OW]

[OW] *Old Westminster*

Secretary to the Governing Body and Bursar: M Walsh

Head Master: P S J Derham, MA (*History*)

Under Master: J H Kazi, MA (*English*)

Deputy Head (*Academic*): R R Harris, MA (*Geography*)

Deputy Head (*Co-curricular*): N Page, BA (*French, Russian and Spanish*)

Deputy Head (*Boarding & Community*): J J Kemball, BSc (*Biology*)

Head of Upper School: Miss C M Leech, MA (*French and Spanish*)

Director of Teaching and Learning: P Sharp, MA, MSc (*Physics*)

Assistant Staff:
* *Head of Department/Subject*
R Agyare-Kwabi, MSc, PhD (*Electronics)
E Alaluusua, MA (*Art*)
J L Allchin, BA MA (*Art*)
H A Aplin, BA, PhD (*Russian)
K Y Au, MMath (*Mathematics*)
S T Bailey, MA (*Theology and Philosophy*)
H L Barton, BA (*History*)
S J Berg, BA (*Spanish)
S G Blache, PhD (*French)
A Bottomley (*Mathematics*)
P A Botton, BSc (*Chemistry*)
M R Bradshaw, MA (*Chemistry*)
G P A Brown, MA, DPhil (*History*)
J H Brown, BA (*Economics*)
M V Bustamante-Jenke, BSc (*Computer Science*)
I T Butler, BA (*Mathematics*)
L Carabantes (*Spanish Assistant*)
P J Chequer, DipPA (**Director of Drama*)
J L Chidgey, BA, MA (*Product Design)
B Choraria, MPhys (*Physics*)
S E Clarkson, MSt (*English, US University Advisor*)
D W F Coles, BSc (*Mathematics*)
T R Cousins, BA, MMath (*Mathematics*)
E T A Coward, BA, MSci (*Chemistry)
S Crow, BA (*Art)
S N Curran, BA (*English*)
M C Davies, MA (*Mathematics)
A J Derham, (*Learning Support*)
T E Durno, MA, PhD (*English*)
T P Edlin, MA (*History*) [OW]
R J Evans, PhD (*Biology)
F D Elliot (*Mathematics*)
N A Fair, MA (*Economics*)
A E Farr, MA (*English)
G Franco Castro, BA (*Spanish and French*)
G M French, MSc, MRSC, LTCL, FRSA (*Chemistry*)
W D Galton, BA (*Mathematics*)
T D Garrard, BA (**Director of Music*)
R L L Goodman, BA, MSt (*History of Art*)
A Graham-Brown, BA (*Drama*)
A J Granville, PhD (*German*)
B E J Gravell, BA (*Classics, DofE Award – Gold*)
A K Griffiths, BA, MA (*German and French*)
V Guichard, MA, PhD (*French Assistante*)
P A Hartley, BSc, PhD (*Biology*)
G D Hayter, MMath (*Mathematics*)
D R Hemsley-Brown, BSc, MIEE (**Electronics and Technology*)
R J Hindley, MA, CMath (*Director of IT)
G St J Hopkins, MA (*Registrar; Music*)
O T W Hopwood (*French and German*)
J J Hughes, BSc, MA (*Geography)
R M Huscroft, MA, PhD (*History)

J A Ireland, MA (*Classics*)
K E Ireland, MSc (*Study Skills Coordinator*)
D A Jones, BA (*Classics*)
G K Jones, MA (**French and Russian*)
S M Joyce, BSc (*Biology, Head of Fifth Form*)
N G Kalivas, BSc, DPhil (*Mathematics*)
J D Kershen, MA (**Sport and PE*) [OW]
C M C Kingcombe, BSc (*Biology and Chemistry*)
R A Kowenicki, MA, MSci, PhD (*Chemistry*)
E A Lewis, BA (*Classics*)
Dr J E D Lillington, MA, PhD (*Chemistry, Physics*)
F Lofts, (*Italian*)
L A Lorimer, BA, MA (*Mathematics*)
E Lutton, MSc, MA (*Mathematics*)
L D MacMahon, BA (*German and French*)
G D Mann, BA, MSt (*History, Master of the Queen's Scholars*)
A Marquez, BA (*Spanish Assistant*)
D J McCombie, BA, MSt, DPhil (*Classics*)
P L Michel, MA (*French Assistant*)
J Moore, BA (*Biology*)
L C M Murphy, MA, LLM (*English*)
A E A Mylne, MA (**Classics*)
L J Newton, BSc (*Economics*)
S Page, BA, MSc (**Computer Science*)
T D Page, MA (*Religious Studies*)
M R Parry, MA, PhD (*History*)
H J Prentice, MSci, MA, PhD (**Physics, DofE Award – Silver*)
S E Quintavalle, MA (*Physics*)
C D Riches, BEd, MSc (**PE, Rowing; History*)
M N Robinson, BA (*Chemistry*)
J Rogers (*Japanese*)
S C Savaskan, BA, MMus, DPhil (**Academic Music*)
N J Simons, MMath, DPhil (*Mathematics*)
B J Smith, MA (**Wellbeing, French*)
K W Smith, MA (*Learning Support*)
P C L Smith, BSc (*Mathematics*) [OW]
W T Stockdale, MA (*Geography, Head of Lower Shell*)
L Tattersall, BSc, MA (*Mathematics*)
A Theodosiou, BA (*Modern Greek*)
A C Tolley, BA (*Mathematics*)
J M Tomasi (*Physics*)
K D Tompkins, BA (*English, Head of Public Examinations*)
C J R Ullathorne, MA, MSci (*Physics, *Science*)
R C Wagner, BA, PhD (*Mathematics*)
H E Wagstaff, BA (*Economics*)
R S Wait, MA (*English*)
Dr K A P Walsh, BSc, PhD (*Physics*)
B D Walton, BA (*History of Art*)
H Wang, BSc, MA (*Chinese*)
J A Ward (*Music*)
G D Ward-Smith, MA, PhD (*History*)
G W Warner, (*Arabic*)
The Revd G J Williams, MA (*Chaplain*)
J C Witney, MA, MIL (**Modern Languages*)
J G Woodman, BA (*Art*)
T D W Woodrooffe, BA, BTh, MA (**Theology and Philosophy*)
S D Wurr, BA (*Geography*)

Houses and Housemasters:

Boarding House for Queen's Scholars:
College: G D Mann

Boys' Boarding and Mixed Day Houses
Grant's, 2 Little Dean's Yard: N A Fair
Rigaud's, 1 Little Dean's Yard: Dr R Kowenicki

Mixed Boarding and Mixed Day Houses:
Liddell's, 19 Dean's Yard: Dr R Agyare-Kwabi

Busby's, 26 Great College Street: P A Botton

Girls' Boarding and Mixed Day House:
Purcell's, 22 Great College Street: Dr G D Ward-Smith

Day Houses:
Ashburnham, 6 Dean's Yard: B D Walton
Dryden's, 4 Little Dean's Yard: T P J Edlin
Hakluyt's, 19 Deans' Yard: Mrs L C M Murphy
Milne's, 5A Dean's Yard: Dr P A Hartley
Wren's, 4 Little Dean's Yard: Ms B Choraria

Librarian: Mrs C Goetzee
Archivist: Miss E Wells

Westminster Under School

Master: M O'Donnell, BA, MSc Arch, EdM, PGDE, FRSA
Deputy Master: D R Smith, MA (*History and RS*)
Assistant Master (Pastoral): D S C Bratt, BA (*Maths*)
Assistant Master (Academic): Miss S Wollam, BSc (*Science*)
Assistant Master (Extra-Curricular): M J Woodside, BSc (*Science and History*)

Mrs L Adams, BA, Dip Counselling (*School Counsellor*)
Mrs E-L Allison, BA, MA (*English Support*)
Mrs A C Apaloo, MA (**Religious Studies*)
I Baillie, ACTC, MBA, Pg Dip Adv Net (*ICT Consultant*)
Ms E Beauclerk, MA, BA (*Teaching Assistant*)
A J P Busk, Dip Fine Art (*Art, Games*)
O T Campbell Smith, MA, MSc (**Geography, Head of Year 8*)
C R Candy, MA (*French, English, 8C Form Teacher*)
Mrs L R Chacksfield, BA, MA (**PSHE, English*)
Miss S E K Corps, BSc (*Science*)
P Daly BA, MA (**Classics, Games, 7D Form Teacher*)
A J Downey, BA, MA (*Latin, Greek, Games*)
Miss M E Ellis, BEd (**Mathematics, Games, 8E Form Teacher*)
G Gougay, BA (*French, Games, 6G Form Teacher*)
I D Hepburn, BA, MA (**Director of Sport, 6H Form Teacher*)
C H W Hill, MA (**Drama, English*)
G K Horridge, PhD (**History, Games, 8H Form Teacher*)
Ms F M Illingworth, BA (**Art & 3D Design*)
S R H James, BA (*Latin, Greek, Games, Vincent Editor*)
Mrs V James, BEd (*Librarian, Art*)
Miss A E A Johnson (*Geography*)
Mrs D L F Jones BA, MEd (**Learning Enrichment*)
Miss E R Marr, BA (*English, 5M Form Teacher*)
E Matthews, M Eng (*Mathematics, 5M Form Teacher, Enterprise Coordinator*)
Mrs M Raikes, BEd, Dip Counselling (*Religious Studies*) [Maternity cover]
Miss H Roome, BSc (**Science, 7R Form Teacher*)
P A Rosenthal, BA (**English, Games, 8R Form Teacher*)
D Shaw, BSc (*Sport, Head of Year 7*)
D R Smith (*History, Religious Studies*)
S Singh, BSc (**ICT, 7S Form Teacher*)
S Thébaud, BSc, MA (**French, Games, 7T Form Teacher*)
Mrs R Thorn, BMus, MMus (*Assistant Director of Music, Head of Years 5 and 6*)
Miss L Timms, BSc (*Mathematics, 5T Form Teacher*)
Miss H L Verney, BSc (*Head of Junior Forms, 3V Form Teacher*)
J S Walker, BEd, LRAM, FRSA (**Director of Music*)
Miss C Wheeler-Bennett, BSc (*4W Form Teacher, Geography*)
Miss H Wellman, BSc (*4H Form Teacher, PSHE, Geography, Drama*)

Administration:
PA to the Master: Mrs O Unterhalter, BA

Registrar: Ms A-M McCarthy
Receptionist and Admissions Assistant: Miss S Tindley, BA
Financial Secretary: Mrs M Waggett
School Matron: Miss L Blanchard, BA
Personnel Bursar: Mrs S Parsons, BA

Winchester College

College Street, Winchester, Hampshire SO23 9NA
Tel: 01962 621100 (Headmaster and Office)
             01962 621200 (Bursar)
             01962 621247 (Admissions)
email: admissions@wincoll.ac.uk
website: www.winchestercollege.org
Twitter: @WinColl

Motto: '*Manners Makyth Man*'

Winchester College is a boys' boarding school of approximately 700 pupils. Founded in 1382 by William of Wykeham, it has the longest continuous history of any English school. Wykeham planned and created a double foundation consisting of two Colleges, one at Winchester and the other (New College) at Oxford. The two Colleges are still closely associated.

Academic study. At Winchester College, academic expectations are high, and success is achieved through a curiosity and love for learning. A Winchester education combines cultural studies in Div with a curriculum of examined subjects.

Div. Div is at the heart of a Winchester College education. It defines the liberal character of the academic life of its pupils. In Div, pupils engage in discussion and debate, and embrace the idea of learning for its own sake, unrestrained by an examination syllabus.

In Years 9 to 11, Div provides pupils with an introduction to the broad sweep of Western History, from classical antiquity to the modern age. It also encompasses English literature and language, the History of Science and Art, Religious Studies and PSHEE.

In the sixth form, each Div teacher determines the programme, and the material selected for inclusion is equally likely to be artistic, literary, philosophical, political, sociological, art-historical, ethical, religious or musical.

The Curriculum.

GCSEs: The majority of pupils complete a minimum of nine GCSEs and IGCSEs (all graded 9–1).

In addition to Div, pupils begin at Winchester in Year 9 studying Mathematics, Biology, Chemistry, Physics, French or German, Geography and Latin. They also study one of the following: Ancient Greek, Spanish, Russian or Chinese, and choose two subjects from Art, Design and Music: Towards the end of Year 9, pupils express their preferences for GCSE study. The compulsory subjects (in addition to Div) are English, Mathematics, Latin, French or German, and two or three Sciences. Pupils also choose from among the following to bring the total to nine: History, Geography, Ancient Greek, Art, Design, Music, Spanish, Russian and Chinese.

Pre-Us: Pupils in sixth form study three Cambridge Pre-U subjects alongside Div. Pre-U offers a rigorous academic qualification and an excellent preparation for university study. It provides both learners and teachers with a great deal of flexibility, and speaks well to the educational philosophy embodied in Div. There is generally less prescription than at A Level, and the Pre-U is very good at training soon-to-be undergraduates by fostering the development of student responsibility and independence. Assessment provides differentiation at the highest level.

Scholarships and Exhibitions.

Boys who have already been offered a conditional place at the school but demonstrate exceptional academic ability are encouraged to apply for an Academic Scholarship. This is known as Election.

Election is taken instead of the Winchester Entrance Exam. It is a unique and academically-challenging selection process involving both written examinations and interviews. Election typically takes place at the school over three days in the April or May of Year 8.

Those boys who are successful at Election are awarded either:

• A Scholarship – boys are offered a place in College, the oldest of the school's boarding houses. On joining the school, they are known as Scholars and are distinct by the gowns they wear.

• An Exhibition – boys are publicly recognised for their academic ability and accept their existing offer of a place in one of the school's other boarding houses.

• Headmaster's Nominations – an award where a boy has not previously been offered a conditional place at the school or been successful in gaining an Academic Scholarship, but whose exam results are strong enough to gain a place in the school. He will subsequently be offered a place in one of the school's boarding houses.

Music Scholarships are available to any candidate who shows exceptional musical talent.

Winchester offers two main types of music awards:

• A Scholarship – offering free tuition in two instruments (including, if appropriate, singing)

• An Exhibition – offering free tuition in one instrument

In addition, up to three Choral Scholarships and one Organ Scholarship are available for 16+ entrants only. These carry free tuition in two instruments, one of which must be singing or the organ.

Auditions for a Music Scholarship are designed to establish an all-round view of musical ability. The audition includes a short 15 minute performance and 10 minutes of practical tests. Informal pre-auditions are also available for candidates from the Asian region not currently in a UK school. These take place in Hong Kong each January.

The Director of Music can give advice about all aspects of Music Scholarships and is pleased to see potential candidates at any time after they are nine years of age. Full details of Music Scholarships can be found on the school's website. For further information and an entry form, please contact the Music School Administrator on jma@wincoll.ac.uk or by calling 01962 621123.

Sports Scholarships offer successful candidates at 13+ specialist coaching sessions, a regularly assessed strength and conditioning programme, and a dedicated tutor from the Sports Department to help a boy achieve his sporting goals while maintaining a sensible and sustainable routine in the school.

Successful candidates will be invited to an assessment day, designed to understand a boy's all-round sporting ability. The day is typically split in to three parts and looks at physical, technical and mental agility.

Full details of Sports Awards can be found on the school's website. For further information, please contact the Admissions Team (sportsawards@wincoll.ac.uk) or by calling 01962 621164.

Bursaries. Winchester College is committed to maintaining the founder's original intention of offering a Winchester education to any boy who would benefit from it, regardless of their financial circumstances.

The bursary offered to each family is means-tested and reflects individual circumstances. To allow the widest range of pupils to attend the school, awards range from 5% to

100% of the school fee, and for those on the largest bursaries, this may include additional support for a laptop, books, exam fees or trips.

The school also awards *Scholarships and Exhibitions* for those boys with exceptional academic, musical or sporting talent. Unlike Bursaries, Scholarships and Exhibitions do not automatically carry a remission on school fees, however free individual tuition is provided for sportsmen and musicians.

For more information, please read the Guidance on Bursaries on the school website. Alternatively, please contact our Bursary team on 01962 621271 or by emailing bursaries@wincoll.ac.uk.

Sixth Form entry. A small number of places are offered each year to boys joining the Sixth Form from other schools. There is an Open Day in September. Examinations and interviews take place in Winchester in November each year. Enquiries should be sent to the Deputy Registrar (admissions@wincoll.ac.uk).

Fees per term (2018–2019). Boarders £13,304 per term (£39,912 p.a.). There is an entrance fee of £500.

Boarders. Winchester College is a full boarding school for boys. Boarding at Winchester gives boys an unmatched experience of focused learning and friendship. Discussions in class can continue in the house, instilling a lifelong love of debate. In consultation with parents and boys, the school accommodates boys with care, getting to know them first through a personal admissions process.

There are approximately 60 boarders in each House.

The Housemasters are:

College: Mr Ian Fraser

Chernocke House: Mr James Fox

Moberly's: Mr Sam Hart

Du Boulay's: Dr Andrew Savory

Fearon's: Mr Matthew Winter

Morshead's: Dr Jamie McManus

Hawkins': Dr James Hodgins

Sergeant's: Mr David Yeomans

Bramston's: Mr Stephen Rich

Turner's: Mr Christopher Good

Kingsgate House: Dr Mark Romans

Boys should be registered any time after their eighth birthday and before the end of Year 5. They are usually at least 13, but under 14, on 31 August in the year of entry to the School but exceptions may be considered in special circumstances. Places are offered after tests and an interview in Year 6. The Registrar holds a Reserve List, which includes the names of late applicants, but it is essential to have a place at another school until a firm place at Winchester has been confirmed.

The entrance examination covers the normal subjects; particulars and copies of recent papers may be obtained from the Deputy Registrar.

Term of entry. Usually September.

Alumni, Winchester College Society. Secretary: A F J Roe, Donovan's, 73 Kingsgate Street, Winchester SO23 9PE.

Charitable status. Winchester College is a Registered Charity, number 1139000. The objects of the charity are the advancement of education and activities connected therewith.

Visitor: The Bishop of Winchester

Warden: C J F Sinclair, CBE, BA, FCA

Sub-Warden: A Sykes, MA

Fellows:

J B W Nightingale, MA, DPhil

Professor C T C Sachrajda, FRS, PhD, FInstP, CPhys

P Frith, MD, FRCP, FRCOphth

Major-General J D Shaw, CB, CBE, MA

C M Farr, MA

A N Joy, MA

N E H Ferguson CBE, FSA Scot, BSc, MBA

W E J Holland, BA, FCA

W E Poole, MA, DPhil, FSA

M Young, MA

The Hon Sir S W S Cobb, QC

Dr M Ryan

Bursar and Secretary: S P Little, MA, FCA

Headmaster: **T R Hands**, BA, AKC, DPhil, FKC

Second Master: N P Wilks, MA, ARAM

Deputy Headmaster (Academic): P M Herring, MA

Director of Studies: T N Thomas

Undermaster: Dr J P Cullerne

Registrar: A C Shedden, BEd

Deputy Registrar: Mrs P C McComb

Wisbech Grammar School

Chapel Road, Wisbech, Cambs PE13 1RH

Tel:	01945 583631
	01945 586750 Admissions
Fax:	01945 476746
email:	office@wisbechgrammar.com
website:	www.wisbechgrammar.com
Twitter:	@WisbechGrammar
Facebook:	@WisbechGrammar

Founded during the turbulent reign of Richard II in 1379, Wisbech Grammar School was established by a society of local merchants, the Guild of the Holy Trinity, to provide education for poor boys of the town. Now a fully co-educational day school, it draws around 500 pupils aged 4 to 18 from the three counties of Cambridgeshire, Norfolk and Lincolnshire.

Occupying a prime site on the North Brink, one of England's most handsome Georgian streets and a magnet for film makers, the School – the finest in Fenland – is set in 34 acres of magnificent grounds in a conservation area. Open, friendly and welcoming, the School is small enough for staff to know all the pupils individually but large enough to provide an impressive range of opportunities. The traditional emphasis on the pursuit of academic success is complemented by a sensitive and highly effective pastoral care system. All members of the Senior School and Magdalene House Preparatory School are encouraged to develop their confidence and unlock their true potential, both inside and outside the classroom, as well as engaging with the wider community.

Development. The ongoing development programme has included a dedicated 6th Form centre and a floodlit, all-weather Astroturf pitch, as well as the refurbishment of the science laboratories and an upgrade of the information technology infrastructure. A new £2.5m refectory opened in 2015 and a major expansion of the on-site playing field provision has recently been completed. State-of-the-art tennis courts now offer floodlit space for evening games. The old dining hall has become The Studio offering dance and performing arts space for pupils and the wider community. Two more classrooms and a new hall have been constructed for the rapidly expanding preparatory school, which takes its name from Magdalene College. The Cambridge college has enjoyed a close connection with the Grammar School for over 350 years and the Master and Fellows appoint two of their number to the governing body.

Senior School admission. The main entry is at age 11 by a competitive entrance examination. The test, which consists of verbal and non-verbal reasoning, spatial, quantitative tests and English, is designed to discover potential. Pupils can also enter at 2nd, 3rd and 4th Form levels. The test, which consists of mathematics and English, is designed to discover potential. Pupils can also enter at 2nd, 3rd and 4th Form levels. Offers of 6th Form places are made on the basis of interview and a report from a pupil's current school.

Fees per term (2018–2019). Senior School £4,449; Magdalene House Preparatory School £3,099–£3,199.

Bursaries and Scholarships. Wisbech Grammar School offers a bursary programme which provides financial assistance to pupils who would not otherwise be able to take up the offer of a place, allowing them to achieve their full potential. Bursaries are means tested and will require the parents to make a detailed statement of their income and assets. Awards range from 5% to 85%. In exceptional cases, an award of 100% may be granted. The School also offers Scholarships for children entering Year 7, Year 9 and Year 12. Scholarships are awarded to children who excel in a number of areas (Academic and All-Rounder); this includes financial support and may be awarded alongside a bursary. Application forms for Bursary Assisted Places are available from the Admissions Team: admissions@wisbechgrammar.com.

Travel to School. The School's catchment area embraces King's Lynn, Hunstanton, Downham Market, March, Whittlesey, Peterborough and Spalding and Long Sutton. School buses run from a number of these places, visiting villages en route, and there is a late bus for pupils involved in after-school activities. The School is also well served by local buses.

Teaching and learning. The School aims to foster a love of learning and to provide an environment which nurtures talent and breeds success. In recent years the expansion of the teaching staff has helped to reduce class size and foster more individual learning. There is a high regard for the traditional disciplines, but the School is also ready to open up exciting new fields of study. An extensive academic curriculum in the first three years of the Senior School includes opportunities to sample a broad range of subjects. One pupil has recently reached the national finals of the Foreign Language Spelling Bee competition. The options system at GCSE ensures a broad-based curriculum as well as allowing pupils to play to their strengths. In the 6th Form, the subject range is extensive and pupils have their first chance to take business studies, economics, government and politics, and graphics. The School also provides support which allows bright pupils with learning difficulties and disabilities to rise to the challenge of a rigorous academic education.

The 6th Form experience. The School has a first-class track record in enabling pupils to realise their university and career aspirations. Entrusted with a greater degree of independence, 6th Formers are encouraged to make their mark and develop leadership qualities, both within the house system and at a wider level. The 6th Form centre provides a fine facility for the School's most senior pupils.

Creative and performing arts. The flourishing music department provides practical opportunities for pupils to develop their creative talents. Nine visiting instrumental and vocal tutors give individual tuition to nearly a fifth of the pupils, and there are numerous opportunities to join in choirs, wind and steel bands and perform in the annual concerts and community charity events.

The vibrant Drama department encourages every pupil in the School to take part in at least one major production during their School career as either performer or technician, to appreciate live performance and embrace wider opportunities such as competing in national competitions, or becoming part of the Edinburgh Fringe Festival. Pupils enjoy considerable success with their Trinity College, London qualifications in all Acting and Speaking disciplines whilst Dance and Musical Theatre are recent additions to our portfolio. Classroom Drama and extra-curricular projects, such as student-directed work, ensure that all benefit from the art of entertainment, and provide a creative strategy for managing life's complex demands.

The art and design department is a highly visible presence in the School, mounting exhibitions on-site and at the Reed Barn at the neighbouring National Trust property, Peckover House, and talented artists and designers regularly win places at the top art colleges.

A competitive spirit. The Assistant Head Sports and Partnerships ensures that teams enjoy the challenge of a competitive fixture list against schools across the eastern counties and in the Midlands, and Wisbech Grammar School takes pride in punching above its weight. An extensive inter-house programme also allows pupils of all abilities to develop their competitive spirit. The main games for boys are rugby in the Michaelmas term and hockey and rugby sevens in the Lent term, together with cricket, athletics and tennis in the Trinity term. Girls play hockey in the Michaelmas term and netball and rugby sevens in the Lent term and rounders, tennis, cricket and athletics in the Trinity term. For pupils above the 3rd Form who are not involved in a major team game, the options range from badminton and basketball to archery and spinning. The facilities include a full-sized sports hall, a fitness suite and an extensive on-site floodlit Astroturf pitch, together with generous playing field provision. Pupils also enjoy access to a covered swimming pool, a sports hall and a fitness centre at a neighbouring leisure centre.

Beyond the classroom. Wisbech Grammar School believes in learning on location. The biology department has recently run a field class in Galapagos, and the 5th Form went on a recent expedition to Borneo with a Madagascar expedition in the pipeline. Geographers have explored the west coast of the United States and there are frequent art trips to New York. There is a flourishing exchange with the Willibrord Gymnasium in Emmerich, and the French department has added a GCSE study trip to Normandy and an A Level cross-curricular visit to Paris for the annual chateau trip. Pupils also criss-cross the country for hands-on learning, and excursions such as the 3rd Form trip to Shakespeare's Globe or the Royal Shakespeare Theatre run regularly. Around 130 pupils participate in the Duke of Edinburgh's Award, with those at the highest level mounting expeditions to the Lake District, Snowdonia and Mont Blanc. The Senior School adventure begins with an outdoor activity weekend for the 1st Form.

Closer to home, 6th Formers hone their business skills in the Young Enterprise scheme, regularly reaching the regional finals. Clubs such as language leaders, riding and grow, cook, eat help to stretch the mind and develop life skills. Members of Caritas, the charity and community service team, reach out to those in need, both on their doorstep and across the globe, and the School hosts an annual party for local pensioners.

Magdalene House Preparatory School caters for pupils from Kindergarten to Prep 6. (*For further details see entry in IAPS section.*)

Old Wisbechians Society. Further information about the society can be obtained from the Admissions Team at the School, to whom requests for the school magazine, *Riverline*, should be sent. News of past pupils is published on the School website: www.wisbechgrammar.com.

Charitable status. The Wisbech Grammar School Foundation is a Registered Charity, number 1087799. It exists to promote the education of boys and girls.

Governing Body:

Chairman: Dr D Barter, MB BS, MRCP, FRCPCH, DCH
Vice Chairman: Mr C Goad, BSc, ACA

Fellows appointed by the Master, Magdalene College, Cambridge:
Prof J Raven, MA, PhD Cantab, MA Oxon, LittD Cantab, FSA, FRHistS

Mrs J Bodger BEd
Mr R Calleja, MD, MSc Urol, FRCS Urol
Dr K Hart, MBChB, FRCPCH
The Venerable Hugh McCurdy, BA, Archdeacon of Huntingdon and Wisbech
Mr I MacLachlan
Dr C Mair, BSc, BVetMed, MRCVS
Mrs E Morris, LLB
Dr Q Wong, MBBS, FRCGP, DRCOG, Dip Palliative Medicine

Clerk to the Governors: Mrs Kerry Massen (*Headmaster's PA*)

Senior Team:

Headmaster: Mr C N Staley, BA, MBA

Bursar: Mrs N J Miller
Senior Deputy Head – Magdalene House: Mrs K Neaves, BEd
Deputy Head Academic: Mr P G Logan, BSc
Deputy Head Pastoral: Mr P W Timmis, BSc
Human Resources Manager: Mrs S M Simmons, FCIPD
Head of Marketing and Admissions: Mrs S A Taylor
Assistant Head Academic Administration: Mrs V Garment, BA, MA, NPQSL
Assistant Head Academic Leadership: Dr S J Miller, BSc, PhD, DIC
Assistant Head Co-Curricular: Dr K J Mann, BA, PhD
Assistant Head Teaching & Learning: Mr R D Killick, BSc
Assistant Head Sports & Partnerships: Mr P J Webb, BA

Lower School (1st, 2nd & 3rd Forms):
Mr T W Calow, BA (*Head of Section*)
Mrs A L Sloan, BSc, MA (*Deputy Head of Section*)

Middle School (4th & 5th Forms):
Mr A Duncan (*Head of Section*)
Mrs A S Ogston, BSc (*Deputy Head of Section*)

Upper School (6th Form):
Miss K L Taylor, BA (*Head of Section*)
Dr S J Miller, BSc, PhD, DIC (*Assistant Head Academic Leadership*)
Mr A C Laybourne, MSc (*Deputy Head of Section*)

Heads of Departments:
Mrs Emma Simmonds (*Academic PE*)
Mrs Susan Cooper, BA (*Art and Textiles*)
Miss Deborah Cook, BSc (*Biology*)
Dr Gary Paine, BSc, PhD (*Chemistry*)
Mr Mark Arnold, BEng (*Computer Science*)
Mr Robert Frost, BEd (*Design Technology*)
Mrs Susan Duncan, BSc (*Drama*)
Mrs Vicky Garment, BA, MA, NPQSL (*Economics & Business Studies*)
Mrs Harriet Kember-Whitfield (*English*) [*Acting Head*]
Mrs Alison Sloan, BSc, MA (*Food & Nutrition*)
Mr Guy Nunnerley, BSc (*Geography*)
Mr Tim Chapman, MA (*Government & Politics*)
Mr Sam Emerson, BA (*History*)

Mrs Claire Harding, PG Dip, AMBDA, MDG (*Learning Support – Prep School*)
Dr Emma Stanley Isaac, BSc, PhD, NASENCo (*Learning Support – Senior School*)
Mrs Kirstie Harrison, BSc (*Mathematics*)
Miss Rebbecca Davies, BSc (*Head of Lower School Mathematics*)
Mr Thierry Jestin, MA (*Head of Lower School Modern Foreign Languages*)
Ms Elizabeth Semper, MA (*Modern Foreign Languages*)
Mrs Jane Missin, BA (*Music*)
Mr Al Duncan (*Performing Arts*)
Dr Alexander Shillings, MSci, PhD (*Physics, Head of Upper School Science*)
Miss Joanne Gomm, BSc (*Psychology*)
Mrs Sarah Fox, BA, MSc (*Head of Lower School Science, Prep 5 and 6 Science*)
Mr Phillip Webb, BA (*Sport*)

Sports Department:
Mr Phillip Webb, BA (*Assistant Head Sports & Partnerships*)
Mr Alexander Laybourne, MSc (*Head of Rugby*)
Mrs Andrea Glover, BEd (*Head of Hockey*)
Mr Neil Taylor (*Head of Cricket*)
Mrs Samantha Goodier, BSc (*Head of Netball*)
Mrs Sally Webb (*Head of Swimming and Athletics*)
Mrs Heidi Milton (*Sports Coach*)
Mrs Andrea Eggleton (*Sports Coach*)
Mrs Emma Simmonds (*Head of Academic PE*)
Mr Joss Linney, BSc (*Academic PE*)
Mr James Williams (*PE/Sports Coach*)
Mr Freddie Whatling (*Sports Coach/Instructor*)
Mr Sean Fox (*Archery*)
Mr Samuel Coe (*Strength & Conditioning Coach*)
Mrs Claire Taylor (*Physiotherapist*)

Music Department:
Mrs Jane Missin, BA (*Head of Music*)
Visiting Teachers:
Mrs Sarah Garford (*Woodwind*)
Mr Ivan Garford (*Piano and Bass*)
Mrs Claire Harding, GRSM, ARCM (*Piano and Oboe*)
Mrs Michele Larkin (*Singing*)
Mr Kevin Steward (*Brass*)
Mr John Savage (*Drum and Guitar*)
Mr Rhodri Williams-Wandoch (*Violin*)
Mrs Sally Parnell (*Cello*)
Michele Larkin (*Musical Theatre*)

Teaching Staff:
Mr Mark Arnold, BEng (*Computer Science, Mathematics, Head of Computer Science*)
Mrs Amy Beck, BA PGCE (*Prep 4*)
Mr Thomas Calow, BA (*German, French, Head of Lower School*)
Mr Tim Chapman, MA (*History, Government & Politics, Head of Government & Politics*)
Miss Alison Clayton, BA (*English*)
Mr Samuel Coe (*Strength & Conditioning Coach*)
Mr Christopher Cole, BSc (*Physics, Chemistry*)
Miss Deborah Cook, BSc (*Biology, Science and Sport, Head of Biology*)
Mrs K Cook, BA, MA, PGCE (*Prep 2*)
Mrs Susan Cooper, BA (*Art and Textiles, Head of Art and Textiles*)
Mrs Tina Crawley, BEd, MEd (*Prep 3, Leader of Teaching and Learning – Prep School*)
Mrs Sarah Cross, BA (*English*)
Miss Rebbecca Davies, BSc (*Mathematics, Head of Lower School Mathematics*)
Mr Al Duncan (*Drama, Head of Middle School*)

Mrs Susan Duncan, BSc (*Drama, Speech & Communications, Head of Drama*)

Mrs Andrea Eggleton (*Sports Coach*)

Mr Sam Emerson, BA (*History, Head of History*)

Mrs Karen Fairbrother, BEd (*Prep 4, Assistant Deputy Head – Prep School*)

Mrs Louise Feaviour, BA (*Art and Textiles*)

Mrs Emma Fenn, BA (*KS1*)

Mrs Sarah Fox, BA, MSc (*Biology & Science, Head of Lower School Science*)

Mr Sean Fox (*Archery*)

Mr Robert Frost, BEd (*DT, Head of Design & Technology*)

Mr Dominic Garfoot, BSc (*Geography, Sport, Head of Outdoor Learning, Deputy EVC, Head of House, DofE Coordinator*)

Mrs Vicky Garment, BA, MA, NPQSL (*Business and Economics, Assistant Head Academic Administration, Head of Economics and Business*)

Mrs Andrea Glover, BEd (*Sports Coach, Head of Hockey*)

Miss Joanne Gomm, BSc (*Psychology, Sport, Head of Psychology, Head of House*)

Mrs Samantha Goodier, BSc (*PE/Sports, Head of House, Head of Netball*)

Mrs Claire Harding, PG Dip, AMBDA, MDG (*Peripatetic Piano & Oboe, Head of Prep Learning Support*)

Mrs Kirstie Harrison, BSc (*Mathematics, Head of Mathematics*)

Mr David Hyland, BA, MA (*Prep 5*)

Mr Thierry Jestin, MA (*French & Spanish, Head of Lower School MFL*)

Mrs Alison Kelly, BA, PGCE (*Prep 6*)

Mrs Harriet Kember-Whitfield (*Acting Head of English, Head of Lower School English*)

Mr Russell Killick, BSc (*Geography, Assistant Head Teaching & Learning*)

Miss Jennifer Lasouska, BSc, PGCE (*Biology, Chemistry*)

Mrs Ashleigh Lawrence, BA (*Religious Studies, Lead Teacher Religious Studies*)

Mr Alexander Laybourne, MSc (*Business Studies, PE/Sports, Deputy Head 6th Form, Head of Rugby, Careers*)

Mr Joss Linney, BSc (*Academic PE*)

Mr Paul Logan, BSc (*Mathematics, Deputy Head Academic*)

Dr Kevin Mann, BA, PhD (*History, Assistant Head Co-Curricular*)

Mrs Gemma McMullen, BA (*Prep 4*)

Dr Stuart Miller, BSc, PhD, DIC (*Biology, Assistant Head Academic Leadership*)

Mrs Heidi Milton (*Sports Coach*)

Mrs Jane Missin, BA (*Music, Head of Music*)

Julie Nicholson, BA (*English*) [maternity cover]

Mr Guy Nunnerley, BSc (*Geography, Head of Geography, Lead Educational Visits Coordinator*)

Mrs Amelia Ogston, BSc (*Mathematics, Deputy Head Upper School, PSHCE Coordinator, Child Protection Officer*)

Mrs Emma Oram, BA, PGCE (*Reception, EYFS Leader*)

Mrs Jane Page, BEd (*Prep 5*)

Dr Gary Paine, BSc, PhD (*Chemistry, Head of Chemistry*)

Mr Inigo Rodriguez, BA (*Spanish, Head of House*)

Mrs Claire Sandall, BA (*Prep 5*)

Ms Elizabeth Semper, MA (*Modern Foreign Languages, Head of MFL*)

Dr Alexander Shillings, MSci, PhD (*Chemistry, Head of Physics, Head of Upper School Science*)

Mrs Emma Simmonds (*Head of Academic PE*)

Mrs Monika Skinner (*German*)

Mrs Alison Sloan, BSc, MA (*Food & Nutrition, Deputy Head Lower School, Head of Food & Nutrition*)

Miss Olexandra Solomka, BA (*DT*)

Dr Emma Stanley Isaac, BSc, PhD, NASENCo (*Chemistry, Science, Head of Learning Support – Senior School*)

Mr Mick Stump (*Art*) [p/t]

Mrs Claire Taylor (*Physiotherapist*)

Miss Kate Taylor, BA (*Geography, Head of 6th Form*)

Mr Neil Taylor (*PE/Sports, Head of Cricket*)

Mr Chris Thursby, BA, MA (*Mathematics, Director of Examinations*)

Mrs Kate Timmis, BA (*English, Head of English*) [maternity leave]

Mr Peter Timmis, BSc (*Physics, Deputy Head Pastoral*)

Mrs Michaela Tooke, BSc, PGCE (*Food & Nutrition*)

Mr Phillip Webb, BA (*PE/Sports, Assistant Head Sports & Partnerships*)

Mrs Sally Webb (*Head of Swimming and Athletics*)

Mr Freddie Whatling (*Sports Coach/Instructor*)

Mrs Jill Whiteman, CertEd (*Prep 1*)

Mr James Williams (*PE/Sports*)

Headmaster's PA: Mrs Kerry Massen/Mrs Michele Busby

Withington Girls' School

Wellington Road, Fallowfield, Manchester M14 6BL

Tel: 0161 224 1077
Fax: 0161 248 5377
email: office@wgs.org
website: www.wgs.org
Twitter: @WGSManchester
Facebook: @withingtongirlsschool

Motto: *Ad Lucem ~ Towards the light*

Independent (formerly Direct Grant).

Since its foundation in 1890, Withington has remained relatively small and now has around 720 pupils, 155 of whom are in the Junior Department and 155 in the Sixth Form. This size allows a friendly, intimate environment together with a broad and balanced curriculum. Withington provides a wide range of opportunities for girls, helping them to achieve their potential, academically, socially and personally. Withington attracts pupils from a wide geographical area and from many different social and cultural backgrounds, producing a diversity in which the school rejoices.

The School's A Level and GCSE results have been consistently outstanding. Girls who gain a place as a result of the entrance examination normally take GCSE/IGCSE examinations in 9/10 subjects, followed by 3 or 4 A Levels. An exciting and varied Enrichment programme offers Sixth Formers core elements such as financial literacy, PSHE and professional skills plus a range of choices from astronomy to mosaics and Eastern Philosophy. In addition to the Enrichment Programme, which all Sixth Formers follow, many also complete an Extended Project Qualification (EPQ). Studies are directed towards encouraging a love of learning for its own sake, frequently going beyond the confines of the examined curriculum, as well as towards the ultimate goal of University entrance, including Oxford and Cambridge (18% of the cohort in 2018).

The School enjoys excellent facilities and has an ongoing programme of major developments. Recent projects have included a purpose-built Junior School building, a central, enclosed 'Hub' area at the heart of the school and an expanded and refurbished suite of university-standard Chemistry laboratories, all of which were completed in 2015. During 2018 a significant new sports facilities development was completed, reflecting the school's ongoing commitment to the promotion of physical activity for girls, one of the school's founding principles.

Withington fosters all-round development and the girls' academic studies are complemented by an extensive range of extracurricular activities. Music is strong and very popular; there is a comprehensive range of choirs and orchestras, involving all age groups. Drama also thrives with regular productions including original works. Girls play a variety of sports, including hockey, lacrosse, netball, rounders, tennis, athletics and football. Pupils are regularly selected for county and national squads and there are regular sports tours within Europe and further afield such as the USA and South Africa. In addition to fixtures with other schools, games players compete within the School's House system. The four Houses, named after Withington's founders, also provide a focus for dramatic, musical and other activities.

The Duke of Edinburgh's Award scheme and the Young Enterprise scheme, Model United Nations conferences, voluntary work in the local community, science, mathematics, linguistics Olympiads and a wide range of academic extension activities, residential activity weekends, foreign trips and local fieldwork all feature prominently in the School's provision. Numerous extracurricular clubs and societies include: Model United Nations, debating, zumba, yoga, robotics, film making, app development, dance and chess. Awareness of the wider world is encouraged and girls have a strong sense of social responsibility, participating in many fundraising activities and maintaining special links with a hospital and two schools in Kenya. Each year groups of girls give up their holiday time to participate in community projects in Uganda and The Gambia; others participate in World Challenge expeditions (to Malaysia and Borneo in 2016 and Sri Lanka in 2017). Preparation for life after school starts early and involves a programme of careers advice, work experience and UCAS application guidance. Older girls work with younger girls in numerous ways, through the House system, extra-curricular activities, peer support and mentoring.

Visitors are warmly welcomed at any time. Open Days are held in the Autumn term. A substantial number of means-tested Bursaries are awarded annually together with awards from various external Trusts. Entrance at age 7–11 is by Entrance Assessment/Examination, held in January, together with interview (11+ entry only) and report from current school. Admission to the Sixth Form is by interview and is conditional upon GCSE results. For entry at other points, please don't hesitate to contact the Admissions Team for further information.

The School has a thriving alumnae network with regular events and many alumnae offering help and inspiration to current pupils. The School engages in a number of projects with local State schools and has strong links with the local community. Withington was named as The Sunday Times Parent Power Top Independent Secondary School of the Year 2009/10 and the Financial Times Best Value Independent Day School in 2012. Consistently named as the top secondary school in the north west by the Sunday Times, The Tatler Schools Guide named Withington as a Runner-Up for Public School of the Year 2015.

Fees per term (2018–2019). Senior School £4,084, Junior School £3,065. LAMDA and individual instrumental music lessons are charged separately.

Charitable status. Withington Girls' School is a Registered Charity, number 1158226. It aims to provide an exceptional quality of opportunity, to encourage independence of mind and high aspirations for girls from seven to eighteen.

Board of Governors:
Chair: Mr M Pike, LLB
Mr D Illingworth, BA, FCA (*Hon Treasurer*)

Mr M Adlestone, OBE, FGA
Dr J Allred, MB ChB, MRCGP, DRCOG, DFFP
Mr A Chicken, BA, MEd, FRSA
Professor I Grigorieva, PhD
¶Mrs D Hawkins, DL, JP, LLB
Mrs J Kinney, Fd Sc, LLB
Ms M Michael, BA, NPQH, LLE
Mr A Pathak, BSc
Mr H Sinclair
¶Mrs S Stuffins, BA, MSc, MRICS

¶ *Alumnae*

Headmistress: **Mrs S J Haslam**, BA Lancaster (*English*)

Deputy Head: ¶Ms J M Baylis, MA Manchester (*English and Drama*)

Director of Studies: Mr I McKenna, BA Manchester (*Religious Studies*)

Assistant Head: Dr S E Madden, PhD Newcastle (*Biology*)

Bursar: Mrs S Senn, BSc Hull, ACA

Full-time Teaching Staff:
* *Head of Department/Subject*
Mrs L Bradshaw, MA Cantab (**Science, *Physics*)
Miss K L Browning, BA London (*Geography*)
¶Miss D Bruce, BA Birmingham (**Religious Studies*)
Miss M Cahill, BA Leeds (*History*)
Miss J Carter, Leeds (*Physical Education*)
Mrs E Corrigan, MSc Durham (**Biology*)
Mr A Cumberford, BA Oxon (**German*)
Ms C J Davies, BA Hull, MA Open University (**English*)
Mr K Eckersall, BSc Leicester, MA Durham (*Chemistry*)
Mrs C E Edge, MA Leeds (*English*)
Mrs S E Fletcher, BEd Brighton (*Mathematics*)
Mr C Forrest, MPhys Manchester (*Physics, Enrichment**)
Miss E Hall, BA Sheffield (*English*)
Mrs S E Hamilton, MA Aberdeen (*Geography*)
Mrs J Healey, BSc Newcastle (**FTT*)
Mrs S Hetherington, BA Leeds Beckett (*Physical Education*)
Miss A R H Holland, BMus Birmingham (*Music, *PSHCE**)
Mrs J C Howling, MA Cantab (**Classics*)
Mrs N Kimpton-Smith, BA Durham (*History, Religious Studies*)
Mrs A Kusznir, Dip Mech Moscow (*Mathematics*)
Dr E A Maisey, PhD London (*Chemistry*)
¶Mrs Y T Menzies, MA Salford (*French*, German*)
Miss K Mottershead, BA Brighton (*Physical Education*)
Mrs S I Mounteney, BSc London (**Mathematics*)
Miss A Noya, BA Santiago de Compostela (*Spanish*)
Mrs E O'Neal, BEd Leeds Polytechnic (**Physical Education*)
Mr A Parry, BSc Manchester (*Mathematics*)
Mrs E K Robinson, MA Cantab (*Classics*)
Mrs G E Sargent, BMus London (**Music*)
Mr A Snowden, BSc Warwick (**ICT*)
Mrs N Toubanks, BSc Manchester (**Economics*)
Dr C P G Vilela, PhD Lisbon (**Chemistry*)
Miss N A West, BA Manchester (*English, *Enrichment**)

Junior School:
Head of Junior School: ¶Mrs E S K Burrows, MA St Andrews (*Geography*)
Mr M Dunn, BSc Sheffield (*Year 6*)
Mrs K Williams, BA Victoria, Canada (*Year 6*)
Miss J Arschevir, MA Liverpool (*Year 5*)
Mrs A Harris, MSc MMU (*Year 5*)
Miss H Dillon, BA Manchester (*Year 5*)
Miss L Gorman, BA Edge Hill (*Year 4*)
Mrs H Stallard, BA Newcastle-upon-Tyne (*Year 4*)

Miss L Geoghegan, BA York (*Year 3*)
Mrs B Lowe, BSc Northumbria (*Year 3*)

Part-time Teaching Staff:
Mrs C Air, BA Oxon (**History*)
Mrs L Berry, BA Manchester (**Drama*)
Mrs S Birch, BEd Edge Hill (*Junior School, FTT, Drama*)
Mrs J W Bowie, MA Dundee (*English*)
Mr M Boyle, BSc Wales (*Biology*)
¶Mrs J Buckley, BA Durham (**Geography*)
Mrs H Carey, MChem Manchester (*Chemistry*)
Mrs A Collard, BSc Durham (*Mathematics*)
Mrs R Corner, MA Exeter (*Drama*)
Mrs N Cottam, BSc Durham (*Biology, *Careers*)
Mrs F Cotton, BA Heriot-Watt (**Design & Technology*)
Miss K Easby, MA Manchester (*Classics*)
Mrs R Fildes, MA MMU (**Art*)
Ms A Furlong, MA St Mary's (*English*)
Ms A Godwin, BA Oxon (*Learning Support*)
Mrs Z Goldman, BA Manchester (*Design Technology*)
Mrs A Humblet, BA University of Dijon (*Spanish*)
Mrs J Johnston, BA MMU (*Art*)
Dr Z Kenny, PhD Edinburgh (*Biology*)
Mrs V Kochhar, BSc Exeter (*Mathematics*)
Mrs E Lee, BSc Manchester (*Physics*)
Ms M Lopez, BSc Pennsylvania (**Spanish*)
Miss C McGregor, BSc Manchester (*Biology*)
Mrs N Morgan, BMus Lancaster (*Music*)
Mrs D Odeyinde, BSc Queen's Belfast (*Learning Support*)
Mrs B O'Neal, MSc MMU (**Psychology*)
Mrs C Ositelu, DEA-ès-L Nantes (*French*)
Mrs S J Rigby, BA Nottingham (**Learning Support*)
Mrs S Roberts, MA Manchester (*Physical Education*)
Mrs A Siddons, BA Bath (*German*)
Dr J Smiles, PHD Manchester (*Chemistry*)
Mrs K Smith, BSc Royal Holloway (*Biology*)
Miss R Smith, MA Goldsmiths (*Music*)
Mrs R Statter, BSc Warwick (*Mathematics*)
Mrs J Stockton, BA Leeds (*English*)
Mrs Z Taylor, BA MMU (*Art*)
Dr E L Terrill, DPhil Oxon (*Mathematics*)
Mrs J Wagstaffe, BA Nottingham (*Spanish*)
Mrs J C Wallis, BA Leeds (**Politics*)
Mrs N Watson, BA Leeds (*FTT, Careers*)

PA to Headmistress: Mrs A L Adams, BA Sheffield Hallam
Librarian: Mrs H Brackenbury, MA Sheffield
Assistant Librarian: Mr D Whelan, BA MMU
Archivist: Miss H Brown, MA MMU
School Nurse: Mrs J Lees, RGN
School Counsellor: Miss S Horsfall, BSc Newcastle, Dip GPTI
Examinations Officer: Mrs S Breckell, BSc Dundee (*Mathematics*)
Assistant Examinations Officer: Mrs A Collard, BSc Durham (*Mathematics*)
Development Director: Mrs T Leden, BSc Surrey
Director of Admissions and Marketing: Mrs C Dow, BA Johannesburg
Admissions Officer: Ms J Ellis, BA Bath
Network Manager: Mr A Lockett, BSc Bradford
HR Manager: Mrs N Byrne, BA Huddersfield
Officer Manager: Mrs N Baguley, BA MMU
Site Manager: Mr M Morris, NEBOSH
Catering Manager: Mrs S Cartledge, HCIMA MMU

Woldingham School

Marden Park, Woldingham, Surrey CR3 7YA

Tel:	01883 654206
email:	registrar@woldinghamschool.co.uk
website:	www.woldinghamschool.co.uk
Twitter:	@WoldinghamSch
Facebook:	@woldinghamschool.co.uk

Founded in 1842 by the Society of the Sacred Heart, Woldingham is a leading independent boarding and day school for girls aged 11–18 and one of the oldest girls' schools in the UK. Woldingham School's grounds are among the most extensive in England; its beautiful 700-acre estate is just 20 miles from London and there is a fast and direct train link to the station in the school grounds (25 minutes). Woldingham is also conveniently located just 20 and 45 minutes from Gatwick and Heathrow Airports respectively. Woldingham was awarded '*excellent*' in all areas by the Independent Schools Inspectorate in 2018 and The Good Schools Guide described Woldingham as a '*delightful school with pupils to match, benefiting from first class leadership*'.

Woldingham's strong sense of community is deeply ingrained and academic fulfilment and personal development go hand in hand. Woldingham girls understand about courage and integrity and develop into young women who achieve academic success and become positive influences in the world. Woldingham is a Catholic school which welcomes girls of all faiths or none.

Teaching is outstanding and Woldingham has an excellent track record of GCSE and A Level results, achieving 61% A*–A at A Level and 67% 9–7/A*–A at GCSE in 2018. Students gain places at a range of top universities, predominantly Russell Group and Oxbridge.

Pastoral care is widely regarded as exceptional; Woldingham's unique THRIVE programme promotes emotional well-being and enables every girl to develop the growth mindset, resilience and self-worth to truly enjoy her successes and learn from her setbacks. Boarding facilities are excellent, with small dormitories for the younger girls and individual study bedrooms from Year 10 upwards. Full, weekly and flexi boarding are available and the school has a balance of pupils from London, Surrey and overseas.

Education at Woldingham extends well beyond the classroom. Woldingham's co-curricular programme is rich and varied, with over 80 clubs on offer across the week and throughout the weekend; girls are encouraged to balance their study with activity. Athletes compete at local, regional and national level, and are helped by the extensive grounds which provide a wide range of excellent sporting facilities. Artists can be bold and experimental in the purpose-built art studio, while the Performing Arts Centre boasts an impressive 600-seat auditorium. Around this the Music and Drama departments are based; both see girls performing regularly and at the highest standard.

Admissions. Main entry is via the Woldingham School Assessment in the autumn prior to entry for 11+, 13+ (standard and deferred entry) and 16+ candidates.

Scholarships. We offer the following academic and co-curricular scholarships, designed to recognise exceptional achievement, intellectual curiosity and persistence:

Academic, Art, Music, Drama, Sport and All Rounder Scholarships are offered at 11+, 13+ and 16+. In addition, a Local Girl Scholarship is offered at 11+ and a Science Scholarship at 16+.

Bursaries. We are committed to providing bursaries, depending upon the financial and other pertinent circumstances of applicants. They are intended for girls who demonstrate strong academic potential and where the financial circumstances of the family will make attending Woldingham impossible.

Fees per term (2018–2019). Years 7 & 8: Boarding £11,190, Day £6,860. Years 9 to Upper Sixth: Boarding £12,180, Day £7,480. Flexi boarding (all Years): £60 per night (max. 2 nights per week, per term). Sixth Form Direct Entry carries a premium of £500 per term for boarders and £250 per term for day pupils.

Charitable status. Woldingham School is a Registered Charity, number 1125376.

Chairman of Governors: Mr Robert Parkinson MA Oxon

Headmistress: Mrs A Hutchinson, MA Oxon

Senior Deputy Head: Mrs M Giblin, BA, HDipEd Maynooth

Deputy Head Academic: Ms N Weatherston, BSc Newcastle

Deputy Head Pastoral: Mrs J Brown, BEd CNAA

Head of Sixth Form: Mr P Abbott, BSc Cardiff

Head of Marden: Miss C Owen, BA Royal Holloway London

Director of Finance, Resources & Operations: Mr S Hopkins, MA Oxon, FCA

Marketing Director: Mrs S Jordan, MA Cantab

Registrar: Mrs L Underwood

Heads of Departments:
Art: Miss C Reay, BA Manchester Metropolitan
Classics & Latin: Mr T Hayward, MA SOAS
Computer Science: Mr T Rattle, BA Exeter
Design & Technology: Mr D Wahab, BA Brighton
Drama: Miss S Williams BA Middlesex
EAL: Mrs T Carrilero, BA Spain
Economics & Business: Mr W Bohanna, BA UEA
English: Mrs J Vivian, BA Wales, MEd Newcastle
French: Mrs C Maillot, BA equiv France
Geography: Mr D Lock, BA London
German: Mr V Ceska, BA Czech, MA France
Government & Politics: Mrs K Payne, BA Dunelm
Higher Education & Careers: Mrs B Chambers, BA Leeds
History: Miss G Noble BA Exeter, MEd Cantab
History of Art: Mr A Cullen, BA SOAS
Learning Enhancement: Ms R Moorvan, BA S Africa, MEd OU
Mathematics: Mrs M Kazi-Fornari, MA Oxon
Media Studies: Mr S Maunder, BA Sheffield
Music: Mr J Hargreaves, BA Ebor, MMus, FRSA
Personal, Social & Health Education: Miss A O'Neill, BEd London
Physical Education: Mrs C Treacy, BSc Gloucestershire
Psychology: Miss R Collinson, BSc Psych, BMus, PG Dip RCM
Spanish: Mr A Lopez, BA Oviedo
Theology: Mr A Ross, BA Lancaster, AIDTA [B]
Science & Biology: Mrs S Baldwin, BSc London
Chemistry: Dr R Yu, BA, MSc Cantab, Dr rer nat Dresden, Germany
Physics: Mrs K Connor, BSc East Anglia

Wolverhampton Grammar School

Compton Road, Wolverhampton, West Midlands WV3 9RB

Tel: 01902 421326
email: info@wgs.org.uk
website: www.wgs.org.uk
Twitter: @WGS1512
Facebook: @Wolverhampton-Grammar-School-Official
LinkedIn: /WGS-Old-Wulfrunians-and-Friends

Wolverhampton Grammar School was founded in 1512 by Sir Stephen Jenyns – a Wolverhampton man who achieved success as a wool merchant, became a member of The Merchant Taylors' Company then Lord Mayor of London. He decided to benefit his home town by founding a school "for the instruction of youth in good manners and learning". The school retains close links with the Company.

Wolverhampton Grammar School is an independent, selective day school for boys and girls aged 7–18 from a wide catchment area throughout the West Midlands, Staffordshire and Shropshire.

In 2011, the school opened a junior school (Wolverhampton Grammar Junior School) for students aged 7–11. The Junior School has proved exceptionally popular with parents advised to apply early to avoid disappointment.

The school's mission is to deliver education that transforms lives as well as minds, as individual as every child, within an environment that's like no other. The school delivers a personalised curriculum to provide an education and learning experience that is unique. Students achieve excellent GCSE and A Level exam results alongside an experience that includes the largest range of co- and extra-curricular activities available in the area.

The school was inspected in February 2017 and was judged to be 'excellent' in all areas. The report can be read on the ISI website: www.isi.net.

Buildings. The stunning 23-acre site includes a purpose-built Sixth Form Centre and a £3.8 million Arts & Drama Centre home to the Viner Gallery and Hutton Theatre. A Sports Centre and floodlit Astroturf pitches provide some of the best sporting facilities in the area, with a new Sports Pavilion unveiled in 2012 providing panoramic views of the sports fields. Chemistry and Physics laboratories that have been refurbished to the highest modern standards. State-of-the-art ICT facilities provide Wi-Fi internet access to all parts of the school and all teachers use iPads and app technology to enhance the learning experience.

Admission. The School accepts applications to the Junior, Senior and Sixth Form (Year 3 to Year 13) throughout the year, although new students usually join the school in September. The school's own Year 7 entrance tests are held in the preceding January. For the Sixth Form: offers of places are made subject to GCSE results and interview.

Fees per term (2018–2019). Junior School £3,457 Senior School and Sixth Form £4,554.

Entrance Scholarships. There are a number of options available which offer support with fees, including a range of Bursaries and Scholarships. The awards vary according to the level of family income and are reviewed annually so please contact Jane Morris, Admissions Registrar on 01902 421326 or email jam@wgs-sch.net for further details.

Assistance with Fees. The School offers a number of means-tested bursaries to children from less affluent families who can demonstrate that they will benefit from the opportunity of an education with Wolverhampton Grammar School. Bursaries are reviewed annually so please contact

Jane Morris, Admissions Registrar on 01902 421326 or email jam@wgs-sch.net for further details.

Curriculum. The curriculum is delivered using a two-week timetable. Supported by over 100 termly extra and co-curricular activities, it covers a broad range of academic subjects that includes three language choices and Classics. Sixth Formers have a choice of A Level subjects and Cambridge Technical qualitifications. Sixth Formers usually take 3 or 4 subjects and this can also be supported by an Extended Project Qualification (EPQ) as well as structured work experience and HE/UCAS advice and guidance. Students go on to excellent universities including Oxford, Cambridge and other Russell Group institutions.

Games and Outdoor Activities. Wolverhampton Grammar School offers the largest range of extra-curricular activities, clubs, societies, trips, international expeditions and sport tours of any independent school in the area. Sport has a long tradition at the school and students compete at city, regional and national level. The 23-acre site includes rugby, cricket, hockey and football pitches, netball courts, an all-weather Astroturf and athletics track as well as a fully equipped sports centre with multi-gym and indoor courts for badminton, squash and nets. A 'sport for all' attitude exists in games and PE, where the staff endeavour to match the student to a sport or activity in which they can succeed. There is a commitment to the highest standards of skill and sportsmanship but the emphasis is also placed on enjoyment. The school participates in The Duke of Edinburgh's Award scheme and there are opportunities to undertake field trips and foreign exchanges. There is a rigorous outdoor education programme. The School also boasts Fives Courts as well as a purpose-built climbing wall and sports pavilion offering panoramic views of large outdoor sports fields.

Dyslexia. The School's OpAL (Opportunities through Assisted Learning) department is designed to allow bright children with Specific Learning Difficulties (Dyslexia) to enjoy the challenge of a first-rate academic education. OpAL students have consistently achieved exceptional GCSE and A Level grades – consistently above the national average.

Arts and Other Activities. Purpose-built facilities for art, music and drama provide the best venues possible for exhibitions and school productions. The school boasts a purpose-built art gallery known as the Viner Gallery, which is used by students and commercial artists alike. A large contemporary theatre known as the Hutton Theatre is home to exceptional performances by students from across the School. The location of the music department at the heart of the school ensures the sound of singing, ensemble and band music is always heard on campus. There is a wide variety of extra-curricular clubs and activities giving students the opportunity to discover and cultivate new interests, both inside and outside the classroom. A Community Service programme and an active student Charity Fundraising Committee ensure that all students are involved in working for the good of others.

Pastoral Care. The school is proud of the pastoral care and support it offers to its students and has an Assistant Head dedicated to lead Pastoral support across School. In the Junior and Middle Schools care is provided by a form tutor under the overall responsibility of the appropriate Heads of Schools. Regular consultations are held with parents including an annual parents' survey supported by full and frequent reports. An important forum is the Student Parliament which consists of elected representatives from all year groups who are encouraged to voice concerns and suggest improvements to the running and organisation of the school. The weekly meetings, with the Head plus one other member of staff in attendance, are run by an elected Chair and Secretary.

Charitable status. Wolverhampton Grammar School Limited is a Registered Charity, number 1125268.

Chairman: Mr James E Sage

Directors, Council and Trustees:
The Mayor of Wolverhampton (*ex-officio*)
Mr Matthew Armstrong
Mr Nick Berriman
Mr Chris Bill
Mrs Anne-Marie Brennan
Revd Sarah Cawdell
Mr Robin Cooper (*ex-officio USA*) [OW]
Dr Manisha Gowan-Gopal
Dr Stephen J L Gower, Appointed by the University of Birmingham [OW]
Mr Rod Grainger
Mr John Harper
Mr Peter A Hawthorne, CBE [OW]
Mr David Hughes
Mr Mike Hughes
Mrs Kate Lawrence
Professor Keith Madelin
Mr Peter Magill, Appointed by the Merchant Taylors' Company
Mr Yusuf Malik
Mr Anthony Phillips, Appointed by the Old Wulfrunians Association [OW]
Mr Jay Patel
Mr Stuart Ross
Mr Carl Tatton
Mr Simon Walford
Mrs Christine Wood

[OW] *Old Wulfrunian*

Head: **Mrs Kathy Crewe-Read**, BA Wales

Deputy Heads:
Mr Nic J C Anderson, BA Leeds (*Mathematics*)
Mr Toby R Hughes, MA, MPhil Queens' College Cambridge, PGCE Homerton College Cambridge (*Geography*)

Assistant Head Curriculum: Mr Alex P Yarnley, BA Hull (*Mathematics*)

Assistant Head Pastoral: Miss Claudine Jones, BA Nottingham Trenty, Dip RSA (*OpAL*)

Assistant Head Academic Administration: Mr Jonathan R Wood, BA Royal Holloway London, MA Ed Bangor (*OpAL, Peer Support and Exams Officer*)

Head of Junior School: Mr Dan Peters, BMus Birmingham (*Music*)

Deputy Head of Junior School: Miss Jill R Trevor, BA Wales

Teaching Staff:
Miss Lauren Austin, BSc Oxford Brookes (*WGJS*)
Mr Tom Baker, BSc Edinburgh (*Head of Geography*)
Mr Mark Benfield, BA Leeds, GCD Birmingham (*Head of English*)
Miss E A Bowater, BA Birmingham City (*Head of Art*)
Dr Neil J Bradley, BSc PhD Nottingham (*Mathematics*)
Miss Rebecca Bradley, BSc Hons Cardiff Metropolitan (*Head of Girls' Games*)
Mrs Sarah F Brentnall, BA Birmingham (*Modern Foreign Languages*)
Mr Nick Brown, BSc Hons Exeter (*Head of Mathematics*)
Mrs Katy Brown, MA Cambridge (*WGJS*)
Mr Andrew P Carey, BA London (*Head of Chemistry*)
Mr Russell B Charlesworth, BA Lady Margaret Hall Oxford (*Head of History*)

Mrs R E Clancy, BA Birmingham (*Head of Careers, Deputy Head of L6th Form and English*)

Mr Steve M Clancy, BSc Loughborough (*HOY 10, Boys' PE, Games and English*)

Mrs Victoria J Clarke, BA Cambridge (*Geography*)

Mr Francis Cooney, BSc Brunel (*Physics*)

Mrs Clare L Cooper, BA Royal Holloway London (*WGJS*)

Mr Truan J Cothey, BSc Lancaster (*WGJS*)

Mr Nigel H Crust, BA Bangor (*Deputy Head of U6th Form, Head of Boys' Games*)

Mrs Melanie Cuthbert, BA UCE Birmingham (*Director of Academic Music*)

Mrs Lynn D'Arcy, BA Wolverhampton (*WGJS*)

Mrs Anna L Dalton, BA Nottingham Trent (*WGJS*)

Mr J G David, BA Newcastle-upon-Tyne (*History*)

Mrs Helen V David, MChem York (*Chemistry*)

Mrs Rachael Davies, BA Hons Birmingham City (*Art*)

Mrs Laura Dixon, BSc Cardiff (*Science*)

Mr Christopher Doman, BSc Hons Newman Birmingham (*WGJS*)

Ms Liz Duncan, BEd Hons Warwick (*Mathematics*)

Mrs Kathy A Dyer, BA Gloucestershire (*Psychology and Girls' Games*)

Mrs Kath L Finn, BA Manchester (*Head of Theology and Philosophy*)

Dr Karen J Flavell, BSc PhD Wolverhampton (*Biology*)

Mr Andrew Fowler, MA Magdalen College Oxford (*Music*)

Mrs Diana S Gibbs, BA Bristol (*WGJS*)

Mrs Amelia Grant, BSc Open (*Geography*)

Mr James Griffiths, BA Liverpool John Moore's (*WGJS*)

Mrs Petra D Grigat-Bradley, Erstes und Zweites Staatsexamen, Ruhr-Universität Bochum (*Modern Foreign Languages*)

Mrs Gemma Guest, BA Hons UCE Birmingham (*Art*)

Ms Nikki T Guidotti, BA Anglia Polytechnic University (*Music*)

Mr Jonathan Hall, BA Newcastle upon Tyne (*HOY 7 and English*)

Mr Edward D Hamill, BSc Glasgow (*Science*)

Mrs Elizabeth S N Harris, BA Southampton (*Head of Modern Foreign Languages*)

Mrs Amy Hughes, BEd Cambridge (*WGJS*)

Mr Steve M Jackson-Turnbull, BA, MA Huddersfield (*HOY 9 and Design & Technology*)

Mr Adam Jones, BSc Hons Birmingham (*Head of Monitoring & Interventions for Mathematics*)

Mr Robert Jagger, BA Liverpool (*English*)

Mr Peter Johnstone, BA Hull (*Head of Psychology*)

Mr Theo King, ICC, Senior Coach (*Games, i/c Cricket*)

Mr Scott Li, BSc Warwick (*Head of KS5, Mathematics*)

Mr Ryan Lovatt, MA Liverpool (*Physics*)

Mrs Pav K Mahey, BA UCE Birmingham (*Economics and Business Studies*)

Mrs Patrizia Manzai, BA Turin (*Modern Foreign Languages*)

Mr Robert W Mason, BA Nottingham (*Modern Foreign Languages*)

Mr David Matkin, BSc Coventry (*OpAL*)

Mr Nick P Munson, BA Birmingham (*Head of Physics*)

Mrs Rachel E Munson, BA Leeds (*Modern Foreign Languages*)

Mr Simon L J O'Malley, BA Wolverhampton (*Head of Design & Technology*)

Mr Simon P Palmer, Senior Coach (*Girls' Hockey Coach*)

Mr Mark R Payne, BA Warwick (*English*)

Dr Ryan Pounder, PhD MChem Warwick (*Chemistry*)

Mrs Claire L Ray, BA Luton (*HOY 8 and Girls' PE*)

Mr Andrew Reddish, BA Sunderland (*Head of ICT and Computer Studies*)

Miss Naomi Roberts, BA Plymouth (*WGJS*)

Mr Jim P Ryan, BEd Crewe & Alsager College, MEd, Adv Dip SNE Open University, AMBDA, SpLD APC (*HOY 11 OpAL*)

Mr Gordon L Smith, BEd Loughborough (*Design & Technology*)

Mr Tom D Smith, BA Strathclyde (*Head of Economics and Business Studies*)

Mr Liam Taylor, BA Reading, MA Birmingham (*History*)

Mrs Ruth Taylor-Briggs, BA, PhD, Birmingham (*Head of Classics*)

Mr Ian H M Tyler, BA Saskatchewan, MEd Birmingham, Dip DA RADA (*Director of OpAL, SENCO, English and Theatre Studies*)

Mrs Fran E Wainwright, BSc Hertfordshire, PGCE Wolverhampton (*Mathematics*)

Mrs Diana M Ward, BA, MA Birmingham (*Art*)

Miss Emma L Watson, BA Manchester (*Physics*)

Miss Emma Yates, MA Leicester (*WGJS*)

Miss Rachel Young, BA Warwick (*Head of Biology*)

Mrs Beverley Young, BA Reading (*Religious Studies*)

Bursar: Mrs Penny Rudge
Head's PA: Mrs Caroline Harris

Woodbridge School

Burkitt Road, Woodbridge, Suffolk IP12 4JH

Tel:	01394 615000
	01394 382673 (The Abbey Prep)
Fax:	01394 380944
email:	admissions@woodbridgeschool.org.uk
website:	www.woodbridgeschool.org.uk
Twitter:	@woodbridgesch
Facebook:	@woodbridgeschool

'*Everyone happy, everyone confident, everyone successful.*'

Situation. Woodbridge is an attractive market town on the River Deben, opposite the site of the famous royal Saxon ship burial at Sutton Hoo. Timber-framed buildings dating from the Middle Ages, and Georgian facades draw many visitors to the town throughout the year as does the Aldeburgh Festival at the nearby international Snape Maltings Concert Hall. Excellent sailing facilities are available on the River Deben. Woodbridge is seven miles from the Suffolk coast and close to the continental ports of Felixstowe and Harwich. The rail journey to London takes a little over an hour.

History and Buildings. Woodbridge School was originally founded in 1662. The scholars were to be taught "both Latin and Greek until thereby they be made fit for the University (if it be desired), but in case of any of them be unapt to learn those languages …they should be taught only Arithmetic, and to Write, to be fitted for Trades or to go to Sea". They were also to be "instructed in the principles of the Christian Religion according to the Doctrine of the Church of England".

For 200 years, the School existed in cramped quarters in the town until its incorporation with the Seckford Trust. Endowment income then enabled it to move to its present undulating site overlooking the town and the River Deben and to begin the steady expansion and development which have accelerated over the last 25 years. The School has been fully co-educational for nearly four decades. The school has an on-site professional theatre, the state-of-the-art 350-seat Seckford Theatre. Other notable facilities include stunning on-site sports facilities including an all-weather pitch, the recently refurbished Britten Pears Music School and superb art and design facilities.

Woodbridge has had close links with the local community and, through its outstanding Music and Science, with Finland, France, Spain, The Netherlands, Hungary and Germany. Woodbridge has a British Council International School Award for its international links, pupils are able to go on cultural exchange to countries as diverse as Australia, Japan, India and China and also to Europe.

The Abbey prep school is based in a beautiful house dating from the 16th Century in the town, adjacent to which two large new buildings have been added. Taking pupils from 7–11, it has full use of the Senior School sports dome, tennis courts, etc. (*For further details, see entry in IAPS section.*) There are currently 137 pupils in the Abbey prep school.

Queen's House, the pre-prep department for 65 pupils aged 4–6, is based on the edge of the senior school site but will move to The Abbey site from September 2019.

Organisation. There are approximately 600 pupils in the Senior School. The Senior School (11–18) numbers 290 boys and 279 girls, with a Sixth Form of about 200. There is a co-educational Boarding House for pupils aged 13+. A Day House system exists with a Junior House for 11 year old entrants and four other Day Houses for those aged 12–16. All Sixth Form day pupils are based in the Sixth Form Centre.

Teaching. The curriculum at Woodbridge is a traditional academic curriculum, combining breadth with a strong focus on the major academic disiplines. The school's unique and innovative teaching approach, Learning@Woodbridge. This enables every pupil to not only acquire essential knowledge, but also empowers them to know how to learn better and become more independent.

Music, Games and Activities. Music is at the heart of much of the life of the School. Over 350 music lessons are given every week and a large number of pupils concerts and recitals each year, large and small, offer pupils opportunities to perform at all levels. Some 45% of pupils study at least one instrument.

Woodbridge is a chess centre of excellence, representing England at the world chess championships.

Riding, athletics, cross country, shooting and hockey are real strengths. Other main games are rugby and netball in the winter; cricket, also tennis and rounders in the summer. The Sports Hall has facilities for most indoor sports.

The first-class Combined Cadet Force embraces Army, RAF, and Royal Navy Sections. The extensive variety of clubs and societies includes The Duke of Edinburgh's Award scheme. All 11 and 12 year olds follow the Seckford Scheme which paves the way for these, and many other, activities.

Careers. The School offers comprehensive careers advice and there is an annual careers fair. There are close links with county and university careers departments, alongside an extensive alumni network accessible through Graduway.

Chapel and Religious Education. The School has a strong Christian ethos and pupils attend Chapel every week. There is an annual Confirmation Service.

Admission. Every child is invited to attend a taster day. Entry to the senior school is 11+, 12+ and 13+ by examination in January, prior to entry, plus interview and reference from current school. There are tests in English, Mathematics and Verbal Reasoning. Admission to Queen's House pre-prep is by assessment. Entry to The Abbey is by taster day and assessment. A reference from the current school is also sought.

Registration Fee: £50 (day), £100 (boarding). Acceptance Fee: £300 (day), £500 (UK boarding), £9,995 (overseas boarding).

Fees per term (2018–2019). Day: Pre-Prep (Queen's House) £3,247–£3,463; Prep (The Abbey) £3,950–£4,991; Senior School: Years 7–8 £5,082; Years 9–13 £5,500. Boarding: £10,295.

Scholarships and Bursaries. Due to its generous endowment, the School is able to offer remission of up to 100% of fees to pupils whose parents have incomes in the lower and middle ranges through Awards and/or Means-Tested Bursaries.

Academic Scholarships are available for entry at 11+, 13+ and 16+. These are awarded on the results of the annual entrance examinations at 11+ and 13+ and on the basis of interview and GCSE results at 16+.

Music scholarships are available on entry at 11+, 13+ and 16+ to candidates with considerable musical ability who also have a definite commitment to music at the school.

Drama scholarships are available on entry at 11+, 13+ and 16+ to applicants with considerable dramatic ability, and award holders must study Drama to at least GCSE level.

Art scholarships are available at 11+, 13+ and 16+ to pupils with considerable artistic ability, and award holders must study GCSE or A Level Art as appropriate.

Sport scholarships are available for entry at 11+ 13+ and 16+. In making these awards the school is ideally looking for candidates who excel in two or more team sports played at county or regional levels, although excellence in individual sports may be considered too.

All-round Awards can be offered at 11+, 13+ and 16+ to those who have are talented in one or more areas.

Chess Awards are available to candidates with considerable ability who have a definite commitment to chess at school. Potential and experience are both taken into account.

Charitable status. The Seckford Foundation is a Registered Charity, number 1110964. Its aims are to give education for "poor children" by the provision of scholarships and fee remissions out of charity funds, and to maintain "the elderly poor" by providing a subsidy out of the charity for the Almshouses and Jubilee House.

Governing Body: The Trustees of The Seckford Foundation

Chairman: R Finbow, MA Oxon

Headmaster: **Dr R Robson**, BA Hons, PGCE, MA, EdD

Deputy Head (*Academic*): Ms N E King
Deputy Head (*Pastoral*): Miss S Norman

Assistant Staff:
Head of Music: C M Milton
Head of Geography: Miss J A Gill
Head of Computing: J A Hillman
Head of Art: J L Hutchinson
Head of MFL: Mrs L R Chandler
Head of Classics: Mrs A Wright
Head of Chemistry: Mrs A Hillman
Head of Biology: Dr L V Rickard
Head of History: N E Smith
Head of Drama: Miss G Mayes
Head of Mathematics: E Turner
Head of Academic PE: Miss N L Sanders
Director of Sport: I J Simpson
Head of Religious Studies: Miss E Tattoo
Head of Design: Mrs D Cracknell
Head of Economics and Business Studies: J M Percival
Head of English: Dr A E Renshaw
Head of Physics: J D Morcombe

Bursar: G E Watson
School Medical Officer: Dr J P W Lynch
Headmaster's Secretary: Miss C Shaw

The Abbey and Queen's House
Woodbridge Prep and Pre-Prep Schools

Head of Prep and Pre-Prep: Mrs N Mitchell
Deputy Head of Prep: Mrs C M T Clubb
Deputy Head of Pre-Prep: Mrs S Lindsay-Smith

Assistant Staff:
Reception Class Teachers: Mrs K Spalding and Mrs M N Kiley
Year 1 Class Teachers: Mrs L Smith, Mrs A King and Mrs J Duncan
Year 2 Class Teachers: Mrs H Cory, Mrs K Start and Mrs L Ford
Year 3 Class Teachers: Mrs S Griffiths and Mrs P A Martin
Year 4 Class Teachers: Mrs J O Chamberlain, Mrs S K Cox-Olliff and C French
Year 5 Class Teachers: M R Fernley and L M Palin
Year 6 Class Teachers: Miss G R Ballam and C S Smith
Head of Spanish: Mrs L Verona
Head of Performing Arts: Mrs J Rayner
Head of Games: M C Wheelhouse

Woodhouse Grove School

Apperley Bridge, Bradford, West Yorkshire BD10 0NR

Tel: 0113 250 2477
Fax: 0113 250 5290
email: enquiries@woodhousegrove.co.uk
website: www.woodhousegrove.co.uk
Twitter: @woodhouse_grove
Facebook: @woodhousegroveschool

Motto: '*Bone et fidelis*'

Woodhouse Grove was founded in 1812 and is a co-educational day and boarding school for pupils aged from 3 to 18 years. Boarding pupils are taken from the age of 11 years.

Our hard work has been recognised by the Independent Schools Inspectorate inspection in March 2017 which rated Woodhouse Grove as Excellent. The inspectors came away with very clear evidence of the Grovian Values that we seek to promote. They recognised our outstanding academic and co-curricular programme and our aim to ensure that all our pupils reach their full potential.

At Woodhouse Grove, we appreciate that every child is a unique individual and this is at the heart of everything we do. We aim to motivate pupils academically and beyond the classroom and to provide an educational environment designed to allow students to fully participate in school life.

We offer a rich, challenging and dynamic curriculum and want our students to ask questions of the world around them with an open mind; to have the character to listen to others, but also to stand up for their beliefs. We encourage our pupils to 'give back' to their community and we believe that this well-rounded, diverse approach is the key to building academic and personal confidence. Ultimately, our objective is to provide our students with the drive and aspiration to become the very best version of themselves that they can be.

Set in idyllic grounds near Leeds, the school is opposite Apperley Bridge train station and within four miles of Leeds Bradford Airport. We have high standards and an all-encompassing approach to education and our outstanding facilities reflect this. A recording studio, 230-seater theatre, sports halls, swimming pool and climbing wall are all within our 70-acre campus.

Numbers. There are 751 pupils in the Senior School including 83 boarders and a Sixth Form of 193 students. Brontë House (age 3–11 years) has 358 pupils.

Buildings. Our facilities include a purpose-built sports centre with a multi-functional sports hall, a fitness suite, a dance studio, a 25m competition swimming pool, squash courts, floodlit outdoor courts, floodlit all-weather pitch, performing arts centre and climbing wall. We have fully equipped science laboratories, a new state-of-the-art DT and Art centre, a spacious music and drama block, language suite and fully-equipped IT rooms. We have a modern spacious Sixth Form centre and refurbished boarding houses to provide a separate sixth form annexe for boys.

Sport. We have approximately 40 acres of playing fields including grounds for Cricket, Rugby, Football and Athletics as well as indoor Squash, Basketball and Swimming facilities. There are several all-weather Tennis Courts, a floodlit outdoor court for Netball and Tennis and a floodlit all-weather pitch.

Music. 33% of pupils have instrumental or vocal tuition and pupils can perform in a wide variety of music, drama and dance groups. Accredited exams offered include ABRSM & Trinity Guildhall Speech and Drama. There are a number of high-profile annual performances taking advantage of the dedicated theatre and recording studio. Music tours take place every two years. Sixth form courses are available in Music and Music Technology.

Curriculum. Boys and girls can enter the Senior School at any age but mainly at the age of 11, 13 and 16 and the curriculum is arranged to provide a seamless transition through from Brontë House and upwards through the Sixth Form to University entrance. A wide range of GCSE (and IGCSE) courses are offered and currently we are offering 28 subjects at A Level. Specialist support is offered to meet EAL, dyslexia and other learning needs. All students get the chance to study French, Spanish and German. The campus is served by full-site Wi-Fi.

Sixth Form Entry. Places are available for students who want to come into the School at the Sixth Form stage subject to entry requirements.

Scholarships and Bursaries. Scholarships can be applied for directly from the headmaster for academic, all-rounder, art, sport and music. In addition, bursaries can be awarded following the offer of a place, in cases of financial need (plus allowances for children of ministers and of service personnel). Extras include excursions and extra tuition, such as music.

Admission. Places are offered subject to availability and based on our own entrance exam, in-school interview and previous school report. Pupils are usually accepted in September, although arrangements can be made for entry throughout the school year.

Brontë House is our Preparatory School and takes boys and girls during the term that they turn three. Ashdown Lodge Nursery & Reception takes pupils on a day or part-day basis, all year round.

Fees per term (2018–2019). Main School: £9,300–£9,340 (full boarders), £8,720–£8,875 (weekly boarders), £4,440–£4,525 (day). Brontë House: £3,300–£4,000 (day). Ashdown Lodge Nursery and Reception: £3,000 (full day), £1,870 (half day). Fees include all meals, books, stationery, examination fees and careers tests.

Extra Subjects. There is a wide range of extra subjects available including individual music lessons, singing, speech and drama, dancing, extra sports coaching, debating, Duke of Edinburgh's Award, photography and fencing.

Old Grovians Association. *Secretary*: Mrs Heather Garner, email: foundation@woodhousegrove.co.uk.

Charitable status. Woodhouse Grove School is part of the Methodist Independent Schools Trust, which is a Registered Charity, number 1142794.

Governors:
Mr A Wintersgill, FCA (*Chairman*)
Mr M Best, ACA
Mr S Burnhill, BSc
Mr R S Drake, LLB Hons, ACIArb
Rt Revd C P Edmondson
Mrs P M Essler, BSc
Dr G H Haslam, MBChB
Mr R C Hemsley, FCA, MA
Ms P Kaur, MSc
Mr F J McAleer, BA Arch, Dip Arch, RIBA
Prof M Manogue, BDS, MDSc, PhD
Mr M Pearman, MA
Mr I M Small, BA, DipEd
Revd Dr R L Walton, MA, EdD
Revd P Whittaker, BA
Mrs G Wilson, CertEd

Staff:

Headmaster: J A Lockwood, MA

Deputy Head (Academic): E J Wright, BSc
Deputy Head (Pastoral): A M Cadman, BA
Deputy Head: Mrs E Nulty, BA
Assistant Head (Boarding and Compliance): S P Vernon
Assistant Head (Curriculum): Mrs E Ainscoe
Assistant Head (Organisation): K D Eaglestone
Assistant Head (Pupil Welfare): Mrs F L Hughes
Assistant Head (Teaching and Learning): Mrs D L
   Shoesmith-Evans
Chaplain: Revd D H Bonny, BA, BD
Clerk to the Governors & Finance Manager: D Ainsworth,
   BA, ACA
Operations Director: Mrs V Bates, ACA

* *Head of Department*
† *Head of House*

Mrs E Ainscoe, MA (*Biology*)
Miss F Alimundo, BSc (*Geography*)
Mrs C Allday (*Learning Support*)
Dr J Allday, PhD, MA (*Information Technology*)
J Allison, BA (**Design Technology*, †*Vinter*)
S Archdale (*Speech and Drama*)
Miss A Barron, BA (*German*)
Mr N Barr, (*PE and Games,*†*Stephenson*)
E Bean, BSc (*Physics)
A Cadman, BA (*PE*)
J Carter, BA (*History, *RE*)
Mrs P N Charlton, MA (*Art & Design*)
Miss E Corson, BA (*Modern Foreign Languages*)
A N Crawford, BA, ARCO (*Music, Mathematics,*
   †*Findlay*)
Miss C Couper, BA (**Drama and Theatre Studies*)
Mrs K Curtis, BSc (*PE and Games*)
T Davis, BA (*Chemistry)
M Dobson, BSc (*PE and Games*)
K Eaglestone, BSc (*Mathematics*)
Mrs J L Edger, BSc (*Physics*)
Mrs H Fisher, MA (*Psychology)
Miss L Follos, BA (*Design Technology*)
R I Frost, BEd (*PE and Games)
Mr C Garbutt, BSc (*Biology*)
Mrs K L Goodwin-Bates, MA (*English & Media Studies*)
Miss C Gray (*Learning Support*)
Miss S Harder, BSc (*Physics*)
D Hole, BSc (*Chemistry*)
Miss L Holloway, BA (*History & Religious Studies*)
Mrs F L Hughes, BEd (*French*)
Miss L Hughes, BA (*English*)
Dr A Ingham, BSc (*Biology*)
A Jarvis, BA (*Modern Languages*)

Miss C D Jemmett, BA (*English*)
A Jennings, BA (**Religious Studies*)
Mrs K Jennings, BEd (*PE)
R Johnson, BA (*English & Media Studies*)
Mrs A Kerr, BSc (*Mathematics*)
Mr D King (*Director of Sport*)
P Lambert, BA (*Modern Foreign Languages*)
Miss E Landy, BSc (*Chemistry, Biology*)
S Lomax, BA (*Mathematics*)
Mr P Madden (*History & Religious Studies*)
O Mantle, BA (*IT*, **Business Studies and Economics*,
   †*Atkinson*)
Miss F McLean, (*English with Media Studies*)
Mrs H Mitchell, BA (**Modern Foreign Languages*)
P J Moffat, BA (*Geography*)
Miss B Monk, BA (*ESOL, *Learning Support)
M F Munday, BA (*Geography*)
Mrs C Nott, MA (*Mathematics)
Mrs E Nulty, BA (*Business Studies and Economics*)
Miss L Oakley, BA (*English)
Mr P Oatridge, (*Maths*)
Miss C Pearce, BA (*PE and Games, Geography*)
A J Pickles, BA (**Art & Design*)
Mrs H Priestley (*Drama and Dance*)
Mrs L Richardson, BSc (*Biology)
J B Robb, BA (**Religious Studies*)
Miss J Russell, BA (*IT*)
Mr T Ryder (*PE, Games and Biology*)
Mrs R Sharpe, BA (*English and Media Studies*)
Mrs D L Shoesmith-Evans, BA (*Humanities)
Mrs D Smith, BA (*Design and Technology*)
Mrs L Smith, BA (*Modern Foreign Languages*)
Miss H Spiller, BA (*Art*)
C Softley, BA (*PE*)
Mrs C Spencer, BA (*Business Studies and Economics*,
   †*Towlson*)
D Sugden, BSc (*Mathematics*)
Miss G Thompson (*PE and Games*)
J P A Tedd, MA (*Music)
Mrs R Vernon, BA (*PE*)
S Vernon, BA (*PE*)
Mrs R Warner, BA (*Politics, History*)
Mrs P L Watson, MA (*Business Studies, IT*)
Mrs L Watmough (*Business Studies*, †*Southerns*)
Mrs R Wickens, BA (*Geography)
G Williams, BSc (*Science)
K Wilson, BA (*English Studies*)
E Wright, BSc (*Mathematics*)

Headmaster's Secretary: Mrs S Hargrave
Registrar: Mrs J Amos

Brontë House
Headmaster: S Dunn, BEd
Deputy Head: Mrs S Chatterton, BEd
Director of Studies: Mrs N Woodman, MPhil
KS1 Coordinator: Mrs H J Simpson, BA
Foundation Stage Coordinator: Mrs A Hinchliffe, BA

Worth School

**Paddockhurst Road, Turners Hill, West Sussex
RH10 4SD**

Tel: 01342 710200
Fax: 01342 710230
email: admissions@worth.org.uk
website: www.worthschool.org.uk

Twitter: @worthschool
Facebook: @worthschool
LinkedIn: /worth-school

Worth is a Catholic Benedictine boarding and day school for boys and girls aged 11–18. It is a truly distinctive school, known for its strong community values, friendly atmosphere and the excellence of its all-round education. The School has been under the leadership of Mr Stuart McPherson (formerly at Eton College) since September 2015 and in the Head Master's words is: "a place where we seek to uncover and ignite children's passions and talents. The path a life takes often begins at school, and this is why we do not just provide education, we offer learning with heart and soul, and this gives Worth a difference of kind that sets us apart."

This magnificent school is in the heart of the Sussex countryside, about halfway between London and Brighton, and less than 15 minutes from Gatwick airport. We are ideally placed to allow students to sample some of the cultural highlights that Britain has to offer, while providing a beautiful environment in which to learn.

In an Independent Schools Inspectorate (ISI) Report in November 2017, Worth was judged to be excellent – the highest possible grade – for the quality of the pupils' academic and other achievements and personal development. In January 2011 we had a full Ofsted inspection on provision for Boarders at Worth. The school was found to be 'Outstanding' and no recommendations were made. A review by the *Good Schools Guide* in 2017 concluded that "This school has everything going for it..."

The school offers a broad curriculum, where students can opt for the International Baccalaureate Diploma or A Levels. The School has offered the IB since 2002 and a pre-IB course was introduced for non-UK students in Year 11 in 2015. Examination results are excellent and pupils enter the best universities in the UK and abroad, including Oxford, Cambridge, Russell Group universities and Ivy League institutions.

The wider curriculum is rich and varied with a huge range of activities, societies, lectures and trips from which to choose. There is also a lively sporting programme which has produced students of national and county standard, and the school's reputation for performing arts is outstanding.

History. Worth School is situated in the midst of the beautiful 500-acre Worth Abbey estate on a ridge of the Sussex Weald that had formerly been the property of the first Lord Cowdray. The estate was purchased in 1933 by a group of monks from Somerset who opened a prep school for boys. The prep school was evacuated during the Second World War and a senior school was founded in 1959.

Worth welcomed girls into Years 7 and 9 in September 2010. They joined other girls in an already thriving co-educational Sixth Form, and the School has been fully co-educational since 2012 with girls integrated into all aspects of school life.

Courses of study. At GCSE level, students usually take ten subjects. The compulsory core is: English, Mathematics, Sciences, French or Spanish or German (plus PE and SMSC). Two or three options are chosen from: Art, Drama, Design Technology, Economics, Classical Civilisation, French or Spanish or German as a second language, Geography, History, ICT, Latin, Music and Photography. Tuition is available (for an additional fee) in Greek, Italian and Chinese to GCSE and A Level.

There is a wide choice of subjects at A Level: Art, Biology, Business Studies, Chemistry, Drama, Economics, English, French, Geography, German, History, ICT, Maths and Further Maths, Music, Music Technology, Physics, Physical Education, Photography, Politics, Psychology and

Spanish. There is also the opportunity to take the Extended Project Qualification (EPQ).

Alternatively, Sixth Form students may study the International Baccalaureate. This involves the study of six subjects, three at Higher Level and three at Standard Level. Students study one subject from each of the following groups:

Group 1: English, German, Italian

Group 2: English, French, German, Greek, Italian (ab initio), Latin, Spanish (also ab initio)

Group 3: Economics, Geography, History, Philosophy, Psychology

Group 4: Biology, Physics

Group 5: Mathematics (HL), Mathematics (SL), Mathematical Studies (SL)

Group 6: Music, Theatre Arts, Visual Arts, Chemistry, French, History, Economics, Greek

Sixth Form students may also choose to study for Oxbridge entrance and a number gain places at either Oxford or Cambridge.

A Catholic school. Worth believes that each person is on a spiritual journey and that the school should support them wherever they are on that journey, and try to encourage a faith which will sustain pupils in later life. Over half of the 620 students at Worth are from Roman Catholic families, and there are a significant number of Christians from other denominations. Equal members of the community in every way, non-Catholic pupils have no difficulty integrating in the school and bring a different perspective which is most welcome. The School Chaplaincy team includes a part-time Anglican Chaplain, as well as Catholic Chaplains and lay members. Everyone is expected to subscribe to the School's Benedictine values which include Hospitality, Service, Worship and Community among others.

There are prayers each day in Houses, whole-school worship each Wednesday and Mass every Sunday for those boarding over the weekend and for local families.

Pastoral Care. Care of each student is of central importance throughout the School, as evidenced by our 'Outstanding' Ofsted grading for Boarder provision. Each pupil is a member of a House and has a personal tutor who monitors work progress and assists the Housemaster/Housemistress with overall care. The House support structure also includes a Chaplain and a matron, supported by an assistant matron in each of the Boarding Houses. There is a counsellor who is available to pupils. The Benedictine tradition of community life underpins everything. Many staff families live on-site and parents are welcomed as integral to the school. There are regular points of contact, with parent-teacher consultations, meetings, social events and active support from the Friends of Worth (the parents' association).

Sport. Worth loves its sports. The main sports are: rugby, football, hockey, netball, cricket, tennis and athletics. Other sports played at competitive level include fencing, squash, golf, basketball, lacrosse and swimming, and sports are also available through school clubs and activities (see below). There is a floodlit Astropitch, a nine-hole golf course, squash courts, tennis courts, fencing salle, dance studio and fitness suite. The School also makes use of the excellent athletics facility and 50m swimming pool at a multi-sports centre nearby.

Performing Arts. Music is important at Worth. There is a flourishing choir that is involved in tours and recordings as well as regular appearances in the Abbey Church. Parents, local friends and students join the Choral Society for at least two concerts each year (performing such works as Requiems by Fauré and Duruflé). The School orchestra performs regularly, as does the Jazz Band. The annual House Music, Battle of the Bands and Worth Unplugged competitions provide all pupils with an opportunity to perform and encourage an interest in music.

Drama also flourishes with regular productions at all levels and the standard of performance is exceptional. There are three major productions a year, taking place in the purpose-built Performing Arts Centre which comprises a 250-seater theatre, box office, drama office and workshop, dressing rooms, recording studio, a sound-proofed 'rock room', rehearsal rooms, a recital room and music classrooms.

Extracurricular activity. On Wednesday afternoons every pupil participates in one or more activities, ranging from Age Concern and photography to sailing, clay pigeon shooting, and polo. There is a horse riding school for students and there are stables on the campus. Worth is also a centre of excellence for The Duke of Edinburgh's Award scheme. There are lectures by external speakers and a wide array of trips, visits and exchanges both at home and abroad.

Admissions Policy. Entry at 11+: Entrance tests in English, Maths and Non-Verbal Reasoning are held in January each year. Offers are based on test results, a report from the student's current school and an interview with the Head Master. Annual promotion is subject to the pupil having shown satisfactory academic performance as determined by the Head Master, and a good disciplinary record.

Entry at 13+ (Year 9) for 2020: Admission at 13+, after visits and registrations, is via the ISEB Common Pre-Test, taken either at Worth or at Prep schools in the Autumn Term of Year 7, and Worth's additional assessment days. Admission for overseas candidates is via separate assessment tests and interviews held in their own countries.

Entry at 13+ (Year 9) for 2021: Admission at 13+, after visits and registrations, is via the ISEB Common Pre-Test, taken either at Worth or at Prep schools in the Autumn/Spring Term of Year 6, and Worth's additional assessment days. Admission for overseas candidates is via separate assessment tests and interviews held in their own countries.

Entry at 16+: Admissions is by means of reports and references from the candidate's current school, assessments and interviews held at Worth during the year prior to entry. Entry is competitive, and successful applicants will usually be predicted to gain top grades in most of their GCSEs or equivalent examinations, but we recognise the central value of Art, Drama, Music, Sport and other co-curricular activities, and enthusiasm in these fields is expected and encouraged.

For further information on Admissions please contact the Registrar on 01342 710231.

Scholarships. Scholarships are prestigious awards available to candidates demonstrating outstanding promise and ability in the spheres of Academic Study and/or Music. They are awarded in order to assist in creating and sustaining a culture of the love of learning and academic ambition throughout the School.

Exhibitions are available for candidates with outstanding promise in Art, Drama or Sport and have the same objective as scholarships in the specific areas to which they apply. While most awards will be subject to means-testing, a limited number of non means-tested awards may be allocated each year to the most able applicants in each category.

Bursaries are awarded to assist access to candidates whose parents support the School's values and ethos and who can both benefit from and contribute to the School's educational offering.

In these and in all cases the School's limited financial resources will be applied only to those parents who genuinely need them. Thus it may well occur that a Scholarship or Exhibition offer carries no financial advantage.

Scholarships and Exhibitions are awarded on the basis of competitive entry examinations and careful scrutiny of references. Scholars and Exhibitioners are offered tailored programmes and opportunities to develop their talents to the full. They are expected to act as role models who promote their area of excellence in the School. All awards are won in open competition and are made solely on merit. Candidates must be registered with the School prior to entering the award process.

The number and value of Scholarship and Exhibition awards in any year will depend on the number and calibre of applications. Pupils may apply for up to three awards. The continuation of any award will depend upon continued good behaviour and outstanding progress. All Scholarships and Exhibitions are reviewed at the end of every school year.

Parents seeking financial assistance must submit a formal application for bursary assistance when the Scholarship or Exhibition application is submitted.

For further information on scholarships and bursaries, please see the School website.

Fees per term (2018–2019). Years 9–13: Boarding £11,230, Day £7,910; Years 7 & 8: Boarding £7,070, Day £5,320, Flexi Boarding (boys only) £6,750.

Friends of Worth. The parents of children at Worth run their own programme of social events to which all parents are invited. Typical events are coffee mornings, drinks receptions and a bi-annual ball.

Worth Society. All Worthians are entitled to join the alumni society which organises events as well as assisting with individual work experience and ongoing careers guidance. Contact Mary Lou Burge at worthsociety@worth.org.uk.

Charitable status. Worth School is a Registered Charity, number 1093914. Its aims and objectives are to promote religion and education.

The Abbot's Board of Governors comprises both monks and laity:
President: The Rt Revd Dom Luke Jolly, BA
Chairman: Mr Tim Pethybridge, MA
The Revd Dom Mark Barrett, MA, PhD
Mr David Buxton, BA, MTh, MA
Dr Bridget Dolan, QC
Mr Benedict Elwes, BSc
Mr Jeremy Fletcher, BA
Mrs Henrietta Fudakowski, BA
Mr Peter Green, Cert RE, MA
Dom David Jarmy, Cert Theol, PGCE
Mrs Fiona Newton, BA, PGCE
Mrs Helen Parry, BSc, FCIS
Dr Ralph Townsend, MA

Head Master: Mr Stuart McPherson, MA

Second Master: Mr André Gushurst-Moore, MA
Deputy Head (*Academic*): Mr Simon Fisher, BA
Deputy Head (*External*): Mr Gordon Pearce, MA
Deputy Head (*Pastoral*): Mrs Louise Chamberlain, BSc
Assistant Head (*Co-Curricular*): Mr Julian Williams, BSc, MA, Dip TESL
Senior School Chaplain: Dom Peter Williams
School Bursar: Mr Paul Bilton, MA, FCA

Teaching Staff:
* *Head of Department/Subject*

Miss Ellen Affleck, BA (*Sports Graduate Assistant*)
Mr Paul Ambridge, BA (*Physics*)
Mrs Esme Atkinson (*Librarian*)
Mrs Frances Baily, MSc (**Physics*)
Mr Matthew Ball, BSc (*Science and Games*)
Miss Jo Barnes (*Games & Physical Education*)
Mrs Andrea Beadle, BA, MA (*German, German Assistant*)
Mr Jonathan Bindloss, BA (**Christian Theology and Philosophy, Theory of Knowledge*)
Mr Stuart Blackhurst, HND (*Head of Digital Strategy*)
Mr Andrew Brinkley, MA (*History, Butler Housemaster*)

Mr Lewis Brito-Babapulle, MA (*Director of Music*)
Mr Joe Brock, BSc (*Physics*)
Ms Amanda Brookfield, BA, MA (*Director of Careers and Higher Education, English*)
Mrs Caroline A Brown, BA, MA (*Religious Studies*)
Mrs Sophie Bruton, BA (*French*)
Mrs Caroline Burton, MSc (*Biology*)
Mr David Burton, BEd (*Director of Sport*)
Mrs Lucinda Button, BA (*Art & Design*)
Mrs Katie Camp, BA (*Art*)
Miss Iria Carnota (**Spanish*)
Mr Raj Chaudhuri, BCom, ECB Level 4 (*Master in charge of Cricket*)
Mrs Minakshi Chaudhuri, BA (*Activities Manager*)
Mrs Cheryl Cheeseman, RCN, Dip Paeds (*Head Nurse, Medical Department*)
Mr Paul Cheeseman, BA (*Design Technology*)
Miss Sarah Clarke, BA (*History*)
Mrs Dawn Clubb, BA, MA (**English*)
Mr Daniel Collins, LLB (*Head of Football*)
Mr William Crénel, LLCE (*French, St Bede's Housemaster*)
Mrs Claire Cross, BA (*Religious Studies, St Catherine's Housemistress, SMSC Coordinator*)
Mr Damian Cummins, BA (*Physical Education, Rutherford Housemaster, Senior HsM*)
Mrs Sue Cummins, BA (*Mathematics, Games, Junior Rutherford Housemistress*)
Mr Simeon Dann, BA, MA (*Religious Studies*)
Mrs Jayne Dempster, BSc (*Mathematics*)
Mr Stephen Doerr, BA (*Learning Support, Mathematics*)
Mr Matthew Doggett, MA, MSci (**Mathematics, Science*)
Mr Jeremy Dowling, BEd (*Mathematics*)
Mr John Everest, BA (*Photography*)
Mr Simon Faulkner, BA (*Head of Hockey, Games & Physical Education*)
Mrs Sarah Flint, BA (**Modern Foreign Languages, *French*)
Mr Jonathan Fry, BA (*Economics, Farwell Housemaster*)
Mrs Rose Fry, BA (*Learning Support*)
Dr Barbara Gehrhus, Diplomchemiker, PhD (*Chemistry*)
Mr Benjamin Gray, MA, BSc (*Religious Studies*)
Dr Bruna Gushurst-Moore, BA, MSt, PhD (*English, St Anne's Housemistress*)
Mr Edward Hall, BSc (*Economics & Politics*)
Mrs Karolina Hall, BA (*English as an Additional Language*)
Miss Juley Hudson, BA, MA (**Art*)
Mrs Siobhan Isaacs, BA (*Games & Physical Education, Assistant Director of Sport*)
Ms Melanie Kendry, MA (*English*)
Mrs Emma Kenyon, BA (*French*)
Mrs Andrea Kirpalani, BSc (**Science, Senior Teacher*)
Mrs Kerrie-Anne Langendoen, BSc (*Learning Support*)
Miss Naomy Larkin, BA (*English*)
Mrs Catherine Latham, BSc, MSc (*Head of Learning Support and SENCO*)
Mr Andrew Lavis, BA (**Geography*)
Mr Alex Leadbeater, BA (*Assistant Director of Music*)
Miss Lucy Lockwood, BA (*Music Technology*)
Mrs Natalie Lynch, BA (*Director of Drama*)
Mr Mark Macdonald, BSc (*Geography, Chapman Housemaster*)
Mr Alick Macleod, MSc (*Geography, Gervase Housemaster*)
Mrs Helen Macleod, BA (**History, Extended Essay Coordinator*)
Mr David Marks, MA, BA (*English as an Additional Language*)
Mr Dominic Marshall, BA (*Religious Studies*)
Mrs Gemma McCabe, BSc (*Mathematics*)

Ms Anna Mester, MSc (**German, Spanish*)
Mr Alan Mitchell, BSc (*Games & Physical Education*)
Mrs Maria Molinero, BA (*Spanish*)
Mr Bruce Morrison, Bed (*Games & Physical Education*)
Mr Robin Moss, BSc (*Chemistry & Science*)
Mrs Sheena Nasim, MA (*Economics & Business Studies*)
Mrs Deanna Nicholson, BSc (*Mathematics, Physics*)
Mrs Fiona Norden, BA (*English*)
Mr Peter O'Kang, BEng (*Mathematics*)
Miss Fran O'Neill, BA (*Religious Studies*)
Mr Andrew Olle (*Games & Physical Education*)
Mr Andrew Oxley, BSc (*Science*)
Mr Gordon Perera, BA (*Mathematics*)
Mr Richard Phillips, BSc (**Economics and Business Studies*)
Ms Alessandra Pittoni, Laurea in Lingue (*Italian*)
Dr Duncan Pring, MA, PhD (*Economics & Business Studies, Head of Careers*)
Miss Kate Reynolds, BSc (*Biology*)
Ms Linda Rice, BA, MA (*Learning Support*)
Mr Thomas Richardson (*Head of Rugby*)
Mr Liam Richman, BSc (*Mathematics, Austin Housemaster*)
Mr Theo Rivers, BSc (*Sports Graduate Assistant*)
Mr Philip Robinson, MA (*Classics*)
Miss Eleanor Ross, BSc (*Chemistry*)
Ms Victoria Sadler, MA (*Geography*)
Dr Peter Scott, MA, PhD (**Biology*)
Mrs Sarah Smith, BA (*English*)
Mrs Rebecca Steinebach, BA (*Modern Languages, St Mary's Housemistress*)
Mr Philip Towler, MA (**Classics*)
Mr Dan Weaver, BA (*Design Technology, ICT*)
Mr James Williams, BSc (*Physics*)
Ms Naomi Williams, BSc (**Psychology, IB Coordinator*)
Mr Ben Young, BA (*Graduate Language Assistant*)

Registrar: Mrs Lucy Garrard
Head Master's Secretary: Mrs Samantha Braund
Medical Officers: Dr R Harvey, Dr S Ferrier
Lead Nurse: Cheryl Cheeseman, SRN, Paediatric Dipl
Nurses:
Jo Doyle, EN
Julia Horner, RN
Lorna Lindo, RN
Helen Paine, RN
Angela Wayt, RN

Wrekin College

Wellington, Shropshire TF1 3BH

Tel:	Main: 01952 265600
	Headmaster's Office: 01952 265602
	Admissions: 01952 265603
Fax:	01952 415068
email:	admissions@wrekincollege.com
website:	www.wrekincollege.com
Twitter:	@WrekinCol
Facebook:	@WrekinCollege

Motto: '*Aut vincere aut mori*'

Wrekin College was founded in 1880 by Sir John Bayley and in 1923 became one of the Allied Schools, a group of six independent schools including Canford, Harrogate Ladies' College, Stowe and Westonbirt.

The College is situated in an estate of 100 acres on the outskirts of the market town of Wellington. We pride ourselves on the excellent quality of our staff, as well as the excellent quality of our facilities, and we measure our achievements not only by our examination results, but also by the whole development of individuals within the school. Being a relatively small school, about 400 pupils, the quality of relationships is good and enables a purposeful atmosphere to prevail in which pupils can achieve their potential, both in academic and extra-curricular activities. Our facilities include a purpose-built Theatre, a double Sports Hall, Astroturf and 25m indoor swimming pool, together with all the expected classrooms, ICT facilities and a dedicated Sixth Form Centre. The new, purpose-built Business School opened in 2017 providing a unique combination of teaching and real-life engagement in an office-style setting. Teaching is expert and disciplined. Co-educational since 1975, there are 7 Houses, which cater for both day and boarding pupils, and these include dedicated junior Houses for the 11 to 13 intake. Everyone eats together in a central dining room and a Medical Centre is available to all pupils. The Chapel is central to the school both geographically and in the impact it makes on the ethos of the school.

Admission. Boarders and day pupils are admitted at 11+ or 13+ after passing the Entry Examination or Common Entrance. There is also a Sixth Form entry based on GCSE achievement. Entry into other years is dependant on places being available.

Term of entry. The normal term of entry is the Autumn Term but pupils may be accepted at other times of the academic year in special circumstances.

Academic Matters. The core purpose of the school is teaching and learning to support each child in reaching their academic potential. Wrekin is proud of its strong academic record, based on stimulating intellectual curiosity, providing excellent and inspiring teaching, and making learning exciting. Our guiding principle is to help every child achieve the most they are capable of, to prepare them for the competitive world they will enter, and to give them a lasting sense of the pleasure and value of learning that will enrich their future lives.

Classes are small, typically no more than twenty for the younger pupils and between eight and fifteen at A Level. Our teachers are experienced, expert and approachable, and give a great deal of time to pupils both inside and outside the classroom. Our tutoring system means each pupil has personalised academic support throughout the year. Our Support for Learning staff can help those with additional needs, and our enrichment programme stimulates and stretches our more able students.

Our curriculum is constantly reviewed in the light of changes in educational policy and philosophy, but we are committed to offering our pupils a solid and broad academic foundation. We offer a wide range of subjects for GCSE, A Level and BTEC exams, and guide pupils in choosing subjects that suit their interests, abilities and future plans. Our Head of Careers advises pupils throughout their time at school, and the Head of Sixth Form offers expert advice on university applications.

Sport. For a small school, our sporting prowess is remarkable. We aim for very high standards in our core sports and a very wide range of options – up to twelve different sports in any term. Our sporting philosophy is based on a pyramid, with elite athletes at the top (including our national level gymnasts, swimmers, athletes and cross-country runners) and minor sports to appeal to all at the base. We believe in excellence but also in participation – sport for all, and for life.

Educating the Whole Person. The outdoors is one of Wrekin's most valuable classrooms. The skills learned and adventures experienced during pupils' participation in the Combined Cadet Force and the Duke of Edinburgh's Award scheme stay with them for life. Both are enthusiastically supported by highly dedicated staff, and the take up among our middle year pupils is impressive. We are very proud that Wrekin's 'completion rate' at all levels of the scheme is substantially above the national average.

What happens on the sports pitch and in the music rooms, the theatre and the art studios is just as important a part of a Wrekin education. The range and quality of activities available to every pupil is outstanding, especially for a school of this size. Our pupils' development and achievements in these areas are supported by wonderful facilities and highly dedicated staff.

Scholarships and Bursaries. *Academic Scholarships* are awarded at our normal entry points of 11, 13 and 16. Candidates should be under 12, under 14 or under 17 on September 1st of the year in which they will enter the school. Age may be taken into account when comparing candidates, so that those who are young for their year are not disadvantaged.

Music and Art/Design Scholarships take place in November (11+/16+) and February (13+). As for all other scholarships, Music and Art Awards will not exceed twenty five per cent of the fees. However, Music Scholarships carry with them a specified amount of free instrumental and/or vocal tuition. Candidates must also satisfy the school's normal academic entry requirements.

Sports Awards: Sports Scholarships may be awarded to candidates with outstanding ability in Sport. Applicants must attend a sports assessment day and satisfy the school's normal academic entry requirements. Candidates should be capable of a very significant contribution to the sporting success of Wrekin College. Typically candidates will have representative success at regional or National level.

Pendle Awards may be offered to all-rounders who have high academic standards and excellence in other areas such as sport, music or art. Those seeking a Pendle Award must sit the academic Scholarship Examination, either at 11+, 13+ or 16+ level and meet scholarship standard in at least one other area.

Bursaries may be awarded on entry and can be awarded in addition to a scholarship. All bursaries are means tested and could in some circumstances cover the whole school fee.

For further information please visit our website www.wrekincollege.com.

Fees per term (2018–2019). First and Second Forms: £4,940 (day); £7,120 (weekly boarding); £9,120 (full boarding). Third-Sixth Forms: £5,975 (day); £8,440 (weekly boarding); £10,680 (full boarding).

Music lessons £23 per 30-minute session; Extra Tuition £23 per 30-minute session.

We offer a 10% discount to serving members of the Armed Forces; to children of Old Wrekinians; and for a second full-time boarder from the same family. When three siblings are enrolled in Wrekin College/The Old Hall School each child attracts a 20% remission in fees.

Old Wrekinian Association. A flourishing Wrekinian Association of over 3,500 members exists to make possible continuous contact between the School and its old pupils, for the benefit of both and to support the ideals and aims of the school. It is expected that pupils will become members of the Old Wrekinian Association when they leave Wrekin.

Charitable status. Wrekin Old Hall Trust Limited is a Registered Charity, number 528417. It exists to provide independent boarding and day co-education in accordance with the Articles of Association of Wrekin College.

Visitor: The Rt Revd The Lord Bishop of Lichfield

Governors:
R J Pearson, BSc (*Chairman*)

A J Dixon, LLB
J A Grant, BSc [OW]
M Halewood, BEng, CEng, MICE, MAPM [OW]
A J Heber-Davies
P A T Hunt
A B Huxley [OW]
C Jones [OW]
P Mack, BSc, ACA, CTA
R Mottram
T Shaw, BSc, MRICS [OW]
D Malyon, BSc

[OW] *Old Wrekinian*

Headmaster: T Firth, BA Hons

Senior Deputy Head: Mrs S E Clarke, BA, FRGS

Deputy Head (Teaching and Learning): Mrs A Wright, BSc

Assistant Head (Planning): Dr G Roberts, BSc, PhD
Assistant Head (Co-Curricular): D Winterton, BA
Director of External Relations: Mrs A Nicoll

Head of Sixth Form: T Southall, BSc

Bursar: Mrs Y K Thomas, MBA, FCA

Assistant Staff:
† *Housemaster/mistress*

J Ballard, BSc	D McLagan, BA
Mrs H E Berry, CertEd	J Mather, BSc
P J Berry, BA	Mrs H Milton, BA
Dr. R Bliss	F Milton, BA
Mrs H Bibby, BA	R B Nayman, BA
Miss L Boffey, BSc	R Norval, BSc
†A J I Brennan, BA	Mrs E M Perry, BSc
†H S R Brown, BA	J G Phillips, BA
Miss B Camargo Castillo, FyL	Mrs C A Ritchie-Morgan
	Miss R Salano Marin, BA
Mrs K Carter, BSc	J Shaw, BA
Mrs F Coffey, BSc	Mrs J Shindler
†Mrs M Crone, BA	T A Southall, BSc
†Mrs K Davies, BSc	P M Stanway, BSc
R Edge, BSc	Mrs C Thust, BSc
Miss R Evans, BA	P Trahearn, BA
A Francis-Jones, BSc	A J Ware, BSc
J C Frodsham, CertEd, Adv DipEd	Mrs M N J Warner, BSc
	Mrs A E Wedge, BSc
Miss A V Gardener, BA	Ms G T Whitehead, BA Oxon
Miss J Harris, BSc	
A R Hurd, BSc	Dr A Woodshore, BA, MA, PhD
Mrs A Jagger, BA	
A Knight, BSc	Miss A Williams, BSc
†Mrs J D Kotas, BA	†I Williamson, BA
K B Livingstone, BA	†D J Winterton, BA

Support for Learning:
Mrs H Berry
Ms M Beattie
Ms H Ingoldby, BA, TEFL
Mrs J M Lloyd, BSc, MEd, DupELS, AMBDA, TEFL, APC SpLD Patoss, TPC SpLD Patoss
Mrs A H Livingstone, MA, RSA CELTA
Mrs J Roberts, BA, BSc, TEFL
French Assistant: Mrs F Kennedy

Visiting Music Staff:
J Burgess (*Flute*)
Miss K Burningham, MA, Dip ABRSM (*Piano & Organ*)
M Buxton, LRSM (*Piano*)
A Clark, GSRM, ARCM, CertEd (*Piano*)
M M Davey, MA, FRCO, LRAM, ARCM Organ Scholar of Corpus Christi College Cambridge
O James

C J Jones, BMus (*Piano, Clarinet and Saxophone*)
L Jones, BA, RNCM (*Violin*)
Miss Y Kagajo, MMus, PG Dip (*Piano*)
Ms J Magee, MA, GRSM, LRAM, ARCM, ABSM (*Cello*)
P Parker (*Guitar*)
A Pinel, ARCM, ARCO (*Organ*)
G Santry (*Drums*)
M Svensson, BMus (*Head of Strings*)
Ms R Theobald, LRAM, ALCM (*Piano, Oboe & Singing*)
Miss A Tiffin, RNCM, PG Dip (*Voice*)
G Wilkes, ALCM, LLCM, GLCM (*Brass*)

Games:
Mrs C A Ritchie-Morgan (*Head of Games*)

Sports Coaches:
D Ashley (*Hockey*)
Mrs K Bennett (*Girls' Games*)
D Clarke (*Swimming*)
G Davies (*Cricket*)
M Easter (*Rugby*)
S Floyd (*Hockey*)
B Gleeson (*Cricket*)
V Harrhy (*Boys' Games*)
K Holding (*Fencing*)
S Jenkins (*Basketball*)
R Oliver (*Cricket*)
Mrs R Reilly (*Swimming*)
A C Sammons (*Rugby*)
C J Sheperd (*Cricket*)
G Singh (*Cricket*)
Mrs C Still (*Gymnastics*)
M Stinson (*Cricket*)
L Swann (*Cricket*)
Miss V Woodman (*Netball*)
M de Weymarn (*Cricket Umpire*)

Medical Officers: Dr D Allen

CCF:
SSI & Outward Bound Activities Instructor: RQMS, E J Fanneran, late RA
Secretary OWA: M de Weymarn
Archive OWA: M Joyner MSc

Deputy Bursars:
Facilities: B C Crone
Operations: P Rowles

Chaplain: Revd M Horton, MA Cantab, MA Oxon, CertTh, DipTh

Admissions Registrar: Ms R Curel
Headmaster's Personal Assistant: Mrs P Bottomley

Wycliffe College

Bristol Road, Stonehouse, Gloucestershire GL10 2AF

Tel:	01453 822432
Fax:	01453 827634
email:	senior@wycliffe.co.uk
website:	www.wycliffe.co.uk
Twitter:	@WycliffeCollege
Facebook:	@WycliffeCollege
LinkedIn:	/wycliffe-college

The School was founded in 1882 by G W Sibly and placed on a permanent foundation under a Council of Governors in 1931.

Location. Wycliffe College is a thriving day and boarding school set in a stunning 60-acre safe campus, with no busy roads to cross, for 707 girls and boys, including around

350 boarders across the Prep and Senior Schools. The elegant main house is surrounded by first-class teaching facilities, extensive sports pitches, homely and welcoming boarding accommodation and extensive social areas such as a café available for all pupils at the senior school.

The Preparatory School (under its own Headmaster) is on a separate, adjacent campus with extensive facilities including plenty of outdoor spaces, sensory garden, dedicated drama facilities and indoor swimming pool.

Conveniently located in the South West of England midway between the famous cities of Bath and Cheltenham, Wycliffe is within easy reach of international airports such as Heathrow, Bristol and Birmingham as well as major road and rail connections. The school is under two hours from London by car (M4 motorway) or train (direct line to the local station).

Organisation. Senior School 13–18: 247 Boys, 174 Girls, 224 Boarders, Sixth Form 160. Class sizes vary from 3–15 pupils. Preparatory School 2–13: 123 Boys, 124 Girls.

Admission. Pupils are admitted at key entry points following interview and assessment, via CAT testing or Scholarship examinations at 13+ and via GCSE or Scholarship examinations into the Sixth Form. A one-year pre-A Level is offered to pupils joining from overseas.

Scholarships and Bursaries. Thanks to the generosity of Trustees, Old Wycliffians and Friends of Wycliffe, awards are available offering a reduction of up to 40% of the fees. These may be supplemented in cases of financial need up to a maximum of 90%.

For 13+ entry a candidate must be under 14 on 1 September of year of entry and sit the examination in the Spring Term.

For 16+ entry, examinations are held in the Autumn prior to arrival or by arrangement.

At other ages, applications to be made to the Registrar.

Awards are made to candidates with academic talent or potential and also specifically in music, art, design technology, drama and excellence in sports (including cricket, rugby, football, girls' hockey, netball and squash).

Special awards are also available to (a) those with all round merit, (b) children of serving members of the Services school fees fixed at CEA + 10% of school fees, (c) vegetarians.

Fees per term (2018–2019). Senior School: Boarders £11,740 new Sixth Form entrants £12,190, Development Year £12,705; Day pupils £6,645–£6,995. Preparatory School: Boarders £6,875–£8,885, Foundation Year £8,565–£9,420, Residential Short English Course £850 per week; Day pupils: £3,225–£5,265.

It is the College's aim to keep extras to a minimum but may include expeditions, exam fees and certain Society subscriptions.

GCSEs are usually taken three years after 13+ entry. The School offers a wide range of subjects supported by outstanding tutorial practices. Four modern languages and four sciences are among those on offer to students who may make a free choice at age 14.

A Levels. Most students choose four subjects to study in the Lower Sixth or one of three available BTEC courses. Most students then continue to study three subjects in the second year to A2 Level. Apart from the traditional subjects, the following are also on offer to A2 Level: Art and Design, Design Technology, Japanese, Psychology, Film Studies, Government and Politics, Computer Science, Theatre Studies, Music, Sociology and Physical Education. In addition, the EPQ is available along with expert Career and University Advice. Wycliffe provides SAT preparation and is the SAT accredited centre in the South West. Oxbridge preparation is also available.

One Year GCSE programme/Pre-A Level Development Year. Some international pupils choose to join the Development Year (DY) at Wycliffe before embarking on the full two-year A Level programme. This is because they wish to improve their English and experience a range of subjects while living and working in a traditional British boarding school.

DY pupils study a broad range of subjects including English, Maths and the Sciences and many can take up to six GCSEs as well as a range of ESOL exams. During the year they also receive an introduction to some A Level subjects, in preparation for Sixth Form. The DY students are part of all the house, sports, and social activities in which they can build friendships and improve their language skills. Included in the timetable, students benefit from expert tuition in English as a Second Language.

Music. A purpose-built music school including a dedicated Music Technology suite with enthusiastic staff enables high standards to be achieved. Music is taken at GCSE and A Level; several pupils each year continue their music studies at the Conservatoires and universities. There are two choirs, numerous large ensembles and bespoke chamber ensembles developing a high level of performance in all styles of music. Associated Board Examinations are taken every term as well as Trinity and Rock school exams. The School hosts professional concerts and dramatic productions annually as well as the School's own artistic output.

Sport. Our sports and physical education programme gives opportunities to develop talents and skills and to enjoy sport as a team member, individual or for recreation. We recognise and support gifted sports players and have the facilities to offer a wide range of sports such as rowing, rugby, hockey, fencing, football, netball, squash, badminton, basketball, swimming, cricket, tennis, athletics, health and fitness, yoga, equestrian, shooting, and cross country.

Training for Service is available via the Combined Cadet Force, Duke of Edinburgh's Award scheme, Leadership Courses, and the Wycliffe Charitable Organisation.

International Travel is regularly organised for varied groups; trips can enhance academic study, provide exchanges with our sister schools in America and Japan, be part of the Comenius partnership with schools in Europe or specific sporting or musical tours. Pupil trips and exchanges are arranged for those studying foreign languages.

School Societies. Among those available are Cookery, Chamber Choir, Music, Christian Union, Creative Writing, Photography, Drama Workshops, Theatre Trips, Voluntary Work, Philosophy, Language, Debating, Art, Computing, Scrabble, Squash, Shooting, Choral, Instrumental Music, First Aid, Investment Club, Bee Club, Sewing, Student Magazine, UKMT, MOOC and Equestrian.

Houses. Wycliffe's House system promotes a strong sense of community, building staunch friendships and promoting healthy competition, and ensuring high levels of personal and pastoral care. There are seven Houses which quickly become 'home from home' all with dedicated study areas and three Sixth Form Halls of Residence, each with study-bedrooms and en-suite facilities. A brand new £6m Boarding House with state-of-the-art boarding facilities including en-suite for every pupil and featuring the latest security and safety systems opened in September 2017 and has since won the British Boarding School's 'Boarding Extension or Refurbishment Award'.

Tutors. Each pupil has a House-based tutor in the Lower School and a specialist tutor in the Sixth Form. Supported by a Housemaster/Housemistress, Tutor, Chaplain and Head of Year, each pupil gains maximum advantage towards personal fulfilment in a community noted for its friendly and caring support.

Sunday Specials. Brunch is a highlight of Sunday morning and a variety of activities, both at the College and locally, are organised for boarders.

Religion. Christian interdenominational, all faiths welcome. Confirmation classes, Christian Fellowship group and daily worship in keeping with this generation are an integral part of College life.

Medical Centre. 24-hour attendance is provided by qualified staff. The Health Centre is nearby. Special dietary requirements for health or faith are met by first-class catering facilities.

Careers Guidance forms a vital department which is recognised as a centre of excellence. The College has its own experienced Careers Manager who is available to advise and support students throughout the school day. The Careers Library is well-equipped with information on careers and entrance to Higher Education. The school offers SAT preparation for American Universities.

Teacher Training. Wycliffe has been selected as a training centre for teachers, reflecting the high esteem in which the College is held.

Alumni. Our thriving community supports OWs and parents through open communication, engagement and networking. We hold multiple events throughout the year from global drinks receptions to local dinner dances, sports events, plays and recitals.

For more information please use the following ways to make contact with the Wycliffian Society:

Facebook: https://www.facebook.com/WycliffeCollegeTWS
Website: http://www.wycliffe.co.uk/the-wycliffian-society
OW Registrar: Tel 01453 820439
Email: TWS@wycliffe.co.uk

Charitable status. Wycliffe College Incorporated is a Registered Charity, number 311714. It exists to provide education for boys and girls.

Council of Governors:

President: S P Etheridge, MBE, TD, JP, MBA, FIFP, CFP, FCII, ACIArb

Chair of Governors: Brigadier {Retd} R J Bacon, MBA, Chartered FCIPD, FCMI, CMILT

Vice Presidents:
J C H Pritchard, DipM
J R E Williams, FCA

Vice Chairs:
Mrs S J Lacey, MEng, BA Hons
I H Paling, BMet, MMet

S K Collingridge, BA Hons, LLB
Mrs C Duckworth, MA Hons
Mrs L C Duncan, BSc PGCE
W R Garrard, MBA, BSc Hons
S F Lloyd, BSc Hons, Est Man, MRICS
G May BA, MA Oxon
Mrs A L Palk, MBE, BA Hons
J Slater, FRICS

Director of Finance & Operations & Company Secretary: T P Wood, BA Hons, FCA

Head: N J Gregory, BA, MEd

Senior Deputy Head: P Woolley, BA, PGCE (*Politics*)
Deputy Head (Academic): S V Dunne, BA, PG DipJ, PGCE (*Media Studies*)
Deputy Head (Pastoral), Designated Safeguarding Lead: Mrs E A Buckley, BSc, PGCE (*Physical Education*)
Assistant Head (Academic): Mr P J F Martin, BSc Hons, PGCE (*Mathematics*)

Head of Sixth Form, Head of Higher Education and Careers, Contingent Commander, CCF: M J Archer, MA (*Chemistry*)
Head of Lower School: Mrs S V Collinson, BA, PGCE (*Business Studies*)
Director of ICT: B Ittyavirah, BSc, MSc, PGCE (*ICT*)
Chaplain: The Reverend J M McHale, BTh, BA, PGCE (*RS*)

House Staff:
Collingwood House Junior: Mrs N Bryant, BSc, PGCE (*Chemistry*)
Collingwood House Senior: S Costello, BSc, PGCE, MEd (*Head of Psychology and Sociology*)
Haywardsend: Mrs L Nicholls, BA, PGCE (*Geography*)
Haywardsfield: I Russell, BSc, PGCE (*Mathematics*)
Ivy Grove: Mrs J L Smith, BSc, PGCE (*Chemistry*)
Lampeter House: Mrs G Tavner, BA, PGCE (*English*)
Loosley Halls: T P Larkman, BSc Hons, PGCE (*Geography*)
Robinson House: A C Naish, BSc, PGCE (*Sport*)
Ward's House: A M Golightly, BA, MA, PGCE (*Head of Drama*)

Teaching Staff:
Mrs A Attwell, BA Hons, MA, PGCE (*English*)
R O Beamish, BA, PGCE (*Head of Digital Creative Arts*)
F Blackwood, BSc, PGCE (*Mathematics*)
Mrs M Bray (*Italian & Spanish*)
G C Brown, BSc, PGSE (*Computer Science*)
Miss C E Browne, BA, PGCE (*English*)
Ms S Carter, BA, PGCE (*ESOL*)
J P Clements, BEng, PGCE (*Curriculum Leader Science and Head of Physics*)
Mrs A K Cobbs, BA, PGCE (*Head of Mathematics*)
G P Constable, BA, QTS (*Business Studies & Economics*)
Mrs C R L Conway, BA, MA, QTS (*History*)
Mrs J Cottrell, BA, PGCE (*SEN*)
Mrs K Cox, BA Hons, MSc, PGCE (*Mathematics*)
E M Crownshaw, BA, PGCE (*Physics*)
G M Davies, BA Hons, MA, PGCE (*Assistant Director of Music*)
W H Day-Lewis, BA DiELTA, PGCE (*Head of Development Year*)
Mrs S M Dudley, BSc, PGCE (*Head of Girls' Games*)
Mrs E Dytham, BA Hons, PGCE (*Head of Learning Support*)
Miss K F Elliott, BA, PGCE (*Head of ESOL*)
A J Finebaum, BEng, PGCE (*Mathematics*)
G G Flower, Cert Higher Ed Sports Coaching (*Director of Rowing*)
Mrs S Flye, BSc, PGCE (*Mathematics*)
J R Gallagher, BA Hons (*History*)
B W Gannon, BSc, Level 3 Cert Cricket Coaching QCF (*Sport*)
S R Garley, BAF (*Fencing Coach and CCF*)
Mrs N Golightly, BEd (*Drama*)
Miss N Green, BA, PGCE (*Head of Art & Design*)
Mrs N J Halford Scott, BA, PGCE (*Head of History*)
A J J Hamilton, BSc, PGCE (*Head of Physical Education*)
C J Hancock, BA, PGCE (*Head of RS*)
Mrs M Hardwick, MA, PGCE (*French & Spanish*)
J C Harford, Level 3 Coach Squash (*Director of Squash*)
A J Hart, BSc, MEd, PGCE (*Mathematics*)
T A Hayes, BA Hons, PGCE (*Design & Technology*)
W H Helsby, BA, RSA DipTEFL, PGCE (*ESOL*)
Mrs A J Hodges, BSc, MSc, PGCE (*Mathematics*)
Mrs R Honeywill, BA, Cert Ed (*French & German*)
S J Hubbard, BA (*Art & Design*)
Mrs L J James, BSc, PGCE (*Mathematics*)
M J Kimber, New Zealand Coaching Cert, ECB Level 1, RFU Levels I & II (*Head of Boys' Games*)

Mrs J H King, BSc, PGCE (*Science*)
M J Kingscote, BA, PGCE (*Head of English*)
Mrs S Knight, MChem, PGCE (*Chemistry*)
Mrs L Knighton-Callister (*Biology, EPQ*)
Mrs E S Lambert, BA, PGCE (*English*)
D Lester, BA Hons, MEd Applied Linguistics (*MFL*)
W Luecke, Diplom-Volkswirt, PGCE (*Business Studies & Economics*)
Mrs E Lunch, BSc, PGCE (*Mathematics*)
J Lunch, BSc Hons, PGCE (*Boys Games*)
M Martinez, PGCE (*Spanish*)
Mrs M I McGregor, PG Dip (*German*)
Mrs B K Miller, BA, BSC, MA (*International University Applications Coordinator*)
Mrs C Moran, BA, Celta (*ESOL*)
J S Murphy, BA (*Digital Creative Arts*)
Mrs L Newton, BA, PGCE (*Head of Business Studies & Economics*)
Miss A P Norman-Walker, BA Hons (*Art & Design*)
Miss A Nowak, BA Hons, PGCE (*English*)
J J O'Sullivan, PGCE (*Economics*)
H C Parker, BSc, PGCE (*Computer Science*)
K G Patrick, BA Hons, HDipEd (*History*)
R Pender, BSc, PGCE (*Head of Geography*)
Mrs H S Phelps, BA, BSc, MSc (*Psychology and Sociology*)
Mrs V Ralph, BSc, PGCE (*Biology & Chemistry*)
Miss S K Revie, BA, PGCE (*Head of Japanese*)
Dr R K Rose, MA, MSc, PhD, PGCE (*Head of Chemistry*)
Mrs G L Russell, BA, PGCE (*Director of Music*)
P D Scott, MBioChem, PGCE (*Mathematics*)
Miss H Sherwood, Level 2 Cert Hockey Coaching QCF, Level 1 Cert Teaching Swimming (*Sport*)
Mrs N Stephens-Mikesch, PGCE (*Head of German*)
B D Taylor, BSc (*Director of Sport*)
Mrs H Thompson Uno, BA, MA, CELTA (*Japanese*)
Mrs S L Trainor, HDipEd, PGCE (*Biology*)
B A Urquhart, BA Hons, PGCE (*MFL*)
Mrs M G Vidal, BSc Hons, PGCE (*Physical Education*)
M L Waller, BSc, PGCE (*Physics*)
G J Wheeler, BEd (*Head of Design & Technology*)
I L Williams, BSc, PGCE (*Head of Biology*)
M A Williams, BEd Foundation (*Resident Squash Coach*)
Mrs L Wisbey, BA, PGCE (*Head of Spanish*)
Mrs L A Wong, BSc, RSA Dip TEFLA, PGCE (*ESOL*)
Ms L E Wood, BA Hons, PGCE (*ESOL*)
Miss H Woodham (*School Staff Instructor/CCF*)
Mrs R A S Wordsworth, BA (*Art & Design*)
Mrs K Worsdell, BA Hons, PGCE (*English*)
Mrs J Wright, BA, PGCE (*PE, Games & Head of BTEC*)
Dr D York (*Physics*)

Teaching Support Staff:
R Feather, BA, PGCE (*Academic Data & Exams*)
Mrs S A Hodgkins (*Senior Librarian*)
Mrs M Holden, MA HRM (*Careers Education Manager*)

Visiting Music Staff:
Mrs S Blewett, FTCL, LTCL, LWCMD (*Flute*)
Mr M Bucher, Dip Perc (*Percussion*)
Miss B M Collins, BMus Hons
Mr M Coldrick, Dip OS, AGSM (*Percussion*)
Mrs M Cope, GMus, LTCL, Cert ABRSM (*Piano*)
Mrs D Denton, BA Hons RCO (*Piano*)
Mr I Dollins, BMus, ARCM (*Voice & Piano*)
Mrs V Green, GRSM, ARCM, LRAM (*Piano & Double Bass*)
Ms C Hill, BMus, PG Dip (*Violin*)
Ms S L Holmes, BMus Hons
Mrs S Jee, MA Oxon, LTCL, PGCE (*Recorder*)
Mr A Jones, BA Hons (*Guitar*)
Miss J Orsman, GBSM (*Violin & Viola*)

Mr G Rees, Dip Trpt (*Brass*)
Mr M Sharp, BMus (*Piano*)
Mr D Thompson, MA, BA Hons (*Piano*)
Mrs L Thompson, BMus Hons, ARCM, CertEd (*Cello*)

Medical Officers and Staff:
Mrs J Lewis (*School Nurse*)
Mrs P Norman (*School Nurse*)

Administration:
Director of Finance and Operations and Company Secretary: Mr T P Wood, BA Hons, FCA
Director of Marketing and Admissions: Mrs T Nichols, BA Hons, MA
Human Resources Manager: Mrs W Jenkins, MBA, CIPD
Estates Bursar: M Rickard
Wycliffian Society Manager: Mrs V Vicary, MA
Admissions Manager: Mrs F Lawson-Best
Marketing Manager: Miss K M J Smith, BA Hons
Head's PA: Mrs C J Philp

Preparatory School:
(*see also entry in IAPS section*)

Headmaster: A Palmer, BEd, MA
Headmaster's Wife: Mrs J Palmer, Cert Ed (*SENCo to Lower Prep, General Subjects Teacher*)
Deputy Head: Mrs S J Owenson, BSc, PGCE, PhD
Director of Pastoral Care: Mrs L Askew, LAMDA (*Head of Drama*)

Teaching Staff:
D Aherne, BSc Hons, PGCE (*Assistant Head, Lower School*)
S J Arman, BEd (*Head of Shaftesbury, Head of History and RS*)
Mrs J Baylis, NVQ3 (*Lower Prep Assistant*)
Mrs K Bierer, BA Hons, Support Teaching Cert Level 3 (*Lower Prep Assistant*)
Mrs C Bish, BA (*Year 2 Teacher*)
Mr T Bloodworth, BSc, PGCE (*Head of Boys Games*)
Mrs H Bloodworth, BA Hons, PGCE (*Head of PE, Head of Girls' Games*)
Mrs S Bond, BEd Hons (*Reception Teacher, EYFS Lead*)
D Broadhead, BA, PGCE (*Languages Teacher*)
Mrs C Brown, BA, PGCE, TESOL (*Head of Lincoln, Head of Modern Foreign Languages*)
Mrs K C Buckley, BSc, PGCE (*Year 1 Teacher*)
Mrs A Cleere, BEd, ASA Level 2 (*General Subjects Teacher*)
Mrs S Collins, BA Hons (*Lower Prep Assistant*)
Mrs C A Curtis, BSc Hons, PGCE (*Mathematics*)
Mrs S Davis, TEFL, CELTA (*ESOL Teacher*)
Miss L Dracup, BA QTS, ALCM (*Lower Prep Teaching Assistant*)
Mrs N Ely, BTEC National Diploma, BTEC First Diploma (*Middle Prep Assistant*)
Mrs E Flake, BEd (*Director of Studies Teaching; General Subjects Teacher*)
M F Folkard, BSc (*Sports Coach*)
Miss J Florio, BSc, PGCE (*Maths and Science Teacher*)
Mrs N Gaunt, BEd, OCR Level 5 (*SEN Teacher, Games Teacher*)
R Gaunt, BA QTS (*Head of Mathematics*)
Mrs N Gidman BA, QTS (*Year 5 Teacher*)
C Guest, BSc, PGCE (*Head of Scott, Head of SEN*)
Mrs R Hanson, BA, PGCE (*Head of Grenfell, Year 5 Teacher*)
T Holroyde, BSc, PGCE (*Head of Science*)
R Irwin, BSc, PGCE (*Director of Studies Learning, Year 5 Teacher*)
Miss C Lewis, BA (*Year 3 Teacher*)
Mrs J Maloney, BA Hons (*Reception Teaching Assistant*)

Mrs Y Martin, BEd Hons (*Year 2 Teacher*)
Mrs E Muszasty, BA (*Head of English*)
Miss M Muszasty (*Middle Prep Assistant*)
Madame M Perhirin, BA Hons, PGCE (*Lower Prep French Teacher and Lower Prep Assistant*)
Miss M Potts, BA (*Head of ICT, Data and Exams Manager, Gifted and Talented Coordinator*)
Mrs J Seyburn BA, MA, PGCE (*English and Humanities Teacher*)
A Sinclair, BA, PGCE (*Year 3 Teacher*)
Mrs C Stanley, BA, PGCE, Cert SpLD (*SEN Teacher*)
M Stopforth, BA, PGCE (*Head of Art & DT*)
Mrs R Taylor, BA, PGCE (*Director of Music*)
Mrs C Viggers, BSc, PGCE, Lifeguard (*Sports Coach*)
Miss R H Willis, BA, PGCE

Boarding House Staff:
Mrs L Field (*Housemistress*)
Miss K Thomas (*Housemistress*)
Mrs J Swirski (*Matron*)
Mrs K Yates (*Matron*)
Mrs G Rumming (*Matron*)
Mrs J Saynor (*Matron*)

Day Matrons:
Mrs M Coombs, British Red Cross First Aid at Work Cert
Mrs S Phillips, British Red Cross First Aid at Work Cert, GCS Foundation to Counselling

Administration Staff:
Admissions Manager: Miss B Armstrong
School Secretary: (*to be appointed*)
Headmaster's PA: Mrs S Rogers

Nursery:
Mrs C Marsh, NNEB, C&G Child Care 0–7, FDEY (*Nursery Manager, Lower Nursery Teacher*)
Mrs A Hawes, BA Hons, Early Years Safeguarding Lead (*Deputy Nursery Manager, Upper Nursery Teacher*)
Mrs K Holmes CACHE Level 3 Dip (*Lower Nursery Teacher*)
Miss L Chapman, NVQ3 (*Nursery Assistant*)
Miss A Chivers, NVQ3 (*Nursery Assistant*)
Miss A Harcourt, CYPW Intermediate (*Nursery Assistant*)
Miss R Hursthouse, NNEB Level 3 (*Nursery Assistant*)
Miss C Holmes, NVQ3 (*Nursery Assistant*)
Miss S Johnson, NVQ3 (*Nursery Assistant*)
Mrs M Young, NVQ3 (*Nursery Assistant*)

Wycombe Abbey

High Wycombe, Buckinghamshire HP11 1PE

Tel: 01494 897008
email: registrar@wycombeabbey.com
website: www.wycombeabbey.com
Twitter: @wycombeabbey
Facebook: @wycombeabbey

Motto: *In Fide Vade*

Founded in 1896.
Numbers on roll. 631 Girls: 574 Boarding; 57 Day Girls.
Age range. 11–18.
Aims. Wycombe Abbey is a global leader in outstanding education and modern boarding. The School is committed to creating tomorrow's women leaders and has a long tradition of academic excellence. The culture of the School stimulates and inspires throughout the day, seven days a week, empowering girls to achieve their very best, academically and socially. In our happy and close community, each girl is known, and cherished, as an individual.

Location. Near the centre of High Wycombe, five minutes' drive from the M40. It is a 30-minute journey from Heathrow Airport and a 90-minute journey from Gatwick Airport by road.

Buildings. The School buildings are all within the extensive grounds of 170 acres which include playing fields, woods, gardens and a lake.

Boarding Houses. There is a Junior House for UIII. At LIV, girls move to one of nine Houses where they remain until the end of the Lower Sixth. In the final year all girls move to the Upper Sixth House where they are encouraged to prepare for university life.

Religion. Wycombe Abbey is a Church of England foundation with its own Chapel. All girls attend morning prayers and a Sunday Service. (Roman Catholic girls can attend Mass and Jewish girls may receive instruction from a Rabbi.) Christian principles inform the whole ethos of the School and a resident Chaplain oversees spiritual matters and plays a central role in pastoral care.

Curriculum. The Lower School curriculum includes the study of English, English Literature, History, Geography, Religious Studies, French, German, Spanish, Latin, Greek, Mathematics, Biology, Chemistry, Physics, Information Technology, Art, Cookery, Drama, Music, Singing, Personal, Social and Health Education and PE. In the Sixth Form, Economics, History of Art, Classical Civilisation, Government and Politics, Psychology and Physical Education are also available. Critical Thinking AS is compulsory. Girls are prepared for the IGCSE, GCSE, AS and A2 Level examinations, Pre-U and for university entrance. Girls proceed to leading universities in the UK with about 30–40% going to Oxbridge and a handful to America.

Teaching facilities are very good and have been extended and upgraded over recent years.

Physical Education. The School has excellent outdoor facilities, including five lacrosse pitches, a full-size multipurpose floodlit Astroturf pitch, an athletics track and twenty tennis courts which can be used for netball in the winter. The Davies Sports Centre is a state-of-the-art sports complex including a six-lane 25m swimming pool, well-equipped fitness suite and four glass-backed squash courts. Girls are taught lacrosse, netball, tennis, athletics, swimming, gymnastics and dance. A huge range of extracurricular sports and activities is also available.

Music. There is a strong tradition of music-making with outstanding facilities for tuition and for recitals. About three-quarters of the girls study at least one musical instrument and are taught by a large team of visiting specialists who provide tuition in a wide range of instruments, including voice. There are many opportunities for performing in orchestras and ensembles. In addition, there is a strong tradition of singing; the Chapel choir plays a central role in Chapel worship and undertakes biennial overseas tours.

Drama. As well as class Drama, GCSE and A Level Drama, extracurricular Speech and Drama lessons are also available from Year 8 in groups of approximately six girls and from Year 10 in pairs or solo. LAMDA examinations take place in the fully-equipped 436-seater proscenium arch theatre and generally culminate in a Grade 8 Gold Medal in the final year. There are extracurricular production opportunities at various points throughout the year, several girls annually get into the National Youth Theatre and alumnae include Naomi Frederick, Rachel Stirling and Polly Stenham.

Art, Craft, Design & Technology. Girls can pursue their interests in these subjects at weekends when the studios are open, as well as in curriculum time. Visiting artists provide workshops at weekends to give girls a broad experience in the subject.

Other Activities. A wide range of clubs and societies, usually led by girls, are very popular as are the numerous social events with leading boys' schools.

Fees per term (2018–2019). The fees for boarders are £12,980 (£9,735 for day boarders). They are inclusive and cover, in addition to the subjects and activities already mentioned, lectures, concerts, most textbooks and stationery.

Admission. Girls are admitted at the age of 11 or 13. Application should be made well in advance. The suggested procedure is given in the prospectus information booklet.

Sixth Form Entry: Competitive entry by examination for a limited number of places. Application must be received at least fifteen months prior to the proposed date of entry.

Scholarships and Bursaries. Lower School Entry: A variety of Scholarship and Exhibition awards are available for candidates under 12 and under 14 on 1 September of the proposed year of entry.

Some awards are also available for candidates entering the Sixth Form.

Music: Scholarships and Exhibitions of varying value are available to candidates under the age of 14 on 1 September of the proposed year of entry. A Music Scholarship is also available to girls entering the Sixth Form.

Bursaries: A number of means-tested bursaries are available. Bursaries are held subject to the satisfactory conduct and progress of the recipient.

For further information, please contact the Director of Admissions.

Charitable status. The Girls' Education Company Limited is a Registered Charity, number 310638. Its aim is the provision of first class education for girls.

Governing Council:

Vice Presidents:
Mr A M D Willis, LLB, FCIArb
Mrs C M Archer, MA

Chairman:
Mr P P Sherrington, LLB, LLM, FCIArb

Council Members:
Lady Sassoon, MA
The Hon Mrs Justice Carr, DBE
Mr D P Lillycrop, LLB, FCMI
The Rt Revd Dr A Wilson, MA, DPhil, Bishop of
   Buckingham
Mrs D Rose, MA
Dr L Fawcett, MA, DPhil
Mr R Ashby, MSc, BSc Eng, ARSM, FRICS
Mr R Winter, BA, FCA
Mr J W Bailey, ACA
Mr P Lewis, MA, MBA
Mr S C Henderson, MA
Dr C Godlee, BSc, MB BChir
Mr T Clarke, BA, BBus
Dr J MacDougall, BA, MB BChir, MRCOG, MD, FRCOG,
   MA

Staff:

Senior Leadership Team:

Headmistress: **Mrs R Wilkinson**, MA Oxon, PGCE, MEd,
   Dip SpLD

Chief Operating Officer and Clerk to the Council: Mr N
   Campbell, MBA Cranfield
Senior Deputy Head (*Staff*): Mr J Mercer-Kelly, MChem
   Oxon, PGCE, PGDES
Deputy Head (*Academic*): Miss E Boswell, MA Oxon,
   PGCE Roehampton
Deputy Head (*Operational*): Miss R A Keens, BEd
   Liverpool

Deputy Head (*Pupils*): Mr J Jones, MA Sheffield
Director of Sixth Form: Mr J Franks, MA Cantab, GTP e-
   Qualitas
Head of Boarding: Mrs A Spillman, BA Open, BSc Exeter,
   PGCE Greenwich

Director of Innovation and Learning: Mr D Vaccaro, MA
   Cantab
Director of Curriculum Management: Mr M Welch, MEng,
   BA Cantab, PGCE Nottingham
Director of Admissions: Mrs S Langdale, BA Dunelm

For a full staff list, please visit our website.

HMC International

ALPHABETICAL LIST OF SCHOOLS

HMC Schools in Europe

The British School of Brussels

Pater Dupierreuxlaan 1, 3080 Tervuren, Belgium

Tel: 00 32 2 766 04 30
Fax: 00 32 2 767 80 70
email: admissions@britishschool.be
website: www.britishschool.be
Twitter: @BSB_Brussels
Facebook: @britishschoolbrussels
LinkedIn: /the-british-school-of-brussels

Creation. The British School of Brussels (BSB) was founded in 1969 as a non-profit making organisation in Belgium and was opened in 1970 by HRH The Duke of Edinburgh. It is run by a Board of Governors, comprising distinguished British and Belgian citizens from both the professional and business worlds, together with parent and staff representatives.

Site. The school occupies a beautiful site of ten hectares, surrounded by woodlands and lakes near the Royal Museum of Central Africa in Tervuren, which is 20–25 minutes by car from the centre of Brussels. The site belongs to the Donation Royale, the Foundation which manages the estates left to the Belgian people at the beginning of the 20th century by King Leopold II.

Facilities. The school has excellent modern facilities, including a science and maths centre, networked IT suites, all with internet access and Wi-Fi. Students in most year groups are issued with either their own iPad or laptop computer. The school has dance and drama studios as well as nine science laboratories, four art studies and three technology workshops, including a state-of-the-art design & technology workshop and food & nutrition rooms, comprehensive modern languages and humanities suites and a self-service cafeteria. There is an Early Childhood Centre for children of 1–3 years also on campus. The school has developed its sporting facilities extensively and has a multipurpose sports hall, gymnasium, fitness suite and dance studio. It is the only international school in Belgium to have its own swimming pool that opened in September 2016.

Organisation. The British School of Brussels is an independent, fee-paying, non profit-making international school. The School is a co-educational, non-selective day school for students from 1 to 18 years of age, with over 1,350 currently on roll. Approximately 34% of the students are British and there are 70 other nationalities represented. Our curriculum, both in the Primary and Secondary Schools, is a British-based curriculum, adapted to suit the needs of our European context and international students. In the Secondary School, students sit GCSE/IGCSE examinations at the end of Year 11 (aged 16). Senior students then have the choice of three pre-university qualifications: the International Baccalaureate (IB) Diploma (with English/French or English/Dutch bilingual options), GCE A Levels or BTEC courses in business, sports, applied science and hospitality prior to moving on to Higher Education in the UK, Belgium or beyond. Provision is also made for Oxbridge tuition. Our examination results, year on year, are very impressive for a non-selective school. In 2018 our students achieved 100% pass rate in A Levels with a 99% pass rate in IB Diploma and BTEC. Students successfully graduate to some of the top universities around the world.

BSB has an established French/English bilingual programme for children aged 4–14 years to complement its English-medium teaching. We introduce the teaching of Spanish, German or Dutch as optional additional languages in the Secondary School. We have developed programmes to help students with learning differences and to help students who join us with little or no English skills. The school also employs a counsellor.

Sports and Extracurricular Activities. Use of the extensive sports facilities (purpose-built sports centre with gym, sports hall, fitness suite, dance studio and 25m indoor swimming pool) together with all-weather artificial pitches, grass pitches, floodlit training area, four outdoor tennis courts and a 240-seat Brel Theatre. In addition to curricular sport, a wide range of competitive sports is offered: athletics, cricket, cross country, gymnastics, hockey, rugby, football, swimming and tennis, as well as recreational activities such as basketball and golf. The school participates very successfully in the International Schools Sports Tournaments (ISST) and ISGA (Gymnastics).

Music and Drama. The Music Department houses an extremely well-equipped music technology studio, a recording studio and a rehearsal studio for the School's orchestras, concert bands and instrumental ensembles. Individual instrument lessons are available from visiting specialist teachers, and take place in the suite of music practice rooms. The school is the largest Associated Board centre in Europe. Each year up to fifteen drama productions – including student-directed performances – are presented across the full student age range. The Theatre has its own workshop and Green Room, as well as a more intimate studio space that seats 80.

Careers. The school has the highest expectations of its student population and advice on careers, as well as higher and further education opportunities, is of vital importance to the further development of the students. The school takes part in many careers conventions and has its own international higher education and careers team.

Fees per annum (2018–2019). From €27,550 (Reception) to €35,250 (Years 10–13).

Past Students' Association. The school has a growing association of Alumni and has its own official BSB Alumni Facebook page. Please visit the Alumni section of the school website (www.britishschool.be) to see how to subscribe to the alumni newsletter and follow the school on Twitter and LinkedIn.

Patron:
Her Excellency the British Ambassador to the King of the Belgians

Chairman of the Board: Mr Ian Backhouse

Principal: Ms Melanie Warnes

Vice Principal and Head of Primary School: Mr Neil Ringrose

Vice Principal and Head of Secondary School: Mr Gary Minnitt

The British School of Paris

38 quai de l'Ecluse, 78290 Croissy sur Seine, France

Tel: 00 33 1 34 80 45 90
Fax: 00 33 1 39 76 12 69
email: info@britishschool.fr
website: www.britishschool.fr

Twitter: @BritishSchParis
Facebook: @BritishSchParis

Age Range. 3–18.

Number of Pupils. 800 (Boys and Girls)

Fees per annum (2018–2019). Senior School €27,152–€29,516; Junior School €18,261–€24,762.

The BSP provides, in a caring environment, a high-quality British-style education for international students, to enable them to become caring citizens and to lead fulfilling lives.

Located just 15 kilometres from Paris, the School caters for English-speaking children of over 50 nationalities (about 30% are British) from ages 3–18. It is a not-for-profit association in France and is presided over by a governing body under the patronage of His Excellency the British Ambassador to France.

The **Junior School** provides education for primary aged children from 3–11 years. The purpose-built Junior School is located very close to the Senior School along the leafy banks of the river Seine. There are 35 classrooms accommodating up to 500 pupils, as well as 4 bespoke classrooms and 2 activity areas that are dedicated to our foundation stage/nursery section. Studies are based on the English National Curriculum with emphasis on English, Maths and Science, and of course, the French language. Being a holistic educator the BSP has a strong co-curricular base with a special focus on music and drama as well as a large variety of sports. (*For further information about the Junior School, see entry in IAPS section*).

The **Senior School**, which caters for pupils aged from 11–18 years, is situated beside a beautiful stretch of the Seine in Croissy sur Seine. The buildings, with the exception of two nineteenth century houses, have been built since 1990. The Science and Technology block provides excellent facilities for Science, Information Technology, Electronics and Design. There are six large, well equipped science laboratories. The other classroom blocks house Humanities, Art, Business Studies, Modern Languages, Music, English and Mathematics. Other facilities include a generously staffed and resourced student career guidance programme, a library, IT labs, a refectory, a large sports hall and fitness centre. Students enter at the age of 11 and for the first three years, a broad general education is maintained in line with the National Curriculum. Pupils are prepared for the GCSE and A Level examinations in a comprehensive range of subjects.

Music and drama are an integral part of school life; the music centre includes teaching and practice facilities as well as a well-equipped electronic studio. Specialist teachers visit the School to provide individual lessons in a wide range of instruments. Children take the Associated Board exams at regular intervals.

The School has had considerable sporting success over the years, winning the International Schools' Sports Tournament competition in girls' field hockey, and boys' rugby. Our international fixture lists provide an incentive to gain a place in school teams. As well as local matches our teams travel regularly to Belgium, Holland and the UK.

Small overall numbers, modest class sizes and a supportive pastoral system all help new pupils integrate quickly. Our examination results are outstanding. At A Level over 33% of all grades were A* and A and 97% of all grades at GCSE were between A* and C in 2018. These results compare very favourably with high-calibre schools in the UK. Most students continue their education at prestigious universities in the UK, USA, France and worldwide. BSP students have been successfully admitted to the Universities of Cambridge and Oxford, London School of Economics, University of Pennsylvania, Stanford University, McGill University, Universidad de Madrid, Seoul National University, L'Université de la Sorbonne, to mention but a few.

Chairman of Governors: Mr E Coutts

***Headmaster*: Mr N Hammond**

Head of Senior School: Dr J Batters

Head of the Junior School: Mr M Potter

Registrar: Mrs V Joynes

King's College
The British School of Madrid

Paseo de los Andes 35, Soto de Viñuelas, Madrid 28761, Spain

Tel: 00 34 918 034 800
Fax: 00 34 918 036 557
email: info@kingscollege.es
website: www.kingscollegeschools.org
Twitter: @Kings_Soto
Facebook: @Kings-College-The-British-School-of-Madrid
LinkedIn: /King's College, Soto de Viñuelas

King's College is a British co-educational day and boarding school founded in 1969. It is the largest British curriculum school in Spain and the first school to have had full UK accreditation through the Independent Schools Inspectorate. The Headteacher is an international member of HMC, while the school is a member of COBIS, NABSS and BSA.

The school is governed by the Board of Directors and School Council which is composed of distinguished members from the business and academic communities.

The Vision of King's College, is "to be at the forefront of British education internationally" as well as to provide students with an excellent all-round education while fostering tolerance and understanding between young people of different nationalities and backgrounds.

King's College, Soto de Viñuelas caters for more than 1,500 pupils between the ages of 20 months and 18 years (Pre-Nursery to Year 13) and stands on a 12-acre site in a residential area about 25 km from the centre of Madrid near the Guadarrama mountains and surrounded by open countryside. It is well connected to the city centre by motorway and rail. There is an optional comprehensive bus service to the city of Madrid and its outlying residential areas and all routes are supervised by a bus monitor.

Facilities. There are extensive, purpose-built facilities which include 7 science laboratories, 2 libraries, an art studio, 3 computer centres with multimedia stations, and 2 music rooms. All classrooms are fitted with interactive whiteboards and there are computers in all Primary classrooms. The school offers a purpose-built Early Learning Centre, an Auditorium with seating for over 350 people and a Music School with 6 rooms for individual or small group tuition. The sports facilities include a 25-metre indoor heated swimming pool, a floodlit multi-purpose sports area, football pitches, basketball and tennis courts, a gymnasium with fitness centre and a horse riding school. Future development includes plans for a covered sports hall.

Tenbury House, the school boarding residence, opened in September 2011 and offers brand new purpose-built accommodation for up to 44 boarders. The residence is located in the school grounds and offers pupils a breakfast room, kitchen, laundry, work room, lounge, TV room, storage and easy access to the new AstroTurf pitch and sports facilities.

Curriculum. Pupils at all three King's College schools in Madrid follow the English National Curriculum leading to

(I)GCSE, GCSE, AS and A Level examinations. A wide range of subjects is available. All pupils learn Spanish. The school has a reputation for high academic standards and excellent examination results with students going on to top universities in Britain, USA and Spain amongst others.

An Oxbridge preparatory group works with the most able students to prepare university applications. There is a very experienced Careers and University Entrance Advisory Department for all students.

Activities. King's College has choirs, musical ensembles and drama groups, which participate in numerous events throughout the year. Pupils are encouraged to explore their capabilities in the areas of music and the arts from a very early age.

Sports play an important role at the school and pupils are encouraged to take part in tournaments and local competitive events, in addition to their normal PE classes. King's College currently has football, basketball and swimming teams participating in local leagues, and also takes part in inter-school championships in athletics and cross-country.

There is a programme of optional classes which includes horse riding, ballet, judo, Spanish dancing, swimming, tennis, tuition in various musical instruments, performing arts and craft workshops.

Admission. Pupils entering the school at the age of 7 or above are required to sit entrance tests in English and Mathematics and possibly other subjects, while younger candidates are offered a review by the Head of Admissions in each school. For those applying to the Sixth Form, admission depends on the results of the (I)GCSE examinations, or equivalent.

Fees per term (2018–2019). Tuition: €2,592–€4,530 excluding lunch and transport. Boarding (including tuition): Full €7,796–€8,501.

Scholarships. The school offers a small number of scholarships to Sixth Formers selected on academic merit.

Further information may be obtained from The Director of Admissions at the School: Rebecca Conlon, rebecca.conlon@ kingsgroup.org.

Headteacher: **Matthew Taylor**, MA Oxon, MA London, PGCE, MRCIEA

Deputy Headteacher: Nicola Lambros, BSc Birmingham, MEd Roehampton, PGCE Brunel

Head of Secondary Department: Christopher T Parkinson, BEd Hons Crewe and Alsager

Director of Studies: James Slocombe, BSc Hons Bath, PGCE Bristol, MA OU

Head of Primary Department: Paula Parkinson, BA Hons Newcastle, PGCE Manchester

Deputy Head of Primary: Adele Dickson, LLB, PGDE

Head of Spanish Studies: Sara Fernández, Lic Filología Hispanica UCM

Head of Boarding: Hanan Nazha, BA QTS London

Head of Admissions: Rebecca Conlon, BSc Hons Kent, MSc London Metropolitan University

Other HMC International Schools

Africa

Kenya

Peponi School
PO Box 236, Ruiru 00232, Kenya
email: info@peponischool.org
website: www.peponischool.org

Headmaster: **Mark Durston**

South Africa

Michaelhouse
Balgowan 3275, Kwazulu-Natal, South Africa
email: info@michaelhouse.org
website: www.michaelhouse.org

Rector: **Paul Fleischack**
From April 2019: Antony Clark

Zimbabwe

Peterhouse
Private Bag 3741, Marondera, Zimbabwe
email: rector@peterhouse.co.zw
website: www.peterhouse.co.zw

Rector: **Howard W Blackett**

Asia

Brunei Darussalam

Jerudong International School
PO Box 1408, Bandar Seri Begawan BS8672, Negara
Brunei Darussalam
email: enrol@jis.edu.bn
website: www.jis.edu.bn

Principal: **Barnaby Sandow**, BSc Eng Durham, PGCE
Exeter

China

Dulwich College Beijing
89 Capital Airport Road, Shunyi District, Beijing
101300 PRC, China
email: info@dulwich-beijing.cn
website: www.dulwich-beijing.cn

Headmaster: **Mr Simon Herbert**

Hong Kong

Harrow International School
38 Tsing Ying Road, Tuen Mun, New Territories, Hong
Kong
email: info@harrowschool.hk
website: www.harrowschool.hk

Head: **Ms Ann Haydon**

India

The British School, New Delhi
Dr Jose P Rizal Marg, Chanakyapuri, New Delhi 110021,
India
email: britishschool@british-school.org
website: www.british-school.org

Director: **Vanita Uppal**, OBE

The Cathedral & John Connon School
6 Purshottamdas Thakurdas Marg, Fort Mumbai 400
001, India
email: cajcs@mtnl.net.in
website: www.cathedral-school.com

Principal: **Mrs Meera Isaacs**

The Doon School
The Mall, Dehradun 248001, Uttaranchal, India
email: hm@doonschool.com
website: www.doonschool.com

Headmaster: **Mr Matthew Raggett**

The International School Bangalore
NAFL Valley, Whitefield-Sarajapur Road, Near
Dommasandra Circle, Bangalore –562 125, Karnataka
State, India
email: school@tisb.ac.in
website: www.tisb.org

Principal: **Dr Caroline Pascoe**

Woodstock School
Tehri Road, Mussoorie, Uttarakhand 248179, India
email: communications@woodstockschool.ac.in
website: www.woodstockschool.in

Principal: **Dr Jonathan Long**

Indonesia

The British School Jakarta
Bintaro Jaya Sector 9, Jl Raya Jombang - Cileduk,
Pondok Aren, Tangerang 15227, Indonesia
email: principal@bsj.sch.id
website: www.bsj.sch.id

Principal: **Mr David Butcher**

Malaysia

Kolej Tuanku Ja'afar
Mantin, 71700 Negeri Sembilan, West Malaysia
email: principal@ktj.edu.my
website: www.ktj.edu.my

Principal: **Dr Glenn Moodie**

Marlborough College Malaysia
Jalan Marlborough, 79200 Isjander Puteri, Johor, Malaysia
email: marlborough@marlboroughcollege.my
website: www.marlboroughcollegemalaysia.org

Master: **Alan Stevens**

Singapore

Tanglin Trust School
95 Portsdown Road, Singapore 139299
email: admissions@tts.edu.sg
website: www.tts.edu.sg

Chief Executive Officer: **Mr Craig Considine [HMC]**

Head of Infant School: Mrs Paula Craigie [IAPS]

Head of Junior School: Mrs Clair Harrington-Wilcox [IAPS]

Head of Senior School: Mr Allan Forbes

(*See entry in IAPSO section*)

Thailand

Shrewsbury International School
1922 Charoen Krung Road, Wat Prayakrai, Bang Kholame, Bangkok 10120, Thailand
email: enquiries@shrewsbury.ac.th
website: www.shrewsbury.ac.th

Principal: **Christopher Seal**

Australia and New Zealand

Australia

Anglican Church Grammar School
Oaklands Parade, East Brisbane, Queensland QLD 4169, Australia
email: reception@churchie.com.au
website: www.churchie.com.au

Headmaster: **Dr Alan Campbell**

Camberwell Grammar School
PO Box 151, Balwyn, VIC 3103, Australia
email: headmaster@cgs.vic.edu.au
website: www.cgs.vic.edu.au

Headmaster: **Dr Paul Hicks**

Geelong Grammar School
50 Biddlecombe Avenue, Corio, VIC 3214, Australia
email: principal@ggs.vic.edu.au
website: www.ggs.vic.edu.au

Principal: **Ms Rebecca Cody**

Haileybury
855 Springvale Road, Keysborough, VIC 3173, Australia
email: admissions@haileybury.vic.edu.au
website: www.haileybury.com.au

Principal: **Derek Scott**

Kincoppal-Rose Bay School of the Sacred Heart
New South Head Road, Rose Bay NSW 2029, Australia
email: reception@krb.nsw.edu.au
website: www.krb.nsw.edu.au

Principal: **Mrs Maureen Ryan**

The King's School
PO Box 1, Parramatta, NSW 2124, Australia
email: headmaster@kings.edu.au
website: www.kings.edu.au

Headmaster: **Anthony L George**

Knox Grammar School
2 Borambil Street, Wahroonga, NSW 2076, Australia
email: contact@knox.nsw.edu.au
website: www.knox.nsw.edu.au

Headmaster: **Scott James**

Melbourne Grammar School
Domain Road, South Yarra, Melbourne, VIC 3004, Australia
email: mgs@mgs.vic.edu.au
website: www.mgs.vic.edu.au

Headmaster: **Roy Kelley**

Methodist Ladies' College
207 Barker Road, Kew, Victoria 3101, Australia
email: college@mlc.vic.edu.au
website: www.mlc.vic.edu.au

Principal: **Miss Diana Vernon**, BA, PGCE, MACE, MACEL

St Leonard's College
163 South Road, Brighton East, VIC 3187, Australia
email: stleonards@stleonards.vic.edu.au
website: www.stleonards.vic.edu.au

Principal: **Mr Stuart Davis**

Scotch College
1 Morrison Street, Hawthorn, VIC 3122, Australia
email: scotch@scotch.vic.edu.au
website: www.scotch.vic.edu.au

Principal: **I Tom Batty**

The Scots College
Victoria Road, Bellevue Hill, NSW 2023, Australia
email: reception@tsc.nsw.edu.au
website: www.tsc.nsw.edu.au

Principal: **Dr Ian P M Lambert**

Shore School
PO Box 1221, Blue Street, North Sydney, NSW 2059, Australia
email: headmaster@shore.nsw.edu.au
website: www.shore.nsw.edu.au

Head: **Dr Timothy Wright**

Wesley College
577 St Kilda Road, Melbourne, VIC 3004, Australia
email: principal@wesleycollege.net
website: www.wesleycollege.net

Acting Principal: **Mr Richard Brenker**

Central, North and South America

Argentina

St Andrew's Scots School
Roque Saenz Peña 654, 1636 Olivos, Buenos Aires, Argentina
email: administration@sanandres.esc.edu.ar
website: www.sanandres.esc.edu.ar

Head: **Gabriel Rshaid**

St George's College North
C. Rivadavia y Don Bosco, Los Polvorines 1613, Buenos Aires, Argentina
email: info.north@stgeorges.edu.ar
website: www.stgeorges.edu.ar/north

Headmaster: **Oliver Proctor**

St George's College Quilmes
Guido 800, CC2 (1878), Quilmes, Buenos Aires, Argentina
email: infoquilmes@stgeorges.edu.ar
website: www.stgeorges.edu.ar

Headmaster: **Ian D Tate**

Brazil

St Paul's School
Rua Juquiá 166, Jardim Paulistano, São Paulo SP 01440-903, Brazil
email: spshead@stpauls.br
website: www.stpauls.br

Head: **Ms Louise Simpson**

(*See entry in IAPS section*)

Chile

The Grange School
Av Principe de Gales 6154, La Reina, 687067, Santiago, Chile
email: rectoria@grange.cl
website: www.grange.cl

Rector: **Rachid R Benammar**

(*See Grange Preparatory School entry in IAPS section.*)

Europe

Cyprus

The English School
PO Box 23575, 1684 Nicosia, Cyprus
email: head@englishschool.ac.cy
website: www.englishschool.ac.cy

Headmaster: **Mr David Lambon**

Czech Republic

The English College in Prague
Sokolovska 320, 190-00 Praha 9, Czech Republic
email: office@englishcollege.cz
website: www.englishcollege.cz

Headmaster: **Dr Nigel Brown**

The Prague British School
K Lesu 558/2, 142 00 Praha 4, Czech Republic
email: info@pbschool.cz
website: www.pbschool.cz

Head of Senior School: **Michael Bardsley**

Head of Primary Schools: **John Bagust**

Greece

Campion School
PO Box 67484, Pallini, Athens 153 02, Greece
email: satherton@campion.edu.gr
website: www.campion.edu.gr

Headmaster: **Stephen W Atherton**

St Catherine's British School
PO Box 51019, Kifissia GR 145 10, Greece
email: headmaster@stcatherines.gr
website: www.stcatherines.gr

Headmaster: **Mr Stuart Smith**

Italy

The British School of Milan
Via Pisani Dossi 16, 20134 Milan, Italy
email: info@sjhschool.com
website: www.britishschoolmilan.com

Principal & CEO: **Dr Chris Greenhalgh**

St George's British International School
Via Cassia, La Storta, 00123 Rome, Italy

email: secretary@stgeorge.school.it
website: www.stgeorge.school.it

Principal: **David Tongue**

Netherlands

The British School in The Netherlands
Vrouw Avenweg 640, 2493 WZ, Den Haag, The Netherlands

email: admissions@britishschool.nl
website: www.britishschool.nl

Principal: **Kieran Earley**

Headteachers:

Junior School Diamanthorst: Angela Parry-Davies (*IAPS Member*)

Junior School Leidschenveen: Karren van Zoest

Junior School Vlaskamp: Sue Aspinall

Senior School Voorschoten: Paul Topping

Portugal

St Julian's School
Quinta Nova, 2775-588 Carcavelos, Portugal

email: ccoelho@stjulians.com
website: www.stjulians.com

Head: **Dr Nicola Mason**

Spain

The British School of Barcelona
Cognita Schools Group
Carrer de la Ginesta 26, 08860 Castelldefels, Barcelona, Spain

email: school@bsb.edu.es
website: www.britishschoolbarcelona.com

Principal: **Mr Jonathan Locke**

Switzerland

Aiglon College
CH-1885 Chesières-Villars, Switzerland

email: info@aiglon.ch
website: www.aiglon.ch

Head Master: **Mr Richard McDonald**, MA Oxon, PGCE

Middle East

Bahrain

St Christopher's School
PO Box 32052, Isa Town, Kingdom of Bahrain

email: office.principal@st-chris.net
website: www.st-chris.net

Principal: **Dr Simon Watson**

Head of Junior School: **Mr Ian Fellows**, BEd, NPQH

Oman

British School Muscat
PO Box 1907, Ruwi, Muscat PC112, Sultanate of Oman

email: admissionsoffice@britishschoolmuscat.com
website: www.britishschoolmuscat.com

Principal: **Mr Kai Vacher**

Qatar

Doha College
PO Box 7506, Doha, State of Qatar

email: seniorexec@dohacollege.com
website: www.dohacollege.com

Principal: **Dr Steffen Sommer**

United Arab Emirates

Brighton College Abu Dhabi
PO Box 129444, Abu Dhabi, United Arab Emirates

email: admissions@brightoncollege.ae
website: www.brightoncollege.ae

Head Master: **Mr Simon Corns**

The British School Al Khubairat
PO Box 4001, Abu Dhabi, United Arab Emirates

email: head@britishschool.sch.ae
website: www.britishschool.sch.ae

Headmaster: **Mr Mark Leppard**, MBE

(*See entry in IAPS section*)

Dubai College
PO Box 837, Dubai, United Arab Emirates

email: dcadmin@dubaicollege.org
website: www.dubaicollege.org

Headmaster: **Mr Michael Lambert**

Jumeirah English Speaking School
PO Box 24942, Dubai, United Arab Emirates

email: jess@jess.sch.ae
website: www.jess.sch.ae

Director: **Mr Mark Steed**

Head Teacher, JESS Jumeirah Primary: **Mr Asa Firth**

Head Teacher, Arabian Ranches Primary: **Mr Darren Coulson**

Headmasters' and Headmistresses' Conference

Associates

In addition to Full membership (open to Heads of independent schools in the UK and Ireland) and International membership (open to Heads of independent schools overseas), HMC also elects a small number of Associates each year.

HMC Associates are either heads of high-performing maintained sector schools proposed and supported by HMC divisions or influential individuals in the world of education, including university vice-chancellors and academics, who endorse and support the work of HMC.

The following is a list of current HMC Associates:

BRIDGET TULLIE
Batley Grammar School, Batley, West Yorkshire
website: www.batleygrammar.co.uk

DR STUART D SMALLWOOD
Bishop Wordsworth's Grammar School, Salisbury, Wiltshire
website: www.bws.wilts.sch.uk

ANDREW MOSS
Gordon's School, Woking, Surrey
website: www.gordons.school

ROBERT J MASTERS
The Judd School, Tonbridge, Kent
website: www.judd.kent.sch.uk

DAVID HUMPRHEYS
Methodist Independent Schools Trust, London NW1
website: www.methodisteducation.co.uk

RUSSEL ELLICOTT
Pate's Grammar School, Cheltenham, Gloucestershire
website: www.pates.gloucs.sch.uk

PETER MIDDLETON
Welbeck – The Defence Sixth Form College, Loughborough, Leicestershire
website: www.dsfc.ac.uk

CLARE WAGNER
West London Free School, London W6
website: wlfs.org

JILL BERRY
Educational Consultant

DR BRENDA DESPONTIN
Former Head

PART II
Schools whose Heads are members of the Girls' Schools Association
ALPHABETICAL LIST OF SCHOOLS

512

The following schools, whose Heads are members of both GSA and HMC, can be found in the HMC section:

Benenden School
Berkhamsted
Bromley High School
Cheltenham Ladies' College
Downe House
Francis Holland School, Regent's Park
Francis Holland School, Sloane Square
The Godolphin and Latymer School
James Allen's Girls' School (JAGS)
King's High School
Monmouth School for Girls
Moreton Hall
Newcastle High School for Girls

Norwich High School
Queen Anne's School
Queenswood School
Roedean School
St Albans High School for Girls
St Helen & St Katharine
St Mary's School Ascot
St Mary's Calne
Sherborne Girls
Withington Girls' School
Woldingham School
Wycombe Abbey

GSA
GEOGRAPHICAL LIST OF SCHOOLS

Individual School Entries

Abbot's Hill School

Bunkers Lane, Hemel Hempstead, Herts HP3 8RP

Tel: 01442 240333
email: registrar@abbotshill.herts.sch.uk
website: www.abbotshill.herts.sch.uk
Twitter: @AbbotsHill
Facebook: @AbbotsHillSchool
LinkedIn: /abbot's-hill

Motto: *Vi et Virtute*

Founded 1912.

Abbot's Hill School is an Independent Day School for girls aged 4–16 years. Our Day Nursery and Pre-School caters for girls and boys from 6 months. The school is situated in 76 acres of parkland on the edge of Hemel Hempstead.

A great emphasis is placed on providing a complete and balanced education. We have a strong record of academic success. Throughout the school, pupils are taught in small classes in which excellent teaching and personalised support ensure that everyone is inspired to exceed their potential.

We pride ourselves on our pastoral care. The sense of being part of an extended family is frequently commented on by pupils, parents and staff alike. In such a nurturing environment, pupils grow naturally in confidence, are happy to embrace new challenges and eagerly take on increasing responsibilities. Pupils leave Abbot's Hill fully equipped to take on with passion the challenges and opportunities life has to offer.

With small classes and a high teacher to pupil ratio, the school aims to develop the academic and creative talents, social skills and confidence of each pupil. Every pupil benefits from being known personally by the Headmistress and teaching staff who seek to create a happy and caring environment.

Senior School. The Senior School is based in a spacious and comfortable 19th Century house, which, combined with purpose-built teaching blocks, Science, Sport, Performing Arts and ICT suites, provides our pupils with first-class facilities.

Curriculum. During the first three years, a broad programme based on the National Curriculum is followed, encompassing both academic and creative subjects. Each girl's potential and progress is carefully monitored by both teaching staff and a personal tutor. Subjects studied include English, Maths, Science, French, Spanish, Geography, History, Media Studies, Information and Communication Technology, Religious Studies, Music, Personal, Social, Health, Economic and Citizenship Education, Art and Design, Drama, Food Technology and Physical Education.

In Years 10 and 11, a core GCSE curriculum of up to 8 subjects is followed with girls choosing up to three further subjects.

Music and Performing Arts. The school has very strong Music and Performing Arts Departments with excellent facilities. The Performing Arts building includes studios for dance, drama and music as well as a theatre. The School Choirs and Orchestra perform regularly in concerts, recitals, plays, musicals and various functions throughout the year and there is a school production each year.

Sports. The school has a strong sporting tradition. There is a well-equipped Sports Hall, lacrosse pitches, grass and hard tennis courts, and a swimming pool. The main sports played are Lacrosse, Netball, Athletics, Tennis, Rounders and Swimming. All girls are encouraged to participate in the sporting opportunities at Abbot's Hill and currently there are a number of girls who have reached County and National standard in selected sports.

Extracurricular Activities. Many activities and clubs are held outside of school and these vary in range from Dance, Art, The Duke of Edinburgh's Award scheme, Music, Speech and Drama and all sports.

Admission. Admission to Abbot's Hill is by Entrance Examination, interview, and a report from the previous school.

Scholarships and Bursaries. Academic, Art, Drama, Music and Sport scholarships are available giving 5–10% reduction in fees. Means-tested Bursaries are also available.

Fees per term (2018–2019). Senior School: £6,172 (Years 7–11); Prep School: £3,588–£4,507 (Reception to Year 6); Nursery: from £54 per day.

Prep School. Abbot's Hill Prep is situated in the same grounds as the Senior School. The Prep School provides Pre-Preparatory and Preparatory education for girls aged 4 and above. Abbot's Hill Nursery and Pre-School welcome boys and girls from 6 months of age. The Prep mixes the formal setting of the classroom with the wealth of opportunity provided by our physical surroundings. Children are given the freedom in which to grow, learn and play. Classrooms and corridors are bright and well decorated with children's work reflecting the diversity of the curriculum.

The Prep School plays a very important role within our school community and is an integral part of the school as a whole. It is our aim at Abbot's Hill to nurture the whole child, thus enabling our pupils to develop their talents whether they be academic, artistic or sporting. Specialist teaching is introduced from a child's earliest days; French, Music and PE are introduced in the pre-school year. This is added to as a child progresses to include Drama, Games, ICT and Geography. By the time a girl reaches Year 5 she is being completely subject taught and is able to adapt to moving around whilst being supported by a class teacher.

The small class sizes at Abbot's Hill Prep enable individual needs to be recognised and met early with the minimum disruption. For those who need extra support this is offered within the classroom setting or one-to-one as appropriate. Gifts or talents for a particular area of learning can be extended and developed to their potential.

The wider curriculum plays a key role. Educational visits are an integral part of the teaching programme and children are regularly taken on visits to galleries and museums to enhance their learning experience. Outside visitors lead workshops at school for year groups or the whole school as appropriate. The extracurricular programme is wide ranging and ever changing. It currently includes such wide-ranging pursuits as languages, trampolining, gardening and board games as well as a wealth of musical and sports clubs.

Further information. Abbot's Hill welcomes visits from prospective parents and pupils. If you would like to visit the School, please contact the Registrar for an appointment on 01442 240333 or email registrar@abbotshill.herts.sch.uk.

Charitable status. Abbot's Hill Charitable Trust is a Registered Charity, number 311053, which exists to provide high quality education for children.

Chairman of the Governing Body: Mrs J Mark, BA Hons, QTS

Headmistress: **Mrs E Thomas**, BA Hons, PGCE, NPQH

Head of Prep School: Mrs S Stephen, BEd Hons, QTS

Head of Senior School: Mrs S Doyle, BEd Hons

Bursar: Mrs C Korniczky, BA Hons, ACA

Registrar: Miss A Cooper

Adcote School

Little Ness, Shrewsbury, Shropshire SY4 2JY

Tel:	01939 260202
Fax:	01939 261300
email:	office@adcoteschool.co.uk
	admissions@adcoteschool.co.uk
website:	www.adcoteschool.org.uk
Twitter:	@AdcoteSchool
LinkedIn:	@Adcote-School-for-Girls

Age Range. 7–18.

Number in School. 200 Girls.

Adcote School is a thriving boarding and day school for around 200 girls currently. Despite its imposing exterior, we are proud of our welcoming, friendly and unpretentious reputation. We are fortunate to be located in a beautiful and safe rural setting with a magnificent Grade I listed building, with 30 acres of beautifully landscaped parkland surrounding the school. These wonderful gardens provide an incredibly safe, secure and idyllic backdrop to this historic school. Adcote has begun a multimillion pound project of modernisation and investment in the school – the most significant development in Adcote's 109 year history. New facilities completed by 2015 include new classrooms, four science labs, catering facilities, boarding accommodation, sports hall, art and textiles block.

Perhaps Adcote's greatest achievement is the variety and breadth of education that it provides for its pupils. Both day girls and boarders benefit from excellent tuition in a range of activities including tennis, horse riding, gymnastics and swimming as well as plenty of healthy competition with local schools in netball, hockey and other sports. Every year, as the GCSE and A Level examination results come in, we are proud of the achievements of each girl and of our school. The excellent results and high league table ranking reflect the hard work of the girls, excellent teaching and the support of parents and families.

Every girl at Adcote, when she leaves the school, should feel she has achieved all she can both academically and intellectually.

Curriculum. Adcote is committed to fostering the achievement of all our girls, without undue pressure. Self-confidence and poise distinguish our pupils whose teachers are dedicated to cultivating the strengths of each girl. Adcote produces confident, enquiring and well-rounded girls who are equipped to play full and constructive roles in an ever-changing society.

Years 7, 8, and 9 follow a broad curriculum which ensures that there is continuity and progression together with sufficient flexibility to respond to individual needs and interests.

The GCSE and IGCSE programme taught in Years 10 and 11, includes the core subjects of English Language, English Literature, Mathematics, ICT (Cambridge Nationals), PE (non-examined) and PSHE (non-examined), plus at least one Science and 7 other subjects from a range of 16 options choices. IGCSE qualifications are internationally recognised by schools, universities and employers as equivalent to, or even slightly more challenging than, UK GCSEs. They are an excellent preparation for A/AS Level courses.

Adcote's outstanding academic results at A Level, Oxbridge success, and entry to other top Universities, accounts for the recent and growing number of pupils in the Sixth Form. The Sixth Form requires each girl to follow her specialist subjects in depth. In Lower Sixth (Year 12), most girls choose to take four A Level subjects from a list of 21 options, in addition to PSHE and PE, which are compulsory but non-examined. In the Upper Sixth (Year 13) three subjects are usually continued to full A Level (A2). As part of ongoing investment in buildings and facilities, the school has recently created a dedicated Sixth Form Centre.

Performing Arts. The school places great emphasis on Music, Dance, and Drama as well as a range of other activities. All the performing arts are included in the core curriculum to age 14, and thereafter voluntarily. Instrumental playing is much encouraged, there are several choirs in the school which practice regularly and there are extracurricular workshops in dance and drama, and performances several times a year.

Activities. All girls participate in a wide range of activities, including rowing, fencing, Chinese, Russian, Yoga, gardening and horse riding. Sport plays an important part in the life of the school. The school regularly plays hockey, netball, rounders and tennis, with gymnastics being particularly strong. Outward bound programmes also play an important part of life at Adcote, as do interesting weekend activities, and trips away from school. There is an interesting programme of weekly activities for boarding students. A new sports hall was built in 2014 for use by all pupils.

Pastoral Care. The school's size means that the children, staff and parents really get to know each other. There is a tangible sense of community, creating a warm and enabling family atmosphere. Boarders are looked after by Housemistresses and the resident staff, and all girls have a personal tutor, responsible for individual welfare and academic progress. Great importance is attached to understanding the individual and developing personal abilities so that girls meet the demands of the modern world with confidence and good judgement. There is a range of full and weekly boarding options.

Fees per term (2018–2019). UK/Domestic Students: Day Girls £3,047–£4,946; Weekly Boarders £5,754–£8,251 Full Boarders £6,539–£9,032.

Reductions are made in fees of second and subsequent sisters. Bursaries are available for children from the clergy or from Forces families. There are scholarships for academic excellence. The school welcomes applications from girls whose parents cannot afford the fees in full or in part. In line with our aim as a Charity to provide public benefit the school offers means-tested bursaries to outstanding pupils who would not otherwise be able to benefit from the education we provide. The school offers a wide range of discretionary and means-tested bursaries each year to pupils.

A prospectus and further details may be obtained from the Admissions Assistant: admissions@adcoteschool.co.uk.

Adcote is a private limited company. Registered Office: 11th Floor, Centre City, 5–7 Hill Street, Birmingham, B5 4UA. Company Registration No. 10067403.

Headmistress: **Mrs D Browne**, BA Hons Wales, PGCE Exeter, MEd Gloucestershire, NPQH

Deputy Head: Miss L Hudson, BEd Hons Bedford

Head of Prep School: Mrs N Candler, BA Hons Birmingham, PGCE Wolverhampton (*Prep School*)

Head of Student Services: Mrs J Greenwood, BA Hons
Wales, PGCE Manchester
Head of Assessment & Learning and Head of Sixth Form:
Mrs N Tribe, BEng Hons Liverpool John Moores, PGCE
Wolverhampton (*Science, Maths*)
Middle School Coordinator: Mrs K Gardner, BSc Hons
Nottingham, PGCE Loughborough
Head of Enrichment: Mr C Farmer, BEng Hons Coventry,
PGCE (*Head of ICT, ICT Manager*)
Director of Sport: Miss A Pugh BSc Hons Loughborough,
PGCE Birmingham
PSHE Coordinator: Miss S Roberts, BA Hons Chester,
PGCE Aberystwyth
Bursar: Mr Richard Walker
Chaplain: Reverend L Burns

Academic Staff:
Mr D Barker, BSc Hons Manchester, Cert Ed
Wolverhampton (*Physics*)
Mrs E Barnett, BSc Hons Glasgow, PGCE Bristol (*Science*)
Mr C Bunn, BMus Hons Royal Academy, PGCE Edge Hill
(*Music*)
Mrs N Candler, BA Hons Birmingham, PGCE
Wolverhampton (*Junior School*)
Miss H Collier, BA Hons Edge Hill (*Prep School*)
Miss S Dodd, BA Hons Northumbria (*Languages*)
Mr C Farmer, BEng Hons Coventry, PGCE (*Head of ICT,
ICT Manager*)
Mrs K Gardner, BSc Hons Nottingham, PGCE
Loughborough
Mrs J Greenwood, BA Hons Wales, PGCE Manchester
Miss L Hudson, BEd Hons Bedford
Ms E Labbe BA Hons Wolverhampton, PGCE Edge Hill
(*Performing Arts*)
Mrs J Lewis, BSc Hons Newcastle, PGCE Leeds
(*Chemistry*)
Mrs K Newth, BEd Hons Chester (*Prep School*)
Ms L Nixson (*Assistant Director of Sport*)
Mr A O'Connor, BA Middlesex, PGCE Carmarthen, Dip
TEFL/ESP London (*SENCO*)
Mr I Phillips, BSc Hons Leeds, PGCE Aberystwyth (*Head
of Science*)
Mrs M Pragg, BA Hons Swansea, PGCE Keele (*Head of
English*)
Miss A Pugh, BSc Hons Loughborough, PGCE
Birmingham (*Director of Sport*)
Mrs L Richards, BSc Hons Leicester, PGCE Leicester
(*Mathematics*)
Miss S Roberts, BA Hons Chester, PGCE Aberystwyth
(*History*)
Miss E Stephenson, BSc Hons City, PGCE London (*Exams
Officer*)
Mrs N Tribe, BEng Hons Liverpool John Moores, PGCE
Wolverhampton (*Science, Mathematics*)
Miss M Warner, BSc Hons Huddersfield, PGCE
Birmingham (*Textiles*)
Mrs S Warner, BA University of Wales (*English*)
Mrs H Wrobel, BA Hons NE Wales, PGCE Chester (*Art*)
Mrs M Wylde, BA Hons Coventry (*Business Studies*)

Music Staff:
Mrs E Bouyac, BA Hons, MA, PGCE (*Singing*)
Mrs Robinson, ARCM (*Violin*)
Mrs R Glossop, LRAM, LTCL, Dip Mus Huds, PGCE
(*Piano*)
Mr A Jones, BA Hons Leeds (*Guitar*)
Mrs K Langdon (*Woodwind*)
Mrs O Lewis, Academy of Music, Moscow (*Piano*)
Mrs L Le Boutillier (*Singing*)
Ms K Turpin (*Singing*)
Mr R Lewis (*Strings*)

Sports/Extra-Curricular Staff:
Mr D Hiam (*Fencing*)
Mrs L Cooke (*Cookery*)
Ms K Crosland (*K Pop*)

Support Staff:
Finance Manager: Mrs M Modebe
Financial Assistant: Miss E Stirton
Financial Assistant: Mrs H Jones
School Secretary/Headmistress's PA: Miss E Brown
Commercial Events Manager: Mrs P Peplow-Freer
Admissions and Communications Assistant: Miss K
Wakenshaw
School Receptionist/Admin Assistant: Mrs K Lenc

Teaching Assistants:
Mrs L Hughes
Mrs S Hawkins

Head of Boarding and Admissions: Ms N Jones

Boarding House Matrons:
Mrs W Edwards
Mrs S Okell
Mrs E Richardson

Medical Officer: Miss J Mansell

Science Technician: Mrs A Wright
IT Technician: Mr T Weaver

Alderley Edge School for Girls

Wilmslow Road, Alderley Edge, Cheshire SK9 7QE
Tel: 01625 583028
Fax: 01625 590271
email: jbedigan@aesg.co.uk
website: www.aesg.co.uk
Twitter: @schoolforgirls
Facebook: @Alderley-Edge-School-For-Girls

Age Range. 2–18.
Number in School. Nursery, Pre-School and Reception
39; Junior School 128; Senior School 276; Sixth Form 63.
Fees per term (2018–2019). Nursery £2,705; Pre-School
£2,290; Key Stage 1 £2,800; Key Stage 2 £3,300; Senior
£4,150, Sixth Form £4,150.

Alderley Edge School for Girls provides girls with outstanding pastoral support, innovative teaching, a broad curriculum and a fantastic array of extra-curricular
opportunities. Each girl is nurtured and supported in small
classes and it is our priority that each girl reaches her individual potential and becomes the best she can be.

We value the successes and achievements of all our girls;
both academically and in other contexts, from dance to
drama, music to sport. Girls leave as confident, articulate
and mature young women who can achieve in the world
beyond our school gates.

Alderley Edge School for Girls is a community. All our
girls, from those in Nursery at the age of two, through to
Sixth Form at the age of 18, feel safe and secure and benefit
from being in a school positioned in a vibrant village environment.

The School is a high-achieving, academic and dynamic
school which fosters the well-being of each individual
within an exciting, challenging and supportive environment.
We recognise commitment, hard work and success, setting
the girls the challenges they need to develop their talents to
the full.

We are proud of our school and its Christian values, yet
respect the beliefs of others in our community. We believe in

social justice for all and feel a sense of responsibility for those less fortunate, for whom we provide support both locally and globally through our fundraising and community service.

The School has recently been awarded *Apple Distinguished Status* after a huge development in Technology Enhanced Learning. Girls bring their own iPads into school to enrich their learning experience. Each teacher is also given his/her own iPad to support their teaching. The School has also integrated Apple TVs into classrooms, corridors and the newly-built fitness suite.

In January 2018 the Independent Schools Inspectorate (ISI) undertook a Regulatory Compliance Inspection at Alderley Edge School for Girls. We are delighted to report that the School was found to be fully compliant with all ISI regulations with no recommendations.

We are a proud member of the Girls' Schools Association and we value the importance of an all-girls education and the benefits this provides for our students. There are numerous opportunities for girls to develop both team working and leadership skills and to help guide the school and their peers. In this way our students learn important life skills which prepare them for the world of work and they leave us as impressive young women who make a difference.

Admissions. The Early Years Department caters for girls from 2 years. Admission for girls to the Junior School is at 4/5 years old. Admission to the Senior School is at 11 years by Entrance Examination and interview.

The Arts. *Music*: A very large percentage of pupils learn a musical instrument and examinations may be taken. The school runs 4 choirs, 2 orchestras, a jazz band and numerous smaller instrumental ensembles including string groups, a brass group and 5 different woodwind groups. Many cups have been won in local festivals and pupils perform in local youth orchestras.

Drama and Dance: Both are offered. The majority of pupils are involved in school productions and all pupils participate in House and other productions. There are four dance squads which rehearse weekly and holiday courses in Dance and Drama are also on offer.

Facilities. In creating a new school we achieved our objective to remain small enough to care for every child's needs and yet the school enjoys all the benefits and resources of a much larger school. A multimillion pound investment programme has provided a new Senior School and a completely refurbished Junior School. Facilities include a climbing wall, fitness suite, six superbly equipped science laboratories, brand new netball courts and pavilion, four ICT suites with online facilities throughout the school, language suite with language laboratory, Humanities block with Business Studies centre, competition-size sports hall, gymnasium, Performing Arts centre, chapel and a library with breathtaking views over the Cheshire Plain. In addition there is a modern and well-appointed Sixth Form centre – including a dedicated ICT suite – to accommodate the increasing number of girls in our Sixth Form. There is also a recently developed Sixth Form coffee bar.

Scholarships and Bursaries. Several Academic scholarships and scholarships for Music are awarded at 11+, 13+ and 16+. Art and Sport scholarships are available at 11+. Bursaries are also available (income linked).

Charitable status. Alderley Edge School for Girls is a Registered Charity, number 1006726. It exists to provide education for children.

Chair of Governors: Mrs S Herring

Headmistress: Mrs Helen Jeys, BA Durham

Deputy Headmistress: Mrs C Wood, BA Hons, PGCE Leicester

Director of Studies: Mrs C Millar
Head of Junior School: Ms B Howard, BEd Hons Exeter
Head of Lower School (*Years 7–8*): Mrs J Barker
Head of Year 9: Miss M Moss
Head of Upper School (*Years 9–11*): Ms L Telford
Head of Sixth Form: Mr J Russell
Bursar: Mr S Malkin
Registrar: Mrs J Bedigan

Heads of Department:

Art: Mrs M Billington
Business Studies: Mrs R Hilsley
Chemistry: Dr D Hughes
Classics: Mr P Tandler
Design Technology: Mrs K Bryan
Drama: Mrs C Foster
English: Mrs C Polley
Food Technology: Mrs C Leigh
Geography: Mrs R Hawkes
History: Mr D Wilson
ICT: Mr J Chadwick
Mathematics: Mr S Cunliffe
Modern Foreign Languages: Mrs I Jones
Music: Mrs A Pattrick
Physical Education: Miss L McConville
Physics: Mrs K Torr
Psychology: Mrs A Raval
Religious Education: Miss R Stokwisz
Science: Dr D Hughes

Badminton School

Westbury-on-Trym, Bristol BS9 3BA

Tel: 0117 905 5200
Fax: 0117 962 3049
email: admissions@badmintonschool.co.uk
website: www.badmintonschool.co.uk

Motto: *Pro Omnibus Quisque Pro Deo Omnes*

Founded 1858. Non denominational.

Badminton is an independent girls' boarding, weekly boarding and day school situated in a 15-acre site in Westbury-on-Trym on the outskirts of the university city of Bristol.

Age Range of Pupils. 3 to 18.

Number of Pupils. 475.

Number of Staff. Full-time teaching 37, Part-time teaching 16. Teacher to Pupil ratio is currently 1:7.

Educational Philosophy. Whilst the school retains an outstanding academic record, its focus continues to be on nurturing the girls' natural curiosity and fuelling their passion for learning. The enduring excellence that Badminton girls achieve, stems from the positive atmosphere in the School and the holistic approach to education, as well as the exceptional relationships between staff and pupils, which are mature, friendly and based on principles of courtesy and mutual respect. Teachers are highly-qualified specialists in their field and encourage girls to develop academic confidence and to become independent learners by taking responsibility for their work and progress. The most important feature of academic life at Badminton is the resounding philosophy that it is the norm to ask questions, to seek help and, above all, to enjoy learning.

It is a characteristic of Badminton girls that they are thoughtful individuals, able to evaluate information and decide for themselves. This approach extends beyond their studies and into the day-to-day life of the School, where girls are given a wide range of opportunities to grow, develop and express themselves in an enormous range of activities. Staff also enjoy sharing their enthusiasm for their subject and often involve girls in projects and competitions in the local community and nationally.

The Badminton community gives girls a chance to develop an understanding of the viewpoints of others and to think about contributing to the world around them. Girls leave Badminton ready to face the changing and challenging wider world and, when they do, they take with them a strong network of lifelong friends developed through a wealth of shared experiences.

Boarding. The size of the campus and community at Badminton gives a homely and vibrant feel to the School. This, coupled with excellent pastoral care, leaves no scope for anonymity, but rather lends itself to strong mutually supportive relationships between girls as well as between girls and staff.

The boarding accommodation is split into three areas (junior, middle and Sixth Form) so girls get a good sense of progression and development as they move up through the school. Full-time, weekly or flexi boarding are offered and day girls are welcome to flexi board, allowing girls to easily combine their academic schedules with the many activities that are on offer after school and at weekends.

Bartlett House offers cosy bedrooms for boarders in Years 5–8 and easy access to gardens and play areas. Sanderson House, a modern boarding house opened in 2008, accommodates boarders in Years 9, 10 and 11. The Sixth Form Centre provides the Lower Sixth and Upper Sixth with a more independent environment in double or single studybedrooms. In each House, boarders have the support of a resident Housemistress, Assistant Housemistresses and Resident Tutors and there is a broad range of clubs and activities on offer every day as well as a full weekend programme.

The School's enrichment programme is extremely important in the overall development of the pupils and girls participate in many activities and are encouraged to do so. The activities offered vary depending on the interests of the girls; some have an academic bias, others let the girls explore their creative interests. Girls are very much encouraged to enjoy and value their own and their peers' successes and triumphs in every area of life.

Curriculum. The School's broad curriculum provides a rich and varied experience for the girls. Through Art, Drama and Music programmes, each girl has many opportunities to express her individuality and develop her own unique identity. In an increasingly global society, the importance of languages has never been greater and girls have the opportunity to study Mandarin and Greek in addition to more traditional languages such as French and Latin.

Small classes ensure that all the girls receive individual help and attention from their teachers. Badminton girls are proactive and independent learners; they are not afraid to take intellectual risks and are always happy to ask questions. The emphasis at Badminton is on a holistic education, not narrowly academic, and both the curriculum and the timetable are constructed to create a balance between academic achievement, personal development, life skills and other enterprising activity.

Academic Record. Badminton has a fine academic record at GCSE, AS and A Level. The GCSE and A Level pass rate is 100%. Sixth Form leavers go on to study at some of the top universities and Music Conservatories in the UK and overseas, including Oxford, Cambridge and the Royal Academy of Music and further afield.

Facilities. All the facilities of the school are on site and include a 25m indoor swimming pool, international-sized astro pitch, 7 tennis and 4 netball courts, gymnasium and fitness suite as well as a fully-equipped Science Centre, Creative Arts Centre and self-contained Sixth Form Centre.

There are extensive fiction, careers, music and art libraries as well as a Music School.

Music, Drama and Creative Arts. All girls are involved in the Arts, both within the curriculum and as extracurricular activities, and the School attaches great importance to the development of musical and artistic talent.

Music is extremely popular at Badminton with over 85% of all pupils studying at least one musical instrument. There is a wide range of choral and instrumental groups to join including Junior and Senior Choir, Schola (choral group), orchestra, swing band, string ensembles, woodwind ensembles and other mixed musical groups. With visiting peripatetic teachers, all of whom are professional musicians, the students can study any instrument of their choice. There are a wide variety of performance opportunities including informal concerts and concerts for the local community.

There are several drama productions every year including plays directed and produced by the girls. Many girls take optional Speech and Drama lessons and LAMDA examinations.

There is an excellent Creative Arts department, with a wide choice of subjects for the girls to pursue including Fine Art, Pottery and Sculpture, Textiles, Design, Jewellery-making and Photography.

Clubs and Societies. A wide range is offered including: Extended Project Qualification, The Duke of Edinburgh's Award, Italian GCSE, Sports Leaders Award, Leith's Cookery Course, Modern Languages, Debating, Drama, Musical Theatre, Mandarin, Cookery, Young Enterprise, Art and Crafts, Science Outreach and The Prince's Trust.

Games and Activities. Specialist PE teachers and coaches offer timetabled and optional sport including Hockey, Tennis, Netball, Swimming, Athletics, Rounders, Gymnastics, Badminton, Basketball, Self-Defence and Judo.

Optional extras. All girls participate in activities which include the full choice of Games, Creative Arts and Clubs as above and boarders have the opportunity of additional activities at weekends.

Badminton is fortunate in being sited on the outskirts of the university city of Bristol; regular visits are arranged to concerts, lectures and theatres and there is considerable contact with Bristol University. Community and voluntary work is strongly encouraged, with girls assisting with Science Outreach and reading in local primary schools, volunteering in local hospitals and charity shops.

Admission. Girls sit the Senior School entrance assessments in the November or January prior to year of entry. Entrance assessments are taken in English, Mathematics as well as an online reasoning test. Girls are also interviewed by a senior member of staff and the girl's current school is asked to provide a reference.

Girls sit Sixth Form entrance papers in the November in the year prior to joining. They choose two academic subjects they are intending to study for A Level and also sit an online reasoning test. They too will be interviewed by a senior member of staff and the girl's current school is asked to provide a reference.

Prospective Junior School pupils are assessed by spending a day in the school during which they are observed and assessed informally by staff and the Junior School Headmistress, Mrs Emma Davies. This also helps them to make initial relationships with their prospective peers and gives them a real taste for life at Badminton. From Years 3–6 the tests are more formal and written papers in English, Maths, Reading and a Reasoning test are completed during the assessment day. Entry for Little Acorns (our pre-reception class) is by appointment with the Junior School Headmistress, Mrs Emma Davies, and girls will also have a short observation session in our Little Acorns class.

Prospective parents are encouraged to visit the school individually or attend one of our Open Mornings. To obtain a prospectus and arrange a visit, please contact the Admissions Department via email at admissions@badminton school.co.uk or call 0117 905 5271.

Scholarships. Academic, Music, Sport and All-Rounder scholarships are available for girls entering Badminton in Years 7, 9 and 12. A STEM Scholarship is also available in Years 7 and 9 and an Art Scholarship is available in Years 9 and Year 12. Scholarships for entry into the upper end of the Junior School are also available. Parents of girls who are awarded scholarships are also eligible to apply for a means-tested Bursary.

Scholarship application forms and more information can be obtained by emailing our Admissions Department at admissions@badmintonschool.co.uk.

Bursaries. Bursaries are means-tested and awarded on the basis of parents' financial circumstances. Application forms may be obtained by emailing admissions@badminton school.co.uk.

Fees per term (2018–2019). Day: Juniors £3,250–£3,745. Seniors £5,475. Boarding: Juniors £7,100–£8,315, Seniors £10,150–£12,525.

Forces families in receipt of CEA or an equivalent civilian allowance receive 20% remission of fees.

Charitable status. Badminton School Limited is a Registered Charity, number 311738. It exists for the purpose of educating children.

Chairman of Governors: Mr Bill Ray

Clerk to the Governors, Secretary and Director of Finance and Operations: Ms E Sandberg, LLB Hons

Headmistress: **Mrs R Tear**, BSc Hons Exeter, MA London, PGCE London

Deputy Head: Dr P Bennett, MA Durham, PGCE Buckingham, PhD Bristol

Director of Studies: Mr S Dalley, BA Hons Exeter, MA Bristol

Director of Welfare: Mrs J Scarfe, BA Wales

Head of Junior School: Ms E Davies, BA Hons Cardiff, PGCE

Executive Assistant to the Headmistress: Mrs S Brown

Bedford Girls' School

Cardington Road, Bedford, Bedfordshire MK42 0BX

Tel: 01234 361918
email: admissions@bedfordgirlsschool.co.uk
website: www.bedfordgirlsschool.co.uk
Twitter: @BedfordGirlsSch
Facebook: @BedfordGirlsSch
LinkedIn: /bedford-girls'-school

Foundation – The Harpur Trust.

"Let me keep an open mind so I understand as much as I can in my lifetime and not reach the limits of my imagination."

Bedford Girls' School is a dynamic, forward-thinking selective independent day school for girls aged 7–18. As an exceptional school, we value creativity and innovation highly. From Year 3 to Sixth Form, it is our belief that learning should be exciting and lifelong, so that girls leave us fully equipped academically, personally, emotionally and morally fulfilled individuals capable of achieving their full potential in every aspect and at every stage of their lives.

Part of the Harpur Trust, we offer both the International Baccalaureate and A Level to Sixth Formers. Whichever course of study our student elect to take post-16 our philosophy lies in equipping them with critical thinking skills and the attributes of the IB learner profile from the moment they join us, whether in the Junior or Senior Schools. As a result, we find that the natural curiosity of the girls is heightened and sharpened and they are extremely engaged with their own learning. Our girls excel academically; we are an outstanding sports school and have an excellent reputation for Music and the Creative Arts.

The atmosphere of our school is unique and exciting. Classrooms fizz with energy and enthusiasm and each day brings forth new discoveries and achievements. We would be delighted to welcome you to visit, either for one of our Open House events or a private tour, to experience at first hand a true flavour of life at Bedford Girls' School. Please visit www.bedfordgirlsschool.co.uk for further information or contact our Admissions Team: Tel: 01234 361918, email: admissions@bedfordgirlsschool.co.uk.

Admissions. Entry to the Junior School is based on online assessment in Mathematics, English and a creative writing task. Entry to the Senior School is based on interview, online assessments in Mathematic and English, and a Verbal Reasoning paper. Sixth Form entry is based on interviews, Verbal Reasoning, and GCSE results. A Reference from the Head of the student's current school is required for all candidates.

Fees per term (2018–2019). Junior School (7–11 years) £3,146; Senior School (11–16 years) £4,421; Sixth Form (16–18 years) £4,421.

Charitable status. Bedford Girls' School is part of the Harpur Trust which is a Registered Charity, number 1066861.

Chair of Governors: Ms T Beddoes

Head: **Miss J MacKenzie**

Senior Deputy Head: Mr J Gardner

Deputy Head – Pastoral: Ms E Teale

Assistant Head: Mrs K Jones
Assistant Head: Mrs N Keeler
Assistant Head: Mrs S Mason-Patel
Director of Sixth Form: Dr J Walters

Head of Bedford Girls' School Junior School: Mrs C Howe

Blackheath High School
GDST

Vanbrugh Park, London SE3 7AG

Tel: 020 8853 2929
email: info@bla.gdst.net

Junior Department:
Wemyss Road, London SE3 0TF

Tel: 020 8852 1537
Fax: 020 8463 0040
email: info@bla.gdst.net

website: www.blackheathhighschool.gdst.net
Twitter: @BlackheathHigh
Facebook: @BlackheathHighSchool
LinkedIn: /Blackheath-High-School

Founded in 1880.

Blackheath High School is part of the Girls' Day School Trust (GDST), the UK's leading network of independent girls' schools. As a charity that owns and runs 23 schools and two academies, it reinvests all its income in its schools. For further information about the Trust, visit www.gdst.net.

Blackheath High School is a selective, independent day school for girls aged 3–18 situated in Blackheath, South East London. We enjoy an enviable 'village' like location, within the Royal Borough of Greenwich and have a long history of educating a rich social and cultural blend of students, that reflects the cosmopolitan character of London itself.

Rated 'excellent' in all areas in the latest ISI inspection, academic success is at the heart of what is offered at Blackheath High School. Fuelled by our aspirational culture, students make exceptional progress, with excellent public examination results and a range of ambitious and interesting university destinations. This is achieved through the provision of an innovative and interesting curriculum that challenges and inspires students and nurtures a love of learning. Alongside our core curriculum there are unique opportunities such as Astronomy GCSE at the Greenwich Royal Observatory and our bespoke academic enrichment programme – The Wollstonecraft. Optional courses are designed to engage and inspire, covering topics as diverse as: the culture and history of Tibet; an introduction to architecture and designing a radio programme for Radio 4 Woman's Hour.

Within the core curriculum, girls are able to choose two languages from Mandarin, German, French and Spanish and study these all through to year 13 and great value is placed upon the girls broadening their horizons beyond the school with a range of exciting trips and work experience opportunities. A strong focus on science and technology subjects ensures that our students defy the national trends in terms of numbers of girls applying for science and technology subjects. Strong role models and a curriculum that is well supported by the latest technology, including iPads, digital radio stations and 3D printing, inspire ever-growing numbers of girls to pursue ambitions related to computing, science and design. This is a school where girls are encouraged to discover their passions and teachers support and challenge girls in pursuing their aims.

Enviably located between beautiful Royal Greenwich Park and stunning Blackheath, the school is located over three sites: separate Junior and Senior Schools and a dedicated sporting facility in Kidbrooke Grove that enables us to ring-fence curriculum time for the girls' sporting activity. With a multimillion pound investment in our Senior School facilities completing in 2018, the opportunities available to the girls will continue to grow. Adding to our recently refurbished dedicated Sixth Form Centre 'Westcombe House', the redevelopment will include a state-of-the-art library, creative arts centre, science labs and entrance building to enhance the opportunities already on offer through our theatre, dance and drama studios, language lab, science suite and teaching rooms.

Individuality is cherished and there is a culture of open-mindedness and harmony. Teachers pride themselves on their superb knowledge of the girls and the positive relationships that are fostered in the school. This is a community where older girls mix readily with younger and the atmosphere of open-mindedness and tolerance is genuine and tangible. These excellent relationships are founded upon the staff's willingness and desire to provide a superb and wide-ranging co-curricular programme. From overseas trips to exotic destinations like Peru and Beijing, to clubs designed to appeal to every girl, like 'crochet collective', 'Samba Band' or 'Iron Woman running club', the co-curricular programme builds vital life skills and cements positive and productive relationships. Our strong focus on 'putting girls first', as part of our founding mission, ensures that this is a

school where girls take pride in their talents and ability and ignore gender stereotypes.

As described in the ISI report, the school provides an educational experience that is "stimulating and extraordinarily supportive, conducive to the highest standards of teaching and learning".

Admission to the school is by examination and interview; scholarships and bursaries are available. Regular Open Days are held in the autumn and spring terms, but visitors are always welcome and the Head likes to discuss each girl's particular needs individually with pupils and parents. Please telephone our Admissions Secretary on 020 8557 3009 for a prospectus and to arrange a visit.

Curriculum. We offer a broad choice of subjects at GCSE and an even wider choice at AS and A Level. An education at Blackheath High School inspires and equips girls to strive for personal excellence in all their endeavours: intellectual; physical; creative; cultural; social and moral. We prepare and empower girls for the future by providing an atmosphere in which academic curiosity is cultivated, confidence is built and a balanced, open-minded outlook is nurtured.

As an all-through 3–18 school, we have the luxury of being able to design a curriculum entirely tailored to these aims in every key stage.

Fees per term (2018–2019). Senior School £5,498, Junior Department £4,506, Nursery £3,507. The fees cover the regular curriculum, school books, stationery and other materials, choral music, and games, but not optional extra subjects, school visits or lunch.

Bursaries. The GDST makes available to the school a number of bursaries. The bursaries are means tested and are intended to ensure that the school remains accessible to bright girls who would profit from our education but who would be unable to enter the school without financial assistance.

Scholarships. A number of scholarships are available to particularly gifted girls for entry at 11+, 13+ or the Sixth Form. These are awarded on academic or sporting, musical and artistic merit as measured by the entrance examination and scholarship assessment days. Particulars of the examination are available from the Admissions Officer, email: admissions@bla.gdst.net.

Charitable status. Blackheath High School is part of The Girls' Day School Trust, which is a Registered Charity, number 306983.

Chairman of Local Governors: Mr David Atterbury Thomas

Head: **Mrs C Chandler-Thompson**, BA Exeter, PGCE

Deputy Head (Pastoral): Mrs C Maddison, BA Staffordshire, MSc Leicester, PGCE

Deputy Head (Academic): Mr S Henderson, BMus Goldsmiths, PGCCE Dunn

Director of Finance & Operations: Mr R Ryan, AAT, DSBM

Assistant Head (Co-Curricular & Enrichment): Mrs C Pheiffer, BA London, QTA

Assistant Head (Teaching and Learning): Mrs N Argile, BSc Newcastle, MSc, PGCE

Head of Junior School: Mrs S Skevington, LLB Hons Sheffield, PGCE EYP

Head of Sixth Form: Mrs K Elliott, BSc Cardiff, PGCE

Admissions Officer: Mrs F Nichols, BA London

Bolton School Girls' Division

Chorley New Road, Bolton, Lancs BL1 4PB

Tel:	01204 840201
Fax:	01204 434710
email:	seniorgirls@boltonschool.org
website:	www.boltonschool.org/seniorgirls
Twitter:	@BoltonSchool
Facebook:	@boltonschool.org
LinkedIn:	/bolton-school

Bolton School Girls' Division was founded in 1877 as the High School for Girls and quickly gained a reputation for excellence. In 1913 the first Viscount Leverhulme gave a generous endowment to the High School for Girls and the Bolton Grammar School for Boys on condition that the two schools should be equal partners known as Bolton School (Girls' and Boys' Divisions).

Bolton School is a family of schools, where children can enjoy an all-through education, joining our co-educational Nursery or Infant School before moving up to our single-sex Junior and Senior Schools with Sixth Forms. We are strong believers that girls and boys from 7+ perform best in a single-sex environment, but one where there are co-educational activities – the best of both worlds.

The School occupies a stunning 32-acre site and the Girls' Division Senior School contains over 770 day pupils. The co-educational infants' school, Beech House, offers an education for 225 pupils aged 4–7 and up to a further 200 girls are educated in the Girls' Division Junior School (age 7–11). In the Senior School 200 girls typically attend the Sixth Form.

Bolton School Girls' Division seeks to realise the potential of each pupil. We provide challenge, encourage initiative, promote teamwork and develop leadership capabilities. It is our aim that students leave the School as self-confident young people equipped with the knowledge, skills and attributes that will allow them to lead happy and fulfilled lives and to make a difference for good in the wider community.

We do this through offering a rich and stimulating educational experience which encompasses academic, extra-curricular and social activities. We provide a supportive and industrious learning environment for pupils selected on academic potential, irrespective of means and background.

Facilities. Housed in an attractive Grade II listed building the school has an impressive Great Hall which seats 900 people, spacious corridors, a theatre, two Resistant Materials workshops, two Textile studios, two Food Technology rooms, four computer rooms, seven laboratories, three Art studios and two fine libraries staffed by two qualified librarians and their staff. In September 2013, the Sixth Form moved into the purpose-built £7m Riley Sixth Form Centre, where girls and boys share a Common Room, cafe and learning areas equipped with the very latest technology. The girls' dining room was completely redeveloped in the Summer of 2015.

Besides its own fully-equipped gym, the Girls' Division shares the award-winning Careers Department, the Arts Complex and Sports Hall, a 25-metre swimming pool, extensive playing fields, the Leverhulme Sports Pavilion and an outdoor pursuits facility at Patterdale Hall in the Lake District. Pupils also have the option of spending a week undertaking sailing lessons in the Irish Sea on Tenacity of Bolton, a boat built by pupils in the Boys' Division.

Beech House Infants' School. The curriculum, though based on the National Curriculum, extends far beyond it. Specialist teaching is provided for older pupils in Physical Education and Music and all children are taught French. The school has recently moved to purpose-built state-of-the-art premises and in addition to its own resources, Beech House benefits from the use of Senior School facilities such as the swimming pool, playing fields and Arts Centre.

The Girls' Junior School. There are 2 classes in each of Years 3–6. In September 2010, the junior girls moved into their new £5m school which has its own hall, laboratory, art and design facility, IT suite and library, as well as large classrooms. Besides following the National Curriculum with Senior School specialists teaching PE, Music and French, pupils have additional opportunities. The many clubs and wide range of extracurricular activities ensure a full and well-balanced programme.

The Senior School. The curriculum encompasses all the National Curriculum but also offers the study of two modern languages, the classics and a wide range of modules in Technology. At age 11 all girls follow a similar weekly timetable. The twelve subjects offered are: Art, English, French, Geography, History, Classical Studies, Mathematics, Music, PE, Religion and Philosophy, Science and Technology. All pupils in Year 9 begin to study GCSE Biology, Chemistry and Physics. The above list does not fully show the great variety of opportunities available which also include: Athletics, Biology, Chemistry, Computer Graphics, Dance, Drama, Earth Science, Electronics, Food Technology, Gymnastics, Information Technology, Lacrosse, Netball, Physics, PSHE, Resistant Materials Technology, Rounders, Swimming, Tennis and Textiles Technology. This breadth is maintained to GCSE with a second language, German, Latin or Spanish, being offered in Year 8. In Years 10 and 11 we also offer Archery, Badminton, Basketball, Climbing, Fitness/Gym sessions, Football, Rounders, Unihoc and Volleyball.

GCSE. There is extensive choice at GCSE. All follow a common curriculum of English, English Literature, Mathematics, Biology, Chemistry and Physics (with an option to consolidate down to Dual Award Science at the end of Year 10) together with non-examined courses in Information Technology, PE, and Religion and Philosophy. Personal aptitude and inclination are fostered by allowing a maximum of 11 GCSEs: the core subjects plus options chosen from Art, Biology, Business and Communication Systems, Chemistry, Food Technology, French, Geography, German, Greek, History, Information Technology, Latin, Music, Physics, Religious Studies, Resistant Materials Technology, Spanish and Textile Technology. Essential balance is maintained by requiring all to include one Humanity and one Modern Language, but the choice is otherwise entirely free.

The Sixth Form. Flexibility is a key feature of the Sixth Form. Teaching in the Sixth Form is in smaller groups and single-sex teaching remains the norm, although in a very few subjects co-educational arrangements are in operation. Students choose from a list of approximately 30 AS courses. Breadth is promoted further by our complementary Curriculum Enrichment Programme. All students have the opportunity to follow a range of non-examined courses as well as Physical Education (sports include golf, football, life-saving, rugby, self-defence, tennis and yoga). Links beyond school include the Community Action Programme and Young Enterprise scheme, as well as opportunities with Business Awareness and Work Experience.

Students in the Sixth Form have greater freedom which includes wearing their own smart clothes, exeat periods and having their own Sixth Form Centre away from the Senior School. Joint social and extracurricular events are regularly organised with the Boys' Division. There are opportunities for students to assume a variety of responsibilities both within the school and in the wider community. Increasing personal freedom within a highly supportive environment helps students to make the transition to the independence of the adult world. Some students stretch themselves by taking the AQA Baccalaureate qualification.

Almost all students (95%) go on to Higher Education (10% to Oxford and Cambridge).

Music and Drama are popular and students achieve the highest standards in informal and public performances. The wide variety of concerts and productions may take place in the Arts Centre, the Great Hall or the fully-equipped Theatre, all of which make excellent venues for joint and Girls' Division performances. The School regularly performs at Manchester's Bridgewater Hall.

Personal, Social and Health Education, and Citizenship. PSHE and Citizenship are targeted in a variety of ways and coordinated centrally. Some issues may be covered within departmental schemes of work while others will be discussed in the informal atmosphere of form groups led by the form tutor. Those areas which require specialist input are fitted into longer sessions run by experts from outside school.

Careers. The Careers Department helps prepare students for adult life. It is staffed by two experienced assistants and has a resource centre giving access to all the latest information. The extensive programme starts at age 11 and includes communication skills, work sampling, and support in making choices at all stages of schooling. In addition, girls prepare their CVs and applications to Higher Education with the individual help of a trained tutor.

Extra-curricular Activities. Patterdale Hall, our outdoor pursuits centre in the Lake District, offers many activities including abseiling, gorge walking, orienteering and sailing on Lake Ullswater. Awards are regularly made to enable individuals to undertake a variety of challenging activities both at home and abroad while every year, the whole of Year 9 as well as many older girls embark on The Duke of Edinburgh's Award scheme. In 2017 the School won the Queen's Award for Voluntary Service, the MBE for organisations. In addition to the annual exchanges for Modern Languages students, we also offer a wide range of educational and recreational trips both at home and abroad. All have the opportunity to follow a wide range of non-examined courses of their choice, including Physical Education.

Admission. Entrance to the school is by Headteacher's report, written examination and interview in the Spring term for girls aged 7 and 11. New girls are also welcomed into the Sixth Form. Applications to other year groups are welcomed and spaces may be available depending upon migration.

One in five Senior School pupils receives assistance with their fees through the School's own bursaries. Non-means-tested Scholarships are also awarded to those pupils who achieve highly in the Entrance Examination.

Fees per term (2018–2019). Senior School and Sixth Form £3,992; Infant and Junior Schools £3,193. Fees include lunches.

Charitable status. The Bolton School is a Registered Charity, number 1110703. Under the terms of the Charity it is administered as two separate Divisions providing for boys and girls under a separate Headmaster and Headmistress.

Chairman of Governors: M T Griffiths, BA, FCA

Headmistress: Miss S E Hincks, MA

Deputy Head: Mrs L D Kyle, BSc
Assistant Head: P Linfitt, BSc, MEng
Assistant Head: Ms H Bradford-Keegan, MA (*Curricular and Extracurricular Achievement*)
Assistant Head: Mrs C Winder, MA (*Head of Sixth Form*)
Assistant Head: Ms M Teichman (*Head of Upper School*)
Assistant Head: Mrs A Field, BA (*Head of Middle School*)

Senior School:

Heads of Departments:

Art, Design & Technology: Miss J A Fazackerley, BA
Careers and Higher Education: Miss L Jones, BA
Classics: Mrs J Hone, BA
Economics & Business Studies: Miss L Jones, BA
English: Miss R Sutcliffe, BA
Food Technology: Mrs N James, BA
Geography: Ms S Noot, BA
History: C Owen, MA
ICT: Mrs S Brace, BSc
Learning Support Coordinator: Mrs A Elkin, BA
Mathematics: G Heppleston, BSc
Modern Languages: Mrs A Shafiq, BA
French: C Fico, BA
German: Ms R McQuillan, BA
Spanish: Mrs A Shafiq, BA
Music: Mrs A Price, MA
Physical Education: Mrs K A Heatherington, BA
Religion and Philosophy: Mrs K E Porter, BA
Resistant Materials: Miss R Langley
Science: Dr A Fielder, BA
Biology: Mrs A D Furey, BSc
Chemistry: Ms M Teichman, BSc
Physics: Mr R Ball, BSc
Psychology: Mrs J Sanders, BSc

Instrumental Music Staff:
Brass, Cello, Clarinet, Flute, Guitar, Oboe, Organ, Percussion, Piano, Saxophone, Singing, Violin.

Lower Schools:

Junior Department (Age 7–11):
Head: Mrs C Laverick, BSc
Deputy Head: Mrs H Holt, BEd

Beech House (Age 4–7):
Head: Mrs T Taylor, BEd
Deputy Head: Mrs J Mees, BSc

Brighton & Hove High School
GDST

The Temple, Montpelier Road, Brighton, East Sussex BN1 3AT

Tel:	01273 280280
Fax:	01273 280281
email:	enquiries@bhhs.gdst.net
website:	www.bhhs.gdst.net
Twitter:	@BHHSGDST
Facebook:	@BrightonHoveHighSchool

Founded 1876.

Brighton & Hove High School is part of the GDST (Girls' Day School Trust). The GDST is the leading network of independent girls' schools in the UK. As a charity that owns and runs 23 schools and two academies, it reinvests all its income in its schools. For further information about the Trust, see p. xxiii or visit www.gdst.net.

Additional information about the school may be found on the school's website and a detailed prospectus is available from the school.

See also Brighton & Hove Prep GDST entry in IAPS section.

Number of Pupils. 370 Girls in the Senior School (age 11–18), including 50 in the Sixth Form; 230 in the Prep School (age 3–11).

Location. The school stands in its own grounds in the centre of the city of Brighton and Hove. It is about half-a-mile from Brighton Railway Station and pupils come in from Lewes, Haywards Heath and Lancing by train. It is easily reached by bus from all parts of Brighton and Hove.

The Prep School is housed in premises in Radinden Manor Road. The Senior School is in the Temple, a gentleman's residence built by Thomas Kemp in 1819 which has been considerably altered and enlarged to offer all modern amenities, most recent of which is a Sports Hall and Dance Studio. There is a self-contained Sixth Form Centre and the school owns a Field Centre on the River Wye in mid-Wales.

Curriculum. The school course is planned to provide a wide general education. Girls are prepared for GCSEs and in the Sixth Form a wide choice of A Level subjects is offered in preparation for universities and other forms of professional training.

The school has an all-weather hockey pitch at the Prep School site with facilities for hockey, rounders, netball and tennis. Gymnastics and dance are also taught with swimming for junior forms, and senior forms choose from activities including badminton, cricket, netball, water sports and dance.

Fees per term (2018–2019). Senior School £4,669–£4,807, Prep School £3,037–£3,411, Nursery £2,397.

The tuition fees cover the regular curriculum, school books, stationery and other materials, choral music and sport, but not optional subjects. There is compulsory catering up to year 10, invoiced termly.

The fees for extra subjects (instrumental music and speech and drama) are shown in the prospectus.

Admission at all ages is by interview and test/entrance examination, except at 16+ where GCSE qualifications are essential. The main entry points are 3+, 4+, 11+ and 16+, though occasional vacancies occur at all ages.

Scholarships and Bursaries. The GDST has made available to the school a number of scholarships and bursaries. The bursaries are means tested and are intended to ensure that the school remains accessible to bright girls who would profit from our education but who would be unable to enter the school without financial assistance.

Trust Scholarships are available on merit, irrespective of income, to internal or external candidates for entry at 11+ or to the Sixth Form.

Charitable status. Brighton & Hove High School is part of The Girls' Day School Trust, which is a Registered Charity, number 306983.

Chair of Local Governors: Mrs J Osler

Head: Jennifer Smith, MA Glasgow, MEd

Deputy Head (Pastoral): Ms W Fox, BA Durham

Head of Prep School: Mrs S Cattaneo, BA, Cert Ed Sussex

Head of Sixth Form: Mrs O Pianet, BA Brighton

Registrar: Mrs E Manning, BSc Sheffield

(Full staff list available on the school's website.)

Bruton School for Girls

Sunny Hill, Bruton, Somerset BA10 0NT

Tel: 01749 814400
Fax: 01749 812537
email: admissions@brutonschool.co.uk

website: www.brutonschool.co.uk
Twitter: @BrutonSchool
Facebook: @Bruton-School-for-Girls

Established in 1900 and set in beautiful Somerset countryside, overlooking Glastonbury Tor, Bruton School for Girls is a day school for girls and boys aged 3–7 and a day and boarding school for girls aged 7–18. Around 30% of the pupils board and full, weekly and flexi boarding options are available. The teaching week is Monday to Friday with no Saturday lessons.

Sunny Hill Preparatory School comprises the Pre-School, Pre-Prep and Prep School. Boarding is available for girls from the age of 7 years old. Reception, Year 1 and Year 2 classes are co-educational until the age of 7. A low pupil to teacher ratio and good relationships enable creative and dedicated teachers to make the most of the inquisitive childhood years and ensures that every pupil receives quality individual attention. Pupils develop strong learning habits. In a broad curriculum, they explore the exciting world of science, IT, humanities, French, music, DT and creative arts. Mathematics and English programmes build firm foundations for purposeful learning. Girls receive specialist teaching in Years 5 and 6 in Maths, Science, History and Geography. The Early Years Foundation (Nursery to Reception) has an 'Outstanding' Ofsted rating. A weekly enrichment programme broadens the pupils experience and often includes outdoor education and forest school, drama, cooking and problem solving. *(See also entry in IAPS section.)*

The **Senior School** is a thriving community of girls age 11–16 years who are taught in separate year groups Senior 1–5. Girls joining the Senior School come from a wide variety of local, national and international schools, as well as from Sunny Hill Prep School. Offering a broad and balanced curriculum, girls usually study 9–10 subjects at GCSE. We have an excellent academic reputation, which is especially notable as we are a non-academically-selective school. We consistently score highly on the 'added value' measure which shows that each girl significantly exceeds her expected grades. Additional learning support is available from specialist Skills Development teachers where appropriate.

The **Sixth Form** offers excellent preparation for university, with tutorial support and individual study programmes and a weekly lecture programme in the Autumn and Spring terms. An extensive range of A Levels is complemented by the Extended Project Qualification (EPQ), extension studies and extracurricular activities which include public speaking and the Leiths Certificate in Food and Wine. Career and Higher Education advice feature prominently at this stage. Many girls entering the Sixth Form transfer from the Senior School and are joined by students from local and international schools.

Why choose BSG? We are passionate about, and experts in, girls' education. We believe in offering our girls an education that will equip them to grow intellectually, think independently and become confident and responsible young women. What really sets us apart is our focus on each girl as an individual. We are proud that our size means we get to know each and every girl personally. It is this academic and pastoral support that means we can help each girl to reach her full potential and become the most amazing person she can be.

Academic and Personal Expectations. Academically, the school has high expectations and most girls gain places at their first-choice universities, many of which are Russell Group and other prestigious establishments including Oxford and Cambridge. The girls are encouraged to have self-belief, to set challenging goals, display independence of thought and enjoy learning for its own sake.

There are many opportunities for leadership and the development of personal and social skills, particularly in the Sixth Form, where students may take up the role of prefect or hall captain.

Location. Set on a 40-acre campus in beautiful countryside, the school is close to the Somerset, Wiltshire and Dorset borders, and has easy access to the M3/A303 corridor between London and the South West. Bristol, Bath, Salisbury and the south coast are all within approximately one hour's travel. Castle Cary station, served by London Paddington-Exeter express trains, is 4 miles away and Templecombe on the line to London Waterloo is 10 miles. Transport is available from London Heathrow, Bristol International and other airports. A network of daily buses serves the school from surrounding areas.

Boarding. Our boarding houses provide comfortable and well-appointed accommodation appropriate to the different age ranges of pupils. Facilities include common rooms, kitchens and dining areas. All the houses have Wi-Fi. Younger girls share a room with two/three other girls, while Senior girls either share a room of two or have their own study-bedroom. Sixth formers all have individual study-bedrooms and enjoy an increased degree of independence that aims to bridge school and university. The boarding houses are situated on the school campus and girls are cared for by experienced Housemistresses and house staff. A variety of weekend activities is offered and, as boarders are full boarders, there is always lots going on at weekends.

A high standard of catering is provided, with a wide variety of choice. Specific dietary needs are catered for.

Extracurricular Activities. Art, Drama, Music and Sport feature strongly. The outstanding success of the Art department is reflected in work displayed around the school. The Hobhouse Studio Theatre provides a professional-standard performance space for productions and 'speech and drama' presentations. There is a wide range of opportunities for both instrumental and choral performance, with choirs performing music across a range of styles and numerous instrumental groups, including a school orchestras and a jazz band. The sports department offers a wide range of activities in which every girl can participate either competitively or for her own enjoyment. There is a full fixture list of competitive matches in the traditional sports of hockey, netball, swimming, athletics and tennis. Tennis coaching, horse riding, self-defence, yoga and individual exercise regimes are available. There is also the popular Duke of Edinburgh's Award programme. Having been awarded the Eco-Schools Green Flag, many girls participate in the Eco Club and assist with the schools recycling programme. In the Preparatory School, all pupils from Reception to Prep 6 participate in Forest School.

Entry. There is open entry into the pre-prep and preparatory school from which pupils normally progress seamlessly into the senior school. The senior school entry process includes the school's own diagnostic assessments or Common Entrance. Entry into the Sixth Form is by interview and GCSE or equivalent qualifications.

Fees per term (2018–2019). Day: £5,935 (Senior School and Sixth Form), £4,255–£4,372 (Preparatory School), £2,835 (Foundation Stage). Boarding: £7,843–£10,110 (full), £7,300–£9,455 (weekly boarding inc Sundays).

Scholarships and Bursaries. Bruton School for Girls has a range of scholarships which are offered on entry to the Senior School at 11+, 13+ and Sixth Form including academic, all-round, music, art, sport and drama.

Governors' Exhibitions (means-tested) exist to support those pupils whose families would find difficulty in meeting the full fees and are awarded on entry to the Senior School and Sixth Form.

Charitable status. Bruton School for Girls is a Registered Charity, number 1085577, and a Company Limited by Guarantee. It exists to provide education.

Chairman of Governors: Mr D H C Batten

Headmistress: **Mrs Nicola Botterill**, BSc, MA, PGCE, NPQH, FRGS, FRSA

Deputy Head: Mrs Rachel Robbins, BA, PGCE

Director of Teaching and Learning: Mr Will Talbot-Ponsonby, BSc, MA, PGCE

Head of Preparatory School: Mrs Helen Snow, BEd

Bursar: Mr A H D Harvey-Kelly

Director of Admissions: Mrs Carrie Crook

Burgess Hill Girls

Keymer Road, Burgess Hill, West Sussex RH15 0EG

Tel:	01444 241050
Fax:	01444 870314
email:	registrar@burgesshillgirls.com
website:	www.burgesshillgirls.com
Twitter:	@BHillGirls
Facebook:	@BurgessHillGirls
LinkedIn:	/burgess-hill-girls

An independent day and boarding school or girls age 2½ to 18 years, founded in 1906 by Miss Beatrice Goode. Our school has a Nursery (accepts boys), Junior School, Senior School and Sixth Form. To fully appreciate our school come for a visit and talk to the students, they will be delighted to show you around. (*See also Burgess Hill Girls Junior School entry in the IAPS section.*)

General. The ethos of the School is to provide a caring, challenging and supportive atmosphere which encourages young people to use their initiative, be inquisitive and creative and develop responsibility and independence. Boys are welcome in the nursery. Our school is a community in which girls flourish; from age 4 the focus is firmly on girls and the way they learn. They develop self-esteem and confidence and go on to make a positive contribution in their chosen professions. We have small classes with fully qualified, professional staff dedicated to catering for the needs of each individual child. The School has established a reputation for excellence in Music, Sport, Art, Textiles and Drama and achieves impressive academic results. We are consistently highly ranked nationally and regularly lead the field in Sussex. We believe that education for life involves much more than academic success alone. Girls can, and do, strive for excellence wherever their talents lie.

School Facilities. The Senior School offers specialist teaching rooms including: a state-of-the-art language suite equipped with computers and specialist software for personalised listening and speaking; a Music room equipped with the latest Apple Mac composition software; Music practice rooms; two Art studios with an exhibition area, Art library and a kiln area; a Drama studio; a fully-equipped Media suite; two modern Chemistry labs; a specialist Textiles room and Technology workshop; a Learning Resource Centre and enhanced outdoor PE facilities with tennis courts and an Astroturf training area. The Performing Arts facilities have been extended with a glazed, curved entrance foyer.

The Junior School's facilities include a Learning Hub which incorporates a library, large learning space and access to iPads and interactive electronic screen. The Junior School also offers fully-equipped subject-specific classrooms

rooms for Music, ICT, Art, Science and Technology and access to all the sports facilities on the main school campus. The Infants are based in a building with bright, open classrooms and have their own hall and library. The Infants and Juniors have an exciting playground with a wooden adventure trail and outdoor classroom.

The Sixth Form centre includes a seminar room, contemporary classrooms, a study room with ICT facilities, a higher education library, a music practice room, two common rooms and a new student kitchen. All curriculum areas are well served with appropriate specialist accommodation, either in the Sixth Form Centre or in the Senior School complex for Art, Drama, Music, Media, PE, Science, Technology and Textiles. All classrooms are equipped with interactive whiteboards, and suites of laptop computers ensure that technology is available when and where needed.

The school has two Edwardian boarding houses with bedrooms and common rooms which are spacious, light and pleasantly furnished.

Curriculum. The curriculum is broad and challenging and relevant to the needs of young people. There is a wide choice of subjects both at GCSE and A Level with many extracurricular activities.

ISI Inspection 2014. The Senior School report recognises the many strengths of the Senior School's provision. Each phase of the school is praised, with comments such as: *The quality of teaching is excellent. The achievements of all pupils, including those with SEND or EAL, are excellent. The curricular and extracurricular programme makes an excellent contribution to the pupils' success ...The personal development of the pupils is excellent. Pupils are confident and articulate, having high levels of self-esteem.*

The Senior and Junior Schools' Inspection reports can be viewed on www.isi.net.

Entrance Procedures. Entrance to either the Junior or Senior School is by examination and school reference. Senior girls are also interviewed by the Head. Scholarships are awarded each year for academic and/or musical excellence into Years 3–6 inclusive, 7, 9 and the Lower Sixth. Sport/Creative scholarships are available for students entering Year 7, 9 and the Lower Sixth. The Margaret Morris All-Rounder Scholarship is available to girls entering Year 9.

Fees per term (2018–2019). Senior School: £4,850–£6,400 (day girls); £9,850–£11,400 (boarding). Junior School: £1,840–£4,750 (day girls).

Old Girls' Association. Now operates through the school and is under development. Please contact the school for further information.

Charitable status. Burgess Hill School for Girls is a Registered Charity, number 307001.

Chairman of Governors: Dr Alison Smith, MB ChB, MRCGP

Head: Mrs E Laybourn, BEd Hons

Bursar: Mr G Bond

Head of Junior School and Deputy Head of School: Mrs H Cavanagh, BA Hons QTS

Assistant Head, Academic (Teaching & Learning): Ms R Flint, MA Hons, PGCE

Assistant Head, Pastoral & Boarding: Miss N Donson, BMus Hons, PGCE

Head of Sixth Form: Mr W O'Brien-Blake, BA Hons, MSc, QTS

Head of Futures: Mrs J Edey, MA Hons, PGCE

Deputy Head of Junior School: Mrs S Collins, BA Hons, PGCE

Nursery Manager: Mrs S Roberts, BA Hons, PGCE

Heads of Departments:
Art: Ms E Levett, BA Hons, PGCE
Biology: Miss M Bramley, BSc Hons, PGCE
Economics and Politics: Ms D Flatman, MA Hons, PGCE
Chemistry: Mrs J Medcalf, BSc Hons, PGCE
Classics & Latin: Miss J Jones, BA Hons, PGCE
Computer Science: Mr R Stanway, BSc Hons, PGCE
Design & Technology: Mrs B Bradley, BEd Hons C&G
English/Media: Miss R Flint, MA Hons, PGCE
Speech & Drama: Mrs E Cassim, MA Hons, PGCE
French: Mrs I Martin, Licence Maîtrise, DDT
Geography: Mrs J Ponting, MA, BSc Hons, PGCE
German: Mrs J Edey, MA Hons, PGCE
History: Mr T Clarke, BA Hons, PGCE
Learning Resource Centre: Ms Y Akehurst, BA
Mathematics: Mr R Stanway, BSc Hons, PGCE
Music: Mr D Black, BEd, QTS, BMus, MMus,
Physical Education & Games: Miss S Clapp, BA Hons QTS
Physics: Mr A Gillaspy, BSc Hons, PGCE
Psychology: Mrs J Scopes, BSc Hons, GTP
Religious Studies: Miss S Cull, BA Hons, PGCE
Spanish: Mr J Montesinos, BA Hons, PGCE

Head of Events: Miss C Driscoll
Registrar: Miss C Laybourn
Housemistresses:
Mrs S Beels (*Head of Avondale*)
Ms A Arshad-Mehmood, BA Hons (*Head of Silverdale*)
School Nurse: Mrs L Hall, RGN
Careers Adviser: Mrs J Edey, MA Hons, PGCE

Bury Grammar School Girls

Bridge Road, Bury, Lancs BL9 0HH

Tel:	0161 696 8600
Fax:	0161 763 4658
email:	communications@burygrammar.com
website:	www.burygrammar.com
Twitter:	@BuryGrammarSch
Facebook:	@BuryGrammarSchoolGirls
LinkedIn:	/burygrammarschools

Motto: *Sanctas Clavis Fores Aperit*

The School, formerly housed in the precincts of the Parish Church of St Mary the Virgin, was first endowed by Henry Bury in 1634, but there is evidence that it existed before that date. It was re-endowed in 1726 by the Revd Roger Kay and moved to its current site in 1966. The school is a selective grammar school which aims to provide a first-class academic and extracurricular education; to nurture the whole person in a safe, stimulating, challenging and friendly community in which each individual is encouraged to fulfil her potential; and to prepare each girl for an adulthood of fulfilling work, creative leisure and responsible citizenship.

Numbers of Pupils. Infants: 140; Girls: 514 aged 7 to 18.

Admission, Scholarships and Bursaries. Admission is by examination and interview. Most girls join the school at either age 7 or 11, although, subject to places being available, admission is possible at other ages. A number of means-tested bursaries, based on academic performance and financial need, are awarded each year.

Fees per term (2018–2019). Senior School £3,585; Junior School £2,664.

Facilities and Development. Bury Grammar School has a distinguished history of excellence dating back to the 1570s. Proud of its historic links with the town of Bury and the surrounding area, Bury Grammar School possesses a full range of modern facilities. These facilities enable the School to offer a broad and rich academic curriculum and extra-curricular programme. Since 1993 the Junior School has occupied its own site opposite the Senior School. Junior School pupils are able to take advantage of the additional specialist facilities and resources in the Senior School. A new Learning Resource Centre, consisting of a Library, extensive ICT provision and private study facilities, was opened in 2002, and a new Art Centre in 2004. State-of-the-art Science laboratories were completed in 2010 and a new university-style Sixth Form Centre for both girls and girls opened in September 2014. In September 2016 brand new sports facilities were opened to include a 3G artificial pitch and a multi-use games area so that sports can continue in inclement weather. Bury Grammar School is constantly striving to improve its facilities and to provide the best possible educational experience for all its pupils.

Pastoral Care. Bury Grammar School prides themselves on excellent pastoral care and their ability to work together, as a family, to nurture and care for every individual. They care for and respect their students and, in turn, they expect them to care for and respect others. The BGS philosophy for pastoral care is simple: BGS students should be happy, secure and ready for all that life has to offer. BGS offers individualised pastoral support for every student and are always keenly aware that it is a privilege to work alongside young people. BGS is fortunate to have on site a highly dedicated and skilled School Health Team who work closely with pupils, parents and staff to ensure that the medical, health and wellbeing needs are met. BGS also offers the services of a qualified counsellor who is on site on a weekly basis to provide confidential support and advice to those students who need it. Each girl has a Form Tutor who has primary responsibility for her pastoral care and for oversight of her academic progress and extra-curricular programme. Form Tutors are led by Heads of Year who also oversee a girl's academic progress. There is also a strong House system for a wide range of sporting, musical and cultural interhouse competitions.

Curriculum. Bury Grammar School is immensely proud of its traditions and is happy to be a modern school, continually embracing new technologies and innovative teaching methods. BGS is a leading school in the area where pupils continually reach outstanding academic standards, achieving exceptional examination results at GCSE and A Level and gaining places on competitive courses at elite universities. In response to the increasing demands of newly-reformed GCSE and A Level qualifications, BGS has introduced a new enhanced curriculum model throughout the School to strengthen further the quality of education it offers – ensuring breadth alongside academic challenge – to enable pupils to obtain the very best examination results of which they are capable and to open doors to even greater opportunities in the future. It also delivers an enhanced extra-curricular and co-curricular offering, to maintain the School's strong tradition of nurturing fully-rounded individuals.

Art. Well-equipped facilities in BGS' Schools allow all BGS pupils to develop skills in print making, ceramics, sculpture, painting, drawing, textiles, new media and animation. There are frequent visits to galleries, both locally and further afield. Pupils' artwork is proudly displayed throughout the school and BGS hosts regular exhibitions which are opened to the School community.

Music and Drama. Music is an important part of school life. As an academic subject it is offered at GCSE and A Level. At least three major musical events take place each year. Visiting peripatetic teachers teach over 170 pupils. Girls have the opportunity to involve themselves in musical groups such as orchestra, concert band, dance orchestra and festival choir. As well as this, girls can take part in show-stopping musical productions which showcase the incredible musical talents of girls and boys across both Senior Schools and Sixth Form.

Physical Education and Games. Bury Grammar School has long had a tradition of sporting excellence and engagement. Superb sports facilities on the 45-acre campus means that all students have the opportunity to engage in purposeful and competitive sporting activity on site throughout the week. All sporting activities aim to allow our pupils to participate recreationally or to compete locally, regionally, and even nationally! Our excellent sporting facilities include:

- 18-metre indoor swimming pool
- 50-metre high jump, long jump and triple jump track
- A new suite of artificial playing surfaces, including exceptional 3G all-weather pitches for football, rugby, cricket, futsal and hockey
- Two multi-use games areas
- Tennis and netball courts
- Full sized volleyball and basketball courts

Outdoor Education. In the Senior School, the Outdoor Activities programme includes an outdoor pursuits course for all Year 7 girls. Bury Grammar School Girls is also delighted to be able to offer participation in the Duke of Edinburgh's Award scheme and World Challenge Expeditions.

CCF. The Bury Grammar School CCF was established in 1892 and is one of the oldest CCFs in the country. Originally affiliated to the local regiment, the Lancashire Fusiliers, the Contingent is now affiliated to the Royal Regiment of Fusiliers and the cadets wear its badge and hackle with pride. The current strength of the Contingent is 214 cadets. The CCF helps the girls develop qualities such as self-discipline, resourcefulness and perseverance, a sense of responsibility and skills of management and leadership.

Careers. The Careers Department aims to provide all girls with access to the information and advice they need to make informed and sensible decisions about their futures. In addition to an excellent careers library, guidance is provided by individual interviews. There are regular careers conventions and mock interview mornings. All girls are also required to complete a period of work experience during Year 10.

Bury Grammar School Old Girls' Association. The BGS journey carries through to our Old Girls' Association; friendships formed at Bury Grammar School really do last a lifetime. Secretary: Suzanne Gauge, email: suzanne.gauge@btinternet.com

Charitable status. Bury Grammar Schools Charity is a Registered Charity, number 526622. The aim of the charity is to promote educational opportunities for girls and girls living in or near Bury.

Governing Body:
Chair of Governors: Mrs G Winter
Vice Chair of Governors: Mr M Edge

Mr M J Entwistle	Mr A H Spencer
Mrs S Gauge	Mr S Wild
Mrs C Hulme-McGibbon	Mr D Baker
Mr A Marshall	Mr D Long
Dr J G S Rajasansir	

Bursar and Clerk to the Governors: Mrs J Stevens, BFocFC, ACA

***Principal of The Bury Grammar Schools, Headmistress of Bury Grammar School Girls:* Mrs J Anderson**, BA, MEd, PGCE

Assistant Principal, Director of Academic Provision: Mrs V Leaver, BSc (*Geography*)
Head of Sixth Form: Mr S Prest, MA (*History & Politics*)

Senior Deputy Head, Staff Development & Digital Strategy:
   Mrs H Campion, BA (*Head of Business Studies and
   Economics*)
Deputy Head – Administration and Enrichment: Mrs S
   Fielden, BSc (*Biology*)
Deputy Head – Pastoral: Mrs R Newbold, BSc (*Physical
   Education & Geography*)

Teaching Staff:
Mr M Ahmad, BSc (*Physics*)
Mr B Alldred, MSc (*Mathematics*)
Mr M Andrews, BA (*Director of Sport – BGSB*)
Mr D Ashworth, BA (*ICT*)
Dr A Austin, PhD (*Mathematics*)
Miss E L Bailey, BSc (*Biology*)
Mrs C Banks, Licence (*Modern Foreign Languages*)
Miss G Barber, BSc (*Mathematics*)
Mrs L Barron (*Swimming*)
Dr E Bennett, PhD (*Chemistry*)
Mrs C Bevis, BA (*History*)
Mrs M Boulton, BA (*CDT*)
Mr M R Boyd, BA (*Head of French*)
Miss R Britton, BMus (*Music*)
Mrs M Bonilla-Marti, Licence (*Modern Foreign
   Languages*)
Mrs S G Cawtherley, BA (*Religious Studies, Head of Fifth
   Year*)
Miss R Charlesworth, BA (*Drama and English*)
Miss C Clarke, BA (*English*)
Mr M Cooper-Latham, BSc (*Biology*)
Mr P F Curry, BSc (*Head of Physics*)
Miss A Davenport, BA (*English*)
Mrs V Davitt, BA (*Food and Nutrition*)
Mrs F Dickson, BMus (*Music*)
Mrs K Dowling, BSc (*Mathematics*)
Miss J H Downing, BMus (*Director of Music*)
Mrs M Eady, BA (*Physical Education*)
Mr J Eastham, BA (*History, Head of Third Year*)
Miss J Elliot, BA (*English*)
Mr R Entwistle, BSc (*Biology*)
Mrs D Evans, BA (*Religious Studies*)
Mrs G L Fern, BSc (*Chemistry*)
Miss V L Frisby, BA (*French*)
Miss K A Gore, BA (*Head of Art*)
Miss E Gumbley, BSc (*Mathematics*)
Mr G Hall, BSc (*PE & Sport, Head of Second Year*)
Mr O Griffiths, BSc (*Physical Education*)
Miss O Halstead, BA (*History and Politics*)
Mrs R Hartley, BA (*Economics and Business Studies*)
Mr M J Hone, MA (*Head of History & Politics*)
Mr P Howard, BA (*Mathematics*)
Mrs S J Howard, BA (*French & German, Head of First
   Year, E-Safety Officer*)
Ms U Imtiaz, BA (*Modern Foreign Languages*)
Mrs L Irwen, BA (*Chemistry*)
Miss L Jackson, BSc (*Chemistry*)
Miss R Jones, BA (*Classics*)
Mrs J Kay, BA (*History*)
Mrs K Kershaw, BA (*Art*)
Mrs K Lewis, MSc (*Physics*)
Mrs K Lynch, BA (*English*)
Mr P Meakin, BSc (*Head of Computing*)
Ms C McDermott, BA (*Psychology*)
Mrs G Mehta, BA (*Geography*)
Mrs R Newbold, BSc (*Physical Education and Geography*)
Mr D T Newbury, BSc (*Geography, Head of Fourth Year*)
Mrs E Nicholls, BEng (*Physics*)
Mrs S Norman, BMU (*Music*)
Mr P O'Sullivan, BA (*Head of Mathematics*)
Mrs H Poulson, BA (*English*)
Mrs J Rumboldt, BA (*Religious Studies*)
Mr T Seed, BA (*English*)

Mrs J Slade, BSc (*Physical Education*)
Mrs J G Smith, BA (*English*)
Miss E A Stansfield, BA (*English, Head of Third Year*)
Mrs A Tait Hanlon, MSc (*Psychology*)
Miss V Tandon, BSc (*Mathematics*)
Mrs G Taylor, BA (*Modern Foreign Languages*)
Mrs S Taylor, BSc (*Chemistry and Careers*)
Mrs T J Taylor, MA (*Head of Geography*)
Ms J Tomkinson, BSc (*Geography*)
Mr A D Watts, BSc (*Head of Biology*)
Mrs M Whitlow, BA (*Economics and Business Studies*)
Mr B Wong, PhD (*Chemistry*)
Dr J Yates, PhD (*Chemistry*)

*Head, Kindergarten, Infant School and Girls' Junior
   School*: Mrs C Howard, CIPS

Deputy Head, Girls' Junior School: Mrs J Daly BSc

Teaching Staff:

Mrs S Aylin, BA	Mrs S Hill, BA
Miss K Bird, LLB	Mrs R Hankinson, BA
Mrs K Booth, BEd	Mrs D Jones, BEd
Mrs A Bye, BSc	Mr R McGadie, BSc
Mrs J Daly, BSc	Mrs H Scourfield, BEd
Mrs F Gray, BMus	Mrs K Temple, BEd
Miss J Hall, BA	

Head of Admissions: Mrs S Lewis

Channing School

The Bank, Highgate, London N6 5HF

Tel:	020 8340 2328 (School Office)
	020 8340 2719 (Bursar)
Fax:	020 8341 5698
email:	info@channing.co.uk
website:	www.channing.co.uk
Twitter:	@ChanningSchool
Facebook:	@ChanningSchool

At Channing everything is possible!

Channing School is unique in providing an education
based on the principles of two Unitarian sisters who, more
than 130 years ago, founded a school for girls in Highgate,
North London.

In a changing world of uncertainty and pressure, girls
find at Channing an oasis of calm purpose, where pupils are
encouraged to think for themselves, and to keep an open
mind. Our academic results are among the best in the country and our most recent Independent Schools Inspectorate
(ISI) awarded Channing the highest possible ratings in all
categories, concluding that 'The quality of pupils' achievements and learning is exceptional'.

Each girl is treated as an individual and valued for her
achievements and efforts, whether they be sporting, musical,
theatrical, intellectual, spiritual or academic ...or none of
the above. Sometimes the greatest lessons are learned from
the kindness of others and we recognise and encourage this,
too.

Every member of the school belongs to a warm, supportive community and this includes all our pupils, staff, parents, alumnae and many friends. Many visitors comment on
the indefinable 'feel' of the school, its very special atmosphere and unique ethos.

Number of Pupils: Junior School – 315 pupils; Senior
School (including Sixth Form) – 630 pupils.

The School is situated in Highgate Village, in attractive
grounds, and offers a balanced education combining a traditional academic curriculum with modern educational devel-

opments. The complex of old and new buildings has been constantly adapted to provide up-to-date facilities, and there are strong links with the local community and local schools.

Girls usually take nine or ten subjects to GCSE and there is a wide range of A Level choices, including Physics, Further Maths, Politics and Theatre Studies. The Junior School has its own building – the elegant family home of Sir Sydney Waterlow, one-time Lord Mayor of London – set in spacious gardens, and is notable for its happy and secure atmosphere.

Most girls learn at least one musical instrument and there are frequent concerts and theatrical productions. The school is fortunate in its gardens, open space and its facilities. The school has invested £13m in new facilities including a Sixth Form Centre with bespoke study facilities, a state-of-the-art Sports Centre, a Music School and a magnificent Performing Arts Theatre.

Entry is by assessment at 4+, an examination/assessment and interview at 11+ and predicted GCSE results and interview at 16+. In addition, entry is subject to a satisfactory report from the applicant's current school. Entry assessments for occasional vacancies that arise for other years are age appropriate.

Further information can be obtained from the School prospectus and the Sixth Form prospectus available from the Registrar and the school website (www.channing.co.uk).

Scholarships and Bursaries. Academic Scholarships are offered at 11+. Academic awards are also offered to Sixth Form entrants, based on predicted GCSE grades and contribution to the school or as a result of interview and predicted GCSE grades for external candidates. Music Scholarships are offered at 11+ and 16+. These cover up to 50% of the tuition fees and lessons in school on one instrument for a year (renewable). Art Scholarships are offered to Sixth Form entrants based on submission of a portfolio of work. Bursaries are offered at 11+ and 16+. Please see the school website for further details.

Fees per term (2018–2019). Junior School (Reception to Year 6) £5,870; Senior School (Years 7–13) £6,470.

Charitable status. Channing House Incorporated is a Registered Charity, number 312766.

Governors:
Ms C Leslie, LLB Bristol (*Chair*)
Mr J Alexander, FCA
Mr G Algar-Faria, MSc Durham
Mr A Appleyard, BSc Reading (*Vice Chair*)
Mrs J Burns, BA Southampton
Revd D Costley, BA Open University
Mrs J De Swiet, MA Cantab
Miss D Patman, FRICS, ACIArb
Ms B Rentoul, MA Yale
Mr W Spears, MBA London
Dr A Sutton, MRCGP
Mrs A Thomas, PGDE Cambridge
Mr C Underhill, MNAEA
Dr I Wassenaar, MA, DPhil
Dr R Williams, BSc, MSc, PhD

Bursar & Clerk to the Governors: Mr R Hill

Headmistress: Mrs B M Elliott, MA Cantab (*Modern Foreign Languages*)

Deputy Head: Mr A J Underwood, MEd Cantab (*Theology*)
Director of Studies: Ms J Newman, MA UCL (*Economics*)

* *Head of Department*

Miss S Adewale, BEng UCL (*Chemistry*) [part-time]
Miss C Arnold, BSc Nottingham (*Biology*)
Ms S Beenstock, BA Leeds (*English*) [part-time]

Miss L Bellingham, MA London (*Drama and Theatre*) [part-time]
Mrs G Bhamra Burgess, MSc SOAS (*Economics, Head of Year 11 and Sharpe House*)
Mrs S Blake, BSc Bristol, MA London (*Geography, Young Enterprise Coordinator*)
Mr P Boxall, GRSM, ARCO Royal Academy of Music (*Director of Music*)
Mr A Boardman, BA Hons Durham (*Geography, Assistant Head – Teaching and Learning*)
Ms J Bramhall, MA Oxon (*Geography*)
Dr M Bremser, BA Wellesley, USA, MPhil, DPhil Oxon (*English, *Critical Thinking*) [part-time]
Ms K Cronk, BA New York (*Learning Support Assistant*)
Mr P Daurat, BEd Huddersfield (*Mathematics*)
Mrs W Devine, BA Reading (*Politics*)
Ms S Della-Porta, BEd Wollongong Australia (*Director of Physical Education and Sport*)
Dr N Devlin, DPhil Oxon (*Classics, EPQ Coordinator*) [part-time]
Ms C Dodsworth, OCR Dip SpLD, MA SEN UCL (*SENCO*) [part-time]
Miss S Donington, MA Leeds (*Second in English*)
Mrs S Elliot, MA Cantab (*Classics*)
Miss P Evernden, MA Cantab (*English*)
Mr S Frank, BSc Birmingham (*Biology*)
Miss S-L Fung, BSc Coventry (*Physics*)
Mrs C Garrill, BA Leicester (*Politics*) [part-time]
Mr P Gittins, BA Wolverhampton (*Art, *PSHE, Head of Year 9 and Spears House*)
Mr D Grossman, BSc Hons Manchester (*Assistant Head – *Director of Science, Technology and Engineering*)
Mr A Haworth, MA RCA (*Art*)
Mr G Headey, BA Durham (*Religious Education*)
Mrs B Hernandez, BA Hons Alicante Spain (*Spanish, French*) [part-time]
Ms J Hill, BA Hons Royal Conservatoire of Scotland (*Drama and Theatre*)
Mr M Holmes, BSc Hons City (*Information and Communication Technology*)
Miss A Hosseini, BSc UCL (*Chemistry*) [part-time]
Miss L Hunter, BA London (*History, More Able Coordinator*)
Ms K Hurst, MA East Anglia (*Drama and Theatre*) [part-time]
Mr R Jacobs, BA Oxon (*Physics*)
Mrs H Kanmwaa, BA Oxon (*English*)
Mrs A Kennedy, MSc London (*Chemistry, Oxbridge Coordinator*) [part-time]
Ms C Kyle, BA Jt Hons Nottingham (*Assistant Head – *Director of MFL and Leader of Adelante Strategy*)
Ms J Kung, BA USYD Australia, DipEd MU Australia (*History, Director of Sixth Form*)
Mrs C Leigh, MEd Cantab (*English*) [part-time]
Miss Z Lindsay, BA Leicester (*History*)
Ms R Marmar, BSc Queen Mary (*Chemistry*)
Ms T MacCarthy, BSc Hons Edinburgh (*Second in Mathematics*)
Ms S Mackie, BA Oxon (*Art*) [part-time]
Mrs S Mahmood, BEd University of Alberta Canada (*Chemistry*) [part-time]
Ms S Melvin, BA Oxon, MA MPhil Columbia (*Classics*)
Mr P Martini-Phillips, BA Hons Leicester (*History*)
Miss E Moor, BA Durham, FRGS (*Geography*)
Ms E Pavlopoulos, LLB King's/Paris I, MA Ed Open (*Careers*)
Miss V Penglase, BA Hons London, RHBNC (*Drama and Theatre*) [part-time]
Miss I Ramsden, MSc City London (*Senior School Librarian*)
Mr D Riggs-Long, BSc Imperial (*Mathematics*) [part-time]

Miss A Romero-Wiltshire, BA Nottingham (*French*)
Ms A Rozieres, MA Grenoble France (*French*)
Ms M Ruiz-Pena (*Spanish Language Assistant*)
Mrs D Shoham, MSc, LSHTM (*Biology*) [part-time]
Dr C Spinks, PhD Manchester (*Chemistry*)
Ms A Stöckmann, MA Westfaelische Wilhelms Germany
  (*German*)
Miss I Taylor, BA Bristol (*Classics*)
Mrs K Thonemann, MA Oxon (*Mathematics*) [part-time]
Mrs J Tomback, MA London (*History, Head of Year 7 and
  Secondary Transition*)
Mr C Waring, BS Strathclyde (*Spanish*)
Ms O Watts, BA London (*Art*)
Ms E Wijmeersch, MA Ghent Belgium (*Physical
  Education*)
Ms K Wilkinson, BA East Anglia (*English*) [part-time]
Mrs R Williams, BSc Hons UCL (*Mathematics, Assistant
  Director of Sixth Form*)
Mr P Williamson, BEd Huddersfield (*Mathematics*)
Ms M Yun, BSc London (*Mathematics [part-time], Duke
  of Edinburgh's Award Manager*)
Miss L Zanardo, BA, BMus Ed Australia, Grad Dip
  Australia (*Assistant Director of Music, Head of Year 10
  and Waterlow House*)
Ms N Zekan, BEd RMIT Australia (*Physical Education,
  Head of Year 8 and Goodwin House*)
Mrs D Zuluaga De La Cruz, MA Valenciennes France
  (*French*) [part-time]

Junior School Staff:
Head of Junior School: Miss D Hamalis, BEd Hons
Miss C Bolton, BA Northampton (*Junior School Physical
  Education Teacher*)
Miss F Bury, MA France (*Spanish, French*) [part-time]
Miss C Clancy, BEd Institute of Education (*Classroom
  Teacher Year 1*)
Miss K Collins, BA St Mary's (*Classroom Teacher
  Reception*)
Mrs C Constant, MA Greenwich (*Deputy Head Year 1*)
Miss A Conway, BA Tel Aviv (*Drama*) [part time]
Miss R Corkindale, BA Glasgow (*Head of Junior School
  Physical Education*)
Miss E Evans, LLB Leeds (*Classroom Teacher Year 6*)
Mr R Fellows, BA Plymouth (*Classroom Teacher Year 5*)
Miss A Frost, BEd Leeds (*Classroom Teacher Year 4*)
Miss G Gerstein, BA Birmingham (*Classroom Teacher
  Year 1*)
Mrs L Hudson, BA Southampton (*DT & Art, ICT*)
Mr L Ip, BSc Southampton (*Director of Studies Year 4*)
Mrs T Luxford, BA Middlesex (*DT & Art*)
Ms R McGinnety, BA Cantab (*Classroom Teacher Year 6*)
Miss A McLennan, BA Leeds (*Classroom Teacher Year 3*)
Mrs K Miller, BA Birmingham (*Classroom Teacher Year
  2*)
Miss M Pepper, LTCL (*Head of Music Junior School*)
Miss A Phipps, BEd Middx Polytechnic (*Classroom
  Teacher Year 2*)
Mrs C Rand, CertEd (*Classroom Teacher, Year 1*) [part-
  time]
Mrs K Rattenbury, BMus Manchester (*Music*) [part-time]
Mr C Rich, MA St Andrews (*Classroom Teacher Year 5*)
Miss S Snowdowne, BEd Plymouth (*Classroom Teacher
  Year 3*) [part-time]

Mrs S Ahmed (*Teaching Assistant Art & D T*) [part-time]
Mrs A Done (*Teaching Assistant Year 3*) [part-time]
Miss B Drayton (*Teaching Assistant Reception*)
Mrs D Galli (*Teaching Assistant Year 2*) [part-time]
Mrs K Hadjipateras (*Teaching Assistant Reception*) [part-
  time]
Miss M Holmes (*Teaching Assistant Year 3*) [part-time]
Miss V Houry (*Teaching Assistant Year 5*)
Ms S Ibrekic (*Teaching Assistant Reception*) [part-time]

Miss K Johnson (*Teaching Assistant Reception*) [part-time]
Miss S Litiu (*Teaching Assistant Year 2*)
Mrs R Maloumi (*Teaching Assistant Reception*)
Ms R McEwan (*Teaching Assistant Year 1*)
Miss M O'Hara (*Teaching Assistant Year 4*)
Miss L Nelson (*Teaching Assistant Reception*)
Mrs R Pieri (*Teaching Assistant Year 1*) [part-time]
Ms C Jupp (*Librarian*) [part-time]

Visiting Teachers:
Miss J Bacon, MA Oxon, PG Dip RAM (*Head of Vocal
  Studies, Voice*)
Mr A Bailey, MMus (*Clarinet*)
Mrs H Bennett, BMus Hons (*Trumpet*)
Miss S Bircumshaw, GRSM Hons (*Violin Junior*)
Mrs M Bradbury-Rance, MA (*Voice*)
Mr A Brown, Dip TCL (*Percussion*)
Mrs K Collier, BMus (*Clarinet*)
Mrs P Capone, AGSM (*Piano*)
Mrs M Cartwright, BMus (*Double Bass*)
Miss R Chapman, BA (*Singing*)
Mr G Cousins, BMus Hons (*Guitar*)
Mrs L Dodds, Dip ABRSM, BMus Hons (*Cello*)
Mr N Harrison, GRSM, SRCM (*Bassoon*)
Miss J Herbert, BA (*Cello*)
Mrs H Jolly, GRSM (*Flute*)
Ms M Keogh, ARAM (*Harp*)
Mr A Khan, LTCL (*Guitar*)
Mrs L Knight, MA (*Singing*)
Miss A Leighton, BA Hons (*LAMDA*)
Mrs P Malloy, LRAM, ABRSM (*Violin/Viola*)
Miss N Myerscough, ARAM (*Head of String Studies,
  Violin*)
Miss E Owens, BA (*LAMDA*)
Miss C Philpot, LRAM (*Oboe*)
Miss H Shimizu, BMus (*Piano*)
Miss A Szreter, BA (*Singing*)
Ms A Thomas, BMus (*Flute*)
Miss C Thompson, LRAM (*Violin*)
Mr T Travis, BMus (*Saxophone*)
Ms R Stockdale, BMus (*Flute*)
Miss S Vivian, LTCL, Dip (*Singing*)
Miss J Watts, FRCO, GRSM, LRAM (*Piano*)
Mr A White, MMus, MA (*Lower Brass*)

Cobham Hall

Brewers Road, Cobham, Kent DA12 3BL

Tel:	01474 823371
Fax:	01474 825906
email:	enquiries@cobhamhall.com
website:	www.cobhamhall.com
Twitter:	@CobhamHall
Facebook:	@CobhamHall

Cobham Hall is an international boarding and day
school for 180 girls aged between 11 and 18. Founded in
1962, Cobham Hall is an all-girls Round Square school with
both boarding and day pupils in the United Kingdom.

Situation. The School is set in 150 acres of historic parkland. Situated in North Kent, close to the M25 and adjacent
to the M2/A2. Thirty minutes from London, 60 minutes
Heathrow, 50 minutes Gatwick and Stansted, 60 minutes
Dover and Channel Tunnel, 10 minutes Ebbsfleet International Eurostar Railway Station (17 minutes to St Pancras, 2
hours Paris).

School Buildings. This beautiful 16th century historic
house was the former home of the Earls of Darnley. There
are many modern buildings providing comfortable accom-

modation for study and relaxation. Brooke and Bligh Houses are separate buildings within the school grounds offering Lower and Middle School and Sixth Form accommodation in single or twin study-bedrooms, many with en-suite facilities. Both Houses have common rooms with a kitchen and computer room.

Curriculum. In Years 7 to 9, girls follow the English National Curriculum. In Years 10 and 11, girls study for GCSE and IGCSE qualifications. Sixth Form study a broad curriculum with a wide range of A Level subjects, Cobham Hall Theory of Knowledge, Extended Project Qualification and The Duke of Edinburgh's Award or Service.

Sixth Form. The Sixth Form numbers 45–50 students. Academic tutorial groups are spread across the two years and facilitate interaction between students. There are exceptional leadership opportunities, including election to the Student Leadership Team which plays a significant part in the management of the school. University destinations include Aston, Bath, Central St Martins, Cumbria, Durham, Edinburgh, Essex, Exeter, Greenwich, University College London, Leeds, Loughborough, Lancaster, LSE, Manchester and Nottingham Trent, Royal Conservatoire of Scotland, Warwick, as well as Oxford and Cambridge.

Sporting and other activities. The School's main sports are Tennis, Swimming, Hockey, Athletics and Netball. There are seven hard tennis courts, six netball courts, a large, indoor multi-sports complex, including fitness centre, dance studio and a heated indoor swimming pool, which is in use throughout the year. Horse riding and golf may be taken as 'extras'. A wide variety of extracurricular activities is available.

Careers. High-quality Careers Guidance and personal support is offered across Lower and Middle School and in the Sixth Form by School staff. Activities in partnership with external providers include Futurewise Profiling, Interview Training and an annual "Dragons Den" Day.

Round Square. The School is a member of this international group of schools, which subscribes to the philosophy of educationalist Dr Kurt Hahn. Annual conferences are attended by a school delegation including Sixth Formers. In recent years these have been held in Australia, America, Canada, India, Singapore, South Africa, Transylvania and Germany. Younger students attend Round Square conferences in the UK and Europe. Students have the opportunity to visit other member schools on an exchange programme as well as visit other countries by taking part in service projects and relief work organised by the Round Square.

Health. Residential trained nursing staff providing 24-hour medical care.

All Terms. Two Exeat Weekends and a Half Term break.

Admission. Admission is by the School's own entrance assessments which can be taken on Entrance Assessment Days in October (Lower/Middle School) and November (Sixth Form) or at a girl's own school. Girls normally enter the School between the ages of 11+ and 13+ and follow a course leading to GCSE level at the end of the fifth year and to the International Baccalaureate Diploma at the end of the seventh. Girls wishing to enter the Sixth Form should achieve a good standard of GCSE or equivalent examination passes.

Scholarships. Scholarships are available for 11+, 13+ and Sixth Form entry.

11+: Academic, Art, Drama, Music and Sport.

Candidates for Academic Scholarships who demonstrate outstanding potential at Entrance Assessment Day will be invited back to sit a General Scholarship paper. Candidates for other scholarships will have an audition/assessment on Entrance Assessment Day.

13+: Academic, Art, Drama, Music and Sport.

Candidates for Academic Scholarships who demonstrate outstanding potential at Entrance Assessment Day will be invited back to sit scholarship papers. Candidates for other scholarships will have an audition/assessment on Entrance Assessment Day.

Sixth Form: Academic, Art, Music, Theatre and Physical Education.

Sixth Form Scholarships are awarded for two years, covering the Sixth Form. Application is via Cobham Hall Sixth Form Scholarship Application Form. A letter of application must also be submitted to the Headmistress by the student. Candidates will also sit a scholarship paper/audition in a subject they intend to study in the Sixth Form and have a personal interview with a member of staff.

For further information contact Admissions on 01474 823371.

Bursaries. Special bursaries are available for boarders from British Services families, diplomats and those families working for UK Charitable Trusts overseas and charitable bursaries for very able children from certain areas. For further information, contact Admissions.

Fees per term (2018–2019). Day girls: £6,077–£7,401. Boarders: £9,182–£11,517.

Old Girls' Association. Known as the Elders' Association. There is a representative committee which meets regularly either in London or at the School. The Chairman is Mrs Tracey Balch, email: tracey.balch@outlook.com or elders@cobhamhall.com.

Charitable status. Cobham Hall is a Registered Charity, number 313650. It exists to provide high quality education for girls aged 11–18 years.

Governing Body:
Mr M Pennell (*Chairman*)

Mr C Sykes	Mrs S McRitchie
Mr G Smith	Dr K O'Neill-Byrne
Mr J Dick	Mrs S Webb
Mrs P Tebbitt	

Staff:

Headmistress: Ms M Roberts, BA Hons Birmingham

Bursar: Mr D Standen, BSc Bradford
Deputy Headmistress and Head of Boarding: Mrs W Barrett, BSc London
Head of Sixth Form: Mrs M Thompson, BSc London (*Biology*)
Director of Studies: Mrs S Carney, BEd Exeter
Head of Middle School: Mr K Eyers, TDip Canterbury Christ Church
Assistant Head of Middle School: Mr P Hosford, BSc Thames Polytechnic (*Physics*)
Head of Lower School: Mrs E Wilkinson BA London

* *Head of Faculty*

English:
*Miss J West, BA Oxford, MA Oxford
Miss J Stevens, BA Hull
Mrs F West-Lindsay, BA Reading

Mathematics:
*Miss T Afolayan, MA Cantab
Mrs W Barrett, BSc London
Mrs C Sheehan, BA Greenwich
Mrs R Hillier, BA Exeter

Science:
*Mr J Fryer, BSc Leicester, MA Kent (*Biology*)
Mrs M Thompson, BSc London (*Biology*)
Mr P Hosford, BSc Thames Polytechnic (*Physics*)
Mr A Kirkaldy, BSc Wales, PGCE Southampton (*Chemistry*)

Art:
*Mrs K Walsh, BA Kent Institute of Art & Design
Mrs A Lockheart, BA Illinois State University, PGCE
   London

Drama:
Mrs C Gorman
Miss N Elliott, BMus, MMus
Mrs C Ruby, BA Hons Guildford School of Acting under
   the University of Surrey

Economics:
Mr S Parmar, BSc Kingston, MBA Accredited OU, PGCE
   Canterbury Christ Church, NLP Coaching Academy

Film Studies:
Mrs F West-Lindsay, BA Reading

Geography:
Mrs S Carney, BEd Exeter
Miss V Kipling
Mrs R Keys, BA Hons Plymouth

History:
*Miss A Williams, BA Brasenose College Oxford
Mr N Bushell, BA York

IB Coordinator:
Mrs M Thompson, BSc London (*Biology*)

Computer Science/ICT:
Mr K Eyers, TDip Canterbury Christ Church

Latin:
Dr P Marin, BA, MA USA, MPhil Oxon, PhD Dublin

Modern Foreign Languages:
*Miss J Caro Quintana, Licenciada en Filologica Inglesa,
   Valencia, Spain, PGCE Exeter
Mrs E Wilkinson, BA London
Mrs M Gutierrez, Licenciada en Lenguas Extranjeras
   Columbia, GTP Christ Church
Mrs T Russell, BA La Sorbonne, PGCE Lancaster

Music:
Miss P Clements, BA London
Mr M Haas, BA Michigan, MMus London

Physical Education:
Mrs K Hooper, BA Greenwich
Miss D Fautley, BSc Herefordshire

PSHE:
Miss P Clements, BA London
Mrs A Lockheart, BA Illinois State University, PGCE
   London

Psychology:
Mrs K-A Hickmott, BSc Middlesex

Theory of Knowledge:
Mrs K-A Hickmott, BSc Middlesex

EFL:
*Mrs A M R Deacon, BA Birmingham, PGCE Nottingham,
   CELTA St Giles

Student Support Department:
*Ms J Konec, BA London, PGCE London, OCR Level 7
   Diploma
Mrs R Hillier, BA Exeter
Miss M Frost, BA Hons Canterbury Christ Church
   (*Teaching Assistant*)
Mrs D Berry, HLTA BA, MA (*Teaching Assistant*)
Mrs J Balson, BTEC Level 3 (*Teaching Assistant*)

Careers:
Sixth Form: Mrs M Thompson, BSc London (*Biology*)
Middle School: Mr K Eyers, TDip Canterbury Christ
   Church

Lower School: Mrs E Wilkinson, BA London

Librarian:
Mrs P Geater

Laboratory Technician:
Mrs Erika Howard

Art Technician:
Mrs L Hunt

Computer Support:
Mr D Wright (*Network Manager*)

Boarding Staff:
Mrs W Barrett, BSc London (*Head of Boarding*)
Mrs D Didzinskiene, BA Šiauliai Univ Lithuania, MS
   Vytautas Magnus Univ Lithuania (*Day Housemistress*)
Mrs D Jackson, RGN/RSCN (*Resident Nurse/
   Housemistress*)
Mrs C Fenice (*Housemistress*)
Miss A Ukachi-Lois (*Graduate Housemistress*)
Miss I Rabot (*Graduate Housemistress*)
Miss Cristina Valero Ballo (*Graduate Housemistress*)
Miss Laura Urtet Pech (*Graduate Housemistress*)

Visiting Staff for:
Cello, Clarinet, Double Bass, Drums, Flute, French Horn,
Guitar, Keyboard, Oboe, Percussion, Piano, Recorder, Sax-
ophone, Trombone, Trumpet, Tuba, Viola, Violin, Drama,
Voice and Communication, Ballet, Self-Defence and Ten-
nis.

Administration:
Registrar: Mrs J Shelley
Assistant Registrar: Mrs H Standen
Marketing Assistant & Elders' Liaison Representative: Mrs
   J Booth
Marketing Assistant: Mrs T Reid
Receptionist: Mrs C Coster
Headmistress's PA: Mrs K Theobald
Deputy Head's PA: Mrs S Slater
Director of Studies's PA: Mrs J Elliman
School Secretary: Mrs S Hawkins
Bursar's Secretary: Mrs J Brace
Accounts Administrator: Mrs K Pinder, FMAAT
Accounts Assistant: Mrs S Thompson
Maintenance Foreman: Mr J Best
Grounds Foreman: Mr T Gilbert

Cranford House

Moulsford, Wallingford, Oxfordshire OX10 9HT

Tel: 01491 651218
Fax: 01491 652557
email: admissions@cranfordhouse.net
website: www.cranfordhouse.net
Twitter: @CHSMoulsford
Facebook: @CranfordHouse

Cranford House is a non-selective independent day
school for girls aged 3–16 years and boys 3–11 years. It has
an excellent reputation for providing its 440 pupils with a
balanced, all-round education within a warmly nurturing
environment. Set in over 14 acres of rural South Oxfordshire
the small class sizes, close community and committed staff
ensure each pupil is ably supported and challenged to
achieve their full potential. The school was rated as 'Excellent' in all categories in its ISI Inspection of November
2014. The Early Years Foundation Stage was rated as 'Outstanding'. In September 2020, the school will open a new
Sixth Form, allowing pupils to stay till the age of 18, and

boys will be welcomed into the Senior School in Years 7 and 12.

At Cranford House, the aim is to encourage pupils to achieve their full potential, becoming motivated, confident and happy individuals, recognising the importance of respect and support for others, but ready to seize life's opportunities.

The Early Years Foundation Stage (EYFS) encompasses Nursery and Reception, catering for boys and girls aged 3–5 years. Pupils benefit from a large, off-site Nursery School in a beautiful setting with plenty of green space for free-flow activities and learning. There are many links to the main school site for integration with Reception, swimming lessons and whole-school productions and activities.

The Junior School comprises Years 1 to 6. Juniors benefit from Senior School facilities and specialist subject teachers are used in a variety of disciplines. The school's all-inclusive approach sees all pupils taking part in competitive sports matches from Year 3 upwards. Lesson content is based on the National Curriculum, but supplemented to ensure pupils develop their own collaborative, reflective and reasoning skills and abilities. Results are excellent. Responsibility is offered at a young age through posts such as Junior Head Girl and team captains.

In the Senior School, girls follow a common core curriculum, as well as an extensive range of extra-curricular opportunities. While the school is non-selective, academic ambition for each pupil is high and every child is supported in achieving to the very best of their ability. In the 2016 Sunday Times Parent Power league tables, Cranford House was rated 3rd nationally for its GCSE results in the small schools, no sixth form category.

Pupils benefit from an excellent pastoral offering, key to which is a vibrant House system which encourages both a sense of community and leadership. On reaching Year 11, pupils enjoy further positions of responsibility. The school has extensive recreational facilities and games fields. In winter, hockey, football and netball are played, and in summer, tennis, rounders, cricket and athletics. Swimming takes place on site. Dramatic, musical and dance productions are an important aspect of school life and all are encouraged to take part.

In addition to the extensive range of enrichment activities offered throughout the school, all pupils have the opportunity to join educational trips and excursions. For Senior pupils, Bronze and Silver levels of The Duke of Edinburgh's Award scheme are offered, in addition to far-flung expeditions with World Challenge. Opportunities for overseas travel are also offered through exchanges, ski and sports trips and choir tours. School transport operates over a wide area throughout both Berkshire and Oxfordshire.

Scholarships, bursaries and awards are offered for Year 7 entry into Senior School.

Fees per term (2018–2019). £3,500–£5,680.

Charitable status. Cranford House School Trust Limited is a Registered Charity, number 280883.

Board of Governors:
Mrs N Scott-Ely (*Chair*)
Mr R Fisher (*Chair Finance & General Purposes Committee*)
Mrs L Kilroy (*Chair of HR & Remuneration Committee*)
Mr P Thomas (*Education Committee*)
Mr Jim Clarke (*Health and Safety*)
Mrs A Page (*Safeguarding & Prevent*)
Mrs A Gray (*SEN & EYFS*)
Mr P Tollett (*Chair of Bursaries and Scholarships Committee*)

Head: **Dr James Raymond**, PhD, BA Hons, PGCE, NPQH

Senior Deputy Head: Ms S Wilson, MA OU, BSc Brunel, QTS
Deputy Head (Academic & SENCo): Mr C Ellis, MA, MEd, BA Hons, PGCE
Deputy Head (Junior School): Mrs A Stewart, BA Hons, PGCE
Director Finance & Operations: Mrs E Taylor, MA
Deputy Head (Director of Studies): Mr R Barker, BSc Hons, PGCE
Director of Music: Mrs J Powell, BA Hons, Dip Adv Studies RAM
Assistant Head (Pastoral): Mrs M Carter, BA, PGCE

Senior School Teaching Staff:
Mrs N Butler, BA Hons, CAPES
Mr S Cowley, BA Hons, PGCE
Mrs S Day, BA Hons, PGCE
Mrs L Gifford-Guy, BMus Hons
Mrs K Heard, BA Hons, PGCE
Dr K Hill, PhD, BSc Hons, QTS
Miss A Holbrook, BSc Hons, PGCE
Mrs N Horn, BA, MSc, PGCE
Mrs D Keoghan, MA, BA
Mrs R Lanyon, MSc, PGCE
Mrs L Lawson, BA Hons, PGCE
Mrs A Macmillan, PGCE MFL
Mrs J McCallum, MA, PGCE
Mr K McIntyre, BSc
Mrs E Mean, BA, PGCE
Mr T Mean, BA Hons, PGCE
Mrs A Mir, MA, BA Hons, PGCE
Mrs G Mitcham, MA, PGCE
Miss P Newton, MSc, BSc, PGCE
Miss A Robson, MA, PGCE
Mrs J Turner, BA Hons, PGCE
Mr R Tyler, BA Hons, PGCE
Mrs N Tiedeman, BA Hons, PGCE
Mr J Winters MA Hons, PGCE
Mrs A Watkins-Cooke, BEd
Mrs D Cranton, BA Hons, PGCE
Mr C Morrison, BSc
Mrs S Sear, BA Hons, PGCE
Mrs B Graham, BSc Hons, PGCE

Junior School Teaching Staff:
Head of EYFS: Mrs K Knight, BA Hons, EYPS
Head of Key Stage 1: Mrs C Bennett, BA Hons, EYPS
Head of Key Stage 2: Mr T Mean, BA Hons, PGCE
Mrs G Bone, MA Hons, PGCE
Mrs L Breeze, BSc, PGCE
Miss R Carpenter, BA Hons, PGCE
Mrs A Diamond, BEd Hons
Mrs B Graham, BSc Hons, PGCE
Mrs A Greedy, BEd Hons
Miss E Hanson, MA Hons, PGCE
Miss R Hudson, BA Hons, PGCE
Mrs N I'Anson, BEd Hons
Mr T Mean, BA Hons, PGCE
Miss C Oliver, BA Hons, PGCE
Miss C Millar, BA Hons, PGCE
Mrs J Morris, BA Hons, PGCE
Mr C Morrison – BSc
Mrs K Raymond, BA Hons, PGCE
Miss H Stanley, BA Hons
Miss V de Trense, BA Hons, PGCE
Mr G Vickers-Jones, BA Hons, PGCE
Mrs A Watkins-Cooke, BEd
Mrs D Cranton, BA Hons, PGCE
Mr C Morrison, BSc
Mrs S Sear, BA Hons, PGCE
Mrs B Graham, BSc Hons, PGCE

Nursery Teaching Staff:
Head of EYFS: Mrs K Knight, BA Hons, EYPS
Mrs L Hayne, BTEC Childhood Studies
Mrs A John, NVQ3
Miss S Swift, NVQ3

Learning Support:
Miss D Smale, BA Hons, BSc Hons

Croydon High School
GDST

**Old Farleigh Road, Selsdon, South Croydon, Surrey
CR2 8YB**

Tel:	020 8260 7500
Fax:	020 8657 5413
email:	seniors@cry.gdst.net
	admissions@cry.gdst.net
website:	www.croydonhigh.gdst.net
Twitter:	@CroydonHigh
Facebook:	@CroydonHighSchoolGDST

Founded in 1874, the school's original site was in Wellesley Road Croydon but is now situated in the leafy suburb of Selsdon.

Croydon High School is part of the GDST (Girls' Day School Trust). The GDST is the leading network of independent girls' schools in the UK. As a charity that owns and runs 23 schools and two academies, it reinvests all its income in its schools. For further information about the Trust, see p. xxiii or visit www.gdst.net.

For over 140 years, Croydon High School has provided a superb all-round education for girls, around the Croydon area and further afield. The school combines tradition with a forward-looking, supportive and nurturing atmosphere where every girl is encouraged and supported to achieve her personal best. The school welcomes girls from a wide range of backgrounds; excellent pastoral care ensures that each girl is known as an individual.

Croydon High offers girls a wide range of extracurricular opportunities ensuring that each can find something she enjoys. The school regularly achieves local, regional and national success in Sport; its Arts are also outstanding, with a vibrant Music department offering opportunities to musicians at varying ability levels to develop their talents in all musical genres. Termly productions involve students across all year groups and young artists are motivated and inspired to develop their creative talents in different media.

The school aims to develop confident young women with wide ranging interests and abilities who have also achieved excellent academic results. Emphasis is placed on ensuring that girls are happy and fulfilled in whatever career path they choose for the future.

Number of Pupils. Senior School (aged 11–18): 360 girls (including 110 in the Sixth Form). Junior School (aged 3–11): 240 girls (including 17 in the Nursery).

Facilities. The purpose-built school has outstanding facilities; including specialist music rooms, a drama studio, a language laboratory, 5 computer suites, 10 science laboratories, design technology room and a recently refurbished sports block incorporating sports hall, gym, indoor swimming pool, fitness room and dance studio. The school is surrounded by spacious playing fields with netball/tennis courts, athletics track and an all-weather hockey pitch.

The Junior School, which has its own Nursery, is in an adjacent building on the same site, sharing many of the excellent facilities. It also boasts a state-of-the-art 4D immersive learning room, where girls can experience sound

and sights that inspire them to produce highly imaginative written and verbal work.

The Sixth Form have their own suite of rooms, including a common room and quiet study area, adjacent to the school library and excellent Further Education and Careers resources are available on site.

Curriculum. Most girls take 10 GCSE subjects with the aim of providing a broad and balanced core curriculum which keeps career choices open. Over 23 subjects are offered at A Level including Government & Politics, Economics, Latin and Physical Education. Almost all girls proceed to University, and, each year, a number are offered places at Oxbridge or to read Medicine

Admission. A whole school Open Day is held annually in October and a Sixth Form Open Evening also in October. An Open Event for both Junior and Senior Schools is held in May. Tours and private visits are welcome and can be arranged at any time through the Junior and Senior Admissions Registrars.

The school admits girls to the Junior School on the basis of either individual assessment (younger girls) or written tests (girls of 7+ and above). Selection procedures are held early in January for Juniors and assessments for Infants are held during the Autumn and Spring Terms for entry in the following September.

For entrance to the Senior School in Year 7, the school holds Entrance Tests in December for entry in the following September. All successful applicants are interviewed and references are taken up.

Entrance Tests are held in January for Year 9 entry in the following September.

For the Sixth Form, the school interviews applicants and requests reports from the present school. A Sixth Form Open Evening is held in October and Scholarship and Bursary applicants sit an examination in December.

Further details on the admissions process are available on the website or via the Registrar, admissions@cry.gdst.net.

Fees per term (2018–2019). Senior School: Years 7–9 £5,353, Years 10–13 £5,552; Junior School: Nursery (full time) £3,280, Reception £3,917, Years 1–2 £3,975, Years 3–4 £4,320, Years 5–6 £4,393.

Scholarships and Bursaries. Following the ending of the Government Assisted Places Scheme, the GDST has made available to the school a number of scholarships and bursaries.

Academic scholarships are available for entry at 11+ or to the Sixth Form. Music, art & design, drama and sports scholarships are also available at 11+ and 16+.

For entrance at Year 9, the school offers two Academic Plus scholarships to applicants joining from other schools, who have chosen to be assessed academically and in one of the following subjects; art, music, drama or sport.

Bursaries are means tested and are intended to ensure that the school remains accessible to bright girls who could not otherwise benefit from the education we offer. These are available to Senior School girls only.

The school has a vibrant and active Old Girls Network – The Ivy Link – which supports the school in numerous ways, including offering careers and mentoring connections.

Charitable status. Croydon High School is part of The Girls' Day School Trust, which is a Registered Charity, number 306983.

Chairman of Local Governors: Mr A Spiro

Headmistress: **Mrs E L Pattison**, BA Leeds

Deputy Head, Welfare Systems and Innovation: Mr D King, BA Oxford

Deputy Head, Academic: Mr C Burnie, MA Cambridge

Assistant Head, Curriculum: Mr M Pickering, BA, MSc Manchester

Head of Junior School: Mrs S Bradshaw, BA Bristol

Director of Marketing: Mrs F Cook, BSc Southampton

Derby High School

Hillsway, Littleover, Derby DE23 3DT

Tel: 01332 514267
Fax: 01332 516085
email: headsecretary@derbyhigh.derby.sch.uk
website: www.derbyhigh.derby.sch.uk
Twitter: @DerbyHighSchool
Facebook: @derbyhighUK
LinkedIn: /DerbyHighSchool

Derby High School is an independent day school conveniently situated in the Derby suburb of Littleover which educates boys and girls aged 3 to 11 and girls only from 11 to 18.

Academically, the school regularly achieves the best results in the county, however a Derby High education is about much more than academic results. Whether your child is musical, creative, analytical or sporty, at Derby High each student's individual strengths are identified to help them achieve their potential in a fun, friendly and supportive atmosphere.

There are 500 pupils in school of whom 300 are in the Senior School, which is for girls only, and 200 are in the Infants and Juniors which are both co-educational.

The Primary Department follows an enhanced national curriculum course. KS1 and KS2 take internal assessments. ASPECTS are used for pre-school and INCAS for Year 5. There is considerable enrichment in the curriculum with a wide variety of sports, music, drama and other activities available both within the curriculum and at club time.

The Senior School offers courses in Art and Design, Biology, Chemistry, Design Technology, Drama, Business, English Language and Literature, French, General Studies, Geography, German, History, Food & Nutrition, ICT, Mathematics, Further Maths, Music, Physical Education, Psychology, Physics, Religious Studies, Spanish and Theatre Studies. The curriculum is enhanced by activities such as the Engineering Education Scheme, Young Enterprise, The Duke of Edinburgh's Award and World Challenge. Sports, drama and music are also strengths, with pupils gaining recognition at county and national level.

The main points of entrance are at pre-school, Reception, Year 3, 11+ and 16+ where Scholarships and Assisted Places are available. Entrance is by examination and interview. Entrance at other ages is by assessment and takes place by arrangement.

The school has an active Christian ethos and broadly follows the teaching of the Church of England, but pupils of all faiths are welcomed and valued.

Examinations. Pupils are entered for ASPECTS, INCAS, GCSE and GCE AS and A Level examinations, some Sixth Form pupils take the EPQ. The school takes part in INCAS and MidYIS testing. Short course GCSE ICT is taken by all pupils. Many pupils have individual music lessons and take music examinations through the Associated Board of the RCM. LAMDA is offered in the Junior School, leading to examinations. The Young Enterprise examination may be taken by Company members.

Games. Hockey, Netball, Rounders, Tennis, Swimming, Athletics, Short Tennis, Tag Rugby, Football and Trampolining are major sports.

Fees per term (2018–2019). £2,114–£4,290.

Charitable status. Derby High School Trust Limited is a Registered Charity, number 1007348. It exists to provide education for children.

Governors and Foundation Governors:
Chairman: Mr G Jones
Mrs J Bullivant
Dr R Faleiro
Ms H Barton
Dr V Churchhouse
[1]Mr M R Hall, DL, Hon D Univ, FCA, FCMA, FCT
Mrs R Hughes, BA, ACIB
Mr T Ousley
Mr P Rowley
Mr J Atwal
Mrs S Sandle
Ms F Apthorpe
Reverend Alicia Dring (*Bishop's representative*)

[1] *Foundation Governor*

Head: **Mrs A Chapman**, MA Open University, BA Hons Nottingham, PGCE Warwick

Deputy Head: Miss A Jordan, BA Hons Wolverhampton, PGCE Keele

Head of Sixth Form & Assistant Head: Mrs C Bellman, BA Hons Oxford, MA Oxford, PGCE Oxford

Assistant Head: Mr A Maddox, MMath Oxford, PGCE Oxford, PGDES Oxford

Assistant Head: Mr A Lee, BA Hons Salford, PGCE Leicester

Chaplain: Ms J Whitehead, MA Sheffield, BA Hons Nottingham

Bursar: Mrs M Mitchell, BA Hons, ACA, ICAEW

* *Head of Department*

Miss A Allum, BSc Hons Brunel, PGCE Brunel (*Physical Education*, *PSHE)
Mrs K Aydi, BSc Aberdeen, PGCE Bath (*Biology)
Dr G Bhattacharyya, BA Hons Cambridge, PhD Cambridge, PGCE Oxford (*Physics*)
Mrs A Bodycombe, BA Hons Central St Martin's College of Art & Design, MA Coventry, PGCE OU (*Art, Design Technology*)
Mr J Buckley, BSc Hons York, PGCE York (*Mathematics*)
Mrs S Bussey, BSc Econ Hons Aberystwyth (*Information Resources Manager*)
Miss R Coates, BA Hons University of Bath, PGCE Oxford (*French*)
Mrs E Davies, BA Hons Nottingham Trent, PGCE Loughborough (*Food & Nutrition*)
Mr R Dodson, MEng Hons Bristol (*Mathematics)
Mrs N Driver, BEd Hons Lancaster (**Religious Studies*, *Head of Years 7–9*)
Mrs J Fraser, BSc Hons Derby, PGCE Nottingham Trent (*Psychology*)
Mr J Gallagher, BA Hons Durham, PGCE Nottingham (*Geography)
Mrs S Goodman, BSc Hons Sheffield, PGCE Sheffield (*Physical Education, Deputy Head Sixth Form*)
Mrs J Hancock, BEd Hons Manchester Metropolitan (**Physical Education*)
Mrs K Hewitt, BSc Hons Birmingham, PGCE Leeds (*Biology, Food & Nutrition*)
Mrs S Hilton, BA Hons Brighton, PGCE Brighton (**Business, ICT*)
Mrs L Hough, BSc Hons Brunel, CertEd (**Design Technology, Art & Design Graphics*)

Miss S Kelliher, BA Hons Dublin, PGCE Birmingham (*German*, *French*, *MFL*)

Mrs N Ley, BSc Hons Loughborough, PGCE Loughborough (*Mathematics*)

Mrs M Martinez Hernandez, BA Salamanca, PGCE Madrid (*Spanish*)

Mrs S Martin-Smith, HND Swansea, BA Hons Swansea, PGCE Swansea (*Art*, *Textiles*)

Dr S Mathews, BA Hons Sheffield Hallam, MSc Manchester, PhD Manchester (*History*)

Dr J Myers, BSc York, PGCE Leics, PhD Edinburgh (*Chemistry*)

Dr J A Nelmes, BSc Hons London, PGCE Nottingham, PhD Loughborough (*Physics*, *Chemistry*)

Mrs J Orr, BSc Hons Ulster, PGCE Nottingham Trent (*Physics*)

Mr C Quichaud, BA Hons Birkbeck London, PGCE King's College London (*French*, *Spanish*)

Miss M Render, BA Hons Hull, PGCE Hull (*English*, *SENCO*)

Miss C V Riley, BSc Hons Leeds, PGCE Leeds (*Chemistry*, *Head of Years 10 & 11*, *DofE Award*)

Mrs M Roe, BA Hons Nottingham (*Geography*, *DofE Award*)

Mrs L Seymour, BA Hons, PGCE Notts (*German*)

Mrs E Smith, BA Hons Loughborough, PGCE Loughborough (*Drama*, *English*)

Mrs F Supran, BA Hons Manchester, PGCE Oxford, Cert TEFLA Oxford Brookes (*English*, *Drama*)

Mr E Temple, MusB Hons Manchester, PGCE Manchester (*Director of Music*)

Mrs J Webster, MA Hons Cambridge (*English & Psychology*)

Mr S Williams, BSc Hons Birmingham, PGCE Nottingham (*Mathematics*, *ICT*)

Miss L Wilson, BA Hons Manchester, PGCE Manchester (*Religious Education*, *History*)

Mrs C Wood, BSc Hons Manchester, PGCE Nottingham (*Biology*)

Primary School:

Head of Primary: **Mrs M Hannaford**, BEd Hons Derby, MA Ed OU, NPQH

Mrs R Youngman, BEd Hons Derby, NPQML (*Primary Assistant Head*)

Miss A Bailey, BEd Hons QTS Derby

Miss L Baker, BA Hons Derby, PGCE Derby

Mrs J Bowden, BA Ed Primary Reading

Mrs C Courtney-Hale, BA Ed Hons Wales, MA Ed Loughborough (*EYFS Coordinator*)

Mrs A Dowell, BSc Hons, QTS Newman Coll of HE

Mrs S Evans-Bolger, BA Hons QTS, MA Ed BG University College Lincoln

Mrs R Ford, BA Hons Leeds, PGCE Primary Bradford

Mrs J Foster, BEd Hons Derby

Mr R Gould, BA Hons Wolverhampton, PGCE Birmingham City

Mrs R Hill, BSc Hons Liverpool, PGCE Nottingham

Miss S Holmes, BA Primary Education QTS Leeds

Mr C Horne, BEd Primary Hons Derby

Miss D Hyland, BA Hons Birmingham, PGCE Birmingham

Miss H Law, BA Hons Nottingham, Primary PGCE Manchester

Mrs R Lesley, BMus Hons Birmingham, PGCE Birmingham

Miss L Pitt, BA PrimEd Birmingham

Mrs J Swainston, BEd Hons Sheffield (*Primary Coordinator*)

Mrs A Trindell, BSc Hons QTS BG University College Lincoln

Durham High School for Girls

Farewell Hall, Durham DH1 3TB

Tel:	0191 384 3226
Fax:	0191 386 7381
email:	enquiries@dhsfg.org.uk
website:	www.dhsfg.org.uk

Durham High School for Girls aims to create, within the context of a Christian ethos, a secure, happy and friendly environment within which pupils can develop personal and social skills, strive for excellence in academic work and achieve their full potential in all aspects of school life.

- Highly qualified, specialist staff.
- Excellent examination results.
- Continuity of education from 3 to 18 years.
- Entry at 3, 4, 7, 10, 11 and 16.
- Superb modern facilities include state-of-the-art Science/ICT/Library Block and Performing Arts Suite.
- Academic, Music, Performing Arts, Art, Drama and Sports Scholarships.
- Financial assistance available at all stages.

Number on roll. 411 day pupils.

Age range. Seniors 11–18; Juniors 7–11; Infants 4–7; Nursery from age 3.

Entry requirements. Assessment, formal testing and interview if age is applicable. Sixth form entry is dependent on the level of achievement at GCSE.

Junior House (age range 3–11). A purpose-built Nursery provides a stimulating environment for children aged 3–4 years. Children may start the day after their 3rd birthday. Early Years Funding available. Superb Outdoor Learning environment.

Junior House follows a topic-based curriculum linked to the National Curriculum which enables girls to enjoy every aspect of learning and discovery. Form teachers encourage and support a high standard of achievement in all areas of the curriculum and promote a feeling of warmth and security.

Extra-curricular activities include: Choirs, Orchestra, Wind Band, Instrumental Tuition, Debating, Textiles Club, Drama, Hockey, Rounders, Netball, Tennis, Ballet, Karate, Chess, Amnesty Club, Dance and Drama. A range of sports fixtures are made with other schools.

The immediate environment plays an important role in stimulating learning and regular visits are made to the theatre, museums and places of educational interest.

Senior House Curriculum. The curriculum is designed to be enjoyable, stimulating and exciting, providing breadth and depth in learning.

- Wide choice of options at GCSE and A Levels.
- Languages: French, Spanish, Latin and Classical Greek.
- Separate and Dual Sciences.
- Personal and Social Education programme.
- Careers Education and Guidance.
- UCAS and Oxbridge support

Extra-curricular activities include regular visits abroad, foreign exchanges, visits to the theatre, art galleries, museums and concerts. There is also a thriving programme of Music, Drama and Sport, as well as a flourishing Duke of Edinburgh's Award scheme and debating clubs.

The Sixth Form. The Sixth Form of 61 girls takes a full and responsible part in the life and organisation of the school. A wide range of A and AS Level subjects is available. Girls usually take 3 or 4 subjects in L6 and 3 in U6, with an option of an EPQ.

Fees per term (2018–2019). Nursery £1,380*, Infants (Reception–Year 2) £2,290**–£2,960, Juniors (Years 3–6) £3,270, Seniors (Years 7–13) £4,375.

*Fees for hours above the 15 hours per week provided by the Early Years Funding.

**Fees for 4 year olds qualifying for Early Years Funding.

Extra subjects. Greek, Speech and Drama, Astronomy and Music (piano, strings, brass, woodwind, singing).

Scholarships and Bursaries. Means-tested Scholarships are available at at 7+, 11+, 14+ and 16+.

At 11+ a number of academic Open Scholarships are offered and bursaries are available in cases of financial need. There is also the Barbara Priestman award of £600 per annum for daughters of practising Christians. Scholarships (Academic, Performing Arts, Sport and Music) are awarded at 11+ and financial help is available at all stages from age 11.

At 13+ Academic, Music, Performing Arts and Sport Scholarships are available.

At 16+ there are a number of academic scholarships available to external and internal candidates. Music scholarships are also available at 16+, as well as Performing Arts, Sports and an Art Scholarship.

Transport. Transport is available from most local areas and the school is also accessible by public transport.

After School Care. After School Care is available until 5.30 pm and is free of charge (there is a charge for Nursery children).

Further information. The Head is always pleased to welcome parents who wish to visit the school. For further information and a full prospectus please contact the School on: tel: 0191 384 3226; fax: 0191 386 7381; website: www.dhsfg.org.uk; email: enquiries@dhsfg.org.uk.

Charitable status. Durham High School for Girls is a Registered Charity, number 1119995. Its aim is to create a friendly, caring community based on Christian values and to encourage academic excellence.

Governors:
Mrs M Cummings, BA (*Chairman*)
Mr S Cheffings (*Vice Chairman*)

Mrs K Barker	Revd J Logan
Mrs E Berry	Mr I Meston, BTh Min
Miss L Clark, BEd, MA	Mr R Metcalfe
Dr C English	
Dr M Gilmore, MA, PhD	Mr A Ribchester, MBE, FCA
Dr M Hyder	
Mr A Lake	Mrs P Walker

***Headmistress*: Mrs S Niblock**, MA Oxon, MA OU, MEd OU (*English*)

Deputy Head: Mrs J Tomlinson, BSc Newcastle (**Biology*)

Assistant Head: Mrs L Ibbott, BA Cardiff (**English; Marketing and Development*)
Assistant Head: Mrs K Morrey, MA Durham (*History*)

Head of Junior House: Mrs K Anderson, BEd

Bursar: Mr D Payne, BSc London, ACA

Senior House:
* *Head of Department*
Dr N Alvey, MPhys, PhD Kent (**Physics*)
Mr A Cartmell, BA OU, BSc Southampton (*Mathematics*)
Miss G Casey, BA Cantab (*Modern Languages, Librarian*)
Mr R Coates, BA Dunelm (*History*)
Mrs P G Clarke, BSc Cork (*Physics*)
Miss G Colon, BA Hons London (*Modern Languages*)
Mrs C I Creasey, BA Dunelm (**Geography*)
Mrs A Jenkinson (*Physical Education*)

Mrs J Flavell, MA Cambridge (**Science, Chemistry*)
Mrs E Gentry, BSc St Andrews (*Science*)
Mrs S Green, LLB Cardiff (*Careers Coordinator*)
Mrs J Golding, BA OU (*English*)
Dr L Hardy, PhD London (*Music*)
Mrs A Hawkins, BA London (*English, Sociology*)
Miss N Hill, BA Leeds (**Modern Languages*)
Mrs D Jackson, BA Sheffield (*Geography*)
Mrs A Jenkinson, BEd Leeds Metropolitan (*Physical Education*)
Mrs M Kenyon, BSc York (*Chemistry*)
Mrs C Kelly, BSc York, MSc Sunderland, MA Dunelm (*Mathematics*)
Mrs C Lawrence-Wills, BA Cantab (**Music*)
Mrs A Lee, BA Manchester (*Learning Support*)
Mrs J Lonsdale, BA, MA Leeds (**Drama*)
Mrs L Lowes, MA Newcastle (**Director of Sport*)
Mrs K Measor, BA Sunderland, MA OU (*Business Studies and Economics*)
Mrs L Middleton, BA Dunelm (**Religious Education*)
Mrs C Murray, MA Oxon (**Classics*)
Mrs J Newby, BSc Warwick (**Biology*)
Mrs H O'Neill, BA Hons Dunelm (*Modern Languages*)
Mr J Priest, MSc Bath (**Mathematics*)
Mrs D Rabot, MA Ed Sunderland (*ICT*)
Revd Dr S Ridley, MA Oxon, EdD Dunelm (*Classics*)
Miss A Schofield, BSc Northumbria (*Physical Education*)
Mrs J Shaw, BA Manchester (*Mathematics*)
Mrs J V Slane, BSc Surrey (*Physical Education*)
Mr D Smith, MA Oxon, CertTh York (**History and Politics*)
Miss J Sneddon, BA Hons, MA Edinburgh (**Art and Design*)
Mrs R Stephenson, BA Newcastle (*English*)
Mrs J Sutcliffe, BA Wimbledon (*Art*)
Ms D Todd, BA Hons Sunderland (**English*)
Revd B Vallis, BA Cambridge, BA Theology Dunelm (*Chaplain and Religious Education*)
Mrs C Wheeler, BA Dunelm (*Psychology, Head of Sixth Form*)
Mrs B Wildish, MA Newcastle (*Mathematics*)

Junior House:
Mrs R Booth, BMus Manchester
Mrs E Brothers, BSc Sheffield (*Deputy Head*)
Mrs S Cehic, BSc York
Mrs J A Coxon, BEd Liverpool (*Physical Education*)
Mrs P Everett, BEd Hons Cambridge
Mrs K A Hall, BA Central Lancashire
Mrs C M Hopper, BA Nottingham
Mrs L Mock, BA Dunelm
Miss S Rose, BSc Wales, MSc London, MA Durham
Mrs K Tozer, BEd Canterbury
Mr G Wright, BA Hons Sunderland

Junior House Support Staff:
Miss A Dobson, BA Dunelm
Mrs A Maddison, NNEB Durham
Mrs C Gorman
Mrs M Harrison
Mrs J Tipple, MEng Sheffield Hallam (*After School Care*)

Visiting Staff:
Mrs B Bailey (*Suzuki Violin*)
Mrs R Barton-Gray (*Cello*)
Miss V Bojkova, Diplomas in Conducting & Piano Performance (*Singing and Piano*)
Mr Bovill (*Drum Kit and Percussion*)
Miss S Innes, BMus, LRAM (*Violin & Viola*)
Mrs F Preston (*Woodwind*)
Mr G Ritson, GRNCM, PPRNCM (*Brass*)
Ms H Saunders (*School Counsellor*)
Miss R J Shuttler, BA, MMus, LTCL (*Piano*)

Miss C Smith, BA, FRSA (*Clarinet & Saxophone*)
Mr R Woods (*Guitar*)

Administrative Staff:
Head's PA: Mrs A Thompson
Administrator: Mrs J Ridley
Marketing/Publicity: Mrs A Wright
Librarian: Miss G Casey, BA Canterbury
Assistant Bursar: Mr P Atkinson
Accountant: Mrs C McAdams
ICT Systems Manager: Mr J Kerton
ICT Technician: Mr P Cass
Reception: Mrs P Steele, Mrs C Gillham
Catering Manager: Mrs A Hibbart
Laboratory Manager: Mrs L Foskett, MChem York
Laboratory Technician: Dr D Wiles, BSc, DPhil Dunelm
Laboratory Assistants: Miss J Cummings, Miss L Tinnion
Performing Arts/Art Technician: Mr N Raine, BSc
    Newcastle, BEd Sunderland
Caretaker: Mr K Riding
Assistant Caretakers: Mr D Wilson, Mr P Tennant, Mr A
    Brack

Edgbaston High School

Westbourne Road, Edgbaston, Birmingham, West Midlands B15 3TS

Tel: 0121 454 5831
Fax: 0121 454 2363
email: admissions@edgbastonhigh.co.uk
website: www.edgbastonhigh.co.uk

This independent day school, founded in 1876, attracts girls both from the immediate neighbourhood and all over the West Midlands. They come for the academic curriculum, the lively programme of sporting, creative and cultural activities, and for the individual attention and flexibility of approach.

Personal relationships at EHS are of paramount importance. Parents, both individually and through their association, give generously of their time to support our activities; while staff, through their hard work and good relationship with the girls, create an atmosphere at once orderly and friendly.

Organisation and Curriculum. There are three departments working together on one site which caters for over 950 day girls aged two and a half to eighteen. One of the features of EHS is the continuity of education it offers. However, girls can be admitted at most stages. Staff take special care to help girls settle quickly and easily. Pupils enjoy a broadly based programme which substantially fulfils the requirements of the National Curriculum and much more.

The Pre-Preparatory Department, known as Westbourne, offers facilities for about 100 girls aged two and a half to five in a spacious, purpose-built, detached house. The staff aim to create an environment in which they can promote every aspect of a girl's development. A brand new Nursery (part of the £4 million Octagon building) was opened in February 2005.

The Preparatory School accommodates over 350 girls from 5+ to 11 in up-to-date facilities, among them a new IT suite, Science Laboratory, Library and Design Technology Centre. A full curriculum, including English, Mathematics, Science and Technology, is taught throughout the department.

The Senior School caters for about 500 girls aged 11+ to 18. Girls follow a well-balanced curriculum which prepares them for a wide range of subjects at GCSE and A Level.

Examination results are very good with high grades distributed across both Arts and Science subjects. The vast majority of girls in the Sixth Form of over 100 proceed to Higher Education. Every year girls obtain places at Oxbridge and Russell Group Universities.

Extra Curricular Activities. Girls can take part in a broad range of activities including art, ceramics, Mandarin, drama, Duke of Edinburgh's Award, music, sport and Young Enterprise. There are clubs during the lunch hour and after school. Instrumental music lessons are available. There is a strong music tradition in the school. Girls go on visits, expeditions and work experience in this country and abroad. We encourage girls to think of the needs of others.

Accommodation. There is a regular programme of improvements to the buildings. An exciting new multi-purpose hall, The Octagon, was opened in February 2005. A floodlit all-weather surface was opened in Summer 2006. The school has its own indoor swimming pool, 12 tennis courts and 8 acres of playing fields. Work on extended Sixth Form accommodation, a new library and fitness suite, at a cost of £3.5m, was completed in January 2011. In August 2016 the school completed a building development designed to enhance the Preparatory School. At a cost of £1.6 million, the project has resulted in a newly extended library, Art room and large welcoming Reception space. A multi-purpose building, the Hexagon, was completed in early 2018. In September 2018, the Sports Pavilion underwent a refurbishment.

Location. The school is pleasantly situated next to the Botanical Gardens in a residential area, 1½ miles south-west of the city centre. It is easily accessible by public transport and also has its own privately run coaches.

Fees per term (2018–2019). £2,767 (5 days); Prep £2,864–£4,023; Senior £4,258.

Scholarships and Bursaries. Academic Scholarships are available at 11+, awarded on the basis of performance in the entrance examination. Sixth Form Academic Scholarships are awarded based on examination and interview.

Two Music Scholarships are also offered annually: one at 11+ and one at 16+. 11+ candidates must sit the main entrance examination in October and then have written, aural and practical tests. Candidates at 16+ attend an audition and interview in January.

At 16+ there are further scholarships for Art, Performing Arts and Sport awarded to girls of outstanding ability. Assessments take place in January.

A Bursary fund exists to help girls of good academic ability in financial need to enter at 11+ and the Sixth Form and to assist those whose financial circumstances have changed since they entered the Senior School. Bursaries may cover part or full fees. All scholarships can be combined with means-tested bursaries in cases of need.

Further information. Full details may be obtained from the school. Parents and girls are welcome to visit the school by appointment.

Charitable status. Edgbaston High School for Girls is a Registered Charity, number 504011. Founded in 1876, it exists to provide an education for girls.

President: Sir Dominic Cadbury, BA, MBA

Vice-Presidents:
Mr Duncan Cadbury, MSc
Mr I Marshall, BA
Her Honour Judge Sybil Thomas, LLB

Council:
Chairman: Mr J D Payne, BSc, MRICS
Deputy Chairman: Mrs C Fatah, RGN

Ms H J Arnold, BSc
Lord Bhattacharyya, KB, CBE

Mrs S A England Kerr
Mr I Griffiths, MA Cantab, MA, PGCE, CEng
Mrs A E S Howarth
Dr J Leadbetter, PhD, BSc, AFBPsS, CPsychol
Mrs V Nicholls, Chartered MCIPD
Mr G I Scott, MA Oxon
Mrs S Shirley-Priest, MA, MRICS
Mrs J Tozer, LLB, BD

Representing the Old Girls' Association:
Mrs L Lucas

School Staff:

Headmistress: Dr Ruth A Weeks, BSc, PhD Birmingham

Deputy Head Academic: Mrs S-E Rees, MA Oxford
Deputy Head Pastoral: Mrs A Cirillo-Campbell, BA UCE
Deputy Head Curriculum: Miss J Rance, BSc Manchester, MEd Birmingham

School Management Team:
Mrs L Batchelor, BSc Birmingham (*Senior Teacher, Co-Curricular*)
Mrs M Khuttan, BSc Keele (*Senior Teacher, Teaching and Learning*)
Mr P Smith (*Senior Teacher, Academic Pathways*)

* Head of Department/Subject Leader

Ms G Ajmal, BA Wolverhampton (*English, Head of Year 8*)
Miss M Aznar-López, BA Birmingham (*Spanish, French, DofE Bronze Coordinator*)
Mr J Ball, BSc Birmingham (*Mathematics*)
Miss M Barbet, Licence d'Anglais Université de Clermont-Ferrand, France (*French, Spanish*)
Mrs L Batchelor, BSc Birmingham (*Senior Teacher Co-Curricular*)
Mr D Berman, MA Oxford (*Science; Octagon Technician*)
Mrs A M Brookes, BSc Brunel (**Chemistry*)
Mrs C Cardellino, BA Leicester (**German*)
Mrs J Chalmers, BA York (*Mathematics*)
Mrs A Cirillo-Campbell, BA Birmingham (**ICT, Senior Teacher Digital Strategy*)
Mrs A Coley, BA Northampton (*Food & Nutrition and Textiles, Charity Coordinator*)
Miss J Cox, BA Newcastle upon Tyne (*RS and History*)
Dr E Cruice, BSc Sussex, PhD Birmingham (*Science*)
Mr N Day, BA Huddersfield (*History*)
Mr M Dukes, BA Wolverhampton (**Art, Director of Visual Communications*)
Mrs Z Ehiogu, BA University East London (*Physical Education, Head of Year 12, PSHEE and Study Skills Coordinator*)
Mrs C A Evans, Cert Ed Anstey College of Physical Education (*Physical Education*)
Mrs S Flitter, MA Oxford (*Classics*)
Mr A Flox-Nieva, Licenciado en Filología Inglesa, Castilla, Spain (**Spanish*)
Mrs J Forrest, BSc Open University (*Biology*)
Miss S Glover, BA Nottingham (**History*)
Ms D Graham, BSocSc Birmingham, Grad Dip Psych Aston (**Psychology and Sociology*)
Mr P Gray, MA Ohio, USA (**English*)
Miss J P Harrison, BA Southampton, MA Birmingham (*English, *Critical Thinking, Higher Education Advisor, Examinations Secretary*)
Miss M Hayday, BA Hull (**Religious Studies, Head of Year 9*)
Mrs J Hayward, BSc Newcastle-upon-Tyne (*Mathematics*)
Mrs S Hewison, BA Ed Exeter (*Physical Education, Assistant Head of Year 9*)
Mrs H Howell, GBSM, ABSM, Birmingham (*Music*)

Mrs K Hughes, BA Durham (**Geography, Assistant Head of Year 11*)
Miss K Jacks, BA Durham (*Physical Education, Assistant Head of Year 7*)
Mr M James, BA Northumbria (*Art*)
Mrs R Jarvis, MusB Music Manchester (*Music*)
Mrs J Johnson, BA Aberystwyth (**MFL, Gifted & Talented Coordinator*)
Miss N Jones-Owen, BA Manchester Metropolitan (*English, *Media Studies, Head of Year 7*)
Mrs A Lacey, BSc East Anglia (*Senior Teacher, *Science*)
Mr S Lane, BA Plymouth (**Drama*)
Mrs A Lee, BSc Birmingham (*Mathematics, Assistant Head of Year 10*)
Mrs S Lynch, BSc Sheffield, MA Sheffield (*Science*)
Mr P Malone, BA Sheffield (*ICT, Business Studies*)
Miss K Massey, BSc Reading (*Geography*)
Mrs R J Matthews, BSc Aberystwyth (*Science, Biology*)
Mrs K McAlister, MA Oxford (**Classics*)
Miss M P Monet-Rossetti, BA Open University (*French, German*)
Mrs L Mooney, BA Wolverhampton (*Food & Nutrition and *Textiles, Head of Year 11*)
Miss S H Mullett, BA Nottingham (*Art*)
Mrs K E Newling, BSc Birmingham (*Mathematics*)
Mrs R Norman, BSc Liverpool (**Mathematics*)
Miss S O'Hare, MA St Andrews (*English, Head of Year 10*)
Mrs S Park, BA Cardiff, MPhil Cardiff (*English*)
Mrs G Parsons, BSc University of Wales Institute, Cardiff (**Physical Education, Head of Year 13*)
Mrs L Parsons, BSc Coventry, MSc Coventry (*Psychology*)
Mr C J Proctor, BA Swansea (*English*)
Dr A Rajp, PhD Birmingham (**Biology, *Chemistry*)
Miss R Richardson, BA Reading (*History, *Critical Thinking, Higher Education Advisor*)
Mr K Robson, BMus Conservatoire Birmingham, MA Huddersfield (**Music*)
Mrs S Rowntree, BA Salford (*Drama*)
Dr D Royal, BSc UCL, PhD UCL (*Physics*)
Miss C Roye, BSc Loughborough (*Physical Education, Assistant Head of Physical Education*)
Mr J Sabotig, BSc Birmingham (**Physics, Head of Houses*)
Mrs D Saddington, Cert Ed Nottingham Trent (*Food & Nutrition and Textiles*)
Mrs H Sahota, BSc Birmingham (*Mathematics*)
Dr Y Shang, BSc Peking, China, MSc Beijing, China, PhD Loughborough, BA Jinan, China (*Mandarin*)
Mrs J Shutt, BA Keele (**Business and Economics, Head of Careers*)
Mr R Skilbeck, BA Leeds College of Music (*Music*)
Mrs A Smith, BA Birmingham (*English*)
Mr P Smith, BA Staffordshire (*Senior Teacher Academic Pathways*)
Mr N Southall, BSc BCU Birmingham, MA BCU Birmingham (*Music, Assistant Head of Music*)
Mrs C Syer, BSc Oxford Polytechnic (**Food & Nutrition and Textiles*)
Mr S Thomas, BA Cambridge, MPhil Cambridge, MA Cambridge (*Mathematics*)
Mr M Tomaszewicz, BSc Birmingham (*Science*)
Miss S E Vann, BEd De Montfort (*Physical Education*)
Miss H Welsh, BSc Portsmouth (*History, English, PSHEE and Head of Academic Support*)
Mr M Wiggins, BA Birmingham (**Religious Studies, *Sociology*)
Mr D Wilkins, BA Birmingham (**English*)
Miss R Williams, MusB Manchester (*Music*)
Miss E Wood, MA Edinburgh (*Classics, Assistant Head of Year 8*)

Librarian: Miss V Jones, BA Brunel

Library Assistant/Examinations Officer: Mrs J Hall, BSc
Surrey

Head of ICT Systems, Development and Management: Mr
A Matloob, BSc BCU
Network Manager: Mr A Ijaz

Language Assistants:
French: Ms M Romero
German:
Spanish: Miss C Gonzáles

Technicians:
Art: Miss A Birch, BA Southampton
Food & Nutrition and Textiles: Mrs C Harris
Science:
Mr J Coley, BSc Northampton
Mrs A Duvnjak, BSc Coventry, MSc Birmingham
Miss V Gutzmore, BSc OU, HND

D of E Silver and Gold Coordinator: Mrs S Griffiths

Visiting Staff:

Music:
Pianoforte:
Ms E Cockbill, MA, LLCM, ALCM
Mrs L Kitto, GBSM, ABSM, LTCL
Miss M Morris, MMus, Birmingham; LRSM
Mrs C J Purkis, GBSM, ABSM, LRAM
Flute:
Miss H Jones, BA
Mrs S Wilson, BA
Clarinet/Saxophone:
Miss M Harper, GRNCM, ARMCM
Mr J Meadows, BA, ABSM
Horn:
Mrs C Butler, BMus Birmingham
Violin/Viola:
Miss A Chippendale, BMus
Mr M Owen, LRAM
Cello:
Miss J Carey, GRSM, ARCM
Guitar:
Miss L Larner, BMus
Brass:
Mrs M Brookes, DRSAMD
Percussion:
Mr J Groom, BMus
Singing:
Mrs S Allsop, ARCM, ABRSM
Miss S Purkis, BMus
Mr R Skilbeck, BMus
Theory:
Mrs K Stocks, BMus, ARCM
Miss M Harper, GRNCM, ARMCM

Fencing:
Professor P Northam, BAF

LAMDA Teachers:
Mrs T Bolt
Ms C Fidler, BA, LRAM, FETC, IPA
Mrs J Foley

Life Saving: Rose Link

Gym Club: Mrs S Hewison

Administrative Staff:
Headmistress's PA: Ms G Franchi
Finance Director: Mrs B Kail, CIMA
Head of Marketing & Development: Mrs A Rowlands, BSc
Lancaster
Senior School Admissions Secretary: Mrs H Head
Preparatory School Admissions Assistant: Mrs A Jackson

Nurses:
Mrs M Al-Ani
Mrs H Heyes
Mrs J Irving, RGN, SCM

Facilities Manager: Mr S Watson, MHCIMA

Preparatory School:

Head: Mrs S Hartley, BEd Bristol

Deputy Heads:
Mrs A Aston, BSc Birmingham
Miss C Robinson, BA Exeter

Mrs A M Collins, BEd Birmingham
Mrs S Crompton, BSc Leeds
Mrs A Dawes, BSc Cardiff
Miss S Dawes, BSc Leeds
Miss R Deacon, BSc Newman College
Mrs S Donelly
Mrs S Draper, BSc Swansea
Miss C Dugdale, BSc Leeds Metropolitan
Mrs C Eveleigh, BSc Bath
Mrs S Flitter, MA Oxford
Mrs J Goodyear, BA Ed Worcester College of Higher
Education
Mrs C Hennous, BA
Mrs L Hobbs, BSc Birmingham
Miss S Howarth, BSc Worcester College of Higher
Education
Mrs L Humble, BA Swansea
Mrs H Jones, BA Swansea
Mrs J Knott, BA Birmingham
Miss K McKee, BA Sussex
Miss V Nelsey, BA Hull
Miss F O'Connor, BEd Wolverhampton
Mrs M Poade, BA Reading
Mrs F Scott Dickins, BA London
Mrs G Villiers Cundy, BEd Bath
Mrs K Waterworth, BSc Aston
Mrs F Watson, BA Leeds
Mrs V Woodfield, BEd UCE Birmingham

Librarian: Mrs N Ash

Teaching Assistants:
Mrs D Audley
Mrs M Bracey
Mrs G Draysey
Mrs N Mohamed
Mrs J Russon

Preparatory School Nurse: Mrs H Heyes
Preparatory School Technician: Mr P Flynn
Preparatory School ICT Coordinator: Mr N Hartley

Before School Care Supervisor: Mrs C Harris
School Support and After School Care Supervisor: Mrs M
Henry
School Support and After School Care Assistants:
Miss E Clinton
Mrs J Eyres
After School Care Assistants:
Miss L Osborne
Mrs M Rees

Administration Staff:
Prep School Secretary: Mrs V Angrave
Prep School Secretary: Mrs K Williams

Pre-Preparatory Department:
Mrs L Bowler, BA Leicester
Miss V Brenner, BA St Martin's College, Lancaster
Mrs J Goodman, BA Birmingham
Mrs D A Kennedy, BEd West Midlands College of Higher
Education

Mrs H Robinson, BEd University of Wales
Mrs H Skidmore, BA Trinity College, Carmarthen

Teaching Assistants:

Mrs R Aulak	Mrs F Green
Miss S Collins	Mrs C Holliday
Mrs J Corbett	Mrs A Knight
Mrs E Cornelius	Mrs J Redden
Mrs H Coulson	Miss A Sanzari
Mrs D Deakin	Mrs P Varma

Before School Care Supervisor: Mrs H Coulson
Before School Care Assistant: Mrs C Holliday

After School Care Supervisor: Mrs R Aulak
After School Care Assistants:
Miss E Clinton
Mrs M Hart
Mrs P Varma

Visiting Staff:

Ballet: Miss D Todd

Farnborough Hill

Farnborough Road, Farnborough, Hampshire GU14 8AT

Tel:	01252 545197
Fax:	01252 513037
email:	admissions@farnborough-hill.org.uk
website:	www.farnborough-hill.org.uk
Twitter:	@FarnboroughHill
Facebook:	@Farnborough-Hill

Motto: *In Domino Labor Vester Non Est Inanis*

Farnborough Hill is a leading independent Catholic day school for 550 girls aged 11 to 18. The school was established in Farnborough in 1889 by The Religious of Christian Education and is now an educational trust. It welcomes girls of all Christian denominations, other faiths or no faith, who are supportive of the ethos. Farnborough Hill is committed to the education of the whole person in a happy, caring Christian community in which each individual is valued.

Academic standards are high with students usually taking ten GCSE subjects and three A Level subjects. The vast majority then go on to Higher Education. The school is a member of Inspiring Futures and there is a well-equipped Careers department and a specialist Careers teacher.

Farnborough Hill offers a wide range of extracurricular activities and is especially renowned for its reputation in music, sport, drama and art.

The school's impressive main house, once the home of Empress Eugenie, has had modern purpose-built facilities added. These include a sports hall, indoor swimming pool, newly refurbished laboratories, drama studio, IT suites, art and design technology centre, a music suite, a chapel, an all-weather hockey pitch and extensive playing fields.

Although within a few minutes' walk of both Farnborough Main and Farnborough North railway stations, the school is situated in 65 acres of parkland and woodland with magnificent views over the Hampshire countryside. Girls come from Hampshire, Surrey and Berkshire with many travelling by train or by school coach.

Admission. Entry is by examination taken in January for the following September.

Scholarships and Bursaries. The school offers academic, music, sports and art and design scholarships and also bursaries for parents who are in need of financial assistance. Academic scholarships are offered for entry at 11+.

One of these is reserved for a Roman Catholic student. In addition music, sport and art and design scholarships are awarded at 11+. Sixth Form scholarships are awarded for academic achievement, excellence in the performing arts, the creative arts and sports. An additional scholarship is awarded by Farnborough Hill Old Girls' Association.

Fees per term (2018–2019). Tuition: £4,932.

Further information. The prospectus is available from the Director of Admissions. The Head is pleased to meet prospective parents by appointment.

Charitable status. The Farnborough Hill Trust is a Registered Charity, number 1039443.

Board of Governors:
Mrs Claire E Hamilton (*Chair*)
Mr Tim J Flesher (*Deputy Chair*)
Mr Mark R Bernard

Mrs Ann Berry	Mrs Julie L Micklethwaite
Dr Cathryn Chadwick	Mrs Gillian Rivers
Mr Chris J Fowler-Tutt	Mrs Margaret Welford
Mr Tony L Grace	Mrs Janet Windeatt
Mr Gerry J McCormack	

Head: **Mrs Alex Neil**, BA Southampton, PGCE Canterbury, MA Oxford Brookes

Deputy Head – Academic: Mrs Zoe Ireland, BA Manchester Met, PGCE Reading
Deputy Head – Pastoral: Miss Pippa Sexton, BA Swansea, PGCE Oxon, MA Herts
Assistant Head – Assessment and Reporting: Mr Peter Forrest-Biggs, MA London, QTS CfBT
Assistant Head – Head of Sixth Form: Mr Craig McCready, BSc PGCE Queen's Belfast

Mr Joseph Adams, BA PGCE Sussex (*Music and Mathematics*)
Mrs Elizabeth Aitchison, BA QTS Chichester (*Physical Education*)
Mr Erik Anders, BA PGCE Reading, MA Royal Holloway (*Drama*)
Miss Denise Andrews, BSc Cardiff, PGCE Homerton (*Biology and Chemistry*)
Mrs Christina Balsom, State Exams Luneburg, Germany (*German*)
Mrs Susan Batt, BSc Glasgow, QTS GTP (*Computing and ICT*)
Mrs Katherine Bell, BA Bristol, PGCE Soton (*History*)
Mrs Denise Brennan, BA, Higher Diploma PGCE Limerick (*Art & Design and Photography*)
Mrs Joanne Brereton, BA Soton, PGCE Reading (*Geography and History*)
Dr Milly Bright, BSc Sierra Leone, MSc PhD Birmingham (*Chemistry*)
Mrs Georgina Brocklehurst, BSc UWIST, PGCE OU (*Mathematics*)
Mrs Olivia Brophy, BSc LSE, PGCE Institute of Education (*English*)
Miss Fionnuala Burke, BA Kent QTS (*French and Spanish*)
Mrs Rosemary Byrne, BA South Glamorgan Institute, Art TCert Goldsmith's College (*Art & Design, Photography*)
Mrs Sarah Campbell, BA Dunelm, PGCE Oxon (*English*)
Mrs Susana Camprubi-Reches, BA Barcelona, MEd Cardiff, PGCE Barcelona (*Spanish*)
Mrs Kim Cappleman, BSc Exeter, QTS GTP (*Mathematics*)
Miss Helen Clutterbuck, BSc PGCE Warwick (*Biology, Chemistry, Physics*)
Mrs Karen Davis, BSc London, PGCE Surrey (*Mathematics*)
Mrs Maria Davy, BA Surrey, PGCE St Mary's (*RE, Philosophy and Ethics*)

Mrs Helen de Mattos, BA PGCE Roehampton, MA Royal Central School of Speech and Drama (*Drama*)

Mrs Beverley Dunnage, BA Birmingham, PGCE Soton (*Geography*)

Mrs Laura J Evans-Jones, BA Royal Holloway, MA PGCE Roehampton (*English*)

Mrs Ludivine Fitzwater, Licence Valenciennes, QTS CiLT (*French*)

Mrs Lesley Gildea, BA PGCE York, MSc Edinburgh (*History*)

Mr Phillip Gillingham, BA Reading, PGCE Bath (*History/ Government & Politics*)

Mrs Anne Goddard, BEd Bath (*Design & Technology*)

Mrs Madeline Greene Lally, BA MSc UCL (*English*)

Mr Simon Haddock, BSc UEA, PGCE Institute of Education (*Psychology*)

Mrs Emily-Jayne Harrison, BA QTS Brighton (*Physical Education*)

Mrs Susie Haynes, BSc Imperial, PGCE Reading (*Chemistry and Physics*)

Mrs Jessica Hocking, BA Exeter, PGCE Surrey (*Mathematics*)

Mrs Lynda Hooper, BSc Liverpool, QTS GTP (*Mathematics*)

Mrs Katja Jackson, BEd Bedford (*Physical Education*)

Mr Andy Johnson, BA UCA (*Art & Design, Graphics*)

Mr Keith Johnson, MA Cantab, DipEd Oxon (*Greek*)

Miss Faye Kelsey, BA QTS St Mary's (*Physical Education*)

Ms Nicole Kirby, BA UCL, MA OU, PGCE Surrey (*English*)

Mrs Victoria Kirby, BSc St Mary's, PGCE Brunel (*Physical Education*)

Ms Carmel Landowski, BA Bangor, QTS (*Classics*)

Mrs Elizabeth Larkin, BA Northumbria, PGCE Reading (*Design &Technology*)

Miss Camilla Lawson, BA W Surrey College of Art and Design (*Art & Design*)

Mr Emanuele Maccherini, BA MA Siena, QTS (*Classic Civilisation and Latin*)

Mrs Sue Macey, BSc UMIST, PGCE Cantab (*Chemistry*)

Mr William Maxwell, BSc Exeter, PGCE Portsmouth (*Mathematics*)

Mrs Vivian McCarthy, BA Cork, PGCE Oxon (*RE, Philosophy & Ethics*)

Mr Matt McCarthy-Brown, BSc PGCE Exeter (*Computing and ICT*)

Mrs Pauline McFadden, BSc, Higher Diploma PGCE Galway (*Computing and ICT, Science*)

Miss Lucy Miller, BA Reading, PGCE UWE (*Business Studies and Economics*)

Mrs Jane Moseley, BSc Surrey QTS (*Mathematics*)

Ms Jacqueline Munnings, BSc Plymouth, PGCE Sussex (*Biology*)

Miss Danni O'Laoire, MA Nottingham, PGCE King's (*Classic Civilisation*)

Mrs Anna Payne, BSc BCHE, PGCE Bristol (*Geography*)

Mrs Claire Peilow, BA Exeter, QTS UEL (*Drama*)

Miss Katriona Pengelley, BA Nottingham, MA PGCE Institute of Education (*Classic Civilisation and History*)

Mrs Joanne Quinlan, BA Luton, PGCE Manchester Met (*Spanish, German and French*)

Dr James Quinnell, BA Winchester, MA PhD Dunelm, PCGE Lancaster (*English*)

Dr Simon Rawle, MA DPhil Oxon, PGCE Kingston (*Physics*)

Miss Hannah Rowsell, BA Exeter, PGCE Oxon (*Geography*)

Mrs Anne Smith, MA PGCE Cantab (*Mathematics*)

Mrs Lynn Storrie, BSc Salford, PGCE Manchester (*Biology*)

Mrs Pippa Sutton, BA PGCE Oxon (*Mathematics*)

Mrs Colleen Swire, BEd St Mary's Belfast (*RE, Philosophy and Ethics*)

Dr Ian Taylor, BA MSt DPhil Oxon (*Music*)

Mr Scott Temple, MChem PGCE Sussex (*Chemistry and Physics*)

Dr Andrew Tytko, BSc PhD Leeds, MA Dunelm PGCE Kingston (*Business Studies and Economics*)

Miss Lucy Warwick, BMus Manchester, Dip ABRSM, PGCE (*Music*)

Mr Ralph Wellington, BA Exeter, PGCE Birmingham (*RE, Philosophy and Ethics*)

Miss Polly White, BA UCL, PGCE King's (*French and Spanish*)

Mrs Lori Winch-Johnson, BA Hertfordshire, MSc PGCE Surrey, CCRS Dip Perf Coach Newcastle (*English, Learning Support Coordinator*)

Dr Christina Wood, BSc Dunelm, DPhil Oxon, GTP Reading (*Physics*)

Mrs Taryn Zimmermann, BA Leeds, PGCE Manchester (*German and Spanish*)

Librarian and Website Manager: Mrs Joanna Wood, MA Cantab, DipLIS London

Matron: Mrs Lucinda Forster-Knight, RGN and Mrs Nicola Condren, RGN

Bursar: Cmdr Mike Robertson, BSc Hons, ACIPD

Director of Admissions: Mrs Clare Duffin, BA Hons, FCIM Chartered Marketer

Chaplain: Mrs Nelle Dalton, BA, MDiv

ICT Coordinator: Mr André Labuschagné

Examinations Officer: Mrs Charlotte Barlow, BA Hons

Gateways School

Harewood, Leeds LS17 9LE

Tel:	0113 288 6345
Fax:	0113 288 6148
email:	gateways@gatewaysschool.co.uk
website:	www.gatewaysschool.co.uk
Twitter:	@Gatewaysschool
Facebook:	@gatewaysschool

Gateways School is an independent school, founded in 1941, located in a delightful rural area on a 20-acre site in Harewood village between Leeds and Harrogate. The Early Years and Prep settings are fully co-educational and the High School is becoming co-educational when it welcomes its first boys into year 7 from September 2019.

The school has international status in recognition of its work in promoting multiculturalism, global issues and internationalism. The school has an active Community Outreach programme which organises several events throughout the year to raise funds for charities supported by the school, while the proactive Environment club, and its commitment to green issues, has contributed to Gateways' ongoing status as a Green Flag school.

The ethos and objectives of Gateways School are to provide, within a structured framework, the opportunities and encouragement for every pupil to achieve his or her personal best. The environment is safe and caring, with outstanding pastoral care. Pupils develop self-confidence, self-discipline and a breadth of interests.

Teaching and Learning. Gateways consistently achieves excellent academic results and its Value Added scores see it placed within the top 10 schools nationally every year. The headline results for the 2018 examination season are as follows:

GCSE

- 57% of all examinations were graded 7 and above. Nationally the figure is just 21%.
- 16% of all examinations were graded at level 9, four times the national average
- 1 in 3 students achieved Grade 7(A) or above in eight or more GCSEs

This data means that in The Telegraph's league table for small independent schools, Gateways is placed at number 7 in the country.

A Level

- 49% of all examinations were graded at A*/A. The national figure is 26%.
- 100% of all examinations were graded A*–E
- 95% of all year 13 students progressed to their 1st or 2nd choice University

This data means that in The Telegraph's league table for small independent schools, Gateways is placed at number 5 in the country.

Gateways consistently achieves such great results because it limits it's class sizes up to the end of Key Stage 3 to the educational optimum range of 14–18 pupils. At GCSE the average number of pupils in a class is reduced to 10 and at A Level it is further reduced to an average of 5. High levels of individual attention result in huge success for all our pupils.

The curriculum at Gateways is broad and challenging and pupils are always encouraged to think for themselves, and to become inquiring and independent learners. A wide range of subjects is offered at GCSE and A Level.

The Stella programme ensures that the most able pupils are challenged and support is available to help individuals with specific learning needs.

Pupils participate in a variety of extra-curricular activities including Drama, Music, Sport, The Duke of Edinburgh's Award scheme, The Archbishop of York Young Leaders Award and Community Outreach.

Facilities. The school has an ongoing programme of development to renew and enhance its facilities. Recent projects include The Terrace Music Suite with recording studio. There is a state-of-the-art Performing Arts Centre, extensive playing fields, tennis courts, well-equipped Sports Hall and Dance Studio, the Cox-Simpson Library and specialist facilities for Science, Mathematics, Languages and Business Studies.

The Gateways Community. The Friends of Gateways and The Old Gatewegians Association both play an active role within the school community.

Location and Transport. Gateways School is set in 22 acres of beautiful parkland in the village of Harewood, just north of Leeds. The former Dower House of the Harewood Estate forms the heart of the School. Gateways is within easy reach of Harrogate, Wetherby, Leeds, Ilkley, Otley and the surrounding villages. A comprehensive school transport service is available.

Scholarships and Bursaries. The school has a programme of Scholarships which are awarded through examination or assessment and interview depending on the type of scholarship applied for. Academic, Sports and Arts (including Music, Drama, Dance and Art & Design) Scholarships are awarded to pupils who demonstrate exceptional ability. In addition, an Exhibition Scholarship is awarded for all-round contribution to school life, high standards across the curriculum and in extra-curricular areas. The value of the Scholarships will be up to a maximum of 25% of the tuition fee.

A limited number of means-tested bursaries are available.

Fees per term (2018–2019). Sixth Form £4,538; High School: £4,538 (Years 9–11), £4,508 (Years 7–8); Prep School: £3,406 (Years 4–6), £3,345 (Year 3), £2,830 (Years

1–2), £2,815 (Reception), Pre-Reception & Nursery fees are available on request. Lunch: Reception to Lower 1 £265 per term, Upper 1 to Sixth Form £280 per term.

Charitable status. Gateways Educational Trust Limited is a Registered Charity, number 529206. It exists to offer a broad education to girls and boys aged 2–18 in an environment where they are encouraged to strive for excellence to achieve their full potential.

Governing Body:
Chairman: Mr R Barr, BA Hons, MSc, MBA
Professor D Hogg, BSc Hons, MSc Hons, DPhil
Mr S Watson, BA
Mrs G Brennan, BA Hons, PGCE
Mr R Webster, BSc Hons, MRICS
Mrs L Atkinson, BA, PGCE
Prof M Brennan, BA Hons, MA, PGCE, DPhil

Senior Staff:

Headmistress: Dr Tracy Johnson, BSc, PhD, PGCE

Deputy Head: Mrs K Titman, MA Ed, BEng, PGCE (*ICT*)
Head of Preparatory School: Mrs H Wallis, BA Hons, QTS TASC
Head of Sixth Form: Mr M Davison, BA Hons, PGCE

Mr C Adegboro, BSc, MSc, PGCE (*Head of Mathematics*)
Miss K Ashurst, BSc Hons, PGCE (*Head of Science, Physics*)
Mrs C Bartle, NNEB (*Head of Early Years*)
Mrs L Braithwaite, BA Hons, PGCE (*Subject Leader of PE*)
Mrs L Brown, BA Hons, PGCE (*Subject Leader of German*)
Mrs M Burns, BA Hons, PGCE (*Head of English*)
Mrs S Crawshaw, BA Hons, MA, PGCE (*Subject Leader of Art*)
Miss F Feeney, BA Hons, PGCE, PG Cert SENCO, TEFL, CCET, CPT3A (*Head of Learning Support*)
Mr I Lenihan, BA Hons, MA, PGCE (*Director of Music*)
Mr D Reeves, BA Hons, PGCE (*Subject Leader of Religious Studies*)
Mr S Scholfield, BA Hons (*Head of Prep Games & PE*)
Mrs F Wilson, BA Hons, PGCE (*Head of MFL, Leader of Teaching & Learning*)
Mrs K Wilson, BA Hons, MA (*Head of Drama*)
Mrs L Wood, BSc Hons, PGCE (*Designated Safeguarding Lead & Child Protection Officer*)

Finance Director: Mr J Halliday, ACA
Registrar: Miss F Sellars
School Nurse: Mrs D White, RGN

Haberdashers' Aske's School for Girls

Aldenham Road, Elstree, Herts WD6 3BT

Tel:	020 8266 2300
Fax:	020 8266 2303
email:	theschool@habsgirls.org.uk
website:	www.habsgirls.org.uk

Motto: *Serve and Obey*

This School forms part of the ancient foundation of Robert Aske and is governed by members of the Worshipful Company of Haberdashers, together with certain representatives of other bodies.

Haberdashers' Aske's School for Girls is situated on a site of over 50 acres, and has an excellent reputation for academic, sporting and musical achievements. Entry to the Junior School is at 4+ or at 7+; and to the Senior School, at 11+ and Sixth Form. The academic results are outstanding, a reflection of able pupils who enjoy learning and thrive on a full and challenging curriculum.

Facilities are first-class with a brand new Dining Room, Performance Space and Learning Resources Centre and a very wide range of extra-curricular activities. Sport, music, drama, art and debating thrive and there are many other opportunities for leadership within the school community including the Duke of Edinburgh's Award scheme, the Community Sports Leadership Award and a very active community service programme. Life at Habs is busy and challenging, embracing new technology, for example, digital language labs, touchscreen interactive whiteboards and remote access to all electronic work areas via the intranet, alongside old traditions, which include the celebration of St Catherine's Day as patron of the Haberdashers' Company. Work has begun on the creation of a new STEM hub and new Drama Studio, both opening in Spring 2019.

Over 110 coach routes, shared with the Haberdashers' Aske's Boys' School next door, bring pupils to school from a thirty-mile radius covering north London, Hertfordshire and Middlesex. The provision of a late coach service ensures that pupils can take part safely in the wide range of the many clubs and societies organised after school. The St Catherine Parents' Guild, the school's parents' association, provides enormous support to the school through fundraising and social events.

Junior School. There are approximately 325 day pupils in the Junior School, with two parallel classes from Reception to Year 6.

Pastoral Care: Class teachers and Learning Support assistants maintain close contact with pupils and their parents. It is very important that our pupils feel happy and comfortable. Every adult has a responsibility for the pupils' welfare and security and there are many layers of care in place. From the outset, through the behaviour code, pupils are encouraged to be friendly, polite and caring to everyone else in the community, whether adults or children, and there is strong peer support. There are two nurses, a counsellor and two individual needs specialists, all of whom are able to provide support and to ensure each pupil understands her unique importance in the school community. Where appropriate, older pupils have responsibility for younger ones and Senior School Sixth Formers regularly help Juniors in the classroom. A programme of PSHE (personal, social and health education lessons) covers important issues of self-development and allows pupils to reflect on their responsibilities to each other and the wider community. Many parents are involved in the classroom, clubs and outings.

Spiritual and Moral Education: Habs is a school with a Christian tradition which welcomes the rich diversity of faiths within the community. Assemblies are held for the whole school twice a week and on other days are separate for Key Stage One and Key Stage Two. Values, themes, stories and reflections are drawn from a range of sources including cultures, traditions and faiths. Once a year selected classes perform an assembly to which their parents are invited. Parents are also very welcome to attend assemblies on major occasions such as St Catherine's Day and are often invited to speak to the pupils in assemblies on an area of their expertise or experience relevant to the pupils. Pupils also take part in many charitable ventures throughout the year, raising money and enhancing their awareness of lives in the wider world.

Enrichment: There is a wide range of over 30 clubs covering our pupils' interests in sport, music, arts and crafts, languages, science, maths, creative writing, reading, games and puzzles, cookery and gardening. Visits linked to the curriculum are arranged for every class and there are regular visitors to school such as theatre companies, historical re-creations, authors, illustrators, musicians and scientists. Joint events with the Boys' School occur at intervals throughout the year for the different age groups.

Sport: We have first-class sports facilities, including a sports hall, gymnasia, netball and tennis courts, a swimming pool and ample playing fields. The curriculum provides a core of gymnastics, dance, swimming, netball, tennis, athletics and rounders. Teams in netball, cricket, football, gymnastics, rounders and pop lacrosse compete against other schools.

Performance Arts: Concerts and drama productions are a major part of school life, showcasing the wide range of creative talent amongst our pupils. Our Performance Space provides many opportunities to explore and extend their interests in the performance arts. There are two major drama productions annually: an Infant production for all those in Reception and Key Stage One, and a dramatic production for Year 6. The annual Spring Concert showcases all the musical groups and ensembles as well as a massed choir of all Key Stage Two pupils. The summer Chamber Concert features performances from many of our musical ensembles. Informal lunchtime concerts occur at least once a term for Year 4 to 6 soloists or duets. Our pupils' own art and design work is displayed around the school.

Curriculum: There is a broad and challenging curriculum with the provision of opportunities for outdoor, active and independent learning, with plenty of practical tasks and problem solving, to enable pupils to develop their bright young minds. Fun is a vital ingredient. There are curriculum evenings for parents to learn about the school's approach to particular subject areas and how they can best support their daughters at home and work in true partnership with the school.

The Early Learning Goals of the Foundation Stage are met through a balance of child-initiated opportunities and teacher-led activities. There is a daily range of stimulating, play-based activities which prompts pupils to ask questions, to discover, to wonder and to learn new skills. No homework is set in Reception or Year 1 so that pupils can enjoy the precious childhood pleasures of imaginative play and being read to by a parent when they get home. Music, French and daily PE lessons are taught by specialist teachers. Phonics teaching enables pupils to make rapid progress with reading and to gain an easy independence in their writing, while the foundations of mathematical thinking are laid through carefully selected practical tasks.

Extensive use is made of IT throughout the Junior School, with a dedicated IT Suite enabling an exciting Computing curriculum, including coding and robotics. In addition, each pupil has an iPad which she can use in class under the supervision of the teacher. The use of mobile technology is not meant to replace traditional learning but to supplement and enhance it and, in some cases, to open up whole new ways of learning for the pupils.

Creativity is fostered in music and dance, in art, design technology, literacy activities, drama and role play. The school grounds provide a rich environment for building knowledge about the world of nature as well as space to develop physical skills and pupils spend one afternoon a week in our on-site Forest School.

At Key Stage One, curriculum subjects are English, mathematics, science, history, geography, religious studies, French, Spanish, ICT, art, design technology, music, PSHE and physical education, including swimming. Fostering a love of reading is paramount. A little homework is introduced in Year 2.

As pupils progress through Key Stage Two they encounter more subject specialists. Science lessons, which are taught in the well-equipped laboratory, strongly feature practical and investigative work. The Art Room is a magnificent space for the creation of stunning works of art, while pupils can feel transported to another culture as soon as they step into the Languages Room and they are introduced to German for the first time.

Senior School. There are approximately 870 day students aged 11–18 in the Senior School.

Pastoral Care: In such a big and busy school, care for each individual is deeply important so that all can flourish and fulfil themselves in every way. Looking after them is a pastoral team consisting of the Deputy Head, Heads of Section, Form Tutors, a School Nurse, a Counsellor and an Individual Needs Specialist. The provision of pastoral care is designed to help students make decisions and to care about others within the framework of a very diverse community. There is an outstanding range of opportunities for their personal development and to help them consolidate a system of spiritual beliefs and a moral code. The welfare of students is of paramount importance and it is the responsibility of all members of staff, teaching and support staff, to safeguard and promote this. From the moment a student joins the school, emphasis is placed on the partnership with parents so that, hand-in-hand, school and parents can support each child, operating on a basis of trust and with people she knows from the start.

Spiritual and Moral Education: Haberdashers' is a school with a Christian tradition which welcomes the rich diversity of faiths within the community. Every day begins with the whole school meeting in an assembly or House meeting to reinforce the school's values and its sense of community. These meetings are often led by the students themselves. Once a week there are separate faith assemblies: Christian, Hindu, Jain and Sikh, Humanist, Jewish or Muslim. Students can choose which one they attend. Holy Communion takes place twice a term. Roman Catholic Mass is celebrated each half term, either in the Girls' or the Boys' School. Students may pray at lunchtime in a room set aside for them to do so. Students organise and run many charitable events within their Houses throughout the year. This enhances their awareness of the wider world as well as raising funds for charities small and large, at home and abroad.

Enrichment: There is a wide range of clubs on offer in the Senior School, including art, creative writing, cricket, dance, debating, design technology, drama, football, maths, philosophy, science, and swimming; there are also campaigning groups such as Amnesty International and the Animal Welfare Society. Trips and visits include a Year 7 adventure holiday and various trips abroad, with language exchanges, work experience, and study visits. Subject specific trips in the UK and abroad include field trips, theatre visits, trips to sites of historical importance, museums and art galleries, music and sports tours.

Sport and Performance Arts: The core curriculum includes gymnastics, dance, swimming, lacrosse, netball, tennis, athletics and rounders. For older students, there are additional options in self-defence, basketball, volleyball, football, step-aerobics, trampolining, badminton, weight-training, judo, life-saving, synchronised swimming, water polo, golf and squash. There are clubs in a range of sports for recreational enjoyment as well as for the teams. There are major drama productions in all sections of the school and symphonic concerts showcasing a variety of ensembles including three orchestras, wind and jazz bands, percussion groups, flute choirs, and rock bands as well as recitals and chamber concerts. There are annual Drama and Music Festivals; occasionally, there are joint productions and orchestral concerts with the Boys' School. Students' painting, sculpture and design installations are displayed around the school.

Opportunities for leadership and challenge are valued and encouraged. Activities include: The Duke of Edinburgh's Award; Tall Ships; Community Service; Community Sports Leader's Award; European Youth Parliament; Model United Nations; English Speaking Union; and the Oxford Union.

Curriculum: The school follows its own wide-ranging academic curriculum tailored to the needs of its very able pupils. It preserves the best of a traditional education whilst responding positively to curricular developments. Much emphasis is placed on developing the students' ability to think and learn independently, nurturing an intellectual resilience and self confidence which will prepare them for the world beyond school. In all subjects, the curriculum aims to be something that inspires the students and stimulates discussion and ideas. A high value is placed upon creativity, imagination and the opportunity to pursue topics beyond the confines of the exam specifications. The school is not required to follow the National Curriculum but draws upon the best practice of what is happening nationally and in other schools. In the first three years of the Senior School, students follow a set curriculum, studying French, Spanish and German on a carousel and then choosing two to continue with into Year 8. As they progress through the school they are given greater choice and the opportunity to personalise their curriculum to suit their needs and interests. Thus the GCSE curriculum has space for up to four optional subjects. In the Sixth Form the girls have a free choice of subjects from the 23 subjects on offer. At each level, the curriculum is designed to prepare them for the opportunities, responsibilities and experiences of the next stage of their education and their lives.

Fees per term (2018–2019). Senior School £6,131; Junior School £5,660. A number of scholarships are awarded annually and means-tested financial assistance (up to full fees) is also available for students entering at 11+ or 16+.

Charitable status. The Haberdashers' Aske's Charity is a Registered Charity, number 313996. It exists to promote education.

Clerk to the School Governors: Mr C M Bremner

Headmistress: Miss B A O'Connor, MA Oxon

Personal Assistant to the Headmistress: Mrs B Cohen

Senior Deputy Head: Mr Robert James-Robbins, BA London
Deputy Head (Pastoral): Mrs L Winton, BA Manchester
Deputy Head (Academic): Dr F Miles, BA Cantab

Director of Finance and Operations: Mr D Thompson, BA Manchester, ACIB

Assistant Heads:
Mrs R Davies, BA Cardiff (*Head of Sixth Form*)
Mr A Doe, BA Oxon (*Acting Head of Middle School*)
Mr D Thakerar, BA London (*Acting Head of Upper School*)
Mrs S Wright, MA Cantab (*Acting Head of the Junior School*)
Miss G Mellor, BA Exeter (*Director of Wellbeing*)
Mrs S Ashton, BSc Keele (*Staff Development*)
Mr D Sabato, BA Nottingham (*Pupil Experience, Teaching & Learning*)
Mr T Scott, MA Cantab (*Development & Marketing*)
Mr E Stock, MPhys Oxon (*Director of E-Learning*)
Mr S Turner, BSc Brunel (*Pupil Experience, Extracurricular*)

Head of Careers and Higher Education: Mrs L Mee, BSc London

Library:
Miss F Hackett, BA Loughborough

Teaching Staff:
* *Head of Department*

Art:
*Miss K Shaw, BA Manchester
Mrs S Deamer, BA Manchester
Mrs D Hobbs, BA Lancaster
Mrs S Wiseman, MA London

Classics:
* Miss A Dugdale, MA Oxon
Mr M Barr, BA Cantab
Mrs E Bowyer, BA Cantab
Miss E Desmond, BA Nottingham
Mr A Doe, BA Oxon
Dr G Brunetta, MA Udine
Mrs R Pittard, BA Cantab

Design and Technology:
*Mr M Squire, BSc South Bank
Miss C Marshall, BA Portsmouth
Mr J Oliver, BA Warwick
Mr S Turner, BSc Brunel

Drama:
*Ms L Wallace, BA London
Ms E Bridgeman-Williams, BA Middlesex

Economics:
*Mrs K Healer, MEd Cantab
Mr R Henry, BA Galway

English:
*Miss I Condon, BA Manchester
Miss Z Bowie, MA London
Mrs F Graves, MA Leicester
Miss S Innocenti, BA London
Mrs L Jeffcock, BA Oxford Brookes
Mrs A Leifer, BA Birmingham
Dr F Miles, BA Cantab
Mrs K Nash, MA Cantab
Mr D Thakerar, BA London
Ms S Walton, BA Oxon
Mrs L Winton, BA Manchester

Geography:
*Miss S Nanji, BA London
Mrs S Ashton, BSc Keele
Miss E Hargreaves, BSc Exeter
Mrs M McCarthy, BA London
Mrs C Needham, BSc Loughborough
Miss H Wakefield, MSc Loughborough

History:
*Mr R Yarlett, BA Leicester
Mr K Davies, MA London
Mrs R Davies, BA Cardiff
Miss A Efstathiou, LLB Cardiff
Mr P Harper, MA Oxon
Mr D Heyman, BA Oxon
Ms L Mesrie, BA Birmingham
Mr D Sabato, BA Nottingham
Mrs C Wilding, BA Bristol

Individual Educational Needs:
Ms A Baker, BA Oxford Brookes

IT:
Mr A Mahmoud, MSc South Bank
Miss C Wright, BSc Pennsylvania

Mathematics:
*Mr C Howlett, BSc Dunelm
Mrs I Barrett, BSc Manchester
Miss L Chelliah, BSc Kent

Mr T Doherty, BSc Newcastle
Mrs N Gohil, BEng Aston
Mrs R Gourdin, MSc Leeds
Mrs S Lee, BSc Manchester
Mrs V Lees, BSc Cardiff
Mrs G Malik, BSc Herts
Mrs L Mee, BSc London
Mrs R Patel, BSc London
Mrs S Patel, BSc London
Mr N Salter Perez, BA Oxon
Mrs R Sandu, BSc Bucharest
Mrs L Woodville, BSc York

Modern Languages:
*Mrs I Fanning, MA London (*Spanish*)
Sr J Carbonell, MA London
Ms C Fenn, BA Edinburgh (* *French*)
Frau E Green, BA Oxon
Miss C Janin, BA Reims
Miss G Mellor, BA Exeter
Mme H Robinson, BA Cantab
Sra M Salvatierra-Romero, BA Seville, Spain
M M Smeaton, BA Leeds
Frau A Tebb, BA Oxon (*German*)
Miss H Terretta, BA Bristol
Ms K Ting, BA Taiwan

Music:
*Mr A Phillips, MMus London
Miss C Turner, BMus Manchester (*Assistant Director of Music*)
Mr D Davies, BA Keele
Mr T Scott, MA Cantab
Ms A Turnbull, LRAM
and 25 visiting teachers

Physical Education:
*Miss N Garvey, BA Leeds
*Miss T Dawson, BEd Greewich
Miss H Millns, BSc Leeds Beckett
Miss L Scott, BSc Exeter
Miss L Watts, BA Leeds
Miss C Wright, BSc Pennsylvania
Ms E Wright, MEd Mary Washington, USA

Politics:
*Mrs C Wilding, BA Bristol

PSHCE:
*Mr D Davies, BA Keele

Psychology:
*Mrs L Woodville, BSc York

Religion and Philosophy:
*Mrs K Opie, MA London (*Deputy Head of Sixth Form*)
Ms L Childs, BA Manchester
Mrs S Evans, MA Oxon
Miss A Walker, BA Durham

Science:
*Miss N Percy, BSc Leeds (*Director of STEM*)
Miss S Adat, BSc Nottingham
Dr K Bridge, BSc Loughborough (*Physics*)
Dr H Burgess, MA Cantab
Mrs Dabby-Joory, BSc Southampton
Miss E Dinsey, BSc London
Mr P Duddles, BEng Warwick
Miss E Frankel, BSc Nottingham
Mrs N Ghinn, BSc Nottingham
Mrs L Gupta, LLB Keele
Dr J Harvey-Barrett, BSc Newcastle (*Biology*)
Miss R Lane, BA Cantab
Miss L Lilley, BSc Durham
Mrs Z Makepeace-Welsh, MA Oxon
Dr M Mirza, BSc Brunel

Mrs C Press, BSc Leeds
Dr C Ruddick, BSc Exeter
Mr C Shaw, BSc London (*Chemistry*)
Mr R Shopland, BA Exeter
Ms M Smith, MPH Nottingham
Mr E Stock, MPhys Oxon

Junior School:
Acting Head: Mrs S Wright, MA Cantab
Acting Deputy Head: Mrs L Patel, BSc Middlesex
Miss C Chapman, BA East Anglia
Mrs S Collins, MA Kingston (*ICT Specialist*)
Mrs E Davies, BA Brighton (*Individual Needs*)
Mrs K Ede, BA Bournemouth
Mrs L Flynn, BSc Southampton
Miss E Galvin, BA Warwick
Mrs C Gibson, BSc Worcester
Mrs L Gill, BA London
Mrs S Hayes, BA Durham
Mr N Hobley, BSc Oxford Brookes
Miss K Keith, BA Bournemouth
Mrs L Liddelow, BEd Exeter
Mrs A Mack, BEd Brighton
Mrs E Miller, BA Hertfordshire
Mrs J Millman, BEd Leeds
Mr M Mitcham, BA London (*MFL Specialist*)
Mrs J Nicholas, BA Newcastle
Miss R Nutkins, BA Exeter
Mrs S Odysseos, BA Birmingham
Mrs F Pick, BEd West of England
Mrs C Prendergast, BA Brighton
Miss L Ryan, BA Brighton
Mrs C Sawkins, BA Surrey
Mrs S Summers, BA Manchester (*Individual Needs*)
Mrs M Tatman, BA Hertfordshire
Ms S Tersigni, BA Middlesex
Mrs J Whiteley, BMus Sheffield

Harrogate Ladies' College

Clarence Drive, Harrogate, North Yorkshire HG1 2QG

Tel: 01423 504543
email: admissions@hlc.org.uk
website: www.hlc.org.uk

Harrogate Ladies' College is a Boarding and Day school for 300 girls aged 11–18. Situated within the College campus, Highfield Pre School is a Pre School for over 70 boys and girls between the ages of 2–4. Highfield Prep School, which opened in 1999, is a Day Prep school for over 200 boys and girls between the ages of 4–11.

Location. The College is situated in a quiet residential area on the Duchy Estate about 5 minutes' walk from the town centre and is easily accessible by road and rail networks. Leeds/Bradford airport is 20 minutes' drive away. Harrogate itself is surrounded by areas of natural interest and beauty.

Accommodation. Approximately half of the pupils are full boarders. Houses are arranged vertically with mixed age groups from Year 7 to Year 12. Year 13 pupils enjoy a greater sense of independence in their own accommodation called Tower House. This contains a large, modern kitchen, comfortable lounges and relaxation areas and girls have individual study-bedrooms. Each house has a Housemistress and Assistant Housemistress who are responsible for the well-being of the girls. There is a well-equipped Health Centre with qualified nurses.

Curriculum and Examinations. The College aims to provide a broad-based curriculum for the first three years in line with National Curriculum requirements. This leads to a choice of over 28 subjects at GCSE, IGCSE and A Level. Each girl has a form tutor who continuously monitors and assesses her development.

Facilities. The central building contains the main classrooms, hall, library, and dining rooms, and a Sixth Form Centre with studies, seminar rooms, kitchens and leisure facilities. The College Chapel is nearby. An extension provides 8 laboratories for Physics, Chemistry, Biology and Computer Studies. Three dedicated computer suites, provision in the boarding houses and throughout the school, form an extensive computer network. Sixth Formers have network access using their own laptops from studies and bedrooms. Additional facilities for specialised teaching include Art, Textiles, Photography, Design and Technology, Drama and Home Economics/Food Technology.

Our award winning Business School is where girls are able to enjoy the academic study of Economics, Business Studies and Psychology in a state-of-the-art business-like environment which helps prepare young women of today for the global world of tomorrow.

Sport. The College has its own sports hall, a full size indoor swimming pool, gymnasium, fitness centre, playing field, netball courts, 9 tennis courts and 2 squash courts. Girls are taught a wide range of sports and may participate in sporting activities outside the school day. Lacrosse and netball are played in winter, and tennis, rounders, swimming and athletics are the main summer physical activities. Extracurricular sports include badminton, basketball, fencing, golf, horse riding and gymnastics.

Sixth Form. The College has a thriving Sixth Form Community of 140 pupils. Girls have a choice of 26 courses at A Level. There is a broad range of general cultural study. In preparation for adult life, Sixth Formers are expected to make a mature contribution to the running of the school and many hold formal positions of responsibility. Personal guidance is given to each girl with regard to her future plans and most pupils choose to continue their education at University.

Religious Affiliation. The College is Christian although pupils of other religious denominations are welcomed. We focus on inclusion, mutual respect and understanding of people of all faiths and of no faith.

Music. A special feature is the interest given to music and choral work both in concerts and in the College Chapel, and the girls attend frequent concerts and dramatic performances in Harrogate. There are Junior and Senior choirs, orchestra, string, wind and brass groups.

Scholarships. Academic, Art, Textiles, Music, Choral, Drama and Sport scholarships are available.

Fees per term (2018–2019). Boarding £9,705–£12,170; Day £5,345. Fee remissions are available for girls with a sibling at Harrogate Ladies' College or at Highfield Prep School.

Entry. Entry is usually at age 11, 13 or at Sixth Form level. Entry is based on the College's own entrance examination and a school report. Sixth Form entry is conditional upon GCSE achievement and an interview with the Principal.

Charitable status. Harrogate Ladies' College Limited is a Registered Charity, number 529579. It exists to provide high-quality education for girls.

Chair of Governors: Dame Francine Holroyd

Principal: **Mrs Sylvia Brett**, MA London, BA Dunelm

Director of Finance: Miss Rebecca Henriksen, MA Edinburgh, ACA
Director of Admissions and Marketing: Mrs Sarah Bowman, MSc Stirling, BA UWE
Head of Highfield: Mr James Savile, BEd Southampton

Deputy Head Academic, Senior Resident: Miss Claire
Preece, BSc Manchester, MA OU
Deputy Head Pastoral and Boarding: Mrs Sarah Parker,
MA Oxon
Assistant Head, Head of Lower School: Mrs Joanna Griffin,
BA Bristol
Assistant Head, Head of Middle School: Mrs Fran Irvine,
BEd Bedford
Assistant Head, Head of Sixth Form: Dr Rebecca Ashcroft,
BA PhD Huddersfield

Headington School

Oxford, Oxfordshire OX3 7TD

Tel: 01865 759100
           Admissions: 01865 759 861/113
Fax: 01865 760268
email: admissions@headington.org
website: www.headington.org
Twitter: @HeadingtonSch
Facebook: @HeadingtonSchool

Headington is a highly successful day and boarding
school in Oxford for 832 girls aged 11–18 with a Preparatory School for 252 girls aged 3–11 occupying its own site
just across the road. (*See Headington Preparatory School
entry in IAPS section.*)

The school offers girls from Nursery to Sixth Form an
unrivalled opportunity to pursue academic, sporting and
artistic excellence in a caring and nurturing environment.

Founded in 1915 and set in 23 acres of playing fields and
gardens, our superb facilities provide the perfect backdrop
for teaching and learning that extends way beyond the classroom and curriculum. We encourage participation in all
aspects of sport and culture, teamwork and leadership, challenging girls to discover and explore their own potential and
achieve more than they thought possible.

Consistently in the premier league of academic schools in
the UK, life at Headington is about much more than exam
results. Through the sheer breadth of subjects and activities
at Headington and the option to study for the International
Baccalaureate, we aim to educate the complete individual,
giving girls the confidence and self-awareness to compete,
contribute and succeed at school, university and in their
adult lives.

Facilities. Headington offers a superb range of facilities
to day girls and boarders to support and enhance their learning. Our Music School has superb acoustics, along with
teaching rooms, a recording studio and electronics studio.
The 240-seat Theatre, run by a professional team who provide expertise in set design, lighting and sound design, is
home to the School's Drama Department. The Art School
includes four art studios and a photography darkroom. Our
Dance and Fitness Centre benefits from a fully-equipped
gym, training rooms and a large dance studio. Other sports
facilities include a floodlit all-weather pitch, sports hall and
25m indoor swimming pool. In 2016, the School opened its
state-of-the-art Library, complete with 'sonic chairs' where
girls can listen to music, lectures or vocabulary without
speakers and without disturbing their neighbours and interactive tables for group working. An extended and refurbished Sixth Form Centre is due to open in early 2019.

Curriculum. In Years 7 and 8 girls are taught in four
classes of around 20 each, which increases to six slightly
smaller classes in U4 after 13+ entry. They study Art, Biology, Chemistry, Computing, Dance, Drama, English, Fashion and Textile Design, Food and Nutrition, French, Spanish
and German (there is an introduction to all three languages

in the Year 7 and then girls choose two of these languages to
continue in Year 8), Games, Geography, History, Latin,
Mathematics, Music, Physical Education, Physics, Religious Studies. By Year 9 they choose two subjects from Art,
Dance, Drama, Fashion & Textile Design and Music. Most
girls study ten GCSE or IGCSE subjects, with eight core
subjects plus two chosen from a list of 17 others. The majority of students move into the Sixth Form from the Middle
School and many new girls, both day and boarders, also join
us at this stage. Headington offers both A Levels and the
International Baccalaureate Diploma in the Sixth Form.

Physical Education. From Olympic rowers to recreational dancers, Headington offers a genuinely inclusive
approach to PE and extracurricular sport and encourages
each girl to enjoy sport at the level that suits her. PE is taught
throughout the school and many girls choose to study PE to
GCSE. They can choose from more than 30 different sporting activities, from Dance and Fencing to Equestrian and
Trampolining. Games such as Hockey, Netball and Athletics
are played competitively against other schools and girls
have the chance to represent the school across a range of
abilities. More than 70 girls currently compete at county
level and beyond and the School enjoys national success in a
wide range of sports. Our rowers compete at the very highest level, with the school consistently triumphing at the
National Schools' Regatta. More than 150 of our girls row
and regularly go on to represent Great Britain at international competitions.

Music. At Headington every girl has the opportunity to
enjoy music both within the curriculum and beyond. Five
hundred individual music lessons take place each week and
28 visiting teachers offer girls the opportunity to learn a
wide range of instruments. The Senior School has numerous
orchestras, choirs and ensembles, varying from those for
which there are no auditions to the exceptional Chamber
Choir, which has made numerous recordings and toured
overseas.

Drama. The 240-seat Theatre is home to a thriving
Drama Department. There is a busy programme of productions each year and girls of all ages become involved in all
aspects of theatre, from writing and producing their own
plays, to lighting, costume and make-up. As well as a curriculum subject lower down the School, Drama is an option at
GCSE, A Level, or as part of the International Baccalaureate. Many girls also elect to take private Guildhall Speech
and Drama exams in school.

Dance. At Headington the state-of-the-art Dance facilities provide a multitude of opportunities for every girl.
Dance is part of the curriculum in the Lower School and a
Games option throughout the School. The Dance Department was established in 2015 and outside the classroom
there is a huge range of dance options, from Ballet to Street
Dance and Contemporary. As well as annual Dance Shows,
the Headington Dance Company competes in local and
national competitions.

Extracurricular activities. More than 50 extracurricular
activities take place every week during lunchtime, before
and after school. A wide choice of subjects, sports, interests
and hobbies ranges from The Duke of Edinburgh's Award
and Drama to Astronomy and Young Enterprise and
includes such diverse pastimes as debating and colouring for
mindfulness. Headington has a very successful Combined
Cadet Force, with around 60 cadets from L5 and above in
our Army detachment.

Higher Education and Careers. Whether they have
chosen to study for A Levels or the International Baccalaureate Diploma, girls continue to higher education, heading
to leading universities in the UK and abroad or to competitive school leaver programmes. A significant number of
girls choose Oxbridge each year; some head for medical or

veterinary college and others take up Art Foundation courses. Girls graduate from a wide range of arts and science degrees in subjects as diverse as civil engineering, architecture, classics and natural sciences. Detailed assistance on choice of universities is given in the Sixth Form along with special programmes for Medicine, Veterinary Science, Oxbridge, Law and Architecture. A careers programme is in place throughout the School.

Boarding. Headington has always been a boarding school and just over a quarter of the school – around 200 girls – board with us today. The five boarding houses provide the girls with a 'home from home' where, supported by a team of highly experienced staff, they learn to develop into mature and independent young people. Many of our boarders come from the UK and we are also very proud of our international boarding community, made up of more than 30 nationalities from all over the world. There is a choice of flexible boarding options for girls aged eleven and upwards with full, weekly and half-weekly boarding all on offer.

Entrance. The main entry points to the Senior School are at 11+, 13+ or, for the Sixth Form, 16+. Girls are occasionally able to join at other ages if places become available. Girls enter the school at 11+ via our own examination day and interview in December. Girls at UK prep schools sit the ISEB pre-tests in Year 6 or 7 for entrance at 13+, then Common Entrance in Year 8. Other 13+ candidates sit the School's own examination papers in Year 8. Sixth Form entrance examinations and interviews are held in the November before the proposed year of entry and include a general entrance paper and a critical thinking skills assessment.

Our registration fees for the Prep School are £95 (UK) and £150 (overseas based families) and for the Senior School are £125 (UK) and £250 (overseas based families). For information about admissions, please check our website, www.headington.org, or contact our friendly admissions team who will be happy to help.

Fees per term (2018–2019). Senior School: Full Boarders: £11,628–£12,762; Weekly Boarders: £10,122–£11,122; Half-Weekly Boarders: £8,005–£8,788; Day Girls: £5,884–£6,417.

Scholarships and Bursaries. Scholarships are awarded for academic achievement, art, dance, drama, music and sport. These awards recognise talent and achievement and most do not provide any fee reduction or financial reward, although there are a small number of special academic and music scholarships available to the highest achieving candidates at 11+, 13+ and 16+ entry. The Headington Access Programme (HAP) supports talented girls who would benefit from all that the School has to offer but who may not be able to access a Headington education without some form of financial assistance. Means-tested bursaries of up to 100 per cent of fees are available for local day girls who achieve high marks in our entrance examinations and are awarded at 11+, 13+ and in the Sixth Form.

Charitable status. Headington School Oxford Limited is a Registered Charity, number 309678. It exists to provide quality education for girls.

Governing Council:
Chair of Governors: Mrs Sandra Phipkin ACA
Vice Chair of Governors: Miss Margaret Rudland, BSc
Dr Susan Burge, OBE, BSc, BM, DM, FRCP
Professor Katya Drummond, MA Oxon, PhD
Mr Steven Harris, BSc, ACA
Lady Nancy Kenny, BA, PGCE
Mrs Penelope Lenon, BA Hons
The Revd Darren McFarland, BA Hons, BTh
Miss Bryony Moore, MBA
Mrs Carol Oster Warriner, MA Oxon

Dr Kate Ringham, BA Hons, PhD
Mrs Sallie Salvidant, Cert Ed, BEd Hons
Mr Stephen Shipperley

Company Secretary: Mr Richard Couzens, MBE, MA Cranfield

Clerk to the Council: Miss Emma Saville

Headmistress: Mrs C Jordan, MA Oxon

Head of Prep: Mrs J Crouch, BA Keele, MA London, NPQH
First Deputy Head (Academic): Dr J Jefferies, BSc, PhD Exeter
Second Deputy Head (Staff, Admissions & Marketing): Mrs C Knight, BSc Strathclyde
Deputy Head (Co-curricular): Mr S Hawkes, BA Brunel
Deputy Head (Pastoral): Miss A Proctor, BA Oxon, MSc Dunelm
Bursar: Mr R Couzens, MBE, MA Cranfield

Heathfield School
Ascot

London Road, Ascot, Berkshire SL5 8BQ

Tel: 01344 898343
Fax: 01344 890689
email: registrar@heathfieldschool.net
website: www.heathfieldschool.net
Twitter: @HeathfieldAscot
Facebook: @HeathfieldSchool
LinkedIn: /heathfield-school

Introduction. Pioneering high standards in girls' education since 1899, the boarding and day school provides outstanding education for girls in beautiful surroundings less than an hour from London in the heart of Berkshire near the world-famous Ascot Racecourse.

The school combines exemplary standards of pastoral care with a personalised academic curriculum which adds value to every girl's achievements to provide a holistic education for girls aged 11–18.

Not only is Heathfield firmly on the academic map but it also produces county and national sportswomen and talented artists, photographers, actors, musicians and dancers.

Heathfield is headed by Oxford English Language and Literature graduate Mrs Marina Gardiner Legge, previously the school's Director of Studies, who is dedicated to excellence in all areas of the school under her leadership. Mrs Gardiner Legge was appointed Head in September 2016.

In 2016, the school also boosted its growing reputation for the STEM (Science Technology Engineering and Maths) subjects with the completion of a state of the art STEM facility, officially opened by Lord Robert Winston.

Atmosphere and Ethos. The school's aim is to help every student get the most out of life by providing the very best intellectual stimulation, physical challenges and pastoral care. The school is founded on Church of England principles but welcomes all faiths.

Pastoral Care. Heathfield's strength is in its size meaning each girl is supported throughout her school career and can never slip under the radar. Pupils are overseen by a dedicated team of academic staff, Housemistresses, Heads of House and prefects. They work together to provide the highest level of pastoral care. Teachers will meet with your daughter regularly to discuss her particular needs and to ensure she is achieving her maximum potential.

Curriculum. Heathfield offers variety in terms of the subjects on offer as well as fundamental excellence in all the traditional subjects. At A Level, girls can choose from twenty-four subjects plus EPQ (Extended Project Qualific-aiton). Extras such as the Leiths Basic Certificate in Food and Wine and the Duke of Edinburgh's Award are also offered. The school is famous for its excellence in the creative arts and enjoys a unique link with the University of the Arts, London. It has also won a record five Good Schools Guide awards for Art and Design Photography at A Level.

Activities. The St Mary's Theatre and the Sports Hall are always hives of activity and there are many other co-curricular activities: frequent museum and theatre trips, field trips and overseas visits.

Sport. Heathfield's outstanding facilities include a large multi-purpose sports hall, a dance studio, five lacrosse pitches, six tennis/netball courts and a 25m indoor heated swimming pool. The school competes successfully at lacrosse, netball, swimming, rounders, athletics and various equestrian disciplines including polo. Girls have represented the school regionally, nationally and internationally in a variety of sports.

Boarding Accommodation. Boarding accommodation is first-class. From Form IV onwards, all girls have single rooms. For more freedom and independence, the Upper Sixth live in Wyatt House which contains two fully-equipped kitchens and areas in which to study and socialise.

Medical Welfare. Three nursing sisters and the school doctor are in charge of the girls' medical welfare, supported by Heads of House, Housemistresses and Tutors. The Heads of House or Housemistresses are available at all times for any parental concerns.

New Facilities. A state-of-the-art STEM (Science, Technology, Engineering and Maths) block opened in January 2016 and a digital recording studio opened in 2017. A new Sixth Form Centre is planned for 2019.

Admission. Admission points are 11+, 13+ and Sixth Form. Occasional places may be available in other year groups. Applicants are assessed in Maths, English and NVR and have a short interview. Common Entrance examinations are also used as a guide, if they are taken. Entry into the Lower Sixth Form is via predicted GCSE grades and interview. Deferred entry is also available and international students wishing to apply are guided through the procedure step by step by our Admissions team. For further information see: www.heathfieldschool.net

Scholarships and Bursaries are awarded. Scholarships are worth £750 per annum. Bursaries are means tested and are awarded at the Headmistress's discretion. Armed Forces discounts are also available.

Fees per term (2018–2019). Senior (Forms III–UVI): Boarding £12,210, Day £7,600. Lower (Forms I–II): Boarding £11,920, Day £7,395.

Charitable status. Heathfield School is a Registered Charity, number 309086. It exists to provide a caring boarding education leading to higher education for girls aged between 11 and 18.

Board of Governors:
Chairman: Mr Tom Cross Brown, MA Oxon, MBA Insead
The Rt Revd Dr Jonathan Baker, Bishop of Fulham, MA Oxon, MPhil, Dip Theol
Mrs Sally-Anne Barrett
Mr Guy Egerton-Smith, FRICS
Mr Robert Gregory, BSc Hons Sussex
Mrs Rosemary Martin, MEd, NPQH
Mr Richard Pilkington
The Hon Mrs Peter [Frances] Stanley
Mrs Sally Tulk-Hart
The Revd Canon Dr Philip Ursell, BA Wales, MA Oxon

Senior Leadership Team:

***Headmistress*: Mrs M Gardiner Legge**, MA Oxon, PGCE Hong Kong

Bursar: Mrs R Frier, BSc Hons Bristol, FCA
Director of Studies: Mr D Mitchell, MA Hull, MSc York, BA Hons Warwick, PGCE UWE
Director of Pastoral and Co-Curricular Activities: Mrs K de Ferrer, MA Leeds, BA Hons USA, PGCE London
Director of Sixth Form: Mr J Hart, MA London, BA Hons London
Director of Boarding: Mr John Gale, MSc Oxford, BSc Plymouth, PGCE Exeter
Director of IT: Mr M Taylor, BSc Eng London, PGCE Greenwich, MBCS, CITP
Director of Marketing & Admissions: Ms A Morgan, MCIM, MIDM
Director of Development: Mrs E Boryer, BSc Hons Bristol

Chaplain: Fr D Clues, BD Hons London, Cert Theol Oxon, PGCE London (*Chaplain*)
Academic Staff:
+ *Head of Faculty*
* *Subject Leader/Teacher in Charge*

Art & Textiles:
+*Mrs E Feilen, MA Goldsmiths, BA Hons ECA, PGCE Cambridge
Miss H Smith, BA Hons Aberystwyth, PGCE Bath Spa (*Art*)
Miss J Losq, MA UCL, BA Hons Cambridge, BA Hons RCA (*Art*)
Mr B Crawshaw, BA Hons Glasgow (*Art Technician*)
Mr S Lisseman, BA Hons Ravensbourne University London Fashion and Textiles, MA Central Saint Martins Fashion Design (*Designer in Residence*)

Business:
*Mrs G Kendall, BA Hons Reading, PGCE London, D&B Diploma in Credit and Financial Analysis

Cookery:
*Mrs M Blackburn, BEd Hons Cardiff
Miss P Fairclough, BA Hons Oxford Brookes, Adv Cert Leiths Food & Wine

Dance:
Mrs N Shaw, BA West Sussex, ALAM, RAD TC, AISTD

Drama and Theatre Studies:
*Mrs L Halcrow, BA Hons, PGCE Central Sch of Speech & Drama
Mrs K de Ferrer, MA Leeds, BA Hons USA, PGCE London
Mrs N Shaw, BA West Sussex, ALAM, RAD TC, AISTD (*also Dance*)

English:
*Mrs S Shirwani, MA Oxon, BA, MA London, GTP Reading
Mrs C Fowler-Whale, BA Hons Canterbury, MA Kent, PGCE Reading (*Highly Able & Scholarship Coordinator*)
Miss C Jackson, BA Exeter, PGCE Exeter

Geography:
*Mrs L Worrall, BSc Hons Kingston, PGCE Kingston
Miss C McSwiggan, MA Dublin, BA Hons Dublin, PGCE Canterbury

History & Politics:
*Dr C Bradshaw, PhD St Andrew's, MA St Andrew's, BA Hons Exeter, PGCE Gloucester
Mr D Mitchell, MA Hull, MSc York, BA Hons Warwick, PGCE UWE

Mr J Hart, MA London, BA Hons London
Miss C McSwiggan, MA Dublin, BA Hons Dublin, PGCE
  Canterbury

History of Art:
*Ms J Meeson, BA Hons East Anglia

ICT:
*Mrs R Millns, BA Joint Hons Wales, Postgraduate
  Management Certificate Wales, GTP RBWM (*Careers
  & Outreach*)

Latin & Classical Civilisation:
+*Mr A Valner, MA Nottingham, BA Nottingham, PGCE
  London
Dr D Stobart, PhD Cambridge, PGCE Utrecht

Mathematics:
+*Mrs Z Benjamin, BSc Hons Reading, PGCE Bath
Mr G Benjamin, MSc Bath, PGCE Bath
Mr J Doyle, BA Canberra, Dip Ed Canberra
Miss K Johnson, Teaching Cert Nottingham

Modern Foreign Languages:
*Mr F Troublé, MA Paris, PGCE London, Bccomm DUT
  de Commerce (*MFL Coordinator*)
*Mrs A Pullen, BA Hons Cordoba (*Spanish*)
Mrs F Rayner, MA Strasbourg, PGCE Oxford Brookes
  (*French & Spanish*)
Miss M Armstrong, BA Hons Dublin, Higher Dip Ed
  Dublin (*French*)
Miss M Plaquin (*French Assistant*)
Miss F Garcia, MSPE Malaga (*Spanish Assistant*)
Mr T Chatzivadaris, MA London, BA Athens (*Greek*)
Ms K Davies, PGCE Oxford Brookes, Dip Teaching
  (*German*)
Mr K Forrester, BA Tokyo (*Japanese*)
Ms A Khoursheen, MA Surrey, BA Aleppo, Dip
  Translation Aleppo (*Arabic*)
Mrs M Strain, Dip Foreign Languages Moscow (*Russian*)
Ms S Zhou, BA Birmingham, BA Beijing (*Chinese*)

Music:
*Mrs J Dance, BA Hons Birmingham, PGCE Birmingham,
  LRAM (*Director of Music*)
Miss S M Kong, MA Birmingham City, BA Hons UCSI
  University Malaysia, PGCE Buckingham, Adv Piano
  Studies Franz Liszt Academy of Music, FTCL (*Assistant
  Director of Music*)
Mr S Ash, Dip Music New York (*Drums*)
Mr K Bulford, BA Hons Swansea (*Drums*)
Mr N Charlton, BA Hons Mus Ed, LTCL (*Cello*)
Ms L Head, LTCL, FTCL (*Brass*)
Mrs L Elliott, BA Mus RSAMD Glasgow (*Harp*)
Mr P Ford, BA Hons Open & London, MMus Conducting
  Surrey (*Piano*)
Mrs R Heathcote, BMus Hons Kent, PGCE Reading
  (*Oboe*)
Mr A Hooley, CMI Level 4 & 5 in Management and
  Leadership (*Clarinet*)
Mr G Horton, BEd London (*Singing*)
Miss S Jubert, BMus Hons, PGCE Oxford Brookes (*Piano*)
Miss A Kryvanos, BMus Hons Royal Welsh College of
  Music and Drama (*Guitar*)
Mrs J Minns, LTCL Flute Trinity College of Music,
  ABRSM (*Flute/Piano*)
Miss H Woodruff, BMus Hons Ohio USA, MA Reading,
  MA London (*Flute*)

Photography:
*Miss K White, BA Hons Oxford Brookes, ABIPP
Mrs M Butler, BA Hons TVU (*Photography Technician*)

Physical Education:
+Miss W Reynolds, BEd Hons Liverpool

*Miss C Willimott, BA Hons Southampton, PGCE
  Hertfordshire (*Head of Sport*)
Miss J Talbot, BPhysEd Otago, NZ (*PE*)
Mrs C Papadopoulos, BSc Hons Surrey, PGCE Brunel (*PE*)
Mrs G Glimmerveen (*Equestrian*)
Mr A Turner, LTA, CCA, BTCA (*Tennis Coach*)
Mr A Moir, LTA Registered, Registered Professional
  BTCA (*Tennis Coach*)

PSHE:
*Mrs A Diaz, BA Hons Open, Cert Ed Cambridge

Psychology:
*Mr C Confait, BSc Hons Essex, GTP/PGCE Kingston

Religious Studies:
*Ms K Oster, Fil Mag Linkoping, PGCE Cambridge
Fr D Clues, BD Hons London, Cert Theol Oxon, PGCE
  London

Science:
+*Miss C Wells, BSc Hons Bath, PGCE Exeter (*Science
  Coordinator, Assistant Director of Studies*)
Mr J Lawson, MSc Leeds, MPhys Hons USA, PGCE Leeds
  (*Physics*)
Mrs B Clench, BSc Penn State, Secondary Education
  Certification State of PA (*Chemistry*)
Ms L Johnson (*Biology*)
Mrs A Ellis, BEd Bedford (*Science*)
Mrs A Milner, HND Applied Biology Ulster, Bsc Biology/
  Ecology Ulster (*Senior Science Technician*)
Mr I Whitehurst, BA Surrey (*Science Technician*)

Teaching & Learning Support:
Spectrum Learning Support & EFL
*Mrs R Colley, BA Hons Oxford Brookes, PGCE
  Roehampton, SpLD Level 5, CPT3A, TEFL London
  (*SENCo*)
Mrs S Simpson, BEd Birmingham, Postgraduate Diploma
  in Dyslexia & Literacy York
Mrs M Battleday, HLTA Maths, NOCN Speech and
  Language, ADHD, Dyspraxia, Dyslexia
Mrs A Jones, HLTA Maths, Diplome de Langues Paris
Dr M Snow, PhD London, MA Hons Aberdeen, MSc
  Robert Gordon, PGDip Aberdeen, CELTA, FHEA, EFL

Teaching Support & Coordinators:
Mrs N Tenorio (*Examinations Officer*)
Mrs H Fernandes, MSc Sheffield, BA Hons Brighton
  (*Librarian*)
Mrs D Hunt (*Duke of Edinburgh's Award Coordinator*)
Mrs G Glimmerveen (*Equestrian Coordinator*)
Mrs M Butler, BA Hons TVU (*Photography Technician*)
Mrs A Milner, HND Applied Biology Ulster, BSc Biology/
  Ecology Ulster (*Senior Science Technician*)
Mr I Whitehurst, BA Surrey (*Science Technician*)

Pastoral:
*Mrs K de Ferrer, MA Leeds, BA Hons USA, PGCE
  London (*Director of Pastoral*)
*Mr J Hart, MA London, BA Hons London (*Director of
  Sixth Form*)
Mrs A Ellis (*Deputy Director of Sixth Form*)
Mr A Valner, MA Nottingham, BA Nottingham, PGCE
  London (*Head of House, Austen*)
Mrs C Fowler-Whale, BA Hons Canterbury, MA Kent,
  PGCE Reading (*Deputy Head of House, Austen*)
Miss J Talbot, BPhys Ed Otago, NZ (*Head of House, de
  Valois*)
Mrs M Battleday, HLTA Maths, NOCN Speech and
  Language, ADHD, Dyspraxia, Dyslexia (*Deputy Head of
  House, de Valois*)
Miss K White, BA Hons Oxford Brookes, ABIPP (*Head of
  House, Seacole*)

Miss C Jackson, BA Exeter, PGCE Exeter (*Deputy Head of House, Seacole*)
Mr J Doyle, BA Canberra, Dip Ed Canberra (*Head of House, Somerville*)
Mr G Benjamin, MSc Bath, PGCE Bath (*Deputy Head of House, Somerville*)
Mrs L Worrall, BSc Hons Kingston, PGCE Kingston (*Head of Lower School*)
Mrs A Diaz, Cert Ed Cambridge, BA Hons Open (*Day Girls Coordinator*)

Boarding:
Mr J Gale, MSc Oxford, BSc Plymouth, PGCE Exeter (*Director of Boarding*)
Miss M Armstrong, BA Hons Dublin, Higher Dip Ed Dublin (*Deputy Director of Boarding & Teaching Housemistress*)
Miss P Sutton, Dip Teaching & Learning Canterbury NZ, BA Hons Winchester (*Teaching Housemistress Lower School*)
Miss S Crafer, NNEB, RSH (*Boarding Manager*)
Ms A Brooks (*Housemistress, Form IV*)
Mrs J Liepa, BA Hons London, PGCE Middlesex (*Housemistress, Form V*)
Miss S Broomfield (*Housemistress, LVI Form*)
Mrs P Munro, BSA Boarding Diploma (*Housemistress, UVI Form*)
Mrs P Kerley (*Housemistress, UVI Form*)
Mrs S Bush, BA Hons Exeter, PGCE Exeter (*Evening Housemistress*)
Mrs S Jackson (*Evening Assistant Housemistress*)
Miss E R Carling, Resident Scholar, BA Varsity College, Durban
Miss I Crocker, Resident Scholar, BA University of Oregon

Surgery:
Sister M Couzens, RGN (*Senior Nursing Sister*)
Sister E Warrington, RNC (*Nursing Sister*)
Sister L Brazel, RGN, BSc Hons London (*Nursing Sister Weekends*)
Miss S Lambert, BSc, PG Dip, MSc, HCPC, MCSP, AACP (*Physiotherapist*)
Ms M Jemmett, BSc Hons London, HE Dip Counselling Bucks (*School Counsellor*)

Support Staff:

Administration:
Mrs A Hoo (*PA to the Headmistress*)
*Mrs C Bradberry (*Administration Supervisor & PA to the Director of Studies*)
Mrs V Williams, BA Hons Durham, CPRS (*PA to the Directors of Pastoral & Co-curricular*)
Miss E Bridge (*Receptionist & School Administrator*)
Mrs D Chapman (*School Administrator*)

Bursary:
*Mrs R Frier, BSc Hons Bristol, FCA (*Bursar*)
Mrs L Farrin (*Deputy Bursar*)
Mrs D Davies (*Accounts Administrator*)
Mrs V Boxhall (*Accounts Administrator*)

Development:
Mrs E Boryer, BSc Hons Bristol, AMAC Manchester, Cert SDL CMI Manchester (*Director of Development*)

Marketing & Admissions:
Ms A Morgan, MCIM, MIDM (*Director of Marketing & Admissions*)
Mrs I Hutchings, BSc Hons Open (*Registrar*)
Ms E Massey (*Marketing & Events Assistant*)
Ms J Woodhams (*Admissions Assistant*)

Fellowship:
Mrs R Farha (*Fellowship Coordinator*)

IT Systems:
Mr M Taylor, BSc Eng London, PGCE Greenwich, MBCS, CITP (*Director of IT*)
Mr S Rendall, BSc Hons UWE (*IT Administrator*)
Mr A Simon (*IT Technician in Residence*)

Facilities:
Mr S Bennett (*Facilities Manager*)
Mr P Brown (*Foreman*)
Mr A Roberts (*Electrician*)
Mr A Lata (*Facilities*)
Mr S Climpson (*Head Groundsman*)
Mr C Lynch (*Apprentice Groundsman*)

Housekeeping:
Mrs R Tatum, NVQ Business Mgmt, Dip Music Ukraine (*Housekeeping Manager*)
Ms H Beacham (*Housekeeping Supervisor*)
Mrs D Prendergast (*Housekeeping Supervisor*)
Mr J Badley (*Housekeeping Cleaner*)
Miss L Beaugie (*Housekeeping Cleaner*)
Mrs L Brown (*Housekeeping Cleaner*)
Miss S Carter (*Housekeeping Cleaner*)
Miss L Conway (*Housekeeping Cleaner*)
Mrs L Jefferys (*Housekeeping Cleaner*)
Miss D Jennings (*Housekeeping Cleaner*)
Mrs I Kwiatwowska (*Housekeeping Cleaner*)
Mrs C Ledwich (*Housekeeping Cleaner*)
Mrs S Mason (*Housekeeping Cleaner*)
Mrs I Plank (*Housekeeping Cleaner*)
Mrs N Vis (*Housekeeping Cleaner*)
Mrs S Waghorn (*Housekeeping Cleaner*)

Drivers:
T Chivers (*Driver*)
G Coxell (*Driver*)
K Gregory (*Driver*)
S Luckhurst (*Driver*)
G Martin, BA Hons Nottingham Trent (*Driver*)
K Matthews (*Driver*)
P Walton (*Driver*)

Swimming Pool:
Mr D O'Toole (*Swimming Pool Manager*)

Hethersett Old Hall School

Norwich Road, Hethersett, Norwich, Norfolk NR9 3DW

Tel: 01603 810390
email: enquiries@hohs.co.uk
website: www.hohs.co.uk
           www.hohs-blog.com
Twitter: @HOHS_tweets
Facebook: @HethersettOldHallSchool

Hethersett Old Hall School, founded in 1938, is located in 16 acres of beautiful Norfolk countryside in the heart of East Anglia, just minutes from Norwich city centre.

The school is a charitable trust administered by a Board of Governors, which is in membership of AGBIS. The Headmaster is a member of GSA and the school is also in membership of BSA.

The school provides education for around 180 pupils aged between 3 and 18 years old. The school is co-educational from age 3–11 and girls only from age 11 (Year 7). Full, weekly and flexi boarding is available for girls from age 9 (Year 5). The school welcomes international students. Younger boarders live in the historic main house and sixth formers have their own separate building. All girls are cared for by resident house staff who organise an exciting programme of evening and weekend activities.

Aims. Hethersett offers a friendly, supportive community in which each child is encouraged to develop their academic, creative and practical skills and to become self-reliant, tolerant and concerned for others.

Curriculum. Classes are small and teaching staff are well qualified, well informed and enthusiastic.

The Preparatory School is situated in modern, purpose-built accommodation with a dedicated play area. In Lower Prep (pupils age 3–7) the key skills of reading, writing and numeracy are developed in a stimulating atmosphere that builds on children's natural inquisitiveness and enthusiasm for learning.

The Upper Prep department (pupils age 7–11) provides a thorough grounding in the core curriculum. Sport, drama and music feature strongly in each year's programme of study. There are many opportunities for pupils to compete against other schools in swimming galas and games fixtures.

Pupils in the Senior School are offered a broad range of academic, technological and creative subjects. Their achievements at GCSE are consistently high. Support, advice and individual care throughout the senior school enables pupils to be confident in planning their future education and careers.

Sixth Form. From 2018, the school is offering greatly reduced fees to widen accessibility to its excellent Sixth Form. Over 20 AS and A Level subjects are offered, from the unusually creative combination of art, photography and art textiles to a range of highly academic subjects. All Sixth Formers also take a Level 3 business qualification to enhance employability. The majority of sixth formers choose to go on to university after benefiting from dedicated personal guidance from staff in choosing courses, completing their UCAS form and composing their personal statement. Since 2007, all applicants have gained entry to their first-choice university to study subjects as diverse as clergy training, astrophysics and interior design.

The EPQ (Extended Project Qualification) is well established at the school and has proved popular with universities as it fosters research skills. Most Sixth Formers also achieve the Gold Duke of Edinburgh's Award.

Buildings and Facilities. The school has excellent teaching facilities with bright, modern, purpose-built teaching blocks. The senior school teaching blocks feature an ICT suite, science laboratories, an art and technology suite with photography dark room, design technology and food and nutrition rooms. Pupils also benefit from the dedicated music rooms, 'The Barn' for drama, an indoor heated swimming pool, tennis courts, sports fields, gardens, woodland and an orchard. Sixth formers have their own common room, kitchen, study room with designated individual study space for each girl and careers library. The boarding facilities include bright, attractive accommodation for younger girls with en-suite bathrooms. Older girls move onto single study-rooms and sixth formers are housed in their own separate building.

Recreational Activities. The school offers a wide range of recreational activities and optional extras which includes drama, dance, choir, orchestra, rock band and individual musical instrument tuition, sport clubs – swimming, tennis, football, rugby, badminton, trampolining, shooting, rounders, hockey and netball. The majority of senior school girls successfully take part in The Duke of Edinburgh's Award scheme, achieving their Bronze, Silver and Gold awards. There is also a wide range of clubs including Rock Band, Maths, Art, Drama, Bird Club and Green Club.

Entrance. Entry is by the school's own assessment designed to give staff an indication of the child's stage of development, and to ensure they are able to meet the demands of the curriculum. The assessment focuses on maths, English and a reasoning test. Entry to the Sixth Form is by interview, school record and assessment. For further information or to obtain a prospectus please contact the Registrar.

Bursaries. Means-tested bursaries are available to enable pupils to attend the school who meet the entry criteria but who cannot afford the fees. These awards may be up to 100% of fees. They are limited in number and their award is discretionary.

Fees per term (2018–2019). Nursery fees (age 3–4) vary according to the length of the term and are charged at £32.07 for a morning session and £50.20 for a full day. Lower Prep Department (age 4–7) £3,344; Upper Prep Department (age 7–11): £3,905 (day), £6,000 (weekly boarding from age 9); £6,850 (full boarding from age 9); Senior School (Years 7–11): £5,210 (day), £8,020 (weekly boarding); £9,760 (full boarding); Sixth Form (Years 12–13): £3,500 (day), £6,310 (weekly boarding), £8,050 (full boarding). All day fees include a cooked lunch.

Nursery fees (age 3–4) vary according to the length of the term and are charged at £30.80 for a morning session and £48.00 for a full day. Lower Prep Department (age 4–7) £3,225; Upper Prep Department (age 7–11): £3,775 (day), £6,490 (weekly boarding from age 9); £8,170 (full boarding from age 9); Senior School: £5,035 (day), £7,750 (weekly boarding); £9,430 (full boarding). Sixth Form fees will be greatly reduced from September 2018 – please ask for details. All day fees include a cooked lunch.

Charitable status. Hethersett Old Hall School is a Registered Charity, number 311273. It exists to provide a high quality education.

Chairman of Governors: Mr Martin Matthews

Headmaster: **Mr Stephen G Crump**, MA

Deputy Headmistress: Mrs Joanna Collin

Senior Housemistress: Miss Alison Kirkham

Financial Administrator: Mrs Helen Eastwood

Head's Secretary: Mrs Susan Potts

Registrar: Mrs Linda Jones

Howell's School Llandaff GDST

Cardiff Road, Llandaff, Cardiff CF5 2YD

Tel:	029 2056 2019
Fax:	029 2057 8879
email:	admissions@how.gdst.net
website:	www.howells-cardiff.gdst.net
	www.howellscoedcollege.gdst.net
Twitter:	@HowellsSchool
Facebook:	@Officialhowells

A magnificent Victorian gothic building right on the edge of the great, green expanse of Llandaff Fields, Howell's School Llandaff GDST has a tremendous sense of roominess for a city school, with a swimming pool, tennis courts and newly-opened sports pavilion and all-weather sports pitch on the five-acre site.

Visionary Principal Sally Davis presides over excellent academic results, and in August 2018, GCSE students did particularly well in the science subjects. 88% of all science entries graded 9–8 (the equivalent of an A*). In Biology, 92% of all results were level 9–8, in Chemistry, 88% were level 9–8, and in Physics 83%.

Across the board, the results at Howell's were excellent, making it the top school in Wales at GCSE. 50% of students taking Drama and Music were graded Level 9–8/A*. In total, 63 students sat GCSEs at the school this year, and an impressive 53% of all GCSE grades were at Level 9–8/A*, with a combined Level 9, 8, 7/A*–A rate of 74%.

In the Co-Ed College, of the 73 students sitting A Levels in 2018, 26% of all results were the highest A* grade, with 74% receiving A*–B grades. Six students achieved all A*s, and 30% of students achieved all A* and A grades. 100% of students studying Further Mathematics achieved an A*, 100% of those studying Music achieved an A*, and all those studying Mathematics achieved at A*–B.

Student numbers. 756: Nursery 34; Prep School 230; Senior School 316; Co-Educational Sixth Form College 176.

Founded in 1860 as a school for girls, the school was built by the Drapers' Company from the endowment left in 1537 by Thomas Howell, son of a Welshman, merchant of London, Bristol and Seville and a Draper.

Howell's School Llandaff is part of the Girls' Day School Trust GDST. The GDST is the leading network of independent girls' schools in the UK. As a charity that owns and runs 23 schools and two academies, it reinvests all its income in its schools. For further information about the Trust, visit www.gdst.net.

Howell's School puts great value on a rich and varied life outside of the classroom, with enrichment activities running from Photography to Philosophy, Song Writing to Synchronised Swimming. The extensive Enrichment Programmes, together with impressive Wellbeing and Laureate Programmes, make Howell's a special place to learn and develop in an exciting, creative and thriving environment. The school's strong Leadership Team, talented and dedicated teaching and support staff, wonderful young people and committed and interested parents are what make Howell's unique.

The Nursery at Howell's is situated in Roald Dahl's childhood home and takes inspiration from its famous former occupant. Girls who enter the nursery experience a safe, family atmosphere, making the transition from home to nursery a relaxed and happy one. The Prep School radiates an atmosphere in which every child is valued and nurtured. Great emphasis is placed on developing the self-identity, self-esteem and self-confidence of every girl.

When entering the Senior School, girls are encouraged to develop skills of self-analysis and reflection, and choose the learning methods that suit them best, whilst teachers challenge and motivate them towards an appetite for lifelong learning. Howell's aims to help students acquire skills essential to tackling a competitive and rapidly changing world. The established co-educational college has a proven track record for excellence in and out of the classroom, and offers students an exceptional learning experience with flexible teaching styles designed to manage the transition between school and university.

Curriculum. All National Curriculum subjects including Welsh are taught at Key Stages 1, 2 and 3. In Year 7, French, Spanish and Welsh are on offer. Latin is introduced in Year 8. First language Welsh is taught on demand. There is a broad range of subjects available in the College. Examinations in a number of AS subjects are taken at the end of Year 12. Active learning styles are an essential part of the classroom experience, and the curriculum is made more diverse by:

- Educational visits, locally and abroad
- Visiting authors, poets, musicians, artists and lecturers
- Special activity weeks focusing on particular areas of the curriculum

Extracurricular activities. Howell's aim is to fulfil the potential of all the students in all areas, which it achieves through a rich extracurricular programme. Extracurricular opportunities include:

- Orchestras, choirs, chamber and jazz groups
- Reading and reviewing, eco, science, mathematics, history, geography, language and religious and cultural clubs
- Concerts, plays, a drama festival and eisteddfodau
- Tennis, hockey, rounders, swimming, athletics, cross-country, netball, rugby and football teams
- The Duke of Edinburgh's Award, Envision and Interact
- Quiz, public speaking and debating teams
- Community service and fundraising for charities

The school seeks to support the widest range of students' needs through specialist dyslexia teaching at our on-site Dyslexia Institute satellite, and through an extensive and comprehensive careers programme.

Admission. A selection process operates for all points of entry. Contact Admissions for further details.

Fees per term (2018–2019). Co-Ed College: £4,690; Senior School: £4,461; Prep School: Years 3–6 £3,396, Rec–Year 2 £3,329, Nursery £2,585. Fees quoted are inclusive of non-residential school trips. Lunch: £205.33 (Nursery to Senior School).

Scholarships and Bursaries. Bursaries, which are means-tested, are available in the Senior School and in the Co-Ed College; these are intended to ensure that the school remains accessible to bright students who would benefit from our education, but who would be unable to enter the school without financial assistance.

Details of scholarships and bursaries are available, on request, from the school.

Charitable status. Howell's School Llandaff is part of The Girls' Day School Trust, which is a Registered Charity, number 306983.

Chairman of Governors: Mrs S Thomas

Principal: **Mrs S Davis**, BSc London

Deputy Principal: Mrs J Ashill, BEd Swansea

Deputy Principal: Mrs N Chyba, BA London

Assistant Principal: Mrs C Darnton, BEd Hons West Glamorgan, MSc Leicester

Director of Finance and Operations: Mr R C Read, OBE, CDir

Director of External Relations: Mrs V Yilmaz, BA

Ipswich High School

Woolverstone, Ipswich, Suffolk IP9 1AZ

Tel:	01473 780201
Fax:	01473 780985
email:	admissions@ipswichhighschool.co.uk
website:	www.ipswichhighschool.co.uk
Twitter:	@IpswichHigh
Facebook:	@ipswichhighschool

Founded in 1878, Ipswich High School has a long-standing reputation for offering an exceptional education and experience to pupils. We lead the way in education with an innovative and personalised curriculum, allowing the right amount of flexibility and support for each individual. We provide a strong, vibrant and thriving educational community for children aged 3 to 18, allowing our pupils to succeed and grow at all stages of their school education.

Our beautiful 84-acre campus is located in Woolverstone, just outside Ipswich. The spacious site has superb facilities such as a theatre, ICT suites, a 25m swimming pool, Sixth

Form suite, cookery rooms, dedicated music rooms and floodlit AstroTurf pitches. We also capitalise on our outstanding natural surroundings; our woodland provides an outdoor learning area for the Prep School, offering a unique, proactive learning experience in an ever-changing environment.

From September 2018, we are offering the Diamond Model of education. This model is seen as an approach which not only gets the very best from pupils, but also from teaching staff, as they are able to tailor their professional techniques for girls and boys. The model offers the benefits of the single-sex classroom for 'pre-teen and lower-teen' students, whilst gaining from the social benefits of a co-educational school at other ages. The Diamond Model recognises that, as girls and boys reach their teenage years, they approach their learning in different ways. Boys, for example, are more spatially aware, and girls have well-developed verbal skills.

At Ipswich High School we pride ourselves on the academic excellence of our pupils. Year after year, their exam performances are a testament to both their incredible hard work, and the stimulating learning environment that we are able to provide. Once again, we see a steady increase in our GCSE results, a trend for the last seven years. In 2018 we celebrated yet another fantastic set of exam results at both A Level and GCSE. At A Level, 70% of our pupils' grades were awarded A*–C, with 100% of our Year 13 cohort accepting a place at their first-choice university. At GCSE, 26% of our pupils' results were awarded 9 or A*, the highest in Suffolk. 64% of our pupils' grades were awarded 9–7 or A*–A, an absolutely fantastic achievement. Year on year we have had the best GCSE results in the region.

Our Enrichment programme is embedded within the school day and offers a wealth of diverse and engaging activities to our pupils, with over 80 enrichment activities on offer throughout the year. These activities give your child the opportunity to further develop a variety of skills, promoting growth and enthusiasm. Enrichment begins for our pupils in our Prep School and runs all the way through Sixth Form. Our school timetable allows us to add nine enrichment periods a week, varying from midday sessions to sessions that close out the school day.

We welcome pupils from across Suffolk, Essex and South Norfolk, many of whom travel to school using our extensive coach network. We are proud to develop pupils who are inspirational, respectful, courageous, ambitious and have real integrity.

Admissions. Admission to the Pre-Prep is on the basis of an informal assessment in a play situation. Entry to the Prep School is on the basis of an informal assessment or written test. Entry to the Senior School involves interviews, written tests and a school report. Sixth Form entry is on the basis of interviews, GCSE results and a school report.

Fees per term (2018–2019). Prep School: Pre-Prep including Reception £2,923, Years 1–2 £3,098, Years 3–6 £3,444; Senior School & Sixth Form: Year 7–9 £4,708, Years 10–13 £4,774.

Scholarships. Scholarships are highly sought after and are reserved for those candidates believed to be of an exceptional standard.

We offer Year 7 and Year 9 Scholarships to the value of 10% of fees. These are offered to those who excel in academia, sports, drama, art and music. These Scholarships are offered to the top performing Senior School candidates who demonstrate outstanding ability.

We offer two Year 12 Scholarships, The Orwell Scholarship and the Elliston Award. The Orwell Scholarships are awarded to both external and internal Sixth Form candidates on the basis of ability, potential and qualities necessary to make a significant and ongoing contribution to the quality of school life. The Elliston Awards are up to the value of 50% of our school fees to suitable applicants, who meet our criteria, from each state-funded school in Essex or Suffolk. We will also consider applications from pupils currently receiving bursaries to attend other independent schools.

Headmistress: **Ms Oona Carlin**

Head of Prep School: Mrs Eileen Fisher

Registrar: Ms Rebecca Geoghegan

Kilgraston School

Bridge of Earn, Perthshire PH2 9BQ

Tel:	01738 812257
Fax:	01738 813410
email:	headspa@kilgraston.com
website:	www.kilgraston.com
Twitter:	@kilgraston
Facebook:	@kilgrastonschool

Kilgraston is an independent boarding and day school for girls aged 5 to 18 years. It is an all-through school comprising Junior Years, Senior School and Sixth Form.

The Independent School Awards named Kilgraston UK Independent School of the Year in 2011, making it Scotland's first school to be awarded this accolade. In 2014, Kilgraston received the Sunday Times Scottish Independent School of the Year award. Most recently the school has been named the Sunday Times top-performing independent school in Scotland for Intermediate 2, Highers and Advanced Highers and won the best-schools.co.uk award for the top-performing independent school for Highers in Scotland.

Kilgraston is set in a Georgian mansion house located in 54 acres of stunning parkland three miles from the centre of Perth with Edinburgh and Glasgow only an hour away. The school has benefited from extensive recent investment in facilities including a state-of-the-art science centre, a sixth form study centre, a 25m indoor swimming pool complex, and floodlit astroturf hockey pitch and tennis courts. Kilgraston is also the only school in Scotland with an on-site equestrian centre incorporating a 60m x 40m floodlit arena with show jumps.

Visitors to Kilgraston are struck by its warm and welcoming atmosphere, and the sense of community and friendship across the year groups. Staff know each pupil individually, and are proud of the well-rounded girls who thrive in a range of curricular and co-curricular activities. Kilgraston's Sacred Heart ethos is central to school life, providing a firm foundation for personal growth and individual contribution, whilst welcoming girls of all faiths and none.

The Curriculum. Kilgraston follows the Scottish educational system with all the girls studying a broad curriculum before selecting subjects to continue at National 5 (GCSE equivalent). Over 18 subjects are offered at Higher/Advanced Higher (A Level equivalent). Kilgraston has a record of high academic achievement and the girls gain entrance to top UK and international universities including Oxbridge. In 2015, Kilgraston was named the Sunday Times top-performing Independent School in Scotland for Intermediate 2, Highers and Advanced Highers. In 2016, Kilgraston was named top performing independent school for Advanced Highers by best-schools.

Music, Art and Drama play an important part of life at Kilgraston. The Music Department alone has 14 individual teaching rooms, a recording studio and two large music rooms designed to suit all needs. There are also many oppor-

tunities for pupils to perform throughout the year by participating in orchestra, string orchestra, fiddle, woodwind and
brass groups or one of several choirs.

The Art Department is housed in the top of the mansion
with superb views across the Ochil Hills and the school
boasts an impressive number of past pupils who are practising artists.

Sports and recreation are catered for within a superb
sports hall including a climbing wall and fitness gym. The
extensive grounds incorporate the indoor 25m swimming
pool, nine floodlit all-weather courts, playing fields and athletics track. Whilst the main sports are hockey, netball, tennis, rounders, swimming and athletics other sports include
football, touch rugby, skiing, cricket, badminton, yoga,
karate, fencing, aerobics, ballet, modern dance and highland
dancing. Fixtures and competitions are also arranged against
other schools throughout the year. Kilgraston also hosts the
Scottish Schools' Equestrian Championships every Spring.

Kilgraston is divided into houses which compete against
each other in games, music and debating. The girls can also
take part in The Duke of Edinburgh's Award scheme and are
encouraged to use all the facilities not only for curriculum
lessons but also for leisure activities.

Kilgraston Junior Years is for pupils aged 5–12. The
boarders live in the newly refurbished Butterstone House.
All of the pupils benefit from the many facilities of the
Senior School. (*See separate entry in IAPS section.*)

Admission is normally interview and school report.
Entry to the Junior Years is by interview and assessment.

Means-tested bursaries are available on application.
Scholarship Examinations are held in early February and
awards are also offered each year as a result of outstanding
performance in the Academic Scholarship Examinations.
Scholarships are also offered in Art, Music, Drama and
Sport.

Fees per term (2018–2019). Senior: Day £5,880, Boarding £10,045, Junior Years: Day £3,630–£4,600, Boarding
£7,675.

Charitable status. Kilgraston School Trust is a Registered Charity, number SC029664.

Chair of Governors: Mr Timothy Hall

Senior Leadership Team:

Headmistress: Mrs D MacGinty, BEd Hons, NPQH,
DipMonEd

Bursar: Mr B Farrell, BCom, HDE, ACIS
Deputy Head: Mrs C A Lund, BA Hons, MA, MA Ed Man,
PGCE
Head of Pastoral Care & Boarding: Mrs G McFadden
Head of Junior Years: Mrs A Fidelo, Dip Ed
Director of Communications and Sport, Head of L4: Mrs P
Stott, MBE

Academic & Pastoral Staff:
Mrs J Baird (*Classroom Assistant/Playground Supervisor*)
Ms C Blackler, BSc Hons (*Science Technician*)
Mrs S Birrell, MSc, BA Hons, PGCE Primary (*Head of
Support for Learning*)
Mrs A Bluett, BA Hons, PGCE (*Head of Latin & Classics*)
Miss E Boxall (*Residential Assistant*)
Mrs A Caldwell, BSc Hons, PGDE (*Mathematics*)
Mr C Campbell, MA, PGDE (*Head of History & Modern
Studies, Year Head L6 & Head of Inchcolm*)
Mr E Connolly, BSc Hons, PGDE (*Director of Science*)
Ms D Cooper, MA Hons (*Junior Years Form Teacher*)
Mrs E Cran, BEd Hons (*Physical Education*)
Mme I Dépreux, BA Hons, Maitrise, PGCE (*French*)
Mrs A Dunphie, BSc Hons, PGCE (*Mathematics & Head
of Business Management*)
Miss R Elliot, BHSAI (*Equestrian Instructor*)

Mrs P Ferguson, MA Hons, PGCE (*Learning Support
Teacher & Junior Years Form Teacher*)
Mrs H Ferry, BEd Hons (*Head of Physical Education*)
Mr A Fynn, MA Hons, PGDE (*Head of Modern
Languages*)
Mrs K Guthrie, MA Hons PGCE, CELTA (*ESOL*)
Mrs S Hewett, MSc, BSc Hons, PGCE (*Physics*)
Mrs S Hewitt, BA (*Swimming Development Manager*)
Miss S Howett (*Assistant Residential Mistress, Mater*)
Mr S Johnston, MA, BA, PGDE (*Religious Studies*)
Mr T Kearns, MA Oxon, MA Ed, Dip Lit, PGCE (*Head of
English*)
Miss C Laidlaw, MA Hons (*Chaplain*)
Mr D Laird (*Duke of Edinburgh's Award Coordinator*)
Mrs E Lyle, BA Hons, PGDE (*Spanish and French*)
Miss R MacLean, BHSPI (*Equestrian Manager/Riding
Instructor*)
Miss G Macleod, BA Hons, PGCE (*Head of Art & Design*)
Dr J Mathers, BSc Hons, PhD (*Science Technician*)
Mr J McAuley, BA Hons (*Director of Music*)
Mrs D McCormick, BSc Hons (*Science, Year Head U6 &
Head of Kinnoull*)
Mr D McFadden, BEd Hons, PGCE (*Social Sciences*)
Ms A MacPhee (*Junior Years Form Teacher*)
Miss R MacLean, BHSPI (*Equestrian Manager/Riding
Instructor*)
Mrs M Malloch (*Junior Years Learning Assistant*)
Ms P Martin, BA Hons (*Art*)
Mrs K Megahy, NVQ Early Years Care and Education
(*Classroom Assistant*)
Ms S Muller, Bachelor of Social Work, PGCE (*Residential
Mistress, Mater*)
Mr G Murch, BMus Hons, PGCE (*Music*)
Mrs L A Murray, RGN, SCM (*Matron*)
Miss C Neave (*Residential Assistant*)
Mrs D Neville, MA Hons, PGDE, CELTA (*Head of ESOL*)
Miss E Norton (*Residential Assistant*)
Miss C Ogg (*Equestrian Assistant*)
Mrs A O'Hear, BSc Hons, PGCE Biology (*Year Head U5
& Head of Moncreiffe*)
Mrs L Oswald, BEd Hons (*Mathematics, History, Year
Head U4 & Head of Arran*)
Dr C Phillips, BA Hons, MA, PhD, PGCE (*Head of
Geography*)
Miss A Pitkin (*Residential Mistress, Barat/Swinton*)
Mrs E Rodger, BEd Hons (*Physical Education*)
Mrs M Saunders, BA Hons (*English*)
Mrs K Scott, BHSPI (*Equestrian Instructor/Assistant*)
Mrs L Scott, BA (*Head of Drama*)
Mrs L Sidey, BA (*Classroom Assistant*)
Mrs L Smith (*Assistant Residential Mistress*)
Mrs S Speed, BSc Hons, PGCE (*Head of Mathematics &
Computer Science*)
Miss B Spurgin, MA Hons (*Librarian*)
Mrs E Stewart, Dip Ed (*Junior Years Form Teacher*)
Miss L Watt (*Assistant Boarding Mistress*)

Administration:
Miss A Gibb, HNC (*Headmistress's PA*)
Mrs S Harrison (*School Secretary*)
Mrs C Heaton-Armstrong (*Receptionist*)
Mrs A Johnstone, BA Hons (*Head of Admissions*)
Mrs A Macdonald, LLB, Dip LP, HNC (*Data Manager and
Examinations Officer*)
Mrs A McHugh, BEd Hons (*Receptionist*)
Mr G Muirhead, BSc Hons (*ICT Manager*)
Mrs L Sidey, BA (*Receptionist*)
Ms T Stack (*Junior Years School Secretary*)
Catering Manager: Mr D Macdonald
Facilities & Transport Manager: Mr M Richmond, BSc,
MSc

Finance:
Mrs K Mackie (*Finance Assistant*)
Mrs A Roger (*Assistant Bursar*)
Housekeeping Staff:
Miss O Fraser, Mrs L Friars (*Housekeeping Supervisor*),
Miss L Holden, Mrs C Hunter, Mrs A Kenny, Mrs D
McDonald, Mrs A McCallum, Mrs P Ptak, Mrs J
Sinclair, Mrs K Smith, Miss A Todd, Mrs D Townsley
Language and Activities Manager: Ms S Littlejohn, BA
Hons
Maintenance/Grounds/Security/Transport Team:
Mr S Anderson, Mr S Cameron, Mr R Carter, Mr J Fenton,
Mr M Gunn, Mr S Kettles, Mr J Marshall, Mr I Shepherd
(*Maintenance Supervisor*)
Marketing Manager: Mr D Milner, BA Hons

King Edward VI High School for Girls

Birmingham

Edgbaston Park Road, Birmingham B15 2UB

Tel: 0121 472 1834
Fax: 0121 471 3808
email: enquiries@kehsmail.co.uk
website: www.kehs.org.uk

Independent, formerly Direct Grant.

Founded in 1883, the School moved in 1940 to its present buildings and extensive grounds adjacent to King Edward's School for Boys. There are 601 girls from 11 to 18 years of age, all day pupils.

Curriculum. The curriculum is distinctive in its strong academic emphasis and aims to inspire a love of learning. The purpose of the curriculum is to help girls realise their full potential. Excellence is sought in aesthetic, practical and physical activities as well as in academic study. Our aim is to achieve a balance of breadth and depth, with dropping of subjects postponed as long as possible so that girls may make informed choices and have access to a wide range of possible careers.

In **Year One** all girls take English, Mathematics, separate Sciences, Religious Studies, French, Latin, History, Geography, Music, Art and Design, Drama, Information Technology, Games, Swimming, Dance and Creative Skills.

In **Years Two and Three** all girls take English, Mathematics, separate Sciences, Religious Studies, French, Latin, German or Spanish, History, Geography, Music, Art and Design, Information Technology, Physical Education, Creative Skills.

Core subjects in **Years Four and Five** are English Language, English Literature, Mathematics, at least two Sciences, but they can take three, Latin, French. Girls then choose from 3 option blocks their other GCSE subjects. Another modern language can be taken as a two-year GCSE course.

In the **Sixth Form** girls choose four A Levels from a wide range of subjects, all Arts, or all Sciences or a mixture of the two. Stress is placed on breadth at this level. The school also offers Critical Thinking in the Upper Sixth as well as the Extended Project Qualification. Various philosophical, scientific and practical topics are explored in short courses.

All girls follow a course in personal decision-making in which they explore and discuss a wide range of issues which call for personal choice and which helps develop life skills.

Religious and moral education are considered important. Academic study of them is designed to enable girls to be informed and questioning. There is no denominational teaching in the school in lessons or morning assembly. Girls of all faiths or of none are equally welcome.

Girls take part in Physical Education, until the Upper Sixth Form where it is voluntary, with increasing choice from gymnastics, hockey, netball, tennis, rounders, dance, fencing, badminton, squash, fives, swimming, athletics, basketball, volleyball, self-defence, aerobics, archery, health related fitness. We have our own swimming pool, sports hall and extensive pitches, including two artificial hockey areas.

In addition to the music in the curriculum, there are choirs and orchestras which reach a high standard. These are mostly joint with King Edward's School. Individual (or shared) instrumental lessons, at an extra fee, are arranged in school in a great variety of instruments. Some instruments can be hired. Individual singing lessons can also be arranged.

A large number of clubs (many joint with King Edward's School) are run by pupils themselves with help and encouragement from staff. Others (e.g. Drama, Music, Sport) are directed by staff. Help is given with activities relating to The Duke of Edinburgh's Award scheme. Some activities take place in lunch hours, others after school and at weekends.

As part of the school's commitment to developing an awareness of the needs of society and a sense of duty towards meeting those needs, girls are encouraged to plan and take part in various community service projects as well as organising activities in school to raise money to support causes of their choice.

A spacious careers room is well stocked with up-to-date information. Individual advice and aptitude testing is given at stages where choices have to be made. The Careers Advisor has overall responsibility but many others are involved with various aspects. Girls are encouraged to attend conferences, gain work experience, make personal visits and enquiries. Old Edwardians and others visit school to talk about their careers. There is good liaison with universities and colleges of all kinds. Virtually all girls go on to higher education. A wide range of courses is being taken by Old Edwardians.

Admission of Pupils. Entry is normally for girls of 11 into the first year of the school in September. Applications must be made by September the year before they are due to start secondary school. The entrance examination is held early October. Girls should have reached the age of 11 years by 31st August following the examination. Girls are examined at the school in English and Mathematics. The syllabus is such as would be normally covered by girls of good ability and no special preparation is advised.

Girls from 12 to 15 are normally considered only if they move from another part of the country, or in some special circumstances. Applications should be made to the Registrar. Such girls can be admitted during the first three years if there is a vacancy.

There is an entry into the Sixth Form for girls wishing to study four main A Level subjects. Application should be made to the Principal by the end of January in the preceding academic year.

Fees per term (2018–2019). £4,296.

Scholarships and Bursaries. The equivalent of up to a total of two full-fee scholarships may be awarded on the results of the Governors' Admission Examination to girls entering the first year, with a maximum of 50% for any individual scholarship. These are independent of parental income and are normally tenable for 7 years.

Means-tested Bursaries are available for girls entering the school at 11+ and 16+.

Charitable status. The Schools of King Edward VI in Birmingham is a Registered Charity, number 529051. The purpose of the Foundation is to educate children and young persons living in or around the city of Birmingham mainly by provision of, or assistance to its schools.

Governing Body: The Governors of the Schools of King Edward VI in Birmingham

Principal: Mrs A Clark, MA Cantab, PGCE

Vice Principal: Ms Susan Pallister, BA Birmingham, MA York, NPQH, PGCE
Vice Principal: Mrs Neelam Varma, BSc & MA Warwick, PGCE
Vice Principal: Mr Martin Lea, BSc Sheffield, PGCE
Director of Sixth Form: Mrs Joanna Whitehead, BSc Birmingham, PGCE
Acting Assistant Head (Administration): Mr Andrew Duncombe, MA Cantab, PGCE
Assistant Head & Head of Middle School: Mrs Kam Sangha, MBA UCE, PGCE Warwick
Head of Lower School and 3rds Coordinator: Mrs Sarah Shore-Nye, BA Swansea, PGCE

Teaching Staff:
Mrs Rachel Arnold, MA Cantab, PGCE
Mrs Marcia Atkins, MA Reading, QTS
Dr Victoria Bailey, BSc Cardiff, PhD Cardiff, PGCE
Mr Nicholas Bassett, BA, MA Kingston, PGCE
Mrs Marion Bellshaw, BSc Westfield College London, PGCE
Mrs Susan Bhagi, BSc Birmingham, PGCE
Dr Sheila Blain, BA, MA Cantab, PGCE
Miss Sarah Blanks, BA Birmingham, GTP, QTS
Mrs M Cas Britton, BA London, PGCE
Mrs Gemma Buck, BSc Nottingham, PGCE
Miss Angela L Buckley, BA Oxon, GTP, QTS
Mrs Gillian K Chapman, BEd Chelsea School of Human Movement
Dr Jonathan Chatwin, BA Hull, MA Hull, PhD Exeter, PGCE
Mrs Rebecca M Coetzee, MA Cantab, PGCE
Mr Timothy O Cooper, BA Bristol, PGCE
Mrs Kate Cowan, BSc Glasgow, MRes Glasgow, MA Ed OU, PGCE
Mrs Rita D'Aquila, Master Cert Ed Catania
Mr Roger Devey, BSc Derby, PGCE
Mrs Jennifer Douglas, BA Hons Sheffield, PGCE
Miss Penny Evans, BA Hons Exeter, PGCE
Mrs Lois Fisher, MA Nottingham
Mme Laurence D Franco, Maîtrise LLCE Montpellier III, PGCE
Mr Mike Gilbert, BA USC
Mr Neil Haines, BA Kent, MA Nottingham, PGCE
Mrs Fiona Hall, MA Oxon, PGCE
Mrs Gemma Hargreaves, BSc Cardiff, PG DipEd
Dr Stephanie J T Hayton, BSc, PhD Newcastle, PGCE
Mr James Heather, BSc Birmingham, PG DipEd
Mr Simon Holland, BA Warwick, PGCE
Mrs Katherine Howes, BA Birmingham, PGCE
Ms Sara Huxley-Edwards, BA Birmingham, PGCE
Dr Rachel M Jackson-Royal, BA King's College London, MA London, PGCE, PhD Birmingham
Mr Tom Jarvis, MusB Manchester, PGCE
Mrs Alexandra John, DMM Bury, PGCE
Mr Harry J Kavanagh, MA Cantab, PGCE
Mrs Helen D Kavanagh, BA Bristol, PGCE
Miss Roselyne R Laurent, Diplome de technicientrilingue Haute Alsace, PGCE
Mrs Victoria J Law, BA Hons Oxon, PGCE
Dr Andrew Limm, BA, PhD Birmingham, PGCE
Mr Findlay Mackinnon, BA Strathclyde, PGCE
Mrs Jaspal K Mahon, BSc London, PGCE
Mrs Aurore Marquette, BA, MA France, MPhil, PGCE
Mrs J E Moule, BA Durham, PGCE

Mrs Elena Norman, BA Hons USSR, QTS Wolverhampton
Miss Jill Oldfield, BSc Durham, PGCE
Miss Sarah Platt, BSc Manchester, PGCE
Mrs Christine Pollard, BSc Nottingham, PGCE
Dr Manish Popat-Szabries, BSc City, MA Warwick, PhD Warwick, PGCE
Miss Rebecca Priest, BA Aberystwyth, PGCE
Miss Hannah Proops, BA Central School of Speech & Drama, GTP, QTS
Mr Rimmy Ridges, BSc Warwick, PGCE
Miss Kathryn Rollason, BSc York, PGCE
Ms Michelle N Sanders, GRSM, ARCM Royal College of Music, PGCE
Mr Richard T Sheppard, BEng Manchester, PGCE
Dr Matthew Simpson, PhD Birmingham, MSc Birmingham, GTP QTS
Mrs Marta Soldevilla, BA Oviedo, PGCE
Dr Daljit Suemul, BSc Hons Polytechnic of North London, PhD Polytechnic of North London, PGCE
Mr Jack Symes, BA Liverpool, PG Dip Ed Birmingham, MA Liverpool
Dr Bernard L Tedd, BSc London, MA Mgt Ed, PhD Leicester, PGCE, AKC
Mrs Beverley Thompson, BSc Sheffield Polytechnic, PGCE
Mrs Adele Waites, BA Hull, MA Birmingham, PGCE
Miss Katharine Williams, MA Cantab, MA Ed Birmingham
Miss Catrin E Woods, BA Warwick, QTS

Librarian: Mr Adam Rogers
Principal's PA: Mrs Debbie Macleod
Admissions Registrar: Mrs C Oakes
Matron: Mrs Julie Kent

The Kingsley School

Beauchamp Hall, Beauchamp Avenue, Royal Leamington Spa, Warwickshire CV32 5RD

Tel:	01926 425127
Fax:	01926 831691
email:	schooloffice@kingsleyschool.co.uk
website:	www.thekingsleyschool.com

Independent Day School for Girls aged 3 to 18, and boys up to 11 years, founded in 1884.

For over 130 years The Kingsley School has had an excellent reputation for high academic standards and first class pastoral care. What sets The Kingsley School apart from other schools is its distinctive family ethos and friendly atmosphere. We are immensely proud of the fact that everyone who visits us remarks on the happy staff-student relationships and the sense of community it fosters. At Kingsley, pupils have a positive and purposeful approach to learning. The atmosphere is unique; enthusiastic and approachable teachers inspire pupils to learn; behaviour is excellent and pupils are challenged and supported according to individual need. Where practical, we aim to personalise the curriculum so that pupils can reach their potential whatever their gifts and talents.

The Kingsley **Preparatory School** is friendly and purposeful and offers a rich, vibrant and creative Curriculum for girls and boys aged 3–11. Outstanding teaching encourages a love of learning by providing a balance between the sound foundations for academic progress with character-building creativity. Kingsley has a well-established core curriculum in which the focus is on excellence within English, mathematics and science, supported by bespoke teaching in music, drama, modern foreign languages and physical education. In support of the core curriculum we have developed an exciting Creative Curriculum which sets our pupils a challenge; to explore and discover the real world. Most girls progress to The Kingsley Senior School, and boys move on to the next stage with self-assurance, some having been awarded scholarships for entry into local schools.

The **Senior School** provides continuity of academic and pastoral care. We offer a broad, balanced and stimulating academic experience. The curriculum at Kingsley is structured to maximise progress, building on girls' prior learning to encourage creativity, intellectual curiosity and independence. Our GCSE results are excellent, with high attainment year on year. At GCSE our curriculum provides opportunities for girls to study examinations in the core subjects of English, mathematics and the three separate sciences, as well as in the humanities subjects, the performing arts, physical education and modern foreign languages. The school delivers an academically rigorous timetable, yet has the flexibility and scope to offer additional subjects such as Latin and classical civilisation. Girls also experience a range of design subjects, for example food technology and textiles. Academic standards are high, with the 2018 GCSE results showing a 100% pass rate at grades 9 to 4 in at least 5 subjects, of which 23% of were at grades 8 to 9, and 11% achieving grade 9.

The Kingsley School's **Sixth Form** provides a wide range of opportunities for all students. We offer a high-quality A Level curriculum and cater for a wide range of interests and post-16 aspirations. Students' academic achievements are outstanding and the diversity of their goals is embraced, with most progressing to their first-choice university, choosing to take apprenticeships within prestigious commercial organisations or studying further Higher Education courses. In the 2018 A Level exams over a third achieved A* to A grades. Recent leavers' destinations include Medicine at UEA, Law at Leeds and Liverpool, Medieval and Modern Languages at Cambridge, Dentistry at Bristol, English at Cardiff, Geography at Leeds, Maths at Swansea, Marine Zoology at Newcastle, Nursing at King's College London, Music at Edinburgh and Birmingham Conservatoire and a Fashion and Retail Apprenticeship at Harrods, London.

Kingsley offers many enrichment activities which both extend and enhance the curriculum. The inclusive programme is designed to engage each pupil allowing them to enjoy new experiences in addition to developing essential life skills. There is a diverse selection of clubs and activities on offer. Opportunities include The Duke of Edinburgh's Award, Young Enterprise and World Challenge schemes. There are a variety of trips and visits, both local and international, for example theatre trips, an art and Spanish visit to Barcelona, geography trips to Iceland and the West Coast of the USA and a choir tour of Tuscany.

Sport and physical education are a vital part of life at Kingsley; each child is encouraged to achieve their personal best. We recognise that mental and physical fitness go hand in hand to develop wellbeing and academic potential. Sport helps to develop resilience, teamwork and leadership skills and lifelong health and fitness. Each week there is an inclusive programme of extracurricular sports offered before school, during lunchtimes and at after-school clubs. We compete regularly against local and regional opposition, with thriving sports teams. Kingsley also runs its own competitive riding squad and a thriving and award-winning ski team.

We offer tuition in the performing arts leading to national music and drama qualifications. There are Kingsley choirs and musical ensembles and bands with regular opportunities to perform and showcase talent; both Prep and Senior School have annual musical theatre and drama productions.

Fees per term (2018–2019). Preparatory School: £3,533 (Reception to Year 2), £4,115 (Years 3–6). Senior School & Sixth Form: £4,418.

Scholarships and Bursaries. Academic, art, music, drama, sport and performing arts scholarships are available at 7+, 11+, and 16+.

Bursaries are available.

Our fleet of 11 school minibuses serves a wide area and before and after-school care is available.

Charitable status. The Kingsley School is a Registered Charity, number 528774. It exists to provide high-quality education for girls aged 3 to 18 and boys up to 11 years.

Governors:
President: Mr A Noble
Chair: Dame Y Buckland

Mr L Brown	Mrs M Hicks
Mr N Button	Mr D Loudon
Mr A Bye	Mr A Maher
Mr D Cleary	Mrs C Rigby
Mrs C Ellis	Mrs E Smith
Mrs L Greaves	Mr J Strain

Clerk to the Governors: Mrs M Griffin

Head Teacher: Ms H Owens, BA, PGCE, NPQH

Deputy Head (Pastoral): Mrs J Bailey, BA, MEd, CertEd

Assistant Headteacher (Curriculum): Mrs R Rogers, BSc, PGCE,, MA

Head of Preparatory School: Mrs R Whiting, BA, MA, PGCE, NPQSL

Head of Sixth Form: Mrs D Morgan, BA, PGCE

Staff:
* *Head of Department*

Art:
*Mr E Lax, BA, PGCE
Mrs R Whiting, BA, MA, PGCE, NPQSL

Classics:
*Ms I Peace, BA, PGCE

Design & Technology:
*Mrs C Dempsey, BEd
Mrs K Hughes-O'Sullivan, BEd, MA
Miss C Shephard, BSc, PGCE

Economics & Business Studies:
*Mrs M Bennett, BEd, MA

English and Drama:
*Mrs A Alton, BA, PGCE
Mrs D Morgan, BA, PGCE
Mrs J Hillson, BA, PGCE, MA
Ms H Owens, BA, PGCE, NPQH
Mrs J Rhodes, BA QTS

Geography:
*Mrs K Ahmed, BA, PG DipEd
Mrs J Bailey, BA, MEd, CertEd
Mrs R Rogers, BSc, PGCE

Health and Social Care:
Mrs S Mace, BA, PGCE

History:
*Miss C Parry, BSc Econ, PGCE

ICT:
*Mrs M Bennett, BEd, MA
Mrs C Dempsey, BEd
Mrs S Mace, BA, PGCE
Mrs M Roberts, BEd, MA

Mathematics:
*Mr T Spillane, BSc, PGCE
Mrs P Davies, BSc, PGCE
Mrs L Laubscher, HED SA QTS
Dr A Smith, BA, PhD, PGCE

Modern Languages:
*Mr I Stickels, BA, PGCE
Mrs C Cocksworth, BA
Mrs T Connor, BA
Mrs H Foulerton, BA, PGCE
Miss M Mahé, Maîtrise Litt et Lang, Lic de Lang

Performing Arts:
*Mr J Smith, BMus, PGCE
Mrs K Buckingham, LSDE LAMDA
Mrs A Vallance, BA QTS (Dance)

Personal and Social Education:
*Mrs K Hughes-O'Sullivan, BEd, MA

Mrs K Ahmed, BA, PG DipEd
Mrs J Bailey, BA, MEd, CertEd
Mrs C Dempsey, BEd

Physical Education:
*Miss S Windsor, BEd
Mrs J Bailey, BA, Med, CertEd
Mrs S Bates, BA, CertEd
Mrs K Close
Mrs J Davies, BEd
Mrs E Macleod, BA

Psychology:
*Mrs S Mace, BA, PGCE
Mrs K MacLeod, BSc, Cert Teach

Preparatory School:
Head: Mrs R Whiting, BA, MA, PGCE, NPQSL
Mrs G Adair, BN, PGCE
Mrs R Bhangal, BA, NCFE
Miss J Clark, BA, PGCE
Mrs L Conniff, BA QTS
Mrs C Divers, BA QTS
Miss H Fennell, BA Primary QTS, PG SENCO
Ms C Gardner, TA Qual
Miss C Harris, BSc, PGCE
Ms C Hayward, NNEB
Mrs S Holmes, BA QTS

Careers:
Mrs S Bennett

Duke of Edinburgh's Award:
Manager: Mrs L Laubscher, HED SA QTS

Academic Learning Support:
*Mrs L Payne, BA, SEND PG
Mrs R Athwal, BSc, MEd, PGCE
Mrs C Cocksworth, BA
Ms J Harper, BA MSocSc, Adv Dip
Mrs Y Raja, Dip
Mrs S Smith, BA, PGCE

Learning Resources Centre:
Mrs E Smith, BA

Finance Office:
Mr B Cheney (*Head of Finance*)
Mr D Falp (*Senior Finance Assistant*)
Mrs S Punj (*Finance Assistant*)
Mrs M Adamo (*Finance Assistant*)

Administration:
Mrs J Bostock (*PA to Headteacher*)
Mrs A Griffiths (*Admin and Receptionist*)
Mrs K Parker (*Prep School Admin and Receptionist*)
Ms J Prosser (*Premises Manager*)
Mrs S Tsang (*Exam Secretary/Cover Administrator*)
Mrs M Wright (*Admin and Receptionist*)

Marketing and Admissions:
Mrs S Hill (*Registrar*)
Mr J Farrington-Smith (*PR & Marketing Manager*)
Mrs A Gardner (*Digital & Marketing Assistant*)
Miss K Sutton (*Admissions Assistant*)

School Nurse:
Mrs T Ball, SRN, BSc Hons

Philosophy, Ethics and Religion (PER):
*Miss R Bubb, BA, PGCE
Mrs K MacLeod, BSc, Cert Teach
Mrs K Ahmed, BA, PG DipEd

Science:
*Dr C Robertson, BSc, PhD, PGCE
Mrs S Bains MSc, PGCE
Mrs S Bacon, BSc Hons, PGCE
Mrs S Baker, BSc, PGCE
Mrs A Hawthorn BEng MSc, PGCE
Mrs L Lane, BSc, PGCE
Miss G Reid, BSc, PGCE

Miss M Knight-Adams, BSc, PGCE
Mrs C Lopez, BA, MA (*Spanish*)
Ms T Markwell, BA, PHCE
Mrs E Murphy, BA, PGCE
Mrs B O'Reilly, BMus, MMus, PG Dip Perf (*Music*)
Miss S Slater, BA, PGCE
Miss E Smith, BA (*Drama*)
Mrs J Thompson, BA Early Years

Wellbeing Counsellor:
Mrs P Thomas, BSc, Dip Psych, PG Dip, Registered MBACP

Lady Eleanor Holles

Hanworth Road, Hampton, Middlesex TW12 3HF

Tel: 020 8979 1601
Fax: 020 8941 8291
email: office@lehs.org.uk
website: www.lehs.org.uk
Twitter: @LEHSchool

This Independent Girls' School is one of the oldest in the country, founded in 1710 in Cripplegate under the Will of the Lady Eleanor Holles. In 1937, the school moved to purpose-built premises in Hampton. Numerous additions to the building have enabled the school to increase to some 930 girls, aged from 7 to 18 years, who enjoy a wealth of specialist facilities and the use of 24 acres of playing fields and gardens. Nine science laboratories, Learning Resources Centre, Sixth Form Library, a Product Design suite, extensive computing and multimedia language facilities and a dedicated Careers area are complemented by grass and hard tennis courts, netball courts, 5 lacrosse pitches, track and field areas and a full-sized, indoor heated swimming pool refurbished in 2017. A Boat House, shared with Hampton School, was opened in October 2000 and a large Sports Hall, adjacent to the swimming pool, in September 2001.

September 2012 saw the opening of a new Arts Centre consisting of a 300-seat theatre, new Music and Art Departments, Sixth Form Common Rooms, followed in September 2013 by a new dining room, a new suite of classrooms, two dedicated Drama Studios, a Conference Room and The Friends' Courtyard.

In 2018 the Gateway Building opened with a state-of-the-art Computing suite, and Product Design facilities. Both of these subjects are now offered at A Level.

Both the Junior and Senior Schools are equipped with a lift for the disabled.

The School's Statement of Purpose embodies the original aim, to encourage every girl to develop her personality to the full so that she may become a woman of integrity and a responsible member of society. It also emphasises the value of a broad, balanced education which gives due importance to sport, music and the creative arts in general, whilst providing the opportunities for girls to achieve high academic standards within a framework of disciplined, independent study.

The Curriculum. In Years 7–9 girls take two modern foreign languages, Latin, separate sciences, dedicated computing lessons and a PSHE programme which continues throughout the school. Selection rather than specialisation for GCSE allows girls to respond to individual abilities and attributes, and every girl continues to experience a broad education in which as few doors as possible are closed. A large sixth form of about 200 girls means that a wide choice of Advanced Level subjects is offered. Most girls will study four or five subjects in L6th, proceeding to A Level with three or four. The girls have the option of taking the Extended Project Qualification, and a great deal of emphasis is placed on leadership roles and extra-curricular activities. All sixth form students move on to further training, the majority to universities, and there is a sizeable Oxbridge and North American contingent annually. The formal Careers programme, which begins in Year 9, continues throughout the school and uses external specialists, parents, past pupils,

ECCTIS and other computer programmes, as well as the School's own, trained staff.

Extra-Curricular Activity. A key strength of the school is the range and diversity of its flourishing extra-curricular provision. Some 120 clubs run each week ranging from Music, Drama and Sports to Outward Bound and subject clubs, all aiming to stimulate further and inculcate a love of learning outside the classroom: 'The Other Half'. Sixth Formers lead a number of groups which focus on various political, environmental and ethical issues, including 'Model United Nations', 'Amnesty' and Eco-Squad. Girls are encouraged to take the initiative to form their own clubs with a Medic Group, Law Society and Book Club formed in the recent past. The school is very much at the heart of the local community and has developed a wide range of activities to ensure that students are aware of their social responsibilities, including Service Volunteers which works with disadvantaged local school children and the elderly, and running numerous activities in local primary schools, including language and drama clubs. Pupils are strongly encouraged to participate in extra-curricular activities.

The Junior School (190 pupils aged 7–11) is accommodated in a separate building in the grounds which was extensively renovated and refurbished in 2003. It is an integral part of the whole school community and uses many of the specialist facilities available for Seniors.

(*See entry in the IAPS section for more details.*)

Entrance. Pupils may enter the Junior School from the age of 7, and the Senior School at 11 years. LEH Junior School pupils are guaranteed places in the Senior School (other than in exceptional circumstances). Girls with good academic ability may apply for direct entry to the Sixth Form. All external applicants must sit the School's competitive entrance examinations, which are held in November for Sixth Form entry and January (7+ and 11+) each year, for admission in the following September. There are no internal hurdles for entry to Sixth Form. Registration and Entrance Examination Fee: £100.

Scholarships and Bursaries.

11+ Entry Academic Scholarships: On average ten awards are offered each year. These are expressed as percentages of the full fee and will thus keep pace with any fee increases. Awards are non-means-tested and usually 10%. The awards are based on performance in the school's own Entrance Examinations and subsequent interview.

Governors' Bursaries: Candidates who sit entrance papers at any stage from 11+ onwards may be considered for a bursary award. These are available for up to 100% of fees, plus extras, and are means tested and subject to annual review.

Sixth Form Academic Scholarships: Ten Scholarships worth 10% of fees over the two years of Sixth Form study are offered to internal and external candidates who sit the Sixth Form Entrance and Scholarship Examination in November before the year of proposed entry.

Music Scholarships: Both Major and Minor Awards for Music are available at 11+ and 16+. These are for 10% and 7.5% of fees respectively, plus free tuition on one instrument. Candidates must satisfy academic requirements in entrance papers before being invited to a music audition. Full details are available from the school.

At 16+ only, Scholarships are also available in Art, Sport, Drama and STEM (one in each) for girls who propose to take A Level in the subject in the case of Art.

Fees per term (2018–2019). £5,576 in the Junior School; £6,732 in the Senior School. Fees are inclusive of books and stationery and exclusive of Public Examination fees.

Former Pupils' Association. Holles Connect. Address for communications: Alumnae Administrator c/o Lady Eleanor Holles; email: alumnae@lehs.org.uk

The Cripplegate Schools Foundation

Chairman of the Foundation: Mr C S Stokes

Vice-Chairman: Mrs W J Wildman, BA, PGCE, Dip Counselling

Governors:
Mr S R Kamat, MBA, MS
Mr D H King, BSc FCA
Mr N D Lewis, LLB
Dr S McCormick, MA, PGCE, PhD, FRSB
Mrs A Meyric Hughes, BA, PGCE, MA
Mr R J Milburn, MA, FCA
Ms C Millis, Chartered FCIPD
Miss C V Thomas, BSc, AADip, ARB, RIBA
Mrs C Thomas, BA Hons
Sister P Thomas, BEd Hons, MA

Clerk to the Governors: Mrs S Whitehouse, BA

Head Mistress: Mrs Heather G Hanbury, MA Edinburgh, MSc Wolfson College Cambridge

Deputy Head: Mrs Lindsey Hughes, BA Warwick

Head of Junior School: Mrs Paula Mortimer, BEd Westminster College Oxford

Director of Finance: Mr Michael Berkowitch, BSc, JD

Senior Assistant Head: Mr Matt Williams, BA City of London Polytechnic

Senior Assistant Head Pastoral and Co-curricular: Mrs Amanda Poyner, BSc Exeter, MBA

Assistant Head Pastoral LVI/UVI: Mr Mark Tompsett, MA Selwyn College Cambridge

Assistant Head Pastoral LV/UV: Mrs Hilary Ndongong, MA St Edmund Hall Oxford

Assistant Head Pastoral III-UIV: Mrs Katie Sinnett, BA Peterhouse Cambridge

Director of Studies: Mr Dave M Piper, BA King's College London

Director of Development and Communications: Mrs Jenny Blaiklock, MA St Hilda's College Oxford

Senior School

Art and Design:
Miss S Pauffley, BA Goldsmiths London (*Head of Art*)
Mr L Curtis, BA Slade School of Art, MA Royal College of Art
Miss H Peat, BA Loughborough College of Art and Design
Ms A E Seaborn, BA Winchester School of Art
Miss S White, BA University of the Arts

Classics:
Miss F Ellison, MA Girton College Cambridge (*Head of Classics and Head of LVI*)
Mrs R Brown, BA Durham (*Head of UV*)
Miss K C Eltis, BA Balliol College Oxford
Miss E Lewis, BA University College London
Mr D Piper, BA King's College London (*Assistant Head – Director of Studies*)

Computing:
Miss R Crisa, BSc Brunel, MSc St Mary's (*Head of Computing*)
Mrs D Bakre, BArch BKPS College of Architecture Pune India, MBA The Citadel USA
Mr J South, BA Goldsmiths London; MA Roehampton (Manager Digital Teaching & Learning):
Mrs P M Stewart, BSc Bath

Design Technology:
Miss A M Travers, BEd Surrey (*Head of D&T*)
Mrs A-M Angliss, BEd Trinity College Dublin
Mrs H Boczkowski, BSc Bath Spa
Mrs G Bell (*D&T Assistant*)

Drama and Theatre Studies:
Dr B J Tait, BA CSSD, PhD Royal Holloway London
   (*Director of Drama & Theatre Studies*)
Miss G Guttner, BA Kent
Miss S Torrent, BA Greenwich
Mrs P Tate (*Music and Drama Administrator*)

Economics:
Miss A J Matthews, BA Leicester (*Head of Economics and
   Careers*)
Miss D A Self, BSc Brunel

English:
Mr T-S Li, BA University College London, MPhil St
   Edmund's College Cambridge (*Head of English*)
Mrs K Mackichan, BA Leeds (*Deputy Head of English*)
Miss H Barnett, BA Durham (*Head of UVI*)
Mrs H M Ndongong, MA St Edmund Hall Oxford
   (*Assistant Head Pastoral Upper School*)
Ms J Parry, MA St Andrews
Mrs U Renton, MA Aberdeen
Mrs C Richardson, BA Reading
Miss A-M Wright, MA Aberdeen

Geography:
Mr L M Tresserras, BA Southampton (*Head of Geography*)
Miss R Ling, BA Christ Church Oxford
Mrs R Lockett, BA Southampton (*Head of LIV*)
Miss A Perlowska-Goose, BSc Reading

History of Art:
Miss A Lindsay, BA Manchester (*Head of History of Art*)

History and Politics:
Miss N Randall, MA York (*Head of History and Politics*)
Mr N Allen, BA Nottingham
Mrs A M Bradshaw, MA St Andrews
Ms K Crosby, BA Brunel
Ms J FitzGerald, BA Newcastle, MA Central School of
   Speech & Drama
Mrs L Harding-Anderson, BA Warwick
Mrs L D Hughes, BA Warwick (*Deputy Head*)

Mathematics:
Mrs J Manns, BSc Sheffield (*Head of Mathematics*)
Mr C Ralphs, BEng Birmingham (*Deputy Head of
   Mathematics*)
Mrs N Banerjee, BA Delhi
Mr M Deacon, BSc Exeter
Miss H Doshi, BSc City University London
Mrs S Leigh, BSc Edinburgh (*Head of UIV*)
Mrs M Najjar, BSc University College London
Miss R Nicholl, BSc King's College London
Mr C O'Brien, BSc Limerick
Mrs A Poyner, BSc Exeter, MBA (*Senior Assistant Head
   Pastoral and Co-curricular*)
Mrs M Read, BSc Durham
Mr C Sin, BSc MSc Cardiff
Mrs K Sinnett, BA Peterhouse Cambridge (*Assistant Head
   Pastoral Middle School*)
Mr M J Williams, BA City of London Polytechnic (*Senior
   Assistant Head*)

Modern Languages:
Mrs Y Wiggins, BA Staatsexamen Universität Würzburg
   (*Head of MFL and German*)
Mrs V M Kean, BA Leeds (*Head of French*)
Mrs U Arrieta, BA Deusto, Bilbao (*Head of Spanish*)
Mrs A Buck, Licenciada en Filología Anglogermanica
   Universidad de Valencia (*Spanish and German*)

Ms N Murray, BA Leeds, MA Leeds (*French*)
Mrs N J Rees, MA New Hall Cambridge (*Spanish and
   Special Educational Needs*)
Miss D L Robbins, MA St Andrews (*French*)
Mrs A Rowe, BA Nottingham (*French and German*)
Mr M Russell, BA St Catherine's College Oxford (*German,
   Head of LV*)
Mr M Tompsett, MA Selwyn College Cambridge (*German,
   Assistant Head Pastoral*)

Music:
Mrs M Ashe, MA St Catherine's College Oxford (*Director
   of Music*)
Mr B G Ashe, BA York, PGCE, LRAM (*Composer in
   Residence*)
Miss N Redman, BMus Manchester, MMus GSMD (*Head
   of Thirds*)
Miss C Sheppard-Vine, BMus Birmingham, MMus
Mr E Zuckert, MMus Royal College of Music, BMus
   Royal Conservatoire of Scotland
Mrs P Tate (*Music and Drama Administrator*)

Natural Sciences:
Miss H Airbright, BSc Reading (*Biology*)
Miss A Boland, BSc St Mary's (*Head of Psychology*)
Mr A Brittain, BSc Canterbury Kent (*Physics*)
Mrs N C Camilleri, BSc Manchester (*Physics*)
Mrs J Crook, BSc Nottingham (*Chemistry*)
Mrs P Earl, BSc Swansea (*Biology*)
Mrs K M Ellis, BSc Durham (*Physics*)
Mr A Hayter, BSc Durham (*Head of Chemistry*)
Mr J James, BSc East Anglia (*Chemistry*)
Mrs S Jansz, BSc Bangor (*Chemistry*)
Mr N Johnson, MSc Nottingham (*Physics*)
Mrs H Lenox-Smith, BSc University College London
   (*Biology*)
Mr R Mangion, BSc King's College London (*Chemistry*)
Miss L Mercer, BSc Edinburgh (*Biology*)
Ms L Monteil, BSc Manchester (*Psychology*)
Mrs C R Nicholls, BSc Cardiff (*Biology*)
Ms C Packer, BSc University College London (*Chemistry*)
Miss V Ranjan, BSc Durham (*Biology*)
Mrs F Rosier, BSc Bath MRSB (*Head of Biology*)
Ms P Shoebridge, BA Sussex, MA St Mary's (*Psychology*)
Mrs V Whiffin, MEng Southampton (*Head of Physics*)

Philosophy and Religious Studies:
Miss L Prothero, BA Harvest Bible College, Melbourne,
   Australia, MA University College London (*Head of
   Philosophy and Religious Studies*)
Mr T Lightfoot, BA Reading, MPhil Regents Park College,
   Oxford
Miss A Lindsay, BA Manchester (*Head of History of Art*)
Miss D Self, BSc Brunel

Physical Education:
Mrs N Budd, BSc Brighton (*Director of Sport and Outward
   Bound Activities*)
Mrs R Crane, BA St Mary's Twickenham (*Assistant
   Director of Sport*)
Miss E Carlstedt-Duke, BSc University of West of England
   (*Head of Netball*)
Miss E Harrison, BA Durham
Miss P Hawkins, BA Brighton
Miss S Meakings, BSc (*Lacrosse Coach*)
Miss C Wilson, BA University of Notre Dame, Australia
Mrs N Crowther (*Duke of Edinburgh's Award, CCF
   Coordinator*)

Product Design:
Mr S G Bicknell, BSc Brunel, PG Dip (*Head of Product
   Design*)
Mr D Smeaton, BEng Southbank Polytechnic

Rowing:
Mr A Smith (*Head of Rowing*)
Mr S Larner, BSc Imperial College London, MOst British
    School of Osteopathy, PG Dip (*Assistant Head of
    Rowing*)
Mr J Clay, BA Bath, MA Cantab
Mr A James, BSc Cardiff
Ms A Leake, BA Newcastle
Mr J Moon
Mr J Stoddart, BSc
Mr J Thomas, BEng Cardiff
Mr D Fehily
Mr C Shankster (*Boat House Supervisor*)

PSHE:
Mrs A-M Angliss, BEd Trinity College Dublin (*Head of
    PSHE*)
Mrs A Bradshaw, MA St Andrews
Mrs S Leigh, BSc Edinburgh

Learning Support:
Miss M Christodoulou, BA Middlesex, MA Durham,
    PGCert Dyslexia and Literacy (*Head of Learning
    Support*)
Mrs N Rees, MA New Hall Cambridge

Learning Resources Manager:
Mrs L Payne, BA California, MA San Francisco, MCILIP
Mrs C Didiot-Cook (*Assistant*)

Senior School Administrative Staff:
Head Mistress's Personal Assistant: Miss E Clinton, BA,
    PGCE
Registrar : Mrs A Siddiqui, BSc, MSc
HR Manager: Ms N Dimotrova, Assoc CIPD
School Office Manager: Mrs S Austyn
Estates Manager: Mr M Walburn, MRICS, C.Build E
    FCABE
Finance Manager: Mr S Robinson, AAT, Member ACCA

Junior School

Head of Junior School: Mrs P Mortimer, BEd Westminster
    College Oxford
Deputy Head of Junior School: Mrs R Yates, BA Trinity
    College Cambridge, LLM

Teaching Staff:
Mrs J E Allden, BSc London (*Chelsea College*), MSc
    Kingston
Miss V M Barnes, BA Kingston
Mrs S L Bartholomew, BSc St Mary's [maternity leave]
Mrs M M Bass, BEd Natal
Mrs J Deverson, BEd Oxford Brookes
Miss L Evans, BA Kingston
Mrs M Frampton, BEd Exeter
Mrs S Grant-Sturgis, BA Exeter
Mrs S Harding, BEd De Montfort
Mrs K Hide, BEd La Sainte Union College of Education
Mr A Hopkins, BSc Portsmouth
Mrs L Kent-Skorsepova, MA Comenius University,
    Bratislava
Mrs C Lyne, Dartford College of Physical Education, BA
    OU
Mrs S Marr, BEd West of England [maternity leave]
Mr J Miller, BSc Durham, MSc UCL
Mrs N Rees, MA New Hall Cambridge
Mrs K Sehgal, BA St Mary's
Mrs M Walker, BA Canterbury Christchurch (*Director of
    Studies Junior School*)
Mrs L Cowin (*Teaching Assistant*)
Ms P Evans (*Teaching Assistant*)

Junior School Administrative Staff:
Personal Assistant to the Head of Junior School: Miss J
    Chudleigh

Junior School Secretary: Mrs J Rees

School Nurses:
Senior School: Sister S Brew, RGN
Junior School: Nurse L Parker, RCN

School Counsellors:
Senior School: Mrs G Young BA, MBACP, Higher
    Diploma in Counselling
Senior School: Ms T Albekoglu, BA Psychodynamic
    Practice, PG Dip
Junior School: Mrs R Ticciati, SRCN, SRN, MBACP

Leicester High School for Girls

454 London Road, Leicester LE2 2PP

Tel: 0116 270 5338
Fax: 0116 270 2493
email: enquiries@leicesterhigh.co.uk
website: www.leicesterhigh.co.uk
Twitter: @LeicesterHigh
Facebook: @Leicester-High-School-For-Girls

The school is a Trust with a Board of Governors in membership of AGBIS and the Headmaster belongs to the GSA.

Leicester High School is a well-established day school for girls situated in lovely grounds on the south side of the city. Founded in 1906 as Portland House School, it now comprises a Junior Department of approximately 110 girls (3–9 years) and a Senior School of approximately 250 girls (aged 10–18) sited on the same campus.

The Headmaster is responsible for both the Junior Department and Senior School. The staff are well-qualified specialists and the school is renowned for both its academic excellence and extra-curricular programme. At present 18 subjects are offered at GCSE Level and 21 subjects at A Level.

Facilities. The premises are a combination of modern purpose-built units and the original Victorian house, skilfully adapted to its present purpose. The facilities of the School have been systemically improved and updated over recent years. The school has a Junior Department and a Senior School in separate buildings on one site. The Junior Department has its own hall, library, IT suite, garden, playground and outdoor learning area. The Senior School has a central gym, library, drama/dance studio, ICT suites, language computer suite, 6 science laboratories, art and design studio, separate sixth form area and food studies room set around an award-winning courtyard garden. The school benefited from a £3.7m extension in 2010. The 3-acre grounds of the school have tennis and netball courts within extensive gardens.

Religion. The school has a Christian foundation but welcomes girls of other faiths or of none.

Admission. All candidates over the age of 7 are required to pass an entrance examination for admission into the Junior and Senior sections. Direct entry into the Sixth Form is dependent on GCSE results. Entrance into the Early Years Unit is by assessment. A registration fee of £85 is payable for all applicants.

The Headmaster is always pleased to meet parents of prospective pupils and to show them around the school. All communications should be addressed to the Admissions Officer from whom prospectuses, application forms and details of fees may be obtained.

Fees per term (2018–2019). £2,995–£4,065.

Extras. Individual Music lessons, Speech and Drama, and Ballet are offered.

Scholarships and Bursaries. The Headmaster's Scholarship is a five-year scholarship for entry into Year 7 for an academic girl. All those interested must sit the January Entrance Examination. Registering for the examination costs £85.

Scholarships are awarded to any student – either existing Year 6 or external candidates – on the basis of performance in the Year 7 examination papers in English and Mathematics sat on Entrance Examination day in January.

The LHS Sixth Form Scholarship: A scholarship of up to 50% is available to one, exceptional girl joining the Sixth Form. A personal statement, grades and references will be requested and shortlisted girls will be invited to attend an initial interview with the Head of Sixth Form and the subject heads of her chosen A Levels. If successful at this initial interview, girls will be invited to attend a final interview with the Headmaster.

Girls entering the Sixth Form from a state school, and resident in Leicestershire or Rutland, have been invited to apply for a Sir Thomas White Scholarship, which is 100% fees-only funded for two years. The School has had seven Sir Thomas Scholars in recent years.

A small number of Bursaries are available from Year 6 onwards up to the value of full fees.

Charitable Status. Leicester High School Charitable Trust Limited is a Registered Charity, number 503982. The Trust exists to promote and provide for the advancement of education based on Christian principles according to the doctrines of the Church of England.

Board of Governors:
Chair: Mrs M Bowler, JP, BA Hons
Vice-Chair: Mr T Leah, BA, NPQH
Mr J Allen, FCA
Mr M Dunkley, LLB, TEP
Mrs K Mayes, BSc, FCA
Mrs M Neilson, BEd
Mr J Tomlinson, FCA, MA
Mrs S Siesage, BA, PGCE, MBA, NPQH

Clerk to the Governors: Mrs E Mackay, AAT

Headmaster: Mr A R Whelpdale, BA, NPQH

Deputy Head: Miss D E J Wassell, BA

Assistant Head: Mrs D Solly, MSc, BSc

Head of Years 6 and 7: Nurse Abby Cox
Head of Years 8 and 9 (with overview of KS3): Mrs D Morgan, BSc
Head of KS4: Mrs J Rose, BEd
Head of Sixth Form: Ms K Purewal, BSc

Teaching Staff:
* Head of Department

Careers:
*Miss E Tyler, BSc

Computing and Information Technology:
*Mr A Tighe, BSc

English:
*Mrs K Penney, BA
Mrs H Rees, BA
Miss D E J Wassell, BA

Expressive Arts:
Mrs E Bott, BA (*Art and Design*)
Miss E Ikin, BA (*Art and Design/Photography*)
Mrs J Rose, BEd (*Drama, Head of KS4*)
Mr M Haynes, MMus (*Music*)

Food Studies:
*Mrs J Whalley, BSc

Geography:
*Mrs K Haresign, BA
Mrs V Reed, BA

History and Politics:
*Miss A Paul, MA
Mrs F Lodder, MA
Mr A Whelpdale, BA, NPQH

Mathematics:
*Mr M Pinnick, BSc
Mrs K Keary, BSc
Mr A Stewart, BEng
Mrs D Solly, MSc

Modern Languages:
*Mrs L Soto, MA (*Spanish and French*)
Mrs C Dwyer, BA (*Spanish and French*)
Mrs M Watkiss, BA (*Spanish and French*)
Mrs G Wheeler, BA (*French*)

Personal, Social, Health and Citizenship Education:
*Mrs D Morgan, BSc (*Head of KS3 Years 7–9*)

Physical Education:
*Mrs K McCarthy, BSc
Miss S Watson, BA

Religious Studies:
*Mrs E Brookes, BA

Science:
Mrs D Morgan, BSc (*Chemistry*)
Mrs H Rai, BSc, MSc (*Biology*)
Dr N Singleton, BSc, PhD (*Chemistry*)
Miss E Tyler, BSc (*Biology and Physics*)
*Dr M Wheeler, BSc, PhD (*Physics and Chemistry*)

Social Science:
Mrs K Haresign, BA (*Economics*)
Miss N Perveen, BSc (*Psychology and Sociology*)
Miss K Purewal, BSc (*Psychology*)

Special Educational Needs and Disabilities Coordinator:
Mrs P Oaten, MA

More Able Coordinator:
Mrs A Wall

Heads of House:
Mrs E Bott, BA

Duke of Edinburgh's Award/Adventure Service Challenge/ Outdoor Education:
Miss S Watson, BA

School Bursar: Mrs E J Mackay, AAT
Accountant: Mrs K Allen, BA, FCA
Finance Officer: Mrs J Garner, AAT
Headmaster's PA: Ms S Davies
Admissions Officer: Mrs A Hailes
Receptionist: Mrs K Clark, BTec
Admin Officer: Mrs K Kotadia
Examinations Officer: Mrs A Wall
Head of Marketing and Admissions: Ms A Costello, BA, MSc, PG Dip CIM
Librarian: Mrs S Timms
ICT Network Manager: Mr A Collins
IT Technician: Mr R Rai
School Nurse: Mrs A Cox, Dip HE, RN
Laboratory Technicians: Mrs M Cupac
Art Technician: Miss R Winder
Site Manager: Mr D Parmar
Caretakers: Mr G Neary, Mr M Bird
Groundsman: Mr P Dunn

Visiting Staff:
Mrs H Barwell (*Dance*)
Mrs W Boswell (*Piano*)

Mr N Bott, BA (*Drums, Electric Guitar*)
Ms J Bound (*Singing*)
Mrs J Bound, GBSM (*Piano*)
Mrs J Butterworth (*Yoga*)
Mrs K Loomes, FIDTA (*Ballet*)
Mr J Pagett, BA (*Guitar*)
Mrs C Pitchford, LRAM (*Violin*)
Miss E Stanier, BA (*Speech & Drama*)
Miss C Sullivan, BA (*Speech & Drama*)
Mr M Wells (*Tae Kwan Do*)

Junior Department:

Head of Department: Mrs S J Davies, BA Ed
Assistant Head: Mrs P Gascoigne, BA
Early Years Coordinator: Miss C Pow, BA

Class Teachers:
Y5: Mrs C Dryland, BA
Y4: Mrs S Wayman, BEd
Y3: Mrs S Hague, BA and Mrs P Gascoigne, BA (*and
    Junior PE Coordinator*)
Y2: Miss A Parkinson, BSc
Y1: Miss E Stell, BA
YR: Miss C Pow, BA
YF: Mrs J Jethwa, NVQ5

EYFS:
Miss S Barton, NNEB
Mrs L Boyer, NNEB
Mrs L Dunn
Mrs S Gray, NNE

Learning Support Assistants:
Mrs A Cobley
Mrs P Jackson, NNEB
Mrs N Sturmey, NVQ5

Administrator: Mrs M Singh, NVQ

Leweston School

Sherborne, Dorset DT9 6EN

Tel: 01963 210691
Fax: 01963 210786
email: admin@leweston.dorset.sch.uk
website: www.leweston.co.uk
Twitter: @LewestonSchool
Facebook: @Leweston

Leweston School is a co-educational boarding (full, weekly and flexi) and day school. From 2019 the school will be adopting a 'diamond model' with teaching in Science, Maths and some sport taking place in single-sex classes. With this model the school provides the opportunity to combine the academic benefits of single-sex education with the all-round advantages of co-education.

Situated in 46 acres of beautiful Dorset parkland, 3 miles south of Sherborne, the school offers all the advantages of both the traditional and modern in education with excellent facilities, particularly in the Sciences, Design & Technology and Sport. The school is also a Pentathlon GB Modern Pentathlon Training Academy, and one of only 9 in the country, thanks to its impressive record in the field of multisport disciplines. The school runs dedicated training programmes for these disciplines and hosts a number of popular training camps and competitions throughout the year. There is also a popular and successful Equestrian team who are NSEA Regional Points League winners for the third year running. Leweston pupils achieve outstanding results in many sports as representatives of the school, the county and Team GB.

Founded by the Religious of Christian Instruction in 1891, the school is a Catholic foundation but has a large percentage of pupils from other denominations. There are approximately 195 pupils in the school of whom around 80 are boarders. The ethos of the school is based on a wide social mix with a spread of talents, firm but friendly discipline and a keen sense of Christian and moral values. The Head is forward looking with a strong sense of leadership and vision. The school has a Lay Chaplain and pupils are expected to attend Chapel once a week. Preparation for confirmation is available for both Catholic and Anglican pupils.

The academic standard of the school is high. At both GCSE and A Level pass rates are consistently over 95% and the school's reputation for excellence in Music and Drama runs parallel with academic achievement in Sciences and the Arts. Each year pupils gain places at leading universities and go on to read a wide range of degrees. The real success of the school, however, is achieved by realising the full potential of each individual pupil; much emphasis is placed upon the rich extracurricular offering, which helps to discover and nurture a wide range of talents.

Teachers are dedicated and imaginative, including specialist teachers for Dyslexia and EAL. The school's special quality is its ability to encourage in each pupil a sense of her own worth and ability. Pupils are outgoing, well-mannered and unstuffy. While Leweston has a high proportion of day pupils, the school is fully committed to boarding, offering a wide programme of activities in the evenings and at the weekends.

The school has close links with the Sherborne Schools and there are many combined social, recreational, musical and cultural activities. Sherborne is an attractive historic abbey town with few of the distractions of a large city but at the same time, it is served by regular Network Express trains to and from London and good road links to Salisbury, Exeter and Bath.

Leweston Prep (IAPS) for girls and boys aged 3 months to 11 years, with boarding provision from age 7, is situated on the same campus, thus offering continuity of education to age 18. The early years provision includes French, Spanish and weekly swimming lessons from Nursery and was recently award outstanding in all areas by Ofsted. The school hosts a weekly Forest School Playgroup and Toddler Swimming Group. (*For further details, see entry in IAPS section.*)

Scholarships are awarded at 11+, 13+ and Sixth Form entry. Academic scholarships are available as well as Music, Art/Design, Drama, Sport, Equestrian and Pentathlon. Dates of examinations: Late November for Sixth Form scholarships, late January for others. Further details and entry forms can be obtained from the Registrar or found on the school website.

Fees per term (2018–2019). Full Boarding £8,350–£10,185; Weekly Boarding (4 nights) £7,265–£8.045; Weekly Boarding (5 nights) £7,680–£8,460; Day £5,140. Flexi Boarding (including supper): £55–£68 per night.

Charitable status. Leweston School Trust is a Registered Charity, number 295175. It is a charitable foundation set up for educational purposes.

Governing Body:
Mr Chris Fenton (*Chair*)
Mr I Stanton (*Deputy Chair*)

Dr N Bathurst	Mr J Massey
(*Safeguarding*)	Canon R Meyer
Mr C Comyn	Mr H Tatham
Mrs C Gill	Mr D McKechnie
Mrs S Gordon Wild	

Head: Mrs K Reynolds, LLB Bristol, PGCE Bath

Deputy Head Academic: Mr G Smith, BSc Hons Open University, PGCE (*Mathematics*)

Assistant Head Pastoral/Head of Careers: Mrs E Massey, BSc Hons Oxford Brookes, PGCE Chichester (*Mathematics*, *EPQ*)

Bursar: Lt Col Gus Scott-Masson

Lay Chaplain and Director of Boarding: Mrs Lu Worrall

Teaching Staff:

Classics:
Mrs L Gammon, BA Hons Warwick (*Head of Classics*, *Head of Years 10 and 11*)
Mr M Burton-Brown, TD, MA Oxon (*Greek*)

English and Drama:
Miss S Evans, BA Hons Sheffield, PGCE London (*Head of English and Drama*)
Miss J Ateyo, BA Hons Leeds, MA London, PGCE Oxon (*English, Head of Sixth Form*)
Mr C Thomas, BA London, PGCE Cambridge, MA London (*Drama*)
Mrs K Pankhurst, HND Theatre and Performing Arts, PGCE (*Speech and Drama*)
Mrs J Ogilvie, PG Dip Dyslexia & Literacy York (*Head of Individual Needs*)
Mrs A Croy, BA Hons Newcastle, PGCE Edinburgh (*Individual Needs Teacher*)

Modern Languages:
Mr R Dillow, BA Hons Cantab, MA Cantab (*Head of Modern Languages*)
Mrs G Gotke, BA Hons London, PGCE Kent (*Spanish, French and Italian*)
Mrs L Vandyck, BA Hons Ealing (*German*)

Geography:
Mrs A Dencher, BA, MA, PGCE Cantab (*Head of Geography*)
Ms S Lilly, MA Hons Aberdeen, PGCE, MSc Southampton (*Geography*)

Home Economics:
Mrs E Hobson, BA Hons De Montfort, PGCE St Mark and St John Plymouth (*Home Economics*)

Mathematics:
Mrs L Newnham, BSc Bristol, PGCE Oxford Brookes (*Head of Mathematics*)
Mrs E Massey, BSc Hons Oxford Brookes, PGCE Chichester (*Mathematics*, *EPQ*, *Head of Sixth Form*)
Mr G Smith, BSc Hons Open University, PGCE (*Mathematics*, *Deputy Head Academic*)
Mr A Okai, MSc, PGCE Portsmouth (*Mathematics*)
Dr E Pyke, MEng (*Mathematics*)

Religious Studies:
Ms C O'Toole, BA Hons London, PGCE, Catholic TCert Liverpool (*Head of Religious Studies*, *PSHE Coordinator*)
Mrs E Littlechild, BA Hons York, PGCE Twickenham (*Religious Studies, Health and Social Care, Head of Years 8 and 9*)
Mrs A Griffiths, BD London, PGCE Exeter (*Religious Studies, Health and Social Care, Head of Year 7*)

Psychology:
Mrs S Hunt, BA Hons Bournemouth, PGCE Exeter (*Head of Year 7*)

Science:
Mr P Ainsworth, BSc Hons, PGCE (*Physics*)
Mrs R Dawson, BSc Hons Bristol, PGCE Cambridge (*Biology*)

Dr O Kemal, BSc Hons, PhD London, PGCE Surrey, MRSC (*Head of Chemistry*)
Dr C Maunder, BSc Hons London, PhD Bristol, PGCE Open University (*Chemistry, Biology*)
Mrs A Valentine, BSc Hons Swansea, PGCE London (*Head of Physics*)
Dr R Whale, BSc, PhD Birmingham, PGCE Exeter, CChem, MRSC (*Chemistry*)
Mr S Whittle, BSc (*Head of Biology*)

Economics and Business Studies:
Mrs L Bruller (*Head of Economics and Business, Senior Academic Boarding Tutor*)

ICT:
Mrs L Christy-Clover, BSc Hons CITM Open University (*ICT*)

History:
Mr M Hayward, BA Hons Oxon (*Head of History, History of Art*)

Art, Design and Technology:
Mrs J Lacey-Scott, BA Hons Winchester School of Art (*Head of Art and Design*)
Mrs A Wright, MA Royal Academy of Art (*Art and Design*)
Miss L Robinson, BA Hons Glamorgan (*Art*)

English as an Additional Language:
Mrs J Taylor, BA Hons Bath Spa, CELTA (*Head of EAL*)

Physical Education:
Mrs S Guy, BA Hons Keele, PGCE Hull (*Director of Sport*)
Mr K Pool, BSc (*Physical Education*)
Mr A Slater, BA Auckland (*Physical Education*)
Mr M Flaherty, NVQ Management Level 4 (*Head of Swimming and Pentathlon*)
Ms A Parnell (*Swimming Pool Manager*)
Mr D Barlow, BSc Hons Nottingham, MSc London, PGCE Birmingham (*Physical Education*)
Mr M Long, LTA Coach (*Tennis*)
Mr T Prideaux-Brun (*Tennis*)

Music:
Dr R Milestone, MMus, BA Hons Wales, PhD Leeds, LRSM (*Director of Music*)
Miss S Stockel (*Singing*)
Mrs C Bryan (*Singing*)
Miss A Wilmshurst (*Brass*)
Mr A Chester (*Guitar*)
Mrs W Partridge (*Guitar*)
Mr P Huddleston, BTech (*Percussion*)
Miss C Jackson, GTCL, ARCM, LTCL (*Flute*)
Ms S De-Batts (*Flute*)
Mr D Price, LRAM (*Violin, Viola*)
Mrs N Price, GRSM Hons, ARCM, LRAM (*Pianoforte, Bassoon*)
Mrs M Riquelme Toomey (*Piano*)
Mrs R Dudley-Smith (*Piano*)
Mr A Serna (*Violoncello*)
Mrs A Slogrove, BA Hons, LRSM, PGCE (*Piano*)
Ms K Whatley (*Harp*)
Ms A Whittlesea (*Recorder*)
Mrs A Law (*Oboe*)
Mr H Jackson (*Organist*)

Marketing & Admissions Manager: Miss C Worsley
Registrars: Mrs C Damant and Mrs C Godman-Dorington
Academic Administrator: Mrs J Wells
Head's PA: Miss N Holmes

Loughborough High School

Burton Walks, Loughborough, Leicestershire LE11 2DU

Tel:	01509 212348
Fax:	01509 215720
email:	high.office@lsf.org
website:	www.lsf.org/high
Twitter:	@LboroHigh
Facebook:	@LboroHigh

Loughborough High School is an 11 to 18 school of approximately 580 day girls with a large Sixth Form numbering around 160. We are part of Loughborough Schools Foundation, a charitable Foundation of four Independent Schools and a Nursery operating under a single Board of Trustees and Directors. The Foundation comprises Loughborough High School, Loughborough Grammar School, Loughborough Amherst School, Fairfield Prep School and Loughborough Nursery.

Established in 1850, Loughborough High School is one of the oldest girls' grammar schools in England located on a delightful 46-acre site close to the town centre with many first-rate facilities, which are being added to and improved continuously.

We have an excellent reputation for our academic, cultural and sporting achievements, and for the quality of our pastoral care. Pupils are encouraged to be well-mannered, happy and self-reliant individuals and are presented with schooling opportunities that enable them to become the best version of themselves.

Since we are a comparatively small school, we are able to know our pupils as individuals and this leads to a strong community spirit. In providing a strong academic education in a disciplined atmosphere we hope to enable each girl ultimately to enter the career of her choice. We believe that our academic curriculum and extra-curricular activities nurture our pupils and encourage them to become active citizens of a modern world.

Further details about the school can be obtained by contacting the school's Registrar.

School Curriculum. Applied Science, Art, Biology, Business, Chemistry, Classical Civilisation, Computer Studies, Drama, Economics, English, French, Games (hockey, netball, tennis, rounders and athletics), Geography, German, Greek, Gymnastics, History, History of Art, Latin, Mathematics, Modern Dance, Music, Physical Education, Physics, Politics, Religious Studies, Sociology, Spanish, Food, ICT, Psychology and Theatre Studies. Careful note is taken of the National Curriculum with additional subjects included within the curriculum to provide breadth and depth.

Fees per term (2018–2019). £4,183. Music (individual instrumental lessons): £232.50 (for 10 lessons).

Scholarships and Bursaries.

Academic Awards: The Governors offer a number of scholarships at 11+ which are awarded on academic merit. All candidates are considered for these awards without the need for any further application.

Music Awards: Music Scholarships are available to musically promising and talented pupils who are successful in the Entrance Examinations. Auditions are held around the time of the Entrance Examinations.

Bursaries: Means-tested Foundation Bursaries of up to 100% remission of tuition fees are available. These awards are normally made only to those entering at 11+ and 16+.

Further details of all these awards are available from the School.

Charitable status. Loughborough Schools Foundation is a Registered Charity, number 1081765, and a Company Limited by Guarantee, registered in England, number 4038033. Registered Office: 3 Burton Walks, Loughborough, Leics LE11 2DU.

Governing Body:

Chairman: Mr G P Fothergill, BA

School Board Chairs:
Professor A Dodson, BSc Hons, PhD, DSc
Professor J Ketley, BSc Hons, Phd Bham, CBiol, MSB
Mrs G Richards, BA Hons, MEd, Hon EdD
Admiral Sir Trevor Soar, KCB, OBE, DEng Hon, FCMI

Co-optative Governors:
Mr P Alexander
Professor R Allison, BA, PhD
Mrs E K Critchley, MA Oxon
Professor J Feather, MA, PhD, FRSA
Mrs M Gershlick
Lady Jennifer Gretton, DVCO, JP, LLD Hon, DUni Hon, Hon DLitt
Mr R Harrison, MA Cantab, Dip Arch, RIBA
Mr P M Jackson, FIMI
Mr A D Jones, BA, FCA
Mrs R J E Limb, OBE, MA Cantab
Mr P Middleton, MA Oxon, BA Hons Oxon
Mrs A Murphy, MA
Mrs P O'Neill, MA Cantab
Mr P Snelling
Mr J Stone
Mrs Louise Webb, BSc Hons

Nominated Governor: Sister C Leydon

Ex-Officio Governors:
Dr A de Bono, MA, MB, FRCGP, FFOM (*Bursary Committee*)
Dr P J B Hubner, MB, FRCP, DCH, FACC, FESC (*Bursary Committee*)
Mr H M Pearson, DL, DUniv Hon, BA Econ (*Bursary Committee*)

Senior Leadership Team:

Acting Head: Mr S A I Thompson, MA Lon

[*Deputy Head*: Mr S A I Thompson, MA London]
Director of Studies: Dr S Jackson, BSc, PhD UMIST, CChem, MRSC
Assistant Head (*Curriculum*): Miss C Hitchen, MEng Newcastle
Assistant Head (*Pastoral*): Miss V Standring, BSc Chester

Head of Sixth Form: Dr C Burnett, BEng, EngD Swansea
Head of Year 11: Mrs G Nightingale, BSc Sheffield
Head of Year 10: Mrs H Wilson, BSc Sheffield
Head of Year 9: Miss J Anguiano Gomez, BSc, MRes, MEd Granada
Head of Year 8: Miss E Rees, BSc Leeds
Head of Year 7: Mrs J Day, BSc Manchester
Sixth Form Coordinator (*Academic*): Mr J Travis, BSc Leeds
Sixth Form Coordinator (*Pastoral*): Miss A Quemby, BSc Northumbria at Newcastle

Staff:
* *Head of Department*

Art:
*Mrs K Murphy, BA Ulster
Miss M Bidgood, BA MA Nottingham

Artist in Residence (*Digital Media*): Mr M Leger, BA University College Falmouth

Careers:
*Dr C Burnett, BEng, EngD Swansea

Mrs R E F Burn, MA Cambridge
Dr D Cladingboel, BSc, PhD Southampton

Classics:
*Mrs R E F Burn, MA Cambridge
Mr S Forde, BA University College Cork
Mrs L McPherson, BA Nottingham

Drama:
*Ms S E Boon, BA Plymouth Dartington
Miss R Hooper, BA Liverpool

Economics and Business:
*Ms D McDonald-Mansell, BSc Manchester
Mr P Lodhia, BA Nottingham

English:
*Miss E Bancroft, BA Oxford
Mrs J Evans, BA University College London
Mrs L Harrison, BA Leeds Met
Mr J Martin, BA Wales
Mrs F Moore, BEd De Montfort Bedford
Mrs A Palmer, BA Chester
Mrs M Woolley, BA Leicester

Food:
*Mrs E Harvey, BA UC Birmingham
Mr R Lewis, BSc Nottingham Trent

Geography:
*Mr A Moreton, BA Manchester
Mrs J Day, BSc Manchester
Miss A Forster, BA Nottingham
Miss V Standring, BSc MSc Chester

History:
*Dr E C Eadie, BA Birmingham, DPhil Oxford
Mrs J Bower-Gormley, BA Hull
Dr D Cornell, BA PhD Durham

Information & Communications Technology:
*Mr J Singh, BA Coventry
Mrs C Winship, BSc Reading

Mathematics:
*Mrs J Beardsley, BEng Surrey
Miss C Andrews, BEng Derby
Mr P Lodhia, BA Nottingham
Miss C Hitchen, MEng Newcastle
Miss R Mistry, BSc Warwick
Mr G Needham, MA Liverpool
Miss E Rees, BSc Leeds
Miss C I Shawcross, BSc Loughborough
Mrs R Slade, BSc Surrey
Mr N Stevens, BSc York

Modern Languages:
*Mrs A Lee, BA Nottingham
Miss J Anguiano Gomez, BSc, MRes, MEd Granada
Mr D Gough, BA Sheffield
Miss C Pellejero, MA La Rioja
Mrs E Raouf, BA Salford
Mrs M West, MA Swansea

Language Assistants:
Miss L Miano (*French Assistant*)
Miss M Cordón (*Spanish Assistant*)
Miss S Cormehic (*German Assistant*)

LES Music School:
*Mr R J West, BA Durham, MSc Herts, LGSMD, LRSM,
    PG Cert Mus Tech
Ms N Bouckley, BA Durham
Mr N Ellum, BA Keele
Mr C Price, BA
Miss C Revell, BMus Huddersfield
Mr S A I Thompson, MA London

Personal, Social, Health & Citizenship Education:
*Mrs J Conway, BA MA Ulster

Physical Education:
*Miss N Attwood, BSc Staffordshire
Miss S Griffin, BSc Loughborough
Miss S James, MA Loughborough
Miss A Quemby, BSc Northumbria at Newcastle
Miss V Standring, BSc MSc Chester

Politics (LGS):
*Mr M I Dawkins, BA De Montfort, MA De Montfort
Miss S H Jenkins, BA UCL

Psychology:
*Mrs A Kenyon, BA Hull
Miss E Rees, BSc Leeds

Religious Studies:
*Mrs J A Lewis, BA Nottingham
Mrs A Justice, BEd Warwick
Miss G Thomas, BA Wales

Science:
*Mrs J E Stubbs, BSc Nottingham
*Mrs M Ghaly, BSc Teesside
*Mrs J Pellereau, MA Cambridge, MSc Loughborough,
    CSci Teach
Dr D Cladingboel, BSc PhD Southampton
Miss E Coady, BSc Sheffield
Dr J Downing, BSc, PhD Bristol
Dr S Jackson, BSc, PhD UMIST, CChem, MRSC
Mrs H Wilson, BSc Sheffield
Mrs G Nightingale, BSc Sheffield
Miss C Page, BSc Newcastle Upon Tyne
Mrs J Peart, Grad Dip Phys Guy's
Dr N Simmonds, BSc, MRes, PhD Leicester
Miss C E Todd, BSc Manchester
Mr J Travis, BSc Leeds
Dr A Williamson, BSc, PhD Imperial College London

Learning Support:
*Ms E Johanson, BA Bradford
Mrs Jennifer Walker, CACHE Level 3

Librarian: Mrs G Burton, BLS Loughborough

Matron:
Mrs A Cannon, RGN
Mrs S Chad-Smith, RGN

Examinations Officer: Mrs S English, Level 4 Professional
    Certificate for Managing Examinations
E-Learning Coordinator: Mrs C Winship, BSc Reading
PR, Communications & Events Manager: Ms L E Shipman
Registrar: Miss A M Anderson, BSc Aston
PA to the Headmistress: Miss C Hughes, BA Leicester
Data and Policy Manager: Miss A Burrows, MA Bangor
School Secretary: Mrs A Cox
Diary Manager and Receptionist: Ms H Ingham
Receptionist and Reprographics Technician: Ms J Calow
Art/Food Technician: Mrs J Pheby
Humanities Technician: Mrs A Shepherd, BA Sunderland

LHS Caretakers:
Mr R de Silva Guerreiro
Mr R Boby

Charity Coordinator: Ms L E Shipman
Duke of Edinburgh's Award Coordinator (LHS): Miss R
    Bull
Voluntary Service Unit Coordinator: Dr A Williamson,
    BSc, PhD Imperial College London

Laboratory Technicians:
Mrs E Fraser, BSc DMU
Mrs K Bedwell, BSc De Montfort, MSc Loughborough

Mrs L Deamer, BSc Loughborough
Mrs L Hirst, BTEC The People's College of FE

ICT Support:
Mr S Dickman

Bursary Staff:
Chief Operating Officer: Mr J Doherty, ISBA
PA to Chief Operating Officer: Mrs K Payter
Director of Operations: Mr R Grant
Finance Director: Mr R Harker, BA Coventry, FCA

Facilities Manager: Mr D Fenn
Secretary to the Board: Mrs R Brutnall, BA Birmingham
Commercial and Marketing Director: Mrs G Collicutt, BA
   Nottingham
IT Director: Mr R Smeeton
H & S and Compliance Officer: Mr G Leeson, BA
   Northumbria
HR Manager: Mrs K James
Development and External Relations Director: Mrs J
   Harker
LES Shop Manager: Mrs J Gurney
Catering Operations Manager: Mrs J L Johnstone
Catering Manager Fairfield Kitchen: Mrs F Coltman

Manchester High School for Girls

Grangethorpe Road, Manchester M14 6HS

Tel:	0161 224 0447
Fax:	0161 224 6192
email:	administration@mhsg.manchester.sch.uk
website:	www.manchesterhigh.co.uk
Twitter:	@mhsg
Facebook:	@ManHighSG

Established in 1874, Manchester High School for Girls (MHSG) has a long and proud history of educating women who have gone on to change the world.

Its alumnae include the famous suffragette sisters, Sylvia, Christabel and Adele Pankhurst, through to present-day business leaders such as Nicola Mendelsohn, Vice-President of Facebook EMEA, and Clara Freeman, the first female Executive Director of Marks and Spencer.

As a 'through' school, Manchester High enables girls to enjoy a seamless and settled education from their infant years through to the early days of adulthood. Whatever stage of school life they are at, students find Manchester High a vibrant and stimulating environment, where their classmates, not just the teachers, support and encourage them.

The School is committed to developing fulfilled and balanced individuals through diverse extra-curricular activities, and exceptional Well Being and Futures programmes.

Girls benefit from a wide and varied learning experience that is full of opportunity, and they are challenged and supported to achieve their personal best. This is a testament to the school's public examination results which are, year on year, some of the best in the country.

At MHSG, artistic and sporting talents are nurtured and students enjoy a diverse range of extracurricular activities. These are complemented by superb modern facilities which include a state-of-the-art Sixth Form Centre with lecture theatre, common room and study area, a sports complex, a fitness suite, a dance studio, all-weather sports pitches, a multi-purpose auditorium, a drama studio and a purpose-built Music House. Instrumental and Speech & Drama lessons are optional extras.

Highly skilled and committed staff strive to ensure that every MHSG student leaves the School a well-educated young woman, with highly-developed interpersonal skills and a broad range of interests. The School encourages girls to respect themselves and others; developing responsible global citizens who have a positive impact on the world.

Students at Manchester High come from a wide range of backgrounds and this rich social and cultural mix gives the School a warm and friendly feel. The girls learn about the importance of social responsibility with charity, voluntary and community work strongly encouraged.

Entry to the Reception class is by assessment while an entrance examination is set for the Juniors and Year 7. From time to time vacancies in other year groups can become available, but the main entry levels are at ages 4, 11 and 16. Sixth Form assessment is by interview and GCSE qualifications.

MHSG is committed to providing education to academically gifted girls regardless of circumstance. In the Senior School financial assistance is offered through a limited number of part or full means-tested bursaries. One or more scholarships may be awarded for excellence in performance in the entrance tests taken at the age of 10 or 11 for admission to the Senior School in September. Such scholarships will be awarded on merit only, not on the basis of parental income, and will provide part remission of fees. Music, Sports and Dance scholarships are also available.

Further details and a prospectus are available from the Registrar.

The Reports of the ISI Inspections from 2010 and 2016 can be viewed on the School's website.

Fees per term (2018–2019). Seniors £3,958, Juniors £2,950, Infants £2,904.

Charitable status. Manchester High School for Girls is a Registered Charity, number 1164323. The aim of the charity is the provision and conduct in Manchester of a day school for girls.

Board of Governors:
Chairman: Mrs S E Spencer, BA
Dr A Ahmed, DCH, DRCOG, DFFP, MRCGP
Mr A Bland, FCA, FABRP
Mrs S Beale, BA, PG Cert, AMBDA, MA
Mr A Clarke, FCA
Lady R Cooper, OBE, PhD
Mrs L Earnshaw, BSc
Mrs M Grant, Cert Ed
Mrs S Klass, MA Oxon
Mrs D Kloss, MBE, LLB, LLM, Hon FFOM
Ms M Lowther, BSc Hons, MBA, CIMGT, FCIB, LLD
Professor R W Munn, PhD, DSc, FRSC
Mrs C V F Sargent, BSc
Mr C J Saunders, OBE, MA, FSI
Mr K S Yeung, MBE

Hon Treasurer: Mr A Clarke, FCA

Head Mistress: Mrs A C Hewitt, BSc, NPQH

Deputy Heads:
Ms J L Hodson, MA Cambridge, BA Cambridge (*Biology*)
Mrs A P Goddard, BA Thames (*Theological Studies*)

Assistant Heads:
Dr M Leach, BA Oxford, PhD Durham, PGCE Edge Hill
   (*Director of Co-Curriculum, Physics*)
Mrs S Norton, BA UC Berkeley USA, MA Mills College
   USA (*Director of Sixth Form Studies, English*)

Staff:
* *Head of Department*
§ *Part-time*

Mr S Banks, BA Salford (*Modern Languages*)
§Mrs P Bell, BA Leeds Polytechnic (*Art & Design
   Technology*)
Mrs C Bennett, BSc Staffordshire (*Physics*)

Mr A Bradley, BMus Birmingham (*Music*)
Miss M Bowler, BEd Hons Sheffield (*Physical Education*)
Mrs D Brown (*Dance & PE*)
Ms J Burley, BA Liverpool (*English*)
Dr A Bushell, PhD, MChem Manchester (*Chemistry*)
Mrs A G T Chambers, BA West Surrey College of Art & Design, ATC (*Art & Design Technology*)
Mrs K Chisnall, BSc Bradford (*Business/Economics, ICT*)
Mr J Clarke, BA, MPhil Manchester (*History*)
Mrs E S Counsell, BA Leeds, MSc Birmingham (*French, German*)
Mrs R Daly, BA Durham (*Geography*)
§Mrs T Davey, BA University of Wales (*English*)
Dr L Deignan, MA, BSc Newcastle (*Biology*)
Mrs E A Diamond, BA Birmingham (*Religion & Philosophy*)
Mr B Eaton, BSc Manchester (*Physics*)
Mrs J L Fordham, Cert Ed Manchester (*Art & Design Technology*)
§Miss E Forshaw, BA Durham (*Psychology*)
Mr K Gilkes, BSc Bolton (*ICT*)
Mr O Goulding, BSc Surrey (*Biology*)
Mr A Guinan, MChem Leeds (*Chemistry*)
Miss S Hadley, BA Liverpool (*Psychology*)
§Miss C Hannan, MA Cantab (*Classics*)
§Mrs J Haves, BA De Montfort Leicester, PGCE (*Drama*)
Mr F Heywood, BSc Nottingham, MSc UMIST (*Mathematics*)
Dr R E Hoban, BSc, PhD Newcastle (*Chemistry*)
Mr S P Holmes, BSc Nottingham (*Mathematics*)
Ms E Hudson, BA Hull (*English*)
Mrs P Inglis, BSc Manchester (*Chemistry*)
Mr D L Jones, BSc Manchester (*Mathematics*)
Mr A Kingsley, BA Leeds (*Modern Foreign Languages*)
Miss K Large, BSc Leeds (*Chemistry*)
Mrs K Loughrey-Davies, BA Warwick (*English*)
§Miss K Martin, BA Birmingham, MPhil Birmingham (*History*)
Mr P McDaid, BSc Nottingham (*Physics*)
Mrs L McDonagh, BSc Manchester Metropolitan (*Physical Education*)
Mrs S A Moores, BA Cardiff (*Modern Languages*)
§Mrs C Morell, BA Hull (*Psychology*)
Miss K Mottershead, BA Manchester Metropolitan (*Physical Education*)
Mrs S Newman, BEd Leeds Metropolitan (*Physical Education*)
Mr B Norris, BSc Cardiff (*Mathematics*)
Mr P J O'Brien, BA Hull (*German, *Modern Foreign Languages*)
§Mrs E Othen, MA, MPhil, Cambridge (*Classics*)
§Mrs C J Ousey, BA Southampton (*English*)
§Miss J Parker, BSc Imperial College London (*Biology*)
Mrs C Pattison, BSc Newcastle (*Mathematics*)
Dr C M Poucher, BSc, PhD Leeds (*Biology*)
Mrs M Price, BA Manchester (*English*)
Ms A N Protheroe, BSc Swansea (*Mathematics*)
§Mrs C Purvis, BA Lancaster (*Religious Studies*)
Mr M Randall, BA CNAA, MA Leicester (*Business Economics IT*)
§Mrs S Reynolds, BA UCL, MSc Kingston (*Geography*)
Miss H Robinson, BSc Heriot-Watt (*Mathematics*)
Mr D Rose, BA, MA Kent (*English*)
Miss S C Rowley, BA Staffordshire (*Physical Education*)
Mrs P Scott, BA Duncan of Jordanstone College of Art (*Art & Design Technology*)
Dr R Smither, BSc Bath, MPhil, PhD Cambridge (*Biology*)
§Mrs J Taylor, BA Manchester (*Philosophy & Literary Studies*)
§Mrs R Thompson, BA, MPhil Birmingham (*Spanish*)
§Mrs D E Troth, BA Exeter (*History*)

Mr S R F Vance, BA Manchester (*Art & Design Technology*)
Miss R Ward MA, BMus Manchester (*Music*)
§Mrs J Watson, BSc Newcastle-upon-Tyne (*Geography*)
Miss J Welsby, BA Manchester (*Classics*)
Mrs C Wilkes, BA Sorbonne, MA Rennes (*Modern Languages*)
Mrs C Zakaria, BA King's College London (*Spanish, French*)

Preparatory Department Staff:

Head of Preparatory Department: Mrs H Mortimer, BSc, MEd

Mrs K Adam, BSc Sheffield Hallam
Mrs R A Anderson, BEd Glasgow
Mrs V Baird, BSc Lancaster
Miss J Bingham, BA UMIST
Mrs C Callanan, BA MMU
Miss S Diamond, BEd Cantab
Mrs S Edale, BA Derby
Miss L Flaherty, BSc Liverpool John Moores
Miss J H Floyd, BA Charlotte Mason College
Mrs C Harnett, BSc UMIST
Mrs M R Heggie, BMus, BEd New South Wales
Mrs E Mason, BA Nottingham
§Mrs S Oliveira, BA Manchester
Mrs J C Philip, BA Manchester
Miss F Sanderson, BA Manchester Metropolitan

Bursar: Mr J P Moran, FCCA
Registrar: Mrs P Percival
PA to Head Mistress: Mrs K Joynes
Librarian: Miss Z Hawker, BA Liverpool, MSc Northumbria
Archivists: Mrs G Hobwson, BSc Hons Salford, MA Salford and Mrs P Roberts, BA Hons Durham
School Medical Officer: Dr J Herd, BM BS, DFFP, DRCOG, MRCGP
Clerk to the Governor: Mrs S Hutton, BA Manchester

Manor House School, Bookham

Manor House Lane, Little Bookham, Surrey KT23 4EN

Tel:	01372 457077
Fax:	01372 450514
email:	admissions@manorhouseschool.org
	admin@manorhouseschool.org
website:	www.manorhouseschool.org
Twitter:	@ManorHseSchool
Facebook:	@manorhousesch

Motto: "An individual approach to academic success."

Manor House School, Bookham is a selective independent day school for girls aged 4–16 with a co-educational nursery.

Founded in 1920, the school is a charitable trust located partly in a Georgian building and set in seventeen acres of parkland in the Surrey commuter belt. A range of local minibus routes operate before and after school each day. The day boarding system operates from 8.00 am to 6.00 pm.

Manor House School provides a caring yet challenging environment with an extensive co-curricular enrichment programme that develops confidence in students to seek new experiences and instils the qualities of courage, kindness and integrity.

The school maxim 'An individual approach to academic success' is brought to life by ensuring that every girl can fulfil her potential in whichever subject areas or activities it lies.

Girls learn together at their own pace, develop the confidence to take risks, choose any field of study without stereotypical influence, grow in emotional intelligence and show compassion for others while honing life and leadership skills for the future. But most importantly, develop into happy, confident and successful young women.

The excellent facilities include a purpose-built spacious Art/Textiles studio, Music and Drama Room and Home Economics facility, a recently refurbished ICT suite, language laboratory, fit-for-purpose Science block, and Sports/Theatre/Assembly Hall in addition to a further main hall in the Manor House itself. The School has excellent sports facilities which include an open-air heated swimming pool, five floodlit tennis and netball courts, hockey and rounders pitches, and an athletics track.

Manor House girls follow a wide curriculum throughout their school career and generally take 9.5 or 10.5 GCSE subjects achieving consistently strong academic results and being highly sought after by sixth form destinations. There are typically over fifty extracurricular clubs and activities taking place during any one term and these are an important part of school life.

Pastoral care is a particular strength of the school. Senior girls are caring role models for younger pupils and there is a flourishing peer support group.

Admission to the Senior Department is by the School's own Entrance Examinations, which are held in the second week of January prior to the September entry. Other main entry points are at Reception Class and Year 3 although the school welcomes mid-year applications to other entry years, subject to the availability of places. Selection is determined by successful completion of an age-appropriate taster and assessment day. Offers are made following the outcome of this process at the discretion of the Headteacher.

Scholarships and Bursaries. There are two major and two minor academic scholarships open to girls entering the senior department at 50% and 40% of basic annual tuition fees. There are also sports scholarships and scholarship/s in the Creative and Expressive Arts valued at up to 30% of the basic annual tuition fee. Scholarships are awarded based on performance in the Entrance Examinations and attendance at one of two Scholarships Day in November. For an application pack, please contact: admissions@manorhouse school.org.

Means-tested bursaries may also be applied for and further details are available from Mr C Burton, Director of Finance and Operations at cburton@manorhouseschool.org.

Fees per term (2018–2019). Tuition: From £3,085 (Reception Class) to £5,801 (Seniors). For Nursery fees, please apply directly to admissions@manorhouse school.org.

Charitable status. Manor House School is a Registered Charity, number 312063. It exists for the promotion of children's education according to their academic, social, sporting and musical abilities.

Senior Leadership Team:

Headteacher: Ms T Fantham, BA Hons, MA, NPQH

Deputy Head: Mr S Hillier, BSc Hons, PGCE, NPQH
Director of Finance & Operations: Mr C Burton, Hons BCompt
Head of Key Stage 4 (Seniors): Miss S Brodie, BSc Hons, MSc
Head of Key Stage 3 (Seniors): Mrs T Evans, BSc Hons, MSc, PGCE
Head of Prep: Miss S Lopez, BSc Hons, MSc, PGCE

Admissions and Marketing: Ms M Fowell, H Dip Marketing, CIAM Dist

Heads of Department
Art: Mrs T Williams, BA Hons, PGCE
Drama: Mrs T Williams, BA Hons, PGCE
English: Mrs E Mayes, BA Hons
Geography: Miss C Grindrod, BSc Hons, PGCE
History: Miss R St Johnston, MA Hons, PGCE
Technology and Food Science: Mrs P Knight
Latin and Classical Civilisation: Mrs L Stephens, BA Hons, PGCE
Academic Advancement: Ms M Hinkley
Mathematics and ICT: Mr P O'Neill
Modern Foreign Languages: Mrs A Wright, BA Hons, H Dip Ed
Music: Mrs J Harman, BA Hons, PGCE
Physical Education: Miss H Jones
Religious Studies:
Science: Mrs S Brodie, BSc Hons, PGCE

The Marist School – Senior Phase

Kings Road, Sunninghill, Ascot, Berkshire SL5 7PS

Tel: 01344 624291
Fax: 01344 874963
email: admissions@themarist.com
website: www.themarist.com
Twitter: @Marist_School
Facebook: @themarist

Independent Day School for Girls aged 11–18 founded in 1870 by The Marist Sisters. The school has been at the current site since 1947 and is set in 55 acres of private woodland in the village of Sunninghill near Ascot.

Number of Pupils. 285 girls.

Mission Statement. To be a centre of excellent education where outstanding teaching and pastoral care underpins academic success; this combined with the development of the whole person equipping children and young adults with the capacity to succeed in their life's journey.

Strengths.
• Strong reputation for academic excellence as well as sport, drama, music and creative arts.
• Able to offer a wide range of both academic and extracurricular activities.
• Strong emphasis on pastoral care, spiritual and personal development; care and consideration for others.
• Small class sizes to enhance individual progression and recognition.
• The school is renowned for its high standards regarding moral values, community spirit, respect and care. This is in line with the overall ethos of The Marist order which has a worldwide presence, providing a truly international dimension to a girl's education.

Facilities. Indoor swimming pool, Multi-purpose Sports Hall, dedicated Sixth Form suite, comprehensive ICT suite, Music and Drama block, Language Laboratory, Ceramics Studio & Darkroom, AstroTurf Multi-Sports Surface and Learning Resource Centre.

Academic Curriculum. Art, Biology, Business Studies, Classical Civilisation, Chemistry, Drama/Theatre Studies, Economics, English, French, Geography, German, History, ICT, Italian, Latin, Mathematics (also Pure & Mechanics, Pure, Statistics, Pure & Statistics), Music, Personal, Social & Health Education, PE, RE, Religious Studies: Philosophy & Ethics, Science, Spanish, Sports Studies, Textiles, Food

Science, Psychology, Photography and Government & Politics.

Sixth Form. The school offers a total of 26 subjects at A Level. Year 12 students will study 4 four subjects in their first year (in certain circumstances some students can take 5). Girls will decide which 3/4 subjects they wish to continue on to final exam.

Extracurricular Activities. Art, Athletics, Choir, Clarinet & Saxophone Ensemble, Drama Club, Duke of Edinburgh's Award, Flute Group, French Films, Greek (Ancient), Guitar Group, History Films, Hockey, Human Rights, ICT, Latin, Library Club, Literacy, Netball, Orchestra, Polo, Prayer Group, Public Speaking/Debating, Rock Band, Science, Strategy/Numeracy, Swimming, Swing Band, Textiles, Tennis, Young Enterprise. Please check the school website for up-to-date lists.

Results. 2018: A Level: 53% of all grades were A*–A; GCSE: students achieved 54% A*–A/9–7.

Admission. Entrance examination tests in (1) English, (2) Mathematics and (3) Cognitive Abilities, (4) Personal Portfolio, (5) Interview with the Principal and (6) Reference from Primary/Preparatory Headteacher.

Sixth Form Entry. A minimum of 7 GCSEs A*–C grade or above, preferably B grade in subjects to be studied.

Fees per term (2018–2019). £4,870. Extra benefits: Generous sibling discount scheme (4th and any subsequent children free), after school care provided.

Scholarships. Year 7 and Sixth Form Academic, Art, Drama, Music and Sport scholarships are available.

Preparatory School. The Preparatory Phase of The Marist School is on the same campus which is for girls aged 3–11. (*For further details, see The Marist School – Preparatory Phase entry in the IAPS section.*)

Affiliations. Girls' Schools Association (GSA), Catholic Independent Schools Conference (CISC), Silver Artsmark, Eco-Schools award and Healthy School.

Charitable status. The Marist School is a Registered Charity, number 225485. The principal aims and activities of The Marist School are religious and charitable and specifically to provide education by way of an independent day school for girls between the ages of 3 and 18.

Chair of Governors: Mrs A Nash

Principal: Mr K McCloskey, BA Hons, PGCE, MA

Senior Vice Principal: Mrs W Reed, BA Hons, PGCE

Heads of Department:
Art: Mrs R Ellwood
Artistic Director: Mr R McAllister
Classics: Mrs A Osmond
Drama: Ms E White
Economics/Business Studies: Mr P Rowley
English: Mrs L Lutton
Food Science: Mrs G White
Geography: Mr E de Grande
History: Mr A Baker
ICT: Mrs J Shill
Mathematics: Miss C Vardon
Modern Foreign Languages: Mrs R Beckh
Music: Mrs L Karakurt
Psychology: Mrs J Cope
Physical Education: Mrs J Bishopp
Religious Education: Miss L Vaughan Neil
Science: Mrs A Costello
Textiles: Ms S Bowley

Head of Sixth Form: Ms N Fenning

Marymount International School

George Road, Kingston-upon-Thames, Surrey KT2 7PE
Tel: 020 8949 0571
Fax: 020 8336 2485
email: admissions@marymountlondon.com
website: www.marymountlondon.com

An Independent boarding and day school for girls ages 11–18 (grades 6–12). A member of GSA, CIS, NCGS and MSA (USA).

Established in 1955 by the Sisters of the Religious of the Sacred Heart of Mary, Marymount International School welcomes girls of all faiths and traditions. The School is proudly IB with outstanding results and a 100% pass rate.

A vibrant, garden school with 250 students (of which 75 are boarders), the overall student to teacher ratio is 6:1 and the average class size numbers 11 students. Teaching is innovative, student centred, and flexible, enabling students to remain motivated and achieve their full potential. The journey of each girl to find her gifts and voice is explored and supported.

The school provides an intellectually stimulating and emotionally secure environment in which the academic, social and personal needs of each individual student may be met. Education is seen as a continuous process of growth in awareness and development towards maturity in preparation for participation in the world community. Each student's schedule is individually tailored to the subjects she wishes to follow. All classes are taught in English and additional languages on offer for native speakers include German, Spanish, French, Japanese, Chinese, Korean, Italian and Arabic.

With over 40 nationalities in the School, students are fully prepared for life in a global setting and develop an essential understanding of and respect for the richness of cultural difference.

Facilities in the beautiful seven-acre campus include a Fab Lab (the first in a UK School), refurbished Main House with a Grade 11/12 Diploma Lounge, Library, Sports Hall, Auditorium, Science Centre, Music Centre and Tennis Courts. New art classrooms have been recently added. The Dining Hall and boarding facilities have also been updated recently. We are twenty minutes from downtown London with easy accessible public transportation.

Curriculum. Students are prepared for the International Baccalaureate Diploma (ages 17–18, grades 11–12) by the IB Middle Years Programme (ages 11–16, grades 6–10). Marymount was the first British school to be accepted to teach the MYP, which stretches students with challenging, interdisciplinary projects, a variety of visual and performing arts offerings, real world simulations and a STEAM focus.

The School has taught the IB Diploma since 1979 and has outstanding results in its delivery. The IB diploma syllabus leads to UK university admission and US college credit. In 2018 over 80% of students applying in the UK gained places at Russell Group Universities and other competitive colleges in the United States and in Europe.

The school programme also includes the option to visit a variety of other world cities designed as educational trips and to participate in RSHM Festivals within our Global Network of Schools in Paris, Rome, Lisbon, and New York among others.

The school is within a half-hour drive of Heathrow Airport and conveniently located for M25/A3 road links to Gatwick Airport.

Admission. Previous school reports, teachers' recommendations, placement testing in English and Mathematics and interview.

Fees per annum (2018–2019). Tuition: £23,775 (Grades 6–12). Boarding Supplement: Grades 6–12: £14,930 (5-day), £16,650 (7-day).

Charitable status. Marymount International School is a Registered Charity, number 1117786. It exists for the promotion of education.

Headmistress: **Mrs Margaret Frazier**, BA Dartmouth College, USA

Deputy Head, IB Coordinator: Mr Nicholas Marcou, BA Hons York, PGCE Roehampton, MA St Mary's Twickenham

Deputy Head-Compliance, Designated Safeguarding Lead and Theory of Knowledge: Ms Annah Langan, MA Hons Glasgow, MA St Mary's Twickenham, PGCE Roehampton

Assistant Headmistress, English: Ms Anna-Louise Simpson, BA Hons Southampton, MSc Southampton, QTS

Bursar: Mr Alan Fernandes, MBA, BSc Surrey

Middle School Coordinator, Pastoral Life Coordinator: Mrs Geraldine Donnelly, BA Barry, USA

Director of Admissions: Mrs Mary Burke Tobias, BA Connecticut College, USA

Director College Counseling: Ms Victoria Mast, BA Hons Durham, PGCE Buckingham

Director of Spiritual Life: Mrs Emma Burke

Faculty:
Mr João Barroca, BSc Hons Portugal, MBA Spain
Mr Malcolm Blake, BSc Sheffield, PGCE Reading
Ms Monika Boothby-Jost, RUHR Germany
Dr Eamon Byers, BA Hons Belfast, MA Hons Belfast, PhD Belfast
Ms Raquel Cagigas, BA Spain, QTS
Mr Alex Clanios, BSc Northumbria
Mr Stephen Clarke, MA Hons Glasgow, PGCE Glasgow, TESOL
Dr Alexandre Delin, BA Brittany, MA Brittany, PGCE Wales, PhD Paris
Ms Francesca Denton, Royal Academy of Dance
Mr Joe Dodd, BA Hons UCL, MA Hons UCL
Mr James Elden, BSc Kent, PGCE Canterbury Christ Church Kent
Ms Sandra Forrest, BA Denison University, US, MA NYU, PGCPSE Open University
Ms Lucia Franjo-Garcia, BA Autónoma University, Madrid
Ms Dolores Garcia Suarez, BA Spain, MA King's College London
Ms Lauren Gregory, BA Mississippi USA, MEd North Texas USA
Ms Linda Holland, BSc Hons QMC London, MSc Birkbeck, PGCE Chelsea, CBiol, MSB, FRES
Ms Christina John, BSc Kerala, MSc Kerala, MPhil
Mr Damian Kell, MA Oxford
Ms Linda Kelly, BA Hons Bradford, PGCE Nottingham
Mr Steven Klurfeld, MAT New York
Ms Sarah Openshaw, BA Hons Bristol, TEFL Cambridge, PG Dip South Bank
Mrs Nathalie Pengilly, BA Hons Lyon, France, MA Hons Lyon, France, PGCE Thames
Ms Ulrike Richter, BA Hons Sussex, MA Sussex, QTS
Mr Jerome Ripp, BA, MA Oxford, BSc Open
Mr Jim Robertson, BA Hons Kingston, QTS
Mrs Helena Sansome, BA Hons, HDipEd Dublin, BPhil Liverpool, MLitt Oxford
Ms Katrina Schieber, BA Queensland, Dip Ed Queensland
Mr Mitsuo Shima, BA Meiji Gakuin, Cert Japanese as a Foreign Language
Ms Bethany Kandemir, MA Cambridge, PGCE, CELTA, MA Sheffield, QTS

Ms Cathy Stockall, BA Royal Holloway and Bedford New College, PGCE
Ms Kellie Symons, BSc Arizona, USA, MBA California USA, QTS
Ms Helen Szymczak, BA Dramatic Art Hons AFDA South Africa, ATCL, MA London
Ms Joanne Taylor, BA Cambridge, MA Cambridge
Mr Alexis White, BA Hons Oxford, PGCE St Mary's University
Dr Alwyn Williams, BA, MSc Hons UEL, PhD Sydney
Ms Huiping Wu, BA Liaoning China, MA Liaoning China, PGCE Westminster

Residential Houseparents:
Mrs Paula Horton, (*Head of Boarding*)
Ms Fiona Pendergrast
Ms Jolly Chou
Ms Martina Michalcova
Ms Dervla McMorrow

Mayfield School

The Old Palace, Mayfield, East Sussex TN20 6PH
Tel: 01435 874623 (Headmistress and Secretary)
           01435 874600 (School)
           01435 874642 (Admissions)
Fax: 01435 872627
email: enquiry@mayfieldgirls.org
website: www.mayfieldgirls.org
Twitter: @mayfieldgirls
Facebook: @mayfieldgirls

Mayfield is a leading independent boarding and day school for girls aged 11 to 18 set in the beautiful, and easily accessible, Sussex countryside less than an hour from central London. Described by the Independent Schools Inspectorate as "outstanding" and by Country Life as "one of the finest schools in the land", a Mayfield education combines academic rigour, breadth of opportunity and a strong sense of community. The School has an excellent academic record, exceptional pastoral care and an extensive co-curricular programme. Individuality, independence of thought and intellectual curiosity are nurtured and the School encourages equally the intellectual, creative, physical, emotional and spiritual development of each pupil.

Mayfield is successful in unlocking and developing the unique potential and talent of each girl. Every pupil is accepted for who she is and is instilled with the confidence to find her strengths, wherever they may lie, and develop them in an inspiring and nurturing environment. Mayfield's ethos reflects its Catholic foundation and encourages integrity, initiative, respect and a commitment to be the best you can be within a vibrant and inclusive community, which welcomes all. Mayfield is a lively, happy and successful School and Mayfield girls develop a lifelong love of learning, a range of transferable skills that will prepare them for their future and friendships that will last a lifetime.

Founded in 1872 by Cornelia Connelly and her Society of the Holy Child Jesus, the School continues to fulfil its Founder's vision to educate young women to respond to the needs of the age. This is achieved through an innovative and stimulating curriculum, an extensive range of co-curricular opportunities and a strong and supportive pastoral foundation.

Curriculum. Mayfield's curriculum, both within taught lessons and beyond them, is designed to create an environment in which questioning, reflection, risk-taking and the freedom to learn from mistakes are all encouraged. Inspirational teaching, from highly-qualified and dedicated staff, enables girls to flourish and excel, reflecting the equal value placed on every subject and the breadth of curriculum offered. In Years 7, 8 and 9 pupils enjoy a broad curriculum with core subjects – English, Maths, the sciences, Religious Studies, Geography, History, Physical Education and ICT – complemented with a variety of languages and lessons in Art, Music, Drama, Textiles (to Year 9), Ceramics and Food and Nutrition. Time each week is also specifically dedicated to the spiritual and pastoral education of the girls in the form of assemblies, liturgies and Mayfield's innovative Life Skills Programme.

To ensure an excellent basis for further study and a wide variety of career options, all pupils in Years 10 and 11 follow a compulsory common core, comprising English Language and English Literature, Mathematics, at least one language, Religious Studies and Science (separate or trilogy). Most pupils study between 10 and 11 subjects at GCSE, selecting from a wide range of optional subjects including Art & Design, Classical Civilisation, Greek, History, Geography and Drama.

ICT, Physical Education and Games are also an integral part of the timetable. Physical Education options range from traditional sports including Hockey and Netball, Cricket and Tennis to other activities including Water Polo, Fitness Room, Circuit Training, Volleyball and Badminton. In addition, there are clubs in Hockey, Netball, Swimming, Dance, Tennis, Athletics and Rounders. As part of the ICT course, all girls study for a BCS Application in IT Skills Level 2 Qualification.

The guiding principles of Sixth Form study (Years 12 and 13) at Mayfield continue to be breadth and depth and it is not unusual for girls to combine Mathematics and Science subjects (consistently the most popular choices at A Level) with Ceramics, Art or a language. Pupils choose up to four A Levels from a wide selection of over 30 options. In addition, the Sixth Form benefits from the School's Enrichment Programme, enabling girls to develop valuable life and critical thinking skills from a wide variety of options, including Global Perspectives; Science in Society; Farming and Land Management; Diploma in Culinary Skills and The Art of Effective Communication. Pupils also have the opportunity to complete Mayfield's Erasmus Research Project on a topic of their choice, which is excellent preparation for higher education. The School's state-of-the-art Sixth Form Centre is an inspirational learning space, with an individual study area allocated to each pupil, dedicated group work spaces and excellent resources, providing a first-rate transition to university.

Mayfield has an excellent record of outstanding examination results and girls invariably perform well above expectation, however, the School's focus is not exclusively to this end and it encourages a balanced approach to academic studies and the development of the whole person.

Mayfield girls receive excellent careers advice and guidance throughout their school career as an integral part of the curriculum and this prepares them very well to make excellent, confident choices. Almost all pupils progress to higher education, the vast majority to Russell Group universities including Oxbridge and, increasingly, to overseas universities particularly in the USA and Europe. They study a wide variety of subjects, from Architecture to Zoology, with a regular stream of engineers, medics and vets, lawyers and economists. The School has a highly engaged alumnae community throughout the world, which is a valued support network for advice on further study and career options.

Co-curricular Activities. An extensive co-curricular provision at Mayfield accompanies learning in the classroom and girls are positively encouraged to try new activities, ranging from Riding (in the School's first class equestrian centre), Fencing and Kick Boxing to Textiles, Debating and Journalism, Cricket, Astronomy and Dance. The School's 'Actions Not Words' Programme, reflecting Mayfield's motto and incorporating the Duke of Edinburgh's Award scheme, provides opportunities to be involved in service in both the local community and overseas, ensuring that faith in action continues to be an important part of Mayfield life.

There are significant opportunities to become involved in the creative and performing arts. Mayfield has outstanding Ceramics facilities and teaching and has produced international and award-winning ceramicists. Similarly pupils can develop their skills in art and textiles and benefit from a variety of exhibitions and workshops throughout the year.

Mayfield has an impressive reputation for music and, with a significant number of girls learning a musical instrument, there are opportunities to perform in the School Orchestra and in the many ensembles. In addition, Mayfield's acclaimed school choir, Schola Cantorum, performs regularly in prestigious venues in the UK and internationally, including the Vatican, Westminster Cathedral, St Paul's Cathedral and Westminster Abbey.

Pupils also have the opportunity to develop their drama skills performing in the wide variety of drama productions throughout the year, together with Drama Club, LAMDA and theatre workshops.

Admissions. The main entry points are at 11+, 13+ and 16+, with applications considered for occasional places in other years. Entry at 11+, 16+ and in other years is based on the School's Entrance Assessments; at 13+ on the School's Entrance and Scholarship Assessments or Common Entrance Examination and Scholarship Assessments.

Registration fee: £125

Fees per term (2018–2019). Full Boarders £11,300, Day girls £7,000.

Scholarships and Bursaries. Academic Scholarships and Gifted and Talented Scholarships are available for entry at 11+, 13+ and 16+. Scholars are identified through a programme of examination and assessment and are expected to show a high degree of aptitude in their chosen discipline. Scholarships are offered on merit.

Means-tested bursaries up to 100% of the cost of a day or boarding place are available.

Charitable status. Mayfield School is a Registered Charity, number 1047503. It exists to provide education for girls in keeping with its Catholic foundation.

Governors:
Lady Davies of Stamford, MA Oxon, MBA (*Chairman*)
Dr Christopher Storr KSG, MA, PhD, FRSA (*Deputy Chairman and Chairman of Governance Committee*)
Mrs Marion McGovern (*Chairman of Education Committee*)
Mr Chris Buxton, BA, ACA (*Deputy Chairman and Chairman of Finance and General Purposes Committee*)
Miss Julia Bowden, BA, PGCE, MBA
Sister Maria Dinnendahl SHCJ, BA, MA Oxon, BA, Lic Phil
Mrs Sara Hulbert-Powell, BA
Mrs Rhona Lewis, MA
Mrs Maureen Martin, BA, PGCE
Mrs Marlane Mellor, BSc, ACMA
Mr Tim Reid, LLB
Sr Paula Thomas SHCJ, BEd, MA
Mr Eddie Walshe OBE, PhD, BSc

Headmistress: **Miss A M Beary**, MA, MPhil Cantab, PGCE

Deputy Head (Pastoral & Boarding): Mrs N C Green, BA, MA, PGCE, MBA

Senior Managers:
Director of Studies: Mrs A R Bunce, BSc, PGCE
Bursar: Lt Col [ret] A H Bayliss, MA Cantab, CEng, MICE
Head of Sixth Form: Mr J G Filkin, BA Oxon, MA, PGCE
Head of Middle School: Mrs J M Stone, BSc, MSc, GTTP
Head of Lower School: Mr P F G Christian, BA Dunelm, MA, PGCE
Director of Co-Curricular: Mrs A C Glubb, BA, CIM DipM, PGCE, OCN Level 3 Dyslexia, QCF Level 4 Dip Career Information & Advice
Director of Development: Mrs C A Saint, BA Dublin, PG Dip

Teaching staff:

Art:
Miss J Thackray, BA, PGCE (*Head of Department*)
Miss H Oliver, HND, BA
Mrs A Sivyour, BA, PGCE

Ceramics:
Mr T Rees-Moorlah, BA, PGCE, QTS (*Head of Department*)
Mrs Y McFadyean, BA
Mr D Stafford, BA 3D Design Ceramics, MA Ceramics (*Artist in Residence*)

Classics:
Mrs D Downing, BA, MA (*Head of Department*)
Mrs E Aherne, MA, BA Oxon
Dr A Towey, MA Cantab
Mrs V Williams, BA, MA, MSc, PGCE, QTS

Drama & Theatre Studies:
Mrs S Gerstmeyer, BA, GTP, QTS (*Head of Department*)
Mr D Smith, BA, PGCE

Economics & Business Studies:
Mrs A Cox, BSc, PGCE (*Head of Department*)
Mrs C Bryan, BA, MA, PGCE

English:
Mrs N Evans, BA, PGCE (*Head of Department*)
Mrs L Parrett, BA, PGCE, MSc (*Deputy Head of Department*)
Mrs C Cox, BA Oxon, PGCE
Mrs E Crawley, BA, PGCE, Cert SpLD, EYPS
Mr J Filkin, BA Oxon, MA, PGCE
Mrs J Leslie, BA, PGCE

ESOL:
Mrs K Kilvington, BA, MA Oxon, MSc, Dip TEFLA (*Head of Department*)
Mrs C Gibson, BA CELTA
Mrs A Maimi, BA, CELTA, QTS
Mrs J D Sandoval, MA, Dip TEFLA

Food & Nutrition:
Miss E Theobald, BSc, PGCE, QTS (*Head of Department*)
Mrs C Davies, CNAA, BEd, PGCE
Mrs S Rothero, BEd, CertEd
Mr D Walker (*Catering Manager and Head Chef*)

Geography:
Mr S Gough, BSc, PGCE (*Head of Department*)
Mrs V Williams, BA, MA, MSc, PGCE, QTS
Mrs F Morris, BEd

History:
Mr D Warren, BA, PGCE (*Head of Department*)
Miss L Hunt, BA, PGCE

History of Art:
Dr J Weddell, BA Arch Hons, MA, PhD (*Head of Department*)
Mr J Davis, BA, MA, MSc, ARHistS, PGCE, Dipl Counselling, MBACP

Information Technology:
Mrs L Bartlett, BA, QTS, Dip RSA (*Years 7–11 Head of Department*)
Mrs S Howie, BSc, PGCE

Learning Support:
Mrs E Martin, BA, PG Cert, MA (*Head of Department*)
Mrs M Bushell, BA, PGCE
Mrs J Cordner, BA, TEFL
Mrs S Fuller, BSc Speech Pathology and Therapy
Mrs A C Glubb, BA, CIM DipM, PGCE, OCN Level 3 Dyslexia, QCF Level 4 Dip Career Information & Advice

Librarian:
Mrs J Gabriel, BA, MA

Mathematics:
Mrs A Pullinger, BSc, PGCE (*Head of Department*)
Ms A Demetriou, BSc, PGCE (*Deputy Head of Department*)
Mr W Clarke, BSc, PGCE
Mrs S Howie, BSc, PGCE
Dr E Keyman, BSc, MSc, DPhil, QTS
Mrs L Motoc, BSc, PGCE
Mrs J Stone, BSc, MSc, PGCE

Modern Languages:
Mrs R Testa, BA, PGCE (*Head of French*)
Mrs M Criado, BA, PGCE (*Head of Spanish*)
Mrs A Boyle, BA
Ms H Christin
Mrs A Fernandez, BA, CAP
Mrs N C Green, BA, MA, PGCE, MBA
Mrs A Maimi, BA, CELTA, QTS
Mrs N Maslova, PGCE
Mlle C Richard, BA, MA, MA, PGCE

Music:
Dr M J C Ward, MA Cantab, MPhil, PhD (*Director of Music*)
Miss L Le Riche ATCL, BMus, MMus, PGCE
NB. the Music Department also includes c.20 visiting music teachers

Physical Education:
Miss N Lydall, BA, PGCE, QTS (*Head of Department*)
Miss S Auer, BA, PGCE
Mrs G Fletcher, BA, MA, PGCE
Mrs J Jones, BA, QTS, Dip RSA
Mrs H Miller, BA, PGCE
Miss E Starr, BSc
Mrs P Whitby, BA, QTS

Politics:
Ms C Bryan, BA, MA, PGCE (*Head of Department*)

Psychology:
Mrs D Buchner, BA, HDE, BA, CBT Diploma (*Head of Department*)

Religious Studies:
Dr D Coughlan, MSt Oxon, MA Cantab, PhD (*Head of Department*)
Mr P Christian, BA Dunelm, MA, PGCE
Mrs C Smith, BA, PGCE
Mrs K Sunderland, BRelSc, Cert Ed, QTS
Mrs E Warnett, BA, MA, PGCE

Riding:
Miss J Barker, BEd, BHSII J, CertEd (*Director of Riding*)

Sciences:
Mrs J Mahon, BSc, PGCE (*Head of Biology and overall Head of Science*)
Ms A Mistry, BSc, PGCE, MA (*Head of Chemistry*)
Mr D Bullock, BSc, MA, PGCE

Mrs A Bunce, BSc, PGCE
Dr D Corvan, BSc, PGCE, MSc, PhD (*Head of Physics*)
Mrs R Davies, BSc, PGCE
Mrs J Gradon, BA Cantab, PGCE
Miss R Jackson, BSc Dunelm, PGCE
Miss B Lumborg, BSc, PGCE
Mr S Senior, BSc, PGCE

Textiles:
Mrs T Budden, Dip Fashion Design & Construction (*Head of Department*)
Miss J Alcaraz, BA Textile Design, CELTA
Mrs H Robertson

Technicians:
Mrs E Brown, MIBiol (*Biology*)
Mrs S Chapman (*Food & Nutrition*)
Mr J Fuggle (*Ceramics*)
Mrs J Mackenzie (*Chemistry*)
Miss H Oliver (*Art*)
Mrs J Pyett (*Physics*)
Mr D Stafford (*Ceramics*)

Careers Coordinator: Mrs A C Glubb, BA, CIM DipM, PGCE, OCN Level 3 Dyslexia, QCF Level 4 Dip Career Information & Advice
Examinations Officer: Mr A Welford
Gifted & Talented Coordinator: Mrs K Kilvington, BA, MA Oxon, MSc, DipTEFLA
STEM Coordinator: Mrs R Davies, BSc, PGCE

Housemistresses, Pastoral & Medical Staff:

Leeds House (*Years 7 and 8*):
Mrs Elizabeth Crawley, BA, PGCE, Cert SpLD, EYPS (*Housemistress*)
Miss P Kotesovska (*Assistant Housemistress*)
Mrs C Jones (*Day Matron*)

St Gabriel's House (*Years 9, 10 and 11*):
Mrs P Whitby, BA QTS (*Housemistress*)
Mrs C Jones (*Day Matron*)

St Michael's House (*Years 9, 10 and 11*):
Mrs K Sunderland, BRel Sc, Cert Ed, QTS (*Housemistress*)
Mrs J Mead (*Day Matron*)

St Dunstan's House (*Years 12 and 13*):
Mrs C Smith, BA, PGCE (*Housemistress*)
Mrs J Mead (*Day Matron*)

Graduate Assistants:
Miss B Atkinson, BA
Miss J Coppinger, BA
Miss R Johnson, BA
Miss S Purcell Gilpin, MSci

School Doctor:
Dr A Fyfe, Woodhill Surgery, Mayfield

Senior Nurses:
Mrs D Streeter, RGN
Ms A Winter, RGN, RSCN
Mrs C Slade, RCN

Sixth Form:
Head: Mr J Filkin, BA Oxon, MA, PGCE
Deputy Head: Ms C Bryan, BA, MA, PGCE

Middle School:
Head: Mrs J Stone, BSc, MSc, PGCE
Year 9 Senior Tutor: Miss S Auer, BA, PGCE
Year 10 Senior Tutor: Mrs A Maimi, BA, CELTA, QTS
Year 11 Senior Tutor: Ms A Demetriou, BSc, PGCE

Lower School:
Head: Mr P Christian, BA Dunelm, MA, PGCE
Senior Tutor: Mrs Y McFadyean, BA

Chaplaincy:
Lay Chaplain: Miss P Cronin, MA

Society of the Holy Child Jesus (*at Mayfield*):
Sr Teresa Joseph Barret
Sr Maria Dinnendahl
Sr Jean Sinclair

The Maynard School

Denmark Road, Exeter, Devon EX1 1SJ
Tel: 01392 355998
email: admissions@maynard.co.uk
website: www.maynard.co.uk
Twitter: @MaynardSchool
Facebook: @The-Maynard-School
LinkedIn: /the-maynard-school

The Maynard is a leading independent day school in Exeter, for girls aged 4–18. We are the third oldest girls' school in the country, founded in 1658 by Sir John Maynard. Girls and boys learn differently and we are experts in educating girls; our long history is testament to our ability to bring out the best in each and every one of them.

Ethos. Our vision is to be a leading school in the UK, committed to educational excellence in a caring and happy environment that fosters a lifelong love of learning. Our mission is that our team of inspiring teachers will instil in each individual the confidence to excel academically, socially and morally. Through an educational experience designed specifically for girls, we are able to give them the skills and the courage to go out into the world and make a real difference.

Numbers. There are approximately 415 day girls in the School, of whom 100 are in the Pre-Prep and Junior School and 100 in the Sixth Form.

School Buildings. The School is set in a leafy area of central Exeter in Devon, five minutes from the centre of the city. The extensive buildings include a separate Sixth Form Centre; a purpose-built block for Science, Mathematics, and Computing; well-equipped Food & Nutrition and Textiles Rooms; Music and Art Rooms and a Performing Arts Theatre which also serves as a gym, and an impressive Sports Hall which provides full-scale indoor facilities. The Junior School and Pre-Prep are situated within the grounds and are fully equipped for the education of girls aged 4–11 years.

Curriculum. The curriculum is academically rigorous and maintains a good balance between Arts and Science subjects. English, Mathematics, the Sciences and Sport are particular strengths; full scope is given to creative and practical activities, as well as ICT skills. The School prepares all girls for University, including Oxford and Cambridge. A carefully developed programme of careers advice, begun at 11+ and continuing through to the Sixth Form, ensures that all pupils are individually guided in subject options with their long-term career interests at heart. The Maynard Aspire programme is an enrichment initiative for high achieving students in Upper 5 (Year 11) and the Sixth Form who are ready to develop their skills in a wider context as they make decisions about their future career paths.

Examinations. Candidates normally take 9 subjects at GCSE and 3 at A Level. Students are fully prepared for Oxford and Cambridge University Entrance.

Physical Education. Hockey (outdoor and indoor), Netball, Badminton, Basketball, Volleyball, Fencing, Dance and Gymnastics are offered in the winter terms; Tennis and Rounders are played in the Summer Term. Training is given in Athletics and Swimming is part of the normal timetable for all girls during the Summer Term. Besides its excellent indoor facilities and the three hard courts in its own grounds, the School has access to a playing field a short walk away and is close to three swimming pools and an Astroturf playing area. The school has an extensive fixture programme in Netball, Hockey, Indoor Hockey, Badminton, Basketball, Tennis, Swimming, Athletics and Rounders. Teams have regularly reached national standard. In addition, The Maynard has a strong extra-curricular programme of outdoor pursuits including the Ten Tors, the Duke of Edinburgh's Award and Exmoor Challenge.

Admission. All admissions, except Pre-Prep, are subject to an Entrance Assessment graduated according to age and held in January each year for entry in the following September. Pre-Prep admissions attend a Taster Day where they are informally assessed. Entry into the Sixth Form is by interview.

Fees per term (2018–2019). Pre-Prep: Reception £2,095, Years 1–2 £2,430; Junior School: Years 3–5 £3,670; Senior School: Years 6–13 £4,416. Fees include wraparound care from 8.00 am to 5.30 pm. Reception fees include lunch.

There is a generous Sibling Discount Scheme.

Scholarships and the Maynard Award Programme. A range of Academic, Sport, Music and Creative Arts Scholarships are available for senior school entry at 11+, 13+ and Sixth Form. In addition, the Maynard Award Programme is a new initiative which offers opportunities to girls from all sectors of the community. Three free places are available for entry into our Lower 6th.

Further Information. The Prospectus and Scholarship and Maynard Awards information are available from the Admissions Office. Visitors are very welcome by appointment, and tours and taster days can be arranged for girls considering the school. Email: admissions@maynard.co.uk; Tel: 01392 355998.

Old Maynardians. Email: RachaelBoard@maynard.co.uk.

Charitable status. The Maynard School is a Registered Charity, number 1099027. It exists to provide quality education for girls.

Governors:
Lady Jan Stanhope (*Chair*)
Sarah Randall Johnson
Mr Nick Bruce-Jones
Miss Wendy Manfield
Mrs Wendy Dersley
Mr Christopher Gatherer
Mr Henry Luce
Ms Lynn Turner
Dr Caroline Pascoe
Mrs Jane Chanot
Ms Sarah Witheridge
Mr James Dart
Mr Alan Gibbons
Cllr Cynthia Thompson
The Lord Mayor of Exeter (*ex officio*)

Senior Leadership Team:

Headmistress: Miss S Dunn, BSc Hons Exeter, NPQH

Director of Sixth Form: Mr T Hibberd, MA Cambridge
Director of Studies: Dr P Rudling, MA Cambridge; MSc, PhD Exeter
Assistant Head: Mrs Caroline Leigh BSc Hons Birmingham
Assistant Head: Mr M Loosemore, BA Hons Southampton (*Head of English*)
Head of Junior School: Mr Steven Smerdon, BEd Exeter

Pastoral Lead: Mrs P Wilks, MA Oxford (*History*)
School Business Manager: Mrs S Gardner
Marketing Manager: Mrs J Conway, BSc Hons Southampton

Teaching Staff:

Full-time:
Ms J Bellamy, BA Hons Manchester (*Head of Drama*)
Mr B Dunford, BSc Roehampton, PGCE Plymouth (*ICT*)
Mr J Friendship, BA Bristol, One Planet MBA Exeter (*ICT*)
Mr A Ganley, BA Hons Nottingham (*Drama*)
Mrs C Gorrod, BA Hons Surrey (*Junior School*)
Mrs N Haworth, BA Hons Birmingham (*Junior School Teaching Assistant*)
Dr R Henderson, MMath Hons Durham, PhD East Anglia (*Mathematics*)
Ms A M Hurley, MA London (*Art*)
Mrs D Lewis, BA Hons Cheltenham (*Careers, Exams Officer*)
Mr J Lodge, BSc Hons Sussex (*Physics*)
Miss T Lothingland, MA Exeter (*EAL*)
Mrs V Martin, BA Hons Hull (*English*) [maternity cover]
Miss C Morton, BA Jt Hons Sheffield (*Spanish*)
Miss K Parsons, BSc Nottingham (*Geography*)
Mrs I Powell, BSc Hons, MSc, Rennes (*French*)
Mr P Richards, LL.B Southampton (*Lead Teacher of Economics*)
Mrs A Rowley, BA Hons Liverpool (*English, Head of Upper 3*)
Mrs R Smith, BA Hons PGCE Primary with Music Specialism (*Junior Music*)
Mrs C Smith, MA Tours (*Head of Modern Foreign Languages*)
Mrs K Spelman, BA Hons Oxford, MA London (*Classics, History*)
Mrs M Stuttaford, MA Exeter, BA Hons Exeter (*German*)
Mrs V Willcock, BSc Hons City University London (*Year 2 Teacher*)
Miss N Wintle , BA Ed Hons Exeter, National SENCO Masters Level Qualification (*SENCO*)
Mrs S Wood, BA Ed Exeter (*Physical Education*)
Mrs V Woulfe, BSc Hons Keele (*Mathematics*)
Ms J York, BSc Hons Bath (*Biology*)

Part-time:
Mr G Banks, BA Hons Leeds (*English*) [maternity cover]
Ms J Bellamy, BA Hons Manchester (**Drama*)
Mrs C Finnegan, BA Hons Central Saint Martins (*Food & Nutrition, Textiles*)
Mr A Ganley, BA Hons Nottingham (*Drama*)
Mrs C Gorrod, BA Hons Surrey (*Pre-Prep*)
Dr R Henderson, MMath Hons Durham, PhD East Anglia (*Mathematics*)
Ms A M Hurley, MA London (*Art*)
Mrs D Lewis, BA Hons Cheltenham (*Careers, Exams Officer*)
Miss T Lothingland, MA Exeter (*EAL*)
Miss C Morton, BA Jt Hons Sheffield (*Spanish*)
Miss K Parsons, BSc Hons Nottingham (*Geography*)
Mrs I Powell, BSc Hons MSc Rennes (*French*)
Mr P Richards, LLB Southampton (*Lead Teacher of Economics*)
Mrs A Rowley, BA Hons Liverpool (*English, Head of Upper 3*)
Mrs R Smith, BA Hons, PGCE Primary with Music Specialism (*Junior Music*)
Mrs C Smith, MA Tours (*French, Spanish*)
Mrs K Spelman, BA Hons Oxford, MA London (*Classics, History*)

Mrs A Weeks, BSc Hons Loughborough (*Physics*)
Miss N Wintle, BA Ed Hons Exeter, National SENCO
  Masters Level Qualification (*SENCO*)
Mrs S Wood, BA Ed Exeter (*Physical Education*)
Mrs V Woulfe, BSc Hons Keele (*Mathematics*)
Ms J York, BSc Hons Bath (*Biology*)

Non-Teaching Staff:
Mr A Ayre (*Chef Manager*)
Mrs G Baker (*Kitchen Assistant*)
Miss L Blake (*Part Time Finance Assistant*)
Mr D Bratt (*Gardener*)
Mrs E Bremner (*Marketing Assistant*)
Mrs R Board, BA Hons Warwick (*Head of
  Communications*)
Mrs Claire Chudley (*Home Economics Assistant*)
Mrs M Craig (*SLT Administrator*)
Mrs Z Cunningham (*Human Resources Advisor*)
Mrs M Davey, DipHE Exeter, BSc Hons Plymouth, BA
  Hons Kent (*School Nurse*)
Mrs L Drake (*Office Administrator*)
Miss M Ellis (*Archivist*)
Mrs R El-Nashar, MA Edinburgh (*PA to Deputy Head &
  Director of Studies*)
Mr M Everhard (*Estate Dept*)
Mrs M Green (*Finance Assistant*)
Mrs H Halpin, BSc Hons Surrey (*Resources Manager*)
Mr P Hancock (*Estates*)
Mrs G Hannaford (*Kitchen Assistant*)
Miss C Harrison (*Kitchen Assistant*)
Mrs W Holt, BEng Plymouth (*Science Technician*)
Mrs J Hourihan, BSc Birmingham, 2 x BA Hons Open
  University, PG Dip Info & Lib Studies Robert Gordon
  University (*Librarian*)
Mrs O Jelinkova (*Cleaner*)
Mrs J Jephson (*Art Technician*)
Miss L Jones (*Head's PA*) [maternity leave]
Mrs M Kaan, BA Hons Bangor, MA Lancaster (*Facilities
  Administrator*)
Mrs K Jones (*Kitchen Assistant*)
Miss K Kovacova (*Cleaner*)
Miss H Lloyd (*Junior School Administrator*)
Mrs G Lovelock (*Mini bus driver*)
Mr A Matthews (*Bus Driver*)
Mrs K Matthews (*Cleaner*)
Mrs L Mitchell (*Chemistry Technician*)
Mrs Munro (*School Registrar*)
Mrs L Oldfield (*Admissions Assistant, Data Manager*)
  [maternity leave]
Mr B Pugh (*Cleaning Supervisor*)
Mrs G Pugh (*Assistant Cleaning Supervisor*)
Mrs F Purchase, BSc Hons, Exeter (*Graduate Learning
  Support Mentor*)
Mr M Reid (*Graphic Designer*)
Mrs J Pinniger (*Counsellor*)
Mrs K Sanders (*Resources Assistant*)
Mrs J Street (*Admissions Assistant*)
Mr D Sutton (*Bus Driver*)
Mr M Tribble (*Chef*)
Mrs T Turner (*Receptionist*)
Mrs J Wallis (*Kitchen Assistant*)
Mr J Wicksteed, BSc Hons St Andrews (*IT Systems
  Manager*)
Mrs H Wright (*Science Technician*)

Visiting Staff:
Mrs C Austin (*Oboe*)
Mrs S Barlow (*Dance*)
Mrs D Broomfield (*Choirs*)
Mrs E Bucci (*Netball Coach*)
Dr H Catterick (*Kick-Boxing, Martial Arts Instructor*)

Mr D Cottam (*Guitar*)
Mrs H Edwards (*Netball Coach*)
Ms C Conner (*Gymnastics Coach*)
Mrs N Fitzgerald (*Badminton Coach*)
Ms S Fernandez-Temino (*Aerobics Coach*)
Ms J Gall (*Clarinet*)
Mrs A Higgins (*Piano, Bassoon*)
Miss M Hiley (*Percussion*)
Mrs S Hill (*Singing, Flute*)
Ms K Howard (*Creation station after school club*)
Miss T Jeffery (*Yoga Instructor*)
Miss A Kettlewell (*Singing*)
Mr N Lawrence (*Singing*)
Mrs P Leonard (*Speech & Drama*)
Ms C Sanz Planchart (*Tennis Coach*)
Mr J Martin (*Outdoor Education*)
Mr A Nuthall (*Brass, Saxophone*)
Mr C Pettet (*Singing*)
Mr R Porch (*Piano Tuner*)
Mr T Ross (*Flute*)
Mr J Rycroft (*Lead Tennis Coach*)
Mr T Simpson (*Martial Arts*)
Mrs V Taylor (*Outdoor Education*)
Mrs A Tillson-Hawke (*Violin, Viola*)
Ms I Woollcott (*Double Bass*)
Mr C Worcester (*Basketball Coach*)

Merchant Taylors' Girls' School
Crosby

80 Liverpool Road, Crosby, Liverpool L23 5SP

Tel: 0151 949 9366 (Admissions)
Fax: 0151 932 1461
email: admissionsmtgs@merchanttaylors.com
website: www.merchanttaylors.com
Twitter: @MerchantsCrosby
Facebook: @merchanttaylorscrosby

Motto: *Concordia Parvae Res Crescunt*

The Senior Girls' School was opened in 1888 on the site which had been occupied by the Boys' School for over 350 years. The original grey stone building, erected in 1620, is still in daily use as the Library.

We are a famous school with an enviable reputation and we are determined to remain true to the guiding principles of our founder, John Harrison, citizen and Merchant Taylor of London, to provide an outstanding academic education to pupils from the surrounding area. The Guild of Merchant Taylors in London is one of the twelve great City Livery Companies that survived from medieval times. Merchant Taylors' are proud of their historical links to the company and still welcome visitors from the Company every year.

Over the years extensions have been made to the school that include a Fitness Suite, Science Laboratories and a Sixth Form Centre. The Centenary Hall provides ample accommodation for concerts, plays and sports. The School is beautifully situated approximately 8 miles from Liverpool and within 10 minutes' walk of the Sefton coastline. There are netball and tennis courts on the premises with a playing field and the joint schools' multimillion pound sports centre. The Centre incorporates a Sports Hall suitable for a variety of indoor sports, dance and fitness studios, a refreshment area and classrooms. A new entrance was built in 2009 to include a new reception area and an art gallery space called The Vitreum. This gallery has been used to showcase pupils' work as well as exhibitions from local, national and international artists.

The girls receive a broad academic education. Subjects included in the curriculum are Art, Biology, Chemistry, Classics, Drama and Theatre Studies, Economics, English Language and English Literature, French, Geography, German, Government and Politics, History, Home Economics, Information Technology, Latin, Mathematics, Music, Physical Education, Physics, Psychology, Religious Studies and Spanish.

Merchant Taylors' is a family of Schools with a brother school just a mile down the road. There is a separate Primary School situated in a self-contained building near to the Main School with girls aged 4–11 and boys aged 4–7. This recently underwent a £5.5 million redevelopment which was completed in December 2014. The Senior Girls' School age range is 11–18. There are at present 944 pupils at both schools.

We are proud of our family of schools and our academic excellence, pastoral care, outstanding sport and the array of extra-curricular activities that we offer.

Fees per term (2018–2019). Tuition: Senior School £3,798; Junior School £2,839, Infant School (ages 4–7) £2,755.

Examinations. The 11+ Entrance Exam takes place in January. There are papers in Maths and English and Verbal Reasoning. The papers are common to both the Boys' and the Girls' Schools.

The Music Examinations taken are those of the Associated Board of the Royal Schools of Music, The London College of Music, Trinity Guildhall.

Parent Teachers' Association. *Chairperson:* Heather Brown, c/o The School.

Old Girls' Association. *Hon Secretary*: Mrs S Duncan, 'Fairhaven', The Serpentine South, Liverpool L23 6UQ.

Charitable status. The Merchant Taylors' Schools Crosby is a Registered Charity, number 1125485, and a Company Limited by Guarantee, registered in England, number 6654276. Registered Office: Liverpool Road, Crosby, Liverpool L23 0QP.

Governors:
Chairman: Mrs B Bell, CBE, LLB Hons, FCLIT, FSOE, FIMI, FIRTE
Mr J Cartwright, BSc
Mr C Cowling, BSc, FIA, FIMA, CSci, CMath
Mrs K Crewe-Read, BSc, PGCE
Mr D S Evans, LLB, MA Oxon
Dr Je A Fox, MBChB, DRCOG, MRCGP, FRCGP
Mrs S Gascoigne, BEd Hons
Miss A Gervasoni, MBA, BHSc Hons, ALMC, LLCM
Mr J Hepworth, MRICS
Ms L C Martin Wright, ONC, JP, DL
Mr S A Wilkinson, BA, FCA
Mr D Yip, MA, IoD

Clerk to the Governors & Director of Finance and Operations: Mrs Lynn Hill
Accounts: Mr D Norton

Headmistress: Mrs C Tao, BSc Surrey, MSc LSE

Deputy Headmistress: Mrs M L Bush, MA Liverpool, BMus Hons Wales, FRSA, NPQH, PGCE
Head of Sixth Form: Mr F Lawell
Head Upper School: Mrs A Wadsworth
Head of Lower School: Mrs B Jones
Head of Year 7: Mrs E Moore

Admissions Officer: Mrs S Barrington

PA to Headmistress: Mrs J Baccino

Merchant Taylors' Primary School, 'Stanfield':
Head of School: Miss E Lynan, BA Hons, PGCE, MAST
Maths Specialist Teacher

Admissions Officer and Head's PA: Mrs M Langham
Receptionist: Mrs N McKie-Thomson

More House School

22–24 Pont Street, London SW1X 0AA

Tel:	020 7235 2855; Bursar: 020 7235 4162
Fax:	020 7259 6782
email:	office@morehouse.org.uk
website:	www.morehouse.org.uk

More House is an independent Catholic day school of up to 220 girls, aged 11–18. The school was founded in 1953 by the Canonesses of St Augustine; since 1969 it has been under lay management as a charitable trust.

Located in the heart of Knightsbridge in central London, the school provides an advantageous proximity to some of the city's best museums and galleries.

Aims of the School.

- To establish an environment where pupils and staff are valued and supported as individuals and where their rights and dignity are maintained.
- To foster an ethos of spiritual growth, not only for those within the Roman Catholic Church, but also for those who adhere to other Christian traditions and other faiths.
- To develop the spiritual, academic, and cultural potential of each pupil to the full at every stage of their school career in such a way that this development will continue throughout their life.
- To encourage intellectual curiosity and pride in achievement.
- The school expects all its members to act with integrity, to display a concern for justice, and to be sensitive to the needs of other people.

Ethos. More House is a small and happy community, in which a generous pupil to teacher ratio ensures each student is fully supported, nurturing their talents and abilities so that they may reach their full academic and personal potential.

Pupils leave More House armed not only with the qualifications they need to pursue the courses and careers of their choice, but with a confidence, composure, and grace that will stay with them and carry them through the rest of their lives.

Religious Affiliation. Although the school has a Catholic foundation, pupils of all faiths or no faith are welcome. More House provides a safe and inclusive environment that fosters mutual respect and understanding of all faiths or the absence of one.

Curriculum. The maximum class size at More House is normally sixteen, streamed where necessary in mathematics, science, and languages. Class sizes decrease further up the school, numbering between one to ten students in A Level classes. This ensures the needs of each individual student are catered for.

The school curriculum offers a wide variety of subjects at all levels. In the first two years, all pupils study mathematics, science, English, French, German, Latin, history, geography, history of art, religious studies, information technology, drama, art, physical education, classical civilisation, music, dance, and study skills. Spanish is added in year 9, offering the possibility of taking two modern languages at GCSE, where the core curriculum of mathematics, science, English language and literature, and religious studies is supplemented by four further options.

The Advanced Level courses offered are structured around each pupil's choice of subjects. New options available at this stage are business studies, economics, psychology, and textiles. Further breadth of study is achieved through an enrichment programme, which includes study for the EPQ (Extended Project Qualification).

Most girls leaving the sixth form proceed to higher education and then to careers in a variety of fields.

Extracurricular. More House offers an impressive number of extracurricular clubs that take place before, during, and after school.

The PE department offers several extracurricular activities, including climbing, swimming, rowing, netball, rounders, hockey, football, and cricket. Their successful league results are a testament to the talent and dedication of the department – the under 13 and under 15 teams are borough champions in netball, and the under 13 team are borough champions in indoor cricket.

The music department runs several talented choirs and chamber choirs, who perform in concerts regularly throughout the year. Furthermore, the combined choirs go on a yearly tour in the Autumn term – recent destinations have included Madrid, Paris, Rome, Malta, New York, Vienna, and Budapest.

The drama department stages several productions throughout the school year and a school musical every two years in an external venue. Recent productions have included *A Little Princess: The Musical*, *Macbeth*, *A Midsummer Night's Dream*, and *Guys and Dolls*.

Other extracurricular clubs offered include: dance, debating, circuit training, science, foreign film, Sporcle, 7-minute workout, 3-song workout, netball shooting, drama, band, percussion, retro games, dream catcher crafting, multi-skills, ukulele, eco, guitar, art, horrible histories, prayer, running, chess, swimming, book, scrabble, Italian, and Mandarin, to name a few.

Facilities. The school occupies two adjoining, nineteenth-century, Queen Anne style houses. The buildings retain many of their original architectural features and charm, but have been modernised to include purpose-built facilities. These include four science laboratories, two computer rooms, a chapel, a library, and a drama and dance studio. The recently renovated sixth-form centre features a bright and spacious common room, communal kitchen, and two study rooms.

Physical education and extracurricular sport take place in Battersea Park, Hyde Park, Imperial College London, Fulham Reach Boat House, and St Mary's Paddington – all a short walk or short coach ride away.

Admission. Admission is primarily for entry in year 7, with occasional places available across other years. More House is part of the London 11+ Consortium – details can be found on the school website. Entry at 11+ is by examination, coupled with an interview with one of the Co-Heads. £130 registration fee.

Fees per term (2018–2019). £6,650 including school meals.

Scholarships and Bursaries. Academic, Music, Drama, Art, and Sports scholarships are awarded at 11+ and sixth form, based on merit. Bursaries are also available, based on means-testing.

Charitable Status. More House Trust is a Registered Charity, number 312737. It exists to provide an academic education for girls aged 11 to 18 within the framework of a Catholic Day School.

Governing Body:
Chairman: Mr J J Fyfe, BSc Birmingham
Vice-Chairman: Mrs S Shale, BA Birmingham, FCA

Mr P I Ewings, BA Belfast, Solicitor of the Supreme Court [England and Wales]
Ms N Patel, BA Nottingham Trent, MCIPD, CQSW
Mrs S Sturrock, BMus London, ARCM
Mr K Lake, BA London
Mr W Ralston-Saul
Mr L Mayol-Navarrete, LLB Granada, PhD Cardiz

Clerk to the Governors: Mrs A Barker, BA UCLAN

Co-Head: **Mrs A Leach**, BSc Liverpool
Co-Head: **Mr M Keeley**, BMus London

Director of Studies: Mrs J Boulter, BA London
Director of Pastoral Care: Miss S Brown, BA Bristol

Senior Teachers:
Miss K Devine, BA Bristol
Mr T Robertson, BSc Leeds
Mr J La Frenais, BSc Leeds

Bursar: Ms S Meadows, BA Manchester, FCCA, FCSA

Chaplain: Father Lawrence Nam

PA to the Headmaster and Registrar: Mrs J Barnwell
Communications Officer: Miss L Scotting, BA London, MA London
Marketing Officer: Miss S Xiberras, FdA London
School Secretary: Miss A Tharma, BA London

Academic Departments:
* *Head of Department*

Art:
*Miss K Devine, BA Bristol
Ms D Rigby, MA Chelsea
Miss H Yate BA, MA London, PGCE London

Business Studies and Economics:
*Mrs P Revell, BA Wellington

Classics:
*Mrs R Gilbertson, MA St Andrews
Mrs R Tunnicliffe, BA London, MA London

Drama:
*Miss V Jackson, MA London
Mrs S Fischer, BA Birmingham, BA LAMDA

English Language and Literature:
*Mrs L Garwood, BA Durham
Mrs J Boulter, BA London
Mr P Hegarty, BA London
Miss L Kempin, BA Leeds

History:
*Mrs B Cain, BA Lancaster
Mr F Young, MA St Andrews, MSc PhD Edinburgh

History of Art:
*Mrs B Hunt, BA Scotland, MBA Scotland

Geography:
*Mr J La Frenais, BSc Leeds
Mr C Reilly, BA Galway IRL

Information Technology:
Mrs A Leach, BSc Liverpool

Mathematics:
*Mr M Ginever, BSc Exeter
Mrs J Mullins, MSc Cape Town
Mr T Robertson, BSc Leeds
Ms O Soltani, BA Ternopil

Modern Foreign Languages:
*Mr M Caroll, BA Belfast
Miss S Brown, BA Bristol
Miss C Gremillet, BA Barcelona, MA Bristol
Miss N Stojanovic, MA Paris

Music:
*Miss E Calderwood, BMus London
Miss K Radzvilaite, BMus MA London
Mr M Keeley, BMus London

Physical Education:
*Miss S Minto, BSc Brunel, QTS
Mrs K Mercer, BSc Exeter
Miss E Hails, BA Leeds Beckett

Psychology:
Ms E Aldous, MA Austria, MBA Leicester

Religious Studies:
*Miss D Reid, BA Belfast
Miss O Henvey, BEd Belfast
Ms K Gulin, MA Sweden

Sciences:
*Ms J Mazewski, BSc Massey, MSc Massey
*Miss I Wijewardana, BSc London
*Miss C Davidson, BSc York
Miss S Tahhan, BEng London

Support for Learning:
* Mrs C Alexander, BA Keele
Miss S Gunner, BA Roehampton
Mrs M Tomlinson, BA Manchester

Mr G Minica (*Network Manager*)
Ms F Bunting, BSc Nairobi, PGD London (*Science Technician*)

Peripatetic staff:
Ms D Matthews Forth, RAD TC, BBO TD, IDTA T, IDTA M
plus various instrumental teachers

North London Collegiate School

Canons, Canons Drive, Edgware, Middlesex HA8 7RJ

Tel: Senior School: 020 8952 0912
             Junior School: 020 8952 1276
email: office@nlcs.org.uk
website: www.nlcs.org.uk
Twitter: @NLCS1850
Facebook: @nlcs1850

North London Collegiate School was founded by Miss Frances Mary Buss in 1850 to provide an education for girls that would equal that of boys and it produced many of the first women graduates. Since its foundation the school has continued to provide an outstanding education for girls.

It is a unique school that combines academic excellence with a vibrant extracurricular life, an international outlook, glorious facilities and a warm community. We are proud of our tradition of producing independent, often pioneering, young women with the drive and confidence to make the most of opportunities and a difference in the world. That was the vision of the school's founder and it remains true of the school today. Although steeped in tradition, the school has always helped to pioneer women's education and constantly looks to improve the education offered. That is why we have enjoyed the accolade of being named the leading Independent Secondary School of the Year twice in the last decade.

Examination success is only part of the picture. Art, music, drama, dance, sport, community service projects and over 30 clubs and societies create a vibrant atmosphere and help girls to flourish and enjoy their time at North London. Every girl matters and the pastoral care at the school ensures pupils feel supported and valued throughout their time here.

North London Collegiate School enjoys the beauty, space and safety of a parkland setting within London. The school provides an ambitious education for girls from a wide range of social backgrounds. The very best of academic teaching is coupled with the widest range of extracurricular activities to help the pupils fulfil their potential.

There are approximately 1,080 girls at North London Collegiate School: 120 in the First School aged from 4+ to 7, 190 Juniors aged 7–11, and 770 in the Senior School aged 11–18, of whom 235 are in the Sixth Form.

The school's academic record is outstanding. It has twice been named as *The Sunday Times* "Independent School of the Year" and *The Daily Telegraph* has described it as the most consistently successful academic girls' school in the country. Results in 2018 were again consistent with the school's academic profile. Over 94% of A Level entries in principle subjects were A*–B grades, with 85% of students gaining straight A* or A grades in all subjects taken.

Sixth formers at North London Collegiate are in the top 4 per cent of students worldwide in the internationally recognised International Baccalaureate.

45 girls were offered places at either Oxford or Cambridge, with 100% of students who applied receiving offers from Russell Group institutions. Our students also received 17 offers to study at Ivy League or equivalent institutions in the US. This reinforces the Sutton Trust's report published in 2011, which placed North London first nationally for the proportion of students gaining places to highly-selective universities.

The GCSE 2018 results were equally outstanding, with 77.5% of all entries were awarded a 9 – the top grade.

The facilities at the school are first class, designed to offer the girls every opportunity to develop themselves both academically and socially. These facilities include lacrosse pitches, all-weather tennis courts and a Sports Centre with indoor swimming pool and fitness centre.

The Performing Arts Centre, with a 350-seat auditorium, orchestra pit, galleries and rehearsal rooms, hosts over 35 productions a year. Music and Drama are strong, with opportunity for all to take part in productions, choirs and orchestras. The music programme includes challenging pieces for the most able, with such events as the National Chamber Group competition where the school has won the Founder's Trophy as the most successful competing school on several occasions. On the campus are a Music School, Drawing School and Design Technology Block, all situated around the lake, where waterlilies in the summer make it the ideal place to relax during the long lunch interval. Alternatively, girls may visit the beautifully light and spacious four-floor library.

There is an extensive school coach scheme.

Full details of Open Days and Taster Afternoons are on the school's website.

Bursaries. Enabling bright girls from all backgrounds is central to the ethos of the school. Many bursaries are offered to girls who do well in the 11+ test and those entering the Sixth Form, whose parents can demonstrate financial need.

Scholarships. A number of Academic Scholarships, up to the value of 50% fees, are awarded each year based on the results of the 11+ and 16+ entrance examinations and interviews.

A number of Music Scholarships, up to the value of 25% fees, are awarded at 11+ each year.

Fees per term (2018–2019). Senior School: £6,676; Junior School: £5,641.

Charitable status. The North London Collegiate School is a Registered Charity, number 1115843. It exists to provide an academic education for girls.

The Governing Body:
Mr T Suter, MA (*Chairman*)
Mr K M Breslauer, BSc, MBA
Mrs S Carter, BSc Hons, Associate CFA
Mrs E Davis, BA, Dip ONL
Mr A Emmanuel, BSc, MD, FRCP, FRCPE
Mr A Fox, MA, MD, MSc, MB BS, DCH, FRCPCH, FHEA, Dip Allergy
Mr J Herlihy, MA, FCCA
Mr S Jaffe, BSc Hons, FCA
Mr P Linthwaite, MA
Mr P Needleman, MA, FIA
Mrs E A Raperport, BA, FCT
Professor Brian Young, BA, MA, DPhil

Chief Operating Officer: Mr I Callender

Headmistress: Mrs E S Clark, MA Cambridge, PGCE

Deputy Head – Academic: Mr P Dwyer, BA Oxon

Deputy Head – Pastoral: Dr H Bagworth-Mann, BA Brunel, PhD Brunel

Director of Studies and Administration: Mr M Burke, BA Newcastle, MA Durham

Head of Junior School: Mrs J M Newman, BEd Cantab

Assistant Heads:
Teaching and Learning: Mrs J Bedi, MA Cantab
Enrichment: Mr H Waddington, MA Cantab, MPhil Cantab FRGS
Senior Tutor: Dr C Jackson, PhD Glasgow
Professional Development: Mr R Sykes, BA Manchester
Communities: Mrs M Fotheringham, MA Oxon
Head of Sixth Form: Mr C Cockerill, BSc London
Head of Upper School: Mrs E Wells, BSc York, MPhil Cantab
Head of Middle School: Dr R Ferguson, BSc Bath, PhD Bath

Director of University Admissions: Mrs K Hedges, MA Cantab

SEN Advisor: Ms L. Timm, MChem Oxon

Director of IB: Ms M Copin, MA Cantab

Careers Advisor: Mr H Linscott, BA London, MA London

Heads of Academic Departments:
Art and Design: Mr J Robinson, BA Nottingham Trent
Classics: Mrs D O'Sullivan, BA Cantab
Economics: Mrs S Dean, BSc London, MSc London
English: Mr D James-Williams, BA London, MA Open
Drama: Miss D Gibbs, BA Surrey
Geography: Mr A Murray, BA London, MA London
History and Government & Politics: Dr S Goward, BA Surrey, MA London, MSc Aberystwyth, PhD Oxford Brookes
Information Technology: Dr A P Cripps, PhD London
Mathematics: Ms M Copin, MA Cantab
Modern Languages & Spanish: Ms D Mardell, MA Cantab, MEd Cantab
French: Miss K Bonnal, Maîtrise Avignon
Italian: Mr P Langdale, MA Oxon
Russian: Mr P Chadwick, BA Cantab, MA Toronto
German: Dr J Baughan, BA Bristol, MLitt Bristol, PhD Exeter
Music: Mr C Ham, BA Cantab, MMus Royal Northern College of Music
Physical Education: Miss G Aldcroft, BA Liverpool
Religious Studies & Philosophy: Mr J Holt, BA Durham, MA Open
Biology: Miss K Wilson, BSc York
Chemistry: Dr A Potter, PhD London
Physics: Mrs N Timoshina, MSc Moscow

PA to the Headmistress: Mrs D Daum

The pupil teacher ratio is 11:1

Notre Dame School

Burwood House, Cobham, Surrey KT11 1HA
Tel: 01932 869990
email: office@notredame.co.uk
website: www.notredame.co.uk
Twitter: @NotreDameCobham
Facebook: @NotreDameSchoolCobham
LinkedIn: /notredamecobham

Notre Dame School is an independent Roman Catholic day school for girls aged 2–18 and boys aged 2–7. We welcome families of all faiths and none.

At Notre Dame Senior School we offer a holistic, personalised and nurturing education in a secure and stimulating environment. Our girls are at the centre of everything we do. Their physical and mental well-being is as important as their academic achievements – pastoral care is embedded at the heart of our whole approach to education.

We are always looking to improve and all staff are encouraged and supported in continually striving to enrich the educational experience. We have a range of dynamic strategies which together assure the delivery of an exemplary all-round education, as recognised across the board in our 'Excellent' ISI Inspection Report in 2017.

A detailed teaching and learning quality assurance programme is in place, which focuses on five categories; teaching, learning, differentiation, behaviour and assessment. Year-on-year tracking shows impressive rises in all five areas. 'Learning walks' and marking reviews allow middle and senior managers to monitor standards and share good practice. The focus on assessment and collaborative marking has included pupils in the process and given them greater ownership over their own academic progress.

The Lestonnac Approach is our fully embedded resilience strategy which has been further enhanced recently with the appointment of a student Counsellor. The Counsellor is not only available to counsel girls on an individual basis but is actively looking to promote positive social and emotional wellbeing throughout the whole school.

Sport and the Arts are the heart and soul of the school. The opening of our state-of-the-art, all-weather pitches (hockey, netball, tennis and athletics) in 2017 took our sporting facilities to new heights and we are further enhancing our field sports on newly acquired land. Our professional 360-seater theatre stages numerous and varied productions and performances each year and a new Art block is imminent to further enrich our highly successful Art and Textiles curriculum.

It is the integration of all these strands – academic challenge, quality of teaching and learning, student and teacher collaboration, well-being and resilience and excellence in Sport and the Arts, which allows us to fulfil our aim of providing an exemplary holistic education. Our academic value added (in top 8% nationally) and examination results (52% A*/A grades at A Level) speak for themselves and are particularly impressive given our broad intake.

Notre Dame is built on 400 years of educational experience: The Company of Mary Our Lady was founded in Bordeaux in 1607 to educate girls, and Notre Dame is one of some 300 educational foundations around the world that now come under this umbrella. To ready our pupils for the wider world, to live life to the full, we believe that our shared mission and purpose help our children to aspire to be the best they can be in in all their endeavours, during their school years and beyond.

ISI Inspection 2017. The full report can be viewed on the school website: ISI-Inspection-Report.

Transport. Notre Dame is excellently located – two minutes from the A3/M25 junction, 10 minutes from Walton, Weybridge, Cobham or Esher, and 20 minutes from Guildford, Wimbledon and Putney. Private school coaches for girls from Year 3 upwards – flexible single/return journeys – from Clapham, Putney and Fulham to Esher, Woking and Weybridge and many stops in between.

Admission. Usual entry points: Year 7 (age 11), Year 9 (age 13) and Year 12 (Sixth Form). Occasional places are sometimes available in other year groups.

Registration: Registration Form and payment of £100 registration fee.

Assessment: The 11+ entrance examination held in early January – Maths, English and Non-Verbal Reasoning. Closing date for entries typically in the November previously. Approximately half of intake at 11+ comes from Notre Dame Prep.

11+/13+/Sixth Form scholarships awarded in Art, Music, Drama and Sport. Academic scholarships also awarded based on performance in entrance examination.

For occasional vacancies: candidates invited to attend Taster Day, to include assessments and time with prospective classmates. Assessments can be arrange overseas as necessary.

As a rough guide, intake sits in the top 50% of the ability range.

Prep School. For further information about Notre Dame Prep School, please see entry in IAPS section.

Fees per term (2018–2019). Senior School £5,590; Prep School £1,345–£4,535.

Charitable status. Notre Dame School Cobham is a Registered Charity, number 1081875.

Chair of Governors: Mr Gerald Russell

Executive Team:

Head Teacher (*Senior School***): Mrs Anna King**, MEd, MA Cantab, PGCE, FRGS

Head Teacher (*Prep School*): Mrs Amelie Morgan MA, BA Hons, PGCE

Bursar: Ms Louise Ayling, BSc Hons, MA Oxon, PGCE, FCA

Senior Leadership Team:
Executive Team [as above]
Assistant Head – Curriculum: Ms Sarah Badger, BSc Hons, PGCE
Assistant Head – Teaching and Learning: Mr Michael Coackley, BA Hons, PGCE
Assistant Head – Sixth Form: Miss Janine Harber, BA Hons PGCE
Assistant Head – Pastoral: Mrs Amanda Windibank, BA Hons, PGCE
Assistant Head – Prep: Mrs Clare Barber, BSc Hons, PGCE
Head of EYFS: Miss Melanie Lehmann, BA Hons, EYPS
Head of Infants: Miss Geraldine Deen, BA Hons, QTS
Pastoral Director – Prep: Miss Rebecca Golding, BA Hons, PGCE

Estates Manager: Mr Anthony Madigan

Admissions Manager: Mrs Beccy Johnson, MA Oxon, Dip Stat

Alumnae Officer: Mrs Ros Roberts, NUJ, BACB, IoD

Notting Hill and Ealing High School
GDST

2 Cleveland Road, Ealing, London W13 8AX

Tel:	020 8799 8400
email:	enquiries@nhehs.gdst.net
website:	www.nhehs.gdst.net
Twitter:	@nhehs

Founded 1873.

Notting Hill and Ealing High School is part of the GDST (Girls' Day School Trust). The GDST is the leading network of independent girls' schools in the UK. As a charity that owns and runs 23 schools and two academies, it reinvests all its income in its schools. For further information about the Trust, see p. xxiii or visit www.gdst.net.

An academically selective, independent day school for girls aged 4 to 18. Separately housed and run Junior Department (ages 4+–11) and Senior Department (ages 11+–18) on the same site.

Pupils and Location. Approximately 900 pupils. 590 in the Senior School (153 in the Sixth Form) and 310 in the Junior Department. Transport links are excellent (Ealing Broadway station is nearby and several buses stop outside the school). Girls come from Ealing and all over west London.

Ethos. This is a school with a long tradition of academic excellence and creativity within an exceptionally warm and supportive environment. Notting Hill and Ealing girls are well grounded, confident and independent. They are proud of their school and value kindness and laughter, fun and friendship. This is a place where tolerance and mutual respect are nurtured; where you can be yourself. With a wide variety of activities and opportunities, and a strong emphasis on charitable giving, everyone can enjoy being part of a vibrant community and express their passion for learning, and for life.

Pastoral Care. The system of pastoral care is overseen by the Deputy Head – Pastoral working through the Heads of Year and Form Tutors. The Head also takes a personal interest in all pupils. The result is a well structured system that is sufficiently flexible to support every girl and to ensure that she is treated as a whole person with individual strengths and needs. In the Sixth Form the tutor team is led by the Head of Sixth Form and her deputy.

Curriculum. Throughout the Junior and Senior Schools our curriculum is broad and balanced and encourages independence of learning and thought. In Years 7–9 everyone follows courses in English, History, Geography, Mathematics, Physics, Chemistry, Biology, Design Technology, Computer Science, Religious Studies, Art, Music, and Drama. In Year 7 all girls study Mandarin plus a second modern language (French, German or Spanish). In Year 8 Latin also becomes available. Girls usually take ten subjects at GCSE, including a compulsory core of English Language and Literature, Mathematics, 3 Sciences and a Modern Language. 26 subjects are offered at A Level. Most girls take 3 or 4 subjects. Those who wish may also take the Extended Project Qualification which is highly regarded by university admissions tutors. Each department runs a special programme to support UCAS applications and there is additional support for those applying to Oxbridge or particularly competitive universities. There are also lessons in personal health, ethical and social issues appropriate to each age and stage. Physical Education is taught throughout the school.

The Sixth Form. Our sixth formers play an important role in the school. They enjoy the independence of their own new Sixth Form Centre with common rooms, outdoor space for relaxing, café and fitness centre. They take responsibility for many extra-curricular activities such as organising clubs and act as mentors for girls in the lower years. Additional leadership opportunities are offered by the House system, and voluntary and charity work. All go on to Higher Education and, with excellent results (94% achieving grades A*, A or B in 2018, with 65% of grades being A*/A and 26% of grades being A*), successfully secure places at their choice of university (including Oxford and Cambridge).

Extra-Curricular Activities. As well as covering a wide variety of sports and activities connected with art, drama and music these range from computer animation to competing in the London-wide Hans Woyda Maths competition and from debating to The Duke of Edinburgh's Award scheme.

We take full advantage of everything London offers, with visits to theatres, museums, galleries, performances, and conferences incorporated into the curriculum. Trips abroad are arranged for modern languages, geography, history, art and art history, politics and economics. There is an annual ski trip.

Careers Advice. All girls are enrolled in the Inspiring Futures Futurewise programme which entitles all students to careers help and advice until the age of 23. Sixth formers receive extensive support with university applications, including mock interviews. The GDST Alumnae Network, the unique resource from the GDST, offers each student access to a database of former GDST students, who will give advice and support on careers (including helping with work experience) and universities. An annual Careers Evening typically featuring senior representatives from almost 70 different professions and occupations is organised by the Parents' Guild.

Creative Arts. There are three orchestras, three choirs, and many chamber and ensemble groups. School productions offer opportunities either to perform or to work with production, lighting, sound, costume and staging. Art thrives within the curriculum and through various art clubs. It also contributes to work in design technology and various aspects of ICT, such as web design and animation projects.

Sport. Sport is taken seriously with success in local fixtures and championships, and we encourage participation and enjoyment at all standards. On site facilities include all-weather pitch, four-court sports hall, dance studio and indoor swimming pool. Lifeguard training is available for sixth formers. Aerobics, self-defence, kick boxing and football are among the extra-curricular sports clubs currently available.

Fees per term (2018–2019). Junior School £4,771, Senior School £6,187.

The fees cover the regular curriculum, necessary school books, normal public examination fees, membership of the Futurewise scheme including the Morrisby careers aptitude test, stationery and other materials, but not optional extra subjects or school meals. Fees for extra subjects including instrumental music, speech and drama, are shown in the prospectus. Certain off-site sports are charged for separately, as are school trips.

Scholarships and Bursaries. Academic and music scholarships are available at 11+. At 16+ there are academic awards as well as awards for Physical Education, Drama, Art, and an All-Rounder scholarship.

Means tested bursaries are available in the Senior Department only. Application should be made via the school.

Admission. Usually at 4+, 7+, 11+ and 16+, by appropriate test and/or interview.

Occasionally, vacancies may become available in other year groups.

Charitable status. Notting Hill and Ealing High School is part of The Girls' Day School Trust, which is a Registered Charity, number 306983.

Chairman of Local Governing Board: Ms Sue Blyth

Head: Mr Matthew Shoults, MA, PGCE

Deputy Head – Pastoral: Mrs Rebecca Irwin, BA, PGCE
Deputy Head – Academic: Mr Alex Smith, MA, MEd, PGCE

Head of Junior Department: Mrs Silvana Silva, BEd Hons

Nottingham Girls' High School
GDST

9 Arboretum Street, Nottingham NG1 4JB

Tel:	0115 941 7663
Fax:	0115 924 0757
email:	enquiries@not.gdst.net
	admissions@not.gdst.net
website:	www.nottinghamgirlshigh.gdst.net
Twitter:	@NottmGirlsHigh
Facebook:	@FriendsofNGHS
LinkedIn:	/Friends of Nottingham Girls High School

Founded 1875.

Nottingham Girls' High School is part of the GDST (Girls' Day School Trust). The GDST is the leading network of independent girls' schools in the UK. As a charity that owns and runs 23 schools and two academies, it reinvests all its income in its schools. For further information about the Trust, see p. xxiii or visit www.gdst.net.

Additional information about the school may be found on the school's website and a detailed information pack may be obtained from Central Admissions at the school.

Number of Pupils. Senior School 581 (including 143 in the Sixth Form); Junior School 250.

A selective day school, NGHS is on a single site adjacent to a park in the middle of Nottingham. The original Victorian houses have been modernised and there have been extensive additions to create a well-resourced school. The Junior School is housed in separate buildings on the same campus as the Senior School, and has been extended to include a library and ICT learning resources centre as well four additional classrooms. A major programme of refurbishment in the Senior School has included refitting the science laboratories, food technology and design technology. A state-of-the-art performing arts centre was opened in December 2016.

There is a self-contained Sixth Form Centre providing a large coffee shop-style common room and recreational area. The tutorial rooms are light and airy, and fully equipped with the latest technology.

The school grounds include an all-weather sports pitch, climbing wall, outdoor learning area, gymnasium, sports hall and fitness suite. There is also a sizeable sports field close to the school. The modern dining hall has excellent facilities for providing a wide choice of snacks and meals throughout the day.

Although examination results are among the best in the country, the school believes that education for life involves much more. Leadership, confidence, teamwork, flexibility and reliability are among the qualities increasingly demanded in today's ever changing society. Everyone is encouraged to take the opportunity to participate fully in a wide range of enrichment activities to develop skills and qualities that will lead to a happy, successful and fulfilling life.

At all ages, it is hoped that the girls will enjoy their studies. The school provides a lively, stimulating learning environment to encourage girls to discover the excitement and satisfaction of high academic achievement coupled with growing knowledge and understanding.

Curriculum. The curriculum is designed to give a broad academic education and due regard is paid to the National Curriculum. In the Junior School as well as following a pattern of work designed to help develop a confident grasp of core skills, the girls benefit from a stimulating and challenging integrated creative curriculum with enrichment experiences firmly embedded into teaching and learning. Girls take complete internal assessments in Year 6 and results are consistently very high. There is liaison with the Senior School staff, helping to ensure continuity for pupils at 11+. In the Senior School girls are prepared for GCSE, AS and A2 Levels, with almost all girls proceeding to university.

Girls at all ages follow a comprehensive programme of personal and social development including aspects of careers, citizenship, health and sex education, current affairs and environmental issues.

Throughout the school girls are encouraged to develop their physical skills and the school has an excellent sports record; teams regularly win trophies at City and County level with many being selected to compete at regional or national level.

Admissions. At 4+ entry, small groups of girls are invited to come into school and take part in a number of activities together to see if they are ready for school. Entry at 11+ is by interview and a written test which includes English, mathematics and verbal reasoning and is designed to determine potential and understanding. Most of the existing students stay on at 16+ and a number of students are admitted into the Sixth Form from other schools. The entry requirement is 8 GCSE subjects at an average of grade B, with grades A or B in any subject to be studied in the Sixth Form as specified by the department. This is supported by individual interviews and a report from the current school. The school will consider applications for admission into most year groups if there are available places.

Fees per term (2018–2019). Seniors (excluding lunch): Years 7–13 £4,527; Juniors: Rec–Year 6 (inc lunch) £3,473. The fees cover non-residential curriculum trips, school books, stationery and other materials, games and swimming, but not optional extra subjects.

Scholarships and Bursaries. The GDST makes available a substantial number of bursaries. These are means tested and intended to ensure that the school remains accessible to bright girls who would profit from our education but who would be unable to enter the school without financial assistance. Up to 100% of the tuition fee may be awarded. Bursary application forms are available through Central Admissions at the school.

A limited number of academic scholarships are available each year for entry to the Senior School at both 11+ and direct into the Sixth Form. The value of a scholarship is to a maximum of 10% of the current tuition fee. Scholarships are awarded solely on the basis of academic merit and no financial means test is involved. A Performing Arts Scholarship is available at 11+. Music scholarships are available from Year 10.

Charitable status. Nottingham Girls' High School is part of The Girls' Day School Trust, which is a Registered Charity, number 306983.

Chairman of Local Governors: Mrs Jean Pardoe, OBE, DL

Headmistress: **Miss J Keller**, BA

Deputy Head: Ms K Handford-Smith, MEd

Assistant Heads:
Mrs R A Halse, BSc
Mrs L M Wharton-Howett, BA

Head of Junior School: Mrs L Fowler, BA Ed

Director of Finance and Operations: Mr J C Dunn, ACA

Central Admissions:
Mrs S M Webb-Bowen
Mrs C L Haddow

Oxford High School
GDST

Belbroughton Road, Oxford, Oxfordshire OX2 6XA

Tel: 01865 559888
Fax: 01865 552343
email: oxfordhigh@oxf.gdst.net
website: www.oxfordhigh.gdst.net
Twitter: @OxfordHighSch
Facebook: @OxfordHighGDST

Motto: *Ad Lucem.*

Oxford High School is an independent day school for girls founded in 1875. It is Oxford's oldest girls' school and is located in the heart of Oxford. It is part of the Girls' Day School Trust (GDST) which is at the forefront of educational innovation, teaching over 20,000 girls across the UK in 25 schools and is the leading network of independent girls' schools in the UK.

Tatler describes OHS girls as 'charming, witty and creative' and with outstanding results and a 'have a go' attitude, it remains true to its heritage of pioneering girls' education, and achieved 'Exceptional' in its 2016 ISI inspection.

Pupil numbers. 900: Junior School 300, Senior School 600.

The school is on three sites in North Oxford. Already extremely well resourced, the Senior School has a sports hall, indoor swimming pool, The Mary Warnock School of Music, and separate purpose-built centres for all other subjects and the Sixth Form. The school is networked with well-equipped ICT areas. Exciting new developments are in the pipeline with a brand new Sixth Form and Arts centre due to open in Spring 2020 with state-of-the-art teaching and learning space, dedicated sixth-form campus style areas, an auditorium to enable NT-Live type events and a new art teaching and gallery space.

Curriculum. Girls are prepared for GCSE and A Level. Sixth-formers choose from 24 subjects and their timetable is individually tailored around their choice of subjects. Mandarin is a compulsory language for Year 7 along with French. The school offers 8 languages including Latin and Ancient Greek. Approximately 30% proceed to Oxbridge annually. Many girls take examinations in Music, and Speech and Drama, as well as belonging to the Duke of Edinburgh's Award scheme and Young Enterprise. The 360 Programme for Sixth Form offers an innovative and academically challenging programme designed to prepare girls for life at university and beyond.

Admission. The main points of entry are at Reception, Year 3, Year 7, Year 9 and Year 12. Contact our Admissions team for details (admissions@oxf.gdst.net or 01865 318500).

Fees per term (2018–2019). Reception: £3,000 (plus lunch £229); Year 1 and Year 2: £3,406 (plus lunch £229);

Years 3–6: £3,889 (plus lunch £273); Senior School (Years 7–13): £5,182 (plus lunch £273 for Years 7–11). Lunch is compulsory for girls from Reception to Year 11 and optional for Sixth Form girls only, who have the freedom to go to Summertown, Oxford or eat in school.

The fees cover the regular curriculum textbooks, stationery and other materials, educational visits, choral music, games and swimming, but not optional extra subjects.

Bursaries. The School offers bursaries. These are means-tested and ensure that the school remains accessible to bright girls who would profit from the education provided, but who would be unable to enter the school without financial assistance. Bursaries are available at Year 7, Year 9 and Year 12 entry to the Senior School and a confidential application can be made to the GDST. If your family's assessable income and resources are below £85,000 a year, you may be eligible for some support.

Scholarships. Scholarships for Year 7 and Year 9 entry in Art, Drama, Sport, Music, Academic and the Head's Scholarship. Year 12 scholarships in Art, Academic, Drama, Music, Sport and the Head's Scholarship.

Charitable status. Oxford High School is part of The Girls' Day School Trust, which is a Registered Charity, number 306983.

Chairman of School Governing Board: Mrs L Ansdell

Head: Dr P D Hills

Deputy Head – Students and Staff: Dr S Squire

Deputy Head – Academic: Dr P Secker

Head of Junior School: Mrs K Gater

Director of Admissions: Mrs H Griffiths

Registrar: Mrs D Cullen

Palmers Green High School

104 Hoppers Road, London N21 3LJ

Tel: 020 8886 1135
Fax: 020 8882 9473
email: office@pghs.co.uk
website: www.pghs.co.uk
Twitter: @PGHSGirls
Facebook: @palmersgreenhighschool
LinkedIn: @palmers-green-high-school

Motto: *By Love Serve One Another*

Palmers Green High School, founded in 1905 by Miss Alice Hum, has provided an exceptional education for over 100 years. At PGHS we specialise in educating girls, challenging them to achieve their full potential within our warm and friendly school environment.

The school motto, "By Love Serve One Another" was carefully chosen and it still epitomises our special ethos where individuals are nurtured, successes are celebrated and their contribution to the community is greatly valued.

We provide an inspiring, challenging and supportive environment through which all pupils are given opportunities to be inquisitive, independent and develop a lifelong love of learning.

PGHS is a very special 'through-school' where pupils progress in a familiar setting and benefit from seamless transitions across the key stages in the Lower and Senior Schools. There is an authentic feeling of being one family where strong friendships are formed and extend beyond year groups.

All sections of the school, from the Nursery through to the Seniors, enjoy being part of our 'one school' community. Preps use the same facilities as the GCSE students in some subjects e.g. Art, Music, PE and D&T, and Years 5 & 6 enjoy Science in the laboratories. Throughout, small class sizes and excellent teaching enable rapid progress, whilst exciting extra-curricular activities encourage girls to develop into well-rounded individuals.

Our purpose-built Nursery is designed for 3–4 year old girls, most of whom transfer to Reception at PGHS. Lower School classes from Reception though to Year 6 benefit hugely from the encouragement and expertise of their class teachers and teaching assistants. Favourable teaching group sizes, light and airy classrooms and access to senior school facilities all lead to an inspirational learning environment. This is enriched by specialist teaching in Art, Design & Technology, Drama, French, Spanish, Music and PE – frequently in half-class groups.

In Senior School small class sizes (an average of only 10 at GCSE) and a broad range of extra-curricular activities enriches the girls' experience. In 2018, 53% of GCSE/IGCSE grades were A*/9/8 and 79% were A*/9–A/7, placing them amongst the top performers in the country.

Former pupils enjoy coming back to share their news with recent leavers currently following Sixth Form courses at Henrietta Barnett, St Michael's, Latymer, Dame Alice Owen's, King's College Mathematical School, Woodhouse Sixth Form, North London Collegiate, Aldenham, Channing, Downe House, Headington and Roedean. Popular University destinations include Birmingham, Bristol, Cambridge, Durham, Exeter, Glasgow, King's College London, Liverpool, London School of Economics, Manchester, Nottingham, Oxford, Sussex, University College London, University of East Anglia and Warwick.

Ranked second in The Sunday Times national league table for small independent schools, parents can be reassured that Palmers Green High School girls not only attain excellent results in relation to their abilities and aptitudes, but also grow in confidence and poise as members of this very special school community.

Fees per term (2018–2019). Nursery: £3,195 (Full time), £1,960 (Part time); Reception–Year 2 £3,710; Years 3–6 £3,970; Years 7–11 £5,310.

Scholarships. Academic scholarships, bursaries and Music awards are available to candidates aged 11+ for entry in September.

Entrance. Admission to all forms is by test and interview, the main intakes being at 3+, 4+ and 7+ and 11+.

Charitable status. Palmers Green High School Limited is a Registered Charity, number 312629. It exists for the education of girls.

School Council:
Chairman: Mr Dermot Lewis, FCIB IAC, Banker
Mr John Atkinson, Chair of Buildings Committee, Special interest in Health & Safety
Miss Anna Averkiou, Chair of Risk Mitigation Committee
Mrs Melanie Curtis, Vice Chair of Governors, Chair of Education Committee
Miss Alexia Eliades, Special interest in EYFS
Mrs Bronwen Goulding, Special interest in Safeguarding
Mr Robert Keys
Mr Jeremy Piggott
Mrs Karen Tidmarsh, Special interest in Safeguarding
Mr Jeffrey Zinkin, Chair of Finance & General Purposes Committee

Headmistress: Mrs Wendy Kempster, BSc Reading, PGCE (*Mathematics*)

Bursar: Mrs Angela Monty, MAAT

Deputy Head (Designated Safeguarding Leader): Mrs Karen Thompson, BA Denver, Colorado (*ICT, PSHEE and RE*)

Assistant Head: Miss Hannah Lucas, BSc Sussex, MSc, PGCE (*Lower School Class Teacher*)

* *Head of Department*

Mrs L Aghassi, CertEd Middlesex (**Computing*)
Miss R Begum, MA Cantab (**English*)
Mrs H Bhundia, Dip Playgroup Practice (*First Aid Coordinator, Teaching Assistant*)
Mrs M Brent, MA Cantab, GTP London Institute (**Geography*)
Mrs B Broad, BEd Leeds (**Physical Education*)
Miss T Fan Cho, MSc London, PGCE (*Science*)
Miss T Fong Cho, MSc London, PGCE (*Science*)
Mrs E Christodoulou, BA Middlesex, PGCE (*Lower School Class Teacher*)
Mrs K Conlon, MSc London, BSc London (*Librarian*)
Mrs A Davey, BA Leeds, PGCE (*English*)
Mr A Desai, BEng, BEd India, OTTP, PGCE (*Mathematics*)
Mrs H Dodi, NCFE CACHE Level 3 (*Teaching Assistant*)
Mrs C Doe, BA East Anglia, MA Ed Open, PGCE (**Careers and PSHEE*)
Dr J English, BA Southampton, MMus London, PhD Cantab, PGCE Manchester (*Music*)
Mrs H Eve, BA Bristol, PGCE (**Drama*)
Miss L Gelsthorpe, BA Manchester, MSc Salford, PGCE, (*Lower School Class Teacher*)
Mrs K Gil, CACHE Level 3 (*Nursery Assistant*)
Miss S Govani, BA London School of Economics, PGCE Oxford (**History*)
Mrs S Hagi-Savva (*Assistant School Secretary, Teaching Assistant*)
Mrs S Harney, BEd Cantab, (*Head of Nursery*)
Mrs E Hassan, NVQ3 (*Lower School Teaching Assistant*)
Miss E Hemsley, BA Birmingham School of Acting, QTS King Edward's Consortium (*Drama and English*)
Miss J Henry, BA Newcastle, MA, PGCE (**Art*)
Mrs S Kazim, BSc Middlesex PGCE (**Science*)
Mrs B Kennedy, BSc Loughborough, CertEd (*Design & Technology*)
Senora M Laratonda, MA London, BEd Buenos Aires, PGCE (*Spanish*)
Mrs E Logan, BA Middlesex, PGCE (*Art*)
Mr J Matthews, BMus Cardiff, LTCL (**Music*)
Mrs M Mehran, BSc North London (*Science Technician*)
Mrs A Michael, NNEB (*Nursery Assistant*)
Mrs R E Morrison, BA Warwick, PGCE, AMBDA UCL IOE (*Individual Needs Coordinator*)
Miss J Newman, BA London, PGCE (*French and History*)
Mrs M Nicolaou, NVQ3 (*Teaching Assistant*)
Mme K Parry-Garnaud, Licence Anglais Tours France, BA Sunderland (**Modern Foreign Languages*)
Mrs J Pauk, BA Aberystwyth, PGCE (*Lower School Class Teacher*)
Mrs C Pearson, BSc London, PGCE (**Mathematics*)
Mr A J Pepper, BSc Loughborough, CertEd (**Design and Technology*)
Mrs H Pestaille, BA Middlesex, PGCE (**Geography*)
Miss V Rich, BSc Bedfordshire, PGCE (*Lower School Class Teacher*)
Miss K Robinson, BA London, PGCE (*Lower School Class Teacher*)
Miss L Selley, BA Brighton (*Physical Education*)
Mrs M Sinfield, CACHE Level 3 (*Lower School Teaching Assistant*)
Ms A Singh, BA London (*Examinations Officer & Individual Needs Teaching Assistant*)
Mrs M Suleyman, NVQ3 Childcare (*Reception Teaching Assistant*)

Miss O Tennant, BA Manchester, GTP Middlesex (*Lower School Class Teacher, French*)
Mrs S Turanli, BSc London, PGCE (*Physical Education*)
Mrs M Wing, BSc Transylvania, PGCE Middlesex (*Mathematics*)
Mrs K Woods-Shelley, BA Middlesex, PGCE, LLAM (*Drama*)

Visiting Staff – Instrumental Tuition:
Clarinet/Saxophone: Mr J Matthews, BMus, LTCL
Flute: Ms K Bircher, BA, FTCL
Piano: Mrs B Cimen
Singing: Ms E Jeffrey, BA, PGCE
Violin/Viola: Miss V David, AGSM
Violin/Viola: Miss G Austin, LRAM, Dip RAM

Administrative Staff:
PA to the Headmistress/Admissions Officer: Mrs L Mount
Office Manager: Miss V Bennett
School Secretary: Mrs A Dudley
Assistant School Secretary: Mrs S Hagi-Savva
Assistant to the Bursar: Mrs D Hadjicostas, MICM
Assistant to the Bursary Department: Mrs M Soudah
Marketing Officer: Mrs D Simmons, BA Bournemouth, Dip Marketing CIM, AMDIS Diploma in Schools' Marketing
Caretaker: Mr G Munian
Caretaker: Mr D Singh
Lunchtime and Outdoor Supervisor: Mr F McLoughlin

Pipers Corner School
High Wycombe

Great Kingshill, High Wycombe, Bucks HP15 6LP

Tel: 01494 718255
email: theschool@piperscorner.co.uk
website: www.piperscorner.co.uk
Twitter: @PipersCornerSch
Facebook: @PipersCornerSchool

At Pipers Corner all girls, from Pre-Prep through to Sixth Form, are supported and challenged to achieve their full potential. In our nurturing and encouraging environment personal development is as important as academic success and every girl is stretched as much outside as inside the classroom. We aim to know each girl as an individual and identify, develop and support her talents and strengths.

Set in 96 acres of beautiful Chiltern countryside, the school is less than one hour from central London (40 minute rail links to Marylebone Station in London), 4 miles north of High Wycombe and 2 miles from Great Missenden.

We offer exceptional pastoral care, an extensive range of extra-curricular activities and small class sizes. Our superb facilities include an Arts Centre with 280-seat theatre and café, Sixth Form Centre, sports hall, swimming pool and triple-court astro.

Academically successful, our students progress to further study at some of the country's top higher education institutions. In 2018 there was a 100% pass rate at A Level, with 43% of all results at grades A*/A, and 70% of results at grades A*–B. At GCSE 97% of results were at grades A*–C (9–4) and 45% were at grades A*/A (9–7).

Fees per term (2018–2019). £2,960–£6,130.

Scholarships and Bursaries. Pipers Corner girls are extremely successful in many areas of achievement. In recognition of this success, the Governors are keen to encourage girls' potential and to widen access to ensure that as many talented girls as possible are able to take advantage of the excellent education that Pipers Corner can provide.

Girls from any primary school, as well as girls from Pipers Corner Prep Department may apply for an 11+ Scholarship for entry into the Senior School in up to two of the following areas: Academic, Art, Drama, Music and PE.

Means-tested Bursaries are also available up to a maximum of 100% of fees (including any Scholarship award).

The Jessie Cross Award – for an all-rounder at 11+ – is a means-tested award of up to 100% of fees, available to a deserving student currently educated in a maintained primary school who shows promise in a number of areas. Students applying for the award would need the recommendation of their Headteacher and would also need to provide supporting evidence of their achievements and involvement in their school, church or community.

Applications for Scholarships and Bursaries must be received by the end of October of the year preceding the intended entry to the School. Entrance Assessments are held early in January and potential scholars will be invited back shortly afterwards for further interview and assessment. Prior to this girls will also be invited in to school for an entrance interview with the Headmistress.

Sixth Form Academic Major and Minor Scholarships: Girls from any secondary school as well as girls from Pipers Corner may apply for a Sixth Form Scholarship. Scholarship applications will be considered for any of the subjects offered at A Level. Girls who apply for a Scholarship may be awarded either a Major or Minor Scholarship for study in the Sixth Form. Neither of these Awards are means-tested.

A limited number of Jessie Cross Foundation Awards are available to girls joining our Reception class. The number we are able to award will vary year on year depending on the circumstances of the candidates and the available budget. The Foundation Awards are means-tested and can have a value of up to 100% of fees. The Award is given for the duration of Pre-Prep education (Reception to Year 2). Please contact the school for further details.

Charitable status. Pipers Corner School is a Registered Charity, number 310635. It exists to provide high quality education for girls.

Visitor: The Rt Revd The Lord Bishop of Buckingham

Chair of Governors: Lady Allison, MA
Mr A Cannon, BA Hons
Ms E J Carrighan, MA, MBA
Mr M F T Harborne, CBII
Mrs J B Ingram, BA Hons, JD
Mr F W Johnston, BA Hons, FCA (*Associate Governor*)
Professor P B Mogford
Ms H F Morton, MA, MSc, CEng
Reverend H E Peters, BSc Hons, FdA
Lady Redgrave, BSc Hons, MBBS, MSc SEM
Mr H B P Roberts, BSc Eng, FCA
Mrs J Smith, BEd, MSc, DipM
Mr P B Wayne, MusB, NPQH

Headmistress: Mrs H J Ness-Gifford, BA Hons, PGCE

Deputy Head (Academic): Mrs T Smith, BA Hons, MA, PGCE

Deputy Head (Pastoral): Ms R Tandon, BA Hons, MSc, PGCE, PGDip

Assistant Head (Pastoral): Mrs E Cresswell, BA Hons, PGCE

Assistant Head (Academic): Mrs C Derbyshire, BSc Hons, PGCE

Head of Prep Department: Mr D Leith, MBA

Bursar and Clerk to the Governors: Colonel G R Pearce, MBE

Director of Admissions & Marketing: Mrs F Knight, BA Hons

Director of Digital Strategy: Mr A Rees, BSc Hons, PG Dip

Portsmouth High School
GDST

25 Kent Road, Southsea, Hampshire PO5 3EQ

Tel:	023 9282 6714
email:	admissions@por.gdst.net
website:	www.portsmouthhigh.co.uk
Twitter:	@portsmouthhigh
Facebook:	@PortsmouthHigh

Founded 1882.

Portsmouth High School is part of the Girls' Day School Trust (GDST). The GDST is the leading network of independent girls' schools in the UK. As a charity that owns and runs 23 schools and two academies, it reinvests all its income in its schools. For further information about the Trust, see p. xxiii or visit www.gdst.net.

Additional information about the school may be found on the school's website and a prospectus pack is available from the Admissions Registrar at the school.

Number of Pupils. 350 are in the Senior School (11–18), 150 in the Prep School (rising 3–11).

Portsmouth High School is a community of learning committed to academic excellence and preparing girls to be the leaders of tomorrow. Each girl is encouraged to develop her own voice and her own views and to understand and build on her strengths. A broad based education encourages each girl's talents and potential to the full in an atmosphere of achievement and excellence. Characteristic of the GDST philosophy, Portsmouth High School has a profile of sustained achievement, strong relationships with the local community and outstanding pastoral care. Situated close to the sea, the school draws pupils from an extensive area of Hampshire, West Sussex and the Isle of Wight. All major transport providers serve the area. The school received the highest category in each section of the Independent Schools Inspectorate Report 2015. The school underwent a four-day inspection in April 2015 which looked at the following criteria: the success of the school, the quality of academic and other achievements, the quality of the pupils' personal development and the effectiveness of governance, leadership and management. In each section the school was ranked "excellent".

The Senior School provides a broad and balanced education that prepares girls to specialise at A Level and the Sixth Form provides a perfect bridge to higher study. The Senior School is accommodated in the original building; a capital investment programme has seen the development of a Sport, Design Technology and Geography building on the senior school site.

A partnership with the University of Portsmouth means the school has joint use of the Langstone sports ground facilities, including a floodlit synthetic turf pitch and a multi-use games area; the site is just 2 miles from the school. In addition, the school site facilities include a Sport England standard sports hall, with climbing wall, 4 hard tennis courts and 6 netball courts. Sixth Form students do not wear uniform, but have a 'Dress for Work' code. Sixth Formers have a recently refurbished Sixth Form Centre with a large common room, kitchen, study rooms and IT room.

The Prep School. This is a school where intellectual curiosity is developed and where girls enjoy learning through a range of opportunities both inside and outside the classroom. The Prep School is located 2 minutes' walk away in a wonderful period house with extensive gardens including 4 netball courts, an outdoor classroom and a range of other indoor and outdoor facilities. Major investment in the Prep School saw the completion of an award-winning Pre-Prep building and science discovery lab. With the addition of a Pre-Prep (Nursery) class which, along with Reception, was judged "Excellent" in all categories in the school's ISI inspection (2015), the school is able to offer continuity of education throughout the Foundation Stage.

The Curriculum. The aim at Portsmouth High School is to foster in each girl the confidence to take risks and tackle new challenges within an atmosphere of ambition and enterprise, by providing appropriate teaching, advice and support. The focus on girls' learning is reflected in the design of learning spaces; the use of digital technology; a challenging and rewarding curriculum and a focus on pupils taking responsibility for their learning and having the confidence to take intellectual risks.

Co-Curricular Activities. There is an extensive programme of co-curricular activities in both the Prep and Senior schools. The lunchtime and after-school clubs range from dance to public speaking. There is an enthusiastic involvement in music, art, sport and drama with many performances and fixtures throughout the School calendar for Prep and Senior girls. Senior Girls have the opportunity to become involved in The Duke of Edinburgh's Award scheme as well as a Sixth Form Seminar Group and Enrichment Programme. There are regular overseas music, and other, tours.

Admission Procedures/Entrance Examinations. At 11+ and 13+ entry the examinations in mathematics and English are designed to test potential rather than knowledge. Prior to the 11+ examinations all girls take part in a series of team activities in school. At 13+ girls take part in a Shadowing Day and are interviewed by the Headmistress. Sixth Form entry is based on having at least 7 GCSEs at grade B/ 6 or above. Most subjects will require at least grade A/7 as a prerequisite for A Level study and applicants are invited for interview. Entry into the Prep School is based on assessments and examinations dependent on age.

Fees per term (2018–2019). Senior School £4,662, Prep School from £2,500–£3,296.

The fees in the Prep School cover wrap-around care from 7.30 am to 6.00 pm daily. The fees also cover the regular curriculum, school books, non-residential curriculum trips, stationery and other materials, public examinations, choral music, games and swimming. The fees for extra subjects, including individual lessons in instrumental music and speech training, are shown in the Admissions Handbook.

Scholarships and Bursaries. The GDST makes available to the school a number of scholarships and bursaries. Bursaries are means tested and are intended to ensure that the school remains accessible to bright girls who would be unable to enter the school without financial assistance.

Academic and Music Scholarships are available for 11+, 13+ and Sixth Form, with Art, Drama and Sport Scholarships available in the Sixth Form. HSBC scholarships are also available for Sixth Formers.

Charitable status. Portsmouth High School is part of The Girls' Day School Trust, which is a Registered Charity, number 306983.

Chair of the School Governing Board: Mrs A McMeehan Roberts, BA

Headmistress: Mrs J Prescott, BSc Cardiff, PGCE, NPQH

Deputy Head (Pastoral): Mrs H Trim, MSc Leicester, BSc Southampton

Deputy Head (Academic): Mr J Paget-Tomlinson, BA Reading, MA King's College

Headmaster, Prep School: Mr P Marshallsay, BA Education

Admissions Registrar: Mrs C Thompson

Princess Helena College
United Learning

School Lane, Preston, Hitchin, Hertfordshire SG4 7RT

Tel:	01462 432100
Fax:	01462 443871
email:	office@princesshelenacollege.co.uk
website:	www.princesshelenacollege.co.uk
Twitter:	@PHCPreston
Facebook:	@PHCPreston
LinkedIn:	/Princess Helena College

Motto: *Fortis qui se vincit*

Princess Helena College is a day and boarding school for girls aged between 11 and 18. The College is located in Hertfordshire and set in over 100 acres of rolling hills, fields and beautiful woodland. This, combined with its close proximity to London, enriches the girls' educational experience.

History. Founded in 1820 we are one of England's oldest academic girls' schools. We are extremely proud of our heritage and aim to maintain high academic standards and respect for traditional values. The school was founded for daughters of officers who had served in the Napoleonic Wars and daughters of Anglican priests. We now encourage this tradition by offering bursaries to daughters from families that are in the forces and the clergy.

Ethos. At Princess Helena College, we believe every girl is an individual and aim to inspire her to achieve both her academic and personal goals. We choose to remain a small school because we strongly believe this unique approach provides many benefits in academic, extracurricular and pastoral areas. The educational benefits include a flexible curriculum and small classes. Both result in individual attention and excellent value-added attainment. A smaller school allows teachers to understand girls' individual learning styles, to recognise their particular strengths and weaknesses and to set individual learning targets. Pastoral care is strengthened by excellent relations between pupils and staff, which result in a strong family atmosphere. Knowing our girls well allows us to encourage them to take risks, safe in the knowledge that we will support them. This allows every girl to be challenged, to achieve and to grow. Within a small school your daughter's chances of being selected for a team, a place in the orchestra, a part in a play or a position of responsibility are far higher. Having the opportunity to take part or perform in these activities will increase her confidence and self-belief. The value of this should not be underestimated.

Facilities. As well as an idyllic and safe learning environment, Princess Helena College has excellent educational facilities. The main building is a beautiful Queen Anne mansion that lies in fine Gertrude Jekyll gardens and over 100 acres of parkland. Over the past 5 years the school has invested heavily in developing the facilities for all girls: a Sixth Form area has been added, the boarding house has been renovated and there are plans for a Performing Arts Centre. Other developments include a new science centre, art and design studios, a fitness suite and a refurbished learning resources centre.

Curriculum. We offer every girl the opportunity to excel within a varied and stimulating curriculum. Taught in small classes by highly-qualified and enthusiastic teachers who are dedicated to supporting each girl's talents and interests, our girls attain high levels of academic excellence and confidence. Girls are taught in sets that rarely exceed 18 and their potential and progress is carefully monitored.

The lower school curriculum (Years 7–9) consists of English, French, Spanish, Mathematics, Computing, Biology, Physics, Chemistry, History, Geography, Religious Education, Music, Drama, Physical Education, Art and Design. There are also programmes in PCC (PSHEE, Citizenship and Careers) and General Studies.

In Years 10–11, girls study their chosen GCSE subjects, following much consultation with staff and parents. On average, girls study between 8 and 10 GCSE subjects.

In the Sixth Form, A Level courses are available in all the traditional academic subjects, as well as Business Studies, Economics, Dance, History of Art, Media Studies, Psychology and Photography. Extensive career and Higher Education support and advice is provided; in addition our one-to-one mentor scheme monitors the girls' academic progress and welfare.

In 2017, 26% of girls received A* at GCSE, 56% A*–A and 97% A*–C.

A flexible approach to boarding. Princess Helena College is a vibrant community made up of boarders and day girls. We offer a very flexible approach to boarding and full, weekly, and flexible boarding are well established. Day girls can choose to stay into the early evening to make full use of the optional extended school day, participating in supervised prep or one of the numerous after school activities.

The Arts. Princess Helena College is particularly strong in Art & Design, Dance, Drama, Music and Speech & Drama. Girls may enter examinations in all these areas. Dance is a hugely popular activity, with girls learning jazz, modern, ballet, Irish and tap. Most of the school is involved in some form of musical activity, with many girls participating in one of the many different music groups or ensembles. Plays are staged throughout the year and there are regular joint productions with neighbouring boys' and co-educational schools.

Sport. In addition to timetabled lessons, there are sports activities on weekdays after school and on some Saturdays. Girls participate in a wide range of sports including lacrosse, netball, tennis, athletics, badminton, cross-country, rounders and swimming in our own swimming pool. Girls are given the opportunity to participate in competitive sport, recreational sport and fitness – we aim to encourage all girls to find an activity they will enjoy at school and in the future.

Extra-curricular activities. Life is busy at Princess Helena College – there is an exciting array of extra-curricular activities and clubs, which form part of our exciting SCITLLE (Serve, Create, Inspire, Thrive, Lead, Learn, Explore) programme. Girls can choose to join in with these activities either during their extended lunch break or after school. From photography to public speaking, from language club to life-saving and from touch-typing to trampolining, there is an activity for everyone. The Duke of Edinburgh's Award scheme is also a popular activity, with many girls attaining Gold, Silver and Bronze awards each year.

Religion. Girls attend the nearby village church of St Martin's in Preston, which is also used for the school's Confirmation Services. Although the school's affiliation is to the Church of England, girls of other denominations and religions are welcomed.

Location. Set in over 100 acres of rural parkland the school offers an easily accessible location within a safe and beautiful environment. The school is situated 30 minutes north of London between the A1 and the M1, just 5 minutes from the market town of Hitchin. Our excellent transport links include rail access (35 minutes to King's Cross station) and proximity to several airports (Luton 15 mins, Stansted 45 mins and Heathrow 60 mins). There is an extensive network of school bus routes to Ashwell, Brookmans Park, Cuffley, Digswell, Enfield, Gustard Wood, Hadley Wood, Harpenden, Hertford, Hitchin, Kimpton, Little Wymondley, London Colney, Luton, Potters Bar, St Albans, Stevenage, Welwyn and Wheathampstead.

Admission. We welcome girls aged 11–18. Most girls join the school at age 11 (Year 7), but there are also entrants at age 13 (Year 9) and the Sixth Form (Year 12). Please contact Melanie Harper, Registrar (01462 443888) for a prospectus or to find out the date of our next Open Day. All girls must sit either the school's own Entrance Exam or the Common Entrance Exam. Sixth Form places are conditional on GCSE results.

Fees per term (2018–2019). Day Girls: Years 7 and 8 £5,536; Years 9–Sixth Form £6,741. Weekly Boarding or Full Boarding: Years 7 and 8 £7,885; Years 9–Sixth Form £9,800. Flexible Boarding: Year 7–8 £60 per night, Years 9–Sixth Form £70 per night. Overseas Boarders additional fees: £775 for weekend activities and £800 for EAL lessons. Fees include fruit at break, hot lunch, afternoon tea, stationery, and supervised prep from 4.15 pm to 5.55 pm. Boarding fees additionally include breakfast, supper and laundry. Most SCITLLE activities are also included.

Scholarships and Bursaries. All girls applying to Princess Helena College who have achieved a high enough level of attainment in the entrance examinations in January will be invited to sit a further test and interview for an Academic Scholarship. Scholarships are also awarded to students who have achieved a high enough level of attainment in the Year 9 school examinations. Academic Scholarships are also available in the Sixth Form and are dependent on GCSE results. There are also Scholarships available in Art, Drama, Dance, Music and Sport. Bursaries of 10% are available for daughters of clergy and members of the armed forces from Year 7 onwards. Sibling bursaries of 5% of fees are awarded from Year 7 onwards to the younger daughter, ceasing when only one daughter remains. Means-tested bursaries are also available to prospective girls.

Charitable status. Princess Helena College is a Registered Charity, number 311064. It was founded in 1820 for the purposes of education.

Patron: Her Majesty the Queen

President: HRH The Duchess of Gloucester

Governing Body:
Chairman: Mr David Prosser, BSc, FCA, MSt Cantab
Vice-Chairman: Mrs Louise Smith, BSc
Treasurer: Mr Ian Chambers, BSc, FCA

Clerk to the Governors and Bursar: Mr Andrew MacFarlane, BSc, MSc, FCMI, VR

Headmistress: Mrs Lynda Corry, BEd Wales, Dip Eng, NPQH

Deputy Head: Ms Rachel Poston, BSc, PGCE

Registrar: Ms Melanie Harper

Putney High School

GDST

35 Putney Hill, London SW15 6BH

Tel: 020 8788 4886
email: putneyhigh@put.gdst.net
website: www.putneyhigh.gdst.net

Putney High School is one of the UK's leading schools with a reputation for academic excellence combined with outstanding opportunity. Girls aged 4–18 develop into inspired learners, well-supported within a warm and vibrant community that allows girls to flourish, both inside the classroom and beyond.

Founded in 1893, Putney High School has been at the forefront of educating girls for 125 years. Part of the Girls' Day School Trust (GDST), the leading network of independent girls' schools in the UK, Putney has a proud tradition of innovative, ambitious teaching that nurtures talent and prepares pupils for a complex 21st century world. The GDST is a charity which owns and runs 23 schools and two academies and all income is reinvested in its schools. For further information about the Trust, see p. xxiii or visit www.gdst.net

The most recent Independent Schools Inspectorate report, which awarded Putney the highest possible grading in every category, concluded: "A spirit of innovation, openness and creativity" pervades Putney High School.

We develop a culture of intellectual agility, with girls stretched, challenged and supported by staff keen to nurture the same sense of academic curiosity that they themselves enjoy. Students have fun and can take risks, secure in the knowledge they are in a safe environment. We lead in digital innovation – all girls have their own iPads from year 7 onwards.

We want girls to have a voice, to take ownership in all aspects of their school life.

Students go on to some of the best universities around the world, from Stanford in the USA to Oxford, Cambridge, LSE and Durham amongst others, as well as to music conservatoires and art colleges.

Facilities. A Performing Arts Centre with professional sound and lighting showcases the wealth of talent in Drama, Music and Dance. A boathouse on a prime stretch of the Putney embankment builds on the growing success and popularity of our rowing. Our state-of-the-art Sixth Form Centre incorporates cutting-edge technology as well as offering cafés, a rooftop terrace and a professionally-equipped fitness centre only for Sixth Form use. Cross-curricular links are strong and there are plans for STEAM subjects to be brought further together in a new, purpose-built Science, Music, Drama and Debating centre.

Curriculum. Well-qualified, specialist staff provide continuity of education from Reception through to A Levels at 18. Girls are welcome to enter the school at 4+, 11+ and 16+ or in other years if an occasional vacancy arises.

In the Senior School, the girls follow a broad and balanced curriculum, which includes Latin, Classics and Greek, French, Chinese (Mandarin), German, Spanish, Arabic, Italian and Design Technology. On entering the GCSE years, all girls study the core subjects plus Biology, Physics and Chemistry and at least one modern language. They are also able to choose from a wide list including Art, Computing, DT-Textiles, DT-Resistant Materials, Drama, Geography, History, Music, PE and RS. At A Level these subjects may be supplemented by others such as Business, Economics, Politics, History of Art, Further Mathematics and Psychol-

ogy. Students can also complete an Extended Project Qualification on a topic of their choice.

Music. Putney is renowned for excellence in music and has a well-equipped and hugely successful department. Large numbers learn a musical instrument and many are accomplished musicians, studying at the junior conservatoires and/or are members of nationally auditioned choirs and orchestras. Private tuition is available in all instruments and voice. Girls have many opportunities to participate in music – orchestras; chamber groups, brass groups, four Senior Choirs and a Junior Choir and many smaller ensembles. There are even pop concerts and a Year 9 Opera.

Sport. Putney High School promotes a 'sport for all' policy, encouraging all pupils to participate for enjoyment, fitness and fun. At the same time, we compete at county, national and international level, and have a reputation for nurturing elite performers. As well as facilities on site, the school uses off-site grounds at Wimbledon Rugby Football Club and Barn Elms. All girls have lessons in netball, lacrosse, gymnastics, tennis, cricket (Years 7–10) and athletics. Rowing is introduced in Year 9 and is a popular extra-curricular club from Year 7. Other clubs include dance, badminton, trampolining, cross country and fencing. Tennis, lacrosse, netball, rowing, cross country, gymnastics, athletics and sports acrobatics teams all compete successfully nationally.

The Junior School promotes a love of learning through active, exciting experiences within and outside the classroom. We aim to develop mental agility through high quality, inspirational teaching. Philosophy and debating develop critical thinking skills. Every pupil from Year 1–6 has a timetabled Opening Minds lesson to teach learning dispositions which will help her to thrive – resilience, resourcefulness, creativity, perseverance and tenacity.

There are 1020 pupils, of whom about 700 are in the Senior School (ages 11–18), which includes a Sixth Form of around 180, with 320 in the Junior School (ages 4–11).

Fees per term (2018–2019). Senior School £6,300, Junior School £5,212.

The fees cover the regular curriculum, school books, stationery and other materials, choral music, games and swimming, but not optional extra subjects or special sports. All pupils below the Sixth Form take school meals for which the charge is £202 per term (Reception–Year 2) and £239 per term (Years 3–11). The fees for instrumental tuition are available on the website.

Financial Assistance. We are committed to offering opportunities to bright girls whose parents would not be able to afford the fees. The GDST has its own means-tested Bursary Scheme. Bursaries are available in Senior School and Sixth Form.

Scholarships. Academic, music and sports scholarships are available to internal or external candidates (up to 50% of fees) for entry at 11+. At 16+ we provide academic, art, design, drama, music, and sports scholarships, as well as travel scholarships in modern languages and science.

Charitable status. Putney High School is part of The Girls' Day School Trust, which is a Registered Charity, number 306983.

Governors:

Mr Jason Bacon, BA Vermont American History, Literature and Politics

Mrs R Bell, BSc UCL Human Science, MSc Stirling Public Relations

Mrs C Boardman, MA Cantab Natural Sciences, MBA City (*Chair of the LGB*)

Ms A Di Marco, MA Cantab, MBBS King's, Guy's & St Thomas', MRCS Eng, AKC King's College London Medical Sciences

Ms C Lux, MA Oxon Modern History
Mrs M Matley, MA Oxon Modern Languages
Prof C Ozanne, BA MA Oxon, DPhil Ecology
Mr Neal Scambler, BSc Hons MRICS
Ms A Scott-Bayfield, MA Cantab, Solicitor of the Supreme
    Court

Headmistress: **Mrs S Longstaff**, BA Dunelm, MA Bath

Deputy Head Pastoral: Mrs H Armstrong, BA Nottingham
Head of Junior School: Mrs P Page-Roberts, BEd Hons
    Chichester
Director of Sixth Form: Ms E Barden, BSc Durham

Queen Mary's School
A Woodard School

**Baldersby Park, Topcliffe, Thirsk, North Yorkshire
YO7 3BZ**

Tel: 01845 575000
email: admin@queenmarys.org
website: www.queenmarys.org
Twitter: @QueenMarysSch
Facebook: @Queen-Marys-School

Queen Mary's is an outstanding day and boarding school
for girls aged 3 to 16 and boys aged 3 to 7. The school has a
unique family atmosphere with friendliness and concern for
others being an important part of the school's ethos. The
country setting provides a safe haven for girls to thrive and
develop self-confidence.

Location. Queen Mary's is situated at Baldersby Park in
a beautiful Grade 1 Palladian mansion, with 50 acres of
grounds, including formal gardens, playing fields, and riding stables. Despite its idyllic surroundings, it is only 2
miles from Junction 49 of the A1 and within ten minutes of
Thirsk railway station. York and Harrogate are within easy
reach and so are Leeds/Bradford and Teesside airports.
Minibuses, each covering a twenty-five mile radius, transport girls to and from home on a daily basis.

The Curriculum. Pupils at Queen Mary's are offered a
great deal in terms of breadth and depth of learning. Generous time is given to core subjects, English, mathematics, science and modern languages, but strong emphasis is also
placed on the supporting subjects – geography, history, religious studies, classics, ICT, design technology, music, art
and a varied programme of physical education. Classes are
kept deliberately small, which means that every girl can
receive plenty of support from her teachers. The school has
an excellent learning support department for those pupils
who have specific learning difficulties. The two years leading up to GCSE are full and focused, with most girls taking
ten subjects at GCSE. The public examination results are
outstandingly good and the school is one of the highest
achieving non-selective schools in the country.

Pastoral care. All girls in school have personal tutors
who oversee the academic, social and emotional development of each of their tutees. Building self-confidence and
developing the individual talents of each pupil is seen as a
vital aspect of the education offered. Each girl is encouraged
to be self-reliant from an early age and pupils are taught a
real concern for the needs of others. Girls in their final year
at Queen Mary's undertake a number of important responsibilities to help the school community function smoothly.

Boarding. Queen Mary's offers a number of boarding
options to suit the needs of parents and their daughters.
Those who choose to board may be weekly or full boarders.
The experience of boarding is considered to be valuable for
all girls and, when space permits, day girls may board on a

nightly basis to fit in with extracurricular commitments or
parental need. The boarding accommodation is all within the
main building and the girls find their dormitories cheerful
and comfortable. The full boarders, who stay at weekends,
enjoy a broad range of activities and trips, often much to the
envy of those who go home. The Housemistress, together
with her colleagues, looks after the general health of the
girls, while the school nurse and the school doctor oversee
all medical care.

Extracurricular Activities. An impressive range of
extracurricular activities is available to all members of the
school community. Choral and orchestral music are both
huge strengths of the school, as well as sport, with hockey,
lacrosse and netball being played in the winter terms and
tennis, rounders and athletics in the summer. Facilities
include a modern indoor swimming pool and AstroTurf
pitch. Drama, debating and The Duke of Edinburgh's Award
are highly popular choices and the all-weather outdoor riding facilities allow more than 90 girls to ride each week.
Children enjoy the opportunity to tackle the climbing wall,
canoe on the adjacent River Swale or participate in very
popular pheasant-plucking club.

Religious Affiliation. The school is part of the Woodard
Corporation, an Anglican foundation which promotes Christian education and high academic and pastoral standards
within all its schools. The school has its own Church of
England chapel. The school Chaplain prepares girls for confirmation. Girls of other denominations are welcome.

What happens after GCSE? Specialist careers advice is
offered throughout the senior school and well-informed staff
support the girls as they seek to make applications and progress on to some of the most prestigious sixth forms in the
country. Each senior girl is able to choose a school or sixth
form college which can offer her exactly the courses and
educational environment she requires for her continuing
studies. A healthy proportion of the girls join their new
schools as scholars.

Scholarships. Scholarships are offered at 11+, 12+ and
13+ to those candidates who show particular academic flair
or have special talent in Music, Sport or Art. Examinations
are held during the Spring Term.

Entrance. By interview with the Head. Entry can be at
most stages, subject to availability. An up-to-date prospectus can be sent upon request. Visit www.queenmarys.org for
more information.

Fees per term 2018–2019. Day: Nursery £32 per half-
day session; Reception £2,840; Years 1–2 £3,105; Year 3–6
£5,140; Years 7–8 £5,575; Years 9–11 £6,325. Full Boarding: Years 3–6 £7,345; Years 7–8 £7,770; Years 9–11
£8,630. Weekly Boarding: Years 3–6 £7,030; Years 7–8
£7,455; Years 9–11 £8,300.

Charitable status. Queen Mary's School (Baldersby)
Ltd is a Registered Charity, number 1098410. It exists to
educate children in a Christian environment.

Chair of Governors: Mr T E Fielden, BA Hons, FCA

Head: Mrs Carole Cameron, MA, PGCE, NPQH, FRGS

Deputy Head: Mrs Deborah Hannam Walpole, BEd Hons

Queen's College, London

43–49 Harley Street, London W1G 8BT

Tel: 020 7291 7070
Fax: 020 7291 7090
email: queens@qcl.org.uk
website: www.qcl.org.uk

Queen's College was the first institution to provide an academic education and qualifications for young women. It was founded in 1848 by F D Maurice, Professor of Modern History at King's College, and was housed originally at 45 Harley Street.

Today it is a thriving school of 375 girls aged from 11–18, of whom 90 are in the Sixth Form. Queen's College Preparatory School (020 7291 0660), which opened in 2002 at 61 Portland Place, takes girls from age 4–11.

Queen's College is situated in Harley Street, combining the beauty of four eighteenth century houses with modern facilities for science, languages, art, drama, music and computer science, as a well as a Hall and gymnasium. Two libraries, in the care of a graduate librarian, offer the students some 10,000 books, and we also preserve a unique archive recording the history of the College.

Curriculum. Class sizes rarely exceed twenty and the normal size of a year group is 55–60, divided into three forms. The year group is streamed for Mathematics and French during the first year and at a later stage for English, Latin and science.

The curriculum is wide, including four modern languages, as well as Latin, Greek and classical civilisation. Girls usually take nine or ten subjects at GCSE, and the three sciences are taught separately. At A Level it is possible to study History of Art, Economics, or Government and Politics as well as the subjects already taken at GCSE.

There is a comprehensive programme of sport offered. There is a well-equipped gym on site and outdoor games take place at Paddington Recreation Ground. Girls play netball, football, rounders, and tennis; there are thriving clubs before and after school for swimming, running and other leisure pursuits. Dance and PE are offered at GCSE. Regular sports fixtures are arranged against local schools. The Duke of Edinburgh's Award is organised at bronze and silver levels. Individual music lessons are offered in all instruments including voice, and the musical or dramatic productions and jazz concert are highlights of each year.

The location of the College means that theatre and other educational visits in London are an integral part of the curriculum, complemented by opportunities to travel abroad or to other parts of the country. Every summer Year 7 visit Northumberland for a week and in recent years groups of girls have visited France, Greece, Germany, Italy, America and Japan. There is at least one ski trip each year, usually run jointly with Queen's College Preparatory School.

Almost all girls leaving Queen's proceed to university, including Oxford or Cambridge, and several students each year choose to take an Art Foundation course at one of the London colleges. Former students are prominent in medicine, education, writing and the media; they retain contact with each other and the college through the Old Queen's Society, which also gives bursaries to families in financial need.

Pastoral Care. Queen's College prides itself on its friendly and informal atmosphere, highly valued by girls, parents and staff. Pastoral care is strong and we have a full-time nurse to support the work of form tutors and pastoral staff. A specialist in various special educational needs works individually with pupils once the need has been identified. We send reports to parents every half-term and hold regular Parents' Evenings; contact with parents benefits from the use of email by all members of staff. Parents also support the College through membership of the Parents' Association, giving practical and some financial assistance to College functions.

Admission. The College is a member of the London 11+ Consortium. Candidates for Year 7 entry sit the London 11+ Consortium entrance examination and are invited to attend an interview. As well as high academic standards we value

enthusiasm and creativity, and academic, music and art awards are available to 11+ entrants.

If vacancies arise we also welcome applicants at other ages, particularly after GCSE, where there is a long-standing tradition of accepting students to undertake their A Level education at Queen's. Some scholarships are available on entry at this stage. Means-tested bursaries are available at all points of entry.

Fees per term (2018–2019). £6,375.

Charitable status. Queen's College, London is a Registered Charity, number 312726. It exists to provide education for girls. It is an Anglican foundation, open to those of all faiths or none who are prepared to subscribe to its ethos.

Patron: Her Majesty The Queen

Visitor: The Rt Revd and Rt Hon the Lord Bishop of London

Council:
Chairman: Professor Alison While, BSc MSc PhD London, RGN, RHV
Vice Chairman: Mr Matthew Hanslip Ward, MA Cantab
Mr Seth Bolderow, MSt Oxon, BA Exeter
Mr Richard Ford, BSc LSE
Mrs Alexandra Gregory, BA Exeter, ACA
Mr John Jacob, BSc Southampton
Ms Holly Porter, MA Cantab, MA RCA, RIBA, FRSA
Mr Paul Reeve
Mrs Danielle Salem, BA Farnham
Mrs Rhiannon Wilkinson, MA Oxon, MEd Manchester

Bursar and Secretary to the Council: C P Morton, BA Durham, MBA Cranfield

***Principal: R W Tillett**, MA Cantab*

Headmistress of Queen's College Preparatory School: Mrs E Webb, BA London

Senior Tutor: M J Wardrop, MChem Oxon, FRSC

Pastoral Deputy Head: Dr S J Abbott, BA MA PhD Reading

Assistant Head: E A Wilkins, MA Oxon, MA Cardiff

Registrar: Miss F A Murdoch, BSc Portsmouth

Queen's Gate School

133 Queen's Gate, London SW7 5LE

Tel:	020 7589 3587
email:	registrar@queensgate.org.uk
website:	www.queensgate.org.uk
Twitter:	@Queens_Gate
Facebook:	@133queensgate

Queen's Gate School is an independent day school for girls between the ages of 4 and 18 years. Established in 1891, the school is an Educational Trust situated in five large Victorian Houses within easy walking distance of Kensington Gardens, Hyde Park, Stanhope Gardens and the Museums of South Kensington.

The aim of the school is to create a secure and happy environment in which the girls can realise their academic potential and make full use of their individual interests and talents. The School encourages the development of self-discipline and creates an atmosphere where freedom of thought and ideas can flourish.

Close cooperation with parents is welcomed at every stage.

There is no school uniform except for PE and for the Junior girls, a top coat in winter and blazer and boater in summer. There is a dress code and girls are expected to wear clothing and footwear suitable for attending school and taking part in school activities.

Curriculum. Girls follow as wide a curriculum as possible and generally take GCSE in ten subjects that must include English, Mathematics, Science and a modern language.

An extensive range of AS/A Level subjects is offered. Four AS Levels are studied in the first year and three of these are taken at A2 Level.

Games. Netball, Hockey, Tennis, Swimming, Rowing, Athletics, Basketball, Horse Riding, Cross-Country, Biathlon and Dance.

Admission. By test and interview in the Junior School; by London 11+ Consortium entrance examination; by the School's own entrance examinations for entry to other years in the Senior School. Applicants for the Sixth Form are expected to have passed a minimum of six GCSEs at A Grade with A grades required in those subjects they wish to pursue to A Level.

Registration fee: £125.

Fees per term (2018–2019). £6,170–£6,850.

Board of Governors:
Mr Michael Cumming (*Chairman*)
Mrs Laura Marani (*Deputy Chairman*)
Mr Jonathan Dobson
Mr William Gillen
Mrs Reica Gray
Dr Jill Harling
Mr Gary Li
Mr Joseph McNeila
Mr Peter Trueman
Mrs Manina Weldon

Principal: Mrs R M Kamaryc, BA Hons, MSc, PGCE

Deputy Principal: Dr P Bennett, MA

Senior School:

Director of Pastoral Care: Ms C A Yates, BEd, MA
Director of Academic Administration & Compliance: Miss B Ward, BEd Hons
Director of Teaching & Assessment and Head of Upper School: Mr M Crundwell, BSc Hons, MPhil Lon, MEd Dist, QTS
Director of Academic Development: Mrs Z Camenzuli, BA, MA Oxon, PGCE

Head of Sixth Form: Dr M Lee, BSc, PhD Lon
Head of Form UV: Mrs S Sexon, BA, MA, QTS
Head of Form V: Mr A Cohen, MA, PGCE
Head of Form IV: Mr R Moss, BA Hons, PGCE
Head of LIV: Miss M Butt, BSc Hons, PGCSE
Head of Remove: Miss C Spencer, BSc Hons, PGCE

Art & Design:
Mr S Mataja, BA, PGCE
Ms M Vazquez, BA, MA, PGCE
Miss N Sitko, MFA Poznan Academy of Fine Arts

History of Art:
Ms I Cornwall-Jones, MA Hons, PGCE

Biology:
Mrs P Garty, BSc, PGCE
Miss L Coulton, BSc Hons, PGCE
Mr I Gallagher, BSc Hons, PGCE
Miss B Ward, BEd Hons

Careers Education & Guidance:
Ms I Cornwall-Jones, MA Hons, PGCE
Mrs S Sexon, BA, MA

Chemistry:
Mrs C Mayne, BSc, PGCE
Mr A Selkirk, BSc, BComm, PG Dip Teaching secondary
Mrs V Manson, MChem, PGCE
Miss C Spencer, BSc Hons, PGCE

Classics:
Miss A Mitropoulos, BA, MPhil, PGCE
Dr P Bennett, MA
Mr R Moss, BA Hons, PGCE
Miss C Fox, BA Hons, PGCE
Mrs N J Clear, BA Hons, PGCE

Computing:
Ms E Adler, MA, PGCE
Ms M Butt, BA Hons, PGCE

Design & Technology:
Mrs V Thompson, BSc, PGCE
Mr J Francis, BA Hons, PGCE
Miss E Oppong, BA Hons, PGCE

Drama & Theatre Studies:
Ms L Arthur, MA Hons, MA RADA/London, Dip Teaching NZ
Miss F Sutherland, BDiv Hons, MA RADA London, PGCE, LGSM

LAMDA:
Ms J Doolan, MA

Economics:
Mr M Smith, MA, PGCE

English:
Mrs E Burnside, MA, BA, PGCE
Miss R Davies, BA, PGCE
Ms C A Yates, MA, BEd
Mr M Spicer, BA, BEd
Miss S Cadwallender, MA GTTP

French:
Mme F Collombon, Maîtrise Langues Etrangeres Appliquées, Licence Anglais Langues et Civilization, PGCE
Mme S Riglet, BA Hons, CAPES IUFM Paris, PGCE
M P Solomons, BA, MA, LLP
Mme F Leuluan, BA, PGCE

Geography:
Mr M Crundwell, BSc Hons, MPhil Lon, MEd Dist, QTS
Dr M Lee, BSc, PhD Lon
Mrs Z Camenzuli, BA, MA Oxon, PGCE
Miss S Scott, BSc Hons, PGCE, PCET, MEd
Mrs M Stonehill, BA, MTeach

German:
Frau I Atufe-Kreuth, MA Mag Phil, Cert Ed

History:
Mrs J S Ditchfield, MA Hons, PGCE
Mrs S Sexon, BA, MA, QTS
Mrs M Stonehill BA, MTeach

Italian:
Mr S Mocci, MA, PGCE

Mathematics:
Dr P Williams, MA
Dr P Bennett, MA
Ms P Howe, BA Hons Oxon
Mrs R Kamaryc, BA Hons, MSc, PGCE
Ms A Helm, BSc, PGCE
Mr A Chaudhry, BSc, PGCE, Med

Mr I Maclean, BSc, PGCE
Mr J Lechmere Smith, Int Dip, Grad Dip, QTS

Music:
Mr E Liepa, BMus Hons
Ms L Sansun, MA, LRAM, MTC
Miss G McHenry, BA QTS Hons

Physical Education:
Miss C Hurlbatt, BA Hons, PGCE
Miss B Ward, BEd Hons, BEd Hons
Miss E Pillow, BA Hons
Miss M Johson, BA, MSc
Miss G McLister, BSc
Mr A Labourt
Ms J Marshall, BSc, PGCE
Mr G Marton (*Head of Rowing*)
Mr V Meshkov (*Fencing*)

Philosophy:
Mr A Cohen, MA, PGCE

Physics:
Dr J Mercer, PhD, BSc Hons, ARCS, PGCE
Mr T Wong, BSc, PGCE

PSCHE:
Mrs E Aston, BA, MSc, PGCE

Psychology:
Miss S Palframan, BSc, PGCE

Religious Studies:
Mr A Cohen, MA, PGCE
Mrs M Stonehill, BA, MTeach
Mrs N J Clear, BA Hons, PGCE
Ms S Robertson-Glasgow, BEd Hons, MA Ed, Adv Dip Ed
Mrs C White-da Cruz, BA Hons, PGCE, MLitt

Sociology:
Mrs H Hutton, BA, PGCE [Maternity Leave]
Miss E Aston, BA, MSc, PCSE [Maternity Cover]

Spanish:
Sta S Gomez, Licenciada en Filología

Laboratory Technicians:
Mr D I Swan, BSc Hons, MRSC
Mr M Sell, MSc

Art & DT Technicians:
Mr K Lynn, BA Hons
Miss R Band, BA

Librarian/VLE Coordinator: Mrs E Scott, BA, MSc LIS, US Teaching Certificate

SEN Coordinator: Ms S Robertson-Glasgow, BEd Hons, MA Ed, Adv Dip Ed

Debating: Mr T Barclay

EAL: Mr G Brinkworth, TESOL, PCSEi

Catering & Maintenance – Senior and Junior School:
Catering Manager: Miss C Osunde
Housekeeper: Mrs S Lewis
Assistant Housekeeper: Mrs T Iacono
Maintenance Manager: Mr J Newman
Caretaker: Mr M Ward

Junior School:
Director of the Junior School: Mr J Denchfield, BA Hons PGCE
Preliminary & EYFS Coordinator: Miss E Allan, BA, BEd, PGCE
Transition: Miss G Philips, BA
IB & KS1 Coordinator: Miss E Smith, BA, MA, PGCE
IA & KS2 Coordinator & Children's Literacy Advisor: Miss J Hasler, BEd Hons

IIB & Senior Tutor: Mrs C Makhlouf, BEd Hons
IIA: Miss M McCann, BA Hons, BEd, MEd; Miss K Jonczyk, BA, MA
III Form & Director of Studies: Miss L Coles, BA, PGCE
Assistants: Mrs M Kolnikaj, Mrs S Leigh, Mrs Y Meneely, Mrs L Menez, Mrs J Van Loon, MSc
French Coordinator: Mme F Leluan, BA, PGCE
French:
M P Solomons, BA, MA, LLP
Mr E Bonner, MA Music
Italian: Miss C Podavitte, Dottoressa in Archeologia, Milano
Spanish: Sta S Gomez, Licenciada en Filologia
German: Frau I Atufe-Kreuth, MA Mag Phil, Cert Ed
Music Coordinator: Mr E Bonner, MA Music
Art & Design Coordinator: Miss N Sitko, MFA Poznan Academy of Fine Arts
Science Coordinator: Mrs C Mayne, BSc, PGCE
LAMDA: Ms J Doolan, MA
Learning Support: Ms S Robertson-Glasgow, BEd Hons, MA Ed, Adv Dip Ed
Librarian: Miss C Podavitte, Dottoressa in Archeologia Milano

Peripatetic Music Staff – Senior and Junior School:
Bassoon: Miss C Marroni, Dip ABRSM, MPerf
Clarinet/Saxophone: Miss R Davies, MA, BMus, LRSM
Cello, Theory: Ms V Evanson, BA, MMus
Flute: Miss A Burrows, RCM Cert of Higher Education; Miss C Vincent, BMus Hons
Guitar: Mr J Lofving, MA, BMus First Class
Harp: Miss F Orme, BMus Hons
Percussion: Miss K Stephenson, BA Hons Music
Piano/Theory: Mrs M A Tham MA, MM, PG Dip RAM, BMus Hons, FLCM, LLCM, LRAM, LMusA, ATCL
Piano: Mrs G Haynes, Dip in Piano Ed and Accomp
Singing:
Mrs S Mailley-Smith, BMus Hons, RCM, PG Dip dist Opera
Ms L Sansun, MA, LRAM, MTC
Violin/Viola: Mr G Irwin, BA, MPhil, PGCE

Support Staff:
Bursar: Mr J Cubitt, ACCA
Finance Manager: Ms O Lynn, BCom, ACCA
Bursar's Assistant: Lady Wilkinson
Registrar: Mrs C Roberts-Beresford, BA
PA to the Director & Junior School Secretary: Miss P Jackson
School Archivist: Miss C Podavitte, Dottoressa in Archeologia Milano
ICT Network Manager: Mr H Hirani
Principal's PA: Mrs S Evans, BA Hons
Principal's Assistant: Mrs C Bickford
Senior School Secretary: Mrs L Hayes, BSc Hons
Communications Officer: Miss A Hinds, MA
Alumni Fundraising & Events Officer: Miss L de Bie, BA Hons
ICT Assistant: Mr S Siktar

Redmaids' High School

Westbury Road, Westbury-on-Trym, Bristol BS9 3AW

Tel: 0117 962 2641
email: admissions@redmaidshigh.co.uk
website: www.redmaidshigh.co.uk
Twitter: @RedmaidsHigh
Facebook: @redmaidshighschool
LinkedIn: /redmaids'-high-school

Redmaids' High was formed from the merger of two of the South West's finest girls' schools – The Red Maids' School and Redland High School for Girls.

Our combined history of over 500 years provides proven experience and expertise, feeding into our forward-looking, 'this girl can' ethos.

Our academic record is excellent and our students excel in a diverse range of subjects. But we are so much more than the sum of our exam results. By prioritising development of the whole girl, giving breadth and depth of knowledge and experience, as well as an international mindedness, we aim to equip girls to become the leaders of tomorrow. The scholarships and bursaries we offer ensure that any able and ambitious girls in the region are given the chance to truly flourish.

Redmaids' High became the first International Baccalaureate (IB) World School in Bristol, winning accreditation in 2008. Ten years on, we have guided our Sixth Formers to world-beating IB Diploma results, alongside our established and successful A Level programme. Both courses are highly valued by universities and employers and generate rich and diverse learning throughout the school.

Opportunities here extend far beyond the classroom. Girls are given the chance to become exceptional public speakers who excel in local and national competitions; future game-changing scientists, engineers and mathematicians; adventurers, who spend time caving, kayaking and competing in local and national sporting fixtures. We support and encourage them to be whoever they want to be.

We have the experience and expertise that enable our girls to shine whilst helping them understand the importance of curiosity, collaboration and possibility.

Our first-class facilities provide the very best learning environments, allowing girls to excel not only academically but also in sport, drama, art and music. Technology makes a central contribution to the way students work and learn – we use iPad technology in the classroom to create dynamic and independent learning environments. In addition, the international links developed over recent years and the thriving alumnae network are an integral part of the school and a hugely valuable asset for the students.

All this adds up to Redmaids' High School being one of the finest girls' schools in the UK for girls aged 7 to 18. The opportunities and facilities – combined with excellent teaching – equip young women with the skills and confidence to truly make their mark in today's world.

Character. The school provides a positive and purposeful learning environment where everything is focused on the girls; where there is no dilution of attention to their needs as young women; and where they are offered all the opportunities and hold all the responsibilities.

Facilities. The site at Westbury-on-Trym, Bristol, just beyond the Clifton Downs, provides an inspirational backdrop for learning, with space for girls to relax and enjoy. The 12-acre campus has a spacious, rural feel, despite being just a few miles from the city centre.

At the centre of the Senior School campus is Burfield House, built in the 19th century as a private family home. Today it houses classrooms, offices, the Pearson Library, Dining Hall and main school reception.

Redland Hall, opened in September 2017, provides a modern performance space and auditorium, complete with flexible seating, first-class lighting and acoustically engineered sound systems. It also houses new classrooms, additional music practice rooms and an area for serving refreshments at key school events.

The contemporary, self-contained Sixth Form Centre, opened in 2011, provides a university-style, independent learning space for Years 12 and 13.

Exceptional sports facilities are a hallmark of the school. On site at Westbury-on-Trym and at the 27-acre sports grounds at Golden Hill, girls have international-standard, all-weather pitches for hockey, athletics and tennis. They take part in netball, basketball, fencing, judo, dance and gymnastics in the multi-use Sports Hall and use the outdoor netball courts and separate grass pitches for football, running, athletics and rounders.

A detached former stable block is home to the music department, and includes teaching and rehearsal space. Students can also access specialist recording equipment and individual workstations with keyboards and Apple computers.

Six fully-equipped, modern laboratories provide everything the Science Department needs, while the Art Department has room to be creative with two large studio spaces, a computer suite and a library.

Extended Day. Girls can arrive from 7.45 am and stay until 6.00 pm, at no extra charge. Breakfast can be bought on an ad-hoc basis and supervised homework and extra-curricular activities take place until 5.30 pm. Clubs and societies include: current affairs, choirs, orchestras, Harry Potter club, the Duke of Edinburgh's Award scheme, film production, drama and many sports clubs.

School Life. The School Council and Sixth Form leadership positions encourage students to take responsibility for others. Peer support systems, clubs run by older students and staff, and charitable fundraising demonstrate the pupils' involvement in their community. Assemblies celebrate pupils' all-round achievements, examine topical issues and offer opportunities for thought, reflection and spiritual exploration.

Curriculum. For the first three years, all Redmaids' High students follow a broad and balanced curriculum. Mathematics is taught in sets from Year 7 and separate Sciences from Year 9. In Year 7, all girls study two languages from a choice of French, German, Russian and Spanish. In Years 10 and 11, we select the best mix of qualifications from GCSE and IGCSE to prepare the girls for the next steps in their education..

Sixth Form. Redmaids' High was the first school in Bristol to offer Sixth Formers the choice of A Levels or the International Baccalaureate (IB) Diploma. Students take three or four linear A Levels, with exams at the end of Year 13. Most girls enrich their A Level experience by taking an additional qualification such as an EPQ, Duke of Edinburgh's Gold award, Astronomy GCSE, or a Level 3 Food Science or Sports Leaders award. IB Diploma students select six subjects, three each at Higher and Standard level, which they take together with compulsory core topics of Theory of Knowledge, Creativity Activity Service, and the Extended Essay. Final IB Diploma exams also take place at the end of the two year course.

Redmaids' High Sixth Formers enjoy excellent teacher relationships and the independence of a modern, purpose-built Centre with dedicated teaching, seminar and common rooms, café, quiet study area, ICT facilities and careers library. Students achieve their full academic potential through high-quality teaching and developing habits of independent study and academic rigour. Almost all students go on to study at university, including Oxbridge. Sixth Formers take on many leadership roles within school and develop a broader understanding of the wider world through a varied community service programme. They also follow a Futures Programme to prepare them for life beyond school and receive individual careers advice.

Fees per term (2018–2019). Years 7 to 13: £4,810. Curricular school trips are included in this fee. Lunch is compulsory for Years 7 to 9 and is invoiced termly. Other extras are individual music lessons, speech and drama lessons, optional non-academic trips, and any one-to-one tuition for those with individual needs.

Admission to Senior School. All students are admitted on the basis of an entrance examination, interview and headteacher's report. Key points of entry are at Year 7, 9 and 12. The entrance exam for Years 7 and 9 is held in January for admission the following September. Entry can take place into other years, subject to availability. For further information, contact the Admissions team.

Scholarships. Scholarships are available to girls who show true potential, a dedication to learning and a lot of ambition in any subject. They are available for entry into Years 7, 9, 10 and 12 for both internal and external candidates. They may also be awarded to exceptional students entering at other stages.

Bursaries. The unique founding origins of Redmaids' High mean the school can offer a number of fully and partially-funded places. As a broad guide, most bursaries offer up to 50% discount on the fees, although two fully-funded places are available each year.

Junior School. *See Junior School entry in IAPS section.*

Charitable status. Redmaids' High School is a Registered Charity, number 1105017. It has existed since 1634 to provide an education for girls.

Governing Body:

Chairman: Mr Andrew Hillman

Vice-Chairman: Mrs Elizabeth Clarson and Mrs Rosemary Heald

Mrs Katie Atkins	Mrs Thelma Howell
Mr Mike Davies	Mr Christopher Martin
Mrs Val Dixon	Mr Richard Page
Mrs Sally Dore	Mr Timothy Phillips
Mr James Fox	Mrs Gilly Rowcliffe
Mr Andrew Hardwick	Mrs Anne Taylor
Mr Mike Henry	

Senior School:

Headmistress: Mrs Isabel Tobias, BA Hons New Hall Cambridge

Deputy Head: Mrs Laura Beynon, MA Durham

Deputy Head: Mrs Kate Doarks, BSc Hons Bristol

Assistant Head Sixth Form and International: Mr Jon Cooper, MA Hons St Andrews

Assistant Head Co-curricular: Dr Alice England, PhD Sheffield

Assistant Head Staff: Mr Tom Johnston, BA Hons Bath College of Higher Education

Assistant Head Pastoral: Mrs Jacklyn Turner, BSc Hons Aston

Director of Finance and Operations: Mr M Marshall, FCMA

Junior School:

Headteacher: Mrs Lisa Brown, BSc Hons Leicester

PA to Headmistress: Mrs Jenny Bell

PA to Director of Finance and Operations: Mrs Susannah Wooldridge

Admissions Registrar:

Mrs Lynn McCabe (*Juniors*)

Mrs Sarah Baker-Patch & Mrs Antonia Firebrace (*Seniors and Sixth Form*)

Roedean Moira House Girls School

Upper Carlisle Road, Eastbourne, East Sussex BN20 7TE

Tel:	01323 644144
Fax:	01323 649720
email:	admissions@roedeanmoirahouse.co.uk
website:	www.roedeanmoirahouse.co.uk
Twitter:	@moirahouse1875
Facebook:	@moirahouse

Motto: *Nemo A Me Alienus*

Foundation. Moira House was founded in 1875 in Surrey. The School moved to its present site in 1887. The founders, Mr and Mrs Charles Ingham, were regarded in their time as gifted pioneers in the field of female education. In 1947 the School became an Educational Trust.

Situation and Facilities. Situated in Eastbourne with views over the sea, the grounds open directly onto the Downs which provide magnificent walking country and offer opportunities for expedition work and field studies. There are extensive playing fields with facilities for Tennis, Cricket, Soccer, Hockey, Netball and Athletics, a 25-metre indoor heated swimming pool and an excellent all-weather sports hall. Each subject has its own resource base. Eastbourne is a thriving cultural centre containing 3 theatres, an art gallery and a concert hall.

Faith. The School is interdenominational.

Organisation. *Junior School* (IAPS): The Junior School has provision for 120 day girls. We offer boarding starting from the age of 9. (*See Junior School entry in IAPS section.*) Our Nursery welcomes boys and girls and we also have a Baby Unit.

Senior School: The Senior School has provision for 140 boarders and 150 day girls.

Boarding Houses: Boston House Boarding has recently been completely refurbished to a high standard, housing all of our boarders and with a dedicated team of House assistants, led by the Head of Boarding, fostering a true sense of community. Sixth Formers are allocated their own rooms and have access to their own common spaces. Plans are to refurbish School House Boarding next year, which will double capacity. Emphasis is placed upon a full range of extra-curricular activities, both in the evenings and at weekends.

Curriculum. *Junior School*: We offer a wide curriculum, based on the National Curriculum and a belief that children learn best when happy and stimulated, whilst also preparing for transfer to the Senior School.

Senior School: The formal academic courses follow a broad curriculum offering 22 subjects leading to GCSE, AS and A Level and University Entrance. At GCSE we offer English Language, English Literature, Mathematics, Business Studies, Biology, Chemistry, Physics, Computing, French, German, Spanish, Latin, History, Geography, Religious Studies, Music, Economics, Mandarin, Photography, Drama, Art and Design, Design/Technology, Physical Education and Food Technology.

Sixth Form: A Levels are offered in Art, Craft and Design, Biology, Business Studies, Chemistry, Theatre Studies, Economics, English Literature, Further Mathematics, Geography, History, ICT (Applied), French, German, Spanish, Latin, Mathematics, Music, Photography, Physical Education, Physics, Psychology, and Religious Studies.

Careers Counselling. We have a strong programme of Careers Counselling, led by our Careers Counsellor.

Drama and Music. Drama and Music have always been strengths of Roedean Moira House. We are aware of the part Speech and Drama play in the development of clear communication and creative expression. There are a number of School productions and concerts each year, and school choirs take part in performances throughout Sussex. We also enter the local festival of Music and Drama and proximity to Glyndebourne gives girls a chance to have their first taste of opera at an early age. As well as regular class music lessons, there is every opportunity to learn a musical instrument, and the exams of the various musical examining bodies are taken. There is also a state-of-the-art recording studio. There are also overseas tours, including recently to Paris.

Physical Education and Sport. We provide excellent facilities and opportunities. The main sports are Swimming, Netball, Tennis, Athletics and Hockey, and teams represent the School in these and in cricket and football. In addition, coaching is given in Sailing, Riding, Squash, Dance, Golf and Badminton, to name a few.

Activities. Activities are considered an essential part of the curriculum. Many activities are offered, including: Drama, Music, Trampolining, Chess, Local History, Sailing, Down-walking, Environmental Studies, Poetry/Play Reading, Table Tennis, Duke of Edinburgh's Award, Mandarin, Japanese, and Debating. Girls are also encouraged to be aware of the needs of others. Senior girls work regularly with local charities. There are annual expeditions both within this country and to Europe and the School has links with French, German and international schools of a similar nature to ours.

Health. The school doctor holds regular surgeries at the School and there is a residential School Nurse.

Entry. Entry to the Senior School is by English, Maths and Non-Verbal Reasoning entrance tests, interview and review of previous school reports and references. Admission to the Junior School is by Taster Day and review of school reports and references, and is a rolling process at any age; to the Senior School admissions is usually at 11–13+ and 16+.

Scholarships and Bursaries. *Junior School*: Principal's Awards are available for entry to Years 3 to 6, in recognition of all-round talent.

Senior School: Standard Scholarships: Academic and Subject Specialist Scholarships are available at 11+, 13+ and 16+ entry, and are typically awarded up to the value of 5 – 50%. Where appropriate, these awards may be supplemented with a Bursary. Eastbourne Scholarships: these are combination awards specifically for girls applying from the state sector and living within 20 miles of the school, who are currently in the top 2% of their class for English and Maths. They combine an Academic scholarship with a means-tested bursary, and together can be awarded up to the value of 70 – 100%. These awards are open to 11+, 13+ and 16+ entry.

Fees per term (2018–2019). Senior School: £4,730–£6,020 (Day Pupils); £8,200–£9,835 (Weekly Boarders); £8,985–£11,140 (Full Boarders). Junior School: £3,115–£4,370 (Day Pupils); £7,305 (Weekly Boarders); £8,155 (Full Boarders).

Charitable status. Moira House Girls School is a Registered Charity, number 307072. It exists to provide quality education for young women.

The Council:
Chairman: Mr Andrew Pianca, FCA
Ms Jenny Barnard-Langston, BA, MA, Dip Couns, JP
Mr Patrick Henshaw, BSc Hons, MRICS, MaPS
Ms Anne-Marie Martin, MBE, BSc, MSc
Mrs Camilla Nightingale, BA, MBA
Mrs Teresa Outhwaite, BA, PG Dip
Mrs Vivien Smiley, BA
Mr Ian Sperling-Tyler, BSc, FCCA
Dr Henry Fajemirokun, MA Oxon, PhD

Senior Leadership Team:
Principal: Mr Andrew Wood

Head of School: Mrs Elodie Vallantine, BA Hons, PGCE

Head of Junior School: Mrs Cecy Kemp, BSc, Dip RE

Head of Teaching & Learning: Mrs Olivia Barber, BA, BSc Hons, PGCE

Head of Sixth Form: Mrs Ruth Harris-Moss, BA Hons, PGCE

Director of Pastoral Care and Scholars: Dr Rebecca Swingle Putland, DMA, MM, BM, BA

Nursery Manager: Mrs Sarah Hughes, BA Hons Early Years

Head of Boarding and Welfare, Residential Nurse: Mrs Jo Talkington

Head of Operations: Mr Simon Hicks

Head of Admissions and Marketing: Ms Emilie Whitmore

Rye St Antony

Pullen's Lane, Oxford OX3 0BY

Tel: 01865 762802
email: enquiries@ryestantony.co.uk
website: www.ryestantony.co.uk
Twitter: @RyeStAntony
Facebook: @RyeStAntony

Motto: *Vocatus Obedivi*

First-class teaching, excellent facilities and a wide programme of extra-curricular opportunities support Rye St Antony pupils in discovering who they are and who they have it in them to become.

Recent inspections have given the school top rankings: 'Outstanding' by Ofsted and 'Excellent' in all areas inspected by the Independent Schools Inspectorate (ISI Inspection Feb 2017). Set in a beautiful twelve-acre site only one mile from the centre of Oxford, Rye helps pupils seek excellence in the recognition that every pupil is an individual with talents to be developed. Academic standards are high, and we never forget that wider life skills are also important to prepare our pupils for a happy, fulfilling and successful life.

Rye St Antony is a school of 315 pupils that provides an environment both safe and stimulating in which every individual is considered a valued member of the community. Everyone is encouraged to respect others and to consider their opinions; no one is overlooked. Pupils have access to the best and most varied opportunities for enrichment which challenge them, develop their characters and help them to be independent, determined and resilient. Each year almost every member of Sixth Form achieves her preferred university place, and destinations range from History at King's College London, to Engineering at Christ Church Oxford, to Computer Science at Sheffield, to French and Film Studies at Bristol. Those with particular talent in music have been supported to apply for choral or organ scholarships at Oxbridge. The school really does bring out the best in each pupil, helping all pupils discover the subjects about which they are passionate and enabling them to take their first steps towards a rewarding future.

We have day places for girls aged 3–18 years and boys aged 3–11 years. Rye St Antony offers full, weekly and flexible boarding options, including occasional boarding days to help each pupil to fully participate in all that the school has to offer.

Of the 315 pupils, 115 are in the Prep School (ages 3–11) and 200 are in the Senior School (ages 11–18). Of the 40 members of Sixth Form, all prepare to continue their studies at university. In recent years the average UCAS points score per candidate has been 115; half of our A Level grades have been A*, A or B.

The school is highly regarded for its happy and purposeful atmosphere and its strong sense of community. The school's aim is to help each pupil develop the intellectual curiosity and skills, the emotional understanding and resources, the ability to work independently and with others, and the personal, social and spiritual values that will lead to personal fulfilment and the ability to contribute something of value to the world.

Religious Life. The school's sacramental life is of central importance, the Eucharist uniting the school with Christ and his church. Several Oxford priests act as the school chaplains and celebrate school masses at the beginning of each term and on Sundays in term time. Religious education is an integral part of the school curriculum.

Senior School Curriculum. Academic standards and expectations are high, pupils are offered many opportunities in music, art, drama and sport, and there is a busy programme of evening and weekend activities.

In the Senior School all pupils follow a broad and balanced common course for the first three years, comprising English, Mathematics, Physics, Chemistry, Biology, Religious Education, French, History, Geography, Technology, Information and Communications Technology, Art, Graphic Communication, Music, Drama and Physical Education. There is a full PSHE programme.

Seventeen subjects are offered as GCSE subjects. For the two-year GCSE course pupils usually study 10 subjects, a mixture of options and core subjects.

In Sixth Form three or four A Level subjects are chosen from over twenty or more options. We also offer Leiths Extended Certificate in Professional Cookery and BTEC Business.

Careers Guidance. The school's careers advisory service provides help and guidance for all pupils, and there is a formal programme of careers advice throughout Years 9, 10 and 11 and Sixth Form. Almost all pupils go on to university and are helped to investigate thoroughly the Higher Education and careers options open to them, careful guidance being given concerning their applications and interviews. The support of the Head, the Head of Sixth Form and other senior staff is available at all stages. Work experience placements are organised, and pupils are encouraged to make particular use of this option at the end of their GCSE courses. Visiting speakers give lectures on various higher education and careers topics and visits to appropriate conferences and exhibitions are arranged regularly.

Prep School Curriculum. The Prep School and Senior School are closely linked, and Prep School pupils are steadily introduced to the specialist teaching and facilities of the Senior School. In the early years the teaching of most subjects is undertaken by the class teachers. In Years 5 and 6 pupils are taught by subject teachers, some of whom also teach in the Senior School, and this arrangement gives them the benefit of specialist teaching and encourages them to develop a feeling of confidence and continuity when the time comes for them to move into the Senior School. Use of the Senior School facilities is particularly valuable in Science, Art, Music, Physical Education and Drama. There is a Prep School Library in Langley Lodge, and older Prep School pupils may also use the King Library in the Senior School.

Performing Arts. The school has a strong tradition of debating and public speaking, and pupils have many successes to their credit in city, county and regional competitions. A major drama production each year, and various smaller presentations give pupils the opportunity to develop their skills in performing, directing, lighting, sound, stage design, costume design and make-up. There are frequent visits to Stratford, London and regional theatres including the Oxford Playhouse. The majority of pupils learn one musical instrument and some learn two or more; there are two choirs, one orchestra and several smaller ensembles, and some pupils are often members of the Oxford Girls' Choir, the Oxford Youth Chamber Choir, the Oxford Schools' Symphony Orchestra, the Oxfordshire Youth Orchestra and the Thames Vale Orchestra. Instruments learnt include piano, violin, viola, 'cello, flute, oboe, clarinet, trumpet, bassoon, saxophone, French horn, guitar and percussion. Through musical productions, concerts and the liturgy there are many opportunities for pupils to contribute to the musical life of the school. In Drama pupils prepare for the examinations of the London Academy of Music and Dramatic Art (LAMDA), and in Music, they prepare for the examinations of the Associated Board of the Royal Schools of Music (ABRSM).

Sport. The school has an indoor sports centre, good playing fields, all-weather hard courts and an outdoor heated swimming pool. The principal winter sports are netball and hockey; the principal summer sports are tennis, swimming, athletics and rounders. Girls compete regularly in local, county and regional tournaments.

Duke of Edinburgh's Award. The school has an outstanding record in The Duke of Edinburgh's Award, each year about 20 girls achieving the Bronze Award, 10 girls or so achieving the Silver Award and several more girls achieving the Gold Award. The purpose of the Award is to give challenge, responsibility and adventure to young people, thus encouraging them to develop initiative and team skills.

Visits. Fieldwork, conferences, lectures, art exhibitions, plays and concerts give girls an interesting programme of visits within the UK. Visits abroad include study courses, exchanges, sports tours and skiing holidays, and the school regularly hosts visiting groups from schools overseas.

Health. The School Nurses work closely with the School Medical Adviser who sees girls at the nearby Health Centre. Dental and orthodontic treatment can be arranged locally, and the John Radcliffe Hospital is five minutes away.

Admissions. Applicants to the Prep School are invited for a taster day and during the day will sit a mathematics and English assessment in the classroom setting. 11+ and 13+ applicants will be invited for an entrance day during which they will take assessments in English and mathematics. All other applicants to the Senior School will sit assessments relative to their year. Admission to the Sixth Form is by interview, school report and GCSE results. International applicants will assessed by interview, level of English and assessments relative to their year.

Scholarships. Scholarships are available at 11+, 13+ and 16+.

Fees per term (2018–2019). Senior School: Full Boarders £8,645; Weekly Boarders £8,230; Day Pupils £5,110. Prep School: Full Boarders £7,410; Weekly Boarders £7,000; Day Pupils £3,290–£4,065.

Charitable status. Rye St Antony School Limited is a Registered Charity, number 309685, to provide for the education and welfare of pupils, in accordance with the school's aims.

St Augustine's Priory School

Hillcrest Road, Ealing, London W5 2JL

Tel: 020 8997 2022
Fax: 020 8810 6501
email: admissions@sapriory.com
website: www.sapriory.com
Twitter: @staugustinesp
Facebook: @StAugustine's_Priory
LinkedIn: /st-augustine-s-priory

Motto: *Veritas*

St Augustine's Priory is a Catholic, independent day school for girls aged 3–18 and also welcomes boys in the nursery. The school was founded in France in 1634 by Lady Mary Tredway to provide a haven where young English women could be provided with an independent education. Moving to Ealing in 1914–15, to its current location, the School follows the philosophy expounded by its Patron, St Augustine of Hippo: children (and for that matter adults) achieve their best when they are happy.

Our vision is for girls to leave St Augustine's equipped with an outstanding academic education and also with the full range of skills required to lead an effective and fulfilling life as women. As part of their journey, in a girls' school environment, they will acquire the skills of self-knowledge, of reflection, of intellectual risk-taking, of persuasiveness and team-building and of emotional strength as well as a cultural fabric for their enriched enjoyment of life. Our team of dedicated and enthusiastic teachers, teaching assistants and support staff care for the girls and encourage them in all aspects of their education and development.

Number of Pupils. There are approximately 474 girls aged from 3–18 (50 in the Sixth Form).

Location. The School is well served by public transport, with Central and Piccadilly line connections within a ten-minute stroll, Ealing Broadway Underground and main line station approximately 20 minutes' walk away and buses stopping nearby. The School sits in an idyllic setting of thirteen acres, with views across to the South Downs.

Admission. St Augustine's Priory is a unique and vibrant community; the best way to understand it is to come and look around the school and meet the pupils, Headteacher and staff. During the application process we invite Parents to visit us on Open Day during the Michaelmas and Lent Terms and you are also warmly invited to visit the school for a private appointment at other times.

St Augustine's Priory operates a selective entry procedure. Selection is based upon academic merit and potential, which is assessed through an entry examination, an interview at the school and references from the candidate's previous school. Our selection process is designed to identify pupils who are able to benefit from our balanced and well-rounded education and to make a positive contribution towards the life of the school. Admission to the Preps is via interview in the Michaelmas Term. Girls in the Junior School move up seamlessly into the Senior School. External candidates for 9+, 10+ 11+, and 13+ sit entrance examinations on our Selection Day in January.

Those wishing to join the Sixth Form are invited to visit the school and meet with the Director of Sixth Form. Interviews are then conducted by the appropriate Heads of Department along with the Headteacher and offers are sent out with conditional GCSE pass requirements.

Faith. St Augustine's Priory is a Catholic Independent Day School for Girls. The Chapel is at the heart of school life and is used for assemblies, weekly Masses and as a place for moments of quiet reflection and prayer. We also welcome girls from other religions and faiths and learn from them.

Pastoral Care. Children from all backgrounds and all races, with a wide range of gifts, make up the community which is St Augustine's Priory. From their first day, girls become part of a community which respects the beliefs and customs of its members and learns to work together. When problems arise and questions need to be asked, we encourage a very personal approach.

Curriculum. We offer an extensive and balanced curriculum including PSHEE, and offer 20 subjects at GCSE and IGCSE and 23 subjects at AS and A2 Level. Girls will usually take ten or more subjects at GCSE.

Priory 6 (Sixth Form) and Careers. Priory 6 facilities include a common room, ICT suite, kitchen and balcony overlooking the South Downs. The Head Girl and Deputy Head girls have their own office.

We expect girls to think about their next steps and to make informed decisions at every stage of their development. Priory 6 students are supported by the Careers Coordinator and Head of UCAS who provide advice and guidance. We work with the students to consider their many future options, assisting with university and course selection, preparation for Oxbridge and other university applications and subsequent interviews. This process is supplemented by a fortnightly programme of guest speakers and a biennial Careers Evening.

Working with Form Tutors and the Director of Priory 6, every girl is expected to examine her own strengths and to explore possibilities suitable for her interests and personal abilities. Talks, conferences, seminars, courses and University Open Days allow all our students to keep abreast of opportunities on offer. The school is a member of Inspiring Futures.

All of this support builds on the guidance received throughout the school. When our girls leave here for university, they take with them not only impressive qualifications but also kindness, an understanding of, and the ability to adapt to, the world in which they live, the confidence to succeed in whatever they choose to do and above all, friendships which will last them through life.

Co-curricular Activities. A wide variety of co-curricular activities aim to ensure spiritual, moral, social and cultural development of all pupils, and to enable students to develop their talents to the full by searching for excellence. Girls will develop and practise new skills, integrate with children across year groups and be challenged and encouraged to take risks. Clubs on offer include chess, yoga, life drawing, photography, Cipher and French conversation. The school excels in its extremely popular sports activities fielding winning teams in hockey, netball, swimming and cross country.

Whilst Drama forms part of the curriculum we also stage a biennial major production in the Spring at Questors Theatre, which allows involvement by the whole Senior School. We offer LAMDA, qualifications in Acting, Speaking Verse and Prose and Speaking in Public. A Musical Theatre club is run for Preps and a Drama club for Juniors.

Music flourishes throughout the school with girls taking part in school orchestras, ensembles, choirs and concerts. A wide range of private musical instrument lessons are also on offer.

Art is outstanding and the girls' work is displayed throughout the school. An annual Art Exhibition is held each summer and is open to the public, and the department makes use of visits to the many theatres, museums and galleries in London.

A majority of girls complete The Duke of Edinburgh's Bronze, Silver and Gold Awards. Visits to Iceland, New York and Salamanca enrich Modern Foreign Languages and Geography learning, as well as History visits to Berlin, sports tours to Paris and Holland and ski trips to Italy and Canada.

Facilities. St Augustine's Priory offers superb amenities including a full-size floodlit all-weather astroturf pitch, floodlit competition-sized netball court and indoor sports hall set in stunning 13-acre grounds. In 2017 the school enhanced, expanded and modernised its School Hall complete with acoustics and sound-proofing.

In addition to sporting facilities, our 13 acres include a dedicated Prep meadow, orchards, Sixth Form Rose Garden, outdoor stage and Priory Farm which homes chickens, micro-pigs and sheep. The state-of-the-art Science Wing opened in 2007 with four laboratories and dedicated Senior and Junior music and drama rooms. A new Nursery block was completed in 2011. To complement this there are two IT suites, music practice rooms, Senior and Junior Art rooms, a Sixth Form Art studio and separate photography studio, Modern Languages Academy, dedicated Sixth Form areas, private studies and seminar rooms, and Scriptorium. Kitchens are on site and the Chef and catering staff serve fresh cooked lunches daily.

Fees per term (2018–2019). Nursery: £1,662 (5 mornings/afternoons), £3,677 (full time), Preparatory Department £3,903, Junior Department £4,368, Senior Department £5,231.

Additional information may be found on the school's website and a more detailed prospectus may be obtained from the School.

Charitable status. St Augustine's Priory School Limited is a Registered Charity, number 1097781.

Board of Governors:
Mrs C Copeland (*Chair of Governors*)
Mrs C Phillips, LLB
Mrs F Baker, MA
Ms J Burbury
Mr B Cassidy
Mr J Davies
Deacon A Clark, BA, BD
Mr P D'Arcy, BSc, MRICS
Dr T Donovan
Mr H Parmar
Mr F Steadman, BA

Senior Leadership Team:

Headteacher: Mrs S Raffray, MA, NPQH

Deputy Head Seniors: Mrs M-H Collins, MA Oxon, PGCE (*Designated Safeguarding Lead Seniors*)
Deputy Head (Academic) Seniors: Ms C MacAllister, ALCM, BA, ACA, PGCE
Director of Sixth Form: Ms F Hagerty, BA, PG Dip, LAMDA
Deputy Head Juniors: Mrs K Knowles, MA (*Designated Safeguarding Lead Juniors*)
Head of Preps and Pre-Preps: Miss E Keane, BA (*Designated Safeguarding Lead Preps and Pre-Preps*)
Bursar: Mr J Powell, BA

Art:
Miss C Eng, BSc, PGCE, TEFL
Mrs K Mackay, BA, PGCE (*Co-curricular Coordinator, Juniors & Seniors*)
Mrs A Wright, BA, PGCE
Mr A Cook, BA (*Art Technician*)

Business & Economics:
Ms C MacAllister, ALCM, BA, ACA, PGCE

Classics:
Dr G Carleton, MA, PhD (*Head of Classics*)
Mrs H Maclennan, BA Cambs, PGCE (*Oxbridge Coordinator*)

Co-Curricular Activities:
Ms F Hagerty, BA, PG Dip, LAMDA (*Director of Sixth Form*)
Mrs K Mackay, BA, PGCE (*Co-curricular Coordinator, Juniors & Seniors*)

Drama:
Ms C Brown, BA, GTP (*Head of Drama*)
Ms F Hagerty, BA, PG Dip, LAMDA (*Director of Sixth Form*)
Miss M Hewitt (*LAMDA*)
Ms L Mcmullin (*LAMDA*)

English:
Mrs M Eaton, BA, PGCE (*Head of English*)
Mr N Elder, BA, PGCE
Mrs M King, BA, PGCE

Geography:
Mr I Chappory, BA, PGCE (*Head of Geography*)
Miss M Keep, BA, PGCE

Government & Politics:
Mr P J Murphy, BSc, MEd, PGCE (*Head of Social Sciences, Director of UCAS*)

History:
Miss P Trybuchowska, MA Oxon (*Head of History*)
Mr P Ferguson, BA, PGCE
Mrs C. Lunn, BA, PGCE

IT:
Mr M Dellow, BSc, PGCE (*Head of ICT and Computing*)

Juniors:
Miss P Brown, BA, PGCE
Ms P Cattigan, BSc, PGCE
Miss N Daya, BA, PGCE
Mrs K Knowles (*Deputy Head Juniors; Designated Safeguarding Lead Juniors*)
Mr F Lennon, BEd
Mrs H Round, BA, PGCE
Mrs L Tomlinson, BA, PGCE

Languages:
Mr A Alejandro, MA, PGCE (*Head of Modern Languages*)
Ms F Assemat, MA, PGCE
Mrs E Cebotari, BA, PGDE
Ms M De Lahitte, BA, PGCE
Miss A Gandi, MA, PGCE
Mrs S Okafor, BA, PGCE

Learning Support:
Mrs K Davis (*Prep and Pre-Prep LSA*)
Miss F Johnson, MA, NA SENCO, ALCM
Mrs A Rai, LLB (*Support in Learning Assistant*)
Mrs Z Thackray, BA (*Learning Support Teacher*)
Mrs C Young, Mont Cert, BA (*Support in Learning Assistant*)

Mathematics:
Mr U Ahmed, BSc, PGCE
Mrs J Bennet, MA, PGCE Oxon (*Head of Mathematics*)
Mr N Harnett, MChem, PGCE
Miss K Khairoun, BSc, PGCE

Music:
Dr G Higgins, BMus, MA, PGCE, CRCO (*Director of Music*)
Miss R Westley, BMus, PGCE

Nursery & Preps:
Miss J Corr, CACHE Level 3 Childcare & Education (*EYFS Practitioner*)
Mrs C Costello, BEd
Mrs L Cvetkova, CACHE Level 3 Dip Children & Young People's Workforce (*EYFS Practitioner*)
Miss L Halton, NNEB (*Teaching Assistant*)
Mrs A Islam, FdA (*Level 5 Teaching Assistant*)
Miss E Keane, BA (*Designated Safeguarding Lead Preps and Pre-Preps*)
Mrs L Lubowiecka, BA, PGCE
Mrs N Morris, NNEB (*EYFS Practitioner*)
Miss H Nikolova (*EYFS Practitioner*)
Mrs P O'Connell, DPP (*Teaching Assistant*)
Mrs R Van Der Merwe, BA, PGCE

PE:
Miss A Cross, BEd
Mrs H Gosling, BSc, PGCE (*Director of Sport*)
Miss L Hales, BA, PGCE
Mrs C Lindsay
Miss S Nowakowska, MEd, PGCE

Psychology:
Ms G Taher, BSc, PGCE

RE:
Mrs L McDermott, BA, PGCE (*Head of RE*)
Mrs C Flannelly, BA, PGCE

Science:
Miss A Burrell, BSc, PGCE (*Second in Science*)
Mr F Green, MSc, ARCS, PGCE
Mr M Kane, BSc, PGCE (*Head of Science and Physics*)
Mrs G Pugh, BSc, PGCE
Mr A Stylianou, BSc, MRSC, PGCE
Mr P Thomas, BSc, MEd, MCIEA, PGCE (*Head of Chemistry, Examinations Officer*)

Sixth Form:
Ms F Hagerty, BA, Dip LAMDA (*Director of Sixth Form*)
Mr P J Murphy, BSc, MEd, PGCE (*Head of Social Sciences, Director of UCAS*)

Sociology:
Mr P J Murphy, BSc, MEd, PGCE (*Head of Social Sciences, Director of UCAS*)

Welfare Staff:
Mrs R Finnegan, RGN (*School Nurse*)
Mrs R Good, BSc, PGCE, Dip Therapeutic Counselling (*Counsellor and Play Therapist Consultant*)

Peripatetic Staff:
Ms R Aspinall, BMus, TCM (*Harp*)
Mrs E Curran, MGR (*Piano*)
Miss E Ferrari, ALCM (*Singing*)
Mrs S Hatch, BMus (*Drum, Percussion*)
Miss E Jackson, MA, GMus, ARCM (*Violin, Viola*)
Mr I Judson, LWCMD, ALCM (*Flute*)
Mr C Smith, BMus, LRAM (*Brass*)
Mrs J Warren, GTCL (*Cello*)
Mrs S Watson (*Clarinet, Saxophone*)

Technicians:
Miss P Morrison, BSc (*Laboratory Technician*)
Mr A Cook, BA (*Art Technician*)
Mr S Wood (*Senior ICT Support Technician*)

Administration:
Ms J Sathananthan (*HR & School Office Manager*)
Mrs K Bhatti, MSc Econ, ACLIP, DipLis (*Librarian*)
Miss C Costello, BA (*Admissions & Communications Assistant*)
Mrs C Cox, BSc Econ (*Design Manager*)
Miss D Cebotari (*Saturday Receptionist*)
Ms M King, BA (*Communications Administrator*)
Mrs J Lanek (*Domestic*)
Miss T Hosten-Sandyi (*Office Assistant*)
Miss L Masih (*Marketing Officer & Events Manager*)
Mr P Martin, BA (*ICT & Data Services Manager*)
Miss L Naylor (*Finance and Examinations Assistant*)
Miss V Norris (*Receptionist*)
Mrs A Ross (*Receptionist*)
Mrs G Savic, BA (*Registrar and Head of Communications*)
Mrs T Sumpter, RGN, AMSPAR (*PA to the Headteacher*)
Mrs G Vymeris MA (*Assistant Bursar*)

Estates:
Mr C Mortimer, BSc (*Head Groundsman*)
Miss M Gelderblom (*Minibus Driver*)
Mr M Raffray (*Premises Officer*)
Mr I Smith (*Groundsman*)

St Catherine's School
Bramley

Station Road, Bramley, Guildford, Surrey GU5 0DF

Tel:	01483 893363
Fax:	01483 899608
email:	schooloffice@stcatherines.info
	admissions@stcatherines.info
website:	www.stcatherines.info
Twitter:	@stcatsbramley

Founded as a Church of England School for Girls in 1885, welcoming both day girls and boarders, St Catherine's is one of the UK's premier girls' schools. The location, just three miles south of Guildford and surrounded by miles of countryside offers space and green vistas and yet, is within one hour of central London and Heathrow Airport.

In The ISI Report, October 2016, We were pleased to receive '*Excellent*' in all three focus areas. Wherever the Inspectors visited from PP1 to the U6, and from Day to Boarding, they encountered girls and staff who were proud to represent St Catherine's. A recurring theme of the Report was the close teamwork between the girls and their teachers. '*Pupils attitude to learning are exemplary. Teachers create an ambience of encouragement in which learning thrives*'.

According to The Sunday Times, St Catherine's is positioned in the top 5 schools in the country sending students to the UK's most highly selective universities. Superb examination results are testament to the quality of teaching and learning, where students are not afraid to show enthusiasm and ambition. Lessons are taught in well-appointed classrooms by subject specialists. In 2018, 90.4% of girls achieved A*–B at A Level and 83.2% achieved Grades 9–7 at GCSE.

With extensive playing fields, superb sports facilities and an auditorium which boasts better acoustics than many London venues, it is no surprise that St Catherine's is always buzzing with life after the teaching day is over.

A well-established House system underpins the whole School, allowing new girls to feel at home very quickly, encouraging an ethos of care and concern for others as well as a friendly competitive spirit.

The outstanding results gained by our students in public examinations secure them places at the top universities, in competitive disciplines like medicine and veterinary science, law and languages. This success comes not only as a result of the fine quality of the teaching, but is also due to the individual attention received by every girl. St Catherine's places great emphasis on creating a happy environment where every girl is encouraged to work hard to maximise her talents. The atmosphere is friendly and one in which children can develop and grow in a very stimulating environment.

Pivotal to the life of St Catherine's are the six school Houses. The girls' loyalty and affection for their Houses is impressive with memories of inter-house plays, competitions and matches enduring long after School days have ended.

A broad and varied curriculum allows all pupils to participate in many challenging and rewarding extracurricular activities. As a Church of England School girls are encouraged to think of others and impressive sums of money are raised for charity each year. The School has its own beautiful chapel which is used by the girls on a daily basis.

The School's flexible approach to boarding makes it increasingly attractive to busy, professional families; the ISI team picked out boarding as one of the outstanding features of St Catherine's. The School welcomes both weekly and full boarders who enjoy a busy and exciting programme. The Four cornerstones of boarding at St Catherine's: Expert care from experienced and highly trained boarding staff; a huge raft of on-site activities with superb facilities; a friendly and welcoming community; and, last but not least, boarding at St Catherine's represents excellent value for money.

Facilities include 3 lacrosse pitches, a multi-purpose sports hall, fitness suite and indoor pool. The auditorium provides superb acoustics for our musical and theatrical productions, better than many London venues. The Sixth Form girls have their own Library which provides a perfect study environment right at the heart of the School. The Anniversary Halls and the Speech Hall Library were officially opened by the School's patron, HRH The Duchess of Cornwall; the first Baron Ashcombe, the Duchess's Great-Great Grandfather was one of the original founders and benefactors of St Catherine's.

Activities Week is held each year in the Summer Term when every girl in the School participates in a variety of programmes organised to both support the curriculum and offer challenges not normally met in the classroom. Pupils participate in outward bound ventures, an industrial heritage tour to the north and midlands, modern language courses in France, Germany and Spain, whilst Sixth Formers focus on university choices. Activities Week costs are included in the fees.

International links are also very important. St Catherine's has an exchange programme with St Catherine's Melbourne, Australia and there are also links with schools in Kenya, South Africa and Afghanistan.

St Catherine's has an unrivalled reputation in art, music, sport and drama; photography and textiles are popular options amongst the Sixth Form, and younger girls are encouraged by an enthusiastic Art and Design department to take advantage of the superb facilities, and join many after-school clubs.

Music is an important feature of school life, with numerous choirs, orchestras and concert bands rehearsing each week and performing regularly. There are in excess of 600 individual music lessons taking place each week where over half the girls learn to play a musical instrument. There are flute choirs, string quartets, recorder groups and ensembles to cater for all levels of ability. Concerts and recitals are held regularly. The Jennifer Bate Organ Academy and the Jennifer Bate Organ Scholarship in conjunction with Guildford Cathedral and the Andrew Lloyd Webber Foundation. The School boasts two organs, one in the School Chapel and a second in the Preparatory School.

Many girls go on to represent their county in netball, lacrosse, swimming, squash and athletics. Every girl is encouraged to take part in sport at school, whatever her level of expertise. The PE Department regularly fields four or five teams for lacrosse and netball, allowing every girl who wishes to play competitively the opportunity to do so.

Drama and Theatre Studies are extremely popular options and all girls are encouraged to audition for the annual middle and senior school plays. As well as acting opportunities, pupils are also offered the opportunity to help backstage and front of house and learn many valuable skills as a result. LAMDA classes are offered to all year groups. With the opening of the impressive new performance halls including state-of-the-art lighting and acoustics, facilities for Theatre are second to none. St Catherine's also has its own very popular School of Dance.

The Preparatory School: most girls join at 4 with a limited number of places available in other years. It aims to support families in helping younger pupils develop a strong sense of values, high standards of behaviour and consideration to others, as well as achieving excellent academic success. The girls benefit from specialist teaching, combining the best of traditional methods with modern technology to prepare them for the Entrance Examinations to all Senior Schools at 11+, including St Catherine's.

St Catherine's is situated in the heart of the attractive Surrey village of Bramley, three miles south of Guildford which has a main line station (Waterloo 35 minutes). The school operates a return bus service to Guildford Station Monday to Friday and there is a Friday evening bus service to London for weekly boarders. There is easy access to Heathrow and Gatwick and travel arrangements are made for overseas boarders. Close proximity to London allows frequent visits to theatres and galleries and the miles of countryside on our doorstep is an asset to the many girls who take part in The Duke of Edinburgh's Award scheme.

Fees per term (from January 2019). Day Girls: £2,995 (Pre-Prep 1), £3,630 (Pre-Prep 2), £4,285 (Pre-Prep 3), £5,060 (Prep School), £6,125 (Senior School).

Boarders: Middle and Senior Boarding and Tuition £10,095.

Fees include the Activities Week programme for Senior School girls and lunches for all pupils aged 4–18.

Entry. This is by Entrance Examination held in January. The Preparatory School also holds its entrance assessments in January.

Scholarships and Bursaries.

11+: There are four Academic Entrance Scholarships available for pupils at age 11. These are awarded on the results of the Entrance Examination. Two scholarships are for 20% of the fees payable and the other two are for 10% of the fees. These run through the Middle School and can be extended through the Sixth Form at the discretion of the Headmistress and in consultation with the teaching staff.

Upper 5 and Sixth Form (Year 11): The following scholarships are awarded during the Summer Term of the girls' Lower Fifth (Year 10). Selection for the awards is based on the results of the June examinations at the end of the Lower Fifth, performance throughout the Lower Five year, a Scholarship Examination paper, and an interview.

There are several internal academic Sixth Form Scholarships: these are scholarships of 20% of the fees payable to run for three years (through Upper 5 and the Sixth Form).

Sixth Form Scholarships: These are scholarships of 20% of fees. However, this group can be extended by a mix of additional 20% or 10% awards depending on the performance of the candidates and the recommendations of the awarding panel.

The Clare Gregory Memorial Sports Scholarship: This is awarded for sporting prowess and is for 20% of the day fees in the Sixth Form.

The Sixth Form Art and Textiles Scholarship: There is an Art and Textiles Scholarship to the value of 20% of the School Fees, awarded during the Autumn Term of Upper 5.

The Sixth Form Drama Scholarship: There is a Drama Scholarship to the value of 20% of the School Fees, awarded during the Autumn Term of Upper 5.

Scholarships for New Entrants to the Sixth Form: There are up to three external academic scholarships of up to 20% of fees and these are awarded, at the discretion of the Headmistress, to new pupils joining the School in the Sixth Form. The Sixth Form Art and Music Scholarships may be applied for by external applicants by the end of October each year.

Music Scholarships and Awards:

An *11+ Music Scholarship* of 20% of the fees and tuition on one instrument may be awarded annually upon entry to an 11+ candidate adjudged by the Director of Music and the independent adjudicator to have strong musical talent. A second Music Scholarship of 10% of fees and tuition on one instrument can be awarded in years where the field of applicants is particularly strong. Applications should be made by November and auditions are in January. A *Sixth Form Music Scholarship* is awarded to a pupil entering the Sixth Form – from within the School or as an external applicant – to the value of 20% of the School Fees.

The Jennifer Bate Organ Scholarship, offered in conjunction with Guildford Cathedral, is awarded in alternate years to a girl who is already a good organist or shows potential. This award is typically for 20% of fees payable, but may involve means-tested bursary assistance if appropriate.

Further Music Awards which cover music tuition, exam fees and sheet music on a range of musical instruments from chapel organ to piccolo and voice are available to pupils in the Senior School. Some are specifically for those wanting to take up less 'popular' instruments. Auditions for Awards take place at the same time as Music Scholarship auditions

Bursaries: Means-tested bursaries are available to external applicants which may cover up to 100% of the fees payable. For further details please contact the Business Manager.

Prospectus and School Visits. Please apply to the Registrar. The Headmistress will be pleased to see parents by appointment.

Charitable status. St Catherine's School Bramley is a Registered Charity, number 1070858. It exists to provide education for girls in accordance with the principles of the Church of England.

Governing Body:
Chairman: Mr Peter Martin, BA, FRGS, FCCA
Mr Albert Alonzo, BSc, PhD
Mr Michael Bustard, JP, FICPD
Mr A Carruthers, BCom Hons
Prof Finbarr Cotter, MBBS, FRCP[UK], FRCPath, FRCP[I],PhD
Mrs Penny Crouch, LLB
Mrs Karen Farrell
Mrs Clare Johnstone [Dr Clare Higgens], MRCS, LRCP, MBBS, MD, FRCP
Dr Michael Jordan, MA, MB BChir, FRCA
Dr Janet McGowan, MBBS, FRCA
Mr Andrew Pianca, FCA
Mrs Sue Shipway
Mr Jonathan Tippett, BSc, FCA, TEP
Mr Denis Ulyet, MRICS BSC

Headmistress: **Mrs Alice Phillips**, MA Cantab

Acting Business Manager: Mr Robert Kinnison
Head of Boarding: Mrs Alice Phillips, MA Cantab
Director of Studies: Mrs Jacki Deakin, BSc UCL, PGCE
Senior Housemistress: Mrs Kirsty Meredith, BA Hons London, AKC, PGCE
Director of Staff: Mrs Claire Wyllie, MA Dunelm, PGCE
Head of Sixth Form: Mrs Kate Hawtin, BA Dunelm, PGCE
School Administrator: Mrs Sheila Kelsall, MA Open, BSc Hons Open, PGCE
Head of Prep School: Miss Naomi Bartholomew, MA London, BEd Cantab, QTS, MA London
Deputy Head – Curriculum: Mrs Julie Micklethwaite, BEd Hons Roehampton
Deputy Head – Pre-Prep: Miss Emily Jefford
Deputy Head – Staff: Mrs Wendy Gibbs, BEd Hons Winchester

Marketing Director: Mrs Gill David, BA Manchester, PGCE
Development Director: Ms Pippa Carte, BD, MA
Association Director: Mrs Dawn Pilkington, BA

Chaplain: Revd Dr Benjamin McNair Scott, BA, MA, PGCE, CELTA, PhD

School Housemistresses:
Ashcombe: Mrs Amanda White
Merriman: Mrs Rosa McQuade
Midleton: Mrs Kirsty Meredith
Musgrave: Mrs Penny Harris
Russell-Baker: Mrs Izzy McLean
Stoner: Mrs Simone Berry

Boarding Housemistresses:
Bronte: Mrs Helen Hobourn
Symes: Mrs Helen Harkness
Keller: Mrs Isabel Cook
Sixth Form: Mrs Vic Alexander

Heads of Departments:
Art: Mr Alexander Perry-Adlam, BA Hons Liverpool John Moores, Cert Ed
Biology: Mrs Claerwen Patterson, MA Oxon, PGCE
Careers: Mrs Sue Weighell, BA Hons Birmingham, QTS Business Studies

Chemistry: Mrs Nicola Austin, MChem Oxon, QTS
Classics: Mrs Jessica Ashby, BA Cantab, PGCE
Drama: Mrs Sally Gallis, BA Ed Plymouth, QTS
Design Technology: Mr Alastair White, BA Hons Winchester
Economics/Business Studies: Mr Nigel Watson, BA Hons Ealing College of Higher Education, PGCE
English: Mr Jonathan Worthen, MA Oxon, PGCE
Examinations Coordinator: Mr Carl Gladwell, BA London
French: Mrs Catherine Peel, BA Oxon, PGCE
Food and Nutrition: Mrs Nicola Genzel, BA Hons Roehampton, PGCE
Geography: Mrs Sophie Mackness, BSc Hons London, PGCE
German Dr Elodie Nevin, MA Oxon, PhD, QTS
History: Mrs Gill David, BA Manchester, PGCE
History of Art: Miss Emily Ward , BA, MA Teaching Western Australia
ICT: Mrs Sandra Morris, BSc Surrey, QTS
Librarian: Mrs Kathryn Bainbridge, MA Loughborough, BA Hons, CILIP
Study Skills Coordinator: Mrs Caroline Warren, BA Hons, Lancaster, PGCE
Mathematics: Mr Alasdair Wright, BSc Hertfordshire, PGCE
Director of Music: Mr Matthew Greenfield, MEng Oxon, QTS
Physical Education: Mrs Nancy Moore, BA Wales, PGCE
Physics: Dr Kathleen Puech, BSc PhD Dublin, PGCE
Politics: Mr Carl Gladwell, BA Hons London, PGCE
Psychology: Mrs Jean Arrick, BSc Hons Liverpool, PGCE
PSHE: Mrs Amanda White, BSc Hons Wales, PGCE
Religious Studies: Mrs Cecilia Townley, MA London, BA Sheffield, PGCE
Spanish: Mrs Carol Ann Van Deventer, BA, MA, Initial Teaching Cert, New York
Textiles: Mrs Margaret Maunder, BEd Hons Leeds, PGCE

Administration:
Senior School Registrar: Mrs Clare Woodgates
Prep School Registrar: Mrs Sally Manhire
PA to the Business Manager: Mrs Diane Haeffele
PA to the Headmistress: Miss Toppy Wharton
Office Manager: Miss Sally Marshall

St Catherine's School

Twickenham

Cross Deep, Twickenham, Middlesex TW1 4QJ

Tel: 020 8891 2898
Fax: 020 8744 9629
email: admissions@stcatherineschool.co.uk
website: .www.stcatherineschool.co.uk

Motto: Not Words But Deeds

Age Range. Girls 3–18 years.
Number in School. 446 Day Girls.

Founded in 1914 by the Sisters of Mercy, St Catherine's moved from its original site to its current location in 1919. Now under lay management, St Catherine's is a Catholic School in the ecumenical tradition, and pupils of all denominations are welcome.

Aims. Catholic ethos – a commitment to values-based education informs our aim to provide a broad and balanced curriculum within a stimulating and supportive environment which encourages and challenges girls to strive to be the best they can be. Success is achieved through personal responsibility, high expectations and a close partnership between parents and school. Emphasis is placed on self-discipline, responsibility and the importance of respect for others. Since we are a relatively small school with small class sizes the staff know the pupils as individuals and there is a strong sense of community which promotes academic success.

Situation. The school enjoys an enviable position, located next to the River Thames. It is a short distance from the centre of Twickenham and approximately 10–15 minutes' walk from Strawberry Hill and Twickenham Stations. Both have regular services to London (Waterloo), Surrey, Berkshire and Middlesex. There are also a number of local bus routes.

Entrance. Main points of entry are at 3, 5, 7, 11 and 16 but girls are accepted at any stage subject to availability. Places at the school are usually awarded on the basis of an interview, a report from the candidate's previous school and an assessment (examination in the Senior School).

Scholarships and Bursaries. Academic Scholarships are awarded annually at 11+ and 16+. At 11+ girls are invited to sit scholarship papers on the basis of their entrance examination results. At 16+ students are required to sit three examination papers in the subjects they plan to study at A Level. Art, Drama, Music and Sport scholarships are also awarded annually following an audition/assessment and are conditional on the applicant achieving the school's academic requirement for entry.

A limited number of means-tested Bursaries are offered depending on need and funds available.

Curriculum. In the Senior School pupils follow courses in English, Mathematics, Biology, Chemistry, Physics, Religious Education, French, German, Spanish, History, Geography, Drama, Music, Art, Food Technology, ICT and Physical Education. All of these subjects are offered at GCSE with the addition of Economics, Psychology, Textiles and Photography. Most pupils study ten subjects to GCSE level. All of the above subjects are available at A Level, with the addition of Politics, Graphics, Further Mathematics and Sociology.

There is a strong commitment to Sport, Music, Drama and extracurricular activities. The school has its own hockey pitch and indoor swimming pool as well as tennis and netball courts. Sports include swimming, netball, athletics, hockey, tennis, gymnastics, trampolining and rounders and our pupils achieve considerable success at county, regional and national level.

Music plays an important part in the life of the school; all pupils are encouraged to participate in choirs, orchestras and ensembles, and there is a varied programme of concerts and informal performances each term.

Drama is popular and, as well as opportunities to perform in school productions, regular theatre visits take place during the year.

Buildings. The Preparatory and Senior departments are on one site. The buildings include a large multi-purpose hall as well as a smaller assembly hall, well-stocked Prep and Senior Libraries, three ICT Suites, a spacious Art and Photography Suite and a Food Technology Room. The Music Centre has class and individual practice rooms. There are fully-equipped laboratories for Physics, Chemistry and Biology. A large programme of new building has recently added extra teaching blocks, a Sixth Form Centre, Drama Studio and Fitness Suite.

Extracurricular Activities. These play a significant role in the life of the school. Activities include the Duke of Edinburgh's Award scheme, Badminton, Science Club, Football, Rugby, Rowing, Cross-Country Running, Zumba, Chess and Photography. Trips, both locally and abroad, add to the extensive range of activities on offer. Pupils also take part in community service and fundraising activities.

Fees per term (2018–2019). Inclusive of lunch: Nursery £3,598, Reception £3,847, Years 1 and 2 £3,950, Years 3 to 6 £4,152, Years 7 to 13 £4,970 (excluding examination fees).

Charitable status. St Catherine's School, Twickenham is a Registered Charity, number 1014651. It aims to provide for children seeking education in a Christian environment.

Chair of Governors: Mr Edward Sparrow

Headmistress: **Mrs Johneen McPherson**, MA

Deputy Head: Miss A Wallace, MA, BA, PGCE

Bursar & Clerk to the Governors: Mr I G Stewart, BAcc, CA

Admissions Manager: Mrs A Faulkner, FAPA, PAFSA

St Dominic's Grammar School

Bargate Street, Brewood, Staffordshire ST19 9BA

Tel: 01902 850248
Fax: 01902 851154
email: secretary@stdominicsgrammarschool.co.uk
website: www.stdominicsgrammarschool.co.uk
Twitter: @StDomsBrewood
Facebook: @StDominicsGrammar

St Dominic's Grammar School Brewood provides education for over 180 girls and boys from the ages of 2 to 18.

Development of the 'whole person' is at the heart of our school. We believe each child has special talents and we work to enable them to achieve their full potential within a caring environment. We nurture the pupils academically, socially, creatively and spiritually.

Teaching & Learning. Small class sizes facilitates individual attention so strengths and weaknesses are diagnosed and all work is tailored to match individual's needs. We believe in close partnership with parents, keeping you informed about your child's progress.

Curriculum. We offer a broad and balanced curriculum with enhancement and enrichment. The National Curriculum is taught throughout the school. This is enhanced with additional subjects including performing arts, dance, drama and singing which are integrated into the weekly timetable. We offer a comprehensive range of subjects at AS and A Level.

Expressive Arts. We are renowned for our musical and dramatic excellence. Our contemporary Performing Arts Centre houses a Drama and Dance Studio, a Music Suite and a Recording Studio. Pupils are encouraged to join the choirs, play an instrument, take up dance, singing or tread the boards. Throughout the year there are a variety of performances ranging from the Pre-Preparatory Christmas play, to productions such as *Into the Woods* and *Annie*. The pupils participate in many local and regional competitions, take part in local festivals and public speaking events. Many do LAMDA examinations and all Year 7s take English Speaking Board examinations.

Sports. We offer a broad curriculum including netball, hockey, dance, gymnastics, aerobics, football, volleyball, basketball, badminton, rounders, tennis, golf, athletics and cross-country. Our all-inclusive extra-curricular programmes provide further sporting variety including Zumba, gymnastics, trampolining, modern dance and ballet, with all abilities encouraged to attend.

There is a comprehensive fixtures programme incorporating inter-house events and annual Junior and Senior Sports Days. We take part in ISA sporting events at local, regional and national level.

The facilities include newly-resurfaced netball and tennis courts, hockey, football and rounders pitches and athletics track. We also have an excellent fully-equipped sports hall with new cricket nets and electronic basketball hoops.

Extra-Curricular Activities. Four days a week there is an all-inclusive after-school programme where pupils can undertake a variety of activities ranging from The Duke of Edinburgh's Award scheme to debating, cooking, Young Enterprise, STEM Club and gardening.

Throughout the year, pupils are encouraged to become involved in fundraising for local and national charities. These activities help each child develop a good community spirit with respect and consideration for others.

Pastoral Care. Our outstanding pastoral care system and Christian ethos create an atmosphere which fosters trust and mutual respect between pupils and teachers. Pupils feel relaxed and secure and develop their self-respect, self-confidence, personal discipline and consideration for others.

Examination Results. Our pupils achieve outstanding exam results year on year outperforming the national averages of both comprehensive and independent schools at Key Stage 2, GCSE and A Level. We ranked 25th nationally in The Sunday Times 2018 Parent Power publication.

Facilities. We have a purpose-built Kindergarten and Junior building, which encompasses a Junior Hall, IT room, DT and Art room, Home Economics room and library. The Senior building has fully-equipped science laboratories, IT room and library. All classrooms have networked computers and interactive whiteboards. The Sixth Form and Performing Arts Centre is a modern, state-of-the-art facility housing the latest technology in music, IT and the Performing Arts. It has a common room with terraces and a well-equipped Library with Wi-Fi technology.

Admissions. Although selective, we draw our pupils from a wide ability range, which makes our record of results outstanding. Assessment is made during trial days at school. Entry into Year 7 is dependent on the entrance examination held in October. Applications for all other year groups are considered, depending on availability. A place in the Sixth Form is conditional upon GCSE results.

Fees per term (2018–2019). Reception including lunch £2,278, Year 1 including lunch £2,744, Year 2 including lunch £2,989, Years 3–6 £3,466, Years 7, currently at £2,500, Years 8–9 £4,205, Years 10–11 £4,404, Sixth Form, currently at £2,500.

Scholarships and Bursaries. Scholarships may be available for Preparatory. Academic, Sport and Performing Arts scholarships may be awarded for entry into Years 7 and 12. Art scholarships are available in Year 8. Means-tested Bursaries are also available.

Headmaster: **Mr Peter McNabb**, BSc Hons, PGCE

Bursar: Mr Paul Tudor
Head of Preparatory School: Miss Louise Hovland, BEd Hons
Head of Senior School & Sixth Form (Safeguarding): Mrs Nicola Hastings Smith, BA Hons, PGCE, NPQH
Admissions & Marketing: Miss Neelam Malik, BA Hons

Heads of Faculty:
Mathematics: Mr Richard Brocklehurst, BSc Hons, PGCE
Science and Technology: Mr Ian Henderson, BSc Hons, MRSC, PGCE, QTS
Expressive Arts: Mrs Carol Molin, BA Hons, PGCE, LGSM
Communications: Mrs Nicola Hastings Smith, BA Hons, PGCE, NPQH
Humanities: Mr Gareth Saul, BA Hons, PGCE

St Gabriel's

Sandleford Priory, Newbury, Berkshire RG20 9BD

Tel: 01635 555680
Fax: 01635 555698
email: info@stgabriels.co.uk
website: www.stgabriels.co.uk
Twitter: @StGabrielsNews
Facebook: @stgabrielsnewbury
LinkedIn: /st-gabriel's-newbury

Independent Day School for Girls, in membership of GSA and IAPS.

Number of Pupils. 450.

Academic excellence, high expectation, intellectual challenge and a fulfilling co-curricular life are core values at St Gabriel's. Developing a lifelong intellectual curiosity and securing the very best university places for students is at the heart of this successful school.

From Nursery to Sixth Form visitors recognise the enthusiasm and sense of purpose of both staff and pupils. Some parents choose St Gabriel's because of its reputation for achieving exceptional academic standards; others welcome the individual attention given to all pupils.

Curriculum. The formal curriculum is broad and well-balanced, providing an education that is both traditional and forward-thinking. Small class sizes, an outstanding system of pastoral care and dynamic teaching assist pupils to achieve their full potential both academically and holistically.

To ensure connectivity to the real world and to prepare the students to meet the challenges of the 21st Century workplace, the school has forged strong links with high-tech industry and multinational businesses.

A choice of 27 subjects is offered at GCSE of which English, English Literature, Mathematics, all three Sciences, a Modern Foreign Language (MFL) and a Humanity are compulsory.

At Sixth Form, students choose three subjects to study to A Level from the 27 offered. All students also study for the Extended Project Qualification.

Extra-Curricular Activities. The school provides a wide range of opportunities outside of the classroom. Numerous activities and visits extend and enrich pupils' learning experience throughout the school. The performing and creative arts, sport and a wide range of clubs and societies ensure that girls progress to the next stage of their education with confidence. Whether it is through The Duke of Edinburgh's Award or World Challenge, the girls constantly rise to meet new challenges.

Music. There are two orchestras, four choirs a wide range of ensembles including two string quartets, jazz and rock bands and several woodwind ensembles. Most orchestral instruments may be learned.

Sport. Netball, Hockey, Swimming, Rounders, Athletics, Cricket, Cross-Country, Dance, Equestrian, Gymnastics, Rugby and Tennis.

Facilities. Specialist IT suites, state-of-the-art science laboratories and MFL rooms, multi-disciplinary sports hall, theatre and dance studio.

Christian Community & Ethos. St Gabriel's has a Church of England foundation but girls of other faiths are welcome. A strong moral code and Christian values ensure the girls leave the school as well-balanced, unpretentious, spirited individuals with the confidence to be assertive and decisive with warmth and without arrogance. The girls are always encouraged and supported to resist pressures and to have the confidence to make the right choices.

Supervised Prep. This is provided on a daily basis between 4.00 pm and 6.30 pm.

Scholarships & Bursaries. Academic, Sport, Art, Dance, Drama and Music scholarships are awarded at 11+ and 13+. Sixth Form scholarships are also awarded at 16+. Bursaries covering up to 100% of fees are available through the Montagu Award scheme, which aims to ensure that St Gabriel's is accessible to girls who would otherwise not be able to enjoy the unique education the school offers.

Admission. Entry to the Junior School for children aged 6–10 years is by assessment. An entrance exam is held in November for entry at 11+ and 13+ and girls are accepted in to the Sixth Form on the basis of their GCSE results and an interview.

Fees per term (2018–2019). £5,602–£5,806.

Junior School. (*See entry in IAPS section*).

Charitable status. The St Gabriel Schools Foundation is a Registered Charity, number 1062748. It exists to provide education for girls.

Governing Body:
Chairman: Mr N Garland, BSc Hons

Mr S Barrett	Mr D Peaple
Mrs S Bowen	Mr S Ryan
Mrs J Heywood	Mr M Scholl
Mrs S Hutton	Mrs J Whitehead

Principal: Mr R Smith, MA Hons, MEd, PGCE

Vice-Principal: Mrs A Chapman, BA Hons, PGCE, QTS (*Spanish*)
Bursar & Clerk to Governors: Mrs Penny Setter, BA Hons
Head of Sixth Form: Mrs C Reseigh, BA Hons, PGCE (*French*)
Head of Upper School (*Years 9, 10 & 11*): Mrs E Hammons, LLB, PGCE (*History, Politics*)
Head of Lower School (*Years 7 & 8*): Mrs R Wright, BSc Hons, PGCE (*Physical Education*)
Head of Junior School: Mr P Dove, BA Hons, PGCE (**Thinking Skills*)
Director of Teaching & Learning: Mrs H Trevis, BSocSc Hons, PGCE (**Religion, Philosophy & Ethics*)
Director of Curriculum: Mrs A Chicken, BA Hons, PGCE (*Mathematics*)
Deputy Head of Junior School: Miss A Smith, BEd Hons, QTS (*Form Tutor Year 2, *Computing*)
Sandleford Nursery Curriculum Manager: Mrs C Lawrence, BA Ed, QTS (*Form Tutor Reception*)
Sandleford Nursery Manager: Mrs K Noonan, BA Hons, EYTS
Sandleford Deputy Manager: Mrs M Bullock, NVQ Level 3
Director of Education Partnerships: Mrs W Rumbol, BA Hons, PGCE, DMS (*French, Spanish*)
Compliance Coordinator: Mrs V Vaughan, BSc Hons, QTS (*Mathematics*)
Challenge & Extension (*Senior School*): Mrs A Chicken, BA Hons, PGCE (*Mathematics*)
Challenge & Extension (*Junior School*): Miss A Smith, BEd Hons, QTS (*Form Tutor Year 2, *Computing*)

Senior School Teaching Staff:
* *Head of Department*
Mrs N Archer, BA Hons, PGCE (*English*)
Mrs N Bailey, BA Hons, QTS (*Mathematics*)
Mrs A Beake (*Science Technician*)
Mr F Beake (*Science Technician*)
Mr A Beverly, MA, PGCE (*Religion, Philosophy & Ethics*)
Mrs R Chaplin, BA Hons, QTS (**Drama*)
Mrs G Clarkson, MA, PGCE (*Mandarin Chinese*)
Mrs K Cook (*Art Technician*)
Mrs F Dabrowski, BSc Hons, PGCE (*Chemistry*)

Mrs R Dadds, MTeach, BSc Hons, PGCE (*Psychology, English*)

Mrs D Evans, BSc Hons, PGCE, MinstLM (*Business Studies*)

Ms S Ferretti, Laurea in Lingue, PGCE (*Modern Foreign Languages, Italian, French*)

Mrs C Gwilliam (*Science Technician*)

Mrs R Golding, BA Hons, PGCE (*English*)

Ms S Hall, BA Hons, PGCE (*English*)

Miss E Halstead, BA Hons (*Classics*)

Ms J Hammett, MSc, BSc Hons, PGCE (*Science*)

Mrs R Harvey, BSc, Hons, PGCE (*Geography*)

Mrs K Hastings, BA Hons, PGCE (*Dance*)

Mrs S Haywood Smith, BSc Hons, JEB (*Computer Science*)

Ms M Hunter, MA RCA, BA Hons (*Art, Textiles, Photography*)

Mr M Ives, MA, BA Hons, PGCE (*Classics, Latin, Greek*)

Mrs Taya Johnson, MEng, QTS (*Mathematics*)

Mrs P Joseph, MEd, BA Hons, PGCE (*Physical Education*)

Miss A Keenleyside, BEd Hons (*Art, Textiles, Photography*)

Mrs J Knott, BSc Hons, PGCE (*Design Technology*)

Mr B Lewis, MA Cantab, PGCE (*History, *Politics*)

Mr J Mannion, BA Hons, PGCE (*Computer Science, History*)

Mr G May, BA Hons, QTS (*Physical Education*)

Mrs D McLaughlin, BSc Hons, PGCE (*Physics*)

Mrs Alison Pasternakiewicz, BEd Hons (*Physical Education*)

Mrs H Porter, BSc Hons, PGCE (*Biology, KS3 Science Coordinator*)

Mr S Repacholi, BSc Hons, PGCE (*Chemistry*)

Ms H Rayner, BA Hons, PGCE (*Physics*)

Miss A Roe, MA, BA Hons, PGCE (*Geography*)

Mr R Shah, BSc Hons, PGCE (*Chemistry*)

Mrs L Sharman, BA Hons, PGCE, QTS (*Drama*)

Mrs J Shillaw, BA Hons, PGCE (*History, *Politics*)

Mrs S Sim, BSc Hons, PGCE (*Mathematics*)

Mr P Spurrett, BA Hons, PGCE (*Art*)

Dr P Tebbs, DPhil Oxon (*Music*)

Mrs A Thayer, MA Cantab, BA Hons, QTS (*English*)

Mrs L Tyler, BA Hons, PGCE (*Spanish*)

Mrs S Yeoman (*Technology Technician*)

Miss L Zhu, MSc, BA Hons, PGCE, QTS (*Mandarin Chinese*)

Miss Y Zhang, MSc, BA Hons, PGCE (*Mandarin Chinese*)

Mrs T Zogaj, MA, RCA, BA Hons, PGCE, QTS (*Food & Nutrition*)

Junior School Teaching Staff:
* *Subject Leader*

Miss E Bloomfield, BA Hons, PGCE (*Form Tutor Year 1*)

Mrs S Bloxsom, BA Hons, QTS (*Form Tutor Reception & Year 2, *English*)

Mrs R Chaplin, BA Hons, QTS (*Drama*)

Mrs G Clarkson, MA, PGCE (*Mandarin Chinese*)

Mrs M Davidson, BEd Hons (*Form Tutor Year 4, *English*)

Mrs R Dye, MA, PGCE, QTS (*Form Tutor Year 4*)

Ms S Ferretti, BA Hons, PGCE (*MFL, Italian, French*)

Ms M Gunn, BA Hons, QTS (*Music*)

Mrs K Hastings, BA Hons, PGCE (*Dance*)

Mr R Havercroft, MEng, QTS (*Form Tutor Year 5, *Science, *Mathematics*)

Mrs L Hayes, BA Hons, PGCE (*Form Tutor Year 4*)

Mrs S Haywood Smith, BSc Hons, JEB (*Computing*)

Ms M Hunter, MA RCA, BA Hons (*Design Technology*)

Mrs P Joseph, MEd, BA Hons, PGCE (*Physical Education*)

Mrs J Knott, BSc Hons, PGCE (*Design Technology*)

Mr J Mannion, BA Hons, PGCE (*Computing*)

Mr G May, BA Hons, QTS (*Physical Education*)

Miss H Moth, BA Hons (*Form Tutor Year 3*)

Mrs A Pasternakiewicz, BEd Hons (*Physical Education*)

Miss J Pearmine, BA Hons, PGCE (*Year 6 Form Tutor, *Humanities, *Religion, Philosophy & Ethics*)

Mrs T Stoyanova, NVQ Level 8, QTS (*Art*)

Mrs S Webb, BSc Hons, PGCE (*Form Tutor Year 1, *PSHE*)

Mrs D Wilkinson, BA Hons, PGCE (*Form Tutor Year 2*)

Miss Y Zhang, MSc, BA Hons, PGCE (*Mandarin Chinese*)

Mrs T Zogaj, MA, BA Hons, PGCE (*Food & Nutrition*)

Teaching Assistants:

Mrs C Adams, NVQ Level 3 (*Year 1*)

Mrs Y Brown, CACHE Level 3 (*Reception*)

Mrs Catherine Cockar, QTS (*1–1 LSA*)

Mrs S Ducker (*Year 1*)

Miss A Joseph (*1–1 LSA*)

Mrs G Livingstone, BA Hons, NCFE Level 3 (*Year 2*)

Mrs H Martin, NVQ Level 2 (*Year 1*)

Mrs S Morris, BSc Hons, HLTA (*Year 3*)

Sandleford Nursery Staff:

Mrs L Cox, NVQ Level 3

Miss J Gilpin, CACHE Level 3

Miss L Greetham, NVQ Level 3

Miss K Grineau, CACHE Level 3

Miss M Hamm, NVQ Level 3

Miss F Hughes, CACHE Level 3

Mrs N Kelly, NVQ Level 3

Miss K Lee, NVQ Level 2

Miss S Milligan, CYPW Level 3

Miss A Siddons, NVQ Level 3

Miss T Upham, NVQ Level 3

Visiting Music Staff:

Mrs K Addis (*Double Bass*)

Mr D Birnie, BMus Hons (*Guitar & Drums*)

Mr T Bott, BMus Hons, PG Dip (*Violin*)

Mr N Cole, BA Hons, PG Dip (*Drums & Percussion*)

Mrs J Frith, CT ABRSM (*Flute & Recorder*)

Miss E Gregory, BMus Hons (*Voice*)

Ms L Hayles, BA Hons, PG Dip

Ms M Hendrickx-Nutley, BA Hons, GTC (*Voice*)

Mr M Lijinsky, CT ABRSM (*Piano*)

Mrs H Page, BMus Hons, PGCE (*Piano*)

Mr S Parker, ALCM, LLCM, CT ABRSM (*Clarinet, Saxophone*)

Mrs H Rawstron, BA, LTCL (*Oboe*)

Mrs S Riddex, BA Hons, PGCE, LTCHM, LESMD (*Cello*)

Mr P Tarrant, ARCM, CertEd (*Brass*)

Mrs V Toll, LRAM, CertEd (*Piano*)

Individual Needs:

Mrs M Goodhead, Dip SpLD (*Individual Needs*)

Mrs C Oxley, BSc Ed Hons, Dip SpLD (*Individual Needs*)

Administrative, Support & Facilities Staff:

Bursar's Office:

Mr T Britten (*Site Manager*)

Mrs J Goodman-Mills (*Transport Coordinator*)

Mrs A Morris (*HR & Operations Advisor*)

Mrs A Williams (*Accounts Assistant*)

Mrs S Willson (*Assistant Bursar – Finance*)

School Office:

Ms C Adams (*After School Club*)

Mrs J Benney (*Admissions Manager*)

Miss H Bonney (*After School Club*)

Mrs A Borzoni, BA Hons, PG Dip (*Librarian*)

Mrs H Corkhill, BEd Hons (*Examinations Officer*)

Miss G Crook (*After School Club*)

Mrs B Evans (*Marketing Manager*)

Mrs G Goldsborough (*After School Club*)

Miss C Jackson (*Executive Secretary*)

Mrs A Kail (*Data Manager*)
Mrs J Reehal (*School Nurse*)
Mrs S Tucker (*School Secretary*)

St George's, Ascot

St George's School, Wells Lane, Ascot, Berks SL5 7DZ

Tel: 01344 629920
Fax: 01344 629901
email: office@stgeorges-ascot.org.uk
website: www.stgeorges-ascot.org.uk
Twitter: @stgeorgesascot
Facebook: @stgeorgesascot

Member of GSA, AGBIS, BSA.

St George's Ascot, is a vibrant Boarding and Day school for girls aged 11–18 providing an excellent academic education in a supportive and caring environment.

The school is set in 30 acres of stunning grounds, only 30 minutes from central London and located just off the High Street in Ascot. With outstanding value added, St George's helps girls achieve at least one and a half grades higher at both GCSE and A Level.

St George's is not a narrowly academic school – academics matter but this alone is not what makes a great education. St George's prides itself on offering a much more in-depth approach to learning; preparing our pupils beyond school by developing good communication skills, a love of learning and a willingness to get involved.

Friendly atmosphere, small classes, strong pastoral care and opportunities for individual development make St George's stand out from the crowd.

Curriculum. Small class sizes ensure that every girl is given the right balance of academic challenge and support by inspirational teaching staff, who deliver a wide-ranging and varied curriculum. Girls are given opportunities to excel, not only in traditional subjects but also in Art, Drama, Music and Sport. Team sports are offered in Lacrosse, Netball, Swimming, Tennis, Rounders, Athletics, Squash and Polo.

Academic results at St George's are strong, with the majority of the girls going on to Russell Group universities. All Sixth Form girls take the Extended Project Qualifications in addition to A Levels, and typically one third of the candidates achieve three or more A grades.

Entrance. Entry at 11+ is by our own assessment. A reference from the current school, examinations in English, Mathematics and an online CEM (Centre for Evaluation and Monitoring) test, together with and a short presentation to a senior member of staff take place in the November of Year 6. For entry at 12+/13+, testing takes place in the January preceding entry and applicants will sit papers in English, Mathematics, Science and an online CEM test. Girls will also make a short presentation to a senior member of staff.

Girls considering an application to the Sixth Form will be invited for an interview with the Head of Sixth Form or another senior member of staff. Any offer of a place made will be contingent on meeting our minimum admissions criteria of achieving at least six, 9 to 5 grades at GCSE, with at least a 6 in any subject to be taken at A Level. A wide range of scholarships are available at 11+, 13+ and 16+.

Fees per term (2018–2019). £11,820 Boarding, £7,600 Day.

Scholarships. Scholarships are available at 11+, 13+ and 16+ for outstanding potential, as evidenced by examination results. Academic, Art, Performing Arts, Sport, Music and All Round scholarships and instrumental awards are available at 11+ and Academic Art, Music, Drama, Performing Arts, All Round and Sport scholarships at 13+ and 16+.

Extra Subjects. Other languages (including Mandarin), Music (most instruments), Speech and Drama, Ballet, Modern Stage and Tap Dancing, Individual Tennis, Polo, Riding, Zumba, and Pilates.

Charitable status. St George's School Ascot Trust Limited is a Registered Charity, number 309088. It exists to provide independent secondary girls' education.

Governors:
Mr E Luker, FRICS (*Chairman*)
[2]Mr G W P Barber, MA Oxford, LVO
[2]Mrs D R Brown, MBE
[2]Dr J M Gibbons, BA, MPhil, DPhil
[1]Mr P James
[1]Mrs A Laurie-Walker, BSc MSc Provence
[1]Mr A Mackintosh, BSc Aberdeen, MBA City
[2]Mr A Miles, BSc Durham, PGCE
[1]Mrs R E S Niven Hirst, BArch Newcastle, RIBA [OG]
[1]Mr P Sedgwick, MCSI
[2]Ms A Triccas, MA, BA London

[1] *Member of Finance and Marketing sub-committee*
[2] *Member of Education sub-committee*

Headmistress: Mrs E M Hewer, MA Cantab, PGCE

Bursar and Clerk to the Governors: Mrs J M Wood, JP, BA Exeter, Dip FM

Deputy Head Academic: Mr J V Hoar, BA Hull, PGCE

Deputy Head Pastoral: Mrs H L Simpson, BA Ed Exeter (*Designated Safeguarding Lead*)

Deputy Head Co-Curricular and Connections: Mr A J Wright, MA Oxford, MA London, PGCE (*Deputy Designated Safeguarding Lead*)

Teaching Staff:
* *Head of Department*

Art, Textiles, Photography and Cookery:
*Miss O Antolik, BA Kingston, PGCE
Mrs H Jones
Ms K Gilbert, BA Chichester, PGCE
Mrs A Morgan, BA Dundee, PGCE
Ms E Townsend, BA East Anglia, PGCE

Business and Economics:
*Mr D Wilkins, BSc London, PGCE

Classics:
*Miss L Fontes, BA Leeds, PGCE
Mrs C Phipps, BA Nottingham, PGCE

ICT and Computing:
*Mrs R Belkacem, BSc London, PGCE
Mr Naeem Mohammad, BSc MA Punjab, HDipEd Dublin

Drama:
*Mr A Carroll, BA St Mary's, PGCE
Mrs J Condliffe, BA MA Leeds, PGCE
Mrs E Gregan, BA Liverpool, PGCE
Miss R Johnson, BA Warwick

English:
*Mr N Lee, BD BA MA London, PGCE
Mrs J Condliffe, BA MA Leeds, PGCE
Mrs E Gregan, BA Liverpool, PGCE
Ms M Johnston, BA East Anglia, MA London, PGCE
Ms L Baker, BA Sheffield

EAL:
*Mrs N Anderson, MA East Anglia, PGCE
Mrs S Davies, CTESOL
Miss O Kellaris, BA

Geography:
*Mrs S Johnson, BSc Exeter, PGCE
Miss N Stepp, BSc St Mary's, PGCE

History and Politics:
*Mrs D Kratt, BA Reading, PGCE
Mr J V Hoar, BA Hull, PGCE
Mrs M Soni, BA MA Oxford Brookes, GTP [Maternity]
Mr A Wright, MA Oxford, MA London, PGCE
Mr J da Costa, BA Exeter, MA King's College, PGCE

History of Art:
*Miss L Cordingley, BA Warwick, PGCE

Modern Languages:
*Mrs F Burrows, Maitrise Toulouse, GTP
Miss A Figueira, Licence Paris, PGCE
Mrs R Martinez, BA Portsmouth, PGCE
Miss L Fontes, BA Leeds, PGCE

Learning Support:
*Ms M Johnston, BA East Anglia, MA London, PGCE

Mathematics:
*Mr P Wilson, BEng Nottingham, PGCE
Mrs C Lilley, BSc London, PGCE
Mr Naeem Mohammad, BSc MA Punjab, HDipEd Dublin
Mrs S Scholefield, BSc Birmingham, PGCE

Music:
*Mr I G Hillier, GLCM, FLCM, FCSM, FGMS, PGCE
Miss C Mason, LLB Bristol, PGCE

Physical Education:
*Mrs A Earnshaw-Punnett, BA Sheffield City
Miss L Myers, BA Leeds Met, QTS
Miss L Mogford, BA Oxford Brookes
Mrs K Hammond, BEd Chichester
Mrs R Tune, BSc Loughborough, PGCE

SMSC:
*Mrs H Simpson, BA Ed Exeter
Mrs A Morgan, BA Dundee, PGCE
Miss L Myers, BA Leeds Met, QTS
Mrs E Shingles, BSc Brunel, GTP
Miss N Stepp, BSc St Mary's, PGCE

Psychology:
*Mrs E Shingles, BSc Brunel, GTP [Maternity]
Mrs M Langenegger, BA South Africa

Philosophy, Ethics and Religion:
*Mrs M Magill, BA Bristol, MA London, PGCE
  [Maternity]
*Mrs R Graham, BA London, PGCE

Science:
*Mr S Rhodes, BSc Canterbury New Zealand, PGCE
Dr C Alsop, PhD Durham, PGCE
Mr Naeem Mohammad, BSc MA Punjab, HDipEd Dublin
Mrs F Radley, BSc Bristol, PGCE
Ms D Schmidt, BEd MSc Pretoria
Mrs E Shingles, BSc Brunel, GTP [Maternity]
Mrs A Sutton-Jennings, BSc Sheffield, MSc Birmingham,
  QTS

Residential Staff:
Deputy Head Pastoral: Mrs H Simpson, BA Ed
Markham Housemistress: Miss O Kellaris, BA
Knatchbull Housemistress: Miss L Myers, BA, QTS
Loveday Housemistress: Mrs J Condliffe, BA, MA, PGCE
Assistant Housemistress First to Fourth: Miss L Stott
Assistant Housemistress Fifth to Upper Sixth: Miss R
  Johnson, BAL
Tutor in Residence Markham: Miss H Johnson, BSc, MSc
  Cardiff
Teacher in Residence Knatchbull: Miss A Figueira,
  Licence, PGCE

Director in Residence: Miss R Johnson, BA
Artist in Residence: Miss E Finnigan, BA Loughborough
Head Librarian: Ms A Kennedy, BA, MSc

Co-Curricular Staff:
Director of Teaching and Learning: Mr S Rhodes, BSc
  PGCE
Head of Alexander House: Miss N Stepp, BSc, PGCE
Head of Becket House: Mrs K Hammond, BEd
Head of Churchill House: Mr Naeem Mohammad, BSc
  MA Punjab, HDipEd Dublin
Head of Darwin House: Ms A Kennedy, BA MSc
School Chaplain and Charities Coordinator: Revd S Watts,
  BA BDiv
Duke of Edinburgh's Award: Mr D Moran, BA PGD
EPQ: Ms A Kennedy, BA MSc
Schools Partnerships: Mrs F Radley, BSc PGCE

Visiting Staff:
Arabic: Mrs A Surridge, BA, MA
Chinese: Mrs K Baldwin
French: Mrs A Langlois, Maitrise
German: Mrs K Davies, BA, PGCE
Italian: Dr G Galli, BA, PhD
Japanese: Mrs K Forrester, BA
Russian: Mrs M Strain, MA
Spanish: Mrs T Bello, BA
Learning Support: Mrs R Baxter, BA
Mrs J Hooper, BComm
Percussion: Mr R Smith
Guitar: Mr P Williams, BA
Violin: Mr S Perkins, BMus
Double Base: Mr Charlton, BA
Singing: Mr T Carleston, BMus
Mr A Thompson, BA
Miss N Parker, BA East Anglia
Piano: Miss E Krivenko, MMus
Harp: Mrs E Elliott, BA RSAMD
Flute: Mrs S Dunsdon
LAMDA:
Miss A Rooke, BA, GTP
Ms R Moir, BA, PGCE
Tennis: Mr N Ingham
Ballet and Pilates: Ms E Edwards
Modern and Zumba: Ms A Lewis
Squash: Mrs N Leader, BSc
Pilates: Mrs P Brewer

Support Staff:
Bursar: Mrs J Wood, JP, BA, Dip FM
Operations Manager: Mr P Lewis
Finance Manager: Mrs L Foster, FCMA
Accounts Assistant: Mrs T Vickers, BA Brighton
Resources Officer: Mrs T Barber
PA to Headmistress: Mrs J Witt
Secretary to the SLT: Mrs C Reader
Director of Admissions and Marketing: Mrs K Bertram,
  Grad CIPD
Marketing and Design Officer: Miss K Hook
Admissions Assistant: Mrs S Moore, BA, Dip HRM
Receptionist – Mon to Wed: Mrs S Davies
Receptionist – Wed to Fri: Mrs L Hide
Administrator: Mrs A Ardron
Data Manager: Ms A Shevills
Alumnae Officer: Mrs S van der Veen, MA
Domestic Bursar: Miss E Carrington
Deputy Domestic Bursar: Mrs J Burns
Chef: Mr J Eddyvean
Network Manager: Mr A Attan
Theatre Technician: Mr R Pearn, BA
Science Technicians:
Mr P Goldsbrough, BSc
Miss J Letley

Nurse: Mrs N Tomsett, NMC
Counsellor: Miss S Byrne
Listener: Ms E Manners
Chaplain: Revd S Watts, BA, BDiv
Head Librarian: Ms A Kennedy, BA, MSc
Deputy Librarian: Mr D Moran, BA, PGD
Clerk of Works: Mr R Cotterell
Groundsman: Mr P Thompson
Carpenter: Mr H Bowyer
Electrician: Mr C Smith
Maintenance: Mr F Baldwin

St Helen's School

Eastbury Road, Northwood, Middlesex HA6 3AS

Tel: 01923 843210
Fax: 01923 843211
email: enquiries@sthelens.london
admissions@sthelens.london
website: www.sthelens.london
Twitter: @StHelensSchool
Facebook: @sthelensnorthwood

Independent Day School for Girls founded in 1899.

St Helen's School has a commitment to academic excellence that has given us an enviable reputation for 120 years. Our belief in the importance of what we offer girls and young women is both considered and ardent. In a friendly, happy, welcoming, diverse School, set in over 21 acres of beautiful grounds in the heart of Northwood in North London, we provide an exceptional all-round education and develop our pupils and students through excellent academic teaching and by providing vibrant and exciting opportunities to extend their horizons and fulfil their potential.

Strong academic standards prevail in the Prep School, the Senior School and the Sixth Form, and we are extremely proud of our students' academic success – with 94.4% A*–C at A Level this year, 99.2% A*–C in unreformed GCSE subjects and 24% Grade 9s in reformed subjects – although St Helen's is about so much more than outstanding examination results.

We believe in celebrating the School as a community of wonderfully bright, energetic, creative and inspiring young people who contribute much and achieve so well. Our vibrant and varied co-curricular programme provides each girl with the opportunity to discover her talents and her passions. Our pupils, whether they start in Nursery, join us in Year 7, or choose our ambitious Sixth Form curriculum to prepare them for Higher Education, are the future of the School and they, as individuals and as a group, shape it, enrich it and give it its character. A Levels are offered in the Sixth Form, with girls able to choose from 30 subjects and going on to prestigious universities, including Oxford and Cambridge, after comprehensive support through the university applications and preparation process.

Our celebrated Futures Programme enables 6th form students to flourish in their lives beyond school: to develop the resilience, self-confidence, professional and networking skills to become the leaders of tomorrow in their chosen fields. We are proud to offer a comprehensive and personalised programme at St Helen's and in partnership with the Development Office provide a range of networking and mentoring opportunities in the transition to Higher Education and beyond. Underpinning our programme and approach is a commitment to ensuring that all students receive outstanding personalised guidance and are empowered to realise their aspirations. To enable girls to develop the self-awareness, opportunity awareness and career-man-

agement skills to succeed, there are a number of key strands to this programme: Curriculum Provision · Higher Education Planning · Professional Insight and Experience · Personalised Guidance.

With the support and guidance of exceptional pastoral care, girls at all ages and stages become well-rounded and well grounded. Every girl is valued for her unique qualities, with her own interests, strengths, gifts and talents, and we ensure that she is nurtured and supported and that success is as each girl defines it for herself.

By the time they leave us, our young women are confident and independent thinkers. In developing intellectual virtues such as an enquiring mind, openness to risk taking and respect for knowledge, and having developed core skills such as leadership, teamwork, time management, self-discovery, relationship management and building self-esteem alongside social and moral virtues, St Helen's students will not only be ready for university or for a career, they'll be ready to relish the challenges and rewards of a fulfilling life.

Most girls enter the School at one of our main entry points: Nursery (3+), Reception (4+), Year 7 (11+) or the Sixth Form (16+). We are members of The North London Independent Girls' Schools' Consortium

The curriculum is designed to enable every girl to achieve intellectual and personal fulfilment and to develop her talents to the full. We support the aims of the National Curriculum, but offer a wider range of subjects and teach to greater depth, so enabling the girls to explore their interests and talents. The staff are subject specialists whose aim is to inspire a love of their subjects. They help the girls to learn how to study independently and develop good study habits, through stimulating and rigorous teaching. On entry to the Senior School in Year 7, all girls study two modern foreign languages together with Latin. Science subjects are popular at all levels of the Senior School. We expect the girls to study with commitment and to develop qualities of intellectual curiosity and resilience. Music, Art, Drama and Sport are all an integral part of the life of the school and involve every girl. Many also take extra Music, Ballet, Speech & Drama lessons and Sports coaching.

Girls take a full part in the broader life of the school and, through co-curricular activities, discover new interests to complement their academic achievements. Clubs and societies abound, catering for the widest possible range of interests and hobbies, and we have a flourishing programme of optional outdoor and adventurous activities. We are recognised as an independent licensing authority for the Duke of Edinburgh's Award scheme, and many girls successfully complete their Bronze, Silver and Gold Awards. A full range of Combined Cadet Force activities is offered in partnership with Merchant Taylors' School, with whom we also organise 'Phab Week', an annual residential activity week for disabled children. Further co-curricular opportunities include Model United Nations, Young Enterprise and St Helen's University, a pioneering initiative designed to enable all girls in Years 7–9 to pursue wisdom and wellbeing beyond the curriculum and give them the opportunity to discover new interests and passions. The programme has been designed to respond to the needs of the whole student, aimed at developing intellectual virtues such as an enquiring mind, openness to intellectual risk taking and respect for knowledge, alongside social and moral virtues.

St Helen's is located on a spacious 21-acre greenfield site, with a new Prep School Building, Sixth Form Centre and a brand new, state-of-the-art School of Music opened in Autumn 2018. The School is easily accessible on the London Underground Metropolitan Line. Northwood Station is less than five minutes' walk from the school. The School also runs extensive and flexible coach services from the surrounding areas, including Beaconsfield, Watford, Stanmore, Finchley and Ealing.

Our popular Breakfast Club and after-school care programmes allow girls to extend their day in the safety of the school environment, where they are provided with refreshments and their activities are supervised by our qualified staff. The Mint Café, a Sixth Form facility during the school day, is available to all Senior School pupils from 7.30 am and after 4.00 pm.

Fees per term (2018–2019). Senior School £5,816, Prep School £4,613.

Registration Fee: £100.

Scholarships. Academic entry scholarships to Senior School are awarded annually at 11+ and 16+; Music Scholarships and Exhibitions are available at 11+ and 16+ for applicants of exceptional musical ability. Sport Scholarships are available at 11+ and 16+, and Sixth Form Art Scholarships are also awarded. St Helen's is committed to increasing access to girls who would thrive in our environment irrespective of their families' ability to pay the fees by expanding our Bursary provision; an academic Scholarship is awarded each year to a pupil at 14+.

St Helen's Alumnae Relations. Development Director: Ms Zoe Baines, email: zoe.baines@sthelens.london.

Charitable status. St Helen's School for Girls is a Registered Charity, number 312762. It exists to provide quality education for girls.

Council of Governors:

Chairman & Safeguarding Governor: Ms S Woolfson, BSc, FCA
Mrs M Bhandari, LLB, LLM, LPC
Mr N Boghani, BSc Hons, CA
Dr S Gordon, MA, DPhil Oxon
Ms P Mongia, MA, MEng Cantab, CEng, MRAeS, MBA
Mrs A Phillipson, MA Cantab, MBA, PGCE
Dr S M Pitts, MSc, MA, PhD
Mrs E Radice, MA Oxon, Cert Ed
Mr V Sapra, SFA, MBA, CEng, BEng, MICE
Mrs M Weerasekera, Mont Dip, LLB

Headmistress: Dr M Short, BA London, PhD Cantab

Deputy Head Pastoral & Designated Safeguarding Lead: Mrs D Sinclair, MA London
Deputy Head Academic & Deputy Designated Safeguarding Lead: Dr P Arnold, MA, DPhil Oxon
Head of the Prep School & Prep School Designated Safeguarding Lead: Mrs A Lee, MA Oxon
Business Director and Clerk to the Council: Mr M Mackenzie Crooks, BSc Oxford Brookes, MSc, MBA Cranfield

Director of Studies: Mr K Bulman, BSc City, MSc London
Director of Communications: Mrs A Saunders, MA Cantab

Pastoral Head of Sixth Form: Mr H Dymock, BA Durham, MA London
Head of Upper School: Mrs R Reidel-Fry, MPhil, MA Columbia USA, MA London
Head of Middle School: Mrs C Hill, BA Newcastle

Deputy Head, Prep School: Miss E Sami, MEd Herts
Deputy Head, Prep School: Mrs D Smith, BEd Warwick

Development Director: Ms Z Baines, BA Birmingham, MSc LSE

Senior School Staff:
* *Head of Department*

Art:
*Mrs N Smith, BA Sunderland, MA London
Mrs J George, BA Solent, MA London

Mr V Hazeldine, Diploma AD UAL
Mrs J Tibbs (*Technician*)

Classics:
*Dr A Berriman, BA Bristol, PhD Nottingham Trent
Dr P Arnold, MA, DPhil Oxon
Mr H Dymock, BA Durham, MA London
Mrs N O'Hagan, CertEd Westminster, BA Calabria Italy
Mrs S Zheng, BA Warwick

Computer Science:
*Mr M Hoffman, BA S Africa
Mrs C Gaikwad, BSc Bharati Vidyapeeth, India MSc Pune India
Mr P Martin, MA Cantab, LRSM
Mr R Shaikh, BA Brighton

Design & Technology:
*Mr R Shaikh, BA Brighton
Mr S Binning, BA Greenwich
Mrs L Hallam, BA Middlesex
Mrs M Olivera Smith, BSc Brunel
Mrs A Flash, BA Loughborough (*Technician*)

Drama:
*Mrs M Connell, BA Manchester Metropolitan (*Director of Drama*)
Mrs J Barton, BA Oxford Brookes
Mrs K Newby, BA Loughborough [leave of absence]
Mrs D Sinclair, MA London
Mrs H McGreal, BA Salford (*Speech & Drama*)

Economics & Business Studies:
*Mr M Khan, BSc Wollongong Dubai, MSc London
Mr L Casey, BA Wales, MA Middlesex

English:
*Mr R Johnston, BA Liverpool
Mrs Y Afnan, BA Southampton, MA Edinburgh
Ms S Ahmed, BA Essex, MA London
Mrs K Douglas, MA St Andrews
Mr T Gerig, BA Illinois
Miss J Tidd, BA Brighton
Mr A Williams, MA Cantab

Geography:
*Mrs K Whittingham, BSc Keele
Ms J Brew, MA Cantab
Mr D Froggatt, BSc Cardiff
Mr R Pimlott, BA Middlesex

History, Government & Politics and History of Art:
*Mrs J Begum, BA Bedfordshire, MA London
Mrs C Hill, BA Newcastle
Dr N Marx, BA Amherst, MA London, PhD Harvard
Mrs R Reidel-Fry, MPhil, MA Columbia, USA, MA London
Mr A Reynolds, BA Birmingham
Mrs H Sinclair, MA St Andrews
Mr P Whalley, BA Portsmouth

Individual Needs:
*Ms J Halmagyi, MA Debrecen Hungary, MA Middlesex, NASCO Middlesex
Mrs R Bird, BA London
Miss F Khundmir, BSc London
Ms P Vine, BA Exeter

Mathematics:
*Miss C Kerry, BEng London
Mr K Bulman, BSc City, MSc London
Mr K Chohan, BSc Birmingham
Miss G Day, BSc Durham
Dr J Donovan, Med, MSc, PhD London
Mrs J Hurley, BSc Sheffield
Mrs S King, BEng Bristol
Mr B Manivannan, BSc Eng Sri Lanka

Mrs S Michaels, BSc Manchester
Mrs T Onac, BSc London

Modern Foreign Languages:
*Mrs E Serrano, Filologia Inglesa Degree Madrid (*Head of Modern Foreign Languages and Spanish*)
*Mrs E Davis, BA Birmingham, MA Westminster (*Head of German, Deputy Head of Middle School Years 8–9*)
*Mr P Vines, BA UEA (*Head of French, Deputy Head of Upper School*)
*Ms J Lee, MSc London (*Subject Leader Mandarin*)
Mrs G Chuykov, BA Yaroslavl Russia, MA London
Mrs M Ishikawa, MA London
Miss L Louiset, BA MA Antilles
Miss E McKinley, BA Heriot-Watt
Mrs N O'Hagan, CertEd Westminster, BA Calabria Italy, BA Open
Mrs J Orme, BA Durham
Ms K Psihoda, BA London South Bank, MA London Metropolitan
Miss V Radom, Licentiate Paris, MA Jacksonville USA
Mrs A Savell, BA Cantab
Mrs Y Tang
Mrs N Wright, BA Manchester [leave of absence]
Ms M Deng (*Italian Assistant*)
Ms V Dopler (*German Assistant*)
Mrs C Gauci (*Spanish Assistant*)
Mrs B Lee (*Mandarin Assistant*)
Miss R Jin (*Mandarin Assistant*)
Miss P Nisavanh (*French Assistant*)
Dr Y O'Connor (*Japanese Assistant*)

Music:
*Mr P Martin, MA Cantab, LRSM (*Director of Music*)
Ms A Stobart, BA Nottingham, MEd Cantab, LRSM (*Assistant Director of Music*)

Music – Visiting:
Miss A-M Andritoiu, BMus Birmingham Conservatoire, MMus Trinity Laban
Ms C Barry, BA Mod Trinity College Dublin, LTCL
Miss J Chen, BMus, PG Dip Royal Academy of Music
Miss C Cook, BMus New Zealand, MA Wales
Mrs D Ellin, BMus Royal Scottish Academy of Music, PG Dip, LRAM
Mr A Gathercole, GGSM, ALCM Guildhall School of Music and Drama
Mrs S Gregory, LRAM, LTCL
Mr R Halford, GNVQ St Albans
Miss N Hawkins, GLCM, FLCM
Mr D Hester, Dip TCL, LTCL, PDOT Guildhall School of Music and Drama
Mr C Hooker, ARAM, LRAM, Dip RAM
Miss D Kemp, MA Oxon, Dip RCM, ARCM
Miss R Krbilkova, DiS Pardubice Conservatory Czech Republic
Mrs J Maclean, BSc City, LTCL
Mr I Marcus, LTCL
Mr N Martin, Cert NLP
Mr A McAfee, BA Nottingham Trent, PG Cert Trinity College of Music
Ms A Presswood, BMus Manchester, MMus Trinity Laban
Mrs S Stroh, LRAM, PG Dip RAM, BMus Hull
Miss E Tsampa, MA Royal Academy of Music, BMus Athens, LRAM

Physical Education:
*Miss J Hurt, BA Brunel (*Director of Sport*)
*Miss S Chadburn, BSc Sheffield Hallam (*Head of Curriculum PE, Senior School*)
*Mrs D Macey, BSc Brunel (*Head of Co-Curricular PE, Senior School*)
*Miss K Pickering, BA Chichester (*Head of Prep School PE*)

Mrs A Arnot, BEd Bedford
Mrs J Barton, BA Oxford Brookes
Mrs N Barton, BSc Loughborough
Miss H Harding, PTTLS Award
Miss S Heath, BEd Bedford, MA Brunel
Miss N Miller, BSc Leeds Metropolitan (*Deputy Head of Middle School Year 7*)
Miss B Roberts, BA Brighton

Psychology:
*Mrs A Hussain, MSc Brunel (*Subject Leader*)

Religious Studies, Philosophy & Ethics:
*Mr G Bezalel, MSc LSE, MA London (*Head of Academic Enrichment*)
Mr H Dymock, BA Durham, MA London
Miss S Hussey, BA Cantab
Mrs N Jehan, BA Middlesex
Mr E McCartney, BSc London
Mrs A Saunders, MA Cantab (*Director of Communications*)
Miss H Williams, MA Edinburgh

Science:
*Mrs A Adlam, BSc Southampton, MSc Imperial, MInstP (*Head of Science & Physics*)
*Mr M Reynish, BSc York (*Head of Chemistry*)
*Dr C Ryan, MChem Southampton, PhD London (*Head of Biology*)
Miss H Brand, BSc Bristol (*Deputy Head of Sixth Form*)
Mr N Dave, BSc London
Miss N Haridas, BSc London
Ms A James, BSc Durham
Dr C Jones, BSc Nottingham Trent, PhD London
Mr C Le Bas, BSc Edinburgh
Mrs H Lupton, BSc Open
Mrs A Scott, BSc East Anglia
Mrs S Thomas, MSci London
Mrs S Wardley, BSc Southampton
Mrs S Williams, BSc Exeter
Mrs M Wyburn, BSc Bath
Mrs Z Alidina, City & Guilds (*Pharmacy Technician*)
Mrs A Ghosh, BSc Calcutta (*Technician*)
Mrs B Lee, BEng China (*Technician*)
Mrs H Nguyen, BSc, MPhil Leicester (*Technician*)
Dr Y O'Connor, BSc MSc Kyoto Japan, PhD Tokyo Japan (*Technician*)

Library:
*Ms E Howard, BA Leicester, MA Roehampton, Dip Lib Metropolitan
Mrs S Gleave
Mrs R Serbos, BA Sheffield Hallam, MA London

St Helen's Prep School:

Head of Prep School: Mrs A Lee, MA Oxon

Deputy Head, Prep School: Miss E Sami, MEd Herts
Deputy Head, Prep School: Mrs D Smith, BEd Warwick
Phase Leader EYFS: Miss R Cox, BA Ryerson BEd Queen's University Ontario
Phase Leader KS1: Mrs D Roberts, BA Surrey
Phase Leader Years 3 & 4: Miss S Gupta, BA Roehampton
Phase Leader Years 5 & 6: Miss Z Farrell, MA St Andrews

Mrs L Baldwin, BEd Cantab
Mr M Barazi, BA Leeds
Mrs G Bass, MA Cantab
Mrs S Begley, BSc Bangor, MPhil Pontypridd
Miss M Bunce, BSc London
Mrs I Cane, BA Birmingham
Miss E Carey, BA Durham
Mrs H Casingena, LLAM Lamda
Mrs A Cawthorne, BSc Surrey, MA Middlesex

Mrs G Collins, BEd Queen's University Ontario, MA
  Calgary
Miss J Collins, BA Herts [leave of absence]
Miss S English, BA Portsmouth
Mr E Eshref, BA Middlesex
Mrs R Garton, BA Surrey
Miss N Gavigan, BSc Birmingham
Mrs A Groves, BA Brunel
Mr V Hazeldine, Diploma AD UAL
Mrs N Johar, BA Brunel
Ms D Kelly, BA, BEd Sydney
Mrs A Lam, BA Essex
Mrs N Lawson, BA Bath
Mrs R Marshall, BA UEA
Mrs D Moody, BEd Oxon [leave of absence]
Mrs H Morris, BA Winchester
Mrs G Parmar, BA Herts
Mrs M Parry, BA Warwick, MTeach London [leave of
  absence]
Miss K Pickering, BA Chichester (*Head of Prep School
  PE*)
Mrs P Prosser, BEd Durham
Mrs H Sansom, BEd Herts
Ms D Sarnat, BA Tel Aviv (*Head of Prep School Music*)
  [leave of absence]
Mrs J Seddon, BA Middlesex
Mrs R Sirera, BA MA Manchester
Miss J Van Krinks, BA Middlesex
Mrs M Watson, Bmus, LRAM, PG Dip Mus London
  (*Acting Head of Prep School Music*)
Mrs R Wilson, BA Leeds [leave of absence]
Mrs T Wood, BA Surrey
Mrs K Cook BA Exeter
Mrs S Johnson

Ballet Teachers:
Lead Ballet Teacher: Miss J Hale, BA Durham, LRAD,
  AISTD RAD, RTS
Mrs C Gillespie, BA Surrey, LRAD, ARAD, RAD, RTS
  [leave of absence]
Miss R Henry, BA Bath, LRAD, ARAD, RAD, RTS
Miss L Matthews, BA Surrey, LRAD, ARAD, DDE, RAD,
  RTS
Mrs M O'Brien, BA RAD, LRAD
Mrs A Philpott, BA Surrey, LRAD, ARAD, AISTD RAD,
  RTS
Miss S Price, CSB Dip RAD, Dip ARAD, AISTD RAD,
  RTS
Miss S Ross, BA Surrey, RAD, RTS
Miss G Yiannakas, BA Surrey, LRAD, ARAD, RAD, RTS
Miss S Aoki, BSc MSc London ARAD RAD RTS (*Piano
  Accompanist*)
Miss A Tetsuya, BMus London, MMus RCM, Dip
  ABRSM (*Piano Accompanist*)

St James Senior Girls' School

Earsby Street, London W14 8SH
Tel: 020 7348 1777; Admissions: 020 7348 1748
email: admissions@sjsg.org.uk
website: www.stjamesgirls.co.uk

Motto: *Speak the truth. Live generously. Aim for the best.*

Founded in 1975, St James Senior Girls' School is a day
school for 265 pupils aged from 11–18. We are situated on a
spacious site in Olympia, West Kensington, shared with our
own Junior School.

We offer an education which nurtures and enriches the
physical, intellectual, emotional and spiritual development
of our pupils. Our happy, united atmosphere provides the
ideal environment for every girl to discover her own unique
combination of strengths and talents and to 'be the best she
can'.

St James girls are industrious, open-hearted and courageous; they work together, enjoying others' successes as
well as their own. They achieve the highest academic standards and are also encouraged to develop strength through
self-discipline and an ability to live according to an intelligent understanding of what is wise and true. Regular opportunities for stillness and quiet enable pupils to learn to be at
ease with themselves, to appreciate the value of being fully
present and to develop their ability to concentrate.

Our teachers have excellent subject knowledge and give
their time generously to support the well-being and development of their pupils. Relationships throughout the school are
extremely positive and are characterised by a spirit of love,
trust and mutual respect.

Whilst admission to the school is through a selective procedure, the school seeks to admit those candidates who are
able and willing to make good use of the education offered.
We aim to foster creativity and intellectual curiosity, challenging our pupils to achieve excellence. Standards in public
examinations are high: nearly all leavers proceed to Higher
Education degree courses either at university, a specialist
music college or to pursue an art foundation course.

The Curriculum offers a wide-ranging education including PSHEE, SMSC, citizenship, philosophy and religious
studies as well as leadership training, public speaking and
debating. Community Service runs throughout the school.
Careers Guidance is offered to all pupils from Years 7–13.

Subjects available to GCSE/IGCSE: art, biology, chemistry, classical Greek, computer science, drama, English language, English literature, French, geography, history, Latin,
mathematics, music, physical education, physics, religious
studies, Sanskrit and Spanish. Year 7 are taught General Science prior to commencing the three separate sciences in
Year 8. Year 7 also receive lessons in textiles and the Art of
Hospitality.

Subjects offered at A Level: art and design, biology,
chemistry, drama and theatre, English, French, geography,
Greek, history, history of art, Latin, mathematics, further
mathematics, music, physics, psychology, religious studies,
Sanskrit and Spanish. Students also take the Extended Project Qualification, a project which develops research and
independent learning skills.

The Sixth Form. Most pupils stay on to complete their
education in the Sixth Form. This is treated as a very distinct
stage and pupils' growth in initiative and responsibility is
supported and encouraged. The PSHEE and SMSC programme is continued in order to provide support for personal development through a series of talks, debates and
workshops. Emphasis is given to academic excellence and
the cultivation of social awareness and, in particular, leadership skills are developed through assuming responsibility
for younger pupils in the school. In Year 12 students are
offered a community service project abroad to South Africa
to trek in the wilderness and do volunteer work in a Zulu village.

Creative Arts. The performing arts are strong features of
the school. There is a tradition of choral and solo singing, as
well as instrumental music making. Most of our productions
take place in our assembly hall, fully equipped with lighting
and sound. There are several choirs, orchestras and instrumental ensembles and girls are strongly encouraged to take
up individual instruction with one of our visiting instrumental and/or vocal teachers. There are performance opportunities for all pupils every year: the Lower School (Years 7–9)
perform a play one year, a musical the following year and
vice versa for the Upper School (Years 10–13). Recent

Lower School productions include: *The Lion King* (2017) and *Arabian Nights* (2016). Recent Upper School productions include: *Les Misérables* (2017) and *The Wizard of Oz* (2015). Pupils also have the opportunity to perform in the school's Youth Dance Company and music, speech, debating, dance and other artistic competitions. There is also an annual Arts Week during which pupils have the opportunity to take part in various workshops.

Physical Education. Sports and PE is an important part of school life. Athletics, gymnastics, health related fitness, lacrosse, netball, rounders, football, cross country, team building, and tennis are all offered. We have a playground and gymnasium on site and use the facilities at Barn Elms Sports Centre and King's House Sports Ground which are a 15-minute coach journey from the school. There is also an annual Sports Week during which pupils take part in various trips and hear presentations from high profile sportswomen.

Extra-Curricular Activities. Pupils are offered a wide range of clubs including art, classics, cookery, dance, drama, lacrosse, netball, football, karate, politics, rounders, science, The Duke of Edinburgh's Award, ICT, choirs and orchestras. Years 7–11 attend an annual Activity Week with their own class at a variety of locations within and outside the UK. There is a biennial ski trip and a biennial trip to Pompeii. There are also trips to Berlin and Iceland.

Admission. For entry at 11+ girls sit the London 11+ Consortium Entrance examination; at Sixth Form candidates are required to sit an entrance exam and to attain the necessary GCSE grades for A Level study. For occasional vacancies in Years 8, 9 and 10 candidates will need to take an entrance examination.

Fees per term (2018–2019). £6,700.

Bursaries. There are limited funds available for Bursary assistance. Awards are discretionary and based on a full financial enquiry into parents' means by the Bursary Fund Committee. The funds are primarily to assist children already attending St James, but some help may be available to new parents in specific circumstances. Enquiries should be made in the first instance to the Bursar.

Charitable status. The Independent Educational Association Limited is a Registered Charity, number 270156. It exists to provide education for children.

Governors:
Mr Jeremy Sinclair, CBE (*Chair*)
Mrs Koula Ansell, BA Hons
Mrs Jennie Buchanan, Montessori Dip
Mr George Cselko, BA Hons
Mr Aatif Hassan, BSc, CA (*Joint Deputy Chairman*)
Mrs Miranda Munden, BA Hons, PGCE
Mr John Story, FRICS (*Joint Deputy Chairman*)
Mr Hugh Venables, BSc, MBA
Mr Jerome Webb, MA, MRICS
Dr Fenella Willis, MBBS, MRCP, MRCPath, BSc

Headmistress: Mrs Sarah Labram, BA

Deputy Heads:
Mr Bertie Cairns, MA Oxon, QTS (*Academic*)
Ms Charlotte de la Peña, BA, MA, PGCE (*Pastoral*)

Assistant Head: Miss Anna Holliss, BA, QTS

Head of Sixth Form: Mrs Yolanda Saunders, BA, PGCE
Assistant Head of Sixth Form: Mrs Sarah Ashbolt, BA, BA, MA, PGCE

Head of Lower School (*Year 7*): Mrs Melissa George, MA, PGCE
Head of Middle School (*Years 8 & 9*): Mr Steve Allen, MA Cantab, MSci, PGCE
Head of Upper School (*Years 10 & 11*): Mrs Monica Wraith, Dip HND, Cert Ed

Teaching Staff:
Miss Joanna Adamkiewicz, MSc, PGCE (*Teacher of Mathematics*)
Ms Beatriz Aenlle Colado, QTS (*Teacher of Spanish*) [maternity cover]
Mr Stephen Allen, MA Cantab, MSci, PGCE (*Teacher of Chemistry*)
Ms Sarah Ashbolt, BA, BA, MA, PGCE (*Head of Psychology*)
Mrs Edel-Anne Bailey, MA Cantab, QTS, MSt (*Head of English*)
Miss Lauren Berridge, BA, PGDE (*Teacher of PE*)
Mrs Rebecca Candy, MA Cantab, PGCE (*Head of Religious Studies*)
Mlle Mylène Chaudagne, Licence, MA, PGCE (*Head of Modern Foreign Languages, Senior Teacher Pastoral*)
Ms Julia Childs, BA, MA, Dip (*Teacher of English and Learning Support*)
Dr Josef Craven, BA, MPhil, PhD (*Head of History and Citizenship*)
Mr Jonathan Crowe, BA, PGCE (*Teacher of History*)
Mrs Eileen Damzen, BA QTS (*SENDCO*)
Mr Nicholas de Mattos, BA PGCE (*Teacher of Classics*)
Miss Rachel Edmunds, BA, PGCE (*Head of PSHEE, Teacher of English*)
Ms Pauline Flannery, MA, PGCE (*Head of Drama, Senior Teacher Pastoral*)
Mrs Melissa George, MA, PGCE (*Teacher of English*)
Ms Ioanna Georgiou, MSc, MPhil, QTS, FIMA, CMath Teach (*Second in Mathematics Department, Head of Academic Enrichment*)
Miss Lisa Hayat, MA, PGCE (*Head of History of Art*)
Miss Anna Holliss, BA, QTS (*Head of PE*)
Mr Peter Holloway, BA, PGCE (*Head of Music*)
Mr Alastair Horsford, BA, QTS (*Head of Geography, Senior Teacher Academic*)
Mrs Elena Jessup, BSc, MA (*Teacher of Sanskrit*)
Mr Warwick Jessup, BA Oxon, MA, MPhil (*Head of Sanskrit*)
Mr Mark Kerrigan, BSc, PGCE, MTL (*Head of ICT and Computer Science*)
Mrs Sally Kuhrt, BA (*Head of Art of Hospitality*)
Mr Kenneth MacLean, BSc, MSc, PGCE (*Head of Science and Biology*)
Mrs Jane Mason, MA Oxon, PGCE (*Head of Classics*)
Mrs Helena McDowell, BA, QTS (*Teacher of Geography*)
Miss Julie Menon, Licence Maitrise (*Teacher of French*)
Mr Ben Mohammed, BSc, PGCE (*Head of Mathematics, Senior Teacher Academic*)
Miss Annette Morgan, Dip EAL Cambridge Cert (*Teacher of Sanskrit*)
Mrs Yolanda Saunders, BA, PGCE (*Teacher of Classics*)
Miss Niamh Somers, BA, PGCE (*Teacher of Biology*)
Mrs Gordana Tarundzioska, BEd, BSc (*Teacher of Mathematics*)
Mr David Treloar, BA, PG Dip (*Teacher of Art*)
Mrs Lynsey Walters, BA, QTS (*Teacher of PE, Head of Outdoor Pursuits*)
Mr Tomas White, BSc, PGCE (*Head of Chemistry, EVC, School Diary Coordinator*)
Mrs Montserrat Wight-Rahona, BA, QTS (*Head of Spanish*) [maternity leave]
Mrs Monica Wraith, Dip HND, Cert Ed (*Head of Art*)
Mr Stuart Young, BSc, QTS (*Head of Physics, Head of ICT Strategy*)
Mr Henryk Zdzienski, BSc, MPhil, PGCE (*Teacher of Science*)

Support Staff:
Mrs Katharine Boddy, BA, PGCE (*Library Assistant*)
Mrs Alison Buchanan (*Examinations Officer*)

Mrs Selina Coleman, RSci Tech (*Senior Laboratory Technician*)

Mrs Carla Escoto Montero, Psic (*Science Laboratory Assistant and Art Technician*)

Mrs Emily Johnston, AMI Mont Dip, ITEC Dip (*Meditation Programme Coordinator and Well-being Coach*)

Ms Bernadette O'Gorman, RN (*School Nurse*)

Mrs Eleanor Parker, MA (*Librarian*)

Administrative Staff:
Mrs Sue Allen (*Registrar & School Uniform*)
Miss Abigail Davies BA (*School Secretary*)
Miss Kelly Farrell (*Sixth Form Receptionist*)
Miss Hermione Fricker, BA, PG Dip (*PA to Headmistress & Director of Education*)
Mrs Lindsey Kavanagh, BA, MCIM (*Marketing Manager*)
Ms Leah Murray (*Events Manager*)
Miss Mikyla Taylor (*Secretary to the Deputy Heads*)

Bursary:
Mr William Wyatt (*Bursar*)
Ms Dorte Newman (*Finance Manager*)
Ms Charlotte Grinsted, BA (*Accounts*)
Ms Suzette Lindor, AAT (*School Fees Secretary*)
Ms Esiri Mac-Jaja, MA, Assoc CIPD (*HR Manager*)
Ms Loy Phillips, BA (*PA to Bursar*)

Property Management:
Mr Jeff Griffin, MBIFM, Tech IOSH (*Site Manager*)
Mr Salah Chebiouni
Mr Karl Graham
Mr Dushan Jokic

Director of Education:
Mrs Laura Hyde, Cert Ed, MEd

Development Office:
Mrs Kim Brown (*Development Manager*)
Mrs Lindsey Kavanagh (*Development Officer*)
Miss Ellie Mello, BA, MA (*Development Assistant*)

St Margaret's School for Girls
Aberdeen

17 Albyn Place, Aberdeen AB10 1RU

Tel:	01224 584466
Fax:	01224 585600
email:	info@st-margaret.aberdeen.sch.uk
website:	www.st-margaret.aberdeen.sch.uk
Twitter:	@StMegsAbdn
Facebook:	@StMargaretsSchoolForGirls
LinkedIn:	/St-Margaret's-School-for-Girls

Founded in 1846, St Margaret's School is the oldest all-through girls' school in Scotland and the Head is a member of the Girls' Schools Association, Scottish Girls' Schools Group and Schools Leaders Scotland. Education is provided for around 380 girls from Nursery to Sixth Year. The Nursery is within the main building, and boys and girls are admitted from the age of 3 years.

St Margaret's School is conveniently situated in the west end of Aberdeen. The school's excellent facilities include spacious, well-equipped science laboratories, dining room, art studio, an attractive music suite, a fine gymnasium, playing fields and a pavilion at Summerhill. The school has three computer suites, and the whole school is networked.

Aims. We aim to provide a stimulating education for girls in an all-through school where each girl is encouraged to realise her potential in a friendly, caring atmosphere. The school also aims to provide public benefit through the advancement of education. We encourage staff and girls to contribute to the development of Scottish education.

Curriculum. Girls are prepared for National 5, Higher and Advanced Higher examinations of the Scottish Qualifications Authority. National examinations can be taken for awards in music and drama.

The curriculum includes Art and Design, Biology, Business Management, Chemistry, Classical Studies, Computer Studies, Drama, Economics, English (language and literature), Food Technology, French, Geography, German, History, Information Systems, Latin, Mathematics, Modern Studies, Music, Personal and Social Education, Philosophy, Physical Education, Physics, Religious and Moral Education and Spanish.

Girls are encouraged to take part in extracurricular activities which include dance, swimming, drama, debating, computer club, science club, Scripture Union, junior and senior orchestra, woodwind ensemble, junior, senior and chamber choir, The Duke of Edinburgh's Award, Young Enterprise, Highland dancing, chess and Choi Kwang Do.

Admission. Girls are admitted to the School by informal or formal assessment.

Fees per term (2018–2019). Nursery (10 half day sessions) £2,287–£3,660; 1 Junior £2,088–£3,341; 2 Junior £2,220–£3,553; 3 Junior £2,748–£4,396; 4 Junior £2,815–£4,504; 5, 6 and 7 Junior £2,932–£4,691; I to VI Senior £3,308–£5,292

These fees include SQA examination fees and all books and materials for nursery and early years classes; they are payable termly with an option to pay monthly. A reduction is made when three or more siblings attend at the same time.

Means-tested bursaries are available for entry to 6 Junior upwards.

Charitable status. St Margaret's School for Girls is a Registered Charity, number SC016265. It exists to provide a high quality education for girls.

School Council:
Prof Margaret Ross (*Chair*)
Mr J M Baillie, BSc Hons, MEng
Mr A Bannister, BA, CA
Dr R Vij, PhD, MPhil, MA, BA
Mr I F McLennan, LLB, BA Hons Hum, NP
Prof E Gammie, Dip M, BA, CA, PhD
Dr J House, MBBS, MRCGP
Revd Dr R Smith (*ex officio*)
Mrs F Littlejohn (*ex officio*)
Mrs A Everest, BA Hons

Clerk to the Council: Mr A R Mountain

Head: Miss Anna Tomlinson, MTheol Hons, PGCE

Deputy Head: Mrs S Lynch, MA Hons, PGCE (*Modern Languages*)

Senior Staff:
* *Head of Department*
§ *Part-time or Visiting*

Mr R Adair, BSc Hons, PGCE Sec (**Chemistry*)
§Miss J Aitken, BEd (*Physical Education*)
Mrs L Arthur, BSc Hons, MSc, PGCE (*ICT9*)
Mrs T Scott (**Art & Design*)
Ms S Brown, BEd, ATCL (*Music*)
Mrs A Bryce, BSc Hons, PGCE (*Mathematics*)
Mrs S Cooper Weber (*English*)
Mr G Cunningham, MA Hons, PGCE Sec (**Economics and *History*)
Mrs D Dale, MA, PGCE S (*English*)
Miss S Forgie, BA Hons, PGCE (*Modern Languages*)
Mrs V Gerbrandy
Mrs L Goodwin, BEd (**Speech and Drama*)

Mrs L Gurney, LTCL (*Music – Woodwind*)
Mrs L Howitt, BSc Hons, PGDE (*Biology and Chemistry*)
Mrs H Jennings, BD, PGCE (*History, *Philosophy and *RMPE*)
Mrs S Lynch, MA Hons, PGCE (*Modern Languages*)
Ms E MacDonald (*English*)
Mrs S MacFadyen, BSc, PGCE (*Mathematics*)
§Mrs A Miller, BSc Hons, PGCE (**Biology*)
Miss E Moore, BSc Hons Physics, BSc Medical Physics, PGDE (**Physics*)
§Mrs H Nehring, BA, PGCE (*Modern Languages*)
Mrs K Norval, BEd Hons (**Physical Education*)
§Mrs S Stirton, MA Hons, PGDE (*History*)
Mr P Parfitt, BA Hons, MMus (**Music*)
Mrs J Reid, BEd Hons (*Physical Education*)
Mr G Rennet (*Geography and Modern Studies*)
§Mrs J Richardson, BA Hons, PGCE (*Art and Design*)
§Mrs J Robson, GRSC pt11, PGCE (*Chemistry*)
Mrs J Slater, Dip Comm (**Business Mgt, Word Processing, Guidance and PSE*)
Mrs S Smith, BA Hons, PGCE (**Mathematics*)
§Mrs S Hendry, BSc Hons, PGDE (*Biology, Physics*)
§Mrs L Tapper, BSc Hons, PGCE (*Mathematics*)
Mrs S Torrie (**English*)
Mrs M Wiedermann, ATCL, AMusTCL (*Head of Strings*)

Junior Department:
Ms A Dressel, BSc, PGCE
Mrs J Garden, BEd Primary
Mrs N Murray, BSc Hons PGCE (**Head of Junior School*)
Mrs E Gibb
Mrs G Wyatt
§Mrs L Reilly, MA, CertEd
Mrs M Smith, BEd, PGC Inclusive Practice
Mrs P Twigg, BA Hons, PGDE (*Principal Teacher*)
Mrs S Wightman, BEd Hons, PGCE Autism and Learning

Classroom Assistants:
Mrs C Duncan, HNC
Miss G Gray, SVG4 Playwork
Mrs D Gregory, SVQ2 in Care

Nursery at St Margaret's:
Mrs L Dredge
Miss W Fraser, HNC Childcare & Education SVQ Level 3
Miss A Milne
Miss J Minett, BA Hons Childhood and Youth Studies (**Early Years Coordinator*)

Support for Learning:
*Ms L Hawthorn
Mrs J Kerridge
§Mrs J Robson, GRSC pt11, PGCE

Administrative Staff:
Bursar: Mr A R Mountain
Finance Manager: Mrs M Miller
Finance Assistant: Mrs J Smith
PA to Head: Ms K Schmitz
Admissions: Miss N Shepherd
Marketing Officer: Mrs A Ramsay
Alumnae Relations & Events Officer: Mrs F Littlejohn
School Administrator/Receptionist: Mrs M Coutts
ICT Technician: Mr C Morris, BSc Hons
Laboratory Technician: Miss K Mackie, ONC, HNC, Bio Sci
Facilities Manager: Mr D Cordiner
Art Technician: Miss I Andrianova
Janitors: Mr B Henderson & Mr J Grant

After-School Care and Playground Supervision:
Mrs A Cameron
Mrs S Crabb
Miss W Fraser, HNC Childcare & Education SVQ Level 3 (*After-School Care*)

Miss H Limanton
Miss J Minett, BA Hons Childhood and Youth Studies (**Early Years Coordinator*)
Mrs S Flores

There are also visiting instrumental teachers for strings, brass and percussion and three modern language assistants for French, German and Spanish.

St Mary's School
Colchester

Lexden Road, Colchester, Essex CO3 3RB
Tel: 01206 572544 (Office)
01206 594180 (Registrar)
Fax: 01206 576437
email: info@stmaryscolchester.org.uk
website: www.stmaryscolchester.org.uk
Twitter: @stmaryscolch
Facebook: @stmaryscolchester

Motto: *Scientia et Veritas*

St Mary's – a happy, high achieving school
At St Mary's the emphasis is on encouraging pupils to be happy and to make the most of all the opportunities school life brings. When they feel secure and supported, pupils are able to do their best academically and also to develop as individuals, finding confidence, talents and interests that will bring them pleasure and fulfilment throughout their lives.

Lessons at St Mary's are lively and designed to encourage a real enthusiasm for learning among girls aged 3 to 16 (and boys aged 3 to 4 in the Kindergarten). Art, drama, music, sport and all manner of other activities are also entered into with great energy and our pupils' achievements across the board never cease to amaze.

St Mary's has a happy and caring atmosphere. In this very positive culture, pupils are keen to achieve, and this leads to success. St Mary's pupils' GCSE results are consistently among the best in the area – in 2018, 96% of St Mary's GCSE entries were graded four or C or above – and SATs results are well above the national expectations, with many pupils achieving grammar school places and St Mary's Senior School scholarships. All this, despite the fact that St Mary's is not an academically selective school.

"I am always delighted to see our pupils' hard work pay off," says St Mary's Principal Mrs Hilary Vipond, "but what makes me most proud is meeting former pupils who tell me that without the happy and focused education they received at St Mary's they wouldn't be the positive and successful individuals that they are today. They look back on their school days with fondness – 'once a St Mary's girl, always a St Mary's girl'!"

Fees per term (2018–2019). Senior School: £4,795–£4,995; Lower School: £3,260–£4,090; Kindergarten: from £48.30 per day. Fees are inclusive of accident insurance, lunch and drinks (including milk in the Lower School), as well as extra tuition and learning support if required.

Charitable status. St Mary's School (Colchester) Limited is a Registered Charity, number 309266.

Chair of Governors: Mrs M Haddrell

Principal: **Mrs H Vipond**, BSc Hons, MEd, CertEd, DipEd, NPQH

Director of Senior School: Miss A Jones, BEd, NPQH

Director of Lower School: Mrs E Stanhope, GMus, NPQH

Bursar: Mr S Cooke

Registrar: Mrs J Tierney

St Mary's School
Gerrards Cross

Packhorse Road, Gerrards Cross, Buckinghamshire SL9 8JQ

Tel: 01753 883370
Fax: 01753 890966
email: registrar@st-marys.bucks.sch.uk
website: www.stmarysschool.co.uk
Twitter: @StMarysSchoolGX
Facebook: @St-Marys-School-Gerrards-Cross

Badge: *Ecce Ancilla Domini*

Founded by Dean Butler in 1872. Formerly at Lancaster Gate. Established in Gerrards Cross in 1937 as an Independent Day School catering for 340 day girls.

The School is situated in the attractive residential area of Gerrards Cross which is surrounded by beautiful countryside, 20 miles from London, close to the M25 and A40/M40, on the main bus routes and 10 minutes from the Railway Station.

The aim of the School is to provide an excellent academic and rounded education leading on to University for day girls between the ages of 3 and 18 and to enable each of them to develop their own talents and personalities in a happy, caring and purposeful environment, and to become successful, fulfilled adults.

Curriculum. Subjects offered include English Language and Literature, History, Geography, RE, Drama, French, German, Spanish, Business Studies, Economics, Information Technology, Mathematics, Psychology, Chemistry, Biology, Physics, Music, Art & Design, Food & Nutrition, Gymnastics, Hockey, Netball, Tennis, Rounders, Football, Rugby, Swimming, Media, Personal, Social, Cultural and Health Education, Dancing and other sporting activities. Regular trips are made to places of educational interest, field courses are undertaken, foreign visits including a ski trip to the USA are arranged, and there is highly successful participation in The Duke of Edinburgh's Award scheme and Young Enterprise. There is an excellent staff to pupil ratio.

Examinations: Girls are prepared for Entrance to the Universities and Colleges in all subjects; for the General Certificate of Education at AS, A Level and GCSE/IGCSE Level; Associated Board Examinations in Music and examinations in Speech and Drama (LAMDA). The School is an 11+ centre.

The Buildings are a highly attractive mixture of old and new and include two Libraries, Dining Hall, a Science Block with Laboratories, a Geography Room, a large open-plan Art Studio, a Home Economics Room, Textiles Room, two Computer Suites, a modern Sixth Form Centre, Cedar House which opened in 2016, two Music Rooms, Drama Studio, Chapel and two Assembly Halls/Gymnasiums equipped to the highest standards. The Prep Department, in the grounds of the Senior School, comprises an Early Years Centre, Paddington House, and two modern purpose-built blocks, with a Science Laboratory, Hall, Gymnasium, Textiles/Art room and ICT suite. The lovely grounds include tennis and netball courts, a hockey pitch and an athletics lawn. There is a Sport England full-size Sports Hall. Cherry Tree House, a new classroom block, opened in September 2018.

School Hours. The hours are 8.30 am – 3.45 pm. The School year is divided into 3 terms.

Reports are sent to Parents at the end of each term and there are regular Parent/Staff meetings. The School also communicates with Parents via ParentMail.

Fees per term (2018–2019). £1,890–£5,660.

Scholarships and Bursaries. Academic scholarships are available at 7+, 11+ and at 16+ in the Sixth Form. There are also Art, Drama, Music and Sports scholarships at 11+. A means-tested Bursary scheme is in operation.

Charitable status. St Mary's School (Gerrards Cross) Limited is a Registered Charity, number 310634. It provides education for girls from Early Years to A Level in a well-structured, academic and caring environment.

Governors:
Chairman: Mr D Wilson, BA, FCA
Mrs C Bayliss, Cert Ed
Mr D Campkin, ACA, BSc Hons
Mrs C Eilerts de Haan, MSc Chem Tech
Mrs M Hall, MA Cantab, CPA, EPA
Mr N Hallchurch, LLB Hons
Mrs R Martin, MEd, NPQH, FRSA
Mr N Moss, MNAEA
Mrs Helen Phillips, BA Hons

Senior Leadership Team:

Headmistress: Mrs P J Adams, MA Oxon (*French and Spanish*)

Bursar: Mr D Martin, BSc Hons London
Deputy Head: Mrs J Kingston, BSc Hons Cardiff, MPhil Bath (*Chemistry*)
Head of Preparatory Department: Mrs M Carney, BA Hons Galway (*Year 6 Class teacher*)
Director of Studies, Preparatory Department: Miss S Radburn, BA Hons Leeds (*Year 5 Class Teacher*)
Assistant Head Marketing and Communications: Mr J Dodd, MTL Birmingham City (*Business and Economics*)
Assistant Head Academic Transition and Key Stage 3: Mrs J Deadman, BEd Hons Exeter (*PSHCE*)
Assistant Head Staff Development: Mr A Gibb, BA Hons Queens (*English*)
Director of IT and Systems Management: Miss H Snaith, MA Canterbury Christ Church (*ICT*)

Senior School:
Mr A Adams, BSc Hons London (*Physics*, *Chemistry*)
Mrs E Beasley, BA Hons Cambridge (*Geography*)
Mr P Boland, BEng Hons McGill (*Head of Science*, *Physics*)
Mrs K Cork, BA Hons Durham (*Head of Psychology*)
Mr S Cox, BA East Anglia (*Head of Politics*)
Mrs J Davison, BA Hons Leicester (*History*)
Mr P Fernando, BA Hons Nottingham, MLitt St Andrews (*Head of Business and Economics*)
Mrs W Fox, MA Cambridge (*Biology*)
Mrs Z Glenister, BA Hons Newcastle upon Tyne (*Teacher in Charge of KS4, German, French*)
Mrs J Good, Hons Leeds (*Head of Sixth Form, Dance*)
Mr J Heath, BSc Hons Loughborough (*Head of Humanities, Geography*)
Miss R Hillier, BA Hons Sussex (*Director of Enrichment, Senior House Mistress, Religious Studies*)
Miss K Kaaber-Gore, BA Hons Cumbria (*English*)
Mrs K Kalinowski, BA Royal Central School of Speech and Drama (*Head of Drama*)
Mrs I Martin, MA Cambridge (*Biology*)
Mrs E McNally, BA Hons West of England (*Head of English*)
Miss L Murphy, BA UCL (*French, Spanish*)
Ms J Newton, BA Hons The London Institute (*Head of Art*)

Mrs J Phillips, MA Beds (*Head of Expressive Arts and Director of Music*)
Mr I Plunket, BSc Hons King's College London (*Science*)
Mrs F Qureshi, BSc London (*Head of Mathematics*)
Miss K Reid, BEd Hons Brighton (*Mathematics*)
Mrs F Ritchie, BA Hons Exeter (*French, Spanish*)
Mrs E Roberts, BEd Hons Sheffield (*Food & Nutrition, Textiles, Housemistress Kirk*)
Mrs B Sivaramalingam, MA London (*Mathematics*)
Miss H Snaith, MA Canterbury Christ Church (*Director of ICT and Systems Management*)
Mrs K Stansfield, MA York (*Head of History*)
Mrs G Sugrue, BA Hons Northampton, AMBDA PG Cert SpLD L7 (*Support for Learning*)
Mrs B Taylor, PGD Leeds, BA Hons de Montfort, OCR L7 SpLD (*Head of Support for Learning*)
Mrs S Taylor, BA Hons Kent, MA Kent (*French, Spanish*)
Miss E Warburton, BSc Hons Warwick (*Chemistry*)
Mrs R Webster, BA Leeds (*Head of Physical Education*)
Mrs S Wells, MA Ed UCL (*Head of Modern Foreign Languages*)
Mr C Wild, BA Tufts USA (*Mathematics*)
Miss C Wilkins, BA Hons St Mary's Twickenham (*Physical Education, Duke of Edinburgh Coordinator*)
Mrs H Williams, BA Hons Cardiff (*Assistant Head of Sixth Form, Head of Media Studies, English*)
Mrs T Wingfield, MA Oxford Brookes (*Chemistry*)

Preparatory Department:
Mrs A Bishop, LLB Liverpool Polytechnic School of Law (*Music Coordinator*)
Mrs S Brereton, BA Hons Leicester (*Y3 Class Teacher, Mathematics Coordinator*)
Mrs R Brown, BA Hons West of England (*Art*)
Mrs S Burton, BA Leeds (*Teacher of English*)
Mrs M Carney, BA Hons Galway (*Y6 Class Teacher, Head of Prep Department*)
Miss G Connell, BA Hull (*Y1 Class Teacher*)
Mrs L Gibson, NVQ Level 3 (*Teaching Assistant*)
Miss R Heath, BA Winchester (*Y5 Class Teacher*)
Mrs K Hemsworth, BEd de Montfort (*Y5 Class Teacher, Physical Education and 11+ Coordinator*)
Mrs M Keal, Level 4 Dyslexia Certificate (*Learning Support Coordinator*)
Miss S Radburn, BA Hons Leeds (*Y5 Class Teacher, Director of Studies*)
Mrs E Roche, BSc Hons Leeds (*KS2 Art/Design Technology Specialist*) [Maternity Leave]
Miss R Rose, BA Hons Plymouth (*EYFS Teacher, Pre Prep Coordinator*)
Mrs T Smith, Foundation Bucks NVQ Level 3 (*Teaching Assistant*)
Mrs C Stuart-Lee, MA Oxon (*French*)
Miss K Sweeney, BA Hons Plymouth (*Y4 Class Teacher*)
Miss O Trangmar, Art Foundation Bucks New University (*Teaching Assistant*)
Mrs K Williams, Higher Level Teaching Assistant (*Teaching Assistant*)

Non-Teaching Staff:
Mrs Z Arcari, BA Hons (*Head of Marketing*)
Mrs S Chapman, MSc King's College London (*Science Technician*)
Mrs L Chorley (*Administration Assistant*)
Mrs L Dimmock (*Attendance Officer/Receptionist*)
Mr C Gutteridge (*Assistant Caretaker*)
Mrs S Jenkins (*Administration Assistant, First Aid Officer*)
Mrs H Kelly (*Assistant to the Bursar*)
Miss V Leisos, BA Hons UAL (*Art & Food Technician & Administrative Support*)
Mr D Long (*Site Manager*)
Mrs S Murray (*Librarian*)
Mrs M Nemec AAT (*Assistant to the Bursar*)

Mrs C Panayiotou, BA Hons Kent (*Head of Digital Media*)
Mr R Petersen (*Caretaker*)
Mrs Y Rogers (*Examinations Officer*)
Mrs C Sylvester (*PA to the Headmistress*)
Mrs E Szczerbiak (*Registrar*)

St Mary's School
Shaftesbury

Shaftesbury, Dorset SP7 9LP
Tel: 01747 852416 (General Enquiries)
          01747 857111 (Admissions)
Fax: 01747 851557
email: enquiries@stmarys.eu
website: www.stmarys.eu

St Mary's School, Shaftesbury is an outstanding Independent Catholic Boarding and Day School for girls aged 9–18. Situated in the heart of the Dorset countryside, St Mary's offers a very special environment in which girls thrive academically and socially. A strong commitment to traditional values is fostered and girls are inspired to achieve a fulfilling all-round education.

Girls achieve their first-choice University offers as well as Oxbridge success. Inspired to have the courage to face the unexpected and challenge the ordinary, girls are encouraged to think globally and work collaboratively with other Mary Ward and CJ schools globally.

A very happy and friendly school; two-thirds of the school is boarding and everyone here enjoys a real sense of community, staff and pupils alike. Girls are welcome to the main school from age nine.

Situated in 55 acres of beautiful parkland, St Mary's offers a secure learning environment with excellent facilities and a forward-thinking approach. It is less than two hours by train from London; just outside Shaftesbury, it is very accessible for visits and school trips to Salisbury, Bath and the surrounding area.

Houses. There is a junior boarding house and 2 main boarding houses with a modern stand-alone Sixth Form house. Excellent modern facilities include Rookwood – an academic building devoted to English, History, Geography and Learning Support and a new art building, completed in 2014, with conference centre. This is home to Fine Art, Photography, History of Art, Textiles and Ceramics and is an inspiring and creative work space for pupils. The School also has an impressive swimming centre, alongside its excellent sports facilities.

Admission. The School has its own Entrance Examination held in January for 9+, 11+ and 13+ entry. Sixth Form entry is by interview.

Scholarships and Bursaries. 9+, 11+, 13+ and Sixth Form Scholarships available in: Academic, Sport, Music, Dance, Drama and Art. All-Rounder 'Mary Ward' and 11+ Catholic Local Primary School scholarships also available. All offer up to 10% remission of fees and 20% remission for the Catholic Local Primary scholarship, in accordance with parental means.

Scholarship Examinations take place in January.

Fees per term (2018–2019). Boarders £6,695–£10,490, Day Girls £5,400–£6,950.

Aims and Curriculum. The School aims to give girls as broad an education as possible, combining academic, spiritual, personal and extra-curricular elements, to foster independent thinking and the opportunity for each girl to realise her own strengths and potential. Girls achieve outstanding results year on year with the recent GCSE results being the best in eight years.

In Years 5–9 all girls follow a common curriculum which includes, English, History, Geography, French, Latin, Mathematics, Information Technology, Religious Education, Science, Art, Textiles, Music, Singing, PSE and PE. From Year 10 both the core curriculum: English Language and Literature, Mathematics, One Modern Foreign Language, Religious Education and either Triple or Double Award Science; options are arranged to ensure that each girl follows a balanced course suitable for her ability and interests.

22 subjects are offered at A Level in addition to General Studies, General RE, and PE and the Leiths Basic Certificate in Food and Wine as a professional qualification. Some also go on to more vocational forms of Higher Education or pursue their studies in the Creative Arts.

All girls receive individual careers advice and the school arranges Careers Fairs, expert speaker visits and work experience placements.

Music. With a thriving Music Department any orchestral instrument may be learned. In addition there are two school choirs, an orchestra and various instrumental ensembles. Bi-annual choir trips are organised to cities such as Vienna, Rome, Budapest and Venice.

Sport. Winter: hockey, netball, cross country and swimming teams with a wide range of additional activities also available such as dance, badminton, basketball, volleyball, tag-rugby and football. Summer: swimming, tennis, rounders and athletics and also a range of other activities available to choose from. The School has its own Sports Hall, Fitness Suite, floodlit Astroturf and a 25m six-lane indoor swimming pool.

Extra subjects or activities. Speech and drama, dance (taught by the renowned TLW Dance), riding, fencing, tennis coaching, self-defence, archery, Duke of Edinburgh's Award, photography, and a wide range of other clubs and societies including book groups, Forest School, cricket, textiles, debating, beekeeping, science club and many more.

Charitable status. St Mary's School Shaftesbury Trust is a Registered Charity, number 292845. Its aims and objectives are to administer an independent Roman Catholic school education for girls of all denominations.

Governors:
Ms Victoria Younghusband (*Chair*)
Mrs Kathryn Mounde (*Vice Chair*)
Major General Nick Borton
Mr Philip Conrath
Mr Mike Farmer
Mr Peter Geike-Cobb
Sister Gemma Simmonds, CJ
Mrs Janet Watts

Senior Leadership Team:

Headmistress: Mrs Maria Young

Deputy Head (*Academic*): Dr Chris Enos
Acting Deputy Head (*Pastoral*) *& Head of Boarding*: Mrs Susannah Hill
Bursar & Clerk to the Governors: Mrs Sudipa Ghosh
Director of Mission and Ethos: Mrs Jacintha Bowe

Resident Priest:
Father Andrew Moore

Safeguarding Team:
Mrs Louise Phillips (*Designated Safeguarding Lead*)
Mrs Beverley Roberts (*Deputy Designated Safeguarding Lead*)
Mrs Felicity Whyte (*Deputy Designated Safeguarding Lead*)

Head of Sixth Form and Careers:
Mr Dominic Simmons

Teaching Staff by Department:
* *Head of Department*

Art & Design:
*Miss Maxine Bridger (*Photography*)
Mrs Julie Hodge (*Art, Design, Textiles*)
Mr Richard Taylor (*Fine Art*)
Ms Kathy Banneel (*Art Technician*)

Business Studies:
Mr Mike Hayes

Classics:
Mrs Harriet Blanco
Mr Michael Forrester
Mr Dominic Simmons

Drama:
*Mr Chris Sykes (*Performing Arts*)
Mrs Sue Holman

Duke of Edinburgh's Award:
Mr Rod Wiltshire

Economics:
Mr Mike Hayes

English:
*Ms Rosslyn M R Brand
Mrs Hilary Key
Mr Dominic Simmons
Mr Chris Sykes

English for Speakers of Other Languages:
Mrs Cristina Waddington

Examinations Officer:
Dr Chris Enos
Mrs Debbie Whitehead (*Assistant*)

Geography:
*Mrs Daisy Phillips
Mrs Nathalie Boyer-Castle
Mrs Jane Lilley

History:
*Mr Tim Goodwin

History of Art:
Mrs Olha Karamenova

ICT:
*Mrs Kirsten Le Poidevin

Learning Support:
Mrs Rebecca Dixon (*Coordinator*)
Mrs Jacqueline Kaskow
Mrs Sally Trinkler

Leiths Cookery:
Miss Charlotte Archer

Library:
Miss Min Edmonds (*Librarian*)

Lower III:
Mrs Siobhan Cheadle

Mathematics:
*Mrs Louise Phillips
Mr Mike Hayes
Mr Ian Phillips
Mr Rod Wiltshire

Modern Languages:
*Mr Hugo Gardner (*Spanish*)
Mrs Valeria Findlay-Wilson (*Italian*)
Mrs Yuko Leece (*Japanese*)
Mrs Odilia Orue-Green (*Spanish*)

Miss Veronique Raffenne (*French*)
Mrs Fiona Rowland (*French*)
Mrs Cristina Waddington (*Portuguese*)

Music:
Miss Sarah Watton (*Director of Music*)

Peripatetic Music:
Mrs Louise Blyth (*Double Bass*)
Mrs Jennifer Brookfield (*Piano*)
Mrs Angela Caunce (*Piano*)
Mr Peter Caunce (*Violin, Viola*)
Mr James Gilbert (*Percussion*)
Mrs Sacha Langton-Gilks (*Singing*)
Miss Sue Lockyer (*Clarinet, Saxophone*)
Mr Simon Lockyer (*Cello, Double Bass*)
Mrs Jennifer Lucas (*Violin, Ukelele*)
Mr Daren Mayo (*Acoustic/Electric Guitar*)
Mrs Patricia Stewart (*Singing*)
Mrs Catherine Wall (*Flute*)

Personal and Social Education:
Mrs Emily James

Physical Education:
Mrs Nathalie Boyer-Castle (*Director of Sport*)
Mr Lawrence Dalton
Mrs Emily James
Miss Louise Rees

PE Coaching:
Mr Ian Griffin (*Tennis*)
Mr Matthew Haskett (*Hockey*)

Psychology:
Mrs Rita Bauer

Religious Education:
*Mrs Jacintha Bowe
Miss Honoria Connolly
Mr Michael Forrester

Science:
*Mr Martin Lawrence (*Physics*)
Dr Gill Caunt (*Biology*)
Dr Chris Enos (*Chemistry*)
Mrs Annabel Fearnley (*Chemistry*)
Miss Sadie Flower (*Biology*)
Mrs Kirsten Le Poidevin (*Biology*)
Mrs Carol Gray (*Science Technician*)
Mrs Yuko Leece (*Science Technician*)

Speech and Drama:
Mrs Hilary Earle
Mrs Sue Holman

House Staff:
Mrs Susannah Hill (*Head of Boarding*)

Harewell House:
Mrs Felicity Whyte (*Housemistress*)

Hewarth House:
Mrs Emily James (*Academic Housemistress*)
Mrs Maxine Tomlinson (*Boarding Housemistress*)

Mary Ward House:
Mrs Beverley Roberts (*Housemistress*)

Newby House:
Mrs Fiona Rowland (*Housemistress*)

York House:
Mr Lawrence Dalton (*Housemaster*)

Resident Tutors:
Ms Kathy Banneel
Miss Honoria Connolly
Mr Chris Sykes

House Assistants:
Mrs Gina Bent
Mrs Ellen Boote
Mrs Tina Richards
Mrs Heather Sanger
Mrs Sandra Shutler
Mrs Jacky Watts

Nursing Staff:
Mrs Sophie Savage (*Registered Nurse, Senior Nurse*)
Mrs Anita Horak (*Registered Nurse*)

Support Staff:
Mr Calvin Bent (*Premises Manager*)
Ms Felicity Brenan (*Domestic Manager*)
Miss Laura Coffin (*Administration and Office Manager*)
Mrs Kerry Condie (*PA to Headmistress*)
Mr Neil Ford (*IT Manager*)
Mr Cliff Hedger (*Head of Maintenance*)
Mrs Catherine Kelleher (*Director of Admissions*)
Mrs Gill Patterson (*Pool Manager*)
Mrs Sophie Pender-Cudlip (*Director of Communications and Marketing*)
Ms Micaila Vivier (*HR Manager*)
Ms Jeanine Wilkinson (*Finance Bursar*)

St Nicholas' School

Redfields House, Redfields Lane, Church Crookham, Fleet, Hampshire GU52 0RF

Tel: 01252 850121
Fax: 01252 850718
email: headspa@st-nicholas.hants.sch.uk
website: www.st-nicholas.hants.sch.uk

Motto: *Confirma Domine Serviendo*

St Nicholas' School is a small independent day school for girls aged 3–16 and boys aged 3–7. Founded in 1935 in Bransomewood Road, Fleet, the school moved to Redfields House, Redfields Lane, Church Crookham in 1996. Redfields House, a Victorian Mansion, is set in 27 acres of glorious parkland and playing fields.

Bransomewood, the Nursery and Infant department, retains the original name of the road where the school was founded. Being built of natural wood with a wonderful airy atmosphere this building gives light and space to our younger children, creating a calming environment in which they thrive. With an adventure playground set in the woods, a large hall fitted with PE equipment, overlooking the grounds and our experienced teaching staff, it is no wonder the children are so happy.

St Nicholas' Junior department is based in Redfields House itself which keeps the charm of the old family house with its oak panelling and the senior department is located in the newer part of the school behind. All three departments have benefited from several building projects. Both Infant and Junior pupils have Forest School sessions throughout the year that take advantage of the beautiful outdoor learning space.

In December 2000 an Olympic-size sports hall opened with netball and tennis courts, showers, changing rooms and a viewing gallery. This has enhanced the sports lessons and enabled even more sports competitions as well as extra-curricular activities. Badminton, tennis, netball, volleyball and basketball may be played throughout the year.

Spring 2006 saw yet another addition with the opening of the art, design technology and textiles centre, offering three spacious rooms with large work benches, and a kiln for pottery. By having this wonderful new building it opened an opportunity for the school to adapt the old art centre into several music practice rooms. Tuition in the violin, piano, guitar, harp, drums as well singing, woodwind and brass is offered.

In November 2009 The Pritchard Hall, named after the school's founder, was unveiled. The performing arts centre has raked seating for over 330, in the semi round, with an orchestra pit, concerts and plays are staged regularly. The drama department has in addition two studios.

September 2013 welcomed the opening of state-of-the-art laboratories for juniors and seniors. The classrooms include teaching areas as well as practical learning spaces in a bright and welcoming environment.

In 2016 the addition of an all-weather pitch and two new tennis courts complemented the sports facilities. The new sand-based AstroTurf will be floodlit and provide pupils with a multi-use sports facility including hockey, tennis and netball. The tennis courts will also be floodlit. Hockey, athletics, football and rounders take place on the games field and the floodlit courts are used all year round. In 2018, the Junior Department benefited from a new play area.

Pupils come to St Nicholas' from Hampshire, Surrey and Berkshire. School buses operate from Farnham, Odiham, Fleet, Basingstoke, Camberley, Yateley, Aldershot and Farnborough. Situated just off the A287, Hook to Farnham road, junction 5 of the M3 is approximately 4 miles short away.

Religion. The school is a Christian foundation but children of other faiths are welcomed. Assemblies are held each morning. Children are encouraged to show tolerance, compassion and care for others.

Curriculum. St Nicholas' offers an extended day, from 7.30 am to 6.00 pm. Academic standards are high and a balanced curriculum is offered. Small classes place greater emphasis on the individual and pupils are encouraged to achieve their full potential in every area of school life. The curriculum is kept as broad as possible until the age of fourteen when choices are made for GCSE. The option choices vary year by year depending upon the girls' abilities and talents. On average each girl sits ten subjects at GCSE. More than twenty subjects are offered at this level. A carefully structured personal development course incorporates a Careers programme. Our girls move confidently on to enter sixth form colleges or scholarships to senior independent schools. Choir, drama and music thrive within the school and there are frequent performances which enable the girls to develop self-confidence.

Physical Education. Pupils take part in inter-school and local district sports matches: hockey, netball, football and cross-country in winter; and tennis, athletics and swimming in summer. Rounders and cricket are also played.

Entry. Children may enter at any stage subject to interview, school report and waiting list. Scholarships and Bursaries are available. For 11+ candidates there is an entrance examination.

Fees per term (2018–2019). Infants: £3,427 (Reception), £3,594 (Years 1 & 2); Juniors: £4,014 (Years 3–4), £4,092 (Years 5–6); Senior School: £4,786 (Years 7–11). Nursery: £9.30 per hour.

Further Information. The prospectus is available upon request from the Registrar. The Headmistress is pleased to meet parents by appointment.

Charitable status. St Nicholas' School is a Registered Charity, number 307341. It exists to provide high quality education for children.

Chair of Governors: Reverend Tara Hellings

Headmistress: Dr Olwen Wright, PhD Winchester, MA, BA Hons, PGCE

Deputy Head – Pastoral: Caroline Egginton, BEd Hons London

Deputy Head – Academic: Christine Moorby, BSc Hons Southampton, CertEd

Teaching Staff:
Josephine Allen, BA Hons QTS West of England (*Key Stage 2*)
Alison Audino, BEd Hons Bath (*Food Technology*)
Florence Ayache, BA Hons Glamorgan, QTS (*Spanish & French*)
Helen Barnes, BA Ed Hons Exeter (*Key Stage 2*)
Jenny Brackstone, BA Hons Nottingham, PGCE (*Key Stages 3 & 4*)
Sarah Carter, BEd Hons Southampton (*Key Stage 2*)
Janet Coombe, BA Hons Manchester, PGCE (*Geography*)
Joanne Edwards, BA Hons Brunel, PGCE (*Head of History*)
Nicola Dale, BA Hons Surrey, PGCE (*Key Stage 2*)
Deborah Di Carlo, BA Hons Central Saint Martins, PGCE
Josie Downer, BA Hons Leeds, MA King's (*Head of Drama*)
Barbara Edwards, BA Hons Sheffield, PGCE (*English*)
Amy Franke, BMus Hons Surrey, MMus (*Music*)
Naomi Jackson, BA Hons Leeds, PGCE Southampton (*Director of Sport*)
Edwina Grosse, BA Hons Trent (*Head of Art*)
Rosalie Hague, BA Hons Lancaster, PGCE (*Head of English*)
Valerie Helliwell, BEng Hons Liverpool, PGCE (*Head of Mathematics, Examinations Officer*)
Laura Homer, BA Hons Wales, PGCE (*Key Stage 1*)
Pilar Kimber, MA Reading (*Latin & Classical Civilisation*)
Janice R King, BSc Hons London, PGCE (*Head of Biology*)
Alexandra Lawrence, MA Oxon, PGCE (*Head of Modern Languages*)
Deborah Martin, BA Hons Surrey (*Mathematics*)
Julie Merker, BA OU, CertEd (*PE*)
Michelle Morgan, NNEB (*Nursery*)
Paul Nicholls, BA Hons London (*Key Stage 2*)
Virginia Pearson, Perf Cert RAM, LTCL, ARCM (*Part-time music*)
Tracy Perrett, BEd Sussex (*Head of Juniors*)
Benjamin Pont, BMus Hons (*Director of Music*)
Joanna Pont, BMus Hons (*String Tutor*)
Lee Render, BA Hons QTS Surrey (*Head of Infants*)
Lisa Ruffell, BA Hons QTS Surrey (*Key Stage 2*)
Jane Stansbury, BEd Cambridge, PG SpLD Kingston (*Curriculum Support*)
Michelle Strevens, BEd, CNAA (*Foundation Stage*)
Julia Tiley, BA Hons QTS Kingston (*Head of Foundation Stage*)
Jane Tomlinson, BA Hons London, PGCE (*Modern Languages*)
Frances van Heerden, BSc Natal, UED (*Science*)
Suzanne Walch, BA Hons OU (*Head of Curriculum Support*)
Catherine Williams, BA Hons Salford (*Head of IT*)
Xinsheng Zhang, MEd Johannesburg SA (*Chinese Mandarin*)

Peripatetic Music:
Wendy Busby, BMus Hons (*Voice*)
Tamasin Cline, BMus Hons (*Violin*)
Sylvia Ellison, BA Hons, PG Dip RCM (*Oboe*)
Susan Gillis, PG Dip Mtpp, ALCM, LLCM (*Piano*)
Claire Hickling, BMus Hons (*Piano, Flute*)
Claire Hasted, BMus Hons (*Violin*)
Oksana Maxwell, LTCL (*Piano*)
Valerie Mitchell, LRAM (*Piano, Cello*)
Austin Pepper, ALCM (*Brass*)

Eleanor Bowyer, PGCE Drama Middlesex (*LAMDA*)
Rachel Riordan, Adv Teaching RSM (*Saxophone, Clarinet*)
Elizabeth Rockhill, MA Mus Hons GSMD, PG Dip,
    LRAM (*Violin*)

Administration:
Teaching Assistant: Tania Negus
School Nurse: Sarah Watkins, RGN, NNEB
Bursar: Tarn Canning, FCCA
Accounts Assistant: Debbie Smitherman
Headmistress's PA: Dawn Brown, FInstAM, FGPA
Registrar: Katie Grace, BA Hons
School Secretary: Sarah Watkins
Laboratory Technician: Michele Axton, BA OU
Catering: David Clayton – Chartwells, Compass Group
    PLC
Maintenance: Maurrice Readman, Paul Rippingale
Caretaker: Robert Crail
Bus Driver: Robert Crail, Timothy Hunt, Glenn Shearer
Second Hand Uniform Shop: Maureen Mullins
Librarian: Sarah Stokes

St Paul's Girls' School

Brook Green, Hammersmith, London W6 7BS

Tel: School Office: 020 7603 2288
             Admissions: 020 7605 4882
             Business Director: 020 7605 4881
Fax: 020 7602 9932
email: admissions@spgs.org
website: www.spgs.org

Founded in 1904 as one of the first purpose-built schools for girls, St Paul's embraces both tradition and innovation. The emphasis on liberal learning established by the first High Mistress, Frances Gray, and Director of Music, Gustav Holst, finds expression today in an academically challenging curriculum, which encourages intellectual freedom, discovery and the joy of scholarship.

St Paul's is committed to providing an outstanding academic education within a highly supportive environment. Girls regularly achieve exceptional results (over 60% A* at A Level, including Pre-U equivalence, and 92% at GCSE in 2018), but the school aims to teach far beyond the prescribed curriculum, endowing girls with a lifelong love of learning and the necessary tools of scholarship and enterprise. It is also the opportunities outside the classroom which make a St Paul's education distinctive. Most of the 110+ clubs and societies are run by pupils – for pupils – and new ones are created every year to reflect passion and demand. Girls are given leadership opportunities and an environment in which to experiment, innovate and push boundaries. Girls follow a traditional liberal education and are prepared for GCSE and IGCSE in Year 11; alternative school directed courses in art, drama and music are also offered for this age group. Sixth form students are offered 24 subjects at A Level or Pre-U, and are prepared for university entrance by our specialist higher education and careers advisory team. Virtually all students go on to study at major universities in the UK and the USA, with about 40% going to Oxbridge annually. The creative and performing arts are at the heart of school life. Since its foundation music has always been a particularly strong feature with well over half the student body taking instrumental lessons; there are also multiple orchestras, choirs and ensembles on offer. Art and design benefit from studio and workshop facilities and there are several major exhibitions of students' work every year. Drama enjoys a purpose-built theatre and drama studio and any girl can direct her own production. Indeed, facilities are

some of the best offered by a central London school with extensive sporting facilities on site. All girls from Year 7 are placed in small tutor groups of no more than 12 girls to ensure the highest standards of pastoral care. The main ages of admission are 11 and 16. There are currently 759 girls on the roll. The school is committed to making a St Paul's education available to the brightest girls whatever their means and has an active development campaign dedicated to raising funds for that purpose.

Scholarships.
Junior Music Scholarships (11+) to the value of lessons in two instruments/voice, currently worth £1,632 per annum, tenable for five years when scholars will be able to apply for a 16+ scholarship in Year 11 for their final two years at St Paul's. Music exhibitions may also be awarded following auditions at the discretion of the Director of Music. They are based on the value of lessons in one instrument/voice, currently worth £816 per annum and tenable for five years.

Senior Music Scholarships (16+) to the value of lessons in two instruments/voice, currently worth £1,632 per annum, tenable for two years *(choral awards up to the value of one lesson in voice may be available)*. External candidates must be successful in the Senior School entrance examination.

Senior Art Scholarships (16+) of the value of £250 per annum are offered to up to two internal and two external candidates who are currently in their final GCSE year and who, if applying from another school, have previously been successful in the Senior School entrance examination. Candidates take part in a workshop and are also required to submit a portfolio.

Senior Drama Scholarships (16+) of the value of £250 per annum are awarded on the basis of an audition, workshop and interview with our Director of Drama and other drama staff to candidates who show outstanding potential as an actor or director. Please note that scholarship candidates will often study Drama at A Level, however, those able to demonstrate a significant commitment to co-curricular drama will also be considered.

Bursaries. *Junior Bursaries* (11+) to a value of up to full fee remission based on proven financial need subject to annual review are available. Candidates must be successful in the 11+ entrance examination. The number of Junior bursaries available each year will vary.

Senior Bursaries (16+) to a value of up to full fee remission based on proven financial need subject to annual review are available for candidates who have been successful in the Senior School entrance examination and who are currently in their final GCSE year at another school.

Fees per term (2018–2019). £8,297, including lunches and personal accident insurance, and excluding textbooks. The fees per term for new entrants entering at 16+ are £8,920.

Registration & Examination Fee £125.

Charitable status. St Paul's Girls' School is a Registered Charity, number 1119613, and a Company Limited by Guarantee, registered in England, number 6142007 and is governed by its Memorandum and Articles of Association. It exists to promote the education of girls in Greater London. The sole member of the charitable company is the Mercers' Company.

Governors:
Chairman: The Hon Timothy Palmer
Deputy Chairman: Ms Kate Bingham

Mrs Zeina Bain	Mr Tim Haywood
Mr Nicholas Buxton	Mrs Gillian Low
Mr Nicolas Chisholm MBE	Mrs Dervilla Mitchell CBE

Miss Cally Palmer CBE
Mr Robert Palmer
Miss Judith Portrait OBE

Professor Jane Ridley
Dr Julia Riley

High Mistress: **Mrs Sarah Fletcher**, MA Oxon (*History*)

Senior Deputy Head, Director of Studies:
Mr Andrew Ellams, MA Oxon (*Economics*)

Deputy Head, Director of Co-Curricular:
Mr Fred Hitchcock, BA Bristol (*Classics*)

Deputy Head, Director of Pastoral Care:
Miss Sandrine Paillasse, BA Guildhall, MSc Bath (*Modern Languages*)

Deputy Head, Director of People and Diversity:
Ms Helen Semple, MA Edinburgh (*Religious Studies*)

Deputy Head, Director of Senior School:
Ms Josephine Lane, BA Leeds (*English*)

Deputy Head, Director of Strategic Development
Mr Ellis Whitcomb, BSc Birmingham, Postgrad Certificate Cantab (*Physics*)

Mrs Gillian Abbott, MA St Andrews (*Geography*)
Ms Kathryn Arblaster, BA Oxon, MSc MPhil Imperial (*Biology*)
Miss Elizabeth Armstrong, BSc Exeter, MRes Lancaster (*Geography*)
Mr Tom Attenborough, BA Cantab (*English*)
Miss Helen Barff, BA Goldsmiths College, MA Camberwell (*Art and Design*)
Mr Wayne Barron, BA Cantab (*Classics*)
Miss Sandra Barth, BA Martin-Luther-Universität Halle-Wittenberg (*Modern Languages*)
Miss Jessica Basch, BA Eastern MA Eastern (*Physical Education*)
Mrs Sarah Bell, BA Cantab (*Chemistry*)
Mrs Paola Bianchi, MEng Cagliari (*Mathematics*)
Mr Allyn Blake, BSc Imperial (*Mathematics*)
Mrs Lucy Bond, BSc Exeter (*Biology*)
Dr Joanna Bratten BA Steubenville, MLitt, PhD St Andrews (*English*)
Mr Spencer Buksh, BSc London (*Mathematics*)
Mr Matthew Bunning, BA Cantab (*Art and Design*)
Mrs Birgit Cassens, MA Christian Albrechts Universitaet Kiel (*Modern Languages*)
Mrs Rachel Chamberlin, BSc Durham (*Geography*)
Miss Sophie Corthine, BA Durham (*Physical Education*)
Ms Liza Coutts, MA Oxon, MA London (*History*)
Mr Ian Crane, BSc Durham (*Mathematics*)
Mr Alexander Daglish, BA Plymouth (*Art*)
Dr Gary Davies, BSc Nottingham, MSc Cantab, PhD UCL (*Physics*)
Mr Tom Dean, MChem Oxon (*Chemistry*)
Ms Suzanne Debney, BA Rose Bruford (*Drama*)
Miss Marjorie Delage, BA Limoges (*Modern Languages*)
Mrs Sydne Derbyshire, BA Queen's University of Charlotte (*Physical Education*)
Mr Jonathan Dho, BA, MA Oxon, MBA Northwestern (*Chemistry*)
Dr Phoebe Dickerson, BA, MPhil, PhD Cantab (*English*)
Mr Matthew Dickinson, BA Nottingham, GSMD Guildhall (*Music*)
Miss Gill D'Lima, BSc St Andrews (*Mathematics*)
Ms Nicola Doble, BA Oxon, MSc Bath (*Mathematics*)
Mr Michael Donkor, BA Oxon, MA London (*English*)
Mrs Marianna Doria, MChem Oxon, MSc Imperial (*Chemistry*)
Ms Alice Dvorakova, (*Modern Languages*)
Miss Katherine Evans, BA London (*History of Art*)
Miss Emilie Eymin, BA Toulouse, MA Toulouse/London (*Modern Languages*)
Mrs Danu Fenton, BA Oxon, MA Courtauld (*History*)

Miss Isabel Foley, BA London (*Drama*)
Miss Megan Folley, BA Edinburgh (*Physical Education*)
Mrs Anna Foster, BA Oxon (*Economics*)
Miss Kate Frank, BA London, MA London (*Modern Languages*)
Mrs Hannah Fussner, BA Oxon, MA Stanford, USA (*Learning Support*)
Miss Penelope Garcia-Rodriguez, BA Oviedo, Spain, MA London (*Modern Languages*)
Miss Agniete Geras, BA Oxon (*Physics*)
Ms Blanche Girouard, BA Oxon (*Religious Studies*)
Miss Maria Gonzales-Mateos, Single Honours Spanish Cardiff, PhD Wales (*Modern Languages*)
Mrs Cat Graham, BA Oxon (*Religious Studies*)
Mr Roger Green, MA Kent (*Mathematics*)
Miss Claire Halliday, BA Roger Williams (*Physical Education*)
Miss Helen Hancock, BSc Loughborough (*Physical Education*)
Miss Emily Hardy, BA Cantab (*English*)
Miss Sophie Harley-Mckeown, BA Cantab (*History*)
Mr Michael Hennessy (*Physical Education*)
Miss Elizabeth Hodges, BA Wolverhampton Polytechnic, MA Royal College of Art (*Art and Design*)
Dr Anna Holland, BA Oxon, DPhil (*Classics*)
Dr Bernard Hughes, MA Oxon, MMus London, PhD London (*Music*)
Mrs Manuela Knight, BA Milan (*Modern Languages*)
Dr Kingston Koo, BSc Warwick, PhD London (*Physics*)
Miss Chloe Lallyett, BSc Glasgow (*Biology*)
Mrs Nina Lau, BSc London (*Biology*)
Dr Kate Lee, BSc Witwatersrand, MSc Cape Town, PhD London (*Physics*)
Miss Hsiang-Ju Lin, BA Soochow, MA London (*Modern Languages*)
Miss Gill MacMillan, BSc Nottingham Trent (*Physical Education*)
Ms Paula Mahoney-Velez, MA Cordoba (*Modern Languages*)
Mr Rory Malone, BA Harvard (*Economics*)
Ms Silvana Marconini, BA Turin (*Modern Languages*)
Mrs Hélène May, MA aggregation Sorbonne (*Modern Languages*)
Dr Matthew McCullagh, BA, MPhil, PhD Cantab (*Classics*)
Miss Claire McNulty, BEng Imperial (*Mathematics*)
Mrs Nadège Mériau, MA RCA (*Art and Design*)
Mrs Jo Moran, BA London (*Information Technology*)
Dr Joanna Moriarty, BSc Birmingham, PhD Reading (*Biology*)
Ms Rosa Nguyen, BA Middlesex, MA RCA (*Art and Design*)
Mrs Irina Ninnis, BA Moscow and London (*Modern Languages*)
Mrs Jen Noble, MSc Edinburgh (*Geography*)
Mr Leigh O'Hara, BA York, MMus London (*Music*)
Mr Oswald O'Neill, MA Oxon (*History*)
Ms Rosalind Orchard, BSc Cantab (*Biology*)
Mr Dipesh Patel, BSc Bristol (*Mathematics*)
Dr Jonathan Patrick, BA, DPhil Oxon (*English*)
Mr Roger Paul, BA Norwich, ARCO (*Music*)
Mrs Emma Payler-Lodge, BSc London (*Biology*)
Mr Tom Peck, BA Manchester (*History and Politics*)
Miss Heidi Pegler, BA Cardiff, LTCL (*Music*)
Mr Russell Pointin, BSc Bath (*Mathematics*)
Mrs Jocelyne Rapinac, MA Aix-Marseille (*Modern Languages*)
Miss Jessamy Reynolds, MA St Andrews (*Classics*)
Mrs Julie Runacres, MA Cantab, MA London (*English*)
Ms Leonie Rushforth, BA Cantab (*English*)
Ms Kaarin Scanlan, BA Bristol (*Physical Education*)

Dr Jemma Senczyszyn, MChem York, PhD Manchester (*Chemistry*)
Mrs Alexandra Shamloll, MA Cantab (*Mathematics*)
Mrs Holly Shao, BSc Hunan (*Modern Languages*)
Mrs Kate Snook, MA, MPhil St Andrews (*History*)
Miss Lauren Speight, MMath Newcastle (*Mathematics*)
Mr Paul Sperring, MPhil London, MA Warwick (*Religious Studies*)
Miss Hilary Sturt, AGSM, ARCM (*Music*)
Ms Claire Suthren, BA Cantab (*Classics*)
Miss Jessica Tipton, BA Bristol, MA London (*Modern Languages*)
Mr Rupert Try, MA, MSt Oxon (*History*)
Miss Faith Turner, BA York (*English and Drama*)
Dr Damon Vosper Singleton, MMath Oxon, PhD London (*Mathematics*)
Dr Sarah Wah, MA Leeds, DPhil Cantab (*English*)
Miss Mary Wenham, BA Oxon (*Modern Languages*)
Ms Barbara Wesolowska, BA UCL, MA RCA (*Art and Design*)
Miss Alexis White, BMus RNCM, MMus Eastman School of Music (*Music*)
Ms Kirsten Wilson, BA Oxon (*Geography*)
Ms Jane Zeng, BSc Guangzhan, China (*Modern Languages*)

Visiting Music Teachers:
Miss Charlotte Ansbergs, LRAM, Dip RAM (*Violin*)
Mr Edward Barry, Dip Mus, LTCL (*Violin*)
Mrs Emily Bates, BA, MSTAT (*Alexander Technique*)
Ms Lisa Beckley, MA Oxon (*Singing*)
Ms Anna Boucher, BA Durham (*Singing*)
Ms Emma Brain-Gabbott, BA Cantab (*Singing*)
Mr Andrew Brownell, DMusA Guildhall, FRCO (*Piano*)
Ms Alexia Cammish, MA Cantab, MA GSMD, LGSMDT (*Horn*)
Mrs Jane Clark-Maxwell, BMus London, AKC, LTCL (*Singing*)
Mr Adam Cooke, MusB Manchester, MMus GSMD (*Brass*)
Miss Jane Fisher, LTCL, PGCE (*Flute*)
Mr John Flinders, BA York, LGSM (*Piano*)
Miss Carolyn Foulkes, GRSM, LRAM, ARAM, Dip Adv Studies (*Singing*)
Miss Caterina Grewe, BMus, MMus Royal College of Music (*Piano*)
Ms Gill Hopkin, GRNCM, ARNCM, PGCE (*Violin*)
Mr John Langley, BA (*Theory*)
Mr Mornington Lockett, BA (*Saxophone*)
Miss Naadia Manington, BMus, LGSM (*Jazz Piano, Piano*)
Miss Hannah Marcinowicz (*Saxophone, Clarinet*)
Ms Bridget Mermikides, LRAM (*Singing*)
Mr Alexander Mobbs, BMus (*Double Bass*)
Miss Amanda Morrison, BA (*Singing*)
Miss Helen Neilson, BSc, PG Dip Adv RCM, MMus (*Cello*)
Ms Jessica O'Leary, BMus, Dip CSM, LTCL, LRAM (*Violin, Viola*)
Ms Emma Ramsdale, GRSM, LRAM, Dip RAM, ARAM (*Harp*)
Mr Daniel Roberts (*Strings*)
Mr Mark Rose, BMus London, MMus London (*Guitar*)
Mr Neil Roxburgh, Dip RCM, ARCM, ARCT (*Piano*)
Miss Julie Ryan, ARCM (*Trumpet*)
Miss Rachel Shannon, MA Cantab, RAM (*Singing*)
Mr Nicholas Shaw, BA Oxon, Diploma RCO, MMus London (*Organ*)
Ms Janet Shell, BEd Lancaster, AGSM
Miss Erica Simpson, ARAM, ARCM (*Cello*)
Mr James Sleigh, ARCM, Hon ARAM (*Viola*)
Ms Louise Strickland, BMus, MMus, LGSMD (*Recorder*)

Mrs Sarah Stroh, BMus, Dip Dist RAM, LRAM (*Singing*)
Ms Shelagh Sutherland, ARAM, LRAM, STAT (*Piano, Alexander Technique*)
Ms Sarah Thurlow, MMus, Dip RCM (*Clarinet*)
Miss Emma Tingey, LWCMD, ACC PG Dip (*Harp*)
Ms Seaming To, BMus RNCM (*Singing*)
Miss Judith Treggor, BMus Connecticut (*Flute*)
Ms Frith Trezevant, ARCM, LTCL (*Music Education and Speech & Drama*)
Ms Joanne Turner, Dip RCM, ARCM (*Bassoon, Flute*)
Miss Enloc Wu, ARCM, LRSM (*Piano*)
Ms Masumi Yamamoto, MMus QCGU Brisbane, PG Dip RAM, PG Dip TCM, LRAM (*Harpsichord*)
Mrs Fiona York, AGSM (*Piano*)

Director of Operations: Ms Barbara Sussex, BA, MPhil Birmingham
Director of Resources: Ms Katie Kerr, BA York, MCIPD
Assistant to the High Mistress: Ms Zein Al-Rifaii, BA UCL
Head of Admissions: Ms Claire Richardson, MA Cantab
Librarian: Mrs Linda Kelley, BA Manchester, MSc UCE

St Swithun's School

Alresford Road, Winchester, Hampshire SO21 1HA

Tel:	01962 835700
Fax:	01962 835779
email:	office@stswithuns.com
website:	www.stswithuns.com
Twitter:	@StSwithunsGirls
Facebook:	@StSwithunsGirls

St Swithun's is a modern and flourishing educational organisation. The school is set on an impressive and attractive campus of 45 acres in the South Downs National Park on the outskirts of Winchester. It offers girls excellent teaching, sporting and recreational facilities.

The school offers weekly boarding and full boarding and day options for girls aged 11–18. At present the senior school (girls aged 11–18) has 290 day girls and 231 boarders. There is an adjoining Prep School for girls aged 4–11 with a co-ed nursery (*see Prep School entry in IAPS section*).

Ethos. St Swithun's is an 'appropriately academic' school which means that we celebrate intellectual curiosity and the life of the mind, but not to the exclusion of all else. We expect our pupils to develop individual passions and through them to acquire a range of skills and characteristics. These characteristics will include a willingness to take risks, to question and to debate, and to persevere in the face of difficulty. In the words of Samuel Beckett: "Ever tried. Ever failed. No matter. Try again. Fail again. Fail better." If a girl can immediately excel at everything we ask of her, we as educators must set the bar higher.

We want all girls to learn about life beyond the school gates, to appreciate the rich variety of our world, to develop an understanding of compassion and to value justice. We encourage all pupils to become involved in fundraising and community work. They should appreciate how their decisions and their actions can affect those around them.

St Swithun's was founded by Anna Bramston, daughter of the Dean of Winchester, and Christian values underpin our approach to education. We provide a civilised and caring environment in which all girls and staff are valued for their individual gifts and encouraged to develop a sense of spirituality and of kindness. We believe that kindness and tolerance are at the heart of any fully functioning community.

Location. The school is on a rural site in Winchester's 'green belt' but only a short distance from the city centre. It is easily accessible from Heathrow and Gatwick airports and is one hour from London by car (via the M3 motorway). There is a frequent train service to London Waterloo (one hour). We also offer a popular London taxi service from St Swithun's School to London on a Friday evening and a return journey on Sunday.

Curriculum. Girls at St Swithun's benefit from a broad and balanced curriculum that promotes individual choice and achievement. The timetable is designed to enable each pupil to fulfil her intellectual, physical and creative potential through a dynamic range of purposeful lessons and activities.

From their first years here girls are taught to examine social, cultural and moral issues so that they can make informed decisions about their own way of living as well as respecting the values of each individual. The PSHEE & citizenship programme is tailored for each year group and is delivered through a range of school activities and specialist speakers.

All girls follow an enrichment programme known as Stretch. This consists of taught short courses and lectures from visiting speakers. Courses are wide-ranging and topics such as magic and mathematics, biblical Hebrew, cryptic crosswords and French cinema. M5 girls will use Stretch to undertake community service.

Games and PE are taught throughout the school so that girls can participate in a wide range of team and individual sports. Both in lessons and as recreational activities, the emphasis is on personal enjoyment and the development of a healthy, active life, but all pupils receive expert coaching and the most talented individuals and teams are entered into county, regional and national competitions.

Learning support provides bespoke support for individual girls who may be experiencing difficulties in aspects of their academic studies.

Girls take 9 or 10 GCSE exams to allow time for other interests and activities. Everyone takes English language, English literature, mathematics, at least two sciences and one modern foreign language. The girls then choose a further three or four subjects from a choice of 13. Girls are encouraged to take at least one humanity or social science to ensure a breadth of knowledge and skills.

In the sixth form girls are offered 22 subjects from which they choose four at A Level (five if maths and further maths are chosen). Advice is given about the implications for their choice of university, degree course and career to ensure sensible combinations. Some girls choose to follow courses in subjects which are not offered at GCSE. Over half the sixth form study at least one science subject at A Level. Girls normally continue with three of their lower sixth subjects to complete three full A Levels.

In addition, all sixth-formers may choose to do the Extended Project Qualification (EPQ). This is worth half an A Level and is graded from A*–E. The qualification gives girls the opportunity to research an area of personal interest. Universities recognise the value of the skills required for the qualification and it attracts UCAS tariff points. Italian GCSE is also available in the sixth form.

Religion. The school is a Church of England foundation. There are close ties with Winchester Cathedral, where termly services and the annual confirmation and carol services are held. A full-time chaplain prepares girls for confirmation. There is a newly converted chapel at the heart of the school.

Music. From the first hymn in the morning to the final applause on concert nights every day is enriched by music and the school enjoys a fine reputation for the excellence and variety that girls achieve. Through lessons, practice, rehearsals, exams, competitions, performances and cathedral services, the girls are drawn together to make the most

of a busy and ambitious musical life: 75% have instrumental lessons and there is a choice of twenty-two instruments to study. Twenty flourishing school ensembles create a wealth of music and everyone is welcome to join in. Our most accomplished musicians are also cathedral choristers or play in county and national groups. There are endless possibilities at St Swithun's whether it is Renaissance church music, African drumming or 21st century pop music that girls wish to study, listen to, compose or perform. They are taught to appreciate many different styles of music from all over the world and from different historical eras. Learning to compose enables some to express themselves through music and we encourage performing as an integral part of what we offer. Learning a musical instrument and sharing this with an audience requires a high standard of creativity, commitment, technique and courage.

Sports. All girls are encouraged to be involved in sport throughout their time at the school. Sport at St Swithun's has so much to offer, emphasising cooperation, leadership, teamwork, competition and respect. Our girls learn how to deal with success and failure, how to be self-disciplined and how to communicate with each other. We expect every girl to try her best in every area of school life and sport is no exception. Many girls represent their county, region or even country in sports as diverse as lacrosse, fencing, diving, athletics and tennis and we are naturally very proud of these individuals. However, whilst we celebrate success and our teams aspire to excellence, we value effort and sportsmanship as much as winning and we are proud to run first, second and sometimes third teams for all age groups.

Of supreme importance to us is identifying at least one sport to suit each girl so that she will acquire a lifelong enjoyment of exercise.

Facilities. The original school building contains the main teaching rooms and libraries and has been extended and developed to provide specialist areas for languages, information technology, food and textiles and careers. The science wing contains eight fully equipped modern laboratories and project rooms. In addition, there is an art, design and technology centre and a performing arts building was opened in 2003. This has a 600-seat main auditorium and two smaller performance spaces. A new library, careers and ICT facility was opened in 2007.

School Houses. There are 6 boarding houses and 4 day girl houses, each staffed by a housemistress and assistant who take pride in the high level of pastoral care offered to each girl. The junior house is for girls aged 11 who are then transferred to one of the senior houses after a year. They remain in the senior house until they have completed one year in the sixth form. The upper sixth house is for boarders and day girls together, with study-bedrooms for boarders, study facilities for day girls and common rooms and kitchen for all.

Careers. Most girls continue to university, including Oxford and Cambridge, and all continue to some form of higher education and training. Each girl is counselled by one of the team of careers staff in a well-resourced department. Lectures and video presentations are organised frequently and a careers fair held annually.

Leisure Activities. There is an extensive range of co-curricular activities and an organised programme of visits and activities at the weekend. Girls participate in the Duke of Edinburgh's Award scheme, Young Enterprise and local community service work. The sixth form are able to assist with Stretch activities and this can count towards their UCAS tariff. Each year there are drama productions as well as regular drama activities. There are many overseas study and activity trips which include visits to Uganda to meet pupils from St Katherine's, our sister school, volunteer work, language trips, ski trips and watersports holidays.

Health. The school health centre forms part of the main buildings. It is staffed by qualified RGNs and visited by the school doctor twice a week.

Entrance. Entry is by means of a pre-test and the Common Entrance examination for Independent Schools. The majority of girls enter the senior school at the age of 11 or 13 years, but girls are accepted at other ages, including the sixth form, subject to satisfactory tests.

Scholarships and Bursaries. Academic scholarships, carrying a fee subsidy of up to 20%, are available for day girls and boarders entering the school at 11+, at 13+ and to the sixth form.

Music scholarships carry a subsidy of up to 20% and provide free tuition on two instruments; exhibitions provide free tuition on one instrument. Music scholars can apply for a means-tested award of up to 100% of school fees.

Sports scholarships may be awarded each year to suitable applicants at 11+ and 13+. These scholarships will have a maximum value of 20% fee remission.

Bursaries of up to 100% of school fees are available for girls who meet the school's entrance criteria. All bursaries are subject to means-testing.

Fees per term (2018–2019). Senior School: Boarders £11,200; Day Girls £6,855. Prep School: £1,808–£4,657.

Charitable status. St Swithun's School Winchester is a Registered Charity, number 307335. It exists to provide education for girls aged 11–18 years.

Chairman of School Council: Professor Natalie Lee, LLB

Headmistress: Ms Jane Gandee, MA Cantab

Deputy Head Pastoral: Mr Graham Yates, MA Brunel
Deputy Head Academic: Mr Charlie Hammel, AB Princeton, MLitt St Andrews

Admissions Registrar: Mrs Kate Cairns
Assistant Registrar: Mrs Liz Turner

Sheffield High School for Girls
GDST

10 Rutland Park, Sheffield, South Yorkshire S10 2PE

Tel: 0114 266 0324
email: enquiries@she.gdst.net
website: www.sheffieldhighschool.org.uk
Twitter: @SheffieldHigh
Facebook: @sheffieldhighschool
LinkedIn: /Sheffield-High-School

Sheffield High School for Girls is part of the GDST (Girls' Day School Trust). The GDST is the leading network of independent girls' schools in the UK. As a charity that owns and runs 23 schools and two academies, it reinvests all its income in its schools. For further information about the Trust, see p. xxiii or visit www.gdst.net.

Number of Pupils. 972: Infant 102, Junior 185, Senior 467, Sixth Form 218.

The school was opened in 1878 and has occupied its pleasant site in the suburb of Broomhill since 1887. It draws its pupils from all parts of the Sheffield City region. Transport to and from school is available from a wide area.

The Infant School, which relocated to its new home at 266 Fulwood Road in September 2017, is home to Snowdrops Pre-School (including boys), Reception, Year 1 and Year 2 girls. The girls benefit from specialist teachers and teaching facilities, enabling them to develop an early love of music, languages, sport and drama. The facilities on this site include the Infant School Library, Music Rooms, Science Room and Art room where specialist teaching takes place.

The Junior School, based at 5 Melbourne Avenue, is surrounded by outdoor learning spaces as well as easy access to the wider facilities in the Senior School, including sports facilities. Learning is enhanced by enrichment beyond the curriculum, which includes speakers and visitors into school, trips to theatres and museums.

In the Senior School, which is located at 10 Rutland Park, a £3.5 million development programme over the past two years has seen the development of a new Cookery room, a new Drama Studio and a complete refurbishment of the Gym, which now incorporates a state-of-the-art Fitness Suite and accommodation for trampolining, gymnastics and dance.

A separate Sixth Form Centre on Melbourne Avenue, close to the Senior School buildings, offers well-furnished and comfortable common rooms for Years 12 and 13, a Learning Resource Centre with laptops, printer and high speed Wi-Fi, and fully equipped kitchen.

Beyond the School Day. Food and refreshments are available in the dining hall from 7.30 am every morning. In the Infant and Junior School, after-school care is available daily from 3.15 pm until 6.15 pm in Tea Time Club. The cost for Tea Time Club is £7.50 per day. Bookings can be made in advance or on the day if required.

Between 3.30 pm and 5.30 pm every Monday to Friday during term time, Senior pupils can stay in school to devote time to homework tasks or revision. Many pupils also stay in school after 3.30 pm to take part in any of a wide range of activities led by staff and senior students.

Curriculum. School life at Sheffield Girls' centres on an exciting and challenging curriculum. As well as the core subjects of English, Mathematics and Science, the broader Infant and Junior School curriculum includes History, Geography, Drama, Religious Studies and PSHE with specialist teaching in Music, Modern Foreign Languages (French, Spanish or German), Art and Design Technology and Physical Education.

In the Senior School, a challenging and up-to-date curriculum combines the best of traditional, modern, scientific, creative and practical subjects to provide a broad, balanced and inspiring Secondary School education. From Year 7, girls study three separate sciences, two modern foreign languages and Latin (from Year 8) in addition to the standard national curriculum. There is a full range of options in Languages, Humanities and Technical and Aesthetic subjects. Most girls study nine GCSE subjects.

In the Sixth Form, the school offers a bespoke curriculum tailored to the needs of each individual, with a personalised timetable for each girl. The majority of Year 12 students study 3 or 4 A Levels. Students also opt to do the Extended Project Qualification (EPQ).

The school has received a string of prestigious national awards for the exceptional quality of its extra-curricular provision, such as PE Quality Mark with Distinction, Artsmark (Gold), GO4it, ICT Quality Mark, Eco-Schools Award and Career Mark, making it the only school in South Yorkshire to be so accredited for the quality of its careers provision.

The school's sporting teams regularly compete in national finals and teams regularly reach national competition finals in STEM subjects and debating. The School has almost 100 lunchtime and after school clubs, which encourage excellence in sport, music, drama and art, and offers the full Duke of Edinburgh's Award scheme. A varied programme of residential trips and expeditions at home and abroad is offered, including Sport, Music, Foreign Language and Art tours. The School has strong community links and has received four Independent School Awards as well as being shortlisted in two further years. Awards have been for:

Best Independent-Maintained School Collaboration, Outstanding Community Initiative and Best Leadership Team.

Fees per term (2018–2019). Senior School £4,325, Junior Department £3,072–£3,188.

The fees cover the regular curriculum, school books, stationery and other materials, most extra-curricular activities, but not school lunches. Girls are required to stay for school lunches up to Year 7 and these are charged separately per term.

Scholarships and Bursaries. The GDST makes available to the School a substantial number of scholarships and bursaries. In particular, it aims as far possible to focus its support on girls for whom the chance of a GDST education would be a transformative, life-changing prospect.

Bursaries are awarded to pupils in the top 30% of performance in the entrance examinations. All bursaries are means-tested.

Scholarships are awarded on merit, irrespective of financial means. Offers are made based upon performance in the entrance examinations or audition for Year 7, or in the case of Sixth Form scholarships for outstanding ability demonstrated in individual subjects and disciplines. A Scholarship can be combined with a bursary where there is financial need.

Charitable status. Sheffield High School is part of The Girls' Day School Trust, which is a Registered Charity, number 306983.

Chair of Local Governors: Mr Jon Dunn

***Headmistress*: Mrs N Gunson**, BSc MSc Huddersfield

Deputy Head: Mrs S White, BA Sheffield

Senior Teacher, Assistant Head (*Examinations, Assessment and Learning*): Mrs K Boulton-Pratt, MSc Leicester

Director of Sixth Form: Ms Cathy Walker, BA Sheffield

Assistant Head (*Pastoral*): Mrs A Reed, BA Sheffield Hallam

Assistant Head (*Co-Curricular*): Mrs E Rodgers, BEd Liverpool John Moores

Head of Junior School: Mr C Hald, MA York

Director of PR, Marketing and Communications: Mrs A Bouchier, BA Sheffield

Director of Finance and Operations: Mr I Kane, BSc Open University

South Hampstead High School
GDST

3 Maresfield Gardens, London NW3 5SS

Tel: 020 7435 2899
Fax: 020 7431 8022
email: senior@shhs.gdst.net
           junior@shhs.gdst.net
website: www.shhs.gdst.net
Twitter: @SHHSforgirls
Facebook: @SouthHampsteadHighSchool
LinkedIn: /south-hampstead-high-school

Founded in 1876, South Hampstead High School is a selective, independent day school for girls aged 4 to 18 in North West London – a buzzing academic powerhouse with kindness and curiosity at its core. Although excellent results and university destinations place it among the country's top schools, South Hampstead is also known for its forward-looking ethos and an approach that aims to ignite a genuine joy in learning.

The school is well-connected to most London postcodes, close to Finchley Road underground (Jubilee and Metropolitan lines), several overground stations and numerous bus routes. It has approximately 900 pupils, including around 130 in the Sixth Form and 265 in the Junior School. Entry is competitive: at 4+ and 7+ to the Junior School, and 11+ and 16+ to the Senior School. Occasionally vacancies arise at other ages. Full details of the admissions procedures are available at www.shhs.gdst.net.

The Junior School occupies two large houses a few minutes' walk from the main Senior School site. The Senior School is housed in a bright, modern building, designed by Hopkins Architects. Sixth Form students have their own home in Oakwood – complete with its own common room and cafe – in a beautiful, Victorian house, connected to the Senior School. A four-acre sports ground with excellent facilities is a short walk away.

At South Hampstead, the curriculum is designed to provide a secure and imaginative basis for academic progress at each key stage of a pupil's development. The intention is that all girls develop their own enthusiasms and initiative within a broad educational framework and a balanced range of academic, cultural and aesthetic subjects. In the Junior School there is a clear focus on developing literacy and numeracy skills and an integrated approach to the curriculum whereby the focus is on learning across several subjects around a theme. In this way girls develop real depth of knowledge, as well as confidence in key skills such as research, analysing results and interpreting and presenting information. In the Senior School the curriculum has a strong academic spine. The Head teaches Philosophy to all Year 7 pupils, while other subjects on offer include Critical Thinking, Design & Technology, Drama and a choice of French, German, Mandarin and Spanish. The girls also have a weekly double period of enrichment – with choices ranging from electronic music production to photography – providing ample opportunities for pupils to discover new interests and passions.

The Sixth Form offers a range of 23 subjects at A Level and students have a strong track record in the Extended Project Qualification (EPQ). A rich and varied programme of speakers, leadership opportunities, international trips and co-curricular activities ensure that every student has the chance to grow, to give back and to shine. The school's Futures Programme provides a comprehensive framework for supporting pupils with higher education and career choices. Typically around 15% go on to Oxbridge each year, with the vast majority offered their first choice university – primarily to Russell Group universities, but with good numbers to medical school, prestigious art colleges and Ivy League destinations.

Pupils throughout the school participate enthusiastically in an enormous number of co-curricular clubs, societies and activities. Creativity in art, writing, music and drama is strongly encouraged at all stages. There are many orchestras, ensembles and choirs. Tuition in almost any instrument and singing can be arranged and girls are prepared for the examinations of the Associated Board of the Royal School of Music. Large numbers of pupils participate in the Duke of Edinburgh's Award and Young Enterprise business scheme.

Fees per term (2018–2019). Senior School £6,218, Junior School £5,109.

The fees do not include school meals or instrumental/singing lessons.

Scholarships and Bursaries. A number of scholarships and bursaries are available to internal or external candidates for entry at 11+ and to the Sixth Form. The bursaries are means-tested to ensure that the school remains accessible to bright girls who would benefit from a South Hampstead education but who would be unable to enter the school without financial assistance. Scholarships are currently awarded for academic and musical excellence as well as for art and drama in the Sixth Form.

Charitable status. South Hampstead High School is part of the Girls' Day School Trust, a leading network of independent girls' schools, which is a Registered Charity, number 306983.

Local Governors:
Chairman: Mrs H Strange, GRSM, PGCE, RGN
Mrs K Fear
Mrs L Frank, BA
Mr R Freeman, BA, MBA
Prof R Jackman, MA
Miss D Navanayagam, BA
Mrs J Solomon
Mrs M Trehearne, MA, BEd
Mrs V Fox, BSc
Dr V Wass, OBE, BSc

Headmistress: Mrs Victoria Bingham, BA Oxon
(*Classics*)

Deputy Heads:
Ms Z Brass, BA Queen's University Canada (*Economics*)
Mr S Foster, BA Oxon, MA Warwick (*Economics*)
Director of Sixth Form: Mr J Waller, BA Oxon (*PPE*)
Director of Finance and Operations: Mr G Collins-Down, MSc Cardiff (*Business Administration*)

Senior School Teaching Staff:
Mr C Alaru, BA Queensland (*Drama*)
Miss A Aneja, MSc King's College (*Mathematics*)
Mrs J Arundale, BSc Lancaster (*Physics*)
Mr P Arundale, BSc Manchester (*Chemistry*)
Mrs R Banfield, BA Brighton (*Physical Education*)
Mrs A Bartnicka, CLM Granada (*German*)
Mr C Beecroft, BMuS Trinity Laban (*Music*)
Mrs S Bernstein, BSc London (*Physics*)
Miss C Bluck, BA Kingston (*Art*)
Ms A Bokkerink, MA Cambridge (*English*)
Miss A Bolland, BA Cambridge (*Classics*)
Mrs V Boyarsky, BA Cantab, MPhil London (*History*)
Ms R Buttigieg, BSc Malta (*Biology*)
Mr E Cabezas, BA Seville (*Spanish*)
Ms E Chandler-Thompson, MA London (*History*)
Mrs M Claridge, BA Portsmouth (*Design Technology*)
Ms M Cohen Christofidis (*Philosophy*)
Dr S Collisson, BMus Manchester (*Music*)
Mrs G Cooke, BA Brighton (*Physical Education*)
Mrs O Crossley-Holland, BA Oxon (*English*)
Mr S Davis, BSc London (*Mathematics & Statistics*)
Dr M Egan, BA UCL, MA Essex, PhD UCL (*Politics, History and Critical Thinking*)
Ms N Elliot, BA Manhattanville College (*Biology*)
Miss S Ellis, BMus Cardiff (*Music*)
Dr K Etheridge, BA, MSt, DPhil Oxon (*English*)
Miss M Fajardo Duran, QTS, CILT (*Spanish*)
Mrs S Fanning, BSc London, Dip Arch RIBA (*Design Technology*)
Mrs C Finley, CAPES Toulouse (*French and Spanish*)
Mr M Gadgil, BSc OU (*Chemistry*)
Mrs C Gallagher, BSc Leeds (*Biology and Geography*)
Mr N Garrard, MA Cantab, MA Manchester (*English*)
Miss M Greenland, BSc London (*Computing*)
Mr J Hansford, BA York (*Mathematics*)
Miss C Hardy, BA Bath (*Physical Education*)
Mr B Harkins, MA Cantab, MA London (*English*)
Mrs D F Hugh, BA Manchester, MBA (*Modern Languages*)
Miss J Humphreys, BSc Birmingham (*Geography*)

Mr N Hunter, BA Liverpool, MA Goldsmiths London (*Art*)
Ms R Hewes, MA King's College London (*Classics*)
Mrs A Johnson, BA Birmingham (*Theology and Religion*)
Mr T Jones, BA Cambridge (*Mathematics*)
Mrs H Kamps, BSc British Columbia (*Physics*)
Mr A Keiler, BA Leicester (*English*)
Mrs L Kench, BA Oxford Brookes (*Sport*)
Ms N Kennedy, BA (*Theology and Religion*)
Mr R Kerr, BSc Polytechnic of Central London (*Mathematics*)
Ms A Khoursheed, MA Surrey (*Arabic*)
Miss L Knowles, BA Sheffield (*History*)
Miss A Knox, MSci Durham (*Chemistry*)
Mr P Larochelle, BA Massachusetts (*Drama and English*)
Miss Z Levin, BSc Oxford Brooks (*Physical Education*)
Mrs N Liston, MA Oxon (*Geography*)
Mrs A Logan, BSc Wales (*Science*)
Miss S-L Lui, BA Oxon (*Classics*)
Miss N Marchant, BA Cantab (*Classics*)
Ms K Martin, BA De Montfort (*Drama*)
Miss J Matthews, BSc Loughborough (*Physical Education*)
Miss H McDougall, BA Oxon (*History*)
Mrs J Meyer, BSc, MA London (*German*)
Miss C Moffat, BA Warwick (*History and Politics*)
Dr E Morewood, MA Cantab (*Biology*)
Mr M Morgan, BA Leeds Metropolitan (*Geography*)
Mrs P Morgan, MA Cantab (*History*)
Miss S Morgan, BA, MA Norwich (*Art*)
Mr M Morley, BA Lancaster (*French and History*)
Miss A Morton, BA Bristol (*English*)
Dr M Naydenova-Slade, PhD Courtauld (*History of Art*)
Mrs G Nwoko, MA Roehampton (*Spanish and French*)
Mrs S O'Driscoll, BA Cork (*German*)
Dr R Osborne, PhD Imperial (*Physics*)
Mr L Poza, BSc London (*Chemistry*)
Mrs L Raitz, MA Cantab (*French*)
Miss Z Robson, BSc Brunel (*Physical Education*)
Ms R Russo, BSc Durham (*Physics*)
Mrs E J Sanders, BSc Miami (*Geography*)
Miss L Scahill, BA Australian College of Physical Education (*Physical Education*)
Mrs P Shah, BA Oxford (*Mathematics*)
Ms C Simpson, BA Oxford (*Classics*)
Miss K Smith, BA Bath (*Physical Education*)
Mr R Soames, BA UCL (*German and Italian*)
Ms V M Spawls, BSc Westminster (*Biology*)
Miss R Stern, BA London, MA Warwick (*Drama*)
Mr D Suarez, BSc London (*Mathematics*)
Mr C Tanfield, MA Oxon (*Classics and Universities Officer*)
Ms V Teles, MA Institute of Education (*Mathematics*)
Miss C Waghorn, BA Exeter (*Psychology*)
Miss Y Wang, BSc ICL (*Mathematics*)
Ms L Wengrowe, BA Sussex (*History of Art & Cultural Studies*)
Mr C Wharton, BA Oxon (*Economics*)
Mr M Willett, BA Cambridge (*Mathematics*)
Dr C J Woodward, BSc, PhD London (*Biology*)
Ms A Wrigglesworth, BA Loughborough, MA Cambridge (*Design Technology*)

Head of Junior School: Mrs Gabrielle Solti, BA Oxon
Deputy Head of Junior School: Miss L Szemerenyi, BSc Sussex

Junior School Teaching Staff:
Mrs C Atkinson, MA Cantab
Mrs T Bhattaacharya, MA King's College London
Mrs H Blackford, BSc Durham
Miss M Campbell, BEd Edinburgh
Mr C Christensen, BA Middlesex
Miss S Cramer, BSc Leeds
Ms C Grimes, BA Manchester

Ms Z Hammond-Smith, BA Roehampton
Miss S Jenkins, BA Sussex
Ms B Lagaay, BSc Sheffield Hallam
Mrs S-J Lewis, BA London
Mrs L Lougee, BA Durham
Mrs Z Paramour, BA Leeds
Mrs A Ruffini, MA Milan
Mrs S Somers, BA Manchester, MA UCL
Mrs R Sterling, BA Birmingham
Ms J Stewart, BA Oxford Brookes
Mr M Weddell, BEng Brunel

Stamford High School

St Martin's, Stamford, Lincolnshire PE9 2LL

Tel:	01780 484200
Fax:	01780 484201
email:	headshs@ses.lincs.sch.uk
website:	www.ses.lincs.sch.uk
Twitter:	@SpedeNews
Facebook:	@stamfordendowedschools

Motto: *Christe me spede*

Founded by Browne's Hospital Foundation, of Stamford, 1876.

Introduction. Stamford High School is one of three schools within the overall Stamford Endowed Schools Educational Charity, along with Stamford School (boys) and Stamford Junior School, the co-educational junior school.

Numbers and Boarding Houses. There are 633 girls aged 11–18 years including boarders. The main point of entry is at age 11 though applications are welcomed at any stage up to the Sixth Form. Girls who enter through the Junior School progress automatically on to the High School without further competitive entrance testing. Boarders are received from the age of 8 (in the Junior School). There are two Boarding Houses for girls including a Sixth Form Boarding House where the girls have single or shared study bedrooms. The School accepts full, weekly and three-night boarders.

Fees per annum (2018–2019). Day £15,318; Full Boarding £28,446; Weekly Boarding £24,801; 3-Night Boarding £21,552.

These fees include all stationery, textbooks and games. School lunches for day girls are at additional charge.

Registration Fee £100. Acceptance Fee £250.

Extras. Individual music lessons, Speech and Drama, Dancing (Riding for boarders only).

Curriculum. The curriculum is designed to ensure all girls have a balanced educational programme up to age 16 thus avoiding premature specialisation. The National Curriculum is broadly followed but much more is added to the curriculum to make it stimulating and rewarding. Most girls are entered for at least 9 GCSE examinations and continue on to A Level examinations leading to university entry. In partnership with Stamford School, all Sixth Form girls have access to the full range of A Level subjects offered across the two schools providing an exceptionally wide choice of 25 subjects.

Throughout their time in the school girls are prepared for the examinations of the Associated Board of the Royal Schools of Music in music and The London Academy of Music and Dramatic Art for speech and drama. There is much scope for creative activities in Music, Art and Drama and state-of-the-art facilities for Information & Communication Technology, including access to the Internet. The Director of Music for the Stamford Endowed Schools

ensures that the Music Department works very closely with Stamford School providing access to a wide range of activities for orchestras, bands, Chapel Choir and choirs. There are joint drama productions and a Performing Arts Studio.

Sport and Physical Education include Hockey, Netball, Tennis, Swimming, Golf, Judo, Athletics, Volleyball, Basketball, Badminton, Trampoline, Gymnastics and Squash. There is a very full programme of extracurricular activities including Olympic Gymnastics, Athletics and Taekwondo. There is a heated, indoor swimming pool, a Sports Hall and a floodlit artificial hockey pitch. The Duke of Edinburgh's Award Scheme operates at Bronze, Silver and Gold levels with a considerable number of girls taking part each year. There is a thriving, mixed CCF offering RN, Army and RAF sections. There are many school clubs and societies and a thriving weekend activity programme.

Entrance Examinations are held in January.

Scholarships and Bursaries. The Schools offer a range of scholarships for pupils entering into years 7, 9 and 12 (Sixth Form). Scholarships are less common for pupils entering into other years but may at times be available. There are scholarships for Academic, Music, Art, Sports and All-Rounder performance. Means-tested bursaries can be applied for by families of pupils who would otherwise not be able to benefit from a Stamford education. Please see our website for full details.

Charitable status. As part of the Stamford Endowed Schools, Stamford High School is a Registered Charity, number 527618.

Chairman of the Governing Body: Dr Michael Dronfield

***Principal of the Stamford Endowed Schools*: William Phelan**

***Vice-Principal, Head*: Victoria Buckman**

Deputy Head: Andrew Murphy
Director of Studies: Lorraine Johnson
SLT – Pastoral Care: Dominique Evans
SLT – PSD, Events and Trips: Denise Smith
Head of Sixth Form: Christine Hawkins
SES Chaplain: The Revd Mark Goodman

Teaching Staff:
Kirsten Allen (*Geography*)
Diana Ashley (*Art*)
Tessa Bennie (*Head of 6th Form Enrichment*)
Maria Bewers (*PE*)
Michael Blissett (*Head of Classics*)
Caroline Boyfield (*DT*)
Aimee Brock (*Maths*)
Daniel Burke (*Head of Maths*)
Lucy Cade-Stewart (*Classics*)
Elida Calleja Rubio (*Head of Spanish*)
Rachael Carter (*Maths*)
Nicholas Clift (*Spanish*)
Christian Collett (*History*)
Andrew Cox (*Head of Religious Studies*)
Andrew Crookell (*Head of Chemistry*)
Anneke Davies (*Head of Drama*)
Sarah Davies (*Head of History*)
Katie Dexter (*English*)
Yvonne Dias (*Art*)
Jillian Dickson (*Maths*)
Kate Docherty (*Religious Studies*)
Charlotte Echezarreta (*English*)
Alison Gossel (*Home Economics*)
Jennifer Hamflett (*Biology*)
Lynette Harte (*Psychology*)
Annabelle Holland (*Head of Art*)
Julia Husbands (*Physics*)

Nicola Jeffs (*English*)
Anna Johnson (*Maths*)
Anne Johnstone (*Head of Biology*)
Luke Jones (*Religious Studies*)
Emmanuelle Kerbrat (*MFL*)
Rachel Kersey (*Psychology*)
Amy Lewin (*Home Economics*)
Jacqueline Lewis-Gorman (*MFL*)
Alexandra Marsden (*Maths*)
Victoria Maskell (*Head of Psychology*)
Holly McCullough (*English*)
Lucy Meadows (*PE*)
Brenda Murphy (*Coach – Fitness*)
Holly Naismith (*Head of PE*)
Adam Patchett (*Head of Physics*)
Ruth Peterson (*Science*)
Amanda Rackham (*History*)
Catherine Raitt (*PE*)
Elizabeth Salt (*Head of Careers and UCAS*)
Victoria Saunders (*History*)
Kiren Sekhar (*Chemistry*)
Michael Smith (*Head of Geography*)
David Tuck (*Head of Politics*)
Catherine Vié (*Head of French*)
Emma Ware (*Psychology*)
Nicola Watson (*Drama*)
Nigel Webster (*Chemistry*)
Grant Weeks (*Biology*)
Elizabeth Wenban (*Physics*)
Gary Whitehouse (*Head of Learning Support*)
Hazel Williams (*Maths*)
Christopher Williamson (*Maths*)
Karen Wilson (*Head of Food and Nutrition*)
Vivienne Wilson (*Classics*)
Mark Zacharias (*Head of English*)

Music Department:
Giles Turner (*Director of Music*)
Duncan McIlrae (*Assistant Director of Music*)
Stephen Chandley (*Head of Brass*)
Daniel Leetch (*Head of Strings*)

Visiting Music Staff:
Steven Andrews (*Drum Kit, Percussion*)
Jonathan Aughton (*Flute*)
Margaret Bennett (*Singing*)
Karen Bentley (*Cello, Double Bass*)
Tatiana Boison (*Pianoforte*)
Susan Bond (*Singing*)
David Brown (*Clarinet*)
Alexander Crutchley (*Lower Brass*)
Julie Dustan (*Flute*)
Frances Gill (*Saxophone*)
Nicholas Gray (*Electric Guitar*)
Nan Ingrams
Sarah Latham (*Violin, Viola*)
Alexander MacDonald (*Classic Pianoforte*)
Margaret Maclennan (*Pianoforte*)
Anne McCrae (*Bassoon, Pianoforte*)
Elizabeth Murphy (*Violin, Pianoforte*)
Janet Roberts (*Cello*)
Kieran O'Riordan (*Percussion*)
Elizabeth Taylor, BA (*Violin, Viola*)
Nicholas Taylor
Eleanor Turner (*Harp*)
Lynn Williamson, LTCC (*Pianoforte*)

Medical Officer: Dr J Barney, MBChB, DAvMed, DOccMED, MRCGP

Streatham & Clapham High School
GDST

42 Abbotswood Road, London SW16 1AW

Tel: 020 8677 8400 (Senior School)
          020 8674 6912 (Prep School & Nursery)
Fax: 020 8677 2001
email: senior@schs.gdst.net
          prep@schs.gdst.net
website: www.schs.gdst.net
Twitter: @SCHSgdst
Facebook: @SCHSgdst

Motto: *ad sapientiam sine metu*

Streatham & Clapham High School is a distinguished historical foundation. It was founded, as Brixton High School, in 1887 by the Girls' Public Day School Trust as one of its earliest member schools. HRH Princess Louise, Duchess of Argyll opened its buildings in Wavertree Road, London SW2, in 1895, now the site of the Prep School. In 1994 the Senior School moved to Abbotswood Road, London SW16, into the imposing buildings of the former Battersea Grammar School.

The School offers an inspiring, enlightened and intellectually challenging education for its pupils in a lively, vibrant and warmly supportive environment. The family ethos of Streatham & Clapham High School enables its masters and mistresses to know, value and nurture each pupil as an individual. The School celebrates diversity and draws strength from its rich social and cultural mix.

The School's core belief is that all members of its community should be inspired to outperform expectations on a daily basis. The pursuit of excellence is thus the School's defining feature. It nurtures pupils to attain success across the widest spectrum of activity, extending far beyond the conventional 'academic' horizon. In so doing, they learn the beauty of reason, the allure of the aesthetic, and the vitality of the physical. The School's pupils thus learn to navigate the landscape of the human spirit and achieve beyond the realms of expectation.

General information. Streatham & Clapham High School is an independent, academically selective school for girls aged 3–18, with over 760 pupils on the roll. Girls aged 3–11 attend the Nursery and Prep School, located in spacious buildings with outstanding facilities in Wavertree Road in Streatham Hill. The Senior School inhabits a four-acre site focused on a symmetrical 1930s building designed by J E K Harrison, FRIBA in a delightfully tranquil and leafy oasis of south London, next to Tooting Bec Common, where the soundscape is dominated by birdsong.

Many girls live locally and an increasing number walk or cycle to School, encouraged by the School's commitment to sustainable travel. The Senior School is ten minutes' walk from Streatham Hill National Rail station and seventeen minutes from Balham National Rail and Underground. Other pupils come from further afield, including Battersea, Clapham, Wandsworth, Dulwich, Tooting and Brixton. The School is also within easy reach of the theatres, museums and galleries of central London.

Facilities. The School has first-class facilities for learning, providing an environment that enables girls to develop their interests and strengths both inside and outside the classroom. The School keeps up-to-date with new teaching methods and innovative techniques, such as interactive online learning, and use them to engage and extend its pupils. Its facilities include two ICT suites, a music suite including a dedicated music technology suite, a Recital Hall, two design & technology workshops, a full-size indoor

Sports Hall, Dance and Art studios, and sports pitches and tennis courts. In 2017, the school occupied a stunning state-of-the-art sixth-form centre on a new floor on the main building (which constituted the first phase of the £13 million building project), and the final phase of the building work, an architecturally innovative and spacious new dining hall and a striking new reception at the front of the school, together with a fountain atrium, was completed in March 2018. The new facilities have won a number of architecture awards, including the Building Design Awards, a RIBA Award, and the Architects' Journal Retrofit Awards (School Project of the Year).

Academic matters. The ability profile of the School is significantly above the national average, with a proportion of pupils being far above the national average. The School is in the top tier of independent schools in terms of its public examination results. Pupils do well: in 2018 at GCSE, over 17% of results were Grade 9. At A Level, the percentage of grades at A*–B over the past five years has averaged 75%.

Curriculum. The school offers a wide range of subjects. Pupils in the Upper Third, Lower Fourth and Upper Fourth (Years 7 to 9) study the core disciplines of English, Mathematics, and Science. Other subjects offered include Art, Computing, Design & Technology, Drama, French, Geography, History, Italian, Latin, Music, Physical Education, Religious Education, and Spanish. All of these subjects, as well as Ancient Greek, are available at GCSE or IGCSE in the Fifth Form (Years 10 and 11). Pupils in Upper Third and Lower Fourth also follow the 'Learning2Learn' programme that encourages pupils to explore and develop their own awareness of how they approach learning opportunities and how to become more effective and autonomous in their learning.

The School offers a range of subjects for study at A Level, including Art & Design, Biology, Chemistry, Classical Civilisation, Latin, Critical Thinking, Design & Technology, Drama & Theatre Studies, Economics, English Literature, Geography, Government & Politics, History, French, Italian, Spanish, Mathematics, Further Mathematics, Music, Physical Education, Physics, Psychology and Religious Studies. The majority of sixth-form students also pursue the Extended Project Qualification to extend their interests and knowledge. Virtually all sixth-form students proceed to the most competitive Russell Group universities (including Oxbridge).

Enrichment programme ('Kinza'). Kinza, an Arabic term meaning 'hidden treasure', is the unique enrichment programme of timetabled weekly sessions throughout the year. Every Kinza activity is designed to encourage a love and respect for learning for its own sake, utilising the interests and expertise of staff. The activities provide a wide spectrum of choice for each pupil, covering an extremely broad range of activities. In recent years, these have included Mandarin, Anthropology, Robotics, Chess, Law, Meditation, Model United Nations, Cosmology, Kiwi Culture, Podcast Production, To Infinity and Beyond, Urban Wildlife, Magic, and much more. Opportunities to deepen aspects of the broad knowledge acquired through Kinza are afforded through co-curricular trips, individual research, and collaborative working processes in a vertical tutoring system, with younger pupils learning side-by-side with older girls. Each participates in several different activities during the course of the year.

Activities. The School has a thriving co-curricular life, with societies and clubs in the fields of Art, Design and Technology, Classics, English, Geography, History, ICT, Mathematics, Modern Foreign Languages, Science and Religious Studies, as well as more specialised activities such as CCF. There are a very large number of performing arts activities, pupils having the opportunity to perform in a

number of dramatic productions during the school year or to belong to around 15 music ensembles, including choirs and orchestras, which annually lead the School's Carol Service at Southwark Cathedral. Pupils may belong to a legion of sporting clubs (including hockey, netball, rounders, rowing, cricket, football, tag rugby, athletics and much more) and fixtures, and have the opportunity to participate in a number of outdoor educational activities, such as the Duke of Edinburgh's Award. A busy programme of trips and expeditions is scheduled, for instance Classics and Languages trips to Greece and Italy, an annual flagship sixth-form trip to Cambodia, an annual geography trip to Iceland, and music tours of the Continent. Pupils have trekked across the Atlas Mountains in Morocco and reached the Base Camp of Mount Everest. The School's proximity to central London makes possible many excursions to concerts, museums, art galleries and theatres.

Pastoral care. The School does not view outstanding pastoral care as an 'add-on' to its academic programme. Neither does it believe that a 'hothouse' atmosphere is desirable or healthy. The School's core belief is that girls achieve best if they are happy and settled in their social relationships. Hence the 'family' ethos of the School, which holds that the way in which individuals are nurtured and valued is intrinsic to the pupils' progress and success. All pupils are under the care of one of five Heads of House, and all members of staff, up to the Head Master, are easily accessible to pupils. To ensure that the School's social and emotional care is comprehensive and alert, the School has a Deputy Head Mistress with oversight of pastoral matters. In conjunction with the work of the Heads of House and the sixth-form mentoring scheme, this enables the School to identify challenges or problems early and then work with pupils and where necessary their parents to overcome them. It also helps the School to encourage and celebrate real progress and achievement every day. The strong prefectorial system and school council under the leadership of the Head Girl ensure that the pupil voice has suitable influence in shaping the life and work of the School.

Admission. There are six principal admission stages: by assessment for the Nursery (3+ years), 4+ and 7+, and by competitive entrance examination at 11+ and 13+ and at Sixth Form level. Occasional places sometimes arise at any age; interested parents are advised to contact the Registrar. All candidates for 11+ entry are called for interview in the Michaelmas Term. Applicants for 13+ entry will have individual interviews after the 13+ entrance examination.

All senior-school applicants sit the School's entrance examination. The 11+ examination comprises papers in English and Mathematics. Applicants for 13+ entry sit papers in English, Mathematics and Science.

The transfer of a pupil from the Prep to the Senior School is contingent on the School's assessment of the pupil's suitability for admission into the Upper Third Form (Year 7).

Fees per term (2018–2019). Senior School £5,874, Prep School £4,564, Nursery £3,477.

The fees are inclusive of non-residential trips and extras, but exclude the cost of lunch.

Academic scholarships. A number of academic scholarships, worth up to a maximum of 50% of fees, are available for 11+ entrance. They are not means-tested. Awards are made on the basis of individual candidates' performance in the entrance examination and interview. A number of sixth-form academic scholarships are also available, on the basis of a written assessment and interview.

Specialist scholarships. Specialist scholarships are awarded at 11+ in the fields of Art, Sport, Drama and Music (including the Sadie Crawford Music Scholarship, primarily for jazz musicians). Further details are available on the school website.

Bursaries. A small number of means-tested bursaries are available at 11+ and HSBC scholarships are available for students applying for the Sixth Form. All requests are considered in confidence and application forms are available from the Registrar.

The Board of Local Governors:
Mrs F Smith, BA Dunelm, PGCE (*Chairman*)
Mrs R Bailey Packard, BA
Mr R Brent, BA
Miss S Campbell, BA, MA
Mrs R Chowdhury, BA, MSc
Mrs K Eldred
Mrs E Gibson, BA, LLB

Head Master: Dr Millan Sachania, MA Cantab, MPhil, PhD, FRSA

Second Master: Mr R Hinton, BSc Dunelm, PGCE (*Mathematics*)

Deputy Head Mistress: Mrs G Cross, BA, MA. PGCE (*English*)

Assistant Head Master (*Co-Curricular and Partnerships*): Mr A Christie, MA Oxon, PGCE (*Classics*)

Assistant Head Mistress (*Sixth Form*): Mrs S Ridley, BA Dunelm, PGCE (*Classics*)

Assistant Head Mistress (*Academic*): Mrs N Snelgrove, BSc, PGCE (*Mathematics*)

Head of Prep School: Mr T Mylne, BA, PGCE

Director of Finance & Operations: Mr S Puryer, BA

Director of Marketing & Communications: Ms M Beer, BA Columbia, USA

Assistant Masters and Mistresses (*Senior School*):
Mrs Conor Ainsworth, BEd Canterbury NZ, PGCE (*House Mistress, Physical Education*)
Ms Sharon Akintunde, BSc UCL, MSc, GTP (*Head of Chemistry*)
Ms Rebecca Baker, BA Falmouth, PGCE (*Acting Head of Art*)
Mr Paul Baker, BA Colchester, PGCE (*English*)
Mrs Kate Birtwistle, BSc Leeds, PGCE (*House Mistress, Biology*)
Mr Brian Brackrog, BA San Diego, MA (*Head of Economics*)
Mrs Fiona Brent, BA Birmingham, PGCE (*Art*)
Miss Anusha Burton, BA Birmingham, PGCE (*Religious Studies*)
Miss Catherine Casset, BA Paris, MA, PGCE (*French*)
Mr Khalid Chaudery, BSc Strathclyde, MSc, PGCE (*Second in Mathematics*)
Dr Sadaf Choudhry, MEng QMW, PhD, PGCE (*Chemistry, Physics, Lead in Innovation and Research*)
Mrs Amy Cooper, BA Leeds, MA, PGCE (*Head of Art, Lead in Extended Learning, Innovation & Research*)
Mrs Laura Cooper, BA Nottingham, QTS (*Head of Modern Foreign Languages, Head of Careers*)
Mr Andrew Doddridge, BSc UCL, PGCE (*Head of Geography*)
Miss Mariarosa Durello, BA Padua, Italy PGCE (*Italian*)
Ms Bridget Elton, BA Newcastle, PG Dip D&T, PGCE (*Design & Technology*)
Mrs Drina Evans, BSc Edgehill, PGCE (*Computer Science*)
Mrs Mary Evans, BA Exeter, PGCE (*Drama*)
Mrs Ciara Eves, BA St Mary's Twickenham, QTS (*Director of Sport*)
Ms Danielle Feehan, BA Sussex, MA Birkbeck London, PGCE (*English*)
Miss Sarah Fitzgibbon, BSc Leeds, PGCE (*Head of Science, Head of Physics*)

Mrs Jane Flanagan, BA Nottingham, MSc, QTS (*Geography*)
Miss Carole Forber, MMath Dunelm, PGCE (*Head of Transition, Mathematics*)
Mr Paul Frost, BA Lancaster, PGCE, ACMA (*Head of Computing and Digital Learning*)
Miss Carmen Garcia-Gomez, BA Southampton, PGCE (*Spanish*)
Mr Duncan Gould, BA Southampton, PGCE (*English*)
Mrs Rachel Grant, BSc Loughborough, PGCE (*House Mistress, Physical Education*)
Ms Sarah Harmer, BA Cardiff, MA, PGCE, CCET (*Head of Learning Support*)
Mr Tom Heaton, BA Ed Goldsmiths London, QTS (*Head of Design & Technology*)
Ms Fiona Helszajn, BA Edinburgh, PGCE (*Second in Modern Foreign Languages, Spanish*)
Mrs Victoria Henderson-Cleland, BA Bristol (*EPQ Coordinator*)
Mrs Annalisa James, BSc UCL, PGCE (*Head of Biology, Oxbridge & Competitive Universities Coordinator – STEM Subjects & Medicine*)
Ms Georgina Kennedy, BSocSc Birmingham, PGCE (*House Mistress, Geography*)
Mrs Juliana Kirby, BA Leicester, PGCE (*Head of Mathematics*)
Miss Alice Kirrage, MA St Andrews, PGCE (*Head of Classics*)
Mr David Lee, BA Leicester, PGCE (*History and Politics*)
Mr Patrick Lynch, BA London Metropolitan, PGCE (*Design & Technology*)
Miss Lucy MacPhee, BA Dunelm, PGCE (*Classics, Lead in Extended Learning*)
Ms Polly May, BMus Edinburgh (*Director of Music*)
Miss Thuhana Nguyen, BSc Queen Mary London, PGCE (*Mathematics*)
Dr Joshua Newton, BA Reed, USA, MA, PhD Cantab, PGCE (*Head of History, Oxbridge & Competitive Universities Coordinator – Arts & USA applications*)
Ms Irene Obalim, BSc Bristol, PGCE (*Chemistry*)
Mr Duncan Reader, MA Cantab, MSc, PGCE (*Mathematics*)
Miss Laura Ruffman, BA Bath, PGCE (*Physical Education*)
Miss Kathryn Shaw, BA Leicester, MA, PGCE (*Acting Second in English*)
Mr Michael Spooner, BSc Bristol, MA Warwick, PGCE (*House Master, Physics*)
Miss Charis Stubbs, BA Leeds Beckett, MSc, PGCE (*Physical Education*)
Ms Penelope Thane-Woodhams, BA Loughborough, PGCE (*Director of Drama*)
Mrs Carol Tempestilli-Sarti, BA Kingston, MA, PGCE (*Learning Support, History*)
Miss Maria Tsikkinis, BSc Bristol, PGCE (*Physics*)
Dr Esther van Heerden, BA Stellenbosch, SA, BA, BEd, MSc, DPhil, PGCE (*Head of Psychology*)
Ms Lily Vigor, BA Central Saint Martins, PGCE (*Art*)
Mrs Beverley Ward, BA Wales, MA, PGCE (*Religious Studies*)
Ms Jennifer Watts, BD London Heythrop, PGCE (*Head of Religious Studies*)
Mrs Emma Wheeler, BSc Birmingham, PGCE (*Biology*)
Mr Jack Williams BA, MA Oxon, QTS (*English*)
Mr Francis Winston, BA UCC Colchester Institute, MA, PGCE (*Music*)
Mrs Gillian Yamin, BSc Bristol, PGCE (*Geography*)

Head Master's Executive Assistant: Ms Shirley Halms
Registrar: Mrs Phyllis Warner

Sydenham High School
GDST

19 Westwood Hill, London SE26 6BL

Tel: 020 8557 7000
email: senior@syd.gdst.net
website: www.sydenhamhighschool.gdst.net
Twitter: @SydenhamHigh
Facebook: @sydenham.high.gdst
LinkedIn: /sydenham-high-school-gdst

Founded in 1887 by four pioneering women, Sydenham High School is an independent day school for girls aged 4–18 and is part of the GDST (Girls' Day School Trust). The GDST is the leading network of independent girls' schools in the UK. As a charity that owns and runs 23 schools and two academies, it reinvests all its income in its schools. For further information about the Trust, see p. xxiii or visit www.gdst.net.

Pupil numbers. Senior School 415, Prep School 222.

Sydenham High is a school bursting with warmth, creativity, talent and, above all, excellence in all that we do. We pride ourselves on enriching young minds in a way that will endure a lifetime. Providing a first-class education for girls was the aim of our founders and it remains our aim today. The outlook and opportunities for girls may have changed, but our educational goals have not. Our school motto, 'Nyle ye Drede' (Fear Nothing), lies at the heart of all we do. A Sydenham High education is centred on the girl, and academic and pastoral excellence go hand in hand. We want our pupils to have a 'can do' approach and inner strength, so that they are enabled to thrive, succeed and be happy.

We are a school which is small enough to ensure that every pupil is visible, but large enough to have lots going on, and the education on offer here is both aspirational and personalised. We want to empower our girls to face potential challenges with confidence and be resilient in all that they do, so that in an ever-changing world they are able to respond positively to the ever-increasing demands placed on them, both at school and in their future lives.

Curriculum. The school offers a broad curriculum, ensuring all our pupils are stimulated and excited by learning. English and Maths provide solid foundations while languages offered include French, German, Spanish, Italian and Latin. All students study Biology, Chemistry and Physics as separate sciences. Creative and practical subjects include Design Technology, Art, PE, Music and Drama, as well as Computer Science. Humanities include History, Geography, Religious Studies and Classical Civilisation.

In the Sixth Form, there are 26 subjects to choose from: Art, Biology, Chemistry, Computer Science, Design Technology, Drama & Theatre Studies, Economics, English Literature, French, Geography, German, Government & Politics, History, Italian, Latin, Mathematics and Further Mathematics, Music, Philosophy, Physics, PE, Psychology, Religious Studies, Sociology and Spanish. Our 'Next Steps' programme ensures that our students are future confident and are equipped with the knowledge and skills to thrive in higher education and beyond. Our programme includes our Oxbridge and Competitive Courses preparation, where students are given targeted and focused guidance to support them in making applications to Oxford or Cambridge, alongside applications for medicine, veterinary, dentistry and law. Another key feature is our Professional Skills programme which ensures that students are well versed in the soft skills required for the workplace. Alongside this, we offer a huge range of additional curriculum opportunities for our sixth formers including the chance to take part in the Young Enterprise Company programme, volunteering in the local community and leadership responsibilities.

Personalised subject guidance at both GCSE and A Level ensures that our students are fully informed when choosing their options. Bespoke timetabling means we are able to offer students the widest range of subject combinations to suit their interests. There are regular careers events and opportunities for students to broaden their knowledge of career options and students go on to read a range of subjects at competitive universities. The breadth of co-curricular opportunities ensures there is something for everyone, encouraging pupils to get involved and develop key skills. The Performing Arts are an integral part of school life, whilst we offer over 20 sports, including rowing. Involvement in the wider community is encouraged through our successful involvement in The Duke of Edinburgh's Award scheme and charity work and volunteering.

Fees per term (2018–2019). Senior School £5,579, Prep School £4,387.

School fees include examination fees, textbooks, stationery and other materials, choral music, PE and swimming, Inspiring Futures and Careers counselling. They do not include instrumental music, speech and drama, and after-school clubs.

Scholarships and Bursaries. *Entrance Scholarships*: The Girls' Day School Trust provides a number of scholarships each year for entry to the Senior School at 11+ and directly into the Sixth Form. Scholarships are awarded on academic merit and no financial means test is involved.

Bursaries: The GDST provides bursaries which are means-tested and intended to ensure that the school remains accessible to bright girls who would benefit from our education, but who would be unable to enter the school without financial assistance. Bursaries are awarded on the basis of financial need and academic merit. Details can be obtained from our Registrar. It is recognised that occasions will arise when some form of short-term assistance is required – a small fund exists to help pupils taking public examinations in such cases.

Sydenham High School Scholarships: Art, Music, Drama and Sports scholarships may be awarded on entry at 11+ in addition to our academic scholarships.

Charitable status. Sydenham High School is part of The Girls' Day School Trust, which is a Registered Charity, number 306983.

Chair of Local Governors: Ms G Evans

Headmistress: **Mrs K C Woodcock**, BA Bristol, PGCE

Deputy Head (*Staff & Student Development*): Mr K Guest, MA St Mary's Twickenham, PGCE

Deputy Head (*Academic*): Mr C Batty, BSc Bangor, Wales, PGCE

Head of Prep School: Ms C Boyd, BA London, PGCE

Head of Sixth Form: Ms R Parrish, BA Southampton, PGCE

Talbot Heath

Rothesay Road, Bournemouth, Dorset BH4 9NJ

Tel: 01202 761881 Senior School Admissions
01202 763360 Junior School Admissions
01202 755410 Finance
Fax: 01202 768155
email: office@talbotheath.org

website: www.talbotheath.org
Twitter: @TalbotHeathSch
Facebook: @TalbotHeathSch
LinkedIn: /Talbot-Heath-School

Motto: *Honour before Honours*

Talbot Heath is an Independent School for Girls, founded in 1886, and is among the longest-established schools in the Bournemouth area, with over a century of success. It is a Church of England Foundation and pupils of all denominations are welcome. This School is committed to safeguarding and promoting the welfare of children and young people and is also committed to a policy of equal opportunity.

There are some 347 girls in the Main School, of whom 80 are in the Sixth Forms and 40 are Boarders. There is a Junior Department for about 147 girls between the ages of 7 and 11. The Pre-Preparatory department caters for 120 girls aged 3+ to 7.

The school enjoys an attractive wooded site and outstanding facilities for Art, Drama, Music and STEAM subjects, they are an APPLE regional training centre with outstanding ICT provision and extensive modern accommodation for a wide range of sports activities. Talbot Heath is also in the top 5 boarding schools for girls in the UK (Study International 2015) Talbot Heath is also no. 1 tennis school in the UK for girls and no. 4 in the world.

Many believe that the future will be powered by STEAM (Science, Technology, Engineering, the Arts and Maths). The extensive new flexible learning centre, dedicated to interdisciplinary learning with a creative focus, will be the heart of the vision for the future. The centre will include a large auditorium, gallery space, graphic design, robotics, technology, textiles, art, drama and food studios, as well as flexible learning spaces for the use of pupils of all ages. In addition the school is building a covered pool and sports facility as part of this inspirational new complex.

The school follows the best practice of the National Curriculum but does not undertake Key Stage testing at levels 1, 2 and 3.

Examinations. 21 subjects are offered to GCSE (including Core Subjects) and A Level, and girls gain places at a variety of universities, including Oxford and Cambridge, or go on to other forms of higher education or professional training. Dorset's no. 1 performing school.

Admission. Girls are admitted into the Junior School by examination at 7 and above and into the Main School by examination at 11+, 12+ and 13+. The Entrance Examination is held annually in January and girls must be capable of working with those of their own age. Entry to the Pre-preparatory Department requires no examination.

Boarding Houses. St Mary's Boarding House is located in the School grounds, Miss Scarr being in overall charge.

Fees per term (2018–2019). Tuition: Senior School: £4,801; Junior School: £2,201–£3,918; Kindergarten according to sessions. Boarding (in addition to Tuition Fees): £3,563 (full); £3,180 (weekly); flexi: £50 per night; 3 nights £120.

Scholarships and bursaries are available and there is also a discount for daughters of Service families and the clergy.

Charitable status. Talbot Heath is a Registered Charity, number 283708. It exists to provide high quality education for children.

Governing Body:
Chairman: Mrs C Norman
Vice Chair: Mrs C Sutcliffe

Dr T Battcock
Mrs C Edwards
Mrs D Leadbetter
Dr A Main
Mr J Paget

Revd Canon Dr C Rutledge
Mrs C Saunders
Mrs R Small
Mr D Townend

Head: **Mrs A Holloway**, MA Oxon

Deputy Head, Pastoral: Mrs C Stone, BSc Hons Royal Holloway London
Head of Junior School: Mrs E Pugh
Deputy Head of Junior School:

Heads of Faculty Senior School:
Mrs T Magrath, MA York (*English*)
Mrs J Maynard, BSc Hons Nottingham (*Mathematics*)
Mr A Hill, BMus Hons, FTCL (*Creative Arts & Technology*)
Mr M Gibson, BSc Hons Hull (*Science*)
Mrs H Chapleo, BSc Hons Kingston (*Humanities*)
Miss L Marks, BSc Hons Loughborough (*Physical Education*)
Miss A Klemz, PGCE Liverpool

Visiting teachers also attend for Piano, Violin, Violoncello, Double Bass, Flute, Clarinet, Oboe, Bassoon, Horn, Saxophone, Trumpet, Trombone, Tuba, Percussion, Singing, Dancing, Speech Training and Voice Production, English for foreign students, French, Spanish and German Conversation.

Director of Support Services: Mr C Evans
Medical Officer: Dr M Shaw
Director of Finance: Mr G Ives
Head of Admissions: Mrs K Wills
Head's PA/Office Manager/HR Manager: Mrs D Flynn

Tormead School

Cranley Road, Guildford, Surrey GU1 2JD
Tel: 01483 575101
Fax: 01483 450592
email: registrar@tormeadschool.org.uk
website: www.tormeadschool.org.uk
Twitter: @TormeadSchool

Tormead is an academically selective independent day school for around 760 girls from 4 to 18 years of age. Founded in 1905, it stands in pleasant grounds, close to the centre of Guildford. The atmosphere is lively and the teaching stimulating and challenging. Standards and expectations are high and girls leave the school as confident, articulate and self-reliant young women, ready to meet the challenges of university and beyond. Almost all girls leave Tormead to read for degrees at the university of their choice. On average, 10% gain an Oxford or Cambridge place.

An extensive extracurricular programme provides further challenge and opportunity. We believe that a breadth of interests, skills and initiative are an essential complement to academic success for the future lives of our pupils.

The school has a lively and active musical life with orchestras, various chamber groups, ensembles and choirs as well as a highly popular and talented Jazz Band which has undertaken tours to various European countries. Drama, dance, public speaking and debating, Young Enterprise, The Wings of Hope Achievement Award, and Duke of Edinburgh's Award are all very well supported and sixth form girls have the opportunity to travel to Vietnam and Zambia.

A wide range of sports is on offer and there is a busy programme of fixtures in Hockey, Netball, Rounders, Athletics and Swimming in all of which we compete with great success. Gymnastics has been a particular strength for some years with our teams competing successfully at national level.

Fees per term (2018–2019). Reception £2,700, Years 1–2 £2,980, Years 3–4 £4,435, Years 5–6 £4,500, Years 7–13 £5,150.

Scholarships and Bursaries. Academic, Music, Art and Sport Scholarships are offered at 11+ and 16+. Bursaries are available at 11+ and 16+ entry and are dependent on the level of parental income.

Tormead Old Girls' Association. Email: toga@tormead school.org.uk.

Charitable status. Tormead Limited is a Registered Charity, number 312057. It exists to provide education for able girls.

Board of Governors:
Chair: Mrs Rosie Harris, BA, ACA
Mrs Anne Cullum, BA, PGCE, NPQH
Mr Mark Dixon, BSc, PGCE
Mrs Anne Geary
Mr Matthew Howse, LLB
Mr Robert Jewkes, BEng, FIE Aust
Dr Caroline Kissin, MB ChB, MRCP, FRCR
Mr Peter O'Keefe, RIBA, MCIOB, MIMgt
Dr Janet Page, LLM, BSc, MB BS, MRCP, FRCR, MFFLM
Miss Anna Spender, BSc, FIA
Mr John Watkins, FCA
Cllr Jenny Wicks, BA

Bursar and Clerk to the Governors: Miss Helen Davies, MA Oxon, MBA London

Headmistress: Mrs Christina Foord, BA, MPhil, PGCE Birmingham

Deputy Head Academic: Mr Jon Coles, BA Swansea, PGCE UEA, MEd Buckingham (*Geography and IT*)
Deputy Head Pastoral: Miss Tania King, MA Cantab, PGCE Oxon (*English*)

Senior School Staff:
* *Head of Department*

Mr Stephen Baird, BSc Edinburgh, PGCE Brunel (*Head of Geography*)
Mrs Alexandra Barker, BSc Bath, PGCE Kingston (*Mathematics*)
Mrs Helen Boczkowski, BSc QTS Bath (*Head of Food & Nutrition*)
Mr Edward Braun, BEng Birmingham, PGCE Roehampton (*Head of Design and Technology, Examinations Officer*)
Mr Tony Breslin, BA Sussex, PGCE Buckingham (*Head of History, Beacon Coordinator*)
Miss Susan Buchan, MEng Cantab, PGCE Oxon (*Physics, D of E Silver Coordinator*)
Mrs Eleanor Bucknall, MA St Andrews, PGCE Cumbria (*Head of History*)
Mrs Liz Burton, BA Birmingham, PGCE Birmingham (*Mathematics*)
Mrs Jessica Callanan, BA Leeds (*History*)
Dr Victoria Campbell, BA Oxon, DPhil Oxon (*Head of Drama, Oxbridge Coordinator*)
Mrs Susan Clarke, MA Cantab, Dip Lib North London (*Senior School Librarian*)
Miss Megan Cowx, BSc Cardiff Metropolitan (*Physical Education*)
Mrs Laura Crooks (*Learning Support*)
Mrs Serafina Culhane, BA Washington, PGCE Goldsmiths (*Head of IT Curriculum, English, School Magazine Editor*)
Mrs Karen Dabill, BSc Bangor, PGCE Surrey (*Head of Mathematics*)

Mrs Claire Don, MA Oxon, PGCE Roehampton (*Mathematics*)
Mrs Fiona Durrant, BSc Witwatersrand, HE UNISA, QTS Goldsmiths (*Biology*)
Mrs Victoria Dvali, BA Leeds, PGCE Nottingham (*English*)
Mrs Teresa Dyer, BA Swansea, PGCE Institute of Education (*Senior Teacher, Head of Modern Foreign Languages, French*)
Mrs Lana Eagers, BSc Durham, PGCE Cambridge, MEd Cambridge (*Chemistry, Assistant Head of Sixth Form*)
Mrs Sara Elmes, BA King's, PGCE Cardiff (*Religious Studies, Head of PSHE*)
Mrs Danielle Fellowes-Freeman, BA Greenwich, PGCE Greenwich (*Head of Curriculum Physical Education*)
Mrs Charlotte Fentem (*Learning Support*)
Mrs Amanda Ferns, MA Cantab, MSc London (*Assistant Librarian*)
Ms Agnes Franchot, MA Paris (*French Assistante, Junior School French Yr3 – Yr6*)
Miss Charlotte Froomberg, MA Cantab, PGCE Cantab, MA St Mary's (*Head of Religious Studies*)
Miss Hannah Gibbs, BA ITT Secondary Physical Education, QTS St Mary's Twickenham (*Physical Education, Head of Academic Physical Education*)
Mrs Sara Gibbs, BSc Bangor, PGCE Nottingham (*Biology*)
Mrs Julie Glazier, BSc Exeter, PGCE Bristol (*Second in Charge of Mathematics*)
Ms Tamarind Hetherington, MA London, BA London, PGCE Surrey (*Head of Art*)
Mr Martin Holford, BMus Surrey, PGCE Roehampton, ARCO Royal College of Organists (*Assistant Director of Music, Physics*)
Mrs Yvette Hughes, BA Loughborough, SpLD Cert Helen Arkell, SpLD Dip Helen Arkell (*Head of Learning Support*)
Mr Robert Isaacs, BSc St Andrews, PGCE Reading (*Head of Biology, Assistant Head of Sixth Form*)
Mr Christopher Ives, BA Warwick, PGCE Reading (*Head of German, Head of Teaching and Learning*)
Mrs Zoe Jarvis, BA Buckinghamshire, PGCE Sussex, MA King's (*Head of Chemistry*)
Mr Allan Jobling (*Head of Hockey*)
Mrs Samantha Jones, BSc Surrey, PGCE SWELTEC (*Head of Year 11, Geography*)
Mr James Keey, MA St Andrews, PGCE St Mary's (*Religious Studies*)
Mrs Rachel Landon, BSc UEA, PGCE Kingston (*Biology*)
Mrs Emma Lange, BA MBA PGCE Guildford (*German, French*)
Miss Marie Langlet, Licence d'Anglais Toulouse, Maîtrise d'Anglais Toulouse, PGCE Oxon (*Head of Year 8, Head of French*)
Mrs Nicola Ludlow, BA Warwick (*Learning Support Assistant*)
Mrs Geraldine Mackay, BA Rhodes, UED Rhodes (*English*)
Mrs Stella Mariash, BA Reading College (*Art*)
Mrs Fiona Marriott (*Learning Support*)
Mr Anthony Merryweather, BA UEA, PGCE Buckingham, ARCO Royal College of Organists (*Director of Music*)
Miss Stefanie Michalopoulou, BA Leeds, MSc Edinburgh (*Classics*)
Mrs Pauline Moodie, BA Manchester Met, PGCE Manchester (*Head of Spanish, Charity Coordinator, Senior Head of House*)
Miss Mia Morlang, MChem Surrey (*Science*)
Mrs Michelle O'Brien, BEd Chichester (*Director of Sport*)
Miss Imogen Painter, BA Dunelm, PGCE Nottingham Trent (*Head of Year 10, Head of Classics*)

Mr Jonathan Parsons, BA Lancaster, MA Lancaster, PGCE Reading (*Head of English*)

Mr Gary Press, BSc Brunel, CertEd Brunel (*Senior Teacher, Head of Computer Science, Design Technology*)

Mrs Kaethe Reid, MA Trier, PGCE Greenwich (*French, German*)

Mrs Gloriana Riggioni Vargas, BA Open, MRes Central St Martins, PGCE Kingston (*Spanish*)

Mrs Elizabeth Robinson, MA Oxon, PGCE York (*Spanish*)

Mrs Gillian Rodgers, BCom Edinburgh (*Head of Netball, Physical Education*)

Miss Sophie Sheridan, BA UCSB, MA UCL (*English*)

Dr Sarah Smedley, MPhys Lancaster, PhD Cantab (*Physics, Astronomy*)

Miss Madeline Smith, BA Durham, MA Roehampton, PGCE Roehampton (*English*)

Mrs Dorothy Snell, MA Aberdeen, Cert Ed Aberdeen (*Language Assistant German*)

Mr James South, BA London, PGCE Exeter, MA Ed Roehampton (*Head of Digital Learning, History*)

Mr Julian Sykes, BA Westminster, MSc LSE (*Head of Sixth Form, Head of Government and Politics, Debating*)

Mrs Charlotte Tee, BA South Bank, Cert Ed South Bank (*Food and Nutrition*)

Mrs Victoria Thomas, BEd De Montfort (*Physical Education*)

Mrs Lindsey Tidy, BA Chichester, QTS Chichester (*Physical Education*)

Ms Sarah Travis, MA Cantab, PGCE Cantab (*Chemistry, Bronze D of E Coordinator*)

Miss Eleanor Walshe, Nat Dip DIT, Ireland, BSc Greenwich, PGCE St Mary's (*Head of Year 9, Biology*)

Mrs Louise Whitaker, BSc Manchester, PGCE Exeter (*Head of Year 7, Geography*)

Mr Daniel Wilkinson, BMus Huddersfield, Dip Psych Open, PGCE Dunelm (*Head of Psychology*)

Mr Peter Wilkinson, MA Cantab, MSc UCL, MBA Brunel (*Head of Physics, Oxbridge Coordinator*)

Mrs Catherine Williams, BA Cantab (*Head of Economics, Head of Careers and Professional Development*)

Mrs Anna Woodfine, MEng Oxon, PGCE Chichester (*Mathematics*)

Mrs Charlotte Wyatt, BSc Manchester, PGCE Sussex (*Mathematics*)

Junior School Staff:

Mrs Nicola Fry, BA Ed Exeter (*Deputy Head Junior School, Senior Team*)

Mrs Karen Moulder, BEd London, MA Kingston, Dip Lib Surrey (*Deputy Head Junior School, Senior Team*)

Mrs Elizabeth Alderman, BSc Leeds, PGCE Bristol (*Head of KS1, Senior Team*)

Miss Salaidh Insch, BEd Surrey (*Year 6 Class Teacher, Director of Studies Humanities, Senior Team*)

Mrs Jacqueline Johnson, BEd Dunelm (*Year 5 Class Teacher, IT, Director of Studies Science & Maths, Senior Team*)

Mrs Gillian Blackburn, BSc Sussex, Level 7 Dip Helen Arkell (*Head of Learning Support Junior School*)

Mrs Caroline Broadway, BSc Surrey, PGCE Surrey (*Year 4 Class Teacher, Junior School DT*)

Miss Mary Colyer, BSc York, PGCE Cantab (*Year 4 Class Teacher*)

Mrs Laura Crabtree, BSc City of London Polytechnic, PGCE Primary Kingston (*Year 3 Class Teacher*)

Miss Melissa Davies, BA St Mary's (*Reception Teacher*)

Mrs Hilary Ellis, NVQ3 Childcare, Learning and Development Guildford (*Teaching Assistant*)

Miss Kirsty Finch, BA Chichester, QTS Chichester (*Head of Junior School PE*)

Mrs Kerry Fuller (*Teaching Assistant*)

Miss Britta Hogan, BSc Surrey (*Year 5 Class Teacher*)

Miss Jody Howard, BA Nottingham Trent (*Year 6 Class Teacher*)

Mrs Jacqueline Norman, BSc Nottingham, MPhil Reading, NVQ3 Guildford (*Teaching Assistant*)

Miss Louisa Payne, BMus Surrey (*Year 3 Class Teacher*)

Mrs Gertrude Seaborne, BA Malaya, Dip Ed Malaya (*Year 2 Class Teacher*) [Maternity cover]

Mrs Harriet Van Der Byl-Knoefel, BA York, PGCE Roehampton (*Year 2 Class Teacher*)

Mrs Susan Vega, BA Dunelm, PGCE Dunelm, LTCL Trinity College of Music (*Head of Junior School Music*)

Registrar: Mrs Melanie Hobdey
Headmistress's PA: Mrs Christina Francis
Junior School Secretary: Mrs Tricia Kelly/Mrs Nicky Overgaard

Tudor Hall

Wykham Park, Banbury, Oxon OX16 9UR

Tel:	01295 263434
Fax:	01295 253264
email:	admissions@tudorhallschool.com
	admin@tudorhallschool.com
website:	www.tudorhallschool.com
Twitter:	@TudorHallSchool
Facebook:	@TudorHallSchool

Motto: *Habeo Ut Dem*

Tudor Hall is an Independent Boarding School for Girls aged 11–18 years. The school was originally founded in 1850 and moved to Wykham Park in 1946. It is situated in spacious grounds 1½ miles from Banbury Station and is within easy access of London, Oxford, Bicester and Stratford-upon-Avon – M40, Junction 11. This enables the girls to enjoy a wide range of cultural and educational activities.

The school accommodates approximately 250 boarders and 75 day girls. Its buildings comprise a 17th century and an 18th century manor with a modern purpose-built house for Sixth Formers and extensive new facilities. These include laboratories for biology, chemistry, physics and general science; CDT workshop; 2 information technology rooms; language laboratory; modern languages and domestic science rooms; drama studio; music school; studios for art and pottery; textiles room; gym and sports hall. There are tennis and netball courts, a swimming pool, squash courts, astroturf and pitches for hockey, lacrosse and rounders. An extension to the Sixth Form block has been completed, with the original rooms undergoing extensive refurbishment. The Year 10 House has undergone extensive refurbishment and the school benefits from a purpose-built drama studio and sports complex. Work is currently under way on a £5.2 million Teaching Centre designed to provide spaces for the core subjects of Mathematics and English, and specialist classrooms for the creative arts, transforming the teaching provision the school offers.

The curriculum and co-curriculum at Tudor are very broad and provide students with intellectual challenge and the opportunity to expand their horizons. Students are able to develop knowledge and understanding, as well as speaking, listening, literacy and numeracy skills, in a manner which encourages their confidence, gives satisfaction and enjoyment, and allows all to learn and make progress. Students develop a love of lifelong learning and acquire the necessary skills needed for university and adult life. A comprehensive careers programme ensures that students leave armed with pertinent and relevant information and experience to continue to be successful in life beyond school.

Admission is by internal examinations at 11+ and internal examinations and Common Entrance at 13+. Entry may also be made to the Sixth Form where all girls pursue courses leading to higher education or vocational training and they are treated as students. Those entering at 11 are accustomed to being away from home by being housed separately in a smaller environment. Girls are divided into four competitive Houses but residence is with their own age group.

Tudor Hall places great importance on having a friendly atmosphere, a lively and united spirit and high standards. Girls are expected to take an interest in a wide range of activities as well as following a broad educational programme. Involvement in the local community through the Duke of Edinburgh's Award and social service, and participation in events with other schools are encouraged. Debating and public speaking are strong and there is keen involvement in the Young Enterprise Scheme, Model United Nations and European Youth Parliament. Tudor Hall is an Anglican school but members of other religious groups are welcomed. There is a small chapel.

Scholarships and Bursaries. *Academic* 11+/13+ and 16+. These are awarded to candidates entering at 11+ or 13+ on the basis of their performance at Common Entrance and interviews. At 16+ awards are offered on the basis of interview, school report and examination. The value of the award is up to £1,000 per annum. These awards are intended for the support of the pupil's academic interests.

Music 11+/13+ and 16+. These are awarded on the basis of ability and potential at 11+, 13+ and 16+. The value of the award is up to £1,000 per annum to entrants who show outstanding musical ability. Music awards exist in the form of free tuition in one or more instruments for the duration of the student's time at the school.

Art 13+/16+. These are awarded on the basis of ability and potential either at 13+ or 16+. The value of the award is up to £1,000 per annum. These awards are intended for the support of the pupil's Art interests.

Dance 16+. These are awarded on the basis of ability and potential at 16+. The value of the award is up to £1,000 per annum. These awards are intended for the support of the pupil's Dance interests.

Drama 13+/16+. These are awarded on the basis of ability and potential either at 13+ or 16+. The value of the award is up to £1,000 per annum. These awards are intended for the support of the pupil's Dramatic interests.

Sport 13+/16+. These are awarded on the basis of ability and potential either at 13+ or 16+. The value of the award is up to £1,000 per annum. These awards are intended for the support of the pupil's Sporting interests.

Textiles 16+. These are awarded on the basis of ability and potential at 16+. The value of the award is up to £1,000 per annum. These awards are intended for the support of the pupil's Textiles interests.

Bursaries are awarded to new and current parents who are in financial need.

Fees per term (2018–2019). £11,870 for boarders; £7,365 for day pupils.

Board of Governors:
Chairman: Mr John Gloag
Chairman of Finance & General Purposes Committee: Mr John Elliot
Chairman of Education Committee: Mrs Alison Darling
Chairman of Audit Committee: Mrs Kathy Fidgeon
Chairman of the Design Committee: Mrs Victoria Harley
Chairman of Carrdus School Committee: Mr Duncan Bailey

Mr Simon Beale
Mrs Sally Bowie
Mrs Debbie Chism
Mr Jonny Hammond-Chambers
Miss Mary Kinnear
Mr Bob Lari
Mr Charlie Newsome
Mrs Nicky Wilson

Senior Management Team:

Headmistress: Wendy Griffiths

Bursar & Clerk to the Governors (*Interim*): Neil Urquhart
Deputy Head: Clare Macro
Deputy Head (*Pastoral*): Kate Simlett
Head of Sixth Form: David Beaumont
Director of Staff: Susie Jeffreys
Director of Studies: Lucy Keyte
Director of Digital Learning: John Field
Director of Co-Curriculum: Pippa Duncan-Jones

Boarding Staff:
Boarding Coordinator: Jackie Webb
Ashtons Housemistress: Lucy Pickford
Ashtons Deputy Houseparent: Henry Vigne
Inglis Housemistress: Jennifer Ranson
Inglis Deputy Housemistress: Lorraine Logue
Vs Housemistress: Pippa Duncan-Jones
Vs Deputy Housemistress: Deborah Sellers
IVs Housemistress: Sarah Belcher
IVs Deputy Housemistress: Lara Price
IIIs Housemistress: Lucinda Burton-Sims
IIs Housemistress: Sarah Neale
IIs Deputy Housemistress: Camille Garnon
Todd Housemistress: Elizabeth Buckner-Rowley
Todd Deputy Housemistress: Lauren Nightingale
Boarding support: Penny Davies
Boarding support: Carol Edginton
Boarding support: Marilyn Harris
Boarding support: Rachael Knapman

Pastoral:
School Chaplain: John Jackson
School Counsellor: Mahwish Qamar
School Counsellor: Denise Jones

Administrative and Support Staff:
PA to the Headmistress: Jennifer Lewis
PA to the Deputy Head: Helen Holt
PA to Deputy Head (*Pastoral*): Kate Greaves
Data Manager: Brian Wray
Examinations Officer: Richard Moody
Senior Administrative Secretary: Helen Mascall
Administrative Secretary: Peggy Snowden
Administrative Secretary: Katie Donald
Administrative Secretary – Music: Joanne Twelvetrees
Administrative Secretary – PE: Rachael Knapman
Parent & Community Links Coordinator: Amanda Brauer
Educational Visits Coordinator: Kate Martin

Admissions: *Marketing and Communications*:
Registrar: Philippa Drinkwater
Admissions Secretary: Fiona Gaskin
Director of Marketing: Laura Greenwood
Communications Manager: Annabelle Coombs

Bursary:
Finance Manager (*Interim*): Gary Atack
Compliance Manager: Nicole Hamilton
Finance Assistant: Diane Cook
Finance Assistant: Louise Sollis
Administration Assistant (*Bursary*): Carol Edginton

Development and Alumnae Relations:
Head of Development & Alumnae Relations: Rachel Graves

Development & Alumnae Relations Office Administrator:
Rachael Roberts
Alumnae Communications Manager: Lindsay Silver

Grounds: Maintenance and Domestic Services:
Property Services Manager: Graham Butcher
Head Gardener: Andrew Crompton
Facilities Management and Travel Administrator: Caroline
Thomas
Domestic Services Manager: Linda Tubb
Head Chef: Darren O'Neill

ICT Systems and Network:
ICT Systems & Network Manager: Paul Smith
ICT Systems Engineer: Luke Harris
ICT Technician: Melanie Bolton

Technicians:
CDT Technician: Martin Bolton
Senior Science Technician: Alison Montanaro
Science Technician: Linda Stone
Textiles Technician: Amy Pearce

Librarian: Lara Price

Medical:
School Doctor: Dr Nicola Elliott
Nurse-in-Charge: Janet Bonham, RGN
Nurse: Caroline Hutchison, RGN
Nurse: Lindsay Pickering, RGN

Teaching Staff:
David Beaumont, BSc Lancaster, PGCE Herts
(*Mathematics*)
Jo Benlalam, BMus, AKC, PGCE London, Head of Careers
and Academic Music)
Amy Bird, BA Northampton, PGCE UWE Bristol
(*Photography*)
Claire Blackburn, BA De Montfort (*Textiles*)
Amanda Brauer, BA Kent, PGCE Bedford (*Physical
Education*)
Elizabeth Buckner-Rowley, BA Portsmouth, PGCE Leeds
(*Spanish*)
Lucinda Burton-Sims, BA Leeds, PG DipEd Birmingham
(*PSHE*)
Justine Callaghan, BPsych Curtin, DipEd Notre Dame,
Australia (*Mathematics*)
Daniel Carrington, BSc Hull (*Mathematics/Science*)
Alan Christopher, MA Essex, BTEC Kingshurst, HND
Coventry (*Drama*)
Jason Conduct, BSc UCL, PGCE Sussex (*Head of Science
and Physics*)
Sheila Craske, BA Oxon, PGCE MMU (*Head of Art*)
Lindsey Cullen, MA Oxon (*Head of Classics, Head of
Lower School*)
Emma Dathan, BSc De Montfort, PGCE Liverpool (*Head
of Netball*)
Barrie Dolphin, BSc Coventry, MA Sheffield Hallam,
PGCE Wolverhampton (*Head of CDT*)
Gerard Duncan, PGDSST, BPE University of Otago, New
Zealand (*Physical Education*)
Pippa Duncan-Jones, BSc Loughborough, PGCE Leeds
(*Physical Education*)
Ian Edwards, BSc Newcastle, PGCE UEA (*Mathematics,
Academic Administrator*)
John Field, MA, PGCE Oxon (*English*)
Sara Fordy, BA Winchester, PGCE Oxon (*Head of
Textiles*)
Elizabeth Fulton, BA Reading, MA Warwick (*Head of
History of Art*)
Jonathan Galloway, BA Middx, PGCE London (*Head of
Philosophy, Theology and Ethics*)
Alison Gamble, MA London, CPE Law (*Head of Senior
History & Politics*)

Marie Genot, MA Provence, France, PGCE UWE (*French/
Spanish*)
Florence Gifford-Cagnol, MSc Paris, PhD Paris (*Learning
Support*)
Shazia Gleadall, BA Birmingham, PGCE Chester (*Head of
KS3 Religious Studies*)
Elizabeth Gulliver, BA Oxon (*Head of Learning Support,
Psychology*)
Kerri Hadfield, BA Leeds, PGCE Canterbury (*Head of
Geography*)
Jane Haggarty, CertEd Bedford (*Head of Home Economics*)
Louise Harper, BA Dunelm, PGCE Oxon (*Head of KS3
Geography*)
Matthew Harper, BA Oxon, PGCE Warwick (*French/
Spanish*)
Marilyn Harris, BA London, PGCE Bulmershe (*French*)
Kate Hart, BA MMU, PGCE Birmingham (*Head of
PSHEE*)
Monica Jimenez, BA La Rioja, Spain, PGCE Canterbury
(*Head of Spanish*)
Kathryn Joel, BA Warwick, DELTA, TESOL (*EAL
Coordinator*)
Nicola Jones, BA, MA Dunelm, MA Arts & Musical
Theatre London (*Religious Studies, Head of Year IV*)
Matthew Kent, BA Keele, MA, PG DipEd Birmingham
(*2 i/c English*)
Kate Kettlewell, BVSc Bristol, PGCE Oxon (*Biology*)
Lucy Keyte, BA Nottingham, PGCE Warwick (*French*)
Holly Kidman, BA Portsmouth (*Textiles*)
Rachael Knapman, Netball Level 1 Coach UKCC (*Netball*)
Sally Knight, BA Derby (*Business Studies*)
Sadie Lapper, BSc, PGCE Worcester, MSc Oxford Brookes
(*Director of Sport*)
Lindsey Lea-James, BMus, LTCL, ALCM, PGCE
Huddersfield (*Director of Music*)
Lorraine Logue, BA Trinity, Dublin, PGCE University
College Dublin (*Head of Biology*)
James Long, BA, PGCE Liverpool (*Head of Hockey*)
Clare Macro, MA, PGCE Oxon (*Religious Studies*)
Victoria Marsh, BSc Keele, PGCE Exeter (*Head of
Mathematics*)
Sarah Malpass, BSc Sheffield, MSc Dunelm, PGCE
London (*Biology, Science*)
Harriet Millar-Mills, BSc Loughborough, PGCE MMU
(*Mathematics*)
Bev Murphy, BA Wales, MA, PhD, PGCE UEA (*Head of
Junior History*)
Sarah Neale, BA Worcester (*Dance*)
Lauren Nightingale, BA Brighton (*Physical Education,
Dance*)
Pervin Özkan, Licence Tours, France, PGCE Exeter (*Head
of French*)
Charlotte Pemble, BSc, PGCE Worcester (*2 i/c Physical
Education*)
Jonitha Peterpillai, BSc, Warwick MSc, PGCE Oxon (*2 i/c
Mathematics*)
Ryan Pickering, NPLQ, NUCO (*Sporting Facilities &
Physical Education*)
Cherylin Preston, BSc Leicester, PGCE Exeter (*Head of
Chemistry*)
Bob Roberts, BA, MA Warwick, PGCE Lancaster (*Head of
English*)
Lisa Roberts, BA Wales, PGCE Nottingham (*Learning
Support*)
Bronwen Robinson, BEd Worcester, Dip PE (*Dance*)
Ian Robinson, BEng, PGCE Lancaster (*Physics*)
Deborah Sellers, BA, PGCE Nottingham (*History*)
Catherine Simpson, BA, GDL, MPhil Cantab, PGCE
Belfast (*English*)
Elizabeth Smith, CertEd Nottingham (*Learning Support*)

Rachel Smith, BA Wales, PGCE Leicester (*Head of Psychology*)

James Stead, BA Cumbria, PGCE Wales (*Art*)

Justine Stephens, BA London, PGCE Middx (*Head of Drama*)

Holly Thomas, BA Bath, PGCE Coventry (*Head of Modern Languages*)

Richard Thompson, MA Oxon, PGCE London (*Head of Economics & Business Studies*)

Julia Thorn, BA Reading, MSt Oxon (*Classics*)

Henry Vigne, BA London, MA Kent (*History, Home Economics*)

James Wakeley, BSc OU, PGCE Bath (*Computing & IT*)

Kitty Wells, BA London (*Head of Outdoor Education*)

Helen Wilks, PhD Bristol, PGCE Warwick (*Chemistry*)

Layla Williams, BA London, PGCE De Montfort (*Dance*)

James Woodward, BSc Wales, PGCE Exeter (*Biology, Head of Year V*)

Additional Subject and Coaching Staff:

Helen Fryer (*Lacrosse*)
Ginny Steven (*Ballet*)

Tennis:
Godwin Abah
Shola Adebisi
Mark Boden
Pamela Eagles
Jo Kelly
Lee Morton
Charlotte Peckover

Modern Foreign Languages:
Younès El Barhdadi (*French Assistant*)
Kubra Özkan (*French Assistant*)
Belen Sainz-Pardo (*Spanish*)

Music:
Karina Bell (*Harp*)
Bob Evans (*Brass*)
James Foley (*Guitar*)
Jessica Friend (*Singing*)
Sarah Haigh (*Singing*)
Kim Keeble (*Oboe*)
Cliff Pick (*Percussion*)
Kate Pickin (*Piano*)
Miranda Ricardo (*Cello and Piano*)
Beverley Savidge (*Singing*)
Elisabeth Sharam (*Flute*)
Deborah Siepmann (*Piano*)
Kayleigh Skinner (*Singing (maternity leave)*)
Noriko Tsuzaki (*Violin*)
Lucy Tugwell (*Clarinet and Saxophone*)

Speech and Drama:
Susie Lowe
Pippa Phillips

Walthamstow Hall

Senior School:
Holly Bush Lane, Sevenoaks, Kent TN13 3UL

Tel: 01732 451334
Fax: 01732 740439

Junior School:
Bradbourne Park Road, Sevenoaks, Kent TN13 3LD

email: registrar@whall.school

website: www.walthamstow-hall.co.uk
Facebook: @Walthamstow-Hall

Walthamstow Hall is an Independent girls' day school based on two separate sites in Sevenoaks. Founded in 1838, the school celebrated its 180th anniversary in 2018. The Junior School in Bradbourne Park Road takes pupils from age 3–11 years and the Senior School in Holly Bush Lane takes pupils from 11–18 years.

The school has a long established history of preparing academically-able girls for stimulating, purposeful and happy lives within and beyond school. The belief that every student given the right opportunities, encouragement and inspiring teaching can develop an incredible range of skills and talents, is central to the everyday life of the school.

The Headmistress is a member of the GSA (Girls' Schools Association).

The school was judged to be 'Excellent' by the ISI in 2013, excellent being the highest category awarded.

Facilities. Walthamstow Hall is set in its own grounds within the town of Sevenoaks. Girls are taught in light and airy classrooms in buildings specifically designed for learning. The original 1882 Arts and Crafts school building still lies at the heart of the School. During the past 10 years, campus developments have included the building of the Swimming Pool complex, Music, Drama and Design Technology rooms, and a new Student Entrance Hub and Art Gallery. The Ship Theatre was refurbished in 2014, and more recent additions have included the new Sports Centre opened in September 2015, the expansion of provision of Art studios, and a new Sixth Form Centre with additional Science facilities opened in January 2018. The Junior School offers Wrap-Around Care, and benefits from specialist facilities including an ICT Suite, Science Laboratory, Design and Technology, Art and Cookery Rooms and a dedicated Music Centre.

Curriculum. Walthamstow Hall delivers an enriched curriculum which is innovative and flexible, facilitating breadth and individual choice, without sacrificing depth of study. This is brought to life with inspirational teaching.

All girls in their first three Senior School years (7, 8 and 9) follow a core curriculum of 17 subjects, with a second language being added in Year 8. As they progress through to public examinations the flexibility of the curriculum enables girls to study a wide breadth of subjects rather than being shackled by restrictive subject blocks.

Subjects taught up to age 18 include: Art, Biology, Business, Chemistry, Classical Civilisation, Computing, Computer Science, Creative Textiles, Design and Technology, Drama, Economics, English, English Literature, Extended Project Qualification (EPQ), Art (Fine), French, History, Geography, German, Government and Politics, Latin, Mathematics, Additional Mathematics, Further Mathematics, Music, Philosophy & Theology, Physical Education, Physics, Religious Studies, Sociology, Spanish, Art Textile Design, Theatre Studies and Three Dimensional Design.

Girls are prepared for GCSE, IGCSE, A Levels and Cambridge Pre-U. The record of success in public examinations is excellent. In 2018 73% of Pre-U and A Level examinations were passed at grades A*–B, and 92% of I/GCSEs were passed at grades A*–B.

The breadth and flexibility of the curriculum, combined with expert teaching and encouragement to be ambitious, enables students to be highly successful in their post-Sixth Form choices. In 2018 over 75% of the students secured their first-choice places at Universities, Drama and Art Colleges, and on Higher Level Apprenticeships.

Religious Teaching is interdenominational.

Extracurricular Activities. The high profile of Drama, Music, Sports, trips, careers and study skills and personal development, together with an excellent pastoral system, provides further opportunity and support for every girl.

An active policy of 'sport for all' enables both team players and individuals to find the sporting activities that suit them best. Lacrosse, netball, swimming, athletics, badminton, judo, curling and tennis teams achieve highly at local, county and national levels.

A high proportion of students participate in the Duke of Edinburgh's Award scheme, Business enterprise, the school choirs and orchestra and Trinity Drama.

Girls undertake voluntary service within the local community and abroad.

Admission. Admission to the Junior School is via a 'taster' day, which includes age-appropriate assessments. Admission to the Senior School for Year 7, 9 and Sixth Form is through the School's own entrance examinations and interview. Parents are warmly invited to visit the School at Open Mornings in September and March, or on a personal visit.

Fees per term (2018–2019). Senior School and Sixth Form £6,690.

Scholarships. Academic scholarships are awarded annually to the candidates who show the greatest academic potential in the school's own Year 7, 9 and Sixth Form scholarship examinations.

Music and Sport scholarships are also available for Year 7 and Year 9 entry. Drama and Art Awards are offered for Year 9 entry.

Academic scholarships and Art Awards are offered in Sixth Form.

All awards are available to both internal and external candidates.

In addition, a means-tested bursary scheme in the Senior School provides financial help with school fees based on a family's financial circumstances. The scheme includes our Founders' Bursary, which pays nearly 100% of a pupil's school fees throughout their time at the school.

Charitable status. Walthamstow Hall is a Registered Charity, number 1058439. It exists to provide education for girls.

Chair of Governors: Mrs J Adams, BA Joint Hons
There are 16 school governors.

Headmistress: **Miss S Ferro**, BA Hons Oxford, MA, PGCE UCL

Deputy Head: P Howson Esq, BA Hons Plymouth, QTS Kent, AST London (*English*)

Deputy Head: C Hughes Esq, BSc Hons, Cert Ed Loughborough, NPQH (*Mathematics*)

Director of Studies: S Ledsham Esq, MA Oxford, PGCE Sussex (*Physics*)

Head of the Junior School: Mrs D Wood, BSc Hons, PGCE Durham

Senior Teacher, Head of Sixth Form & Careers: Ms E Ancrum, MA Oxford, MPhil Hong Kong, PGCE London (*Economics/Business*)

Senior School:
* *Head of Department/Teacher In Charge of Subject*
Miss J Bateman, MEng Hons Imperial, PGCE Greenwich (*Physics, Mathematics*)
Ms J Bisset, BSc Hons Heriot-Watt, PGTC Edinburgh (*Chemistry*)
Mrs F Boorman, BA Hons, PGCE Kent (*Business*)
*Mrs V Bower-Morris, BA Hons Surrey, PGCE Goldsmiths (*Drama/Trinity Drama*)
*Miss C Bridge, BSc Hons Worcester, QTS Bucks (*PE, Head of Lacrosse*)

Mrs E Brown, BA Hons Leeds, PGCE Brighton (*Art & Textiles*)
*N Buckingham Esq, MA Reading, BA Hons, PGCE London (*Classics, Examinations Officer*)
*N Castell Esq, BMus Hons, PGCE Manchester (*Director of Music; Assistant Head of Lower School*)
J Clements Esq, MusB Hons Manchester (*Music*)
*Mrs J Cox, MA Cambridge, PGCE Open, ATCL (*Biology*)
T Dakin Esq, BSc Hons Bristol, PGCE Sussex (*Mathematics, AGT Coordinator*)
*Mrs S Dalton, BSc Hons Keele, PGCE Canterbury, Dip SpLD Dyslexia (*Learning Support*)
Dr R Davies, BSc Hons, PhD Imperial College, PGCE King's College (*Mathematics/Physics*)
*Mrs P Durrant, BSc Hons Southampton, PGCE London (*Mathematics, Head of Middle School*)
Mrs J Dymond, MSc Sheffield, BA Scotland (*Swimming*)
* *Mrs C Evans, BA Hons Greenwich, QTS* (*Technology*: D&T, Food Technology)
Mrs S Fitzmaurice, BSc Hons, PGCE Manchester (*Biology, Food Technology*)
Miss M Fournier, Licence, Masters Lille (*MFL*)
Mrs K Franzen, BA Hons Durham, PGCE King's College (*Theology &Philosophy, Drama; Assistant Head of Lower School*)
Mrs E García, BA Hons Seville, PGCE Sheffield (*MFL, Assistant Charities Coordinator*)
Miss R Harris, BA Hons Chichester, QTS KMT (*Drama*)
*R Hill Esq, BSc Hons Warwick, PGCE Sussex (*Physics*)
Mrs K Hofmann, MA St Andrews, QTS (*MFL, Head of Lower School*)
Mrs H Hook, BA Hons Aberystwyth, PGCE Cambridge (*English*)
*Mrs C Hughes, BA Hons West Surrey College of Art and Design, BSc Hons Middlesex, PGCE London (*Art & Textiles*)
*Mrs R Hunt, BA Hons Exeter, PGCE King's College (*MFL*)
Mrs S Isted, BA Hons Warwick, PGCE King's College (*Classics*)
*Mrs R Jennings, BSc Hons Southampton, PGCE Open, MICA (*Mathematics*)
*Mrs V Jones, BA Hons, PGCE, Leeds (*Theology & Philosophy*)
Ms M Knight, BA Hons London, PGCE Canterbury (*English*)
*Miss R Leggett, BA Hons with QTS, Brighton (*Director of Sport, Charities Coordinator*)
Miss C Lesieur, BA Hons, MA Hons Amiens, Fr, PGCE UWE (*MFL*)
*Miss S Mehaffey, MA, PGCE Edinburgh (*English, Assistant Head of Sixth Form*)
Mrs L Mortimore, BSc Hons Imperial, PGCE King's College (*Science*)
Mrs C Mulcahy, BA Hons Surrey, PGCE London (*Design & Technology, Art*)
Ms A Murphy, MA Oxford, PGCE East Anglia (*History/ Politics, Oxbridge Coordinator*)
Dr G Pender, MA, MSc Cambs, PGCE Bucks, DPhil UCL (*Physics, Computer Science*)
Mrs E Peters, BSc Hons, PGCE Southampton (*Mathematics*)
Mrs C Platt, BA Hons London, QTS (*MFL*)
*Mrs L Rowell, BA Hons Surrey, PGCE King's College (*Computer Science & ICT*)
Miss F Ryan, BSc Hons London, PGCE Brighton (*PE*)
Mrs L Scott, BA Hons Keele, PGCE Canterbury (*History*)
Mrs A Sherwen, BSc Hons London, PGCE Leeds (*Biology*)
Mrs C Solan, BA Hons London, PGCE Canterbury (*Art & Textiles*)

*C Sullivan Esq, HNC, BA Hons Sussex, NPQL
(*Geography*)

Mrs B Tanner, BA Hons Wales, PGCE Southampton
(*MFL*)

*Mrs L Thomas, MA Open, BA Hons Wales, PGCE Bristol
(*History, EPQ Coordinator, Assistant Head of Middle
School*)

Mrs L von Kaufmann, MA, BA Hons Oxon, PGCE Bristol
(*Geography, Assistant Head of Middle School, Assistant
Head of Careers, Co-Curriculum Coordinator*)

Mrs S Walker, BSc Hons London QTS Greenwich
(*Chemistry*)

Mrs S Whawell, BSc Hons Birmingham, MSc Reading,
PGCE Bristol (*Mathematics, Assistant to the Director of
Studies*)

Mrs R White, BA Hons, PGCE Bristol, MA Hons New
York, PGCE Canterbury (*English*)

Dr S Wilkinson, DPhil Hons Oxon, PGCE King's College
(*Chemistry*)

Dr S Willcox, MA Cambs, DPhil Oxon, SCITT/ATS
Bromley (*Science*)

*S Wilson Esq, BA Hons Sunderland, PGCE London
(*Sociology*)

*Ms O Windle, MA, BA Hons Edgewood College, USA
(*History/Politics*)

*Mrs M Wood, BSc Hons Aberdeen, PGCE London
(*Chemistry, Head of Science*)

Mrs Z Wood, MA Hons St Andrews, PGCE London
(*Theology & Philosophy*)

Mrs N Yates, BA Hons Kent, QTS (*Fine Art &
Photography*)

Visiting Staff:

M Andrews Esq, MM Connecticut, BMus Hons
Westminster (*Piano*)

Mrs C Barnes, MA East London, BSc Hons Anglia, PGCE
Greenwich, Dip SpLD (*Literacy Support*)

Miss C Brand, MMus London, GTCL, ARCM, LRAM
(*Piano*)

B Brooker Esq (*Percussion*)

D Burrowes Esq, BA Hons Leeds, MMus TCM (*Cello*)

R Connell Esq, BA Hons Canterbury, PGCE, ATCL
(*Guitar*)

Mrs R Castell, MusM, MusB Manchester (*Piano*)

Mrs H Clements, Adv Dip Opera, MA, PGA, PGDip,
LRAM, QTS (*Singing*)

Mrs J Dammers, LRAM (*Violoncello; Music
Administrator*)

Mrs B Day, BSc Hons Miami, USA, Hornsby Level 4,
TEFL (*Literacy Support*)

Miss N Dobie, BA Hons First class City University, LTCL,
NCDT, Dip Opera Performance London (*Singing*)

Mrs C Effingham, MA Hons Edinburgh, PGCE King's
College, PG Dip Dys & Lit York (*Literacy Support*)

Mrs A Goff, BSc Hons Leicester, QTS (*Numeracy Support*)

Ms S Graham, LRAM, GRSM Hons, Dip RAM (*Singing*)

Mrs H Greenfield, BMus Hons Birmingham Conservatoire,
LRAM, DPP RAM, Dip CESMD (*Clarinet, Saxophone*)

Mrs J Hamlet, Chelsea Ballet School (*Dance*)

Mrs G Hayward, Dip Music, LTCL, ALCM, Newcastle,
PG Dip Orchestral Studies London (*Singing, Piano*)

Mrs F Hillyar, BMus Hons Royal College of Music, PGCE
Reading (*Piano*)

Miss L Jeffery, BMus Trinity College of Music, PG Dip
Royal Academy of Music (*Flute*)

Miss S Kisilevsky, BA Hons Royal Holloway, MA RCS
(*Trinity Drama*)

Ms E Leather, BA Hons Leeds, PG Dip Mus Guildhall
School of Music, Artist Diploma Cincinnati (*Music
Coach*)

Miss V Longhurst, BMus Trinity College of Music (*Harp*)

Miss A Murray, ATCL, LTCL Trinity College of Music
(*Recorder*)

Mrs V Newman, BA Hons Oxon, PGCE Wales, BSc Hons
Open, Dip SpLD (*Learning Support*)

Ms S Oakley, BA Hons Surrey (*Trinity Drama*)

Mrs S Purton, LRAM (*Oboe*)

Mrs J Rhind, GRSM Hons, LTCL, LRAM, (*Saxophone,
Clarinet*)

Miss H Ross, BMus Hons, PG Dip RNCM (*Violin*)

I Snape Esq, BSc, FCA (*Chess Coach*)

Mrs A Steynor, BA Hons Durham, PGCDM Open,
ABRSM Dip (*Piano*)

D Wallace Esq, BMus Hons Cork, MMus, LRSM (*Violin/
Viola*)

Miss E Wiggins, BMus Hons, LRAM (*Brass*)

T Williams Esq, BA First Class Fine Art Oxon, Art &
Design Foundation (*Songwriting*)

Medical Centre:

Mrs L Mottram, Dip Nursing Studies City University
London

Mrs E Leisinger, Dip Nursing Brighton

Mrs C Baker, MBACP (*School Counsellor*)

Sports Coaches:

K Alexander Esq (*Tennis*)

M Burkett Esq/Miss S Burkett (*Judo*)

Mrs G Cameron, Foundation Degree (*Netball*)

Miss A Carroll (*Gymnastics*)

J Christian Esq, BSc Hons Lincoln (*Lacrosse*)

Mrs J Dymond, MSc Sheffield, BA Scotland (*Swimming*)

S Hadlow Esq (*Taekwon-do*)

P Hill Esq (*Squash*)

Ms A Longhurst (*Taekwon-do*)

Miss J Muggeridge (*Badminton*)

Mrs N Norris (*Netball*)

Miss H Olver (*Sports/Badminton*)

Ms J Powlson (*Tennis*)

D Smith Esq, BA (*Cross Country*)

R Smith Esq, ASA Level 2 Coaching, NPLQ (*Head
Swimming Coach*)

Miss T Verloop (*Dance*)

N Wilkinson Esq, RFU Level 2 Coaching (*Rugby*)

Technical Support and Assistants:

G Burgess Esq, BA Hons King's (*ICT Technician*)

Mrs L Clarke, Dip Natural Sciences, BSc Hons (*Biology
Laboratory Technician*)

P Cole Esq (*Network & Data Manager*)

Mrs A Ford (*Art Technician*)

Mrs R Gardner, BSc Hons Manchester, RPharmSGB Bath,
PGCE Oxford (*Senior Science Laboratory Technician*)

Mlle L Gollunski (*French Assistant*)

A Hayter Esq (*ICT Technician*)

C Hayward Esq, TEC, BTEC, MI Biol, PGCE (*Science
Laboratory & DT/3DD Technician*)

J Mitchell Esq, BEng Hons Surrey (*Drama/Performing
Arts Technician*)

Mrs J Osborne, BSc Hons Oxford Brookes (*Science
Laboratory Technician*)

N Ramsden Esq, (*Duke of Edinburgh's Award Manager,
Artist in Residence/Art Technician*)

Sta M Senero (*Spanish Assistant*)

E Thompson Esq (*ICT Technician*)

Administrative/Support Staff:

Miss B Adiamoh, BSc (*Payroll Administrator*)

Mrs J Alcock, BSc Greenwich (*Estates Manager*)

Ms R Boardman, Management Diploma Canada (*Assistant
Librarian/Archives*)

Mrs J Butler, BA Hons Sheffield (*Marketing and Admissions Assistant*)
Mrs C Buxton, BSc Hons King's College (*Receptionist*)
Mrs O Cornes, BA Hons Bristol (*Marketing Assistant*)
Mrs C Crofts, BA Hons Birmingham, PGCE Greenwich (*Junior School Administrative Assistant*)
Mrs W Fahy (*Junior School Secretary*)
R Heath Esq, BEng Hons Nottingham, MSc Cranfield (*Human Resources Administrator*)
A Jayatilaka Esq, BA Hons, MBA, FCCA (*Finance Manager*)
Mrs A Knight (*Admissions Registrar*)
Ms K Lippiatt (*PA to the Headmistress*)
Mrs H Manning (*Receptionist*)
Mrs S Pelling, BA Hons Keele (*Head of Marketing*)
Mrs C Press (*School Office Manager/Secretary*)
Miss O Rayner (*Admin Assistant, Bursar's Office*)
Mrs S Seeds (*Staff Secretary*)
Mrs L White, MA Brighton, MCLIP (*Lead Librarian/ Archives*)
Mrs H Yates (*Purchase Ledger Clerk*)

Westfield School

Oakfield Road, Gosforth, Newcastle-upon-Tyne NE3 4HS

Tel:	0191 255 3980
email:	westfield@westfield.newcastle.sch.uk
website:	www.westfield.newcastle.sch.uk
Twitter:	@Westfieldschool
Facebook:	@WestfieldSchool
LinkedIn:	/westfield-independent-day-school-for-girls

Westfield is a day school for 380 girls aged 3+ to 18, in Junior and Senior Houses situated on one campus in a very pleasant wooded site of over 6 acres. The School's aim is an uninterrupted education, a high academic standard and a wide curriculum offering scope and stimulus for individual development. There is a vast range of extracurricular activities with particular emphasis on Sport, Outdoor Pursuits, Music, Art and Drama. The Duke of Edinburgh's Award scheme has a high profile and all senior girls are encouraged to participate. In addition to a sound grounding in basic skills, Junior House (3–11) offers specialist teaching in Art, Craft, PE, French and Music. So that every child may be assured of individual attention class sizes are restricted to a maximum of 20. Frequently, classes are further divided into smaller units.

Senior House (11–18), has first rate classroom and laboratory facilities with excellent specialist accommodation for Home Economics and Music. A wide range of subjects is taught by specialists. Initially all girls have lessons in the traditional academic core subjects, in English, Mathematics, Geography, History, Science (taught as 3 separate subjects) and French, as well as in Music, Drama, PE, Food and Nutrition, ICT and Design. German and Spanish are introduced in the second year. Girls are encouraged to aim for breadth in their choice of subjects at GCSE. Most girls achieve 9 passes in the A–C range of the GCSE, a number with straight A and A* passes. There is a carefully structured programme of Careers and Personal and Social Education and a well developed pastoral system.

The Sixth Form occupies a cottage block in the grounds and is under the direction of the Head of the Sixth Form.

There is a full range of AS, A2 and other courses and girls are prepared for University and other Higher Education courses, including Oxbridge, as well as for other courses and for employment. The A level pass rate is always over 90%, ensuring for most girls a place in their first choice of institute of higher education.

Sixth Formers have considerable responsibility within the School in addition to their own thriving academic and cultural life.

Westfield is a member of Round Square, a worldwide association of schools which share a commitment, beyond academic excellence, to personal development and responsibility through service, challenge, adventure and international understanding. Girls from Westfield have the opportunity to attend the Annual International Conference and to participate in exchanges with member schools from all over the world, and in the Round Square International Service Projects in developing countries.

Westfield is totally committed to producing happy, self-confident, well-balanced young women who are international in their outlook and fully prepared to face life in the 21st Century.

Admission to Westfield is by interview and examination. While children of all faiths are accepted, the religious life of the school is based on Christian principles.

Fees per term (2018–2019). In Junior House fees range from £2,690 to £3,585 and in Senior House are £4,530.

Scholarships are available at 9+, 11+, 13+ and Sixth Form, including Academic, Art, Music and PE. Some bursaries are also available in cases of financial need.

Charitable status. Westfield School is owned and administered by the Northumbrian Educational Trust Ltd, which is a Registered Charity, number 528143. It exists for the purpose of education.

Governors:
Chairman: Mrs J Keep, MSCP, SRP
K Bainbridge, BA Hons
A L Dowie, MA
I Greenshields, LLB
I Henderson, BA Hons
Mrs L Keightley, BA Hons
Dr K Manzo, PhD
Mrs J Rowley, BA Hons
Mrs I Smales, MA

Headmaster: J N Walker, BSc St Andrews, MA Manchester Met, PGCE

Deputy Headteacher: Mrs K Quinn, BA Hons Leeds, PGCE

Assistant Head: S Ratcliffe, LLB Newcastle, BA Hons Wimbledon, MFA Michigan

Assistant Head: Mrs W Wise, BA Hons Newcastle, PGCE

Head of Sixth Form: Mrs E Wise, BA Hons Newcastle, PGCE

Art/Design:
S Ratcliffe, S Ratcliffe, LLB Newcastle, BA Hons Wimbledon, MFA Michigan
D Stone, BA Hons Kingston, PGCE

Biology:
Mrs H Morell, BSc Columbia, New York
Mrs J Dudley, BSc Hons Newcastle, PGCE

Business Studies:
Mrs D Carton, BA Hons Leeds, PGCE

Chemistry:
P Russell, BSc Hons Bath, PGCE

Computing:
Mrs C Lloyd BA Hons Liverpool, PGCE

Drama/Theatre Studies:
Mrs E Forster, MA Hons Cantab, PGCE
Mrs N McGowan, BA Hons E Anglia, PGCE

English:
Dr A Leng, BA Hons Reading, MA Reading, PhD
Mrs E Forster, MA Hons Cantab, PGCE

Food & Nutrition:
Mrs L Hender, BA Hons Northumbria

French:
Mrs F Boyce, BA Hons Salford, PGCE
Mrs S Dodds, BA Hons Dunelm, PGCE

Geography:
C Dunn, MA Hons Cantab
Mrs E Gardner, MA Hons Cantab, BA Hons Cantab, PGCE

German:
Mrs F Boyce, BA Hons Salford, PGCE
Mrs E Wise, BA Hons Newcastle, PGCE

History:
Mrs J Harris, BA Hons Northumbria, PGCE

Mathematics:
Dr C Barnett, MMath Newcastle, PhD Dunelm
Mrs L Marshall, BEng Hons Liverpool, PGCE
Mrs F Swift, MA Hons Cantab, MEng Cantab, PGCE

Music:
Dr L Hardy, BA Hons Keele, PhD

Physical Education:
Miss N Baguley, BSc Lancaster, PGCE
Miss M Lamb, BSc Sheffield, PGCE
Mrs K Nicholson BEd Hons Exeter

Physics:
Dr E Corbin, BA Oxon, MSc Newcastle, PhD Newcastle

Psychology:
Miss R Little, BSc Newcastle, MSc Northumbria, PGCE

Religious Studies:
S Shieber, BA Hons Dunelm, PGCE, MA

Spanish:
Mrs F Boyce, BA Hons Salford, PGCE
Mrs S Dodds, BA Hons Dunelm, PGCE

Additional Learning Support:
Mrs E Thompson, BSc OU, PGCE, NASC
Mrs N McGowan, BA Hons East Anglia, PGCE

Junior House:
Assistant Head: Mrs C Baines, BSc Hons UMIST, PGCE

Teachers/Teaching Assistants:
Mrs N Alexanders, BA Hons Newcastle, PGCE
Miss J N Brown, BSc Hons Huddersfield, PGCE
Mrs F Collier, BA Hons Keele, PGCE
Mrs H Dean, BEd Hons Newcastle
Mrs L Kendall BA Hons York, PGCE
Miss R King BSc Hons Dunelm
Miss A McKale NVQ Level 3 Early Years
Miss G McKeating, BEd Hons York
Mrs K Meeson, BSc Hons Northumbria, PGCE
Mrs L McNaught, BA Hons Staffs, NCFE3
Mrs T McQuade, NCFE Level ONC Dyslexia Level 3
Mrs J Slack, BA Hons Hull, PGCE

Admin Staff:
Bursar: J Leese CIPFA
Domestic Bursar: Mrs D Oldroyd
Headmaster's Secretary: Mrs J Jokelson
Junior House Secretary: Mrs A Dryden, BA Northumbria
Laboratory Technician: Dr A Rose

Examinations Officer: Mrs H Morell, BSc Columbia, New York
Marketing Coordinator: Mrs M Brannigan
School Librarian: Dr A Leng, BA Hons Reading, MA Reading, PhD

Westonbirt School

Tetbury, Gloucestershire GL8 8QG

Tel:	01666 880333
email:	admissions@westonbirt.org
	enquiries@westonbirt.org
website:	www.westonbirt.org
Twitter:	@WestonbirtSch
Facebook:	@Westonbirt-School
LinkedIn:	/Westonbirt-Schools

Location. Westonbirt School is a senior day and boarding school set in 210 acres of magnificent parkland in the heart of the Cotswolds, close to the cultural cities of Bath, Bristol and Cheltenham and only 90 minutes from London. The site is shared with co-ed Westonbirt Prep School. Westonbirt School will be welcoming day boys from September 2019 and gradually moving to full co-education.

Philosophy. Westonbirt School encourages every student to achieve their full potential, instilling confidence in a safe, secure and stimulating environment. Students experience exceptional pastoral care and outstanding educational opportunities in a 'greenhouse, not a hothouse' environment. This is achieved through our boarding ethos, which is shared by day pupils, and delivered through a unique educational environment where pupils thrive in a vibrant community with small classes, magnificent grounds and inspiring teachers. Our inclusive ethos means students are admitted for their potential. Academic success is strong yet not sought at the expense of other areas of a pupil's development.

As a Church of England School, with our own Chapel and Chaplain, our Christian ethos underpins all that we do. Strong friendships are formed across year groups and every pupil is guided by nurturing academic and pastoral staff.

Curriculum. All pupils follow the national curriculum and are offered a full sporting timetable with a wide range of extra-curricular opportunities to provide each student with an outstanding, rounded education. The exceptionally able are stretched and challenged through our Gifted and Talented programme and individual help and support is tailored by specialists for those who need Learning Support or English Language Training.

The school has performed consistently well in both GCSE and A Level results. In 2018, at GCSE 12% of papers were graded 9, 27% were graded 8–9 and 46% graded 7, 8 and 9. At A Level, 31% were graded A*–A and 57% A*–B. Excellent results for the inclusive intake of pupils.

Westonbirt is in the top 5% of schools in the UK for value added. This objectively assessed measure conducted by the University of Durham calculates pupils' academic improvement between the ages of 11 and 16. Analysis shows that students at Westonbirt achieve almost a grade higher than expected at entry in each subject at GCSE. Westonbirt is a non-selective school which consistently delivers strong results.

Each student has their own personal tutor, helping students to manage their time and acquire effective study skills from the moment they join until securing their place at university.

Headmistress Natasha Dangerfield has implemented a robust 'Skills for Life' program designed to compliment academic success and prepare young people for the challenges facing them in a global society. The program explores the diversity of the workplace, promotes career achievement and offers practical and financial training for life beyond school.

Music, Drama and Art and Design. The state-of-the-art Music Technology Centre boasts a rehearsal room, fully-equipped Apple technology suite and recording studio. As well as individual lessons, girls have many opportunities to perform regularly in choirs, orchestras or ensembles.

Art and design is a key strength and the school has fully-equipped art and design studios. Pupils regularly achieve places at prestigious design and art institutions such as Central St Martins.

Drama is thriving with outstanding productions every year and our talented pupils performing at the Edinburgh Festival to great acclaim. The Orangery Theatre, with adjacent Green Room and Rehearsal Studio, provides a versatile venue for the performing arts. Individual speech and drama lessons are popular with many pupils successfully performing at competition level.

Sports and Leisure. Westonbirt has extensive grounds and sports facilities, including a £3m modern Sports Centre, 25m indoor swimming pool, full fitness suite, nine-hole golf course, tennis courts, lacrosse pitches, netball, and athletics facilities. The school has an ambitious equestrian team and those keen on equestrian sports may take riding lessons at nearby stables and polo at the neighbouring Beaufort Polo Club. Our sports teachers are experts in their fields; we currently have a UK lacrosse coach and an olympiad swimmer on our PE staff. Many students go on to compete at county and national level.

Extracurricular Activities. Students are inspired to participate in the broad range of extra-curricular activities on offer. Drama, music and dance are particularly popular, but there are many other varied and rewarding options. Older pupils participate in The Duke of Edinburgh's Award scheme, World Challenge or the Leiths cookery school. Planned activities are offered every weekend including cultural, fun and shopping trips, which are open to day pupils as well as boarders. Overseas cultural and world challenge trips broaden pupils' horizons and have recently taken students to France, Italy, Spain, the USA and Peru. Community and fundraising projects are strongly supported and the school has links with other schools in Sierra Leone, Japan and India which Westonbirt pupils have also visited.

Learning Support. The Learning Support Department at Westonbirt School prides itself on a personalised approach to learning. The small specialist team works closely with pupils and all members of staff to provide support and guidance to pupils with learning support needs so that they approach their studies with confidence.

The department is passionate about nurturing the talents of all students identifying their unique qualities, supporting them in developing skills and becoming successful independent learners

ELT (English Language Training). Our English Language Training department offers specialist individual and group lessons. All pupils are assessed on entry to ensure they have the requisite amount of support needed and are taught in mainstream lessons for all other subjects. International students appreciate the supportive and professional ELT department who work closely with all academic staff.

Entrance Requirements. Students normally join the school at 11, 13 or 16, though they may do so at other ages in special circumstances. At 11+ and 13+ they must sit either the Common Entrance Examination or take the school's own entrance papers, attend an interview with the Headmistress, and provide a reference from their current school. Sixth Form entrants must have a minimum of 5 GCSEs at grades A*–C, attend an interview and sit tests in the subjects they intend to study at A Level.

Fees per term (2018–2019). Years 7 to 13: £4,995 for a day pupil, £9,750 for a boarder.

Scholarships and Bursaries. Scholarships are available for those entering Years 7 (11+), 9 (13+) and 12 (16+) and these are given for Academic Excellence, Art, Drama, Music, Sport, Organ and Choral. We also offer the Mary Henderson Performing Arts Scholarship, for all-round excellence in Music, Drama and Dance. These can be each worth up to a maximum of 10% of the current tuition (day) fees. Scholarships may be topped up with bursaries. Bursary application forms are available on request from the Director of Admissions.

Westonbirt School is part of The Wishford Schools Group, www.wishford.co.uk.

Head: **Mrs N Dangerfield**, BA Brighton

Deputy Head Academic: Mrs J Barlow, BSc Birmingham, PGCE Open
Head of Boarding: Mrs L Bradbury, BA
Chief Operating Officer: Mr S Kenny
Director of Admissions: Mrs P Stevenson
Director of Marketing & Digital Communications: Mrs L Brook, BSc Hons, MCIM, CIM Dip
Chaplain: Revd A Monaghan, BA Cambridge, MA Edinburgh

Heads of Department:
Art: Ms M Stockton, BA, MA, PGATC
Business Studies: Mrs J Edwards, BA
Classics: Mr P Holland, BA
Drama: Mr A English, BA, PGCE
ELT: Miss C Lloyd, BA, MA, Cert TESOL
English: Mr A Mew, BA Hons, PGCE
Food & Textiles Technology: Mrs J Bell, BEd
Geography: Mrs N Gill, BA Hons, PGCE
History: Mr I Ahmed, BA, PGCE, MEd
Learning Support: Mrs P Reuter, BA
Mathematics: Mrs J Barlow, BSc, PGCE
Modern Languages: Mrs C Rock, L-ès-L
Music: Mrs N Atwell, BA, PGCE
Physical Education: Mrs L Johnson, BEd
Psychology & Religious Education: Mrs Lisa Allen, BA, PGCE
Science: Miss H Rogerson, MPhys, PGCE

Health & Well-being Centre: Mrs R Etherington, RCN

Housemistresses:
Badminton House: Mrs S Price, BA, MA
Beaufort House: Miss C Crowley
Dorchester House: Miss S Gould
Sixth Form: Mrs L Bradbury, BA Hons, MA, PGCE

Preparatory School:
Headmaster: Mr Sean Price

Assistant Head Organisation & Year 6, Class 6C Form Tutor: Mrs C Clifton
Assistant Head Teaching & Learning, Year 3 Form Tutor, Forest School Leader: Mrs A Dicks
Nursery Leader: Mrs M Belton
Reception Form Tutor: Miss E Palmer
Year 1 Form Tutors: Miss R Lewis and Mrs E Ourahou
Year 4 Form Tutor: Miss P Cole and Mrs K Armitage
Year 5: Miss B Moody
Year 6: Mr B Stirling and Mrs C Clifton
Sport Coordinator: Miss R Bird
SENCO: Mrs C Smith
Swim Programme Lead: Mr R Francis

Wimbledon High School
GDST

Mansel Road, London SW19 4AB

Tel:	020 8971 0900 (Senior School)
	020 8971 0902 (Junior School)
email:	info@wim.gdst.net
website:	www.wimbledonhigh.gdst.net
Twitter:	@WimbledonHigh
Facebook:	@WimbledonHighSchoolGDST

Founded 1880.

Wimbledon High School is part of the GDST (Girls' Day School Trust). The GDST is the leading network of independent girls' schools in the UK. As a charity that owns and runs 23 schools and two academies, it reinvests all its income in its schools. For further information about the Trust, see p. xxiii or visit www.gdst.net.

Pupil numbers. Junior School: 340 aged 4–11; Senior School: 690, including 170 in the Sixth Form.

Wimbledon High School combines academic strength with a firm belief that learning should be fun. Jane Lunnon took up the Headship in September 2014 and says she is "struck by the natural, unaffectedness of the students, their scholarship and their willingness to get involved in all aspects of school life". Results at A Level and GCSE are consistently extremely high, music and drama are a vibrant part of school life and a Director of Sport and Head of Rowing have rejuvenated PE at the school. Activities include World Challenge, Model United Nations and The Duke of Edinburgh's Award, alongside many smaller clubs and societies, from Mah Jong to Coding and Robotics. The older girls often run these themselves.

An innovative programme of pastoral care supports students (and their parents) through what can sometimes be difficult teenage years. Students increasingly gain more responsibility as they move up through the school. Sixth Formers practise leadership through the Student Leadership Team and by mentoring younger girls; there is a peer counselling service and older students help with Literacy, Maths and Latin at local primary schools. The school runs SHINE – the outreach Serious Fun on Saturdays programme as well as Teach Together and volunteering in the community.

Junior and Senior Schools share one central Wimbledon site, with a swimming pool and sports hall, Performing Arts Centre and a centre for design and technology. Project Ex Humilibus is its development project; the school is building a STEAM tower (Science, Technology, Engineering, Arts and Maths) along with a new Sixth Form Centre, assembly hall and dining hall. The playing fields are ten minutes' walk away at Nursery Road (the site of the original All England Lawn Tennis and Croquet Club) providing a full-size, all-weather hockey pitch and five netball/tennis courts. The school believes in nurturing all sporting talent and a fit and active lifestyle is encouraged.

The **Junior School** provides a creative and academic education in a happy and stimulating environment, with specialist rooms for art, music and science, plus a (prototype and whole school) STEAM space. There is a balance of class and specialist subject teaching. An enriched and extended National Curriculum is the foundation, with the school embracing the 'creative curriculum' encompassing various areas of learning at the same time; Spanish and French are taught at various times, as well as Latin. An after-school club offers flexibility to working parents. Sports teams do well, as do the school's chess players and musicians.

The **Senior School** curriculum runs over a two week timetable. In Key Stage 3, girls study English, Mathematics and Sciences; they learn German or Spanish alongside French (Latin is added in Year 8) as well as Geography, History, Religious Studies, PE, Music, Drama, Art, Design & Technology (textiles, product design and cookery and nutrition, on rotation), Computer Science, Study Skills and PSHE (Personal, Social and Health Education).

At Key Stage 4 girls choose 9 GCSE subjects, of which one must be a Modern Foreign Language, with the possibility of adding Classical Greek as a 10th GCSE. PE and PHSE continue. A Global Perspectives course in Year 10 brings breadth beyond the curriculum, and Explore is a series of thought-provoking talks held for Year 10 and above. The school also holds regular Rosewell Lectures for older girls, parents and staff.

In the **Sixth Form,** students may choose from the same subjects on offer at GCSE (except PE – compulsory in Year 12 but non-examined), plus Further Mathematics, Economics, Politics and Classical Civilisation. There is a high uptake of science subjects and in recent years the Extended Project Qualification has been popular. An extensive programme of enrichment (starting in Year 11 and continuing in Years 12 and 13) offers short courses in scores of subjects as well as the opportunity to participate in Community Service. PSHE continues and a comprehensive programme of careers and university entrance advice is offered.

Admissions. 4+ girls are assessed in groups in a nursery-style environment; indication of a girl's potential is the key at this stage, rather than evidence of what has already been learnt.

For 11+ entry, applicants are assessed in two stages. The first is verbal and non-verbal reasoning, in the autumn. Successful candidates from that stage are invited back for stage two in January – creative assessments carried out in small groups and encompassing various problem-solving and creative activities, plus a short writing task. The occasional entry examination for other years tests Maths and English.

16+ assessment comprises entrance exam and interviews. Offers of places are conditional upon GCSE grade 7 or above (A* or A) in candidates' chosen A Level subjects, and a minimum of eight GCSEs (grades 6–9) overall.

Fees per term (2018–2019). Senior School £6,270, Junior School £4,874.

The fees cover the regular curriculum, school books, choral music, games and swimming, but not optional extra subjects.

Scholarships and Bursaries. Academic scholarships are awarded to girls who do exceptionally well in the 11+ exam, worth 5% of the fees. There are also music and sport scholarships at 11+. At 16+ there are scholarships in Art, Drama, Music and Sport, worth up to 10%, as well as Academic scholarships. Details and application forms available on request.

Bursaries take account of academic merit, but all are means-tested. The maximum value is the full fee.

Charitable status. Wimbledon High School is part of The Girls' Day School Trust, which is a Registered Charity, number 306983.

Chairman of the Local Governors: Mr G Williams, BA Econ Manchester

Head: Mrs J Lunnon, BA Bristol

Senior Deputy Head: Ms F Kennedy, MA Oxon

Head of Junior School: Miss K Mitchell, BEd Warwick, MA York (*until July 2019*)

Director of Finance & Operations: Mrs S Lawton, AInstAM Dip

Director of Sixth Form: Dr J Parsons, BMus, MA, PhD Cardiff

Director of Studies: Mrs C Duncan, BSc Sheffield

Director of Academic Administration & Data: Mr B Haythorne, MA Oxon

Director of Co-curricular & Partnerships: Miss J Cox, BSc Brunel

Director of Marketing & Communications: Mrs R Brewster, BA Oxon, MA Leeds

Assistant Head Academic: Ms Suzy Pett, MA Cantab

Assistant Head Pastoral: Mr Ben Turner, BA Hons London

Deputy Head, Junior School: (*to be appointed*)

Wychwood School

72–74 Banbury Road, Oxford, Oxfordshire OX2 6JR

Tel: 01865 557976
Fax: 01865 556806
email: reception@wychwoodschool.org
website: www.wychwoodschool.org
Twitter: @wychwoodschool
Facebook: @wychwoodschool
LinkedIn: /wychwood-school-limited

Wychwood is a unique and friendly day and boarding school for girls, with excellent academic grades and outstanding pastoral care. Situated in the heart of Oxford, the school offers an exceptional education for pupils of all abilities through its small class sizes which allow for extensive individual attention without intense pressure. Established in 1897, individuality has always been more important than conformity at Wychwood and the girls have opportunities for success in many directions.

Curriculum. All girls are expected to take up to 10 subjects at GCSE; most go on to work for A Level and BTEC and University entrance. The lower school curriculum includes: Religious Education, English, History, Geography, Mathematics, Biology, Physics, Chemistry, French, Computing, Textiles, Art, Photography, Music, PHSEE, PE, Spanish (from Year 8), and Drama. Visiting staff teach other optional foreign languages and musical instruments; there is a school choir and chamber groups.

School Council. Day-to-day life is largely controlled by the School Council which meets weekly and consists of staff, seniors (elected by the school) and form representatives. This is a type of cooperative government, the matured result of a long series of experiments, which trains the girls to deal with the problems of community life and gives everyone, in greater or lesser degree according to her age and status, an understanding of, and a voice in, the rules necessary for a sensibly disciplined life.

Sixth Form. Members of Wychwood Sixth have considerable freedom yet play an active part in the life of the school. The choice of subjects at A Level is wide. New BTEC courses have been introduced from September 2018. Classes are small and stimulating. Individual help with university applications and careers is a key feature of Wychwood Sixth. Girls are allowed to be out of school during study periods and on a Friday, students do not start lessons until 9.30 am. There are regular outside speakers and girls attend a variety of lectures, conferences, exhibitions and meetings. Their participation in school plays and concerts as well as School Council is greatly valued. Sixth Form girls may spend approximately 2 hours per week on community

service. Sixth Form boarders have individual study-bedrooms.

Entrance. A personal interview between the Headmistress and both a parent and the pupil is a key part of the selection process. There is an entrance test to satisfy the staff that the girl will benefit from an education of this kind; the opinion of the girl's former school is also taken into account, particularly in relation to non-academic qualities.

Scholarships and Bursaries. Scholarships are offered in art, creative writing, drama, music, sports and academia.

Academic scholarships are awarded on the basis of the entrance examination papers at 11+ and 13+ and on the basis of the results of scholarship papers at 16+. Girls take three scholarship papers in subjects of their choice at 16+ as well as a general paper. At 11+ and 13+ we award major scholarships of £1,000 p.a. and minor scholarships of £500 p.a. At 16+ we award major scholarships of £2,000 p.a. and minor scholarships of £1,000 p.a.

At 11+ non-academic scholarship auditions take place on the day before the entrance examinations; at 13+ they take place in the February preceding entry; at 16+ auditions take place on the day of the entrance examinations.

Creative Arts Scholarships are offered at 11+, 13+ and 16+ to candidates with outstanding ability in Art, Creative Writing or both. We award major scholarships of £1,000 p.a. and minor scholarships of £500 p.a.

Art: Candidates are asked to bring 6 artistic compositions or craft items which will be discussed with the Head of Art. A short unprepared task will also be undertaken.

Creative Writing: Candidates are asked to bring 6 different pieces of writing, including poetry, a story and a description. These will be discussed with the Head of English. A piece of creative writing will also be set.

Drama scholarships are offered at 11+, 13+ or 16+ to candidates with outstanding ability and potential in drama. We award major scholarships of £1,000 p.a. and minor scholarships of £500 p.a. Drama scholars are expected to be grade 3 or 4 level at 11+, grade 5 or 6 level at 13+ and grade 6 or 7 level at 16+. Candidates are asked to perform a prepared piece and discuss their love of drama with the Head of Drama at audition.

Three Music Scholarships are offered: one at 11+, one at 13+ and one at 16+ to cover instrumental tuition for up to two instruments including voice. Music scholars are expected to be grade 3 or 4 level at 11+, grade 5 or 6 level at 13+ and grade 6 or 7 level at 16+. Candidates are asked to play two prepared pieces on their instrument(s) and to do aural tests and sight reading. There is also a single organ scholarship available to cover organ tuition which is awarded to a high-level pianist.

Sports scholarships are offered at 11+, 13+ and 16+ to candidates with outstanding ability and potential in sports. We award major scholarships of £1,000 p.a. and minor scholarships of £500 p.a. Candidates are asked to submit video evidence of their performance in our two main sports of hockey and netball. They will also have an individual interview with the Director of Sport when they will have the opportunity to discuss their achievements and their favourite sports.

Bursaries: There are means-tested bursary funds available for a limited number of pupils in particular financial need.

Fees per term (2018–2019). Boarders £9,300, Weekly Boarders £8,100, Day Girls £5,300.

Charitable status. Wychwood School is a Registered Charity, number 309684. It exists for the education of girls from the ages of 11 to 18.

Staff List:

Headmistress: Mrs A Johnson, BSc Dunelm, PGCE

Deputy Head: Ms B Sherlock, BA, MEd (*English*)
Director of Studies: Mrs A Stacey, BA Hons, PGCE
Head of Wychwood Sixth: Mrs J Sherbrooke, BSc Hons, MSc, PGCE

Miss J Bettridge, TESOL Cert (*EAL*)
Ms M Bridgman, LDS (*Textiles*)
Mrs K Britton, BSc Hons, MBA QTS (*Biology*)
Miss F Centamore, BSc, PGCE (*Director of Sport*)
Mrs C Collcutt, DEUG (*French*)
Mrs M Constance (*Drama*)
Mrs C Crossley, BA Hons, PGCE (*RS*)
Mrs E Dean, MA Oxon, PGCE (*English*)
Dr M Donald, BA Hons, PhD (*Psychology/EPQ*)
Mr P Humphreys, BSc, PGCE, MEd, BSA Cert (*Geography*)
Mr P Ilott, BEng (*Physics*)
Mrs T Jarrett, BA Hons, PGCE (*EAL*)
Mr L Jimenez, LLB, MA (*Spanish*)
Mrs H Kirby, BA Hons, PGCE (*English*)
Mrs M Lord (*Mathematics*)
Mr M Pennington, BA Hons, MA (*Photography*)
Mrs J Sherbrooke, BSc Hons, MSc, PGCE (*History*)
Mrs A Stacey, BA Hons, PGCE (*Chemistry*)
Mrs M Stephenson, BSc Hons, PGCE (*ICT, Careers, SENDCo*) [maternity cover]
Mrs B Stevens, BSc Hons, PGCE (*Mathematics*)
Mrs G Troth, BSc Hons (*Economics & Business Studies*)
Mrs B Walster, BMus Hons, PGCE (*Music*)
Miss A Wardell, BA Hons, MA (*Art & Design*)
Dr J Williams, BA Hons, PGCE, SRN, RSCN (*History of Art*)

Mrs J Bridge (*Office Manager*)
Mrs M Davis (*School Counsellor*)
Mrs C Drummond (*Technician*)
Mrs L Henk (*senior Housemistress*)
Dr C Hornby, MB BChir, MRCGP (*School Doctor*)
Mr M Holland, BA Hons, MA (*Marketing & Admissions Manager*)
Miss S Hussain (*Finance Assistant*)
Mrs C Legg, BA, MSc (*Librarian*)
Miss S Mack (*Assistant Housemistress*)
Miss R Morris (*Receptionist*)
Mr J Mott (*Network Manager*)
Miss J Tyers (*Junior Housemistress, Marketing and Admissions Manager*)
Mrs J Wells (*SEND Teaching Assistant*)
Mr I Williams (*Bursar*)

PART III
Schools whose Heads are members of
The Society of Heads

ALPHABETICAL LIST OF SCHOOLS

The following schools, whose Heads are members of both The Society of Heads and HMC, can be found in the HMC section:

The following school, whose Head is a member of both The Society of Heads and GSA, can be found in the GSA section:

THE SOCIETY OF HEADS
GEOGRAPHICAL LIST OF SCHOOLS

Individual School Entries

Abbey Gate College

Saighton Grange, Saighton, Chester CH3 6EN

Tel: 01244 332077
Fax: 01244 335510
email: admin@abbeygatecollege.co.uk
website: www.abbeygatecollege.co.uk
Twitter: @AbbeyGateColl
Facebook: @AbbeyGateCollege

Motto: *Audentior Ito*

Founded in 1977, Abbey Gate College is a co-educational day school for boys and girls from 4–18 years of age.

Location and Facilities. The senior school is set in beautiful grounds at Saighton Grange some three miles south of the City of Chester. The history of Saighton Grange goes back long before the Norman Conquest, although most of the present building is Victorian. From 1853 the Grange was a residence of the Grosvenor family. Additional facilities include a large Sports Hall, playing fields and an Arts and Media Centre opened in March 2004 by HRH the Duchess of Gloucester. A purpose-built Art and Design & Technology Centre and new science laboratory were completed in Spring 2008 and opened by His Grace the Duke of Westminster. In 2013 developments included a new multi-purpose classroom and drama studio. In 2016 a Sports & Teaching Pavilion was opened, followed two years later by the opening of an all-weather pitch. Future developments include two fully-equipped and cutting-edge laboratories and a new Sixth Form Centre with personal study zones and a range of seminar classrooms.

The Infant and Junior School is situated in Aldford, a picturesque village only two miles from Saighton. Facilities here include a new Foundation and Infant School building opened in 2018, with three spacious classrooms all with covered outdoor areas, a library area, and a space for Learning Enrichment, along with excellent playing fields, an ecology and wildlife area plus a number of other outdoor learning spaces. The Juniors and Infants benefit from shared use of the senior site facilities and specialist staff that teach throughout the age range.

Aims. At Abbey Gate College, our children are at the heart of everything we do. We promote a love of learning, academic ambition and excellence within a welcoming, safe and caring community. We nurture our pupils' potential, encourage aspiration and develop their understanding of the wider world. Together, we strive to make a positive contribution to society. We foster an environment in which achievement and personal development in all contexts are celebrated and endeavour is recognised. Pupils are instilled with a 'can do' attitude giving them the confidence to make a difference and 'Be Someone'.

At Abbey Gate College, we aim to inspire our pupils to:
• Achieve individual academic excellence
• Become happy, confident, fulfilled and resilient young people
• Embrace enrichment opportunities to discover and realise their full potential
• Enjoy learning and be ambitious
• Become tolerant individuals with respect for others
• Develop a strong moral code and be responsible members of society

In achieving these aims, the College builds the self-confidence of pupils and prepares them for the opportunities, responsibilities and experiences in the next chapters in their lives.

Academic Programme. The College aims to provide children with a broad general education through GCSE and A Levels to university or other forms of higher education. In Years 7 and 8 pupils study Art, Drama, English, French, German, Spanish, Home Economics, Geography, History, Mathematics, Music, Physical Education, PSHE, Textiles, Religious Studies, Science, Spoken English, Design & Technology, Information and Communication Technology.

In Years 10 and 11 an option scheme takes effect: within the core, all pupils study English, English Literature and Mathematics, a modern foreign language and at least two Sciences. Study skills are developed and all pupils participate in sport and a rolling PSHE programme. To support their academic curriculum, Year 10 undertake a week's work experience and participate in a Development Course designed to build teamwork, self-confidence, leadership skills and peer mentoring.

Option subjects for GCSE are taken from the following: Art, Biology, Chemistry, Design and Technology, Drama, French, Geography, German, History, Music, Physics, ICT, Spanish and PE.

In the Sixth Form A Level subjects available (according to demand) are: Mathematics, Further Mathematics, English Literature, English Language, History, Government and Politics, Geography, Economics, Business Studies, Physics, Chemistry, Biology, French, German, Art, Music, Product Design, PE, ICT, Psychology and Theatre Studies. Sixth Form students follow a comprehensive PSHE programme, have the opportunity to study AS Citizenship, complete an EPQ (Extended Project Qualification), the AQA Baccalaureate and participate in a range of sports, music and drama at the College.

In the Lower Sixth students may also join the Young Enterprise scheme which gives theoretical and practical knowledge of the business world. They enjoy an active community service programme. A number of outside speakers visit the school and regular trips to theatres, conferences or galleries are arranged. All the Lower Sixth students also attend a study skills and team building course in the Lake District in their first term which supports the transition from GCSE to A Level.

Music. The College is well known throughout Chester and North Wales for the outstanding quality of its music. The Chapel Choir has for several years undertaken weeklong summer visits to Cathedrals in various parts of the country including Ely, Gloucester, St Albans, Ripon, Tewkesbury, Winchester, Durham, York, Bath, Norwich and Hereford, as well as touring overseas: the USA in 2003, Italy in 2009, Belgium in 2010 and Poland in 2013. Annually, the Chapel Choir sings Evensong at St Paul's Cathedral or St George's Chapel, Windsor. The College also has a Concert Band, The Saighton Syncopators dance band, a modern Funk Band and a Barber Shop Group.

Many pupils of all ages take music lessons and with visiting staff are prepared for the Associated Board Examinations.

Drama. There are two major drama productions each year and these can be drama and musical. There is a whole-school production, a Key Stage 3 performance and GCSE and A Level plays. Pupils are also prepared for examinations in Speech and Drama and regularly enter local competitions with great success. All pupils in Years 7–9 participate in the English Speaking Board scheme within the English and Drama curriculum, helping to develop their confidence and public speaking skills. Year 6 Junior pupils also present a summer performance in their final term before moving into Year 7.

Sport. The College has extensive playing fields, tennis courts, a sports hall, a new Sports and Teaching Pavilion with fitness room and state-of-the-art all-weather pitch. The Sports Hall offers four badminton courts, five-a-side soccer, volleyball, basketball, netball, indoor hockey, tennis and cricket nets.

All pupils participate in physical education and games. Boys play rugby, soccer, cricket and tennis; girls play hockey, netball, tennis and rounders. Athletics is popular for both boys and girls and all sports provide full fixture lists for the various College teams. The local swimming pool is reserved each week for sessions with a fully-qualified instructor for the younger pupils.

The College competes in both Regional and National Independent Schools sports events, and has enjoyed great success in athletics and swimming. Pupils are regularly sent for trials for Chester and District and County teams with players selected to represent Cheshire in handball, football, hockey, cricket and rugby. There have been soccer tours to Malta and Spain and recent Hockey tours to South Africa, Germany and Spain. The school's Ski Racing team trains weekly and is involved in many competitions including the annual British Championships in France where individual and team performances have been impressive. A number of pupils already train with the English Schools Ski Squad. The equestrian team has achieved national honours, with riders being selected to represent their country and the college organises a local competition and sponsors a number of pony club or equestrian competitions.

Other activities. The College has a remarkable record of giving generously to Charities and the three Houses serve to raise money through sponsorship; Sixth Formers take a leading role in this. At weekends and during holidays many pupils take advantage of outdoor pursuits and many choose to follow The Duke of Edinburgh's Award scheme; there are over 70 participants at all levels from Bronze to Gold Award.

Our **Infant and Junior School** provides excellence in education with a broad-based curriculum supported by a diverse extracurricular programme that gives children aged 4–11 a wide range of opportunities. These include choir, gymnastics, team games, Spanish, Belleplates, Ju-Jitsu, creative arts and drama to name but a few. There are frequent school trips and excursions that support the school experience, including a Year 6 residential outdoor and adventurous week at Glaramara in the Lake District.

Admission. *Senior School*: Most pupils enter the College at age 11 following an Entrance Examination held in the Spring Term, although where occasional places occur in other year groups, assessments can be made mid year. Each pupil is allocated to one of the Senior School Houses; the house system encourages competition, community and positive attitudes through the allocation of home points.

Junior School: Pupils are admitted to the Junior School by means of short assessment and interview at ages 7, 8, 9 and 10 dependent on spaces being available. It is expected that children already in this part of the school will move directly into the College at age 11.

Infant School: Entry at ages 4, 5 and 6 is also available. Reception places are limited and assessments run on separate occasions throughout the year.

Sixth Form: Priority is given to existing pupils but places are offered to others and are conditional on good results at GCSE.

Scholarships. A number of academic scholarships are available following the results of the Entrance Examination. A comprehensive Bursary Scheme also operates at 11+ and Sixth Form entry offering places to pupils with proven ability or talents who would normally not be able to afford the school fees.

For musical talent awards are offered including Music Exhibitions at Year 7 and Sixth Form level and the Daphne Herbert Choral Scholarship. In addition there are sports awards available at 11+.

Fees per term (2018–2019). Tuition: Infant and Junior School £2,985; Senior School £4,280.

Old Saightonians. All pupils are encouraged to join the Old Saightonians' Association. Further details of the Association can be obtained from the Registrar at the College.

Charitable status. Deeside House Educational Trust is a Registered Charity. number 273586. It exists to provide co-education for children in the Cheshire, Wirral and North Wales areas.

Visitor: His Grace The Duke of Westminster

Chairman of Governors: Mrs F Taylor

Head: **Mrs T Pollard**, BEd Hons, NPQH, MA

Deputy Heads:
Mr D P H Meadows, BA Hons, PGCE (*History*)
Mr G Allmand, BSc Hons, PGCE (*Geography*)

Academic Staff:
Mr J Andrews, BMus Hons, PGCE (*Head of Music*)
Mr A Austen, BSc Hons, PGCE (*Geography*)
Mr K Bailey (*Business and Economics*)
Mr S Ball, PhD, MPhys (*Physics*)
Mrs C Bennett, BA Hons, PGCE (*Modern Foreign Languages*)
Mr M Booth, MA Cantab, PGCE (*Mathematics*)
Miss K Burdon, BSc, PGCE (*Mathematics*)
Mr M Cavallini, BSc Hons, GTP (*Mathematics, Head of Sixth Form*)
Mr C Cutler, BSc Hons (*PE*)
Mr G Darbey, BA, MA, PGCE (*Geography*)
Mr M Dickins, BA, PGCE (*History*)
Mrs S Dolan, BSc Hons, PGCE (*Biology*)
Miss R Falcon, BSc Hons, QTS (*Design and Technology*)
Mrs V Goodwin, MusB Hons, PGCE (*ICT*)
Mr A P Green, BEd (*Mathematics*)
Miss I Greenlees, MPhil Cantab, PGCE (*History & English*)
Mrs S Hall, BA Hons, History, QTS, AMBDA, PGCE (*Learning Enrichment*)
Mrs A Hollis (*MFL*)
Mrs C Houghton, BA Hons, PGCE (*History*)
Mrs C House, BA Hons, PGCE (*Drama*)
Mrs K Jackson, HDE, GTP (*English*)
Miss G Johnson, BSc Hons, PGCE (*Mathematics*)
Miss E Jones, BA Hons (*PE*)
Mrs H Kitchin, BSc Hons, PGCE (*Economics & Business Studies*)
Dr E Leatherbarrow, BSc Hons, PGCE, PhD (*Science*)
Mr D Luckwell (*English*)
Mrs Z Leonard, BA Hons, PGCE (*English*)
Mrs J Lloyd-Johnson, BA Hons, PGCE, MA (*Art*)
Miss H Milloy, BA, MA, QTS (*English*)
Mrs N Moses, BA Hons, PGCE (*English*)
Mrs S Parker, MSc, PGCE (*Geography*)
Mrs L Poyser, BSc, PGCE (*Chemistry*)
Mrs A Prestwich, Maître FLE, PGCE (*Modern Foreign Languages*)
Mr D Rowett, BSc Hons, PGCE (*PE*)
Mrs E Sanders, BEd Hons (*PE*)
Mr D I Stockley, MSc, PGCE (*Design & Technology*)

Mrs S Storrar, BSc (*PE*)
Mr M Tempest, BEng Hons, PGCE (*Physics, Chemistry*)
Mrs G Thomas, BSc Hons, PGCE, MA (*Mathematics*)
Mrs E Worth, MA Hons, PGCE (*Modern Foreign Languages*)

Part-time Staff:
Mrs C Ayton, BA Hons, PGCE, PGC SpLD, AMBDA, APC (*Learning Enrichment*)
Mrs K Baty, MA, PGCE (*English*)
Mrs J Dukes, BEd (*Music*)
Mrs C Garratt, BA Hons (*Modern Foreign Languages*)
Mr K Gray, BSc Hons, PGCE (*Geography*)
Miss A Heaps, BA Hons (*Art*)
Mrs J Heaton, BEd Hons (*Learning Support*)
Mrs F Kay, BSc Hons, PGCE (*Biology & Psychology*)
Mr G Leadsom, BA Hons, PGCE (*Spanish, French*)
Mr D Murphy BSc, PGCE, Dip HE (*Biology, Chemistry*)
Mrs E Sanders BEd Hons (*PE*)
Mrs N Stammers, HND, BA Hons, PGCE (*ICT*)

Infant & Junior School:
Head of Infant & Junior School: Mrs A M Hickey, BSc Hons, PGCE (*Mathematics*)
Academic Lead and Primary School Teacher: Mrs T Jones, BEd Hons, PGCE
Mr P Butcher, BEd Hons
Mrs H Courtney, BEd Hons
Mrs W Richards, BEd Hons
Mrs S Tomlins, BA Hons, PGCE
Mrs C Travis, BA Hons, PGCE
Mrs A Williams, BEd Hons
Miss E Williams, BEd Hons
Miss M Webley, BSc Hons, PGCE, MA
Mrs C Spreyer (*Teaching Assistant*)
Mrs W Jones, (*KS2 Teaching Assistant*)
Mrs G Foulkes (*After-School Care Coordinator*)
Mrs J Rawlinson-Smith (*PA to I&JS Head*)

Musical Instruments Teaching:
Miss K Banerjee (*Piano*)
Mr E Hartwell-Jones, BMus (*Singing*)
Mr A Bowen-Lewis, CT ABRSM, Adv Dip MusTech (*Brass*)
Mr G Macey (*Woodwind*)
Mrs M Parsonage (*Violin*)
Mr J Rowlands, LLB (*Drums*)
Miss R Owen (*Woodwind*)
Mr S Smith (*Piano*)

Mrs C Faithfull, LRAM, FNEA (*Speech and Drama*)

Mrs H Barnes, MEng (*Bursar*)
Mrs S Boyd (*Registrar*)
Mrs K Campion (*Finance Manager's Assistant*)
Mr P Carter (*Head of Learning Enrichment*)
Mr D Duerden (*Head Groundsman*)
Miss C Evans, BA Hons (*Marketing Manager*)
Mr J Giles (*Caretaker*)
Mr R Girven (*Caretaker*)
Mrs S Greening (*Cleaner*)
Mr P Hamilton (*Caretaker*)
Mr M Healy (*Caretaker*)
Mr S Huxley (*Technician*)
Mrs A Ivory (*School Reception*)
Mrs S Knowles (*PA to SLT & Alumni Officer*)
Mrs J Littler (*Librarian*)
Mrs M Macey (*Cleaner*)
Mrs A McCleary (*School Reception*)
Mr A McKeown (*Apprentice Gardner*)
Mrs R Morrison, BA Hons, PGCE (*School Reception*)
Mrs S Okoth (*Cleaner*)
Mrs A Owen (*Examination Officer*)
Mrs A Povey (*Purchase Ledger Clerk*)

Mrs P Rees, FCCA (*Finance Manager*)
Mr P Rowlands, BSc Hons (*Network System Admin Manager*)
Mrs D Roxborough (*School Secretary*)
Miss P Sheckley (*School Nurse*)
Mr J Shenyagwa (*ICT Assistant*)
Mrs K Simons (*PA to Head*)
Mr D Stewart (*Director of ICT*)
Mr R Sutton (*Caretaker*)
Miss C Taylor (*Cleaner*)
Mrs R Upton (*HR & Compliance Manager*)
Miss L Whiteley (*Applications Development Manager*)
Miss S Williams (*Cleaner*)
Mr C Yusuf (*Interim Estates Manager*)
Mrs H Rawson (*Technician*)
Mrs R Freeman (*Art Technician*)
Mr S Horsefield (*DT Technician*)

Abbotsholme School

Rocester, Uttoxeter, Staffordshire ST14 5BS

Tel: 01889 594289 (admissions)
            01889 590217 (main number)
Fax: 01889 591001
email: admissions@abbotsholme.co.uk
website: www.abbotsholme.co.uk
Twitter: @AbbotsholmeSch
Facebook: @abbotsholmeschool

Abbotsholme School is an independent day and boarding school for boys and girls aged 2 to 18, situated in wonderful rolling hills and meadows on the border of Staffordshire and Derbyshire, close to the magnificent Peak District, in the UK. Our 140-acre campus offers the perfect environment to learn, achieve and enjoy a special education that focuses on academic success and character development. With superb facilities, all of our pupils from Pre-Prep through to Sixth Form, have the opportunity to participate and excel in an extensive programme of sports, outdoor education, agriculture and equine activities as well as the creative arts, music and drama. Abbotsholme aims to prepare each pupil for the whole of life through a balanced, flexible and challenging curriculum fostering a sense of self-worth, enthusiasm for learning and ambition for the future.

ISI Inspection. Following its latest inspection in February 2017 by the Independent Schools Inspectorate, the report stated that at Abbotsholme the '*quality of the pupils personal development is excellent*', '*pupils have positive attitudes towards learning*' and '*academic and other achievements are good*'.

Special Characteristics. Membership of the *Round Square* organisation (www.roundsquare.org) provides a strong international perspective. A worldwide and unique association of schools committed to personal growth and responsibility through service, challenge, adventure and international understanding, members share one aim – the full and individual development of every pupil into a whole person.

Our *outdoor education* programme is both well known and well regarded. Its pioneering principles inspired such organisations as the Outward Bound movement, the United World Colleges and The Duke of Edinburgh's Award scheme. With adventures both close to home and internationally, it presents pupils with personal challenges, both physical and mental, and teaches them the importance of taking responsibility for themselves and others. Many pupils are involved in The Duke of Edinburgh's Award scheme and all participate in summer camps and autumn hikes each year.

Abbotsholme is one of the very few schools in England to have a working *farm* upon which pupils are able to learn about animal husbandry and crop management and gain a healthy respect for the environment. In addition to the 70-acre farm, our British Horse Society approved *Equestrian Centre* is a popular place to be for our horse enthusiasts, who happily involve themselves in the upkeep of the stables and yard and can study for NVQ or BHS exams.

All pupils are encouraged to appreciate *Music* in some way, either by learning to play an instrument or taking singing lessons or by simply attending some of the performances that are frequently organised. Both the orchestra and the choir comprise a mixture of staff and pupils, which fosters the special atmosphere so typical of Abbotsholme.

Drama flourishes, in and out of the classroom, with performances in the 120-seat theatre always oversubscribed. All pupils who are keen to be involved, whether on stage or behind the scenes, find regular opportunities to experience the fun and self-discipline characteristic of performance and improvised theatre.

The influence of the *Art* department is evident throughout school, where pupils' painting, drawing, pottery, ceramic, graphic design and 3D creations are permanently on display. In addition many pupils enjoy the facilities of the *Design and Technology* department, which provides excellent opportunities for developing creative design into quality manufacture. Photography is a real strength of the Art department and pupils have access to a traditional darkroom as well as cutting-edge editing equipment.

We believe that the physical and mental disciplines of working together in a team are very important. *Sport* teaches the art of winning and losing with equally good grace, self-reliance and leadership, and the opportunity to compete are grasped by many of our pupils. Sports at Abbotsholme include: rugby, football, hockey, netball, tennis, swimming, athletics, squash, skiing, cross-country, horse riding, badminton and basketball.

Curriculum. Abbotsholme caters for a broad ability range. Academic standards are high with the majority of sixth formers going on to their first-choice university. Breadth and balance shape the curriculum, which aims to develop critical and creative thinking and self-discipline across a wide range of subjects at GCSE and A Level.

Activities. Abbotsholme firmly believes that a school should have a greater purpose beyond preparing students for College or University. As a result we seek not only to help all pupils realise their individual academic potential but also to develop in everyone a sense of responsibility for themselves and others through active participation within the community as well as a sense of adventure through challenges in and beyond the classroom. A comprehensive range of compulsory activities is integral to the curriculum, taking place on four afternoons a week. Each week's activities alternately include Outdoor Education and Farm/Conservation work, commitments to team sports, music and drama.

Home from Home. The boarding experience at Abbotsholme is a happy one, where staff and pupils know each other well and where every individual shares equal responsibility for the community's well being and progress. Small, friendly homes are run by resident houseparents as family units. Younger boarders share bright and comfortable dormitories in threes and fours whilst older pupils have single or shared study-bedrooms. A log cabin village has been added for sixth formers giving them opportunities to experience a greater degree of independence and privacy. Weekly boarding has become a popular option for families with busy lives and for our full boarders, a full programme of weekend activities provides plenty of choice and lots of fun, balancing academic work with social time. Our modern approach to boarding means that sleepover and flexi boarding are also options.

Facilities. These include: dedicated classroom areas for each subject, including specialist science laboratories, art, music, design and IT centres (two suites), a purpose-built studio theatre for drama, sixth form centre, log cabin complex, indoor climbing wall, 70-acre working farm, equestrian centre and manège, film studies and films, a modern, multi-purpose sports hall, extensive playing fields and swimming pool, and a chapel, which combines as the venue for morning assembly as well as concerts.

Fees per term (2018–2019). Day £2,995–£7,495; Weekly Boarding £5,995–£8,925; Full Boarding £7,995–£10,995; Occasional Boarding: £40 per night.

The Abbotsholmians' Club. The Club currently has some 2000 members and is run by a Committee of Old Abbotsholmians, elected yearly. Members receive regular mail-outs, which give contact addresses and details of the adventures of OAs, young and old. There are also regular invitations to events, to help them keep in touch with each other and with current developments at the school. An enormous amount of networking takes place between OAs, often facilitated by the Club, ensuring that friendships are sustained and memories are relived. Website: https://www.abbotsholmians.co.uk.

The Club operates a small Bursary fund specifically aimed at helping to educate sons and daughters of OAs at Abbotsholme.

Abbotsholme Arts Society. The School is host to one of the most respected concert presenters in the country. Although embracing jazz, poetry and drama performances, its core programme of chamber music has brought a Who's Who of big-name musicians to the school over the years – Ashkenazy, Brendel, Galway, Hough, the Amadeus Quartet to name just a few. Pupils are able to attend any of the Arts Society concerts free of charge. Website: https://www.abbotsholmeartssociety.co.uk.

Abbotsholme Parents' Association. Run by parents, for the benefit of parents, children and school, the Parents' Association (APA) aims to help new families settle in and become quickly familiar with Abbotsholme and all that it has to offer. Keen to promote active parental involvement in the school, members regularly organise social activities and fundraising events.

Headteacher: **Mr Robert Barnes**

Deputy Headteacher: Mrs Amy Thornton

Head of Prep School: Mrs Kristy Hankin

Head of Operations: Mr Richard Mayfield

Head of Boarding and Pastoral Care: Mrs Jo Simpson

Headteacher's PA: Mrs Julie Noon

Austin Friars

Etterby Scaur, Carlisle, Cumbria CA3 9PB

Tel:	01228 528042
Fax:	01228 810327
email:	office@austinfriars.co.uk
	admissions@austinfriars.co.uk
website:	www.austinfriars.co.uk
Twitter:	@AustinFriarsSch
Facebook:	@austinfriarsschool

Motto: *"In Omnibus Caritas"*

Austin Friars is a co-educational day school, founded by members of the Order of St Augustine in 1951. It is the UK's only Augustinian school and pupils of all denominations are welcome into the School which provides education for 450 boys and girls aged 3–18.

The 3–18 profile of the School allows pupils more time to respond to the core Augustinian values of Unity, Truth and Love which are enshrined in the way the School goes about its business on a daily basis. The 3–18 model also facilitates a seamless transition from Pre-School to VI Form and presents younger pupils with access to facilities usually the preserve of secondary pupils, such as science laboratories, music suites, specialist sports facilities and design technology workshops.

The quality of pastoral care is one of the School's greatest strengths. Both the Junior and Senior Schools are divided into three Houses with the House being central to the strong sense of a community in which older and younger pupils mix freely.

Studies. The curriculum at all levels is broad and balanced which encourages academic achievement alongside sporting, musical, cultural and creative development, thus allowing each child's talents and potential to be fully pursued. Pupils are encouraged to become increasingly independent learners as they progress through the School with excellent support mechanisms available, on an individual or small group basis, for those pupils with specific learning difficulties who require specialised provision. From age 3 in the Pre-School, pupils benefit from specialist teaching in Music, Drama, French and Spanish. As pupils move up the Junior School, this specialist teaching extends further to include Art, Classics, Philosophy for Children, Science, Design & Technology and Games. In the Senior School, class sizes are small and high standards are expected and achieved through careful monitoring of progress and a commitment by all to outstanding teaching and learning.

Activities. The School is an excellent centre for developing new and existing interests and talents. Some 50+ extracurricular activities are available to pupils both during the School day, and in after-school clubs including Chess, Mountain Adventure, Lego, Duke of Edinburgh's Award, Arts and Crafts, Cookery, Languages, Fencing, Gardening, Young Enterprise and a Debating Society. Music, Speech and Drama have a high profile across all phases of the School. Annually Junior 1 (Year 3) pupils are given a musical instrument to learn and enjoy specialist tuition. Juniors and Seniors take LAMDA Verse and Prose Speaking Examinations achieving consistently high grades. There are regular concerts, musical performances, plays and musicals.

Sport. The school has a full-sized astroturf which is utilised throughout the year and various sports pitches. The range of sporting options available is vast. Gymnastics and fitness are all offered within the activities programme. The pupils regularly achieve county status in their various sports. Qualified and enthusiastic staff provide coaching in team sports from the Junior School upwards, and the School's record in inter-school competition is acknowledged far beyond Cumbria. Annual skiing trips take place.

Admissions. Children are admitted into the Pre-School in the three to four age range following a successful taster session. Entry into the Junior School at all levels, except Kindergarten, is by assessment of English, mathematics and non-verbal reasoning. Entry into Kindergarten is by interview and a taster session.

The Senior School adopts a three-form entry policy. The majority of places are offered at 11+ where pupils sit the Senior School's entrance assessments; entry to the Sixth Form is on the basis of performance at GCSE. Admissions at other ages are considered, subject to availability of places and completion of the entrance assessment. All prospective pupils spend a taster day(s) with their prospective year group.

Fees per term (2018–2019). Pre-School: £6.15 per hour, plus £2.05 for lunch (the EYFS offers government funded hours). Junior School: £2,551 (R–Year 2), £2,810 (Years 3–4), £3,586 (Years 5–6). Senior School: £4,880 (Years 7–10), £4,984 (Years 11–13). Fees are inclusive of lunches.

Charitable status. Austin Friars is a Registered Charity, number 516289. It exists for the purpose of educating boys and girls.

Chairman of Trustees: Mr John Little

Headmaster: **Mr M F Harris**, BSc, PGCE

Deputy Head: Mrs J Thornborrow, BSc, PGCE
Deputy Head (Academic): Mr M C F Fielder, MA, PGCE
Head of VI Form: Mr S Parry, MEd, BSc, PGCE, Dip RSA
Head of Junior School: Mr Chris March, BSc
Bursar: Mr E Swinton, ACIBS
Admissions and Marketing Manager: Miss A Burns, BA

Bedstone College

Bucknell, Shropshire SY7 0BG

Tel: 01547 530303
Fax: 01547 530740
email: admissions@bedstone.org
            reception@bedstone.org
website: www.bedstone.org
Twitter: @BedstoneCollege
Facebook: @BedstoneCollege
LinkedIn: /bedstone-college-bucknell

Motto: *Caritas*

Bedstone College, founded in 1948, is a fully co-educational, independent, boarding and day school catering for children between the ages of 4 and 18 years. The school enjoys a beautiful 40-acre campus within an idyllic setting amongst the south Shropshire hills, close to the ancient and beautiful market town of Ludlow, and within 40 minutes' drive of both Shrewsbury and Hereford.

The school comprises the Junior School (for children aged 4 to 11 years) and the Senior College (for ages 11 to 18 years), all integrated within one campus. Students from age 9 are welcome to board.

Bedstone offers a broad and balanced curriculum with some 18 subjects available at GCSE, AS and A2 Levels. Despite being non-selective and catering to those of all ability levels, Bedstone is proud to boast that over 90% of its Upper Sixth leavers secure places at University with a large majority (80% in 2015) being at their first-choice institution. In the DfE performance tables of 2015, Bedstone was named as the top ranked school for GCSE Ebacc subjects in both Shropshire and Herefordshire.

The College aims to fulfil the potential of every child wherever that potential may lie and, with an average teacher to pupil ratio of 1:8, the smaller class sizes allow individual needs to be catered for. The well-qualified and highly-motivated staff believe that each child has a unique talent which it is their job to find and to nurture.

Bedstone is very aware of the problems that learning difficulties, such as dyslexia, can cause and a nationally recognised Learning Support Department, led by its full-time director with the aid of fully-qualified staff, is central to the help provided. Bedstone is one of just 37 schools (both state and independent) in the UK to be accredited by CReSTeD as a Specialist Dyslexia Unit.

Character of the College. Many children who join Bedstone have done so because their parents feel that the individual strengths of their child have become lost within their current school; that the challenges and opportunities for fulfilling their child's unique talents do not exist, or that they wish for greater pastoral support and guidance for their child. Every parent knows that what they want is the education of the whole child – mind, body and spirit – and Bedstone provides that with its academic and extracurricular programme coupled with its outstanding pastoral care and boarding ethos. Bedstone prides itself on its family atmosphere that students are proud to be a part of.

Accommodation. The main house, Bedstone Court, is a listed building of fine architectural merit and accommodates the Junior and Senior boys' houses. In addition, it houses the administration offices, library, dining hall and sixth form cellar club. The two girls' boarding houses are on the opposite side of the campus with the senior girls accommodated within a purpose-built boarding house and the junior girls within the homely surroundings of a 19th century manor house. All boarding houses have been completely refurbished. All boarding houses have resident staff and their families as houseparents. There is seating for 300 people in the Rees Hall Theatre with full AV facilities. There is a modern well-equipped Sports Hall, Design Technology and Art Centre, Music School, a Medical Centre staffed by RGNs, Fitness Suite, Performing Arts Studio, Learning Support and Counselling facility, a heated swimming pool and a wide range of additional facilities. There is also a social club for the Sixth Form with a weekend bar manned and carefully controlled by teaching staff. The College has a campus-wide wireless LAN.

Religious Education. The formal classroom teaching of Religious Studies follows the National Curriculum which covers all the major world religions. More broadly, the college follows the teachings of the Church of England though other denominations, and children without any religious affiliation, are most warmly welcomed. Children, whose parents wish it, are also prepared for Confirmation by the Chaplain. The College enjoys a strong choral tradition and the Choir enjoys an excellent reputation.

Senior College Curriculum. From the First Form (Y7) to the Third Form (Y9) (when a number join from other Preparatory and Primary Schools) the subjects taught are: Religious Education, English Language and Literature, History, Geography, French, Spanish, Mathematics, Biology, Physics, Chemistry, Design Technology, Art, Music, Physical Education and ICT.

In the Fourth and Fifth Forms, in addition to the Core Curriculum of English, English Literature, Mathematics, one modern foreign language (French or Spanish), the three Sciences, Religious Studies, (and non-examination Physical Education), options are: History, Geography, Art, Business Studies, Music, French, Spanish, Design Technology and Sports Studies. Latin and German tuition are also available off timetable.

Throughout the College, in all classes, we help students achieve the very best that they are capable of and surpass their own expectations. There is no "cramming" at Bedstone and we are not an academic hothouse. However, with the aid of close tutorial support, a well-qualified staff, an excellent staff/pupil ratio, plus, of course, determined effort on the part of the students, good progress and examination success are assured. AS/A2 courses are offered in English, History, Geography, French, Spanish, Business Studies, Art, Design Technology, Mathematics, Further Mathematics, Music, Physics, Chemistry, Biology, Psychology and Sports Studies. The Extended Project Qualification (EPQ) is on offer to all Sixth Form students and provision can be made for preparation in languages such as German, Polish, Chinese and Russian.

The College has its own Learning Support Department. Excellent EAL provision is available for those who require it in addition to pre-sessional intensive English courses, three-year A Level programme, IELTS, IGCSE and subject-specific language support.

Careers. There are specific careers staff and a well-resourced Careers Room. Bedstone makes full use of Inspiring Futures' careers services and all members of the Fifth Form take the Inspiring Futures Psychometric tests and have the opportunity to undertake work experience. Our individual guidance means that, typically, 90% or more of Sixth Former leavers gain entrance to their university of first choice.

Games and Physical Education. There are 15 acres of playing fields, with an excellent Sports Hall, fitness suite, performing arts studio and netball & tennis courts plus an astroturf. The success of the boys and girls in physical activity at school, county and district level has been nothing short of remarkable. The school holds several ISA National Championships in various disciplines including Rugby 7s, Cross Country, Tennis and Hockey.

Rugby, Football, Athletics, Cross-Country and Cricket are the main sports for the boys and Hockey, Netball, Rounders, Cross-Country and Athletics for the girls but they can join in many more. A rotation system ensures that all students, to a greater or lesser degree, have their share of such activities as Basketball, Swimming, Badminton and Tennis. Nor are the individualists forgotten. Horse riding is popular, teams in Biathlon and Triathlon have been successful both regionally and nationally, and there are facilities for Table Tennis and Mountain Biking, whilst the South Shropshire and Powys hills provide excellent opportunities for Duke of Edinburgh's Award activities.

Clubs and Activities. The Duke of Edinburgh's Award scheme flourishes and there is a wide range of out-of-class activity, including splendid dramatic and musical productions, debating, individual music tuition. There are twice weekly 'activities' sessions which offer some 40–50 different clubs over the course of any one year. Pupils are expected to know and observe all College rules and parents to cooperate in seeing that this is done. Prefects play an important part in the pastoral system of the College. There are also a number of trips and visits that take place throughout the year, including visits to some of the most beautiful cities in Europe. Every two years there are major international sports tours for both the boys and the girls.

Bedstone Junior School is for boys and girls aged 4 to 11 years. The school is housed in its own separate accommodation and yet shares all the facilities of the senior school. Science, Modern Foreign Languages, Sport, Art and Music are all taught by senior school subject specialists within specialist areas. There is a specialist gifted and talented mathematics programme for the most able junior school students and talented sports players are developed through specialist coaching from the teachers in the senior college and entry into regional and national competitions.

The Junior School is an integral part of the College and children find the transition to the Senior College seamless. Any child accepted within the Junior School is automatically accepted into the Senior College.

Scholarships. For entry to the Senior College, there is a scholarship examination, held at the College on a Saturday in the early Spring Term. Bedstone offers Academic, Sport, Music, Art, DT and All-Rounder scholarships at 11+, 13+, 14+ and 16+ with the maximum award being up to 25% remission of fees. For local children from maintained schools, who might not have realistically considered Bedstone as an option, there is also the 'Four Counties' Scholarship which is worth up to 50% remission of fees. The school is also able to provide separate means-tested bursaries.

Forces fees discounts available upon request. We also offer scholarships in the Junior School to mirror what is done in the Senior College.

Fees per term (2018–2019). Junior School: Day: Reception to Year 2 (age 4–7) £1,675, Years 3–6 (age 7–11) £3,535; Boarding (Years 5–6, age 9–11) £5,825. Senior School (Years 7–13, age 11–18): Day £4,885, Boarding £8,840.

Governors:
Chairman: Grp Capt [Retd] J P S Fynes
Vice Chairman: Mrs Y Thomas, BSc
Dr M Lawton   Mrs S Phillips
Mr S Stringer   Lt Col [Retd] T Lowry

Headmaster: Mr D Gajadharsingh, BSc, PGCE, CPhys, MInstP, NPQH

Deputy Headteacher Pastoral: Mr J Lynch, BA, PGCE, MA Ed
Deputy Headteacher Academic, Director of Studies: Mr A A Whittall, BA, PGCE
Head of Junior School: Mr J Forster, BSc, MSc
Bursar: Mr A R Gore, AFA

Houseparents:

Boys Boarding:
Pearson House: Mr and Mrs A Whittall
Rutter House: Mr and Mrs O Downing

Girls Boarding:
Bedstone House: Mr and Mrs P Singh
Wilson House: Mr and Mrs M Rozée

Members of Common Room:
Ms J Bartley, BA, PGCE (*Head of Modern Foreign Languages*)
Miss G Kindermann, BA, MA (*Head of EAL*)
Mr C Braden, BEd QTS, PG Dip Man (*Head of Design Technology, Head of UCAS & Careers*)
Mrs E Bryden, BA, PG Dip Perf RCM, MMus, PGCE (*Head of Music*)
Miss L Bullock, BA, PGCE (*Head of History & PHSE*)
Mr E Olive, BSc, PGCE (*Head of Physics*)
Mr D Foreman, BSc, PhD, PGCE (*Head of Biology*)
Mrs S Simmons, MA, PGCE (*Mathematics*)
Mrs C Hunter, CDMVA La Sorbonne (*Modern Foreign Languages*)
Mr O Downing, BA, PGCE (*Head of English*)
Mr J Lowe, MA, PGD Inclusion & SEN, PGCE (*Head of Learning Support*)
Mrs N Newman, BA, MA, PGCE (*English*)
Mrs S Morris, BA, PGCE, Cert TEFL (*Head of Religious Education*)
Mr D P Marsh, BSc, PGCE (*Head of Geography*)
Mr D M Rawlinson, BSc, PhD, PGCE (*Head of Mathematics*)
Mr D M Rozée, BSc, PGCE, MSRC (*Head of Science*)
Mr J P Smith, BA (*Head of Art*)
Mr J R Simpson, BA, QTS (*Sports Studies, Head of Boys' PE & Games*)
Mrs N Williams, BSc, PGCE (*Head of Business Studies*)
Mrs E Coyle, BSc, PGCE (*Science*)
Miss S Ross, BA QTS (*Sports Studies, Head of Girls' PE & Games*)
Mrs J Crouch, BA, PGCE (*Teacher of DT, Maths and Art*)

Junior Department:
Mrs J Richards, BA, PGCE, MA Ed
Mrs S Crabtree, BA, QTS
Mrs R Rawlinson, BSc, MSc, PGCE
Mrs J Williams, BEd

Mrs L Meredith, NNEB

Learning Support:
Mr J Lowe, PGD Inclusion & SEN, PGCE
Miss J Griffiths

EAL:
Ms G Kindermann
Mr C Morris, BA, CELTA

Lay Chaplain: Mr A C Dyball, MA Cantab, Dip Ed

School Medical Team: Mrs N Stead, RGN; Mrs R Revuelto-Barrett
School Counsellor: Mrs Prentice
School Doctors: Dr M L Kiff and Dr A Lempert

Visiting Music Staff:
Mr D Kirk (*Drums*)
Mr D Luke (*Guitar*)
Mrs S Freeman (*Brass*)
Mr J Hymas (*Violin*)
Mrs K Norton (*Piano*)
Mr J Nicholls (*Piano*)
Ms S Lee (*Singing*)
Mr C Lacey (*Woodwind*)

Competitive Houses:
Hopton: Ms J Bartley
Stokesay: Mrs Emma Bryden
Wigmore: Mr J Lowe

Headmaster's PA: Mrs Paula Davis
Accounts Administrator: Mr Paul Downes
Head of Admissions, Marketing & Enterprise: Mr Graeme Neill
Marketing Assistant: Mrs Roz Pacey
Assistant to Head of Admissions, Marketing & Enterprise: Mrs Anne Whittall
IT Manager: Mr S Davis, BSc
Drama: Mrs E Bryden
Receptionist: Mrs W McKee-Wills, Miss J Naprous
Accounts Clerk: Mrs S Gore, BSc
Librarian: Mrs Anne Whittall
Catering / Head Chef: Mr D Ostle
Domestic Supervisor: Mrs D Gough
Transport Manager: Mr P Singh
Maintenance Manager: Mr S Pullen

Beechwood Sacred Heart School

Pembury Road, Tunbridge Wells, Kent TN2 3QD

Tel: 01892 532747
Fax: 01892 536164
email: bsh@beechwood.org.uk
website: www.beechwood.org.uk

Beechwood is an independent co-educational day and boarding school for pupils aged 3–18. Founded in 1915 by the Society of the Sacred Heart. As a Sacred Heart School, it retains sound Catholic values, whilst welcoming pupils from all nations and beliefs.

The Nursery School (age 3–5), Preparatory School (age 5–11) and Senior School (age 11–18) are located in 23 acres of landscaped grounds overlooking open countryside, close to the centre of the historic town of Royal Tunbridge Wells. The Main School is based in a Victorian villa with all facilities located on a single campus. There are 350 pupils on roll.

Boarding is offered for seventy boys and girls in modern and comfortable accommodation on the school campus. Junior boarders share in two or three bedded rooms whilst all sixth-form boarders are allocated single study-bedrooms.

We receive a large number of applications for boarding places each year, so an early application is advised. The School does not operate 'Exeat' weekends.

Beechwood is noted for its genuine family atmosphere. Consideration for others underpins the code of behaviour for all pupils, making Beechwood a happy school with high academic standards being achieved through expectation and challenge, rather than prescription. We are an ambitious, caring school and that sense of confidence and generosity of spirit permeates throughout the school. At Beechwood we prepare our pupils for the future but encourage them to enjoy the present.

Curriculum. In our small classes, teachers stimulate pupils to excel in what they are good at and build confidence in areas they find difficult, from the youngest child in the Preparatory School through to our oldest Senior School pupils. Our Learning Development department supports the individual needs of those pupils who require extra support.

Beechwood provides a broad education. At Key Stage 3 all pupils study a range of subjects. Most subjects are taught in mixed-ability classes of boys and girls. Mathematics is setted from Year 7. French is studied in Year 7, with options to study Spanish and German from Year 8. Academic standards are important and we challenge our pupils to achieve their best. We also encourage our pupils to participate in a wide range of extracurricular activities, trips, and visits.

At GCSE pupils can study ten GCSEs from a wide range of subjects. Biology, Chemistry and Physics ('triple Science') are offered as single subjects and we offer French, German, and Spanish as Modern Foreign Language options. Mathematics, English Language, and English Literature are compulsory at GCSE as well as at least one science subject. This also enables pupils to select from a wider range of options when they construct their GCSE portfolio. Additional English language lessons are provided for international pupils. Pupils participate in a diverse PE curriculum and study PHSCE as part of their personal development.

At A Level, more than twenty subjects are offered including three Sciences, Theatre Studies, Further Mathematics, Business Studies, Photography, Product Design, Psychology, Law, Media Studies, History and Textiles. The Sixth Form curriculum is enhanced by an enrichment course that includes Life Skills and comprehensive Careers and University application advice.

Sixth Formers are encouraged to show initiative and take responsibility. They have opportunities for leadership as prefects and in organising activities for younger pupils. All leavers successfully gain places at university on a wide range of courses.

Examination Results. Beechwood's record in public examinations is particularly impressive for a non-selective school, with a pass rate (A*–C) of around 90% at GCSE and 100% at A Level, and is in the top 25% of schools for value-added performance at A Level.

Sports. Pupils are encouraged to experience a wide variety of sports, the emphasis being on fun and participation. Recent successes include being Kent County Basketball Champions. Sports facilities include hockey and football pitches, netball, basketball and tennis courts, cricket nets, gymnasium, badminton and volleyball courts. We also take advantage of local all-weather pitches.

Preparatory School and Nursery. Adjacent to the Senior School, the Preparatory School and Nursery provide an excellent beginning for every child in a supportive, family atmosphere. The curriculum stimulates enquiry, academic standards being maintained through regular monitoring and assessment. French is studied from Year 1 and all pupils also enjoy cookery lessons. In addition, by sharing the facilities of the Senior School, pupils participate in a wide variety of sports and can represent the school in matches. Extracurricular activities include chess, crafts, gardening and keyboard music making, and many pupils have instrumental music lessons.

Entry Requirements. The school is non-selective academically, selection being based on interview with the Headmaster, previous school report, performance in entrance assessments and confidential reference. All enquiries and applications should be addressed to the Registrar.

Fees per term (2018–2019). Full boarders £9,950; Weekly boarders £8,950; Day pupils £2,895–£5,795.

Scholarships. Academic, Music, Art, Sport and Drama scholarships are available at 11+, 13+ and 16+. Entrance and Scholarship Days take place in January for 13+ and in November for 11+ and 16+ prior to entry the following September.

Charitable status. The Sacred Heart School Beechwood Trust Ltd is a Registered Charity, number 325104.

Governors:
Mrs Constance Williams (*Chairman*)
Sister Moira O'Sullivan (*Vice-Chairman*)
Mrs Gillian Hill
Mr Robert Park
Mr Michael Southern
Mr Michael Stevens
Dr Amanda Turner
Mr Jon Emery

Company Secretary and Clerk to the Governors: Mr Andrew Harvey

Head: **Mrs Helen Rowe**, BA Hons, PGCE

Director of Studies: Mrs Kim Allen, BSc Hons, PGCE
Chaplain: Miss Victoria Gillespie

Staff:

Heads of Division:
Mrs Rebecca Smith, BA Hons, PGCE (*Junior Division*)
Mr Joshua Rowe, BSc, PGCE (*Middle Division*)
Mr Michael Awdry, BA Hons, PGCE (*Senior Division*)

Heads of Department:
Mrs Olga Clarke, PGCE, Maîtrise MA, Licence/Deug BA (*Modern Languages*)
Mr Gary Hatter, MEd, PGCE (*Art*)
Mrs Louise Neill, BSc Hons, PGCE (*Geography*)
Mrs Gwen Goodley, MBA, BA Hons, BSc Hons (*History*)
Mr Angel Sandoval, PGCE, Bs Management (*EAL*)
Mr Jonathan Millward, BSc Hons, PGCE (*Science*)
Mrs Sarah Kershaw, BA Hons, PGCE (*Music*)
Mrs Kim Cook, BEd Hons, Dip Ed, AMBDA (*Learning Development*)
Mr Joshua Rowe, BSc, PGCE (*Physical Education*)
Mrs Candy Prodrick, BD, PGCE (*Religious Education, PSHE*)
Mrs Diana Ringer, BSc Hons, PGCE, MSc (*Mathematics*)
Mr Mark Thomas, BSc Hons, PGCE (*ICT*)
Ms Nicola Phipps, BA Hons, PGCE (*English*)
Mr Sumair Hussain, BA Hons, PGCE (*Drama*)
Mr James Walters, BSc Hons, PGCE (*Design Technology*)

Preparatory School:
Head: Mr John Coakley
Director of Studies: Mrs Teresa Cutts, MA Cantab, PGCE

Head's Secretary: Miss Liz Milner
Head of Marketing and Admissions: Mr Daniel MacDonnell, BA Hons

Bethany School

**Curtisden Green, Goudhurst, Cranbrook, Kent
TN17 1LB**

Tel: 01580 211273
email: admissions@bethanyschool.org.uk
website: www.bethanyschool.org.uk
Twitter: @bethanyschkent
Facebook: @bethanyschkent
LinkedIn: /Bethany-School-Kent

The School was founded in 1866 by the Revd J J Kendon. It is a Charitable Trust administered by a Board of Governors, a member of the Association of Governing Bodies of Independent Schools.

Bethany has 320 pupils, aged 11 to 18. Approximately 30% board on either a weekly or termly basis, with a varied weekend programme of activities available for termly boarders. A generous staff to pupil ratio of 1:8 ensures small classes and high quality pastoral care. Individuals are encouraged to develop their potential to the full in academic and all other respects. Most teaching takes place in modern classroom blocks, the result of an ongoing building development programme. Development in ICT has been a priority at Bethany: a wireless network enables pupils from Year 7 upwards to use laptops across the curriculum. For new Year 7 and 8 pupils joining Bethany, a new Laptop Programme is in place whereby the School offers to pay half for the recommended device.

The Orchard, our dedicated Sixth Form Boarding House, offers single study-bedrooms with en-suite facilities, study rooms for day pupils and communal facilities. Recent additions to the School include a brand new six-lane, 25m indoor swimming pool, a state-of-the-art fitness suite and a new Sixth Form centre as an extension of The Orchard. Our next major project will be a Digital Performing Arts Centre.

Situation. The School occupies a scenic, 60-acre, rural campus in the heart of the Kent countryside, easily accessible from most parts of South East England: an hour from Charing Cross (Marden Station) and easy access to Gatwick and Heathrow Airports, the Channel ports and Ashford and Ebbsfleet International railway stations.

Admission. The normal age of entry is at 11 or 13 by the School's Entrance Assessment and at Sixth Form level based on predicted GCSE grades, but the School welcomes pupils to the Bethany community at other stages if places are available.

Fees per term (2018–2019). Full boarders £9,355–£10,500, weekly boarders £8,650–£9,555, day pupils £5,575–£6,155. Learning Support and English as an Additional Language, if required, incur an additional fee of up to £630 per term.

Scholarships and Bursaries. Academic Scholarships are awarded based on performance in the Entrance Examination. Scholarships are also available in Performing Arts, Creative Arts and Sport at the main points of entry, which are Years 7 and 9 and into the Sixth Form. The Christopher Jackson Scholarship is available for pupils who attend state primary schools local to Bethany, are particularly able and have a capacity for academic excellence. This award is for boys and girls entering Bethany at Year 9 who are aged 14 years or under at the start of the academic year of entry. Means-tested bursaries are also available. Children of members of HM Forces and the Clergy receive a 10% fee discount.

Curriculum. The broad curriculum is based on the National Curriculum. The full range of subjects is taught including Information Technology from 11+ and Spanish from 13+. We have also introduced Mandarin at Year 7, and GCSE Dance. There are 26 GCE A Level subjects, including Economics, Business Studies, Spanish, Government and Politics, Music, Photography, Politics, Textiles, Theatre Studies and Media Studies. Almost all Sixth Form leavers proceed to degree courses at University.

Dyslexia. The Dyslexia and Learning Support department, which enjoys an international reputation, has been supporting pupils at Bethany for over 30 years.

Games and Activities. The School offers a wide range of sporting opportunities and enjoys an extensive fixture list, having established a long tradition of inter-school Sport. Facilities include a Sports Centre, climbing wall, fitness room, three squash courts, tennis courts, an indoor swimming pool and a floodlit AstroTurf. There is also a wide range of clubs and activities. The Duke of Edinburgh's Award scheme is well established at Gold, Silver and Bronze levels.

Music. There are wide-ranging opportunities for instrumental tuition. There are sectional instrumental groups including: a Symphony Orchestra, Rock School, Jazz Band, Concert Band, Brass Consort and a Choir, all making use of the fine Music School with its recording studio and music technology area.

Careers. The School is a member of Inspiring Futures and careers education is an important part of the Curriculum. Sixth Form pupils take part in the Coursefinder Analysis Scheme and receive detailed advice regarding Higher Education and Gap Year opportunities.

Chapel. The Chapel, built in 1878, is the focal point of School life. Bethany welcomes children of all faiths or none, and together they attend Chapel twice weekly.

Charitable status. Bethany School Limited is a Registered Charity, number 307937.

Governors:
Mr Roger Stubbs, BSocSc, CMRS (*Chairman*)
Mrs Wendy Kent (*Vice Chair*)
Mr Peter Askew
Mr David Boniface, MA, MSc
Mr Keith Buckland
Mr Mike Clark, BSc, CEng, MICE, MIStructE
Mr Roger Clark
Mr Andrew Cunningham
Mr Jonathan Fenn, LLB
Dr Robert Hangartner, BSc, MB BS, MBA, FRCPath
Mr Nigel Kimber, BSc, FCA
Mr Robert Pilbeam
Ms Lindsay Roberts, BEd Hons
Mr Kevin Sunnucks

Bursar and Clerk to the Governors: Mr Stuart Harris

Staff:

Headmaster: Mr Francie Healy, BSc, HDipEd, NPQH

Deputy Headmaster: Mr Steven Winter, BA Hons

HR Manager: Miss Toni Carter, Chartered MCIPD

Assistant Head Academic: Mrs Emily Hill, BA Hons, PGCE

Assistant Head Pastoral: Mr Alan Sturrock, BA Ed Hons

Lay Chaplain: Mrs Serena Willoughby

Staff:
Mr Russell Bailey
Mr Alex Bolton
Ms April Bridge
Mr Jonny Brinson, BMus, PGCE (*Head of Music*)
Miss Nicola Brown, BDes, PGDE

Mr Richard Clough (*History, Assistant Housemaster Pengelly*)
Ms Dilys Coley MA (*English*)
Mr Cliff Cooper, MSc
Mr Simon Cuthbert, BA Hons, PGCE
Mr Simon Davies, BA Hons
Mr Simon Duff, BEd, TEFL, NPQML
Mr Alejandro Garcia (*Spanish*)
Mr Sherrick Hamilton, BA Hons
Mrs Kate Harper, BSc Hons QTS, PG Cert SpLD
Mr Tim Hart Dyke, BA Hons, PGCE, DipEd
Mrs Frances Healy, BA, SpLD
Mr Tom Henson, FdA (*TA, Trainee Teacher*)
Mr Phil Hughes, BA Hons, PGCE
Mr Anthony Khan, BA Hons, PGCE
Miss Sam King, BA
Ms Dorothy Li, PGCE (*Mandarin*)
Ms Liz MacRae, BA Hons, QTS
Mr Adam Manktelow, BSc Hons, PGCE
Miss Claire Mills, BEd Hons, PG Cert SpLD
Mr Marcus Norman, BEd Hons
Mrs Claire Pack, BA Hons
Mr Matt Payne, BSc Hons, PGCE
Mrs Rachael Payne, BA Hons, PGCE
Mr Rob Philbin, BSc Hons, PGCE (*Head of Biology*)
Mr Devin Reilly, BSc Hons
Ms Nicola Rendall-Jones (*Head of EAL*)
Mrs Carly Shapland, BA Hons
Miss Fleur-Estelle Shaw, MA, PGCE
Mr Adrian Staiano (*Geography, Assistant Housemaster Kendon*)
Mrs Anne-Marie Sturrock, BEd Hons
Mr Chris Thomas, BSc Hons (*Music, Assistant Housemaster The Mount*)
Mr Mike Thomas, MSc, PhD
Mr James Vickerman, BSc Hons, PGCE
Mrs Jules Wareham, BEd Hons (*Maths & Games, Housemistress Old Poplars, Director of Enrichment*)
Mrs Katy Williams, BSc

Medical Officer: Dr J N Watson, MBBS, MRCGP

Marketing & Admissions Manager: Mrs Ginnie Corbett

Registrar: Mrs Sally Martorell

Headmaster's Secretary: Mrs Andrea Discombe

Bournemouth Collegiate School
United Learning

Senior School:
College Road, Southbourne, Bournemouth, Dorset BH5 2DY

Tel: 01202 436550
email: registrar@bcschool.co.uk

Prep School:
40 St Osmund's Road, Poole, Dorset BH14 9JY

Tel: 01202 714110
email: prep-admin@bcschool.co.uk

website: www.bournemouthcollegiateschool.co.uk
Twitter: @BCSPrep; @BCS_Senior

Bringing Out the Best in Everyone

Bournemouth Collegiate School is a popular and successful independent, non-selective, co-ed Senior School (day and boarding, 11–18), situated in an inspiring location next to Bournemouth's golden beaches, and Preparatory School (day, 2–11) in a spacious woodland setting in Lower Parkstone, Poole.

Parents and pupils are attracted by the small classes, excellent results and outstanding facilities across both sites including indoor swimming pools at both schools.

BCS is an extraordinary place to learn. We are part of a country-wide educational group, United Learning, that seeks 'the best in everyone', and we take that mission very seriously.

We offer an exhaustive extracurricular, sporting and music programme and run a successful Sports Academy for talented athletes. BCS really believes in developing the potential of every pupil and is determined to get the best out of everyone.

The caring, supportive ethos of the school is based on a policy of mutual respect. We encourage independent learning and intellectual curiosity and enable pupils to experience a broad range of experiences which includes numerous trips, seminars, talks by guest speakers and the opportunity for fun, expression and friendship in the many school events on offer.

Fees per term (2018–2019). Prep School: £3,055–£3,775. Senior School: Day Students £4,810; Weekly Boarders £9,060; Full Boarders £9,890.

Scholarships and Bursaries. Scholarships may be offered to pupils who join the school into Year 7 to Year 12. They are awarded to students with all-round excellence or special ability in academia, music, performing arts, art or sport.

Assisted Place Bursaries are available for those entering Year 7, Year 9 and Year 12.

The 'BCS Award' combines academic excellence and the Assisted Place, effectively offering a means-tested academic scholarship, awarding up to a 100% discount on the School fees.

Charitable status. Bournemouth Collegiate School is part of United Learning which comprises: UCST (a Company Limited by Guarantee, Registered in England, number 2780748, and a Registered Charity, number 1016538) and ULT (a Company Limited by Guarantee, Registered in England, number 4439859, and an Exempt Charity).

Headmaster: **Mr Russell Slatford**, BSc, MA Cantab

Senior Deputy Head: Mrs Maria Coulter, BSc Hons, PGCE, NPQH, Dip Ed

Head of Prep School: Miss Kay Smith, BEd, NPQH

Admissions Registrar: Miss Rhiann Bowden

Box Hill School

Mickleham, Dorking, Surrey RH5 6EA

Tel: 01372 373382
          01372 385002 (Registrar for Overseas Admissions)
          01372 384240 (Registrar for UK Admissions)
Fax: 01372 363942
email: registrar@boxhillschool.com
website: www.boxhillschool.com

Affiliations: The Society of Heads, Round Square, BSA, AGBIS, ISBA, BAISC, IBO, DofE, NAGC.

Box Hill School is a co-educational school set in forty acres of grounds in the heart of the Surrey countryside, offering day, weekly and full boarding places for 11–18 year olds. We have a strong educational, artistic and sporting tradition; however, what makes us stand out is that we discover and nurture the talents and abilities of every individual student, so that they can unlock their potential and in doing so, develop confidence and resilience. Box Hill School is proud of its academic attainment and broad curriculum. Academic standards are high given the non-selective approach to education and students achieve above national averages in public exams.

In the Sixth Form, students can choose to study either the IB Diploma Programme or A Levels. Subject combinations are flexible within the constraints of our options timetable system, and we aim to cater for as wide a range of choices as possible.

Box Hill School is a proud founder member of Round Square, an international organisation of over 150 schools worldwide united by a set of 'IDEALS': Internationalism, Democracy, Environmental concern, Adventure, Leadership and Service which are at the core of the school's ethos.

All the Houses at Box Hill School are small and friendly, and students never feel lost or overlooked. The Boarding Houses each board around 20–35 pupils with the majority of boarders' rooms being doubles, particularly at Key Stage 4 and above. First-time Boarders are reassured by the family structure of our Houses and find them easy to settle into. To strengthen the bond between students even further, a central school dining room is provided and students are allocated to competitive group teams for school-wide competitions. Full-time Boarders also enjoy a variety of outings at the weekend. An on-site medical centre is provided, staffed by qualified nurses with two non-resident school doctors on call. Boarders may stay in school during term time, except at half terms. There are no 'exeat' weekends.

We provide strong pastoral support for each student, each one being assigned to a House, complete with common room and kitchen. The Houses are run by teaching House staff and each student is assigned to a personal tutor within their house – a member of teaching staff who supports their academic and pastoral development.

We believe that activities outside the classroom form an important part of education, and all students take part in the extensive timetabled activities programme. As well as this regular programme, younger students take part in expeditions around the UK twice a year. The Duke of Edinburgh's Award is particularly strong in the school. Students have the opportunity to participate in Round Square expeditions, carrying out community based projects in locations including Peru and South Africa. They also have the opportunity to go on an exchange to another Round Square school overseas.

The school has an active Parents Association, comprised of supportive parents and friends of the school who maintain links with the local community as well as running social functions and fundraising events. Parents are strongly encouraged to join.

Special features of the School.
- International opportunities through Round Square membership
- IB World School
- Small classes and a high level of academic support
- Outstanding pastoral care
- Weekly and termly activities for all students from an exciting and wide range of options
- International Study Centre

Courses offered. GCSE: Mathematics, English Language, English Literature, Biology, Chemistry, Physics, Geography, History, Business Studies, Computer Science, French, Spanish, Music, Music Technology, Art, Fashion and Textiles, Drama, Physical Education, Design Technology.

IB: Biology, Environmental Systems, Business and Management, Maths Studies, Chemistry, Psychology, Economics, English Literature, Visual Arts, Geography, History, Mathematics, German, Russian, Italian, French, Spanish, Physics. We aim to offer all other IB approved languages in any year, subject to demand.

A Level: Art, Biology, Business Studies, Chemistry, Economics, English, Further Mathematics, Geography, History, Mathematics, Physics, Psychology.

Sports. Athletics, basketball, cricket, football, hockey, netball, rounders, rugby and tennis as competitive sports but many others as part of the activities programme such as dance fitness, kickboxing, pilates, golf, swimming, volleyball, mountain biking and multi-gym.

Drama, Music and Art. Art students gain excellent examination grades each year, with many going on to be accepted at major art schools. Our purpose-built Music School enables a wide range of musical opportunities within school, including a choir, Year 7 choir, rock band and performance opportunities for individual vocalists and instrumentalists. The school stages senior and junior productions each year and has performed *The Great Gatsby* and an innovative and original festival, *A festival of Music and Mayhem*, in the last academic year. LAMDA coaching is available and the school has an excellent record in these examinations.

Fees per term (2018–2019). Day: £5,950–£6,570; Weekly Boarding: £9,170–£9,600; Full Boarding: £11,230–£13,310.

A fee discount is offered to students who have a parent who is a serving member of HM Armed Forces and to siblings of students currently in the school.

Scholarships. A variety of awards are offered for entry to Box Hill School; the latest information can be found on the school's website. Scholarships are available for those entering Years 7, 9 and the Sixth Form, under the following categories: Academic, Art, Drama, Music and Sport.

Bursaries are available on application following registration and are subject to means-testing and are offered on the basis of a formula laid out in the school's Scholarships and Bursaries Policy which is available on request from the Bursar. All bursaries are reviewed annually.

Method of Entry. Entry is based on an interview, the two most recent reports from the pupil's present school, and written tests in Maths and English. Sixth Form entry is based on report, interview and GCSE predictions. For overseas pupils a personal interview on site is desirable but we are happy to conduct a Skype interview if necessary. Main school entrance ages are 11, 13 and 16 years. Under normal circumstances, we like to meet prospective pupils and their parents or guardians – this also gives you an opportunity to have a look around our campus facilities and meet key staff and students.

Charitable status. Box Hill School Trust Limited is a Registered Charity, number 312082. It exists to promote the advancement of education.

Chairman of Governors: Mr John Banfield

Headmaster: Mr Cory Lowde

Chief Operating Officer: Mr Stuart Ansell

Registrar for Overseas Students: Mrs Kirstie Hammond

Registrar for UK Students: Mrs Claire Jordan

Headmaster's PA: Ms Samantha Jepp-Panteli

Bredon School

**Pull Court, Bushley, Tewkesbury, Gloucestershire
GL20 6AH**

Tel:	01684 293156
Fax:	01684 298008
email:	enquiries@bredonschool.co.uk
website:	www.bredonschool.org
Twitter:	@BredonSchool
Facebook:	@Bredon-School

Age Range. 7–18.

Number of Pupils. 215: Boarders 90, Day 125.

Bredon School is situated in a magnificent 84-acre rural estate and delivers a broad-based education centring upon individual attention and personal recognition. Since the school was founded 56 years ago, it has set out to discover and nurture children's strengths and talents and to support them in overcoming any weaknesses.

Ethos. Bredon educates the whole child through sound, realistic, academic provision, sympathetic pastoral care, regular leadership challenges and a varied sports programme. The small and friendly environment allows children of all ages to thrive and achieve more than they thought possible.

Learning Support. The school is internationally-renowned for its expertise in supporting children with specific learning difficulties, such as dyslexia, dyspraxia and dyscalculia. It is also CReSTeD-accredited, holding Dyslexia Specialist Provision (DSP) status. Within the dedicated Access Centre, an extensive range of specialist software and specialist tuition allows pupils to organise their thoughts, practice their skills and use voice-activation to enhance their individual progress.

Curriculum. Bredon provides a broad academic curriculum at all Key Stages through to GCSE and A Level. In addition Bredon offers extensive vocational programmes at Foundation, Intermediate and Advanced levels. The School Farm offers a vocational route for those interested in pursuing a career in agriculture or land-based studies. Class sizes across the school average 10 in number and the teacher to pupil ratio is 1:5.

Physical & Outdoor Education. In addition to the many sporting opportunities on offer; including frequent competitive fixtures with local schools, there is a fully-equipped gymnasium, a 30-metre sports hall, a climbing wall and bouldering course, a clay shooting ground, plus numerous outdoor sports pitches and cross country running trails. Bredon also has a swimming pool, a canoe launch onto the River Severn, a forest school and thriving School Farm with ponies, rare breed pigs, cattle, sheep, fowl as well as small animals, which add to the amount of time children spend learning outdoors and engaged in practical activity. The school also organises an extensive range of trips and expeditions through the Duke of Edinburgh's Award scheme, and dedicated overnight outdoor education activities.

Clubs and Activities. There are many thriving lunchtime clubs including model making and music activities. In addition, once a week, the afternoon lessons are given over to activities and the children can choose from activities as varied as sailing, cycling, dancing, music, art, cookery, magic club, fencing, engineering, farming and clay pigeon/air rifle shooting.

Boarders. There is provision for boarders from age nine and they are cared for by house parents, creating a real home from home environment. Accommodation is in dormitory-style rooms until Year 11 when boys move into individual study-bedrooms. Girls from Year 11 can choose to have a small individual room or share with a friend. Boarders have an extensive range of after school activities to participate in and there is a lively schedule of weekend events too.

Admissions. Admission is by potential not just attainment, and specialist support is available to pupils with learning difficulties. There is no entrance examination, instead school reports and any specialist reports will be requested and assessed, followed by a 3-day guest visit to the school to assess suitability. A place is usually offered upon completion of a satisfactory guest stay.

Fees per term (2018–2019). Day £3,680–£7,315; Weekly Boarding £8,080–£11,715.

Chairman of Local Governing Body: Mr Aatif Hassan

Headteacher: **Mr Koen Claeys**, BA, GLSE Belgium

Deputy Head Pastoral: Mr N S Allison, BSc, Dip SW, PGCE

Deputy Head Curriculum: Mrs G Hamilton, PGCE

Bursar: Mrs H Archer-Smith, FCA, DChA

Head of Admissions and Marketing: Mrs L Ciaravella, BA Hons

SENCO and Inclusion Coordinator: Mrs K Weston, BSc Hons, PGCE, NASENCO, CPT3A

Admissions Officer: Miss R Jones

Marketing Officer: Mrs E Cutler, BA Hons

The Cathedral School Llandaff
A Woodard School

Llandaff, Cardiff CF5 2YH

Tel:	029 2056 3179
Fax:	029 2056 7752
email:	registrar@cathedral-school.co.uk
website:	www.cathedral-school.co.uk
Twitter:	@cslcardiff

Set in 15 acres of parkland and playing fields within minutes of Cardiff city centre, the Cathedral School was founded in 1880. Acknowledged by Estyn as an "excellent" school (2012), there are currently 800 pupils at the co-educational school between the ages of 3 and 18 years. The Cathedral School is a member of the Woodard Corporation and adheres to a firmly Christian ethos. Pupils of all denominations and faiths are welcomed.

Track record for excellence. At the Cathedral School, our excellent academic results and exceptional co-curricular programme foster the growth of intellectual curiosity, offering enormous breadth of opportunity. High-quality pastoral care and the School's Christian ethos give our students the opportunity to reach their full potential in a vibrant, fun and supportive environment.

Our beautiful campus and our links with Llandaff Cathedral inspire a sense of heritage, whilst our first-class curriculum enables our young people to look confidently to the future.

Nursery, Infants & Juniors. A positive experience of learning in our earliest years at school sets the foundations for being an engaged and successful learner later in life. The classroom is a place of energy and creativity, a place of high expectations within an atmosphere of nurture and encouragement.

Beyond the classroom walls there are extensive opportunities to enjoy competitive sport, especially team games which have busy and challenging fixture lists; opportunities to perform music at an excellent standard including opportunities for boys and girls to join choirs and to sing in Llandaff Cathedral, along with drama, dance and elocution; opportunities to enjoy the outdoors, wildlife, outward bound activities; opportunities to get involved in action for good causes, including environmental awareness and charity work. There are also plenty of inter-house activities to get involved with which create a vibrant atmosphere.

Nearly all pupils transfer into the Senior Section to continue their educational journey through to 18.

The Seniors. At this school we pride ourselves upon being a strong learning community. It is important that everyone feels valued and that they have a meaningful part to play. From the initial Year 7 bonding weekend creating new friendships, to the competitive house system, a mutually supportive environment means that every pupil's skill, interest, talent and potential are nurtured.

Regularly recognised, whether by the schools inspectorate Estyn, or in newspaper league tables, as one of the highest achieving schools in Wales academically, a great emphasis is also placed upon the "co-curricular". For Years 10–13 the Duke of Edinburgh's Award (D of E) is hugely popular and delivered by our own dedicated staff. For Years 7–9, the Head's Award, underpins what we do, recognising character and breadth of achievement and celebrating our pupils' sense of motivation, organisation and willingness to be involved.

The quality of music at the Cathedral School is outstanding. It is our boys and girls who sing Llandaff Cathedral's choral services day by day, and the same excellence of musicianship rubs off in school within a wide range of genres, from the classical to rock and pop, chamber music to jazz. On the sports field a similar appetite for excellence pervades all we do. With a very high coach to player ratio and a busy, competitive fixture list, rugby, football, sevens, cricket, hockey, netball, rounders, cross-country and tennis all thrive here. Equally, participation in public speaking and debating competitions, challenging drama productions and various genres of fine art all add to the opportunities for all pupils to achieve standards which help them grow in confidence.

Sixth Form. We were delighted that our A Level students once again achieved such outstanding results this year, following the introduction of sixth form teaching in 2013. With a 100% overall pass rate, in 2018 our Year 13 students achieved 53% of all grades at A*–A and 75% at A*–B, securing places at the most competitive universities, including Bristol, Cambridge, Durham, Exeter, Imperial, London School of Economics, Oxford, UCL, and Warwick. With a full range of academic subjects available (England Pathway Qualifications), very small classes, highly-experienced staff with close university links, our sixth form culture is ambitious and supportive in equal measure.

Sixth formers are encouraged to engage in the professional mentoring programme, which pairs them with leading professional figures for advice and guidance. Practitioners from a range of professions are regularly invited to address the students and they have the opportunity to network at Cardiff Business Club.

A Level Subjects: Art, Biology, Chemistry, Computer Science, Design & Technology, Drama & Theatre, Economics, English Literature, French, Geography, German, Government & Politics, History, Latin, Mathematics, Further Mathematics, Music, Physical Education, Physics, Psychology, Religious Studies, Spanish, and the Extended Project Qualification (EPQ).

Scholarships & Bursaries. Financial support via means-tested bursaries is available at Year 7 and 12 entry, with scholarships in a range of disciplines from academic to sport and music.

School Transport. School transport is available with bus routes from Castleton, Cowbridge, Caerphilly, Colwinston, Llantrisant and Lisvane. Working parents are helped by

wrap-around care from 8.00 am to 6.00 pm and a holiday club for our pupils and their siblings.

Fees per term (2018–2019). Year 7 & above £4,238, Years 5 & 6 £3,883, Years 3 & 4 £3,447, Reception, Years 1 & 2 £3,022, Nursery £2,595.

Charitable status. The Cathedral School Llandaff Limited is a Registered Charity, number 1103522. It exists to provide a high standard of education for girls and boys underpinned by a caring Christian ethos.

Chairman of the Council: G C Lloyd

Senior Management Team:

Head: **Mrs Clare Sherwood**, MA

Deputy Head Pastoral: Mr Lawrence Moon, BA, MA

Deputy Head Academic: Dr Nathan Horleston, PhD, MSci

Head of Sixth Form: Mrs Catrin Ellis-Owen, BA

Head of Primary: Mrs Sally Walsh, BEd, NPQH

Assistant Head (*KS2*): Mr Chris Morgan, BA

Assistant Head (*EYFS & KS1*): Mrs Karen Price, BA, MA

Assistant Head (*Safeguarding*): Dr Stuart Bailey, PhD, MEng

Bursar: Mr Robert Leek

Claremont Fan Court School

Claremont Drive, Esher, Surrey KT10 9LY

Tel:	01372 467841
email:	info@claremont.surrey.sch.uk
website:	www.claremontfancourt.co.uk
Twitter:	@CFCSchool

Situation. Claremont Estate is one of the premier historic sites in the country. The original house and the famous Landscape Garden were first laid out by Sir John Vanbrugh for the Duke of Newcastle early in the eighteenth century. Later Capability Brown built the present Palladian Mansion for Clive of India. For over a century Claremont was a royal residence and played an important part in Queen Victoria's early years. In 1930 the School acquired the Mansion and now owns 100 acres of peaceful parkland. Esher is only 16 miles from London and almost equidistant from Heathrow and Gatwick airports with access points onto the M25 within 3 miles.

General Information. Claremont Fan Court School is a co-educational day school for pupils from 2½–18 years. The School consists of the Pre-Preparatory and Nursery School for pupils aged 2½–7 years, the Preparatory School for pupils aged 7–11 years and the Senior School for pupils from 11–18 years. Claremont Fan Court is a school with strong Christian values and welcomes pupils from all faiths and none

Aims. To care for and value the potential of every child. With this recognition comes the expectation of high academic achievement and participation in sporting and cultural activities.

Curriculum. The core curriculum provides all pupils with the opportunity to learn the skills and understandings required to continue learning throughout their lives. Emphasis is placed on the acquisition and development of skills in numeracy and literacy while providing a wide and varied range of subjects to stimulate the joy and wonder of learning. These curriculum ideals are delivered in a manner appropriate to the ages of the pupils throughout the Pre-Preparatory, Preparatory and Senior School.

An important element in our teaching philosophy is to understand the link between academic rigour and the value of good character. The academic curriculum ensures that all pupils attain the highest qualifications of which they are capable for entry into university or college.

Many pupils excel in the sporting arena where they develop talents through fixtures against other schools as well as in county or national school championships. Annual tours, both nationally and overseas, give an added dimension to pupils' sporting education.

Music, art and drama are also important aspects of the daily curriculum. All contributions are valued, whether they be leading, supporting or backstage roles, in order for the participants to be given every opportunity for creative thought and individual expression and to develop an awareness of self-worth.

Sixth Form. The Sixth Form is a vibrant and vital part of the School, focusing on 26 A Level courses. It forms a bridge between the years of compulsory schooling and the more independent years of Higher Education. Students take on many responsibilities including leadership and organisational roles which provide an all-round experience of special value to universities, colleges and employers.

At Sixth Form, Claremont Fan Court also welcomes external students, who meet our entry requirements. The sensational new sixth form centre at the heart of the campus opened during the summer of 2018.

Careers. Pupils receive careers advice from Year 8 onwards. All sixth form students have a weekly dedicated Careers lesson, delivered by a specialist Careers teacher. This ensures that all students receive detailed personalised guidance, leading them to courses and career choices that are appropriate for their individual preferences. Interviews are organised for students and conducted by external advisors.

Co-Curricular Activities. Making individual choices in the learning programme and developing a wide range of interests are both necessary preparations for lifelong learning. All pupils are actively encouraged to participate in a wide variety of clubs and enrichment activities, including The Duke of Edinburgh's Award scheme and overseas trips.

Admissions. The main intake of pupils occurs at 2½, 3, 7+, 11+, 13+ and Sixth Form. Places are offered subject to a pupil reaching the School's entry requirements. Applications for entry at other levels are welcome subject to a place becoming available.

Fees per term (2018–2019). Pre-Preparatory and Nursery: Nursery £1,780; Reception–Year 2 £3,560. Preparatory School: Years 3–6 £4,480. Senior School: Years 7–8 £5,510; Years 9–11 & Sixth Form £5,890.

Scholarships. Academic Scholarships are offered at Year 3 and Year 5, to continue through to the end of Year 6, and at Year 7 and Year 9 to continue through to the end of Year 11. Offers are based on a written examination and interview. Sixth Form Academic Scholarships are also available.

All-Round Scholarships are offered at Year 7.

Music Scholarships are available for Senior School applicants. As a guide, scholarship candidates should be working at the following levels before applying: Year 7 – Grade 4, Year 9 – Grade 5, Sixth Form – Grade 6. Sixth Form Scholarships will be awarded for the two-year course. Year 7 and Year 9 Scholarships will be awarded through to the end of Year 11.

Sports Scholarships are awarded for pupils of exceptional sporting ability. Sixth Form Scholarships are awarded for the two years of the course. Year 9 Scholarships are awarded through to the end of Year 11. Tennis Scholarships are also available.

Textiles, Art and Drama Scholarships are available to candidates applying for a Sixth Form place and are awarded for the duration of their two-year course.

Full details about scholarships are available on the school website.

Charitable status. The School is owned and run by an educational foundation with charitable status, Registered Charity number 274664.

Headmaster: **Mr William Brierly**, BSc Hons Southampton, PGCE

Head of Preparatory School: Mrs Helen Hutton-Attenborough, BSc Bristol, PGCE

Head of Pre-Preparatory and Nursery School: Mr Michael Williams, BA Hons Sussex, PGCE, NPQH

Clifton High School

College Road, Clifton, Bristol BS8 3JD

Tel:	0117 973 0201 (School Office)
	0117 933 9087 (Admissions)
	0117 973 3853 (Finance)
Fax:	0117 923 8962
email:	admissions@cliftonhigh.co.uk
website:	www.cliftonhigh.co.uk
Facebook:	@CliftonHighSchoolBristol

Clifton High School, founded in 1877, is a co-educational independent school offering a first-class education to nearly 600 pupils from nursery pre-school (rising 3s) to Sixth Form. Host family boarders are accepted from the age of 16 years. Unique in Bristol, the school has adopted the Diamond Edge Model of education where boys and girls are taught separately in core subjects in Years 7–9 before becoming fully re-integrated in Years 10 and above.

Aims. The school is a community that places importance on knowing each and every member – pupils, parents, staff and old friends. High value is placed on the importance of the individual. The school aims to inspire, support and challenge the individual, enabling pupils to achieve their full potential and excel at their particular talents. The school believes that each and every pupil has a brilliance; within an environment of high expectations, excellent teaching, supportive staff and outstanding pastoral care the school aims to give pupils a rich and varied educational experience where they can realise that brilliance. The school believes that with the privilege of an excellent education comes responsibility, and they aim to send students out into the world who not only have a lifelong passion for learning but who are ready to make a real and positive contribution to society.

Facilities. The school occupies a splendid site in Clifton, near the Downs and Suspension Bridge. The facilities and accommodation are excellent and include a science department with seven laboratories, a STEM room, well stocked libraries and over 250 networked workstations, a multimedia language laboratory, Sixth Form centre and a performing arts theatre and cinema. Sports facilities include a heated 25m indoor swimming pool with spectators gallery, gymnasium featuring a climbing wall and floodlit multi-games courts on site. Professional grade off-site sports facilities, in partnership with the University of Bristol, include an indoor tennis centre (with four courts), ten outdoor courts, newly refurbished 3G pitches and grass pitches for football, rugby and cricket.

Curriculum. Class sizes average 15 in the Early Years and Junior School and 17 in the Senior School.

The *Nursery to Junior Schools* offer an excellent academic, social and moral foundation:

The *Early Years* follow the Foundation Stage curriculum, focusing upon: personal, social and emotional development; communication; language and literacy; problem solving, reasoning and numeracy; knowledge and understanding of the world; physical development and creative development. The children enjoy a myriad of experiences in a safe and stimulating environment. 'By the end of their time in Reception, children's high levels of personal development show that they are extremely well prepared for the next stage of their education.' (ISI Inspection report 2016)

Years 1 and 2, working in an informal atmosphere within a structured framework, focus on high standards of literacy and numeracy, stimulating the children's minds through creative work and challenging projects. The curriculum also includes English, Mathematics, French, IT, Science, History, Geography, Art, Music, Swimming and Games. Pupils in Years 1 and 2 enjoy regular visits to a nearby Forest School throughout the year.

The *Junior Department* gives children a strong grounding in English, Mathematics, Science, ICT, History, Geography, Modern Languages, Music, Art, Drama, Religious Studies, PE, Swimming and Games (Netball, Hockey, Rugby, Football, Tennis, Rounders and Cricket). As children progress through the junior school, a greater number of subjects are taught by specialist teachers, for example Modern Languages, Art, Mathematics, Science, Music, Swimming and PE. Over 40 extra-curricular activities are on offer including Choirs, Orchestra, ICT, Speech and Drama, Dance and Art and Craft, together with a wide range of sports clubs providing opportunities for individual and team sports. Visiting speakers and regular trips to the local area and further afield enhance the curriculum in all departments. Children in the Junior Department also have the opportunity to enjoy a residential trip each year.

The *Senior School* is fully co-educational throughout. Boys and girls are taught separately for English, Mathematics, Physics, Chemistry and Biology in Years 7–9 and together in all other subjects before moving back into fully mixed classes for their chosen examination subjects when they reach Year 10. This is the pioneering Diamond Edge Model of education and Clifton High School is the only school in the Bristol area to adopt this approach. 'Pupils benefit greatly from the small class sizes enabled by the Diamond Edge model in Years 7 to 9 and from the way that teaching is adapted to meet the differing needs of boys and girls.' (ISI Inspection 2016). Year 7–9 pupils study a broad and balanced curriculum including English, Mathematics, Physics, Chemistry, Biology, Computing, History, Geography, modern languages (French, German, Spanish), Latin, Drama, Music, Art & Design, Food & Nutrition, Product Design, Textiles, PE and Personal, Social, and Health Education (PSHE). For study at GCSE there is a common and balanced core of English, Mathematics, separate sciences, humanities and a modern foreign language, in addition to which pupils may select subjects based on their interests and career plans. There is also a newly introduced programme of Life Skills and Competencies which runs alongside the GCSE courses and provides further opportunities for pupils to develop and identify extra skills, qualifications and interests. The school has an excellent academic record at GCSE, AS and A Level. In 2017, 100% of GCSE pupils achieved at least 6 A*–C Grades. 68% of A Level results were at A*–B, 31% above the national average. Throughout the Senior School and Sixth Form pupils have a personal tutor who monitors their academic and social welfare. 'Throughout the school, pupils' personal development is excellent, in line with the school's conviction that promoting their individuality, as well as their achievement is fundamental.' (ISI Inspection 2016)

The co-educational *Sixth Form* is a thriving centre of excellence within the school. The students play an important part in the whole school community, developing their leadership skills through a peer support scheme with younger pupils, the House system, the Pupil Council, the Head's Team, the Eco Club Committee and many other opportunities. Students have a wide choice of A Level subjects. The most able are encouraged to apply for Oxbridge entrance and the vast majority of those who apply gain the offer of a place. All Sixth Form students take part in Futures and Skills which is an enrichment programme designed to offer a range of experiences and also have individual careers guidance sessions. All students have regular one-to-one tutorials. Sixth Form students holding scholarships are encouraged to manage the Scholars' Forum by producing an annual programme of debates and current affairs discussions with other pupils in the Senior School and for inviting speakers in to the school to talk on specific topics of interest.

Host Family Boarding. Clifton High School welcomes international students over the age of 16 to join its Sixth Form and study for their A Levels in the United Kingdom. Whilst studying at Clifton High students live with Host Families who have a very close link to the school. The home boarding scheme at Clifton High is tailored to each student to ensure that they settle well, are supported academically and integrate socially during their time at the School. The International Admissions Officer is on hand as a point of contact for boarders during the school day. The 2016 ISI Inspection rated the quality of boarding as excellent, commenting that the school has the provision to support excellent outcomes for boarders.

Physical Education is a key part of the curriculum, not only for competitive sport, but for promoting a healthy lifestyle through the enjoyment of sport and exercise. In addition to the school's traditional sports of hockey, netball, football, rugby, swimming, athletics, rounders, cricket, tennis and gymnastics, specialist staff also teach a wide variety of other activities including squash, badminton, basketball, climbing, water polo and trampolining. Boys and girls regularly gain county and national honours and both boys and girls sports teams perform strongly in their relevant leagues and tournaments. Player pathways are in place in a number of different sports due to exciting partnerships with the University of Bristol and Bristol Henleaze Performance Swimming Club.

Music and Drama. Virtually any instrument, including voice, may be studied, with some 50 per cent of pupils having individual lessons. Associated Board examinations are taken. There are opportunities to belong to orchestras, wind bands, drama groups and choirs who perform in a variety of concerts and productions throughout the year including some of the highest profile events in the school calendar. In Speech and Drama, a large number of pupils enter LAMDA examinations and consistently achieve outstanding results. Many Clifton High School pupils have gone on to study at top drama schools and are now working within the industry.

Charitable and Extra-curricular Activities. Pupils have a strong sense of social responsibility and are actively involved in various local and national charity fundraising events throughout their school careers. Annual collections amount to several thousand pounds. There is an extensive extra-curricular activities programme throughout the school, responding to pupils' interests. Clubs are split into three categories: Skills Development, Academic Progress and Individual Brilliance. There are over 100 clubs running in the three categories throughout the year, including Fencing, Dance, Water Polo, Tumble Club, Judo Club, Art Club, Orchestra, Climbing Club, Eco Club, App Building and 3D

Printing Club. Clifton High School is particularly successful in running the Duke of Edinburgh's Award and World Challenge expeditions every year. There is a rich programme of trips both home and overseas.

Admission and Scholarships. Entry to the Nursery School, Early Years and Junior School is through in-class assessment by the class teacher and taster session with the relevant class. Entry to the Senior School is dependent on the results of an entrance examination, interview with the Head of School and school report. Pupils in Clifton High School Year 6 also sit the entrance examination to the Senior School. A good number of scholarships are awarded for Year 7 and Sixth Form entry, with flexibility for awards at entry to other year groups. Means-tested school-assisted places are available at all Senior School levels. Music and Sports awards are also available on entry to the Senior School, with sports, performing arts and creative arts awards available in the Sixth Form. Further details may be obtained from the School Registrar and Admissions Manager.

Fees per term (2018–2019). Tuition: Nursery School (5 days) £2,965; Early Years: Reception £3,455, Years 1–2 £3,480; Junior School (Years 3–6) £3,500; Senior School (Years 7–11) £4,985; Sixth Form (Years 12–13) £4,995. Lunch: Years 1–6 £240, Years 7–13 £250. Family Boarding (exclusive of Tuition): £4,500. EAL: details on request from the Home Boarding Coordinator.

Termly fees across the school are inclusive of all compulsory educational visits.

Reductions for siblings concurrently in the school (except where fees are paid by an authority or bursary): 2nd – 7%; 3rd – 15%; 4th – 25%.

Charitable status. Clifton High School is a Registered Charity, number 311736. It exists to provide first-class education for pupils aged 3 to 18 years.

Head of School: Dr Alison M Neill, BSc Hons UCW Aberystwyth, PhD UCW Aberystwyth, PGCE

Director of Finance and Operations: Mr Guy Cowper, BA Hons Warwick, MSc Sheffield

Deputy Heads of School:
Dr Mark Caddy, BSc Hons Warwick, PhD Warwick (*Years 3–6 and Years 10–11*)
Dr Helen Pascoe, BSc Hons Reading, MSc Leicester, PhD Reading, PGCE (*Nursery School–Year 2 and Years 7–9*)

Senior Assistant Head – Pupils, Staff and School Operations: Mr Manolis Psarros, BA Hons Wales, MA Bristol, MEd Bristol
Assistant Head – Teaching Enhancement and Quality Assurance: Mr Christopher Collins
Assistant Head – Pupil Experiences and Outcomes: Ms Louise Brackenbury

Head of Sixth Form: Mr Samuel Adams, MA Cambridge, PGCE
Assistant Head: Sixth Form: Miss Charlotte Allen, BA Hons London, PGCE

Senior Management Team – Assistant to Deputy Head:
Mrs Sarah Barker, BEd Hons UWE (*Nursery School–Year 2*)
Ms Alice Bagnall, BSc Hons UCW Cardiff, PGCE (*Years 3–6*)
Mr Joseph Cozens, BSc Hons Swansea (*Years 7–9*)
Miss Rebecca McInnes, BSc Hons UWIC, PGCE (*Years 7–9*)
Mr Oliver Mullins, BA Hons Birmingham, PGCE (*Years 10 and 11*)
Miss Natasha Widdison, BA Joint Hons Nottingham, PGCE (*Years 10 and 11*)

Lead Support Assistant to Deputy Head:
Mr Samuel Rimmer (*Nursery School–Year 2*)
Mrs Helen Tabb, BA Hons Surrey, QTS (*Years 3–6*)

Child Protection and Safeguarding:
Ms Alison Taylor, BSc Hons Reading, MEd Bristol, PGCE (*Designated Safeguarding Lead – Years 7–13*)
Miss Claudia Mulholland, BSc Hons Swindon, PGCE (*Designated Safeguarding Lead Support – Nursery School–Year 6*)

Senior School Teachers:
* *Head of Department*

Art and Design:
*Mr Paul Ayers, BA Hons Cornwall, MA Falmouth, PGCE
Miss Lisa Davies, BA Hons Leeds
Ms Claire Jaques, BA Hons Plymouth, PGCE, PG Dip Special Education

Art and Textiles:
*Mrs Emma Studd, BA Hons UWE, MA UWE, PGCE

Business Studies:
*Mr Peter Jackson, BA Hons Westminster, PGCE

Latin:
*Mrs Elizabeth Marriott, BA Oxford, MA London, PGCE
Mr Manolis Psarros, BA Hons Wales, MA Bristol, MEd Bristol

Design and Technology:
*Mr Simon Francis BA Hons Bristol Polytechnic, PGCE (*School Curriculum Lead, Product Design*)
*Mrs Bernadette Holton, BA UWE, QTS (*Food and Nutrition*)
*Mr Bryan Murphy, MA Cambridge, PGCE (*Design and Innovation*)

Drama:
*Mr Craig Pullen, BA Hons Manchester Metropolitan, MA Leeds Metropolitan, PGCE
Mrs Susan Johnson-Martin, BA Hons Royal Holloway College London, PGCE

English:
*Mrs Philippa Lyons-White, BA Hons Bristol, PGCE
Mr Samuel Adams, MA Cambridge, PGCE
Mr Christopher Hope, BA Hons Hull, MA Birmingham, PGCE
Mrs Siobhan Hosty, MA Kingston

Geography:
*Mrs Laura Giles, BSc Hons Loughborough, PGCE
Mrs Helen Ellerton, BSc Hons Manchester, PGCE
Mrs Amy Schmid, BA Hons Birmingham, PGCE

History:
*Mr Oliver Mullins, BA Hons Birmingham, PGCE
Miss Charlotte Allen, BA Hons London, PGCE

Computing:
Mr Richard Shelswell, MEng Hons Bath, PGCE

Digital Learning:
*Mr James Webber, BA Hons Sheffield, PGCE

Mathematics:
*Mr Andrew Hillman, BSc Hons Nottingham, PGCE
Mr Christopher Collins, MMath Oxford, PGCE
Dr Mark Caddy, BSc Hons Warwick, PhD Warwick
Mr Andrew Harkin, MSc Dublin Institute of Technology, PGCE
Mr Richard Shelswell, MEng Hons Bath, PGCE
Ms Alison Taylor, BSc Hons Reading, MEd Bristol, PGCE
Mrs Emily Waters, BEng Hons Swansea, PGCE

Modern Languages – French, German and Spanish:
*Miss Helen McKenna, BA Hons York, PGCE (*French*)

*Mrs Tara Harris, BA Hons Newcastle upon Tyne, PGCE (*German*)
*Miss Louise Sobey, BA Hons Portsmouth/Murcia, PGCE (*Spanish*)
Miss Natasha Widdison, BA Joint Hons Nottingham, PGCE (*Modern Foreign Languages*)

Music:
*Mr Andrew Cleaver, BA Hons Lincoln and Hull, QTS (*Head of School Music*)
*Mr Stephen Lea, Graduate Trinity College of Music, Licentiate Trinity College London, MMus Bristol, QTS (*Head of Senior School Music Academic*) [maternity cover]
*Mrs Donia Pieters, BA Hons Brunel, MMus Goldsmiths, QTS (*Head of Senior School Music Academic*)

Physical Education Department:
*Mr James Taylor, BSc Hons Sheffield Hallam (*Head of School Sport and Extra-curricular*)
*Mrs Lynne Reid, BSc Hons Cardiff, PGCE (*Head of School Games, Girls*)
*Mr Thomas Morison, BEd Hons St Mark and St John, QTS (*Head of School Games, Boys*)
Miss Rebecca McInnes, BSc Hons UWIC, PGCE
Mr Mike Wallington BSc Hons Glamorgan, PGCE

Science – Biology, Chemistry, Physics:
*Miss Jennifer England, BSc Hons Exeter, PGCE (*Biology*)
Miss Rebecca Cole, BSc Hons Bath, PGCE (*Biology*)
Mr Joseph Cozens, BSc Hons Swansea (*Biology*)
*Mr Gareth Phillips, MSc Bristol, PGCE (*Chemistry*)
Mrs Louise Brackenbury, BSc Hons UWIC, PGCE (*Chemistry*)
*Mr Paul Griffin, BSc Hons Birmingham, PGCE (*Physics*)
Mr Bryan Murphy, MA Cambridge, PGCE (*Physics*)

Enhanced Learning Department:
*Mrs Gabrielle Pilgrim, BA Hons Reading, PGCE, BDA ATS, SpLD APC Patoss
Mr Frank Allen, BA Hons Nottingham Trent, MEd Queensland, PGCE
Mrs Lucie Bailey, BA Hons Lincoln, RSA CELTA TEFL
Mrs Faith Jameson, BA Hons Warwick, PMP MA SpLD/Dyslexia
Mrs Amanda Swannell, BA Hons Hull, MA UWE, PGCE, PG Dip Dyslexia
Ms Vivienne Swarbrick, BSc UEA, PGCE
Mrs Sue Jones

Nursery School to Year 2 Teachers:
*Mrs Sarah Barker, BEd Hons UWE (*Assistant to Deputy Head, Nursery–Year 2*)
Mrs Donna Andrews, BSc Hons Bath, QTS, EYPS
Miss Angharad Daker, BA Hons UWIC, EYTS
Miss Claudia Mulholland, BSc Hons Swindon, PGCE
Mrs Sarah Manning, BEd Hons Kingston
Miss Kerry Quick, BEd Saint Mark and Saint John, Plymouth, QTS
Mr Samuel Rimmer, BSc Hons Leeds, MSc Brock Ontario, PGCE
Mrs Claire Shaw, BA Hons King Alfred's College, QTS

Year 3 to Year 6 Teachers:
*Ms Alice Bagnall, BSc Hons UCW Cardiff, PGCE (*Assistant to Deputy Head Years 3–6*)
Miss Lucy Buff, BA Hons Liverpool, PGCE
Mrs Hannah Crofts, BEd Hons Winchester
Miss Jesse Dyer, BA Hons Exeter, MSc Bristol
Mrs Pamela Eyles, BSc Hons Bristol, PGCE
Mrs Polly Gibbons, MA Hons St Andrews, PGCE
Ms Claire Jaques, BA Hons Plymouth, PGCE
Mr Charles Lowe, BA/Ed Joint Hons Goldsmiths
Mr David Pye, BA Hons West London Inst of HE, PGCE
Mrs Helen Tabb, BA Hons Surrey, QTS

Teaching Assistants:
Mrs Lindsey Burch, NNEB, NVQ Level 3
Miss Debbie Clements, NNEB
Ms Karen Collins, Level 3 Supporting Teaching and Learning
Mrs Jenni Kerslake, BSc Hons Reading, PGCE, EYPS
Mrs Lucy Motherwell, MA Glasgow, MSc Aberdeen, Level 3 Supporting teaching and Learning
Mrs Iona Payne BA Hons Worcester, QTS
Mrs Emma Takle, NNEB
Miss Selena Wilcox, NNEB

Pupil Welfare Counsellors:
Mrs Jackie Brangwyn, BEd Hons Sussex, MSc Bristol, Diploma
Mrs Jodie Sheward, Diploma City of Bristol College

School Nurse:
Mrs Lindsay Bailey (*Healthcare Practitioner*)
Miss Laura Lynch (*School Nurse*)
Mrs Louise Williams (*Healthcare Practitioner*)

Business Support Staff:
Head's Office:
*Mrs Natalie Cridland (*Head's Personal Assistant and Senior Administration Manager*)

Admissions:
Ms Lindy Scudder (*Registrar and School Admissions Manager*)
Mrs Sarah Maidment (*Admissions International Officer*)

School Office:
Miss Alice Bushell (*Office Manager*)
Mrs Frances Avent (*School Office Administrative Assistant, Quality Assurance, Facilities and Operations*)
Mrs Lucy Mansford (*School Office Events Manager*)
Mrs Punam Kaur (*School Office Administrator*)

Concord College

Acton Burnell Hall, Shrewsbury, Shropshire SY5 7PF

Tel: 01694 731631
Fax: 01694 731389
email: enquiries@concordcollege.org.uk
website: www.concordcollegeuk.com
Twitter: @ConcordCollege
Facebook: @ConcordCollegeUK

Concord College is a highly successful co-educational international school for day and boarding students aged 13–19 providing GCSE and A Level courses. Set in 80 acres of Shropshire parkland, the College combines outstanding facilities with first-rate academic performance. The College is regularly rated in the top 10 schools in the UK. Students are cared for by a dedicated staff in a safe and beautiful environment. Concord is a community that celebrates national and cultural diversity while students and staff are united by the wish to set high standards. The result is a happy and kind community in which students are polite, articulate and conscientious without ever losing their sense of fun.

Number of students. 590 (approximately equal numbers of boys and girls) of whom over 480 are boarders.

Facilities. Facilities at Concord College are impressive. Based around an historic Main Hall, there are many new additions as well as medieval ruins within the grounds. There has been considerable investment in the facilities over the last 15 years.

Lessons are taught in a variety of excellent classroom facilities. The new state-of-the-art Science block was completed in January 2018 and comprises 22 laboratories including a special projects lab. The refurbished and remodelled Castle Block which opened in September 2018 is home to the English, economics and art departments. The academic departments are well supported by a modern library in the Jubilee Building which was completed in 2009.

There is a well-resourced Theatre and Music School, an excellent Sports complex, indoor swimming pool as well as extensive grounds including sports pitches, tennis courts and a high ropes course. Students eat their meals in the College Dining Room and select from a variety of international cuisine. Most students have individual study-bedrooms on campus, many with en-suite bathrooms. Students have a wide variety of facilities including common rooms and a student kitchen.

Education. Teaching at Concord is undertaken in groups that average 16 at GCSE and 14 at A Level. Teachers are experts in their subjects.

At GCSE Biology, Chemistry and Physics are taught as separate subjects and emphasis is placed upon laboratory experience. Other compulsory subjects are English and Mathematics. Optional subjects include Art, Astronomy, Computer Science, Economics, French, German, Geography, History, Music, Statistics, Religious Studies and Spanish.

In the sixth form students normally study at least three A Levels and perhaps one further AS Level. Subjects include Art, Biology, Chemistry, Economics, English Language and Literature, French, Geography, History, Mathematics, Further Mathematics, Music, Photography, Physics and Spanish. There is also an opportunity to study for an EPQ which is an independent research project. All students who do not have GCSE English are expected to study English.

In addition to their teachers, students have an individual tutor with whom they meet daily and who monitors their academic progress. Students also have a Boarding Parent who is responsible for their well-being. There is a comprehensive careers programme to support all students with their university applications in the UK or overseas.

Examination Results and University Entry. The College achieves excellent examination results with 95% A*–B at A Level in 2018, placing Concord 9th in the UK according to The Times league tables. The college has a particularly strong record of placing students into STEM courses at top universities, as well as into UK medical schools. 71% of Concord's 2018 leavers are now attending UK Top 10 universities. In 2018, 20 students won places at Oxford or Cambridge University, 21 at Imperial College London, 23 at UCL and 14 at the LSE.

Selection for Entry. The college selects applicants upon the basis of interviews, school record and entry tests. Overseas applicants are normally required to take the UKiset test at a registered centre in their home country. Students can be accepted for entry at all ages.

Fees per annum (2018–2019). Full Boarding £39,900, Day £14,280. (Boarding fees are payable in 2 instalments.)

Scholarships and Bursaries. A fee reduction of up to 10% of full fees may be available to students who have a particularly strong academic background. For entrants to GCSE classes, scholarship entry tests are administered. General bursaries are also available on request: indeed the College has a 'needs blind' admissions policy for its day students.

Holidays. Half term holidays are nine days long in the autumn and spring terms and 5 days in the summer term. The Christmas holiday is one month and Easter is only two and a half weeks. There is a long summer vacation from the end of June until early September.

The college remains open at half terms (for all students) and during the Easter holiday (for students in Form 5 or the sixth form).

The School Day. Lessons run from 9.00 am to 4.00 pm Monday to Friday with Wednesday afternoon allocated to sport and to a trip to Shrewsbury for senior students. There is compulsory supervised study (prep) each evening Monday to Friday.

Saturday morning is used for whole-college testing. These tests are taken under examination conditions to help students to prepare for their GCSEs and AS and A Levels.

Reports to Parents. These are sent at half term in the first term and subsequently at the end of each term.

Clubs, Sports and Extracurricular Activities. Students at Concord can choose from a multitude of activities. As Concord is an academic school, many clubs and societies have an academic focus and are part of Concord's well-developed super-curriculum, for example the Medics Society, the Philosophy Club and numerous academic discussion groups.

Sports, music, dance and drama are also all available in our own facilities. There is a Sports Hall, squash courts and gymnasium as well as outdoor facilities including football, athletics and tennis. A wealth of sporting activities are on offer ranging from archery to fencing and badminton to volleyball. There is a purpose-built dance studio and a range of gym equipment available for students to use after lessons and in the evenings.

Musicians can have individual instrumental tuition and join one of the chamber groups. Choir and singing lessons can develop all levels of vocal talent. Many other activities are also offered ranging from public speaking and chess to horse riding and charity fundraising. Students take part in Concord's outdoor education programme and the Duke of Edinburgh's Award scheme is also available. Whatever their talents, students are able develop them at Concord.

Charitable status. Concord College is a Registered Charity, number 326279. It exists to provide high quality education for secondary age students.

Chair of the Governors: Dr Iain M Bride

Clerk to the Governors and Bursar: Mrs Barbara Belfield-Dean

Principal: Neil G Hawkins, MA Cantab, PGCE

Vice-Principal (Academic): Tom Lawrence, BA, PGCE
Vice-Principal (Pastoral): Jeremy Kerslake, MA
Head of Lower School: Mrs Rachel Coward, MEd, BEd
Assistant Principal: Phil Outram, PhD, BSc
Assistant Principal: Daniel Wilson, MA
Assistant Principal: Rob Pugh, PhD, BA

Principal's Personal Assistant & Admissions Registrar: Mrs Wendy Hartshorne

Derby Grammar School

Rykneld Road, Littleover, Derby DE23 4BX

Tel:	01332 523027
email:	enquiries@derbygrammar.org
	admissions@derbygrammar.org
website:	www.derbygrammar.org
Twitter:	@derbygrammar
Facebook:	@DerbyGrammarSchool
LinkedIn:	Derby Grammar School

Derby Grammar School is Derbyshire's leading independent day school for boys aged 7 to 18, and girls aged 16 to 18.

Founded in 1995, the School provides a high-quality education for able pupils in Derbyshire, Staffordshire and Nottinghamshire. It has 270 pupils from the age of 7 (Year 3) to 18 (Year 13).

Whilst pupils perform extremely well academically, the School places great emphasis on developing character and leadership skills across and beyond the curriculum.

There is a full competitive sports programme and a wide-ranging and flourishing music scene. There is an extremely strong tradition of charity work and fundraising, featuring ongoing links with a community in Tanzania.

The School has a broad programme of outdoor education, including The Duke of Edinburgh's Award, as well as numerous trips and visits both at home and overseas.

Location and Facilities. The School is set in a superb Victorian parkland site on the edge of the city of Derby, near to the arterial A38 and A50 routes.

The original manor house has been converted and extended with a purpose-built teaching block, Chemistry and Design Technology building. The buildings also house specialist Biology and Physics laboratories and Music and Music Technology rooms and a recording studio.

The School has recently acquired sports facilities that will provide an AstroTurf for hockey, rugby and cricket pitches and a sports hall.

Curriculum. The Junior School follows an enhanced curriculum, providing a strong grounding in all subject areas. In addition, the pupils have specialist teaching in Music, French and Latin.

In the Senior School, all pupils follow a broad common curriculum at Key Stage 3 which includes teaching in each of the separate sciences and two modern foreign languages up to the end of Year 9. Pupils will study 9 or 10 GCSEs, including at least one modern foreign language and the three separate sciences.

Pupils in the Sixth Form can choose from over twenty different A Level subjects and the options process is based around pupil choice rather than being in fixed blocks. In recent years nearly 75% of students have studied at least one science at A Level and over 25% have gone on to study bio-medical, science or engineering degrees at university.

Admissions. Admission to both the Junior and Senior School is through assessment in English, Mathematics and reasoning papers. The main Entrance Examinations are held in January but are available throughout the year.

Open days are held each term, but visits and taster days are welcomed at any time by prior appointment. For further information contact our admissions team on 01332 510030, email admissions@derbygrammar.org or visit the school website.

Scholarships and Bursaries. There are Scholarships available for entry into the Senior School. As well as academic Scholarships we offer specialist Sports, Music and Choral Scholarships which are awarded after successful trials or auditions. Bursaries are available for Junior, Senior and Sixth Form.

Fees per term (2018–2019). £2,941 (Years 3–4), £3,587 (Years 5–6), £4,483 (Years 7–13). There are three terms per academic year.

Charitable status. Derby Grammar School is a Registered Charity, number 1015449.

Chair of Governors: Mr Tim Wilson

Vice-Chair of Governors: Mr Simon Richardson

Head: Dr R Norris, MA Cantab, DPhil Oxon

Deputy Head: Mrs L Reynolds, BSc Hons
Assistant Head and Head of Sixth Form, Miss K Stebbings, BA Hons
Senior Master: Mr P D Hilliam, BA Hons
Head of Lower School: Mr K Clark, BA Hons

Head of Upper School: Mrs V Charnock, BA Hons
Chaplain: Revd P Taylor, BA Hons
School Bursar: Miss J Jameson, MAAT
Admissions: Ms S Green

Senior School Teaching Staff (principal subjects):

Art:
Miss E Sellors

Biology:
Mrs L C Reynolds
Mr I Lowden
Mrs U Ahtamad

Chemistry:
Dr A Buckenham
Mrs S Burton

Classics:
Mr S Fletcher

Design Technology:
Mr P Lakritz
Ms E Sweet

Economics:
Mrs K Cowgill

English:
Mrs E Collins
Mr I Benjafield
Mr S Penny
Mrs K Watson

Geography:
Mr C Critchlow
Mrs R Taylor

History:
Mr J Taylor
Dr R Norris

Mathematics:
Mr M R Allen
Miss C Bruce
Mrs V Charnock

Modern Languages:
French:
Miss K Stebbings
Miss F Ciaravino

German:
Mrs Schroeder
Mr I Watson

Spanish:
Miss K Stebbings

Music:
Mr N Coley
Mr Wilford

Physical Education:
Mr K Clark
Mr C D Whitworth
Mr J Smyth

Physics:
Mr D Hills
Miss A Trubilina

Religious Studies:
Mr P D Hilliam
Mrs K Lacey

Junior School Staff:
Head of Junior School: Mrs A Sly
Mrs K Genders
Mrs R Hamilton
Mrs E Jackson
Mrs H Monk
Miss R Devine

Dover College

Effingham Crescent, Dover, Kent CT17 9RH

Tel:	01304 205969
Fax:	01304 242854
email:	admissions@dovercollege.org.uk
website:	www.dovercollege.org.uk
Twitter:	@DoverCollege
Facebook:	@DoverCollege
LinkedIn:	/Dover-College

Dover College was founded in 1871 in the historic grounds of the old St Martin's Priory.

We are the closest school to continental Europe, one hour to Central London by train and within easy reach of London's airports.

We are a small, family-style school with a vibrant mix of local and international pupils. We expect academic excellence from our pupils, but also encourage them to find their talents in other areas such as art, drama, music and sport.

Co-education. Dover College (age 3–18) has been fully co-educational since 1975 and the 300+ boys and girls are integrated at all levels. There are 100 boarders.

Organisation. Our Junior School is located in its own comfortable building on the main College campus and accepts day pupils aged from 3–11. Our Senior School is for pupils aged 11–18 and we can accept day, weekly boarding and full boarding pupils. We have two boarding houses for girls and two for boys. Pupils in Years 7 and 8 have their own dedicated house, Priory, to help them with the transition from Junior to Senior School.

Catering. The catering team provides delicious, healthy, well-balanced homemade food and meals are taken in our historic Great Hall.

Curriculum. Our Creative Curriculum has been developed to promote independent learning opportunities and creative thought in all subjects. In particular, it covers linguistic, mathematical, scientific, technological, human and social, physical, aesthetic, creative and cultural education appropriate to the pupils' age and ability. It takes account of national requirements, where appropriate, but creates greater flexibility and choice.

Our core purpose is to inspire academic excellence and personal fulfilment. We encourage and expect high standards and success, fostering a sense of responsibility for self and others. Our aim is that all our pupils leave Dover College thoughtful, qualified, ambitious and ready to make a significant contribution wherever their futures may take them. We hope our pupils will want to give back to society some of the benefits which they have enjoyed through their engagement with education here.

Our pupils have a wide range of academic abilities and talents and we are proud of their successes at GCSE, A Level and throughout the College. Inspirational teaching and small class sizes enable pupils to develop confidence, self-esteem and a love of learning. We encourage all pupils to aspire to excellence, to always push their academic boundaries, no matter how high their academic achievement.

Sixth Form. The Sixth Form is overseen by a Head of Sixth Form and pupils are able to choose A Levels and BTECs. Traditional academic subjects are provided, as are the practical subjects of art, design and technology, textiles, photography, drama and music.

Sixth Formers wear business attire and are given more choice and freedom than junior pupils, being expected to respond positively to their treatment as young adults. A well-equipped Sixth Form Centre is used as a meeting place and social club.

The School's Careers Adviser works in liaison with external agencies to plan, deliver and evaluate an integrated careers education and guidance programme. This enables pupils to gain the necessary knowledge, skills and understanding in order to make informed career plans before attending the universities of their choice.

International Study Centre (ISC). The International Department was started in 1957 and backed at the time by members of NATO, although international boarding has a far longer history than this starting point. The International Study Centre provides intensive English courses for pupils whose first language is not English. These courses vary in length and the aim is to enable all pupils to integrate fully into the life of Dover College as soon as possible after their arrival.

Individual Support. There is an Individual Needs Department in which pupils with learning difficulties (e.g. Dyslexia) receive 1:1 tuition. Each pupil has a member of staff as a personal tutor. The tutor supervises his/her pupils' general academic progress.

Art and Technology. The Art Department is situated in purpose-built accommodation. Fine Art, pottery, textiles and photography are all available. Examination results are always excellent both at GCSE and A Level.

The Technology Department shares the building with Art and is situated in a large, well-equipped, open-plan workshop. Pupils are encouraged to work with a range of materials (wood, plastic etc) and use CAD software. Design Technology is available at GCSE and A Level. There are many opportunities for the students to use the workshop outside curriculum time. Design and Technology also thrives as an activity.

Music and Drama. Music plays a particularly important part in the life of the School. The well-equipped Music School was relocated on site in January 2011 and opened by Julian Lloyd Webber. It comprises high-tech soundproof pods of various sizes for practice, classrooms and recital room. Extracurricular activities are numerous. The Chapel Choir meets three times a week and is the backbone of the many concerts and services, but there are weekly rehearsals for the Choral Society, String group, Windband, Jazz band, and Madrigal group. There is a concert at the end of each term, held in the Refectory, and numerous informal concerts in a variety of locations. A House Music competition takes place annually.

Drama is a very active part of the cultural life of the School, as well as part of the Lower School curriculum; there is a major school production each year together with additional House productions. Drama is offered at A Level and GCSE.

Learning Resources Centre. It provides cutting-edge facilities and resources to all pupils, including Careers information.

Sport. The School's main playing fields are a short distance away; on site are tennis courts, an astroturf, basketball court and an excellent Sports Hall with a fitness suite. Sports include Athletics, Badminton, Basketball, Cricket, Cross Country, Running, Football, Hockey, Netball, Rugby, Sailing, Tennis, Volleyball and various PE activities. Swimming takes place at the indoor swimming pool in the local leisure centre. Golf may be played on local courses and horse riding is also offered locally through the School.

Extracurricular Activities. In addition to sport, pupils have the opportunity of taking part in a wide range of over 50 activities including Adventure Training, Art, Car Mechanic, Chess, Computing, Debating, Duke of Edinburgh's Award, Dancing, Fencing, First Aid, Horse Riding, Language Clubs, Music, Photography, Wine Tasting, Stage Management and Technology. The London West End theatres are within easy reach and regular trips to a variety of productions are made.

Pastoral Care. All pupils benefit from a carefully designed system of outstanding pastoral care. Every Dover College student belongs to a House and Boarders are provided with comfortable accommodation in one of four boarding houses. All Sixth Formers have single study-bedrooms. A Housemaster or Housemistress, supported by a team of tutors, runs each House; it is their role to give pastoral support as well as supervising the pupils' academic progress.

Pupils have access to a fully equipped and professionally staffed Medical Centre, which can accommodate pupils overnight.

Religious Life. College has its own Chapel and is a Church of England school. All pupils are encouraged to respect each other's beliefs and faiths from a position of tolerance and understanding.

Entry. Pupils are typically admitted into the Senior School at 11, 13 or 16 years old, but may come at any age. Most pupils join the College in September, but entry in January and April is possible.

Entry into the Infants and Juniors is by interview and an informal assessment carried out during a "Taster Day" at the school. Entrance into the Senior School at 11+ and 13+ is dependent on previous school reports as well as an interview with the Headmaster. Provision is made for direct entry into the Sixth Form for boys and girls. This is normally conditional upon GCSE results. Further information can be obtained from Admissions.

Fees per term (2018–2019). Junior Day £2,575–£3,550; Senior Day £4,250–£5,350; Senior Weekly Boarding (up to 6 nights per week) £7,000–£8,500; Full Boarding £8,250–£10,500.

Scholarships. Academic Scholarships are awarded by competitive examinations.

Scholarships for Music, Drama, Art, Design Technology, Sport and All-Rounder are available by competitive interview.

Scholarships are available to pupils at 11+, 13+ and 16+ entry. Scholarships are not awarded to pupils in the Junior School.

Sibling Bursaries (10%) and Service Bursaries are automatically awarded. Members of HM Armed Forces and the Diplomatic Service who are eligible for the boarding allowance only pay a parental contribution of 10% of the full boarding fee.

Further details may be obtained on application to Admissions.

Old Dovorian Club. President: Mr Simon Charlier, c/o Dover College.

Friends of Dover College (PTA). Chairman: Mrs Jessica Doodes, c/o Dover College.

Charitable status. Dover College is a Registered Charity, number 307856. The School exists to develop confidence and individual talents.

Chairman of Governors: Mr Michael Goodridge, MBE [Old Dovorian]

Headmaster: Mr Gareth Doodes

Bursar & Clerk to the Governors: Mrs Sarah Greig

Deputy Head of Senior School: Mr Simon Kibler

Director of Studies: Mr David Brooks

Deputy Head (Academic) of Junior School: Mr Brett Fairclough

Deputy Head (Pastoral) of Junior School: Mrs Tracey Mills

Head of International Study Centre: Mr James Carson

Staff Tutor: Mrs Therese Taylor

Registrar: Ms Alison Wilson

PA to the Headmaster: Mrs Jane Skinner

d'Overbroeck's

333 Banbury Road, Oxford OX2 7PL

Tel: 01865 688600
email: sixthform@doverbroecks.com
website: www.doverbroecks.com

Age Range. 11–18 (11–16: day only; 16–18: day and boarding).

Number in School. 598.

Fees per term (2018–2019). Tuition: £5,910 (Years 7–11); £7,950 (Years 12–13). Boarding: £3,000–£4,950.

d'Overbroeck's is a co-educational school in Oxford for students aged 11–18. We are fairly evenly divided between residential and day students in the Sixth Form; but are day only up to the age of 16.

Our academic approach is characterised by small classes (maximum of 10 students per class in the Sixth Form and 15 up to GCSE) and a highly supportive and encouraging approach that builds on each student's strengths and enables outstanding academic achievements.

Teaching is highly interactive and seeks to generate enthusiasm for the subject, sound academic skills and effective working habits – while at the same time providing a thorough preparation for public examinations and ensuring that the learning experience is motivating and fun. The environment is friendly, stimulating and engaging with staff and students working together to achieve the best possible results.

A wide range of sporting and other extra-curricular activities is available to complement the learning in the classroom. Students can take part in numerous school events and performances as well as benefit from the wide range of educational, cultural and social activities which Oxford has to offer. We believe that happiness and success go hand in hand – and throughout the school we do our utmost to ensure that every student is given new opportunities to develop and is encouraged and rewarded – whether in the classroom, on stage or on the sports field.

The Sixth Form is based on a different site from Years 7 to 11 and the value of this is that it allows us to provide a clear sense of progression as students start their A Level studies and begin to make the transition towards university. Many students from other schools also join us for direct entry into our Sixth Form. The new Sixth Form building that opened in September 2017 provides first-class facilities for all subject departments.

We expect high standards of commitment and effort from our students and have a track record of strong GCSE and A Level results, both in absolute terms and on a value-added basis. Students benefit from excellent teaching and a positive approach which enables them to maximise their potential. In 2018, for example, our students achieved 59% grade 9–7 (equivalent to A*–A) at GCSE and 53% grade A*–A at A Level. The overwhelming majority of students go on to university and we have an excellent record of success with entry including Oxford and Cambridge as well as medical, law, veterinary and art schools.

Main Entry Points: at 11+, 13+ and directly into the Sixth Form, post GCSE.

Scholarships: Academic, Art, Music, Drama and Sport.

Principal: **Emma-Kate Henry**, BA, PGCE

Deputy Principal: Jonathan Cuff, BA, MSc (*Religion, Ethics and Philosophy*)

Deputy Principal Academic: Alastair Barnett, BA, PGCE (*History*)

Chief Operating Officer: Nick Woods

Head of Years 7–11: Mark Olejnik, BA, PGCE (*History*)

Head of Sixth Form: Alasdair MacPherson, MA (*English*)

Head of Lower Sixth: Kate Palmer, BSc, PGCE, SDes (*Geography*)

Head of International School: Ted McGrath

Teaching Staff:
* Head of Department or Departmental Coordinator

Katie Amiri, BA, DELTA (*EAL*)
Louise Arnould, BA, PGCE (*Art, Textiles*)
Daniel Austin, BA DELTA (*EAL*)

Kathryn Avent, BA, PGCE (*Sport*)
Rebecca Bates, BSc, PGCE (*Biology*)
Rachel Bayley, BA, PGCE (*Music*)
Thomas Bell, BA, PGCE (*Media*)
Shanti Bharatan, MSc, PhD (*Biology*)
Joe Bibby, BSc, PGCE (*Physics*)
John Blythe, PTLLS (*Photography*)
Dave Borthwick, MChem, PhD (*Chemistry**)
Ursula Boughton, BSc, PGCE (*Mathematics, Independent Learning**)
Christopher Bright, BA, PGCE (*Geography*)
Christophe Brinster, M-ès-L (*French*, Film Studies**)
Kelly Bristow, MSc, PGCE, CPsychol (*Psychology**)
John Butler, BA, PGCE (*Sociology**)
Evelyn Campbell, BA, PGCE (*Mathematics*)
Michelle Cartey, MSc, PGCE (*Chemistry*)
Jennifer Clark, BSc, PGCE (*Chemistry, Science*)
Meghan Clarke, BA, MSc (*Computer Science*)
Jane Cockerill, BA, MEd, PGCE (*Music*)
Amy Coe, BA, PGCE (*Physical Education*)
Andrew Colclough, BA, MA (*Politics**)
Claire Coltellini, MA, PGCE (*French*)
Margaret Craig, BA, MA, FAETC (*History of Art*)
Stephen Creamer, MEng, PGCE (*Chemistry, Physics*)
Charles Currie, MPhys, PGCE (*Physics**)
Chelsey David, BA (*History, Politics*)
Jon-Paul Davies, BSc, MA, PGCE (*Geography**)
Lynn Doughton, BSc, MA (*Biology*)
Dani Fidler, BA, PGCE (*PE*)
Chris Gallop, MChem, DPhil, PGCE (*Chemistry, Science*)
Andrew Gillespie, MA (*Business**)
Nita Goriely, MS, PhD (*Mathematics*)
Agnieszka Gurbin, BA, MA, PhD, ESOL (*EAL*)
Nick Haines, MMathPhil (*Mathematics**)
Marianne Harlock, BA, PGCE (*Psychology*)
Simon Harrison, BA, MA (*Economics**)
Camilla Heath, BA, MA, PGCE (*Economics*)
Holly Hiscox, BA, MA, PGCE (*History*)
Christopher Holland, BA, MPhil (*English**)
Graham Hope, MA, DPhil (*Mathematics*)
Clare Horne, BSc, PhD, PG Dip (*Mathematics*)
Jo Humphreys, BA, MA, PGCE (*Learning Support*)
Fizza Hussain, BA, PGCE (*Drama*)
Anna Irvine, BA, DELTA (*EAL*)
Laura Johnson, BSc, PGCE (*Computing, ICT*)
Adam Johnstone, MA, MSt (*EPQ*, Biology*)
Anne-Marie Jones, BSc, PhD (*Biology*)
Adam Kerr-Boyle, MA, PhD, PGCE (*History, Politics*)
Elena Kolpakova, MSc, PhD (*Russian*)
Susanne Kreitz, PhD (*German**)
Christopher Lacy, BA, TEFL (*EAL*)
Andrew Latcham, BA, DPhil (*History, Politics*)
Jessica Leach, BA, PGCE (*Sociology, Media*)
Cheryl Linton, BSc, PGCE (*Physics*)
Dearbhla Loughran (*Spanish, French*)
Kate MacDonald, BA, DSpLD (*Learning Support*)
David Mackie, BA, MA, DPhil, CPE, PGDL (*Classical Civilisation, Latin, Philosophy**)
Becky Mann, BA, PGCE (*Politics, History**)
Christine Martelloni, MSc (*French*)
Robyn McCall, BSc, PGCE (*Psychology*)
Sarah McSwiggan, BA, PGCE (*English*)
Elina Medley, BA, MA, PGCE (*Photography*)
Lucia Modena, MA, MSc (*Italian*)
Sandra Monger, BA, DELTA (*EAL*)
Alex Newton, BA, MA, PGCE (*Art*)
Jane Nimmo-Smith, BA (*Classics*, Ancient History**)
James O'Connor, BTEC HND (*Music Technology**)
Laura O'Donovan, BA, PGCE (*Business, Economics*)
Stephen O'Keeffe, MA (*Mathematics*)
Leon O'Rourke, BSc, PGCE (*Mathematics*)

Catherine Orme, BA, PGCE (*Biology*)
Lisa Pearson, BSc, MSc, PGCE (*Economics, Business*)
Mark Piesing, BA, PGCE (*Communication and Culture**)
Rosalinda Polato (*Italian*)
Robert Pollard, BA, TESOL, PGCE (*History, Politics*)
Martin Procter, BA, PGCE (*Physical Education**)
Richard Poyser, BA, PGCE (*Music**)
Wendy Rawding, BA, PGCE (*Art*)
Nick Reeves, MA, PGCE (*Art*, History of Art*, Photography**)
Imogen Rhodes, BA, PGCE (*Physics*)
Jonathan Richards, BSc, PGCE (*Physical Education**)
Naomi Richards, BA, PGCE (*History*)
Angus Roberts, BA, MA, MSc, PGCE, CEng (*Mathematics, Physics*)
Sara Roberts, BA, MA (*English*)
Ana Rodriguez Nodal, BA (*Spanish*)
Emily Rugg, BA, PGCE (*Mathematics*)
Emily Saddler, BA, PGCE (*English, Drama*)
Jacob Savage, BSc, PGCE (*Computer Science**)
Helen Self, BA, PGCE (*English*)
Aleksandra Selkovaja, BSc, MSc, PGCE (*Mathematics*)
Joan Shaw, BSc (*Physics*)
Sarah Shekleton, BA, MA, PGCE (*Mathematics**)
Lianne Skriniar, DipTCL (*Music*)
Jennifer Skym, BA, PGCE (*Geography*)
Bethany Slater, BA, PGCE (*Mathematics*)
Janey Su (*Mandarin*)
Joe Swarbrick, BA, PGCE (*Drama**)
Ben Symington, BA, MMath (*Mathematics*)
Alison Talbot, BA, MSc (*EAL**)
Jaimie Tarrell, BEd (*Biology**)
Rachel Thanassoulis, MA, PGCE (*English**)
Emma Tinker, BA, MA, PhD (*Film Studies*)
Michael Vanden Boom, MSc, PhD (*Mathematics*)
Katie Vingoe, BA, PGCE (*SEND & Well-being Coordinator*)
Rie Wakayama, BA (*Japanese*)
David Wareham, BA, MA, DELTA (*EAL*)
Rebecca Watkins, BA, MA, PGCE (*English, Drama*)
Natasha Wertheim, BA, PGCE (*Religion, Ethics and Philosophy**)
Paul Wheeler, BSc, PGCE (*Geography*)
Stephen Wheeler, BA, Dip TESOL (*EAL*)
Tricia Whitby, BA (*Geography*)
Clare Wildish, BA (*Business Studies*)
Helen Wilson, BA, PGCE (*Art*)
Henry Winney, MA, PGCE (*Chemistry, Biology*)
Sharon Wyper, BA, PGATC, MA (*Art*)
Jonathan Young, BA, BSc (*Business**)
Elena Zambrano (*Spanish*)
Marta Zborowska, MA, TEFL (*EAL*)

Sport & Extra-Curricular Activities:
Jonathan Richards, BSc, PGCE (*Physical Education**)

Registry:
Years 7–11: Rob Barker
Sixth Form: Lynne Berry, Anna Mitchell, Rebecca Wood

Boarding Office:
Kate Higgins
Emma Brett

School Counsellor: Charlie Morse-Brown, Kiki Glen

Higher Education & Careers Coordinator: Adam Kerr-Boyle, MA, PhD, PGCE

Principal's PA: Tracy Roslyn, BA, DipRSA

Dunottar School
United Learning

High Trees Road, Reigate, Surrey RH2 7EL

Tel: 01737 761945
email: info@dunottarschool.com
website: www.dunottarschool.com
Twitter: @dunottarschool
Facebook: @Dunottar

The aim of Dunottar is to offer an outstanding education to boys and girls and, through excellent teaching and high levels of individual support, to enable pupils to achieve added value which is amongst the top 10% of schools in the UK. Dunottar is a vibrant, co-educational secondary school which, as part of United Learning's family of schools, shares the group's core values of ambition, confidence, determination, creativity, respect and enthusiasm along with the objective of bringing out the "Best in Everyone". Dunottar celebrates achievement in its broadest sense resulting in a community of happy, confident pupils who achieve their first choice ambition for their future education and employment.

The School was founded in 1926 and joined United Learning in 2014. It is situated in 15 acres of gardens and playing fields on the outskirts of Reigate, convenient to mainline stations and bus routes. The main building is a handsome Palladian mansion and purpose-built wings include additional classrooms, art and design suites, the main hall, Sixth Form common room, a 25-metre heated indoor swimming pool and large sports hall. Outdoor space includes a sports field, several courts and woodland trail and arrangements with Old Reigatian RFC and Salfords CC extend the off-site sporting facilities. Building work has begun on a state-of-the-art Sixth Form Centre, which will be ready for use at Easter 2019.

Religion. The School holds the Christian ethos paramount and welcomes children from any denomination or none.

Curriculum. The school offers a broad education and preserves a balance between arts and science subjects. Early specialisation is avoided, though some subject options become necessary from the beginning of the GCSE year. Subjects include English Language and Literature, Mathematics, French, Spanish, History, Geography, Religious Studies, Biology, Physics and Chemistry, Business and Economics, Design and Technology, Computer Science, Physical Education, Drama, Food and Nutrition, Music and Art and Design. Dunottar has strong sporting and music traditions. Teaching is given in a wide range of musical instruments and pupils are encouraged to join the orchestras, music groups and choirs. A busy fixtures list offers many opportunities for competitive sport and 'sport for all' is encouraged within school and through the co-curricular programme. Rugby, football, athletics, netball, lacrosse, swimming, cricket and rounders are amongst the sports on offer. Co-curricular clubs are designed to broaden horizons and encourage new skills, hobbies and interests and range from current affairs debating to science based groups such as 'dissection club' and sports including badminton and swimming. Students also participate in The Duke of Edinburgh's Award scheme at Bronze, Silver and Gold levels.

Careers. Dunottar offers an interesting and varied careers programme for pupils, from online careers research tools through to careers networking lunches and suppers. The school welcomes a range of speakers from a diverse range of fields to offer our pupils an insight into application processes, daily life of employees and the skills employers are looking for.

Examinations taken. GCSE and A Levels, Associated Board of the Royal School of Music, London Academy of Music and Dramatic Art, Imperial School of Dancing, Royal Society of Arts.

Admissions. The admissions process at Dunottar is designed to identify those pupils who will thrive at the school. The admissions process is as friendly and relaxed as possible. The main intake is in Year 7 and Year 12, with a limited number of places available for Year 9 entry. We are happy to consider pupils joining into other year groups where spaces are available. Prospective pupils can be registered at any time prior to the registration deadline. For Year 7 entry pupils should be registered before 30th November of the year prior to entry and assessments take place in January of the year of entry. Applications for entry to Year 12 are usually required by 31st January in the year of entry. The Admissions Department are happy to answer any questions about the admissions process.

Fees per term (2018–2019). £5,345 (Year 7 to Year 13).

Scholarships. Academic Scholarships are awarded annually in Year 7 to those who reach the highest standard in the entrance tests. Year 12 scholarships will be awarded to those who reach a high standard in the scholarship papers. Year 12 scholarship examinations take place in November. Some scholarships are also available in Year 7 and Year 12 for those who show exceptional promise and talent in Music, Art, Design & Technology, Performing Arts and Sport. Further particulars may be obtained from the Admissions Department.

Charitable status. Dunottar School is part of United Learning which comprises: UCST (a Company Limited by Guarantee, Registered in England, number 2780748, and a Registered Charity, number 1016538) and ULT (a Company Limited by Guarantee, Registered in England, number 4439859, and an Exempt Charity).

Chair of Board of Governors: Dr R Given-Wilson

***Headmaster*: Mr M Tottman**, MA Oxon, MBA

Senior Leadership Team:
Deputy Head Pastoral, Designated Safeguarding Lead: Mr M Broughton, BA Hons Worcester
Deputy Head Teaching & Learning: Mrs P Smithson, BA Combined Hons Exeter, PGCE, MEd
Director of Studies: Mrs R Stringer, BA Hons Warwick, PGCE

* Head of Department

English:
Mr M Broughton, BA Hons Worcester
Mrs J Bolt, MA, BA Hons Sussex, PGCE Roehampton
*Ms K Lewis, MBA De Montfort, BEd Hons Sunderland
Mrs P Smithson, BA Combined Hons Exeter, PGCE, MEd
Miss R Wilshaw, BA Hons Keele, PGCE Bath, MA

Mathematics:
Ms N Budgen, BComm Durban SA, PGCE (*Assistant Head of Lower School*)
Mrs L Chessell, BSc Hons Durham, PGCE
*Mrs R MacTavish, BSc Hons York, ACMA, CSBM, PGCE
Ms H Needler, BA Hons York, PGCE
Mrs S Ryde, BSc Bristol, PGCE

Science:
Miss C Davis BSc Imperial College, PGCE
Mrs H Davison, BSc Hons Southampton, PGCE (*Second in Science*)
Mrs C Hammond, BSc Hons UCL, PGCE, PGCP, MEd Cantab (*Head of Sixth Form*)

Mr D McColl
*Mrs R Pope, BSc Hons Nottingham PGCE
Mrs J O'Dwyer, BSc Hons Durham, PGCE
Mrs S Sagar, MSc Coventry, BSc Hons Birmingham, PGCE

Foreign Languages:
Mrs S Bartlett-Rawlings, BA Hons Open University, PGCE
*Ms M Hurriaga, MEd Cantab, PGCE, LLb Complutense
Mrs C Pennels, BSc Hons Surrey, PGCE
Mrs A Robertson, BA Hons Bristol, PGCE (*Head of Lower School*)

Computing:
*Mrs S Berry, BSc Hons Exeter, PGCE
Mrs S Goldring, BSc Hons Cardiff, MSc UCL, PGCE

Design & Technology:
*Mrs F L Exley, BSc Hons Brighton, PGCE

Geography:
*Mrs S Thorne, BA Hons Leicester, PGCE
Mrs N Jackson, BSc Hons Sheffield, PGCE, Head of Upper School

Economics & Business and Government & Politics:
Mrs K Hurrell, BA Hons, PGCE
*Mrs N Wintle, MA Oxon, PGCE

History:
*Mrs J Boden, MA St Andrews, PGCE, FCTT
Miss S Colman, BA Hons Exeter, PGCE
Mrs R Stringer, BA Hons Warwick, PGCE

Art & Design:
*Ms B Horn BA Hons WSCAD, PGCE
Mr J Kopiel, BA Hons UEL, MA RCA, PGCE

Music:
Mr T Lowe, BMus Hons GSMD, MA, Dip RAM, PGCE
Miss E Pettet, BMus Hons Surrey, PG Cert GSMD, PGCE, Dip ABRSM (*Director of Music and Director of Co-Curricular*)

Drama:
Mrs T Jago, BA Hons Hull, PGCE (*Head of Performing Arts*)

Photography:
*Mr M Huxley, BSc Hons Westminster, PG Dip PGCE

Physical Education:
Mr M Everett, BSc Hons Brighton, PGCE
Miss N Grant, BSc Hons Loughborough, PGCE
Mr S Manning, BA Hons Exeter, PGCE (*Director of Sport*)
Mr J Myers, BSc Hons Chichester, PGCE
Mrs E Pieters, BA Hons Brighton, QTS (*Head of Girls' Sport*)

Psychology:
*Mr D Kokott
Mrs S Williams, BSc Kingston, PGCE

Religious Studies & Philosophy:
*Mr P Cooper, BA Nottingham, PGCE Brighton
Mrs K Wells, BA University of Wales Lampeter, PGCE

Food & Nutrition:
*Mrs R Macintyre, BA Hons East London, PGCE
Mrs C Champion
Mrs S Giblin (*Assistant*)

Careers:
*Miss R Wilshaw, BA Hons Keele, PGCE Bath, MA

Special Needs:
Mrs A Aylwin, RSA Dip SpLD (*Special Needs Coordinator*)
Mrs K Hanlon, BSocSci Hons Keele

Ms S Saward, BA Hons London, PG Dip Dyslexia and Literacy, AMBDA, LTCL, QTS, CELTA, Deputy SENCo

Counsellors:
Mrs J Gumm (*School Counsellor*)

Peripatetic Staff:
Mrs S Dembinska, BA Christchurch, Performance Diploma Trinity (*Piano*)
Mr S Hill (*Guitar*)
Mr G Morrison, GGSM, Dip Adv Studies Performance (*Flute*)
Mrs A Morse–Glover (*Recorder*)
Miss L Nagioff, Dip NCOS (*Violoncello*)
Mr J Park (*Drums*)
Mr C Thompson, BA Hons East Anglia, MTC (*Voice, Piano*)
Miss C Walford, AISTD Dip (*Dance*)
Mr C Watts (*Drama*)

Support Staff:
Mrs C Allison, RGN (*School Nurse*)
Dr R Ashworth, BSc Hons, PhD Brighton (*Senior Science Technician*)
Mr A Cotton (*Estates Manager*)
Mr G Davies (*Finance Officer*)
Mrs M Dennehy (*Catering Manager*)
Mrs A Doman, CIM Chartered Institute of Marketing (*PA to SLT*)
Mrs S Edwards (*Head of Admissions*)
Mrs S Fribbance (*Finance and Admin Manager*)
Mrs J Hyden (*Maintenance*)
Mrs J Jones (*School Secretary*)
Mrs C Kendrick (*PA to Headmaster*)
Mr A Kerr (*Data Manager*)
Mrs L Longstaff (*Examinations Officer*)
Mrs S Machacek (*Laboratory/Art and DT Technician*)
Mrs L Moon (*Accounts Assistant*)
Mr T Stevens, BSc Hons Staffordshire (*Network Manager*)
Mr E Thomas (*Operations Manager*)
Mrs R Tottman (*Admissions & External Relations Manager*)
Mrs G Wiles, BSc Hons Aston (*Director of Marketing*)
Mrs L Wootton (*HR Associate*)

Ewell Castle School

Church Street, Ewell, Surrey KT17 2AW

Tel: 020 8394 3561 (admissions)
          020 8393 1413 (main office)
Fax: 020 8786 8218
email: admissions@ewellcastle.co.uk
website: www.ewellcastle.co.uk
Twitter: @EwellCastleUK
Facebook: @EwellCastleSchool

Ewell Castle is an independent, co-educational day school in Surrey, twenty minutes from London. It was built as a castellated mansion in 1814. It offers a Nursery, Pre-Preparatory School, Preparatory School, Senior School and a Sixth Form.

The gardens and playing fields of the Senior School cover some fifteen acres and were once part of Nonsuch Park. The Senior School is accommodated at The Castle. The Preparatory School occupies two other premises in Ewell village: Chessington Lodge, a Georgian house minutes from The Castle; and Glyn House, the former Rectory to the parish church, opposite the Senior School. The School, which was founded in 1926, is registered as an educational charity and is administered by a Board of Governors, which is in membership of AGBIS (Association of Governing Bodies of Independent Schools). The Principal is a member of The Society of Heads and the Head of the Preparatory School is a member of IAPS (Independent Association of Prep Schools).

The school comprises approximately 550 pupils in total with 350 pupils in the Senior School and 200 pupils in the Preparatory School.

Buildings. The school is located on three sites within the village of Ewell, accommodating The Preparatory School (Chessington Lodge: co-educational 3–7 years; Glyn House: co-educational 7–11 years) and the Senior School (The Castle: co-educational 11–16 years and the Sixth Form co-educational 16–18 years). Academic departments are well resourced and accommodated. A new building on The Castle site (completed August 2011) provides six new classrooms, purpose-built kitchen and dining/assembly area, Sixth Form cafeteria, cloakrooms and office accommodation. Other recent developments include: major refurbishment of the Library (The Castle), new hard play area (Glyn House), the building of a new Nursery building and establishment of new garden area (Chessington Lodge). The new Music Pavilion, completed in Spring 2017, incorporates classrooms, a recording studio, a music technology suite and a recital room.

Vision. The vision of our School is to **Inspire** and **Nurture** our pupils to **Achieve**, within a happy, family friendly atmosphere.

Ethos. Ewell Castle is a happy school with an atmosphere of purposeful, academic work. Care, consideration, honesty, integrity, fairness and tolerance are valued. Self esteem is enhanced and all aspects of personal development are fostered. With an ethos in which each child's achievements are acknowledged, valued and celebrated, students thrive academically as a result of the small class sizes, a varied and stimulating curriculum, an extensive extracurricular programme and strong support systems.

Values. Integrity, Trust, Respect, Responsibility, Determination

Organisation. The Preparatory School is co-educational and accepts pupils from three years. Most pupils transfer to the Senior School, whilst others go to a range of Independent and selective/non-selective schools at 11+. The Sixth Form has been co-educational since September 2013 and the Senior School became fully co-educational in September 2015.

Curriculum. National Curriculum requirements are incorporated into Senior and Preparatory School schemes, although the broad and flexible curriculum extends beyond such criteria. Breadth at KS3 (11–13 years) is replaced at KS4 (14–16 years) by a core of Mathematics, English, Science and Religious Studies, supplemented by a wide ranging option scheme covering the languages, arts, humanities and technologies. There is an increased range of subjects available at AS and A Level in the Sixth Form

Work experience is undertaken by pupils in Year 11. Specialist HE/Careers guidance is available from Year 9 within the Senior School.

After the Sixth Form the majority of pupils proceed to universities and colleges, with most pupils achieving their first choice of institution.

Extracurricular Activities. The principal sports are rugby, football, hockey, netball and cricket. In addition there are numerous pursuits which include: athletics, badminton, basketball, table tennis, skiing, and tennis. There is an extensive music and drama programme and other activities such as The Duke of Edinburgh's Award scheme. Regular language, sports and field trips embarked for America, Austria,

Belgium, France, Germany, Iceland, Ireland, Italy and Spain in recent years.

The school benefits from an active PTA known as the PSFA.

Admissions. Boys and girls are admitted to the Preparatory School at the age of three. There are no entry requirements at this stage. Older children are invited to attend the school for a day's assessment within a class, during which time they may undertake tests in English & Mathematics.

At the Senior School the standard points of entry are at 11+, 13+ and 16+. Subject to availability, there may be places at other levels. Entry requirements include interview, report from previous school, written assessments and a Taster Session. At 13+ and 16+ the assessments may take the form of Common Entrance or GCSE respectively.

Visitors are welcome to the school on scheduled Open Days or by appointment. Individual assessments are held by arrangement. Scholarship assessments are undertaken in January each year.

Scholarships. Scholarships are available for pupils entering the school at 11+, 13+ and 16+. At 11+ awards are made on the basis of competitive examination/assessment in the designated category. In the case of 13+ and 16+ awards are likely to be made on the basis of Common Entrance and GCSE performance respectively. Awards are made for Academic excellence and also in the categories of Art, Design and Technology, Drama, Music, and Sport.

Fees per term (2018–2019). Senior School £5,564, Preparatory School £3,814, Pre-Preparatory School £3,375, Nursery & Reception £2,884.

Preparatory School. *For further information, see Ewell Castle Preparatory School entry in IAPS section.*

Charitable status. Ewell Castle School is a Registered Charity, number 312079. The aim of the charity is to achieve potential and excellence over a broad field: in academic, in sport, in the arts, and in numerous other extracurricular activities and aspects of school life.

Chairman of the Governing Body: Mr D Tucker QPM

Principal: Mr Silas Edmonds, BA Hons, MA, NPQH

Head of Preparatory School & Vice Principal: Ms S Bradshaw, BEd
Acting Deputy Head of Senior School & Vice Principal: Mr S Leigh, BA, PGCE
Acting Director of Studies & Assistant Principal: Ms C Hoddell, BEd
Deputy Head of Preparatory School & Assistant Principal: Mrs S Fowler, BSc, PGCE
Bursar: Ms J Abraham, BSc, FCCA
Marketing, Development & Alumni Manager: Ms C Hernandez, BA, CIM Grad Dip

Heads of Department:
Art & Design & Photography: Ms D Carrick, BA, QTS
Business: Mrs R Rudd, BA,QTS
Computing and Information Technology: Mr M Scott, BEd (*Acting Head*)
Design Technology: Ms D Sarmiento, MA, BA, GTP
Drama: Mr L Bader-Clynes, BA, RADA
Economics: Mrs R Rudd, BA, QTS
English: Ms K Wallace, BA, PGCE
Geography: Mrs R Owen, BSc, QTS
History & Classics: Mr J C W Blencowe, BA, PGCE
Learning Support, SENCo: Mrs C Buckley, BA, PGCE
Mathematics: Mr D Vijapura, BSc, PGCE
Modern Foreign Languages: Miss P Hernandez, Licence LLC, PGCE (*Deputy DSL*)
Music: Mrs V Edwards, MA, BMus, PGCE
Politics: Mrs E Harrison, BA, PGCE
Physical Education: Mr N Turk, BSc, GTP

Science: Mr K Hungsraz, BSc, QTS
PSHEE: Mr K Peto, BA, PGCE
Psychology: Mr J D'Souza, BSc, PGCE
Philosophy, Religious Studies and Ethics: Mrs V
　Ikwuemesi, MA, BEd

Principal's PA: Mrs K El-Dahshan, BA
Registrar: Mrs T Wilkins

Farringtons School

Perry Street, Chislehurst, Kent BR7 6LR

Tel:　　020 8467 0256
email:　fvail@farringtons.kent.sch.uk
website:　www.farringtons.org.uk
Twitter:　@FarringtonsSch
Facebook:　@Farringtons-School

Farringtons School is situated in 25 acres of green belt land in Chislehurst, which provide attractive surroundings while still being within easy reach of London (25 minutes to Charing Cross), the South Coast and Gatwick airport (45 minutes) and Heathrow airport via the M25 (1½ hours).

The School is committed to providing a first-class education for pupils of all ages in a caring community which supports all its members and helps each pupil to achieve his or her full potential both academically and personally. After-school care is available until 6.15 pm.

The curriculum offered is that of the National Curriculum, with a wide range of GCSE and A Level subjects available. Nearly 100% of Sixth Form leavers customarily go on to degree courses at Universities or Higher Education Colleges. Academic standards are high from a comprehensive intake of pupils and in 2018 a 97% pass rate was achieved at A Level.

The excellent facilities include a Technology building, a large Sports Hall with Dance Studio and Fitness Suite, splendidly-equipped Science and Modern Language departments, a well-stocked library, Careers Room, indoor heated swimming pool and extensive playing fields, as well as a School Chapel, where the School regularly comes together.

The main sports are netball, tennis, football, rugby, swimming and athletics, but badminton, volleyball and table tennis are also undertaken and other extracurricular activities available include The Duke of Edinburgh's Award scheme, various choirs and instrumental ensembles, gymnastics, dance, ballet, drama club, fencing, etc.

To obtain a prospectus and further information or to arrange a visit, contact the Registrar.

Fees per term (2018–2019). Day: £3,250 (Pre-Reception full time), £4,010 (Junior), £4,870 (Senior); Weekly Boarding £9,950, Full Boarding £10,560.

Charitable status. Farringtons School is part of the Methodist Independent Schools Trust, a Registered Charity, number 1142794. It exists solely to provide a high-quality, caring education.

Governing Body:
Chairman: Mr A Harris
Vice-Chairman: Mrs R L Howard

Members:

Ms K Davies	Mr S Richardson
Miss M Faulkner	Mr W Skinner
Mr R Hinton	Dr A Squires
Mrs J King	Mr M Vinales
Mr A Raby	

Bursar and Clerk to the Governors: Mrs Sally-Anne
　Eldridge

Headmistress: Mrs Dorothy Nancekievill, MA, BMus,
　PGCE, HonARAM

Deputy Head: Mr N Young
Head of Junior School: Mr J Charlton
Assistant Head Senior School: Mrs R Frances
Assistant Head Senior School: Mr L Garwood
Head of Sixth Form: Mrs V Jackson
Chaplain: Reverend Dr J Quarmby
Registrar: Mrs B Thompson (*Day*), Mrs F Vail (*Boarding*)

* *Head of Department*

English:	*Humanities*:
*Miss S Bliss	Mr D Barrett
*Mrs L Bowdery	Mr C Catling
Mr B Coultard	*Mr G Curran
Mrs S DiStefano	Mr A Essex
Mrs S Freeston	Mr K Jones
Ms L Hirsh	Mrs L Mortimer
Miss D Humphrey	Ms N Robertson
Mrs M Kershaw	
Mr S Message	*Business, Finance &*
Mrs K O'Neil	*Technology*:
Mrs D Scott	Mrs R Ashworth
	Mr E Case
Mathematics:	Mr J Gardner
Ms J Bagshaw	*Miss K Ootim
Mr N Chandler	Mr S Owen
*Mr F Gray	Mrs L Williamson
Mrs I Haider	
*Mrs Z Hanson	*Creative Arts*:
Mr T Kyle	Mrs G Allen
Revd Dr J Quarmby	*Miss R Azulay
Mr N Varley	Miss N Lubrani
	Mr R Matthews
Science:	Miss K Speakman-Brown
Mrs J Daws	Mrs S Watson
*Mrs P Garton	
Dr N Haughey	*Music*:
Mr I Kimuli	*Mr N Rayner
Mrs V Owen	Mrs P White
Miss A Sobota	
Mrs L Sriram	*Learning Support*:
Dr J Taylor	Ms C Curtis
	Ms K Miles
Modern Languages:	*Mrs D Rabot
*Mlle I Mosqueron	Mrs J Pyle
Mrs R Frances	Mrs A Vinales
Mr J Hernando	
Mrs M Kershaw	*Sport*:
Mrs V Millett	Mr A Doherty
Mrs N Pasquie-Taylor	*Mr C Doyle
Mrs H Razii-Rydall	Miss C Hemmings
Mr P Scowen	Mrs G Ody
Ms V Jackson	Mrs J Sherwood
Ms S Wolage	Mr B Suverkrop
	Miss E Whitehead
Junior School:	
Ms F Alexander	Ms J Howard
Ms S Austin	Ms S Johnson
Mrs G Bastos	Ms H Kearns
Mrs L Benjamin	Mrs L Long
Mrs P Brookman	Miss F Ody
Mrs S Carter	Mrs N Pasquie-Taylor
Miss S Cox	Miss K Randall
Mrs C Crouser	Mrs H Reynolds
Mrs J Cryan	Mrs H Roberts
Mrs T Devaux	Mr T Ruffle
Mrs V Fox	Miss S Seager
Ms C Frisby	Mr J Shimmin
Mrs A Gibson	Ms C Steel
Mrs H Hill	Ms K Streeter

Mr B Suverkrop
Mrs A Vinales
Mrs S Walker

Ms S Watts
Miss L Vinales

Boarding Staff:
Mrs S Arnold
Mrs S Collier
Mrs C Bowstead
Miss V Lang

Miss A Rutherford
Miss I Smith
Mr B Suverkrop

Fulneck School

Pudsey, Leeds, West Yorkshire LS28 8DS

Tel: 0113 257 0235
Fax: 0113 255 7316
email: enquiries@fulneckschool.co.uk
website: www.fulneckschool.co.uk
Twitter: @FulneckSchool
Facebook: @FulneckSchool

Fulneck School was established on 1 September 1994 by the merger of Fulneck Boys' School and Fulneck Girls' School, both originally founded in 1753, by the Moravian Church (a very early Protestant Church which has two schools in England and many more abroad) as part of a settlement on the slopes of a valley within the Green Belt on the outskirts of Pudsey. Leeds and Bradford are both nearby and the School has easy access to the motorway network and airports.

The School is a registered charity and the Provincial Board of the Moravian Church is the Trustee of the School. The Governing Body provides a range of professional expertise and is in membership of AGBIS (Association of Governing Bodies of Independent Schools). The Principal is a member of The Society of Heads and the Head of the Junior School is a member of IAPS (Independent Association of Prep Schools).

Originally founded for the education of the sons and daughters of ministers and missionaries, the school nowadays provides an education for approximately 350 pupils from all backgrounds. Most of the pupils live in West Yorkshire and travel daily to School, but approximately 75 of them are boarders including some who board weekly and return home from Friday evening to Monday morning.

The School is co-educational and provides a modern, academic curriculum based on Christian principles. Fulneck Sixth Form offers 20 A Level subjects and the school has an outstanding record of success in public examinations. Class sizes rarely exceed 20 and most teaching groups are smaller; in the Sixth Form groups seldom exceed 10.

Buildings. The main buildings of the School are part of the original settlement, yet other buildings on the campus have been added over the years (most recently these include a new Junior Library with ICT facilities, a new self-contained Sixth Form Centre, performing arts building and a totally refurbished teaching block). The boys' boarding accommodation has been extended and improved. Extensive playing fields and tennis courts are located on the site, which adjoins Fulneck Golf Club, and looks over to the Domesday village of Tong.

Pastoral Care. The staff work closely and effectively together, sharing in the duties and recreational needs of the School. The School Nurse, who is medically qualified, and other house staff take care of the boarders in conjunction with the resident teaching staff and the Principal, who also lives on the campus. Weekly and flexi boarding are offered in addition to full boarding.

Sport. Netball, Hockey, Football, Rugby, Cricket, Athletics and Tennis are the main games of the School, but Basketball, Badminton, Cross-Country Running, Golf, Rounders, Swimming, Table Tennis and Martial Arts are all available to the pupils as part of a rapidly expanding programme of outdoor pursuits. Teams of various ages, in most sports, have full fixture lists with neighbouring schools. Dance classes are also run.

Activities. Music education is very strong with choirs and bands in the junior and senior school, and other orchestral groups. The Choirs perform often to the public. Drama is actively pursued with pupils involved in both lessons and Theatre Workshop productions.

There are a number of clubs and societies such as Art, Computer, Cooking, Golf, Orienteering, Hockey, Netball, Table Tennis, Forensic Club, Theatre Workshop, Science, Gardening, Eco Friends, Dance and Martial Arts.

The Duke of Edinburgh's Award scheme is available to pupils over the age of 14, together with a wide range of trips and residential visits, walking and skiing. The school has regularly participated in World Challenge expeditions.

Careers. The Head of Careers is on hand to advise, and the Library stocks most of the available literature on the whole range of courses and careers. All pupils complete a period of work experience at the end of Year 10.

Foundation Stage/Key Stage 1. This is housed within the main building and caters for children from the ages of 3 to 7.

Junior School (Key Stage 2). The Junior School is self-contained and caters for pupils from the ages of 7–11. Once a pupil is admitted he or she will usually progress into the Senior School, after assessment at age 11. The Junior School has access to many of its own specialist facilities for Science, Art, Technology, Music, IT and Library, as well as to the Senior School sports facilities.

Learning Support Unit. Specialist staff provide help on an individual or small group basis to children with dyslexia or other learning differences. The Unit is CReSTeD approved and has repeatedly confirmed its 'DU' status, the highest grade awarded to mainstream schools.

Parents and Friends Association. There is a flourishing organization which acts as a fundraising body, and also supports the School in a variety of other ways. This is a living example of the belief that education is a partnership between home and school.

Admission. Admission to the school is welcomed at any age depending on the availability of places, although the main intake is at the ages of 3, 7 and 11. Direct entry to the Sixth Form is also possible. Means-tested academic bursaries and other scholarships are available.

Fees per term (2018–2019). Junior School Day: Nursery (mornings only) £1,520; Foundation Stage (full day) £2,465; Years 1 & 2 £2,675; Years 3–6 £3,315; Weekly Boarding: £6,150; Full Boarding £6,680; Flexi Boarding £40 per night. Senior School: Day £4,375; Weekly Boarding £7,675; Full Boarding £8,485; Flexi Boarding £40 per night.

Fulneck Former Pupils' Association. Mr D Robbins, Fulneck School, Pudsey, West Yorkshire LS28 8DS.

Charitable status. Fulneck School is a Registered Charity, number 251211. It exists to provide a traditional, Christian education for boys and girls between the ages of 3 and 18.

The Governing Body:
Mrs L Jordan (*Chair*)
C J Stern (*Vice-Chairman*)
Revd M Newman
D Scott
Mrs A Roberts

Mrs L Johnson
Mr C Smith
Mr B El-Haddadeh

Principal: **Mr Paul Taylor**

Vice-Principal, Head of Senior School: Mrs Gemma Carver

Vice-Principal, Head of Junior School: Mr Chris Bouckley, BEd

Bursar: Mrs K Thompson

Hampshire Collegiate School
United Learning

Embley Park, Romsey, Hampshire SO51 6ZE

Tel:	01794 512206 (Senior School)
	01794 515737 (Prep School)
Fax:	01794 518737
email:	info@hampshirecs.org.uk
website:	www.hampshirecs.org.uk
Twitter:	@hampshirecs
Facebook:	@hampshireschool

Hampshire Collegiate School is a welcoming community. Its core purpose is that each child is the best that they can be, equipping children with the competence to succeed academically, the confidence to be their own character and instil in them a compassion for the world. The school is nestled in 130 acres of private parkland, which includes woodlands, playing fields, tennis courts, astroturf pitches, a swimming pool and a golf course. It also runs a comprehensive sailing programme with its own boats moored at Lymington.

Constitution. Over 450 pupils, with approximately 300 in the Senior School and Sixth Form and 160 in the Prep School.

Boarding. Flexi, weekly and full-time boarding is available from 11+. The Heads of Boarding reside in the Boarding House. The house family includes dedicated nurses and matrons who specialise in the welfare and medical needs of all boarders.

Curriculum.

Prep School: A broad curriculum is offered, including French, Music, Information Technology, Design Technology and Physical Education taught by specialists and throughout the school the children take part in Learning Outside the Classroom (LOC).

Senior School: The GCSE curriculum offers a choice of many subjects (including separate subject sciences).

Sixth Form: More than 20 A Level subjects are available and a Pre-A Level for international students whose first language is not English. All students are expected to take an Extended Project Qualification.

Further details can be found at www.hampshirecs.org.uk

Co-curricular and enrichment. The school has an extensive co-curricular programme which includes rugby, football, cricket, hockey, golf, sailing, netball, cross country, basketball, swimming, tennis, athletics and golf. The school has a thriving Drama, Art and Musical life. All Senior School pupils are encouraged to undertake The Duke of Edinburgh's Award scheme.

Higher Education & Careers. The school runs a regular series of industry career evenings, its own Higher Education Conference and International University Conference. Year 12 students benefit from an MBA Experience and all Sixth Form students attend termly Nightingale Lectures (black-tie events with eminent guest speakers).

Admission procedures.

Nursery: No formal assessment

Prep School: Entry at any age from 4 to 11. Informal assessment.

Senior School: Entrance assessments, interview and a suitable reference from the head teacher of the pupil's current school.

Sixth Form: Offers made usually on the following conditions: A minimum of 5 GCSE grades at A*–C (9 to 5); GCSE grade B (6) or above in subjects to be studied at A Level; and a suitable reference from the head teacher of the pupil's current school.

Scholarships. Scholarships are available at 11+, 13+ and 16+ and are awarded for: Academic, Art, Music, Design Technology, Drama and Sport.

Fees per term 2018–2019. Nursery: £2,833 (full time). Prep School £3,366–£3,864; Senior School: £5,253 (day), £8,925 (UK & EU boarding), £9,812 (Non-EU Boarding). Please refer to www.hampshirecs.org.uk/admissions/fees for further information.

Local Governing Body:
Professor R Thomas (*Chairman*)
Mr C M Canning
Mr R Butler
Mr S Neilson
Mrs K Smith
Mrs P Smithson

Headmaster: **Mr Cliff Canning**, BA Hons, BD Hons, HDipEd, NUI

Deputy Head: Mr Jose Picardo, MA, PGCE
Bursar: Major Richard Amey, PG Dip, MCGI, FCMI
Head of Prep School: Mrs Sarah Phillips, BSc, QTS
Assistant Head (Academic): Mr Steve Bowyer, MA, PGCE
Assistant Head (Pastoral): Mrs Leah Goodey, BA, PGCE
Assistant Head (Co-Curriculum): Mrs Elaine Morgan, BA, PGCE
Director of Marketing, Admissions & Communications: Mrs Charlotte Welland, BA

Highclare School

10 Sutton Road, Erdington, Birmingham B23 6QL

Tel:	0121 373 7400
Fax:	0121 373 7445
email:	enquiries@highclareschool.co.uk
website:	www.highclareschool.co.uk

Founded 1932.

Age Range. 2–18 years Co-educational.

Number of Pupils. 560.

Fees per term (2018–2019). £2,795–£4,215.

Location. The School is situated on three sites on the main road (A5127) between Four Oaks, Sutton Coldfield and Birmingham. The Senior Department and Sixth Form, is on direct train and bus routes from Birmingham City Centre, Tamworth, Lichfield and Walsall as well as being serviced by our own buses. There are two Primary Schools, known as Highclare Woodfield and Highclare St Paul's. Wrap-around care operates from 7.30 am until 6.00 pm for the parents who require it. Holiday cover is available for Pre-School only. The ethos of the school lies in the encouragement of individual excellence for each pupil, outstanding pastoral care and a belief in the education of the 'whole person'.

Organisation. Four departments:

Nursery and Preparatory Department (age 2 to 7 years, girls and boys) caters for children from 2 years and, although an independent unit, it has the support of facilities and resources of the Preparatory Department. MFL is taught from Pre-School 2.

Junior Departments (age 7+ to 11 years, two co-educational departments). The Junior Departments, with classes of up to a maximum of 22 pupils, follow National Curriculum guidelines. Pupils also have the benefit of specialist tuition in MFL, PE/Games and Music. Other foundation subjects are taught by subject and by class teachers. Entry by School's own assessment procedure.

Senior Department (age 11 to 16, co-educational). The full curriculum is covered at KS3. At GCSE all students study English Language and English Literature, Mathematics, Combined Science or separate sciences, and a modern foreign language, (French, German or Spanish) with a wide choice of options. In addition pupils also study PSHCE. Physical Education, Music and Performing Arts also form important parts of the curriculum. Through a wide programme of enrichment activities every child has the opportunity to enjoy activities beyond the academic. Entry by School's own assessment procedure.

Sixth Form (age 16+). The Sixth Form is co-educational and accepts external candidates as well as pupils transferring from Highclare Senior School. A wide range of A Level subjects is available for study alongside the extended project qualification, with excellent pastoral, higher education and careers guidance available. The timetable is structured to meet the individual requirements of each student.

All parts of the School participate in extensive lunchtime and after-school activities.

The School is multi-denominational. Further information may be obtained from the School or the website and prospective parents are always welcome to visit. Open mornings are held throughout the year including school-in-action days on all three sites.

Charitable status. Highclare School is a Registered Charity, number 528940.

Chair of Governors: Mrs L Flowith

School Leadership Team:

Headmaster: Dr R Luker, PhD Sheffield Hallam, MA, BA Hons, PGCE Madeley

Head of Senior School: Mrs A Moore, BA Hons UCE, PGCE Birmingham

Head of Junior Schools: Mrs P Bennett, BA Hons Liverpool, PGCE Liverpool

Business Manager: Mrs M P A McGoldrick, MSc Manchester, BA Hons Manchester, MAAT, AInstAM Dip

Deputy Head of Senior School: Mrs A Healey, BSc Hons Durham, PGCE Durham

Senior School Staff:

Head of Senior School: Mrs A Moore, BA Hons UCE, PGCE Birmingham

Heads of Departments:
Art: Mrs V Hughes, BA Hons Birmingham, PGCE Birmingham
Business Studies: Mrs A Green, BSc Econ Aberystwyth, PGCE Warwick
Design & Technology: Mrs H Good, BEd Hons Worcester
Drama: Mrs M Sharman-Everton, BA Hons Birmingham QTS
English: Mrs K J Dawson, BA Hons Exeter, PGCE Oxford
Geography: Mrs S Cassell, BA Hons Oxford, PGCE Keele
History: Miss M Watson, BA Hons Durham, MA Warwick, PGCE Glos
Home Economics: Mrs A Cobbold, BEd Bath
Information Technology/Computing: Mr L Sneary, BSc Hons Brunel, PGCE Brunel
Law: Mrs N Stead, LLB Cardiff

Mathematics: Mr S Parkinson, BSc Hons Southampton, PGCE Birmingham
Modern Languages: Mrs J Lightfoot, BA Hons Newcastle, PGCE Warwick
Music: Miss A Cassells, BMus Hons Cardiff, PGCE Birmingham
Psychology: Mrs A Thorpe, BSc Hons Aston, PGCE Wolverhampton
Physical Education: Mrs A de Sousa-Bartlett, BEd Hons St Mary's College
Religious Studies: Mrs J Palmer, BSc Hons Open, PGCE Birmingham
Science: Mrs S Dudley, BSc Hons Leics, PGCE Bath
Sociology: Dr D Edwards, BA Hons Liverpool, PGCE Leics, MA, PhD Manchester

Posts of Additional Responsibility (*Senior*):

Assistant Head of Senior School: Mrs S Cassell, BA Hons Oxford, PGCE Keele
KS5 Coordinator/Head of Sixth Form: Mr S Parkinson, BSc Hons Southampton, PGCE Birmingham
KS4 Coordinator/Gifted & Talented Coordinator: Mrs A de Sousa-Bartlett, BEd Hons St Mary's College
KS3 Coordinator/Gifted & Talented Coordinator: Mrs H Good, BEd Hons Worcester
Learning Support – KS3, 4, & 5: Mrs K Johnson, BEd Hons Leeds

Junior Schools Staff:

Head of Junior Schools: Mrs P Bennett, BA Hons Liverpool, PGCE Liverpool
Deputy Head of Junior Schools: Mrs J Griffiths, BA Hons, QTS York, MA Wolverhampton

Highclare St Paul's:
Assistant Head and KS2 Coordinator: Mr C Gordon, BSc Hons Wales, PGCE Newman
KS1 Coordinator: Mrs J Ford, BA Hons Leicester
EYFS Coordinator: Mrs J Harris, MA, PSC, BA Hons ECS Birmingham EYPS

Highclare Woodfield:
Assistant Head and KS2 Coordinator: Mr P Greenfield, PGCE Cumbria, BSc Hons Manchester
KS1 Coordinator: Mrs K S Tidman, BA Hons UCE, PGCE
EYFS Coordinator: Mrs L Bayliss, BA Hons Liverpool, MARCA, PGCE Birmingham QTS

Support Staff:
Business Manager: Mrs M P A McGoldrick, MSc Manchester, BA Hons Manchester, MAAT, AInstAM Dip
Marketing Coordinator: Mrs D Pulisiciano
Admissions Registrar: Mrs L Madden
Facilities Manager: Mr D Underwood
ICT Systems Manager: Mrs S Robinson

Hill House School

Fifth/Sixth Avenue, Auckley, Near Robin Hood Airport, Doncaster, South Yorkshire DN9 3GG

Tel: 01302 776300
Fax: 01302 776334
email: info@hillhouse.doncaster.sch.uk
website: www.hillhouse.doncaster.sch.uk
Twitter: @HillHouseSchool

Hill House was founded in 1912 and now occupies the site of the former RAF Officers' Quarters of RAF Finningley. The school provides a seamless, fully co-educational day education from age 3 to 18, and aims to provide a top-class holistic education where extra-curricular success and personal development stand alongside academic excellence. Hill House was named Independent School of the Year 2012–13.

Number of Students. There are 700 pupils, with an equal number of boys and girls.

Education. Children enter the School at 3 years of age via Nursery where structured play and learning are the order of the day. As children progress through the School there is a gradual change to subject based teaching in specialist rooms, in preparation for GCSEs at 16 and A Levels at 18. Upon leaving the Junior School children enter a full house system for pastoral care. All main school subjects are offered, including individual Sciences, French, Spanish and Latin.

Facilities. The whole school is based in a historic building with new, purposely renovated classrooms. The site includes a large hall, dining room and theatre. In 2011 Hill House Sixth Form was launched, housed in its own new Sixth Form Centre, including classrooms, coffee shop and large common room. A new Music School contains practice rooms, a recording studio and a performing studio. 2013 saw the opening of the school's new sports grounds at Blaxton. In 2015, the blue Astroturf Paver Hockey Pitch was opened, and in 2017 a new Dining Hall was created.

Extra-Curricular Activities. Music, Drama, Art and Sport play an important part in the life of the School. Throughout the year over 100 academic, recreational, musical and sporting activities per week are also offered in extra-curricular time. The major sports undertaken include rugby, netball, hockey, cricket, and tennis. There is a competitive fixture list including a number of overseas tours. There are two orchestras and five choirs within the school, who enjoy the newly-built Music School. Drama productions and concerts are undertaken on a regular basis. Residential trips and sports tours are undertaken at most age levels.

The School Day. School opens at 8.00 am, with lessons from 9.00 am to 4.00 pm. Activities run from 4.00 pm, and a before and after school club operates from 7.30 am and until 6.00 pm. The school operates a five-day week, with a full games afternoon for all ages above 7. There are some activities and fixtures at weekends. Sixth Formers also have an Internship Afternoon, where they spend time at local businesses, hospitals etc.

Fees per term (2018–2019). £2,900–£4,400 according to age. Fees include lunch and most extras.

Scholarships. Scholarships are available at 11+ for Academic, Sport, Art, Music and Performing Arts, and at 16+ for Academic and Leadership.

Charitable status. Hill House School Limited is a Registered Charity, number 529420.

Governors:
Mrs V Cusworth (*Chair*)
Dr A Cooper

S Colbear	Dr M Fraser
R De Mulder	Mrs J Jameson
N Ebdon	R Leggott
Dr D Eggitt	J Sprenger
Mrs J Fearns	M Wilson-MacCormack

Headmaster: **David Holland**, MA Cantab

Deputy Head: Mrs Belinda McCrea, MA Cantab
Assistant Head: Mrs Caroline Rogerson, BSc Hons
Head of Junior School: Mr Jonathan Hall, BEd Hons
Senior Master: Mr Simon Hopkinson, BA Hons
Deputy Head of Junior School: Mrs Charlotte Leach, BA Ed Hons
Bursar and Clerk to the Governors: Mrs Karen Kidney, ACMA Hons

Heads of Departments:
Mr Emilio Bayarri-Torres, BEd Hons (*Head of Modern Languages*)
Mr Mark Brannan, BSc Hons (*Head of Science*)
Mr Mark Cadman, BA Hons (*Director of Music*)
Mr Richard Dorman, BA Hons (*Head of History*)
Mr Graham Green, MA (*Head of Geography*)
Dr Kurt Johnson, PhD (*Head of English*)
Mrs Wendy Parkhurst, BA, MA (*Head of Art*)
Mr James Ross, BSc Hons (*Director of Hockey*)
Mrs Mahjabeen Thomas, BSc Hons (*Head of Mathematics*)
Mr Martin Webdale, BSc Hons (*Director of Rugby*)

Housemistress (*Field House*): Mrs Mahjabeen Thomas, BSc
Housemaster (*Master House*): Mr Peter Shipston, BA, MA
Housemaster (*New House*): Mr Christopher Barnett, BEng Hons
Housemaster (*School House*): Mrs Christine Havard, BA Hons

Kingsley School
Methodist Independent Schools Trust

Northdown Road, Bideford, Devon EX39 3LY

Tel:	01237 426200
Fax:	01237 425981
email:	admissions@kingsleyschoolbideford.co.uk
website:	www.kingsleyschoolbideford.co.uk
Twitter:	@KSBideford
Facebook:	@KingsleySchoolBideford

Kingsley School Bideford, a single campus Co-educational Boarding and Day school for pupils aged 0 to 18, is committed to discovering, nurturing and celebrating the talents and achievements of each and every one of its pupils. This commitment makes it the ideal school for families, from the UK and overseas, who believe that every child is an individual, worthy of individual attention and encouragement.

As a relatively small school of around 420 boys and girls from Nursery to Sixth Form, Kingsley's atmosphere is like that of a large family where everybody knows each other well. The school's philosophy encourages personal qualities such as courage, generosity, honesty, imagination, tolerance and kindness. In addition, we develop the students' wider interests and skills in sport, music, art, and drama. Overall, a Kingsley education develops the individual character and talents of each and every student both inside and outside the classroom.

Location. Kingsley School is situated in the beautiful North Devon market town of Bideford, a historic port beside the estuary of the River Torridge. The spectacular scenery of the North Devon coast and beautiful beaches are on our doorstep and there is easy access to the National Parks of Exmoor and Dartmoor. The North Devon link road, which passes close to Bideford, provides a direct route to the M5 motorway.

Organisation. Kingsley School is entirely co-educational and comprises a Senior School with approximately 200 pupils, aged 11 to 18 years and a Prep School with approximately 130 pupils aged 2½ to 11 years, as well as 50 in our Nursery which offers wrap-around care for children from 8 weeks to 3 years old. The Learning Development Centre, with a nationwide reputation for outstanding dyslexia provision, serves around 25% of the school's pupils.

Site and Buildings. Situated on a beautiful 25-acre site, the School has two Boarding Houses for boys and one for girls, all of which have immediate access to extensive playing fields, an all-weather hockey pitch, netball and tennis courts.

In recent years an ambitious programme of building has led to the provision of first-class facilities for sport, ICT, drama, gymnastics, art and science. The Library provides an excellent environment for study, research and career guidance.

Curriculum. Senior School pupils study a core of subjects, including English, Mathematics, Biology, Chemistry, Physics, Modern Languages and Religious Studies. Subjects such as Geography, History, Art, ICT, Food & Nutrition, Design & Technology, Drama, Music, Sport and PSE complete the programme of study for Years 7–9.

For GCSE, in addition to the core subjects, other courses include Design & Technology, Food & Nutrition, Computer Science, Physical Education, Art, Engineering, Statistics, Drama, Geography, History and Music.

In the Sixth Form, there is a wide choice of AS, A Level and vocational subjects including English Literature, Mathematics, Biology, Chemistry, Economics, Physics, Geography, History, Art, Modern Foreign Languages, Hospitality, Psychology, Business Studies, Performance Arts, Photography, Sport and Music. Tuition in English for speakers of other languages is also available.

Sport and Physical Education. All pupils, girls and boys, are encouraged to participate in a large variety of sports including rugby, hockey, netball, cross-country, handball, cricket, gymnastics, badminton, basketball, football, rounders, tennis, judo, swimming and health-related fitness. The Judo Academy has a unique link with the elite Team Bath, and the School's gymnasts compete at a local, regional and national level. Kingsley School is also home to the Devon Handball Squad – recently the girls' handball team came second in the Handball Nationals. A number of our students are on the England and GB squad path for handball.

Clubs and Activities. There is an extensive range extra-curricular activities which are organised and supervised by staff. Among the most popular is The Duke of Edinburgh's Award scheme, choir, orchestra, judo, computing, art, music, climbing and surfing. Numerous expeditions and field trips, both in the UK and abroad, are organised each year. Musicals, plays and concerts are regularly presented in the school's purpose-designed theatre.

Careers. From Year 9 onwards, pupils are offered a planned programme of careers education and guidance as part of the tutorial programme. This is complemented by presentations from visiting professionals, visits to careers events and close contact with Careers Advisers from Connexions Cornwall and Devon. All pupils have access to the latest careers information in the School Library.

Religion and Pastoral Care. In common with every Methodist Group School, Kingsley has a Christian ethos and welcomes children of all religious denominations, as well as those without religious affiliation. In addition to their Year Heads, all pupils have a personal Tutor who is responsible for monitoring their academic progress and personal wellbeing. For Boarders, care is also the responsibility of the Housemaster or Housemistress.

Admission. Boys and girls are admitted to the Nursery from the age of 3 months. Entry to the Prep and Senior Schools is by interview and taster day. Assessment for academic scholarships is made through written tests in Mathematics, English and Science, as well as a verbal reasoning test. For pupils with recognised learning difficulties entry is by interview together with an up-to-date educational psychologist's report. 13+ admission is through our own Entrance Examination or Scholarship Examination. For older pupils, an interview together with a report from their present school is required.

Prospectus. The Kingsley School prospectus is available from the Registrar, Mrs Louise Wivell, email: admissions@ kingsleyschoolbideford.co.uk, tel: 01237 426200 or online via the school's website: www.kingsleyschoolbideford.co.uk. Visitors are most welcome to tour the School by appointment.

Scholarships. Entrance Scholarships are offered annually for pupils joining Year 7 and Year 9 on the basis of the results of entrance tests held in the preceding January. Awards are also available where candidates show outstanding ability in Music, Art, Drama, and Sport. Sixth Form Academic Scholarships are awarded on the basis of GCSE performance.

Fees per term (2018–2019). Prep School: Day (including lunch): £1,980 (Reception), £2,080 (Years 1 and 2), £2,590 (Years 3 and 4), £3,345 (Years 5 and 6); Boarding (from Year 4): £5,580 (weekly), £7,385 (full). Senior School: Day (including lunch) £4,220–£4,460 Boarding: £8,945 (full), £6,995 (weekly).

Charitable status. Kingsley School, Bideford is part of the Methodist Independent Schools Trust, which is a Registered Charity, number 1142794.

Governors:
Chairman: Mr David Pinney

Dr Mike Cracknell	Mr John Tomalin
Mrs Sue Fishleigh	Mrs Jane Woodhams
Mrs Jane Hellier	Mr Ian Huggett
Mr Richard Holwill	Mt Patrick Hamilton
Mr Andrew Laugharne	Ms Jamie Turner
Mr Michael Portman	

Ex officio:
Mr Peter Rigby, Senior Executive Officer and Director of Finance, Methodist Independent Schools Trust
The Revd Canon Graham Thompson, Chairman of Plymouth and Exeter District of the Methodist Church

Head: **Mr Pete Last**, BA Hons Cantab, Ad Dip Ed London, MEd Buckingham

Head of Prep School: Mr Andrew Trythall, BA

Deputy Head & Director of Studies: Dr Susan Ley, BSc, PhD

Deputy Head and Head of Pastoral Care: Mr Jon Dickinson

Senior School Teaching Staff:
* *Head of Department/Subject*

Mr Chris Beechey, BA, MA, ACIEA (*Head of History, Religious Studies*)
Mrs Michele Borsten, BA, MA (*Head of Drama, English*)
Miss Gemma Braunton (*PE & Games, Gymnastics Coach*)
Mr Simon Cannon, MA (*Chemistry*)
Mr Matt Child, MEng (*Head of 6th Form, Head of Engineering*)
Mr Leigh Crossman, BA (*Head of Music, Drama, Theatre Technician*)
Mr Jon Dickinson, BA (*Deputy Head, Head of Art & Photography, Applied Art & Design, Head of Upper School*)
Miss Rosalyn Dyer, BSc (*Mathematics, ICT*)
Miss Sarah Gosai, BA (*Food Science*)
Mrs Christine Hamilton, MA (*Head of Maths*)
Mr Ian Holleran, BSc (*Head of Science, Physics*)
Mrs Sarah Huxtable, BSc (*Science*)
Ms Stephanie Lofthouse, BSc (*Psychology, Science*)
Miss Kathryn Makepeace, BA (*Head of English*)
Mrs Natalie Marquet-Georgiou, MA, BA (*English*)
Mr Simon Mathers, BSc (*Head of Boys' PE & Games, Science*)

Miss Sarah Parsons, BSc (*Mathematics, Careers Coordinator, Head of Lower School*)
Ms Diana Percy, BA, MEd (*Head of EAL*)
Mr Neil Phillips (*Physics*)
Mrs Hilary Roome, BEd Cambridge (*Technical Sport*)
Mrs Barbara Sochon, BEd, Adv Dip SEN (*Dyslexia Centre, EAL*)
Mrs Linda Stella, BA (*Geography, Outdoor Ed, DoE, Head of Boarding*)
Miss Kat Timms, BA (*Chaplain, Art & Photography, PE, Applied Art & Design*)
Mrs Sandrine Toubin-Whale, DEUG Licence, BA (*Head of French, EAL, Houseparent Belvoir*)
Mr Simon Ward (*PE & Games, Judo Coach*)
Mr Steve Whaley, BSc (*Head of Geography*)
Miss Caroline Williams, BA (*Head of Spanish, EAL*)
Mrs Louise Wivell, BA (*Head of Business Studies*)

Prep School Teaching Staff:
Mr Andrew Trythall, BA (*Head of Prep School*)
Miss Gemma Braunton (*PE and Games*)
Dr Jennie Cousins, BA, MA, PhD (*MFL*)
Miss Emma Ford, BA (*Class Teacher*)
Miss Sarah Gosai, BA (*Food Technology*)
Mr Simon Mathers, BSc (*PE and Games*)
Mrs Melanie Smithson, BEd (*Class Teacher*)
Mrs Linda Stella, BA (*Geography*)
Mrs Elaine Thorne, BA (*Class Teacher*)
Mr Simon Ward (*PE and Games*)
Mrs Emma Wilson, BA Ed (*Class Teacher*)
Mr Paul Wilson, BSc (*Class Teacher, Forest Schools*)
Miss Rachel Wilson, BA (*Class Teacher*)

Pre-School Staff:
Mrs Elaine Henry, Montessori Cert Teaching
Mrs Kim Curtis BTEC Nat Diploma
Mrs Mary Lock, Montessori Cert Teaching
Miss Catherine Smith, NVQ, Children's Nursing, Level C
Miss Alison Sunman, Foundation Degree Early Childhoood Studies
Miss Sian Wade, BTEC Level 3 Childcare & Learning Development

Nursery Staff:
Miss Harriet Dare, Nat Dip Children's Care Learning & Development Level 3 (*Acting Nursery Manager*)
Miss Chloe Elliott, Nat Dip Children's Care Learning & Development Level 3 (*Deputy Nursery Manager*)
Miss Clare Heard, Level 3 BTEC Nat Dip Children's Care Learning and Development (*Deputy Nursery Manager*)
Miss Sophie Baglow, BA Early Childhood Studies Level 6
Miss Loren Braund, BA Early Childhood Studies Level 6
Miss Emma Cunneen, CACHE Dip Children and Young People's Workforce (*Level 3*)
Miss Eilish Hodgson, Nat Dip Children's Care Learning & Development Level 3
Miss Samantha Loates, BTEC Nat Cert Children's Care Learning and Development Level 3
Miss Eloise McPake, BTEC Childcare Learning & Development Level 3
Miss Chelsea Rockey (*Trainee Nursery Nurse*)
Mrs Naomi Russell, NVQ Level 3 Children's Care Learning & Development
Miss Saskia Scott, BTEC Nat Dip Children's Care Learning & Development

Head of Marketing: Mrs Lucy Goaman, BA, MA, MCIM
Finance Director: Mr Stephen O'Brien
Admissions: Lou Wivell
ICT Technician: Mr Jon Hector
Exams Officer & Data Systems/Web Manager: Mrs Fo Edmonds, BA
Head's PA: Ms Sandie Hall
Logistics Administrator: Mrs Ann Neale

Prep Secretary: Mrs Diane Smart
Student Support Services & Stationery Manager: Mrs Wendy Flint
Food Technology Technician: Mrs Katharine Stone
Senior Science Laboratory Technician: Mrs Philippa Veillet
Matron: Mrs Judith Barnes

Lichfield Cathedral School

The Palace, The Close, Lichfield, Staffordshire WS13 7LH

Tel:	01543 306170
Fax:	01543 306176
email:	thepalace@lichfieldcathedralschool.com
website:	www.lichfieldcathedralschool.com

Age Range. 3–18.

Number of Pupils. 470 including 39 Cathedral choristers.

Fees per term (2018–2019). Tuition: £1,765–£4,605; Instrumental Music Tuition: £245 per instrument per term.

Our mission is to be an internationally recognised school that serves its local area by creating an inclusive school community devoted to Christian ideals of learning, raising the aspirations of each of its members and fulfilling their potential in body, mind and spirit. Founded in 1942 principally as a boarding school for the choristers of Lichfield Cathedral, the school has since grown considerably and now provides all through education for boys and girls aged 3 to 18.

The ethos of the school is that of a community where Christian values are upheld and, whilst most pupils are members of the Church of England, children of other denominations and religions are welcomed.

The school occupies two main sites: the Junior Years are located 3½ miles north of Lichfield city centre in six acres of countryside at Longdon Green, while the Middle and Senior Years occupy several buildings in the Cathedral Close, one being the magnificent 17th century Palace, the home of the Bishops of Lichfield until 1952.

The link with the Cathedral remains strong with a twice-weekly school service, as well as concerts and services throughout the year. The 18 boy choristers (aged 7–13) and 19 girl choristers (aged 10–15) are supported by scholarships provided by the Cathedral Chapter and the school. Former choristers continue their choral training in Cantorum, the scholarship-based youth choir. Academic, art, drama, sport and music scholarships are available to internal and external students entering Year 7 (11+), Year 9 (13+) and Sixth Form.

Learning in the Early Years Foundation Stage is planned around half-termly topics and the children take part in a range of activities which are balanced between adult-led and child-initiated opportunities. Activities are carefully structured to challenge children, encouraging them to develop confidence and the skills needed to solve problems. The outdoor facilities offer children an exciting environment in which to explore and investigate, and we ensure children have the time for free play.

Forest School is a popular element of the curriculum up to Year 9 that provides a holistic, individualised approach to outdoor learning, with a strong focus on developing self-esteem, confidence, communication skills and social and emotional awareness.

The spirit of intellectual enquiry is at the heart of teaching and learning at the school. Academic results are strong, particularly at GCSE and A Level. Throughout Key Stages 1 to 3, pupils follow a broad and balanced curriculum of English, Mathematics, Science, Computing, French, Spanish, German, Latin, History, Geography, Religious Studies, Art, Design, Music, Drama, Physical Education and Games and Personal, Social and Health Education. ICT skills are developed across every subject.

We offer a wide range of GCSE subjects, including Art and Design, Biology, Business Studies, Chemistry, Computing, Design Technology, Drama Studies, English Literature, English Language, French, Geography, German, History, Mathematics, Music, Physical Education, Physics, Product Design, Religious Studies and Spanish. The same subjects are offered at A Level with the addition of Computer Science, Economics, Further Mathematics, Government & Politics, Law, Music Technology, Philosophy and Ethics, Psychology, Sociology and Drama. BTEC qualifications are available in Applied Law, Criminology, Business and Sport & Exercise Science.

A co-curriculum of 'Beyond the Classroom' activities ensures students are well-rounded and gain valuable skills for higher education, employment and life outside school. Extra-curricular activities every day after school cover a wide range of subjects from chess to cooking and from Taekwondo to tennis. Several orchestras and ensembles are extremely active, as are the five main school choirs.

The unique, whole school Ethical Leadership Programme helps pupils and students to develop both the life skills and the strength of character to succeed in the world beyond education.

All pupils have access to a rich variety of both residential and day trips as well as pupil exchanges, overseas expeditions and cultural immersion opportunities. Many are directly linked to the curriculum, but the benefits to pupils go far beyond the purely educational. The Duke of Edinburgh's Award scheme is thriving, along with Young Enterprise.

The school has a long-term association with the Waterloo Schools Project in Sierra Leone; Sixth Form students lead the fundraising efforts for the Waterloo Schools Project in Sierra Leone and as part of World Challenge.

Parents are welcome to contact the school for a tour and a meeting with the Head or to attend the any of the school Open Events held throughout the year.

Charitable status. Lichfield Cathedral School is a Registered Charity, number 1137481.

Governors:
Chairman: Mr C Hopkins, MBE, BA, MBA
Mrs C Abbott, BA
The Very Revd A Dorber, BA, MTh, Dean of Lichfield
Mrs N Dawes, OBE
The Revd Canon P Hawkins, MA Oxon, BPhil, CQSW, BTh
Mrs J Mason, PGCE
The Revd Canon A Stead, BA, MA
Mr C Rickart, BA Hons, PGCE
Mrs C Tonks, BA
Mrs N Roy
Mr R Oakley

Head Teacher: **Mrs Susan Hannam**, BA Hons, MA, PGCE

Deputy Head: Mr A Harrison, BEd Hons QTS
Assistant Head, Pupil Support & Guidance: Mrs J Reynolds, BSc Hons, PGCE
Head of Early Years Foundation Stage: Mrs A M Stevens, BEd
Head of Junior Years: Mrs J M Churton, BSc Hons, PGCE
Key Stage 2 Coordinator: Mrs A Lomas, BEd Hons

Head of Years 7–9: Mr S Lane, BEd Hons
Head of Years 10–11: Mrs M Godwin, BA Hons, PGCE
Head of Sixth Form: Mr A Sherrington, LLB, PGCE

Mrs L Borenstein (*Director of Music*)
Mr M Turner, BSc Hons, PGCE (*Head of Sport*)
Mrs J M Sedgley, BA Hons, PGCE (*Head of English*)
Mr L Guffick, MA, MSc, BSc Hons, PGCE (*Head of Mathematics*)
Mrs M Gardner, BSc Hons, PGCE (*Head of Science*)
Mrs N Smith BA Hons, PGCE (*Head of Modern Foreign Languages*)
Mrs I Johnson, BA Hons, PGCE (*Head of Religious Studies*)
Mrs B A Dunne, BA, PGCE (*Head of Drama*)
Mrs S E Whatley, BA Hons, PGCE (*Head of Art and Design*)
Mr J Gardiner, BA Hons, PGCE (*Head of Computing*)
Dr P Jones, BA, MRes, PGCE, PGCES, PhD (*Head of History*)
Mr M Amison, BSc Hons, PGCE, MSc, FRGS (*Head of Geography*)

School Chaplain: Revd Dr T Plant, MA Hons, MPhil, PhD

Longridge Towers School

Longridge, Berwick-upon-Tweed, Northumberland TD15 2XQ

Tel: 01289 307584
Fax: 01289 302581
email: enquiries@lts.org.uk
website: www.lts.org.uk
Twitter: @LongridgeTowers

Motto: *Carpe Diem*

The school occupies a Victorian Mansion set in 80 acres of woodland in the beautiful Tweed Valley and enjoys excellent road and rail links with England and Scotland. Daily school bus services operate within a radius of 30 miles from the school.

Longridge Towers, refounded in 1983 under its founder and President, the late Lord Home of the Hirsel, has grown from 113 pupils to nearly 300 pupils. It is probably unique in offering the close personal relationships between pupils, staff and parents which creates a genuine 'family atmosphere'. The school has a reputation for turning out well-rounded and confident young people, the vast majority of whom continue their education at university.

Alongside the excellent academic results, the school offers many opportunities through its sporting and extra-curricular enrichment activities. All of these combine to give all pupils the chance to participate and acquire a variety of skills.

Sport figures strongly in the life of the pupils and many gain representative honours at county and national level in a variety of sports, such as rugby, hockey, cross-country running, athletics, tennis and cricket. Art, Music and Drama are also very popular and successful activities.

Entry. The school caters for a wide spectrum of abilities among its pupils who are taught in small classes. Special provision is made for the needs of pupils with mild dyslexia and for the small proportion of pupils for whom English is their second language.

Assessments upon entry to the Junior and Senior Departments in Mathematics and English are diagnostic and have no fixed pass mark.

The school is divided into 2 departments, Junior and Senior, and caters for pupils throughout their school career, from three to eighteen years. Pupils may enter at any age provided that a vacancy exists. Classes are small with less than 20 pupils per teaching set, reducing to about half this in the Sixth Form.

Activities. Longridge Towers is a school where the development of the pupils outside the academic sphere is considered to be vital. Every afternoon there is an extensive Enrichment programme offering a wide range of activities including: archery, rocket making, lacrosse, football, computer construction, dance, karate, judo, drama, kick boxing, creative writing, wildlife and gardening, young engineers, science club, debating, along with many others. The major team games are rugby, hockey, tennis, cross-country running, athletics and cricket. Many senior pupils participate in the Duke of Edinburgh's Award scheme. The musical activities within the school are varied and numerous. There are five Choirs, two Orchestras and various instrumental groups. Almost a third of the pupils take private instrumental lessons and the taking of grade examinations is encouraged. Over half of the pupils also take LAMDA examinations. No visitor to the school could fail to be aware of the variety and excellence of the artwork on display which includes clay modelling and photography.

Public Examinations. Sixteen subjects are offered at GCSE level, including Physics, Chemistry and Biology and 19, including Economics, Psychology, Sports Studies and Drama, are offered in the Sixth Form at A or AS Level.

Parents receive reports half-yearly and three-weekly Grade Cards ensure that they are kept up to date about their children's progress.

Boarding. The Boarding House and pastoral care are in the hands of resident non-teaching house parents. There is medical and dental care. Pupils have access to telephones and email and may send or receive fax messages using the facilities in the school office. Boarders may attend on a weekly or termly basis from age 8 years onwards. At weekends the boarders participate in a wide range of activities.

Scholarships and Bursaries. Academic awards at various levels are available annually to pupils aged 9–14 and 16 (into Sixth Form). Music, Sports and All-Rounder Scholarships are also available to pupils aged 11–14 and 16.

Bursaries are available to children of serving members of the Armed Forces.

Bursaries are also available to pupils; the value of these is determined after consideration of a statement of parental income.

Fees per term (2018–2019). Full Boarders: £8,780 (Junior), £9,250 (Senior). Weekly Boarders: £6,700 (Junior), £7,200 (Senior). Day pupils: Government funded Nursery with charges for extra hours, £3,100 (Junior age 5–7), £4,050 (Junior age 7–11), £4,550 (Senior age 11–18).

Charitable status. Longridge Towers School is a Registered Charity, number 513534. It exists to provide an academic education for boys and girls.

Board of Governors:
Chairman: Mr A E R Bell

Mr A Birkett	Mr J Hutchison
Mr T Bramald	Mrs A Marshall
Mrs J Coats	Mrs J M McGregor
Mrs D Dakers	Dr E C Miller
Mrs C E G Davies	Mr J Robertson
Mr J A Houston	

Headmaster: **Mr J C E Lee**, MA Hons, ACA, PGCE

Deputy Head: Mr P Whitcombe, BSc, PGCE

Head of Junior Department: Mrs S Maddock, BEd

Deputy Head of Junior Department: Mrs S Bullen, BA, SENCO

Senior Teachers:
Mrs I Cheer, BA, BSc, Cert HSC, Dip HSW (*Music, Pastoral, SENCO*)
Mr I Dempster, BEd (*History, Games, Examinations*)
Mr P Dodd, BEng, DIS, PGCE (*Mathematics, Operations*)

Teaching Staff:
Ms D Bryden, BEd (*Junior Department*)
Mr M Caddick, BA, PGCE (*German*)
Mrs C Cairns, BA Hons (*Junior Department*)
Dr N Dalrymple, PhD, MLitt, BA, PGCE (*Director of Learning*)
Mr R Davie, BSc, PGCE (*Mathematics, Computing*)
Mrs S Douglas, BA (*Junior Department*)
Mrs A Gettins, BA (*Librarian, English*)
Mr R Glenn, BSc, PGCE (*ICT Coordinator*)
Mrs N Green, BA, PGCE (*EFL*)
Mrs H Heath, BA Hons, PGCE (*Junior Department*)
Mrs L Johnson, BA, MA, PGCE (*English*)
Mr R Johnson, BA, MA, PGCE (*English*)
Mr C Johnston, BA (*Geography*)
Mr D Kendall, BEd (*Mathematics*)
Dr D Hardy, MA, PhD, LRSM, QTS (*Music*)
Mrs J Masey, BSc, PGCE (*Science*)
Mrs B Mayhew, BA, PGCE (*French/Spanish*)
Miss J McCalvey, BSc, PGCE (*Science*)
Mrs E McCorquodale, BA (*Art*)
Ms H McDaniel, BTL (*Junior Department*)
Mrs R Mole, BSc, PGCE (*Junior Department*)
Mrs L Monkman, BA, QTS (*Junior Department*)
Mr R Moscrop, BA, QTS (*Junior Department*)
Mrs S Murray, BA, PGCE (*Junior Department*)
Mrs L Peters, BEd (*Girls Games, Sports Studies*)
Miss K Phillips, BA (*Drama/Speech & Drama*)
Mr M Pugh, BSc, PGCE (*Physics*)
Mr E Roney, BSc, MSc, PGCE (*Biology*)
Mr P Rowett, BA (*RE, History, Geography*)
Mrs R Scalici, BA (*Junior Department*)
Mrs E Shaw, BA, PGCE (*Girls Games, Sports Studies*)
Mr A Skeen, BA, QTS (*Economics, Games*)
Mrs G Skeen, BSc, QTS (*Junior Department*)
Mrs M Smith, BSc, PGCE (*PE, CDT*)
Mr A Westthorp, BEng, PGCE (*CDT, Computing*)
Mrs K Westthorp, MA, PGCE (*French*)
Mrs D Whitcombe, MA, PGCE (*English*)
Mrs A Young (*Teaching Assistant, Sport*)

Boarding Staff:
Mr G Hattle (*Senior House Parent*)
Mrs L Patterson (*House Parent*)
Mrs A Ireland (*Residential Senior House Parent*)
Mr M Short (*House Parent*)

Matron: Mrs M Hattle, RGN

Administration:
Bursar: Mr S Bankier, BA, FCMA
Bursar's PA: Mrs E Crossan
Assistant Bursar: Mrs L Mason, BSc, ACMA
Accounts Assistant: Mrs A Krzeminska, BA, MA
Head's PA: Mrs C Craze BSc
PA to Head of Junior Dept: Mrs A Allis, BA
IT Manager: Mr D Mulholland
Registrar/Marketing Manager: Mrs M Burns
Reception: Mrs C Jobson, MA
Site Manager: Mr E Sutherland

Luckley House School

Luckley Road, Wokingham, Berkshire RG40 3EU

Tel: +44 (0)118 978 4175
Fax: +44 (0)118 977 0305
email: registrar@luckleyhouseschool.org
website: www.luckleyhouseschool.org
Twitter: @LuckleyHouse
Facebook: @LuckleyHouseSchool
LinkedIn: /Luckley House School

Luckley House School is a co-educational day and boarding school located in beautiful Berkshire. The current numbers are 275 pupils aged 11 to 18. The majority are day pupils, but approximately 30 are either full or weekly boarders. Pupils are selected on the basis of an entrance examination and interview. The main age of entry is at 11 years, 13 years and into the Sixth Form. Our in-house transport service covers a wide area, with late drop-offs for students wishing to stay for prep or after-class activities. We offer a transport service to West London, to provide an excellent option for families looking for weekly boarding away from the city.

Luckley was founded on its present site in 1918. In 1959 it amalgamated with Oakfield School, established in 1895 in the Lake District. Initially the school was administered by the Church Society but in 1969 it became an independent educational trust. A gracious Grade II listed Edwardian country house forms the centre of the school, which is on a 14-acre site with views of the countryside and woodlands.

We have high expectations for all our pupils, achieving excellent academic results and we are proud of our exceptional added-value record.

Luckley boasts fantastic facilities: the school is set in beautiful, safe and secure grounds, with modern classrooms, new science laboratories, contemporary boarding accommodation, a state-of-the-art music centre and stunning performing arts centre and conference theatre, well-equipped art studios and a large sports centre with extensive playing fields, tennis courts, fitness suite, climbing wall and fully-sprung dance floor.

Curriculum. The curriculum is broad and challenging with pupils taking 9.5 subjects for GCSE. A wide variety of A Level courses is offered and almost every student goes on to higher education as a preparation for careers in, for example, languages, medicine, engineering, law, business and design.

The school has a well-deserved reputation for Art, Drama, Music and Sport and offers a range of other activities including computing, debating, riding, The Duke of Edinburgh's Award scheme, Combined Cadet Force and Young Enterprise. Boarders and Day students are encouraged to join in this extensive programme of extracurricular activities during the extended day slot from 4.00–5.30 pm. Instrumental lessons, Singing, Speech and Drama are offered as additional subjects.

Boarding. Weekly and flexi boarding offer the opportunity to experience the fun of boarding while keeping close links with home and avoiding long daily journeys. Full boarding, with an extensive weekend activity programme, can provide a stable and secure education for pupils whose schooling would otherwise be interrupted. Living accommodation for all boarders is situated in the Main House and Cornish House.

Ethos. Luckley House School is built on the Christian foundations of love and service. We enable our students to thrive in a secure and encouraging environment, thereby equipping each pupil to be resourceful and resilient, and ready to take on the challenges and opportunities that lie ahead.

Fees per term (2018–2019). Full Boarders £9,694, Weekly Boarders £8,985, Day Pupils £5,540.

Scholarships and Bursaries. Scholarships are awarded at 11+ on the results of the Entrance Examination and on entry to the Sixth Form. Music, Drama, Art and Sports scholarships are also available.

Means-tested Bursaries offering a reduction of up to 80% of fees are offered. Forces Bursaries are also available.

Charitable status. Luckley House School Limited is a Registered Charity, number 309099. It offers day and boarding education for pupils on the basis of Christian values.

Governing Body:
Reverend G Curry (*Chair*)

The Lady Farmer	Mr R Scurlock
Dr V Houghton	Mrs C Tao
Mr B Gardiner	Mrs L Horrocks
Dr J Ledger	Mr D Kratt
Mr A Imlay	

Head: Mrs J Tudor, BSc Hons UCL, MA Ed Open University

Bursar: Mr N Patterson, MSc
Deputy Head Pastoral (*Lower School*): Mrs S Hills, MSc London, BEd Hons Leeds
Deputy Head Academic: Mr I Vallance, BEd Bristol, MA Ed London South Bank
Deputy Head Pastoral (*Upper School*) *and Head of Sixth Form*: Mrs C Gilding-Brant, BA Brighton

Academic Departments:
* *Head of Department*
** *Director of Department*

Art:
*Mr R Battrick, BA Hons Loughborough, MA Cardiff (*Assistant Head of Sixth Form*)
Mrs A Venables, BA Hons Oxon

Classics:
Dr R Freeman, PhD St Andrews

Computer Science:
Mr D Beasley, BSc Hons Southampton

Design Technology & Engineering:
*Mrs C McCafferty, HND CertEd MlfL QTLS (*Assistant SENCo*)
Mr D Savage, BA Humberside (*Senior Teacher, Pastoral Care Years 9, 10 & 11*)

Drama & Theatre Studies:
**Mrs E Brown, BA Hons Wales (*Head of Transition*)
Mrs J Harris, BA Hons Reading
Visiting Staff: Mr I Cullen

Economics & Business Studies:
Ms L Stephens, BA Hons York

English:
*Mrs C Rees, BA Hons Belfast, MA York, MEd Bath
Miss D Bahbra, BA Hons Surrey, MSc Leicester
Mrs A Chick, BA Hons Hull
Mrs K Clutterbuck, BA Hons Royal Holloway
Mrs E Simpson, BA Hons Portsmouth (*EAL Teacher*)

Food Preparation and Nutrition:
Mrs S Gibson, BSc Bath

Geography:
* Mrs K Knight, BA Hons Oxford Brookes
Miss B Eveleigh, BA Hons, MA Ed Exeter
Mr G Cromb, BSc Hons London

History:
*Mr P Maynard, BA Hons Portsmouth
Mrs V Stratton, BA Hons York

Mathematics:
*Miss R Duncan, BSc Hons Surrey
Mrs N Dawson, Higher Diploma University of Natal, South
  Africa
Mr S McGonnell, BEd Hons Bristol
Mr I Vallance, BEd Bristol, MA Ed London Southbank
Miss L Walls, BSc Hons Sussex

Modern Languages:
*Miss H Ryan, BA Hons Southampton, MEd Exeter
Mrs H Hinz, BA Hons, MA Hull (*PSHE Coordinator*)
Miss K Intxaurbe, BSc Hons Spain
Mrs L Simmonds, BA Jt Hons Exeter

Visiting Staff:
Mrs K Baldwin (*Chinese*)
Mrs S Huddleston (*Spanish Conversation*)
Mrs C Paisley (*German Conversation*)
Mrs L Porter (*French Conversation*)
Mrs S Rose (*Russian Tutor*)

Music:
**Mrs J Ellwood, GRSM Hons, Dip RCM, PGCA Perf
  RCM, QTS Reading
Mrs J Clark, BMus Hons London, LRSM, PGCE
Mr A McKenna, BMus, BEd, ARCT

Visiting Staff:
Mr N Charlton, BA Hons, LTCL (*Cello*)
Mrs H Cheng, MMus, Dip RCM, ARCM (*Piano*)
Mrs J Clark, BMus Hons London, LRSM, PGCE (*Flute*)
Mr M Davies, BMus, LRAM ,ARCM, LWCMD (*Singing*)
Mr J Ellwood, Dip GBSM, ABSM (*Brass*)
Mr A Gwilt, BA Hons (*Clarinet, Saxophone*)
Mr M Kelly, Dip RCM ARCM (*Violin, Viola*)
Mr J Mitchell, HDip, ACM (*Guitar*)
Mrs L Roper, MSc (*Singing*)
Mrs M Stallwood, Cert Music (*Classical Guitar*)
Mr A Fujimoto, MMus (*Drum*)

Physical Education:
**Mrs K Hobson, BA Hons Brighton
Miss J Cumming, BA Hons Wales (*Senior Teacher,
  Pastoral Care Years 7 & 8*)
Mrs C Gilding-Brant, BA Brighton
Mrs S Hills, MSc London, BEd Hons Leeds Polytechnic
  (*SENCo*)
*Mr M Humphrey, BSc Hons Portsmouth (*Head of Boys'
  Sport*)
Outdoor Education: Mr P Hills

Psychology:
Mrs H Strivens, BSc Hertfordshire
Mrs C Gilding-Brant, BA Brighton

Religious Studies:
*Mrs K Matsuya, BA Hons Durham
Miss T Matthews, BSc Hons Open University
Mrs S Kearns, BA Hons Wales

Science:
*Mrs H Buck, BSc Hons York (*Head of Science*)
Mr S Bond, MA Oxon (*Head of Physics*)
Mrs F Blackmore, BEng Brunel
Dr R Jones, PhD Aberdeen (*Head of Biology*)
Dr W Ross, PhD Imperial College London (*Head of
  Chemistry*)
Mrs J Tudor, BSc Hons London, MA Ed Open University

Textiles:
Mrs C McCafferty, HND CertEd MlfL QTLS (*Assistant
  SENCo*)

Learning Support:
Mrs S Hills, MSc London, BEd Hons Leeds Polytechnic
  (*SENCo*)
Mrs C McCafferty, HND CertEd MlfL QTLS (*Assistant
  SENCo*)
Mrs S Wakelin, BSc Surrey (*SEN Tutor*)
Mrs B Beaup, MA Admin Surrey, Trinity Cert TESOL
  (*EAL Tutor*)

Support Staff:
Mr N Patterson, BA.Hons, BSc, MSc (*Bursar*)
Mrs N Hall, CIPD (*HR Manager & PA to the Head*)

Marketing, Admissions & Development:
Mrs D Ennis, CIM Dip (*Marketing, Admissions &
  Development Manager*)
Mrs C Crombie (*Registrar*)
Mrs S Hawkins (*Alumnae, Events Coordinator, Careers*)
Mrs S Humphreys (*Centenary Coordinator*)

Boarding:
*Mr D Savage & Mrs S Savage (*Houseparents*)
Miss J Cumming, BA Hons University of Wales (*Assistant
  Housemistress*)
Mr I Vallance, BEd Bristol, MA Ed London Southbank
  (*Housemaster*)
Miss K Dworkin, BSc Oxford Brookes (*Graduate
  Boarding and Sports Assistant*)
Miss G Cole, BSc Hons Royal Holloway (*Graduate
  Boarding and Teaching Assistant*)

Catering:
Miss E Coogan (*Chef Manager*)
Mrs A Williams (*Chef de Partie*)
Mr S Taylor (*Chef de Partie*)
Miss S Hill (*Commis Chef*)

Estates:
Mr S Kulan (*Maintenance Manager*)
Mr G Steele (*Maintenance Assistant*)
Mr S Holland (*Maintenance Assistant/Caretaker*)

Examinations:
Mrs L Cox (*Examinations Officer*)
Mr G Wilkins (*Examination Invigilator*)
Mrs C Sowton (*Examination Invigilator*)

Finance:
Mrs R Stevens, BA Hons Sheffield Polytechnic, ACA
  (*Finance Bursar*)
Mrs J Fowler, BSc Hons De Montfort (*Finance Assistant*)

Human Resources:
Mrs N Hall, CIPD (*HR Manager*)
Mrs S Norman (*Administrative Assistant*)

Library:
Mrs R Maskelyne, BA Hons Reading, MA UCL (*Senior
  Librarian*)
Mrs D Godfrey (*Assistant Librarian*)

Medical Care:
Mrs L Lan, RGN (*School Nurse*)

Reception:
Mrs S Hawkins (*School Secretary*)
Mrs J Leatherby (*School Secretary*)

Classroom Assistants/Technicians:
Mrs N Allaway (*Science Technician*)
Mrs K Crawshaw (*Science Technician*)
Miss S Hitchcock (*Photography Assistant*)
Mrs N Partner (*D&T Technician*)

Technical Services Team:
Mr D Wilkinson (*ICT Technician*)

Theatre:
Mr O Bamber (*Theatre Manager*)

LVS Ascot

London Road, Ascot, Berkshire SL5 8DR

Tel: 01344 882770
email: registrar@lvs.ascot.sch.uk
website: www.lvs.ascot.sch.uk
Twitter: @lvsascot
Facebook: @LVSAscot

LVS Ascot is a non-selective, co-educational day and boarding school of over 800 pupils aged 4–18. It is an all-through school so pupils can begin their school career at LVS Ascot at age 4 and remain there until they complete Sixth Form.

Exam results in 2018 saw nearly 10% of GCSEs graded A* or equivalent, with 99% of students who achieved 5 or more A*–C grades gaining passes in both maths and English. LVS Ascot also recorded an increase in A* grades at A Level, with an overall pass rate of 98.3%.

Numbers. Infant & Junior School 183, Senior School 635 (including 171 in Sixth Form), boarding approximately 192.

Organisation. Pupils aged 4 to 11 (Years R to 6) are taught in the Infant & Junior School, in separate classes each with a class teacher. Houses are used for sports and other competitions. Junior School pupils may board from Year 3 (age 7) and join a mixed House (Kew House), which is an integral part of the Junior School buildings.

Senior School pupils, aged 11 to 18 (Years 7 to 13), are placed in tutor groups and a school House, with a tutor who monitors their pastoral care and oversees their academic performance. Students are taught in ability groups with a maximum class size of 20. Boarders are accommodated in four separate boarding Houses, each supervised by House-masters/mistresses: Kew (junior house) is mixed for pupils from Year 3 to Year 7; Osborne (girls' house) for pupils from Year 8 to Year 11; Hampton (boys' house) for pupils from Year 8 to Year 11; Blenheim (mixed sixth form house) for pupils in Years 12 and 13.

Location. LVS Ascot is north of the A329, close to Ascot Racecourse and Royal Windsor. The school is easily accessible from the M3, M4 and M25 motorways as well as Heathrow and Gatwick airports. The school bus service connects with trains at Ascot Station, as well many surrounding towns within a 20 miles radius including locations in West London.

Facilities. LVS Ascot is a modern day and boarding school in the UK. The purpose-built facilities, set in 25 acres of landscaped grounds, include: boarding accommodation and classroom blocks, a sports centre, all-weather pitch, indoor swimming pool, fully-equipped 250-seat theatre and a music technology suite. LVS Ascot hosts over five-hundred networked computer workstations, with every classroom equipped with ICT resources for digital and interactive learning. Wireless networking provides additional facilities for centrally-managed student laptops, eBooks and other devices in a secure environment. There is a dedicated Sixth Form Centre, and a Learning Resource Centre, that has an extensive range of books and journals.

Curriculum. The curriculum is broad and based on the national curriculum "plus". Pupils follow a common core curriculum of English, Mathematics, Science, one/two foreign languages, plus PE and PSHE. Science is taught as separate subjects. At GCSE, students select their choices from: Business Studies, Technology, Art & Design, Geography, History, Food Technology, Music, Drama, Media Studies, Economics, Physical Education, Computer Science, Spanish, German or French.

A wide range of A Level and vocational options are provided, including Mathematics, Physics, Chemistry, Biology, Music, Geography, History, Economics, Business Studies, English, Art & Design, Theatre Studies, Design & Technology, Media Studies, Photography, Psychology, French, Spanish, German, ICT, Computer Studies, Engineering and Physical Education.

Sport. The school has superb indoor and outdoor facilities with a large Sports Hall, dance studio with ballet bars, a 25-metre swimming pool and a well-equipped gym as well as rugby, football and hockey pitches, tennis courts and an all-weather pitch. The school has achieved considerable success in providing County, Regional and National standard players in a wide range of sports. Whilst all pupils play team games such as Rugby, Football, Cricket, Hockey, Tennis, Netball, Basketball or Athletics in their early years, the range of options widens as pupils become older to encourage fitness for life, with opportunities such as skiing, skating, polo, fencing and playing squash.

Clubs and Activities. LVS Ascot is an accredited Duke of Edinburgh's Award training centre and runs a vibrant and popular award scheme. Alongside this there is a range of co-curricular activities such as music ensembles, newspaper club, riding, canoeing, rowing, climbing, cookery, animation and film club. In September 2015 LVS Ascot Junior School introduced a range of 25 co-curricular after-school clubs.

Admissions. There is no entrance examination; reports are requested from a student's current school. All students are interviewed prior to acceptance. Prospective students and their families are welcome to visit the school. Personal tours can also be arranged by appointment.

Open Days 2018–2019.

Saturday 17th November 2018 – Infant & Junior, Senior and Sixth Form

Wednesday 6th February 2019 – Infant & Junior and Senior School

Saturday 16 March 2019 – Infant & Junior, Senior and Sixth Form

Wednesday 8th May 2019 – Infant & Junior, Senior School and Sixth Form

Saturday 15th June 2019 – Infant & Junior, Senior School and Sixth Form

Fees per term (2018–2019). Infants £3,330; Junior: £3,988 (day), £8,522 (boarding); Senior: £5,657 (day), £10,077 (full/weekly boarding); Sixth Form: £5,969 (day), £10,488 (full/weekly boarding).

Scholarships and Bursaries. Academic, Music, Art, Drama, Sport Scholarships are available at Year 7 entry and various Scholarships are available for entry to the Sixth Form (Year 12).

Fee discounts and Bursaries are available to assist parents working in the Licensed Drinks Trade, MoD and British Diplomats. Third child discount is also available.

Charitable status. The Society of Licensed Victuallers is a Registered Charity, number 230011. It exists to provide education for boys and girls.

Patron: Her Majesty The Queen

Director of Education: Mr I Mullins, BEd Hons, MSc, MBIM

School Principal: **Mrs C Cunniffe**, BA Hons, MMus, MBA

Head of Infant & Junior School: Mrs R Cox, BA Hons, PGCE

Deputy Head Pastoral/Head of Boarding: Mrs Karen Olliver

Deputy Head, Head of Sixth Form: Dr P Hodges, PhD, BSc, MSc, PGCE

Deputy Head Academic Development & Co-curricular: Mr C Jenkins, BA Hons, PGCE

Vice Principal, Director of Studies: Mr B Padrick, BA, MTS Hons

Housemasters/mistresses:

Boarding Houses:
Housemaster of Kew: Mr A Cruz, BA
Assistant HM of Kew: Mr J Sivier, BA Hons
Housemistress of Osborne: Mrs B O'Grady, BA Hons
Assistant HM of Osborne: Ms G Els, BA
Housemaster of Blenheim: Mr T Jarrett, MA, PGCE
Assistant HM of Blenheim: Mr W Truter, BSc, PGCE
Housemaster of Hampton: Mr J Wilder, FASC, BMus Hons, PGCE
Assistant HM of Hampton: Mr T Wyndham-Smith

Day Houses:
Housemistress of Brake: Mrs T Bason, BA, PGCE
Housemistress of Buchanan: Mrs C Robinson, MA
Housemaster of Coburg: Mr J Curtis-Nye, BSc Hons, MA, AHEA, PGCE
Housemistress of Hart: Mrs R Sandford, BA Hons
Housemistress of Kennington: Mrs G Windsor, BA Hons, PGCE
Housemistress of Melbourne: Miss J Clark, BA Hons, PGCE

Designated Safeguarding Leads:
Mrs K Olliver, BA Hons, HDE (*Senior School*)
Mrs R Cox, BA Hons, PGCE (*Junior School*)

Child Protection Officers:
Mrs T Bason, BA Hons, PGCE (*Snr*)
Mrs W Sales-Mint, BSc (*Snr*)
Mrs L Rawlinson, BEd Hons (*Jnr*)

Heads of Departments:
Art and Design: Mrs R Sandford, BA Hons
Business Studies: Mr R Furse, BA Hons, PGCE
Drama: Mrs G Windsor, BA Hons, PGCE
English and Media Studies: Ms S Quant, BA Hons, MA, PGCE
Additional Learning Needs (ALN): Mrs J Pearce, BA Hons, PGCE
Geography: Mrs D Finch, BA Hons
History: Mr A Kydd, BA Hons, PGCE
Information Technology: Mr S Panayi, BSc Hons, PGCE
Law: Mr K Towl, LLB, PGCE
Mathematics: Mr R Bignell, MBA, BSc Hons
Modern Foreign Languages: Mr J Curtis-Nye, BSc Hons, PGCE, MA
Music: Mr J Bryant, BA, MMus, ALCM
Philosophy & Religion: Mr S Martin, BA Hons, PGCE
Physical Education: Miss E Bunyan, BA Hons
Psychology: Mr J Paterson, BSc Hons
Science & Technology: Mrs S Catlin, BSc, PGCE
Learning Resource Centre: Mrs E Keeler, MA Hons, PG Cert, MCLIP

Infant & Junior School:
Head of Infant & Junior School: Mrs Rachael Cox, BA Hons, PGCE
Assistant Head of Junior School: Mrs L Rawlinson, BEd Hons

Administrative Staff:
Examinations Officer: Mrs R Jacobs
Principal's PA: Mrs C Gedge
Marketing: Mrs P Smith
Registrar: Mrs M Buttimer
Senior School Administrators: Miss H Austin, Mrs N Smith

Senior School Reception: Mrs L Reddy
Head of Junior School's PA: Mrs D Pearce

Milton Abbey School

Milton Abbas, Blandford Forum, Dorset DT11 0BZ

Tel: 01258 880484
email: admissions@miltonabbey.co.uk
website: www.miltonabbey.co.uk
Twitter: @MiltonAbbey
Facebook: @MiltonAbbeySchool

Foundation. Milton Abbey was founded in 1954 and comprised 211 pupils at the start of the 2018–19 academic year. In 2018 a second girls' house was opened, reflecting an increased proportion of girls across each year group since going fully co-educational in 2012.

Milton Abbey has a unique ability to deliver a truly bespoke education, due to our small size and exceptional team of teaching and pastoral staff. We tailor each child's education to make the most of his or her individual skills and talents so that they can achieve the best possible results, both inside and outside the classroom.

Care, guidance and carefully targeted support in learning is available wherever required, resulting in greater confidence and enhanced self-esteem. We inspire pride in pupils' individual work, whether in sport, academia, the creative arts or in our range of outdoor and practical subjects. Milton Abbey gives pupils the opportunity to study GCSEs, A Levels, BTECs or a combined programme, offering one of the widest range of subjects in the independent sector.

Everyone has a great involvement in school life, with 89% of children representing the school in a sport or pursuit last year. Lasting and fulfilling friendships are forged, and everyone has the chance to get to know one another.

Situation. Our picturesque grounds and stunning surroundings offer space, yet safety and security, providing an inspirational setting for learning. The Dorset towns of Blandford and Dorchester are located nearby and used for weekend outings and activities, along with the coastal towns of Weymouth, Poole and Bournemouth.

Buildings. The Great Abbey is our School Chapel, and our dining room, the Abbot's Hall, dates back to the medieval era. Outside the mansion house, modern facilities include contemporary boarding houses, a music school, art studio, creative media and IT buildings, a 370-seat theatre, School Farm, all-weather pitches, an indoor heated 25-metre pool, cricket pavilion, golf course, and other leisure facilities.

Organisation. Milton Abbey is proud of its full-boarding status and of the comprehensive extracurricular and weekend programme this allows. Boarding pupils go home for a long weekend twice a term, three half term breaks and three longer holidays.

On joining the School, every boarding pupil is assigned to a House; a close-knit community where year groups are fully integrated. Each House has a team of resident staff and matrons to help provide a home-from-home environment. Milton Abbey has five boarding Houses: Athelstan, Hambro and Tregonwell for boys, and Damer and Hodgkinson for girls.

Our provision is all-encompassing and encourages every pupil to lead a fulfilling and rewarding life during their time here. Hard work and academic determination are balanced with a comprehensive programme of activities and social events.

Curriculum. All pupils follow a broad and balanced curriculum up to age 16, predominantly consisting of GCSEs, with some Level 2 BTECs also offered. The Sixth Form provides a wide range of academic, technical and vocational courses including traditional A Levels, BTECs and top-up GCSEs.

Music. A wide variety of individual tuition is available for singers or musicians. Singing is a strong and popular part of school life.

Clubs and Societies. We run a comprehensive programme of engaging and rewarding extracurricular activities. Activities for both Lower School and Sixth Form pupils take place twice a week on Tuesday and Thursday afternoons and cater for a wide range of interests. From cookery courses to mechanics, and textiles to School Farm Club, there is something for all to enjoy. There is a termly programme of fun and competitive inter-House activities for pupils to take part in. The School's thriving CCF contingent holds regular camps in the holidays, as well as expeditions at home and abroad.

Most weekends offer an opportunity for a pupil to choose from caving, climbing, sailing, windsurfing and canoeing. Pupils undertake a range of extracurricular and volunteering activities every Wednesday afternoon, designed to broaden their interest.

Games. Autumn: Rugby, Football and Hockey. Spring: Hockey, Netball, Lacrosse and Cross Country. Summer: Cricket, Athletics, Tennis and Rounders. All year round: Swimming, Golf, Rifle Shooting, Basketball, Cycling (road and mountain), Sailing, Polo, Riding, Canoeing and Clay Pigeon Shooting.

Admission. Most pupils join the School at age 13 in the Third Form. Level 1 papers at Common Entrance are accepted but Milton Abbey also welcomes those who have not been prepared for Common Entrance. A satisfactory report from the pupil's current school will also be required.

Those with Special Educational Needs will be asked to come for pre-assessment with the Head of Learning Support, to make sure that the School can offer them the correct level of support.

For entry into the Sixth Form, candidates attend an assessment day, as well as completing an assessment paper. Candidates should have a good GCSE pass in the subjects he or she is intending to take for A Level and a satisfactory report from their current school.

Fees per term (2018–2019). Lower School: Boarding £12,850, Day £6,750. Sixth Form: Boarding £13,350, Day £7,250.

Scholarships. Several Scholarships are awarded annually. Including academic scholarships in Music, Drama, Art and DT. Sport scholarships are also offered in traditional and individual sports, including special programmes for Golf and Road Cycling. Scholarships can also be awarded at Sixth Form entry level. Bursaries may also be considered in cases of need.

Charitable status. The Council of Milton Abbey School Limited is a Registered Charity, number 306318. It is a charitable Trust for secondary education.

Governors:
I G Bromilow, MSc, PhD (*Chair*)
Mrs J H Simm, MA, FCA, JP (*Vice Chair*)
N S Boulton, MA
Ms K S Butler, MA
Col O J H Chamberlain, QVRM, TD, DL [OM]
M J Dyer
P W McGrath, MA, MW [OM]
M D L Noyce, MCSI [OM]
L J Rake, BA Oxon, FLS

[OM] *Old Miltonian*

Visitor: Revd Canon C W Mitchell-Innes, MA

Senior Management Team:

Head: Judith Fremont-Barnes, MA, MEd

Deputy Head: Matthew Way, BSc Hons, MEd
Assistant Head (*Pupil Progress*): Chris Barnes, BA
Assistant Head (*Teaching and Learning*): Natalie Perry, BSc Hons, MSc
Assistant Head (*Pupil Welfare & PHSE*): Ruth Butler, BA Hons
Assistant Head (*Boarding*) *& Registrar*: Matthew Porter, BA Hons
Bursar & Clerk to the Governors: Julian Litchfield, FCIPD
Head of Finance: Stephen Lane, BSc, ACA
Head of Admissions: Claire Low

Academic Management Team:
Natalie Perry (*Chair*) and Chris Barnes [see above]
Curriculum Manager: Rebecca Barton, BSc
Head of Sixth Form: Dr Josh Bradbury, BA, MA, PhD
Head of Learning Support: Hayley Chipman, BA
Director of Digital Learning: Angela Giesens, BSc, MA

House Management Team:
Athelstan Housemaster: Will Fraser, MA
Damer Housemistress: Emma Williams, BA
Hambro Housemaster: Henry Stoot, BA
Hodgkinson Housemistress: Liz Always, BA
Tregonwell Housemaster: Christopher Hill, BA

Directors/Heads of Department:
Art & Photography: Sara Burton, BA
Countryside Management & Land Based Studies: Elisabeth Carr, BSc
Creative Media: Angela Giesens [see above]
Enterprise, Economics & Entrepreneurship: Rebecca Barton [see above]
Design & Technology: James Ratcliffe, BA
Drama: Liz Bemment, BA
English & Communication Studies: Karen Baney, BA
Geography: Torie Morley, BSc
History: Chris Barns [see above]
Hospitality: Leonie Monaghan, BA
Mathematics: Stephen Phillips, BSc
Media Studies: Dr Josh Bradbury [see above]
Modern Languages: Christophe Douchet, Maitrise DP
Music: Nikki Budd, BA
Psychology: Natalie Perry [see above]
Religious Studies: Revd Jo Davis, BA, MTh, PGCert
Science: Nick Anderson, BSc
Sport: Ben Lawes, BSc
Sport BTEC and PE GCSE: Fran Porter, BSc

Other Key Contacts:
Head's PA: Georgie Woolgar
ICT Manager: Tim Chandler, BA
Facilities Manager: Christian Palmer, BIFM, CMI
Events Manager: Andrew Kennedy
Head of Marketing & Communications: Nick Cloke, BA, MCIPR
Chaplain: Revd Jo Davis [see above]
SENCO: Ruth Dal Din, BSc
Milton Abbey Association (*Alumni*) *Manager*: Hugo Mieville, BA, MA, PG Dip

Mount House School

Camlet Way, Hadley Wood, Barnet, Hertfordshire EN4 0NJ

Tel: 020 8449 6889
Fax: 020 8441 5632
email: admissions@mounthouse.org.uk

website: www.mounthouse.org.uk
Twitter: @MountHouseSch
Facebook: @mounthouseschoolofficial

Age Range. 11–18 co-educational.
Number in School. 190 Day Girls & Boys.
Fees per term (2018–2019). £5,010.

Mount House School provides co-educational excellence, where everyone is known, cherished and challenged.

Centred around the historic Mount House it is a school that aims to create confident, articulate independent learners in an environment in which each individual is valued and their unique talents identified and nurtured during their time with us. The overarching aim is that Mount House is a happy and successful school for girls and boys to achieve excellent public examination results and secure places at top universities when they leave having completed their A Levels.

Mount House though is not just about examination results and as a consequence of their time with us, the girls and boys will develop the skills required to help them grow into capable adults with a sense of self-worth. All of this must be seen within the context of a personalised approach to each individual that brings success without stress.

Mount House has developed a set of values that will provide the benefit of preparing our pupils and students for life after Mount House. We are looking for all our students to become: adaptable; supportive; principled; inquisitive; resilient and excellent in every way. It is important to us that each of these values is integrated into all aspects of life at Mount House.

In addition to recent investment in Science, Sixth Form, ICT and the Library this year plans for a new Sports Hall and extra classrooms are awaiting application approval so that building work can begin.

What Mount House offers girls and boys is a modern, inspirational and challenging curriculum with exceptional teaching and learning; excellent sports provision; creative learning spaces and a community that works together.

Boys began joining Mount House School in September 2018 in First Form (Year 7) and Lower 6th and will work their way through the school ensuring it is fully co-educational in September 2022. We believe what we have to offer is unique in North London and Hertfordshire. If you would like to find out more please do not hesitate to visit our website www.mounthouse.org.uk or call our admissions team on 020 8449 6889. We very much look forward to welcoming you to our great school.

Board of Directors:
Mr Colin Diggory (*Chairman*)
Mr Emil Gigov
Mr Toby Mullins (*Director and Principal*)
Ms Isabel Dolan (*Director of Finance*)

School Staff:

Principal: Mr Toby Mullins, BA Hons, MBA

Deputy Head Academic: Dr M Wall, BSc Hons, PhD, PGSE
Head of Sixth Form: Mr C McCormick, BA Hons, MA, PGCE
Finance Director: Ms I Dolan
Head of Marketing & Admissions: Mrs C Thrift

* *Head of Faculty*
† *Head of House*

Ms Thelma Agyepong, MA, BA Hons (*Textiles*)
Ms Shameem Akhtar, BA Hons, PGCE (*Geography)
Mr Phillip Allman, BA Hons, PGCE (*Sociology*)
Mrs Satbir Allman, MA, PGCE (*Sociology*)

Mr Jerome Boonzaier, BCOM, HDE Post Grad (*Business)
Mr James Brookes, BA Hons, GDL (*English*)
†Mrs Charlotte Carpenter, BA Hons, GTP, SRT (*Art & Design*)
Mrs Maria Christou (*Careers*)
Ms Sue Colebrook (*Learning Support*)
Mrs Abisoye Da Rocha, BA Hons, PGCE (*French and Spanish*)
†Ms Katy Evans, MA Advanced Theatre, BA Hons (*Drama*)
Ms Linzi Fairweather, BSc Hons QTS (*Director of Sport*)
Mrs Kathryn Fallon, BA Hons, MLDP, PGCE (*Classics*)
Mr Patrick Gallagher, BSc Hons, MSc (*Mathematics)
Mr Ali Hosseinian, BEng Hons, PGCE (*Mathematics*)
Mr Tom Klidzia, GMus Hons, BSc Hons, PGCE (*Psychology*)
Mrs Melani Lazouras, BA Hons, PGCE (*MFL)
Mrs Rebecca MacDonald, MA Hons, PGCE (*English)
Ms Eleonora Mariottini, Class 3 University, Italy QTS (*Spanish*)
Mrs Daisy Martin, BSc Hons, MSc, PGCE (*Chemistry*)
Mrs Danuta Mela, GLCM, PGCE (*RE*)
Mrs Androulla Melekis, BA Hons, PGCE (*Inclusion EAL*)
Mr Jacob Menelaou, PhD, MA Theo, MA, BA Philology (*Latin & Classics*)
Mr Peter Pandelis, BSc Hons, PGCE (*Computing*)
Mrs Bernadette Rodgers, BA Hons, GTP (*Home Economics*)
Mr Graham Scobie (*Physics)
†Miss Patrice Smyth, BSc Hons, PGCE (*PE*)
Ms Elizabeth Somerville, BA Hons Fine Art, PGCE (*Art & Design*)
Mrs Robyn Stern, BEd FETP (*Biology*)
Ms Qin Wang, MA SOAS (*Mandarin*)
Ms Ombretta Veronese (*English*)
Mr Sam Whitehouse, BA Hons, PGCE (*Music*)
Greetje Wijnstok, BEd (*Mathematics*)

Admin:
Mrs Ashita Bavisha (*Examinations Officer*)
Mrs Monica Dixon (*Art Technician*)
Mr Alex Erotocritou (*IT Network Manager*)
Miss Lauren Hine (*Marketing and Admissions Assistant*)
Mr Chris Heaney (*Site Manager*)
Ms Karen Hunt (*Finance Administrator*)
Mrs Sheila Lamsley (*Receptionist pm*)
Mrs Suzanne Linsey-Mitellas (*Principal's PA*)
Mrs Renata Panak (*Science Technician*)
Mrs Esther Rayner (*Receptionist am*)
Mrs Annie Swynnerton (*International Admissions*)
Mr Danny Webster (*Assistant Site Manager*)

Myddelton College

Peakes Lane, Denbigh, North Wales LL16 3EN
Tel: +44 (0)1745 472201
email: admissions@myddeltoncollege.com
website: www.myddeltoncollege.com
Twitter: @MyddeltonCol
Facebook: @MyddeltonCollege

Age Range. 9–18.
Number in School. 230 pupils.
More than just an Education. "Being a great school requires more than just providing the best possible education, it requires a different view of what education is". At Myddelton College, we take the broadest possible view of education and our students, whether boarders or day students, are exposed to a wide range of activities that encom-

pass the whole experience of what it means to be human. Yes, there are the academic subjects there, with high standards and even higher expectations of success (because a strong academic background is a necessity in today's global community), but beyond that, a Myddelton College student will be expected to develop interests in sporting, creative, aesthetic and cultural areas. But alongside that, there is the need for breadth and balance – which is why the education provided at Myddelton includes the extra activities, and why every student is expected to be involved in all aspects of College life.

Myddelton College is about providing a pastoral care structure that goes beyond basic welfare. At Myddelton we focus on developing and maturing the individual, both emotionally and intellectually. Myddelton College students will have an international perspective as members of the global village. Vitally, it is about preparing young people for life beyond College: helping them gain access to their chosen university, helping them to be fully prepared for the life they will lead beyond, and then equipping them to become suitably qualified and confident to lead, to serve, to be a good influence – wherever life takes them.

21st Century Learning. Upon joining us, all students at Myddelton College will need to purchase a touch screen device. Using these devices as part of their everyday work and learning will become second nature to our students, as we help to prepare them for life after school. We place a huge importance on the use of technology in order to offer a richer and more realistic 21st century experience for our students.

As a Microsoft Global Showcase school, we are proud to be innovators in education, building a 21st century curriculum, so that our students leave with the skills required to be successful, whatever the future holds. With 5 Microsoft Innovative Educator Experts on staff, we know that the use of technology is the very best it can be. The fact that our curriculum is seen as an example of the very best use of technology, globally, is a real strength.

Learning through the Outdoors. Our 'Learning through the Outdoors Programme' will enable all students to undertake a wide range of activities designed to help them develop the leadership skills that collaboration and teamwork in the physical environment provide. Whether that's through joining our Cadet Force, the Duke of Edinburgh's Award programme or training with our triathlon team, our students will learn the skills that will see them through their lives.

Physical sports should encourage a young person to extend themselves and see themselves as a physical being – by building a programme that includes climbing, caving, orienteering and triathlon sports, young people have a wider exposure to what they are capable of. Alongside this, a broad, general and inclusive fitness programme, supported by measurable, observable and repeatable results, is a core part of our provision. This programme prepares the young people for any physical contingency – not only for the unknown but for the unknowable, too.

Sixth Form. Our rigorous Sixth Form curriculum will provide the opportunity to study a wide variety of Cambridge International A Levels subjects valued by high performing universities and employers alike. All taught by a highly qualified and experienced team of subject specialist in small class sizes. Believing it is important for students to present more than a suite of examination results, we offer a broad range of enrichment courses, enhanced by our extensive facilities.

There is a range of full and weekly boarding options.

Fees per annum (2018–2019). UK/Domestic Students: Day Pupils £9,000–£12,000; Boarders £25,500–£28,100. International Students: Boarding £36,600.

Reductions are made in fees of second and subsequent siblings. Bursaries are available for children whose parents or guardians are key workers or from Forces families. There are scholarships for academic, sporting, music, drama, artistic or technological excellence. The college welcomes applications from pupils whose parents cannot afford the fees in full or in part. The college offers a wide range of discretionary and means-tested bursaries each year to pupils.

A prospectus and further details may be obtained from the UK Admissions Manager: admissions@myddelton college.com.

Headteacher: Mark Roberts, BSc, PGCE

Senior Deputy Head and Head of 21st Century Technology: Stuart Ayres, BSc, MSc, QTS
Deputy Head: Alicia Davies, BSc Hons, MSc, PGCE
Assistant Headteacher – Director of Learning: Andy Allman, BA Hons, MA, PGCE, QTS
Assistant Headteacher – Director of Studies: Ian Lloyd, BSc Hons, PG Cert, QTS
Assistant Headteacher – Director of Sport and Outdoor Learning: Nat Churchill, BSc Hons, PGCE

Heads of Faculty:
Head of English: Alan Biles-Liddell
Head of Science: Neil Bentley
Head of STEM-B: Paul Greene, MChem, PGCE, QTS
Head of Humanities: Joanne Orchard, BA Hons, PGCE
Head of Performing Arts: Laura Hughes, PGCE
Head of EAL and Languages: Joanna Davies, CELTA, Graduate Diploma
Head of Student Development Centre: Nikki Pritchard

Heads of House:
Andrew's: Mike Pearson, BSc, QTS
David's: Natasha Williams, BSc Hons, PGCE, QTS
George's: Edie Shemilt-Griffiths, BA Hons, PGCE
Patrick's: Gail Jones, BA Hons, PGCE

Teaching Staff:
English: Catherine Halford
Art/Technology: Gail Jones, BA Hons, PGCE
Physics: Tanya Owen, BSc, PGCE
Physics: Owen Jones, BSc
Chemistry and Physics: Ruth Cunliffe
Maths: Philippa Gillespie-Jones, BSc, PGCE
Maths: Sarah Vowles
Further Maths: Peter English, MA
Spanish: Miriam Alos
Business Studies: Edie Shemilt-Griffiths, BA Hons, PGCE
EAL: Iryna Graham, PGCE, MEP
Economics: John Hamilton
Humanities: Natasha Williams, BSc Hons, PGCE, QTS
Economics: John Hamilton
Humanities: Natasha Williams, BSc Hons, PGCE, QTS
EAL: Iryna Graham, PGCE., MEP
Prep School: Katie Gresley-Jones, BA Hons, PGCE, QTS, SEN Coordination
Prep School: Annie Williams
Sport: Mike Pearson, BSc, QTS
LTTO: Jack Stanyer, BSc Hons, PGCE

Boarding Staff:
Housemaster (Stanley's): Kyle Scott, BD Hons, PGCE, QTS
Housemistress (St George's): Stephanie Redfern-Jones, MA Hons, MA
Houseparent: Philippa Gillespie-Jones, BSc, PGCE
Houseparent: Jack Stanyer, BSc Hons, PGCE
Houseparent: Ayrun Edwards

Houseparent: Paul Greene, MChem, PGCE, QTS

Support Staff:
UK Admissions Manager: Carly Roberts
Finance Assistant: Sue Downes
College Secretary: Nicola Evans
Operations and Commercial Manager: Lisa Hitchen, BA
  Hons, CIM Dip M
Alumni Liaison Officer: Wendy Grey-Lloyd

Newcastle School for Boys

Senior School:
34 The Grove, Gosforth, Newcastle-upon-Tyne NE3 1NH
Tel: 0191 255 9300
Fax: 0191 213 0973
email: enquiries@newcastleschool.co.uk

Junior School:
30 West Avenue, Gosforth, Newcastle-upon-Tyne NE3 4ES
Tel: 0191 255 9300
Fax: 0191 213 1105
email: info@newcastleschool.co.uk

website: www.newcastleschool.co.uk

Age Range. 3–18.
Number of Boys. 400.
Fees per term (2018–2019). £3,163 (Reception), £3,655 (Years 1–2), £3,769 (Years 3–6), £4,616 (Year 7 and above).

Newcastle School for Boys is now established as the only independent school in the north east providing continuous education for boys from ages 3 to 18. Situated in Gosforth, Newcastle-upon-Tyne, the Senior School site on The Grove covers 5 acres of playing fields and buildings that currently house Years 7 to 11. Opposite the Senior School Years 12 and 13 are now housed in their own dedicated Sixth Form Centre, opened in September 2017. Our Junior School is housed on nearby sites on West Avenue and North Avenue. The School currently has 380 pupils on role from Nursery to Year 13.

The academic curriculum starts in the Infants and provides boys with opportunities for stretch and challenge from the outset. This leads through the Juniors to GCSE and A Level qualifications in a wide range of disciplines at the Senior School and Sixth Form.

Pastoral care is outstanding throughout the school and boys receive plenty of individual attention so that they grow in confidence and independence.

Newcastle School for Boys believes strongly in enhancing learning beyond the classroom and runs an extensive trips and visits programme with great emphasis being placed on this in the junior and infant departments. Residential and day visits are offered to all pupils from age 5 onwards and culminate in major overseas trips and Duke of Edinburgh's Gold Award expeditions in the Sixth Form.

Senior School. The Senior School starts at Year 7 (11+) and runs through to Year 13 (18+).

We generally run two classes per year group and offer an enhanced curriculum leading up to GCSE, where most boys sit 10 subjects. The Senior School provides an extensive co-curricular programme of music, drama and a wide range of sports, including a number of major overseas trips. The School enhances its sporting provision through the use of a number of excellent local facilities including at South Northumberland Cricket Club and Northern Rugby Club.

Sixth Form. The School has established a successful and growing Sixth Form offering students a wide choice from a traditional AS and A Level structure. The Sixth Form provides the learning and support the boys need to achieve their best possible academic and personal outcomes.

Entrance and Scholarship Examinations are offered in January for boys entering Year 7 (11+), Year 9 (13+) and Year 12 (16+). Entry at other points is possible following a full academic assessment and interview.

Junior School. The learning environment across our Junior School is tailored to the needs of the younger boys, taking into account their energy and enthusiasm for challenge and discovery. The curriculum offered is a blend of the traditional and the innovative, and is designed to balance the need for adventure and fun, while maintaining progress in numeracy and literacy. The boys are provided with opportunities to develop their individual academic talents and to pursue their creative goals. Excellence is also pursued in the sporting arena where boys have opportunities including soccer, rugby, cricket, golf and fencing.

Regular drama performances and musical productions encourage teamwork and build confidence from an early age.

Breakfast club and after-school clubs and activities provide full 'wrap-around' care,

Charitable status. Newcastle School for Boys is a Registered Charity, number 503975.

Chairman of Governors: T J Care,

Headmaster: **D J Tickner**, BA, MEd

Deputy Head: G Hallam, BSc

Deputy Head: A Newman, BA

Head of Sixth Form: A Caulfield

Head of Junior School: T White

Bursar: C Dobson, FCCA

Ockbrook School
Derby

The Settlement, Ockbrook, Derbyshire DE72 3RJ
Tel: 01332 673532
email: enquiries@ockbrooksch.co.uk
website: www.ockbrooksch.co.uk
Twitter: @ockbrookschool
Facebook: @Ockbrook-School

Motto: *In Christo Omnia Possum*

Founded in 1799.

Independent Day and Boarding School for boys and girls aged 2–18. Member of The Society of Heads, IAPS and AGBIS.

Situation. Situated in the heart of the Midlands, Ockbrook School lies equidistant between the historic towns of Derby and Nottingham and is easily accessible from the motorway network, rail and air transport. The School is set in a superb rural position overlooking the Trent Valley and it is surrounded by its own estate including landscaped gardens, grounds, playing fields and farmland. This setting, and the high standard of facilities within it, provides an excellent environment for learning …free from urban noise and distractions.

Pupils. There are c400 pupils, who are divided between the Primary School (age 2–11) and Senior School (age 11–18). Boarders are accepted from the age of 11 years for entry into Year 7 or above.

Ethos. We aim to develop individual potential and self worth through stimulating and positive relationships and through an understanding of Christian values so that our pupils are prepared for the changes they will face in their future lives. We believe that education should be a partnership between School, pupils and parents. To this end we provide comprehensive feedback on progress in the classroom and welcome family and friends at our extracurricular drama productions, concerts, sports events, open door days and acts of worship.

Curriculum.

Primary School:

Early Years (Ages 2–5). A dynamic programme of language, numeracy and scientific activities provide a secure foundation for later conceptual development.

Key Stage 1 (Years 1 & 2). The core subjects of Mathematics, Science and English are covered in addition to nine other subject areas including French and Information Communications Technology.

Key Stage 2 (Years 3–6). Study for the core of subjects continues with additional experience in nine other subjects including Dance, Drama and Gymnastics.

Teachers' assessments are carried out throughout both Key Stages and form the basis of internal assessment procedures for progression through to the Senior School at 11+.

Senior School:

Lower School (Years 7–9). Pupils study the core subjects and a broad range of additional subjects including ICT, French, Spanish, German, Drama and PSHCE (Personal, Social, Health & Citizenship Education). From Year 9 students follow IGCSE courses in Mathematics and the three sciences.

Upper School (Years 10–11). At GCSE level all pupils study Mathematics, English Language and English Literature, plus additional subjects; there is a wide range of options.

Sixth Form. Students usually study 3 subjects in Sixth Form, although Further Mathematics can be studied as an additional A Level. A wide range of subjects is available and students can opt to do an additional EPQ. Great emphasis is placed on the development of Life Skills which help to develop the competencies so necessary for adult life, whilst adding to the breadth of study. The vast majority of pupils leaving the Sixth Form proceed to higher education, including Oxbridge.

Sport. As well as the core PE subjects the school has a strong tradition in sport, i.e. athletics, cross country, netball, swimming and rounders etc. Teams of various ages, in most sports, have full fixture lists with neighbouring schools and the School is proud of its County and National representatives. We are also a member of the Sports Leaders Award Scheme.

Activities. The Duke of Edinburgh's Award scheme is available to pupils over the age of 14, together with a wide range of trips and outdoor holidays, walking, canoeing and skiing. Other activities include Young Enterprise, Wilderness Expertise, Community Service, chess, debating, and numerous other clubs or societies. A School Holiday Club also operates from the School.

Music and Drama. Many pupils learn musical instruments and a large number play to a high standard. Opportunities are provided by the Primary and Senior choirs, orchestras, chamber choir, strings group, and wind band. Performance venues include Westminster Abbey, Manchester, Derby and Barcelona Cathedrals, Ojab-Haus Aigen, Salzburg, Salzburg Cathedral, Pfarrkirche Bad Ischl Salzburg and Chatsworth House, Derbyshire. There is a wide range of dramatic productions each year providing as many pupils as possible with the chance of developing their dramatic talents.

Art and Design & Technology. Great emphasis is given to the development of creative talent both as academic subjects and interests. Out-of-class involvement is strongly encouraged.

Fees per term (2018–2019). Tuition £2,985–£4,390. For Boarding fees please contact the Registrar.

Admission. *Primary School*: Entry is decided as a result of a combination of interview, assessment day and school report (if applicable).

Senior School: Entry is decided as a result of a combination of interview, assessment, school report and if necessary an entrance examination held throughout the year and in January for Year 7 and Year 12.

Sixth Form: Entry is decided as a result of a combination of interview, school report, predicted GCSE grades and ultimately a good performance in the GCSE examinations.

Scholarships and Bursaries. Scholarships are available for Academia, Sport, Art, Drama and Music (including voice) for Year 7 and Sixth Form entry. A Head Teacher's Award is also available for all-round achievement. Bursary applications are considered by way of a full means test which may also include a home visit assessment. Full details are available from the Registrar, Mrs J Sheldon, email: enquiries@ockbrooksch.co.uk.

School Prospectus. A prospectus and registration details may be obtained from the Registrar, details as above, or on the school website: www.ockbrooksch.co.uk. Parents are encouraged to visit the School and appointments may be made by contacting the Registrar.

Charitable status. Ockbrook School is a Registered Charity, number 251211.

Governing Body:
Chair of Governors: Mrs A Redgate, LLB
Deputy Chair: Mr J Luke
Mr J Bailey
Revd J Kreusel
Dr G Lamming, FRCOG
Dr V Poultney, MEd
Mr C Purcell, BA Hons, MCIPR
Mrs M Ralph, MEd, MCollP
Mrs G Taylor, FCA

Clerk to the Governors: Mrs J Buckley

Leadership Team:

Headmaster: **Mr T Brooksby**, BEd Crewe & Alsager, NPQH

Head of Primary & Music Coordinator: Mrs S Worthington, BA Exeter
Deputy Head: Mrs H Springall, BA Newcastle, MA Open, NPQH
Deputy Head of Primary & ICT Coordinator: Mr R Beach, BA Sussex
Head of Lower (Years 7–10): Mrs S Wood, BA Hull
Head of Upper (Years 11–13): Mr N Gupta, BSc MAPSE Leicester
Head of Achievement and Progress: Mr A Walsh, BA Huddersfield

Early Years:
Mrs S Taylor, BA Scarborough (*Head of Early Years*, EY SpLD)
Mrs N Felstead, BA Loughborough [Maternity Leave]
Miss G Cresswell, BA Nottingham Trent [Maternity Cover]

Primary Department:
Mrs S Breedon, BA Nottingham (*English Coordinator*)
Mrs J Cresswell, BEd College of St Mark & St John

Mrs L Ireland, BEd Derby (*PSHCE Coordinator*)
Mrs M Lamell, BA Newcastle (*Drama*)
Mrs H Marsden , BEd Derby (*History, Geography & RS Coordinator*)
Mrs K Morris, BA Norwich School of Art & Design (*Art, DT Coordinator*)
Mrs J Mullineux, BEd Bedford College (*Physical Education, Dance, Humanities*)
Mrs B Thornton, BEd Derby (*Science Coordinator*)
Mr D Williams, BEd Bangor (*PE Coordinator*)
Mrs P Ward, CertEd Kesteven

Senior Department:
Mrs L Archibald, BA Leeds (*Food Technology & Head of Careers*)
Mrs J Bacall, BA Sheffield Hallam (*English*)
Mrs F Birkbeck, BA Edinburgh, MEd (*Psychology*)
Ms K Chetwin, BSc London, BA Nottingham (*Science & Business Studies*)
Ms K Cleland, MA Glasgow (*English*)
Miss L Colgan, BA Plymouth (*Drama*)
Mrs L Coggle, BSc Sheffield (*Mathematics & Head of Boarding*)
Mrs R Dwight, BSc Loughborough (*Geography*)
Mrs F Faulkner, BSc Newcastle (*ICT*)
Mrs C Fletcher-Eton, BSc Loughborough (*Religious Studies*)
Mrs M Lamell, BA Newcastle (*Drama*)
Mrs C McBeth, BEd MSc Loughborough (*SENDCo*)
Mrs J McGahey, BA Leeds (*Fine Art, Art & Design, Art Textiles*)
Mr J McNaughton, MA Cambridge (*Geography*)
Mrs E Marsh, BSc Leeds (*Physics, Sciences*)
Mrs J Moses, BA Nottingham (*Modern Languages*)
Mrs S Mitchell, BA Hull (*English*)
Mrs K Moorhouse, BSc Loughborough (*Physical Education, Dance*)
Mr R Moorhouse, BSc Loughborough (*Physical Education*)
Mr B Mistry, BSc Loughborough (*Chemistry*)
Mrs A M Newton, BSc Essex (*Mathematics*)
Mrs R O'Reilly, BA Liverpool (*Physical Education, Dance*)
Mrs S Price, BSc York (*Chemistry/Sciences*)
Miss A Renow, BA Leicester, MEd Nottingham (*History*)
Mr T Sands, BA Sheffield Hallam (*Product Design*)
Mrs S Scott, BSc Hertfordshire (*Biology*)
Mrs A Sidery, BEd Nottingham (*English*)
Mr E Swindell, BMus, MMus Manchester (*Director of Music*)
Mrs P Theaker, BSc Nottingham (*Mathematics*)
Mrs J Wakefield, BSc University of Wales (*ICT*)
Mrs M Watkins, BA Leeds (*Modern Languages*)
Mrs S West, BA Birmingham (*Drama*)
Mrs A Wright, BA Derby (*History*)

Support Staff:
Head Teacher's PA: Miss C McMain
Business Manager: Mrs E Green
Operations Manager: Mrs J Buckley
Registrar: Mrs J Sheldon
Finance and HR Assistant: Mrs N Brierley
Administrator: Miss L Lambord
Administrator: Mrs S Everill
Network Manager: Mr A Crowter

Boarding Houses Staff:

Mrs M Cooper	Miss G Hawkins
Mrs S Cooper	Mrs W Holmes
Miss J Cresswell	Mrs C Horspool
Mr A Evans	Mrs L McClay
Mrs R Gascoigne	Miss H Naylor
Mrs J Halford	Miss M Spectrum

Ms D Sycamore
Miss K Sharratt (*Boarding Coordinator*)
Mrs K Taylor

Classroom Assistants:

Mrs C Bowers	Mrs A Kenyon, NNEB
Miss C Brewster	Mrs J Leighton, NNEB
Mrs S Cooper, Cert EYP	Mrs C Newby, BSc
Mrs J Federici	Mrs K Nutty
Mrs S Hawksworth, NNEB	Mrs S Payne
Mrs A-M Heaps	Mrs M Shawcross
Mrs L Holmes, BTEC	

Nurse: Mrs L Tanser, RN

Technicians:
Mrs S Cullen, BSc (*Combined Science*)
Miss V Betesta

Librarian: Mrs C Purcell, BSc, MSc

Our Lady's Abingdon Senior School

Radley Road, Abingdon, Oxfordshire OX14 3PS

Tel:	01235 524658
Fax:	01235 535829
email:	office@olab.org.uk
website:	www.olab.org.uk
Twitter:	@OLAabingdon
Facebook:	@OLAabingdon

Motto: *Age Quod Agis – Whatever you do, do it well*

Founded in 1860 by Mother Clare Moore of the Sisters of Mercy, Our Lady's Abingdon (OLA) is an independent, Catholic day school, for boys and girls aged 3–18. The school welcomes pupils of all faiths and none who wish to benefit from its nurturing and outward-looking ethos. OLA offers outstanding pastoral care and a wide range of academic and co-curricular activities, ensuring that pupils are confident and engaged and leave school excited about their next steps in life.

Small class sizes allow staff to get to know every single pupil, giving them the support and encouragement they need to fulfil their academic and personal potential.

Following our ISI Inspection in 2015 OLA received an excellent report, which noted in particular that: '*The school is successful in providing a good quality of education and meeting its aim to encourage respect for the individual and, through this, to develop self-confidence. Throughout the school pupils are well-motivated, communicate easily and have well-developed skills for learning. Pastoral care is excellent.*'

Numbers. There are 311 pupils aged 11–18 in the Senior school and 75 pupils aged 3–11 in the Junior section, which is on the same site under its own headteacher, Erika Kirwan. (*See Junior School entry in IAPS section.*)

Facilities and Buildings. Bright, spacious classrooms and an excellent library provide a pleasant ambience conducive to study and learning. Extensive grounds surround the buildings, providing an attractive setting in which pupils can play and relax during breaks. Sports facilities include football and rugby pitches, a multi-use games area, tennis courts, a sports hall, hockey and athletics provision and a 25-metre indoor swimming pool. The school has benefited from a refurbished Nursery and new dining rooms and a 70 seater cafe, with other recent building projects including a Design & Technology centre, an auditorium and library, the latest in ICT equipment and additional Science laboratories. The Music department benefits from new facilities to aid composition and support the wide variety of instruments taught in the school.

Curriculum. The school teaches a balanced range of subjects both academic and practical during the first three years. Latin is a core subject in Y7 and 8. Pupils usually take 10 or 11 subjects at GCSE, including English Language and English Literature, Mathematics, Science (Combined Science or Biology, Chemistry and Physics), Religious Studies and French or Spanish. Options are chosen from the Humanities to Classics and Physical Education. Three subjects are studied in the Sixth Form, with many students taking the opportunity to take the EPQ (Extended Project Qualification) in the Lower Sixth. Some take Further Mathematics as a fourth A Level. The great majority of Sixth Form students go on to Higher Education, but some have also succeeded in gaining places on highly competitive professional placement programmes. There is also support throughout the school for pupils with special educational needs and for pupils for whom English is not their first language.

Co-curricular activities. The school provides an extensive programme of co-curricular activities including drama, music, art, public speaking and many forms of sport. Sailing is particularly popular. Buses run later on three evenings a week to accommodate these activities and to allow for supervised homework. There is also a strong commitment to local community schemes and an impressive record in the Duke of Edinburgh's Award scheme and Young Enterprise. OLA has regularly been accredited with the British Council's International School Award for the links it has fostered with schools in Uganda.

Fees per term (2018–2019). Senior School: £5,350; Junior School: £3,158–£4,383.

Admission. Through the school's own Entrance Examination at 11 and 13; pupils require at least 5 GCSEs at Grade 5 for entry at Sixth Form level with at least Grade 6 in the subjects they wish to study at A Level. Pupils interested in entering the Sixth Form for whom English is a second language must in addition have achieved a minimum level of 6.5 in IELTS for each category. Pupils may join in any year if a place is available with the exception of Years 11 and Upper Sixth.

Pupils may apply for Scholarships for entry to Year 7, Year 9 and the Sixth Form. Candidates may also apply for bursaries, which are awarded at the discretion of the Governors.

Charitable status. Our Lady's Abingdon Trustees Limited is a Registered Charity, number 1120372, and a Company Limited by Guarantee, registered in England and Wales, number 6269288.

Board of Governors:
Chairman: Mr E McCabe, MA Oxon, MBA
Mr T Ayling, MA Oxon
Dr L Bergmeier, PhD, CBiol, MRSB, FHEA
Mr J Cunliffe, MA Oxon
Mrs A Freeman, BEd
Mr A Hearn, MNAEA
Revd J McGrath, STB, MA
Ms L Mills, BA, BSc
Mr F Peck
Sr P Roker, MA Cantab
Mrs H Ronaldson
Mrs M Shinkwin, BA, MA Ed, NPQH
Dr E Wheaton, BA, MA, PhD
Mr P Williams, MA Oxon
Dr Jacqueline Woodman, MB ChB, MRCOG, MA, MEd Ed, DPhil Oxon

Bursar & Clerk to the Governors: Mr P Karian, CIPD

Leadership Team:

***Principal*: Mr S Oliver**, BA Birmingham, MLitt St Andrews, PGCE Cantab

Deputy Head: Mr N Hathaway, BA Sheffield, PGCE Leicester, PG Dip Ed Warwick
Deputy Head, Academic: Mrs S Robson, BSc Manchester, NPQSL, PGCE Portsmouth
Bursar: Mr P Karian, CIPD

Year Tutors:
Sixth Form Tutor: Mr D Willcock, MA Oxon
Year 11 Tutor: Mr A Jackson, BA, PGCE Gloucestershire, MSc Nottingham
Year 10 Tutor: Mrs C Sharkey, BA De Montfort, PGCE UWE
Year 9 Tutor: Mr L Allen, BSc, PGCE Cardiff
Year 8 Tutor:Mr P Hudson, BSc, PGCE London
Year 7 Tutor: Mrs E Irving, MA, PGCE

Heads of Departments:
Art: Mrs H Holden, BA Oxford Brookes, BA, PGCE Limerick, MSt Oxon
Careers: Mr C Sissons, BEd
Classics: Miss P Smith, BA Oxon
Design & Technology: Mr N Humphreys, BEd Wales
Drama: Dr E Lawson BA MA Loughborough, PhD Canterbury
Economics & Business Studies: Mrs L Webster, BA Nottingham, Grad Dip, MEd Sydney
English: Mrs K Thompson, MA St Andrews, PGCE Leeds
Geography: Mr A Jackson, BA, PGCE Gloucestershire, MSc Nottingham
History: Mr A Weekes, BA, PGCE Swansea
Learning Support: Mrs L Barr, BA, MA, PGCE London, MSt Oxon
Mathematics: Mrs A Knight, BSc Nottingham, PGCE Cantab
Modern Languages: Mme H Pang, MA Versailles St Quentin
Music: Mr N Farrow, MA Oxon
Physical Education (Girls): Mrs M Barnett, BA Chichester
Physical Education (Boys): Mr L Allen, BSc, PGCE Cardiff
PSHE: Ms S Martin-Morrissey, BA Leeds, PGCE, NASENCO London
Psychology: Mrs J James, BSc, PGCE, GTP
Religious Studies: Mr D Willcock, MA Oxon
Science: Mr A Easton, BSc, PGCE Reading
Textiles: Mrs C Sharkey, BA De Montfort, PGCE UWE

Admissions Registrar: (*to be appointed*)
Marketing and Communications Manager: Mrs H Alderman, BA Brighton
Principal's PA: Mrs J Braley, BSc Bradford
School Business Manager: Ms T Wheatley

The Peterborough School
A Woodard School

Thorpe Road, Peterborough PE3 6AP

Tel:	01733 343357
	Bursar: 01733 355720
Fax:	01733 355710
email:	office@tpsch.co.uk
website:	www.thepeterboroughschool.co.uk
Twitter:	@PeterboroughSch

The Peterborough School is the City's only independent day school for boys and girls from Nursery to Sixth Form.

Situated in beautiful surroundings in the heart of Peterborough, the School enjoys excellent road and rail links. The School is a member of the Woodard Corporation, the largest group of Church of England Schools in England and Wales.

Situation and Buildings. The School is located in beautiful secluded grounds, near the centre of Peterborough, 50 minutes by fast train from King's Cross and easily accessible by road from the A1, A14 and A47. The elegant Victorian house is the centre of a modern, purpose-built complex of classrooms, laboratories, Music School, Art Block, Sixth Form Centre, Library and a modern Computing Suite. The Sports Facility was completed in September 2012.

The Preparatory School. Boys and girls are admitted into the Reception Class from the age of 4+. The whole range of Key Stage subjects is covered in addition to a variety of other subjects and activities, e.g. Reasoning, French and other languages. Some subjects are taught by specialist staff from the Senior School. There is emphasis on academic standards, good manners, Physical Education, Music and Drama.

The Senior School. The curriculum of the Senior School is characterised by small classes and an emphasis on individual guidance and target-setting. A balanced programme leads to high achievement at GCSE. English, Mathematics, Sciences, Religious Education, Games and PE remain compulsory throughout; Languages, Computer Science, Food Tech, History and Geography, Art, Art Textiles and Design Technology, Music, Drama and Physical Education form the matrix of options. Spanish has recently been added to the curriculum.

External candidates are selected from the entrance examinations and opportunities for Scholarships exist at Year 7 and Sixth Form entry.

The School has a modern Computing Suite with state-of-the-art equipment, including iPads and laptops. All classrooms are networked.

There are specialist laboratories for all sciences and a new Sixth Form science lab.

In the Sixth Form students usually take three A Level subjects but may in some circumstances undertake four. These are linear qualifications, with examination at the end of the two-year course of study: there are no AS examinations available at the end of the Lower Sixth. In addition to their academic studies, Sixth Formers undertake a significant enrichment programme that includes volunteering, the Extended Project Qualification (EPQ) and an electives programme.

As a School with pupils from Reception and children in the Nursery from 6 weeks and above, older pupils have many opportunities to develop a sense of involvement and responsibility, and carry out valuable service in the wider School community. Business sense is developed through the Young Enterprise scheme, in which the School is very successful. The Duke of Edinburgh's Award Scheme is also prioritised.

The Nursery. The Peterborough School Nursery offers daycare for children aged from 6 weeks to 4 years. Optional lessons include French, Ballet and Key Sports.

Religion. Weekly Communion Services are held and attendance is compulsory, although participation is optional.

Music and Drama. The music of the School, in particular its choral tradition, is renowned and the School benefits from holding its own Music Festival. Tuition in singing, piano and all orchestral instruments is available. Major theatrical and musical productions take place several times a year, and the School presents an Art & Design Exhibition each summer.

Games and Physical Education. The pupils achieve outstanding success in team and individual sports and athletics. Many pupils have represented the county, the region,

and Team GB. The School estate is spacious with several pitches and all-weather courts. The many and varied sporting facilities of the city are within easy reach for swimming, rowing and athletics. The School is benefiting from the major development of its Sports Facility, including a Fitness Suite and Climbing Wall.

Extra-curricular Activities. Many clubs and societies operate in extra-curricular time, and field visits and excursions illuminate classroom work. Many pupils undertake the Duke of Edinburgh's Award Scheme at both Bronze and Gold levels, with outstanding success and the School has its own St John Ambulance division. Cubs, Scouts and Beavers are also run from the School.

Fees per term (2018–2019). Reception/Infants £3,314; Years 3–6 £4,051; Years 7–13 £4,956.

Lunches/snacks are paid in addition; they are compulsory and annualised.

Scholarships. Academic, Art, Music and Sport are the main scholarships available to those entering Year 7. Woodard All-rounder Scholarships are also available for Senior students at the Headmaster's discretion. Sixth Form Academic Scholarships are also available. Please apply to the Registrar for more information.

The Peterborough School Alumni (Westwoodians' Association). Secretary: Mrs Ivana Zizza who is based at the School.

Charitable status. The Peterborough School Limited is a Registered Charity, number 269667. It is an independent school which exists to promote the education of children.

School Council:
Chairman: Ms L Ayres, LLB
Revd Canon I Black, BA, MDiv
Mrs P Dalgliesh
Mrs L Frisby
Mrs K Hart, BA Hons
Mr P Hayes
Prof C J Howe, MA, DPhil, FLS
The Rt Revd R Ladds, SSC, Provost of Woodard Schools
Mrs H Milligan-Smith, LLB Hons
Mrs E Payne
Mr P Simmons
Mr P Southern, FRICS
Dr J S Thompson, LMSSA, MBBS, DRCOG

Head: **Mr A Meadows**, BSc Hons Manchester, NPQH

Bursar: Mr N A Johnson, MA, FCMI
Deputy Headmaster: Mr R Cameron, BA Hons Southampton
Head of the Preparatory School: Mrs A-M Elding, MA OU, BEd Hons Derby
Head of Pastoral Care: Mrs E Rivers, BSc Hons London
Director of Sixth Form: Mr A Stroud, BA Hons Oxon
Chaplain: Revd T Sherring, MTh Oxon, BA Exeter

Staff:
Miss H Adams, BSc Hons (*Mathematics*)
Mrs L Andrew, BEd Hons (*Preparatory*)
Mr P Baldwin, BA Hons (*Preparatory*)
Mr K Bingham, BA Hons (*Preparatory*)
Mr C Brocklesby, BA Hons (*Geography*)
Mrs K Brocklesby, BSc (*Mathematics*)
Mrs H Brookes, BA Hons (*English*)
Miss A Buxcey, BA Hons (*Religious Education*)
Mrs C Castell, BA Hons (*Physical Education*)
Miss Z Chappell, BA Hons Cantab (*Preparatory*)
Miss S M Clarkson, BA Hons Cantab (*History*)
Miss H Clisset, BA Hons (*Dance*)
Mr G Cloke, BSc Hons (*Preparatory*)
Miss S Cummings, BA Hons (*Chemistry*, *Head of Key Stage 4*)

Mrs K Davis, BSc Hons (*Chemistry, Head of Key Stage 3*)
Mrs R Ditcher, BSc Hons (*Preparatory*)
Mr S Dyer, BA Hons (*Economics, Business Studies*)
Mrs J Evans, Licence Limoges (*French*)
Dr L Fox-Clipsham, PhD, BSc (*Science*)
Mrs L Grinyer, BA Hons (*English*)
Mrs R Hampson, BA Hons (*Art, Textiles*)
Mr A Harwin, BA Hons (*Art*)
Miss C Johnson, BSc Hons (*Biology*)
Mrs E Kay, BSc Hons (*Physical Education*)
Mr C King, BSc Hons, CMath, MIMA (*Mathematics*)
Ms A Kupara, BA (*Computing & Digital Strategy*)
Mr S Law, BSc Hons (*Physics*)
Miss L McChlery, BEd (*Preparatory*)
Mrs L McClarnon, BEd Hons (*Preparatory*)
Mrs H McKillop, BA Hons GB SM, LTCL (*Music*)
Mr C McManus, MA, BA Hons (*History*)
Mr J Marsden, BSc Hons (*Physical Education*)
Miss J Martin, BA Hons (*Physical Education*)
Mrs G Mason, OND Hotel & Catering (*Food Technology & Preparatory Teaching Assistant*)
Mr D Moxon, BSc Hons, MSc (*Psychology*)
Mrs S Noone, BEd (*Preparatory*)
Mrs E Porsz, BA Hons (*Physical Education*)
Ms E Potbury, BA Hons (*French*)
Mrs A Quy, BSc Hons (*Preparatory*)
Mrs J Roberts, BA Hons (*English*)
Ms S Robinson, BEd Hons (*Preparatory*)
Mr P Schavier, Masters Degree (*German*)
Mrs R Shang, BA Hons (*Drama, PSHE*)
Mrs M Silvester, BSc Hons (*Mathematics*)
Mrs A Skelton, BA Hons (*Preparatory*)
Miss C Steward, BA Hons (*Preparatory*)
Mr M Twigg, BA Hons (*Product Design*)
Mrs C Wagner-Lees, BA Hons (*German*)
Mrs S Ward, BSc Hons, PGCE (*Head of Individual Learning*)
Mrs L Wisdom, BSc (*Geography*)
Mrs J Young, BSc Hons (*Physical Education*)

Instrumental Music/Speech & Drama :
Miss K Birtles, BMus Hons (*Flute & Oboe*)
Mr R Brain, BA Hons, MA (*Director of Choral Music*)
Mr J Cranfield, BA Hons (*Guitar*)
Ms T Doyle, MNATD (*SPeech & Drama*)
Mr S Hamper, Army School of Music (*Percussion*)
Mr R Haylett, BA Hons Cantab (*Singing*)
Mr M Jewkes (*Jazz Piano & Saxophone*)
Mrs M McAuliffe, Dip ABRSM (*Violin*)
Mr C Patterson, GRNCM, PPRNCM, ARCM (*Trumpet*)
Mrs P Samuels, LGSM Cert Acting GSMD (*Speech & Drama*)
Miss E Smith BMus Hons (*Lower Strings*)

Administrative Officers:
Head's PA: Mrs J Farrow
Marketing Manager/Registrar: Mrs L Pengelly
Development Manager/Assistant Registrar: Mrs I Zizza
Administration/HR Assistant: Mrs Z Vickers
Administrative Assistant: Miss E Nicholson, BA Hons
Accounts: Mrs J House BA Hons, Mrs R Forman
Domestic Bursar: Mrs Z Clark
Estate Manager: Mr C Lang
Laboratory Technician: Mrs A Albon, BSc
Art Technician: Miss H Senior, BA Hons
Network Manager: Mr L Taylor
IT Technician: Mr K Rossall
Food Technology Technician: Mrs V Tobin
LRC Manager: Mrs C Thomson
Receptionist: Mrs R Adcock

Teaching Assistants & Supervisors:
Mrs A Brennan

Miss C Callow
Mrs W Cohen
Miss F Cupoli
Ms E Drew, BA Hons
Mrs Z Green
Miss C Hudson
Mrs E Penniston, BA Hons
Miss D Pepper
Mrs J Reade
Miss D Skelton
Mr R Westbrook

Medical Staff:
Mrs F Aylmore, BSc Hons (*Senior Nurse*)
Mrs K Shepherd, DN, RM
Mrs M Lay, BSc Hons (*School Counsellor*)

Pitsford School

Pitsford Hall, Pitsford, Northamptonshire NN6 9AX

Tel: 01604 880306
Fax: 01604 882212
email: office@pitsfordschool.com
website: www.pitsfordschool.com
Twitter: @Pitsford_School
Facebook: @PitsfordSchool

Age Range. 4–18 Co-educational.
Number of Pupils. 300 boys and girls.
Fees per term (2018–2019). Junior School: £2,825–£4,582; Senior School: £4,902. Lunches: £304.

The School was founded in 1989 to offer a traditional Grammar School standard education to boys in Northamptonshire. Today, the School still offers the same high standards of education but to boys and girls from 4–18 years of age.

In April 2016 the school opened its brand new £2 million sports centre, complete with large sports hall, café and a state-of-the-art fitness suite.

Pastoral Care. The School's academic success is complemented by effective pastoral support. By keeping class sizes small, a friendly, family atmosphere is evident, allowing pupils to grow and develop in confidence as they progress through the School.

Admissions. Reception, Year 7 and Sixth Form are the most common years of entry to the School, although pupils may be admitted in other years when required, if space is available.

Entry to Key Stage 1: pupils are invited to spend a day with their current year group to ensure they are happy in their future surroundings.

Entry to Key Stage 2: pupils are invited in for an Assessment.

Entry to the Senior School: Prospective pupils are invited to sit the School's own entrance test.

It is expected all pupils will take 9 or 10 GCSEs before transferring to the Sixth Form at the end of Year 11.

The Sixth Form is structured to provide a stepping stone from the discipline of Senior School to the demands of Higher Education. Sixth Formers take a full part in the life of the School and have many positions of responsibility.

Sport and Extracurricular Activities. Rugby, netball, cricket, rounders and tennis are just some of the sports played throughout the School. In addition, the School's Cross Country Team enjoys ongoing success when competing against other Schools. The Pitsford Run is a well known local event.

Numerous Extracurricular Activities are on offer to pupils throughout the School:

Junior School activities range from the School Council to the English Speaking Board (ESB) and from rugby and netball to art and craft.

Senior School pupils have over 60 activities to choose from. Most Activities take place on site, however the School's excellent location means that a number of activities such as sailing, kayaking and fishing are available just a short distance from the School. All are extremely popular.

Music. Music is an integral element of school life at Pitsford School.

Musical Recitals are held in Pitsford Hall every Thursday lunchtime and in addition, the School holds Four Evening Concerts per year. Individual music lessons are available in a wide range of instruments and group participation and performance opportunities include; woodwind, guitar, percussion, strings, sax and flute ensembles and two choirs.

A number of Junior and Senior plays take place throughout the year, ranging from Shakespeare to Musicals.

Charitable status. Northamptonshire Independent Grammar School Charity Trust Limited is a Registered Charity, number 298910.

Governing Body:
Chairman: Mr A Tait

Mr M Adams	Mr K Mason
Mr J Brown	Mr A Moodie
Mr S Coleman	Reverend S Trott
Mrs J Harrop	Mrs S Burditt
Mr J Hartshorne	Mr M Gaskell

Headmaster: Dr Craig Walker

Deputy Head: Mrs F M Kirk, BA, MEd

* Head of Department

Mr O Auckland, BA Hons (*Junior School*)
Mrs C Ball (*Junior School*)
Mrs C Cabrera-Alvarez (*Modern Languages*)
Mrs F L Care, MA (*Mathematics*)
Mrs L A Chacksfield, BEd (*PE and Games**)
Mr M Cole (*PE and Games*)
Mme M H Conroy, BA (*Junior School*)
Mrs J Cowie, BA (*Junior School*)
Mrs A Cowling, BSc Hons (*Biology and Chemistry*)
Mrs J M Drakeford, BSc (*Chemistry and Biology**)
Dr J Ewington, BSc Hons, MSc, PhD (*Physics**)
Miss E Gant, BMus Hons (*Director of Music**)
Mrs S E Goode, BSc Econ (*Junior School*)
Mr Harrison, MA, PGCE (*History**)
Miss S M Jackson, BSc (*Head of Sixth Form, Chemistry*)
Mrs F Jeffrey, BA Hons (*Asst Head EYFS/KS1, Junior School*)
Mrs L Jones, BA (*Junior School*)
Mr M Kefford, BA (*PE and Games*)
Mrs C King, BA (*EFL*)
Mrs F M Kirk, BA, MEd (*English, General Studies*)
Mrs J M Leeke, BSc (*Mathematics*)
Mr M J Lewis, BSc, FRGS, FRMetS, CGeog (*Geography*, Careers & Higher Education*)
Mrs L M Lyon, BEd (*Modern Languages*)
Ms M F McQuilkin, BA (*Art**)
Mr D Jones (*Geography and Games*)
Mrs J Middlewood, BA (*Spanish*)
Mrs L Oseni (*Head of English*)
Mr J Smorfitt, BA (*Economics**)
Mr C L Stoner, BSc, MSc, Dip CEG (*Mathematics**)
Dr A Templeton, BSc, MSc, PhD (*Physics*)
Mrs H Thorne, BA, PGCE, CTABRSM (*Junior School Music*)
Mrs S Ellis (*History and Religious Studies*)

Mr F B Vié, Licence d'histoire, PGCE (*Modern Languages**)
Mrs C Whiting, MA (*ICT**)
Mrs J Willmott, BEd (*Head of Junior School*)
Miss L Woodford (*English*)

Bursar: Mr C Bellamy
Admissions: Mrs O Smallwood

Portland Place School
Alpha Plus Group

56–58 Portland Place, London W1B 1NJ

Tel:	020 7307 8700
Fax:	020 7436 2676
email:	admin@portland-place.co.uk
website:	www.portland-place.co.uk
Twitter:	@PortlandPlaceHd
Facebook:	@PortlandPlaceSchool

Portland Place School was founded in 1996 in response to demand in central London for a mixed school that provided for pupils from a broad range of backgrounds and abilities.

Age Range. 10–16 Co-educational.

Number of Pupils. Over 250 Day Pupils on average (60% boys and 40% girls).

Fees per term (2018–2019). £7,040.

Aims and Philosophy. Portland Place School is an independent school for boys and girls, located in the heart of central London. It was founded with a particular purpose in mind: to be an alternative to the intense, large, examination-focused independent day schools of which there are many in London.

We believe that exceptional teaching, combined with a modern curriculum inside and outside the classroom, provides the best stimulus for children to become inquisitive, open-minded and creative learners and achieve beyond exams.

We cater for a wide range of abilities and learning styles, achieving strong results at GCSE. At Portland Place School we focus on best preparing our students for any path they wish to take, inclusive of A Level courses, BTEC, Foundation courses and apprenticeships.

More importantly, our students come to school with a smile and are proud to be part of the Portland Place School community.

Location and Buildings. Portland Place is ideally located right in the centre of the capital, less than five minutes' walk from Regent's Park (where much of the outdoor sporting activities take place) and ten minutes' walk from Oxford Circus. The school is housed in two magnificent Grade II* listed James Adam houses in Portland Place with a separate Art, Drama and Science building and a Senior School building close by in Great Portland Street. The buildings have been refurbished to an exceptionally high standard. Classrooms are supplemented by specialist rooms for drama, photography and computing.

Curriculum. The curriculum at Portland Place is developed from the English National Curriculum and offers a flexibility that puts the pupil first. Homework is supervised until 5.00 pm for those who want or require it and each pupil has a homework diary that details the homework programme for each week. Each child takes part in a comprehensive programme of physical education. Pupils in Years 5–9 have four PE sessions per week. Full advantage is taken of its central London location and excellent local facilities available. The outdoor programme takes place in neighbouring Regent's Park and includes athletics, hockey, football, rugby, tennis and cross-country. Indoor sports include basketball and fencing. Pupils represent the school in numerous matches against other London schools and in national tournaments. Class music is a compulsory part of the curriculum in Years 5–9 and all pupils are encouraged, if they do not already play one, to take up a musical instrument and take advantage of the team of visiting instrumental teachers.

Sport and Extracurricular Activities. Our central London position means that we have easy access to world-class facilities. All children are encouraged to participate in an interesting and varied physical education programme. Portland Place School offers a wide range of popular sport including: athletics, basketball, cricket, cross country, fencing, football, hockey, netball, rounders, swimming, tennis and rugby. Outdoor sports take place in Regent's Park less than a ten-minute walk from the school. Indoor activities including basketball and fencing take place at the University of Westminster gym just minutes away in Regent Street. Swimming is at the Seymour Centre, and in the summer we have nets at Lords indoor school. Optional after-school sport activities abound with senior and junior clubs for matches held with schools across London and the UK.

There is a wide and expanding range of extracurricular activities that are offered at the end of afternoon school. Whole school productions, concerts, chamber groups and small dramatic workshops take place throughout the year and clubs ranging from politics and debating to games and Christianity all thrive throughout the year. During the last week of the summer term all pupils take part in an Activities Week that includes outdoor adventure centres and overseas trips.

Admission. Entry to the school (usually at 10+, 11+, and 13+) is by examinations in English and Mathematics and interview. Interviews for September entry are held in the Autumn term prior to entry and the school's entrance examination is in January.

Governance. Portland Place School is part of the Alpha Plus Group of schools.

Senior Management Team:

Headmaster: Mr David Bradbury, MSc Keele, MA Open, MInstP, CPhys (*Mathematics and Physics*)

Deputy Head (*Academic*): Ms Julia Findlater, MEd St Mary's Twickenham, BA Hons Sussex, PGCE (*English*)
Director of Studies: Ms Lucy Price, MA Edinburgh, PGCE (*Classical Civilisation and History*)
Head of Sixth Form: Mr Paul Jones, BA Leeds, PGCE (*Head of 6th Form/Media and Film*)
SENDCO: Miss Patricia Halcakova, BSc London, MA (*SENDCO*)

Teaching Staff:
Mrs Ambreen Baig, BA Hons Queen Mary London, PGCE (*English*)
Miss Danielle Beattie, MSc Queen Mary London, MRSC, PGCE (*Chemistry*)
Ms Carole Bignell, BA Hons Middlesex (*Learning Support Assistant*)
Miss Sarah Birtles, BA Hons UAL, PGCE (*Design and Technology*)
Miss Christina Boyle, BA Hons York, PGCE RNCM/MMU (*Music*)
Ms Katie Burnett, BEd Queensland University of Technology (*Physical Education*)
Mr Oliver Burton, BA East Anglia, PGCE UCL (*English*)
Miss Charlotte Butler, BA Hons Leeds, PGCE (*History*)

Ms Maeve Byrne, BComm Hons Dublin, PGCE (*Business Studies & Economics*)
Mr Juan Caballero Cabello, BA, CAP, PGCE, MA London, MEd Barcelona (*MFL, ICT and Maths*)
Ms Arabella Campbell, BSocSc Manchester, PGCE Exeter (*KS2 Teacher*)
Mr Patrick Capel, BA Rhodes, BA Hons Stellenbosch
Miss Theodora Chen, MA Cambridge, PGCE Anglia Ruskin (*Mathematics*)
Mr David Chivers, BA Cumbria, PGCE (*Drama*)
Dr Robert Dyer, PhD Imperial College London (*Biology*)
Mr Anthony Elliot, PGCE Bedfordshire (*Mathematics*)
Mr Michael Flack, PG Filmmaking Dip (*Media, Film Studies*)
Miss Daciana Florea, BEd Oradea Romania (*EAL*)
Mrs Emily Galvin, BA UCL, MA Royal Holloway, PGCE (*SEN*)
Mr Steven Hill, MA Roehampton, PGCE (*Music*)
Miss Jaimie Hubner, BA, MTeach Secondary Sydney (*English*)
Miss Hannah Johnston, BSc Hons St Andrews, PGCE (*Geography*)
Mr Matthew Jones, BA London, PGCE (*Art*)
Mrs Natalie Keen, BA Hons Manchester, PGCE (*English*)
Mr Joe Kubik, BA Hons St Mary's Twickenham, PGCE (*Physical Education*)
Mr Thomas Lalande, BA Bordeaux, PGCE (*French and Spanish*)
Mrs Caroline Lambert, BA Lancaster, PGCE (*Drama*)
Dr Luca Lapolla, PhD Birkbeck London, PGCE Worcester (*Italian*)
Miss Phoebe Lewis, BA Hons Newcastle Upon Tyne, PGCE (*History*)
Miss Christine Linton, BA Hons UAL, PGCE (*Design & Technology*)
Miss Charlotte Magniez, BA MA Boulogne-sur-Mer, GTP (*French and Spanish*)
Mr Adrian Martjiono, BSc London, PGCE (*Chemistry*)
Ms Tanya Nicholas, BA, BSc Hons Monash Australia, GDE OTTP (*Science*)
Miss Lauren O'Donnell, BA Hons Queen Mary London, PGCE (*English*)
Miss Teffany Osborne, BA Hons Slade (*Art*)
Ms Anita Philipovszky, BA Hons Universita di Roma La Sapienza, PGCE UCL (*Italian*)
Ms Ruth Picado, BA Coruna Spain, PGCE (*Spanish*)
Mrs Julie Rider, BSc London, GTP (*Physical Education*)
Mr Scott Rider, BA Hons Brunel, PGCE (*Physical Education*)
Mr Pardeep Sagoo, MSci Imperial College London, GTP (*Biology/Chemistry*)
Miss Sara Segerstrom, BEd Kalmar Sweden, PGCE (*Head of Mathematics*)
Mr Phillip Stanway, BA Manchester Metropolitan, PGCE (*Physical Education*)
Ms Alison Stringell, PG Slade, PGCE Goldsmiths (*Art*)
Mr Toni Tasic, BA Hons UCL, PGCE (*English*)
Mr Steve Thompson, BSc Plymouth, PGCE (*Physics*)
Ms Melanie Thorne, HDE Ed Natal, QTS Middlesex (*Business Studies*)
Dr Klaus Wehner, MA LCP (*Photography*)
Ms Nuria Waithe, BSc Westminster, PGCE IOE (*Psychology*)
Miss Natalie Whittle, BA Hons Chichester, PGCE (*Physical Education*)
Dr Nader Yazdi, MSc Leeds, PhD UCL, MBA Imperial (*Computing and ICT*)
Ms Paulina Zalesny, Dip Philiology Rzeszowksi (*SEN*)

Visiting Music Teachers:
Mr Nick Bentley (*Brass*)
Mr Adam Blake (*Guitar*)
Miss Zrinka Bottrill (*Classical Piano*)
Mr Jay Jenkinson (*Strings*)
Mr Sam Jesson (*Drums*)
Mr Darren McCarthy (*Guitar*)
Mr Mike O'Neill (*Jazz Piano*)
Mr John Slack (*Guitar*)
Mr Balint Szekely (*Violin*)

Administration and Support Staff:
Mr Gary Brazier (*Reception/Administrator*)
Ms Gail Buranathai (*Reception/Administrator*)
Ms Vicki Bromley (*Finance Officer*)
Mrs Mrs Belinda Carvalho (*Librarian*)
Ms Louise Gannon (*Creative Arts Technician*)
Mrs Anna Kashoumeri (*Reception/Administrator*)
Mrs Trish Kilby (*Reception/Administrator*)
Ms Golnar Narvani (*Head of Marketing*)
Mrs Caroline McNamara (*Exams Officer*)
Mrs Bronagh Preston (*Admissions Registrar*)
Mr Kim Wykes (*Science Lab Technician*)
Ms Laura Young (*PA to Headmaster*)

Caretaking Staff:
Mr Michael Murphy (*Premises Manager*)
Mr John Himana (*Maintenance*)
Mr Jay El Mouden (*Assistant Caretaker*)

The Purcell School

Aldenham Road, Bushey, Hertfordshire WD23 2TS

Tel: 01923 331100
Fax: 01923 331166
email: info@purcell-school.org
website: www.purcell-school.org
Twitter: @PurcellSchool
Facebook: @PurcellSchool

The Purcell School is one of the world's leading specialist centres of excellence and has a national and international reputation in the education and training of exceptional young musicians. It is the oldest specialist music school in the UK, having been founded as the Central Tutorial School for Young Musicians in 1962. It moved to its current site in Bushey, on the outskirts of London, in 1997.

There are around 180 students, boys and girls, aged from 11 to 17, with over 80 in the Sixth Form. All students are means-tested on entry to the School and are able to receive scholarships of up to 100% under the Government's Music and Dance Scheme, or from the School's own Bursary Fund.

The Purcell School exists to provide young musicians of exceptional promise and talent with the best possible teaching and environment in which to fulfil their potential, irrespective of their background. It has consistent success in national and international competitions and has an extensive programme of outreach and community work. The majority of students progress to music conservatoires although a small number each year elect to go to university to study both music and non-musical subjects.

The Music Department at The Purcell School aims to provide:

- A stimulating and challenging musical environment, at the heart of which is an individually tailored programme for every student. We try to ensure that both the balance of musical studies and the balance between musical and academic work are fine-tuned to suit each student.

- A flexible timetable, designed to enable students to practise. Students in Years 7 to 8 are able to practice up to 3 hours each day on their first study. In Years 9 and 10 that rises to 3–4 hours and Sixth Formers are able to do 4–5 hours or even more, depending on their academic commitments. We provide practice supervisors, themselves graduate musicians, who work with students up to Year 11 to ensure they use their practice time effectively. Our experienced and expert Music Specialist Teachers set practice goals and teach practice strategies.

- Twice-weekly contact with the student's first study specialist teacher for a total of up to 2 hours' tuition. All our music specialist teachers have considerable experience of working with motivated young musicians and have proven ability in enabling their students to succeed. Many of them also teach at the London conservatoires.

- An enriched musical programme that includes chamber music, orchestras, piano classes, choirs and aural and theory training. Frequent performing opportunities range from daily lunchtime concerts at School and in the surrounding area to formal recitals around the UK and in the capital's leading venues. Students can audition for the chance to play concertos with the School's orchestras, to give solo and chamber music recitals at the Queen Elizabeth Hall, Cadogan Hall, Wigmore Hall, Purcell Room, Milton Court Concert Hall, Kings Place and other prestigious venues.

- Visits from the world's leading musicians for masterclasses, recitals, courses and collaborative projects to enhance the work of our regular teachers.

- An academic programme which (as far as possible) is organised around each student's musical commitments, whilst still enabling students to achieve the necessary examination grades and all-round education to pursue a musical career if they choose, or to otherwise enjoy a successful future.

- Pastoral care which is provided by professionals who understand the demands on and needs of performing musicians. This includes dedicated boarding staff, a School nurse, physiotherapist and independent counsellor.

- A supportive and sympathetic peer group, keen to help each other to achieve their potential. We are well aware of the benefits of living in a musical environment in which all students understand and support each other, and this is an approach which we actively foster.

Academic Studies. The School aims to achieve a balance between musical studies and an all-round general academic education. Music comprises a significant proportion of the timetabled time depending on age and needs. The remainder of time is spent studying a range of subjects including Mathematics, English, Sciences, Modern Languages and Humanities. Students at The Purcell School are encouraged to regard their academic studies as an essential complement to their performing skills; the curriculum aims to nurture a rich cultural hinterland for each young person, such that their musicality is deepened as a result.

The size of the School ensures that classes are generally small. This allows for a great deal of individual attention from experienced and dedicated teachers.

All students are set homework each day and time is allocated in the boarding houses each evening for this to be completed. Students' academic progress is closely monitored and parents receive frequent progress reports.

Boarding. The Purcell School is international in its outlook and welcomes students from all over Britain and from all over the world. Over 79% are boarders, all of whom live on the School campus.

The youngest students live in Avison House. Sunley House (girls) Graham House (girls) and Gardner House (boys) all provide superb, up-to-date boarding facilities.

Members of the Sixth Form can use their rooms for practice as well as for study. In addition to the Houseparents, resident practice supervisors help the students to maintain their busy musical schedules.

In each half of the term there is normally an Exeat weekend when all students go home or to their guardian or to friends. There is also a half-term period in each of the three terms.

Admission. Entrance is by musical audition and interview – please see the School website for further details. The Registrar, Ms Karen Eldridge, can answer queries.

Fees per term (2018–2019). Day £8,656; Boarding £11,025.

Bursary funding is available, for those students who meet the eligibility criteria, under the Department for Education Music and Dance Scheme, and there is the possibility of means-tested financial support from the School for those who do not. Parents are welcome to consult the Bursar for guidance.

Charitable status. The Purcell School is a Registered Charity, number 312855. It aims to offer specialist musical training, combined with an excellent general academic education, to children of exceptional musical ability.

Royal Patron: HRH The Prince of Wales

Patrons:
Sir Simon Rattle, CBE, OM (*President*)
Baroness Warnock, DBE (*Vice-President*)
Vladimir Ashkenazy, CBE
Sir Andrew Davis, CBE
Donatella Flick
Dame Kiri Te Kanawa, DBE
Evgeny Kissin
Dame Fanny Waterman, DBE

Governing Body:
Sir Roger Jackling, KCB, BCE (*Chairman*)
Charles Beer, MA (*Chairman of Finance and General Purposes Committee*)
Professor Timothy Blinko, BMus Hons, MMus, Dip RCM
Jonathan Eley, MA
James Fowler, MA (*Chairman of Education Committee*)
Janice Graham, ARCM, AGSMD, ACT
Professor Colin Lawson, CBE, MA, MA, PhD, DMus, FRCM, FRNCM, FLCM, RAM
William McDonnell, BA
Dr Rebecca Mooney, DPhil, MSt, MA
Ian Odgers, MA
Mark Racz, BA, MFA Hon, FBC, Hon RAM
Joanna Van Heyningen, OBE, MA, MA, Dip Arch, RIBA
Kirsty Von Malaisé, BA Hons, MA

Principal: Paul Bambrough

Deputy Principal Academic: James Harding
Deputy Principal Pastoral: Christine Rayfield
Bursar: Aideen McNamara

Music Department:

Director of Music: Paul Hoskins

Head of Strings: Charles Sewart
Pál Banda (*Cello*)
Aiste Dvarionaite Berzanskiene (*Violin*)
Leon Bosch (*Double Bass*)
Alexander Boyarsky (*Cello*)
Sarah-Jane Bradley (*Viola*)
Tony Cross (*Alexander Technique*)
Tony Cucchiara (*Violin*)
Alda Dizdari (*Violin*)
Tanja Goldberg PhD (*Violin*)
Sadagat Mamedova-Rashidova (*Violin*)
Francesco Mariani (*Guitar*)

Jean Mercer (*Alexander Technique*)
Julian-David Metzger (*Cello*)
Nathaniel Vallois (*Violin*)

Head of Keyboard: William Fong
Lidia Amorelli (*Piano*)
Justas Dvarionas (*Piano*)
David Gordon (*Harpsichord & Improvisation*)
Caterina Grewe (*Piano*)
Gareth Hunt (*Piano*)
Jianing Kong (*Piano*)
Alla Kravchenko (*Piano*)
Ching-Ching Lim (*Piano*)
Tessa Nicholson (*Piano*)
Danielle Salamon (*Piano*)
Tatiana Sarkissova (*Piano*)
Deborah Shah (*Piano/Accompanist*)
Daniel Swain (*Accompanist*)
Patsy Toh (*Piano*)
Nafis Umerkulova (*Piano*)

Daphne Boden (*Harp*)
Tony Cross (*Trumpet*)
Daniella Ganeva (*Percussion*)
Kevin Hathaway (*Percussion*)
Tom Marandola (*Voice*)
Charlotte Seale (*Harp*)
Jill Washington (*Voice*)
Stephen Wick (*Tuba*)

Head of Wind, Clarinet: Joy Farrall
Joy Farrall (*Clarinet*)
Amy Green (*Saxophone*)
Graham Hobbs (*Bassoon*)
Barbara Law (*Recorder*)
Anna Pope (*Flute*)
Melanie Ragge (*Oboe*)
Stephen Williams (*Clarinet*)

Head of Jazz: Simon Allen
Sebastiaan De Krom (*Jazz Drums*)
David Gordon (*Jazz Piano*)
George Hogg (*Jazz Trumpet*)
Trevor Mires (*Jazz Trumpet*)
Chris Montague (*Jazz Trumpet*)
Steve Waterman (*Jazz Trumpet*)

Head of Composition: Alison Cox
Jacques Cohen
Brain Elias
Simon Speare

Head of Academic Music: Andrew Williams
Alison Cox
John Goldie-Scot
Edward Longstaff
Christine Rayfield

Head of Music Technology: Aidan Goetzee

Academic Staff:
Dr Kristian Angelov (*Philosophy and Theology*)
Dr Margaret Brookes (*Chemistry, Head of Science*)
Paul Elliott (*Drama, Head of German*)
Panos Fellas (*Physics*)
James Harding (*English*)
Deborah Harris (*Juniors*)
Jocelyne Hazan (*French*)
Katherine Higgins (*Head of EFL*)
Saleem Izhar (*Mathematics*)
Andrew Leverton (*Head of English*)
Jane Malan (*English, History*)
Darrell Pigott (*Head of History*)
Nadine Sender (*Head of Art*)
Adam Simmonds (*English*)
Alexandra Stone (*Head of Mathematics*)

Ziggi Szafranski (*Drama, Head of Sixth Form*)
Martin Whitfield (*Mathematics*)
Sally-Ann Whitty (*Head of Learning Support*)
Elizabeth Willan (*Head of Modern Languages, Head of French*)
Dorothy Withers (*Biology*)

Head of Sport: Christopher Lehane

Boarding Houses:
Avison Houseparent: Jane Malan
Gardner Houseparent: Dr Kristian Angelov
Graham Houseparent: Rachel Branch
Sunley Houseparent: Dr Margaret Brookes
Sunley House Resident Assistant and Practise Supervisor: Alicja Herma
Graham House Resident Assistant and Practise Supervisor: Ana Perez
Gardner and Avison House Matron: Annette Cook
Sunley House Day Matron: Susie Hunter
Gardner and Graham Day Matron: Katharine Mendes da Costa

Administration Staff:
PA to the Principal: Shirley Clark
Deputy Bursar: Jo Wallis
School Office: Caroline Fletcher, Antonia Holmes, Jannice Raw
Administrator & Overseas Student Coordinator: Louise Wigodsky
Catering: Holroyd Howe Independent Limited
Concerts Administrator: Bethany Wickens
Concerts Manager: Jane Hunt
Development Assistant: Celia Findell
Development Assistant: Emma McGrath
Development Manager: Ruth Blake
Estates Manager: Tina Little
Exams Officer: Andrea Alexander
Finance Manager: Susan Pickard
ICT Network Manager: Simon Kingsbury
Music Timetabler: Fiona Duce
Physiotherapist: Sarah Upjohn
PR & Communications Manager: Susannah Curran [maternity leave]
PR & Communications Manager: Katie Millman [maternity cover]
Registrar: Karen Eldridge
School Nurse: Hilary Austin
Science Technician: Hawreen Osman
Technology Technician: Tom Bell
UA Technician: Matthew Brownlee

The Read School
Drax

Drax, Selby, North Yorkshire YO8 8NL
Tel: 01757 618248
Fax: 01757 617432
email: enquiries@readschool.co.uk
website: www.readschool.co.uk

Age Range. Co-educational 3–18 (Boarding 8–18).
Number in School. Total 200: Day 170, Boarding 30; Boys 125, Girls 75.

The school is pleasantly situated in the rural village of Drax and is very convenient for main rail (Doncaster, York, Leeds) and road access (M62, M18, A1). Manchester is the nearest international airport (1½ hours distant). It is a relatively small school where children are well known to each other and to the staff.

The school has been a focal point for education in the Selby-Goole area since the 17th century and is celebrating its 350th anniversary throughout 2017. There has been a school on the same site since 1667 and it is proud to be one of the oldest educational establishments in the UK. The school has been co-educational since 1992 and offers a wide range of academic studies at GCSE and A Level, together with a full programme of Sports, Drama, Music, CCF and recreational activity. There is one class in each Prep School year from Pre-School to Year 6. There are two classes in each of the Senior years (7–11). There is a small Sixth Form (40 pupils) following AS and A Level courses. High standards are expected in all aspects of endeavour, and in behaviour and manners.

Facilities. In addition to the refurbished Edwardian buildings there continued to be steady developments in the facilities and accommodation throughout the 1980s and 1990s. These include the fine Moloney Hall, Ramsker classrooms, Sports Hall, Coggrave Building for the Prep School (Years 3–6), in addition to internal developments, especially in the provision of IT which has recently been upgraded. In 2009 a new Creative Arts Centre was provided for Art, Design Technology and Food. More recently, the biology and physics labs have been fully refurbished, as has the Memorial Library. In the summer of 2011 a stunning upgrade of the Sports Hall was implemented. The girls' boarding accommodation was moved onto the main school site in 2015 and underwent a complete renovation with new bathrooms, common room and improved facilities. Over the summer of 2016 the MUGA was completely relaid and refurbished and a new building to house the music department was opened in May 2017.

Fees per term (2018–2019). Boarders: £7,581–£9,482; Day: £2,819–£4,132.

Admission. An offer of a place in the school is made after interview (and verbal reasoning and mathematics tests for admission to the Senior School) and satisfactory report from the pupil's current school.

Charitable status. The Read School is a Registered Charity, number 529675. It exists to provide a proper education for boys and girls aged 3–18.

Chairman of Governors: Peter Watt

Head: **Mrs R A Ainley**, MA Oxon (*Modern Languages*)

Deputy Head: M A Voisey, BA (*English*)

Assistant Head, Curriculum: Ms C M Palmer, BSc, MSc (*Mathematics*)

Teaching Staff:
S Ashworth-Lilley, BSc (*Psychology*)
P J Budd, BSc (*Physics*)
Miss J Bullock, BSc, MSc (*Head of Science, English Additional Language*)
Ms S L Campbell, BSc (*Prep School*)
Mrs S Chambonnet, BA (*Head of MFL*)
Miss C Cross, BA (*Head of Sixth Form, English*)
M Dell, BSc (*Head of Mathematics*)
Mrs L Fairhurst, BA (*EYFS Teacher*)
B Garrard, BSc (*Head of PE and Games*)
D I Gisbourne, BSc (*Director of ICT, Mathematics*)
Ms H Hewson, BA (*English*)
Mr G Hill, BA (*Head of Junior School*)
Mrs K Ives, BA (*Spanish*)
Mrs E Jackson, BSc (*Mathematics, Science*)
Mrs P Kavanagh, BA (*Business Studies*)
Mr J Matthews (*Prep School & Sport*)
Mrs B J Maunsell, BA (*Drama*)
Mrs S Morrell, BEd (*History, Religious Studies, PSHE Coordinator*)
Miss F M Newman, BA (*Prep School, KS3 Art, Dance*)

Mrs K E Patrick, PG Dip Counselling, PG Dip SEN, MA
  (*Head of Inclusive Learning*)
C S Patrick, BSc (*Specialist Tutor*)
Mrs S Prosser, BA (*PE and Games*)
Mrs S Rothwell-Wood, BEd (*Head of Creative Arts,
  Design Technology, Food*)
Mrs S Scholefield, BSc (*Head of Humanities*)
Mrs C Sawicki (*Deputy EYFS*)
Dr J Staves, BSc, PhD (*Chemistry*)
Mrs R M Wake, BA (*Head of Prep School*)
Miss J Reid, BA (*Art*)
Mrs C M Wynne, BEd (*Deputy Head Junior School*)
Mrs X Zambrano BA (*Psychology*)

Reddam House Berkshire

**Bearwood Road, Sindlesham, Wokingham, Berkshire
RG41 5BG**

Tel: 0118 974 8300
Fax: 0118 977 3186
email: reception@reddamhouse.org.uk
           registrar@reddamhouse.org.uk
website: www.reddamhouse.org.uk
           http://inspirededu.co.uk/our-schools
Twitter: @reddamhouseuk
Facebook: @reddamhouseuk

Reddam House Berkshire is a co-educational independent day and boarding school, which inspires excellence in education for students from three months to 18 years old. This newly restructured through-school, which has been divided into four sections – Early Learning School, Junior School, Middle School and a Senior School – is set in a majestic parkland of 120 hectares comprising extensive playing fields, woodland and a lake.

While its historic buildings are situated in a beautiful and secure rural estate, the school is conveniently located between Reading and Wokingham in the royal county of Berkshire, a vibrant location with very easy access to the M3, M4, Heathrow and London.

The former Bearwood College was acquired by the Inspired Group (see further below) in September 2014, and under its new banner, it has been selected as the group's flagship school among its expanding network in the UK and Europe.

The Reddam House philosophy and formula for success are based on the quality and depth of the school's curricular, cultural and sporting activities and – above all – on the uncompromising selection of outstanding teaching staff, in full recognition that the rapport between teacher and student is the strongest influence on an individual child's development and on the overall success of a school.

As part of the Inspired Schools, Reddam House has its origin in South Africa and has opened other schools in Sydney, Australia. In both countries the schools have achieved singular success – both in terms of the well-rounded quality of person introduced to the world and in academic ranking: they top the league tables in South Africa and are among the top ten schools in New South Wales. They are also extremely successful in the diversity and quality of their co-curricular activities: music, dance, drama, public speaking and a wide range of sports. They are also true to their motto: 'We Shall Give Back', instilling a strong sense of civic engagement, which holds a special appeal to students and parents.

Academic Structure. At Reddam House we expect each student to achieve his or her best, working to an academic programme, which is individually targeted and continuously

monitored. It provides a structured, supported and demanding academic challenge appropriate to each student's capacity. The academic curriculum is based on and exceeds the guidelines of the National Curriculum. In the years up to GCSE, we provide a programme which offers choice, breadth of experience and the opportunity to develop particular academic skills, which are then further developed in greater depth at A Level. The individual attention and specialised teaching that continues into the Sixth Form enable an enviable success rate of entry into first-choice universities.

Pastoral and Boarding Arrangements. Daycare and education are available for children from 3 months to 18 years with boarding from 11–18. Once joining the Middle/Senior School the following day/boarding arrangements are available:

• Full boarding with continuous care and involvement for seven days a week.
• Weekly boarding with the chance to go home at weekends once school commitments have been fulfilled.
• Occasional or flexible boarding for limited or irregular periods to help busy parents.
• Study and Supper sessions or late stays.

Sport and Activities. All students take part in a wide range of games and activities outside the classroom. They enjoy a breadth of experience as well as being expected to discover specific areas in which to excel.

Everyone takes part in physical activities on most days. Sports and games give the students physical fitness, personal and team skills and recreation. They offer many opportunities to find a sense of achievement. On-site sports and activities take place on the extensive playing fields and grounds; facilities include a fully-equipped gymnasium, newly-refurbished indoor pool and a floodlit artificial hockey pitch. Few schools can boast such a varied estate.

Combined Cadet Force: All students in Year 9 and 10 join the Combined Cadet Force (CCF). Cadets learn self-reliance and teamwork, and develop their own leadership skills. The CCF also provides an unrivalled opportunity to experience outdoor pursuits. Two camps are held during holiday periods each year. The annual adventure training expedition provides boys and girls with the opportunity to experience environments that test and challenge their characters whilst under the supervision of highly qualified staff. Many cadets choose to continue their service in the cadet force during their fifth and sixth form years. At this time they take on the extra responsibilities of being senior cadets. The experience they gain from taking an active role in teaching and helping younger cadets provides a valuable insight into the qualities required of leaders.

The Duke of Edinburgh's Award: All students in Year 9 are encouraged to start The Duke of Edinburgh's Award at bronze level. Senior students are encouraged to continue with both silver and gold awards. The scheme provides students with an ideal opportunity to develop their own skills, fitness and commitment to others whilst fostering self-confidence and personal esteem.

Music: Music is part of the life of every student, non-specialist and specialist alike. Everyone participates in music events including the House Singing Competition and the Choral Society. There are regular informal and formal concerts given by instrumentalists and singers. All students are encouraged to take up instrumental and vocal lessons with professional peripatetic musicians. Regular visits to concerts and other musical outings take place.

Theatre and Drama: Our Theatre represents the very best that is available for the pursuance of music and dramatic arts. A busy programme of concerts, recitals and plays ensure that this 350-seat auditorium is continually in use. All students are encouraged to make a contribution to these productions. Student performers are supported by their peers as theatre technicians, lighting and sound engineers, stage crew and scenery builders. Drama is for all, and all have their part to play in the many productions.

Specialist tuition leading to LAMDA Speech and Drama grades and awards is available. These help to develop confidence and competence in acting, public speaking and general communication.

All students undertake a course in Public Speaking from Years 7 to 9 allowing the development of vital oratory skills.

Dance: Dance is an exciting and vibrant part of school life. Whether students decide to study GCSE or A Level Dance or enjoy dance outside the curriculum, there is a class for everyone. A variety of dance styles are taught outside the curriculum, including, Ballet, Contemporary, Jazz and Street Dance allowing the truly passionate to share their commitment and flair through performance.

Facilities. The splendid Mansion House is the centre of the school, around which all our other buildings are located. Historic rooms house modern facilities.

The Cook Library is situated in the former drawing room, one of the most beautiful rooms in the Mansion. It has a collection of both fiction and non-fiction books for loan and reference use.

The need for modern technology is supported by an excellent IT backbone. All departments in the school have Apple TVs and Wi-Fi is available throughout the school, and ongoing investment in digital technology for teaching and learning is integral to the restructuring process undertaken by Reddam House.

The range of further facilities for students at Reddam House is extensive. Extensive sports pitches, netball courts, a swimming pool, tennis courts, weight-training room and rifle range are all found immediately adjacent to the main building.

The Early Learning School and Junior Schools are located close to the main Victorian Mansion House, in a thoughtfully converted, listed Coach House. The splendid surroundings of the wider campus combined with the intimate security of the Coach House allow children safely to explore, discover and learn. The Reggio Emilia approach to teaching young children introduced by Reddam House puts the natural development of children as well as the close relationships that they share with their environment at the centre of its philosophy – something which is uniquely enabled by the school's parkland setting.

Admission. Entry is normally 0+, 3+, 5+, 11+, 13+ and the Sixth Form, but applications at other ages are accepted, subject to vacancies. Assessment is by interview, assessment and by Common Entrance where appropriate. Entry to the Sixth Form is normally conditional upon the achievement of a minimum of 5 GCSEs at B grade or above.

Fees per term (2018–2019). Early Learning School: From £58.30 (short day), £72.25 (full day); Junior School (Reception to Year 6): £3,400–£4,380; Senior School (Years 7–13): Day £5,760, Weekly Boarding: £9,025 (Years 7–9), £10,405 (Years 10–13); Full Boarding: £9,555 (Years 7–9), £10,935 (Years 10–13).

Scholarships. A significant number of Academic, Dance, Drama, Music, Art and Sports Scholarships are offered each year for entry at 11+, 13+ and 16+.

Board of Governors:
Dr Stephen Spurr (*Chairman*)
Mrs Clarissa Farr
Mr Mark Ledermann
Mr Graham Able
Mrs Jane Emmett

Principal: **Mrs Tammy Howard**

Head of Senior: Dr Mike Milner
Head of Middle: Mr James Day
Head of Junior: Mrs Cassie Morris
Head of ELS: Mrs Holly Leather
Director of Learning: Mrs Kay Dain
Deputy Head Middle/Senior: Mrs Nat Holsgrove-Jones
Deputy Head Junior: Mrs Suzanne Whitcher
Business Manager: Mr James Bell

Rishworth School

Rishworth, West Yorkshire HX6 4QA

Tel: 01422 822217 (Main School)
Fax: 01422 820911
email: admissions@rishworth-school.co.uk
website: www.rishworth-school.co.uk
Twitter: @RishworthS
Facebook: @RishworthSchool

Rishworth is an exceptionally friendly, caring community, in which pupils are as strongly encouraged to rejoice in each other's achievements as to take pride in their own. The School succeeds in combining a disciplined environment with a relaxed and welcoming atmosphere.

While pupils are at Rishworth, we try to ensure that, in addition to the knowledge and skills acquired through academic study, they develop:

• A love of learning and the will to succeed.
• A sense of responsibility, self-discipline, purpose and fulfilment.
• A capacity for both self-reliance and cooperation.
• An appreciation of certain personal virtues and spiritual values, such as honesty, dependability, perseverance, commitment, humility and respect for others.

General organisation. Founded in 1724, Rishworth is a co-educational day and boarding school comprising a nursery for children from age 3, a Junior School, Heathfield, which has its own separate site where children are taught up to the age of 11, and the Senior School up to age 18. Rishworth is a Church of England foundation, but welcomes children of all faiths, or of none. Numbers stand at about 480 pupils, of whom over 50 are boarders.

Facilities and Location. Superbly located in 130 acres of a beautiful Pennine valley, the School has a mix of elegant older buildings and excellent modern facilities including a capacious sports hall with fitness suite, a separate, newly-redeveloped Sports Club with 25-metre indoor swimming pool and squash courts, a large expanse of games pitches, a music block, 3 modern ICT suites, wireless (and cabled) Internet and Intranet connection across the whole site, a Performing Arts Theatre, a centre dedicated to sixth-form study, freshly-refurbished boarding houses and newly-installed, state-of-the-art science laboratories.

Access to the School by road is easy, with the M62 within five minutes' drive. School buses run to the Halifax, Todmorden, Rochdale, Oldham and Huddersfield areas.

Welfare and Pastoral. The unusually high degree of attention afforded to pupils by small teaching groups, the careful monitoring of progress, coordinated pastoral support and a close working partnership with parents enables pupils to build on their strengths and allows specific needs to be addressed. Each boarding pupil is under the direct care of a Housemaster or Housemistress, who is ably supported by assistant staff in each boarding house.

Teaching. Taught by a dedicated staff of qualified specialists, the curriculum, both academic and non-academic, is broad and stimulating, and offers every pupil the chance to be challenged and to excel. A general curriculum, broadly in line with the National Curriculum, is followed until Year 9, after which pupils select GCSE options in consultation with their parents, tutors and subject teachers. A Level, Diploma and BTEC options are also selected via consultation.

Support is given by qualified specialists for certain special needs including dyslexia and English where this is not the pupil's first language.

Broader Education. In order to help our pupils to become the confident, balanced and considerate young men and women we wish them to be, we encourage participation in a wide range of activities outside the classroom.

Sports are well appointed and well taught, and each term boys and girls enjoy excellent results. The School also has a justly high reputation in music and drama.

Other activities range from The Duke of Edinburgh's Award to golf, skiing, and many others.

Boarding. We have no dormitories. Boarders (from age 10 or 11, and sometimes age 9) are accommodated in individual study-bedrooms, almost all single or double occupancy, which allow pupils their personal space. These are located in spacious houses, overseen by house staff. The boarding houses have recently undergone major refurbishment which has ensured that the character of the historic buildings has been retained alongside the provision of top-rate modern amenities. A full programme of activities is arranged for the evenings and weekends, and there are good recreational facilities reserved for the boarders, including dedicated social areas.

Admission. Places in the Junior School, Heathfield, are given, subject to availability, on individual assessments appropriate to each applicant's age and previous education. Entrants for Rishworth at Year 7 are asked to sit the School's own entrance assessment, which also forms the basis for the award of scholarships.

Those who wish to join the School at other stages are assessed individually.

Fees per term (2018–2019). Reception to Year 2 £2,155; Years 3 to 6 £3,160; Years 7 & 8: £3,870 day, £9,170 full boarding, £8,325 weekly boarding; Years 9 to 13: £4,220 day, £9,995 full boarding, £9,100 weekly boarding. The School operates a number of schemes, including monthly payments, to ease the financial burden on parents.

Scholarships and Bursaries. Scholarships & Bursaries are available, the former on merit, the latter for demonstrable financial need. The extent to which these awards can be offered will also be determined by other factors, such as the School's own circumstances and the nature of a given cohort of applicants.

Scholarships may be awarded, up to a value of 50% of Tuition fees, for excellence in academic work, sport, music or drama. For Year 7 entry scholarships, applicants are formally assessed. For Year 12 entry, awards are made on the basis of an individual's past record (including examination results).

Most awards are made to applicants at these entry levels. However, suitable candidates at any stage will be considered.

Substantial discounts are available for siblings of pupils in the School, for children of serving members of the Armed Forces and of ordained members of the Church of England. Bursaries may also be available in cases of financial need.

The Old Rishworthian Club maintains a fund for the grant of scholarships to children of ORs.

For more information contact the Registrar.

Charitable status. Rishworth School is a Registered Charity, number 1115562. It exists to provide education for boys and girls.

Visitor: The Most Reverend The Lord Archbishop of York

Honorary Governor: A J Morsley, Esq

The Governing Body:
Revd Canon H Barber (*Chairman*)
Mrs J C Slim
T M Wheelwright, Esq
Mrs D M Whitaker, JP (*Vice Chair*)
Revd T L Swinhoe
W P Hodgson, Esq

Bursar and Clerk to the Board of Governors: J Clague, BA Hons, FCA, CTA

Teaching Staff:

Headmaster: Dr Paul Silverwood, BA Hons, MA Cantab, PhD, QTS, CChem

Director of Marketing: Mrs S J Stamp, BSc (*Geography*)
Director of Studies: S Ogden, BSc (*Geography*)
Director of Teaching and Learning: Dr J Ladds, MChem, PhD, MEd (*Science, Assistant Head of Sixth Form*)
Head of Middle School: Ms J Sheldrick, BSc (*DSL, Science, Food & Nutrition*)
Head of Heathfield and Acting Deputy Head: A M Wilkins, BA, MA Lit, MA Hist

* *Head of Department*

Mrs E Allison BA (*Head of Early Years, Key Stage 1, Reception Teacher Heathfield*)
A P Anderson (*PE and Sport*)
Mrs M T Arbelo-Dolan, BA (*Spanish*)
D Baker, BEd (*Deputy Head, Key Stage 2 Teacher, Mathematics Coordinator Heathfield*)
S Barrott, BA (*Key Stage 2 Teacher, Science Coordinator Heathfield*)
*R A Beecher, BA (*Economics, Business Studies, EPQ Coordinator*)
*P Bell, BA, MSc (*ICT & Computing*)
C Brass, BSc (*Key Stage 1 Teacher, Learning Support Heathfield*)
*Ms A Burtonwood, MEd (*Music*)
G Davies, BSc (*Mathematics*)
*M Davies, BA, MSc (*Geography*)
*Mrs C Devney, BA, BSc (*Learning Support*)
Mrs L Eastwood, BEd (*Key Stage 2 Teacher*)
*Mrs K Fraser, BA (*Art, Head of Lower School*)
Miss S Greenwood, BA (*Foundation Stage Teacher, Humanities Coordinator Heathfield*)
Mrs E Gregory, BA (*History*)
*Mrs C Hall, BA, DipEd (*Food & Nutrition, Assistant Housemistress Wheelwright, Careers Coordinator*)
*P Heap, BA (*Drama*)
C D Holmes-Roe, BA, MA (*History, Resident Housemaster of Slitheroe*)
Mrs J Howcroft, BSc, MSc (*Mathematics*)
Mrs J Hudson, BA (*Key Stage 2 Teacher, Learning Support, English Coordinator Heathfield*)
Mrs V Hutchinson, BA (*RE Coordinator, Key Stage 2 Teacher Heathfield*)
Mrs N I'Anson, BA (*Year 1/ Reception Teacher Heathfield*)
Ms K A James, LLB (*EAP, Resident Housemistress Wheelwright, i/c Girls' Boarding*)
*Mrs K Jones, BSc (*Mathematics*)
P W Jones, MA Cantab (*Science Advisor, Teacher i/c Biology*)
*Mrs B Ladlow, BSc (*Psychology*)
Ms J Marsden, BA (*English, Drama*)
*Miss B Martin, BSc (*Psychology*)
Mrs R C McGarry, BA (*English, RS*)
S H J McGarry, BEng, MSc (*Science, Teacher i/c Physics*)
Mrs L Meredith, BA, ARCM (*Music, English, Teacher i/c Provision for Academically Most Able*)

Mrs R Millington, MA Cantab (*Science*)

Mrs S Moore, BA (*English*)

Miss M Needham, BA (*Art, Design Technology*)

Mrs R Ogden, BEng (*Mathematics*)

Ms D O'Shea, BA (*EAP*)

E Redmond, BEd (*Key Stage 2 Teacher, ICT Coordinator Heathfield*)

*P I M Robinson, BEd (*Business Studies, Head of Sixth Form, UCAS & HE Coordinator, Enhanced Curriculum, EPQ*)

Mrs K Rose, BA (*Key Stage 2 Teacher Heathfield*)

*M E Siggins, BA (*English, General Studies*)

*G M Smith, BA (*Modern Languages*)

C Stone (*PE and Sport, Assistant Housemaster of Calder*)

*A J Thomas, BSc (*Director of Physical Education and Sport, Resident Housemaster of Calder, i/c Boys' Boarding*)

*Mrs J Thompson, BA (*EAP*)

Miss L V Turner, BA, MA (*French, EAP*)

Mrs F Wagstaff, BA (*Design Technology*)

Ms L Watkins, BA, MA (*English*)

Mrs L E Wood, BSc (*Physical Education & Sport, PSHCE Coordinator*)

Teaching Assistants, Coaches, Tutors and Boarding Staff:

Mrs J Bridges, BA (*Teaching Assistant, Forest School Heathfield*)

M Brown, NVQ 2 (*Teaching Assistant Heathfield*)

Ms V Callagher, BA (*Foundation Stage Key Person Heathfield*)

Ms H Calverley (*Sports Coach*)

Mrs H Hoyle, BA (*Teaching Assistant Heathfield*)

Mrs P Pritchard, NVQ3 (*Out-of-School Care Manager, Teaching Assistant Heathfield*)

Mrs G Putnam, BA (*Teaching Support Heathfield*)

Mrs C Robinson, BA (*Teaching Assistant, Learning Support*)

Mrs G Sunderland, SRN (*Senior Teaching Assistant, Marketing Heathfield*)

Librarian: Mrs C Ellis, MA, BSc, MCLIP

Administrative Staff:

Bursar: J Clague, BA Hons, FCA, CTA

Registrar: Mrs J Sutherland

Headmaster's PA: Mrs S Billington

Matron: Mrs D K Robinson

Ruthin School

Mold Road, Ruthin, Denbighshire LL15 1EE

Tel: 01824 702543
Fax: 01824 707141
email: registrar@ruthinschool.co.uk
website: www.ruthinschool.co.uk
Twitter: @ruthinschool
Facebook: @RuthinSchool

Motto: *Dei gratia sum quod sum*

Ruthin School was originally founded in 1284. Refounded in 1574 by Gabriel Goodman, Dean of Westminster, and granted a Royal Charter, the School is a centre of academic excellence in North Wales.

The School is co-educational with around 360 pupils, comprising 240 boarders and 120 day pupils. The emphasis is on academic excellence and providing an environment to gain our students entry to the very best universities in the UK. Good manners, personal discipline and respect for others are of supreme importance, as is a thorough grounding in

central subjects of the curriculum. We believe that social responsibility can be developed in a small community with a family atmosphere, comprising a wide range of academic and other talents. This is reflected in our entry policy. Ruthin School is committed to providing an education of the highest quality, endeavouring to develop the potential of all its pupils in all spheres of education. The pupils develop self-confidence through recognising and building upon their strengths as well as identifying and striving to improve their weaknesses. They are thus prepared to face the challenges of the changing world beyond school.

Organisation. Places (both day and full boarding) are offered to boys and girls from the age of 10.

The six boarding houses – Archbishop Williams, Ellis, Goodman, Russell, Trevor and Wynne – have their own House system under the guidance of resident Housemasters and Housemistresses.

Admission. The normal method of entry to the School is by interview, examination and reports.

Activities. A wide range of non-curricular activities is provided and has included fitness training, basketball, swimming, yoga, judo, Taekwondo, drama, rock climbing, sailing and canoeing, mountain biking, weight training, table tennis, badminton, conservation, gardening and tennis. Boys and girls are encouraged to participate in the Duke of Edinburgh's Award scheme at the age of 14 until they have completed the Bronze Award; several go on to complete the Silver and a few aspire to the Gold Award. Over half the pupils receive individual instrumental tuition from the professional music staff. A programme of excursions is organised for boarders in the evenings and at weekends and these are open to all pupils.

Bursaries and Awards. In addition to academic awards, remissions are available for siblings, children of members of the armed forces, and of Old Ruthinians.

Curriculum. A wide curriculum is offered and includes English, Mathematics, History, Geography, Latin, separate Biology, Physics and Chemistry, Art, Music, Computer Science, French, Mandarin and Spanish. Astronomy and Economics are added at GCSE level. Further Mathematics is taught in the Sixth Form.

An option scheme operates for Form 4, but English, Mathematics, Physics, Chemistry, Biology are compulsory.

Careers. Guidance begins in the Senior School and a comprehensive programme evolves through Forms 4 and 5 and the whole of the Lower Sixth is devoted to research and visits before university applications are made. All members of the Sixth Form who wish to enter university are successful. Work experience is undertaken in Form 4 and the Lower Sixth.

Games. Rugby, basketball, football, cross-country, netball, tennis and athletics all feature in the coaching programme.

Fees per annum (2018–2019). Day £11,000–£14,000; Boarding £34,500. Fees are payable twice yearly, at beginning of August and February. British parents have the option to pay monthly by Direct Debit.

Transport. The School provides daily transport to and from the North Wales coast, the Chester area and the Wrexham area. Transport is provided for boarders from Manchester airport to the School, at the beginning and end of each term.

The Old Ruthinian Association fosters close links between past and present pupils of the School.

Charitable status. Ruthin School is a Registered Charity, number 525754. It exists to provide education for boys and girls.

Visitor: Her Majesty The Queen

Council of Management:
Chairman: Mrs J Oldbury
C W Conway
Revd J S Evans
Dr T Kerrigan
Dr G H Roberts
J E Sharples
His Honour Judge I J C Trigger

Principal: **T J Belfield**, MA Cantab

Vice-Principal: I Welsby, BSc, MIBiol, PGCE, DipEd

Assistant Principal – Academic: Miss S Frencham, BSc, PGCE

Assistant Principal – Assessment, Inspection, Procedures: Dr A W Hughes, BEng, PhD, PGCE

Assistant Principal – Universities, Careers, Alumni: Mrs J I Morton, BSc, PGCE

Assistant Principal – Pastoral: I M Rimmer, BSc, PGCE

Teaching Staff:
J S Bartlett, BSc, PGCE
Mrs S M Bellis-Whitworth, BA, MA, PGCE
N J R Blandford, BA, MA, PGCE
Mrs E T Brodzinska, LLB, MA, DELTA
Mrs E M Brown, BA, MA Ed, PGCE, TEFL, AMBDA
B Cribb, BA, PGCE, MEd
Mrs R Crowther, BA, PGCE
Dr D G Edwards, BA Hons, DPhil
I G Evans, BA, PGCE
Mrs S J Eve, BSc, PGCE
Dr N Fairbank, PhD
Miss P Foster, BA, PGCE, DELTA
Dr I Franjic, BSc, MSc, PhD
Dr G H Green, BSc, MA, PhD
J P Hamer, BA, PGCE
Dr M D Hannant, PhD, PGCE
Mrs I Haywood, BSc, MBA, PGCE
J R Henry, BA, PGCE
M H L Hewer, MA Oxon, DipEd
L Hogan, BSc, PGCE
Miss R Howlett, BSc, PGCE
Mrs K Hughes, BA, PGCE
G N Johnson, BSc, MSc, PGCE
Dr K M Johnson, BSc, PhD
Mrs M Kenworthy, BSc, PGCE
Miss K A McCord, MA, PGDE
Mrs S Morley, BEd, CELTA
M A Orchard, BSc, PGCE
D A Owen Booth, MGCI, BEd, DipHE
C Perry, BSc, PGCE
Mrs C Peters, BSc, PGCE
M S Robinson, BA, MA Oxon, PGCE
C Sennett, DRSAMD, PGCE
S D Stark, BSc, MEng, PGCE
R A Wadon, BSc, PGCE
Miss J Warriner, BSc, MEng, MA, PGCE
Miss H Webb, BSc, PGCE
Miss D A Williams, BSc, PGCE
M A Williams, BA, MPhil
Dr M Wilton, BSc, PhD, PGCE
Miss S C Wright, BEng
Miss L Zhao, BA, PGCE

Registrar and PA to the Principal: Mrs S E Williams
Finance Administrator: Mrs J Rainford
School Medical Officer: Dr T Kneale
School Nurse: Mrs T Beaver, RGN, RSCN
School Nurse: Mrs C Bland, RGN
School Nurse: Mrs S Fitzsimmons, BSc, RSCN
School Nurse: Mrs J Wordsworth

St Christopher School

Barrington Road, Letchworth Garden City, Hertfordshire SG6 3JZ

Tel: 01462 650947
Fax: 01462 481578
email: admissions@stchris.co.uk
school.admin@stchris.co.uk
website: www.stchris.co.uk
Twitter: @StChris_School
Facebook: @StChrisLetchworth
LinkedIn: /st-christopher-school-letchworth-garden-city

Fully co-educational from its foundation in 1915, St Christopher has always been noted for its friendly informality, breadth of educational vision, good academic standards and success in developing lifelong self-confidence. St Chris aims for its students to develop competence and resourcefulness, social conscience and moral courage, a capacity for friendship and a true zest for life.

There are over 550 pupils aged 3 to 18. Boarders can start from age 10. Full and Weekly Boarding are available for pupils from Year 6 to Sixth Form.

When the School was founded in 1915 the Daily Herald reported that the School was based 'not on the sameness of children, their conformity to type, but on their differences'. This concept of treating children as individuals was revolutionary at the time and continues to be one of the distinctive characteristics of a St Chris education.

St Chris is a champion for progressive education and is known for its forward-thinking, creative and supportive environment. Pupils are supported to reach their potential academically, socially and in the activities they pursue.

The School provides for children of average to outstanding ability. All who are admitted to the Junior School (for 3 to 11 year olds) may continue through the Senior School, subject to performance. Entry to the Sixth Form is dependent on GCSE results and the ability to cope with the A Level programme.

Academic Programme. The Nursery dovetails the National Early Years Curriculum (EYFS) with the very best of Montessori Practice to provide a real educational experience within a caring and nurturing environment in the Early Years Centre.

Close attention is given to the transition to the Junior School which follows a programme that includes extensive enrichment built around the core elements of the National Curriculum. The Junior School offers small classes and a wide range of opportunities. Subject specialists teach modern languages, music and sport and the children at the top of the Junior School spend one afternoon a week in the Senior School to prepare them for their onwards move.

In the Senior School a wide-ranging programme continues to the age of 16, including the study of sciences to Double Award GCSE or GCSE in all three Sciences. In Modern Languages there are exchanges with schools in France or Spain. The creative and expressive arts are particularly encouraged and the School has been awarded the Arts Council Artsmark Gold award.

The Sixth Form. Although St Christopher is not a large school, the Sixth Form is a good size (numbering around 100) with excellent facilities in its Sixth Form Centre. Over 20 A Level courses are on offer with all the usual Arts and Science subjects and, in addition, Computer Science, Psychology, Film Studies and Design 3D. There is a lively extracurricular programme.

Learning through experience. There is an emphasis on learning through experience both with regard to academic subjects and more generally. There are many opportunities for practical and community work and for outdoor pursuits. At the end of the Summer Term the timetable is suspended for all pupils to undertake an extended project, generally away from the School campus. Each year two groups of Sixth Formers visit development projects in the Indian desert province of Rajasthan. There are also long-standing international projects in Ladakh. As a result of these the School was awarded the International School Award by the Department for Education through the British Council. The Vege Centre, the School's cookery centre, opened in 2011 and cooking is an important part of life at St Chris.

A humane and global outlook. There is no uniform (except for games). All children and adults are called by their first names. Internationalist and green values are encouraged and St Chris holds the Eco-Schools Award. People of different religions and of none feel equally at home; there is a period of silence in every assembly.

Self-Government. The School is founded on democratic principles and every voice is valued. Everyone, child and adult, is represented on the School Council which is chaired by an elected senior pupil. The elected Major Officials and Committees look after different aspects of community life. The informality of the School encourages openness: children speak up for themselves – and for others.

Treating children as individuals. From the outset the School has sought to treat children as individuals. In consequence, the ethos is an encouraging one and suits children who enjoy a broad education and who will thrive in a non-competitive academic environment where each child is asked to do their best, rather than being compared to their peers.

Creative and Performing Arts. The School has an excellent tradition in these areas and has fine purpose-built facilities that reflect this. There are several productions a year in the Theatre which has tiered seating and full technical resources. Similarly there are regular concerts and recitals in the Music Centre. A Music Technology Suite opened in 2007. In the Arts Centre there are studios for fine art, design and ceramics, as well as a photography dark room. Sixth Form work students have individual areas as in art college and a lecture theatre.

Technology and Computing. The School benefits from a modern ICT Centre and online resources for teaching and learning are standard. GCSE and A Level Computer Science and Robotics and Programming Clubs give lots of options.

Clubs and Societies. There are plentiful activities for pupils to join in with, taking place after School and at weekends. Staff share their enthusiasms and pupils too can take the lead in their own areas of interest.

Health, Fitness and Physical Education. The diet is broad and healthy and considerable pride is taken in the catering. There is a full-time nurse with relief staff on call. The PE programme is full and varied, making use of the extensive grounds including playing fields, gym, sports hall, all-weather surface and a 25m indoor swimming pool. Matches take place against many other schools.

Full collaboration with parents. The Parents' Circle was founded in 1921 and the School has, throughout, valued the close involvement of parents who are welcome in the School, not just for consultation about their children but also to take part in evening classes and in sharing the many performances, events and information evenings. We want parents to share in the education of their children and in the School community.

Boarders. There are 50 full and weekly boarders living in 2 boarding houses. The provision for younger pupils is in cosy, traditional rooms in the heart of the School. Year 10 and 11 students are in a modern, light extension which has recently been renovated. Most students have their own rooms. Sixth Form students are in a separate house on the School grounds and have individual rooms and study facilities. Boarding at St Chris has a family feel with all students under the supervision of resident Houseparents. There is a busy weekly programme of weekend and evening activities. Weekend activities almost always involve a trip away from school. All meals are provided by the School, however, cooking facilities for snacks are available to students. Older students also have use of a full kitchen and cook for a weekly supper club.

Day Pupils. Day pupils benefit from the residential nature of the community, sharing in the evening and weekend life and taking meals in the School when they wish. Sixth Formers have their own study areas in the Sixth Form Centre.

Fees per term (2018–2019). Day Pupils £1,530–£6,025; Full Boarding £10,550; Weekly Boarding £8,225. There are discounts for second and subsequent children, so long as they have an older sibling in the School. A range of financial assistance is available through a Bursary Scheme.

Admission Procedure. The most usual admission points are the Nursery or Reception class, or Years 4, 5 or 6 in the Junior School, or Year 7 and Year 9 in Senior School, or Year 12 in the Sixth Form. From Nursery to Year 3 in the Junior School assessment involves a taster day. Year 4 to Year 6 in the Junior School involves a taster day and a Cognitive Ability Test. Year 7 to 10 involves a Cognitive Ability Test and an interview with the Head. Sixth Form entrance involves an interview and is conditional on GCSE results. Art and Academic Scholarships are available for entry into Years 7, 9 and 12.

Situation and Travel. The School has an attractive 25-acre campus on the edge of Letchworth Garden City with excellent transport links. The A1(M) is a mile away and there are direct train lines to London (King's Cross, 35 minutes) and Cambridge (25 minutes). Luton Airport is 25 minutes and Heathrow 60 minutes by car. The School runs bus services to surrounding areas including North London and Cambridge.

Old Scholars. The Membership Secretary of the St Christopher Club is David Cursons who can be reached c/o The School.

Charitable status. St Christopher School is a Registered Charity, number 311062. It exists to provide education for boys and girls, aiming to treat all as individuals and to develop their proper self-confidence.

Board of Governors:
Bertie Leigh (*Chair*)
Sarah Kilcoyne (*Vice-Chair*)

Dasha Nicholls	Sophie Nolan
(*Safeguarding*)	John Simmonds
Emma-Kate Henry	Rabinder Singh
Peter McMeekin	Ben Walker

Head: **Richard Palmer**, BEd, FRSA

Deputy Head & Designated Safeguarding Lead: Rich Jones, BA
Second Deputy (Academic Director): Andy Selkirk, MBA, BSc, DipPhy, PGCE
Director of Pastoral Care: Gavin Fraser-Williams, BA, MA
Director of Activities: Byron Lewis, BSc
Head of Junior School and Early Years: Katie Wright, BA

Admissions:
Marketing and Communications Manager: Rhiannon Butlin, BA, MSc
Registrar: Kate Allan, BA
Admissions Assistant: Sarah Davis, BA

Bursary:
Bursar, Company Secretary & Clerk to the Governors: William Hawkes, MA
Assistant Bursar: Lucy Coddington

Senior School Teaching Staff:
Sebastian Aguilar, BSc (*Geography, Careers Coordinator*)
Alaine Anderson, BSc, MEd (*Head of Maths*)
Lizzie Anstice-Brown, BA, MA (*Art, Artist in Residence*)
Bruce Balden, BA (*Maths*)
Rebecca Belson, BSc (*Food & Nutrition, Science*)
Emma Bennett-Jones, BA, CELTA Level 4, (*Head of EAL/ English, Resident Tutor*)
Simon Cockle, BA, MA (*English*)
Michael Collins, BA, MA, PGCE (*History, Politics*)
Wendy Cottenden, Cert Ed (*Head of PSHE, Cookery*)
Sarah Davies, BSc (*Mathematics*)
Chris Drayton, BSc (*Mathematics, Outdoor Pursuits*)
Adam Eldin, BSc (*Head of Computer Science*)
Gemma Fernandez, Licence University of A Coruna (*French, Spanish*)
Nicolas Fowler, BSc (*Geography*)
Gavin Fraser Williams, BA, MA (*Craft, Design & Technology*)
Martin Goodchild, GRSM, LRAM, PGCE (*Director of Music*)
Janine Hall, BA (*Art, Art Technician*)
Ian Hughes, BA (*Head of PE & Games*)
Helen Hunt, BSc (*Biology*)
David Ilott, BA, Dip Ed (*Head of English, Head of EFL*)
Anne-Marie Knight, BA, MA (*Music, PSHE*)
Kate Kreyenborg-Nichols, BSc (*Biology*)
Andrew Lambie, MA (*Chemistry*)
Charlotte Leeke, BSc (*Geography*)
Byron Lewis, BSc (*ICT, Director of Activities*)
Penny Main, BA, MA (*History, English, Head of Sixth Form*)
Mario May, BA, MA, PhD (*Head of History & Politics, Humanities Faculty Coordinator*)
Jack Maydom, BSc (*PE & Games*)
Isabelle Mills, Licence d'Anglais, PGCE (*French, Spanish*)
Helen Ogilvie, PhD, MSc, PGCE (*Chemistry*)
Angeles Ojeda, Licendiada (*Spanish, German*)
Susanne Okulitch (*English, Media Studies*)
Andy Owen, BSc, PGCE (*Physics, Head of Science Faculty*)
Jennifer Petit, BSc (*Physics*)
James Robertson, BA (*CDT*)
Emma Roskilly BA, PGCE (*English, Head of Media Studies*)
Jennifer Savage, BA, MA (*Geography, Music, Drama*)
Andy Selkirk, MBA, BSc, Dip Phy, PGCE (*Second Deputy – Academic Director, Biology*)
Emma Semple, BA, MA, PGCE (*Head of Arts Faculty*)
Cyrille Simon, Maître (*Head of MFL, Faculty Coordinator*)
Allan Simpson, BA (*Music Technology*)
Claire Slater, BEng (*Maths*)
Rebecca Sweeney, BA, MA (*English*)
Rebecca Twiston-Davies, BA Hons (*Art*)
Maria Walker, BSc (*Mathematics*)
Ben Wall, BSc, PGCE (*Head of Craft, Design & Technology*)
Jeremy Wallis, BSc, MA (*Economics*)
Jenny White, BEd (*Director of PE & Games*)

Rebecca Wilson, BA, PGCE (*English, ICT*)
Susan Woollard, BSc, MSc (*Psychology, Science*)
Jonathan Wright, BSc (*PE, Games*)
Naz Yeni, BA, MA (*Drama*)

Junior School and Early Years Centre Teaching Staff:
Head of Junior School and Early Years: Katie Wright, BA
Deputy Head of Junior School: Zareena Subhani, BA
Deputy Head of Early Years Centre: Lesley Farrell, HNC
Bryan Anderson, BEd
Marcia Bonanni, BA
Sarah Brown, Maria Montessori Diploma
Louise Day, BSc
Andrew Duffell, BA
Christine Hawkes, BEd
Clare McComb, BA (*Individual Needs Coordinator*)
Lyn McGregor, BEd (*PE & Games*)
Carly Ougham, BA
Claire Plain, BA
Jim Sands, BSc
Rebecca Simon, BSc
Coralie Skerman-Gray, BEd
Eleanor Snow, BSc
Lydia Somerville, BA
Iain Wheeler, BA Hons (*Year 5, E Group*)
Jennifer Whale, BA (*Junior School Resources*)
Avril Harker, BA (*After School Care Organiser*)
Teaching Assistants: Natalie Allen, Sarah Gardener, Gemma Horwood, Roxanne Jackson, Anita Moore, Chloe Palmer, Natasha Paxton, Lucy Pinkstone, Joanna Pitts, Denise Sheelan, Corrine Toller

Librarian: Linda Aird, BA, Dip Lib, MCLIP
Performing Arts Technician: Mike Li
School Nurse: Caroline Dorrington
Assistant School Nurse: Gina Williams

Individual Needs:
Karen Hoyle, BA, Cert Dyslexia and Literacy (*Joint Head of Individual Needs*)
Elizabeth Miller, BEd, Dip RSA SpLD (*Joint Head of Individual Needs*)

Boarding Houseparents:
Arundale: Chris and Cecilia Drayton
Arunside: Iain Coyne and Ruth Miller

St Edward's School

Cirencester Road, Charlton Kings, Cheltenham, Glos GL53 8EY

Tel: 01242 538600
Fax: 01242 538610
email: reception@stedwards.co.uk
website: www.stedwards.co.uk
Twitter: @StEdwardsChelt
Facebook: @StEdwardsSchoolCheltenham

Motto: *Quantum Potes Aude*

St Edward's is a lay-run, co-educational Catholic day school for 11–18 year olds of all denominations. Awarded 'Excellent' in all 8 categories in its 2015 ISI inspection, St Edward's prides itself in offering a full curricular and extra-curricular programme to all its pupils, to enable them to succeed in whatever field they choose. A broad range of subjects is offered at GCSE, together with 24 subjects at A Level. The broad range of subjects ensures that pupils are taught in small class sizes, enabling each pupil to receive individual attention.

Admission. The main entry to the Senior School is at age 11. Pupils can also join the School at age 13 and into the Sixth Form and entry is by exam. Scholarships are available for entry into Year 7, 9 and 12.

Fees per term (2018–2019). £4,850–£5,920. Discounts are offered for the third, fourth and subsequent children.

The Senior School offers means-tested Bursary-Scholarships for entry at age 11, scholarships for academic excellence, art, music, drama and sport. For entry into Year 10 scholarships are available for academic excellence, art, music, drama, sport and design and technology. Scholarships for entry into Sixth Form are available for academic excellence, art, music, drama and sport.

Old Edwardians' Association. Secretary: Mrs P Hemming, St Edward's School, Cirencester Road, Charlton Kings, Cheltenham, Gloucestershire GL53 8EY.

Further information is available on the School's website, www.stedwards.co.uk. A School prospectus is available on request from the Admissions Manager and Headmistress's PA. You are warmly invited to arrange a visit to the School by telephoning her on 01242 538600.

Charitable status. St Edward's School is a Registered Charity, number 293360.

Chairman of Trustees: Dr Sue Honeywill

Headmistress: **Mrs Pat Clayfield**, BSc, PGCE

St James Senior Boys' School

Church Road, Ashford, Surrey TW15 3DZ

Tel:	01784 266 930
	01784 266 933 (Admissions)
Fax:	01784 266 938
email:	admissions@stjamesboys.co.uk
website:	www.stjamesboys.co.uk

St James Senior Boys' School, founded in 1975, is registered as an educational charity and is administered by a Board of Governors. The Headmaster is a member of The Society of Heads and the Independent Schools Association. The school is a member of the International Boys' Schools Coalition (IBSC). These Associations require that excellence is assured by regular inspections by the Independent Schools Inspectorate which is itself monitored by Ofsted.

The school has 416 students – all boys, aged between 11 and 18.

The school relocated from its site in Twickenham in 2010 and now resides in the magnificent Victorian/Gothic building which once housed St David's School in Ashford, Surrey, set in 32 acres of grounds. This move has provided the physical space necessary for every boy to develop his sporting, artistic and dramatic talents in addition to working in high-quality classrooms and state-of-the-art laboratories.

Aims and Values. St James Senior Boys' School offers a distinctive education that unites a unique philosophical ethos with academic excellence and outstanding skills for life.

At St James we believe that every child is a pure and perfect being; it is our job as educators to help the pupils in our care to discover and express their individual talents and reveal their brilliance. With this room to grow and blossom each boy develops in body, mind and spirit.

Although academic potential is important to us, pupils at St James are not selected solely on their examination performance; we are also interested in strength of character, future potential and emotional intelligence. We are looking for a boy with a spark, who gives freely of themselves whether in the classroom, on the stage or the sports field.

We are known internationally for our championing of Meditation and Mindfulness, something we have been successfully practising for 40 years. Each boy has the opportunity to connect with their inner being in periods of Quiet Time each day. This makes an enormous difference to pupil development and academic achievement.

We also like to offer the pupils in our care the opportunity to push themselves beyond any self-imposed limits, and our beautiful 32-acre site certainly enables a wealth of sports, drama, music and other extracurricular activities to flourish. Activities offered include: Cadets, The Duke of Edinburgh's Award, Sailing Club, Mountain Biking and Kayaking on our lake!

At St James we wish to produce young men who can question with sharp minds, who can contemplate in quietude, who can find their way ahead with wisdom and moral discrimination and who can meet others with open-hearted compassion.

St James is ideally located with easy access from Central London and the South West London Suburbs through to the Thames Valley.

Academic Standards and Successes. Academic standards are high, but we also measure success to the extent that boys surpass their own expectations. 2018 results were: GCSE: 100% pass rate, 9–7 36%, 9–4 98%; A Level: 100% pass rate, A*ABC 91%.

Extracurricular Activities. Boys are offered an adventure pursuits programme designed to challenge the young men in terms of fitness, endurance, courage, leadership skills, service, self-esteem and confidence. Cadets (239 Para detachment), The Duke of Edinburgh's Award, Skiing, Sailing Club, Climbing Club, Community Service and Task force are among the activities offered.

Educational Trips. These are fairly regular and frequent for the Lower School, but there is an Activities Week in March when Year 7 enjoy an adventure break in the UK; Year 8 go to Greece to further their studies of Classical Civilisation; Year 9 travel the pilgrims way to Santiago de Compostela, and Year 10 spend some time in Lucca in Italy for leadership training and aspects of teamworking, then move on to Florence to study Renaissance art and architecture.

Philosophy. Each class throughout the school has one period of Philosophy per week. The boys are opened up to the great ideas relating to human values and relationships. Broadly, the themes prepare boys through different stages of development – Years 7 to 8: the correct use of mind, the power of attention; Years 9 to 11: aspiring to a great vision of Man and exploring human relationships and personal mastery; Years 12 to 13: living the philosophical life, making it practical, the importance of service.

Meditation and Quiet Time. The importance of inner stillness is recognised in the school, with two 5 minute periods of Quiet Time every day. During this time, boys can meditate, pray, read something of value or just be still. Every lesson begins and ends in a quiet moment of stillness and rest.

Admissions. The standard entry is at 11+, 13+ and 16+. Boys applying for entry to Year 7 take an Entrance Exam in January and also are all interviewed by a member of the Senior Management Team shortly afterwards. Boys are not judged solely on their exam results for the Headmaster favours selection by character and their ability to express themselves. At 13+, students are required to pre-test at either 11+ or 12+ level (in Y6 or Y7). We welcome applications to our Sixth Form at 16+. Very good GCSE performance and satisfactory interviews will be the basis of selection.

Fees per term (2018–2019). £6,310.

Open Days and Visits. Every year we hold Open Days in October. We also encourage parents to come and see the school in action at one of the school's tours. Please book by online at www.stjamesboys.co.uk.

Charitable status. The Independent Educational Association Limited is a Registered Charity, number 270156.

Chairman of Governors: Jeremy Sinclair

Headmaster: **David Brazier**, BA Hons, PGCE, MSc

Deputy Headmaster Pastoral: Charles Neave, BA, Grad Dip Ed, Grad Dip Mus, QTS (*English*)
Deputy Headmaster Academic: Dr Richard Bustin, BSc, PGCE, MA, PhD (*Geography*)
Assistant Headmaster: David Hipshon, BA Hons, MPhil Cantab, PhD, PGCE (*History*)
Head of Sixth Form: David Beezadhur, BA Hons, MA, GTTP (*Ancient History*)
Head of Upper School (*Years 9–11*): James Johnson, BSc Hons, PGCE (*Science*)
Head of Year 7: Adam Hooper, BEng Hons, PGCE (*Physics*)
Head of Year 8: Peter Rodgers, BSc, PGCE (*PE*)
Academic Director: Lorraine Soares, MSc Hons, PGCE (*Chemistry*)

Academic Staff:
Lauren Aubrey-Mills, BEd (*Mathematics*)
Paul Bahia, BSc Hons, PGCE (*Mathematics, Economics*)
Kevan Bell, MA, MSc, BEd (*Sports Performance Director*)
Gillian Bloor, MA (*English*)
Zoe Boland, BA Hons (*Latin, Greek*)
Stuart Bridge, BA Hons, PGCE (*German, French, Assistant Head Upper School*)
Frank Byrne, BEng Hons, PGCE (*Head of Physics*)
Anne-Helene Choimet, BA France, PGCE MFL (*French, German*)
Arjun Deb, BSc (*Mathematics*)
Sarah Ford, BSc Hons, PGCE (*Chemistry*) [maternity leave]
Richard Fraser, BA Hons (*Mathematics*)
Suki Gill, BSc Hons, MSc (*Head of IT*)
Rishi Handa, MA, BSc Hons, PhD (*Head of Sanskrit, Classical Greek, Religious Studies*)
Charlotte Hooper, BA Hons, PGCE (*English*)
Anisah Hussain, BA Hons, MA, PGCE (*Head of Classics*)
Samuel Jackson, MA Cantab, PGCE (*Director of Music*)
William Jeffreys, BA (*Physical Education*)
Nic Lempriere, MA, PGCE (*Head of English, Deputy Head of Sixth Form*)
Keith Lovell, Cert Ed (*Head of Design Technology*)
Pardeep Marway, BSc Hons, PGCE (*Head of Science, Designated Safeguarding Lead*)
Paolo Militello, MA (*Spanish*)
Marco Piotti, MSc, PGCE (*History*)
Charles Protheroe, BA Hons (*Religious Studies, English*)
Caroline Pugh, BA Hons, PGCE (*Head of Drama (maternity leave)*)
Virginie Quartier, BA GLSE (*Belgium*) (*Head of Languages*)
Terrence Radloff, BA Hons (*Geography*)
Adam Rood, BA (*Drama*)
Julia Russell, BA Hons, GTTP (*Art (Art of Science Coordinator)*)
Oliver Saunders, BA Hons, GTTP (*Head of History*)
Mark Saunders, BA, HND Art & Design (*Head of Art*)
Tammy Taylor, BA (*Librarian*)

Joanna Thorn, BSc Hons (*English*)
Ben Wassell, BSc Hons, GTTP (*Director of Sport and PE*)
Michaela Weiserova, MSc (*Head of Mathematics*)
Steven Whitehouse, BSc, PhD, PGCE (*Mathematics*)
Sandra Williams, BEd (*Head of Business Studies, Careers Coordinator*)
Carlene Williams-Harvey, BSc (*Mathematics*)

Learning Support:
Christine Davies
Angela Hall
Sarah-Jane Hipshon, BA Hons Lit Open, OCR Level 5 Dip SpLD
Carola Robinson-Tait (*Learning Support Specialist Teacher*)
Marion Sudell
Cora Wren, Cert Ed, BA Hons, OCR Level 5 Dip SpLD (*SENDCo*)
Alice Wood, BA Hons, PGCE, NASENCO Award UCL (*SENDCo*)

Support Staff
Headmaster's PA: Nina Patel
Assistant to the Deputy Head: Cecilia Leggett
Receptionists: Sindy Bahia, Monica Lacey
Matron: Alison Jefferies RSCN
Estates Manager: Adam O'Higgins
Caretakers: Nicholas Freddino, Mark Freddino, Tim Prendergast
Groundsman: Stephen Fidler
Registrar & Marketing Manager: Sarah Harris BA Hons
Examinations Officer: Reshma Kanani
Lab Technicians: Anil Sud, Lorraine Haysom
Art Technician: Dominique Holt BA Hons PGCE
Health & Safety Officer: Charles Neave
Designated Safeguarding Lead: Pardeep Marway
Events Managers: Lisa Canderton, Claire Pestana
Sixth Form Cover Supervisor, School Staff Instructor (CCF): Tim Paul

Bursar's Department:
Bursar: William Wyatt
PA to the Bursar: Loy Phillips

St John's College

Grove Road South, Southsea, Hampshire PO5 3QW

Tel:	023 9281 5118
Fax:	023 9287 3603
email:	info@stjohnscollege.co.uk
website:	www.stjohnscollege.co.uk

Founded in 1908 by the De La Salle Brothers, St John's College seeks to provide an excellent all-round day and boarding education to boys and girls of all abilities. Children of all Christian denominations, those of other faiths and those with no formal religious affiliation but who are in sympathy with the values of the school are welcome. The College became fully independent and decoupled from the De la Salle Trust in September 2015, but continues to provide an academic education based on the spiritual and moral ethos of the Founder John Baptist De La Salle.

St John's is a thriving co-educational day and boarding school for pupils aged 2 to 18 (boarding from Year 5). Number of Pupils: 581 including 90 Boarders.

Situation. St John's College campus is located in the heart of Southsea, an attractive and thriving seaside suburb of Portsmouth. The College's extensive sports fields are located on the outskirts of the city, with transport provided to and from that site.

Approach and Ethos. Academically, St John's College is a non-selective school, its aim being excellence for every pupil according to their personal potential. All children who are able and willing to benefit from the curriculum provided are welcome to join the school community. The school's academic record – by all measures – is outstanding.

The pastoral care offered to boarders and day pupils is of very high quality. The commitment of the staff to the welfare and progress of each pupil is second to none. In return, honest effort and application is expected from the children – in order to meet the challenging standards set in academic work, sporting endeavour, behaviour and self-discipline.

Nursery. The Nursery (Little St John's) is located within the Junior School. It has its own entrance and secure playground. The Nursery caters for children aged from two to four years. The children are actively involved in a carefully constructed pre-school programme. Great emphasis is placed on creative artwork, outdoor play and educational visits – as well as on acquiring foundation skills and concepts relating to Numeracy and Literacy.

Junior School. The Junior School is also located within the main College campus. This enables younger children to make daily use of all the College's excellent facilities and to benefit in some areas from specialist tuition by Senior School staff. The broadly-based curriculum incorporates and extends the National Curriculum. Great emphasis is placed on English, Mathematics and Science – which is taught in well-equipped laboratories. Musical talent is also carefully nurtured, with all pupils learning a musical instrument from the age of seven. The Junior School Choir and Orchestra provide opportunities for ensemble playing and performance.

Senior School. The Senior School curriculum again incorporates and extends the National Curriculum. All subjects are taught by appropriately qualified specialists in well-resourced subject areas. A wide range of GCSE subjects is offered alongside IGCSE Maths, English and Science. Instrumental tuition is encouraged and the Senior School Choir and Orchestra are open to all pupils. Sport – principally rugby, cricket, hockey and netball – is strong at all levels. Pupils' progress in all areas is assessed formally each half-term, with formal examinations being held twice yearly.

Sixth Form. As they progress into the Sixth Form, older students are enabled and encouraged to become independent and self-motivated learners – in preparation for Higher Education. The teaching and pastoral staff continue to work closely with parents, who are kept fully informed of progress and achievement. A wide range of A Level subjects is offered. The College ensures a good student to teacher ratio, allowing for close and constant monitoring of the performance and effort of each student. Preparation for Oxbridge entry is available, and students are also offered practice interviews for university and job applications and a full careers service.

Beyond the formal curriculum, a wide range of sporting, academic, dramatic, cultural and social activities is available. The Politics Society, administered predominantly by Sixth Form students, enjoys a national reputation.

Admission. Pupils are accepted and placed on the basis of a formal assessment and previous reports.

Fees per term (2018–2019). Junior School: Day £3,075–£3,285, Years 5 & 6 UK Boarding £8,695, Years 4, 5 & 6 Overseas Boarding £9,580. Senior School: Day £4,030, UK Boarding £8,695, Overseas Boarding £9,580.

Occasional Boarding (including bed, breakfast, evening meal): £42 per day.

Music fees are extra.

Scholarships and Bursaries. Academic and other scholarships and bursary awards are available.

Charitable status. St John's College, Southsea is a Registered Charity, number 1162915.

Chairman of Governors: Mr R Staker

Head of College: Mrs M Maguire, BSc, PGCE

Deputy Head: Mr M Renahan, BA Hons HDE, MEd
Head of the Junior School: Mr T Shrubsall, MA Ed, BH
Assistant Head Academic: Mr A Martin, MEng, ACGI, Fri, PGCE
Assistant Head Pastoral: Mr M Round, BSc, PGCE
Senior Master: Mr M Hooper, BA Hons, PGCE
Bursar: Mr C Inigo-Jones, MA Hons, FCA
Estates Manager: Mr R Phillips
Head of Development and Marketing: Mrs S Travis, BA Hons
Admissions Registrar: Mrs J Mengham

Heads of Department:
Art and Design: Ms J Carr, BA Hons, PGCE
Design and Technology: Mr B Horrod, BSc Hons, PGCE
Economics & Business Studies: Ms M Faulkner, BSc
English: Mrs L Lynas
Geography: Mr McBeath, BSc
Government & Political Studies: Dr G D Goodlad, PhD, BA
History: Mrs K Audsley, BA, MA
ICT & Computing: Mr T Harris, BSc, QTS
Learning Support: Mrs L Fillery, BA, Dip SpLD
Mathematics: Mr T Fairman
Modern Languages: Mr A Jackson
Music: Miss V Francis, BA Hons, PGCE
Physical Education: Mr K Long
Religious Studies: Mrs J Turner, BA, MA
Sciences: Mr A Martin, BSc

Head's PA: Mrs C Withers

St Joseph's College

Belstead Road, Ipswich, Suffolk IP2 9DR

Tel:	01473 690281
Fax:	01473 602409
email:	admissions@stjos.co.uk
website:	www.stjos.co.uk
Twitter:	@MyStJos
Facebook:	@StJosephsCollegeIpswich
LinkedIn:	/St-Joseph's-College-Ipswich

St Joseph's College is a vibrant day and boarding school, for girls and boys aged 3 to 18. Its Nursery, Prep, Senior and Sixth Form provision offers a broad, well-rounded and all-through education.

Located on a 60-acre parkland site near to the centre of Ipswich, the College is situated just ten minutes' walk from Ipswich train station or alternately just a five-minute drive from the A12/A14 interchange.

Traditional values are at the heart of the school community which, at the same time, is forward-thinking as it meets the challenges of an ever-changing world. Pupils are provided with every opportunity to develop their talents to the full, growing up in a happy and fulfilling environment guided by Christian values, where all are valued and encouraged.

Ethos. St Joseph's feels different and that's the way we like it. Our uniqueness is shaped by our ethos, which combines Christian values with a distinctive approach to supporting and nurturing children individually within a friendly, family environment. Along with the pursuit of excellence, this approach is reflected in all aspects of life at the College, academic, sporting and cultural.

Developments. The second phase of the College's ambitious Building for the Future plans came to fruition in September 2016 with the opening of a state-of-the-art Sixth Form Centre, combining 21st century technology with light, space, serenity and colour.

Eight years earlier, the innovative Prep School building was formally opened. This fascinating curved building with its Maltings-style wind-catcher towers provides a highly stimulating environment for pupils between 3 and 11 years of age and is equipped with the latest technological and physical resources.

In September 2015 a new Technology Centre opened and in March 2014 a floodlit Astroturf, new changing rooms, a spectators viewing facility and function suite were added to the school's facilities within its 60 acres. in 2018 a new meeting space was created – The ARC. Named for the school's three core values (Aspiration, Respect, Confidence), The ARC provides a formal assembly area which can also be used for concerts, art exhibitions and social gatherings.

ISI Inspection. In March 2013, the College received an excellent ISI inspection report.

All areas of EYFS were judged to be outstanding. The quality of pupils' spiritual, moral, social and cultural development; pastoral care and quality of teaching; the curriculum and extra-curricular provision; and pupils' achievement were all excellent. ISI judged that '*all children make excellent progress and achieve better than age-related expectations in all areas of learning.*'

The arrangements for pastoral care and boarding were also judged to be excellent. '*A well-developed network of support, with clear lines of communication, provides the basis for pastoral care throughout the school and supports the pupils' excellent personal development. The family community is an obvious strength of the college. Pupils value the kindness and support that staff show them and enjoy positive relationships with all.*'

Judgements on achievement and teaching and learning included: '*Standards in the EYFS are high and pupils continue to make good progress towards their GCSE exams, where results are good. Pupils' personal and social development are excellent, in accordance with the Christian values which permeate the life of the college. Teachers have good subject knowledge and the most successful teaching promotes academic rigour and uses a variety of methods and resources. The pupils' performance in extra-curricular activities is frequently outstanding. They have had significant successes in sport, particularly rugby and cricket, but also in drama, music and art.*'

The most recent Inspection of Boarding in 2016 confirmed it was fully compliant and found no action points – in line with the most recent quantitative inspection in 2013, which deemed it excellent.

Boarding. We offer flexible, weekly and full boarding in family-run, spacious and warm boarding houses. The College has two boarding houses which provide both single and shared rooms, with kitchen, study and recreational facilities.

Curriculum. The curriculum is designed to provide a broad and balanced education for all pupils from 3 to 18. Strong foundations in the core skills of reading, writing and numeracy are laid down in the Infant Department through innovative programmes such as Read Write Inc and Singapore Mathematics. The Junior section continues the process of preparing the children for their secondary education by concentrating further on the core skills. In addition to these subjects, Science, French, Music and PE are taught and the children are introduced to a wider curriculum, including Design & Technology, Art, History, Geography, RE, IT and Games.

The Senior School prepares pupils for entrance to universities, other forms of higher education and the professions. Pupils are set according to ability in certain subjects. In Years 7 to 9, the emphasis continues to be placed on the core subjects whilst developing knowledge, skills and experiences necessary for the GCSE courses. The languages studied at the College include French and Spanish.

GCSE studies maintain a broad and balanced curriculum, but with the introduction of a degree of specialisation. Mathematics, English Language & Literature, Double Science Award and RE are compulsory. Once again core subjects continue to be set by ability. To cater for developing interests and abilities, there is a wide range of further choices from Food Technology and Photography to History, Spanish and Business Studies.

The majority of our pupils continue into the Sixth Form to complete their A Level or BTEC courses before going on to university or into apprenticeships or the workplace. There is a wide range of subjects available in the Sixth Form: Art (Fine Art), Biology, Business Studies, Chemistry, Drama & Theatre Studies, Economics, English, French, Geography, History, Mathematics, Further Mathematics, Music, Photography, Psychology, Physics, Product Design, Sociology and Spanish. We offer the General National Vocational Qualification (BTEC) in Applied Science, Business Studies, Creative Media, ICT & Sport, together with diverse sporting and other leisure and cultural opportunities. St Joseph's also offers the Extended Project Qualification.

A Learning Support department operates throughout the College to provide support individually or in small groups for students of all abilities with specific learning needs and differences.

There is comprehensive careers guidance from Year 9 and extensive help with university admission in the Sixth Form.

Extra-Curricular Activities. Sport, Art, Music and Drama are strongly encouraged, together with participation in the Duke of Edinburgh's Award scheme. A large number of extra-curricular clubs meets weekly – with a choice of over 100 in total. Regular ski trips, activity holidays and language exchanges are organised throughout the College. There is also a Year 9 exchange programme with two leading schools in Sydney, Australia.

Admission. Entry to the College is normally at 3+, 7+, 11+, 13+ and the Sixth Form, with applications for vacancies at other ages, subject to spaces being available. The entry process includes an interview, a Taster Day in the school, a formal assessment and a report from the applicant's previous school. For the Sixth Form, the academic assessment is replaced by GCSE results.

Fees per term (2018–2019). Nursery: £56.70 (per full session); Infants (Reception to Year 2) £3,095; Juniors (Years 3–6) £4,020 (day); Senior School: Years 7–8: £4,750 (day), £8,330 (weekly boarder), £8,715 (full boarder/EEA), £8,715 (overseas boarder); Year 9: £5,050 (day), £9,105 (weekly boarder), £11,265 (full boarder/EEA), £11,590 (overseas boarder); Years 10–11: £5,050 (day), £9,105 (weekly boarder), £11,265 (full boarder/EEA), £11,590 (overseas boarder); Sixth Form: £5,050 (day), £9,105 (weekly boarder), £11.265 (full boarder/EEA), £11,590 (overseas boarder).

Scholarships and Bursaries. The College offers a number of Academic Scholarships each year for different points of entry, as well as Scholarships for Music, Art, Drama and

Sport. Bursaries are also available in cases of need. Please contact the Admissions team for further information.

Charitable status. St Joseph's College is a Registered Charity, number 1051688. It exists to provide high quality education for children.

Governing Body:
Chair: Mr Perry Glading
Vice Chair: Mr Richard Stace, LLB

Mr John Button	Mr Anthony Newman
Prof Penny Cavenagh	Mr Matthew Potter
Mrs Renata Chester	Mrs Vicky Fox
Mr Philip Dennis	

Senior Leadership Team:

Principal: Mrs Danielle Clarke, BA Hons, NPQH

Vice Principal, Pastoral & Boarding: Mr Fergus Wilson, BSc Hons, PGCE
Vice Principle, Student & Staff Education: Dr Martin Hine, BEd Hons, PhD, FRSA, NPQH
Vice Principle, Academic: Mr Sacha Cinnamond, BA Hons, MA
Assistant Principle, Pastoral, Boarding, International: Mrs Gina Rowlands, BA Hons, PGCE, PG Dip
Assistant Principle, Director of Sport & Extra Curricular: Mr Anthony O'Riordan
Assistant Principal, Art & Academic: Mrs Vicki Harvey, BA, Dip Ed, PGCE
Assistant Principal, Head of Prep School: Mrs Vanessa Wood, BA Hons, PGCE
Head of Sixth Form: Dr Jen Stimson, BA Hons, MSc, PhD, PGCE
Bursar: Mrs Deborah Baber

Senior School Heads of Faculty and Pastoral Leads:
Mr M Frost (*Head of ICT & Computing*)
Miss L Cunningham (*Head of Learning Support*)
Mr C Branch (*Head of Prep School Sports*)
Mrs S Daley (*Assistant Director of Sport, Head of Girls' Sport*)
Mr M Grigg (*Head of Boys' Sport, Head of Rugby*)
Mrs H Green (*Head of English*)
Mrs A Hall (*Head of Upper School*)
Miss L Hassell (*Head of Science*)
Mr C McNicholas (*Head of Humanities*)
Mrs K Brown (*Head of MFL*)
Mrs A Willis (*Head of PSHEE*)
Mr C Fletcher (*Head of Lower School*)
Mr N Walkinshaw (*Head of Mathematics*)
Ms S Comley (*Head of EAL*)

Prep School:
Mrs L Wright (*Head of EYFS & Infants, Nursery to Year 2*)
Mrs D Searle (*Deputy Head*)

Scarborough College

Filey Road, Scarborough, North Yorkshire YO11 3BA

Tel:	01723 360620
Fax:	01723 377265
email:	admin@scarboroughcollege.co.uk
website:	www.scarboroughcollege.co.uk
Twitter:	@Scarboroughcol1
Facebook:	@ScarboroughCollege

Motto: *Pensez Fort*

Scarborough College, founded in 1896, is a thriving co-educational day and boarding school for children aged 3–18 with an exceptional academic pedigree and an unrivalled reputation for making the most of every child's potential. The College, its Prep School and Pre-School all share the same site. Our beautiful campus overlooks the spectacular North Yorkshire coast and is ten minutes' walk from the centre of the stunning seaside town of Scarborough. The boarding houses are merely a 15 minute walk from the beach. The College has fine views overlooking the South Bay of the town and Scarborough Castle.

Although the ethos of the College is firmly based upon wholesome traditional principles we have a progressive approach to education, which has led to us offering the International Baccalaureate in our Sixth Form for the past ten years, a qualification that is highly prized throughout the world. This year the College features as one of The Times Top 50 Independent Schools in the UK – something our staff, pupils and parents are very proud of. Our average staff to student ratio of 1:8 ensures we develop the full potential of every child.

Superb facilities including 20 acres of sports pitches, a fully floodlit AstroTurf, a performing arts centre with 400-seater theatre, sports hall and neighbouring 18-hole golf course all ensure a truly first-class education can be delivered to nurture the talents of all.

Scholarships for academic performance, sport, music and as an 'all-rounder' are awarded at all entry points. Means-tested bursaries are also available.

Admission. *Prep School*: Admission is by visit to the school and an interview with the Head of Prep School. Taster days can be arranged.

Senior School: Admission at age 11 is following an Entrance Assessment and interview. Admission at all other ages is subject to recommendation from the previous school, an interview and satisfactory performance in a general assessment.

Sixth Form: Admissions are subject to the achievement of a minimum of five GCSEs at Grades A* to C and an interview with the headmaster. *Overseas Students* are required to submit: school reports for the previous two years; academic certificates, if appropriate (GCSE or equivalent and any other exams taken); written reference from the Head of current/previous school. They are also required to sit our English and maths assessments and undergo an interview either during a visit to the school or via Skype. Scholarships and bursaries are available.

Senior School. Students join us in all year groups with especially high numbers of new arrivals in Years 7, 9 and 10 for GCSE, Year 11 for our bespoke Pre-IB course and the Lower Sixth for the IB Diploma.

Students in Years 7, 8 and 9 study three modern languages and three sciences, providing them with a firm foundation for further study. Along with English and maths, they also study traditional subjects including history, geography, music, art, religious education, classics, ICT, drama, and design and technology. Further options appear as GCSE subject choices in Year 10.

A dedicated Learning Support and English as an Additional Language team of staff ensures all individual needs are fully met.

Sport, music, and drama are very important parts of the daily College life with over 50 clubs and societies on offer every year. Horse riding is particularly popular and the College has both a Surf Academy and Golf Academy.

Prep School. Our educational vision is simple: the pursuit of excellence in every aspect of school life in an environment which will develop active, questioning, confident, thinking children.

At the core of our school is a traditional academic approach and a challenging curriculum. We provide the best pastoral care and support for every child. We also pride ourselves on the breadth of our education inside and outside the classroom. Dedicated subject specialists deliver a stimulating programme including art, drama, design technology, French and music, as well as daily games and outdoor pursuits. The enrichment programme is rich and varied.

In addition we offer free wrap-around care before and after school for our busy working parents plus a fun and caring Holiday Club for those who need additional child care support.

Sixth Form and the IB Diploma. The International Baccalaureate Diploma programme provides our Sixth Form students with a stimulating and challenging post-16 curriculum. Our experience has shown that the IB encourages the development of inquisitive, critical and reflective thinkers who engage fully in the learning process to acquire knowledge. 29 separate subject course options are available.

In our Sixth Form, students develop a new relationship with their teachers within a university-style tuition setting. They have many opportunities to show and develop their leadership skills and become very involved in the School Council, hosting and organising school, house and social events as well as prefect duties and helping younger students in roles such as mentors and sports coaches. There is a rich programme of visiting speakers and exchange visits, and they have their own dedicated Study Centre, Café and Common Room. This is a caring, friendly and warm environment which is a great place to develop and grow into inquisitive and confident young adults.

Boarding. There are three traditional and charming boarding houses at Scarborough College, offering boarding accommodation for pupils aged 11–18 years from all around the world. These really do provide a warm family environment with a home-from-home feeling for all our students, both British and foreign.

A busy programme of weekend entertainment is planned each term to keep the students active. More spontaneous events also include house barbecues, impromptu sports, trips to the beach, go karting, mountain biking, surfing and cinema trips, just to name a few.

Our boarding staff are all experienced members of staff with families of their own, so know how challenging and demanding teenagers can be from time to time, but also are very caring, understanding and sympathetic to the needs of each and every individual child.

Day Pupils benefit from all of the extras that being part of a boarding school brings, including the opportunity for occasional boarding. The school bus service operates daily to Bridlington, Whitby, Driffield, Malton and Pickering.

For further up-to-date information on the school, please visit the College's website.

Fees per term (2018–2019). Senior School: £4,394–£4,898 (day), £5,739–£6,480 (Weekly boarding), £7,347–£8,267 (UK and MOD boarding), £7,953–£8,803 (EU boarding), £8,569–£9,486 (Overseas boarding). Prep School: £2,496–£4,010 (day).

Charitable status. Scarborough College is a Registered Charity, number 529686.

Governors:
Dr J Renshaw (*Chairman*)
A S Green (*Deputy Chairman*)

Mr M Baines	Mr J M Green
Mr J Cliffe	Mr R Guthrie
Mr J Cook	Mr R Marshall
Mr S Fairbank	Dr I G H Renwick
Mr N Gardner	Mr J Rowlands
Mrs V Gillingham	

Senior Management Team:

Headmaster: Mr Guy Emmett

Head of Prep School: Mr Chris Barker

Deputy Head: Mrs Helen Devine Costa

Director of Studies: Mr Simon Harvey

Assistant Head – Academic Administration: Mr James Fraser

Business Manager & Clerk to the Governors: Miss Alison Higgins

Shebbear College

Shebbear, North Devon EX21 5HJ

Tel:	01409 282000
Fax:	01409 281784
email:	registrar@shebbearcollege.co.uk
website:	www.shebbearcollege.co.uk

Shebbear College is a day and boarding school for boys and girls between the ages of 3 to 18 years. Set in 85 acres of beautiful Devon countryside, the school, which was founded in 1841, offers superb facilities and plenty of room to run around in a very safe and healthy environment. The school is part of the Methodist Independent Schools Trust and embraces all faiths as it welcomes pupils from all over the world. The secure, happy family atmosphere at Shebbear, free from urban distractions, offers pupils full, weekly, or occasional boarding and day education. We aim to instil self-confidence in all our pupils, we teach them to be self-disciplined and they leave the College with excellent qualifications, many of our Sixth Form leavers achieving places at their chosen universities. Shebbear College offers all our pupils "A foundation for life".

Pupil Numbers. In the Senior School there are around 280 pupils, of whom around 80 are boarders, and around 80 pupils in our Prep School. We also have a thriving preschool offering the new 30 hours funding.

Situation and Location. Shebbear College borders on Dartmoor National Park and stands in 85 acres of unspoilt countryside. It can be easily reached by main road and rail links; only 40 miles west of Exeter and 40 miles north of Plymouth. Both cities have their own regional and international airport.

Buildings. The main College buildings include Prospect House, Lake Chapel, Beckly Wing, Shebbear College Prep School, Science Department, Music Centre, Sixth Form Centre, Language Centre and Sports Hall. All classrooms have interactive whiteboards. There are 2 Senior boarding houses and 1 Junior boys boarding house. The Junior girls have a separate area within the Senior girls house.

In recent years there has been an impressive record of school building projects. The latest work has been to build a full-size all-weather pitch and multi-gym. A new Prep School extension houses new classrooms and Assembly Hall. Two new buildings have now been completed – a new Music Centre and a new Sixth Form Centre.

Admission. The Pre School accepts boys and girls from the age of 3 and from the age of 5 they move into our Prep School. Entrance into Form 1 in the Senior School from other schools is by assessment in January for entry in September. Depending on availability we can consider in year entries. Entry into the Sixth Form is conditional upon GCSE performance.

Houses. Every pupil belongs to a House – Ruddle, Thorne or Way. These Houses organise activities and games competitions throughout the year. Our boarders also belong to an additional boarding house – Pollard House for Senior boy boarders, Pyke House for Junior boy boarders and Ruddle House for girl boarders – each having a Senior Houseparent and two assistants who live in. The House Tutors watch each child's progress academically as well as their general development.

Curriculum. All pupils at Shebbear College follow the National Curriculum until the age of 14. A wide choice of subjects is available in the following two years, leading to GCSE, but everyone is obliged to take English, Mathematics, Science and, usually, a foreign language. In the Sixth Form there is not only a wide choice of A2 and AS levels, but there is particularly flexible timetabling which enables students to mix Arts and Science subjects. We also offer a variety of BTech courses which pupils can study alongside A Levels and / or the Extended Project Qualification (EPQ).

Sport. With more than 25 acres of playing fields, modern sports hall with multi-gym, dance studio, cricket nets, all-weather pitch, tennis and netball courts, pupils have the security to exercise within the school grounds confidently. The main games covered for the boys are rugby, football, hockey and cricket, in which we have fixtures with most of the major schools in the South West of England. For the girls, we have teams in netball, hockey, rounders and tennis. All pupils are also offered tennis, basketball, athletics, cross-country, badminton and table tennis. All pupils up to the 4th Form have one afternoon of games plus an additional one period of PE every week.

Music and Drama. Pupils are strongly encouraged to participate in music and drama. Our choir has over 40 members and our orchestra, which represents most instruments, also has over 40 members. Players perform regularly in concerts and instrumental ensembles. Every term candidates proudly achieve Honours and Distinctions with The Associated Board of the Royal School for Music or Trinity College London. Also, every term, a theatrical production is performed to a very high standard. Following successful completion of A Levels at Shebbear College, we regularly have pupils going on to the Cardiff University School of Music and other prestigious Conservatoires.

Societies and Activities. All pupils participate in at least 4 afternoons a week of extra-curricular activities. This widens their interests and develops their self-confidence. The list of activities is endless and includes the usual and unusual. Many pupils enjoy getting involved with Ten Tors training, hillwalking, camping, sailing, canoeing, and surfing. The Army-run Ten Tors Challenge is proving to be very popular and many pupils are involved in the Duke of Edinburgh's Award scheme.

Careers. Careers advice is taken very seriously. Staff help our students prepare for their chosen career. The College is a member of Inspiring Futures. Individual attention is given at appropriate levels and a team of Old Shebbearians covering many professions visits the school regularly and helps with work experience and placement.

Scholarships and Bursaries. On application, scholarships and bursaries are awarded at the discretion of the Headmaster.

At 11+: All candidates take the Entrance and Scholarship Assessments in January.

At 13+: The Scholarship Examination is held in the Spring Term. Awards are also made following assessment results.

For Sixth Form candidates, scholarships and bursaries are awarded on the basis of interview, school report and GCSE performance.

Further details may be obtained from the Registrar.

Fees per term (2018–2019) Prep 1 and 2 £1,745. Prep 3 and 4 £2,745. Prep 5 and 6 £3,162. Senior School: Day £4,325, Weekly Boarding £4,750–£4,995, Full Boarding £6,250–£8,775.

Charitable status. Shebbear College is a Registered Charity, number 306945. It exists to provide high quality education for children.

Chairman of the Governors: Mr M J Saltmarsh

Headmaster: Mr S D Weale

Deputy Head Pastoral/Head of Boarding/Designated Safeguarding Lead: Mr M Newitt
Assistant Head/Head of Lower School: Mrs F Lovett
Head of Upper School: Mr J Sanders
Head of Prep School: Mr M Foale
Bursar & Clerk to the Governors: Mrs S Day

Heads of Departments:
Academic Support: Miss L Body, BA Hons, PGCE, NASENCo Award
Art: Mr A Barlow, BA Hons SIAD, Dip AD, LSDC, PGCE
Business Studies: Mr L Oxenham, BA Hons PGCE, MSc
Chemistry: Mr G Drake, BSc Hons
English: Mrs F Shamsolahi, BA Hons
Media: Mrs F Lovett, BA Hons
Drama: Mr J Pomroy, BA Hons, PGCE, MEd
English as a Second Language: Mrs A Vassilaki, BA Hons
Director of Sport: Mr A Steel, BSc Hons GTP
Geography: Mrs L Douglas, BA HMS UDE
Head of Science: Mr S Clewley, BSc Hons, PGCE
History & RS: Mr M Rogers, MA Hons, BA Hons, PGCE
ICT: Ms M Davies, BSc Hons, MSc
Mathematics: Mr S Trask, BEng Hons, PGCE
Music: Mr K Parker, GRSM
Careers: Mrs J Aliberti, BA Hons, PGCE
Modern Languages: Mrs C Fanet, BA, MA, PGCE
PSHE: Mr M Newitt & Mrs F Lovett
Psychology: Dr H Riley, BSc Hons, MSc, PhD, D Clin Psy

Headmaster's PA/Registrar: Miss N Giddy

Sibford School

Sibford Ferris, Banbury, Oxon OX15 5QL

Tel: 01295 781200
Fax: 01295 781204
email: admissions@sibfordschool.co.uk
website: www.sibfordschool.co.uk
Twitter: @SibfordSchOxon
Facebook: @Sibford-School

Founded 1842. A Co-educational Independent Boarding (full, weekly, and flexi) and Day School. Membership of The Society of Heads, BSA, AGBIS.

There are 398 pupils in the school aged between 3 and 18: 306 pupils in the Senior School and 92 pupils in the Junior School. There are 85 teachers plus visiting staff.

Curriculum. Sibford School offers an extensive, innovative and diverse education where pupils are encouraged to 'live adventurously'. Broad and balanced curriculum which reflects our view that while some may have talent for maths or history others may be gifted in the arts or horticulture. Renowned dyslexia tuition and support for a small number of pupils with other learning difficulties.

Junior School (age 3–11): wide-ranging curriculum with an emphasis on outdoor education. Literacy, numeracy, science and technology skills are emphasised alongside art, music, drama and PE. Enriched Curriculum in Year 6 with Senior School Staff. Specialist teachers help individual children with specific learning difficulties. No SATS.

Senior School (age 11–16): all pupils follow courses leading to GCSE, in a curriculum expanding on the National Curriculum. Information Technology is introduced at an early age and the use of laptop computers is widespread.

Dyslexic pupils have special tuition in small groups on a daily basis. Highly regarded Support for Learning Department provides specialised support within the timetable. Personal and Social Development runs through the school.

Sixth Form (age 16–18) students take A Levels and/or BTEC Diplomas. The Sixth Form curriculum leads to higher education, and offers a particularly wide range of opportunities for further study. In 2018 24% of leavers gained places at Russell Group Universities.

Overseas pupils are welcomed into the school community. The school has a specialist ESOL department and English as an additional language is taught by ESOL qualified teachers.

Entry requirements. Admission is by interview and internal tests. Where applicable a report from the candidate's current school is required. No religious requirements.

Examinations offered. A Level, GCSE, BTEC Diploma, Associated Board Music Examinations, LAMDA, Oxford and Cambridge IELTS Examinations.

Academic and leisure facilities. Exceptional Performing & Creative Arts in purpose-built facilities. Multi-purpose Sports Centre, including brand new state-of-the-art Climbing Wall. 25m indoor swimming pool. Well-equipped Library and Information Technology Centres. Design Technology Centre. Separate Sixth Form Centre. Wide range of indoor and outdoor activities. 50 plus-acre campus set in beautiful North Oxfordshire countryside. Three boarding houses (for girls, boys and sixth form). Easy access to Stratford, Oxford, Cheltenham, Birmingham, London.

Religion. Established as a Quaker school, Sibford welcomes pupils of all faiths, backgrounds and nationalities, encouraging in each of them genuine self-esteem in a purposeful, caring and challenging environment.

Fees per term (2018–2019). Full Boarders £9,359–£9,548, Weekly Boarders £8,718–£8,890, Flexi Boarding £60 per night, Day Pupils £4,818–£4,913. Junior School: Day Pupils £3,060–£3,703. The fee for a full term of learning support is £1,707.

Scholarships and Bursaries. The School offers general Academic scholarships and specific scholarships in Art, Music and Sport. A limited number of bursaries is offered to both Quaker and non Quaker children. Limited bursary support is available for UK boarders in Years 7–8.

Charitable status. Sibford School is a Registered Charity, number 1068256. It is a company limited by guarantee under number 3487651. It aims to give all pupils a vehicle to educational and personal success.

Chair of School Committee: Seren Wildwood

[1] *Postgraduate Teaching Qualification*
§ *Part time Staff*
† *House Parent*

Head: Toby Spence, BA, MEd [1]

Assistant Head (*Curriculum*): John Charlesworth, MSc [1]
Assistant Head (*Pastoral*) *and Designated Safeguarding Lead*: Tracy Knowles, BA Ed [1]
Assistant Head (*Learning and Teaching*): Anna Jo Mathers, BA [1]
Head of Sixth Form: Cate Mallalieu-Needle, MA, NPQH [1]
Head of Junior School: Edward Rossiter, BSc, PG Dip Social Sciences, MEd [1]
Senior Teacher, Junior School: Nicholas Hadley, BA [1]

Senior School:
Michelle Aylott (*Textiles*)
Simon Baker, BSc [1](*Head of Key Stage 4, Head of Geography, Enrichment Week Coordinator, EcoSchools Coordinator, Head of Houses*)
Victoria Baker, BA [1](*English, Head of Boarding*)
§Katie Bertie (§*Dyslexia Teacher, English*)
David Brassett, (†§*Assistant to PE department*)
Simon Chard, BA [1](*PE, Vocational Education*)
Tara-Louise Cheetham (†§*PE Teacher*)
Frances Claydon, B Nursing (§*Teaching Assistant*)
Hannah Copping, BSc [1](§*Geography*)
Emma Crocker, BA [1](§*Design Technology, Head of Home Economics*)
Tamsin Cygal, BSc [1](*Science*) [maternity leave]
Darren de Bruyn, B Bus Admin [1](*Assistant Head of Sixth Form, Head of Business Studies, PSHE Coordinator KS5*)
Matthew Dibbens (*Peripatetic Music Teacher*: Drums)
Frances Eason, Dip Theatre Design/Craft, Cert Ed Post 16 (*Teaching Assistant*)
Helen Earle, BSc [1](§*Mathematics*)
James Elliot, BSc [1](*Science*)
Debby Evans, Cert Ed PCE, Cert SpLD (*Head of ICT, BTEC Quality Nominee*)
Claire Ferley, BSc (§*Joint Acting Head of PE*)
Richard Ferley, BSc [1](§*Joint Acting Head of PE*)
Rebecca Flynn, BA, MA, CTEFL (§*Psychology, ESOL Dyslexia*)
Andrew Foakes, BA, MA [1](*Head of Media, English, Head of House*)
Barry Fowkes (*Peripatetic Music Teacher*)
Andrew Glover, Dip SpLD, BA, Dip TEFL [1](*ESOL*)
Sarah Haig Rees (*Peripatetic Music Teacher*)
Cath Harding, BSc [1](§*Head of Science*)
Catherine Harnett (*Teaching Assistant*)
Jane Harper, BSc (*Teaching Assistant*)
Deborah Holroyd, BSc, MA Ed [1](§*Science*)
Adam Hosler (*Mathematics Teacher*)
Fiona Hudson, BA, Licenciate Trinity College Music [1](*Head of Music*)
John James, BA [1](§*Ceramics*)
Pippa Jones (§*Teaching Assistant*)
Jane Kenehan (*Teaching Assistant, Dyslexia*)
Tracey Leigh, MA [1](*Head of Art*)
Victoria Macaulay, MSc [1](*Head of Key Stage 3, 2nd in Science*)
Neil Madden BA [1](*Head of Drama, Head of House*)
Michael Maguire (†*Teaching Assistant*)
Andrea Mardon (*LAMDA Teacher*)
Joanna Mayes, BA, Cert TEFL, Cert Ed (§*ESOL*)
Harriet Meddows (*Head of Mathematics*)
Sarah Moffat (*Peripatetic Music Teacher*)
Isabelle Murphy (*Teaching Assistant*)
Ingar Noble, Dip Clinical & Pathological Psychology (*Teaching Assistant*)
Moira Oliver (§*Teaching Assistant*)
Linda Phillips, BSc, MA [1](*Mathematics, Joint Coordinator Duke of Edinburgh's Award*)
Sally Pickering, BA, Dip TEFL [1](*Head of ESOL*)
Barney Porter (*Assistant to Music department, Teaching Assistant*)
Greg Prosser (*Peripatetic Music Teacher*)
Sarah Read (*Business and Economics*)
Verity Redrup (*Science*) [maternity cover]
Jay Riley (*Peripatetic Music Teacher*)
Lee Riley (*PE Teacher with responsibility for Senior School PE*)
Jeremy Ross, MA [1](*History, RS, Joint Coordinator Duke of Edinburgh's Award*)
Sue Sabin (*SfL Teacher*)

Jon Seagroatt (*Peripatetic Music Teacher*)
Lois Self, BA (*Careers Coordinator*)
Jessica Shalders [1](*§PE*)
Elizabeth Sharam (*Peripatetic Music Teacher*)
Deborah Siepmann (*Peripatetic Music Teacher*)
Zoë Simms, BA, MA, AKC [1](*Head of RS, Philosophy & Ethics, Charities Coordinator, Quaker Outreach*)
Deborah Simpkins, BA [1](*Modern Foreign Languages*)
Claire Skitt (*Mathematics*)
Annie Smith, BSc, Cert Dyslexia & Literacy [1](*Assistant Head of Support for Learning*)
Jill Spence (*PE teacher with responsibility for Junior School PE*)
Penelope Spring, BA [1](*English teacher, PGCE mentor*)
Catherine Stockdale, MA SEN [1](*Head of Support for Learning*)
Greg Symes (*Head of Design & Technology*)
James Topp (*Peripatetic Music Teacher*)
Noriko Tsuzaki (*Peripatetic Music Teacher*)
Valerie Vet (*Peripatetic Music Teacher*)
Sally-Anne Ward (*Head of English*)
Allison Warrillow, BA [1](*Assistant Head of PE, Head of House*)
Belinda Webb (*Peripatetic Music Teacher – Drums*)
Jayne Woolley, BA, Cert Ed (*§Dyscalculia*)
Harry Wragg (*§Horticulture*)
Marcel Zidani (*Peripatetic Music Teacher*)

Sibford Junior School:
Head of Junior School: Edward Rossiter, BSc, PG Dip Social Sciences, MEd [1]
Margaret Allen, BA [1](*Year 4*)
Helen Arnold, BA [1](*Year 3*)
Rachel Bee, BMus [1](*§Music*)
Rebecca Edwards, BSc, MA Ed [1](*Years 1 & 2*)
Anna Hadley (*After School Care*)
Nicholas Hadley, BA [1](*Senior Teacher, Year 6*)
Jason Harris (*Outdoor Environment Facilitator*)
Helen Hoy, BA [1](*Head of Early Years Foundation Stage*)
Jane Kenehan (*Teaching Assistant, Dyslexia*)
Nicola Key, BA Education (*Senior Early Years Assistant*)
Amanda Levett, BA [1](*§Junior School Dyslexia teacher*)
Alice Pennell, BEd (*Year 5*)
Lois Self, BA [1](*Teaching Assistant, Senior School Careers Coordinator*)
Helen Sinton (*Early Years Assistant*)
Claire Solesbury (*§Teaching Assistant*)
Susan Spillett, BA (*Teaching Assistant*)
Katy Stotesbury, BA [1](*Year 5*)
Hazel Sykes, BA [1](*§Year 6, Dyslexia*)
Jayne Woolley, BA, Cert Ed (*§Dyscalculia*)

Business Manager: Peter Robinson, Health and Safety, Estate & Business Management
Admissions: Elspeth Dyer
Marketing: Ali Bromhall

Stafford Grammar School

Burton Manor, Stafford, Staffordshire ST18 9AT

Tel: 01785 249752
Fax: 01785 255005
email: headsec@staffordgrammar.co.uk
website: www.staffordgrammar.co.uk

Motto: *Quod tibi hoc alteri*

Number in School. There are 304 pupils (11–18 years) of whom 153 are boys and 151 girls. There is a Sixth Form of 88. Stafford Preparatory School has just over 100 pupils.

Stafford Grammar School is housed in a fine Victorian manor house, designed by Augustus Pugin, standing in 47 acres of grounds with sports pitches, tennis courts and extensive additional specialist accommodation. Sixteen acres of sports land have recently been developed to further enhance outside sport provision.

Curriculum. In Year 7 and Year 8 all pupils follow a common course consisting of English, Mathematics, Science, French, German, Geography, History, Music, Art, Drama, Computing, Design, Technology, Religious Education and Physical Education. Year 9 sees Science divide into separate subjects.

Pupils in Years 10 and 11 study nine or ten subjects at GCSE: English (2), Mathematics, Science (triple award) and a language, together with three further subjects chosen from a whole range including humanities and practical subjects. Physical Education continues and Careers and Life Skills are introduced.

There is setting in Mathematics from Year 8, Science from Year 9 and English from Year 10. Other subjects are taught in mixed ability groups. Classes are kept small so that pupils can receive individual attention.

In the Lower Sixth Form students study three or four A Level subjects (AS) leading to three or four A Level subjects (A2) in the Upper Sixth Form. Approximately 20 A Level subjects are available.

Creativity and the Arts. The School has an extensive Art and Design Department. Pupils' powers of observation and awareness are developed through practical skills and theoretical studies involving areas as varied as painting, printing, 3-D work, photography and textiles. There are frequent competitions and exhibitions of work as well as projects linked with other departments.

Music plays an important part in the life of the School. There is an orchestra, a concert band and choirs which perform on many occasions in musicals, church services and concerts. Ensembles, both instrumental and vocal, are encouraged. Pupils have the opportunity to learn to play a wide range of musical instruments with tuition provided by peripatetic teachers. The bi-annual music trips abroad are well supported.

Drama enables pupils to gain confidence and self-understanding. It is particularly effective in the early years in the School. Two annual School Plays are major productions on the School's excellent stage and involve a large number of pupils. Recent productions include *Les Misérables, West Side Story and Fame.*

Art and Drama are available at both GCSE and A Level.

Peripatetic LAMDA tuition is available from Grade 1 to Gold Medal (Grade 8). LAMDA students also attend local drama festivals.

Sport and Activities. Whilst competitive sport plays a prominent part in School life, the emphasis is also on preparation for future leisure time.

The School has outstanding sports facilities and the following sports are available: Soccer, Hockey, Rugby, Cricket, Tennis, Badminton, Basketball, Netball, Volleyball, Athletics, Gymnastics, Rounders, Table Tennis, and Health-related Fitness, as well as Swimming. The School has an extensive fitness suite.

The School plays a large number of matches against other schools, both state and independent, and is fully involved in local leagues. Individuals regularly secure places in Staffordshire and Midlands teams.

Our range of activities is deliberately wide since we believe that every child is good at something and that it is our job to discover and develop talent in any direction.

There are many Clubs and Societies of widely differing kinds and a large number of pupils are working for The Duke of Edinburgh's Award scheme.

At present there are 15 inter-House competitions. These range from Technology to Public Speaking and from Football to Hobbies, and include some which are specifically for younger pupils.

The intention of these is not only to enable as many pupils as possible to represent their Houses, but also to stress that we value excellence in any area.

Pastoral Care. In its pastoral organisation, the School seeks to nurture the potential of every child giving both support and encouragement in an overt and practical way. The School is divided into three houses, the Head of House being the key figure in the academic and personal development of each child. Tutor groups are kept small and are based on the House to maintain continuity and to strengthen communal bonds. Tutors maintain strong links with each pupil using a programme of active tutoring which includes scheduled interviews. We place great emphasis on close contact with parents, believing that lack of progress and other problems are best addressed jointly and as early as possible.

In the Sixth Form a slightly different system operates. Although retaining the same House Tutor, the pupil will have a Form Tutor from a specialist team of Sixth Form Tutors. Additionally one of the Senior Teachers is attached to this team. Further to this is the opportunity for each pupil to choose a Personal Tutor with whom to build a special rapport.

Sixth Form. The Sixth Form is the ideal environment in which to foster confidence, responsibility, leadership, initiative and self-discipline.

The keynote of the Sixth Form is freedom with responsibility. At this stage pupils still need help in planning their time and in establishing good working habits, and the guidance of an understanding tutor can mean the difference between success and failure. There is an extensive UCAS programme which includes Oxbridge preparation.

Careers. Considerable attention is paid to career advice, and there are frequent visits by speakers from industry and the professions. From Year 10 onwards, individual advice is given by our own careers staff, and pupils are also encouraged to consult the County Careers Service.

Religion. Although we welcome pupils of all faiths, or none, the School is a Christian foundation.

The School seeks to live by the Christian ideal, in particular by being a community in which members genuinely care about each other.

Admission. Entrance is by examination and interview in order to ensure that pupils have sufficient reasoning ability to be able to attempt GCSE in a reasonable range of subjects.

Entrance to the Sixth Form is by GCSE results and interview.

Scholarships and Bursaries. The Governors have allocated funds to enable pupils of exceptional ability or limited means to join the school.

Fees per term (from January 2019). Grammar School: £4,260 excluding lunch; Preparatory School (including lunch): Reception–Year 2 £3,484, Years 3 & 4 £3,673, Years 5 & 6 £3,819.

Stafford Preparatory School opened, in purpose-built accommodation, in September 2007 admitting pupils into Years 5 and 6. A Year 4 class was admitted in September 2008, a Year 3 class in 2009, Years 1 and 2 in September 2012, and a Reception class in 2014. Stafford Preparatory School provides exciting opportunities for pupils to prepare for selective senior school education at Stafford Grammar School or elsewhere.

Charitable status. Stafford Independent Grammar School Limited is a Registered Charity, number 513031. It exists to provide education for children.

Patrons:
The Right Hon The Earl of Shrewsbury
The Lord Stafford
The Right Hon The Earl of Lichfield

Governing Body:

B Baggott (*Chairman*)	D Pearsall
Mrs J Causer	Mrs P Pearsall
Mrs J Colman	Mr T Carson
Revd J Davis	Mr J Johnson
B Hodges	A Wright
J Lotz	

Headmaster: M R Darley, BA

Head of Senior: L H Thomas, BA
Director of Curriculum: Dr P A Johnson, BSc, PhD
Senior Teacher: R C Green, BA

Assistant Staff:

C Anderson, BSc	Mrs T A Hollinshead, BSc, MSc
Mrs E Ayirebi, BA	
M Azeem, BA	Mrs K Horsley, BA
D R Beauchamp, BSc	A C Johnson, BSc
G Beckett, BSc	G R Lamplough, BMus
Miss K Butler, BA, MA	D Mole, BA
C Cooke, BA	Mrs K Owen-Reece, BA
Ms K Farmer, BA	Mrs E L Paton, BA
Mrs K Fletcher, BA	Mrs P H Patrick, BSc
S Godwin, MSc, BA	Mrs D Shaughnessy, BA, MA
Mrs R Godwin-Bratt, BSc	
J Grace, BSc	Mrs C Slater, BA
Mrs L J Griffiths, BA	Mrs S Smith, BA
Mr S Gunnell, BA	Mrs J Stace, BA
Miss H Hackett, BSc	Ms C Taig, BSc
Miss G Hague-Jones, BA	Miss J Wedgwood, BSc
L J Harwood, BEd	Mrs A L Weetman, LAES

Chaplain:
Prebendary R Sargent, MA
Revd J Davis, MBE, KStJ, BA, MA

Bursar: J Downes

Headmaster's Secretary: Mrs R Sheridan

Stonar

Cottles Park, Atworth, Wiltshire SN12 8NT

Tel:	01225 701740
Fax:	01225 790830
email:	office@stonarschool.com
website:	www.stonarschool.com
Twitter:	@StonarSchool
Facebook:	@StonarSchool

Co-educational Day and Boarding School from Nursery to Sixth Form.

Ethos. Stonar combines an impressive all-round education, with a wide-ranging curriculum and a wealth of extra-curricular activities. Pupils go on to achieve outstanding academic results, with almost all pupils gaining their first choice of university course in 2017 and 2018. Stonar develops the talents of every individual, enabling pupils of all abilities to achieve their potential across and beyond the formal curriculum. There is a positive work ethic and excellent pastoral care. Curiosity, confidence and independence are encouraged so that pupils leave school well-equipped for the challenges of adult life and keen to contribute to the wider community.

Curriculum. A talented and committed staff offers pupils a broad and flexible curriculum. Prep Children follow the IEYC and IPC. In Years 10 and 11, pupils study GCSEs and iGCSEs, with an individual choice from wide-ranging options in addition to the core of Science, Maths, English, a foreign language and RS. 'Able and Talented' pupils are identified throughout school and opportunities to extend their learning exist both within the curriculum and in extra-curricular activities. The BHS and UK CC courses are available to pupils in Year 11 and the Sixth Form and a broad range of A Levels is also available.

Considering our broad academic intake, Stonar's results are outstanding and pupils go on to university courses ranging from Medicine, Law and Accountancy to Geology, Veterinary Science and Music. Talented artists proceed to a variety of Art Foundation Courses. Young riders take up careers in eventing or go for the Equine Studies option.

Extra-curricular Activities. The school's internationally renowned Equestrian Centre provides tuition for all ages and abilities. Facilities include indoor and outdoor arenas, cross country training fields and a hacking track. The Equestrian Centre has the top level of BHS accreditation and is also a Pony Club centre.

The Sports Hall, indoor Swimming Pool, AstroTurf, Theatre, Music, Sixth Form & Arts Centre offer first-class opportunities for sport, music and drama. A timetabled tutorial period provides a rolling programme of careers advice, health education, study skills, first aid, self-defence and citizenship. An extensive programme of after-school activities includes academic, sporting and life skills options which challenge and extend pupils' development. In the Sixth Form, pupils enjoy debating, dance, film studies, aerobics and a Cookery Course including the Leiths Toolkit. The Duke of Edinburgh's Award scheme flourishes at Stonar.

Boarding. Boarders live in comfortable, family-style houses, each with internet access. Pupils of any religion and of all nationalities are welcomed and can work towards IGCSE English, if this is not their first language.

Admission. Straightforward entrance procedures via Stonar entrance examinations in early January and school report at appropriate ages.

Fees per term (2018–2019). Prep Day £2,832–£3,818; Senior Day £5,100–£5,500; Prep Boarding £7,318; Senior Boarding £10,135.

Scholarships and Bursaries. Year 7 & Year 9 Entry: Academic, Art, Drama, Sport, Music and Riding Scholarships are offered. Scholarship assessments take place in January following the Entrance Examination.

Sixth Form Entry: Academic, Art, Drama, Sport, Music and Riding Scholarships are available. Scholarship examinations, assessments and interviews held in November.

Means-tested Bursaries are available. A Forces Bursary is available to Senior School boarders whose parents are current serving members of HM Forces.

Governance. Stonar is a part of NACE Educational Services Limited, Company Registration No. 8441252, Registered Address: 17 Hanover Square, London, United Kingdom W1S 1HU.

Chairman of Board of Directors:
Mr Daniel Jones, NACE UK Ltd

Head: **Dr Sally Divall**, MA, PhD, PGCE

Bursar: Mrs Claire Sparrow, BA Hons MBA ACMA

Deputy Head: Mrs Nicola Hawkins, MSc, BSc Hons, PGCE

Director of Studies: Mrs Alison Rivers, BSc Hons, PGCE

Senior Staff:
§ *Part-time*

Mrs S Aikman, BA Hons, PGCE (*Head of Modern Foreign Languages*)
Mrs N Battley, BA Hons, PGCE (*Dance*)
Mrs C Bennett, BA Hons, PGCE (*Head of Sixth Form, Geography, RS*)
Mrs K Bouchard, BSc Hons, PGCE (*Science*)
Mr S Boxall, MA, PGCE (*Subject Leader of History*)
Mrs T Brain, BA Ed Hons (*English and Drama*)
§Mrs J Brighouse, BA Hons, PGCE (*French, EAL*)
Miss A Catt, BA Hons, GTP (*EAL*)
Miss S Cholmondeley, MEng Hons, PGCE (*Head of Maths and Computer Science*)
Mrs S Cross, BA Hons, PGCE (*Art & Photography*)
Miss H Culverhouse, BSc Hons, PGCE (*PE and Games*)
Mr A Curtis, MSc, BSc Hons, PhD (*Head of Careers, Psychology*)
Ms E Davies, BSc Hons, PGCE (*Subject Leader of Biology*)
Mrs C Deans, MA, TEFL Dip (*Head of EAL*)
Mr J Dyde, BA Hons, PGCE (*Head of English*)
§Mrs T Gates, BA Hons, PGCE, PG Dip (*Learning Support*)
Mr N Goodall, BA Hons, MMus, PGCE (*Director of Music, ICT*)
Mr R Hobson, BSc Hons, PGCE (*PE & Games*)
Mrs K Leach, BSc Hons, PGCE (*Science*)
§Mrs S McQueen, BA Hons PGCE (*EAL*)
Miss S Meehan, BA Hons, PGCE (*Assistant Director of Music, English*)
Mr D Messenger, BSc, PGCE (*Maths*)
Mr R Miller, BA Hons (*Director of Sport and PE*)
Mrs S Moore, BSc Hons, PGCE (*Maths, Houseparent of Hart*)
Mrs L Noad, BA Hons (*RS, Houseparent of York*)
Mr A O'Hanlon, BA Hons, PGCE, PG Dip (*Head of Art & Photography*)
Mrs J Phillips, MA, PGCE (*Head of Learning Support*)
Mrs A Rigby, MA, BA Hons, PGCE (*French and Spanish*)
Mrs B Russell, MLD, BA Hons, HLTA, ELSA (*Learning Support*)
Mrs A Sawyer, BA, PGCE (*Latin*)
Mrs J Slark, BSc Hons, PGCE (*Subject Leader of Business*)
Mrs L Smith, BSc Hons, PGCE (*Head of Geography*)
Mrs T Tilley, BSc Hons, PGCE (*PE, Biology, Houseparent of Ganbrook*)
Mrs F Villaba-Carrasco, MA, PGCE, PG Dip (*Spanish & French*)
Mr C Walker, BA Hons, PGCE (*Subject Leader of Drama*)
Mrs S Walker, BEd Hons (*Learning Support Assistant*)
Mrs R Wells, BSc Hons, PGCE (*Science/Chemistry*)
Mr D Wicks, MSc, BSc Hons, PGCE (*Head of Science, Physics*)
Mrs J Wigley, BLib Hons, MCLIP (*Learning Resources Supervisor*)
Ms J Wigley, BA Hons QTLS (*Subject Leader of Food and Nutrition*)
Mrs R Windridge, MA Ed, PGCE (*Learning Support*)

Prep School:

Head of Prep: Mr M Brain, BA Ed Hons
Deputy Head of Prep: Mr D Lee, MA, BA Hons (*Year 6 Tutor*)
Miss L Allen, Level 3 Dip (*Teaching Assistant*)
Mrs V Clarkson, BTEC (*Learning Support*)

Mrs S Crouch, NNEB, EYFS (*Reception Class Teaching Assistant*)
Mr D Gower, BSc Hons, PGCE (*Year 5 Tutor*)
Mrs S Gower, BA Hons, PGCE (*Reception Tutor*)
Mrs S Jackson DfA Level 5 (*EYFS Assistant*)
Mr G James, BA Hons, PGCE (*Year 2 Tutor*)
Mrs F Liddle, BEd (*Teaching Assistant*)
Mrs H Mittra, BSc Hons, PGCE (*Year 4 Tutor*)
Miss K Osborne, BA Ed Hons (*Year 3 Tutor*)
Mrs J Redsull, NNEB (*Forest School Leader*)
Mrs J Skinner, BA Hons, PGCE (*Year 5 Tutor*)
Mrs M Tober, MEd (*Year 1 Tutor*)

Nursery:
Nursery Manager: Mrs M Urbieta Irastorza, QTS
Miss S Davies, Level 6 Dip (*EYFS Nursery Deputy*)
Mrs J Redsull, NNEB (*Forest School Leader*)
Miss E Fiducia-Brookes, Level 4 Dip (*EYFS Assistant*)
Miss J Tyler, BA Hons (*EYFS Assistant*)

Equestrian Centre:
Mr D Scaife, FBHSI, BE AcCoach UKCC Level 3 (*Director of Riding*)
Miss J Chilcott, BHSII (*Senior School Instructor*)
Miss J Foster, BHSAI (*Prep School Instructor*)
Miss E Halsey, BHSII (*Assistant Director of Riding*)
Mr N Hubbard (*Yard Manager*)
Mrs E Sowels (*Equine Secretary*)

Stover School

Newton Abbot, South Devon TQ12 6QG

Tel: 01626 354505 (Main switchboard)
          01626 359911 (Registrar)
          01626 335240 (Finance Office)
Fax: 01626 361475
email: mail@stover.co.uk
website: www.stover.co.uk

Stover School is a leading independent, co-educational, non-selective, day and boarding school for pupils aged 3 to 18. It is set in 64 acres of beautiful and historical grounds in the heart of Devon's glorious countryside between the foothills of Dartmoor and the South West Coastline. In the last ISI Inspection the School was judged as fully compliant and in the previous quality inspection as excellent in teaching, pastoral care, welfare, health and safety, quality of leadership and management and governance.

Stover School delivers a cutting edge Research Based Learning Curriculum across the entire age range while retaining a healthy focus on traditional Christian morals, values and manners. Happy children are at the very centre of the school's ethos, reflecting the robust system of pastoral care. Children who feel safe, valued, respected and who trust those around them are free to focus on learning to their maximum potential.

Pupils are encouraged, motivated and supported in achieving their aspirations in all areas of the academic and broader curriculum. Successes are celebrated wherever they occur, be that in Bushcraft, French, Hockey, Science, Fencing, Art or Computer Programming.

The extensive activities and enrichment programmes ensure that everyone can enjoy, develop and challenge themselves. In this relatively small school every pupil is well known. The strong House system provides a framework for pupils to develop a sense of collectiveness within the supportive environment. Pupils learn respect for themselves and others through the teaching of moral values and good standards of behaviour.

The aim is to ensure that every child enjoys their experience at Stover School, having achieved the best they are capable of in the broadest education sense and having equipped themselves with the qualifications and skills required for future success and fulfilment.

Recent developments include a refurbished Art Studio, Sixth Form Centre and boarding accommodation, a newly established tennis academy, the creation of a music ensemble practice suite and recording studio, the establishment of a clay shooting and rifle range and the arrival of the first vegetable beds, chickens and beehives, coupled with an outdoor classroom.

Examinations. Public examinations set by all examination boards include GCSE, BTEC and A Level. Music examinations are set by the Associated Board of the Royal Schools of Music. Speech and Drama examinations are set by LAMDA. Sixth Form pupils can also take CoPE and CSL/HSL qualifications, set by ASDAN and Sports Leaders UK respectively.

Physical Education. Hockey, rugby, netball, table tennis, football, rounders and cricket are the core team games. Individual sports include athletics, gymnastics, golf, tennis, badminton and cross country. Other sports throughout the year include adventure development, orienteering, shooting and dance.

The school has extensive grass pitches, six tennis courts (3 floodlit and one cover all-weather), a 9-hole golf course, cross-country tracks, clay pigeon and rifle range and cricket nets. We run a full range of school sports activities, clubs and fixture lists for both Senior and Prep.

Optional subjects. In addition to a wide variety of activities organised by Stover's own staff there are specialist peripatetic staff for instrumental and voice tuition, speech and drama, riding, fencing, judo, golf, clay pigeon and rifle shooting and tennis coaching.

Fees per term (2018–2019). Preparatory School: Day: Reception £2,740, Years 1–3 £2,800, Years 4–6 £3,480. Weekly Boarding: Years 4–6 £6,150. Full Boarding: Years 4–6 £7,070. Senior School: Years 7–13: £4,260 (day), £7,400 (weekly boarding), £8,730 (full boarding);

Entrance and Scholarships. Compatibility of new pupils is assessed through a Head's interview, school tours, a series of taster days and submission of previous school's full written report. Academic, Music, Sport and Arts Scholarships are available and can be sat at point of entry or on our Scholarship Assessment Day in January. In addition, means-tested bursaries are available. Stover School, in association with Plymouth University, also offers the Excellence in Mathematics Scholarships to International students. This attracts a 10% remission of fees at Plymouth University for the duration of the Undergraduate Degree course (3 years).

Health. Nursing care is provided by our on-site Matron who is a Registered General Nurse. All boarders are registered with the school's GP.

Old Stoverites. c/o Stover School.

Charitable status. Stover School Association is a Registered Charity, number 306712. Stover School is a charitable foundation for education.

Chairman of Governors: Mr S Killick, ND, ARB

Headmaster: **Mr R W D Notman**, BCom Birmingham

Deputy Head: Dr J Stone, BSc Wales, MEd Open, PhD S'ton, HDipEd, Dublin
Head of Preparatory School: Mr D Burt, BA Keele

Senior Leadership Team:
Mr R W D Notman, BCom Birmingham (*Headmaster*)
Mr D Burt, BA Keele (*Head of Preparatory School*)
Dr J Stone, BSc Wales, MEd Open, PhD S'ton, HDipEd Dublin (*Deputy Head*)

Mr P Jenkins (*Bursar*)
Mrs H Notman, BSc, UMIST, MSc Ed Res Manchester
  (*Senior Teacher, Pastoral*)

Middle Leadership Team Senior School:
Mr C Baillie, BSc Keele (*Head of Sixth Form*)
Mr S Griffin, BEd Cheltenham & Farnborough (*Head of
  Years 7, 8 & 9*)
Mrs D Robinson, BA, Twickenham (*Deputy Head of Sixth
  Form*)
Mrs E Machin, BA Manchester (*Head of Years 10 & 11*)

Senior School Teaching Staff:
Dr D Allway, BSc MSc PhD, Manchester (*Head of
  Science*)
Mr C Baillie, BSc Keele (*Science & Head of Sixth Form*)
Mr J Balfour (*Head of Drama*)
Mrs E Barnes, BEd Bath (*Head of Home Economics*)
Mr P Barter, BA Exeter (*Head of Humanities, Duke of
  Edinburgh's Award Coordinator*)
Mr J Brown (*Science*)
Mr S Cocker, BSc QTS Marjon (*Head of Mathematics*)
Miss R Cocks (*Geography*)
Mrs A Coster, BA Exeter (*Sport*)
Mrs T Craven, BA QTS Brighton (*Head of Sport*)
Miss E Evans, BA Exeter (*French & German*)
Mr G Forsyth, BA Sheffield, TEFL (*English*)
Mrs R Fenton, BA Manchester (*Head of English & Media*)
Mr G Foxley (*Head of Modern Foreign Languages*)
Mrs K Gardner, BA Nottingham (*History*)
Mr S Griffin, BEd Cheltenham & Farnborough (*Geography
  & Sport, Head of Years 7, 8 and 9*)
Mr A Hardy, BSc Kent (*Mathematics*)
Mr J Hartley, BA Exeter (*Head of Business Studies*)
Mr M Halse, BA Exeter (*Head of Boys' Sport*)
Miss J Henwood, BSc Bath (*Mathematics*)
Mrs C Howard, BA Wales (*Head of Art & Photography*)
Dr L LeTissier, BA Exon, BSc Plymouth, PhD Exon (*Head
  of Psychology*)
Mrs E Machin, BA Manchester (*Director of ICT & Head of
  D&T (Graphics), Head of Years 10 & 11*)
Miss A Morgan, BSc Wales (*Biology*)
Mrs A Richards, BSc Ed Exeter (*Head of Physics*)
Mrs D Robinson, BA Twickenham (*PE, Deputy Head of
  Sixth Form*)
Mrs B Seward, BA Middlesex (*Philosophy & Ethics*)
Mrs C Sewell, BA, MA Edinburgh (*German*)
Mrs A Stone, BA Angers, HDipEd Dublin, CELTA (*Head
  of EAL*)
Mr J Tizzard, BMus DipEd Cardiff (*Head of Music*)
Mrs C Wightman, BA Wolverhampton (*Art*)
Revd F Wimsett, BA Wales, Dip Th Dunelm (*School
  Chaplain & RE*)

Tettenhall College

**Wood Road, Tettenhall, Wolverhampton, West
Midlands WV6 8QX**

Tel: 01902 751119
Fax: 01902 793000
email: head@tettcoll.co.uk
website: www.tettenhallcollege.co.uk
Twitter: @TettColl
Facebook: @TettColl

Motto: '*Timor Domini Initium Sapientiae*'

Tettenhall College offers a remarkable opportunity for
your child's education in the UK; set in a stunning location
with outstanding facilities our boarders live as part of a true
family community where your child will be happy, safe and
cared for. This really is "home from home" and family is at
the heart of all we do.

We place emphasis on developing individual strengths in
pupils of all abilities and our caring staff create a nurturing
environment, with small class sizes and excellent pastoral
care. Boarders are a diverse mix of British and international
pupils and all enjoy a close relationship with the staff that
live on site to look after them.

Outside the classroom, there are many opportunities for
extracurricular activities such as music, drama, sport and
charity work. Boarders benefit from weekend activities and
cultural visits (there are no exeat weekends) which makes
leisure time enjoyable and enriching and staff are always
there to share our pupils' successes and help them with any
problems.

Tettenhall is a thriving school where pupils in all years
exceed expectations whether that be their reading levels in
Preparatory School, GCSE examinations or A Levels in
Sixth Form. Leavers' destinations include some of the most
prestigious names in the educational world – Oxford, Cambridge and RADA to name a few. Alongside academic
achievement pupils are involved in a full programme of
exciting extracurricular activities and opportunities which
we believe develops the whole individual.

Situation and Buildings. Set in over 30 acres of beautiful woodland grounds, with outstanding sporting facilities,
Tettenhall College is a blend of historic buildings and modern amenities where pupils thrive within a caring family
atmosphere. Located in the picturesque village of Tettenhall,
yet only 40 minutes from Birmingham International Airport,
the School is one of the leading independent day and boarding schools in the region catering for girls and boys from 2
to 18 years.

Amenities include a brand new Sixth Form and Study
Centre, an indoor heated Swimming Pool, Sports Hall,
Squash Courts, Sports Pavilion and floodlit artificial courts
for football, netball, tennis and hockey. There are two
cricket squares and playing fields for rugby, football and
athletics.

Religion. Services in the College Chapel are interdenominational.

Entry. The school accepts girls and boys. Entry to the
Senior School (age 11–18) is normally by way of assessment in Mathematics, English and Non Verbal Reasoning.
By arrangement with the Headmaster, pupils may be interviewed and tested according to their individual needs.

Organisation. Senior School (Years 7 to 11 and the Sixth
Form) and the Preparatory School (Reception to Year 6) are
divided into four Houses which compete in activities, work
and games. The Nursery comprises Day Nursery and Pre-
School from the age of 2 to 4.

Senior School & Sixth Form Curriculum. Years 7 to 9
in Senior School are designed to give our pupils a sound
basis for studies at GCSE and beyond.

As well as a strong emphasis on the core subjects of
English, Mathematics and Science we consider languages to
be important, and so offer French and Spanish. Creativity
abounds in our Art, Music and Drama programmes, and History and Geography lessons teach pupils about our world,
both past and present.

Computing offers exciting possibilities to understand and
control new technologies. Physical Education and Games
encourage health and fitness, as well as providing opportunities to acquire and develop skills and attitudes to individual endeavour and teamwork. Add to the mix the moral and
ethical dimensions discussed in PSHE and Religious Education and you have an academic programme that is broad and
balanced, enjoyable and intellectually demanding.

In Year 9, Business and Electronics are introduced to
ensure that pupils experience all of our GCSE subjects

before choosing which subjects they wish to study further. EAL is offered as a specialist subject throughout Senior School.

The A Level years are academically challenging and entry into the Sixth Form (Years 12–13) is dependent on appropriate success levels at GCSE: the minimum entry requirement into the Sixth Form at Tettenhall College is six GCSEs at grade B or above. Our A Level curriculum offers a wide range of subjects, with small class sizes ensuring the best possible results.

For further information on the curriculum subjects offered in the Senior School and Sixth Form, please visit our website.

Careers. Extensive advice is given by the Head of Careers and every Sixth Former is assigned a Personal Tutor to guide and support them over the two years. This is enhanced by many visits and seminars throughout the year from external organisations such as universities and local companies. In addition the School is supported by Old Tettenhallians who will come in to host career talks and seminars.

Societies and Activities. All pupils are encouraged to become fully involved in the life of the community and to play a part in the social and cultural organisations.

Pupils take part in The Duke of Edinburgh's Award scheme, working for Bronze, Silver and Gold Awards. In addition to the sporting opportunities, school plays and musicals are produced each year; there is a house festival of Performing Arts and the Music Department has a deservedly strong reputation for its quality of performance and opportunities. All senior pupils take part in the extended day programme where activities range from climbing and mountain biking to the Extended Project Qualification for our older pupils

Preparatory School. The Preparatory School is housed separately in a purpose-designed building opened in 2002. It shares a number of the facilities with Senior School and Senior School Staff help with games and specialist teaching.

The curriculum goes far beyond the confines of the national curriculum. Younger pupils are taught by a form teacher with an emphasis on the acquisition of key skills in Literacy and Numeracy. As children move through the years they are introduced to teaching from subject specialists.

Athletics, Cricket, Netball, Hockey, Rounders, Rugby, Soccer, Swimming and Tennis are the main sports and all pupils have PE and two afternoons of games each week. Extracurricular activities change regularly but include clubs in all the previously mentioned sports.

Fees per term (2018–2019). Senior School: Full Boarders: £9,790 (Years 7–9), £10,533 (Years 10–13); Weekly Boarders: £8,714 (Years 7–9), £9,358 (Years 10–13); Day Pupils: £4,627 (Years 7–13). Preparatory School: Day Pupils £2,431–£3,477.

Scholarships and Bursaries. Senior School Academic Scholarships may be offered to outstanding boys and girls. Scholarships are also awarded for Music, Art, Drama, Performing Arts and Sport.

Means-tested Bursaries are available. There is a reduction in fees for the children of the Clergy and members of HM Forces as well as children of former pupils.

The Old Tettenhallians' Club. Membership is automatic on reaching 18 years of age.

Charitable status. Tettenhall College Incorporated is a Registered Charity, number 528617. It exists to provide a quality education for boys and girls.

Chairman of Governors: Mr Jeremy F Woolridge, CBE, DL, BSc Hons

Senior Leadership Team:

Headmaster: D C Williams, BA Hons, MSc

Bursar: C Way, BSc Hons
Deputy Head (Academic): Mrs R Samra-Bagry, BSc Hons, PGCE
Deputy Head (Pastoral): J Shipway, BSc, MA Hons
Head of Preparatory School: S Wrafter, BA Hons
Assistant Head Preparatory School, Years 3 to 6: Ms M Lofting, BA Hons, MA
Assistant Head Preparatory School, EYFS to Year 2: Mrs D Kane, BA Hons, PGCE

Thetford Grammar School

Bridge Street, Thetford, Norfolk IP24 3AF

Tel: 01842 752840
email: scsec@thetgram.norfolk.sch.uk
website: www.thetfordgrammar.co.uk
Twitter: @ThetGram
Facebook: @thetfordgrammarschool

Thetford Grammar School is a co-educational independent day school that teaches pupils aged 3–18. We are one of the oldest schools in the country and have been educating young people since the 7th century. Our pupils benefit from an academically robust, yet rounded education that includes a range of extracurricular activities and a strong pastoral system. We understand that children learn best when they are relaxed and at ease and our school is very much focused on providing an environment that encourages this. Children flourish at Thetford Grammar School because they feel safe and supported.

Buildings and Situation. Situated close to the centre of Thetford, the school occupies a well-established site graced by several buildings of architectural interest and the ruins of a medieval priory. There are extensive playing fields with a refurbished pavilion within walking distance of the main buildings, as well as an award-winning Sixth Form Centre built around the original Cloisters.

Organisation. Prep Department pupils (age 3–11) are taught in their own premises with independent facilities. Older Prep pupils have contact with specialist teachers in several subject areas and benefit from similar integration into many other aspects of school life. Main School education from 11 follows a two-form entry pattern in core subjects to GCSE. Sixth Form students play a full part in the life of the school.

Curriculum. Prep Department teaching follows National Curriculum lines with strong emphasis on the English/Mathematics core and the range of specialist subjects in support. Music and Drama are important, while a full programme of PE and Games allows for the development of team sports and individual fitness.

Main School education through to GCSE is based on a common core of English, English Literature, Mathematics, a Modern Language (French or German) and the Sciences. Options allow students to develop skills and interests in History, Geography, RS, Business Studies, Languages, the Expressive Arts, Physical Education and Technology. IT is strongly represented across the curriculum. AS and A2 courses are offered in all these subjects. Mathematics and Science lead a strong pattern of results at this level and Sixth Form students proceed to university degree courses.

Sport and Extracurricular Activities. The life of the school extends widely from the classroom into sport, community service, dramatic and musical presentation.

Winter sports are Rugby, Football, Hockey, Netball and Cross-Country with Cricket, Tennis, Rounders and Athletics in the Summer. Popular indoor sports such as Basketball, Aerobics, Badminton, Volleyball and Gymnastics are also followed. Sixth Form students are able to enrol in the local gym which is situated opposite the school.

A majority of pupils take part in training for The Duke of Edinburgh's Award scheme. A lively concert programme supports individual instrumental tuition and choral rehearsal while opportunities for theatre are provided termly by House and School productions.

There is a varied programme of curricular and extracurricular clubs and trips including expeditions and foreign visits.

Admission. Admission into the Prep Department follows a day in school with the appropriate year group during which an assessment is made. Admission into Main School is by formal examination with interview and school report. Sixth Form entrance is on the basis of interview and school report, with subsequent performance at GCSE taken into consideration. The main Entrance Examination is held in January but supplementary testing continues throughout the year. Full details from the Admissions Officer, admissions@thetgram.norfolk.sch.uk

Fees per term (2018–2019). Prep Department: Reception–Year 2 £2,750, Years 3–6 £3,908; Main School £4,555, including books and tuition but excluding uniform, lunches, transport, examination entry fees and some specialised teaching such as instrumental music lessons. Nursery funding of 15 per week is available and there are fee awards for Service families across the school.

Scholarships and Bursaries. Bursaries can be available from Year 3 upwards. Scholarships of an honorary nature may be awarded to the top performers in the entrance examinations. Music scholarships are available on entry in Year 7 or 9 which will provide free instrumental or voice tuition. Scholarships, Academic, Art, Drama, Music and Sport are also available into the Sixth Form, Year 7, Year 9 and Year 3 for both internal and external candidates. These can provide a reduction in fees for two years and are awarded as the result of a scholarship paper sat in December or in recognition of outstanding GCSE performance in the summer. Details of all awards may be obtained from the Head.

Head: **Mr Michael Brewer**, BA, PGCE

Head of Sixth Form: Ms L Pearson, BA Oxford Brookes, Cert Ed

Head of Preparatory Department: Mrs N Peace, BA Bishop Grosseteste

Academic Staff:
Mrs A Alecock, BA Manchester
Miss E Bailey, MEd Cambridge, PGCE
Mrs T Beukes, BSc Stellenbosch SA
Mrs S Cornell (*Head of Drama*)
S Braden, BSc RMCS Shrivenham
Mrs J Bull, BA Leicester, PGCE
Mrs H Butler-Hand, BA, MEd Cantab
Mrs S Collins
Mrs R Dimminger, Dip Ed Bulawayo
Miss D Dunsmore, BSc Cambridge, PGCE
M Foreman, BEd Nottingham
Mrs J Foreman, BA Warwick
M Glassbrook, BSc Northumbria, PGCE
Mrs T E Granger, BSc Wolverhampton, PGCE
Miss C Griffiths, BA LCC, PGCE
M Hill, BA Bedfordshire
Mrs H Pringle, BA Teesside Polytechnic
Mrs C Salt, BEd Exeter
Miss A Sherring, BA Camberwell School of Art

J Snipe, BSc Bristol, PGCE
Miss F Travers, BA Nottingham Trent
Mrs R Vincini-Smith, BA Brighton, PGCE
A Ward, BSc London, PGCE
Mrs P Weyers, MMus Wales, PGCE
Miss M Warton, BA Bristol, PGCE
Mrs L Wingham, BA London, PGCE

LAMDA:
Ms G Irving, MA Lancaster, PGCE

Teaching Assistants:
Ms A Graca
Mrs K Hill
Miss Cecily White
Miss Emily Bell

Learning Support:
Mrs K Jones, BSc QTS, Dip SpLD, AMBDA, SpLD APC Patoss
Mrs P Ballard, BEd Southampton
Mrs V S Webber, BA Open University

Visiting Music Staff:
Mrs N Absolum (*Piano*)
Mrs S Brotherhood (*Woodwind*)
M B Clarke, BA Sussex, MA Illinois (*Clarinet, Saxophone*)
Ms F Levy, LLCM TD, ALCM (*Violin*)
A H Salazar, GSMD, PGC, PG Adv Dip TCM (*Voice*)
J Rowland (*Drum Kit and Jazz Piano*)

Administrative Staff:
Mrs C Huggins (*Accounts Secretary*)
Mr J Law (*Examinations Officer*)
Mrs C Sadler (*HR and Admin Assistant*)
Mrs C Reynolds (*Senior School Secretary*)
Miss H Higgins (*Receptionist*)
Mrs J Settle (*Librarian*)
Mr A Koch (*Apprentice Accounts Assistant*)
Mr A Small (*Apprentice Business Administrator*)

Technicians:
Mrs S Grimwood (*Art*)
Mrs A Kingsnorth, BSc London, PGCE (*Science*)
D Simpleman, BSc Southampton (*ICT*)

Tring Park School for the Performing Arts

Tring Park, Tring, Hertfordshire HP23 5LX
Tel: 01442 824255
Fax: 01442 891069
email: info@tringpark.com
website: www.tringpark.com

Tring Park School for the Performing Arts is a co-educational boarding and day school for pupils aged 8–19.

Number in School. Boarders: Boys 108, Girls 261. Day: 142.

Tring Park School for the Performing Arts stands at the forefront of specialist performing arts education in the UK. At Tring Park talented young people from 8–19 specialise in Dance, Acting, Musical Theatre or Commercial Music and receive a full academic education to GCSE and A Level where Tring Park offers up to 24 A Level subjects. Entrance is via audition and scholarships are available for Dance via the Government's Music and Dance Scheme. School scholarships and bursaries are available for Drama and Musical Theatre.

Pupils perform in Tring Park's Markova Theatre as well as in London, throughout the UK and Europe. Performances have included *To Dance with the Gods, Jesus Christ Super-star*, *Guys and Dolls* and *Cabaret*. Tring Park provides ballet dancers for the Christmas productions of *Nutcracker* and *Le Corsaire* with English National Ballet and for ENB's production of *Swan Lake* at the Royal Albert Hall. Several pupils have played the part of Billy in *Billy Elliot* in London and on tour, others have joined the cast of *Matilda* and performed the role of Gavroche in the London production of *Les Misérables*.

Alumni success.

Daisy Ridley – Rey in *Stars Wars The Force Awakens*

Lily James – *Cinderella, War and Peace* and *Romeo and Juliet*

Lily James and **Jessica Brown Findlay** – *Downton Abbey*

Bryony Hannah and **Helen George** – BBC's *Call the Midwife*

Drew McOnie – awarded an Olivier Award for Best Theatre Choreography

Caroline Finn – Artistic Director of National Dance Company Wales

Max Westwell – Principal with English National Ballet

Tyrone Singleton – Principal with Birmingham Royal Ballet

Tring Park also celebrates considerable academic success with students entering Russell Group universities and another who was awarded a Scholarship to study English at Churchill College, Cambridge.

Fees per term (2018–2019). Prep School: Boarders £8,425, Day £4,955. Age 11–16: Boarders £11,135, Day £7,125. Sixth Form Entry: Boarders £11,920, Day £7,885. Sibling discount 10% of termly fees. Forces discount available on request.

Aided places for Dance are available under the Government's Music and Dance Scheme. School scholarships are available for Drama and Musical Theatre.

Charitable status. The AES Tring Park School Trust is a Registered Charity, number 1040330. It exists to provide vocational and academic education.

Board of Governors:
Chairman: Mr Michael Geddes
Mrs Mary Bonar
Ms Alice Cave
Mr John Clark
Mr Michael Harper
Mr Mark Hewitt
Mrs Angela Odell
Mr Eric Pillinger
Mrs June Taylor
Mr Daniel Zammit

Principal: **Stefan Anderson**, MA Cantab, ARCM, ARCT

Deputy Principal: Anselm Barker, MSt Oxon, BA Harvard

Director of Vocational Studies: Elizabeth Odell, BA, AVCM, AISTD, FDI, QTS

Director of Dance: Rachel Rist, MA, FRSA
Deputy Directors of Dance: Antony Dowson & Lorraine Jones

Director of Drama: Edward Applewhite, BA Hons
Deputy Director of Drama: Heather Loomes, BA Hons
Deputy Director of Drama: Dominic Yeates

Director of Music: Elizabeth Norriss, BMus Hons, PGCE, ALCM
Head of Commercial Music Course: Harmesh Gharu, MA, BMus Hons, PGCE

Director of Musical Theatre Course: Donna Hayward, FISTD

Deputy Director of Musical Theatre Course: Simon Sharp, BA Hons, PGCE

Director of Performance Foundation and Theatre Arts Course: Louisa Shaw

Director of Academic Studies: Brian Liddle, MEd, PGCE, BSc Hons
Deputy Director of Academic Studies: Anu Mahesh, PhD, MSc Hons, PGCE
Head of Sixth Form: Edward Hawkins

Marketing Director: Miriam Juviler, ARAM, LRAM
Fundraising Director: Dawn Adam

Head of Learning Support: Suzanne Kennedy, BA Hons, PGCE, MA, NPQH, SpLD, SENCOs

Trinity School

Buckeridge Road, Teignmouth, Devon TQ14 8LY

Tel:	01626 774138
Fax:	01626 774138
email:	registrar@trinityschool.co.uk
website:	www.trinityschool.co.uk

Foundation and Ethos. With a joint Anglican/Catholic foundation, Trinity School's Christian ethos and family atmosphere are complemented by a commitment to excellence in both academic and personal development. With recent inspections by both ISI and Ofsted rating the School as 'Outstanding' in many areas, the School has successfully demonstrated a determination to deliver the best education possible for the pupils in its care.

Pupil Body. Over 300 pupils from age 3 to 19 years, with over 50 boarders.

Location and Facilities. The School offers excellent facilities in a very attractive environment with panoramic views of Lyme Bay. Facilities include a purpose-built Design Technology building, IT laboratories, a Music Centre, a Science block, a Food Technology Centre, en-suite boarding accommodation for Sixth Formers, indoor and outdoor tennis facilities, a 25m heated swimming pool, and an Art Centre. The School is very well connected by road and rail, with the nearest railway station being under a mile away and on the London main line.

Academic Record. At the upper end of our ability profile, we have a proven track record of sending pupils to Russell Group universities. We have gained 6 Good School Guide Awards for performance in English, Business Studies and Science. Prep pupils' performance considerably exceeds expectations at KS1 and KS2. 95% of Sixth Form students in recent years have progressed to university or apprenticeships. A mix of BTEC and A Level subjects are taught (inc all facilitating subjects) in the Sixth Form.

Pastoral Care and Welfare. The quality of the School's pastoral care is an established and considerable strength as proven by the recent inspections. Our Anglican/Catholic ethos permeates all that we do. We believe that for care to be effective, it is essential that school and family work closely together – the relationship needs to be dynamic, honest and built on mutual trust and understanding. This approach, and the fact that Trinity provides education for girls and boys of all ages, helps to generate the School's warm, 'family' atmosphere.

Personal Development. Extensive sporting, cultural, charitable and leadership opportunities are available at all ages: rich musical life with yearly musical productions involving Prep and Senior department pupils; South West Junior Choir of the Year 2011 and 2012; one of the most active CCF sections in the country; Ten Tors and DofE regulars; Lawn Tennis Association centre of excellence with one national LTA champion and regular Independent Schools Association (ISA) champions; in swimming, athletics, cross country, tennis – Prep and Senior.

Admissions. Trinity is a non-selective school, so there are no entrance examinations required for entry. Assessments are carried out for new students in order to gauge ability and tailor education. Scholarships are by open competition at 11+, 13+ and 16+, for academic, music, art, drama, sport and all-rounder Notre Dame Awards (selection in January). Bursaries and HM Forces Bursaries.

Fees per term (2018–2019). Tuition (day pupils) £2,585–£4,100; Boarding: £6,315–£8,530 (weekly), £6,850–£9,259 (full), £6,990–£9,925 (international students).

Charitable status. Trinity School is a Registered Charity, number 276960.

Patrons:
Rt Revd Mark O'Toole, Bishop of Plymouth
Rt Revd Robert Atwell, Bishop of Exeter

Chairman of Governors: Mr Simon Brookman

Headmaster: Mr Lawrence Coen, BSc Hons Aberystwyth

Deputy Head: Mrs Wendy Martin, BSc Hons Kent, PGCE Kent

Senior Department:
Mr Mark Acher, BSc Hons Sheffield, PGCE Nottingham (*Senior Tutor, Geography*)
Miss Kate Ashfield (*Assistant Head of MD Boarding House*)
Mrs Lucy Atkins, BA Hons Exeter, PGCE Exeter (*Subject Leader English*)
Mrs Angela Bingham, BA Hons Sheffield, PGCE Nottingham (*Learning Support and Mathematics*)
Mrs Claire Bird, BA Hons Lancaster, MA Open, PGCE Exeter, TEFL Cert (*Director of Learning Humanities Faculty*)
Mrs Anna Brown, BA Hons Glamorgan, PGCE Bristol (*Deputy Head of 6th Form, Subject Leader Business Studies*)
Mrs Julia Bryant, MEd Open, BSc Hons London, PGCE Exon, ADSNEd, PGDPD (*Director of Studies, Subject Leader Psychology*)
Mr Patrick Cairns, BEd Liverpool (*Subject Leader Art*)
Mrs Pauline Cartwright (*Teaching Assistant*)
Mrs Sheridan Couch, BAEd Hons Exeter (*Subject Leader Physical Education*)
Mr Tim Crompton, Dip ABSM, GBSM UCE, PGCE UCE (*Subject Leader Music*)
Mrs Kathryn Crook, Dip TEFL, LTCL Trinity (*Subject Leader EAL*)
Mrs Geraldine Davis, BA Hons UWE Bristol, PGCE UWE (*Head of Key Stage 3, Maths, Psychology*)
Mr Edward Donaldson, BTech Ireland, PGCE Truro (*Director of Learning Technology Faculty*)
Mr Joost van Es, BSc Hons Durham, PGCE Brighton (*Physics, Boarding Tutor*)
Ms Sarah Evans, MA History Oxon, PGCE Oxon (*Subject Leader History*)
Mrs Emma Firth, BA Hons Nottingham Trent, PGCE Roehampton (*Art, Textiles and Food Technology*)
Mrs Jana Fischer, BEd Leipzig, Germany (*Head of Chapel Boarding, German*)
Mr Darrel Jones, BSc Hons Liverpool, PGCE Liverpool (*Director of Learning Science Faculty*)
Mr Robert Larkman, BEd Hons Plymouth (*Head of Key Stage 4, Physical Education*)
Mr Guy Martin, BSc Hons London, PGCE London (*Head of Sixth Form, Geography*)

Mrs Shani Mason, Diploma Level 3 Support Teaching & Certificate Counselling Skills (*Teaching Assistant*)
Mrs Jane McConkey (*Teaching Assistant*)
Mrs Emily McEwen, BA Hons Oxford Brookes, PGCE Roehampton (*English*)
Mrs Tessa Nicol (*Teaching Assistant*)
Mrs Claire Palmer, BA Hons Swansea, PGCE Nottingham (*Subject Leader Spanish, EAL*)
Lt Cdr Geraldine Poulet-Bowden RNR, BSc Hons Imperial College, ARCS, PGCE Exeter, CPhys, MIoP (*Head of CCF*)
Lt Gerard Poulet RNR, Lic ès Lettres Lille, MA Exeter (*CCF*)
Mrs Heather Rabone, BSc Hons, PGCE SEN (*Subject Leader Learning Support – SENCO*)
Mrs Nicola Smith, BA Hons Glamorgan, PGCE Leeds (*Subject Leader Performing Arts*)
Mrs Giulietta Swift, BA Hons Bristol, PGCE Bath (*Subject Leader ICT*)
Mrs Fiona Tamlyn, BEd Hons Cambridge (*Learning Support – Assessment SENCO*)
Mr Stephen Tew, BEd Hons Westminster College Oxford (*Subject Leader ICT*) [maternity cover]
Dr Bronwen Trimming, BSc Hons Swansea, PhD Manchester, PGCE Exeter (*Chemistry and Religious Studies*)
Mrs Chryssa Turner, BEd Hons Exeter (*Examinations Officer, Boarding Tutor*)
Mr Ben Whittles, BSc Hons East Anglia, PGCE Canterbury Christ Church (*Subject Leader Geography, Boarding Tutor*)

Preparatory Department:
Mr Mike Burdett, BEd Oxford (*Acting Head of Preparatory Department*)
Mr Sean Lovett, BEd Primary Physical Education Plymouth (*Acting Deputy Head of Prep Dept, EYFS/KS1 Coordinator, Physical Education, Head of MD Boarding House*)
Mrs Karen Brazier (*Teaching Assistant*)
Mrs Hannah Broom, BA Early Years Open (*Teaching Assistant Reception*)
Miss Laura Brown, BA Hons Exeter Education Studies, BSL Level 3, Cued Speech Level 2, MSI Intervenor (*Deaf Inclusion Worker*)
Mrs Hannah Cassidy, BA History of Art and Archaeology London, PGCE Exeter (*Art Teacher*)
Mrs Joanna Davey, NVQ Level 3 (*Prep Lodge Early Years Key Worker*)
Mrs Julie Drewett, Cambridge Open College Level 3 (*Teaching Assistant*)
Mr Simon Fisher, BSc Hons Wales, PGCE Wales (*Sports Coordinator, Year 5 Teacher*)
Mrs Lyndsey Ganner, BA Hons Primary Advanced Early Years – QTS, NVQ Early Years Care and Education (*Year 1 Teacher, English, Thrive*)
Miss Emma Hawley (*Teaching Assistant*)
Mrs Zoe Hughes, BA Hons Classics Reading, PGCE Plymouth (*Year 3 Teacher*)
Ms Tracey Loveridge, NNEB, FNATD Mod & Tap, LNATD Ballet (*Teaching Assistant, ESB Tutor, Drama*)
Mrs Laura Lovett (*Teaching Assistant*)
Mrs Kelly May, BA Hons Exeter, PGCE Exeter (*Reception Teacher, French & Spanish Coordinator*)
Mrs Natalie Miller, BEd Early Years Brighton (*Year 1 & 2 Teacher*)
Miss Jennie Moss, BA Hons Exeter, PGCE Plymouth (*Director of Learning Int and Performance Studies, Year 6 Teacher, KS2/3 Girls' Sport*)
Mrs Dee Owens, NNEB (*Prep Lodge Early Years Key Worker*)

Miss Nicola Piggott, BTEC, CACHE (*Prep Lodge Early Years Key Worker, Asst Head of Chapel Boarding House*)

Mrs Sarah Robbins, BEd Exeter (*Year 4 Teacher*)

Mrs Kate Sutton, BA Hons London PGCE Kingston (*Year 5 & 6 Girls' Teacher, English, Forest School*)

Ms Karen Weir, BA Hons Open, Cued Speech Level 1 & 2, CACDP, British Sign Language NVQ6 (*Deaf Inclusion Worker*)

Administration:
Bursar: Mr Shaun Dyer, BA Portsmouth
Registrar: Mrs Maria Kerr
Headmaster's PA: Mrs Lindsey Lloyd-Jacob
Academic Administrator: Mr John Turner
Head of Prep's PA: Mrs Lisa Paget

Welbeck – The Defence Sixth Form College

Forest Road, Woodhouse, Loughborough, Leicestershire LE12 8WD

Tel: 01509 891700
Fax: 01509 891701
email: helpdesk@dsfc.ac.uk
website: www.dsfc.ac.uk

Welbeck Defence Sixth Form College aims to provide an environment in which young people from all backgrounds can reach the very highest academic and personal standards in pursuit of a career as a Technical Officer within the Armed Services and the Civil Service. Welbeck's history began in September 1953 at Welbeck Abbey, near Worksop in Nottinghamshire, as a Sixth Form College for potential Engineering Officers for the British Army. The Defence Training Review of 2002 resulted in the decision to expand the College across all three Armed Services as well as the Defence Engineering and Science Group (DESG), and in September 2005 Welbeck – The Defence Sixth Form College opened at its new purpose-built site in Woodhouse, Loughborough. Welbeck is the first stage of the Defence Technical Officer and Engineer Entry Scheme (DTOEES) which sponsors students to study their A Levels at Welbeck and then move on to partner Universities to study Technical or Engineering degrees. Students receive an annual bursary of £4,000 whilst at University, and once they have graduated they will enter Initial Officer Training with the service that has sponsored them through the scheme or, in the case of DESG, they will enter the Graduate Training Programme.

Welbeck is a full boarding establishment offering a technically focused A Level education. There are approximately 175 places available for Year 12 students who have passed the selection for sponsorship by one of the three Armed Forces or the Defence Engineering and Science Group. The College will also accept a limited number of applications from private students.

Situation. Welbeck College is situated on a 36-acre site in the charming rural setting of Charnwood Forest in Leicestershire. Welbeck has a spacious campus with state-of-the-art facilities and amenities.

Approach and Ethos. Our aim is to provide all students with an outstanding education that will enable them to achieve A Level results that will qualify them to continue to the next stage of the DTOEES scheme – an engineering or technical degree at a top university.

Welbeck educates its students in the broadest sense of the word; it offers a programme of intellectual, personal and physical development specifically designed to meet the needs of today's modern Armed Forces. Pupils will have innumerable opportunities to develop their understanding of leadership and of success, and in doing so will leave the College better equipped for life in the Armed Forces. As you would expect, there is a strong emphasis on core military skills and values. Additionally, sport plays a prominent role for all students with College teams regularly securing regional, and occasionally national, honours. At Welbeck, such an education is founded on moral integrity, responsibility and a genuine sense of service, which together lead to inculcating the core skills of leadership which are not only strong in our community but enduring.

Our students come from all over the United Kingdom and from a variety of backgrounds. The vast majority of them have never boarded before, but find themselves surrounded by others who are in the same position. Pastoral care at Welbeck is outstanding, and through House Staff and personal Tutors all individual students are supported throughout their time at the College. Welbexians are ambitious and motivated, and thrive in an environment with other like-minded individuals who have the same drive and determination to succeed and make the most of each and every opportunity. Students leave the College resolute, skilled in communication and with their ambitions extended, having shared excellence and involvement in the many and varied experiences offered by the College.

Admission. To apply to Welbeck, and subsequently the Armed Services, candidates should be medically fit UK, Commonwealth or Irish citizens aged between 15 and 17 years and six months on 1st September in the year of entry to the College. Commonwealth citizens are required to have 5 years residency in the UK prior to application. Certain other single-service conditions may apply and will be outlined at the time of application. To join Welbeck as a DESG Civil Service student candidates must be British citizens or hold dual nationality, one of which must be British. To join the Welbeck Private Scheme (WPS), applicants must show a strong commitment to develop themselves both personally and academically at Welbeck, and are also required to meet the academic, medical and fitness criteria of the MOD Sponsored students.

Requirements for successful candidates will include an A/7 in Maths, B/6 in Physics and C/4 in English Language at GCSE or the equivalent qualifications.

All MoD candidates are required to attend a Service Selection Board prior to entrance to Welbeck. Welbeck Private Scheme (WPS) candidates undergo a similar selection process at Welbeck.

Fees. *MoD students*: Tuition is paid for by the Ministry of Defence. Parents or guardians are required to make a contribution towards the cost of their child's maintenance which covers board, lodging and the value of clothing and services provided. *Welbeck Private Scheme*: Fees per term £6,666.

Chair of Governors: Air Vice-Marshal C J Luck, MBE, MA, MPhil, RAF – Commandant Joint Services Command and Staff College and Chief Executive of the Defence Academy

Principal: Mr J P Middleton, MA Oxon

Westholme School

Meins Road, Blackburn, Lancashire BB2 6QU

Tel: 01254 506070
Fax: 01254 506080
email: secretary@westholmeschool.com
website: www.westholmeschool.com

Westholme School comprises: Nursery (Boys and Girls from the age of 3 months), Infant School (Boys and Girls aged 3–7), Junior School (Boys and Girls aged 7–11), Senior School (Boys and Girls aged 11–16) and Sixth Form (Boys and Girls aged 16–18).

There are currently 756 day pupils at Westholme: 528 in the Senior School and Sixth Form, 196 in the Infant and Junior Departments, and 32 boys and girls in the Nursery.

Westholme School is administered by a Board of Governors which includes three nominated Governors representing current parents. Although the school is non-denominational, its Christian foundation is regarded as important, the emphasis being placed on the moral aspect of Christian teaching.

Senior School, Sixth Form. The aim of the Senior School is to provide an atmosphere in which each pupil can develop his or her abilities to the full and can excel in some field of activity. There is constant effort to widen interests and to instil a strong sense of individual responsibility. Most students continue to the Sixth Form and then move on to Higher Education. Most pursue degree courses, a significant number at Oxford and Cambridge.

The Senior School offers an academic curriculum in English Language and Literature, Mathematics, Biology, Chemistry, Physics, Geography, History, French, German, Mandarin, Spanish, Design Technology, Food Preparation, ICT, Textiles, Art, Photography, DT, Physical Education, Business Studies, Classical Civilisation, Drama, Latin, Music, Ethics, Philosophy & Religion (EPR), Psychology, Sociology and Theatre Studies. Most of these subjects can be taken for the GCSE examination and at A Level.

Set in the countryside to the west of Blackburn, Westholme School offers excellent facilities. The premises have been regularly upgraded to give purpose-built accommodation for specialist subjects such as Art, Design and Information Technology and Music; seven modern laboratories support the three separate sciences. Sporting facilities include a sports hall, indoor swimming pool, brand new all-weather pitch and tennis courts and a large playing field with running circuit. The full-sized professional theatre opened in 1997, seats 500 and offers students outstanding production resources. The Learning Resource Centre has open-access multimedia giving students full research facilities. The Sixth Form wing opened in September 2003 complete with lecture theatre, common room, café and classrooms.

The Performing Arts are a special feature of the school. There are several school choirs and girls have the opportunity to learn a string, brass or wind instrument and to play in the school orchestras or wind ensembles. Co-curricular drama includes the full-scale spectacular musical, in the round productions, club and house competitions, while make-up and costume design are popular options at GCSE.

School societies and house teams meet on most days during midday break and girls are encouraged to participate in a variety of activities and in their house competitions. These provide younger girls with opportunities beyond the curriculum and older students with the chance to assume a leadership role.

Westholme Nursery & Infant School, Westholme Junior School. There is close cooperation between these schools and with the Senior School. A family atmosphere allows children to learn in a supportive and happy environment. Firm academic foundations are laid with the emphasis upon the basic skills of literacy and numeracy. Excellent facilities afford ample teaching space and resource areas; the Junior School has three halls, music rooms and specialist provision for Information Technology. Co-curricular activities include public speaking, orchestra, choir, sports, societies and school visits. Music and sport are taught by specialists and all Departments use the swimming pool, sports hall, athletics track and outdoor pitches at the Senior School.

Admission. Pupils usually enter the school in September. Entry to the Junior and Senior Schools is by examination, and to the Infant School by interview. The normal ages of entry are at 2, 3, 4, 7, 11 and 16.

In view of the demand for places, parents are advised to make an early application.

The Principal is happy for prospective parents to visit the school during normal working hours; appointments may be arranged through the Registrar, from whom application forms are available. Annual Open Days are held in October and other open days are held in the spring and summer terms.

Private coaches run from Accrington, Blackburn, Bolton, Burnley, Colne, Chorley, Clitheroe, Darwen, Leyland, Preston, Standish, Ribble Valley, South Ribble, the Rossendale Valley and Wigan.

Fees per term (from January 2019). Senior School £3,760; Junior School £2,915; Infant School: £2,710; Pre-School £2,890; Nursery (age 2–3 years) £200 pw; Nursery (age 3 months–2 years) £220 pw.

Scholarships are available for entry into Year 3, Year 7 and Year 12 for students who show good academic ability and various Bursaries are available (means-tested).

Charitable status. Westholme School is a Registered Charity, number 526615. It exists for the education of children between the ages of 3 months and 18.

Governing Body:
Chairman: Mr B C Marsden, FCA
Vice Chairman: Mr P Forrest, MRICS, FCIOB
Mr M Abraham, BEd
Mr S Anderson, BA Hons, FCA
Mr J Backhouse, LLB Hons
Mr D J Berry, BA, FCMA, MIBM
Dr R Dobrashian, MBChB, FRCR
Mrs J Meadows, BSc Hons, ACA
Mr O McCann, BA Hons
Mrs L Robinson, BA Hons, MA
His Honour E Slinger, BA
Mr J R Yates, BSc

Clerk to the Governors: Mr J Backhouse, LLB Hons

Principal: **Mrs Lynne Horner**, BA Hons, PGCE

Commercial Director: Mrs Vivienne Davenport, MA Oxon

Deputy Headteacher, Curriculum: Miss Francine Smith, BSc Hons Brunel, PGCE, FRSA

Deputy Headteacher, Pastoral: Mrs Jude Gough, BA Hons Wolverhampton, PGCE, MISTC [Maternity Leave]

Assistant Head, Pastoral: Mrs C Hornby, BSc Hons Staffordshire [Maternity Cover]

Assistant Head: Mrs Z Kenealy, MEng, BA Hons Cambridge

Headteacher, Infant and Junior School: Mrs R E Barnett, BA Hons, MA, PGCE

Windermere School

Patterdale Road, Windermere, The Lake District, Cumbria LA23 1NW

Tel: +44 (0)15394 46164
Fax: +44 (0)15394 88414
email: admissions@windermereschool.co.uk

website: www.windermereschool.co.uk
Twitter: @windermeresc
Facebook: @Windermereschool

A small and friendly school, with an emphasis on challenge through adventure and academic excellence.

Windermere School, is an independent co-educational boarding and day school, founded in 1863, and is an Educational Trust administered by a Board of Governors. It is divided into the Senior School (ages 11 to 18) and the Infant and Junior School (ages 3 to 11).

Located in the heart of the English Lake District National Park, our school offers a rich environment in which pupils can achieve academic and personal excellence. It has the beauty and tranquillity of a wooded campus overlooking the mountains and lake, along with a lakefront boathouse, beach and watersports centre. The amenities of the vibrant resort of Windermere are within minutes of the school. Even with its breathtaking location, the school has easy access to the motorway network, main rail lines and major airports.

Adventure activities and watersports opportunities are provided for each pupil with nationally recognised certificates from organisations including the Royal Yachting Association and British Canoeing. This combined with the rich literary and cultural heritage of the Lake District provides a unique setting for academic study and self-development; thus the motto Vincit qui se Vincit, *One conquers, who conquers oneself.*

The Senior School and Sixth Form is located on a mountainside campus overlooking the lake, with the Infant and Junior School campus and watersports centre nearby. The school owns over fifty acres in the Lake District National Park. There is a modern Sixth Form Boarding House with single and double study-bedrooms, plus a lodge-style Boys Boarding House with magnificent views south and west over Lake Windermere and the mountains, and a traditional girls dormitory in Browhead, formerly a private estate.

Numbers. There are approximately 400 pupils in total. The Senior School has approximately 275 pupils, of whom 60% are boarders. The size of the community has the advantage of providing a friendly atmosphere of understanding and fosters good staff-pupil relationships. Many members of the teaching staff hold additional qualifications in outdoor adventure. There is a 4-house system for competitions and games.

Curriculum. The curriculum offered at Windermere School reflects the belief that students should be exposed to as many opportunities as possible and leave the school as well-rounded individuals. It is tailored to the needs of each child, with small class sizes. Each pupil is provided with a personal tutor that stays with them throughout their years at the school, to oversee work on a daily basis and act as an advocate. One year and two year GCSEs and IGCSEs are taken in Years 10 and 11. Sixth Form students undertake the internationally recognised International Baccalaureate Diploma or International Baccalaureate Careers Programme.

There are qualified staff and programmes in place for Special Educational Needs, English as an Additional Language, and Gifted and Talented pupils.

Music, Art, and Drama play an important part in the life of the school. There are two choirs, and individual instruction leading to chamber groups and orchestra. Students are prepared for the written and practical music exams of the Associated Board of the Royal Schools of Music. The school participates in regional Music Festivals. The Central School of Speech and Drama and LAMDA's examinations are also taken in Speech and Drama. Art, Pottery and Design Technology provide considerable scope and opportunity. The Art Studios contain facilities for History of Art and an

Art History Library. Drama classes are included in the curriculum, and there are several productions staged each year.

Extra-Curricular Activities. Windermere School's watersports centre, Hodge Howe with over 160 metres of lakefront on the shores of Windermere, hosts a wide range of activities during the school's timetabled curriculum, and as part of the extra-curricular activity programme. The centre has accreditation from British Canoeing and the Adventure Activities Licensing Authority, as well as being a Royal Yachting Association Teaching Centre. In 2018, the School was announced as a British Youth Sailing Recognised Club by the Royal Yachting Association for its race training. Windermere was the first school in the UK to be awarded this status.

There are traditional competitive sports teams in hockey, netball, tennis, athletics and more. Many students play for regional and national teams, as well as for the school.

Service. Windermere School has a strong tradition of Community Service where pupils are active participants. The most high profile is the Thussanang Project with many staff and pupils travelling to South Africa each year to contribute to projects. The school supports many other charities including local Hospices, Young Carers, NSPCC, Save The Children Fund and works with regional Rotary Clubs.

Religion. The school is Christian in outlook and welcomes other denominations.

Medical. The health of the pupils is under the care of appointed school Doctors and two School nurses. There is a regular clinic, and dispensary twice daily.

Societies. More than 40 Clubs and Societies provide a variety of interests for out-of-school hours.

Uniform. Senior School – Girls wear blue kilt/trousers and striped blazer plus light blue blouses and optional navy jumper. Boys wear dark grey trousers, navy blue blazer, white shirt and school tie with optional navy jumper. Home clothes may be worn at weekends. The Sixth Form wear dark suits and they may wear home clothes in the evenings and at weekends.

Infant and Junior School – Girls wear blue kilt/trousers and striped blazer plus light blue blouses in the winter. In the summer the kilt is worn with a blue and white flowered short-sleeved blouse and blue sleeveless slipover or summer dress. Boys wear grey trousers, pale blue shirts and sweater, the school tie and blazer.

Boarding. There is a strong boarding tradition at Windermere School that benefits the whole school community. Each Boarding House has live-in staff supervised by a House Mistress or House Master. Each evening, academic staff oversee prep and are available for extra tuition and advice. There are weekend activities both on campus and with staff-led excursions throughout the Lake District and beyond. It is a safe and caring extended family environment where pupils can excel both academically and personally.

Round Square. The School is a member of the international Round Square group of schools. Exchanges and Overseas Service Projects are regularly arranged between the schools involved in Australia, Canada, Germany, India, Switzerland, South Africa and USA and Brunei.

Infant and Junior School. The nearby Infant and Junior School is in the care of a Head, and takes boarders from age 8, along with day children up to Year 6. The Infant and Junior School is fully integrated with the Senior School giving continuity of teaching programmes and use of joint facilities.

Entry. Pupils are accepted into the Senior School from Prep and Junior schools at age 11+, or by direct entry into the Sixth Form. In other circumstances students may be accepted at other times. In the Infant and Junior School, pupils are taken at various stages from Nursery onwards.

Visitors are welcome at anytime during the year, and Open Days are held once a term.

Fees per term (2018–2019). *Average* Day Fees (including lunch): Reception £2,535, Years 1–2 £3,395, Years 3–6 £5,010, Years 7–8 £5,245, Years 9–11 £5,820, Years 12–13 £5,925.

Average Weekly Boarding Fees: Years 3–6 £8,040, Years 7–8 £8,810, Years 9–11 £9,950, Years 12–13 £10,050.

Average Full Boarding Fees: Years 3–6 £8,495, Years 7–8 £9,325, Years 9–11 £10,445, Years 12–13 £10,445.

Average International Students: Years 3–6 £8,495, Years 7–8 £9,325, Years 9–11 £10,445, Years 12–13 £10,445.

Discounts are available for Forces families eligible for the MOD Continuity of Education Allowance (CEA).

Scholarships. Scholarships are available for entry in Years 7, 9 and 12. For more information please visit the school's website or contact Admissions.

Charitable status. Windermere Educational Trust Limited is a Registered Charity, number 526973, with a mission to provide education of the highest quality.

Acting Chair of Governors: Mr J Dearden

Head: **Mr Ian Lavender**, MA Oxford, BA Hons Oxford, NPQH

Deputy Head Pastoral: Miss J Parry, MPhil, BSc Hons Liverpool, PGCE Manchester

Deputy Head Academic: Mrs E Vermeulen, BA Hons Birmingham, PGCE Lancaster

Head of Elleray Campus: Mrs R Thomas, BA Hons Music Huddersfield, PGCE Newcastle

Administrative Staff:
School Business Manager: Mrs S Ross
Head's PA: Mrs J Jones
School Secretary: Mrs S Dougherty
Head of Admissions/Marketing: Mrs J Gallon

The Yehudi Menuhin School

Stoke d'Abernon, Cobham, Surrey KT11 3QQ

Tel: 01932 864739
email: admin@menuhinschool.co.uk
website: www.menuhinschool.co.uk
Twitter: @menuhinschool
Facebook: @yehudimenuhinschool

The Yehudi Menuhin School was founded in 1963 by Lord Menuhin and is situated in beautiful grounds in the Surrey countryside, close to London and within easy reach of both Gatwick and Heathrow.

The School provides specialist music tuition in stringed instruments, piano and classical guitar to 80 musically-gifted boys and girls aged between 8 and 19 and aims to enable them to pursue their love of music, develop their musical potential and achieve standards of performance at the highest level. The School also provides a broad education within a relaxed open community in which each individual can fully develop intellectual, artistic and social skills. We are proud that our pupils develop into dedicated and excellent musicians who will use their music to inspire and enrich the lives of others and into friendly, thinking individuals well equipped to contribute fully to the international community.

Music. At least half of each day is devoted to musical studies. Pupils receive a minimum of two one-hour lessons each week on their first study instrument and at least half an hour on their second study instrument. Supervised practice is incorporated into the daily programme ensuring that successful habits of work are formed. All pupils receive guidance in composition and take part in regular composers' workshops and concerts. Aural training and general musicianship studies are included in the music curriculum. To awaken feeling for good posture, training in Alexander Technique is provided. GCSE and A Level Music are compulsory core subjects for all pupils.

Regular opportunity for solo performance is of central importance to the musical activity of the School, and pupils also perform chamber music and with the String Orchestra. Concerts are given several times each week within the School and at a wide variety of venues throughout the United Kingdom and overseas. The most distinguished musicians have taught at the school, including Boulanger, Perlemuter, Rostropovich and Perlman. Lord Menuhin visited the school regularly. Selection of pupils is by stringent audition which seeks to assess musical ability and identify potential. Special arrangements are made for applicants from overseas, who account for around half of the School's pupils.

The School opened a state-of-the-art Concert Hall in 2006 seating 315 with outstanding acoustics. Concerts and outreach programmes are now presented in this new facility. New purpose-built Music Studios opened in September 2016.

Academic Studies and Sport. The curriculum is designed to be balanced and to do full justice to both the musical and the general education of each pupil. Academic studies including the understanding of art, literature and science are considered vital to the development of creative, intelligent and sensitive musicians. All classes are small with excellent opportunities for individual attention, and as a result GCSE and A Level examination grades are high. To broaden their artistic and creative talents, all pupils work in a wide variety of artistic media including painting, ceramics and textiles. Pupils from overseas with limited English receive an intensive course in the English Language from specialist teachers.

The extensive grounds allow plenty of scope for relaxation and sport, including tennis, dance, badminton, football, running, swimming and yoga. An indoor swimming pool was opened in 2010.

An International Family. The international reputation of the School brings pupils from all over the world who find a happy atmosphere in a large musical family. Pupils live in single or shared rooms and are cared for by the resident House Staff and Nurse. New en-suite single rooms for senior pupils were provided in the girls' house in September 2015; similar facilities in an extension for the boys' house opened in September 2016. Special attention is paid to diet with the emphasis on whole and fresh food.

Fees and Bursaries. All pupils fully resident in the UK are eligible for an Aided Place through the Music and Dance Scheme which is subsidised by the Department for Education (DfE). Parents pay a means-tested contribution to the school fees based on their gross income assessed on a scale issued by the DfE. Pupils from overseas pay full fees for two full calendar years until they acquire the residence qualification needed for support through the Music and Dance Scheme. The school has some bursary funds available to assist with fees for pupils until they become eligible for the Music and Dance Scheme.

Admission. Entry to the School is by rigorous music audition, and prospective pupils are auditioned at any time during the year. Candidates may audition at any age between 7 and 16.

Charitable status. The Yehudi Menuhin School is a Registered Charity, number 312010. It exists to provide musical and academic education for boys and girls.

President: Daniel Barenboim

Vice-Presidents:
Barbara R-D Fisher, OBE
Sir Alan Traill, GBE, QSO
The Hon Zamira Menuhin Benthall

Governor Emeritus:
Daniel Hodson
Anne Simor

Music Patrons:
Sir András Schiff
Steven Isserlis, CBE
Tasmin Little, OBE

Governors:
Chairman: Richard Morris
Vice-Chairman: Geoffrey Richards

Dominic Benthall	Stuart Mitchell
Lord Norman Blackwell	John Pagella
Jonathan Deakin	Alice Phillips
John Everett	Vanessa Richards
Andrew Hunter Johnston	Dr John Scadding
Anna Joseph	Veronica Wadley
Oscar Lewisohn	Jonathan Willcocks

Staff:

Head: **Mrs Kate Clanchy**, MA Cantab, MBA INSEAD, MA London

Director of Music: Oscar Colomina i Bosch, PhD RAM, MMus, BMus GSMD, BMus Valencia

Director of Studies: David Bruce, BSc, PGCE

Interim Bursar: Simon Browning, BA Hons, FCMA

Development Director: (vacancy)

Head of Pastoral Care: Joanne Field, RN, RM

Academic Staff:

Art and Craft: Patsy Belmonte, BA Hons
Biology and Science:
Karen Lyle, BSc Hons, PGCE
Jenny Dexter, BSc Hons, PGCE
English & Drama:
Alan Humm, BA Hons QTS
French & German: Didier Descamps, MA
German & Russian: Petra Young, MA MSc London
History: Sarah Howell, BA Hons, PGCE
Jeanne Rourke, BA Hons, PGCE
Junior Subjects: Tony Chipps, BA Hons, PGCE
Philippa Brown (*Teaching Assistant*)
Mathematics: David Bruce, BSc, PGCE
Sarah Lee, BSc Hons, PGCE
English as an Additional Language: Naomi Roberts, BSc Hons, BA Hons, MA, PGCE, RSA TEFLA Cert & Dip
Japanese: Akiko Kubo, BA
Chinese: Xiang Yun Bishop, BA, MA, TCAFL
Spanish: Nuria Lopez-Costa
Turkish: Ayla Turacli
PE and Fitness: Fraser Dewar, BSc Hons, PGCE
Yoga: Jennifer Garcia, BMus Hons
Dance: Katie Brewer

Music Staff:

Violin:
Natalia Boyarsky, Dip Solo Performance & Teaching
Lutsia Ibragimova, Dip Solo Performance Baroque Violin, Teaching

Akiko Ono, 1st Cert Dip Mus & Perf Arts Vienna
Diana Galvydyte, MMus RCM, BMus

Violin/Viola:
Boris Kucharsky, MMus

Violin Assistants:
Akerke Ospan
Elliott Perks, BMus Hons
Oscar Perks, BA Hons Cantab
Anna Ziman, BMus Hons
Tereza Privratska, MMus, BMus

Cello:
Thomas Carroll, ARCM
Bartholomew LaFollette, BMus, MMus

Cello Assistant:
Matthijs Broersma, BMus Hons, MA Mus Perf

Double Bass:
Caroline Emery, LTCL, GTCL, Cert Ed

Guitar:
Richard Wright, GRSM Man, ARMCM

Guitar Assistant:
Laura Snowden, MMus, MPerf

Piano:
Ruth Nye, MBE, Dip Mus Perf Melbourne Conservatory
Marcel Baudet, Groningen Conservatory

Piano Assistant:
Miho Kawashima BMus Hons MA

Piano Supporting Study:
Mariko Brown, BMus Hons, LGSM (*Piano 1st Study*)
Alexis White, MMus Piano Perf and Literature, BMus

Harpsichord:
Carole Cerasi Hon ARAM

Harp:
Thea Butterworth, BMus Hons

Staff Pianists:
Nigel Hutchison, BMus Hons
Svitlana Kosenko, Baccalaureate Diploma
Nathan Williamson, BMus, Master Mus Dist, Master Musical Arts Yale

Chamber Music:
Dr Ioan Davies, PhD MA Cantab

Orchestra:
Dr Oscar Colomina I Bosch, PhD RAM, MMus, BMus Hons GSMD

Chance to Play:
Elliott Perks, BMus Hons

Choir:
David Condry, BA

Interpretation through Improvisation:
David Dolan, BMus, MMus

Composition:
John Cooney, BMus Hons, Cert Adv St RCM & GSMD, Hon ARAM

General Music:
Grace Gates, MMus, BMus Hons
Marco Galvani, MMus RAM, BA Hons Oxon
Damian leGassick, PG Dip Surrey
Matthew Taylor, MA Cantab, Dip RAM

Alexander Technique:
Angela Bradshaw, MSTAT, DMU, DCR R

Pastoral Staff:
Housemaster, Harris House: Fraser Dewar, BSc Hons,
    PGCE
Housemistress, Music House: Joanne Field RN RM
Assistant Housemaster: Marco Galvani, MMus RAM, BA
    Hons Oxon
Assistant Housemistress: Jeanne Rourke, BA Hons, PGCE
School Nurse: Pollyanna Richardson, RN Child Dip

Support Staff:
Registrar and Head's PA: Cheryl Poole, BA Hons
Music Administrator: Catharine Whitnall, MA Cantab,
    LTCL
Receptionist & School Secretary: Lisa Guy, BA Hons,
    PGCE
Examinations Officer: Jeanne Rourke, BA Hons, PGCE
Partnership & Outside Events Officer: Tamas Reti, BMus
    Hons
Music Admin Assistant: Dave Greenwood
Music Librarian: Marta Gonzalez Bordonaba, BMus
Practice Supervisor: Debbie Stennett
Science Lab Technician: Delphine Wellington

Bursary:
Accountant: Mark Armstrong, ACCA, BSc Hons
Accounts Assistant: Philippa Stanfield, BSoc Sci Hons
Compliance Officer: Alison Packman
HR Officer: Corinne Spencer MCIPD

Marketing & Communications:
Marketing Manager: Sarah McDonald, BA Hons

Development:
Development Director: Vacancy
Head of Philanthropy: Vacancy
Development Assistant: Amy Mitchell, BMus Hons
Estates:
Estates Manager: Brian Harris
Assistant Estates Manager: Steve Foden

Catering:
Catering Manager: Jean Labourg
Senior Chef: Jo Busby
Commis Chef: Samuel Bartlett
Kitchen Porter: Paulo Trindade Fernandes

Menuhin Hall:
Menuhin Hall Manager: Alice Benzing, BA Hons
Menuhin Hall Admin Assistant: Sian Gandhi, BA Hons,
    PGCE
Menuhin Hall Box Office Manager: Penny Wright
Menuhin Hall Box Office Assistants:
Wendy Gabriel
Clive Stevens
Menuhin Hall Technical Manager: Brian Fifield
Part-Time Assistant Technical Managers:
Alex Baily
Al Forbes
Dominic Mackie
Menuhin Hall Bar and Holiday Course Supervisor: Jon
    Griffin
Menuhin Hall Bar Staff:
Alex Baily
Charly Brough
Oliver Dean
Grace Evans
Wendy Gabriel
Diana Glassett
Lisa Guy
Anna Larson
Clive Stevens
Adrian Whyte
Clive Stevens
Grace Evans

The Society of Heads

Alliance Members UK

MARY-CLARE STARTIN
Head, Berkhamsted Boys
Berkhamsted Boys School, Berkhamsted, Herts
email: enquiries@berkhamsted.com
website: www.berkhamsted.com

TITUS EDGE
Headmaster
Gordonstoun School, Gordonstoun, Elgin, Moray
email: admissions@gordonstoun.org.uk
website: www.gordonstoun.org.uk

JONATHAN SHAW
Head, King's Ely Senior
King's Ely, Ely, Cambridgeshire
email: enquiries@kingsely.org
website: www.kingsely.org

DUNCAN MURPHY
Headmaster
Kingswood House School, Epsom, Surrey
email: office@kingswoodhouse.org
website: www.kingswoodhouse.org

JOHN DOBSON
Headmaster
Stoneygate School, Great Glen, Leics
email: school@stoneygateschool.co.uk
website: www.stoneygateschool.co.uk

MARK HEYWOOD
Principal
The Royal School, Wolverhampton, West Midlands
email: info@theroyal.sch
website: https://theroyalschool.co.uk

Alliance Members Overseas

DR WALID EL-KHOURY
Principal
Brummana High School, Brummana, Lebanon
email: info@bhs.edu.lb
website: www.bhs.edu.lb

HECTOR MacDONALD
Principal
The English School of Kyrenia, Bilim Sokak, Beylerbeyi,
Northern Cyprus
email: info@englishschoolkyrenia.org
website: www.englishschoolkyrenia.org

JON MURRAY-WALKER
Headmaster
Greensteds International School, Nakuru, Kenya
email: office@greenstedsschool.com
website: www.greenstedsschool.com

DEBORAH DUNCAN
Principal
The Junior and Senior School, Nicosia, Cyprus
email: contact@theseniorschool.com
        contact@thejunior school.com
website: www.thejuniorandseniorschool.com

KOEN RINGOOT
Head
Leerwijzer School, Oostduinkerke, Belgium
email: info@leerwijzer.be
website: www.leerwijzer.be

MARK DURSTON
Headmaster
Peponi School, Ruiru, Kenya
email: info@peponischool.org
website: www.peponischool.org

VALERIE MAINOO
Principal
The Roman Ridge School, Accra, Ghana
email: enquiries@theromanridgeschool.com
website: www.theromanridgeschool.com

DR CHRISTIAN BARKEI
Principal
St George's International School, Luxembourg
email: info@st-georges.lu
website: www.st-georges.lu

DAVID YOUNG
Head of School
TMS School, Richmond Hill, Ontario, Canada
email: admissions@tmsschool.ca
website: www.tmsschool.ca

PART IV
Schools whose Heads are members of the Independent Association of Prep Schools

ALPHABETICAL LIST OF SCHOOLS

The following school, whose Head is a member of both IAPS and ISA, can be found in the ISA section:

Ballard School

IAPS
GEOGRAPHICAL LIST OF SCHOOLS

IAPS Member Heads and Deputy Heads

Individual School Entries

Abberley Hall

Worcester WR6 6DD

Tel: 01299 896275
Fax: 01299 896875
email: office@abberleyhall.co.uk
website: www.abberleyhall.co.uk
Twitter: @abberleyhallsch

Chairman of Governors: Mr James Tanner

Headmaster: **W J Lockett**, BA, PGCE

Deputy Headmaster: N Richardson, BSc Hons

Age Range. 2–13.
Number of Pupils. 230: Prep School 164, Pre-Prep & Nursery 66 (132 Boys, 98 Girls; 90 Boarders, 140 Day Pupils).
Fees per term (2018–2019). Prep: Boarders £8,125, Day Pupils £3,890–£6,470. Pre-Prep & Nursery: £2,678–£3,260.

Abberley Hall is co-educational. It is situated 12 miles north-west of Worcester, with easy access to the M5. It is a boarding and day school and nursery for boys and girls aged 2–13 years (boarding from 8 years), and is set in 100 acres of gardens and wooded grounds amid magnificent countryside.

Pupils are prepared for all Independent Senior Schools. Although there is no entry examination, the school has a strong academic tradition with consistently good results in scholarships and Common Entrance, thanks to a highly-qualified staff, favourable teacher/pupil ratios and small classes. This also helps encourage the slower learners, for whom individual attention is available.

The school's facilities include an indoor swimming pool, chapel, library, music school and concert studio, two science laboratories, technology room, DT centre and extensively equipped computer centre, art studio and pottery rooms, multi-purpose hall with permanent stage, rifle range and climbing wall, sports hall, hard tennis courts, Ricochet court and ample playing fields for the major games and athletics, including a large Astroturf pitch. The school also owns its own French chalet where children go on three-week blocks for total immersion into the French language and way of life.

The pupils are also encouraged to take part in a wide range of hobbies and activities including archery, chess, fishing, golf, horse riding, fencing, model-making, printing, ballet, mountain-biking, woodwork and many more.

The school aims to combine a friendly atmosphere with the discipline which enables pupils to achieve their full potential and learn to feel responsibility for themselves and others.

Charitable status. Abberley Hall is a Registered Charity, number 527598. Its aim is to further good education.

Abercorn School

Early Years:
28 Abercorn Place, London NW8 9XP
Tel: 020 7286 4785
email: admin@abercornschool.com

Pre Prep:
The Old Grammar School, 248 Marylebone Road, London NW1 6JF
Tel: 020 7723 8700
email: togs@abercornschool.com

Prep:
38 Portland Place, London W1B 1LS
Tel: 020 7100 4335
email: portland@abercornschool.com

website: www.abercornschool.com

High Mistress: **Mrs Andrea Greystoke**, BA Hons

Headteacher: **Mrs Dusty Fretwell**

Age Range. 2½ to 13+ Co-educational.
Number of Pupils. 350.
Fees per term (2018–2019). £3,340–£6,685. Fees include all extras, apart from lunch and school transport.

For more than 30 years, Abercorn School has proudly offered children from the age of 2 and a half to 13 years the perfect balance of a rigorous academic curriculum, delivered in a warm and nurturing environment in central London.

The school has gained an enviable record of achievement for both boys and girls graduating at 11+ and 13+. We guide both pupils and parents through the education process to ensure our pupils attain the highest standard and meet their potential.

The children are continuously evaluated, supported and challenged in order to foster their individual talents and skills. We are firm believers in traditional values and standards, including excellent pastoral care. However, we are committed to embracing the best of what the 21st century offers, and preparing each child to face the challenges of the modern world with confidence and competence.

Happiness is an essential prerequisite to the acquisition of knowledge. At Abercorn learning is serious but fun!

'Pupils are extremely well prepared for the responsibilities, opportunities and experiences of the next chapter of their lives.' *Independent Schools Inspectorate 2018.*

Discover Abercorn, uncover their future.

Aberdour School

Brighton Road, Burgh Heath, Tadworth, Surrey KT20 6AJ
Tel: 01737 354119
email: enquiries@aberdourschool.co.uk
website: www.aberdourschool.co.uk
Twitter: @aberdourschool

The School is an Educational Trust run by a Board of Governors.

Chairman of the Governors: Mr R C Nicol, FCA

Headmaster: **Mr S D Collins**, CertEd

Senior Deputy Headmistress: Mrs T Thomas, BEd Hons
Deputy Headmaster: Mr C Hoy, BA Ed
Head of Pre-Prep: Mrs A Terry, BA Hons

Age Range. 2–13.

Number of Pupils. 360 Day Boys and Girls.

Fees per term (2018–2019). £1,405–£4,840 inclusive.

Children are taken at 2 years old into the Pre-Preparatory department and transfer to the Preparatory school at age 7. Children are prepared for all the major Senior Schools and many scholarships have been won. There is a school orchestra and a concert band as well as a school choir. There are ample playing fields, climbing wall, two all-weather areas, a large sports hall and indoor heated swimming pool. There are two science laboratories, a design technology room and an Arts & Innovation Centre with a STEM room, languages studio, classrooms, music rooms, VR and Creativity studio and dance studios. All the usual games are coached and the general character of the children is developed by many interests and activities. Aberdour offers a uniquely personalised education with its own distinct curriculum.

Charitable status. Aberdour School Educational Trust Limited is a Registered Charity, number 312033. Its aim is to promote education.

Abingdon Preparatory School

Josca's House, Kingston Road, Frilford, Abingdon, Oxon OX13 5NX

Tel: 01865 391570
email: admissions.manager@abingdonprep.org.uk
website: www.abingdon.org.uk/prep
Twitter: @abingdonprep
Facebook: @abingdonprep

The School was founded in 1956. In 1998 it merged with Abingdon School to become part of one charitable foundation with a single Board of Governors.

Chairman of the Governors: Adrian Burn

Headmaster: **Craig Williams**, MA Oxon, PGCE

Age Range. Boys 4–13.

Number of Pupils. 250 Day.

Fees per term (2018–2019). £4,030–£5,540.

Main entry points are at age four and seven, although entry into other years is sometimes available. The majority of boys move on to the senior school, Abingdon. Pupils for whom Abingdon School is appropriate, will receive an offer for entry to Year 9 at Abingdon School at the end of Year 5 at Abingdon Prep. For these pupils there will be no pre-test and the offer is not dependent on Common Entrance, hence an end to the double testing that was previously in place and that is a requirement for boys from other prep schools. This offer will be based on the continuous assessment of pupils and is conditional on the pupil maintaining his profile of achievement in Years 6–8 at Abingdon Prep. Boys not moving on to Abingdon are prepared for other senior school entrance examinations.

Abingdon Prep is a thinking and learning school – as well as a teaching school. Pupils enjoy a happy and stimulating environment where they are encouraged to develop self-reliance and a sense of responsibility. Considerable emphasis is placed on helping pupils to develop good working patterns together with sound organisational and learning skills.

The School enjoys extensive facilities including dedicated art, drama, ICT, music, CDT and science suites and a multi-purpose sports hall and swimming pool. The School benefits from extensive grounds with woodland, gardens, adventure play areas an all-weather pitch and acres of sports fields.

The extracurricular activities are a major strength of the school outside the classroom. The excellent amenities enable every child to participate in a wide range of sports and activities. There are regular fixtures against local schools in the main school sports of rugby, football, cricket, tennis and athletics. All pupils swim at least once a week. There is a range of after-school clubs, which includes amongst many others, orchestra, choir, art, science, karate, golf, fencing, gardening, chess and drama.

A regular number of academic, music, drama and all-rounder awards are gained every year to senior schools – the majority to the senior school, Abingdon.

A large number of trips are organised for all year groups during the year and the oldest boys go abroad for a week on completing their examinations.

Charitable status. Abingdon School is a Registered Charity, number 1071298. It exists to provide for the education of children aged 4–18.

Aldenham Preparatory School

Aldenham Road, Elstree, Herts WD6 3AJ

Tel: 01923 851664
email: prepschool@aldenham.com
website: www.aldenhamprep.com

Chairman of Board of Governors: Mr J T Barton

Head of Preparatory School: **Mrs V Gocher**, MA

Age Range. 3–11.

Number of Pupils. Total 171: 89 Boys, 82 Girls.

Fees per term (2018–2019). Prep: £4,657; Pre-Prep: £4,234; Nursery: £31.00 per morning or afternoon session, £63 per day, £3,250 per term (five full days).

At Aldenham Preparatory School, we provide a warm, happy and nurturing environment where quality learning takes place and the needs of each individual child are fulfilled.

The Preparatory School is a co-educational day school encompassing the Nursery (3–4 years), the Pre-Prep Department (4–7 years) and the Prep Department (7–11 years). It forms an integral part of the main school which was established in 1597 and remains on the same glorious site, set in over 110 acres of countryside yet only 13 miles from the centre of London.

Our primary aim is to provide an excellent all-round education, presenting all of our pupils with exceptional opportunities. The school is dedicated to ensuring the flexibility for each child to develop their own individual abilities, whether they are academic, creative or sporting. We offer high-quality teaching from enthusiastic, motivated and caring staff.

An inspection commissioned by the Independent Schools Inspectorate (ISI) praised the school for being "...*a lively, happy community in which young children thrive. They benefit from a high standard of education and very good care in all year groups. Children's attitude to learning and their behaviour are exemplary. Relationships between children and staff are friendly and courteous.*"

Small class sizes (a maximum of 23 in the Pre-Prep and Prep) and expert teaching from an early age ensure that academic attainment is high. The requirements of the National Curriculum and preparation for 11+ entrance exams are blended into a broad based curriculum. This along with an excellent staff to pupil ratio enriches our children's learning and encourages them to work to the very best of their ability.

Extensive extracurricular provision including Cookery, Fencing, Chess, Choir and Karate and specialist teachers in

French, Drama, Music and Sport enrich the children's education.

The accommodation for both Pre-Prep and Prep Departments is first class with pupils having access to their own DT and art room, library, music and drama suite, computer room and three-acre playing field. We are also able to share the Aldenham School campus as a whole, enabling us to enjoy use of the extensive grounds and facilities, including the sports complex, artificial turf pitch, chapel, dining hall, and theatre. (For further information about the senior school, see Aldenham School entry in HMC section.)

We have high expectations of all our pupils and encourage initiative, independence and self-confidence. We also insist on good manners and consideration for others, as a result there is a strong sense of community at Aldenham.

Entry is primarily at rising 3 and 4+, although there are also a number of places available at 7+.

Our excellent established Nursery facilities provide a structured lively and stimulating introduction to Aldenham School with morning and afternoon classes or full days.

All our children find themselves well equipped and prepared for the next stage of their education with many moving on to Aldenham Senior School.

Charitable status. The Aldenham School Company is a Registered Charity, number 298140. It exists to provide high quality education and pastoral care to enable children to achieve their full potential in later life.

Aldro

Lombard Street, Shackleford, Godalming, Surrey GU8 6AS

Tel:　01483 813530 (Headmaster)
　　　01483 813535 (Admissions)
　　　01483 810266 (School Office)
email:　hmsec@aldro.org
website:　www.aldro.org
Twitter:　@AldroSchool
Facebook: @AldroSchool

Chairman of the Governors: Mr B R Kirkpatrick, MA, FCA

Acting Headmaster: **Mr Chris Rose**, BEd

Age Range. 7–13.
Number of Boys. 220: 50 boarders, 170 day boys.
Fees per term (2018–2019). Boarding: Form 3 £7,782, Forms 4–8 £8,427. Day: Form 3 £5,848, Forms 4–8 £6,493.

Aldro is a boys' independent day and boarding prep school set in a beautiful rural location yet within a mile of the A3 and 45 minutes of central London, Gatwick and Heathrow airports.

Aldro aims to offer boys an exceptional all-round education in a happy, purposeful community. It has a Christian foundation and this underpins the values and ethos of the school. Each school day starts with a short service in the lovely Chapel, beautifully converted from an eighteenth century barn.

The school is fortunate in having a spacious site including a lake and about 20 acres of playing fields. We have our rowing lake, the new sports centre, four all-weather tennis courts, two shooting ranges, swimming pool and a croquet lawn. The Centenary Building opened in 2000 and houses most of the classrooms, the ICT centre, an outstanding library and, in the basement, changing rooms and a large common room. The Crispin Hill Centre incorporates a Music School and theatre. Two science laboratories and the

Art and Design Technology Centre have been developed in eighteenth century buildings either side of the Chapel. The Argyle Building including a new dining hall and kitchen was opened in late 2003. The dormitories in the main building have recently been refurbished. The boarders enjoy high-quality pastoral care and a varied programme of activities in the evenings and at weekends.

In the classroom, there is a balance between the best traditional and modern approaches, whilst firm and friendly encouragement of each individual has led to an outstanding academic record of success at Common Entrance and Scholarship level. Forty academic awards have been won in the last four years (2016 being a record breaking year) to leading schools such as Charterhouse, Eton, Sherborne, Winchester, Radley, Tonbridge and Wellington College.

Aldro is committed to giving boys real breadth to their education and much emphasis is placed on extracurricular activities. There are many opportunities for the arts, with a good record of success in Art and Music scholarships – 20 awards have been won in the past four years. An astounding 200 boys learn musical instruments and there are three choirs, brass group, and numerous more ensembles. Drama also features prominently with several productions each year.

The major sports are rugby, soccer and hockey in the winter, with cricket in the summer. Athletics, tennis, swimming, cross-country running, polo, sailing and shooting are secondary sports and high standards are achieved. A huge range of activities are available including badminton, dodge ball, pioneers, bottle digging, fly fishing and pétanque. The school has an enviable record for Chess with 9 teams winning National championships in the past five years.

Boys at Aldro are treated as individuals with talents to develop. They lead cheerful and purposeful lives, and are well-prepared for a wide range of leading senior schools.

'Bringing out the best in boys' is what Aldro has been achieving through the generations. There is a focus on excellence and achievement, whether that is in the classroom, music room or on the sports field. Aldro prepares boys for the rest of their lives.

Charitable status. Aldro School Educational Trust Limited is a Registered Charity, number 312072. It exists to provide education for boys.

Aldwickbury School

Wheathampstead Road, Harpenden, Herts AL5 1AD

Tel:　01582 713022
email:　j.felgueiras@aldwickbury.org.uk
　　　　e.warrington@aldwickbury.org.uk
website:　www.aldwickbury.org.uk
Twitter:　@aldwickbury
Facebook: @aldwickburyschool

Chair of Governors: J Bromfield, MBE, BA, PGCE

Headmaster: **V W Hales**, BEd Hons Exeter

Deputy Head: C Schanschieff, BSc Hons Exeter

Age Range. 4–13.
Number of Boys. Prep School: 260 (including up to 26 weekly boarders). Pre-Prep: 120.
Fees per term (2018–2019). Day Boys: Pre-Prep £4,370–£4,515, Years 3–8 £4,825–£5,405. Weekly Boarding Fee: £32.90–£38.50 per night.

Aldwickbury is a day and boarding school set in 20 acres on the outskirts of Harpenden. Aldwickbury is a boys' school that focuses on boys' education, their growth and development. We allow them to flourish in an environment that challenges and stimulates them whatever their interests, passions or talents. Our teaching mixes traditional approaches together with modern ideas and methods; interactive whiteboards have been installed in all departments.

The school provides an extensive extracurricular programme for the boys. Music, art and drama are well catered for with an emphasis on involvement as well as the desire for excellence. There are plays and concerts providing performance opportunities for all age groups, both formally and informally. A games session is held every day for all boys in Years 3–8 and teams in all the major sports at every level. The school has an excellent reputation at all sports and has had national recognition in skiing, swimming, athletics, tennis and soccer in recent years.

The school has excellent facilities based around a large Victorian House. Purpose-built teaching blocks, including a modern pre-prep department, ensure that the education is of a high standard. Other facilities include an indoor swimming pool, tennis courts, gymnasium and playing fields. Recent additions to the buildings have been a library, dining room and changing rooms. A new hall complex including a new music department, performance space and classrooms was completed in 2014; in 2016 the science labs were refurbished and the Coach House renovation providing a new Art and DT department was finished.

The boys move onto a wide range of senior schools, both day and boarding. The recent results at Common Entrance, entry tests and scholarships have been a reflection on the good teaching that the boys receive.

The Pre-Preparatory Department is accommodated in a building opened in 2001.

Charitable status. Aldwickbury School Trust Ltd is a Registered Charity, number 311059. It exists to provide education for children.

All Hallows School

Cranmore Hall, East Cranmore, Somerset BA4 4SF

Tel:	01749 881600 (School Office)
	01749 881609 (Admissions)
email:	info@allhallowsschool.co.uk
website:	www.allhallowsschool.co.uk
Twitter:	@AllHallowsSch
Facebook:	@allhallowssch

Head: **Dr Trevor Richards**, CPsychol

Age Range. 3–13 Co-educational.
Number of Pupils. 256: 140 Boys, 116 Girls.
Fees per term (2018–2019). Boarding £7,785; Day: £2,560 (Rec–Year 2), £4,815 (Years 3 & 4), £5,090 (Year 5 & 6), £5,135 (Years 7 & 8). A range of scholarships and bursaries are available. There are no compulsory extras.

The all-round personal development of children has long been at the heart of the vision and ethos at All Hallows. The school passionately promotes an individualised and holistic approach to learning that seeks to inspire each child to fulfil their potential, with happiness and well-being at the heart of everything the school does. The dedicated and experienced team at All Hallows works in partnership with parents to prepare children for the ever changing world they are growing up in and for the lives they will lead, nurturing and encouraging them to live responsibly and compassionately and to embrace with energy and enthusiasm the fantastic opportunities that lie ahead. This approach is proving outstandingly successful with superb pupil outcomes and the

children known for being exceptionally well-prepared for their senior schools.

All Hallows pioneered boarding co-education for preparatory school age children and the school continues to be innovative with the recent appointment of dedicated boarding staff who are fresh and ready to welcome the children into the boarding house at the end of the day. Boarding was rated '*Excellent*' in all areas in the latest integrated inspection report in 2014, with ISI recognising the school in all areas as "*of exceptionally high quality*" noting that "*children are exceptionally well cared for*".

Christian principles are integrated into daily life so that all faiths are welcomed into the life of this Roman Catholic foundation. Energetic and family-orientated staff, many of whom reside in the school, provide for the academic and pastoral welfare of the children.

The school has a mix of boarders and day pupils with many day pupils flexi boarding on a regular basis. There is an extensive programme of activities and prep for all children each evening after school, with weekend and holiday highlights. An innovative Saturday enrichment programme for Years 6, 7 and 8 comprises an ever broader range of extracurricular activities including photography, young enterprise, bush craft and more.

The school enjoys regional and national sporting success both at a team level and on an individual basis. A comprehensive programme of competitive fixtures enables children of all abilities to play against local opposition in the traditional team sports. Excellence within a framework of sport for all is the school's aim. The Tennis Academy carries an LTA Clubmark for excellence and is available to every child in the school as well as siblings and parents. It also has strong links with the Tennis Performance Centre in Bath.

Exceptional facilities for creativity allow the children and staff to discover talent and develop potential. A state-of-the-art Creative Centre offers the children fantastic design facilities including 2D and 3D design packages, 3D printing, laser cutting, animation, digital photography and fantastic 'making' opportunities. Music and the Arts thrive, ranging from the grace of the Chapel Choir to the creativity and performance of dance and drama. All Hallows also enjoys Forest School status, this fresh learning approach brings immense benefits and the outdoor environs are an integral part of the curriculum at the school, helping to foster the skills and wider perspective that truly encourage innovation, risk-judging and positive risk-taking, self-belief, ambition and a genuine sense of optimism.

All Hallows' independent status enables parents and the Head to select the most appropriate senior school to suit a particular child's needs and talents. In the last few years, pupils have gone to over forty different senior schools. In 2018, 65% of the leavers gained a scholarship or award to their senior school.

Charitable status. All Hallows is a Registered Charity, number 310281. The school is a Charitable Trust, the raison d'être of which is the integration of Christian principles with daily life.

Alleyn Court Preparatory School

Wakering Road, Southend-on-Sea, Essex SS3 0PW

Tel:	01702 582553
Fax:	01702 584574
email:	office@alleyn-court.co.uk
	admissions@alleyn-court.co.uk
	head@alleyn-court.co.uk

website: www.alleyn-court.co.uk
Twitter: @AlleynCourt; @AlleynCourtPE

Headmaster: **Mr Rupert Snow**, BEd Hons, NPQH

Age Range. 2½–11.
Number of Pupils. 300 Boys and Girls.
Fees per term (from April 2018). £1,086–£4,243 according to age.

Alleyn Court was founded in 1904 by Theodore Wilcox and is a non-selective, co-educational day school, for children aged 2½–11. It has recently converted to become a Charitable Trust.

Alleyn Court provides an exciting and wondrous educational adventure, where outstanding learning is present at every opportunity. We educate children from age two to eleven years old so they emerge as respectful, responsible, resilient, resourceful and reflective young people; children who are thoroughly prepared for the rigorous challenges facing them in their secondary school of choice; children who have the bravery and confidence to really thrive in lives filled with exciting and diverse challenges.

Set amongst fourteen acres of woodland and playing fields, with our own, large pond and historic walled garden, the school enjoys a secluded and peaceful environment which lends itself perfectly to our experiential curriculum.

We celebrate curiosity, discourse, effort and investigation. This results in individuals who know themselves well, have diverse and interesting personalities, and who thrive on challenging opportunities, having developed effective and robust work ethics. We believe in developing children who are morally strong and creative problem-solvers.

Alleyn Court has an excellent reputation for its breadth of curriculum, academic achievement, outstanding competitive sporting success, and familial pastoral care. A happy and relaxed atmosphere, family ethos and strong sense of community underpin the purposeful approach to school life and activities.

The school is split into three sections: two parallel Pre-Preparatory departments – one located on the main school site in Thorpe Bay and the other on the original school site in Westcliff – offer an education based on Montessori principles for children aged 2½–5 years in the EYFS. The Junior School (Years 1–3) offers class-based teaching with specialist teaching in French, Art, PE/Sports, Drama, Music and IT. The Senior School maintains this profile in Year 4, and in Years 5 and 6 subject specialist teaching in all subject areas thoroughly prepares children for a broad range of entrance exams and the CSSE 11+. All year groups have 2 parallel classes, which rarely rise above 20 children. Children are accepted for entry into any year group, providing that spaces are available. French and Music is taught from age 4, with specialist teaching for Art, French, Music and PE from Year 1 upwards. All lessons in Years 5 and 6 are taught by subject specialists in dedicated subject rooms.

Academic facilities on the main school site are expansive to suit an academically strong, subject specialist environment. Part of the school site around the pond has recently been developed to create a Woodland School and outdoor classroom to offer more practical and skills-based learning. Our ESR programme (Education for Social Responsibility) also encourages and develops study skills, critical and lateral thinking, problem-solving and philosophy for children.

The school offers extensive provision for sport (with an expansive fixture list) and extracurricular activities, with a splendid variety of clubs before and after school, as well as during morning and lunch breaks. Sports facilities include our large, picturesque, on-site playing fields, sports hall, cricket nets, netball and tennis courts, a woodland cross-country course and a smart pavilion with changing rooms, kitchen and function room.

The performing arts are also well provided for with a dedicated music block which houses a classroom and music practice rooms. Additional indoor and outdoor facilities provide space for drama and LAMDA activities, where children develop their self-confidence, presentation skills and prepare for productions, exams, local festivals and competitions.

Our wonderful in-house catering team source local produce to create delicious meals in our state-of-the-art kitchen and we strive to provide a family atmosphere in all we do. The organisational pressures on many working families are eased through our breakfast club and assisted prep provision, which helpfully extend the school day and provide specialised support for children.

Scholarships and means-tested bursaries are available, up to an annual limit, for pupils with academic, sporting, musical, dramatic or artistic talent.

Alleyn's Junior School

Townley Road, Dulwich, London SE22 8SU
Tel: 020 8557 1519
email: juniorregistration@alleyns.org.uk
website: www.alleyns.org.uk

Chairman of Governors: Mr Iain Barbour

Head: **Mr Simon Severino**, MA Hons, PGCE

Registrar: Mrs Felicity Thomas

Age Range. 4–11.
Number of Pupils. 240 boys and girls.
Fees per term (2018–2019). Reception to Year 2 £5,787; Years 3–6 £6,027 including lunches, out of school visits and one residential trip per year for Years 3–6.

The school is part of the foundation known as 'Alleyn's College of God's Gift' which was founded by Edward Alleyn, the Elizabethan actor, in 1619.

Opened in 1992 to provide a co-educational Junior School for Alleyn's School and sharing the same excellent green site, Alleyn's Junior School provides a happy and lively environment in which well-motivated boys and girls follow a broad and academic education. Boys and girls work together with their teachers in a calm and structured way to develop their potential and self-confidence as they pursue the highest standards across a curriculum which embraces many opportunities for Art, MFL, Drama, Music, Computing and a wide range of sports. Entry to the school is at 4+, 7+ and 9+. The overwhelming majority of children move on to Alleyn's senior school at 11+.

Within small classes and with a balance of class and specialist subject teaching, children are set clear and challenging targets for their learning. Children perform at above average level in KS1 and KS2 tests. The school enjoys a strong extracurricular life offering children varied and exciting opportunities to extend their learning beyond the classroom.

Progress is carefully monitored and individual differences appropriately met. Competition has its place in the encouragement of the highest academic, artistic and sporting standards, but it is always tempered by an emphasis on values of thoughtfulness, courtesy and tolerance. All members of the school community are expected to maintain high standards in their behaviour, manners and appearance, showing pride in themselves and their school.

The school enjoys excellent support from its parent body. Regular meetings and reports keep parents informed of academic progress and pastoral matters and The Alleyn's Junior School Association works tirelessly to promote social cohesion within the school and to support the charity, sporting, dramatic and extracurricular programmes.

Charitable status. Alleyn's School is a Registered Charity, number 1161864, and a Charitable Company Limited by Guarantee, registered in England and Wales, number 09401357. Registered office: Townley Road, London SE22 8SU.

Alpha Preparatory School

21 Hindes Road, Harrow, Middlesex HA1 1SH

Tel: 020 8427 1471
email: sec@alpha.harrow.sch.uk
website: www.alpha.harrow.sch.uk

Chairman of the Board of Governors: I Nunn

Headmaster: **C J W Trinidad**, BSc Hons, PGCE

Age Range. 3–11.
Number of Pupils. 160 boys and girls (day only).
Fees per term (2018–2019). Inclusive of lunch, with no compulsory extras: Nursery £1,500–£2,425; Pre-Preparatory £3,400; Main school £3,750.

The School, situated in a residential area of Harrow, was founded in 1895, and in 1950 was reorganised as a non-profit-making Educational Charity, with a Board of Governors elected by members of the Company; parents of pupils in the School are eligible for membership.

The majority of children enter the Main School at the age of 4 by interview and assessment but there can also be a few vacancies for older pupils and here entry is by written tests, dependent upon age.

There is a full-time staff of 16 experienced and qualified teachers, with additional part-time teachers in instrumental Music. The main games are Football and Cricket, with cross-country, athletics, tennis and netball. Extracurricular activities include Piano and Violin and Guitar instruction.

Religious education, which is considered important, is non-sectarian in nature, but follows upon the School's Christian foundation and tradition; children of all faiths are accepted.

Outside visits to theatres and museums form an integral part of the curriculum and during the Lent Term pupils in Year 6 visit the Isle of Wight.

Regular successes are obtained in Entrance and Scholarship examinations, with many Scholarships having been won in recent years.

The School has its own Nursery (Alphabets) for children aged 3 in the term of entry.

Further details can be obtained from the Registration Secretary.

Charitable status. Alpha Preparatory School is a Registered Charity, number 312640. It exists to carry on the undertaking of a boys and/or girls preparatory school in Harrow in the County of Middlesex.

Altrincham Preparatory School

Marlborough Road, Bowdon, Altrincham, Cheshire WA14 2RR

Tel: 0161 928 3366
email: admin@altprep.co.uk
website: www.altprep.co.uk

Headmaster: **Mr A M Whittaker**, BEd, FCCT

Age Range. 2+–11.
Number in School. 320 Day Boys.
Fees per term (2018–2019). £2,205–£2,880.

With an engaging curriculum designed to capture the imaginations of its boys and a reputation for outstanding academic, musical and sporting achievements, Altrincham Preparatory School is widely regarded as one of the very best schools for 2–11 year olds in the North-West.

Altrincham Preparatory School believes in delivering academic excellence and its boys go on to some of the best selective grammar schools in the region, including Altrincham Grammar School and The Manchester Grammar School. Yet while recent examination results are hugely impressive – 92 per cent of Year 6 boys have an offer for a Grammar School place in September 2016 – Altrincham Preparatory School is also a music school, an arts and technology school and a sports school. The culture of participation means the boys want to be part of everything and two full-time specialist PE teachers have guided the boys to national finals in a range of sports.

Altrincham Preparatory School is described as "excellent" in the latest ISI report (February 2016) with the broad overall provision "enriching the pupils' educational and personal experience, enabling them to develop their talents happily and fruitfully." The ISI was also impressed by the boys' positive approach to their studies, while the "high quality teaching" was reflected in "good and often rapid progress and significant academic achievement". Pastoral care is at the centre of everything it does.

Altrincham Preparatory School is committed to providing such high-quality education in a happy, safe and state-of-the-art environment. The brand-new Early Years Foundation Stage Centre at Bank Place opened in 2015 with a beautiful 16-place Nursery for boys aged 2 and above feeding into the Pre-School. Boys there are able to access the adjacent Bell Field for outdoor exploration, while the use of Bowdon Cricket, Hockey and Squash club's facilities means games can take place on high-quality artificial and grass surfaces. With bright, well-equipped and attractive classrooms, Altrincham Preparatory School is welcoming, nurturing, and most important of all, happy.

Amesbury

Hazel Grove, Hindhead, Surrey GU26 6BL

Tel: 01428 604322
email: n.holmes@amesburyschool.co.uk
website: www.amesburyschool.co.uk

Chairman of the Governors: Tarquin Henderson

Headmistress: **Sheina C Wright**, BA Hons, QTS, NPQH

Age Range. 2–13.
Number of Pupils. 361.

Fees per term (2018–2019). Prep School: £4,895–£5,305; Pre-Prep: £3,465; Early Years (Pre-Nursery to Reception): from £32.90 per session.

Amesbury is a co-educational day school founded in 1870 and is the only co-educational Prep school in the Hindhead/Haslemere area. The main building is unique, as the only school to be designed by Sir Edwin Lutyens, and stands in its own 34-acre estate in the heart of the Surrey countryside.

We are a family school, keen for siblings to study together and to feel equally valued irrespective of their aptitudes and abilities. There is no competitive entry. Entry is based on registration plus a visit – not a formal assessment but the opportunity for child and school to get acquainted.

Classes are small guaranteeing individual attention. Study programmes currently lead to senior school entrance and scholarship examinations at 11+ and at 13+. We have a proud tradition of academic, sporting and artistic achievement. The school has excellent purpose-built facilities with a new Visual Arts Facility opened in September 2015.

We pride ourselves on sending children to the best senior schools in the country at both 11+ and 13+. Amesbury's academic record is excellent with an average of 20% of pupils receiving senior school scholarships. "Many a school may claim to be 'academically rigorous'. Not all would also make such a virtue out of also being 'relaxed' …this one does." (Good Schools Guide).

In addition to a compelling academic record, Amesbury has a thriving Performing Arts Department: "Music embraces everything from formal chapel choir to semisecret bands formed each year, strutting stuff at annual concert. There's plentiful dance and drama including ambitious takes on Shakespeare" (Good Schools Guide). As for sport, the site is 34 acres, with an all-weather astro, indoor sports hall and an all-school tennis programme. Our Extra Curricular programme runs a whole host of activities including Mandarin Chinese, Judo, Golf, Chess, Music Technology, Drama and many more.

Amesbury understands its role as part of your family life. We believe weekends should be your time; there is no Saturday school and prep can be done at school. We offer Breakfast Club and After School Care. Our Pre-Nursery and Nursery offer early drop-offs, late pick-ups and holiday care.

ISI Inspection 2017.

The quality of the pupils' academic and other achievements is excellent.

• Pupils of all abilities make excellent progress during their time at school.

• Pupils are highly independent and confident communicators, who keenly articulate their views and opinions to enhance their learning.

• Pupils have extremely well-developed study skills and relish opportunities for analytical and hypothetical thinking in their learning.

• Pupils have outstanding attitudes to learning and enjoy the breadth of the curriculum.

The quality of the pupils' personal development is excellent:

• Pupils develop high levels of confidence and warmly embrace new challenge.

• Pupils speak passionately about all that the school provides and the strong support that staff provide.

• Pupils have excellent moral awareness and a mature understanding towards the importance of positive behaviour.

• Pupils' empathy towards the needs of their peers is exemplary.

Focused Compliance:

Eight standards are reviewed and the highest accolade one can hope for is that the school will be found to be compliant in all eight areas. Amesbury was found to be fully compliant.

Open Mornings take place in October, February and May.

Charitable status. Amesbury School is a Registered Charity, number 312058. It exists to provide education for boys and girls. It is administered by a Board of Governors.

Ardingly College Prep & Pre-Prep Schools
A Woodard School

Ardingly, Haywards Heath, West Sussex RH17 6SQ

Tel:	01444 893200 (Prep)
	01444 893300 (Pre-Prep)
email:	registrar@ardingly.com
website:	www.ardingly.com

Chairman of School Council: Mr J Sloane, BSc

Headmaster: **Mr H Hastings**, BA Hons, MEd Oxon

Deputy Head: Mr J Castle, BA Hons

Head of Pre-Prep: Mrs H Nawrocka, MSc, PGCE

Age Range. Pre-Prep 2–7, Prep 7–13.

Number of Pupils. Pre-Prep 101, Prep 302.

Fees per term (2018–2019). Day Pupils: Reception, Years 1 & 2 £3,065; Years 3 & 4 £4,370; Years 5 & 6 £5,180; Years 7 & 8 £5,250. Boarding (in addition to day fees) £300–£1,100 (1–4 nights). Casual boarding: £36 per night.

Ardingly College Prep School is the Preparatory School for Ardingly College Senior School (*see entry in HMC section*).

Ardingly College Prep School is set within 250 acres of glorious Sussex countryside, which it shares with the Senior School and Pre-Prep. The School is co-educational and has over 400 pupils from Pre-Nursery to Year 8 (ages 2–13). The Prep School benefits from the College's Chapel, Music School, Dining Hall, Gymnasium, Sports Hall, Indoor Swimming Pool, 2 Astro Pitches, Medical Centre and School Shop. Girls and boys are admitted into the Pre-Prep from the age of 2, and into the Prep School from the age of 7. The Prep School offers weekly boarding to children from Year 3 with pupils taking an option of anything from one to four nights a week. There is an extensive after-school care provision which includes activities that run until 7.00 pm for all pupils. The School (Prep and Pre-Prep) offers nursery care from 7.00 am to 7.00 pm for 50 weeks of the year.

The extracurricular activities include Drama Club, Fencing, Lego Club, Dance, Swimming Clubs, Orchestra, Jazz Club, Mandarin Club, Forest School, as well as numerous Sports Clubs. The School has recently launched its own News Show.

Children are prepared for Common Entrance in the core subjects, but follow our own Humanities curriculum which links with the programmes of study in the Senior School.

Girls play hockey, netball and rounders and football. Boys play football, hockey and cricket. In the summer both girls and boys enjoy athletics. Cross country and swimming take place throughout the year. The School has had much success recently on a national scale in swimming, fencing and athletics.

Religious Education is in accordance with the teaching of the Church of England.

Details of Scholarships and Bursaries available may be obtained from the Registrar.

A new character and skills initiative known as 'Shaping My World' is due to be launched in June. The School prides itself on encouraging independence.

The Farmhouse Pre-Prep provides children with the perfect introduction to their education. Safely yet idyllically situated within the College estate, our Pre-Preparatory is housed within carefully restored Grade 2 listed Victorian farm buildings. We have full use of the College facilities, including the swimming pool, sports hall, playing fields, chapel and full medical on-site care. The school grounds provide us with a wealth of resources for many different purposes including Forest School.

We aim to lay the basic foundations – academic, social, physical and spiritual – upon which every child can build a sound education, all within a vibrant, caring and yet challenging atmosphere.

The Farmhouse caters for children from 2 to 3 years in our Pre-Nursery, 3 to 4 years in our Nursery and from 4 to 7 in the Pre-Preparatory classes. The Pre-Preparatory children are taught in classes of about 16 pupils, whilst the Nursery may cater for up to 25 children (full day available).

The Farmhouse has its own highly qualified staff and access to a range of specialist staff. French is taught from the age of 4 years and a wide variety of sport is included in the curriculum.

After-school activities include Hockey, Ballet, Football, Chess, Tennis, Modern & Tap dance and Lego Clubs.

The School is open from Monday to Friday 7.00 am to 7.00 pm. There are no boarding facilities at this age.

Charitable status. Ardingly College Limited is a Registered Charity, number 1076456. It exists to provide high quality education for boys and girls aged 2–18 in a Christian context.

Ardvreck School

Crieff, Perthshire PH7 4EX

Tel: 01764 653112
Fax: 01764 654920
email: office@ardvreck.org.uk
          admissions@ardvreck.org.uk
website: www.ardvreckschool.co.uk
Twitter: @ArdvreckSchool
Facebook: @Ardvreck-School

Chairman of the Governors: Major-General Michael Riddell-Webster, CBE, DSO

Headmistress: **Mrs Ali Kinge**, BA, PGCE, BCAv

Age Range. Co-educational 3–13.
Number of Pupils. 107. Main School: 29 Full Boarding, 10 Step-up Boarding, 61 day. Little Ardvreck 17.
Fees per term (2018–2019). Main School: £7,495 (boarders), £4,987 (day); Little Ardvreck £2,335.

Ardvreck School is an independent boarding and day preparatory school for boys and girls aged 3–13.

Ardvreck stands in 42 acres of Perthshire countryside on the edge of Crieff having been purpose built and founded in 1883. The School has a long tradition of providing academic excellence as well as outstanding achievement in sport and music. There are 17 full-time and 3 part-time members of the teaching staff and classes are no larger than 16. Health and domestic arrangements are under the personal supervision of the Head of Pupil Welfare who is assisted by three full-time Matrons (two resident) and one qualified school Nurse. The School Doctor visits regularly.

Boys and girls are prepared for senior schools throughout Britain. In recent years, all have passed the Common Entrance to their schools of first choice both North and South of the border and over 50 scholarships have been awarded in the past four years.

Children aged 3–7 join Little Ardvreck before joining Junior House at the age of 8. The Nursery runs every morning for 3–4 year olds and After School Club until 6.00 pm is provided.

Rugby, netball, hockey, cricket, rounders, tennis and athletics are the main sports and on several Saturdays in the summer, pupils are provided with picnic lunches enabling them to explore the surrounding countryside, accompanied by members of staff, where they can study the wildlife, fish in one of the rivers or lochs, climb, sail or canoe. Other activities include golf, riding, mountain biking, skiing and shooting in our own purpose-built range. Outdoor pursuits are a regular fixture on the Ardvreck calendar with a range of activities on offer including munro bagging, canyoning, white water rafting and climbing of every kind.

A modern and well-equipped Music School provides the best possible opportunities for music-making. There is an orchestra and choir, both of which regularly participate in both school and local music events. Visiting music specialists teach the full range of instruments including the bagpipes. Music and drama play an important part in the life of the school and a major production is staged annually with several smaller productions and numerous concerts taking place throughout the year. Ardvreck boasts the largest prep school pipe band in Scotland.

There is a heated, indoor swimming pool (all children are taught to swim), an Astroturf surface for hockey, tennis and netball, and a superb sports hall.

Most full-time staff live within the school grounds and a special feature of Ardvreck is that there are three houses – one for the Juniors, one for the senior girls and one for the senior boys. The senior houses are where pupils gain a little more independence and are encouraged to show greater personal responsibility in readiness for the transition to senior schools.

Some boarders live overseas and they can be escorted to and from Scottish airports; all necessary documentation can be handled by the School if required.

Admission is by a meeting with the Headmistress and an overnight or day 'taster'. Financial assistance is available through means-tested bursaries.

Charitable status. Ardvreck School is a Registered Charity, number SC009886. Its aim is to provide education for boys and girls.

Arnold House School

1 Loudoun Road, St John's Wood, London NW8 0LH

Tel: 020 7266 4840
email: office@arnoldhouse.co.uk
website: www.arnoldhouse.co.uk

Chairman of the Board of Governors: Dr M Badenoch, BSc, MBBS, DCH, DRCOG, MRCGP

Headmaster: **V W P Thomas**, BEd, MA

Age Range. 5–13.
Number of Boys. 270 (Day Boys only).
Fees per term (2018–2019). £6,344 including Lunch.

Arnold House is an independent day school for boys founded in 1905.

Most boys join the school in Year 1 after their fifth birthday. A few join at other ages.

The Arnold House website gives full details of recent developments in the school's curriculum and facilities. These include the complete refurbishment and extension of the main teaching facilities at Loudoun Road. At the school's 7 acres of playing fields at Canons Park, Edgware, the existing pavilion hall has been adapted to become an auditorium seating 150 with a fully-equipped stage and associated facilities. The Canons Park Activity Centre has become an important addition to the excellent facilities at Loudoun Road.

Boys transfer to their chosen independent senior schools at the age of 13. Arnold House has an enviable record of success in placing each boy in the school that is right for him. More than half of the boys move on to the most sought-after London day schools: City of London, Mill Hill, St Paul's, UCS and Westminster. Others transfer to renowned boarding schools: Bradfield, Eton, Harrow, Marlborough, Radley, Rugby, Tonbridge, Wellington and Winchester have been popular destinations in recent years. Arnold House takes a long view of a boy's education. Academic breadth, a balance between study, sport, music, the arts and activities together with excellent pastoral care constitute the foundations of the school's philosophy and success.

Charitable status. Arnold House School is a Registered Charity, number 312725. It exists to provide education for boys in preparation for transfer to senior independent schools at 13.

Ashdown House

Forest Row, East Sussex RH18 5JY

Tel: 01342 822574
email: secretary@ashdownhouse.com
website: www.ashdownhouse.co.uk

The School is part of The Cothill Trust.

Headmaster: **Mike Davies**

Age Range. 4–13 Co-educational.
Number of Pupils. 101.
Fees per term (2018–2019). Boarding: £9,150 (Years 3–8); Day: £6,700 (Years 7–8), Day: £6,100 (Years 5–6), £4,950 (Years 3–4), £2,990 (Reception, Years 1–2).

The School (mainly full boarding in Years 6–8) with most day pupils begging to board by Year 5 or 6 is a Latrobe house situated in its own grounds of 40 acres, on the edge of the Ashdown Forest. We have an indoor sports hall, theatre and music centre, new Science Block and well-equipped ICT provision. There is an indoor swimming pool, three tennis courts, a golf course and open countryside surrounding us for field studies and adventure.

An escorted train to London and back on exeat weekends and half terms and easy access to Gatwick & Heathrow airports make us a popular choice for London parents and families living abroad.

Every child in Year 7 spends the first half of the autumn term in the Château de Sauveterre – a wonderful opportunity to improve their written and oral French, as well as to develop personally and socially and experience life in France at first hand.

There are 31 full-time members of teaching staff, most of whom live within the grounds. Music of all kinds is studied under resident and peripatetic teachers and Art, DT and ICT

are part of every child's curriculum. Scholarships are regularly won in all disciplines.

Games. Major sports for boys are cricket, soccer, rugby; the girls play netball and rounders, and hockey and athletics are played by both girls and boys. In addition there are huge numbers of other sporting opportunities, including swimming, tennis, riding, golf, squash, archery and cross-country.

The Headmaster and his wife, supported by houseparents, matrons and a State Registered Nurse look after all pastoral and domestic arrangements.

Charitable status. The Cothill Educational Trust is a Registered Charity, number 309639.

Ashfold School

Dorton House, Dorton, Bucks HP18 9NG

Tel: 01844 238237
Fax: 01844 238505
email: registrar@ashfoldschool.co.uk
website: www.ashfoldschool.co.uk
Twitter: @AshfoldSchool

Chairman of Governors: Mr Hugh Taylor

Headmaster: **Mr Colin MacIntosh**, MA Hons

Age Range. 3–13 Co-educational.
Number of Pupils. 160 boys, 120 girls (day pupils and flexi/weekly boarders).
Fees per term (2018–2019). Weekly boarders £6,730; Day £5,170–£5,615; Pre-Prep £3,175–£3,810.

Ashfold is an independent day, weekly and flexi boarding school for boys and girls aged three to thirteen years. Set in thirty acres of stunning grounds in rural Buckinghamshire, the School is located within easy reach of Thame, Princes Risborough, Oxford, Bicester and Aylesbury. The nearest mainline station with regular connections to London Marylebone and Birmingham is just 15 minutes away. Ashfold is a busy and vibrant place with a reputation as a friendly, family-orientated school.

Founded in 1927, Ashfold is a country prep school offering the very best in both traditional and innovative teaching. The School's extensive facilities include a purpose-built Pre-Prep Building, sports hall, full-sized astroturf and a heated outdoor pool. A new Art & Design Centre opened in January 2016 with state-of-the-art facilities for design technology, cookery & nutrition, art, ceramics and textiles.

Most children join the School in the Pre-Prep Department and move on to top independent senior schools at 13+. Ashfold has a strong academic record and in recent years, on average, more than 40% of the Sixth Form have achieved scholarships or awards to their chosen schools.

The School offers an excellent all-round education with outstanding opportunities for sport, art, music and drama as well as a wide-ranging programme of extracurricular activities.

In the School's latest inspection by the Independent Schools Inspectorate in 2015, the following areas of the School's provision were all rated 'excellent': pupils' achievements and learning; curricular and non-curricular provision; teaching; the spiritual, moral, social and cultural development of pupils; pastoral care; boarding; governance; and leadership and management.

Charitable status. Ashfold School Trust is a Registered Charity, number 272663. It exists to provide a quality preparatory school education, academically and in other respects, for all the children entrusted to its care.

Ashford Prep School
United Learning

Great Chart, Ashford, Kent TN23 3DJ

Tel:	01233 620493
Fax:	01233 636579
email:	coxr@ashfordschool.co.uk
website:	www.ashfordschool.co.uk
Twitter:	@AshfordSchool
Facebook:	@AshfordSchool

The Prep School of Ashford School, a co-educational day and boarding school for ages 0–18.

Chairman of School Council: Mr W Peppitt, MRICS

Head: **Mrs P Willetts**, BPE

Deputy Head – Teaching and Learning: Mrs R Clifford, BSc

Deputy Head – Pastoral: Mr C Neesham, BA

Age Range. 3–11.
Number of Pupils. 416: 202 Boys, 214 Girls.
Fees per term (2018–2019). Day: Nursery: £753 (one full day per week), £3,000 (full-time); Reception–Year 2 £3,500, Years 3–6 £5,000.

Ashford Prep School is part of United Learning and as such has benefited from significant recent investment, including extensive refurbishment and new facilities. The school believes in the importance of focusing on the development of the individual through a broad education in which every child can find success whilst developing confidence, motivation, self-esteem and emotional intelligence.

Situated in a rural setting, Ashford Prep School lies in some 25 very attractive acres. The School enjoys both classroom-based and excellent specialist teaching with well-designed facilities for science, art, music, PE, ICT and design technology. The School is fully networked and has exceptional provision for ICT with ACTIVboards in all classrooms, iPads accessible in all lessons, a computer room capable of accommodating entire classes and broadband access to the Internet throughout. We have recently celebrated the opening of our new floodlit all-weather astro and sports fields, which includes three cricket squares and four rugby pitches, and we are looking forward to the opening of our sports pavilion in the coming year.

The thriving Nursery operates on a flexible basis and the school offers full, wrap-around care from 7.30 am to 6.30 pm for all our children. The school operates Mondays to Fridays. Holiday Clubs operate during school breaks.

Throughout the school, team sports include rugby, hockey, netball, football, rounders, athletics and cricket. Regular fixtures are held with other local schools. Children also participate in PE and swimming as part of their curricular programme.

An extensive range of co-curricular activities is provided, both at lunchtime and after school. Individual music tuition with a wide range of instruments is available. Music, drama, dance and public speaking are all important opportunities; productions and presentations are performed by all age groups to a high standard and take place throughout the year. The choir and orchestra meet regularly.

A programme of educational trips and visits provides a stimulating and important addition to the all-round education and development of the 'whole' child and the costs of these are included in the fees.

An inspection by the Independent Schools Inspectorate in March 2014 declared the whole school 'outstanding' or 'excellent' in every category.

Children normally progress to Ashford Senior School (*see HMC entry*) without the need to take an entrance test, unless they wish to sit scholarship exams. The Prep School has had considerable success in preparing children for scholarships to leading independent schools as well as other entrance tests including the 11+.

Charitable status. Ashford Prep School is part of United Learning which comprises: UCST (a Company Limited by Guarantee, Registered in England, number 2780748, and a Registered Charity, number 1016538) and ULT (a Company Limited by Guarantee, Registered in England, number 4439859, and an Exempt Charity).

Avenue House School

70 The Avenue, Ealing, London W13 8LS

Tel:	020 8998 9981
email:	school@avenuehouse.org
website:	www.avenuehouse.org
Twitter:	@avenue_house

Co-educational Day School.

Proprietor: Mr David Immanuel

Headteacher: **Mr Justin Sheppard**, BA Hons, PGCE

Age Range. 4–11.
Number of Pupils. 80.
Fees per term (2018–2019). £3,920.

Avenue House School provides a small, caring environment where children gain the confidence to flourish in all areas of the curriculum. Good manners, mutual respect and a caring community are prevalent at all times.

Children are taught in small classes conducive to the development of an excellent work ethos and achieve high standards in academic subjects as well as an appreciation and understanding of Drama, Art, Music and Sport.

Avenue House School does not test children on entry to Reception as we feel that each child develops at their own individual rate. All pupils are monitored and assessed individually throughout the year and meetings between parents and school are frequent as we believe a positive approach leads to excellence.

Children have access to our own small library and small hall for the younger children. The school has laptop computers with wireless broadband internet connection and whiteboards are installed throughout.

Pupils are prepared for the competitive entrance examinations to the London Independent Day Schools.

Avenue House School is proud of the many high-standard musical and drama productions that are performed throughout the year by children from Reception to Year 6.

Physical Education is an important part of our curriculum and all pupils go swimming every week. Children in Reception and Year 1 have Physical Education in our Gymnasium and small playground. From Year 2 the children have weekly sports lessons at Trailfinders Sports and Leisure Club. The traditional annual sports day for the whole school is also held. The children are also involved in inter-House matches.

Extra-curricular activities form a valuable and key part of our education. Apart from the daily homework club other activities include football, drama, guitar, Junior & Senior choir, Junior & Senior ICT, art, ballet, Mad Science, French and gardening (Summer Term). For Years 5 and 6 we also have lunch-time clubs which include Debating, School Magazine and Mathematics Club.

Educational visits play an important role in helping children relate their class work to the real world. For this reason pupils are taken on outings each term where they can benefit from having first-hand knowledge of London and its surrounding areas. Children have the opportunity to go on residential trips which include Dorchester, France, the Isle of Wight and Black Mountain in Wales.

Avenue Nursery & Pre-Preparatory School

2 Highgate Avenue, Highgate, London N6 5RX

Tel: 020 8348 6815
email: office@avenuenursery.com
website: www.avenuenursery.com

Principal: **Mrs Mary Fysh**

Head: **Mrs Sarah Tapp**

Age Range. 3–7 Co-educational.
Number of Pupils. 75.
Fees per term (2018–2019). £2,600–£4,900.

The ethos of the School is the happiness of every child through a secure, friendly and exciting environment. The provision of a wide and different extracurricular programme of activities from pottery to ice skating contributes considerably towards achieving this aim. The high staff/child ratios enable children to learn and achieve in small groups thus progressing successfully throughout the curriculum. External assessments (PIPS) are introduced in the Nursery and continued through Reception, Year 1 and 2. The results are collated and provide a useful means of tracking the progress of each child: it also aids the planning and learning needs of different children. The School is non-denominational and children of all denominations or none are welcome. Children are made aware of major religious festivals including Christmas.

Pre-Nursery children enter the School when rising 3. The staff ratio is 1:6 and the children enjoy participating in many different activities designed to promote speech and language skills, hand/eye coordination and learning to interact with peers and adults. The large garden provides many opportunities for physical activities, role play and social interaction.

The Nursery takes children from the age of 3+ for five mornings a week and the staff ratio remains at 1:6. The children build on the skills they have learned in Pre-Nursery and are also introduced to letters and numbers. Pottery is added to the curriculum plus visits off site to places of interest.

The Reception Class is divided into two groups according to age. These groups are taught Literacy and Maths in groups of 9 and the work is differentiated so that each child is able to achieve at the level appropriate to them. French and trampolining are added to the curriculum. Children remain at school until 3 pm and bring a packed lunch.

The Year 1 and 2 children's respective class teacher remains with them throughout Key Stage 1 to ensure a seamless transition from Year 1 to 2 greatly benefiting the children's preparations for their future 7+ assessments. The classes follow a curriculum based on the National Curriculum but designed to enable each child to progress towards a successful outcome at 7+. Ice skating is added to the extra-curricular timetable.

Children leave the School at varying stages. Some of the girls leave at 4+ and others at 7+. Boys generally stay until 7+. We have built up good relationships with other schools in the area and as members of the IAPS (since November 2009) enjoy meeting and visiting member schools.

Aysgarth School

Bedale, North Yorkshire DL8 1TF

Tel: 01677 450240
email: admissions@aysgarthschool.co.uk
website: www.aysgarthschool.com
Twitter: @AysgarthSchool
Facebook: @aysgarthschool

Chairman of Governors: J M P D Stroyan

Headmaster: **Mr Rob Morse**, BEd Hons De Montfort

Assistant Headmaster: Mr Philip Southall, BA Hull, PGCE St Mary's Twickenham

Age Range. 3–13.
Number of Pupils. 203. Pre-Prep Department: 44 boys and girls aged 3–8. Prep School: 159 boys aged 8–13.
Fees per term (2018–2019). Boarders (full and weekly) £8,630, Day £6,630, Pre-Prep £2,700–£3,585.

The Prep School is a boarding school for boys set in 50 acres of grounds in North Yorkshire about 6 miles from the A1. It attracts boys from all over the UK, and boys go on to the country's leading independent senior schools, many of them in southern England. Some boys start as day boys or weekly boarders to enable them to adjust to boarding gently. For exeats, boys can be escorted on trains from Darlington to the north and south and there are coaches to and from Cumbria and Lancashire.

Boys of all abilities are welcomed and academic standards are high. All boys are prepared for Common Entrance and several gain scholarships. Before entry, each boy is assessed to ensure that any special needs are identified early and given fully integrated specialist help where necessary. Class sizes are typically around 12. There is a newly equipped computer centre and every teacher has a laptop to link to digital projectors and interactive whiteboards in most classrooms.

The activities in which boys can participate are enormously varied. The facilities include a new heated indoor swimming pool, a modern sports hall, tennis, fives and squash courts, 17 acres of excellent playing fields and a floodlit all-weather pitch. Cricket, Soccer and Rugby Football are the main school sports, and there are opportunities to participate in a wide range of other sports. Music is one of the strengths of the school with more than 75% of boys playing a musical instrument and several boys have been awarded music scholarships. There are three choirs and the school musicians have regular opportunities to perform both in the school and locally. Each term different year groups produce a play or musical. Art and Craft and Design & Technology are taught by specialist teachers.

The school has a fine Victorian chapel, and boys are encouraged to develop Christian faith and values in a positive, caring environment. Pastoral care is the first priority for all staff. The headmaster and his wife, a housemaster and his wife and three matrons, are all resident in the main building. A wide range of exciting activities in the evenings and at weekends ensure that boys are keen to board, and they are encouraged to do so particularly in their last two years as preparation for their next schools.

The school aims to encourage boys to be well mannered and courteous with a cheerful enthusiasm for learning and for life and a determination to make the most of their abilities.

There is also a flourishing Pre-Prep Department including a Nursery for day boys and girls aged 3 to 8.

Charitable status. Aysgarth School Trust Limited is a Registered Charity, number 529538. Its purpose is to provide a high standard of boarding and day education.

Bablake Junior School and Pre Prep

Junior School:
Coundon Road, Coventry, West Midlands CV1 4AU

Tel:	024 7627 1260
Fax:	024 7627 1294
email:	jhmsec@bablakejs.co.uk
website:	www.bablake.com/junior
Twitter:	@BablakeJunior
Facebook:	@BablakeJunior

Pre Prep:
8 Park Road, Coventry, West Midlands CV1 2LH

Tel:	024 7622 1677
Fax:	024 7623 1630
email:	bablakepreprep@bablakejs.co.uk
website:	www.bablake.com/pre-prep

Chairman of Governors: Mrs J McNaney

Headmaster: N A Price, BA Hons, PGCE

Deputy Head: Mr L Holder, BEd
Head of Pre Prep: Mrs T Horton, BEd Hons Cantab

Age Range. 3–11.
Number of Pupils. 350 Day Pupils.
Fees per term (2018–2019). £2,376–£2,981.

Bablake Junior School offers an outstanding educational experience that allows children to thrive. Pupils enjoy coming to school and are given broad opportunities to develop and learn. They acquire skills and interests that will equip them for their future learning and for life.

We are a school where children are nurtured as individuals. This helps them to achieve all that they are capable of academically, creatively and on the games field. Excellent learning support is offered to those who may not be achieving their potential. Most of our pupils continue their education at Bablake until they complete their A Levels. (*See Bablake School entry in HMC section.*) Throughout the school, we help our pupils make the most of their abilities and the outstanding opportunities that exist here for them.

We follow a broad and balanced curriculum – lessons are interesting and our academic results excellent. Our teachers' commitment to helping everyone achieve their potential is reflected in the support of our parents and the hard work our pupils put into their studies. All achievement – academic, creative or sporting – is recognised and celebrated. The support and respect of the community helps all children achieve their best.

Pupils receive expert coaching in a wide variety of sports and have the opportunity to take part in many activities. We believe in participation and the pursuit of excellence and all children have the opportunity to represent the school in fixtures. We share the swimming pool, fields, sports hall and astroturf with our Senior School and make use of Bablake's fantastic theatre and other specialist facilities. Taking part in

a wide variety of activities builds confidence and reinforces positive child development.

Children may join Bablake Pre Prep in the September after they turn 3. The Pre Prep offers a happy, homely and stimulating environment where thorough and considered preparation takes place for the challenges ahead. Later admission to the Pre Prep and Junior School is available at any time should space exist. An assessment of a pupil's potential takes place before entry.

Charitable status. Coventry School Foundation is a Registered Charity, number 528961. It exists to provide education for boys and girls.

Badminton Junior School

Westbury-on-Trym, Bristol BS9 3BA

Tel:	0117 905 5271
Fax:	0117 962 3049
email:	admissions@badmintonschool.co.uk
website:	www.badmintonschool.co.uk

Chairman of Governors: Mr Bill Ray

Headmistress: Mrs Emma Davies, BA, PGCE

Age Range. 3–11.
Number of Girls. 132.
Fees per term (2018–2019). Day: £3,250–£3,745 inclusive of lunch and extended day. Boarding (from Year 5): £7,280–£8,315.

Educational Philosophy. Children learn best when they are interested, happy and supported in their work. Our girls thrive in a stimulating environment where high standards of work and behaviour are expected. All subjects in the Junior School are taught by enthusiastic subject specialists in classes of up to sixteen pupils. We provide a welcoming and friendly atmosphere so that all of our girls feel emotionally secure and we encourage them to develop their own particular talents and interests. Key notes in our philosophy are the development of self-confidence, a healthy respect for one another and the nurturing of curious, critical minds.

We believe children enjoy being kept busy and acquiring new skills and so we try to create a balance between academic work in the classroom, plenty of physical exercise, a range of extra-curricular activities and opportunities for recreational and creative play. The girls are given the opportunity to explore and develop their language skills and study French, Latin, German and Spanish whilst additional languages, such as Mandarin and Italian, are offered in after-school clubs.

Facilities. The Junior School is well appointed with light airy classrooms, dedicated rooms for Art and Music, a Science laboratory, and an ICT suite. We have a well-stocked library and an Assembly Hall in which various activities including ballet, drama and musical concerts take place. There is a wonderful, secure adventure playground which the girls make the most of during break and lunch times.

Being on the same campus as the Senior School, the girls make use of all the facilities on site which include the 25m indoor swimming pool, gymnasium and the all-purpose sports pitch. There are excellent facilities for music, which plays an important part both inside and outside the curriculum.

With our extended day facilities we aim to provide a warm and caring environment to suit the needs of all our pupils and their parents. Every day clubs such as gardening, chess, drama, art or playground games take place after school and girls are welcome to stay on for prep or late stay until 5:45 pm, at no additional cost

For further information on Badminton School, see entry in GSA section. A prospectus is available on request from our Admissions Department (admissions@badminton school.co.uk).

Charitable status. Badminton School Limited is a Registered Charity, number 311738. It exists to provide education for children.

Bancroft's Preparatory School

High Road, Woodford Green, Essex IG8 0RF

Tel: 020 8506 6751
          020 8506 6774 (Admissions)
Fax: 020 8506 6752
email: prep.office@bancrofts.org
website: www.bancrofts.org

Chairman of the Governors: Prof P Kopelman, MD, FRCP, FFP

Head: **J P Layburn**, MA

Assistant Head, Co-Curriculum & Compliance: M Piper, BA
Assistant Head, Teaching & Learning: N Thomas, BCom, MA
Assistant Head, Operational & Pastoral: Mrs L Life, BA

Age Range. 7–11.
Number of Pupils. 125 girls, 138 boys.
Fees per term (2018–2019). £4,917.

Bancroft's Preparatory School was established in September 1990 in the attractive grounds of Bancroft's School in Woodford Green (*see entry in HMC section*) and became a member of IAPS in 2000. Academic results are excellent and places are much sought after – the school is heavily oversubscribed with numbers of registrations rising year by year.

The Prep School has its own distinct character within the Bancroft's community and has the advantage of being able to use the excellent Senior School facilities including the sports hall, music facilities, Chapel, catering facility and hard play area. The School has recently expanded with an impressive new wing providing a further three classrooms, a performing arts studio for drama, music and dance, a science/design & technology room, a new front entrance and reception area as well as a children's adventure play area. This expansion has enabled the school to reduce its class sizes; the School now has three forms in each of its four year groups.

The school seeks to provide an education enriched by a vibrant, multicultural environment. Pastoral care is seen as key and the happiness of all the children is fundamental. Assemblies link with PSHE and focus on key values – such as treating others as you would like to be treated and going "the extra mile". The school constantly seeks to encourage children to feel part of a happy and caring community.

Regular charity work is seen as very important and through it children gain an appreciation of the advantages on offer to them and so develop a sense of compassion for the world beyond Bancroft's.

The class teacher has a central role to play and there is an emphasis on specialised teaching in the top two years, so that staff can pursue their subject passions to the benefit of the children. Academic standards are high with a broad, structured curriculum including French, Humanities, Creative Thinking, PSHE, Drama, Music, Games, Swimming,

PE and Art. The Prep School wants its bright pupils to have fun and "to sparkle" while they learn so that they will derive a lifelong love of learning.

As well as establishing a strong academic base, the school is very much concerned with an holistic approach for each child – encouraging good manners, respect for others and a keen sense of humour. Children take part in a great variety of extracurricular activities at lunch times, after school and at weekends. Older children are given the opportunity to take on responsibilities around the school – every child becomes a Monitor at some stage in their final year. The school hopes that the children will in time become successful adults who will make a difference in the 21st century.

Children are assessed for entry at the age of six/seven, visiting the school in small groups and testing by the Head and Head of Transition is friendly and low key. Once accepted, pupils have guaranteed transfer to Bancroft's Senior School (on the same site) at the age of eleven. Bancroft's Prep School offers up to two Francis Bancroft's means-tested awards for pupils entering the School at the age of 7 each year. These are awarded based on disclosure of family finances and performance in the entrance tests; these only cover Prep School fees.

The administration of the Prep School and Senior School are closely linked and the Head and Assistant Head of the Prep School are members of the Senior Management Team of Bancroft's School.

In 2013 the Prep School was inspected and the school was delighted with the excellent report in which they were awarded the top grade in most areas. The full report can be read by visiting the ISI website: www.isi.net.

Charitable status. Bancroft's School is a Registered Charity, number 1068532. It exists to provide a rounded academic education for able children.

Barfield School & Nursery

Guildford Road, Farnham, Surrey GU10 1PB

Tel: 01252 782271
Fax: 01252 781480
email: admin@barfieldschool.com
website: www.barfieldschool.com

Barfield School is part of the Cothill Trust.

Chairman of the Board of Trustees: Dr Ralph Townsend

Headmaster: **Mr James Reid**, BEd Hons

Age Range. 2–13 Co-educational.
Number of Children. 190.
Fees per term (2018–2019). Prep £4,600–£4,750, Pre-Prep £3,220–£3,400, Nursery £1,116–£3,880.

Barfield School, set in 12 acres of beautiful grounds, was awarded "Excellent" in all eight areas of inspection by the ISI in 2016. The school is co-educational and takes children between the ages of 2 and 13 years.

The Nursery is an integral part of the school and is bright and airy, with plenty of green space. Open 50 weeks of the year from 8.00 am to 6.15 pm, experienced and qualified staff nurture, encourage and support all the children, ensuring they feel both happy and secure in our care. The children have use of all the school facilities and access to specialist teachers for swimming and music.

Barfield School has an excellent reputation for high academic standards and caring staff. Facilities include an Auditorium, ICT Suite, Library, Music and Music practice rooms, Cookhouse, Art and DT rooms. The school has a flourishing PE and Outdoor Pursuits Department, with most major and minor sports covered. There is a magnificent indoor heated swimming pool and children are encouraged to participate in a wide range of extracurricular activities. Activity courses are run throughout the school holidays and are enjoyed by children from Reception to Year 8.

Children are taught in small classes and are prepared for Common Entrance and Scholarship examinations, as well as Grammar School entry.

Visitors are always welcome. Please contact the school.

Charitable status. Barfield School is part of the Cothill Trust, which is a Registered Charity, number 309639.

Barlborough Hall School

Preparatory School to Mount St Mary's College

Park Street, Barlborough, Chesterfield, Derbyshire S43 4ES

Tel:	01246 810511
email:	headteacher@barlboroughhallschool.com
website:	www.barlboroughhallschool.com
Twitter:	@BarlboroughHall

Chair of Governors: Fr Adrian Porter SJ

Headteacher: **Mrs Karen Keeton**

Age Range. 3–11 Co-educational.
Number of Pupils. 210.
Fees per term (2018–2019). £2,645–£3,595.

Barlborough Hall School is a co-educational preparatory school in the Jesuit Catholic tradition, welcoming pupils aged 3–11 of all denominations. The preparatory school to nearby Mount St Mary's College (11–18), Barlborough is set in over 300 acres of parkland.

Barlborough became a school in 1939 and is built around an Elizabethan manor house which now houses many of the teaching rooms. The school encourages children to develop their talents in many different areas: academic, social, spiritual and physical with a strong focus on the individual. Academically, pupils achieve success through small classes, low pupil to teacher ratios and setting from Year 3 onwards. Teaching facilities ensure that children receive a traditional preparatory school education and include a science laboratory, technology lab and ICT suite. Pupils learn French from Nursery and most pupils learn Latin in Years 5 and 6.

All pupils receive pastoral care and academic tutoring through their form teachers, under the leadership of the Key Stage Coordinators. There is a clear sense of progression from Pre-Prep, situated in its own distinct area with its own playground, to the Upper School, which allows pupils to develop greater independence but still within a nurturing environment. There is a Jesuit chaplain who works closely with the teachers on the Chaplaincy team.

Emphasis is placed on developing the whole person, and the school enjoys an impressive reputation for its sport and music. There is an indoor heated swimming pool, dance studio and extensive games fields, and pupils enjoy a wide range of sports. Barlborough Hall is well-established on the rugby, football, hockey and netball circuit and plays regularly against other schools. Many pupils learn instruments from skilled peripatetic teachers and the school's music teacher leads prize-winning choirs and an orchestra. Drama also flourishes, with a major production every year in the school's theatre.

There are many extracurricular activities, allowing pupils to develop their interests in a wide range of fields. Pupils are encouraged to take part in at least two activities a week and have the option to attend Saturday school, where they are able to enjoy hobbies in a more relaxed environment or practise for team sports. The wide range of activities available includes Chess, Ballroom Dancing, Art, Drama and Touch Typing. Pupils can also stay after school every evening to do homework under teacher supervision.

For further details of the admissions process and a prospectus, please contact the admissions team at admissions@ barlboroughhallschool.com.

Barlborough Hall pupils can automatically transfer at age 11 to Mount St Mary's College (*see entry HMC section*).

Charitable status. Mount St Mary's is a Registered Charity, number 1117998.

Barnard Castle Preparatory School

Westwick Road, Barnard Castle, County Durham DL12 8UW

Tel:	01833 696032
Fax:	01833 696034
email:	prep@barneyschool.org.uk
website:	www.barnardcastleschool.org.uk

Chairman of Governors: Mr P Mothersill

Head: **Mrs Laura Turner**, MA

Age Range. 4–11 years.
Number of Pupils. 187 girls and boys, including 9 boarders.
Fees per term (2018–2019). Prep: £6,710 (Boarders), £3,465 (Day). Pre-Prep: £2,288.

Barnard Castle Preparatory School is the junior school of Barnard Castle School and offers an all-round, high-quality education for boys and girls aged between 4 and 11 years. The School offers both day and boarding places and is situated in a beautiful setting on the edge of a traditional English market town.

The campuses of the two schools are adjoining, allowing shared use of many excellent facilities. At the same time the Preparatory School is able to provide a separate, stimulating environment, with small classes, a wide range of extracurricular activities and an exciting school excursion programme. The school has recently benefited from an extensive building and refurbishment programme. This has included the construction of 3 new classrooms and a Science Laboratory.

The School is well served by a bus network system and a breakfast club and after-school supervision is readily available. The boarders reside in a newly developed boarding house, which creates a warm and friendly environment supported by a full range of facilities including the School's medical centre. Flexi boarding from 2–4 nights is also available.

Our Director of Studies oversees a carefully designed, broad and balanced curriculum. Sport, drama and music occupy important places in the life of the School. All children have numerous opportunities to participate in each of these, as well as in an extensive co-curricular programme. The School also offers a qualified learning support service to those children who require further assistance.

Charitable status. Barnard Castle School is a Registered Charity, number 1125375. Its aim is the education of boys and girls.

Barnardiston Hall Preparatory School

Barnardiston, Nr Haverhill, Suffolk CB9 7TG

Tel:	01440 786316
Fax:	01440 786355
email:	registrar@barnardiston-hall.co.uk
website:	www.barnardiston-hall.co.uk

Headmaster: **Mr K A Boulter**, MA Cantab, PGCE

Deputy Headmaster: Mr T Cooper, MEd, BA Hons, PGCE

Registrar: Mrs L P Gundersen

Bursar: Mrs A Gregory

Age Range. Co-educational 6 months–13 years.
Number of Pupils. Day 180, Boarding (full and weekly) 27.
Fees per term (2018–2019). Day Pupils £1,400–£4,465; Weekly Boarders £6,170; Full Boarders £6,695.

Barnardiston Hall, set in 36 acres of grounds on the borders of Suffolk, Essex and Cambridge, offers an individual all-round education for boys and girls, both day and boarding. High standards are achieved by small classes taught by graduate and teacher-trained staff, a caring approach and close liaison with parents.

The School has good facilities, including a Nursery, a Pre-Preparatory Block and Art Room / CDT complex, a very modern and well-equipped computer room, assembly hall, music room, science laboratory, library, tennis/netball courts, astroturf and extensive sports fields. For the boarders, the dormitories are bright, uncluttered and home-like.

The curriculum is designed to allow pupils to reach Common Entrance standards in the appropriate subjects. The best of traditional methods are mixed with modern ideas to provide an enjoyable and productive learning environment. French and computers are taught from the age of 3; Latin from age 7. The School is CReSTeD registered. It has received outstanding gradings in ISI reports for both welfare and education. Pupils go on to a wide range of secondary schools.

Sports in the Michaelmas and Lent Terms are hockey, swimming (Pre-Prep only) and cross-country/orienteering for all pupils, rugby for the boys and netball for the girls. During the Summer, all do athletics, cricket/rounders, and tennis/short tennis. The School has won the National Orienteering Championships for the last six years.

There is a wide range of clubs and societies including 3 choirs, an orchestra, recorders, chess, painting, drama, carpentry, air rifle, cookery and pottery. Ballet, speech and drama, piano, guitar, woodwind, violin, brass, string and singing lessons are also offered.

Throughout the term, there are weekend activities for boarders (optional for day pupils) which include mountain walking. Derbyshire Dales at 6, Ben Nevis at 8, camping, visits to museums/historic buildings and other places of interest and theatre trips. There is an annual trip to Europe. Some pupils aged 7+ have reached Everest Base Camp.

Barrow Hills School

Roke Lane, Witley, Godalming, Surrey GU8 5NY

Tel:	01428 683639
email:	info@barrowhills.org
website:	www.barrowhills.org
Twitter:	@BarrowHills
Facebook:	@Barrow-Hills-School

Chairman of the Governors: Mrs Justine Voisin

Headmaster: Mr Sean Skehan, BA, PGCE, MA, NPQH

Age Range. 2–13.
Number of Pupils. 220.
Fees per term (2018–2019). Tuition: £3,344–£5,120 (including meals). Nursery and Kindergarten according to sessions.

Barrow Hills School believes in having a long and happy childhood. This demands the highest standards of pastoral care and academics, underpinned by core values. We follow the Catholic ethos of education: educate the whole child, find out what they are good at and celebrate this in the school community. To achieve this aim we have a broad and deep curriculum, increasingly specialist taught, as children progress through the school. Ability in specific subject areas is identified and supported. We are a 'totally connected' school and have provided Samsung tablets with digital s-pens for every child in the prep department. Access to tablets is also provided for younger pupils along with Wi-Fi, large screen digital displays and air printers across the school. Resources are cloud based and we have our own encrypted site on Google, running Google apps for education. Our children have a full childhood; they are encouraged to be themselves and take risks with their learning. All we do is underpinned by our values of kindness, honesty, empathy, fortitude and charitable works. Music and theatre is in our DNA and our children are part of a culture that sees everyone, every year, be part of a production. Sport matters too, and by Year 3 all children have five hours of sport a week including, whenever possible, competitive matches against rival schools. The major team sports are: hockey, netball, rounders, tennis, cricket, swimming and some lacrosse for girls; football, rugby, hockey, swimming and cricket for boys. We offer an 11+ scholarship programme with scholarships in Art, Music, Drama, Sport, Academic and All-Rounder for exceptional candidates worth up to 30% of fees. We have strong links with excellent senior schools, in particular with King Edward's Witley, our partner school, and many of our children are awarded scholarships. We are proud of our 100% success at Common Entrance with all children gaining entry to their chosen senior school at 13+. We offer broad range of extracurricular activities and a comprehensive programme of educational and residential visits.

Barrow Hills School is an independent co-educational Catholic day school for children of all denominations aged 2 to 13 years. Our main building is an attractive Arts and Crafts house, and we have 33 acres of beautiful gardens, playing fields and woods in the Surrey Hills countryside. We are close to Guildford, Godalming and Haslemere. Key entry points: Nursery, Kindy, Reception, Year 3 and Year 7.

Charitable status. Barrow Hills School Witley is a Registered Charity, number 311997.

Bassett House School

60 Bassett Road, London W10 6JP

Tel:	020 8969 0313
email:	info@bassetths.org.uk
website:	www.bassetths.org.uk
Twitter:	@bassetths
Facebook:	@Bassett-House-School

Motto: *Quisque pro sua parte ~ From each to the best of his or her ability*

Chairman of Governors: Mr Anthony Rentoul

Head: Mrs Philippa Cawthorne

Age Range. 3–11 Co-educational.
Number of Pupils. 190.
Fees per term (2018–2019). Nursery (5 mornings) £2,950, Pre-Prep £5,900, Prep £6,150.

Bassett House School was founded in 1947 and takes both boys and girls from the age of 3 or 4 until age 11. Entry is, in the younger years, non-selective and the school has some 190 pupils in thirteen classes.

Philippa Cawthorne, the headmistress, believes she has "yet to meet a child who isn't naturally curious. It's our job to develop this curiosity so it becomes a lifelong love of learning." The school believes in a regime of creativity, encouragement and reward, but firstly ensures every child feels secure and welcome. Children blossom when they feel happy and valued, and nurturing individuality is at the heart of the school's teaching philosophy – this leads to outstanding results.

Bassett House School also teaches the value of endeavour and of staying power, of developing social skills and forming respectful relationships. It has an extensive programme of extra-curricular activities and clubs, day outings and residential trips, as well as a lively schedule of music, drama and sports.

Bassett House provides a thorough and broad educational grounding following the national curriculum and embracing different teaching techniques (including Montessori). The school has invested heavily in the latest classroom technology to give teachers additional tools to make learning lively, fun and effective. It has specialist teachers in maths, English, science, computing, French, music, physical education, art/design technology, eurhythmics, Latin and dance.

The school was built towards the end of the 19th century and what was originally designed as a large family house now provides modern spacious and airy classrooms. The school premises include use of a separate annex comprising an assembly hall with a stage and gymnasium, three classrooms, a kitchen and a garden. The main school building has a playground and the school also uses excellent local play and sports facilities.

Beachborough

Westbury, Nr Brackley, Northants NN13 5LB
Tel: 01280 700071
Fax: 01280 704839
email: office@beachborough.com
website: www.beachborough.com

Chairman of Governors: Mrs S Barrett

Headmaster: Mr Christian Pritchard, MA, BA Hons QTS

Age Range. 2½–13.
Number of Children. Main School 225 (40% flexi boarding), Pre-Prep 150.
Fees per term (2018–2019). Prep School: Years 5–8 £5,615, Years 3–4 £5,150, Reception, Years 1 & 2 £3,576. Nursery £301 per session per term. Flexi boarding from £35 per night.

Beachborough is a friendly and energetic Independent Prep School ideally situated on the borders of Buckingham-

shire, Oxfordshire and Northamptonshire. We provide an outstanding all-round education for around 300 boys and girls, a quarter of whom take advantage of our flexible boarding provision. We are large enough to have a diverse and lively community, yet small enough for each individual to be known and nurtured.

We believe that a good prep school education will give children opportunities that will equip them intellectually, physically, culturally and emotionally for the challenges of the twenty-first century. At whatever stage your child joins us, be it Early Years (pupils aged 2½ to 5), Pre-Prep (pupils aged 6 to 7) or Prep School (pupils aged 8 to 13) they will be warmly welcomed into the school. We are not obsessed with reflecting on past glories or the latest headline-grabbing news, but have an active desire to find each child's individual talent and help them surpass their personal best. Our parents use words such as inclusive, nurturing and rounded to define our school, so if you share in our belief that happy children thrive, please come and visit.

Charitable status. Beachborough is a Registered Charity, number 309910.

The Beacon

Chesham Bois, Amersham, Bucks HP6 5PF
Tel: 01494 433654
email: office@beaconschool.co.uk
website: www.beaconschool.co.uk
Twitter: @Beacon_School
Facebook: @beaconschoolamersham

Chairman of the Governors: David M Hollander

Headmaster: William T Phelps, MA New York, BA AKC King's College London

Age Range. 4–13.
Number of Boys. 530.
Fees per term (2018–2019). Upper School (Years 7 & 8) £5,750, Middle School (Years 5 & 6) £5,500–£5,700, Lower School (Years 3 & 4) £5,250, Pre-Prep (Years 1 & 2) £4,300, Reception £3,950.

The Beacon is an independent day school for boys aged 4 to 13 years. The Beacon prepares boys for secondary education through a curriculum that offers both richness and diversity of opportunity. From the earliest steps in initial learning, to independent success in competitive examinations, the priority is to ensure sound academic development, within a happy and stimulating environment. The Beacon is proud to prepare its boys for entry to over 26 senior independent day and boarding schools, with a variety of academic, music, drama, art and sport scholarships being won each year. The school also enjoys impressive success at 11+ for entry into Buckinghamshire Grammar Schools.

The ethos of The Beacon is encapsulated in the words: *Traditional Values, Contemporary Education, World-Class Experience.* Over 500 boys are educated in extremely well-resourced buildings; a blend of old: 17th century farmstead and barns; and new: including a 200-seat Theatre, a Design and Technology Suite, Food Technology Room, Science Laboratories, Drama Studio, Music Technology Suite, two Libraries, a large Sports Hall and an AstroTurf, set in attractive surroundings, with 16 acres of playing fields.

There are three Reception classes with a maximum of 18 boys in each. Each class teacher has an assistant.

There is a second entry point in Year 3 at age 7, when boys join the Lower School and a fourth class is added. Class sizes are a maximum of 20. Boys study a broad range of subjects, including International Studies from Year 2 to Year 5, examining nine of the world's most spoken languages and associated cultures, including Mandarin and Russian, Spanish and French.

The third entry point is in Year 7 at age 11, where boys are prepared for the Prep School Baccalaureate, Common Entrance and scholarship examinations to many leading independent Senior Schools. In Year 8, boys take on leadership roles and demonstrate greater responsibility and independence.

Sport at The Beacon is all-inclusive and exemplifies teamwork, emphasising the school ethos that everybody matters. Boys regularly compete at County level in cricket, hockey, tennis, swimming and rugby. The Beacon has an excellent record of success in the many national and regional competitions.

The Music Department has numerous choirs (including a parents choir), ensembles and clubs, individual music scholarship mentoring and music technology work on LogicPro. There are 26 visiting music teachers with over 300 weekly music lessons taking place. Beacon Voices choirs tour regularly to countries around the world.

Performing Arts is another key strength of the School, with every boy given a chance to perform throughout the year in a range of productions, showcases, playlets and also at The Edinburgh Festival.

Charitable status. The Beacon Educational Trust Limited is a Registered Charity, number 309911. It exists to provide education for boys.

Beaudesert Park School

Minchinhampton, Stroud, Gloucestershire GL6 9AF

Tel: 01453 832072
email: office@bps.school
website: www.beaudesert.gloucs.sch.uk
Twitter: @beaudesertpark • @beaudesertsport
Facebook: @Beaudesert-Park-School

Chairman of Governors: M C S-R Pyper, OBE, BA

Headmaster: **C Searson**, BA

Age Range. 3–13.
Number of Pupils. Weekly and Flexi Boarders 146, Day Boys and Girls 180, Pre-Prep Department 108.
Fees per term (2018–2019). Nursery from £1,915 (5 mornings or 3 days); Reception £3,065; Years 1 & 2 £3,188; Year 3 £4,200; Year 4 £4,967; Years 5–8 £5,887. Boarders (Years 5–8) £7,559. Flexi boarding £38 per night. All fees include lunch. Boarding and flexi boarding fees also include breakfast and supper.

The School was founded in 1908 and became an educational trust in 1968.

Beaudesert Park is a preparatory school for boys and girls from 3–13. There is a strong academic tradition and all pupils are encouraged to work to the best of their ability. There is great emphasis on effort and all children are praised for their individual performance. Pupils are prepared for Common Entrance and Scholarship examinations. They are given individual attention in classes which are mostly setted not streamed. Over the last five years an average of 12 scholarships a year – academic, art, music, sport and technology – have been awarded to leading independent senior schools. The teaching staff, all of whom take a personal interest in the children's welfare, consists of 84 full-time teaching staff and 21 peripatetic staff, of which 19 are music teachers, and the other two are LAMDA teachers.

Good manners and consideration for others are a priority. Beaudesert strives to create a happy and purposeful atmosphere, providing for the talents of each child in a wide range of activities – cultural, sporting and recreational. There are thriving music, drama, art and pottery departments. Sporting activities include cricket, football, rugby, hockey, netball, rounders, tennis, swimming, athletics, golf, badminton, fencing, dance, judo, riding and sailing. A wide number of societies and clubs meet each week, with a choice of 30+ extra-curricular activities on offer each term.

The school is very well equipped with a brand new library and a very high spec, multi-functional performing arts centre (shortlisted for a RIBA award when launched), as well as three science labs, indoor and outdoor swimming pools, sports hall, art studio and design technology department. There are also astroturf tennis courts and hard courts which are situated in beautiful wooded grounds within the 30-acre site, as well as 15 acres of sports fields. The school stands high up in the Cotswolds adjoining 500 acres of common land and golf course. Despite its rural location, the school is within half an hour of the M4 and M5 motorways and within easy reach of the surrounding towns of Gloucester, Cheltenham, Cirencester, Swindon, Bath and Bristol.

Charitable status. Beaudesert Park is a Registered Charity, number 311711. It exists to provide education for boys and girls in a caring atmosphere.

Bede's Preparatory School

Duke's Drive, Eastbourne, East Sussex BN20 7XL

Tel: 01323 734222
email: prep.school@bedes.org
website: www.bedes.org
Twitter: @bedesprep
Facebook: @bedesprepschool

Co-educational day and boarding school with Nursery and Pre-Prep departments.

Chair of Governors: Mrs Geraldine Watkins, JP

Headmaster: **Giles Entwisle**, BA Hons

Deputy Head: Ben Purkiss, BSc Hons

Age Range. 3 months–13 years Co-educational.
Number of Pupils. 363: Prep 234, Pre-Prep 44 (166 Boys, 112 Girls); Nursery 85; Boarders: 23.
Fees per term (2018–2019). Boarding £2,750 (in addition to Tuition); Tuition: Prep £4,680–£5,800, Pre-Prep £3,410. Nursery prices per session.

Bede's Prep School, founded in 1895, is situated in Eastbourne, on the South Coast with spectacular views of the sea. It takes a couple of minutes to reach the beach from the school and the principal playing fields are in a wide natural hollow nestling in the South Downs.

Boarders sleep in cosy bedrooms in a house that has a real family feel and are looked after by dedicated and caring staff. Both winter and summer weekends are filled with an exciting variety of activities and special celebrations take place on the children's birthdays.

Pupils are prepared for Common Entrance and the more able are tutored to sit scholarships to independent senior schools. Last year 95% of pupils chose to continue their education at Bede's Senior School (*see HMC section entry*).

Bede's offers academic, sport, music, dance, art and drama scholarships and bursaries for children from the ages of 7 to 12 years.

Pupils from the age of 4 are given Information Technology lessons at least once a week in a Computer Centre which is constantly updated to keep at the forefront of educational technology. French and Music, Short Tennis and other Sports are also introduced to children in this age group.

In 2009 a beautiful new building overlooking the sea and housing new kitchens and dining room and eight new classrooms opened.

In January 2016, a newly expanded nursery facility opened with a state-of-the-art baby unit for babies from 3 months upwards and expanded provision for toddlers. This was followed by the launch of the school's Pre School Scheme with two classrooms, a messy activity area and free flow access to a new outside play area.

The Art Department is very strong, opening for afterschool activities to encourage young talent. Music also plays an important role at Bede's. There is a thriving orchestra and the majority of pupils learn one or more instruments, with children as young as six playing in recorder groups. Informal concerts take place during the school year and there are also several choirs.

Drama forms an integral part of the school. The Pre-Prep produces a Christmas play and there are frequent productions throughout the year for older children to take part in.

Sport at Bede's is taken seriously. Boys play soccer, rugby, hockey, cricket, tennis and athletics and the major sports for girls are netball, hockey, rounders, athletics, cricket and tennis. All the pupils use the indoor 20-metre swimming pool. The fixture list is very comprehensive and, whilst the top teams enjoy a high standard of coaching and performance, special emphasis is placed on ensuring that the other teams also have the opportunity to play matches against other schools. The Sports Hall covers two indoor tennis courts and is used to house a huge variety of sports. Wet weather activities include badminton, basketball, climbing and table tennis. Children also regularly use facilities at the Senior School nearby.

There is a Learning Enhancement department staffed by qualified learning support staff which can cater for pupils who require additional or particular support. The school also has an EAL centre which is run by highly trained and experienced staff. Gifted children are placed on a Curriculum Enhancement Programme to maximise their potential.

The School operates a comprehensive programme of activities after lessons which children are encouraged to participate in ranging from fencing to cookery and basketball to art masterclasses.

The school runs a comprehensive coach and minibus service locally and transport to and from Gatwick and Heathrow airports is arranged by the transport department.

Entry to Bede's Prep School is by interview.

Charitable status. St Bede's School Trust Sussex is a Registered Charity, number 278950. It exists to provide education for boys and girls.

Bedford Girls' School Junior School

Cardington Road, Bedford, Bedfordshire MK42 0BX

Tel: 01234 361918
email: admissions@bedfordgirlsschool.co.uk
website: www.bedfordgirlsschool.co.uk
Twitter: @BedfordGirlsSch
Facebook: @BedfordGirlsSch

Foundation – The Harpur Trust.

"Let me keep an open mind so I understand as much as I can in my lifetime and not reach the limits of my imagination."

Chair of Governors: Ms T Beddoes

Head of Bedford Girls' School: Miss J MacKenzie

Head of Bedford Girls' School Junior School: Mrs C Howe

Age Range. 7–11.
Number of Pupils. 230 Girls.
Fees per term (2018–2019). £3,146.

Bedford Girls' School is a dynamic, forward-thinking selective independent day school for girls aged 7–18. As an exceptional school, we value creativity and innovation highly. From Years 3 to Sixth Form, it is our belief that learning should be exciting and lifelong, so that girls leave us fully equipped academically, personally, emotionally, and as morally fulfilled individuals capable of achieving their full potential in every aspect and at every stage of their lives.

This journey begins in the Junior School where our expert teachers recognise and ignite the curiosity of each individual girl, harnessing her natural curiosity and fuelling her confidence to develop her own thoughts, opinions and talents. In consequence, pupils not only excel academically but also as well-rounded, insightful, caring girls with a joy and passion for life and learning.

The atmosphere of our school is unique and exciting. Classrooms fizz with energy and enthusiasm and each day brings forth new discoveries and achievements. We would be delighted to welcome you to visit, either for one of our Open House events or a private tour, to experience at first hand a true flavour of life at Bedford Girls' School. Please visit www.bedfordgirlsschool.co.uk for further information or contact our Admissions Team: Tel: 01234 361918, email: admissions@bedfordgirlsschool.co.uk.

Admissions. Entry to the Junior School is based on online assessment in Mathematics, English and a creative writing task. Entry to the Senior School is based on interview, online assessments in Mathematics and English, and a Verbal Reasoning paper. Sixth Form entry is based on interviews, Verbal Reasoning, and GCSE results. A Reference from the Head of the student's current school is required for all candidates.

Charitable status. Bedford Girls' School is part of the Harpur Trust which is a Registered Charity, number 1066861.

Bedford Modern Junior School

Manton Lane, Bedford, Bedfordshire MK41 7NT

Tel: 01234 332513
email: info@bedmod.co.uk
website: www.bedmod.co.uk
Twitter: @BedfordModern
Facebook: @BedfordModernSchool

Chair of Governors: Sally Peck, OBE

Head of Junior School: Mrs J C Rex, BA Hons, PGCE

Deputy Head of Junior School: Mrs P S Pacyna, BA Hons, QTS
Director of Studies: Mrs K Harpin, BA Hons
Junior School Head's Assistant: Mrs K Smith
Head of Junior School Sports Development; Mr T W Bucktin, BSc, PGCE

Age Range. 7–11 Co-educational.
Number of Pupils. 253 (M: 55%; F: 45%).
Fees per term (2018–2019). £3,257.

The Junior School is housed in its own separate building adjacent to the Senior School. Facilities include specialist rooms for Art and Science, ICT, Design Technology and a newly refurbished Library, with designated Year 3 classrooms and play area and a superb state-of-the-art School Hall.

The whole site overlooks the School playing fields and the Junior School has extensive views over the Ouse Valley. Many of the Senior School facilities are available to the Junior School, including full use of the playing fields, Sports Hall, Gymnasium, covered and heated Swimming Pool and all-weather pitches. The Howard Hall provides facilities for full-scale drama productions and use is made of the Music School.

There is a strong musical, dramatic and sporting tradition.

Students are admitted to the Junior School at ages 7, 8, 9 and 10, after taking tests, some of them on computer, in January each year in English, Maths and non-verbal reasoning. Students proceed to the Senior School at 11, unless special circumstances prevent this.

(*See Bedford Modern School entry in HMC section.*)

Charitable status. Bedford Modern School is part of the Harpur Trust which is a Registered Charity, number 1066861. It includes in its aims the provision of high quality education for boys and girls.

Bedford Preparatory School

De Parys Avenue, Bedford MK40 2TU

Tel: 01234 362216
email: prepadmissions@bedfordschool.org.uk
website: www.bedfordschool.org.uk
Twitter: @bedfordschool
Facebook: @Bedford-School

Chairman of Governors: Sir Clive Loader, KCB, OBE, ADC, FRAeS

Headmaster: **Mr Ian Silk**

Deputy Head (*Academic*): Mr Jonathan Egan

Age Range. 7–13.
Number of Boys. Day Boys 384, Boarders 16, Weekly Boarders 5.
Fees per term (2018–2019). Day £4,111–£5,387, Full Boarding £7,316–£8,689, Weekly Boarding £6,973–£8,346.

Bedford Prep School is a thriving and vibrant independent day and boarding school for boys aged 7–13.

We believe that boys learn best when they're happy, confident, and their curiosity is stimulated, so we feel it's paramount that learning is fun, creative, inspirational and active. We also recognise boys learn differently from girls and this informs our teaching.

Whether it's music and the arts, science and technology, language and literature, or sports and games, boys are encouraged to learn new skills and embrace new experiences.

Visit our classes and you'll find boys thoroughly engaged in their learning, inspired by challenge, competition, high expectations and risk within a safe environment. Our expectations are high but achievable, and our curriculum encompasses and transcends the National Curriculum, uniting traditional practice with innovative teaching and the best of the creative and academic.

Our extensive campus offers boys outstanding academic, sporting, music, drama and art facilities. We share the swimming pool, recreation centre, playing fields, Astro and tennis courts with the Upper School and make use of the school's fantastic theatre and other specialist facilities.

Working with each and every boy, we help them to develop their sporting talents. We provide expert coaching in a wide variety of sports, including rugby, hockey, cricket, golf, skiing, horse riding, cross country, swimming, badminton and rowing.

Creative arts are a big part of school life, with boys taking part in concerts, exhibitions and performances throughout the year. In our dedicated music building, with a state-of-the-art music technology suite and well-equipped practice rooms, many of our boys learn to play one or more instruments.

Boys can also get involved in a broad range of extracurricular activities: from cookery to steel band, chess to canoe building – there is something for every boy.

A full range of wrap-around care options is available to working parents. Boys can stay at school, free of charge, until 5.45 pm in our Late Room or join one of our before and after school 'Day Plus' sessions.

Eagle House, our purpose-built junior boarding house, is a real home from home for our boarders, who flourish in its warm, family atmosphere. Full, weekly, flexi and occasional boarding is available, enabling boys and their parents to find an option that is just right.

Admissions. Entrance assessments for the Prep School are held during the Spring Term and all boys are assessed in English, Maths and underlying ability. We will also request a report from your son's current school.

We recommend that families come and visit us to see the school in action and meet the boys and staff. Please call admissions on 01234 362216 or email: prepadmissions@bedfordschool.org.uk to arrange a visit or request a prospectus.

Charitable status. Bedford Preparatory School is part of the Harpur Trust, which is a Registered Charity, number 1066861.

Beechwood Park

Markyate, St Albans, Hertfordshire AL3 8AW

Tel: 01582 840333
Fax: 01582 842372
email: admissions@beechwoodpark.com
website: www.beechwoodpark.com
Twitter: @BWPSchool
Facebook: @BWPSchool

Chairman of Governors: Mr G Freer

Headmaster: **Mr Edward Balfour**, BA Hons, PGCE

Age Range. 3–13.
Number of Pupils. 538: 50 boarders (aged 9–13), 269 day boys and 219 day girls (aged 3–13), including 41 preschool children at the Woodlands Nursery which is housed in new purpose-built premises on the main school site.
Fees per term (2018–2019). Day pupils: Senior £5,510, Middle £4,445, Junior £4,345, Reception £3,675. Boarders (up to 4 nights per week in addition to day fees) £1,310. No compulsory extras. Fees are inclusive of lunches, most trips and visits.

Beechwood Park occupies a large mansion, with a fine Regency Library and Great Hall, in 37 acres of surrounding grounds, which provide ample space for the Forest School.

Modernisation has added Science laboratories, computer suites, Design Technology workshop, gymnasium and sports facilities, including a large sports hall and two squash courts, hard tennis courts, an all-weather pitch and two heated indoor swimming pools. Boarding House with modern facilities and spacious common rooms. Two purpose-built classroom blocks house the Middle and Junior Departments. The Music Department has a song room, 14 practice rooms and a newly-opened Music Technology Suite. A large Performance Hall provides space for assemblies and the many music and drama productions.

Many day pupils use private buses serving Harpenden, St Albans, Dunstable and the surrounding villages. Many subsequently convert to boarding under the care of the Houseparents, Mr and Mrs R Humphreys.

Class size is around 20 (15 in Reception); major subjects are setted from Year 5 onwards. There is a resident Chaplain. The Director of Music has a staff of visiting instrumentalists in a flourishing Music Department.

The number of scholarships gained each year and Common Entrance results affirm a high standard of work, against a background of wide ranging extracurricular activities.

Football, Rugby, Cricket (boys and girls) Netball, Hockey, Swimming, Athletics and a Sport for All programme, which includes an unusually wide range of minor sports, are all coached by well-qualified PE Staff.

Charitable status. Beechwood Park School is a Registered Charity, number 311068. It exists to provide education for boys and girls from 3–13.

Beeston Hall School

West Runton, Cromer, Norfolk NR27 9NQ

Tel: 01263 837324
email: office@beestonhall.co.uk
website: www.beestonhall.co.uk

Chairman of Governors: T E Leicester

Headmaster: **W F de Falbe**, BA Hons, PGCE

Bursar: Mrs S Lubbock

Age Range. Co-educational 4–13 years.
Number of Pupils. 150: 60 Boarding, 90 Day Pupils. 76 Boys, 74 Girls.
Fees per term (2018–2019). Boarding: £6,300 (Year 3), £8,180 (Years 4–8); Day Pupils: £2,950 (Pre-Prep), £4,190 (Year 3), £6,090 (Years 4–8).

Beeston Hall was established in 1948 in a Regency house set in 30 acres in North Norfolk, close to the sea and surrounded by 700 acres of National Trust land. Beeston has a reputation for being a cheerful, family school, with a focus on achievement arising out of happiness and confidence. Kindness and courtesy, alongside hard work and awareness of others, underpin all aspects of life at Beeston, where children are encouraged to maximise their potential and think and act for themselves.

The strength of the pastoral care system ensures that every child is closely watched over and cared for. Beeston has a boarding ethos (the majority full or weekly), with flexi for those progressing towards boarding; most children experience boarding before they leave.

Relatively non-selective, Beeston is proud of the value it adds, with most moving on to boarding schools such as Ampleforth, Eton, Downe House, Framlingham, Gresham's, Harrow, The Leys Cambridge, Oakham, Oundle, Queen Margaret's York, Radley, Repton, Rugby, Stephen Perse,

Shrewsbury, Stowe, Tudor Hall and Uppingham – and Norwich School, of course. The school enjoys great success at scholarship level, with over 66 scholarships won in the last 6 years.

In addition to the usual examinable subjects, art, music, DT, computing, PHSE, reasoning and theatre studies are all timetabled, providing children with a wealth of opportunities to find activities in which they can excel. Qualified EAL staff support overseas pupils and the Learning Support department of five qualified staff give help on a one-to-one basis and in the classroom.

Every child takes part in at least one production each year, with an emphasis on developing confidence through participation and presentation. Three choirs and ten music groups meet each week and over 80% of the school learn a musical instrument.

The school is equally proud of its record on the sports field where all children are coached, regardless of ability, by a dedicated team of staff, and are given the opportunity to represent the school. In 2016 cricket was introduced for girls and in 2017 they won 13 of 16 fixtures; both Under 11 and Under 13 girls reached IAPS national hockey finals as well. In addition to the usual major sports, children compete in cross country, athletics, swimming, tennis, fencing and sailing (IAPS champions in 2018), whilst a comprehensive activities programme provides opportunities to suit all tastes: shooting, martial arts, circus skills, archery, minibridge, chess, Scottish reels, yoga, cooking, scouts or coding, to name a few.

The **2017 ISI Inspection Report** comments thus: *"Pupils' attitudes to work are outstanding, nurtured by the high expectations of staff ...many awards also reflect pupils' exceptional achievements in areas such as sport, music, art, drama ...Pupils can apply their outstanding numeracy skills effectively across a range of subjects ...Pupils show outstanding social skills and are highly respectful of people ..."*

Religious denomination: Mainly Church of England; 15% Roman Catholic.

Charitable status. Beeston Hall School Trust Limited is a Registered Charity, number 311274. It exists to provide preparatory education for boarding and day boys and girls.

Belhaven Hill School

Belhaven Road, Dunbar, East Lothian EH42 1NN

Tel: 01368 862785
email: secretary@belhavenhill.com
website: www.belhavenhill.com
Facebook: @BelhavenHill

Joint Chairs of Governors: Camilla Gray-Muir & Alexander Dewar

Headmaster: **Henry Knight**, BA, PGCE, MEd

Age Range. 7–13 Co-educational.
Number of Pupils. 61 boys, 62 girls. Boarders 83, Day 40.
Fees per term (2018–2019). Boarding £7,920. Day: £5,625 (Form 6: £3,840).
Religion. Non-denominational.

Overlooking the sea in an idyllic East Lothian location, Belhaven Hill School is an independent full boarding and day school for boys and girls from 7 to 13 years. Since its establishment in 1923, the school has focused on developing well-rounded, happy, confident children through a strong academic curriculum, lots of sport and a broad extracurricular programme. Ideally placed just off the A1, it is close to both a mainline London-Edinburgh railway station, is only 30 miles from central Edinburgh and less than an hour to Edinburgh airport.

A full boarding and day school, Belhaven Hill has a long tradition of providing a first class all-round education before sending its pupils far and wide to all the leading public schools in both England and Scotland. These include Ampleforth, Eton, Fettes, Glenalmond, Harrow, Loretto, Marlborough, Merchiston, Oundle, Radley, Rugby, Sherborne, Stowe, Tudor Hall and Uppingham. Committed and enthusiastic members of staff work with small classes of between 10–16 pupils. There is ample opportunity for scholarship and extended work, resulting in an excellent number of awards being gained every year. A strong learning support department with three dedicated, trained staff provides one-to-one and small group tuition.

Belhaven Hill pupils are renowned for being happy children and this is in no small part due to the outstanding pastoral care provided. The majority of staff live on site and the policy of the governors has been to keep the school comparatively small in order to retain a family atmosphere. The boys are housed in the original main building and the girls in a separate, purpose-built house. The pastoral system revolves around the four patrols, with each pupil being looked after by their form teacher in the junior years and a personal tutor higher up the school. A full-time School Nurse and a team of matrons (day and night) take care of the children around the clock. The Headmaster's Wife is in overall charge of the pastoral care.

The school has an excellent reputation for sport with rugby, netball, hockey, cricket, rounders, tennis and athletics, making up the main part of the sporting programme. Swimming takes place from April to October in the school's heated outdoor pool. In addition many opportunities abound for a wide variety of other recreational activities: skiing, surfing, horse riding, golf on the adjacent links course and gardening for those who want to grow their own produce in the school's walled garden. An extensive Activity Programme offers something for everyone to discover and enjoy such as charity work, debating, 'mastermind', knitting, model-making, computer programming and coding, cookery, crafts, chess, Taekwondo, fencing, Girls' rugby, water polo, Highland dancing and reeling to name but a few.

Music and Drama flourish at Belhaven and every child has ample opportunity to perform in regular concerts and productions throughout the year. A stand-alone music building houses a vibrant department which caters for a wide range of instrumental ensembles and choirs. A high proportion of the children play one or more instruments, with specialist tuition provided by a team of peripatetic music staff.

The school is well resourced with purpose-built facilities, including an outdoor heated swimming pool, floodlit all-weather pitch, playing fields, sports hall, specialist music and art schools, attractive teaching rooms, two ICT suites and a library.

Belhaven begins with the belief that every child is an individual who has a talent and that it is their mission to foster both their individuality and abilities. To achieve these aims it places the child at the core of everything it does. By providing an environment that promotes enjoyment, exploration and nurturing of curiosity, each child grows to understand that they too are responsible for their learning, alongside staff and parents. As a result they grow to value and respect those around them, delighting in the achievements of others as well as their own. Qualities such as courtesy, tolerance, honesty and perseverance are all encouraged and celebrated, with the children understanding that it is better to have had a go and fail, than never to have tried at all.

Whether they are day pupils or boarders, all children benefit from a boarding school ethos of community and friendship, where challenges are plenty, but where a sense of fun and enjoyment pervades all.

The school welcomes a seven year-old entry and has an outdoor education element into its junior curriculum where children can learn more about their environment through practical, hands-on learning experiences.

Means-tested bursary support is available. Fee concessions are available for children of members of the armed forces. For a prospectus and more information please see our website www.belhavenhill.com or contact Alex Farquhar at secretary@belhavenhill.com.

Charitable status. Belhaven Hill School Trust Ltd is a Registered Charity, number SC007118. Its aim is to educate children in the full sense of the word.

Belmont
Mill Hill Preparatory School

The Ridgeway, Mill Hill Village, London NW7 4ED
Tel: 020 8906 7270
Fax: 020 8906 3519
email: office@belmontschool.com
website: www.millhill.org.uk/belmont

Interim Chair of the Court of Governors: Mr Elliot Lipton, BSc Hons, MBA, FRSA, FRICS

Head: Mr Leon Roberts, MA, PGCE

Senior Deputy Head (*Pastoral*): Mr P Symes, BSc, PGCE
Deputy Head (*Operations*): Mr J Fleet, BSc, PGCE
Deputy Head (*Academic*): Miss J Harrison, BSc, PGCE

Age Range. 7–13 Co-educational.
Number of Pupils. 285 Boys, 256 Girls.
Fees per term (2018–2019). £6,033 per term; £18,099 per annum.

Belmont Mill Hill Preparatory School is situated in the Green Belt on the borders of Hertfordshire and Middlesex, just ten miles from Central London. A part of the Mill Hill School Foundation which is set in 160 acres of beautiful grounds, Belmont stands in about 35 acres of its own woods and we take advantage of the truly rural environment by extending our learning to our own nature reserve and our Eco Garden. We provide a happy, secure and rich learning environment for boys and girls aged 7 to 13, the majority of whom move on at the end of Year 8 to the senior school, Mill Hill, which educates boys and girls from age 13 to 18.

At Belmont we have created a rigorous and diverse curriculum that goes well beyond the National Curriculum and gives your child the chance to excel in many areas. Our curriculum runs seamlessly through every school in the Foundation, and is designed to prepare your child for life in the 21st century. It teaches children to think creatively and critically, and builds flexible skills for a fast-changing world of new technologies. Our teachers are highly skilled, motivated and love their work. We use both traditional teaching and learning methods, and innovative approaches using IT, inquiry based projects and peer-to-peer learning.

The school has its own secure play areas and adventure playground and we regularly make use of the further facilities on offer at Mill Hill School, including sports fields, Five Courts, swimming pool and theatre.

The usual age of entry is at 7+ or 11+ but 8+, 9+ and 10 + entry is considered as vacancies occur.

Charitable status. The Mill Hill School Foundation is a Registered Charity, number 1064758. It exists to provide education for boys and girls.

Belmont Grosvenor School

Swarcliffe Hall, Birstwith, Harrogate, North Yorkshire HG3 2JG

Tel: 01423 771029
email: admin@belmontgrosvenor.co.uk
website: www.belmontgrosvenor.co.uk
Twitter: @BelmontGrosveno
Facebook: @BelmontGrosvenor

Chair of Governors: Mr Gordon Milne

Head: **Mrs Sophia Ashworth Jones**

Age Range. 3 months–11 years Co-educational.
Number of Pupils. 148.
Fees per term (2018–2019). Prep £3,610, Pre-Prep £3,050, Pre-Reception £350–£3,050. Nursery: Under 2s £31.50–£62.00 per session; Over 2s £29–£54 per session.

Belmont Grosvenor School is a magical place – a caring, friendly school where every child is nurtured and made to feel special.

Along with its Magic Tree Nursery, Belmont Grosvenor caters for boys and girls from three months to 11 years and is set in 20 acres of beautiful countryside just three miles from the centre of Harrogate, North Yorkshire.

One of our greatest strengths is the continuity of education we offer. We provide a rich, diverse, happy, and supportive learning environment, fostering each child's intellectual, creative, sporting, and personal development.

We encourage our children to enjoy and respect learning, to develop as effective communicators and as independent, critical thinkers and decision-makers, accept challenges, and appreciate and respect differences.

Each child at Belmont Grosvenor is valued both as an individual and as a member of the school community, and we offer them a range of educational opportunities to fulfil their ambitions and potential.

It is our goal that Belmont Grosvenor School children learn to live as informed, concerned and responsible members of society.

Our 20 acres of grounds ensure our children learn both inside and outside the classroom – our Forest Schools area is well used with weekly lessons on the timetable for Nursery youngsters to Year 2. We have the prestigious Silver Learning Outside the Classroom Mark which recognises how BGS uses its grounds, buildings and environment, and enhances the outdoor learning with clubs, trips and visits.

Learning outside the classroom is embedded in the school's curriculum and all children, from the youngest in Magic Tree Nursery to Year 6, make full use of its fields, woodland and outdoor facilities, which include an outdoor classroom and a logged Forest School area complete with parachute roof and campfire.

Belmont School

Feldemore, Holmbury St Mary, Dorking, Surrey RH5 6LQ

Tel: 01306 730852
Fax: 01306 731220
email: admissions@belmont-school.org

website: www.belmont-school.org
Twitter: @BelmontPrep
Facebook: @BelmontPreparatorySchool
LinkedIn: /helen-skrine-a33526134

Chairman of the Governors: Mr N Butcher

Headmistress: **Mrs H Skrine**, BA Hons Exeter, PGCE London, NPQH, FRSA

Age Range. 2–13.
Number of Pupils. 229 Boys and Girls: Day, Weekly and Flexible Boarding.
Fees per term (2018–2019). Day Pupils: Kindergarten, Transition & Pre-Reception (per morning/afternoon) £313, Reception £3,130, Years 1–2 £3,670, Years 3–4 £5,150, Years 5–6 £5,240, Years 7–8 £5,310. Boarding: £545 (1 night per week), £1,080 (2 nights per week), £1,565 (3 nights per week), £2,030 (4 nights per week, Monday to Thursday), £2,255 (5 nights per week, Sunday to Thursday).

Founded in London in 1880, the School is now established in 65 acres of wooded parkland overlooking the picturesque village of Holmbury St Mary, between Guildford and Dorking. The main house, Feldemore, was completely refurbished in the early 1990s so that the school now boasts an historic building with a purpose-built interior. Outstanding facilities include a brand new Early Years building, impressive sports hall, a well-equipped theatre, a state-of-the-art computer suite, newly-refurbished Science lab and woodland adventure courses. These, together with our friendly, talented staff and confident, happy boys and girls, make Belmont the very best choice you could make for your child.

We offer co-educational day education for boys and girls aged 2 to 13, and optional weekly boarding or flexible boarding arrangements.

Children qualify for 15 hours of Early Years funding from the term following their third birthday until the term following their fifth birthday. Extended day care is also available from 7.30 am until 6.30 pm.

Here, every child matters and we look to develop children as individuals, seeking to inspire and to unfurl the hidden strengths of every boy or girl. There is a happy, industrious atmosphere and high expectations pervade throughout all aspects of school life. In addition, we have a challenging curriculum and an extensive array of extracurricular opportunities which together are designed to captivate the imagination. Creativity is a particular strength of the school. The teaching staff is well qualified and healthy pupil: staff ratios have enabled us to develop a flexible setting system within a relatively small school.

We prepare children for Common Entrance and Scholarship examinations to a wide range of schools, and will assist children in preparing for other Senior Schools that have their own admissions procedures.

The curriculum covers all the required Common Entrance subjects plus Drama, Art, DT, IT, Music, PSHCE, PE and Games. Sports include Netball, Rugby, Football, Cross-Country, Hockey, Tennis, Swimming, Cricket, Athletics and Rounders.

Children in Year 1 and above attend for a half day or full day visit prior to entry. Further details can be obtained from the Registrar, Charlotte Smith on 01306 830852 or admissions@belmont-school.org.

Charitable status. Belmont School (Feldemore) Educational Trust Limited is a Registered Charity, number 312077.

Berkhamsted Pre-Prep

Chesham Road, Berkhamsted, Hertfordshire HP4 2SZ

Tel: 01442 358188 (Pre-Prep)
          01442 358276 (Berkhamsted Day Nursery)
email: preprepoffice@berkhamsted.com
website: www.berkhamsted.com
          www.berkhamsted.com/day-nursery/
Twitter: @BerkoPrePrep
Facebook: @berkhamstedschool

Chairman of Governors: Mr G C Laws

Principal: Mr Richard Backhouse, MA Cantab

Headteacher, Pre-Prep: **Ms Karen O'Connor**, BA, PGCE, NPQH

Age Range. 3–7 years Co-educational. Day Nursery: 5 months–3 years.
Number in School. 110 Boys, 91 Girls.
Fees per term (2018–2019). £3,455–£3,555 (including lunch).

Berkhamsted Pre-Prep is a co-educational independent day school for ages 3–7. Berkhamsted Pre-Prep offers a balanced approach to learning where children are equally nurtured and challenged to extend themselves. Taking risks and being adventurous in all aspects of school life underpin an ambition to aim high with integrity, for every individual child. The extensive grounds and innovative approach to learning which develop not only knowledge but also the skills of being a learner, ensure that the children bound into school excited and hungry to learn more. The family atmosphere, where experienced staff place pastoral care and wellbeing at the heart of school life, provides children with a safe and secure environment to grow emotionally and socially. In addition, children have opportunities to learn French, music, drama, dance, sport and art, all taught by specialist teachers, as well as an outdoor education that takes full advantage of our exceptional grounds.

Knowing that future success is dependent on the firm foundations of academic and personal growth, the excellent educational start at Pre-Prep enable children to progress through the family of schools at Berkhamsted and beyond, with key skills of leadership, independence and high levels of communication. Pupil voice and placing the child at the centre is seen in all aspects of school life with the evidence being considerate, empathetic and confident children who embrace every day with curiosity and a smile.

After-school clubs, outings and trips further enhance an exciting curriculum and extend children's experiences. Wrap-around care, from 07.30 to 18.30, supports parents and provides a healthy breakfast and home-from-home experience after a long day. Mini BASECAMP, our holiday activities camp at the school designed for 3–5 year olds, is also available every holiday from 07.30 to 18.30.

Berkhamsted Day Nursery (0–3+ years) is open 50 weeks per year from 07.30 to 18.30, and is situated on the school site. Children can join Berkhamsted Day Nursery from 5 months of age and can move on to Berkhamsted Pre-Prep, which is just next door. Berkhamsted Day Nursery caters for children up to the September that they begin in the Nursery class at Berkhamsted Pre-Prep (when they can use the school's out-of-hours clubs).

In June 2016, the Independent Schools Inspectorate found the quality and standards of the early years provision at Berkhamsted Day Nursery and Berkhamsted Pre-Prep to be '*outstanding*' across all five key areas. The ISI also concluded that "*All children make excellent, continuous progress in relation to their individual starting points and capabilities due to the nurturing and supportive environment that recognises each child as an individual*".

Berkhamsted Prep

Doctors Commons Road, Berkhamsted, Hertfordshire HP4 3DW

Tel: 01442 358201/2
Fax: 01442 358203
email: prepadmin@berkhamsted.com
website: www.berkhamsted.com/prep
Twitter: @berkhamstedprep
Facebook: @berkhamstedschool
LinkedIn: /berkhamstedschool

Chairman of Governors: Mr G C Laws

Principal: Mr R P Backhouse, MA Cantab

Head: **Mr J Hornshaw**, BEd Hons, MEd, NPQH, FInstLM

Deputy Head: Mr P D Whitby, BA, MA

Age Range. 7–11.
Number of Pupils. 162 boys, 179 girls.
Fees per term (2018–2019). £4,685–£4,990.

Berkhamsted Prep School is part of Berkhamsted School, a school with a 'Diamond' structure that combines single-sex and co-educational teaching. Boys and girls are taught together at the Pre-Prep (Haresfoot site) from age 3 to 7, and at the Prep (Doctors Commons Road site) from age 7 to 11. They are then taught separately from age 11 to 16 (Berkhamsted Boys and Berkhamsted Girls), before coming back together again in a joint Sixth Form.

Berkhamsted Prep School offers first-class facilities for the 7 to 11 age group, in conjunction with the highest standards of teaching and educational development. All classes offer a happy, caring environment where children are encouraged to investigate and explore the world around them. Classes at all levels have access to computers. Key features include a multi-purpose hall, modern dining facilities and a full range of specialist classrooms (e.g. Science laboratory, a DT and an ICT suite with mobile device accessibility for all year groups, Drama Studio, new Food Technology and Art classrooms). The school has also added a netball court, Eton Fives courts and an outdoor learning area. The Prep School also has use of Senior School facilities including extensive playing fields, tennis and netball courts, a Sports Centre, a swimming pool and a 500-seat theatre.

All children are encouraged to develop to their full potential and grow in confidence and independence. The School's general approach is progressive, while retaining traditional values and standards; courtesy and politeness towards others are expected at all times. Academic achievement is of great importance, but the emphasis on other activities such as sports and music ensures that pupils receive a well-rounded education.

The most recent ISI Inspection Report (September 2017) found that the school was excellent in all areas, in particular in terms of the quality of pupils' academic and other achievements and also their personal development.

A wide range of voluntary extracurricular activities is offered at lunch-time, the end of the school day, including art, drama, music and sport. Choirs and orchestras perform in concerts and services throughout the year and school teams compete successfully in a variety of sports.

Berkhamsted Schools Group is committed to supporting working parents and offers wrap-around care from 07.30 to 18.30 each day. In addition, the school operates a holiday care facility, BASECAMP, which offers a variety of courses from multi-activity to specialist sports and cookery each holiday with extended care available from 07.30 to 18.30 each day.

Charitable status. Berkhamsted Schools Group is a Registered Charity, number 310630.

Bickley Park School

---

24 Page Heath Lane, Bickley, Bromley, Kent BR1 2DS

Tel:	020 8467 2195
Fax:	020 8325 5511
email:	info@bickleyparkschool.co.uk
website:	www.bickleyparkschool.co.uk
Twitter:	@bickleyparksch
Facebook:	@bickleyparksch

Chairman of Governors: Mr M Hansra

Headmaster: **Mr P Wenham**, MA Cantab, PGCE

Age Range. Boys 2½–13, Sibling Girls 2½–4.
Number of Pupils. 383 Boys, 6 Girls.
Fees per term (2018–2019). From £2,330 (Nursery) to £4,980 (Boys in Years 4–8). There are no compulsory extras.

Bickley Park School, founded in 1918, is a 13+ boys-only day school which occupies two spacious and attractive sites in Bickley: the Prep Department at 24 Page Heath Lane and the Pre-Prep Department at 14 Page Heath Lane. The school has excellent facilities to complement the original Victorian buildings, including a five-acre sports field, large sports hall, swimming pool, Design Technology and Art Studios.

The EYFS Department (rated as outstanding in the school's last inspection) provides a first-class foundation before the children progress to their final two years in Pre-Prep.

In the Prep Department, the children are introduced to more specialist teaching and setting for Mathematics, English, Science and French. The curriculum is built around Four Quadrants of Learning that espouse academic rigour alongside exceptional opportunities in the wider curriculum.

The majority of children leave at 13+ to attend some of the UK's leading independent schools, whilst a small number leave at 11, usually to join local Grammar Schools.

The school is very outward-looking and enjoys a vibrant community feel.

Charitable status. Bickley Park School Limited is a Registered Charity, number 307915. It exists to provide a broad curriculum for boys aged 2½–13 and girls aged 2½–4.

Bilton Grange

Dunchurch, Rugby, Warwickshire CV22 6QU

Tel:	01788 810217
Fax:	01788 816922
email:	admissions@biltongrange.co.uk
website:	www.biltongrange.co.uk
Twitter:	@biltongrange
Facebook:	@biltongrangeschool

The school is registered as an Educational Trust under the Charities Act and is controlled by a Board of Governors.

Chairman of Governors: Charles Barwell OBE

Headmaster: **Alex Osiatynski**, MA Oxon, PGCE

Deputy Headmaster: Paul Nicholson, BA Hons, PGCE
Bursar: Nick Winther
Assistant Head Pastoral: Antoinette Keane, BA Hons
Assistant Head Academic: Greg Das Gupta, BSc, BCom, PGCE
Assistant Head Boarding: Mark Tovey, BEd Hons
Head of Pre Prep: Katie Gedye, BA, QTS
Registrar: Liz Graham, BSc Hons
International Admissions Registrar: Caroline Morgan, MA Oxon

Age Range. 4–13.
Number of Pupils. 284 boys and girls of whom 84 are full, weekly, or flexi boarders. Preparatory (8–13 year olds): 186 pupils; Pre-Preparatory (4–8 year olds): 98 pupils.

Bilton Grange School was established in 1887 and is one of the foremost co-educational prep schools in the country. Set in 90 acres of heritage parkland, woods and sports fields, dominated by a 19th Century Pugin mansion, the school prides itself on bringing out the very best in every child. Children are extremely happy, and in a nurturing, inspiring and caring environment, confidently find their true potential.

Bilton Grange offers a diverse range of opportunities all designed to support individual accomplishments. Here, children share common values of respect, awareness of others and courtesy. They are usually 'all-rounders', willing to take advantage of all the opportunities open to them – be it on the sports field, in the classroom or on an adventure weekend. The school builds on the proven advantages of the traditional prep school curriculum – small class sizes, a broad range of subjects, and specialist teaching staff – with innovative approaches to teaching and learning, using technology as appropriate, but also the magnificent 90-acre site to the fullest extent to enhance pupils' education.

The school is very proud of its pupils' accomplishments. Bilton Grange is non-selective and yet maintains the highest standards in every arena, all with a remarkable sense of relaxed informality. Children are entered for the Common Entrance Examination and go on to top senior schools across the UK including Rugby, Oundle, Eton, Repton, Oakham, Bloxham and Uppingham. Every year a large number of pupils win awards and scholarships to senior schools and, in recent years, all Year 8 leavers have gone on to the senior school of their choice.

Full, weekly and flexible boarding are offered with over 50 boys and girls boarding on a full and weekly basis. Together the team of House Parents and Matrons create a nurturing environment where children can feel comfortable, safe and secure, whether they are staying for an occasional night a week or full boarding.

The School offers unrivalled facilities, as well as fully resourced classrooms, Science laboratories and a Design Technology workshop. Bilton Grange maintains a theatre, library, Music School, chapel, sports hall, 25-metre indoor heated swimming pool, nine-hole golf course, shooting range and a floodlit artificial grass hockey pitch situated within Pugin's walled garden. The School has seen great sporting success in recent years at a regional and national level. The creative arts are a big part of school life with scholarship successes and creative achievement across Music, Art, Drama and Design Technology.

Fees per term (2018–2019). Preparatory: Full Boarding £8,830, Weekly Boarding £8,190, Day £5,720–£6,480, Pre-Preparatory: £3,360–£4,030.

There are fee discounts for Services children.

Bursaries and academic scholarships are awarded annually, with the scholarship competition open to internal and external candidates in Year 6 to commence in Year 7. Bursaries are awarded on the basis of financial need. This annual application process gets under way in September and details are available on the school website.

We encourage all prospective parents and children to visit the school to see and experience teaching and learning of the highest standards in an inspiring setting.

Charitable status. Bilton Grange Trust is a Registered Charity, number 528771. It exists to provide education for boys and girls.

Birchfield School

Albrighton, Wolverhampton, Shropshire WV7 3AF

Tel:	01902 372534
Fax:	01902 373516
email:	office@birchfieldschool.co.uk
website:	www.birchfieldschool.co.uk
Twitter:	@BirchfieldSch
Facebook:	@Birchfield-School

Chair of Governors: Mrs T K Carver

Headmistress: Mrs Sarah Morris, BA Hons, PGCE

Age Range. 4–13.

Number of Pupils. 120: Pre-Prep (age 4–7) 47, Prep (age 8–10) 57, Senior (age 11–13) 16.

Fees per term (2018–2019). Under 5s £2,275; Reception & Year 1 £2,925; Year 2 £3,920; Years 3 to 8 £4,750.

Birchfield School is now fully co-educational with 50 girls and 70 boys. The last Independent Schools Inspectorate report in March 2012 highlighted the first-class education delivered by the School. The School obtained the highest descriptor 'excellent' in the following key areas: Boarding; Extracurricular provision; Pastoral Care; Leadership and Management; Overall Achievements of the Pupils; Pupils' Personal Development; and Quality of the Pupils' Achievements and Learning.

Birchfield's academic staff consists of many subject specialists who operate from well-equipped classrooms and modern facilities such as a Lego Innovation Centre, Music suite, Science laboratory, Design and Technology workshop and Art studio, library and Food Technology room. There are two ICT suites with networked PCs. iPads are used throughout the School.

Sport is a fundamental part of school life and with superb playing fields and an outdoor swimming pool, Birchfield enjoys an excellent sporting reputation. Birchfield also has a floodlit synthetic sports surface which is used for a variety of sports and by all age groups.

Birchfield also encourages self-expression through Music, Drama, Art and Design Technology. Art is a considerable strength of the School. The Music Department holds regular concerts and our musicians have performed with professional bodies in major productions. The pupils are also involved in a wide range of extra-curricular activities.

The School has a well-resourced Learning Enhancement department with two members of staff who provide excellent support for pupils with special educational needs. For those demonstrating strong academic prowess a scholarship form is in place during the final years.

In recent years senior pupils have achieved numerous scholarships and awards. One in three leavers at 13+ leaves with an award. There is a rich and challenging programme for pupils up to the age of 13, including the opportunity to board in the final years. When the time comes to say goodbye, senior pupils are prepared for entry into a wide range of independent senior schools and local grammar schools which best suit the individual's needs.

There is a full-time school matron. Birchfield has a fine reputation for its all-round holistic education.

Set in 20 acres of attractive grounds and playing fields, Birchfield School is close to Wolverhampton and Telford and boasts excellent transport links.

Co-educational nursery Prepcare (managed by Prepcare LLP) operates on the Birchfield School site and welcomes children from 6 weeks to 4 years old, all year round (except weekends and Bank Holidays) from 8.00 am until 6.00 pm.

Charitable status. Birchfield School is a Registered Charity, number 528420.

Birkdale Prep School

Clarke House, Clarke Drive, Sheffield S10 2NS

Tel:	0114 267 0407
Fax:	0114 268 2929
email:	prepschool@birkdaleschool.org.uk
website:	www.birkdaleschool.org.uk
Twitter:	@BirkdalePrep
Facebook:	@BirkdaleSchool

Chairman of Governors: P Houghton, FCA

Head of Prep School: C J Burch, BA, PGCE

Age Range. 4–11.

Number of Boys. 250 day boys.

Fees per term (2018–2019). Pre-Prep Department £2,900; Prep Department £3,555. Lunch included.

Birkdale Prep School is Sheffield's only school specialising in quality education and care exclusively for boys. Continuous education is offered from 11–18 at Birkdale Senior School (Co-educational Sixth Form).

Birkdale Prep School is based at Clarke House, situated in a pleasant residential area near the University and close to the Senior School. The school has a firm Christian tradition and this, coupled with the size of the school, ensures that the boys develop their own abilities, whether academic or otherwise, to the full.

The Pre-Prep Department is based in a new building, Belmayne House. The facilities are outstanding and designed specifically to meet the needs of 4–7 year olds. Specialist subject teaching across the curriculum starts at the age of 7 and setting in the core subjects in the final two years enhances, still further, the pupil to teacher ratio.

The school has its own Matron and pastoral care is given high priority. Boys are encouraged to join a wide variety of clubs and societies in their leisure time. Music plays a significant part in school life, both in and out of the timetable. There is a large choir, brass band and orchestra and there are strong choral links with Sheffield Cathedral where many of the choristers are Birkdalians.

Cricket, Association and Rugby Football are played on the School's own substantial playing fields, which are within easy reach of the school. A broad range of activities is available as part of the extensive extracurricular programme.

The majority of boys pass into the Senior School.

Charitable status. Birkdale School is a Registered Charity, number 1018973, and a Company Limited by Guarantee, registered in England, number 2792166. It exists to provide education for boys.

Bishop's Stortford College Prep School

Maze Green Road, Bishop's Stortford, Hertfordshire CM23 2PH

Tel: 01279 838607
email: psadmissions@bishopsstortfordcollege.org
website: www.bishopsstortfordcollege.org
Twitter: @BSCollege
Facebook: @bishopsstortfordcollege

Chairman of Governors: Mr G E Baker, BSc, MRICS

Head: **Mr W J Toleman**, BA

Age Range. 4–13.
Typical Number of Pupils. 50 boarders and 410 day pupils.
Fees per term (2018–2019). Full Boarders £7,109–£7,714; Overseas Boarders £7,428–£8,034; Weekly Boarders £7,034–£7,637; Day £4,678–£5,243; Pre-Prep £3,030–£3,089. There are no compulsory extras.

Bishop's Stortford College is a friendly, co-educational, day and boarding community providing high academic standards, good discipline and an excellent all-round education.

There are 50 full-time members of staff, and a number of Senior School staff also teach in the Prep School. As the Prep and Senior Schools share the same campus, many College facilities (music school, sports hall, swimming pool, all-weather pitches, dining hall, medical centre) are shared. The Prep School also has its own buildings containing a multi-purpose Hall, laboratories, IT centre, library, art room and classrooms. In 2013 the Dawson Building was opened, enhancing and extending the Prep School facilities.

The Prep School routine and curriculum are appropriate to the 7–13 age range, with pupils being prepared for Common Entrance and Senior School Scholarships, although most children proceed to the College Senior School. There are 23 forms streamed by general ability and setted for Maths. High standards of work and behaviour are expected and the full development, within a happy and friendly atmosphere, of each child's abilities in sport and the arts is actively encouraged. A strong swimming tradition exists and many of the staff are expert coaches of the major games (rugby, hockey, cricket, netball, rounders, tennis and swimming). The choirs and orchestra flourish throughout the year, and two afternoons of activities provide opportunities for pupils to participate in many minor sports, outdoor pursuits, crafts, computing and chess. Six major dramatic productions occur every year.

A Pre-Prep for 4–6 year olds was opened in 1995 and new purpose-built accommodation was opened in September 2005.

The Prep School is run on boarding lines with a six-day week and a 5.00 pm finish on four days with Wednesdays ending at 4.00 pm and Saturdays at 3.00 pm. The 7 and 8 year olds have a slightly shorter day and their own dedicated building.

Entry tests for 7, 8, 9, 10, 11 year olds are held each January. Scholarships are available at 10+ (Academic and Music) and 11+ (Academic, Music, Art and Sport), as is Financial Assistance.

Charitable status. The Incorporated Bishop's Stortford College Association is a Registered Charity, number 311057. Its aims and objectives are to provide high quality Independent Day and Boarding education for boys and girls from age 4 to 18.

Bishopsgate School

Bishopsgate Road, Englefield Green, Surrey TW20 0YJ

Tel: 01784 480222 (Admissions)
           01784 432109 (School Office)
email: headmaster@bishopsgatesch.uk
           office@bishopsgatesch.uk
           admissions@bishopsgatesch.uk
website: www.bishopsgate-school.co.uk
Twitter: @BishopsgateSch

Chairman of Governors: Mr T Eddis

Headmaster: **Mr Rob Williams**, MA Hons Edinburgh, PGCE Bedford

Age Range. 3–13.
Number of Pupils. 372.
Fees per term (2018–2019). £5,126 (Years 5–8), £4,469 (Years 3–4), £3,741 (Years 1–2), £3,297 (Reception), Nursery: £1,805 (5 mornings), £1,425 (5 afternoons).

Set in 20 acres of beautiful woodland, close to Windsor Great Park, Bishopsgate is blessed with a glorious learning environment. The heart of the school remains as a large, Victorian house, but many additional modern buildings have been added over the past 15 years with the creation of dedicated Upper and Lower School building offering parents outstanding on site facilities for their children.

In 2013, the School completed the development of a four-lane 25 metre swimming pool and swimming is included in the curriculum from Nursery. During the same year, additional new classrooms were added in the Windsor Lower School Building along with a state-of-the-art Design & Technology suite. In addition, a major investment to upgrade the IT Suite included touch screen computers and the procurement of laptops and Chromebook for our pupils. In 2014, the School completed an extension to the Dining Room followed by a major refurbishment of the Science Classroom. Most recently, the completion of a major upgrade of the School All Weather Facility, the Performing Arts Studio, the building of a new cricket square, and the redevelopment of the current all-weather surface has vastly enhanced the facilities.

In early summer 2016, an extension to the Music House increased the number individual teaching rooms and the music classroom. At the same time, major improvements were made to the School Kitchen, the administrative offices in Main Building, and a significant improvement to the School's IT equipment and infrastructure. These developments and other future projects are part of the Governors long term plan to ensure Bishopsgate continues to offer excellence in teaching along with progressive facilities.

Children may enter Bishopsgate from the age of rising 3 into our Nursery. Some children may already be 4 when they join in September if their birthday falls in the Michaelmas term. Our trained staff and well-equipped Nursery ensure that each child is given the best possible start to life. There is a warm family atmosphere as we recognise how important it is for children to feel happy and secure. We place great emphasis on building a solid foundation of social skills and a love of learning, which will enable each child to settle confidently into school life. A wide variety of activities is on offer with plenty of opportunities for healthy outdoor learning, including Forest School.

Beyond Nursery, a class teacher remains at the core of each child's learning. Emphasis is placed on establishing a firm foundation in literacy and numeracy, but the curriculum is broad with a range of educational visits planned to enrich and extend the children's learning. The teaching of French,

Music, PE, Singing and Dance is provided by specialist teachers. Good use is made of our glorious grounds as a learning resource.

Form-based teaching continues in Years 3 and 4, but by Year 5 all teaching is by subject specialists. Programmes of study in Upper School are full and varied, covering the traditional academic subjects as well as Art, Design, Music, Computer Studies, PSHE and Physical Education. The children are prepared carefully for entrance to a range of senior schools and we are proud of our record of success. We prepare children for 11+ entry to senior schools, but we hope our children will remain with us to 13 and participate in the exciting Prep School Baccalaureate.

In Upper School, opportunities to represent the school in sports teams, plays, choirs and instrumental groups are all part of the 'Bishopsgate Experience'. In addition, a busy programme of extracurricular activities ensures that all children have the opportunity to shine at something.

Music plays an essential part in the life of the school with many of our pupils enjoying individual music lessons. There are choirs and ensembles. Participation by children of all abilities, with ample opportunities to perform, is our aim. Drama productions, dance and public speaking events all provide additional occasions when the children can develop their presentation skills.

Our vibrant Art and Design Department occupies a spacious studio equipped with a kiln for ceramics and a printing press for design projects. There is an annual art exhibition for both Lower and Upper School and the children's work is displayed proudly around the school and in our annual School magazine. There is a popular after-school Art club for children and regular weekend workshops with professional artists.

Team Games, Rowing, Athletics, Dance, Tennis, Gymnastics, Judo, Taekwondo, Swimming and much more are all included in a varied and exciting sporting programme within the school day. An extensive programme of inter-school fixtures is arranged each term and we like to see as many parents in support as possible! We like to win, but our priorities are participation, enjoyment and teamwork.

A prospectus and further details can be obtained from the Admissions Office.

Charitable status. Bishopsgate School is a Registered Charity, number 1060511. It aims to provide a broad and sound education for its pupils with thorough and personal pastoral care.

Blackheath Preparatory School

4 St Germans Place, Blackheath, London SE3 0NJ
Tel: 020 8858 0692
Fax: 020 8858 7778
email: contact.us@blackheathprepschool.com
website: www.blackheathprepschool.com

Co-educational Day School.

Chairman of Governors: Mr Hugh Stallard

Headmistress: Mrs P J Thompson, BA Hons, PGCE, BDA Dip

Age Range. 3–11.
Number of Pupils. 173 Boys, 205 Girls.
Fees per term (2018–2019). Nursery: £2,580–£4,165; Reception–Year 2 £3,960; Years 3–6 £4,310.

The school is located in an attractive residential area close to Blackheath village, overlooking the heath itself and borders of Greenwich Park. The five-acre site includes attractive playing fields, cricket nets, tennis courts and two playgrounds, providing enviable sporting opportunities and room for children to play.

A most attractive learning environment includes specialist rooms for Science, ICT, Art, DT, Maths and Music. A spacious multi-purpose hall and music suite enhance the opportunities for Music, Drama, Sport and extracurricular activities. Over 40 activities are offered in a wide-ranging extracurricular programme.

Most children join the school in the nursery at the age of three and progress through the Pre-Prep (4–7) and Prep (7–11) before leaving to transfer to selective senior schools. Academic standards are high and pupils are well prepared for selection at 11 and achieve consistent success in obtaining places at their first choice of grammar or independent senior school. On average over the last five years more than 50% of Year 6 pupils have been awarded academic scholarships each year and a plethora of pupils are awarded scholarships in Art, Music, Drama and Sport.

The form teacher of every class is responsible for the pastoral welfare of each child. In the Nursery and the Pre-Prep the key worker and the form teacher are primarily responsible for teaching the children. However, there is a strong emphasis on specialist teaching from the very beginning. Music, French, PE, Drama and Dance are introduced in the Nursery. As the children progress through the school, more specialist teachers are responsible for Art, ICT, Design Technology, Maths, English and Science. The quality of teaching has been recognised as one of the many strengths of the school and pupils display real pleasure in their learning.

The school positively encourages parental involvement in the daily life of the school. The strong ethos and vision of the school is underpinned by the vibrant enthusiasm of all involved and by the very strong sense of community.

The Blue Coat School

Somerset Road, Edgbaston, Birmingham B17 0HR
Tel: 0121 410 6800
email: admissions@thebluecoatschool.com
website: www.thebluecoatschool.com
Twitter: @bcsbirmingham
Facebook: @bluecoatbirmingham
LinkedIn: /Blue-Coat-School-Birmingham

Founded 1722. Co-educational Day Preparatory School.

Chairman of Governors: Mr B H Singleton

Headmaster: Mr N G Neeson, BEd Hons, NPQH

Age Range. 2–11.
Number of Pupils. The total enrolment is 602 children. Buttons Nursery and Pre-Prep have 273 girls and boys from 2–7 years, while Prep has 329 from 7–11 years.

There is a graduate and qualified full-time teaching staff of 48, and 11 part-time teachers.

Fees per term (2018–2019). Pre-Prep: £2,717–£3,468; Prep: £4,092–£4,238. The fees quoted include lunches and morning and afternoon breaks. Over 50 extracurricular activities are available, some of which are charged as extras.

Assisted Places are available to children with a demonstrable need, entering Years 3 and 4.

Scholarships are offered for academic and musical excellence at age 7 (entry to Year 3).

The School is set in 15 acres of grounds and playing fields just 2 miles from the centre of Birmingham. Its well-designed buildings and facilities include an AstroTurf pitch, a purpose-built Nursery, Chapel, a Year 6 Hub, a spacious auditorium and a superb multi-purpose Sports Centre with a 25m indoor swimming pool and two brand new studios. Morning and After-school care is available. In Prep this is provided in two spacious, purpose-designed Houses.

Additional features include the Library Resource Centre and specialist facilities for Science, Art, Design and Technology, Music, Media Studies and ICT. All the classrooms have an IWB, and the school is very well equipped with Apple and Windows computers including desktops, laptops and tablets.

Children are prepared for scholarships and examinations to prestigious local schools. The school enjoys particular success in the 11+ examinations to Birmingham's grammar schools and the schools of the King Edward VI Foundation. The Statutory Framework for the Early Years Foundation Stage is followed for children aged 2 to 5, and the National Curriculum is incorporated at Key Stages 1 and 2 as part of a wider academic structure.

The school is well known for its Music. The robed Chapel Choir is affiliated to the RSCM, and there are five further choirs and a significant number of instrumental groups and ensembles. Musicals, concerts and recitals feature in abundance, involving the great majority of the children. Over 300 instrumental lessons are given weekly.

The main sports are Hockey, Netball, Rounders, Rugby, Soccer, Cricket, Athletics and Swimming. The teams enjoy considerable success in inter-school competitions and all children have the opportunity to develop their skills.

A dynamic Friday afternoon Enrichment Programme allows senior children the chance to broaden their horizons as they follow a TED (Thinking, Exploring, Doing) programme, which includes a choice of practical and sporting activities such as Debating, Philosophy, Team-building, Forest School, Gardening and Squash. Co-curricular activities include Gymnastics, Judo, Ballet, Drama, LAMDA, Science and Chess. Lessons in the classroom are complemented by outings including field courses and residential trips.

Charitable status. The Blue Coat School Birmingham Limited is a Registered Charity, number 1152244, and a Company Limited by Guarantee, registered in England, number 8502615.

Blundell's Preparatory School

Milestones House, Blundell's Road, Tiverton, Devon EX16 4NA

Tel: 01884 252393
Fax: 01884 232333
email: prep@blundells.org
website: www.blundells.org

Chairman of Governors: Mr C M Clapp, FCA

Headmaster: **Mr A D Southgate**, BA Ed Hons

Age Range. 2½–11 years.
Numbers of Pupils. Boys and Girls: Prep (aged 7–11) 127; Pre-Prep (aged 2½–7) 77.
Fees per term (2018–2019). Prep: £3,980–£4,065 (Lunch £315); Pre-Prep: £1,960–£2,930 (Lunch £280); Nursery: £18.50 per session (Lunch £5.60 per day).

Blundell's Preparatory School is a family school and all the staff adopt a personal interest in every child and work in partnership with the parents. The school places great emphasis on children being happy, secure and confident, thus offering individuals every opportunity to achieve their full potential within a caring family atmosphere.

The School has been established for over seventy years and is part of the Blundell's Charitable Trust. It enjoys its own separate site within the very extensive Blundell's campus. This rural setting is within easy reach of the market town of Tiverton and is conveniently placed less than ten minutes from the M5 motorway and Tiverton Parkway Station.

The School has an excellent reputation for providing the essentials. Sound academic standards are based on providing the core subjects of Maths, English and Science taught to an extremely high standard. Added to this is the bonus of a wide range of supplementary subjects, well taught by specialist teachers. The School has recently had a major redevelopment and a significant extension. This includes a fully-equipped Art & Design Centre and a Food Technology Suite.

Drama, music and art flourish at Blundell's Preparatory School with all the children participating fully both in lessons and as part of extracurricular activities. Specialist music teachers offer an extensive variety of different instruments. The Drama and Music department have their own dedicated facility.

The sports department has an enviable reputation of producing good all-round sporting pupils, as well as nurturing and extending those with talent. Amongst the sports offered are rugby, football, netball, hockey and cross-country in the winter and cricket, tennis, athletics and swimming in the summer. The Preparatory School has access to the extensive sporting facilities within Blundell's campus.

There is an comprehensive choice of extracurricular activities offered to the pupils which includes ballet, chess, fencing, golf, art, judo, bushcraft club and woodwork.

Children at Blundell's Prep School do not have to sit a formal entrance exam to gain entry to the Senior School. Children who wish to move to Year 7 will be able to do so as long as the school is confident, through the wealth of assessment data already held by the Prep School and shared with the Senior School, that they can be suitably catered for. Parents will be kept fully informed prior to Year 6 if there is any question surrounding that. All children who do not attend Blundell's Prep are required to sit the Entrance exams which take place in the January of Year 6.

(*See also Blundell's School entry in HMC section.*)

Charitable status. Blundell's School is a Registered Charity, number 1081249. It exists to provide education for children.

Bootham Junior School

Rawcliffe Lane, York YO30 6NP

Tel: 01904 655021
email: junior@boothamschool.com
website: www.boothamschool.com
Twitter: @BoothamSchool
Facebook: @BoothamSchool
LinkedIn: /bootham-school

Clerk to the School Committee: Stephen Sayers

Head: **Helen Todd**, BA Hons, MA Ed, QTS

Age Range. 3–11 Co-educational.
Number of Pupils. 140.
Fees per term (2018–2019). £2,715–£3,455 inc lunch for full-time pupils.

Bootham Junior School stands apart by treating each member of its community, in a practical application of Quaker principles, as equally important. We welcome all faiths or none, encouraging our children to develop their own convictions while learning to respect those of others. The Independent Schools Inspectorate reports '*A sense of calm and a quiet pace to the working of the school that enables individuals to flourish*'. Although our children are as boisterous as any others, and, indeed, enjoy a tolerance to behave as children, quietness is important. The values of cooperation, community, and quietness grow from the Quaker tradition, but they resonate with the modern world of work, where teams find solutions individuals can't, where knowledge is seen as interrelated and not separate, and where values-driven responses earn our respect.

At Bootham Junior School, we aim to encourage a life-long love of learning and inspirational teaching is a good place to start. Equally important is the mutual high regard and understanding that children and teachers enjoy. This relationship provides the very best environment for learning to take place. High standards are achieved because children feel happy, confident, motivated and respected. Education is more than examination preparation; it is about unlocking potential skills and aptitudes. We want our children to find their particular strengths: through sport, through music, through the Arts, through outdoor education, through social debate and action.

Bootham Junior School has a beautiful sports field, a swimming pool at the senior school dating from 1912 and hard courts for tennis and netball. The range of sports taught include: gymnastics, dance, athletics, netball, tennis, swimming, football, basketball, cricket and rounders. Our Director of Music has a range of musical groups including: two choirs, orchestra, flute group, string group, clarinet group and recorder group. Individual music lessons are also available in all instruments should parents wish it. Engagement with the community is in line with a Quaker sense of responsibility and extends to children's activities too. Drama flourishes both within and beyond the formal curriculum. Regular productions of plays and musicals cater for different age groups and allow talents to be explored, nurtured and showcased. Children also take part in LAMDA schemes for recital and public speaking. Our Outdoor Classroom is an extremely well-used resource and all children have the opportunity to take part in residential experiences, from nursery age onwards. We believe in building adaptable, resilient young people who can respond to the world around them. Whatever their interests, this is the place where all our children can find inspiration and where they will be inspired. The small size of our school means that everyone has the chance to try something new. The result is a sense of personal achievement both in and outside the classroom.

Charitable status. Bootham School is a Registered Charity, number 513645.

Boundary Oak School

Roche Court, Wickham Road, Fareham, Hampshire PO17 5BL

Tel:	01329 280955
email:	registrar@boundaryoak.co.uk
	office@boundaryoak.co.uk
website:	www.boundaryoakschool.co.uk
Twitter:	@boundaryoak
Facebook:	@boundaryoak

Head: **Mr James Polansky**, MA Cantab, PGCE

Age Range. 2–16.

Number of Pupils. 24 Boarders, 183 Day Pupils.

Fees per term (2018–2019). Boarding Supplement (Years 3–11): £2,009 (Weekly boarding 5 nights); £2,654 (Full boarding 7 nights). Day Pupils: £2,983–£4,829 (Reception–Year 11), Pre-School: £2,983 (full time). Sessions available.

The school was founded in 1918 and moved to Roche Court in 1960. A new 99 year lease was secured in 1994. The school is set in 22 acres of pleasant, self-contained grounds between Fareham and Wickham in Hampshire and enjoys extensive views of the countryside around.

The Pre-School takes children from the age of 2 to rising 5 and this group is housed in a purpose-built centre offering the most up-to-date facilities. This department is structured to the needs of this age group and the day can extend from 8.00 am to 5.30 pm.

The Pre-Prep Department has its own purpose-built buildings and other facilities within the school, and caters for children from rising 5 to 8 years of age (Reception to Year 3).

At 8 years the children move to the Preparatory Department where they remain until they are 13 (Year 8). From here they move to Seniors in Year 9 where they are introduced to our GCSE subjects. Full, weekly and flexi boarding are offered to all from the age of 7 years and the school has a policy of admitting boarders in a flexible system that is of great benefit to all. Pupils are prepared for a wide number of independent schools throughout the United Kingdom in a friendly and caring environment.

Apart from the historic main house of Roche Court where the boarders live, there is the Jubilee Block of classrooms, two laboratories, the Widley Block, Library and the Music Centre. The School has an ICT Suite and a purpose-built Art and Design Technology Centre that incorporates work areas for Photography, Pottery and Carpentry. The school has a fine Assembly Hall that is also used for Drama and Physical Education.

As well as extensive playing fields with woods beyond for cross country and an all-weather AstroTurf pitch which incorporates football, hockey, netball and tennis courts, there is an outdoor swimming pool and the indoor Fareham Pool is within very easy reach.

Most sports are taught and there is a wide selection of clubs and activities run in the school for both day and boarding pupils including judo, horse riding, art, camp craft, chess, shooting and many more.

For a copy of the prospectus and details of scholarships and bursaries, please apply to the Registrar, email: registrar@boundaryoak.co.uk or look at our website www.boundaryoakschool.co.uk.

Bradford Grammar Junior School

Keighley Road, Bradford, West Yorkshire BD9 4JP

Tel:	01274 553742
Fax:	01274 553745
email:	chsec@bradfordgrammar.com
website:	www.bradfordgrammar.com
Twitter:	@KerryLHowes
	@bradfordgrammar
Facebook:	@bradfordgrammarschool
LinkedIn:	/bradfordgrammar

Chairman of the Board of Governors: Lady L Morrison, LLB

Headmistress: **Miss K L Howes**, BSc, MSc

Age Range. 6 to 11.

Number of Pupils. 96 boys, 85 girls.

Fees per term (2018–2019). £3,305.

Bradford Grammar Junior School is a selective school for boys and girls aged 6 to 11, holding no catchment boundaries and a strong reputation for specialist teaching.

The school seeks to inspire happy, respectful and grounded children, who are ready for the transition to Senior School. The school's aim is to provide exceptional care in a relaxed atmosphere so that each child can thrive.

Location. Bradford Grammar Junior School is located at the same site as the Senior School at Keighley Road, Bradford. It is housed in an original seventeenth century manor house called Clock House.

Specialist facilities. The school offers pupils a wide range of specialist facilities, including a swimming pool, theatre, instrumental music tuition and dedicated Computer Science and Design Technology rooms. Full use is made of the Senior School facilities including Science laboratories, Sports facilities and Art rooms.

Specialist teaching. In Years 2, 3 and 4 (age 6 to 9) pupils are taught the majority of subjects by form teachers and are based in their classrooms, with specialist teaching for Art, Modern Foreign Languages, Music Computing, and Games. In Years 5 and 6 pupils have increasing input from specialist teachers utilising the extensive facilities throughout the whole school.

Co-curricular Activities. The Junior School offers a wide and varied range of co-curricular activities which mainly take place during the lunch break. All pupils are encouraged to participate in at least two different activities each week. These may include: netball, hockey, rugby, swimming, cross country, cricket, football, rounders, athletics, table tennis, dance, design technology, computing, lego, craft, art, board games, gardening, choir, orchestra, wind band, string group, rock band, guitar group and samba band.

Pastoral Care. Form Teachers are closely involved with the wellbeing of the children in their form and all of our teachers have a good knowledge of, and relationship with, the pupils. We encourage open communication between school and home and hope parents will keep in close contact with us. A child's progress and happiness are our priorities. We promote good manners and respect for others throughout the School and believe that this is an important aspect of all pupils' education.

After Care. Bradford Grammar Junior School provides before and after school care from 7.45 am to 6.00 pm.

Transport Links. The school organises private coach transport for pupils travelling to and from Huddersfield, Halifax, Bramhope, Horsforth, Rawdon, Wharfedale and Oxenhope. It is situated a short walk from Frizinghall Railway Station, which is on the Airedale and Wharfedale lines. There are half-hourly rail services, taking approximately 30 minutes, to Leeds, Skipton, Ilkley and Apperley Bridge.

Entry. The school is selective and takes a number of pupils each year for entry from Year 2 (age 6 to 7) through to Year 6 (age 10 to 11).

Entry to Years 2, 3 and 4 (age 6, 7 and 8) is by assessment. Entry to Years 5 and 6 (age 9 and 10) is by entrance examination and involves tests in Maths and English.

Pupils who progress from Bradford Grammar School Junior School to the Senior School are not required to sit the 11+ entrance exam. The close relationship between the two schools enables a smooth transition from Junior to Senior School.

Charitable status. Bradford Grammar School (The Free Grammar School of King Charles II at Bradford) is a Registered Charity, number 529113. It exists to provide education for children.

Brambletye

Lewes Road, East Grinstead, West Sussex RH19 3PD

Tel: 01342 321004
email: schooloffice@brambletye.com
website: www.brambletye.co.uk
Twitter: @brambletweet
Facebook: @brambletyeschool

Chairman of Governors: Mr P J Lough, MA, PGCE

Headmaster: **Mr Will Brooks**, BA, PGCE, MBA Ed

Age Range. 2½–13 Co-educational.

Number of Pupils. 301 day/boarding pupils.

Fees per term (2018–2019). Boarders £8,235–£8,425; Day Pupils £6,205–£6,910; Pre-Prep: £3,335 (Years 1 & 2), £3,205 (Reception), Nursery £2,825 (5 full days).

Brambletye is an independent day and boarding Preparatory School for boys and girls aged 7–13 years, situated in beautiful grounds in rural Sussex. There is a Pre-Preparatory/Nursery department which takes boys and girls from the age of 2½ years to the age of 7 years.

Brambletye is a large country house in its own wooded estate of 140 acres, overlooking Ashdown Forest and Weir Wood Reservoir. The school stands one mile south of East Grinstead. Gatwick Airport is only 20 minutes by car and Heathrow is an hour away. London is 30 miles by road and 50 minutes by rail. There is escorted travel to and from London at the beginning and end of all exeat weekends and half-term holidays.

The school has outstanding academic, sporting, music, drama and arts facilities. These include a new modern classroom block, 2 redeveloped science laboratories, an up-to-date Arts Room and Design Technology workshop, an extensive Library, an ICT room, a large theatre and music rooms. There is also a Sports Hall, tennis and netball courts, two squash courts, a swimming pool, a golf course and several playing fields. We aim to produce happy, confident, well-rounded children who work hard, enjoy drama, games and music, play a part in some of the numerous societies and hobbies, and take a full share in the daily life of the school. These facilities in conjunction with high quality teaching staff, generate regular awards for the children from the schools that inherit them.

Brambletye has always been run along family lines, with a distinctive warm and friendly atmosphere. Traditional values such as high standards of manners and good behaviour provide a platform for academic and personal development. As a co-educational day and boarding school, pupils enjoy and benefit from living and working in a community. At weekends, there is a full programme of activities for the boarders and children are encouraged to make constructive use of their spare time. The environment is inspirational and pupils develop a love of learning which creates a positive interaction with the staff and a curiosity about the world around us.

The Nursery and Pre-Preparatory Department is situated in a self-contained purpose-built state-of-the-art building. The main aim of the Department is to provide a secure, friendly and structured environment in which all children are encouraged to achieve their full potential and to develop at their own rate.

Children may join the Nursery class at the age of two and a half before progressing to Reception at four. Boys and girls transfer to the Preparatory Department at the age of seven. All children acquire the basic skills, while following the breadth of the National Curriculum. Religious Studies, Physical Education, Art, Music, Science and Technology are all integrated into the weekly timetable. Children have swimming lessons throughout the year in the indoor pool, and teachers from the Preparatory Department visit regularly to teach Music and to coach games. The Pre-Prep has an exciting School in the Woods project.

Enquiries about admissions, our scholarships and bursary programme are welcomed throughout the year. Brambletye offers generous discounts for Armed Services Families. Please contact the Headmaster's Secretary for a prospectus.

Charitable status. Brambletye School Trust Limited is a Registered Charity, number 307003. It aims to provide an all-round education for the children in its care.

Brentwood Preparatory School

Middleton Hall, Middleton Hall Lane, Brentwood, Essex CM15 8EQ

Tel: 01277 243239 (ages 3–7)
          01277 243333 (ages 7–11)
Fax: 01277 243340
email: prepadmissions@brentwood.essex.sch.uk
          prep3–7@brentwood.essex.sch.uk
          prep7–11@brentwood.essex.sch.uk
website: www.brentwoodschool.co.uk

Chairman of Governors: Sir Michael Snyder, DSc, FCA, FRSA [OB]

Headmaster: **Mr K J Whiskerd**, BA, PGCE

Head of Early Years and Key Stage 1: Mrs V Audas, BEd

Age Range. 3–11.
Number of Children. Prep 409.
Fees per term (2018–2019). Nursery £2,412, Prep £4,824.

Brentwood Preparatory School has its own buildings and grounds quite distinct from Brentwood School (qv) but close enough to share the use of its chapel, indoor swimming pool, Sports Centre and world-class athletics track.

The co-educational Preparatory School, which opened in 1892, educates children from age 3 to 7 in the spacious Higgs Building with very well-equipped classrooms. Entrance is by an informal assessment at age 3.

Older children, aged 7 to 11, are based in Middleton Hall, an elegant building which has its own extensive grounds, sports pitches and all-weather Astroturf. Entrance is at age 7 by an academically-selective test and candidates come from a wide range of schools. Small class sizes and a team of well-qualified teachers provide a caring and challenging environment. Specialist rooms for art, design technology, drama, French, ICT, music and science provide outstanding facilities and a stimulating environment in which children can thrive.

There is an extensive programme of house and inter-school sports matches. Three choirs, two orchestras and a variety of ensembles perform regularly both in and out of school. Every child has the opportunity to take part in a major drama production. There is a wide range of lunchtime and after-school clubs, and a late stay scheme for children to complete homework at school. Many day visits to museums and places of interest complement school-based work and children enjoy annual residential trips in the holidays.

The Preparatory School has a strong academic tradition and a reputation for providing an excellent all-round education. The vast majority of pupils transfer to the Senior School (founded in 1557) at age 11.

The Preparatory School was last inspected in 2013 by the ISI and received a superb report with inspectors giving 'excellent' findings in every category of school life. Inspectors reported that "*the School is successful in meeting its aims and offers a high quality educational experience to its pupils ...The pupils' achievements are particularly notable in mathematics, literacy, music, art and drama*". The School fulfils its aims "*to encourage pupils to develop a lifelong love of learning and to strive for the highest academic standards in the classroom ...Teaching is well planned with a high degree of awareness of the differing needs of all the pupils ...Extremely well planned, lively lessons ensure pupils of all ages thoroughly enjoy their learning and provide stimulus and challenge*".

The report continued: "*The teachers' subject knowledge is excellent in all subjects and pupils benefit from specialised teaching in a wide range of subjects. Teachers have very high expectations for pupils, and praise and encouragement are used to good effect. All staff know their pupils well and the excellent relationships are marked by mutual respect, creating an environment conducive to learning and exemplary behaviour from pupils in class.*"

Charitable status. Brentwood School (part of Sir Antony Browne's School Trust, Brentwood) is a Registered Charity, number 1153605. It exists for the purpose of educating children.

Brighton & Hove Prep
GDST

Radinden Manor Road, Hove, East Sussex BN3 6NH

Tel: 01273 280200
email: prepenquiries@bhhs.gdst.net
website: www.bhhs.gdst.net
Twitter: @BHPrep
Facebook: @BrightonAndHovePrep

Chair of Local Governors: Mrs Jen Smith

Head: **Mrs Sian Cattaneo**

Age Range. Girls 3–11.
Number of Pupils. 190.
Fees per term (2018–2019). £3,037–£3,411, Nursery £2,397.

The Prep School of Brighton & Hove High School stands on a large site in Hove. It benefits from an extensive purpose-built site which provides many specialist areas such as a new well-equipped IT suite, a large refurbished science lab, bright and airy art studio, and a spacious music room with several practice rooms. Despite our urban site we make the most of our green areas with an extensive all-weather play area and pond and our astroturf and netball courts are great additions to the PE opportunities.

Our Nursery, which takes girls from age three, is very much part of the BHHS community and almost all girls transfer to the Reception class. We have a significant intake at Year Three and girls are then prepared for transfer to our Senior School at the end of Year Six. (*See Senior School entry in GSA section.*)

The ethos of the school is firmly centred on the benefits of a girls-only education. We believe that girls are more independent, focused, self-motivated and that relationships are more positive in a girl-centred setting. We put a strong emphasis on a rounded education and believe that the confidence built at an early age with a range of opportunities and experiences provides a great platform for girls for the future.

We currently run several choirs, an orchestra and other musical opportunities. We offer a wide PE curriculum which includes the opportunity to be involved in inter-school matches. Drama and Art are also well resourced and girls often get involved in local events such as the Brighton Festival.

We pride ourselves on having a strong relationship with parents and readily involve them in the life of the school. We continue to build positive links with the community with a number of outreach projects. We are the holder of the prestigious Green Flag which reflects our eco work and commitment to energy saving and eco awareness. Despite the short distance between the sites we often use the opportunity to have whole-school events, such as an annual dance show for Years 3–13.

Charitable status. Brighton & Hove High School is part of The Girls' Day School Trust, which is a Registered Charity, number 306983.

Brighton College Nursery, Pre-Prep & Prep School

Prep:
Walpole Lodge, Walpole Road, Brighton, East Sussex BN2 0EU

Tel: 01273 704210
email: prepoffice@brightoncollege.net

Nursery & Pre-Prep:
Eastern Road, Brighton, East Sussex BN2 5JJ

Tel: 01273 704259
email: preprepoffice@brightoncollege.net

website: www.brightoncollege.net
Twitter: @BCNPPS
Facebook: @BCNPPS

Chairman of Governors: The Lord Mogg, KCMG

Headmaster: **John Weeks**, BA

Senior Deputy Head: Joanne Wergan, BA, PGCE

Deputy Heads:
Jane Ashfold, BSc, PGCE
Lois Griffiths, BPharm, PGCE

Head of Nursery & Pre-Prep: Jo Williams, BEd, MA

Registrar: Alison Westbrook, BA, PGCE

Age Range. 3–13.
Number of Pupils. Nursery & Pre-Prep 220, Prep 307.
Fees per term (2018–2019). From £3,350 (Reception) to £6,450 (Year 8).

Brighton College Nursery, Pre-Prep & Prep School is a co-educational school, which offers a broad curriculum taught to high standards by dedicated and energetic staff. The Nursery & Pre-Prep cares for children from 3–7 years in a purpose-built building with playing fields, overlooking the sea. The Prep is situated adjacent to the College on its own site. Both sites are urban, but enjoy close proximity to the sea, the Downs and the vibrant sports and culture of Brighton, where an annual arts festival is held in May. Some of the excellent facilities provided by Brighton College are shared; these include the Chapel, swimming pool and sports hall (new building due 2019), two areas of playing fields, a purpose-built Performing Arts Centre and the Great Hall, which doubles as a large theatre for the annual Prep musical.

The Nursery & Pre-Prep offers specialist lessons in art, music, French, Mandarin, PE, games and swimming on its own well-equipped site. The Prep has many specialist rooms including a well-equipped ICT suite, a large design technology room, art room, science laboratories, home economics room, library and hall.

Pastoral care is very strong and a culture of kindness is commonplace and reinforced in assemblies, within the curriculum and during form time or tutor meetings for older pupils. The motto from Nursery to Year 8 is 'Be Good. Be Kind. Be Honest. Be the Best You'.

Academic standards are high and are one of the foundations upon which school life is built, along with the broad range of subjects and activities. A variety of teaching methods is used – the key principle being that children enjoy their lessons and thus develop a love for learning.

Learning Support teachers can provide specialist teaching on a 1:1 basis or in small groups for pupils with an identified need.

Sport is a very important part of the life at the school. Girls and boys games teaching begins in Year 1 and includes netball, hockey, rounders, football, rugby, cricket, athletics and swimming.

The school is well known for its strength across the performing arts. Thirty-five visiting music teachers provide tuition for a large number of pupils who learn a wide variety of instruments. There are two orchestras, a concert band and three choirs organised by the music department.

Drama clubs and coaching are available from Year 2 and there are opportunities for children to perform during the academic year through assemblies, recitals, Chapel services and annual drama productions and musicals. The Brighton College School of Dance is thriving and many pupils attend classes after school during the week and on Saturdays.

The school runs a large number of clubs and activities after school and at lunchtimes for pupils from Year 2 and there is a range of school bus routes for pupils from Year 4. Children attending Nursery can stay for optional, themed afternoons which include yoga, French and art.

The Admissions team hold termly events for prospective pupils and their families or can arrange individual visits. Open Mornings, taster days and themed mornings take place throughout the year, alongside assessment days for pupils wishing to join from Year 1. For details of events, assessment procedures, scholarships available at 13+ and bus routes, please contact the Registrar on prepadmissions@brightoncollege.net or 01273 704343.

Charitable status. Brighton College is a Registered Charity, number 307061. It exists to provide high quality education for boys and girls aged 3–18.

BGS Infants and Juniors

Elton Road, Bristol BS8 1SR

Tel: 0117 973 6109
Fax: 0117 974 1941
email: admissions@bgs.bristol.sch.uk
website: www.bristolgrammarschool.co.uk
Twitter: @bgsbristol
Facebook: @bgsbristol

Chairman of Governors: Romesh Vaitlingam, BA Hons Oxon, MBE

Headmaster: **Peter R Huckle**, BA, MEd

Assistant Head: Mrs Veryan E Rookes, BSc Hons, PCGE
Assistant Head: Adam M Turpin, BA Hons, PGCE

Age Range. 4–11.

Number of Pupils. 336. Infants 108; Juniors 228

Fees per term (2018–2019). Juniors: Years 3–6 £3,320. Infants: Years 1 & 2 £3,085, Reception £2,825. Fees include Lunch.

BGS Infants and Juniors is an independent co-educational day school. It was founded in 1900 and since 2010 has offered Infant as well as Junior provision. The School occupies self-contained buildings on the same site as the Senior School, Bristol Grammar School (*see entry in HMC section*). Its own facilities include a Hall, Library, Music, Art, Science and Technology rooms. Some facilities are shared with the Senior School, particularly the Sports Hall, Performing Arts Centre and Dining Hall. The School now thrives on the happy and purposeful demands of approximately 340 girls and boys aged 4–11 years.

Entry into BGS Infants is by an informal assessment session. Entry for the Junior School is by test and is normally at seven or nine years old (entry to other age groups is subject to the availability of places). Peloquin bursaries are awarded annually and are means-tested. Children who have been members of the School since the start of Year 5 or earlier are offered places in the Senior School following continuous assessment of their progress; other children take the normal Senior School entrance test.

BGS Infants and Juniors aims to provide a rich, broad and balanced curriculum while also maintaining a nurturing environment for children to flourish. The School encourages all pupils to develop their own ideas, giving support so they gain skills and confidence and offering challenges to stretch their thinking. Many subjects are taught by subject specialists, including specialists from the Senior School. Music, art, dance and drama are particularly encouraged with the annual MADD Evening being a particular highlight. There are many clubs and activities including Origami, Lego, Gardening, Animation, Russian, Ukelele, and Chicken Club, as well as extra sports and musical opportunities. One afternoon per week is dedicated to the Activity programme, where children can choose a new challenge or a favourite hobby. In addition, all children in the Infant School, and many Juniors, take part in Forest School and have violin tuition. The children have many opportunities to develop leadership and responsibility; the Infant and Junior School Councils meet regularly with the Headmaster and there is a Charity Committee as well as an Eco-Committee.

A wide range of sports is offered to the pupils at the School's superb playing fields at Failand with its state-of-the-art pavilion. The impressive purpose-built Sports Hall on the main campus provides facilities for indoor PE. Pastoral care is provided by the Form Tutors and Assistant Heads, supported by all teaching staff and the Headmaster. Form Tutors take a lead in ensuring that children are learning and progressing well. A prosperous House system produces many friendships between age groups, with mentors and buddies showing new pupils the ropes, making sure that things are running smoothly for them. This leads to a strong sense of family and community within the School owing much to the warm and trusting relationships between children with each other and with their teachers.

Charitable status. Bristol Grammar School is a Registered Charity, number 1104425. The object of the Charity is the provision and conduct in or near the City of Bristol of a day school for boys and girls.

Brockhurst School

Hermitage, Newbury, Berkshire RG18 9UL

Tel: 01635 200293
email: registrar@brockmarl.org
website: www.brockmarl.org.uk

Headmaster: **D J W Fleming**, MA Oxon, MSc

Age Range. 3 to 13.

Number of Boys. 154 Boys (including 74 Boarders).

Fees per term (2018–2019). Boarding £7,975, Day £3,550–£5,950. Pre-Prep School (Ridge House): £3,550 (full-time). Temporary Overseas Boarders £8,600.

Established in 1884, Brockhurst is situated in 500 acres of its own grounds in countryside of outstanding beauty, but is only four miles from access to the M4. The school is located on the same site as Marlston House Girls' Preparatory School which occupies separate, listed buildings. Boys and Girls are educated separately, but the two schools join forces for drama, music and many hobbies. In this way, Brockhurst and Marlston House aim to combine the best features of the single-sex and co-educational systems: academic excellence and social mixing. The schools have built up a fine reputation for high standards of pastoral care given to each pupil within a caring, family establishment. (*See also entry for Marlston House School.*)

The Pre-Prep School, Ridge House, is a co-educational department for 75 children aged 3 to 6½.

Boys are prepared for entry to all Independent Senior Schools and there is an excellent scholarship record.

All boys play Soccer, Rugby, Hockey and Cricket and take part in Athletics, Cross Country and Swimming (25m indoor heated pool). Additional activities include Riding (own ponies), Fencing, Judo, Shooting (indoor rifle range) and Tennis (indoor court and three hard courts). Facilities for gymnastics and other sporting activities are provided in a purpose-built Sports Hall. Year 7 pupils make a week-long visit to a Château in France as part of their French language studies.

The school is currently building a new dedicated Music School and Theatre to open in the Summer Term 2014. Music and art are important features of the curriculum and a good number of pupils have won scholarships to senior schools in recent years.

Where appropriate, pupils can be transported by members of staff to and from airports if parents are serving in the armed forces or otherwise working overseas.

Bromsgrove Preparatory & Pre-Preparatory School

Prep:
Old Station Road, Bromsgrove, Worcs B60 2BU

Tel: 01527 579679

Pre-Preparatory:
Avoncroft House, Hanbury Road, Bromsgrove, Worcs B60 4JS

Tel: 01527 579679

email: admissions@bromsgrove-school.co.uk

website: www.bromsgrove-school.co.uk
Twitter: @BromsSchool
Facebook: @BromsgroveSchool

Chairman of Governors: Mr Paul West, QPM

Headmistress: **Mrs Jacquelyne Deval-Reed**, BEd

Age Range. 3–13.
Number of Pupils. Prep School (7–13): 231 day boys, 209 day girls, 42 boy boarders, 37 girl boarders. Pre-Preparatory & Nursery (3–7): 120 boys, 121 girls.
Fees per term (2018–2019). Nursery: £2,950 (full-time); Pre-Prep: £2,660–£2,930; Prep: £3,880–£5,035 (day), £8,080–£9,965 (full boarding), £5,895–£7,130 (weekly boarding).
Forces Bursaries and, from 11+, scholarships are available.
Bromsgrove Preparatory School feeds the adjacent 950-strong Senior School. (*See Bromsgrove School entry in HMC section.*) The sites covering 100 acres offer exclusive and shared facilities, with a combined Prep and Senior Performing Arts Complex opened in November 2017, which gives outstanding performance and rehearsal facilities to the School. A new purpose-converted boarding house for 70 boys and girls was opened in 2012. This allows the School's youngest boarders to live together in modern and comfortable surroundings. Other recent improvements include a new suite of classrooms, an upgrading of the dining hall, a new science laboratory, refurbishment of the library, main hall and sports hall. Pupils have access to a flourishing Forest School. Teachers working in both Senior and Preparatory Schools ensure continuity of ethos and expectation.
Academic, sporting and cultural facilities are extensive and outstanding.
Pupils are admitted at the age of 7+ with another substantial intake at 11+ but pupils, including boarders, are admitted throughout the age range up to 13. Admission to the School is by Entrance Test (English and Maths) supported by a report from the current school. Year 5 and 6 pupils are assessed during the course of the year; the outcome of these assessments allow them to be guaranteed a place in Bromsgrove Senior School two years later. Pupils admitted at age 11 are also guaranteed entry to the Senior School.
Prep School boarding is flourishing and the junior boarding house is a lively, homely environment where pupils are cared for by resident houseparents and a team of tutors. The School aims to make a boarder's first experience of life away from home enjoyable and absorbing.
Parents can choose either a five or six day week for their children. All academic lessons are timetabled from Monday to Friday, with Saturdays offering an optional and flexible programme of activities and sports fixtures. The School has a national reputation in a number of sports.
The aim of the School is to provide a first-class education, which identifies and develops the potential of individual pupils, academically, culturally and socially. It prepares them to enter the Senior School with confidence.
In the Preparatory School, there is a purposeful and lively atmosphere. Mutual trust, respect and friendship exist between staff and pupils. The high quality and dedication of the teaching staff, favourable teacher to pupil ratio and regular monitoring of performance ensure that the natural spontaneity and inquisitiveness of this age group are directed purposefully. The 2016 ISI Inspection found the School to be excellent in every category. The pastoral care system is rooted in the School's Christian heritage and firmly founded on the form tutor. It is designed to ensure that every pupil is recognised as an important individual and that their development is nurtured.

The School has its own feeder Pre-Preparatory School which takes children from the age of 3. The clear majority of children transfer to the Prep School at the end of Year 2. Situated just a mile away in the spacious tree-lined grounds of an old manor house, the Pre-Preparatory School has spacious and light classrooms, equipped with interactive whiteboards. High teacher to pupil ratios and small class sizes ensure each pupil's individual needs are met.
Charitable status. Bromsgrove School is a Registered Charity, number 1098740. It exists to provide education for boys and girls.

Brontë House
The Junior School of Woodhouse Grove

Apperley Bridge, Bradford, West Yorkshire BD10 0PQ
Tel: 0113 250 2811
Fax: 0113 250 0666
email: enquiries@brontehouse.co.uk
website: www.woodhousegrove.co.uk
Twitter: @BronteHouse_
Facebook: @woodhousegroveschool

Chairman of Governors: A Wintersgill, FCA

Headmaster: **S W Dunn**, BEd

Headmaster's Secretary and Admissions: Mrs C Richardson
Deputy Head: Mrs S Chatterton
Director of Studies/Key Stage Two Coordinator: Mrs N S Woodman
Key Stage One Coordinator: Mrs H J Simpson
Foundation Stage Coordinator: Mrs A Hinchliffe

Age Range. 3–11 Co-educational.
Number of Pupils. 358 Boys and Girls.
Fees per term (2018–2019). £3,300–£4,000 (day). Ashdown Lodge Nursery and Reception: £3,000 (full day), £1,870 (half day). Fees are graduated according to age. The day fee covers an extended day from 7.30 am to 6.00 pm; there are no extra charges for breakfast, tea or the majority of supervised activities after lessons.
At Brontë House we welcome children to Ashdown Lodge, our Early Years setting, during the term that they turn three.
The School is situated in its own grounds, a short distance from the Senior School, close to both Leeds and Bradford and with easy access to Leeds/Bradford Airport and the Yorkshire Dales National Park.
Our hard work has been recognised by the Independent Schools Inspectorate inspection in March 2017 which rated Brontë House and Woodhouse Grove as Excellent. The inspectors came away with very clear evidence of the Values that we seek to promote. They recognised our outstanding academic and co-curricular programme and our aim to ensure that all our pupils reach their full potential.
During their time in Foundation Stage, we aim to develop a child's ability and self-confidence, encouraging good behaviour and consideration for others. Children are provided with a stimulating programme of learning and play within a calm and relaxed atmosphere, providing a framework for every individual to fulfil their potential ready for the next stage of their education.
The EYFS curriculum is followed, beginning in Nursery and lasting for two years. Language and literacy, mathematics, knowledge and understanding of the world, physical and

creative development are promoted in preparation for the transfer to Key Stage One.

By encouraging a child's intellectual, creative, sporting and personal development, we aim to get the best from our children in the classroom, on the games field, in music, drama and all other activities. We also offer bushcraft lessons to all pupils, appropriate to their age, where they learn about the outdoors, nature and survival skills. The broad academic curriculum covers a wide range of subjects, including foreign languages, but with particular emphasis on ensuring a strong foundation in reading, writing, mathematics and science.

As children progress through the school they are encouraged to take increasing responsibility and to show consideration for others. Friendship, trust and courtesy are promoted so our children have a sound foundation as they move up to Woodhouse Grove at the end of Year Six.

We aim to encourage every pupil to develop his or her potential by participating in a variety of activities both as part of the curriculum and extracurricular. As they progress through the school, sport plays an increasingly significant role in the life of the children and there are plenty of opportunities for pupils to be involved in team games and individual sports, which encourage not only physical achievement but also a healthy outlook for enjoying school life to the full.

As with sports, music and drama also play an important part of life at Brontë House. All children are encouraged to learn an instrument. The music curriculum is a mixture of traditional and modern with opportunities for composing and performing. There are many choirs and ensembles and the children are regularly offered the chance to take part in concerts and festivals. Housed in spacious rooms on the top floor of Brontë House, our children are given excellent opportunities to develop musically and creatively.

Charitable status. Woodhouse Grove School is part of the Methodist Independent Schools Trust, which is a Registered Charity, number 1142794.

Brooke Priory School

Station Approach, Oakham, Rutland LE15 6QW

Tel: 01572 724778
email: admissions@brooke.rutland.sch.uk
website: www.brooke.rutland.sch.uk
Twitter: @Brooke_Priory
Facebook: @brookepriory

Headmaster: **Mr R Outwin-Flinders**, BEd Hons

Age Range. 2 to 11 years (co-educational).
Number of Pupils. 192: 149 (age 4+ to 11); 38 (Nursery, age 2 to 4).
Fees per term (2018–2019). £2,670–£3,190.
Staff. There are 20 graduate and qualified members of the teaching staff.

Brooke Priory is a day Preparatory School for boys and girls. The school was founded in 1989 and moved into its own purpose-built building in February 1995. Since then it has doubled its classroom provision, established a Nursery, fully-networked Computer Suite, state-of-the-art Resources Centre, Theatre, Art & DT Studios, individual Music Practice Rooms, Sports Hall and use of Oakham School's sports pitches, astroturf and swimming pool.

Brooke Priory provides a stimulating, caring environment in which children are encouraged to attain their highest potential. Class sizes average 16, in parallel forms, and chil-

dren are grouped according to ability in Mathematics and English (reading and spelling).

The school delivers a broad and varied curriculum, where every child will participate in Art, Drama, French and Music. Over 60% of children in the Prep Department enjoy individual music lessons and are encouraged to join one of the Choirs and Ensembles.

The curriculum is enriched with a variety of trips, visits (and residential trips for Forms III–VI) which support learning in the classroom.

In recent years, the school has enjoyed 100% pass rate at 11+ to independent schools and local select entry grammar schools. Some children are offered scholarships to independent schools each year including academic, music and sport. In 2018, 2 academic and 1 music scholarships were awarded to children progressing to Oakham School and Stamford High School (SES). Children progress to senior schools as confident and independent learners.

Sport is an important part of the curriculum. Children swim weekly throughout the year and are coached in a wide variety of games by specialist staff. The main sports are Soccer, Rugby, Hockey, Netball, Cricket, Rounders, Tennis and Athletics.

The original Brooke Priory, which is situated just 1 mile outside Oakham, is set in 30 undulating acres and everyone, from the Nursery to Year VI, visits regularly for Welly Days.

The school offers a wide choice of extracurricular activities.

Before and after school care is available and holiday clubs are enjoyed by many children. Many holiday courses specialise in sport, dance/drama and music and each course is followed by a short presentation to the parents.

Broughton Manor Preparatory School

Newport Road, Broughton, Milton Keynes, Buckinghamshire MK10 9AA

Tel: 01908 665234
Fax: 01908 692501
email: info@bmprep.co.uk
website: www.bmprep.co.uk

Chairman of the Governors: Mr David Pye, BA Hons, Cert Ed, MA Ed Dist, HETC, SEDA III, FRSA

Headmaster: **Mr James Canwell**, BA Hons, PGCE

Deputy Head: Mrs Rachel Smith, BA Hons PGCE
Deputy Head: Mr Jeremy Smith, BA Combined Studies QTS

Age Range. Nursery 2 months–2½ years. Pre-Prep 2½–7 years. Preparatory Department 7+–11 years.
Number of Pupils. 350 Day Pupils.
Fees per term (2018–2019). Nursery (per week): £295 (babies under 1 year), £305 (1–2½ years). Pre-Preparatory: £4,120 (2½–5 years), £4,260 (6–7 years). Preparatory £4,660 (8–11 years).

Broughton Manor Preparatory School is a well-established, family-owned school, with two sister Pre-Preparatory and Preparatory schools based across Milton Keynes.

Opening hours are 7.30 am to 6.30 pm for a 35-week academic year and a total of 46 weeks per year, enabling children of working parents to join play schemes in school holidays and to be cared for outside normal daily school hours.

Staff are highly qualified and committed to delivering the very best teaching and levels of care. Academic standards are "excellent", as rated in the most recent ISI Inspection, with pupils being prepared for entry to senior independent schools locally and nationally and to grammar schools. Teaching is structured to take into account the requirements of the National Curriculum, with constant evaluation and assessment for each pupil. Scholarships are offered for those with all-round academic and sporting abilities from the ages of 7+.

Housed in a modern purpose-built building, all departments also have their own outside soft play and extensive playground areas; there is a multi-purpose sports hall and Astroturf court.

State-of-the-art facilities include an Art workshop, high-tech CTS Suite and Science laboratory.

Additional facilities at The Farm, the school's Environmental Studies Centre, include a fully-equipped fitness room, dance and music studio, arts and craft room and CTS suite. Outside there are a weather station, large pond and polytunnels.

Music and Sport play an important part in the life of the school. Concerts are held, and a wide variety of sport is played, with teams competing regularly against other schools, and additional clubs are held for those wanting to learn specialist activities such as karate and ballet.

The school aims to incorporate the best of modern teaching methods and traditional values in a friendly, caring and busy environment, where good work habits and a concern for the needs of others are paramount.

Bruern Abbey School

Chesterton House, Chesterton, Oxfordshire OX26 1UY

Tel: 01869 242448
Fax: 01869 243949
email: secretary@bruernabbey.org
website: www.bruernabbey.org

Chair of Governors: Mrs Sarah Austen, BA Hons

Headmaster: **Mr J Floyd**, MA, PGCE

Age Range. Boys 7–13.
Number of Pupils. 150.
Fees per term (2018–2019). Day £8,430, Boarding £10,142, Flexi Boarding £59 per night.

Bruern Abbey School is unique in the marketplace because it is the only school in the country that caters exclusively for children diagnosed with learning difficulties and prepares them for Common Entrance to mainstream public schools; learning difficulties should not preclude academic success. ISI has stated that 'pupils are successfully educated in a secure and nurturing environment where they are given every possible help and encouragement to overcome the challenges presented by their specific learning difficulties'. Bruern provides a tailored education in beautiful surroundings and maintains high expectations for the academic future. We aim to enhance boys' self-esteem, in the firm belief that confidence is the key to academic success. A recent Crested report stated that 'Bruern Abbey is a unique school with its own special way of delivering an all-round education for its pupils. It successfully prepares boys for the Common Entrance Examination whilst at the same time developing each boy into a happy and confident individual'.

In most other respects, Bruern models itself on traditional preparatory schools, with breadth to the curriculum, including French to Common Entrance, full and varied sports, activities and cultural programmes, and the adherence to good manners, self-discipline and common courtesy. We encourage boys to share their aspirations and their anxieties. Ofsted has stated that 'the school has an incredibly warm and compassionate approach to all the boys' and also that 'pastoral care is exceptional – very understanding and caring staff'.

At Bruern we place great emphasis on experiencing all that prep school life has to offer; specialist teaching should not mean missing out on all the fun. We also make every effort, despite our somewhat diminutive size, to give the boys an action-packed time – be it musical, theatrical, cultural or sporting.

Bruern differs from traditional preparatory schools in many ways which allow our boys to succeed at Common Entrance and be ready for life beyond. These are regarded as the 'pillars' upon which the School's ethos and reputation, founded by the Principal in 1989, still stand, not to be compromised under any circumstances, and ingrained within the mission statement. They are not necessarily in any order of priority, but are:

- a clear focus on literacy and numeracy, with nine periods each of English and Mathematics a week. We have approximately twice as many English and Maths lessons as standard prep schools for all our Junior School boys, and there are two teachers in each class for these key subjects;
- small classes (eleven pupils or fewer) which allows boys more individual attention in class;
- limited withdrawal for remedial support, as boys needs are met in class;
- the extensive use of IT as a tool with which to deliver the curriculum;
- the use of laptops in lessons. For those who have difficulty in expressing themselves as swiftly or as coherently on paper as they do in speech, this is an absolute godsend;
- the teaching of reading as a distinct curriculum subject and
- the importance attached to good food and to finding the time for children within their busy schedule to eat, talk, play and relax together without the distraction of television or electronic games.

The Buchan School

Castletown, Isle of Man IM9 1RD

Tel: 01624 820481
email: admissions@kwc.im
website: www.kwc.im

Chairman of the Governors: N H Wood, ACA, TEP

Headteacher: **Mrs Janet Billingsley-Evans**, BSc

Age Range. 4–11.
Number of Pupils. 168 (91 boys, 77 girls).
Fees per term (2018–2019). Day only: £3,270 (P1–P3), £4,140 (Forms 1–4).

After more than a century of independence, mainly as a Girls' School, The Buchan School amalgamated, in 1991, with King William's College to form a single continuous provision of Independent Education on the Isle of Man.

As the Preparatory School to King William's College (*see entry in HMC section*), The Buchan School provides an education of all-round quality for boys and girls until the age of 11 when most pupils proceed naturally to the Senior School although the curriculum meets the needs of Common

Entrance, Scholarship and Entrance Examinations to other Independent Senior Schools.

The school buildings are clustered round Westhill House, the centre of the original estate, in fourteen acres of partly wooded grounds. The whole environment, close to the attractive harbour of Castletown, is ideally suited to the needs of younger children. They are able to work and play safely and develop their potential in every direction.

Classes are small throughout, providing considerable individual attention. A well-equipped Nursery provides Pre-School education for up to 65 children. At the age of 5, boys and girls are accepted into the Pre-Preparatory Department. They work largely in their own building in bright, modern classrooms and also make use of the specialist Preparatory School facilities where they proceed three years later.

The School is particularly well-equipped with ICT facilities extending down to the Pre-Prep Department. There is a Pavilion with fields marked out for a variety of team games and a multi-purpose area which is used for Netball, Tennis and Hockey.

There is emphasis on traditional standards in and out of the classroom, with an enterprising range of activities outside normal lessons. Music is strong – both choral and instrumental – and there is energetic involvement in Art, Drama and Sport.

The school strives for high academic standards, aiming to ensure that all pupils enjoy the benefits of a rounded education, giving children every opportunity to develop their individual talents from an early age.

Entry is usually by Interview and School report (if applicable) and the children may join The Buchan School at any time, providing there is space. The School is a happy, friendly community where new pupils integrate quickly socially and academically.

Charitable status. King William's College is a Registered Charity, number 615. It exists for the provision of high quality education for boys and girls.

Buckingham Preparatory School

458 Rayners Lane, Pinner, Middlesex HA5 5DT

Tel: 020 8866 2737
email: office@buckprep.org
website: www.buckprep.org
Twitter: @BuckinghamPrep
Facebook: @buckinghamprep

Chairman of Governors: Mrs Lynn Grimes

***Headmistress*: Mrs Sarah Hollis**

Age Range. Boys 3–11.
Number of Pupils. 123.
Fees per term (2018–2019). £3,200–£4,100 (includes lunches).

Buckingham Preparatory School (BPS) is a small school which offers its pupils an extremely high level of academic education and pastoral care. An ISI inspection in May 2017 rated BPS as "Excellent" and "Outstanding" in each and every aspect of our offering in every part of the school.

Our teaching staff have been universally praised for their "constantly warm and encouraging guidance" and pupil progress is put down to our teachers' "highly effective use of clear explanations" and "because all teachers focus strongly on improving individual pupils' learning and achievement".

With a maximum class size of 18 throughout the school, individual attention is guaranteed.

BPS pupils consistently achieve excellent academic results due to the inspirational teaching, commitment and professionalism of its highly qualified teaching staff. Each year, Year 6 pupils gain offers to the major Independent and Grammar schools in the area and beyond. In the majority of cases, this is to the boys' first-choice schools, often with scholarships.

BPS also prides itself in its results in other areas of the curriculum; areas which are vital in building confidence and self-esteem. Achievement in sport, music and drama is excellent. The pupils regularly take part in local fixtures, often winning inter-school tournaments in cricket, unihoc, football, rugby swimming and cross-country, and other sports. A thriving choir and orchestra, school concerts and plays allow the pupils plentiful opportunities for performance. Many pupils play an orchestral instrument.

The Expressive Arts Week, when pupils have the opportunity of participating in approximately 14 categories of events, is also a focal point of the academic year allowing all boys from the very youngest to demonstrate their individual talents.

The School also believes in forging a strong Parent/Teacher partnership so that parents feel they have a vital role to play in the education of their child. A thriving Parent/Teacher Association also organises as many as three major fundraising events during the academic year which are always well supported and are highlights of the year.

At BPS we do not select pupils based simply on their current academic abilities, but on their desire to learn and achieve. We believe in potential. We believe that if your child wants to succeed, then we will enable him to do so.

Charitable status. The E Ivor Hughes Educational Foundation is a Registered Charity, number 293623.

Burgess Hill Girls – Junior School

Keymer Road, Burgess Hill, West Sussex RH15 0EG

Tel: 01444 241050
email: registrar@burgesshillgirls.com
website: www.burgesshillgirls.com
Twitter: @BHillGirls
Facebook: @BurgessHillGirls
LinkedIn: /burgess-hill-girls

Chairman of Governors: Dr Alison Smith MB, ChB, MRCGP

Head: Mrs E Laybourn, BEd Hons

***Head of Junior School*: Mrs H Cavanagh**, BA Hons, QTS

Deputy Head of Junior School: Mrs S Collins, BA Hons, PGCE

Age Range. Girls 2½–11.
Number of Pupils. 133.
Fees per term (2018–2019). £1,840–£4,750.

Burgess Hill Girls is a day and boarding school for girls between 2½ and 18 years. We welcome boys into our Nursery (2½ to 4 years).

The school stands in 14 acres of beautiful grounds close to the centre of Burgess Hill town. It is a five minute walk from Burgess Hill railway station and transport is provided to collect girls from outlying areas of East and West Sussex.

It is small enough that pupils are known as individuals yet large enough to offer breadth, choice and opportunity. Girls are able to strive for excellence wherever their talents lie and the mix of ages, working together on the same site, gives the school a special character. The aim of the school is to provide each girl with the opportunity to realise her potential and the focus is firmly on girls and the way they learn.

The Junior School provides a broad, varied and stimulating curriculum within a warm and caring environment. Every girl is helped to reach her full potential socially, physically, emotionally and intellectually. Whilst academic achievement is important, the school aims to educate young people for life, providing education in the broadest sense.

The Junior School offers small classes and subject teachers for music, sport and languages. It has an excellent reputation for Music and the Junior School Choir has been invited to sing at St Paul's and Chichester Cathedrals.

All Junior pupils take part in sports, with daily PE lessons. There are many opportunities to play against other schools in a range of sports and many pupils achieve sporting success at local, county and national level.

The Junior School offers fully-equipped subject-specific classrooms for Music, ICT, Art, Science and Technology and access to all the sports facilities on the school campus plus a Learning Hub incorporating a library – a large learning space with access to iPads and an interactive electronic screen.

The Infants and Nursery are based in the Little Oaks building with bright, open classrooms and have their own hall and library. The Infants and Juniors have an exciting playground with a wooden adventure trail and outdoor classroom. The Nursery has an equally exciting specific outdoor play area.

Entrance to the Junior School is by examination and school reference. Scholarships are awarded each year for academic and/or musical excellence into Years 5–6 inclusive.

ISI Inspection 2014. The inspection team reported that:

"Pupils achieve high levels of knowledge, understanding and skills in curriculum subjects and extracurricular activities. Pupils come happily to learn in an environment where they feel safe and secure and where they are valued for their unique personalities and qualities."

"Pupils are well-educated and their levels of achievement are excellent ...pupils of all abilities make good progress. Pupils' attainment ...is judged to be high in relation to national age-related expectations. They achieve excellent learning skills ...effectively equipping them for the next stage of their education."

"Excellent arrangements are in place for the pastoral care of the pupils. Tolerance and understanding are at the heart of their daily interactions. The curriculum is highly effective ...making a significant contribution to pupils' achievements ...supported by an excellent range of extracurricular activities."

The inspectors also commented on our parents *"who are overwhelmingly supportive of all aspects of the school ...overwhelmingly positive about the school and the support their children are given"*.

The inspectors found that *"strong dynamic leadership"* with clear *"vision and determination"*, coupled with *"excellent strategic planning and high levels of self-evaluation are key elements to ensure success"*.

The full report can be viewed on www.isi.net.

Charitable status. Burgess Hill Girls is a Registered Charity, number 307001 (formerly known as Burgess Hill School for Girls).

Bute House Preparatory School for Girls

Bute House, Luxemburg Gardens, Hammersmith, London W6 7EA

Tel: 020 7603 7381
Fax: 020 7371 3446
email: mail@butehouse.co.uk
website: www.butehouse.co.uk

Chairman of Governors: Mr S Wathen

Head: **Mrs Helen Lowe**, BA, LGSM

Age Range. 4–11.
Number of Pupils. 310 Day Girls.
Fees per term (2018–2019). £5,486 inclusive of lunches.

Bute House overlooks extensive playing fields and is housed in a large bright modern building. Facilities include a science laboratory, art room, technology room, music hall, 2 drama studios, multi-purpose hall and a large well-stocked library. A well-qualified, enthusiastic and experienced staff teach a broad curriculum which emphasises both the academic and the aesthetic. Information Technology is an integral part of the curriculum and the school has a wireless network. The classrooms are all equipped with multimedia machines. Laptops are also widely used for individual or class work. Monitored access to the internet is available. French and Spanish are taught from Year 1.

Sports include swimming, gymnastics, dance, tennis, lacrosse, netball and athletics which are taught on excellent on-site facilities. Full use is made of all that London has to offer and residential trips further afield are also offered to older girls.

Girls are encouraged to take full part in the school life from an early age. There is a democratically elected School Council and regular school meetings run by the girls when all pupils are able to put forward their views as well as to volunteer for duties around the school. A wide variety of extracurricular activities is available.

The school aims at academic excellence in a non competitive, happy environment where girls are encouraged to be confident, articulate and independent and where courtesy and consideration are expected. There is a flourishing Parents Association. Entry is by ballot at age 4 and by assessment at age 7.

Caldicott

Crown Lane, Farnham Royal, Buckinghamshire SL2 3SL

Tel: 01753 649300
email: registrar@caldicott.com
website: www.caldicott.com
Twitter: @CaldicottSchool
Facebook: @Caldicott.School

Chairman of the Board of Governors: M S Swift

Headmaster: **Jeremy Banks**, BA Hons, MEd

Age Range. 7–13.
Number of Boys. 105 Boarders and 136 Day Boys.
Fees per term (2018–2019). Year 7 and 8 Boarding: £9,229; Year 5 and 6 Boarding: £8,306; Year 5 and 6 Day: £6,260; Year 3 and 4 Day: £5,611.

Caldicott is a day and boarding country prep school for boys aged 7–13 in South Buckinghamshire. Situated in 40 acres of magnificent grounds, we are just 15 miles from Heathrow Airport and 30 minutes from West London, operating a daily return bus service from Chiswick, Brook Green, Notting Hill and the local area. We pride ourselves on our warm community where our pupils are happy and feel valued.

We have the reputation as one of the best prep schools in the UK with an excellent record in preparing boys for scholarships and Common Entrance to top UK public schools including Eton, Harrow, Radley and Wellington. We have a strong and dynamic staffroom of dedicated and inspirational teachers and professionals. As a result, we have high academic standards and expectations, an outstanding record in art, sport, music and drama scholarships, excellent pastoral provision and a wide range of extra-curricular activities in which all boys can take part.

Our sports fields and facilities are second-to-none and recent sporting successes are numerous. At national level, we have the distinction of being the final winners of the Rosslyn Park National Schools Sevens Tournament Prep Competition (2015 and 2016), winners of the 2016 RNCF Cricket Shield U13 National Competition for Prep Schools and winners of the 2017 U13 IAPS Ski Championships.

Boarding is caring, fun, and an integral part of the school community. Boys live and work together in a friendly, supportive environment, build lifelong friendships and develop independence before they go on to their senior schools at 13+. Boarding is optional in Years 5 and 6 and compulsory in Years 7 and 8, to prepare boys for public school.

We endeavour to harness the best of the school's traditions and values within a forward-looking and innovative approach and within a caring and supportive environment. We ensure boys always aim to do their best, are modest in victory and gracious in defeat, to be givers rather than takers and to be proactive rather than sit back and watch.

Our aim is to broaden boys' interests and develop their personal qualities so that Caldicotians leave fully prepared for the challenges that lie ahead. Senior schools commend us for our well-mannered, considerate, confident boys who have high personal, moral and spiritual values and are striving to become their very best.

Charitable status. Caldicott is a Registered Charity, number 310631. Its purpose is to provide education for the young.

Cameron House

4 The Vale, London SW3 6AH

Tel: 020 7352 4040
Fax: 020 7352 2349
email: info@cameronhouseschool.org
website: www.cameronhouseschool.org

Founded in 1980.

Principal: **Miss Josie Cameron Ashcroft**, BSc, DipEd

Headmistress: Mrs Dina Mallett, BA Ed Hons

   Age Range. 4–11 Co-educational.
   Number of Pupils. 120.
   Fees per term (2018–2019). £6,155.
Based in a beautifully designed Edwardian building, just steps from London King's Road, Cameron House School prides itself on sending pupils to some of the most sought-after schools in the country.

At 11, boys go on to Latymer, Emanuel, Alleyn's, City of London, Colet Court, Westminster Under and other day and boarding schools, and girls leave for St Paul's, Godolphin and Latymer, Queen's Gate, Francis Holland and City of London, as well as a number of other day and boarding schools.

The school is designed to be completely child-centred, modern and warm, creating the right atmosphere for learning. Yet it is not a hot house: its programme is designed to develop each child's personality and to stretch his or her individual talents. A high teacher to pupil ratio is essential to Cameron House's success. Excellent provision is made for children of exceptionally high IQ, or unusual ability, e.g. a Native French Speakers' Club, and Artists' Group.

The aim is to instil a firm sense of self, a passion for exploration and a freedom to express creativity, balanced by good manners, kindness and a selfless interest in others.

One of the first tasks is to foster a joy of reading, which Cameron House believes is the best foundation in each class. All pupils can access the school's own intranet, interactive whiteboards, class sets of laptops and the extensive computer suite.

From their earliest years, music, art, drama and sport form an integral part of the children's school life and excellent local facilities allow the pupils to engage in a wide variety of sports. Unusually, a large majority of children learn karate, which builds physical confidence. Verbal communication skills are also developed, leading to English Speaking Board Examinations or Guildhall Examinations. Other popular clubs are Lunchtime Latin, Touch Typing, Tennis, Chess, Ballet, Tap and Fencing, to name just a few.

Three active choirs, as well as singing and percussion classes, composition and musical appreciation classes, and individual instrument lessons, lead to grade examinations of the Association Board of the Royal Schools of Music.

There is a genuinely open dialogue between parents and teachers, also fostered by The Friends of Cameron House. This contributes to the welcoming feel of the school. The Headmistress of Cameron House is always delighted to give parents a tour of the school so that they can experience its special qualities for themselves.

Cargilfield School

45 Gamekeeper's Road, Edinburgh EH4 6HU

Tel: 0131 336 2207
Fax: 0131 336 3179
email: admin@cargilfield.com
website: www.cargilfield.com
Twitter: @cargilfield

Chairman of the Board of Governors: Mr David Nisbet, BA Hons

Headmaster: **Mr Rob Taylor**, BA, PGCE

Assistant Headmaster: Mr David Walker, BA Hons

Deputy Heads:
Mrs Emma Buchanan, MEd, BEd
Ms Anjali Dholakia, MA Hons, Dip LP, PGDE
Mr Ross Murdoch, BEd Hons

   Age Range. 3–13.
   Number of Children. 310.
   Fees per term (2018–2019). Boarding: £6,481 (weekly). Day Pupils: £5,281, Pre-Prep £3,427, Nursery £2,017–£3,427.

Cargilfield is the oldest independent boarding and day prep school in Scotland, for more than 300 boys and girls, aged 3–13 years. Each child has an extensive range of opportunities to learn, explore and discover before they leave Cargilfield to join leading senior schools across Edinburgh, Scotland and the whole of the UK with no particular tie to any school. Children leave with confident, lively minds, secure values and a sense of identity and community spirit that serves them well for their future lives. We achieve this by delivering a broad and challenging education in a supportive and caring family-led environment. As a prep school, Cargilfield offers your child a chance to reap the benefits and flourish as one of the oldest pupils in the school with positions of responsibility and significance. Without the influence of much older pupils, we can limit the influences that force children to grow up faster than we want and develop instead, qualities of courtesy, self-reliance and assurance.

A small prep school means we get to know our pupils well so that we can guide them towards a senior school that will best suit their needs and reflect your priorities for their education. Small classes, good teaching and high expectations mean that we can achieve high standards for a range of abilities. In addition, a broad curriculum, both inside and outside the classroom, will develop your child's all-round abilities. We play sport every day from age 8 onwards and offer regular opportunities for music, art, design and drama. This is supported by over 40 different clubs, looking to inspire new talents and a wide range of interests. Try flytying or snowboarding, highland dance or computer coding.

As your child grows through the school, there are opportunities to challenge and stretch them further with opportunities to join evening activities, to board on a weekly or flexible basis or to join us on weekend camps or school-based activity weekends.

Charitable status. Cargilfield School is a Registered Charity, number SC005757.

Carrdus School

Overthorpe Hall, Nr Banbury, Oxfordshire OX17 2BS
Tel: 01295 263733
email: office@carrdusschool.co.uk
website: www.carrdusschool.co.uk

Chairman of Governors: Mr J S G Gloag

Headmaster: Mr Edward Way, BSc Hons

Deputy Head: Mr Mark Tetley, BA Hons

Age Range. Boys 3–8, Girls 3–11, Nursery Class for children 3–4½.
Number of Day Pupils. 120 (101 girls, 19 boys).
Fees per term (2018–2019). £245–£3,875. Sibling discount: £75 per term.

Carrdus School is a prep school for girls and a pre-prep school for boys. The large house stands in 11 acres of beautiful grounds.

The teaching staff consists of nine full-time qualified teachers and fifteen part-time specialists. Boys are given a good grounding for their preparatory schools and 7+ or 8+ entrance exams. Girls take 11+ entrance exams. The school has an excellent record of success in examinations, regularly sending girls to well-known independent senior schools, with many achieving Academic Scholarships.

There is a heated outdoor swimming pool, two tennis courts, an Art Studio, Science Lab and a purpose-built Sports Hall. Sport, Music, Drama and Art are highly valued

in the curriculum. There are regular sessions of Outdoor Learning for all children. Daily use is made of Tudor Hall's extensive facilities.

The aim of the school is to produce confident, well-disciplined and happy children, who have the satisfaction of reaching their own highest academic and personal standards. This is possible for an organisation run by teachers for children, flexible enough to achieve a balance between new methods of teaching and sound traditional disciplines.

Charitable status. Carrdus School is part of Tudor Hall School, which is a Registered Charity, number 1042783.

Casterton, Sedbergh Preparatory School

Kirkby Lonsdale, Cumbria LA6 2SG
Tel: 015242 79200
email: hmpa@sedberghprep.org
website: www.sedberghprep.org
Twitter: @Sedbergh_Prep
Facebook: @SedberghPrep
LinkedIn: /casterton-sedbergh-preparatory-school

Chairman of Governors: Hugh M Blair

Headmaster: Mr Will Newman, MA

Age Range. 6 months–13 years Co-educational.
Number of Pupils. 200.
Fees per term (2018–2019). Day £2,770–£5,395, Full Boarding £6,875–£7,970, Weekly Boarding £6,475–£7,530.

Casterton, Sedbergh Preparatory School is situated in the spectacular rural location of the Lune Valley between the Lake District and Yorkshire Dales. There is no rush to grow up here but, the foundations are laid for nurturing the resilience our children need as young adults and the tenacity essential for achieving high standards. This is evident in the unrivalled activities' programme and around the clock personal care, which is offered to our children. Breadth of opportunity and depth of involvement is what sets us apart. Maths competitions, explosions and dissections in Science lessons, pony care at our stables and collecting eggs from the School chickens – all these create outstanding Prep School memories for the young people in our care. Above all, we incubate a sense of success in each and every one of our pupils.

Facilities at our Prep School are first class and include a high-spec Design, Technology and Engineering Department, seven Science specific laboratories, floodlit astro and tennis courts, a theatre, heated pool, equestrian centre and an iMac and iPad suite. Our three boarding houses – Beale, Thornfield and Cressbrook – are very much 'home from home' environments, with all houses having space for music practice and a kitchen for preparing those all-important snacks! Very few Prep Schools dovetail their education with lectures and activities in the way we do here at Sedbergh Prep. Likewise we balance our academics with outdoor learning; we are creating a School farm and pupils consult with the School Chef about growing vegetables and herbs in their Secret Garden. We are excited by the curiosity and thirst for learning that each child, regardless of their academic ability, naturally displays. We work hard to allow each child the time to question and develop their thoughts independently, leading to fresh discoveries in an innovative learning environment. Each child is actively taught to 'own' their learning because all our teachers plan their lessons using three strands – discovering, applying and communicating. To support this, we have recently introduced a Digital Enhanced Learning strategy, including SOLE (self organised learning environment) lessons. This encourages our children to use what they have learnt and to create their own ideas, which are then communicated to their peers. The end result is the celebration of learning – a reward in its own right! One of our strengths is a focus on the individual. We are not a School of rote and regurgitation. Rather, we understand that a child's future success is dependent upon their ability to use what they know in a variety of creative ways, most of which we, as teachers could never have imagined. Every area of School life, therefore, provides fantastic opportunities for creativity of all kinds. Day in, day out, we encourage our pupils live our ethos of 'give it a go and try your best' in order to help them develop a level of resilience and determination that will give them the best chance of overcoming challenges, in all areas of their schooling and beyond. We are responsible for making memories and we are determined to make these as special as possible.

Caterham Preparatory School

Harestone Valley Road, Caterham, Surrey CR3 6YB
Tel: 01883 342097
email: prep.reception@caterhamschool.co.uk
website: www.caterhamprepschool.co.uk

Chairman of Governors: J E K Smith, CBE

Headmaster: **H W G Tuckett**, MA Ed

Age Range. 3–11 years.
Number of Pupils. 288: 152 Boys, 136 Girls.
Fees per Term (2018–2019). Pre-Preparatory £1,950–£3,385. Preparatory £4,320–£5,020. Lunch: £220 (Nursery), £230 (Pre-Preparatory and Preparatory).

The School stands in 200 acres of grounds in the green belt on the slopes of the North Downs, approximately 1 mile outside Caterham.

The curriculum offers the normal range of subjects, including Technology, Theatre Studies and Science, in well-equipped classrooms. In addition, French is taught from age 4. There is a full PE programme, including Soccer, Netball, Cricket, Rounders, Athletics, Tennis, Swimming and Gymnastics. Regular use is made of the sports hall, astroturf and 25m indoor swimming pool.

Over 30 clubs and co-curricular activities take place each week, including Computer Club, Sailing, Drama, Short Tennis, Taekwondo, Needlework, Choir, Orchestra and facilities for instrumental tuition.

All classrooms are equipped with their own multimedia computers and are fully networked with screened internet access. There are also separate ICT Suites in both Prep and Pre-Prep, with 20 computers each.

For entry to the Pre-Prep and Prep School, pupils are invited to visit the school to meet the Headteacher and attend an entrance assessment day. All children for entry to the Pre-Prep (from Reception to Year 2) are informally assessed within the classroom during their entrance assessment day.

The entrance examinations for the Prep School (Year 3 to Year 6) consist of written papers in English and Mathematics, as well as oral language and reading assessments. A report is also requested from the pupil's current school prior to an offer of a place being made.

The Preparatory School enjoys close liaison with Caterham School, to which pupils normally proceed at age 11.

Charitable status. Caterham School is a Registered Charity, number 1109508.

The Cavendish School

31 Inverness Street, London NW1 7HB
Tel: 020 7485 1958
email: admissions@cavendish-school.co.uk
website: www.cavendishschool.co.uk
Twitter: @CavendishSchool
Facebook: @The-Cavendish-School

Chair of Governors: Mrs M Robey

Headmistress: Miss Jane Rogers, BA Hons, PGCE, Dip Sci Ed

Age Range. Girls 3–11; Sibling Boys 3–7.
Number of Children. 255 Day Pupils.
Fees per term (2018–2019). Nursery depending upon number of sessions: from £2,780 (mornings only) to £4,800 (full time). Reception–Year 6: £4,900. Fees include lunch.

The Cavendish School is a small, friendly IAPS school for girls aged three to eleven and sibling boys aged three to seven. The school is situated near Regent's Park in the heart of Camden Town with its excellent public transport links. The Cavendish has a Christian ethos and welcomes pupils of all faiths and none.

The school is non-selective at entry. We provide manageable class sizes and high teacher-pupil ratios so that the foundations of a good education and effective study habits are laid from the beginning.

Through a broad and balanced curriculum we provide personalised learning and much specialised teaching which allows our pupils to flourish. Many gain entry and scholarships to top senior schools at 11+.

There is an extensive programme of extracurricular activities, after-school care services and flexible arrangements for nursery-age pupils.

We are very strong in music, drama and art. Class music is taught by specialists; instruction is available in a wide variety of instruments and we have a thriving orchestra and choirs.

The school is housed in well maintained Victorian buildings and a modern wing with purpose-built ICT facilities. It has recently expanded into a new building which contains a further five classrooms and a 230-seater multi-use auditorium.

The school maintains close links with the local community in a variety of ways both charitable and educational.

Our most recent inspection report by the Independent Schools Inspectorate awarded us 'excellent' in all areas and is available to read via our website.

Charitable status. The Cavendish School is a Registered Charity, number 312727.

Charlotte House Preparatory School
Nursery, Pre-Prep & Preparatory School for Girls

88 The Drive, Rickmansworth, Herts WD3 4DU
Tel: 01923 772101
email: office@chpschool.co.uk
website: www.charlottehouseprepschool.co.uk
Facebook: @CharlotteHousePrepSchool

Chairman of Governors: Mr David Baker

Headmistress: **Miss P Woodcock**, BA Hons QTS

Age Range. 3–11.

Number of Pupils. 140 Girls.

Fees per term (2018–2019). £1,155–£4,195.

Charlotte House is a forward-thinking dynamic school built on traditional values. This winning combination means we instill in our girls all the social and academic tools they need to become independent, successful, confident and caring women.

Our pupils aspire to be the best. We help them discover their talents and encourage them to persevere when they meet challenges. To aid this we teach them a varied curriculum and they are fortunate to have specialist teachers right the way through the school commencing in Nursery.

We are passionate about the learning that goes on outside the classroom walls, whether it is their manners as they move around the school, discovering mini beasts in our beautiful garden or meeting up with their French pen pals in France; we provide the girls with a wealth of experiences to learn more about themselves and the world around them.

Charlotte House encourages the girls to be confident so that they meet challenges head on. We enter many academic and sporting inter-school competitions. We encourage the girls to be confident on stage with termly class assemblies and each girl is involved in an annual play.

At Charlotte House, we recognise the importance of strong links between home and school and provide many opportunities for parents to visit us and find out more about their daughter's progress.

Charlotte House has an excellent record at Secondary Transfer and we have a thorough programme in place to ensure both the girls and their parents feel supported and ready for the challenges secondary transfer poses. Our girls go on to a wide range of schools including state and private schools and the secondary schools often comment on how pleased they are to welcome our girls as they know they will be of a high calibre.

We are a dynamic school whose girls achieve great things!

Charitable status. Charlotte House School Limited is a Registered Charity, number 311075.

Cheam School

Headley, Newbury, Berkshire RG19 8LD

Tel:　　01635 268242
　　　　Registrar: 01635 267822
Fax:　　01635 269345
email:　registrar@cheamschool.co.uk
website:　www.cheamschool.com
Twitter:　@CheamSchool

The School, originally founded in 1645, is a charitable trust controlled by a Board of Governors.

Chairman of Governors: R Marsh

Headmaster: **M J S Harris**, BSc Loughborough, PGCE

Assistant Headmaster: T C Haigh, BA Birmingham, PGCE

Age Range. 3–13.

Number of Pupils. 90 boarders, 410 day children.

Fees per term (2018–2019). £9,210 Boarders; £3,980–£6,590 Day children.

The School became co-educational in September 1997. A merger with Inhurst House School, formerly situated at Baughurst, and which relocated to the Headley site in 1999, offers parents the opportunity for education from 3–13+ for their sons and daughters.

Bursaries are offered annually for 8 year olds.

Classes are small (maximum 18) and pupils are prepared for the major senior independent schools with Eton, Harrow, Radley, Winchester, Marlborough, Bradfield, Wellington, Downe House, St Mary's Ascot, St Mary's Calne and Sherborne Girls' featuring frequently. Recent improvements include excellent facilities for Design Technology and Information Technology, a dedicated Science Building, a refurbished Chapel and Teaching Block, a Music School, a Sports Hall and much improved boarding facilities. Dormitories are comfortable, carpeted and curtained. A new Astro-Turf opened in September 2017.

Rugby, Soccer and Cricket are the major team games for boys; Netball, Rounders, Cricket, Tennis and Hockey for girls. A heated outdoor swimming pool, 6 all-weather tennis courts and a 9-hole golf course in the extensive 80-acre grounds allow a wide range of other sports and pastimes to be enjoyed.

The School is situated half way between Newbury and Basingstoke on the A339 and is within easy reach of the M3 and M4 motorways and the A34 trunk route from Portsmouth, Southampton and Winchester to Oxford and the Midlands. London Heathrow Airport is within an hour's drive.

Charitable status. Cheam School Educational Trust is a Registered Charity, number 290143. It provides high-class education for boarding and day pupils; traditional values; modern thinking; education for the 21st century.

Cheltenham College Preparatory School

Thirlestaine Road, Cheltenham, Gloucestershire GL53 7AB

Tel:　　　01242 522697
Fax:　　　01242 265620
email:　　prepadmissions@cheltenhamcollege.org
website:　www.cheltenhamcollege.org
Twitter:　@cheltprep
Facebook: @cheltprep

President of Council: Mr Bill Straker Nesbit

Head: **Mr Thomas O'Sullivan**, LLB Hons Durham, PGCE Cambridge

Age Range. 3–13.

Number of Pupils. 400 (40 boarders, 360 day boys and girls).

Fees per term (2018–2019). Boarders £6,085–£7,930; Day Boys and Girls £2,725–£6,105.

Cheltenham College Preparatory School is a co-educational preparatory school from 3 to 13. The Pre-Prep Department, Kingfishers, is located in a separate purpose-built wing.

The school stands in a beautiful 15-acre site near the centre of Regency Cheltenham; the town itself being well served by both motorway and rail networks. Pupils enjoy a brand new, dedicated Science and Technology Centre with university grade Science labs and state-of-the-art technology equipment including a laser cutter and 3D printer. Around the school, other excellent facilities include: an art studio, extensive ICT suites, music school, large multi-purpose Assembly Hall, and woodland Forest School. It also benefits from the College's amenities including the stunning College Chapel, spacious sports complex with a 25m indoor swimming pool, floodlit astroturf all-weather pitches, athletics track, squash courts, tennis courts, and fully-equipped Science laboratories.

The curriculum is wide and stimulating with all pupils being prepared for 13+ Common Entrance and Scholarship examinations. In addition to the normal academic subjects, all pupils study Art, Music, PE, Information Technology, and Design & Technology, all led by a team of professional and dedicated teachers.

A wide range of sports are available including: rugby, cricket, hockey, cross country, netball, badminton, athletics, golf, gymnastics, squash, ballet, sailing, skiing, horse riding, fencing, archery, swimming, tennis and orienteering. Sporting skills are taught from an early age and include swimming for the whole school.

The Boarding House aims to provide a 'home from home', with excellent pastoral care and a wide range of extracurricular activities under the supervision of the House Parents. The boarding facilities themselves are large and airy, with plenty of pictures, toys and colourful duvets making the place warm and homely. Regular contact with parents is encouraged with frequent exeat weekends, with flexi boarding being a popular option for children from Year 3 up. Progress reports are issued three times a term and either formal parent/teacher meetings are held or full reports issued at the end of each term.

Visitors are warmly welcomed and further information is available from the Prep Admissions team, who arranges school tours, Taster Days, entry assessments and meetings with the Head.

Charitable status. Cheltenham College is a Registered Charity, number 311720. It exists to provide education for boys and girls.

Chesham Preparatory School

Two Dells Lane, Chesham, Bucks HP5 3QF

Tel: 01494 782619
Fax: 01494 791645
email: secretary@cheshamprep.co.uk
              registrar@cheshamprep.co.uk
website: www.cheshamprep.co.uk

Chairman of Governors: Mr Nick Baker, BA Hons, PGCE

Headmaster: **Mr Jonathan Beale**, BEd Hons, PGCE

Age Range. 3–13.
Numbers of Pupils. 400 boys and girls.
Fees per term (2018–2019). £3,090–£4,800 (inc lunch).

Chesham Preparatory School has a well justified reputation for being an incredibly friendly school where boys and girls work hard, behave well and achieve wonderful things. The most recent ISI report (2016) is glowing in its praise for a school in which, "The quality of the pupils' achievements and learning is excellent. The pupils' attitude to their work and learning is exemplary."

Founded in 1938, Chesham Prep has developed into a flourishing co-educational school. As a partially selective school which educates pupils from 3 to 13 years of age, it champions the strong belief that boys and girls of Prep school age should be educated together. They thrive in the holistic, caring environment and there is a real emphasis on

ensuring that every child fulfils his or her potential whatever his or her varied strengths.

In September 2011 the school was delighted to announce the opening of its nursery – extending the provision offered to children rising 3 years old. From that early age, the children are well prepared for a smooth transition into their Reception class and, very importantly, they feel part of the Chesham Prep family.

The school boasts excellent success rates at 11+ Grammar school entry, as well as 13+ Common Entrance to senior independent schools. All pupils benefit enormously from the wonderful years of personal development at Chesham Prep.

Sports teams are highly skilled and competitive, while there is a fabulous choir and orchestra, as well as a wide range of opportunities for involvement in the creative arts. Children are encouraged to express themselves with joy and passion!

Above all, it is the aim of Chesham Preparatory School to inspire children with a love of learning and a confidence to make the most of their abilities.

To find out more or to arrange to visit the school, please visit our website: www.cheshamprep.co.uk.

Charitable status. Chesham Preparatory School is a Registered Charity, number 310642. It exists to provide education for boys and girls.

Chigwell Junior School

Chigwell, Essex IG7 6QF

Tel: 020 8501 5721
Fax: 020 8501 5723
email: admissions@chigwell-school.org
website: www.chigwell-school.org
Twitter: @chigwellschool

Chairman of the Governors: Mrs S Aliker, BA, MBA, ACMA

Head of the Junior School: **Mr A Stubbs**, BA, PGCE

Age Range. 4–13.
Number of Pupils. 508 Day Pupils.
Fees per term (2018–2019). £3,995–£5,995 inc Lunch/ Tea.

The Junior School is housed in a purpose-built building on the same site as the Senior School only 7 miles from the heart of London. It shares the use of a wide range of activities and facilities including Chapel, Science laboratories, Music School, Arts and Technology Centre, Theatre, Gymnasium, Swimming Pool, Sports Hall and 100 acres of playing fields.

The curriculum and administration of the Senior and Junior Schools are very closely linked and are overseen by the Headmaster.

Pupils sit a written test for entry to the Junior School and are normally admitted to the Senior School without further examination. (*See Chigwell School entry in HMC section.*)

A Pre Prep opened in September 2013 for 4–7 year old children in a purpose-built building. Entry is by assessment.

Charitable status. Chigwell School is a Registered Charity, number 1115098. It exists to provide a rounded education of the highest quality for its pupils.

Chinthurst School

52 Tadworth St, Tadworth, Surrey KT20 5QZ

Tel: 01737 812011
email: info@chinthurstschool.co.uk
website: www.chinthurstschool.co.uk
Twitter: @ChintSchool
Facebook: @ChinthurstSchool

The School is an Educational Trust, administered by a Board of Governors.

Chair of Governors: Mr Marc Benton

Headteacher: **Miss Cathy Trundle**, BA Hons QTS

Age Range. Rising 3–11.
Number of Pupils. 190.
Fees per term (2018–2019). Green Shoots: £357 per morning session, £1,070 (3 sessions min). Kindergarten: £1,785 (5 sessions min). Lower School £3,670 (inc Lunch); Upper School £4,950 (inc Lunch).

Chinthurst School is a leading co-educational school for children aged 3 to 11 years and is part of the Reigate Grammar School (RGS) Family. Children proceed to a range of top independent and state schools and can benefit from early offer entrance arrangements to RGS in Year 5, should this be their chosen path. Outstanding 11 plus results reflect a challenging and diverse curriculum delivered within a caring environment where each child is encouraged to reach their potential.

An education of considerable depth and breadth is delivered within an atmosphere of respect, nurture and, importantly, fun. All pupils are encouraged to be ambitious and to reach the best standards they can, not only academically, but in all areas of extracurricular activity. However, children are valued for who they are, not just for what they achieve and enjoyment and enthusiasm to learn are key. From the beginning, they are encouraged to have a caring attitude towards others and to develop confidence and interpersonal skills and this provides the framework from which they become responsible, adaptable and independent adults.

The children's horizons are broadened through excellent provision of Music, Drama, Art and DT. There is a range of music ensembles and choirs for the children to enjoy and plenty of opportunity to showcase their musical talents. Drama is a strength throughout the school and this is reflected in outstanding results in LAMDA drama exams. The children excel at sport and dedicated specialist teachers work hard to find a sport that each child enjoys. Sports teams are of an excellent standard and after-school clubs give the children a chance to develop their skills further. This is evident in the numerous successes on the sports field and in the pool.

Charitable status. Chinthurst School is a Registered Charity, number 271160 A/1.

The Chorister School

Durham DH1 3EL

Tel: 0191 384 2935
email: registrar@thechoristerschool.com
website: www.thechoristerschool.com
Twitter: @TheChoristerSchool

Chairman of Governors: The Dean of Durham, The Very Revd Andrew Tremlett

Headmaster: **Mr Ian Wicks**, BEng Hons, PGCE

Age Range. 3–13.
Number of Pupils. 170 (30 Boarders, 140 day pupils, including 40 in the Nursery and the Pre-Prep.) The school became co-educational in 1995 and there are girls in every year group.

Fees per term (2018–2019). Choristers (including piano lessons) £3,840, Full/Weekly Boarders £7,320, Day Pupils £4,275, Pre-Prep £3,840, Nursery £25 per half day session. Reductions are available for children of CofE clergy, serving members of the armed forces, children of Durham University staff, children of former pupils and for younger siblings. Scholarships available at entry to Year 7. Fees are inclusive of all normal requirements; there are no compulsory extras.

The Chorister School is in an outstanding situation in a World Heritage Site tucked behind Durham Cathedral. Quiet and secluded it is a haven in the centre of Durham City. Whilst it is the school for the choristers who sing in the renowned Cathedral Choir, over eighty per cent of pupils are not choristers.

Pastoral care is the responsibility of all members of staff. The needs of the boarders are attended to by a dedicated team led by the Housemistress, Housemaster and Headmistress. Before and After School Care is available from the Nursery onwards and there is a wide range of after-school activities including: Art, Ancient Greek, Textiles, Rowing, Gardening, Choirs, Dance, Film Club, Sports, Speech and Drama, Music Ensembles and World Challenge. Flexible boarding is also available.

Our curriculum introduces French from Pre-Prep level, where each of the classes has its own class teacher. In the Prep School class-teaching of the core curriculum is gradually replaced by subject-specialist teaching as children are prepared for Common Entrance and Scholarship examinations to senior schools. The school has a reputation for academic success, but cherishes all its pupils, whatever their academic attainment. The curriculum, which includes RE, PE, swimming, Art, Technology and Music, is designed to ensure that academic edge does not lead to academic narrowness.

Games are an important element in the curriculum. The Chorister School competes at various levels with other schools in athletics, cricket, netball, hockey, rounders, rugby, football and swimming. Badminton, volleyball, basketball, tennis, indoor football and netball (in our large Sports Hall) are also played. The Chorister School has its own sports fields, tennis court and play areas, and uses the indoor swimming pool at Durham School.

Individual instrumental music lessons are available in almost all instruments, and all pupils take class music in which they sing and learn about musical history, musical instruments, simple analysis and some famous pieces.

Entry is by English and Maths test graded according to age or by informal assessment during a 'taster' day, as seems best for the age of the individual child. Competitive auditions for aspiring Choristers are held regularly, with pre-audition training sessions offered by appointment.

Next School. Children move from The Chorister School to a wide range of maintained and independent secondary schools throughout the North East and further afield. The school advises and guides parents in the appropriate choice of next school and aims to secure a successful transition for every pupil. In the past ten years every child has won a place to the senior school of choice, with an average of 60% winning an academic or subject scholarship or a competitive entry place.

Charitable status. The Chorister School and Durham Cathedral enjoy charitable status (exempt from registration) and the school exists to provide boarding education for the choristers of Durham Cathedral and day or boarding education for other children aged 3–13.

Christ Church Cathedral School

3 Brewer Street, Oxford OX1 1QW

Tel:	01865 242561
Fax:	01865 202945
email:	schooloffice@cccs.org.uk
website:	www.cccs.org.uk

Chairman of Governors: The Very Reverend Professor Martyn Percy, Dean of Christ Church

Headmaster: **Mr Richard Murray**, BA, MA

Age Range. 3–13 (Co-ed Nursery).

Number of Boys. 20 boarders, all of whom are Cathedral Choristers (who must board), and 135 day pupils.

Fees per term (2018–2019). Day boys (including lunch) £5,523; Pre-Prep £2,563–£3,890 (including lunch); Cathedral Choristers £3,486; Probationer Choristers: £3,853 (Chorister fees are subsidised by the Cathedral); Nursery £1,889–£2,606 (inc EY Funding).

Christ Church Cathedral School is a day Preparatory and Pre-Preparatory School for Boys with a Co-ed Nursery.

The School provides Choristers for the choirs of Christ Church Cathedral and Worcester College, and is governed by the Dean and Canons of Christ Church, with the assistance of lay members drawn from the city's professional community, some of whom are past or current parents.

It was founded in 1546 when provision was made for the education of eight Choristers in King Henry VIII's foundation of Christ Church on the site of Cardinal Wolsey's earlier foundation of Cardinal College. In the latter half of the nineteenth century, at the initiative of Dean Liddell, father of Alice Liddell, the inspiration for 'Alice in Wonderland', the boarding house was established at No 1 Brewer Street, and in 1892, during the Headship of the Reverend Henry Sayers, father of Dorothy L Sayers, the Italian Mediaeval scholar and creator of Lord Peter Wimsey, the present building was erected.

The School is centrally situated off St Aldates, two hundred yards from Christ Church. It therefore enjoys the unique cultural background provided by Oxford itself as well as beautiful playing fields on Christ Church Meadow. Buildings include a former residence of Cardinal Wolsey and the Sir William Walton Centre, which contains a recital hall and spacious classrooms.

Charitable status. Christ Church Cathedral School Education Trust is a Registered Charity, number 1114828.

Churcher's College Junior School and Nursery

Midhurst Road, Liphook, Hampshire GU30 7HT

Tel:	01730 236870
Fax:	01428 722550
email:	ccjsoffice@churcherscollege.com
website:	www.churcherscollege.com

Chairman of Governors: M J Gallagher, Dip Arch Hons, RIBA, MIoD, FIMgt

Head: **Mrs F Robinson**, BA, MA

Age Range. 2¾–11 Co-educational.

Number of Pupils. 225 (excluding Nursery)

Fees per term (2018–2019). £3,305–£3,530 excluding lunch.

Churcher's College Junior School and Nursery is the perfect place to start your child's learning journey.

We are a haven for learning and adventure with a 'have a go' philosophy and an overarching aim for each child to reach their personal best inside and outside the classroom. With a broad and rich curriculum, the children enjoy a range of subjects and fully seize the array of opportunities on offer. From the academic to the activities that feed the soul, the children love it here.

Set just off the South Downs in Liphook, Hampshire, your child can experience a real countryside childhood and then make a very smooth transition at eleven years old as she/he moves to the Senior School in Petersfield. We fully support each child at every step of the entrance process. Every child's happiness is paramount to their achievement and we pride ourselves on our high-quality pastoral care, excellent teaching and learning, all within a warm, family atmosphere.

The Nursery. Nestled in the grounds of our Junior School, Churcher's College Nursery is a warm and creative environment where children are encouraged to explore, question and discover. Every child is unique and we want to give each boy and girl every opportunity to grow and flourish in a safe and nurturing environment so that they become happy, self-confident and thoughtful children who respect each other and the wonderful natural space they are sharing.

Pastoral. Happy children make happy learners. We strive to create a secure and friendly place of learning in which our children feel valued and where they can grow personally, socially, spiritually and intellectually. Class teachers take responsibility for day-to-day pastoral care. Heads of School support pupils, parents and staff. Our close-knit community enables us to talk freely with parents and vice versa. We work hard to make sure pupils thrive here. The House system fosters great community spirit, allowing friendships to form between year groups.

Academic. Academic rigour is at the heart of our teaching.

Junior Curriculum: A broad and balanced curriculum, combining academic, creative and cultural elements, gives children a varied day and also develops a lifelong love of learning in preparation for Senior School and beyond.

Nursery and Reception: Pupils in the Nursery and Reception Class follow the Early Years Foundation Stage curriculum.

Sport. We offer a broad range of sports to help develop fitness and skills, teamwork and a healthy attitude towards competition through PE and Games. There are many opportunities to represent the school in a variety of matches from Year 2 onwards. The pupils learn a great deal from these: etiquette, collaboration, organisation, sportsmanship. They enjoy the experiences immensely.

Music and Drama. The Arts play a significant role throughout school life at the Junior School.

Music is integral throughout school life and is a dynamic and engaging department at the Junior School. Music is made accessible to all pupils, whatever their abilities, whether being inspired for the first time or developing existing skills. With plenty of performance opportunities, the pupils' confidence is positively built. From the harp to trombone, individual music lessons are available at extra cost.

Drama plays a key part in helping our pupils to gain confidence and to develop their imagination and communication skills. There are a number of dramatic performances throughout the year. The Infants are all involved in a wonderful Nativity performance and a summer production. At key points during their Junior years, year groups work together to perform a production. Assemblies and workshops also provide more opportunities for pupils to unleash their dramatic flair and build every child's confidence.

Adventure. Building confidence and self-esteem is important for all of our children. We do this by providing challenging and adventurous activities that include the opportunity to take risk in a controlled environment. This is achieved through our Outdoor Adventurous Activities Programme and embedding Learning Outside the Classroom throughout the curriculum. From onsite campfire events to residential trips off site, the children relish the opportunity to learn outside their comfort zone. Children remember these adventures and experiences fondly.

Clubs and After-school Activities. Pupils at Churcher's are encouraged to be involved in a wide range of activities, to broaden their interests and try new things. There is a great deal of choice, with activities ranging from sports and drama to music and dance. We love giving our children every opportunity to discover something a bit different or try out a new activity, and we find they thoroughly enjoy doing so.

Charitable status. Churcher's College is Registered Charity, number 1173833, and a Charitable Company Limited by Guarantee, registered in England and Wales, company number 10813349.

City of London Freemen's Junior School

Ashtead Park, Surrey KT21 1ET

Tel:	01372 822474 (PA)
	01372 822423 (Admissions)
Fax:	01372 822415
	01372 822416 (Admissions)
email:	admissions@freemens.org
website:	www.freemens.org

Co-educational day school.

Chairman of Governors: Mr Roger Chadwick

Head: **Mr Matt Robinson**, BA Hons, MA, MEd

Age Range. 7–13.
Number of Pupils. 388.
Fees per term (2018–2019). Tuition £4,466–£4,914.

The City of London Freemen's Junior School was established formally in 1988 as an integral part of Freemen's and it prepares girls and boys for entry to the Senior School in Year 9. The School is located on a magnificent 57-acre site in Ashtead Park, Surrey, where the many outstanding facilities are available to all pupils (*see separate entry in HMC section*).

With its broad based curriculum and modern purpose-built facilities, the Junior School offers a challenging and unique atmosphere for all. There is a Junior School Head with specialist teaching staff and a clearly defined academic and pastoral structure to ensure that all pupils know what is expected of them. The Junior School encourages young pupils to develop their strengths and discover new skills and

passions in an environment of kindness, honesty and fun. There are usually 20 pupils in each of the three parallel classes in each year group. In Year 7 the year groups rises to four classes. Junior pupils benefit greatly from seeing their Form Prefects, who are Sixth Formers from the Senior School, on a daily basis.

For the first four years, in Key Stage 2, Heads of Year work in liaison with the subject coordinators and the Heads of Senior School Departments to ensure that the programmes of work are compatible and progressive. The aim is to establish a secure foundation in traditional core subjects within a curriculum which will broaden experience and excite the imagination of each child. In Years 7 and 8 the teaching programme is managed by the Heads of the Senior School Departments using specialist teachers for all of the subjects. Whilst academic excellence throughout the Junior School is still a major aim, there is also an enrichment programme and a very full programme of extracurricular activities including drama, music and sports.

Fully integrated into whole school routines, the Junior School takes full advantage of Ashtead Park's facilities. Extensive playing fields, the floodlit all-weather pitch and the sports hall ensure that the sports facilities available are second to none.

There are three Houses in the School providing pastoral care and supervision whilst also promoting healthy competition in many activities. In both the Senior and the Junior School outstanding work and good progress, inside and outside the classroom, are recognised by the award of appropriate merits and distinctions.

Admission to the Junior School is through entrance examination, interview and feeder school report. Progression to the Senior School is based on continuous assessment with no separate qualifying entrance test and as such is almost always automatic for Junior School pupils. Pupils are constantly reviewed and can be assured that they will move through to the Senior School with many familiar faces around them.

Claremont Fan Court Preparatory and Nursery School

Claremont Drive, Esher, Surrey KT10 9LY

Tel:	01372 465380
email:	prepschool@claremont.surrey.sch.uk
website:	www.claremontfancourt.co.uk

Chair of Governors: Mr Gordon Hunt, MA Kingston, Adv Dip Ed Exeter, Cert Ed Belfast

Head: **Mrs Helen Hutton-Attenborough**, BSc Bristol, PGCE

Age Range. 2½–11 Co-educational.
Number of Pupils. 350.

Claremont Fan Court Preparatory and Nursery School is fortunate to be situated within a hundred acres of beautiful Grade One listed landscape. Whilst offering the advantages of a Preparatory School that is run and organised independently, we also have the benefit of sharing facilities and expertise with our Senior School; most children choose to transfer seamlessly on to the Senior School, taking advantage of an education through to Sixth Form.

The Pre-Preparatory and Nursery School have their own self-contained building, where children flourish in the spacious, purpose-built classrooms, surrounded by the delights of wooded parkland. Here our youngest children have the freedom to grow and develop in a secure and healthy environment. The partnership between home and School is strong, with shared values for life taught in a supportive, caring atmosphere. An emphasis on the early acquisition of knowledge and skills in literacy and numeracy, within the context of a stimulating and creative curriculum, prepares the children well for the onward move to the Preparatory department in Year 3.

The Preparatory School is housed in the historic Stable Court and backs onto an idyllic Walled Garden, originally built by Sir John Vanbrugh in 1708. Within this heritage building, children benefit from a progressive educational philosophy that combines the best of old fashioned rigour with contemporary practice.

No two days are the same at the Preparatory School and the children arrive with a smile on their face and a skip in their step. Our dynamic curriculum offers each child the opportunity to develop their unlimited potential both in and outside the classroom. The ethos of our school promotes tolerance, respect and friendship; kindness underpins our actions and thus children love their time here, knowing that they are valued as individuals within our tight knit community.

From the earliest days in Nursery, through to Year 6 and the move on to the next stage of their education, each child is known to us. Academic progress and pastoral care are inspired and provided in equal, excellent measure by our dedicated staff team. With a forward thinking curriculum, incorporating traditional academic delivery with creative, sporting and musical activities, and a rich programme of character development, Claremont Fan Court Preparatory School is a school where children blossom and achieve more than they believed possible.

Fees per term (2018–2019). Pre-Nursery (2–5 mornings) £760–£1,900; Nursery (5 mornings per week) £1,780; Full-time Nursery, Reception, Year 1 and Year 2 £3,560; Years 3–6 £4,480.

Charitable status. The Claremont Fan Court Foundation Limited is Registered Charity, number 274664.

An ongoing development programme has provided this fully co-educational school with outstanding facilities for sport, music, drama and the arts, while the 62-acre parkland campus, in beautiful rural Dorset, is the ideal environment for young ones to experience a true childhood as they grow. A state-of-the-art building was opened in 2008 comprising five classrooms and two Science laboratories. An adventure playground, complete with pirate ship, has recently been built, and the ballpark has been updated.

The 'all through' provision means there is a comfortable transition between schools and Prep pupils can make a worry-free step up to Senior School accompanied by a soothing sense of familiarity.

The school is proud of its long association with HM Forces and offers a number of service bursaries. There are also children from expatriate families and the school is well versed in handling overseas travel arrangements.

Small classes and individual attention ensure speedy progress and each day at Clayesmore is further enriched by the superb facilities and exciting activities. Younger children spend most of their time with their Form Teacher but by age 10, children are taught by specialist subject teachers. In the upper school the children are put in sets for Mathematics and English, with some streaming taking place in Science, Humanities and Languages, to allow them to proceed at their own pace. Though the pressure of academic work increases as examinations approach, every child experiences a full range of Art, Music, ICT, Design Technology and Games as well as vital play and relaxation time.

Clayesmore has an outstanding reputation for supporting pupils with dyslexia. Regular staff training means that the work of the Learning Support specialists is understood and reinforced by subject staff and form teachers.

When they are ready to move on to the next stage of their education, pupils are prepared for Common Entrance and Senior School Scholarship examinations.

Charitable status. Clayesmore School is a Registered Charity, number 306214. It exists for the purpose of educating children.

Clayesmore Preparatory School

Iwerne Minster, Blandford Forum, Dorset DT11 8PH

Tel: 01747 813155
email: admissions@clayesmore.com
website: www.clayesmore.com
Twitter: @clayesmoreprep

Chairman of Governors: Mr J Andrews, LLB

Head: **Mrs J S Thomson**, BA, MBA, FRSA

Age Range. 2–13 years.
Number of Pupils. 217 (Boarders 56, Day 161).
Fees per term (2018–2019). Boarders: £5,890 (Year 3), £8,370 (Years 4–8). Day Pupils: £2,570 (Pre-Prep), £4,410 (Year 3), £4,750 (Tear 4), £6,250 (Years 5–8).

Filled with a warm, friendly atmosphere, Clayesmore Prep offers excitement and opportunity at every turn with the aim of developing the unique gifts of every pupil. Founded in 1929 at Charlton Marshall House by R A L Everett, the Prep School moved to Iwerne Minster in 1974 and now nestles side by side with the thriving Senior School. There is also a Nursery and Pre-Prep, with their own snug self-contained home, where little ones learn and develop through play and via a host of activities led by specialist teachers.

Clifton College Pre-Preparatory School

Guthrie Road, Clifton, Bristol BS8 3EZ

Tel: +44 (0)117 3157 591
             +44 (0)117 911 5785 (Admissions)
Fax: +44 (0)117 3157 101
email: prepadmissions@cliftoncollege.com
website: www.cliftoncollege.com
Twitter: @Clifton_College
Facebook: @CliftonCollegeUK
LinkedIn: /clifton-college

Chairman of College Council: Mrs Alison Streatfeild-James MA

Headmistress: **Joanne Newman**, BSc, MSc, PGCE

Age Range. 2–8.
Number of Pupils. 172.
Fees per term (2018–2019). 2 year olds (3–5 full days) £2,204–£3,674; 3–4 year olds (3–5 full days) £2,004–£3,340; Reception (5 full days) £3,340; Year 1 £3,545; Years 2–3 £3,900.

Clifton College Pre-Preparatory School, part of the main Preparatory School, is independent of Clifton College in terms of running and organisation. However, it benefits from being governed by the same Council and enjoys the considerable advantages of sharing many of the College's extensive facilities. These include the swimming pool, sports hall, gymnasium, multi-activity hall, Chapel and Theatre. The School is situated in two buildings either side of a superb playground with a variety of play equipment.

The School caters for children in the Foundation Stage (Nursery and Reception), Key Stage 1 (Years 1 and 2) and Year 3, the first year of Key Stage 2. The Nursery has up to 60 children on roll, with a staff to pupil ratio of 1:4 for 2-year-olds and from 1:6 for 3-year-olds. Attendance in the Nursery may be either five mornings, three days or full-time for 3-year-olds and a minimum of two sessions for 2-year-olds. The Nursery staff are either qualified teachers or Early Years practitioners.

There are two classes in Reception and Year 1, and three classes in Years 2 and 3, each with a class teacher and teaching assistant. In all, there are 22 full-time and 15 part-time staff. Qualified specialist class teachers deliver a topic-based curriculum, with specialist teachers for Music, Dance (Ballet, Jazz Dance, Tap), Sport, French, Mandarin and IT. Piano and instrumental lessons are available from Year 2, and all children in Years 2 and 3 learn the recorder, strings and sing in the choir. Some sports activity takes place every day.

Life at the Pre-Preparatory is busy and exciting. Year 2 and 3 pupils may take part in a range of co-curricular activities at lunchtimes or after school, when around 16 clubs and societies are held. These change termly and include a variety of sports, street dance, sewing club, craft club, science club, ukulele club, book club and lego club etc. Termly services and concerts are held in the Chapel, and an annual musical is performed in the Redgrave Theatre. There is a full programme of visits and outings for all ages, including a youth hostelling trip for Year 3.

Recent investment has seen the creation of an outdoor area leading from the reception classrooms. This is designed to give reception classes easy access to an outdoor space which they can use to extend and enhance their learning.

Another exciting provision is the Forest School at our Beggar's Bush Sports Ground. All year groups, from Nursery to Year 3, visit Forest School and it provides a range of stimulating outdoor experiences for the children, enabling them to learn, achieve and develop confidence through curriculum-linked activities and free exploration of the natural woodland.

Charitable status. Clifton College is a Registered Charity, number 311735. It provides boarding and day education for boys and girls aged 2–18.

Clifton College Preparatory School

The Avenue, Clifton, Bristol BS8 3HE

Tel: +44 (0)117 3157 502
          +44 (0)117 911 2643 (Admissions)
Fax: +44 (0)117 3157 504
email: prepadmissions@cliftoncollege.com
website: www.cliftoncollege.com
Twitter: @Clifton_College
Facebook: @CliftonCollegeUK
LinkedIn: /clifton-college

Chairman of College Council: Mrs Alison Streatfeild-James, MA

Headmaster: Mr Jim Walton, BA

Age Range. 8–13.

Number of Pupils. 311.

Fees per term (2018–2019). Boarders (from Year 4) £8,060–£9,550; Flexi Boarders (3 nights from Year 4) £5,435–£6,855; Day Pupils £4,410–£5,820.

A wide range of subjects is included in the normal curriculum and pupils are supported and encouraged to achieve across the breadth of subjects available. Small class sizes, first-class facilities and teaching excellence enable pupils to reach their academic potential and beyond. The school features in the Sunday Times Top 100 independent preparatory schools list, but the individual successes of pupils are equally important.

The majority of pupils go on to the Upper School, but a number are prepared for and win scholarships to other schools. Over 60 awards have been won in the past three years.

The administration of the School is entirely separate from the Upper School, but some facilities are shared, including the Chapel, Theatre, Sports Complex, Indoor Swimming Pool, Gymnasium, Squash and Rackets Courts and 90 acres of playing fields. This includes an Olympic-standard water-based Hockey pitch, a 3G pitch, an indoor Tennis and Netball Centre and a new Activity Centre. The School has its own Art & Design Centre and possesses one of the most advanced Information Technology Centres in the West of England.

The single-sex system operates for both boarders and day pupils. Two Houses cater for the boarders, each under the supervision of a Housemaster or Housemistress assisted by wife or husband, Tutors and Matrons. The remaining six Houses cater specifically for day pupils. In September 2012, a new purpose-built facility was opened containing two Houses, and a large dance studio with light rigging and a sprung floor. All other Houses are fully renovated.

Out-of-school activities supplementing the main School games are many and varied, the aim being to give every child an opportunity to participate in an activity from which he or she gains confidence and a sense of achievement.

The youngest boys and girls (aged 2–8) work separately in the Pre-Preparatory School next door, under the care of their own Head and teachers. (*See separate IAPS entry for Clifton College Pre-Preparatory School.*)

Charitable status. Clifton College is a Registered Charity, number 311735. It provides boarding and day education for boys and girls aged 2–18 years.

Clifton School and Nursery
The Pre-prep School of St Peter's School, York

Clifton, York YO30 6AB

Tel: 01904 527361
Fax: 01904 527304
email: enquiries@cliftonyork.org.uk
website: www.cliftonyork.org.uk
Twitter: @PhilHardyCPS
Facebook: @clifton.school.and.nursery

Chairman of the Governors: Mr W Woolley

Head: Mr Philip Hardy, BA Northumbria, PGCE

Deputy Head: Mrs Antonia Clarke

Age Range. 3–8 co-educational.
Number of Pupils. 115 boys, 94 girls.

Fees per term (2018–2019). Nursery (full time) £2,660; Reception, Years 1 & 2: £2,875; Year 3: £3,080. Nursery Education Grant accepted for 3 and 4 year olds.

With 47 green acres in the heart of one of the country's most magnificent cities, Clifton School and Nursery offers an vast and stimulating learning environment. As part of the St Peter's School family, Clifton represents the start of an exciting and rewarding learning adventure.

Curriculum. An exciting and dynamic thematic skills-based curriculum is covered, which offers variety, challenge and opportunities for everyone to discover what they love. Small classes, individual attention and a huge range of after-school activities enable high standards to be achieved. French is offered to all children from Nursery upwards.

Music and Drama. All children throughout the school have ample opportunity to be creative and express themselves. Nursery children have a session of music and movement, and all other classes have weekly lessons with a dedicated music teacher. From Year 2, children have the opportunity to learn to play a variety of instruments in personal lessons. Each year there are opportunities for children to participate in performances to a wider audience. All classes have weekly drama lessons, and there is the opportunity for Y2 and Y3 to do speech and drama as an after school activity.

Sport and Co-Curricular Activities. Physical Education starts in the Nursery. As children grow older, games and swimming are added. The pupils at Clifton School and Nursery have access to the impressive sports facilities at St Peter's School. Co-curricular activities include: Art, Drama, Animation, Ballet, Karate, Explorers, Lego and The Green Team

Assessments. Throughout Nursery and Reception, children work towards achieving the Early Learning Goals, culminating in the completion of the Foundation Stage Profile. Work is assessed continuously and children's progress is discussed at monthly staff meetings. Incas is used in Years 1 to 3 for assessment purposes which informs future planning. There is ongoing communication between parents and staff through a reports system, invitations to visit the school and parent evenings.

An ISI Inspection in April 2017 found St Peter's School 3–18 to be 'excellent' in all areas for the quality of its education – the highest grading that any school can achieve.

Charitable status. St Peter's School, York, is a Registered Charity, number 1141329. It exists to provide education for boys and girls.

Cokethorpe Junior School

Witney, Oxfordshire OX29 7PU

Tel:	01993 703921
Fax:	01993 773499
email:	admin@cokethorpe.org
website:	www.cokethorpe.org.uk
Twitter:	@CokethorpeSch
Facebook:	@CokethorpeSch

Chairman of Governors: Mr R F Jonckheer, LLB Hons

Headmaster: D J Ettinger, BA, MA, PGCE, FRSA

Head of Junior School: Mrs N A Black, BA

Age Range. 4–11 Co-educational.
Number of Pupils. 124.
Fees per term (2018–2019). £4,200 Reception–Year 2, £4,500 Years 3–4, £4,700 Years 5–6. Fees include lunch.

Staff. 21 full-time and 2 part-time qualified and enthusiastic staff teach the 9 classes.

Location. Cokethorpe Junior School is set in 150 acres of beautiful Oxfordshire parkland, two miles from Witney and ten from Oxford. It was established in 1994 and occupies the elegant Queen Anne Mansion House that is at the heart of Cokethorpe School. The Junior School retains its own identity, independence and distinct character, allowing the children to flourish, develop confidence and feel valued, whilst having the advantage of being part of a wider community with the Senior School.

Facilities. Whilst self-sufficient in most respects, the Junior School benefits from having access to the Senior School facilities, especially the all-weather pitches, Sports Hall and other sports facilities, performing arts, science laboratories, ICT resources and the splendid Dining Hall. There is also a dedicated play area, library, art room and music room.

Aims. Excellence is at the heart of Cokethorpe School with success measured by the progress of the individual. Teaching and learning extends beyond the classroom and participation is encouraged across all aspects of school life, challenging each child to aim higher, try harder and discover their own potential. Children in the Junior School are excellent company, great fun, hardworking and eager to be involved in all the School has to offer. It is a firm belief at Cokethorpe that children have individual talents, and providing a range of opportunities for them to discover new skills and passions is essential. Whether it is an appetite for academic challenge, a creative flair, a musical ear or natural athleticism, the variety provided by the academic and extra-curricular programme ensures that children experience a host of new activities and are inspired to pursue those they enjoy.

Curriculum. The Junior School offers a fully balanced curriculum with the focus on developing high standards and providing intellectual challenges. Children receive vital foundations for study in small classes and in a positive and purposeful learning environment. Whilst the National Curriculum is followed, the freedom to offer breadth is fully embraced. Trips and events support work done in the classroom and also help children meet the School's high academic, behavioural and social expectations.

Enrichment. Sport and The Arts play a strong part in the Junior School. Children participate in team sports on two afternoons a week, including competitive fixtures, and time is also found for other sports such as swimming, tennis, judo, golf, modern dance and ballet. There are drama productions each year and it is often the case that every child has a speaking or singing role. In addition they have the opportunity to take part in concerts and recitals throughout the year. The dedicated art room is a riot of colour and creativity with displays decorating the corridors and classroom walls.

The School enjoys a particularly close relationship with parents and there is a strong Parents' Association.

Entry. There is no formal assessment for entry to the Reception although children will be invited to spend either the day or half day in School. For entry to Years 1 to 6, children are invited to an Assessment Day, during which they will complete an assessment appropriate to their age. Individual arrangements for assessment can be made throughout the academic year. Reports are also requested from the child's current school or nursery. Early registration is recommended as places are limited. The majority of pupils continue to Cokethorpe Senior School, with many going on to achieve scholarships in the Senior School. (*See Cokethorpe School entry in HMC section.*)

Charitable status. Cokethorpe Educational Trust Limited is a Registered Charity, number 309650.

Colfe's Junior School

Horn Park Lane, London SE12 8AW

Tel: 020 8463 8239 Junior Head
            020 8463 8266 Junior Office
email: junioroffice@colfes.com
website: www.colfes.com
Twitter: @ColfesSchool
Facebook: @ColfesSchool

Chairman of the Governors: Mr Matthew Pellereau, BSc, FRICS

Head of the Junior School: **Miss C Macleod**, MSc

Deputy Head: Mrs K Dempster, BEd
Head of KS2: Mrs V Welch, BA, Cert Ed
Head of KS1/EYFS: Mrs S Gurr, BEd Hons
Director of Studies: Mr M Heil, BEd

Age Range. 3–11.
Number of Pupils. 450 boys and girls.
Fees per term (2018–2019). Junior School, KS2 £4,665 (excluding lunch); KS1 £4,410 (including lunch); EYFS £4,221 (including lunch).

Colfe's Junior School is an independent day school for boys and girls 3–11. Entrance is academically selective. The Junior School offers a broad curriculum and aims to provide an excellent all-round education. Small class sizes and a team of well-qualified teachers provide a caring and vibrant environment. Children normally enter at the ages of 3 or 4, although the occasional vacancy arises at other times.

For the children starting school it is the beginning of an exciting and inspiring journey; this begins in our Nursery and Reception classes which together form the Early Years Foundation Stage (EYFS). Children gain confidence and thrive in a warm, friendly and nurturing atmosphere where they feel secure and valued. Through a specialised play-based curriculum teachers plan for a rich learning environment which provides opportunities for the children to flourish in all aspects of their development. In Years 1 and 2 children begin to study all National Curriculum subjects, building on the skills, knowledge, understanding and experience gained during their time in Nursery and Reception. Moving into KS2 the focus shifts to three aspects of every child – talent, potential and character. Strong curriculum and expert teaching is underpinned by a rich programme of music, art, sport, drama, outdoor pursuits. Each pupil belongs to a House and they compete to earn the most points, helping them to develop a real sense of community.

The majority of Junior School pupils transfer to the Senior School at the end of Year 6, providing they achieve the qualifying standard.

The Junior School is housed in modern purpose-built accommodation with spacious and well-equipped classrooms. Excellent library facilities and specialist accommodation for art and design, ICT and science provide pupils with a stimulating environment in which to learn. Full use is made of the school's swimming pool, sports centre, visual and performing arts centre and extensive on-site playing fields.

PE specialists teach a wide range of sports and there is an extensive programme of House and inter-school sports matches. A school choir, orchestra, strings group and numerous ensembles perform frequently both in and out of school. Drama productions normally take place each term. There is a wide range of after-school clubs on offer (over 50 each week for the 7–11 year olds) and a Breakfast Club from 7.30 am and Late School scheme until 6.00 pm each day.

Charitable status. Colfe's School is a Registered Charity, number 1109650. It exists to provide education for children.

Collingwood School

3 Springfield Road, Wallington, Surrey SM6 0BD

Tel: 020 8647 4607
email: secretary@collingwoodschool.org.uk
website: www.collingwoodschool.org.uk
Twitter: @Collingwood_Sch
Facebook: @Collingwood-School

Headmaster: **Mr Leigh Hardie**

Age Range. 3–11 Co-educational.
Number in School. Day: 100.
Fees per term (2018–2019). £1,660–£2,975 (reduction for siblings).

Collingwood was founded in 1928 and became an Educational Trust in 1978.

It is a school that has deliberately remained small in order to foster a very friendly and caring environment.

Our aim is to give children a first-class academic and sporting education while at the same time instilling the virtues of courtesy, respect and consideration for others. These traditional values, coupled with a modern, relevant education, make Collingwood the happy, purposeful and unique place that it is.

We offer an exciting range of subjects including ICT, French and Spanish. Currently we have over twelve extra-curricular activities taking place each week including street dance, drama, football, gardening, judo and sewing. Children are also able to learn to play a musical instrument such as piano, keyboard, drums, violin, cello, guitar or recorder. We also offer a breakfast, after-school and holiday club.

Although we are a non-selective school, many of our children over the years have gained entry into the local Grammar or Independent Selective Schools.

For a prospectus or to arrange a visit, call Mrs Goff, the Headmaster's PA, on 020 8647 4607.

Charitable status. Collingwood School Educational Trust Ltd is a Registered Charity, number 277682. It exists to promote and foster a sound education for boys and girls aged 3–11 years.

Colston's Lower School

Park Road, Stapleton, Bristol BS16 1BA

Tel: 0117 965 5297
Fax: 0117 965 6330
email: admissions@colstons.org
website: www.colstons.org
Twitter: @colstonsschool
Facebook: @Colstons-School

Chair of Governors: Mr T Ross

Head of Lower School: **Mr D A H Edwards**, BEd, MA

Deputy Head: Mr M Weavers, BEd Hons
Head of Juniors: Mr O Barwell, BA Hons
Head of Pre-Prep: Miss S Evans, BEd Hons

Age Range. 3–11.
Number of Pupils. 230 Day Pupils.

Fees per term (2018–2019). £2,560 (Reception, Years 1 & 2) to £3,160 (Years 3 & 4) and £3,475 (Years 5 & 6) plus catering charge £215.

Colston's Lower School is located in Stapleton village which is within the city of Bristol. It is less than one mile from Junction 2 of the M32 and therefore easily accessible from north Bristol and South Gloucestershire. In addition to its own specialist facilities for Science, ICT, Music, Design & Technology, Art and Games, the Lower School has full use of facilities at the neighbouring Upper School including 30 acres of playing fields, theatre, concert hall and sports centre.

At the end of Year 6 pupils move from the Lower to the Upper School (see entry in HMC section). They work in small classes on a broad and engaging curriculum that extends and enthuses a community of highly active learners. It incorporates the full range of academic subjects together with French, Design and Technology, ICT, Art, Music, Forest School and competitive sports. A wide range of co-curricular activities such as climbing, golf and ballet are also available. The School benefits from a highly efficient Learning Support Unit for those needing additional support and a Gifted and Talented program for those who show particular strengths.

The creative arts flourish in the Lower School, with a choir and orchestra, regular concerts, school plays and music competitions. A large number of children also play musical instruments, with specialist teachers providing weekly tuition.

In addition to PE lessons there are two afternoons of junior games each week. The boys principally play rugby, hockey and cricket, and the girls play hockey, netball and rounders. Pupils also enjoy opportunities to take part in football, tennis, athletics and badminton. All juniors are encouraged to take part in competitive sports fixtures, and sports tours are also arranged.

The school also has its own excellent Forest School site which is used every week for outdoor learning.

Colston's Lower School offers a wide range of clubs and activities, and pupils are able to stay on at school under supervision for an extended day or start with Breakfast Club. There are numerous visits and trips including skiing and adventure activities.

Charitable status. Colston's School is a Registered Charity, number 1079552. Its aims and objectives are the provision of education.

Copthorne School

Effingham Lane, Copthorne, West Sussex RH10 3HR

Tel: 01342 712311
email: office@copthorneprep.co.uk
website: www.copthorneprep.co.uk
Twitter: @copthorneprep
Facebook: @copthorneprep

Chairman of Governors: K Bell

Headmaster: C J Jones, BEd Hons

Deputy Head: N Close

Age Range. 2–13.
Number of Boys and Girls. 350 (20 Boarders).
Fees per term (2018–2019). Day: Reception £3,080, Year 1 £3,175, Year 2 £3,230, Year 3 £4,260, Year 4 £4,675, Years 5–8 £5,365. Weekly Boarding £5,855. Termly Boarding £7,955. Occasional Boarding £28 per night.

Copthorne is a flourishing IAPS Prep School with approximately 350 boys and girls aged from 2 to 13. The school has grown by over 75% within the last 5 years. Children are prepared for Independent School Scholarships or Common Entrance. In the last 5 years Copthorne children have been awarded 48 Scholarships or Awards to a variety of Senior Schools.

We believe that, in order to learn, children must be happy and feel secure in their environment. Copthorne Prep School is full of happy children and the environment is caring but still allows children the freedom to develop as individuals.

The school helps to develop each child's confidence, to raise self-esteem and to make children feel good about themselves. Nothing does this more than children enjoying success in all areas of school life. This is why Art, Music, ICT, DT, Drama and Sport are all just as important as the pursuit of academic excellence.

We provide opportunities for children to achieve success in all areas of the curriculum and we always celebrate their achievements.

We recognise that all children have talents, and every child is encouraged to realise their true potential, whatever that may be, in whatever area of school life.

We demand and set high standards, and our children respond by always giving of their best.

Put simply, our mission is to:

Develop **C**onfidence – Provide **O**pportunity – Realise **P**otential – in every single child.

The school is very proud of its history of over 100 years, and retains all the important traditions of the past whilst developing a very forward thinking approach. The children receive a "child-centred" education, where their individual needs come first, in an environment that is "parent-friendly", with very high levels of communication and pastoral care.

Charitable status. Copthorne School Trust Limited is a Registered Charity, number 270757. It exists to provide education to boys and girls.

Cottesmore School

Buchan Hill, Pease Pottage, West Sussex RH11 9AU

Tel: 01293 520648
Fax: 01293 614784
email: office@cottesmoreschool.com
website: www.cottesmoreschool.com
Twitter: @cottesmoreprep
Facebook: @cottesmoreprepschool

Headmaster: T F Rogerson, BA Hons, PGCE

Age Range. 4–13.
Number of Pupils. 150.
Fees per term (2018–2019). Prep: £5,991 (Day), £9,095 (Boarding); Pre-Prep: £3,199–£4,267.

Cottesmore is a co-educational preparatory school offering Day and Full Boarding for boys and girls in West Sussex. It is situated a mile from Exit 11 of the M23, ten minutes from Gatwick Airport and one hour from Central London and Heathrow Airport.

In September 2009 the school opened a Pre-prep Department.

Curriculum. Boys and girls are taught together in classes averaging 14 in number. The teacher to pupil ratio is 1:9. Children are fully prepared for Common Entrance and Scholarship examinations.

Music. The musical tradition is strong – more than 80% of children learn a variety of instruments; there are three Choirs, a School Orchestra and several musical ensembles.

Sport. The major games are Association Football, Rugby, Cricket, Hockey, Swimming, Tennis, Netball, Athletics and Rounders. Numerous other sports are taught and encouraged. They include Archery, Riding, Basketball, Shooting, Billiards, Short Tennis, Canoeing, Snooker, Cross-Country Running, Squash, Table Tennis, Gymnastics, Trampoline, Golf, Windsurfing and Judo. The School competes at a national level in several of these sports.

Recent Developments. Our Technology Centre houses a constantly developing Information Technology Suite, a Design Technology room for metal, woodwork, plastic and pneumatics, a Craft room, Kiln, two Science laboratories and Art Studio.

Hobbies and Activities. These include Pottery, Photography, Stamp Collecting, Chess, Bridge, Model-Making, Model Railway, Tenpin Bowling, Gardening, Rollerblading, Ballet, Modern Dancing, Drama, Craft, Carpentry, Printing, Cooking and Debating.

The boys and girls lead a full and varied life and are all encouraged to take part in as wide a variety of activities as possible. Weekends are a vital part of the school life and are made busy and fun for all.

Entry requirements. Entry is by Headmaster's interview and a child's last three terms' school reports. For a prospectus and more information, please write to or telephone the Registrar, Lottie Rogerson.

Coworth Flexlands School
United Learning

Valley End, Chobham GU24 8TE

Tel: 01276 855707
email: secretary@coworthflexlands.co.uk
             registrar@coworthflexlands.co.uk
website: www.coworthflexlands.co.uk
Twitter: @CoworthFlexSch
Facebook: @CoworthFlexSch

Chairman of Governors: Mr Gordon Hague

Headmistress: Miss Nicola Cowell

Age Range. Girls 3–11 years; Boys 3–7.
Number of Pupils. 125.
Fees per term (2018–2019). £3,315–£4,470.

Coworth Flexlands School is an independent Prep School & Nursery offering high-quality education for girls to age 11 and boys to age 7. Our pupils have specialist teaching across a broad spectrum right from nursery upwards.

Set in beautiful grounds between Chobham, Windlesham and Sunningdale, the school is ideally located to provide our students with a stimulating environment to develop their skills and abilities. Our two forest school practitioners and outdoor classroom set in the woods enable the children to have a real hands-on learning experience.

Coworth Flexlands is renowned for academic excellence. The girls move on to top senior schools in the UK, with many gaining scholarships each year. Our boys head off to local prep schools well prepared for their new challenges.

The school offers the convenience of optional wraparound care and clubs for busy parents from 7.30 am to 6.00 pm and a wide range of on-site holiday activities.

Charitable status. Coworth Flexlands School School is part of United Learning which comprises: UCST (a Company Limited by Guarantee, Registered in England, number 2780748, and a Registered Charity, number 1016538) and ULT (a Company Limited by Guarantee, Registered in England, number 4439859, and an Exempt Charity).

Crackley Hall School

St Joseph's Park, Kenilworth, Warwickshire CV8 2FT

Tel: 01926 514444
Fax: 01926 514455
email: post@crackleyhall.co.uk
website: www.crackleyhall.co.uk
Twitter: @CrackleyHallSch
Facebook: @crackleyhallandlittlecrackersofficial

Co-educational Nursery and Junior School.

Headmaster: **Mr Robert Duigan**, BComEd, MEd

Deputy Head: Mr Duncan Cottrill, BSc, PGCE
Assistant Head – Early Years Foundation Stage and KS1:
  Mrs Susan Glen-Roots, BEd
Assistant Head – Co-curricular and Cross Phase Liaison:
  Mr Charles Lamprecht, BEd

Age Range. 2–11 years.
Number of Pupils. 275.
Fees per term (2018–2019). Junior School: £3,096–£3,296. Nursery: £255 per week (full time, term time only), £249 per week (full time, all year).

Crackley Hall is a co-educational independent Catholic day school which welcomes pupils of all denominations. The school is part of The Princethorpe Foundation comprising Little Crackers Nursery, Crackley Hall School, Crescent School and Princethorpe College.

Crackley Hall continues to go from strength to strength following the merger with Abbotsford School in September 2010. Under the leadership of Headmaster, Robert Duigan, pupil numbers have risen considerably and we are now well known for our high academic standards, sporting provision and excellence in the performing arts.

In 2017 the ISI Inspectors judged the school to be 'excellent' in every area.

Building work that provided more classrooms, specialist teaching rooms for Art and Music, greatly enhanced IT, Science and Technology suites, and improved sports changing rooms was completed in 2013, and the second phase of major development, a new multi-purpose hall with additional teaching space, was completed in Spring 2016.

Situated on the outskirts of Kenilworth, Crackley Hall occupies a pleasant and safe setting with playing fields a short distance across the road. An extended day facility is offered; pupils may be dropped off from 7.45 am and can stay at school until 6.00 pm. Nursery attendance times are flexible, with term-time and year-round (51 weeks) places available.

Crackley Hall bases its care for individuals on the sound Christian principles of love and forgiveness; children become strong in the understanding of themselves and others. There is a keen sense of community between pupils, staff and parents. We encourage fairness, freedom, friendship and fun.

Small class sizes promote individual attention. The curriculum is based on national guidelines, but pupils are encouraged to achieve well beyond these targets. During the early years, great emphasis is placed on developing key skills in reading, writing, speaking, listening, mathematics and science. The learning of tables and spellings is actively developed through simple homework tasks. Specialists teach Art, Design Technology, French, Music, Games, ICT and RE. Recent investment has resulted in specialist teaching rooms for Art and Music, greatly enhanced IT, Science and Technology suites and improved sports changing facilities.

Sports are very strong with football, rugby, cricket, hockey, netball, tennis, athletics, swimming, rounders, trampolining, gym and karate all available. There is a strong and thriving music department and all pupils together with members of the choir, choral group and orchestra participate in concerts and stage productions to enrich their learning and to build confidence and self-esteem. Pupils have the opportunity to study a wide range of individual instruments under the guidance of a team of peripatetic staff and specialist teachers offer classes in music theatre, speech and drama and dance. Other activities are offered before and after school as well as during lunch breaks including art, chess, craft, ICT, Mandarin, cookery, rock school, Lego, Latin, Irish dancing, brass, climbing, sewing and mindfulness.

Admission is through interview with the Head, assessments in English and Mathematics, and a taster day at the school. We also ask for a reference from the child's current school. The admission information is considered as a whole so that as accurate a picture as possible of the child can be obtained. The pastoral elements are as important to us as academic ability.

Parents are welcomed into school for Friday morning assembly when the children's good work is celebrated. An active Parent Teacher Association organises social and fundraising events. Pupils are encouraged to maintain their links with the school by joining the Past Pupils' Association.

Charitable status. The Princethorpe Foundation is a Registered Charity, number 1087124. It exists solely for the purpose of educating children.

Craigclowan Prep School

Edinburgh Road, Perth PH2 8PS
Tel: 01738 626310
Fax: 01738 440349
email: head@craigclowan-school.co.uk
website: www.craigclowan-school.co.uk
Twitter: @craigclowan
Facebook: @craigclowan

Chairman of Governors: Bill Farrar

Headmaster: John Gilmour

Bursar: Tom Kerrigan
Admissions & Marketing: Jennifer Trueland

Age Range. 3–13.
Number of Pupils. 221: 107 boys, 114 girls.
Fees per term (2018–2019). £4,220.

Craigclowan provides a warm and nurturing environment for boys and girls aged 3–13. Set in stunning grounds with magnificent views over Perthshire, the school has a distinguished history and a reputation for the highest standards and expectations.

Our learning environment delivers a modern and distinctive education within a framework of proven traditional values, effectively balancing the best of old and new in education. Grant funding is available for Pre-school pupils and particular attention is paid to the transition period as our Pre-school children begin their primary education. Every pupil is encouraged to achieve their all-round potential, both

academically, on the sports field and in more than 50 extra-curricular activities on offer. These range from skiing, on the school's own dry ski slope, to judo, metafit, bushcraft skills, mountain biking and fencing. The school is a hive of activity and our outdoor classroom, all-weather training ground, sports fields, Forest School and new trim trail are in daily use. With an average class size of 12 pupils, and a friendly, caring and supportive ethos, staff are able to get to know the children closely and treat them as individuals in all they do. When it comes to moving on to senior school, our children head to a wide range of top UK schools, both north and south of the border, many having been awarded scholarships.

Our fleet of minibuses collects children from across the region in the mornings. To assist working parents, our Breakfast Club is open from 7.30 am and free after-school care is available for all children until 6.00 pm daily. We also operate a number of holiday activity camps throughout the year including multi-activity camps and hockey, cricket and tennis coaching.

Charitable status. Craigclowan School Limited is a Registered Charity, number SC010817. It exists to promote education generally and for that purpose to establish, carry on and maintain a school within Scotland.

Cranford House Junior School

Moulsford, Wallingford, Oxfordshire OX10 9HT
Tel: 01491 651218
Fax: 01491 652557
email: admissions@cranfordhouse.net
website: www.cranfordhouse.net
Twitter: @CHSMoulsford
Facebook: @CranfordHouse

The School is a Charitable Trust run by a Board of Governors.

Chair of Governors: Mrs Natalie Scott-Ely

Headmaster: Dr James Raymond

Head of Junior School: Mrs Alison Stewart

Head of Nursery & EYFS: Mrs Kim Knight

Age Range. 3–11 Co-educational.
Number of Pupils. 205.
Fees per term (2018–2019). £3,500–£4,725.

Cranford House's co-educational Junior School has a reputation for excellence, as well as a unique approach to education that is modern and progressive. Our innovative curriculum is delivered in a stimulating environment, underpinned by traditional values, within a warmly nurturing community.

We have a strong set of values that underpins everything we do here at Cranford House. We believe in caring for the development of the whole person and ensuring every child reaches their fullest potential whilst ensuring that the education we provide enables our boys and girls to become well-adjusted young adults in the future.

Children are admitted from the age of three into the Cranford House Nursery School. The large, spacious purpose-built Nursery offers plenty of green space for free-flow play and learning. With an on-site Forest School, weekly swimming lessons and specialist coaches for sports, the children thrive and make great progress in their learning. In the September of the year they turn five years old, children move into Reception on the main school site. Nursery and Reception children follow the Early Years Foundation Stage curriculum.

The curriculum in Years 1 to 6 is founded on the National Curriculum, but supplemented to ensure children learn to develop resilience, independence, collaborative, reasoning and reflective skills. Junior pupils benefit from Senior School facilities and specialist subject teachers are used in a variety of subjects, including Sport, Music and Languages. Results in the Junior School are excellent.

With an all-inclusive emphasis very much in evidence throughout the school, all Junior pupils take part in school drama productions, learn a wide variety of musical instruments and benefit from a full choir, chamber choir and orchestra. Sport is equally inclusive at Cranford House, with competitive sport being provided for all, regardless of ability, and an incredible array of sports and activities on offer. In addition, an extensive programme of extracurricular clubs and activities ensures the widest possible range of opportunities and the all-round development of our pupils.

Responsibility is offered at a young age through posts such as House Captains and team captains.

Charitable status. Cranford House School Trust Limited is a Registered Charity, number 280883.

Cranleigh Preparatory School

Horseshoe Lane, Cranleigh, Surrey GU6 8QH

Tel:	01483 542058
Fax:	01483 277136
email:	ekkr@cranprep.org
website:	www.cranprep.org
Twitter:	@CranleighPrep
Facebook:	@CranPrep

Chairman of Governors: Mr Adrian Lajtha, MA, FCIB

Head: **Mr Neil Brooks**, BA Hons QTS

Age Range. 7–13.

Number of Pupils. 340 (40 Boarders, 300 Day).

Fees per term (2018–2019). Boarders £8,085; Day Pupils: £5,160 (Forms 1 & 2), £6,695 (Forms 3–6). These are genuinely inclusive and there are no hidden or compulsory extras.

The School stands in its own beautiful and spacious grounds of 40 acres. Cranleigh Preparatory School is a coeducational boarding and day school. A teaching staff of 59 enables classes to be small. The Head and his wife live in the school, as do the boys' Housemaster and his family and the girls' Housemistress and her family. They are fully involved with the health and happiness of the boys and girls, together with pastoral staff, including matrons. A great source of strength is the close partnership with Cranleigh School 'across the road', with both schools sharing an innovative 7–18 programme across sport, music and computing. The Preparatory School has use of Senior School sports facilities, including an indoor pool, artificial pitches, the stables and golf course.

The boys and girls are prepared for Common Entrance and many scholarships are won. Through these exams about three quarters of the children move on to Cranleigh School and the remaining one quarter to a wide variety of other independent senior schools.

Boarding life is busy and fun, with a wide array of exciting activities on offer. There is the opportunity to board all week or flexi board for two or more nights during the week; all pupils return home every weekend and there is a weekly bus service to and from London.

The curriculum is broad, balanced and covers all and more than that laid down by the National Curriculum. The School teaches Computing, and technological problem solving is encouraged. Art, Food Technology, Design and Music are included in the curriculum at all levels. Individual instrumental lessons are available and peripatetic music staff teach at both schools. There are choirs, orchestras, bands and several ensembles. Boys and girls are given every incentive to develop spare time interests and a choice of activities is built into the timetable.

The School is fortunate to have excellent facilities including a full-sized artificial pitch, a large Sports and Drama Hall, a Dance Studio, a Music School and very light, airy classrooms. The School has just opened a brand new teaching block, housing three new Science laboratories, two Art Studios and state-of-the-art Design and Food Technology areas. Boarding accommodation is bright, cheerful and fully modernised, with ongoing additions and improvements to the facilities.

Rugby, football, hockey, netball, cricket, athletics, tennis, swimming, rounders, squash, cross country, basketball, fencing, riding, golf, Eton Fives, archery and badminton, are among the sports.

Normal entry age is at 7 or 11. Places are sometimes available in the intervening year groups.

Charitable status. Cranleigh School is a Registered Charity, number 1070856, whose Preparatory School exists to provide education for boys and girls aged 7–13.

Cranmore School

Epsom Road, West Horsley, Surrey KT24 6AT

Tel:	01483 280340
Fax:	01483 280341
email:	admissions@cranmoreprep.co.uk
website:	www.cranmoreprep.co.uk

Chairman of Governors: Mr M J G Henderson, FCA

Headmaster: **Mr M P Connolly**, BSc, BA, MA, MEd

Deputy Head: Mr B Everitt, BSc, MEd, PGCE
Assistant Head of Senior Dept: Miss J Schembri, BA, PGCE
Head of Junior Dept: Mrs F Nicholson, BEd

Age Range. 2½–13 Co-educational.

Number of Pupils. 430 Day Pupils.

Fees per term (from January 2019). Nursery (term time) from £1,530; Junior Department £4,275; Senior Department £5,100.

The School is equidistant between Leatherhead and Guildford and is easily accessible from Cobham, Esher, Weybridge, Dorking and Woking with school transport available. Normal entry points are Nursery, Reception and Year 3 (7+); entry is non-selective in the early years and assessments are held for 7+ entry. There is a Scholarship programme for 7+ entry offering Academic, Sport and Music Scholarships. The most recent Inspection awarded the school top grades in every category including 'Outstanding' for the Early Years (Nursery and Reception).

Cranmore Nursery (from age 2½) offers both term-time and all-year-round attendance. It has its own dedicated accommodation which includes several rooms and outdoor learning area. The Junior Department (4–8 years) offers all children access to tremendous resources including the sports hall, gymnasium, swimming pool, forest school and music facilities. Pupils enter the Senior Department at 8+ years and are taught by specialist subject teachers. For National Curriculum Year 7 we create Scholarship and Common Entrance classes. Cranmore's academic standards are high and pupil development enables all pupils to fulfil their individual potential.

Children are prepared for entry to a wide range of senior schools. We have an impressive track record in Common Entrance and in our pupils gaining Scholarships to a wide variety of prestigious schools. Pupils at the upper end of the school (Years 7 and 8) are given significant additional opportunities with a broad curriculum including Philosophy, Latin, Greek, Spanish and Current Affairs culminating in an impressive post-Common Entrance programme.

An ongoing programme of investment over several years has given the school many outstanding facilities based on the extensive 25-acre site. These include a £250,000 redevelopment of the Cranmore Nursery outdoor learning area, Multi-Activity Games Area including netball court, complete car park redevelopment, a forest school, refurb of 25m swimming pool, new hospitality suite, teaching block with 3 large well-equipped science labs, and 2 ICT suites. The sports facilities include: a MUGA (multi-use games area), a sports hall, gymnasium, 25m swimming pool, 4 astro tennis courts and hockey pitch, 5-a-side astro, 9-hole golf course, large playground with rubberised surface, 3 squash courts and fitness room plus extensive playing fields.

Sports teams compete in galas, tournaments at local and national level; Inter-School and Inter-House competitions allow all pupils to take part. All children have the opportunity to represent the school at one of the main sports. Rowing, golf, tennis, judo, skiing and many other sporting clubs operate. There is a thriving extracurricular programme ranging from Archery to Science Technology. Many other out-of-school activities are offered including annual PGL, watersports and skiing trips.

The Drama, Speech and Music school offers every pupil the opportunity to learn an instrument, sing in a choir and play in a wide variety of ensembles and orchestras.

Cranmore is a Catholic school, welcoming families from all religious backgrounds and none. Our Christian ethos is central to supporting every child's development and values such as trust, tolerance, care and concern for others really matter in our community.

Charitable status. Cranmore School is a Registered Charity, number 1138636. It exists to provide education for children.

Crescent School

Bawnmore Road, Bilton, Rugby, Warwickshire CV22 7QH

Tel:	01788 521595
Fax:	01788 816185
email:	admin@crescentschool.co.uk
website:	www.crescentschool.co.uk
Twitter:	@CrescentSchRug
Facebook:	@cres.school

Chair of Governors: Mrs Liz Griffin, BSc, PGCE, CTC

Headmaster: Mr Joe Thackway, BA Hons, PGCE

Deputy Head: Mrs Bryony Forth, BSc Hons, PGCE
Assistant Head: Mr Alan Webb, BEd Hons
Senior Teacher: Mrs Sarah Lowe, BEd Hons
Finance Manager and Registrar: Mrs Helen Morley, ACIB

Age Range. 4–11.
Number of Pupils. 159 Day Boys and Girls (83 boys, 76 girls).

Fees per term (2018–2019). £2,968–£3,238.

The Crescent School is an independent co-educational preparatory school for day pupils aged 4–11 years. It merged with the Princethorpe Foundation in September 2016 joining the other schools in the Foundation – Little Crackers Nursery, Crackley Hall School and Princethorpe College. In addition, there is a Nursery on site for children from the age of 6 months to pre-school run by Pathfinders for 51 weeks of the year.

The school was founded in 1948, originally to provide a place of education for the young children of the masters of Rugby School. Over the years the school has steadily expanded, admitting children from Rugby and the surrounding area. In 1988, having outgrown its original premises, the school moved into modern, purpose-built accommodation in Bilton, about a mile to the south of Rugby town centre. The buildings provide large and bright teaching areas, with a separate annexe housing the Nursery and Reception classes. There are specialist rooms for Science, Art, Design Technology, ICT and the Performing Arts. In addition, there is also a spacious Library and Resource Area. The multi-purpose hall provides a venue for daily assemblies, large-scale music-making, is fully equipped for physical education and has all the necessary equipment to turn it into a theatre for school productions. The school is surrounded by its own gardens, play areas and sports field.

The requirements of the National Curriculum are fully encompassed by the academic programme and particular emphasis is placed on English and mathematics in the early years. All pupils receive specialist tuition in Information and Communication Technology, Music and Physical Education. Specialist teaching in other subjects is introduced as children move upwards through the school. Spanish is introduced in Reception, followed by French in Year 4 and Latin in Year 5. The pupils are prepared for the local 11+ examination for entry to maintained secondary schools, including local grammar schools, and specific entrance examinations also at 11+ for independent senior schools.

The performing arts are a particular strength of the school and lessons are given in speech and drama, singing, percussion, musical theory and appreciation and recorder playing. Instrumental lessons (piano, brass, woodwind and strings) are offered as an optional extra. There is a school choir, orchestra, brass, string and wind ensembles and recorder groups.

Charitable status. The Princethorpe Foundation is a Registered Charity, number 1087124. It exists solely for the purpose of educating children.

The Croft Preparatory School

Alveston Hill, Loxley Road, Stratford-upon-Avon, Warwickshire CV37 7RL

Tel:	01789 293795
email:	office@croftschool.co.uk
website:	www.croftschool.co.uk

Principal: Mrs L K M Thornton, CertEd London

Chairman of the School's Governing Committee: Mrs Vanessa Aris, MBE, MSc

Headmaster: Mr M Cook, BSc Hons, PGCE

Deputy Headmaster: Mr E Bolderston, BSc Hons, PGCE

Age Range. 3–11.
Number of Pupils. 403: 215 boys, 188 girls.
Fees per term (2018–2019). £583–£4,071.

The Croft is a co-educational day school for children from 3 to 11 years old, situated on the outskirts of Stratford upon Avon. Founded in 1933, the School occupies a large rural site with superb facilities and extensive playing fields, offering children some of the most exciting educational opportunities in the area. There is also a nature conservation area with lake.

A family-based school, The Croft provides specialist teaching in small groups, where good discipline and a wider knowledge of the world around us, both spiritual and geographical, is encouraged. Music, Sport and Drama each play an important part in the curriculum. The resulting high educational standards provide the all-round excellence which is at the heart of the School.

In 2012, the School opened its 600-seat Theatre and fully-equipped 400m² Sports Hall. Mundell Court was completed in 2009 – a two-storey building providing additional, spacious teaching areas for ICT, DT and Mathematics. It also incorporates a small-scale performance space.

Children are prepared for 11+ entry either to the local Grammar Schools or Senior Independent Day Schools, or to go on to Boarding Schools.

Entrance requirements. Children can be accepted in the Nursery from the age of 3 years. Children above Reception age are assessed.

Crosfields School

Shinfield Road, Reading, Berks RG2 9BL

Tel: 0118 9871810
email: office@crosfields.com
website: www.crosfields.com

Chairman of Governors: Mr N Habgood

Headmaster: **Mr Craig Watson**, BEd, MA

Deputy Headmaster: Mr Simon Dinsdale, MA Ed Open, BA Hons Chichester, FLCM, LTCL, LLCM, FISM, PGCE Open

Age Range. 3–13.
Number of Pupils. 554.
Fees per term (2018–2019). £3,438–£5,053 including lunches, school visits and after-school care for Years 2–8. There is an additional charge for children in Nursery, Reception and Year 1 who remain in school after 4.15 pm.

Crosfields School is a co-educational day preparatory school based in Shinfield, Reading. It offers a first-class education with opportunities for all for boys and girls aged 3–13 years. Academically the school is excellent. Pupils progress quickly in small class sizes where they receive individual attention from dedicated teaching staff. Pupils move on to a range of senior schools and there have been a good number of scholarships and exhibitions in recent years and also an excellent record of entry to Reading School.

Facilities within the 40 acres of grounds are unrivalled at prep school level in the area, with a modern library, ICT suite, theatre and music complex, sports hall, indoor swimming pool, cricket nets and even a 6-hole golf course. The main sports for boys are Football, Rugby and Cricket with Netball, Hockey and Rounders for girls. Mixed football and tag rugby are played by both girls and boys and there is a wide range of extracurricular hobbies and clubs from Year 3 upwards including Cookery, Golf, Drama, Judo, Dance and Fencing. A new Food Technology room opened in May 2009.

The school offers bursary awards of up to 100% of the fees at 11+ entry.

Charitable status. Crosfields School Trust Limited is a Registered Charity, number 584278. The aim of the School is solely to provide education for children between the ages of 3 and 13.

Culford Preparatory School

Bury St Edmunds, Suffolk IP28 6TX

Tel: 01284 728615
Fax: 01284 728631
email: admissions@culford.co.uk
website: www.culford.co.uk
Twitter: @CulfordSchool
Facebook: @OfficialCulfordSchool

Chairman of Governors: Air Vice Marshall S Abbott, CBE, MPhil, BA

Headmaster: **M Schofield**, BEd

Age Range. Co-educational 7–13.
Number of Pupils. 182 (Day), 40 (Boarders).
Fees per term (2018–2019). Day £3,875–£5,075, Boarding £7,495–£7,995, International Boarding £7,675–£8,215.

Admission is by entrance examination at all ages, though the majority of pupils enter at age 7 or 11 and scholarships are available at 11+.

Culford Prep School has its own staff and Headmaster, but remains closely linked to the Senior School. This allows the School to enjoy a significant degree of independence and the ability to focus on the particular needs of prep school age children while benefiting from the outstanding facilities and community spirit of Culford.

Facilities. Culford Prep is situated in its own grounds, within Culford Park. The heart of the School is the impressive quadrangle at the centre of which lies the Jubilee Library. Other facilities include two science laboratories and two state-of-the-art ICT suites which, in common with the rest of the Prep School's classrooms, have networked interactive whiteboards.

Outside Prep have a mix of playing fields for all the major sports and the perennially-popular adventure playground. Prep School pupils also have free access to Culford's magnificent Sports and Tennis Centre with its 25m indoor pool, indoor tennis courts, artificial turf pitches, fitness suite and sports hall.

Teaching & Learning. Prep School pupils are given a thorough grounding in the essential learning skills of Mathematics and English and the enhanced curriculum broadens beyond the confines of the National Curriculum. Work in the classrooms is augmented by an extensive Activities Programme which offers pupils a wide range of opportunities and experiences, including trips out and visits from guest authors and experts in their field.

Music and drama play a significant part in Culford Prep School life, and a variety of theatrical performances, choirs and ensembles are performed each year, either in Prep's own hall or in Culford's purpose-built Studio Theatre. Specialist speech and drama lessons are also offered.

Boarding. Prep School boarders live in Cadogan House, a mixed boarding house located next to the School overlooking the playing fields. Boarders are able to take advantage of a comprehensive programme of weekend activities and are looked after by a team of dedicated staff under the direction of the Housemaster. Recent trips have included visiting Harry Potter World, the Oasis Camel Park and the North Norfolk Coast.

Religious affiliation. Methodist: pupils from all faiths, and those of none, are welcome.

Charitable status. Culford School is part of the Methodist Independent Schools Trust, which is a Registered Charity, number 1142794.

Cumnor House School
Cognita Schools Group

Boys School:
168 Pampisford Road, South Croydon, Surrey CR2 6DA

Tel: 020 8660 3445
Fax: 020 8645 2619

Girls School:
1 Woodcote Lane, Purley, Surrey CR8 3HB

Tel: 020 8660 3445
Fax: 020 8660 9687

email: admissions@cumnorhouse.com
website: www.cumnorhouse.com
Twitter: @WeAreCumnor
Facebook: @WeAreCumnor

Headmaster – Nursery and Boys School: **Mr Daniel Cummings**

Headmistress – Girls School: **Mrs Amanda McShane**

Age Range. Boys 4–13, Girls 4–11. Co-educational Nursery 2–4 years.

Number of Pupils. Prep & Pre-Prep: 360 Boys, 185 Girls. Nursery: 149.

Fees per term (2018–2019). £3,545–£4,460 (including lunch and school trips).

Cumnor House School for Boys is one of Surrey's leading Preparatory Schools and prepares boys for scholarships and common entrance examinations to leading senior independent schools and local grammar schools.

Scholarships have been won recently to Charterhouse, Epsom, Dulwich, Harrow, Tonbridge, Westminster and the local senior independent schools, Caterham, Trinity and Whitgift.

Music, Sports, Art and Drama play a large part in the life of the School and all contribute to the busy, happy atmosphere.

Choir, sports tours and matches, ski trips, regular stage productions and a broad spectrum of clubs and options, give the boys the opportunity to pursue a wide range of interests.

This school is located in a residential area in South Croydon with access to good transport links.

Entry requirements: Taster Day with Assessment.

At **Cumnor House School for Girls** our main aim is to give parents and their daughters as much choice as possible when selecting their senior schools in Year 6. This journey starts in the Early Years; by developing confidence and a positive attitude to learning, we lay vital foundations for the future.

Practical experiences complement the curriculum and encourage the love of learning needed to embrace the academic, cultural, sporting and musical opportunities that Cumnor House School for Girls provides. The girls are encouraged to develop all their interests and talents, both within the extensive curriculum and through involvement in a wide range of clubs and activities.

Scholarships have been won recently to Caterham, Croydon High, Ewell Castle, Old Palace, Reigate Grammer,

Royal Russell, Streatham and Clapham High, Sutton High and Woldingham.

The school is located in a quiet, leafy, private road in Purley – a hidden gem of a school!

Entry requirements: Taster Day with Assessment.

Cumnor House Sussex

Danehill, Haywards Heath, West Sussex RH17 7HT

Tel: 01825 790347
email: registrar@cumnor.co.uk
website: www.cumnor.co.uk
Twitter: @cumnorhouse
Facebook: @cumnorhouse

Chairman of Governors: Niall FitzGerald

Headmaster: **C St J S Heinrich**, BA Hons, PGCE

Deputy Headmaster & Bursar: M N P Mockridge, BSc Hons, PGCE

Age Range. 2–13.

Number of Pupils. 390: 203 boys, 187 girls; 102 in the Pre-Prep; 40 in Nursery, 69 boarders.

Fees per term (2018–2019). Boarding: Full £7,750, Weekly £7,545; Day: Years 5–8 £6,510, Year 4 £5,750, Year 3 £4,995, Year 2 £3,950, Year 1 £3,495, Reception £2,995 (£2,245 above free entitlement)

At Cumnor Nursery, we provide flexible childcare for 2–5 year old children from 7.00 am to 7.00 pm, five days a week for 50 weeks of the year. This is offered as either 'term-time only' or a 'full-time' childcare provision. Daily rates range from £29.95 to £66.70 per day (non-funded rate) depending on sessions hours.

We aim to provide a happy and purposeful atmosphere in which children learn to set themselves high standards and live by the school motto 'Aim High, Be Kind, Dare to be Different'. Individuality is encouraged and equal esteem is given to achievements in and out of the classroom.

The School has a strong tradition of scholarship success, and many scholarships are awarded each year to a wide range of senior schools across academic, all-round, art, drama, equestrian, leadership, music, sport and design technology.

We offer the children many opportunities for involvement in sporting and cultural activities. All girls and boys in the Prep school play sport every day. Each term children are given a choice of 20 or so supervised hobbies, from which they choose three. Much music and drama takes place – 95% of pupils in the Prep school learn an individual instrument and the choirs, orchestra and ensembles perform regularly. There are two orchestras, a strings group, wind band, as well as much singing and ensemble work. Each Summer term 50 or more children are involved in the annual production of a Shakespearean play which takes place in our open air theatre, 'the gloaming'. In 2017 our new state-of-the-art science, technology, engineering and maths centre, called 'The Peake' was formally opened by NASA scientist, Dr Gary McKay and a pioneering schools programme launched simultaneously highlighting the importance of creativity and innovation in helping to solve global problems using science, technology, engineering and maths. The former science classroom has been converted into a Library space designed by the pupils. Our rebuilt Sussex barn is used as a Music School and a purpose-built theatre complex operates as a local arts centre for concerts, lectures, exhibitions and winter term plays. Set in 65 acres of fields and woodland, the school has an international standard all-weather surface, a Sports Hall, four tennis courts, a heated outdoor pool and a 25m indoor pool. Football, Rugby, Cricket, Netball, Hockey, Rounders and Athletics are all part of the sporting mix with 20 or so teams involved every Wednesday and/or Saturday in matches. Former farm buildings have been converted into blocks for music practice, art, ICT and home economics with the addition of new boarding wings, new kitchens and a laundry room in the main school building. All classrooms have interactive whiteboards and all children in Years 6 and above are provided with iPads. The boarding staff includes a full-time qualified nurse. Boarding, which is entirely elective for pupils in Years 7 and 8, is on a bi-weekly basis allowing time for full weekends both at home and at school.

Charitable status. Cumnor House School Trust is a Registered Charity, number 801924. It exists for the advancement of education.

Dair House School

Bishop's Blake, Beaconsfield Road, Farnham Royal, Buckinghamshire SL2 3BY

Tel: 01753 643964
email: admissions@dairhouse.co.uk
website: www.dairhouse.co.uk
Twitter: @DairHouseSchool
Facebook: @dairhouse

Chairman of Governors: Mrs Jane Masih

Headmaster: **Mr Terence Wintle**, BEd Hons

Age Range. 3–11 Co-educational.
Number in School. 135 Day pupils.
Fees per term (2018–2019). £1,725–£4,345.

Located on the A355 in Farnham Royal we are conveniently placed for the Farnhams, Gerrards Cross, Beaconsfield, Stoke Poges and surrounding villages.

Dair House School offers an exciting and personalised education to boys and girls from 3–11 years old.

We take pride in our warm, friendly, individual care, catering for each child's abilities. We provide our children with a firm sense of belonging and a sure foundation from the start in classes which are no larger than 19.

The school has excellent facilities with a new Learning Resource Centre which incorporate books and an ICT suite, a new dining room, new offices and a recently decorated School Hall. Each class is fully resourced with interactive whiteboards and computers. Our Nursery houses a 65" Smart Screen.

Dair House School is situated in wonderful tree-lined grounds with a large sports field and an all-weather sports surface.

We offer a breakfast club from 7.30 am and an after-school tea club until 6.00 pm, as well as a plethora of lunchtime and after-school activities.

Charitable status. Dair House School Trust Limited is a Registered Charity, number 270719. Its aim is to provide 'a sure foundation from the start'.

Dame Bradbury's School

Ashdon Road, Saffron Walden, Essex CB10 2AL

Tel: 01799 522348
email: office@damebradburys.com
website: www.damebradburys.stephenperse.com
Twitter: @DameBradburys

Dame Bradbury's is a co-educational day school, founded in 1525. It is a school of the Stephen Perse Foundation, Cambridge.

Chairman of Governors of the Stephen Perse Foundation: Mr J Dix

Principal of the Stephen Perse Foundation: Miss T Kelleher

Head of Dame Bradbury's: **Mrs Tracy Handford**, MA

Age Range. 3–11.
Number of Pupils. 250 day boys and girls.
Fees per term (2018–2019). Kindergarten: Full day £2,850, 5 mornings £1,450 (children should be registered for a minimum of three morning sessions per week). Reception: £3,725; Years 1–2: £4,000; Years 3–4: £4,400; Years 5–6: £4,600. Lunch is included for all children in Kindergarten to Year 6.

Every child that joins us takes an individual journey at Dame B's, through which they flourish and succeed. Set in the beautiful town of Saffron Walden, we pride ourselves on getting to know every child and their family.

We are not afraid to do things differently. Our approach, in both Pre-Prep and Prep, encourages young people to become independent thinkers – preparing them for life way beyond school.

Whilst our school has a history dating back to 1317, our facilities in the heart of Saffron Walden are definitely 21st century, from our beautiful sports grounds, modern sports hall and astroTurf to our inspiring library, theatre and art studio.

Creativity and fun is everywhere – in our Forest School and inspiring art facilities, as well as in our clubs. From ballet to photography, rugby to rock band – there's something to capture the imagination of every child.

From 3 to 11, our pupils share a willingness to experiment, to question and to take on new challenges. They leave us full of enthusiasm, equipped with a love of learning and ready to take their next steps in life.

As part of the Stephen Perse Foundation, we offer a natural route into the Senior School in Cambridge and our children are already used to visiting for joint activities, trips and projects. The Independent Schools Inspectorate describes Dame B's as "outstanding" and says that Years 1 and 2 and the Prep "provide an outstanding education that challenges and motivates pupils in equal measure".

Danes Hill

Leatherhead Road, Oxshott, Surrey KT22 0JG

Tel: 01372 842509
email: registrar@daneshill.surrey.sch.uk
website: www.daneshillschool.co.uk

Chair of Governors: Mr Hugh Monro

Headmaster: **Mr William Murdock**, BA, PGCE

Age Range. 3–13 co-educational.
Number of Children. 860.
Fees per term (2018–2019). £2,205–£6,427.

As a co-educational school, Danes Hill prepares boys and girls for Scholarship and Common Entrance examinations to senior schools. A high academic record (57 scholarships to senior schools awarded in 2018) combines happily with a strong tradition of sporting prowess, to ensure that all children are exposed to a kaleidoscope of opportunity on a peaceful 55-acre site set well back from the main Esher-Leatherhead road. The Pre-Preparatory Department takes children from 3 to 6 years and is situated separately, but within easy walking distance of the Main School.

Extensive facilities include 2 state-of-the-art IT suites, a science block with 6 fully-equipped laboratories, a high-tech Art and DT centre, and new studio theatre. Both Pre-Prep and Main School sites have covered swimming pools.

The curriculum is broad and a wide range of extra-curricular activity is encouraged. Languages are a particular strength of the school. All children learn French and Spanish from age 3. All scholars and some Common Entrance pupils also study Latin. Scholars are encouraged to sit one or more modern foreign languages at GCSE in their final year.

Pastoral care and pupil welfare are closely monitored. The school's Learning Support Centre provides a high level of support both for those with specific learning difficulties as well as running a programme for the exceptionally gifted and talented.

Residential and day trips are seen as an essential part of the school experience. The school operates language trips to centres in Spain and France. The annual Trips Week is a very special feature of the school calendar with over 500 children leaving the site to a range of residential destinations in the UK and abroad. There are also annual ski trips, as well as choir, rugby, netball and hockey tours.

Sport is a major strength and specialist games staff ensure that all the major sports are expertly coached. A floodlit astroturf pitch allows all-weather training and team spirit is valued alongside ability. There are extensive programmes of inter-school fixtures for all age groups. Every child is encouraged to participate. We also arrange annual games dinners for the senior teams and their parents to celebrate the end of each season. In-house Easter and Summer holiday activity courses are also very popular options with the pupils.

Charitable status. Danes Hill School (administered by The Vernon Educational Trust Ltd) is a Registered Charity, number 269433. It exists to provide high-quality education for boys and girls.

Daneshill School

Stratfield Turgis, Hook, Hampshire RG27 0AR

Tel: 01256 882707
Fax: 01256 882007
email: office@daneshillprepschool.com
website: www.daneshillprepschool.com

Headmaster: **Mr Jim Massey**, BSc Hons

Age Range. 3–13.
Number of Pupils. Day Boys 124, Day Girls 139.
Fees per term (2018–2019). Nursery on application; Reception £3,650, Year 1 £3,750, Year 2 £4,060, Year 3 £4,370, Years 4–8 £4,935. Lunch included. There are no compulsory extras.

Founded in 1950, Daneshill has always prided itself on the collective qualities of its teaching staff and their ability to interact with pupils and deliver a stimulating learning experience.

Set in a beautiful, rural location close to the Hampshire-Berkshire border the School provides the perfect environment and atmosphere for each pupil to grow and prosper as an individual with a strong set of core values.

Academically the Daneshill curriculum has always maintained the expectations of the national curriculum while also

offering so much more in respect of what we would regard as real education. Traditional values form the basis of a learning experience that engenders an enthusiasm for knowledge and encourages hard work as a means to academic success. This broadly-based curriculum also allows the development of high academic achievement to sit comfortably alongside our enthusiasm for pupils to become actively involved in all areas of the performing arts as well as the pursuit of sporting excellence.

Our aim has always been to develop enthusiastic learners who will make a strong contribution to their senior schools as good citizens and as pupils who are prepared to work hard in order to achieve success. This is certainly made easier by the children at Daneshill who possess a self-confidence and natural carefree joy which makes them a pleasure to teach. Each of them is a living testament to our belief that self-esteem is crucial to their development and success. We are also justifiably proud of the way our pupils exude courtesy, honesty, warmth and respect for others. They develop responsible attitudes to learning and life, and are a credit to themselves and their families.

Visitors to the School will be made very welcome and straight away they will experience the atmosphere that makes Daneshill unique.

Davenies School

Beaconsfield, Bucks HP9 1AA

Tel: 01494 685400
Fax: 01494 685408
email: office@davenies.co.uk
website: www.davenies.co.uk
Twitter: @DaveniesSchool
Facebook: @DaveniesSchool

Chairman: Mr N Edwards

Headmaster: **Mr Carl Rycroft**, BEd Hons

Age Range. 4–13.
Number of Boys. 335 (Day Boys only).
Fees per term (2018–2019). £3,995–£5,800.

Davenies is a thriving IAPS day school for boys aged 4–13. Our ethos and philosophy enable the boys to make the most of their preparatory years, supported by high-quality pastoral care, a broad and stimulating curriculum and numerous extra-curricular opportunities.

Davenies has its own distinct character and from their earliest years children are encouraged to relish the learning experience.

We are committed to an education both in and out of the classroom, thereby enabling the academic, artistic, musical, creative and physical potential of each child to flourish. This school is a warm, caring and happy one, where self-esteem is nurtured and grown; we believe that by fostering a wide range of interests and passions we provide the boys with every opportunity to develop in confidence. Our high-quality teachers have an excellent track record of preparing children for life at the country's leading senior schools and beyond.

Enterprises such as the unique Davenies Award Scheme and the permeation of technology in our teaching and learning ensure we offer a truly independent educational experience.

At Davenies, our outstanding facilities support us in providing a positive learning experience with our own language of learning that nurtures each boy's understanding of how he learns. Davenies' boys are polite and friendly with their own individual characters, personalities, passions and interests.

Charitable status. Beaconsfield Educational Trust Ltd is a Registered Charity, number 313120. It exists to provide high standards and the fulfilment of each child's potential.

Dean Close Pre-Preparatory School

Lansdown Road, Cheltenham, Gloucestershire GL51 6QS

Tel:	01242 258079
Fax:	01242 258005
email:	squirrels@deanclose.org.uk
website:	www.deanclose.org.uk
Twitter:	@DeanCloseSchool
Facebook:	@DeanCloseSchool

Chairman of Governors: Mrs K Carden

Headmistress: **Dr C A Shelley**, BEd, PhD

Age Range. 2–7 Co-educational.
Number of Pupils. 145.
Fees per term (2018–2019). £2,747–£2,842.

Dean Close Pre-Preparatory School is a co-educational, Christian family school which occupies the same campus as Dean Close Preparatory and Dean Close School and is, therefore, able to share their outstanding facilities including the swimming pool, sports hall, tennis courts, theatre and art block.

The Pre-Preparatory School is based in a purpose-built school building opened by Lord Robert Winston in June 2004. The School has a large hall surrounded by classrooms on two floors. There are two playgrounds – one for the Nursery and Kindergarten and one for Reception and Years 1 and 2.

The curriculum within the Pre-Preparatory School offers a wide range of learning opportunities aimed at stimulating and nurturing children's development and interests in an intellectual, physical, spiritual, social and emotional sense. Speech and Drama, Dance, Tennis, Music, Orchestra and Choir are some of the extracurricular activities available. All children participate in Forest School, which inspires creativity, thinking skills and cooperation, together with a love of the natural world.

Charitable status. Dean Close School is a Registered Charity, number 1086829.

Dean Close Preparatory School

Lansdown Road, Cheltenham, Gloucestershire GL51 6QS

Tel:	01242 258000
email:	dcpsoffice@deanclose.org.uk
website:	www.deanclose.org.uk
Twitter:	@DeanCloseSchool
Facebook:	@DeanCloseSchool

Chairman of Governors: Mrs K Carden

Headmaster: **Mr Paddy Moss**

Age Range. 7–13.
Number of Pupils. 307: Boarding Boys 34, Boarding Girls 35, Day Boys 128, Day Girls 110.

Fees per term (2018–2019). Boarders £6,420–£8,455, Day Boarders £4,547–£7,008, International Boarders £7,193–£9,011 Day Pupils £3,788–£6,250.

Dean Close Preparatory School is a co-educational, Christian, family school which occupies the same campus as Dean Close School and is, therefore, able to share the outstanding facilities. These facilities include: 25m swimming pool, amphitheatre, shooting range, performance hall, 550-seat theatre and chapel. There are also extensive playing fields and sports facilities including hard tennis courts, floodlit astroturf hockey pitches and the new sports hall, which houses indoor tennis and cricket nets, as well as a large gymnasium and dance studio.

The Prep School also has its own teaching blocks and Music School, and a £4.5m building which opened in autumn 2013. This contains an additional 360-seat theatre and 8 teaching areas located over two floors, with a dedicated IT suite and drama rooms.

The new building also contains a music suite, which links to the existing Music School, and comprises 6 music practice rooms including a dedicated guitar room. The building has a formal reception area where parents and visitors are welcomed into the School.

There are two additional classroom blocks. One consists of 10 specialist teaching rooms including 2 laboratories and a computer centre. The other has 7 purpose-built classrooms, together with day house facilities, a staff Common Room, a new Library and an Art and Technology block. There is also a separate dining hall and kitchens.

Although the Preparatory School is administered by the same Board of Governors as the Pre-Prep and the Senior School, it has its own Headmaster and staff. There are 48 teaching staff who either hold degrees or diplomas in education. As well as a dedicated Director of Music, Director of Sport and Director of Drama. The music department is also supported by a team of excellent peripatetic music teachers specialising in a variety of instruments.

Pupils in Years 7 and 8 are taught in ability based form classes. All pupils follow an Independent Curriculum, aligned to the Common Entrance for: English, Mathematics, Biology, Chemistry, Physics, French, History, Geography, Religious Studies and Spanish. Pupils in the top two forms study Latin from Year 7.

The School has three boarding houses one for girls, one for boys and a mixed boarding house for the younger children. Each boarding house has a team of resident Houseparents, 2 House Tutors and a resident matron.

The day pupils are accommodated in three purpose-built houses. Each is run by a Housemaster/Housemistress, assisted by House Tutors.

The main games for boys are rugby, hockey and cricket, and for girls, hockey, netball, cricket and tennis. Swimming, athletics and cross-country running are also taught and use is made of the School's covered playing area. Golf and horse riding are available nearby.

A wide range of additional activities is also available: camping, canoeing, hillwalking, orienteering, judo, climbing, cooking, watercolour painting and all forms of dance, to name but a few.

With a Prep School population of 307, the sense of family-like community is developed in such a way that it is possible for every child to know each other and to be individually known, valued and cared about. The Prep School offers Foundation, Art, Drama, Music, Academic, Sports and Design and Technology scholarships at 11+ and educates the Choristers who sing Evensong at Tewkesbury Abbey.

Charitable status. Dean Close School is a Registered Charity, number 1086829. It exists to provide education for children.

Denstone College Preparatory School at Smallwood Manor

A Woodard School

Uttoxeter, Staffs ST14 8NS
Tel: 01889 562083
email: enquiries@denstoneprep.co.uk
website: www.denstoneprep.co.uk
Twitter: @Denstone_Prep
Facebook: @denstonecollegeprep

Custos: Matthew Ellias

Headmaster: **Jeremy Gear**, BEd Hons

Age Range. 2–11.
Number of Pupils. 90 Boys, 49 Girls.
Fees per term (2018–2019). £3,395–£4,300.

Denstone College Preparatory School at Smallwood Manor is a co-educational Nursery and Day School for children aged 2 to 11, set in 50 acres of beautiful woods and parkland just south of Uttoxeter on the Staffordshire/Derbyshire border.

The aims of the school are:

• To ensure that every child enjoys coming to school and that each individual's potential is fully realised.

• To educate the whole child so that academic achievement goes hand in hand with developing spiritual, cultural and physical maturity.

• To emphasise traditional Christian values of good manners and responsible behaviour.

• To provide a stimulating programme of activities to encourage children to develop skills and interests which will make their school careers successful and rewarding.

• To lay a firm foundation for further education.

As a Woodard School, Denstone College Preparatory School has strong ties with Denstone College and has enjoyed an excellent reputation for preparing children for 11+ Entrance Examinations and Scholarships. Our pupils enjoy excellent sports facilities which include: a covered heated swimming pool, a gymnasium, superb sports pitches and two hard tennis courts. Rugby, Hockey, Football and Netball are the main winter games; Cricket and Rounders are the main summer games.

Denstone College Preparatory School has a fine modern Chapel and our award-winning choir sings regularly in Music Festivals and local churches. Each child learns the violin for a year and a large percentage of our pupils learn at least one musical instrument to a high standard. Our peripatetic music team provide opportunities for pupils to learn brass, woodwind, strings, piano and voice. The school has a string group, wind band and various musical ensembles. Many of our pupils, past and present, sing in the National Children's Choir of Great Britain. Last year 20% of the NCC were our current pupils. The School is currently experiencing the most successful period in its prestigious history, with 73 scholarships and exhibitions being awarded by senior schools over the past four years.

We offer an exciting range of clubs and activities after school including: Forest School, Archer, Water polo, Fencing, Orienteering, Police Cadets, Rock Climbing, LAMDA, Beginners French (for adults and children together), Origami, Cookery and Modern Pentathlon. Our after-school care extends from 8.00 am until 6.00 pm.

Charitable status. Smallwood Manor Preparatory School Limited is a Registered Charity, number 1102929. It aims to provide a Christian education for boys and girls aged 2 to 11.

Devonshire House Preparatory School

2 Arkwright Road, Hampstead, London NW3 6AE
Tel: 020 7435 1916
email: enquiries@devonshirehouseprepschool.co.uk
website: www.devonshirehouseschool.co.uk
Twitter: @DHSPrep

Headmistress: **Mrs S Piper**, BA Hons

Age Range. Boys 2½–13, Girls 2½–11.
Number in School. 650: 340 Boys, 310 Girls.
Fees per term (2018–2019). £3,375–£6,200.

Devonshire House School is for boys and girls from three to thirteen years of age and the School's nursery department, the Oak Tree Nursery, takes children from two and a half. The academic subjects form the core curriculum and the teaching of music, art, drama, computer studies, design technology and games helps to give each child a chance to excel. At the age of eleven for girls and thirteen for boys the children go on to their next schools, particularly the main independent London day schools.

Devonshire House pursues high academic standards whilst developing enthusiasm and initiative. It is considered important to encourage pupils to develop their own individual personalities and a good sense of personal responsibility. A wide variety of clubs and tuition are available in ballet, judo, yoga, Mandarin, chess, speech and communication and in a range of musical instruments. High standards and individual attention for each child are of particular importance.

The School is located on the crest of the hill running into Hampstead Village and has fine Victorian premises with charming grounds and walled gardens.

Dolphin School

Waltham Road, Hurst, Berkshire RG10 0FR
Tel: 0118 934 1277
Fax: 0118 934 4110
email: omnes@dolphinschool.com
website: www.dolphinschool.com
Twitter: @DolphinSch
Facebook: @dolphinschoolhurst

Founded in 1970.

Head: **Adam Hurst**

Age Range. 3–13.
Number of Pupils. 203: 112 Day Boys, 91 Day Girls.
Fees per term (2018–2019). Nursery £3,390 (9.00 am to 3.00 pm, 5 days); Reception £3,545; Years 1–2 £3,920; Years 3–4 £4,630; Years 5–8 £4,690.

We believe that children have special gifts and talents, which too often remain hidden forever. Dolphin School offers an environment which encourages these gifts to flourish. Children leave Dolphin with confidence in themselves, a strong sense of individualism, the ability to adjust well in school and social situations, at least one area in which they can feel pride in their own achievement and a strong sense of curiosity and enjoyment in learning. Throughout life, in an ever more quickly changing world, they will have the skills and the confidence successfully to pursue their ambitions and interests and to lead happy and fulfilled lives.

Dolphin children are allowed to develop as individuals and encouraged to fulfil their various potentials in small classes under the careful guidance of specialist teachers. Abundant academic, artistic, social and sporting stimulation is provided through an extremely broad, well-rounded programme. We encourage lateral thinking and the ability to cross reference. Expectations for all children are high and academic rigour is a key component in all lessons.

Dolphin School provides the friendly, family atmosphere of a small school. All members of staff are actively concerned with the pastoral care of all the children, but each form teacher assumes special responsibility for the daily well-being and the overall progress of a very small group of children. In addition children in their final three years have a personal mentor. Class sizes average twelve to sixteen. Children learn both to talk and listen to each other, to evaluate and tolerate the opinions of others and to take pride in each other's achievements. They are also encouraged to accept responsibility and to develop their leadership abilities.

Courses offered. Children are taught by graduate specialists from age seven in most subjects. In the early years we provide a firm grounding in English-based skills throughout all humanities subjects. French begins in Nursery, Mandarin in Year Five, Latin in Year Six and Spanish and Greek in Year Seven. Laboratory science is taught from age seven. Mathematics, geography, history, ICT, earth studies, classical studies, art, design technology, drama, music and PE are taught throughout the upper school. Architecture, astronomy, philosophy, thinking skills, religious education and current affairs are also on the curriculum.

Activities. A unique strength of Dolphin School is our residential field trip programme in which all children participate from age seven. The work related to these trips forms major sections of all departmental syllabuses. Principal annual field trips visit East Sussex, Dorset, Ironbridge, North Wales, Northumbria, Normandy, Ireland and Italy, while departments organise residential trips to Boulogne and Stratford. We also offer an extensive mountain-walking programme. We have a large number of trained British Mountain Leaders. Staff and children participate in a graded fell walking programme. Locations range from the Lake District and Brecon Beacons to Snowdonia and the Alps. We also organise sports tours and a "custom made" adventure week in North Wales.

We believe in 'hands-on' learning, whether in or outside the classroom, and children participate in a very wide range of day trips to museums, theatres, archaeological sites and many other venues.

Almost all costs associated with field, walking and day trips are included in the fees, as are lunch-time and after-school clubs which include: athletics, tennis, short tennis, judo, rounders, cricket, embroidery, computing, swimming, football, netball, gymnastics, craft, hockey, chess, cross-country, rugby, art, table tennis, orchestra, windband, string group, choir, orienteering, gardening, cookery and drama.

We field teams at all levels in football, rugby, cricket, chess, netball, rounders, tennis, swimming, cross-country, athletics, hockey and judo. We are well represented at county level.

Facilities. Our hall offers a splendid venue for school concerts and plays. We stage several major productions each year. Grounds include a swimming pool, all-weather tennis, hockey and netball courts, and playing fields. Cricket matches are played at Hurst, a neighbouring county standard ground.

Entry. Nursery at age 3+, Reception at age 4+, and throughout the Upper School as places become available.

Internal and external scholarships are available to children aged 12–13 in the performing arts, art, creative writing and sport. Academic bursaries are also available.

Examination results. Our examination results are very strong and we regularly win scholarships (academic, drama and sport) to senior independent schools, including Wellington College, Abingdon, The Abbey, Queen Anne's and Leighton Park. We have a thriving Old Delphinian organisation. Most past pupils gain good degrees with several going on to Oxbridge.

The Downs Malvern

Brockhill Road, Colwall, Malvern, Worcs WR13 6EY

Tel: 01684 544 108
Fax: 01684 544 105
email: registrar@thedowns.malcol.org
website: www.thedownsmalvern.org.uk
Twitter: @DownsMalvern
Facebook: @TheDownsMalvern

Chairman of Governors: Reverend Kenneth E Madden, BA, PGCE

Headmaster: Alastair S Cook, BEd Hons, FRGS, IAPS

Age Range. 3–13 years Co-educational.
Number of Pupils. 258 children.
Fees per term (2018–2019). Full Boarding £4,880–£7,534; Weekly boarding £4,298–£6,630; Flexi boarding £39.00 per night; Day £4,043–£5,692; Pre-Preparatory £2,369–£3,207; Early Years: £24.22 per am/pm session, £48.44 per day (8.30–3.30), £53.04 per day (8.30–5.00).

The Downs Malvern is a busy, vibrant and successful co-educational preparatory school for boarding and day children aged between 3 and 13 years, offering an outstanding education.

Located 3 miles west of Malvern, 4 miles east of Ledbury, 15 miles from the M5 motorway, on the main line from Paddington and served by Malvern College transport, the Downs is situated on the Herefordshire side of the Malvern Hills on a striking rural 55-acre campus in Colwall.

The Downs Malvern strives to exceed the confines of the National Curriculum in academic, as well as cultural, sporting and social accomplishments. The school offers a broad curriculum challenging the academically gifted and supporting those with special needs. The School was subjected to an Independent Schools Inspectorate (ISI) inspection in 2015 and was considered to be "*an excellent School*". The full inspection report is available on the School website.

The Early Years and Pre-Prep have now settled into their newly refurbished building. Six years after a seamless move over to the Prep Department at 7 years old, pupils will move on to Year 9 at Malvern College, or to their preferred senior school to complete their school education.

Year 8 pupils have moved on to a variety of independent senior schools on the basis of scholarship or Common Entrance examinations and, whilst the option to go on to a wide variety of independent schools is still there, the direction has changed. The Downs is the main feeder school for Malvern College and the emphasis in Years 7 and 8 is not only a preparation for scholarships and Common Entrance, but also to allow a smooth transition to the College academically and socially.

Sports, especially team games, are a significant part of the curriculum, as are Music and Art. 80% of the pupils learn to play a musical instrument. There is also a wide and expanding Hobbies programme that includes Railway Engineering as well as Speech and Drama, Dance, Design Technology and Art.

Boarding. The refurbished Boarding House provides a home for up to 60 boarders. Boarding can be full, flexi or a one-off experience with a published programme of evening and weekend activities. All boarders are looked after by a caring staff, dedicated to their welfare. A boarding inspection carried out by the ISI in November 2015 found the provision of boarding care at The Downs to be "*excellent*".

Facilities. There is a wide range of facilities including a 300-seat capacity Concert Hall, self-contained Music and Art buildings; new Science laboratories; a new Design and Technology suite, Pottery studio and wired computer network with whiteboards. A new sports complex is supplemented by an astroturf Hockey pitch, 3 Netball/Tennis courts and 55 acres of grounds set aside for games pitches, Forest School lessons and relaxation. The school has its own narrow gauge steam railway! Plans are under way for a new indoor 25 metre Swimming Pool.

11+ Scholarships and Exhibitions, as well as being awarded to pupils who show academic excellence, are also awarded to pupils who show academic competence as well as having a particular talent in Art, Music, Drama or Sport.

Bursaries are available offering assistance to parents subject to completion of a means test form.

Charitable status. The Downs, Malvern College Prep School, trading as The Downs Malvern, is a Registered Charity, number 1120616. It exists to provide education for girls and boys from 3–13 years.

The Downs Preparatory School

Wraxall, Bristol BS48 1PF

Tel: 01275 852008
email: office@thedownsschool.co.uk
website: www.thedownsschool.co.uk
Twitter: @TheDownsSchool

Chairman of Governors: M A Burchfield

Headmaster: **Marcus Gunn**, MA Ed, BA, PGCE, IAPS

Age Range. 4–13.
Number of Pupils. 281: 167 boys, 114 girls.
Fees per term (2018–2019). £3,615–£5,475 including lunch.

The Downs Preparatory School was founded in 1894 on the parklands of Bristol, otherwise known as the Downs. The school moved to the estate of Charlton House, its present site, in 1927. The Headmaster at the time, Mr Wilfred Harrison, stated that the relocation was because of the "incessant roar of traffic" and the "nerve-racking turmoil of the city". As a consequence of his vision, today at the end of a long meandering drive, three miles from the turmoil of a busy city, approximately two hundred and eighty children

excel in the stunning rural environment of The Downs School.

Our children enjoy a vibrant all-round education that is stimulating, challenging and exciting. Academic study is important and we expect all our pupils to adopt a healthy work ethic and achieve high standards, but we believe that to truly educate it is essential to embrace the creative, the physical and the spiritual as much as the intellectual.

At The Downs we embrace a strong set of traditional values and expectations. Childhood is cherished; our young children wear wellies, climb trees and make dens. They make elaborate daisy chains, delight in playing conkers and relish bushcraft cooking. The sophisticated world of mobile devices and adolescence remains at the front entrance for later life. Within this healthy, happy and wholesome environment we seek to nurture unaffected good manners, we embrace grace and humility, and we applaud the qualities of friendship, excellence and respect. We encourage and have high regard for individuality, we endorse aspiration and we celebrate success. Essentially, however, quality of character is considered equally as important as achievement.

Class sizes are small (ideally 18). Pupils are prepared for the major independent senior schools with Badminton, Clifton College, Bristol Grammar School, Queen Elizabeth's Hospital, Millfield, Marlborough, Sherborne, King's College Taunton and Winchester featuring regularly. The pupils follow the Common Entrance Syllabus, a programme that enables the school to make the most of its independence to the benefit of the pupils. The traditional disciplines of English, Maths, Science and French form the core studies. The Foundation subjects of History, Geography and Religious Education are taught independently. These are complemented by a range of contemporary subjects such as Computer Science, Spanish, (Latin optional) and the Theory of Music and Etiquette.

Sport is of an exceptional standard, but there is a team for everyone; it is not unusual to field twenty teams or more at one time. All the major team sports are played. The Performing Arts are valued highly and standards are impressive: 85% of pupils play instruments, choir is compulsory in the Prep School, over 50% of the school attend Speech and Drama lessons, productions are continual, Dance in its many forms is popular and the vibrant Art Department provides for all styles.

Excellent facilities include a purpose-built Pre-Prep, new classroom block, theatre, two IT suites, woodwork centre, extensive playing fields, Forest School, huge Sports Hall, 2 astroturf pitches, and outdoor swimming pool. Significant work to extend the facilities for the Performing Arts is under way.

An independent Prep School, The Downs does not feed any particular senior school. Over the last decade our children have moved on to numerous schools including the best and most demanding in the country. Considerable time is taken to get to know these schools in order that we can provide constructive and objective advice to interested parents. This consultative process is evidently successful, as it is extremely unusual for a child not to gain entry to a school of their first choice, indeed many of our pupils are awarded scholarships.

Visitors are warmly welcomed. The School Registrar, Caroline Crew, is very happy to assist interested parents at their convenience.

For further information or to arrange a visit to see the children at work and play, please contact The School Office on 01275 852008.

Charitable Status. The Downs School is a Registered Charity, number 310279. It was established for the education of boys and girls aged 4–13.

Downsend School

Cognita Schools Group

1 Leatherhead Road, Leatherhead, Surrey KT22 8TJ

Tel:	01372 372311
Fax:	01372 363367
email:	admissions@downsend.co.uk
website:	www.downsend.co.uk
Twitter:	@DownsendSchool
Facebook:	@DownsendSchool
LinkedIn:	/downsend-school

Headmaster: **Mr I Thorpe**, BA Ed Hons Exeter, MA Ed Open

Deputy Head: Mr G S Watts, BA Hons London, PGCE
Head of Upper School: Mr K Newland, BSc Hons Surrey, PGCE
Head of Lower School: Mrs C Kirkham, BA Hons London, PGCE
Assistant Head (*External Relations*): Mr J Albert, BSc Hons Kingston, MA Ed, QTS

Age Range. 2–13 co-educational.
Number of Pupils. Day: Age 2–6: Boys 138, Girls 124; Age 6–13: Boys 256, Girls 168.
Fees per term (2018–2019). Pre-Preparatory £1,030–£3,845, including lunch for full-time pupils and 'Early Birds', 'Little Lates' and Extended Day facilities. Preparatory: £4,250 (Year 2), £5,145 (Years 3–8), including lunch. Sibling discounts apply for more than one child in Reception or above.

Downsend is a co-educational day school for children aged between 2 and 13 years.

The preparatory school stands on a pleasant, open site just outside the town, surrounded by its own playing fields, tennis courts, Astro pitch, cricket nets and sports pavilion. The Sports Complex includes a large indoor swimming pool and sports hall. The comfortable and vibrant library, expanded networked ICT provision, bespoke facilities for Design Technology, Textiles and Food Technology, a Music Suite (complete with sound proof practice rooms) and Drama Room extend the curriculum to support children's learning and development.

Pre-Preparatory (age 2 to 6). There are three co-educational pre-preparatory school sites in Ashtead, Epsom and Leatherhead. Pupils work in a welcoming and stimulating environment, in small classes, where a strong focus on education builds solid foundations in Numeracy and Literacy. Dance and Drama, French, Music and Swimming are all taught by specialists and enhance the curriculum across all year groups. An enhanced afternoon programme, further supported by a wide range of after school clubs including Spanish, is also on offer. An extended day facility provides complimentary 'Early Birds' and 'Little Lates' facilities each day from 8.00 am to 5.30 pm (6.00 pm at Epsom & Leatherhead Pre-Prep), which is especially useful for working parents. Leatherhead Pre-Prep also offers a breakfast club from 7.30 am for a small charge (includes breakfast). At the age of 6 the children move on to Downsend Preparatory School where they are joined by children from other local independent and state schools.

Preparatory (age 6 to 13). Founded in 1891, Downsend is an established academic prep school preparing children for Common Entrance, Scholarship and Senior School examinations. The school is a thriving community where

children are encouraged to develop their talents both in and outside the classroom. A huge variety of extra-curricular opportunities are offered to allow children to try new activities during and after school.

The standard of work is high and the school is particularly proud of its scholarship record with over 200 being achieved since 2014 to some of the top senior schools in the area.

There is a broad and engaging curriculum. Our approach to learning sees English, Science, Maths, Languages, Humanities, Art and Technology being lifted off the pages of textbooks and worksheets though creativity and enthusiasm. In addition to the normal Common Entrance subjects children study Art, Drama, Food Technology, ICT, Music, Design Technology, Textiles and PSHE. There is a termly curriculum collapse day for STEAM projects. Parents are kept informed of their children's progress through regular parents' evenings and termly reports and are welcome at all times to communicate with teaching staff and the management team.

The school has a strong reputation for music, with regular and varied concerts throughout the year, as well as orchestras and choirs for the Lower and Upper School. A large number of children learn musical instruments and all pupils in Year 3 enjoy the instrumental scheme where they try different instruments before choosing which one to learn for the rest of the school year. Drama is equally important and there is a production at the end of each term. Pupils can take part in a full range of sports not only in school but also at local, regional and national level. Regular visits occur outside school and trips abroad are also offered.

The holiday club scheme, Downsend+, gives pupils access to exciting and absorbing workshops, courses, themed days and thrilling days out. Run by qualified Downsend staff, this provision is available to children aged 4–13 from 8.00 am to 5.30 pm, including breakfast, lunch and tea as appropriate. Downsend Pre-Prep+ is also available as a dedicated facility for Downsend children aged 2–5 and is held at Leatherhead Pre-Prep.

Dragon School

Bardwell Road, Oxford OX2 6SS

Tel:	01865 315405
Fax:	01865 311664
email:	admissions@dragonschool.org
website:	www.dragonschool.org
Twitter:	@thedragonschool
Facebook:	@DragonSchoolOxford

Chairman of Governors: Professor R W Ainsworth

Headmaster: **Dr Crispin Hyde-Dunn**, MA Oxon, PGCE, MA Ed, NPQH, PhD

Age Range. 4–8 (Pre-Prep), 8–13 (Prep).
Number of Pupils. 824. Pre-Prep: 217 (127 boys, 90 girls). Prep: 608 (364 boys, 244 girls); Day: 379 (216 boys, 163 girls); Boarders: 228 (148 boys, 81 girls).
Fees per term (2018–2019). Day £3,996–£7,045; Boarding £10,205.

The Dragon is a co-educational boarding and day school in Oxford which offers an outstanding educational experience for both boys and girls from 4 to 13 years. The school's distinctive approach encourages enquiry, confidence and enthusiasm in a quintessentially English school environment. Recognised as individuals, children are encouraged to try everything and express themselves. Highly-qualified staff foster a culture of learning how to learn which promotes academic, sporting and creative excellence. A non-selective school, pupils win numerous scholarships and awards to excellent senior schools.

The Dragon's beautiful campus and dedicated Pre-Prep are located just north of central Oxford – the oldest University City in the world.

The Curriculum. Teaching is tailored to the needs of each pupil and their learning styles and motivations. Teachers aim to inspire, motivate and challenge to help children take ownership of their own learning.

Games & the Arts. The Dragon supports children's development, coordination, movement and performance through sport and exercise. Children observe, explore and learn through drawing, painting, printmaking, sculpture and ceramics in Art, and to experiment with a range of materials and electronics in Design Technology. There are 20 sports on offer, including sculling, fencing, girls' and boys' football, golf, cricket and judo.

Pastoral Care. The Dragon strives to create a happy, secure and stimulating learning environment in which all members of the school community can grow and develop as individuals. The Dragon is a Family Links School and follows the Nurturing Programme which is a way of educating children and adults which enhances self-awareness, personal empowerment, self-esteem and empathy. The Deputy Head of Social and Emotional Learning supports this whole-school approach which extends beyond the classroom to all staff, children and parents.

Boarding. Boarding options begin from age 8, in small, family-run boarding houses. The family feel within the boarding community is strengthened by boarders returning to their Houses throughout the school day.

Future Schools. 47 Scholarships and Awards offered for senior schools in 2018 including: all-rounder, academic, music, sport, art and drama and DT. Dragons go on to a vast range of senior schools, notably: Eton, Rugby, Harrow, Marlborough College, St Edward's Oxford, Radley, Oundle, Winchester, Wellington, Wycombe Abbey, Cheltenham Ladies' College, Stowe School and Bradfield College. Preparatory years at the Dragon lay the firm foundations of a successful education at senior schools in the UK and beyond.

Headmaster's Philosophy. At the Dragon, new talents are uncovered and ambitions nurtured; friendships are forged and challenges embraced. Every child is valued and every achievement celebrated. A strong scaffold for academic excellence is provided by our cutting-edge curriculum and outstanding teaching, equipping our pupils for smooth transition to their senior schools and beyond. We promote kindness and tolerance, we encourage a sense of service to others, and we teach children to respect and nurture their own wellbeing.

Outstanding Characteristics. The 2014 ISI inspection rated the Dragon as outstanding; and teaching and learning as 'exceptional'. The School ethos hinges on a dynamic balance of relaxed unpretentiousness and academic discipline.

For further information or to arrange a visit please contact Dr Kate Heath, Registrar, on 01865 315405 or admissions@dragonschool.org.

Charitable status. The Dragon School Trust Ltd is a Registered Charity, number 309676. It aims to provide education for boys and girls between the ages of 4 and 13.

Duke of Kent School

Peaslake Road, Ewhurst, Surrey GU6 7NS

Tel:	01483 277313
Fax:	01483 273862
email:	office@dokschool.org
website:	www.dukeofkentschool.org.uk

Chairman of the Governing Body: Mr Richard Brocksom

Head: **Mrs Sue Knox**, BA Hons UCNW, MBA Cranfield, GradDipEd & MEdLead Macquarie University Sydney

Age Range. 3–16.
Number of Pupils. 309.

Set in inspirational grounds high in the Surrey Hills, surrounded by forest land, Duke of Kent School provides an excellent co-educational option for pupils from 3 to 16 years. Coming from Guildford, Horsham, Dorking and surrounding local villages, many pupils use the School minibus service.

Extended day arrangements for those pupils who wish to arrive before or stay beyond the end of lessons (7.30 am to 7.30 pm) provide families with exceptional flexibility. At the end of the School day, pupils can choose to complete their Prep at school under supervision or at home, and can also choose from a varied programme of sport, academic and social activities.

The small size of the School enables us to know our pupils very well and to ensure that all pupils can reach their potential. All pupils receive the appropriate combination of academic challenge and support to enable them to achieve. A Duke of Kent School pupil is expected to contribute and participate to the very best of his or her ability, take an active role in community life and take responsibility for his or her learning. Our able and committed teaching and support staff work in partnership with pupils and their families. The expectation is that each pupil will strive to achieve a string of 'personal bests': in the classroom, on the sports field, in personal development, in exploring the arts and in a wide range of activities. We focus on each child's attitude to learning in order to ensure that they are fully equipped to make maximum progress. Teaching and learning is supported by a well established 1–1 iPad programme and supported by our dedicated fibre optic line.

Pupils are prepared for GCSE/IGCSE examinations in the context of a curriculum which aims to take pupils above and beyond exam preparation. There is a focus throughout the School of encouraging pupils to adopt a growth mindset in order to become successful learners. Building on the work of our Prep School in which Creative Curriculum provides excellent stretch and challenge for pupils, our rigorous GCSE programme prepares pupils for A Level and university study and sparks what may be lifelong intellectual passions. Learning beyond the classroom, whether on educational visits or through outdoor learning on site, is a crucial aspect of our pupils' experience. Personal development receives close attention. Our pupils develop confidence and self-esteem from opportunities to lead and to serve. Kindness is expected and encouraged from pupils of all ages.

The School maintains a busy fixtures calendar at all ages. We have extensive playing fields, an all-weather turf pitch, all-weather tennis courts, a swimming pool and a full-sized sports hall. More than half of our pupils are learning a musical instrument. Music and Drama activities take place in a purpose-built Performing Arts Hall with facilities for Music Technology. The quality of Art on display and in production is a particular strength of the School.

In 2018, 97% of our pupils achieved the benchmark of 5 GCSE passes, including IGCSE Languages and Mathematics, and 47% of all grades achieved were 7/8/9 (the equivalent of A or A*), which is a tremendous accomplishment for an inclusive school. In recent years our pupils have gone on to successful courses of further study at day schools, boarding schools and colleges, both locally and further afield.

Prospective pupils are invited to attend a visit day during which they will be interviewed by the Head or another senior member of staff, and will take a range of cognitive tests (CAT4). No preparation is required for our admissions testing. We are looking for evidence of enthusiasm and willingness to get fully involved in our lively community.

Fees per term (2018–2019). £2,320–£6,030.

Charitable status. The Duke of Kent School is a Registered Charity, number 1064183.

Dulwich Prep Cranbrook

Coursehorn, Cranbrook, Kent TN17 3NP

Tel:	01580 712179
Fax:	01580 715322
email:	registrar@dulwichprepcranbrook.org
website:	www.dulwichprepcranbrook.org
Twitter:	@DPCranbrook
Facebook:	@DPCranbrook

Chairman of Governors: Mrs C Nash

Headmaster: Mr Paul David, BEd Hons

Age Range. 3–13.

Number of Boys and Girls. Day and Boarding: 279 (Upper School), 191 (Little Stream), 64 (Pre-Prep).

Fees per term (2018–2019). Day: £6,050 (Years 5–8), £5,140 (Years 2–4), £3,895 (Year 1), £3,760 (Reception), Nursery: £3,160 (full day), £1,990 (mornings). Boarders: from £28 per night.

The School, which is one mile from the country town of Cranbrook, has extensive grounds (50 acres) and offers a broad and varied education to boys and girls from 3 to 13+. To ensure that children receive the personal attention that is vital for this age range the School is divided up into three separate, self-contained, departments. These are Nash House (3–5 year olds), Little Stream (5–9 year olds) and Upper School (9–13 year olds). Each department has its own staff, teaching equipment, sports facilities, playgrounds, swimming pools, etc. Pupils are prepared for Common Entrance or Scholarship examinations to any school of their parents' choice, and there is a strong emphasis on up-to-date teaching methods. The wide scope for sporting activities – Football, Rugby, Cricket, Hockey, Netball, Rounders, Athletics, Cross Country, Swimming, Tennis – is balanced by the importance attached to Art, DT, Drama, ICT and Music. Over 200 pupils learn the full range of orchestral instruments. There are two Orchestras, Wind and Brass Bands, Jazz Band, and four Choirs. The boarders are divided into two houses, boys and girls, each under the care of House staff. The happiness of the boarders is a particular concern and every effort is made to establish close and friendly contact between the School and the parents. There is a flourishing Parents Association, and regular meetings are held between staff and parents.

The School is a Charitable Trust, under the same Governing Body as Dulwich Prep London, although in other respects the two schools are quite separate. The link with Dulwich College is historical only.

Charitable status. Dulwich Prep Cranbrook is a Registered Charity, number 1174358. It exists for the provision of high quality education in a Christian environment.

Dulwich Prep London

42 Alleyn Park, Dulwich, London SE21 7AA

Tel:	020 8766 5500
Fax:	020 8766 7586
email:	admissions@dulwichpreplondon.org
website:	www.dulwichpreplondon.org

The School was founded in 1885 and became a charitable trust in 1957 with a board of governors.

Chair of Governors: Mrs C R Randell

Headmaster: **M Roulston**, MBE, MEd

Age Range. Boys 3–13, Girls 3–5.

Number of Boys. 870 day boys, 16 girls.

Fees per term (2018–2019). Tuition: Day boys £4,358–£6,438 inclusive of lunch (there are no compulsory extras).

Dulwich Prep London is an independent prep school with a national reputation for excellence.

While we are essentially a boys' school, with about 870 pupils aged between 3 and 13, we start with the Early Years Department which also caters for girls. There are four other sections to the school: the Pre-Prep (Years 1 & 2), the Lower School (Years 3 & 4) and the Middle & Upper Schools (Years 5 & 6 and 7 & 8).

At 13+ our boys go on to more than fifty excellent day and boarding schools throughout the country. Alleyn's, Harrow, Dulwich College, Eton College, Marlborough College, Tonbridge, St Paul's, Wellington College, Westminster and Winchester College are just a selection of our leavers' destination schools. In the 2017–2018 academic year our leavers gained more than 70 academic, musical, artistic and sporting scholarships and awards.

Situated in SE21, we have the very best in educational facilities. These include very spacious classrooms, science block containing 3 labs, a DT suite, a cookery suite and an observatory, a dedicated music school, a large sports hall, a studio theatre, 3 ICT suites, a superb art studio, a six-lane 25m swimming pool and more than 25 acres of playing fields, quite unique given our privileged location.

Some of the opportunities available to our pupils are:

- We run more than 25 sports teams each term with the top teams regularly doing well in national competitions. Recent sports tours include cricket to South Africa, football to Italy, rugby to Ireland.
- More than 700 individual music lessons take place every week and boys have opportunity to perform regularly in a range of groups and ensembles.
- Approaching 30 groups perform regularly in our own 300 seat concert hall. Many also appear on the programme for our gala concerts at prestigious venues such as St John's, Smith Square and Southwark Cathedral.
- We provide more than 100 clubs and extra-curricular activities, stimulating boys' intellectual and sporting interests.
- We run residential trips for pupils in Years 4–8 within the curriculum that are built in to the fee structure. 15 more trips, ranging from cultural visits to skiing, are offered during the holidays.
- Drama productions are staged by forms and year groups from Reception to Year 8.

Charitable status. Dulwich Prep London is a Registered Charity, number 1174356. It exists to provide education for boys.

Dumpton School

Deans Grove House, Deans Grove, Wimborne, Dorset BH21 7AF

Tel:	01202 883818
Fax:	01202 848760
email:	secretary@dumpton.com
website:	www.dumpton.com
Twitter:	@dumpton
Facebook:	@dumpton
LinkedIn:	/dumpton-school

Chairman of Governors: Mr H Cocke

Headmaster: Mr A W Browning, BSc, PGCE, MA Ed, CChem, MRSC

Age Range. 2–13.
Number of Pupils. Girls and Boys: 221 aged 7–13 and 100 aged 2–7.
Fees per term (2018–2019). Prep School (Years 3–8) £5,283; Pre-Prep (Reception, Years 1 & 2) £2,948; Nursery charged at £6.50 per hour. The school week is from Monday to Friday. All fees include meals and there are no compulsory extras.

Dumpton School is a co-educational day school for pupils aged 2 to 13 years. The school is set in a beautiful rural setting with 26 acres of grounds but is nevertheless only one mile from Wimborne and school buses run daily to and from the nearby towns of Bournemouth, Poole, Dorchester, Wareham, Ringwood and Blandford.

Despite record numbers in the school, class sizes are small. Children enjoy excellent teaching as well as incomparable opportunities for Music, Art, Drama and Sport in which the school excels. Dumpton is renowned for its caring approach in which every child is encouraged to identify and develop his or her abilities and personal qualities as fully as possible. This safe and supportive environment sees the children thrive and reach their full potential. The framework of family and Christian values emphasises the importance of teamwork and mutual respect that pervades the school. It is a very happy and successful school and children regularly win scholarships to their Senior Schools or places at the local Grammar Schools. Over the past eight years, Dumpton pupils have been awarded over 192 scholarships to schools such as Bryanston, Canford, Clayesmore, Millfield, Talbot Heath and Sherborne.

Recent developments have included a new multi-purpose Performing Arts venue complete with music recital room, a new outdoor adventure playground for the Prep School, a new Science and Maths Block, a full-size floodlit Astroturf, a covered swimming pool, a new Art, Design and Food Technology Centre, an outdoor classroom, climbing wall and environmental area, complete with ponds, pontoons, beehives and pupil allotments. In addition, the school has been awarded Green Flag status by Eco-Schools for 2 years running as well as the South West Environmental Award for 2018. The building of a new state-of-the-art sports hall is under way and due to be completed in 2019.

The school motto 'You can because you think you can', lies at the cornerstone of teaching at Dumpton and our aim is for pupils to leave us having reached their full potential, as confident communicators and appreciating good manners and tolerance.

For a copy of the prospectus, please apply to the Headmaster's Secretary.
Charitable status. Dumpton School is a Registered Charity, number 306222. It exists to provide education for boys and girls.

Dunhurst
Bedales Prep School

Alton Road, Steep, Petersfield, Hampshire GU32 2DR

Tel:	01730 300200
email:	admissions@bedales.org.uk
website:	www.bedales.org.uk
Twitter:	@DunhurstSchool
Facebook:	@bedalesschool
LinkedIn:	/bedales-school

Chairman of Governors: Matthew Rice, BA

Head: Colin Baty, BA Ed

Deputy Head (*Pastoral*): Aaron Gardner

Director of Teaching & Learning: Andy Wiggins, BA Kent, PGCE Portsmouth

Age Range. 8–13.
Number in school. 202 pupils: 104 boys; 98 girls; 61 boarders
Fees per term (2018–2019). Boarders £8,310; Half Boarding (3 nights) £7,405; Day: £5,640–£6,255. Flexi Boarding available.

John Badley founded Bedales School in 1893 to educate through head, heart and hand. When Dunhurst was added in 1902 as the prep school, Badley's philosophy on education continued. Dunhurst is a unique school: a warm inclusive atmosphere in which relationships are built on trust, tolerance, respect, support and care; a stimulating curriculum that has breadth and depth; a school where children experience the joy of discovery and learning and a wealth of opportunity.

The academic curriculum aims to offer challenge through innovative teaching that inspires the pupil and focuses on the individual. Confidence grows as the children grow, and with it their desire to question and discuss. The school's distinctive approach to learning helps children excel academically. Learning through doing lies at the heart of the educational ethos.

The creative and performing arts, sport, the outdoor work programme and the diverse wealth of activities on offer ensure that every pupil can develop new interests and skills important to them.

Relationships throughout the Dunhurst community are warm and informal but this goes hand in hand with a strong philosophy of respect and courtesy. A global understanding is nurtured in the pupils through a wide range of outreach projects and fundraising initiatives; Dunhurst pupils are encouraged to see themselves through the context of a wider world.

Dunhurst engenders inquisitiveness in pupils so they are prepared for the academic rigour of IGCSEs, Bedales Assessed Courses (BACs), A Levels and beyond. It isn't all about getting results; there is depth to pupils' learning because of Dunhurst's diverse curriculum. The creative and performing arts, sport, the outdoor work programme and the wealth of activities on offer ensure that every pupil can develop new interests and skills.

Matches against other schools take place regularly in athletics, cricket, football, hockey, netball, rounders, rugby, swimming and tennis. A wide range of other sports and outdoor activities is also offered, including judo and golf.

Dunhurst makes full use of the first-rate facilities at Bedales which include the Bedales Olivier Theatre, a Sports Hall, floodlit netball and tennis courts, an all-weather pitch and covered swimming pool. This and the similarity of ethos, makes for an easy transition for pupils moving from Dunhurst to the Senior School at the age of 13.

There is a strong boarding community at Dunhurst. Many of the older pupils are full boarders and provision is made for flexible boarding for day pupils.

Applicants for both boarder and day places sit residential entrance tests. The main points of entry are at 8+ and 11+. Entry at other ages is dependent on the availability of places.

For information about Dunannie, the Pre-Prep (3–8 years), see the Bedales entry in HMC section.

Charitable status. Bedales School is a Registered Charity, number 307332. It exists to provide a sound education and training for children and young persons of both sexes.

Durlston Court

Becton Lane, Barton-on-Sea, New Milton, Hampshire BH25 7AQ

Tel: 01425 610010
email: registrar@durlstoncourt.co.uk
website: www.durlstoncourt.co.uk
Twitter: @durlstoncourt
Facebook: @DurlstonCourt

Chairman of Governors: Mr Chandra Ashfield

Headmaster: Mr Richard May, BA, PGCE

Age Range. 2–13 Co-educational.
Number of Pupils. 300 Day Pupils.
Fees per term (2018–2019). Kindergarten £27.48 per morning or afternoon session, £51.02 a day, £2,995 (Reception–Year 2), £4,395 (Year 3), £5,445 (Years 4–8).

Durlston Court Prep School is a happy and successful school for children aged 2–13 years from across the New Forest and surrounding areas. The school prides itself on providing a first-class, all-round, Prep School education in an inspiring and nurturing environment.

Excellence, integrity and challenge are fostered as core values of the Durlston Family. Our children are prepared to face challenges and to fully engage and thrive in the world of today and tomorrow.

A preparatory school prepares a child for the next stage in his or her educational journey. We are proud that we do this so well. Durlston Court has a long-standing reputation for all-round educational excellence, confirmed by the highest inspection rating possible. We focus on good manners and behaviour whilst promoting tailor-made challenge in all areas for each child within the Durlston Family – a cohesive and mutually supportive unit. We look forward to encouraging the mindset and skills that will enable all to flourish post-Durlston.

Our children will be ready for the future – any future – and we will be proud of each and every one of them.

Academic Success 2017–2018:
- 100% success rate to Canford School was achieved.
- 100% success rate to King Edward VI Southampton was achieved.
- 100% pass rate in Year 8 Common Entrance Examinations.
- No. 1 in Hampshire and Dorset in Sunday Times 'Top 100 Prep Schools' list.

- In the past 2 years Durlstonians have been awarded Scholarships in areas including Academics, Sports, Performing Arts, Music, Art and All-Round as they transferred to Senior Schools.

Bus services cover routes from: Beaulieu, Boldre, Bournemouth, Bransgore, Brockenhurst, Burley, Christchurch, Highcliffe, Ferndown, Milford on Sea, Mudeford, Lymington, Lyndhurst, St Leonards, Southbourne, Sway, Ringwood.

Parents are most welcome to visit the school by making an appointment or by attending an Open Morning.

Further details of the school are available by visiting the school's website or by contacting registrar@durlstoncourt.co.uk

Charitable status. Durlston Court School is a Registered Charity, number 307325, which exists to provide quality education for children from 2–13 years.

Durston House

12 Castlebar Road, Ealing, London W5 2DR

Tel: 020 8991 6530
Fax: 020 8991 6547
email: info@durstonhouse.org
website: www.durstonhouse.org

Co-Chairmen of Governors: Mr K Mahoney, BSc, MRICS & Mr D G Henshall

Headmaster: Mr N I Kendrick, MA, BEd Hons

Deputy Head: Mr W J Murphy, BA, DipTch
Bursar: Mrs J Twyford
Director of Studies: Mr D Stock, BSc Hons St Mary's, PGCE
Head of Complementary Curriculum: Mrs C Green, MA, BA, QTS
Head of Junior School: Mr S W Perkins, BEd Hons
Head of Pre-Prep: Mrs N Sharma, BA Hons UCE, PGCE

Age Range. 4–13.
Number of Boys. 394 Day Boys.
Fees per term (2018–2019). £4,160–£5,060.

Durston House is a leading London prep school, with a long history of academic success and a fine record of preparing boys for Senior School. This is reflected in the Scholarships won at many prominent senior schools. The school began life in 1886 and has, from its earliest years, enjoyed a strong academic reputation and encouraged keen sporting and lively cultural interests. We take pride in the true and visible diversity of our community and embrace pupils and staff from all ethnic, cultural and religious backgrounds.

We are very proud of the boys at Durston House. We are very proud of their success as people. The emphasis is on high standards of work and targets that are commensurate with each pupil's personal development. A boy's education here is shaped by the development of his character, his curiosity to learn and discover more, and his expanding capability. These three concepts – Character, Curiosity and Capability – are the cornerstones of his success at Durston House and his success in life. The development of fine young men, who achieve great things, is the aim and reward for any boys' school. That such achievement is made, in a spirit of humility and quiet determination, is testimony to the values of the whole Durston House community.

Durston House has three classes of about sixteen boys in each year group. We have many specialist teachers along with generous ancillary staffing and learning support for specific needs. Throughout the school there are Activities

Programmes offering a wide range of cultural, recreational and sporting pursuits. Both playing field complexes have floodlit all-weather facilities and there has been much sporting success in recent years. Extensive use is made of local facilities, especially for drama and swimming. There are fixtures with other prep schools, full participation in IAPS events, and regular expeditions at home and abroad. Entry into the Reception year is in order of registration and is non-selective. For all other years, entry assessment procedures are in place.

The educational experience at Durston House is one that countless parents seek for their sons. It is well-rounded and thorough, holistic and specific. It speaks to the very core of who we are as people: to be human is to grow. At Durston House, the manner in which this growth is guided is one of relaxed, quiet integrity of purpose, allowing boys the freedom to develop themselves. This is the essence of our ongoing success as a school.

Charitable status. Durston House School Educational Trust Limited is a Registered Charity, number 294670.

Eagle House

Crowthorne Road, Sandhurst, Berkshire GU47 8PH

Tel: 01344 772134
email: info@eaglehouseschool.com
website: www.eaglehouseschool.com
Twitter: @EagleHouseSch
Facebook: @EagleHouseSch

Chairman of Governors: H W Veary, Esq

Headmaster: **A P N Barnard**, BA Hons, PGCE

Age Range. 3–13.
Number of Children. 380: 60 Boarders, 320 Day Children.
Fees per term (2018–2019). Prep School: £8,110 (boarders), £5,830–£6,035 (day pupils). Pre-Prep: £3,860. Nursery: £2,250 (5 mornings including lunch).

Eagle House is a co-educational, boarding and day Prep, Pre-Prep and Nursery located in Berkshire. The school's superb grounds and excellent facilities are the background to an experience where success, confidence and happiness are paramount. The school is proud of its academic record, preparing children for a host of top independent schools and boasting a diverse and robust curriculum. In December 2017 the school received an 'excellent' rating in all areas from the ISI Inspectorate.

Younger pupils follow the International Primary Curriculum and our older children have embarked on a new Humanities curriculum that links subjects through topics and themes. Great teaching, new technology and a focus on the basics mean that children make good progress and love to be in the classroom. Independent learning is a focus for all children and our Extended Project programme helps drive inquisitive minds.

Eagle House offers a diverse and varied extra-curricular programme and we unashamedly offer lots as part of our Golden Eagle activities experience. Children benefit from a huge range of opportunities in sport, music, drama, art, outward bound and community programmes. Busy children are happy and fulfilled children and we like to think that all pupils are Learning for Life.

Learning for Life means that children benefit from the best all-round education. They can feel confident in the classroom, on the games field, on stage, in the concert hall and in the community. Everyone is given the chance to stretch themselves in every area. Challenge is an important part of growing up and at Eagle House we learn that success and failure are both positive experiences.

Bright learning environments, outdoor learning areas and wonderful sporting facilities are important, but it is the community that shapes a young person. Through the excellent pastoral care and tutor system, coupled with a buddy structure, ensuring children have an older pupil to support them, Eagle House seeks to develop wellbeing from the youngest to the oldest.

Recognising how to be a positive influence within a community is also part of the Eagle House journey. Through our wonderful Learning for Life programme that teaches children about themselves and the wider community, we aim to make all our pupils responsible and independent as well as able to show empathy and understanding towards others. Time for reflection in chapel and assemblies also improves the way we look at the world and mindfulness sessions help us all take stock.

Boarding is a popular option and allows children to experience a varied evening programme of activities as well as being part of a vibrant and caring community. Boarding encourages independence, but it is also great fun and whether full, weekly or flexi, boarders have the most wonderful time.

We often say that Eagle House children have the time of their lives and we firmly believe this. Learning for Life at Eagle House opens the doors to all sorts of opportunities and this results in children who are highly motivated and enthusiastic in all they do. Eagle House buzzes with achievement and laughter – not a bad way to grow up!

Charitable status. Wellington College is a Registered Charity, number 309093. Eagle House School is owned by Wellington College and is part of the same charity registration.

Eaton House Belgravia Pre-Prep, Prep and Nursery

3–5 Eaton Gate, Belgravia, London SW1W 9BA

Tel: 020 7924 6000
email: admissions@eatonhouseschools.com
website: www.eatonhouseschools.com
Twitter: @eatonhousesch
Facebook: @eatonhouseschools

Head: **Mr Huw May**

Age Range. 3–11, Boys.
Number of Pupils. 240.
Fees per term (2018–2019). Pre-Prep £5,950; Prep £6,900; Nursery prices according to sessions attended.

Traditional in tone, but modern and welcoming in outlook, Eaton House Belgravia Pre-Prep has achieved some of the most outstanding 7+ and 8+ Pre-Prep results in London. In 2018, some 40% of 7+ and 8+ pupils received offers to Westminster and St Paul's, amongst other fine schools. This was the best result for 5 years. We are non-selective and as the *Good Schools Guide* (2018) points out, 'This would be an impressive record for a selective school'.

We are equally ambitious for our Prep School, which opened in 2017, taking up the baton for 8-year-old boys who wish to sit the 11+ examinations. With an outstanding teacher to pupil ratio and an exceptional degree of personal input towards exam preparation, each pupil will receive a first-class education and achieve the senior school of his choice. We have high aspirations for every boy, and the progress that they will make in their three years at EHB Prep school will be remarkable.

In view of our all-round excellence in academic teaching, pastoral care and value-added extras Eaton House Belgravia was the winner of a Highly Commended Award in the Boys' School of the Year category in the Independent School of the Year Awards.

According to the *Good Schools Guide* (2018), Mr Huw May, the Headmaster of both the Pre-Prep and Prep is 'Ambitious for his school, shows vision and is full of enthusiasm for developing each boy's all-round potential, emotionally as well as academically'. To help with this, the school offers the boys personalised learning plans that allow the brightest to be fully stretched and help to be given to those that need it.

The day starts and ends in a traditional way, with a handshake with the Headmaster. Pre-Prep boys will learn Composition, Comprehension, English, French, Grammar, ICT, Reading, Mathematics, Music, Non-Verbal Reasoning, Science, Spelling, Phonics, PSCHEE, RS, and Verbal Reasoning. In addition, the boys will have lessons in Drama, Games and Art, and enjoy a number of educational trips each year.

For Prep boys, the subjects covered will be Art, Computing, Design Technology, Drama, English, French, Geography, History, Latin, Maths, Music, PSHEE, Science, Theology, Philosophy & Religion.

Beyond academics, sport and the performing arts are both central to our school life. A combination of onsite PE lessons and offsite games and swimming sessions enable our boys to develop key sports skills.

Most of our boys have individual music lessons and some play several instruments to a very high standard by the time they leave us. We have regular Music Assemblies in school and termly Music Competitions in which boys can showcase their talents. Our big annual musical production is enjoyed by many students and boys can win Colours in music, singing, drama, the arts and sports for outstanding service to the school.

Boys are attached to one of four Houses when they arrive and there is great House solidarity across all the years. Sport is an integral part of life at school, whether boys are representing the school or their House, or simply learning to be part of a team. The boys will engage in sports such as football, cricket, rugby and athletics every day as we strongly believe that it is essential for a healthy lifestyle. All boys have a chance to enter competitions and challenges throughout the year.

At 4.00 pm, boys can take advantage of over 30 clubs, which vary according to age. These include: Newsround Club; Book Club; History Club; Classics Club; Fun French; Computer Coding Club; Debate Club; Chess Club; Football Club; Karate Club; STEM (Science, Technology, Engineering and Maths).

The happiness of our pupils is incredibly important to us, and pastoral care is the cornerstone of everything we do. Our Buddy System helps to integrate the newest boys into the school from the first day. The House system provides another layer of support and guidance. The form teacher is the key person who ensures the boys are supported in their emotional development and parental involvement is welcomed.

We encourage every generation of Eaton House Belgravia boys to be recognisable for the strength of their intelligence and their moral integrity. We want them to try everything, to be confident and adaptable, persevering where necessary. We want them to want to make a difference in the world, to be responsible, kind and considerate and to look after each other. We want the boys to thrive on the personalised learning plan they have prepared together with the teacher and to have fun!

Eaton House The Manor Girls' School

58 Clapham Common Northside, London SW4 9RU

Tel: 020 7924 6000
email: admissions@eatonhouseschools.com
website: www.eatonhouseschools.com
Twitter: @eatonhousesch
Facebook: @eatonhouseschools

Headmaster: **Mr Oliver Snowball**

> **Age Range.** 4–11.
> **Number of Pupils.** 225 Girls.
> **Fees per term (2018–2019).** £5,381.

Eaton House The Manor Girls' School has had an outstanding year academically. Pupils were awarded 11 scholarships to London day and boarding schools, in part as a result of what the Good Schools Guide, 2017, acknowledges as 'passionate and dynamic teaching'. Our stimulating classroom environment promotes intellectual curiosity and we prize both academic exploration and risk-taking highly. As a result, 'Teaching is highly effective in promoting pupils' excellence and attainment', according to a recent ISI report.

Our girls typically leave us for a range of top schools including St Paul's Girls' School, Godolphin & Latymer, Wycombe Abbey, St Mary's Calne, St Mary's Ascot, James Allen's Girls' School, Putney High School, and many more. Beyond academics, our girls are happy, calm, emotionally intelligent, balanced, kind and mannerly. As we are non-selective at entry, interest is keen and early application is advised, with registration accepted from birth.

The Headmaster, Mr Oliver Snowball, wants the girls to have an adventure at school and to be intellectually challenged to their maximum potential. Beyond that, he would like each girl to feel that they are known, nurtured, challenged, and to have a genuine love of learning and a deep-rooted respect for people and places by the time that they leave the school.

Sport is very important in the life of the school. Being regularly active enhances the girls' physical and emotional health and they have access to excellent facilities, both indoors and outdoors. We enjoy fielding teams in a range of sports such as Hockey, Netball, Gymnastics and Cross Country. In addition, House matches provide a great deal of excitement and healthy competition for the girls as there is strong House spirit throughout the school.

In the arts, we teach our girls how to generate original and meaningful ideas for themselves and actively encourage them to produce fresh, imaginative responses. There are always plays for the girls to shine in every year and they are held in our full-sized theatre, complete with professional lighting and elaborate costumes. New specialist teachers have strengthened our offering in Drama, Music and the Arts and they are bringing the girls up to an exceptionally high standard very quickly. In addition, we also offer speech and drama lessons leading to outside examinations.

The art department is a very exciting place and girls are encouraged to experiment with a wide range of media. In music, instrumental activities have included a Musical Ensemble Club which has grown to 25 members and a String Ensemble which is setting a very impressive standard. The Form 2 Junior Choir includes every girl in the year, while the Senior Choir, open to years 3–6 now has over 60 members. The singing group Bel Canto, drawn from Forms 4–6 with entry by audition, was invited, once again, to sing at Westminster Abbey's annual Christingle Service – a big honour.

The school day is very busy and at 4.00 pm the girls can take advantage of a range of 33 clubs, some with Pre-Prep boys, such as Choral Club. We can truly say there is something for everybody when it comes to clubs.

For us, pastoral care is about understanding and supporting each individual girl and being there for her in every way, Our House system, excellent form teachers and visible senior management team all combine to ensure that each girl feels known and supported throughout her learning journey at Eaton House The Manor Girls' School. There really is a 'sky is the limit' approach to learning and all our pupils are encouraged to use their intelligence in a dynamic way to demonstrate quick, reasoned and engaging responses to the world about them.

The school is non-selective at age 4; there are English and Maths assessments for older girls. Parents wishing to enrol their children in the School are advised to register them at birth.

Eaton House The Manor Pre-Preparatory School

58 Clapham Common Northside, London SW4 9RU

Tel: 020 7924 6000
email: admissions@eatonhouseschools.com
website: www.eatonhouseschools.com
Twitter: @eatonhousesch
Facebook: @eatonhouseschools

Headmistress: **Mrs Nicola Borthwick**

Age Range. 4–8.
Number of Pupils. 220 Boys.
Fees per term (2018–2019). £5,381.

Eaton House The Manor Pre-Prep is an academic school for boys aged 4–8 which feels like a family, yet it offers the perfect blend of traditional values and a forward thinking education.

The majority of the Pre-Prep boys go directly on to Eaton House The Manor Prep School on the same site, where they stay until they are 13. The quality of an Eaton House The Manor education means that all of the boys leaving the Prep school go to their first choice of senior school, including Eton, Winchester, Westminster, Dulwich College and Tonbridge. Every year a number of our Eaton House The Manor Prep boys win top scholarships to some of the finest schools in the UK, including, in 2018, a highly-prized John Colet Scholarship to St Paul's School.

The foundations of this success are built at the Pre-Prep, where younger boys discover a love of learning that lasts. At Eaton House The Manor Pre-Prep, we firmly believe that it is no coincidence that children learn best when they feel happy and secure. Our aim is to give the boys a smooth and confident transition into the Prep school.

An 'open door' policy means that parents can feel fully involved, confident in the knowledge that boys are being treated as unique individuals. Boys are taught to be kind, considerate, thoughtful and mannerly, as well as to always strive to do their best both academically and personally.

Our approach, which teaches according to ability in small groups, means that we succeed in bringing out the best in each individual child, attaining the highest academic results possible. We encourage both independent and cross-curricular learning in our topic work and lessons are fun, exciting and active – perfectly suited to young boys.

We are a very sporty school, with beautiful Clapham Common on our doorstep providing the perfect venue for team games such as rugby, football and cricket. Sport is a central part of school life and there are a variety of sports and sports clubs beyond the core curriculum. Sport helps the boys' physical and emotional health as well as teaching them to be part of a team representing their school and their House.

Every boy is part of a team and that is very important for building confidence, team spirit and sociability. In addition, drama, art and music are greatly enjoyed by all our pupils. They are all seen as fundamental in developing communication skills and confidence. We have a full-size theatre with technical rig and our boys (and parents) enjoy the many wonderful productions that we put on, complete with elaborate theatrical costumes and effects.

Exceptional pastoral care ensures that the years spent at Eaton House The Manor Pre-Preparatory are happy and inspiring, enabling every boy to fulfil his potential. The warm and friendly teaching staff understand and support the boys so that they grow in self-belief. The buddy system helps to integrate the newest boys into the school from the very beginning and the House system provides another layer of support and guidance.

This year we introduced 'learning habits' that have been very successful in teaching boys how to mindfully adopt the best character traits. It is crucial that we do our best to prepare children to flourish in this very competitive, fast-changing world and we believe that our learning habits of empathy, courage, open-mindedness, good judgement, curiosity, kindness, collaboration and perseverance will help the boys to succeed later in life.

Admission to Eaton House The Manor Pre-Preparatory School is non-selective and on a first-come, first-served basis into the Reception (Kindergarten) Year. Parents wishing to enrol their children in the school are advised to register them at birth.

Eaton House The Manor Preparatory School

58 Clapham Common Northside, London SW4 9RU

Tel: 020 7924 6000
email: admissions@eatonhouseschools.com
website: www.eatonhouseschools.com
Twitter: @eatonhousesch
Facebook: @eatonhouseschools

Headmistress: **Mrs Sarah Segrave**

Age Range. 8–13.
Number of Pupils. 220 Boys.
Fees per term (2018–2019). £6,581.

Eaton House the Manor Prep takes boys aged from ages 8–13. It has achieved exceptional results in 2018, and pupils have moved on to a range of top day and boarding schools. There have been a number of scholarships, including a coveted John Colet Scholarship to St Paul's. We have great aspirations for every child, and the progress they make in their five years at EHTM Prep school is remarkable.

Our boys are prepared for entry to the finest day and boarding schools, including Eton, Westminster, Tonbridge, Dulwich College, King's Wimbledon, and many more.

Most of our pupils transition directly from the Pre-Prep where registration is recommended from birth. However, a good proportion of boys join us from other schools at 8 and it is always worth asking about occasional places further up the school, including 11+ entry.

If the boys do brim with academic confidence, it's in part due to the exceptional pastoral care provided by the school. The Headmistress, Mrs Sarah Segrave, is committed in her belief that, on her watch, every boy will be recognised as an individual and his potential maximised.

Our boys are prepared in all the core subjects for the finest day and boarding schools in the UK. They take a whole range of classes including Art, Computing, Design Technology, Drama, English, French, Geography, History, Latin, Maths, Music, PSHE, Science, and Theology, Philosophy and Religion. With a staff ratio of 1:9 our boys get all the specialist input that they need, whether they are aiming for scholarships, Common Entrance or entry to London day schools at thirteen.

We want the boys to be inspired academically by their time at school. This is why we aim to provide stimulating, challenging lessons supported by an exceptional level of pastoral care. We encourage boys to think for themselves, to engage fully in class discussions and to take pride in their work.

Eaton House The Manor Preparatory offers a diverse range of extracurricular activities that go far beyond the classroom. The Manor Preparatory boys can often be seen out and about, whether exploring London's world-class museums and galleries, taking advantage of the school's prime location or playing out on Clapham Common. The school works to combine fun and learning activities by planning regular special trips both at home and abroad. One very special event this year involved a number of our oldest pupils completing the Three Peaks Challenge, climbing Ben Nevis, Scafell Pike and Snowdon in 24 hours and raising £11,243 for the Great Ormond Street Hospital children's charity.

Every day after school, the boys have a huge range of clubs on offer. For autumn 2018 these include Art, DT, Newspaper, Music Theory, Spanish, Drama, Football Squad, Fitness and Circuits, French for Advanced Speakers, Creative Science, Code Breaking, Basketball, Movie Making, Classic Film Club, Yoga, Wallace Chess, Football, Politics and Current Affairs, Stem Science Club, the Shakespeare Project, Running Club, The Big Questions Breakfast Club, the 100th Wandsworth Cubs and Sports Club. When it comes to clubs we can truly say there is something for everybody!

At Eaton House The Manor, pastoral care is of the highest importance. Knowing the boys, sharing their highs and lows and being there for them in every way is a fundamental cornerstone of our philosophy and intrinsic to all we do. Perhaps this is why the pupils follow their teachers in being so kind and caring. A recent ISI Report commented, 'The pupils have an excellent moral understanding. They demonstrate an outstanding natural courtesy and consideration towards everyone.'

Sport is an integral part of life at school, whether representing school or House, or simply learning to be part of a team. In winter, we field as many as 20 teams a week, for both home and away matches in football and rugby, and in summer we excel at cricket, athletics and other field sports. This sporting prowess is nurtured by specialist coaches with formidable professional CVs, and it proves useful beyond Prep school when boys are trialling for their senior schools.

At Eaton House The Manor, we are as musical and artistic as we are sporting! The musical life at the Manor is vibrant, with nearly three-quarters of our boys playing at least one instrument, sometimes several, to a high standard. Musical boys can join our Choir, Vocal Ensembles, Brass Group, Orchestra or Woodwind Group and can have the

opportunity to join in House Music Competitions, which include singing. There are also special Music Assemblies attended by parents where boys can showcase their often quite exceptional progress on individual instruments.

In addition, over the last year we have introduced Year Group Recitals. In these recitals, each boy has the opportunity to play their instrument or to sing. There are no auditions and they are open to all abilities, giving all the boys a chance to make music together even if music is not their primary focus.

Every boy within the school has weekly drama lessons, and many become involved in complex and sophisticated theatrical productions. At Eaton House The Manor Preparatory School there are first-class facilities available for the arts, including a state-of-the-art theatre with full technical rig. In the Prep School, the boys perform at a high level. The wide range of performance opportunities enable boys to share their talents with the community, allowing them to showcase what they have learned in their drama lessons. There is a well-established and popular Drama Club and regular concerts, musical ensembles and art exhibitions that allow the boys to develop self-expression and gain in confidence.

Mrs Segrave argues that a school is not a building, a curriculum or a timetable. Rather, it is a place where children grow intellectually and emotionally, guided by teachers who are determined that children succeed and are happy. As one former pupil wrote, 'The thing that I will miss the most is the atmosphere, how everyone is so happy and so encouraging.'

Eaton Square Belgravia

79 Eccleston Square, Pimlico, London SW1V 1PP

Tel: 020 7931 9469
Fax: 020 7828 0164
email: registrar@eatonsquareschool.com
website: www.eatonsquareschool.com

Principal of Eaton Square Schools Group & Headmaster of Eaton Square Belgravia: Mr Sebastian Hepher

Age Range. 2–11 Co-educational Prep School and Senior School age 11–18.

Number of Pupils. 550.

Fees per term (2018–2019). Nursery £1,678–£5,995, Pre-Prep £6,950, Prep £7,300. Senior £7,495–£7,750.

Contact. *Pre-Prep & Prep*: Penelope Stitcher, Registrar, email: registrar@eatonsquareschool.com

Nursery: Lyndsay Salaman, Nursery Registrar, email: nursery@eatonsquareschool.com

Senior School: Jules Day, email: registrar@eatonsquaremayfair.com

Ethos. Eaton Square School is one of the few co-educational day schools in the heart of London offering Nursery, Pre-Preparatory, Preparatory and Senior education. The School maintains high standards and encourages in every child an enthusiasm for learning, good manners, self-discipline and, in all things, a determination to do their best and realise their potential. The 2016 ISI inspection report found the school to be Excellent in all categories and highlighted the pupils' personal development as "outstanding". The School offers a stretching, challenging approach to learning that emphasises achievement and builds confidence. Great emphasis is placed on experiential learning including ski trips, classical tours of Rome and Pompeii, survival skills in the mountains of Scotland and a week's French immersion spent in a French château in Normandy in Year 7.

Academic Life. The Class Teachers teach general subjects to their classes up to the age of 10. Thereafter, specialist subject teachers continue the curriculum in preparation for the Common Entrance Examinations for senior English Independent Schools, for girls at age 11 and for both boys and girls at age 13. A wide range of subjects are encompassed in the curriculum. ICT is introduced from the age of 3 and it is an integral part of the syllabus. In addition, all Prep School classrooms are equipped with interactive whiteboards and data projectors.

Pupils are prepared for entry into both selective London Day schools and leading Boarding schools through London Day School examinations at 11+ and Common Entrance examinations at 13+. See below for information about the Upper School. Mayfair.

Sport & the Arts. Sport and Physical Education include Swimming, Fencing, Gymnastics, Football, Rugby, Cricket, Hockey, Sailing, Skiing and Tennis and the School has successful teams competing against other London and national schools. The School regularly wins National Awards for its swimming success. Music is a flourishing department within the School. Appreciation of music, singing, composition, music theory and recorder tuition are taught by specialists at all ages. There are active School Choirs, an orchestra and a variety of ensembles that rehearse throughout the week. Instruction in Music, Art and Design Technology is included for all children from Nursery School upwards, as part of the Curriculum. Drama is integrated within the curriculum and each child takes part in at least two public productions every year. The Prep School production for children in Years 5–6 is held at a West End Theatre during the Summer Term.

Upper School. An independent, co-educational day school for children ages 11 to 18. We are located in a beautiful Grade I listed building on Piccadilly, opposite Green Park in the heart of London.

We are the only senior school in Mayfair, a stone's throw from the hundreds of acres of green space afforded by the Royal Parks. The education we provide has a traditional British foundation, but a modern and international outlook.

Eaton Square School is part of the Dukes Education Group. Dukes Education is a family of schools and education organisations based in the UK. We bring together schools that are diverse in their offering, and yet united as outstanding examples of teaching and learning.

Edge Grove

Aldenham Village, Radlett, Herts WD25 8BL

Tel:	01923 855724
Fax:	01923 859920
email:	office@edgegrove.com
website:	www.edgegrove.com
Twitter:	@EdgeGrove
Facebook:	@Edge-Grove

Chair of Governors: Mr Ian Elliott

Headmaster: **Mr Ben Evans**, BA Hons

Age Range. 3–13.

Number of Pupils. Day: 196 (Pre Prep), 305 (Prep); Boarders 21.

Fees per term (2018–2019). Day: Pre Prep £2,310–£4,220; Prep £4,847–£5,645; Boarding supplements: Weekly Boarding £2,260; Flexi Boarding: £560–£2,075.

Edge Grove is a vibrant and successful day and boarding school for boys and girls aged 3–13 years. It is set in 48 acres of parkland, only 15 miles from central London and conveniently located close to the M1 and M25 motorways. Our wonderful setting and facilities ensure our children are exposed to a wide range of experiences and develop confidence in a challenging, fun and inspirational environment. The school was inspected by the Independent Schools Inspectorate (ISI) in September 2015 who rated it 'excellent' in all areas. The ISI stated that at all stages of the school "the quality of pupils' academic and other achievements is excellent. Key factors supporting high achievement are the extensive and innovative curriculum, pupils' understanding attitudes towards their learning and excellent teaching." They observed that pupils are "articulate and highly effective listeners. They are diligent in their approach to lessons and their behaviour is exemplary."

The Pre Prep at Edge Grove caters for children between the ages of 3 and 7. The Edge Grove Pre-School is located in a purpose-built building close to the main school site and can accommodate up to 40 children aged 3–4 years. The Pre Prep (Reception to Year 2) is situated within the main school grounds, close to the main Preparatory school. Class sizes are no more than 20, supervised by a teacher and teaching assistant. A broad curriculum is offered with French, Music, Sport and Forest School taught by specialist teachers.

Pupils move on to a wide variety of senior independent schools across the country and the school has an excellent record of Scholarship and Common Entrance success. Music and Art are also particularly strong and Edge Grove is a leading player in the world of prep school sport. There is a great range of after-school activities on offer every day until 6.00 pm.

Facilities include an outdoor learning hub with a gazebo and stage; two Forest School sites; an adventure playground; a language classroom with a dedicated 'virtual language lab'; Chromebooks throughout the school and 1:1 from Year 5; iMacs for music technology; a fully-equipped textiles room and two science laboratories; and purpose-built and state of the art facilities for Home Economics. Sports facilities include a 20-metre heated swimming pool; vast playing fields with ten junior football fields; a 3-court badminton Sports Hall; an AstroTurf hockey pitch; two tennis/netball courts and six outdoor/four indoor cricket nets.

Weekly and flexi boarding is available at Edge Grove to children in Years 3–8. The boarding community is housed in the original building of the school in contemporary, comfortable dormitories organised by age. The Headmaster and his family live in the main building as do the Head of Boarding, Housemistress and Gap Students, all of whom work to maintain the smooth running of the boarding community and to enhance the quality of life of the boarding pupils.

Charitable status. Edge Grove School Trust Ltd is a Registered Charity, number 311054.

Edgeborough

84 Frensham Road, Frensham, Farnham, Surrey GU10 3AH

Tel:	01252 792495
Fax:	01252 795156
email:	office@edgeborough.co.uk
website:	www.edgeborough.co.uk

Twitter: @edgeborough
Facebook: @edgeborough

Chairman of Governors: Mr Jeremy McIlroy

Headmaster: **Mr Daniel Thornburn**

Age Range. 2–13.
Number of Children. Boarders 36, Day 198, Pre Prep 58, Nursery 50
Fees per term (2018–2019). Years 5–8 £5,845, Years 3–4 £5,245, Pre Prep Years R–2 £3,580. Weekly Boarding (4 nights): £32.00 per night.

Edgeborough is a co-educational Independent School for children aged 2–13, with day and weekly boarding. The school is situated within 50 acres of rolling countryside in Frensham, Surrey.

Edgeborough offers a carefully balanced, all-round education with a focus on outdoor learning, which aims to develop skills, interests and an aspiration within pupils to do anything and everything to the best of their ability. A strong and enthusiastic team of experienced specialist teachers enrich the curriculum, while small class sizes ensure that each child's progress is recognised and encouraged.

Boarding at Edgeborough enhances the overall experience of pupils in the school and is a vital factor in creating a vibrant family atmosphere. Boarding at Edgeborough offers a modern take, providing a safe, home-from-home environment. It is an exciting opportunity to stay overnight with friends, while the schedule is as flexible as possible to tailor the experience to each family's needs.

Excellent educational opportunities at Edgeborough enable pupils to regularly gain scholarships to prestigious senior schools. During the past academic year, 20 Edgeborough pupils were awarded scholarships to the senior school of their choice for excelling in sports, art, drama, music and all-round skills.

A range of extra-curricular activities and clubs provide the opportunity for teachers to nurture and develop pupils' self-esteem. Our vast outdoor space is ripe for discovering and is a constant source of enjoyment for pupils. The specialist facilities help make learning fun, enriching the academic, social and cultural aspects of school life. Facilities include state-of-the-art ICT and music suites, an art and pottery studio, libraries full of cheer, a fully-equipped indoor theatre, dance and drama studios, a large sports hall, floodlit astro pitches and a heated swimming pool.

Charitable status. Edgeborough Educational Trust is a Registered Charity, number 312051.

Elm Green Preparatory School

Parsonage Lane, Little Baddow, Chelmsford, Essex CM3 4SU
Tel: 01245 225230
Fax: 01245 226008
email: admin@elmgreen.essex.sch.uk
website: www.elmgreen.essex.sch.uk

Principal: **Mrs A E Milner**, BTech Hons, MSc, PGCE

Age Range. Co-educational 4–11 years.
Number of Day Pupils. 220.
Fees per term (from April 2018). £2,948.
Religious affiliation. Non-denominational.

Elm Green was founded in 1944 and enjoys a lovely rural setting, surrounded by National Trust woodland.

Children enter in the September after their fourth birthday and in their final year are prepared for scholarships, entry to other independent schools and for entry to maintained schools. Many of the pupils take the Essex 11+ and the school has an excellent record of success in this examination.

The school maintains a high standard of academic education giving great emphasis to a secure foundation in the basic subjects whilst offering a wide curriculum with specialist teaching in many areas.

Information technology and design technology form an integral part of the curriculum and there are flourishing art, music and PE departments. The school competes successfully in a wide range of sports – football, rugby, netball, swimming, cricket, gymnastics, athletics, rounders and tennis.

There are many extra-curricular activities and all the children are encouraged to work and to play hard in order to fulfil their potential.

The school aims to foster intellectual curiosity and to encourage individual and corporate work. Kindness and thought for others are given a high priority.

The Elms

Colwall, Malvern, Worcestershire WR13 6EF
Tel: 01684 540344
email: office@elmsschool.co.uk
website: www.elmsschool.co.uk
Twitter: @theelmsschool
Facebook: @TheElmsSchool

Founded 1614.

Chairman of the Governors: T N Hone, MA, MBA

Headmaster: **C Hattam**, BA, MA

Age Range. 3–13.
Number of Pupils. 169. Boys 95, girls 71
Fees per term (2018–2019). Full board £8,160; Flexi Boarding £7,200, Day £6,500; Pre-Prep (3–7) £3,090–£4,515. Fees are payable termly. There are no compulsory extras.

The Elms is run as a charitable, non-profit making company with a Board of Governors. Children are taken in the Main School from the age of rising 8 and there is a Montessori and Pre-Preparatory Department for 3–7 year olds.

An experienced staff and small classes ensure individual attention for every pupil and a high academic standard is maintained to CE and Scholarship levels. Small numbers create a family atmosphere with comfortable accommodation and a resident Headmaster and staff. One of the many advantages of being an independent, preparatory school is that the children are guided through the process of carefully selecting the senior school that is right for them.

Impressive gardens, fields and woodland with stream surround the school, set at the foot of the Malvern Hills, and include fine playing fields for Rugby, Football, Hockey, Cricket, Athletics, Netball, Tennis, Rounders and Triathlon. Facilities include Indoor Heated Swimming Pool, Floodlit AstroTurf, Manège, Theatre, Sports Hall, Tennis Courts, Laboratories, ICT Suites, Design and Technology Room and Art Room. The children manage a small farming enterprise and many ride on school ponies or bring their own.

Bursaries and Scholarships are available.

Charitable status. The Elms (Colwall) Limited is a Registered Charity, number 527252. It exists to provide education for boys and girls.

Eton End School

35 Eton Road, Datchet, Slough, Berkshire SL3 9AX
Tel: 01753 541075
email: admin@etonend.org
website: www.etonend.org

Chairman of Board of Governors: J Clark, Esq

Headmistress: Mrs Sophie Banks

Age Range. 3–11 Co-educational.
Number of Pupils. 215: 155 girls, 60 boys.
Fees per term (2018–2019). Nursery: £1,980–£3,180; Pre-Prep £3,275–£3,520; Prep £3,880–£4,185. Fees exclude lunch.

The school is a day school set within six acres of spacious grounds. Having been set up in 1936 to educate the children of Eton Masters, it is a school which successfully merges tradition with a forward-thinking approach. All the classrooms are purpose built and modern, including specialist rooms for subjects such as Art & Design, Music, Science, School Library and IT Suite with touch-screen computers. There is a large well-equipped gymnasium/performance space, two hard tennis/netball courts, and a large sports field. Outdoor learning is a core part of the curriculum at Eton End, with outdoor classrooms, a pond and nature trails accessible. Children spend break time in the surrounding woodland, building dens and enjoying the beautiful space available. Pupils leave after the 11+ Entrance Examination with many often gaining Scholarships. Small classes allow each child to reach their maximum potential in a happy caring environment.

Charitable status. Eton End School Trust (Datchet) Limited is a Registered Charity, number 310644. The aim of the charity is to provide a well-balanced education for children whose parents wish them to attend Eton End School.

Eversfield Preparatory School

Warwick Road, Solihull, West Midlands B91 1AT
Tel: 0121 705 0354
Fax: 0121 709 0168
email: enquiries@eversfield.co.uk
website: www.eversfield.co.uk

Chairman of Governors: Dr T Brain

Headmaster: Mr R Yates, BA, PGCE, LPSH

Age Range. 2¾–11 Co-educational.
Number of Pupils. 336.
Fees per term (2018–2019). £1,432–£3,677 according to age and inclusive of lunch, books and swimming lessons.

Eversfield is a Day Preparatory School on an attractive five-acre site in the centre of Solihull preparing boys and girls for entry to the leading Independent Senior Schools in the Midlands. The school was founded in 1931 and its mission is to provide an outstanding, broad education within a safe, caring, happy, family atmosphere where the talents of every child are valued and nurtured.

The curriculum focuses on academic excellence whilst also retaining the breadth which nurtures the creative, sporting, technical and social skills and potential of each child. There is a wide and varied range of lunchtime and after-school extracurricular and holiday activities. Eversfield promotes high moral standards and responsible attitudes based upon clear and relevant Christian teaching. A strong sense of community exists where small classes, a well-ordered routine and good pastoral support help pupils to feel secure and develop their self-confidence.

On-site facilities include specialist rooms for art, design & technology, science, food technology, music and computing. Sporting facilities comprise a gymnasium, extensive playing fields and all-weather courts. In addition September 2015 saw the opening of a brand new Sports and Performing Arts Centre with an indoor heated pool. This state-of-the-art building has three badminton courts, indoor cricket nets and is also marked for netball. The customised lighting and sound system, theatre curtains, modular staging and retractable seating for over 200 make it the perfect venue for performances.

Charitable status. Eversfield Preparatory School Trust Limited is a Registered Charity, number 528966. It is under the direction of a Board of Governors and exists to carry out the work of an Independent Preparatory School.

Ewell Castle Preparatory School

Glyn House, Church Street, Ewell, Surrey KT17 2AP
Tel: 020 8394 3579
Fax: 020 8394 2220
email: enquiries@ewellcastle.co.uk
website: www.ewellcastle.co.uk
Twitter: @EwellCastleUK
Facebook: @EwellCastleSchool

Chairman of Governors: Mr D Tucker, QPM

Principal: Mr Silas Edmonds, BA Hons, MA, NPQH

Head of Preparatory School: Ms S Bradshaw, BEd Hons

Deputy Head of Preparatory School & Assistant Principal: Mrs S Fowler, BSc, PGCE

Age Range. 3–11.
Number of Pupils. 200 Boys and Girls.
Fees per term (2018–2019). £2,884–£3,814.
Vision. The vision of the School is to **Inspire** and **Nurture** our pupils to **Achieve**, within a happy, family friendly atmosphere.
Ethos. Ewell Castle is a happy school with an atmosphere of purposeful, academic work. Care, consideration, honesty, integrity, fairness and tolerance are valued. Self-esteem is enhanced and all aspects of personal development are fostered. With an ethos in which each child's achievements are acknowledged, valued and celebrated, students thrive academically as a result of the small class sizes, a varied and stimulating curriculum, an extensive extracurricular programme and strong support systems.
Values. Integrity, Trust, Respect, Responsibility, Determination.

Ewell Castle Preparatory School is an independent co-educational day school, located on two sites in the heart of Ewell Village. Nursery to Year 2 pupils (3–7 years) are based at Chessington Lodge in Spring Street, while Years 3 to 6 (7–11 years) are based at Glyn House in Church Street, opposite the Senior School (co-educational 11–18 years), with which a close liaison is maintained.

Those entering the Nursery may attend for a half-day (minimum three sessions per week) until they are ready for full-time education. There are no entry requirements for Nursery children, but older pupils attend the school for a day's assessment, which will include assessment through lesson observation. The majority of pupils at Glyn House proceed to the Senior School and a number of aided places and scholarships are available at 11+, 13+ and 16+ entry. All pupils are prepared for entry at 11+ to selective state schools. The National Curriculum is incorporated within a broad curriculum.

The creative arts play an important part in school life. Apart from the timetabled music lessons, there is the opportunity for pupils to learn a variety of instruments under professional teachers. Drama productions take place regularly. Pupils' art work can be seen on display in the local community and is always to be found decorating the school walls. All pupils join in various sporting activities as part of the weekly curriculum. In addition, a wide variety of activities are available after school and during the holidays.

All pupils use the five acres of attractive gardens and playing fields at Glyn House for outdoor play and games lessons. In addition, Preparatory School pupils benefit from full access to the excellent sporting facilities, including a sports hall and playing fields, on the 15-acre site at The Castle. The main games are football, netball, hockey, cricket and tennis. There are also athletics and cross country events, including a school sports day. All pupils receive swimming instruction.

Outside speakers include police liaison officers and actors and authors who conduct workshops with pupils. A number of visits occur to places of interest which are relevant to a particular area of study. There are regular school visits abroad.

The school also enjoys close links with St Mary's Church, where regular assemblies are held throughout the year.

The Preparatory School aims to provide a caring, responsive and stimulating environment in which pupils are able to fulfil their potential. Hard work and high standards together with courtesy and consideration to others are of prime importance.

Charitable status. Ewell Castle School is a Registered Charity, number 312079. It exists to provide education for boys and girls.

Exeter Cathedral School

The Chantry, Palace Gate, Exeter, Devon EX1 1HX

Tel: 01392 255298
Fax: 01392 422718
email: reception@exetercs.org
website: www.exetercathedralschool.co.uk
Twitter: @ECSPrepSchool
Facebook: @ExeterCathedralSchool

Chairman of Governors: Mr Derek Phillips

Headmaster: James Featherstone, BA Hons, PGCE

Age Range. 3–13.
Number of Pupils. 18 full/weekly boarders, 35 regular flexi boarders, 263 day pupils.
Fees per term (2018–2019). Tuition: £2,375 (Reception–Year 2), £3,604 (Years 3–4), £3,739 (Year 5), £3,959 (Years 6–8). Lunch: £192 (Reception–Year 2), £243 (Years 3–8). Full Boarding (6/7 nights a week) £2,470. Flexi boarding is also available.

Founded in 1179, the Cathedral School provides 36 Boy and Girl Choristers for Exeter Cathedral and educates the other pupils to the same high standard.

Entry is normally at age 3 into the Nursery (the School is a member of the Government's Early Years Funding Scheme) or at age 7 or 8 years into the Prep School, though pupils may join the school at any stage, subject to place availability.

Voice Trials for Cathedral Choristers are usually held in January each year, or by arrangement. There are 18 scholarships available for Boy Choristers and 18 for Girl Choristers to the value of 25% of the tuition fee.

Pupils are prepared for senior school entry to both independent and maintained schools and the School has a proven track record of academic, music, art, drama and sports scholarship success.

There are no Saturday lessons, though day pupils sometimes join boarders in weekend or after school activities. The curriculum encompasses all National Curriculum and Common Entrance subjects, including Modern Foreign Languages and Latin.

In the Michaelmas Term, rugby and netball are the team sports. Netball, soccer and hockey are played in the Lent Term. During the Trinity Term, cricket, rounders, athletics and swimming are all pursued competitively. Swimming takes place all year round.

Musical activities, including school choir, orchestra and ensembles for string, woodwind, brass and jazz instrumentalists are available to all pupils in the prep school.

Daily morning worship takes place in the Cathedral or in The Chapter House led by the Headmaster, School Chaplain or a member of the Cathedral Clergy.

The buildings are located around the Close and include a Science Laboratory, a gym, music and drama school, as well as a large portion of the 14th Century Deanery. There is a Food Technology Centre, Design and Technology Department and Computer Centre.

For games, use is made of first-class facilities at Exeter University as well as other playing fields and swimming baths situated short distances away in the city.

Charitable status. Exeter Cathedral School is a Registered Charity, number 1151444.

Exeter Junior School

Victoria Park Road, Exeter, Devon EX2 4NS

Tel: 01392 258738 Headmistress
            01392 273679 Registrar
Fax: 01392 498144
email: admissions@exeterschool.org.uk
website: www.exeterschool.org.uk
Twitter: @ExeterSchoolUK

Co-educational Day School.

Chairman of Board of Governors: Mr A C W King

Headmistress: Mrs Sue Marks, BSc, PGCE

Age Range. 7–11.
Number of Pupils. 188: 104 Boys, 84 Girls.
Fees per term (2018–2019). £3,975 (includes lunch which is compulsory).

Exeter Junior School is housed in a spacious, Victorian building in the grounds of Exeter School. The close proximity of the Junior School to the Senior School enables the pupils to take full advantage of the facilities on site, which include a chapel, music centre, science laboratories, sports hall with dance studio, fitness suite and squash courts, indoor swimming pool, playing fields, all-weather astroturf arena and tennis courts.

In addition to this the Junior School retains its own playground and green space, therefore giving the School a separate and clearly recognisable identity.

Liaison between Junior and Senior staff is a positive feature of this thriving Junior School.

The School aims to offer, in academic, cultural and sporting terms, the widest possible range of opportunities thus helping each pupil to identify the activities which will give the greatest scope for development and fulfilment in years to come. Music, drama, art, sport and expeditions all have an important part to play in the life of the school.

The majority of pupils enter the school at age 7 or 9, and entrance is by informal assessment in January. This includes a report from the child's previous school, classroom sessions in the company of other prospective pupils, literacy and numeracy tasks. Pupils may enter the school at other ages where space is available.

Pupils are offered an academic programme which incorporates the National Curriculum model with the addition of French which is introduced from Year 3.

Specialist teaching is offered from the outset, with the additional support of Senior School staff in Science, French, German, Spanish, Music, Sport and Latin.

A wide variety of clubs are available during the week including art & craft, dance, modern languages, calligraphy, sewing, football, hockey, netball, rugby, chess and drama. After-school care is available until 5.30 pm.

(*For further information about the Senior School, see Exeter School entry in HMC section.*)

Charitable status. Exeter School is a Registered Charity, number 1093080. It exists to provide education for children.

Fairfield Prep School

Leicester Road, Loughborough, Leics LE11 2AE

Tel: 01509 215172
Fax: 01509 238648
email: Fairfield.office@lsf.org
website: www.lsf.org/fairfield
Twitter: @LboroFairfield
Facebook: @LboroFairfield

Chairman of the Governors: Mr G P Fothergill, BA

Head: **Mr A Earnshaw**, BA Lancaster, NPQH

Age Range. 3–11.
Number of Pupils. 236 Boys, 218 Girls – all day pupils. (Numbers exclude Kindergarten.)
Fees per term (2018–2019). Pre-Prep £3,502, Upper Prep £3,552. Lunches and individual music lessons extra.

Fairfield is the prep school of Loughborough Schools Foundation, a foundation of four schools comprising: Loughborough Grammar School (boys aged 10–18, day and boarding) – *see HMC entry*, Loughborough High School (day girls aged 11–18) – *see GSA entry*, and Loughborough Amherst School (from September 2019 co-educational age 4–18, day) – *see ISA entry*, which became the foundation's fourth school on 1 September 2015. The schools operate under one governing body and are situated on two neighbouring campuses in the town. The Foundation also includes The Loughborough Nursery for children from 6 weeks to 4 years.

In 2014, the school embarked on an ambitious new building project to provide pupils with additional space and improved accommodation, including new classrooms for pupils in Reception and Years 1–3, an extended gymnasium with spacious changing rooms for pupils and staff, a specialist arts and craft room, an additional performance hall, designated main entrance and essential office space. It also houses a brand new purpose-built Kindergarten unit for children aged 3+ during term time, which can cater for up to 44 children.

Fairfield's partnership with pupils, parents and the wider community ensures every child is given the ability to reach their full potential through a combination of academic, cultural, sporting and artistic opportunities.

Learning is extended through a wide range of activities, utilising iPads and other technologies, along with specialist teaching in science, ICT, modern foreign languages, PE, and music. Music is a vital part of the school's culture and the facilities available to pupils are second to none. All Year 2 pupils follow a course in instrumental playing, and children in the Upper Prep have the opportunity to have individual instrumental lessons with one of the Foundation Music department's peripatetic staff. In September 2015, the Music department became the only All-Steinway School in the Midlands, demonstrating the foundation's commitment to providing pupils with the very best instruments on which to learn, practise and perform.

Fairfield provides access to an extensive range of extracurricular activities. There are a greater number of sports, and more teams, clubs and opportunities for extracurricular music on offer than ever before. Practically every single member of staff at the school runs at least one extracurricular session, ensuring that our programme of activities meets the diverse and ever-changing interests of our pupils.

In a nurturing, happy atmosphere, children are guided along their educational journey through purposeful, academic work and are constantly encouraged to succeed. Staff help develop each child's confidence, courtesy and self-worth so they grow stronger, not only as individuals, but also as members of their local community. By taking individual differences into account, the successful Fairfield Preparatory School pupil of today acquires the skills and values which allow them to make a valuable contribution to the success of the senior schools, and through their lives, to the society of tomorrow.

The Headmaster is happy to show prospective parents around the school by appointment. Further information can be found on the school website at www.lsf.org/fairfield.

Charitable status. Loughborough Schools Foundation is a Registered Charity, number 1081765, and a Company Limited by Guarantee, registered in England, number 4038033. Registered Office: 3 Burton Walks, Loughborough, Leics LE11 2DU.

Fairstead House School

Fordham Road, Newmarket, Suffolk CB8 7AA

Tel: 01638 662318
email: registrar@fairsteadhouse.co.uk
website: www.fairsteadhouse.co.uk

Chair of Governors: Dr Patrick Round

Head: **Dr Lynda Brereton**, BSc, PhD, PGCE

Age Range. Co-educational 3 months – 11 years.
Number of Children. 182.
Fees per term (2018–2019). Tuition (including lunches): Reception, Year 1 & 2 £3,249, Years 3–6 £3,537. Please visit our website for information on current Nursery fees.

Fairstead House is situated in the heart of Newmarket and offers a combination of an excellent academic education with an emphasis on creativity and imagination in a caring, happy community with a unique family ethos, closely linked to the local community.

From Nursery onwards, we offer a broad and stimulating curriculum which provides the children with a solid foundation for their onward journeys to senior schools in both Independent and State sectors. The curriculum is complemented by Art, DT, Music, Drama and Sports.

Pupils take part in a variety of sports such as rugby, football, cricket, hockey and netball. All children play rounders and take part in cross-country running and athletics.

Extracurricular Speech & Drama lessons are available, as is private tuition in a wide selection of musical instruments. Children may join the Fairstead House Orchestra or Choir and take part in the many theatrical productions that are held at School.

A programme of development has ensured the provision of first-class facilities throughout the School including a state-of-the-art Music & Drama Centre with specialist facilities, an ICT suite, iPads, interactive whiteboards in every classroom and a dedicated Science & DT area.

As well as a breakfast club and after-school care club providing wrap-around care, there is a diverse range of after-school activity clubs available. A Holiday Club is also available for all children out of term time.

Throughout the year, pupils go on a variety of trips and excursions, both day and residential. The residential trips to Norfolk and Snowdonia for the older pupils are designed to encourage independence and cultivate a spirit of adventure as well as personal responsibility and development.

Charitable Status: Fairstead House School Trust Limited is a Registered Charity, number 276787. It exists to provide education for boys and girls.

The Falcons Schools
Alpha Plus Group

Boys Nursery and Pre-Prep:
2 Burnaby Gardens, London W4 3DT

Tel:	020 8747 8393
Fax:	020 8995 3903
email:	admin@falconsboys.co.uk
website:	www.falconsboys.co.uk

Boys Prep:
41 Kew Foot Road, Richmond, Surrey TW9 2SS

Tel:	020 8948 9490
Fax:	020 8948 9491
email:	admin@falconsprep.co.uk
website:	www.falconsprep.co.uk

Girls School:
11 Woodborough Road, Putney, London SW15 6PY

Tel:	020 8992 5189
Fax:	020 8752 1635
email:	admin@falconsgirls.co.uk
website:	www.falconsgirls.co.uk

Head Teacher, Girls School: **Mrs Sara Williams-Ryan**, L-ès-Lettres Geneva, MA

Head Teacher, Pre-Prep Boys School: **Mr Andrew Forbes**, BA Hons, Dip Ed

Head Teacher, Prep Boys School: **Miss Olivia Buchanan**, BSc Hons, MEd, PGCE

Age Range. Boys School: 3–7 (Pre-Prep), 8–13 (Prep); Girls School 3–11.

Number of Pupils. 280 Boys; 85 Girls.

Fees per term (2018–2019). Boys School: £2,825–£5,945. Girls School: £2,860–£5,235.

The Falcons Schools enjoy a well-deserved reputation for excellence. Results to the leading London Day Schools are impressive, as too is the specialist teaching on offer throughout the schools. The schools provide a safe outdoor space for play and sport and a school hall for gym, assemblies and lunch. Nearby sports facilities are used to enhance an exciting sports program. There are well-equipped libraries, music rooms, ICT suites, with a much-admired art and science facility. Our overriding emphasis is on achieving excellence in numeracy and literacy whilst offering a broad and creative curriculum. The Falcons is a uniquely caring and stimulating environment, where learning is seen as fun and the pursuit of excellence is embraced by all.

Farleigh School

Red Rice, Andover, Hampshire SP11 7PW

Tel:	01264 710766
Fax:	01264 710070
email:	office@farleighschool.com
website:	www.farleighschool.com
Twitter:	@FarleighSchool

Chair of Governors: Mr Keith Abel

Headmaster: **Fr Simon Everson**

Age Range. 3–13. Boarding from age 7.

Number of Pupils. 99 boarders (53 boys, 46 girls), 352 day: including 20 flexi boarders; 108 in Kindergarten and Pre-Prep.

Fees per term (2018–2019). Boarders: £8,495 (Years 7 and 8), £7,660 (Years 4–6), £7,330 (Year 3); HM Forces boarders £7,225 (Years 3–8); Day pupils: £1,720–£6,530 (Years 4–8), £6,250 (Year 3).

Farleigh is a contemporary, Catholic, co-educational boarding and day school, which welcomes children of all faiths, or none. Situated in a stunning Georgian country house standing in 70 acres of magnificent parkland and landscaped woodland in the Test Valley of Hampshire, near Andover, Farleigh is just over an hour from London and within easy reach of Southampton and London airports.

High standards are achieved both in and out of the classroom and excellent academic results are the norm, with leavers going on to a large number of leading senior schools and many obtaining scholarships.

Farleigh has outstanding facilities, which now include an all-weather pitch (opened in 2016) and a new purpose-built music school (opened in 2017) with 12 practice rooms, recital hall, rehearsal room, sound proof 'rock' room and recording studio. The Junior and Senior Boarding Houses have also undergone significant refurbishment. There is a spacious and light Art and Design Technology building, computer rooms with state-of-the-art technology, theatre with tiered seating, spacious recreation rooms, a fine Chapel, gymnasium, 22-metre heated indoor swimming pool, tennis courts, squash courts and separate purpose-built Pre-Prep and Kindergarten with its own landscaped and secure playground. Opened in September 2012 were two new buildings, which accommodate four new classrooms, three new science laboratories and a food technology room, as well as additional circulation space with a well-lit ball play area and a small amphitheatre to the rear of the existing Farleigh theatre.

The teaching staff is complemented by a committed pastoral team including Year Heads, House Parents and three matrons who are qualified nurses. Many staff are resident, giving the school a welcoming family atmosphere, often commented upon by visitors. The latest Ofsted inspection (2010) of the school's boarding provision was "Outstanding" in all six areas inspected, "with no recommendations". The inspectors added, "This is a very caring school that is child-centred and achieves high standards throughout."

The school provides a vibrant and active evening and weekend activity programme for boarders. Regular dinner nights, barbecue parties, annual X-Factor competition, theatre trips, quiz nights, and bowling are just some of the weekend events organised for pupils. Weekday activities include bushcraft, forest school, cooking, cycling, community service, judo, golf, archery, yoga, winter cricket nets, swimming, water polo, tennis and additional sport sessions.

Drama, music and art play an important part in school life with two-thirds of the school learning at least one musical instrument and a third of the school taking up LAMDA drama lessons. A programme of major musical productions and informal concerts take place throughout the year and the children's artwork is displayed around the school.

The major sports for boys are rugby, football, cricket, athletics and cross country; for girls they are netball, hockey, cricket, athletics and cross country. Swimming lessons and extra tennis coaching are offered throughout the year.

Charitable status. Farleigh School is a Registered Charity, number 1157842. It exists for the purpose of educating children.

Felsted Preparatory School

Braintree Road, Felsted, Essex CM6 3JL

Tel:	01371 822610
Fax:	01371 822617
email:	prepadmissions@felsted.org
website:	www.felsted.org
Twitter:	@felstedprep
Facebook:	@felstedschool
LinkedIn:	/Felsted School

Chairman of the Governors: Mr J H Davies

Head: **Mr S C James**, BA Hons, PGCE

Age Range. 4–13 Co-educational.
Number of Pupils. 513 pupils (of which 5 are full-time boarders, 15 weekly and 61 flexi boarders).
Fees per term (2018–2019). Day: Prep £4,475–£5,940, Pre-Prep £3,095. Weekly Boarding £7,750, Full Boarding £8,155, Flexi Boarding (1–4 nights) £49.50–£117.00 per week.

The staff, excluding the Headmaster, consists of over 50 full-time qualified teachers and there are additional part-time teachers for instrumental music and games. There are six matrons and two sisters in charge of the Medical Centre.

The School was rated 'excellent' in every category by the Independent School Inspectorate at its latest inspection, in addition to a legacy rating of 'Outstanding' by Ofsted for EYFS and Boarding.

The Preparatory School, set in its own area on the main Felsted School campus, has all its own facilities, including a modern well-equipped library, an excellent theatre/assembly hall, music practice rooms, a multi-purpose sports hall,

open-air heated swimming pool and floodlit, multi-purpose, hard play/games area. Use is made of Felsted School's extra amenities at regular times so that indoor swimming, two Astroturf hockey pitches, small-bore rifle shooting, squash courts, a new state-of-the-art Music School and another indoor sports hall are also available to the pupils. Pupils in Years 7 and 8 also lunch at the senior school every day as part of a smooth transition process to senior school.

Rugby, football, netball, hockey, cricket, tennis, swimming, athletics and cross country are the major sports. Music plays an important part in the School's life, with an excellent Chapel Choir. Regular instrumental, orchestral and rock concerts are given and those children showing particular talent can study at the Junior Guildhall on Saturdays, subject to passing their auditions. The School has a deserved reputation for its drama productions, while Art, Design and Technology, PSHE, and Computing are part of the weekly timetable. Out-of-class activities include public speaking and debating opportunities, horse riding, chess, football, golf, karate, public speaking, aerobics, cookery and dance/ballet, among others.

Pupils joining at 11+ can be guaranteed assured transfer to Felsted School at 13, as can pupils of a similar age already at the Preparatory School, following successful completion of assessment tests. The majority of pupils proceed to Felsted School itself, but a number regularly move on to other major independent senior schools, having taken Common Entrance, and there is an excellent record of academic, art, music, sport, drama and Design & Technology scholarships. (*For further information about Felsted, see entry in HMC section.*)

Academic and Music Scholarships and Mary Skill Awards are open to pupils joining Felsted Preparatory School at ages of 11+ in the September of the year of entry. Top-up bursaries may also be available on a means-tested basis. One 100% bursary is available each year to a child who meets the right criteria and is given at the discretion of the Head.

Charitable status. Felsted School is a Registered Charity, number 310870. It exists to provide education for boys and girls.

Feltonfleet School

Byfleet Road, Cobham, Surrey KT11 1DR

Tel:	01932 862264
Fax:	01932 860280
email:	office@feltonfleet.co.uk
	admissions@feltonfleet.co.uk
website:	www.feltonfleet.co.uk

Chair of Governors: Mr Giles Ashbee

Headmistress: **Mrs Shelley Lance**, BD, PGCE

Registrar: Mrs Jackie Williams, BA Hons

Age Range. 3–13.
Number of Pupils. Nursery/Pre-Prep 87, Years 3–8 307, of whom 54 are Boarders.
Fees per term (2018–2019). Boarders £7,017, Day Pupils £3,933–£5,775; Nursery £2,106.

Feltonfleet School was founded in 1903 and became an Educational Trust in 1967. The School is situated in 25 acres of scenic grounds close to the M25 between Heathrow and Gatwick Airports. There are 56 full-time and 4 Gap Year members of the teaching staff. The School became fully co-educational in September 1994 and offers both weekly boarding (Monday to Friday) and day education, as well as a flexible boarding option. There is a flourishing, purpose-built Pre-Preparatory Department called Calvi House.

Academics. In 2018 academic results were high, with record breaking results in Common Entrance including 23 Senior School Scholarships. The staff team are 100% committed to drawing out the best in each and every child and this is really shining through in Feltonfleet's results.

Ethos. The school ethos is based upon the three areas of Positive Learning, Positive Living and Positive Leading, underpinned by our four School Values of Honesty, Responsibility, Respect and Kindness. It is the School's strongly held belief that, if children are happy, they will fulfil their potential and, by recognising the individual in a child, this is more likely to happen, which is why it is committed to fostering a small school atmosphere centred on family values, but also keeping academic achievement at its heart. The School places the children first, meets each child's needs on an individual basis, encourages and nurtures the positive aspects of 'self': self-discipline, self-confidence, self-motivation, self-reliance and self-esteem. High-achieving children, irrespective of their real potential, are those who have a high self-esteem – without it very little can be achieved.

Pastoral. Caring for each other matters at Feltonfleet. From a child's first day, the adult community provides care, direction and confidence. The form tutor is the welcoming face on a daily basis and a secure link with daily routine, a familiar and reassuring presence, a trusted confidant and role model. Small classes make quality pastoral care much more certain. Once pupils join the Main School, the Head of Year provides further direction and guidance. The boarding house is run by two house parents, seven boarding house tutors and two matrons who promote the personal, family atmosphere on which Feltonfleet prides itself.

Entry. Children are admitted from the age of three into the Nursery in the Pre-Preparatory Department. Moving into the Main School at the age of seven, they are joined by a further 34 children, and are prepared for Common Entrance or Scholarship examinations to a wide range of independent senior schools. In the Main School there is a staff to pupil ratio of 9.5:1 with an average class size of 18.

For entry into the Main School pupils are required to sit an entrance assessment and interview. Academic, Art, Music, Drama, DT, All-Rounder and Sports Scholarships are offered at 11+.

Facilities. A brand new, state-of-the-art, 200-seat Performing Arts Centre opened in May 2015, where dramatic productions, dance shows and music are performed by all year groups. Well-equipped Science, Art, DT and Digital Learning Departments and Library. The Pre-Prep, Calvi House, has its own hall, gardens and outdoor classrooms. There are landscaped play areas throughout the school and a stunning tree house, pond and wildlife area with bird hide.

Sport. The Sports Department prides itself on its ability to encompass both excellence and sport-for-all within a very busy prep school environment. All pupils receive high quality teaching and coaching in a variety of sports and activities in a positive and safe learning environment. Facilities include a magnificent sports hall, sports fields, a 15m indoor swimming pool, a shooting range for air and .22 rifles, a large floodlit Astro pitch and a climbing wall.

Games played are rugby, football, hockey, netball, athletics and cricket.

Extra-Curricular Activities. The School has an active policy of preparing children for the challenges of today's world and an exceptional activities programme is offered to all pupils during the school day as often as possible. Pupils in the main school are offered the opportunity to attend residential activity courses as well as subject-related overseas trips. In the final two years pupils attend residential leadership courses. After Common Entrance examinations, Year 8 pupils take part in a varied programme of activities, lectures and trips in preparation for leaving Feltonfleet and moving on to their senior schools.

Charitable status. Feltonfleet School Trust Limited is a Registered Charity, number 312070.

Fettes College Preparatory School

East Fettes Avenue, Edinburgh EH4 1QZ

Tel: +44 (0)131 332 2976
Fax: +44 (0)131 332 4724
email: prepschool@fettes.com
website: www.fettes.com
Twitter: @Fettes_College
Facebook: @FettesCollegeFettesPrep

Chairman of Governors: I M Osborne

Chairman of Preparatory School Committee: H Bruce-Watt

Headmaster: **A A Edwards**, BA Hons, PGCE

Age Range. 7–13.
Number of Pupils. 214: 34 boarders, 180 day pupils; 105 boys, 109 girls.
Fees per term (2018–2019). Boarders £8,070, Day Pupils £5,500, including all meals and textbooks.

Fettes Prep School lies within the Fettes College grounds – 80 acres of parkland in the heart of Edinburgh. Although housed in separate buildings about 200m away from the main Fettes College building, the Prep School has all the advantages of the excellent facilities of Fettes College but with the ability to be a complete campus in its own right. Due to expansion in the school roll, William House was completed in 2009 – a state-of-the-art teaching block with superb eco credentials.

Their HMIe inspection had superb results with both Fettes Prep and Fettes College deemed as 'sector-leading'.

The Boarding houses of Iona (girls) and Arran (boys) offer a safe, secure and happy environment. The pastoral staff; housemaster, housemistress, matron and resident tutor, are of the highest calibre and dedicate themselves to creating a secure and happy home.

The curriculum is structured to reflect the strengths of the Curriculum for Excellence, the National Curriculum of England and Wales and IAPS guidance. A strong emphasis is placed on a sound and thorough grounding in the traditionally important subjects of Maths and English as well as specialists subjects such as Science, Art and Languages being taught by specialist teachers. Class sizes remain small to allowing individual attention for each child.

Formal coaching is given to boys in rugby, hockey, athletics and cricket and to girls in hockey, netball, rounders, athletics and tennis. Each year pupils from the school represent their district in these sports and others. Swimming is also taught as are judo, fencing, squash and shooting (the vast majority taking place on campus). There are over 30 activities and clubs ranging from climbing to origami.

Music and Drama flourish. The School Choir and School Orchestra give concerts each term, and choirs and instrumental groups participate successfully in musical competitions. Year group concerts, too, are regularly held. Each year there is a large-production School Play, younger pupils produce their own pantomime, and shorter plays are performed in French and Latin. The art department continues to excel and every pupil within the school has their work displayed.

There are annual trips abroad to bring learning to life and other tours are regularly organised. All twelve year olds receive leadership training and the top two year groups are involved in a programme designed at the school to increase and improve skills in various areas including resourcefulness, initiative and personal challenge.

Entrance. Entrance at the age of seven, eight or nine is by assessment tests and at 10+, 11+ and 12+ by the Entrance Examinations, taken in late Jan/early Feb. All applicants can apply for a means-tested bursary which can cover up to 100% of the fees. There is a finite amount of funding available each year and therefore not all applicants will be successful. Bursaries are awarded independently of any Scholarship or Award.

All candidates who are applying for entry into the 1st Form at 11+ years of age, will automatically be considered for a Junior Scholarship. The results of the Entrance Examinations will determine who receives a Junior Scholarship.

These Scholarships are awarded for academic or all-round excellence and there is great kudos associated with being a scholar of The College. They can also attract reductions of up to 5% of the fees and these reductions are not related to parents' financial circumstances. A Music award can also be applied for at 11+ and 12+ entry.

Further information and a prospectus can be obtained from the Registrar (Tel: +44 (0)131 311 6744, email: admissions@fettes.com) who will be very happy to arrange a visit.

Charitable status. The Fettes Trust is a Registered Charity, number SC017489.

Finton House

171 Trinity Road, London SW17 7HL

Tel: 020 8682 0921
email: admissions@fintonhouse.org.uk
website: www.fintonhouse.org.uk
Twitter: @FintonHouseSch
Facebook: @Finton.House.School

Co-Founders: Terry O'Neill and Finola Stack founded Finton House in 1987.

Chair of Governors: Mr Mark Chilton

Headmaster: **Mr Ben Freeman**

Age Range. 4–11.
Number of Pupils. 140 Boys, 180 Girls.
Fees per term (2018–2019). £5,126–£5,196.
Entrance. No testing at 4+ – first come/first served.
Exit. Boys and Girls at 11 for London Day, Prep or Boarding.

Aims to provide a broad education, embracing technology and outdoor learning, encouraging children to live a healthy life in order to flourish in a rapidly changing world. Academic subjects, music, art, computing, design and technology, languages and sports are all taught to a very high standard. High success rate in entrance exams to good 11+ senior schools, mainly London Day plus some boarding schools, and a third of leavers winning scholarships and awards. Strong policy of inclusion with a percentage of children with special needs. Employs a Speech and Language Therapist, an Occupational Therapist and teaching assistants in most classrooms. A stimulating environment which encourages all children to learn and gain confidence in their own abilities. Non-denominational but instils values such as

respect, honesty, cooperation, forgiveness, resilience and self-discipline.

Charitable status. Finton House is a Registered Charity, number 296588. It exists to provide an broad, inclusive education for children.

Foremarke Hall
Repton Preparatory School

Milton, Derbyshire DE65 6EJ

Tel: 01283 707100
email: registrar@foremarke.org.uk
website: www.foremarke.org.uk
Twitter: @foremarkehall

Chairman of Governors: Sir Henry Every

Head: **Robert Relton**, BEd Hons

Age Range. 3–13.
Number of Pupils. 412: Boys: 28 boarders, 180 day; Girls: 19 boarders, 185 day.
Fees per term (2018–2019). Prep Day: Years 3–4 £5,298, Years 5–6 £5,960, Years 7–8 £6,620. Prep Boarding: Years 3–4 £7,252, Years 5–6 £7,912, Years 7–8 £8,573. Flexi Boarding prices available on request. Pre-Prep: Years 1–2 £3,591, Reception £3,240, Nursery £3,080 (full-time), £308 per session.

Foremarke Hall is under the control of the Governors of Repton School. Boys and girls are prepared for all Independent Schools but most choose to continue to Repton.

The school is situated in a fine Georgian mansion surrounded by 55 acres of woods, playing fields and a lake. The facilities include all that the school requires including a new classroom building to house mathematics, three science laboratories, sophisticated computer technology with full-time IT specialist, an extensive library run by a chartered librarian, an indoor competition-sized swimming pool, a sports hall and a floodlit sports artificial turf surface.

The £6m Quad Development houses a contemporary music facility, a new language laboratory, many new classrooms, a new art block complete with kiln, a designated ICT suite for design and technology and a Greenpower garage for Foremarke's award-winning electric cars.

Great importance is attached to pastoral care where boarders have their own dedicated staff and space for themselves. There is an imaginative and varied programme of activities making most use of the grounds including outdoor pursuits. The games programme is extensive and includes athletics, cricket, football, hockey, rounders, netball, swimming and tennis. We also have an extensive and varied after-school activities programme.

We seek to bring out the most in every pupil, to provide a rounded education and a range of experience and skills that will be a preparation for life. We value our 'family atmosphere' and strong sense of community, the spacious grounds and happy environment.

Foremarke is situated in undisturbed countryside on a 55-acre site in the centre of England. It is easily reached by road from the M1/M6/M5 via the A50, by rail to East Midlands Parkway, or from nearby Birmingham and East Midlands airports.

Charitable status. Repton Preparatory School is a Registered Charity, number 1093165. It exists to provide high quality education for boys and girls.

Forest Preparatory School

College Place, Snaresbrook, London E17 3PY

Tel: 020 8520 1744
Fax: 020 8520 3656
email: prep@forest.org.uk
website: www.forest.org.uk
Twitter: @ForestSchoolE17
Facebook: @ForestSchoolE17

Co-educational Day School.

Chairman of Governors: David Wilson, LLB

Head: James Sanderson, BMusPerf Hons Elder Conservatorium, BMus Adelaide, FRSA

Age Range. 4–11.
Number of Pupils. 278.
Fees per term (2018–2019). £4,365–£5,009.

Forest Preparatory School is part of Forest School (HMC), with which it shares a 50-acre site at the foot of Epping Forest on the East London/Essex border. Its aims are to offer an education of high quality, and to encourage and develop each child academically, physically and creatively. In the Pre-Prep, pupils are taught in small co-educational classes. From the age of 7, pupils are taught in single-sex classes, and at age 11 they proceed to the Senior Section of Forest School (*see separate entry in HMC section*).

Entry to the school is by selection, at 4+ by means of an informal assessment and at 7+ by entrance examination.

The Pre-Prep Department is co-educational, with forms of 16 pupils who are taught predominantly by form teachers and supported by classroom assistants. ICT, music, drama, Mandarin, swimming and PE are taught by specialist teachers. From the age of 7, forms become single-sex with 22 pupils in each. Form teachers teach the main curriculum subjects, while specialists teach modern foreign languages – Mandarin, Spanish and German – ICT, art, music, drama, dance, design and technology, physical education, swimming and games.

Academic standards, sport and music are all strengths of the school in equal measure. The main sports played are football, cricket, netball and rounders, and teams compete locally and regionally. Athletics, swimming and cross-country are all coached to a high standard. The musical life of the school is enriched by its choirs, orchestra and several chamber groups, and all pupils in Years 3 and 4 are provided with free tuition in a musical instrument. There are endless opportunities for pupils to perform in concerts or recitals throughout the year, and Chapel services, form assemblies and school competitions provide occasions for public speaking and performance. A full-time Librarian runs the Prep School Library. Activities take place at lunchtime, before school and after school, with a wide variety of extra-curricular clubs on offer. Breakfast club commences at 7.30 am and after-school care is available until 6.00 pm each day. Forest School also has an extensive school bus service in operation.

Charitable status. Forest School, Essex is a Registered Charity, number 312677. The objective of the school is education.

Forres Sandle Manor

Sandleheath, Fordingbridge, Hampshire SP6 1NS

Tel: 01425 653181
email: office@fsmschool.com
website: www.fsmschool.com
Twitter: @fsmschool
Facebook: @fsmschool

Acting Head: **Mr Jody Wells**

Age Range. 3–13.
Number of Pupils. Prep: 168 (100 boarders, 100 boys, 68 girls). Pre-Prep: 49 (all are day children, 32 boys, 17 girls).
Fees per term (2018–2019). Boarders: £8,085 (Years 5–8), £7,780 (Year 4), £6,635 (Year 3); Day pupils: £5,925 (Years 7 & 8), £5,705 (Years 5 & 6), £5,410 (Year 4), £4,815 (Year 3), £3,030 (Years 1 & 2), £2,885 (Reception). Early Years Education Entitlement provider.

At Forres Sandle Manor, we believe that "Happy Children Succeed".

You may imagine, with a line like that, Forres Sandle Manor (or FSM as we are known) is some kind of holiday club dedicated to keep the children smiling and entertained. However, this is a surface sort of happiness. The sort of happiness FSM means comes from knowing that you are liked and respected by your peers and your teachers. It comes from knowing that no matter what your skills and talents, or indeed your lack of them, you will be helped and supported to do the best that you can in order to reach your own particular star.

From the Nursery all the way up to Year 8 there are many stars at FSM. Naturally there are those who excel in particular areas of the curriculum or indeed one of the many extra-curricular activities, and these children are enrolled into our Gifted and Talented Programme. Some of these children may also attend the fabulous, nationally renowned, Learning Support Centre which also provides essential support for those who learn differently when and where required. Not all children are all-rounders after all.

Considering they are a small, non-selective school, in the last three years FSM children have achieved 40 scholarships and awards to leading public schools across the country. Children have gone on to Eton, Sherborne, Sherborne Girls, Stowe, Bryanston, Marlborough, Canford, as well as a host of other leading public schools up and down the UK. Add to this the success FSM children achieve in sport and music both regionally and nationally and more often than not against much larger schools!

The Independent Schools Inspectorate visited in May this year and FSM were delighted that they found the school to be 'Excellent' in all areas. Indeed, one of their key findings was that 'pupils have outstanding attitudes to learning and are determined to succeed'. Happy children …

At FSM each and every child is supported by our skills based, creative curriculum which allows every single child to contribute to the plans of what they will be learning as a class. We believe that it is only when children have some ownership of their learning that they are able to fully engage with it so that it is meaningful and relevant to them.

None of this happens by accident. FSM have exceptional resources; at the heart of the school is the manor house, which is surrounded by 35 acres of playing fields, woods and streams. Our facilities are the same as you would expect to find at a leading prep school; an astro pitch, a multi-purpose sports and performance hall, our Forest School, a 25-

metre heated swimming pool as well as much more! Our most important resource, however, is our staff. The teachers at FSM are passionate about what they do and in all areas they actively seek out and nurture raw talent in whatever field that may be.

Life at FSM starts at the Pre-Prep, where children can join the Nursery during the half-term when they turn 3. The first years of school are vital and it's fundamental that they are of the very highest standard. It is at this time that children learn how to learn; that their curiosity is harnessed through meaningful and purposeful play and that they develop the neural pathways that will serve them for the rest of their lives. It is in these valuable years that a child's dispositions and attitudes to learning are developed and that children learn to take risks, to persevere, to explore and to ask questions, as well as the social and communication skills which can only develop through being with others.

FSM provides an environment which nurtures and encourages the developing child at this special time in their lives. We don't believe in hot-housing. We feel that's the way to produce rapid, but weak growth. Instead we allow children the most precious thing of all – time. It is only through sustained, active learning, that a child is able to become absorbed, make connections to past experiences, develop higher order thinking skills and truly learn.

The Music school produces amazing results and every child is encouraged to try an instrument and experience performance in many different areas. Drama is timetabled for all children from Year 3 and above. We encourage all the children to get up and perform as often as they can. It's a fantastic way of building up their self-confidence and by the time they get to Year 8, standing up in front of an audience becomes second nature.

Sport is played everyday, apart from Thursdays and there is always a full fixture list on Wednesday and Saturday afternoons. Every child has the opportunity to represent the school at some point, with our best sportsmen and women competing at County and National level.

Academically, FSM leads the way in its innovative approach to teaching. Many of the techniques used here have now been adopted by Prep Schools across the country and we are justifiably proud of the fact that every Year 8 has always been successful in achieving their first choice senior school. Always! Not only that, but the children win more than their fair share of scholarships and awards. We spend much time liaising with senior schools, children and parents to ensure that we match the child to the senior school, academically, pastorally, creatively, on the sports field and socially. As we are not a feeder school, we have the freedom to do just that – the children come first.

Much of the family atmosphere surrounding the school comes from the fact that at its heart, FSM is a boarding school; almost two thirds of the children in Years 3 to 8 are full or weekly boarders, and we have a waiting list of children eager to try! The recent Ofsted report supports our claim to have 'the Best Boarding House in the World' by grading it as "outstanding". The level of care shown by the pastoral team isn't just saved for the boarders though. The Senior Houseparent, and her team, extend their support not only to all the children but their parents as well. There is no segmentation between day children and boarders. Day children can also take part in the numerous hobbies and activities on offer at the end of the school day and we often invite our day children in to join in our legendary Wednesday nights; our boarders also get invited out to stay with day children at the weekends.

FSM excels in their care of children from HM Forces families as well as other overseas based families and have done for many, many years. We always have a large number of children staying in at the weekend who look forward to the planned activities as well as having a bit of "chill time"! The school office is excellent at, and very used to, handling any overseas travel arrangements.

It is difficult to single out any one particular area and be able to say that FSM excels in this or that; perhaps this is where the uniqueness of FSM lies. We hope that to really get a feel for the school, you will come and visit us and as you walk around the beautiful manor house and amazing grounds you will also think that, actually, "Happy Children Succeed" isn't a clever advertising gimmick after all. It really is at the heart of everything we do.

Charitable status. Forres Sandle Manor Education Trust Ltd is a Registered Charity, number 284260. It exists to provide first-class education for boys and girls.

Fosse Bank School

Mountains Country House, Noble Tree Road, Hildenborough, Kent TN11 8ND

Tel: 01732 834212
email: admissions@fossebankschool.co.uk
              headteacher@fossebankschool.co.uk
website: www.fossebankschool.co.uk
Twitter: @FosseBankSchool
Facebook: @FosseBankSchool

Chair of Governors: Mr Mark Waddington

Headmistress: **Miss Alison Cordingley**, LTCL, PGCE, NPQH

Admissions Officer: Mrs Louise Taylor

Age Range. 2–11 Co-educational.
Number of Pupils. 115.
Fees per term (2018–2019). £3,445 (Reception) to £4,286 (Year 6).

Founded in 1892, Fosse Bank School including Little Fosse Nursery (available from the term in which the child turns 2 years old) offers an excellent academic education combined with a truly supportive, friendly and stimulating environment in which children learn and flourish.

Wrap-around care is offered for fifty weeks a year from 7.30 am to 6.00 pm. With ample off-road parking, parents take advantage of the ten-minute walk to park at school and walk to Hildenborough railway station

Parents and children appreciate the excellent pastoral care. We celebrate each success and encourage every child to be the best that they can be. The importance of good manners is emphasised and our children have a reputation for being confident, articulate and well-behaved. The school is a strong family community and is located in a beautiful Grade II listed building with 28 acres of parkland and boasting a range of wonderful facilities including an indoor heated swimming pool, tennis courts, sports hall, Mongolian Yurt and well-resourced Early Years. With research clearly demonstrating the link between physical learning and academic success, weekly Forest School sessions offer a unique educational experience using the outdoor environment of our woodland as a classroom,

Academic Studies. Our children achieve excellent academic results accepting offers of places at selective state and independent schools every year. Our Kent 11+ results are excellent. In the Early Years we give the children a solid foundation based on the Early Years Foundations Stage. Further up the school we extend the National Curriculum, offering many enriching learning experiences. Music, PE,

Forest School and French are taught by specialists so that high standards are achieved in all subject areas. With recorder, violin and ukulele lessons as part of the curriculum, children are given frequent opportunities to perform and share their musical talents.

Extra-Curricular. A wealth of activities are available after school for all children, such as orchestra, science club, cookery, cross-country running, ballet, football, choir, karate, Lego and construction and many others. We also have a dynamic after-school care facility, the Phoenix Club which provides lively activities from 3.30 to 6.00 pm.

Entry Procedure. Fosse Bank is not academically selective at entry, although the Headmistress reserves the right to make a decision as to whether the applicant's learning needs can be managed within the School's normal provision. All children are required to attend a Taster Day before an offer may be made.

Charitable status. Fosse Bank New School is a Registered Charity, number 1045435.

Framlingham College Prep School

Brandeston Hall, Brandeston, Woodbridge, Suffolk IP13 7AH

Tel:	01728 685331
Fax:	01728 685437
email:	admissions@framcollege.co.uk
website:	www.framcollege.co.uk
Twitter:	@FramPrep
Facebook:	@framcollege
LinkedIn:	/framlingham-college

Chairman of Governors: Air Vice-Marshal T W Rimmer, CB, OBE, MA, FRAeS, FRGS, RAF Retd

Headmaster: **Mr Matthew King**

Senior Team:
Deputy Head Co-Curricular: Mr Bruce Wilson
Deputy Head: Pastoral: Mrs Joanna Coventry-King
Deputy Head: Academic: Mr Darren Bilton
Head of Junior Prep: Mr James Loveridge
Head of Pre-Prep & Nursery: Mrs Ruth Steggles
Head of Boarding: Mr Ed Marland

Age Range. 2–13 Co-educational.
Number of Pupils. 260.
Fees per term (2018–2019). Full Boarding £36 per night, Day £5,067.50 (inc lunch), Pre-Prep: Day £2,912 (inc lunch), Nursery: £35 (full day session inc lunch), £17 (half day session exc lunch).

A prep school education should be rigorous and challenging, but it must also be creative, vibrant and, above all, fun. At a time when schools so often surrender their individuality in the face of rigid testing and regulation, we believe passionately that children should be able to carry on doing the stuff that children ought to be doing for as long as they possibly can.

For that reason, a Framlingham College Prep School education remains every bit as diverse as it was when the school was established in its idyllic, rural haven nearly seventy years ago. From sports pitches to laboratories and from Art and Design to Music, Drama and Technology you'll find children confidently expressing themselves and discovering new talents. They work hard but always enjoy their learning and they carry that passion with them for life.

While we are understandably proud of our impressive academic record, we know that long-term success is built on broader qualities and values. Well-being, resilience and citizenship feature highly amongst these. Framlingham College Prep School is a happy, nurturing school where children feel valued and inspired. We celebrate difference and encourage pupils to communicate respectfully, to work well together and, above all, to care for those around them and the world beyond. We value kindness and service every bit as highly as academic prowess and all-round talents.

However, it is not just the children that are prioritised and happy parents are a crucial part of the learning partnership. With the flexibility of our extended days and our innovative Brandeston+ boarding programme, we are better equipped than ever to build an education around the lives of busy families.

Our aim at Framlingham is to develop independent, well mannered, positive individuals who stand out from the crowd in all the right ways, but also know the value of the team. The young men and women who move on from the Prep School do so as confident, well-balanced youngsters, all-rounders in every sense. We are preparing children not just for exams, but also for life.

Do not hesitate to swap the virtual world for the real one and pay us a visit. You'll soon discover why Framlingham College Prep School pupils are so proud of their school and why we are so proud of them.

Various scholarships are available for 11+ and 13+ entrants.

Charitable status. Albert Memorial College is a Registered Charity, number 1114383. It exists for the purpose of educating children.

The Froebelian School

Clarence Road, Horsforth, Leeds LS18 4LB

Tel:	0113 258 3047
email:	office@froebelian.co.uk
website:	www.froebelian.com
Twitter:	@FroebelianS
Facebook:	@FroebelianSchool
LinkedIn:	/FroebelianSchool

Chair of Governors: Mrs Rosey James

Head: **Mrs Catherine Dodds**

Age Range. 3+ to 11+ years (3–4 years half days, optional afternoons).
Number of Pupils. 189 (96 boys, 93 girls).
Fees per term (2018–2019). £1,740–£2,595. Compulsory extras for full-time pupils, such as lunches and swimming, amount to approximately £260 per term.

Bursaries (income-related fee reduction) may be available.

Religious Affiliation: Christian, non-denominational.

Entry Requirements: Interview and assessment; written tests for older children.

Entry is usually at 3+, but limited places are sometimes available throughout the school.

Every child is respected as an individual and pupils are encouraged to reach their full potential in the purposeful atmosphere of this caring, disciplined school. High standards are achieved in all areas of the school – academic work, creative arts, music, sport, behaviour and manners. Early progress in language and mathematics is sustained and broadened in the junior curriculum, which includes French, information and design technology, drama and outdoor pursuits.

The school enjoys an envied reputation for success in entrance and scholarship examinations at 11+. Froebelian is the only school in Leeds to appear consistently in The Sunday Times list of 'Top 100' schools. A flourishing Parent Teacher Association supports the school and a growing database helps to keep former pupils in touch.

Situated to the north-west of Leeds, and close to Bradford, the school is well served by major transport links. 'Wrap-around' care is available from 7.30 am to 6.00 pm in the form of Breakfast Club, Little Acorns and Homework and Activities Club and there is a holiday club during the summer break.

Charitable status. The Froebelian School is a Registered Charity, number 529111. It exists to provide education of the highest quality at affordable fee levels.

Garden House School

Turk's Row, London SW3 4TW

Tel:	020 7730 1652 (Girls)
	020 7730 6652 (Boys)
email:	info@gardenhouseschool.co.uk
website:	www.gardenhouseschool.co.uk

Principal: Mrs J K Oddy, BA Hons

Headmistress – Upper School: **Ms Annie Lee**, BMus, PGCE, MA
Headmistress – Lower School: **Mrs Julia Adlard**, BA Hons, Dip Montessori
Headmaster – Boys' School: **Mr Christian Warland**, BA Hons

Age Range. 3–11 Girls, 3–11 Boys.
Number of Pupils. 290 girls, 198 boys, taught in single-sex classes.
Fees per term (2018–2019). Kindergarten £5,900 Reception–Year 6 £7,300–£7,600. There is a 10% reduction for siblings.
Buildings and facilities. The School is housed in a light, airy listed building in Chelsea. Original artwork hangs in every classroom and facilities include libraries for different age groups, a ballet/performance/drama hall and dedicated science and art rooms.

Sport is played in various locations close to the School. The school has its own garden within the grounds of the Royal Hospital where children enjoy science lessons and attend a Gardening Club.

School drama productions are staged at the Royal Court Theatre in Sloane Square.

Aims, ethos and values. Garden House provides a thorough, balanced education in a lively and purposeful environment. Our children achieve strong academic results in a calm, constructive manner, being encouraged to have inquiring and independent minds. We teach our boys and girls separately, delivered in teaching styles relevant to the difference audiences. Emphasis is placed not only on academic, sporting and artistic excellence but on manners and consideration to others. Our Kindness Code is adhered to and constantly re-emphasised.

Curriculum. English, Mathematics, Science, History, Geography, Religious Education, French (from Kindergarten), Latin, Computing, Life & Culture, Current Affairs, Art, Drama, Singing and Music, Dancing, Fencing and Physical Education (netball, tennis, rounders, gymnastics, swimming, athletics, cricket, hockey, rugby and football). We have many sports squads, sports clubs and matches. The Learning Support Department helps both children with special needs and those who are gifted, catered for in small groups, taught by two full-time and many visiting specialist teachers. 80% of children learn at least one musical instrument. The School runs four choirs and a chamber orchestra.

A diverse range of early morning and after-school clubs include Chess, Coding, Debating, Harry Potter, Lego, Maths Monsters, Music Technology, French, Spanish and German to name a few of the fifty on offer every week.

Benefiting from our central London location, visits to museums, galleries and churches form an essential part of the Curriculum, as do annual field study and outward bound trips. Girls and boys spend a week in France after CE and boys enjoy a camping expedition among others including Outpost trip, a geography and science trip, a Bushcraft trip. The choir sings around the country; this year at Stratford-upon-Avon in a combined music/drama trip.

School Successes. Girls are prepared for the Common Entrance, with the majority leaving for the premier girls' Schools, 60% to leading London senior Schools, 40% to major boarding schools. Some boys leave us at 8, having been well prepared for entrance to leading London Prep Schools and 10% to top boarding Preps. Other boys remain at Garden House, being educated to the age of 11. Our children achieve several scholarships each year.

Entrance. We encourage you to visit the School. Girls and boys join Garden House in September after they reach 3 or 4 years of age. A Registration Form can be obtained from the School Office and once completed and returned with the relevant fee, your child's name is placed on the Waiting List. Entry interviews are held one year before entry. We look forward to welcoming you and your children to Garden House School.

Gatehouse School

Sewardstone Road, Victoria Park, London E2 9JG

Tel:	020 8980 2978
Fax:	020 8983 1642
email:	admin@gatehouseschool.co.uk
website:	www.gatehouseschool.co.uk

Acting Head: **Mrs Sevda Korbay**, BA Hons, MA, GTP

Age Range. 3–11 Co-educational.
Number in School. 450 Day Pupils.
Fees per term (2018–2019). £3,870–£4,075.

Gatehouse School is an Independent Co-educational School for girls and boys aged 3 to 11.

Founded by Phyllis Wallbank, in May 1948, in the gatehouse of St Bartholomew, the Great Priory Church near Smithfield London, the School was a pioneer of much that is now generally accepted in education. Gatehouse is based on the Wallbank plan whose guiding principle is that children of any race, colour, creed, background and intellect shall be accepted as pupils and work side by side without streaming or any kind of segregation with the aim that each child shall get to know and love God, and develop their own uniqueness of personality, to enable them to appreciate the world and the world to appreciate them.

Gatehouse is now located in Sewardstone Road close to Victoria Park and continues to follow this philosophy.

The Nursery is accommodated in a self-contained building with an outdoor play area. Pupils follow a balanced curriculum of child-initiated and teacher-led activities.

Lower Juniors are taught most subjects by their own qualified teacher and assistant, but have French, PE and Music with a specialist teacher.

In Upper Juniors from the age of 7, teaching is by subject and is conducted by highly qualified specialist staff. This is a special feature of Gatehouse and gives children from an early age, contact with subject specialists, not available to many children until secondary school.

We send children to schools such as City of London boys and girls, Forest, Bancroft's and Highgate, often with scholarships.

Charitable status. Gatehouse Educational Trust Limited is a Registered Charity, number 282558.

Gayhurst School

Bull Lane, Gerrards Cross, Bucks SL9 8RJ

Tel: 01753 882690
Fax: 01753 887451
email: enquiries@gayhurstschool.co.uk
website: www.gayhurstschool.co.uk

Chair of Governors: Mrs C Shorten Conn

Headmaster: **Mr G R A Davies**, BA Hons, PGCE, MEd

Age Range. 3–11 Co-educational.
Number of Children. 306.
Fees per term (2018–2019). £4,053–£5,146 (inclusive of lunch). Nursery: £26–£78 per session.

Gayhurst is a happy, thriving and vibrant independent preparatory school for girls and boys aged 3–11. For over 100 years the school has endeavoured to bring out the best in every child in its care by focusing on individual talents and supporting children to achieve their full potential. Since becoming co-educational in 2008, Gayhurst has built a reputation as a family school, providing first-class co-education in Gerrards Cross.

Life at Gayhurst is engaging and exciting with regular activities organised to enrich the education of its pupils. Children are encouraged to participate in sport, with a busy programme of fixtures against other schools. Creativity is evident throughout the school with opportunities to learn an instrument, become a member of one of the many musical ensembles or take part in the annual year group drama productions. There are also numerous visits to places of interest on both day and residential trips.

Gayhurst strives to ensure that pupils are given every opportunity to achieve the best start in life. The school's commitment to continual improvement and development means that the children benefit greatly from the facilities offered on the school's five acre site, including IT rooms, Science laboratories, woodland adventure playground and an all-weather AstroTurf.

Pupils consistently achieve strong academic results progressing to both local Grammar Schools and to Senior Schools, day and boarding, in the Independent sector.

Headmaster, Gareth Davies says, "Pupils' social and personal development is enhanced by the co-educational experience that they get at Gayhurst. In my experience, boys and girls enjoy learning and socialising together and at such a young age, the elimination of gender stereotypes and access to different perspectives and ideas proves only to be beneficial. The family ethos, excellent pastoral care, support and guidance from our caring staff and parent partnership also reinforce the children's positive experiences at school".

For more information about the school, or to arrange a visit, please contact the Registrar on 01753 279140 or email enquiries@gayhurstschool.co.uk.

Charitable status. Gayhurst School Trust is a Registered Charity, number 298869.

Giggleswick Junior School

Giggleswick, Settle, North Yorkshire BD24 0DG

Tel: 01729 893100
Fax: 01729 893150
email: juniorschool@giggleswick.org.uk
website: www.giggleswick.org.uk
Twitter: @GiggJunior
Facebook: @GiggleswickJuniorSchool

Chairman of Governors: Mrs H J Hancock, LVO, MA

Head: **Mr James Mundell**, LLB, PGCE University of Wales Cardiff

Head of Early Years: Mrs Julie Middleton, BA Hons QTS Lancaster
Head of Boarding: Mrs C Gemmell, BEd Manchester Polytechnic
Headmaster's Secretary: Mrs S E Driver

Age Range. 3–11 Co-educational.
Number of Pupils. 80.
Fees per term (2018–2019). Boarders (Years 5–6): £7,080 (full), £6,365 (5-night flexi), £5,470 (3-night flexi). Day Pupils: £4,255 (Years 3–6), £2,655 (R–Y2).

Boys and girls from the age of three up to eleven flourish in the busy, vibrant and supportive community of Giggleswick Junior School, where the happiness and progress of every child is an absolute priority. Our idyllic setting in the Yorkshire Dales gives life at the School a real sense of adventure and discovery, giving children the space and freedom to grow as individuals and develop a lifelong love of learning.

We welcome day pupils across all years and full and flexi boarders in Years 5 and 6. The boarding ethos of the wider school creates a unique homely atmosphere and the extended day allows children the time to develop their individual talents with 19 clubs and activities a week including 70 specialist music lessons, 40 dance sessions, 40 French sessions and 136 sports fixtures each year.

All pupils in Years 1 and 2 learn a stringed instrument as part of the Foundation Strings Scheme. In Years 3 to 6 over 75% of pupils take lessons on at least one instrument.

We set high academic standards to nurture all levels of ability, with a strong focus on personal and social development and helping young children to become independent learners. Our pupils benefit from small classes, specialist teaching and excellent IT provision, allowing us to provide a tailored learning programme for each child.

In Year 6 our pupils study 15 different subjects a week and everyone learns two modern languages. 100% of pupils achieved or exceeded national expectations in English in Year 3 and 88% achieved or exceeded national expectations in Key Stage 1 Maths.

Children have plenty of opportunity to learn outdoors in our forest school, to grow food and plants in our garden and to learn a respect for nature by taking care of our pets in school. The Junior School shares its campus with the Senior School, providing access to some of the best school facilities in the region including an indoor swimming pool, a mountain bike trail, floodlit AstroTurf, two indoor sports halls, an Observatory, The Richard Whiteley Theatre and Giggleswick School Chapel.

We were delighted to be voted 'One of the UK's Top 10 Best Value Prep Schools' by the Daily Telegraph, acknowledging our outstanding teaching and learning facilities alongside highly affordable fees.

To help busy, working parents and families travelling from across the region, we provide daily bus services on seven routes covering a 45-minute radius of the School. Areas include Kirkby Lonsdale, Grassington, Skipton, Ilkley, Colne, Clitheroe and the Lune Valley.

"Team spirit and trust thrive within the school's friendly community. Pupils were keen to report that theirs is a trusting and friendly school. Courtesy and kindness prevail throughout the setting and behaviour is exemplary." Independent Schools Inspectorate (ISI) 2015

Charitable status. Giggleswick School is a Registered Charity, number 1109826.

Glebe House School

Cromer Road, Hunstanton, Norfolk PE36 6HW
Tel: 01485 532809
Fax: 01485 533900
email: ghsoffice@glebehouseschool.co.uk
website: www.glebehouseschool.co.uk
Twitter: @GlebeHS
Facebook: @GlebeHouseSchoolandNursery

Chairman of the Governors: Mr Nicholas Crane

Headmaster: **Mr Louis Taylor**, BA, PGCE

Age Range. 6 months to 13 years.
Number of Children. 45 Boys, 48 Girls, Nursery 79.
Fees per term (2018–2019). Prep £4,430; Pre-Prep £2,772. Weekly boarding: £320–£745 (1–4 nights).

Glebe House School and Nursery was founded in 1874 as a preparatory school and is surrounded by 12 acres of playing fields with a stunning new Nursery building.

The Junior School children are accommodated in a purpose-built building. The Senior School has specialist areas for all academic subjects and music, sport and drama are a significant part of a child's life at Glebe House. Our 25-metre indoor heated swimming pool, astroturf pitch for hockey, tennis and netball, adventure playground, gym, music school and performance hall all help to ensure that the core academic subjects are supported by a balanced and stimulating curriculum. Lessons finish at 3.30 pm (Pre-Prep), 4.10 pm (Prep) but breakfast club, after-school activities, cooked tea and supervised prep provide day care from 7.30 am to 6.30 pm.

Aims and Values. At the heart of Glebe House is our emphasis on supporting and valuing the individual. We encourage the traditional values of courtesy, consideration for others, self discipline and a desire to contribute to society.

Academic Life. We are committed to high academic standards, harnessing the best of modern educational practice. Class sizes remain small and every child is encouraged to achieve their full potential. Close supervision, with one-to-one support where necessary, is maintained and progress is carefully monitored through regular standardised testing and classroom assessments. The broad curriculum both incorporates and exceed national requirements, including offering a second modern language in addition to French from year six. Glebe House enjoys a high success rate at Common Entrance and in Independent Scholarship Examinations and with this solid foundation our pupils move confidently on to a wide range of senior schools.

Sport and Activities. We offer a wide sporting programme aimed to encourage fitness and a healthy enjoyment of sport that will remain with the children for life. Rugby, hockey and cricket are the main sports for boys and hockey,

netball and rounders for girls. We also encourage involvement in many activities including athletics, cross country, football, golf, swimming and tennis. The lunchtime and after-school activity programme is varied and includes sporting, dramatic, artistic and musical groups as well as others such as Mandarin Chinese. We offer a wide range of activities during the summer holidays, including ball sports, swimming, craft, music and drama workshops, tennis, and sailing.

Pastoral Care and Boarding. Relations between children and staff are respectful but relaxed and the children know they are free to talk to all staff, one of the great advantages of a school this size. All pupils belong to one of three houses and have a tutor who sees them each morning and is the first point of contact for parents. Good communication is crucial and we operate an open door policy to parents. The school offers 35 weekly boarding places and flexibility in choosing from one to four nights.

Travel. Our minibuses pick up in the morning and take home at 4.15 pm and 6.00 pm to King's Lynn and surrounding areas.

Further Information. Prospective parents and children are most welcome to contact the School Registrar, email: tjf@glebehouseschool.co.uk, to meet the Headmaster and tour the school.

Charitable status. Glebe House School Trust Limited is a Registered Charity, number 1018815.

The Gleddings Preparatory School

Birdcage Lane, Savile Park, Halifax, West Yorkshire HX3 0JB
Tel: 01422 354605
Fax: 01422 356263
email: thegleddings@aol.com
website: www.thegleddings.co.uk

Headmistress: **Mrs P J Wilson**, CBE

Age Range. 3–11 Co-educational.
Number of Pupils. 192.
Fees per term (2018–2019). £2,910.

"The Gleddings is very special. It is precious to several generations of families in the locality and beyond. We are now educating the children of our past pupils. We consider it a great privilege to do so.

The staff and I remember, all of the time, the trust that parents bestow in us. We promise our best efforts for every child.

Our academic results speak for themselves but The Gleddings is about much more. We develop self-discipline, self-respect and confidence within The Gleddings' unique "YOU CHOOSE" ethos. We encourage children to THINK! and to learn how to learn."

Jill Wilson, Headteacher.

Godolphin Prep

Laverstock Road, Salisbury, Wiltshire SP1 2RB
Tel: 01722 430652
Fax: 01722 430651
email: prep@godolphin.wilts.sch.uk
website: www.godolphin.org

Chairman of Governors: Mr M J Nicholson

Headmistress: **Miss J Miller**, BA, MEd

Head of Admissions: Mrs C Florence

To view a full list of the staff, please visit the website: www.godolphin.org.

Age Range. 3–11.
Number of Pupils. 100.
Fees per term (2018–2019). Full boarding £8,410; 5-day Boarding £7,180, 3-day Boarding £6,240; Day: £4,645 (Years 4–6), £3,690 (Year 3), £2,385 (Years 1–2), £2,375 (Reception).

Godolphin is a very special school, which offers a broad education for girls from 3–18. Our whole school ethos is unique in Salisbury and it ensures the girls move from one stage of their education to the next.

Godolphin Prep provides a supportive and stimulating environment with a strong academic ethos. Godolphin girls are happy and confident. They flourish because of the excellent pastoral care and the close partnership between staff and parents.

The whole school approach is reinforced through strong links with the Senior School and the three competitive Houses that girls belong to from Nursery to the Upper Sixth.

Flexi and Full Boarding is available. Prep boarders, from the age of seven, are an integral part of the whole school boarding community and are supported by specialist boarding staff in a bespoke boarding house. The Walters House staff help and support them with every aspect of school life from homework and uniform to laundry and music practice.

Sharing the site with the Senior School means we offer outstanding facilities such as our art and design department, the swimming pool, theatre, science and technology labs and sports pitches. We also share staff expertise and this enables us to offer a wide variety

We also share staff expertise an this enables us to offer a wide variety of after school activities which include fun cookery, Lego robots, kick boxing, choir, science club, Zumba, yoga and orchestra.

To find out more about Godolphin Prep, visit us on one of our Snapshot Days when you can experience a typical school morning. For dates and further information visit www.godolphin.org.

Godstowe Preparatory School

Shrubbery Road, High Wycombe, Bucks HP13 6PR

Tel:	01494 529273
	01494 429006 Registrar
Fax:	01494 429009
email:	schooloffice@godstowe.org
website:	www.godstowe.org
Twitter:	@GodstoweSchool
Facebook:	@GodstoweSchool

Motto: *Finem Respice*

Chairman of the Governors: K Allner, BA Econ

Headmistress: **Ms S Green**, BSc Econ, PGCE

Age Range. Girls 3–13, Boys 3–7.
Number of Pupils. Preparatory: 335 (boarding and day). Pre-Preparatory: 102.
Fees per term (2018–2019). Boarders £8,215, Day Children £3,600–£5,540. Nursery: £1,725–£3,450.

Since its foundation in 1900, Godstowe Preparatory School has been at the forefront of education. It has a distin-

guished tradition as the first British boarding preparatory school for girls, in a foundation that includes Wycombe Abbey, Benenden and St Leonards.

Today, Godstowe is a flourishing boarding and day school with 435 pupils, enjoying an unparalleled academic reputation. It has a Pre-Prep department for boys and girls aged between three and seven, and a Preparatory School for girls from seven to thirteen years old. Class sizes are small allowing children to benefit from individual attention.

A new indoor swimming pool opened in Autumn 2018. The school underwent an ISI inspection in June 2018 and was regarded as 'excellent' in every respect.

Academic Record. Godstowe enjoys an excellent and unparalleled academic reputation amongst British independent schools. Despite its non-selective entry policy, Godstowe consistently achieves unrivalled academic results. In 2018, 34 scholarships and distinctions were awarded. By the age of nine, pupils are taught by specialists in 16 subjects across the curriculum. Language teaching includes French, Spanish and Latin. Sport, ICT, art and music are all outstandingly taught within first-rate facilities.

Boarding. Girls' boarding life is focused within three houses in the grounds, one of which is a dedicated junior house. Each has three resident staff and a warm and supportive atmosphere. A combination of professional and caring staff and beautifully refurbished accommodation ensures a safe and relaxing environment. Each house has its own garden, reinforcing the feeling of 'going home' at the end of the school day. Weekends are packed full of activity and fun, with many weekly boarders often choosing to stay at School for the weekend.

The **Enrichment Curriculum** offers 50 after-school activities each week, most of which run after school between 4.30 pm and 6.30 pm. The 'E-Curriculum' gives children the chance to try many exciting and challenging new pursuits including poetry writing, judo, cooking, Chinese Mandarin, football and debating. In addition, supervised homework sessions are offered every evening. Day children may join the boarders for breakfast and supper. Other than those sessions supervised by outside instructors all activities are offered free of charge. An Enrichment programme is also in place for Pre-Prep children.

Charitable status. The Godstowe Preparatory School Company Limited is a Registered Charity, number 310637. It exists to provide education and training for young girls and boys.

Grace Dieu Manor School & Nursery

Grace Dieu, Thringstone, Leicestershire LE67 5UG

Tel:	01530 222276
email:	admissions@gracedieu.com
website:	www.gracedieu.com

Chairman of Governors: Mr R Gamble

Headmistress: **Mrs Margaret Kewell**

Age Range. 0–11 Co-educational.
Number of Pupils. 247.
Fees per term (2018–2019). £3,595–£3,784.

Grace Dieu Manor School & Nursery, for children aged 12 weeks to 11 years, is often described as a hidden gem. Nestling in 120 acres of idyllic parkland, just 15 minutes from Loughborough, Coalville and Ashby de la Zouch, children have acres of space to grow, learn and play.

All that we offer, both inside and outside of the classroom, is rooted in our goal to develop the whole person. This is what makes us distinctive and, as a Catholic School that welcomes all faiths, permeates through our whole school community.

We offer small classes with specialist teaching in Sport, Music, Art, Drama and Languages, and we are justifiably proud of our strong academic reputation. This year, 94% of our pupils won places to their first-choice senior school, and every year pupils win scholarships to a range of different schools across the region.

Learning is all encompassing at Grace Dieu. A lot of our learning opportunities happen outside of the classroom – in our Forest School, on the sports pitch, on school trips or during extra-curricular activities. Whilst our pupils excel academically, this doesn't come at a cost of a fully-rounded education. Our focus is very much on developing the whole person, going far beyond just intellectual development. We place equal importance on developing every child's physical, moral, spiritual and aesthetic development, meaning that, as well as other vital character traits, our pupils develop confidence, courtesy, creativity and capability.

We have extensive sports facilities on site – including a swimming pool, sports hall and numerous outdoor courts and pitches. We are also specialists in Outdoor Learning and our Forest School is an integral part of our curriculum. Pupils enjoy den building, foraging, campfire cooking, storytelling and nature watching – as well as taking some of their other subjects outside (from measuring trees for Maths, to studying plants for Science). We even have our own chickens and alpaca herd! The opportunities for outdoor fun and learning are boundless – thanks to our expert teaching staff and our stunning and expansive setting.

We understand just how busy family life can be. Our Nursery is open 51 weeks a year. Families can use a range of flexible bus routes and we offer free and flexible wraparound care from 8.00 am to 6.00 pm, as well as a breakfast club from 7.30 am.

Children are able to join Grace Dieu at any time in the school year, depending on our space and availability. Children are invited to a visit day where they will be informally assessed so that we know whether they will be happy and thrive at Grace Dieu. The level of this assessment varies depending on their age of entry.

Charitable status. Grace Dieu Manor School is a Registered Charity, number 1115976.

Grange Park Preparatory School

13 The Chine, Grange Park, London N21 2EA

Tel: 020 8360 1469
Fax: 020 8360 4869
email: office@gpps.org.uk
website: www.gpps.org.uk

Day School for Boys and Girls.

Chair of Governors: Mr Amit Metha

Head: Miss Flavia Rizzo, BSc, PGCE, MA

Age Range. 3–11
Number of Children. 90.
Fees per term (2018–2019). £3,534–£3,561.

Grange Park Preparatory School is a long established, happy and successful school that provides a broad and stimulating education. It is situated in the pleasant residential area of Grange Park.

We remain committed to educating boys and girls in a small school with small class sizes, thus allowing every child to be known as an individual. The children enjoy a broad curriculum taught by experienced staff who encourage excellence in all areas of school life.

We also have a Nursery class for boys and girls aged 3 and 4. Nursery staff and children have access to the excellent resources available at GPPS, including outside space, the gym and a cooked lunch for those children staying the whole day. The children follow the Early Years Curriculum with additional specialist teaching in French, Dance, Drama and Music.

In KS1 the children are taught mostly by form teachers with specialist teaching being introduced gradually in KS2. From Reception specialist teachers teach games, French, music, dance and drama. Individual music tuition is available from Year 1.

In Key Stage 2 preparation for 11+ state selective and independent secondary schools starts from as early as Year 3, where children undertake verbal and non-verbal reasoning as part of the curriculum. In addition, from the summer term in Year 4, children wishing to sit for selective schools attend extra prep classes, thus equipping them with the tools to achieve their maximum potential in terms of academic attainment. Every year we are proud to announce that our Year 6 children do extremely well in the secondary school entrance exams, with some being awarded scholarships.

Children enjoy a very busy school life and benefit from an excellent variety of extra-curricular activities, including LAMDA, Judo, horse riding and chess, further enriching their experience and creating lifetime memories.

The school has a healthy eating policy. Lunches are cooked in school using only fresh ingredients; no processed food is used. There is always a vegetarian option and salads and fresh fruit are available daily.

Places for Reception are offered after the Headteacher has met with parents and their child. Children taking up chance vacancies in other classes will be invited to spend a day in school to ensure they will fit into the class successfully.

Before leaving GPPS every child will have been given a responsible role at some level, instilling in them a sense of duty and ingrained confidence, preparing them for today's challenges.

Grange Park Preparatory School is a part of The Inspired Learning Group, company number 11458444,

The Granville School

2 Bradbourne Park Road, Sevenoaks, Kent TN13 3LJ

Tel: 01732 453039
email: secretary@granvilleschool.org
website: www.granvilleschool.org

Chairman of Governors: Mr J Sorrell

Headmistress: Mrs Louise Lawrance, BPrimEd Hons

Age Range. Girls 3–11, Boys 3–5.
Number of Pupils. 200.
Fees per term (2018–2019). Kindergarten (mornings only) £1,954 (mornings only) or £3,356 (all day), Recep-

tion, Years 1 & 2 £3,953, Year 3 £4,471, Years 4, 5 & 6 £5,037. Lunch included.

Breakfast Club (7.45 am until the start of school day) £5.40 per session, After School Care (until 6.00 pm) £14.35 per session

Extras: Private Lessons: Singing, Pianoforte, Violin, Cello, Oboe, Clarinet, Flute, Recorder, Brass, LAMDA, £220 per term. Shared Lessons: Ballet £72.00 per term.

The Granville School was founded on VE Day, 8th May 1945, with the Dove of Peace and Churchill's victory sign chosen to form the school crest.

The Granville is an exceptional school which combines the very best of a Prep school tradition with a vibrant, forward-looking outlook where change is embraced and innovation celebrated. Girls aged three to eleven, and boys aged three to four, thrive on individual attention and achieve their best in a happy, secure and stimulating environment. Our highly-qualified, specialist teachers make learning enjoyable, develop inquiring minds and raise levels of expectation.

The school maintains Christian principles and traditional values within a broad and stimulating curriculum. The Granville has a strong record of academic achievement and children are prepared for 11+ entry into independent schools and state grammar schools. Granville pupils excel in music, art, drama and sport. There is a wide range of extra-curricular activities available for all age groups.

The school is set in five acres of garden and woodland close to Sevenoaks Station. The original house and new buildings enable pupils to enjoy a high-quality learning environment with light and airy classrooms. The Granville has its own indoor heated Swimming Pool, a Sports Hall, Science Lab, Studio for Music and Drama, French room, ICT Suite, individual teaching rooms and Junior and Senior Libraries. A new building, opened in January 2014, provides high-quality Early Years facilities together with a large Art and DT room. Outside facilities include three netball/tennis courts, sports/playing field, junior activity playgrounds and a woodland classroom. Plans are under way to further develop the Hall, Computing Suite and Performing Arts Studio.

Means-tested bursaries are available on request.

Charitable status. The Ena Makin Educational Trust Limited is a Registered Charity, number 307931. Its aim is to run any school as an educational charity for the promotion of education generally.

Great Ballard

Eartham, Chichester, West Sussex PO18 0LR

Tel:	01243 814236
Fax:	01243 814586
email:	office@greatballard.co.uk
website:	www.greatballard.co.uk
Twitter:	@GreatBallard
Facebook:	@GreatBallardSchool

Headmaster: **Mr Richard Evans**, BEd Hons, Adv Dip Ed Mgt, IAPS

Age Range. 2–13 co-educational.

Number of Children. 125: 53 Boys, 72 Girls (including 43 in Pre-Prep and approximately 35 flexi boarders).

Fees per term (2018–2019). Day: Prep School £4,630–£5,310, Pre-Prep £2,860–£3,220. Boarding: Weekly (4 nights) £5,670, Full (7 nights) £8,220–£8,840. Nursery:

£35.50–£37.50 (morning only), £40.50–£42.50 (morning or afternoon with lunch), £52.00–£56.50 (all day, including lunch). Boarding fee discounts for HM Forces. The school offers a limited number of Scholarships for children with exceptional abilities. These awards can be supplemented by a means-tested bursary.

The school is located in 30 acres of wonderful countryside in the South Downs National Park between Chichester and Arundel. The school itself is based around a stunning eighteenth century house surrounded by glorious woodlands which are a feature of the impressive school grounds, which the children are allowed to explore and where they love to build dens in the woods.

Children are prepared for Senior School entrance exams, as well as for 13+ Common Entrance and Scholarship examinations to a wide range of Independent Senior Schools. The emphasis is on providing children with numerous opportunities to identify their talents and ensure that they all achieve their potential both inside and out of the classroom. The average number of children in a teaching group in the prep school is 12. A small number of International Students are welcomed who benefit from the family-centred community and are able to enjoy their first overseas boarding experience in a small, friendly, family atmosphere.

Outdoor activities include: Soccer, Rugby, Hockey, Cricket, Netball, Rounders, Tennis, Athletics, Swimming, Golf, Mountain Biking, Trampolining, Volleyball and Forest School. In addition, there is a growing outdoor education and country pursuits programme.

Facilities include: multi-purpose gym and hall, libraries, a computerised science laboratory, dance/drama studio, indoor heated pool, extensive sports fields, tennis courts, cricket nets and an astro practice area. In addition, there is a fantastic Forest School. ICT facilities have recently been upgraded and a brand new ICT suite is now in use. Tablet computers are also increasingly used throughout the school. A wide range of extra-curricular clubs are enjoyed which give all children the opportunity to experience a wide variety of activities. There are also visits to France for intensive language studies as well as exciting outdoor education residential trips for most year groups in the Prep school.

Children showing real potential in Art, Drama or Music are able to take advantage of excellence classes, a range of instruments are taught and with choirs and various ensemble groups, many children participate in festivals, sit musical exams and enjoy performing in concerts.

Drama is a timetabled subject and every child appears in a form and school play at some time during the year. LAMDA classes are also offered. Cookery is also on the timetable as well as a popular after-school activity.

Art is a significant strength of the school; many children build up quality portfolios to take to their next school and scholarships are won regularly. The constantly changing displays throughout the school show both the quality of work and the children's enthusiasm for Art.

The Pre-Prep Department, for children aged 2–7, is housed in a walled garden area with plenty of space for play activities. The curriculum is delivered by well-qualified, enthusiastic form teachers with extra input from Prep School specialists in PE, music, swimming and drama. The school also offers a Holiday Club for Pre-Prep children which operates during school holidays. Little Ballard Nursery is very much a part of the whole school – children have full access to the whole school grounds and are able to take part in swimming, Forest School and specialist music lessons. They are involved in school events such as sports day, harvest festival and Christmas celebrations.

The 'after-hours' club, for children from nursery age upwards, enables parents to work a full day. This involves both a breakfast club from 7.45 am and after-school supervision to 6.00 pm.

Boarding remains popular and many children take advantage of the very flexible arrangements the school offers. Boarding facilities are in the Grade II listed House in small, cosy dormitories. The Headmaster and his family together with other members of staff live in the House, giving the boarding community a homely feel.

The happiness and safety of our children remain priorities. This is supported by the ISI Inspection report that states that "*the quality of relationships between the pupils and staff is outstanding*".

Great Ballard is a traditional, but forward-looking school where proven values and high standards and expectations of behaviour are the norm; it is undoubtedly a hidden gem and well worth a visit!

Great Walstead School

East Mascalls Lane, Lindfield, Haywards Heath, West Sussex RH16 2QL

Tel: 01444 483528
email: GWmail@greatwalstead.co.uk
website: www.greatwalstead.co.uk
Twitter: @greatwalstead

Chairman of the Board of Governors: M Searle

Headmaster: C B Calvey, BEd Hons

Deputy Head: J Sutherland, BEd

Director of Studies: Emma Scotland, BMus Hons, PGCE, NPQSL

Age Range. 2½–13.

Number of Pupils. 387: Main School 262; Pre-Prep 70; Nursery and Reception (EYFS) 55.

Fees per term (2018–2019). Tuition: Nursery £423 per day (inc EYFE), Reception £2,685; Pre-Prep £3,220–£3,750, Main School £4,750–£5,170.

Founded in 1925 by Mr R J Mowll in Enfield, the school moved to its present location in the heart of Sussex two years later. Staff and pupils came to a large country house set in over 260 acres of fields and woodland, where children could learn and play in unspoiled surroundings.

From these beginnings, Great Walstead has developed into a thriving co-educational prep school, catering for children from 2½ to 13 years of age. It is a school which values children as individuals and regards it as vital that each child develops his or her potential – academically, creatively, socially and spiritually. Above all, the school is built on the strong values of Christian Faith, Success, Communication, Environment and Dedication, creating an essential foundation for the whole of a pupil's education and life.

The Early Years Foundation Stage incorporates Nursery and Reception classes, welcoming children from the age of 2½ until it is time to enter the Pre-Prep at 5. It provides a full, rich and varied Early Years education, laying firm foundations in basic skills and understanding for future learning. They share a dedicated outdoor learning and play space with a giant covered sandpit, mud kitchen and music area.

The Pre-Prep covers the ages from 5 to 7 within its own section of the school. It has its own library, ICT suite and play area. The aim here is to ensure that the foundation skills of reading, writing and maths are taught while, at the same time, teachers add a breadth of interest through specialist lead classes in French, computer skills, PE and Music.

Children enter the Junior School at 7. For the next two years they will have a class teacher who supervises them closely for a good proportion of the day, but have specialist teachers for French, Music, ICT, Art, Craft, Design & Technology, Sport and PE. They have games or outdoor activities each day and gradually learn to become more independent.

Children in the senior age group, from 9 to 13 years of age, are taught by graduate specialist teachers in preparation for the Common Entrance examination and senior school scholarships at 13. In the past ten years, Great Walstead pupils have won over 200 scholarships or awards to senior schools and in the last four years over 50% of pupils gained such success. Facilities in the Senior School include two computer rooms with 21 linked PCs, a well-equipped science laboratory, and a fine Library.

The 269 acres of farmland, playing fields and woodland make many outdoor activities possible. The woods host learning activities in Eco-School and Forest School and fun exercises in camp-building, as well as teddy bear picnics for the younger children. In the summer, the older children camp out overnight. In addition, the purpose-built challenge course gives enormous pleasure all year round for all ages.

The Art, Craft and Design Technology department is housed in old farm buildings, which have been adapted to make workshops and studios; the lessons form an integral part of the curriculum for all children. New in 2016, the Great Walstead Farm is a wonderful addition to the curriculum, providing insight and hands-on experience of both horticultural and agricultural farming methods.

The school's extensive grounds allow a wide range of major sports. Swimming is possible all year round in our own heated pool. We have a superbly equipped sports hall and facilities including a wonderful new AstroTurf. Match Day on Wednesdays is a central weekly event with emphasis on sportsmanship, healthy competition and sport for all. All children (Years 3–8) have the opportunity to be involved in competitive sport at least once per season. Those children not involved in match fixtures on a particular week are able to access a carousel of indoor and outdoor activities, including: cookery, pottery, archery, art, ICT, woods games, gardening and a variety of sports.

The school has a Learning Development department where specialist staff are able to give the extra support required. The department helps children with all their learning needs whether helping with a specific difficulty or extending those children who are gifted and talented.

Music has long been a strength at Great Walstead, with a high proportion of the children learning instruments and playing in groups, bands and orchestras. Singing is encouraged from Nursery upwards. Drama is also an important part of the Arts here. All children are given the opportunity to act, with both major productions and form performances.

Matron, the school nurse, tends to the health of the children in the whole school. The school, through the Keep and Wrap Around Care, provides flexible holiday, pre- and after-school care, as well as other holiday activities to meet the needs of today's parents.

Parents are always made most welcome at the school. There is a thriving parents' organisation called FOGWA (Friends of Great Walstead Association) which provides a number of successful social events and raises substantial sums for the benefit of the school.

Academic, Music and Sports Awards are offered at 9+, and Academic, All-Rounder, Art, Drama, Music, Performing Arts and Sport Scholarships at 11+.

Charitable status. Great Walstead School is a Registered Charity, number 307002. It exists to provide a good education on Christian foundations.

Greenfield

Brooklyn Road, Woking, Surrey GU22 7TP

Tel: 01483 772525
email: schooloffice@greenfield.surrey.sch.uk
website: www.greenfield.surrey.sch.uk

Chairman of Governors: Mrs Janet Day

Headteacher: **Mrs Tania Botting**, BEd, MEd

Age Range. Rising 3 to 11 years.
Number of Pupils. 83 day girls, 116 day boys.
Fees per term (2018–2019). £1,921–£4,495.

Greenfield is a non-selective co-educational school for children aged from rising 3 to 11 years. We aim to offer every possible opportunity for children to reach their full potential and recognise that all children have talents and strengths in many different areas. We are proud of our academic and non-academic successes and have a strong track record of achieving scholarships to a wide range of senior schools for music, art, sport, and academic excellence.

At Greenfield we believe that a happy child will learn. Therefore, we provide a secure and caring environment working closely with our parents, to enable the children to develop their confidence and self-esteem and prepare them for the next stage of their education and future.

We attach importance to traditional values, promoting courtesy, respect, tolerance, empathy, humility and consideration for others.

Greenfield has high standards but we also appreciate the need to strike a happy balance between work and play and the formal and informal. There is an excellent ratio of adults to children throughout the school enabling children to receive individual attention and children are often taught in small groups. Visitors are welcome to visit the school at any time and appointments can be made by calling the school office. To request a copy of the prospectus, please visit the school website or call the school office.

Charitable status. Greenfield is a Registered Charity, number 295145. It aims to offer an excellent all-round education to children of all abilities.

Gresham's Prep School

Holt, Norfolk NR25 6EY

Tel: 01263 714600
            01263 714575 (Nursery and Pre-Prep School)
Fax: 01263 714060
email: prep@greshams.com
website: www.greshams.com
Twitter: @Greshams_School
Facebook: @greshamsschool

Chairman of Governors: Mr M Goff

Acting Head: **Mrs C Braithwaite**, BA Ed Hons, QTS

(*For a full list of governors and Heads of Departments, please refer to Gresham's Senior School entry in the HMC section.*)

Age Range. 2–13.
Number of Pupils. 325 (including Nursery & Pre-Prep).
Fees per term (2018–2019). Boarders (from Year 3) £8,450, Day £6,030, Day (Years 3 and 4) £4,890. Pre-Prep School: £3,350–£3,590.

Gresham's Prep School is part of the family of Gresham's Schools, which is located in the busy market town of Holt in a beautiful and tranquil part of north Norfolk. Some pupils enter the school from the Nursery and Pre-Prep School, which is based in the Georgian town of Holt, a quarter of a mile from the Prep School, but many others enter the school from elsewhere. Most pupils move on to Gresham's Senior School, but the school has a very good record of winning scholarships and gaining entry to other major Independent Schools.

The school has excellent facilities including extensive playing fields, an Art and Technology Centre, a drama hall, a modern and well-equipped Music School and science labs. Use of the Auden Theatre, Chapel, astro pitches, swimming pool, sports hall and the recently opened Outdoor Activity Centre and other excellent sports facilities are shared with the Senior School.

Boarders stay in modern, comfortable boarding houses; Crossways House (girls) or Kenwyn House (boys). Flexible boarding is available and is extremely popular.

The school prides itself on the breadth of its curriculum. Sport, Performing Arts and Drama and Music play an important part in the lives of all pupils. The school has built up a considerable reputation in these areas in recent years. There is a wide range of extra-curricular activities available in the evenings, which changes on a termly basis.

Above all, the school wants children to enjoy the process of growing up and developing their talents to the full and to establish the strong roots that will help them become self-assured and well-balanced adults.

Entry Requirements. Entry is by assessment in Mathematics and English and a reference from the child's previous school. Entry is possible into all year groups.

Scholarships are available for entry into Year 7. Art, Drama and Performing Arts, Music and Sport are worth up to 10% of the fees. Academic Scholarships are worth up to 50% of the fees. Britten Instrumental and Vocal, Organ and Instrumental Scholarships are also available. All scholarships may be supplemented by a means-tested bursary.

Nursery and Pre-Prep School. Co-educational, age 2–7 years, day pupils only.

Headmistress: Mrs S Hollingsworth.

The Nursery and Pre-Prep School is housed in the beautiful setting of Old School House within the town of Holt and within walking distance of the Prep School. It is a vibrant and dynamic school which works to create an environment where happy, relaxed, calm, courteous and curious children can flourish and be their best. Children benefit from a broad and balanced curriculum, which also includes specialist teaching in music, drama, languages, ICT and sport within the school day.

Charitable status. Gresham's School is a Registered Charity, number 1105500. It exists for the purpose of educating children.

Grimsdell
Mill Hill Pre-Preparatory School

Winterstoke House, Wills Grove, Mill Hill, London NW7 1QR

Tel: 020 8959 6884
Fax: 020 8959 4626
email: office@grimsdell.org.uk
website: www.millhill.org.uk/grimsdell

Co-educational Pre-Preparatory Day School.

Chairman of Court of Governors: Dr Amanda Craig, MBBS, DRCOG

Head: **Mrs Kate Simon**, BA Hons, PGCE

Senior Deputy Head: Mrs Jenny Ticehurst, BEd Hons
Assistant Head Teaching & Learning: Miss Yuka Matsushita, BA Hons, QTS
Assistant Head Early Years: Mrs Emily Jenner, BA Hons, PGCE

Age Range. 3–7 Co-educational.
Number of pupils. 96 Boys, 92 Girls
Fees per term (2018–2019). £4,965 (full day), Nursery: £2,692 (mornings only), £2,284 (afternoons only).

Grimsdell, Mill Hill Pre-Prep is situated in the Green Belt on the boarders of Hertfordshire and Middlesex and just ten miles from Central London. A part of the Mill Hill School Foundation which is set in 160 acres of beautiful grounds, we make extensive use of the outdoors in all subject areas and 'Forest School' has a firm place within our curriculum. We provide a happy, secure and rich learning environment for boys and girls aged 3 to 7. Belmont, Mill Hill Preparatory School, is less than a quarter of a mile away and educates pupils from age 7 to 13, the majority of whom move on to the senior school, Mill Hill, which educates boys and girls from age 13 to 18.

We pride ourselves on the exciting and creative curriculum we offer. The children who come here are inspired to learn whilst being encouraged to explore and enjoy their childhood. The boys and girls at Grimsdell learn through hands-on experience. With the support and guidance of professional, caring staff and excellent resources and equipment, each child is encouraged to reach their full potential. Our approach combines traditional skills of reading, writing and mathematics with the breadth and balance offered by an enhanced Early Years Foundation Stage and KS1 Curriculum. Every pupil can enjoy many opportunities offered by learning through Science, Technology and Computing, Art, Drama, Music, PE and French lessons.

The school is housed in a large Victorian building with its own secure play areas and adventure playgrounds, taking advantage of further facilities on the Mill Hill site including a Forest School area, sports fields, swimming pool and theatre.

The usual age of entry is at 3 and 4 years old, but 5 and 6 year olds are considered as vacancies occur. It is expected that most children will pass to Belmont at the end of Year 2.

Charitable status. The Mill Hill School Foundation is a Registered Charity, number 1064758. It exists to provide education for boys and girls.

Guildford High School – Junior School
United Learning

London Road, Guildford, Surrey GU1 1SJ
Tel: 01483 561440
email: guildford-admissions@guildfordhigh.co.uk
website: www.guildfordhigh.co.uk
Twitter: @guildfordhigh
Facebook: @GuildfordHigh

Chairman of Local Governing Body: Mr D Perrett

Head of Junior School: **Mr Michael D Gibb**, BA Hons London

Deputy Head of Junior School: Mr Toby W Day, BA Hons Southampton

Age Range. Girls 4–11.
Number of Pupils. 285.
Fees per term (2018–2019). Reception, Years 1 and 2 £3,528, Years 3–6 £4,581.

Awarded the 'Sunday Times Independent Prep School of the Year 2015–16', and the 'Best School for Pastoral Care in The Week Magazine 2018', the Junior School at Guildford High School is situated on the same site as the Senior School. It is a modern, bright, self-contained school with the third floor especially dedicated to art, music, science, IT and the Library.

The girls normally start in the Reception classes (4 years) or at Year 3 (7 years), however, they are welcome in any year group depending on spaces available, and work their way through the Junior School with natural progression on to the Senior School at Year 7 (11 years).

The breadth and depth of the curriculum encompasses 15 fast paced subjects, with an embedded thinking skills programme. Three modern foreign languages are included, with Spanish starting in Year 1 for the five year olds. Music, drama and sport play an important part in the curricular and co-curricular programmes. Specialist teachers and resources are employed throughout the Junior School. Parents and teachers work closely together to ensure excellent differentiation and a nurturing environment with strong pastoral care.

Guildford High School Junior School girls are confident, happy and well-prepared for entry to the Senior School. (*See Guildford High School Senior School entry in HMC section.*)

Charitable status. Guildford High School Junior School is part of United Learning which comprises: UCST (a Company Limited by Guarantee, Registered in England, number 2780748, and a Registered Charity, number 1016538) and ULT (a Company Limited by Guarantee, Registered in England, number 4439859, and an Exempt Charity).

The Haberdashers' Aske's Boys' Preparatory & Pre-Preparatory School

Butterfly Lane, Elstree, Hertfordshire WD6 3AF
Tel: 020 8266 1779
email: prepoffice@habsboys.org.uk
website: www.habsboys.org.uk
Twitter: @habsboys
Facebook: @habsboys

Chairman of The Aske Board: Mr S Cartmell, OBE
Chairman of Governors: Mrs M Chaundler, OBE

Headmaster: Mr A R Lock, MA

Head of Preparatory School: **Mr M E Rossetti**, MA

Head of Pre-Preparatory School: Mrs V Peck, BSc

Deputy Head: Mr J Evans, MA
Deputy Head Pastoral: Mrs C Griggs, DSD Cert Ed Dramatic Studies
Senior Teacher: Mrs H Pullen, BEd

Age Range. Prep 7–11; Pre-Prep 5–7.

Number of Boys. Prep 219, Pre-Prep 72.

Fees per term (2018–2019). Pre-Prep £5,113 (including lunch); Prep £6,782.

The Preparatory School at Habs has been the top-performing independent boys' school in the country. It is vibrant with the energy and curiosity of over 200 boys aged 7–11 from a wide range of local schools and communities. It is a very special place to work and play.

It is housed in a purpose-designed building, opened by HRH The Princess Margaret, Citizen and Haberdasher, in 1983, on the same campus as the Senior School. The bright, cheerful classrooms provide a welcoming and stimulating environment. The Prep enjoys a unique mix of family atmosphere and close links with the Senior School. The boys are able to share the wonderful facilities and grounds of the Senior School, including the Sports Centre, the heated indoor Swimming Pool, the Music School and the Dining Room. The Pre-Prep School is located six miles north of the school at How Wood, near St Albans.

The Prep building has completed an extensive refurbishment. This includes a brand new library and state-of-the-art teaching facilities.

The relationship between the Preparatory staff and their forms is close and friendly, within a context of firm discipline. In this environment, brimming with opportunities, the school ensures an education of breadth and depth extending well beyond national guidelines.

Sport and games play a major role in the boys' week, offering fitness and fun to all. Indeed, the sporting ethos of team spirit and fair play underpins the whole structure of Prep School life.

The arts spring to life in a wealth of musical, dramatic and artistic activity, guided by specialists whose passion for their subject is matched by the enthusiasm of their pupils.

Every boy is a musician for at least one year when he studies an orchestral instrument of his choice, free of charge, through the Music Scheme; many of these fledgling musicians eventually make their way into the Senior School's First Orchestra.

There are many clubs and societies; however boys with some special interest often start their own, supported by staff, and eagerly attended by those of like mind. Some boys also stay on to enjoy extra play time with their friends or to do their homework and to have tea. The After School Care Facility is equipped with bean bags, games and sports equipment.

Boys are admitted each September after assessments to the Pre-Prep at the age of 5+ and to the Prep at 7+. Boys are expected to move into the Senior School at 11. Most boys will flourish in the Senior School as they have in the Prep, and the transition is made as natural as possible. A qualifying examination assures candidates that the Senior School is right for them and they are given help preparing for the different pace and rhythms they will find there. (*For further details, please see entry in HMC section.*)

Charitable status. The Haberdashers' Aske's Charity is a Registered Charity, number 313996. It exists to promote education.

Chairman of Governors: Anthony Fobel, Esq

Headmaster: **C Godwin**, BSc, MA

Age Range. 4–13.

Number of Pupils. 460 Day Boys.

Fees per term (2018–2019). £6,265–£6,455 (inclusive of lunch).

Founded in 1889, the school is on three sites within close proximity. The majority of boys join Reception or Year 1 at the age of 4 or 5, but a few places are occasionally available in later years. The average class size is 18.

The school's buildings are spacious and well-appointed, and resources are good. There has been considerable investment over the last ten years in the school's fabric and facilities, and there is a continuing programme of improvements planned, including a well-advanced programme of ICT development. The Junior School (Years 1–3) is undergoing a programme of continuous refurbishment and provides up-to-date computing, science and music facilities. The Senior School boasts a modern library, spacious music, DT, pottery, computing facilities and changing rooms. Boys in the Junior School use the sports hall, located in the Senior School, and have lunch in the dining hall which serves the whole school.

From the Junior School, boys transfer to the Middle School for Years 4 and 5. During that time they make the transition from classroom based teaching to subject based teaching. Boys are taught by subject specialists from Year 5.

The Hall prides itself on the breadth of education it offers. Senior School boys study Life Skills, Art, Drama, Music, Pottery, ICT, Design Technology and Current Affairs within the timetable and there is a broad range of after-school activities. Music and Drama are considerable strengths within the school. Team games, soccer, rugby and cricket are played mainly at the Wilf Slack Memorial Ground, and in recent years fencing and skiing have developed as sporting strengths. A major development of the Wilf Slack Playing Fields includes two all–weather surfaces, upgraded pitches and a well-appointed pavilion to provide a high-quality facility. Hockey, squash, athletics, golf and other sports are also offered.

The school is not linked with any particular senior school. Two-thirds of the boys proceed to London day schools, such as Westminster, St Paul's, Highgate, City of London and UCS, and others proceed to leading boarding schools such as Eton, Harrow, Winchester and Tonbridge. In recent years numerous academic scholarships have been won at these and other schools. Other awards have been won in areas such as music and sport.

Means-tested bursaries are available at 8+ and a number of boys apply at these entry points from London primary schools.

The school was last inspected in 2016 and the report may be found on the school's website.

Charitable status. The Hall School Charitable Trust is a Registered Charity, number 312722. It exists entirely for the purposes of education.

The Hall

23 Crossfield Road, Hampstead, London NW3 4NU

Tel:	020 7722 1700
Fax:	020 7483 0181
email:	office@hallschool.co.uk
website:	www.hallschool.co.uk
Twitter:	@the_hallschool

Hall Grove

London Road, Bagshot, Surrey GU19 5HZ

Tel:	01276 473059
Fax:	01276 452003
email:	office@hallgrove.co.uk
website:	www.hallgrove.co.uk

Twitter: @hallgroveschool
Facebook: @hallgroveschool

Headmaster: **A R Graham**, BSc, PGCE

Age Range. 3–13.
Number of Children. Pre-Preparatory (age 4–7) 129. Preparatory (age 7–13) 321.
Fees per term (2018–2019). Day fees: Pre-School (mornings) £1,950, Reception–Year 2 £3,600, Lower Juniors (Years 3 & 4) £4,300, Upper Juniors (Years 5 & 6) £4,600, Seniors (Years 7 & 8) £4,900. Weekly Boarding: £1,325 supplement per term. Pre-Paid Flexi Boarding: £30 per night. Casual boarding: £40 per night. Sibling discount.

Hall Grove is a happy, vibrant school of over 445 boys and girls aged 3–13 with a separate pre-school in its grounds for those aged 3 and 4. Weekly/Flexi boarding is offered for up to 12 pupils. The main entry ages are 3, 4, 7 and 11.

The school was founded in 1957 by the parents of the current Headmaster. At its centre is a most attractive Georgian house set in beautiful gardens and parkland. Recent additions have provided some modern rooms and specialist teaching areas, an impressive computer facility and new classroom blocks. Despite this building programme, the character and atmosphere of a family home has been retained.

The academic standards are high and there is a very strong emphasis on Sport and Music. A wide range of activities flourish; woodwork, ceramics, food technology, drama and a host of major and minor sports including soccer, rugby, hockey, netball, rounders, cricket, tennis, athletics, swimming, golf, judo, basketball, badminton and dance. Riding and stable management is an added attraction.

Optional 'Half Boarding' extends the school day to 8.00 pm for Years 6, 7 and 8. Some may stay overnight on a regular basis. There is also provision for after-school care and a full programme of evening activities.

Hall Grove has its own residential field study centre situated on the South Devon coast called Battisborough House and there are many field trips and expeditions both in Devon and overseas. Battisborough is available for hire by other schools and can accommodate up to 60 in comfort.

Hallfield School

Church Road, Edgbaston, Birmingham B15 3SJ

Tel: 0121 454 1496
Fax: 0121 454 9182
email: office@hallfieldschool.co.uk
website: www.hallfieldschool.co.uk
Twitter: @HallfieldSchool
Facebook: @HallfieldSchool
LinkedIn: /hallfield-school

Governing Body: The Hallfield School Trust

Chairman of Governors: K Uff, MA, BCL of Gray's Inn, Barrister

Head Master: **Mr Keith Morrow**

Age Range. 3 months to 11 years.
Number of Pupils. 570 Day Boys and Girls.
Fees per term (2018–2019). Pre-Prep: Transition £3,264 (5 days per week), Foundation to Year 2 £3,650; Prep School: £4,340 (Years 3–6). Lunches are included in the fees.

Since 1879, Hallfield School has offered an exceptional education for boys (and since 1995, boys and girls) which

makes it the leading preparatory school in the Midlands and possibly the country. It is now a flourishing and highly successful co-educational day school.

However, the success of a school should not be judged simply on academic results. To the contrary, the School has always nurtured a strong 'hidden curriculum' which cannot be measured by league tables – where courtesy, manners, self-discipline and respect are valued and reinforced. It is this strong hidden curriculum which underpins everything that takes place at the School: 'happy children are successful children'.

The School's aims are clear and concise:

- To provide a happy, secure and purposeful environment based on Christian principles, whilst welcoming children of all faiths to the School.

- To develop each child's full potential in academic, social, emotional, cultural and sporting areas.

In 2016–2017 a record number (37) scholarships were awarded to the leading Independent Schools in the Midlands and 83% of Leavers were successfully offered places at selective Local Authority Grammar Schools.

However, Hallfield is more than just successful results at 11+ Examinations. We have top-class athletes across the board and this year, one of our leading chess players became a national champion, winning the Under 9 tournament in the British Chess Championships.

Also, the Young Shakespeare Company joins us every year for a week during the summer term working with Year 6 children to produce an exceptional interpretation of one of Shakespeare's classic plays, most recently "A Midsummer Night's Dream".

There is something for everyone at Hallfield, but high standards are expected in everything the children take part in. Excellence and success are celebrated at every opportunity through Year group or School assemblies and, of course, the end of year School Prize Giving.

Hallfield strives for children to become happy, confident, independent learners and prepares them for their secondary education in an ever-changing world.

Charitable status. Hallfield School Trust is a Registered Charity, number 528956. It exists for the purpose of providing education for children.

Halstead Preparatory School for Girls

Woodham Rise, Woking, Surrey GU21 4EE

Tel: 01483 772682
email: registrar@halstead-school.org.uk
website: www.halstead-school.org.uk

Chairman of Governors: Mr J Olsen

Headmistress: **Mrs P A Austin**, BA Hons London, LTCL Trinity College of Music, PGCE, NPQH

Age Range. 2–11 years
Number of Pupils. 220 Girls.
Fees per term (2018–2019). Nursery (flexible) from £924; Reception (Kindergarten) £3,600; Year 1 £3,800; Year 2 £3,850; Years 3 and 4 £4,650; Years 5 and 6 £4,800.

Girls thrive in the calm, purposeful and happy atmosphere at Halstead with a good balance of study and fun and the opportunities to establish friends and many happy memories.

Halstead is delighted to have been recognised as 'excellent' in every aspect by the Independent Schools Inspectorate.

"The school meets its aims very successfully, providing a comfortable and homely environment where pupils are well known, treated as individuals and gain the confidence to thrive and fulfil their potential. From the Early Years Foundation Stage onwards, they achieve highly both in their academic work and in their activities outside the classroom, and have a great appetite for learning. This is thanks to the relevant and interesting curriculum and enthusiasm and expertise of teachers."

"Relationships throughout the school are excellent, and both pupils and their parents say it feels like a happy family."

"The school has a strong track record of success in entrance exams for prestigious local schools. Almost all pupils consistently gain places at their first choice of (senior) schools, with a considerable number being awarded scholarships."

Established in 1927 Halstead is situated in a leafy part of residential Woking. The main school building is a large Edwardian house to which modern facilities have been added including a purpose-built Food Technology, Design Technology and Art Room.

Prospective parents are very welcome to attend an Open Morning or, if more convenient, please make an appointment to meet Mrs Austin and see our happy, nurturing and secure school in action.

Charitable status. Halstead (Educational Trust) Limited is a Registered Charity, number 270525. It exists to provide a high quality all-round education for girls aged 2+–11.

Hampshire Collegiate Prep School
United Learning

Embley Park, Romsey, Hampshire SO51 6ZA

Tel: 01794 515737
email: info@hampshirecs.org.uk
website: www.hampshirecs.org.uk
Twitter: @hampshirecs
Facebook: @hampshireschool

Chairman of the Local Governing Body: Professor Richard Thomas

Headmaster: Mr Cliff Canning, BA Hons, BD Hons, HDipEd, NUI

Head of Prep School: **Mrs Sarah Phillips**, BSc, QTS

Age Range. 2–11 Co-educational.
Number of Pupils. 170 day pupils
Fees per term 2018–2019. Nursery: £2,833 (full time excluding EYE funding). Prep School: £3,366 (Reception, Years 1 and 2); £3,864 (Years 3–6). Please refer to www.hampshirecs.org.uk/admissions/fees for further details.

Hampshire Collegiate School is a welcoming community. Its core purpose is that each child is the best that they can be, equipping children with the competence to succeed academically, the confidence to be their own character and instilling in them a compassion for the world.

The school is nestled in 130 acres of private parkland, which includes woodlands, playing fields, tennis courts, astroturf pitches, a swimming pool and a golf course. It also runs a comprehensive sailing programme with its own boats moored at Lymington.

The Nightingale Nursery operates for 48 weeks of the year, offering an exciting introduction to learning to ensure that each child will love going to school. From the early years, children are encouraged to be resilient in their approach and take responsibility for their learning adventures. They leave the nursery with a calm confidence and independence; the perfect learning foundation.

A broad curriculum is offered, including French, Music, Information Technology, Design Technology and Physical Education taught by specialists and throughout the school the children take part in Learning Outside the Classroom (LOC). This is part of the curriculum and introduces the children to learning experiences that engage them in finding out more about their environment, making use of the school orchards, allotments, an outdoor classroom and an amphitheatre, all within the school's 130-acre private parkland estate.

There is a strong tradition of musical achievement in the school with many children taking individual music lessons in a wide variety of instruments. They also have the opportunity to participate in the school choir or orchestra. Hampshire Collegiate Prep School also offers a choral scholarship in association with Romsey Abbey.

Children compete in a wide range of sports within curriculum time and as part of the busy House and fixture programme. Drama is promoted via its inclusion within the weekly timetable for all children, annual LAMDA preparation and regular productions. Each year the school's 10 and 11 year-olds undertake residential visits. Year 5 experience geographical studies and outdoor pursuits on the Isle of Wight, whilst Year 6 travel to a Normandy château.

The Hampshire School, Chelsea

Pre-Preparatory and Preparatory:
15 Manresa Road, London SW3 6NB
Tel: 020 7352 7077

Early Years:
5 Wetherby Place, London SW7 4NX
Tel: 020 7370 7081

email: info@thehampshireschoolchelsea.co.uk
website: www.thehampshireschoolchelsea.co.uk

Head: **Dr Pamela Edmonds**, EdD, MEd, BEd Hons

Age Range. 3–13.
Number in School. Day: 150 Boys, 150 Girls.
Fees per term (2018–2019). £4,370–£6,285.
Founded in 1944 and located in the London Borough of Kensington and Chelsea, just a stone's throw from the King's Road, The Hampshire School, Chelsea provides the top-class education one would expect from a traditional British preparatory school, combined with a caring approach and family feel. An independent, interdenominational day school, we cater for boys and girls between the ages of rising 3 and 13. Through personal attention from their dedicated staff and a stimulating curriculum, The Hampshire School ensures that learning is fun and that every child feels confident and valued.

In January 2009, the Pre-Preparatory and Preparatory sections made a successful move to a spacious and beautiful new site in Chelsea's old Public Library at 15 Manresa Road, London SW3. The Early Years children are based in a recently renovated Victorian town house on Wetherby Place. The children are provided with the 'home away from home' secure and nurturing environment they need at this tender young age. The EYFS curriculum is followed, with the school putting emphasis on the children becoming happy, confident and polite learners who are engaged and enthusiastic in their education.

A broad-based and balanced curriculum is provided by experienced and passionate staff. Children are given every opportunity to develop individual talents as fully as possible; a wide range of academic subjects being supported by a high level of instruction in music, art, physical education as well as the core subjects. Children are encouraged to study the history and development of their environment and culture by means of regular visit to museums, art galleries, exhibitions and places of interest.

The main school's excellent facilities include a galleried library, gymnasium, science laboratory, art and design studio, fully equipped stage, and garden.

There are a wide range of extracurricular activities offered, from judo, gymnastics, fencing and dancing to art, languages and music, as well as many in between, such as media, radio station, ukulele and cross stitch.

The school has been successful in preparing pupils for examination and scholarship entry into leading day and boarding senior independent schools. Great emphasis is placed on developing each child's individual talents. Children excel academically at The Hampshire School, Chelsea. In recent years, pupils successfully navigate the 11+ or 13+ Common Entrance Examinations to gain entry to their first-choice schools including City of London, Dulwich College, Westminster, Stowe, Ibstock Place and Latymer, to name a few.

Hampton Pre-Prep & Prep School

Gloucester Road, Hampton, Middlesex TW12 2UQ

Tel: 020 8979 1844
email: admissions@hamptonprep.org.uk
website: hamptonprep.org.uk
Twitter: @Hampton_Prep

Chairman of Governors: J S Perry, BA

Headmaster: **Mr Tim Smith**, BA, NZ Dip Tchg, MBA

Age Range. Boys 3–11, Girls 3–7.
Number of Pupils. 224.
Fees per term (2018–2019). Kindergarten (3–4 years): £2,010 (mornings), £4,020 (all day). Pre-Prep (4–7 years): £4,255. Prep (7–11 years): £4,645 including lunch for full day pupils.

The Prep School moved into its new state-of-the-art building in March 2016. The School is situated in a quiet, leafy part of Hampton and is easily accessible by road and rail. The School merged with Hampton School in September 1999. Both schools are served by the same Board of Governors and the Headmaster of Hampton Prep reports to the Headmaster of Hampton School. The amalgamation produces economies of scale from which Hampton Prep benefits. Boys transfer to senior schools at 11+.

Although there is no expectation for pupils to select Hampton as their first-choice secondary school, approximately 50% of our boys transfer there each year. Since September 2004 Hampton has been offering Assured Places for 11+ entry. These can be gained from Year 2 through to the end of Year 5 via an ongoing programme of assessment of the boys. In addition, those boys who perform very well in the 11+ Hampton entrance examinations, but who do not gain an award from Hampton, will be considered for the W D James Award made by Hampton Prep, which will be in the form of a reduction in the child's first term's fees at Hampton.

The Pre-Prep is housed on its own site in the homely atmosphere of two linked residential houses offering space and security. Rooms are well-appointed and there is one class per year group of 22 pupils. The Prep School is two-form entry with 18 pupils per class. The Preparatory School, which backs onto an attractive public park, has undergone significant redevelopment, the old buildings have been demolished and the remainder of the site re-landscaped. The new facilities have played a large part in the transformation of the School, its academic life included. Major school sports are Football, Rugby and Cricket. An extensive programme of co-curricular activities includes: art club, chess, drama, judo, yoga, computing, Warhammer/Lego and a variety of minor sports. There is a School choir, an orchestra, and a flourishing tradition of drama. Individual music tuition is also provided.

Parents share in the life of the School as fully as possible and there exists a very active Parents' Association.

Please contact the School Office for a prospectus.

Charitable status. Hampton Pre-Prep & Prep School is part of the Hampton School Trust, which is a Registered Charity, number 1120005. It exists to provide a school in Hampton.

Handcross Park School

London Road, Handcross, West Sussex RH17 6HF

Tel: 01444 400526
email: info@handxpark.com
website: www.handcrossparkschool.co.uk
Twitter: @HandcrossPark
Facebook: @handcrosspark

Where potential is nurtured and success is celebrated in a friendly learning environment.

Chairman of Governors: M Templeman

Headmaster: **R C M Brown**, BA Hons, MA, PGCE

Head of Nursery & Pre-Prep: Mr J Gayler, BSc Hons QTS
Senior Deputy Head (Pastoral): Ms E Lyle, BSc USA, QTS UK
Deputy Head (Academic): Mr A Falkus, BSc Hons QTS

Age Range. 2–13 Co-educational.
Number of Pupils. 379: Boys 205, Girls 174.
Fees per term (2018–2019) Nursery according to number of sessions; Pre-Prep £3,230–£3,450; Prep £4,270–£6,360; Weekly boarding £5,370–£7,480; Full boarding (EU) £6,030–£8,130; Flexi boarding (2 weekday nights per term) £660; Full boarding (non-EU) £11,110–£12,670.

Handcross Park is part of the Brighton College family of schools, offering a Pre-Preparatory and Preparatory School education, set in beautiful surroundings but conveniently located just off the A23 and close to Haywards Heath, Horsham, Gatwick and Crawley. The School provides a first-class education for children from 2 to 13 in a happy family atmosphere within a caring Christian framework.

The School unashamedly takes pride in the pursuit of excellence for all its pupils. Alongside academic endeavour, staff believe ardently in educating children to become well-rounded, compassionate and articulate citizens.

The modern Nursery, situated in the Pre-Prep and accommodated in well-designed and purpose-built classrooms, offers a wonderful environment in which to begin the exciting adventure of a child's school career. Activities are specially designed to help young minds investigate and find solutions for themselves and the cleverly planned classrooms allow children the opportunity to pursue interests both inside and outdoors. With an excellent staff to pupil ratio throughout the Early Years and small class sizes right the way through the school, the emphasis is on helping the individual to flourish as part of a supportive, vibrant and happy community.

Handcross Park has a proven academic record with over half of its Year 8 pupils gaining scholarships to Brighton College and other top Senior Schools both locally and further afield. We are proud of our 100% pass rate at Common Entrance and our excellent scholarship success over the years. But as well as a deep and broad knowledge of the curriculum, pupils also develop an understanding of the role they can play in society as informed and caring citizens.

Alongside the provision of a high quality academic education for all children, the School's highly-qualified, friendly staff focus on nourishing the creative, musical and sporting aptitudes of the pupils. The School boasts an all-weather pitch, a recently refurbished, vibrant Music School, a brand new Art & Design Studio, excellent sports coaching and facilities and well-equipped Science, IT and Design Technology Rooms, pupils are offered the best opportunities to foster and showcase their talents.

The 'home away from home' accommodation at Handcross Park has been refurbished, revamped and rejuvenated resulting in growing boarding numbers and a necessary extension to the Boarding House to cater for these additional numbers. With a variety of activities to choose from the focus is on having fun in a structured environment. Flexi (2 consecutive nights), weekly (Monday–Friday) and full boarding options are available and flexible pre and after school care offered to day parents.

Handcross Park was inspected in June 2014 and in the resulting inspection report achieved top rating across every area.

Charitable status. Newells School Trust is a Registered Charity, number 307038. Handcross Park School exists to provide a high-quality education to children aged 2 to 13.

Hanford School

Child Okeford, Blandford Forum, Dorset DT11 8HN

Tel: 01258 860219
Fax: 01258 861255
email: office@hanfordschool.co.uk
website: www.hanfordschool.co.uk
Twitter: @HanfordDorset
Facebook: @HanfordSchool

Chairman of Governors: Mrs L Sunnucks

Headmaster: **Mr R Johnston**, BA

Age Range. 7–13.
Number of Girls. 100.
Fees per term (2018–2019). Boarders £7,500, Day Girls £6,250.

Hanford School, located between Blandford and Shaftesbury in Dorset, was founded in 1947 by the Revd and Mrs C B Canning. It is housed in a beautiful 17th Century Jacobean manor house set in 45 acres of land in the Stour valley. The amenities include a Chapel, Laboratories, a Computer Room, a Music School, an Art School, a Gymnasium, a Swimming Pool, a Handwork Room, two Netball/Tennis Courts (hard) and an indoor covered Riding School.

Girls arrive from the age of seven onwards and leave at 13 after taking Common Entrance. Hanford is non-selective and prides itself on bringing out the best in each and every girl. Pupils are prepared for entry to Independent Senior Schools including: Marlborough, Bryanston, St Mary's Shaftesbury and Sherborne Girls.

Hanford believes children should be children for as long as possible, climbing trees, building dens, riding ponies and playing in the garden. Giving girls free time is something Hanford has always believed in as it encourages girls to become lost in their own imagination and develop creatively. Hanford recently took the decision to switch off all 'Smart devices', iPhones, tablets etc. during term time. Unplugging the girls from social media, games and communications was not done to protect them but to encourage them to make their own fun; they will have plenty of time to use social media but a relatively short time in which to be silly, fun-loving children. The girls use their free time to play games such as British Bulldog, riding the Hanford ponies, tending the chickens, gardening or climbing trees.

Hanford teaches girls to combine having fun with working hard. A strong and committed teaching staff seeks to bring out the best in each and every girl. This combination of fun and hard work pays dividends when it comes to Common Entrance and Scholarships. There have been 21 scholarships awarded in the past three years – evidence of this successful formula. Class sizes are small, normally 10–12, and there is learning support available if required. Alongside the core curriculum girls are taught handwork, where they make their own school uniform skirt, and Art Appreciation (Art Apre) where they can begin to understand and appreciate the cultural world around them. Music has always been central to life at Hanford with almost all girls learning at least one instrument or joining one of the choirs or folk group; music composition is also offered as an activity.

Sport is also strong at Hanford. Last summer term the rounders, tennis and athletics teams were all county champions. Hanford is perhaps most famous for its ponies and stables with most girls choosing to have riding lessons and some testing their equestrian skills at local and national events including tetrathlons.

Hawkesdown House School

27 Edge Street, Kensington, London W8 7PN

Tel: 020 7727 9090
email: admin@hawkesdown.co.uk
website: www.hawkesdown.co.uk

Preparatory Day School for Boys and Girls.

Headmistress: **Mrs J A K Mackay**, BEd

Admissions Secretary: Mrs S Zazzarino

Age Range. 3–11.
Number of Pupils. 120.
Fees per term (2018–2019). £5,450 (age 3), £6,030 (age 4), £6,390 (age 5–11).

Early literacy and numeracy are of prime importance and the traditional academic subjects form the core curriculum. A balanced education helps all aspects of learning and a wide range of interests is encouraged. The School places the greatest importance on matching pupils happily and successfully to potential schools and spends time with parents ensuring that the transition is smooth and free of stress.

Sound and thorough early education is important for success and also for self-confidence. The thoughtful and inspirational teaching and care at Hawkesdown House ensure high academic standards and promote initiative, kindness and courtesy.

The School provides an excellent traditional education, with the benefits of modern technology, in a safe, happy and caring atmosphere. Many of the pupils coming to the School live within walking distance and the School is an important part of the Kensington community.

There are clear expectations and the pupils are encouraged by positive motivation and by the recognition and praise of their achievements, progress and effort. Individual attention and pastoral care for each of the pupils is of great importance.

Hawkesdown House has a fine building in Edge Street, off Kensington Church Street.

Religious Denomination: Non-denominational; Christian ethos.

Parents who would like further information or to visit the School and meet the Headmistress, should contact the School Office for a prospectus or an appointment.

The Hawthorns School

Pendell Court, Bletchingley, Surrey RH1 4QJ
Tel: 01883 743048
Fax: 01883 744256
email: admissions@hawthorns.com
website: www.hawthorns.com
Twitter: @HawthornsSchool
Facebook: @hawthornsschoolbletchingley

Chair of Governors: Mr B Dyer

Headmaster: A E Floyd, BSc, PGCE

Age Range. 2–13.
Number of Pupils. 540 Day Pupils.
Fees per term (2018–2019). From £710 (Nursery 2 mornings) to £4,960.

The Hawthorns is a co-educational day school for ages 2 to 13 where a love of learning and the development of character gives children the confidence to embrace life. Children pass on very successfully to a wide range of academically selective day and boarding senior schools. Old Hawthornians look back at their start at The Hawthorns with great loyalty and affection.

We believe that happy children learn, so instilling a lifelong love of learning and a strong sense of self-belief are the cornerstones of our curriculum. Set in a wonderful location, our education offers challenge and sets high expectations to shape our young people into engaged and articulate contributors.

The Early Years Foundation Stage Curriculum builds upon the natural curiosity evident, developing confidence, questioning and independent thinking. Curiosity about the world is fostered through diverse opportunities in and out of the classroom and through expert teaching. As children grow up, each transition from year to year is carefully managed. Special Needs and More Able Coordinators oversee the progress of every child. As children reach the top of the School they are ready for the Compass Curriculum which allows them to explore the full range of academic subjects, gain excellent knowledge and develop the learning skills that will set them up for senior school and life.

Charitable status. The Hawthorns Educational Trust Limited is a Registered Charity, number 312067. It exists to provide education for girls and boys of 2 to 13 years.

Hazelwood School

Wolfs Hill, Limpsfield, Oxted, Surrey RH8 0QU
Tel: 01883 712194
email: bursar@hazelwoodschool.com
website: www.hazelwoodschool.co.uk

Chair of Governors: Mrs Annabel Lark

Head: Mrs Lindie Louw

Deputy Head (*Academic*): Dr Carolyn Orr
Deputy Head (*Pastoral*): Mr Russell Shepherd
Assistant Head (*Lower School*): Mr James Walton
Assistant Head (*Nursery and Early Years*): Mr Howard Garlick

Age Range. 6 months–13 years Co-educational.
Number of Pupils. 570.
Fees per term (2018–2019). Day Pupils from £3,325 (Reception) to £5,300.

Founded in 1890, Hazelwood stands in superb grounds, commanding a magnificent view over the Kent and Sussex Weald.

Pupils enter at age 4 into the Pre-Prep or at 7+ to the Prep School, joining those pupils transferring from the Pre-Prep to the Prep School. Entry at other ages is possible if space permits. Hazelwood School's Nursery and Early Years, open all year round for children from 3 months to 4 years, opened in September 2009 on the Laverock site which offers unrivalled accommodation and facilities.

A gradual transition is made towards subject specialist tuition in the middle and upper forms. Pupils are prepared for the Common Entrance examinations at 11+ and 13+, and also for Scholarships to Senior Schools. Over 200 academic, all-rounder, sporting, music and art awards have been gained since 1995. The school has a balanced curriculum with Forest Schools and Philosophy for Children sitting alongside the more traditional subjects of Maths, English, Science and Modern Languages.

Extracurricular activity is an important part of every pupil's education. Excellent sports facilities, which include games fields, heated indoor swimming pool, gymnasium and many games pitches, tennis courts and other hard surfaces, allow preparation of school teams at various age and ability levels in a wide range of sports. A fully-equipped Sports Hall was completed in May 2004. Our aim is that every pupil has an opportunity to represent the School. In September 2016 the new Baily Building was opened containing 14 classrooms, a Recital Room, a Food Tech Kitchen, a Lower School Art Room and a 450-seat auditorium, The Bawtree Hall. In 2016 the school was crowned IAPS National Champions at U11 Netball. The U9 Rugby team was unbeaten in their National Finals.

Art, Technology, Music and Drama are also strengths of the school. Our Centenary Theatre incorporates a 200-seat theatre, music school and Chapel. All our pupils are encouraged to play an instrument and join one of the music groups catering for all interests and abilities. Further extracurricular activities include tap, ballet and jazz dance, judo, art, gymnastics, scuba, debating, fantasy football, Forest Skills, computing, Lego modelling and chess. In the summer term of 2017 the school introduced Ultimate Frisbee and Quidditch into its after-school club repertoire.

Our pupils develop a curiosity about the world in which they live and a real passion for learning. Most importantly of all they become confident learners, mature and articulate individuals who love coming to school each day. The school's Community Fund was set up to benefit from pupil and parent fundraising. Each year, grants totalling £8,000 are awarded to community organisations with an educational bias. It is hoped, during 2017–18, to establish a strong association with schools in Tanzania through the charity, Champion Chanzige.

Charitable status. Hazelwood School Limited is a Registered Charity, number 312081. It exists to provide excellent preparatory school education for girls and boys in Oxted, Surrey.

Hazlegrove

Sparkford, Yeovil, Somerset BA22 7JA

Tel: 01963 440314
email: office@hazlegrove.co.uk
website: www.hazlegrove.co.uk
Twitter: @HazlegrovePrep
Facebook: @HazlegrovePrep

Senior Warden: Lt General [Ret'd] A M D Palmer, CB, CBE

Headmaster: **Mark White**, MA Hons, PGCE

Deputy Headmaster: Vincent Holden, BSc Hons, MEd

Head of Pre-Preparatory Department: Hannah Strugnell, BSc Hons, PGCE

Age Range. 2½–13.
Number of Pupils. 367 boys and girls of whom 97 are boarders. Preparatory (7–13 year olds) 297 pupils; Pre-Preparatory (2½–7 year olds) 72 pupils.
Fees per term (2018–2019). Preparatory: Boarders £6,886–£8,787 (fees are inclusive, with few compulsory extras); Day pupils £4,654–£5,937. Pre-Preparatory: £2,928. Nursery: Morning session £30, Afternoon session £20, Lunch £9.
Scholarships and Bursaries. Academic Scholarships are available for entry at 11+. Armed Forces Bursaries are also available to serving members.

Hazlegrove is located within a 200-acre park and is based around a country house built by Carew Hervey Mildmay in 1730. The entrance to the school is situated on the A303 roundabout at Sparkford. The Preparatory School has a strong boarding ethos. This is reflected in the full days, Saturday morning lessons from Year Four and the full range of activities for boarders, and those day pupils who wish to join in, during the evenings and at weekends. The school was judged "Excellent" in all nine areas of assessment in its last ISI Inspection in 2015.

Hazlegrove is a happy and purposeful school with a strong tutor system. The curriculum provides a varied and exciting experience for pupils as they progress through the school and includes Art, Food Technology, Design and Technology, Drama, Music and Outdoor Education. Latin and Mandarin are introduced in Year 5. The main sports are Rugby, Hockey, Cricket, Netball, Rounders, Tennis, Athletics and Swimming. Squash, Golf, Horse Riding, Judo and Karate are also available among other activities.

Streaming and setting is introduced as pupils progress through the school with a scholarship stream in the top two years. Pupils are entered for Common Entrance or Scholarship Examinations. About half go to the senior school, King's School Bruton. Others move on to major secondary schools such as Bryanston, Eton, Sherborne, Sherborne Girls, Millfield, King's College Taunton, Marlborough and

Winchester. Between 25 and 30 scholarships and awards are gained by pupils each year. Extra support is available to those pupils who have specific learning difficulties or who are gifted.

Pupils have achieved considerable success at regional and national level in recent years through sport, in team and individual performances, in drama and in music.

Hazlegrove has outstanding facilities. These include a state-of-the-art new Teaching and Learning Centre, a Theatre, a Sports Hall, a 25m Indoor Heated Pool, two Squash Courts, the Design Centre, three award-winning Libraries, an excellent Music School and a comprehensive Wi-Fi network. Outside, the extensive playing fields are complemented by two synthetic pitches, tennis courts, eight all-weather cricket nets and for golf, a 6-hole course, a putting green and driving nets. A full-time tennis coach ensures best use of the hard tennis courts and the second synthetic playing surface – both with flood lighting. The adventure playground is equipped with a timing device so pupils can compete for the Tarzan award.

Pastoral care for Boarders is provided by three sets of House Parents, four Matrons and a Nurse. Other resident staff provide additional support. The school has considerable experience of meeting the needs of pupils whose parents are in the Services or who live in expat communities working overseas. Flexible boarding can also be arranged to meet individual needs.

The school shop, which is on site, provides most necessary clothing and games kit.

Pre-Preparatory Department. Located in a purpose-built facility within the grounds, the Pre-Prep provides a carefully structured curriculum which encourages the development of the basic skills within a balanced programme of learning and play. The children enjoy Forest School and specialist teaching for French, drama, music, games and tennis. In addition to making full use of the Prep School facilities, the Pre-Prep enjoys its own Rainbow Room dedicated to Science, Art and Investigation, an adjacent gardening area and extensive climbing equipment in the playground. After school care is available.

Charitable status. King's School, Bruton is a Registered Charity, number 1071997. It exists to provide education for children.

Headington Preparatory School

26 London Road, Headington, Oxford, Oxfordshire OX3 7PB

Tel: 01865 759400
Fax: 01865 761774
email: prepadmissions@headington.org
website: www.headington.org
Twitter: @HeadingtonPrep
Facebook: @HeadingtonSchool

Chairman of Board of Governors: Mrs Sandra Phipkin, ACA

Headmistress: **Mrs J Crouch**, BA Hons Keele, MA Hons London, NPQH

Age Range. Girls 3–11.
Number of Pupils. 250.
Fees per term (2018–2019). Day: £1,336–£4,694.

Headington Preparatory School occupies its own three-acre site just two minutes' walk from Headington School and one mile from the centre of Oxford.

The Prep School's friendly, family atmosphere means girls develop as happy individuals with a sense of responsibility and self-awareness, enjoying a wealth of experiences inside and out of the classroom as part of an outstanding education.

In September 2016, an outdoor play area was created for the Early Years and Foundation Stage department. It includes a mound with a tunnel, extended climbing equipment with climbing wall, cargo nets and bridges and new all-weather flooring. This Centenary Campaign project also included a revamp of the nursery classrooms with new flooring, new lighting, redecoration and a two-storey role play area. A new playground for the older girls was opened in September 2018.

We have a wide range of extracurricular facilities including a gym and specialist art and design facilities, as well as a substantial performance space for music and drama, and a refurbished library. Our adventurous art and design curriculum allows girls to explore their imaginations through painting, drawing, clay-work and model-building and there are many exciting opportunities for girls in drama and music. We want all our girls to enjoy a variety of musical activities and we are quick to spot and nurture talent. From the age of seven, girls have the chance to learn at least one musical instrument and many of our girls play at a very high standard. All girls are taught to read music in both treble and bass clef through our keyboard scheme which is for Reception and Year 1. Theory clubs are offered to continue and support their learning.

In sport, specialist staff deliver a broad and balanced programme with a total of 12 different sports on offer. Girls are encouraged to try new activities and discover new talents to achieve their full potential, with many taking part in county level tournaments.

The school day runs from 8.30 am to 3.30 pm, with an extended day from 7.45 am to 6.00 pm. There are a large number of after-school clubs and activities from Fencing to Coding and Trampolining and aftercare runs every day incorporating a range of activities, tea and prep.

Entry to the Prep School is in order of application from nursery to 6+, with priority given to girls with siblings already at Headington, and by examination from 7+. The majority of pupils continue to Headington School, with a number of girls awarded scholarships every year. (*See Headington School entry in GSA section.*)

Charitable status. Headington School Oxford Limited is a Registered Charity, number 309678. It exists to provide quality education for girls.

Heath Mount School

Woodhall Park, Watton-at-Stone, Hertford, Hertfordshire SG14 3NG

Tel: 01920 830230
Fax: 01920 830357
email: registrar@heathmount.org
website: www.heathmount.org
Twitter: @heathmountsch

The school became a Trust in September 1970, with a Board of Governors.

Chairman of Governors: Mrs J Hodson

Headmaster: Mr C Gillam, BEd Hons

Senior Deputy Head: Mr M Dawes

Age Range. 3–13.

Number of Pupils. 256 Boys, 226 Girls. Flexi/Sleepover boarding offered.

Fees per term (2018–2019). Boarding (1–4 nights): £575–£1,970. Tuition: Nursery £2,300–£3,850, Pre-Prep £4,445, Years 3–6 £5,745, Years 7–8 £5,935.

There is a reduction in fees for the second and subsequent children attending the School at the same time.

Heath Mount School is situated five miles from Hertford, Ware and Knebworth, at Woodhall Park – a beautiful Georgian mansion with 40 acres of grounds set in a large private park. A dedicated Nursery and Pre-Prep and a new Lower School are situated a short walk from the main house. The fabulous facilities are inspiring – excellent sports facilities include a sports hall, covered swimming pool, an all-weather pitch for hockey and tennis, netball courts and cricket nets. The main house contains an imaginatively developed lower ground floor housing modern science laboratories and rooms for art, pottery, textiles, film making, food technology and design technology. There is a further information technology room and well-stocked research and fiction libraries. The boys board in a wing of the main house and the girls in a dedicated house in the adjoining park. Resident boarding house parents provide a welcoming environment for both the boys and girls.

The School has an excellent academic record, as well as outstanding art and sport and some of the finest school music in the country. Illustrating this, in 2018, forty-two of the 13+ leavers achieved scholarships to their senior schools across a range of areas.

Charitable status. Heath Mount School is a Registered Charity, number 311069.

Heatherton

Copperkins Lane, Amersham, Buckinghamshire HP6 5QB

Tel: 01494 726433
email: enquiries@heatherton.com
website: www.heatherton.com
Twitter: @HeathertonSch
Facebook: @HeathertonSchool

Chairman of the Governors: Mr G C Laws (Chairman of Berkhamsted Schools Group)

Principal: Mr R P Backhouse, MA Cantab

Head: Mrs D Isaachsen, BEd Hons, MEd

Age Range. Girls 3–11, Boys in Nursery only.
Number of Pupils. 143 Girls, 11 Boys.
Fees per term (2018–2019). £1,995–£4,445 inclusive of all but optional subjects.

Founded in 1912, Heatherton is set in an attractive green and leafy location on the outskirts of Amersham.

Heatherton provides an excellent all-round education. An experienced staff of specialist teachers encourage each child's individual academic and emotional development. High standards are achieved across a broad curriculum with small classes (max 20), a caring ethos and a close relationship with parents.

At 11 pupils progress to both local independent girls' senior schools and Buckinghamshire grammar schools. Excellent results are produced at all stages of school performance tests and the girls are tracked from an early age, both pastorally and academically.

Musical, artistic and sporting talents flourish at Heatherton. A thriving orchestra, individual instrument lessons and many drama, ballet and music productions are an important part of life in a school year. Art and design skills are celebrated in display and exhibitions, both internally and externally. Each pupil is offered a wide range of sporting activities – swimming, netball, gymnastics, dance, athletics, tennis, lacrosse and cross country.

An extensive range of educational visits and activities in the UK and Europe are organised each year. The school has recently introduced an additional Enrichment Curriculum to its pupils' timetables, offering the girls exciting opportunities to expand their knowledge, with topics as diverse as mindfulness, team-building and Tudor cooking.

In September 2015, the Heatherton Nursery became Co-Educational, providing for both boys and girls. Heatherton has been recognised for its '*outstanding quality of provision*' in the Early Years Foundation Stage. Its '*calm, purposeful environment*' and '*a host of stimulating learning opportunities*', were just some of the features highlighted by the Independent Schools Inspectorate who are now citing Heatherton's EYFS as an example of very best practice. Heatherton remains a girls' school from Reception class to Year 6.

Following a merger with Berkhamsted School in 2011, Heatherton pupils are increasingly enjoying the benefits of initiatives such as joint curriculum days, music and drama workshops, sports coaching and residential trips in partnership with Berkhamsted Prep, as well as access to the significant resources and infrastructure of the Berkhamsted Schools Group.

Charitable status. Heatherton House School is a member of the Berkhamsted Schools Group, which is a Registered Charity, number 310630.

Heathfield
The Junior School to Rishworth School

Rishworth, West Yorkshire HX6 4QF

Tel: 01422 823564
Fax: 01422 820880
email: gbattye@heathfieldjunior.co.uk
website: www.rishworth-school.co.uk

Motto: *Deeds Not Words*

Chairman of the Board of Governors: Canon Hilary Barber

Head: **Mr A M Wilkins**, BA, MA, MA

Age Range. 3–11 co-educational.
Number of Pupils. 120 day boys/girls and 50-place Foundation Stage Unit. Boarding is available from Year 5: details on request.
Fees per term (2018–2019). Day: Reception–Year 2 £2,155; Years 3–6 £3,160.
Staffing. 11 full-time teaching and 5 part-time teaching; 2 NNEB staff and 4 teaching assistants; additional teaching support in physical education and specialist teaching in music, art, PE, dance, ICT and drama; specialist peripatetic staff provide expert individual tuition in Music and the Arts.
Location. Heathfield stands in its own substantial grounds and enjoys an outstanding rural position in a beautiful Pennine location with easy access via the motorways to Manchester and Leeds.
Facilities. Well-equipped classrooms; Foundation Stage Unit and purpose-built Infant classes; designated teaching rooms for Music, Science, Art and Design Technology; modern ICT Suite; Library; a multi-purpose Hall for assemblies and productions; heated indoor swimming pool; netball court and football/rugby pitch; Pre/After School Care and Holiday School available. The extensive grounds are used for a wide variety of academic and other purposes.

Aims. To provide a stimulating and challenging environment in which individual attainment is nurtured, recognised and celebrated.

To ensure each child receives their full entitlement to a broad, balanced curriculum which builds on a solid foundation in literacy and numeracy.

Curriculum. An extensive programme of study which incorporates the Foundation Stage, Key Stage 1 and Key Stage 2. An emphasis on developing an independence in learning and analytical thinking through Literacy, Numeracy, Science, French, History, Geography, Religious Studies, Design Technology, Information and Communications Technology, Music, Art and Physical Education.

Extra-Curricular Activities. Includes activities such as: Drama, Choir, Orchestra, Baking, Brass, Recorder and String Groups, Steel Pans, Art, Board Games; Sports include Swimming, Rounders, Netball, Football, Rugby, Cross-Country, Cricket, Fencing, Athletics, Gymnastics, Hockey and Biathlon.

Extensive fixtures list of sports for boys and girls.

Each term there are plays and musical concerts incorporating most children in the School. Residentials include Outdoor Pursuits, Camping and Environmental Studies.

Charitable status. Rishworth School is a Registered Charity, number 1115562. It exists to provide education for boys and girls.

Hereford Cathedral Junior School

28 Castle Street, Hereford HR1 2NW

Tel: 01432 363511
email: enquiry@herefordcs.com
website: www.herefordcs.com
Twitter: @Herefordcs1
Facebook: @HerefordCathedralSchool

Chairman of Governors: Rear Admiral P Wilcocks CB, DSC, DL

Headmaster: **C Wright**, BSc, MSc, MEd

Age Range. 3–11.
Number of children. 244.
Fees per term (2018–2019). £1,485–£2,125 (Nursery), £2,676 (Reception), £2,730 (Year 1–2), £3,440 (Years 3–6).

Hereford Cathedral Junior School provides an outstanding education in the heart of the city. With small class sizes, specialist staff and strong pastoral care, pupils' individual needs are easily addressed. Excellent teaching is at the heart of the School, and with a strong reputation for Sport, Music, Drama and Art children are encouraged to make the most of the opportunities on offer.

Entry is into the Nursery or Reception, but a number of children join other year groups. Almost all children continue through to the senior school. The staff are well qualified and the maximum class size is 18. In the junior forms all subjects are taught by specialists. French is taught from the age of 4.

Music plays an important part in the life of the school with the Cathedral Choristers being educated at the school and a team of over twenty peripatetic music teachers. There are two school choirs and an orchestra.

An extensive programme of clubs and activities is offered during lunchtime and after school aimed at giving all children opportunities to develop their talents. After-school care is also available.

The games fields are on the banks of the River Wye with expert coaching being given in the main sports of cricket, football, rugby, hockey, netball, rounders, athletics and swimming.

There is an active PTA organising a wide programme of social and fundraising activities.

The Little Princess Trust founded in memory of former pupil, Hannah Tarplee, was started at the school and provides hair pieces for children who lose their hair through cancer treatment.

The School was founded in 1898 and now occupies listed Georgian and Medieval buildings in Castle Street at the East End of the Cathedral with facilities including specialist music rooms, an Art and DT centre, an ICT suite and an extensive library. The Moat, a purpose-built nine-classroom building to house the Pre-Prep, opened in 2003.

Charitable status. Hereford Cathedral School is a Registered Charity, number 518889, and a Company Limited by Guarantee, registered in Cardiff, number 2081261. Its aims and objectives are to promote the advancement of education.

Hereward House School

14 Strathray Gardens, London NW3 4NY
Tel: 020 7794 4820
email: office@herewardhouse.co.uk
website: www.herewardhouse.co.uk

Headmaster: **Mr P J E Evans**, MA

Deputy Headmaster: Mr N Arnold, BA Ed
Director of Studies: Ms E B Olsen, MA, PGCE
Head of Middle School: Miss N Scaffidi, BEd
Head of Junior School: Mrs R Batchelor, BSc, PGCE
Bursar: Mr A Jenne, BA
Headmaster's PA/Admissions: Mrs S Eaves

Age Range. 4–13.
Number of Pupils. 171 Day Boys.
Fees per term (2018–2019). £5,500–£5,650.
Hereward House provides a warm and welcoming atmosphere in which every child feels valued, secure and thrives. The school works hard to create a stimulating, purposeful and happy community, within which boys are encouraged and assisted to develop academically, morally, emotionally, culturally and physically. The school's aim is for boys to enjoy their school days yet at the same time be well prepared for the demands of Common Entrance and Scholarship examinations.

The school's academic success is built upon excellent teaching and the highly individual educational teaching programmes created to meet individual boy's needs. Great care is taken to ensure that a boy gains a place at the school which is right for him.

Boys are prepared for the Common Entrance and Scholarship examinations to highly sought after independent schools, both day and boarding. Two-thirds of boys proceed to top London Day Schools, such as City of London, Highgate, St Paul's, UCS and Westminster, others to leading boarding schools such as Eton, Harrow and Winchester. Scholarships and Awards have been won by our boys to several of the above schools.

The school takes pride in the breadth of education it offers. Music plays a major role in the boys' education. Almost all boys learn at least one instrument, most of them two or even three. There is a full school orchestra which gives a performance each term. Weekly concerts are held throughout the year.

Team Games play an integral part in the sports syllabus. We regularly field teams against other schools and have an enviable record of success in cricket, football and cross-country running. Swimming, tennis, hockey and athletics are included in our sports programme.

Art, pottery and drama have a valued place in the syllabus. Chess, judo, fencing, coding, yoga, ICT and music theory are among the clubs available to the boys.

Herries Preparatory School

Dean Lane, Cookham Dean, Berks SL6 9BD
Tel: 01628 483350
Fax: 01628 483329
email: office@herries.org.uk
website: www.herries.org.uk
Twitter: @Herries_School
Facebook: @herriesschool

Chair of Governors: Mr George Stinnes

Headmistress: **Mrs Fiona Long**

Age Range. 3–11 Co-educational.
Number of Pupils. 110 Day Boys and Girls.
Fees per term (2018–2019). £3,070–£3,600.
Herries has a delightful location alongside National Trust land and is close to Maidenhead and Marlow. Small class sizes enable each child to receive individual attention and to flourish in a secure environment. The curriculum is broad and balanced and there is a wide range of extracurricular clubs including football, street dance, judo, cookery, archery and horse riding. Instrumental music lessons are available. Wrap-around care is available to all pupils from 7.30 am until 6.00 pm Monday to Friday. Herries has a distinctive family atmosphere and happy pupils who progress to the grammar, state and independent secondary schools of their choice.

Curriculum. The National Curriculum is covered and we teach beyond the levels expected of children in each age group. Class teachers deliver the core and foundation subjects in Key Stage 1 while there is subject specialist teaching in all subjects in KS2.

Examinations. Children are assessed through the NFER testing scheme and a variety of standardised tests. Emphasis is placed on preparing pupils for their next school of choice and the timetable includes 'Thinking Skills' which helps pupils learn to cope with a variety of different tests and exams.

Facilities. Set in a beautiful building which was the house in which Kenneth Grahame wrote 'The Wind in the Willows', the nursery occupies a purpose-built and spacious suite of rooms. ICT is taught in a specialist room with the latest computers and software. Class rooms are equipped with interactive Smart Boards and there is an excellent library. Games are played at the National Sports Centre at Bisham Abbey, only a few minutes away by coach; swimming at Wycombe Leisure Centre; cricket at Cookham Dean Cricket Club; athletics events at Braywick Sports Centre.

High March School

23 Ledborough Lane, Beaconsfield, Bucks HP9 2PZ

Tel: 01494 675186
Fax: 01494 675377
email: office@highmarch.bucks.sch.uk
          admissions@highmarch.bucks.sch.uk
website: www.highmarch.co.uk

Established 1926.

Chairman of the Governing Board: Mr C Hayfield, BSc, FCA

Headmistress: **Mrs S J Clifford**, BEd Hons Oxon, MA London

Age Range. Girls 3–11, Boys 3–4.
Number of Pupils. 298 day pupils.
Fees per term (2018–2019). £1,910–£4,935 inclusive of books, stationery and lunches, but excluding optional subjects.

High March consists of 3 school houses set in pleasant grounds. Junior House comprises Nursery and Key Stage 1 classes, ages 3–7 years, whilst Upper School covers Key Stage 2, ages 7–11 years. Class sizes are limited. Facilities include a state-of-the-art 20-metre indoor heated swimming pool, a well-equipped Gymnasium, as well as Science, Music, Art, Poetry, Design Technology, Drama, Information Technology rooms and a Library. Recent refurbishments include large extensions to the Art Room and Science Laboratory and re-landscaping of all the Upper School's outside space to include a new Adventure Playground, new Netball courts and an outdoor learning classroom. The playground at Junior House was re-landscaped in Summer 2015 and Summer 2016 and now includes a Sensory Garden as well as new play equipment.

High March is within easy reach of London, High Wycombe, Windsor and within a few minutes' walk of Beaconsfield Station.

Under a large and highly-qualified staff and within a happy atmosphere, the children are prepared for Common Entrance and Scholarships to Independent Senior Schools and for the 11+ County Selection process. All subjects including French, Latin, Music, Art, Technology, Speech and Drama, Dancing, Gymnastics, Games and Swimming are in the hands of specialists. The academic record is high but each child is nevertheless encouraged to develop individual talents.

There is an Annual Open Scholarship to the value of one-third of the annual fee tenable for 3 years.

Highfield & Brookham Schools

Highfield Lane, Liphook, Hampshire GU30 7LQ

Tel: 01428 728000 (Highfield Prep)
          01428 722005 (Brookham Pre-Prep)
email: headspa@highfieldschool.org.uk
          admissions@brookhamschool.co.uk
website: www.highfieldschool.org.uk
Twitter: @HighfieldSch
Facebook: @HighfieldBrookham
LinkedIn: /highfield-and-brookham-schools

Chairman of Directors: Mr W S Mills

Headteacher, Highfield (*Prep*): **Mr Phillip Evitt**

Headteacher, Brookham (*Pre-Prep*): **Mrs Sophie Baber**

Age Range. 3–13.
Number of Children. 450.
Fees per term (2018–2019). Day Pupils £3,700–£7,175; Boarders £7,950–£8,750.

Discounts are available for siblings and Forces families.

Highfield and Brookham are charming country prep and pre-prep schools offering an exceptional all-round education for children aged 3–13. Set within 175 acres of stunning grounds, the schools are ideally located only an hour from London, on the borders of Hampshire, Surrey and West Sussex. For our thriving community of boarders, there is also a weekend shuttle service to London.

The schools enjoy outstanding academic success, and one of the great features of Highfield is the supportive, collaborative process it provides to parents in helping them identify the right Senior School for their child. Highfield feeds the top Senior Schools in the country and enjoys a flawless track record of securing every child's place at their first-choice school, as well as an excellent scholarship success rate.

There is an abundance of sport played by pupils at Highfield and Brookham, and sport is an integral part of the broad curriculum we offer. Our specialist coaches work with children right from Nursery, and by Year 2 they have the opportunity to take part in matches against other schools, both home and away. Alongside extensive playing fields we have an indoor swimming pool, squash court, tennis courts, golf course, cross-country course and a sports hall. Children enjoy games lessons every day with weekly fixtures on Wednesdays and Saturdays, as well as weekly physical education and swimming lessons.

In general, the facilities at the schools are enviable and enable us to offer an enormous breadth in the curriculum, as well as a plethora of extra-curricular activities. Facilities include a music school, art school, new science and DT labs and a renovated theatre, nursery and indoor swimming pool.

Above all, our pupils are happy and fulfilled. There are fields and woodlands to explore and trees to climb; it's a place where children really can still be children. Whether you eventually choose day or boarding, co-educational or single-sex, Highfield and Brookham provide a wonderful and relevant experience for your child, ensuring they leave us as happy and well-rounded individuals, full of enthusiasm to tackle the next stage of their learning journeys.

Highfield Preparatory School

West Road, Maidenhead, Berkshire SL6 1PD

Tel: 01628 624918
Fax: 01628 635747
email: office@highfieldprep.org
website: www.highfieldprep.org

Chairman of Governors: Mr Peter Campbell, MA, MSc, Chartered FCIPD

Headteacher: **Mrs Joanna Leach**, BEd Hons, NPQH

Age Range. 3–11.
Number of Pupils. Approximately 140 girls. Class sizes: average 15, maximum 22.

Picture your daughter at Highfield Preparatory School, the leading independent girls' school in Maidenhead. It offers a great start to the life of learning in a safe, secure and academically stimulating environment.

We believe, that in the important primary years, girls learn best in girls' schools. They learn by doing, listening, exploring and experimenting. The girls are given daily opportunities to explore, question, try, investigate, discover, apply and have fun. This all starts in the Nursery where the girls learn to develop confidence and independence.

Our girls achieve well beyond national expectations and move on to some of the best Grammar and Independent schools in the area at 11+, often achieving academic, sports and music scholarships. We also offer a wide range of after-school clubs including ICT, Mandarin, Street dance, Futsal and Self-defence.

From Nursery to Year 6, we offer extended day care from 7.45 am to 6.00 pm, have an all-year round holiday club, serve hot lunches every day and our fees are highly competitive. The entry process is non-selective. We are located close to Maidenhead train station.

Come and see for yourself why Highfield Prep offers #myfirstclasseducation. A prospectus is available on request from our Registrar on 01628 624918.

Fees per term (2018–2019): Reception to Year 6: £3,075–£4,060. Nursery: £3,245* (full-time inc lunch) – please call for current prices for morning and afternoon sessions. Lunch: Reception to Year 6 £354.

*Nursery Education Funding (NEF) is currently available for all 3 and 4 year olds attending a setting registered within the RBWM. Highfield Preparatory School is a registered setting. We offer the free entitlement NEF in 3-hour morning and afternoon sessions (maximum 30 hours per week).

Free wrap-around care for Nursery children. For girls in the nursery we offer a free Breakfast club and free after-school care in The Den for each full day they attend school. That means we can care for your daughter from 7.45 am until 6.00 pm. This package is only available on the days where children attend a morning and an afternoon session combined.

Your daughter will receive a nutritional breakfast on arrival and a sandwich tea is served at 4.30 pm as part of our after-school club. This is in addition to the cooked lunch that she will receive when she attends a full day in Nursery.

Wrap-around Care costs for Reception–Year 6. £3.15 for breakfast (7.45 am – 8.25 am). Breakfast available from 8.00 am to 8.15 am. £9.35 for the Den from after school until 6.00 pm. Includes a snack tea and activity programme.

Charitable status. Highfield Preparatory School is a Registered Charity, number 309103. It exists to provide an all-round education for girls.

Highgate Junior School

3 Bishopswood Road, London N6 4PL

Tel: 020 8340 9193
email: jsoffice@highgateschool.org.uk
            pre-prep@highgateschool.org.uk
website: www.highgateschool.org.uk

Chairman of Governors: Bob Rothenberg, MBE, BA, FCA, CTA, MAE

Principal of Junior School: **S M James**, BA, MA

Principal of Pre-Preparatory School: Mrs D Hecht, PDCE

Age Range. 3–11 Co-educational.
Number of Day Pupils. Junior (age 7–11): 400 boys and girls; Pre-Prep (age 3–7): 130 boys and girls.
Fees per term (2018–2019). Junior School: £6,410; Pre-Preparatory School: £6,055 (Reception–Year 2), £3,020

(Nursery). Fees are inclusive of lunch (exc Nursery) and the use of books.

Pupils are prepared for Highgate School only. (*See entry in HMC section.*)

Entry to the Pre-Preparatory School is by individual assessment for entry at 3+. Entry to the Junior School is by test and interview at the age of 7. Transfer to the Senior School is at 11+.

The Pre-Preparatory School and the Junior School are both housed in self-contained buildings, located in Bishopswood Road, N6.

The School is well situated close to Hampstead Heath and has excellent facilities as the result of an ongoing development programme. There are several acres of playing fields attached; the Mallinson Sports Centre (which includes a 25-metre indoor pool) is shared with the Senior School, and a newly completed all-weather sports pitch.

A broad and balanced curriculum is followed with art, drama, music, games, ICT and design technology all playing an important part.

Charitable status. Sir Roger Cholmeley's School at Highgate is a Registered Charity, number 312765. The aims and objectives of the charity are educational, namely the maintenance of a school.

Hilden Grange School
Alpha Plus Group

Dry Hill Park Road, Tonbridge, Kent TN10 3BX

Tel: 01732 351169 / 01732 352706
email: office@hildengrange.co.uk
website: www.hildengrange.co.uk
Twitter: @HildenGrange
Facebook: @HildenGrange

Headmaster: **J Withers**, BA Hons

Deputy Head: Mrs R Jubber, BSc, HDE

Age Range. 3–13 Co-educational.
Number of Pupils. 340: 240 Boys and 100 Girls.
Fees per term (2018–2019). Prep School £5,025, Pre-Prep £3,690, Nursery: £48.40 per day. Lunches are provided at £230–£265 per term.

Hilden Grange provides a friendly, secure and stimulating environment where children enjoy learning and participating in all aspects of school life.

We offer high standards of teaching and learning, excellent pastoral care and outstanding opportunities in art, music, drama and sport. Both inside and outside the classroom we strive to help each child achieve their own level of excellence – to do their best.

Though links are especially strong with Tonbridge and Sevenoaks, boys and girls are prepared for all Independent Senior Schools and Grammar Schools at 11+ and 13+. We have an impressive record of success in this area. Examination results rank among the highest in Kent, and in the past ten years, all pupils gained entry to their chosen school at 13. Boys and girls who show special promise sit for scholarships to the school of their choice, and our track record in this area is excellent. 146 scholarships have been gained in the past ten years in areas as diverse as music, drama, technology and sport as well as traditional academic scholarships. Pupils benefit from specialist teaching in all subjects from Year 3, dedicated staff, and class sizes that average 16.

The School stands in about eight acres of attractive grounds in the residential area of North Tonbridge. Boys and girls are accepted into the Nursery at 3+ or at 4+ into the Pre-Preparatory Department within the school grounds, and at 7 into the main school. Tonbridge School Chorister awards may be gained; at present there are twelve Choristers.

There is an outdoor heated swimming pool, a dedicated Sports Hall, all-weather tennis courts, Science Laboratories, Music Rooms, an Art and Design area, a Library, a Learning Support Area, a dining hall and two Information Technology Rooms, with networks of personal computers. An extensive building program was completed in September 2012 providing new education and communal facilities which are enjoyed by the whole school.

The Headmaster, staff and children welcome visitors and are pleased to show them around the School.

Hilden Oaks Preparatory School & Nursery

38 Dry Hill Park Road, Tonbridge, Kent TN10 3BU

Tel: 01732 353941
email: secretary@hildenoaks.co.uk
website: www.hildenoaks.co.uk
Twitter: @HildenOaks
Facebook: @Hilden-Oaks-Preparatory-School-Nursery
LinkedIn: /hilden-oaks

Chair of Governors: Mr D Walker

Headmistress: **Mrs Katy Joiner**, NNEB, BEd Hons, QTS, MEd

Age Range. 3 months–11 years Co-educational.
Number of Children. 190.
Fees per term (2018–2019). Reception: £3,200, Years 1 & 2: £3,600, Years 3 & 4: £4,100, Years 5 & 6: £4,300.

Hilden Oaks School, founded in 1919, became an Educational Trust in 1965. It is located in a residential area of north Tonbridge and the Trust owns all the land and buildings.

Hilden Oaks prides itself on being a happy, family school where every child is helped and encouraged to develop their potential and independent learning in a caring, stimulating and purposeful environment. We maintain high academic standards while expecting good manners and consideration to others at all times. This is reflected in the active parents' association, close liaison between parents and staff and the school's close involvement with the local community.

In the Pre-School and Pre-Prep, children are given a solid foundation upon which they can build, with additional specialist teachers for Computing, French, Music and PE. The Prep school has specialist teachers for Science, Computing, French, Music and PE. All forms are taught by form teachers for the core subjects.

Our pupils enjoy taking part in Music and Drama with regular opportunities to perform. They also enjoy competitive sport in house matches and against other schools. Extracurricular activities include Choir, Drama, Art, Computing and Games. A late room operates where children are provided with tea. Prep is supervised for the older children while the younger children can relax and play.

All pupils are prepared for both the Common Entrance examination at 11 and the 11+ examination for entry to grammar schools. Our results in these examinations put us among the top prep schools in Kent.

Hilden Oaks offers a challenging and supportive environment designed to inspire children to life-long learning.

Charitable status. Hilden Oaks School is a Registered Charity, number 307935. It exists to provide education for children.

Hoe Bridge School

Hoe Place, Old Woking, Surrey GU22 8JE

Tel: Prep School: 01483 760018/760065
           Pre-Prep: 01483 772194
Fax: 01483 757560
email: enquiriesprep@hoebridgeschool.co.uk
           enquiriespreprep@hoebridgeschool.co.uk
website: www.hoebridgeschool.co.uk
Twitter: @HoeBridgeSchool

Co-educational Preparatory and Pre-Preparatory School.

Chairman of Governors: Ian Katté

Headmaster: **Christopher Webster**, MA, BSc Hons, PGCE

Deputy Headmaster: Adam Warner, BA Hons

Head of Pre-Prep: **Mrs Linda Renfrew**, MA, PGCE

Age Range. 2½–14.
Number of Children. Prep 265, Pre-Prep 215.
Fees per term (2018–2019). Day: Prep £4,510–£5,115 (including lunch); Pre-Prep £1,980–£3,600 (including lunch).

Hoe Bridge School is set in a perfect location on the outskirts of Woking surrounded by 22 acres of beautiful grounds and woodland and is only 25 minutes from London.

At the heart of Hoe Bridge stands the stunning 17th century mansion, Hoe Place. Hoe Place is steeped in history and was once the favourite retreat for Lady Castlemaine, one of the mistresses of King Charles II. Major development has taken place over the past few years and the school now boasts outstanding 21st century facilities. These facilities are second to none and we are immensely proud of the successes and achievements of our children as they take full advantage of all that is available to them here. The children are equally proud to call Hoe Bridge their school.

The Pre-Prep department is located in its own purpose-built building and achieved 'Outstanding' throughout at our last inspection. From Nursery to Year 2 the creative curriculum followed at the Pre-Prep enables the children to learn through play, adventure, discovery and experience.

Transition to the Prep Department is seamless and as children mature they become increasingly independent learners in preparation for the move to senior school. The results achieved by the children across the ability range are outstanding leading to success at some of the country's leading schools. The pupils are inspired by dedicated staff, lessons are rigorous and interactive and achievement is excellent.

Alongside the academics sport, music, art and drama play a major part throughout the school and children excel in many areas: end-of-year productions; sporting excellence achieving national success in netball and hockey, county success in cricket and football; individual musical success in national youth orchestras and choirs and a spectacular annual art exhibition. Scholarships in all these areas are won every year to a variety of schools across the country. "The pupils' successes in academic work, sport and music, both individually and in groups, are due to their excellent attitudes to learning." Latest ISI Inspection Report.

Senior pupils in Years 7 and 8 take part in regular extracurricular activities such as Bush Craft weekends, French trips, cricket and netball tours and are challenged by preparing and presenting a gourmet meal to their parents. It is at this stage of their time at Hoe Bridge that they take on extra responsibility becoming prefects and role models to the younger children.

The atmosphere of every school is unique and we consider the strength and attraction of Hoe Bridge to lie in the atmosphere here. Created by the staff and children it combines warmth, care, good relations and pride in achievement. The children spend ten years at Hoe Bridge. These are formative years and they should be ten happy and rewarding ones and our aim is to do the very best for each child. Standards and targets are realistic, though set as high as possible. The bright are challenged and the less able supported; we endeavour to instil confidence in all our children. Visitors are amazed how happy the children are, how determined they are to succeed and how much they care about each other.

The School has an extremely good reputation and we are constantly striving to preserve the atmosphere, improve our results and explore all possibilities for enriching both the School and the children.

Charitable status. Hoe Bridge School is a Registered Charity, number 295808. It exists to provide a rounded education for children aged 2½–14.

Holme Grange School

Heathlands Road, Wokingham, Berkshire RG40 3AL

Tel:	0118 9781566
Fax:	0118 9770810
email:	school@holmegrange.org
website:	www.holmegrange.org
Twitter:	@HolmeGrangeHead
Facebook:	@holmegrange

Chairman of Governors: A Finch, Former Company Director

Head: **Mrs Claire Robinson**, BA, PGCE, NPQH

Deputy Head: Mr Matthew Jelley, BA Hons, PGCE, MEd

Age Range. 3–16 Co-educational.

Number of Pupils. 491: 263 boys, 228 girls.

Fees per term (2018–2019). Little Grange Nursery £1,950–£3,395; Pre-Preparatory: £3,625 (Reception), £3,690 (Years 1–2); Prep: £4,625 (Years 3–4), £4,735 (Years 5–8), £4,850 (Years 7–8), £4,995 (Years 9–11) with an option to pay over 10 months. Reductions for second and subsequent children.

Holme Grange is a co-educational day school for girls and boys aged 3–16 years. The school provides pupils with a toolkit to live their lives and when they eventually enter the adult world, they will do so well prepared with a real-life foundation for every challenge they will face. Set in 21 acres of Wokingham countryside, Holme Grange offers a unique educational journey in an idyllic setting, delivering a creative experience, sporting prowess and academic excellence.

The School occupies a large country mansion, to which many additional facilities have been added over recent years, including outdoor classrooms, two additional science laboratories, food technology room, common room and additional classrooms. At the start of the 2016–17 academic year we saw the opening of a 300-seat Performing Arts Theatre, Music School and Drama Suite and a new block housing a dining room, kitchens and eight additional classrooms. An extension to the Sports Hall has also been completed.

Further classrooms have been newly added to enhance the Senior School facilities and new Reception class facilities will be in place for September 2019. A dedicated Prep Science Lab has also opened for the start of the 2018–19 academic year.

The School is set in an idyllic environment of just over 20 acres of grounds comprising grass pitches, all-weather surfaces, swimming pool, Cricket, Football, Hockey and Rugby pitches, Netball and Tennis courts, 3 Forest schools and woodland walks for the children to explore. Specialist teaching and facilities for Music, Art and Technology, Dance, Performing Arts, Science, ICT and Sport enhance our fully comprehensive provision and support the individual development of all our pupils. Holme Grange is one of the first schools in the area to have gained Forest School status and has a number of qualified Forest Leaders on the Staff, thus allowing opportunities for children to achieve and develop confidence and knowledge through hands-on learning in a woodland environment. The recent erection of a second Polytunnel provides opportunities for pupils to learn about sustainable education whilst the development and expansion of the School farm with its goats, pigs, chickens and ducks enable the pupils to learn about life cycles and animal husbandry in a very hands-on manner.

Little Grange is an established Nursery for 3 and 4 year olds equipped to the highest standard located in its own safe and secure environment within the School grounds, providing flexible education either part or full day including lunch and tea. There is the facility for all children to stay to 5.50 pm.

We welcome and cater for pupils with a wide range of ability. Entry is based upon an assessment day where baseline assessment tests are taken in verbal and non-verbal reasoning. This entry process is designed to identify pupils who are able to benefit from our balanced and well-rounded education. We aim to foster confidence and a love of learning across the age range. Pupils are accepted from the start of the term in which they turn 3 providing outstanding continuous education up to and including GCSE, and also preparing students for the Common Entrance examinations. July 2018 saw our first full cohort of GCSE students and the school celebrated record results with over half of all grades (58%) being 9–7, the old A*–A. The school achieved a 90% pass rate across the board.

The Headteacher is assisted by a highly qualified and experienced teaching staff with classroom assistants in the Pre-Prep and NNEB assistants in Little Grange. There is an Accelerated Learning Centre giving help to those children with special needs.

The School's policy is to set high standards, to establish good all-round personalities and to give inspiration for each pupil's life. Our aim is to create an environment where every child can thrive. Our Mission is to inspire achievement beyond the bounds of expectation within an environment where every child can succeed. A bold statement but one that we believe every child deserves. We appreciate children's differences and respond to their individual needs. In 2013 we were awarded the prestigious NACE Challenge Award for More Able, Gifted and Talented Pupils in recognition of the high quality work by the whole school in challenging all pupils to achieve their best, gaining re-accreditation In 2017. Only 36 other schools in the country have achieved this elevated status.

At Holme Grange we offer excellence in personalised learning – a rare school that caters equally well for pupils at both ends of the academic continuum. We believe in our pupils and instil a belief in themselves.

We develop intellectual character through our learning habits and the ethos throughout the school is one of warmth and friendliness – questioning; divergent thinking and the freedom to learn from mistakes are all encouraged. Pupils are inspired to take responsibility for their own learning, develop good work habits and gain a sense that learning can thrill and invigorate.

We deliver a rounded education by providing opportunities in sport, the arts, languages, technology and a wide range of activities, maximising opportunities for success for all. We hope to inspire your child both in and outside of the classroom. At Holme Grange School, we foster self-reliance, self-discipline and self-confidence in a caring community where children gain interests and characteristics that give them a head start for life.

We will not only unlock your child's potential but will also foster within them, a passion for learning. Our pupils are prepared to succeed in an ever changing, competitive world. We offer challenge, we strive to inspire, develop confidence, provide opportunity and realise potential in every child up to the age of 16.

We are committed to providing the very best education. Academic standards are excellent. Life in our school is a journey of exploration and discovery. We are a holistic school offering an all-round education, bursting with life and vitality.

The School is a Trust, administered by a board of Governors who have considerable experience in education and business.

Charitable status. Holme Grange Limited is a Registered Charity, number 309105. It exists to serve the local community in providing an all-round education for boys and girls.

Holmwood House Preparatory School

Chitts Hill, Lexden, Colchester, Essex CO3 9ST

Tel: 01206 574305
Fax: 01206 768269
email: headmaster@holmwood.house
website: www.holmwood.essex.sch.uk

Headmaster: **Alexander Mitchell**, BA Hons, LLCM, PGCE

Age Range. 4–13 Co-educational. Nursery: 6 months to 4 years.

Number of Pupils. 300.

Fees per term (2018–2019). Day Pupils £3,380–£5,965; Boarding: £35 per night. 5 nights boarding for the price of 4. All fees are inclusive; there are no compulsory extras. Nursery fees dependent on hours attended.

Holmwood House was founded in 1922 and stands in 30 acres of grounds only 2 kms from Colchester town centre. Children of all abilities are welcomed and are prepared for the Common Entrance examination and for scholarships to senior independent schools both locally and nationally.

The principal aim of the school is genuine all-round education with high academic standards at its core. Small class sizes, well-qualified staff, superb facilities and high-quality leadership ensure pupils at all levels make excellent progress. The Pre-Prep department enjoys spacious and modern accommodation and with *Forest School*, the children benefit even more from the beautiful grounds through a programme of outdoor learning. Specialist teaching starts in Reception (languages, music, PE, games, swimming) and this increases by age 6/7 (art, science, sports teams). In the Prep school, specialist teaching in all subjects offers pupils an outstanding range and depth of curriculum. Children are

increasingly encouraged to take personal ownership of their learning through creative, collaborative and independent activities in all subjects. Pupils' progress is carefully monitored and the relationship between parents and school is an important partnership. Excellent Learning Support is available when required and all teachers have a highly developed understanding of learning needs, ability levels and strategies to enhance progress.

Facilities include 15 acres of sports fields; vibrant, well-equipped classrooms; five squash courts; indoor heated swimming pool; state-of-the-art sports hall; six tennis courts (two covered); floodlit tarmac play area; 2 adventure playgrounds; a permanent stage with sound and lighting systems; superb Art and Design facilities incorporating print and ceramic workshop; separate music facilities. The majority of pupils study at least one musical instrument. There are four well-equipped science laboratories. The ICT facilities, networked to all classrooms including two ICT suites a mobile suite of 130 chromebooks, 40 tablets and various display equipment, also supports pupils' learning.

The extensive sports programme in which every child takes part from age 7, is delivered through generous scheduled sessions of instruction in afternoons and evenings and weekly matches against other schools are a strong feature of the week. Classes and compulsory games are all timetabled conventionally; as are 'preps' – supervised homework. An impressive activities programme provides opportunities for pupils to experience a wide range of options; e.g. archery, fencing, kung-fu, design technology, cookery, knitting, jewellery design, athletics, squash, tennis, badminton, dance and much more. Music and drama flourish particularly, ranging from the large-scale productions to the smaller ensembles.

Flexi boarding is a popular option open to all pupils from Year 5 upwards and is a great start for those children who plan to go on to a senior boarding school, where they can gain a boarding experience in familiar surroundings with their friends, to develop the necessary confidence. There is a wide range of opportunities and activities for boarders to explore and during boarding time, pupils have use of all of the school's facilities, as well as a large cinema-style TV screen for special sports events and lectures, pool tables, table football, air hockey and table tennis.

Pastoral care is excellent and the family atmosphere is palpable. Pupils enjoy exceptionally good relationships with their teachers and the supportive atmosphere encourages them to make the most of their abilities and the abundance of opportunities on offer. Children at Holmwood House are comfortably confident, display excellent manners and have a thirst for learning. The school's guiding principles of care, courtesy and consideration provide a framework in which children can develop their values, emotional intelligence and sense of citizenship within this and the wider community.

Wrap-around care is offered as an option for children from Reception to Year 3 from 7.30 am, up until 6.00 pm, with one member of staff for every 8 children. Pupils in Year 4 upwards also have the option to be dropped off at 7.30 am and all Prep pupils stay until 6.10 pm at no extra cost; this is mandatory for Years 6–8.

Holmwood House Nursery caters for children from 6 months to 4 years. A flexible service is offered so that children can attend either during Holmwood House term only, or for any number of different sessions and options. The Nursery is open for 48 weeks in the year.

We would be pleased to send our prospectus and to welcome visitors to the school.

Holy Cross Preparatory School

George Road, Kingston-upon-Thames, Surrey KT2 7NU

Tel: 020 8942 0729
email: admissions@holycrossprep.com
website: www.holycrossprepschool.com

Headmistress: **Mrs S Hair**

Age Range. 4–11.
Number of Girls. 250.
Fees per term (2018–2019). £4,332.
Location. The school is situated on a private estate in an attractive area of Kingston Hill.

Facilities. The building, the former home of John Galsworthy, is of both historical and literary interest and provides excellent accommodation for two classes in each year group through the school from Reception to Year Six. The school contains a state-of-the-art sports and performing arts hall, library, Design and Technology facility, Music suite, ICT suite, science and cookery room, art room and 14 classrooms all with computers.

The 8 acres of stunning grounds include two tennis/netball courts, hockey pitch, running track and three large playing areas which have play equipment, including adventure climbing frames. In Spring 2019 the school is opening a floodlit All Weather Pitch and a large sports pavilion. There is a nature trail and ecology area, together with a fountain within the ornamental lawns and a pond which is well used in science lessons.

Educational Philosophy. The school was founded by the Sisters of the Holy Cross, an international teaching order who have been engaged in the work of education since 1844. A sound Christian education is given in an Ecumenical framework. The children are happy, cared for and well disciplined. The emphasis is on developing the God-given gifts of each child to their fullest potential, in a stimulating, friendly atmosphere where high standards of work, behaviour and contribution to the well being of the school community are expected. The school was named Sunday Times Prep School of the Year in 2014.

Curriculum. There is a broad and dynamic curriculum providing a high standard of education. Specialist teaching in French, Music, Physical Education, drama, art and Information Technology. The school has a first rate record of success in Common Entrance and in preparing pupils for top Senior Independent, High and Grammar Schools. The varied extra-curricular activities include ballet and dance, drama, pottery, art and design, music (including cello, piano, flute, clarinet, violin and guitar), sports, technology, languages, debating, judo, tennis, and chess.

Charitable status. Holy Cross Preparatory School is a Registered Charity, number 238426. It is a Roman Catholic School providing excellence in Christian education to local children.

"I don't believe we could have found a better school in the country to bring out the best in both our sons."

Chairman of Governors: Dr Inderpreet Dhingra, BSc Hons, PhD, MBA, FSI

Head: **Mr John Towers**, MA, PGCE, NPQH, FRSA

Age Range. 3–13.
Number of Boys. 350.
Fees per term (2018–2019). Senior Department and Year 3 £4,400; Junior Department (1st and 2nd Year) £3,770; Early Years Department: Reception £3,040, Nursery: £3,040 (full day), £2,070 (mornings only). Lunches: £320 (Seniors and Juniors), £280 (Nursery and Reception).

Homefield is a preparatory school for 350 boys aged 3 to 13, and 60 staff, housed in an extensive purpose-built complex with well-equipped science laboratories, large Art, DT and Music suites, complemented by a spacious Early Years Department, a well-resourced Computing Department and a two-acre adjoining playing field.

Founded in 1870, Homefield has its roots in the 19th century and its branches in the twenty-first. The School has cemented its powerful academic reputation by continuing to achieve a 100% pass rate at Common Entrance to 46 senior schools over the last 10 years. Every year scholarships are won to senior independent schools for academic, musical, sporting, artistic and all-round accomplishment in the last three years.

Throughout the School's development it has been very careful to preserve the original family ethos and intimacy, together with its reputation for academic excellence, the breadth of extra-curricular sporting, musical and artistic provision and first-class pastoral care. We pride ourselves on achieving fulfilment of individual potential, the openness of communication, the provision of specialist teaching at the earliest appropriate opportunity (French, ICT, Music and Sport from the Foundation Stage), our commitment to best practice and all-round academic, musical, dramatic, sporting and artistic achievements. *"Pupils make a strong contribution to their learning through their highly motivated and enthusiastic attitudes. The quality of pupils' achievements and learning is excellent."* (ISI Inspection, March 2013.)

The school has county or national representatives in table tennis, squash, tennis, athletics, swimming, soccer, rugby, cricket and chess.

Awareness of others is encouraged and the pupils are involved in many fundraising charity events. A wide range of opportunities are available to extend gifted pupils and learning support is available for children with special needs.

We offer academic, sporting, art and music scholarships as well as occasional bursaries.

Daily minibuses run to and from Wimbledon and Purley/Carshalton.

Breakfast and after school clubs are available.

Charitable status. Homefield Preparatory School Trust Limited is a Registered Charity, number 312753. It exists to provide education for boys.

Homefield Preparatory School

Western Road, Sutton, Surrey SM1 2TE

Tel: 020 8642 0965
Fax: 020 8642 0965
email: registrar@homefieldprep.school
website: www.homefieldprep.school
Twitter: @HomefieldSchool
Facebook: @homefield.school

Hornsby House School

Hearnville Road, London SW12 8RS

Tel: 020 8673 7573
email: school@hornsbyhouse.org.uk
website: www.hornsbyhouse.org.uk

Chair of Governors: Mr Huw Davies

Headmaster: **Mr Edward Rees**, BA Ed Hons

Age Range. 4–11.

Number of Pupils. 209 Girls, 226 Boys.

Fees per term (2018–2019). £4,760 (Reception to Year 2), £5,115 (Years 3 to 6). Lunch: £265 per term.

Hornsby House is a thriving IAPS co-educational prep school in Wandsworth, southwest London. At their most recent inspection in October 2016, the Independent Schools Inspectorate judged Hornsby House pupils' overall achievement as "excellent" and found that "pupils achieve highly from the wide ranging curriculum that provides for all abilities". Pupils' personal development was described as "excellent" and stated that "pupils have high levels of self-esteem, positive relationships, healthy lifestyles and social awareness". Hornsby House provides a nurturing environment where attainment and happiness are key aims and the children achieve outstanding educational outcomes as a result. In 2016 our Year 6 children won 40 scholarships and awards between them. There are three classes in each year group, a generous staff to pupil ratio and around 430 pupils in the school. Entry into Reception classes is unassessed and is on a first-come, first-served basis with priority being given to siblings. Children wishing to enter the school in year groups above Reception are required to attend an assessment.

There is an extensive co-curricular programme with over 50 clubs, as well as before and after school care. Over half the children in the school play a musical instrument and a third sing in one of the three choirs. Sport is a central part of the curriculum, the staffing level is excellent and the benefits of teamwork are seen clearly in school life as a whole. The school has an outstanding IT infrastructure, with four classrooms set up as e-learning suites and 120 iPads used to support the children's learning. The majority of leavers go to one of seven London day schools: Dulwich College, JAGS, Alleyn's, Emanuel, King's College School Wimbledon, Streatham & Clapham High School and Whitgift. The remainder move on to other day or boarding schools.

To arrange a visit to see the children at work, please contact the Registrar.

Charitable status. Hornsby House Educational Trust is a Registered Charity, number 800284.

Horris Hill

Newtown, Newbury, Berks RG20 9DJ

Tel: 01635 40594
email: registrar@horrishill.com
website: www.horrishill.com
Twitter: @HorrisHill

Chairman of Governors: Ms M B Lund

Headmaster: G F Tollit, BA Hons

Deputy Headmasters:
A W Rendall, BA Hons, PGCE
F J Beardmore-Gray, BA Hons, PGCE

Age Range. 7–13.

Number of Boys. Boarders 100, Day 20.

Fees per term (2018–2019). Full Boarders £9,150; Transition Boarders (4 nights per week) £7,950; Day Pupils £5,600.

Horris Hill is one of the leading boys' prep schools in the UK. The school's emphasis is on the development of the whole boy, without compromising the 130 year record of academic excellence. Horris Hill School has a unique ethos

which develops every boy as an individual and provides a rigorous and extensive academic, sporting, musical and artistic foundation.

We deliver success by achieving places and awards at the very best senior schools and developing boys with impeccable manners, good humour, kindness and self-confidence. Recent awards to senior schools have included – Academic at Winchester, Eton and Marlborough, Outstanding Talent at Harrow, Music and Drama at St Edward's Oxford and Milton Abbey, Sport at Millfield, Charterhouse and Sherborne.

We believe that the period from 7–13 years of age are the most critical in any boy's life. These are the years where the foundations of the men they can become are laid. At such a crucial stage in their cultural development, we believe that an all-boys school provides the optimal setting where boys will exercise their intellectual inquisitiveness, free to explore all avenues, building self-confidence and awareness in a safe and encouraging environment.

We offer a wide variety of sports and extra-curricular activities, so that every boy has the opportunity to develop interests away from the classroom. The main sports are Rugby, Football, Cricket, Hockey and Tennis. We also have our own golf course, train and modelling room, swimming pool, squash court and cross-country course. For boys with green fingers, we have our very own Kitchen Garden. We also offer LAMDA for budding performers, Judo, Sailing, Clay Pigeon Shooting, Mandarin and a hugely successful Chess Club.

To see for yourself what a difference a Horris Hill education could make for your son, please come and visit us. Simply email registrar@horrishill.com to arrange an appointment. We look forward to welcoming you to Horris Hill.

Charitable status. Horris Hill Preparatory School Trust Limited is a Registered Charity, number 307331. It exists to prepare boys for the Senior Independent Schools.

Hunter Hall School

Frenchfield, Penrith, Cumbria CA11 8UA

Tel: 01768 891291
Fax: 01768 899161
email: office@hunterhall.cumbria.sch.uk
website: www.hunterhall.co.uk

Chairman of Governors: Mr Peter Kirk

Headmistress: Mrs Donna Vinsome, BEd Hons, MA

Deputy Head: Mrs Antonia Taylor, BA Hons, QTS
Foundation Stage Manager and KS1 Coordinator: Mrs Georgina Griffiths, BEd Hons
Bursar: Mr David White, BA Hons, FCCA

Age Range. 3–11 co-educational.

Number of Pupils. 85.

Fees per term (2018–2019). £2,583 Lower School (Reception to Year 2), £2,993 Upper School (Year 3 to Year 6) including after-school activities. Nursery paid per hour.

Hunter Hall School has grown rapidly from its inception over 32 years ago into a thriving and vibrant community, providing high quality education for children aged 3 to 11. Its location is idyllic, in imaginatively converted farm buildings on the outskirts of Penrith and only 2 km from the M6, providing easy access to the attractions of the Lake District and the north of England generally.

It is providing a range of experiences that is important at Hunter Hall and staff recognise that effective learning can take place in a variety of situations. Within the classroom, creativity and independence is emphasised, and the objective is to provide the children with the knowledge, skills and confidence to prosper, not only whilst at Hunter Hall, but also in the schools that they will subsequently join. In the Foundation Stage, the activities that are undertaken are determined by the children, originating from their own interests and needs, then facilitated by the staff. The aim is to stimulate curiosity, interest and excitement in learning, and to encourage self-discipline and develop confidence. These qualities extend as the children move through the school, with the emphasis on providing them with a range of skills to help them to recognise that they have the ability (and courage) to think for themselves. In addition, perseverance and cooperation are especially valued, creating a warm, friendly and almost tangible sense of community within the school.

The curriculum is broad, and specialist subject teaching is provided from Year 3. Class sizes are small. Teaching facilities are excellent. Pupils are encouraged to take responsibility for their own progress and to set themselves challenging targets.

Children at Hunter Hall spend a great deal of time outdoors and, indeed, beyond the school boundaries. The environment in the local area lends itself admirably to geographical and historical investigation, as well as providing an unrivalled stage for exploration and adventure as part of our outdoor learning sessions. Participation in Art, Drama and Music is extremely active, with extensive representation at local festivals. The variety and quality of sport that is on offer is equally remarkable, and Hunter Hall children have received wide-ranging recognition at local and national level in recent years.

This is a happy school, in which a Christian ethos of tolerance and respect for each other is dominant. Children (their parents) and staff enjoy spending time here and contributing to the development of the community.

Charitable status. Hunter Hall School Ltd is a Registered Charity, number 1059098.

Hurlingham School

Main School:
122 Putney Bridge Road, Putney, London SW15 2NQ

Tel: 020 8874 7186
Fax: 020 8875 0372
email: office@hurlinghamschool.co.uk
website: www.hurlinghamschool.co.uk

Nursery and Pre-Prep:
The Old Methodist Hall, Gwendolen Avenue, Putney, London SW15 6EH

Headmaster: **Mr Jonathan Brough**, BEd Hons Cantab, NPQH, FCollT

Age Range. 2–11 Co-educational.
Number of Pupils. 326 in main school; up to 100 more in nursery.
Fees per term (2018–2019). Main School: £5,430–£5,650; Nursery & Pre-Prep from £2,228.
Location and Facilities. Hurlingham is a non-selective independent preparatory school on two sites in Putney, the main campus situated in very close proximity to Wandsworth Park. The modern and spacious buildings provide excellent facilities which include bright classrooms, a large gym and dance and drama studios, as well as a science laboratory, art studio and several music rooms. Recreational space includes a large playground with climbing wall and an adventure playground.

Ethos. The School's ethos is to provide a happy, secure atmosphere in which children flourish both academically and personally. Experienced and enthusiastic teachers provide opportunities for the children that strongly promote creativity and independence of thought, essential attributes for a child growing up in the 21st Century. Self-confidence, self-discipline, self-motivation, self-esteem and above all a thirst and enjoyment for learning are nurtured.

Academic. The curriculum is broad, with the aim of providing a balanced and rounded education in which every child is treated as an individual and is encouraged to make the most of their particular talents. The important skills of reading, writing and numeracy are given a high priority in everyday teaching; these are delivered through many exciting cross-curricular topics which bring the children's learning alive and allow them to make sense of the world around them. All children on the main site learn French and Spanish in Reception, then choose one for the remainder of their time in school. Latin is taught from Form IV; Thinking Skills and many aspects of Design Technology, including Ceramics, are also greatly enjoyed across the school.

Sport. Hurlingham children are fit and healthy, and all boys and girls participate enthusiastically. Seasonal team games skills are taught in football, rugby, hockey, netball, cricket, gym and athletics. Numerous matches are organised with other local schools throughout the sporting year. Every Summer Term the whole school joins in with traditional Sports Day activities, and a family picnic lunch.

Music. Hurlingham has an excellent music department. The youngest children are encouraged to sing, play simple instruments and enjoy performing. For older pupils there are many opportunities to learn individual instruments, play in ensembles and participate in music concerts. There are several, very popular and talented, choirs and ensemble groups.

Pastoral Care. Strong pastoral care is a very important feature of life at Hurlingham. All staff foster an intimate and welcoming environment centred on family values, with a clear focus on good manners and respect for one another. The House System, School Council and various pupil committees provide the children with wonderful opportunities to support each other and express their views about their own school.

Clubs. Children are encouraged to participate in a wide range of clubs which include: art, ballet, chess, drama, karate, music, modern dance, pottery and science. Older children are able to do their homework in school if parents wish.

Starting Out. A newly-refurbished nursery close to the main site provides cutting-edge pre-school experiences, including a unique 1:4 forest school option. Children begin their life on the main campus in Reception which, although contained within the school building, is a separate area allowing children to feel part of the whole school but not overwhelmed by it. The three parallel classrooms all have direct access on to the playground, thus enabling the teaching of the curriculum to extend outside. There is also a cosy dedicated activity hall for Reception pupils which provides space for all three forms to join together for group activities, regular access to computers and a quiet place for reading.

Entry. For entry to Nursery and Reception there is no entrance test or interview. Places are offered in order of registration, although siblings, and those living within 1.2 km of the school, are given priority. Older children are invited to spend a day at Hurlingham and take part in lessons in order to assess their academic ability. Scholarships are available for children joining from 7+ onwards.

School Visits. Appointments should be arranged with the school office. There is an underground car park which visitors are welcome to use.

Hurstpierpoint College Preparatory School
A Woodard School

Chalker's Lane, Hurstpierpoint, West Sussex BN6 9JS

Tel:	01273 834975 (Prep and Pre-Prep)
Fax:	01273 836900
email:	prepadmissions@hppc.co.uk
website:	www.hppc.co.uk
Twitter:	@Hurst_Prep
Facebook:	@HurstCollege

Chairman of Governors: Mr A Jarvis, BEd, MA, FRSA

Head of Prep School: **I D Pattison**, BSc Southampton

Deputy Head of Prep School: N J Oakden, BA Wales, NPQH, MEd Buckingham

Heads of Years:
Reception–Year 2: Mrs D Ross, BEd Brighton
Years 3–4: Mrs A E Oakden, MA St Andrews
Years 5–6: Mr N J Oakden, BA Wales, MEd Buckingham, NPQH
Year 7: Mrs T Preen, BSc Southampton
Year 8: Ms K A Pattison, BA Wales

Admissions Officer: Mrs C Treadaway

Age Range. 4–13 Co-educational.
Number of Pupils. Prep 298; Pre-Prep 57.
Fees per term (2018–2019). £2,398–£5,355. There are no compulsory extras.

The Prep and Pre-Prep Schools of Hurstpierpoint College (*see entry in HMC section*) share a beautiful 140-acre campus with the College. Although both Schools operate independently of the Senior School, having their own timetable, staff, buildings and Heads, the schools work closely together to offer a first-class programme of education for boys and girls from the age of 4 to 18.

Hurst's Pre-Prep School for children aged 4–7 opened in 2001. It occupies a self-contained unit with well-equipped classrooms and a new outdoor play area, built in 2016. There is one class for each year group.

The Prep School has joint use of many of the College's superb facilities, including a 25m heated indoor swimming pool, theatre, drama and dance studios, music school, large sports hall, tennis courts and three full-size AstroTurf hockey pitches.

The aim of the Prep and Pre-Prep is to provide an outstanding education in a secure and happy environment.

The academic programme is exciting and innovative, with independent learning and mobile technology at the heart of our teaching and learning. The children are provided with an excellent grounding in the more traditional subjects and, as they progress through the school, they are encouraged to take more responsibility for their learning in order to develop the qualities and skills required for academic success in the Senior School.

The Sports programme is extensive with Netball, Hockey, Rugby, Football, Rounders, Cricket, Swimming,

Tennis and Athletics on offer. In addition there is a wide-ranging activity programme which caters for the interests of all pupils.

The Music, Drama and Dance Departments are also very strong; about half the pupils learn musical instruments. The Preparatory School choir performs at the weekly Chapel service. There are at least three musicals or plays each year involving many children throughout the School.

The College has a dedicated Medical Centre with fully-qualified staff.

Each year a number of scholarship awards are available for entry into Year 7 (11+).

Charitable status. Hurstpierpoint College is a Registered Charity, number 1076498. The College provides a Christian education to boys and girls between the ages of four and eighteen.

Ipswich Preparatory School

3 Ivry Street, Ipswich, Suffolk IP1 3QW

Tel:	01473 282800
Fax:	01473 400067
email:	prepadmissions@ipswich.school
website:	www.ipswich.school

Chairman of Governors: Mr H E Staunton, BA, FCA

Headteacher: **Mrs A H Childs**, BA QTS, PGC PSE, Dip Ed, MA

Age Range. 3–11.
Number of Pupils. 263.
Fees per term (2018–2019). Years 4–6 £4,116; Year 3 (inc lunch) £4,328; Reception, Years 1 & 2 (inc lunch) £3,950; Nursery (inc lunch): £34.56 per am/pm session, £65.36 per whole day.

The Preparatory School has its own staff and Headteacher. It is located just across the road from the Senior School (*see Ipswich School entry in HMC section*). The School opened The Lodge Day Nursery in January 2018, providing excellent childcare for children aged 3 months to 3 years and this is situated on Ivry Street.

The School seeks to provide a learning environment which allows pupils to develop skills and personal qualities. The curriculum is planned to encourage the children to develop lively, enquiring minds and appropriate emphasis is placed on securing for each child a firm foundation of skills in literacy and numeracy. The broad, balanced curriculum offered provides a breadth of experience which is suitable for children of primary age. High academic standards are reached by the pupils, but in addition, they are encouraged to develop skills in music, art, drama and sport.

Children's happiness is considered essential and the School works closely with parents to ensure a partnership which provides the best possible care for all girls and boys.

The School enjoys the advantage of sharing Senior School facilities such as playing fields, sports hall, swimming pool, theatre/concert hall and the Chapel. The Prep School has its own Art, Design Technology, ICT and Science facilities.

Charitable status. Ipswich Preparatory School is part of Ipswich School, which is a Registered Charity, number 310493. It exists for the purpose of educating children.

James Allen's Preparatory School

East Dulwich Grove, London SE22 8TE

Tel:	020 8693 0374
email:	japs@jags.org.uk
website:	www.jags.org.uk
Twitter:	@JAGS_Prep
Facebook:	@JAGSschool

Chair of Governors: Mrs Frances Read, MA Cantab, FCA, MSI

Head: **Miss Finola Stack**, BA Hons, MA Ed Open, PGCE, Mont Dip

Age Range. Girls 4–11.
Number of Pupils. Day: 302 Girls.
Fees per term (2018–2019). £5,434.

James Allen's Preparatory School (JAPS) is an independent day school for girls aged between 4 and 11, offering a high quality of education provided by a team of skilled, motivated and dedicated teachers and support staff. The curriculum is broad and well-balanced and enriched by a varied and interesting programme of extra-curricular clubs and activities.

Warmth, happiness and vitality are at the heart of everything we do at the Prep school. Children are encouraged to work to the best of their abilities, but we also want them to have fun and be curious in their learning. We see the primary years as vital to the success of any child's education.

The school has an excellent staff-to-pupil ratio and provides specialist teachers in Art, DT, ICT, Music, PE and Science from Year 3. In French the children are taught from 4 years of age onwards using the immersion method. Prep school girls enjoy specialist teaching for most of their subjects whilst regularly being taught by their Form Teacher. Our newly-designed Computing suite along with the Science, Design Technology and Art rooms enable girls to enjoy practical activities. Enriching our exciting and diverse curriculum is an extensive range of extra-curricular activities to develop and extend the girls' own interests, teamwork and leadership skills.

The Pre-Prep School (for pupils aged 4–6) is housed in a separate Edwardian building with a large outside green space, including a sensory garden and Forest Schools activities. The Middle School (for pupils aged 7–11) is a large, modern building on the same site as the senior school sharing the facilities (the theatre, swimming pool and games fields). The recently opened (2018) James Allen's Community Centre offers exceptional musical opportunities for the school and local community.

Pupils normally enter the school in the year in which they are 4 or 7 on 1 September. Assessments take place the preceding January. 36 places are available for 4+ entry and 12/15 places available for 7+ entry. At 11, girls normally progress to JAGS where JAPS girls regularly win many scholarships. (*See JAGS entry in HMC/GSA section.*)

JASSPA is the James Allen's Saturday School for the Performing Arts for pupils from JAPS and many other local schools. This is entirely voluntary and complements the week's activities: music lessons, dance and drama are all offered.

Charitable status. James Allen's Girls' School is a Registered Charity, number 1124853. The purpose of the charity is the conduct at Dulwich of a day school in which there shall be provided a practical, liberal and religious education for girls.

Keble Prep

Wades Hill, Winchmore Hill, London N21 1BG

Tel:	020 8360 3359
Fax:	020 8360 4000
email:	office@kebleprep.co.uk
website:	www.kebleprep.co.uk

Chairman of Governors: Mr David Fotheringham

Headmaster: **Mr Mark Mitchell**, BSc Hons, PGCE

Deputy Head: Mr P Gill, BA Hons

Age Range. 4–13.
Number of Boys. 220 Day Boys.
Fees per term (2018–2019). £3,990–£5,080.

As confirmed by the ISI Inspectors in 2012, the warm and friendly atmosphere that exists at Keble ensures that the boys are well-motivated, keen to learn and able to mature at their own pace. Strong pastoral care is regarded as a key element in the boys' overall development and well-being, along with the encouragement of courteous and considerate behaviour.

The academic staff comprises 23 qualified graduate teachers, 5 classroom assistants and 2 Learning Support teachers. The buildings are well maintained and facilities are regularly updated. The school has an ambitious ICT development programme.

The average class size in the school is 15, although many classes are taught in half-groups and sets as the boys progress through the school. Boys follow the Foundation Stage in Reception. General subject teachers cover the academic curriculum in Years 1 to 4, with subject specialists following on from Year 5 onwards. The National Curriculum is used as a guide to curriculum development. Art, Music, PE, ICT, PSHE and Games are introduced at appropriate stages and are included within the timetable. Boys are encouraged to learn a musical instrument, sing in the choir, perform in plays and concerts, and play an active part in the wide range of sports on offer.

Football, rugby and cricket are the major team games. Further opportunities exist to participate in hockey, swimming, basketball, athletics, cross country and tennis. There is a wide range of lunchtime and after-school activities and clubs, including drama, gardening and chess. There are also numerous educational outings and four residential trips.

Boys are not required to pass an assessment to gain entry into the school at Reception. Boys wishing to join the school at a later stage in Year 1 or above are assessed in order to ensure that they will fit comfortably into their new surroundings.

Boys are prepared for entry to senior independent schools through Common Entrance and Scholarship examinations at 13+. The school has a strong record of success in placing boys in the senior school which is right for them. In recent years, these schools include Aldenham, City of London, Haberdashers' Aske's, Highgate, Haileybury, Mill Hill, St Albans, St Columba's, University College and Westminster.

Charitable status. Keble Preparatory School (1968) Limited is a Registered Charity, number 312979. It exists to provide education for boys.

Kensington Prep School

GDST

596 Fulham Road, London SW6 5PA

Tel: 020 7731 9300
email: enquiries@kenprep.gdst.net
website: www.kensingtonprep.gdst.net

Founded in 1873.

Kensington Prep School is part of the GDST (Girls' Day School Trust). The GDST is the leading network of independent girls' schools in the UK. As a charity that owns and runs 23 schools and two academies, it reinvests all its income in its schools. For further information about the Trust, see p. xxiii or visit www.gdst.net.

***Head*: Mrs Caroline Hulme-McKibbin**, BEd Hons Cantab

Age Range. 4–11 years.
Number of Girls. 295.
Fees per term (2018–2019). £5,731.

Since 1997 the School has been based in Fulham. The school is set in an acre of grounds and has large bright classrooms with specialist rooms for ICT, Art, Drama, Music, Science and Design Technology. The large playground provides fantastic play facilities, netball and tennis courts and a pond for environmental studies.

We have just completed an innovative £2.7m building project 'Creating Spaces for Growing Minds' transforming the school, providing ground-breaking facilities for independent exploration, self-directed learning and collaborative work. These include spacious classroom breakout areas with retractable doors, a high-tech 'Explore Floor', multimedia recording studio, and an Eco-Greenhouse. The specialist Drama, Art, Science and ICT suites have also been refurbished and the school is fully accessible throughout for pupils with two new lifts.

The school aims to provide an excellent, broadly-based but strongly academic curriculum. Independence, individuality and questioning thinkers are encouraged. Girls enjoy challenging and interesting work in a stimulating and caring environment, whilst being prepared for entry to leading boarding and day schools at 11+.

The School achieved the highest possible grades across the board in the recent Inspection by the Independent Schools Inspectorate and the quality of pupils' achievements and learning was rated 'exceptional'. Kensington Prep was named 'Independent Prep School of the Year' by the Sunday Times Parent Power for 2009–10 in recognition of its "consistently strong academic results, inspiring leadership and innovative curriculum".

Entry to the School is selective and the main entry points are at 4+ with a small intake at 7+. Occasional places do occur throughout the School from time to time.

Charitable status. Kensington Prep School is part of The Girls' Day School Trust, which is a Registered Charity, number 306983.

Kent College Junior School

Harbledown, Canterbury, Kent CT2 9AQ

Tel: 01227 762436
email: registrarjuniorschool@kentcollege.co.uk
website: www.kentcollege.com
Twitter: @AndyCarterKentC
Facebook: @kentcollege
LinkedIn: /kent-college-canterbury

Chair of Governors: Lorna Cocking

Executive Head Master: Dr D J Lamper, EdD Hull, BMus, MA London, AKC

***Junior School Head Master*: A J Carter**, BEd Hons

(Full staff list can be found on the Kent College website)

Age Range. 3–11 Co-educational.
Number of Pupils. Juniors (Day and Boarding) 156.
Fees per term (2018–2019). Juniors: Boarders £8,412; Day Pupils (including lunch): Year 6 £5,337, Year 5 £5,277, Year 4 £5,137, Year 3 £4,629, Year 2 £3,626, Year 1 £3,605, Reception £3,330, Nursery: £2,740 (5 full days).

GREAT – the foundation stones to educational success.

The GREAT programme (which stands for Gifted, Really Enthusiastic, Able and Talented) offered by the unrestricted curriculum structure at the Nursery, Infant and Junior School at Kent College is key to early success. Setting in core subjects is designed to accelerate progress and gives children the option to develop particular skills, be they academic, art, drama, music or sport. All children are on individualised programmes to maximise their academic potential and are set for English and Maths according to their needs and talents rather than their chronological age.

Parents can also choose for their child to enjoy more focus in a particular area: academic challenge; Kent Test preparation; art; design technology; drama; music or sport. Students do not have to sit the Kent Test, however, those that do enjoy excellent results. Scholarships to senior schools are targeted and in recent years there has been a success rate of over 50%.

Whilst the school day finishes at 4 pm there is a full range of after-school clubs and activities, which all the children can enjoy until 6 pm each evening. There are also holiday activity weeks meaning the school is open for at least 47 weeks a year.

Boarding places are available on a full, weekly or occasional basis and accompanied travel home is available to London's St Pancras station.

All in all a win-win situation resulting in the students being well equipped for senior school education and parents given the peace of mind so that they can focus on their busy working lives.

Charitable status. Kent College, Canterbury is part of the Methodist Independent Schools Trust, which is a Registered Charity, number 1142794. The School was founded to provide education within a supportive Christian environment.

Kew College

24–26 Cumberland Road, Kew, Surrey TW9 3HQ

Tel: 020 8940 2039
Fax: 020 8332 9945
email: enquiries@kewcollege.com
website: www.kewcollege.com

Chairman of Governors: Mr David Imrie

***Head*: Mrs Marianne Austin**, BSc Hons, MA Hons, ACA, PGCE

Age Range. 3–11 Co-educational.
Number of Pupils. 296.
Fees per term (2018–2019). £2,350–£4,050.

Kew College was established in 1953 and was made into a charitable trust in 1985 by its founder, Elizabeth Hamilton-Spry, to ensure the long-term continuity of the school. The school's ethos is to ensure all pupils have an excellent grounding in the basics, but with a strong emphasis on areas such as art, music, drama and sport to develop the whole child.

Kew College's style is described as traditional, yet imaginative and the atmosphere is happy and lively with a team of enthusiastic, caring and dedicated staff to help fulfil each child's potential. Pupils enjoy excellent facilities including specialist ICT and science labs. The ISI inspection in October 2010 concluded that '*Pupils achieve well across the curriculum and extra-curricular activities, and standards are exceptionally high in all aspects of English and Mathematics. The quality of their reading, writing and mathematical skills is in advance of their years. Pupils also exhibit great creativity, particularly in art work. Pupils display enthusiasm for their lessons and good learning skills. Pupils' personal development and the school's arrangements for welfare, health and safety are outstanding. Pupils develop into exceptionally moral beings. Pupils leave the school as well-balanced personalities. The school is a caring community where pupils are thoughtfully and skilfully looked after by the pastoral care of the whole staff, which contributes strongly to their personal development.*' In the Early Years Foundation Stage the inspectors commented that '*Children are happy and secure and their needs are met well. Careful attention is given to children's welfare and safety; their exemplary behaviour and excellent personal development are strengths.*'

Beyond the core curriculum pupils enjoy participating in lively mixed-year clubs within school on Friday afternoons including graphic design, origami, Sudoku and table tennis. A wide range of weekly after-school clubs includes chess, computer, debating, STEMKids, fencing, handball and jazz dance, with arts and crafts and little golfers for the younger pupils. There are also school choirs, a wind band and string orchestra. The school takes full advantage of its London location for educational visits. There are residential field trips in Years 3, 4, 5 and 6. In their final term, Year 6 pupils enjoy a week-long stay at a château in France improving their language skills, cultural knowledge and doing outward bound team activities.

At 11+ pupils not only achieve places through competitive entrance examinations to selective London day schools but also win a good number of awards.

Charitable status. Kew College is a Registered Charity, number 286059.

Kew Green Preparatory School

Layton House, Ferry Lane, Kew Green, Richmond, Surrey TW9 3AF
Tel: 020 8948 5999
email: secretary@kgps.co.uk
website: www.kgps.co.uk

Chairman of Governors: Mrs Sanela Smith

Headmaster: Mr Jem Peck

Age Range. 4–11 Co-educational.
Number of Pupils. 280.

Fees per term (2018–2019). £5,857.

Kew Green Preparatory School is housed in an attractive building and grounds directly next door to the Royal Botanical Gardens. The front of the school overlooks Kew Green, which is used for games and the back of the school has a good-sized playground which looks onto the River Thames.

In a non-pressurised, caring environment, KGPS produces excellent academic results, sending its pupils to London's best independent senior schools.

The children are encouraged to use philosophy and ethical thinking throughout the curriculum, which includes English, maths, science, French, RE, music, design & technology, art, games/PE and computer studies. All Upper School children attend a summer term Residential Week where cross-curricular studies are applied in a non-urban environment.

There are many after-school clubs and sports activities including three choirs, an orchestra and rock band. Individual tuition is offered in piano, violin, brass, woodwind, cello, saxophone, guitar, drums and singing.

An 8.00 am to 6.00 pm All-Day Care service is offered to parents at an extra charge.

The school is noted for its warm, happy atmosphere where parents play a full part in enriching the curriculum and social life. Off-site visits and guest workshops presented by noted visitors are a regular feature of education at Kew Green.

The school is always heavily over-subscribed and registration is recommended from birth. A prospectus can be downloaded on the school website and the registration form is now online.

Kilgraston Junior Years

Bridge of Earn, Perthshire PH2 9BQ
Tel: 01738 812257
Fax: 01738 813410
email: junioryears@kilgraston.com
website: www.kilgraston.com
Twitter: @kilgraston
Facebook: @kilgrastonschool

Chairman of Board of Governors: Mr Timothy Hall

Head of Kilgraston School: Mrs Dorothy MacGinty

Head of Junior Years: Mrs Anne Fidelo

Age Range. Girls 5–12.
Number of Pupils. 54 Girls.
Fees per term (2018–2019). Day £3,630–£4,600, Boarding £7,675.

Kilgraston Junior Years is the junior school for Kilgraston, a leading boarding and day school for girls aged 5–18 in Scotland. Located in its own building, the Junior Years is surrounded by 54 acres of stunning parkland in Bridge of Earn, three miles from the centre of Perth, 45 minutes from Edinburgh and an hour's drive from Glasgow.

Admission to Kilgraston Junior Years is by interview. Girls are able to progress to Kilgraston Senior School, or prepare for scholarship exams for Kilgraston and Common Entrance exams for other schools. The academic standard is high with all pupils completing the Junior Years and achieving a place in their senior school of choice.

Pupils are taught by class teachers until the age of nine, with specialist teachers for PE, French, music and drama. Form teachers hold pastoral responsibility for the pupils and classes are small with provision for additional support needs. From age ten, the curriculum becomes more specialised with increasing input from specialised subject staff and use of the facilities in the Senior School. Pastoral care is the responsibility of a tutor.

The core academic curriculum is enhanced by a wide range of co-curricular subjects. While academic excellence is a priority, art, drama and music flourish and are an important feature of life at Kilgraston. Classrooms are well equipped and modern IT facilities are spread throughout the school. Opportunities are provided throughout the year for pupils to perform in groups or as soloists and they compete successfully in local festivals and events. The girls have the opportunity to take LAMDA, Associated Board and Trinity examinations. There is an annual production involving all pupils.

Sports and recreation thrive within the superb Sports Hall, which includes a climbing wall and gym. Pupils benefit from a 25m indoor swimming pool, 9 floodlit all-weather courts, playing fields and athletics track. Kilgraston is the only school in Scotland with an equestrian facility on campus and it also hosts the Scottish Schools Equestrian Championships each year.

The school's main sports are: hockey, riding, netball, tennis, rounders, swimming and athletics, and fixtures are regularly played against other preparatory schools. The school has an excellent skiing record.

Kilgraston Junior Years has a pastoral House system. Inter-House competitions and challenges in games, music and debating provide an opportunity for friendly competition and fun. The family atmosphere in the newly refurbished boarding area, Butterstone, is enhanced by the wide range of weekend activities that make use of the superb local facilities in and around Perthshire.

Charitable status. Kilgraston School Trust is a Registered Charity, number SC029664.

Kimbolton Preparatory School

Kimbolton, Huntingdon, Cambs PE28 0EA

Tel: 01480 860281
Fax: 01480 861874
email: prep@kimbolton.cambs.sch.uk
website: www.kimbolton.cambs.sch.uk
Twitter: @KimboltonSchool
Facebook: @KimboltonSchool

Motto: *Spes Durat Avorum*

Chair of Governors: C A Paull, MPhil, FCA

Headmaster: **J P Foley**, BA, NPQH

Age Range. 4–11 Co-educational.
Number of Children. Approximately 300.
Fees per term (2018–2019). £3,290–£4,295 (including lunch). A 2% discount is applied if fees paid by termly direct debit.

Mission Statement. Kimbolton School creates a caring, challenging environment in which pupils are encouraged to fulfil their potential and are given opportunities to flourish in a wide variety of curricular and extra-curricular interests.

We provide a close family environment where young people are educated to be tolerant, socially responsible and independent of mind, equipping them for our changing world. We are a community that challenges pupils to discover their talents, develop socially and excel.

Our Preparatory School is located at the western end of Kimbolton village in a mix of modern and Victorian buildings, while our Senior School is based at the opposite end of the village in Kimbolton Castle in 120 acres of parkland and playing fields. We are very much one school: the curricula of the Prep and Senior Schools are aligned; our warm, caring ethos starts at the Reception Year and continues through to the Upper Sixth; and some of our staff teach at both the Prep and Senior Schools.

Our normal entry points for the Prep School are 4+, 7+ and 9+, but we accept pupils into other year groups and/or at times other than September when space permits, subject to passing an appropriate assessment.

Pupils join our Reception year and are then split into two classes in Year 1 and Year 2. Years 3–6 have three classes each. Each has its own class teacher and pupils throughout the Upper Prep also benefit from a good deal of specialist teaching. We have provision for academically gifted children and provide one-to-one and small group tuition as needed.

We offer an extensive range of trips, visits and competitions to complement the curriculum, as well as regularly welcoming visiting speakers. From Year 4 onwards, children have the option of participating in residential trips.

There is a vibrant musical scene throughout Kimbolton School. The majority of children in Years 3–6 take individual music lessons in addition to class music; those in Years 1 and 2 may opt for small group string sessions. Performance opportunities abound, with formal and informal concerts plus an annual orchestral afternoon.

Lower Prep is located in Aragon House, a purpose-built facility for 4–7 year olds, which provides a safe, welcoming and happy environment. Children in Lower Prep also use the facilities on offer throughout the Prep School. Children automatically progress to the Upper Prep, with the expectation that at age 11 pupils will continue to the Senior School. (*See entry in HMC section*).

The Prep School has, on its own site, a dining hall, library, digital suite, assembly hall, music teaching and practice rooms, science laboratory, art and design technology room and sports hall, as well as large, light and airy classrooms. There is a full-time nurse on site.

Our outdoor facilities include tennis and netball courts, 400m grass athletics track, rounders fields, floodlit all-weather pitches, plus football, hockey and cricket pitches. Pupils also enjoy regular access to the first-class facilities at the Senior School, including a 25-metre swimming pool. We have a full programme of sports fixtures and tournaments and have achieved notable successes across a range of sports.

Out of hours options provide high-quality support to working parents. Children may arrive for breakfast at 7.30 am and our 'Kim Club' facility is available after school until 6.00 pm. There is also an extensive range of extra-curricular activities, clubs, and supervised prep to extend the school day. Many of our children use our daily bus service to travel to and from school.

Kimbolton Preparatory School was inspected by ISI in 2011.

Charitable status. Kimbolton School Foundation is a Registered Charity, number 1098586.

King Edward's Junior School
Bath

North Road, Bath BA2 6JA

Tel:	01225 463218
Fax:	01225 442178
email:	junior@kesbath.com
website:	www.kesbath.com
Twitter:	@KESBath
Facebook:	@kesbath

Chair of Governors: Mrs W Thomson, MEd, BEd Hons, LLCM TD

Head Teacher: **Mr G Taylor**, BA Ed, NPQH

Age Range. 7–11 Co-educational.
Number of Pupils. 196.
Fees per term (2018–2019). £3,750.

Our award-winning, purpose-built Junior School on the same North Road site as the Senior School is extremely well equipped for learning, with dedicated specialist teaching rooms for Science, Art, Design Technology and Music and a state-of-the-art ICT Suite and Technology Centre, all housed around a lovely central library. The School also includes a large multi-purpose hall and dining room.

Externally, the Junior School has its own adventure playground, dipping ponds, wildflower garden and multi-sport play area, an Activity Trail, as well as access to the Meadow, a delightful and spacious area with beautiful views over Bath.

The Junior School is an integral part of the King Edward's foundation and is governed by the same Board. It joins with the Senior School in major events, such as the Founder's Day Service in Bath Abbey, and shares various games facilities and specialist teaching staff.

All children learn the strings (violin, viola, cello and double bass) in Year 3, recorder in Year 4, whole class orchestra/band and Gamelan in Year 5 and Steel Pans in Year 6. Well over half of the children learn additional instruments under the tutelage of a strong peripatetic music team. A mixture of French, German and Spanish is taught throughout the School while purpose-built facilities in Art, Science, Technology and IT, coupled with specialist teaching, ensure high standards of achievement in those areas. The School is a very busy one renowned for its co-curricular programme. The wide variety of activities on offer include table tennis, gymnastics, fencing, judo, chess, dance, Eco Club and Crafty Club. This is not to mention the various musical and instrumental groups and the many opportunities to play rugby, football, hockey, netball, cricket, basketball, tennis, rounders, cross country and athletics. Frequent educational trips are arranged in and around the local area and during the summer Activities Week; residential trips for Years 3–6, include destinations such as France and Devon. Sporting tours also take place each year.

The House system plays a central role in the life of the School. All children belong to one of four Houses and take part in many events and competitions during the year.

Pre-Prep & Nursery and Senior School. For details of the Pre-Prep and Nursery please see separate IAPS entry and for Senior School details please see King Edward's School's entry under HMC.

Charitable status. King Edward's Junior School is part of King Edward's School Bath which is a Registered Charity, number 1115875.

King Edward's School Pre-Prep and Nursery
Bath

Weston Lane, Bath BA1 4AQ

Tel:	01225 421681
Fax:	01225 428006
email:	pre-prep@kesbath.com
website:	www.kesbath.com
Twitter:	@KESBath
Facebook:	@kesbath

Chair of Governors: Mrs W Thomson, MEd, BEd Hons, LLCM TD

Head Teacher: **Ms J Gilbert**, BEd Hons, NPQH

Age Range. 3–7.
Number of Pupils. 107.
Fees per term (2018–2019). £2,790–£3,385.

King Edward's Pre-Prep and Nursery offers an exciting and stimulating world in which to start school life. A desire to make learning 'irresistible' in a nurturing environment is at the heart of everything we do. Personalised learning, combined with academic rigour, ensures that every child thrives and is provided with the extension and support that they need. New initiatives, fresh challenges, concerts, trips, visiting experts and inspiring projects all help to enrich our broad and creative curriculum.

Ethos. *Child focused* – First and foremost we want every child to feel safe, encouraged and happy in school. We place children at the centre of learning, creating a close match between your child and the curriculum. This helps to increase a child's eagerness to learn, builds self-esteem and encourages positive attitudes.

Family focused – Visitors to the Pre-Prep often remark on the wonderful 'family feel' that they sense in the school. We work very hard to be as family-focused as possible and are very fortunate to have such supportive parents; we are never short of volunteers for the many school trips that the children enjoy and for all the varied events that take place. It is lovely to see not only parents but grandparents taking an active role in the school.

Outdoor focused – At King Edward's the outdoor environment is a natural extension of the classroom and we are proud of our status as a Forest School. As well as allowing children to engage directly with the environment, outdoor learning also brings together many different elements of the curriculum and enriches school life.

Facilities. Our Pre-Prep and Nursery is situated in a beautiful Victorian house close to Royal Victoria Park, Bath. In addition to the light and airy classrooms, we have a well-equipped gymnasium and school hall with stage. There is also a specialist music room, ICT suite, Teddy's Lodge for pre and after school care, a newly enhanced art room and library. Children make full use of the spacious and safe grounds to the rear of the main house, with a dedicated outdoor cedar lodge classroom, storytelling corner, surfaced playground, wooden fort, wooded area and climbing frame. There is also a designated gardening area with greenhouse, where the children cultivate their own vegetables. There is also a magical sensory garden and playing field for team games.

Junior School and Senior School. For details of the Junior School please see separate IAPS entry and for the Senior School please see King Edward's School's entry under HMC.

Charitable status. King Edward's Pre-Prep and Nursery is part of King Edward's School Bath which is a Registered Charity, number 1115875.

King Henry VIII Preparatory School

Kenilworth Road, Coventry CV3 6PT

Tel: 024 7627 1307
Fax: 024 7627 1308
email: headteacher@khps.co.uk
website: www.khps.co.uk

Chairman of Governors: Mrs Julia McNaney

Head: **Mrs Gill Bowser**

Age Range. 3–11 Co-educational.
Pupils. 500 Day Boys and Girls.
Fees per term (2018–2019). Nursery: £29 per morning (excl. lunch), £39 (incl. lunch), £49 all day (incl. lunch), Reception–Year 2 £3,087 (incl. lunch), Years 3–6 £2,981 (excl. lunch).

King Henry VIII Preparatory School is part of Coventry School Foundation, which includes King Henry VIII Senior School and Bablake School (3–18).

The School is situated on two campuses a short distance from each other on the south side of Coventry.

Swallows Campus, opposite Coventry Memorial Park, educates children aged 3–7 in classes of 16 (from Reception onwards). The campus occupies a beautiful 3½ acre site with a wealth of facilities, including its own Swimming Pool, Sports Hall, Music Department, Library, ICT Suite, Art & Design Centre, All-weather surface and play areas. Its main building dates to the 17th century. The majority of teaching is provided by class teachers, giving young children a continuity of approach. A number of specialist teachers are provided as children progress through Key Stage 1 in Music, Games and Swimming and Art & Design Technology from Reception. A strong tradition of pastoral care exists at the School. Fundamentally, the School seeks to be a happy place where individuals can grow and express themselves. We recognise that each child is unique and will have their own developmental path: we are committed to helping pupils to develop at the appropriate times, in the direction of their talents and interests, and to ensure that all children feel safe and secure

Hales Campus occupies a portion of the main King Henry VIII School site. The main building was purpose-built in 1996 and provides an excellent range of modern facilities for children aged 7–11 including its own Sports Hall, Music Department, Library, ICT Suite, Art & Design Room, Science Laboratory and play areas. Some facilities are shared with the senior school, including games fields and a 25-metre indoor swimming pool.

Children are taught from Year 5 by specialist teachers for all subjects in classes of around 20. The School seeks to encourage and develop a range of gifts and talents amongst its pupils (academic, artistic, creative and sporting). It has high academic standards and aspirations but the timetable is broad with plenty of extra-curricular activities.

King Henry VIII Preparatory School is a feeder school for King Henry VIII School (11–18) and therefore tries to ensure that each child offered a place has a good chance of passing the senior school entrance examination taken at the age of 11 during Year 6. King Henry VIII Senior School is academically selective and accepts pupils who work at a level typically well above age-related expectations. The main points of entry to King Henry VIII Preparatory School are at the ages of 3, 4 or 7. Children may gain admission to the school at other ages subject to there being vacancies in specific year groups. Once a child has been accepted at the School, education at King Henry VIII Preparatory School may be continued by the child up to the age of 11, without there being any examinations to prevent progress through the School. After the point of entry any assessments undertaken are to monitor progress and guide teachers' planning to ensure that the curriculum is well matched to the needs of individuals.

The school is not academically selective for children joining in Nursery and Reception. However, all children must show a good level of competency for their age in spoken English and have sufficient independence to meet their personal needs.

Children joining the school in Years 1 and 2 will be assessed during individual 'taster days'.

Children joining the school from Year 3 onwards are assessed more formally by way of an Entrance Assessment.

Our broad and balanced sports curriculum, alongside a strong extra-curricular programme of activities, provides opportunities for all children to succeed in sport. We aim to develop a love of being physically active, enable all children to engage in sport at a level appropriate to each individual and give opportunities for children to play in a competitive environment.

There is a very strong music tradition at King Henry VIII Preparatory School and many opportunities for children to develop their musical talents. Music lessons are taught by a music specialist from Nursery upwards. Children in Years 3 and 4 participate in our choirs. Optional choirs are available in Years 2, 5 and 6. In addition to classroom music and singing, children can learn solo instruments in school. We have a number of talented peripatetic music teachers who deliver high-quality tuition during the school day. Children learning solo instruments (in or out of school) have the opportunity to join one of the many extra-curricular music clubs and groups which take place before, during and after school. There are also solo performance opportunities in concerts throughout the year.

Scholarships are awarded to existing pupils based on formal and informal assessments at the end of Year 3 in the form of discounted fees. There are a limited number of bursaries available at entrance from Year 3 onwards (7+). These are awarded on the basis of financial need and subject to passing the entrance exam.

The School has a vibrant extra-curricular activities programme which may be accessed by pupils from Reception onwards, this includes both lunchtime and after-school clubs. Before-school care (from 7.45 am) and after-school care (up to 6.00 pm) are available daily during term time. The school runs holiday clubs for children aged from 3–11, starting at 8.00 am and continuing until 5.30 pm, during school holidays.

School trips and educational visits are regarded as an important aspect of each child's experience at school. These include visits to local places of interest, usually associated with programmes of study, but also residential trips for each year group from the age of 7 onwards, including one to France in Year 5.

Confide Recte Agens – Have the confidence to do what is right. The school motto is the driver for the moral compass we aim to develop in our pupils. We promise that the best interests of the child will always be at the heart of our decision making.

King Henry VIII Preparatory School has a Christian tradition, in keeping with the other schools in the Coventry

School Foundation, however children from all faiths and cultural backgrounds are warmly welcomed. Tolerance, forgiveness and understanding between people of different religions, races, backgrounds and countries are imperatives in a modern world. Children are taught that differences between people and places help to make the world a wonderful and fascinating place. King Henry VIII School has an association with Coventry Cathedral and is a member of its Community of the Cross of Nails which seeks international peace and reconciliation.

Charitable status. Coventry School Foundation is a Registered Charity, number 528961. Its aim is to advance the education of boys and girls by the provision of schools in or near the City of Coventry.

King's College School, Cambridge

West Road, Cambridge, Cambridgeshire CB3 9DN

Tel:	01223 365814
email:	office@kcs.cambs.sch.uk
website:	www.kcs.cambs.sch.uk

Chairman of Governors: The Revd Dr S Cherry

Head: **Mrs Y F S Day**, BMus Cape Town, MMus London, GDL College of Law

Deputy Heads:
Mr T Hales, BA Hons
Miss C Greenlaw, BA

Age Range. 4–13 Co-educational.

Number of Pupils. 404 day pupils, 35 boy boarders including 27 choristers.

Fees per term (2018–2019). Weekly Boarders £8,070; Choristers £2,665; Day Pupils £5,185; Pre-Prep £4,080.

King's College School is a leading independent prep school with 413 boys and girls aged 4–13. We are large enough to provide a full range of options and facilities, but small enough to give a 'family feel' where the teachers can get to know all the children.

The school enjoys an excellent academic reputation, with a pleasing number of leavers winning scholarships to senior schools in various disciplines.

Situated close to the centre of Cambridge, the School is ideally placed to combine the strengths of traditional academic and cultural excellence with modern and innovative educational ideas.

Admission. Prospective parents are invited to come to King's for an individual tour of the School with the Registrar. Entry to all year groups is by assessment and by taking into account current school reports (Years 1–8).

Curriculum. Our curriculum embraces the Common Entrance and Independent Schools Scholarship syllabuses, as well as meeting the requirements laid down in the National Curriculum. We also teach French from the age of 4, Latin from age 9, and Greek to some older children. Standards of literacy and numeracy are high at King's. While external examination success is the final goal, children are encouraged to develop a sense of achievement, enjoyment and attainment of potential in all subjects. The School has a history of winning numerous academic, art, music, drama and sports awards annually.

Choristers. In 1441 Henry VI founded King's College and decreed that there should be 16 choristers to sing at services in his chapel. Now over 550 years later, our choristers are famed throughout the world and each year millions of listeners and viewers tune in on Christmas Eve to enjoy the 'Festival of Nine Lessons and Carols' from King's College Chapel. For more information about the choir and choristerships at King's please visit our website: http://www.kcs.cambs.sch.uk/kings-choristers.

Facilities. The Wiles Centre for Technology has first-class facilities for ICT and DT. The Performing Arts Centre includes 16 music rooms and a multi-purpose hall used for plays and concerts; it also doubles as a fully-equipped gym.

A modern classroom block contains 2 well-equipped science labs as well as classrooms for modern languages, English and maths; our purpose-built library houses over 15,000 books.

Music. King's has a strong tradition of musical excellence and encourages pupils to participate on all levels. We have many choral and instrumental groups including 2 orchestras of some 80 players each and about 40 chamber groups.

Sports. Our new sports and cultural centre is now complete and includes facilities for badminton, netball, basketball, cricket, dance, concerts, lectures and assemblies. We also have two large playing fields, tennis courts, a heated outdoor swimming pool, floodlit astroturf, and two recently-built squash courts. Games include Rugby, Football, Hockey, Cricket, Girls' Cricket, Netball, Rounders, Athletics, Tennis, Squash, and Swimming.

Activities. Drama, Art, Computing, Craft, Touch-typing, Spelling, Gardening, DT, Gymnastics, PE, Chess, Science, Wildlife Explorers, Library, Orienteering, Yoga, Ballet, Spanish, Electronics, Karate, Jazz Dance, Street Dance, Airfix, Ballet, Cookery, Cross Stitch, Spelling, Board Games, French Films, and Mandarin Chinese.

Staff. The Head is assisted by 51 full-time and 22 part-time teachers. There are 40 full or part-time music staff.

Bursaries. Means tested bursaries are available for Primary School children applying for places in Years 3 or 4.

Leaving King's. Pupils are prepared for local senior school entrance assessments as well as for Common Entrance and academic scholarship examinations. Most children are offered places at their first-choice senior school and many achieve scholarship awards.

Charitable status. King's College School is an integral part of King's College, Cambridge, which is a Registered Charity, number 1139422. Its aim is to provide an excellent education for girls and boys of mixed ability aged 4 to 13.

King's College Junior School

Wimbledon Common, London SW19 4TT

Tel:	020 8255 5335
Fax:	020 8255 5339
email:	jsadmissions@kcs.org.uk
	HMJSsec@kcs.org.uk
website:	www.kcs.org.uk
Twitter:	@KCJSWimbledon

Chairman of the Governing Body: Lord Deighton, KBE

Headmaster: **Dr G A Silverlock**, BEd Hons, MLitt, PhD

Age Range. 7–13.

Number of Boys. 460 (day boys only).

Fees per term (2018–2019). £5,980 (Years 3–4), £6,510 (Years 5–8).

The Junior School was established in 1912 as an integral part of KCS, to prepare boys for the Senior School. It shares with it a common site and many facilities, in particular the Music School, the Art, Design and Technology School, the

Dining Hall, the Sports Hall, the swimming pool and extensive playing fields. For the rest, Junior School boys are housed in their own buildings. The Priory, rebuilt in 1980, contains twenty-three classrooms, including specialist rooms for languages, mathematics, history, geography, information technology and multimedia work. The youngest age groups have their own special accommodation in Rushmere, a spacious Georgian house whose grounds adjoin the Junior School. The School also has its own purpose-built library, science laboratories and well-equipped theatre and assembly hall.

The School is separately administered in matters relating to admission, curriculum, discipline and day to day activities. There are thirty-six members of staff in addition to those teaching in specialist departments common to both Schools.

The work and overall programme are organised in close consultation with the Senior School to ensure that boys are educated in a structured and progressive way from 7 to 18, having the benefit of continuity, while enjoying the range and style of learning that are best suited to their age.

Boys come from both maintained and pre-preparatory schools and are admitted at the age of 7, 8, 9 or 10. Entry is by interview and examination.

Charitable status. King's College School is a Registered Charity, number 310024. It exists to provide education for children.

King's Ely Junior

Ely, Cambridgeshire CB7 4DB

Tel: 01353 660732
Fax: 01353 665281
email: admissions@kingsely.org
website: www.kingsely.org/Junior
Twitter: @kings_ely

Chairman of the Governors: Mr J Hayes

Head: Mr R J Whymark, BA Ed Hons

Age Range. 7–13.
Number of Pupils. Boarders: 28 Boys, 10 Girls; Day: 159 Boys, 144 Girls.
Fees per term (2018–2019). Boarding £7,564–£7,985; Day £4,744–£5,177.

King's Ely Junior has its own specialist teaching staff and its buildings are part of the main school campus. The facilities of King's Ely Senior are freely available to King's Ely Junior boys and girls.

There is a family boarding house for boys and girls up to the age of 13 and a separate boarding house for the boy choristers of Ely Cathedral who are all pupils at King's Ely Junior. Each has its own Housemaster or Housemistress, assisted by House Tutors and experienced Matrons. Both Houses have recently been refurbished and offer excellent boarding facilities.

During the school day all children are divided into four equal-sized co-educational 'Houses' for pastoral and competitive purposes. Each of these 'Houses' is staffed by a Housemaster or Housemistress and several House Tutors.

Entry to King's Ely Junior for boys and girls is through assessment tests and interview. The main two entry points are Year 3 (age 7) and Year 7 (age 11) but pupils may start in any year providing there is space. The main assessment weeks are in January, although it is common to assess for entry at other times of the year. Exceptional children for

Year 7 entry may be invited to take the King's Ely Junior Scholarship examination. A broad preparatory school curriculum is followed and all pupils are prepared for the relevant transfer examination. While the great majority proceed to King's Ely Senior in Year 9, pupils can also be prepared for other Independent Schools.

The main games for boys are Rugby, Football, Cricket and Tennis, and for girls they are Hockey, Netball, Cricket and Tennis. Both boys and girls are involved in Athletics and Cross-Country Running. There is a Swimming Pool, a well-equipped Sports Hall, a full-size all-weather hockey/tennis area, and excellent playing fields. Rowing is offered throughout the academic year from Year 8 onwards. A wide-ranging programme of extra-curricular activities is also offered. All pupils have the opportunity to learn one or more of a wide variety of musical instruments. There are several Junior School Orchestras, and choral and ensemble music are taught. The Junior School musicians regularly tour abroad. The School has its own Music School and Technology Centre, and access to the Senior School's new £1 million Recital Hall and Music School. Years 7 and 8 enjoy a new £1.2m block of seven classrooms and a science laboratory, plus recreational and study facilities.

The School is also justly proud of its art and drama, which are taught in their own studios, and of its excellent computer facilities.

Charitable status. The King's School, Ely is a Registered Charity, number 802427. It exists for the provision of education.

King's Hall School
A Woodard School

Kingston Road, Taunton, Somerset TA2 8AA

Tel: 01823 285920
Fax: 01823 285922
email: schooloffice@kingshalltaunton.co.uk
            admissions@kingshalltaunton.co.uk
website: www.kingshalltaunton.co.uk
Twitter: @KingsHallSchool
Facebook: @Kings-Hall-School

Headmaster: **Mr J T S Chippendale**, BSc Joint Hons

Director of Finance and Operations: Mr S C Worthy, BA, MBA
Deputy Head (Academic): Mrs J Brazier, BSc Hons
Deputy Head (Pastoral): Mr S Watson, BA, BSc
Head of Pre-Prep: Mrs C Luckhurst, BEd Hons
Head of Boarding: Mrs C Masters
Director of Admissions: Mrs K Rippin
Chaplain: The Revd M A Smith, BA, Dip Th

Age Range. 2–13 Co-educational.
Number of Pupils. 153 boys, 147 girls; including 40 boarders.
Fees per term (2018–2019). Preparatory: Day £3,220–£5,500, Full/Weekly Boarding £6,150–£7,995, Pre-Prep £2,575–£2,675.

King's Hall School is a leading Pre-Prep and Prep school with around 300 girls and boys. Set in a beautiful countryside location surrounded by farmland, the school is only a couple of minutes' drive from the centre of Taunton. The school respects traditional values and boarding is a strong feature, which contributes to the tangible family atmosphere that exists in the school. Children enjoy a challenging all-round education in a progressive and stimulating environment. King's Hall has a partner senior school, King's College, Taunton, and the two schools benefit from having their own independent sites, furnished with excellent age-appropriate facilities and attitudes to maximise the opportunities for the children in our care. There is a close working relationship between King's Hall and King's College and the vast majority of pupils move on there at age 13. Scholarships are available for pupils with exceptional ability. These are awarded at 11+ and continue at King's College, Taunton up to age 18.

King's Hawford

Hawford Lock Lane, Claines, Worcester, Worcestershire WR3 7SD

Tel: 01905 451292
Fax: 01905 756502
email: hawford@ksw.org.uk
website: www.ksw.org.uk
Twitter: @KingsHawford

Chairman of the Governors: H B Carslake, BA, LLB

Headmaster: **J M Turner**, BEd Hons, DipEd, ACP

Age Range. 2–11.
Number of Pupils. 297.
Fees per term (2018–2019). £2,448–£4,407 (excluding lunch).

King's Hawford is a junior school to the historic King's School, Worcester, and is set in twenty-three acres of parkland situated on the northern outskirts of Worcester. The school is accommodated within an elegant and recently refurbished Georgian house surrounded by well-maintained playing fields, with tennis courts, a heated enclosed swimming pool, a multi-purpose sports hall and performance space and secure play area for younger children. Academic results are excellent. The school has a strong focus on outdoor learning, with an outdoor classroom, a traversing wall, 2 forest school areas and trees that children can climb. Children are taught to navigate the adjacent canal in the school's katakanus. The childrens' weekly radio show is posted on the website. The school has recently purchased a Double Decker Bus that has been converted into an amazing library for the children to enjoy.

There are extensive opportunities for a wide range of extra-curricular activities and there is a busy calendar of music, drama, sport, dance and many other clubs. Sports include Rugby, Association Football, Cricket, Hockey, Netball, Rounders, Athletics, Tennis, Cross-Country and Swimming. The school has been awarded the prestigious Artsmark Gold.

The Pre-Prep department accepts children from age 2–6 and the Junior department from age 7–11.

Charitable status. The King's School Worcester is a Registered Charity, number 1098236. It exists to provide a broad education for a wide range of children from 2–11 years.

King's House School

68 King's Road, Richmond, Surrey TW10 6ES

Tel: 020 8940 1878
Fax: 020 8939 2501
email: schooloffice@kingshouseschool.org
website: www.kingshouseschool.org

Established in 1946, the School was constituted as an Educational Trust with a Board of Governors in 1957.

Chair of Governors: Mrs Christine Laverty

Head: **Mr Mark Turner**, BA, PGCE, NPQH

Age Range. Boys 3–13 (Co-educational Nursery).
Number of Pupils. 450.
Fees per term (2018–2019). Nursery Department £2,370–£2,610; Junior Department £4,315–£5,005; Senior Department £5,560 (all fees inclusive of lunch excluding Nursery).

We believe the King's House School is a very special place and are very proud of what we have on offer here and what we do.

We are a lively, busy, happy School and one where we feel that the boys (and girls in our wonderful Nursery) thrive. Our aim is to offer a broad education to all our pupils, enabling them to develop their academic, social, sporting and artistic attributes. This breadth and balance on offer is we believe one of the strengths of the School.

The academic side underpins the education here with the emphasis on the core areas in the early years spreading to an increasing range of subjects by the top end of the School. The destination schools of our leavers show that the boys are achieving well academically.

We believe very much that King's House is a community; we pride ourselves on strong pastoral care and an environment where the children feel happy. The positive relationships that we enjoy with our parents and the local community and our links to Rwanda are all key to our sense of responsibility.

The School is based on three sites on Richmond Hill and also benefits from its own extensive playing fields in Chiswick. The three main School sites have spacious state-of-the-art facilities. The School also enjoys the advantages of having close access to London with all the educational opportunities that affords.

King's House is a friendly, caring and supportive School. We have a strong sense of community both within the School and with our parents but we are also keen to play a role in the local and global community and to develop our pupils' sense of awareness of the world around them.

King's House is a lively, busy and happy School and we aim to give each child a broad academic and balanced education. We provide an environment in which the children feel secure and are able to flourish; offering opportunities to take part and develop in all areas, so that the needs of each individual are catered for.

King's House is non-selective at our two main entry points, Nursery and Reception, and this means we have a range of pupils and abilities. We believe that boys benefit from staying in the prep environment until they are 13 years old before moving on. Their final two years here allow them to grow up and develop a sense of responsibility, taking on roles around the school. The boys are well-prepared for the transition to their senior schools.

King's House is proud of its traditions and history. Its principles and standards are founded on Christian values although the school is not aligned to any particular religion, and welcomes pupils of all religions and backgrounds.

For more information visit the school's website or contact our Registrar, Sally Bass, on 020 8940 1878 or bass.s@kingshouseschool.org.

Charitable status. Kings House School Trust (Richmond) Limited is a Registered Charity, number 312669. It exists for the education of children.

King's St Alban's School

Mill Street, Worcester, Worcestershire WR1 2NJ

Tel:	01905 354906
Fax:	01905 763075
email:	ksa@ksw.org.uk
website:	www.ksw.org.uk
Twitter:	@KingsStAlbans
Facebook:	@KingsStAlbans

Chairman of the Governors: H B Carslake, BA, LLB

Head: R A Chapman, BSc

Age Range. 4–11 Co-educational.

Number of Pupils. 193.

Fees per term (2018–2019). £2,336–£4,226 excluding lunch.

Education is about far more than academic learning, although that is still our primary purpose. At King's St Alban's we aim to develop the whole child, encouraging each girl and boy to explore their capabilities, find fresh challenges and discover spheres in which they can excel.

King's St Alban's, an established school with a purpose-built Pre-Preparatory Department, is located near to Worcester Cathedral on a separate site adjacent to the Senior School. In the grounds stand the Chapel, the main buildings of the Junior School with the Pre-Preparatory Department on an adjacent, self contained site. The school has a large hall, a dedicated Science Laboratory, an IT suite, an Art and Technology Room, well-stocked Libraries and Music Rooms, all of which supplement the usual amenities of a preparatory school. In addition, use is made of Senior School facilities, which include an indoor Swimming Pool, a fully equipped Sports Hall, Dance Studio, Fitness Centre, the Music School, Playing Fields, and a purpose-built Theatre.

We work hard to discover talent and develop it to the full. Music, Art, Dance and Drama play an important part in the life of the school. King's St Alban's supports an Orchestra, Wind Band, Flute Choir and String and Recorder groups with most children playing at least one musical instrument. In the Junior School nearly all children are involved in the school's Choir and there is a smaller Chamber Choir. The annual Carol Service is held in the Cathedral with concerts and musical evenings held each term in the Theatre and Chapel. A major whole-school production is staged annually in the Theatre with several smaller workshop productions taking place during the year.

The staff comprises a mix of men and women, all of whom are experienced and well qualified. In addition there are various visiting music and sport specialists.

The main sports are Rugby, Netball, Soccer, Hockey, Cricket and Rounders with Swimming, Cross-Country, Orienteering and Tennis also featured. Matches are arranged with other schools and excellence is sought, but participation of all girls and boys is the main objective. A thriving inter-House competition provides further opportunities for all to enjoy competition.

Beyond the classroom an extensive programme of after-school activities is available with opportunities varying each term, examples are Art & Craft, Science, Fencing, Ball Skills, Latin, Chess and Swimming. Children from across the school spend time each year at the school's Outdoor Activity Centre in the Black Mountains.

King's St Alban's is academically selective and pupils are expected to progress to the Senior School, subject to a satisfactory performance in their examinations at the age of 11. The main assessment of candidates for the Junior School takes place in early February for entry the following September, but assessments can be arranged on an individual basis throughout the year, when required. The tests cover English, Mathematics and Verbal Reasoning.

There are a small number of Scholarships and Bursaries available from the age of 7, as are Choral Scholarships for Cathedral Choristers.

Charitable status. The King's School, Worcester is a Registered Charity, number 1098236. It exists to provide high quality education for girls and boys.

Junior King's School

Milner Court, Sturry, Canterbury, Kent CT2 0AY

Tel:	01227 714000
email:	office@junior-kings.co.uk
website:	www.junior-kings.co.uk
Twitter:	@JuniorKingsSch

Chairman of Governors: The Very Revd Dr R A Willis, BA, Dip Th, FRSA, Dean of Canterbury Cathedral

Headmistress: Mrs Emma Károlyi

Age Range. 3–13.

Number of Pupils. 342 (60 Boarders; 282 Day Pupils, including 76 Pre-Prep).

Fees per term (2018–2019). Boarders £8,570; Day Pupils £5,620–£6,245; Pre-Prep £3,715 (including meals).

Junior King's was founded in 1879 as the preparatory school to The King's School Canterbury, which can trace its roots back to the sixth century when St Augustine established a monastery in Kent.

Set in eighty acres of attractive countryside, just two miles from Canterbury city centre, Junior King's pupils enjoy a calm, happy and purposeful atmosphere drawing upon a rich Christian heritage. Girls and boys from the ages of three to thirteen years achieve their potential, both inside and beyond the classroom, whatever their ability.

The school has an outstanding reputation for academic excellence and scholarship due to a varied and stimulating curriculum. This is supported by first class teaching and opportunities to enjoy a wide range of sports, music, drama and extra-curricular activities.

The school is in the grounds of Milner Court, a 16th century Manor House This historic building, along with a Kentish Oast House used by the Pre-Prep, a newly-refurbished Tithe Barn used for theatre and musical productions, and a flint stoned church for services and assemblies has been sensitively augmented over the years. Other impressive facilities include specialist art, science, ICT and design suites.

Spacious and comfortable boarding accommodation for around 80 boarders with social rooms, kitchens and games rooms are at the heart of the school in the main building.

The school has a fine reputation for music, both instrumental and choral, as well as for art, design and drama. The school year includes a programme of concerts, recitals and exhibitions involving children of all ages.

In 2013, Mr Hugh Robertson, MP and Minister of State for Sport, Olympic Legacy and Tourism opened a stunning new all-weather sports pitch and tennis courts. In 2016, a magnificent new music school was officially opened by Dr Harry Christophers, CBE, OKS.

A large and modern sports hall is used for PE lessons, basketball, volleyball, badminton, and netball, as well as indoor hockey, soccer and tennis. Rowing and sailing take place on nearby lakes. Pupils make use of the large indoor swimming pool at the senior school.

For boys, cricket, soccer hockey and rugby are the main team games, while girls play netball, hockey and rounders. Athletics, tennis and fencing are joint pursuits.

Children can join the Nursery from the age of three in our impressive purpose-built 'Little Barn'. In its delightful Kentish Oast House setting, the Pre-Prep has its own spacious hall, library and seven bright classrooms complete with the latest ICT facilities. Outside, pupils have their own extensive adventure playground as well as sharing the main school facilities such as the sports hall, tithe barn, sports fields and dining hall.

Junior King's pupils progress at 13+ to The King's School Canterbury and other leading public schools, with a sense of achievement, maturity and self-confidence. Academic standards are high and the record of success in Scholarships and Common Entrance is outstanding.

(*See entry for The King's School Canterbury in the HMC section.*)

Charitable status. The King's School of the Cathedral Church of Canterbury is a Registered Charity, number 307942. It exists to provide education for boys and girls.

King's Rochester Preparatory School

King Edward Road, Rochester, Kent ME1 1UB

Tel:	01634 888577
Fax:	01634 888507
email:	prep@kings-rochester.co.uk
website:	www.kings-rochester.co.uk
Twitter:	@Kings_Rochester
Facebook:	@KingsRochester
LinkedIn:	/king-s-school-rochester

Chairman of Governors: Ms J A Shicluna, MA Oxon

Headmaster: **Mr Tom Morgan**, BMus Hons RCM, QTS

Age Range. 8–13.
Number of Pupils. 250.
Fees per term (2018–2019). Boarders £7,320, Day Pupils £4,395–£4,985 (including lunches).

Admission between 8+ to 12+ is by interview and report from present school as well as Entrance Examinations in English, Mathematics and Verbal or Non-Verbal Reasoning. Many children also join at 11+ and sit either our November or March 11+ Assessment Tests in English, Mathematics and Non-Verbal Reasoning.

Scholarships are awarded (partly from the Cathedral, partly from the School) to Cathedral Choristers (boys at age 8 and girls at age 10) and King's (30%) or Governors' Exhibitions (means-tested up to 100%) to those whose performance in the Entrance Examination merits it.

The Preparatory School is an integral part of King's Rochester, founded in 604 AD by Justus, a Benedictine monk, the first Bishop of Rochester. The Cathedral is at the heart of the School's life with a weekly School service and every day the Choristers maintain the tradition of choral singing at the world's oldest Choir School. When the School is not in the Cathedral a religious assembly is held at the Preparatory School.

The School is a member of the Choir Schools' Association.

Set in Rochester Town Centre, the Preparatory School building overlooks the beautiful Paddock, one of the School's large playing fields. The teaching block consists of 12 classrooms, 2 Science Laboratories, a Computer Suite, Language Laboratory and a Library with over 6,000 volumes. Other facilities such as the Design and Technology Centre, Art Centre, Music School, Indoor Swimming Pool and Sports Halls are shared with the Senior School which virtually all pupils join following the internal Entrance Examination. The King's Rochester Sports Centre, just 10 minutes away, provides pupils with nine external tennis/netball courts, a large gymnasium, a fitness gym, physio suite and changing rooms.

The Preparatory School has a small number of boarders who are housed either in School House for boys, or St Margaret's House for girls. Boarding, both full and weekly, is available for boys and girls from 11+.

The curriculum is broad and balanced. In Year 8 science is taught as three separate subjects, French, German and Spanish are the modern languages, and Latin is taught to the A stream from Year 7. A full programme of CPSHE is given to all pupils. Individual educational support tuition and EFL is available if required.

All pupils enjoy the benefit of two full afternoons a week of Games in addition to a PE lesson for most year groups. Major sports include Rugby, Hockey, Cricket, Netball, Athletics, Tennis and Swimming. There is a wide range of extra-curricular activities at the end of the school day.

Choral and instrumental music is strong throughout the School. Many of our pupils learn one or more musical instruments and strong results are achieved in Associated Board examinations. Each year the Drama Club presents a play or musical held over three nights. Recently productions have required casts in excess of fifty and have been wonderful opportunities for pupils to show their dramatic and musical skills. Amongst latest productions have been *Peter Pan, The Roman Invasion of Ramsbottom, Honk!, The Caucasian Chalk Circle, Olivia, Bendigo Boswell, Homer's Odyssey, Under Milk Wood, Bugsy Malone, In Holland stands a House* and *Little Shop of Horrors*.

Charitable status. King's School, Rochester is a Registered Charity, number 1084266. It is a Charitable Trust for the purpose of educating children.

Kingshott

St Ippolyts, Hitchin, Hertfordshire SG4 7JX

Tel:	01462 432009
email:	pa2head@kingshottschool.com
website:	www.kingshottschool.com
Twitter:	@Kingshottsch
Facebook:	@KingshottSchool

Chairman of Governors: Mr David Keast

Headmaster: **Mr Mark Seymour**, BA, BSc, CertEd

Age Range. 3–13.
Number of Pupils. (All Day) Prep (7–13): 153 Boys, 95 Girls; Pre-Prep (4–7): 91 Boys, 76 Girls; Nursery (3–4): 19 Boys, 16 Girls.
Fees per term (2018–2019). (including Lunch) Nursery £2,030–£2,740, Pre-Prep £3,580, Prep £4,370.

Kingshott, founded in 1930, occupies a large Victorian building, with major recent classroom additions, in 23 acres of attractive grounds on the outskirts of Hitchin. Luton, Letchworth, Baldock, Stevenage, Welwyn and the A1(M)

Motorway are all within a 10 mile radius. The school has continued to invest in new facilities including a stand-alone Nursery building, Pre-Prep, Middle School (for Years 3–5) and most recently a purpose-built Prep School.

Kingshott, a Charitable Educational Trust, with a Board of Governors, welcomes all denominations. Children are encouraged to work towards and realise their individual potential – academic, creative, sporting – and to this end there is a happy friendly atmosphere, with strong emphasis on manners and being part of the wider community.

Kingshott offers a wide range of academic subjects including Latin, French, DT, Drama and ample curriculum time for PE and Games. This is complemented by a full and varied after-school programme.

There is a strong and successful sporting tradition which includes Football, Rugby, Cricket, Hockey, Netball, Rounders, Tennis, Swimming, Cross Country and Athletics. The School has a fabulous new sports and drama hall, its own covered, heated swimming pool, astroturf pitches, hard play areas and extensive playing fields.

Many pupils stay for Prep each evening, and there is opportunity for involvement in a wide variety of After-School Hobby activities. The School also offers a Breakfast Club and After-School Care is also available until 5.30 pm for Pre-Prep pupils.

Academic, Music, Art and Sports Scholarships to Senior Independent Schools are gained each year, and Common Entrance results are very sound, with virtually all children accepted by their first-choice schools.

Entry for Reception and beyond is by assessment, appropriate to age.

Registration for Nursery and Pre-Prep is advisable several years before required admission.

Charitable status. Kingshott School Trust Limited is a Registered Charity, number 280626. It exists to provide education for boys and girls.

Kingswood House School

56 West Hill, Epsom, Surrey KT19 8LG

Tel: 01372 723590
Fax: 01372 749081
email: office@kingswoodhouse.org
website: www.kingswoodhouse.org

The school is an educational trust, overseen by a board of governors.

Chairman of Governors: Christopher Shipley, LLB Hons, MBA

Headmaster: **Duncan Murphy**, BA Hons, MEd, FRSA, FCMI, FCollT

Age Range. Boys 4–16.
Number of Pupils. 210 day pupils.
Fees per term (2018–2019). Reception–Year 2 £3,580, Years 3–8 £4,660, Years 9–11 £4,950. Free after-school care provided until 5.00 pm.

Founded in 1899, the school moved to its current site, a large Edwardian house in a leafy suburb of Epsom, just outside the town centre in 1920 and with excellent transport links.

At Kingswood House, we have long enjoyed an outstanding reputation as a leading preparatory school for boys. Our new senior department opened in September 2016, thereby extending our exceptional academic and pastoral provision

through to GCSE. We offer a genuine all-round education, underpinned by exciting curricular and co-curricular opportunities, with a strong emphasis on character development and preparation for life beyond the school gate. We are ambitious for our boys and challenge each individual to achieve their potential in a conducive environment of small classes and high expectations.

Accredited as "excellent in all areas" in our last ISI inspection, Kingswood House is also endorsed by the Independent Association of Preparatory Schools (IAPS) and the Society of Heads (SoH).

Our values promote tolerance, respect and friendship and we welcome families from all faiths, or none. We offer a well-rounded education and a purposeful, supportive ethos in which each child will grow in independence, resilience and self-esteem. All boys are encouraged to participate in every aspect of school life. A rich variety of opportunities, both inside and outside the classroom, engenders an avid natural curiosity and propagates a willingness to try new things.

With the advent of our flourishing Senior Years, parents are able to consider their options carefully, secure in the knowledge that Kingswood House offers an excellent pathway for the boys through to GCSE. We are also developing KHS for the future and have recently built an impressive Lower Prep and Upper Prep Department. The new "Peter Brooks" building, boasting customised teaching accommodation for our Senior Years, opened in September 2018.

You are warmly invited to explore the benefits of a KHS education online, or better still, in person.

Charitable status. Kingswood House School is a Registered Charity, number 312044. It exists to provide educational support in the form of bursaries for the parents of children in need.

Kingswood Preparatory School

College Road, Lansdown, Bath BA1 5SD

Tel: 01225 734460
Fax: 01225 734470
email: kpsreception@kingswood.bath.sch.uk
website: www.kingswood.bath.sch.uk
Twitter: @KWS_Prep
Facebook: @KingswoodSchool

Chairman of Governors: **Mr T Westbrook**

Headmaster: **Mr Mark Brearey**, BA Hons, PGCE

Deputy Head: Ms Helen Worrall
Head of The Garden Nursery and Head of EYFS: Mrs A Ballanger
Head of Key Stage One: Miss Rebecca Howe
Senior Teacher, Girls Wellbeing & Pastoral: Mrs Marie McGlynn
Senior Teacher, Health and Safety: Mr David Murphy
Senior Teacher, Academic Number 2: Mrs Alexandra St Quintin

Age Range. 9 Months–11 Years.
Number of Pupils. 327: Prep: 115 boys, 69 girls; Pre-Prep: 43 boys, 46 girls; Nursery: 31 boys, 23 girls; 9 Boarders.
Fees per term (2018–2019). Nursery, Reception, Years 1 and 2: £3,334 (Nursery part-day pro rata); Years 3–4: £3,929; Years 5–6: £3,991. Boarding: £7,861–£8,240 (full), £6,603 (weekly).

Kingswood Prep School is the Preparatory School for Kingswood School, Bath. It is part of the Kingswood Foundation and each year over 95% of pupils move on to Kingswood School, through examination in January, at the end of Year 6.

Kingswood School is the oldest Methodist educational institution in the world, having been founded by John Wesley in 1748. Both Preparatory and the Senior Schools have extensive linked sites on Lansdown hill overlooking the world-famous city of Bath.

At Kingswood Preparatory School we are passionate about children's learning and combine high academic standards with a core of kindness that permeates every corner of our School. Our aim is to create a happy, caring community based upon Christian principles in which all individuals can develop respect for themselves and for others.

In September 2018, 'The Garden At Kingswood' was opened, welcoming children from nine months old for 50 weeks of the year. Secluded by woodland, The Garden is situated at the heart of the Prep School's expansive 100-acre parkland estate. Outdoor education is a vital part of life at Kingswood Prep School and the Nursery children will be able to explore the School's beautiful grounds and enjoy the age-specific play areas that lie right outside of their bespoke Nursery rooms.

We provide the children with a rich variety of academic, sporting, creative and social experiences. By doing so, we hope to give them the opportunity to develop their personalities and potential in an atmosphere of enthusiasm, enjoyment, security and care for fellow pupils.

As well as our regular Extra-Curricular Programme which currently contains over 80 weekly options, the school offers regular opportunities to participate in Music, Drama and Sport. We are able to use certain senior school facilities such as the swimming pool, the astroturf hockey pitch and the theatre. The Prep School shares 56 acres of playing fields with the seniors.

The Pre-Prep facilities are vibrant and stimulating, and our curriculum helps children to flourish through our enthusiastic and supportive teachers. During Years 3–6, we offer a broad and rich learning experience, combining the best of primary practice with high specialist teaching. We are proud of our warm, friendly, family atmosphere and all that we achieve within it.

The boarders live in High Vinnalls which offers all types of boarding to boys and girls aged between 7 and 11. Adjacent to the school and its superb surroundings, it has been acclaimed as a model for what boarding houses for young children should be like, in terms of its homely atmosphere and facilities.

Charitable status. Kingswood Preparatory School is a Registered Charity, number 309148. It exists for the purpose of educating children.

Knighton House

Durweston, Blandford, Dorset DT11 0PY

Tel: 01258 452065
Fax: 01258 450744
email: enquiries@knightonhouse.co.uk
website: www.knightonhouse.com
Twitter: @knighton_house
Facebook: @knighton.house.school

Joint Chairs of Governors: Mr Ian Weatherby & Mr Paul Slight

Head: Mr Robin Gainher, BSc Hons

Age Range. Girls 3–13, Boys 3–7.

Number of Pupils. Prep School: 80; The Orchard, Pre-Prep and Nursery (co-educational): 41.

Fees per term (2018–2019). Boarders £5,800–£7,600; Day: Prep £3,750–£4,950, Pre-Prep £2,700, Nursery: £2,325 (full time but excluding Early Years funding). There are no compulsory extras.

Established in 1950, Knighton House is an exceptional friendly day and boarding school for girls aged 7–13 with an 'outstanding' co-ed pre-prep for children aged 3–7.

Knighton House keeps pace with the expectations of the 21st Century, whilst nurturing its unique traditional values. As one of the few remaining all-girls prep schools, we pride ourselves on our pastoral care and the opportunities we offer girls through a crucial developmental stage of their life. We encourage independent thinking and learning and outdoor play is a key part of the school day. In a delightful country setting, the school provides a safe but challenging environment in which children can discover their strengths, take risks and make friends. Boarding is entirely flexible and ponies and pets are all welcome.

The small classes and high staff to pupil ratio ensures individual attention. The scholarships and awards won from Knighton House reflect academic, musical, artistic and all-rounder prowess; there is a strong artistic and musical tradition. Team sports and swimming have an all-year-round place in the timetable. There are many extracurricular activities including riding from our own stables, triathlon, tetrathlon, dance, drama and outdoor environmental pursuits.

This careful balance of academic subjects and extracurricular activities encourages all aspects of personal growth. The size of Knighton House ensures that each pupil is known by everyone; each girl has an identity and is respected for her individuality.

Knighton House feeds a wide range of senior schools, both co-ed and single-sex.

Charitable status. Knighton House School Limited is a Registered Charity, number 306316.

Knightsbridge School

67 Pont Street, London SW1X 0BD

Tel: 020 7590 9000
Fax: 020 7589 9055
email: registrar@knightsbridgeschool.com
website: www.knightsbridgeschool.com

Principal: **Mr Magoo Giles**

Head: **Ms Shona Colaço**

Age Range. 4–13.
Number in School. 430.
Fees per term (2018–2019). £6,500–£6,900.

Knightsbridge School is a preparatory school offering a broad, balanced and challenging curriculum to prepare both boys and girls for entry to senior day and boarding schools.

Pupils are encouraged to play hard, work hard in the Junior School and work hard, play hard in the Senior School, and make the most of every opportunity open to them to achieve their full potential. They are taught all National Curriculum subjects to a high standard, and modern languages from nursery age upwards.

The school fosters a strong sense of community, and provides a supportive and warm environment. Small classes, overseen by highly qualified, dynamic and enthusiastic staff, will ensure that boys and girls benefit not only academically but also personally. By developing their self-esteem and confidence they will grow into happy, independent all-rounders of healthy body and healthy mind.

Located in the heart of Central London, the school is housed in two magnificent mansions. The premises have undergone an extensive renovation and upgrade programme. Teaching facilities include well-equipped and modern class-rooms, a new science laboratory, an information and com-munication technology suite, music rooms, and a performing arts studio and a new library, as well as a fully catered kitchen and dining area.

Sports facilities include a gymnasium on site and the diverse and challenging sports programme makes use of local venues such as Burton's Court, Battersea Park, St Luke's recreational grounds, the Queen Mother Sports Cen-tre and Hyde Park.

Entry to Knightsbridge School is by informal interview of both parents and children at the appropriate level. Pro-spective boys and girls for Year 1 and above will be expected to spend a day of assessment at the school in their relevant year group, and a report from the Head of the appli-cant's current school will be required.

Lady Barn House School

Schools Hill, Cheadle, Cheshire SK8 1JE

Tel:　　　0161 428 2912
email:　　info@ladybarnhouse.org
website:　www.ladybarnhouse.org
Twitter:　@LadyBarnHouse
Facebook: @ladybarnhouseschool

Headmaster: **Mr M Turner**

　Age Range. 3–11.
　Number in School. Day: 238 Boys, 244 Girls.
　Fees per term (2018–2019). Nursery: £2,521 (all day), £1,675 (mornings only); KS1 & KS2: £2,880. Lunches £199 per term.

W H Herford, minister and educational pioneer, founded the school in 1873. His vision was to establish a co-educa-tional school that promoted happiness, academia, whilst embracing a Christian ethos. Today, Herford's vision still drives our thriving, family-orientated community. Boys and girls flourish, learning side by side, in an exceptional educa-tional setting.

We combine the latest educational thinking with tried and tested traditional methods. Pupils are gradually nurtured and developed so that they can confidently face their future with knowledge, understanding and the ability to be independent. Music, sport, drama, languages, outdoor adventure and a wide range of other clubs, trips and residential visits enhance our curriculum.

Pupils are prepared and supported for their 11+ entrance exams; they then move on to the best and most appropriate senior schools.

Lady Barn House School is a truly special educational institution where each and every pupil experiences success and reaches their potential. It remains one of the North West's most prestigious independent primary schools.

The School is a Charitable Trust. Bursaries are available for entry into Year 3 and above.

Charitable status. Lady Barn House School Limited is a Registered Charity, number 1042587. It exists to provide education for boys and girls.

Lady Eleanor Holles Junior School

Burlington House, 177 Uxbridge Road, Hampton, Middlesex TW12 1BD

Tel:　　　020 8979 2173
　　　　　Registrar & Senior School: 020 8979 1601
Fax:　　　020 8783 1962
email:　　junior-office@lehs.org.uk
website:　www.lehs.org.uk
Twitter:　@LEHSchool
Facebook: @LEHSchoolOfficial

Chairman of Governors: Mr C S Stokes

Head Mistress: Mrs H G Hanbury, MA, MSc

Head of Junior School: **Mrs Paula Mortimer**, BEd

　Age Range. 7–11.
　Number of Pupils. 188 day girls.
　Fees per term (2018–2019). £5,576.

Lady Eleanor Holles Junior School is housed in its own separate building in one corner of the school's spacious twenty-four-acre grounds. Junior School pupils make full use of the school's extensive facilities, such as the newly renovated heated indoor 25m pool, Sports Hall and floodlit netball courts. (*See The Lady Eleanor Holles School's entry in the GSA section for more details.*) They also take advan-tage of a fleet of school coaches serving most of West Lon-don and Surrey.

The school is academically selective, with most girls joining in Year 3. Entrance exams in English and Maths are held the January before entry. The vast majority of Junior School pupils are given guaranteed places in the Senior School.

The school's teaching is firmly based on the National Curriculum and there are specialist teachers for Science, Art, French, IT, Music and PE from the beginning. The school is very well resourced and staff use a wide variety of teaching styles and activities to ensure pace, stimulation and progression.

There is a wide range of extracurricular activities so girls can develop their own interests and abilities, and all achievements and progress are valued and praised.

Extracurricular clubs include Drama, Chess, Gardening and various Art, Music and Sports activities.

Whilst LEH is a broadly Christian foundation, it wel-comes girls of all faiths, and none. School Assemblies, some of which are performed by the girls for their parents, may feature Hindu, Islamic Sikh or Jewish festivals and stories, as well as Christian.

In 2003, Burlington House, the home of the Junior School, was the subject of a very extensive programme of extension and renovation, and now boasts superb facilities for a 21st-century education. Amongst the main improve-ments were four spacious new Practical Rooms for Art, DT and Science; two new Computer suites; a well-stocked and welcoming Library; and larger, brighter classrooms.

The staff work hard to establish and maintain a caring, supportive atmosphere in which girls feel confident to be themselves, to respect and care for everyone in the commu-nity, to be proud of their achievements and to persevere with things they find challenging. Pastoral care is a priority and we are proud of the happy, lively, hard-working pupils of the Junior School.

Charitable status. The Lady Eleanor Holles School is a Registered Charity, number 1130254.

Lambrook

Winkfield Row, Nr Ascot, Berkshire RG42 6LU

Tel: 01344 882717
email: registrar@lambrookschool.co.uk
             info@lambrookschool.co.uk
website: www.lambrookschool.co.uk
Twitter: @lambrookschool
Facebook: @lambrook

Chairman of Governors: Tom Beardmore-Gray, MA, FCA

Headmaster: Jonathan Perry, BA Hons, PGCE Cantab

Deputy Head: Daniel Cox, BA, MSc
Deputy Head: Nina Kingsmill Moore, HDE, MEd

Age Range. 3–13.
Number of Children. 540.
Fees per term (2018–2019). Prep: Weekly Boarding £7,366–£7,888; Day £6,056–£6,579. Pre-Prep: Day £4,104. Nursery: £1,875–£3,750.

Lambrook is a thriving independent preparatory day and boarding school (weekly and flexi boarding), home to 540 boys and girls. From our children's beginnings in our Nursery through their Pre-Prep and Prep education, we immerse them in a world of experiences forging the academic and life skills they will need to soar into their young adult lives. Our children excel at their Common Entrance examinations, with many securing prestigious scholarship awards, enabling them to progress to the leading independent senior schools in the country.

The Lambrook experience offers inspiration at every turn: inside the classroom, in our expansive 52-acre grounds and within the architecture of our historic school site, which blends the beauty of our 19th Century buildings with state-of-the-art specialist facilities. We are proud of our rich history of success and to have received an 'excellent' rating across the board from the Independent Schools Inspectorate.

Academic rigour is married with an enviable list of extra-curricular activities to feed young curious minds. On any day, the School is awash with activity on the sporting, musical and theatrical fronts that seek to draw the best out of each and every one of our pupils. Whilst opportunities abound at Lambrook, we recognise the vital role we also play in raising happy children. They have one opportunity for the education that will form the basis of their lives, and at the same time, one childhood: our aim is to keep a happy balance between the two.

We are situated in the Berkshire countryside near Ascot and are easily accessible from central London, the M4, M3 and M40 motorways. We provide transport services across the local area and also to and from West London.

Charitable status. Lambrook School Trust Limited is a Registered Charity, number 309098. Its purpose is to provide an excellent education for boys and girls.

Lancing College Preparatory School at Hove

A Woodard School

The Droveway, Hove, East Sussex BN3 6LU

Tel: 01273 503452
email: hove@lancing.org.uk
website: www.lancingcollege.co.uk
Twitter: @LancingPrepHove
Facebook: @LancingPrepHove

Co-educational school for children aged 3–13 years.

Chairman of Governors: Dr H O Brünjes, BSc, MBBS, DRCOG, FEWI

Head: Mrs K Keep, BEd Hons

Age Range. 3–13 Co-educational.
Number of Pupils. 255.
Fees per term (2018–2019). £1,320–£5,325 (including lunch).

Lancing College Preparatory School at Hove is situated on a superb 7-acre campus in the heart of Hove.

We aim to inspire a desire for excellence, to develop independent, searching minds and to foster creativity. We encourage the children entrusted to us to explore and achieve their potential, academically and creatively. Academia is rightly important to us but of equal importance is our pupils' personal development.

Whilst proud of our traditions, we are also a forward-thinking school, looking to build upon our past successes to achieve even greater heights in the future. By the time our pupils leave, they will have acquired a confidence and a self-belief, together with a set of values that will remain with them throughout their lives.

Our pupils are taught by our fully-qualified staff of 27 and enjoy wonderful facilities including a brand new school hall and new library (both in 2017), fully-equipped science laboratory, art design and technology room and music teaching spaces. Outside, our leafy grounds include an adventure playground and an all-weather area for the coaching of our main sports: cricket, football, hockey, netball, rounders, rugby and tennis. Our pupils also benefit from the extensive cultural and sporting facilities at Lancing College. From September 2018, older children take part in the modern foreign language programme learning Spanish or German at Lancing College.

Charitable status. Lancing College is a Registered Charity, number 1076483. It exists to provide education for boys and girls.

Lancing College Preparatory School at Worthing

A Woodard School

Broadwater Road, Worthing, West Sussex BN14 8HU

Tel: 01903 201123
email: worthing@lancing.org.uk
website: www.lancingcollege.co.uk
Twitter: @LancingPrepWthg
Facebook: @lancingprepworthing

Co-educational day school for children aged 2–13 years.

Chairman of Governors: Dr H O Brünjes, BSc, MBBS, DRCOG, FEWI

Head: Mrs H Beeby, BH, PGCE, MA

Age Range. 2–13 Co-educational.
Number of Pupils. 194.
Fees per term (2018–2019). £2,705–£3,820 (5 days including lunch). Wraparound care for Pre-Prep children is available at an extra charge and is free of charge for Prep children.

Lancing Prep Worthing is based in a lovely Georgian manor house on a site of two acres, with space to run and play, in the Broadwater area of Worthing. It is located some six miles from Lancing College.

We nurture in all our pupils a love of learning to enable them to maximise their academic potential. Our broad and balanced curriculum is enriched with high quality creative and physical activities to provide a vibrant learning environment. Drama and Music are thriving; every year our children gain many awards in public competitions and have an impressive track record in external examinations.

Our pastoral care is excellent and the twin themes of loving learning and kindness to one another run throughout our school community. In working and playing together, within the framework of a Christian community, our children develop a sense of service to each other, and the world beyond the school gates, which will characterise their future lives. We hope they will learn that they can effect positive change and make a difference in the world.

The pupils are taught by our staff of 20, plus classroom assistants, in bright and airy classrooms. The school campus has undergone upgrades since joining the Lancing College family of schools in 2014, with a refurbished hall, where freshly-cooked lunches are served daily, a popular Food and Nutrition room, new library and a brand new drama studio in 2017. Outdoor space comprises hard courts and a large grass field for the coaching of our main sports: cricket, football, hockey, netball, rounders and tennis. Our children also benefit from sharing the extensive cultural and sporting facilities at Lancing College. From September 2018, our older children take part in a modern foreign language programme learning Spanish or German at Lancing College.

Charitable status. Lancing Prep at Worthing is a Registered Charity, number 1155150. It exists to provide education for boys and girls.

Lanesborough School

Maori Road, Guildford, Surrey GU1 2EL

Tel:	01483 880650
Fax:	01483 880651
email:	office@lanesborough.surrey.sch.uk
website:	www.lanesborough.surrey.sch.uk
Twitter:	@lanesboroughSch
Facebook:	@Lanesboroughschool

Chairman of Governors: Mrs S K Creedy, MA Cantab

Head: **Mrs C Turnbull**, BA Hons, MEd

Age Range. 3–13.
Number of Boys. 355 day boys.
Fees per term (2018–2019). £3,630–£5,090.

Lanesborough is the Preparatory School of the Royal Grammar School and the choir school for Guildford Cathedral. Cathedral choristers qualify for choral scholarships.

The main entry points are Nursery, Reception and Year 3. Many of the pupils gain entry to the Royal Grammar School at age 11 or 13, whilst others are prepared for Scholarship and Common Entrance examination to senior Independent schools at 13.

The School is divided into four Houses for House competitions. Pastoral care and supervision of academic progress are shared by the Head, Housemasters, Form and subject teachers. Extra-curricular activities include music, art, chess, drama, computer club, judo, fencing, tennis, basketball, science and general knowledge.

Music is a strong feature of the life of the school, which is a member of the Choir Schools Association. In addition to the Cathedral Choir, there are senior and junior choirs, an orchestra, wind and string groups. Private tuition by qualified peripatetic teachers is available in most instruments. There are music concerts and the school Carol Service at the Cathedral has achieved wide acclaim. Music scholarships to Independent senior schools are gained each year.

Art plays an important part in the curriculum also, with boys receiving tuition throughout the school.

A new performance space will further enhance drama productions.

Games are association football, rugby, cricket, athletics, swimming, basketball, hockey and badminton. There is a school field, gym and astroturf. A brand new, purpose-built Sports Hall opened in September 2016, and a bespoke performance space for drama and music.

Regular school visits are undertaken to local places of interest. School parties also go abroad, e.g. for skiing, watersports, football and on cultural visits.

The Pre-Preparatory department (for boys aged 3–7 and including a Nursery unit) is housed in a separate building (Braganza House), but shares many of the facilities of the main Prep School.

There is an active and very supportive Parents' Association.

Charitable status. RGS and Lanesborough is Registered Charity, number 1177353, and a Company Limited by Guarantee, incorporated in England and Wales, Company number 10874615. Registered Office High Street, Guildford, Surrey, GU1 3BB.

Langley Preparatory School at Taverham Hall

Taverham, Norwich, Norfolk NR8 6HU

Tel:	01603 868206
email:	admissions@taverhamhall.co.uk
website:	www.taverhamhall.co.uk
Twitter:	@TaverhamHall
Facebook:	@LangleyPrepTH
LinkedIn:	/taverham-hall-preparatory-school

Motto: *Conanti Dabitur ~ through effort we succeed*

Chair of Governors: Lt Col Mark Nicholas MBE

Headmaster: **M A Crossley**, BEd Hons, NPQH, MHFA Instructor

Deputy Heads:
E Wood, BSc PGCE
S Menegaz, Maîtrise in English Literature & Language, PGCE
C Franklin, BA Hons, PGCE, MA

Age Range. 2–13.
Number of Pupils. 371: Prep 227, Pre-Prep 99, Pre-Prep Early Years 45.
Fees per term (2018–2019). Day: Prep £3,915–£4,725 (inc lunch); Pre-Prep £3,425 (inc lunch). Pre-Prep Early Years (per session): £34.20 (morning), £48.00 (all day); Weekly Boarding £6,105.

Langley Preparatory School at Taverham Hall, originally founded in 1921, is a co-educational IAPS, ISA and BSA day and flexi/weekly boarding school set in 100 acres of beautiful woodland conveniently situated near Norwich whilst offering school transport for those living further afield. Scholarships are available from age 7 (Year 3) in the areas of music, sport, academic and art and open mornings take place each term. Under the leadership of its experienced Headmaster, the School has received six outstanding inspection reports covering the areas of EYFS, Boarding as well as the all-round education provided by the School. The Headmaster is also a mental health first aid instructor, a District Representative for 63 independent schools and a regular inspector of schools.

The School's aim is to develop children who are resilient, independent, confident, caring and well-mannered. This takes place in a nurturing environment with a rich and broad curriculum where high levels of pastoral care are in place. As a result pupils recognise the value of their responsibility in the learning process. In addition, both the school's Council and Boarders' Forum provide pupils with a voice and an opportunity to play an active role in the school's community.

Pastoral care and personalised learning. The school is dedicated to providing outstanding pastoral care for its pupils in a vibrant, warm and friendly atmosphere. Every child is different and how pupils learn is just as important as what they learn. The school's Growth Mindset culture from Early Years onwards recognises that pupils can change and grow throughout their lives and that there is no limit to their potential. Teaching staff will help identify a pupil's learning style, set personalised targets and tailor teaching to the individual, ensuring pupils have every opportunity to achieve their personal best and become an empowered independent learner. As pupils approach Year 8 and scholarship examinations, there is a greater move towards independence. Pupils take increased responsibility for their learning and conduct, as well as obtaining leadership roles within the school, including Prefect status and mentoring Year 3 pupils when in Year 8. In Years 7 and 8 pupils embark on the Prep School Baccalaureate, an academic framework which seeks to reward achievement in a range of subjects as well as the development of lifelong skills sought after by senior schools and beyond. Their final year culminates in an exciting leavers programme with a clear focus on fun, adventure and teamwork. High pupil achievements contribute to the school's excellent record for placing Year 8 pupils at their preferred senior schools in addition to obtaining a high number of senior school scholarships each year.

Pre-Prep for ages 2 to 7. Children in the Pre-Prep department are heard to read every day and those in the Early Years and Reception classes follow the school's own bespoke curriculum. This curriculum draws on the strengths of the nationally recognised Early Years curriculum whilst crucially offering children, who are ready, the opportunity to read and write at a younger age and to develop their mathematical skills beyond the current levels of expectation.

Awards and life skills. The school is the proud recipient of the prestigious NACE Challenge Award, which recognises the excellence of its provision for able and talented pupils, as well as its fourth consecutive Gold Schools Games Mark based on its 'sport for all' philosophy, the high level of attainment, inclusivity and provision for sport in addition to the school's contribution to the wider community. Pupils are offered 4–5 hours each week of PE and Games lessons including weekly sporting fixtures, termly tournaments and competitions at local, regional and national level. The school has a dedicated Mental Health First Aiders team which demonstrates the importance it places on wellbeing whilst the school's holistic approach to education is further enhanced through its fully integrated outdoor Forest School lessons. Langley Preparatory School at Taverham Hall is the first in Norfolk to receive the esteemed FSA Recognised Forest School Provider Award as a result of the

quality of the work its Forest School Leaders undertake with their pupils who simply love the freedom to explore the 100 acres of beautiful wooded parkland.

Art and Drama. Creative thinking and imagination are further developed through the School's performing arts programme which offers a wide range of opportunities within Music, Drama and Art which is taught to all pupils in the School. A purpose-built Music and Art block houses the latest interactive whiteboards as well as state-of-the-art music recording and composing equipment.

Extended day. Choice and flexibility are central to what the school is able to provide for families. This includes length-of-day options, after-school clubs, day and flexible boarding opportunities and lift sharing/school transport provision. Sibling discounts and means-tested bursaries may be available for some families, whilst scholarship opportunities exist for those in the Prep School.

Inspection Reports and Awards can be viewed via the school's website: www.taverhamhall.co.uk.

Langley Preparatory School at Taverham Hall's Open Mornings take place in September, January and May.

Charitable status. Langley Preparatory School at Taverham Hall is a Registered Charity, number 311270.

Latymer Prep School

36 Upper Mall, Hammersmith, London W6 9TA

Tel:	020 7993 0061
email:	registrar@latymerprep.org
	admin@latymerprep.org
website:	www.latymerprep.org
Twitter:	@LatymerPrep

Chairman of Governors: Ros Sweeting, LLB

Principal: **Ms Andrea Rutterford**, BEd Hons, Dip SpLD

Age Range. 7–11 Co-educational.
Number of Pupils. 164 Day Pupils.
Fees per term (2018–2019). £6,110.

Latymer Prep School, led by its own Principal, was granted independence by the Governors of the Latymer Foundation in 1995 – the Centenary Year of Latymer Upper School on its present site. Previously the Prep School had been run as a very successful department of the Upper School and the relationship remains an extremely close one with all children usually expected to proceed to the Upper School.

The school is academically selective and pupils are taught the full range of subjects following National Curriculum guidelines, but to an advanced standard. Classes are kept small (20) which allows for close monitoring and evaluation of each pupil's progress and well-being. Means-tested academic scholarships are available.

The school is well resourced and has attractive facilities in two elegant period houses adjacent to the River Thames. Catering, sports and theatre facilities are shared with the Upper School.

A main feature of the school is its friendly and caring atmosphere which offers close pastoral support to each individual pupil. Academic achievement is strong, but in addition, all staff and pupils contribute to an extensive range of activities featuring Sport, Music, Art and Drama. The school has 3 large choirs and its own orchestra. Opportunities exist for all pupils to participate in concerts, plays and inter-school sporting events.

The major sports are soccer, rugby, cricket, tennis, athletics, hockey and netball. There is also a thriving swimming club (the school has its own pool). Karate chess, drama and bridge are just some of the clubs which take place after school. There is an Arts Week, plus a residential to Norfolk for Y5 and a residential to Italy for Y6 pupils.

There is a Parents' Gild and opportunities occur frequently to meet with staff socially. Visits for prospective parents occur throughout the year and can be arranged by telephoning for an appointment.

Charitable status. The Latymer Foundation is a Registered Charity, number 312714. It exists to provide an opportunity for able pupils from all walks of life to develop their talents to the full.

Laxton Junior School

East Road, Oundle, Peterborough PE8 4BX

Tel: 01832 277275
email: info@laxtonjunior.org.uk
website: www.laxtonjunior.org.uk
Twitter: @LJS_Head
Facebook: @LaxtonJunior

Governors: The Worshipful Company of Grocers

Chairman: Mr Robert Ringrose

Head: Mr Sam Robertson, MA Cantab, PGCE

Deputy Head: Miss Janet Bass, BA Hons, Dip TEFL, PGDPSE

Age Range. 4–11.
Number of Children. 255.
Fees per term (2018–2019). £3,740–£4,100 (including lunches).

Opened in 1973 and part of Oundle School, Laxton Junior is a co-educational day school for children aged 4–11 years. In September 2002 Laxton Junior moved into a new building which caters for 280 pupils. The school has 14 forms of no more than 20 pupils, each with a fully qualified Form Teacher. The curriculum includes Art & Design, Computer Skills, MFL, Music, PE and Performing Arts as well as the major academic subjects. Emphasis has always been placed on the individual child and the importance of each doing their best at all times, according to their ability. Children are prepared for entrance examinations for Independent Senior Schools in the area; Kimbolton, Oundle, Oakham and Stamford Schools being the key schools.

The new building has a large multi-purpose hall which is used for PE, Music and Performing Arts as well as concerts, school plays and social events The school has its own games fields and netball courts plus all children receive swimming instruction each week in the Oundle School Pool. The main games are football, rugby, cricket, netball, rounders, hockey and athletics plus coaching in tennis.

In Year 2 all pupils have the opportunity to play the violin or cello as part of the curriculum. From Year 3 the recorder is introduced, plus additional time is given for choir, orchestra and learning other musical instruments. The school also has an Education Support Unit which monitors all pupils' development and helps individuals with specific difficulties.

The aims of the school are to encourage the formation of good work habits and good manners, to lay the foundations for the development of self-discipline, self-confidence and self-motivation and to offer the children the opportunity of experiencing the satisfaction of achievement.

The partnership of home and school in the education of the child is strongly emphasises and all parents are members of the Parents' & Friends' Association.

Laxton Junior School was inspected in February 2014. The report is available on the school website.

Charitable status. Oundle School is a Registered Charity, number 309921. It exists to provide education for boys and girls.

Leehurst Swan School

19 Campbell Road, Salisbury SP1 3BQ

Tel: 01722 333094
email: registrar@leehurstswan.org.uk
            reception@leehurstswan.org.uk
website: www.leehurstswan.org.uk

Chairman of Governors: Mr Richard Thorp

Headmaster: Mr Stuart Morgan-Nash, BSc Ed, MEd

Age Range. 4–16 Co-educational.
Number of Children. 275.
Fees per term (2018–2019). Senior School £4,805; Prep School £2,900–£3,720.

Leehurst Swan is an independent day school, just 10 minutes' walk from Salisbury city centre, which has been inspiring and educating pupils for over 100 years. We are the only independent day school in Salisbury offering education for girls and boys from Reception to GCSEs. The benefits of an all-through education are widely recognised, eliminating the problems of transfer between the stages of education. A co-educational environment also encourages the development of excellent social skills. We celebrate the best of the old while embracing the latest innovations and technology.

The school has small classes, a family atmosphere, and an environment that inspires and motivates pupils to achieve their best. The individual attention pupils receive reflects the ethos of Christian values and respect for the individual. Many children face social obstacles in education and find school a stressful experience. At Leehurst Swan we nurture our pupils as they navigate their way on life's journey; stressing the importance of respect, good manners and self-control.

Pupils in the Prep enjoy state-of-the-art teaching facilities and have specialist teaching in key subjects and use dedicated ICT, Science, Music, Art, and Design Technology suites. The children are prepared for 11+ examinations for entry into the local grammar schools and for entry into the Leehurst Swan Senior school.

The Senior pupils normally pursue studies in ten GCSE subjects and academic results are excellent. The school equally values and nurtures creative and sporting talent awarding scholarships in these areas in addition to academic scholarships.

Individual lessons are arranged in a wide range of musical instruments leading to Associated Board examinations.

In 2017, Leehurst Swan achieved the grade of 'Excellent' in every aspect of educational quality; the highest possible outcome from the Independent Schools Inspectorate (ISI).

The inspectors reported, "The quality of the pupils' personal development is excellent. Pupils of all ages are happy and confident individuals who feel supported by the school community."

Further comments included: "The quality of the pupils' academic and other achievements is excellent. Pupils of all ages make excellent progress."

Leehurst Swan welcomes visitors to the school to come and see them at work and play.

Charitable status. Leehurst Swan Limited is a Registered Charity, number 800158. It exists to provide education for children.

Leicester Grammar Junior School

London Road, Great Glen, Leicester, Leicestershire LE8 9FL

Tel:	0116 259 1950
Fax:	0116 259 1951
email:	friell@leicestergrammar.org.uk
website:	www.lgs-junior.org.uk
Twitter:	@LGS_Junior
Facebook:	@LeicesterGrammarJuniorSchool

Chair of Governors: Dr Sarah M Dauncey, MRCGP

Headmistress: **Mrs C Rigby**, BA

Age Range. 3–11 Co-educational.
Number of Pupils. 385.
Fees per term (2018–2019). Years 3–6 £3,745; Kinders to Year 2 £3,531; Kinders Part-time £2,330.

Leicester Grammar Junior School was founded in 1992 when Leicester Grammar School Trust took over educational responsibility for Evington Hall, an independent school run by the Sisters of Charity of St Paul.

The school is a selective, co-educational day school with a Christian Foundation. It acts as the junior school to Leicester Grammar School and is the first stage in a continuous education from 3 years through to A Level. In September 2008 both the Junior and Senior schools relocated to a new purpose-built campus SW of the city of Leicester. Thus, the school now encompasses the full 3–18 age range on the one site.

The school provides a stimulating, disciplined, happy environment where each child is encouraged to aim for the highest standards in everything they do and take a full and active part in all aspects of school life. It operates as an extension of the family unit within which the staff act with firmness and fairness. Respect and consideration underpin school life. Pupils are encouraged to develop a caring and responsible attitude to others, leading to good manners and acceptable behaviour.

The children benefit from not only academic success and development but also from excellent musical, sporting and dramatic involvement within a broad and well balanced curriculum.

Music is a particular strength of the school and plays an important part in the life of every child. From the beginning as 3 year olds, children are taught by a music specialist. Pupils have the opportunity to learn a variety of instruments and there is a particularly strong Infant String Scheme; children as young as five or six years of age learn to play the violin or cello. The school orchestra and ensembles perform at festivals, concerts and assemblies. There are also many choral opportunities within the Junior and Infant choir which are often linked with Drama. A number of boys and girls are also members of the Leicester Cathedral choir and enjoy weekly training sessions with the Cathedral Master of Music.

In 2004 the school received the Sportsmark Gold Award in recognition of the quality of sport within the curriculum and extracurricular. The PE and Games provision aims to develop skills in team and individual games, gymnastics, dance, swimming and athletics. The main team games are rugby, football and cricket for the boys and netball, hockey and rounders for the girls. After-school clubs offer additional sporting opportunities such as tennis, badminton, table tennis and cross country.

Admissions. Pupils are admitted at all ages between 3+ and 10+ although the vast majority enter in the September following their third or fourth birthday (Kinders or Reception). Following a visit to the school an Application Form is offered. When the form is returned a date for assessment is set. Parents wishing their children to be admitted to the Infant Department at times other than in September are invited to bring their child to school to spend part of a day with the class he or she would join. Class teachers then carry out an assessment to determine whether or not the child will be able to integrate into the year group.

Charitable status. Leicester Grammar School Trust is a Registered Charity, number 510809.

Leweston Prep School

Sherborne, Dorset DT9 6EN

Tel:	01963 210790
Fax:	01963 210648
email:	enquiries@leweston.dorset.sch.uk
website:	www.leweston.co.uk
Twitter:	@LewestonSchool
Facebook:	@Leweston

Chair of Board of Governors: Mr Chris Fenton

Head of Leweston School: Mrs Kate Reynolds, LLB Bristol, PGCE Bath

Head of Leweston Prep: **Miss Alanda Phillips**, BA Hons Winchester, PGCE, MA Ed

Age Range. 3 months–11 years Co-educational.
Number of Pupils. 103: 73 Girls, 30 Boys.
Fees per term (2018–2019). Day: Reception–Year 1 £1,975, Years 2–3 £2,595, Years 4–5 £3,220, Year 6 £3,840. Boarding: £5,755 (weekly), £6,900 (full). Nursery (per day): £51.00–£53.50 (all day 08:00–18:00 including food); £25.50–£28.00 (1 x 5 hr session 08:00–13:00 or 13:00–18:00); Breakfast Club 07:30–08:00: £4.50.

Setting. Leweston Prep School is an independent Catholic school for boys and girls with boarding provision for girls from Year 3 and above. The school is situated in forty-six acres of Dorset parkland three miles south of Sherborne and occupies an enviable setting in a skilfully converted former Coach House providing a unique range of bright spacious classrooms. The beautiful rural site is shared with Leweston School, offering continuity of education right through to A Level. The Prep enjoys the benefit of many excellent facilities including a modern, well-equipped Art and Design Centre, an all-weather sports pitch, a swimming pool, a large sports hall, tennis courts and extensive playing fields. As a result of the integration with Leweston School in 2014, Prep pupils now take advantage of the specialist teaching in Languages, Art, Maths, Home Economics, Music and Sport that is provided by the Senior School. The parkland setting offers many opportunities for study and recreation. An accredited Forest School opened in September 2017 and every year group will have a Forest School session once a week.

Ethos. Traditional excellence in teaching is combined with modern facilities and resources in a stimulating, happy and purposeful environment. The school motto 'Gaudere et Bene Facere' (Rejoice and Do Well) exactly reflects the importance of high academic standards together with artistic, musical and sporting excellence achieved in an atmosphere of joy and vibrancy. Each child is encouraged to develop individual talents within the caring and supportive school community. Small class sizes, a friendly family ethos, and traditional values of work and behaviour are appreciated by parents. Full and flexi boarding options provide flexibility for pupils to enjoy a wide variety of extracurricular activities, whilst no Saturday morning school allows for rest and relaxation. Wrap-around care is available from 8.00 am to 6.00 pm.

Curriculum. Programmes of study encompass the National Curriculum without being constrained by it. Basic subjects are taught to a high standard concentrating on literacy and numeracy acquisition in the early years before expanding into a broader curriculum in Years 3–6. Well-qualified class teachers and specialist subject teachers foster independent learning and encourage the development of problem solving and investigative skills in all areas of the curriculum. Academic standards are high and many pupils gain awards to senior school.

There is a strong tradition in the creative arts and sport. Music, Drama and Performing Arts are taught within the curriculum. A high percentage of pupils learn to play musical instruments and take additional Drama. There is a school orchestra and choir and many opportunities throughout the year for performance and grade examinations in both Music and Drama. All pupils in Years 4–6 undertake English Speaking Board assessments. Individual and team sports are considered important as part of the healthy, active lifestyle and the school enjoys a particular reputation for hockey and cross-country. The school is one of only nine Pentathlon Academies in the UK and is regarded as a centre of excellence by Pentathlon GB. Art, Ceramics and Design Technology are taught by specialist teachers using the exceptional facilities in the Art and Design Centre.

Charitable status. Leweston School Trust is a Registered Charity, number 295175. It exists to provide for children a contemporary education in the Catholic tradition.

Littlegarth School

Horkesley Park, Nayland, Colchester, Essex CO6 4JR

Tel: 01206 262332
Fax: 01206 263101
email: office@littlegarth.essex.sch.uk
website: www.littlegarth.essex.sch.uk
Twitter: @LittlegarthPrep
Facebook: @LittlegarthPrep

Chairman of Governors: Mr J Henderson, MA Oxon, PhD

Headmaster: **Mr Peter Jones**, BEd Hons

Deputy Head: Mrs Lynda Turner, BA Hons

Age Range. 2½–11.
Number of Pupils. Day: approximately 173 Boys, 138 Girls.
Fees per term (2018–2019). £821–£3,723.

Littlegarth has grown steadily following the School's move to our current premises of Horkesley Park in 1994. The Grade II listed Georgian house is situated in delightful Stour Valley countryside, designated as an Area of Outstanding Natural Beauty. The 30 acres of School land boast a number of purpose-built teaching rooms, including a multi-purpose Sports Hall, Science Laboratory, and numerous classrooms. A brand new purpose-built facility opened in January 2018, which provides outstanding specialist

teaching rooms for music, drama and art, a large library incorporating a computer room, a learning support room and six substantial new teaching rooms. These facilities provide the children with increased opportunities to develop a wide range of skills, supported by our exciting and broad curriculum.

Outdoors, we make good use of our sports field with up to eight pitches and four outdoor cricket nets. Our outdoor play area has climbing and activity structures and a vegetable garden with a recent extension to the green area enhancing the natural space around our covered outdoor reading areas. Our innovative adventure woodland provides an excellent environment for nature walks and Forest School activities, which run from Nursery through to Year 4. This area has been enriched by the planting of wildflower meadows and the erection of an outdoor stage which will allow for productions and concerts by the children.

Children from the age of two are provided with excellent specialist teaching in Drama, French, Music and Sport. Small class sizes ensure that children receive a high level of individual attention and the Early Years Foundation Stage (EYFS) framework provides a springboard for individualised learning which continues throughout the school. Pre-Prep teachers provide a firm foundation in the core subjects, supported by caring teaching assistants and learning support staff. In Year 3, the number of lessons taught by subject specialist teachers increases and from Year 4 all timetabled lessons are taught by subject specialists.

Pastoral care is one of the key strengths of Littlegarth, as highlighted in our inspection report. Year 6 children are given considerable opportunities to take on responsibilities and further develop their self-confidence as Prefects, supporting children and staff in a variety of ways.

The School produces many plays each year and strong drama links with the local community are being forged. As well as running the school library, parents are also actively involved in running a wardrobe department and there is a flourishing 'Friends of Littlegarth' parent body.

A wide variety of clubs and extra-curricular activities are available each day and the School also provides pre and after school care.

Charitable status. Littlegarth School Limited is a Registered Charity, number 325064. It exists to provide education for children.

Lochinver House School

Heath Road, Little Heath, Potters Bar, Herts EN6 1LW

Tel: 01707 653064
Fax: 01707 663828
email: registrar@lochinverhouse.com
website: www.lochinverhouse.com
Twitter: @LHSPrep

Chairman of the Governors: William Moores

Headmaster: **Ben Walker**, BA Hons

Age Range. 4–13.
Number of Boys. 350 Day Boys.
Fees per term (2018–2019). £3,725–£4,895 with no compulsory extras.

The academic staff consists of 36 qualified and graduate teachers, Laboratory, ICT, DT technicians, Teaching Assistants and a Matron.

The school, founded in 1947, is situated in a pleasant residential area on the edge of green belt land in South Hertfordshire, and yet is conveniently placed for access to London. At the heart of the school is a late Victorian house. Facilities on our 8½ acre site are extensive and include a purpose-built Pre Prep Department, separate Sports Hall, Gymnasium & Theatre, Music Centre, two Science Laboratories and specialist IT, DT, and Art rooms. Lochinver is fully advanced with IT including an exciting project which provides iPads to older boys.

Boys are prepared for Common Entrance and Scholarship examinations to a wide range of top day and boarding Independent Schools.

The school has its own extensive playing fields on site, including an all-weather, Astro pitch. The major sports: Football, Rugby, Cricket, Athletics and Basketball are complemented by opportunities to take part in a very wide range of further sports and physical activity. All boys learn to swim whilst they are at the School. Residential trips take place both within the UK and overseas, such as skiing in Europe, a Classics trip to Italy and a Rugby Tour to South Africa. During their time at the school each boy will spend some time in France as this is an important and much valued part of the French Curriculum. There are opportunities for the boys to also study Spanish, Latin and Russian.

Music, Art, Drama, Design Technology and PE are part of the timetabled curriculum for all boys. The school encourages boys to learn at least one musical instrument and currently 75% of the children are doing so. There is a School Orchestra, Junior and Senior Choir, together with a variety of instrumental Groups. Parents appreciate our provision of extended care at both ends of the day.

The school is a non-profit making Educational Trust administered by a Board of Governors.

Charitable status. Lochinver House School is a Registered Charity, number 1091045. It aims to provide a quality education.

Lockers Park

Lockers Park Lane, Hemel Hempstead, Hertfordshire HP1 1TL

Tel:	01442 251712
Fax:	01442 234150
email:	secretary@lockerspark.herts.sch.uk
website:	www.lockerspark.herts.sch.uk

Chairman of Governors: C Lister, BSc Hons, MBA

Headmaster: **C Wilson**, BA Cantab, PGCE

Admissions: Mrs S Johnson

Age Range. 4–13. The Pre-Prep is co-educational and the Prep is boys only.

Number of Pupils. 170 children, of whom 45 are boarders or flexi boarders.

Fees per term (2018–2019). Boarders £8,350, Day Boys £3,650–£5,795. Day fees include the flexible day, which runs from 7.30 am to 7.30 pm with the option to have breakfast, stay for supper and participate in evening activities at no extra cost.

Further details are outlined in the prospectus, available on application.

Lockers Park is located in 23 acres of parkland above the town of Hemel Hempstead, only five miles from both the M1 and M25 motorways. It lies within easy access of London (Euston 30 minutes) and all four of its airports; consequently the School is well accustomed to providing the necessary help and support to parents living both in Britain and abroad.

The main school building, purpose-built in 1874, is situated in grounds which are perfect for children, with well-maintained playing fields surrounded by woodland areas which easily occupy even the most active. There has been a steady process of modernisation over the past two decades and the School boasts first-class, all-round facilities: the Mountbatten Centre, which provides eight excellent specialist classrooms including a well-equipped ICT centre; an attached Science and Technology Building, containing two spacious laboratories, technology classroom and fully-fitted workshop; an exceptional art and pottery centre and a well-resourced library.

A purpose-built Pre-Preparatory School opened in September 2015 and admits both boys and girls while the main Prep School remains firmly committed to a boys-only education.

Sports facilities are of a high calibre and include a fully-fitted sports hall, two squash courts, a recently refurbished heated swimming pool, two tennis courts, an all-weather sports surface and cricket nets, a shooting range and a nine-hole golf course.

Lockers Park is proud of its academic and musical records; its success in both scholarships and Common Entrance examinations to 45 different schools in the past ten years reflects this well. The average class size is 14 and the pupil to teacher ratio a very healthy 1:7. The Music Department is well known; encouragement is given to every boy to find an instrument which he will enjoy and most gain proficiency in at least one. There is a full orchestra, wind, brass and jazz bands, a string ensemble and two choirs. The number of senior school scholarships of all types awarded to Lockers Park is considered high.

Drama plays a large part in school life with at least two major productions each year together with junior plays, school assembly productions, charades and public speaking debates.

At Lockers Park, there is a real family atmosphere, there is always someone to whom a boy can turn and great care is taken to ensure the happiness of every child. Boys are safe, happy, fit and well looked after. While day boys enjoy all the facilities and opportunities of a boarding school, boarding is fun; dormitories are warm and friendly rooms and opportunities for a variety of enjoyable weekend activities are immense. With day boys and boarders alike, great care is taken over the personal development of each individual.

Bursaries & Scholarships. Lockers Park is committed to offering financial help to deserving candidates, subject to financial resources. Scholarships are available, which may be increased with a means-tested bursary.

Charitable status. Lockers Park School Trust Ltd is a Registered Charity, number 311061. It aims to provide an all round, high quality education on a non-profit making basis.

Longacre School

Hullbrook Lane, Shamley Green, Guildford, Surrey GU5 0NQ

Tel:	01483 893225
email:	office@longacreschool.co.uk
website:	www.longacreschool.co.uk
Twitter:	@longacreschool
Facebook:	@longacreschool

Headmaster: **Mr Matthew Bryan**, MA PGCE Cambridge, MA MSc Oxford

Age Range. 2½–11.

Number of Pupils. 250+ boys and girls.

Fees per term (from January 2019). £1,700–£5,100.

Are school days really the happiest days of your life? Many Longacre pupils would answer "Yes!" The cheerful and purposeful atmosphere at Longacre is apparent as soon as you enter the school. Here, children are valued as individuals and are encouraged to fulfil their potential in every facet of school life. Personal and social development is highly valued, enabling pupils to grow in confidence as they mature.

The Head and staff believe that children learn more effectively when they are happy, and that excellent academic results can be achieved without subjecting pupils to hothouse pressure. The fact that Longacre pupils gain a range of scholarships, and that they transfer successfully to senior schools of parental choice, shows that this approach is definitely working.

Academic progress is closely monitored and regularly tested. Small classes (maximum eighteen) enable pupils to be taught at an individual level, with increasing subject specialist tuition as children progress through the school. Alongside the core curriculum, Longacre offers a wide range of sporting opportunities, stimulating off-site visits and exciting workshops. There are after school clubs every evening, ranging from cooking to judo, and regular masterclasses for able pupils.

Set in a beautiful rural location on the outskirts of the picturesque village of Shamley Green, between Guildford and Cranleigh, the school offers a wonderful environment for young children. The school buildings comprise the original large 1902 house plus modern, purpose-built classrooms standing in nine acres of grounds. Facilities include a brand new sports hall and astroturf, sports fields, gardens, woodland and an adventure playground.

Longacre is a community where parents are welcome. The school has a thriving and supportive PTA and parents are kept well informed about school events and their children's progress through a weekly newsletter, formal and informal meetings and written reports. The Head and staff work closely with parents to ensure that their children are happy, successful and fulfilled.

To arrange a visit, please call 01483 893225.

Lorenden Preparatory School

Painter's Forstal, Faversham, Kent ME13 0EN

Tel: 01795 590030
email: office@lorenden.org
website: www.lorenden.org
Twitter: @LorendenSchool
Facebook: @lorendenschool

Chairman of Governors: R Boyd-Howell

Headteacher: Mrs K Uttley, BA Hons, PGCE

Age Range. 3–11 Co-educational.

Number of Pupils. 120.

Fees per term (2018–2019). £2,880–£4,180.

Lorenden is situated in the village of Painter's Forstal between Faversham and the North Downs and within easy driving distance of Canterbury, Whitstable, Ashford and Sittingbourne; an idyllic position in the heart of the Kent countryside.

The school's avowed aim is to develop self-disciplined thoughtful children with a cheerful 'can do' attitude to life and a strong sense of fair play, exemplified through the motto 'We Care. We Share. We Strive. We Succeed'.

All round expectations are high and academic results are excellent. At eleven children either transfer to local grammar schools, or continue in independent education. The school places great emphasis in ensuring each individual is nurtured according to their strengths, and advice to parents on senior school choice is carefully tailored to each child, with parents then able to make the best decision. Able children are awarded major academic, sports or art scholarships annually to a range of senior schools.

Music is a great strength of the school and sports results are remarkably good. Every child 'gets a go' and resilience is the name of the game.

This is a school that needs to be experienced to be truly appreciated: a friendly, family environment where visitors are always delighted by what they find.

Enquiries concerning places and admissions should be made to the Secretary.

Charitable status. Lorenden School is a Registered Charity, number 1048805.

Loretto Junior School

North Esk Lodge, 1 North High Street, Musselburgh, East Lothian EH21 6JA

Tel: 0131 653 4570
Fax: 0131 653 4571
email: juniorschool@loretto.com
website: www.loretto.com
Twitter: @lorettohead
Facebook: @lorettoschool

Chairman of Governors: Mr Peter McCutcheon

Headmaster: Dr Graham R W Hawley, BSc Hons, PGCE, PhD

Head of Junior School: Mr Andrew Dickenson

To view Loretto Junior School's Staff Directory, please visit www.loretto.com/staff-directory

Age Range. 5–12.

Number of Pupils. 164.

Fees per term (2018–2019). Day: £3,060–£5,300; Year 4–7 Full Boarding £7,445; Year 7 Flexi Boarding (3 nights per week) £6,320.

Loretto has a whole-School approach and 'The Nippers' enjoy the same safe, supporting and stimulating environment as Senior School pupils, with closer adult supervision. They also benefit from the exceptional shared facilities such as the playing fields, Theatre, Sports Hall, Music School and Chapel. Occasional and Flexi Boarding are possible for pupils aged 11 and over.

A small School, big on heart, big on ambition.

- One of Scotland's leading schools.
- Scotland's oldest boarding school, founded in 1827.
- An independent, private boarding and day school for girls and boys, from 0 to 18 years.
- Set in a safe, leafy, spacious, 85-acre campus in Musselburgh; the school enjoys all the advantages of its rural setting.
- Globally connected, with the convenience and opportunities of being just 9 kilometres / 6 miles from Edinburgh, its international airport, rail and road networks.

- Offering the traditional British / English curriculum of GCSEs and A Levels, and ranked in the top 7% of schools nationally for A Level.
- 97% of pupils enter the University of their choice, such as Oxford, Cambridge, St Andrews, and Durham.
- Welcoming 600 pupils, 400 in the Senior School, 200 in the Junior School and Nursery.
- An excellent staff to pupil ratio (1:7)
- Every pupil is known personally, and can grow and develop wherever their interests lie.
- A distinctive emphasis on the full development of the individual in mind, body and spirit.
- Exceptional facilities, bespoke to learning and teaching, sport, drama, dance, art and music.
- Extensive Sports programme with specialised coaches in major sports including Cricket, Hockey, Lacrosse, Rugby and more
- An industry-leading Golf Academy with indoor and outdoor centres, providing every pupil with an unmatched opportunity to develop their talent.

Admission. Loretto School's Admissions procedure aims to ensure that boys and girls who join Loretto are able to be happy, successful and secure within its academic, cultural and pastoral environment, whether they are boarders or day pupils.

Pupils can enter 'The Nippers' at age 5 and are prepared for entrance and scholarship assessments, mostly to Loretto at 12+.

The selection criteria include provision of satisfactory evidence, through the School's own age-appropriate assessment tests, of academic ability sufficient to access the School curriculum, and a satisfactory reference from the applicant's current school. Loretto is academically selective but also recognises the central value of co-curricular activities, and enthusiasm in these fields is expected and encouraged.

Scholarships and Bursaries. A range of Bursaries are available for entry to the Nippers, usually at 10+ and 11+.

To find out more, please visit www.loretto.com or contact the Admissions Department, Tel: 0131 653 4455 or email: admissions@loretto.com.

Loretto Senior School. Please see Loretto School's entry in the HMC section.

Charitable status. Loretto School is a Registered Charity, number SC013978.

Loyola Preparatory School

103 Palmerston Road, Buckhurst Hill, Essex IG9 5NH

Tel:	020 8504 7372
Fax:	020 8505 5361
email:	office@loyola.essex.sch.uk
website:	www.loyola.essex.sch.uk

Chair of Governors: Mrs A M Fox

Headmistress: Mrs Kirsty Anthony, BA Hons, PGCE

Age Range. 3–11.
Number of Boys. 168.
Fees per term (2018–2019). £3,295 (inc lunch).

Loyola Preparatory School is a long established school educating boys for over a century, originally as part of St Ignatius College. As a caring Catholic School it welcomes boys of all denominations offering a weekly mass to celebrate faith, ethos and values.

As a boys-only school, Loyola focuses its teaching techniques to harness the attention of boys by applying the extensive studies made into 'the ways boys learn best'. These practices encourage greater stimulation and enjoyment which is demonstrated by their overall behaviour and results.

Loyola has a high teacher to pupil ratio, facilitated by enthusiastic and committed teachers, supported by a generous quota of quality teaching assistants.

Loyola boys are encouraged to be kind and respect each other, with the older boys acting as role models for the younger boys. Year 6 boys are given Prefect responsibilities as well as the opportunity to be elected to the position of Head Boy and Deputy Head Boy. All boys regularly take part in community events including fundraising for national and local charities.

Loyola supports their boy's progression for the next step in their learning journey by preparing them for entrance and scholarship exams with English and Maths being taught in small ability sets from Year 3 upwards.

The curriculum covers all the normal primary subjects and includes German, science and computer studies. There are schola, choir and orchestra opportunities available in school, with additional tuition for piano, strings, woodwind, brass and guitar.

Loyola is proud of its range of sporting activities for the boys, aided by a large all-weather pitch on site. Sporting activities include soccer, cricket, rugby, swimming, athletics and sailing (Year 6) of which many are available during the school day and others offered as an after-school club.

During their time at the school, Loyola boys experience a wide range of trips and activities including a 5-day residential trip (Year 6), a 4-day trip to Kingswood in Norfolk (Year 5), together with many day trips across the school years selected to stimulate and enrich their learning experience.

The school prospectus is available on the school website and prospective parents are welcome to telephone for an appointment to be given a personal tour of the school.

Charitable status. Loyola Preparatory School is a Registered Charity, number 1085079. The school is established in support of Roman Catholic principles of education.

Lucton Prep School

Lucton, Leominster, Herefordshire HR6 9PN

Tel:	01568 782000
Fax:	01568 782001
email:	admissions@luctonschool.org
website:	www.luctonschool.org
Twitter:	@LuctonSchool
Facebook:	@Lucton-School
LinkedIn:	/lucton-school

Headmistress of Lucton School: Mrs Gill Thorne, MA, BA Hons, PGCE, LLAM

Head of Prep School: Mr David Bicker-Caarten, MBA

Age Range. 6 months–11 years.
Number in School. 135.
Fees per term (2018–2019). Day £2,350–£3,300, Weekly Boarding £7,500, Full Boarding £9,295.

Lucton Prep School is on the same site as Lucton School, which was founded in 1708. Lucton provides pupils with an excellent all-round education which aims to bring out their full potential. Pupils benefit from small classes, a friendly atmosphere and an idyllic rural location. The Prep

School pupils benefit from the Senior School's extensive facilities, including a modern indoor swimming pool, sports hall and an equestrian centre. Lucton accepts boarders from Year 3 and has a good mix of day pupils, weekly boarders and full boarders.

Taught in small classes, with no combined year groups, the pupils benefit from a very high degree of individual attention.

The Lucton Nursery accepts babies from the age of 6 months and with the extra early and late sessions, nursery children may be dropped off from 8.00 am and collected as late as 6.00 pm.

The vast majority of Lucton Prep School pupils continue through to the senior part of the school. (*See full details in Lucton School's entry in the ISA section.*)

School Facilities. The school is set in 55 acres of beautiful Herefordshire countryside. Facilities on site include:

- Separate junior and senior libraries
- Science laboratories
- ICT rooms
- Design and technology workshop
- Tennis courts
- Indoor swimming pool
- Indoor sports hall
- Games fields
- Equestrian centre.

Boarding pupils are housed in modern buildings and the Prep School boarders are all in dormitories in their own junior house. They have the opportunity to move into their own rooms in the Senior School.

Admissions. Admission can take place at any time of the year by interview and assessment. Prospective pupils are always invited to spend a taster day in the school without obligation. Examinations for academic scholarships are held in January each year.

Affiliations. The Head of Lucton Prep School, part of Lucton School, is a member of the The Independent Association of Prep Schools (IAPS); the Headmistress of Lucton School is a member of the Independent Schools Association (ISA); and Lucton School is in membership of the Boarding Schools' Association (BSA).

Charitable status. Lucton School is a Registered Charity, number 518076.

Ludgrove

Wokingham, Berks RG40 3AB

Tel:	0118 978 9881
Fax:	0118 979 2973
email:	office@ludgroveschool.co.uk
	registrar@ludgroveschool.co.uk
website:	www.ludgrove.net
Twitter:	@_Ludgrove

Chairman of Governors: P D Edey, QC

Head: **S W T Barber**, BA Durham, PGCE

Registrar: Mrs Olwen Dennis-Jones

Age Range. 8–13.
Number of Boys. 190 Boarders.
Fees per term (2018–2019). £9,150.

Ludgrove is a thriving full boarding boys prep school situated in 130 acres of beautiful grounds in Berkshire. It is a magical place to spend five years of childhood, where outstanding pastoral care lies at the heart of everything.

The principal aims of the school are for boys to grow and develop in a happy caring environment, to explore and expand their potential and to learn to develop an awareness and concern for others around them. We aim to prepare our boys to meet the demanding challenges they will experience at the next stage of their education with confidence and good humour.

We are unashamedly ambitious for every boy and are proud of our strong academic record. In recent years we have sent over 70% of boys on to Eton, Harrow and Radley, in addition to other distinguished public schools. The boys have a wealth of opportunities: a stimulating curriculum, exceptional facilities and a vibrant extra-curricular programme with exposure to music, drama, sport and art.

Our extensive facilities include a stunning 350-seat theatre, purpose-built science laboratories, art, pottery and CDT department, a refurbished sports hall and well-stocked library, in addition to the impressive 120 acres of grounds incorporating numerous games pitches, a 9-hole golf course, squash courts, fives courts, an astroturf, tennis courts, a 20m indoor pool and adventure playground.

Charitable status. Ludgrove School Trust Limited is a Registered Charity, number 309100.

Lyndhurst House Preparatory School

24 Lyndhurst Gardens, Hampstead, London NW3 5NW

Tel:	020 7435 4936
email:	office@lyndhursthouse.co.uk
website:	www.lyndhursthouse.co.uk

Headmaster: **Andrew Reid**, MA Oxon

Age Range. 4–13.
Number of Day Boys. 165.
Fees per term (2018–2019). £6,190–£6,910 (including lunch and outings).

There is a full-time teaching staff of 30, with classroom assistants for the first four years and learning support across the year groups. Entry is at 4+, or 7+ following interviews and assessment. All boys stay to 13+, and sit the Common Entrance Exam or Scholarship to the Independent Senior Schools. Lyndhurst is a friendly and lively traditional boys' school, with its own special atmosphere and character. The environment is warm and friendly, small and familiar in feel, yet full of bustle, activity and purpose. Strong foundations laid in the early years are followed by small sets in the top three years to provide the School's excellent record of success in transfers to London day schools and major public schools further afield. In addition to high academic expectations, there is a strong emphasis on sporting activity and achievement, as well as art, music, drama and computing. Lyndhurst House – a full, rich life in a personal, individual and friendly environment.

Lyonsdown School

3 Richmond Road, New Barnet, Hertfordshire EN5 1SA

Tel:	020 8449 0225
email:	enquiries@lyonsdownschool.co.uk
website:	www.lyonsdownschool.co.uk
Twitter:	@LyonsdownSchool
Facebook:	@LyonsdownSchool

Headmaster: **Mr C Hammond**, BA Hons, PGCE

Age Range. Girls 3–11, Boys 3–7.

Number of Pupils. 200.

Fees per term (2018–2019). Pre-Reception: £1,421–£2,597; Reception–Year 2 £3,250; Years 3–6 £3,553.

Lyonsdown School is a small, friendly school for girls aged three to eleven and boys aged three to seven. The school is a member of both IAPS and ISA and is situated in the leafy suburb of New Barnet, within easy access to the North Circular and both Northern Line and mainline rail services.

Lyonsdown nurtures both potential and ability, allowing all pupils to thrive and achieve personal excellence. The school is non-selective at entry. Year 6 girls and Year 2 boys gain entry and scholarships to top senior schools, both independent (day and boarding) and selective maintained schools.

Class sizes are small with high teacher to pupil ratios, ensuring that both teaching and pastoral care are of the highest standard. A broad and balance curriculum provides personalised learning and a great deal of specialist teaching. This allows pupils to flourish and, with guidance, discover their abilities, whatever they might be.

Lyonsdown has significant strengths in Music, Drama and Art with recent successes coming in the North London Music Festival and the ISA Art competition and being shortlisted for the National ISA awards. The school runs two lively and popular choirs and individual instrumental lessons are taught by visiting specialists.

"Lyonsdown learning" is at the heart of the school and the pupils develop those skills that will prepare them for their senior school and a life of learning beyond. They are critical thinkers, exploring their lessons and activities with independence, responsibility and imagination.

The school is housed in a beautiful Edwardian building with modern facilities that include a discovery garden, library and dedicated classrooms for Art, Computing, Music and Science. Sport is both popular and important at Lyonsdown and the school makes good use of its own purpose-built hall and local facilities for PE and Games.

An extensive extra-curricular programme, including breakfast and after-school clubs, maypole dancing, street dance and fencing runs throughout the year. Visiting speakers, theatre groups and workshops are very popular with pupils and parents alike. The school makes excellent use of its location with trips into London a regular feature of the calendar and Year 5 and 6 pupils enjoying an annual residential activity trip.

Specialist learning support is also provided to those pupils who need additional focus, be it a specific need such as dyslexia, or for those who need a temporary boost. More able girls and boys have their learning extended in lessons and in a variety of additional activities, and pupils of all abilities are challenged.

Lyonsdown is an inclusive community with a Christian ethos, welcoming a diverse mix of pupils of all faiths. The school is a community of learning and the partnership between home and school is of central importance. Regular communication ensures parents are well-informed and celebrates the pupils' many successes.

Charitable status. Lyonsdown School Trust Ltd is a Registered Charity, number 312591.

Magdalene House Preparatory School
Wisbech Grammar School

North Brink, Wisbech, Cambs PE13 1JX

Tel:	01945 583631 (Pupil Services/Reception)
	01945 586750 (Admissions)
Fax:	01945 586781
email:	pupilservices@wisbechgrammar.com
website:	www.wisbechgrammar.com
Twitter:	@WisbechGrammar
Facebook:	@WisbechGrammar

Chair of Governors: Dr D Barter, MBBS, FRCP, FRCPCH, DCH

Senior Deputy Head – Magdalene House: **Mrs K Neaves**, BEd, TDip

Age Range. 4–11 co-educational.

Number of Pupils. 145 day pupils.

Fees per term (2018–2019). £3,099–£3,199. Means-tested bursary support is available.

Magdalene House Preparatory School is the prep section of Wisbech Grammar School and caters for pupils from Reception to Prep 6. Great emphasis is placed on reading, writing and numeracy, and the pupils follow a broad-based curriculum. The pupils have access to many of the excellent senior school facilities, including the science laboratory, food & nutrition room, sports hall, music and theatre. They also have their own library, a dedicated computer room and a light and spacious hall. Specialist teaching is offered in science, music, modern foreign languages, food & nutrition, music, physical education and games, computing and drama. Many children receive peripatetic music lessons and participate in musical groups. Opportunities for performance in drama and music, nativities, musicals, assemblies and informal concerts, are regular features. In October, Prep 6 pupils sit an entrance examination for the senior school. (*See Wisbech Grammar School entry in HMC section.*)

Sporting opportunities abound and a full timetable of fixtures against other schools is arranged. The main boys' team sports are rugby, hockey and cricket, whilst the girls play hockey, netball and cricket. Members of the under 11 rugby and hockey teams enjoy an annual long weekend tour.

A varied after-school programme for both juniors and infants provides the opportunity to develop sports and leisure skills, as well as artistic and musical talents. A supervised homework club also runs each day.

Field trips, activity days at local museums and visits by theatre groups and outside speakers lie at the heart of the curriculum. Prep 4, 5 and 6 enjoy an annual residential visit to an educational activity centre.

Generally children are admitted to the Reception class at the beginning of the school year in which they reach the age of 5, but entry into all year groups is possible throughout the year. All children registering are invited to spend a day in school when they are assessed in a manner appropriate to their age. Candidates for entry are also welcomed at all other stages of the prep school age range.

All enquiries should be made to the Admissions department at Wisbech Grammar School.

Charitable status. The Wisbech Grammar School Foundation is a Registered Charity, number 1087799. It exists to promote the education of boys and girls.

Maidwell Hall

Maidwell, Northampton, Northamptonshire NN6 9JG

Tel: 01604 686234
Fax: 01604 686659
email: thesecretary@maidwellhall.co.uk
website: www.maidwellhall.co.uk
Twitter: @MaidwellHall
Facebook: @Maidwell-Hall

Chairman of the Governors: R H Cunningham, Esq

Headmaster: **R A Lankester**, MA Cantab, PGCE

Age Range. 7–13.
Number of Pupils. 123: 109 Boarders, 14 Day pupils.
Fees per term (2018–2019). £8,960 Boarding, £5,835 Day.

Maidwell Hall is a co-educational boarding school with some day pupils. Occupying a substantial 17th Century hall the school is situated in beautiful countryside and is characterized by its rural location and by 44 acres of grounds. It is a Christian school and the teachings of Jesus Christ are central to the moral and spiritual education of the children. Every Sunday morning the school worships in the parish church on the edge of the school grounds. The school aims to encourage all the children to discover and develop all their talents through the academic curriculum, the games programme, Music, Art, Drama and an impressive range of hobbies and activities. The school's happy atmosphere is based on a clear framework of rules and conventions with strong emphasis placed on good manners and a traditional code of behaviour and courtesy.

The school is organized as a 7 day-a-week boarding school with a comprehensive programme of club activities in the evenings supplemented by a choice of outings or school based free-time activities on Sundays. There is a weekly boarding option for Year 4. The children benefit greatly from the freedom and security of the school's spectacular grounds including its famous arboretum (wilderness) and its large lake for fishing and boating. Leave-outs occur every 2 or 3 weeks and run from Friday midday until Monday evening and each term contains a long half-term break. Pastoral care for the boarders is the direct responsibility of the Headmaster and his wife, the Housemaster and the team of Matrons and other residential staff. In addition each pupil has an individual tutor.

Pupils are prepared for Common Entrance to the major independent senior schools (typically Eton, Harrow, Oundle, Radley, Rugby, Shrewsbury, Stowe, Uppingham and Winchester) and every year several sit scholarships. In addition to core subjects all pupils study Art, Design, ICT, Latin, Music and Religious Studies and there are also timetabled lessons in PE, Swimming, PSHE, and Drama. There is a specialist carpentry shop which operates as a club activity.

The school has a strong reputation for sport. The major games for the boys are rugby, football, hockey and cricket and there are also matches against other schools in athletics, cross-country running, golf, squash, swimming and tennis. The major games for girls are hockey, netball, tennis and rounders. Teams are entered for riding events and the Pytchley hunt meets at the school every year. There is a successful school shooting team. In the Summer and Autumn there is sailing once or twice a week. In addition to impressive games pitches, sporting facilities include a multi-purpose sports hall with climbing wall, a squash court, a 6-hole golf course, astroturf, hockey pitch, tennis courts and a heated indoor swimming pool. There is particular emphasis on outward bound activities and leadership. There is a strong musical tradition and most pupils play one or two musical instruments; there is a thriving church choir and strings, wind and guitar groups. There are regular concerts throughout the year and each year there is a major school play.

Charitable status. Maidwell Hall is a Registered Charity, number 309917. It exists for the purpose of educating children.

Maldon Court Preparatory School

Silver Street, Maldon, Essex CM9 4QE

Tel: 01621 853529
email: enquiries@maldoncourtschool.org
website: www.maldoncourtschool.org

Principal: **Mrs L F Guest**, BEd Hons

Headteacher: Mrs E Mason

Age Range. 1–11 co-educational.
Number of Pupils. 141 Day pupils.
Fees per term (2018–2019). Reception £3,117.10; Years 1–6 £3,162.70 for the first child, with sibling discounts.

Welcome to Maldon Court Preparatory School, a small, happy and caring school community where young children can flourish in a positive and supportive environment. Originally established in 1956, the school has maintained its vision of being run as a family-owned, friendly school with high expectations and standards.

Children here are encouraged to develop in all aspects of the broad and balanced curriculum. Each pupil is valued as an individual and allowed to develop at their own pace. Strengths and weaknesses are identified at an early age and our dedicated staff ensure that every child is challenged and supported to achieve their full potential through exploring the huge range of possibilities open to them.

Within this framework of close care and encouragement, Maldon Court delivers a first-class education, laying down strong foundations for the future. At the same time, great emphasis is placed on pastoral care, which is strengthened by a close partnership with parents and a strong family atmosphere that is evident throughout the school. The success of this ethos is reflected in the school's achievement of 'excellent' (the highest inspection rating) in every area in 2013. We are also delighted to have been graded 'Outstanding' in our Ofsted Nursery inspection in May 2017 and 'Outstanding' in our Nursery ISI Inspection in May 2017.

There is a love of sport at Maldon Court which has been nurtured and developed by the dedicated members of our PE Department. We aim for high levels of physical fitness and coordination, in turn fostering confidence and encouraging participation from children at all levels. The school enters teams both locally and nationally in a wealth of sporting events and competitions, and currently holds the title of 'District Track and Field Athletics Champions'.

At the end of their time at Maldon Court, we are proud to see our boys and girls emerge as articulate, well-informed and interesting young people, comfortable in their abilities, buoyed by their achievements, ambitious and well equipped for the challenges that lie ahead.

The Mall School

185 Hampton Road, Twickenham, Middlesex TW2 5NQ

Tel: 020 8977 2523
Fax: 020 8977 8771
email: admissions@themallschool.org.uk
website: www.themallschool.org.uk

Chairman of Governors: R J H Walker, BSc

Headmaster: D Price, BSc, MA, PGCE

Deputy Head: J Fair, BA

Age Range. 4–13.
Number of Boys. 290 day boys.
Fees per term (2018–2019). Reception–Year 2 £4,080, Years 3–8 £4,589.

Founded in 1872, for over 140 years we have been preparing boys for a range of the leading independent London day and boarding senior schools. Many scholarships have been secured by our boys (35 in the last 5 years) in a wide range of disciplines including Academic, Sport, Art, Drama, Choral, All-rounder and the highly coveted John Colet Award for St Paul's.

Boys are welcomed at 4+, as well as at 7+, and are taught by a well-qualified staff consisting of 29 full-time and 3 part-time members, in an average class size of 18. We teach a broad curriculum, including Art, DT, Music, and Drama, in addition to sport and PE.

Cricket, Rugby, Football, Swimming and Athletics are the main sports played at the school. We have our own outstanding 25m indoor swimming pool and a state-of-the-art Sports Hall which opened in January 2014.

Music and Drama are warmly encouraged at the Mall School. There are 2 choirs and 2 orchestras with a large variety of ensembles and visiting teachers for piano, strings, guitar, woodwind and brass.

To help working parents, we provide wraparound care from 7.30 am to 6.00 pm with an extensive range of after-school clubs, such as chess, judo and art clubs.

In addition to bright modern classrooms, facilities include science laboratories, music practice rooms, IT suite, library and a new creative and performing arts centre which provides a 160-seat theatre and large-sized art and design technology studios. A morning minibus service is in operation which brings boys to school from the Teddington, Kingston, Richmond, St Margarets, Twickenham and Isleworth areas.

The Pre Prep is housed in an old Victorian Vicarage, a five-minute walk from the Prep school. This building was refurbished in 2015 and a new outdoor interactive play area was opened in September 2016.

The Mall School prospectus is available via the website or the Headmaster's PA. Early application is advisable as the school is non-selective for entry into Year R and there are only limited places available via assessment at 7+.

The school currently has boys up to Year 8, but from the summer term 2020, all boys will leave at the end of Year 6.

Charitable status. The Mall School Trust is a Registered Charity, number 295003. It exists to promote and provide for the advancement of the education of children.

Maltman's Green

Maltmans Lane, Gerrards Cross, Bucks SL9 8RR

Tel: 01753 883022
Fax: 01753 891237
email: office@maltmansgreen.com
website: www.maltmansgreen.com
Twitter: @MaltmansGreen
Facebook: @MaltmansGreenSchool

Headmistress: Mrs J Pardon, MA, BSc Hons, PGCE

Age Range. 2–11.
Number of Girls. 420.
Fees per term (2018–2019). £1,860 (5 mornings Nursery)–£5,090.

Complimentary Stay & Play Sessions: Saturday 26 January 2019, Saturday 18 May 2019.

Open Mornings: Friday 8 February 2019, Friday 22 March 2019, Friday 14 June 2019.

Our Approach. At Maltman's Green we believe in the pursuit of excellence whilst maintaining a sense of enjoyment. Girls are inspired to do their best inside and outside of the classroom through an exceptional academic curriculum and extensive extra-curricular opportunities. We prepare girls for the modern world through a relevant, adaptable and innovative approach that is supported by a foundation of traditional values. Our girls are given every opportunity to succeed across multiple disciplines, fostering confidence and self-belief, and empowering them for whatever future awaits.

We believe that the emotional, social and physical well-being of our girls is paramount. By providing a personalised learning experience in an encouraging and nurturing environment, we ensure our girls feel happy, confident and valued – a perfect foundation from which children can flourish. This ethos has been recognised by the ISI who applauded our "outstanding" pastoral care.

Games and The Arts. Our sports provision is an outstanding feature of the School, with dedicated facilities and daily lessons. All girls enjoy friendly tournaments between houses, within year groups and against other local schools. Those with the talent and inclination can progress to squad level to compete regionally or nationally with exceptional results. Music is a very important part of life at Maltman's Green. Specialist teaching, exceptional facilities and lots of choice give our girls plenty of opportunity to explore and showcase their musical talents. Over 100 girls participate in our various choirs and we have nine different musical instrument lessons available as well as a variety of instrumental ensemble groups. Drama too has a big part to play in school life where regular performances and workshops give girls a strong sense of confidence and creative expression.

Achievements. Our girls are encouraged to be independent thinkers, to challenge themselves and to always try their best. Maltman's Green provides a firm foundation, preparing girls to face senior school and beyond with confidence, determination and a lifelong love of learning. This is reflected in our impressive 11+ results – an 80% pass rate in 2018 – and a record number of scholarships being awarded to Independent Senior Schools.

Outstanding Characteristics. 2018 marks our 100th Anniversary and, since the School was founded in 1918, we have seen numerous developments and upgrades to our facilities, including dedicated subject classrooms, a 6-lane, 25-metre indoor swimming pool, a multi-use gymnasium, a state-of-the-art theatre space and a dedicated 2–3 year olds daycare centre.

Charitable status. Maltman's Green School Trust Limited is a Registered Charity, number 310633.

Manor Lodge School

Rectory Lane, Ridge Hill, Shenley, Hertfordshire WD7 9BG

Tel:	01707 642424
Fax:	01707 645206
email:	enquiries@manorlodgeschool.com
website:	www.manorlodgeschool.com

Chair of Governors: Mr D Arnold, MBE

Head: **Mrs Alyson Lobo**, BEd Hons

Age Range. 3–11.

Number of Pupils. Nursery (age 3) 18; Infants (age 4–7) 181; Juniors (age 7–11) 222.

Fees per term (2018–2019). Nursery £3,440; Infants £3,700; Juniors £4,100.

There are three forms of 18–20 children in Reception to Year 6 inclusive. We have specialist teachers for French, PE, IT, DT, Art, Drama, Science (Years 5 & 6), and Music, as well as numerous instrumental teachers for piano, brass, woodwind, percussion and strings. All staff are fully qualified.

The main school building consists of an 18th century manor house and extension which offers classrooms, French, Science, Art, IT, DT and a hall. A magnificent new building housing further classrooms and a sports hall/theatre provides additional space for sports, music and the performing arts.

The cottage at the end of the drive houses our Nursery. The children must be siblings of pupils in the main school and are eligible to attend from the term in which they turn three.

Our classrooms are bright and well-equipped and the standard of work displayed is very high. We aim to provide excellent teaching and learning opportunities within a caring environment in which high standards of behaviour and good manners are encouraged and expected. We thus ensure that all pupils achieve their full potential and are prepared for entry to senior schools, both independent and state.

Music plays an important part in the life of the school. There are several choirs, an orchestra, jazz band and various ensembles and almost half the children in school learn an instrument. Music is of course linked to our Drama activities. Reception to Year 5 children take part in at least two performances a year, and in Year 6 the children have a theatre experience in our brand new hall. Art is of a particularly high standard and the children use a variety of media, producing excellent original work. We strongly believe in children being allowed a childhood and with this in mind, have created an all-weather Outdoor Learning area and will endeavour to create an environment that makes it simple to integrate traditional learning with an outdoor space. Our aim is to create physical spaces where students are able to develop key concepts that help meet their well-being needs. The twelve acres of grounds also include pitches, an all-weather court and play areas with climbing activity equipment and other outdoor toys. The children are offered a wide range of sporting activities including football, rugby, hockey, cricket, netball, rounders, swimming and athletics.

Our caterers provide a delicious selection of fresh, healthy lunches and cater for a number of dietary requirements.

Extra activities available at the school include chess, drama and ju-jitsu. There are numerous clubs run by the staff after school until 4.30 pm, for example, cooking, football, rugby, cricket, netball, dance, athletics and choir.

Charitable status. Manor Lodge School is a Registered Charity, number 1048874. The school exists to provide an education which will maximise the potential of the girls and boys in our care.

The Manor Preparatory School

Faringdon Road, Abingdon, Oxon OX13 6LN

Tel:	01235 858458
Fax:	01235 559593
email:	admissions@manorprep.org
website:	www.manorprep.org
Twitter:	@ManorPrep
Facebook:	@ManorPrepSchool

Chair of Board of Governors: Mr Shaun Forrestal

Headmaster: **Mr Alastair Thomas**, BA Hons, PGCE

Age Range. Girls and Boys 2–11.

Number of Pupils. 358 Day Pupils: 75 boys and 283 girls.

Fees per term (2018–2019). £4,260–£5,190.

Founded in 1907 and situated in Abingdon, the Manor Preparatory School is an independent co-educational day school that welcomes boys and girls aged 2–11.

The school has a wonderfully happy, creative atmosphere where every individual is valued and nurtured to reach their potential. The Manor's most recent ISI Inspection took place in April 2017, with every area of school life receiving the highest possible rating of 'Excellent'. Inspectors commented that "Pupils approach every day with an overwhelming passion to learn and develop."

This is in part due to the exceptionally caring and invigorating tone of the school, where laughter is an essential part of the school day, and also by children's personal development being further strengthened by staff who act as excellent role models. Every child is encouraged to push themselves to new challenges and fulfil their own potential, resulting in outstanding results academically, on the sports field, and in creative and performing arts.

The school has an excellent record in ensuring leavers move on to the next school that is perfectly suited to each individual. Scholarships, awards and exhibitions feature highly in all areas.

Completion of a new Sports Hall in September 2018 underpins the exciting development programme that is underway, and extends even further the breadth of opportunities that are on offer to the children.

The school aims to simplify the logistics of family life as well, and so have created an extensive daily bus service covering Oxfordshire, Berkshire, Buckinghamshire and Wiltshire, and fully flexible wraparound care.

For further information please visit our website www.manorprep.org or contact Mrs Karen Copson, Director of Admissions and Communications on 01235 858462 or admissions@manorprep.org.

The Marist School – Preparatory Phase

Kings Road, Sunninghill, Ascot, Berkshire SL5 7PS

Tel: 01344 624291
Fax: 01344 621566
email: admissions@themarist.com
website: www.themarist.com
Twitter: @Marist_School
Facebook: @themarist

Independent Day School for Girls.

Chair of Governors: Mrs A Nash

Principal: Mr Karl McCloskey, BA Hons, PGCE, MA

Vice Principal (*Prep*): **Mrs Jane Gow, BEd Hons**

Age Range. 3–11.
Number of Pupils. 164 girls.
Fees per term (2018–2019). £3,260 (Nursery) – £3,980 (Year 6).
Mission Statement. The aim of the school is to:
- provide a caring community where learning is guided by strong Christian values;
- promote excellence where all are encouraged to reach their full potential.

Strengths of the school:
- Early Years and Preparatory departments tailored to the specific needs of the girls at each stage of their education.
- Caring, well qualified and professional staff dedicated to developing happy, secure and stimulated girls.
- Curriculum designed to achieve all the foundation/early years learning goals.
- Able to offer a wide range of both academic and extracurricular activities.
- High achievement in gym, ballet, art, judo, drama, choir and music.
- Strong emphasis on pastoral care, spiritual and personal development; care and consideration for others.
- Small class sizes to enhance individual progression and recognition.
- The school is renowned for its high standards regarding moral values, community spirit, respect and care. This is in line with the overall ethos of The Marist order which has a worldwide presence, providing a truly international dimension to a girl's education.
- Girls are taught to consider and help those less fortunate than themselves through involvement in a wide range of local, national and international charity projects.

The Marist Preparatory School is able to offer your daughter a complete and fulfilling education in the security of a single-sex environment, from the age of 3 to 11. We welcome all Christians and those supporting our ethos. We are renowned for our happy and caring ethos, where pastoral care is considered paramount. Your daughter will be treated as an individual and encouraged to achieve her full potential in every area. We have a strong academic record but we also place a strong emphasis on extracurricular activities which help to develop important qualities such as self-confidence, individual creativity and teamwork.

The Marist School consists of three phases – Preparatory, Senior and Sixth Form – which are all on the same campus. *For further details, please see The Marist School – Senior Phase entry in the GSA section.*

Charitable status. The Marist School is a Registered Charity, number 225485. The principal aims and activities of The Marist School are religious and charitable and specifically to provide education by way of an independent day school for girls between the ages of 3 and 18.

Marlborough House School

High Street, Hawkhurst, Cranbrook, Kent TN18 4PY

Tel: 01580 753555
Fax: 01580 754281
email: registrar@marlboroughhouseschool.co.uk
            frontoffice@marlboroughhouseschool.co.uk
website: www.marlboroughhouseschool.co.uk
Facebook: @Marlborough-House-School

Marlborough House was founded in 1874 and is registered as an Educational Trust with a Board of Governors.

Chairman of Governors: H Somerset

Headmaster: **M Ward**, BEd Hons

Deputy Head: Ms V Coatz, BEd Hons
Assistant Head (*Academic*): Mrs P Archer, BA Hons, GTP
Head of Senior School: J Ridge, BA Hons, PGCE
Head of Middle School: Mrs C Walker, BA Hons, PGCE
Head of Nursery & Pre-Prep: Mrs R Reid, BSc Hons, GTP
Head's PA: Mrs M McTrusty

Age Range. 2¾–13 Co-educational.
Number of Pupils. 330.
Fees per term (2018–2019). Prep £6,020, Pre-Prep £2,910–£3,555, Nursery according to number of sessions. Flexi boarding: from £31 per night. No compulsory extras.

Marlborough House School is an independent Preparatory School for boys and girls. The School is fully co-educational creating a friendly, family atmosphere for children between the ages of 2¾ and 13. We are a community where our values, with mutual respect at their core, are at the heart of everything we do. Happy, confident children are keen to learn, to push themselves and to achieve more. It is our job to help children achieve academically but, much more than this, we also want to nurture children to become well-rounded, enthusiastic, self-confident and fulfilled young people. We believe in high expectations, the value of knowing each child as an individual and providing a breadth of experiences but above all this is our commitment to making sure children here are happy – because we know that only then will they achieve their goals.

Marlborough House is situated in the village of Hawkhurst in beautiful countryside on the Kent/Sussex border, near the town of Cranbrook. The fine Georgian house is set in 35 acres of superb gardens, playing fields, lawns and woodland. The School has a self-contained Pre-Prep department, Chapel, Computer Centre, large Sports Hall, 2 Performance/Dance Halls, superbly equipped Science Laboratory, Art, Pottery and Design Technology Department, Music Rooms, Swimming Pool, a .22 Rifle Shooting Range, Forest School and 2 large all-weather games surfaces.

With our 50+ qualified teaching staff we aim to produce well motivated, balanced, confident children who know the value of hard work, and who will thrive in their next schools and the modern world beyond. Our classes are small and the children are prepared for leading independent day and boarding schools and Kent Grammar schools, whilst those showing special promise are supported to sit scholarships.

Encouragement is given to each child to experience a wide variety of activities. In addition to the traditional sports of Cricket, Rugby, Soccer, Hockey, Athletics, Tennis, Netball and Rounders, opportunities are provided for Music (with around 12 peripatetic music teachers visiting the school each week, children can learn a wide range of instruments and join the many groups and choirs), Art (in many different media), Pottery, Drama, Ballet, Technology, Computing, Shooting, Sailing, Golf, Swimming, Fencing and Judo. The club programme is extensive with over 70 clubs offered in the course of a year.

The website is detailed and informative and the school also has a very active Facebook page.

Charitable status. Marlborough House School is a Registered Charity, number 307793. It exists to provide education for children.

Marlston House School

Hermitage, Newbury, Berkshire RG18 9UL

Tel: 01635 200293
email: registrar@brockmarl.org
website: www.brockmarl.org.uk

Headmaster: **Mr D J W Fleming**, MA Oxon, MSc

Age Range. 3–13.
Number of Girls. 169 Girls (including 65 Boarders).
Fees per term (2018–2019). Boarding £7,975, Day £3,550–£5,950. Pre-Prep School (Ridge House): £3,550 (full-time). Temporary Overseas Boarders £8,600.

Established in 1995, Marlston House is situated in 500 acres of its own grounds in countryside of outstanding beauty, only four miles from access to the M4. The school is situated beside Brockhurst Boys' Preparatory school and occupies separate listed buildings. Boys and girls are taught separately, but the two schools join together for drama music and activities. In this way Brockhurst and Marlston House combine the best features of the single-sex and co-educational systems: academic excellence and social interaction. The schools are proud of the high standard of pastoral care established within a family atmosphere. (*See also entry for Brockhurst School.*)

The Pre-Prep School, Ridge House, is a co-educational department of Brockhurst and Marlston House Schools for 75 children aged 3–6 years, and is situated on the same site in new self-contained, purpose-designed accommodation.

Girls are prepared for entry to a variety of leading Independent Senior Schools through the ISEB Common Entrance and Scholarship Papers at 11+ and 13+.

All girls play Netball (outdoor and indoor courts), Hockey, Rounders and Tennis (outdoor and indoor courts) and take part in Athletics, Cross Country and Swimming (25m indoor heated pool). Additional activities include riding (own equestrian centre), fencing, judo, shooting (indoor rifle range), dance and ballet. Facilities for gymnastics and other sporting activities are provided in a purpose-built Sports Hall. Year 7 pupils make a week-long visit to a Château in France as part of their French studies.

Music and Art are important features of the curriculum and a number of girls have won scholarships and awards to senior schools in these subjects recently. The school is currently building a new dedicated Music School and Theatre to open in the Summer Term 2014.

Transport is provided by the school to and from airports and between Newbury and Paddington stations. Pupils are accompanied by school staff to their destinations.

Mayfield Preparatory School

Sutton Road, Walsall, West Midlands WS1 2PD

Tel: 01922 624107
email: info@mayfieldprep.co.uk
website: www.mayfieldprep.co.uk

Administered by the Governors of Queen Mary's Schools.

Chair of Governors: Mrs J Aubrook

Headmaster: **Mr Matthew Draper**, BA, PGCE

Age Range. 2–11 Co-educational.
Number of Pupils. Day: 108 Boys, 101 Girls.
Fees per term (2018–2019). Main School £2,900; Pre-Nursery £1,740.

A co-educational day school for children aged 2 to 11+, set in a listed building with beautiful surroundings and playing fields. A purpose-built Science/Art building opened in November 2000.

The self-contained Nursery Department accepts children at 2+.

A fully qualified Staff with full-time ancillary support throughout KS1 ensures that the individual child receives maximum attention.

The main aim at Mayfield is to encourage intellectual excellence. Children experience a thorough grounding in literacy and numeracy skills.

Through stimulating courses of correctly-paced work the school specialises in the preparation of the children for Grammar and Independent School entrance examinations at 11+.

Our children achieve excellent results, but it is always borne in mind that the individual child's needs are met by matching achievement to potential. All children are expected and encouraged to develop daily in confidence and security.

We believe in a balanced curriculum, and at Mayfield practical and non-academic activities additionally provide interest and varied experiences in Sports, Art, Music, ICT, DT, Dance, Drama and Public Speaking.

Good manners are expected at all times, as well as a happy and whole-hearted participation in the life and studies offered by the school.

Merchant Taylors' Prep

Moor Farm, Sandy Lodge Road, Rickmansworth, Herts WD3 1LW

Tel: 01923 825648
Fax: 01923 835802
email: office@mtpn.org.uk
website: www.mtpn.org.uk
Twitter: @MTSPrep
Facebook: @MerchantTaylorsPrep

Chair of Governors: Mr C P Hare

Head: **Dr Karen McNerney**, BSc Hons, PGCE, MSc, EdD

Deputy Head: Mr Tony McConnell, MA Hons, PGCE, FHA
Deputy Head: Mr Andrew Crook, BA Hons, PGCE

Age Range. 3–13.
Number of Pupils. 360 Day Boys.

Fees per term (2018–2019). £3,556 (Nursery full-time), £5,081 (Reception, Years 1 and 2), £5,333 (Years 3–8).

The School is located amidst 14 acres on a former farm in an idyllic park and woodland setting. The Grade II listed buildings have been stylishly converted to provide a complete and unique range of classrooms and ancillary facilities. The medieval Manor of the More, once owned by King Henry VIII and used as a palace by Cardinal Wolsey, was originally located within the grounds and provides some interesting and historical associations.

The School is divided as follows: an off-site Nursery & Reception School for children aged 3+ and 4 + based at Merchant Taylors' School; then on the Merchant Taylors' Prep School site, there is the Pre-Prep (Year 1 to Year 2) and the Prep Department (Year 3 to Year 8).

Pupils are admitted to the school after an assessment by Heads of Section. The main entry is into Nursery at 3+ when boys are admitted in the September after their third birthday. We also have a small 4+ and 7+ entry. Pupils are expected to remain until the age of thirteen. Parents of pupils at the Prep School will be given an assurance at the end of Year 5 as to whether their son will be able to progress to Merchant Taylors' School at the end of Year 8. Continuity scholarships are awarded to some pupils in the Prep School in Year 6.

Work of a high standard is expected of everyone. The curriculum is interpreted as richly as possible and includes Technology, Music, Art, Drama, Physical Education and Games. We focus on a genuinely holistic education that emphasizes values and dispositions as much as academic skills. The School has a fully-qualified and experienced staff team that complements modern teaching facilities including The Sir Christopher Harding Building for Science and Technology with two state-of-the-art laboratories, a new Art Design Technology workshop that opened in 2018, an ICT suite and a Learning Resource Centre. A 200-seat theatre with tiered seating and a separate music school provide a Centre for the Performing Arts. A Centenary Trail and outdoor classroom accommodate a range of outdoor learning activities. A bespoke nursery school was opened in the grounds of Merchant Taylors' School in April 2008 known as The Manor. Additional classrooms were added as part of our centenary celebrations in 2010. In 2014 a new dining hall, kitchen and common room were added. In September 2016, the Reception Year joined the Nursery in The Manor to create a specialist Early Years Foundation Stage.

Swift access to London by train from nearby Moor Park Station (Metropolitan line) allows easy access to places of historical and cultural interest as well as concerts and lectures.

While the Christian tradition on which the life of the School is based is that of the Church of England, all Christian denominations and other faiths have always been welcomed.

There is an extensive programme of extra-curricular activities in which all pupils are encouraged to take part. A key feature of the School's ethos is a strong tradition of caring, both for those within our community and for the wider community through regular charitable activities.

Rugby Football, Hockey, Association Football and Cricket are the principal team games. Athletics, Golf, Swimming, Tennis, Table Tennis and other sports are also coached. The School has the benefit of a fully-equipped Sports Hall with indoor cricket nets and a floodlit Astroturf facility.

The School has a flourishing Parents' Association which arranges social and fundraising activities, and an association for former pupils, The Old Terryers.

Charitable status. Merchant Taylors' School is a Registered Charity, number 1063740.

Micklefield School

10 Somers Road, Reigate, Surrey RH2 9DU
Tel: 01737 224212
email: office@micklefieldschool.co.uk
website: www.micklefieldschool.co.uk
Facebook: @MicklefieldSchoolReigate

Chair of the Council: Mrs J M Hamilton, LLB Hons, LLM

Headmistress: **Mrs L Rose**, BEd Hons, Cert Ed, Dip PC

Bursar: Mr P Flowerday, FFA, FIPA

Age Range. Rising 3–11.
Number of Pupils. 234 (106 boys, 128 girls).
Fees per term (2018–2019). £1,120–£3,975. Lunches: £225–£230.

'*Micklefield recognised the individuality in my twins and helped them realise their potential socially and academically.*'

'*Micklefield has helped my boys build confidence and self-esteem in a friendly and secure environment.*'

'*My children have flourished at Micklefield.*'

These quotes from current and former parents sum up the very special education offered at Micklefield School. Established in Reigate 108 years ago, we offer small classes, taught by qualified staff and qualified subject specialists. We cater for boys and girls from the age of rising 3 up to the age of 11, preparing them for Common Entrance and other examinations. The children enjoy academic success and have an excellent record in examinations for entrance to senior schools including Scholarship Awards.

In addition to the normal academic subjects, the curriculum includes design technology, computing, dancing, drama, French, netball, hockey, tennis, athletics, swimming, football, rugby and cricket. The school also has its own Sports Ground within 250 yards in St Albans Road.

The children take an active part in a variety of musical and theatrical activities and excel in sports. Dramatic productions and concerts provide opportunities for everyone to display their talents. We encourage participation in drama festivals, sports fixtures, the School's orchestra and choirs. Visits to concerts, theatres and museums are organised together with residential activity holidays for the older children. After-school care is available for children from Reception age.

Visit the website or telephone for a prospectus on 01737 224212. Mrs Rose, the Headmistress, is always pleased to show prospective parents around by appointment.

Charitable status. Micklefield School (Reigate) Limited is a Registered Charity, number 312069. It exists to provide a first-class education for its pupils.

Millfield Prep School

Edgarley Hall, Glastonbury, Somerset BA6 8LD
Tel: 01458 832446
Fax: 01458 833679
email: office@millfieldprep.com
website: millfieldschool.com
Twitter: @millfieldprep
Facebook: @millfieldprep

Chair of Governors: Mr Roland Rudd

Head: **Mrs Shirley Shayler**, MA, BSc Hons, PGCE

Tutor for Admissions: Mrs Fiona Gordon

Age Range. 2–13.
Number of Boys and Girls. 253 Boys, 196 Girls.
Fees per term (2018–2019). Prep: Full and Weekly Boarding £9,460, Day £3,605–£6,235. Flexi Boarding: £1,090 (2 nights), £1,635 (3 nights), £2,180 (4 nights). Occasional boarding: £59 per night. Pre-Prep: Day £2,835.

The school is administered by the same Board of Governors and on the same principles of small-group teaching as Millfield (made possible by a staff to pupil ratio of approximately 1:8) which ensures breadth and flexibility of timetable. It has its own attractive grounds of 185 acres some four miles from the Senior School, and its extensive facilities include games fields, art, design and technology centre, drama hall, music school, science laboratories, sports hall, AstroTurf, gymnasium, golf course, tennis courts, squash courts, sport pavilion, equestrian centre on campus, 25-metre indoor swimming pool, three IT laboratories and chapel. The pupils also have access to some of the specialist facilities at Millfield including a water-based astro, Olympic-sized swimming pool, tartan athletics track and indoor tennis centre.

The Pre-Prep department, taking children from 2–7, moved onto the Prep school site in 2004 so that the school now offers an education for children from ages 2–13, after which the majority of pupils transfer to Millfield. The small class sizes allow the individual pupil to be taught at his or her most appropriate pace. The range of ability within the school is comprehensive and setting caters for both the academically gifted and those requiring additional learning support.

The curriculum is broadly based and provides a balance between the usual academic subjects and the aesthetic, musical and artistic fields. Junior pupils study French and in Year 6 there is a choice of Spanish or French plus a taster in Latin for more able pupils. In Years 7 and 8 there is a choice of French, Spanish and Latin. Children may choose either one or two foreign languages, dependent on ability. Pupils are also given a choice of extra-curricular languages: we are currently offering Mandarin (these languages vary depending on demand). Science is taught throughout the school and as three separate subjects from the age of 10.

There is a full games programme organised by qualified teachers of physical education, with the help of other staff. The programme includes Athletics, Basketball, Climbing, Cross Country, Cricket, Fencing, Football, Golf, Hockey, Netball, Riding, Rounders, Rugby, Sailing, Squash, Swimming, Tennis, Outdoor Pursuits and Multi-Sports to name but a few. Over 80 different clubs are available.

Within Music we offer two Choirs, an Orchestra, Wind Band and 19 different music ensembles ranging from rock bands and brass bands to cello club. Over 250 pupils learn at least one musical instrument. There are regular opportunities for performance and all pupils are coached in performance and presentation skills. Highlight events include themed large ensemble evenings such as the annual Rock and Pop Concert, Summer Concert, Saturday morning breakfast masterclasses with visiting international artists and the traditional annual whole school House Singing competition.

Boys and girls can start from the age of 2 and up to the age of 12 and they come from over 20 different nationalities and widely differing backgrounds. Admission usually depends on interview, assessment and reports from the previous school. We award a number of Academic, Art, Chess, Music and Sports Scholarships each year for entry into Years 6, 7 and 8. We also welcome applications for scholarships from good all-rounders: boys and girls who have reached a good standard academically and show promise in specific areas such as Art, Music or Sport.

There are five boarding houses for pupils aged 7 years and above (three for boys and two for girls). Each house is under the care of resident houseparents and assistant houseparents. The Medical Centre is staffed by 3 qualified nurses, a physiotherapist, and the School Doctor attends daily.

Charitable status. Millfield is a Registered Charity, number 310283. The Millfield Schools provide a broad and balanced education to boys and girls from widely differing backgrounds, including a significant number with learning difficulties, and many for whom boarding is necessary.

Milton Keynes Preparatory School

Tattenhoe Lane, Milton Keynes, Buckinghamshire MK3 7EG

Tel:	01908 642111
Fax:	01908 366365
email:	info@mkps.co.uk
website:	www.mkps.co.uk

Chairman of the Governors: Mr David Pye, BA Hons, Cert Ed, MA Ed Dist, HETC, SEDA III, FRSA

Principal: Hilary Pauley, BEd

Headmaster: **Simon Driver**, BA, PGCE

Vice-Principal: Patricia Cave, BEd

Age Range. Nursery 2 months–2½ years. Pre-Prep Department 2½–7 years. Preparatory Department 7+–11 years.
Number of Pupils. 470 Day Pupils.
Fees per term (2018–2019). Nursery (per week) £295 (babies under 1 year), £305 (1–2½ years). Pre-Preparatory Department (per term): £4,120 (2½–5 years), £4,260 (6–7 years). Preparatory Department (per term): £4,660 (8–11 years).

Milton Keynes Preparatory School is a well-established family-owned school, with two other schools in the group, in Milton Keynes: one is a preparatory school and one is a pre-preparatory school and nursery.

Opening hours are 7.30 am to 6.30 pm for a 35-week academic year and a total of 46 weeks per year, enabling children to join play schemes in school holidays and to be cared for outside normal daily school hours.

Staff are highly qualified and committed to delivering the very best teaching and levels of care. Academic standards are "excellent", as awarded by recent Inspections, with pupils being prepared for entry to senior independent schools locally and nationally and to local grammar schools. Teaching is structured to take into account the requirements of the National Curriculum, with constant evaluation and assessment for each pupil. Scholarships are offered from Year 3 for those with excellent academic and sporting abilities.

Housed in purpose-built accommodation, all departments have their own outside soft play and extensive playground areas and there is a large astroturf court. The Nursery and Pre-Prep department have extended artificial grass terraces for year-round activities and learning.

Specialist facilities include a Music Technology Studio, IT Suite, Science Laboratory, D&T and Art rooms and a superb sports hall.

Additional facilities at The Farm, the school's Environmental Studies Centre, provide a fitness suite, music and dance studio, art and crafts facility, plus a brand new, state-of-the-art outdoor learning resource centre and raised beds for gardening.

Music and Sport play an important part in the life of the school. Concerts are held, and a wide variety of sport is played, with teams competing regularly against other schools. Additional extra-curricular clubs are offered in the Preparatory and Pre-Preparatory Departments.

The school aims to incorporate the best of modern teaching methods and traditional values in a friendly, caring and busy environment, where good work habits and a concern for the needs of others are paramount.

The Minster School
York

Deangate, York YO1 7JA

Tel: 0844 939 0000
Fax: 0844 939 0001
email: school@yorkminster.org
website: www.minsterschoolyork.co.uk

Chair of Governors: The Very Revd Vivienne Faull, Dean of York Minster

Acting Headteacher: **Mlle Sophie Schoukroun**, MA, MA, MA, BA Hons

Age Range. 3–13 Co-educational.
Number of Pupils. Preparatory 115; Pre-Prep Department 65.
Fees per term (2018–2019). Prep £3,466, Pre-Prep £2,266 (full day). Choristers receive substantial Scholarships, ranging between 60%–100%.

The Minster School was originally founded in 627 AD to educate singing boys. It is now a fully co-educational preparatory and pre-preparatory school, which includes a Nursery department. Its most recent ISI inspection report highlighted the Nursery teaching and provision as 'Outstanding' and the school overall was judged to be 'Excellent'. Teaching throughout the whole school was singled out as a particular strength and the achievement, attitude and behaviour of the pupils were warmly praised.

The Nursery and Pre-Prep departments are housed in their own accommodation with gardens, playgrounds and an ICT suite for junior pupils' use. French is taught from Year 2 upwards. In the prep school, teaching is delivered by well-qualified subject specialists. With computers in all classrooms, an IT suite, science lab, art room and DT suite the school is well equipped to deliver a broad curriculum. On our 8-acre sports fields, games are taught by school staff and professional coaches. Regular fixtures for boys and girls teams are arranged throughout the year. The major sports are football, hockey, netball, cricket and athletics. In addition to the normal academic curriculum, there is a flourishing music department and all orchestral instruments are taught. Pupils' levels of musical achievement are very high though there are no academic or musical tests to join the school.

Lunch and after-school care are not charged as extras and a wide variety of extracurricular activities is available, e.g. sewing, chess, ballet, fencing, judo, art and craft, model-making, drama and sports clubs etc.

Of the 180 children in the School, 20 boys and 20 girls are choristers who sing the services in York Minster in return for a substantial scholarship. Pupils are prepared for Common Entrance and Senior Independent School Scholarships. Many children gain music, art and academic scholarships to their senior schools.

Monkton Prep School

Combe Down, Bath BA2 7ET

Tel: 01225 831200
Fax: 01225 840312
email: mpsadmissions@monkton.org.uk
website: www.monktoncombeschool.com
Twitter: @monkton
Facebook: @MonktonCombeSchool

Chairman of Governors: Professor H Langton, RGN, RSCN, RCNT, RNT, BA Hons, MSc

Headmaster: **Mr M Davis**, BEd

Head of Pre-Prep: Mrs C Winchcombe, BEd Hons, MA Ed

Deputy Head: Mrs H M Grant, BEd

Age Range. 2–13.
Number of Pupils. Boarders 40, Day 175, Pre-Prep 115.
Fees per term (2018–2019). Reception £3,245; Years 1 and 2 £3,340; Years 3 to 6 £3,920–£5,050; Years 7 and 8 £5,710. Boarding: Years 3 to 6 £7,630–£7,920; Years 7 and 8 £8,230.

There are no extra charges except for learning a musical instrument and specialist activities. There are reductions in fees for the children of clergy and HM Forces.

The School became fully co-educational in September 1993 and has full flexi boarding arrangements that cater for both boys and girls from the age of 7. It stands in its own grounds on a magnificent site with the city of Bath on one side and the Midford valley on the other. The buildings include a modern classroom block, a theatre for drama and music with 12 music practice rooms, a sports hall, an indoor 25-metre pool, science laboratories and dance studio. The Coates Building incorporates an art studio, design technology workshop, a learning resource centre, seminar room and ICT suite. There are 20 acres of grounds, 3 all-weather netball courts, extensive playing fields as well as an all-weather hockey pitch.

The Pre-Prep, for ages 2–7 is on the same site as the Prep School, with light and airy classrooms which all have direct access to the outdoor space.

The School has a strong musical tradition and flourishing Art and DT Departments. There are numerous choirs, an orchestra, a band and various other instrumental groups. Drama also plays an important part in school life.

Rugby, Hockey and Cricket are the major boys' games; Netball, Hockey and Rounders are the major girls' games. All pupils take part in Gymnastics, Swimming, Athletics and Cross-Country. Squash, Badminton, Dance and Judo are also available. There is a full programme of matches. All pupils take part in a variety of hobbies and activities sessions which include imaginovation, Bevers, gardening, cross-country running, cookery, gymnastics (run by external professionals Baskervilles Gym) and fun science to name but a few.

Boys and Girls are prepared for Common Entrance and Scholarship exams to Independent Senior Schools. At least three-quarters of them proceed to Monkton Senior School and a quarter to a wide range of other Independent Senior Schools.

Over the years Monkton has educated many children from families who are working overseas, especially HM

Forces families. We make special arrangements for them and are well used to meeting their various needs.

The School finds its central inspiration and purpose in its Christian tradition. The caring, family ethos is underpinned by a large number of resident staff, including the Headmaster and his wife.

Charitable status. Monkton School is a Registered Charity, number 1057185. Its aim is to provide education for girls and boys aged 2 to 18, in accordance with the doctrine and principles of the Church of England.

Monmouth School Boys' Prep

The Grange, Hadnock Road, Monmouth NP25 3NG

Tel: 01600 715930
email: boysprep.enquiries@habsmonmouth.org
website: www.habsmonmouth.org/boysprep
Twitter: @Habsmonmouth
Facebook: @Habsmonmouth

Chairman of Governors: Mr A W Twiston-Davies

Head: **Mr N Shaw**, MA

Age Range. 7–11.
Number of Pupils. 132 boys.
Fees per term (2018–2019). Day £3,697, Boarding (from age 7) £6,760.

Monmouth School Boys' Prep welcomes day and boarding pupils aged 7–11 to The Grange – where we focus on developing enthusiastic, inquisitive, resilient boys with high aspirations.

We provide the friendliness and close pastoral care of a small school together with the outstanding resources of a large school through our close association with Monmouth School for Boys.

The curriculum is carefully planned around boys' learning styles to develop solid academic foundations. Our engaging subject-specialist teaching staff inspire and motivate the children to learn with a sense of fun and enjoyment.

We add the excitement of new subjects and areas of exploration, both in and out of the classroom. Boys make the most of the outstanding facilities on offer for sports, culture and the arts.

Through our unique Monmouth Model, boys also benefit from the many and varied joint activities with the Girls' Prep: school trips and expeditions, joint social and co-curricular events and shared community projects. There is a sense that anything is possible, ensuring a confident step up to the senior school.

In their final year, pupils take the General Entry Assessment for Monmouth School for Boys. Almost without exception, the boys have a 100% pass rate and a significant number gain scholarships and other awards – academic, music and sport.

In 2014 a full school inspection by ESTYN (Her Majesty's Inspectorate for Education and Training in Wales) graded the school as "Excellent" (the top grade) in every key question and in every quality indicator.

Aims. We aim to provide an excellent education as the foundation for future achievement and to develop personal qualities of confidence, independence and social conscience.

Location. In February 2009, we moved into new, purpose-built premises at The Grange, next to Monmouth School Sports Club with its own 25-metre swimming pool and all-weather pitch.

Facilities. Our building has light, spacious, well-equipped classrooms, each of which opens out onto the play area, as well as a large hall, library, art studio, science laboratory, computer suite, music room and music studios. We have newly-equipped kitchens and the grounds provide a safe, spacious area for recreation, games and outdoor projects. In addition, we share the facilities of Monmouth School for Boys, including the School Chapel, large playing fields (25 acres), sports complex, new sports pavilion, drama studio and performing arts centre – the Blake Theatre.

Staffing. We have 10 full-time and five part-time staff who teach the eight classes, in addition to peripatetic teachers and specialist coaches for extra-curricular activities.

Curriculum. Our curriculum is broad and varied and takes account of, though is not constrained by, the National Curriculum. We teach English, mathematics, science, Latin, humanities, information and communication technology and computing, history, geography, religious education, art, design technology, music, physical education, games, drama, French and study skills.

Extra-curricular activities. We have a full programme of activities which take place both in the lunch break and after school. This includes rugby, football, cricket, tennis, swimming, golf, karate, cross-country running, string orchestra, wind band, choir, fencing, art, gardening, modern foreign languages, computing and chess. There is a good record of boys playing at county and national level in rugby, cricket, fencing and chess.

Entry is usually at 7+ following assessment, though due to the larger new premises recruitment is currently across all year groups.

Charitable status. William Jones's Schools Foundation is a Registered Charity, number 525616. Its aims and objectives are to provide an all-round education for boys and girls at reasonable fees.

Monmouth School Girls' Prep

Inglefield House, Hereford Road, Monmouth NP25 5XT

Tel: 01600 711205
             01600 711104 (Admissions)
Fax: 01600 711118 (Admissions)
email: girlsprep.enquiries@habsmonmouth.org
website: www.habsmonmouth.org/girlsprep
Twitter: @Habsmonmouth
Facebook: @Habsmonmouth

Chairman of Governors: Mr A W Twiston-Davies

Headmistress: **Mrs H Phillips**, BA Hons, BEd

Age Range. Girls 7–11. Boarding from age 7.
Number of Pupils. 145.
Fees per term (2018–2019). Day £3,697, Boarding £6,760.

Monmouth School Girls' Prep welcomes day and boarding pupils aged 7–11 to Inglefield House and focuses on developing inquisitive, resilient, spirited girls with high aspirations.

Entry to the school is by entrance assessment and a discussion with the Headmistress to ensure each pupil will be able to access the curriculum. This is carefully planned to take a wide range of learning styles into account, to accommodate the needs of learners and to ensure solid academic foundations.

A love of learning and a curious, enthusiastic attitude to life are the cornerstones of producing independent, confident girls who also have a very strong sense of responsibility and consideration for others.

We are set in an Area of Outstanding Natural Beauty and our girls make the most of the superb facilities on offer.

Through our unique Monmouth Model, girls also benefit from the many and varied joint activities with the Boys' Prep: school trips and expeditions, joint social and co-curricular events, and shared community projects. There is a sense that anything is possible.

Our engaging staff inspire and motivate the children to learn with a sense of fun and enjoyment.

Teaching is broadly classroom based in Years 3 and 4 but is supplemented by specialist teaching in Humanities, Physical Education, Modern Foreign Languages, Music, Drama and Science.

Residential trips in the UK and abroad are effective in broadening our girls' horizons and increasing their sense of independence throughout the school.

Girls in Years 5 and 6 receive the finest tuition from our subject-specialist teachers. Access to facilities, including Science laboratories, ICT suites, Home Economics facilities and the Design Technology studios, will prepare the girls for the smooth transition into the senior school. We encourage girls to maximise their potential and achieve their academic and all-round potential.

Young girls at the school can build self-confidence through taking part in performing arts, while individual music lessons and the school orchestra, choir and string sections offer them a chance to flourish. We teach a wide range of dance as part of PE and within the extended curriculum.

Bringing enjoyment and enthusiasm to sport is another of our central aims. Sport plays a big part in school life. We have specialist PE teaching and a large number of extra-curricular clubs and fixtures each week.

We nurture a love of team sports and to balance this with other activities which the girls can continue to enjoy into their adult lives. Making the most of our membership of IAPS and ISA, our girls compete at national level in a variety of sports, including hockey, netball, gymnastics and fencing. Girls reap the benefits of using the senior school sports facilities, including the 25-metre swimming pool, gymnasium, full-sized sports hall and artificial pitches.

Boarding creates a real sense of community throughout Monmouth School Girls' Prep, where children thrive in a safe and friendly environment.

We award a number of scholarships each year to girls moving on to the senior school. (*For further details see Monmouth School for Girls' entry in the HMC section*).

Charitable status. William Jones's Schools Foundation is a Registered Charity, number 525616.

Moor Park School

Richard's Castle, Ludlow, Shropshire SY8 4DZ

Tel: 01584 876061
Fax: 01584 877311
email: head@moorpark.org.uk
website: www.moorpark.org.uk
Twitter: @moorparkludlow
Facebook: @MoorParkSchool

Chairman of Governors: Julian Rogers-Coltman

Headmaster: Mr Charlie Minogue, BSc Hons, PGCE

Deputy Head: M. J-M Collin

Age Range. 3 months to 13 years.
Number of Pupils. 190.
Fees per term (2018–2019). Boarding £7,120–£8,530, Day £2,060–£5.745.

Founded in 1964, Moor Park is an IAPS, Catholic, co-educational boarding and day school accepting children from 3 months to 13 years of age. A family atmosphere pervades, resulting in happy, rounded and grounded children.

Children often start in the Tick Tock Nursery (from 3 months) at Moor Park which provides a secure environment for our very youngest children. The Nursery has recently moved into a brand new facility and has been rated 'Outstanding' in all areas (Ofsted 2016). The children then transfer to the Pre-Prep Kindergarten in the term that they turn 3. They are then carefully prepared to start more formal schooling by a team of well-qualified and caring staff. Our Early Years provision was graded as 'Outstanding' by ISI in May 2016. All our children make full use of the 85 acres of stunning grounds but Moor Park is not just about getting muddy and exploring. Our children gain entry to the full range of schools nationally and have been awarded an extraordinary number of scholarships in recent years. These include academic and extra-curricular awards to some of the top senior schools in the country. It is also worth saying that Moor Park is emphatically not simply an academic hothouse and is a school where children of all abilities thrive. All of this is underpinned by a carefully maintained culture of kindness which ensures that all children are valued for who they are. Passionate teachers and an average class size of around 14 also make a difference.

Not every child can be good at everything but every child can be good at something and finding something for every child is something that we take seriously. Moor Park's facilities and, more importantly, enthusiastic and dedicated staff ensure that the school is well placed to get the best out of every child. A highlight of each term is the Big Weekend, for which we were shortlisted in the 2014 Independent Schools Awards.

Charitable status. Moor Park School is a Registered Charity, number 511800, which exists to provide education for young people.

Moorfield School

Wharfedale Lodge, 11 Ben Rhydding Road, Ilkley, West Yorkshire LS29 8RL

Tel: 01943 607285
email: enquiries@moorfieldschool.co.uk
website: www.moorfieldschool.co.uk
Twitter: @MoorfieldIlkley
Facebook: @Moorfield-School

Moorfield is an Education Charitable Trust and the Headmistress is a member of IAPS.

Chairman of Governors: Mr Martin Alton

Headmaster: Mr Paul Baddeley

Age Range. 2–11 Co-educational.
Number of Pupils 125 Girls and Boys.
Fees per term (2018–2019). Nursery £25.00 per session; Main School £3,200 including lunch.
Staff: 12 full-time, 16 part-time.
Religious affiliation: Interdenominational.
Excellence in Education inspiring Kindness, Confidence & Creativity

Moorfield School is situated in a beautiful setting on the edge of Ilkley Moor. It prides itself in providing inspirational teaching within a giving and caring school. Independence and individuality are encouraged and confidence nurtured. The whole child is important and we work together to grow hearts, minds and strength of character.

Our child-led approach to teaching and learning from ages 2 to 6 is unique and results show that children at the end of Reception (90%) are way above the national average (67%) across the curriculum.

Further up the school, high standards in English and Maths are the bedrock of academic success enabling all our pupils to get into their secondary school of choice. Outstanding teaching from a vibrant staff gives pupils confidence to succeed in all subjects. With specialist teaching in many subjects, pupils are given the opportunity to develop skills and interests in Drama, Music and Sport, Art, Cookery and Bushcraft.

Support for working parents is provided by offering wrap-around care in term time from 7.45 am to 6.15 pm and throughout school holidays from 8.00 am to 4.00 pm.

Pupils leave Moorfield with a secure foundation of learning, a strong work ethic and the confidence to be successful.

Moorfield is recommended by The Good Schools Guide.

Charitable status. Moorfield School Ltd is a Registered Charity, number 529112.

Moorlands School

Foxhill Drive, Weetwood Lane, Leeds LS16 5PF

Tel: 0113 278 5286
email: info@moorlands-school.co.uk
website: www.moorlands-school.co.uk
Twitter: @MoorlandsHead
Facebook: @MoorlandsLeeds

Headteacher: **Jacqueline Atkinson**, GMus Hons, PGCE, MEd

Age Range. 2–11 Co-educational.
Number of Pupils. 141 Day Boys and Girls.
Founded in 1898, Moorlands School is dedicated to providing a first-class education for girls and boys aged 2 to 11 years in a warm, friendly environment.

The school is conveniently located off the Ring Road at Weetwood Lane, yet sat in beautiful grounds providing all the outdoor space (and off-road parking) required for children to play in a safe and secure environment. The school boasts fantastic wrap-around care facilities (included in the fees from the term after pupils turns 5 years old), excellent teaching standards, on-site swimming pool and small class sizes.

Moorlands is a full member of the Methodist Independent Schools Trust (MIST) bringing with it the benefits of membership of a large network of independent schools.

The aim of the school is to develop the full potential of every child within a happy and caring environment fostered by small classes and the professional skills of a highly qualified staff. Strong links between the parents and the school are encouraged to facilitate the provision of an effective education.

Admission is by assessment and observation. Pupils are accepted at 2 years old for entry into the Nursery and are expected to progress through the school in preparation for entry to senior independent day and boarding schools. The school has a well-developed specialist facility to provide assistance to pupils with any learning issue such as dyslexia or to gifted children.

Blended with this traditional core of academic work is offered a comprehensive range of sporting activities, outdoor education and a wide range of musical and extra-curricular pursuits.

At Moorlands, we have a simple yet beautiful motto, 'Intrepide', or 'be brave'! In school, we talk about how being brave or intrepid takes many forms. Being brave isn't always a grand gesture; sometimes it simply means 'having a go', such as attempting that difficult question, offering an answer in class when you're not quite sure or trying something new. This culture of intrepidness allows children to try new things in a safe, nurturing and stimulating environment.

Religious affiliation: Methodist.

Fees per term (2018–2019). Early Years £2,995, Reception £3,132, Years 1 and 2 £3,142, Lunch £200; Years 3 to 6 £3,497–£3,522, Lunch £220.

Charitable status. Moorlands School is a Registered Charity, number 529216. It exists to provide children with the finest education possible, using the best resources in an environment of care.

Moreton Hall Preparatory School

Mount Road, Bury St Edmunds, Suffolk IP32 7BJ

Tel: 01284 753532
email: office@moretonhallprep.org
website: www.moretonhallprep.org

Chairman of the Board of Governors: Neil Smith

Headmaster: **C E Moxon**, BA, PGCE

Age Range. 4–13.
Number of Pupils. Boys 54, Girls 34.
Fees per term (2018–2019). Boarding: £7,500 (full), £6,475 (weekly). Day: £2,900–£4,775.

Moreton Hall Prep School is a warm and welcoming school, set in an impressive historic building with 30 acres of attractive grounds. Sporting standards are high with daily games sessions. Results in team sports are impressive: #SmallSchoolBigResults. Rugby, soccer, hockey, cricket, netball and tennis form the major sports. There is an outdoor, heated swimming pool and a large sports hall. A second, indoor swimming pool and squash courts are available for use at the adjacent health club.

The staff to pupil ratio is high with an average class size of 14 pupils. Pupils are prepared for Year 9 Scholarship or Common Entrance examination to the full range of Senior schools; prestigious Academic, Music and Sporting awards are all achieved regularly. High importance is also placed upon Music and Drama. The majority of pupils learn a musical instrument and perform regularly in concerts; there are plays in each section of the school and weekly lessons in Speech and Drama are available.

The school accepts boarders from the age of 8 and day pupils from age 4. Weekly and flexible boarding arrangements are also popular. The Headmaster is the resident Houseparent and they are supported by a residential matron, other staff and gap students. The centre of Bury St Edmunds is a five-minute walk away, Cambridge is under an hour away and London is two hours by road or rail. The School can arrange transport to and from airports.

Moreton Hall Prep School has a Catholic tradition but welcomes children of all denominations. Financial support is available through means-tested bursaries. Scholarships are available at 11+ in Sport and Music.

For further information, please access our website or ring the office to arrange a visit or taster day.

The school is a member of CISC.

Charitable status. Moreton Hall School Trust Limited is a Registered Charity, number 280927. It exists to provide high quality education for boys and girls.

Moulsford Preparatory School

Moulsford-on-Thames, Wallingford, Oxfordshire OX10 9HR

Tel: 01491 651438
email: pa.registrar@moulsford.com
website: www.moulsford.com
Twitter: @Moulsford
Facebook: @Moulsford

The School is a Charitable Trust controlled by a Board of Governors.

Chairman of the Board of Governors: Mr E L A Boddington

Headmaster: **B Beardmore-Gray**, BA Hons, QTS

Age Range. 4–13.
Number of Boys. 34 Weekly Boarders, 325 Day Boys.
Fees per term (2018–2019). Day Boys £3,805–£5,685, Weekly Boarders £7,120. These fees are all inclusive but individual coaching in music, judo, golf and fencing is charged as an extra.

The School has its own river frontage on the Thames, spacious games fields and lawns and is situated between Wallingford and Reading.

Boys are prepared for the Common Entrance and Scholarship examinations to the top independent schools in the country. An experienced and well qualified staff ensures that a high standard is achieved academically, musically, artistically and on the games field.

The principal games are rugby football, soccer, tennis and cricket. Other sporting activities include athletics, swimming, sailing, judo, golf and gymnastics. The school is proud of its fine academic and sporting reputation which has been built up over many years.

Charitable status. Moulsford Preparatory School is a Registered Charity, number 309643.

Mylnhurst Preparatory School & Nursery

Button Hill, Woodholm Road, Ecclesall, Sheffield S11 9HJ

Tel: 0114 236 1411
Fax: 0114 236 1411
email: enquiries@mylnhurst.co.uk
website: www.mylnhurst.co.uk

Left IAPS Dec 2018. A Catholic Foundation Welcoming Families of All Faiths – maximising the potential of your children through partnership within a challenging and supportive Catholic Christian Community.

Headmaster: **Mr C P Emmott**, BSc Hons, MEd, MBA

Age Range. 3–11 Co-educational.
Number of Pupils. 200.
Fees per term (2018–2019). £3,250

Situated in extensive private grounds, Mylnhurst provides a state-of-the-art teaching environment supported by our outstanding school facilities, which include a 25m pool, dance studio, sports hall and Apple Mac suite.

With a strong emphasis on school-parent partnership, Mylnhurst embraces your high expectations and ensures each child benefits from an exciting and stimulating curriculum.

Top performing Sheffield School in the Times Top 100.

Be assured of a very warm welcome and the opportunity to work closely with our committed and talented staff. So, whether it be an informal chat or a school open day, we look forward to sharing our vision with you and discussing the exciting future of your children.

Charitable status. Mylnhurst Limited is a Registered Charity, number 1056683.

Naima JPS

21 Andover Place, London NW6 5ED

Tel: 020 7328 2802
email: secretary@naimajps.co.uk
website: www.naimajps.org.uk

Chair of Governors: Mrs Sabine Howard

Headmaster: **Mr J W Pratt**, GRSM Hons, CertEd

Age Range. 2–11 Co-educational.
Number of Pupils. 175 girls and boys.
Fees per term (2018–2019). £2,690–£4,515.

Naima JPS is centred on the belief that an excellent secular education and strong Jewish grounding are mutually attainable. As such, our twin goals merge as we aspire to prepare our children for a successful life in society imbued with Torah values. We aim to provide a secular education on a par with the top national private schools with a curriculum that extends beyond the minimum guidelines provided by the National Curriculum. As a private school, we provide both the environment and teaching resources to monitor each individual, and to help children of all abilities to reach their full potential.

Naima JPS challenges all children, together with their parents, no matter what their level of religious observance, to pursue ongoing spiritual growth as individuals. We encourage children on their journey to spiritual maturity in a harmonious and nurturing community environment of tolerance, respect and care for one another.

The school has a one-form entry. Given that class sizes seldom exceed 22 and the favourable ratio of teachers and assistants to children – as little as 1:5 depending on the age and need – programmes of learning have the flexibility for differentiation. The school has a high number of particularly able children with specific intellectual gifts.

During the crucial early years at school it is important that children define themselves by things they can do well. Self-esteem, that essential by-product of success, empowers strength and gifts. Once children understand how their minds work, as they learn in many different ways, they can feel comfortable about entering any environment and mastering it. Children who truly understand, value and like themselves are better equipped to flourish and embrace fresh challenges. Confidence through success contributes to strong identities that welcome new horizons. Resiliency, discovery, independence and spiritual maturity are nurtured at all levels. At Naima JPS education is not about coveting garlands for the few, but ensuring that all children reach their full potential.

Charitable status. Naima JPS is a Registered Charity, number 289066.

The New Beacon

Brittains Lane, Sevenoaks, Kent TN13 2PB

Tel: 01732 452131
Fax: 01732 459509
email: admin@newbeacon.org.uk
website: www.newbeacon.org.uk

Chairman of the Governors: Mr James Thorne

Headmaster: **Michael Piercy**, BA Hons

Age Range. 4–13.
Number of Boys. 380. Predominantly Day Pupils, but a small element of flexi boarding is retained from Monday to Thursday.
Fees per term (2018–2019). £3,700–£5,295. Fees include lunches.

Boys are prepared for both grammar and senior independent schools, and enjoy considerable success at 11+ and 13+, with many achieving scholarships (including music, sport, art and drama) to a wide range of first-class senior schools.

The School divides into Senior, Middle and Junior sections in which boys are placed according to age and ability. Initiative is encouraged by organising the School into 4 houses or 'companies'. The well-equipped main School building is complemented by several modern, purpose-built facilities: separate Pre-Prep and Junior School buildings for boys aged 4–9; a Sports Hall with modern changing facilities; a multi-purpose, astroturf sports pitch; a Theatre; a heated indoor Swimming Pool; a centre for Art and Music; and modern facilities for Science and Technology. Soccer, Rugby Union and Cricket are the major games. During the summer months Tennis and Athletics are available. Swimming and Shooting are available all year round. A very extensive range of extra-curricular activities is offered (including many interesting and exciting trips) together with a programme of Pre and After School care. Music, sport, art and drama at the School are highly regarded.

A limited number of music and academic bursaries are offered subject to means-testing.

Charitable status. The New Beacon is a Registered Charity, number 307925. It exists to provide an all-round education for boys aged 4–13.

New College School

Savile Road, Oxford OX1 3UA

Tel: 01865 285560
email: office@newcollegeschool.org
website: www.newcollegeschool.org

Governors: The Warden & Fellows of New College Oxford

Headmaster: **N R Gulliver**, MA, FRSA

Age Range. 4–13 years.

Number of Boys. 161 Day Boys, including 22 Choristers.

Fees per term (2018–2019). Reception £3,290, Year 1 £3,961, Years 2–4 £4,863, Years 5–8 £5,317, Choristers £1,921.

New College School was founded in 1379 when William of Wykeham made provision for the education of 16 Choristers to sing daily services in New College Chapel. Situated in the heart of the city, a few minutes' walk from the College, the school is fortunate in having the use of New College playing fields for sport and New College Chapel for school services.

The staff consists of some 22 full-time teachers and a full complement of visiting music teachers. Boys are prepared for the Common Entrance and Scholarship Examinations for transfer to independent senior schools at age 13. In the final year there is a scholarship form and a common entrance form. The school broadly follows the national curriculum subjects, but also teaches French, Latin, Design Technology and Greek.

Sports, played on New College Sports Ground, include soccer, hockey, cricket, rounders, athletics and rugby. Activities include archery, art, craft, pottery, design, chess, sport, computer, drama, and science clubs. There is a Choral Society for parents.

Music plays a major part in school life with orchestra, ensembles, concert and junior choirs and form concerts, in addition to individual tuition in a wide range of instruments. A optional Saturday morning music education programme is followed by boys from Year 5 upwards.

Boys are admitted by gentle assessment to the Pre-Prep Department at 4 years and to the Prep School at 7 years. Potential Choristers are tested between the ages of 6 and 7 at annual voice trials.

Newbridge Preparatory School

51 Newbridge Crescent, Wolverhampton, West Midlands WV6 0LH

Tel: 01902 751088
email: office@newbridgeprepschool.org.uk
website: www.newbridgeprepschool.org.uk

Chairman of Board: Mrs H M Hughes

Headmistress: **Mrs S Fisher**, BEd Hons

Age Range. Girls 2–11. Boys 2–7.
Number of Pupils. 157.
Fees per term (2018–2019). £1,800–£2,760 including dance, recorder, drama, gym, netball, singing for various year groups.

Newbridge Preparatory School, founded in 1937, occupies a super site on the outskirts of Wolverhampton, convenient for parents travelling from Telford, Bridgnorth, Shropshire, and Stafford.

The school is divided into Lower School (Pre-Nursery–Year 2) and Upper School (Years 3–6). Upper School is housed in the main building which is a substantial house set in huge, beautiful mature gardens. There are specialist facilities in Art and Design, ICT, Science, Music and PE. The school also has netball and tennis courts.

The staff to pupil ratio is high. Specialist teaching takes place in Key Stage Two in English, Mathematics, Music, Science, French, PE, Dance and Drama. In Key Stage One: Dance, PE, Music and French.

Lower School enjoys a separate Nursery and a new building for Pre-Nursery to Year 2. There is a sports hall.

Children with Special Needs are well supported and nurtured.

Upper School girls take drama and dance and enter examinations. They also enter the annual local festival for Music and Drama.

The school offers a Breakfast Club (7.30 to 8.00 am), an Early Club (8.00 to 8.30 am), an After-School Club (3.15 to 6.00 pm) and a Holiday Club (8.00 am to 5.30 pm).

Standards are high in all areas of the curriculum. Senior School results are excellent. Places are gained at local selective Independent and Maintained Schools but also Boarding Schools. Sporting, Academic and Speech and Drama Scholarships are attained for entrance into Senior School. Once examinations are complete, Year 6 follow an exciting STAR (Summer Term Activities Refreshed) curriculum using and developing skills previously taught. Girls leave Newbridge well equipped to face the challenges of a Senior School.

Educational visits take place each term. Nursery children enjoy a Forest School experience. Residential visits occur in Years 3–6. The visits vary from outdoor activities and challenges and cultural visits to London and France.

Emphasis is placed on traditional values, personal development and responsibility. The curriculum is very broad, including many opportunities in Sport, Dance, Drama and Music.

Our school mission statement is: Aiming High, Building Bridges and Preparing for Life.

Children are taught to do their best in all areas, strive for a challenge and succeed at their own level.

Emphasis is placed on self-discipline, inclusion, equal opportunity and respect.

Charitable status. Newbridge Preparatory School is a Registered Charity, number 1019682. It exists to advance the education of children by conducting the school known as Newbridge Preparatory School.

Newcastle Preparatory School

6 Eslington Road, Jesmond, Newcastle-upon-Tyne, Tyne and Wear NE2 4RH

Tel: 0191 281 1769
Fax: 0191 281 5668
email: enquiries@newcastleprepschool.org.uk
website: www.newcastleprepschool.org.uk

The School was founded in 1885 and is now a Charitable Trust with a Board of Governors.

Chair of Governors: Mr Richard Appleby

Head Teacher: Ms Fiona Coleman

Age Range. 3–11.
Number of Pupils. 280 Day Pupils (180 boys, 100 girls).
Fees per term (2018–2019). Reception & Year 1: £3,645, Years 2 & 3: £3,704, Years 4–6: £3,769.

The School is situated in a residential part of Newcastle with easy access from all round the area.

Newcastle Preparatory School is a fully co-educational day school for children aged 3 to 11 years. It is a warm, caring environment in which all pupils are encouraged to reach their full potential.

Children may join 'First Steps' at NPS from the age of 3 years. 'First Steps' is an exciting and colourful nursery with

excellent resources and well qualified staff who look after the needs of each individual.

At age 4, children make the easy step into School where they experience many 'steps to success'.

The curriculum offered throughout school is broad and balanced so that children enjoy learning in a variety of ways. French is taught from the age of 4 with music and PE being taught by specialist teachers. As children progress through School they become independent learners, following a varied timetable and class sizes are small to provide individual attention.

Music is an important part of life at NPS. There is a choir and a lively swing band.

Sporting achievements too are very good. There is a purpose-built Sports Hall and a wide range of sport is offered with extracurricular activities including rugby, football, cricket, hockey, netball, athletics, tennis and swimming.

Also there are many clubs and activities to enrich the curriculum, e.g. Drama, Dance, Chess, Philosophy, Art, ICT, Design, Food Technology and there is an effective School Council as well as a Buddy System.

Outdoor learning is offered throughout the school. In 2017 a dedicated Forest School area was opened and pupils also run a a local allotment.

The variety of opportunities ensures that the children leave NPS well equipped for an easy transition to senior school. The academic results are very good and the children receive an all-round education, so that they are confident, eager learners.

Charitable status. Newcastle Preparatory School is a Registered Charity, number 528152. It exists to provide education for boys and girls.

Newland House School

Waldegrave Park, Twickenham TW1 4TQ

Tel: 020 8865 1234
email: admissions@newlandhouse.net
website: www.newlandhouse.net
Twitter: @newlandhouse
Facebook: @Newland-House-School-Twickenham

Founded in 1897, the school was privately owned until 1971 when the Newland House School Trust was formed. It is a charitable Educational Trust with a Board of Governors.

Chairman of Governors: D Ridgeon

Head: D A Alexander, BMus, Dip NCOS

Age Range. 3–13.
Number of Pupils. 282 Boys, 189 Girls.
Fees per term (2018–2019). Nursery from £2,290, Pre-Prep £3,848, Prep £4,306. Lunch is included in the Fees.

Newland House School is a co-educational day preparatory school set in a residential area on the Twickenham-Teddington border. In September 2017 the school also opened a nursery school for children aged 3 to 4. The school is ideally situated for parents in the Richmond, Kingston and Hampton areas and is very close to the river Thames.

The school currently occupies approximately 5 acres with grounds that provide sports facilities, including an all-weather pitch. The school is also fortunate to have daily access to the nearby National Physical Laboratory Sports Ground.

The school is divided into Nursery, Pre-Prep, which provides for children in Reception (EYFS) to Year 2, and Prep for children in Years 3 to 8. A new Pre-Prep school building was opened in autumn 2016 immediately adjacent to the Prep School providing an innovative and unique learning environment for pupils using leading sustainable design and the latest technology. Following the move to the new premises, the additional space has enabled the school to offer a three-form intake, with an additional 20 places available in Reception from September 2016.

The school's main intakes are at the age of 3 (Nursery) and age 4 (Reception) which are non-selective. Places may also become available in other age groups throughout the school year.

The Prep School has well-appointed, airy classrooms with a traditional feel, a large gymnasium/assembly hall, dining room, separate senior and junior libraries and two well-equipped science laboratories. There is an Art and Design Technology block, as well as a purpose-built Music block. The school has a substantial computer network, including a state-of-the-art computer suite.

The staff currently consists of 34 full-time teachers, and 10 classroom assistants, mostly in the Pre-Prep School. Children are well prepared for the Common Entrance and Scholarship examinations to Independent Schools. During the ISI Inspection in 2013, the school was found to be 'excellent' in many areas. In particular, the opportunities which the school provides for academic achievement and learning, as well as pastoral care and pupils' personal development, were clearly recognised.

There is a strong music department staffed by 19 visiting music staff who teach a variety of instruments. There are 5 choirs, several wind and brass ensembles, 2 orchestras and a jazz band who have the opportunity to perform at a variety of external venues.

The main games for boys are Rugby, Football and Cricket with Netball, Hockey and Rounders for girls. All children from the age of 7 have the opportunity to swim throughout the year. The teams take part in a range of leagues and competitions and there is an annual cricket tour to South Africa.

The school is committed to providing a broad and balanced curriculum and an environment that fosters enquiring minds. A wide variety of extra-curricular activities is available including, fencing, golf, chess, and badminton. The school also provides a Breakfast Club from 7.30 am each morning and an After-School Club until 6 pm.

Charitable status. The Newland House School Trust Limited is a Registered Charity, number 312670. It exists to promote and provide for the advancement of education for children of either sex or both sexes.

Newton Prep

149 Battersea Park Road, London SW8 4BX

Tel: 020 7720 4091
Fax: 020 7498 9052
email: admin@newtonprep.co.uk
website: www.newtonprepschool.co.uk
Twitter: @NewtonPrep
Facebook: @NewtonPrepSchool

Chairman of Council: Dr Farouk Walji

Head: Mrs A E Fleming, BA, MA
head@newtonprep.co.uk

Administration & Finance Manager: Mr P Farrelly
bursar@newtonprep.co.uk

Admissions Registrar: Mrs Susan Symes
registrar@newtonprep.co.uk

Age Range. 3–13.
Number of Pupils. 650+: 50% Boys, 50% Girls.
Fees per term (2018–2019). £3,100–£6,565.
Average size of class: <20.
The current teacher to pupil ratio is 1:11.
Religious denomination: Non-denominational.

Newton Prep is a vibrant school which offers a challenging education for inquisitive children who are eager to engage fully with the world in which they are growing up. The school aims to:

- inspire children to be adventurous and committed in their learning;
- provide balance and breadth in all aspects of a child's education: intellectual, aesthetic, physical, moral and spiritual;
- encourage initiative, individuality, independence, creativity and enquiry;
- promote responsible behaviour and respect for others in a happy, safe and caring environment.

Entry requirements. Siblings are given priority when allocating nursery places; other nursery places are awarded by lottery, while ensuring an even balance of boys and girls; children joining Reception are assessed individually: a gentle process, with offers made during October half term in the year before entry. Older children come to an assessment morning in the Spring Term (on a case-by-case basis at other times) during which they will be assessed in reading, maths and some diagnostic, age-appropriate reasoning tests. Scholarships and means-tested top-up bursaries are available in and after Year 3.

Examinations offered. All entrance examinations to senior schools, Common Entrance and scholarships at 11, 12 and 13. Children leave to go to top London day schools, with a significant minority now going up the boarding route. We pride ourselves on the quality of guidance offered by our dedicated Senior School Transfer Deputy Head and, every 2 years, we organise a Senior Schools Fair attended by over 75 schools. Throughout each school year, Heads from top public schools come for our popular Newton Forum evenings, along with an array of top-flight speakers from other fields of life: politics, the film world – even the spiritual sphere, as when the Dalai Lama hosted a children's conference at the school.

"Bright children, exceptional opportunities."
First-time visitors to the school are invariably impressed by the scale and range of the secondary-school-level facilities and by the wide open outdoor spaces enjoyed by the children on a large site so close to the centre of London. As well as the three school gyms there are two huge outdoor spaces for PE/Games and free play: behind the school, an all-weather pitch and, in front, a large, tree-fringed playground for the littler children. The school also has a large garden with a wildlife area and an activity area with a pirate boat.

Newton Prep occupies an early 20th-century elementary school building, which has been extensively remodelled internally, and behind which stands large modern extensions containing classrooms, the dining hall and kitchen, two gymnasiums, a 300-seat auditorium and a state-of-the-art recital hall (along with a recording studio and a music technology suite). The top floor of the Edwardian building provides one large general-purpose space as well as two art studios. Below are two floors of classrooms, including three collegiate-style science labs, three ICT suites and a library that is the envy of the many visiting authors, who all say it is one of the most vibrant and popular reading spaces they have come across in a school.

Despite the excellence of their education, Newton Prep children are notable for their lack of arrogance and entitlement. The kindness and generosity shown by the pupils towards their peers is remarkable and the engagement between the older children and the little ones is heartwarming, especially when it comes to inter-house events, when children up and down the school are united by their love for their house!

Newton is not a blazers and boaters kind of school. As one current parent put it, *"Newton combines a quirky nature and knowledge of families with great space and facilities ...All the teachers understand my (very different) children, the management is open to fresh ideas and the school is large enough to accommodate variety."*

Norland Place School

162–166 Holland Park Avenue, London W11 4UH

Tel:	020 7603 9103
Fax:	020 7603 0648
email:	office@norlandplace.com
website:	www.norlandplace.com

Headmaster: **Mr P Mattar**

Age Range. Girls 4–11, Boys 4–8.
Number of Children. 235.
Fees per term (2018–2019). £5,369–£6,024.

A Preparatory school founded in 1876 and still standing on the original site in Holland Park Avenue. Children are prepared for competitive London day schools and top rate boarding schools. The curriculum is well balanced with an emphasis on English, Mathematics and Science. Music, Art and Games are strong. The school contains a Library in addition to specialist Music, IT, Science and Art Rooms.

Early registration is essential.

Northbourne Park

Betteshanger, Deal, Kent CT14 0NW

Tel:	01304 611215
Fax:	01304 619020
email:	admissions@northbournepark.com
website:	www.northbournepark.com
Twitter:	@northbournepark
Facebook:	@Northbourne-Park-School

Chairman of Governors: Mrs Stephanie Aiyagari

Headmaster: **Sebastian Rees**, BA Hons, PGCE, NPQH

Age Range. Nursery – 13 Co-educational.
Number of Pupils. 176 boys and girls, including 56 boarders.

Northbourne Park is a co-educational day and boarding school set in 100 acres of beautiful park and woodland in rural Kent, close to Canterbury and within easy reach of central London, Eurostar and Gatwick Airport.

We provide children with a first-class education focusing on the individual needs of every child, inspiring them to succeed across a wide range of learning experiences. We offer each child the freedom and space, together with countless opportunities, to grow in confidence and succeed.

Academic. From the Nursery and Pre-Prep through to the Prep School all our pupils gain confidence in their learning, and through inspirational teaching from dedicated staff, the pupils adapt well to an engaging and stimulating curriculum with a real sense of achievement. Although non-selective,

we consistently achieve 100% pass rate in examinations – entry to top Independent Senior and local Grammar schools, LAMDA and the Associated Board of the Royal Schools of Music. Many of our pupils gain scholarships to prestigious Senior Schools.

Northbourne Park's unique Language Programme helps every child develop foreign languages in an integrated learning environment. French is introduced at 3 years and we have a unique Bilingual programme for French pupils joining Years 7 and 8 who study the French academic curriculum. The result is a clear advantage when they move on to Senior Schools.

Sport. We are passionate about sport and through an excellent sports programme the pupils develop key skills and learn the importance of teamwork and leadership. There are many opportunities to try a variety of sports from the traditional to the more diverse such as archery and trampolining.

Creative Arts. We nurture a love for all the Arts. Many pupils learn one or more instrument in our purpose-built Music suite. They have the opportunity to take part in the choir, band, orchestra, string and brass groups performing regularly within the school and the local area. Other opportunities include LAMDA lessons, regular drama productions and Public Speaking that ensure pupils are articulate and confident in their performances. Artistic talents are encouraged through a range of media including sculpture, costume design, film-making on iMacs and pottery.

Community. Pupils are provided with a first-rate level of pastoral care in safe and nurturing surroundings with a real family atmosphere. Our welcoming boarding community provides a home-from-home environment and a continuous boarding service at weekends throughout the term. Boarders enjoy regular excursions and activities, and the accompanied services to London and Paris provide opportunities for weekends at home.

Extracurricular. We provide the pupils with a fun and extensive programme of clubs that help develop their interests and skills in hobbies that can endure long into adult life. Love of the outdoors and respect for the environment begins in the Pre-Prep and develops through into the Prep School with fun physical adventures. Whether they are playing in the woods, camping out overnight or following our pioneering Outdoor Education Programme, children love Northbourne Park life.

Fees per term (2018–2019). Boarders: £6,995 (weekly), £8,100 (full); French Programme £8,495. Day Pupils: £2,544–£3,570 (Pre-Prep), £4,180–£5,585 (Years 3–8). Sleepover £42 per night. Fees include customary extras and many extracurricular activities. We offer bursaries and a wide range of scholarships. Sibling, HM Forces and Clergy discounts are generous and popular.

Charitable status. Northbourne Park is a Registered Charity, number 280048.

Norwich School, The Lower School

30 Bishopgate, Norwich NR1 4AA

Tel:	01603 728439
email:	admissions@norwich-school.org.uk
website:	www.norwich-school.org.uk

Chairman of Governors: P J E Smith, MA, FIA

Master of the Lower School: **J K Ingham**, BA

Principal Deputy Head: A Wilson, BSc, MSc
Deputy Head (Academic): C M W Parsons, BSc
Head of Pre-Prep: A Barclay, BA

Age Range. 4–11.

Number of Pupils. 248.

Fees per term (2018–2019). £3,666–£4,925.

The Lower School is the Infant and Junior Day School for Norwich School (*see entry in HMC section*). It is delightfully located in the Cathedral Close, between the East End of the Cathedral and the River Wensum. The Cathedral Choristers are educated at Norwich School, which is a member of the Choir Schools' Association.

The Lower School provides depth and breadth of education through a challenging curriculum. It seeks to recognise, nurture and develop each pupil's potential within an environment which encourages all-round emotional, physical, social and spiritual growth and to foster positive relations between pupils, teachers and parents. The dedicated teaching staff is committed to providing a stimulating programme of active learning which has rigour and discipline but avoids unnecessary pressure.

With one form in Reception to Year 2, two forms in Years 3 and 4 and three forms in Years 5 and 6, the Lower School is the ideal size for ensuring a lively environment within a warm family atmosphere. The main building has bright, spacious areas for activities and lessons. As well as the library, there are specialised facilities for science, art, technology and ICT. There is an excellent play area in addition to the adjacent, extensive playing fields. A new Infant department opened in September 2018 offering bespoke facilities for the EYFS and Key Stage 1 curriculum.

A wide range of extra-curricular activities and school trips is offered. Music is a strong feature of school life. Many pupils choose to learn a musical instrument and participate in the various instrumental music groups. Rugby, netball, hockey, cricket, rounders and tennis are taught and the games programme is designed to encourage pupils of all abilities to enjoy games and physical activity.

The School aims to attract pupils who will thrive in a challenging academic environment and is therefore selective. All pupils are assessed by age-appropriate means. There is a one-form entry at 4+, 5+ and 6+, two-form entry at 7+ and a small number of places is available each year at 8+, 9+ and 10+. The prospectus and application forms are available from the Admissions Registrar, Tel: 01603 728449.

The vast majority of pupils from the Lower School progress to the Senior School at age eleven, and the curriculum is designed to prepare the pupils effectively for the next stage of their Norwich School education.

Charitable status. Norwich School is a Registered Charity, number 311280.

Notre Dame School
Preparatory School

Burwood House, Cobham, Surrey KT11 1HA

Tel:	01932 869990
email:	office@notredame.co.uk
website:	www.notredame.co.uk
Twitter:	@NotreDameCobham
Facebook:	@NotreDameSchoolCobham
LinkedIn:	/notredamecobham

Chair of Governors: Mr Gerald Russell

Head of Prep: Mrs Amelie Morgan, MA, BA Hons, PGCE

Assistant Head: Mrs Clare Barber, BSc Hons, PGCE
Head of EYFS: Miss Melanie Lehmann, BA Hons, EYPS

Head of Infants: Miss Geraldine Deen, BA Hons QTS
Pastoral Director: Miss Rebecca Golding, BA Hons, PGCE

(*For full list of Preparatory School staff, see Notre Dame School's GSA entry.*)

Age Range. Girls 2–11, Boys 2–7.

Number of Pupils. 200 Girls, 18 boys.

Fees per term (2018–2019). Nursery £1,345–£3,385 Reception £3,570, Prep 1 & 2 £4,190, Prep 3–6 £4,535.

Bursaries. A limited number of assisted places and bursaries are offered subject to income and asset tests.

Notre Dame School is an independent Roman Catholic day school for girls aged 2–18 and boys aged 2–7. We welcome families of all faiths and none.

The 2017 ISI Inspection judged Notre Dame Prep School to be 'Excellent' across the board. The Prep School was shortlisted in the Strategic Education Initiative of The Year category in the TES Independent School Awards 2018, and has been shortlisted for Independent School of The Year for Sporting Achievement in the Independent Schools of The Year 2018 Awards.

At Notre Dame School we have created a curriculum that encompasses the academic, creative, physical, moral, and intellectual challenges expected of all good schools, but also the fun, laughter and community needed to enable happy children to learn, to develop confidence and to feel fulfilled. A caring and trusting family relationship completes the balance, so that children can thrive and flourish.

Our children participate in many sporting activities, making full use of our on-site all-weather hockey, netball, tennis and athletics facilities, indoor arena, swimming pool and extensive fields. We encourage them to sing and play instruments in concerts and events in our wonderfully acoustic chapel, perform in our fully equipped 370-seat professional theatre, and enjoy our 24 acres of beautiful, rural parkland.

Prep School pupils benefit from a vibrant, bespoke humanities curriculum to develop thinking skills, moral foundation and knowledge. Meticulously planned and delivered English programmes and a 'mastery' approach to Mathematics are yielding excellent outcomes for our pupils. Girls are taught by specialist teachers for a number of subjects, including Music, Science (Juniors), Art, Drama, Dance, Spanish and PE. We are fortunate to have dedicated teaching spaces for Dance, Music, Drama, ICT and Art, as well as a fully-equipped Science Laboratory. Our girls leave the Prep School excellently equipped to take on their next challenge and nearly all progress to our Senior School.

Our outstanding Nursery welcomes boys and girls from the age of two and follows the Early Years Foundation Stage Guidance. As well as their own classrooms, outdoor play areas and Forest School, children access all of the school's sporting facilities and theatre and enjoy specialist teaching for Music, Dance, Spanish and Swimming.

Notre Dame is built on 400 years of educational experience: The Company of Mary Our Lady was founded in Bordeaux in 1607 to educate girls, and Notre Dame is one of some 300 educational foundations around the world that now come under this umbrella. To ready our pupils for the wider world, to live life to the full, we believe that our shared mission and purpose help our children to aspire to be the best they can be in all their endeavours, during their school years and beyond.

ISI Inspection 2017. The full report can be viewed on the school website: ISI-Inspection-Report.

Transport. Notre Dame is excellently located – two minutes from the A3/M25 junction, 10 minutes from Walton, Weybridge, Cobham or Esher, and rarely more than 20 minutes from Guildford, Wimbledon and Putney. Private school coaches for girls from Year 3 upwards – flexible single/return journeys – from Clapham, Putney and Fulham to Esher, Woking and Weybridge and many stops in between.

Admission. Usual entry points: Early Years (age 2), Reception (age 4) and Year 3 (age 7). Occasional places are sometimes available in other year groups.

Registration: Registration Form and payment of £50 registration fee.

Assessment: Children are invited to attend a Taster Day, to include observation/assessment and time to get to know prospective classmates. As a rough guide, intake sits in the top 50% of the ability range.

Senior School. For further information about Notre Dame Senior School, *please see entry in GSA section*.

Charitable status. Notre Dame School Cobham is a Registered Charity, number 1081875.

Notting Hill Preparatory School

---

95 Lancaster Road, London W11 1QQ

Tel:	020 7221 0727
Fax:	020 7221 0332
email:	admin@nottinghillprep.com
	l.tate@nottinghillprep.com
website:	www.nottinghillprep.com

Co-Chairs of Governing Body:
Mr John Mackay
Mr John Morton Morris

Headmistress: Mrs Jane Cameron, BEd Hons

Age Range. 4–13 Co-educational.
Number of Pupils. 370.
Fees per term (2018–2019). £6,600.

NHP is a co-ed Prep School in the heart of Notting Hill, West London. It was created through the cooperation of parents and teachers and this partnership with parents is a cornerstone of the philosophy of the school. It operates on a split site, Reception to Year 2 being housed in a fine Victorian School House and Years 3–6 in a magnificent modern building providing, in addition, school hall/dining room, music practice rooms, science lab and computing suite. Years 7 and 8 have moved to exciting new premises on Portobello Green which also offer a music centre, an art and DT studio and an additional dining facility, and in the future, an additional science lab.

Our aim is to educate children in the truest sense of the word – to light a fire, not simply fill the bucket. Driven by our Thinking School approach, and delivered by dynamic and inspiring teaching, we strive to develop a passion for learning that will carry our pupils through their school years and beyond.

We create an environment where children's views and ideas are respected and encouraged. We believe that the classroom should be a place where pupils feel safe to challenge and be challenged.

When children do not fear being wrong, they are ready to express their own views, test out new ideas and take risks. At NHP, we celebrate making mistakes, and learning from them, as the path to deeper learning. We nurture the hardy attitudes and habits that will serve our children now and in later life. We develop in our pupils the ability to problem solve and become independent learners. We focus on their ability to cooperate, to think and act collaboratively and to show consideration for the feelings and needs of others.

We are a preparatory school and believe in academic rigour, preparing our pupils comprehensively for entrance exams to all the major London day schools at 11+ or 13+, as well as boarding schools at 13.

Alongside academic achievement, we also believe in the innate joy of childhood and we encourage children to follow their passions inside and outside of the classroom.

Music and performance are particular features at the school, with creative staff producing original material for plays and concerts. There are four choirs, an orchestra, chamber groups and bands and over two-thirds of the pupils learn a musical instrument.

A wide and varied sports programme using local facilities as well as our own on site gym ensures that children develop and perfect skills in the major sports (football, netball, hockey, rugby, cricket, athletics and swimming). Opportunities for displaying these skills are provided by frequent fixtures arranged with local schools.

Regular school trips enhance all aspects of the curriculum. Full use is made of the many and varied opportunities London offers to extend children's knowledge of their environment, their culture and their history.

NHP is noted for its open, friendly and happy atmosphere and its strong sense of being part of a wider community. Courtesy, kindness and appreciation of a diversity of talents, abilities and needs are defining values of the school's ethos.

The school is heavily oversubscribed and places are offered following a ballot.

Nottingham High Infant and Junior School

Waverley Mount, Nottingham NG7 4ED

Tel:	0115 845 2214
email:	juniorinfo@nottinghamhigh.co.uk

Lovell House Infant School:
13 Waverley Street, Nottingham NG7 4DX

Tel:	0115 845 2222
email:	lovellinfo@nottinghamhigh.co.uk
website:	www.nottinghamhigh.co.uk

Chairman of Governors: David Wild

Head: Mrs C Bruce

Deputy Head (*Academic*): Miss L Thorpe
Deputy Head (*Pastoral*): Mr C Cordy

Age Range. 4–11 Co-educational.
Number of Pupils. 276 Day pupils.
Fees per term (2018–2019). Infant School £3,393; Junior School £3,947.

Nottingham High Infant and Junior School has been co-educational since September 2016, with girls across all year groups.

The **Junior School** is housed in purpose-built premises on the main school site, having its own Classrooms, ICT Suite, Library, Art Room, Science Laboratory, Dining Hall and more. In 2018 our impressive new Junior School redevelopment was completed, expanding the number of classrooms, introducing a brand new spacious and contemporary library, improving our outdoor play areas, and much more.

Entrance Assessments are held in January, based around the core subjects of Mathematics and English, including reading, along with some measures of general ability. The tests are all set at National Curriculum ability levels appropriate for each age group.

The Junior School has an experienced and well-qualified staff. The curriculum is designed for those who expect to complete their education at Nottingham High School. The subjects taught are Religious Education, English, Mathematics, History, Geography, Science, French and PSHE. Full provision is made for Music, Art, Design Technology, Information Communication Technology, Swimming, Physical Education and Games.

The Junior School has its own Orchestra and about 100 pupils receive instrumental tuition. All Year 3 pupils play an instrument of their choice. A Concert and School Plays are performed annually. A wide range of supervised activities and hobbies takes place during every lunch time.

School games are Association Football, Netball and Rugby with some Hockey and Cross Country in the winter, Cricket and Tennis in the summer.

Lovell House Infant School opened in September 2008 for children in Reception, Year 1 and Year 2. Lovell House is situated across the road from the main High School in its own secure and self-contained grounds. The school has been completely refurbished and upgraded recently to provide state-of-the-art classrooms and facilities, and extensive play areas, all in a friendly, home-from-home surrounding. In fact, the main school building is very much like a large house, making the transition between nursery and the early stages of a formal school education so much easier.

Classes are deliberately kept small (a maximum class size of 18), so that our teachers are able to devote time to the children as individuals. The majority of subjects are taught by class teachers, although specialist teachers are used for ICT, Swimming, Music, French and Spanish. All subjects are taught in an integrated curriculum to allow time for play and problem-solving activities to take place.

Beyond the classroom we offer an excellent range of extracurricular activities giving real breadth to our curriculum. We make full use of some of the Nottingham High School facilities, such as the swimming pool, the extensive games fields and both the music and drama facilities. Thus whilst Lovell House is largely self-contained we are also able to use the High School's wider facilities to expand the horizons of the children in our care.

Entry to Lovell House is by assessment; the admissions process is designed to assess the numeracy and literacy skills of the children applying for a place in Years 1 and 2, and a range of activities are used to assess the potential for learning for those applying for a place in Reception. In addition, all children are invited to school for a final classroom-based assessment where they are observed completing practical activities.

As part of Nottingham High School, Lovell House not only benefits from the continuity of education and community from entry at age 4 right through to A Level at age 18, but also from the extensive recreational and cultural facilities provided by the High School.

Charitable status. Nottingham High School is a Registered Charity, number 1104251. It exists to provide education for boys and girls between the ages of 4 and 18 years.

Oakfield Preparatory School

125–128 Thurlow Park Road, West Dulwich, London SE21 8HP

Tel: 020 8670 4206
email: lbraim@oakfield.dulwich.sch.uk
            admissions@oakfield.dulwich.sch.uk
website: www.oakfield.dulwich.sch.uk
Twitter: @OakfieldPrep

Headmaster: Mr Patrick Gush, BEd Hons

Head of Pre Prep: Mrs Moyra Thompson, MA Cantab, PGCE, NPQH

Age Range. 2–11.
Number in School. Day: 201 Boys, 183 Girls.
Fees per term (2018–2019). Years 1–6: £3,595 including lunch. Early Years Foundation Stage fees according to sessions and Early Years funding where applicable.

Oakfield School was founded in 1887 and is today a modern co-educational prep school which prepares children for the entrance examinations of London and countrywide independent senior schools.

The School is arranged into three groups, the Nursery (age 2–3), Foundation Years and Year 1 (age 3–6) and Years 2–6 (age 6–11). Each age group has its own self-contained building and facilities. The School site of nearly three acres allows space for play and games and older children use the nearby playing field where games sessions are played. Children aged five to eleven swim once a week under instruction.

Entry to the 2+ Nursery is by observation. Once accepted the child will progress automatically into the Foundation Years (subject to the admissions policy) and Main School. Entry at 3+ and 4+ is also by observation. Entry at 7+ follows an assessment and observation in a class setting.

Prospective parents – and children – would be very welcome to visit Oakfield during a school day on an Open Morning.

Old Buckenham Hall School

Brettenham Park, Ipswich, Suffolk IP7 7PH

Tel: 01449 740252
Fax: 01449 740955
email: admissions@obh.co.uk
website: www.obh.co.uk
Twitter: @OBHSchool
Facebook: @OBHSchool

Chairman of Governors: N Bullen, BA Hons

Headmaster: **D Griffiths**, BA

Deputy Head: Mr D Farquharson, BA Hons, PGCE

Age Range. 3–13.
Number of Pupils. 85 Boarders; 63 Day Pupils; 35 Pre-Prep; 20 Nursery.
Fees per term (2018–2019). Full and Weekly Boarders £7,352–£8,370; Transitional Boarding: £5,507–£8,098; Day £5,090–£6,424; Pre-Prep inc Nursery £136–£3,167.

OBH was founded in Lowestoft in 1862 and moved in 1937 to Old Buckenham in Norfolk. In 1956, the school moved to its present site in Brettenham Park, Suffolk, which is 4 miles from Lavenham and 18 miles from Ipswich. The school became an Educational Trust in 1967.

All pupils progress to a wide range of senior schools via the scholarship and Common Entrance route. The school has a fine history of achieving scholarships and entrance to top public schools including Oundle, Uppingham, Downe House, Benenden, Harrow, Eton and Rugby.

The staff to pupil ratio is approximately 1:8 giving an average class size of 14. All members of staff, including part-time staff, contribute to a wide range of afternoon, evening and weekend extra-curricular activities – where every child has the opportunity to participate. Activities on offer include art and DT clubs, tennis, dance, drama, music, football, karate, music, climbing, remote control cars, cookery, gymnastics and horse riding.

Winter sports include hockey and netball for the girls, and hockey and rugby for the boys. There is also a structured football activity programme for both boys and girls. All pupils swim throughout the year (in our own heated outdoor pool in the summer and at a local swimming pool in the winter months). In the summer girls and boys play cricket and take part in athletics. The school offers excellent tennis facilities with pupils receiving specialist tennis coaching on six tennis courts and a purpose-built, state-of-the-art Astroturf. The school also has a squash court and a 9-hole golf course.

Boarding continues to grow in popularity and the opening of the new junior boarding house, Spero, is proving a phenomenal success. The youngest pupils at OBH are able to benefit from a warm, nurturing boarding environment, whilst being in the care of very experienced and caring staff. The boarding model is flexible, offering children the opportunity to board anything from 1 night a week to full boarding on an eleven-day cycle. Children boarding at the weekend enjoy a varied programme of exciting activities such as campfires and wide games by torch light, the 'Great OBH Bake Off', 'Bush Tucker Trials', a Masquerade Ball and trips out to the coast and other local attractions.

Children develop a wide range of life skills through the outdoor education programme – the OBEs (Old Buckenham Explorers) for pupils in Years 3–8 and the MBEs (Mini Buckenham Explorers) for pupils in the Pre-Prep. The construction of two outdoor classrooms has proved to be very innovative and exciting – where children learn to camp, shelter, cook and learn vital survival skills in preparation for Bronze, Silver and Gold expeditions.

The school stands in 80 glorious acres and offers children a chance to grow and develop in a wonderful, healthy environment, whilst also being equipped to deal with all the demands of modern life.

The school prospectus can be obtained on application to the Registrar.

Charitable status. Old Buckenham Hall (Brettenham) Educational Trust Limited is a Registered Charity, number 310490. It exists to provide education for boarding and day pupils.

The Old Hall School

Stanley Road, Wellington, Shropshire TF1 3LB

Tel:	01952 223117
Fax:	01952 222674
email:	admissions@oldhall.co.uk
	enq@oldhall.co.uk
website:	www.oldhall.co.uk
Twitter:	@oldhallschool
Facebook:	@The-Old-Hall-School

Chairman of the Governors: Mr R J Pearson, BSc

Headmaster: **Mr Martin C Stott**, BEd Hons

Age Range. 4–11.
Number of Pupils. 220: 116 boys, 104 girls.
Fees per term (2018–2019). Lower School: £2,770 (Reception), £3,050 (Years 1–2); Upper School (Years 3–6): £4,355.

Founded in 1845, The Old Hall School is a co-educational day school (4–11 years), which is housed in spectacular premises, located alongside Wrekin College. The school offers first-class facilities; a double sports hall, 25-metre

indoor swimming pool, Astroturf and grass pitches offer an excellent sports and games environment, whilst specialist music and drama areas help to promote high standards in the performing arts. A suite of specialist learning support rooms reflects the School's commitment to the needs of the individual. First-class facilities have also been created for preschool care and the education of children from the age of three months.

The broad curriculum is enriched by a dedicated team of professionals who encourage pupils to fulfil their potential in a happy and secure environment.

Through the academic curriculum and caring pastoral system, the school aims to lay solid foundations in the development of well-motivated, confident and happy individuals who are always willing to give of their best on the road to high achievement.

Charitable status. Wrekin Old Hall Trust Limited is a Registered Charity, number 528417.

The Old School Henstead

Toad Row, Henstead, Nr Beccles, Suffolk NR34 7LG

Tel:	01502 741150
email:	office@theoldschoolhenstead.co.uk
website:	www.theoldschoolhenstead.co.uk

Headmaster: **Mr W J McKinney**, MA Hons, PG Dip, MA Ed

Age Range. 2½–11.
Number in School. 100 Day Boys and Girls.
Fees per term (2018–2019). £2,330–£3,359; Nursery fees from £23.30 for 3 hours to £48.70 per day; early years funding accepted.

"Our children are so happy at Henstead …""Exceptional teaching standards and a wealth of opportunities across the whole academic, arts and sports spectrum." "…inspiring staff whose dedication is reflected in such highly-motivated and well-rounded children". These are typical comments from the school's parents.

The school is committed to realising the potential of all its pupils, creating a place of learning that inspires children to excel in and make their own special contribution to the global environment that awaits them. Henstead children know not just what to learn, but how to learn it; they are interested and interesting and they have the words to prove it.

Whilst focusing on the core subjects, the teaching at The Old School Henstead ensures that every pupil maximises his or her potential. The curriculum is designed to inspire and challenge all pupils, with teaching adapted to meet their varying needs. The school's aim is to teach children how to grow into positive, responsible people, who can work and cooperate with others, whilst developing knowledge and skills in order to achieve their true potential. Above all, the school believes in making learning fun, to engender a love of lifelong learning in every child that passes through the school. Small class sizes, excellent teaching and an insistence on traditional values of hard work and good manners help all pupils at The Old School Henstead to achieve high academic standards. The school caters for pupils of all abilities, offering specialist support where needed at both ends of the ability spectrum. In Early Years (Reception) and the Lower School (Years 1 and 2), the children are taught in their class base by their class teacher for the majority of subjects. In the Upper School, from Year 3 onwards, the majority of subjects are taught by subject teachers. Assessment for learning plays a vital role in ensuring that every pupil makes excellent progress. Pupils are encouraged to take responsibility for their own learning, to be involved as far as possible in reviewing the way they learn, and to reflect on how they learn – what helps them learn and what makes it difficult for them to learn. Children learn French from Nursery up and Latin in Year 6.

In the Early Years Foundation stage the school aims to give each child a happy, positive and fun start, so that he or she can establish solid foundations on which to expand and foster a deep love of learning. This is done through the seven areas of learning and supported by the school's outstanding outdoor learning environment.

After-school clubs take place every day. The activities on offer vary from term to term. The school has a thriving Pony Club and Tennis Club as well as other sports and arts clubs.

There is an active house system that encourages pupils to interact and collaborate with pupils outside their own year group. The School Council has two elected representatives from every year from Reception to Year 6.

Music-making is a very important part of life at The Old School Henstead. The school choirs rehearse every week and lead the singing in the daily assembly and at regular services at St Mary's Church. In addition to this, the school has, over the years, been very proud of the achievements of the choir at local, regional and national music festivals.

The school believes passionately in sport for all. All pupils are expected to take part in competitive sport, representing the school in a range of sports. Outdoor Education is an important part of the curriculum, for it is inclusive, builds confidence and encourages supervised, sensible risk-taking and learning opportunities that are as varied and challenging as those enjoyed indoors. In sport, teams and individuals compete against local schools and further afield in both regional and national competitions.

In keeping with The Old School Henstead's focus on building pupils' confidence, social skills and awareness of others, the Drama syllabus provides an approach which is both structured and adventurous. With drama games, improvisations, role play and practice of specific elements of Drama, the children are equipped to meet not only the challenges of regular performance and presentation within the broader curriculum of the school, but also in their ensuing educational experience. The Junior and Senior Summer Shows, the traditional climax to the year, are produced at an exceptional level of professionalism by talented and dedicated staff and include every child from Nursery to the top of the Senior School, at an appropriate level of performance. LAMDA tuition is also offered in the Upper School.

Religious affiliation: The school is underpinned by a Christian ethos, but accepts children of all faiths and none.

Charitable status. The Old School Henstead Educational Trust Limited is a Registered Charity, number 279265. It exists to provide education for boys and girls.

Old Vicarage School

48 Richmond Hill, Richmond, Surrey TW10 6QX

Tel:	020 8940 0922
Fax:	020 8948 6834
email:	office@oldvicarageschool.com
website:	www.oldvicarageschool.com

Chairman of Governors: Mr G Caplan

Headmistress: **Mrs G Linthwaite**, MA Oxon, PGCE

Age Range. 4–11.
Number of Pupils. 200 girls.

Fees per term (2018–2019). £4,740.

The Old Vicarage school is a non-selective girls' prep school based in a beautiful Grade 2* listed "castle" on Richmond Hill. The School was established in 1881 and became a Charitable Educational Trust in 1973. Whilst retaining traditional values, there is a clear vision for the future and teaching and facilities combine the very best of the old and the new. Girls are admitted to the school into one of the two Reception forms in September following their fourth birthday. Older girls may be admitted further up the school if a vacancy arises, following a day spent at the school to ensure it is a good fit for them. Girls are expected to remain until the age of 11, being prepared for Common Entrance Examinations at 11+ and for entry to the London Day Schools. A good range of academic, sporting, drama and arts scholarships to senior schools has been awarded to girls over the years.

Work of a traditionally high standard is expected of the girls and they are challenged and supported in classes of up to 15 girls, encouraging self esteem and enabling them to fulfil their potential. Girls in the Lower School are taught by a Form Teacher, with some specialist input. Girls in the Upper School are taught by subject specialists who impart a real enthusiasm and love for their subject areas. They will also have a form tutor to provide the pastoral support the school is known for. A system of older buddies, prefects and the Student Council ensures that all girls feel an integral part of the school from the beginning.

Music and drama are active throughout the school. Individual music tuition is provided in a wide range of instruments in purpose-built facilities and active choirs sing at numerous competitions and collaborations. All girls take part in at least one dramatic production a year, as well as in assemblies to which parents are invited.

The major sports are netball, hockey, cricket, rounders, athletics and swimming and the school has close access to state-of-the-art facilities in the surrounding area as well as our own gym and playground. Girls compete in fixtures against other schools from Year 3 and have had notable successes in recent years in borough-wide championships.

Extra-curricular activities cater to a range of interests and include art, photography, sports, computing, cooking, craft and drama clubs. All girls in the Upper School attend a residential trip to Sussex, Dorset, Oxfordshire or France and up to fifty join the biennial ski trip to Italy.

Charitable status. The Old Vicarage School is a Registered Charity, number 312671.

The Oratory Preparatory School

Goring Heath, Reading, South Oxfordshire RG8 7SF

Tel:	0118 9844511
Fax:	0118 9844806
email:	office@oratoryprep.co.uk
website:	www.oratoryprep.co.uk
Twitter:	@OPS_OratoryPrep
Facebook:	@oratoryprepschool

Chairman of the Board of Governors: M W Stilwell Esq

Headmaster: **R Stewart**, BA, MA

Age Range. 2–13.
Number of Pupils. 400 (260 boys and 140 girls), including 15 full, weekly or flexi boarders and 100 in the Pre-Prep department.

Fees per term (2018–2019). Boarders: £7,051 (weekly boarders), £8,174 (full boarders); Day £5,481; Pre-Prep:

£3,422 (all day), Kindergarten (5 sessions) £1,700; 'Little Oaks' Nursery £72 per day, £37 per pre-booked morning session.

Our school provides an enriched education to boys and girls aged 2 to 13. Set within 65 acres of Oxfordshire countryside with outstanding facilities, we nurture happy, balanced, confident and inquisitive children.

Our commitment to the pastoral care, wellbeing and all-round development of each child, combined with an ethos of broad-minded and inclusive learning lies at the heart of the school. This is reflected in our creation of a Deputy Head of Pastoral Care. The school strives to strike a balance between encouraging children to step out of their comfort zone, seek adventure and develop resilience, while ensuring that they feel fulfilled, secure and supported.

A focus on outdoor learning and expression through sport, music, art and drama are central to the self-confidence and self-discovery of our children. This includes Forest School from the age of two, science experiments in our Woodlands, art classes in our gardens and outdoor musical productions. Performing Arts flourishes through LAMDA, and the Distinctions across the board tell the story of further personal growth and character building among our pupils.

The school boasts an Astroturf for an array of sporting fixtures, including hockey, lacrosse and rounders. The 25-metre indoor swimming pool for Year 3 onwards is the venue for galas and a starting point for Mini-Triathlons. The smaller pool for children from Kindergarten upwards allows for weekly lessons.

The children have so many opportunities to discover themselves and their talents through our after school activities programmes, including fencing, archery and dance, alongside clubs for art, science and decoding.

Our popular Saturday Enrichment Programme focuses on the broader development of each individual and their horizons, offering a wealth of modules from interview practice and presentation skills, to outdoor living skills and history on their doorstep, alongside Bee keeping and cycle proficiency courses. The newly introduced Leadership Programme specifically for Year 8 extends the range of physical and mental challenges we offer our youngsters.

The school's Boarding House is made all the richer for its mix of nationalities with pupils in Year 4 upwards from China, Spain, France and Nigeria.

Charitable status. The Oratory Schools Association is a Registered Charity, number 309112. It exists to provide general, physical, moral and religious education for boys and girls.

Orchard House School

16 Newton Grove, London W4 1LB

Tel: 020 8742 8544
email: info@orchardhs.org.uk
website: www.orchardhs.org.uk
Twitter: @orchardhs

Chairman of Governors: Mr Anthony Rentoul

Headmistress: Mrs Maria Edwards

Age Range. Girls and Boys 3–11.
Number of Pupils. 277: 142 Girls, 135 Boys.
Fees per term (2018–2019). Nursery (5 mornings) £2,950, Pre-Prep £5,900, Prep £6,150.

Orchard House School, with Bassett House and Prospect House, is part of the House Schools Group. It provides an excellent all-round education for boys and girls from 3 to 11,

preparing them for the competitive entry examinations for the London day and country boarding schools whilst maintaining a happy, purposeful atmosphere.

There is an emphasis on teaching traditional values tailored for children growing up in the 21st century. Uniform is worn and good manners are expected at all times. Children shake hands with the staff at the end of each day and are encouraged to take part, with the deputy head or headmistress, in describing the school to prospective parents and other visitors. Appetising lunches are provided and all food is cooked freshly on site each day.

The main premises were designed by the well-known architect Norman Shaw and built around 1880; the building is Grade 2 listed. The school enjoys a corner site in Bedford Park and the classrooms have good natural lighting as well as overlooking a large playground.

Children aged 3 or 4 are admitted on a first come, first served basis. Occasional places higher up are filled following assessment. The Montessori method is used to deliver the Early Years Foundation Stage curriculum; at KS1 and KS2 the curriculum is based on the National Curriculum and the demands of the future schools. Specialist teachers are employed for many subjects and support teachers provide one-on-one or small group tuition where necessary. Staff turnover is low.

Orchard House is proud of the excellent results the children achieve at their future schools which include many of the most academic schools in this country. The school is within easy reach of St Paul's schools, Latymer Upper, Hampton School, Notting Hill & Ealing High School and Godolphin & Latymer and many pupils have taken up places at one of these schools.

The school boasts state-of-the-art ICT resources and attractive playgrounds/garden with all-weather surfaces. The children make good use of additional local facilities to enhance their Sport and Drama lessons.

Orchard House participates in the Nursery Education Grant. There are occasional means-tested scholarships available through the House Schools Trust for children entering Year 4. See www.houseschoolstrust.org.

Orchard School

Higham Road, Barton-le-Clay, Bedfordshire MK45 4RB

Tel: 01582 882054
email: admin@orchardschool.org.uk
website: www.orchardschool.org.uk

Chair of Friends: Mrs Mindi Byrne

Head Teacher: Mrs Anne Burton, MEd Cantab, Cert Ed, HV SRN

Deputy Head: Miss Louise Burton, BEd Hons Cantab, QTS

Co-educational Day School.
Age Range. 4–9 years; Nursery for children aged 0–4.
Number of Pupils. Preparatory School 65; Nursery 30.
Fees per term (2018–2019). Tuition (inc lunch) £2,713.45. Breakfast Club £3.84 per day. After School Club (inc tea) £8.23 per day.
Location. Orchard School is a Preparatory School for boys and girls, ideally situated on the outskirts of a large village in south Bedfordshire.

The School has been established for 14 years, and the Nursery for 25 years. Located in a beautiful setting and backed by the Barton Hills (thought to be The Delectable Mountains in Pilgrim's Progress) both School and Nursery are surrounded by rolling countryside that hosts an abundance of wildlife.

Ethos. The school's motto – "to be the best that you can be" is reflected in all areas of school life. Orchard's aim is to enable each child to value and strive for the highest levels of achievement, and to nurture a pride in success. Praise and encouragement are the primary motivational tools employed, tempered by the recognition that every child develops at their own pace. Skillful and careful observations are undertaken by the teaching team to help the children meet and surpass key learning targets. The school also encourages an 'esprit de corps' and a sense of true belonging. Emphasis is placed on the moral, social and personal development of all pupils in order to expand their confidence and self-esteem.

100% academic success. The school boasts an exemplary academic record with (for example) a 100% pass rate into the nearby Harpur Trust schools in Bedford.

The combination of a progressive, structured, yet genuinely friendly family atmosphere creates an ideal environment for the children to thrive both academically and in other activities that they pursue.

Activities. We encourage each child to experience as wide a range of activities as possible; for example, music lessons, choir, ballet, dance and philosophy.

A comprehensive sporting programme including swimming and rugby is also included within the well-rounded curriculum. Further opportunities include craftwork, running, lacrosse, badminton and recorder are offered via lunchtime and after-school clubs. There are several visits a term across all year groups to complement topic learning and to provide a real-life context to the subjects being studied. Years 3 and 4 also enjoy residential trips to specialist adventure-based facilities where activities such as abseiling, kayaking and raft building help increase fun, team spirit and pupil confidence.

Friends of Orchard. Orchard is proud of its strong and supportive parent base and there is a well-established 'Friends of Orchard School' group which organises social gatherings and fundraising events, further enhancing the friendly and family inclusive atmosphere at the school.

Bursaries. Bursaries are available for year 3 and above.

Summary. Our aim is to develop well-motivated and confident children who are considerate to others, well-mannered, who know the value of hard work.

We are happy to say that virtually all Orchard School pupils have been proven to excel at their subsequent schools and seats of learning.

Orley Farm School

South Hill Avenue, Harrow on the Hill, Middlesex HA1 3NU

Tel: 020 8869 7600
Fax: 020 8869 7601
email: office@orleyfarm.harrow.sch.uk
website: www.orleyfarm.harrow.sch.uk

The school is a Charitable Trust administered by a Board of Governors.

Chairman of Governors: Mr C J Hayfield

Headmaster: **Mr T Calvey**, BA Ed Hons

Age Range. 4–13 Co-educational.
Number of Pupils. 495 Day pupils, including 189 in Pre-Prep (age 4 to 7).

Fees per term (2018–2019). Pre-Prep £4,720; Years 3–4 £5,018; Years 5–8 £5,445 (inclusive of lunch).

At Orley Farm School we are in the fortunate position of being a London day school blessed with boarding school acreage and facilities. Founded in 1850, the school has grown and developed to become one of the leading and largest co-educational prep schools in Greater London. Entry is by assessment at 4+ and when occasional places appear in the rest of the school. The academic journey of the children begins in Reception and ends when pupils transfer successfully to their senior schools – at the end of Year 6 for some of our girls and Year 8 for both girls and boys attending more traditional senior schools. Pupils enter a range of very impressive senior schools, including Eton, Haberdashers' Aske's Boys and Girls, Harrow, John Lyon, Merchant Taylors', Northwood College, North London Collegiate, Notting Hill and Ealing, Royal Masonic, St Helen's, St Paul's, Westminster and Wycombe Abbey to name but a few. However, most impressively, Orley Farm has served over 61 senior schools over the past 5 years. We pride ourselves in finding the right future step for every child. Scholarships are regularly awarded to our senior pupils – 51 awards were offered in 2017–2018.

Success, happiness and future fulfilment start with a deep love of learning. So firmly do we believe in this philosophy, that we have invested £9 million in our facilities (a Music and Drama School, three state of the art Science Laboratories, a new Humanities department, a new Dining Hall and at the very heart, a cutting edge Library). Whilst some schools are binning books, we are buying more, and investing heavily in our environment to accompany a focused drive on study skills for life. Solid foundations are setting, not only in our new buildings, but also in the hearts and minds of a generation of young learners.

'Breadth, Balance & Excellence …The Orley Farm Way!'

Alongside academic excellence, we pride ourselves on giving pupils experiences and opportunities that foster a lifetime and love of learning. All pupils are expected to contribute to the broader curriculum and a packed programme of Drama, Art and Music and Design & Technology. Over 200 individual music lessons take place each week and are supported by many musical groups and choirs. Productions, concerts and competitions offer all pupils the chance to showcase their talents and dedication in a variety of different settings.

Sport plays a very large part in our school life. We have over thirty six acres of land and full use is made of this in providing a venue for training and matches. Pupils will compete internally and externally in athletics, cricket, football, hockey, netball, rounders and rugby. In addition basketball, cross-country, fencing, fives, gymnastics and tennis also thrive through activities, clubs and matches. A Gym, Sports Hall and full-sized AstroTurf pitch enable our strong PE and Games Department to help our pupils develop their sporting talents.

This rich blend of curricular and co-curricular education is exemplified by our Expeditions Week. All pupils and staff from Year 4 and above travel to a variety of venues to spend a week extending their curriculum in a host of new challenges and adventures.

Orley Farm School is located in North West London close to Harrow on the Hill and is only twenty minutes on the Metropolitan Line from Baker Street Station.

Entry to this exciting place of learning is by assessment. For further details contact the Registrar, Mrs Julie Jago, on 0208 869 7634.

Charitable status. Orley Farm School is a Registered Charity, number 312637.

Orwell Park

Nacton, Ipswich, Suffolk IP10 0ER
Tel: 01473 659225
Fax: 01473 659822
email: headmaster@orwellpark.org
website: www.orwellpark.co.uk
Twitter: @OrwellParkSch
Facebook: @orwellpark

Chairman of Governors: James Davison, BA

Headmaster: **Adrian Brown**, MA Cantab

Age Range. 2½–13.
Number of Pupils. Prep: 229: 133 Boarders (58 girls, 75 boys); 96 Day Pupils (41 girls, 55 boys). Pre-Prep: 69 (29 girls, 40 boys).
Fees per term (2018–2019). Prep School: Weekly Boarding: £7,207 (Year 3), £8,005 (Years 4–9); Full Boarding: £8,135 (Year 3), £8,667 (Years 4–8); Day Pupils: £5,621 (Year 3), £6,230 (Years 4–8). Pre-Prep Day Pupils: £29 per session (Nursery), £2,700 (Reception), £3,000 (Year 1), £3,840 (Year 2).

Pupils are prepared for all Independent Senior Schools (local day and national boarding) via the Scholarship or Common Entrance Examinations (37 awards in 2016). The school has a thriving Pre-Prep School, which is housed in a new, state-of-the-art building containing a large hall, six classrooms and music and ICT rooms.

The timetable is especially designed to be very flexible, with setting in most subjects, a potential scholars' set in Year 7 and a scholarship set in Year 8. The curriculum, both in and out of the classroom, is unusually broad. Children are encouraged to enjoy their learning and good learning support is offered. Thinking Skills and other opportunities for academic enrichment are also offered, including a weekly evening lecture programme to challenge the older children. There is a host of extracurricular activities (just under 100) run by permanent or visiting staff.

About 90% of the school learn a musical instrument and the school has a number of orchestral and ensemble groups. Drama is strong and all children have opportunities to perform regularly in school productions. All children take part in annual Reading and Public Speaking Competitions.

The very large Georgian style building and 110 acres of grounds (sandy soil) on the banks of the River Orwell have the following special features: 21 recently refurbished themed dormitories, 22 bright classrooms with modern audio-visual equipment, beautiful Orangery used as an Assembly and Lecture Hall, 2 ICT suites, large Design Centre including metal, wood and plastic workshop plus electronics, mechanics, home economics, radio and model-making areas, Music Technology Room, Music Room and 40 Practice rooms, 2 Laboratories plus associated areas, brand new Library, Art Room including large pottery area and kiln, Observatory with 10' Refractor Telescope, Photographic Room, 17 Games pitches and one Astroturf pitch, one Multi-Use Games Area, large Sports Hall with permanent stage, Climbing Wall, Games Room, large heated Swimming Pool, 3 Squash Courts, 5 Hard Tennis Courts, Nine-hole Golf Course (approximately 1,800 yards) and a purpose-built Assault Course.

Good sports coaching is given and fixtures are arranged in the following sports: Rugby, Hockey, Cricket, Netball, Rounders, Tennis, Athletics, Squash, Sailing, Swimming and Cross-Country Running. Emphasis is also placed on individual physical activities and we offer a wide range including Gymnastics, Fencing, Ballet, Canoeing, Sailing,

Modern Dance, Karate, Riding and Clay Pigeon Shooting. The school owns its own canoes and dinghies.

The School aims to introduce the pupils to a broad and varied set of experiences and opportunities. It tries to see that every activity, whether academic, sporting, social or character building, is properly taught using the best possible facilities and that each is conducted in an atmosphere which is friendly but disciplined. Children are encouraged to feel comfortable taking risks and to be confident without being arrogant. The school has introduced some key initiatives this year. Under the overarching value of integrity, it has introduced core values: kindness, collaboration, courage, spirit and respect. Each term assemblies focus on a different value and posters in classrooms reinforce the values for pupils.

Charitable status. Orwell Park School is a Registered Charity, number 310481. It exists to provide education for boys and girls.

Our Lady's Abingdon Junior School

St John's Road, Abingdon, Oxfordshire OX14 2HB
Tel: 01235 523147
Fax: 01235 530387
email: officejs@olab.org.uk
website: www.olab.org.uk
Twitter: @OLAabingdon
Facebook: @OLAabingdon

Chairman of Governors: Mr Edward McCabe, MA Oxon, MBA

Headteacher: **Ms Erika Kirwan**, MA Cantab, PGCE London, MTeach London

Deputy Headteacher: Miss Brigid Meadows, GTCL Hons, LTCL, PGCE

Age Range. 3–11 Co-educational.
Number of Pupils. 75.
Fees per term (2018–2019). Years 5 and 6 £4,383, Years 3 and 4 £3,653, Years 1 and 2 £3,158. Early Years (Nursery/Reception) £3,158 or £315.80 per session per term.
Staff: 16 full time and 5 part time. Specialist teaching in Mathematics, English, Science, French, PE, Art, Design Technology and Music.

Our Lady's Abingdon Junior School is a small friendly school with a strong sense of community. Children are treated as individuals and nurtured so that they can achieve to the best of their abilities. Education is not just about academic results, although these are important to us. We offer a broad curriculum so that our children have the opportunity to excel in Art, Music, Drama and Sport. Moreover, we seek to develop every aspect of our children's character so that they go on to their chosen Senior School as confident, resilient learners who are curious about the world around them.

Our Catholic ethos is at the heart of everything we do and is reflected in the positive relationships that exist between the members of our school community, and the encouragement given to each individual child to be the best that they can be.

The report from our ISI Inspection in 2015 praised the wide range of extra-curricular subjects we offer and also commented on the specialist teaching that we are able to provide.

Pupils are self-aware, reflective and well-grounded, recognising their responsibilities to one another and to their community.

Pupils throughout the school, including the most able and those with SEND or EAL make good progress in relation to their ability.

Within the EYFS, the children's personal development is excellent. They behave extremely well at all times taking turns and sharing without prompting from adults. Many examples of kindness were seen during the course of the inspection.

Location. Our Lady's Abingdon Junior School is part of the larger Our Lady's Abingdon, which is a 3–18 school located in the market town of Abingdon. The school occupies its own buildings adjacent to the Senior School and has the advantage of maintaining its own distinct character and ethos, whilst being able to share the extensive facilities and specialist staff on offer in the Senior School. (*See also Senior School entry in The Society of Heads section.*)

Facilities. Bright, spacious classrooms, a well-equipped library, a recently refurbished ICT suite and other specialist rooms provide a stimulating environment conducive to the teaching and learning of our pupils. Sports facilities include a number of tennis courts, a Junior School gymnasium, a sports field and a 25-metre indoor swimming pool. The Junior School has the advantage of sharing a number of the Senior School facilities, including science laboratories and D&T workshops, and the children also benefit from specialist lessons taught by Senior School teachers. The newly-refurbished Nursery area is a well-resourced provision on two floors – a peaceful and relaxed classroom area on the first floor and a purpose-built kitchen and "wet" area on the ground floor leading to a large and excitingly resourced outdoor garden area. This provides a gentle yet exciting introduction to school where the children learn through play and discovery to develop their social and learning skills.

Curriculum. Throughout the school we believe that all children have the right to experience a broad and balanced programme of subjects, which provides continuity and progression, and takes into account pupils' individual differences and needs. Children have lessons in Maths, English, Science, Computing, Geography, History, RE, Art, Design Technology, Music, French and PSHE. In the older year groups, much of this teaching is done by specialist staff.

Children in the EYFS setting follow the Early Years Foundation Stage curriculum and are assessed according to the EYFS profiles. We are members of the Local Authority Early Years Partnership which enables parents to receive a grant that can be offset against school fees.

Extracurricular Activities. The Junior School provides a wide programme of extracurricular activities including drama, music, art, many forms of sport, ICT, D&T, cooking, creative play and African Drumming to name but a few. These clubs operate from 3.20 pm until 4.00 pm each evening and are available to all children from Reception through to Year Six. A supervised homework session is also available for those who require it. Children in Nursery and Reception visit Forest School on Friday mornings; older children in the school can attend Forest School Club at lunchtimes. The School Council, which meets regularly each term, is an integral part of the way in which we involve the pupils in the decision-making processes in the school.

Admissions. Our Lady's Abingdon Junior School considers for admission any pupil for whom it is able to provide an appropriate education. The main intake is at the age of 3 or 4, although pupils may be accepted into any Year Group where there are vacancies, at the discretion of the Headteacher. Pupils are selected on the basis of application, previous reports (where applicable) and parents' interview. Pupils may also be asked to visit the school on one or more days prior to the term in which the place is required. The school will wish to ascertain the previous attainment of

pupils entering years Four, Five and Six and this is done by formal testing in Mathematics and English.

Charitable status. Our Lady's Abingdon Trustees Limited is a Registered Charity, number 1120372, and a Company Limited by Guarantee, registered in England and Wales, number 6269288.

Packwood Haugh

Ruyton XI Towns, Shrewsbury, Shropshire SY4 1HX

Tel:	01939 260217
Fax:	01939 262077
email:	hm@packwood-haugh.co.uk
website:	www.packwood-haugh.co.uk
Twitter:	@packwoodhaugh

Chairman of Governors: D R Stacey

Headmaster: Paul H Reynolds, BA Hons, PGCE, MEd Oxon
Headmaster from April 2019: Robert Fox

Deputy Heads:
Mr R Chambers, BA, MEd
Mrs S Rigby, BA Hons, PGCE, Dip SpLD

Age Range. Co-educational 4–13.
Number of Children. 196. Boarding: 48 boys, 24 girls. Day: 67 boys, 32 girls. Pre-Prep 25.
Fees per term (2018–2019). Boarding: UK £7,810, International £8,810; Day £4,240–£6,110, Pre-Prep (Acorns) £2,935. No compulsory extras. Extras available on request.

Set in the heart of the Shropshire countryside, between Shrewsbury and Oswestry, Packwood Haugh is a co-educational day (4–13) and boarding (7–13) school which provides an excellent all-round education in a happy and caring environment. Children benefit from a wide range of academic, sporting, musical, artistic and cultural activities which encourage them to develop enquiring minds and an enthusiasm for learning. The school espouses an atmosphere of cooperation and understanding between pupils, staff and parents and encourages good manners and consideration towards others at all times.

Packwood has always striven for academic excellence; class sizes are small (average 13) and children are prepared for all the major independent schools across the country winning a number of academic, music, sports, art and all-rounder scholarships and awards each year. The school has a thriving pre-prep department (Packwood Acorns), which takes children from Reception.

The school's facilities are superb; a state-of-the-art sports hall allows for fencing, indoor tennis, badminton, indoor cricket nets, judo, gymnastics and five-a-side football. Incorporated in the building are fully equipped CDT and Art departments and a linked computer suite. A 280-seat theatre is used for assemblies, concerts and drama productions throughout the year.

As well as the classrooms in the main school buildings and a purpose-built new block, there are three science laboratories, two libraries, a year 8 study area and two further computer suites. Park House, which accommodates Packwood Acorns and girls' boarding, is a short distance from the main school building.

Packwood has a very strong sporting tradition. Set alongside 66 acres of grass playing fields, there is a newly resurfaced full-size, floodlit AstroTurf pitch, an additional hard court area, 10 tennis courts, two squash courts, an indoor, heated swimming pool and a 9-hole golf course. In the winter terms the boys play rugby, football and hockey while the girls play netball, hockey and lacrosse. There is also cross-country running on a course within the grounds. In the summer the boys play cricket, the girls play rounders and cricket, and all take part in tennis, athletics and swimming.

Additional facilities include Forest School, a shooting range and an equestrian cross-country course as well as an adventure playground.

Charitable status. Packwood Haugh is a Registered Charity, number 528411. It exists to provide day and boarding education for boys and girls from the age of 4 to 13.

Papplewick

Windsor Road, Ascot, Berks SL5 7LH

Tel:	01344 621488
Fax:	01344 874639
email:	schoolsec@papplewick.org.uk
	registrar@papplewick.org.uk
website:	www.papplewick.org.uk
Twitter:	@PapplewickAscot

Chairman of Board of Governors: Brigadier {Retd} A R E Hutchinson, JP

Headmaster: **T W Bunbury**, BA University College Durham, PGCE

Age Range. 6–13.
Number of Boys. 214 97 Boarders, 117 day boys.
Fees per term (2018–2019). Boarders £9,915; Day Boys: £5,485 (Year 2), £7,185 (Years 3–4), £7,615 (Years 5–6).

Papplewick is a boys only, day, weekly and full boarding school with an exceptional Scholarship record to top Independent Schools. Day boys do prep at school and come into board from the Summer term of Year 6. Happiness comes first and kindness is a priority here. Three very popular daily transport services run to and from London, one from Chiswick, one from Brook Green and one from near the Millennium Gloucester Hotel. Also, a daily service runs to and from Maidenhead/South Bucks. Situated between the M3 and M4, the school boasts easy access to London airports. A new Year 8 stand-alone boarding house has now opened with two Year 5 classrooms underneath and staff accommodation.

Papplewick exists to provide a high-quality education where – for all our academic, cultural and sporting success – the happiness of the boys come first, and kindness is a top priority.

Papplewick has recently been awarded Tatler's Prep School of the Year 2018.

Charitable status. The Papplewick Educational Trust is a Registered Charity, number 309087.

The Paragon
Junior School of Prior Park College

Lyncombe House, Lyncombe Vale, Bath BA2 4LT

Tel:	01225 310837
Fax:	01225 427980
email:	reception.paragon@priorparkschools.com
	rbraithwaite@priorparkschools.com

website:	www.priorparkschools.com
Twitter:	@ParagonBath
Facebook:	@TheParagonJunior

Chair of Governors: Mr Michael King

Headmaster: **Mr Andrew Harvey**, BA Hons, PGCE

Registrar: Mrs Rebecca Braithwaite

Age Range. 3–11 years.
Number of Pupils. 150 Boys, 120 Girls.
Fees per term (2018–2019). Juniors (Years 5–6) £3,500 including lunch; (Years 3–4) £3,415 including lunch; Infants (Years 1–2) £3,250 including lunch; Reception £3,085 including lunch. Nursery (full time) £2,915 including lunch, part time according to sessions. Sibling discounts available. Registration Fee (non-refundable) £100.

25 experienced and qualified teachers.

The Paragon is an independent, co-educational day school based in a beautiful Georgian house situated a mile from the centre of Bath. The school is set in eight acres of beautiful grounds with woodland, conservation areas, lawns and streams. It's the perfect 'outdoor classroom' and we use it right across the curriculum. We also enjoy regular access to the superb sport, science, D & T and drama facilities at our Senior School, Prior Park College.

Several factors help create the 'distinctive Paragon atmosphere'. One is undoubtedly the homely feel that comes from being based in a beautiful, former family home. Then there's our Christian ethos and strong pastoral care, as well as our belief that school at this age is about being stimulated and inspired, about laughter and spontaneity – in short, about having fun. We may be a private school and we certainly expect high standards of behaviour but we're anything but stuffy and grey.

We offer a broad curriculum taught in small classes by teachers with real passion. Academic life at The Paragon cultivates a love of learning and encourages independent and creative thinking. Our results are impressive. Our children consistently achieve well above the national average and many Year 6 children win senior school scholarships. Our facilities include a library, large gymnasium/dining hall, ICT suite, nursery with secure indoor and outdoor play areas, art studio, modern languages and music rooms.

Sport is particularly strong at The Paragon. Our sports teams take part, with considerable success, in a wide range of tournaments and festivals. We also offer a vast range of sports clubs that all children can join regardless of ability. Prior Park College offers us an indoor swimming pool, AstroTurf and grass pitches, tennis courts, athletics track and sports centre.

The Paragon's extracurricular programme is extensive. Staff run more than 60 lunchtime and after-school clubs that range from pottery and chess to film-making and cross-country running. The school also enjoys an enviable reputation for Music. All children receive weekly music lessons from a specialist teacher. In addition, visiting instrumental teachers offer tuition in a wide range of instruments. We offer an excellent choice of extracurricular music activities including the orchestra, two choirs, a wind band, brass group, flute choir, string ensemble, African drumming group and an ever-growing Samba band.

The Paragon is proud of its consistently impressive academic results but we strive for much more than success in exams. We believe in developing the whole person – physically, spiritually, and emotionally as well as intellectually. As W B Yeats said: "Education is not filling a bucket but lighting a fire".

Charitable status. Prior Park Educational Trust is a Registered Charity, number 281242.

Parkside

**The Manor, Stoke d'Abernon, Cobham, Surrey
KT11 3PX**

Tel: 01932 862749
Fax: 01932 860251
email: head.pa@parkside-school.co.uk
website: www.parkside-school.co.uk
Twitter: @parksideprep
Facebook: @parksideprep

Chairman of Governors: Robin Southwell

Acting Head: **Ms Nicole Janssen**, BA Hons, PGCE,
  NPQH

Deputy Head: Mrs M McMurdo

Age Range. Boys 2½–13. Co-educational Nursery.
Numbers. 308: Prep 188, Pre-Prep 53, Nursery 67.
Fees per term (from January 2019). Day Boys £5,564,
Pre-Prep £4,055, Nursery £858–£3,410.

Parkside was founded in 1879 and became a Charitable
Trust in 1960. The School moved from East Horsley to its
present site of over 40 acres in 1979, its centenary year.
Since the move the Governors have implemented a continual development programme which has included a purpose-
built, well-equipped Science Block, extending the main
building to provide more Pre-Prep accommodation and a
Music School with a large classroom and six practice rooms.
An excellent Swimming Pool and Sports Hall complex with
a stage for drama offers unrivalled facilities in the area. In
addition, a £2m Classroom Block was built about 10 years
ago to further enhance the facilities in the school. The
Design Technology Department, Nursery and ICT suite are
housed in a delightful Grade II Listed Barn which has been
completely and skilfully refurbished to provide spacious,
well-lit classrooms and workshops. A second Computer
Room has been linked to the main network in recent years
and the Art and Music facilities have been further expanded.

The school is large enough to be flexible and offer setting
in major subjects yet small enough for each pupil to be
known and treated as an individual. On average there are 15
pupils in a Set and the teacher to pupil ratio is 1:8. All teaching staff are highly qualified and there is a low staff turnover. Each boy is a member of a House and this helps to
stimulate friendly competition for work points and many
other inter-house contests.

The National Curriculum is followed to prepare all boys
for entry to Senior Independent Schools by Common
Entrance and Scholarship examinations. All boys pass to
their first choice Senior Schools and our results in these
examinations are impressive. Over the past few years many
Academic, Art, Music and Sporting Scholarships have been
won. Our curriculum is broad based and all boys are taught
Art, Music, PE and Technology in addition to the usual
Common Entrance subjects. There is a School Choir, a
School Orchestra and several smaller musical groups, and
over one third of the boys are receiving individual tuition in
a wide variety of musical instruments. During the year, there
are many opportunities for boys to perform in musical and
dramatic productions.

The School has a fine sporting record and, over the past
few years, many tournaments in different sports and at different age groups have been won. In addition, a number of
boys have gone on to represent their County and Country in
various sports. The main sports are football, hockey and
cricket, but boys are able to take part in rugby, swimming,
athletics, tennis, cross-country running, basketball and judo.

An extensive Wednesday afternoon and After School Activity Programme (including supervised homework sessions) is
available with over 40 different activities on offer, from gardening to kayaking, and table tennis to golf. Many boys
have also represented the school at a high level in chess. The
beautiful estate and the River Mole, which runs through the
grounds, are also used to contribute to the all round education each pupil receives both in and out of the classroom.

Unusually for a Preparatory School, Parkside has a large
and active Old Boys Association which runs many sporting
and social events during the year.

Further details and a prospectus are available on application to the Head's PA, Lindre Scott, via email: head.pa@
parkside-school.co.uk.

Charitable status. Parkside School is a Registered Charity, number 312041. It exists to provide education for children between the ages of 2½ and 13 years.

Pembridge Hall School
Alpha Plus Group

18 Pembridge Square, London W2 4ED

Tel: 020 7229 0121
email: contact@pembridgehall.co.uk
website: www.pembridgehall.co.uk

Headmaster: **Mr Henry Keighley-Elstub**, BA Hons,
  PGCE

Age Range. 4–11.
Number of Girls. 416.
Fees per term (2018–2019). £7,415.

Pembridge girls take advantage of a vast array of learning
experiences, both inside and out of the classroom. Pembridge Hall offers a 'three-dimensional education', believing that it is only by creating an environment in which
teaching is inspiring and imaginative that girls will thrive.
Sport and the Arts feature strongly on the curriculum.

Teachers, girls and parents work in a close partnership,
ensuring that each girl is happy and achieving her maximum
potential in every area of school life. Girls transfer at the end
of Year Six to some of the finest senior day and boarding
schools in the country.

Pennthorpe School

**Church Street, Rudgwick, Nr Horsham, West Sussex
RH12 3HJ**

Tel: 01403 822391
Fax: 01403 822438
email: enquiries@pennthorpe.com
website: www.pennthorpe.com
Twitter: @PennthorpeSch
Facebook: @PennthorpeSchool

Happy to Learn

Chairman of the Governors: Mr Mark Lucas

Headmistress: **Mrs Alexia Bolton**, MEd, MA, BA Hons,
  QTS, PCPSE

Age Range. Co-educational 2–13.
Number of Pupils. 250 Day Pupils.
Fees per term (2018–2019). £690–£5,535.

Pennthorpe School in West Sussex lies close to the Surrey border, midway between Guildford and Horsham. The school is committed to high standards in all it does. Pennthorpe also recognises that putting the fun into the fundamentals of school life encourages the children to maximise their learning potential.

Pennthorpe has an outstanding record of 13+ Common Entrance successes, with regular academic, art, music and Performing Arts scholarships won to a number of senior schools in Sussex, Surrey and beyond. Many have also won all-rounder scholarships which reflects the school's commitment to developing its pupils into well-balanced youngsters and it is this outlook, along with the principle of putting the fun into the fundamentals, that drives Pennthorpe forward.

Developing all-rounders means offering choice, and from the very earliest stages when the two year-olds join the Pennthorpe Kindergarten, the emphasis is on breadth, both academic and outside the classroom.

The Pennthorpe Sports Department offers a wealth of sporting activities and competitive opportunities: soccer, netball, rugby, hockey, rounders, cricket and athletics are regular features on the termly fixtures calendar, while gymnastics, climbing, judo, tennis, basketball, archery and many others are available as part of the huge range of after-school options.

Pennthorpe is committed to the Arts. From the age of five, every pupil enjoys weekly Performing Arts lessons in our own dance and drama studio. There are also specialist-taught music lessons for all, including access to composition programs such as Garage Band in the iMac suite; these, along with four choirs, an orchestra, individual instrumental tuition, termly concerts and various productions involving every child in the school, provide many performing opportunities.

Pennthorpe also enjoys a cutting edge Art and Design Centre outstandingly equipped to fire the creative spirits of its pupils. The school's long-standing reputation for artistic excellence is now backed up by a 21-station iMac suite, photography studio and design room. With animation, web design, advanced programming and photo editing all embedded within the curriculum, all children can find their own ways to express their imaginations.

Complementing and building upon the classroom work, Pennthorpe's Flexiday programme of after-school activities aims to bring even more chances for every boy and girl to find their strengths and shine. Whether it is developing their computer skills, throwing a pot, scaling the climbing wall or tapping to the rhythm in the dance studio, there's something for everybody.

A continuous programme of major capital investment is under way. A recently completed Pre-Prep building with 6 new classrooms, a state-of-the-art kindergarten and large multi-purpose hall has transformed the academic life of our younger pupils. In addition to this, our new Art and Design Centre opened its doors in February 2012 and plans are already laid for a new Performing Arts and Music Centre. This is a school that never stands still!

If you would like to see how your child could thrive in this busy, happy and successful school, ask for a prospectus, visit our website (details above) and then book a visit: the Headmaster and all the staff and children will make you very welcome. There are generally two Open Mornings each term and the Headmaster is also happy to welcome parents for individual visits at any time.

Charitable status. Pennthorpe School is a Registered Charity, number 307043. It exists to provide an excellent education for boys and girls and to benefit the community.

Perrott Hill

North Perrott, Crewkerne, Somerset TA18 7SL

Tel: 01460 72051
email: admissions@perrotthill.com
website: www.perrotthill.com
Twitter: @perrotthill
Facebook: @PerrottHillSchool

Chairman of Governors: Lord Bradbury

Headmaster: Mr Alexander McCullough, BA Hons Dunelm, PGCE, NPQH

Age Range. 3–13.
Number of Pupils. 126 boys and 92 girls, of whom 41 are full, weekly or flexi boarders.
Fees per term (2018–2019). Boarders: £6,625 (weekly), £7,845 (full), £8,230 (overseas); Day pupils £1,750–£5,435.

Perrott Hill is a co-educational day and boarding school and is registered as an Educational Trust. Set in 25 acres of beautiful grounds in the heart of the countryside, near Crewkerne on the Somerset/Dorset border, it is served by excellent road and rail networks.

Perrott Hill is a thriving country preparatory school where children settle quickly and learn in confidence. Class sizes are small, with an average of 12 children to a form; the pupils being streamed from Year 5 onwards. Staff are dedicated and highly qualified. Facilities now include an all-weather sports area, a purpose-built sports hall, a theatre, a DT/art school, a computer centre, a new music school opened in September 2016, games fields, swimming pool and extensive Forest School. Our new Science Laboratory and Tinker Lab were completed in September 2017.

The Nursery and Pre-Prep are housed within the converted stable courtyard next to the main school buildings, which gives the younger children their own safe, secure environment whilst allowing them to take advantage of the grounds and facilities of the Prep School. There is an emphasis on outdoor learning including weekly sessions in our on-site Forest School.

Music, Drama and Art are taught within the timetable alongside core curriculum subjects. The choir and orchestra perform at charity concerts, in competitions and school functions and the choir has recently toured Venice. There are drama productions every term.

Teaching is class-based until Year 5 and subject-based in the upper school, where all lessons are taught by specialist teachers. French, Music, IT and PE, however, are taught by specialists throughout the school.

Each child, boarding or day, has his or her own pastoral and academic tutor, while the welfare of the boarders is supervised by Ms White and Mr Sheldon. They are ably assisted by a dedicated and enthusiastic boarding staff (many of which live on site).

Sport is played every day, and matches take place on most Wednesdays as well as on Saturdays for the senior part of the school. Emphasis is placed upon skills and team work and games played include rugby, football, hockey, netball, cricket, tennis, rounders, swimming and cross-country running. The school takes part in national events, such as the IAPS Ski Championships, IAPS Sailing Regatta and the National Small Schools Rugby Sevens. Optional extras include fencing, carpentry, archery, karate, horse riding, ballet, speech and drama, cookery, Spanish, golf and craft.

Perrott Hill combines extremely high standards of academic and pastoral care. All children were offered a place at the school of their choice and scholarships have been awarded for academic, artistic, sporting, dramatic, musical, equine and all-round ability. In 2016, over half of all leavers won awards or scholarships to their schools of choice. These included Blundell's, Canford, King's College Taunton, Leweston, Millfield, Queen's College Taunton, Sherborne Girls, Sherborne, Taunton School and Wellington School. Other destinations include Harrow, Winchester, Eton, Bryanston and King's Bruton. Academic, music, sport, art, drama and all-rounder Scholarships are offered annually in February to children in Years 3–6.

The combination of countryside, space, a family atmosphere and a forward-looking academic programme creates an ideal environment for children to thrive both academically and in their leisure pursuits – we warmly invite you to come and see the school in action.

Charitable status. Perrott Hill School Trust Limited is a Registered Charity, number 310278. It exists to give high quality education to boys and girls.

The Perse Pelican Nursery and Pre-Preparatory School

92 Glebe Road, Cambridge CB1 7TD

Tel: 01223 403940
Fax: 01223 403941
email: pelican@perse.co.uk
website: www.perse.co.uk

Chairman of Governors: Sir David J Wright, GCMG, LVO, MA

Headmistress: **Mrs S Waddington**, BSc, MA

Age Range. 3–7.
Number of Pupils. 150.
Ethos. We aim to awaken a thirst for learning, helping children to develop an understanding and enjoyment of the world around them. The children are enthusiastic and inspired by the opportunities on offer and delight in meeting challenges and taking risks whilst benefiting from a safe and secure environment. They learn through a range of play-based activities as well as more formal methods of learning and have many opportunities to develop their independence.

Our aim is to ensure that the children in our care are sociable, rounded, confident and inquisitive. We are proud of our broad, challenging, enticing curriculum and the spirit with which our pupils approach their learning.

Admissions. The main entry point for the Pelican is Nursery, which is for children who are three years old by 1 September in the year of entry. There are also a few spaces available for extra children in Reception. Selection takes place in the January of the year of intended entry for Nursery and in the September in the year prior to entry for Reception.

History. The buildings of the Nursery and Pre-Prep began life in 1911 as a boarding house for the Upper School. The School has been sympathetically extended inside and out, so that it provides exceptional space and excellent facilities, yet still feels like a home from home.

School life. Our pastoral care is second to none; every single child in the School is known to all and is valued for their individual characteristics. All achievements are celebrated.

Classroom routines are quickly established from the start of a child's time at the Pelican, and from day one they feel they belong. Every class benefits from a full-time teaching assistant who works alongside the teacher.

Dance, Games, Languages and Music are all taught by specialist teachers. An inclusive choir is open to everyone in Years 1 and 2 and a range of music ensembles are formed each year appropriate to the needs of the children in those year groups at the time. Our musicians regularly perform in regional and national festivals.

The children relish challenge and aim high, knowing that there is always someone to support them. We work in partnership with parents to nurture children's interests and provide opportunities to develop their potential. Pupils begin to acquire essential skills through play, topic work and a wide range of experiences and activities.

A rounded education. Regular school trips bring learning to life and being close to the centre of Cambridge the School is able to take advantage of trips to local museums and wildlife parks.

Out of school care. Children may be dropped at school from 8.00 am and may stay until 5.30 pm each day. We run an extended range of after school clubs catering to all tastes, from ballet to science, chess to football, and drama to gymnastics. In addition, children may attend our own holiday club, known as Club Pelican, which runs for 7 weeks of the year: five weeks in the summer holidays and one week in each of the Christmas and Lent holidays.

Moving on. By the end of Year 2, children are ready to move onto the Prep with confidence and enthusiasm. Their move is gradual and carefully managed.

Fees per term (2018–2019). Full-time (Reception, Years 1 and 2) £4,510, Part-time Nursery (six sessions per week) £2,924. Additional Nursery sessions: £40 per session. Nursery children attend a minimum of six sessions per week (two of which must be afternoons) but may attend up to 10 sessions per week.

Charitable status. The Perse School is a charitable company limited by guarantee (company number 5977683, registered charity number 1120654) registered in England and Wales whose registered office is situated at The Perse School, Hills Road, Cambridge CB2 8QF.

The Perse Preparatory School

Trumpington Road, Cambridge CB2 8EX

Tel: 01223 403920
email: prep@perse.co.uk
website: www.perse.co.uk

Chairman of Governors: Sir David J Wright, GCMG, LVO, MA

Head: **James Piper**, BA Hons, PGCE, MEd

Age Range. 7–11.
Number of Pupils. 284.
Ethos. At the Prep we are committed to helping your child develop as a confident, smiling, interesting and interested individual. Our School has a strong academic edge, attracting an outstanding group of specialist staff who encourage in the children academic curiosity and a love of learning. Prep children thrive on challenges outside the classroom with great emphasis placed on developing breadth and balance through first-rate sport, clubs, music, art, drama and outdoor pursuits. Excellent pastoral care is at the heart of our work and ensures that our children feel completely at ease and secure in their surroundings.

Admissions. The main entry point to the Prep is Year 3 (7+) with about 25 places available. Admissions to Years 4, 5 and 6 is dependent on availability of places with about 3 places available in each year. Entrance tests assess the applicant's abilities in English, Maths and reasoning, and a reference from the child's current school is also sought. Selection for all year groups takes place in mid-January of the year of intended entry.

Facilities. The Prep is set in spacious mature parkland on Trumpington Road. Traditional and modern buildings are successfully combined on site, from the Victorian Leighton House to the 'New School' classroom block, and the Science block which opened in 2017. The Prep has nine acres of playing fields on its doorstep, including a full-size Astro-Turf.

Educational success. The Prep is an academically selective school with pupils of above average ability who relish challenge. Most pupils progress to the Upper School in Year 7. Pupils follow a broad curriculum which promotes intellectual curiosity and a love of learning, and we nurture creativity through a vibrant programme of drama, music and art.

The depth of academic ability throughout the School allows intellectual curiosity to flourish and pupils thrive on challenges both inside and outside the classroom. Enjoyment of learning, mutual respect and the celebration of achievement characterise life at the Prep and as a result children become independent, confident and responsible.

A supportive environment. Pastoral care is first class: Form Teachers, Heads of Year and the Assistant Head (Pastoral) all support pupils, who have access to a medical room, with a qualified nurse, and to our counselling service.

A rounded education. We make good use of technology, based on our philosophy that it should be effective, meaningful and engaging. Resources include a dedicated ICT suite, a music technology room and bookable laptops and iPads. All classrooms are equipped with SMART boards and PCs. Staff can access the school Wi-Fi (with age appropriate filtering) and we use SharePoint as our Virtual Learning Environment.

We encourage every pupil to make the most of our extra-curricular provision. There is a wide range of lunchtime and after school clubs – more than 70 currently. Music is strong with over 30 different ensembles (including numerous choirs and an orchestra comprising of a quarter of the School). Sport is a major part of a Prep education, and all children compete, whether in House Matches or against other schools. The games programme (football, rugby, cricket, netball, athletics, tennis and hockey) is designed to encourage all pupils to enjoy games and physical exercise. Music plays an important part in the curriculum and wider life of the School. The majority of pupils learn a musical instrument and there are choirs, orchestras and numerous instrumental groups, where there are many opportunities for the children to perform publicly.

Moving on. The School plans carefully for a smooth transition to the Upper School. Year 5 and 6 pupils spend days on the Upper site as part of their subject learning, helping to prepare them for the move up.

Fees per term (2018–2019). £5,235.

Bursaries. Means-tested bursaries are available for families of limited means, ranging from 5% to 100% of annual tuition fees.

Charitable status. The Perse School is a charitable company limited by guarantee (company number 5977683, registered charity number 1120654) registered in England and Wales whose registered office is situated at The Perse School, Hills Road, Cambridge CB2 8QF.

The Pilgrims' School

The Close, Winchester, Hampshire SO23 9LT

Tel: 01962 854189
Fax: 01962 843610
email: admissions@pilgrims-school.co.uk
          info@pilgrims-school.co.uk
website: www.thepilgrims-school.co.uk
Twitter: @PilgrimsSchool
Facebook: @PilgrimsSchool

Chairman of Governors: The Very Revd Catherine Ogle, Dean of Winchester

Headmaster: **Mr Tom Burden**, MA Oxon

Age Range. Boys 4–13.
Number of Pupils. 260 Boys (90 boarders/weekly boarders, 114 day boys, 56 boys in Pre-Prep).
Fees per term (2018–2019). Boarders £8,110, Day boys £6,050–£6,415, Pre-Prep £3,685.

Preparing boys for a broad portfolio of independent schools, with a significant number moving to Winchester College each year. Cathedral Choristers and Winchester College Quiristers are educated at the school and receive scholarships and bursaries up to the value of the full boarding fee together with free tuition in one musical instrument. All boys whether musical or not receive excellent academic and musical tuition, and the sporting tradition is equally strong. The school is noted for its happy family atmosphere, with a major focus on each boy finding his passion and talents, whether they be academic, sporting or artistic. Boarding is a popular option, either full or weekly. All enquiries about the school or singing auditions should be addressed to the Registrar.

Charitable status. The Pilgrims' School is a Registered Charity, number 1091579.

Pinewood

Bourton, Shrivenham, Wiltshire SN6 8HZ

Tel: 01793 782205
email: office@pinewoodschool.co.uk
website: www.pinewoodschool.co.uk
Twitter: @pinewoodprepsch

Headmaster: **Philip Hoyland**, BEd Exeter

Deputy Head: Colin Acheson-Gray, BEd

Age Range. 3–13.
Number of Pupils. 400 Boys and Girls (104 regular boarders, 28 weekly boarders) of which Nursery and Pre-Prep: 105.
Fees per term (2018–2019). Day £3,100–£5,965 inclusive, with no compulsory extras. Weekly Boarding supplement: £1,455.

Pinewood is set in 84 acres of rolling countryside. The School offers a quality, family-based environment where children are encouraged to think for themselves and a strong emphasis is placed on self-discipline, manners, trust and selflessness. Resources include a purpose-built Music School and Science Labs, a flourishing Pre-Prep and Nursery, Art and Design Workshops, Research and Reference Library, ICT Rooms, Astroturf and a state-of-the-art Sports Hall. Fortnightly exeats. Regular or weekly boarding from Year 5 upwards.

Excellent academic results are achieved through a mixture of traditional and forward-thinking teaching within a happy, friendly and stimulating learning atmosphere. Outside trips are frequent and visiting speakers prominent. Great success in Music, Art and Drama.

Sport is keenly coached and matches are played at all levels on our picturesque playing fields, which incorporate a nine-hole golf course. There is a wide range of activities and clubs both for day children and, in the evening, for boarders.

Pinewood is a school where staff, parents and children work together to find and realise the potential in every child.

Exit Schools: Marlborough, Cheltenham College, Bradfield, Radley, St Edward's Oxford, Cheltenham Ladies, Sherborne, Sherborne Girls, Rendcomb, Wellington College, St Mary's Calne, Dean Close, Monkton Combe, Tudor Hall.

Charitable status. Pinewood is a Registered Charity, number 309642. It exists to provide high quality education for boys and girls.

Plymouth College Preparatory School

99 Craigie Drive, The Millfields, Plymouth, Devon PL1 3JL

Tel: 01752 201352
email: prepschool@plymouthcollege.com
           jlearmouth@plymouthcollege.com
website: www.plymouthcollege.com
Twitter: @PlymouthCollege
Facebook: @PlymouthCollege

Chairman of Governors: D R Woodgate, BSc, MBA

Headmaster: C D M Gatherer, BA Keele

Age Range. 3–11 Co-educational.
Number of Pupils. 200.
Fees per term (2018–2019). Infant Department: Kindergarten £2,560, Reception £2,665, Years 1 & 2 £3,150. Junior Department: Years 3–4 £3,380, Years 5–6 £3,535.

Plymouth College Preparatory School is a co-educational school for children from 3–11 years. The school was founded in 1877 and is within a few minutes' drive of Plymouth College senior school.

The primary academic aim of the school is to prepare children for entry to Plymouth College at the age of 11, ensuring that they are articulate and have taken full advantage of an education designed to stimulate the development of each child both intellectually and socially.

There are sixteen full-time and six part-time members of staff, including specialist teachers in Mathematics, English, Science, Information Technology, Design Technology, Geography, History, Art, Music and French. There is a wide range of extracurricular activities.

There are two libraries, a computer room, a well-equipped laboratory, art room, theatre, music room and a sports centre.

Further information and application forms can be obtained from the Registrar, direct on 01752 831911, and appointments to view the school are welcomed.

Charitable status. Plymouth College is a Registered Charity, number 1105544. It exists to help children fulfil their wish to achieve a higher standard of education.

Pocklington Prep School

West Green, Pocklington, York, East Yorkshire YO42 2NH

Tel: +44 (0)1759 321228
Fax: +44 (0)1759 306366
email: enquiry@pocklingtonprepschool.com
website: www.pocklingtonschool.com
Twitter: @PockPrep
Facebook: @PocklingtonSchool
LinkedIn: /pocklington-school

Chairman of Governors: Mr T A Stephenson, MA, FCA

Head of Pocklington Prep School: Mr I D Wright, BSc Hons, PGCE, NPQH

Age Range. 3–11 co-educational.
Number of Pupils. 220.
Fees per term (2018–2019). Day Pupils £2,604–£4,085; Full Boarders £7,682 (Year 3 Junior Boarder £6,734); 5-day Boarders £7,131 (Year 3 5-day Boarder £6,122).

Pocklington Prep School is the Prep School of the Pocklington School Foundation, a supportive and caring community that has been thriving in the heart of rural Yorkshire for 500 years. The school shares a 50-acre rural site on the edge of the market town of Pocklington with Pocklington School. This gives even the youngest pupils access to specialist teaching facilities for sports (astroturf pitches), music and the arts (purpose-built theatre) and plenty of space to play. Classes at Pocklington Prep School are intentionally small, ensuring good individual support.

Good road and bus services from York and Hull are supplemented by the school's own minibus services. Full, weekly and flexible boarding options are available. Junior boarders live in modern single-sex houses. Boarders have a dedicated programme of weekend and after-school activities in addition to the normal school calendar.

Our aim is to ensure that every child who leaves our school is '*Inspired for Life*'. We aim to give our pupils the care and encouragement they need to flourish into confident boys and girls who are inspired for lifelong learning so that when our pupils move on to their senior schools they are well prepared for the challenges ahead.

The formal curriculum reflects the new Primary School Review with the emphasis on creativity and enjoyment. Pocklington Prep School offers a secure and happy environment in which pupils are actively encouraged to express their natural talents and curiosity while developing their confidence in the core skills of reading, writing and numeracy to meet the challenges ahead.

A child's journey through the Prep School begins from the age of three years, when children are first able to access our Pre-School provision, which offers flexible full and half day sessions and provides the perfect opportunity for us to help children become 'school ready' through personalised learning in a nurturing environment.

Children in the Pre-Prep (Pre-School to Year 2) are taught through a thematic approach by a team of dedicated and caring staff. Each term children explore all areas of the curriculum through a different topic which is planned to appeal to children's interests and evoke questions and a desire to learn. Each topic is brought to life with educational visits to exciting locations and a themed learning environment, where a mixture of adult-led and child-initiated activities stimulate children's thirst for learning. Children in the Early Years Foundation Stage (Pre-School and Reception) are provided with vibrant learning experiences, which fulfil the requirements of the EYFS Framework and are paced to meet the needs of each individual child. In a structured educational environment, children learn through play, whilst being overseen and supported by experienced staff who offer guidance with a smile.

Transition into Prep is smooth as this themed approach to learning continues throughout Years 3 and 4, with a gradual increase in the number of discrete lessons taught.

From Year 5 the curriculum focuses on core subjects including English, maths and science but history, geography, art and design technology, music, ICT, religious studies and Modern Foreign Languages also play a prominent part, together with swimming, PE and Games. Initially, forms are balanced in ability, with teachers taking care to ensure that individual children can progress at a pace according to need. From Year 5 onwards pupils are taught in ability groups in maths and English.

A wide range of sporting, cultural and other activities supports the curriculum. Pupils visit an outdoor education centre in the Yorkshire Dales, take part in fieldwork and leadership/team challenges and make full use of the excellent attractions in the area.

Games played include rugby, hockey, football, netball, cricket, tennis and rounders – with clubs and teams in athletics, swimming and trampoline also. PE and swimming form part of the weekly timetable for all pupils.

House competitions include music, art, drama, chess, creative writing, general knowledge and sport.

Extra activities take place at lunchtimes and after school and include art, computing, choir, drama, chess, orchestra, trampoline, language clubs, swimming and team coaching.

Pocklington Prep School has a strong musical tradition with a successful choir and orchestra. Individual music tuition takes place throughout the age range. Full use is made of the Tom Stoppard Theatre to perform in concerts, plays, sketches and musicals – some jointly with the senior school.

Entry Requirements: Entry to the Pre-Prep at 4+ is by informal interview and assessment. All pupils internal and external are assessed at 7+ to ensure that they are progressing in line with their peer group. Nearly all pupils go on to Pocklington School at the end of Year 6 (age 11+). Progress is automatic for Prep School applicants provided there are no concerns about a child's behaviour or ability, which have previously been communicated to parents prior to the date of the entrance assessment. New entrants are required to sit the Pocklington School 11+ Entrance Examination.

Charitable status. The Pocklington School Foundation is a Registered Charity, number 529834.

Port Regis

Motcombe Park, Shaftesbury, Dorset SP7 9QA

Tel:	01747 857800
Fax:	01747 857810
email:	admissions@portregis.com
website:	www.portregis.com
Twitter:	@PortRegisSchool
Facebook:	@PortRegis

Chairman of the Governors: Mr Oliver Hawkins

Headmaster: **Mr Stephen Ilett**, MA Oxon, PGCE

Age Range. 2–13.
Number of Pupils. Boarders: 141 (Boys 94, Girls 47); Day Boarders: 164 (Boys 109, Girls 55).

Fees per term (2018–2019). Boarders £8,950; Day £2,990–£6,450. Weekly and Occasional Boarding options are available.

Port Regis is a co-educational day and boarding school for children aged 2–13. Located in the beautiful Dorset countryside, the school provides the perfect environment in which boys and girls can flourish and enjoy school.

Port Regis is located in 150 acres of parkland in the stunning Dorset countryside and enjoys a beautiful campus with facilities that are second to none in the Prep school world. Extensive woodland with nature trails sits alongside lawns, several ponds and a lake, so that the children can enjoy the space and freedom of the grounds. There are also 35 acres of games pitches, a nine-hole (18 tees) golf course, hockey pitch, hard tennis and netball courts, a 25m indoor swimming pool, a rifle range and an indoor sports complex, which includes two sports halls. An equestrian centre is conveniently situated close to the School.

The school's enviable reputation attracts the best teaching staff from all over the country. We are extremely fortunate to have an immensely accomplished team of staff dedicated to achieving this and who provide the happy, family atmosphere in which a child can realise their full potential.

Port Regis is extremely proud of its 100% Common Entrance success record and the high number of scholarships and awards won to senior schools every year. Learning Support is available for children with mild-to-moderate specific learning difficulties.

Extensive opportunities are provided for Music (about three-quarters of the School learn an instrument), Drama (there are up to six productions a year), and Art (in a wide choice of media), with Woodwork, Electronics, Riding, .22 Rifle Shooting, Karate, Gymnastics and Canoeing included in a list of over 70 hobby options. Major team games are Rugby, Hockey, Soccer, Netball, Cricket and Rounders. Inter-school, county and national standard competitions are entered. Home and abroad trips take place.

The high standard of boarding provision is an impressively strong feature of the school, which explains why so many boys and girls choose to board (awarded 'Outstanding' by Ofsted following their recent boarding inspection). The school was inspected by the Independent Schools Inspectorate (ISI) in June 2014 and was rated 'Excellent' in every single judgement.

Open Mornings take place each term and include tours of the school with pupils. Personal visits are also available.

Academic, Music, Gymnastic, Sport and All-Rounder entrance scholarships may be awarded annually. The School also has a wealth of experience in dealing with HM Services Families and offers special awards to children of HM Services Families.

Charitable status. Port Regis School Limited is a Registered Charity, number 306218.

The Portsmouth Grammar Junior School

High Street, Portsmouth, Hampshire PO1 2LN

Tel:	023 9236 4219
Fax:	023 9236 4263
email:	juniorschool@pgs.org.uk
website:	www.pgs.org.uk
Twitter:	@PGS_Junior
Facebook:	@PGJS1732

Chairman of the Governors: Mr W J B Cha, BA

Head of the Junior School: **Mr P S Hopkinson**, BA, PGCE

Deputy Head: Mr J Ashcroft, BSc, PGCE
Head of Nursery: Mrs K Moore, BA, QTS

Age Range. 4–11. Nursery: 2½–4.
Number of Day Pupils. 227 boys, 179 girls.
Fees per term (2018–2019). Reception, Years 1 and 2: £3,411; Years 3 and 4: £3,597; Years 5 and 6: £3,784. (Fees quoted include direct debit discount.)

The Junior School is an integral part of The Portsmouth Grammar School under the general direction of the Governors and Head. Children from 4–9 years are educated within bright and spacious classrooms that occupy a discreet space on the whole school site. The 9–11 year old pupils are educated in the historic original school building which stands in in close proximity to the main school site.

The Junior School's organisation is distinct under its own Head, with 29 full-time, 18 part-time members of staff, and 18 teaching assistants.

The main three-form entry is at 4+ with an additional Form added at Year 5 to maintain class sizes of 20 and under. Pupils leave at 11 years, the majority moving on to The Portsmouth Grammar Senior School.

Whilst emphasis is placed on the core subjects of English, Maths and Science there is a bespoke and creative curriculum which includes; Geography, History, Religious Studies, ICT, Modern Foreign Languages, the Performing Arts, Design Technology, Philosophy, Physical Education, Games and PSHE. In addition, many pupils receive tuition in a wide range of musical instruments. There are specialist rooms for Art, DT, Music and Drama, plus a Science Laboratory and two Information Technology Centres.

A strong pastoral system and curriculum ensures all pupils are cared for and feel happy and settled in the school environment. The Junior School Learning Tree promotes key values and thinking skills to support the personal development of every child.

The school also provides a wide choice of co-curricular activities to enrich the pupil's learning. Currently over 30 different club activities are offered. An innovative string scheme enables all Year 3 pupils to experience a free term's tuition in learning the violin or cello and a brass scheme offers a similar opportunity in Year 4. Residentials are organised for children in Years 2 to 6 and there is also a ski trip and a sports tour for upper juniors.

Games include Rugby, Football, Netball, Hockey, Rounders, Cricket, Athletics, Tennis and Swimming. The Junior School has its own learner swimming pool and uses the Grammar School's excellent 16-acre playing fields at Hilsea, which include a floodlit Astroturf pitch.

It also has access to the Grammar School's Sports Hall, Music School and Theatre.

The Nursery offers up to 70 places in any one session. The architect designed building provides the children, aged from two years six months, with exciting opportunities to learn through play and exploration. All staff have early years specialism, the Head of Nursery being a fully qualified primary teacher with Early Years expertise. The Nursery School offers provision for 45 weeks a year.

Charitable status. The Portsmouth Grammar School is a Registered Charity, number 1063732. It exists to provide education for boys and girls.

Pownall Hall

Carrwood Road, Wilmslow, Cheshire SK9 5DW
Tel: 01625 523141
email: headmaster@pownallhallschool.co.uk
website: www.pownallhallschool.co.uk
Twitter: @PownallHallSchool
Facebook: @Pownall-Hall-School

Chair of Governors: Mrs Eileen MacAulay

Head: **Mr D Goulbourn**, BA Hons, PGCE Distinction

Age Range. 2–11 Co-educational.
Number of Boys and Girls. 250 (Day Children)
Fees per term (2018–2019). £2,825–£3,325.

Pownall Hall, a preparatory day school for children aged 2 to 11 and set in its own beautiful and extensive grounds, has been established for over 100 years. It is situated on the north-western side of Wilmslow, 12 miles from Manchester and within easy reach of motorway, rail and air travel.

The school has highly-trained teaching staff, who prepare children for the Entrance Examinations to the Independent Day schools in the area. A thorough grounding is given in all academic subjects extending well beyond the confines of the National Curriculum. An excellent mixture of traditional and modern techniques is used through the implementation of cutting-edge technology in and around every classroom. In Key Stage 2 each major subject has specialist teaching staff and subject rooms including a fully-equipped Science Laboratory, Art Studio, D&T Studio, Maths, English, Information Technology, and MFL rooms and, in addition, a computer-aided Library. Mandarin, French and German are taught from the age of two.

Pownall Hall School has two pre-school years with children entering the Nursery from the age of 2 and transferring to Kindergarten at the age of 3. From here the pupils then enter Reception and go through the school to Year 6 by which point the school will have guided parents as to where best for their child to continue their education at the age of 11.

At Pownall Hall there is an excellent staff to pupil ratio throughout the school, ensuring that pastoral care is of a very high level and also supporting the learning of children of all abilities, in conjunction with a specialist SEND provision. Children are taught in small class sizes, gaining from the individual attention they receive.

Great importance is attached to Sport, Music and Drama in order to develop the rounded education that allows all children to achieve, wherever their ability lies. The school has its own well-equipped theatre where all children perform on stage during the year. Music is offered as part of the curriculum and also additionally through a full range of peripatetic teaching staff, providing chances for the children to perform in and outside school. As well as subject specialist rooms with an outstanding range of specialist equipment, the implementation of mobile technology for both staff and children provides opportunity for outstanding teaching and learning across the school.

The facilities for sport are very impressive with the school having its own extensive grounds, alongside a fully-equipped Sports Hall, Astro Pitch and both outdoor and indoor facilities for Netball, Hockey, Football, Rugby, Tennis and so much more.

All children experience outdoor learning, with Forest School, Extra-Curricular clubs, day and residential trips arranged as well as utilising our on-site woods for free-flow teaching and learning at all ages. Children in Years 3 to 6 also experience outdoor pursuits at a range of well-equipped sites which enhance their learning experiences. There is an extensive provision of co-curricular clubs, complementing our out-of-hours Breakfast Club and After School Care. Holiday Club runs on site throughout the year.

The school received an outstanding Full Inspection Report in 2017 and an outstanding EYFS Inspection in 2014.

Charitable status. Pownall Hall School is a Registered Charity, number 525929. It exists to provide education for boys and girls, aged 2–11 yrs.

The Prebendal School

52–55 West Street, Chichester, West Sussex PO19 1RT

Tel: 01243 772220
email: office@prebendalschool.org.uk
website: www.prebendalschool.org.uk

Chairman of Governors: The Very Reverend Stephen Waine, Dean of Chichester Cathedral

Head: **Mrs Louise Salmond Smith**, BA East Anglia, MMus Hull, PGCE Gloucestershire, MBA Keele

Deputy Head Academic: Mr T Bromfield, MA, BEd
Deputy Head Pastoral: Mr I Richardson, BMus, MMus, FTCL, ARCO
Bursar: Mr M Chapman, MA, MBA
Chaplain: Reverend Dr I Smale BA, MA, PhD

Age Range. 3–13.
Number of Pupils. 144 pupils in total (including 16 full boarders and 3 weekly boarders): 110 in the Prep School (Years 3–8) and 34 in the Pre-Prep (Nursery-Year 2).
Fees per term (2018–2019). Full Boarders £7,430. Day Pupils: Years 5–8 £5,165; Years 3–4 £4,790. Weekly Boarding: £1,535 in addition to Day Fee. Pre-Prep £2,720–£3,155. Nursery: £8.15 per hour. Compulsory extras: laundry and linen for Full Boarders.

The Prebendal is the oldest school in Sussex and has occupied its present building at the west end of the Cathedral (though with later additions) for hundreds of years. The Cathedral Choristers are among the pupils educated at the school and they receive Choral Scholarships in reduction of fees. Music and Academic Scholarships are open to boys and girls entering the school. Sibling Bursaries are awarded as well as Scholarships for children entering Year 7. Forces families can also apply for fee remission awards. Year 8 Leavers achieve an impressive range of Scholarship awards to a range of prestigious senior schools every September.

There are excellent playing fields in the heart of the city. The sports are football, hockey, netball, cricket, girls' cricket, athletics, tennis, rugby and rounders. Younger children enjoy Beach School and the school unveiled a new outdoor classroom and amphitheatre in September 2018. The Pre-Senior Baccalaureate has been introduced along with Quadrivium, a programme of academic excellence for children in Years 6–8. Pupils in Year 8 use iPads as an additional tool to enrich their learning.

Approximately 95% of the children learn to play musical instruments and the school has a large range of ensembles and choirs along with Concert Band and 1st Orchestra. There are many optional extras and after-school clubs, such as Forest School and Sailing. Flexi boarding is a popular choice and there is a growing demand for the extended day programme, from Breakfast Club to supper, for busy families.

Former pupils, parents and staff are known as The Prebendal Associates and events are held regularly throughout each academic year. The School also has its own Toddler Group on Wednesday morning during term time. The Head of The Prebendal School, Mrs Louise Salmond Smith, took up the post in September 2017.

Charitable status. The Prebendal School is a Registered Charity, number 1157782. Registered Company No. 09038149.

Prestfelde

London Road, Shrewsbury, Shropshire SY2 6NZ

Tel: 01743 245400
email: office@prestfelde.co.uk
website: www.prestfelde.co.uk
Twitter: @prestfelde
Facebook: @prestfelde
LinkedIn: /Prestfelde

Shrewsbury's Co-educational Prep School for all aged 3–13.

Chairman of Governors: Mr Stuart Hay, MB ChB, FRCS, FRCS Orth

Head: **Mrs F Orchard**, GTCL Trinity College, PGCE Reading

Age Range. 3–13.
Number of Pupils. 306 (195 boys, 112 girls).
Fees per term (2018–2019). Flexi Boarding: £32 per night, Day: Year 8 £5,380, Years 6–7 £5,340, Year 5 £5,275, Year 4 £5,075, Year 3 £4,335, Year 2 £3,320, Year 1 £3,240, Reception £3,190, Nursery £1,700 (5 mornings).

Supported by the nurturing environment that Prestfelde provides, children and their parents benefit from first-class facilities and a highly progressive and inclusive education. We pride ourselves on providing the best school experience a child can have, one that enriches their happiness in school, enables them to pursue their individual interests and develop confidence to grow into the person they want to be. Our excellent teachers build trusting relationships and impart their knowledge through inspirational teaching and learning experiences. Guiding and transforming pupils through a broad range of experiential learning, children at Prestfelde gain the skills, qualities and knowledge to set them up to succeed. The site extends over 30 acres and backs onto countryside with top-class playing fields which form an integral part of the excellent sporting facilities.

Academic highlights are underlined by the level of success and quality of scholarships gained by pupils in the final year group. In 2018, Year 8 pupils achieved 85% A–C pass rates at Common Entrance and were 100% successful in gaining places to their first-choice senior schools. Each year pupils gain scholarships to a number of aspirational independent schools, covering every section of the curriculum from art, design, technology and drama to music and sport. Equally pupils choosing to progress to maintained schools are very well prepared for the next stage of their education, having been encouraged to adopt a positive work ethic.

Whilst many pupils maintain high levels of competitive sport in their disciplines, we recognise the importance of children enjoying the challenges of team sport at school. Outstanding coaching and mentoring in football, netball, rugby, lacrosse and cricket have encouraged pupils to become outstanding team players. Additional hours of coaching in these and other sports, together with physical education lessons, swimming (on site) and outdoor fitness by specialist coaches, enhance the physical well-being of Prestfelde pupils, resulting in the enjoyment of competition in a variety of sporting environments.

The extra-curricular offering at Prestfelde is designed to build on children's experiences with the aim of improving outcomes in all areas of their learning. Purposefully building on pupils' interests, we aim to light that spark for learning and developing talents. Activities range from bushcraft and outdoor gardening to construction and minecraft. Pupils enjoy the many and varied inter-house competitions and the friendly rivalry enhances the will to achieve.

Charitable status. Prestfelde School is a Registered Charity, number 1102931. It aims to provide education for boys and girls.

Prince's Mead School

Worthy Park House, Kings Worthy, Winchester, Hampshire SO21 1AN

Tel: 01962 888000
email: info@princesmeadschool.org.uk
website: www.princesmeadschool.org.uk

Chairman of Governors: Mr B Welch

Headmaster: **Mr Peter Thacker**, BA Hons, PGCE, FRGS

Age Range. 4–11 co-educational.
Number of Children. 246 Day Boys and Girls.
Fees per term (2018–2019). £3,480–£5,315.

Established in 1949, Prince's Mead is a Day Preparatory School on the outskirts of Winchester. The school follows an innovative curriculum that prepares young people for what lies ahead in an every changing world. Children are encouraged to acquire sound working habits, an enthusiasm and hunger for knowledge and a desire to achieve their full potential. The pleasures and responsibilities of school life are an integral part of development and we encourage collaboration, independence and leadership qualities. Extensive playing fields and a strong sporting ethos encourage children to participate in competitive sport. The Performing Arts Department is also significant in developing the skills of all our children. The school is alive to the children's needs both now and in the future. Our Mission Statement, 'Preparing the Children of Today for the Opportunities of Tomorrow' is at the core of all we do within the school and beyond.

Girls are prepared for 11+ Common Entrance and Scholarships to a wide variety of Independent Schools. Boys are prepared for entry to local Independent Day and Boarding schools at age eleven. Each academic year, our Year 6 pupils are offered places in many different senior schools. In 2017 a record 38% of pupils received scholarships and awards to their chosen senior schools. Our children also enter the excellent Secondary Schools in the Winchester area.

The curriculum is innovative with such subjects as Team Building, Debating and Philosophy sitting alongside the more traditional areas of study. An extensive range of extra-curricular activities enhance and enrich development.

Bursaries (financial assistance) are available from Year 3 upwards.

Charitable status. Prince's Mead School is a Registered Charity, number 288675. It exists to provide education for boys and girls.

Prospect House School

75 Putney Hill, London SW15 3NT

Tel: 020 8780 0456
email: info@prospecths.org.uk
website: www.prospecths.org.uk
Twitter: @prospecths

Managing Governor: Mr J A Rentoul

Head: **Mr Michael Hodge**, BPrimEd Rhodes QTS

Age Range. 3–11 co-educational.
Number of Pupils. 320 day pupils.
Fees per term (2018–2019). Nursery (5 mornings) £2,950, Reception–Year 2 £5,900, Years 3–6 £6,150.

Prospect House School occupies two large buildings on Putney Hill situated just a short walk apart. Children aged 3 to 7 years occupy the Lower School building at 76 Putney Hill and children aged 7 to 11 years are based in the Upper School at 75 Putney Hill. They both have large grounds, including an all-weather sports pitch. There are multi-purpose halls where assemblies, music recitals, gymnastics and drama productions take place. There are dedicated rooms for music, ICT and special needs with art and DT also having provision within the school.

Most children join the school at 3 or 4 years of age, although occasionally there are places for older children. Selection for entry at 3 is by date of registration, with preference being given to brothers and sisters of children already in the school. An equal balance of boys and girls is kept throughout the school. There is also a good balance of male and female staff.

Although the school does not have selective entry at age 3 or 4, the academic track record is very strong. The curriculum includes all National Curriculum subjects, with the addition of French from the age of three. There are numerous specialist teachers and children from Nursery are taught by specialists for music, PE, French, ICT and dance. Children are prepared for a wide range of leading day and boarding schools for entry at 11 years of age, with some children taking academic, music and sports scholarships. There is a wide and varied sports programme with many fixtures against other preparatory schools and children from Year 3 upwards attend training sessions at a nearby sports ground under the guidance of qualified teachers.

The school was awarded 'Best Primary School' in the UK in 2009–10 for the teaching and use of ICT.

Clubs after school cater for many interests and visiting teachers also provide a wide range of individual music lessons. Children are taken on educational visits to London and the surrounding area every term, with residential field study trips being undertaken in the final three years.

Quainton Hall School

Hindes Road, Harrow, Middlesex HA1 1RX

Tel: 020 8861 8861
email: admin@quaintonhall.org.uk
website: www.quaintonhall.org.uk
Twitter: @QuaintonHall

Chairman of Governors: The Reverend V Baron, BSc, MA

Headmaster: **Mr Simon Ford**, BEd Hons

Age Range. Boys and Girls 2½–13.

Number of Pupils. 235.

Fees per term (2018–2019). £3,500–£4,320.

Established in central Harrow at the end of the nineteenth century, Quainton Hall is an IAPS Preparatory School for children between the ages of two and a half and thirteen. We have our own Nursery for girls and boys from two and a half to four, our Pre-Prep for girls and boys from four to seven and our Middle and Senior School for girls and boys from seven to thirteen. The children continue on to take 13+ entrance examinations and transfer at the end of Year 8 to a range of senior schools, mostly in North and North West London, though some go further afield and into boarding, where desired. To assist them in doing this, they undertake the Common Entrance (CE) curriculum, starting in Year 6. A number of pupils choose to leave at 11+, moving on to both independent and grammar schools. The majority of the girls leave at 11+ and transfer to North West London schools.

Quainton Hall provides a broad and balanced education, within a secure and caring environment and with a definite Christian ethos. Our children are valued as individuals and their learning experiences are stimulating. We recognise that children need to feel safe and secure in order to be motivated to learn. However, our curriculum is designed to do much more than prepare children for the next stage in their education; we teach skills and foster attitudes and values which will be of lasting benefit throughout their lives. We provide an extensive extra-curricular programme of activities, visits to places of interest and we invite speakers and theatre groups into school during the course of the school year.

Creativity, communication, teamwork, determination and a sense of the value and dignity of others are just some of the attributes we prize at Quainton Hall and where children grow to develop an understanding of the wider world, of those in need and have opportunities to raise funds for a range of charitable causes.

The life and work of the school is planned to enable children to shine in those areas and activities that they are good at and to reach their full potential. All members of staff have this objective as their aim. We also encourage the notion that learning is fun and that the acquisition of knowledge brings its own rewards. All that we do is conducted in an atmosphere and ethos that is personal, caring and family-orientated. We promote good order and self-discipline, consideration and tolerance towards others as well as personal motivation and group endeavour.

Charitable status. Quainton Hall School, under the Trusteeship of Walsingham College (Affiliated Schools) Limited, is a Registered Charity, number 312638. It exists to provide a sound education within a definite Christian framework.

Queen Elizabeth's Hospital (QEH) – Junior School

Berkeley Place, Clifton, Bristol BS8 1JX

Tel: 0117 930 3087
email: juniors@qehbristol.co.uk
website: www.qehbristol.co.uk

Chairman of Governors: D A Smart, BSc, FCA

Junior School Headmaster: **D M Kendall**, BA

Age Range. Boys 7–11.

Number of Pupils. 90 day boys.

Fees per term (2018–2019). £3,218. Fees include pre- and after-school supervision until 5.00 pm.

The QEH Junior School was opened in September 2007 and is located in gracious Georgian town houses in Upper Berkeley Place backing onto the Senior School, which means it can share its first-class facilities including science, drama, music and sport. The cultural facilities of the city, such as the city museum and art gallery, are also on its doorstep.

Pupils travel to the school from across the region and there is a hub for public transport on the nearby Clifton Triangle. The school also offers timed parking facilities for parents in the adjacent West End multi-storey car park, to pick up and drop off pupils, at no extra cost.

As part of the only boys' school in the city, QEH Juniors is unique in Bristol. Being small, it focuses on the individual, fostering a love of learning whilst nurturing the interests and talents of each boy. In addition there is a wealth of extra-curricular activities available.

The school is a happy place with strong pastoral care, academic excellence, and high standards where the educational experience is designed to be relevant and meaningful for every single child. Each boy leaves recognising himself as a lifelong learner.

Boys can therefore enter in Year 3 or Year 5 though places occasionally become available in other Years. Boys are expected to move into the Main School at 11. (*See QEH entry in HMC section.*)

Charitable status. Queen Elizabeth's Hospital is a Registered Charity, number 1104871, and a Company Limited by Guarantee, number 5164477.

Queen's College Junior School
Taunton

Trull Road, Taunton, Somerset TA1 4QS

Tel: 01823 278928
email: junioradmissions@queenscollege.org.uk
website: www.queenscollege.org.uk
Twitter: @QueensTaunton
Facebook: @queenstaunton

Chairman of Governors: Mr Mark Edwards

Headmistress: **Mrs Tracey Khodabandehloo**

Deputy Head: Mr Dick Wilde
Curriculum Director: Mrs Teri Underwood
Head of Pre-Prep: Miss Samantha Horner
Head of Nursery: Miss Elizabeth Hayes

Age Range. 0–11.

Number of Pupils. 175 with 18 children in the Junior boarding house.

Fees per term (2018–2019). £2,630–£4,330 (day); £4,885–£7,350 (boarders); £6,350–£8,890 (overseas boarders).

Queen's College is a co-educational boarding and day school on the outskirts of Taunton, Somerset, with fine views across the playing fields to the surrounding hills.

The Pre-Prep School educates pupils up to the age of 7 and the Junior School educates pupils up to the end of Key Stage 2 (NC Year 6). Children aged 11+ will usually be admitted directly to the Senior School (*see Queen's College entry in HMC section*).

The Junior School is run as an independent unit but shares many of the excellent facilities of the adjacent Senior School. Known especially for its outstanding pastoral care and real focus on individual children, there is no doubt that pupils here are extremely happy. Specialist subject teachers, high academic standards and a sense of fun are setting this school apart from its competitors and the outstanding Head-mistress whose excellent communication skills are admired universally means that parents are flocking towards this lovely, friendly school with its excellent facilities. Definitely on the up.

The House parents are kind, sympathetic and organise a wealth of activities for those away from home. Matrons read bedside stories and arrange fun weekend trips and with lots to do in the evenings the children are kept really busy and involved. Many children come from Armed Forces families and Queen's is well versed in settling pupils whose families have been posted abroad and keeping in contact. Emphasis is made on creating a family-style, homely atmosphere in which the pupils can relax and unwind. Lovely, bright bedrooms and living areas with lots of games.

For every pupil the aim of the School is to find areas in which each child can succeed and develop self-confidence to help them really shine. Using different learning styles, reinforcing classroom learning with external trips and visits and a practical approach means that the children here are really inspired and enjoy their school and make excellent friendships.

The principal games are rugby, hockey and cricket for the boys, with hockey, netball and rounders for the girls. Tennis, swimming and athletics matches also take place. Fullest use is made of the excellent sporting facilities of the School, particularly the Sports Hall, tennis courts, heated indoor swimming pool and floodlit Astroturf. The school has achieved national success in hockey, cross country, swimming, athletics and riding this year and all abilities are welcomed. A new hockey academy opened last year.

After-school activities include Board Games, Cookery, Chess, Computer Club, Drama, Gardening, Specialist Music Groups, Model Making, Photography, Puppets, and Fun Swim. Also arranged at an extra charge are Dancing, Speech and Drama, Climbing and Riding. Junior music is outstanding with many opportunities to play in groups and festivals and the performing arts is a real strength of the school with the Taunton Speech and Drama Festival run at Queen's.

Free before and after-school care is available every day until 5.45 pm and holiday clubs operate.

The Pre-Prep day school is in its own purpose-built building and there is a Nursery School and Highgrove Nursery for children aged 0–3 years. Nursery and Reception are rated as outstanding and it is not difficult to see why. Outdoor gardens and facilities are superb with plenty of room to run and climb and many different things are happening at once in the classrooms. Innovative teaching methods, getting the children involved as well as teaching the foundations in small class sizes with specialist teachers means that the children have tremendous attention and support and really do achieve their potential.

Nearly all the children move on from one section of Queen's College to the next; there is no further qualifying examination.

Charitable status. Queen's College is a member of the Methodist Independent Schools Trust, which is a Registered Charity, number 1142794, and a Company, number 7649422.

Radnor House Sevenoaks – Prep School

Combe Bank Drive, Sundridge, Kent TN14 6AE
Tel: 01959 564320
Fax: 01959 560456
email: enquiries@radnor-sevenoaks.org
website: www.radnor-sevenoaks.org

Twitter: @radnorsevenoaks
Facebook: @radnorsevenoaks

Chairman of Board of Directors: Mr Colin Diggory, BSc Hons, PGCE, MA, EdD, CMath, FIMA, FRSA

Head: Mr David Paton, BComm Hons, PGCE, MA

Head of Prep School: Mrs Beth Cordrey, BSc Hons, PGCE

Age Range. 3–11 Co-educational.
Number of Pupils. 230.
Fees per term (2018–2019). Preparatory School £3,620–£4,590 (Lunch £245). Nursery: £65 (full day), £35 (half day).

Radnor House Sevenoaks School was founded in 1924. The Prep School is a flourishing independent school that stands in 28 acres of gardens and grounds, on the Kent/Surrey borders within easy reach of the centre of Sevenoaks. (*See also Radnor House Sevenoaks School entry in ISA section.*)

The Prep School is housed in an original stable block and affords a unique environment in which the children feel secure and comfortable. Specialist teaching rooms include those dedicated to ICT, French, Music, PE, Speech and Drama. The Hall includes a permanent stage with sound and lighting systems. The older pupils have access to a purpose-built Performing Arts Studio and the senior school's Science and Technology Centre. The ICT suite, networked to all classrooms, allows full class access at any time.

EYFS Nursery classes are housed within the courtyard area, which has recently undergone refurbishment to provide first-class facilities for both indoor and outdoor activities, including a specially designed Secret Garden.

Beech Walk with its secure adventure play area gives the children greater freedom at break times. There are two playing fields and five outdoor tennis and netball courts. A purpose-built Sports Hall allows for the teaching of multi-sport activities and inter-school fixtures. All pupils, including the Nursery, use the indoor heated swimming pool weekly throughout the year.

Academic standards are high. All pupils at Radnor House Sevenoaks gain automatic entry to the senior school and sixth form without re-assessments.

Drama and Music flourish in the school. Pupils have many opportunities to perform throughout their time in the Prep, from large drama productions to musical ensembles. The majority study at least one musical instrument from Year 3.

A highly dedicated staff team takes care of the academic, physical, pastoral and extracurricular needs of the pupils. We are committed to academic excellence for all our pupils. We work together to raise the self-esteem of each child. We pay particular attention to the development of thinking skills and positively encourage independent learning. We actively promote the development of a strong home-school partnership through parent consultations, information evenings and social events. We also recognise the importance of Music, Speech, Drama, Art and Sport in the life of the developing child. The school is distinguished by the high standard of pastoral care it offers. We nurture every individual.

Radnor House Sevenoaks is committed to safeguarding and promoting the welfare of children. We achieved an 'outstanding' rating across all areas of the school at our ISI inspection in 2015.

Ravenscourt Park Preparatory School

16 Ravenscourt Avenue, London W6 0SL
Tel: 020 8846 9153
email: secretary@rpps.co.uk
website: www.rpps.co.uk

Chairman of Governors: Mr Kevin Darlington

Headmaster: **Mr Carl Howes**, MA, PGCE

Deputy Head: Mr Simon Gould, BA Hons QTS
Deputy Head (*Teaching and Learning*): Miss Charlotte Ashworth, BA Hons, PGCE

The full staff list is available on the school website.

Age Range. 4–11 co-educational.
Number of Pupils. 417 boys and girls.
Fees per term (2018–2019). £5,857.

This non-selective school provides education of the highest quality for boys and girls, preparing them for transfer to the best independent schools at 11 years of age. The Lower School caters for pupils aged 4–7 and the Upper School for 7–11 years. All pupils are housed in one of the three main buildings that make up the RPPS site. The addition of the Gardener Building is home to a theatre, a state-of-the-art science laboratory and an art studio. The secure site includes a large play area, a newly refurbished outdoor learning area for Early Years and the school makes use of the extensive facilities of Ravenscourt Park which it adjoins.

The curriculum includes French, humanities, music, art and craft, RE and PE for all pupils in addition to the usual core subjects. In the Upper School the majority of subjects are taught by specialists. All Upper School pupils attend a Residential Week where studies across the curriculum are applied to a non-urban environment.

There are many after-school clubs and sports activities, as well as three choirs and two orchestras. Individual tuition is offered in piano, harp, violin, brass, woodwind, cello, saxophone, clarinet, flute, percussion and singing. The drama productions and concerts are a highlight of each school year.

A Day Care service, before and after school, is offered to parents at an extra charge.

The school is noted for its warm, happy atmosphere where parents play a full part in enriching the curriculum and social life. Off-site visits and guest workshops presented by noted visitors are a regular feature of education at RPPS.

The school is very popular in the local area and registration is strongly recommended on the child's first birthday. A prospectus and registration form may be obtained from the school secretary. Open Mornings take place each month (dates are available on the school website).

The school was inspected by ISI in March 2016 and received 'excellent' in all the categories. The full inspection report is available on the school website.

Redcliffe School

47 Redcliffe Gardens, London SW10 9JH
Tel: 020 7352 9247
email: registrar@redcliffeschool.com
website: www.redcliffeschool.com
Twitter: @RedcliffeSchool
Facebook: @redcliffeschool

Chairman of the Board of Governors: Mr Roger Flynn

Headmistress: **Mrs Sarah Lemmon**, BA Hons, Mont Dip EYPS

Age Range. Boys 3–11, Girls 3–11.
Number of Pupils. 160 Day Pupils (65 boys, 95 girls)
Fees per term (2018–2019). £5,910. Nursery: £3,330 (morning class), £2,220 (afternoon class), £5,580 (full day).

Easily accessible from all parts of central and West London, Redcliffe is a small, friendly school with highly motivated, confident and happy children. Emphasis is placed on a combination of hard work, good manners and plenty of fun within a framework of traditional values of perseverance, courage and resilience. The balanced curriculum includes Maths, English, History, Geography, Science, IT, Art, Religious Education, Current Affairs, Music, Physical Education and Drama. French and Spanish are taught throughout the school. Individual attention encourages the pursuit of high academic standards and we are proud that our children gain places at their first choice of senior or prep school, including Colet Court, Sussex House, St Philip's, Downe House, Benenden, St Mary's Ascot, Queen's Gate, Godolphin & Latymer, City of London, JAGS and Francis Holland. Every class has at least two hours of specialist-taught Physical Education each week including tag rugby, netball, rounders, cricket, athletics and swimming. After-school activities include cookery, gymnastics, ballet, computer skills and drama. Music is a strength of the school with visiting instrumental staff and a high standard of performance. Parents are encouraged to be involved with the school through Open Assemblies, Parents' discussion groups and workshops, the Parents' Committee and regular meetings with the teachers.

Redcliffe Robins is our nursery class for children rising 3 and has access to all of Redcliffe's resources and facilities to help prepare the children for entry to the main school. Each day has a balanced timetable of phonics, mathematical skills, art and craft, music, drama and PE with ample opportunity for structured free play and the development of social skills.

Children are assessed at three years of age for entry to the main school at four. Entry for subsequent years is by assessment. Tours of the school are held weekly during term time by appointment with the school office. Open Days take place in the autumn and summer terms.

Charitable status. Redcliffe School Trust Ltd is a Registered Charity, number 312716. It exists to provide a high standard of education for children within a caring environment.

Reddiford School

38 Cecil Park, Pinner, Middlesex HA5 5HH
Tel: 020 8866 0660
Fax: 020 8866 4847
email: office@reddiford.org.uk
website: www.reddiford.co.uk

Chairman of Governors: Mr G Jukes OBE

Head: **Mrs J Batt**, CertEd, NPQH

Age Range. 2 years 9 months to 11.
Number of Pupils. Prep: 94 Boys, 60 Girls; Pre-Prep: 41 Boys, 35 Girls; Early Years: 42 Boys, 38 Girls.

Fees per term (2018–2019). Nursery: £1,620 (mornings only), £2,871 (all day), Foundation £3,450, Reception £3,740, Pre-Prep £3,755, Prep £3,855.

Reddiford School has been established in Cecil Park, Pinner since 1913. Whilst the school maintains its Church of England status, children from all faiths and cultures are welcomed. Throughout the school the ethos is on respect for one another. Reddiford prides itself on being a town school based in the heart of Pinner; a few minutes' walk from local transport facilities.

Reddiford possesses a fine academic record, preparing its pupils for entrance at 11+ into major independent schools, many at scholarship level. There is a high teacher to pupil ratio ensuring small classes leading to a friendly caring environment where all children are valued.

The Early Years Department is situated in its own building and caters for children from 2 years nine months to rising 5 years. It offers a stimulating and attractive environment where children are encouraged to be independent and active learners. The Early Years Department follows the Early Years Foundation Stage Curriculum. There is a choice of full or half day provision.

The Pre-Prep Department builds on the knowledge and skills acquired in the Early Years placing the emphasis on developing confidence and the ability to learn and work independently and with others. The Pre-Prep Department has its own computer suite and interactive whiteboards in classrooms. There is specialist teaching in French, Music and PE from reception upwards and all children are taught to swim.

In the Prep Department children are taught by specialist teachers in properly resourced subject rooms. There is a fully-equipped science laboratory, dedicated art and music rooms and an ICT suite. Pupils are prepared for entry to the many prestigious senior schools in the area, a process which involves consultation with parents from an early stage.

There is an extensive programme of extra-curricular activities throughout the school including: sports (football, cricket, netball, gymnastics), languages (French, Latin, Mandarin), art and science. We also offer before and after school care, with a prep club for older children.

Assessments for Reception upwards require the child to be in school for the day. They complete English and Mathematics assessments and their ability to cope with the educational and social demands for the year group are evaluated.

Charitable status. Reddiford School is a Registered Charity, number 312641. It exists to provide education for boys and girls.

Redmaids' High Junior School

Grange Court Road, Westbury-on-Trym, Bristol BS9 4DP

Tel: 0117 962 9451
Fax: 0117 989 8286
email: junioradmissions@redmaidshigh.co.uk
website: www.redmaidshigh.co.uk
Twitter: @RedmaidsHigh
Facebook: @redmaidshighschool

Chairman of Governors: Mr Andrew Hillman

Headteacher: Mrs Lisa Brown, BSc Hons Leicester, PGCE Oxford Brookes

Headteacher's PA/Admissions: Mrs Lynn McCabe

Age Range. 7–11.

Number of Girls. 150 Day Girls.

Fees per term (2018–2019). £3,270 plus lunch.

At Redmaids' High Junior School, girls receive an outstanding educational experience. Our mission is for your daughter to wake up every morning eager to be at school. Small class sizes and a family atmosphere make that a reality.

We set the bar high academically, stretching our pupils to ensure they become the best they can be. Each week, time is given to all subjects in our broad curriculum. Alongside the core areas, the foundation subjects and creative arts are just as valued. Sport is integral to our timetable, instilling positive attitudes towards physical activity, and bringing teamwork and specific skills leading to success in competitive fixtures.

Our single-sex setting means no dilution of attention to the needs of the girls as young women. They are offered all the opportunities, hold all the responsibilities, and enjoy everything in their path without any self-consciousness or stereotypical judgement.

Extra-curricular activities are an essential part of the Redmaids' High experience. Girls learn resilience and determination through trying new things. Whether it is playing chess, football or hockey, taking part in a concert or book group, joining art or fencing clubs, caving on the Mendips or sailing in Bristol docks, they enjoy busy, active and purposeful days.

We value diversity and embrace internationalism; we are forward thinking in our teaching, preparing our pupils for an ever-changing technological future filled with careers that have not even been dreamed of yet.

The House system enables girls to work and make friends with children in all year groups. There is a happy and relaxed atmosphere within the school, with easy access for parents to speak to teachers, a regular discussion group with the headteacher and many social events bringing families, staff and pupils together.

Assessment of pupil progress is built into every subject area. We moved away from SAT testing some years ago, preferring Durham University's INCAS test for monitoring performance and progression, and individual target setting.

Pastoral care is one of our major strengths. New pupils are supported by a buddy system and through school meetings and class activities, pupils learn about good citizenship, taking responsibility for themselves, for each other and for the care of their community and their environment.

Close links are fostered between the Junior and Senior schools. Pupils benefit from use of a science laboratory, extensive PE facilities including an all-weather pitch, shared dining facilities and award-winning catering. At age 11, transition occurs to the Senior School (conditions apply) having sat the entrance examination and competed for academic, sport and music scholarships alongside those joining from other schools. (*See Redmaids' High School entry in GSA section.*)

The School occupies a spacious site nestled in a quiet residential neighbourhood. We have a mix of well-maintained traditional and purpose-built buildings including a library, music room, art studio and lofty assembly hall, plus a large garden for outdoor play complete with sports and climbing equipment.

Admission: The main points of entry to the Junior School are in Years 3 and 5, with assessments beginning each year in November. Potential Year 3 pupils are assessed in pairs, with girls spending half the day in class and half working alongside the headteacher. Year 5 and 6 taster days are conducted in groups. Interested families are encouraged to visit the school individually or at one of our collective events.

Charitable status. Redmaids' High School is a Registered Charity, number 1105017.

Reigate St Mary's Preparatory and Choir School

Chart Lane, Reigate, Surrey RH2 7RN

Tel:	01737 244880
email:	office@reigatestmarys.org
website:	www.reigatestmarys.org
Twitter:	@rsmprepschool
Facebook:	@ReigateStMarys

Chairman of Governors: Mr James Dean

Headmaster: **Marcus Culverwell**, MA Ed

Age Range. 3–11.
Number of Pupils. 346 (181 boys 165 girls).
Fees per term (2018–2019). Green Shoots £1,110 (3 mornings min), Kindergarten £1,850 (5 mornings), Reception to Year 2 £4,000, Years 3–6 £4,950.

Reigate St Mary's is an independent day school for boys and girls aged 3–11. It is the nursery and junior school of Reigate Grammar School (RGS). Set in 15 acres of beautiful parkland and sports fields, the older children also benefit from the facilities of Reigate Grammar School including the swimming pool and a further 32 acres of sports grounds.

An education of considerable depth and breadth is provided within a disciplined, happy and caring environment. All pupils are encouraged to be ambitious, to reach the best standards they can in their academic studies, in sport, in art, in music and in other performing arts.

A love of learning, a zest for life and development of a caring and understanding attitude towards other people are central to the ethos of the school. High value is placed on good relationships and developing inter-personal skills to enable our pupils to become responsible, adaptable, independent people in a changing world. With an emphasis on growth mind-sets, integration of IT into the curriculum, opportunities for public speaking and debate, plus the chance to really engage in socially responsible activities, pupils are truly being prepared for the real and rapidly changing world. They are valued for who they are, not just for what they achieve.

Children who are on track for a successful secondary school career at Reigate Grammar do not have to sit the 11+ examination. Instead, they benefit from an early offer entrance arrangement in Year 5.

The school was rated 'Excellent' in all areas following an ISI Inspection in January 2016 which reported that "Pupils throughout the school are well educated, in accordance with its aims of achieving excellent standards in all areas of pupils' studies. They have high levels of knowledge, skill and understanding across all areas of learning" – "Pupils appreciate the strong Christian ethos that pervades the school, whilst also celebrating and learning to respect those of different faiths, in line with wider British values. Pupils' moral awareness is outstanding".

As a member of the Choir Schools' Association, Reigate St Mary's has a traditional choir of boys and girls under the direction of a Head of Choral Music. Choral scholarships are offered by the RGS Godfrey Searle Choir Trust.

RGS Springfield

Britannia Square, Worcester WR1 3DL

Tel:	01905 24999
email:	springfield@rgsw.org.uk
website:	www.rgsw.org.uk
Twitter:	@RGSSpringfield
Facebook:	@RGS-Springfield

Chairman of Governors: Mr Quentin Poole

Headmistress: **Mrs L Brown**, BA Hons, PGCE

Age Range. 2–11 Co-educational.
Number of Pupils. 145.
Fees per term (2018–2019). £2,720–£4,182 including lunch and wrap-around care.

Introduction from the Headmistress. "I am delighted to have this opportunity to welcome you to RGS Springfield, with its wonderful family atmosphere and nurturing co-educational environment, which together creates a uniquely friendly school.

Our aim is to ensure that children develop their full potential academically, socially and emotionally in a safe, caring environment.

All our pupils benefit from individual care, small class sizes, professional and dedicated teaching; all of which help children become confident, secure and considerate of the needs of others.

The school has scored highly in recent inspections, rated as consistently outstanding by Ofsted and ECERS and excellent in all areas by ISI inspectors (March 2015 and is fully compliant March 2018). There are a wealth of academic and extra-curricular opportunities to provide children with an enriching and stimulating environment, preparing them for the challenges of the 21st century, underpinned by traditional family values. The new digital learning programme adds a new dimension to classroom learning.

The school has wonderful grounds, which allow pupils to play outside in all weathers, learn from the natural environment and take part in all the fun that Forest School offers; wellies are very much encouraged!

The school, tucked away within the beautiful Georgian Britannia Square in the heart of Worcester, will provide a safe and happy place for your child to grow and develop. This website conveys only some of the ethos and spirit of RGS Springfield. Please visit us and see for yourself the happy, smiling faces of children having fun and learning in a stimulating environment. We are very much a happy family.

I look forward to welcoming you in person to our school."

Overview. RGS Springfield is the co-educational junior school for RGS Worcester (*see HMC entry*). The school educates children between the ages of 2 and 11 and is situated within a large, beautiful Georgian Town House and gardens in the centre of Worcester.

High academic standards are expected as the children prepared to enter RGS Worcester at 11. There is a wide range of extra-curricular activities on offer and, while the school is noted for academic, creative and sporting excellence, it is of the greatest importance that the children are encouraged to be kind, considerate and well-mannered.

In 2009 an extensive refurbishment was undertaken to restore and develop the original historic site, Springfield, providing excellent modern facilities including art, design technology, science and ICT rooms alongside large, airy and warm well-equipped classrooms.

The school is set in three acres of maintained grounds and offers fantastic games facilities and outdoor space, including an extended Forest School, Walled Garden and Paddock Play Area.

Charitable status. The Royal Grammar School Worcester is a Registered Charity, number 1120644.

RGS The Grange

Grange Lane, Claines, Worcester WR3 7RR

Tel: 01905 451205
email: grange@rgsw.org.uk
website: www.rgsw.org.uk
Twitter: @rgsthegrange
Facebook: @RGS-The-Grange

Chairman of Governors: Mr Quentin Poole

Headmaster: G W Hughes, BEd Hons

Age Range. 2–11 Co-educational.
Number of Pupils. 350.
Fees per term (2018–2019). £2,720–£4,182 including lunch.

Introduction from the Headmaster. "Welcome to a nurturing school with a big personality.

Giving a child the best possible foundations for a bright future is a true privilege. Our fantastic facilities give pupils tremendous scope for achieving the academic, sporting and creative excellence that we encourage. Just as important is the safe, secure and caring framework that we provide, giving children the support and self-belief they need to make their own individual strides forward.

I get huge satisfaction from seeing each one cross barriers and shine in a way that is uniquely theirs and with two children myself, I know the pride parents feel when they see their child thriving.

I look forward to helping your child thrive too."

Overview. RGS The Grange is one of two co-educational junior schools for RGS Worcester (*see HMC entry*). The school educates children between the ages of 2 and 11 and is situated in open countryside three miles north of Worcester in Claines.

High academic standards are expected as the children are prepared to enter RGS Worcester at 11. There is a wide range of extra-curricular activities on offer and, while the school is noted for academic, creative and sporting excellence, it is of the greatest importance that the children are encouraged to be kind, considerate and well-mannered.

The school has scored highly in recent inspections, being acknowledged as 'outstanding' and 'excellent' in all areas by ISI inspectors (March 2015). The Digital Learning Programme adds a new dimension to classroom learning across all three RGS schools and RGS The Grange is a leading school of excellence for computer science.

RGS The Grange provides excellent modern facilities including specialist art, design technology, science, food technology, French and Computing & IT rooms alongside large, airy, well-equipped classrooms.

The school is set in 50 acres of grounds and offers exceptional games facilities and outdoor space, including a full-sized floodlit Astroturf, cricket pavilion, Forest School, traverse wall and adventure play area.

Charitable status. The Royal Grammar School Worcester is a Registered Charity, number 1120644.

The Richard Pate School

Southern Road, Leckhampton, Cheltenham, Glos GL53 9RP

Tel: 01242 522086
email: hm@richardpate.co.uk
website: www.richardpate.co.uk

Chairman of Trustees: Mr John Parker

Headmaster: **Mr R A MacDonald**, MEd, BA

Deputy Heads:
Mrs S Wade
P Lowe

Age Range. 3–11 Co-educational.
Number of Pupils. 300 (approximately an equal number of boys and girls).
Fees per term (2018–2019). Nursery: £1,160 (5 mornings), £1,542 (any 3 full days), £2,056 (any 4 full days), £2,570 (5 full days). Preparatory: £2,610 (Reception), £2,775 (Year 1), £2,950 (Year 2). Junior: £3,145 (Year 3), £3,285 (Year 4), £3,495 (Year 5), £3,650 (Year 6).

Hot lunches are provided and included in the fees, except for 'mornings only' nursery.

The School, occupying an 11½ acre semi-rural site at the foot of the Cotswold escarpment, is part of the Pate's Grammar School Foundation which is a charity founded by Richard Pate, a Recorder of Gloucester, in 1574.

It is a non-denominational Christian school which in its present form began in 1946. The aim of the school is to provide a high academic standard and continuity of education up to the age of 11 years. The curriculum is broadly based with strong emphasis being attached to music, art, drama and sport, for these activities are seen as vital if a child's full potential is to be realised.

Facilities include a music centre with individual practice rooms; a fully equipped computer suite; an all-weather astroturf with floodlights and a woodland area with enclosed pond for environmental studies. There is also a specialist wing with science labs, language suite and art studio. After-school care is available through until 5.30 pm.

At present the School is divided into three sections: Nursery 3–4 years; Preparatory Department 4–7 and Junior 7–11. Entrance is dependent upon the availability of places but most pupils join the school at the commencement of the Nursery, Preparatory or Junior Departments.

No entry tests are taken by younger pupils but interviews and selective tests are used for assessing pupils aged 6 years and upwards. A small number of 7+ scholarships are awarded each year.

The teaching takes full account of national curriculum guidelines with children in the upper part of the school following the normal preparatory school curriculum leading to Common Entrance and Scholarship at 11+. Pupils leave at age 11 for local Grammar Schools and a variety of independent secondary schools, particularly those in Cheltenham.

The Headmaster is assisted by two deputies and 18 fully qualified teachers including specialists in Latin, French, Art/Design, Science, Music and Learning Support. The School employs music and dance teachers, who prepare children for participation in various competitions, in particular the Cheltenham Festival.

Charitable status. The Pate's Grammar School Foundation is a Registered Charity, number 311707.

Richmond House School

170 Otley Road, Leeds, West Yorkshire LS16 5LG

Tel:	0113 2752670
email:	enquiries@rhschool.org
website:	www.rhschool.org
Twitter:	@RHSchoolLeeds
Facebook:	@RHSchoolLeeds
LinkedIn:	/richmond-house-school

Chair of the Board of Governors: Mrs G Galdins

Headteacher: **Mrs Helen Stiles**

Age Range. 3–11.

Number of Day Pupils. 227 boys and girls.

Fees per term (2018–2019). Nursery: £1,950 (half days only), £3,050 (full time, including lunch), Reception to Year 6 £3,050, Lunches £220.

Richmond House School is an independent co-educational preparatory school providing an excellent standard of education for children aged 3 to 11 years within a happy, stimulating, family environment.

At Richmond House School, a team of dedicated staff is committed to giving each child the opportunity to develop into confident, hard-working and successful individuals.

All pupils are given the chance to learn and achieve across a broad range of activities and subject areas and the talents of each child are nurtured. The breadth of activities offered aims to challenge pupils, build self-confidence and lead pupils to discover new interests and skills.

The School boasts outstanding 11+ exam success with pupils having their choice of senior school and a substantial number being awarded scholarships.

In addition to strong academic credentials, Richmond House School is committed to providing all pupils with the opportunity to excel in other areas. The School is situated in 10 acres of land, providing excellent sports facilities and offering pupils a wide range of sports to choose from. The School also provides specialist teaching in Music, Art, Design Technology, ICT, Languages, Outdoor Learning and Science.

Pastoral Care is an important aspect of school life at Richmond House School. Our Assistant Head is responsible for leading Pastoral Care and works closely with staff, pupils and parents to ensure the well-being and progress of all pupils.

Excellent Pre and After School Care and an easily accessible car park and drop-off zone are available for busy families.

Charitable status. Richmond House School is a Registered Charity, number 505630. It exists to provide high quality education for boys and girls aged 3–11 years.

Riddlesworth Hall Preparatory School

Hall Lane, Nr Diss, Norfolk IP22 2TA

Tel:	01953 681246
Fax:	01953 688124
email:	hmsec@riddlesworth-hall.com
website:	www.riddlesworthhall.com

Acting Head: **Mrs Sally Judd**, BSc, PGCE

Age Range. Girls 2–13, Boys 2–13. Girls Boarding from age 7–13. Boys boarding from age 7–13.

Number of Pupils. 17 Boarders, 72 Day, 17 Nursery.

Fees per term (2018–2019). Full Boarders – price on request; Weekly Boarders £5,841.20; Day (inc Lunch): Years 3–8 £2,206.20; Years 1–2 £1,606.20; Nursery & Reception: £142.50 per am/pm session, lunch £181, £1,606.20 full-time inc lunch.

Riddlesworth Hall, situated in a magnificent country house on the Norfolk/Suffolk border, provides an excellent all-round education. The aim is to develop each child's potential to the full in all areas – academic, sport and creative arts.

Riddlesworth Hall has excellent art and pottery studios, science, domestic science and technology laboratories, a computer room, music and drama rooms and a refurbished gymnasium. French and Mandarin are taught from Reception. A range of sports is taught to all levels and regular fixtures are played against other schools.

The care of the children is in the hands of the Principal who is resident, supported by Houseparents and residential staff. International boarders frequently join the School to benefit from a truly British educational experience.

The School is non-selective but exerts academic rigour and expects a high academic standard of its pupils.

Extras include speech and drama, ballet and riding. There is a very active music department with choirs, orchestra, various ensembles and a recorder group.

There is a wide variety of clubs and activities including golf, dance, ball skills, gym and cookery.

Self-reliance, self-discipline and tolerance are encouraged, and good manners are expected. We value individuality and endeavour.

Ripley Court School

Rose Lane, Ripley, Surrey GU23 6NE

Tel:	01483 225217
Fax:	01483 223854
email:	head@ripleycourt.co.uk
website:	www.ripleycourt.co.uk
Twitter:	@RipleyCourtPrep
Facebook:	@ripleycourtschool1

Chairman of Governors: J Evans, BA

Headmaster: **A J Gough**, BSc UED Rhodes, BSc Hons, MA Open, MBPsS

Deputy Head: G P Ryan, HDE Cape Town

Age Range. 3–13 Co-educational.

Number of Pupils. Day: 261: Upper Court (Y5–Y8) 111; Middle Court (Y3–Y4) 61; Little Court (R–Y2) 74; Nursery (age 3+) 15.

Fees per term (2018–2019). Years 5–8 £4,720; Years 3–4 £4,530; Years 1–2 £3,470; Reception £3,250; Nursery/Transition £3,100 full-time or £1,550 part-time (min 5 sessions).

The main intakes are Nursery, Reception and there are a few places in Year 3. Children may enter at other times if there is space. They are prepared for 11+ pre-testing and for Common Entrance and Scholarship Examinations for a wide range of independent senior schools. There is a very high academic standard and many Scholarships are won for academic performance as well as for sport, music and art. Nevertheless there is also a studious avoidance of cramming – the children are allowed a childhood! In addition to the academic subjects, PE, Music, Art and Food Technology are a part of every child's timetable. Forest School sessions are also taught on site from Nursery to Year 4. There are opportunities for all in orchestral, choral and dramatic productions – the school prides itself on ensuring every child can participate in all areas, including in competitive sports fixtures.

Facilities include a library, science laboratories, a gymnasium, computer suite, art, music and food tech rooms. There are banks of iPads to support learning. There are 20 acres of playing fields, on which Football (Association and Rugby), Hockey, Netball, Cricket, Tennis (2 hard, 2 grass courts), Athletics and Rounders are played in season. Swimming and Life Saving are taught in a large, covered, heated swimming pool.

Little Court is the Pre-Prep Department which also uses all the facilities and much teaching expertise. The nursery, known as "The Ark", delivers specialist tuition in French, music, swimming and dance.

School transport serves Woking, Pyrford and West Byfleet.

Charitable status. Ripley Court School is a Registered Charitable Trust, number 312084. It aims to educate children and prepare them well for entry to their next school and for adult life. It offers scholarships as well as bursarial scholarships and bursaries on a means-tested basis. It is not-for-profit and all surplus funds are used to improve provision and facilities.

Roedean Moira House Junior School

Upper Carlisle Road, Eastbourne, East Sussex BN20 7TE

Tel: 01323 636800
email: admissions@roedeanmoirahouse.co.uk
website: www.roedeanmoirahouse.co.uk
Twitter: @moirahouse1875
Facebook: @moirahouse

Chairman of School Council: Mr Andrew Pianca, FCA

Principal: Mr Andrew Wood

Head of Junior School: **Mrs Cecy Kemp**

Age Range. Girls 0–11, Boys 0–4.
Number of Pupils. 115.
Fees per term (2018–2019). £3,115–£4,370 (Day Pupils); £7,305 (Weekly Boarders); £8,155 (Full Boarders).

Roedean Moira House is set within 15 acres of attractively landscaped grounds, on the outskirts of the historic town of Eastbourne on the South Coast of England, and recently joined the prestigious Roedean Group of Schools. Founded initially in 1875, Roedean Moira House welcomes girls from the age of six months to eleven in the Junior School and boys in the Nursery, with full, weekly or flexi boarding offered from the age of 9. The Junior School shares the site with the Senior School for girls aged eleven to eighteen. (*See entry in GSA section.*)

The Junior School aims to provide a broad and balanced curriculum and activity programme, ensuring equal access and opportunity so that children can celebrate and strive for excellence. We believe that children will learn if they feel happy and secure, and if their natural curiosity is aroused. They learn best when they are actively involved in the learning, with skilled teachers to guide them. As a school our aim is to provide an atmosphere and a richness of experience

within which each child's unique qualities can flourish. Our emphasis is on the importance of individual development, helping each child to realise her maximum potential. We aim, therefore, to set high standards for each child so that they are constantly challenged to develop further their skills and understanding.

Curriculum. The Foundation Stage and National Curriculum form the basis of what is taught but with the flexibility of specialist teachers and creative learning and teaching strategies. The curriculum aims to develop critical and creative thinking and self-discipline. Education at this stage is a foundation for the future and as broad as possible, combining the modern technology of interactive whiteboards and an ICT suite with all areas of the curriculum. Teaching is in small groups and is strong throughout. The girls enjoy mixed-ability classes but are grouped according to ability in Maths.

EAL, SEN, Sport, Drama, French, Swimming and Music are all taught or supported to an exceptional level by specialists. The Junior School has three choirs and all the children are involved in productions, concerts and creative arts presentations across the year. Most of the children take individual music lessons on a variety of instruments.

PE and Swimming form part of the curriculum and the girls have been particularly successful in competitive challenges. The girls enjoy the facilities of a 25m heated indoor swimming pool, a sports hall and extensive playing fields and netball and tennis courts.

The school has recently created a wonderful outdoor classroom / Junior playground facility which includes a stage, a mini-astro and climbing wall.

Extracurricular. The school offers daily care from 8.00 am until Afternoon Activity Club at 6.00 pm. There is a fleet of buses which can transport children to and from home each day.

A wealth of extracurricular activities enriches the experience of the pupils. The activity programme includes Dance, Short tennis, Trampolining, Gymnastics, ICT club, Environmental Studies club, Sewing club, String ensemble and a wide variety of sporting clubs.

Charitable status. Moira House Girls School is a Registered Charity, number 307072.

Rokeby School

George Road, Kingston upon Thames, Surrey KT2 7PB

Tel: 020 8942 2247
email: rokebyschool@rokeby.org.uk
website: www.rokebyschool.co.uk
Twitter: @RokebyPrep
Facebook: @rokebyprepschool

Maxim: *Smart, Skilful and Kind*

Chair of the Governors: Mrs Deirdre Davidson

Headmaster: **Mr J R Peck**

Age Range. 4–13.
Number of Boys. 370.
Fees per term (2018–2019). £4,637–£5,774 (including lunch and morning snack, books, day trips and some residential trips, personal accident and dental insurance and all compulsory extras).

Rokeby has an outstanding record of success in Common Entrance and Scholarships to leading Independent Senior Schools. Boys are accepted at 4+ to the Pre-Prep and at 7+ to the Prep School.

In recent years a fabulous two-storey, energy-efficient new building was opened by HRH Princess Alexandra. It has six spacious classrooms, a multi-purpose Performing Arts Hall, as well as other lovely spaces built to house Reception, Year 1 and Year 2 boys. The spacious and exciting playground area is enjoyed by all year groups and includes an outside classroom, an adventure playground with balance wall and an area for gardening club to grow seeds and encourage wildlife.

Science is taught in three well-equipped Laboratories. There is a large Computer Room and a spacious Art and Design Technology Centre. Football, Rugby, and Cricket are played while other sports include Swimming, Athletics, Hockey and Basketball. There are two large Halls and an Astroturf. A full activities programme is available for boys from Chess Club to Golf. The Music Department provides Orchestra, Ensembles and four Choirs and there are fourteen visiting peripatetic teachers, who work within a sound-proofed music block.

There are a number of educational school trips arranged as well as trips overseas, including France, Italy, Iceland and a number of overseas sports tours, including Sri Lanka, Canada and Holland. The school operates a bus service to the Wimbledon, Putney, Barnes and surrounding areas.

Charitable status. Rokeby Educational Trust Limited is a Registered Charity, number 312653. It exists to provide an excellent education for boys aged 4–13.

Rose Hill School

Coniston Avenue, Tunbridge Wells, Kent TN4 9SY
Tel: 01892 525591
Fax: 01892 533312
email: admissions@rosehillschool.co.uk
website: www.rosehillschool.co.uk
Twitter: @rosehillschool
Facebook: @RoseHillSchool

Chairman of Governing Body: Mr Charles Arthur

Head: Ms E Neville, BA Hons, MEd

Age Range. 3–13.
Number of Pupils. 146 Boys, 115 Girls.
Fees per term (2018–2019). £5,075 (Years 3–8); £3,775 (Reception–Year 2); £2,200–£2,635 (Kindergarten).

Rose Hill School is an inspiring place to learn: a warm, caring school with inspirational teachers, an enriching curriculum, first-class facilities and creative indoor and outdoor learning spaces.

A modern school rich with tradition, we offer a rare mix: academic excellence; sporting achievement; exceptional pastoral care and the freedom to explore the creative arts. Set in 18 acres of grass and woodland, the school has countryside on its doorstep and yet the town centre is just five minutes away.

With 260 pupils, everyone knows each other well. All the faces in the corridor are familiar and every teacher knows every pupil. This friendly and supportive family atmosphere means that children feel happy and secure and provides them with the confidence to embrace new challenges and opportunities with gusto.

A wide spectrum of co-curricular activities, including music, art, sport, drama and design, makes it possible for every child to fulfil his or her potential, whilst the school supports and nurtures their emotional and academic growth – helping them develop the leadership skills that will play a vital part in their future lives.

Expectations are high and pupils are encouraged to make the most of every day. Together, pupils, teachers and staff apply themselves with enormous energy to create a truly stimulating environment for learning.

Charitable status. Rose Hill School is a Registered Charity, number 270158. It aims to provide a high-quality education to boys and girls aged 3–13.

Rosemead Preparatory School and Nursery

70 Thurlow Park Road, West Dulwich, London SE21 8HZ
Tel: 020 8670 5865
email: admissions@rosemeadprepschool.org.uk
website: www.rosemeadprepschool.org.uk

Headmaster: **Mr Philip Soutar**, BA Ed Hons

Age Range. 2½–11.
Number of Pupils. Day: 160 Boys, 190 Girls.
Fees per term (2018–2019). £2,246–£4,230.

Rosemead is a well-established preparatory school with a fine record of academic achievement. Children are prepared for entrance to leading independent London day schools and local grammar schools at age 11, many gaining awards and scholarships. The school has a happy, family atmosphere with boys and girls enjoying a varied, balanced curriculum which includes Maths, English, Science, Spanish, Computing, Performing and Creative Arts, Physical Education and Humanities. Music and Drama are strong subjects with tuition available in most orchestral instruments and various music groups meeting frequently. A full programme of Physical Education includes gymnastics, most major games, dance and (from age 6) swimming. Classes make regular visits to places of interest and three residential study courses are arranged for the children in the Prep department. Main entry to the school is at Nursery (age 2½), following an informal assessment, and at National Curriculum Year 3, following a formal assessment. The school is administered by a Board of Governors elected annually by the parental body.

All religious denominations welcome.

A small number of bursaries are available from Year 3.

Charitable status. Rosemead Preparatory School (The Thurlow Educational Trust) is a Registered Charity, number 1186165. It exists to provide a high standard of education in a happy, caring environment.

Rowan Preparatory School
United Learning

6 Fitzalan Road, Claygate, Esher, Surrey KT10 0LX
Tel: 01372 462627
Fax: 01372 470782
email: school.office@rowanprepschool.co.uk
website: www.rowanprepschool.co.uk
Twitter: @Rowan_Prep
Facebook: @RowanPreparatorySchool
LinkedIn: /rowan-preparatory-school

Rowan is a dynamic, happy school, which prepares girls (aged 2–11) for the challenges they will face in life, helping them to develop compassion, respect and a lifelong love of learning. We value all our girls as individuals and attach great importance to the quality of teaching and learning that is at the very heart of our philosophy on education.

Chairman of the Local Governing Body: Mrs Jo Marr

Headmistress: **Mrs Susan Clarke**, BEd, NPQH

Age Range. 2–11 (Pre-Preparatory age 2–7, Preparatory age 7–11).

Number of Pupils. 330 Day Girls.

Fees per term (2018–2019). Nursery (5 mornings) £1,458; Kindergarten (5 mornings) £1,905; Reception–Year 6 £3,730–£4,950.

In 1936, Miss Katherine Millar was determined to breathe new life into the English educational system. She wished to create an environment which inspired a passion for learning. The doors of Rowan were opened wide to enable girls to develop a strong sense of self and establish lasting friendships. Three quarters of a century on, Katherine Millar's core values are firmly established in the school. Girls achieve personal excellence in a warm, family environment.

As our motto says 'Hic Feliciter Laboramus'. Here we work happily.

The school is located on two sites very close to each other in a leafy part of Claygate. Rowan Brae accommodates the Nursery and Pre-Prep and Rowan Hill, the Prep.

Upon entering the Brae you cannot fail to notice the warm, friendly and happy atmosphere. The stimulating learning environment, both indoors and outdoors, creates an inspiring and engaging place to learn. Outstanding lessons and excellent resources allow all pupils to thrive and reach their potential. Girls in Year 2 are fully prepared for the seamless transition and exciting challenges which lay ahead at the Hill.

Girls at the Hill develop a thirst for knowledge, an appreciation of all subject areas and a deeper understanding of how to analyse and apply information across different areas of learning and in everyday life. The varied creative and outdoor curriculum continues to stimulate and inspire in all subject areas of day-to-day learning. Dynamic and challenging lessons, adapted to suit the girls' needs ensure that they can truly achieve personal excellence. There is a superb ICT Suite, which is funded by the very supportive parents association, The Friends of Rowan, and well-equipped playgrounds and adventure walkways with a wooded area called The Spinney, which is held in great affection by the girls.

Admission in the Early Years is non-selective. Early registration is advisable if a place in the pre-prep is to be assured. Girls wishing to enter at other stages will be invited for a Taster Day where they will experience a day in the life of Rowan, involving assessments in maths and English.

Girls are prepared for entry to a wide variety of senior independent day and boarding schools. There is an excellent record of 100% of girls moving on to a first-choice senior school with 30 scholarships being offered this year for academic, music, sports or art.

Rowan offers a broad-based curriculum of work so that each pupil is able to develop her own talents and maximize her potential through an adventurous learning approach. The school welcomes visiting speakers and performers to enhance the curriculum. Day trips are also included in each term and the annual residential trips to Sayers Croft, The Isle of Wight, European ski resorts and France are both popular and highly educational in content. In addition, a wide variety of clubs are offered before and after school and at lunchtimes; they include drama, chess, art, science, foreign languages and a host of sports and musical activities. In addition, breakfast club and after-school prep clubs are available to support families.

Rowan has an outstanding Music Department with all girls singing in a choir and playing the recorder. In addition, three-quarters of girls at the Hill play a further instrument. There are various ensembles, which the girls can also join in preparation for the orchestra. Girls at Rowan Brae are invited to play the violin or 'cello as part of the school's String Initiative during Year 1, a fantastic opportunity to learn about music and performance.

The school has excellent sporting opportunities and achievements. Girls have the chance to represent the school both locally and nationally for sports such as swimming, gymnastics, tennis and biathlon. Games are developed throughout the school with girls taking part in their first matches from Year 2.

Rowan is very proud of its art, providing stunning displays around both the Brae and the Hill expressing the girls' individuality and excellent capabilities.

With small classes on both sites and strong pastoral care it is Rowan's aim to provide the essential early grounding in a happy, stimulating and secure environment where every child's needs are catered for.

Prospective parents are asked to make an appointment to view the school during a normal working day or to attend one of the Open Mornings held each term. Girls entering the school at 7+ will be invited to take part in an assessment day which takes place in January.

Assisted places are available and details may be obtained upon request from the school Registrar.

Charitable status. Rowan has a Local Governing Body that plays an active and supportive role in the school. Rowan is part of United Learning which is an educational trust controlled by a Board of Governors and chaired by Mr Richard Greenhalgh which comprises: UCST (a Company Limited by Guarantee, Registered in England, number 2780748, and a Registered Charity, number 1016538) and ULT (a Company Limited by Guarantee, Registered in England, number 4439859, and an Exempt Charity).

The Rowans School

19 Drax Avenue, Wimbledon, London SW20 0EG

Tel:	020 8946 8220
email:	office@rowans.org.uk
website:	www.rowans.org.uk

Chairman of Governors: Mr Darren Johns

Head: **Mrs J Hubbard**, MA, BA Hons, PGCE, PG Dip SEN

Age Range. 3–7 Co-educational.

Number of Pupils. 128.

Fees per term (2018–2019). Kindergarten £2,635, Reception, Year 1 and Year 2 £4,390.

The Rowans School was inspected by the Independent Schools Inspectorate (ISI) in October 2013 and was given a rating of "Excellent" in every area, the highest rating possible.

The School is one of the few independent co-educational schools in the area and is situated in a quiet road in Wimbledon, with beautiful grounds and large landscaped gardens, including its own sports court which has recently been upgraded with MatchPlay II multi-sport surface. We pride ourselves on providing a nurturing, welcoming and happy start to school life. We have a long-standing reputation for academic and all-round excellence and sport, music and the creative arts contribute strongly to the school's lively curriculum.

The focus of our curriculum is to build strong academic foundations, encouraging a love of learning and enabling our children to discover and develop their personal strengths and talents. We prepare children for the 7+ examinations to many of the London Day Schools and have a highly successful track record of sending pupils to the top local prep schools. Class sizes are typically 16–20 children, with at least one teaching assistant in every class. Music, French and Sport are taught by specialist teachers and children are offered the opportunity of learning violin, piano, recorder and taking part in our choir.

The school takes full advantage of its location with frequent outings for each year group to museums, theatres and the local community. The School has received a prestigious award from The British Council for its commitment to helping young people gain the cultural understanding and skills they need to play an active role in a global society.

The School is very much a family school, with a warm, friendly, child-centred atmosphere.

Charitable status. The Rowans School is owned by Shrewsbury House School Trust, which is a Registered Charity, number 277324.

The Royal Masonic School for Girls
Pre-School, Pre-Prep and Prep Departments

Rickmansworth Park, Rickmansworth, Herts WD3 4HF

Tel:	01923 725337 (Cadogan House Pre-Prep and Prep Department)
	01923 725316 (Ruspini House Pre-School)
Fax:	01923 725532
email:	prep@royalmasonic.herts.sch.uk
website:	www.rmsforgirls.org.uk

Chairman of Governors: Professor J Brewer

Head: Mr K Carson, MPhil Cantab, PGCE

Head of Cadogan House Pre-Prep & Prep Departments:
   Mr I Connors, BA Hons, NPQH

Head of Ruspini House Pre-School: Mrs V Greig

Age Range. Ruspini House: 2–4 Co-educational. Cadogan House: Girls 4–11.

Number of Pupils. Ruspini House 62; Cadogan House 235.

Fees per term (2018–2019). Cadogan House: Boarders (Years 3–6): £7,075 (Full), £6,705 (Weekly); Day Pupils: £3,825 (Reception, Years 1 and 2), £4,430 (Years 3–6). Ruspini House: please visit our website for range of fees.

Ruspini House is a small, friendly, caring community within the larger RMS family, guided by the same inclusive and nurturing ethos.

Housed in totally refurbished, modern and bespoke facilities and sharing our stunning grounds, Ruspini House welcomes boys and girls from 2 to 4 years. The youngest RMS pupils quickly settle into the stimulating, happy and supportive environment where all children are encouraged to reach their full potential through a healthy balance of learning and play.

We follow the principles of the Early Years Foundation Stage Curriculum and focus on each child's individual needs and talents. We encourage each child to develop at their own pace and they are well prepared for entry into their first school.

Recognised by the ISI as outstanding (2014), Ruspini House lays firm foundations for a love of learning. Boys and girls develop independence, curiosity and enthusiasm, learn good manners, courtesy and consideration for others within a busy and supportive framework, where they are challenged and have fun at the same time.

Cadogan House is the stunning, spacious and refurbished home of the RMS Pre-Preparatory and Preparatory Departments for girls aged 4 to 11 years. Recognised as excellent in all areas, Cadogan House is a warm and vibrant community alive with the buzz of happy, enthusiastic and motivated young learners, each of whom is valued as an individual.

The girls benefit from all of the facilities afforded by our magnificent site, including a designated Outdoor Learning Area. We have Forest School status, giving pupils experiences which complement traditional classroom learning, while building self-esteem, confidence and well-being.

The learning opportunities are exceptionally broad with outstanding teaching from both subject specialists and class teachers. Small class sizes ensure that teachers quickly get to know the girls and focus on nurturing their individual talents and strengths to enable them to become well-rounded independent young people. In Pre-Prep, English and Maths are taught each day as individual subject areas, whilst Science and Humanities are covered through cross-curricular work. In Years 3 to 6, girls study English, Mathematics, Science, Art, DT, French, Geography, History, Computing, Music, PE, PSHCE and Religious Studies, with several subjects taught by subject specialists.

Extra-curricular activities abound and sport and Performing Arts have a high profile; girls receive five PE lessons per week, including Swimming, Gymnastics and Dance, and all girls receive music and singing lessons each week, with most playing at least one musical instrument.

Above all, Cadogan House girls learn to exemplify the core RMS values of courtesy, compassion, and respect for others.

Charitable status. The Royal Masonic School Limited is a Registered Charity, number 276784.

Royal Russell Junior School

Coombe Lane, Croydon, Surrey CR9 5BX

Tel:	020 8651 5884
Fax:	020 8651 4169
email:	juniorschool@royalrussell.co.uk
website:	www.royalrussell.co.uk
Twitter:	@Royal_Russell
	@RRS_Sport
Facebook:	@RoyalRussellSchool
LinkedIn:	/royal-russell-school

Patron: Her Majesty The Queen

Chairman of Governors: Mr A Merriman

Headmaster: **Mr James C Thompson**, BA QTS St Mary's Twickenham

Deputy Head: Mrs Ruth Bannon
Deputy Head: Mrs Sarah Pain
Assistant Head: Mr Varun Footring

Age Range. 3–11.
Number of Pupils. 179 Boys, 147 Girls.

Fees per term (2018–2019). Upper Juniors: £4,555 (Years 3–4), £4,740 (Years 5–6); Lower Juniors: £3,720 (Reception–Year 2), Nursery £2,240–£3,720.

The Junior School stands on a magnificent campus extending to over 110 acres, which it shares with Royal Russell Senior School (11–18 years). (*See Royal Russell School entry in HMC section.*)

The school is well served by road, tram and rail links and is one of the few co-educational schools in the South London area.

There is a fully-qualified teaching staff of 35. The school has a broad curriculum which seeks to blend the highest standards of academic work with a wide range of co-curricular activities.

There are opportunities for all pupils to participate in football, netball, hockey, swimming, trampolining, gymnastics rounders, cross-country and cricket as team sports. There is an extensive fixture list of matches against other schools and Royal Russell regularly competes regionally and nationally, with significant success.

Artistic development extends to include full dramatic and musical productions, and many pupils learn musical instruments. All forms of art, design and technology are actively encouraged.

There are excellent teaching facilities with the latest interactive technology, which are complemented by Science Laboratories, Music School, Art Room, Computer Suite, School Chapel and a Performing Arts Centre with a 200-seat Auditorium. For sport, the impressive facilities include a large Sports Hall, Gymnasium, floodlit all-weather pitch for hockey and tennis, multi-use games area, netball courts, 4 grass pitches for athletics, football and cricket and an indoor swimming pool. There is also a Forest School and adventure playground.

The majority of the pupils join the school at 3 years into the Nursery, and transfer to the Senior School at 11+. Candidates for entry to the Lower Juniors and Early Years are assessed informally, while all other entrants sit assessments in English, Mathematics and Cognitive Ability appropriate to their ages.

Prospective parents are very welcome to come and meet the Headmaster and to tour the school, by appointment.

Charitable status. Royal Russell School is a Registered Charity, number 271907. It exists solely to provide education to girls and boys.

Rupert House School

90 Bell Street, Henley-on-Thames, Oxon RG9 2BN

Tel: 01491 574263
email: office@ruperthouse.oxon.sch.uk
website: www.ruperthouse.org
Twitter: @ruperthouse
Facebook: @RupertHouseSchool

Chair of Governors: Mr C Lowe

Head: **Mrs C Lynas**, MA Hons English St Andrews, PGCE, MA Child Development London, NPQH

Age Range. Girls and Boys 3–11.
Number of Pupils. 152.
Fees per term (2018–2019). From £1,927 for 3 year-olds (5 mornings) to £4,710.

Rupert House School is a leading independent pre-prep and prep school situated in the centre of Henley-on-Thames. Welcoming boys and girls from 3 to 11 years old, the school provides first-class education with a broad curriculum and a wide range of extra-curricular activities. Children benefit from small class sizes with a focus on the individual pathway, in a creative, nurturing environment.

The school has a reputation for traditional values, good manners and strong academic standards, with 100% of their Year 6 girls this year achieving a place at their first choice senior school. The strength and breadth of the curriculum is reflected in range of scholarships the girls attain, including Academic, Sport, Art, Music and Drama. This year the school's twelve Year 6 pupils won a very impressive fifteen scholarships between them as well as 2 prizes for Art and 1 award for Science from their senior schools. Of course, the progress made by all children is equally valued, with children moving forward with appropriate support in small classes to fulfil their potential, whatever their starting point.

A town school set in beautiful gardens, with playing fields and a Forest School to its name, Rupert House prides itself on its stimulating and varied curriculum, which includes Outdoor Education and many residential trips. Drama at the school is ambitious, with impressive productions at the Kenton Theatre, and Music is a joy and a strength. The sporting timetable allows for a good number of games lessons and their fixture list throws down the gauntlet to local prep schools with increasing success. Swimming happens year-round and other sports include Football, Rugby, Netball, Gymnastics, Tennis, Cross-Country and Hockey, Athletics, Cricket and Rounders.

The school's brand new all-weather pitch will be fully operational in September 2018. It will represent a significant expansion of sporting provision for all existing and prospective pupils, providing a top quality surface that can be used for hockey, netball, football, tag rugby and mini-tennis.

The school has successfully introduced the PSB (Prep School Baccalaureate), an assessment model that focuses on the development of the values, skills, attitudes and behaviours required for children to succeed and flourish in an ever-changing world. Children are encouraged, recognised and celebrated in their achievements and directly prepared for the next step of their educational journey.

Rupert House's two minibuses cover Henley and Marlow, complementing the school's wrap-around care for working parents. This includes Breakfast Club from 7.30–8.15 am and Homework Club/After-Care from 3.45–5.50 pm.

Bursaries are offered to children from Reception through to Year 6 and a range of scholarships is available for places in the Upper School (Year 3 and above).

Charitable status. Rupert House School is a Registered Charity, number 309648. It exists to provide quality education for boys and girls.

Russell House

Station Road, Otford, Sevenoaks, Kent TN14 5QU

Tel: 01959 522352
email: head@russellhouse.kent.sch.uk
website: www.russellhouseschool.co.uk
Twitter: @RussellHouseSch
Facebook: @RussellHouseSchool

Head: **Mr Craig McCarthy**

Age Range. Co-educational 2–11.
Number of Pupils. Approx 200.
Fees per term (2018–2019). Russell Robins (Under 3s) £760 (2 mornings), Nursery Department £2,020 (5 mornings), Transition £2,090 (5 mornings), Reception £3,610,

Years 1–2 £3,995, Year 3 £4,180, Year 4 £4,450, Years 5–6 £4,590. Fees are inclusive of lunch.

Russell House is a family-friendly school for girls and boys aged from 2 to 11.

We have a reputation for achieving excellent academic results in a warm, caring and inclusive atmosphere where every child has access to a myriad of opportunities for extra-curricular activities.

Many of our pupils are successful in the 11+ examination, gaining entry to the local grammar schools, and others pass on to independent schools such as Sevenoaks. We have a consistently good record in gaining scholarships, both academic and music which goes hand in hand with an ethos which encourages individuality, self-expression, curiosity to learn and the ability to challenge accepted wisdom.

The school is careful to cultivate a calm, happy atmosphere and there is also a strong emphasis on building skills for the future and developing a sensitive awareness of the world beyond the school.

Ryde School with Upper Chine Junior School

Queen's Road, Ryde, Isle of Wight PO33 3BE

Tel: 01983 612901
email: junior.office@rydeschool.net
website: www.rydeschool.org.uk
Twitter: @rydeschool
Facebook: @rydeschool2013

Chairman of the Board of Governors: Christoph Lees, MB BS, BSc, MD

Head: **Mrs Linda Dennis**, BEd

Age Range. 2½–11.

Fees per term (from January 2019). Tuition: Foundation Stage – please see School website; Pre-Prep £2,545–£3,520; Junior School £4,265. Boarding (excluding tuition): £5,310 (full), £4,260 (weekly). Rates for payment by Direct Debit. Lunch included.

Scholarships may be awarded on merit to external or internal candidates for entry at 9+. All scholarships may be supplemented by bursaries, which are means tested.

Ryde Junior School with Fiveways provides an ambitious, happy and supportive environment, one in which children thrive and develop a lifelong love of learning. They benefit from a varied and relevant programme of study supplemented by enriching extracurricular activities as we seek to prepare our pupils for an exciting future in an ever-changing world.

Ryde Junior School caters for children aged 2½–11 years. Fiveways, in its own separate building, is home to the Foundation Stage and Early Years. Through creative and imaginative teaching in new purpose-built classrooms, a sound foundation of key skills is established. They receive the support of a well-qualified and dedicated staff, enjoying a full range of specialist facilities including a continually upgraded IT facility, with Internet access across the school, a Creative Centre, Science Laboratory, Music room and Theatre.

A broad, balanced and rich curriculum is followed. Pupils have the unique opportunity to study and develop a love of languages from an early age. As the original host school for the Isle of Wight Literary Festival Schools programme, our children benefit from the thrill of visiting authors, poets and script writers. Pupils are encouraged to develop their full range of talents. In Music they are able to compose and perform. Many pupils undertake individual instrumental lessons. There are choirs, music groups and an orchestra. As well as the weekly classroom drama lessons, we enter children into LAMDA examinations and they take part in shows and festivals across the Island. Art and Design Technology are taught as discrete subjects and clubs, competitions and exhibitions also allow the children to develop their talents. Sports teams start at U8 level and we compete successfully against Island and mainland prep schools in netball, hockey, rugby, football, athletics (indoor and outdoor), cricket, rounders and cross country. Every child will be able to sail by the end of Year 6 and swimming and tennis also make up part of our extensive sports programme. Our new outdoor education programme and stunning new classroom provides an inspirational environment for the children to learn, grow and develop. There is a full and wide ranging programme of clubs and activities (which changes each term) during lunchtime and after school, offering something for everyone.

Our Senior School is on the same campus, enabling us to benefit from the use of a Sports Hall and pitches. Careful liaison between the staff and induction days in the summer term effect a smooth transition for our pupils to the Senior School (*see entry in HMC section*).

The Junior School takes weekly and full boarders who, together with Senior School boarders, have use of the range of facilities available at the Bembridge campus, situated in some 100 acres on a beautiful clifftop site approximately six miles from Ryde. Transport is provided to and from the school during the week.

Charitable status. Ryde School with Upper Chine is a Registered Charity, number 307409. The aims and objectives of the Charity are the education of boys and girls.

Rydes Hill Preparatory School

Rydes Hill House, Aldershot Road, Guildford, Surrey GU2 8BP

Tel: 01483 563160
email: admissions@rydeshill.com
website: www.rydeshill.com
Twitter: @rydeshillprep
Facebook: @RydesHill

Chairman of the Governors: Mr Dermot Gleeson, MA Cantab

Headmistress: **Mrs Sarah Norville**

Age Range. Girls 3–11, Boys 3–7. Nursery class for children 3–4.

Number of Day Pupils. 145

Fees per term (2018–2019). Reception to Year 6: £2,933–£4,461 including lunch.

Rydes Hill Preparatory School and Nursery has an exceptionally caring, family atmosphere. It has a thriving Nursery and is a Catholic School which welcomes children from all denominations and offers an excellent start academically and socially. Located in a beautiful Georgian house with a panelled Library, vaulted Dining Hall, Victorian Conservatory and galleried, panelled Entrance Hall, Rydes Hill offers beautiful surroundings in which children achieve their full potential.

Although Rydes Hill Preparatory School and Nursery is non-selective academically, it achieves outstanding results and received an "Excellent" rating in every category in the most recent ISI Inspection in June 2017. "*Pupils' achieve-*

ments and progress are strongly influenced by teaching that provides inspiration and challenge for pupils, and employs well-planned learning tasks, suitably matched to their needs. They (pupils) show excellent spiritual and moral awareness which lie at the heart of extremely positive relationships they form with each other. Pupils show outstanding attitudes to work and study. They enjoy learning for its own sake, and derive great satisfaction from working hard and doing their best." This follows the previous ISI Inspection in June 2011 where the School also achieved outstanding results and received the top rating in every category.

Experienced and dedicated teachers encourage self-esteem and help pupils excel. Year after year, a high percentage of Year Six pupils are awarded scholarships to leading senior schools, many receiving offers at multiple schools. Music, French, Ballet, Drama, Science, Sport including swimming at Surrey Sports Park in its Olympic Standard Pool. Every pupil performs in one of the school's annual productions and the creative arts are major strengths of the School with our pupils winning every category of a recent inter-school art competition.

Extra-Curricular activities include: Science Club, Art Club, Coding Club, Speech and Drama, Ballet, Junior and Senior Choirs, Orchestra, Instrumental Music Tuition (Pianoforte, Clarinet, Flute, Violin, Trumpet, Guitar, Cornet, and Cello), Tennis, French, Netball, Football, Gymnastics and Cross Country Clubs. The children are offered the opportunity to take part in matches and races from Year 2 onwards and both our Senior and Junior Choirs sing at various events throughout the year.

An extended school day is available from the 7.30 am Breakfast Club to the 6.00 pm Stay & Play Club, which includes a healthy afternoon tea. Supervised homework sessions are also offered every day. The Nursery has recently launched all-year-round places.

Charitable status. Rydes Hill Preparatory School and Nursery is a Registered Charity, number 299411. It exists to ensure excellence in all aspects of education.

St Albans High School Prep

Codicote Road, Wheathampstead, Hertfordshire AL4 8DJ

Tel: 01582 839270
Fax: 01582 839270
email: Prep@stahs.org.uk
website: www.stahs.org.uk
Twitter: @STAHSPrep

Chair of School Council: Mrs H Greatrex, BA, MSc Hons, ACA

Head of the Prep School: **Mrs Judy Rowe**, BEd

Age Range. Girls 4–11.
Number of Pupils. 300.
Fees per term (2018–2019). Reception £4,930 (inc Lunch), Years 1 and 2 £5,200 (inc Lunch); Years 3–6 £5,200 (exc Lunch).

The Prep School for St Albans High School for Girls is a very popular, academically selective school, with a welcoming family atmosphere, offering outstanding pastoral care. St Albans High School is uniquely placed in being able to offer all the advantages of a continuous education in two very different settings. From the ages of 4–11, the girls have the freedom to grow and develop in an attractive rural environment, before moving on to the more urban setting of the Senior School, close to the heart of the City of St Albans.

The Prep School is set in 18 acres of grounds within the village of Wheathampstead. It has large playing areas, a meadow and school woods, where girls engage in Forest school activities.

The curriculum is broad, embracing the National Curriculum and beyond. A central focus is placed on thinking skills, creativity and independent learning. Excellent facilities include an ICT suite and Science lab. New technologies are used to support learning, with SMART boards, laptops, iPads and Kindles, in addition to the computers in the ICT suite. Pupils at the Prep School use the school swimming pool located at the Senior School.

It is a happy and exciting school with a wide variety of activity days and educational visits throughout the school year. There is an extensive range of clubs including Art, Speech and Drama, Dancing, Sports, Orienteering, Karate, Fencing, Chess and Coding. Music is a real strength of the school and there are many music groups, choirs and an orchestra. Enrichment groups extend and support learning and there are opportunities for highly talented pupils to join with Senior School girls for events.

The School provides a supportive, challenging and creative environment, where girls work hard, are very successful academically and enjoy learning.

Open Days. Prep School Open Morning: Friday 5 October 2018; Prep Snapshot: Friday 9 November 2018.

Charitable status. St Albans High School for Girls is a Registered Charity, number 311065.

St Andrew's Prep

Meads, Eastbourne, East Sussex BN20 7RP

Tel: 01323 733203
Fax: 01323 646860
email: admissions@standrewsprep.co.uk
website: www.standrewsprep.co.uk
Facebook: @StAndrewsprepEB

Open Mornings: Friday 8 and Saturday 9 February 2019, 9.30 am to 12 noon.

Chairman of the Governing Body: Mr P A J Broadley

Head: **Mr Gareth Jones**

Age Range. 9 months–13 years.
Number of Pupils. 254 (Prep School), 126 (Pre-Prep and Nursery).
Fees per term (2018–2019). Full boarding £8,340; Weekly Boarding £7,370; Flexible boarding – supplements from £23 per night; Day children: £5,825 (Years 5–8), £5,565 (Year 4), £5,050 (Year 3), Pre-Prep £3,350. Nursery sessions: We offer the EYEE grant and sessions start from £21 for 3 to 4 year olds claiming the EYEE grant. For 2 to 3 year olds, sessions start from £33. For babies aged 9 to 24 months, sessions start from £34. Sessions run from 8.00 am to 1.00 pm, 1.00 pm to 6.00 pm, 8.00 am to 4.00 pm and 8.00 am to 6.00 pm. Please contact the Registrar for more details.

St Andrew's is positioned within 12 acres of beautifully tended grounds at the foot of the South Downs and is just a five minute walk to the beach. The school, founded in 1877, has a highly qualified teaching staff and children are taught in classes with a maximum size of 20 and an average number of approximately 16. A number of children in the Prep department are boarders and the school operates a popular scheme of flexi boarding allowing day children to stay any number of nights during the week on a flexible basis.

The Head is supported by 2 Deputy Heads (Pastoral and Academic) and a strong management team. All children in the school have a Form Teacher or Form Tutor who is responsible for their pastoral welfare and academic progress. Each section of the school has its own Head (Nursery and Pre-Prep, Junior, Middle and Senior), who coordinates, together with the Deputy Heads and Academic Directors, the overall pastoral and academic work of the staff.

In addition to the expanse of playing fields, St Andrew's benefits from its own indoor swimming pool, newly refurbished netball and tennis courts and a new state-of-the-art sports hall and dance studio which was opened by Baroness Tanni Grey-Tompson in September 2016 to provide excellent sporting provision for its pupils. During the summer 2018 the boarding house was also refurbished together with the Pavilion which now forms a superb space for hosting events and presentations as well as a Senior Common room for pupils in Years 7 and 8.

There are three computer/iPad suites equipped with up-to-date software and hardware including a wireless network connection. There is an interactive whiteboard in every classroom. The equipment in the Pre-Prep suite is designed specifically for children from 3 to 7 years of age.

Other facilities include a modern purpose-built music block, an extensively equipped research and resource centre, a chapel, a Forest School and a creative arts centre with an art studio and design and technology facilities. The school strongly encourages music and drama and more than three quarters of the children play instruments and participate in orchestras, bands and choirs.

As well as music, drama is a timetabled subject and plays take place every term.

From the age of nine, children are taught by subject specialists. French is taught from the age of 5 and Latin is introduced from the age of 9. Children are introduced to working on computers from the age of two. The breadth of the curriculum means that, while the requirements of the National Curriculum are fulfilled, the children are able to experience a variety of other stimulating activities.

Accelerated sets exist from Year 5 to provide more challenging opportunities for those who are academically gifted. Academic, art, drama, music, and sports awards have been achieved to many major senior schools and over the past five years almost 140 scholarships have been won by St Andrew's pupils. The charity running St Andrews's Prep amalgamated with Eastbourne College in 2010 and the two schools are part of the Eastbourne College Charity. The school benefits from the use of College facilities including astroturf pitches, a contemporary performing arts centre and specialist staff. Approximately 65–70% of St Andrew's Prep leavers each year progress to Eastbourne College. However, it should be noted that although the schools are inter-dependent, they are also independent of each other and the Headmaster of St Andrew's advises on any number of other schools too, as appropriate to each individual.

There is a wide range of activities on offer. The Co-Curricular programme, which runs for children in Years 5 to 8, offers opportunities for all children to develop areas of interest and strength or to discover new ones. Each activity offered has its own educational objectives and challenges designed to improve children's skills and broaden their horizons. Optional Saturday morning activities for Years 4 to 8 pupils are also very popular. An extensive programme of after-school activities has always been a strong feature of St Andrew's. This starts at the Pre-Prep and runs through to Year 8.

The school's strong sporting reputation manifests itself in national honours regularly achieved in many different sports. Specialist coaches are employed to teach the skills required for all to enjoy participating in team games and opportunities are available to anyone wishing to represent the school.

Charitable status. Eastbourne College Incorporated is a Registered Charity, number 307071. The aim of the Charity is the promotion of Education.

St Andrew's School

Buckhold, Pangbourne, Reading, Berks RG8 8QA

Tel: 0118 974 4276
email: admin@standrewspangbourne.co.uk
website: www.standrewspangbourne.co.uk
Twitter: @StAndrewsSch
Facebook: @StAndrewsSch

The School is an Educational Trust controlled by a Board of Governors.

Chairman of Governors: Mrs Felicity M Rutland

Headmaster: **Mr Jonathan Bartlett**, BSc QTS Brunel

Age Range. 3–13. Weekly Boarding from age 7.
Number of Pupils. 300 including weekly boarders.
Fees per term (2018–2019). Flexi Boarders £32.50 per night – £1,120, Day Pupils £3,620–£6,050. Nursery from £1,810 (5 mornings).

The School is fully co-educational and set in over 50 acres of private wooded estate and parkland.

The Curriculum includes all the traditional CE and Scholarship subjects and there is emphasis on Music, Speech and Drama and Modern Languages. Senior School preparation and Study Skills are an important part of the senior pupils' timetable and Information Technology is well resourced.

Academic and Sporting standards are high. A brand new Sports Centre with indoor swimming pool was opened in January 2018 alongside a full-size Astro pitch.

Charitable status. St Andrew's (Pangbourne) School Trust Limited is a Registered Charity, number 309090. It exists to provide education for boys and girls.

St Andrew's School, Woking

Church Hill House, Wilson Way, Horsell, Woking, Surrey GU21 4QW

Tel: 01483 760943
email: hmsec@st-andrews.woking.sch.uk
            admin@st-andrews.woking.sch.uk
website: www.st-andrews.woking.sch.uk
Twitter: @StAndrewsWoking
Facebook: @standrewsschoolwoking

Chairman of Governors: Major General James Gordon

Headmaster: **Mr Adrian Perks**, MSc

Deputy Head: Mr Jonathan Spooner, MA Hons

Age Range. 3–13 co-educational.
Number of Pupils. Total: 300 Day pupils. Pre-Prep and Nursery 121.
Fees per term (2018–2019). Prep £4,340–£4,975. Pre-Prep £1,263–£3,665.

St Andrew's School was founded in 1937 and is an established, respected and thriving co-educational Prep school, set in 11 acres of grounds within a quiet residential area approximately half a mile from Woking town centre. The

School seeks to create a nurturing and happy environment of trust and support in which all pupils are encouraged and enabled to develop their skills, talents, interests and potential to the full – intellectually, physically and spiritually, regardless of social circumstances, age or religion.

Within St Andrew's walls children feel secure and confident and are highly motivated to perform to the best of their ability in all aspects of school life. They are competitive without losing sight of their responsibility to share and they are justifiably proud of their school and their own personal achievements. In a world of changing values, self-confidence and a solid grounding are essential building blocks for life. St Andrew's hopes to provide all their children with this basic foundation as they prepare for the bigger challenges that follow. Children are prepared for entrance and scholarship exams to a wide range of independent senior schools and there are specialist teaching facilities for all subjects including science, ICT, music and art. The curriculum is broad and the school places great emphasis on music, sport and the arts.

St Andrew's is very proud of its excellent on-site facilities including an all-weather sports surface, sports pitches, tennis courts, cricket nets and outdoor heated swimming pool. We are very fortunate to enjoy the benefits of carefully designed school grounds that incorporate facilities to meet the needs of the children's physical and social development. Main school games are football, hockey, cricket, netball and rounders. Other activities include, cross-country running, swimming, tennis and athletics.

Children can be supervised at school from 8.00 am and, through our extensive after-school activities programme for Year 3 and above, until 6.00/6.30 pm most evenings during the week. There is also an after-school club from 4.00 pm to 6.00 pm (chargeable) for Pre-Prep, Year 3 and Year 4 children.

Children are assessed for entry into Year 2 and above. Contact the School for more information regarding scholarships and bursaries.

Charitable status. St Andrew's (Woking) School Trust is a Registered Charity, number 297580, established to promote and provide for the advancement of education of children.

S. Anselm's

Stanedge Road, Bakewell, Derbyshire DE45 1DP

Tel:	01629 812734
Fax:	01629 814742
email:	headmaster@anselms.co.uk
website:	www.sanselms.co.uk
Twitter:	@SAnselmsPrep
Facebook:	@s.anselms

The School is an Educational Trust.

Chairman of Governors: R Howard

Headmaster: **P Phillips**, BH Hons London, MA Ed, PG Cert SpLD, NPQH

Age Range. 3–16.

Numbers. College (age 13 to 16) 22 boys, 19 girls, Prep School (age 7 to 13) 86 boys, 71 girls. Pre-Prep (age 3 to 7) 53 boys and girls.

Fees per term (2018–2019). Boarders: £8,700, Day: College £4,450; Prep £5,700–£6,900; Pre-Prep £3,650–£4,150.

Welcome to S. Anselm's School, the only independent co-educational prep school in Derbyshire. Situated in the heart of the glorious Peak District it offers outstanding academic, sporting and extra-curricular opportunities to all pupils. We actively welcome children of all abilities to the school and pride ourselves on cherishing each individual child and allowing their full potential to shine through.

S. Anselm's sits on the crest of a hill in the heart of the Peak National Park – a beacon of excellence in all it does. All parents seek an environment where their children can remain children for as long as possible. Here at S. Anselm's it is just so. Through everything we do this ethos remains steadfast. We are proud of our tradition and are not ashamed to say that the values we hold dear are the very reason this school is quite unique.

With an 18-acre campus in the Peak District the children are surrounded by beauty and opportunities to explore. We have 5 netball courts, an indoor swimming pool, a recently renovated sports hall, a theatre with a permanent stage, a dedicated music block, 3 fully equipped science laboratories, 2 art rooms, a new innovations centre and a newly developed library. The school is forward looking in its approach to IT having invested heavily in it over the last 2 years with iPads for learning, fully interactive whiteboards and Wi-Fi throughout the school.

The boarders enjoy a varied programme of activities including the debating club and fiercely fought tournaments of dodgeball. Those who learn music practise for 20 minutes every evening and cocoa and toast every night give a homely feel to bedtime.

Here our pupils are encouraged to be themselves; they are genuinely excited about learning and have a real thirst for knowledge. They thrive in the music and art rooms, and on the games field and stage. Pupils adore this school and are justly proud of all they do. They love learning and there is a true sense of fun.

Our small class sizes mean our staff can plan their teaching to ensure every pupil is treated as an individual. Each child is cared for and nurtured in every way they need. Our teaching staff simply want the very best for all our pupils and will do all they can to help them achieve their own personal best.

At the very centre of our values is creativity – whether through the individual or the community. It is creativity in thought and every aspect of life that sets a S. Anselm's pupil apart from others. We encourage our children to be creative in their thinking and their play and strongly believe in the importance of nurturing an environment where they can fully and confidently explore their individuality. This is a kind, caring and tolerant school and we are quite sure this wonderful environment will make a lasting impression on all who visit.

Charitable status. S. Anselm's is a Registered Charity, number 527179. It exists to provide an excellent all-round education for boys and girls.

St Anthony's School for Boys
Alpha Plus Group

90 Fitzjohn's Avenue, Hampstead, London NW3 6NP

Tel:	020 7435 3597 (Junior House)
	020 7435 0316 (Senior House)
	020 7431 1066 (Admissions)
Fax:	020 7435 9223

email: PAHead@stanthonysprep.co.uk
website: www.stanthonysprep.org.uk

Headmaster: **P M Keyte**, MA Oxon

Age Range. 4–13.
Number of Boys. 300 Day Boys.
Fees per term (2018–2019). £6,335–£6,475 including lunches.

Founded in the 19th century and now set in the heart of Hampstead village, St Anthony's is an academic IAPS preparatory school for boys between the ages of 4 and 13. It is Roman Catholic, but welcomes boys of other faiths. The majority of boys transfer at 13, via scholarship or CE, to leading independent senior schools including Westminster, University College School, KCS Wimbledon, Habs, Merchant Taylors', St Paul's, Mill Hill, Highgate, Harrow, Eton, City of London, Ampleforth, Stonyhurst, Sevenoaks, Bedales, Tonbridge, Winchester, Charterhouse and Oundle. A number of boys also transfer to leading state Catholic schools such as The Cardinal Vaughan and The London Oratory. It is one of the prestigious Alpha Plus Schools whose CEO is Mark Hanley-Browne, a distinguished former Headmaster. Recently, a sister school, St Anthony's School for Girls, has been opened and works closely to provide an equivalent excellent education.

The school accommodation consists of two large Victorian houses in close proximity. Both have their own grounds and separate playgrounds. There are eight forms in the Junior House, where boys range in age from four to eight, and ten forms in the Senior House, where boys range in age from eight to thirteen. The Senior House has a specialist Design and Technology room, a Music room, a Dance & Drama studio, a computer suite, a Science laboratory and a swimming pool.

All boys receive Religious Education lessons twice a week. The course, which centres on Catholic beliefs and practices, but includes aspects of other faiths, is followed by all pupils. The school's spiritual dimension is regarded as highly important and it exists within a liberal and inclusive atmosphere. Most pupils attend mass about three times each term.

The school curriculum is stimulating and challenging: for example, it is possible for boys to study five foreign languages. All pupils study French and Mandarin from Year 1; Latin, Greek and Arabic are available from Year 6. The arts have an important place in the school with a majority of boys learning to play a musical instrument and all boys involved in drama. Sport is a further strength of the school with some pupils achieving success on a national stage. The school has use of a superb local sports club, at Brondesbury, with extensive facilities. It has recently introduced Computer Programming and Robotics courses have been very successful and pupils can study Philosophy from Year 4 upwards.

St Anthony's still retains its famous commitment to fostering individuality with alumni such as David Suchet, Anthony Gormley and Bombay Bicycle Club underlining its notable commitment to the liberal arts. Recently, pupils have been awarded Music scholarships to Westminster, Eton, Harrow, Highgate, Brighton College and UCS. Academic and Art scholarships have also been gained at Winchester, St Paul's, Habs, UCS, Merchant Taylors', Stonyhurst, City of London Boys and Mill Hill. Boys have also achieved Sports awards at City of London Boys and Mill Hill.

The school works hard to instil in its pupils a sense of social responsibility and charity fundraising is a key feature of school life. A former pupil was awarded the Gusi Peace Prize (Asian equivalent of the Nobel) and the school continues to finance a kindergarten in southern India. Much work is also done with local charities.

St Aubyn's School

Bunces Lane, Woodford Green, Essex IG8 9DU

Tel: 020 8504 1577
Fax: 020 8504 2053
email: school@staubyns.com
website: www.staubyns.com
Twitter: @st_aubyns
Facebook: @St-Aubyns-School

The School was founded in 1884 and is governed by a Charitable Trust.

Chairman of the Governors: Mr A Botha

Headmaster: **Len Blom**, BEd Hons, BA, HDE Phys Ed, NPQH

Deputy Head: Marcus Shute, BEd

Age Range. 3–13+.
Number of Children. 525 Day.
Fees per term (from April 2018). £1,790 (Nursery) to £4,065 (Seniors) fully inclusive.

St Aubyn's provides an all-round preparatory education for children aged 3–13. The School is non-selective at its main point of entry for children aged 3 and 4. There are assessment tests for older children, principally at ages 7+ and 11+.

Classes are small, taught by well-qualified, dedicated staff. Nursery and Reception children are also supported by teaching assistants. Qualified nurses deal with all medical issues and emergencies.

The School offers a wide-ranging curriculum within a traditional framework, encompassing all National Curriculum requirements. French is introduced from Nursery onwards and Latin from Year 6. French, Music and PE are specialist-taught from an early age. All subjects are specialist-taught from Year 6.

Children progress to a range of selective, independent and state schools at 11+ and 13+. Pupils gain a range of scholarships at both 11+ and 13+. Recent awards include several academic scholarships as well as awards in Sport, Technology, Music and Drama. In 2018 a total of 16 awards were gained by a total of 14 children.

The School is pleasantly situated on the borders of Epping Forest, yet is close both to the North Circular and the M11. There are three departments within the School: Pre Prep including EYFS (3+, 4+, 5+, 6+); Middle School (7+, 8+, 9+) and Seniors (10+, 11+ and 12+) and each has its own base and resources. Facilities are extensive with 8 acres of grounds, large Sports Centre, all-weather pitches, fully-equipped Performing Arts Centre and Music School, Science Laboratory, Art and Design and Technology Studio, Library, Dance and Drama Studio and two IT Suites. A computer network runs throughout the school. Games include football, cricket, hockey, rugby, tennis, netball, athletics and swimming, all coached to a high standard.

The Director of Music leads a thriving department, with a School orchestra and various instrumental groups and choirs. Children are regularly involved in performances both within and outside the School.

In January 2017 we opened our world-class, purpose-built, state-of-the-art Nursery facility and currently the School is expanding its changing room facilities.

St Aubyn's School is a registered charity. All income from fees is for the direct benefit of its pupils. Two scholarships are available at 11+. The primary criterion for the award of a scholarship is academic ability, though special talent in music, technology, art, sport, etc may be taken into account. There is a bursary scheme at 7+.

Charitable status. St Aubyn's (Woodford Green) School Trust is a Registered Charity, number 270143. It exists to provide education for children.

St Benedict's Junior School

5 Montpelier Avenue, Ealing, London W5 2XP

Tel: 020 8862 2250
email: enquiries@stbenedicts.org.uk
website: www.stbenedicts.org.uk
Twitter: @stbenedicts
Facebook: @StBenedictsSchool
LinkedIn: /st-benedicts-school

Governing Body:
The Governing Board of St Benedict's School

Headmaster: Mr R G Simmons, BA Hons, PGCE

Deputy Head: Mrs T Scott, BEd

Age Range. 3–11 Co-educational.
Number of Pupils. 273.
Fees per term (2018–2019). Nursery: £2,885–£5,340; Pre-Prep: £4,330; Junior School: £4,810.

St Benedict's is London's leading independent Catholic co-educational school, in leafy Ealing. Within a caring, happy community, St Benedict's has strong academic standards, with considerable ambition for future academic success. The Junior School and Nursery offers a holistic education for children aged 3 to 11, which continues through the Senior School and Sixth Form. St Benedict's, which welcomes children of other Christian denominations and faiths, is committed to supporting all children to develop their full potential.

Inspirational teaching and exceptional pastoral care are at the heart of the education we offer.

The Junior School and Nursery provide a supportive, friendly and vibrant co-educational environment in which to learn. In the Nursery a carefully-planned and child-centred programme enables and extends learning and development. The Junior School provides a broad and balanced curriculum based on a rigorous academic core. Sharing excellent facilities with the Senior School, and participating in a programme of cross-curricular activities, helps ease the transition at 11+ to the Senior School, which is on the same site.

There are extensive opportunities in music, art, sport and drama. St Benedict's has a proud sporting tradition, which promotes the highest sporting aspirations while encouraging everyone to enjoy sport, fitness and teamwork. Music is excellent, with several choirs (including the renowned Ealing Abbey Choir) and many instrumental ensembles. A wide range of co-curricular activities is offered, and an after-school club is available at the Junior School.

There has been huge investment in building and facilities at St Benedict's. Having opened our new Sixth Form Centre and Art Department in 2015, a new Nursery and Pre-Prep

Department opened in September 2017, providing our youngest pupils with a first-rate learning environment.

St Benedict's School is unique. Come and visit and see what we have to offer. You can be sure of a warm Benedictine welcome.

Charitable status. St Benedict's School Ealing is a Registered Charity, number 1148512, and a Charitable Company Limited by Guarantee, registration number 8093330.

St Bernard's Preparatory School

Hawtrey Close, Slough, Berkshire SL1 1TB

Tel: 01753 521821
Fax: 01753 552364
email: registrar@stbernardsprep.org
website: www.stbernardsprep.org

Headteacher: Mr N S Cheesman, BEd

Assistant Heads:
Mrs A Underwood
Mrs A Verma

Age Range. 2½–11 co-educational.
Number of Pupils. 261.
Fees per term (2018–2019). £2,950–£3,515.

St Bernard's Preparatory has a unique ethos. We are a Catholic school, teaching the Catholic faith and living out the Gospel values which are shared by all faiths and are the foundation of all our relationships and the daily life of our school. We welcome and embrace children of all faiths and we recognise and celebrate our similarities and differences, developing mutual respect, understanding and tolerance.

We recognise the value and uniqueness of each individual, both child and adult. We celebrate the talents and gifts of each child and enable them to develop to their full potential spiritually, morally, academically, socially and physically. Our children are happy, courteous, confident, articulate young citizens, committed to the ideal of service to others.

We work in partnership with parents, recognising that they are the first and best educators of their child. We consider ourselves to be very privileged that parents have entrusted us with the care and education of their child. We ensure that parents are kept fully informed of their child's progress.

We are committed to offering a broad, balanced, creative and challenging curriculum, enriched by experiences and opportunities which enhance and consolidate the learning process. Small class sizes enable our team of highly qualified, caring, committed and enthusiastic teachers to be responsive to the needs of the individual child ensuring continuity and progression for all our children. We have developed a wide and varied range of after-school activities which broaden the curriculum and enrich the children's lives. Children are encouraged to develop new skills.

We are proud of our reputation as a school with a strong ethos and nurturing pastoral care coupled with academic excellence reflected in consistently outstanding results in local and national tests.

Our school motto 'Dieu Mon Abri' meaning 'God is my Shelter', is an inspiring reminder of God's love for each one of us. The three swords represent 'Love, Work and Prayer' which underpin and permeate the life of our school.

St Catherine's Preparatory School

Bramley, Guildford, Surrey GU5 0DF

Tel: 01483 899665; Senior School: 01483 893363
Fax: 01483 899669
email: prepschool.office@stcatherines.info
website: www.stcatherines.info
Twitter: @stcatsbramley

Chairman of the Governing Body: Mr Peter J Martin, BA, FRGS, FCCA

Headmistress: Mrs Alice Phillips, MA Cantab

Head of Preparatory School: **Miss Naomi Bartholomew**, MA London, BEd Cantab

Age Range. 4–11.
Number of Pupils. 256 Day Girls.
Fees per term (from January 2019). £2,995 (Pre-Prep 1), £3,630 (Pre-Prep 2), £4,285 (Pre-Prep 3), £5,060 (Prep School).

Girls are accepted from the age of 4 to 11 when they take the Entrance Examinations for entry to Senior Schools.

Charitable status. St Catherine's School Bramley is a Registered Charity, number 1070858, which exists to provide education for girls in accordance with the principles of the Church of England.

St Cedd's School

178a New London Road, Chelmsford, Essex CM2 0AR

Tel: 01245 392810
email: info@stcedds.org.uk
website: www.stcedds.org.uk

Chair of Governors: Mrs F Marshall

Head: **Mr M Clarke**, BEd Hons Cantab

Age Range. 3–11 Co-educational.
Number of Pupils. 400.
Fees per term (2018–2019). £2,850–£3,505 including educational visits, curriculum-linked extra-curricular activities, 1–1 learning support, lunch and the majority of after-school clubs.

St Cedd's School, founded in 1931, is a leading co-educational day school for children aged three to 11. The grounds and facilities create a vibrant and purposeful learning environment where children are encouraged to become independent, confident and caring individuals. A St Cedd's School education focuses on high standards of literacy and numeracy within an expansive academic broad and balanced curriculum, supplemented by a superb programme of sport and an extraordinary creative output of music and the performing arts. PE, Music, Art and MFL are taught by specialist teachers from Pre-School; Swimming and Recorders are introduced in Year 2 and International Studies is studied in Years 5 and 6. Following the 11+ entry and Independent School Examinations, a baccalaureate-style curriculum in Year 6 leads to the HOLDFAST Award which celebrates the breadth of children's achievements and talents. Music is a particular strength of the school with outstanding individual instrumental examination results. St Cedd's School is a Choir Schools' Association School and a member of the Chelmsford Choral Foundation. This link to Chelmsford

Cathedral provides opportunity for our choirs to perform at Choral Evensong.

The grounded confidence the pupils have as a result of excellent teaching and differentiated learning in a happy and supported environment, where children have fun and are encouraged to take risks, results in great personal achievements. Our girls and boys aspire to the highest levels of attainment and we can boast a successful track record of outstanding results at entry to Grammar Schools and scholarships to Independent Senior Schools.

Breakfast is available from 7.30 am and there is an extensive array of after-school activities with wrap-around care in our TLC provision until 6.00 pm.

Charitable status. St Cedd's School Educational Trust Limited is a Registered Charity, number 310865. It exists to provide education for girls and boys.

Saint Christina's RC Preparatory School

25 St Edmund's Terrace, London NW8 7PY

Tel: 020 7722 8784
Fax: 020 7586 4961
email: headteacherspa@saintchristinas.org.uk
website: www.saintchristinas.org.uk

Headteacher: **Mr Alastair Gloag**, BA

Age Range. Girls and Boys 3–11.
Number of Pupils. 134 girls, 13 boys.
Fees per term (2018–2019). £4,500 (inclusive).

Saint Christina's was founded in 1949 by the Handmaids of the Sacred Heart of Jesus. At Saint Christina's, children experience the joy of learning and the wonder of God and His Creation. Our purpose at Saint Christina's is to create an environment where children enjoy learning and where each individual experiences respect and acceptance enabling them to become the balanced person they are called to be.

As a School we take pride in the excellent examination results which we achieve. We value most of all our strong sense of community. We seek to ensure that children feel appreciated for themselves as individuals as much as their achievements. We believe that confidence can only grow in an atmosphere of trust and safety.

Boys are prepared for entrance tests for day and boarding schools.

Girls are prepared for Common Entrance Examination and entrance exams to day and boarding schools.

The School is purpose built in a pleasant location within a short walk of Primrose Hill and Regent's Park. Prospective parents are warmly invited to visit the School.

Charitable status. Saint Christina's is a Registered Charity, number 221319.

St Christopher's School
Hove

33 New Church Road, Hove, East Sussex BN3 4AD

Tel: 01273 735404
Fax: 01273 747956
email: hmsec@stchristophershove.org.uk
website: www.stchristophershove.org.uk

Chairman of Governors: Mr A J Symonds, FCIS

Headmaster: Mr J A S Withers, BEd Cantab

Age Range. 4–13 co-educational.
Number of Pupils. 303.
Fees per term (2018–2019). £2,790–£4,240.

Since its foundation in 1927, St Christopher's School has expanded to become a highly successful academic preparatory school, located in the middle of Brighton & Hove, England's youngest and most vibrant city.

St Christopher's School aims to provide a traditional academic education within a supportive family environment where individual talents are developed to produce confident, articulate and well-balanced children. Pupils regularly obtain top academic scholarships and awards for art, music, drama and sport. St Christopher's is a Brighton College school and many of its pupils go on to Brighton College.

Entry to the School is at 4+, however, places are occasionally available in other age groups. In the Pre-Prep, pupils are taught mainly by their form teachers. Particular emphasis is placed upon reading, writing and mathematics, but the curriculum is broad and a wide range of subjects is taught by specialist teachers, including French, Mandarin, Latin, Science, Music, Art, ICT, PE and Games.

Pupils move into the Middle School in Year 4, where the curriculum reflects the syllabuses of the Common Entrance and Brighton College Academic Scholarship Examinations. Formal homework is introduced at this stage. In the Upper School (Years 7 and 8), all subjects are taught by specialists, who make full use of the interactive ICT suite, music technology suite, science laboratory, art studio and library. A variety of educational day trips, an annual residential visit to France and sports trips ensure that children receive a broad and stimulating educational experience.

The boys achieve an enviable record of success in football, rugby and cricket and the girls match that success in hockey, netball and rounders. The musical life of St Christopher's is enriched by three choirs and the choice of a wide variety of instrumental and vocal tuition. All pupils are encouraged to perform on stage as part of a wide programme of drama and the development of confidence is a central aim of the school. A wide range of extra-curricular activities is on offer. After-school care is available until 5.30 pm each evening.

The Headmaster is always delighted to welcome prospective parents. Please contact the Registrar to arrange a visit.

Charitable status. St Christopher's School, Hove is a member of the Brighton College Family of Schools and is a Registered Charity, number 307061

St Columba's College Preparatory School

King Harry Lane, St Albans, Hertfordshire AL3 4AW
Tel: 01727 862616
Fax: 01727 892025
email: headofprep@stcolumbascollege.org
website: www.stcolumbascollege.org

Chairman of the Governors: Mrs J Harrison, BEd

Dean: Brother Daniel St Jacques SC, BA, PGF HG Dip Counselling, MBACP

Head: **Mrs R Loveman**, BSc

Age Range. 4–11.

Number of Pupils. 235 Boys.
Fees per term (2018–2019). Reception–Prep 2 £3,494 Prep 3 £4,097, Prep 4–6 £4,519. Fees include personal accident insurance. Additional charges are made for coaches and consumables.

The Prep School is an academically selective Catholic Day School which strives to create a welcoming community in which each boy is valued as an individual and endeavours to promote positive relationships based on mutual respect and understanding. There is a rigorous academic curriculum with an extensive range of extra-curricular opportunities. A full curriculum and sports programme is offered at Key Stage 1 and 2.

Admissions at age 4 and 7 years. Entry requirements of the school is by assessment; at age 7+ assessment is via maths, mental arithmetic, perceptual reasoning, creative writing and reading; at age 4 assessment takes place informally using a standardised test and in context in a classroom situation. Subjects include: English, Mathematics, Science, Drama, RE, French, History, Geography, IT, PE, Games, Music, Art and Design Technology.

Examinations: Pupils progress at 11+ to St Columba's College on the same site, or to other senior schools.

Academic facilities include: modern form rooms with specialist facilities for Science, IT, ADT, Music, PE, Games, RE and French, and a professionally staffed extensive library.

Sports facilities include: Rugby/Football pitches, Cricket nets and square. A swimming pool and athletics track are adjacent to the site.

There are means-tested bursaries at Prep level and a number of scholarships available to Prep School boys on entry to St Columba's College Senior School. These include academic and music scholarships.

(*See also St Columba's College entry in HMC section.*)

Charitable status. St Columba's College is a Registered Charity, number 1088480. It exists to provide a well-rounded Roman Catholic education for pupils from 4–18 years of age.

St Dunstan's College Junior School

Stanstead Road, London SE6 4TY
Tel: 020 8516 7225
email: jsoffice@sdmail.org.uk
website: www.stdunstans.org.uk

Chairman of Governors: Mr Peter Coling, FRICS

Head of Junior School: **Mr Paul Cozens**

Age Range. Co-educational 3–11.
Number of Pupils. Pre-Preparatory (3–7) 133, Preparatory (7–11) 168.
Fees per term (2018–2019). Nursery £3,377, Pre-Preparatory £4,304, Preparatory £4,923–£5,423. Fees include lunch.

The Junior School is an integral part of St Dunstan's College and prepares boys and girls for the Senior School (age 11–18) (*see entry in HMC section*). It shares with it a common site and many facilities. In particular the Refectory, Great Hall, Sports Hall, indoor Swimming Pool and playing fields increase the opportunities for all pupils in curricular and extra-curricular activities. For other work the Junior School pupils have their own buildings. The Pre-Preparatory Department is located in a Victorian house which has been beautifully converted for the specific needs of the 3–7 year olds. The Preparatory Department has its own teaching area with an art room and activity room. Junior School pupils also benefit from dedicated facilities for Music, Information Technology and Library within the respective main College departments.

We provide an excellent all-round education with special emphasis upon the development of a high level of literacy and numeracy. The curriculum is also designed to promote learning and appreciation of Science, Humanities, Music, Art, Design and Technology, Information Technology, Drama, Languages and Skills for Life. French, German and Spanish are all taught in the Junior School and the Humanities and Science are delivered through the International Primary Curriculum. Games and Physical Education play an important part in the growth and development of each pupil and the children follow an extensive programme of activities. The children's learning is enhanced by a variety of visits and residential school journeys.

Boys and girls are encouraged to take part in various clubs and activities as part of the College's Forder Programme. As well as activities before and after school hours and at lunch times, from Year 3 there are timetabled sessions across the week during which pupils choose activities from a range of options from music, art and sport groups to extension sessions, ICT and drama.

A caring and friendly environment is provided by small class sizes and a dedicated team of well-qualified class teachers and support staff. In addition to being taught many subjects by their class teacher, Preparatory Department pupils have the advantage of being educated by specialists in Art, Music, Languages, Physical Education and Games.

An effective strong partnership exists between the home and school and parents are encouraged to participate in their children's education and the life of the Junior School. Regular contact is maintained between school and the home to ensure that parents are aware of their child's academic and social progress.

Boys and Girls are admitted at all ages from 3+ to 10+ but principally at 3+ and 4+ (Nursery and Reception) and at 7+ (Year 3).

Charitable status. St Dunstan's Educational Foundation is a Registered Charity, number 312747. It exists to provide education for boys and girls.

St Edmund's Junior School
Canterbury

Canterbury, Kent CT2 8HU

Tel: 01227 475601 (Admissions)
           01227 475600 (General Enquiries)
email: admissions@stedmunds.org.uk
website: www.stedmunds.org.uk
Twitter: @stedscanterbury
Facebook: @StEdsCanterbury

Chairman of Governors: Air Marshal C M Nickols, CB, CBE, DL, MA Cantab, FRAeS

Head of the Junior School: **Dr E L Margrett**, BA Hons Bristol, MA London, EdD Sussex, CCRS Roehampton, PGCE London

Head of the Pre-Prep School: Mrs J E P Exley, BEd Hons CCCU

(*Full staff list is available on the school's website*)

Age Range. 3–13.
Numbers of Pupils. 168. Boarders: School House 15, Choir House 23; Day Pupils: Boys 69, Girls 61.

Fees per term (2018–2019). Junior School: Boarders £8,876, Weekly Boarders £8,089, Choristers £7,809, Day pupils: Years 7 & 8 £5,198, Years 5 and 6 £5,107, Years 3 and 4 £5,032. Pre-Prep: Forms 1 & 2 £3,618, Reception £3,130, Nursery £2,549.

Pupils may enter at any age from 3 to 12. Boarding begins at the age of 11.

The Junior School and the Pre-Prep School are closely linked with the Senior School (*see entry in HMC section*) but have their own identity. The Junior School uses some Senior School specialist staff, particularly in the teaching of Science, Music, Art, Technology and shares with the Senior School such amenities as the Chapel, concert theatre, sports facilities and swimming pool. There is a full-time school Chaplain. Domestic arrangements, including health and catering, are under centralised administration.

Boarding in School House offers a family experience in a stimulating environment where the individual is valued. The Canterbury Cathedral Choristers, who are St Edmund's pupils, live in the Choir House situated in the precincts of Canterbury Cathedral.

Scholarships and bursaries. Academic, music, drama, sport, and all-rounder awards are available for applicants aged 11. Cathedral choristerships are available for boys from age 7. Fee concessions are also available as detailed in the Senior School entry in HMC section.

Charitable status. St Edmund's School Canterbury is a Registered Charity, number 1056382. It exists to educate the children in its care.

St Edmund's Prep School

Old Hall Green, Ware, Herts SG11 1DS

Tel: 01920 824239
email: prep@stedmundscollege.org
website: www.stedmundscollege.org
Twitter: @stedmundsware
Facebook: @stedmundscollege.org

Chairman of Governors: Mr Patrick J Mitton, MSc

Head: **Mr S Cartwright**, BSc Hons Surrey

Deputy Head: Dr F J McLauchlan, MA PhD Cantab
Assistant Head: Mr G Duddy, BEd Wales
Head of EYFS: Mrs V Penfold, BA London Metropolitan

Age Range. 3–11 Co-educational.
Number of Pupils. 213.
Fees per term (2018–2019). Day (inc Lunch): £1,599–£4,610.

St Edmund's Prep, founded in 1874, is a co-educational, independent Catholic Nursery, Pre-Prep and Prep school, situated in beautiful surroundings of wood and parkland in Old Hall Green, easily accessible from the main thoroughfares of Hertfordshire. The school embraces family values to lay the foundation for a happy and successful life. Education is seen as a joint venture involving staff, parents and children.

When you arrive at the Prep you will experience a welcome from us all that invites you and your child to be part of a very special community.

Guided by the principles of our Catholic faith and acknowledging Christ as our leader and teacher, we strive for excellence and creativity in forward-thinking education. We commit ourselves to the preparation of our children by instilling in them a sense of responsibility and strive to ensure that they leave St Edmund's Prep with a solid foundation on which to build their future in the College and beyond.

Small class sizes allow focused attention to ensure that your child becomes a confident learner both inside and outside the classroom. Our facilities shared with the College and our committed teachers ensure our pupils have the experiences they need to develop fully in all aspects of their lives. With a heritage and ethos deeply rooted in the Catholic tradition, we welcome families from all faiths who will appreciate the all-round education that we offer.

The school has a broad, balanced curriculum and it seeks to cater for the individual child at the different stages of their development. The curriculum offered is intended to improve the learners' knowledge, introduce them to a wide range of educational experiences and develop skills needed to deal critically and creatively with the world.

For students who join in or before Year 4 there is the possibility to not sit the entrance examination for the College at 11+, thus offering straight-through entry.

The Prep is proud holders of the Gold sports mark for Sport and the England Arts Council Silver award.

The Prep is committed to healthy living and we deliver this through daily home-cooked, well-balanced meals; fresh fruit is provided at break times and sport and activity for all is a priority.

Extracurricular is the norm in the Prep with a stimulating, fun range of activities run every day from chess club to junior cadets; from cookery in dedicated facilities to sport.

A breakfast and tea-time club is offered and a school bus service runs for children over 7 in Year 3.

We are fortunate to share facilities with St Edmund's College and as a result the Prep children have an opportunity to use the floodlit astroturf, all year round use of the indoor swimming pool, a large gymnasium as well as acres of grounds which the children, with supervision, can explore.

We are committed to being leaders in education in these changing times. We invite you to join us as a member of St Edmund's Prep.

Charitable status. St Edmund's College is a Registered Charity, number 311073.

St Edmund's School

Portsmouth Road, Hindhead, Surrey GU26 6BH

Tel: 01428 609875
Fax: 01428 607898
email: admissions@saintedmunds.co.uk
website: www.saintedmunds.co.uk
Twitter: @excellentsteds
Facebook: @sainteds

Chairman of Governors: Mrs J Alliss

Headmaster: **A J Walliker**, MA Cantab, MBA, PGCE

Age Range. 2–16 Co-educational.
Number of Pupils. Senior, Prep and Lower Prep: 400 day pupils.
Fees per term (2018–2019). Lower School £3,195–£4,597; Prep and Senior £5,582; Flexi Boarding Fee: £40 per night; Nursery from £750 (three afternoons) to £2,835 (full week) not including EYFS funded hours.

The fees are inclusive of all ordinary extras including supervised prep, orchestra/choirs, games, swimming, lectures, optional Saturday activities etc, as well as a free hour of after-school care activities for children in the Lower Prep.

Scholarships and means-tested bursaries are available.

We are a fully co-educational school with an unusual flexible boarding option, from one-off nights to midweek boarding. Through a rich curriculum, small teaching groups and exemplary pastoral care, St Edmund's seeks to provide an excellent all round education by encouraging its pupils to achieve their very best in all that they do. "I like St Ed's, I can be myself." These words, spoken by one of our pupils, capture much of what we strive to do at St Edmund's: to instil in every child a sense of self-esteem and belonging by building on their own talents, opening their eyes to new ones and giving them focused and personal support whenever it is needed. Academically, it is an approach that continues to pay dividends, with our pupils going on to a wide range of senior schools at both 11+ and 13+ and 16+ including St Edmund's Senior.

Yet of equal importance are the discoveries, excitements and good old-fashioned fun that St Edmund's Lower Prep and Prep create inside our 40 beautiful acres with facilities including an immaculate 9-hole golf course, indoor swimming pool, cross-country running course, games fields, rifle range, a floodlit all-weather sports pitch and Dance and Drama Studio. The list of co-curricular activities is endless at St Ed's, from cooking to rock-climbing, scuba-diving to den building and from street dance to rifle shooting, including our unique optional Saturday Activity programme that allows us greater depth in the number of activities on offer to our pupils.

St Edmund's Senior School offers a rare and unique educational experience for those who join us. In contrast to the many larger institutions available, our dedication to small teaching groups and our strong sense of community creates an environment where pupils' confidence can be invigorated. Through high-quality teaching and resources, our aim is to provide our pupils with an inspiring and notable experience that naturally encourages an appreciation for lifelong independent learning. Our broad curriculum across Forms 7 to 11 presents a firm foundation upon which to make future educational choices, and our distinctive tutorial system enables our pupils a platform to discuss progress and achievements as well as any pastoral issues that require guidance and consideration. St Ed's Senior pupils have their own common room, library, kitchen, garden and study areas. Our GCSE results are posting 95% of pupils gaining A* to C grades in 2017 and 96% of pupils gaining A*–C in 2018.

During our latest Independent Schools Inspection, the report noted, "The quality of St Edmund's pupils' achievements and learning is 'Excellent'. Pupils' have positive attitudes to learning and they are well motivated. They show exemplary behaviour and their care for each other is special".

Charitable status. St Edmund's School Trust Limited is a Registered Charity, number 278301. Its aim is the education of children.

St Edward's Preparatory School

London Road, Charlton Kings, Cheltenham, Glos GL52 6NR

Tel: 01242 388550
email: prepschool@stedwards.co.uk
website: www.stedwards.co.uk
Twitter: @StEdwards_Prep
Facebook: @StEdwardsSchoolCheltenham

Co-educational Day School.

Chairman of Governors: Dr Sue Honeywill

Headmaster: **Mr S McKernan**, BA Hons, MEd, NPQH

Age Range. 1–11 years.
Number of Pupils. 297.
Fees per term (2018–2019). £2,590–£4,325.

St Edward's Preparatory School is an independent co-educational Catholic Foundation welcoming pupils of all denominations from 1 to 11 years. We provide a supportive family atmosphere in which pupils are encouraged to develop their individual potential – academic, social, physical, creative and spiritual – in preparation for their secondary education. The school is situated on the edge of Cheltenham in forty-five acres of beautiful parkland. Our facilities are truly exceptional and give our pupils opportunities for practical experience rarely available in a preparatory school, as well as enabling us to provide an unusually wide range of after-school activities. Class sizes are small which ensures the pupils receive plenty of individual attention. With a strong focus on mathematics, science, English and ICT results are good with children going to local grammar schools, successful entrance into St Edward's Senior School, many obtaining scholarships, and other independent schools. Sport is particularly strong as is music, drama and art. A new Drama Studio has enhanced our provision in this area.

Our Kindergarten is open all year round and provides a secure and stimulating introduction to school life. Kindergarten children have their own IT area where they can use dedicated software packages and explore creativity using iPads. Children move from here into our purpose-built Pre-Prep School with small classes and a rich range of extra-curricular activities. St Edward's Preparatory School provides the best possible start for a child's educational journey. In 2013 our Early Years Foundation Stage was awarded an "Outstanding" classification in every area – an exceptional achievement.

Charitable status. St Edward's School is a Registered Charity, number 293360.

St Faith's School

Trumpington Road, Cambridge, Cambridgeshire CB2 8AG
Tel: 01223 352073
email: info@stfaiths.co.uk
website: www.stfaiths.co.uk
Twitter: @St_Faiths
Facebook: @StFaithsSchool
LinkedIn: /st-faith's-school-cambridge

Chair of Governors: Mrs A Brunner

Headmaster: N L Helliwell, MA, BEd Hons

Deputy Head: J P Davenport

Age Range. 4–13.
Number of Pupils. 545.
Fees per term (2018–2019). £4,220 (Pre-Prep), £5,180 (Years 3 and 4) £5,315 (Years 5 to 8).

St Faith's, founded in 1884, is a co-educational day school for children aged 4–13 set in 9 acres of grounds on the south side of Cambridge, approximately one mile from the city centre. Our pupils also have access to a further 20 acres of sports fields just 2 minutes' walk away.

At St Faith's each child is taught, developed and nurtured, to equip them well for life, whatever path they choose to take. Passionate teachers share their knowledge, explore new ideas, challenge the status quo and instil a lifelong passion for learning. Teaching styles are tailored to meet each individual child's needs. Lessons are accessible, engaging and challenging for all pupils. Top-down excellence in all lessons ensures we continually stretch our pupils to achieve more than they thought possible. Our academic curriculum is ground-breaking in its innovative content and has been commended by institutions including Cambridge University, and the Times Educational Supplement awarded us 'Strategic Education Initiative of the Year' (2018) for the introduction of Engineering to the curriculum.

Exemplary, innovative and forward-facing academic subjects are interspersed each day with sporting endeavours, musical experiences, artistic creations and dramatic performances. Assemblies, tutor time and plenty of playtime ensure children have a chance to express themselves away from the classroom. Owing to small class sizes, exceptional teachers and the above average ability of our children all subjects follow an accelerated curriculum and the vast majority of pupils work at a higher level commensurate with their age.

Our green and spacious site, located in the heart of Cambridge, together with extensive playing fields, provide some of the best facilities of any prep school. Every classroom is equipped with modern teaching technology. The shelves in our library brim with over 12,000 volumes with relevance to our youngest and most mature readers. Engineering suites provide access to tools and equipment beyond many inventors' wildest dreams. Fully-equipped science laboratories and computer suites are used by all year groups. Our new £2m STEM Hub includes state of the art science laboratories, flexible large indoor spaces for interdisciplinary projects, a rooftop greenhouse and a night sky viewing platform.

Our broad sporting education is not simply a focus for sporting glory and trophy collection, though in 2017/18 20 St Faith's teams competed in National Finals with 35 children now National Champions. We believe sport is a conduit for developing mental as well as physical fitness. The losing as well as winning of sporting fixtures builds mental resilience and is an emotive demonstration of getting out of life what you put in. Of course team work is omnipresent in many sporting events and as such our pupils learn to revel in team as well as individual accolades, better preparing them for their futures. Drama and the performing arts are tools not only for teaching children a lifelong love of the arts but for promoting self-belief and confidence.

St Faith's pupils stand out as confident, articulate, grounded and courteous, attributes which will stand them in good stead for their futures.

St Faith's is part of The Leys and St Faith's Foundation and although each year approximately half of the children move on to The Leys at the end of Year 8, others prepare for entry to a variety of schools, mainly independent, with an average of 28 scholarships awarded.

Charitable status. The Leys and St Faith's Schools Foundation is a Registered Charity, number 1144035. The aim of the charity is the provision of first-class education.

St Francis School

Marlborough Road, Pewsey, Wiltshire SN9 5NT

Tel: 01672 563228
email: admissions@st-francis.wilts.sch.uk
           schooloffice@st-francis.wilts.sch.uk
website: www.st-francis.wilts.sch.uk
Twitter: @stfrancispewsey

Chair of Governors: P Humphries-Cuff

Headmaster: D W T Sibson, BA Ed Hons Durham

Age Range. 0–13.
Number of Boys and Girls. 275: 136 Boys, 139 Girls.
Fees per term (2018–2019). Reception–Year 8: £2,841–£4,276 including lunch. Nursery Fees available on application.

St Francis is a co-educational day school which takes children from the age of 0 to 13. Established in 1941, the School which is a charitable trust with a board of governors, is situated alongside the Kennet and Avon Canal in the lovely Vale of Pewsey some five miles south of Marlborough. Pupils travel from a wide area of mid-Wiltshire; daily minibus services operate from Marlborough and Devizes. Wrap-around care is available for all pupils, from 7.45 am until 6.00 pm.

Providing every child with the opportunity to fulfil his or her full potential is a feature of the school. Staff ensure that they are very positive and encouraging in their teaching. Should a child be found to need some form of specific learning assistance then appropriate help will be given. The facilities are constantly being improved. The modern Burden Block provides a Library, Design Technology room, ICT room and specialist subject teaching rooms, as well as form rooms.

The curriculum is delightfully diverse enabling the older pupils to have, for instance, CDT, Pottery, Drama, Computing, Choir and Swimming all in their normal weekly timetable. Languages are also a key part of the curriculum: French is taught from the age of three, Latin is introduced in Year 6. The majority of the pupils take up individual musical tuition and a wide range of instruments is available. Many pupils enter local music and public and choral speaking competitions.

The pupils are offered plenty of opportunity to develop and excel in their sport. All the major sports are taught both outdoors on the playing fields and also inside the Hemery Hall which doubles as a sports hall and a drama theatre. Regular matches take place against other schools and a policy of 'sport for all' allows all pupils to be involved.

Little Saints Nursery caters for children from 0 to 4 years of age for 51 weeks a year (both term time and full-time contracts are available). Little Saints Nursery makes use of all the facilities including the school's garden playground and woods.

The school grounds are also home to some more unexpected residents; six years ago sheep and chickens were introduced to the site, joined more recently by pygmy goats and a flock of ducks. Frankie's Farm is very popular with pupils; they especially look forward to lambing in the spring term.

Results are excellent. The pupils are mainly entered for the local senior schools, St Mary's Calne, Godolphin, Dauntsey's, Marlborough College, Stonar and Warminster, but scholarships and common entrance are also taken for boarding schools further afield. Awards are regularly achieved to all of the aforementioned.

Please write, telephone or email for a prospectus, or ask to visit and tour round the school. The Headmaster will be happy to oblige.

Charitable status. St Francis is a Registered Charity, number 298522. It exists solely to provide education for boys and girls.

St Gabriel's
Junior School

Sandleford Priory, Newbury, Berkshire RG20 9BD

Tel: 01635 555680
Fax: 01635 555698
email: info@stgabriels.co.uk
website: www.stgabriels.co.uk
Twitter: @StGabrielsNews
Facebook: @stgabrielsnewbury

Chairman of Governors: Mr N Garland, BSc Hons

Principal: Mr R Smith, MEd, MA, PGCE

Head of Junior School: Mr P Dove, BA Hons, PGCE

Age Range. 6 months – 11 years Co-educational.
Number of Pupils. 199.
Fees per term (2018–2019). £3,556–£4,778.

Sandleford Nursery lies at the heart of St Gabriel's and provides high-quality nursery care and Early Years education for children aged 6 months to 4 years. Sandleford Nursery offers flexible full or part-time care with an extended day provision across 50 weeks a year. At the age of four, the majority of Sandleford Nursery children move through into the Reception class of the Junior School.

The Junior School is situated adjacent to the Senior School in 54 acres of parkland on the southern outskirts of Newbury.

Subjects taught include English, Mathematics, Science, Art, Computing, Dance, Drama, Humanities (History, Geography), Modern Foreign Languages (French, Spanish, Italian, Mandarin), Music, Outdoor Education, PE, Religious Studies, Technology (Food Technology, Design Technology) and Thinking Skills and PSHE.

The excellent range of facilities includes a multi-discipline sports hall, theatre, dance studio, junior science laboratory, library, orienteering courses and woodland trails. There are 2 computing classrooms and newly-refurbished, state-of-the-art science laboratories.

Sport plays an important and integral role in the life of the school and there is a comprehensive fixtures list from Year 3 to Year 6. In 2018 St Gabriel's Junior School achieved School Games Gold Award for their commitment to sport. The wide range of sports includes: Athletics, Basketball, Cricket, Cross-Country, Dance, Football, Gymnastics, Hockey, Netball, Rugby, Rounders and Tennis are included in the curriculum for all pupils. Swimming takes place during the Summer Term in the outdoor heated swimming pool.

Music holds an equally high profile. As well as curriculum Music lessons, there is a wide range of co-curricular music-making for all pupils with an interest in the subject. Many pupils learn instruments in school and they are given numerous opportunities to perform at concerts ranging from informal lunchtime events to major end of term extravaganzas.

In addition, pupils are offered a wide range of co-curricular activities, including Art Club, Ballet, Chess Club, Choir, Climbing Club, Creative Writing Club, Drama, Football, Film Making Club, Gymnastics, Judo, Music Theory, Recorder, Science Club, Trampolining Club and Training Orchestra. Pupils in Years 3–6 are also elected onto a School Council and a Digital Leadership Team.

Prospective pupils entering Years 1 and 2 are assessed by the class teacher and subject staff; prospective pupils entering Years 3 to 6 are assessed by the Individual Needs Department. Pupils who apply for entry to Year 6 will also be assessed on their ability to pass the 11+ entrance examinations to the Senior School.

Boys are prepared for Common Entrance Examinations and the majority of girls progress through to the Senior School at the age of 11, at which point entry is by entrance examination and interview. (*For further information about the Senior School, see St Gabriel's entry in GSA section.*)

Charitable status. The St Gabriel Schools Foundation is a Registered Charity, number 1062748. It exists to provide education for girls and boys from age 6 months to 11 years.

St George's Junior School, Weybridge

Thames Street, Weybridge, Surrey KT13 8NL

Tel:	01932 839400
Fax:	01932 839401
email:	contact@stgeorgesweybridge.com
website:	www.stgeorgesweybridge.com
Twitter:	@sgweybridge
Facebook:	@stgeorgescollegeuk

Chairman of Board of Governors: Mr J Lewin [from Nov 2018]

Headmaster: **Mr A J W Hudson**, MA Cantab, PGCE, NPQH

Age Range. 3–11.

Number of Pupils. 617.

Fees per term (2018–2019). Nursery: £1,795 (mornings only), £2,945 (full days); Reception–Year 2 £3,390; Years 3–6 £4,655. Lunches (compulsory): £250.

St George's Junior School is a fully co-ed Roman Catholic Day School, and most pupils attending the Junior School normally belong to one of the mainstream Christian traditions. The School was established in 1950 by a Religious Order of Priests and Brothers known as "The Josephites" who maintain a keen interest in the future of the School. Pupils who are 'rising three' are admitted into the Nursery, after which children can be admitted to any year group, subject to available spaces.

While the majority of the pupils at the school come from around North Surrey, some 10% of the pupils are from countries as far away as Australia, New Zealand, Hong Kong, South Africa, Brazil, Canada, USA as well as from most European countries including Russia. The School operates a very extensive bus service and an option for parents using cars to drop off their children at either the Junior School in a 'Kiss and Drop' or the College, using the minibus shuttle service.

In September 2000, the Junior School moved from its previous co-located site a mile down the road, to its present 50-acre site on the outskirts of Weybridge close to the River Thames. Huge development has taken place since then, most notably, a new Kitchen and Dining Room – The Mulberry Hall – in 2008, and a state-of-the-art Lower Years building for children aged 3–7 – The Ark – which was opened and blessed by Cardinal Cormac Murphy-O'Connor in 2016, at the same time as a new Performing Arts Centre. Along with the recent development of a Forest School and the Eco Garden, as well as extra playing fields for cricket, rugby and rounders, the Master Plan has given the Junior School first-rate facilities which provide the children with a wonderful start to their education.

The Junior School has a genuinely happy atmosphere in which every pupil is respected and treated as an individual. The Headmaster considers the staff, pupils and parents to be constituent parts of an extended family. The School has always placed great emphasis on the importance of maintaining excellent channels of communication between members of staff, parents and pupils.

The size of classes ensures that the School is a learning community by creating the correct balance between pupil interaction and pupil-teacher contact. The pupils in the top two years of the School are taught by subject specialists. French is offered to all pupils from Year 1. The School was described in an ISI report (2011) as having pupils whose "personal qualities are excellent and the emphasis on promoting the values of the Josephite tradition results in pupils who are well mannered, polite and welcoming", and was found to be fully compliant in its most recent Inspection in 2017. In May 2018, the Diocesan Inspection report noted that 'the school's pastoral care is a particular strength' and the 'teachers manifest an enthusiasm for sharing their love and knowledge of subject, and communicate high expectations'.

All pupils are assessed on entry and when they leave at the end of Year 6 the vast majority transfer to St George's College. over 200 scholarships, including music scholarships, have been won by pupils in Year 6 since 1989. In 2018, 9 Academic, 5 Sports and 2 Art Scholarships along with 2 Music Exhibitions were awarded.

While the pursuit of academic excellence is highly valued, the Mission Statement of the School stresses the importance of pupils being the very best versions of themselves. The School requires its pupils to have high moral values especially those of its school motto: "Honesty and Compassion".

The Junior School has four Houses which compete against each other across a wide range of activities inside and outside the classroom including Music, Public Speaking and Sport.

Extracurricular and other enrichment activities are, likewise, considered to play an important role in the educational development of children. The extensive range of activities include dance (ballet, modern and tap), gymnastics, and clubs based on the academic subjects taught in the School. Since September 2013, Mandarin has been offered to Upper Years pupils. Pupils are taken to places of educational interest regularly including theatre, music and art trips, and there is an annual Book Week during which pupils meet and listen to visiting authors and story-tellers. In 2017, the School hosted its own Literature festival, inviting over 500 children from local schools to attend.

Considerable emphasis is placed on the Creative and Performing Arts. Pupils have dance lessons throughout the school with specialist ballet and tap dance lessons being a compulsory part of the curriculum for all pupils up to the end of Reception Year. The school stages six major drama productions a year. All children in Year 2 learn the violin and recorder as part of the music curriculum. There is an orchestra, choirs and various ensembles. Individual music lessons are very popular, with over 50% of the children in Years 3 to 6 learning at least one additional instrument. In 2016–17, an Instrumental Tuition Scheme was implemented which subsidises free peripatetic lessons for all children in Years 3 or 4, in order to encourage them to take up strings, woodwind or brass instruments, which has been a great success. Concerts take place at least once a term, and music lessons are supported by the use of the latest computer-based technology. Pupils have achieved considerable success at Public Speaking Competitions and achieve a very high level of attainment in their external Spoken English, LAMDA and instrumental music exams. In 2018, the Year 6 pupils choosing to take LAMDA exams achieved 23 Distinctions and 12 Merits, while Year 5 pupils gained 8 Distinctions in their ESB exams.

Apart from its own sports facilities on site comprising an artificial sports pitch, netball and tennis courts, a sprung floor gymnasium and a swimming pool, the School has use of 20 acres of outstanding sports facilities at the College including three floodlit netball courts/tennis courts, a floodlit artificial surface for hockey, a four-court indoor tennis centre, three floodlit French clay courts, a sports hall, gym and a tartan athletics track.

The Junior School has a track record of great sporting success. In 2018, in Hockey the U11 girls were IAPS National Champions, and were U11 IAPS Champions in Netball. In gymnastics, the U9 and U10 girls were Team runners-up in the ISGA 2-piece National Championships, while the U9s were Team runners-up in the 4-piece. The boys were U11 IAPS Regional (London and SE England) Hockey Champions and gained third place in the ISGA 2- and 4-piece National Championships. Other successes include many Tennis wins and the U9, U10 and U11 boys and U11 girls winning the District Cross Country competition with the U8 and U9 girls' teams coming third.

In the midst of this tangible success, the Junior School prides itself on ensuring that all pupils from Year 3 upwards have the opportunity to represent the school at least once each term in one of the mainstream sports, i.e. Rugby, Hockey and Cricket for boys and Netball, Hockey and Rounders for girls. Participation in National Swimming and Gymnastics competitions are also becoming increasingly popular, as well as Girls' Cricket.

School lunches, which are compulsory for children in Upper Nursery staying on for afternoon activities and for all from Reception Year onwards, are prepared on site and eaten in the dining room which can seat 320 people. Upper Nursery children can opt to stay until 5.00 pm each day, while the School offers a free supervised waiting facility each weekday evening during term time until 5.00 pm for children in Reception and Years 1 and 2. Children in Years 3–6 can sign up for clubs which continue until 5.00 pm as well.

For the last few years, the School has usually had more applications for places than it can accommodate in all year groups. When vacancies do occur, pupils are admitted as long as they meet the School's entry criteria and successfully complete an assessment day at the School, as well as receiving a satisfactory report from their current school where this is appropriate. Priority is afforded to siblings and Roman Catholics.

Charitable status. St George's Weybridge is a registered Charity, number 1017853. The aims and objectives of the charity are the Christian education of young people.

St George's School

Windsor Castle, Windsor, Berks SL4 1QF

Tel: 01753 865553
email: enqs@stgwindsor.org
website: www.stgwindsor.org

Patron: Her Majesty The Queen

Chairman of the Governors: The Revd Canon Dr H E Finlay, MA, PhD

Head Master: **Mr William Goldsmith**, BA Hons Durham, MSC Oxford, FRSA

Deputy Head: Mr Kevin Wills, BSc Hons, PGCE

Age Range. 3–13 Co-educational.
Number of Pupils. 320 (20 boarders).
Fees per term (2018–2019). Weekly Boarders £6,900, Upper School £4,960–£5,558, Choristers (Boarding) £3,573, Lower School £3,348–£4,960, Kindegarten £1,751–£3,348.

St George's School was established as part of the foundation of the Order of the Garter in 1348 when provision was made for the education of the first choristers. In 1893 the School moved into the Georgian building of the former College of the Naval Knights of Windsor situated between the mound of the Castle and the Home Park. Expansion followed with the admission of supernumerary (non-chorister) pupils. Extensions were made to the buildings in 1988 and 1996, the latter of which allowed for the opening of a Pre-Preparatory Department and Nursery. In 1997 girls were admitted to the School for the first time, entering both the Pre-Prep and the main school, and five years later the school became fully co-educational. A new building accommodating Music rooms, Modern Languages and Year 4 and 5 classrooms, was opened in Spring 2006 by HRH Princess Alexandra. The school is a central part of the Foundation of the College of St George, within Windsor Castle. The current structure of the school is divided into the Lower School (EYFS to Year 3) and the Upper School (Year 4 to Year 8)

St George's School has a long and proud tradition of academic and musical excellence alongside impressive art, drama and sport. Many pupils gain academic, all-rounder and music awards to some of the country's leading independent schools; in recent years these have included Eton, Hampton, King's Canterbury, Rugby and Winchester. The curriculum is stimulating, broad and varied. In addition to the teaching of core subjects, French is introduced to Nursery children with the addition of Latin and Spanish in Year 6. Specialist teaching in PE and Music is provided from the Nursery upwards and in Art, DT and Drama from Year 3.

Facilities for games are excellent with pitches and playing fields on the Home Park Private, an indoor swimming pool, a recently resurfaced tennis and netball court and a gymnasium. Several areas of the school buildings have recently undergone refurbishment, including the creation of a Design Technology workshop and new Science laboratories opened by HRH The Earl of Wessex. In 2013, a new Food Technology teaching room was opened and in 2015 there was a significant updating of the ICT suite. Enhanced Music facilities now include an Apple networked Music teaching room and recording studio.

The School seeks to pursue the highest standards and aims to develop happy, self-confident children who are encouraged to achieve their potential whilst at St George's. There is a strong family ethos within the school community where each child's talents and skills are identified and nurtured. Pastoral care is excellent and each class teacher and form tutor knows the children in their care extremely well. There are frequent parents evenings for all pupils in the school, and parents are regularly invited to support their children in plays, concerts and sports fixtures and to attend school services in St George's Chapel, Windsor Castle. Indeed the ISI Integrated Inspection report in February 2016 rated the school as being 'Excellent'.

Communications are excellent: two railway stations, the M25, M3, M4 and M40 are all close by and Heathrow is just fifteen minutes away.

Charitable status. St George's School, Windsor Castle is a Registered Charity, number 1100392. Its purpose is the education, either as boarding or day pupils, of children of pre-preparatory and preparatory school age and of the choristers who maintain the worship in the Queen's Free Chapel of Our Lady, St George and St Edward the Confessor in Windsor Castle.

St Helen's College

Parkway, Hillingdon, Middlesex UB10 9JX

Tel: 01895 234371
email: info@sthelenscollege.com
website: www.sthelenscollege.com

Principals:
Mr D A Crehan, ARCS, BA, BSc, MSc, CPhys, MEd
Mrs G R Crehan, BA, MA, PGCE

Head Teacher: **Mrs S Drummond**, BEd Hons, MLDP

Age Range. 2–11 co-educational.
Number of Pupils. 381 Day Pupils.
Fees per term (2018–2019). £3,200–£3,950.

St Helen's College has been described by inspectors as a 'Haven of Harmony' and was deemed 'outstanding/excellent' in all 12 areas in its most recent educational quality inspection. It is a happy, family-run school, based on three enduring values: Love, Harmony and Growth.

The aims of St Helen's College are to develop as fully as possible each child's academic potential, to provide a wide, balanced, stimulating and challenging curriculum, and to foster true values and good character based on moral and spiritual principles. The children enjoy a purposeful and happy 'family' atmosphere and are taught by committed, professional, specialist teachers.

Children are prepared for independent senior schools and local grammar schools, and records of success are very good indeed. In addition to the academic subjects, sport, music and drama play an important part in the lives of the children.

An extraordinarily wide range of extra-curricular activities is offered, and pupils enjoy outings, day and residential, to many places of interest. There is a school bus, breakfast club, after-school club and summer school, and a holiday club which runs throughout the year.

Individual tours for prospective parents are run during term time and on regular Open Mornings. Please telephone 01895 234371 to make an appointment.

St Hilary's Preparatory School

Holloway Hill, Godalming, Surrey GU7 1RZ

Tel: 01483 416551
email: registrar@sthilarysschool.com
website: www.sthilarysschool.com
Twitter: @StHilarysSchool
Facebook: @St-Hilarys-School-Trust

Chair of Governors: Mr Richard Thompson, BSc Hons, MBA

Headmistress: **Mrs J Whittingham**, BEd, Cert Prof Prac SpLD

Age Range. Boys and Girls 2–11. Boys currently leave St Hilary's at 7+ years, but from September 2019, we will welcome boys into Year 3 in a phased plan to be fully co-educational by September 2022.

Number of Pupils. 250 Day Pupils.

Fees per term (from January 2019). Including lunch: Reception £3,499, Year 1 £3,834, Year 2 £4,499, Year 3 £4,634, Years 4 to 6 £5,148. Kindergarten £30.50 and Nursery £32.00 per am/pm session with lunch extra.

St Hilary's is an independent preparatory day school which provides a stimulating, safe environment in which boys and girls can develop, be happy and flourish.

Situated in the heart of Godalming, St Hilary's prides itself in providing an outstanding all-round education, equipping pupils not only with strong academic standards but also the essential qualities and skills required beyond their time at our school. Ultimately we strive to ensure that all our pupils develop a real thirst for learning.

The Independent Schools Inspectorate judged our main school to be 'Excellent' in all areas in December 2016 and our Early Years Foundation Stage achieved 'Outstanding' at its last inspection.

Every child enjoys the benefits of well-qualified, enthusiastic staff and a broad curriculum combined with splendid facilities. Amenities include well-equipped classrooms, music wing, spacious hall for the performing arts, science room, library, modern ICT suite, design & technology and art studios, all-weather pitch, and the Hiorns Centre for drama and ballet. Small class sizes allow children to achieve their best in a dynamic and vibrant environment.

Outside the classroom, pupils can enjoy the woodland through Forest School and play opportunities with the very popular Taurus Trail and exciting adventure play area. Pupils share a love of growing things in our gardens and appreciate the safe, beautiful surroundings.

Physical Education features highly at St Hilary's. The department gives all pupils equality of opportunity to participate in a broad range of activities. All pupils experience a variety of competitive and challenging situations. Our House system encourages healthy competition with matches, a swimming gala and sports days.

Children are given the opportunity to participate in a wide, varied number of extra-curricular activities, such as, gardening, football skills, drama, science, art, pottery, textiles, debating, First Aid, French, chess, gym, cross country, judo, cricket, dance, tap, choirs, woodwind, string ensemble, percussion, orchestra, recorder groups and violin.

Speech & Drama is a highly popular option for many with pupils preparing for LAMDA (London Academy of Music and Dramatic Art) examinations. The school takes advantage of its ideal location and access to London for visits to galleries, museums and theatres.

Parents are guided in next school options and have the opportunity to make informed choices at a time when a child's true academic potential can be accurately predicted and talents in other areas identified. We have an excellent reputation in securing first-choice schools for our pupils when they leave. Our leavers successfully move on to prestigious schools; every year many obtain academic, art, music, sport and drama scholarships.

Please do come and visit us; we will be delighted to welcome you and discuss your child's education. We hold a number of Open Days throughout the year when you can see the school in action; please visit our website for more details.

Charitable status. St Hilary's School Trust Limited is a Registered Charity, number 312056. It exists to provide education for children.

St Hilda's School

High Street, Bushey, Hertfordshire WD23 3DA

Tel: 020 8950 1751
email: secretary@sthildasbushey.co.uk
              registrar@sthildasbushey.co.uk
website: www.sthildasbushey.com
Twitter: @StHildasBushey
Facebook: @sthildasbushey

Chairman of Governors: Mr T Barton, LLB Hons

Headmistress: **Miss S J Styles**, BA, MA

Age Range. Girls 2–11, Boys 2–4.
Number of Pupils. 130 Day Girls. Co-ed Nursery.
Fees per term (2018–2019). Prep School: £4,004–£4,281. Nursery fees upon application according to sessions chosen.

St Hilda's is an Independent Day School for girls aged 4–11, with a full-time nursery for boys and girls aged 2–4. It was founded in 1918 and has occupied its present 5-acre site since 1928. The Victorian house at the centre of the school has been continually improved, adapted and extended to provide an excellent educational environment. This includes a nature garden area, tennis courts, an indoor heated swimming pool, a large all-purpose hall, science laboratory, technology laboratory and computer suite. We teach a wide range of subjects to a high academic standard in a secure and happy environment in which every pupil can develop their academic and personal potential. We offer a broad and challenging curriculum in which art, drama and music play an important role. There is also a wide range of extra-curricular activities, including ballet, seasonal sports activities, ICT, languages and drama. Pre-school and after-school care is offered from 07.30 until 18.30 Monday to Friday during term time.

Charitable status. St Hilda's School is a Registered Charity, number 298140. It exists to provide education for girls.

St Hugh's

Carswell Manor, Faringdon, Oxon SN7 8PT

Tel: 01367 870700
Fax: 01367 870707
email: headmaster@st-hughs.co.uk
              registrar@st-hughs.co.uk
website: www.st-hughs.co.uk

Chairman of Governors: P G Daffern

Headmaster: **A J P Nott**, BA Hons, PGCE

Age Range. 3–13.
Number of Pupils. 350: 15 Weekly Boarders, 245 Day Pupils (of whom over 50% flexi board); Pre-Prep (including Nursery) 90. (Boy-Girl ratio approximately 3:2, both boarding and day).
Fees per term (2018–2019). Upper School: Weekly Boarders £8,005, Day £6,695; Middle School: Weekly Boarders £7,470, Day £6,160; Pre-Prep £3,885–£4,240. (All fees inclusive, with very few compulsory extras).

The School's main building is a fine Jacobean house with extensive grounds. Boys and girls are prepared for Common Entrance and Scholarship examinations to senior independent schools. The school is organised into four departments:

Nursery (3–4), Pre-Prep (4–6), Middle School (7–8) and Upper School (9–13). Careful liaison ensures a strong thread of continuity throughout the school. The main entry points are at 3, 4, 7 and 9.

The School is not an academically selective school and both welcomes and accepts children from all backgrounds and a wide range of academic abilities. We aim to foster confidence and a love of learning across this range: an impressive pre-test, scholarship and CE record and the provision of integral specialist support both bear testimony to our inclusive approach. The arts and sport feature strongly and pupils are encouraged to develop their talents and interests as broadly as possible.

St Hugh's is described by the Good Schools Guide as a school which "personifies what is best in prep school education".

Charitable status. St Hugh's is a Registered Charity, number 309640. It exists to provide a centre of excellence for the education of children.

St Hugh's

Cromwell Avenue, Woodhall Spa LN10 6TQ

Tel: 01526 352169
email: office@st-hughs.lincs.sch.uk
website: www.st-hughs.lincs.sch.uk
Twitter: @sthughslincs
Facebook: @sthughslincs

Chairman of Governors: J Harris

Headmaster: **C A Ward**, BEd Hons

Age Range. 2–13.
Number of Pupils. 174. 58 boys, 50 girls. Pre-Prep: 16 boys, 21 girls. Nursery: 29 children.
Fees per term (2018–2019). Boarding £6,250; Day £4,480–£4,976; Pre-Prep £2,960. The fees are fully inclusive.

St Hugh's School was founded by the Forbes family in 1925, became a Charitable Trust in 1964 and has continued to prosper over the years administered by a forward-thinking Governing Body.

Today the School is fully co-educational, offering both day and boarding places. The Headmaster is assisted by 21 qualified and experienced teachers. Through its Headmaster the School is a member of IAPS (The Independent Association of Prep Schools) as well as the Boarding Schools' Association.

Boys and girls are prepared for the Common Entrance and Scholarship examinations. The School's academic record is excellent, with regular awards being gained to major Independent Schools, as well as places in Lincolnshire Grammar Schools. Children with special learning needs are treated sympathetically within the mainstream, with support from specialist staff. The aim of the School is to give every child a good all-round education and to discover and develop his or her own particular talents.

The major school games for boys are rugby, hockey and cricket, and for girls netball, hockey and rounders. Both boys and girls can also enjoy cross-country, tennis, athletics and swimming. There is an annual Sports Day. All children have PE each week with time set aside for instruction in gymnastics and swimming. Skills in games such as basketball and badminton also form the basis of these lessons.

The school lays heavy emphasis on extra-curricular activities, sport of various kinds, music, the visual arts and drama. All teachers are expected to help in some way with this. There is also a strong and continuing Christian tradition at St Hugh's, where children are encouraged to consider what they believe and develop a faith of their own within the context of regular acts of Christian Worship.

The school has excellent facilities including a modern sports hall, an assembly hall with stage and lighting, a heated indoor swimming pool, extensive playing fields including an all-weather pitch, a fine library, dedicated classrooms and a large Music, Design and ICT studios. The facilities are continually being updated and added to.

Weekly and flexi boarders are accommodated in a well-appointed House under the close supervision of a Houseparent. Dormitories and common rooms are bright and cheerful and recognition is given to the importance of children having a place where they can feel at home and relaxed at the end of the day. Contact with parents and guardians is well maintained. Minibus transport for day pupils is provided from Boston, Louth, Skegness, Lincoln, Market Rasen and Sleaford.

The Pre-Preparatory department caters for approximately 40 children aged from 4 to 7 and is located in its own building with separate play area and staff.

The Nursery for children aged between 2 and 4 is attached to the Pre-Prep and accommodates approximately 45 children.

Charitable status. St Hugh's School (Woodhall Spa) Limited is a Registered Charity, number 527611. It exists to provide a high standard of education and care to pupils from the age of 2 to 13.

St James Prep School

Earsby Street, London W14 8SH

Tel: 020 7348 1794
email: admissions@stjamesprep.org.uk
website: www.stjamesschools.co.uk/prepschool

Chair of Governors: Mr Jeremy Sinclair

Headmistress: **Mrs Catherine Thomlinson**, BA Hons

Age Range. Boys 4–11. Boys can then transfer to St James Senior Boys' School (*see entry in The Society of Heads section*) or other senior schools.

Girls 4–11. Girls then transfer to St James Senior Girls' School (*see entry in GSA section*) or other senior schools.

Number in School. 125 Boys and 127 Girls.

Fees per term (2018–2019). Reception and Years 1, 2 and 3 £5,970, Years 4–6 £5,475.

St James provides an inspiring education. The Prep School is situated on a large Central London site and the beautiful Victorian building provides an Assembly Hall/Theatre, Gym and large airy classrooms. The playground has a climbing wall and pretty cloister gardens.

The curriculum is imaginatively and carefully balanced and, together with the impressive level of commitment from the teaching staff, high academic standards of reading, writing and arithmetic are achieved and above all a love of knowledge. Art, Drama and Music are taught with enthusiasm and results are outstanding; children sing daily and morning assemblies bring joy and a sense of unity throughout the school.

An interest and knowledge in that which is common to all traditions is cultivated. Every class has a weekly Philosophy lesson during which they explore virtues such as consideration, friendship and truthfulness. The school's philosophy curriculum is available on the website, together with curriculum details of all subjects taught.

Team sports, gymnastics or athletics are played daily and full use is made of good facilities both within school and locally. A rota of after-school clubs offers a rich choice of activities, including Ballet, French, Fencing, Cricket, Netball, Rugby and Yoga.

Creative residential holidays are organised each year for children in the Upper Prep School (7+ years) to places such as New Barn in Dorset, Chartres in France and to Northumberland, where History, Geography and Geometry become a living experience and time is enjoyed out of London with their friends and teachers.

Boys and girls are taught separately with frequent joint activities such as plays, concerts and outings. Educating the children about the environment is part of the school's wider curriculum. The Reception classes are involved with the Forest Schools programme and from Year 3 the children visit Minstead Study Centre in Dorset, where they learn about the environment and look after livestock.

The obvious happiness of the children flows from the full education offered and a level of attention and care from teachers that has become a St James trademark.

Charitable status. The Independent Educational Association Limited is a Registered Charity, number 270156. It exists to provide education for boys and girls.

St John's Beaumont

Priest Hill, Old Windsor, Berkshire SL4 2JN

Tel: 01784 494053
Fax: 01784 494048
email: kmasterson@sjb.email
website: www.SJBWindsor.uk
Twitter: @SJBHeadmaster
           @SJBAway
           @SJBBoarding
           @SJBSports
Facebook: @SJBWindsor

Chairman of Governors: T R Cook

Headmaster: **G E F Delaney**, BA Hons, PGCE

Age Range. 3–13.

Number of Boys. 300 (60 Full, Weekly, Tailored Boarders; 240 Day Boys).

Fees per term (2018–2019). Boarding £9,573; Weekly Boarding £8,106; Tailored Boarding £7,580–£7,892; Day Boys £4,249–£6,244; Pre-Preparatory (Nursery–Year 1) £3,264.

St John's Beaumont is a Roman Catholic Jesuit boarding and day preparatory school for boys. The aim is to encourage well-rounded young men who can develop the confidence and open-mindedness to make the most of every opportunity and challenge that life will offer to them. It is important to us that boys demonstrate the same commitment to challenge as they do to areas that naturally inspire and interest them. Our curriculum is broad and invites the boys to think about life from a wider perspective: one that piques their interest and challenges them to see relationships and circumstances from a more sensitive and intelligent perspective. Classes are small and boys can receive individual attention according to their needs and abilities. There is a great emphasis on the academic and pastoral development of the boys and as a result the curriculum and teaching approach is planned very much with boys in mind. All boys study a rich variety of subjects within the curriculum and this is further supported by an excellent extra-curricular program for boys of all ages, including; rowing, rock climbing, philosophy, chef academy, golf and scuba diving. Boys are prepared for entry to a wide range of day and boarding schools including some of the top independent schools in the country and have won many scholarships in recent years.

The first purpose-built prep school in England, this pretty Victorian building stands in 70 acres on the edge of Windsor Great Park. It has a state-of-the-art sports hall and impressive ICT facilities endorsed by Microsoft awarding the school Beacon status. There is a dedicated science and art block, music school, concert hall and 25-metre indoor swimming pool. Games are played every day and the school particularly excels at rugby, cricket, tennis and swimming. The school's pool is also used by other schools and the local community. Wireless technology is available in classrooms enabling access to individual tablets and there are interactive whiteboards in all classrooms.

The boys have daily opportunity for religious practice, as well as formal instruction and informal guidance.

An illustrated prospectus is available from the Headmaster, who is always pleased to meet parents and to show them round the school.

Charitable status. St John's is a Registered Charity, number 230165. It exists to provide education for boys.

St John's College Infant and Junior School

Grove Road South, Southsea, Hampshire PO5 3QW
Tel: 023 9281 5118
email: info@stjohnscollege.co.uk
website: www.stjohnscollege.co.uk

Chairman of Governors: Mr R Staker

Headmaster: **Mr R A Shrubsall**, MA Ed

Head of Pre-Prep: Mrs C Davies, BA Hons QTS

Age Range. Co-educational 2–11 years.
Number of Pupils. 150.
Fees per term (2018–2019). Junior School: Day £3,075–£3,285; Years 5 & 6 UK Boarding £8,695.

St John's College is an independent school founded to provide an academic education in a Christian environment. The College is fully co-educational, day and boarding, with approximately 600 pupils and students ranging in age from 2 to 18. We offer a continuous range of education, starting in the Nursery and progressing through the Junior and Senior schools to the Sixth Form. We are a Christian school but welcome pupils of all faiths and also those with no religious beliefs.

The Junior School is a self-contained unit but located on the main College campus. The Junior School enjoys the use of many excellent facilities: a sports centre, theatre, computer suite, library, science laboratory and music room. The attractive site is complemented by 40 acres of well-maintained playing fields, located on the outskirts of the city.

A broadly balanced and extended curriculum is offered, encompassing all aspects of the National Curriculum at Key Stages 1 and 2. Close staff liaison ensures a smooth automatic transition for pupils into the Senior School at age 11. The Early Years Foundation Stage is covered in Nursery and Reception Year (known as Little St John's).

The Junior School has a fine academic, musical and sporting tradition and there is a wide range of extra-curricular clubs which run during lunchtimes and after school. Educational and character-building residential trips are offered at holiday times.

St John's is committed to developing the whole person, but at the very heart of all that we do is teaching and learning. Our academic record is a very good one and the commitment of our staff to each pupil is outstanding.

A prospectus and further details are available from the Admissions Registrar.

St John's College School

73 Grange Road, Cambridge, Cambs CB3 9AB
Tel: 01223 353532 Reception
                 01223 353652 Admissions Secretary
Fax: 01223 355846
email: shoffice@sjcs.co.uk
                 bhoffice@sjcs.co.uk
website: www.sjcs.co.uk

Chairman of Governors: Mrs Sarah Kerr-Dineen

Headmaster: **Mr Neil R Chippington**, MA, MEd, FRCO

Age Range. 4–13.
Number of Children. 454 girls and boys (including 21 Chorister and 7 Non-Chorister boy and girl boarders).
Fees per term (2018–2019). Choristers £2,690; Day Boys and Girls (4–13) £3,875–£5,110 (according to age); Boarders £8,070. Bursaries available for Choristers.

Profile. St John's prides itself on the quality of the academic and pastoral care it provides for each child. Through relaxed and friendly relations with children in a well-structured environment rich with opportunity; through close monitoring of progress; through communication and cooperation with parents; through expert staffing and, above all, through a sense of community that cares for the strengths and weaknesses of each of its members, St John's has consistently achieved outstanding results exemplified by over 70 scholarships during the last three years. Whilst its Choristers maintain the tradition of choral services and tour the world, St John's status as an Expert Centre for ICT, and other innovations, ensure the school's commitment to the future. Mr Neil Chippington joined St John's as the new Headmaster in September 2016, having been Head at St Paul's Cathedral School in London.

Entry. At 4–7 by parental interview; at 7–12 by parental interview, report from previous school and, as appropriate, assessment.

Curriculum. The curriculum surrounds the core of formal skills teaching with a breadth of enrichment and extension for each child's talents. In addition to the usual subjects including specialist taught DT, ICT, Art, Music, Dance and Drama, and PE for all pupils, the following are also available: French (from 4+), Latin (from 9+), Greek (optional from 11+), Spanish (11+). Pupils prepared for CE and Scholarship examinations. Philosophy and Study Skills are now regularly taught to pupils in certain year groups and all pupils are being introduced to Mindfulness.

Leavers. Virtually all go to senior independent day or boarding schools. The School works closely with parents to assist them in finding the best school for their child.

Consultation. Tutorial system (1 teacher to 10 pupils) with daily tutorial session timetabled. Half yearly academic assessments, end of year examinations, termly Parents' Evenings and weekly staff 'surgery' times.

Sports. Athletics, Badminton, Basketball, Cricket, Cross Country, Football, Golf, Gymnastics, Hockey, Netball, Rounders, Rowing, Rugby, Short Tennis, Squash, Swimming, Table Tennis, Tennis. All games are timetabled and therefore given significant status. All major sports strong.

Activities. Numerous clubs including Art, Chess, Dance, Drama, Pottery, Sketching, Design Technology, Craft, Information Technology, Maths games and puzzles, Magic, Touch-typing, Cycling Proficiency, General Knowledge, Debating, Poetry, Sewing and Wardrobe. College Choir of international status, Chamber Groups, Orchestras, School Chapel Choir, Junior Chamber Choir, Parents' Choir, Major theatrical productions, e.g. *The Sound of Music, Hamlet*, and theatrical opportunities for all children. A range of visits relating to curriculum plus French, Classics, skiing and outward bound trips.

Facilities. School on two sites with facilities used by all pupils.

Byron House (4–8). Outstanding facilities including Science, DT Centre, two large suites of networked PCs, newly-designed Library, Drama Studio, Gym, Hall, and specialist Music wing. The Byron House site has also been redeveloped and the children can now use the newly landscaped and planted 'Forest Garden'. The site has completely redesigned classrooms and a large learning space for child-initiated learning and digital learning. The rooms are fitted with bespoke, streamlined storage. Investigative and collaborative skills have been fostered by the use of the new 'working walls' and 'writeable tables'.

Senior House (9–13). The Senior House site has been completely redeveloped. In addition to existing facilities such as the Chapel, Theatre, Gymnasium Science Laboratory, Art Room, ICT Room, Swimming Pool and Music School, the site boasts 14 new classrooms, an outstanding Library, a new DT and Computer Control and Graphics facility, a second Science Laboratory, a new Drama Studio, new Music facilities, a Quiet Garden, a new Multi-Sports Court and changing block, extensive storage and excellent staff facilities.

Boarding. From age 8. Girl and boy boarders form an integral part of life at St John's and benefit from all the School's facilities whilst living in the homely, caring atmosphere of a brand new Boarding House which was completed in Spring 2011. The Boarding House accommodates up to 40 boys and girls. These improved facilities include recreation areas, a library, TV, table tennis and use of all Senior House facilities. Day boarding and 'Waiters' facilities allow the School to be flexible to the needs of parents and children alike.

Charitable status. St John's College School is part of St John's College Cambridge, which is a Registered Charity, number 1137428.

St John's School

Potter Street Hill, Northwood, Middlesex HA6 3QY

Tel:	020 8866 0067
email:	office@st-johns.org.uk
website:	www.st-johns.org.uk
Twitter:	@stjsnorthwood

Chairman of Governors: Lady A Harding

Headmaster: **Mr M S Robinson**, BSc, PGCE Loughborough

Age Range. 3–13.
Number of Boys. 350 Day Boys (Prep 221; Pre-Prep and Nursery 129).
Fees per annum (2018–2019). Nursery £10,420; Pre-Preparatory £14,050; Preparatory £15,110.

Facing South, on a 35-acre site, we have outstanding views over London. Since the Merchant Taylors' Educa-

tional Trust took the School under its wing, impressive development has taken place. St John's has gained a gymnasium and changing block, two science laboratories, a six classroom Pre-Prep Department and a Junior classroom block. Another major development provided an Assembly Hall/Theatre, an Art Studio, Design & Technology Workshop, ICT Centre and a new Music Department. At the same time, other areas of the School were refurbished creating specialist teaching areas for English, French, History, Geography and Mathematics. We also acquired an area of grassland and woodland for ecological and environmental study, to add to our extensive playing fields and formal gardens.

A major extension of our Pre-Preparatory Department provided Nursery facilities, an Information Technology Suite and Library. Extra play area, including an 'indoor quiet area' and a Forest School, have also been created for our Pre-Prep and Nursery pupils. Our playing fields have been transformed with the construction of a large, all-weather multi-purpose sports area. At the same time, our four rugby pitches and athletics track were levelled and provided with excellent drainage and irrigation. Most recently, we have created a small Golf Course.

Most of the boys enter the School at either the age of three into the Nursery or at four into the Pre-Prep and there is a separate entry into the Prep School at seven. St John's has an excellent record of success in scholarship and senior school entrance examinations. Boys are prepared for all independent schools, however, our links with Merchant Taylors' School, Northwood, are particularly strong.

Although the School was originally a Church of England foundation, boys of all religions and denominations are welcome.

Charitable status. St John's School, part of the Merchant Taylors' Educational Trust, is a Registered Charity, number 1063738. It exists for the purpose of educating boys.

St Joseph's In The Park School

St Mary's Lane, Hertingfordbury, Hertfordshire SG14 2LX

Tel:	01992 513810
email:	admin@stjosephsinthepark.co.uk
	marketing@stjosephsinthepark.co.uk
website:	www.stjosephsinthepark.co.uk
Twitter:	@fromthepark

Chair of Governors: Mrs Pauline Maile

Head: **Mr Douglas Brown**, BA Hons

Age Range. 3–11 Co-educational.
Number of Pupils. 160.
Fees per term (2018–2019). Pre School (Kindergarten and Nursery) (full-time) £3,053 (fees are pro-rata for more or fewer sessions), Reception, Year 1 & Years 2 £4,020, Lower Juniors Y3 to Y4 £4,179, Upper Juniors Y5 to Y6 £4,203, Woodlands Learning Support Centre Y3 to Y6 £5,633. All fees are inclusive of books, stationery and lunches.

St Joseph's In The Park is a single-form entry, co-educational school for children between the ages of 3 and 11 years. Founded in 1898, it is one of the oldest Independent Schools in the area.

Set within 40 acres of Hertingfordbury Park on the outskirts of Hertford, St Joseph's In The Park has not only a celebrated reputation for high academic standards, but also a particularly outstanding tradition in pastoral care and a family environment. Our latest ISI inspection judged us to be

'Excellent' in all areas. This is the highest possible accolade from the largest inspection body for independent schools. The Inspectors noted that *"the pupils' achievement is excellent. It is underpinned by high quality teaching and a vibrant curriculum"*; in addition, the *"pupils thrive in the school's atmosphere of hard work, enjoyment and effort"*.

Through each Key Stage the children experience an exciting curriculum. The core focus of Literacy, Mathematics and Science is supported by a themed approach to some of the Foundation Subjects.

Our environment permits children to develop and learn in a contemporary educational setting which includes:

- a designated Wrap Around Care room providing an extended day, starting with Breakfast Club from 7.30 am and After School Care until 6.00 pm with a light tea at 4.30 pm. Wrap Around Care Fees are additional to school fees.
- the Woodlands Department of Learning, established in 1998, is specifically arranged to respond to the needs of those children who have some difficulty with English or Mathematics or because of a general requirement for support for a specific learning difficulty such as dyslexia or dyscalculia.
- a Wednesday afternoon programme of technology, art and sport for Juniors which changes every half term during the year and may be enriched to include scuba diving, textiles, photography, cookery, golf, forest school, skiing and street dance delivered by specialists. After exams our Year 6 are offered an Opportunities Week, which is intended to prepare them for life beyond St Joseph's and support their individual development;
- two choirs and music lessons in dedicated music rooms that include singing, guitar, drums, clarinet, violin and piano, ensuring that music is enjoyed throughout the school;
- an Art & Design room to provide a bespoke area for creativity;
- a separate Science Room providing space for discovery, taught by a dedicated Science Teacher;
- healthy-eating menus on a three-week rotation providing nut-free, nutritious and varied meals all prepared in the school kitchen by experienced and long-standing catering staff;
- extensive woodland setting within beautiful parkland that provides a wonderful environment for our children to learn and develop outdoors;
- an outdoor heated swimming pool, sports field and large, multi-purpose hall for drama, dance, concerts and sports;
- on-site dedicated car park.

A prospectus which further illustrates the distinctiveness of the school is available on request.

Charitable status. St Joseph's In The Park School is a Registered Charity, number 1111064.

St Lawrence College Junior School

College Road, Ramsgate, Kent CT11 7AF

Tel: 01843 572912
email: jsoffice@slcuk.com
website: www.slcuk.com
Twitter: @slcMain
Facebook: @slcukofficial

Chairman of the Council: Mr David W Taylor, MA Oxon, PGCE, FRSA

Head: **Mrs Ellen Rowe**, BA Hons, PGCE, IAPS

Age Range. 3–11.

Number of Pupils. 200 boys and girls, a dozen of whom are boarders.

Fees per term (2018–2019). Boarders £8,985, Day £2,565–£4,010.

St Lawrence College Junior School offers a supportive, caring environment, based on traditional Christian values, in which children are given every opportunity to fulfil their potential. Academic expectations are high, but realistic and open-minded. Personal attention is given within small classes where talents are recognised and needs are catered for. All pupils benefit from 'Outdoor Adventures' lessons as part of the curriculum.

Most pupils transfer to the Senior School at 11+, and scholarships are regularly earned. There is also an excellent record of success at securing places in the highly-selective local grammar schools.

The Junior School is based in an attractive Victorian building in a peaceful corner of the 45-acre St Lawrence College campus. Its own independent facilities include a Music Department and Performance Hall, Science Lab, Art Studio, Learning Resources Centre, adventure playgrounds, tennis courts and spacious playing fields. Membership of the wider College community gives pupils the best of both worlds, and they are able to share many of the Senior School's excellent specialist facilities, including the Sports Centre and Theatre. Boarders enjoy living in Kirby House, a modern, purpose-built development which offers en-suite accommodation of exceptional quality.

The wide range of sports on offer includes rugby, hockey, cricket, netball, football, athletics, cross-country and swimming. There are plenty of fixtures against other schools, but, most importantly, children learn the value of fitness, cooperative teamwork and good sportsmanship. There is a proud musical tradition, and plenty of scope for drama and the creative arts, including LAMDA lessons. Some extra-curricular activities take place at the end of the school day, but most are concentrated into the popular, informal varied Saturday morning programme.

St Lawrence's Christian heritage underpins all that the Junior School stands for. An atmosphere of trust and mutual respect is based on kindness, forgiveness and consideration for others. There is a strong emphasis placed on thoughtful conduct, courtesy and good manners, and on endowing young people with a clear sense of moral responsibility.

Charitable status. The Corporation of St Lawrence College is a Registered Charity, number 307921. It exists to provide education for boys and girls.

St Leonards Junior School

St Andrews, Fife KY16 9QJ

Tel: 01334 472126
Fax: 01334 476152
email: sljs@stleonards-fife.org
website: www.stleonards-fife.org
Twitter: @StLeonards_Head
Facebook: @stleonardsschool

Chair of the St Leonards Council: Prof Verity Brown, BSc, MBA, PhD, FRSE

Headmistress: **Eve Moran**, BA Hons Hull

Age Range. 5–12.
Number of Pupils. 175 (73 girls, 102 boys).
Fees per term (2018–2019). Day: £2,900 (Years 1–3), £3,469 (Years 4–5), £3,889 (Years 6–7). Boarding (Years 6–7): £7,582.

St Leonards Junior School in St Andrews is the co-educational junior school of St Leonards. The school is administered by the St Leonards Council and educates children between the ages of 5 and 12, from Year 1 to Year 7.

Pupils are prepared for entry to St Leonards Senior School. With specialist teachers and small class sizes, children benefit from individual attention. In addition to a strong academic tradition, drama, music, art, ICT and PE are included in the timetable.

St Leonards Junior School is the first school in Scotland to have be accredited to teach the inspiring International Baccalaureate Primary Years Programme, which encourages boys and girls to develop a love of learning.

Pupils enjoy a dynamic and refreshing way of learning both in and outside the classroom. A wide variety of sports are available, with rugby, hockey, netball, lacrosse, tennis and cricket being the main team activities. Tuition in golf, judo and swimming is also offered.

Outdoor education activities include water sports and beach walks on the East Sands, which is just a four-minute walk from the school grounds. There are also classes in Scottish Country Dancing and ballet.

Charitable status. St Leonards School is a Registered Charity, number SC010904. It exists to provide education to children between the ages of 5 and 18.

St Margaret's Preparatory School

Curzon Street, Calne, Wiltshire SN11 0DF

Tel:	01249 857220
Fax:	01249 857227
email:	office@stmargaretsprep.org.uk
website:	www.stmargaretsprep.org.uk
Twitter:	@StMargaretsPrep

Chairman of Governors: Mr S Adde, BSc

Headmistress: Mrs K E Cordon, GLCM, LLCM TD, ALCM

Deputy Head: Miss C L Jones, CertEd
Head of Pre-Prep: Mrs J Heal, BA Hons QTS EYPS
Head of Learning Support: Mrs H Higgins, BSp & H Th Hons, MPhil, Dip SpLD, Adv Dip SENCO
Bursar: Mr D Boswell, BEd Hons, QTS

Age Range. 3–11.
Number of Pupils. 200 Day: 110 girls, 90 boys.
Fees per term (2018–2019). £1,573–£4,500.
From the Headmistress – Mrs Karen Cordon:

How do you measure an excellent education? Some would argue it's by exam results and a smooth passage to the next school, but I firmly believe that the unquantifiable aspects are every bit as important a benchmark.

St Margaret's is so much more than just a stepping-stone to academic success at 11+. In joining our vibrant community your son or daughter will start a lifelong journey of exploration. We will provide your child with endless opportunities to unearth talents, ignite interests, take risks, and experience failure as well as success. Along the way your son might discover a passion for music, or your daughter may become a gifted sportswoman.

Like you, we aspire for your child to be more than the sum of his or her academic achievement. That's why we place just as much value on building self-confidence and self-esteem, on encouraging self-assessment and personal organisation. These qualities are harder to measure, but they

are the key to your child ultimately being the best he or she can be.

Naturally, you'll be keen to understand what makes St Margaret's special? You will undoubtedly want your children to be happy and enjoy a broad and stimulating education that's rich in opportunities. But St Margaret's is so much more.

The right environment. Your child will learn in a safe, nurturing environment and spend each day in modern, stimulating and purpose-built teaching spaces. 30 acres of campus and off-site facilities mean there's space to explore, learn, play, let off steam, relax, think and grow.

Facilities and opportunities to develop potential. Wherever your child's strengths and interests lie, we have the facilities to support them. Learning spaces are contemporary, vibrant and well-equipped; these have been purpose-built in the last 10 years. These include dedicated specialist teaching rooms; a 25m indoor swimming pool; sports pitches; all-weather Astroturf; Chapel; dining hall; theatre and an outstanding Library and Computer Suite where interactive learning takes place. Additionally, outdoor space is plentiful and children enjoy time spent in the school garden, wildlife area, courtyard classroom or one of the many play areas.

A tailored learning programme. Teaching throughout the school is tailored to meet the needs of the individual child. Children are encouraged to reflect and evaluate their own learning and with support identify their next steps. Specialist teachers offer a wide range of experiences and as a result, our teaching delivers truly personalised learning for each child. An extensive range of mobile technology enhances learning across the curriculum.

Zest and vitality. Your child will join a school with real spirit and energy, which lives each day to the full. We purposefully pack excitement and learning experiences into every moment. Our staff are passionate about teaching and lessons are fun, vibrant and engaging. The children's love of learning is infectious and we hope it'll rub off on you too!

Foundations for life. Of course you want your children to be happy, alongside giving them the best possible start in life. St Margaret's is a place where friendships and special memories are created and where a love of learning is established. Your children will understand that success requires hard work, personal responsibility, respect and consideration for others. These qualities will remain with them, equipping him or her for future challenges and providing an edge in years to come.

I would really like to have the opportunity to find out more about your family and help you decide whether St Margaret's is the right place for your child's exciting journey of adventure and exploration. We welcome visitors at any time of year – please contact us to make an appointment.

St Martin's Ampleforth

Gilling Castle, Gilling East, York YO62 4HP

Tel:	01439 766600
Fax:	01439 788538
email:	headmaster@stmartins.ampleforth.org.uk
website:	www.ampleforth.org.uk/stmartins

Chairman of the Trustees: Mrs Claire Smith

Headmaster: Dr David Moses, MA, DPhil

Age Range. 10 to 13 years.

Number of Pupils. 49 (28 Boarders, 21 Flexi Boarders and Day Children).

Fees per term (2018–2019). Boarding £8,417; Day £5,467.

St Martin's Ampleforth is a boarding and day school which takes boys and girls from the age of 10+ years and prepares them for Common Entrance and Scholarship examinations. It is expected most of the pupils will enter Ampleforth College at 13+.

St Martin's Ampleforth is based in a 14th century castle with spacious and secluded gardens, 18 miles north of York and close to the North Yorkshire Moors National Park.

All Faiths are made most welcome in this Benedictine school. The Chaplaincy team is led by a monk of Ampleforth Abbey.

The highest academic standards are aimed for, within a broad and challenging curriculum. Each pupil's ability is taken into account. Very able children are provided for and coached for scholarships to Ampleforth College and other leading independent senior schools, whilst those with learning difficulties, including dyslexia, are given qualified specialist help. Each form has a tutor responsible for overall progress and pastoral support. Setting is in place from Year 6 and beyond.

There is a striking variety of extracurricular pursuits including Forest School, fencing, golf, shooting, drama, dance, swimming and debating. The School has an enviable reputation for games and fields highly successful teams in rugby, netball, cricket, rounders, hockey, track and field and cross-country running.

Music is strong. Typically, 80% of pupils learn musical instruments and perform regularly. The School provides the trebles for the acclaimed Ampleforth College Schola Cantorum and there is an increasingly successful girls' Schola too. A purpose-built performing arts centre enhances the current provision for choral and instrumental performance as well as fostering drama throughout the school.

Parents are considered part of the School community. They are welcome at any time, especially for matches, other organised events and, of course, for Mass on Sundays and feast days.

Facilities include a sports hall, ICT room, Music School, Language School, all-weather cricket nets, a 9-hole golf course and all-weather floodlit astroturf. The extensive grounds, including woods, lakes and gardens, combine a sense of space and freedom with unrivalled beauty.

Bursaries are available.

Daily transport is provided to and from Pickering, Malton, Kirkbymoorside, Boroughbridge, Easingwold, York and Helmsley.

Charitable status. St Martin's Ampleforth, as part of the St Laurence Trust, is a registered charity, number 1063808 and exists to provide education for boys and girls.

St Martin's School

40 Moor Park Road, Northwood, Middlesex HA6 2DJ

Tel: 01923 825740
Fax: 01923 835452
email: office@stmartins.org.uk
website: www.stmartins.org.uk
Twitter: @stmartinsprep

Chairman of Governors: Andy Harris

Headmaster: David T Tidmarsh, BSc Hons, PGCE

Age Range. 3–13.

Number of Boys. 400 Day Boys.

Fees per term (2018–2019). Main School £5,045; Pre-Prep £4,680; Kindergarten £1,925 (mornings). Bursaries are available, details on request.

St Martin's aims to provide boys aged 3–13 with the breadth of education and experience necessary for them to realise their full potential in a safe and friendly environment. An enthusiastic staff of 40 experienced and well-qualified teachers maintains high academic standards and provides broad sporting, musical and cultural opportunities. The atmosphere is friendly and lively with great emphasis on pastoral care.

The School, which is an Educational Trust, administered by a Board of Governors, prepares boys for entry to all the Independent Senior Schools. One hundred and two Scholarship awards have been won to senior schools during the last five years. The School, which is in a pleasant residential area, stands in 12 acres of grounds. Facilities include a Kindergarten and separate Pre-Preparatory building; two Science Laboratories; a Performing Arts Centre; a Sports Centre including an indoor swimming pool; a playground; two ICT suites; an Art Studio with facilities for Design Technology; 3 Tennis Courts.

Computing, Art, DT, and Music are included in the curriculum for all boys, and a large proportion of the boys in the School learn a musical instrument. There is a varied after-school activity programme for boys to pursue their interests.

There is a pre-school and after-school club from Kindergarten age upwards enabling parents to work a full day.

The School is divided into Patrols for competitions in work and games, and senior boys make a responsible contribution towards the running of the School. Boys are taught football, rugby, cross-country running, hockey, cricket, swimming, athletics and tennis. The school has a fine reputation in inter-school matches.

Charitable status. St Martin's (Northwood) Preparatory School Trust Limited is a Registered Charity, number 312648. It exists to provide education for boys.

St Mary's School, Hampstead

47 Fitzjohn's Avenue, Hampstead, London NW3 6PG

Tel: 020 7435 1868
Fax: 020 7794 7922
email: office@stmh.co.uk
website: www.stmh.co.uk

Chairman of Governors: Mrs Susan McCarron

Headmistress: Mrs Harriet Connor-Earl, BA

Deputy Head: Miss Philippa Walker, BA

Age Range. Girls 2¾–11, Boys 2¾–7.

Number in School. 300 pupils.

Fees per term (2018–2019). Nursery £2,660 (5 mornings a week), £42.50 each additional afternoon per week; Reception to Year 6 £4,915.

St Mary's School Hampstead provides an outstanding and inspirational Catholic education to girls from 3–11 years and boys from 3–7 years.

St Mary's School celebrates the uniqueness of every pupil and their achievements. The rigorous, challenging curriculum places a strong emphasis on high academic achievement within a culture of care and support.

The School aims to instil four key habits of learning in their pupils. The children are encouraged to be risk takers, not only in their play, but also in their learning. They are also taught to be resilient and not to fall at the first hurdle. Staff ask the children to make mistakes because in the process of challenging themselves, they make more academic progress and in turn excel not only in the classroom, but in their own self-confidence. The boys and girls at St Mary's School are respectful, not just of each other, but of themselves. Finally, pupils are encouraged to be reflective, on their faith, their behaviour and their academic work.

The School has recently invested in an extensive refurbishment programme to deliver the most up-to-date and stimulating learning spaces. A key priority has been incorporating the latest technology to bring learning to life with iPads and Google Chromebooks accessible to every pupil. The spacious classrooms are now flooded with natural light and offer innovative flexible seating.

The focus on technology is equally balanced with an emphasis on creative and physical development. Music, drama, art and sports are an essential part of school life and involve everyone. As part of the modernisation programme, the unique and extensive outside space has been enhanced. New climbing equipment has been installed and the full-size netball court has been upgraded allowing football, cricket and tennis to be introduced.

Used together – the integrated technology, the flexible seating and the broad curriculum – the girls at St Mary's are flourishing. They are adopting habits of learning and being encouraged to make independent choices which they can take forward into their secondary education.

Leavers achieve impressive results, gaining offers and Academic Scholarships from the best schools in the country, including City of London School for Girls, Francis Holland School, Highgate School, North London Collegiate, South Hampstead High School, St Mary's Ascot and St Paul's Girls' School.

St Mary's Preparatory School
Melrose

Abbey Park, Melrose, Roxburghshire TD6 9LN

Tel: 01896 822517
Fax: 01896 823550
email: office@stmarysmelrose.org.uk
website: www.stmarysmelrose.org.uk
Twitter: @SchoolMarys

Founded 1895.

Chairman of Governors: Mr G T G Baird

Headmaster: **William J Harvey**, BEd Hons

Age Range. 2–13 co-educational.
Number of Pupils. 180.
Fees per term (2018–2019). Day: Pre-Prep £4,400, Prep £5,350. Weekly Boarding: £6,350.
Curriculum. A healthy variety of subjects including traditional core studies reflecting both the Scottish and English Curriculums (English, Maths, Science, Computer Studies, French, Geography, History, Classics, Latin, Spanish, RE, Art, Music, Drama and PE). The School's intention is to provide a genuinely nourishing environment allowing for the development of the whole child.

Entry requirements. Application by letter or telephone, followed by a visit to the school, if possible, and a tour guided by senior pupils. All pupils can be offered an 'In-day' to help with placement.

Examinations offered. Common Entrance to Scholarship for independent senior schools in Scotland and England.

Academic, sports, games and leisure facilities. Classroom computers, Science Laboratory and a big open Art Room. Theatre-Arts and Assembly Hall for concerts and drama. Spacious games pitches supporting a strong tradition in rugby, cricket, hockey, netball and rounders. There is a cross-curricular Study Support Programme for talented and gifted children as well as for children with Specific Learning Difficulties.

Religious activities. Morning Assembly with hymn-singing and readings, stressing pupil participation and contribution through drama and music.

Charitable status. St Mary's School, Melrose is a Registered Charity, number SC009352. Its aim is to provide education for primary school children.

St Michael's Preparatory School

La Rue de la Houguette, Five Oaks, St Saviour, Jersey, Channel Islands JE2 7UG

Tel: +44(0)1534 856904
Fax: +44(0)1534 856620
email: clt@stmichaels.je
           office@stmichaels.je
website: www.stmichaels.je
Twitter: @stmichaelsprep
Facebook: @St-Michaels-Preparatory-School-Jersey

Headmaster: **M B S Rees**, DipEd, MEd

Senior Deputy Head: L G McAviney, Cert Ed, BEd Hons

Academic Deputy Head: Mrs L M Walsh, BA Hons QTS

Age Range. 3–14.
Number of Pupils. 168 Boys, 143 Girls.
Fees per term (2018–2019). Pre-Prep (Reception, Years 1 and 2) £3,205–£3,655; Juniors (Years 3 and 4) £4,525; Year 5 £4,755; Year 6 £4,990; Years 7 and 8 £5,020. Lunch £298.

Boys and girls are prepared for scholarship and entrance to all Independent Senior Schools. Hockey, rugby, football, gymnastics, netball, rounders, cricket, athletics and tennis are taught on spacious playing fields with pavilion and hard tennis courts which adjoin the school. The school also has a purpose-built Sports Hall (4 badminton court size), indoor swimming pool, gymnasium and dance/drama studio. Regular tours are made to Guernsey and England for sporting fixtures.

The school has flourishing and well equipped computer, art and design technology departments, in addition to networked computers in every classroom. A large variety of clubs and hobbies function within the school and many outdoor activities, including sailing and photography, are enjoyed by the children. Music, drama and art (including pottery), are all encouraged and a wide range of musical instruments are taught. There are three school choirs, two orchestras and a number of ensemble groups. The choirs participate locally and nationally in events and competitions.

For senior children there is an annual Activities Week, which takes Years 6, 7 and 8 to different locations in France and Year 5 take part in island-based activities. Each winter a party of children from Years 3 to 8 ski in Switzerland.

Care, consideration, courtesy and good manners are important aspects of behaviour that the school holds dear.

The academic and physical development, in addition to the spiritual, moral and cultural growth, of the whole child is the main aim of the school and every child is encouraged to do "a little better" than anyone thought possible.

St Michael's Preparatory School

198 Hadleigh Road, Leigh-on-Sea, Essex SS9 2LP

Tel:	01702 478719
Fax:	01702 710183
email:	office@stmichaelsschool.co.uk
website:	www.stmichaelsschool.com
Twitter:	@StMichaelsLeigh
Facebook:	@stmichaelsschool.co.uk

Chair of Governors: Mrs Jane Attwell

Acting Head: **Mrs Kate Mansfield**, BEd Hons Southampton, NPQH

Age Range. Co-educational 3–11 years.
Number of Pupils. 277 day pupils (128 boys, 149 girls).
Fees per term (2018–2019). £1,368–£3,200.

St Michael's is a Church of England Preparatory (IAPS) School founded in 1922 to provide pupils with a well-rounded education based on Christian principles, with children welcomed from other Christian traditions and faiths. The school has its own Chapel.

The school is situated in a popular residential area in Leigh-on-Sea within easy reach of public transport. London is accessible by rail and Fenchurch Street Station is approximately 40 minutes away.

The curriculum offered is broad, balanced and tailored towards the children's needs and it aims to contribute to the intellectual, physical, creative, social and spiritual development of each child. All the children, from Nursery through to Form 6, receive specialist teaching in Music, French and PE with additional specialist teaching in the Prep department. Pupils are prepared for the end of Key Stage standardised attainment tests, 11+ entry to local grammar schools and Entrance or Scholarship examinations for independent schools. High academic standards are achieved throughout the school and the children thrive in a happy but disciplined environment.

St Michael's has a dedicated and well-qualified staff team. Class sizes are small to enable personal attention to be given. The school is well resourced with many specialist areas. Nearby playing fields are used for Games. There is a wide range of extra-curricular activities available, with Music and Drama as particular strengths.

Visits to the school are warmly welcomed.

June 2015 ISI Inspection Report: "Excellent" across all areas of its provision, "Outstanding" EYFS provision.

June 2018 ISI Compliance Inspection Report: The School is compliant across all areas of its provision.

Charitable status. St Michael's Preparatory School is a Registered Charity, number 280688. It exists to provide education.

St Michael's Prep School
Otford

Otford Court, Row Dow, Otford, Sevenoaks, Kent TN14 5RY

Tel:	01959 522137
email:	office@stmichaels.kent.sch.uk
website:	www.stmichaels.kent.sch.uk
Twitter:	@StMichaels_Prep
Facebook:	@StMichaelsPrepSchool

Chair of Governors: Ms Paula Carter

Head: **Mrs J Aisher**, BA Oxon, PGCE London, MCIL

Head of Pre-Prep: Mrs Z Leech, BA Hons, PGCE

Age Range. 2–13 Co-educational.
Number of Pupils. 450.
Fees per term (2018–2019). £790–£4,800.

St Michael's Prep School is a non-selective, co-educational school promoting a rich, varied, broad and balanced education within a Christian context. We challenge and stimulate pupils to achieve their best and strive for excellence in all that they do; fostering in them a sense of wonder and joy in learning, so that they take real pride in their accomplishments. Children are helped to understand themselves as individuals, their feelings and emotions, how they can affect others and to show tolerance and respect for the diversity of the world in which we live, as well striving for individual academic excellence. St Michael's has a strong record of pupils gaining scholarships into Senior Schools.

Culturally the school provides a wide sporting, musical, artistic and dramatic programme to which all pupils are equally entitled and in which all children are encouraged to participate.

We recognise that every child is an individual and aim to promote their happiness, self-confidence and well-being as members of a caring community. Children are given opportunities to make a difference to their school and to the wider world. The school motto: *Perseverance, Wisdom, Gratitude* encapsulates the cornerstone of this education.

St Michael's has been judged excellent in both pupils' academic and personal development and we feel this is a welcome endorsement of what we believe about our school. We attract and retain some of the most excellent teaching and support staff who in turn ensure excellent outcomes for all children.

Pre-Prep is housed in a beautiful purpose-built eco-friendly building, where children learn and play with great joy.

St Michael's is set in 90 acres of the beautiful, rolling North Downs close to Sevenoaks town and the fast train service to central London. Our school is enhanced by a strong Parents and Friends Association and International Parents' Club who welcome international families.

A message from Mrs Jill Aisher our Headteacher:

I very much hope you take the opportunity to discover more about our community by looking at our website and coming to visit us soon. When you choose a school for your children, meeting and talking to pupils and staff is such an important part of knowing in your heart that this is the place where your family will flourish.

My own children, now all grown up, made the move to an independent school and never looked back. There is a confidence, a creativity, a caring soul to pupils at St Michael's; we love to meet children and take them from where they are now to places they never dreamed they would go.

Come and see for yourself. We can't wait to meet you.

Charitable status. St Michael's is a Registered Charity, number 1076999. It exists to provide education for boys and girls.

St Neot's Preparatory School

St Neot's Road, Eversley, Hook, Hampshire RG27 0PN

Tel:	Office: 0118 973 2118
	Admissions: 0118 973 9650
email:	office@stneotsprep.co.uk
	admissions@stneotsprep.co.uk
website:	www.stneotsprep.co.uk
Facebook:	@stneotsprep

Chairman of Governors: Mr S Scott

Head: **Mrs Deborah Henderson**, BA Hons QTS

Age Range. 2–13 years co-educational.
Number of Pupils. 331.
Fees per term (2018–2019). Years 5–8 £5,200, Year 3–4 £4,850, Reception–Year 2 £3,635, Nursery £66 per day (core hours), £42 per morning session, Tiny Tuskers £68 per day (core hours), £37 per morning session, additional hours charged at £8.75 per hour.

St Neot's, founded in 1888, is a happy, vibrant community for boys and girls from 2 to 13 years. The school is situated on the border of Hampshire and Berkshire and is set in 70 acres of beautiful grounds and woodland.

The school's educational philosophy is to inspire children to develop a love of learning in a supportive and happy environment, where each individual is encouraged to achieve their full academic potential and beyond. Children are motivated to discover their full range of talents and to develop the passion to pursue them. They are given the opportunity to embrace challenge, think creatively, develop self-confidence and foster empathy towards others, preparing them both intellectually and emotionally for success in the 21st Century.

We aim to provide the highest standards in teaching and learning, within a well rounded educational experience and St Neot's has a very strong record of success in achieving Scholarships and Awards to numerous Senior Schools.

St Neot's is committed to providing a world of opportunity in every aspect of school life. Stimulating learning environments ensure that engaged pupils work towards the highest academic standards, whilst also enjoying a breadth of experience in sport, music, art, drama and dance.

Emphasis is placed on developing independence, self-confidence, curiosity and collaboration. Forest School and Outdoor Education programmes encourage children of all ages to develop these attributes, which are so vital in the modern world. The St Neot's journey culminates in the Years 7 and 8 leadership programme, which draws together a mix of skills through the core elements of the Prep Schools Baccalaureate (PSB).

Sport is a strength of the school and our state-of-the-art sports complex, comprising sports hall, 25m indoor swimming pool, all-weather astro, cricket nets, hard tennis and netball courts, significantly supplement the extensive playing fields. There is also an on-site mountain bike track and a traversing wall. Judo, dance and tennis are taught by specialist coaches and there are many after-school clubs and activities covering a wide range of interests. Holiday Clubs run in all school breaks and offer a wealth of opportunities, both sporting and creative.

St Neot's holds a Gold Artsmark award, giving recognition to our achievements in art, music, drama and dance. A number of plays, concerts and recitals take place throughout the school year for all age groups, either in the school grounds or in the Performing Arts Centre.

Open Mornings take place termly and details of these can be found on the school website: www.stneotsprep.co.uk. We would also be delighted to arrange an individual tour and a meeting with the Head. Please contact Admissions on 0118 9739650; email: admissions@stneotsprep.co.uk.

Charitable status. St Neot's (Eversley) Limited is a Registered Charity, number 307324. The aim of the Charity is to try to provide the best all-round education possible to as many pupils as possible, with bursarial help according to need.

St Olave's Prep School

106–110 Southwood Road, New Eltham, London SE9 3QS

Tel:	020 8294 8930
Fax:	020 8294 8939
email:	office@stolaves.org.uk
website:	www.stolaves.org.uk

Chairman of Trustees: Mr M D Ireland, MIoD, FRSA

Headteacher: **Miss Claire Holloway**, BEd QTS

Age Range. 3–11.
Number of Pupils. 220 Day Boys and Girls.
Fees per term (2018–2019). Nursery £1,808–£3,616; Reception & Year 1 £3,800; Years 2–6 £4,100.

In a single sentence, the school aims to bring out the best in everyone. It seeks to achieve this aim by providing an all-round education for both boys and girls aged 3 to 11 in a warm and caring environment in which each child can thrive and be happy knowing that each is accepted for who they are.

A Christian ethos permeates the pastoral life of the school, where care for others through thoughtful and responsible behaviour is expected. Praise and encouragement are emphasised and relationships between staff and pupils are relaxed and friendly. A close partnership with parents is sought.

The children in the EYFS (Nursery and Reception) and Pre-Prep (Year 1 and Year 2) are taught in mixed-ability classes where each child's progress is carefully monitored by the Class Teacher. In the Upper School (Years 3–6) the children are set across the year group for Mathematics. Throughout the school individual differences are appropriately met, with the very able and those with mild learning difficulties receiving additional support where this is thought beneficial. The school is noted for the broad curriculum it offers and for its excellent achievements in Music and Drama. A range of sporting activities is taught as part of the curriculum and there is a wide range of after school clubs and activities. Music and PE are taught by specialist teachers from the age of three, French is introduced at four years old and Latin at ten years old. The classrooms are equipped with computers and there is a networked suite which supports all areas of the curriculum. A specialist ICT teacher teaches all year groups from Reception to Year 6. Digital panels and portable devices are used to enhance learning.

St Olave's feeds a wide range of secondary schools and parents are given help in choosing the school most appropriate to meet the needs of their child.

Charitable status. St Olave's School is a Registered Charity, number 312734. It exists to provide high quality education for boys and girls.

St Olave's School, York
The Prep School of St Peter's School, York

York YO30 6AB

Tel:	01904 527416
Fax:	01904 527303
email:	enquiries@stolavesyork.org.uk
website:	www.stolavesyork.org.uk
Twitter:	@StOlavesYork
Facebook:	@stolavesyork

Chairman of the Governors: Mr W Woolley

Master: **Mr A I Falconer**, BA Hons Lancaster, MBA Leicester

Deputy Head: Mr M C Ferguson, HDipEd Capetown College of Education

Master's Secretary: Mrs C Murgatroyd

Age Range. 8–13 co-educational.
Number of Pupils. 209 Boys, 149 Girls.
Fees per term (2018–2019). Day: £4,115–£4,985; Boarding: £7,720–£8,520. Non-EU Boarder: £8,305 (Year 6), £9,155 (Years 7 & 8).

Weekly and flexi boarding are available. Tuition fees include the costs of stationery and textbooks. There are no compulsory extras except for examination fees. Lunches are included in day fees.

St Olave's was founded in 1876. With its own halls, music school, practical subjects workshops, sports hall and magnificently appointed specialist teaching rooms, St Olave's enjoys some of the best facilities for a prep school of its type.

The school puts praise, encouragement and pastoral care of the individual as its highest priority. There is a demanding wide curriculum from the earliest age with specialist subject areas – modern foreign languages, information technology, science and music, amongst others – being taught by specialist teachers from Year 4. Progress is monitored through a regular system of effort grades, and attainment is measured through internal and externally moderated tests.

Boarding is a flourishing aspect of the school, with a co-educational House under the constant care of resident House parents and their own family. Weekly and flexi boarding are also available. There are also five Day Houses.

Music plays an important part in the life of the school with 22 music teachers, two orchestras, a wind band and 14 ensembles playing and practising weekly. Over 200 pupils learn individual instruments, and all are encouraged to join larger groups.

Sport has an equally high profile where football, hockey, cricket, netball, rugby, tennis and swimming are major sports. Athletics, cross-country running, squash, badminton, basketball and volleyball are also available for all. The boys have won the National Schools' Seven-a-Side Rugby tournament four times in the last eleven years and won the National Cricket JET cup. The school has 23 tennis courts, a synthetic pitch and a 25m 6-lane swimming pool.

Drama has an increasing profile, and out-of-school activities flourish through clubs such as science society, chess, photography, art and trampoline.

The vast majority of boys and girls move on to St Peter's and are not required to take the Common Entrance examination.

Entrance assessments are held in January/February each year, and assessments can also be arranged at other times. Entry is possible in most year groups, although the school is heavily oversubscribed at most stages. Means-tested fee assistance is available from age 11.

Charitable status. St Peter's School, York, is a Registered Charity, number 1141329. It exists to provide education for boys and girls.

St Paul's Cathedral School

---

2 New Change, London EC4M 9AD

Tel:	020 7248 5156
Fax:	020 7329 6568
email:	office@spcs.london.sch.uk
website:	www.spcslondon.com

Chairman of Governors: The Very Revd Dr David Ison, Dean of St Paul's Cathedral

Headmaster: **Mr Simon Larter-Evans**, BA Hons, PGCE, FRSA

Age Range. 4–13 Co-educational.
Number of Pupils. Boarding Choristers 28, Day Boys 118, Day Girls 106, Pre-Prep 62.
Fees per term (2018–2019). Choristers £2,912; Day pupils £4,677–£5,035.

There have been choristers at St Paul's for over nine centuries. The present school is a Church of England Foundation dating back over 100 years and is governed by the Dean and Chapter of St Paul's Cathedral and 7 Lay Governors. The broadening of educational expectations and the challenge of curricular developments led the Dean and Chapter to agree to expand the school in 1989 by admitting non-chorister day boys for the first time; a decision which continues to enrich the life of the school and Cathedral. In September 1998, the school admitted girls as well as boys into its new pre-prep department for 4–7 year olds. The school became fully co-educational in September 2002. It offers a broad curriculum leading to scholarship and Common Entrance examinations. In the first three years the work is tailored to individual needs bearing in mind the wide variety of educational backgrounds from which pupils come. The school has an excellent record in placing pupils in the senior schools of their choice, many with music scholarships. Every opportunity is taken to make use of the school's proximity to museums, libraries, galleries, theatres and the numerous attractions which London has to offer.

The 30 chorister boarders are housed on the School site and are fully integrated with the day pupils for all their academic studies and games. The choristers' cathedral choral training offers them a unique opportunity to participate in the rich musical life of St Paul's and the City.

The school was rehoused in the 60s in purpose-built premises on the eastern end of the Cathedral site. Refurbishment projects have added a new music school, art room, IT room, three pre-prep classrooms and games rooms to the existing facilities which include a hall/gymnasium, science laboratory, common room and a TV/video room. All pupils are encouraged to play a musical instrument (most pupils play two) and there are music and theory lessons with school orchestras and chamber groups.

A wide variety of games is offered including field sports at local playing fields and weekly swimming lessons. The children have their own playground and the use of the hall for indoor games and gymnastics.

Admissions procedure: Prospective pupils of 7+ years in September are given academic tests in verbal and non-verbal reasoning, usually in January of the previous academic year.

Pre-Prep children (4+) are assessed in an informal play situation in the November prior to entry.

Voice trials and tests for chorister places are held throughout the year for boys between 6½ and 8½ years old.

St Paul's Juniors

Lonsdale Road, London SW13 9JT

Tel:	020 8748 3461
Fax:	020 8746 5357
email:	spjheadpa@stpaulsschool.org.uk
website:	www.stpaulsschool.org.uk

Chairman of Governors: J M Robertson, BSc

Head: **Maxine Shaw**, BSc London, PGCE Hull, PG Dip Brunel, NPQH

Age Range. 7–13.
Number of Boys. 490.
Fees per term (2018–2019). £6,670.

St Paul's Juniors is the junior division for St Paul's School (*see entry in HMC section*) and attracts bright, enthusiastic boys who are inquisitive and eager to learn.

Working closely alongside St Paul's seniors to inform the curriculum, ensures continuity and a more holistic learning experience, with some teaching staff working across both schools. Pupils at St Paul's Juniors hold a place at St Paul's School and transfer automatically at the end of Year 8, subject to ongoing good work and conduct, rather than a formal examination. Our aim is to offer a broad education to every pupil, along with the opportunity to enjoy a wide range of activities. Music, Art, Drama and Sport are all strong, but additional activities range from history and debating to chess, coding and cookery.

Boys join the School at 7+ and 8+ and 11+. Fifty-four boys join Year 3 into three classes of 18 and a further 18 join them at 8+. Thirty-six boys join in Year 7 creating a total of six classes in Years 7 and 8. Some of these places may be offered to pupils who sit an examination in Year 5 and defer their arrival for one year. This mode of entry is available to boys from maintained primary schools only. Entrance at all levels is by competitive examination and interview. Means-tested bursaries are available at all points of entry.

St Paul's School sits on the south bank of the Thames. The Juniors are in separate but adjacent modern buildings and share many amenities, including the dining hall, sports complex, design & technology workshops and playing fields. St Paul's Juniors has its own main teaching block, hall/theatre, library, two computer rooms, drama studio and music school. Three science laboratories and art & design rooms are situated in a separate building.

Charitable status. St Paul's School is a Registered Charity, number 1119619. The object of the charity is to promote the education of boys in Greater London.

St Piran's

Gringer Hill, Maidenhead, Berkshire SL6 7LZ

Tel:	01628 594300
email:	registrar@stpirans.co.uk
website:	www.stpirans.co.uk

Chairman of Governors: Mrs Kate Taylor

Headmaster: **J Carroll**, BA Hons, BPhilEd, PGCE, NPQH

Age Range. 3–11 Co-educational.
Number of Pupils. 400 day pupils.
Fees per term (2018–2019). £3,619–£5,522. Nursery – 5 full days: £243.57 per week (funded).

St Piran's is a thriving co-educational IAPS day school set amid 10 delightful acres just to the north of Maidenhead town centre. Founded as a small school in Blackheath, London in 1805.

Class sizes are small with a maximum of 18 children. Boys and girls benefit from individual attention in all subjects. They are provided with a wide range of exciting opportunities both inside and outside the classroom. Numerous trips to castles and museums, theatres and shows, history re-enactments, geographical fieldwork and religious sites extend the children's understanding of the world around them. In addition to the academic subjects, pupils take part in a wide range of other activities each week.

Academically, the school offers a broad curriculum at all levels in the school. French starts with our youngest classes where confidence in the spoken language is encouraged. By Year 6 we are introducing Latin and Spanish. The children enjoy specialist teaching in art, games and PE, IT, swimming and music from an early age. We support children with their entrance exams at 11+ to Grammar Schools or other Senior independent schools. Our results over the years have been excellent, supporting our desire to encourage independent thinkers, confident individuals and strong leaders of the future.

The main sports that pupils take part in are rugby, football, netball, hockey, cricket (both girls and boys) and swimming. The school has its own indoor swimming pool and large sports hall. St Piran's also has a dance studio and pupils are encouraged to take an active part in the performing arts. We are blessed with wonderful facilities which serve to enhance the varied sports programmes that we offer the children at all levels.

The school has its own Leadership programme and regular visits off site are arranged for all the children, including residential trips.

Pupils may enter the school at any age, although the main intakes occur at Nursery and Reception. Scholarships and bursaries may be offered after assessment. Please contact the school and an appointment can be arranged to talk to the Headmaster about financial support.

The school is proud of its outstanding record of achievement and the fully rounded education that it provides within a friendly caring atmosphere. We are proud of our Christian tradition and family ethos which foster high expectations and successful, happy children.

Children and parents are warmly invited to visit St Piran's to see for themselves the excellent facilities that we offer and to meet some of the staff and pupils.

Charitable status. St Piran's School Limited is a Registered Charity, number 309094.

St Pius X Prep School

200 Garstang Road, Fulwood, Preston, Lancashire PR2 8RD

Tel:	01772 719937
Fax:	01772 787535
email:	enquiries@st-piusx.lancs.sch.uk
website:	www.stpiusx.co.uk

Chairman of Governors: P Clegg

Headmaster: Mr Andrew Platts

Age Range. 2–11.
Number of Children. 255 Day Girls and Boys.
Fees per term (2018–2019). Main School £2,600, Nursery £250 per week.

The School is administered as a non-profit-making educational trust by a Board of Governors, providing education from 2–11. The children are prepared for the entrance examinations to independent schools and local high schools. The school has an excellent record of scholarships to senior schools and SATS results at KS1 and KS2. The school has a large Nursery division which covers the EYFS in recently-refurbished Nursery rooms. The school is in four acres of its own grounds in a pleasant suburb of Preston. All preparatory curriculum subjects covered.

Sports taught are Association Football, Cricket, Tennis, Hockey, Netball, Rugby, Table Tennis, Rounders, Athletics and Cross Country.

Ballet, piano, clarinet, flute, violin, guitar and singing lessons are some of the optional extras offered. The school has a thriving music centre.

Charitable status. St Pius X School is a Registered Charity, number 526609. Its purpose is to equip the children with an outstanding academic and social education in a Catholic Christian environment, which will enable them to achieve their full potential – the school welcomes pupils of all faiths.

Saint Ronan's

Water Lane, Hawkhurst, Kent TN18 5DJ

Tel:	01580 752271
Fax:	01580 754882
email:	info@saintronans.co.uk
website:	www.saintronans.co.uk
Twitter:	@SaintRonans
Facebook:	@SaintRonans

Chairman of Governors: Mr Colin Willis

Headmaster: Mr William Trelawny-Vernon, BSc Hons

Deputy Head (*Pastoral*): Mr Ross Andrew
Deputy Head (*Academic*): Mr James Green

Age Range. 3–13 fully co-educational.
Number of Children. 430.
Fees per term (2018–2019). Day £3,492–5,984; Weekly boarding (Y4 and above) £7,227. We also operate a flexi boarding system (£38 per night) which can be tailored to individual needs.

Saint Ronan's is a family school as it has been since it was started in Worthing in 1883. It occupies a fine Victorian Mansion set in 249 acres of beautiful Weald of Kent countryside. There are numerous games pitches, hard tennis courts, a golf course and a swimming pool as well as a hundred-acre wood.

With an emphasis on family and pastoral care, the school has a unique and special atmosphere in which staff and children work together to achieve their aims. Small class sizes enable children to gain confidence and interact positively with their peers and the staff.

Academically we have an excellent pass rate at CE and many pupils gain Scholarships to major senior independent schools such as Eton, Sevenoaks, Benenden, Tonbridge, Harrow, King's Canterbury and Eastbourne College; we also prepare children for entry to local Grammar Schools and boast an enviable record. We have had 70 Scholarships in the last three years and a 100% Cranbrook 13+ pass rate.

Music and art play a vital role at Saint Ronan's. We have numerous choirs and ensembles including the Chamber choir and the Chapel choir, and over three-quarters of the children learn at least one musical instrument. We have an excellent orchestra and ensembles for most instruments. Music is thriving and the department regularly achieve scholarships to very competitive schools such as King's Canterbury, Harrow and Eastbourne. The Art and DT departments are flourishing and regularly achieve scholarships.

The major sports at Saint Ronan's are rugby, football, hockey, cricket and netball but we also offer coaching in athletics, tennis, swimming, dance, rounders, judo, golf, fencing, lacrosse and cross country. Sports scholarships are also regularly awarded.

The Nursery and Pre-Prep are very much part of the school, in both location and ethos, and are thriving and dynamic departments taking children from age 3 to 7.

In 2006 we opened a new Nursery, Pre-Prep, Music school and IT suite, in 2010 a new Sports Hall and in 2012 a new DT suite and School Farm. In 2014 we started playing on our new astroturf. A new Drama Studio was built in 2016 and in 2017 a new classroom suite and Library opened. We will open a new DT, Art and Computer suite in 2019.

Charitable status. Saint Ronan's School is a Registered Charity, number 1066420. It exists for the advancement of education of its children.

St Swithun's Prep School

Alresford Road, Winchester, Hampshire SO21 1HA

Tel:	01962 835750
email:	prepoffice@stswithuns.com
website:	www.stswithuns.com
Twitter:	@stswithunsprep
Facebook:	@StSwithunsPrepSchool

Established 1884. Girls day preparatory school with a co-ed nursery. Church of England.

School Council:
Chairman: Professor Natalie Lee, LLB

Headmistress: Mrs Rebecca Lyons-Smith, MBA University College London

Deputy Head: Mrs Katherine Grosscurth, BSc Hons Plymouth, PGCE Exeter
Deputy Head Academic: Mrs Haylie M Saunders, BEd Hons Winchester

Age Range. Girls 4–11, with a co-ed nursery.
Number of Pupils. 184 pupils. Average class size 18. Pupil to teacher ratio 12:1.

Fees per term (2018–2019). Nursery: £1,808 (mornings inc lunch), £3,615 (all day); Reception, Years 1 & 2 £3,615; Years 3–6 £4,657.

Profile. Welcome to St Swithun's Prep School, a school in which every child is known, cherished and at the same time encouraged to be fearless.

In September 2015 we opened the doors to our brand new prep school, which provides a simply spectacular and inspiring teaching and learning environment. It is an environment in which pupils and staff have warm, respectful relationships. The development includes specialist teaching rooms, a science laboratory, an art studio, a media/computing room and, in the final phase, opened in April 2016, a new performing arts space and gym. The children enjoy going to school and the staff relish having the opportunity to share adventures, interests and laughter.

While united in their enthusiasm and energy, the children are all individuals and we encourage them to sample a wide range of experiences so that they each develop individual passions. We look always to celebrate characteristics such as the ability to bounce back from disappointment, to show compassion for others, to rise to challenges and to keep a sense of perspective. We want your children to go home every evening with slightly grubby knees and tales of what they have done at school that day.

Entry. At 3.

Curriculum. Usual subjects taught plus German (from Nursery), art, technology, drama, ICT, music and PE, with due regard for National Curriculum requirements.

Leavers. Girls go on to a range of senior independent schools, with the majority going to St Swithun's Senior School.

Consultation. Biannual reports, regular parents' evenings and PTA.

Sports. Gymnastics, netball, pop lacrosse, rounders, tag rugby, tennis, short tennis, swimming, and athletics.

Activities. These include tennis, art, drama, gymnastics, judo, science, cookery, swimming, football and dance.

Musical concerts and productions are regularly held. Three annual residential trips in Years 4–6, and regular visits from Nursery to Year 6 take place.

Special needs. Qualified Learning Support teacher.

Charitable status. St Swithun's School Winchester is a Registered Charity, number 307335.

'Warm', 'caring', 'happy' – these are the three most popular words used by parents to describe Salisbury Cathedral School. Our unique setting, adjacent to one of England's finest cathedrals, helps to cultivate a strong spiritual awareness and Christian values underpin everything that we do.

Recently merged with Leaden Hall, the school now spans two iconic and beautiful sites within the Cathedral Close. The Junior Department is based on the Leaden Hall Campus with its idyllic riverside setting, while the Prep Department sits on the Palace campus site, complete with its own lake, extensive playing fields and lessons in the thirteenth-century Bishop's Palace.

We believe a child's self-esteem is vital to their success. At SCS, we foster an unpressured environment where pupils are encouraged and congratulated every step of the way, celebrating their achievements and promoting a strong sense of self-worth. Our focus on the individual child means that all staff play a role in discovering strengths and areas that need guidance and support.

This approach works. Our academic results are impressive and consistently out-perform competing schools but, more than this, the children who leave us are confident, self-assured, well-rounded and comfortable in their own skins.

Facilities include: over 20 acres of beautiful grounds, state-of-the-art wooden classrooms, an all-weather sports pitch, tennis courts, swimming pool, outstanding music facilities, a variety of performance spaces, specialist science laboratory, art, design technology and computer suites and extensive playground facilities.

Talented sports staff coach all the major team sports and there are regular fixtures.

There are many after-school clubs open to all children in the Preparatory School. (Quality wrap-around school care is available for children in the Pre-Prep). The boarding house staff operate an "open door" policy to parents, organise many outings and activities and have achieved an enviable reputation for running a truly happy and caring boarding house.

For more information and/or to arrange a visit to the school, please telephone Jane King on 01722 439260 or visit our website.

Charitable status. Salisbury Cathedral School is a Registered Charity, number 309485. It exists to provide high quality education for children.

Salisbury Cathedral School

1 The Close, Salisbury, Wilts SP1 2EQ

Tel:	01722 555300
Fax:	01722 410910
email:	admissions@salisburycathedralschool.com
website:	www.salisburycathedralschool.com
Twitter:	@salisburycathsc
Facebook:	/Salisbury-Cathedral-School

Founded in 1091. Co-educational Day and Boarding Preparatory, Pre-Preparatory and Choir School.

Chairman of Governors: Revd Dr James Woodward

Head Master: Clive Marriott

Age Range. 3–13.
Number of Pupils. Day pupils: 195; Boarders: 35.
Fees per term (2018–2019). Pre-Prep: £4.16 per hour (Nursery), £2,900 (Reception, Years 1 & 2), £4,350 (Year 3). Preparatory School: £5,230 (day), £7,685 (boarding).

Sandroyd School

Rushmore Park, Tollard Royal, Salisbury, Wiltshire SP5 5QD

Tel:	01725 516264
Fax:	01725 516441
email:	office@sandroyd.com
website:	www.sandroyd.org
Twitter:	@SandroydSchool
Facebook:	@sandroydschool
LinkedIn:	@sandroydschool

Chairman of Governors: R G L Thomas, MRICS, FAAV

Headmaster: A B Speers, BSc, MEd

Age Range. 2–13 Co-educational.
Number of Pupils. 140 boarders, 40 day, plus 50 in Pre-Prep, The Walled Garden.
Fees per term (2018–2019). Boarding £8,470, Day £7,000. Year 3: Boarding £6,700, Day £5,200. Pre-Prep

£2,920, Nursery: £24 (per morning), £33 (all day including lunch).

Sandroyd has been a leading boarding Prep school since 1888 and offers an exceptional education in both the Walled Garden Pre-Prep (for children aged 2–7), and in the Prep School (for children aged 7–13).

It is a wonderfully unique family school, set in an idyllic environment, that 'prepares' children in the very broadest sense – offering academic excellence, and so much more. Sandroyd nurtures a child's confidence and self-esteem whilst encouraging each individual pupil to fulfil all aspects of their potential: academic, artistic, cultural, sporting and social.

Sandroyd is unequivocally proud of being a small school and the benefits it offers to all of its pupils. The school's size creates a wonderfully unique family atmosphere, in both the classroom and the boarding house, allowing staff to properly focus on the individual needs of each child at every stage of their education. Indeed, teachers and pastoral staff meet every morning to discuss how to best support each pupil that day.

Sandroyd offers an academically rich and rigorous education that goes far beyond preparing pupils to just pass entrance exams to the country's leading senior schools. Whilst one in four pupils left with a scholarship to their Senior School, the School is focused on inspiring interests and developing talents – both inside and beyond the classroom – from music, dance and drama to a variety of sports which pupils play every day. Pupils are also encouraged to develop the qualities and skills they will need for life beyond their school days through the newly launched 'Strive' programme. This is an integral part of every child's curriculum, consisting of over 50 different activities delivered by specialists, as part of daily 'Strive' sessions.

Sarum Hall School

15 Eton Avenue, London NW3 3EL
Tel: 020 7794 2261
Fax: 020 7431 7501
email: admissions@sarumhallschool.co.uk
website: www.sarumhallschool.co.uk

The School, which has a Christian (Church of England) foundation, is an educational trust with a Board of Governors.

Chairman of Governors: Mr B Gorst

Headmistress: **Mrs Christine Smith**, BA Open, CertEd, RSA SpLD

Age Range. 3–11.
Number of Pupils. 180 Day Girls.
Fees per term (2018–2019). £4,675–£5,060.

Founded in 1929, the school has, since 1995, been housed in new purpose-built premises which provide excellent, spacious facilities, including a large playground, gym, dining room and specialist art, IT, music and science rooms, in addition to a French room, changing room, multi-purpose room and three individual music teaching rooms. The school has recently added a Food Studio to support Food & Nutrition teaching, as well as the wider curriculum.

Girls are prepared for senior London day schools and for 11+ Common Entrance. Girls entering at age 3 are not assessed, but those joining from Year 1 are tested in English and Maths. The school is ambitious for its girls and believes that in a caring, supportive and imaginative environment,

every girl can achieve her potential. They are encouraged to develop a love and interest of learning for itself and awareness that their success in all fields is dependent on their own efforts. Consequently the school has a well-established record of scholarship and examination success. Destination schools include Channing, Cheltenham Ladies' College, City of London School for Girls, Downe House, Francis Holland, Highgate, King's Canterbury, Mill Hill Foundation, North London Collegiate, Oundle School, Queen's College, Queenswood, South Hampstead High School, St Helen's, St Paul's Girls and Wycombe Abbey.

A broad curriculum is followed and a major investment in IT ensures that each girl has access to the latest technology. French is taught from Reception and Mandarin from Year 4, and a comprehensive games programme, which takes place on site, ensures that girls have the opportunity to experience a variety of sports. Strong emphasis is placed on music, art, design and drama. Woodwind, violin, piano, cello and singing are offered. There are also two choirs, an orchestra and ensemble groups. Other extra-curricular activities include theory of music, fencing, junior and senior football, gardening, modern art, nature, netball, tennis, ICT, yoga, philosophy, photography, drama, craft, chess, cooking, classical civilisations, board games and performance.

Charitable status. Sarum Hall School is a Registered Charity, number 312721. Its purpose is education.

Seaford College Prep School
Wilberforce House

Lavington Park, Petworth, West Sussex GU28 0NB
Tel: 01798 867893
email: wilberforce@seaford.org
          jhitchcock@seaford.org
website: www.seafordprep.org

Chairman of Governors: R Venables Kyrke

Head of Prep School: **Mr Alastair Brown**, BEd

Age Range. 6–13 Co-educational.
Number of Pupils. 220.
Fees per term (2018–2019). Day: £3,440–£5,710. Weekly Boarding: £7,170 (Year 6), £7,590 (Years 7 & 8).

Seaford College Prep School (Wilberforce House) is an integral part of Seaford College, having the same board of governors, but with its own buildings, playground and corporate organisation. There is very close cooperation between the two schools and there are many shared facilities such as the games fields, the Music School, Science Department, and Art and Design Department. Wilberforce House is named after Samuel Wilberforce, the son of the anti-slavery campaigner William Wilberforce. Samuel is buried in the grounds of the School's chapel. The School is set in a magnificent 400-acre site adjacent to the South Downs National Park.

The Prep School educates boys and girls from the age of 6 and the vast majority of children continue their education at Seaford College until 16 or 18. The main entry points for the Prep School are at 7+ and 11+ although children are welcome to join the school at any age.

The school aims to nurture a love of learning through a broadly based curriculum and classroom activities are often complemented by day and residential visits. In Years 2, 3, 4 and 5, the majority of lessons are taught by form teachers with subjects such as Music, French, PE/Games and Design and Technology taught by specialist staff. Year 6 are form based for English, Maths, History and Geography with all other subjects taught by subject specialists. From Year 7 all subjects are taught by specialist staff, many of whom also teach in the Senior School. All classrooms are equipped with interactive whiteboards while a Special Educational Needs Coordinator oversees the school's learning support provision which further enhances learning and achievement. The majority of children complete most of their homework in school and the school day finishes at 5.20 pm.

Boarding provision, from Year 6 upwards, is an important aspect of life in the school with the aim being to be as flexible as possible in order to meet parents' and pupils' needs as well as providing a warm and caring home-from-home atmosphere.

Pupils are able to benefit from the impressive range of games facilities on site, including an astroturf hockey pitch, indoor swimming pool and a 9-hole golf course, with practice greens and driving range as well as the services of a golf professional. Expert coaching is provided in the main sports of football, rugby, hockey, cricket, netball, rounders, tennis, athletics and swimming. The school also has excellent facilities for music, art and design and technology.

The standard of pastoral care is high and the school has its own Chaplain who takes a weekly assembly. The Prep School aims to treat each pupil as an individual and to establish the firm foundations necessary for success in the Senior School and beyond. (*See Seaford College entry in HMC section.*)

Charitable status. Seaford College is a Registered Charity, number 277439.

Seaton House School

67 Banstead Road South, Sutton, Surrey SM2 5LH

Tel: 020 8642 2332
Fax: 020 8642 2332
email: office@seatonhouse.sutton.sch.uk
website: www.seatonhouse.sutton.sch.uk
Facebook: @SeatonHouseSchool

Chair of Governors: Mrs J Evans

Headmistress: **Mrs D Morrison**, RSA HDipEd

Age Range. Girls 3–11, Boys 3–4 (Nursery only).
Number of Pupils. Main School 133; Nursery 26.
Fees per term (2018–2019). £1,437–£3,396.

Seaton House School was founded in 1930 by Miss Violet Henry and there is a strong tradition of family loyalty to the school. The School aims to provide children with a thorough educational grounding to give them a good start in their school lives and to instil sound learning habits in a secure, disciplined but friendly atmosphere. The girls, from Year 4, are prepared for various entrance examinations at 11+, both in the London Borough of Sutton and those required by independent day schools with a high percentage of our girls securing grammar school places at Nonsuch High School and Wallington Girls Grammar School. Our highly qualified and committed staff create a stimulating learning environment and small classes ensure that all our girls have the necessary individual attention and encouragement to achieve the highest standards.

We follow the broad outlines of the National Curriculum with generous provision for Music, French and Physical Education. There is a School Orchestra and Choir and, each year, all pupils have the opportunity to take part in dramatic productions. School sports teams enjoy considerable success when they compete regularly against neighbouring schools and each Spring we host our own Netball Tournament. Years

5 and 6 have the opportunity to experience outdoor pursuits during their annual week's residential course, but prior to that in Years 3 and 4 the girls have a one-night/two-day and two-night/three-day residential visit, respectively. The School has excellent Library and ICT resources, while the range of extracurricular activities offered is extremely varied, complementing the established provision of after-school care. There is a daily homework club and after-school care to 6.00 pm, with early-bird arrivals being looked after from 8.00 am.

Pastoral care is of the highest calibre with form staff taking a keen interest in all their pupils. Courtesy, good manners and kindness are expected as the norm and children are encouraged to develop initiative, independence and confidence. There is a strong house system in the main school which stimulates good community awareness.

The prospectus is available upon request and the Headmistress is always happy to meet parents and arrange for them to look around the School.

ISI Inspection. We are delighted to announce that we were judged "Excellent" in all areas by ISI Inspectors in December 2016. Seaton House School was also ranked 4th in the Sunday Times Top 100 Independent Preparatory Schools in England in 2017.

Charitable status. Seaton House School is a Registered Charity, number 800673. It exists to provide education for children.

Sevenoaks Preparatory School

Godden Green, Sevenoaks, Kent TN15 0JU

Tel: 01732 762336
Fax: 01732 764279
email: admin@theprep.org.uk
website: www.theprep.org.uk
Twitter: @Sevenoaksprep
Facebook: @sevenoaksprep

Chairman of Governors: Jan Berry

Headmaster: **Luke Harrison**, BA Hons, PGCE

Head of Pre-Prep: Helen Cook

Age Range. 2½ to 13.
Number of Children. 385 pupils.
Fees per annum (2018–2019). Reception £10,350, Years 1–2 £11,805, Years 3–8 £14,295. Nursery & Kindergarten: £360 per term for one session per week.

Founded in 1919, Sevenoaks Prep School stands on a spacious 25-acre site of playing fields and woodland bordering the 1,000-acre Knole Estate. We welcome girls and boys from 2½ to 13 years of age. Our small class sizes and family atmosphere enables us to build special relationships with the children and their parents.

The curriculum is tailored to the needs of the pupils and their future aspirations. Whilst due regard is paid to the National Curriculum, our children are taught to the highest standard achievable by the individual. To this end, our teachers enhance their Programmes of Study to ensure that every pupil is motivated, challenged and prepared for 11+ or 13+ entry tests to local grammar schools or via Common Entrance examinations and scholarships to independent schools. Our academic achievements are consistently high and our pupils compete successfully for academic, music and other scholarships.

Throughout the school all classes regularly participate in a programme of visits, workshops and field trips to support their learning. Education at Sevenoaks Prep is for life not just the classroom – it is the balance of academic study and co-curricular activities that prepare the children for their future.

The school comprises the Pre-Prep (Nursery–Year 2), and the Prep School (Years 3–8).

Nursery and Kindergarten are staffed by teachers who are specially qualified in Early Years education, with a high teacher to pupil ratio. The education provided is specifically designed to match each child's needs, so that child-initiated play and teacher-directed activities are thoughtfully planned and carefully balanced.

Full-time education starts in the Reception class and from this point, through Years 1 and 2, class teachers and their assistants provide a rich and stimulating environment where curiosity and enthusiasm to learn are fostered.

On entering the Senior School in Year 3, class teaching is continued for core subjects (with specialist teaching for drama, languages, music, ICT, PE and games). By the age of ten, our pupils are taught by specialist teachers in all subjects whilst each class continues to have a form teacher who monitors their progress. Years 7 and 8 are the secondary school years and this is reflected in the teaching and levels of responsibility offered to the children. At Sevenoaks Prep they are at the top of the school and are provided with leadership opportunities and responsibilities. Heads of our destination schools say that children from the Prep enter Year 9 as rounded individuals, confident both academically and socially.

Facilities include a large multi-purpose sports hall, a state-of-the-art drama and music suite, 'Forest School' outdoor education area, and modern Pre-Prep classrooms and hall. A new Cetenary Centre housing science, art, humanities, ICT and a library is under construction. Our location provides a useful and natural extension to our teaching facilities and provide a vast playground, where children are trusted and encouraged to explore safely.

The school provides after-school care until 6.00 pm each evening and the extra-curricular activities are extensive. The school is supported by an active Social Events Committee who regularly arrange social events for parents to meet each other and to raise money for the school.

Sherborne Preparatory School

Acreman Street, Sherborne, Dorset DT9 3NY

Tel:	01935 812097
email:	admissions@sherborneprep.org
website:	www.sherborneprep.org
Twitter:	@Sherborneprep

Chair of Governors: Mr N Jones

Headmaster: **Mr Nick Folland**, BSc Hons, PGCE, MIAPS, MISI

Age Range. 3–13.
Number of Boys and Girls. 260 (Pre-Prep 60, Prep 200).
Fees per term (2018–2019). Boarders: £7,815–£8,180. Day: Nursery £3,020; Pre-Prep £3,020; Prep: £4,675 (Year 3), £5,710 (Years 4–8). Generous discounts available for Forces families and a range of scholarships available from Year 3 upwards (scholarship assessments are held at the beginning of the Spring term each year). Bursaries available on a means-tested basis.

Sherborne Prep School aims to foster independent learning through the teaching of a broader enquiry-based curriculum with an emphasis on study and thinking skills, designed to meet the individual learning styles of the pupils.

The school is an independent co-educational day and boarding school for children aged 3–13 years. Founded in 1858, the School is set in twelve acres of attractive grounds and gardens in the centre of Sherborne and is well served by road and rail links. Although fully independent, it enjoys a long and close association with its neighbours, Sherborne School and Sherborne School for Girls.

The Prep School (Years 3–8) offers a broad education, leading to Common Entrance and Scholarship examinations in the penultimate and final year groups. Despite being non-selective ourselves, over the last five years an impressive 38% of leavers have won scholarships or awards to leading independent schools, including Sherborne School, Sherborne School for Girls, Blundell's, Bryanston, Canford, Charterhouse, Cheltenham Ladies' College, Clayesmore, Downside, Eton, Godolphin, King's Bruton, King's College Taunton, King's School Canterbury, Leweston, Marlborough, Milton Abbey, Monkton Combe, Queen's College Taunton, Radley, Rugby, Taunton and Winchester.

We encourage every child to embrace all the wonderful opportunities on offer and to discover and develop his or her talents and interests to the full. Our children grow to question and reason, so that they are fully prepared to embrace opportunity and fulfil their potential as resilient and responsible members of the community. From September 2018, Forest School has been integrated into the curriculum, offering a great opportunity for pupils to develop curiosity, confidence and independence as well as enriching their knowledge of the natural environment. The Prep offers a full Saturday morning programme of various sporting, artistic, musical and cultural activities, including introductory language classes and informative lectures. At the end of each school day, the pupils can choose to attend an imaginative after-school enrichment and academic support programme until 6.00 pm.

The Pre-Prep Department is housed in a fully-equipped and purpose-built classroom building, with experienced and well-qualified staff, providing an excellent ratio of teachers to children. The children enjoy weekly swimming lessons and a varied programme of after-school activities, including fun fitness, dance, music and circus skills. There is also a thriving weekly toddler group, "Little Preppers", for children between 0 and 3.

The School's ISI report in December 2015 stated The Prep as being 'outstanding' in all areas and praised the School for its success in developing independent learning and positive attitudes to work and study in both boarding and day pupils.

Charitable status. Sherborne Preparatory School is a Registered Charity, number 1071494. It exists to provide an all-round education for children.

Shrewsbury House

107 Ditton Road, Surbiton, Surrey KT6 6RL

Tel:	020 8399 3066
email:	shsoffice@shstrust.net
website:	www.shrewsburyhouse.net
Twitter:	@shrewsburyhouse

Chairman of the Governors: D Johns, BA Hons

Headmaster: **K A Doble**, BA, PDM HR, PGCE, FRSA

Second Master: C Francis, BHum Hons, PGCE

Age Range. 7–13.
Number of Boys. 330 Day Boys.

Fees per term (2018–2019). £6,225.

Shrewsbury House was founded in 1865. In 1979 it became an Educational Trust and is administered by a Board of Governors.

Boys are admitted from 7 years of age and are prepared for entry at 13+, either by Scholarship or Common Entrance, to numerous leading Independent day and boarding schools. There are 42 full-time staff, as well as visiting music staff.

The School aims to educate the whole child by providing unequalled opportunities and support in breadth and depth for the ongoing development of academic, cultural, aesthetic, moral, sporting and practical dimensions of the boys' lives.

Academic work is at the heart of Shrewsbury House. Their aim is to allow each pupil to develop his potential to the maximum. This means setting the highest academic expectations for each boy and then developing the systems to monitor and support his progress. Shrewsbury House believes that this allows pupils to achieve more than they could have imagined. The School follows a broad-based curriculum, allowing for boys to hone their skills in a myriad of subject areas. A large number of the teachers are Subject Specialists, many of whom have taught at senior schools, thereby bringing a wealth of expertise and knowledge to help prepare boys for 'life after SHS'. Whether on the sports field, on the stage, musically, or in the classroom, every boy is encouraged to 'have a go'. Expectations are high and best effort in all pursuits is a given. To this end, for instance: every boy is in a sports team; every boy who wishes to be individually tutored in music may be; every boy performs in at least one concert and one play every year.

The original School building is an Arts and Crafts Victorian mansion; its interior has been adapted, furnished and decorated for modern educational needs. The boys at Shrewsbury House School enjoy wonderful sports facilities based at the main school site and at their dedicated sports ground at Almshouse Lane. They have a covered swimming pool, three senior grass pitches, a state-of-the-art 4G IRB all-weather surface, two further "astro" all-weather surfaces, an indoor sports hall, a hard-standing play area, indoor and outdoor cricket nets and an athletic jump area.

Although much focus and energy is directed towards the delivery of the core sports of Football, Rugby and Cricket, the boys are offered the opportunity of a much broader programme. All boys participate in an extended programme of Swimming as well as following a comprehensive Physical Education (PE) curriculum. This programme includes lessons to enhance physical development, gymnastic ability, racquet skills and athletics technique. Other sports and activities on offer include Hockey, Biathlon, Shooting, Athletics, Tennis, Fives, Basketball, Table Tennis, Badminton, Cross Country, Sailing, Skiing and Judo. The opportunity to compete in other sports is continually being extended and boys from Shrewsbury House have enjoyed success in Golf, Swimming, Athletics, Hockey, Tennis and Sailing.

Shrewsbury House has pupils join from many Pre-Prep schools, including its own Shrewsbury House Pre-Prep (*see Shrewsbury House Pre-Preparatory School entry*) and The Rowans (*see The Rowans School entry*). It also admits a number of boys each year from local state schools.

Charitable status. Shrewsbury House School Trust Limited is a Registered Charity, number 277324. It seeks to provide the best possible learning environment for boys pupils aged between 2 and 13 who have the potential for above-average academic achievement.

Shrewsbury House Pre-Preparatory School

22 Milbourne Lane, Esher, Surrey KT10 9EA

Tel: 01372 462781
Fax: 01372 469914
email: shppoffice@shstrust.net
website: www.shrewsburyhousepreprep.net

Chairman of Governors: Mr Darren Johns

Head Teacher: Mr Jon Akhurst, BA Hons, PGCE

Age Range. 3–7 years Co-educational.
Number of Children. 100.
Fees per term (2018–2019). £2,030–£4,489.

Shrewsbury House Pre-Preparatory School is an IAPS independent day school for boys and girls aged from 3 to 7 years old. It is part of the Shrewsbury House School Trust.

The school aims to nurture and develop the whole child within an exciting environment of academic excellence. It offers a creative and well-balanced curriculum, where inspiring teaching staff help the children to develop lifelong skills and foster a love of learning.

Our school is a happy and welcoming one. It has a purposeful atmosphere and the children learn positive attitudes towards work and play, while building self-esteem, resilience, respect and empathy.

Shrewsbury House Pre-Prep has extensive facilities including modern purpose-built classrooms (all with state-of-the-art interactive whiteboards), an indoor sports hall, a busy and thriving library, a large, well-equipped playground and a heated swimming pool. Children also benefit from regular sports and Forest School lessons at the school's own sports field and pavilion. Creative arts are further developed through strong Art, Music and Drama departments.

Recent popular destination schools at the 7+ stage include Shrewsbury House School and a wide range of London day schools.

Charitable status. Shrewsbury House School Trust is a Registered Charity, number 277324.

Solefield School

Solefields Road, Sevenoaks, Kent TN13 1PH

Tel: 01732 452142
email: admissions@solefieldschool.org
          office@solefieldschool.org
website: www.solefieldschool.org
Twitter: @solefieldschool
Facebook: @SolefieldSchool

Chairman of the Governors: Mr R Clewley

Headmaster: Mr D A Philps, BSc

Age Range. 4–13.
Number of Boys. 150.
Fees per term (2018–2019). £3,990–£4,860 including lunch.

Solefield is a day Preparatory School for boys from 4 to 13, located in the heart of Sevenoaks. Through exceptional teaching, learning and care it prepares boys for entry to a wide choice of independent senior schools including Sevenoaks and Tonbridge at 13, along with Grammar School entry at 11. The curriculum is comprehensive and, along with core subjects and Humanities, also includes subjects such as Latin, Thinking Skills and Politics, Philosophy and Ethics. Extra-curricular endeavours are an essential part of life at Solefield and are well catered for with extensive opportunities in Sport, Drama, Music and Art. Solefield has a strong tradition of academic excellence. Boys are encouraged to value themselves, value others and to value our world. Senior boys gain numerous awards each year to senior schools. Links between parents and the school are a particular strength.

Enquiries concerning places and admissions should be made to the Registrar, Mrs Barbara Volpato.

Charitable status. Solefield School is a Registered Charity, number 293466. It aims to provide a high quality education to boys aged 4–13.

Sompting Abbotts

Church Lane, Sompting, West Sussex BN15 0AZ

Tel: 01903 235960
Fax: 01903 210045
email: office@somptingabbotts.com
website: www.somptingabbotts.com

Principal: Mrs P M Sinclair

Headmaster: **S J Douch**, MA

Bursar: D A Sinclair

Age Range. 2–13 Co-educational.
Number of Pupils. 120.
Fees per term (2018–2019). Day £3,065–£3,935 (including lunches).

The only independent, family-run school in the area!

Set in a magnificent site on the edge of the South Downs, Sompting Abbotts overlooks the English Channel with views towards Beachy Head and the Isle of Wight. The imposing Victorian House has some 30 acres of sports fields, woodlands, gardens and activity areas.

The aim of the school is to provide a well-balanced education in a caring environment, recognizing and developing the individual needs of each child, so that maximum potential academic achievement may be gained. Within the community of the school an emphasis is laid on the cultivation of courtesy, self-discipline and respect for one another in order to engender a happy atmosphere.

The school has a vibrant Pre-Preparatory Department, which includes lively Early Years classes. In the Preparatory Department well-equipped Science Laboratory and Computer Room are enjoyed by all ages. The Art and Drama departments offer wide scope for creativity, and peripatetic teachers provide tuition for a range of musical instruments. Free wrap-around care is provided from 8.00 am to 6.00 pm.

Book your child in for a Taster Day to see what life is like at our wonderful school!

South Lee School

Nowton Road, Bury St Edmunds, Suffolk IP33 2BT

Tel: 01284 754654
Fax: 01284 706178
email: office@southlee.co.uk
website: www.southlee.co.uk

Chairman of the Governors: Mr A Holliday

Headmaster: **Mr Mervyn Watch**, BEd Hons

Age Range. 2–13.
Number of Pupils. 245 Boys and Girls.
Fees per term (2018–2019). £3,327.53–£4,077.90 including lunches.

South Lee enjoys an excellent reputation for its friendly, family atmosphere. The school provides a stimulating and caring environment where children have every opportunity to learn and develop. From an early age, pupils are taught the traditional subjects, emphasising mathematics, science and English but within a wider curriculum that incorporates the use of the latest developments in technology and educational resources.

The school is situated close to the A14, has purpose-built, modern classrooms and specialist teaching areas. Sport is an important part of the curriculum and the school has the use of excellent local facilities

South Lee offers its pupils opportunities for self-expression and individual development through study of the Arts, drama, music and a broad range of outdoor, sporting and extracurricular activities.

The **Nursery**, which caters for children from 2 to 4 years of age, makes learning a fun experience from the very start.

The **Pre-Prep** is essentially class-based, though specialist staff teach French, music, ICT and Physical education.

The **Prep School** is well staffed with experienced teachers. The full range of academic subjects is taught, encompassing the national curriculum and preparing pupils for the Common Entrance 13+ examination.

Charitable status. South Lee exists to educate children from 2–13 years of age. Control is vested in a Board of Governors, the majority of whom are current parents. The school is run as a non-profit making Limited Company and is a Registered Charity, number 310491.

Spratton Hall

Smith Street, Spratton, Northampton NN6 8HP

Tel: 01604 847292
Fax: 01604 820844
email: office@sprattonhall.com
website: www.sprattonhall.com

Chairman: Mr James Coley

Head Master: **Mr Simon Clarke**, BA

Deputy Head Master: Mr Robert Dow, BA Hons, PGCE

Age Range. 4–13 Co-educational.
Number of Pupils. 395+.
Fees per term (2018–2019). Prep £4,650–£5,020, Pre-Prep £3,350. Fees include stationery, lunch, all academic books and most extra-curricular activities.

Set in 50 acres of Northamptonshire countryside, Spratton Hall is a fully co-educational day school for 4 to 13 years old.

Through highly skilled teaching we create an exciting and stimulating environment for learning, and by developing the talents of each child we believe that every pupil can succeed. The children are encouraged to become independent thinkers and to use their own initiative with confidence.

In the happy, caring Pre-Prep Department (from 4 to 7 years old) the girls and boys play imaginatively and grow in confidence. Each child is nurtured to establish a sound social and academic foundation for their future education.

Spratton has an enviable record of success at Common Entrance. Scholarships and awards are frequently won to many of the leading Independent Senior Schools.

The children enjoy a truly all-round education, achieving high academic standards as well as being recognised nationally for their success in sports and the Arts.

There are excellent facilities for Music, Art and Drama. The Performing Arts Centre provides Spratton Hall with a stage, tiered seating and a state-of-the-art sound and lighting system enabling each and every performance to be seen at its best. A wide variety of concerts, productions and exhibitions are enjoyed by all age groups throughout the year.

The Science laboratories, catering facilities and Dining Hall have been completely refurbished. Technology is constantly kept up to date and modernised to reflect the present advances in our society. The Townsend Library and Media centre incorporates books and technology exceptionally well.

The extensive playing fields together with the Jubilee Sports Dome, two all-weather surfaces and a full-size floodlit Astroturf enable all pupils to enjoy a range of sports including rugby, hockey, cricket for both boys and girls, netball, athletics, cross-country and tennis with the Dome allowing for indoor tennis, badminton, gymnastics, dance and ballet.

In November 2016 Spratton Hall's successes were confirmed by an 'excellent' inspection report in every respect by the Independent Schools Inspectorate.

For further information or to arrange a visit to see the children at work and play, please contact The Registrar on 01604 847292 or email registrar@sprattonhall.com.

Charitable status. Spratton Hall is a Registered Charity, number 309925. It exists to provide education for boys and girls.

Spring Grove School

Harville Road, Wye, nr Ashford, Kent TN25 5EZ
Tel: 01233 812337
email: office@springgroveschool.co.uk
website: www.springgroveschool.co.uk
Twitter: @SG_School
Facebook: @Spring-Grove-School-Wye

Chair of Governors: Mrs Dawne Sweetland

Headmaster: Mr W J B Jones, BMus Hons, PGCE
headmaster@springgroveschool.co.uk

Bursar: Mrs Sarah Peirce
bursar@springgroveschool.co.uk

Director of Marketing and Admissions: Mrs Nicky Lee-Browne
admissions@springgroveschool.co.uk

Age Range. 2–11 Co-educational.
Number of Pupils. 214.
Fees per term (2018–2019). £2,092–£4,200.

Spring Grove is a co-educational Day Preparatory School from age 2 to 11. The school was founded in 1967 and is situated on the outskirts of the beautiful village of Wye. The main building is an inspiring late 17th Century house. The facilities include an outstanding Early Years department, Science Room, School Hall, Art Room, a brand new Music Room (2014), well-equipped Classrooms, Computer Room and Changing Rooms. The grounds contain the main school buildings and 15 acres of playing fields. Qualified and graduate staff help prepare the children for entry to Independent

Senior and Grammar Schools. Spring Grove has a strong tradition of academic excellence, exceptionally lively music, drama and art departments, accredited Forest School, and children who are inspired with a sense of wonder about the world. Emphasis is placed on innovative and creative teaching in a caring yet well-structured atmosphere with close contact maintained between parents and teachers. 15 scholarships to senior schools have been awarded in the past two years.

The curriculum includes Music, Drama, Art and Technology, Forest School, PE and extracurricular activities. Athletics, Cricket, Cross-Country (National U11 IAPS Champions in 2011), Football, Hockey, Netball, Rounders and Rugby are the principal games.

Enquiries concerning places and admissions should be made to the Registrar (email: admissions@springgrove school.co.uk, tel: 01233 812337).

Charitable status. Spring Grove School 2003 is a Registered Charity, number 1099823.

Staines Preparatory School

3 Gresham Road, Staines upon Thames, Surrey TW18 2BT
Tel: 01784 450909
email: admissions@stainesprep.co.uk
website: www.stainesprep.co.uk
Twitter: @StainesPrep
Facebook: @Stainesprep

Independent Co-educational Day School founded in 1935.

Chairman of Governors: Mr M Hall

Headmistress: Ms Samantha Sawyer, BEd Hons, MEd, NPQH

School Business Manager: Mrs R McLennan, BA Hons, Assoc CIPD
Marketing & Admissions Manager: Mr P Coll, PG Dip Applied Linguistics

Age Range. 3–11 Co-educational.
Number of Pupils. 187 Boys, 169 Girls.
Fees per term (2018–2019). £3,270–£3,820.

Throughout its history, Staines Preparatory School has maintained a reputation for high standards of education and care. The School aims for all pupils to attain their potential within a secure and happy environment and strives to produce boys and girls who are confident, honest, considerate and courteous. Just as importantly, it must be noted that our fees include residential trips, day trips and lunches and we offer more teaching days than other independent schools.

The School believes in traditional values but is committed to providing the very best in terms of modern facilities and educational methods.

The School's philosophy of *'Educating Today's Children for the Challenges of Tomorrow'* is highlighted by the outstanding achievements of former SPS pupils in their secondary schools.

As Headmistress, Ms Samantha Sawyer said recently, "It is vitally important to the School that all our pupils have the chance to flourish both educationally and personally. Staines Prep provides the foundations for each and every child to strive towards their full potential and enjoy themselves in the process."

The curriculum is based upon the National Curriculum with a sharp focus on the acquisition of literacy and numeracy skills. However, it is given additional breadth by the inclusion of French from Year 2 and Latin/Classical Studies in Years 5 and 6. Sport plays an important role at SPS and there is a regular programme of fixtures against other preparatory schools. Whilst the School believes in competitive sport and has won a number of local tournaments in soccer, netball, cricket and swimming in recent years, it also believes that as many pupils as possible should be given the opportunity to play in matches at various levels. Development of abilities in the Arts is also considered highly important with opportunities provided throughout the School both in the classroom and as extra activities. Subject specialist teaching commences in Year 4 following a series of assessments at the end of Year 3. A regular programme of trips and visits enhance the curriculum and the annual Ski Trip for Year 6 is much enjoyed.

Our Multi-Sports Hall, state-of-the-art teaching and performance facilities along with the The Jubilee Wing, Library, and ICT Suite all indicate the School's commitment to providing the very best facilities as well as education. In addition to the general teaching classrooms there are special facilities for Science, Art, Design and Technology and Special Needs. Hard surfaced playground areas, an all-weather floodlit court and the adjoining playing fields and environmental area provide ample space for sport and recreation.

The School welcomes contact with parents and has a flourishing Friends' Association whose activities strengthen the links between home and school.

After-school wrap-around care is available for pupils of all ages, as well as a minibus service that runs throughout the academic year.

Stamford Junior School

Kettering Rd, Stamford, Lincolnshire PE9 2LR

Tel: 01780 484400
email: headjs@ses.lincs.sch.uk
website: www.ses.lincs.sch.uk
Twitter: @SJS_Head
Facebook: /stamfordendowedschools

Stamford Junior School, along with Stamford High School (girls) and Stamford School (boys), is one of three schools in the historic market town of Stamford comprising the Stamford Endowed Schools. The schools are under a single Governing Body and overall management and leadership of the Principal and allow continuity of education for boys and girls from 3 to 18, including boarding from age 8. Each school has its own Head and staff.

Chairman of Governors: Dr Michael Dronfield

Principal of the Stamford Endowed Schools: Mr W Phelan, MBA

Headmistress: Mrs E Smith, BEd Hons

Age Range. 3–11.
Number of Children. 350.
Fees per annum (2018–2019). Day: Year 0 £9,414, Years 1–2 £10,002, Years 3–6 £12,102; Full Boarding £21,864; Weekly Boarding £19,821; Three-night Boarding £17,415.

The Junior School educates boys and girls up to the age of 11 (including boarders from age 8), when boys move on to Stamford School and girls to Stamford High School. Admission from the Junior School to the two senior schools is based on progress and without further entrance testing.

The Junior School occupies its own spacious grounds, bordering the River Welland, overlooking the sports fields and open countryside, the boarding houses, the sports hall, floodlit artificial hockey pitch and the swimming pool on the same site. It is on the south-west outskirts of Stamford within easy reach of the A1.

Entry to the School is according to registration at 4+ and assessment.

The lively and broad curriculum offers an ILIC-based (Independent Learning and Intellectual Curiosity) foundation to all academic, creative, and sporting subjects. Lessons are stimulating, energetic, and fully engaging so that the natural curiosity of our pupils can flourish. Extensive facilities, sporting opportunities, and the wide-ranging co-curricular programme promote the rounded development that we believe is essential for our children.

There are 26 full-time staff, with specialist teachers in physical education, swimming, art and music, and visiting teachers offering a variety of sports, dance, speech and drama.

There is a purpose-built nursery in the grounds of the school – Stamford Nursery School – offering first-class care and early learning for children aged 3–4. Pupils then head to the adjacent Early Years Reception Classes.

Boarding. The co-educational Boarding House (St Michael's) is run in a homely, family style. Boys and girls are accepted as full or weekly boarders from the age of 8. Occasional or flexi boarding is accommodated where possible and according to family need. A full programme of activities takes place at weekends so that boarders enjoy a rich and varied week.

Stockport Grammar Junior School

Buxton Road, Stockport, Cheshire SK2 7AF

Tel: 0161 419 2405
email: sgjs@stockportgrammar.co.uk
website: www.stockportgrammar.co.uk
Twitter: @stockportgs
Facebook: @stockportgrammar

Chairman of Governors: C Dunn, MA

Headmaster: **T C Wheeler**, BA, MA, FRSA

Age Range. 3–11.
Number of Pupils. 392: 206 boys, 186 girls.
Fees per term (2018–2019). £3,009, plus lunch. Pre-Reception £2,922, plus lunch.

Entry is mainly at 3+ and 4+ following assessment, with occasional places available at other ages. Stockport Grammar Junior School is a happy school, where children are encouraged to develop their strengths. A broad curriculum is taught and academic standards are high. There are specialist facilities and teaching in Science, ICT, PE and Games, Swimming, Music, Art and Design Technology. A large number of pupils learn to play a musical instrument and tuition is available for many orchestral instruments. French and Spanish are taught throughout. All children have swimming lessons in the School's pool. Children can choose to join in the numerous lunchtime and after-school clubs and activities.

The Junior School and the Senior School share the same site. The vast majority of pupils move into the Senior School at 11, having passed the Entrance Examination. (*See also Stockport Grammar School entry in HMC section.*)

Hockey, netball, football, rounders, cricket and athletics are the main sports. Swimming, tennis, cross-country, rugby, archery, canoeing and fencing are also offered. There is a full range of sporting fixtures and regular music and drama productions. All Junior pupils have the opportunity to participate in residential visits, which include outdoor pursuits.

Before and after school care is available and holiday play schemes are run at Easter and in the summer. A Breakfast Club is available from 7.30 am each day.

Facilities are excellent. In addition to specialist teaching rooms, which include a computer room and a science room, the Junior School has its own large all-weather surface along with a sports hall and extensive playing fields.

Charitable status. Stockport Grammar School is a Registered Charity, number 1120199. It exists to advance education by the provision and conduct, in or near Stockport, of a school for boys and girls.

Stonar Preparatory School

Cottles Park, Atworth, Wiltshire SN12 8NT

Tel: 01225 701740
Fax: 01225 790830
email: office@stonarschool.com
website: www.stonarschool.com
Twitter: @StonarSchool
Facebook: @StonarSchool

Chairman of Board of Directors:
Mr Daniel Jones, NACE UK Ltd

Headmaster: **Mr M Brain**, BA Ed Hons

Deputy Head: Mr D Lee, MA, BA Hons

Age Range. 3–11 Co-educational.
Number of Pupils. 122.
Fees per term (2018–2019). Day £2,832–£3,818; Boarding £7,318.

Stonar Prep School is a vibrant and exciting place to be.

Our busy, lively curriculum, delivered by the Prep School's excellent teachers, inspires creativity and intellectual curiosity. Topic-led work brings an exciting dimension to the curriculum, immersing children in a learning experience which builds skills and knowledge across the subjects. The emphasis is firmly on active learning. Pupils enjoy lots of trips and activities which support their learning and keep them stimulated and engaged.

Some pupils show obvious academic ability from an early age; others may need more encouragement. At Stonar Prep we help each child discover their aptitudes and develop their confidence as they experience numerous opportunities within and beyond the classroom. Pupils are encouraged to aim for the best in all that they do, whether it is academic, sporting, creative or performance, and we have high expectations of them.

We encourage the boys and girls to take responsibility for their own learning, behaviour and progress. This helps them become more independent. We involve parents in their child's education at every step along the way; progress is regularly and rigorously reported and the achievements of pupils are recognised and celebrated.

Because the children learn and grow within our secure and nurturing environment, they develop a caring attitude towards each other, their school and the world around them. This is underpinned by the Prep School CARE code which was devised by the children to summarise our school rules:

Communicate kindly
Aim high – always do your best
Respect – treat others as you would be treated yourself
Enjoy – and appreciate what you have.

As part of the NACE Schools group, Prep children have unique opportunities for language immersion, exchanges and links with pupils in Spain and France. Progress is monitored by form tutors so the more able pupils receive challenging tasks that take them beyond their comfort zone; our outstanding Learning Support department is available for girls and boys with specific individual learning needs.

When pupils progress to the Senior School, we ensure that they are ready for the next stage of their education as confident learners equipped with the skills required to thrive.

Governance. Stonar is a part of NACE Educational Services Limited, Company Registration No. 8441252, Registered Address: 17 Hanover Square, London, United Kingdom W1S 1HU.

Stonyhurst St Mary's Hall
Preparatory School for Stonyhurst College

Stonyhurst, Clitheroe, Lancashire BB7 9PZ

Tel: 01254 827073
Fax: 01254 827136
email: smhadmissions@stonyhurst.ac.uk
website: www.stonyhurst.ac.uk
Twitter: @stonyhurstsmh

Chairman of Governors: Mr Anthony Chitnis

Headmaster: **Mr Ian Murphy**, BA, PGCE

Age Range. 3–13 (Boarders from age 8).
Number of Pupils. 279 pupils, of which 65 are boarders.
Fees per term (2018–2019). Day £2,900–£5,700; Weekly Boarding £7,500; Full Boarding £8,800–£9,300.

Stonyhurst St Mary's Hall provides a co-educational preparatory education in the Jesuit Catholic tradition for boarders (age 8–13) and day pupils (age 3–13). Stonyhurst, founded in 1593, is one of the oldest Jesuit schools in the world, and the College and Preparatory School are set within two thousand acres of outstanding natural beauty.

The school has impressive facilities and buildings, however, it will always be the people – children, staff, parents and families that breathe life into Stonyhurst St Mary's Hall. The positive and optimistic vision within the school community is tangible. This is an exciting time for the school and it is thriving. Stonyhurst St Mary's Hall is a special place where children want to be and where relationships between all members of the community are remarkable.

We have a highly personalised approach to the children's learning. All children receive close individual attention and personalised academic tutoring through their class teachers and Playroom (head of year) staff, who meet regularly to monitor pupils' work and progress. Early Years and Key Stage 1 pupils are taught in Hodder House, their own purpose-built building.

Bringing to life their learning in class, teachers and children have access to the artefacts and curator expertise of the oldest museum in the English speaking world, the Stonyhurst Collections. The museum contains over 50,000 objects and books, including a wide and rich collection of Natural History pieces, a first folio by William Shakespeare, Egyptian mummies, fossilised dinosaur dung and a prayer book that was once the property of Mary, Queen of Scots. One of more than 40 clubs and activities on offer to Stonyhurst St Mary's Hall children, the "Young Curators" group gives children the opportunity to handle and categorise these artefacts.

The pupils at Stonyhurst St Mary's Hall are aware of their responsibility to maximise their unique talents and thrive as they engage in the school's broad and innovative activities programme. The school is proud of its strong sporting tradition with high levels of performance in traditional sports, cross country and swimming.

Performing arts is one of the jewels in the school's crown – children of all ages are immersed in curriculum drama lessons and ambitious stage productions utilising the on-site professional standard theatre. The department also works with the London Academy of Music and Dramatic Art (LAMDA), and children may take LAMDA exams in Verse & Prose, Acting and Musical Theatre.

Other unparalleled facilities include a new science lab, an art studio, a swimming pool, a tennis dome for year-round tennis, a sports hall and a professional standard theatre, in which all children have their drama lessons.

The school offers an outstanding boarding experience and sense of belonging. Boarders are under the care of the resident Director of Boarding, supported by a large resident pastoral team and other teaching staff. The boarders enjoy a stimulating and wide-ranging programme of evening and weekend activities. Stonyhurst provides a seven-days-a-week boarding environment, in which the day pupils are able to participate to a great extent if they wish.

Stonyhurst St Mary's Hall is a very safe, nurturing, vibrant and warm-hearted child-centred environment within a beautiful and extensive rural location. The school prides itself on being creative and innovative with a genuine ambition for each individual. It successfully blends high performance with opportunity and engagement for the less confident by being challenging yet supporting in equal measures.

Admission to Stonyhurst Mary's Hall from 3–10+ is by previous school report (where applicable), interview and standardised cognitive assessment. At the 11+ entry level, there is an entrance assessment in English, Maths and critical thinking. Academic, Art, Music, Sport and All-rounder scholarships are awarded at 11+. Almost all children proceed to Stonyhurst College at the age of 13. Further details and a prospectus may be obtained from the Registrar.

Charitable status. St Mary's Hall is a Registered Charity, number 230165. It exists to promote Catholic Independent Jesuit Education within the Christian Community. It also runs its own registered, pupil-led charity, Children for Children, which raises funds for a school in Zimbabwe and other worthy causes.

Stormont

The Causeway, Potters Bar, Herts EN6 5HA

Tel: 01707 654037
email: admin@stormontschool.org
website: www.stormontschool.org
Twitter: @StormontSchool
Facebook: @StormontSchool

The school is administered by a Board of Governors.

Chairman of Board of Governors: Mr A Newland

Headmistress: Mrs S E Martin, BSc

Age Range. 4–11.
Number of Pupils. 180 Day Girls.
Fees per term (2018–2019). £4,100–£4,350 (including lunch). There are no compulsory extras.

The School was founded in 1944 and has occupied its attractive Victorian House since then. There is a spacious, bright, purpose-built Lower School Building, which adjoins the Assembly Hall and Dining Room with a newly-built play area for the younger ages. We provide well-equipped rooms for our Library, Art, Pottery, Design Technology, Science and French. A Millennium Building houses a Drama/Music Studio and an Information and Communications Technology Suite. The school has outdoor tennis courts which double up as netball courts, a two-acre playing field and use of a swimming pool. Our well-qualified and experienced staff prepare the girls for entry to a wide range of both independent and maintained senior schools at the age of eleven, some of whom gain Scholarships at their chosen school.

Charitable status. Stormont School is a Registered Charity, number 311079. It exists to establish and carry on as a school where children may receive a sound education.

Stover Preparatory School

Newton Abbot, Devon TQ12 6QG

Tel: 01626 354505
Fax: 01626 361475
email: schooloffice@stover.co.uk
website: www.stover.co.uk

Chairman of Governors: Mr S Killick, ND, ARB

Head: Mr David Burt

Age Range. 3–11 Co-educational.
Number of Pupils. 142.
Fees per term (2018–2019). Preparatory School: Day: Reception £2,740, Year 1, 2 and 3 £2,800, Years 4, 5 and 6 £3,480. Weekly Boarding: Years 4, 5 and 6 £7,400. Full Boarding: Years 4, 5 and 6 £7,070.

Stover Preparatory School enjoys a beautiful rural setting on the edge of Dartmoor National Park, close to the South Devon coast. Set in 64 acres there is ample space for pupils of all ages to experience the great outdoors, be that through play, nature walks, sport, orienteering, bushcraft, learning in our outdoor classroom or researching the history of our fine old buildings. Stover Preparatory School shares its fine site with Stover Senior School, making transfer at aged 11 years a smooth process for our pupils.

We pride ourselves on our warm, welcoming atmosphere where each individual is nurtured and encouraged to reach their full potential. Visitors frequently comment on the positive, happy feeling they experience upon entering the school. Teachers are aware of pupils' individual needs and provide support in an approachable and friendly manner.

We offer a broad, balanced curriculum with high academic standards, complemented by a wide range of extracurricular activities. Spanish begins in Reception and French is also introduced at Year 3. Languages, PE and music are taught by specialist teachers across the school. All other subjects are taught by the class teacher to enable cross-curricular links to thrive. Underpinning everything we do is our firm belief in Research Based Learning, where students develop their inquiry skills, taking ownership of their learning from a young age. Sport and the Performing Arts play a vital role in each child's development. We have a full fixture list for our U9 and U11 teams as well as involvement with the local Schools' Sports Partnership. Our regular school performances and concerts are a highlight of the calendar. More than 80% of our Prep School pupils choose to participate in the Prep School Choir. In addition, we offer a Pre-Prep Choir and a Chamber Choir for talented pupils in Years 5 and 6. Residential and day trips into our beautiful local environment further complement the curriculum.

Facilities include an extensive Outdoor Classroom, Sports Fields, Tennis Courts, Art room, Music room, Multi-Purpose Hall, Library and ICT suite.

Flexi, weekly and full boarding are available from the age of 8 years. Scholarships are offered at 11+. The majority of our pupils move on to Stover Senior School.

See also Stover School senior entry in The Society of Heads section.

Charitable status. Stover School Association is a Registered Charity, number 306712.

Streatham & Clapham Prep School
GDST

Wavertree Road, London SW2 3SR

Tel: 020 8674 6912
Fax: 020 8674 0175
email: prep@schs.gdst.net
website: www.schs.gdst.net
Twitter: @SCPSgdst; @SCHSgdst
Facebook: @SCPSgdst

Motto: *ad sapientiam sine metu*

Chairman of Local Governors: Mrs F Smith, BA, PGCE

Head: T Mylne, BA, PGCE

Age Range. Girls 3–11.
Number of Pupils. 220.
Fees per term (2018–2019). Prep School £4,564, Nursery (after EYS grant contribution), Full-time £2,029; Part-time £291.

Streatham & Clapham Prep School is a division of Streatham & Clapham High School GDST (*see the entry in the GSA section*), situated on its own extensive campus in Streatham Hill, within a mile of the Senior School. The School provides a specialist academic curriculum as part of a liberal and challenging educational experience for its girls within a caring culture of warm relationships and diversity, all the while nurturing their personal development and confidence. Its facilities include a full-size gymnasium and specialist drama, music, IT, art and design rooms; pupils also regularly benefit from specialist Senior School facilities, for instance its all-weather sports pitch. Admission to the school is by selective assessment, with informal assessment of pupils for Nursery, Reception, Year 1 and Year 2, and an entrance examination for Year 3 candidates. Places in other year groups are occasionally available.

Curriculum. The school's broad and varied curriculum benefits from leading specialist teachers in all areas. Girls enjoy distinctive and invigorating learning through programmes such as Singapore mathematics, Philosophy for Children, the 'Talk4Writing' network, PE, Music, Art, Drama, Computer Science, Design & Technology, Mandarin, French and Latin.

Personal & Pastoral Development. Great emphasis is placed on nurturing well-balanced and considerate individuals, who are ready for the challenges of adolescent and adult life. Strong pastoral and House systems reinforce this ethos,

as do lessons in philosophy, myriad opportunities to build resilience, and overseas residential trips.

Co-curricular Programme & Family Support. The school offers an extensive co-curricular programme with over 30 free clubs as well as other after-school activities, societies and events. Wrap-around childcare is offered from 7.45 am to 5.55 pm, five days a week during term-time. The school is conveniently located near major transport links and also offers five minibus routes serving most of south London.

Stroud School
King Edward VI Preparatory School

Highwood House, Highwood Lane, Romsey, Hampshire SO51 9ZH

Tel: 01794 513231
Fax: 01794 514432
email: secretary@stroud-kes.org.uk
website: www.stroud-kes.org.uk

Chairman of Governors: Mr B Richards

Headmaster: Mr Joel Worrall, BSc

Deputy Head (*Pastoral*): Mr Chris Jackson

Deputy Head (*Academic*): Mrs Sarah Mason-Campbell

Age Range. 3–13.
Number of Pupils. 348: 195 Boys, 153 Girls.
Fees per term (2018–2019). Upper School £5,607, Middle School £5,145, Pre-Preparatory £3,495, full-time Nursery £3,495.

Stroud is a co-educational day school for children aged 3 to 13 years. Pupils are prepared for entrance to Senior Independent or Grammar Schools.

The School stands on the outskirts of Romsey in its own grounds of 22 acres, which include playing fields, a full-sized sports hall, a heated outdoor swimming pool, tennis courts, riding arena, lawns and gardens and a brand new, purpose-built, KS1 building ready for pupils returning in September 2018. The main team games for boys are cricket, hockey, rugby and football, and for girls hockey, rounders and netball. Both boys and girls play tennis.

Music and drama play an important part in the life of the School. A wide variety of instruments is taught and children are encouraged to join the school orchestra. Each year there is a musical production and the Christmas Carol Service is held at the Romsey Abbey.

The Stroud School Association, run by the parents, holds many social activities and helps to raise money for amenities, but its main function is to generate goodwill.

In 2014 a £2.5 million investment included a new kitchen, dining room, as well as an Art/DT/MLF block. Also Included in this project has been a £400K Biomass district heating system.

The Study Preparatory School

Wilberforce House, Camp Road, Wimbledon Common, London SW19 4UN

Tel: 020 8947 6969
email: admissions@thestudyprep.co.uk
website: www.thestudyprep.co.uk
Twitter: @thestudyprep

Chairman of Governors: Mr John Tucker

Headmistress: **Mrs Susan Pepper**, MA Oxon, PGCE London, NPQH

Age Range. 4–11.
Number of Girls. 320 (approximately).
Fees per term (2018–2019). £4,550.

The Study Preparatory School provides a happy and stimulating learning environment for girls from 4 to 11 on two very attractive and well-equipped sites close to Wimbledon Common.

The girls enjoy a rich diversity of experiences, both in and out of the classroom. The school is renowned for its creative ethos, and has been awarded Artsmark Gold status by Arts Council England for the third time in 2018. Each girl is encouraged to do her best academically, and excellent teaching standards encourage academic rigour and challenge. Music and sport are exceptionally strong, while drama, public speaking and a varied clubs programme play an important part. Guest speakers, fundraising events, workshops and school trips all help the children to understand important issues beyond the school gates. Good manners and consideration for others are encouraged at all times. Girls leave at 11+, very well prepared for the next stage of their education, with a zest for learning and many happy memories. Girls receive offers from leading day and boarding senior schools, many with academic or performance scholarships, with over 135 scholarships having been offered over the last five years.

Entry is by ballot at reception and by assessment thereafter. The Study has an assisted places scheme for girls aged 7+. For details contact Joint Educational Trust (JET) on 020 3217 1100.

Charitable status. The Study (Wimbledon) Ltd is a Registered Charity, number 271012. It exists to provide education for girls from 4 to 11.

Summer Fields

Mayfield Road, Oxford OX2 7EN

Tel: 01865 459204
email: admissions@summerfields.com
website: www.summerfields.com
Twitter: @SFSOxford
Facebook: @Summer-Fields-Oxford

Chairman of Governors: A E Reekes, MA, FRSA

Headmaster: **David Faber**, MA Oxon

Age Range. 4–13.
Number of Boys. Prep: 180 boarders, 59 day; Pre-Prep: 41.
Fees per term (2018–2019). Prep: £10,120 Boarding, £7,053 Day. Pre-Prep: £4,000 Reception, £4,500 Years 1 & 2, £5,200 Year 3.

Set in 72 acres of delightful grounds which lead down to the river Cherwell and yet only a few miles from the city centre, Summer Fields is often known as Oxford's *Secret Garden*.

The School has always had a strong academic reputation with Summerfieldians regularly securing scholarships, awards and exhibitions to top independent schools including Eton, Harrow, Radley and Winchester. Each year, boys pass Common Entrance to a wide variety of top public schools.

Huge emphasis is placed on providing the highest standards of pastoral care. Each boy has a personal tutor, who is responsible for his academic progress and social welfare and will be in regular contact with the boy's parents. The boarders live in comfortable Lodges within the school grounds and are looked after by an experienced and dedicated husband and wife team of Lodgeparents. More than 90% of the staff live on site, making a significant contribution to school life both in and out of the classroom.

The Music, Art, Drama, Design Technology, ICT and Sport departments are all impressive. The Choir regularly sing Evensong in Oxford Colleges. They also regularly tour abroad, most recently visiting Malta. At least one Drama production takes place every term in the Macmillan Theatre. Every summer an Art Exhibition of boys' work is held at the school.

The facilities are outstanding, including the new Salata Pavilion, opened in October 2015, which includes purpose-built changing rooms for the boys and a large multi-functional space on the first floor. Within the school there is also a fine library, theatre and chapel; Art, Design & Technology, Music and ICT Centres and a magnificent Sports Hall, with squash and Eton fives courts, a shooting gallery and swimming pool. The extensive outdoor facilities include an astro-turf and tennis courts and all-weather cricket nets, a nine-hole golf course, new adventure playground, the plantation where the boys camp, together with an outside classroom. A huge range of sports, activities and hobbies is on offer to the boys.

In September 2018, Summer Fields opened a new, purpose-built pre-prep school offering an exceptional early education to boys aged 4–7.

8+ Academic and Music Scholarships are available as well as 100% scholarships and bursaries for entry into Year 6 or Year 7.

For further information or to arrange a visit, please contact Mrs Christine Berry, Tel: 01865 459204 or email: admissions@summerfields.com.

Charitable status. Summer Fields is a Registered Charity, number 309683.

Sunninghill Prep School

South Court, South Walks, Dorchester, Dorset DT1 1EB

Tel: 01305 262306
email: info@sunninghill.dorset.sch.uk
website: www.sunninghillprep.co.uk
Facebook: @SunninghillPrepSchool

Chair of Governors: Mr Philip Fry

Headmaster: **Mr John Thorpe**, BSc Hons, PGCE

Age Range. 9 months–13 years.
Number of Children. Baby unit (9 months–2 years 9 months) 5 girls, 6 boys; Nursery (2 years 9 months–4 years) 8 girls, 5 boys; Reception (4–5 years) 7 girls, 8 boys; Junior Prep (5–8 years) 27 girls, 32 boys; Prep School (8–13 years) 35 girls, 34 boys.
Fees per term (2018–2019). £2,950–£5,150. There are no compulsory extras. Nursery: £978 (based on 5 morning sessions per week, inclusive of Early Years Grant).

Sunninghill is a co-educational day school. There are 9 full-time and 16 part-time fully qualified teaching staff.

Founded in 1939, Sunninghill Prep became a Charitable Trust in 1969. It moved to its present site in January 1997 and has its own swimming pool, all-weather sports pitch, tennis courts and extensive grounds. Children are prepared for the Common Entrance examination to any Independent Senior School, and those with particular ability may be entered for scholarships. Over the years the school has attained many academic successes, but the broad curriculum also includes drama, art, craft, music and physical education. Friday Enrichments allow greater cross-curricular links for years 1–8, enhancing their learning further.

Team and individual sports played with PE and Games at least three times a week from years 3–8 and these include hockey, netball, lacrosse and rounders for the girls, and hockey, rugby, association football and cricket for the boys. In the summer term both boys and girls participate in athletics, swimming and tennis.

Out-of-school activities include academic clubs preparing for scholarships, such as the core subjects, humanities and art, plus debating, chess, creative arts, ballet, dance, LAMDA and various music clubs including choir and string quartet. We offer multi sports across a wide age group, all pentathlon sports and swimming and we are a member of the National Sailing Academy, with our own race team. Sunninghill Prep prides itself on its nurturing, family ethos. The school's flourishing Parents' Association ensures that parents and staff all know each other and work together for the good of the children and the School.

The prospectus is available on request or downloadable from our website

Charitable status. Sunninghill Preparatory School is a Registered Charity, number 1024774. It exists to provide education for boys and girls.

Sunny Hill Preparatory School
Bruton School for Girls

Sunny Hill, Bruton, Somerset BA10 0NT

Tel:	01749 814400
Fax:	01749 812537
email:	admissions@brutonschool.co.uk
website:	www.brutonschool.co.uk
Twitter:	@BrutonSchool
Facebook:	@Bruton-School-for-Girls

Chairman of Governors: Mr D H C Batten

Head of Preparatory School: **Mrs Helen Snow**, BEd

Age Range. Day places for Girls and Boys aged 3–7. Day and Boarding places for Girls aged 7–11. No Saturday school.

Numbers of Pupils. 45.

Fees per term (2018–2019). Day: £4,255–4,372 (Preparatory School), £2,835 (Pre-Preparatory School), £22 per session (Pre-School). Boarding (from Year 4): £7,843–£7,960 (full), £7,100–£7,217 (weekly), £8,603 (Overseas Pupils including EAL support).

Ethos. Sunny Hill Preparatory School offers a happy, caring and vibrant atmosphere where children build strong academic foundations and develop personal confidence. Pupils are encouraged to think of others in a community based on mutual respect.

Location. Situated in 40 acres in beautiful countryside, the school is conveniently located on the Somerset, Wiltshire and Dorset borders with easy access to the A303. It shares the campus with the senior school and pupils benefit from specialist teachers and facilities.

Curriculum. A carefully structured and broad curriculum, delivered using an exciting variety of teaching and learning styles, ensures good foundations are laid and high standards are achieved by all. Pupils thrive on a rich mix of activities – including themed curriculum weeks, a comprehensive outdoor education programme, imaginative topic work and educational visits – all encouraging curiosity and a love of learning. A weekly enrichment afternoon includes such activities as Cooking, Drama and Problem-Solving. Creative and enthusiastic teachers inspire and stretch pupils. Pupils are nurtured by an excellent system of pastoral care. Children in the Pre-School and Early Years Class follow the Early Years Foundation Stage curriculum with emphasis on learning through play.

A love of creative and performing arts is encouraged as are opportunities to perform. Facilities include a modern theatre, library, music room, a nature reserve and a meadow. Extracurricular activities may include Ballet, Gymnastics, Orchestra, Hockey, Swimming, Choir and Folk Group.

Sport. Hockey, netball, rounders, tennis, swimming and athletics are taught by specialist PE teachers. Facilities include an astroturf pitch, dance studio and heated outdoor swimming pool. Pupils participate in inter-school competitions.

Boarding. Located on site, the junior boarding wing provides a high standard of care and comfort appropriate to the younger boarders. Girls share a room with two/three others and have their own cosy common room. In the evenings and at weekends, pupils enjoy a full programme of activities.

Spiritual Life. The school is non-denominational with a Christian ethos and welcomes pupils from all faiths or none.

Medical Care. The on-site medical centre is staffed by a medical administrator who is a qualified nurse.

Charitable status. Bruton School for Girls is a Registered Charity, number 1085577, and a Company Limited by Guarantee.

Sussex House

68 Cadogan Square, London SW1X 0EA

Tel:	020 7584 1741
email:	schoolsecretary@sussexhouseschool.co.uk
website:	www.sussexhouseschool.co.uk

Chairman of the Governors: John Crewe, Esq

Headmaster: **Nicholas Kaye**, MA Magdalene College Cambridge, ACP, Hon FCOT, FRSA, FRGS

Deputy Headmaster: Martin Back, BA, PGCE Sussex

Age Range. 8–13.

Number of Boys. 184.

Fees per term (2018–2019). £6,915.

Founded in 1952, Sussex House is situated in the heart of Chelsea in a fine Norman Shaw house in Cadogan Square. Its Gymnasium and Music School are housed in a converted chapel in Cadogan Street. The school is an independent charitable trust. At Common Entrance and Scholarship level it has achieved a record of consistently strong results to academically demanding schools. The school enjoys its own entirely independent character and the style is traditional yet imaginative.

There is a full-time teaching staff of 22. Creative subjects are given strong emphasis and throughout the school boys take Music and Art. Team sports take place at a nearby site and the school's football teams have an impressive record. Cricket is the main summer sport and there are opportunities for tennis, swimming, basketball, indoor football and indoor hockey. All boys have physical education classes and Sussex House is a centre of excellence for fencing and its international records are well known.

Cultural and creative activities play a major role, including theatrical productions in a West End theatre, a major annual exhibition of creative work featuring large-scale architectural models and an annual competition of poetry written by boys. There is a strong bias towards music and an ambitious programme of choral and orchestral concerts. A large number of pupils play musical instruments and there is an impressive record of music awards to senior schools. The school provides a range of sporting and cultural trips.

The school has a Church of England affiliation. There is a school chaplain and weekly services are held in St Simon Zelotes Church, Chelsea. Boys of all religions and denominations are welcomed.

Charitable status. Sussex House is a Registered Charity, number 1035806. It exists to provide education for boys.

Sutton Valence Preparatory School

Church Road, Chart Sutton, Maidstone, Kent ME17 3RF

Tel: 01622 842117
Fax: 01622 844201
email: enquiries@svprep.svs.org.uk
website: www.svs.org.uk
Facebook: @SuttonValenceSchoolKent

Chair of Governors: Lady Vallance, JP, MA, MSc, PhD, FRSA, FCGI

Head: **Miss C M Corkran**, MEd, BEd Hons Cantab

Deputy Head: Mr J Watkins, BSc Hons, PGCE Primary
Head of Pre-Prep: Miss P McCarmick, MA, BSc QTS, AMBDA
Academic Deputy Head: Miss R Harrison, BEd Hons

Age Range. 3–11.
Number of Pupils. 300.
Fees per term (2018–2019). £3,000–£4,610. Lunch £260.

The values of our School community and the happiness of our children are central to everything we do. These provide pupils with a strong feeling of structure and security which enables them to work effectively.

At whichever point children join us they embark on their own journeys, each one different and each one with differing emphasis on the four areas we hold dear: Academic, Co-curricular, Community and Leadership and Service.

By the time they leave us at the age of 11, it is our responsibility to have equipped the children during their formative years with the essentials of character to thrive in an increasingly competitive world. To put firmly in place the qualities which will make them clear thinking, lateral thinking, robust, hardworking, determined and yet kindly citizens, who will go on to influence many people in the coming years.

We have high expectations of ourselves and of our children, both inside and out of the classroom, and we have a long history of successful preparation of children for the next stage of their education, be that for our Senior School, the Kent grammars, or other schools.

None of this should come at the expense of childhood and what the School does so successfully is find that balance between delivering in terms of education, and yet doing so kindly and with many broad, interesting and high-quality opportunities. The School is very proud of its articulate and confident pupils who move on well-equipped to work things out for themselves, so crucial in an increasingly challenging world.

To achieve this we have dedicated Art, Science and ICT facilities and a new Library. Classes are small throughout

the school. The 40 teaching staff are all well qualified and there is an extensive peripatetic staff for music. Special needs are addressed by the SENCO and 3 part-time teachers. The Kindergarten to Year 2 classes all have qualified classroom assistants.

The school is situated in 18 acres of countryside overlooking the Weald and includes a hard and grass play areas, heated outdoor swimming pool, four hard tennis courts, a Sports Hall, a 13-acre games field, a full-size Astroturf and a newly established 'forest school' area, all of which support our co-curricular programme.

A solid foundation in the core subjects of English, Mathematics, Science and ICT is supplemented by Languages, Music, Drama, Art, Design Technology and Sport which are all taught by specialist teaching staff. The co-curricular programme is wide and varied providing many opportunities for children to perform in drama productions and in concerts, occasionally in conjunction with the senior school. Children are prepared for our senior school, Sutton Valence, the local Grammar schools and other independent schools with an 11+ entry.

Cricket, football, hockey, netball, rugby and rounders are the major sports, with athletics, swimming and cross-country also being available. The proximity of the senior school, Sutton Valence, allows the children to benefit from their staffing and facilities, including the use of the Sports Hall, athletics track and the indoor swimming pool. After-school activities include chess club, art, 5-a-side football, gymnastics, drama, craft, croquet, science club, ballet and judo.

The school is a Christian foundation. Assemblies, for celebration, and the use of the local church are an important facet of our lives, with the school's Chaplain visiting regularly. The school provides a fulfilling education for all its children, a thriving network for its parents and a happy workplace for all who dedicate their lives to it.

Charitable status. United Westminster Schools Foundation is a Registered Charity, number 309267. It exists to provide education for boys and girls and provides valuable resources and support.

Swanbourne House

Swanbourne, Milton Keynes, Buckinghamshire MK17 0HZ

Tel: 01296 720264
email: office@swanbourne.org
website: www.swanbourne.org
Twitter: @swanbournehouse
Facebook: @SwanbourneHouse
LinkedIn: /Swanbourne House

The School is a Charitable Trust, administered by a Board of Governors.

Chairman of Governors: Mr J F Willmott

Head: **Mrs J Thorpe**

Age Range. 3–13.
Number of Pupils. Prep: 131 Boys, 92 Girls (27 full/weekly boarders, 50 flexi boarders). Pre-Prep: 35 Girls, 41 Boys. Nursery: 12 Girls, 11 Boys.
Fees per term (2018–2019). Full/Weekly boarding £7,840; Day: Prep £6,120; 7s £4,320; Pre-Prep £3,450; Nursery £470–£2,055.

Established in 1920 and set within 55 acres of stunning Buckinghamshire countryside, Swanbourne House School is a Preparatory School with a difference and one parents of prospective pupils should come and experience before making such a crucial decision for their young child's education.

We aim to be a dynamic, diverse and forward thinking school offering an exemplary service in teaching and learning. Our pupils grow to understand the discipline of study as we ignite the fire for a lifelong love of learning, personal development and reflection. We aspire to develop well-rounded pupils, who rise to mental and physical challenge with optimism, open and enquiring minds, confidence and empathy. We teach children how to think and communicate responsibly and effectively and we give them the freedom and opportunity required to develop their capacity for independent, principled thought. Creativity is strongly encouraged in all areas of school life, not just in the expressive arts. This includes an extensive offering in academics, art, computing, debating, drama, DT and engineering, music and sport.

As a result of the breadth and depth of experience and learning at Swanbourne House, the number of scholarships our Top Year children secure each year in academics, art, drama, DT, music and sport is very impressive indeed. Our Common Entrance results, too, are consistently strong with very nearly all pupils securing their first choice of senior school. We tend to send the majority of our children to Eton, Harrow, Cheltenham Ladies' College, Radley, Bradfield, Stowe, Wellington College, Oundle, Rugby, Oakham, Uppingham, Bloxham, Cheltenham College, Concord, Repton, St Edward's and a number of other leading public schools.

It is noteworthy that a significant and not coincidental number of Old Swanbournians have gone on to be School Captains, Prefects and Sports Captains at their senior schools. They are well-grounded, well-mannered, emotionally intelligent and go on to become highly attractive candidates for the top universities and for future employers.

In a nutshell, we believe our School is exceptional. It is a School that continues to work very hard to earn and deserve its success and enviable reputation. We are there every step of the way on your child's journey through Prep School and we do our best to ensure that each and every child strives to do their best, in every regard, with confidence and determination in a happy, safe and supportive environment, with plenty of time for tree climbing and den building!

Charitable status. Swanbourne House School is a Registered Charity, number 310640.

Talbot Heath Junior School

Rothesay Road, Bournemouth BH4 9NJ

Tel:	01202 763360
Fax:	01202 768155
email:	jsoffice@talbotheath.org
website:	www.talbotheath.org

Chair of Governors: Mrs Christine Norman

Head Teacher: **Mrs Elizabeth Pugh**

Age Range. Girls 3–11.
Number of Pupils. 240.
Our Ethos. We are immensely proud of our pupils and the happy atmosphere, in which there is a genuine love of learning that permeates the school. Being unique in the area in catering for girls from 3–18, the school is one where each individual really matters and is nurtured and valued. The School's motto, 'Honour Before Honours', underpins our community. We care for each other and support one another. Integrity and character lie at the heart of who we are.

We have a strong family atmosphere where all have a chance to achieve at their own level across every area of the broad curriculum. Perhaps, more importantly, the girls are happy and see coming to school as something enjoyable and great fun.

Talbot Heath girls are confident but not arrogant, knowledgeable but not complacent, able to express their opinions but willing to listen to those of others, independent yet supportive, strong yet compassionate, principled but fun. They value what they have and they value others. They are original but can work as a team, are keen to play a role in the wider world but have a strong sense of community.

Being selective we value our academic tradition and encourage hard work, diligence and the creation of a caring community. Pupils are from a range of abilities and emphasis is placed on becoming rounded individuals, experiencing the full breadth of an extensive curriculum and achieving at their own personal level. Home school links are strong and positive which helps to create the caring and supportive environment of which we are so proud. Our results, right from the first steps in EYFS, are outstanding but the school places value on so much more than just results.

Facilities. The Junior School, housed in its own buildings on our woodland campus, is split into two departments, Pre-Prep (age 3–7) and Junior (age 7–11). Apart from large, spacious classrooms, Juniors have their own hall, two dining rooms, computer suites, a library, a studio, a Science room and large outdoor play facilities including woodland trails, playgrounds and an adventure playground.

In addition to this they make use of all the Senior School facilities as they progress through school. These include the dedicated Music School, the Sports Hall, athletics track, all-weather pitches, courts and gym, Science Centre and Creative Arts block. The girls are taught by subject specialists for Music and PE from Reception onwards. Once the girls reach Year 4 they are taught by academic subject specialists for the majority of their curriculum. Every girl has a school ipad and from May 2019 will benefit from STEAM lessons in our state-of-the-art interdisciplinary hub.

Fees per term (2018–2019). £2,201–£3,918.

Charitable status. Talbot Heath School Trust Limited is a Registered Charity, number 283708.

Terra Nova School

Jodrell Bank, Holmes Chapel, Cheshire CW4 8BT

Tel:	01477 571251
Fax:	01477 571646
email:	admissions@tnschool.co.uk
website:	www.tnschool.co.uk
Twitter:	@TerraNovaSchool
Facebook:	@terranovaschool

Chairman of Governors: Mr Will Sillar

Headmaster: **Mr Philip Stewart**

Age Range. 2½–13 Co-educational.
Number of Pupils. 300.
Fees per term (2018–2019). Seniors: Day £4,850–£4,899, Flexi boarding £35 per night, Weekly boarding £100 per week. Juniors: £3,500–£4,200. Pre-Prep: Reception £3,500, Nursery £1,980–£3,300.

Terra Nova is a vibrant and exciting school set in 35 acres of rural Cheshire countryside. The perfect place for a child to grow and develop. The school is steeped in history and values the traditions that form the foundations on which a fresh thinking approach is adopted.

All children in the School are encouraged to develop their talents and realise their potential in the way that best meets their needs and personalities. The wellbeing of every child is at the heart of the School's philosophy, we want them to develop a genuine love of learning, be resilient, optimistic, confident and kind people who can sustain good relationships and make a positive contribution to society.

Boarding. Relationships are further fostered, and independence developed with the opportunity for pupils to board at Terra Nova School in preparation for both Senior boarding schools and future university life. Pupils are enjoying flexible boarding from Year 3 to Year 8. There are currently 35–50 pupils boarding on a regular basis.

Academic Reputation. Terra Nova School prides itself on preparing pupils for the next stage in their education, through a dynamic, vibrant and engaging curriculum taught by world-class educators who have training and experience across the world. All this is achieved making use of the very best resources. Many pupils leave Terra Nova with scholarships at prestigious Schools such as Shrewsbury, Uppingham, Rugby, Repton, Marlborough and Sedburgh. Other pupils have gone on to study at Eton and Oxford.

Facilities. Terra Nova School offers an enviable setting for pupils, perfect for learning outside the classroom through the purpose-built forest school set in our own woodlands, bespoke shooting range, all-purpose floodlit astroturf, tennis courts, Performing Arts Centre and swimming pool. This summer the school has also developed two further facilities, a state-of-the-art Makerspace to enhance our Science, Technology, Engineering, Arts and Mathematics (STEAM) programme and The Hub, a new a vibrant library and resource centre for pupils.

Charitable status. Terra Nova School Trust Limited is a Registered Charity, number 525919. It is dedicated to all round educational excellence for children.

Terrington Hall School

Terrington, York YO60 6PR
Tel: 01653 648227
email: office@terringtonhall.com
website: www.terringtonhall.com
Twitter: @TerringtonHall

Chairman of Governors: Mr Rodger Hobson

Headmaster: **Mr Stephen Mulryne**, BEd Hons

Age Range. 3–13 years.
Number of Children. 175: 91 boys, 84 girls.
Fees per term (2018–2019). Day: £4,665 (Years 5–8), £4,530 (Year 4), £4,430 (Year 3), £2,920 (Year 2), £2,760 (Year 1), £2,610 (Reception & Nursery). Flexible boarding is available at £15 per night.

Terrington is a co-educational day and flexi boarding school situated in the Howardian Hills, an Area of Outstanding Natural Beauty fifteen miles from York.

The main school building, a Georgian rectory, is home to the boarding staff and those pupils staying the night who enjoy family-style dining and plenty of home comforts in the bright and airy accommodation.

The school has a strong flexi boarding community, with over 90 per cent of Years 3–8 pupils opting to stay the night at some point during the school year to make the most of the exciting evening activity programme.

Terrington places special emphasis on preparing pupils for entry into the senior school that best suits each child, whether locally or further afield, day or boarding. Particu-

larly proud of the scholarships won by its pupils for academia, art, sport and drama, the school also places great value in developing young men and women who have the self-belief and confidence to follow their own interests while displaying good manners and consideration for others.

The school enjoys excellent sporting facilities, with eight acres of playing fields, an astroturf facility, tennis courts, an indoor heated swimming pool and sports hall. All major sports are played and an extensive fixture list ensures that every child has ample opportunity to represent the school. Specialist tuition is available in several extra-curricular sport activities, including karate, swimming and tennis. All children have the opportunity to participate in the kayaking and climbing expeditions to the Ardèche and the Alps in Years Seven and Eight.

Teaching facilities are modern and well-equipped and include both computer and science suites. Music, art and drama are an integral part of the curriculum. Tuition is available for most instruments and children are prepared for Associated Board exams. The Junior and Senior choirs perform within school and at local venues, and there is a popular orchestra, rock band and wind ensemble. Drama is particularly well supported by specialist teaching within the curriculum from Nursery to Year 8, and a Drama Club and private lessons are available to pupils wishing to take speech and drama exams.

The School Chaplain is the local Rector who leads the school in worship at the local church every Wednesday morning and takes weekly assemblies at the school. Senior pupils are prepared for Confirmation if they so wish.

The Headmaster, his wife and children live in the school grounds and parents are fully involved in the life of the school which has a flourishing social committee.

Bursaries are available on a means-tested basis.

Charitable status. Terrington Hall is a Registered Charity, number 532362. It exists to provide a quality education for boys and girls.

Thorngrove School

The Mount, Pantings Lane, Highclere, Newbury, Berkshire RG20 9PS
Tel: 01635 253172
email: admin@thorngroveschool.co.uk
website: www.thorngroveschool.co.uk
Twitter: @thorngroveprep
Facebook: @ThorngrovePrep

Proprietors: Mrs and Mrs N Broughton

Headmaster: **Mr A King**, BA Hons QTS Leeds, PDES Leadership and Management

Deputy Head Academic: Mr G Smart, BA Hons Oxford, MA Oxon, GTP, QTS

Deputy Head Pastoral: Mr N Graham, BA Hons Oxford Brookes, PGCE

Age Range. 2½–13 Co-educational.
Number of Pupils. 250 Day Pupils.
Fees per term (2018–2019). Reception–Year 2 £4,690; Year 3 and 4 £5,260; Year 5–8 £5,865.

Thorngrove School was founded in 1988 and is an IAPS co-educational day preparatory school for children aged 2½ to 13 years. The purpose-built facilities are set in former farmland in the village of Highclere, 5 miles south of Newbury and 12 miles north of Andover. Children are prepared for Common Entrance at 13+, from where their paths lead to a wide range of senior day and boarding schools.

The school is set in 25 acres of beautiful, Hampshire countryside. The extensive games fields provide numerous rugby, football and hockey pitches. In addition to this, there is an astro, two new hard courts which are used for tennis and netball and an impressive 3-lane cricket facility (installed Summer 2018). A multi-purpose hall was opened by Robert Hardy in 2007. This provides a wonderful space for music concerts and drama productions as well as indoor PE and games. Either side of the hall are four classrooms and changing facilities. We have a large IT suite and many of the classrooms have interactive whiteboards. There is a dedicated music room in the Senior Block with several practice rooms. The Science laboratory is fully equipped. The Art room is well resourced and has recently been refurbished. Our well-stocked library is located centrally in the main building and we have a full-time librarian. All classrooms are modern, light and airy and some have direct access to the outside. In 2010 a D&T centre was created in the old nursery. In April 2012 a new Nursery was opened to extend our EYFS provision.

Thorngrove offers a unique environment where children can grow and learn independently. We value our intimate and friendly community, and the benefits that it brings; we are proud of our small class sizes and the individual attention we are able to offer to each of our pupils.

The school has a relaxed yet purposeful atmosphere, where working relationships between staff and pupils flourish. We are forward thinking in our approach – ready to adapt to change and technological advancement, whilst at the same time remaining true to traditional values.

Pupils are assessed continuously, and parents are always welcome to discuss their children's progress with staff on a regular basis or at parents' meetings. Above all, our aim is that all our pupils should reach their potential in terms of confidence, creativity and achievement.

The most recent ISI inspection report (May 2013) judged the school to be 'excellent' in all eight key areas. Since then the school has had a Compliance inspection (May 2017) and met all regulations.

Development plans are in place and the next few years will be very exciting.

Thorpe House School

Oval Way, Gerrards Cross, Bucks SL9 8QA

Tel: 01753 882474
Fax: 01753 889755
email: office@thorpehouse.co.uk
website: www.thorpehouse.co.uk
Twitter: @thorpehousesch
Facebook: @thorpehousesch

Chairman of the Governors: Mr David Stanning

Headmaster: **Mr T Ayres**, BA Hons, PGCE

Age Range. Boys 3–16.
Numbers of Pupils. 299 Day Pupils.
Fees per term (2018–2019). Y7–Y11 £5,654, Y3–Y6 £4,795, Y1–Y2 £3,840, Reception £3,650, Nursery £1,825–£2,920.

Thorpe House was founded as a Boys' Prep School in 1923 with the Pre-Prep Department established in 1964. The School became a Charitable Trust in 1986 and in 2006 it increased its age range to become a school catering for boys between the ages of 3 and 16.

Situated on the outskirts of Gerrards Cross, Thorpe House thrives on its 'small school' environment and understanding that each boy is unique. Some are academics, some excel in sport and others in the performing arts and it is that difference that they nurture and value.

The Nursery class takes boys in the September following their 3rd birthday and then many others join Reception the following year. At the end Year 2 boys move to the Prep Department in the main school building where they are taught by the specialist staff in music, ICT, DT, French and PE/Games and specialist teaching in all subjects starts in Year 5.

At the end of Year 6 around half the boys leave to enter local grammar schools. Those who move into the Senior Department are joined by an equal number of new entrants who then form the class groups who will progress through to GCSE, although some move on to independent senior schools at 13 via the Common Entrance or scholarship examinations. Class sizes throughout the school never exceed 16 and are often as small as 12. The school's examination record at GCSE is very strong with a 100% record to date of pupils gaining at least 6 passes at C or above and pupils often gaining a full set of A and A* passes.

Although academic progress and excellence is a fundamental aspect of school life it is far from being the only focus. The boys excel at a variety of cultural activities. Music, drama, art and design technology are popular GCSE courses and boys of all ages enjoy studying these subjects and taking part in practical activities. Well over half of all recent Associated Board Music examination passes have been at Merit or Distinction level and following the latest GCSE Art exhibition one of the pupils was given a commission. The school works closely with the nearby St Mary's Girls' School to give both sets of pupils the opportunity to work together in a number of different cultural activities.

Sport is another central aspect of school life. The school has a seven-acre playing field and an outdoor swimming pool. The main team sports are rugby, football, cricket and athletics and the school puts out teams from Under 8 to Under 16 level against a wide variety of schools from the local area and further afield. These teams are very successful but the school is very proud of its Sport for All ethos and bringing on the less sporty boys is another important aspect of school life.

When the school extended its age range an extensive programme of new building and refurbishment was undertaken and the school now has improved facilities for Science, Art, Design Technology and ICT The school is now able to offer a full and modern range of facilities and all normal school experiences can take place on site. In addition the school runs a very extensive programme of extra-curricular clubs and activities, some of which such as sailing, golf and tennis involve taking advantage of local amenities.

The school offers before and after school care and arrangements to take this up are completely flexible. A bus service is also available to pick up and take home boys from certain areas.

Charitable status. Thorpe House School Trust is a Registered Charity, number 292683. It exists to provide education to boys.

Tockington Manor School

Washingpool Hill Road, Tockington, Bristol BS32 4NY

Tel: 01454 613229
Fax: 01454 613676
email: admin@tockingtonmanorschool.com
website: www.tockingtonmanorschool.com

Twitter: @TockingtonManor
Facebook: @tockingtonmanorschool

Chairman of Governors: G Sheppard

Headmaster: Stephen Symonds, BA Ed Hons

Age Range. Boys and Girls aged 2–13+.

Number of Pupils. 9 Boarders, 102 Upper School Day, 62 Infants, 40 Nursery.

Fees per term (2018–2019). Boarders £6,587–£7,239 (inclusive); Upper School Day £4,354–£5,006 (including meals); Lower School £3,210; Nursery £54.30 per day.

Tockington Manor School and Nursery is an independent co-educational Preparatory school set in 28 acres of lovely countryside in the picturesque village of Tockington, South Gloucestershire. Pupils are welcomed from age 2 to 13+ with boarding available from age 7.

Our small friendly classes and family approach to education provides bespoke learning for every child. We pride ourselves in delivering a varied timetable geared to the needs of each pupil but with emphasis on the core subjects of English, Mathematics and Science. We aim to provide an environment that is positive, supportive and disciplined within a warm, caring family atmosphere. Pupils are encouraged to be confident, considerate and accomplished free thinkers. All pupils take part in all aspects of school life, academic or otherwise, making the most of every moment.

The boarding house has a real family atmosphere and aims to provide a caring environment which promotes the values of honesty, sharing and trust between the children.

The school works closely with parents to prepare every pupil for Common Entrance and Scholarships to appropriate Independent Senior Schools. We have an enviable success rate in delivering entry into their first-choice senior schools, with many being awarded scholarships in Academia, Sport, Music, Drama and Design Technology.

Nursery. Tockington Manor Nursery is set in a recently refurbished converted barn within the school grounds. Each child is encouraged to learn through 'hands on' experience overseen by their dedicated Nursery Practitioner who is specially trained to nurture and extend the development of every child. Children benefit from the wider school facilities, tending to their own "cottage style" vegetable garden, discovering nature and forest skills on "welly walks" or enjoying weekly swimming lessons in the school's indoor heated pool.

The School website has further details or a copy of the School's prospectus is available on request by emailing the Registrar, email: registrar@tockingtonmanorschool.com. The Headmaster will be delighted to give a tour of the School to prospective parents upon request.

Charitable status. Tockington Manor School is a Registered Charity, number 311716.

Tower House School

188 Sheen Lane, East Sheen, London SW14 8LF

Tel: 020 8876 3323
email: admissions@thsboys.org.uk
website: www.thsboys.org.uk

Chairman of Governors: Mr Jamie Forsyth

Headmaster: Mr G Evans, BSc, MA, PGCE

Age Range. 4–13.
Number of Boys. 191.

Fees per term (2018–2019). Reception and Year 1 £4,363, Years 2 and 3 £4,814, Senior School £4,946 (including residential trips and all school lunches).

Originally founded in 1931, Tower House School is now a 21st century centre of excellence for boys from the ages 4–13.

Our boys want to be part of everything. Whether it be sports teams, musical ensembles or our famous drama productions; pupils are enthusiastic because they know they are valued and have an important contribution to make.

Learning takes place both inside and outside the classroom. Weekly Forest School and frequent educational trips help to keep the fun aspect of education firmly in focus.

We are proud of our academic record and boys are prepared for a wide range of senior schools across the country, carefully chosen to suit their academic and extra-curricular strengths.

Tower House pupils characteristically approach the next stage of their educational journey with confidence, humility and distinction.

A prospectus is available online or from the School Secretary.

Charitable status. Tower House School is a Registered Charity, number 1068844.

Town Close School

14 Ipswich Road, Norwich, Norfolk NR2 2LR

Tel: 01603 620180
Fax: 01603 618256 (Prep)
         01603 599043 (Pre-Prep)
email: admissions@townclose.com
website: www.townclose.com
Twitter: @townclose; @townclosehead
Facebook: @towncloseschool

Chairman of Governors: Mr David Bolton, BSc, Dip FBA, FRAgS, FAAV

Headmaster: Nicholas Bevington, BA Hons, PGCE

Age Range. 3–13 Co-educational.
Number of Pupils. Prep 275, Pre-Prep 185.
Fees per term (2018–2019). £2,890–£4,384 including lunch and all single-day educational excursions. No compulsory extras.

Town Close School was founded in 1932 and became a Charitable Trust in 1968. The School is fully co-educational and is situated on a beautiful wooded site near the centre of Norwich. This location provides pupils with space and freedom and contributes substantially to Town Close's reputation as an outstandingly happy school.

There is a team of 57 talented teachers who aim to produce well-motivated, balanced, confident children, who are caring and sociable and who know the value of hard work. The children receive excellent teaching and are prepared for all major senior schools. In recent years, pupils have achieved highly in entrance and scholarship assessments to a range of the country's leading senior schools.

A modern teaching building stands at the heart of the School, containing a large, well-equipped library, an art room, an IT centre and 16 purpose-built classrooms. There are many other outstanding facilities including an indoor heated swimming pool, a high-specification sports hall, a performance hall and a full-size, floodlit Astroturf. Science and DT are taught in specialist buildings and the school places a high value on innovation, engineering and scientific discovery. The Pre-Prep occupies a magnificent converted house on the campus and also contains a multi-purpose hall, kitchens, and a new and purpose-built Nursery wing that opens onto fantastic outdoor facilities.

Nursery and Reception classes follow the Foundation Stage curriculum, an important element of which is outdoor learning. Children progress through a broad and varied programme of activities with a strong emphasis on the development of personal and social skills and on establishing positive attitudes to learning and to school life. Swimming, music and dance are taught by specialist teachers, while the rest of the curriculum is delivered by class teachers, ably supported by well-qualified teaching assistants.

Throughout the children's time at Town Close particular attention is paid to the teaching of good handwriting and spelling. Traditional core skills are valued very highly in addition to promoting children's use of digital technology. IT provision is extensive allowing children to become confident and proficient users. The Pre-Prep pupils use a range of children's software to develop key skills and Prep Department children build on this foundation using more sophisticated software, either in the computer room or on laptops and tablets. All sections of the School have filtered access to the internet across the network. The School Intranet contains interactive activities, images, lesson material and links to carefully selected websites. Interactive whiteboards are used throughout the School to support the curriculum.

Town Close has an excellent academic reputation and is also known for the quality of its sport, music, art, drama and its extensive co-curricular programme. Trips and expeditions form a valuable part of what is offered, and provide the balance essential for a full and rounded education. Activities take place during the lunch hour, after school, and occasionally at weekends. In terms of music, the School has a full orchestra, a variety of choirs and a wide range of ensembles. All children are encouraged to perform with regular high-quality concerts and plays.

Physical Education plays an important part in the development of each child, be they in the Nursery or in Year 8. Emphasis is placed on fostering healthy exercise, as well as encouraging a positive, competitive attitude, individual skills and teamwork. As well as providing all the usual opportunities for the major sports (rugby, netball, hockey, cricket and athletics), coaching is offered in many other sports.

A copy of the School's prospectus is available on request, while a visit to www.townclose.com will provide a fuller picture of the School, including a sight of the most recent inspection report, in which Town Close was given the highest rating in every area.

Charitable status. Town Close House Educational Trust Limited is a Registered Charity, number 311293. It exists to provide education for children.

Truro Preparatory School

Highertown, Truro, Cornwall TR1 3QN

Tel: 01872 272616
email: prepenquiries@truroschool.com
           prepadmissions@truroschool.com
website: www.truroschool.com/prep

Chairman of the Governors: Mr K Conchie

Headmaster of Truro School: Mr A S Gordon-Brown, BCom Hons, MSc, CA SA

Head of Preparatory School: **Miss S L Patterson**, BEd Hons

Key Stage I Coordinator: Mr P Sharp, BEng Hons

EYFS Coordinator: Ms Kate Williams, BEd Hons

Age Range. 3–11.
Number of Pupils. 257: 163 Boys, 94 Girls.
Fees per term (2018–2019). Prep (including lunch): £4,170 (Years 3–4), £4,330 (Years 5–6). Pre-Prep (including lunch): £2,965 (Nursery and Reception). £3,115 (Years 1 and 2).

Optional extras: Individual music lessons, fencing, dance, judo, photography, Bushcraft, badminton, LAMDA (Speech & Drama), Pre-Prep tennis.

Truro School Prep was opened as Treliske School in 1936 in the former residence and estate of Sir George Smith. The school lies in extensive and secluded grounds to the west of the cathedral city of Truro, three miles from Truro School. The grounds command fine views of the neighbouring countryside. The drive to the school off the main A390 is almost 800 metres and Truro Golf Course also surrounds the school, so producing a campus of beauty and seclusion.

The keynote of the school is a happy, caring atmosphere in which children learn the value of contributing positively to the school community through the firm and structured framework of academic study and extracurricular interests. The approach is based firmly in Christian beliefs and the school is proud of its Methodist foundation.

Building development has kept pace with modern expectations and Truro School Prep has its own large sports hall, an indoor heated swimming pool, a design and technology workshop with a computer room adjoined and purpose-built Pre-Prep.

The games programme is designed to encourage all children, from the keenest to the least athletic, to enjoy games and physical exercise. Our excellent facilities and the diverse skill of our staff enable us to offer a rich variety of sporting and recreational pursuits. There are over 70 clubs that run before school, during lunch break or after school from 4.00 pm to 5.00 pm.

There is a strong school tradition in music and drama and the arts. Children may choose to learn a musical instrument from the full orchestral range. Each year the November concert, with Truro School, allows the school to show the community the excellent talents, which flourish in both schools.

Close links are maintained with the Senior School and nearly all pupils progress through at age 11 on the Head's recommendation to Truro School which is the only Independent Headmasters' and Headmistresses' Conference School in Cornwall (*see entry in HMC section*).

The prospectus and further details can be obtained from the Head's Secretary, and the Head will be pleased to show prospective parents around the school.

Charitable status. Truro School is part of the Methodist Independent Schools Trust, which is a registered Charity, number 1142794.

Twickenham Preparatory School

Beveree, 43 High Street, Hampton, Middlesex TW12 2SA

Tel: 020 8979 6216
email: office@twickenhamprep.co.uk
website: www.twickenhamprep.co.uk
Twitter: @twickenhamprep

Chairman of Governors: Mr H Bates

Headmaster: **Mr D Malam**, BA Hons Southampton, PGCE Winchester

Age Range. 4–13.

Number of Pupils. Boys 155, Girls 133.

Fees per term (2018–2019). £3,490–£3,875. Lunch £205–£220.

Founded in 1969, Twickenham Prep is an independent school for boys and girls situated in Hampton. We are a happy, vibrant, and thriving school where every child is valued as an individual and inspired to achieve their full potential, personally, socially and academically. The pupils benefit from small classes, first-class facilities, specialist subject teaching and excellent pastoral care.

Our pupils achieve great success, both academic and extracurricular, moving on to excellent independent secondary schools with regular academic, sporting, musical, art and all-rounder scholarships. We are committed to working in partnership with our parents so that our pupils leave TPS as well-rounded individuals. The girls sit entrance exams at 11+ and the boys Common Entrance at 13+

Our curriculum is based on the National Curriculum with specialist teaching of PE, Games, ICT, French, Music and Think Tank (formerly Mind Lab, an innovative thinking skills programme) from Reception ensuring a balanced educational experience. Art/Design and Technology is introduced in Year 3 and from Year 4 pupils have specialist teaching in all subjects, with Latin being introduced in Year 5. Class sizes are about 18, developing each pupil to their full academic potential and promoting high academic standards. The school is well equipped to cover the full range of subjects, with purpose-built Art/DT, Science and Music facilities and a modern sports hall used for PE and termly productions.

Strong emphasis is placed on participation by all in sporting, musical and extracurricular activities. The school plays a wide range of sports and has recently formed an affiliation with Kempton Cricket Club to provide 10 acres of dedicated sporting facilities for rugby, football, cricket and rounders. The girls also play netball and hockey, with athletics and swimming also part of the sporting curriculum. Music and drama play a large part in the school with full-scale productions and concerts annually involving all pupils. There is a school choir and individual instrumental lessons are taught by visiting specialists.

Twickenham Prep is a leading Chess school and we are also the current National Mind Lab Champions; we have represented the UK for the last 6 years at the International Mind Lab Olympics, held in Turkey this year.

There are also many extracurricular clubs during and after school to choose from, including coding, watersports, chess, Spanish, typing and fencing and we also provide on-site wrap-around care from 7.30 am to 6.30 pm.

Located in Hampton we offer morning minibus services to children living in Kew, Isleworth, Richmond, Twickenham, Teddington, St Margaret's, Hampton Wick, Sunbury and East Molesey.

Entry to the school is non-selective at Reception with limited places available in other year groups subject to an assessment.

Regular Open Days are held and personal tours are available – the pupils and Headmaster would be delighted to show you around. Please contact the school office.

Charitable Status. Twickenham Preparatory School is a Registered Charity, number 1067572. It exists to provide education for boys and girls.

Twyford School

Winchester, Hampshire SO21 1NW

Tel:	01962 712269
Fax:	01962 712100
email:	registrar@twyfordschool.com
website:	www.twyfordschool.com
Twitter:	@TwyfordSchool
Facebook:	@twyfordprep

Chairman of Governors: Mrs F Dunger

Headmaster: **Dr S J Bailey**, BEd, PhD, FRSA

Age Range. 3–13.

Number of Children. 395. Main School: 274 (160 boys, 114 girls, of whom 103 are weekly and flexi boarders); Pre-Prep: 121 (67 boys, 54 girls).

Fees per term (2018–2019). Weekly Boarding £8,184; Day: Prep Years 4–8 £6,503, Year 3 £5,424; Pre-Prep £3,174–£3,651. Fees are inclusive of all outings/trips run during the term. Bursaries are available.

Twyford School is situated at the edge of the beautiful South Downs just two miles from the historic city of Winchester and the M3. Twyford is a family school that aims to offer an all-round top-rate education with a Christian ethos. Boarding is central to life at Twyford. Most pupils start as day pupils, but by the end of their last year many are weekly boarding through the school's flexi boarding system, which makes an excellent preparation for their move to senior school. The contrast between the modern facilities (classrooms, laboratories, music school, creative arts and ICT block, swimming pool and sports centre) and the Victorian chapel and hall creates a rich and stimulating environment.

The school regularly achieves scholarships – 82 awards (academic, art, design, sport and music) in the last 6 years – to major senior schools such as Winchester College, St Swithun's, Canford, Marlborough, Wycombe Abbey, Godolphin, Wellington College, Bradfield, Radley, Sherborne Boys and Sherborne Girls.

Charitable status. Twyford School is a Registered Charity, number 307425. It exists to provide education for children.

Unicorn School

238 Kew Road, Richmond, Surrey TW9 3JX

Tel:	020 8948 3926
email:	registrar@unicornschool.org.uk
website:	www.unicornschool.org.uk
Twitter:	@unicornschool

Chairs of Governors: Mr Phil Hinton and Mr Geoff Bayliss

Headmaster: **Mr Kit Thompson**

Age Range. 3–11.

Number of Children. 171 Day Pupils: 85 boys, 86 girls.

Fees per term (2018–2019). £2,310–£4,240.

Unicorn is a parent-owned IAPS co-ed primary school founded in 1970. Situated opposite Kew Gardens, the school occupies a large Victorian house and converted coach house with a spacious, superbly-equipped playground and garden.

The school has free and unrestricted access to Kew Gardens and the sports facilities at the nearby University of

Westminster grounds are used for games and Pools on the Park for swimming.

Our aim is for Unicorn to be a successful, forward-thinking school that embraces children, staff and parents in an evolving, exciting, dynamic and nurturing community, enriched with creativity and supported by excellent leadership and management. Pupils are encouraged to become independent, responsible, self-aware and confident young people, who reap the benefits of a very broad curriculum to achieve considerable success.

There are 22 children per class, where a variety of teaching methods are used and the children are regularly assessed. Importance is placed upon the development of the individual and high academic standards are achieved. The main point of entry is to nursery at 3+. Children are prepared for entry at 11+ to the leading London day schools, as well as a variety of boarding schools.

There is a specialist IT room and networked computers in every classroom and a bank of iPads to use; a Science and Design Technology suite with interactive whiteboard technology in all classrooms; music rooms, library and a new state-of-the-art fully-equipped Art room.

The curriculum includes Drama, French (from age 5), Art and Music – with individual music lessons offered in piano, violin, cello, drums, clarinet, saxophone, flute, guitar and trumpet, as well as singing. Recorder groups, choirs, an orchestra and a wind band also flourish.

In addition to the major games of football, hockey, netball, cricket, rounders and athletics, there are optional clubs for tennis, squash, ice skating, golf, riding, sailing, musical theatre and karate. Other club activities include arts and crafts, cookery, pottery, chess, riding, sailing, fencing and trampolining. There are regular visits to the theatre and museums as well as the galleries of Central London. All children, from the age of seven upwards, participate in residential field study trips to Surrey, Cornwall and Cumbria.

An elected School Council, with representatives from each age group, meets weekly with the Headmaster and a weekly newsletter for parents is also produced.

A happy, caring environment prevails and importance is placed on producing kind, responsible children who show awareness and consideration for the needs of others.

Charitable status. Unicorn School is a Registered Charity, number 312578. It exists to provide education for boys and girls.

University College School – Junior Branch

11 Holly Hill, Hampstead, London NW3 6QN

Tel: 020 7435 3068
Fax: 020 7435 7332
email: juniorbranch@ucs.org.uk
website: www.ucs.org.uk

Chairman of Council of Governors: Mr S D Lewis, OBE, MA

Headmaster: **Mr L R J Hayward**, MA

Age Range. 7–11.
Number of Boys. 254.
Fees per term (2018–2019). £6,263.
The School was founded in 1891 by the Governors of University College, London. The present building was

opened in 1928, but retains details from the Georgian house first used. It stands near the highest point of Hampstead Heath and the hall and classrooms face south. Facilities include a Science Laboratory, Library, Drama Studio, Music and Computer Rooms, and a Centre for Art and Technology. Boys receive their Swimming and PE lessons in the pool and Sports Hall at the Senior School, 5 minutes' walk away. The Junior School has full use of the 27 acres of playing fields on games days.

Boys enter at 7+ each year and they are prepared for transfer to the Senior School at 11+. (*See entry in HMC section.*)

Charitable status. University College School, Hampstead is a Registered Charity, number 312748. The Junior Branch exists to provide education for boys aged 7+ to 11 years.

University College School Pre-Prep

36 College Crescent, Hampstead, London NW3 5LF

Tel: 020 7722 4433
email: pre-prep@ucs.org.uk
website: www.ucs.org.uk/UCS-Pre-Prep

Chairman of Council: Mr S D Lewis, OBE, MA

Headmistress: **Dr Z Dunn**, BEd, PhD, NPQH

Age Range. Boys 4–7.
Number of Pupils. 110 Boys.
Fees per term (2018–2019). £5,607.
At UCS Pre-Prep, we firmly believe that happiness and self-esteem are the keys to success in every pupil's learning journey. The well-qualified and highly-supportive staff accompany each child on a voyage of educational and social discovery during the first years of school life.

The Pre-Prep fully supports the aims and ethos of UCS: intellectual curiosity and independence of mind are developed, self-discovery and self-expression are fostered and a cooperative and collaborative approach to learning is of great importance.

For every child in our care, we provide a continuously positive and creative learning environment that allows the individual the opportunity to develop personal qualities and talents. Children enjoy specialist teaching in Music, art and Physical Education and the full primary curriculum in well resourced classrooms. The outdoor learning programme takes advantage of the school's allotment and extensive space at the fields. At the end of Year 2, it is hoped that most boys will transfer to the Junior Branch of UCS; this is not automatic and is subject to meeting the required standard in the entrance examination. (*See separate Junior Branch entry.*)

Charitable status. UCS Pre-Prep Limited is a Registered Charity, number 1098657.

Upton House School

115 St Leonard's Road, Windsor, Berkshire SL4 3DF

Tel: 01753 862610
Fax: 01753 621950
email: info@uptonhouse.org.uk
            registrar@uptonhouse.org.uk

website: www.uptonhouse.org.uk
Twitter: @UptonHouseSch
Facebook: @UptonHouseSchool

Chairman of the Council: Mr G O J Story

Headmistress: Mrs Rhian Thornton

Deputy Head: Mrs Kate Newcombe
Head of Early Years: Mrs Sue Bish
Head of Pre-Prep: Mr Craig McEvoy
Head of Prep: Mr Tom Brown

Age Range. Girls 2–11 years, Boys 2–7 years.
Number of Pupils. 240 Day: 190 Girls, 50 Boys.
Fees per term (2018–2019). £1,299–£5,750 (inclusive). Bursaries available.

Our aim at Upton House is to foster a happy and stimulating environment in which each child can prosper academically, socially and emotionally. The school prepares all children for their continuing education and equips them with life skills for the future.

Upton House School was founded in 1936 by benefactors and has evolved over the years to provide a well-equipped modern environment where children thrive.

At Upton House we aim to provide the best possible education for each child. We give encouragement and stimulation to develop their academic abilities and we develop pupils individual strengths, whether it is from our broad curriculum or from our wide range of extracurricular activities. This combined with a loving nurturing environment, develops a set of pastoral values which makes Upton very special.

Our newly-opened arts block houses a music room, an art studio and media room. Our kitchen serves freshly prepared, nutritious meals on site. Facilities also include a fully-equipped IT suite, a drama/dance studio, gymnasium and Nursery music room.

Specialist subjects include PE, French and Mandarin from 3 years old. Educational robots, iPads, laptops, and interactive whiteboards are used across the school to enhance learning. Diverse sporting activities include rowing on the Thames, judo, fencing and ballet.

Boys and girls leaving gain places at a wide range of excellent prep and senior schools and regularly win scholarships.

Entry is non-selective and means-tested bursaries are available for those entering the school.

We provide care from 7.45 am in our Early Birds breakfast club as well as a late day programme until 5.45 pm for children from age 3. A wide variety of clubs are offered in the late programmes as well as teacher-supervised prep for older children.

We have an active PTA which organises many fundraising events through the year and helps to forge close links between the school and parents. Please visit our website for details of forthcoming Open mornings. Personal tours are also welcome.

Charitable status. Upton House School is a Registered Charity, number 309095. It exists to provide an excellent all-round educational foundation for boys and girls.

The Ursuline Preparatory School Ilford

2–4 Coventry Road, Ilford, Essex IG1 4QR

Tel: 020 8518 4050
email: urspsi@urspsi.org.uk
website: www.urspsi.org.uk
Twitter: @URSPSI

Chair of Governors: (*to be elected*)

Head: Mrs Victoria McNaughton

Age Range. 3–11 Co-educational.
Number of Pupils. 145.
Fees per term (2018–2019). Nursery: £3,276 (full-time including lunch, pre- and after-school care, holiday care, minus government funding), Reception–Year 6 £3,276 (including lunch, pre- and after-school care, holiday care).

The Ursuline Preparatory School Ilford is a Roman Catholic day school in the trusteeship of the Ursuline Sisters. The Ursuline Sisters first came to England in 1862 settling at Forest Gate from where they established the school in Ilford in 1903 at 73 Cranbrook Road. The school has since flourished. Formerly part of The Ursuline Academy, The Ursuline Preparatory School Ilford is now a fully independent school in its own right, but continues to share close and valued links with the Academy.

As a Catholic school we firmly believe that Religious Education is the foundation of the entire educational process. Prayers and liturgical celebrations are an important aspect of school life, unifying the hearts and minds of all associated with the school and ensuring we are all working to achieve the best possible education for the children in our care.

We provide a safe, secure and stimulating environment for our pupils to thrive. We recognise each child's unique value and are committed to encouraging self-esteem and developing each child's potential. We encourage the children to become independent learners by building on their curiosity and desire to learn and developing their skills, concepts and understanding.

While the school continues to set its own high standards, we complement these with the integration of the best of the National Curriculum. English and mathematics form the core subjects together with Religious Education, science, history, geography, ICT, PE, drama, design technology, art, music, MFL and stimulating project work. The Performing Arts have a high profile in school and the children are regularly given the opportunity to develop their talents. Well-stocked libraries, audio-visual aids and a state-of-the-art specialist Information Communication Technology department are all available throughout the nursery and school.

We offer a wide range of extracurricular activities including ballet, speech and drama and Irish Dancing. Other clubs and sports clubs including football, cricket, basketball, netball, gymnastics and trampolining are held weekly. Individual instrumental tuition can be arranged for piano, violin, flute, clarinet and saxophone. There is also an award-winning school choir.

All teaching staff are fully qualified, experienced and dedicated to the ideals of the school. They work in close partnership with parents to ensure that each child's special individual needs are recognised. In addition, we have the help of experienced general assistants. Our pupil to teacher ratio is excellent and we are able to engage in small group teaching.

Pre- and after-school care and a holiday club are available. A variety of structured activities is planned for the children enrolled and refreshments are provided.

Charitable status. The Ursuline Preparatory School Ilford is a Registered Charity, number 245661.

Ursuline Preparatory School
Wimbledon

18 The Downs, Wimbledon, London SW20 8HR

Tel: 020 8947 0859
email: headmasterea@ursulineprep.org
website: www.ursulineprep.org
Twitter: @ursulineprep
Facebook: @Ursulineprep

Chair of Governors: Mr Francis Bacon

Headmaster: **Mr Christopher McGrath**

Age Range. Girls 3–11, Boys 3–4.
Number of Pupils. 240+.
Fees per term (2018–2019). £3,605 full-time, £2,205 for part-time Nursery.

Ursuline Preparatory School is an independent Catholic School for girls aged 4 to 11, with an co-educational Nursery for girls and boys aged 3–4 years.

Ursuline Preparatory School is a Roman Catholic school that welcomes children of all faiths and none, in the belief that our ethos will be of benefit to all. The heart of any Roman Catholic school is its Catholic ethos and the commitment it shows to Gospel Values, in Christian service to God and others. As a result, the Ursuline Preparatory School has a strong and very clear ethos and we endeavour to ensure that this ethos will be of benefit to all members of our school community; pupils, staff and families. We will promote Gospel values and seek to develop the spiritual and moral lives of our pupils through the example of St Angela. We are committed to ensuring that every girl will be loved, cared for and believed in. This will create the fertile soil within which all children can flourish. We will promote the ongoing faith formation of all members of our school community, with an emphasis on 'Serviam', in compassionate service to others. We will place equal value on the education of the heart, the mind and the soul, in the sure and certain knowledge that only through the development of all three can you truly become the person you were born to be. We will provide an environment that will help every girl become the best that she can be; the person she was born to be.

The children enjoy a rich diversity of experiences both inside and outside of the classroom. An education that challenges beyond the National Curriculum, with outside visitors hosting workshops, school outings to enhance classroom learning, residential trips to promote teamwork and independence, extensive extra-curricular to extend learning, and fundraising opportunities to promote our ethos of Serviam, are all valuable experiences that help prepare our girls for the next stage of their educational journey and look to the future with confidence, keen to make a difference in the world.

Charitable status. Ursuline Preparatory School, Wimbledon is a Registered Charity, number 1079754.

Victoria College Preparatory School

Pleasant Street, St Helier, Jersey, Channel Islands JE2 4RR

Tel: 01534 723468
email: admin@vcp.sch.je
website: www.vcp.sch.je
Facebook: @VCPJERSEY

Chairman of Governors: B Watt

Headmaster: **Dan Pateman**, BA Hons

Age Range. 7–11.
Number of Boys. 277 Day Boys.
Fees per term (from April 2018). £1,826 (inclusive).

Victoria College Preparatory School was founded in 1922 as an integral part of Victoria College and is now a separate School under its own Headmaster, who is responsible for such matters as staffing, curriculum and administration. The Preparatory School shares Governors with Victoria College whose members are drawn from the leaders of the Island of Jersey with a minority representation from the States of Jersey Education Committee. Members of staff are all experienced and well-qualified teachers, including specialists in Music, Dance, Art, PE and French. Entry to the Prep School is at 7 and boys normally leave to enter Victoria College at the age of 11. The school games are cricket, football, athletics, swimming, hockey, cross-country and rugby. Sporting facilities are shared with Victoria College. Special features of the school are exceptionally high standards of sport, drama, music and French. Many visits, both sporting and educational, are arranged out of the Island.

A separate Pre-Preparatory School (5 to 7 years) is incorporated in a co-educational school situated at JC Prep and offers places for boys whose parents wish them to be educated at both Victoria College and the Preparatory School. Candidates for Pre-Prep entry should be registered at JC Prep, St Helier, Jersey.

Vinehall School

Robertsbridge, East Sussex TN32 5JL

Tel: 01580 880413
Fax: 01580 882119
email: admissions@vinehallschool.com
website: www.vinehallschool.com
Twitter: @vinehallschool
Facebook: @Vinehall-School

Chairman of Governors: Mr W Foster-Kemp, LLB, ACA

Headmaster: **Jonathan Powis**

Age Range. 2–13 co-educational.
Number of Children. 248: 34 boarders, 214 day children.
Fees per term (2018–2019). Prep: Years 6–8: £5,939 (day), £7,736 (full boarding), £7,120 (weekly boarding); Years 3–5: £5,756 (day), £7,547 (full boarding), £6,975 (weekly boarding); Pre-Prep: Reception, Years 1 & 2 £3,185; Nursery (without Early Years funding): £37.15 per morning session, £20.66 per afternoon session, £57.82 per full day session; Nursery (with Early Years funding): £32.98 per full day session.

Founded in 1938, Vinehall School is set within 47 acres of countryside in an area of outstanding natural beauty on the East Sussex/Kent border. A flourishing Nursery and Pre-Prep for boys and girls aged 2 to 7 is situated in a modern, well-resourced and purpose-built building on the same site as the Prep School.

The School's first-class facilities include a magnificent Millennium Building, comprising classrooms, IT suite and library, a science block, music building, art, design and technology centre, a purpose-built theatre with seating for 250, a sports hall and adjoining indoor swimming pool, an Astro-Turf pitch, an adventure playground and a nine-hole golf course.

The curriculum, which is based on the National Curriculum but which extends far beyond, prepares pupils for Common Entrance, local grammar school entrance and scholarship entrance to a variety of independent senior schools. In 2018 25 senior school scholarships were awarded to leaving children. Leavers go on to a wide range of the UK's most prestigious senior schools. In 2018 children went on to 26 different destination schools.

The innovative 'Learning Journey' curriculum (which begins in Year 3), stimulates enquiring young minds. The academic day finishes at 4.40 pm, with a wide range of clubs and enrichment activities until 5.20 pm when school buses depart. On Saturday mornings (apart from exeat weekends) there are optional Clubs and Enrichment activities for pupils in Years 3 to 8. A dedicated learning support team is available for those children who require additional support.

Games and the Arts are an integral part of the Vinehall timetable. Pupils participate in all major team sports and everyone has a chance to represent the School. Girls' sports include netball, hockey, rounders and tennis and for boys, football, rugby, hockey, cricket and tennis. Swimming, gymnastics and athletics are also important sports throughout the year. Creative Arts are also strong, with flourishing Art, Music and Drama departments, all of which exhibit/perform regularly both inside and outside School. Carpentry and wood-turning are also offered.

Boarding is at the very heart of the School and Vinehall has a well-established boarding community, the majority being from Sussex, Kent and London. Temporary, weekly and full boarding are all available and we also offer an accompanied train service to and from London for weekly boarders each Friday and Sunday evening. There is a Junior boarding option for Years 3–6 (four nights per week) with children moving on to full or weekly boarding in Years 7 and 8. There are regular exeat weekends and a full and varied programme of weekend activities.

Charitable status. Vinehall School is a Registered Charity, number 307014. It exists to provide a secure, quality education, in particular for those in need of residential schooling.

Walhampton School

Lymington, Hampshire SO41 5ZG

Tel: 01590 613300
Fax: 01590 678498
email: registrar@walhampton.com
website: www.walhampton.com
Twitter: @Walhamptonprep
Facebook: @walhamptonprep

Chairman of Governors: Mr Jeremy Bennett

Headmaster: Mr Titus Mills, BA Hons

Age Range. 2–13.
Number of Pupils. 370 pupils: 50 boarders, 250 Prep School.
Fees per term (2018–2019). Day £4,375–£5,875; Full Boarding £2,375 (in addition to day fees); Pre-Preparatory £3,000. The only extras are: After-School Club, Riding, Individual Music, Learning Support tuition and Expeditions.

Set within one hundred acres of lawns, lakes and woodland in the idyllic New Forest, Walhampton is an independent day, flexi and full-time boarding school for boys and girls aged 2–13 where academic excellence sits comfortably alongside a distinctive 'Swallows and Amazons' spirit.

With small class sizes and outstanding teaching, Walhampton pupils achieve consistently impressive academic results and around 40% attain scholarships to top senior schools. Pupils are prepared for 13+ Common Entrance and the school has achieved a 100% pass rate over many years.

Over the last five years pupils from Walhampton have gone on to the following schools: Bryanston, Canford, Clayesmore, Eton, Godolphin, King's Bruton, King Edward VI, Marlborough, Radley, Sherborne, St Swithun's and Winchester.

The school has one of the ultimate prep school settings and offers over 60 extra-curricular activities, including sailing on the school's lakes and riding in the on-site equestrian centre.

The Walhampton Express train service brings this remarkable country school closer to London. Boarding staff collect children from Waterloo on Sunday evening and escort them back to Waterloo on Friday for about 6.00 pm. Full, weekly and flexi boarders enjoy the relaxed and homely atmosphere of Bradfield House. Flexi boarding enables children to enjoy all that the school has to offer, while supporting families with busy lives.

The school's location and facilities enable them to offer a broad and dynamic curriculum, which stretches beyond the classroom. Lessons are taught in the kitchen garden, fields and woodland bringing subjects like Maths, English, History and Science to life while making sure sports, music and the arts flourish alongside academic disciplines. In how many other schools would you find the Battle of Trafalgar staged on a lake, or Hastings re-enacted with children in armour on horses?

A warm welcome awaits you at the 2019 open mornings which are on 1st February and 3rd May – contact the School Registrar on 01590 613 303 or at registrar@walhampton.com to make an appointment.

Walthamstow Hall Junior School

Bradbourne Park Road, Sevenoaks, Kent TN13 3LD

Tel: 01732 453815
Fax: 01732 456980
email: registrar@whall.school
website: www.walthamstow-hall.co.uk
Twitter: @WalthamstowHall
Facebook: @Walthamstow-Hall

Chair of Governors: Mrs J Adams, BA Joint Hons

Headmistress of Walthamstow Hall School: Miss S Ferro, BA Hons Oxford, MA, PGCE UCL

Head of the Junior School: Mrs D Wood, BSc, PGCE Durham

Deputy Head Teacher: Mrs R Allen, BSc Hons Wales, MPhil Warwick, PGCE Wales

Director of Studies: Mrs P I Potter, BEd Southampton, Dip MEd Roehampton Institute

Senior Teacher: Mrs C Conway, BA Hons First Class, MA Johannesburg, PGCE Canterbury Christ Church

Head of Pre-Prep Department: Mrs G Watts, MA Hons St Andrews, QTS

Day School for Girls.

Age Range. 3–11.

Number of Girls. 163.

Fees per term (2018–2019). Nursery £315 per session (2–10 sessions per week); Reception–Year 2 £3,925, Years 3–6 £4,950.

Walthamstow Hall Junior School is a happy and vibrant school with a proud tradition of providing the highest quality education for girls aged 3–11 years.

From Reception upwards pupils benefit from being in small classes (up to 20 per class) with two parallel classes in each year group. Optimum-sized classes throughout the Junior School guarantee individual attention, with obvious benefits including a seamless and highly effective preparation for Senior School entrance exams without last-minute cramming and changes to routine.

A well-planned programme of education brings out the potential of each child as she progresses through the Junior School. A broad curriculum is enriched with many co-curricular activities and clubs. Wrap-Around care provision is available from 7.15 am until 6.00 pm every day.

Girls are well prepared for a range of senior schools and have won awards to prestigious independent schools, including Walthamstow Hall Senior School (*see entry in GSA section*). Entry to our Senior School is from 11+, 13+ and 16+ with Awards, Scholarships and Bursaries offered. Equally, our track record in the Kent test is excellent.

Walthamstow Hall was founded in 1838 and is one of the oldest girls' schools in the country. It has built a reputation for all-round excellence and achievements by girls are outstanding. Over recent years, many facilities have been enhanced or added, and our specialist facilities include our ICT Suite and Science Laboratory, Design and Technology, Art and Cookery Rooms, well-stocked computerised Library and dedicated Music Centre. Girls also have access to facilities at the nearby Senior School including the recently refurbished Ship Theatre, Swimming Pool and Sports Centre opened in January 2018. The school is situated in the centre of Sevenoaks within easy reach of road and rail networks.

Warminster Prep School

Vicarage Street, Warminster, Wiltshire BA12 8JG

Tel:	01985 224800
Fax:	01985 218850
email:	prep@warminsterschool.org.uk
website:	www.warminsterschool.org.uk
Twitter:	@WarminsterPrep
Facebook:	@Warminster-Prep
LinkedIn:	/WarminsterSchool

Co-educational, Day & Boarding.

Chairman of Governors: The Right Hon Sir David Latham, QC

Headmaster: P Titley, BEd

Age Range. 3–11 co-educational.

Number of Pupils. 140.

Fees per term (2018–2019). Day: Reception £2,550; Years 1 & 2 £2,755; Year 3 £3,255; Year 4 £3,630; Years 5 & 6 £4,080. Boarding: £7,205.

Conveniently situated on the edge of Salisbury Plain with easy access to London and the South-West, Warminster Prep is a thriving school with a friendly, family atmosphere. Together with our Senior School, we make up Warminster School, providing exciting, high-quality education for children from 3 to 18 years old.

Fully-qualified and dedicated teaching staff deliver a vibrant and stimulating curriculum enriched with many trips and theme days. Our teaching in the Prep School is rich and varied in its styles to suit the diverse variety of children who thrive in our inclusive and holistic environment.

The curriculum is broad and balanced reflecting an ethos that values the development of skills and achievement in all subjects and areas of school life. Whilst the pursuit of excellence in core subjects is very important, Art, Sport, Music, Drama and Technology are also vital areas in building confidence and self-esteem. Scholarships are available from Year 3 upwards as well as for Years 7 and 9 in the Senior School.

Flexible boarding arrangements exist for children from 7 years upwards. Under the auspices of our experienced, dedicated Matrons and House Parents, children enjoy a very high standard of Pastoral care with weekend trips and outings a highlight of the week. A number of children are full boarders, but weekly and flexi boarding are very popular with, and a cost-effective service for, busy working parents. The Boarding Schools Allowance is available for serving members of HM Forces.

Sport is an important part of life at Warminster Prep, with a busy programme of inter-school fixtures in Rugby, Soccer, Hockey and Cricket for boys, and Hockey, Netball and Rounders for girls. In the summer term, children also swim and enjoy Tennis and Athletics.

Warminster Prep has a strong creative tradition in the Arts; performing art in Music, Speech and Drama, visual art in a wide range of media including sculpture and fired clay.

The Prep (and Pre-Prep) School is well-equipped with its own catering and Dining Hall, modern fully-equipped Science lab, ICT suite, sports pitches, AstroTurf, Art and DT studio, well-equipped stage, tennis courts, Music and practice rooms and Library. This is in addition to the superb facilities we share with our adjacent Senior School such as the newly-opened Thomas Arnold Hall, swimming pool, Library, Chapel and Sports Hall. The Courtyard Nursery was opened in 2007 and provides superb accommodation for the Early Years Foundation Stage. The Nursery is oversubscribed and parents are advised to register for places in plenty of time.

We provide, for Day and Boarding children, a wide choice of clubs and activities including a Forest School. These augment our timetabled curriculum and ensure that children can develop their individual tastes and interests alongside more traditionally academic abilities. We include opportunities for foreign travel with our French Trip and Ski Trip.

Interested parents are invited to ring the Headmaster's Secretary for a prospectus and to arrange a visit and free taster-day.

For information about the Senior School, please see entry in HMC section.

Charitable status. Warminster School is Registered Charity, number 1042204, providing education for boys and girls.

Warwick Junior School

Myton Road, Warwick CV34 6PP

Tel: 01926 776418
email: enquiries@warwickschool.org
website: www.warwickschool.org

Foundation Secretary: Mr S T Jones
Chairman of the Governors: Mr A C Firth

Junior School Headmaster: **Mr A C Hymer**, BA, MA Ed, NPQH

Junior School Deputy Headmaster: Mr T Wurr, BA

Age Range. Boys 7–11.
Number of Pupils. 247 day boys.
Fees per term (2018–2019). Tuition: £3,727–£4,183.

Warwick Junior School is situated on a site on the outskirts of Warwick Town adjacent to Warwick Senior School. The buildings are contained within a four-acre site and enjoy the use of the Sports and other facilities of Warwick Senior School. The excellent facilities have been enhanced with the opening of the bespoke Junior science laboratory, new computers in the computer suites and the opening of Warwick Hall, one of the largest and most impressive performance venues in the region.

A Warwick Junior School education nurtures the whole child, helping boys develop confidence and character and to be supportive of their peers. Academic standards are high and in particular participation in a range of activities is encouraged. Each pupil is encouraged to develop his own personality and to realise his own potential.

The curriculum gives a good grounding in English, Mathematics, Science, Design and Technology, Computing, History, Geography, Religious Education, French, Art, Music, Performing Arts, Drama and PE. Many sporting activities are available on the fifty acre campus of Warwick School, which includes a sports hall and indoor swimming pool. Rugby and Football are the main winter sports, with Cricket in the summer, plus Hockey, Athletics, Swimming, Tennis, Badminton and Fencing. The school has won a number of national sporting championships.

The school's creative activities, dramatic productions and musical performances provide a useful focus in the development of many talents within the school. Boys benefit from an extensive co-curricular programme of activity.

Warwick Junior School provides a schedule of Curriculum Support. This support is available both for boys who need some additional assistance in English and/or Maths and also for boys with specific learning difficulties such as dyslexia or dyspraxia.

Extended day facilities are available until 5.30 pm when pupils can either do their homework or enrol in the extensive clubs and activity programme.

Boys are prepared for the Entrance Examination to Warwick Senior School at age 11. The majority of pupils who leave Warwick Junior School gain a place in the Senior School at Warwick. (*See Warwick School entry in HMC section.*)

Further details from the Admissions Team, Tel: 01926 776414, email: admissions@warwickschool.org.

Charitable status. Warwick Independent Schools Foundation is a Registered Charity, number 1088057. It exists to provide quality education for boys.

Warwick Preparatory School

Bridge Field, Banbury Road, Warwick CV34 6PL

Tel: 01926 491545
email: info@warwickprep.com
website: www.warwickprep.com
Twitter: @WarwickPrep
Facebook: @warwickprep

Chairman of the Governors: Mr David Stevens

Headmistress: **Mrs Hellen Dodsworth**

Age Range. Boys 3–7, Girls 3–11.
Number of Children. c. 485.
Fees per term (2018–2019). Nursery: £2,589 (full time, after Nursery Education Funding). Lower School (4–6 years) £3,521; Middle School (7–9 years) £4,035. Upper School (9–11 years) £4,222. (Mid-morning fruit and lunch included.)
Instrumental music tuition optional extra.

Warwick Preparatory School is an Independent School, purpose built on a 4½ acre site on the outskirts of Warwick. It is part of the Warwick Independent Schools Foundation, which includes Warwick School and the King's High School for Girls.

The Prep School has an exceptionally large staff, with specialist tuition in Art, French, Science, Music, Drama, DT, Physical Education and Computing.

Boys and girls are admitted from the age of 3+, subject to the availability of places. At the age of 7, the majority of boys continue to Warwick School, whilst the girls normally remain with us until they are 11.

Entry to King's High School is by a competitive examination and girls at the Prep School are prepared for this. Girls are also prepared for the Common Entrance and any other appropriate examinations for their secondary education.

Early registration is advised if a place in the Pre-Preparatory Dept is to be ensured. Entry to the School at the age of 7 and later requires a satisfactory level of attainment in the basic skills and may be competitive.

Charitable status. Warwick Independent Schools Foundation is a Registered Charity, number 1088057.

Waverley School

Waverley Way, Finchampstead, Wokingham, Berkshire RG40 4YD

Tel: 0118 973 1121
email: info@waverleyschool.co.uk
website: www.waverleyschool.co.uk
Twitter: @waverleyschool
Facebook: @Waverley-Preparatory-School-Nursery
LinkedIn: /waverley-preparatory-school-&-nursery

Chairman of Governors: Mr Blair Jenkins

Head Teacher: **Mr Guy Shore**, BA Hons QTS

Assistant Head: Mr Henry Mitchell

Age Range. 3 months–11 years.
Number of Pupils. 240.
Fees per term (2018–2019). Reception–Year 6 Core day: £2,863–£3,424. Extended day package also available. Nursery according to the broad range of flexible sessions

attended. Wrap-around care available from 7.30 am to 6.00 pm.

Ethos. Providing a family environment with academic excellence and enabling every child to succeed to the best of their ability.

Pupils just love coming to school every morning at Waverley! As soon as you walk in, there is a vibrant buzz of excited children who are happy, thriving and learning.

Our priority at Waverley is to challenge every pupil to achieve academic excellence. We recognise however that only happy children, who feel supported and confident, learn to the best of their ability. Waverley's unique cheerful, nurturing environment enables every child to succeed and reach his or her full potential.

We are very proud of our position as the no. 1 Prep School in Berkshire (The Sunday Times) and no. 14 Primary School in the UK (The Sunday Times) – based upon our strong academic track record. Our school has also been in the Times Top 100 Prep Schools for the past 7 years. Our academic success is also reflected in the exceptional exam results of our Year 6 students and the secondary schools they move on to – most of our students attain scholarships, or places at selective secondary schools.

We operate small class sizes, giving each child individual attention and enabling us to closely monitor every child's progress. Our school is modern and purpose-built, enabling daily school life to flow and function easily. Our family atmosphere means that our teachers not only know every child by name – they also know what makes your child tick. This warm ethos is also visible amongst our children who play with each other freely across the year groups in the playground.

In addition to academic success, we aim to encourage self-discipline, respect, tolerance and kindness and to provide a broad, rich curriculum going far beyond national expectations.

Curriculum. Waverley's curriculum provides children with a solid foundation, particularly in the areas of literacy and numeracy. Pre-prep and Preparatory children engage in a full curriculum of subjects including English, Mathematics, ICT, French, History, Geography, Science and Art.

Gifted and Talented. We have development programmes for gifted and talented children.

Sports. Waverley School's physical education curriculum includes football, rugby, netball, cricket, athletics and rounders. Swimming also takes place throughout the year as part of our ethos that every child needs to learn this life skill. The children regularly take part in sports matches and swimming galas against other local independent schools.

The Arts. We have extremely strong Speech and Drama, and Music (both choral and instrumental) departments. As well as termly productions, the School regularly takes part in local concerts both in the local community and with other schools to build children's self-confidence.

Moving On. The majority of our students attain scholarships, or places at selective secondary schools.

Wellesley House

114 Ramsgate Road, Broadstairs, Kent CT10 2DG

Tel: 01843 862991
Fax: 01843 602068
email: hmsecretary@wellesleyhouse.net
website: www.wellesleyhouse.org

Twitter: @wellesleyschool
Facebook: @wellesleyhouseschool

Chairman of the Governors: Mr P J Woodhouse

Headmaster: **Mr Gavin Franklin**, BA

Age Range. 7–13.
Number of Pupils. 74 Boys, 42 Girls.
Fees per term (2018–2019). Boarding £8,777; Day: Years 5–8 £6,639, Year 4 £5,043, Year 3 £4,077.

Location. The school, which is run by an Educational Trust, stands in its own grounds of 20 acres and was purpose-built in 1898.

Trains run hourly from Victoria Station, London with a high-speed rail link from St Pancras which takes as little as 1 hour 15 minutes or under two hours by road. At the beginning of each term, and at most exeats and half-terms, the school operates coach services between Broadstairs and London via the M2 services. The school also operates a minibus at exeats and half-terms to Brentwood, Charing, near Ashford, and Benenden.

Facilities. The school has a science and technology building, which includes modern science laboratories, an ICT laboratory and a craft room. Other facilities include a library, an indoor heated swimming pool, four hard tennis courts, two squash courts, a modelling room, art room, a music wing, a .22 shooting range, fitness trail, outdoor stage and separate recreation rooms, all of which are in the school grounds. There is a spacious sports hall. The main team games are cricket, Association and rugby football, hockey, netball and rounders. Tuition is also given in fencing, squash, shooting, golf, tennis, archery, judo, scuba and swimming. Ballet, tap, modern dancing and riding are also available.

The girls live in a separate house, The Orchard, within the school grounds, under the care of a housemaster and his wife.

Education. Boys and girls are prepared for all independent senior schools. Those who show sufficient promise are prepared for scholarships and the school has a fine record of success on this front with a third of leavers gaining scholarships in recent years. The curriculum is designed to enable all children to reach the highest standard possible by sound teaching along carefully thought out lines to suit the needs of the individual. In September 2019 Wellesley will be extending the educational provision and will be opening a Pre-Prep.

The Headmaster and his wife are assisted by 21 teaching staff.

Charitable status. Wellesley House and St Peter Court School Education Trust Ltd is a Registered Charity, number 307852. It exists solely to provide education to boys and girls.

Wellington Prep School

South Street, Wellington, Somerset TA21 8NT

Tel: 01823 668700
email: prep@wellington-school.org.uk
website: www.wellington-school.org.uk

Chairman of Governors: Mrs Anna Govey, MSc

Headmaster: **Mr Adam Gibson**, BSc Hons, PGCE, NPQH, Cert Ed Cantab

Deputy Head (*Academic*): Mrs Catherine Aish, BSc, PGCE
Deputy Head (*Pastoral*): Mr Martin Stepney, BA, PGCE

Age Range. 3–11 Co-educational.

Number of Pupils. 220.

Fees per term (2018–2019). Day: £2,110–£3,840.

Wellington Prep School opened in September 1999 in purpose-built accommodation to provide one of the most stimulating educational environments for children anywhere in the country.

Wellington Prep School provides an education of unrivalled quality which both complements and enhances the national reputation of Wellington School and enables us to deliver educational excellence from nursery level through to university entrance. Our school is a place of endeavour, teamwork, integrity and laughter; a place where each child is nurtured.

We value education in its widest sense; making the most of today in order that we can make even more of tomorrow and the days, weeks, months and years that lie ahead. This is 'Learning for Life.' Our education is unbounded, as we encourage our children to be curious, to be creative and to be compassionate. At WPS Learning is not a spectator sport.

We believe that every child deserves to be inspired every day. The qualities our children will need in life are as important as their skills. This is why we have high expectations for each child, nurture and support each child and develop each child's leadership skills. We encourage our children to think independently and to 'have a go', secure in the knowledge that they can learn from mistakes.

While the headline ratio of one fully-qualified and experienced teacher for every ten children in the Prep School is striking, it is the quality of these relationships that really matters and this cannot be gauged by a simple statistic. The range of experiences our teaching team provide for our children is superb. Every person cares deeply about the children in their care and each child's happiness and fulfilment.

Our children benefit from sharing some facilities with our Senior School, giving them access to:

- Eighteen purpose-designed, modern classrooms;
- A large, attractive, central school hall, the hub of our school;
- The most modern and up-to-date education resources;
- Purpose-built ICT suite and library;
- Spacious grounds including a large playground with wooden amphitheatre;
- Our forest school in the Blackdown Hills;
- The Princess Royal Sports Complex;
- Numerous sports pitches, hard courts and the astro;
- An indoor swimming pool.

School is open from 8.00 am and there is an extensive clubs programme followed by STAR club, which is available to all children from 5.00 to 6.00 pm during term time. For children in Reception and older, holiday clubs operate at Christmas, Easter and for six weeks during the summer holidays to accommodate busy working families. Our Nursery setting has a holiday club that runs during some weeks of the Prep School holidays.

Our prospectus is available from the School Registrar and can be requested via our website.

Charitable status. Wellington School is a Registered Charity, number 1161447.

Wellow House School

Wellow, Newark, Notts NG22 0EA

Tel: 01623 861054

email: office@wellowhouseschool.co.uk

website: www.wellowhouse.notts.sch.uk

Twitter: @Wellowhouse

Facebook: @Wellowhouse

Chairman of the Governors: Steve Cooling

Head: **Kirsty Lamb**, BSc Hons, EYPS, QTS

Age Range. 3–13.

Number of Pupils. 150.

Fees per term (2018–2019). Pre-Prep pupils £2,495; Prep pupils £3,495–£3,995. Fees include meals for full time pupils but are charged at £5 per lunch for part-time Pre-Prep pupils. Fees include normal extras. There is a 10% sibling discount.

Wellow House School was founded in 1971 by the Stewart General Charitable Trust. Since 1994 it has been managed as an educational charity by the Directors and administered by a Board of Governors. This co-educational school has an established reputation for high academic standards, a successful sporting record, broad cultural interests and a happy family atmosphere.

The teaching staff are well qualified and experienced, with subject specialists in all subjects from year 4 onwards. A distinctive teaching style places great emphasis on the rapport between teacher and pupil in small classes, without slavish reliance on worksheets and textbooks. Each pupil maintains a file of notes, as a record and for reference. All take pride in honest hard work, confidence through encouragement, courtesy and fair discipline, and a strong sense of belonging. The thriving house points system encourages much voluntary study and is the basis of the disciplinary process. There are visiting teachers for instrumental tuition, tennis, archery, kickboxing, LAMDA and dance.

The school is attractively set in 20 acres of parkland and playing fields on the fringe of the Sherwood Forest village of Wellow. There is easy road access to this heart of Nottinghamshire from Worksop and Sheffield to the north, Mansfield and Chesterfield to the west, Nottingham and Grantham to the south, and Lincoln and Newark to the east. Newark lies on north-south and east-west main line rail routes.

A continuous programme of development has provided purpose-built classrooms, science laboratory, networked computer room, music rooms, library, assembly hall and dining hall to add to the original country house. Recent additions to the school include studios for art and ceramics and a sports hall with indoor cricket nets. There is an indoor heated swimming pool, an all-weather cricket net, and an all-weather tennis court. The Pre-Prep classes are housed in their own building, which is surrounded by play-time facilities. There are close links with the village church.

Children enter the school after an interview visit and a trial day at any age from 3 to 11+ – the oldest often transferring from primary schools. Entrance Scholarships may be awarded annually and means-tested Bursaries can give financial assistance of up to 100% for local children for whom a Wellow education would not otherwise be possible. Pupils are prepared for 11+, Common Entrance and Scholarships to a wide range of Senior Independent Schools, both boarding and day, and there is a continuous programme of assessment and reporting. Over the last 20 years an astounding 100% of pupils have achieved places at their first choice of school post Wellow.

There is a broad physical education programme, with school matches in rugby, netball, football, hockey, cricket, rounders, cross country, swimming and tennis. Day and holiday expeditions for Outdoor Pursuits in the Peak District are popular as well as regular jaunts in the local area.

There is encouragement to participate in Natural History, the Visual Arts, Dance, Drama and Music, and 80% of the pupils learn a musical instrument. Most are involved in the much enjoyed regular concerts.

The school provides activity week cover during the holiday periods in the Pre Prep (it may also include pupils in Y3 and Y4). The Prep runs activity weeks for 7–13 year olds for 2 full weeks in the summer. There are also sports scholarships camps.

Charitable status. Wellow House School is a Registered Charity, number 528234. It exists solely to provide a high standard of all-round education for children aged 3 to 13 years.

Wells Cathedral Junior School

Jocelyn House, 11 The Liberty, Wells, Somerset BA5 2ST

Tel: 01749 834400
Fax: 01749 834401
email: juniorschool@wells.cathedral.school
website: http://wells.cathedral.school

Chairman of Governors: Very Revd Dr John Davies, MA, MPhil, PhD

Head Master: Alastair Tighe

Head of the Junior School: **Julie Barrow**

Registrar: Joanna Prestidge

Age Range. 2–11 years.
Number of Pupils. 167 plus 27 in the Nursery. Girl to boy ratio approximately 1:1.
Fees per term (2018–2019). Day: £2,547–£8,679. Boarding: £7,819–£8,679. Weekly Boarding: £6,774–£7,633.

The Junior School is made up of the Pre-Prep department (age 2–7) and the Junior School (age 7–11). Pupils accepted into the Junior School normally make a smooth transfer to the Senior School at 11 and academic, music and sports scholarships are awarded.

Academic Work. The school prepares children for the academic work in the senior school and takes part in the national tests at the end of KS2, however, the school is not restricted by the demands of the National Curriculum. The aim is to ensure high academic standards within a friendly and stimulating environment.

Children are assessed regularly for both academic achievement and effort, and parents have many opportunities to meet staff and receive information on their child's progress.

Boarding. We offer boarding for pupils in years 4 to 6 (aged 8–11) in the beautiful house and grounds of Beaumont House. It is a priority to create a warm, caring family environment for this age range. The children are very well looked after by a resident family – community living lies at the heart of their daily lives. They all eat breakfast and most evening meals together; the house is extremely spacious and includes excellent facilities, including separate rooms for games, music and relaxing. The house capacity is 14, which ensures a lovely family feel and yet is large enough for the children to form lots of strong friendships.

Creativity. We have close ties to Wells Cathedral and all their boy and girl choristers attend our school, which is set in beautiful grounds just to the north of the cathedral. A number of pupils are specialist musicians who enjoy the expert tuition of the music department, which is one of the four in England designated and grant-aided by the Govern-

ment's Music and Dance Scheme. Scholarships are available.

Drama, music and dance are considered vital activities to bring out the best in children. A full programme of concerts takes place during the year for all age groups as well as big productions and small year group dramas. The school has established drama exchange links with schools in other European countries.

A whole school arts week each summer allows all aspects of creativity to come to the forefront for every pupil. Themes have included the Caribbean, Somerset and China; pupils experience workshops in the areas of art, dance, drama and music. Regular exhibitions and performances are a feature of the school.

Sport. The school has many excellent facilities, such as the sports hall, dance studio, astroturf pitch and swimming pool. Pupils experience a wide range of activities on the games field. Sport is played to a high standard with rugby, cross country, netball, hockey, cricket, swimming, athletics and gymnastics being the main sports; basketball and badminton are also available. A full programme of inter-school matches and house matches is available for all pupils in Year 3 to 6. Many clubs and activities run at lunchtimes or after school.

West Hill Park School

St Margaret's Lane, Titchfield, Hampshire PO14 4BS

Tel: 01329 842356
email: admissions@westhillpark.com
website: www.westhillpark.com

Chairman of Governors: Mr Kevin Murphy, Retired Company Director and former parent

Headmaster: **A P Ramsay**, MSc, BEd Hons

Age Range. 3–13.
Number of Pupils. Prep School (age 5–13): 41 Boarders (21 girls, 20 boys); 255 Day Pupils (105 girls, 115 boys). Early Years (age rising 3 to 5): 30 boys, 27 girls.
Fees per term (2018–2019). Prep School: Day £3,600–£6,220, Boarding supplement £1,500. Early Years: according to sessions attended.

At West Hill Park pupils are prepared for Scholarships and Common Entrance to all Independent Schools.

The main building is Georgian, originally a shooting lodge for the Earls of Southampton, and provides spacious and comfortable boarding accommodation for boys and girls under the supervision of resident Houseparents. Resident matrons, academic staff and a qualified school nurse complete the Boarding team. Also in the main building are the administrative offices, the Library, the Dining Hall and the Assembly Hall with fully equipped sound and lighting equipment and stage. Further excellent facilities include the Art and Design Technology Studios, the Music School, a 25m heated indoor Swimming Pool, a fully-equipped Sports Hall, 2 Science Laboratories, two Computing Suites, the French, History, Maths and Geography Departments with Interactive Whiteboards and the purpose-built Early Years Department with its Outdoor Play Area and Forest School and access to our Beach School Classroom. West Hill Park stands in its own grounds of nearly 40 acres on the edge of Titchfield village. There are sports fields, 5 hard, 3 grass and 5 Astro tennis courts, a floodlit Riding School, a floodlit Astroturf, a cross-country course and in summer a nine-hole golf course.

There are 28 fully-qualified members of the teaching staff. 13 members of staff are resident, either in the main building or in houses in the school grounds, giving a great sense of community to the school.

A strong pastoral care system monitors the individual child's well-being regularly. There is a wide range of activities available in order to encourage children to develop individual skills and talents: choirs, orchestra, dance, aerobics, carpentry, judo, ballet, drama, golf, life-saving, computer club, string group, squash, chess, sailing, fly fishing, riding on school ponies and public speaking, as well as the more intensive training available in the Swim Squad, Tennis Squad and other sporting clubs. The Boarders enjoy many expeditions at weekends as well as fun events at school, such as orienteering, theatre workshops, cycle marathons and games evenings.

Games played include rugby, football, cricket, hockey, tennis, athletics, netball and rounders.

The school has been recently been judged by ISI Inspectors to be 'Excellent' in all areas.

Charitable status. West Hill School Trust is a Registered Charity, number 307343. It exists to educate children.

West House School

24 St James Road, Edgbaston, Birmingham B15 2NX

Tel: 0121 440 4097
Fax: 0121 440 5839
email: secretary@westhouseprep.com
website: www.westhouseprep.com
Twitter: @westhouseschool

Chairman of Governors: S T Heathcote, FCA

Headmaster: **A M J Lyttle**, BA Hons Birmingham, PGCE Birmingham, NPQH

Age Range. Boys: 4–11 years; Co-educational Nursery: 12 months to 4 years.

Number of Pupils. A maximum 230 boys aged 4–11 (Reception to Year 6) plus 100 boys and girls aged 12 months–4 years.

Fees per term (2018–2019). 4–11 year olds: £2,880–£3,908 according to age. The fees include lunches and breaktime drinks. Under 4: fees according to number of sessions attended per week. Fee list on application.

West House was founded in 1895 and since 1959 has been an Educational Trust controlled by a Board of Governors. The school has a strong academic reputation and pupils are regularly awarded scholarships to senior schools at 11+. The well-qualified and experienced staff provides a sound education for boys of all abilities. The National Curriculum has been adapted to suit the aptitudes and interests of pupils and to ensure that it provides an outstanding preparation for entry into selective senior schools. Pupils are taught in small classes which ensures that they receive much individual attention. Specialist help is available for children with Dyslexia or who require learning support. Music teachers visit the school to give individual music tuition.

The school occupies a leafy five-acre site a mile from Birmingham city centre. As well as the main teaching blocks there are two well-equipped science laboratories and a sports hall.

The Centenary Building, opened in 1998, accommodates the art and design technology department, ICT room and senior Library. Extensive playing fields, two all-weather tennis courts and all-weather cricket nets enable pupils to participate in many games and sports. Pupils also enjoy a wide range of hobby activities, and drama and music play important roles in school life.

The school is open during term time between 7.45 am and 6.00 pm. On-site Holiday Clubs are run by members of staff during the holidays.

Charitable status. West House School is a Registered Charity, number 528959. It exists to provide education for boys.

Westbourne House School

Shopwyke, Chichester, West Sussex PO20 2BH

Tel: 01243 782739
email: office@westbournehouse.org
website: www.westbournehouse.org
Facebook: @westbournehouseschool

Chairman of the Governors: Chris Keville

Headmaster: **Martin Barker**

Head of Pre-Prep: Caroline Oglethorpe

Age Range. 2½–13.

Number of Pupils. 350: Boarders 50; Prep Day 210; Pre-Prep 90.

Fees per term (2018–2019). Prep: Day Pupils (Years 3–8) £5,220–£6,115; Boarding (in addition to day fees): Full Boarding International £3,080 (including £1,000 per term for additional English Support), Full Boarding £2,080 (7 nights), Part-Time Boarding: £1,390 (5 nights per week), £1,190 (4 nights per week), £990 (3 nights per week), £685 (2 nights per week), £405 (1 night per week, Years 3 & 4 only). Pre-Prep (Pre-Nursery to Year 2): £1,310–£3,620.

All I am, everything I can be

At Westbourne House, we uncover the magic in each child and ensure they make the most of the world of experiences offered to them here. We develop lifelong learners, cultivating curiosity and rewarding initiative in a kind, caring and happy environment.

Exceptional results

Westbourne House pupils go on to some of the most prestigious schools in the country, including Benenden, Brighton College, Canford, Eton, Harrow, Marlborough, Wellington, Winchester and Wycombe Abbey. Our scholarship record is second to none, with over half our 2018 Year 8 leavers gaining scholarships for outstanding performance in academics, sport, music, choral, dance, art and drama, as well as awards for all-round achievement.

"Pupils here stay kids for longer than those in more urban schools." – Good Schools Guide

Westbourne House is located in 100 acres of parkland in a picturesque location between the sunny South Downs and the south coast, just outside the beautiful city of Chichester. 1½ hours south of London, Westbourne House attracts many families seeking to enjoy the coastal lifestyle. It is easily accessible by train from London and only 45 miles from Gatwick Airport.

We makes sure we give children time to get out in the fresh air and explore the grounds, returning to lessons with muddy knees and renewed spirit; it's key to life here because we know that children who spend time outside are happier, healthier and more creative.

"Teachers have detailed knowledge of the children, allowing carefully-focused support to be provided." –ISI Report

Thanks to small class sizes, our pastoral approach and an exceptional SEN team, we keep a close eye on each child's progress to identify when a child is ready for a challenge and to ensure that extra support is given where needed.

"Exceptional creative talents are evident in many areas." –ISI Report

We give children endless opportunities to find their strengths and shine. Designed to be holistic and stimulating, our curriculum is an unforgettable journey of discovery: science experiments, outdoor adventures, drama, debates, chess, cooking, ceramics, poetry, music, kayaking and a variety of team and individual sports.

Confident, pro-active, collaborative leaders

A recent Independent Schools Inspectorate Report found Westbourne House pupils to "have exemplary leadership skills", to "demonstrate exceptional confidence" and to "show initiative" and "work remarkably well on their own, collaboratively and with their teachers".

"Founded as a family school and the atmosphere remains." – Good Schools Guide

There is a deeply-felt sense of community here. Boarders live in one of seven family-style boarding houses. They enjoy a range of activities, but their favourite time is when they get to take advantage of the grounds, playing games, hanging out and creating lifelong bonds with their friends.

Charitable status. Westbourne House is a Registered Charity, number 307034.

Westbourne School

60 Westbourne Road, Sheffield, South Yorkshire S10 2QT

Tel: 0114 266 0374
Fax: 0114 263 8176
email: admin@westbourneschool.co.uk
website: www.westbourneschool.co.uk

Chairman of the Governors: Mr S Hinchliffe

Headmaster: **Mr John Hicks**, MEd Kingston, BEd Hons Exeter

Bursar: Mrs Vina Khan

Age Range. 3–16.
Number of Pupils. 360 day pupils, boys and girls.
Fees per term (2018–2019). £2,975–£4,250.

The fully co-educational School, founded in 1885, is an Educational Trust with a Board of Governors, some of whom are Parents. The number of entries is limited to maintain small class sizes – with an average class size of 14 throughout the school with a staff to pupil ratio of less than 1:10.

The Pre-School and Junior School are housed in a specially designed and equipped building, staffed by qualified and experienced teachers. French, Music, Drama and Games are taught by specialists. Specialist Science and Technology are introduced from Year 4 (8+), as well as specialist teaching in Computing, Art and Design, and RE. French, Science and Computers are introduced from the age of 4.

In the Junior School, some lessons are taught by specialists in Subject Rooms. There are also ICT, Drama, Art and Music Rooms, Fiction and Reference Libraries, and a Hall with a Stage.

The Senior School provides teaching to GCSE from Year 7 to 11 up to age 16. It has its own campus immediately adjacent to the Junior School. Years 7 and 8 have the benefit of their own designated building with access to all the facilities available in Senior School. The school has a 3-form entry in Year 7 with a scholarship class. External and internal scholarships are taken in January of Year 6. All children are placed in sets in Maths and English from Year 5.

The main aim of the school is to bring out the best in every pupil according to their ability. There is a Department catering for those with Specific Learning Difficulties. Great emphasis is laid on courtesy and a mutual respect for each other.

Art, Music and Drama are strongly encouraged throughout the school, with regular concerts, plays and art exhibitions. Tuition in several instruments is available. A new Drama Studio opened in June 2015 and new Chemistry and Biology laboratories in September 2017.

The main sports are Rugby, Football, Hockey, Cricket, Athletics, Netball, Rounders and Cross-Country Running with regular matches against other schools. There are also opportunities for Short Tennis, Swimming, Basketball, Volleyball, Fencing, Skiing, Badminton, Climbing, Golf and Scuba Diving. Numerous educational visits are on offer with annual trips abroad.

A supervised breakfast club runs from 7.45 am to 8.30 am. Breakfast for pupils and parents is available from 7.55 am and, while the length of day depends on the age of the child, there are after-school facilities for all pupils until 5.15 pm. There is no school on Saturdays.

Charitable status. Westbourne School is a Registered Charity, number 529381. It exists to provide education for boys and girls.

Westbrook Hay Prep School

London Road, Hemel Hempstead, Herts HP1 2RF

Tel: 01442 256143/230099
Fax: 01442 232076
email: admin@westbrookhay.co.uk
website: www.westbrookhay.co.uk
Twitter: @WestbrookHaySch
Facebook: @Westbrook-Hay-Prep-School
LinkedIn: /westbrook-hay-prep-school

Chairman of Governors: Andrew Newland

Headmaster: **Keith D Young**, BEd Hons Exeter

Registrar: Kate Woodmansee

Age Range. Boys 3–13, Girls 3–11.
Number of Pupils. Day: 220 Boys, 100 Girls.
Fees per term (2018–2019). £3,495–£5,030.

Westbrook Hay is an outstanding independent prep school educating boys and girls from rising 3–13 years. The school's beautiful location boasts 26 acres of parkland overlooking the Bourne valley in Hertfordshire, and is just off the A41, between Berkhamsted and Hemel Hempstead. This unique setting offers a secure environment, within which children explore and enjoy all that childhood has to offer.

Through visionary teaching in small classes and with a wonderful mixture of purpose-built facilities and historic surroundings, our children achieve excellent results, enjoy a broad curriculum, and have the all-important confidence to succeed.

The Independent Schools Inspectorate (ISI) carried out a very successful inspection and regarded our school as 'Excellent' and 'Outstanding', the highest possible recognition from the ISI for both age groups.

"Pupil's achievement is excellent and they are very well educated in accordance with the school's aim for pupils to realise their intellectual, social and physical potential."

"The quality of the provision is outstanding. Through excellent understanding of differing developmental stages and careful observations, staff plan challenging and enjoyable work for each child across all learning areas."

Classes are small and each individual is encouraged and helped to achieve their potential. Individuality, honesty, a sense of humour and self-reliance are attributes which are stimulated and valued in this most friendly school, which maintains a caring, family atmosphere.

Lower and Middle School departments prepare children from rising three to eight for entry into the Upper School. Children in Years 3 and 4 are class taught primarily by their form teacher, before a move to a subject-based curriculum in Year 5. The academic focus is based on the curriculum and goals of Common Entrance, together with Senior Schools Entrance and Scholarship examinations. All children follow the National Curriculum subject areas and in many cases extend them.

The facilities of the school have benefited from significant recent improvements including a £2 million lower school building, an art studio with pottery kiln and two new fully equipped Information Technology rooms. A £3 million Performing Arts Centre, with a 300-seat theatre and full music practice and performance facilities is the most recent addition to the outstanding facilities.

Extensive playing fields give ample room for rugby, football, cricket, golf, and athletics. All-weather netball courts and a heated swimming pool are complemented by a purpose-built Sports Hall which provides for badminton, table tennis, cricket nets, five-a-side football, gymnastics and many other indoor sports.

A breakfast club, after-school care and a school bus service are also offered to accommodate the needs of working parents.

Charitable status. Westbrook Hay School is a Registered Charity, number 292537. It exists to provide education for boys and girls.

Westminster Abbey Choir School

Dean's Yard, London SW1P 3NY
Tel: 020 7654 4918
email: headmaster@westminster-abbey.org
website: www.abbeychoirschool.org

Chairman of Governors: The Dean of Westminster

Headmaster: **J H Milton**, BEd

   Age Range. 8–13.
   Number of Boys. Up to 35 all chorister boarders.
   Fees per term (2018–2019). £2,857 inclusive of tuition on two instruments. Additional bursaries may be available in cases of real financial need.

Westminster Abbey Choir School is the only school in Britain exclusively devoted to the education of boy choristers. Boys have been singing services in the Abbey since at least 1384 and the 35 boys in the school maintain this tradition.

Westminster Abbey Choir School is a special place, offering boys from eight to thirteen a unique and exciting opportunity to be a central part of one of our great national institutions. Boys sing daily in the Abbey and also take part in many special services and celebrations both in the UK and abroad.

The small size of the school, the fact that all boys are boarders and the high proportion of staff who live on the premises, allow the School to have an extended family atmosphere.

A full academic curriculum is taught by specialist staff and boys are prepared for the Common Entrance and academic scholarship examinations; most boys win valuable scholarships to secondary independent schools when they leave at 13.

Music obviously plays a central part in the school. Every boy learns the piano and at least one orchestral instrument and there are 15 visiting music teachers. Concerts, both inside and outside school, are a regular feature of the year.

Besides music and academic lessons there is a thriving programme of other activities and there are many opportunities for boys to develop interests outside music.

Sports played include football, cricket, rugby, athletics, hockey, sailing, canoeing and tennis.

Entry is by voice trial and academic tests. Further details are available from Evelyn Neophytou (Headmaster's PA and Admissions Officer). The Headmaster is always pleased to hear from parents who feel that their son might have the potential to become a chorister.

Charitable status. Westminster Abbey is a Registered Charity, number X8259. It is a religious establishment incorporated by Royal Charter in 1560.

Westminster Cathedral Choir School

Ambrosden Avenue, London SW1P 1QH
Tel: 020 7798 9081
email: lauger@choirschool.com
website: www.choirschool.com
Twitter: @WCCSLondon
Facebook: @wccslondon

President: The Most Reverend Vincent Nichols, Archbishop of Westminster

Chairman of Governors: David Heminway

Headmaster: **Neil McLaughlan**, BA Hons

   Age Range. 4–13.
   Number of Boys. 229 (24 Choristers, 205 Day Boys).
   Fees per term (2018–2019). Chorister Boarders £3,362; Day Boys £6,411.

Founded in 1901, Westminster Cathedral Choir School is a day prep and pre-prep school and boarding choir school. Choristers must be Roman Catholic, but day boys of all denominations are welcome.

The school forms part of the precincts of Westminster Cathedral and enjoys such facilities as a large playground and a Grade 1 listed Library. The school has recently undergone a £1.3 million refurbishment, including a brand new playground and boarding facilities.

Choristers and day boys alike achieve a high level of music making. The Choristers sing the daily capitular liturgy in the Cathedral and are regularly involved in broadcasts, recordings and tours abroad. There is also a day boy choir, two orchestras and a substantial programme of chamber music. Boys can learn the piano and any orchestral instrument in school.

The major sports include football, rugby and cricket and the boys travel to Vincent Square, Battersea Park and the Queen Mother Sports Centre for games.

There is a wide range of extracurricular activities available including: chess, computing, debating, fencing, football, judo, drama and a Saturday rugby club.

The school is justly famed for its fantastic food!

Assessment for Choristers is by academic assessment and voice trial, generally in November and February. Day Boy assessments are held in November (pre-prep) and January (7+ and 8+).

Charitable status. Westminster Cathedral Choir School is a Registered Charity, number 1063761.

Westminster Under School

Adrian House, 27 Vincent Square, London SW1P 2NN

Tel: +44 (0)20 7821 5788
Fax: +44 (0)20 7821 0458
email: Louisa.lopes@westminster.org.uk
website: www.westminster.org.uk
Twitter: @WestminsterUS
Facebook: @westminsterUS

Chairman of Governors: The Dean of Westminster, The Very Reverend Dr John Hall

Master: **M O'Donnell**, BA, MSc Arch, EdM, PGDE, FRSA

Deputy Master: D S C Bratt, BA

Age Range. 7–13.
Number of Boys. 272 (day boys only).
Fees per term (2018–2019). £6,448 (inclusive of lunches and stationery).

The Under School is closely linked to Westminster School, sharing the same Governing Body, although it has its own buildings overlooking the beautiful school playing fields in Vincent Square. The school's premises were extended in 2011 with a new dining hall and a specialist suite of Art rooms located in an adjacent building. The current site was also extensively refurbished.

Boys are prepared, though not exclusively, for Westminster through the Common Entrance examinations and "The Challenge", Westminster School's scholarship exams. Most boys proceed to Westminster, but entry into the Under School does not guarantee a place at the "Great School". Each year some boys will go on to other leading senior schools, including Eton and Winchester. There is a strong academic tradition at the school.

The musical tradition is equally strong, with a junior and senior choir, an orchestra, and string, brass and jazz groups. Art is equally strong with new facilities for all kinds of creative activity. The standard of Art is also very high with new facilities for many different areas of creative activity. The Art Department also organises competitions in photography and model-making. There are other school competitions in areas such as public speaking, creative writing, chess and Scrabble. The level of dramatic productions has risen in recent years and there are plays for each year group at different times of the year.

Games are played on playing fields in Vincent Square and although football and cricket are the main sports, there are opportunities to participate in athletics, basketball, cross-country, hockey, rugby, swimming and tennis. Our new sports centre, recently opened in September 2012, provides excellent facilities for all sports and after-school clubs in such activities as fencing, judo, karate, climbing and table tennis.

Approximately 22 new boys are admitted at 7+ and at 8+, and up to 28 at 11+ in September. Means-tested bursaries are available at 11+, as are music scholarships, and many boys apply at this entry point from London primary schools.

Charitable status. St Peter's College (otherwise known as Westminster School) is a Registered Charity, number 312728. It exists to provide education for boys.

Westonbirt Prep School

Westonbirt, Tetbury, Gloucestershire GL8 8QG

Tel: 01666 881400
email: prep@westonbirt.org
website: www.westonbirt.org
Twitter: @westonbirtprep
Facebook: @Westonbirt-Prep-School
LinkedIn: /Westonbirt-Schools

Headmaster: **Mr Sean Price**

Assistant Head (*Organisation*) *and Y6 Form Tutor*: Mrs C Clifton
Assistant Head (*Teaching and Learning*) *and Y2 Form Tutor*: Mrs A Dicks

Age Range. 2–11 Co-educational.
Number of Pupils. 160 day pupils from Nursery–Year 6.

Westonbirt Prep School is a Preparatory Day School and Nursery for Boys and Girls aged 2–11 on the same site as Westonbirt School. It successfully combines the educational quality and individual attention of an intimate family school with the facilities, resources and opportunities of a school many times larger. Westonbirt Prep offers a broad and varied curriculum, with great emphasis placed on sport, music and drama, each delivered by specialist teachers. Committed to making outdoor education part of school life, all year groups attend regular Forest School in the Spinney, a beautiful woodland clearing within the school grounds. A strong family ethos is evident throughout the school and this combination of care and sense of community creates a happy, secure and stimulating environment where boys and girls thrive. Commitment to performance in Music, Drama and the Performing Arts is strong and many pupils play instruments, take singing lessons and participate in school productions.

Location. Set in 210 acres of stunning parkland, shared with Westonbirt School, pupils benefit from the resources of a much larger school while maintaining the atmosphere of a small family setting. The school's idyllic rural location allows pupils the freedom to play and explore in a safe and natural environment, developing imagination and confidence.

The school is located close to Tetbury, within half an hour of the M4 and M5 and within easy reach of Cirencester, Gloucester, Swindon, Bath and Bristol.

Philosophy. Smaller class sizes and the excellent ratio of staff to pupils allow our children to be well supported throughout their development and for their individual abilities to be valued. Boys and girls are praised for their efforts and good behaviour and are encouraged to develop a sense of independence, mutual consideration, manners and respect for others. Our commitment to children's broader personal development combined with a structured preparation for senior school, makes Westonbirt Prep stand out.

Inspirational opportunities. Academic success is strong. Emphasis is also placed on co-curricular activities, particularly Music, Art and Drama. Creativity is fostered and inspirational lessons fire pupil's imaginations.

Sports facilities. With extensive grounds and fine facilities, a broad range of Physical Education and Games are offered so that every child can benefit from the integration of sport within their daily life. Facilities include a 25m indoor swimming pool, well-maintained pitches, netball and tennis courts, cricket, athletics, a nine hole golf course and an equestrian team. All students have weekly swimming lessons in school.

Music. Music is an essential part of school life and is taught to a very high standard. Children have at least two periods of Music per week and many learn instruments in the string, brass, percussion and wind disciplines as well as taking individual singing lessons. Boys and girls often play together in the various ensembles and regularly perform at the Cheltenham Festival of Performing Arts.

Drama. Through Drama lessons, children develop confidence and communication skills. This encompasses clarity, diction, vocal and facial expression and intonation, and an early appreciation of poetry and prose. Individual Speech and Drama lessons are available and your child can work towards the LAMDA competition, Bath and Cheltenham Festival of Performing Arts or the Poetry Vanguard examinations. Children also look forward to participating in annual whole school drama productions.

Fees per term (2018–2019). £2,680–£3,865.

Westonbirt Prep is part of The Wishford Schools Group, www.wishford.co.uk.

Wetherby School
Alpha Plus Group

11 Pembridge Square, London W2 4ED

Tel: 020 7727 9581
email: learn@wetherbyschool.co.uk
website: www.wetherbyschool.co.uk

Headmaster: **Mr Mark Snell**, BA Hons, PGCE

Age Range. Boys 2½–8.
Number of Pupils. 354.
Fees per term (2018–2019). £7,415.

Wetherby School is situated at 11 Pembridge Square and 19 Pembridge Villas. The four Reception classes and Little Wetherby (a boys-only nursery opened in September 2014) are based at 19 Pembridge Villas. Each class occupies a whole floor level and there is a playground at the back for the boys to run around in. The rest of the school in based at 11 Pembridge Square.

Whilst proud of its academic attainments for London Day School entry at 7+ and 8+ and top Boarding Schools, the priority is in producing happy, respectful, thoughtful, sociable and motivated boys. The curriculum is well balanced, with excellent sport, music and art opportunities including specialist teaching rooms for art, ICT, library and music. There is also a wide range of extra-curricular activities available. Wetherby operates a non-selective admissions procedure; registration is at birth.

Widford Lodge

Widford Road, Chelmsford, Essex CM2 9AN

Tel: 01245 352581
email: admin@widfordlodge.co.uk
website: www.widfordlodge.co.uk
Twitter: @widfordlodge

Proprietor: Mrs Louise Gear

Head Teacher: **Miss M Cole**, ACIB, PGCE

Age Range. 2½–11 years.
Number of Pupils. Prep 120; Pre-Prep & EYFS Reception 120; Pre-School Nursery: varies according to number of sessions.
Fees per term (from April 2018). Pre-Prep £2,455, Main School £3,110. All fees include lunch, textbooks, stationery, etc.

Widford Lodge is a co-educational day school situated on the southern fringe of Chelmsford. Founded in 1935 the school aims to provide an all-round education within a happy, caring environment. Children are encouraged to enjoy their time at school, while also learning a sense of responsibility and a positive approach to their role in school and the wider community.

An enthusiastic staff prepare the children for grammar school via the 11+, entrance into senior independent schools through examination or scholarship and local secondary schools. A combination of form tutors, subject specialists and small classes ensure a good academic standard. The curriculum is broadly based and aims to develop a variety of interests, academic, aesthetic and sporting. The school has a well-equipped computer suite and the children are encouraged to use their computer skills in many different ways.

The main part of the school stands in 5 acres of wooded grounds that include a large Victorian house, an outdoor Swimming Pool, a Floodlit Tennis Court, Cricket Nets, Science Laboratory, Design Technology Centre, a room for Modern Foreign Languages and a room for small group work. There is plenty of space for the children to play and to use their imagination. The school also owns 9 acres of playing fields.

The children have the opportunity to play cricket, netball, rugby, hockey, soccer, athletics, swimming, cross-country, tennis, and rounders. Although a small school we are proud of our sporting tradition, which is underpinned by our belief that sport is for all and is ultimately played for fun.

Music, drama and art are all encouraged and a wide range of musical instruments are taught. There is a busy school choir and an annual concert. Speech & Drama is well-established and once a week the whole Prep School go 'off-timetable' and the teaching and learning experience is enriched by such activities as mindfulness, gardening, philosophy and cooking.

From September 2018 we are a Forest School and every child from the Pre-School to Year 6 takes part in a Forest School activity on site each half term.

There are many after-school activities which the children are encouraged to get involved in. These range from sports coaching in all the major games to art & crafts. The children can stay at school until 5.30 pm to do their Prep under the supervision of a member of staff.

Willington Independent Preparatory School

Worcester Road, Wimbledon, London SW19 7QQ
Tel: 020 8944 7020
email: office@willingtonschool.co.uk
website: www.willingtonschool.co.uk

Chair of Governors: Mr R Stewart

Headmaster: **Mr Keith Brown**, MA, BSc Hons, PGCE

Age Range. 4–13.
Number of Boys. 240 (all day boys).
Fees per term (2018–2019). £4,050–£4,880 according to age.

Just a short walk from Wimbledon station, Willington Independent Preparatory School has a proud history of educating boys between the ages of 4–13 since 1885.

The diverse and enriching curriculum offers the boys plenty of depth, academic rigour and creative opportunities. Small class sizes ensure each child is fully supported and catered for. Places and scholarships are gained at top academic senior schools.

Sport (played at our nearby playing fields), art and music are an integral part of life at Willington. The ongoing building programme includes a purpose-built library and the recently-installed climbing wall and new computing suite.

Extra-curricular clubs range from fencing and judo to touch typing and orchestra and a comprehensive programme of educational visits and trips further enhance pupil life.

At Willington, individual strengths are celebrated, effort is rewarded and self-worth fostered, cultivating a quiet confidence that develops boys into exceptional young men.

Charitable status. Willington School Foundation Limited is a Registered Charity, number 312733. Its aim is to devote itself to the continuation and development of the School.

Wilmslow Preparatory School

Grove Avenue, Wilmslow, Cheshire SK9 5EG
Tel: 01625 524246
email: secretary@wilmslowprep.co.uk
website: www.wilmslowprep.co.uk
Twitter: @wilmslowprep
Facebook: @wilmslowprep

Co-ed Day School founded 1909.

Chairman of Board of Trustees: Mr N Rudgard, MA Oxon

Headteacher: **Mrs H Rigby**, BEd Hons, NPQH

Bursar: Miss S J H Davies, BSc Hons, IPFA Hons
Secretary: Mrs S Wragg

Age Range. 3–11.
Number of Pupils. 118 day pupils.
Fees per term (2018–2019). £1,002–£3,780 (lunches extra).

The School is registered as an Educational Trust. It is purpose built and is situated in the centre of Wilmslow in its own spacious grounds. The facilities include an Assembly Hall, Sports Hall, a Science Room, Computer Room with networked PCs, a specialist Art Room with a kiln, two well-stocked libraries and a Classroom Block with its own outdoor area for 3–5 year olds. There is a Tennis/Netball Court, a Sports field with its own stand-alone Sports Hall and new all-weather pitch, and ample play areas.

The School aims to provide wide educational opportunities for all its pupils. It has a long-established excellent academic record and caters for a wide variety of entrance examinations to Independent Senior Day and Boarding Schools.

Wilmslow Preparatory School offers a variety of activities which include Music, Art and Drama. Principal sports include gymnastics, netball, football, cricket, hockey, tennis, athletics and swimming.

There are thirteen qualified and experienced teachers on the staff, as well as a highly knowledgeable and expert team of teaching support staff and management.

Charitable status. Wilmslow Preparatory School is a Registered Charity, number 525924. It exists to provide full-time education for pupils aged between 5 and 11, and part-time or full-time education to kindergarten children from the age of 3.

Wimbledon Common Preparatory School

113 Ridgway, Wimbledon, London SW19 4TA
Tel: 020 8946 1001
email: info@wimbledoncommonprep.co.uk
website: www.wimbledoncommonprep.co.uk
Twitter: @_wcps

Chairman of Governors: Lord Deighton, KBE

Head Teacher: **Mrs Tracey Buck**, BEd Hons

Age Range. Boys 4–7.
Number of Pupils. 168.

Wimbledon Common Preparatory School is a pre-prep school for boys situated in Wimbledon village, south-west London. It was founded in 1919 as a preparatory school for King's College School and other public schools, and moved to its present site in 1957. In 2006 it was bought by King's College School and is now part of their foundation and run by their board of governors.

The school's aims are to provide challenging and exciting teaching; to develop a love of learning; to encourage good study skills; to offer a variety of extracurricular activities; to create a culture which encourages self-confidence and values tolerance, generosity, respect for others and a strong sense of community; to help boys acquire the social skills which will enable them to make a positive contribution to society; to develop sound parent partnerships, and to provide opportunities for boys to reflect upon their relationships with one another, the wider world and their God.

The school educates boys aged from four to seven years, offering Early Years Foundation Stage (EYFS) provision in its Reception classes.

Fees per term (2018–2019). £4,395.

Charitable status. Wimbledon Common Prep School is owned by King's College School, which is a Registered Charity, number 310024.

Winchester House School

44 High Street, Brackley, Northamptonshire NN13 7AZ

Tel: 01280 702483
email: office@winchester-house.org
website: www.winchester-house.org
Twitter: @WHSprepschool
Facebook: @winchesterhouseschool

Chairman of Governors: Mr R S Greaves, BA

Head: **Mrs Emma Goldsmith**, BA

Age Range. 3–13.
Number of Children. 281. Pre-Prep: 67 (41 Boys, 26 Girls); Upper School: 214 (128 Boys, 86 Girls).
Fees per term (2018–2019). Pre-Prep: £2,890–£3,635. Upper School: Day £5,200–£6,410; Boarders £8,110 inclusive.

"The quality of pupils' achievements and learning is excellent." ISI Inspection Report

"A uniquely warm, welcoming environment where my children have truly flourished." Parent

"Low intensity, high academic standards and maximum happiness" Tatler Schools Guide 2018

"Perky children with an unquenchable thirst for life" Tatler Schools Guide 2018

Winchester House School is a friendly and outstanding prep school for boys and girls aged 3–13 with day, occasional and weekly boarding available. Small class sizes and outstanding teachers ensure each child is nurtured and receives individual care to they can thrive and be their best self.

Emma Goldsmith, Head won Best Head of a Prep School in Tatler Schools Guide 2019 and the School was nominated for Best Prep School 2017 in Tatler Magazine.

The new 2020 Vision outlines key changes to the school including stopping academic lessons on Saturday and introducing Sporting Saturdays and Mastery Mornings.

Aim. The aim of Winchester House School is to develop lifelong learners with a spirit of resourcefulness and self-reliance within a warm and purposeful community.

The School. Winchester House School sits in its own 18 acres of sports fields and gardens in the market town of Brackley, midway between Oxford and Northampton and close to the borders of Buckinghamshire, Oxfordshire and Northamptonshire. The school operates three minibus services for day children in the local area and wrap-around care from 7.45 am to 6.30 pm.

Learning. Winchester House has outstanding facilities and small classes. It is non-selective and is proud of developing confident, inquisitive children. The leavers last year gained scholarships to top independent senior schools in the country including Radley, Oundle and Millfield in academic, sport, drama, music and DT. There is also a strong Learning Development department. They recently introduced Independent Learning Tutorials for Years 7 and 8 including subject clinics enabling pupils to take ownership of their learning and develop skills for life beyond Winchester House.

Opportunity. Winchester House has magnificent facilities that include a newly refurbished ICT suite and Art & Design Studios, three separate science labs and two performance spaces. Sports facilities include a full-size AstroTurf, numerous rugby, hockey and cricket pitches, tennis courts, a heated swimming pool, squash courts and a fully-fitted sports hall with indoor cricket nets. Winchester House School offers riding lessons in the after-school curriculum.

There is an extensive after-school activity programme including skiing, golf, dance and STEM Club and it offers a broad range of instrumental music teaching, music groups and three choirs. Recent major dramatic productions have included A Winter's Tale, performed outside in the Upper Quad. The annual candlelit carol service in Hyde Park is a favourite amongst parents and alumni.

Confidence. The school understands that building a child's self-esteem is key to happiness and their ability and desire to learn. The unique Learn to Lead programme teaches leadership and team-building and includes annual expeditions for all children from Year 4 including wild camping and activities in Dorset.

Pastoral. Winchester House has strong pastoral care including a 'Circle of Support', a dedicated Well-Being Mentor and buddy benches in the playground.

Ambition. Winchester House encourages children to take pride in everything they do and live by the school motto: "To be their best self".

Community. There is a strong community at Winchester House. Children are encouraged to show respect and kindness (boarding have a 'Good Egg' cup for being just that) and parents are a valued part of school life, involved in school events such as the Christmas Fair and Easter Egg Hunts.

Charitable status. Winchester House School Trust Limited is a Registered Charity, number 309912.

Windlesham House School

Washington, Pulborough, West Sussex RH20 4AY

Tel: 01903 874700
Fax: +44 (0)1903 874702
email: whsadmissions@windlesham.com
website: www.windlesham.com
Twitter: @WindleshamTweet
Facebook: @windlesham

Chairman of Governors: Adam Perry

Head: **Richard Foster**, BEd Hons

Age Range. 4–13.
Number of Pupils. 194 boarders, 158 day (c. 50/50 boys and girls). Children can board from Year 4.
Fees per term (2018–2019). Prep: Day £5,590–£7,686 (UK & Europe), £7,090–£9,186 (International); Boarding £7,202–£9,272 (UK & Europe), £8,702–£10,772 (International). Pre-Prep: Day £2,995–£3,485.

Windlesham nestles in 65 glorious acres of the South Downs countryside in West Sussex and gives every child the opportunity to reach their potential in whatever sphere of life that may be. Established in 1837 and celebrating its 180th anniversary in 2017, Windlesham was one of the first schools in the country to be established as a preparatory school and in 1967 became the first IAPS co-educational school. Windlesham is one of the few prep schools to have no uniform and our children are not confined to a playground; they make dens, climb trees and camp in the woods and are free to choose what they want to do in their break times.

Today we educate approximately 330 pupils with a broad range of ability. Windlesham traditionally receives outstanding ISI reports which underlines our position as one of the leading prep schools in the world today. We give every child the opportunity to reach his or her full potential in whatever sphere of learning that may be. Although academic excellence is key we also encourage success in sport, music, drama and the arts whilst nurturing a friendly, family-orientated atmosphere with wonderful pastoral care. In March 2018 a new state-of-the-art sports hall and swimming pool were opened which enhance their sporting prowess.

With us children have the time and space to be children, away from the pressures of competition and urban hothousing. Windlesham is set in exceptionally beautiful grounds with magnificent buildings and facilities where children are encouraged to try a host of sports and extra-curricular activities after the academic day and at weekends. The children learn about independence, interdependence and cooperation.

At the top end of the school our overriding aim is to ensure that each child achieves the highest grades they can in their Common Entrance or Scholarship exams to some of the best senior schools in the country, as well as ensuring they follow a balanced and enjoyable curriculum. This year saw a record number of scholarships to senior schools and a 100% success rate at Common Entrance with all candidates gaining places at their first choice of school.

When the time comes to leave Windlesham children do so as confident, curious, clever and above all, kind people who are ready to make a difference in their world. Senior Schools often comment on how well prepared Windlesham children are for the next stage. Some even admit they've got a hard act to follow.

Charitable status. Windlesham House School is a Registered Charity, number 307046. It exists to provide education for girls and boys aged 4–13.

Winterfold House School
Part of the Bromsgrove School Family

Chaddesley Corbett, Worcestershire DY10 4PW

Tel: 01562 777234
email: info@winterfoldhouse.co.uk
website: www.winterfoldhouse.co.uk
Twitter: @winterfoldhs
Facebook: @Winterfoldhs

Chairman of Governors: Mr Paul West

Headmistress: **Mrs Denise Toms**, BA Hons QTS, NPQH

Age Range. 0–13 Co-educational.
Number of Pupils. 350 Day Boys and Girls.
Fees per term (2018–2019). Preparatory £3,650–£4,265; Pre-Prep £2,660–£2,930; Pre-School £2,950 (with nursery funding £1,875).

Set in over forty acres of grounds with views to the Malvern Hills, Winterfold offers excellent facilities which meet the needs of a broad and balanced curriculum. The School is just half an hour from the centre of Birmingham, 10 miles away from Worcester, and a mere 10 minutes from the M5 and M42.

Winterfold is a non-selective school and there are no formal entry requirements or tests. It is a Roman Catholic co-educational day preparatory school but children of all faiths are warmly welcomed and made to feel valued members of the community. The nursery offers day care for babies and toddlers.

The School has an excellent academic record at all levels including National Curriculum Key Stage Tests, Common Entrance and Scholarship. Children are prepared for entrance to both local independent day schools (such as RGS Worcester, King's Worcester, Bromsgrove and the King Edward's schools in Birmingham) and to independent boarding schools such as Shrewsbury, Bromsgrove, Cheltenham College, Malvern College, Stonyhurst and Malvern

St James. There is a highly regarded Learning Support Unit which provides one-to-one help for children with specific learning difficulties such as dyslexia. In 2017, pupils gained Academic, Art, Music and Sports Scholarships at the following schools: Bromsgrove, Shrewsbury, The Priory, RGS, Malvern College, St George's, Malvern St James and Dodderhill.

Winterfold places a great emphasis upon educating the whole child and aims to produce well rounded and confident boys and girls with high moral standards and good manners. In order to develop self-belief, every child is encouraged to achieve success in some area and thus the school fields a number of teams and not just in the main sports of rugby, soccer, cricket, netball, hockey and rounders; but also in sports such as fishing, golf, tennis, swimming, athletics, basketball, fencing and shooting. There are also a large number of clubs and societies and regular visits to theatres and concerts and other places of educational interest providing fullness and breadth to the educational experience.

In recent years, there has been considerable investment into the School which has seen the development of a new classroom block which has eight new classrooms, state-of-the-art Science labs and Art and CDT rooms. The School also boasts a splendid sports hall, new AstroTurf hockey pitches and tennis courts, ICT suite, chapel and a library. The entrance hall and offices have also been updated to offer a welcoming feel to children and parents. Adventure playgrounds cater for the demands of the full age range of pupils. Music and Drama are real strengths of the School and a new Performing Arts Centre is at the heart of Music in the School.

Charitable status. Winterfold House School is part of the Bromsgrove School family which is a Registered Charity, number 1098740. It exists solely to provide education for boys and girls.

Witham Hall

Witham-on-the-Hill, Bourne, Lincolnshire PE10 0JJ

Tel: 01778 590222
email: office@withamhall.com
website: www.withamhall.com

The school was founded in 1959 and was formed into an Educational Trust in 1978.

Chairman of Governors: Mr J W Sharman

Headmaster: **Mr A C Welch**, BEd

Age Range. 4–13.
Number of Pupils. 245: Prep (age 8–13): 101 Boys (60 boarders, 41 day pupils); 67 Girls (47 boarders, 20 day pupils); Pre-Prep (age 4–8): 77 pupils.
Fees per term (2018–2019). Boarders £7,230, Day pupils £5,360, Pre-Prep £3,185–£3,535.

The School is situated in a superb country house setting in the village of Witham on the Hill, close to the Lincolnshire-Rutland border. Boarding is very popular (weekly and flexi are available from Year 4) and benefits from first-class provision within the original Queen Anne house, at the heart of the School.

There is a teaching staff of 40, and additional visiting teachers for instrumental music. The maximum class size is 18 and pupils benefit from outstanding pastoral care across the school. The majority of pupils join at the Pre-Prep stage, and then continue through to Common Entrance. Pupils progress to their first-choice senior school both locally

(Oundle, Oakham, Uppingham and Stamford) and further afield (Eton, Rugby, Repton, Shrewsbury and Stowe). The School has a proud and enviable scholarship record across a range of disciplines, including academic, art, drama, music and sport.

Facilities are outstanding with modern, purpose-built Prep and Pre-Prep teaching areas. Significant developments have taken place in the last three years, the most recent being a superb Sports Centre (that includes a Dance/Drama Studio and Fitness Suite) and new ICT suites. The Stimson Hall, serving as a Concert Hall and Theatre, underpins a strong commitment to both Creative and Performing Arts. Most of the children learn one instrument or more and there are three bands and four choirs. Inclusivity is strong; within sport all Prep pupils represent the school on a regular basis each term. The standard is high, with teams regularly reaching National Finals in Rugby, Hockey, Netball, Cricket and Rounders (IAPS U11 National Champions 2016 and 2018). An Olympic-size all-weather astroturf complements magnificently maintained grass surfaces, including county-standard cricket facilities and a 9-hole golf course. The school has seen considerable growth in numbers in recent years and in almost every year group early registration is recommended.

Charitable status. Witham Hall School Trust is a Registered Charity, number 507070. It exists for the purpose of educating children.

Woodbridge School – The Abbey

Church Street, Woodbridge, Suffolk IP12 1DS

Tel: 01394 382673
email: Abbeyoffice@woodbridgeschool.org.uk
website: www.woodbridgeschool.org.uk

Chairman of the Governors: R Finbow, MA Oxon

Head of The Abbey Prep and Queen's House Pre-Prep: Mrs Nicola Mitchell

Deputy Head of The Abbey: Mrs Christina Clubb
Deputy Head of Queen's House: Mrs Sarah Lindsay-Smith

Age Range. Co-educational 4–11.
Number of Pupils. 202 Day pupils.
Fees per term (2018–2019). Pre-Prep £3,247–£3,463; Prep £3,950–£4,491.

The Abbey is the Preparatory School for Woodbridge School for which boys and girls are prepared for entry. An increasingly small number of pupils go elsewhere. There is a highly qualified teaching staff, with additional visiting music and other specialist teachers. The academic record has been consistently good, with value-added scores showing learning is fully supported: scholarships are won regularly both to Woodbridge and to other schools. The teaching is linked to the National Curriculum and emphasis is placed on pupils reaching their full academic potential whilst also benefiting from a broad education. Emphasis is on learning for life, not just to pass exams and pupils enjoy the unique Learning@Woodbridge programme that encourages them to develop their personalities and learning styles, alongside academics. Pupils are encouraged to be independent learners and the curriculum is structured to support and investigate, enabling pupils to be engaged in their learning and rewarded for their efforts as well as their attainment. Music is regarded as an important part of school life with a large number of pupils receiving individual music lessons and in Year Three all pupils receive strings tuition as well as their class music lessons. Drama and optional LAMDA lessons

are an integral part of the curriculum, encouraging confidence and supporting the curriculum in other areas. In Games lessons boys play rugby, hockey, soccer and cricket and girls play netball, hockey and cricket. Children also have the opportunity to swim, play tennis and take part in athletics, cross-country, dance and horse riding. In lunch breaks and after school, pupils are able to participate in a whole range of extra-curricular activities and hobbies and Mindfulness is incorporated into the curriculum to support pupils with their emotional development.

The School is set in its own beautiful grounds of 30 acres in the middle of the town. As well as a fine Tudor Manor house, it has a well-planned and high-quality classroom and changing room block. Another major development includes a multi-purpose hall and classroom block. Recent developments have included an upgrade of Music, ICT, Art, Drama, Engineering and Science facilities. The grounds are extensive and include playing fields, an all-weather surface games area and a science garden. The Pre-Prep Department is at Queen's House, situated within the Senior School's grounds, a short walk from The Abbey. However, it will move to purpose-built facilities on The Abbey site in September 2019.

Parents of Abbey pupils are eligible to join the Parents' Association and there is close contact maintained between parents and school, with community events the main focus.

Religious affiliation: Church of England (other denominations welcome).

Charitable status. The Seckford Foundation is a Registered Charity, number 1110964. It exists to provide education for boys and girls.

Woodcote House

Windlesham, Surrey GU20 6PF

Tel: 01276 472115
email: info@woodcotehouseschool.co.uk
website: www.woodcotehouseschool.co.uk
Twitter: @woodcotehouse
Facebook: @woodcotehouseschool

Headmaster: David Paterson

Deputy Headmaster: Andrew Monk

Age Range. 7–13.
Number of Boys. 105 (40 full boarders, 40 part boarders, 25 day).
Fees per term (from April 2018). £7,950 (Boarding), £5,950 (Day). No compulsory extras. Scholarship offered at the Headmaster's discretion.

Location. Originally a Coaching Inn on the old London to Portsmouth Road, Woodcote enjoys a beautiful, rural setting in 30 acres of grounds. The school is easily accessible from London and runs 2 daily bus services from SW & W London, 25 miles from Fulham via the M3 (Junction 3), 25 minutes from Heathrow and 40 minutes from Gatwick.

Pastoral Care. Woodcote House has been owned and run by the Paterson family for over 75 years. With a settled and committed staff, most of whom live on site with their own families, Woodcote provides an exceptionally caring and supportive environment for both Boarders and Day Boys. Our unique, graduated approach to boarding has helped solve the modern boarding conundrum faced by parents torn between Full and Weekly options. A strong emphasis is placed on manners, consideration and respect for others. The school has its own Chapel in the woods and parents are welcome to Saturday services, as well as to school matches on Wednesdays and Saturdays (after which legendary Match Teas are served), so there is plenty of opportunity to see their boys and talk to staff and fellow parents.

Academic. There are two forms in each year group, with an average of 10 boys in each class, enabling the staff to offer all boys an enormous degree of individual attention. With SEN and EFL teaching also available, academic standards are high and the school is proud of its 100% Common Entrance and excellent Scholarship record. Woodcote boys go on to a wide variety of independent senior schools and the Headmaster takes particular care in assisting parents to choose the right school for their son.

Music and Drama. 80% of boys learn at least one musical instrument, and the young and innovative Director of Music has ensured that it is considered 'cool' to be in the excellent choir. There is an orchestra and a jazz band and the school holds regular concerts so that the boys are comfortable with public performance, both individually and as part of a group. The school produces a Junior and a Senior Play each year, in which all boys are involved one way or another.

Sports. Rugby, football, cricket and hockey are coached to a high standard and there are teams at all levels of age and ability, with a high success rate for a small school. Individual sports include tennis (the school has five courts), swimming, athletics, golf, judo, fencing, and rifle-shooting.

Hobbies and Free Time. With 'prep' done first thing in the morning, there are numerous opportunities for the boys to pursue hobbies after lessons and games, and each member of staff offers a 'club' during Hobbies Hour on Wednesday afternoons. These activities are also available at weekends, along with the traditional activities of 'hutting' (camp building in the woods), 'cooking' (frying potatoes on camp fires), and overnight camping in the grounds. Boys are also offered the opportunity to be involved in the CCF. Boys are encouraged to read and have a quiet time after lunch each day for this as well as before lights out in the evening.

Ethos. The school motto, "Vive ut Discas et Disce ut Vivas" (Live to Learn and Learn to Live), embodies the school's aim to give all boys a love of learning and to discover and nurture their individual talents in a happy and positive atmosphere.

Woodford Green Preparatory School

Glengall Road, Woodford Green, Essex IG8 0BZ

Tel: 020 8504 5045
email: bursar@wgprep.co.uk
website: www.wgprep.co.uk
Twitter: @wgprep

The School is an Educational Charity and registered company, controlled by a Board of Governors who are also its Directors and Trustees.

Chairman of Governors: Dr E Hare

Head: **Mr Jonathan Wadge**, BA Hons Dunelm, PGCE, NPQH

Age Range. 3–11.
Number of Pupils. 384 (Boys and Girls).
Fees per term (2018–2019). £3,390.
The school provides an exceptional learning environment in which children achieve their best, feeling valued and secure. The School has an outstanding record of success in 11+ examinations to Senior Independent and Grammar

Schools, and demand for places at Nursery (3+) and Reception far outstrips availability. Parents are advised to make a very early application to the school via the website, and are encouraged to attend Open Afternoon and Open Morning events in November and February.

Means-tested Assisted Places, of up to 100% of the full fees, are available for 7+ entry.

Charitable status. Woodford Green Preparatory School is a Registered Charity, number 310930.

Wycliffe Preparatory School

Ryeford Hall, Ebley Road, Stonehouse, Gloucestershire GL10 2LD

Tel: 01453 820470
Fax: 01453 825604
email: prep@wycliffe.co.uk
website: www.wycliffe.co.uk
Twitter: @WycliffePrep
Facebook: @WycliffeCollege

Chairman of Trustees: Brigadier [Retd] Robin Bacon

Headmaster: **A Palmer**, MA, BEd

Age Range. 2–13.
Number of Pupils. Nursery: 39 pupils; Preparatory: 61 boarding, 201 day pupils.
Fees per term (2018–2019). Day £3,225–£5,265, Boarding £6,875–£8,885.

Wycliffe Preparatory School is a co-educational day, boarding and flexi boarding school from 2 to 13 years. The School is administered by the Governors' Advisory Body and the Trustees of Wycliffe (*see Wycliffe College entry in HMC section*), but is a separate unit with its own Headmaster and full-time staff of teachers, house staff and matrons.

A range of Scholarships, both academic and non-academic, are offered by competition annually. There are also bursaries available along with a very generous discount scheme for children from HM Forces families. The vast majority of our pupils go on to the Senior School – in 2018 92% of pupils continued to the Senior School.

Wycliffe is committed to fostering individual learning in all areas of the curriculum and pupils benefit from small class sizes with a high teacher to pupil ratio. One of Wycliffe's aims is to cultivate each pupil's unique talents and to bring out the best in its pupils by creating a supportive learning environment which promotes individual achievements in all fields. Specialist teachers ensure outstanding teaching delivery across the curriculum and a wide variety of extra-curricular activities enables the school to offer a fully-rounded education designed to develop confidence and self-esteem. Drama is taught from Year 1 encouraging pupils to develop their confidence and speaking skills.

Academic excellence is something all pupils are encouraged to attain. Challenge for our Gifted & Talented children is delivered through ensuring more able children are sufficiently stretched in the areas where they have been identified as gifted or talented. In addition to this, further enrichment is delivered through a number of specific Gifted & Talented events that provide children with some exciting and unique learning opportunities. Wycliffe is a member of the National Association for Gifted Children (NAGC) and has recently gained the Gold Star Award.

There is also a dedicated CReSTeD registered SEN Department which supports children who have weaknesses in some areas of the curriculum. The school not only promotes success in the classroom, but prides itself on enabling every child to do well, whether on the sports field, in one of the many drama or musical productions or by taking part in the annual Art exhibition, hosted at the Senior School.

The safe nursery is located within green fields and has its own dedicated outside learning space. The main school campus has excellent facilities designed to reflect the ages of the pupils. Years 7 and 8 are located in a new learning centre with university-style facilities and their own common room. Years 1 and 2 have their own adventure playground. The school also boasts an all-weather pitch, swimming pool, art studio and craft workshop, extensive playing fields, tennis courts, sports hall, studio theatre and music school, two science laboratories, three computer rooms, a covered playground and cafeteria-style dining room. The Preparatory School uses the Chapel, Medical Centre and state-of-the-art Sports Centre at the Senior School. Wycliffe College is the leading school in the UK for Squash and pupils at the Prep take advantage of the dedicated specialist training.

The boarding houses are extremely spacious and the boarders are very well provided for with their own indoor sports facilities, light and large common rooms set within very safe and secure grounds. There are dedicated House staff and members of staff with particular responsibility for the welfare of day pupils. Food is particularly good with a good variety of food including vegetarian. All dietary specialities can be catered for.

As well as the usual range of sport, drama and music, there are clubs, activities and opportunities for outdoor pursuits. A large number of educational trips are also arranged, including a Year 4 trip to Hooke Court, Year 5 to York, Year 6 Sailing, and Year 8 to Boscastle.

Charitable status. Wycliffe College Incorporated is a Registered Charity, number 311714. It is a co-educational boarding and day school promoting a balanced education for children between the ages of 2 and 18.

Yarlet School

Yarlet, Nr Stafford, Staffordshire ST18 9SU

Tel: 01785 286568
email: julia.bryan@yarletschool.org
website: www.yarletschool.org

Chairman of the Governors: Mrs Sarah Tennant

Headmaster: **Mr Ian Raybould**, BEd Hons, ALCM, NPQH

Age Range. Co-educational 2–13.

Number of Pupils. 171 pupils: 94 Girls and Boys in the Preparatory School (aged 7 to 13) and 77 Girls and Boys in the Nursery and Pre-Preparatory School (aged 2 to 7).

Fees per term (2018–2019). £2,535–£4,215. Flexi boarding available (Wednesday and Thursday nights) at £27 per night.

Established in 1873, Yarlet stands in 33 acres of grounds in unspoilt open countryside 3 miles north of Stafford. The school offers small classes, enthusiastic, qualified teachers, excellent facilities and a warm, friendly environment conducive to learning. All teachers keep fully abreast of the National Curriculum guidelines to Key Stage 3 and beyond.

Pupils have access to a wide range of facilities which include a new, state-of-the-art Science Laboratory, an Information Technology Centre, a CDT Centre, a purpose-built Art Studio, an indoor Sports Hall and a Music and Drama Theatre; and extensive outdoor facilities which include a nature walk, including a large wildlife pool, a heated swimming pool, four playing fields (for football, rugby, hockey,

cricket and athletics), three tennis courts, a netball court, an all-weather Astroturf pitch (for football, hockey and netball) and a cross-country running course. These facilities support an extensive sports curriculum, which features a daily games lesson. The Early Years and Key Stage 1 playground areas were redeveloped in June 2015.

Music and Drama complete the picture of a Yarlet education, with termly performances from the Yarlet Academy of Music and the Academy of Performing Arts. The arts are brought to life at Yarlet, inspiring self-belief and creative confidence in all our pupils. Whatever their talent, Yarlet pupils have the chance to shine. Club and extra-curricular activities are a further feature of Yarlet and include art (painting, sculpture and pottery), model-making, music, drama, French culture, chess, photography and fishing.

Yarlet has high expectations of all its children. Children are prepared for entry to a wide variety of senior schools and their achievements in both Key Stage tests and Common Entrance examinations are a source of great pride, as too is the fact that many children leave with a Scholarship award from their Senior School.

Charitable status. Yarlet is a Registered Charity, number 528618. It exists to provide education for boys and girls from 2 to 13.

Yateley Manor Preparatory School

51 Reading Road, Yateley, Hampshire GU46 7UQ

Tel: 01252 405500
Fax: 01252 405504
email: office@yateleymanor.com
website: www.yateleymanor.com

The School is an Educational Trust controlled by a Board of Governors.

Chairman of Governors: Stephen Gorys

Headmaster: **Robert Upton**, BSc Hons, PGCE, MA Ed, NPQH

Age Range. 3–13.

Number of Pupils. Pre-Prep and Nursery: 60 Girls, 80 Boys; Prep: 100 Girls, 160 Boys.

Fees per term (2018–2019). £2,025–£5,100. Fees are fully inclusive of all normal activities, extended supervision from 8.00 am until 6.30 pm, meals, educational visits and residential field trips for Years 5, 6, 7 and 8.

Yateley Manor has a long and successful history of educating girls and boys from the age of 3 to 13.

The development of the Prep School Baccalaureate (PSB), with its focus on rigorous academic standards, coupled with a broad and balanced curriculum, delivers an education for the twenty-first century. The PSB focuses on the vital skills of independence, collaboration and leadership through pupils' thinking & learning, communication and review & improvement and its ethos is embedded throughout the school.

The School's emphasis on educating the whole child is supported by a broad enrichment programme. Activities include chess, dance, horse riding, drama and water sports and the school is always keen to find new opportunities for children to find their talents and strengths.

Nurtured in a warm, friendly and safe environment with excellent facilities and limited class sizes, children are given new experiences to explore, building confidence and stimulating a desire to learn.

Innovative, enthusiastic and committed teachers embrace the different learning styles of children and incorporate varied approaches into lessons. The result is that children may spend a day being Vikings, visiting a Hindu Temple, creating maths games to bolster understanding of probability or fractions or cooking during science to reinforce the difference between physical and chemical changes.

There is a strong culture of continuing professional development with staff regularly attending external courses, as well as weekly after-school workshops and sharing best practice. This ensures the School's innovative and committed staff are constantly challenging their own practice.

A new building housing a state-of-the-art Music School, spacious and light rooms for Art and DT and a new Modern Foreign Languages Department opened in September 2015. The School's superb teaching facilities are complemented by excellent sports amenities including a heated indoor swimming pool, a large sports hall with indoor cricket nets and provision for football, netball and basketball, a gymnasium and several pitches.

The newly developed Woodland Learning Area is an inspirational educational environment which gives children the freedom to explore nature in a hands-on and child-led approach. This helps build confidence, independence and self-esteem as well as giving children new life skills.

The school welcomes children of all ages at any point during the school year. The speed at which children new to the school settle demonstrates the strength of pastoral care. Means-tested bursaries are available.

A network of school coaches serves the surrounding areas including Camberley, Church Crookham, Farnborough, Fleet, Frimley, Hartley Wintney, Hook and Odiham.

Charitable status. Yateley Manor is a Registered Charity, number 307374. It is dedicated to providing the highest quality education for children of the local community.

The school's aim is to encourage children to achieve the highest academic results in a happy atmosphere while promoting self-discipline and caring for others.

The school has excellent facilities which include a multi-purpose hall, library, computer suite, a science laboratory, art room and music centre.

Sporting facilities are excellent with all-weather multi-purpose pitches for netball, tennis and hockey, 15 acres of playing fields for cricket, rugby, soccer, rounders and athletics as well as a 25-metre indoor heated swimming pool.

Our smallholding includes goats, chickens, pigs, sheep and ponies that provide the children with an invaluable opportunity to experience nature first hand. This approach to Outdoor Learning is further enhanced by our 37 acres of parkland, with outdoor classroom, use of local Woodland Trust forest, activity equipment and orienteering trails, mountain biking track, nature pond and fruit orchard.

Pupils are prepared for Common Entrance and Independent School Scholarship. There is a Pre-Preparatory Department for children from age 4 to 7 and a Nursery for children from rising 3.

Charitable status. York House School is a Registered Charity, number 311076. It exists to provide high-quality education to boys and girls.

York House School

Sarratt Road, Croxley Green, Rickmansworth, Herts WD3 4LW

Tel: 01923 772395
email: yhsoffice@york-house.com
website: www.york-house.com
Twitter: @SchoolYorkHouse
          @YHheadmaster

Founded in 1910, York House School is a non-profit making Educational Trust with a Board of Governors.

Chairman of the Governors: Mrs L Keating

Headmaster: **Mr Jon Gray**, BA Ed Hons, PGCE

Age Range. 3–13 Co-educational.

Number of Children. All are Day pupils: 219 Prep, 147 Pre-Prep.

Fees per term (2018–2019). Nursery £315 per session, minimum 4 sessions per week; Reception £3,480; Year 1 £3,835; Year 2 £4,085; Years 3–8 £4,635.

York House School is a well-established, innovative and forward-looking school located in a Queen Anne country house standing in 47 acres of Hertfordshire countryside. The Headmaster is assisted by a fully-qualified and caring staff. Our extended day arrangements enable pupils to attend early-morning clubs and after-school clubs between 7.30 am and 6.00 pm.

IAPS Overseas

ALPHABETICAL LIST OF SCHOOLS

GEOGRAPHICAL LIST OF SCHOOLS

Individual School Entries

The Banda School

PO Box 24722, Nairobi 00502, Kenya

Tel: 00 254 20 5131100
         Mobiles: 00 254 709 951000
email: admissions@bandaschool.com
website: www.bandaschool.com

Chairman of Governors: Mr D G M Hutchison

Headmistress: **Mrs A Francombe**, BEd Hons

Age Range. 12 months–13 years.
Number of Children. 435 (Day).
Fees per term (2018–2019). Tuition: Kshs 614,250 (Years 3–8 including lunches). Sliding fee scale Year 2 and below.

The School was founded in 1966 by Mr and Mrs J A L Chitty. It is 9 miles from Nairobi and stands in its own grounds of 30 acres adjacent to the Nairobi Game Park. Boys and girls are admitted in equal numbers and are prepared for Independent Senior School Scholarship and Common Entrance Examinations to leading secondary schools in the UK, Kenya and South Africa. The Staff consists of 50+ teachers.

Facilities include a purpose-built Early Years section, Science laboratories, ICT rooms, Art rooms, Music rooms, well-equipped hall for Performing Arts, three Libraries, specialist subject rooms for Mathematics, English, MFL, Humanities, Design Technology, Astroturf, two Squash courts and a six-lane 25-metre heated Swimming Pool. High-quality interactive multi-touch screens are available from Reception Classes through our Upper School. Banks of iPads enhance learning for use from Reception to Year 5 inclusive. From Year 6 pupil will require their own iPad as we run an e-learning programme which runs alongside our traditional written language practices.

Sports include Rugby, Football, Hockey, Cricket, Tennis, Swimming, Netball, Rounders, Athletics, Sailing, Squash and Cross-Country. A wide range of extra-curricular activities are available including instrumental and voice lessons, Modern Dance, Ballet, LAMDA, extra tennis, squash, swimming, cross country to name a few.

The British School Al Khubairat

PO Box 4001, Abu Dhabi, United Arab Emirates

Tel: 00 971 2 446 2280
Fax: 00 971 2 446 1915
email: registrar@britishschool.sch.ae
website: www.britishschool.sch.ae
Twitter: @BSAKAbuDhabi
Facebook: @BSAKAbuDhabi
LinkedIn: /british-school-al-khubairat

A member of HMC, IAPS, COBIS, BSME and BSO Inspected.

Chair of Governors: Debby Burton Shaw

Headmaster: **Mark Leppard**, MBE

Head of Secondary School: Teresa Woulfe

Head of Primary School: Elaine Rawlings

Age Range. 3–18.
Number of Pupils. 927 Boys, 927 Girls (all day).
Fees per term (2018–2019). Nursery: AED12,534; Reception–Year 6: AED16,234; Years 7–13: AED21,800.

Founded in 1968 on land generously donated by the late President of the UAE, The British School Al Khubairat is the leading and most established British curriculum school in Abu Dhabi, with a track record of 50 years of academic excellence and exceptional achievement in sport, music, drama and art. With its first-class facilities, experienced British teachers, unparalleled co-curricular activities and inclusive school culture, it provides its students with a proven platform upon which they can grow and be successful.

The School has the highest rating of 'Outstanding' across all six performance standards (ADEK 2018/19) and at the heart of its constitution is its status as a not-for-profit and academically non-selective community school. From Nursery to Sixth Form its aim is to deliver excellence in teaching and learning, bringing everything that is outstanding about the British curriculum to the UAE.

The school provides a dynamic holistic education and it is through this that BSAK supports its students to exceed expectations, ensuring their education becomes the foundation for happiness and success.

The School has the largest choice of 26 A Levels in Abu Dhabi and also provides 3 specialist BTEC courses in engineering, business studies and sport. Also of note is the School's extensive co-curricular programme, leadership enrichment and exceptional pastoral care.

All of these exciting elements are set in a stunning campus and superbly housed in its purpose-built facility, which includes:

- Large, creative classrooms
- A 25m swimming pool
- Learner pool
- Grass pitch
- Two synthetic turf pitches
- Auditorium
- Theatre
- Gym
- Multimedia suites equipped with Apple Macs

The School is under the ongoing patronage of the British Ambassador and is sponsored by His Highness Sheikh Khalifa Bin Zayed Al Nahyan, the current president of the UAE. The board of governors is made up of a British Embassy appointment and parent-elected representatives and the School undergoes regular local and British inspection.

The British School of Paris – Junior School

2 rue Hans List, 78290 Croissy sur Seine, France

Tel: 00 33 1 30 15 88 30
Fax: 00 33 1 73 79 15 71
email: junior@britishschool.fr

website: www.britishschool.fr
Twitter: @BritishSchParis
Facebook: @BritishSchParis

Chairman of Governors: Mr E Coutts

Headmaster: Mr N Hammond

Head of the Junior School: Mr M Potter

Age Range. 3–11 Co-educational.
Number of Pupils. 400.
Fees per annum (2018–2019). €18,261–€24,762.
The Junior School caters for pupils aged 3–11 and is located very close to the Senior School along the leafy banks of the river Seine. This brand new school opened in September 2010; there are 35 classrooms accommodating up to 480 pupils, as well as 4 bespoke classrooms and 2 activity areas that are dedicated to our foundation stage/nursery section. The school was specifically designed to meet the educational and social welfare needs of junior school pupils. It is bristling with new technology and up-to-the-minute IT facilities to assist the pupils' learning and development. The British School of Paris's philosophy of education permeates throughout the Junior School and has at its core the goal of unlocking the potential of all students, by identifying strengths and supporting areas of development, while having fun and enjoying happy and strong social relationships. Studies are based on the British National Curriculum with emphasis on English, Maths and Science, and of course, the French language. Various sports, music, drama and many other extracurricular activities are also provided.
For further details and applications, please contact the Registrar, email: registrar@britishschool.fr.

The English School
Kuwait

PO Box 379, 13004 Safat, Kuwait
Tel: 00 965 22271385
email: registrar@tes.edu.kw
website: www.tes.edu.kw

Owner: Mr Emad Mohamed Al-Bahar

Chair of the Governing Committee: Brigadier Andy Barr

Headmaster: Kieron Peacock

Age Range. 2½–13.
Number of Pupils. 620.
Fees per annum (2018–2019). Nursery (Pre-KG and KG) KD1,741; Pre-Preparatory (Rec, Year 1 and Year 2) KD2,735; Lower Preparatory (Years 3–6) KD3,1350; Upper Preparatory (Years 7 and 8) KD3,435.
The English School, founded in 1953 under the auspices of the British Embassy, is the longest established school in Kuwait catering for the expatriate community. The school operates as a not-for-profit, private co-educational establishment providing the highest standards in education for children of Pre-Kindergarten to Preparatory school age. The school is registered with the United Kingdom Department for Education (DfE No 703 6052) and the Headmaster is a Member of the Independent Association of Prep Schools. TES is an Accredited Member of BSME, of COBIS, and is also accredited as a British School Overseas with the DfE and listed as a "world class British school". Uniquely in Kuwait, the language of the playground is English. The roll is predominantly British, as are the resources and texts. With

the exception of foreign language teachers, the teaching staff are also predominantly British and qualified in the United Kingdom. The number of pupils in the school continues to increase although the average class size remains around 20. The school is housed in well-resourced and spacious, fully air-conditioned premises in a pleasant residential suburb of Kuwait City.
The curriculum is British, contemporary and delivers the best of traditional standards within a broad-based structure. Class teachers are supported by specialist coordinators in Art, Design and Technology, Information Technology, Music, Library and PE and Games. Music is taught to all ages and French is introduced from Year 4. The National Curriculum for England is used as the core for the curriculum, although the most able are challenged and those in need of support benefit from individual tuition. Formal end of key stage assessment takes place in Years 2 and 6. In addition the pupils are prepared for entrance tests to other schools including, where appropriate, Common Entrance Examinations at 11+, 12+ and 13+, and scholarship examinations. Pupils in Years 3–8 use iPads as an integral tool and part of their teaching and learning. Pupils in Year 2 and below have access to banks of school iPads. The school's VLE (Virtual Learning Environment) is also at the heart of the pupils' studies and the development of skills for learning drive the school's innovative approach to teaching and learning.
Responsibility for the school is vested in the Governing Committee whose members serve in a voluntary capacity. The school provides a learning environment within which children develop their individual capacity for achievement to its fullest potential. The school's core values of Confidence, Empathy, Integrity, Positivity and Respect are at the heart of all that it does. Strong emphasis is placed on academic study, together with a wide range of non-academic activities to provide breadth and balance. The school aims to ensure that, by achieving standards at least equivalent and often better than those of competitive private and state schools in Britain, pupils are well prepared for the subsequent stages of their academic development whether in Britain, Kuwait or elsewhere in the world.
In the first instance application for enrolment should be made online via the website – please see drop-down menu: Admissions, Application Form.
The Registrar will confirm receipt of the Online Application Form. If there are places in the year requested, the Registrar will ask for copies of current academic reports and arrange a date for the child/children to be assessed. Where possible for children entering Year 4 and above, part of this assessment will be an online test. Pupils and parents will then be invited to attend one of the school's 'Welcome and Assessment Days' prior to the start of the academic year.

The Grange Preparatory School
Chile

Av Principe de Gales 6154, La Reina, 687067, Santiago, Chile
Tel: 00 562 598 1500
Fax: 00 562 277 0946
email: rectoria@grange.cl
website: www.grange.cl

Co-educational Day School.

Rector of The Grange School: Mr Rachid Benammar

Vice-Rector of The Grange School and Head of Senior: Mr Carlos Packer-Comyn

Head of the Upper Preparatory School: Mr Charles Barton

Head of the Lower Preparatory School: Mrs Carmen Gloria Gomez

Age Range. 4–12.
Number of Pupils. 1,200.
Fees per annum (2018–2019). Approximately £7,235 payable in one annual sum or 11 monthly instalments. There is a one-off incorporation fee payable on entry.

The Grange Preparatory School is the junior section of The Grange, founded in 1928 by John Jackson and based upon the British independent school which he had attended.

The Prep School is divided into the Lower Prep, which takes children from the age of 4 to the age of 8, and the Upper Prep, taking children from 8 to 12. Almost all pupils will transfer into The Grange senior school.

The ethos of the school is strongly based on giving a broad, all-round educational experience to find strengths for each child. The school may be very large but each child is valued as an individual within the team.

Entry to the school is usually at the age of 4, though entry at ages over 4 may be possible as vacancies occur in the course of the year. All teaching is in English except in those areas where the Chilean National Curriculum requires that they be taught in Spanish. The majority of the pupils are Chilean and begin an immersion course in English upon entry.

International assessment criteria are used at various stages of each pupil's career, with NFER testing in English and mathematics. The core curriculum is based largely upon the National Curriculum of England and Wales, fully encompassing and surpassing the local National Curriculum. Teaching is mainly by class teachers, though older children will find themselves being taught by specialists in many subjects. All heads of department are specialists. Approximately 30 of the teachers are expatriates.

Over the last few years strong progress has been made in the areas of Science, Music, Drama and Art and Design Technology, with new rooms having been dedicated to these subjects. There is a comprehensive after-school extracurricular programme in which children from the age of 7 upwards are strongly encouraged to take part.

Hillcrest International Schools

PO Box 24282, Karen 00502, Nairobi, Kenya
Tel: +254 20 883914/16/17 or 254 20 806 7783/4
           +254 724 256 173 or +254 717 969 450
email: admin@hillcrest.ac.ke
website: www.hillcrest.ac.ke
Twitter: @HillcrestKE
Facebook: @HillcrestKE

Chairman of Governors: Mr Bob Kikuyu

Head of Secondary School: Mr John Eveson

Head of Preparatory School: Mrs Vikki Alden

Head of Early Years: Mrs Jackie Leeson

Age Range. 18 months – 18 Years Co-educational.
Number of Pupils. 550 in total across all 3 sections of the school.

Fees per term (2018–2019). Tuition in Hillcrest Early Years from Play Group to Year 1 ranges from Ksh 89,950 to 299,750 including lunch. Tuition in the Preparatory School from Year 2 to Year 8 ranges from Ksh 431,650 to Ksh 569,550. Tuition in Secondary School from Year 9 to Year 13 ranges from Ksh 635,500 to Ksh 671,500. Boarding (in addition to tuition fees): Ksh 275,750 (full boarding); Ksh 175,000 (weekly boarding).

Hillcrest International Schools is a group of schools committed to inspiring each and every child to achieve their own individual personal excellence and to grow to become a valuable member of the global community in which we live. The schools are located on an attractive, purpose-built, 33-acre campus.

Guided by the British Curriculum, we cater for children aged 18 months to young adults aged 18 years. By stimulating each individual's abilities and talents within an atmosphere of mutual respect, we aim to ensure *Semper Prospice* (always looking forward) is a lifelong quest. A valuable boarding resource is offered to children in Prep and Secondary to complement our learning environment and cater for those families who live further afield or juggle work travel with family life.

Early Years: Offering young children a stimulating and creative play-based learning environment in a caring, family-style atmosphere, we foster and nurture a lifelong love of learning and sense of curiosity that lays strong foundations.

Prep: Recognising the uniqueness of each child, we place an emphasis on the development of the whole child and provide pupils of every level with an individualised approach to learning as they develop towards the Common Entrance Exam.

Secondary: Providing a diverse and stimulating environment, we motivate and guide each student to identify their strengths, achieve their individual academic potential at IGCSE, A Level or BTEC and grow into emotionally intelligent independent thinkers.

With over 30 different nationalities represented within the school community, it has a very multinational feel with its pupils drawn from the diplomatic community including the UN, expatriate families on contract, and Kenyan residents. The friendly family spirit and strong communication network that exists between staff, pupils and parents are of particular note.

Extensive information can be found at www.hillcrest.ac.ke.

Kenton College Preparatory School

PO Box 25406, Nairobi, Lavington 00603, Kenya
Tel: + 254 020 3541513
           Cell: 00 254 722 205038 / 00 254 733 687077
email: admin@kenton.ac.ke
website: www.kentonschoolnairobi.com

Chairman of the Governors: C H Banks, Esq

Headmistress: Mrs M Cussans, BA, PGCE, MA

Age Range. 6–13 Co-educational.
Number of Pupils. 365.
Fees per term (2018–2019). Kshs 610,000/-.

Founded in 1924 and transferred to purpose-built accommodation in 1935, Kenton College is one of the oldest schools in the country. Situated in its own secluded grounds of 35 acres, at an altitude of nearly 6000 feet, some three miles from the centre of one of Africa's most cosmopolitan capitals, Kenton is an oasis of calm amidst the rapidly sprawling urban development of the city of Nairobi.

Kenton College is an independent co-educational preparatory school, entry to which is open to both boys and girls of any race or religious persuasion, who have had their sixth birthday before the beginning of the school year in September. Most pupils remain seven years with us and leave in the July following their thirteenth birthday for senior schools in the UK, Kenya or South Africa, having followed a syllabus in the senior part of the school leading to the ISEB Common Entrance Examination. Kenton pupils frequently obtain scholarships to UK or Kenyan senior schools.

The school is based on a strong Christian foundation which is reflected in the warm and caring environment provided for its pupils, wherein positive encouragement is given towards any aspect of school life. Considerable emphasis is placed on character building, discipline and good manners, within a relaxed and happy atmosphere.

We aim for high academic achievements by offering a full curriculum in which the best of traditional and modern approaches are employed. The British National Curriculum provides the framework for our teaching throughout the school. Use is made of specialist subject teaching rooms in the senior school.

The academic day is balanced by opportunities for drama and music for all, together with a wide variety of sports and extra-curricular activities. Traditional British sports are played using our first class facilities which include three tennis courts, a heated swimming pool and a synthetic surface sports pitch.

Many pupils opt for extra activities such as riding, ballet, karate, music tuition, tennis or swimming coaching, speech and drama awards. Trips to facilities found in an international city are combined with expeditions and fieldwork in the unrivalled Kenyan countryside.

Academic subjects are taught by a staff complement of local and expatriate teachers numbering 43. Full use is made of accomplished musicians for music tuition, while recognised Kenyan sportsmen assist with games coaching. The average class size is 18, with 20 the maximum.

King's College School, La Moraleja

Paseo de Alcobendas 5, La Moraleja, Madrid 28109, Spain

Tel: 00 34 916 585 540
Fax: 00 34 916 507 686
email: info.lamoraleja@kingscollege.es
website: www.kingscollegeschools.org
Twitter: @KCS_Moraleja
Facebook: @Kings-College-School-La-Moraleja
LinkedIn: /King's College School, La Moraleja

Headteacher: **Nigel Fossey**, MA Oxon, MA, PGCE, FRSA

Deputy Headteacher: June Donnan, BA Hons Ulster, MEd OU

Upper School Leader: Jacky Walters, BEd Winchester

Lower School Leader: Dhamayanthi Vinthini Sangarabalan, PGCE Edinburgh

Head of Spanish Studies: Pedro García Navarro, Ddo Magistero, Ldo CAFD, CAP Madrid

Head of Admissions: Nuria Sanz, BA, MBA SIU Madrid

King's College School La Moraleja opened in September 2007 and is one of three King's Group schools in Madrid, the first of which was founded in 1969. The Headteacher of

La Moraleja is an overseas member of IAPS and King's College School La Moraleja is also a member of COBIS.

The school is governed by the King's Group Board of Directors and the School Council. These governing bodies are composed of distinguished members from the business and academic communities.

Age Range. 3–15 Co-educational.

Number of Pupils. 500.

It is a co-educational day school catering for approximately 500 boys and girls of some 35 nationalities from Nursery to Year 10. There are 33 fully-qualified British staff and five qualified Spanish language teachers.

The school vision, like its sister schools in Madrid, is to "be at the forefront of British education internationally" and to provide students with an excellent all-round education while fostering tolerance and understanding between young people of different nationalities and backgrounds. It is a happy and inspiring place to learn.

At the age of fifteen, at the end of National Curriculum Year 10, pupils transfer to the school in Soto de Viñuelas to complete their final three years of study. (*See King's College entry in HMC section.*)

Location. This modern, purpose-built school is situated in the superb location of La Moraleja, one of the most highly-regarded residential areas in Madrid. The site is well connected to the city, just off the A1 and a short walk from the La Moraleja Metro station. There is an optional bus service for pupils to the city of Madrid and its outlying residential areas and all routes are supervised by a bus monitor.

Facilities. All classrooms are bright, spacious and house a complement of high-quality resources and technology to encourage interactive learning. The on-site facilities include a library, two ICT suites, science laboratory, music rooms, multi-purpose sports surface, gymnasium and infirmary.

Curriculum. Teachers deliver a broad and balanced curriculum and encourage pupils to put effort into all that they undertake academically, culturally and physically.

Pupils follow the English National Curriculum (leading to IGCSE, GCE AS and A Level examinations once pupils transfer to Soto de Viñuelas). There are Induction English Classes for children over the age of 7 who need to improve their English. There are also Beginners Spanish Classes for international children joining the school. All pupils learn Spanish.

Activities. There are choirs and musical ensembles, which participate in events throughout the year. Pupils are encouraged to explore their capabilities in the areas of music and the arts from a very early age.

Sports play an important role at the school and pupils are encouraged to take part in tournaments and local competitive events, in addition to their normal PE classes. School football and basketball teams compete in the local Alcobendas Leagues and pupils also take part in inter-school championships in athletics and cross-country.

There is a programme of optional classes which includes chess, ballet, judo, Spanish dancing, swimming and tuition in various musical instruments, as well as performing arts, language clubs and craft workshops.

Admission. Pupils wishing to enter Year 3 and above are required to sit entrance tests in English and Mathematics and to present copies of recent school reports. Further information may be obtained from The Head of Admissions, Mrs Nuria Sanz, nuria.sanz@kingsgroup.org.

Fees per term (2018–2019). €2,592–€4,164 excluding transport.

Senior School. At the age of fifteen, at the end of National Curriculum Year 10, pupils transfer to King's College in Soto de Viñuelas to complete their final three years of study. (*See King's College entry in HMC section.*)

King's Infant School, Chamartín

Calle Prieto Ureña 9–11, Madrid 28016, Spain

Tel:	00 34 913 505 843
email:	info.chamartin@kingscollege.es
website:	www.kingscollegeschools.org
Twitter:	@KISChamartin
Facebook:	@Kings-Infant-School-Chamartin
LinkedIn:	/King's Infant School, Chamartín

Headteacher: **Rachel Davies**, BA Hons, QTS, NPQSL

Deputy Headteacher: Gavin Murray, BA Hons History of Decorative Arts and Crafts, PGCE

Head of Admissions: Beatriz Eparaza

Age Range. 3–7 Co-educational.
Number of Pupils. 165.

King's Infant School is a co-educational day school for pupils from Nursery to Year 2 (age 3–7) based in the Chamartín area of Madrid city centre. Chamartín was the original site of the first King's College school opened in 1969. Today King's Infant School is one of nine schools in the King's Group.

The Headteacher of Chamartín is an overseas member of IAPS and King's Infant School is also a member of COBIS.

The school is governed by the King's Group Board of Directors and the School Council. These governing bodies are composed of distinguished members from the business and academic communities.

The Vision of King's Infant School, like its sister schools in King's Group, is to "Be at the forefront of British Education Internationally". The Group's Mission is to provide high-quality British education that delivers a transformative learning experience to all our pupils.

Location. The school occupies a modern, well-equipped and compact campus which caters ideally for young learners. It is well connected by road and public transport and is just a short walk from the nearest Metro station. There is an optional bus service for pupils to and from school which covers the city of Madrid and its outlying residential areas. All routes are supervised by a bus monitor.

Facilities. All classrooms are bright and spacious with high-quality resources and technology to encourage interactive learning. Classrooms are also fully air-conditioned in order to keep pupils cool in the hot summer months.

On-site facilities include:
- Covered play areas for use during summer and winter
- Extended outdoor play areas for Nursery and Reception class
- Mini football and netball pitch
- Music room
- SMART boards in every classroom (Reception–Year 2); IWB for use in Nursery class

Curriculum. Teachers deliver a broad and balanced curriculum, based on the English National Curriculum, and encourage pupils to put effort into all that they undertake academically, culturally and physically. King's Infant School caters for children of a variety of nationalities. There are 10 UK qualified staff, one of whom is a Spanish language teacher, as well as 7 Teaching Assistants and an Educational Psychologist. There are Induction English Classes for children who need to improve their English. There are also Beginners Spanish Classes for international children joining the school. All pupils learn Spanish.

Activities. The school boasts an array of extracurricular activities to complement those already catered for within the curriculum. Pupils are encouraged to explore their capabilities in the areas of music and the arts from a very early age. Sport plays an important role at the school and pupils are encouraged to take part in activity days to build cooperation and confidence in addition to their normal PE classes.

Optional classes include chess, ballet, judo, modern dance, football, skating, Chinese, swimming and tuition in various musical instruments, as well as performing arts.

Admissions. Parents and pupils are invited to meet with the Head of Admissions and the Headteacher on their visit to the school.

Fees per term (2018–2019). €2,592–€2,914 excluding transport.

At the age of seven, at the end of National Curriculum Year 2, pupils transfer to one of two sister schools in Madrid: King's College, Soto de Viñuelas which caters for pupils from Pre-Nursery to Year 13 (age 2 to 18) or alternatively to King's College School, La Moraleja which caters for pupils from Nursery to Year 9 (age 3 to 15). If pupils transfer to La Moraleja, they will later join the main site in Soto de Viñuelas from Year 10 in order to continue their studies leading to IGCSE, GCE AS and A Level examinations. (*See separate entry for King's College School, La Moraleja in IAPS section and King's College's entry in HMC section.*)

Pembroke House

P.O. Box 31, Gilgil 20116, Kenya

Tel:	+254 727108567
	+254 202312323
email:	headmaster@pembrokehouse.sc.ke
website:	www.pembrokehouse.sc.ke

Chairman of Council: Mr Richard Vigne

Headmaster: **Mr Jason Brown**

Age Range. 1–13.
Number of Pupils. 111 boy boarders, 113 girl boarders + Pre-Prep who are day pupils
Fees per term (2018–2019). Nursery Kshs 84,488, Reception Kshs 157,712, Year 1 Kshs 363,300, Year 2 Kshs 581,280, Year 3 to 8 Kshs 726,600 (£654–£5,622).

The school was founded in 1927 and is presently owned and administered by the Kenya Educational Trust Limited. It is situated in over 40 hectares of well-maintained grounds in the Rift Valley at 2,000 metres elevation and is 120 kms from Nairobi. The climate is sunny throughout the year affording many opportunities for an extensive education.

Facilities include a Science Lab, Chapel, Theatre, Swimming Pool, Music School, Library, Art and Design Technology Centre, Computer Room, two Squash Courts and Tennis Courts, access to a neighbouring Golf Course, and a multi-purpose Sports Hall, Stables, Meeting Room and Café. The school has a well-equipped Surgery on site.

The main sports are Cricket, Hockey, Rugby, Rounders and Netball with Tennis, Swimming, Athletics, Squash, Golf, Horse Riding, Sailing, Football and Taekwondo on offer as well.

A full range of clubs and various extras, including individual music instruction, are also offered. Drama is strong with several productions put on each year. The school also has a vibrant and varied weekend programme to support the full boarding ethos of the school. This involves camping and other outdoor pursuits as well as many team building and leadership activities.

Children are admitted from five years as full boarders and are prepared, through the British Curriculum, for the ISEB Common Entrance Examinations which qualifies them for entry to Independent Senior Schools in the UK and South Africa as well as Kenyan schools. The school usually gains numerous academic scholarships and awards each year in addition to music and sports awards. The Learning Support facilities at Pembroke House have been developed over many years and now provide essential help for those who require such assistance. The school currently has children from seven different countries including the United Kingdom.

The average number of pupils in each form is approximately 14, and there is a pupil-teacher ratio of six students per teacher. There are also three qualified Nurses, a Cateress, an Estate Manager, Registrar and a Bursar. Pembroke has a reputation for producing outstanding pupils. The Headmaster and the staff work together to produce kind, well-mannered, balanced children with integrity and courage who try their best at all times. This is the best preparation a child can have.

Peponi House

PO Box 23203, Lower Kabete, Nairobi 00604, Kenya
Tel: 00 254 20 2585710–712, 734881255,
               722202947
email: secretary@peponihouse.sc.ke
website: www.peponischool.org
Facebook: @peponihouseschool

Headmaster: **Mr R J Blake**, BSc Hons, PGCE, NPQH

   Age Range. 6–13.
   Number of Pupils. 370 boys and girls, all day.
   Fees per annum (2018–2019). Kshs 1,896,855.
   Founded in 1986, Peponi House has grown to become one of the leading preparatory schools in East Africa. The attractive and spacious site in Lower Kabete houses all that a thriving prep school requires to get the very best out of the children, both in and out of the classroom. An ambitious building programme has started that will provide the finest school accommodation and that will reflect the school's forward-thinking curriculum. The school was rated as 'outstanding' in all respects in an inspection carried out in February 2018 by SIS.
   We are a multi-cultural community which encourages respect for self and others. Our emphasis is on excellence, through a broad, balanced education which aims to maximise the potential of each pupil as a whole person. To this end, we have outstanding facilities including a 25-metre swimming pool, three hard tennis courts, purpose-built Art and Design Technology rooms and networked PCs in all rooms. Our wireless network now covers the whole site, with excellent bandwidth. In 2017, tablets were introduced, with all children having access to either iPads or LearnPads. A learning platform, also introduced in 2017, allows for clarity of communication between home and school. We have two fully-equipped science laboratories and a new music school. Two new classrooms dedicated to History and Geography opened recently, with a senior RS room. The recently refurbished school library and Computing room occupy an area that is central to the school both geographically and philosophically. These facilities help to complement the excellent work that the children and staff carry out in the well-resourced classrooms. Our extensive use of interactive whiteboards has resulted in the school being elected as a SMART Showcase School.

Whilst always striving for academic excellence, it is central to Peponi's philosophy that education is not limited to the classroom. In addition to the numerous scholarships to senior schools that our pupils have won in the last three years, we have had notable successes in sport, music, art and drama. Peponi teams have won competitions at a national level, with many individuals going on to represent their country.

We follow the British National Curriculum but this is seen very much as a framework for extension. In addition to the core subjects of Literacy, Numeracy, Science and Computing, pupils in the Junior School (Years 2 to 4) also have lessons in Music, PE and Games, Swimming, Kiswahili, Art and DT, tennis and, from Year 3, French. Junior children are taught these subjects by specialist teachers while the class teachers deliver the core subjects and humanities. All children are taught in a way that best suits their individual needs and some children do require additional support. This is carried out by our Learning Support teachers who will help children either individually or in small groups, but mainly through integrated support in the classroom. Our special needs teachers also play a vital role in advising colleagues as to the strengths and weaknesses of particular children so that teaching can be differentiated to suit everyone.

In Year 5, children are taught Humanities and English by their form teachers, who also play a vital pastoral role in preparing the children for life in the senior school. In Year 6, all subjects are delivered by subject specialists. The sciences are taught separately and there is an option for children to study Kiswahili, Spanish or Latin.

We also have a wide and varied range of extra-curricular activities. The whole school joins in the Activity Programme on Friday afternoons, with children from all year groups taking part in activities together. On Mondays, children in Years 5 to 8 take part in HOTS: higher order thinking skills activities.

Our music department flourishes in its own purpose-built accommodation. In addition to weekly class music lessons, the children have the opportunity to play in the orchestra or in one of the ensembles, or sing in either the Junior or Senior Choir. As well as the two major school concerts during the year, all children have the opportunity to perform in front of their peers and parents at our termly "Tea-Time Concerts". The Carol Service and Peponi Schools Concert offer other chances for our choirs to perform and all the children are encouraged to take part in the plays that are staged in December, March and June.

We have children from many different cultures and ethnic backgrounds and we encourage understanding and above all respect for each other. We are a Christian School and the ethos of "Love one another" is a recurring theme in our Monday Assemblies, but we are proud of our multi-faith society where children learn to appreciate and value their differences as well as their similarities.

The school's motto "A School of Many Nations, a Family of One" encapsulates all that we hold most dear. First and foremost, we are a school and the academic side of things lies at the heart of all that we do. However, we are also a family and that makes itself very clear in the day to day life of the school. We have an open door policy with our parents and encourage them to be very active in their support of what we do, either through our energetic PTA or through close consultation with the staff.

At Peponi House, we believe that our role as educators is to give our children the best possible foundation for what lies ahead. We are, after all, a preparatory school and excellent preparation is what we set out to achieve. By the time they leave us, our pupils will be confident young adults who are ready to face the future with poise and self-belief.

The Roman Ridge School

No. 8 Onyasia Crescent, Roman Ridge, Accra, Ghana

Tel: 00 233 302 780456/780457
Fax: 00 233 302 780458
email: enquiries@theromanridgeschool.com
website: www.theromanridgeschool.com

Postal Address:
PO Box GP 21057, Accra, Ghana

Co-educational Day School.

Governors:
Chairman: Dr Frank B Adu Jnr, BA Hons, MBA
Chair, Academic Board: Revd Dr Joyce Aryee, BA Hons,
    PG Cert Public Administration

Principal: **Mrs Valerie Mainoo**, BSc Psych, MA Ed

Head of Middle School: Mr Kwamena Burah
Head of JUnior School: Ms Gloria Dakwa

Age Range. 4–18.
Numbers of Pupils. 241 Boys, 283 Girls.
Fees per term (2018–2019). Junior School (Reception–Class 6): US$1,600; Senior School (Forms 1–5) US$1,900; Sixth Form US$2,000.

Established in September 2002, The Roman Ridge School aims to provide the very best of British Education whilst being firmly rooted in Ghanaian life and culture. The school is a unique facility in Ghana as it offers small class sizes (20), individual pupil attention, a family atmosphere, firm discipline, emphasis on good manners, a sound Christian foundation, a caring environment and a full programme of Sports and extra-curricular activities.

The school is noted for its Individual Learning Programmes and its Special Needs Programmes as well as its dedication to all other pupils including the high ability learners and scholars. Pupils are carefully monitored and assessed regularly in order to achieve academic success, and, parents are encouraged to help in this process.

All teaching is initially based on the English National Curriculum for the Foundation Course and Key Stage One, after which the pupils progress to the 11+ examination, then take the full range of academic subjects at the 13+ Common Entrance & the IGCSE Courses with the Cambridge Board. The school runs a thriving AS & A Level programme and offers a comprehensive range of Courses.

There are thirty classrooms at present, three ICT suites, a Multimedia Centre with a Language lab, two up-to-date Libraries with full audio-visual facilities, E-Learning facilities, junior & senior Science Labs, a Dance Studio, two Art Rooms and sporting facilities. A clinic is on site staffed by a qualified SRN.

Pupils play Football, Basketball, Volleyball, Netball, Hockey and Rounders and also enjoy a very successful Swimming programme. Pupils also benefit from an extensive extra-curricular programme which includes Karate, Ballet, Tennis, Drama Club and a highly successful Choir programme, which includes a Parent Choir. School productions and concerts take place at the end of each term.

The school also runs an excellent internal and external Community Literacy Programme, with Senior Pupils spearheading reading programmes for all age groups.

The school is open on Saturdays for extra work and pupil support programmes, swimming, games, music lessons, art and computer clubs, and special events.

Pupils thrive in The Roman Ridge School and are reluctant to go home at the end of the day.

St Andrew's Preparatory School

Private Bag, Molo 20106, Kenya

Tel: +254 202025708
          +254 735337736
email: officeprep@turimail.co.ke
website: www.standrewsturi.com

Chair of Governors: Mr Mike Moragia

Headmaster: **Mr Fergus Llewellyn**, BA

Age Range. 3–13.
Number of Pupils. 250: 126 Boys, 124 Girls.
Fees per term (2018–2019). Boarding: Kshs 606,500–766,600. Day: Kshs 319,200–498,300.

St Andrew's Preparatory School, Turi, is an international, multicultural, Christian boarding school offering British Curriculum education of the highest standard. The School aims to provide a happy, stimulating, well-rounded educational experience for children. Pupils are encouraged to grow into well-educated, confident, self-disciplined young adults with the potential to be future leaders.

The Prep School together with its Senior School is situated 200 km north west of Nairobi on a beautiful 300-acre estate at an altitude of over 2,000 metres, where the climate is both healthy and invigorating. The School has its own private airstrip within the grounds.

Boarding pupils are accepted from the age of 5 and follow the British National Curriculum and then the Common Entrance Syllabus which prepares them for entry to St Andrew's Senior School and to other independent senior schools in Britain or elsewhere.

The original School, founded in 1931, was destroyed by fire in 1944. It was completely rebuilt and is superbly designed and equipped as a modern purpose-built preparatory school. There are subject rooms for English, Mathematics, French, History, Geography and Science laboratories. Information Technology is an integral part of the curriculum throughout the School with two ICT suites and most classrooms are equipped with interactive whiteboards and data projectors. An exceptionally large Hall is used for plays, concerts and large functions. The average size of classes is 16.

Sports form a key part of school life at St Andrew's School. The grounds and playing fields are extensive. Boys play cricket and rugby; girls play rounders and netball; all play football, hockey, tennis and take part in athletics and cross country. In the newly-opened sports centre there are excellent facilities for a wide range of indoor sports including two glass-backed squash courts and a fitness suite. There are seven school tennis courts and a heated swimming pool, as well as a riding school on site where pupils of all abilities are taught by qualified instructors.

The School has a strong musical tradition. In addition to the many and varied opportunities for music within the curriculum over 80 pupils opt for specialist instrumental tuition in a wide range of instruments. Many of these pupils work towards ABRSM examinations. There are also several specialist music groups who practice and perform together and the Junior and Senior choirs.

A large and well-equipped Art Studio as well as Design Technology and Food Technology rooms allow pupils to express themselves creatively. A wealth of arts and crafts, hobbies and outdoor pursuits are actively encouraged. The School has its own Chapel and aims to give a practical Christian education in a community with high standards and in a supportive family atmosphere.

All staff live within the estate. The teaching staff are all qualified and are committed to the Christian ethos of the School.

St Andrew's Senior School offers a three-year course to IGCSE examinations with excellent academic results, and thereafter students can opt for A Levels at the incorporated St Andrew's College. The School has the same Board of Governors, but its own Headmaster, teaching staff and Management Team.

St Paul's School

Rua Juquiá 166, Jardim Paulistano, São Paulo SP 01440–903, Brazil

Tel:	00 55 11 3087 3399
Fax:	00 55 11 3087 3398
email:	www.stpauls.br/contact
website:	www.stpauls.br
Twitter:	@Head_StPaulsSP
Facebook:	@St-Pauls-School
LinkedIn:	/St-Pauls-School-Sao-Paulo

Chairman of the Board of Governors: Mr Anthony Jezzi

Head: Ms Louise Simpson

Deputy Head: Mr James Diver
Senior Master: Dr Barry Hallinan
Head of Preparatory School: Miss Jassi Grewal
Head of Pre-Preparatory School: Ms Amy Clifford

Age Range. 3–18.
Number of Pupils. 1,109: Pre-Preparatory 232, Preparatory 378, Senior 499.
Fees per annum (2017–2018). R$78,000–R$98,400.

St Paul's School was founded in 1926 and was the first British School in São Paulo. Fully co-educational, with some 1,100 pupils, aged from 3 to 18, it is a school with history and tradition, but which embraces innovation, contemporary values and technological developments. We offer a British curriculum, including the International Primary Curriculum (IPC) and courses up to IGCSE and the International Baccalaureate Diploma. At IB the following subjects are taught in the Sixth Form (and offered as standard and higher levels): Brazilian social studies, English, Portuguese, Spanish, French, mathematics, mathematical studies, physics, chemistry, biology, computer science, geography, environmental systems and societies, film studies, history, economics, business management, theatre, visual arts, and music.

The school prides itself on an excellent enrichment programme ranging from MUN to Duke of Edinburgh's Award, from knitting classes to a robotics programme, from mathematical olympiads to outstanding drama and music. Field trips also form an integral part of the curriculum with every year group from the age of 8 years old going on residential visits throughout Brazil and beyond.

We prepare our pupils within a bilingual and bicultural Anglo-Brazilian community for a global future. We offer a broad and balanced but rigorous curriculum where the individual pupil is at the heart of the teaching and learning. It is our aim to discover the passion and talents of every pupil, and create the right environment to develop these. Pupils leave us confident, assured and well prepared for an exciting life, and a multitude of opportunities, often at top universities.

We are a world-class school; a member of HMC and COBIS and the first officially British government accredited British School Overseas in South America. We are proud of our local, national and international reputation and we constantly strive to improve the opportunities for our pupils and staff.

The school has undertaken an almost continuous programme of building works over the past 20 years as it has gradually grown; this includes extensive refurbishment and extension of the original school building, the creation of a sixth form centre and a multimillion dollar underground state-of-the-art sports centre. In 2016 we celebrated 90 years of excellent education by opening the Queen Elizabeth II academic centre, which houses a learning resources suite, art centre, music recording facilities, and 10 modern science laboratories.

St Saviour's School, Ikoyi
Lagos, Nigeria

54 Alexander Avenue, Ikoyi, Lagos, Nigeria

Tel:	00 234 1 8990153
Fax:	00 234 1 2700255
email:	info@stsavioursschikoyi.org
website:	www.stsavioursschikoyi.org

St Saviour's is an Associate Member of COBIS.

Chairman of Board of Trustees: Mr L N Mbanefo, SAN

Head Teacher: Mr Craig Heaton, BA Hons

Age Range. 4–11 Co-educational.
Number of Pupils. 320.
Fees per term (2017–2018). Naira 944,725.

A truly rounded education is a preparation for life. Grounded on our core values, St Saviour's seeks to provide an education that is challenging, relevant, exciting and delivered in a caring and thoroughly professional manner. We look, unashamedly, for academic achievement in each pupil alongside equal progress in spiritual growth, friendship, independence, confidence and some appreciation of their place in the world and their responsibilities towards others.

Christian principles are integrated into the daily life of the school which is an Anglican foundation. Children of a number of denominations and faiths attend the school and are warmly welcomed. Parents are welcomed as part of the learning cycle; communication with them is regular and their support of the school is exceptional.

The development of the whole child is at the heart of education at St Saviour's. Learning is about developing personal, emotional and social skills as well as being an intellectual and academic process. We aim to help children find their voice – their own unique, personal significance. We encourage them to think about what their contribution will be in the world – how they will try to make a difference as responsible and engaged members of the School community as well as citizens of the world.

St Saviour's has high expectations for all its learners. We pride ourselves on knowing each child as an individual in order to help them make progress. Teachers plan to scaffold success for all learners from their point of entry. This means that learning opportunities are planned so that all students are challenged appropriately, sometimes by providing work that is a little too hard and then providing support systems to enable students to work through their difficulties to achieve success.

Above all, we are interested in the learning process – learning how to learn and how to apply skills and knowledge across an ever-increasing spectrum of experience. From the earliest age we ensure that children have an enjoyable experience of school and are motivated to learn and improve. This positive attitude is supported by a team of highly professional teachers who are themselves engaged in lifelong learning and model effective habits of mind. The curriculum is based on that of the National Curriculum for England and Wales and the International Primary Curriculum adapted to reflect the needs of an increasingly international and multicultural student body We aim to build on the children's background knowledge and experience to equip them with the skills, strategies and a love of learning that will inspire them to succeed whatever the next step on their educational journey.

The school has developed and renewed its own sports facilities over the past few years and now has its own 25m swimming pool and extensive sports field, including football pitch and running track as well as informal play areas. Routinely, about 30 extracurricular Clubs operate after school each week and they are very well supported. Events such as Assemblies, Independence Day, Foundation, KS1 and KS2 Productions, Sports Day, International Week, Flower Show, Fun Day and Harvest Festival add greatly to the school's character. Our support of local orphanages flows from monies raised at some of these events.

Pupils leave the school from Y6 to attend leading Secondary schools in Nigeria and approximately 40% move on to outstanding independent schools in the UK, where they prove to be excellent ambassadors of the holistic education they have received at St Saviour's.

Tanglin Trust School

95 Portsdown Road, Singapore 139299

Tel: 00 65 6778 0771
email: admissions@tts.edu.sg
website: www.tts.edu.sg
Twitter: @TanglinTrust
Facebook: @TanglinTrustSchool
LinkedIn: /tanglin-trust-school

Chair of Governors: Mr Jonathan Robinson

Chief Executive Officer: Mr Craig Considine [HMC]

Head of Infant School: Mrs Paula Craigie [IAPS]
Head of Junior School: Mrs Clair Harrington-Wilcox
[IAPS]
Head of Senior School: Mr Allan Forbes

Age Range. Nursery through to Sixth Form (3–18 years).
Number of Pupils. 2,800 across Infant, Junior, Senior Schools.
Fees per term (2018–2019). S$8,982–S$14,857.
Curriculum. English National Curriculum, A Levels and IB Diploma.

Building on strong foundations. Founded in 1925, Tanglin Trust School provides a unique learning environment to 2,800 students from over 50 different nationalities. We strive to make every individual feel valued, happy and successful. Responsibility, enthusiasm and participation are actively encouraged. We set high expectations whilst offering strong support, resulting in a community of lifelong learners who can contribute with confidence to our world.

Broad and Balanced Curriculum. The English National Curriculum provides the basis for the programmes of study, which are enhanced and enriched to reflect the school's international setting. We are the only school in Singapore to offer both A Levels and the IB Diploma, allowing students to choose a pathway that is best suited to them and

their individual strengths. We have a specialist team of teachers, school counsellors and careers and university guidance counsellors who support and guide students and their parents in making this important choice. A globally recognised, prestigious international school, Tanglin students go on to many of the top universities in the world, with 92% receiving their first choice in 2018.

The Arts. Tanglin has a thriving and vibrant Arts programme with a variety of creative and collaborative opportunities available to our students. Alongside annual showcases, Tanglin also hosts one-off events involving schools across the region.

Sports. Our excellent sporting facilities enable us to provide a wide range of competitive and non-competitive events throughout the year. We also compete in a wide variety of tournaments in Singapore and overseas.

Languages. We encourage a love of languages and an appreciation of cultures. Core languages taught are French, Mandarin and Spanish.

Beyond the Classroom. We firmly believe that children are just as likely to learn outside of the classroom as in it. Our curriculum is enhanced through a multitude of opportunities to inspire including outdoor education trips, special days, service learning and a wide range of co-curricular activities that stimulate and broaden student experience.

Entry. Students entering the school must be fluent in English, residing in Singapore with at least one parent and be able to access the curriculum independently. Prospective students may be required to sit admissions assessments.

Not-For-Profit. Tanglin is a not-for-profit organisation and is registered as an educational charity. All tuition fees go towards the provision of an outstanding education.

Culture. At Tanglin, we create an environment where learning can grow and flourish, and we inspire every individual to be the best they can be. Everyone at Tanglin gets a chance to shine, whether it be in sports, arts or academia. Our students' achievements are celebrated at all levels, in all they do, and lasting values are created.

PART V
Schools whose Heads are members of the Independent Schools Association

ALPHABETICAL LIST OF SCHOOLS

The following schools, whose Heads are members of both ISA and HMC, can be found in the HMC section:

The Grange School	Lingfield College
Ibstock Place School	Princethorpe College
Leighton Park School	

The following schools, whose Heads are members of both ISA and GSA, can be found in the GSA section:

Adcote School	St Dominic's Grammar School
Alderley Edge School for Girls	St James Senior Girls' School
Cranford House	St Mary's School
St Catherine's School	

The following schools, whose Heads are members of both ISA and The Society of Heads, can be found in The Society of Heads section:

Abbey Gate College	Pitsford School
Bedstone College	Portland Place School
Bredon School	Reddam House Berkshire
Derby Grammar School	St Edward's School
Highclare School	St James Senior Boys' School
Kingsley School	Stafford Grammar School
Luckley House School	Tring Park School for the Performing Arts
LVS Ascot	Trinity School
Mount House School	

The following schools, whose Heads are members of both ISA and IAPS, can be found in the IAPS section:

Abercorn School	Lyonsdown School
Alleyn Court Preparatory School	Monmouth School Girls' Prep
Birchfield School	Mylnhurst Preparatory School & Nursery
Collingwood School	Newbridge Preparatory School
Crackley Hall School	Oakfield Preparatory School
Crescent School	The Old School Henstead
Cumnor House School	Reddiford School
Duke of Kent School	Rosemead Preparatory School and Nursery
Gatehouse School	St Edward's Preparatory School
The Hampshire School, Chelsea	St James Prep School
Holme Grange School	St Mary's School, Hampstead
Knightsbridge School	St Michael's Preparatory School
Lady Barn House School	St Olave's Prep School
Langley Preparatory School at Taverham Hall	The Study Preparatory School
Leehurst Swan School	Wilmslow Preparatory School
Littlegarth School	

ISA
GEOGRAPHICAL LIST OF SCHOOLS

Individual School Entries

Abbey College Manchester
Alpha Plus Group Limited

5–7 Cheapside, King Street, Manchester M2 4WG

Tel: 0161 817 2700
Fax: 0161 817 2705
email: admin@abbeymanchester.co.uk
website: www.abbeymanchester.co.uk
Twitter: @AbbeyManchester
Facebook: @AbbeyCollegeManchester

Principal: **Ms L Elam**

Age Range. 15–19.
Number of Pupils. 210.
One Year GCSE, Two Year A Level, One Year A Level Retake and Combined Studies Programme
An independent day school with a college environment

- Year 11, Lower Sixth and Upper Sixth entry
- Very small classes (a maximum of 12 students in each) ensure excellent progress
- Unique one year GCSEs and A Levels for those sitting for the first time or retaking
- A Combined Studies Programme, which is an alternative to A Level and is now accepted by several universities
- High levels of personal support and individual responsibility gives good preparation for university life
- Expert advice is delivered for entry onto all university courses leading to strong relationships with the top universities in Britain
- City centre location means students will benefit from the unlimited arts, business, science, sports and music resources on offer

Flexible learning programmes mean that students can join at any time during the academic year, not just September.

Fees per annum (2018–2019). Year 12 (A Level or Combined Studies) £12,950; Year 13 (A Level or Combined Studies) £12,950; One Year A Level (1 subject) £6,750; One Year A Level (2 subjects) £12,950; Year 11 (GCSE – up to 6 subjects) £12,500.

Fees are inclusive of exam fees.

Abbots Bromley School

High Street, Abbots Bromley, Staffordshire WS15 3BW

Tel: 01283 840232
email: head@abbotsbromleyschool.com
website: www.abbotsbromleyschool.com
Twitter: @AbbotsBromley
Facebook: @abbotsbromleyschool

Chair of Governors: Mrs P Norvall, Cert Ed

Headmaster: **Mr R Udy**, BSc Hons, PGCE

Head of International College: Mrs A Johnson, BA Hons, Cert Ed, Cert Prof St Ed
Head of Preparatory School: Mrs W Gordon, BEd Hons

Abbots Bromley is a thriving boarding and day school for girls and boys aged 3 to 18. Internationally known as a centre of excellence for the creative arts, creativity flows through every facet of the school. From our individualised student-centred teaching to our holistic approach to pastoral care, creativity and passion is evident in everything we do. Set in safe and extensive grounds in the Staffordshire countryside, we are only forty minutes away from Birmingham International Airport.

Abbots Bromley is unique in offering a well-rounded academic education partnered with world-class training in classical ballet and outstanding teaching in music, modern dance, art, musical theatre and equestrian studies.

Beyond the curriculum. Dedicated and well-qualified teachers instil a love of academic learning, inspiring our students to exceed their own expectations. This academic focus is complemented by an ever-increasing range of enrichment opportunities, ensuring all aspects of our students' talents are encouraged to blossom. Our supportive Christian environment nurtures students of all faiths, and enables them to contribute confidently and usefully to society.

Outstanding Pastoral Care. Boarding life is integral to the school, and is a true home from home, with our pastoral care emulating and complementing parental care. Experienced members of staff ensure that our students are both nourished and allowed to flourish. Our catchment covers local, National and International students, and even local students choose to board.

Creativity, Courage, Compassion. It is an exciting time for the school as we expand. As we are now co-educational, we are perfectly placed to offer both boys and girls this caring and creative opportunity to contribute to the thriving Abbots Bromley School Community. At the end of their time at Abbots Bromley, we send out creative, courageous and compassionate young adults ready to play their part on an International stage.

Fees per term (2018–2019). UK Students: Full Boarding £7,177–£8,832, Weekly Boarding £5,850–£7,400, Day £1,551–£5,273. International Students: Full Boarding £8,048–£9,907.

Scholarships. Abbots Bromley offers a variety of scholarships for entry into years 7, 9 and 12. Awards are available for academic, art, dance, equestrian, modern foreign languages (French or Spanish), music, performing arts (either musical theatre or drama) and sport. Academic scholarships carry a maximum remission on academic tuition fees of 10%. All other scholarships carry a remission of up to 5% on academic tuition fees. Some disciplines may also offer additional benefits such as a value towards the cost of materials or specialist lessons.

Charitable status. Abbots Bromley School Ltd is a Registered Charity, number 1103321.

Abingdon House School
Cavendish Education Group

Broadley Terrace, London NW1 6LG

Tel: 020 3750 5526
email: ahs@abingdonhouseschool.co.uk
website: www.abingdonhouseschool.co.uk
Twitter: @Abingdon_House

Headteacher: Ms Tanya Moran

Deputy Headteacher: Mr Matt Archer
Assistant Headteacher: Mr James Banfield
Head of SEN: Ms Susannah Harris
Senior Administrator, Marketing and Admissions: Mrs Claire Essien
Senior Administrator, Finance and Compliance: Mrs Karen Franklin
Senior Administrator, Head of HR: Ms Jenny Fromer

Age Range. 5–16 Co-educational.

Number of Pupils. 62.

Fees per term (2018–2019). £10,750.

Abingdon House School is located in a refurbished Victorian building in London NW1 on four levels with facilities to educate up to 90 pupils aged between 5–16 years of age (Years 1–11). The school has specific expertise in the education of children who have Specific Learning Difficulties. This includes children with Dyslexia, Dyspraxia, Dyscalculia, Social Communication difficulties and associated learning needs.

The school provides a warm, nurturing environment in which the specific individual learning needs of our pupils are addressed through a multi-disciplinary approach. We provide an integrated, whole-school approach to meeting the needs of pupils who are diagnosed with a specific learning difficulty. When diagnosed early in their education, children generally respond well to intense intervention for a period of time, after which it is anticipated they would be able to return to the mainstream.

Effective learning and teaching is based on understanding a child's individual needs, nurturing a child's academic and social development and caring for a child's well-being. The environment is therefore warm and friendly and we are committed to each child's holistic development.

We aim to prepare the children for a return to mainstream schooling through:

- The provision of a holistic and individually tailored education programme.
- A whole-school teaching regime of small classes with teaching assistants, therapists and trained staff using a range of teaching strategies and therapeutic interventions. There is an appropriately low pupil to teacher ratio. Many pupils have integrated successfully into various London day schools.
- Developing, monitoring and implementing an IEP (Individual Education Plan) for each pupil, which details SMART (Specific, Measurable, Achievable, Realistic and Timely) targets and describes the strategies and supports required to achieve those targets.
- Monitoring pupil progress through a rigorous system of assessment and tracking.
- Implementing a consistent system of positive behaviour support.
- Facilitating pupil-centred active learning.
- Placing special emphasis on the development of literacy and numeracy, social skills, language and communication and coordination, sequencing and movement.

Effort and achievement are praised and rewarded to build self-esteem. Merits and stickers are awarded daily. Certificates and rosettes are awarded each week. Pupils are given the opportunity for their efforts and achievements to be recognised and celebrated on a regular basis culminating in an end-of-term Musical Performance and Prize Giving.

We offer a full curriculum. PE/Games take place on a weekly basis at school and in local community facilities. Reading, Literacy and Maths lessons are ability grouped to enable pupils to progress as soon as they are ready. After-school clubs are offered several times a week, for example, ICT, Music, Games and Swimming.

We value teamwork and the partnership between parents and staff. Parent/Teacher meetings are held several times a term. Special Provision staff are available in weekly drop-in sessions.

ACS Cobham International School

Heywood House, Portsmouth Road, Cobham, Surrey KT11 1BL

Tel:	01932 867251
Fax:	01932 869791
email:	cobadmissions@acs-schools.com
website:	www.acs-schools.com/acs-cobham
Twitter:	@ACSintschools
Facebook:	@ACSCobham
LinkedIn:	/ACS-International-Schools-Ltd

Head of School: Simon Leyshon

Age Range. 2–18.

Number in School. Day: 723 Boys, 643 Girls; 153 Boarders.

Fees per annum (2018–2019). Tuition: £7,750–£27,110. Boarding (including tuition fees): 5-Day £38,810–£41,570 (grades 7–12); 7-Day £44,170–£46,930 (grades 7–12).

ACS Cobham is a co-educational school for 1400 students aged 2–18 and 300 expert faculty and staff, representing over 70 nationalities.

The success of the programme at ACS Cobham is based on teamwork, collaboration, and the broad participation of its international community. All students are treated as unique individuals, with equal potential to make a positive contribution to the school. The goal is to instil an enthusiasm for lifelong learning and a sense of global awareness in each student, along with the necessary skills to prepare them for the challenges and changes which lie ahead.

Academic Programme. The academic programme offers both the International Baccalaureate (IB) Diploma and Advanced Placement (AP) courses, creating a curriculum that meets the needs of a broad international student body. ACS graduates have established a tradition of attaining excellent exam results, enabling them to continue their studies at top universities around the world, including the US and UK.

Facilities. Situated on 128 acres approximately 30 minutes by train from Central London, ACS Cobham enrols over 1,400 students. Exceptional facilities include an Early Childhood village; purpose-built Lower, Middle, and High School buildings; gymnasium and cafeteria complex and two world-class boarding houses. All Lower, Middle and High School buildings have separate classrooms, science labs, libraries, computer labs, art and music studios and access to the school's state-of-the-art Interactive Learning Centre.

Enrichment activities. ACS Cobham offers extensive and varied extracurricular clubs and community service activities both locally and internationally, which encourage students to participate in the richness of school life. Students also participate in international theatre arts programmes, maths, literature and music competitions in the UK and across Europe.

Sports. The campus sports programme runs three seasons fielding teams in football, volleyball, cross country, basketball, rugby, swimming, dance, tennis, track & field, baseball, softball and golf. Sports facilities include six tennis courts, an Olympic-sized track, playing fields for football, rugby and baseball, a six-hole golf course, and a Sports Centre with 25-metre competition indoor swimming pool, basketball/volleyball show courts, dance and fitness studios, and a café.

Boarding at ACS Cobham. Over the past 2 years there has been a £10 million investment in a brand new Boarding House, Woodlands as well as the development of our Fields Boarding house to the same standard. Both houses offer premium accommodation and a multicultural ethos that celebrates the diverse student body we serve. The Dormitory provides a home-away-from-home for up to 160 students, aged 12–18. Boarders have single and two-person rooms with ensuite facilities and wireless internet connections; there are student lounges, kitchens, computer and study rooms. Six full-time Dormitory houseparents and over ten resident teaching staff ensure an active yet well-considered programme of pastoral care, friendship and advisor groups, house activities and weekend trips.

Accreditation. ACS Cobham is accredited by the New England Association of Schools and Colleges (NEASC) and is authorised by the International Baccalaureate (IB) to offer the International Baccalaureate Diploma Programme (IBDP). The school holds memberships in the US College Board Advanced Placement (AP) Program, the European Council of International Schools (ECIS), the Council of International Schools (CIS) and the Independent Schools Association (ISA).

Four schools, one world class education. ACS Cobham is part of ACS International Schools. Founded in 1967 to serve the needs of international and local families, ACS International Schools now educates 3,500 students up to age 18, from more than 70 countries, at three London area campuses in England and one in Doha, Qatar.

Contact the Admissions team. The admissions team is available throughout the year to answer questions, book campus visits, and assist families through the enrolment process. Students are accepted in all grades throughout the year, on non-selective criteria.

ACS Egham International School

Woodlee, London Road (A30), Egham, Surrey TW20 0HS

Tel: 01784 430800
Fax: 01784 430626
email: eghamadmissions@acs-schools.com
website: www.acs-schools.com/acs-egham
Twitter: @ACSEgham
Facebook: @ACSEgham
LinkedIn: /ACS-International-Schools-Ltd

Head of School: **Mr Jeremy Lewis**

Age Range. 4–18.
Number in School. Day only: 323 Boys, 281 Girls.
Fees per annum (2018–2019). Tuition: £10,870–£25,360.

Situated on a 20-acre campus 25 miles from central London, ACS Egham is an IB World School for over 600 students (aged 4 to 18), and 160 expert faculty and staff from over 50 countries.

Academic Programmes. ACS Egham is an International Baccalaureate World School and the only school in the UK to offer all four IB programmes: the IB Primary Years (IBPYP), the Middle Years (IBMYP) and IB Diploma (IBDP) Programmes, as well as the IB Career-related Programme (IBCP).

These programmes share a common philosophy and characteristics: they develop the whole student, helping them to grow socially, physically, aesthetically, and culturally; and provide a broad and balanced education that includes science and the humanities, languages and mathematics, technology, physical education, and the arts.

This academic programme challenges students to fulfil their potential, and offers a broad-based selection of courses and levels to meet individual needs and interests. An important characteristic of ACS Egham is individual attention to students' needs facilitated by an exceptionally well-qualified, experienced, and empathetic faculty; many of whom are IB examiners, moderators, and teacher trainers. The success of our programme is reflected in our IB Diploma pass rate over the last ten years, which has enabled our graduates to continue their studies at top universities around the world, including the UK and Europe as well as the US.

ACS Egham runs small class sizes which afford a greater opportunity for individual attention and support for various learning styles. Child Study Teams meet with individual students' teachers, administrators and parents, to ensure that every child is appropriately challenged and encouraged. A Language Coordinator assists families in organising native language lessons.

Facilities. ACS Egham has purpose-built computer and science labs, libraries, spacious classrooms, playgrounds, well-equipped sports centre, with Gym, dance studio and climbing wall, as well as sports fields. To further enhance the teaching programme there is a 21st century Visual Arts & Design Technology Centre and a purpose-built Science wing.

Sport & Extracurricular Activities. ACS Egham offers an extensive range of extracurricular clubs and community service activities both locally and internationally. Students also participate in international theatre arts programmes, maths, literature and music competitions in the UK and across Europe. The Campus sports programme runs three seasons fielding teams in football, volleyball, cross country, basketball, rugby, swimming, dance, tennis, athletics, baseball, softball and golf. We also offer tournament sports competitions across the UK and Europe.

Accreditation. ACS Egham is accredited by the New England Association of Schools and Colleges (NEASC) and is authorised by the International Baccalaureate (IB) to offer the IBPYP, IBMYP, IBDP and IBCP. The School holds memberships in the European Council of International Schools (ECIS), the Council of International Schools (COIS) and the Independent Schools Association (ISA).

Four Schools, One World Class Education. Founded in 1967 to serve the needs of global and local families, ACS International Schools educate over 3,700 students, aged 2 to 18, day and boarding, from more than 100 countries. Our schools – 3 in Greater London and 1 in Doha, Qatar – are all non-sectarian and co-educational.

Contact the Admissions Team. The admissions team is available throughout the year to answer questions, book campus visits, and assist families through the enrolment process. Students are accepted in all grades throughout the year. Partial and full bursaries in Grades 6/year 7, Grade 8/year 9 and Grade 11/year 12 are now available.

ACS Hillingdon International School

Hillingdon Court, 108 Vine Lane, Hillingdon, Middlesex UB10 0BE

Tel: 01895 259771
Fax: 01895 818404
email: hillingdonadmissions@acs-schools.com
website: www.acs-schools.com/acs-hillingdon
Twitter: @ACSintschools
Facebook: @ACSHillingdon
LinkedIn: /ACS-International-Schools-Ltd

Head of School: **Martin Hall**

Age Range. 4–18.
Number in School. Day only: 306 Boys, 264 Girls.
Fees per annum (2018–2019). Tuition: £10,640–£24,400.

ACS Hillingdon is a co-educational, day school for ages 4 to 18, offering the IB Diploma, College Board Advanced Placement (AP) Programme and a US Diploma. The school accepts almost 600 students aged between 4 and 18. The campus is situated on an 11-acre estate less than 15 miles from central London, with another 14 acres of paying fields nearby. A door-to-door bus service covers much of London.

Academic programme. The academic programme offers both the International Baccalaureate (IB) Diploma Programme as well as Advanced Placement (AP) courses, creating a curriculum that meets the needs of our entire international student body. IB scores regularly rank it among the highest achieving non-selective schools in the UK, enabling graduates to continue their studies at top universities around the world, including the UK, Europe and the US.

Facilities. The campus combines a Grade II listed stately mansion with a modern wing housing classrooms, computer labs, an integrated IT network, libraries, cafeteria, gymnasium, auditorium. The Harmony House Centre for International Music houses a digital recording studio, rehearsal rooms, practice studios and a computer lab for music technology.

We opened our new Science Centre in September 2017, which includes seven new laboratories and features a specialist binocular microscope and reflecting telescope among its cutting-edge technology, as well as a electrophoresis unit which students can use to investigate and visualise DNA.

Students will also benefit from the centre's enhanced testing capabilities, such as the high quality Vernier temperature probes, allowing them to conduct advanced scientific experiments. New flexible furniture has also been used throughout the labs to facilitate student collaboration and project work.

A new Middle School technology lab opened in December 2017 with mobile technology at the heart of its design. The tech lab includes projectors and writable walls allowing student work to be shared in real time using mobile devices. Also opened in 2018 is our new STEAM (Science, Technology, Engineering, Arts and Maths) classrooms promoting creative projects and innovation across subjects.

The campus has on-site playing fields, tennis courts and playgrounds, and off-site playing fields for football, rugby and athletics. Local swimming and golf facilities are also used by our students. The sports programme runs three seasons fielding teams in football, volleyball, cross country, basketball, rugby, swimming, dance, tennis, track & field, baseball, softball and golf.

Enrichment. ACS Hillingdon also offers extensive and varied extracurricular clubs and community service activities both locally and internationally, which encourage students to participate in the richness of school life. Students also participate in international theatre arts programmes, maths, literature and music competitions in the UK and across Europe.

Four Schools, One World Class Education. Founded in 1967 to serve the needs of global and local families, ACS International Schools educate over 3,700 students, aged 2 to 18, day and boarding, from more than 100 countries. Our schools – 3 in Greater London and 1 in Doha, Qatar – are all non-sectarian and co-educational.

Contact the Admissions Team. The admissions team is available throughout the year to answer questions, book campus visits, and assist families through the enrolment process. Students are accepted in all grades throughout the year. Partial and full bursaries in Grades 6/year 7, Grade 8/year 9 and Grade 11/year 12 are now available.

Alton School

Anstey Lane, Alton, Hampshire GU34 2NG

Tel: 01420 82070
Fax: 01420 541711
email: enquiries@altonschool.co.uk
website: www.altonschool.co.uk
Twitter: @AltonSchool1938
Facebook: @altonschool1938
LinkedIn: @altonschool1938

Motto: Be the best that you can be

Chairman of Governors: Mr Clive Hexton

Headmaster: **Mr Graham Maher**, BA Hons, PGCE, MA

Senior Deputy Head: Mrs Sally Webb, BEd Hons
Deputy Head: Mr Carl Bingham, BA Hons, PGCE

Age Range. 6 months to 18 years.
Number in School. 488.
Fees per term (2018–2019). Prep £3,383–£4,096, Senior £4,799.

Entrance. Nursery and Prep – non-selective; Senior School – internal exam and interview; Sixth Form – GCSE results and interview.

Details of scholarships on website.

Ethos. Alton School is a co-educational Catholic day school located on the outskirts of Alton in Hampshire. We welcome pupils of all faiths. Our vision is to inspire intellectually brave, morally sound, confident young people who are prepared for life. We are a friendly school with strong pastoral care and an unassuming style. However, we are bold and ambitious in our thinking and in our aspirations for our pupils.

Curriculum. From Nursery through to Sixth Form, we offer a broad, liberal education that attracts boys and girls with a wide range of talents and interests. We regularly win national awards in subjects across the spectrum from Art to STEM. Pupils take an average of ten GCSEs and select three or four subjects at A Level as well as the Extended Project Qualification. Opportunities to stimulate and enrich learning are sought continuously with a variety of day and residential trips offered at all stages.

Academic Results. Results at GCSE and A Level are consistently outstanding. Entry into the Senior School is not based solely on academic achievement so we are particularly proud of the value added to each pupil's achievements.

Pupils outperform expectations based on diagnostic testing, often by a grade or more in every GCSE. In March 2017, the Independent Schools Inspectorate found that "Pupils of all abilities make excellent progress and achieve high standards across all curriculum areas, in line with the school's aim for everyone to 'be the best that you can be'."

Sport. The school enjoys tremendous sporting success and punches far above its weight with both Prep and Senior pupils and teams winning regional and national Independent Schools Association competitions on a regular basis. The major sports for boys are football, rugby, cricket and athletics. For girls, they are hockey, netball, athletics, and rounders. We also have popular tennis, equestrian and ski academies.

International. Our international programme is groundbreaking. We are part of an international network of schools working to deepen understanding of diversity and offer unique opportunities for cultural and language immersion and for exchange in France, Germany, Spain, Colombia and India. A small number of international students join our Sixth Form for one or two terms and fully integrate into school life.

Art, Music and Drama. Musical and dramatic opportunities are strong with various choirs, orchestras, ensembles, jazz groups, concerts and drama productions. Additional tuition in dance, LAMDA and instruments is offered. Art is thriving, with pupils winning a number of national awards.

Enrichment. The school has an extensive enrichment programme with a wide offering of co-curricular activities for all interests. Our voluntary work and fundraising efforts, and the various residential trips offered, are designed to build self-confidence, a caring attitude, and a desire to contribute to the world.

Charitable status. The Alton Convent School Charity is a Registered Charity, number 1071684.

Argyle House School

19/20 Thornhill Park, Tunstall Road, Sunderland, Tyne & Wear SR2 7LA

Tel: 0191 510 0726
email: office@argylehouseschool.co.uk
website: www.argylehouseschool.co.uk

Head: **Mr C Johnson**

Age Range. 2½–16.
Number in School. 250 Boys and Girls.
Fees per term (2018–2019). £2,345–£2,765.

Argyle House School was established in 1884 as a small independent day school for boys and girls, situated in the centre of Sunderland. Students travel from all parts of the region, by our buses, or local forms of transport. The school has maintained its high standards of academic achievement, whilst catering for a wide variety of abilities.

At Argyle House, we believe in the individual, and work with him or her to enable the achievement of each student's potential. This is due to attention to detail by fully qualified and dedicated staff, who help to mould the individual into a well-mannered and accomplished young individual, who will be able to meet future challenges.

Small class sizes and a friendly environment facilitate learning, but not all work is academic, as the school takes an active part in many sporting leagues, both within the school, and locally with other schools. We aim to offer all the facilities of a much larger school, whilst remaining at present student levels to keep the intimacy and friendliness of a smaller school, for both parents and students.

Arts Educational Schools London

Cone Ripman House, 14 Bath Road, Chiswick, London W4 1LY

Tel: 020 8987 6600
Fax: 020 8987 6601
email: rjones@artsed.co.uk
website: www.artsed.co.uk
Twitter: @ArtsEdLondon
Facebook: @artseducational

Founded in 1919.

Headteacher: **Mr Adrian Blake**

Deputy Headteacher: Mrs Claire Parker-Wood
Director of Teaching and Learning: Mr Robert Bannon
Director of Curriculum and Data Management: Mr Thamir Elzubaidi
Director of Sixth Form: Mr Mark Ferrington
Head of BTEC: Mr Myles Stinton

Age Range. 11–18 Co-educational.
Number in School. Day: 201 Girls, 69 Boys.
Fees per term (2018–2019). £5,130–£5,664.

"The UK's Leading Specialist Performing Arts Institution in Academic Achievement" Sunday Times, Parent Power 2007.

100% A Level Pass Rate and outstanding GCSE results.
The Arts Educational Schools London are committed to developing the full potential of each and every pupil. High quality vocational, academic and social education, in a warm, friendly, caring environment, ensures that our pupils feel challenged and fulfilled throughout the whole of their exciting careers at the school.

The school has been educating young performing artists since 1919, and there is no comparable school in the UK. Dancers learn to act and sing, actors learn to sing and dance, musicians learn to do more than play their instruments well, and everyone has the opportunity to be grounded in the visual arts, languages, humanities, sciences, and mathematics.

From Year 7 all pupils follow a course leading to eight or nine GCSEs. All pupils have access to the outstanding performance facilities, rehearsal rooms, proscenium and studio theatres. At Year 12 pupils follow a course of four AS Levels, leading to three or four A Levels, whilst receiving outstanding training in dance, drama, music and musical theatre.

In addition, students in Year 12 can opt to take a Level 3 BTEC in Musical Theatre, Acting, Dance or Production Arts, along with two A Levels as additional courses of study, where they benefit from all the expertise and excellence of the professional performance departments along with the academic reputation and pastoral guidance of the Secondary School.

Former Students of the schools include: Julie Andrews, Samantha Barks, Sarah Brightman, Darcey Bussell, Martin Clunes, Joan Collins, Adam Cooper, Bonnie Langford, Jane Seymour, Hugo Speer, Summer Strallen and Will Young.

Admission is at 11+ and 16+ and occasionally at other ages if places become available.

Charitable status. The Arts Educational Schools is a Registered Charity, number 311087. It exists solely for educational purposes.

Ashton House School

50–52 Eversley Crescent, Isleworth, Middlesex TW7 4LW

Tel: 020 8560 3902
Fax: 020 8568 1097
email: admin@ashtonhouse.com
website: www.ashtonhouse.com

Principal: Mr S J Turner, BSc

Head Teacher: **Mrs Angela Stewart**

Age Range. 3–11.
Number in School. 119 Day Pupils: 71 Boys, 48 Girls.
Fees per term (2018–2019). £2,782–£4,036.
Founded 1930. Proprietors: P A, G B & S J Turner. Entry by interview and assessment. Prospectus on request.

Choosing a school for your child is one of the most important decisions you will be making on their behalf and we fully understand that you want to get it right. At Ashton House we do our very best to deliver a first-class education in a calm and happy atmosphere, where children learn and develop while still enjoying their childhood. Our results at 11 indicate that we are succeeding while our pupils have grown into confident, caring young people ready for the next phase in their education. Our most recent inspection judged the personal development of our pupils to be "outstanding".

Aurora Eccles School

Quidenham, Nr Norwich, Norfolk NR16 2NZ

Tel: 01953 887217
Fax: 01953 887397
email: EcclesSchool@the-aurora-group.com
website: www.the-aurora-group.com/ecclesschool
Twitter: @The_AuroraGroup
Facebook: @AuroraGroupUK

Headteacher: **Mr Chris Brown**

Age Range. 5–18.
Aurora Eccles School is an independent day and boarding school providing specialist education for students aged 7 to 20 who experience difficulties learning in mainstream school environments.

This may be a result of specific learning difficulties around dyslexia and moderate learning difficulties, through to those with higher needs and complexities including communication and interaction difficulties associated with Asperger's Syndrome.

Aurora Eccles School offers the perfect learning environment for each student's needs to be met so they can develop and achieve their full potential, ready when they leave to go on to further education, training or employment.

Specialist teaching, together with small class sizes and a nurturing approach enables students to work at a level and pace that's right for them to achieve their goals. Focus is given to building self-esteem and confidence by implementing strategies to support students' individual needs to engage in education, as well as developing their social and independence skills.

There are many opportunities to take part in a variety of extra-curricular activities including sports and societies, the Duke of Edinburgh's Award scheme and trips.

Our Service & Facilities.
Set in 28 acres of beautiful Norfolk countryside in Quidenham near Norwich, Aurora Eccles School provides:
- Small class sizes and high staff ratios
- Integrated therapy
- Individual tuition and support
- Specialist classrooms for Science, Music, Drama and Art
- Break out areas for quiet time
- Extensive outdoor recreation areas
- Large Sports Fields
- Indoor Swimming pool
- Activity Centre
- High Ropes
- Low Ropes
- Climbing Wall and Forest activities

Ayscoughfee Hall School

Welland Hall, London Road, Spalding, Lincolnshire PE11 2TE

Tel: 01775 724733
email: admin@ahs.me.uk
website: www.ahs.me.uk
Facebook: @Ayscoughfee-Hall-School-Life

Head: **Mrs Clare Ogden**

Age Range. 3–11 Co-educational.
Number of Pupils. 142 Day Pupils.
Fees per term (2018–2019). £1,520–£2,240.
Founded in 1920, Ayscoughfee Hall School is centred around a beautiful Georgian family home. A purpose-built extension complements the already spacious accommodation. The School houses Kindergarten, Infant and Junior Departments and has further developed its facilities to include enlarged classrooms, a dedicated Science/Art Room, Music Department, Cookery Room, Library, a large Sports Hall and a Foreign Language Room.

The guidelines and principles of the National Curriculum are followed in all subjects but go far beyond the basic requirements in order to give each child a broader, more varied understanding. Academic standards are high and progress is well monitored throughout the school. The vast majority of pupils are successful in the Lincolnshire County Council 11+ selection examination and progress to secondary selective school education very well equipped to tackle all subjects. The curriculum is continually reviewed and class teachers are supported by specialist teachers for PE, ICT, languages, music and Forest School. French and Spanish are taught from Reception class.

iPads support learning in the classrooms and pupils receive weekly, dedicated ICT tuition in our up-to-date ICT suite.

The School excels with its music and drama productions over the academic year, in which all children perform in front of their parents and guests.

The school competes successfully in local and regional sports activities, including football, rugby, hockey, netball, cross-country and athletics.

There is a thriving programme of extracurricular activities, including sport, drama, cookery, poetry, textiles, choir, instrumental groups, blogging, code club and Forest School. A wide variety of educational visits is offered, with the older children having the opportunity to participate in alternate cultural and activity trips, accompanied by the staff. Furthermore, regular visits by professional groups and individuals take place in school.

As a small school with small class sizes, we aim to provide a happy and caring environment where the individual child may flourish. We are proud of our academic standards but we also strive to give a broad and balanced education. Above all, we want our boys and girls to use and develop their different abilities and to enjoy the success this brings.

Charitable status. Ayscoughfee Hall School Limited is a Registered Charity, number 527294. It exists to provide education for boys and girls.

Babington House School

Grange Drive, Chislehurst, Kent BR7 5ES

Tel: 020 8467 5537
email: enquiries@babingtonhouse.com
website: www.babingtonhouse.com
Twitter: @babingtonbr7
LinkedIn: /Babington-House-School

Chair of Governors: Mr C Turner

Headmaster: **Mr T W A Lello**, MA, FRSA, NPQH, PGCE

Head of Seniors: Mrs J Brown, MA, BA Hons, PGCE

Age Range. Co-educational 3–18.
Number in School. 370 Day pupils: 112 Boys, 258 Girls.
Fees per term (2018–2019). £4,288–£5,340.

Babington House School is an independent day school for pupils aged 3 to 18 years, situated in a beautiful group of buildings on Grange Drive in Chislehurst, near Bromley and close to Elmstead Woods station.

Our commitment is to provide an academic and well-rounded education with small class sizes which is tailored to the needs of our pupils, believing that bright children benefit from carefully monitored and well-directed learning, where self-discipline is highly prized and where each pupil is known as an individual. This helps Babington House pupils grow into confident, accomplished, creative young people with emotional intelligence and high standards.

Babington is an academic school. Our academic, social and sporting endeavours are underpinned by core Christian values which include a respect for others and an awareness of a purpose greater than ourselves. There is a strong sense of community at Babington House.

Top of the Bromley League tables for Early Years provision for the last two years. Top small independent school in England for A Level results 2018.

In its last inspection Babington House was praised by the ISI for achieving outstanding academic success at all key stages and providing exemplary pastoral care. The boys and girls receive a first-class education in a nurturing and supportive environment, set in pleasant suburban surroundings. Full range of courses for examinations at all levels. "Excellent" in all areas of the school and across every age group from 3–18 (ISI report November 2016).

Specialist facilities for Science, Music, Drama, Art, Sport, ICT, Languages, Maths & English.

Small classes: Maximum size 20 pupils. Careers guidance by a specialist.

Wide range of sports (Athletics, Swimming, Tennis, Netball, Gymnastics, Hockey, Football, Cross Country) and extracurricular activities (Drama, Gym Club, Horse Riding, Cookery, Rock Climbing, Taekwondo, Archaeology Club, Choir, Ballet, Tap, Elocution and Instrumental Tuition).

Charitable status. Babington House School is a Registered Charity, number 307914. It exists to provide exemplary education.

Ballard School

Fernhill Lane, New Milton, Hampshire BH25 5SU

Tel: 01425 626900
Fax: 01425 638847
email: admissions@ballardschool.co.uk
website: www.ballardschool.co.uk
Twitter: @BallardSchool
Facebook: @BallardSchoolNewMilton
LinkedIn: /BallardSchool

Chairman of the Board of Governors: Mr P Goodfellow

Headmaster: **Mr Andrew McCleave**

Age Range. 2 to 16 Co-educational.
Number of Children. 400 day children.
Fees per term (2018–2019). Years 9–11 £5,105 Years 6–8 £4,885, Year 5 £4,720, Year 4 £4,575, Year 3 £4,175. Reception–Year 2 £2,780. Fees include the cost of school lunches and most extra-curricular clubs. Sibling discounts available.

"Pupils are reflective and have high levels of self-esteem and empathy. They are highly successful in displaying these characteristics through academic study as well as the wealth of sporting performing arts and extra-curricular opportunities in which they participate." ISI Inspection November 2017.

Ballard is an award-winning, independent, co-educational day school for children from Nursery to GCSE. We believe in a bespoke education for your child within a nurturing and engaging environment. Set in 32 acres of beautiful grounds located between the New Forest National Park and the Solent on the Hampshire/Dorset border, we are rated 'excellent & outstanding' by ISI.

Ballard pupils achieve excellent examination results with a record set of results in 2018 – 100% A*–C in Maths, English and nine other subjects including all three Sciences. 40% of our pupils gained the top grades of an A*/A (grades 9–7) which is double the National average.

Subject specialist teaching staff, alongside small class sizes and a diverse and inspiring range of activities and trips, nurture self-confidence, aspiration and help develop each child's personality.

A family school with Christian values, Ballard offers inspiring teaching and excellent pastoral care; children are encouraged to take on responsibilities from an early age including a mentoring programme whereby older children help younger children.

There is a wealth of information including our latest GCSE results, and our vision and values on our website – www.ballardschool.co.uk. We have much to offer so please come and visit us soon.

Join our family and fulfil your potential.

"Ballard should not be overlooked by parents wanting a thorough and bespoke education for their children. There is nowhere that offers each individual pupil the opportunity to fulfil their own potential in a lively, sincere environment, rich in the consistent achievement of outstanding results. The school community runs very deep and the children across all year groups are encouraged to 'mix and mentor' which clearly delivers a loyalty within the school community."

"My son's predicted grade for Maths GCSE has gone from a D/C to an A* because of the way he has been taught."

"The attitude at Ballard is very much 'You can do it', not 'Can you do it?'"

"It's been the making of both of our boys."

"You are not just a number."

"Ballard has given me everything I need so that I can go forward and achieve anything I want."

Charitable status. Ballard School Ltd is a Registered Charity, number 307328. It exists for the education of children.

Beech Hall School

Beech Hall Drive, Tytherington, Macclesfield, Cheshire SK10 2EG

Tel: 01625 422192
Fax: 01625 502424
email: secretary@beechhallschool.org
website: www.beechhallschool.org
Twitter: @beechhall_macc
Facebook: @beechhallschool

Headmaster: **Mr J D Allen**, BA Ed Hons, MA, NPQH, FCollT

Head of Infant & Juniors, Pastoral Care: Mrs G Yandell, BA Hons, PGCE, L2 Elklan

Head of Seniors, Curriculum & Assessment: Mr S Gitlin, BSc Hons, PGCE FCollT, L3 Elklan

Bursar: Mr I Percival, BSc Hons

Registrar: Mrs N Lindsay, BA Hons

Age Range. 6 months–16 years.
Number of Pupils. 180.
Fees per term (2018–2019). Infants £3,240, Junior School £3,990, Senior School £4,340. The fees are inclusive of lunches and snacks.

Nursery, Infant, Junior and Senior departments offer education between 8.30 am and 4.00 pm with further supervised sporting and leisure activities available until 5.00 pm. If required, there is supervised care up until 6.00 pm for all children.

Beech Hall is a co-educational Day school situated in spacious and attractive grounds with extensive playing fields, a heated outdoor swimming pool, new food technology lab and many other facilities.

Boys and girls are prepared for entry to a wide variety of Independent Schools and Sixth Form Colleges. Classes are kept small, making individual attention possible in every lesson.

There is a very popular Nursery, Pre-School and Reception department, consisting of children between the ages of 6 months and 5 years under the care of their own specialist teachers. These classes were started with the objective of giving boys and girls a good grounding in reading, writing and arithmetic.

Beech Hall aims to provide a sound all-round education. Rugby, football, hockey and netball are played in the winter terms and in summer, cricket, athletics, and rounders are taught. There is an extensive sporting fixture list covering all sports with children playing representative sport from Year 3 upwards. Swimming is taught throughout the year and other activities include badminton and fives.

The school is situated off the main Stockport–Macclesfield road, within easy reach of Manchester International Airport and the M6 and M62 motorways.

Further details and illustrated prospectus are obtainable from the school or via the school's website.

Beech House School

184 Manchester Road, Rochdale, Greater Manchester OL11 4JQ

Tel: 01706 646309
email: info@beechhouseschool.co.uk
website: www.beechhouseschool.co.uk

Principal: **Mr Kevin Sartain**, BSc Hons, PGCE, Dip Spo Psy, CBiol, FIBiol

Age Range. 2–16 Co-educational.
Number of Pupils. 190.
Fees per term (2018–2019). £1,792–£2,182.

Beech House staff and pupils were delighted on the receipt of the schools latest ISI Educational Quality and Focused Compliance Inspection reports. The School was fully compliant in all areas.

In the Educational Quality Inspection the quality of the pupils' personal development was deemed excellent. The pupils understand how important making the right decision is to their future lives. Pupils are particularly self-disciplined and their behaviour is exemplary, ensuring harmony around school. Pupils take on responsibilities within the school with enthusiasm and maturity.

They feel extremely well known and cared for. Pupils have a strong appreciation of their own culture and that of others and show considerable sensitivity towards those less fortunate than themselves.

The quality of the pupil's academic and other achievements is good. Pupils respond with success to the well-planned initiatives to provide a challenging yet supportive environment to stimulate, maintain and develop a lively enquiring mind. As a result of pupils develop application, purpose, initiative, independence, thought and action. Pupils can adeptly apply their strong numeracy skills across other subjects particularly science. Pupils have excellent literacy and reading skills and express themselves orally extremely well. Pupils with SEND or EL achieve well because they receive appropriate teaching and encouragement to suit their needs. Pupils are determined to succeed and welcome and respond to teachers' advice. They find the best marking extremely helpful in this quest. Pupils recognise that their individual talents are recognised and they are encouraged to develop these.

In the EYFS children make good and often rapid progress in their learning and development. They gain excellent reading and writing skills early in their education.

Bishop Challoner School

228 Bromley Road, Shortlands, Bromley, Kent BR2 0BS

Tel: 020 8460 3546
Fax: 020 8466 8885
email: admissions@bishopchallonerschool.com
website: www.bishopchallonerschool.com
Twitter: @challoner_head

Headteacher: **Mrs Paula Anderson**, BSc Hons, MBA, PGCE

Age Range. 3–18.
Number in School. 360 Day Pupils.
Fees per term (2018–2019). Seniors £3,849, Juniors £3,080, Infants £2,777, Nursery £861 (min 3 sessions), £2,743 (full time).

This is a Roman Catholic Independent Co-educational School for ages 3–18 years.

Happiness, self-fulfilment and personal success are all embraced at Bishop Challoner.

The School welcomes all Faiths.

Admissions to the School follows the successful completion of an entrance examination/assessment and an interview with the Headteacher.

Scholarships and Bursaries are available.

Charitable status. Bishop Challoner School is a Registered Charity, number 1153948. It exists to provide an excellent education for boys and girls.

Bowbrook House School

Peopleton, Nr Pershore, Worcs WR10 2EE

Tel:	01905 841242/841843
Fax:	01905 840716
email:	enquiries@bowbrookhouseschool.co.uk
website:	www.bowbrookhouseschool.co.uk

Headmaster: **Mr C D Allen**, BSc Hons, CertEd, DipSoc

Age Range. 3½–16.
Number in School. Day: 222 124 Boys, 98 Girls.
Fees per term (2018–2019). £1,925–£3,796.

Bowbrook House is set in 14 acres of picturesque Worcestershire countryside yet within easy reach of Worcester, Pershore and Evesham. The school caters for the academic child and also those of average ability, who can benefit from the small classes. All pupils are able to take full advantage of the opportunities offered and are encouraged to participate in all activities. As well as the academic subjects, the school has a flourishing art department, a computer room, hard tennis courts and an open air swimming pool in addition to extensive games fields.

The Pre-Prep department of 3½–8 year olds is a self-contained unit but enjoys the use of the main school facilities.

Whilst stressing academic achievement, the school aims to provide a structured and disciplined environment in which children of all abilities can flourish, gain confidence and achieve their true potential. The small school size enables the head and staff to know all pupils well, to be able to accurately assess their strengths and weaknesses it enables each pupil to be an important part of the school and to feel that their individual attitudes, behaviour, efforts and achievements are important.

There is an extended school day from 8.15 am to 5.30 pm, with supervised prep sessions. There is also an extensive and varied extracurricular programme run by specialist coaches from basketball, gym and dance to kickboxing and fencing.

Braeside School

130 High Road, Buckhurst Hill, Essex IG9 5SD

Tel:	020 8504 1133
Fax:	020 8505 6675
email:	info@braesideschool.co.uk
website:	www.braesideschool.co.uk

Headmistress: **Mrs C Osborn**, BA Hons, MSc, PGCE

Age Range. 2½–16.
Number in School. 200 Day Girls.

Fees per term (2018–2019). £1,290–£4,250.

Braeside School is an independent day school for girls aged between 2½ and 16. Our examination results are routinely excellent and the well-qualified staff are determined to maintain our excellent and distinctive character.

The school sets its own high standards in work and behaviour, aiming to give each pupil a sound moral and intellectual foundation for life. The education provided takes full account of each girl's capabilities and interests, and from the earliest age girls acquire a sense of responsibility and confidence, tempered with a deep consideration for others.

The school is able to offer small class sizes in both the Juniors and Seniors, with the significant advantage of teaching in small groups for many subjects in the Seniors, especially in GCSE options subjects. The high pupil to teacher ratio and individual attention builds confidence both academically and socially, and enables our pupils to reach their full potential.

A range of subject-specific outings, enhancement activities and the opportunity of a residential trip abroad all broaden the educational experience for our students.

Braeside is a happy, united school, where the potential to be part of our close-knit family from 2½ to 16 years old creates a secure and stable atmosphere. Staff and students work collaboratively to ensure that they reach their potential.

Entry, at every age apart from 2, 3 and 4, is by test and interview.

Bridgewater School

Drywood Hall, Worsley Road, Worsley, Manchester M28 2WQ

Tel:	0161 794 1463
Fax:	0161 794 3519
email:	admin@bwslive.co.uk
website:	www.bridgewater-school.co.uk
Twitter:	@BridgewaterScho
Facebook:	@BridgewaterConnected
LinkedIn:	/bridgewater-school-worsley

Chair of Governors: Mr C Haighton, BSc Hons

Headmistress: **Mrs J A T Nairn**, Cert Ed Distinction

Age Range. 3–18 Co-educational.
Number of Pupils. 473: 248 Boys, 225 Girls.
Fees per term (2018–2019). £2,806–£3,741. Lunch is included.

Bridgewater School is a co-educational, independent day school for pupils aged between 3 and 18 years. Established as a boys' school in 1950 and having moved to its present delightful semi-rural setting soon afterwards, the school has since grown considerably – admitting girls and developing a sixth form. We draw pupils from the immediate locality, but also from a much wider area, well served as we are by the motorway network and by other major road links.

Bridgewater is by design not a large school. This enables us to provide small classes and high levels of attention to the needs of individual pupils. We seek to maximise education attainment all through a child's development, not least in the years of external examinations at GCSE and A Level.

In addition to its academic goals Bridgewater seeks to retain the intimate atmosphere it has had since its inception. We greatly value our capacity to offer provision across the full age range, from the nursery years to university entrance, for families wanting this continuity of individual attention for their children.

At the same time, however, pupils must look outward to the wider community and to the society in which they will live as adults. We see it as an integral part of Bridgewater's role to foster high standards of behaviour and self-discipline, as well as to develop an awareness of personal and social responsibility. Vital, too, are the many activities which take place outside the classroom – sport, music, drama clubs and societies, language exchange visits and outdoor activity breaks to name but a sample of the range available.

Entrusting your child's education to a school is a very big decision. We are mindful of our responsibility to justify a parent's decision to send their child to us, and of the need for that child's education to be a partnership between school and home. We aim, by the end of this partnership, to produce rounded, articulate young people who are well prepared for the challenges of adult and business life.

The School governors, staff and pupils share a sense of excitement about Bridgewater's future. The school has developed rapidly in recent years, with splendid new buildings and facilities and a considerable increase in pupil numbers. We have a commitment to continual development and improvement. If you have not yet visited us then may we recommend that you do so soon. We would be delighted to meet you and to show you how much Bridgewater School has to offer you and your child.

Charitable status. Bridgewater School is a Registered Charity, number 1105547.

Bronte School

Mayfield, 7 Pelham Road, Gravesend, Kent DA11 0HN

Tel: 01474 533805
email: enquiry@bronteschool.co.uk
website: www.bronteschool.co.uk

Headmistress: **Mrs Emma Wood**, BA Hons

Age Range. 3–11.
Number in School. 154 Day Pupils: 89 Boys, 65 Girls.
Fees per term (2018–2019). £3,110.

Bronte is a small, friendly, family-orientated, co-educational day school serving Gravesend and surrounding villages. The children are taught in small classes and are prepared for all types of secondary education. In 1999 the school moved to its present building which has since been expanded to accommodate specialist teaching rooms. A broadly-based curriculum and an extensive number of activity clubs provide the children with every opportunity to develop their individual interests and abilities. We achieve excellent 11+ results every year.

The school was awarded Artsmark Gold status in 2013.

Entry is preferred at Kindergarten (age 3) following a parental visit to the school and an interview with the Head. Children joining at a later stage are assessed informally prior to entry.

Buxlow Preparatory School

5/6 Castleton Gardens, East Lane, Wembley, Middlesex HA9 7QJ

Tel: 020 8904 3615
email: admin@buxlowschool.org.uk
website: www.buxlowschool.org.uk

Headteacher: **Mr Darren May**

Director Health and Safety: Mr Michael Aherne
Director of Studies: Mr Stuart Kennedy
Director of Pastoral Care: Ms Sharon Sethi
Director Special Needs and Abilities (*Sendco*): Miss Janine Martin
School Secretary and Headteacher's PA: Mrs Deirdre Hutchinson

Age Range. 2–11 Co-educational, Nursery to Year 6.
Number of Pupils. 79.
Fees per term (2018–2019). Reception £2,990, Years 1–6 £3,110.

Cambridge Tutors College

Water Tower Hill, Croydon, Surrey CR0 5SX

Tel: 020 8688 5284
Fax: 020 8686 9220
email: enquiries@ctc.ac.uk
website: www.ctc.ac.uk

Principal: **Dr Chris Drew**, BSc Sussex, MA Bath, EdD Bath, PGCE, Dip RSA

Age Range. 14–19.
Number of Pupils. 112.
Fees per annum (2018–2019). £22,995 excluding accommodation; up to £31,920 including homestay accommodation or up to £39,990 for boarding accommodation.

2018 A Level results: 47% A*/A and 80% of students entering their first choice universities, mostly Russell Group.

Since 1958 Cambridge Tutors College (CTC) has been offering a very high quality academically focused education to young people from the United Kingdom and from across the world. Fundamental to the College's ethos is small group teaching – our average class size is just over 5 students – and regular testing: students sit weekly tests in every subject, under examination conditions. This combination of small classes, regular testing and expert teaching has proved to be highly successful in giving students the motivation and confidence to succeed.

CTC offers: A Level courses (two-year and 18-month), NCUK International Foundation Year, one-year GCSE course and a one-year pre-GCSE course. CTC also offers one and two-term pre-sessional courses linked to the two-year A Level program.

The College's most recent ISI Inspection report in 2017 was outstanding.

The college enjoys a particularly strong reputation for helping students to gain entry to the UK's most prestigious universities.

Situated in a pleasant parkside location in South Croydon, CTC is just a few minutes' walk from the town centre, East Croydon station and bus and tram routes. It is close to Central London, just 15 minutes away by train, but surrounded by parkland and quiet residential streets.

Facilities and resources are modern and well-appointed. The College has excellent technological infrastructure with fast Wi-Fi, and there is an ambitious development programme in place.

The College's welfare provision includes a team of trained professionals and all students have a personal tutor. A varied weekly programme of sporting and other activities is offered, as well as weekend excursions.

Charitable status. Cambridge Tutors Educational Trust Limited is a Registered Charity, number 312878.

Canbury School

Kingston Hill, Kingston-upon-Thames, Surrey KT2 7LN

Tel: 020 8549 8622
Fax: 020 8974 6018
email: reception@canburyschool.co.uk
website: www.canburyschool.co.uk

Headmistress: **Ms L Clancy**, BEd

Academic Assistant Head: Mrs G Branney, BSc Hons
Pastoral Assistant Head: Mrs P Rich, BA, PGCE
Bursar & Clerk to the Governors: Mrs Lusia Anindita-Beckman, BA Hons, MSc, LLB, PG Dip Law
Head's PA and Registrar: Ms Louise Boggi

Age Range. 11–18.
Number in School. 75 boys and girls.

Founded in 1982, Canbury School is a unique and happy co-educational independent day school for students from the ages of 11 to 18 on the outskirts of London beside Richmond Park. With excellent transport links to the school, students come from various nearby areas such as Barnes, Putney, Wandsworth, New Malden, Richmond, Teddington, Twickenham, Hampton, Epsom, Central London, Surrey and other areas in the South East such as Esher and Effingham. We also welcome overseas students. Located on the top of Kingston Hill, it affords our students the opportunity to experience the vast resources London has to offer such as museums, parks, galleries, and theatres literally via a bus ride. With class sizes of fifteen students or less, enthusiastic teaching, excellent pastoral care and a determination to target the needs of individual students, Canbury School gets the best out of students with a wide range of abilities.

Entry requirements. Educational reports need to be submitted prior to interview with the Headmistress. Assessment day(s) will be arranged to secure entry to the school.

Curriculum. Broad range of GCSE subjects. Functional Skills. BTEC subjects up to Level 3 at KS5. Students are expected to take up to nine GCSEs and/or BTEC level 2 equivalent.

The curriculum in Years 7, 8 and 9 includes the core subjects of English, Mathematics and Science as well as Spanish, Geography, History, Information Technology, Art & Design, Graphics, Performing Arts, PE and Games, Music, Drama, and Personal, Social and Health Education. In Years 10 & 11, Physics, Chemistry and Biology are taken as doubly-certificated GCSE subjects, and GCSE Business Studies, GCSE Photography, Level 2 BTEC Physical Education and BTEC Travel & Tourism are introduced as additional subjects to our option programme. A bespoke Sixth Form curriculum is available including a range of Level 3 BTEC courses in addition to A Levels.

We run a wide range of extracurricular activities and clubs including drama, art, karate, sports and table-tennis.

Canbury School is different in placing emphasis on small classes. No class has more than 15 students. Our aim is to embrace the differences and harness the talents of each student.

Students participate in the school council which is led by our Head Boy and Head Girl. The Prefect Team is responsible for Charity, Sport, Subject areas and Houses. Students are all members of our very active House system led by Heads of Houses from the Prefect team.

Facilities. A small, friendly school with well-equipped classrooms. We have a dedicated Mac computer room, science laboratory, classrooms, Art/DT Studio with pottery area and kiln, playground and a separate Sixth Form building. We access local facilities for a wide range of seasonal sporting activities including athletics, cricket, netball, softball, swimming, watersports, badminton, soccer, hockey, basketball, netball, dance, tennis and rock climbing.

Fees per term (2018–2019). £5,631 (£6,131 Sixth Form). Bursaries are means tested and are available at the discretion of the School subject to satisfactory completion of the School's Bursary Form.

Charitable status. Canbury School is a Registered Charity, number 803766. It exists to provide education to a broad range of children including some of various nationalities who stand to benefit from being in a small school.

Cardiff Sixth Form College

1–3 Trinity Court, 21–27 Newport Road, Cardiff CF24 0AA

Tel: 02920 493121
email: marketing@ccoex.com
website: www.ccoex.com
Twitter: @CSFCOfficial
Facebook: @CardiffSixthFormCollege

Motto: Inspire, Reach and Achieve

Managing Director, Dukes Education Group: Mr Glenn Hawkins

Principal: **Mr Gareth Collier**

Vice Principal: Mrs Victoria Matthews
Acting Director of Studies: Mrs Rebecca Clyde
Director of Marketing and Admissions: Mrs Henrietta Lightwood
Financial Director: Mr Rob Humphreys

Age Range. 14–18 Co-educational.
Number of Students. 320.

Cardiff Sixth Form College's results are outstanding. In 2018 89% of students received A*–A grades, with 96% of students achieving A*–B grades. Excellent teaching, one-to-one support, superb academic materials, nearly double the amount of teaching hours of any other school and developing academic students with programmes designed to enhance their careers is what really makes the difference. The staff offer outstanding one-to-one support, tutorials and academic enrichment on top of their extensive teaching programme.

New for this academic year, CSFC now offers a one-year IGCSE course for students aged 14–16 years. Through a one-year intensive course, CSFC provides a unique opportunity for younger students, many of whom aspire to progress on to the award-winning Sixth Form, to be able to take advantage of the inspirational teaching, excellent career development and modern boarding environment at the top school in the UK. This new course gives students the opportunity to study between six and nine key academic subjects as well as improve their English proficiency in small class sizes with intensive teaching.

Cardiff Sixth Form College has an enviable careers department with five full-time careers advisors, personal tutors and a full-time work experience coordinator. In addition, the College is part of Dukes Education with expertise in medical applications, Oxbridge and Russell Group university placements, giving its students access to top industry specialists from across the professions. A two-year super programme of UCAS support, assistance with university entrance exams, lectures and work experience programmes, interview technique and one-to-one tutoring for personal statements ensures that Cardiff students are expertly prepared for the competitive courses they are applying to.

The College also offers a wide range of super-curricular activities. Internationally, students undertake voluntary and work placement programmes in Malaysia and India, join medical, architectural or finance societies and enter national academic competitions such as science Olympiads, Model United Nations and Maths challenges. The Debating Team's performance this year has been outstanding, coming first in the South Wales round of the Oxford Union Schools Debating Competition and for five years in a row Cardiff students have won NASA's International Space Settlement Design Competition in Florida.

From an extra-curricular perspective, students have plenty of opportunities to get involved with sports, performing and creative arts with highlights including an annual Sports Day, the Cultural Event, Talent Show and annual Glee production. Many are talented musicians and gold awards have been won this year in the Duke of Edinburgh's Award scheme.

Pastoral care is very strong with boarding staff and progress tutors constantly monitoring each student. Boarding accommodation is outstanding with every student having a university-style, single bedroom or studio apartment.

For more information or to find out about upcoming Open Days and the application process, please go to www.ccoex.com

Fees per annum (2018–2019). Day £16,600; Boarding £40,250–£43,750.

Carleton House Preparatory School

145 Menlove Avenue, Liverpool L18 3EE

Tel: 0151 722 0756
email: schooloffice@carletonhouse.co.uk
website: www.carletonhouse.co.uk
Twitter: @carletonhouse

Chair of Governors: Mr Peter Megann

Head Teacher: **Mrs S Coleman**, BEd Hons SLE

Age Range. 3+–11 Co-educational.
Number in School. 189.
Fees per term (2018–2019). £2,591 inclusive of lunch, day trips, Spanish lessons and personal insurance cover.

Located in the leafy suburbs of south Liverpool, Carleton House is Merseyside's leading co-ed Preparatory School (16th in the Sunday Times Parent Power 2016). It is a Catholic school that welcomes children of all denominations.

They can because they think they can truly embodies the spirit of Carleton House. Our school is a lively, vibrant community that gives its pupils a first-class education for the 21st century.

Small class sizes (we endeavour to keep to a maximum of 23) and a high ratio of teaching staff to pupils enable the well-qualified and experienced staff to provide individual attention in a friendly, caring atmosphere. We nurture the development of the whole child – academically, spiritually and in the sporting and cultural aspects of their lives. Through excellent teaching and the close relationship that

exists between school and home, our pupils are challenged, encouraged and supported to achieve their very best.

The implementation of all ten National Curriculum subjects ensures a broad, well-balanced curriculum is followed, but great importance is given to Maths and English as success in these subjects is central to development in other areas. Additional specialist teaching is provided for children requiring support in the basic subjects.

French has been successfully introduced in all classes including Reception with Spanish in the upper years.

All children receive music lessons and individual piano and guitar lessons are also available.

Emphasis is placed on high academic standards with children being prepared for a variety of Entrance examinations at 11 and more than 90% of pupils gain places at selective schools of their choice.

A wide range of sports and extracurricular activities is offered to both boys and girls, including football, netball, cricket, rounders, swimming, chess, lacrosse, singing and speech choir. The children compete in local sporting events as well as choral festivals.

Theatre and educational visits are encouraged along with a residential trip to Shropshire, and Paris for older pupils, which provide field and adventure activities that help build confidence and self-esteem.

Close contact with parents is promoted through regular parent/teacher meetings and reports on pupils progress.

A thriving Parent Teacher Association provides social functions for parents while raising funds for extra equipment.

After-school provision is provided by the 'Kids Club'. This operates daily from 3.30 pm until 6.00 pm and school is open from 8.00 am for early drop-offs.

Parents are welcome to visit the school by appointment.

Further information available from the Head Teacher.

Charitable status. Carleton House Preparatory School is a Registered Charity, number 505310. It exists to provide education for boys and girls.

Castle House School

Chetwynd End, Newport, Shropshire TF10 7JE

Tel: 01952 567600
email: admin@castlehouseschool.co.uk
website: www.castlehouseschool.co.uk
Twitter: @CastleHouseSch

Chairman of Governors: Mrs Carol Gibbs

Headmaster: **Mr Ian Sterling**, BEd Hons Leeds

Type of School. Co-educational day preparatory school.
Age Range. 2–11.
Number of Pupils. 109: 55 girls, 54 boys.
Fees per term (2018–2019). £2,500–£2,950.

Castle House is a friendly day preparatory school with a family feel. It is small enough for everybody to know and be known by everybody else, but offers a full and busy programme.

The school aims to bring the best out of every pupil by providing opportunities to excel and developing confidence to try.

Much importance is attached to the children being kind and considerate to each other, in the belief that happy children work best. We develop positive and courteous behaviour.

The school was founded in 1944 by Miss Zellah Pitchford. Since 1980 it has been a charitable trust, run by a board of governors with varied talents and local interests.

The school's Georgian house, set in delightful gardens, is in the conservation area of Newport in east Shropshire. It serves urban and rural areas, including west Staffordshire, Market Drayton, Eccleshall, Telford and Shifnal.

Pupils are prepared for entrance exams to independent schools and to local grammar schools of which the two in Newport are unique in Shropshire. There is an excellent record of passes and scholarships, from a mixed ability intake, with children achieving their potential and beyond.

The curriculum covers all major subjects, and Art, French, Music, Spanish, ICT, PE, Games, Swimming, Gymnastics and Drama. RE and assemblies are Christian, but non-denominational, encouraging all to join in.

Our flourishing educational nursery for two to four year olds, is open all year from 8.00 am to 6.00 pm.

A rich range of after-school activities includes moviemaking, yoga, crafts, choirs, computers, eco, gymnastics, chess, radio, football, netball, short tennis, cricket and rounders.

Matches are played in traditional team games, cross-country and swimming. Particular success has been achieved in schools' gymnastics, with girls' teams winning silver medals at national level in GISGA (independent schools) competitions. Boys' teams have three times won national under 9 and under 11 titles and the school team has twice won the BSGA under 11 mixed teams Floor and Vault national title.

We see education as a cooperative venture with parents. There are regular progress reports and feedback meetings. Parents are encouraged to bring their concerns to the teachers and there is also a Parents' Forum. The Parents' Association is very well supported.

Further information can be obtained on our website or by telephoning the Registrar at the school.

Charitable status. Castle House School Trust Ltd is a Registered Charity, number 510515. It exists for the provision of high quality education for boys and girls.

Chase Grammar School

Convent Close, Cannock, Staffordshire WS11 0UR

Tel:	01543 501800
Fax:	01543 501801
email:	info@chasegrammar.com
website:	www.chasegrammar.com
Twitter:	@ChaseGrammar
Facebook:	@ChaseGrammar

Acting Principal: **Mr Michael Hartland**, BA Hons, MA Cambridge, PGCE

Age Range. 2–18.
Number in School. 113 Boarders, 208 Day.
Fees per term (2018–2019). Day £1,995–£3,895; Boarding from £7,167. Fees include lunches and most extras.

Independent day and boarding school for boys and girls from 2 years to A Level.

Founded in 1879, Chase Grammar School has been delivering exceptional outcomes for pupils from all backgrounds for the last two centuries and combines high academic standards with holistic and pastoral care.

The school's mission is to develop its pupils into well-rounded, self-assured adults, capable of navigating complex social and cultural environments with confidence. We wish to enable them to learn how to persevere and make appropriate decisions in a range of situations, developing into lifelong learners, who can lead and take responsibility for themselves and others within their community.

Senior school life at Chase Grammar is varied, vibrant and fun. Encouragement, expertise and guidance is ever-present in the pursuit of academic excellence. A wide and varied curriculum offers choice for our pupils and the pastoral care and holistic approach combines to provide an unrivalled nurturing environment for pupils preparing for their GCSEs, A Levels and entry pathways to universities and apprenticeships. The school is highly ranked for academic results, showing that our approach to learning, in which we focus upon the development of character as much as knowledge, really works.

"Pupils of all ages are happy and confident individuals who feel well supported by their teachers" (ISI Inspection Report 2017)

Chase Grammar School teachers are united in their vision to engage the minds and enrich the lives of their pupils with innovative and varied learning programmes. The expectation is that every pupil will capture a deep understanding of, and a keen interest in, their academic subjects.

Chase Grammar School's outstanding academic results and its extensive preparation programme to gear its pupils for higher education and entry to the world's top universities, make this the school of choice for many parents.

As part of its preparation to Higher Education, all pupils receive one-to-one support through the application process to their acceptance. Thorough careers guidance, trips to Universities and visits from university admissions tutors are all part of their programme.

As well as taking pupils from across the county, the school also welcomes pupils from around the world and there is a vibrant boarding community. Pupils are all members of one of our three Houses (named after inspirational local people: education minister Jennie Lee; inventor and chess master Vernon Parton; and physician Frank Tylecote) and are invited to take part in the wealth of after-school and weekend activities and clubs. Boarding opportunities are afforded to every pupil in preparation for independent living at university and beyond.

Parents and carers play an important role in their child's development and at Chase Grammar there are many ways they can get involved with the school. Through detailed reports which are sent home five times each year, parents evenings and regular communication, each pupil's academic progress and attitude to learning is recorded and analysed enabling individual needs to be identified and addressed in a professional and caring manner.

The pupils benefit from small class sizes, a broad academic curriculum, opportunities to study a range of modern and classical languages, a full programme of enrichment activities, one-to-one support from tutors who help them to set targets and meet with them as individuals, and an international environment where different cultures are celebrated and pupils become global citizens who will want to give back to their own communities.

Above all, Chase Grammar School endeavours to educate well-rounded, accountable individuals with the compassion, courage and confidence to engage and excel in any walk of life.

Sport. Football, cricket, hockey and netball are the principal sports with school facilities for tennis, volleyball, basketball, badminton and table tennis.

Music and Drama. A strong team of professional performers and first-rate teachers producing big uptake in the performing arts as extracurricular activities.

School day. 08.40–16.40. Prep school ends at 16.00 with clubs until 16.45. Facilities for early drop-off and late pick-up.

Claires Court

1 College Avenue, Maidenhead, Berkshire SL6 6AW

Tel:	Registrar: 01628 327710
email:	registrar@clairescourt.com
website:	www.clairescourt.com

Principals:
Mr H Wilding, BA, MCIM, FRSA
Mr J Wilding, BSc, FRSA

Head of Senior Boys: Mr J Wilding, BSc FRSA
Head of Junior Boys: Mr D Richards, BEd QTS
Head of Senior Girls: Mrs M Heywood, BEd
Head of Junior Girls: Mrs Kirby, BA QTS
Head of Sixth Form: Mrs S Rogers, BEd, Cert HE, Adv Dip Ex&HS
Head of Nursery: Mrs S Wilding, BA, DPP

Age Range. 3–18.
Number of Pupils. 570 Boys, 300 Girls. Sixth Form: Co-educational 133.
Fees per term (2018–2019). £3,090–£5,580.
Teaching Staff: 207.

Claires Court is a school for families, run by a family, providing education for young people aged 3 to 18 years. Based on three sites across Maidenhead, we are a broad ability 'diamond model' day school where boys and girls are educated separately during their main school years, but come together for trips and visits, whilst the Nursery and Sixth Form pupils benefit from a co-educational learning environment.

It is the feeling of belonging and the school's ethos that helps young people thrive and flourish in our school community. At Claires Court, we treat everyone as an individual, evaluating each child's ability to ensure we can enable them to reach their full potential, helping them achieve great results, whether that is in the classroom, on the sports field or in the creative arena. By offering the best education, strong pastoral care and a wealth of opportunities, our pupils achieve academically, feel valued and have a strong sense of self-belief and self-worth.

Pupils have access to excellent facilities across the sites, with indoor swimming pools, drama studios, extensive playing fields and music suites. Senior pupils have access to top-class facilities for training and playing rugby, football, cricket and hockey through our partnership agreements with local sports clubs. Sailing and rowing are also part of our sport offering with much success in regional and national competitions.

At the core of our learning philosophy are the Claires Court Essentials. Right from Nursery we make learning fun but challenging and from that springboard we focus on developing a variety of skills and behaviours that young people need to be a successful learner and individual in our fast-paced world. As they mature pupils are expected to stretch themselves, push their own boundaries and limitations; we believe it is good to be wrong as long as we learn from that experience and bounce back. We develop boys and girls who are confident and resilient, learners who are critical thinkers and risk-takers, who can solve problems and communicate, as well as be creative and work collaboratively with others.

In the Junior years, the creative, topic-based curriculum inspires a passion for learning and children quickly develop a taste for success. There is a focus on mastering the fundamental skills as well as academic attainment. Further up the school, the breadth and balance of the curriculum allows senior pupils to develop new interests and talents before focusing on their GCSEs.

The Sixth Form offers just as much variety with more than 24 A Level subjects as well BTECs in ICT and Sport. In recent years students have achieved an overall pass rate of 100% and our value added surpasses that of most other Sixth Forms, meaning our students achieve over and above their predicted grades. Alongside this the team also offers development and training for the personal, social and work skills that are desired by universities and employers.

A warm welcome awaits visitors; please come along to one of our regular Open Morning or call the Registrar to arrange an individual tour.

Coopersale Hall School

Flux's Lane, Epping, Essex CM16 7PE

Tel:	01992 577133
Fax:	01992 571544
email:	info@coopersalehallschool.co.uk
website:	www.coopersalehallschool.co.uk
Twitter:	@CoopersaleHSch

Headmistress: **Miss Kaye Lovejoy**, AD BEd, CertEd, BEd Hons

Age Range. 2½–11 Co-educational.
Number in School. 280 Day Pupils.
Fees per term (2018–2019). £1,350–£3,525.

Coopersale Hall School is a thriving, caring local independent school with a high standard of academic achievement and a wide range of activities.

The School offers small class sizes and specialist teachers for ICT, Science, PE, Sport, Music and Drama. We provide a high standard of education and enjoy success in Entrance Examinations at 11 years to a wide choice of Secondary Schools.

We encourage our pupils to develop self-confidence and to take on roles of responsibility as they move up through the school. Creativity is nurtured within a disciplined environment and traditional values such as self-discipline are promoted to maximise our pupils' effectiveness in an ever-changing world.

Coopersale Hall is situated in a large country house that is pleasantly located on the outskirts of Epping, just off Stewards Green Road and only two minutes from Epping High Street. The School has its own private road and stands in some seven acres of landscaped gardens and playing fields.

Entry requirements: Interview and assessment.

Copthill School

Barnack Road, Uffington, Stamford, Lincolnshire PE9 3AD

Tel:	01780 757506
email:	mail@copthill.com
website:	www.copthill.com
Twitter:	@Copthill
Facebook:	@copthill

Principal: **Mr J A Teesdale**, BA Hons, PGCE

Head of School: Mrs Helen Schofield, BA Hons, PGCE
Head of Upper School: Mr Mark Thomas, BEng, PGCE
Head of Lower School: Mrs Anne Teesdale, BEd Hons

Age Range. Co-educational 2–11 years.

Number of Pupils. 300 total: Main School (age 4+ to 11) 240 and Nursery/Pre-School (age 2 to 4) 60.

Fees per term (2018–2019). £3,085–£3,450.

Educational Aims.

- A welcoming, stimulating and happy environment which is friendly, caring and well disciplined, in which every pupil is encouraged to achieve and motivated to succeed.
- An open-door policy, providing the foundations for effective communication and cooperation between Home and School.
- A broad curriculum emphasising the importance of literacy and numeracy and designed to develop lifelong knowledge, skills and attitudes that allow our children to become responsible citizens, independent explorers, creative thinkers, problem solvers, team players and reflective learners.
- An emphasis on using the outdoor environment to engage and inspire our pupils, developing their knowledge, skills and attitudes across the curriculum.
- An excellent preparation for entrance to a wide range of independent and state secondary schools.

Location. Purpose-built, modern facilities set within 350 acres of farmland, including river and woodland. 2 miles from Stamford and the A1 and 15 miles from Peterborough.

School Day. Monday to Friday from 8.35 am to 4.40 pm. Crèche hours from 7.45 am to 6.00 pm. Breakfast and Tea available.

Facilities. Creative Suite, Music Suite, Library, Languages Suite, Sports Hall and playing fields including AstroTurf and a well-established on-site Forest School. High-quality catering facilities offering delicious, nutritionally balanced meals.

Pastoral Care. In addition to their forms, pupils from Year 5 upwards are also placed in small tutor groups in which their progress is closely monitored in preparation for senior school entrance. There is a genuine 'open door policy' throughout the School. Parents' Evenings are hosted twice a year and written reports are distributed at least 3 times a year.

Curriculum. A modern curriculum based on the National Curriculum. Combines traditional and innovative teaching methods. Learning support offered throughout the school where a specific need has been assessed.

Music, Speech & Drama. Music and Drama are taught as part of the curriculum. Regular drama productions encourage all pupils to participate. Pupils can also receive expert individual tuition and perform at school concerts, assemblies and in local music and drama festivals.

Sport. Rugby, Hockey (boy and girls), Netball, Cross-Country, Athletics, Cricket, Rounders, Swimming, Tennis plus many extracurricular sports including Sailing and Archery.

Future Schools. Pupils leave Copthill at 11 years old with great confidence and the ability to think for themselves. Copthill is a truly independent school, offering thorough preparation to a wide variety of independent and state senior schools, both local and national, achieving a large number of scholarships and awards.

Cransley School

Belmont Hall, Great Budworth, Nr Northwich, Cheshire CW9 6HN

Tel:	01606 891747
Fax:	01606 892122
email:	admin@cransleyschool.org.uk
website:	www.cransleyschool.com
Twitter:	@CransleySchool
Facebook:	@CransleySchool

Headmaster: **Mr Richard Pollock**

Deputy Head: Mr Nigel Willetts
Assistant Head (Academic): Mrs Clare Lancaster
Operations Manager: Mrs Clare Holt

Age Range. Co-educational 4–16.

Number in School. Day: 100 Girls, 81 Boys.

Fees per term (2018–2019). £2,641–£3,724.

Set in the midst of beautiful Cheshire countryside, Cransley School really is a very special place to be educated. At Cransley we offer all our children the individual support that allows them to grow in confidence and to discover what makes them unique. Our pupils are given the attention and nurturing they need to excel academically and to reach their full potential. A Cransley education is more than just the excellent academic achievements we produce; we offer our pupils a wide range of extracurricular activities and encourage them to challenge themselves to learn outside of the classroom as well as within. Once again we were thrilled with the GCSE results this year as one of the top performing schools in Cheshire, enabling us to create firm foundations for bright and successful futures for all of our pupils.

Life is never dull at Cransley. There is a wide variety of extracurricular activities available throughout the school – there are three choirs, Duke of Edinburgh's Award expeditions and regular drama performances. Students have a choice of clubs – gymnastics, gardening, languages, rowing, football and rugby to name but a few. There are many sporting opportunities and Cransley teams regularly compete against other schools in the area.

Cransley students enjoy many visits to enrich the curriculum. We also play hosts to visiting theatre groups. We offer residential opportunities – groups have been overnight in London for theatre and museum visits; GCSE Geography students visit Llandudno and the Lake District; activity weekends are particular favourites for both Senior and Junior Department pupils; foreign travel is also on the menu.

Cransley also has a thriving 'Friends of Cransley' – they organise regular events throughout the year which raise valuable funds to support staff and students and also offer a fantastic opportunity for parents to get to know each other.

Cundall Manor School

Cundall, North Yorkshire YO61 2RW

Tel:	01423 360200
email:	head@cundallmanor.org.uk
website:	www.cundallmanorschool.com
Twitter:	@CundallManor
Facebook:	@Cundall-Manor-School
LinkedIn:	/cundall-manor-school

Joint Heads:
Mr John Sample, BSc Hons, PGCE
Mrs Amanda Kirby, BA Hons, PGCE, NPQH

Age Range. 2–16 Co-educational.

Number of Pupils. 383.

Cundall Manor School is a thriving independent co-educational boarding school, catering for nearly 400 boys and girls from two to sixteen years of age. Set in 28 acres of beautiful grounds between Harrogate, Ripon and York, it is easily accessed from the A1(M) and A19.

Cundall Manor School blends the best traditions of honour, integrity and courtesy with up-to-the-minute teaching facilities and approaches. The school has developed a reputation for ensuring that each and every child feels happy, safe, supported and celebrated. Within this environment, children engage fully with the educational challenges and risks that maximise learning and achievement. The rural setting allows pupils to embrace their childhoods while the innovative and unique curriculum provides opportunity for all to develop the confidence, judgement and personal skills that will benefit their futures.

Children are encouraged to participate in a number of sports and events outside of the curriculum including outward bound courses, travel, charity/community work and extracurricular sports. Whilst many children do achieve top standards and awards across academia, sports and music, competing and succeeding at area, county and national level, our aim is to ensure every child has the opportunity to participate in the full range of activities, whatever their level of ability and experience. We do this by cultivating a 'yes' mentality amongst our pupils, encouraging them to engage with the wider world and to think and act independently and without inhibition.

Fees per term (2018–2019). Nursery: £402 (1 full day per term); Reception–Year 2: Day £3,246; Years 3 & 4: Day £5,132, Weekly Boarding £6,771; Years 5–11: Day £5,204, Weekly Boarding £6,843.

Charitable status. Cundall Manor Limited is a Registered Charity, number 529540.

Daiglen School

68 Palmerston Road, Buckhurst Hill, Essex IG9 5LG

Tel: 020 8504 7108
email: admin@daiglenschool.co.uk
website: www.daiglenschool.co.uk
Twitter: @DaiglenSchool

Perstare et Praestare – Persevere and Excel

Head Teacher: **Mrs P Dear**, BEd

Age Range. 3–11.

Number in School. 156.

Fees per term (2018–2019). £3,200–£3,250, sibling discount available. Extras: swimming, music tuition, trips.

Daiglen School is a small preparatory school which provides a happy and secure environment for all pupils. Kindness to others is valued above all, and pupils are polite and considerate with each other as well as with adults. We have a strong sense of family and community, underpinned by warm supportive relationships and mutual respect, which ensures that all pupils are valued and given the chance to shine.

Confident children relish challenge and the school promotes a culture of excellence. We celebrate individual and group successes as children learn the importance of pursuing their ambitions with determination and perseverance. They are inspired to do well both by the infectious enthusiasm of their excellent teachers and by the example of older

children who become their role models. Our pupils flourish in this environment and leave as caring, confident, articulate and well-mannered young people, fully prepared for the next stage in their journey through life. We are justifiably proud of our pupils' academic achievements, as well as those on the sports field and other areas, and a good proportion leave with scholarships to selective independent and state secondary schools.

Founded in 1916, Daiglen School is rich in history and tradition. The school is built around an elegant Victorian house with much of its stained glass and cornices intact. Modern features include a purpose-built gymnasium/hall, art room, science laboratory and ICT suite. It is pleasantly situated on the borders of Epping Forest and is well served by public transport.

Inspection: Daiglen School was inspected in September 2010 and received the highest accolades from the Independent Schools Inspectorate. The team praised Daiglen in glowing terms, awarding the highest possible rating in areas that include pupils' all-round achievement, personal development and the quality of teaching, and declaring the school's Early Years Foundation Stage setting to be outstanding in every respect. The full report is available to read on our website.

Choosing a school is arguably the most difficult decision you will make for your child, and one which will have the greatest consequences in his or her life. Most of our pupils come to Daiglen on personal recommendation from parents of past or present pupils. We encourage a close and mutually supportive partnership with parents. To find out more about us, you can visit our website or make arrangements to visit the school; you will receive a warm welcome.

Charitable status. The Daiglen School Trust Limited is a Registered Charity, number 273015.

Ditcham Park School

Ditcham Park, Petersfield, Hampshire GU31 5RN

Tel: 01730 825659
email: admissions@ditchampark.com
website: www.ditchampark.com
Twitter: @DitchamJuniors
            @DitchamSeniors
Facebook: @DitchamParkSchool

Headmaster: **Mr G D Spawforth**, MA, MEd

Age Range. 2½–16.

Number in School. Day: 217 Boys, 156 Girls.

Fees per term (2018–2019). £2,835–£4,753 excluding lunch.

Situated high on the South Downs, the School achieves excellent results in a happy purposeful atmosphere.

Charitable status. Ditcham Park School is a Registered Charity, number 285244R. It exists for educational purposes.

The Dixie Grammar School

Market Bosworth, Leicestershire CV13 0LE

Tel: 01455 292244
email: info@dixie.org.uk
website: www.dixie.org.uk

Twitter: @DixieGrammar
Facebook: @the.dixie.grammar

Headmaster: **Mr Richard J Lynn**, BA Cardiff

Age Range. 3–18.
Number in School. 475.
Fees per term (2018–2019). Nursery: Daily Rate (inc lunch) £50; Reception, Years 1 and 2 £2,945, Years 3 to 5 £3,340, Year 6 to Sixth Form £4,005. Scholarships, Bursaries, Vouchers/Government Funding, Monthly Payment Scheme available.

The earliest records we have of the School's existence date from 1320, but the School gained its present name when it was re-founded in 1601 under the will of an Elizabethan merchant and Lord Mayor of London, Sir Wolstan Dixie.

The most distinguished of the School's former pupils is Thomas Hooker, founder of Hartford, Connecticut, and Father of American Democracy. The best known of its teachers is undoubtedly Dr Johnson, moralist, poet and author of the famous dictionary, who taught at the School in the mid-eighteenth century.

The main building of today's School was built in 1828 and faces the historic market square of Market Bosworth, making a distinctive landmark. However, in 1969 the School was closed, as new, much larger comprehensive schools found favour.

It was to revive the best aspects of the grammar school tradition that the Leicestershire Independent Educational Trust was formed in 1983, and four years later the School was reopened as a selective, independent, day school for boys and girls of all backgrounds between the ages of 10 and 18. Three years later our Junior School opened, moving to its present premises, Temple Hall in Wellsborough, in 2001, where we have The Pippins Nursery.

The emphasis remains the same as it ever was: to provide an excellent academic education that will be of lasting value to our children as they face the challenges of the future.

Both schools are selective and have academic achievement as their central aim. Music, drama, sport and service are also an integral part of the education offered. Both schools have an interdenominational Christian basis. The relative smallness of the schools ensures that they combine great friendliness with excellent discipline, providing a secure and well-ordered framework in which children can confidently achieve their full potential. We are ambitious for each of them.

The Grammar School offers academic, music, art, sports and sixth form scholarships.

Charitable status. The Leicestershire Independent Educational Trust is a Registered Charity, number 514407.

DLD College London
Alpha Plus Group

199 Westminster Bridge Road, London SE1 7FX

Tel: 020 7935 8411
email: dld@dld.org
website: www.dldcollege.co.uk
Twitter: @DLDcollege
Facebook: @DLDcollege

Principal: **Mr Irfan Latif**

Age Range. 14+ Co-educational.
Number of Pupils. 440 Day and Boarding.

Fees per annum (2018–2019). £23,000.

Part of the Alpha Plus Group, DLD College London was established in 1931. After 10 years located in Marylebone, the College merged with its younger sister, Abbey College, and moved in 2015 to brand new, purpose-built facilities in the heart of London, looking over the River Thames to the Houses of Parliament. With bright, state-of-the-art teaching facilities and secure, on-site student accommodation, all in the centre of the amazing, historic and vibrant city of London, DLD College London is a truly unique college campus, with outstanding facilities including:

- 220 secure, ensuite student bedrooms within the College
- A dedicated wellbeing centre
- Restaurant facilities on site, including a Starbucks franchise
- 6 high specification laboratories
- A creative arts and media faculty featuring art rooms, photography, drama, music and media suites, including a 100+ seat theatre
- Over 40 teaching rooms
- Learning hub, digital hub, study and ICT facilities
- Garden space and third floor roof garden
- Fully air-conditioned classrooms
- Access to shared swimming pool and gymnasium facilities

DLD College is a co-educational London day and boarding school accepting pupils from the ages of 14+. There are over 370 students in the Sixth Form studying A Levels, BTECs or IFP from a choice of over 30 subjects. Most are doing A Levels in the normal way over a two-year period with another cohort joining at the start of Upper Sixth. There are no subject restrictions at A Level. GCSE courses are taught over a one-year period so pupils are able to join at the beginning of Year 11. The average class size is between 6 and 8 students. The College offers a 2-year GCSE Programme for SEN students. The college also offers BTEC programmes in Business, Media Studies and Music Technology.

At DLD we offer an extensive range of co-curricular activities, which includes the prestigious Duke of Edinburgh's Award, as well as many traditional options such as Sport, Music, Drama and Art. Our wide enrichment programme supports our academic curriculum and forms an integral part of the wider education and college experience we offer our students. Our vision is to create all-rounded students, who excel academically and develop further their emotional, inter-personal and social skills. All students are encouraged to participate in one or more of our range of extra-curricular activities. This participation is important for students both as an opportunity for recreation and as an effective way to improve the quality of their UCAS personal statement and CV in the future.

While the atmosphere at DLD is more informal than in mainstream independent schools, rules regarding academic performance are strictly enforced with an emphasis on attendance and punctuality. There are fortnightly tests in each subject and half-termly reports. Parents receive five reports each year and there are two parents' evenings and a parents' social evening.

The teaching staff are highly qualified and chosen not just for their expertise but also for their ability to relate positively to young people. The college aims to make learning interesting, active and rigorous. While clear guidelines are very important to ensure pupils establish a good working routine, the college believes strongly that students respond best when there is a culture of encouragement. Effort, progress, achievement and courtesy are regularly acknowledged and formally rewarded.

Dwight School London

6 Friern Barnet Lane, London N11 3LX

Tel: 020 8920 0600
Fax: 020 8211 4605
email: admissions@dwightlondon.org
website: www.dwightlondon.org
Twitter: @DwightSchoolUK
Facebook: @Dwight-School-London
LinkedIn: /dwight-school-london

Head of School: **Mrs Alison Cobbin**, BA, Dip Ed, MBA

Age Range. 3–18.
Number in School. 350 Boys and Girls.
Fees per term (2018–2019). £1,530–£7,330.

Dwight School London provides a secure, well-ordered and happy environment with the learning process at its core, offering an International Baccalaureate (IB) education for all students in order for them to reach their full potential. Serving a cosmopolitan and diverse North London community, great importance is attached to respect, understanding and empathy with everyone's cultures, religions and backgrounds. Emphasis is placed on development of the individual student with academic, artistic, sporting, creative, practical and social skills being encouraged and individual talents nurtured. We aim to Ignite the Spark of Genius in Every Child.

Students follow the International Baccalaureate curriculum, starting at age 3 with the IB Primary Years Programme, moving on to the IB Middle Years Programme at age 11 and the IB Diploma Programme at age 16. The programmes are designed to encourage the development of learning skills and to meet a child's academic, social, physical, emotional and cultural needs. Through enquiry-based learning and various disciplines, subject interrelatedness is accentuated, preparing students for the pre-university IB Diploma Programme. Within the programme students must study six subjects, a research project, leading to a 4000-word essay, The Theory of Knowledge course, and Creativity, Action, Service (CAS). The CAS programme is a fundamental part of the IB Diploma programme, requiring students to participate in approximately 150 hours of activities both in and out of school.

The Quest Programme is designed for students who need learning support to develop strategies to enable them to successfully access the IB programmes. Through extra support with specialist staff who teach skills such as effective reading, time management, organisational skills, planning of work and revision and exam techniques, students can reach their full potential, further enhanced by the school's low teacher to student ratio.

Students who meet the criteria are accepted for entry at any time throughout the school year subject to space. Full details can be found on the website.

The Upper School has dedicated ICT, music, art, design technology, drama and library facilities. The Lower School has dedicated music, art, library and a multi-purpose hall for sports and drama activities. The school has its own sports fields with tennis courts nearby used by both Upper and Lower School.

Music tuition is incorporated into the curriculum with the addition of individual lessons in a wide variety of instruments such as piano, guitar, drums, woodwind and strings with composition and singing also available. The school has a number of musical ensembles with varying styles from jazz to rock to chamber music and regular concerts highlight the very real talent within the student body.

The students' physical development is considered as important as academic development and the school's sports fields provide excellent facilities for football, cricket, athletics, hockey, tennis and softball. The school's hall, playgrounds and local amenities are also utilised to offer further activities such as basketball, badminton, squash, swimming, table tennis, ice skating and skiing. Matches and tournaments between local schools are regular fixtures.

The school's close proximity to central London allows for numerous trips to the capital's museums, galleries and theatres. A variety of overseas trips are offered, both academic and leisure, including France, Spain, skiing and our sister school, The Dwight School, in New York while the Upper School students have an opportunity to participate in the Model United Nations conferences at The Hague.

Eaton Square Kensington

Preparatory School:
24 Elvaston Place, London SW7 5NL
Tel: 020 7225 3131
Fax: 020 7590 9745
email: registrar.kensington@eatonsquareschool.com

Pre-Preparatory School:
**The Long Garden, St George's Fields, Albion Street,
London W2 2AX**
Tel: 020 7262 1190
email: admissions@hydeparkschool.co.uk

website: www.hydeparkschool.co.uk

Headmistress: **Mrs Trish Watt**

Head of Pre-Prep: **Mrs Nina Firkin**

Age Range. Co-educational: Prep 5–11, Pre-Prep 2–5.
Number of Pupils. Prep 80, Pre-Prep 45.
Fees per term (2018–2019). £3,535–£6,380.

Eaton Square Kensington and its Pre-Prep School occupy two separate and very different sites: the prep is housed in an elegant Victorian building in an excellent location in the heart of South Kensington; the pre-prep is situated in a wonderful large garden in W2, just north of Hyde Park. The prep school takes children aged 5 to 11 years (Year 1 to Year 6) and the pre-prep takes children from 2 to 5 years (Nursery and Reception). The schools have traditional values and our staff expect high standards of both work and behaviour, with kindness and consideration for others being of paramount importance. At the same time, the schools are well resourced with modern equipment and the children are safe, secure and exceptionally well cared for. Both schools are small, cosy, friendly establishments where no individual becomes lost in the crowd. Delicious healthy lunches are prepared by our own cooks who cater for all dietary needs.

One of the main purposes of the prep school is to prepare children for entry into the senior school of their choice. The curriculum consists of all the customary subjects plus our own additions: French from Nursery upwards and Mandarin and Latin from Form 4. We more than compensate for our limited outside space with an extensive PE curriculum including swimming from Reception and outside sports at Hyde Park. We have football and netball teams and play competitive matches against local schools. The children participate in regular trips to the nearby museums and to places of interest further afield. There is a residential trip in Forms 4, 5 and 6. We offer a wide range of after-school activities including fencing, karate, climbing, football, coding, Mini Engineers, netball, mindfulness and philosophy, drama, science and EAL. The children may also take ballet classes as an optional extra and there is excellent provision at both schools for children who do not have English as their first language.

The pre-prep in W2 is a paradise for young children with its wonderful garden and vast sandpit. Whatever the weather, the children have a huge array of resources to exercise their minds and bodies, and the freedom to investigate and experiment under the watchful eyes of our well-qualified and highly-experienced staff. Children who attend the pre-prep are guaranteed places at the prep school and can opt to travel between the sites by school minibus if they wish.

Eaton Square School is part of the Dukes Education Group. Dukes Education is a family of schools and educational organisations based in the UK. We bring together schools that are diverse in their offering, and yet united as outstanding examples of teaching and learning.

Egerton Rothesay School

Durrants Lane, Berkhamsted, Herts HP4 3UJ

Tel: 01442 865275
email: admin.dl@eger-roth.co.uk
website: www.eger-roth.co.uk

A School with a Difference

***Headteacher*: Mr Colin Parker**, BSc Hons, Dip Ed, PGCE, CMath

Age Range. 6–19 years: Poplar 6–11 years; Senior School 11–16 years; Sixth Form 16–19 years.
Number in School. 128 boys, 50 girls.
Fees per term (2018–2019). £5,340–£7,600 (lunches included).

ERS aims to provide an exciting and relevant educational experience for pupils who need that little bit more support from their school, whilst studying a mainstream curriculum.

It focuses especially on students who have found, or would find, it difficult to make progress and succeed within another school – perhaps because of an earlier, negative, educational experience or perhaps because of a specific learning difficulty, such as dyslexia or dyspraxia, a speech and language difficulty or an autistic spectrum condition. If your child has other educational difficulties the school may also be able to help with these.

Children come with a variety of learning styles and use is made of a wide range of teaching strategies in order to match these. The school provides additional levels of support both in the classroom and on an individual basis, varying to suit the need of the child. Throughout the school children are taught in small classes to match their need for support, to the level of teaching and support staff provided. The team of therapists includes Speech and Language, Occupational Therapy, Social Emotional Development and visiting physiotherapists. Our specialist teaching team provide individual lessons in literacy and numeracy.

The Sixth Form provides for students who continue to mature beyond the age of 16 and require an additional amount of support and time in order to enable them to transfer successfully into a further education establishment or employment. The school has developed both one and two year educational programmes within a high-quality, secure and supportive environment, in which students are able to continue to mature, develop and learn whilst studying for additional examinations including GCSE, BTEC, Foundation and ASDAN awards. Examination results enable pupils to enter colleges and sixth forms in both state and independent schools to continue their education before university entrance, if appropriate.

Every child at Egerton Rothesay is seen as a unique person and an individual student. The school aims to make an excellent contribution into the life of each one ensuring that they can be supported in the way that they personally need to maximise their individual learning potential.

The school wants more than just to deliver a curriculum and has a learning skills approach throughout the school – aiming to prepare students not just for school and exams but for life in today's complex society and an ever changing world of work.

A child can often be able and talented in one aspect of the curriculum, yet find it difficult to make good progress in another. Some students will need support for the duration of their time in school, whilst others may only need a short amount of support to address a specific problem or to build confidence.

All activities takes place within an environment offering exceptional pastoral care and spiritual development that is driven and informed by the school's Christian foundation and its Chaplaincy team.

Transport: Egerton Rothesay is also more than just a local school – students travel to the school from all directions, many using the comprehensive bus service that the school runs over a 35-mile radius.

If you think this may be the right type of school for your child you can obtain more information from the Registrar on 01442 877060 or visit the website at www.eger-roth.co.uk.

Fairfield School

Fairfield Way, Backwell, Bristol BS48 3PD

Tel: 01275 462743
email: secretary@fairfieldschool.org.uk
website: fairfield.school

***Headteacher*: Mrs Lesley Barton**, BA Hons, PGCE

Age Range. 2–11.
Number in School. 63 Boys, 38 Girls.
Fees per term (2018–2019). Nursery (full-time), Reception, Years 1–2 £2,640; Years 3–6 £2,915.

Fairfield is an independent day school for boys and girls aged 2–11. The school was founded in 1935 and aims to provide a broad, traditional education. We encourage each child to maximise his or her potential through creating a family ethos in which children feel happy, secure and valued. A fundamental aspect of our ethos is our commitment to small classes, usually of 18–20. Fairfield offers a broad and balanced curriculum, informed by the National Curriculum. Teachers and visiting coaches provide a wide range of extracurricular lessons including music, dance, sport, drama and creative activities. Pupils are prepared for entry into all local independent senior schools as well as for the local maintained sector schools.

For further details please apply to the School Secretary.

Charitable status. Fairfield PNEU School (Backwell) Limited is a Registered Charity, number 310215.

Fairley House School

Junior Department:
218–220 Lambeth Road, London SE1 7JY

Tel: 020 7976 5456
Fax: 020 7620 1069
email: junior@fairleyhouse.org.uk
website: www.fairleyhouse.org.uk

Senior Department:
30 Causton Street, London SW1P 4AU

Tel: 020 7976 5456
Fax: 020 7976 5905
email: senior@fairleyhouse.org.uk

website: www.fairleyhouse.org.uk

Headmaster: **Michael Taylor**, BA Hons, PGCE, FRGS

   Age Range. 5–16.
   Number of Pupils. 189 (128 Boys, 61 Girls).
   Fees per term (2018–2019). £10,609.

Fairley House School is a school for children with Specific Learning Difficulties, Dyslexia and Dyspraxia. The aim of the school is to provide intensive support to help children to overcome difficulties, coupled with a full, rich curriculum designed to bring out children's strengths and talents. Most children return to mainstream schooling after two to three years. Children's learning styles have often not been catered for in their previous school, leading to failure and loss of confidence, but Fairley House offers them a 'level playing field' where everyone has similar difficulties. Children receive a stimulating educational experience integrated with therapy and specialist teaching. Teaching is multi-sensory and children learn Science, Spelling, Geography and History through interesting, hands-on activities. There is a staff to pupil ratio of 1:3.5. This integration is one of the many things that sets us apart as a specialist day school for children with Specific Learning Difficulties.

We emphasise the development of the whole child, helping him or her to gain confidence and self-esteem through an encouraging and nurturing ethos. The children have plenty of opportunities to develop sound academic and social skills and to become independent. At Fairley House, everyone succeeds.

Falkner House

Girls' School:
19 Brechin Place, London SW7 4QB

Tel: 020 7373 4501
email: office@falknerhouse.co.uk

Boys' School:
20 Penywern Road, London SW5 9SU

Tel: 020 7373 2340
email: office20pr@falknerhouse.co.uk

website: www.falknerhouse.co.uk

Principal: **Mrs Anita Griggs**, BA Hons, PGCE

Headmistress, *Girls' School*: Mrs Flavia Rogers, BA Hons, PGCE

Headmistress, *Boys' School*: Mrs Eleanor Dixon, MA Cantab

   Age Range. Girls 4–11, Boys 4–11, Co-educational Nurseries (ages 3–4).

Number of Pupils. Girls: 200. Boys: 90. The Boys' School is growing each year. Current classes from Reception–Year 3. By 2021 this will be Rec-Year 6 and a full school of approx 150 boys.

Fees per term (2018–2019). Girls' School: £6,360; Boys' School: £6,630; Nurseries: £3,260.

Girls' School. Falkner House is unashamedly academically ambitious and pupils achieve notable success at 11+ to the very top day and boarding schools. This is all within a naturally self-policing, civilised atmosphere where the development of self-confidence and happiness are seen as key goals. There is a busy yet friendly environment and as a result pupils have an engaging openness, intellectual curiosity and courtesy beyond their years. "We like them to have ability and oomph" says Mrs Rogers "but not to be sassy or precocious."

Excellent facilities include a science laboratory, art room, library and playground. State-of-the-art IT facilities now include individual iPads integrated into the curriculum. A strong musical tradition lies alongside an excellent sporting record. Pre/post school care is offered, as well as a wide range of after-school activities.

Entrance at 4+ by assessment.

Boys' School. The new Boys' School with a similar ethos and facilities started on a separate site in September 2017.

Falkner House Boys provides an outstanding academic education in a family atmosphere. They offer a unique environment in which children can flourish and are given the opportunity and confidence to excel. Londoners through and through, they embrace the best of British values in the most dynamic and diverse of cities.

One of the most important spaces at Falkner House is the playground – a hardworking space that the school is particularly proud of given its central London location. It helps the boys learn, both directly and indirectly.

Falkner House embraces academic success at any stage of a boy's time at school, whether at 7, 8 or 11+. If they believe that a boy is ready for the 7 or 8+ exam process, and after discussions with the family, they will have a completely tailor-made programme for them to prepare, for success without strain. The years children spend at school are few and precious. The process of teaching and learning is at the heart of the school, and the very reason for its existence. The best teaching, the teaching that Falkner House offers, sets boys off on a lifelong path of satisfying, pleasurable and empowering learning.

Entrance is at 4+ by assessment.

Falkner House Nurseries cater for boys and girls aged 3–4 years. Children thrive in a stimulating atmosphere under the care of professional and thoughtful teachers. Children are encouraged to be curious, to experiment and to learn through play. Specialist staff teach subjects such as music and PE to enrich the nursery curriculum.

Entrance at rising 3 is by date of registration.

Faraday School

Old Gate House, 7 Trinity Buoy Wharf, London E14 0FH

Tel: 020 7719 9342
            020 8965 7374 (Admissions)
email: admissions@faradayschool.co.uk
            head@faradayschool.co.uk
website: www.faradayschool.co.uk

Head Teacher: **Claire Murdoch**

Age Range. 4–11 Co-educational.

Number of Pupils. 104.

Founded in 2009, Faraday is a small but growing independent school in East London located at the unique setting of Trinity Buoy Wharf.

Here at Faraday we offer a traditional approach to primary education with a strong emphasis on the core skills of literacy and numeracy. Although we believe in a traditional approach, our lessons reflect modern thinking on how children learn most effectively and our small classes and quality staff allow for a very personal approach to learning.

Opportunities outside the classroom abound. Through sporting activities, first-class music, art and drama, we encourage every child to find their own particular strength. A wide range of after-school clubs, after-school care and school bus service is attractive to many working parents.

Termly school trips extend the curriculum and develop social skills. Our location on the historic wharf, home to the Faraday lighthouse, Container City and a wealth of creative tenants offers us excellent opportunities for partnerships to extend our pupils' learning. Our partially-covered playground roof, with views over the Thames to the O2 Centre, allows for all-weather play.

Entry into Reception is non selective and based on the date the completed registration form is returned to our Registrar, with siblings given priority. Entry higher up the school is by interview and informal assessment in the classroom. We offer regular open days and welcome private tours.

Faraday was the second of the New Model School Company's schools, offering a low-fee model, based on traditional teaching methods and with a Christian ethos, although we accept children of all faiths or none.

Fees per term (2018–2019). £3,448.

Forest Park Preparatory School
Bellevue Education

Lauriston House, 27 Oakfield, Sale, Cheshire M33 6NB

Tel: 0161 973 4835
email: post@forestparkprep.co.uk
website: www.forestparkprep.co.uk
Twitter: @ForestParkPrep
Facebook: @forestpark

Headteacher: **Mr Nick Tucker**, BEd Hons Prim Ed, MA Ed Leadership & Mgt

Age Range. 3–11.

Number in School. 85 Day Boys, 74 Day Girls.

Fees per term (2018–2019). £2,230–£2,423.

Forest Park occupies a pleasant site in a quiet road surprisingly close to the centre of Sale, easily accessible from motorways and surrounding areas.

The school aims to discover and develop each child's particular abilities by offering a varied curriculum in a stimulating and happy atmosphere. Forest Park has a good pupil to teacher ratio and offers a wide range of subjects with priority given to the traditional disciplines of English, mathematics and science. Pupils from three years of age are taught information technology by specialist staff. Swimming is taught from the age of five and games offered are football, cricket, netball, tennis and hockey. Pupils are taught French from Pre-Prep class. Older children have the opportunity to enjoy residential and activity trips to broaden their knowledge and develop self-confidence.

The confidence and social ease one expects of a private education is a product of the school. Our aim is to develop skills and knowledge through a habit of hard work in a secure and happy environment within a disciplined framework. The school prepares pupils for all independent grammar school examinations and has an excellent record in this respect.

The school prides itself on strong links and communication with a most supportive Parents' Association.

Fyling Hall School

Robin Hood's Bay, Whitby, North Yorkshire YO22 4QD

Tel: 01947 880353
Fax: 01947 881097
email: office@fylinghall.org
website: www.fylinghall.org
Twitter: @Fyling_Hall
Facebook: @FylingHallSchool

Headmaster: **Mr Steven Allen**, BA Hons, QTS

Deputy Head (Academic): Dr Ian Richardson, BSc, MPhil, PhD, PGCE, FGS

Deputy Head (Pastoral): Miss Adele Gilmour, BA, PGCE

Age Range. 4–18.

Number of Pupils. Boarders: Boys 32, Girls 34; Day: Boys 56, Girls 44.

Fees per term (2018–2019). Day: £2,295–£3,151; Weekly Boarding: £3,161–£4,044; Full Boarding: £5,572–£6,865.

Fyling Hall School is one of the oldest recognised co-educational schools in the country. It occupies a spectacular coastal setting within the North York Moors National Park. Pupils may safely enjoy freedom in this beautiful and peaceful rural area.

The buildings centre on a grade two listed Georgian country house in delightfully landscaped gardens incorporating an outdoor theatre overlooking Robin Hood's Bay. Recent expansion has included two new boarding houses, science laboratories and dining room in addition to the purpose-built Junior School. We have also built a spacious multi-functional sports hall and an astroturf recently.

The school is intentionally small due to its desire to educate pupils as individuals. The advantageous pupil to teacher ratio encourages effective learning. The teaching is along traditional lines with an emphasis on 'doing one's best' within a supportive yet challenging environment. A broadly based and well resourced curriculum is followed which reflects recent national initiatives, particularly in the scientific and information technology fields. A wide range of GCSE and A Level courses are offered.

Fyling Hall is a closely knit society with an emphasis on pastoral care and a real sense of communal responsibility. The chief feature is a spirit of confidence and cooperation between staff and pupils in an atmosphere which is natural for growth.

There is no entrance examination, but an interview and a report from the current school are integral parts of the admission process.

Many of the pupils stay to join the Sixth Form, where freedom and responsibility present a balance and are a useful preparation for university life.

The school takes advantage of its natural surroundings in the provision of numerous extra-curricular activities. Fyling Hall has its own ponies and these constitute a much loved part of school life. Climbing, Karate, Duke of Edinburgh's Award and Riding are all popular. The main games are rugby, hockey, cricket and tennis, each with a full fixture list. Music enjoys a good reputation and individual tuition is available in all the usual musical instruments.

Robin Hood's Bay is remarkably accessible despite its rural splendour. Nearby Whitby and Scarborough are both railheads. Teesside Airport and the ferry port of Hull, with their frequent continental connections, are both easily reached. An experienced Secretary is able to advise on all travel arrangements.

Academic standards are high, but other abilities are valued, and aided by the small size of classes it is hoped that all pupils can be encouraged to achieve their maximum potential.

Charitable status. Fyling Hall School Trust Ltd is a Registered Charity, number 507857. It exists for the provision of high quality education for boys and girls.

Gad's Hill School

Higham, Rochester, Kent ME3 7PA

Tel: 01474 822366
Fax: 01474 822977
email: information@gadshillschool.org
website: www.gadshill.org
Twitter: @GadsHillSchool
Facebook: @GadsHillSchoolOfficial

Headmaster: **Mr Paul Savage**, BA Hons, PGCE

Age Range. Co-educational 3–16.
Number in School. 353.
Fees per term (2018–2019). £2,341–£4,391.
Entry requirements. Interview and assessment.
Aim. To provide a good all-round education, to build confidence, establish friendships, to reward success (however small) and to ensure our students leave as mature, self-reliant young people who depart Gad's for the career or University placement of their choice.

Kindergarten (3–6 years). From the very early years in Kindergarten the children are encouraged to learn through play, music and drama. Basic letter and number work is introduced within the nursery and reception class as the children concentrate on the Early Learning Goals. In Year 1 and Year 2 they largely follow Key Stage One of the National Curriculum although in addition; from Reception upwards, all of our children are taught French and also Information and Communications Technology.

Junior School (7–11 years). Our Junior School curriculum seeks to build upon the children's undaunted love of adventure. Literacy, Numeracy and Humanities continue to be taught by Form Tutors however, the children begin to benefit from more lessons delivered by specialist tutors particularly in French, Information Technology, Design & Technology, RE, Games and Drama.

Senior School (11–16 years). Senior School concentrates very much on the preparation for GCSE success and our classes are kept to a maximum of 20 children per class. This way the children benefit from smaller class sizes and consequently our tutors get to know each child as an individual and this enables them to provide the right level of support and assistance. This goes a long way to helping them achieve their goals for GCSEs and A Levels.

Location. Gad's Hill School is centred on the former home of Charles Dickens and is surrounded by beautiful grounds, playing fields and countryside. It is a few minutes'

drive from the A2 and M2, with good access to the Medway Towns, Dartford and Gravesend.

Curriculum. At Gad's we largely follow the National Curriculum although we place a strong emphasis on "communication" with all of our children benefiting from lessons in French, Information and Communications Technology and Drama as well as English. Senior School children progress to take GCSEs in English, English Literature, Maths, French, Design & Technology, Combined Science (Double Award), Geography and GNVQ ICT (4 GCSEs).

Sports and Activities. We concentrate very much on team games (rugby, hockey, soccer, netball, cricket, athletics and rounders) to ensure that our children learn the values of team work and communication. In the Kindergarten and Junior Schools all students take part in weekly swimming lessons. Because of our small class sizes almost all of our children have the opportunity to represent the school in competitive fixtures against other schools. Gad's Hill also has a thriving Combined Cadet Force. Students join the CCF in Year 8 and take part in weekly training sessions as well as termly field days and an annual camp. The CCF allows children to experience fantastic outdoor pursuits, adventurous training and leadership courses and is essentially about doing something different and challenging. Gad's Hill pupils are also able to take part in a variety of after-school activities. These range from academic pursuits to a variety of other sports and Performing Arts.

Charitable status. Gad's Hill School is a Registered Charity, number 803153. It exists for the purpose of educating children aged 3–16.

Gidea Park College

2 Balgores Lane, Gidea Park, Romford, Essex RM2 5JR

Tel: 01708 740381
Fax: 01708 740381
email: office@gideaparkcollege.co.uk
website: www.gideaparkcollege.co.uk
Facebook: @gideaparkcollege

Headmistress: **Mrs Katherine Whiskerd**, BA Hons, PGCE

Age Range. 3–11 Co-educational.
Number in School. 150 Day Pupils.
Fees per term (2018–2019). £3,365.
An established Preparatory school founded in 1917, the current Directors are the granddaughters of the founders.

The main building, a substantial Georgian/Victorian house, accommodates the 7–11 year old children, the school library, assembly room and IT room plus the kitchens. In separate outside classrooms, bounded by lawns and playgrounds, is the Pre-School unit and accommodation for 4–7 year old pupils.

All children are known and treated as individuals with specific talents which are valued and developed. Likewise, identified areas needing extra help and encouragement are recognised.

The broad-based curriculum is delivered by highly qualified, full-time classroom staff using traditional methods, assisted by qualified support staff.

Results in selection procedures at 11+ are of a consistently high standard with scholarships and places awarded at local Independent and Grammar Schools. Our KS1 and KS2 National Assessment Testing reveals standards above the National expectations.

All National Curriculum areas are covered using whole-class teaching methods. Latin and French are introduced in the higher year groups.

A school choir performs on formal occasions.

Local facilities are used for PE, swimming and games lessons. Our House system fosters team spirit and enables each individual to participate in a variety of inter-house competitions as well as inter-school events.

The school has a Christian Foundation and strong links with our local parish church. However, within our diverse community those of other faiths are welcomed and their beliefs respected and festivals celebrated. Our pupils are encouraged to think of others less fortunate than themselves and arrange a variety of fundraising events for charity.

The staff supervise a Morning and After School Club for the convenience of working parents. Those staying complete homework assignments giving quality time for parents and children at home.

New parents are made welcome by our thriving Parents' Association and encouraged to join in the various social events arranged providing a friendship base for them whilst at the school. Their fundraising provides extra equipment and fun occasions for the children.

We encourage all prospective parents to visit the school prior to applying so they may see classes in action and have an opportunity to ask any questions. We consider the partnership between pupils, parents and school to be of paramount importance in enabling each child to reach his/her potential.

Grangewood Independent School

Chester Road, Forest Gate, London E7 8QT

Tel: 020 8472 3552
Fax: 020 8552 8817
email: admin@grangewoodschool.com
website: www.grangewoodschool.com
Twitter: @GrangewoodSch
Facebook: @GrangewoodSchool

Head: **Mrs Beverley Roberts**, BEd Hons, PG Cert SEN

Age Range. 2–11.
Number in School. 20 boys, 15 girls.
Fees per term (2018–2019). Pre-Reception–Year 6: £1,384–£2,100. Nursery: From £1,029.60 (without EY funding) to £2,250.40 (full-time without EY funding).

Early Years Funded hours available from 15 hours – 40 hours FREE (depending on eligibility for 2 year-olds – 5 year-olds).

School Vision Statement: "Unlocking Potential with Excellence as our Hallmark".

Grangewood Independent School, was founded in 1979. We are a Christian, co-educational Prep school that provides a unique and multi-faceted educational experience for children of all faiths, from two to eleven years old.

Our aim is to instil a sense of respect and discipline, develop excellence in academia, whilst inspiring, motivating, and helping our pupils to realise their full potential. The achievement of our pupils in English and mathematics, including those with SEND and EAL, is consistently higher than national norms. Pupils leaving our Reception are articulate, confident and already achieving above national expectations. 'The standard of reading is consistently high throughout the school and exceptional by the time pupils leave …They develop an excellent standard of handwriting,

express themselves clearly on paper and are articulate in discussion.' [ISI, Sept 2013]

To ensure our pupils receive the individual attention they deserve, teaching and learning take place within small class sizes. Our pupils are happy, confident and accustomed to establishing lasting relationships within a positive and peaceful atmosphere. We work closely with parents to identify and nurture interests and talents in our pupils.

All subjects of the National Curriculum are covered by our qualified, experienced and dedicated teaching staff; and our children make tremendous progress in their levels of achievement across the board. We offer French tuition from Pre-Reception and Spanish from Year Five. Our pupils are enabled and encouraged to develop their talents through performances in theatre and concert halls, as well as inter-school events.

Our wide range of extracurricular activities provide extended learning opportunities for our pupils within many areas including sport, art, critical thinking and music. 'All pupils taking external music examinations up to Grade 5 have been successful.' [ISI, Sept 2013]

We provide excellent 'wrap-around' school care with a Breakfast Club and an After-school Club.

We prepare our children for entrance exams, hence, after Grangewood, our children gain bursaries and entrance to independent schools; grammar schools; as well as the more popular academies and maintained schools. Year after year, we say goodbye to confident, happy, well-educated and responsible boys and girls.

We are particularly proud of the opportunity we have to offer flexible hours and assisted places in our EYFS department.

Please visit our website to arrange a visit to our school.

Charitable status. Grangewood Educational Association is a Registered Charity, number 803492.

Grantham Preparatory International School
An IES School

Gorse Lane, Grantham, Lincolnshire NG31 7UF

Tel: 01476 593293
email: contact.grantham@iesmail.com
website: www.tgps.co.uk
Twitter: @tgps_school
Facebook: @GranthamPrep

Head: **Mrs Kathryn Korcz**, BSc Hons, CertEd

Age Range. 3–11 Co-educational.
Number of Pupils. 130.
Fees per term (2018–2019). £2,950–£3,230.

The Grantham Preparatory International School is a non-denominational independent day school for boys and girls between the ages of three and eleven. The school was established in 1981 and moved to a modern purpose-built building in 1987. It is set in nearly four acres of grounds and playing fields and, being close to the A1, it is easily accessible.

The school is owned by International Education Systems. IES is a network of ten schools (three in South Africa, two in the UK, one in Hungary, one in the United States, one in Panama, one in Slovenia and one in Italy). IES's mission is to provide excellence in education provision within an international perspective. Here at The Grantham Preparatory International School we are committed to excellence in all areas of the curriculum, and we aim to provide the best for all our children in a happy family environment. We are now delighted to be a member of the ISA family after being accredited in November 2011.

Our children are prepared for entrance examinations to Independent senior schools and for Grammar school selection examinations. Children benefit from many specialist teachers who bring their own enthusiasm and knowledge to a particular subject. This ensures high academic standards and our broad and balanced curriculum enables our children to experience sport, art, music and drama and have the opportunity to pursue and develop their strengths, achieving their full potential. Specialist music teachers provide individual tuition in a wide variety of instruments.

The school wind band, choir and recital groups continue to delight audiences with their stunning performances. The school has been awarded the Platinum Award for Sport for two years in succession now, 2017–2018 and 2016–2017.

Learning is fun in our Early Years Foundation Unit. In our care, children thrive and make excellent progress in all areas of learning and development. Our last full ISI inspection report (2014) said that in EYFS there was a rich breadth of planned, purposeful activities, both indoors and outside, that enabled the children to develop and learn extremely effectively.

We believe that every child is an important unique individual that should be valued and nurtured during their time with us. We expect our children to leave us at age 11 as independent, confident individuals, tolerant of others and well prepared for the next stage of their education.

Greenbank Preparatory School and Day Nursery

Heathbank Road, Cheadle Hulme, Cheadle, Cheshire SK8 6HU

Tel: 0161 485 3724
Fax: 0161 485 5519
email: office@greenbankschool.co.uk
website: www.greenbankschool.co.uk
Facebook: @Greenbank-Preparatory-School

Headmistress: **Mrs Janet Lowe**, CertEd

Age Range. 6 months–11 years.
Number in School. Day: 85 Boys, 54 Girls. Daycare: 85.
Fees per term (2018–2019). £2,800 including lunches from Reception to Year Six.

Greenbank is an independent co-educational school for pupils aged three to eleven years. A separate Nursery, open fifty weeks of the year, cares for babies and children from six months to four years old.

Greenbank School was founded in 1951 by Karl and Linda Orsborn. Since 1971 the School has been administered by an Educational Trust and is registered with the Department for Education.

Greenbank is situated within extensive grounds, comprises a mixture of traditional and modern buildings including an IT Suite and Library, separate play areas for Foundation, Infant and Junior children, playing fields with a cricket pavilion, an Astroturf area and netball court. 2009 saw the opening of state-of-the-art Science, Art and Music classrooms within a new administration building. Further developments in 2012 include a brand new Preschool offering greater flexibility to parents.

The school day begins at 8.40 am and ends at 3.30 pm, however we provide wrap-around care from 7.30 am until 6.00 pm. The school also runs activity and sports clubs in the holidays.

Through its varied curricular and extracurricular activities the School provides pupils with the opportunity of expanding their natural abilities to the full. Music, drama, sport, computing and educational visits are some of the activities which play their part in providing a well-rounded programme of education. We strive to meet the social, emotional and intellectual needs of all pupils and the success of this philosophy is proven by the consistently outstanding examination results throughout the school, particularly at age eleven.

Charitable status. Greenbank School Limited is a Registered Charity, number 525930.

Greenfields Independent Day & Boarding School

Priory Road, Forest Row, East Sussex RH18 5JD

Tel: 01342 822189
Fax: 01342 825289
email: admissions@greenfieldsschool.com
website: www.greenfieldsschool.com

Head Teacher: **Mr Jeff Smith**, BSc Eng, AMIMechEng

Age Range. 2–18.
Number in School. Day: 70 Boys, 70 Girls. Boarding: 10 Boys, 10 Girls.
Fees per term (2018–2019). Day: £1,060–£3,800, Boarding: £6,190–£7,810. *In July 2012 Greenfields introduced a radical new fees scheme which makes private schooling available for as little as £59 per week (subject to review).*

Greenfields Independent Day and Boarding School is an Independent Schools Association school with a Montessori-based Nursery and a Reception class (forming the Early Years Foundation Stage), an Infant and Junior School, and a Senior School including Sixth Form and long and short-term English as a Foreign Language courses.

Students aged 2 to 18 receive an all-round education for life, using the Cambridge Curriculum from Infants upwards. Greenfields utilises a unique study method which ensures children can apply what they learn for use in life – not just to pass examinations. It has a strong moral code and zero tolerance on bullying, drugs and alcohol.

Fees start from £59 a week. Situated in beautiful grounds, with its adventure playground backing onto the Ashdown Forest itself, the school is a safe and inspirational place to learn.

The main difference between Greenfields and other schools is the unique teaching method it uses. This method isolates the barriers preventing or hindering a child from learning and then provides precise tools to deal with them. Its use allows any child of any ability to learn anything.

There is a high level of open communication between students and staff that helps to prevent failure, bullying or drugs.

Every student is individually programmed and targeted to ensure each one achieves the success they are capable of.

The classes are small and an excellent curriculum, providing core subjects and peripheral studies, is available up to GCSE and Advanced Levels.

A "qualifications" department exists for checking that students have fully understood each step of their studies, and also provides extra help for any student having any trouble in class. There is also an "ethics" department that helps to resolve any personal problems the student may have.

The pre-school has Montessori trained staff who use Montessori materials to ensure the best foundation for the rest of a student's education.

Entry is by tests for literacy and numeracy. There is a pre-entry section for those who need a short programme to catch up and be ready to join their correct class.

Trains take under an hour from London to East Grinstead, which is a ten minute car ride from the school. Gatwick Airport is a twenty minute car ride away.

Charitable status. Greenfields Educational Trust is a Registered Charity, number 287037. The object for which the trust is established is the advancement of education.

The Gregg Preparatory School (formerly St Winifred's School)

17–19 Winn Road, Portswood, Southampton SO17 1EJ

Tel: 023 8055 7352
email: office@thegreggprep.org
website: www.thegreggprep.org
Facebook: @stwinfredsschool

Chairman of Board of Trustees: Mr John W Watts, MCIPS, MILT, AIGEM

Head Teacher: Mrs Jan Caddy, BEd Hons

Age Range. 3–11 Co-educational.
Number of Pupils. 100.
Fees per term (2018–2019). £2,765 (Lunch £155).

The Gregg Preparatory School is a small school, on a pleasant, urban road in central Southampton, close to the university. It exists to make *the most of Individual Talent – nurturing every child*. The school caters for children aged 4–11; the pre-school takes children from age three, including those receiving Nursery Education Funding. The school provides before and after care from 8.00 am until 6.00 pm.

The School aims to provide for the whole child through a varied curriculum, with a wide programme of study and opportunities to develop all aspects of every pupil's talents. The core subjects, English, Maths and Science, as well as the development of ICT skills, are at the centre of learning throughout the school. Pupils are encouraged and helped to develop a disciplined approach to personal study skills at all ages. Group and class activities help everyone to experience cooperative work and gain useful understanding of others skills and feelings.

Details of the curriculum can be found on our website. A structured academic program is covered by all age groups. This is delivered by specialist staff that enable every pupil to achieve their potential. Continuous assessment and tests prepare the upper school pupils for their entrance exams and for further achievement at secondary school.

The School provides regular feedback about pupils' progress at Parents' Evenings and through reports. Weekly newsletters are emailed to parents informing them of events pupils are involved in as well as activities happening within the school. Parents are encouraged to be involved in their children's education where ever possible.

The School is proud of its achievements in music, drama, games, swimming and dance. As well as our own two indoor hall spaces and playground, the school takes advantage of The Gregg School's sporting facilities. Weekly games, swimming and gym/dance sessions with qualified staff are provided, as well as a variety of after-school activities.

Upper school pupils gain valuable experience whilst preparing for Communication examinations. Each year many pupils achieve distinctions and merits but, most importantly, all gain much personal satisfaction and confidence that will help them in later life.

Further opportunities are provided, through extracurricular activities, to develop pupils' individual talents and personal strengths and interests. Monthly Achievement Assemblies celebrate individual and group interests in and out of school as well as focusing on pupils Endeavour and Courtesy within school. These are an opportunity for every individual to learn their own self-worth.

For taster days and further information, please contact the school secretary or visit our website.

Charitable status. The Gregg and St Winifred's Schools Trust is a Registered Charity, number 1089055.

The Gregg School

Townhill Park House, Cutbush Lane, Southampton SO18 3RR

Tel: 023 8047 2133
Fax: 023 8047 1080
email: office@thegreggschool.org
website: www.thegreggschool.org
Twitter: @TheGreggSchool
Facebook: @TheGreggSchool

Chairman of Board of Trustees: Mr John W Watts, MCIPS, MILT, AIGEM

Headteacher: Mrs S Sellers, MSc, BSc Hons, NPQH, PGCE

Age Range. 11–16 years.
Number in School. 300.
Fees per term (2018–2019). £4,275.

The Gregg School is situated to the east of Southampton and set in 23 acres of beautifully landscaped grounds. The School has a unique family atmosphere and an excellent reputation for its outstanding pastoral care. A high value is placed on identifying and developing each child's individual talents and abilities, and small classes, taught by experienced and dedicated staff, ensure that every student has the opportunity to achieve their very best.

A broad and balanced curriculum is supplemented by a wide range of extracurricular clubs and activities, ranging from orienteering to off-road buggy building.

The School's music and drama departments provide a host of opportunities for students to perform to a range of audiences, and the School regularly achieves success in sporting disciplines at both city and county level.

A comprehensive transport service is provided for students living within a 15 mile radius of the School.

Our Trust Partner, The Gregg Preparatory School, offers a high-quality educational experience for children aged 3–11.

Hale Preparatory School

Broomfield Lane, Hale, Cheshire WA15 9AS

Tel: 0161 928 2386
email: mail@haleprepschool.com
website: www.haleprepschool.com

Headmaster: J Connor, JP, BSc, FCP

Age Range. 4–11.

Number in School. Day: 108 Boys, 93 Girls.

Fees per term (2018–2019). £2,620.

Hale Preparatory School is a completely independent, co-educational school for children from the age of 4 to 11.

The school's most recent ISI inspection was in the summer of 2014. The overall summary of the report reads, "*Hale Prep is a very successful school. Throughout, the teaching is excellent and the pupils' industrious approach to their studies is reflected in their rapid progress and substantial academic achievement at all levels. Indeed, in some cases, levels of progress and achievement are exceptional. The pupils reach high standards of personal fulfilment and participate enthusiastically in a wide range of extra-curricular activities. The quality of the pupils' personal development is excellent, reflecting the school's highly effective emphasis on their welfare, safeguarding and well-being.*"

In recent years, the school was considered the Prep School of the Year by the Sunday Times and was referred to in two studies presented to the Department of Education: firstly, on "Best Practice in the Independent Sector" and secondly, as one of five examples of successful private schools.

One of the aims of the school is to develop each child to his or her fullest potential. This can only be achieved in a situation that emphasises a disciplined approach to school work. Teaching is carried out in a formal, traditional manner but one which also incorporates modern teaching aids. Homework is set every night.

The curriculum of the school is designed to create well-rounded children. Thus, whilst 50% of the curriculum is devoted to the core subjects of maths, English and science, all children have weekly lessons in drama, music, dance, art and design, information technology, history, geography, French, Spanish, ethics, physical education/games and Latin in year 6. Additionally, the school offers a range of extra-curricular activities including a dance club, theatre club, fencing, chess, sewing, gardening, choir, orchestra, a range of sports, outdoor pursuit holidays and continental ski trips.

The Hammond

Hoole Bank House, Mannings Lane, Chester, Cheshire CH2 4ES

Tel: 01244 305350
Fax: 01244 305351
email: info@thehammondschool.co.uk
website: www.thehammondschool.co.uk

Principal: **Mrs M Evans**, BA, MA, PGCE, NPQH, FRSA

Age Range. 6–19+.

Number in School. 100 Boarders, 200 Day Pupils.

The Hammond is the leading provider for performing arts education in the North West. Recognised and funded as a centre of excellence by the Department for Education (DfE) under the Music and Dance Scheme (MDS) and also receiving support through the Education Funding Agency's (EFA) Dance and Drama Award (DaDA) Scheme. Accredited by the CDET (Council for Dance Education and Training), The Hammond caters for a wide range of talents and interests. The Hammond has a place amongst the leading schools specialising in the field of dance, drama and music providing pupils with an academic education and training at the highest level in all aspects of the curriculum.

Prep Department takes girls and boys from age 6 to 11.

Education Department takes girls and boys from 11 years to GCSE level.

Drama Department takes girls and boys from 11 years joining the Education Department with additional Drama.

Dance Department takes girls and boys from 11 years joining the Education Department with a Vocational Dance training.

Music Department takes girls and boys from 11 years joining the Education Department with additional Music.

Sixth Form takes boys and girls into the Education Department to study for A/AS Levels, also Diploma Level 6 in Musical Theatre and Dance, BTEC Level 3 in Performing Arts (Acting).

Full boarding is available.

Outreach Programme. The School is acknowledged for its commitment to the community and its varied outreach projects include:

- Hammond Dance Associates – Specialist classes for talented children, selected by audition, 9–16 years.
- Hammond Youth Theatre – weekend drama classes for 4–16 year olds.
- The Hammond's Easter and Summer schools, working with participants drawn from the community.

The Hammond also offers a BA Hons course in Musical Theatre Performance. This course is validated by University of Chester and students who successfully complete the programme will be eligible for a University of Chester award. The three year course will provide specialist vocational studies for a career in the professional world of musical theatre and performance. Its purpose is to nurture and develop the practical skills required to secure and sustain employment as a musical theatre performer. All students must apply through UCAS.

For a prospectus apply to The School Secretary.

Fees per term (2018–2019). £3,850 for education only. Boarding extra £2,950. Prep Department £2,790.

Harvington Prep School

20 Castlebar Road, Ealing, London W5 2DS

Tel: 020 8997 1583
Fax: 020 8810 4756
email: admin@harvingtonschool.com
website: www.harvingtonschool.com
Facebook: @Harvingtonprepschool

Headmistress: **Mrs Anna Evans**, BA Hons, PGCE

Age Range. Girls 3–11, Boys 3–4.

Number in School. 125 Girls, 20 Boys (in nursery).

Fees per term (2018–2019). Early Years £2,175–£4,018; Years 1–6 £4,205.

The School was founded in 1890 and made into an Educational Trust in 1970. Harvington is known for its high standards and happy atmosphere. Classes are small so that individual attention can be given by qualified and experienced staff. An academic education is offered preparing girls for senior school entrance examinations. The school continues to improve specialist facilities and also to provide a mixed nursery class for 3–4 year olds.

It is close to Ealing Broadway station and a number of bus routes.

Prospectus available from the Secretary.

Charitable status. Harvington School Education Trust Ltd is a Registered Charity, number 312621. It aims to subscribe to traditional values in behaviour and academic standards in a happy environment; to encourage a high standard of academic achievement for girls across a broad range of abilities; to encourage girls to develop their potential to the full, both in personal and academic terms; and to create an environment in which pupils will want to learn.

HawleyHurst School

Fernhill Road, Blackwater, Camberley, Surrey GU17 9HU

Tel: 01276 587190
email: info@hawleyhurst.co.uk
website: www.hawleyhurst.co.uk
Twitter: @HawleyHurst
Facebook: @hawleyhurstschool

Principal: **Miss Victoria Smit**

Age Range. Co-educational 2–19 years.
Number in School. 500 Day Pupils.
Fees per term (2018–2019). Prep (Reception to Year 4) £3,625; Seniors (Years 5 to 11) £4,505; Nursery and Sixth Form – see website.

From January 2018 Hawley Place and Hurst Lodge Schools merged to become one entity.

HawleyHurst boasts the benefits of a 'one-school' progression from an outstanding nursery through to a bespoke Sixth Form and further education programmes.

Throughout the school we offer a full academic curriculum enhanced by an aesthetic and creative programme of study. At GCSE and A Level our option choices are diverse offering a strong core subject base with traditional or vocational options. In 2018 HawleyHurst pupils achieved 40% A* to A grades at A Level whilst Year 11 pupils gained 91.6% Level 9–4 grades (including A*–C) at GCSE. Our pupils are supported by a dedicated team of staff who are committed to achieving the very best for their students. The inspectorate considered both schools to have excellent academic standards at their last inspections. By merging the two schools we have created an environment where children are able to follow their chosen academic and vocational paths and maximise their achievements.

HawleyHurst aims to educate students to become responsible citizens, respect their surroundings and tread lightly on the Earth. We aim for children to become successful independent learners, and gain pleasure from their environment whilst contributing to the school and wider community as well as promoting personal growth and development thus achieving personal goals and broadening their life chances.

We aim to provide a holistic approach to education and to place learning, creativity and the building of self-worth at the centre of the school's life. Our secure and purposeful environment enables pupils to develop mentally and physically as far as they are able with the pursuit of excellence in intellectual, physical and cultural activities being the end goal.

We provide a friendly, family atmosphere, conducive to learning, where courtesy, kindness and consideration for others are fostered in all pupils.

In our school, individuals are valued and encouraged to have a sense of their own worth; to show consideration for others and to see learning as a lifelong pleasure. Great importance is attached to personal development through creativity, enhanced self-discipline, good manners and respect for others which are fundamental British values. During their time at HawleyHurst, each pupil will be encouraged to develop these characteristics which are important traditions of our school.

We encourage children to learn through self-expression and participation in order to make the greatest use of their abilities and to channel their creativity to achieve success socially, vocationally and academically.

Whatever your child excels in, HawleyHurst welcomes them to the family.

Heathcote School

Eves Corner, Danbury, Essex CM3 4QB

Tel: 01245 223131
email: enquiries@heathcoteschool.co.uk
website: www.heathcoteschool.co.uk

Headmistress: **Mrs Caroline Forgeron**

Age Range. 2–11+.
Number in School. 90.
Fees per term (2018–2019). £2,880.

Founded in 1935, Heathcote School has achieved a high reputation as a school where every child matters. It is a small, village school that encourages excellence in all areas. However, there is room in this happy school for children of all abilities and parents can be sure that their child's education, at all levels, will be designed to develop their particular potential.

Children may start in our Nursery from 2 years old. We offer wrap-around care from 7.30 am to 6.00 pm and have many extra-curricular activities.

Specialist subject teachers ensure the success of the high teaching standards expected at this school. Many children are prepared for scholarships, entrance examinations and the Essex Selective Schools Examination at 11+. A very high pass rate is attained in these examinations.

The School participates in many sporting fixtures including netball, football and swimming and is particularly successful in horse jumping, cross country and triathlon.

Pupils are expected to show courtesy and consideration at all times and encouraged to develop self-discipline and pride in themselves and their environment. Parents are asked to support the school in this. Regular consultations with parents are held and the Head Teacher is always available for any discussions that parents consider necessary. We have an active and dedicated "Friends of Heathcote School" who regularly hold social events and raise funds for charity and for the school.

For more information please contact us or visit our website.

Heathfield Knoll School and Day Nursery

Wolverley, Kidderminster, Worcestershire DY10 3QE

Tel: 01562 850204
Fax: 01562 852609
email: info@hkschool.org.uk
website: www.hkschool.org.uk
Twitter: @heathfieldknoll
Facebook: @HeathfieldKnollSchool
LinkedIn: /Heathfield-School-and-Day-Nursery

Headmaster: **Mr Lawrence Collins**, MA, PGCE

Age Range. 0–16. Baby Unit for children 3 months plus.

Number in School. 220 Day pupils.

Fees per term (2018–2019). £2,600–£4,155. Pre School: £35 per half day, £47 per full day. Nursery from £34 (part day) to £58 (full day).

Heathfield Knoll School is a co-educational day school with nursery provision, governed by an Educational Trust. The School is situated in spacious grounds in a green belt area north of Kidderminster, within easy reach of Worcestershire, West Midlands and Shropshire.

The curriculum is broadly based and pupils are prepared for GCSE. We also prepare children for the Common Entrance Examination at 13+. Pupils in our Junior School move up to our own Senior School at 11+. Classes are small. Careers guidance is available to senior pupils.

The school is strong in Drama, Music, Art and Sport. A wide variety of team and individual sports is offered with some pupils achieving regional and national standards.

Prospectus available from the Admissions Administrator.

Charitable status. Heathfield Educational Trust is a Registered Charity, number 1098940. It exists to provide excellent educational opportunities at a reasonable cost.

Hemdean House School

Hemdean Road, Caversham, Reading, Berks RG4 7SD

Tel: 0118 947 2590
email: office@hemdeanhouse.co.uk
website: www.hemdeanhouse.co.uk

Head: **Mrs H Chalmers**

Age Range. Girls 4–11, Boys 4–11. Pre-Reception Kindergarten from age 3½.

Number in School. 33 Girls, 25 Boys.

Fees per term (2018–2019). £2,830–£3,100.

Founded in 1859, Hemdean House is a school where traditional educational concepts are highly valued. We look for personal achievement in academic and other spheres, responsible behaviour and consideration for others. We aim to develop the varied talents of each and every child within our structured and caring environment; individual attention has high priority. Small classes help us to achieve our aims. We believe that school and family should work together and have opportunities to meet.

We follow the National Curriculum throughout the school; Mathematics, Science, Information Technology, the Humanities and the Expressive Arts, Modern Languages, Technology and Physical Education are taught throughout the age range. French lessons begin at age 5 and recorder lessons begin at age 7 and many children learn at least one other musical instrument. Drama, Music and Art head a wide range of extra-curricular activities. For the working parent, after-school care is available if required.

National Curriculum Key Stage Tests are excellent with pupils achieving well above the national average. We are delighted to be placed in the Sunday Times Parent Power 2017 rankings as the 29th highest-achieving independent prep school in the country amongst some of the most prestigious schools in the UK.

The school has its own woodland and is proud of its outdoor learning programme and accredited Forest School, which has achieved the coveted Gold Award status from the Woodland Trust.

The school has always been committed to Christian ethics and values, but all faiths are welcomed and understanding and appreciation of the beliefs of others is encouraged.

Admission. Assessment during a day or half-day spent in school according to age. Scholarships and bursaries are available throughout the school.

Charitable status. Hemdean House is a Registered Charity, number 309146. Its aims include academic achievement, the development of every pupil's potential, Christian values and care for others.

Herne Hill School

The Old Vicarage, 127 Herne Hill, London SE24 9LY

Tel: 020 7274 6336
email: enquiries@hernehillschool.co.uk
website: www.hernehillschool.co.uk

Headteacher: **Mrs Ngaire Telford**

Age Range. 2–7.

Number in School. 280 boys and girls.

Fees per term (2018–2019). £2,075–£4,985.

Herne Hill School is the largest independent Pre-School and Pre-Prep in the UK focusing exclusively on 2–7 year olds, i.e. the period research has shown to be the most important educational years in a person's life. Children join Kindergarten in the academic year they become 3 years old. Kindergarten is by far the greatest entry point, followed by Pre-Reception and Reception. There are usually only chance vacancies for Years 1 and 2.

The school is well known as an oasis of happy learning and as the ideal setting for young children to acquire the key values and cognitive, physical, social and emotional skills they will require to lead happy, successful and balanced lives. At 7+, the children graduate to move on to a number of local independent and state schools, 'ready to shine with that special Herne Hill sparkle', as one of the heads of the receiving schools has described his Herne Hill School intake.

The school's grounds and facilities lie tucked away behind St Paul's Church on Herne Hill and combine to provide a 'homely', safe and nurturing feel while at the same time being open, green and deceptively large – the perfect environment for young children to blossom and enjoy discovering how to learn. The buildings consist of an Old Vicarage, recent purpose-built classrooms and a new building which provides a number of additional benefits. These include a large, state-of-the-art Kindergarten room; a modern, multi-functional hall; and a kitchen which produces healthy hot lunches freshly cooked on site daily.

By focusing on Early Years education, Herne Hill School has developed strong expertise in making the critical transition from Nursery to School seamless. Children joining the Kindergarten can avoid the disruption of a 4+ change and enjoy continuity of care for up to five years in what are arguably their most important educationally-formative years. Children joining in Reception benefit from the smooth progression from a play-based learning approach to more structured lessons.

"*Love • Care • Excellence*" encapsulates the school philosophy that love, nurture and a caring environment foster the children's self-confidence, sense of achievement and happiness, thereby stimulating their curiosity and desire to learn. The school's atmosphere lives this philosophy. It is a caring, friendly and stimulating place, and at the same time there is an air of achievement, respect and discipline.

The curriculum is finely balanced to develop all skills and interests of 'the whole child' and take account of each child's individual needs as well as the requirements of the 7+ entry tests – and to make learning fun! It is also designed to develop the skills of independent learning and to sustain the children's innate joy of learning. Music, drama, gym, dancing and French are emphasised and taught by specialists.

The latest ISI inspection report delivered a strong endorsement of the school's ethos, staff, curriculum, *modus operandi* and infrastructure by giving the highest possible rating of 'excellent' or 'outstanding' to *every* aspect of the school. The inspectors deemed overall achievement to be excellent and that pupils demonstrate high levels of success in both their learning and personal development. The full report can be found on www.isi.net.

The school holds two open mornings a year, typically on a Saturday in March and September. Prospective parents may also see the school 'in action' by joining one of the regular tours held during school hours. The school's website contains relevant information about life at the school, its curriculum, the destination of its leavers and some useful links.

Highfield Priory School

Fulwood Row, Fulwood, Preston, Lancashire PR2 5RW
Tel: 01772 709624
email: schooloffice@highfieldpriory.co.uk
website: www.highfieldpriory.co.uk

Headmaster: **Mr J Duke**

Age Range. 6 months–11 years.
Number in School. Day: 130 Boys, 120 Girls.
Fees per term (2018–2019). £2,575.

Highfield is set in 8 acres of landscaped gardens, woodlands and playing fields and is a co-educational preparatory school for children aged 6 months to 11+ years. It is fully equipped with its own established Nursery and prepares children for all Independent, Grammar and Senior Schools in Lancashire, for which it has an excellent academic record.

Class numbers average 20 and children are taught by fully-qualified and experienced staff. Specialist facilities and teachers ensure that children are challenged and fulfilled across the curriculum, most notably in Art and CDT with a new studio in 2005, an ICT suite (since 1994), a Science Laboratory (2006) and, most recently, a Performing Arts Studio in 2013. Children from Nursery through to Year Six are also able to enjoy the school Library, Sports Hall and the school's own nature reserve, Highfield Haven.

The school has strong musical, dramatic and sporting traditions. Every child in the Junior School is given the opportunity to take part in competitive sporting fixtures and to perform in a full-scale dramatic production each year. In addition, Highfield examines the Junior children in the disciplines of Public Speaking, Elocution and Drama twice a year thereby greatly improving the children's eloquence and confidence.

Highfield holds a Step into Quality Award for its Early Years and Foundation Stage and Potential Plus UK's Three Star Gold Membership for its work with Gifted and Talented children. Highfield encourages its pupils to "Aim High" and gives them every opportunity to achieve this.

Highfield offers an extended day from 7.15 am until 6.00 pm. Extra-curricular activities include Ballet, Gardening, Choir, Design, Dance, Judo, Public Speaking, Chess, Spanish, Homework Club and Instrument Tuition. The school is well supported by an enthusiastic Parents Association. Prospective parents, and children, are encouraged to visit the school, have a tour with the Headmaster and to experience a school day.

Charitable status. Highfield Priory School is a Registered Charity, number 532262. It exists to provide independent education to all children between the ages of 6 months and 11 years within Preston and surrounding areas for all who wish to participate and to provide access to the community at large to all sporting, musical and artistic provision within the school.

Highfields School

London Road, Newark, Nottinghamshire NG24 3AL
Tel: 01636 704103
Fax: 01636 680919
email: office@highfieldsschool.co.uk
website: www.highfieldsschool.co.uk
Twitter: @HighfieldsNG24
Facebook: @highfields.newark

Head: **Mr Richard Thomson**, BEd Hons, NPQH

Age Range. 2–11 Co-educational.
Number in School. 150.
Fees per term (2018–2019). £3,065 including lunch. Day Nursery from £15 per three-hour session to £35 per school day (8.30 am – 3.30 pm), £47.50 per full day (7.30 am – 6.00 pm).

Highfields School is situated in fourteen acres of mature parkland and sports fields, an enviable setting for children to enjoy their education. It provides a happy, lively, caring community which allows the children to experience a sense of pride and fulfilment that comes from working to their full potential. Personal responsibility, initiative, good manners and smart appearance are encouraged and developed, in keeping with the School's pledge to combine modern methods with traditional values.

Children enter a structured course of Nursery Education in the term in which they reach the age of three. Children enter the Reception Class before their fifth birthday and proceed through the School in year groups. Each class is taught by its own teacher in the basic subjects. The maximum class size is 24. All members of staff are fully qualified and specialist teachers assist with Art, ICT, Music, PE and Games throughout the School.

Highfields has recently adopted the Cambridge Curriculum which is an education programme designed and administered by Cambridge University for young learners that combines a world-class curriculum, high-quality support for teachers and integrated assessment. By moving the curriculum away from the National Curriculum and SATs examinations, the school has greater flexibility when making decisions about what is important when equipping the children with the skills and knowledge required for them to succeed in a global community.

Highfields has a fully deserved reputation for the quality of its pastoral care.

All children are encouraged to be creative and exhibit a delight in learning. There is the optional opportunity for speech and drama tuition and music lessons including piano, woodwind, brass and strings ensembles, choir, advanced choir, orchestra and band. Peripatetic staff offer individual or joint music tuition in a wide variety of instruments including trumpet, saxophone, violin, cello, flute, clarinet, harp and guitar.

The School offers a wide range of extracurricular activities and sports teams compete against other independent schools as well as local schools. Highfields has fully-qualified staff who teach tennis, hockey, cricket, football, rugby and netball. The School holds an Activemark Gold Award.

All Pre-Prep children have a swimming lesson each week; Prep children enjoy an enhanced PE programme which includes sailing, golf, table tennis and fitness.

Highfields pursues a non-selective admissions policy, but has an excellent academic record, sending most pupils to local selective independent schools or to Grammar Schools in Lincolnshire through 11+ entry.

The School is administered by a Board of Governors, including parent governors.

Charitable status. Newark Preparatory School Company Limited is a Registered Charity, number 528261. It exists to provide and further the education of children.

Hopelands Preparatory School

38/40 Regent Street, Stonehouse, Gloucestershire GL10 2AD

Tel: 01453 822164
Fax: 01453 827288
email: enquiries@hopelands.org.uk
website: www.hopelands.org.uk

Chairman of Governors: Mr R D James

Head: **Mrs Sheila Bradburn**, BA Hons, PGCE

Age Range. 4–11 Co-educational.
Number of Pupils. 80.
Fees per term (2018–2019). £2,096–£2,765.
Charitable status. Hopelands Preparatory School is a Registered Charity, number 1007707.

Howe Green House School

Great Hallingbury, Bishop's Stortford, Herts CM22 7UF

Tel: 01279 657706
Fax: 01279 501333
email: schooloffice@howegreenhouse.essex.sch.uk
website: www.howegreenhouse.essex.sch.uk

Headmistress: **Mrs Deborah Mills**, BA Hons, QTS

Age Range. 2–11 years.
Number in School. 158.
Fees per term (2018–2019). Kindergarten £2,745, Pre-Prep £3,171, Prep £3,931.

Howe Green House offers an education of the highest quality in the widest sense. Facilities are excellent being sited in 15 acres of countryside adjacent to Hatfield Forest. It is a single-stream school which works broadly to the National Curriculum, offering additional French, Latin, Music, Drama and Sport. There is a strong parental involvement within the school whereby parents are actively encouraged to be part of their children's education. The school is seen as a community which fosters an understanding of children's development within both school and home. Children sit external examinations to senior schools both boarding and day and have been highly successful.

Entry to the school is mainly via Acorns Nursery but children are considered for entry to the Junior School by assessment and interview.

Charitable status. The Howe Green Educational Trust Ltd is a Registered Charity, number 297106. It exists to promote and provide for the advancement of education for the public benefit and in connection therewith to conduct a day school for the education of boys and girls.

Hulme Hall Grammar School

Beech Avenue, Stockport, Cheshire SK3 8HA

Tel: 0161 485 3524
email: secretary@hulmehallschool.org
website: www.hulmehallschool.org
Twitter: @HulmeHallGS
Facebook: @Hulme-Hall-Grammar-School

Headteacher: **Mr D Grierson**, BA Ec Hons, MEcon, PGCE

Age Range. 2–16 Co-educational.
Number in School. 200.
Fees per term (2018–2019). £2,695–£3,130.

Hulme Hall Grammar School has an excellent reputation for providing a friendly, warm and positive atmosphere in which all pupils thrive and succeed. Our small class sizes, high quality teaching and superb enrichment programmes ensure that we provide the best possible educational journey for every pupil.

The Pre-School provides an environment where children are happy, secure and confident, instilling them with a love of life and learning.

Our Junior Learning Centre offers an opportunity to learn in an exciting and innovative educational setting. We practise small, group teaching that focuses on each child and uses their areas of interest to engage them in productive learning.

Senior School (11–16 years). The school is well staffed and equipped to deliver a curriculum covering a wide range of academic, creative and practical subjects. An extensive choice of GCSE and other external examination options enables pupils at Key Stage 4 to target optimum qualifications reflecting their personal choice of programme. The staff are consistent in the emphasis they place upon the encouragement of pupils who respond with a highly conscientious approach to their studies, which in turn ensures steady progress and excellent results.

Communication between school and home is given high priority and the regular issue of reports enables parents to monitor closely their child's educational development. At the age of 16, almost all pupils continue with A Level studies.

The school operates a bus service offering an extensive network of services covering a 15 mile radius of the school.

For further information please contact the School Secretary.

Charitable status. Hulme Hall Educational Trust is a Registered Charity, number 525931. The school aims to promote personal, moral, social and academic development of all pupils.

Hurtwood House School

Holmbury St Mary, Dorking, Surrey RH5 6NU

Tel: 01483 279000
Fax: 01483 267586
email: info@hurtwood.net
website: www.hurtwoodhouse.com
Twitter: @hurtwoodhouse
Facebook: @hurtwoodhouse

Headmaster: **C M Jackson**, BEd

Age Range. 16–18.

Number in School. 330 (170 girls, 160 boys).

Fees per term (2018–2019). Boarding £14,476, Day £9,650.

Hurtwood House is the only independent boarding school specialising exclusively in the Sixth Form. It concentrates on the 16–18 age range and offers students a caring, residential structure and a commitment to a complete education where culture, sport, friendship and a full range of extracurricular activities all play an important part. Hugely successful across the whole range of academic subjects, Hurtwood House is also widely recognised as having the best Creative and Performing Arts and Media departments in the country and is therefore especially attractive to aspiring actors, directors, film directors, dancers, singers, artists and fashion designers.

Many students now want to leave the traditional school system at 16. They are seeking an environment which is structured and safe, but which is less institutional and better equipped to provide the challenge and stimulation which they are now ready for, and which is therefore better placed to develop their potential. They also require teaching methods which will prepare them for an increasingly competitive world by developing their initiative and encouraging them to think for themselves.

Hurtwood House has 330 boys and girls. It is a small and personal school, but it is a large and powerful sixth form which benefits from having specialised A Level teachers. The examination results put Hurtwood House in the top independent school league tables, but it is equally important to the school that the students develop energy, motivation and self-confidence.

In short, Hurtwood House is a stepping-stone between school and university for students who are all in the same age group and who share the same maturity and the same ambitions.

The school is situated in its own grounds high up in the Surrey Hills and offers excellent facilities in outstandingly beautiful surroundings.

The Italia Conti Academy of Theatre Arts

Italia Conti House, 23 Goswell Road, London EC1M 7AJ

Tel:	020 7608 0047/8
Fax:	020 7253 1430
email:	admin@italiaconti.co.uk
website:	www.italiaconti.com
Twitter:	@ItaliaContiUK
Facebook:	@italiacontiac

Principal: Mrs Samantha Newton

Vice Principal: **Mr Rod Jones**

Deputy Head: Mrs Glynis Rodgers, BA Ed

Age Range. 10–16.
Number in School. Day 79.
Fees per term (2018–2019). £4,325.

For over a hundred years the Academy has been preparing young people for successful careers in the performing arts it has been aware that the profession expects excellent standards of education and training of its new entrants. Today's Producers and Directors demand that performers entering the industry be versatile and be able to take direction within the theatre, television or film studio.

The four courses offered by the Academy seek to expose students to a wide range of disciplines and techniques in the Dance, Drama and Singing fields working in the mediums of stage, television and recording studio under the careful tuition of highly qualified professional staff.

The courses are as follows:

The Theatre Arts School. For 11 to 16 year olds providing a balanced traditional academic education leading to nine GCSEs with broadly based vocational training in dance, drama and singing.

Performing Arts Course. A three-year Trinity Diploma Course accredited by the CDMT (Council for Drama and Musical Theatre). A three-year Trinity Diploma in Professional Dance accredited by the CDMT. A three-year BA Hons course in Musical Theatre, accredited by the UEL (University of East London).

Entry Requirements. Entry for all the above courses is by audition and assessment.

In addition to the above the Academy offers part-time Saturday classes to children aged 3½ to 18 years in Dance, Drama and Singing. Also offered is a Summer School, one week Performing Arts or Drama courses for those aged 9 to 19.

Charitable status. The Italia Conti Academy Trust is a Registered Charity, number 290261. It exists to promote education in the Performing Arts through both teaching and the provision of scholarships.

King Alfred School

Manor Wood, 149 North End Road, London NW11 7HY

Tel:	020 8457 5200
Fax:	020 8457 5249
email:	kas@kingalfred.org.uk
website:	www.kingalfred.org.uk
Twitter:	@kingalfredsch
Facebook:	@TheKingAlfredSchool

Head: **Robert Lobatto**, MA Oxon, PGCE London

Age Range. 4–18.
Number in School. Primary: approximately 300; Secondary: approximately 350.
Fees per term (2018–2019). Reception, Years 1–2: £5,358, Years 3–6: £6,174, Upper School (Years 7–13): £6,459.

King Alfred School is unique among independent schools in North London. Apart from being all-age (4–18), co-ed and secular, it takes in a range of ability as opposed to its academically selective neighbours in the private sector.

The school's beginnings are unusual: it was founded in 1898 by a group of Hampstead parents and its governing body comprises mainly current and ex-parents. Visitors tend to comment on the pretty site (on the edge of Hampstead Garden Suburb), the "village" layout (carefully preserved by a succession of architects), and the friendly atmosphere – this is a no-uniform establishment and all are on first-name terms. The recent purchase of property across the road has enabled the school to extend classroom facilities.

Academic results are consistently impressive and constantly improving and almost 100% of the KAS Sixth Form go on to university or Art Foundation courses or music colleges and conservatoires, 98% to their first or second choice. The school prides itself on its reputation as a relaxed, informal and vibrant community that achieves academic success within a non-pressured environment.

Bursaries for Year 7 and the Sixth Form are available.

Charitable status. King Alfred School is a Registered Charity, number 312590. It exists to provide quality education for boys and girls.

Kings Monkton School

6 West Grove, Cardiff CF24 3XL

Tel:	029 2048 2854
email:	mail@kingsmonkton.org.uk
website:	www.kingsmonkton.org.uk
Twitter:	@kings_monkton
Facebook:	@kings-monkton-school

Principal: **Mr Paul Norton**

Vice Principal and Head of Primary: Mrs Karen Norton

Age Range. 3–18.
Number in School. 300.
Fees per term (2018–2019). £2,700–£4,068.

Kings Monkton School is a co-educational day school for children from age 3–18. The school is owned by Heathfield Independent Schools and is renowned for its caring and inclusive ethos.

Kings Monkton is one of South Wales's oldest independent schools, having educated generations of local pupils since its foundation in 1870. The school prides itself on its excellent record of academic success, its system of pastoral care with its small classes of 15 and its relations with parents. Pupils are drawn from a wide catchment area including Cardiff, the Vale of Glamorgan, the Valleys and Monmouth, as well as having a number of Tier 4 sponsored international pupils on educational visas. The school is housed in purpose-built accommodation in the centre of Cardiff, close to Queen Street station and to all amenities.

Kings Monkton's primary school has small classes in which young children can receive individual care and guidance. Pupils follow a well-balanced curriculum, designed to develop and stimulate young minds to the full. Children are taught both French and Mandarin and have extensive access to sports.

In the secondary school, pupils pursue a wide curriculum with their progress being carefully monitored and receive strong pastoral support throughout their adolescent years. All pupils are encouraged to strive for high standards in their work and to contribute to the well-being of the community to which they belong. Entry to the school is non-selective, with 15 pupils per class to ensure that all achieve their highest potential.

In 2016 the school opened its new purpose-built sixth form academy with upgraded facilities for psychology, criminology and global perspectives. Students follow a unique Level 3 offering incorporating their learning pathway and co-curriculum. Students are taught in small tutorial groups and in addition to their academic studies participate in a number of other activities including Young Enterprise, Public Speaking and the Extended Project Qualification as part of the school's philosophy of giving its pupils a thorough preparation for life. The minimum entry requirements to the Sixth Form Academy are five GCSE passes at grades A–C. Links with industry and excellent work experience means that pupils are well prepared for university and have the necessary skills to make them stand out in the UCAS application process.

The school works in partnership with many different organisations including Oxford Royale Academy, HSA, Shelley Norton Drama and Wonderland Studios, as well as having close links with China, The Netherlands, Thailand and Spain.

Kirkstone House School

Baston, Peterborough, Lincolnshire PE6 9PA

Tel:	01778 560350
Fax:	01778 560547
email:	info@kirkstonehouseschool.co.uk
website:	www.kirkstonehouseschool.co.uk

Co-Principals: Mrs B K Wyman, Mr E G Wyman, Mr J W R Wyman

Head: **Mrs C Jones**

Age Range. 3–18.
Number in School. 124: 82 boys, 42 girls.
Fees per term (2018–2019). £3,261–£4,000.

Kirkstone House prides itself on being a family run non-selective school where children of all abilities can achieve their full potential in a caring environment. The atmosphere is characterised by its supportive nature and sense of community. Classes are small and pupils and staff know each other well.

There are high aspirations for pupils and the school aims to provide the highest quality of education throughout all years by catering for the full academic range and offering a wide curriculum. Strong emphasis is placed on choice with a wide range of GCSEs and BTEC courses being offered up to the age of 18. There is also a very well established Learning Support Department providing tailored additional assistance including helping pupils to cope with dyslexia.

A wealth of extracurricular activities are enjoyed by many pupils including The Duke of Edinburgh's Award, a thriving Youth Theatre and a range of sporting pursuits. Additionally, a 60-acre site of woodlands and lakes has specific scientific interest and is used for environmental and land-based study.

Lime House School

Holm Hill, Dalston, Nr Carlisle, Cumbria CA5 7BX

Tel:	01228 710225
Fax:	01228 710508
email:	office@limehouseschool.co.uk
	admissions@limehouseschool.co.uk
website:	www.limehouseschool.co.uk
Twitter:	@limehouseschool
Facebook:	@limehouseschooloffice

Headteacher: **Mrs M Robertson-Barnett**, MA Oxon

Age Range. 7–18. Boarders from age 9.
Number in School. Day: 20 Boys, 10 Girls; Boarding: 65 Boys, 40 Girls.
Fees per term (2018–2019). Boarding £7,750–£9,250; Day £3,000–£4,000.
Compulsory extras: Activities, Laundry.

Lime House School is a fully independent co-educational boarding and day school for pupils aged 7 to 18. Our aim is to ensure that each pupil achieves his or her potential both academically and socially, with each child treated individually. Our pupils are cared for in a safe rural environment and every possible attempt is made to ensure that they develop confidence and self-esteem. Boarding is available to all pupils, with the majority being full boarders.

Foreign students whose first language is not English add to the cosmopolitan atmosphere of the school. They are prepared for Cambridge English examinations (KET, PET & IELTS) and follow the same curriculum as all other students.

Games and sport form an important part of school life. All students participate and a wide range of team and individual sports is offered. Most pupils take games to GCSE level, with many continuing to A Level. In 2017 the GCSE pass rate was 100% and at A Level 60% of grades were A* or A.

We would welcome a visit to our school to see it in action. Simply contact the school and we will arrange a time convenient for you.

Loreto Preparatory School

Dunham Road, Altrincham, Cheshire WA14 4GZ
Tel: 0161 928 8310
Fax: 0161 929 5801
email: info.loretoprep@btconnect.com
website: www.loretoprep.org.uk

Headteacher: **Mrs Anne Roberts**, BEd Hons Cantab

Age Range. Girls 3–11.
Number in School. 170 Day Girls.
Fees per term (2018–2019). £2,190.

Loreto Preparatory School, founded in 1909, is a Catholic independent school and is one of many Loreto schools built on the foundations laid by Mary Ward, foundress of the Institute of the Blessed Virgin Mary, according to the vision of St Ignatius of Loyola. It is a modern, purpose-built school standing in pleasant grounds and offering an all-round education by well-qualified staff. The school's primary aim is to provide an environment that enables children to live by the principles of the gospel and in the tradition of the Catholic faith, upholding the values of Mary Ward. The school also seeks to help pupils reach their full potential in all aspects of the curriculum and thus to become happy and confident with an enduring love of learning.

Our recent ISI Inspection was excellent in all areas. The pupils' academic and personal development and other achievements were highly praised. "Pupils view the school as a family and show great respect for each other's culture, opinions and beliefs".

Music, PE, ICT and French are all taught by specialist teachers.

Music plays an important part in the life of the school. We have a school orchestra, and private individual lessons are available in most instruments. The children's dramatic ability and interest are developed through class lessons, theatre visits and regular productions.

Gymnastics, swimming, netball, badminton, cross country and athletics are important elements of our physical education programme and the school participates fully in local and national competitions.

Our ICT facilities are excellent and include a computer suite.

There is a well-stocked, computerised library, allowing pupils to select, issue and return their own books.

We offer a wide range of extracurricular activities including Spanish, Art Club, Zumbatomic, Street Dance, Chess, Football, Cricket, Tennis, Judo, Fencing, Archery and Mad Science.

Visits to the school are welcome by appointment. Open Day is Saturday 9 March 2019. Admission at 3+ is usually by interview and for those wishing to join at 7+ by interview and Entrance Examination.

Charitable status. Loreto Preparatory School is a Registered Charity, number 250607.

Loughborough Amherst School (formerly Our Lady's Convent School)

Gray Street, Loughborough, Leicestershire LE11 2DZ
Tel: 01509 263901
Fax: 01509 236193
email: Amherst.office@lsf.org
website: www.lsf.org/amherst

Headmaster: **Dr Julian Murphy**, DPhil Oxon

Age Range. Girls 4–18, Boys 4–11.
Number of Pupils. Approximately 200+.
Fees per term (2018–2019). Pre-Prep £3,272, Prep £3,353, Seniors £4,063.

Loughborough Amherst School is a Catholic day school that extends a warm welcome to children of all faiths and none. Part of the Loughborough Schools Foundation it educates boys from 4 to 11 and girls from 4 to 18. The focus is very much on the individual child and their personal progress and achievement at all levels. From September 2019, we will be welcoming boys into our Senior School, thereby extending our excellent educational offering to boys and girls from the age of 4 to 18 years.

We hold an open Day in the late September but encourage all prospective parents to see our Senior and Preparatory School departments in action on a normal working day, view our facilities and meet our Headmaster.

At all stages of their education, our pupils receive individual attention in small classes. The emphasis is on giving 'added value' through the patient nurturing of confidence and 'growth mindset' in our pupils, rather than through heavy emphasis on drilling and testing. Our progressive approach to learning and character growth is embodied in the School philosophy we call 'Minerva'.

For a non-selective school our public examination results in 2018 were excellent, with 21.4% A*–A and 57% A*–B at A Level, and 26% A*–A (9–7) and 74% A*–B (9–5) at GCSE. Our Learning Support Department is particularly well-staffed for a school of our size.

Our membership of the Loughborough Schools Foundation places us in a wonderful position, where we can combine all that is best in a small school community with the benefits of the human and physical resources of a campus of over two thousand students. The possibilities are numerous, to give just four examples: our budding musicians have access to one of the finest music schools in the country; our Sixth Formers can choose from twenty-nine A Level courses; our youngest pupils can enjoy outdoor learning in a Forest School; and any future applicants for Oxford, Cambridge or the leading US universities will be able to access subject specialist mentoring from a large body of teaching staff stretching across three schools.

Ninety-nine per cent of our students go on to university to study a wide range of subjects and every year more than 80% of our leavers gain entry to their first choice of university.

We have expanded our sporting opportunities. For example, this year in addition to the traditional sporting teams we now offer morning fitness sessions for all, swimming, basketball, trampoline and football practices with the aim to enter local and ISA competitions. We also run a popular triathlon club. A new astroTurf, sports hall and fitness suite will be operational in the summer of 2019.

The school successfully participates in the Combined Cadet Force (CCF), The Duke of Edinburgh's Award and Young Enterprise schemes.

The School campus is an attractive walled area; an oasis of calm, near the centre of Loughborough. Open days are held during working school days and visitors continually note the happy classroom environment and the mutual respect between pupils, staff and visitors. Some of our pupils are with us from 4 to 18 but others are very welcome to join us at other stages of their education.

The Nursery at the Loughborough Schools Foundation is based on our campus and offers childcare 51 weeks a year from age 6 weeks to 4 years.

For further information visit our website: www.lsf.org/amherst.

Charitable status. Loughborough Amherst School is part of the Loughborough Schools Foundation, which is a Registered Charity, number 1081765, and a Company Limited by Guarantee, registered in England, number 4038033. Registered Office: 3 Burton Walks, Loughborough, Leics LE11 2DU.

Lucton School

Lucton, Leominster, Herefordshire HR6 9PN

Tel: 01568 782000
Fax: 01568 782001
email: admissions@luctonschool.org
website: www.luctonschool.org
Twitter: @LuctonSchool
Facebook: @Lucton-School
LinkedIn: /lucton-school

Headmistress: **Mrs Gill Thorne**, MA, BA Hons, PGCE, LLAM

Deputy Head Academic & Head of Sixth Form: Mr J Goode, MA Cantab, PGCE
Deputy Head Pastoral: Mrs E Niblett, BEd Hons, HDE
Head of Prep School: Mr David Bicker-Caarten, MBA

Age Range. 6 months–19 years.
Number in School. 340.
Fees per term (2018–2019). Day £2,350–£4,575, Weekly Boarding £7,500–£8,825, Full Boarding £9,295–£10,625.

About Lucton School. Founded in 1708, Lucton provides pupils with an excellent all-round education which aims to bring out their full potential. Pupils benefit from small classes, a friendly atmosphere and an idyllic rural location. There are extensive sports facilities and a good mix of day pupils, weekly boarders and full boarders.

Studying at Lucton School. Lucton has a strong academic record and an established tradition of getting the best possible results from each pupil. Subjects taught to GCSE include English language and literature, mathematics, biology, chemistry, physics, information technology, French, Spanish, German, history, geography, business studies, religious education, design & technology, art, music, drama and PE/games.

All the above GCSE subjects and more are available at AS and A2 Levels. The Sixth Form is housed in a new sixth form centre, including a new senior library and well-equipped IT suite.

School Facilities. The school is set in 55 acres of beautiful Herefordshire countryside. Facilities on site include:

- Junior and senior libraries
- Science laboratories
- ICT rooms
- Design and technology workshop
- Tennis courts
- Indoor swimming pool
- Indoor sports hall
- Games fields
- Equestrian centre.

Boarding pupils are housed in modern buildings and senior pupils have individual rooms.

Admissions. Admission can take place at any time of the year by interview and assessment. Prospective pupils are always invited to spend a taster day in the school without obligation. Examinations for academic scholarships are held in January each year.

Affiliations. The Headmistress of Lucton School is a member of the Independent Schools Association (ISA); the Head of Lucton Prep School is a member of The Independent Association of Prep Schools (IAPS); and Lucton School is in membership of the Boarding Schools' Association (BSA).

Charitable status. Lucton School is a Registered Charity, number 518076.

The Lyceum

6 Paul Street, City of London, London EC2A 4JH

Tel: 020 7247 1588
email: admin@lyceumschool.co.uk
website: www.lyceumschool.co.uk

Head Teacher: **Mrs Hilary Wyatt**

Deputy Head Teacher: Miss Alice Riley

Age Range. 3–11 Co-educational.
Number of Pupils. 110.
Fees per term (2018–2019). £5,395.

The Lyceum is a non-selective independent co-educational school conveniently based near Old Street station. At The Lyceum they believe that all children have the potential to achieve and excel. The school provides children with an educational atmosphere and experiences that stimulate, motivate and encourage them to achieve beyond what may be expected.

The Lyceum is a small school with a family atmosphere where children are happy, excited and challenged daily. The children in their care are offered a broad and balanced curriculum with equal emphasis on the arts, physical education, moral and spiritual education as well as academic subjects. They believe that involvement in the arts helps to build confidence and self-esteem, and that a good all-round education leads to high standards.

The Lyceum aims:

- To ensure that each child's talents are discovered and nurtured and they achieve their potential in terms of spiritual awareness, academic achievement and aesthetic appreciation.

- To ensure children go on to a suitable secondary school that matches their academic, emotional and social needs, and where their talents can be nurtured.
- To develop in children the skills which will equip them for the next stage of their lives and to enable them to positively influence their own lives.
- That children and parents look back on their time at The Lyceum as a positive and happy one.
- To ensure all children have access to a broad and balanced curriculum and a range of extra-curricular activities.
- To develop tolerance and understanding towards each other and all members of the wider community.
- To develop curiosity, a drive to learn, confidence, independence and a strong work ethic.
- To develop a positive attitude to behaviour based on traditional manners.
- To develop a responsible and independent attitude towards work and their future roles in society.
- To encourage curiosity and a positive attitude to learning.

The curriculum has a strong emphasis on using local resources, as well as the school's link to a wide range of study centres, experiences of living history and a Year 6 residential visit to a European City, usually Paris or Amsterdam.

Children who attend the Lyceum get to take advantage of their central location including the large range of museums, galleries and concert halls nearby. Children undertake at least one educational visit per half term related to the curriculum. From Year 3 (age 7) upwards children go on residential trips including 'living history' events. In addition to this authors, artists and speakers are invited to speak at the school, to enhance the curriculum.

The Lyceum is part of the Dukes Education group which owns a number of private schools in London, East and South East England. Through Dukes's "Inspiring Learning" programme, we seek to share best practice and ensure the continuing improvement in every child's education.

Lyndhurst School

36 The Avenue, Camberley, Surrey GU15 3NE
Tel: 01276 22895
email: Secretary@lyndhurstschool.co.uk
website: www.lyndhurstschool.co.uk
Twitter: @lyndhurstschool

Headmaster: **Mr Andrew Rudkin**

Deputy Head: Mrs Nicola Price

School Business Manager: Mrs Lesley McCready

Age Range. 3–11 years.
Number in School. Day: 55 Boys, 68 Girls.
Fees per term (2018–2019). Main School £3,195–£4,352. Early Years: £1,830–£3,925 (five full days 8.00 am to 6.00 pm).

Fees include tuition, hot lunches, 2 after-school clubs from a selective list, wrap-around care from 8.00 am to 6.00 pm and all school trips.

We are a small friendly co-educational school with a wonderful family feel. Parents and pupils comment on the 'home from home' atmosphere.

Boys and girls are accepted from the age of 3 years into the happy and friendly Early Years Department, situated in a beautiful house within the school grounds. From here until they leave the school at the age of 11, every care is taken to realise the full potential of each child.

Small class sizes ensure that, whilst teachers really know their pupils and are able to tailor the curriculum to the individual child's needs, pupils are also able to learn from each other in a challenging yet supportive environment. Our experienced staff inspire the children and set high academic standards, we achieve excellent 11+ examination results, including academic scholarships.

We make full use of the excellent local sporting facilities and the Royal Military Academy, Sandhurst. All pupils take weekly swimming lessons and are involved in a wide range of sporting activities.

Music and Drama have a significant presence within the school. We have two choirs and an orchestra, many plays throughout the year and pupils are prepared for the examinations of the Associated Board of Music. We offer an extensive after-school activities programme and wrap-around care from 8.00 am to 6.00 pm.

Entry to the school can be at any age if there is a vacancy.

Happiness is the key ingredient and every child at Lyndhurst is given the chance to shine at something, whether academic, music, sport or art.

Mander Portman Woodward (MPW)
London

90–92 Queen's Gate, London SW7 5AB
Tel: 020 7835 1355
Fax: 020 7259 2705
email: london@mpw.ac.uk
website: www.mpw.ac.uk

Principal: **John Southworth**, BSc, MSc

Vice Principals:
Richard Berlie
Christine Gavin
Petrouchka Stafford

Age Range. 14–19.
Number in School. 600.
Fees per term (2018–2019). £9,529–£10,226.
Mander Portman Woodward (MPW) was founded in 1973 and is one of London's best known independent colleges. Situated in South Kensington, the college is fully co-educational and accepts about 600 students each year.

We offer a highly flexible curriculum of unrivalled depth and breadth, with GCSE and A Levels in over 40 subjects and there are no restrictions on subject combinations at A Level. We also run revision courses over one year, one term and during the Easter holidays.

We are distinctive in many ways, not least with small classes of no more than nine students and our focus on exam preparation, but also in the outstanding personal support for students through our Director of Studies system.

A full team of staff offers specialist university entrance guidance. We have fully equipped media studies, computing and film rooms, plus drama and art studios, a photography darkroom and five science laboratories.

Our extra-curricular programme is comprehensive. Among other options, we offer rugby, football, creative writing, street jazz dancing, basketball, gym membership, conversational Italian, instrumental lessons, debating, Duke of Edinburgh' Award, and community service.

In keeping with our founding principles, our primary focus at all age levels is on academic goals. Entry into the sixth form is dependent on a student's academic record and performance at interview. Almost all pupils proceed to university after leaving, with about 10 each year going to read Medicine. Over the past four years an average of seven of our full-time pupils each year have won places at the Universities of Oxford or Cambridge.

We insist on strict punctuality in the attendance of lessons and the submission of homework and there is a formal system of monthly examinations in each subject throughout a student's career at the school.

Whilst we require pupils to have a strong commitment to academic discipline, our reputation is based on having created a framework in which pupils can enjoy working hard. The environment is friendly, the teachers experienced and enthusiastic and the atmosphere positive and conducive to success.

Maple Hayes Hall School for Dyslexics

Abnalls Lane, Lichfield, Staffordshire WS13 8BL

Tel: 01543 264387
Fax: 01543 262022
email: office@dyslexia.school
website: www.dyslexia.school
Facebook: @Maple-Hayes-Hall-School

Principal: **Dr E N Brown**, PhD, MSc, BA, MSCME, MINS, AFBPsS, CPsychol

Headmaster: Dr D J Brown, DPhil, MEd Psychology of SpLD, MA Oxon, PGCE

Age Range. 7–17.
Number in School. 120 Day Boys and Girls.
Fees per term (from April 2019). £5,205–£6,955.
Maple Hayes is a specialist independent day school approved under the 1996 Education Act as a co-educational school for children of average to very high intelligence who are not achieving their intellectual potential by normal teaching methods.

This school is under the direction of Dr E Neville Brown whose work in the field of learning strategies has achieved international recognition and includes a major breakthrough in the teaching of dyslexic children. Attention is paid to the individual child by teaching the basic literacy and numeracy skills required for the child to benefit from a full curriculum (with the exception of a foreign language). The school had an outstanding Ofsted report in November 2017.

The very favourable teacher to pupil ratio of 1:10 or better ensures a high standard of educational and pastoral care. The children's learning is under the supervision and guidance of a qualified educational psychologist.

Maple Walk School

62A Crownhill Road, London NW10 4EB

Tel: 020 8963 3890
           020 8965 7374 (Admissions)
email: admissions@maplewalkschool.co.uk
website: www.maplewalkschool.co.uk

Head Teacher: **Mrs Sarah Gillam**

Age Range. 4–11 Co-educational.
Number of Pupils. 200.

Maple Walk is a happy, thriving and vibrant independent primary school, for girls and boys aged 4–11, in North West London.

We provide a secure and supportive environment for effective learning and personal development. High standards are pursued in all subjects including English and Maths using traditional teaching methods, alongside an innovative curriculum.

We have a friendly, well-resourced, purpose-built environment with small class sizes, in which children learn and flourish.

Opportunities outside the classroom abound. Through sporting activities, first class music, art and drama, we encourage every child to find their own particular strength.

Termly school trips and residential experiences in Years 5 and 6 extend the curriculum and develop social skills.

Year 6 leavers have been offered places at a range of independent and maintained schools, including St Paul's Girls, Godolphin and Latymer, Christ's Hospital, John Lyon, Frances Holland, Slough Grammar, Notting Hill & Ealing High School, Latymer Upper, Henrietta Barnett and Highgate, to name just a few.

Founded in 2004, Maple Walk was the first of the New Model School Company's schools, offering a low-fee model, based on traditional teaching methods and with a Christian ethos.

Entry into Reception is non selective and based on the date the completed registration form is returned to our Registrar, with siblings given priority. Entry higher up the school is by interview and informal assessment in the classroom. We offer regular open days and welcome private tours.

Fees per term (2018–2019) £3,349.

Mayville High School

35 St Simon's Road, Southsea, Hants PO5 2PE

Tel: 023 9273 4847
Fax: 023 9229 3649
email: enquiries@mayvillehighschool.net
website: www.mayvillehighschool.com

Mayville High School – Excellence through nurture

Headteacher: **Mrs R H K Parkyn**, MA Oxon, MA, PGCE, MCIL

Age Range. 2+ to 16 years.
Number in School. Day Pupils: 246 Boys, 215 Girls.
Fees per term (2018–2019). £2,545–£3,745.
Mayville High School can offer your child a place from the age of 2+ to 16 years. Our close-knit community is divided into the Early Years, Pre-Prep, Junior and Senior Schools. We have a renowned Dyslexia Unit, recognised by CReSTeD, and offer a Gifted and Talented Programme. Our pupils star in numerous ways, and the Mayville family includes pupils, teachers, parents, carers and grandparents.

Mayville, a co-educational day school in Southsea, Hampshire was founded in 1897. There is a strong emphasis on traditional skills, yet Mayville adopts innovative teaching methods to help promote your child's learning. Our size is our strength, big enough to offer pupils a wide range of opportunities, we are small enough to truly treat and know each pupil as an individual.

Mayville provides a learning environment where your child is able to achieve their goals. At Mayville we want children to feel secure and valued: this enables them to take advantage of every opportunity, whether it is academic, social, physical, creative or spiritual.

Mayville sets high standards in all areas. Small class sizes encourage academic success. Boys and girls are taught separately throughout, to best meet their individual learning styles. Over the years Mayville pupils have consistently achieved high standards in GCSE examinations. Flexible teaching, varied resources, support and extension programmes coupled with high expectations help to meet the needs of each individual learner. Art, drama, dance, music and sport play an important part in school life, the latter now enhanced by new playing fields. There are a number of clubs and after-school activities. There is something available to interest everyone.

Early Years (2+ to 5+ years). Our Early Years at Mayville encompass the statutory curriculum of the Foundation Stage; the youngest children are the 2+ year olds (Swans) who are situated in the "Cottage". In the September following their 3rd birthday the Swans graduate to the Kestrels where they complete the second year of their Foundation Stage. Our aim is to ensure that all children feel cherished and secure in a "home-from-home" environment. Our Swan and Kestrels areas have also been awarded the much coveted Flying High for Early Years Accreditation that stamps a seal of excellence on the care we provide.

When you leave your young child for the first time you want them to be cared for as they would at home. In our cosy bright buildings with their own safety surface playgrounds, children are nurtured by qualified Early Years staff. Children sit down together at lunchtime and enjoy freshly cooked nutritious meals. Close proximity to the seafront and local amenities means children are regularly taken out for trips. Our Swan and Kestrel classes are open 50 weeks of the year, 8 am to 6 pm.

For their third and final year of the Foundation Stage the children move into the Reception Class (Lower I) this class provides an early start to literacy and numeracy, and a wide range of activities designed to help them become active independent learners.

Pre-Prep Dept (6–7 years) Key Stage One. The Pre-Prep Department includes Upper I and Lower II. In these classes the curriculum widens to include science, geography, history and ICT as separate subjects. Upper I staff work closely with Lower I in order to affect a smooth transition from the Foundation stage to Key Stage One, while Lower II work closely with the Junior school in order to prepare children for Key Stage Two. All pupils in the Foundation Stage and Pre-Prep benefit from use of the the school's halls for drama, dance and PE. French and Music are taught throughout the Foundation Stage and Pre-Prep Departments.

Junior and Senior Schools. The Junior School accepts boys and girls from the age of 7+. We offer bright airy surroundings, a caring yet disciplined environment and small class sizes. While a strong emphasis is placed on the traditional skills of reading writing and numeracy, children in the Junior School enjoy a varied curriculum. Pupils are taught to appreciate that education is as much about attitudes and values, as it is about academic and sporting success. In the senior school this ethos continues, and pupils are given a wide range of opportunities to excel in: academic, creative, sporting and social settings. Pupils at KS3 follow a full curriculum. This includes thinking skills and first aid, and also study skills seminars. It is Mayville's policy to enter all pupils for their GCSE providing they have completed the course of study and any coursework. Therefore our results, which have been well above the national average for the past ten years, are a true reflection of the efforts of pupils and staff.

At Mayville we believe that confidence is the central building block to success in future life. Our commitment to Global Rock Challenge and membership of our own St John Ambulance cadet unit, allows pupils to develop teamwork and leadership skills. At Mayville we celebrate the many successes of our pupils and encourage their competitive spirit. With three houses, there are a number of inter-house competitions which also promote this. Trips to local, national and international locations are encouraged to broaden the experiences begun in the classroom.

Transport. There are good public transport links into the city from the surrounding areas. School minibuses pick up pupils from the local ferry terminals and train stations.

If you would like a prospectus, to book a tour of the school with the Head teacher, Mr Castle, or to find out about our taster days and entrance procedures, please telephone the school or visit our website. Scholarships are available from Year 2.

Charitable status. Mayville High School is a Registered Charity, number 286347. It exists to provide a traditional education to children from a wide range of academic backgrounds within a caring environment.

Mead School

16 Frant Road, Tunbridge Wells, Kent TN2 5SN

Tel:	01892 525837
email:	office@themeadschool.co.uk
website:	www.meadschool.info
Twitter:	@TheMeadSchoolTW
Facebook:	@themeadschoolTW

Headmaster: **Mr Andrew Webster**

Age Range. 3–11.
Number in School. 242.
Fees per term (2018–2019). Kindergarten £1,456; Infants £3,345; Juniors £3,745.

The Mead School is a thriving, co-educational prep school situated in the heart of Tunbridge Wells. The school, which was rated 'excellent' in all areas in its most recent ISI Inspection Report, is a true community and run as a large family living under one roof.

The Mead's ethos is that a child who is happy and secure in school is one who is going to learn, thrive and aspire. School must be an exciting, fulfilling and safe place where every day, whether you are aged three or eleven, is a new adventure and positively anticipated.

The Mead enjoys a reputation of high academic standards within a caring, happy environment. Children are prepared for the highly-selective Tunbridge Wells and Tonbridge Grammar Schools as well as a wide range of Independent and maintained secondary schools.

The Mead has exceptional music, drama and sport provision and over 30 extra-curricular clubs to choose from. Fully catered provision is offered from 7.45 am to 6.00 pm.

The Mount, Mill Hill International

Milespit Hill, Mill Hill Village, London NW7 2RX

Tel:	+44 (0)20 3826 3333
	+44 (0)20 3826 3366 (Admissions)
email:	office@millhillinternational.org.uk
	registrar@millhillinternational.org.uk
website:	www.millhill.org.uk/international

Motto: Instilling values, inspiring minds

Interim Chair of the Court of Governors: Mr Elliot Lipton, BSc Hons, MBA, FRSA, FRICS

Head: **Mrs Sarah Bellotti**, BEd

Age Range. 13–18 Co-educational.
Number of Pupils. 76.
Fees per term (2018–2019). Day £8,330 including lunch, Weekly Boarding £11,487 (including meals), Full Boarding: £13,513 (Including all meals).

The Mount, Mill Hill International is a co-educational boarding and day school for international pupils aged 13–18. It is situated in the Green Belt on the borders of Hertfordshire and Middlesex, just ten miles from Central London, and forms part of the Mill Hill School Foundation which is set in 160 acres of beautiful grounds. Weekly and full boarding is available for entry at Year 9, Year 10 and Sixth Form. Pupils from all over the world come together in an inspiring school to gain internationally recognised qualifications, a transformational educational and cultural experience.

At Mill Hill International your child will develop habits of mind that will equip them for their educational journey in the UK and prepare them to face the challenges of life in the 21st century with confidence, resilience and creativity. We guide our pupils to seek courage and curiosity within themselves and apply them in all their endeavours. We offer a traditional British educational experience and an academic curriculum up to GCSE/IGCSE and specialist EAL teaching. Pupils for whom English is not their first language receive English language tuition while at the same time studying an appropriate range of other subjects in order to equip them for further study whether at Mill Hill School or elsewhere. Suitable also for British pupils returning to the UK after a period abroad, Mill Hill International offers a Fast Track course which is an English language foundation programme, a year nine course to help pupils prepare for GCSE, an intensive one year GCSE course for pupils entering Year 11 and a two year GCSE programme where students will study between 8 and 12 subjects. In addition, there is a Summer School which offers courses to ages 12–17, combining English learning with academic subjects, including mathematics and science or sport. These core elements are complemented by a varied programme of Creative activity classes including music, drama, IT and art.

Our teaching is rigorous, challenging and exciting and we have high expectations of every pupil. Class sizes are small and all our teachers are qualified or trained in teaching English as an additional language so every pupil can progress quickly. In addition to the impressive resources of the Mill Hill International campus, we use Mill Hill School's sports facilities, including the indoor heated swimming pool, sports hall, theatre and music school. Our pupils are fully integrated with those from Mill Hill School throughout.

Charitable status. The Mill Hill School Foundation is a Registered Charity, number 1064758. It exists for the education of boys and girls.

The Moat School

Bishop's Avenue, Fulham, London SW6 6EG
Tel: 020 7610 9018
email: office@moatschool.org.uk
website: www.moatschool.org.uk

Headmistress: **Clare King**, EMBA, BA Hons, PGCE, Cert SpLD

Co-educational Day School.
Age Range. 9–16.
Number of Pupils. 65 Boys, 15 Girls.
Fees per term (2018–2019). £10,000.

Set within the historic conservation area of Fulham Palace, The Moat School is a specialist school for secondary-age SpLD pupils. Mainstream in structure and specialist in nature, The Moat caters successfully for the needs of pupils with specific learning difficulties. Alongside the curriculum, the school also offers expertise in speech and language therapy, occupational therapy and a school counsellor.

All teachers complete a postgraduate BDA approved course in teaching students with SpLD within their first 2 years of appointment. Qualified Learning Support Assistants accompany pupils throughout their lessons at Key Stage 3, where class sizes are a maximum of 10. Class sizes are even smaller at Key Stage 4.

Multi-sensory teaching is combined with advanced IT provision, each pupil being provided with a laptop computer for use in school and at home. Touch-typing is taught in Year 7 and there is a state-of-the-art wireless network which enables staff and pupils to access the school intranet with its wide range of learning resources and data, as well as the internet.

At Key Stage 3, pupils follow a mainstream curriculum (with the exception of foreign languages) before selecting their GCSE options alongside the core subjects of English, Mathematics and Single or Dual Award Science. The Moat offers excellent facilities for learning, with a suite of Design Technology workshops offering state-of-the-art facilities for Food Technology, Resistant Materials and Graphics. Art, Music, Drama, ICT and Business Studies each have dedicated studios or specialist classrooms.

The Moat has an extensive enrichment programme of extracurricular activities designed to widen experience and develop self-confidence. In Drama, all Year 9 pupils take part in an annual Shakespeare play and there are several productions and workshop performances each year. The Moat's proximity to the River Thames enables pupils to experience rowing as a sport, swimming is popular and 2012 saw the introduction of Martial Arts and boxing. The Duke of Edinburgh's Award encourages pupils to test their own limits and each summer pupils in Years 7, 8 and 9 make a residential visit to an outdoor activity centre to develop independence and leadership skills.

The Moat School is a part of the Cavendish Education Group.

Moon Hall School for Dyslexic Children

Pasturewood Road, Holmbury St Mary, Dorking, Surrey RH5 6LQ
Tel: 01306 731464
Fax: 01306 731504
email: enquiries@moonhallschool.co.uk
website: www.moonhallschool.co.uk

Chairman of Governors: Mr David Baker

Headmistress: **Ms Emma Fraser**, BA Hons QTS, Dip SpLD, Cert Phono-Graphix

Age Range. 7–11.

Number of Children. Approximately 50.

Fees per term (2018–2019). Day Pupils £6,630–£6,895; Boarding Fee in addition payable to Belmont.

Religious denomination: Church of England.

Moon Hall School, Holmbury St Mary caters for boys and girls with SpLD. Accredited by CReSTeD (SP), it has a unique relationship with Belmont Preparatory School (*see separate entry*), sharing its site and excellent facilities. Uniform is common to both schools, and pupils are fully integrated at assembly, lunch and break. They also join together for sport/teams and in dramatic and musical productions. Moon Hall pupils may transfer to Belmont classes when ready, usually into Year 7.

MHS's specialist qualified, multi-disciplinary staff deliver a full curriculum to dyslexic children from Year 3. All are taught to touch-type and are successfully entered for OCR examinations normally taken by those aged 16+. Within the well-designed, purpose-built accommodation, classes contain a maximum of 14 children, subdivided for English and Mathematics. One-to-one tuition is available as needed. Literacy and numeracy teaching is structured and multi-sensory, incorporating material devised by acknowledged experts in the field. The Phono-Graphix Programme is employed at all levels. Study/Thinking Skills are an integral part of our teaching. Great emphasis is placed upon rebuilding self-esteem.

Entry requirements: A full report by an independent Educational Psychologist showing the child to be dyslexic and of at least average intelligence. Assessment and interview at MHS.

After Year 6 children may transfer to a number of suitable mainstream senior schools, or continue their education at Moon Hall College, our own Senior School located in Leigh, near Reigate.

Charitable status. Moon Hall School is a Registered Charity, number 803481.

Moorland School

Ribblesdale Avenue, Clitheroe, Lancashire BB7 2JA

Tel:	01200 423833
Fax:	01200 429339
email:	enquiries@moorlandschool.co.uk
website:	www.moorlandschool.co.uk
Twitter:	@MoorlandSchool1
Facebook:	@MoorlandPrivateSchool

Headteacher: **Mr Jonathan Harrison**, BA Hons, PGCE

Head of Juniors: Miss Kristy Jacks

Age Range. 3 months – 18 years.

Number of Pupils. 200 including 87 boarders.

Fees per term (2018–2019). Day (Reception–Year 13): £1,500–£3,825; Full Boarding: £6,730–£9,000; Weekly Boarding: £5,925–£7,920.

Moorland School is a thriving co-educational day and boarding school located in the historic town of Clitheroe within the picturesque Ribble Valley, in the North-West of England. The school enjoys excellent transport links to Manchester. We have an outstandingly beautiful site with more than 15 acres of grounds. Nearly half of the children at Moorland are boarders and we find it makes for a good social mix with our day pupils from the surrounding area. The opening of our purpose-built new building means our boarders can enjoy modern and spacious facilities, fully equipped with satellite television and Wi-Fi. Moorland can now offer the seamless transition from GCSE to A Level or

BTEC study, through our thriving new Sixth Form Centre, which provides our students with the opportunity to settle in one place rather than having to move from school to school. Furthermore, the School boasts an outstanding elite football and elite ballet, unique to any British boarding school. These courses are led by field professionals in their respective areas.

Admission to Moorland. Parents and children are encouraged to visit the school to meet the Principal and see the school in action. Boarding or Day children are also welcome to attend Moorland for a one or two day 'taster visit'.

Kindergarten & Nursery. As well as having its own indoor soft-play area, the nursery also has a large outdoor play area within its extensive grounds, with unbroken views over Waddington Fell. The Nursery's superb layout of colourful rooms and equipment make it an ideal and exceptional learning environment.

Junior School. The Preparatory Department takes children between the ages of 4 and 11. The children have their own play area and IT suite and benefit from using the facilities of the Senior School such as science laboratories and sports hall.

The children follow Key Stages 1 and 2 of the National Curriculum with particular emphasis on numeracy and literacy. Our small class sizes allow every child to read to the Teacher on a daily basis. French is also included in the Junior curriculum.

The Senior School follows the criteria set down in the National Curriculum. We enter our pupils for the Standard Attainment Tests and for GCSE at the end of Key stage 4.

Football at Moorland. Our FA approved coach, Charles Jackson, is one of the UK's most innovative and well-respected football coaches. He teaches to a Premier League standard. He has worked at Moorland since November 2002. He also worked at the Manchester United Advanced Coaching Centre up to July 2005 and is now the Under 14 academy technical skills Development Coach at Manchester City FC. Mr Jackson is a full-time teacher at Moorland School, teaching children from age 4–18.

Pastoral Care. At Moorland children benefit from continuous pastoral support within a friendly family environment. By day, teaching staff provide continual support within small classes. Evening and weekend care is undertaken by the House Parent team.

More House School

Frensham, Farnham, Surrey GU10 3AP

Tel:	01252 792303
	Admissions: 01252 797600
Fax:	01252 797601
email:	schooloffice@morehouseschool.co.uk
website:	www.morehouseschool.co.uk
Twitter:	@MHSFrensham
Facebook:	@morehouseschoolfrensham
LinkedIn:	/more-house-school-frensham

Headmaster: **Mr Jonathan Hetherington**, BA Hons, MSc Ed QTS

Age Range. 8 to 18.

Number in School. 470: 110 Boarders, 360 Day Boys.

Fees per term (2018–2019). Full Boarding £8,505–£9,535; Weekly Boarding £7,774–£8,803; Day £4,371–£6,126.

More House School occupies a unique position in helping boys with specific learning difficulties in that multi-sensory remediation is applied across the curriculum, through carefully targeted and maintained intervention, and extra help is available in our Learning Development Centre, so that proper support is always available and individual needs met.

It is approved by the Department for Education and has been listed by CReSTeD in their Specialist Schools category. No school can help every child, so we have a very careful selection assessment to ensure that we really can help those who finally enter the school.

Founded 78 years ago, the school is a centre of excellence and prides itself in using the best modern practice to increase confidence and make children feel valued, happy and to fulfil their potential at GCSE, AS, A Level and other public examinations.

Boarding is run by caring staff and is situated in beautiful grounds with ample opportunities for outdoor pursuits. Our activities programme, which offers 18 options each day, encourages all day boys and boarders to make good use of their leisure time. There is a strong sense of community.

There is an ongoing building programme and the facilities are very good in all departments.

The 2016 Ofsted inspection recognises the exceptional progress More House pupils make throughout the school, identifying 'consistently very effective teaching' and 'highly effective support' which enable pupils to 'achieve a gamut of excellent outcomes …not only academic but [that] also relate to pupils' increased confidence, their improved sense of well-being and their ability to form meaningful social relationships'.

We have a comprehensive information pack, hold an annual 'Discover' More House open day in February and welcome new enquiries.

Charitable status. More House School is a Registered Charity, number 311872. A Catholic foundation, open to all denominations, helping boys to succeed.

Moyles Court School

Moyles Court, Ringwood, Hampshire BH24 3NF

Tel: 01425 472856/473197
Fax: 01425 474715
email: info@moylescourt.co.uk
website: www.moylescourt.co.uk

Headmaster: **Mr Richard Milner-Smith**

Please see school website for full Staff list.

Age Range. 3–16
Number in School. Boarders: 22 boys, 11 girls. Day: 76 boys, 84 girls.
Fees per term (2018–2019). Senior Day £4,270–£4,766; Senior Boarding £8,675; Junior Day £2,112–£3,852; Junior Boarding £8,675; Nursery: please contact the school for session rates.

Moyles Court School is non-selective day and boarding co-ed school taking pupils from 3 to 16 years and is housed in a 16th Century Manor house close to Ringwood, set within the beautiful New Forest National Park. It offers individualised learning, affordable fees and traditional core values. The boarding environment at Moyles Court School aims to provide a welcoming and supportive setting where boarders can flourish and develop within a safe and beautiful campus environment. It is an environment in which children grow, where confidence and self-belief are heightened and where values and skills are learnt that will stay with them for the rest of their lives.

We are proud of our academic results, with all our pupils showing that with great effort and determination, from both

teacher and pupil alike, they can secure GCSE results way above their national predictions. However, we are also committed to educating the whole child, on the understanding that academic results will only take you so far in life. Sport, music and drama all flourish here and a vast range of extra-curricular activities ensure children are exposed to an exciting range of opportunities that will help shape and develop them as individuals.

The 2018 GCSE results continue to show the significant improvements being made at the school in recent years Over 90% of pupils gained 5 or more GCSEs at Grade 4 and above (A*–C), with 91% of all grades being above Grade 4 (compared to the national figure of 66.9%). On average each pupil achieved over a grade more than they would normally be expected to achieve

In 2016, Moyles Court partnered with Broadway Education, owned by Lymington family Mark and Jo Broadway, in order to further capitalise on Moyles Court's success. The new strategic relationship complements Broadway Education's portfolio of schools. Broadway Education has a portfolio of three schools: Talbot House Preparatory School in Bournemouth, a successful feeder school for Bournemouth and Poole Grammar Schools; St. Michael's School in South Wales and Bosworth Independent College in Northampton, both of which were listed in the Telegraph Top 100 A Level rankings for 2015. All are respected schools with their own strong identities and leadership teams, and each has a strong reputation for a high standard of learning.

Small class sizes, individualised learning, great teaching, extensive after-school provision, tailored transport and excellent pastoral care provide your children with the best possible start in life. Parents are welcome to book an appointment at any time to see the school and find out why everyone is talking about Moyles Court School. For further details visit the website at www.moylescourt.co.uk or contact Chris Young, Admissions Secretary.

Norfolk House School

4 Norfolk Road, Edgbaston, Birmingham B15 3PS

Tel: 0121 454 7021
email: info@norfolkhouseschool.co.uk
website: www.norfolkhouseschool.co.uk

Headmistress: **Mrs Susannah Palmer**

Age Range. 3–11.
Number in School. 138.
Fees per term (from April 2018). £2,392–£3,460.

Norfolk House School is a Christian Independent day school situated in the pleasant suburb of Edgbaston and is ideally located for pupils and parents all over Birmingham and the surrounding areas.

The school aims to provide individual attention to each pupil, thus enabling each child to fulfil his or her potential. Small class sizes and favourable pupil to teacher ratios culminate in the best possible academic results. Many pupils move on to the various King Edward Schools, or to other Grammar Schools or senior Independent Schools as the direct result of the high standards achieved at Norfolk House.

The syllabus is designed to give each child a general academic education over a wide range of subjects – in line with the National Curriculum; the requirements of the Eleven Plus and the various Entrance Examinations are also taken into consideration.

In addition to education, Norfolk House School aims to instil in each child good manners, consideration and respect for others, and recognition of personal responsibility. Norfolk House is a small school with an emphasis on caring and traditional values, yet forward thinking in outlook. It is a happy school with high attainment, competitive fees and a family atmosphere.

Normanhurst School

68–74 Station Road, North Chingford, London E4 7BA

Tel:	020 8529 4307
Fax:	020 8524 7737
email:	info@normanhurstschool.co.uk
website:	www.normanhurstschool.co.uk
Twitter:	@NormanhurstSch

Headmistress: **Mrs Claire Osborn**, BA Hons, MSc, PGCE

Age Range. 2½–16 Co-educational.
Number in School. 275 Day Pupils.
Fees per term (2018–2019). £1,350–£4,350.

Normanhurst School is a thriving, caring, local independent school with a warm, friendly atmosphere and a wide range of activities offered. The School boasts a high standard of academic achievement with excellent SATs and GCSE results.

We encourage our pupils to develop self-confidence and to take on roles of responsibility as they move up through the school. Creativity is nurtured within a disciplined environment and traditional values such as self-discipline are promoted to maximise our pupils' effectiveness in an ever-changing world.

The School offers small class sizes and a wide range of core and optional subjects up to GCSE, including English, Science, Maths, French, Spanish, Design Technology, Art, History, Geography, ICT, Business Studies, PE, Sport, Music and Drama.

Numerous clubs are provided to strengthen the important social aspect of schooling. These include Football, Netball, Gymnastics, Chess, French, Cross-Country, Dance, and ICT. Homework club and Teatime club are available to all pupils, while tuition on various musical instruments takes place either as an extra-curricular activity during the day or after school.

The School is located in the centre of a tree-lined suburban street with good parking, two minutes from a mainline British Rail station and well-connected bus station.

Entry requirements: Interview and assessment.

Northease Manor School

Rodmell, Lewes, East Sussex BN7 3EY

Tel:	01273 472915
Fax:	01273 472202
email:	office@northease.co.uk
	pa2headteacher@northease.co.uk
website:	www.northease.co.uk

Chair of Governors: Julie Toben

Head: **Ms Claire Farmer**

Type of School. Co-educational day and weekly boarding school.
Age Range. 10–18.
Number of Pupils. 62: 13 Girls, 59 Boys.

Fees per term (2018–2019). Day £7,709, Boarding £10,481.

Northease Manor School is a co-educational specialist school for pupils, aged ten to eighteen, who have autism and/or dyslexia. It caters for both weekly boarders and day pupils. It is approved by the Department for Education, and is set in the South Downs with Grade II listed buildings.

It provides a holistic approach to Specific Learning Difficulties within small teaching groups and provides on-site access to Speech and Language Therapy and Occupational Therapy. Most of the staff have specialist qualifications and benefit from in-house training.

They receive full access to the National Curriculum and benefit from an intensive multi-sensory input which provides for all their literacy and language needs. Detailed pastoral support is given to enable pupils to feel secure and become independent learners. Everything that happens at the school is geared to the needs of the child and to ensure that each pupil experiences success in order to raise self-esteem and self-confidence.

The ethos of the school is based upon respect for the individual and the celebration of success and achievement. All pupils have abilities and talents and it is the school's role to enable every pupil to discover and develop these strengths. Pupils are encouraged to develop their independence. It is "our school" and everybody contributes to its well-being and development. High standards of behaviour are expected, with the onus on partnership between pupils and adults. Mistakes are seen as part of the learning process.

Charitable status. Northease Manor School Trust Ltd is a Registered Charity, number 307005. It exists for the provision of high-quality education for pupils with Specific Learning Difficulties.

Notre Dame Preparatory School

147 Dereham Road, Norwich, Norfolk NR2 3TA

Tel:	01603 625593
email:	secretary@notredameprepschool.co.uk
website:	www.notredameprepschool.co.uk
Facebook:	@notredameprepnorwich

Chairman of Governors: Mr Richard Bailey

Headmaster: **Mr Rob Thornton**, MA Ed

Age Range. 2–11 Co-educational.
Number of Pupils. 210 Day.
Fees per term (2018–2019). £1,955–£2,155.

Notre Dame Prep School was originally founded by the Sisters of Notre Dame de Namur in 1865. The school transferred to its present site in 1971 and is now a Company with charitable status. The school maintains the traditions and the spirit of the Sisters of Notre Dame and the former name and ethos.

As a Catholic school we endeavour to nurture a love of God through Jesus Christ in all the children. The school has an ethos of love and care and embraces children of all faiths.

Children are treated as individuals, respected, nurtured and encouraged to embrace and fulfil their potential in all areas of school life. We have excellent links with High Schools in both the maintained and independent sectors.

The school achieves well above-average results in external tests and has a strong academic reputation. Children are prepared for entry to selective independent schools on request. Subjects include English, Maths, Science, Computing, Design and Technology, Art, Geography, PE, History,

Music, RE, French and Personal, Social and Health Education.

The school has a very strong musical tradition and has a wide range of extra-curricular musical activities on offer including Choir, Chamber Choir, Recorder, Piano, Guitar, Flute, Violin, Saxophone and Clarinet lessons.

Sports include Football, Cricket, Rugby, Netball, Rounders, Hockey, Tennis and Swimming.

The school offers a wide range of extra-curricular activities including Speech and Drama, Chess, Cookery, Debating, Glee Club, Photography, Arts and Crafts, Science, Sewing, Young Explorers, Creative Writing, Badminton and other sports and activities.

All children eat hot dinners at school, which have been fully prepared and cooked on site. We have an After-School Activities Club which runs until 6.00 pm incorporating homework club and games activities for younger children. A light cooked tea is provided for children who stay beyond 4.30 pm. Holiday clubs run throughout most of the main holidays.

Charitable status. Notre Dame Preparatory School (Norwich) Limited is a Registered Charity, number 269003.

Oakhyrst Grange School

160 Stanstead Road, Caterham, Surrey CR3 6AF

Tel: 01883 343344
email: office@oakhyrstgrangeschool.co.uk
website: www.oakhyrstgrangeschool.co.uk

Chairman of Board of Management: Mrs Brenda Davis

Headmaster: **Mr Alex Gear**, BEd

Age Range. 4–11.
Number in School. 147 Day Boys and Girls.
Fees per term (2018–2019). £1,308–£2,867.

Oakhyrst Grange School is an independent, co-educational preparatory day school for boys and girls between 4 and 11 years.

The School was established in 1950 and moved to its present premises in Stanstead Road in 1957. Since September 1973 the School has been administered by a non-profit making trust.

Standing in five acres of open country and woodland and surrounded by the Green Belt, the School enjoys a fine position amongst the Surrey Hills.

The school has a wide and imaginative curriculum, which includes traditional teaching combined with innovative ideas. Small class sizes, with a maximum of 20 pupils, and an excellent teacher to pupil ratio enable pupils to work at their own rate and capabilities whilst being encouraged to meet new challenges.

Our pupils secure the offer of places at prominent senior schools, including scholarships and awards across the range of academic, all-rounder, music, sports and art.

There are many sporting opportunities offered and particularly high standards have been reached in cross-country, swimming, football, judo and athletics where ISA National level has been achieved. The pupils compete in many inter house, inter school and area competitions. The school also has its own heated indoor swimming pool, all-weather floodlit multi-use games area, tennis, netball, hockey and 5-a-side court, sports pitch, cross-country course and gymnasium.

Extra-curricular music lessons are offered and much music making also takes place as part of the normal school timetable. The school has an orchestra in addition to clarinet, flute, guitar, saxophone, violin and trumpet ensembles and a choir, all of whom perform regularly. In 2014, the school was the winner of the National ISA Award for Excellence in the Arts.

In addition to the curriculum the pupils can enjoy an extensive range of clubs and activities throughout the week. At Oakhyrst Grange School we are very proud of our Forest School status. A senior leader is fully trained in Forest School Activities and it is an integral part of our Year 3 curriculum and whole school extra-curricular activities.

Academic excellence is encouraged, every child is expected to attain his or her individual potential. The School helps children to develop into caring, thoughtful and confident adults.

Charitable status. Oakhyrst Grange School Educational Trust is a Registered Charity, number 325043. It exists to provide an all-round education, to give the children success and the best possible start.

Oaklands School

8 Albion Hill, Loughton, Essex IG10 4RA

Tel: 020 8508 3517
Fax: 020 8508 4454
email: info@oaklandsschool.co.uk
website: www.oaklandsschool.co.uk
Twitter: @OaklandsSch

Headmistress: **Mrs S Belej**, BA Jt Hons, Cert Ed

Age Range. 2½–11 Co-educational.
Number in School. 270 Day Pupils.
Fees per term (2018–2019). £1,350–£3,525.

Oaklands is a long-established preparatory school, founded in 1937, and delightfully situated in extensive grounds on the edge of Epping Forest. It provides a firm foundation for girls and boys aged 2½ to 11. Great care is taken in preparing pupils for entrance examinations to their next schools.

A broad curriculum is offered, with early emphasis on literacy and numeracy, ensuring high standards, and great importance is placed on fully developing each child's potential in a secure and caring atmosphere. We have small class sizes and specialist teachers for Science, French, Music, PE, Dancing, ICT, Sport and Drama. A wide range of extra-curricular activities is offered and breakfast club operates from 7.30 am and tea time club continues after school until 6 pm. Parents enjoy easy access to their child's teachers and the headmistress has an open-door policy. Individual music tuition is available, including piano and woodwind instrumental lessons, and singing lessons.

Oaklands is a friendly, happy school where children can enjoy learning and take pride in both their own success and the achievements of others. In addition to the attainment of high standards, pupils build personal qualities of confidence, self-reliance and respect for others, in preparation for the challenges and opportunities of the modern world.

Park School

Queens Park South Drive, Bournemouth BH8 9BJ

Tel:	01202 396640
Fax:	01202 237640
email:	office@parkschool.co.uk
website:	www.parkschool.co.uk
	www.parkschoolnursery.co.uk

Headteacher: **Mrs Melanie Dowler**, BSc Hons, PGCE

Age Range. 2–11.

Number in School. Day: 195 Boys, 169 Girls.

Fees per term (2018–2019). £2,475–£2,985.

Park School is a thriving co-educational junior day school in a pleasant residential area near Bournemouth town centre. Our last full ISI inspection in June 2015 awarded us 'Excellent' across all areas of the School and EYFS and we passed the ISI Compliance Inspection in May 2018 with flying colours.

Pupils are taught in small classes in a caring, happy environment. The school is geared principally towards academic achievement, with an emphasis on nurturing individual progress. At the heart of all we do is the belief that children will achieve their best when they are happy. We foster a positive ethos and the development of the all-round child. This covers not only work in the classroom, but all other aspects of school life: games, music, the arts and other activities. Sport is an important part of Park School life and we use our stunning facility at Dean Park for games lessons and sports fixtures.

Pupils are prepared for entry to Senior Independent Schools and Bournemouth and Poole Grammar Schools through tests at 11+ years. Many children gain scholarships to Senior Independent Schools.

Most pupils join us in the Nursery at 2 years old, but there are occasionally vacancies further up the School. An offer of a place is made only after prospective pupils have been assessed.

Park School Nursery is open between 8.00 am and 6.00 pm Monday to Friday and is open year round with the exception of Christmas week and Bank Holidays.

Park School for Girls

20–22 Park Avenue, Ilford, Essex IG1 4RS

Tel:	Office: 020 8554 2466
	Bursar: 020 8554 6022
Fax:	020 8554 3003
email:	admin@parkschool.org.uk
website:	www.parkschool.org.uk

Head Teacher: **Mrs Androulla Nicholas**, BSc Econ Hons, PGCE

Age Range. 4–16.

Number in School. 170 Day Girls.

Fees per term (2018–2019). Reception £2,265, Pre-Prep £2,500, Prep School £2,615, Senior School: Year 7–9 £3,390, Year 10–11 £3,420.

The School is situated near Valentine's Park in Ilford. It is convenient for road, rail and Central Line tube services.

Our basic aim is to provide a full educational programme leading to recognised external examinations at the age of 16.

We create a caring, well-ordered atmosphere. Our pupils are encouraged to achieve their full academic and social potential. The well-qualified staff and the policy of small classes produce well above the national average GCSE results. We do not offer a sixth form, but the majority of our leavers from Year 11 move to another school to study subjects to A Level. Our students generally secure a place at their first-choice school, in either the Independent or State sector

In addition, the staff and I stress the development of each child as a whole person. We expect every girl to strive for self-confidence in her ability to use her talents to the full and to respect individuality. She is encouraged to make decisions and to accept responsibility for her own actions. The poise that comes from good manners and correct speech, we consider to be highly important. Honesty, reliability, courtesy and consideration for others are prime factors in the educative system.

Interested parents are welcome to visit the school, where the Head Teacher will be pleased to answer their queries.

Charitable status. Park School for Girls is a Registered Charity, number 269936. It exists to provide a caring environment in which we develop our pupils' potential to the full.

The Park School

The Park, Chilton Cantelo, Somerset BA22 8BG

Tel:	01935 850555
email:	admin@parkschool.com
website:	www.parkschool.com
Twitter:	@Park_School
Facebook:	@theparkschoolyeovil

Head: **Mrs J Huntington**, ARAM, GRSM, LRAM, CPSEd

Age Range. 4–18 Co-educational.

Number in School. 160 (84 Boys, 76 Girls).

Fees per term (2018–2019). Day £2,120–£3,500. Weekly Boarding £7,200–£7,700. Full Boarding £7,500–£8,750.

The Park School is a non-selective Independent day and boarding school founded in 1851 in Yeovil, Somerset. We aim to nurture the very best in each of our pupils within a supportive family atmosphere with an emphasis on each individual finding the right path to equip them for the future as fulfilled citizens in an increasingly challenging world.

Pupils flourish in a friendly, caring environment where they benefit from well-qualified staff and small classes. There is a wide and varied curriculum which encourages each pupil to develop his or her own abilities and interests to the full. Twenty-seven acres of private, wooded parkland also allow for a popular Forest School progrgamme and increased outdoor learning opportunities.

In line with the National Curriculum guidelines, senior pupils choose from a wide range of subjects at GCSE and A Level, plus BTEC Sport and NFCE Cookery which are also popular choices.

Academic expectations and standards are high with GCSE students achieving 17% above the national average, all subjects grade 4/C and above. Traditionally the individual sciences are regarded as harder subjects, but our students achieved 100% grades 5–9 in Biology, Chemistry and Physics, as well as in Design Technology and Geography, and in Business Studies which we offered for the first time in 2016–2017.

At A Level our Sixth Form students achieved an overall success rate of 100% pass rate and 78% A*–C grades in exams taken.

Average class sizes are 9–12 in the Prep and 15–22 in the Senior School. EAL is free of charge to all pupils whose first language is not English.

Physical education is an essential part of the curriculum with a wide range of sporting activities including: athletics, badminton, basketball, cricket, football, rugby, hockey, netball and cross-country. The Duke of Edinburgh's Award and the Arts Award scheme are options.

Park School boarders reside in a purpose-built boarding house in the grounds of 27 acres of wooded parkland. The estate offers a safe and secure environment for children to live, learn and develop into young adults.

The School benefits from easy access to roads, mainline rail (to London Waterloo) and local airports for those attending from abroad. Bristol International airport is 45 miles away (around 1 hour 15 minutes' travel time). Mainline rail to London takes around 2½ hours. Transport from the airport is arranged for all boarders who live abroad. Yeovil Hospital is close by and all boarding pupils are registered with a local doctor's surgery, which also provides a weekly on-site surgery when required.

Scholarships. Scholarships are offered in Academic, Art, Drama, Sport and Music. Examinations and interviews are in January for entry into Years 7 and 9. Sixth Form scholarships are in November. Bursaries are offered to families in full-time Christian work, and discounts are offered to members of HM Forces.

Charitable status. The Park School (Yeovil) Limited is a Registered Charity, number 310214. It exists to provide Christian education and care for children aged 4–18 years.

Polwhele House School

Truro, Cornwall TR4 9AE

Tel:	01872 273011
email:	office@polwhelehouse.co.uk
website:	www.polwhelehouse.co.uk
Twitter:	@polwhelehouse
Facebook:	@PolwheleHouse

Headmaster: **Chris Curl**

Age Range. 3–13+.
Number in School. 100.
Fees per term (2018–2019). Day: £600–£4,656, Lunches included; Flexi Boarding (1–4 nights per week): £616–£2,220.

Polwhele House is a beautiful and historic listed building, set in over 30 acres of garden, playing fields, park and woodland. The school enjoys a glorious and secure environment only 1¼ miles from Truro Cathedral.

Uninterrupted education is provided for boys and girls during those important early years from three to thirteen. There is flexible attendance for under-fives who are taught by qualified professionals in Nursery and Reception. The school has an established reputation for high levels of care and excellent teaching.

Although mainly a day school, weekly boarding, day boarding, and after-school care are growing in popularity. The boarders live in the Main House in comfortable surroundings which include a TV lounge, en-suite facilities, quiet areas and garden. The well-being and happiness of each child is the top priority.

This flourishing family school was founded in 1976 and has a continual programme of development, building and refurbishment. Accommodation now includes a separate Pre-Prep and Prep School, built and equipped for art and craft, design technology, sciences, languages and ICT. More recently the EYFS provision was extended with larger rooms and greater free-flow access to the outdoors.

Twenty years ago an equestrian centre was built. There are now five ponies at school and almost half the pupils enjoy riding lessons and some attend competitions.

The school combines modern teaching methods with the best of traditional values. The social development of the child is carefully nurtured to help them to become confident, considerate and polite young people. Polwhele House values each child and a very strong team of skilled and caring staff is able to devote a great deal of time to every pupil in small classes.

Drama flourishes with each child participating in at least one of eight productions a year. Music is an important part of the school life with all pupils singing, and the majority playing an instrument. There are Truro Cathedral Choristerships for boys and Polwhele House Equestrian Scholarships. All the usual team games are coached.

Polwhele House is a Christian, non-denominational school and assembly is considered to be an important part of the day. The school motto is 'Karenza Whelas Karenza', Cornish for 'Love Begets Love'. Boys and girls share the same opportunities and responsibilities in all areas of school life.

The school has a fine record of academic achievement. There is a wide variety of sporting and extracurricular activities to bring out the best in every child. Pupils are prepared for a broad range of schools, and win numerous scholarships, bursaries and exhibitions to senior independent schools.

The Headmaster takes great pleasure in meeting prospective parents and showing them around personally. Polwhele House is not just a school, more a way of life.

Prenton Preparatory School

Mount Pleasant, Oxton, Wirral CH43 5SY

Tel:	0151 652 3182
email:	enquiry@prentonprep.co.uk
website:	www.prentonprep.co.uk
Twitter:	@prentonprep
Facebook:	@prenton.prep

Directors: Mr M J and Mrs N M Aloé

Headteacher: **Mr M T R Jones**

Senior Management: Mrs A Hughes & Miss J Orme

Age Range. 2½–11.
Number in School. Day: 59 Boys, 59 Girls.
Fees per term (from January 2019). £2,710 Infants; £2,835 Juniors; from £830 part-time in Foundation Stage (with free places available for up to 30 hours).

Founded in 1935.

Prenton Preparatory School is co-educational day school for children aged 2½–11 years, situated about a mile from Junction 3 of the M53.

The building is a large Victorian house which has been carefully converted into the uses of a school. There is a large playground and gardens. Facilities include an ICT/Science block and an Art block. The Foundation Stage outdoor play area is a recent addition to the school.

The children benefit from small classes and individual attention in a holistic approach to their education within a disciplined environment which enables them to realise their full potential.

The school offers a wide range of academic subjects with emphasis on the three main National Curriculum core subjects: English, Mathematics and Science. French is taught from an early age and swimming forms a regular part of the curriculum from Year 1 upwards.

Children are prepared for entrance examinations to county, independent and grant-maintained grammar schools, gaining well above-average pass rates.

Child care facilities are available from 8.00 am to 6.00 pm. Clubs are provided at lunchtime and after school. They include football, cricket, computers and technology, karate, swimming, dance, netball, music group, speech & drama and musical instruments.

The school has a wide range of sporting teams that compete in local and regional fixtures and competitions. These include: swimming, water polo, cross-country, football, netball, cricket, rounders and athletics. Several of these teams have been successful enough to qualify for National tournaments in recent years.

Art, drama, dance and music also play an important part in school life and parents and members of the wider school community enjoy the regular performances that are part of the annual calendar.

Priory School

Sir Harry's Road, Edgbaston, Birmingham B15 2UR

Tel: 0121 440 4103/0256
Fax: 0121 440 3639
email: enquiries@prioryschool.net
website: www.prioryschool.net
Twitter: @PrioryEdgbaston
Facebook: @prioryschooledgbaston

Chair of Governors: Ms Heather Somerfield

Headmaster: **Mr Jonathan Cramb**, BA Hons, PGCE, MEd

Age Range. 6 months – 18 years.
Number in School. 480.
Fees per term (2018–2019). £1,628–£4,950.

The school, founded on its present site in 1936 by the Sisters of the Society of the Holy Child Jesus, stands in 17 acres of parkland in the pleasant suburb of Edgbaston, only 2 miles from the centre of Birmingham. The school has extensive playing fields, excellent astroturf tennis courts, a multi gym, athletics facilities and football and cricket pitches. A brand new block of six classrooms with bathroom facilities was added to the campus in October 2018. There are minibuses running to and from school and frequent bus services to all parts of the city.

The school has an excellent Early Years Department on site, which offers care for 51 weeks per annum and accepts children from the age of 6 months. All pupils are able to remain in After Care until 6.00 pm if parents so wish.

The school has a culturally diverse pupil community and instils core Catholic values and attitudes into everyday school life, but welcomes all faiths and none. Pupils are taught by specialist teachers from the age of 9 and in the Senior School the curriculum is broad and balanced with pupils benefiting from small class sizes and individual attention enabling them to make excellent progress in their academic development.

The school, whilst remaining proudly multi-ability, is justly proud of the academic achievements of the pupils. A wide range of subjects is available for GCSE and A Level, with good facilities, including well-equipped Science Laboratories, Language Resources rooms, Information Technology facilities, Sports Centre, Multi-Gym and Performing Arts Suite. The Senior Library and Learning Resources Centre was recently refurbished with the addition of new computers and there will be a new Preparatory School Library and Resource Centre in 2018–19. The school offers support for children with special needs, particularly dyslexia, with specially qualified staff.

A wide range of extra-curricular opportunities are offered across the school. These currently include horse riding, MAD Science, the school newspaper and Duke of Edinburgh's Award scheme to name just a few. Private tuition is also offered in speech, singing and a wide range of musical instruments by peripatetic teachers.

Priory School aims to develop the whole child, so that as well as achieving academic excellence, its pupil grow into confident, articulate, well-rounded individuals.

Entry to the school is by interview, assessment and day visit. Scholarships are awarded at 11+. Bursaries may be awarded in cases of special need.

Parents are warmly welcomed into the school to discuss individual needs. Full details prior to the visit may be obtained from the Admissions & International Relations Coordinator.

Charitable status. Priory School is a Registered Charity, number 518009.

Queen Ethelburga's Collegiate Foundation

Thorpe Underwood Hall, York YO26 9SS

Tel: 01423 333330
email: info@qe.org
          admissions@qe.org
website: www.qe.org

Motto: *To be the best that I can with the gifts that I have.*
Co-educational Day and Boarding School.

Principal: **Steven Jandrell**

Age Range. 3 months–19 years.
Number of Pupils. 1,600.
Fees per term (2018–2019). Day: £1,340–£5,675; Boarding: £10,320–£12,895 (UK students), £12,685–£15,985 (International students).

Now set in more than 220 acres of beautiful North Yorkshire countryside, Queen Ethelburga's has provided students with a vibrant and supportive school community since 1912.

The Collegiate welcomes girls and boys from 3 months and supports them through four schools – Chapter House (3 months to Year 5), King's Magna (Year 6 to 9), The College and The Faculty (both Year 10 to 13).

The QE ethos is centred on supporting each student to be the best that they can with the gifts that they have, by creating the right learning and living environment for them to thrive.

We have a unique offering. We have four individual schools, with their own heads and staff teams, that are small enough to maintain a family atmosphere. This allows staff to know their students thoroughly and successfully guide them through each stage of their formative years.

Our reputation has grown considerably over recent years, and we believe this is due to our drive to ensure that our outcomes for QE students, across all areas of their endeavour and aspiration, match those of the world's best schools.

We place great emphasis on our children growing into resilient, caring, compassionate and confident adults, who develop independence and initiative, and who can take responsibility for their own learning and futures. We provide opportunities for pupils to take part in a range of wider enrichment and extra-curricular activities to help them to gain skills in leadership, teamwork and collaboration, and decision-making.

Our exam results speak for themselves, consistently ranking us amongst the top day and boarding schools in the UK, with students benefiting from incredible study, boarding and leisure facilities as part of campus life.

In 2018, students in the academically-focused College achieved 96% A*/B at A Level and 97% D*/D in the small number of BTECs taken to enrich the A Level programmes (equivalent in university points to A* and A grades at A Level).

The Faculty, which offers a wider range of academic, creative and vocational courses, achieved 91% A*/B at A Level and 64% D*/D in BTECs.

Care is the most important element within the QE community; every member of the Collegiate, staff and student, is responsible for the pastoral care and happiness of the site.

QE offers support and guidance to all students and parents to ensure that we are all working to support individual students needs and equipping them with the right skills, not only to be successful in education, but to excel in their chosen career and life in general. We are focused on developing our students' skills and resilience, whilst nurturing their wellbeing.

Radnor House Sevenoaks School

Combe Bank Drive, Sundridge, Kent TN14 6AE

Tel:	Senior School 01959 563720
	Preparatory School 01959 564320
Fax:	Senior School 01959 561997
	Preparatory School 01959 560456
email:	registrar@radnor-sevenoaks.org
website:	www.radnor-sevenoaks.org
Twitter:	@radnorsevenoaks
Facebook:	@radnorsevenoaks

Chairman of Board of Directors: Mr Colin Diggory, BSc Hons, PGCE, MA, EdD, CMath, FIMA, FRSA

Head: **Mr David Paton**, BComm Hons, PGCE, MA

Radnor House Sevenoaks is an independent school with entry from the term that pupils are 2½ up to the age of 18. it was founded in 1924. (*See also Preparatory School entry in IAPS section.*) In September 2014 the school became co-educational.

Aims and Ethos. Our mission is to inspire pupils to develop their talents and gifts so that they achieve academic excellence and personal success. We provide challenges in learning and opportunities for personal endeavour for all pupils at Radnor House Sevenoaks, so that they develop interpersonal skills, integrity and intellectual curiosity which enable them to reach their full potential in the outside world. The purposeful ethos and commitment to very good quality pastoral care are a distinctive feature of school life. High academic standards are expected.

Location. Situated in a Palladian Mansion built for the Campbell family, Dukes of Argyll and set in superb grounds with 28 acres of parkland just outside Sevenoaks, the school has excellent facilities. The Nursery, Prep School, Senior School and Sixth Form are on the same site and there are many positive links between them, so that all pupils have guaranteed access through the school until they leave at 18.

Curriculum. A modern and broad range of subjects is taught at all age levels. English, Mathematics, Sciences and RE are compulsory at GCSE. In addition pupils can choose from Art, Computer Science, Drama, Economics, English Literature, Geography, History, Mathematics, Modern Languages, Music, PE, Politics, Psychology, RE and Science subjects at A Level. The school boasts strong Art and Music Departments with regular exhibitions and musical performances in which wide participation is achieved. Radnor House Sevenoaks has a well-earned reputation for competitive success in PE and also provides a very wide range of sports and activities to interest all pupils. Swimming in the 25-metre covered pool is a particularly popular activity from Nursery through to Sixth Form.

Admission. Children enter the Prep school in Nursery and Reception. For the Senior School, pupils take the School's entrance examination at 11+ and 13+ Good passes at GCSE are also expected for the A Level subjects of choice in order to join the Sixth Form for external candidates.

Transport. Coach transport is organized for 4 significant routes, to be paid for on a termly basis.

Fees per term (2018–2019). Senior School £5,545–£6,215 (Lunch £295); Preparatory School £3,620–£4,590 (Lunch £245); Nursery: £65 full day, £35 half day (mornings) includes lunch and morning and afternoon wrap care.

Extended Day. We are pleased to be able to offer pre-school and after-school care for all of our pupils from 7.00 am to 7.00 pm (extra charges apply).

Scholarships. The Radnor House Sevenoaks Scholarship programme is open to pupils joining in Years 7, 9 and 12. Rather than the traditional scholarship model, Radnor House Sevenoaks seeks to highlight pupils who embody one or more of the four school values – Excellence, Respect, Courage and Perseverance. Pupils who can demonstrate high levels of one or more of these values in academia, the arts or sport will be considered for a Senior School Scholarship. This attracts a fee reduction of 10% (potentially rising up to 50% through means-testing).

Raphael Independent School

Park Lane, Hornchurch, Essex RM11 1XY

Tel:	01708 744735
Fax:	01708 722432
email:	admin@raphaelschool.com
website:	www.raphaelschool.com

Headteacher: **Ms C Salmon**

Age Range. Co-educational 4–16.

Number of Pupils. Day: 70 boys, 60 girls.

Fees per term (from January 2019). £2,255–£3,250.

Entry requirements. Interview for Early Years and Infants. Entry Tests in English and Maths for Juniors and Seniors.

Aims.

- To develop the academic, social, artistic and sporting potential of each individual within a caring and welcoming school community.

- To foster respect for each other within a multi-cultural school.
- To offer a broad range of educational visits and extracurricular activities.

Location. Raphael is a ten-minute walk from Romford Main Line Station, and a fifteen-minute drive from the A12 or A127 junctions of the M25.

School day. Infants from 8.40 am, Juniors until 3.25 pm and Seniors until 4.00 pm. Our After-School Club looks after pupils until 5.45 pm.

Curriculum strengths. Computer Science, French and Spanish, English and Drama, Maths, History, Geography, Business Studies and Triple or Gateway Double Science.

Sport. We believe in competitive sport, and we offer Soccer, Rugby, Netball, Cross-Country, Swimming, Cricket and Tennis amongst others.

A prospectus containing further information may be obtained from our Office Manager, Anita Hargrove, and all prospective parents are most welcome to visit the school.

Rastrick Independent School

Ogden Lane, Rastrick, Brighouse, West Yorkshire HD6 3HF

Tel:	01484 400344
Fax:	01484 718318
email:	info@rastrick-independent.co.uk
website:	www.rastrick-independent.co.uk
Twitter:	@RastrickSchool
Facebook:	@rastrickindependent

Headmistress: **Mrs S A Vaughey**

Age Range. 0–16 co-educational. Tutorial College 16+.
Number of Pupils. 200.
Fees per term (2018–2019). £2,560–£3,155.

The philosophy of this Independent School is to provide a first-class education for all ages combined with academic excellence. This School and College are also renowned for their superb pastoral care. Situated in a small village in the heart of Yorkshire, this educational campus is flourishing in a historic and beautiful location. A 19th Century Manor House and grounds with extensive, well stocked gardens frame a collection of exquisite buildings which accommodate children and students from birth to eighteen. The academic achievement at Rastrick has been acknowledged as 'Excellent' by ISI and Ofsted. The School has achieved 100% Pass rate at 11+ and 100% A*–C at GCSE. The SATS results are outstanding at all key stages. When it comes to examination results, Rastrick succeeds far above the national and local averages.

The highly qualified team create a vibrant, exciting environment for learning. The pupils have a reputation for manners and discipline which has produced confident, happy, well adjusted young people. Life at this Independent School is extremely successful academically and daily school life is rich and rewarding. There is something very special about the atmosphere and the team at Rastrick.

Walking into the Main School, visitors experience something quite unique. The architecture and design of Rastrick has maintained the atmosphere of the historic buildings and incorporates light, air and space to create a superb learning environment. Children and Students greet invited guests, each other, their teachers and parents with a natural warmth and charm. There is a sense of mutual respect. The structure of a day here is ordered and classes for all ages take place in rooms designed to stimulate learning as well as to showcase

the work being undertaken. Every child learns to take care of themselves and their peers. The pastoral care at Rastrick is outstanding.

In partnership with families, pupils achieve their potential academically but also flourish in Sports and The Arts. The School and College are open all year round to accommodate working parents. The School has taken its place in the centre of the community, taking pride in activities which reflect the daily life of the village of Rastrick.

This educational establishment has experienced a sustained record of academic success and pastoral care. The rapid growth and development of Rastrick has seen considerable investment in buildings and first-class facilities. Rastrick now welcomes Boarders, International Students and students to the Tutorial College for full or part time education beyond age the age of 16. In addition Rastrick is an Examination Centre for Private Candidates.

This environment offers an education which expects success. There is an expectation that discipline, self-worth and good manners will lead to the development of a confident, happy child.

Redcourt – St Anselm's

7 Devonshire Place, Oxton, Birkenhead, Wirral CH43 1TX

Tel:	0151 652 5228
email:	admin@redcourt.net
website:	www.redcourtstanselms.com
Twitter:	@redcourt7
Facebook:	@RedcourtStA

Chair of Governors: Mrs T Cleugh

Headmistress: **Miss R M Jones**

Age Range. 3–11 Co-educational.
Number of Pupils. 124.
Fees per term (2018–2019). £2,240.

Redcourt – St Anselm's is an inclusive school welcoming all children of all abilities. There is no formal entrance examination. Prospective pupils are invited into Redcourt for a day's visit. During the day, Staff will assess the level at which the visiting child is currently working. However, most children join at nursery level. Our aim is to provide each and every child with a sound academic education in an environment which is explicitly Christian and where discipline and care go hand in hand. We endeavour to be aware of each child as an individual and we seek to encourage the development of the whole person. The school operates in an open and friendly manner, becoming something of a second home for its pupils.

The core national curriculum subjects plus RE, History, Geography, Art and Design, PE and Games, Music, ICT and French form the basis of what is taught. Children are prepared for the eleven plus and entrance examinations to grammar and selective independent schools with most children proceeding to Grammar Schools.

Charitable status. Redcourt St Anselm's is part of the Congregation of Christian Brothers which is a Registered Charity, number 254312.

Riverston School

63–69 Eltham Road, Lee Green, London SE12 8UF

Tel: 020 8318 4327
email: office@riverstonschool.co.uk
website: www.riverstonschool.co.uk
Twitter: @Riverstonschool

Chair of Governors: Professor D M Lewis

Headmistress: **Mrs S E Salathiel**

Deputy Headmaster: Mr P D Salathiel

Age Range. 9 months–19 years.
Number in School. Day: 125 Boys, 69 Girls.
Fees per term (2018–2019). £3,099–£4,915 for mainstream pupils in Junior and Senior School.

Riverston School is a small, co-educational, independent day school in South East London for children between the ages of 9 months and 19 years. Riverston was founded in the early 1900s, and in 1927 moved to its present site in Eltham Road, Lee Green. It is centrally located on the A20, close to the A2 and South Circular Roads, served by numerous bus routes and is convenient for mainline railway stations being 20 minutes from London Bridge.

The school stands in nearly three acres of carefully maintained grounds and is built around four imposing Victorian houses. It has modern purpose-built units, incorporating specialist teaching rooms, library, science laboratories, general-purpose hall, ICT suite, music room, Food Technology suite, and most recently a Design Technology room. The school also has a fully-equipped Sports Hall and two large playground areas. The Nursery and Pre-School Departments have their own separate and fully-equipped outdoor play area.

The emphasis is on "Bespoke Learning for Life" and to this end the curriculum encompasses subjects such as textiles, food technology and social communication enabling students to prepare for independent living when school life has ended. Vocational studies are at the core of the Sixth Form curriculum with BTEC courses available in various subjects as well as A Levels being delivered to students who are academically able. We have forged an educational link with Hadlow College in Mottingham where students can study Animal Management.

The school has a well-earned reputation for its teaching of children of all abilities including those who may require learning support or have special learning difficulties. Whilst many pupils may require additional help with their academic work, wherever possible they attend full-time mainstream lessons except for those periods determined by their individual educational programmes when they are taught individually or in small groups.

Riverston has a lively, friendly and cheerful ethos with ideals which are as strong today as they were when first conceived. A traditional school with the mission statement "Bespoke Learning for Life", Riverston endeavours to provide each pupil with an individualised curriculum, promoting a positive self-image and ensuring that all have the chance of maximising their academic potential, whilst encouraging their sporting ability. There is a considerable emphasis on pastoral care for personal happiness and a real sense of community in an environment where staff and pupils know each other very well across the year groups.

Parents are invited to visit the school by appointment only. Details can be found on our website at www.riverston school.co.uk

Rochester Independent College

254 St Margaret's Banks, Rochester, Kent ME1 1HY

Tel: 01634 828115
Fax: 01634 405667
email: admissions@rochester-college.org
website: www.rochester-college.org
Twitter: @rochesterindcol
Facebook: @RochesterIndependentCollege

Principal: **Alistair Brownlow**, MA Hons, MPhil

Age Range. 11–19 Co-educational.
Number of Pupils. 305 (including 90 single room boarding places).
Fees per annum (2018–2019). Tuition: £12,600–£18,900. Weekly Boarding £12,000; Full Boarding: £13,500.

Rochester Independent College is an alternative to conventional secondary education with a happily distinctive ethos. Accepting day students from the age of 11 and boarders from 15, the focus is on examination success in a lively, supportive and informal atmosphere. Students are encouraged to be themselves and achieve exam results that often exceed their expectations. There is no uniform, no bells ring and everybody is on first-name terms. The average class size is eight.

Students enjoy being here and are treated as young adults. We encourage them to search for their own answers, to voice their opinions, to think critically, creatively and independently. They leave not only with excellent examination results but with enthusiasm for the future and new confidence about themselves and their education.

Personal Tutors work closely with students on all courses to give advice about course combinations and help students to ensure that their courses are designed to meet the requirements of university entrance. With such small class sizes individual attention is not only available, it's practically inescapable.

The College has particular academic strengths in the Sciences, Mathematics, English Literature, Social Sciences and the Creative and Visual Arts including Film, Photography and Media.

The College's reputation for academic excellence is founded on over 30 years' experience of rigorous teaching. Students come to us for a variety of reasons and from many different backgrounds. We are not academically selective; our only entrance qualification is an honest determination to work hard. Our results however are always ranked among the best of the academically selective and students secure places at top universities. Direct entry into any year group is possible and the College also offers intensive one year GCSE and A Level courses as well as retake programmes. International students benefit from specialised English Language teaching support.

The College Halls combine the informality of a university residence with the supervision and pastoral support appropriate for young adults. The College offers students the opportunity to thrive in an atmosphere of managed independence and acts as a stepping stone between school and university. All accommodation is on campus and in single rooms.

Rochester Independent College is part of the Dukes Education Group.

Rookwood School

Weyhill Road, Andover, Hampshire SP10 3AL

Tel:	01264 325900
Fax:	01264 325909
email:	office@rookwoodschool.org
website:	www.rookwoodschool.org
Twitter:	@rookwood_school

Headmaster: **Mr A Kirk-Burgess**, BSc, PGCE, MSc Oxon

Deputy Head: Mr R Hick, MA QTS
Head of Senior School: Mrs E Hacker, BA Hons
Head of Lower School: Mrs L Wowk, BA, PGCE
Assistant Head of Lower School: Mrs C Nias, BA Hons

Age Range. Co-educational 3–16 with boarders from age 8.

Number in School. 281: 128 girls, 153 Boys (EYFS 50).

Fees per term (2018–2019). Boarding: £7,750–£9,155. Day: £3,120–£5,200. Nursery: £5.00 per hour (Early Years Education Funding accepted). Flexi and occasional boarding also available.

Hailed by the ISI as an "outstandingly happy and successful school", Rookwood is an independent non-selective day and boarding school for girls and boys aged 3–16 years in Andover, Hampshire.

Described as "warm, welcoming and nurturing", Rookwood is known for its family atmosphere and strong pastoral care which encourages each and every child to achieve their very best with excellent results. In 2018, 97% of students gained five or more 9–4 grades (equivalent to the old A*–C) and an outstanding 100% of students achieved 9–4 in both Maths and English Language.

Set in eight acres of private grounds Rookwood has an impressive range of amenities including a state-of-the-art sports hall, outdoor swimming pool, excellent art and science facilities and a wonderful purpose-built Pre-Prep (currently deemed 'excellent' by the ISI). Both Music and Drama thrive at Rookwood, with every child encouraged to take part, whilst the Physical Education department is equally busy with several pupils advancing to represent their favourite sports at national level in recent years.

In addition to its many tangible achievements Rookwood is committed to delivering excellent pastoral care and takes great pride in seeing its pupils develop into confident, resilient and principled young adults. The School also offers a rich and varied programme of extra-curricular activities for all ages and interests giving pupils the opportunity to develop new skills, discover new passions, grow socially and emotionally and to simply enjoy themselves.

Rookwood's boarding provision was recently rated as 'excellent' in all areas by the ISI with boarders receiving a unique 'home-from-home' experience. Family-style meal times, experienced and supportive boarding staff and busy weekends all combine to ensure that Rookwood's boarders receive the best possible care.

Prospective pupils and their parents are warmly invited to attend one of Rookwood's Open Days (please see website for latest information). Alternatively, if you require any further information or would like to make an individual appointment, please do not hesitate to contact the Registrar directly on 01264 325900.

Admission is by school reports and individual visits. Scholarships are available at 11+ and 7+ and means-tested bursaries.

Rookwood is conveniently situated close to Andover town centre and less than 10 minutes' walk to Andover railway station, with good services to Salisbury, Basingstoke and London Waterloo. By road, there is easy access from the A303 and A343, with the journey from Andover to London taking about one and a half hours. School bus services are also available from Newbury and North West Hampshire.

Charitable status. Rookwood School is a Registered Charity, number 307322. It exists to provide education for children.

Roselyon School

Churchtown Farm, Lanlivery, Bodmin, Cornwall PL30 5BT

Tel:	01726 812110
email:	secretary@roselyonschool.com
website:	www.roselyonschool.com

Head: **Mrs Hilary Mann**, MBA, BEd

Age Range. 3–11 Co-educational.

Number in School. Day: 39 Boys, 37 Girls.

Fees per term (2018–2019). £3,244–£3,914.

Roselyon School is based in the amazing woodlands at Churchtown, Lanlivery. The buildings have been reconfigured to create spacious, light classrooms in a fully accessible school.

The school is proud of its academic strengths and excellent examination results to local senior independent schools and state Grammar schools. It offers a broad curriculum, a variety of sports, music and drama and has an extensive range of extra-curricular activities.

Academic and Music Scholarships and Bursaries are available for pupils in Years 3 to 6, and assessments are usually taken in the Summer Term.

Roselyon is a small, friendly school where a warm family atmosphere is maintained by the committed team of caring staff.

Charitable status. Roselyon School Limited is a Registered Charity, number 306583. It exists to provide quality education to boys and girls. It is a member of the Methodist Independent School Trust.

Ruckleigh School

17 Lode Lane, Solihull, West Midlands B91 2AB

Tel:	0121 705 2773
Fax:	0121 704 4883
email:	admin@ruckleigh.co.uk
website:	www.ruckleigh.co.uk

Headmaster: **Mr Dominic Rhys Smith**, MA Oxon

Age Range. 3–11.

Number in School. Day: 125 Boys, 115 Girls.

Fees per term (2018–2019). £1,065–£3,040.

Ruckleigh is an independent day school offering education to boys and girls between the ages of 4 and 11 with a Nursery Department catering for children from the age of 3.

Although a high standard of work is expected this is related to the individual child, and the school is able to provide opportunities within a wide range of academic ability. Each child has every chance to develop his or her talents to the full, often resulting in achievements beyond initial expectations.

The comparatively small classes mean that every child is well known individually throughout the school creating a friendly environment.

Pupils are guided into habits of clear thinking, self-reliance and courtesy. Sound practical judgement, sensitivity towards the needs of others, and a willingness to "have a go" are the qualities that the school seeks to promote.

Rushmoor School

58–60 Shakespeare Road, Bedford MK40 2DL

Tel:	01234 352031
email:	admissions@rushmoorschool.co.uk
website:	www.rushmoorschool.co.uk
Twitter:	@RushmoorSchool
Facebook:	@RushmoorSchool

Chair of Governors: G M Bates, OBE, JP

Principal: I M Daniel, BA, NPQH

Age Range. Boys 2–18, Girls 2–10.
Number in School. 367 Day Pupils.
Fees per term (2018–2019). £2,195–£3,674.

Rushmoor has grown and improved by investing greatly to provide excellent facilities. In partnership with our Alliance school, St Andrew's School Bedford, we appreciate the importance of selecting the right school for your son or daughter; childhood is something which can be experienced only once. With this in mind, and the belief that children learn best when they feel happy and secure, we aim to develop in our pupils a lifelong interest in learning – one which encompasses the full range of intellectual, cultural, artistic and sporting achievements of our society.

We believe in individual care and attention. Visitors to the school are impressed by the friendly, positive attitude of the pupils and their energetic sense of purpose. The staff are caring and understanding, yet know the importance of effort and personal discipline in enabling pupils to achieve the highest academic standards.

At the school we ensure that all children have opportunities to develop their intellectual, physical and creative gifts, across a broad and balanced curriculum. Children in Reception and Junior classes benefit greatly from a wide range of specialist teachers.

We emphasise the individual, recognizing that all children are different and value each child in their own right. Encouraging children to develop their strengths improves their self-esteem, enabling them to find their role in the community. We promote children's personal development, encouraging lively and enquiring minds, respect for others and a high regard for truth. The stability of continuous education, spanning ages 2 to 18 years, is a major factor in helping us achieve this.

At Rushmoor we pride ourselves on our ability to integrate children with Specific Learning Differences within mainstream school life, whilst still providing extended challenges for our gifted and talented pupils. We believe that every child should be allowed to embrace any aspect of the curriculum. Enabling children to receive support without undermining their confidence amongst their peers is of primary importance.

Rushmoor has a fine reputation in sport and boasts a highly successful record with many pupils gaining county and national honours. In 2016 Rushmoor won the ISA Award for Outstanding Provision in Sport. Children have also gained much success in national and local drama competitions and festivals.

In 2014 Rushmoor was a finalist in the ISA Awards for excellence and winner of the 'Financial Innovation' category.

Prospective parents and children can tour the school at any time and 'taster days' can be arranged. Come and experience our caring ethos which enables our children to develop the confidence and flexibility which allows them to face the demands of modern life. To view our excellent inspection report please visit our website.

Charitable status. Rushmoor School Limited is a Registered Charity, number 307530. It exists to provide education.

Sacred Heart School

Mangate Street, Swaffham, Norfolk PE37 7QW

Tel:	01760 721330/724577
Fax:	01760 725557
email:	info@sacredheartschool.co.uk
website:	www.sacredheartschool.co.uk

Headteacher: **Sister Francis Ridler**, FDC, BEd Hons, EYPS

Age Range. 3–16 Co-educational.
Number in School. 91 Day Pupils, 4 Girl Boarders.
Fees per term (2018–2019). Boarders: Termly £8,000, Weekly £6,285–£6,740; Day: £2,965 (Lower School); £3,940–£4,395 (Seniors).

Assistance with fees: Academic, Music, Art, Sport, All Rounder (Boarder) Scholarships for Year 7 (11+). Some bursaries available.

Entry requirements: Non-selective, Assessments, School Report and Interview.

Religious Affiliation: Roman Catholic (other denominations welcome).

Staff: 9 Full Time, 13 Part Time, 10 Learning Support.

The Sacred Heart School was founded by the Daughters of Divine Charity in 1914. The Sisters and lay staff work together to provide a safe and caring environment where Christian values are upheld.

Principally a day school, the school is now co-educational. Pupils study for eight to eleven GCSEs gaining consistently high A–C grades. At 16, the pupils have gained the confidence and self-possession which makes them much sought after by all Sixth Form Centres and other Independent Schools. There is a limited number of boarding places for girls aged 8–16 as well as the opportunity for flexi boarding.

All pupils are encouraged to develop their gifts in Music, Drama, Art and Sport, and the School has a fine record of success in all these areas.

Facilities include a Sports Hall, Swimming Pool and Arts Centre with Theatre, Art and Music Rooms and a Pottery Workshop.

A very active Parents' Association, loyal past pupils and parents network, together with highly-qualified Staff provide the energy, enthusiasm and friendly atmosphere which characterises the school community.

Before and after school care is available and Nursery Vouchers are accepted for the Little Pedlars Pre-School.

Charitable status. The Daughters of Divine Charity is a Registered Charity, number 237760.

Sacred Heart School

Mayfield Lane, Durgates, Wadhurst, East Sussex TN5 6DQ

Tel: 01892 783414
email: admin@sacredheartwadhurst.org.uk
website: www.sacredheartwadhurst.org.uk

Chair of Governors: Mr Anthony Moffatt

Head Teacher: Mrs Hilary Blake, BA, PGCE

Age Range. 2–11 Co-educational.
Number of Pupils. 120.
Fees per term (2018–2019). £2,785.

Sacred Heart School is a small independent Catholic primary school and Nursery, nestling in the heart of the Sussex countryside.

We welcome boys and girls from 2–11 and with pupil numbers around 100 we have the opportunity to know each child individually, to recognise and encourage their strengths and support them in overcoming areas of difficulty.

Our pupils enjoy a high degree of academic success, regularly obtaining places at their first choice of school, including passes at 11+ and Scholarships.

Courtesy and care for each other are important values nurtured at Sacred Heart School where children play and work well together.

Charitable status. Sacred Heart School, as part of the Arundel and Brighton Diocesan Trust, is a Registered Charity, number 252878.

St Andrew's School
Bedford

Kimbolton Road, Bedford MK40 2PA

Tel: 01234 267272
email: standrews@standrewsschoolbedford.com
website: www.standrewsschoolbedford.com
Twitter: @StAndrewsBeds
Facebook: @standrewsschoolbedford

Chairman of Governors: Mr G Bates, OBE, JP

Principal: Mr I M Daniel, BA, NPQH

Deputy Head: Mr A R Jones
Assistant Head Pastoral: Mrs S Stott

Age Range. Girls 6 weeks to 18 years, Boys 6 weeks to 11 years.
Number of Pupils. 250.
Fees per term (2018–2019). £1,866–£3,674.

Founded in 1896, as a boarding school for girls, St Andrew's School is a charitable trust run by a Board of Governors. It is now a day school and nursery for girls between 6 weeks and 18, and for boys from six weeks to 11. In September 2013 a close working partnership between St Andrew's School and Rushmoor School was formalised to increase educational opportunities, joint ventures and the sharing of best practice. A joint Sixth Form has been in operation since September 2016.

St Andrew's School is located in central Bedford and is based around two large Victorian houses that have seen modernisation and various additions to meet the needs of our pupils. Most recently a complete refurbishment of the Physics Laboratory has been undertaken to support the strong interest of our pupils in science.

Our vision is to continually combine the best of traditional values with being at the forefront of educational advancement. Children in Reception and Junior classes benefit from a wide range of specialist teachers. By Year 9 our pupils are fully prepared to make informed choices for GCSE study.

The school's key aim is to provide the best possible standard of education and an appropriate level of challenge and support to allow each individual pupil to develop fully both academically and personally. Our GCSE results invariably demonstrate a very high degree of "value added". The high achievement at GCSE allows girls to study at competitive entry Sixth Forms, upper schools and colleges.

The older and younger girls form strong bonds outside the classroom through vertical tutor groups in Years 7–9, a pupil led House system, School Council and a wide range of co-curricular opportunities. These include team and individual sports, music, drama, science, ICT and art clubs. We offer a full range of outdoor and residential opportunities including the Blue Peris Mountain Centre and The Duke of Edinburgh's Award scheme.

Our community is a safe and peaceful environment which is both dynamic and caring, and which promotes strong values and mutual respect. To view our excellent inspection report, please visit our website.

We offer a limited number of means-tested bursaries and scholarships for pupils who excel in a particular field.

Charitable status. St Andrew's School (Bedford) Limited is a Registered Charity, number 307531.

St Anne's Preparatory School

154 New London Road, Chelmsford, Essex CM2 0AW

Tel: 01245 353488
email: headmistress@stannesprep.essex.sch.uk
website: www.stannesprep.co.uk

Headmistress: Mrs F Pirrie, BSc, PGCE

Age Range. 3+–11+.
Number of Children. 160.
Fees per term (2018–2019). £2,600–£2,700.

St Anne's is a co-educational day school, with its own excellent nursery facility. Established in 1925, the school is conveniently situated in the centre of Chelmsford. The building is a large Victorian house, which has been carefully converted into the uses of a school. Extensive lawned areas, astroturf, playground and Nursery play area provide ample space for both recreation and games lessons. In addition, older pupils benefit from the use of the excellent sports facilities at the nearby Essex County Cricket Club.

The children benefit from small classes and individual attention in a disciplined but happy environment, which enables them to realise their full potential. Provision is made in the school for the gifted as well as those pupils less educationally able. Classrooms are bright and well equipped and the teachers are chosen for their qualifications, experience and understanding of the needs of their pupils.

St Anne's combines modern teaching with the best of traditional values. The school maintains a high standard of academic education giving great emphasis to a secure foundation in the basic subjects whilst offering a wide curriculum with specialist teaching in many areas.

Examination results at both KS1 and KS2 levels are excellent and many pupils gain places at the prestigious Grammar and Independent schools in the county.

The school offers a wide range of extra-curricular activities and an excellent after-care facility is available for all age groups. St Anne's is rightly recognised for its friendly and supportive ethos. Parents are particularly supportive of all aspects of school life. Visitors are always welcome.

St Christopher's School

6 Downs Road, Epsom, Surrey KT18 5HE

Tel:	01372 721807
email:	office@st-christophers.surrey.sch.uk
website:	www.st-christophers.surrey.sch.uk
Twitter:	@StChrisEpsom

Headteacher: **Mrs A C Thackray**, MA, BA, Dip Mus

Age Range. 3–7.
Number in School. 180.
Fees per term (2018–2019). £3,355 (Full time including lunch), £1,700 (5 mornings).

St Christopher's School (founded in 1938) is a co-educational nursery and pre-preparatory school for children from 3–7 years.

Set in a quiet residential area a short distance from the centre of Epsom, it has attractive secure grounds with gardens and play areas. The school was found to be "excellent" in all eight areas of its 2016 ISI Inspection.

St Christopher's main purpose is to support children and parents through the early years of education. We offer a carefully managed induction programme to school life and, subsequently, a broad and challenging education within a happy, caring and secure family environment. Above all we aim to offer your child the best possible start to their education.

The children are prepared to enter a wide range of Surrey schools and we maintain a very high pass rate in a variety of entrance tests.

Breakfast Club opens at 7.45 am and After-School Care is available until 6.00 pm Monday to Friday. There are also a number of after-school clubs.

St Christopher's enjoys the support of an active parents association that organises a wide variety of social and fund-raising events.

For further information please contact the school. Parents are welcome to visit the school by appointment with the Headteacher.

Charitable status. St Christopher's School Trust (Epsom) Limited is a Registered Charity, number 312045. It aims to provide a Nursery and Pre-Preparatory education in Epsom and district.

St Christopher's School

71 Wembley Park Drive, Wembley Park, Middlesex HA9 8HE

Tel:	020 8902 5069
email:	admin@stchristophersschool.org.uk
website:	www.stchristophersschool.org.uk

Headmaster: **Mr Paul Musetti**, MA, MEd

Age Range. 2–11.

Number in School. 46 Boys, 64 Girls.
Fees per term (2018–2019). £3,002–£3,302. Sibling discounts available.

Entry requirements: Interview and Assessment.

St Christopher's School, a large Victorian building on Wembley Park Drive, offers a caring family atmosphere coupled with an equal emphasis on good manners, enthusiastic endeavour and academic excellence. The School, originally a Christian foundation dating from 1928, welcomes children of all faiths and cultures.

Caring and supportive staff provide a well-structured, disciplined and stimulating environment in which children are nurtured and encouraged to develop the necessary skills – academic, social and cultural – so that when they leave us at the age of 11 they can be certain of future success. All children at St Christopher's are equal and we emphasise the qualities of equality, justice and compassion. Children benefit from a curriculum that offers both breadth and depth, an activity programme that teaches skills and develops talents, and a pastoral programme that develops social responsibility.

The full range of academic subjects is taught based on an enriched National Curriculum. Sports and Music are seen as central elements in school life with sports matches, regular concerts and an annual carol service. In addition there is a variety of clubs and activities both at lunchtime and after school; these include Arts & Crafts Club, Book Club, Booster Club, Choir, Cookery, Gardening, Needlecraft, Netball and Recorders.

Children are prepared for the full range of examinations at 11 years. Historically leavers have gained entry to a wide range of excellent schools including Haberdashers' Aske's Boys' and Girls' Schools, Merchant Taylors', Northwood College, St Helen's, North London Collegiate, Henrietta Barnett, Queen Elizabeth's Boys' School, City of London Boys and Girls, UCS, Aldenham, John Lyon, St Paul's Girls' School and South Hampstead High.

St Christopher's offers both Pre-School and After-School Care, from 8.00 am until 6.00 pm.

Please phone for an appointment to view the school. We look forward to welcoming you.

St Clare's, Oxford

139 Banbury Road, Oxford OX2 7AL

Tel:	01865 552031
Fax:	01865 513359
email:	admissions@stclares.ac.uk
website:	www.stclares.ac.uk/our-courses/international-baccalaureate

Principal: **Mr Andrew Rattue**, MA Oxon, MA London, PGCE London

Vice Principal Pastoral: Susan Tawse, BSc Edinburgh, PGCE
Vice Principal Academic: Cormack Kirby, BA Leeds, PGCE, MEd Bristol

Age Range. 15–19 Co-educational.
Number of Students. 265.
Fees per annum (2018–2019). Boarding £39,977, Day £19,207.

Established in 1953, St Clare's is an Oxford-based international school with the mission "to advance international education and understanding". We embrace internationalism and academic excellence as core values. St Clare's is a co-educational day and boarding school which has been offering the International Baccalaureate Diploma for over 40 years, longer than any other school or college in England. Students regularly achieve the maximum 45 points, achieved by only 0.2% of candidates worldwide and a quarter achieve scores high than 40 points, placing them in the elite top 5% globally.

Students from over 40 countries study at St Clare's with a core group of British students. The caring atmosphere is informal, positive and friendly with an equal emphasis on hard work, tolerance and developing personal responsibility. Each student is paired with a personal tutor who oversees their welfare and progress and is the first point of contact for parents.

St Clare's has an especially wide range of IB Diploma subjects on offer at Higher and Standard level and, in addition, currently teaches 28 different languages. For students not yet ready to begin the IB Diploma, a Pre-IB course is offered with regular entry points throughout the year. As part of the Creativity, Activity, Service requirements of the Diploma there is an extensive programme of social, cultural and sporting activities and students are encouraged to take full advantage of the opportunities that Oxford provides.

In July each year we run a 3-week introduction to the IB Diploma. Unusually, St Clare's is also authorised by the IBO to run IB workshops for teachers.

St Clare's is located in an elegant residential area which is part of the North Oxford Conservation Area. It occupies 28 large Victorian and Edwardian houses to which purpose-built facilities have been added. The campus is made up of classrooms, dining room, the popular Sugar House café, music department and activities department plus library (over 35,000 volumes), an IT suite and a Careers and Higher Education Information Centre. Stunning new buildings in college grounds and gardens provide science laboratories, prep rooms and a mathematics department, plus two new boarding houses arranged around a quad with a beautiful new art studio. There is Wi-Fi throughout both the academic facilities and student houses which are no more than five minutes' walk from the central campus. All students are automatically enrolled as members of the Oxfordshire Health and Racquets Club nearby.

We welcome applications from UK and international students. Entry is based on academic results, interview and confidential school report. There is a competitive scholarship and bursary programme awarded by examination, interview and group exercises.

St Clare's had a highly successful ISI Intermediate Boarding and Welfare inspection in 2016 and a full ISI Integrated inspection in March 2013. The reports may be accessed via our website.

Charitable status. St Clare's, Oxford is a Registered Charity, number 294085.

St David's School

23–25 Woodcote Valley Road, Purley, Surrey CR8 3AL

Tel: 020 8660 0723
email: office@stdavidsschool.co.uk
website: www.stdavidsschool.co.uk

Head Teacher: **Miss Cressida Mardell**

Age Range. 3+–11.
Number in School. 164 Day: 79 boys, 85 girls.
Fees per term (2018–2019). £2,125–£3,550 (including lunch).

We look forward to welcoming you to our happy and creative school, where we aim to achieve the highest academic standards. At St David's we offer a rich and stimulating curriculum, delivered by a talented and caring staff, giving your child the best possible start. The School has undergone many changes and developments since its foundation in 1912 and celebrated its 100th birthday in 2012. Please visit our website to find out more about all the exciting things that have been going on.

The small school atmosphere is, we believe, a strength and reassuring to parents and children alike. We aim to balance nurture with independence to equip your child to succeed academically and we are extremely proud of our results. Please do contact us to experience the warm inspiring environment that is the "St David's Family". Please telephone the School Office to arrange an appointment and we look forward to showing you round our school.

St David's participates in the 15 Hour Government Funding and accepts Childcare Vouchers.

Charitable status. St David's (Purley) Educational Trust is a Registered Charity, number 312613. It aims to provide a quality education for boys and girls from 3+ to 11 years old. Bursaries are awarded in cases of financial hardship.

St Dominic's Priory School

Station Road, Stone, Staffordshire ST15 8EN

Tel: 01785 814181
email: info@stdominicspriory.co.uk
website: www.stdominicspriory.co.uk
Twitter: @stdomsinstone

Chair of Governors: Mr Mark Burton

Headteacher: **Mrs Rebecca Harrison**

St Dominic's Priory School is an independent Catholic school, educating boys and girls from pre-school to 16 years.

We are proud of our strong academic tradition alongside our reputation for nurturing individuals. Our high-quality teaching and small classes create an environment in which true potential can be maximised at all times.

Due to the redevelopment of the school site, the school is introducing two-form entry into the Senior School from September 2019.

Location. Centrally located within North Staffordshire, the school is situated in the picturesque canal town of Stone, Staffordshire, within easy reach of Newcastle-under-Lyme, Stoke-on-Trent, Stafford, Uttoxeter, Cheadle and the surrounding villages. We provide school transport from a number of locations and Stone Railway Station is only a 5 minute walk from school.

Aims and Ethos. Our school mission statement is: Living and Learning with Christ as our Guide. We aim to create a love of learning in a friendly and happy environment, nurture individuality and instil in our students a sense of community spirit rooted in gospel values. We wish to provide each child with tools that will equip them to not only succeed academically, but contribute positively to a society in which values of justice and compassion are paramount.

St Dominic's welcomes children of all faiths and ethnic origins and within our school community diversity is recognised and respected.

We are ranked as one of the top-performing non-selective schools in the area. Once again our students achieved fantastic examination results in their end-of-year GCSE in 2018, which only highlights the school's strong academic tradition and reputation for giving an excellent all-round education. Students leave St Dominic's with superb academic grades, self-confidence and friends for life.

Religion. St Dominic's Priory is a Catholic school where children of all faiths are welcomed.

The Arts. The school excels in the creative and performing arts and our busy programme of sport, cultural events, visits and activities ensures that there is something for everyone at St Dominic's. Pupils regularly take part in public speaking competitions, productions, festivals, concerts, recitals and exhibitions, both within and outside the school.

Sport. The school has a strong sporting tradition. Sports include badminton, hockey, netball, volleyball, gymnastics, athletics, cricket, football, table tennis, tennis, cross-country running, climbing, sailing, trampoline and tri-golf.

Extra-Curricular Activities. Numerous clubs and activities are held after school and during lunchtimes for both the Prep and Senior Schools. These include the Duke of Edinburgh's Award, fencing, musical theatre, choir, and percussion ensemble.

Admission. Please contact Louise Lloyd, our admissions officer on 01785 814181 ext 2 or email admissions@stdominicspriory.co.uk or visit the website.

Scholarships and Bursaries. Scholarships are awarded irrespective of financial means in the senior school. As from 2019 our Governing Body is offering an additional Academic scholarship to the value of £4,000 per annum to an exceptionally talented student; this will be offered alongside several other Academic scholarships.

All students entering year 7 the following academic year, are automatically entered for the Academic scholarships, they also have the opportunity to apply for our Performing Arts, Music, Art and Sport scholarships.

Bursaries are available if bursary funds are available and depending on the financial, compassionate or other circumstances of applicants.

Fees per term (2018–2019). Pre-School: £27 per session (36 weeks, 9.00 am to 1.00 pm), £42 per day (36 weeks, 9.00 am to 3.30 pm), £2,520 per term; Reception £3,035; Primary 1–6 £3,374; Seniors £3,702 (exc lunch), £3,836 (inc lunch).

Further Information. The school welcomes visits from prospective parents and students. For more information please telephone the school office on 01785 814181.

Charitable status. St Dominic's Priory is a Registered Charity, number 271922, providing quality education for boys and girls aged 3 to 16 years.

St Gerard's School
Bangor

Ffriddoedd Road, Bangor, Gwynedd LL57 2EL

Tel: 01248 351656
Fax: 01248 351204
email: sgadmin@st-gerards.org
website: www.st-gerards.org
Twitter: @stgerardsbangor
Facebook: @St-Gerards-School-Trust

Chairman of the Governing Body: Dr P Thomas

Headteacher: Mr C Harrison

Age Range. 4–18.
Number in School. Day: 87 Boys, 88 Girls.
Fees per term (2018–2019). £2,350–£3,565.

Founded in 1915 by the Congregation of the Sisters of Mercy and relocated to Ffriddoedd Road in 1917, this co-educational school is now a lay trust and has just celebrated its centenary year at this site. The school welcomes pupils of all denominations and traditions and has an excellent reputation locally. It has consistently attracted a high profile in national league tables also.

Class sizes in both junior and senior schools ensure close support and individual attention in order to enable all pupils to achieve their full academic potential, within an environment which promotes their development as well-rounded individuals with a keen social conscience.

The curriculum is comprehensive – pupils in the senior section usually achieve 9/10 good GCSE grades, going on to A Level and to university.

Charitable status. St Gerard's School Trust is a Registered Charity, number 1001211.

St Hilda's School

28 Douglas Road, Harpenden, Hertfordshire AL5 2ES

Tel: 01582 712307
email: office@sthildasharpenden.co.uk
website: www.sthildasharpenden.co.uk

Head: **Mr D Sayers**, BA Hons, QTS

Age Range. 3–11.
Number in School. 180 approximately.
Fees per term (2018–2019). £3,845 (Forms II to VI including lunch), £3,805 (Reception & Form I including lunch), Nursery: £2,205.

St Hilda's School, situated in a residential site of 1¼ acres, has its own swimming pool, hard tennis/netball court and adjacent playing field. It also has a fully-equipped stage, a suite of music rooms, a dedicated computer suite, a science lab, a purpose-built EYFS unit, an art room, and six new classrooms.

A broad, well-balanced curriculum covering the requirements of the National Curriculum prepares girls for the Common Entrance and other senior independent school entrance examinations. Girls also enter State secondary schools if desired. Latin and French are taught to all pupils, and German and Spanish sessions are also available.

The school is well known for its high musical standards with almost all pupils learning an instrument, many two or three. The standards in drama, art and sport are also consistently high.

A prospectus is available on application to the School Secretary.

St James' School
A Woodard School

22 Bargate, Grimsby, North East Lincolnshire DN34 4SY

Tel: 01472 503260
Fax: 01472 503275
email: enquiries@saintjamesschool.co.uk
website: www.saintjamesschool.co.uk
Twitter: @StJamesSchoolGY
Facebook: @stjamesschoolgrimsby

Headmaster: **Dr John Price**, BSc Hons, PhD

Director of Senior School: Mr J D Hampson, BSc Hons, PGCE
Deputy Head Academic: Mr S Hutton, BSc
Head of Preparatory Department: Mrs H Boardmas, MA
Head of Pre-Preparatory Department: Mrs C Fillingham, Cert Ed Salzburg
Director of Boarding: Mr I Hughes, BA Hons
Bursar: Mr A Major
Child Protection Officer and Head of Safeguarding: Mrs J Sopp

Age Range. 2–18.

Number in School. Boarders: Boys 20, Girls 14. Day: Boys 115, Girls 87.

Fees per term (2018–2019). Tuition: Prep School: Reception £1,725 to Year 6 £2,725, Senior School £3,795, Sixth Form £2,850. Boarding: £2,000 (weekly), £2,850 (termly).

St James' School, Grimsby provides an excellent day and boarding education for children aged 2 to 18 years. The School is co-educational and a fully incorporated Member of the Woodard Corporation.

Pupils benefit from an extremely supportive environment that creates a rich and rewarding educational experience. Our highly qualified and dedicated teaching staff have the ability and experience necessary to be able to inspire and enthuse every pupil. This teaching excellence, along with the small class sizes, equips our pupils with the knowledge, skills and understanding they require to reach their academic potential.

All pupils are given the opportunity to take part in a vast range of extracurricular activities above and beyond the traditional sporting programme: from Sailing, to Karate, Horse Riding and Golf. Every pupil has a talent and such experiences ensure that we are able to discover that talent and ultimately develop the most important things, which are confidence and self-esteem.

The School offers academic, musical, sporting and all-round scholarships as well as means-tested bursaries.

The School operates a morning bus service calling in at villages from the Louth and Brigg areas and an evening service back to Brigg.

Charitable status. St James' School Grimsby Ltd is a Registered Charity, number 1099060. It exists to provide education for boys and girls.

St John's School

47–49 Stock Road, Billericay, Essex CM12 0AR

Tel:	01277 623070
Fax:	01277 654288
email:	registrar@stjohnsschool.net
website:	www.stjohnsschool.net
Twitter:	@StJBillericay
Facebook:	@StJBillericay

Headmistress: **Mrs Fiona Armour**, BEd Hons

Age Range. 2–16.

Number in School. Day: 199 Boys, 146 Girls.

Fees per term (2018–2019). £1,776–£4,500.

From the moment a child enters St John's, whatever their age, they are treated as an individual. Our passion is to ensure that when a child leaves our school they have fully achieved their potential. Set in a beautiful setting across 8 acres of land overlooking Lake Meadows Park in Billericay,

St John's is ideally located for public transport links and is only a five minute walk from Billericay train station.

Pupils benefit greatly from lessons with specialist teachers. In the Kindergarten, children have weekly lessons in Music, IT, PE and Design and Technology (DT). In the Junior School, pupils study verbal and non-verbal reasoning and have additional specialist teachers for subjects such as Games and PE, Art, Music, IT and French. Senior School pupils follow a broad curriculum, which leads to GCSE courses commencing in Year 10. Subjects include English, English Literature, Maths, Statistics, Double Science, Triple Science, Art, Drama, French, Spanish, Geography, History, Music, PE, Food Technology, RE and Computing. Pupils make excellent progress throughout the school and GCSE pass rates are consistently high.

Sport is not only an integral part of our curriculum but also part of our extracurricular programme. Our Sport England standard Sports Hall hosts a wide range of activities including trampolining, cricket, table tennis, badminton, and basketball to name but a few. We have a proven track record in field events with pupils participating at the ISA National events.

A wide range of extracurricular clubs and activities are offered including, karate, cookery, dance, multi-skills and homework club. Pupils have the opportunity to participate in instrumental lessons, perform in the school orchestra and join the choir. In addition, performing arts, both musical and drama, are a pivotal part of our school, with fantastic success rates for our LAMDA examination entrants. A number of day and residential trips are offered each year. We also offer an annual skiing trip for the pupils in the Senior School.

A child's education is one of the most important factors in their well-being and success. We instil all the virtues of politeness, integrity and consideration of others into our pupils, creating a magical atmosphere where learning, creativity and success is enjoyed by everyone. Although our academic success over the years has been exceptional, we are equally proud that we have educated thousands of children who are confident, successful and who genuinely make a positive contribution to society when they leave.

Means-tested scholarships are available for Year 7 places in the Senior School. For more information and to arrange a tour of the school, please contact Mrs Cox, Registrar on 01277 623070 or by email to registrar@stjohnsschool.net.

St Joseph's Convent School

59 Cambridge Park, Wanstead, London E11 2PR

Tel:	020 8989 4700
email:	enquiries@stjosephsconventschool.co.uk
website:	www.stjosephsconventschool.co.uk

Chair of Governors: Sr Catherine Quane

Headteacher: **Mrs Sheila Birtles**

Age Range. 3–11.

Number in School. 143 Day Girls.

Fees per term (2018–2019). £2,260.

Charitable status. Institute of Our Lady of Mercy is a Registered Charity, number 290544.

St Joseph's Park Hill School

Padiham Road, Burnley, Lancashire BB12 6TG

Tel: 01282 455622
email: office@parkhillschool.co.uk
website: www.parkhillschool.co.uk

Chair of Governors: Mrs Catherine McDermott

Head Teacher: **Mrs A Robinson**, BEd Hons

Age Range. 3–11 Co-educational.
Number of Pupils. 79
Fees per term (2018–2019). £2,127.

St Joseph's was founded by the Sisters of Mercy in 1913 and has operated from its present site since 1957.

It is a small school with a warm, friendly atmosphere where the children are known personally by all the staff. We have a broad, enriched curriculum which provides many activities and opportunities, both sporting and musical. The children enjoy their learning experience and are encouraged to do their best, achieving excellent results.

The Catholic ethos permeates all areas of the school. Pupils learn to care for each other, and respect different cultures. We welcome children from all faiths.

The school has the benefit of extensive grounds and offers a morning and after-school service as well as a 3-week summer school.

Charitable status. St Joseph's School is owned by The Institute of our Lady of Mercy which is a Registered Charity, number 290544.

St Joseph's Preparatory School

Rookery Lane, Trent Vale, Stoke-on-Trent, Staffordshire ST4 5RF

Tel: 01782 417533
email: enquiries@stjosephsprepschool.co.uk
website: www.stjosephsprepschool.co.uk

Chair of Governors: Mrs L Atherton

Head: **Mrs S D Hutchinson**, BEd

Age Range. 3–11 Co-educational.
Number of Pupils. 160 Day Pupils.
Fees per term (2018–2019). £2,535–£2,680.
Charitable status. The Congregation of Christian Brothers is a Registered Charity, number 254312.

St Joseph's School

St Stephen's Hill, Launceston, Cornwall PL15 8HN

Tel: 01566 772580
email: registrar@stjosephscornwall.co.uk
website: www.stjosephscornwall.co.uk
Twitter: @StJosephsSch
Facebook: @StJosephsSchoolLaunceston

Head Teacher: **Mr Oliver Scott**

Deputy Head Academic: Mr Sam Matthews
Deputy Head Pastoral: Mrs Rosemary O'Brien
Junior Head: Mr Henry Matthews

Bursar: Mr Ian Barton
Registrar: Miss Rebecca Walker

Age Range. 4–16 Co-educational.
Number in School. 216.
Fees per term (2018–2019). £900–£4,625.

St Joseph's School, Launceston is an award-winning Independent Day School for boys and girls from 4–16.

St Joseph's has a truly unique atmosphere. The school's small size means that it is possible both to keep sight of strong family values, giving children the confidence necessary to succeed, and to allow staff and pupils to work happily together. Due to the high teacher to pupil ratio, St Joseph's is able to encourage each pupil to reach his or her full potential through positive encouragement and commendation.

In both the Junior and the Senior school, St Joseph's provides an excellent academic education for all, regardless of ability and background. Our individualised academic curriculum runs alongside a wide variety of extra-curricular activities that challenge, stimulate and inspire all pupils to unlock their potential in a safe and supportive environment. St Joseph's offers equal prospects to every individual and it is the positive response to the school's ethos that sees pupils rising to challenges both within the classroom and as highly valued members of the wider school community.

St Joseph's GCSE pupils achieve superb results. An exceptional 90% of pupils gained the required 5 passes at grades 4–9 or A*–C including Maths and English in 2017 and 85% in 2018. This is a remarkable achievement as St Joseph's is a non-selective school, meaning there is no entrance exam and admission is possible at any time throughout a child's education. Fees are set at levels which offer tremendous value for money, particularly in light of what is on offer to all the pupils at the school and our excellent academic results.

Academic and Sports Scholarships are offered from age 7+ and Music Scholarships from 11+. Bursaries are available and considered on an individual basis.

An extensive daily bus service (8 bus routes) allows pupils from a wide area of Devon and Cornwall to attend St Joseph's.

St Joseph's School offers a number of open events throughout the year for prospective parents. To arrange an individual visit please contact the Registrar. Further information can be found at www.stjosephscornwall.co.uk or by contacting the Registrar on 01566 772580, registrar@stjosephscornwall.co.uk.

Charitable status. St Joseph's School is a Registered Charity, number 289048.

St Joseph's School

33 Derby Road, Nottingham NG1 5AW

Tel: 0115 941 8356
email: office@st-josephs.nottingham.sch.uk
website: st-josephs.nottingham.sch.uk
Twitter: @StJosephsNG1
Facebook: /St-Josephs-Independent-School-and-Nursery

Head Teacher: **Mr A E Crawshaw**

Age Range. 1–11 years.
Number in School. 74 Boys, 59 Girls.
Fees per term (2018–2019). £2,703 (Main School Reception to Year 6). Nursery fees on application.

A co-educational day school providing the very highest standards to children of all abilities. Children receive individual attention in small classes. The curriculum is planned to encourage children to develop lively, enquiring minds with emphasis on literacy and numeracy. Music and Drama have a high profile in the school.

Sports include Football, Netball, Cricket, Rounders, Tag Rugby, Swimming, and Squash.

Extra-curricular activities include Archery, Dance, Ballet, Chess, Piano, Recorder and Football.

It provides a happy and caring environment in which children can develop their full potential both socially and academically. The school is Roman Catholic but welcomes children of all faiths.

Charitable status. St Joseph's School Nottingham is a Registered Charity, number 1003916.

St Margaret's Preparatory School
Cognita Schools Group

Gosfield Hall Park, Gosfield, Halstead, Essex CO9 1SE

Tel:	01787 472134
Fax:	01787 478207
email:	admin@stmargaretsprep.com
website:	www.stmargaretsprep.com
Twitter:	@StMargsPrep
Facebook:	@StMargaretsPrep

Headmaster: Mr Callum Douglas

Age Range. 2–11.
Number of Pupils. Day: 90 Boys, 105 Girls.
Fees per term (2018–2019). £3,150–£3,946.

St Margaret's is an ISA accredited school which specialises in the needs of children from 2 to 11 years.

Academically, St Margaret's provides excellence beyond the national standard expected, stretching each child to the best of their individual ability, but not at the expense of a happy, full and varied childhood. Although we annually gain academic, music, art and sports scholarships to senior schools, the emphasis is on an all-round education, encompassing the academic needs, enriching aspects such as social integration and encouraging other interests of each individual.

Typically, a child at St Margaret's will have two afternoons a week of coached sport as well as a PE lesson, extra coaching sessions before school and at lunchtime for the keen and able, and numerous after-school clubs. These clubs encompass a whole range of activities including fencing, seasonal sports, speech and drama, golf, photography, choirs and ensembles, short tennis and music composition – the list goes on. They are regarded as an important and integral part of school, broadening their horizons. With a purpose-built ICT suite, art studio, music practice rooms, science lab and seven acres of grounds in a wonderful parkland setting, the children have every opportunity to excel in their chosen sphere or to experience the fun of a new challenge.

One of the school's specialities is music. We offer individual lessons with 13 peripatetic music teachers on a vast range of instruments. Every child who learns an instrument is encouraged to join a choir or ensemble and the orchestra. Drama plays a big part too, and children participate in numerous concerts and plays throughout the year. There are trips to galleries, concerts, museums, as well as taking part in festivals, competitions and local events.

Our extensive curriculum provides the children with the social confidence and academic ability to achieve their potential and to move on to their chosen senior schools as able and well-rounded individuals.

St Michael's School

Bryn, Llanelli, Carmarthenshire SA14 9TU

Tel:	01554 820325
Fax:	01554 821716
email:	admissions@stmikes.co.uk
	office@stmikes.co.uk
website:	www.stmikes.co.uk
Twitter:	@StMikes
Facebook:	@St-Michaels-School

Headmaster: **Benson Ferrari**, MA, PG Cert, BA Hons, FRSA, FCIEA

Deputy Head: Kay Francis, BSc Hons, PGCE

Head of Prep School: Adrian Thomas, BSc Hons, PGCE

Age Range. 3–18.
Number in School. 415: 216 boys, 199 girls.
Fees per term (UK resident students from January 2018). Tuition: Preparatory School £1,688–£2,739; Senior School £3,774–£4,123. Full Boarding: Years 7–10: £8,400 (twin), £9,300 (single); Years 11–13: £9,000 (twin), £9,900 (single). Weekly Boarding: Years 7–10: £6,776 (twin), £7,480 (single); Years 11–13: £7,216 (twin), £8,184 (single). Sibling allowances available. International Students per annum (2018–2019): Twin room: Years 7–8 £22,800, Year 9 £24,600, Years 10–11 (GCSE) £24,600. Years 7–11 single room supplement £500. Sixth Form (A Level) £27,800 (single en-suite room).

St Michael's combines great learning and excellent pastoral care as part of a well-rounded education. The school has a traditional approach to learning, which does not mean it lives in the past, but places emphasis on the importance of hard work and homework in the school curriculum. The high academic standards of the school are reflected in the National League Tables. In 2017 the school was ranked a Top 20 school in The Times Top 100 Co-Educational Schools in the UK, the same year we were top school in Wales for GCSE results and in 2018, our A Level results saw us reach 63rd of all independent schools in the Daily Telegraph.

No school can build up such a strong reputation without a competitive, but well-disciplined atmosphere and a highly-qualified and dedicated staff. This is where we feel St Michael's is particularly fortunate.

Our boarding houses are excellent: Parc House for Years 7 to 10 is a handsome and historic mansion set in an acre of grounds in the village of Llangennech nearby and Tenby House is a purpose-built, on-site, state-of-the-art, 31-bedroom boarding house for those in Years 11 to 13. Both houses offer a high standard of comfort where every pupil feels safe, happy and protected. Pupils are accommodated in well-furnished and equipped, single en-suite or shared study-bedrooms. The houses provide spacious recreation rooms and pleasant grounds in which pupils may relax, play or watch TV.

We have well-equipped computer laboratories where pupils have access to a computer each from 3 years of age. Languages taught in the school are French, Spanish, Welsh and Chinese (Mandarin).

The school has an envied reputation for its academic achievement but is also proud of the wide range of traditional games and activities it offers. Pupils from Year 10 onwards pupils can also take part in The Duke of Edinburgh's Award scheme to Gold Award standard. We have a large choir and school orchestra and pupils may take music examinations at GCSE and A Level.

One of the main reasons behind the school's success is the thorough grounding that pupils receive in the 'basics' – English, Mathematics, IT/Computing and Science in the Prep and Pre-Prep Schools, continuing into the Senior School.

We have enjoyed outstanding sporting success over the last few years in netball, rugby, football, tennis, cricket and athletics.

Every pupil is encouraged to develop their full potential whether in academic work or in all the extracurricular activities on offer.

St Nicholas House School

Yarmouth Road, North Walsham, Norfolk NR28 9AT

Tel:	01692 403143
email:	info@stnicholashouse.com
website:	www.stnicholashouse.com
Twitter:	@StNicksHouse
Facebook:	@St-Nicholas-House-Prep-School-Nursery

Headmaster: **Mr Philip Oldroyd**, BA, PGCE

Age Range. 2–11 co-educational.
Number of Pupils. 75.
Fees per term (2018–2019). £2,047. Lunch: £230 per term.

Our aim is to **engage** our children in their learning and **inspire** them by **challenge** and competition within a **nurturing** environment. Our expectations are high but realistic, uniting traditional practice with innovative teaching including the best of creative and academic practice. We provide a tremendous all-round education for every pupil.

The intimate atmosphere is a particular strength of the school and enables us to build warm relationships with the children and their parents. Our class sizes allow for more individual attention from staff who value and understand every child and spend quality time with them to enhance their learning. The family feel of the school is evident and our children clearly benefit from being members of a small community.

Pupils leave us confident and well mannered, with essential life skills such as the ability to interact with people of all ages and work independently or as part of a team. Education here is for life not just the classroom.

Saint Nicholas School

Hillingdon House, Hobbs Cross Road, Old Harlow, Essex CM17 0NJ

Tel:	01279 429910
email:	office@saintnicholasschool.net
	admissions@saintnicholasschool.net
website:	www.saintnicholasschool.net
Twitter:	@SaintNicksSch
Facebook:	@saintnicholasschoolharlow

Headmaster: **Mr D J Bown**, BA Hons, PGCE, MA, NPQH

Age Range. 2½–16.
Number in School. 403 Day Pupils: 212 Boys, 191 Girls.

Fees per term (2018–2019). Reception, Years 1 & 2 £3,325. Years 3,4 & 5 £3,455. Years 6,7 & 8 £3,850 and Years 9, 10 & 11 £4,215. Pre-school fees £24 per session.

In 2014 Saint Nicholas School celebrated 75 years of excellence. Saint Nicholas is situated in a delightful rural location and combines a fresh and enthusiastic approach to learning with a firm belief in traditional values.

The academic record of the school is excellent, reflected in high pupil success rates in all competitive examinations. The dedicated team of staff involves itself closely with all aspects of pupils' educational progress and general development. High standards of formal teaching are coupled with positive encouragement for pupils to reason for themselves and develop a high degree of responsibility.

As part of the school's commitment to providing affordable, quality care to children in the community, Little Saints Pre-School opened its doors in September 2014 to children from 2½ years old. Recent building developments include magnificent junior and infant department buildings, theatre, science and technology centre, swimming pool and sports hall, and new on-site catering facilities opened in January 2015.

Main sports include hockey, netball, tennis, football, rugby, cricket, swimming, athletics and gymnastics. Optional extras include ballet, individual instrumental lessons, karate, performing arts and Spanish classes.

Charitable status. Saint Nicholas School (Harlow) Limited is a Registered Charity, number 310876. It exists to provide and promote educational enterprise by charitable means.

St Peter's School

52 Headlands, Kettering, Northamptonshire NN15 6DJ

Tel:	01536 512066
Fax:	01536 416469
email:	st-petersschool@btconnect.com
website:	www.st-peters.org.uk

Headmistress: **Mrs M Chapman**, MA Ed, BA Hons, PGCE

Age Range. 3–11.
Number in School. Day: 61 Boys, 64 Girls.
Fees per term (2018–2019). £2,636–£3,500.

Established in 1946, St Peter's is a small day school set in secure and beautifully green grounds in a quiet residential area of Kettering. It offers a sound education based upon Christian values for boys and girls from the term of their third birthday to age 11. Pupils are thoroughly prepared for entry to a secondary school of their choice and have a high rate of success in Entrance and Scholarship Examinations. In addition to fulfilling the requirements of the National Curriculum the school emphasises the importance of Music, Art, Sport and Information Technology in its programme. The School has a French teacher and French is introduced in the Nursery.

St Peter's School is a lively, friendly school with a strong family atmosphere where children are encouraged to develop to the full their individual strengths and talents. It aims to promote a respect for traditional values, a sense of responsibility and a concern for the needs of others. Each child is encouraged and nurtured to fulfil their own potential. Inspection reports detail the excellent progress made together with a strong extra-curricular activity timetable.

Charitable status. St Peter's School is a Registered Charity, number 309914. It was originally incorporated in

1946 with an intention to maintain and manage a school for boys and girls in the town of Kettering. In addition to this it provides local employment and seeks to source from the local community wherever economically viable.

St Philomena's Catholic School

Hadleigh Road, Frinton-on-Sea, Essex CO13 9HQ
Tel: 01255 674492
Fax: 01255 674459
email: generalenquiries@stphilomenas.com
website: www.stphilomenas.com

Co-educational Day School.

Chair of Governors: Mrs Josephine Geldard

Headteacher: **Mrs Barbara McKeown**, DipEd, CTC

Age Range. 4–11.
Number of Pupils. 88: 46 girls, 42 boys.
Fees per term (2018–2019). £2,080–£2,500.
St Philomena's is situated in a pleasant coastal area close to the beach. The school has a Catholic foundation and ethos, welcoming all traditions, faiths and denominations. Children flourish in the tangible family atmosphere throughout the school.

Very good attitudes to learning are promoted for the mixed ability intake. Pupils strive for high academic standards and have achieved a very good record in 11+ selection examinations for both the grammar schools in the maintained sector and secondary schools in the independent sector.

Staff are fully qualified, experienced and dedicated professionals who communicate well with parents. Very high standards in pupil behaviour are maintained – pupils are caring and courteous with each other and towards adults.

There is a wide range of extra-curricular activities including sports clubs, science club, Scrabble, chess, art, cycling proficiency and ICT. Tuition is offered for a wide range of musical instruments including, piano, violin, drums, guitar, flute, clarinet, trumpet and saxophone. Music lessons with a music specialist take place throughout the school and there are recorder lessons for whole classes. There are weekly swimming lessons and French lessons available for Key Stage 2. The school choirs have achieved outstanding success in local and national competitions in recent years.

Emphasis is given to physical education. There are representative teams for football, hockey, cricket, rounders, netball, and cross country (numbers permitting). Tennis is taught to the senior children.

All children are encouraged to speak confidently and to express themselves clearly. All children from 7+ participate in an annual oral communication assessment adjudicated externally. Parents are invited to regular concerts, plays, class presentations and class assemblies.

Charitable status. St Philomena's Catholic School is a Registered Charity, number 298635. It exists to provide Roman Catholic children and those of other denominations with the opportunity to reach the highest possible standards in every area of school life.

St Piran's School, Hayle

14 Trelissick Road, Hayle, Cornwall TR27 4HY
Tel: 01736 752612
email: admin@stpirans.net
website: www.stpiranshayle.net

Headteacher: **Mrs Carol A de Labat**, BEd Hons, CertEd

Age Range. 4–16.
Number of Pupils. 70.
Fees per term (2018–2019). £922.50–£2,360.
Established in 1988, St Piran's School is set in attractive and well-maintained premises which, at present, accommodate around seventy children, aged from four to sixteen. It is a friendly, well-ordered community with a positive ethos where pupils make good friendships with each other and relate well to staff. Pupils are treated with respect and valued equally. They have a clear sense of right and wrong. There is a good sense of community within the school and new pupils are quickly made to feel welcome. The school places a strong emphasis on good manners and politeness.

The curriculum is broad and balanced and helps to prepare the children for the next stage in their education. A wide variety of after school and lunchtime clubs provide additional activities and experiences for pupils of all ages. Educational visits to local places of interest and annual residential visits (for Year 5 and up) further enrich the curriculum.

From Years Five and Six there is greater emphasis on subjects being taught by specialists. Class size remains low, with the maximum class size being twelve. Well-qualified, conscientious and hard-working staff teach children in a supportive learning environment. Children are given the opportunity to explain their ideas and be involved in activities. There is a very well-equipped and effectively-organised computer suite, which ensures that the children are at the cutting edge of technology.

We offer our senior pupils all of the opportunities, including the Duke of Edinburgh's Award scheme, offered by larger secondary schools.

St Teresa's School

Aylesbury Road, Princes Risborough, Buckinghamshire HP27 0JW
Tel: 01844 345005
email: office@st-teresas.bucks.sch.uk
website: www.st-teresas.bucks.sch.uk

Joint Head Teacher: **Mrs Jane Draper**, BEd Hons
Joint Head Teacher: **Mrs Yasmin Roberts**, BA Hons, GTP

Age Range. 3–11.
Number in School. 110.
Fees per term (2018–2019). Reception to Year Two £2,995 (first child), £2,810 (siblings). Year Three to Year Six £3,055 (first child), £2,866 (siblings).
At St Teresa's we pride ourselves on our loving ethos, where all children are valued and nurtured to become the best that they can be. Each child is unique and we are committed to lighting the spark so that all our children love learning, overcome challenges, experience success and achieve academically, spiritually, physically, artistically, musically and socially.

St Teresa's is a co-educational Catholic school which was founded in 1945 and we welcome children of all faiths or none. Our school is closely linked to the Parish of St Teresa's and is in the small town of Princes Risborough, situated in the beautiful Chilterns in Buckinghamshire, close to the Oxfordshire border.

The size of St Teresa's is a huge advantage; staff know every child by name and nobody is overlooked. Indeed, it is by getting to know the children well that we can help them to develop their individual gifts and abilities. Many of our parents comment on how St Teresa's feels like a family. Our Year Six pupils take on stewardship roles, which encourages this ethos. The responsibility of these roles helps our children prepare for their move to Secondary Schools, which include the local Grammar Schools, state school and a wide range of independent schools, to which many of our pupils have been offered scholarships this year.

Through our curriculum we aim to plan and provide many exciting learning experiences and opportunities through daily teaching, visitors, trips both locally and further afield, including residential trips for our older pupils. Our children are taught by enthusiastic and committed teachers and support staff. We are fortunate to have specialist teachers in many subjects including PE, music and French and these teachers work with our children from Pre-school upwards. We offer many extra activities such as: individual music lessons; various clubs including craft, music, logical games, Latin and chess; sports clubs; tournaments and matches; as well as a school production and other performance opportunities. We also provide a breakfast club before school and an after-school club, which includes supervised homework for our Key Stage Two children.

Prospective parents are always welcome to make an appointment to visit the school and please see our website for forthcoming Open Mornings. When you visit our school we are sure you will notice the happy and busy working environment and the enthusiastic participation of our children, which we think reflects the aims and values of the school.

St Winefride's Convent School
Shrewsbury

Belmont, Shrewsbury, Shropshire SY1 1TE

Tel: 01743 369883
Fax: 01743 369883
email: st.winefrides@btconnect.com
website: www.stwinefrides.com

Headmistress: **Sister M Felicity**, BA Hons

Age Range. 4+–11. Nursery: 3+–4.
Number in School. Day: 67 Boys, 76 Girls.
Fees per term (from April 2018). £1,495–£1,570.

St Wystan's School

High Street, Repton, Derbyshire DE65 6GE

Tel: 01283 703258
Fax: 01283 703258
email: head@stwystans.org.uk
website: www.stwystans.org.uk

Twitter: @StWystans
Facebook: @St-Wystans-School-and-Nursery

Head teacher: **Mrs K Hopkinson**, MA Ed

Age Range. 2½–11.
Number of Pupils: Day: Boys 41 Girls 61.
Fees per term (2018–2019). £2,885. Compulsory extras: Lunch £290.

St Wystan's is an independent preparatory day school for girls and boys aged 2½ to 11 years of age. We are only a short distance from Burton-on-Trent and the city of Derby. Nottingham and Uttoxeter are within 25 minutes of the school.

At St Wystan's, every child is recognised and cherished for their individual strengths and characteristics, in an inspiring teaching and learning environment. Small class sizes encourage a thirst for learning where pupils and staff have warm, respectful relationships. The children enjoy going to school and the staff relish having the opportunity to share laughter, adventures and interests. Indeed, each pupil's individual talents and strengths are recognised and utilised ensuring all achieve their full potential, in a vibrant, busy yet nurturing environment.

St Wystan's is a thriving non-selective school that prides itself on its reputation for producing happy, confident and successful children. Each individual in our school community is extremely special to us and we continually strive to create a varied and stimulating environment, so they can develop, be happy and flourish. Specialist teaching in Music, Physical Education and French is introduced from Nursery through to Year 6 and we are proud of our strong pastoral care and extra-curricular activities.

Our school was founded in 1926 and is situated in the heart of Repton. St Wystan's School and Nursery prides itself in providing outstanding holistic education, equipping pupils not only with strong academic standards and behaviour, but also the essential qualities and skills required beyond their time at our school. We are proud of our strong links with many local secondary Independent and State schools. Our children have an excellent reputation for securing scholarship offers and securing first-choice secondary schools at a time in which a child's true academic potential can be accurately predicted and talents in other areas acknowledged.

St Wystan's enjoys an excellent reputation in music, sport and drama with pupils progressing to regional and national championships in football, swimming, cross country and athletics. Many pupils have instrumental tuition and there is a thriving school choir and orchestra.

St Wystan's runs a very popular pre-school and after-school care facility. Children can arrive at school from 7.30 am and be looked after at school until 6.30 pm.

Scholarships are offered for 7+ entry to Year 3 and bursaries are available.

Free taster days are available.

Charitable status. St Wystan's School Limited is a Registered Charity, number 527181. It exists to provide a quality education for boys and girls.

Salesian College

119 Reading Road, Farnborough, Hampshire GU14 6PA

Tel: 01252 893000
Fax: 01252 893032
email: office@salesiancollege.com
website: www.salesiancollege.com

Twitter: @SalesianFboro
Facebook: @Salesiancollegefarnborough

Headmaster: **Mr Gerard T Owens**, MA Hons, PGCE

Age Range. Boys 11–18 years, Girls 16–18. Co-educational Sixth Form.
Number in School. 623.
Fees per term (2018–2019). £3,987.

As a Catholic school in the Salesian tradition, the College provides a Home that welcomes; a Church where Gospel values are shared and lived out on a daily basis; a School which educates for Life and prepares for future success and realisation of individual potential; and a Playground where personal, social, moral, sporting and cultural enrichment, beyond the academic curriculum, takes place and where lasting friendships are formed. Therefore, the formation of character and the development of social conscience are at the heart of our mission. Students of other Christian denominations and religious faiths are warmly welcomed.

Salesian College forms well-educated, happy and well-rounded, confident young men and women; good Christians; honest citizens who are comfortable with themselves and those around them. Students are decent, courteous, selfless people; well equipped to take their place in and make a significant contribution to society.

Staff are caring and provide an excellent all round education. Salesian has outstanding levels of academic, cultural, spiritual and physical achievement, exemplary student behaviour and a caring ethos. We are a happy and highly successful school.

Although selective, we admit students of a wide range and believe in the pursuit of excellence for all. As such it caters excellently for all levels of ability, providing stretch for the most able and support for those with additional learning needs.

Excellent relationships between staff and students, and the students themselves, are a key feature of the College which seeks at all times to provide a holistic approach to the education and formation of those entrusted to our care.

The recent ISI Inspection report rated Salesian College as excellent in all areas, stating that *"The excellence of academic achievement owes much to the excellence of the curriculum and the teaching. Pupils find the collaborative approach of the teaching staff very helpful and supportive. Teachers know their pupils extremely well; they plan their lessons carefully to include a variety of approaches which succeed in engaging pupils' interest and, in almost all cases, in enabling them to maintain strong progress"*.

The school has its own chapel, chaplaincy and resident chaplain.

Prospective parents are always welcome to make an appointment to visit the College while in session. Please see our website for up-to-date details.

Charitable status. Salesian College Farnborough Limited is a Registered Charity, number 1130166. It exists to provide education in North East Hampshire and neighbouring counties.

Salterford House School

Salterford Lane, Calverton, Nottinghamshire NG14 6NZ
Tel: 0115 965 2127
email: office@salterfordhouseschool.co.uk
website: www.salterfordhouseschool.co.uk

Principal: **Mrs Marlene Venables**

Age Range. 3–11.
Number in School. Main School 56: 31 Boys, 25 Girls. Kindergarten and Pre-Prep 13: 7 Boys, 6 Girls.
Fees per term (2018–2019). £2,600–£2,630.

Salterford House is situated in rural Nottinghamshire, in a 4.5 acre woodland setting, and aims to provide a happy, family atmosphere with small classes, in order to equip children academically and socially to cope with the demands of any type of education which might follow.

Although the school is mainly Church of England, all faiths are accepted. 75% of pupils go on to senior independent schools such as Nottingham Boys' High School, Nottingham Girls' High School, Trent College and Hollygirt.

Sports include Cricket, Tennis, Swimming, Rounders, Rugby, Lacrosse, Netball, Climbing, Football, Hockey, Golf and Skiing.

The school produces 3 concerts a year and there is a recorder Group and Choir. Individual tuition in Speech and Drama, Piano, Flute, Clarinet, Guitar, Violin and Percussion is available.

Dance lessons including Ballet and Jazz/Street Dance are available.

All classrooms are equipped with computers.

Staff are easily available for discussion. Regular contact is maintained with parents via Parents Evening and newsletters.

Sancton Wood School

1–2 St Paul's Road, Cambridge CB1 2EZ
Tel: 01223 471703
email: office@sanctonwood.co.uk
website: www.sanctonwood.co.uk
Twitter: @SanctonWood
Facebook: @SanctonWood

Headmaster: **Mr Richard Settle**, BA Hons, PGCE

Age Range. 1–16 Co-educational.
Number of Pupils. 250.
Fees per term (2018–2019). £3,435–£4,490.

Sancton Wood is a school where every child finds their niche. Our small, supportive and close-knit community is often likened to a family – a kind, tolerant, school where everyone can find their place and be valued.

Our class sizes are similarly small at just 16 pupils, creating fabulous learning environments, where our teachers have time for individual pupils, where they feel comfortable airing their ideas, where imaginations soar.

Our exam results are excellent by any measure. In recent years they have been second to none in some league tables. But the school is not just about exam results; art, music, sport and a wealth of other activities are all important aspects of life here, and play their part in making well-rounded students with their lives in balance.

Sancton Wood School is part of the Dukes Education group which owns a number of private schools in London, East and South East England. Through Minerva's "Inspiring Learning" programme, we seek to share best practice and ensure the continuing improvement in every child's education.

Shapwick School

Shapwick Manor, Shapwick, Nr Bridgwater, Somerset TA7 9NJ

Tel:	01458 210384
email:	office@shapwickschool.com
	admin@shapwickschool.com
website:	www.shapwickschool.com
Twitter:	@ShapwickSchool
Facebook:	@shapwickschool

Principal: **Mr Adrian Wylie**, BEd, PG Dip, NPQH

Deputy Principal: Mrs Hellen Lush

Assistant Principal: Mr Gareth Wright (*Head of Boarding*)

Assistant Principal: Mr Graham Hilliard (*Head of Estates*)

Age Range. 8–18.

Number in School. Boarders: 36 boys, 17 girls; Day: 26 boys, 20 girls.

Fees per term (2018–2019). Boarders £8,733–£10,100, Day £6,327–£6,624.

Shapwick is a specialist school for boys and girls whose education would otherwise be impaired by a specific learning difficulty (SpLD). The School provides a caring and supportive atmosphere, staffed by specialist teachers across a wide curriculum offering the structured help needed by students who have dyslexia, dyscalculia, dyspraxia and associated needs. Students take up to 8 GCSE subjects and the aim is to teach to their strengths whilst their weaknesses are being overcome and their confidence grows. Supplementary courses, such as Study Skills, Keyboard Skills, and careers advice are also undertaken. The School has a full range of specialist classrooms, including three laboratories, computing rooms, design centre, art rooms, library, sports hall, recreation room and games field. Students are involved in a wide range of extracurricular activities, the Duke of Edinburgh's Award and games fixtures, to complement the formal curriculum.

Prospective entrants need a recent Educational Psychologist's report diagnosing a specific learning difficulty together with a current school report followed up by a visit to Shapwick School.

Sherborne International

Newell Grange, Sherborne, Dorset DT9 4EZ

Tel:	01935 814743
Fax:	01935 816863
email:	reception@sherborne-international.org
website:	www.sherborne-international.org
Twitter:	@SherborneInter
Facebook:	@sherborneinternational
LinkedIn:	/Sherborne-international

Principal: **Mr Tim Waters**, MA MSc Oxon

Age Range. Co-educational 11–17 (Boarding 11–17).

Number in School. 140 boarders: 70 boys, 70 girls.

Fees per term (2018–2019). £10,712 (Years 7 & 8), £13,525 (Years 9, 10 and 11), £14,617 (1 Year I/GCSE).

Founded by Sherborne School in 1977, Sherborne International educates girls and boys aged 11–17 from all over the world, preparing them for the best possible British education. A small school of 150 pupils with over 20 nationalities, we have successfully placed thousands of former students at the UK's elite boarding schools.

With our in-depth understanding of international students' needs and very small class sizes (maximum 8 students), we provide a high-quality, personalised learning experience, covering academic, linguistic and cultural education. Our aim is to provide the best possible introduction to the UK education system and ensure each student reaches a high level of academic achievement.

Students on our school term courses typically stay here for between one term and three years. Our short courses, including intensive spring revision courses and summer courses last 2–8 weeks.

Sherborne International is accredited by The British Council and The Independent Schools Association. It is a member of COBIS, ECIS, ISA, BSA and English UK.

We offer a range of courses for international students with an academic focus on improving English and knowledge of subjects. All our teachers are qualified or trained to teach English as well as their specialist subjects.

Our courses include junior preparation where students follow a broad range of subjects from the national curriculum. I/GCSE courses can be taken over one or two years with the flexibility of joining in September, January or April.

Our non-examined Pre-Sixth Form Course can be entered for one or two terms in January or April and helps students develop a range of academic skills to better prepare them for sixth-form study.

Our Summer School Courses are for international students aged 8–17. The courses are intensive and academic with an extensive choice of sports, activities and excursions. We also offer Spring Revision Courses.

In 2018, 80.1% of our students gained A*–C/9–4 at I/GCSE/GCSE and 77% of our year 11 students gained band 6 or above in their IELTS exams.

We pride ourselves on one of the best staff to student ratios in the world, with experienced house parents, supported by teams of residential house tutors responsible for the well-being and happiness of students 24 hrs a day. This also allows us to offer a wide variety of sports, activities and excursions to keep students active and happy. We have a doctor available every morning, so medical care is always available.

Girls and boys live in separate houses and most have a single or double bedroom. We aim to ensure students sharing speak a different language. New for 2018 is a refurbished boarding house with en-suite facilities. Houses have Wi-Fi and common rooms with TVs, DVD players and games consoles. Desktop computers are also available with access to printers. Most weekends have a busy leisure programme on Saturday and Sunday and evenings are also well structured.

The School has impressive sporting and musical facilities, including a 25-metre swimming pool, fitness centre, tennis courts, dance studio, sports hall and sports fields.

Sherrardswood School

Lockleys, Welwyn, Hertfordshire AL6 0BJ

Tel:	01438 714282
Fax:	01438 840616
email:	headmistress@sherrardswood.co.uk
website:	www.sherrardswood.co.uk
Facebook:	@sherrardswoodschool.co.uk

Headmistress: **Mrs Anna Wright**

Head of Prep: Mr Mark Self
Assistant Head – Academic: Mrs Koulla Theodoulou
Assistant Head – Pastoral: Mrs Nicci Venn

Age Range. 2–18.
Number in School. Day: 172 Boys, 146 Girls.
Fees per term (2018–2019). £3,461–£5,371.

Sherrardswood, founded in 1928, is a co-educational day school for pupils aged 2–18. The School is set in 28 acres of attractive parkland two miles north of Welwyn Garden City. The Prep Department is housed in a beautiful 18th century building whilst the Senior Department occupies a purpose-built facility. Games fields, tennis courts and woodlands trail are available on the Lockleys site for both departments.

Entry to the school is by interview and individual assessment. A broad curriculum is offered to GCSE level and a wide range of A Level subjects is available. A range of sport and extracurricular opportunities is available, both within the school day and out of school hours.

The recent ISI inspection confirmed that Sherrardswood is achieving its aims and that the quality of education and pastoral care is outstanding.

Charitable status. Sherrardswood School is a Registered Charity, number 311070. It exists solely to provide independent education for boys and girls aged 2–18.

Shoreham College

St Julian's Lane, Shoreham-by-Sea, West Sussex BN43 6YW

Tel: 01273 592681
Fax: 01273 591673
email: info@shorehamcollege.co.uk
website: www.shorehamcollege.co.uk
Twitter: @ShorehamCollege
Facebook: @shorehamcollege

Headmaster: **Richard Taylor-West**, MA Sussex, BA, AKC King's College London, PGCE

Age Range. 3–16.
Number in School. 234 Day Boys, 142 Day Girls.
Fees per term (2018–2019). £3,250–£5,050.

Shoreham College is a school that cares – it values its children as individuals, knows them well, and ensures that they feel safe, secure and happy. Within a warm friendly environment, it instils traditional values of good manners and courtesy and teaches the children to respect themselves, their peers and their community.

Teachers encourage pupils to enjoy being children, which allows them to grow. They nurture, guide, support and inspire them to develop academically, emotionally, and spiritually and are rewarded by seeing them grow into confident young adults, ready to take on the challenges of life.

Adopting a broadly non-selective approach means that the College is committed to providing a first-class all-round education to children of varied ability, ensuring that every child can achieve their potential. Ambitious for them, we ensure that they are appropriately challenged: the gifted and talented extended and children with learning differences given what they need to thrive.

We look forward to welcoming you.

Charitable status. Shoreham College (The Kennedy Independent School Trust Limited) is a Registered Charity, number 307045. It exists to provide high-quality education for boys and girls.

Slindon College

Slindon House, Top Road, Arundel, West Sussex BN18 0RH

Tel: 01243 814320
email: registrar@slindoncollege.co.uk
website: www.slindoncollege.co.uk
Twitter: @SlindonCollege
Facebook: @SlindonCollege
LinkedIn: /slindon-college

Headmaster: **Mr Mark Birkbeck**, BEd Hons, NPQH

Age Range. 8–18.
Number in School. 20 Boarders, 60 Day Boys.
Fees per term (2018–2019). Boarders £10,760, Day Boys £7,265.

Slindon College is an independent day and boarding school for boys aged 8–18, set in the historic Slindon House, located in the South Downs National Park.

With unrivalled views of the south coast, the 14-acre setting provides the backdrop to a stimulating, broad and balanced educational experience for students of all academic abilities, taking into account their strengths and talents.

Slindon House was built on the historical site of the Summer Palace of the Archbishop of Canterbury. It went through several transitions before being given to the Kempe family by Queen Mary Tudor. In 1948 the house was given as part of the Slindon Estate to the National Trust and Lingfield School moved in from their Surrey home; the school changed name to Slindon College in 1972 under a new charitable trust.

The College has:

- Teachers with specialist training, knowledge, experience & skills in differentiating the curriculum and utilising multi-sensory teaching methodologies with augmentative teaching approaches for all students to help them believe, inspire, succeed.
- A high teacher to student ratio, so that teaching and learning can be consistently monitored and evaluated. Small teaching groups allowing for more interactions with the teacher, greater opportunities for 1:1 teaching, a greater variety of instructional approaches and more social and academic engagement. Assisted technology available in every classroom.
- Target setting which is measurable and achievable, yet challenging to the student, with regular reviews. We have the determination and ability to enable every student to reach their potential, whatever their previous educational experience, through a broad selection of GCSEs and vocational qualifications which are available at Key Stage 4 and 5. We have managed to surpass the national average for value added year on year.
- An extensive, full time, academic support team with a breadth of expertise including: English as an Additional Language, specialist Dyslexia teaching, SaLT, SEAL and Occupational Therapy.
- A range of trips to supplement and enrich the curriculum wherever possible and to provide an experiential education offer that links to post-educational experiences. The College will put an emphasis on preparation for life after College, tailored to the potential of each student. All students are encouraged to participate in work experience from Year 10 onwards.
- A small boarding team, who offer the comfort of family life whilst developing individual living skills. An outstanding pastoral support system, allowing every student

to be listened to in a calm living/learning environment supported by a tranquil setting.

- A reward system, not only for academic achievement and progress, but also for personal development. Regular celebration assemblies, encouraging greater participation with the local community and encouraging external speakers with a wealth of experiences to share with the students and enhance their wider understanding of the world.
- An enrichment program which offers opportunities for self-exploration and calculated risk taking, in activities such as: Duke of Edinburgh's Award Scheme, Greenpower electric car racing (national competition) and Forest School. We offer a wide range of sport facilities including swimming pool, multi-use games area and playing fields.
- Regular entries into national art competitions, key links to South Downs Planetarium and The Chichester Festival Theatre.

Parents are encouraged to be actively involved in their child's education with regular contact with the College team.

We support the traditional values of: honesty, respect for others and hard work through our pastoral team, PSHE curriculum and links to the local community. The House system is driven by these values and the practice of vertical grouping, allows opportunities for mentoring and modelling of these traditional values.

Snaresbrook Preparatory School

75 Woodford Road, South Woodford, London E18 2EA

Tel:	020 8989 2394
email:	office@snaresbrookprep.org
website:	www.snaresbrookprep.org
Twitter:	@SnaresbrookPrep
Facebook:	@SnaresbrookPrep
LinkedIn:	/snaresbrook-prep-school-ltd

Head: **Mr Ralph Dalton**

Age Range. 3½–11.
Number in School. 165.
Fees per term (2018–2019). £3,019–£4,038.

Snaresbrook Preparatory School is a vibrant independent day school for boys and girls aged from 3½ to 11 years. Founded in the 1930s, the school occupies a substantial Victorian building, once a large private family home – something that contributes to the strong community spirit within the school. We aim to cultivate an intimate, caring family atmosphere in which children feel secure and valued. Snaresbrook Values have been introduced and embedded by the current Head – they include Respect, Enjoyment and Excellence. The values are posted all around the School and even on the hopscotch in the playground!

The Nursery is extremely popular and is our main point of entry. A key reason for this is the experience of the Head of Nursery who has worked at the School for over 20 years. Most children join the school at age 3½ and stay with us until they reach 11 when they leave for their senior schools.

We provide a rounded education covering every aspect of your child's early development. The curriculum has broadened in the last few years and is designed to prepare pupils for life as well as entrance and scholarship examinations to senior independent and grammar schools. The curriculum includes Mathematics, English, Science, Current Affairs, ICT, Art, DT, Music, Drama, French, Spanish, PE/Games, RE, Wellbeing and PSHEE. Latin and Swimming are intro-

duced in the Juniors. Year 6 pupils undertake the Adventure Service Challenge in preparation for The Duke of Edinburgh's Award undertaken at senior school.

Areas such as Music, Drama, Sport, ICT and Languages are very strong and are led by passionate specialists. Ambitious School Development Plans have moved the School forward. At age 11, we find that Snaresbrook children are confident, cheerful and courteous, with a good sense of community and a readiness to care for each other and the world around them. They have learned how to work in the ways that suit them best, are receptive to teaching and are well prepared for the next stage of their education and development. We see ourselves as joint trustees, with parents, of the young lives in our care, bearing equal responsibility for their happiness, wellbeing and development.

In 2017 Snaresbrook came through its Regulatory Compliance Inspection fully compliant and without any action needed. The School also had record results at 11+ with the 19 children in Year 6 being offered a total of 18 Scholarships as well as the highest ever number of places at top independent schools including the City of London Schools, Forest, Chigwell and Bancroft's as well as Grammar Schools.

Anyone interested in the School is encouraged to contact the office to book a personal tour.

Steephill School

off Castle Hill, Fawkham, Longfield, Kent DA3 7BG

Tel:	01474 702107
email:	secretary@steephill.co.uk
website:	www.steephill.co.uk
Twitter:	@steephillonline
Facebook:	@Steephill-School

Head Teacher: **Mrs Caroline Birtwell**, BSc, MBA, PGCE

Age Range. 3–11 co-educational.
Number of Pupils. 120.
Fees per term (2018–2019). £3,140. Pre-School Fees are pro rata.

Steephill School is a very successful School based on its academic, sporting and musical achievements. In 2017, 100% of Year 6 pupils gained entry to a selective school; many children won awards at music festivals and there were numerous successes at inter-school sports. In its 2013 ISI inspection report the school was given an "excellent" rating in Pastoral Care, Curriculum, Extra-Curriculum and the Spiritual, Moral, Social and Cultural Development of pupils. In 2016, the School was 100% compliant with Independent School Standards.

The School believes in high-quality teaching within a disciplined but relaxed atmosphere. The School holds traditional values and beliefs; working with and supporting each other is an important part of the ethos. There are close links with the church opposite the School. Four services per year are held there and the Rector takes a fortnightly assembly. The setting is very rural despite being only a few minutes' drive from the M2 and 5 miles from the M20 and M25. The School enjoys beautiful views of the countryside with very little traffic nearby.

The classes are a maximum of 16 and with only 120 pupils in the School, there is a close liaison between all members of the school community: children, staff, family members and governors. Parents are welcomed into the School and work closely with the teachers. There is regular feedback to parents on children's progress. Parents are also active in Friends of Steephill School, the Parents Association, to provide social and fundraising activities.

The children join the School aged 3 in the Pre-School and they leave at age 11. The curriculum is designed to support all abilities to achieve academically and in all the broader aspects of education such as drama, the arts and sports. Information Technology has been developed well over the last few years and is being continually updated.

There is a large selection of extracurricular activities at lunchtime and after school. Our Gardening Club is one of the more popular together with the choir, instruction on musical instruments, dance and football. We are very fortunate to have large grounds with a superb sports field, despite being a small school.

There is a care facility both before and after school so we are open from 7.00 am to 5.30 pm. The School is also very proud of the lunches. All the food is sourced from local shops: butcher, baker and greengrocer. The meals are carefully balanced and freshly made.

Charitable status. Steephill School is a Registered Charity, number 803152.

Stratford Preparatory School

Church House, Old Town, Stratford-upon-Avon, Warwickshire CV37 6BG

Tel: 01789 297993
Fax: 01789 263993
email: secretary@stratfordprep.co.uk
website: www.stratfordprep.co.uk
Facebook: @stratfordprep

Motto: *Lux et Scientia*

Principal: Mrs C Quinn, MBA, BEd Hons

Headmaster: **Mr Neil Musk**, MA, BA Hons, PGCE

Age Range. Preparatory School 4–11 years. Montessori Nursery School 2–4 years.

Number in School. Main School: 37 Boys, 47 Girls; Nursery School: 6 Boys, 4 Girls.

Fees per term (2018–2019). Junior forms £3,760; Infant forms £3,460; Reception £3,200; Nursery School: £2,880 (full-time), £1,440 (5 mornings). Compulsory extras: Lunch £150.

Stratford Preparatory School is situated in the heart of the historic town of Stratford-upon-Avon. The Preparatory school opened in September 1989 and has developed around a large town house. An additional detached house within the school's grounds provides accommodation for the Reception and Nursery children, a gymnasium, a science room and design and technology room.

The school was judged 'Outstanding' in all areas in its 2017 ISI Inspection.

The Nursery implements the Montessori philosophy of learning which encourages a structured learning environment. French and ballet are taught from the age of 2 years.

The main school offers a broad balanced learning plan adapted to the individual needs of the children using traditional teaching methods and with specific reference to the National Curriculum. All children are entered for the 11+ and independent school entrance examinations.

The school offers a high level of pastoral care and attention to personal development.

Physical education activities include: sailing, swimming, football, cricket, tennis, netball, rounders, ballet and athletics.

There are opportunities for the children to learn a variety of musical instruments. The school has two choirs and an orchestra.

Reduction in fees is offered for families with two or more children in the School.

The Headmaster is pleased to provide further details and meet prospective parents.

Study School

57 Thetford Road, New Malden, Surrey KT3 5DP

Tel: 020 8942 0754
Fax: 020 8942 0754
email: info@thestudyschool.co.uk
website: www.thestudyschool.co.uk

Headmistress: **Mrs Donna Brackstone-Drake**, BA Hons, PGCE, NPQH, MBA

Age Range. Rising 3–11 Co-educational.
Number in School. Day: 71 Boys, 72 Girls.
Fees per term (2018–2019). Nursery (mornings only) £1,669, Reception & Year 1 £3,421, Years 2–6 £3,910. Additional Nursery afternoon sessions available each day of the week: £268 per afternoon, until 3.00 pm, per term or £213 per afternoon, until 1.30 pm, per term. All fees include a cooked school lunch. The school belongs to the Early Years Funding Scheme for 3 and 4 year olds; we do not offer the extended funding.

Since 1923 we have successfully given our children a firm foundation in reading, writing and number skills, whilst also teaching French, Spanish, Music, Art and Games. Science, Geography, History, Design and Technology and ICT play an important part in the curriculum, with interactive whiteboards in every classroom and a full set of iPads and laptops which augment the curriculum.

Small classes allow us to stretch the most able pupils, whilst giving all our children individual attention.

Popular After-School Clubs include Football, Infant Rugby, Art, Computer Coding, Drama, Zumba, Winter and Summer Sports, Choir, Modern Foreign Languages and Cookery. Individual instrumental music tuition is also available. We have Before School Care from 7.45 am and After School Care until 6.15 pm. All classes go on a school trip once a term and Years Four, Five and Six attend residential activity and field study courses and language trips abroad.

We provide a caring and stimulating atmosphere in which our children thrive. After Year Six they leave us to enter such schools at Kingston Grammar School, Wallington Boys' School, Non-Such Girls' School, Hampton School, the High Schools at Wimbledon, Sutton, Putney and Surbiton and both Tiffin Schools.

Please visit our website: www.thestudyschool.co.uk.

The Swaminarayan School

260 Brentfield Road, Neasden, London NW10 8HE

Tel: 020 8965 8381
Fax: 020 8961 4042
email: admin@tssuk.org
website: www.swaminarayan.brent.sch.uk

Chairman of Governors: Mr Piyush Amin

Headteacher, Senior School: **Mr Nilesh Manani**, BSc Hons, FRSA, PGCE

Headteacher, Prep School: Mr Umesh Raja, BSc, PGCE, NLP Masters, NPQH

Age Range. 2½–18.
Number of Pupils. 416: 234 boys, 182 girls.
Fees per term (2018–2019). £3,475–£4,653.

The Swaminarayan School was founded in 1991 by His Holiness Shree Pramukh Swami Maharaj to provide education along the lines of independent British schools, whilst reinforcing Hindu culture and tradition. It is a non-profit making, co-educational school for children aged two and a half to eighteen years.

The school admitted its first eighty or so Prep School pupils in September 1992 and the Senior School took its first intake the following September. Now there are just under 500 pupils in the school and already students from the school have gained admission to Cambridge, Oxford, Imperial, Warwick, UCL, LSE and King's.

Since those early days excellent progress has been made in all areas. The most striking aspect that always attracts comment from visitors is the purposeful atmosphere, both in classrooms and throughout the school. Teachers are able to help pupils achieve their full potential because of the generous staff to pupil ratio, excellent behaviour of pupils and commitment from parents.

Resources and premises have also improved beyond recognition with modern libraries and computer rooms for each school. Former students from those early days dropping in to meet their teachers are amazed by the transformation!

On the curriculum front, the school has taken up the most desirable elements of the National Curriculum while developing the best practices of independent education. The cultural subjects unique to the school give it a special dimension – students have lessons in the Indian Performing Arts up to Year 8 and all students whose mother tongue is Gujarati study it up GCSE and all study Religious Education in Hinduism up to GCSE level.

In addition to their timetabled LAMDA lessons, PE lessons and club afternoons, pupils are involved in a range of extracurricular activities such as public speaking, sports, drama, dance and much more. An extensive programme of instrumental lessons, both Indian and European, is also on offer to all pupils. The school arranges regular day trips to museums, parks and other places of educational interest. The Duke of Edinburgh's Award scheme and residential outings are also a feature of the school. Whilst continuing to deliver a value based, broad and balanced curriculum, the school excels academically. Each year its excellent GCSE and A Level results put it at the top of Brent Performance tables. In The Daily Telegraph list of top independent schools, TSS has been consistently placed amongst the top ten performing schools in the country. Twenty years of vision, investment and hard work from trustees and governors, teaching and non-teaching staff as well as commitment from parents and pupils have made this a school to be proud of. The next ten years will see the school reaching even greater heights.

Charitable status. The Akshar Educational Trust is a Registered Charity, number 1023731.

Sylvia Young Theatre School

1 Nutford Place, London W1H 5YZ
Tel: 020 7258 2330
email: info@syts.co.uk
website: www.syts.co.uk

Principal: Mrs Sylvia Young OBE

Headteacher: **Ms Frances Chave**, BSc, PGCE, NPQH

Age Range. 10–16.
Number in School. Day: 72 Boys, 165 Girls. Weekly boarding is available with host families at an additional cost.
Fees per term (2018–2019). Key Stage 2 & 3 (Years 6, 7, 8 & 9): £4,720; Key Stage 4 (Years 10 & 11): £4,820.

The School has a junior department (Year 6 only) and a secondary department (Years 7–11). We aim to provide an appropriately balanced academic and vocational experience for our students. We are proud of the caring and well disciplined environment that prevails and promotes a very positive climate of individual success.

Academic subjects are delivered by highly qualified staff to the end of Key Stage 4.

GCSE Examination subjects include English, English Literature, Mathematics, Combined or Triple Science, Art, Drama, Music, Media Studies, Spanish and History.

Theatrical training is given by experienced professional teachers. Pupils are prepared for examinations in Speech and Drama – LAMDA (London Academy of Music and Dramatic Art). Entry is by audition with academic ability assessed.

Thames Christian School

Wye Street, London SW11 2HB
Tel: 020 7228 3933
Fax: 020 7924 1112
email: info@thameschristiancollege.org.uk
website: www.thameschristianschool.org.uk
Twitter: @ThamesCSchool
Facebook: @Thameschristianschool

Head: **Dr Stephen Holsgrove**, PhD

Age Range. 11–16 Co-educational.
Number of Pupils. 124.

Thames Christian School is the choice for parents who want their child to achieve academically and thrive holistically in a smaller, relational and diverse learning environment. Thames delivers high-quality tailored education and dedicated pastoral care so that children can achieve great grades, good character and become the best they can be.

At Thames we believe that the teenage years are a valuable time to lay the foundations for success in life. Alongside academic achievement, we emphasise the importance of learning to make good choices, build positive relationships and develop the resilience to overcome challenges. Each pupil is valued as a unique and gifted individual and this, combined with small well-behaved classes, enables our dedicated teachers to develop each pupil's talents and inspire them to achieve.

Thames Christian School is an independent co-educational secondary school in Battersea. From September 2020 the school will be accommodated in a new purpose-built facility with a three-stream entry and our own sixth form.

Pupils achieve excellent results, considerably outperforming the national average and have no difficulty gaining places at top independent and grammar schools' sixth forms. Whether your child enjoys science, humanities, languages, the arts, sport or technology, we offer choices to suit them. Options include separate sciences, computer science, music, graphics, drama and PE. Pupils have opportunities to participate in a vibrant programme of co-curricular activities, external competitions and local and international trips, including our award-winning trip to Africa.

ISI Inspection Report, March 2015:

"Behaviour is excellent and pupils feel safe, secure, valued and well supported."

"Performance across the subject range at GCSE is markedly higher than that predicted from their prior attainment."

"Almost all pupils achieve places at their first choice of schools or colleges for post-16 education, some achieving scholarships at highly competitive independent schools."

"Pupils with dyslexia make significantly greater progress, achieving on average nearly a grade higher than the average for pupils with similar abilities."

The best way to find out if our school is suitable for your child is to see for yourself what we have to offer at one of our Open Days. Alternatively please do phone 020 72283933 to make an individual appointment to see the school, especially if it is for immediate entry.

For further information please visit: www.thameschristianschool.org.uk

Fees per term (2018–2019). £5,260.

Charitable status. Thames Christian College Ltd is a Registered Charity, number 1081666.

Thorpe Hall School

Wakering Road, Thorpe Bay, Essex SS1 3RD

Tel: 01702 582340
Fax: 01702 587070
email: sec@thorpehallschool.co.uk
website: www.thorpehall.southend.sch.uk

Headmaster: **A Hampton**, BA Hons, LTCL, MEd, NPQH

Age Range. 2–16 years.
Number in School. Approximately 340 girls and boys.
Fees per term (2018–2019). £3,000–£4,200. Nursery: £24.25 per session (excluding EY funding).

Thorpe Hall School is a co-educational independent day school, pleasantly situated on green belt land on the outskirts of Southend-on-Sea, Essex. The buildings are modern and purpose-built.

Communications to London are good via the A13 and A127 and the Liverpool/Fenchurch Street railway lines. The nearest station is approximately 10 minutes' walk.

Founded in 1925, the school has been educating children for 80 years and consistently achieves excellent academic results at Key Stage 1, 2, 3 and GCSE with special emphasis being placed on the traditional values of good manners, behaviour, dress and speech.

On Monday, Tuesday and Thursday each week the school day is extended by one hour to enable all children to access library and computer facilities as well as having the opportunities to participate in Sport, Music, Drama, Mathematics and French or simply to do their homework in a suitable and supervised environment.

Refurbishment of the Science, Modern Languages, Information Systems and Resources Centre facilities has greatly enhanced the learning opportunities for all pupils.

A new building was recently completed, which houses a Theatre, Technology rooms, an extra ICT suite and an excellent Modern Art area. These new facilities ensure that Thorpe Hall School has the most modern, up-to-date and technologically advanced facilities of any independent school in South East Essex.

Thorpe Hall School has an orderly, disciplined and caring ethos that caters for the social and academic needs of children – Pre-Nursery, Nursery, Reception, Infant, Junior and Senior – not only between the hours of 9.00 am to 4.00 pm but also offers sporting opportunities in golf, tennis, karate, netball, horse riding and football at weekends and during holiday times. Youngsters have the opportunity to join our Beavers, Cubs and Scout groups while senior pupils can become involved in the Duke of Edinburgh's Award scheme.

The Charitable Trust status enables fees, which are very competitive, to be kept to a minimum. Nursery vouchers are accepted and some bursaries are available. The School is regularly inspected by the Independent Schools Inspectorate.

Charitable status. Thorpe Hall School Trust is a Registered Charity, number 298155. It exists to provide good quality education for boys and girls in South East Essex.

Tower College

Mill Lane, Rainhill, Merseyside L35 6NE

Tel: 0151 426 4333
email: mrsogrady@towercollege.com
           office@towercollege.com
website: www.towercollege.com
Facebook: @towercollege

Principal: **Mrs A C O'Grady**

Vice-Principal: Mrs P Knox
Registrar: Miss C McNamara
Bursar: Mr M Taylor

Age Range. 3 months – 16 years.
Number in School. Day: 191 Boys, 140 Girls.
Fees per term (from April 2018). £2,324–£2,704.

Tower College is a non-denominational Christian Day School housed in a beautiful Victorian mansion set in 11 acres.

We believe children thrive in our safe and secure environment where they do not have to conform to a peer group. They are free to become their best selves, to achieve the best possible academic results and are given every opportunity to excel in Sport, Art and Music

Charitable status. Tower College is a Registered Charity, number 526611.

The Towers School

Upper Beeding, Steyning, West Sussex BN44 3TF

Tel: 01903 812185
Fax: 01903 813858
email: admin@thetowersschool.org
website: www.thetowersschool.org
Twitter: @TheTowersSchool
Facebook: @TheTowersSchool

Headmistress: **Mrs Clare Trelfa**

Age Range. Girls 4–16, Boys 4–11.

Number in School. 176.

Fees per term (2018–2019). Tuition: £2,730–£3,850.

The Towers School, a Roman Catholic school for girls aged 4–16 and boys aged 4–11 years in the beautiful setting of the South Downs, is owned by a Community of Sisters. At the heart of The Towers Community is Christian love; all people of whatever race, colour, creed or status are welcome, and have equal worth and opportunity. We aim to celebrate the dignity of each individual pupil. Our motto "Always Faithful" upholds the qualities of honesty and trust, responsibility, self-discipline and forgiveness. Pupils are encouraged to achieve their full potential in everything they do, developing a love of learning and seeking "wholeness". Mathematics and science subjects are particular strengths, and the school has three times won the Whitbread Prize for GCSE results. The GCSE pass rate is consistently high and reflects a quest for high academic standards. There is a keen interest in music and drama and a major musical is produced annually. The school's achievements in sport bear witness to a fine tradition, especially in tennis, where the school has won the Sussex Shield five times; netball and gymnastics are also very strong. The on-site covered and heated pool is a real asset and is enjoyed by all ages.

Find enjoyment and fulfilment at affordable fees!

Charitable status. The Towers Convent School is a Registered Charity, number 229394. It exists to provide quality education for girls and boys.

Trevor-Roberts School

55–57 Eton Avenue, London NW3 3ET

Tel:	020 7586 1444
email:	trsenior@trevor-robertsschool.co.uk
website:	www.trevor-robertsschool.co.uk

Headteacher: **Mr Simon Trevor-Roberts**, BA

Age Range. 5–13 Co-educational.

Number in School. 170 Day Pupils: 100 boys, 70 girls.

Fees per term (2018–2019). £5,100–£5,600.

Trevor-Roberts School was founded in Hampstead in 1955 by the headmaster's late father and moved to its present site in 1981. The school is made up of two departments but operates as one school and occupies two adjacent much-adapted late Victorian houses in Belsize Park. In addition to on-site facilities, the school makes use of nearby playing fields and a local leisure centre swimming pool.

Central to the education provided is the school's aim for all pupils to become happy and confident individuals who fulfil their potential. Strong emphasis is placed on personal organisation and pupils are encouraged to develop a love of learning for its own sake. In a happy, non-competitive atmosphere, pupils are well cared for and teachers' responses are tailored to the individual needs of pupils. It is the School's strong belief that much can be expected of a child if he or she is given self-confidence and a sense of personal worth and does not feel judged too early in life against the attainment of others.

High success rates throughout the school are achieved through small classes, individual attention and specialist teachers. The standards achieved enable almost all pupils to gain places in their first choice of school at either 11+ or 13+ into the main London day schools and academically selective independent boarding schools. In recent years a number of pupils have been awarded academic, art and music scholarships to these schools. The school aims to make pupils

prepared for this process and give them the confidence to enjoy the academic challenges they will be offered.

The school provides a broad range of curricular and extra-curricular activities, contributing to pupils' linguistic, mathematical, scientific, technological, social and physical development in a balanced way. Aesthetic and creative development is strongly encouraged through art, drama and music. In the Senior Department the syllabus is extended to include Classical History, Latin, Greek and Mandarin. The curriculum is enriched at all stages by a variety of one-day educational visits as well as by residential trips for Years 5–8 on activity trips, a sailing weekend, geography field trips and visits to Belgium.

A range of extra-curricular activities and sporting opportunities appropriate for boys and girls of all ages is offered two afternoons a week and after school. The school's founder believed passionately in music and drama as a means of developing pupils' confidence and self-esteem and both subjects are a strong feature of the school today. All classes prepare and perform two drama performances each year in which every pupil has a speaking and/or singing part.

Pupils thrive in a caring family atmosphere where the emphasis is on individual progress and expectation, and where improvement is rewarded as highly as success. It has a broadly Christian tradition, but welcomes pupils of all faiths and of none.

Ursuline Preparatory School

Great Ropers Lane, Warley, Brentwood, Essex CM13 3HR

Tel:	01277 227152
Fax:	01277 202559
email:	headmistress@ursulineprepwarley.co.uk
website:	www.ursulineprepwarley.co.uk

Headmistress: **Mrs Pauline Wilson**, MBE, MSc

Age Range. 3–11.

Number in School. Day 180.

Fees per term (2018–2019). £2,150–£4,005.

Founded in the early 1930s, the Ursuline Preparatory School enjoys a reputation as a happy family school, where pupils strive to give of their best in all areas of school life. Consequently, much emphasis is placed on encouraging the children to develop to the full their individual talents and interests, as well as fostering in each pupil a strong sense of well-being, self-reliance and team spirit. This is achieved by the frequent use of praise, by adherence to an agreed policy of consistent and fair discipline, and by the high standards, moral code and caring attitudes deriving from the strongly Catholic ethos which underpins the life of the whole school.

The Ursuline Preparatory School has well qualified and very experienced teachers and support staff. It is committed to offering to all its pupils the distinct advantages of a broad and balanced curriculum. This includes following the National Curriculum, in addition to affording many other opportunities such as the provision of French, Spanish and Information Technology to all children from 4 years upwards, Swimming Lessons, and also Extension classes where this is deemed appropriate.

A comprehensive range of extracurricular activities are offered to the pupils. These are often taught by specialist staff and include subjects such as Theatre Club, Art Appreciation, Computing, Photography, Sewing, Chess, and Speech and Drama as well as many Instrumental Classes and Sporting Activities, with which the School has considerable success in gaining individual and team awards at competition level.

The School successfully prepares children for entry to local and national independent schools, Grammar Schools or local Secondary Schools, including the Ursuline High School.

The relatively small size of the School allows for very close contact between staff, pupils and parents and provides each child with the opportunity to fulfil his or her academic potential. The pupils are encouraged to follow their own interests and to develop a sense of self-confidence and self-worth which will hopefully remain with them throughout their lives, allowing them to reflect the school motto: *A Caring School that strives for excellence.*

Charitable status. The Ursuline Preparatory School is a Registered Charity, number 1058282, which is non-profit making and managed by an independent board of voluntary trustees. It exists to provide Roman Catholic children and those of other denominations with the opportunity to reach the highest individual standards possible in every area of School life.

The Webber Independent School

Soskin Drive, Stantonbury Fields, Milton Keynes, Buckinghamshire MK14 6DP

Tel: 01908 574740
Fax: 01908 574741
email: registrar@webberindependentschool.co.uk
website: www.webberindependentschool.com
Twitter: @WebberIndie
Facebook: @The-Webber-Independent-School
LinkedIn: /Webber-Independent-School

Headmistress: **Mrs Hilary Marsden**

Age Range. 4–18.
Number in School. 191.
Fees per term (2018–2019). Reception (4–5 years full-time places only) £3,010; Years 1–2 £3,050; Years 3–4 £3,160; Years 5–6 £3,390; Years 7–9 £4,090; Years 10–11 £4,135; Years 12–13 £4,235.

The Webber Independent School is a modern private day school for boys and girls aged 4 to 18, and is situated near Central Milton Keynes.

The School delivers Real World Learning and has a strong record of academic success in STEAM-related subjects, including Science, Technology, Arts and Mathematics. It has established links with the Business & Enterprise community, which benefit students with access to top global employers. Students are challenged to become independent thinkers within a supportive community to enable growth and discovery, building resilience and critical thinking skills to help prepare for their future. Webber Independent helps its students discover their strengths and individual talents whilst instilling its young people with a growth mindset, building the confidence required to become successful global citizens, and to meet the challenges of the modern world. The School focuses on the attributes that are highly prized in higher education and the modern workplace, such as initiative, confidence, perseverance, collaboration and leadership.

What we offer:
- Innovation in Real World Learning and Entrepreneurial skills
- Five star rated by the School Guide
- Excellent ISI Report

- One of the top performing schools in Milton Keynes
- Outstanding results at GCSE and A Level
- Wide variety of extra-curricular activities
- Individualised learning and small class sizes
- Excellent pastoral care – a welcoming, family-centred environment

West Lodge School

36 Station Road, Sidcup, Kent DA15 7DU

Tel: 020 8300 2489
Fax: 020 8308 1905
email: info@westlodge.org.uk
website: www.westlodge.org.uk

Chair of Governors: Mrs Chris Head-Rapson

Head Teacher: **Mr Robert Francis**, BEd Hons

Age Range. 3–11.
Number of Pupils. 163 Day Boys and Girls.
Fees per term (2018–2019). £1,825–£3,050.

West Lodge was founded in 1940 and is now an educational trust. The main building is an extended Victorian house, well adapted to use as a school, whilst still retaining its homely atmosphere. Facilities include a new extension, incorporating a science/cookery room and art room/crèche, which can also be used together as an additional hall facility, a fully-equipped gymnasium, Astroturf surface, music rooms and a computer suite. There are eight classes of up to 21 pupils, one class in each year group from Nursery through to Year 6. The staff to pupil ratio is extremely high and the children are taught in smaller groups by specialist teachers for many subjects. The school is open from 8.15 am and an after-school crèche and homework club operate until 5.30 pm.

The school has a strong academic tradition and a purposeful atmosphere permeates each class. The National Curriculum is at the core of our teaching but it is enhanced and enriched by the inclusion of a wider range of subjects. These include: English, mathematics, science, French, information technology, design technology, history, geography, religious education, music, art and craft, physical education and games, swimming and drama.

Great emphasis is placed on a thorough grounding in basic learning skills, with literacy and numeracy seen as key elements in the foundation, upon which future learning will be built. Particular care is taken to extend the most gifted children and support the less able. West Lodge has a consistent record of a high level of entry to local authority selective schools and independent schools.

Music has a particularly high profile within the school and all of the children are encouraged to develop their talents. Well-qualified peripatetic staff teach both group and individual lessons and children of all ages are encouraged to join the school orchestras and choir. Concerts and dramatic performances are staged regularly and parents are warmly invited to attend.

Sports of all sorts are taught and in 2014–15, in particular, the School was thrilled to achieve competitive success at national level in netball and at a local level in kwik cricket.

The school promotes a caring attitude between all its members and aims to help each child towards the achievement of self-control and self-discipline. The Head Teacher and the class teachers know each of the children well and the excellent pastoral care and family atmosphere are major features of the school.

Home-school links are strong and the open door policy gives parents immediate access to members of staff should worries occur. The school also has strong contacts with the local community.

Extracurricular activities are given the highest priority and clubs run each afternoon after school. Regular school outings form part of the curriculum for all children, the older pupils enjoying residential visits.

Charitable status. West Lodge School Educational Trust is a Registered Charity, number 283627. It exists for the provision of high quality education for boys and girls between 3 and 11 years.

Westbourne School

Hickman Road, Penarth, Vale of Glamorgan CF64 2AJ

Tel: 029 2070 5705
email: enquiries@westbourneschool.com
website: www.westbourneschool.com
Twitter: @WestbourneS
Facebook: @WestbourneSchool

Principal: Dr Gerard Griffiths

Head of Prep School and Nursery: Mrs Joanne Chinnock
Deputy Head of Senior School (*Pastoral*): Mr Colin Laity
International Baccalaureate Coordinator: Ms Lisa Phillips and Mrs Jodi Barber
Finance Director: Mr Gary Hughes
Admissions Manager: Mrs Susan Tester Jones

Age Range. 2–18.
Number in School. 83 Boys, 85 Girls.
Fees per term (2018–2019). £2,700–£4,490 (payable in advance). Fees include textbooks, sporting activities and examination charges. Boarding and/or Home Stay £33,750 per year, fully inclusive of tuition fees, accommodation during term time, daily breakfast, lunch and dinner, guardianship costs and annual airport transfers. Westbourne Nursery accepts children from 2 years and is open for 51 weeks a year at a cost of £47.50 per day from 8.00 am until 6.00 pm.

Westbourne develops well-rounded young scholars who go on to the best universities in the UK and around the world, with the skills, knowledge, confidence and character to become leaders of the future in their chosen fields. Westbourne has ranked 1st in the UK for four years in a row and 90% of our graduates go to Russell Group universities. This experience is gained in the safe, picturesque and affluent seaside suburb of Penarth, in Cardiff, which the Sunday Times ranks as one of the Top 10 best places to live in the UK and the EU Quality of Life Survey ranks as the 3rd best European capital city; the perfect blend of modern metropolis, suburban safety, seaside and countryside.

Westbourne offers the International (IB) Diploma Programme in sixth form and GCSEs and IGCSEs, from Year 10 for Standard Entry and from Year 9 for Advanced Entry (the latter allows students to study a wider range of subjects which is excellent preparation for the IB). Places for Year 8 and below are on request and Westbourne can accept students from as young as 2 years old. We can also support an 'accompanying adult' visa for international parents of students under 12 years old

Founded in 1896, our reputation for academic excellence has been established for 122 years. Having ranked 1st in the UK in league tables for the last four year in a row, Westbourne has secured its place as one of the UK's most successful and academically elite schools.

Our IB average is 36–38 points, with two-thirds of all Higher Level grades being 7s and 6s, and two-thirds of students receiving a Bilingual Diploma.

Our GCSE results are equally impressive with 40% of all grades being 9s and 8s (the old A*); 20% the new, harder, grade 9 and a further 20% grade 8s. This up to 5 times the UK average.

In our 2018 inspection, Westbourne was rated 'Excellent' in all five inspection categories.

A disciplined, caring context is maintained and ample opportunity is given for a variety of sporting activities.

Entry into IB1 (International Baccalaureate) is based on GCSE Results and an interview with the Principal, Westbourne offers a Pre-IB foundation year option for students who may require additional preparation; entry into Year 9 is by Common Entrance at which a 50% pass is required. Otherwise entrance is by interview and two day induction.

Penarth is a small seaside town on the outskirts of Cardiff, with excellent transport links. Pupils are normally drawn from Penarth, Sully, Cardiff, Barry, Cowbridge and the Vale of Glamorgan. There is a convenient train service to Penarth and the School has minibuses running each day from The Vale of Glamorgan, Cowbridge, Barry and Cardiff.

Westville House School

Carter's Lane, Middleton, Ilkley, West Yorkshire LS29 0DQ

Tel: 01943 608053
email: hub@westvillehouseschool.co.uk
website: www.westvillehouseschool.co.uk
Twitter: @WestvilleHouseS

Chairman of Governors: Mr Adam Holdsworth

Head Teacher: Mrs Nicola Hammond, BA Hons, PGCE

Age Range. 2–11.
Number of Pupils. 100.
Fees per term (2018–2019). £1,920–£3,325.

Perched on the top of a stunning hillside location, with views across to The Cow and Calf, lies Westville House School, Ilkley's foremost provider of independent education. The gleaming white school building stands proud in acres of grounds and exudes fun, strong values, pride in tradition and a strong belief in the Westville family.

Originally based down in the town centre, the school relocated to its current site over 20 years ago and has gone from strength to strength, developing fantastic education facilities. Inspirational classrooms are to be seen throughout the school; specialist science, art and music classrooms along with a sophisticated IT suite, a state-of-the-art sports hall with attached playing fields and most recently a forest classroom stimulate learning and encourage fun.

From the minute a child begins their journey at Westville house they are valued for who they are. The Early Years Unit, which takes children from 2 years, devotes masses of energy to building foundations that will set the children up for life. Each child has education tailored to their needs – for those who are very able there is masses to challenge, whilst for those who need a little bit of extra help there is huge encouragement and a clear development of an excitement about learning.

Children progress through the Pre-Prep department (ages 2–7) and then on through the Prep department (ages 7–11). They emerge as well-rounded, confident, and above all very happy children whose memories of their time at Westville prompt them to return year after year.

Academics are brilliant here and the school is consistently ranked in the Sunday Times Top 100 Prep Schools in the UK – a fantastic achievement for a small non-selective school. Children regularly achieve scholarships to many independent senior schools and gain entrance to the local selective grammar schools.

Academics aside, there is a whole host of extracurricular activities designed to have something to suit every child. The school is particularly strong in swimming and cross country; drama and dance produce some excellent school productions. Music, in the form of choirs and instrumental lessons, is encouraged and the school ensemble is always seen as great fun. As the children progress through the school new activities and experiences are opened up to them – canoeing, fencing, first aid, street dancing – all geared to ensure that Westville children are totally prepared for their journey on to the senior school of their choice.

Having recently undergone a £1 million development and refurbishment programme, Westville House now has a brand new, state-of-the-art Early Years facility situated in beautiful woodlands, new media suite, new library, new ICT suite and a brilliant new Hub entrance hall which has become the heart of the school.

The school's motto '*Quotidie Opus Novum – something new every day*' really does sum up the excitement of coming to Westville House – the beginning of a lifelong education where an appetite for learning is something to be nurtured and enjoyed.

Charitable status. Westville House School is a Registered Charity, number 1086711.

Westward School

47 Hersham Road, Walton-on-Thames, Surrey KT12 1LE

Tel: 01932 220911
Fax: 01932 242891
email: admin@westwardschool.co.uk
website: www.westwardschool.co.uk

Proprietors: Mr & Mrs David Townley

Headmistress: **Mrs Shelley Stevenson**, BEd Hons

Age Range. 3–11 Co-educational.
Number of Pupils. 150.
Fees per term (2018–2019). £1,250–£2,690.

Whitehall School

117 High Street, Somersham, Cambs PE28 3EH

Tel: 01487 840966
email: office@whitehallschool.com
website: www.whitehallschool.com
Facebook: @Whitehall-School

Principal: **Ms Rebecca Hutley**, BA Hons

Age Range. 6 months to 11 years.
Number in School. 90 Day children: 43 boys, 47 girls.
Fees per term (from April 2018). £1,065–£2,860.
'*A Unique School in Rural Cambridgeshire: A Dynamic, Forward-Thinking environment.*'

Set in extensive grounds with excellent facilities, Whitehall School provides a small, family environment where children are supported to achieve their best academically whilst also developing personality, creativity and social consciousness.

The school consists of an Edwardian house and 18th Century coach house and is set within approximately 1.5 acres of stunning grounds. Facilities include a covered heated swimming pool, playground, sensory garden, games field, library and iPad suite.

Small class sizes to a maximum of 16 allow us to support children to access the curriculum at their own pace on a 'Vertical Pathway', catering for the specific needs of each child so that they excel. Our Individual Performance Programme allows us to work in partnership with parents to encourage children to become active, independent learners.

Windrush Valley School

The Green, Ascott-under-Wychwood, Oxfordshire OX7 6AN

Tel: 01993 831793
email: info@windrushvalleyschool.co.uk
website: www.windrushvalleyschool.co.uk
Facebook: @Windrush-Valley-School

Headteacher: **Mrs A Douglas**, BA Hons, QTS

Age Range. 3–11 Co-educational.
Number of Pupils. 76.
Fees per term (2018–2019). £2,335.

Windrush Valley School is a lively, happy community in which boys and girls thrive. Its rural location provides access to all the amenities of a beautiful Cotswold village including the 12th century church and playing fields. The school is non-selective; admission is by interview with the Headmaster.

Before- and after-school care extend the school day from 8.00 am to 6.00 pm with a wide range of after-school clubs/societies.

The small number of children with special educational needs are taught under the supervision of specialist staff.

The school plays competitive sports in a wide range of games. Class groups are organised on a chronological age basis and the curriculum exceeds the requirements of the National Curriculum. Excellent examination results enable pupils to achieve their first choice of school on transfer to secondary education and help maintain its listing as a 'Times' top 100 preparatory school.

Woodlands School
Great Warley

Warley Street, Great Warley, Brentwood, Essex CM13 3LA

Tel: 01277 233288
Fax: 01277 232715
email: admissions@woodlandsschools.co.uk
website: www.woodlandsschools.co.uk

Headmaster: **Mr David Bell**

Age Range. 3 months–11 years.
Number in School. 140.
Fees per term (2018–2019). £3,009–£4,796.

Woodlands School at Great Warley is set in attractive, spacious grounds, with excellent facilities for outdoor activities. The school also uses the extensive facilities of our sister school at Hutton Manor.

It is the School's principle aim to ensure that all the children are happy and secure and are as successful as possible. They are encouraged to work hard and to show kindness and consideration to their peers. The resulting ethos of the School is one of warmth, support and mutual respect.

The School provides an exciting learning experience which enables the pupils to achieve full academic potential and to develop qualities of curiosity, independence and fortitude. Classes are small. The school aims to develop high levels of self-esteem and a good attitude to learning. The School has an excellent record in public examinations. Pupils are highly successful in gaining places at the schools of their choice. Examination results in Music and LAMDA are also excellent.

A varied programme of team and individual sports aims to offer something for everyone.

There is a strong music tradition and a variety of dramatic and musical concerts and productions are staged throughout the year for children of each age group.

Modern languages are taught to a very high standard, with French introduced at the age of 3 and Spanish in the Upper School.

Pastoral care is a major feature. An 'Open House' policy is in place for parents, which results in any concern being dealt with promptly and effectively.

It is the School's view that the education of the whole child is the most important priority and is confident that the learning experience it provides is fun, truly stimulating and memorable.

The school has a nursery facility offering places for children from 3 months to 3 years who will then progress automatically into Kindergarten.

Pupils are highly successful in gaining places at the schools of their choice. Examination results in Music and LAMDA are also excellent.

A varied programme of team and individual sports aims to offer something for everyone.

There is a strong music tradition and a variety of dramatic and musical concerts and productions are staged throughout the year for children of each age group.

Modern languages are taught to a very high standard, with French introduced at the age of 3 and Spanish in the Upper School.

Pastoral care is a major feature. An 'Open House' policy is in place for parents, which results in any concern being dealt with promptly and effectively.

It is the School's view that the education of the whole child is the most important priority and is confident that the learning experience it provides is fun, truly stimulating and memorable.

The school has a nursery facility offering places for children from 3 months to 3 years who will then progress automatically into Kindergarten.

Woodlands School
Hutton Manor

428 Rayleigh Road, Hutton, Brentwood, Essex CM13 1SD

Tel: 01277 245585
Fax: 01277 221546
email: admissions@woodlandsschools.co.uk
website: www.woodlandsschools.co.uk

Head Teacher: **Mrs Paula Hobbs**, BEd

Age Range. 3–11 Co-educational.
Number of Pupils. 140.
Fees per term (2018–2019). £4,054–£5,317.

Woodlands School at Hutton Manor is set in attractive, spacious grounds, with excellent facilities for outdoor activities. The school also uses the extensive facilities of our sister school at Great Warley.

It is the School's principle aim to ensure that all the children are happy and secure and are as successful as possible. They are encouraged to work hard and to show kindness and consideration to their peers. The resulting ethos of the School is one of warmth, support and mutual respect.

The School provides an exciting learning experience which enables the pupils to achieve full academic potential and to develop qualities of curiosity, independence and fortitude. Classes are small. The school aims to develop high levels of self-esteem and a good attitude to learning. The School has an excellent record in public examinations.

INDEX OF ENTRANCE SCHOLARSHIPS

Academic Scholarships

Academic Scholarships .../cont'd

PAGE

Art Scholarships

PAGE

Dance Scholarships

PAGE

Drama Scholarships

Bursaries

Bursaries .../cont'd

GEOGRAPHICAL INDEX OF SCHOOLS

OVERSEAS SCHOOLS

ALPHABETICAL INDEX OF SCHOOLS